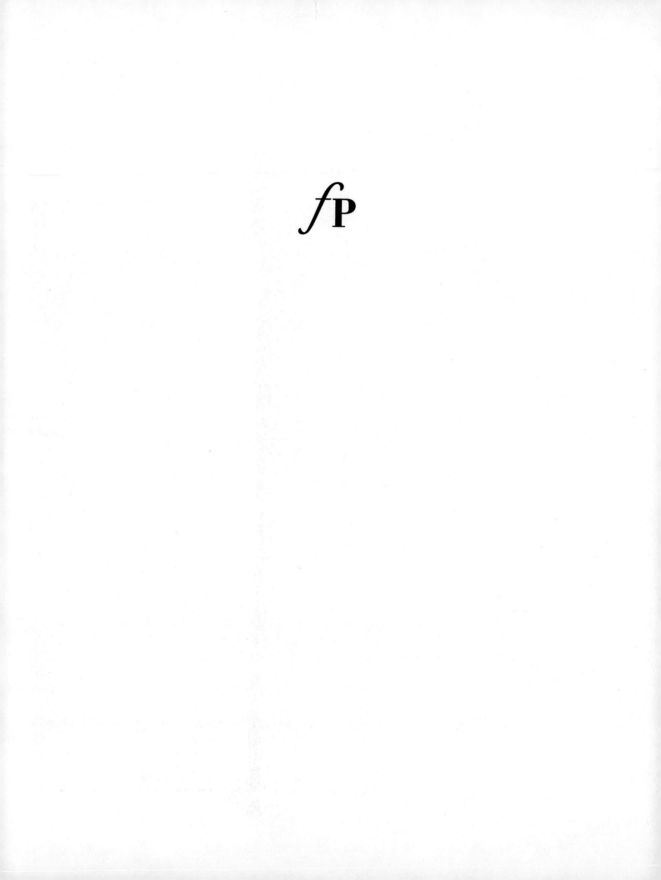

The Bass Handbook of Leadership

THEORY, RESEARCH, AND MANAGERIAL APPLICATIONS

Fourth Edition

Bernard M. Bass
with Ruth Bass

FREE PRESS

New York   London   Toronto   Sydney

*f*P

Free Press
A Division of Simon & Schuster, Inc.
1230 Avenue of the Americas
New York, NY 10020

This Free Press hardcover edition November 2008

FREE PRESS and colophon are trademarks of Simon & Schuster, Inc.

For information about special discounts for bulk purchases, please contact Simon & Schuster Special Sales at 1-800-456-6798 or business@simonandschuster.com

Manufactured in the United States of America

10 9 8 7 6 5 4 3 2 1

Library of Congress Cataloging-in-Publication Data is available.

ISBN-13: 978-0-7432-1552-7
ISBN-10:   0-7432-1552-4

Foreword to the Fourth Edition

Without a doubt, *Bass & Stogdill's Handbook of Leadership* has been the most widely used and cited reference book in the study of leadership. Even though there has been a dramatic increase in leadership books of all kinds, including reviews of research and other handbooks, I am quite certain that the impact of this, the fourth edition of the *Handbook*, will be equal to or greater than the last edition. Why?

For leadership scholars, the *Handbook*, in its three earlier editions, has been *the* primary reference book—our bible for all things leadership. I consult the *Handbook* on a nearly daily basis, so much so that it is the only book that has a permanent place on my work desk. I will retire my third edition to a shelf and replace it with this fourth edition.

The *Handbook*, thanks to the exacting detail of Bernie Bass, is a thoroughly comprehensive and well-organized review of the voluminous (and growing) leadership literature. To grasp the enormity of this task, two-thirds of all psychological and management research on leadership has been published since the last edition of the *Handbook*. The comprehensive nature of the *Handbook* means that scholars can find reviewed here research on nearly every leadership topic imaginable.

The longevity of *Bass & Stogdill's Handbook of Leadership*, third edition, provided a bridge between the earliest research on leadership and the research that was being conducted at the time it was published. All too often, researchers are unable (or unwilling) to search the archives for elusive copies of early leadership research. This fourth edition of the *Handbook* covers the research history and brings it up to date. The fact that Bernie Bass has lived (and published in) the past seven decades means that scholars can use the *Handbook* as a tool to trace modern research from the present back to its earliest roots.

Finally, the *Handbook* is well written and arranged and provides a coherent structure to leadership. Leadership is a topic that has been studied from many perspectives by scholars from a myriad of disciplines. While the greatest contribution of the *Handbook* has been the sheer volume of information packed between its covers, it is Bass's thoughtful organization and structure that help organize and define what is known about leaders and leadership.

Bernard M. Bass, one of the founders of the social scientific investigation of leaders and leadership, left us in 2007. Although he made enormous contributions to the field, this edition of the *Handbook* is Bernie's most impressive gift to the leadership community.

As someone who has followed Bernie around at conferences, as he scurried from one leadership session to another, collecting copies of presentations and making connections with leadership scholars, I know firsthand that Bernie Bass's heart and soul are in this handbook. His home office was crammed with copies of leadership books, journals, and papers, with his wife Ruth providing good organization to what otherwise would have been a mountainous clutter. It is very fitting that Ruth Bass, who contributed so much to Bernie's life and his work, be a recognized co-author on this edition.

Bernie's knowledge of leadership and related topics were truly encyclopedic. The knowledge of leadership research and theory that was inside Bernie Bass's head could fill a dozen or more volumes the size of this *Handbook*. He had a very difficult time deciding what should be included, and he regretted greatly all that had to be left out. There are, after all, only so many pages that fit between a single cover.

Although I have consulted the *Handbook* countless times in my work, I also have had the good fortune of

v

being able to consult Bernie directly on particular leadership topics, and he always had the answer. Those of us who study leadership and the many more who are deeply concerned about the practice of leadership in the world owe an incalculable debt to Bernie Bass.

As you get to know this edition of the *Handbook*, I am sure you will appreciate Bernie Bass's legacy, and this final gift, as much as I do.

Ronald E. Riggio
Kravis Leadership Institute
Claremont McKenna College

In Memory of Bernard M. Bass

On October 11, 2007, during the final stages of the production of the fourth edition of the *Handbook of Leadership*, Bernard M. Bass passed away. Bernie, who was 82 years old, was distinguished professor emeritus in the School of Management at Binghamton University (State University of New York) and a member of the academy of Senior Professionals at Eckerd College in Florida. He was also the founding director of the Center for Leadership Studies at Binghamton and founding editor of *The Leadership Quarterly* journal. In the seven decades after 1946, he published over 400 journal articles, book chapters, and technical reports; plus 21 books and another ten books that he edited.

He was a consultant involved in executive development for many of the Fortune 500 companies and delivered lectures and workshops in over 40 countries. He also lectured and conducted workshops pro bono for wide variety of not-for-profit organizations, including religious organizations, hospitals, government agencies, and universities. His work has been cited thousands of times and he received millions of dollars in research grants. Translations of his work have appeared in French, German, Spanish, Portuguese, Italian, and Japanese.

In addition to authoring the *Handbook of Leadership*, Bernie focused for 25 years on research and applications to management development of transformational leadership. Bernie was honored with many awards for lifetime achievement by several professional organizations, including the Distinguished Scientific Contributions Award from the Society for Industrial and Organizational Psychology and the Eminent Leadership Scholar Award from the Leadership Network of the Academy of Management. A Festschrift in his honor was held in 2001.

He is survived by his wife, Ruth, who was instrumental in the completion of the *Handbook of Leadership*; his daughter Audie; his daughter Laurie and her husband, Steve; his son Robert and Robert's wife Maryanne and their three daughters, Rebecca, Megan, and Lauren; his son Jonathan and Jonathan's wife Patricia, with their three sons Joshua, Jeremy, and Jonathan Jr., and Jonathan Jr's. wife Christie and their two children.

"Bernie was first and foremost a great scholar, scientist, and researcher—the greatest leadership scholar of the last 50 years—but he was also a generous, kind, and humorous human being. The field has lost a great scholar; I have lost a friend, colleague, and mentor."

Francis J. Yammarino, Ph.D.
SUNY Distinguished Professor of Management
Director, Center for Leadership Studies
School of Management
State University of New York at Binghamton

"Bernie was a giant in advancing the field of leadership for over seven decades. He was also a close friend to many colleagues around the globe, a mentor of the highest caliber, and an extraordinary thinker. The field of leadership would not be as advanced as it is today without his enormous contributions to theory, research, and of course the *Handbook of Leadership*."

Bruce Avolio, Ph.D.
Clifton Chair in Leadership
Director, Gallup Leadership Institute
Department of Management
College of Business
University of Nebraska–Lincoln

"For me, leadership is social influence, and therefore Bernie Bass was my leader. Without knowing it, he played a major role in my becoming a leadership scholar 20 years ago, the most significant and fruitful move in my professional life. In the 1980s, the field of leadership studies was half dead and badly needed invigoration. We were lucky that a scholar of Bernie's caliber was around to provide the needed invigoration. He is perhaps the person most responsible for the thriving of the field in the last 25 years. He was truly a luminary."

Boas Shamir, Ph.D.
Dean, Faculty of Social Sciences
The Hebrew University
Mount Scopus
Jerusalem, Israel

"Bernie was a fabulous mentor. The opportunity to work with him shaped my career in many positive ways. I continue 25 years later to pursue leadership research. This interest started with Bernie's passion for transformational leadership."

Leanne Atwater, Ph.D.
Chair, Department of Management
School of Global Management and Leadership
Arizona State University

"I harbor most pleasant and appreciative memories of Bernie. His intellectual depth, the broadness of his interest in organizational issues, the strict scientific approach to the study and analysis of these problems have always struck me. Also, his organizational and editorial energy and care were conspicuous."

Pieter J.D. Drenth, Ph.D.
Emeritus Professor, Work and Organizational Psychology
Vrije Universiteit
Amsterdam, The Netherlands

"Long before I met Bernie Bass, I was very aware of the fact that he had an enormous impact on my discipline of industrial/organizational psychology and on the particular area of leadership. His *Handbook* was really the "bible" for leadership scholars. It was the source for all things leadership, and it has always had a very special place on my bookshelf."

Ronald Riggio, Ph.D.
Henry R. Kravis Professor of Leadership and Organizational Psychology
Director of the Kravis Leadership Institute
Claremont McKenna College

"I currently teach a history of management thought class and we have people we study whom we call 'giants.' Bernie was certainly one of these and has served as a giant role model for my students and for me. His work on transformational leadership has transformed the field, and, I feel confident, has brought many young scholars into it. His work on the various *Handbook* revisions is the gold standard of the field . . . I have also been impressed with the many other innovative contributions he made to the leadership, management, and psychology fields. He was always ahead of the curve. Along with these accomplishments, he has mentored a number of doctoral students and young professors who have gone on to make major contributions in their own right."

Jerry Hunt, Ph.D.
Horn Professor of Management
Founding Director, Institute for Leadership Research
Texas Tech University

"To me, Bernie represents the model of a true scholar: interested in the content, thorough, clear. I've seen people attack relentlessly if their work is at all questioned—not Bernie. True scholar that he was, he was always more interested in furthering the development of the field than 'defending his personal glory,' if I can put it that way. He really has made a tremendous impact on our field."

Deanne N. Den Hartog, Ph.D.
Professor of Organizational Behavior
University of Amsterdam Business School
Amsterdam, The Netherlands

"He opened a new and truly scientific way to look at what I was doing that has served me very well in my 40–year career in my field. To my way of thinking, that is the role of true scientist, scholar, and leader."

Fred Dansereau, Ph.D.
Professor of Organization and Human Resources and
 Associate Dean for Research
School of Management
State University of New York at Buffalo

"Of course the pinnacle of his career was the development of Transformational Leadership, including the articulation of the conceptual space and the development of measures to tap these concepts."

Martin G. Evans, Ph.D.
Professor Emeritus
Rotman School of Management
University of Toronto

Acknowledgments

Many fellow scholars, colleagues, staff, and students helped in the planning of and data collection for this fourth edition of the *Handbook of Leadership*, beginning in 1989 at the Center for Leadership Studies (CLS), School of Management at Binghamton University (State University of New York). Leading scholars of leadership research such as Chet Schriesheim and Fred Fiedler, as well as Robert Wallace, former senior editor of Free Press, reviewed Bass and Stogdill's third edition to suggest ways of improving the fourth edition, along with updating the literature. My faculty colleagues at CLS—Bruce Avolio, Fran Yammarino, David Waldman, and Leanne Atwater—also made useful suggestions and helped frame the decision to maintain and expand the single reference list. Over the 18 years during which the fourth edition was in preparation, I received useful feedback from readers. One example stands out: Native American readers pointed out that in the third edition, Native Americans were seen as a severely impoverished group, when in fact by the 1990s, they had overcome much adversity and were making important economic, educational, and cultural strides. The opening of gambling casinos on Native American lands became a major source of revenue and enabled extensive investments. Much had changed for the good in their lives. Google was another source of unpublished ethnic information.

Secretarial staff and students helped greatly in locating and copying articles and technical reports. Particularly important was CLS secretary Wendy Kramer.

When it came time to finish the final draft of the manuscript of the fourth edition. I was aided immensely by two CLS professors at Binghamton University, Kim Jaussi and Shelly Dionne and their Ph.D. students, Becky Jestice, Jung Hwan Kim, Betsy Carroll, and Mike Palanski, as well as my wife, who all put a great deal of energy into locating and completing fully and partly missing references. They were an important source of support in preparation of the final reference list.

Writing was expedited by my ability to work directly on the computer. It was a new experience trying to get the results to the publisher using the exacting format and instructions I was required to supply. But thanks to Ruth Bass, my wife of 61 years and a self-taught computer buff, it was possible to do this. I remain deeply grateful for her efforts in this regard as well as for her editorial suggestions for the text and her encouragement as the final manuscript unfolded. Without her assistance, the task would never have been completed.

Bernard M. Bass
St. Petersburg, Florida

Contents

Preface to the Fourth Edition

What's new in the fourth edition? Much has happened on the world scene over the past 18 years in international relations, politics, psychology, science, and technology, which is reflected in the leadership and leadership research that have appeared during these years. Increasingly, imaginative leadership is required. Globalization, climate change, and a single superpower, the United States, have become salient issues, along with the expansion and consolidation of the European Union. China and India have joined Japan as major economic powers and contributors to science and technology. The Arab world and the Middle East are now major players in international political life. Militant Islamists have spawned terrorism, civil wars, and massacres like the World Trade Center catastrophe of September 11, 2001, as well as overreaction by governments, particularly that of the United States. In reaction, national security has been strengthened with some loss to individual freedom. But a successful war on Al-Qaeda, the largest and best-organized network of terrorism, has been fought, reducing the network to small splinter groups still pursuing a philosophy of terrorism but lacking a central base and stripped of the means to easily communicate or coordinate their efforts.

In the 18 years since the publication of the third edition, the study, application, and practice of leadership have burgeoned. Business, government, and nonprofit agencies, plus community, education, military, and health organizations have increasingly made leadership a core concept in meeting the challenges of the last decade of the twentieth century and the first decade of the new millenium. There was a 100% increase in leadership research and applications in the United States and a 300% increase in management consultants during this period. Academic courses and curricula on leadership proliferated. In 1990, the same year that the third edition of the

Handbook of Leadership appeared, the *Leadership Quarterly* was first published, followed over the next 10 years by almost 200 new articles. Also new during the 1990s were the *Journal of Leadership Studies* and other new sources on leadership research, applications, and practice. The domination in leadership research and theory by the United States and Britain has changed, spawned by a growing diversity of publications from Holland, Sweden, Spain, and Russia. Japan, China, Korea, Singapore, and India have become other rich sources, along with Canada, Australia, New Zealand, and South Africa.

The subject index of the fourth edition reflects the emergence of new terms and concepts, some likely to be fads but others likely to survive as important innovations. Cognitive models of leadership have become as important as behavioral ones. Personal traits of leadership are back in vogue, bolstered by innovations in genetics. Leaders are both born and made. But situational differences remain of consequence. The "new leadership" of vision and transformation has become as important to leadership as the conception of leadership as an exchange of reward for following the leader. Also new are concentrations on strategic and virtual leadership.

In the last quarter of the twentieth century we saw a rise of interest in the charisma of those in everyday affairs and leadership positions join the interest in world-class figures, politicians, and CEOs. There was a spin-off and application to transformational, visionary, and value-based leadership. Empirical work was greatly expanded as a consequence of Robert House's 1976 theory of charisma and James Burns's 1978 exposition on transformational leadership.

Ralph Stogdill conceived the *Handbook of Leadership* and published its first edition in 1978. Soon after, he asked me to collaborate on the second edition but died before the work could begin. I carried on alone with the second edition, published in 1981 as the *Stogdill's Handbook of Leadership* and the third edition in 1990, published as the *Bass & Stogdill Handbook of Leadership*. This fourth edition still includes some of Ralph's work in two of its 36 chapters. In the final preparation, my wife, Ruth Bass, assisted editorially and applied her skills at research and use of the computer.

Illustrating the new developments are three new chapters added to the *Handbook*. Chapter 9 is dedicated to the ethics of leadership. Chapter 22 deals with transformational leadership. Chapter 24 focuses on strategic and executive leadership. In the same way, in addition to the updated chapters, many new sections address topics like heritability, accountability, authenticity, and virtual leadership. At the same time, space limitations required some reduction in pre-1990 content and details, but generally theories, conclusions, comments, and citations from the earlier literature have been maintained in the text and endnotes. Reflecting the changes in leadership research over the years, the fourth edition proportionally involves fewer short-term studies of leaders and follower relations at the micro level. More is presented at the macro level, of leaders as senior executives and heads of organizations, and the meta level of leaders of societies. Here, more effort has been made to include findings from political science, sociology, and history. As in the third edition, I have included content from prepublished and unpublished manuscripts and an increased number of paper presentations, especially from the annual meetings of the Academy of Management and the Society for Industrial and Organizational Psychology. Books used tend to be limited to those that have some research base and are not just anecdotal accounts.

Most compendiums on leadership like the *Encyclopedia of Leadership* (2004) are collections of essays from many authors selected by the editors. These have the advantage of having been prepared and published quickly; they present many different points of view. They are disadvantaged, however, by duplication and a lack of integration. The *Handbook of Leadership* has a single author, who hopefully has avoided duplication, included a sufficient number of alternative points of view, and provided a continuing integration of the literature. Unfortunately, much more time has been required for data collection, review, and writing.

The third edition, published in 1990, was handwritten, then typed and printed as galley pages and eventually page proofs. This fourth edition was written more efficiently on a personal computer. The file was sent to the publisher on CDs to provide the page proofs for publication.

Plan of the Fourth Edition

The fourth edition of 36 chapters is in nine parts. In Part I, the *Handbook* expands the beginning chapters from the previous editions, addressing the history, definitions, and concepts of leadership. These are followed by taxonomies, theories, models, and methods of leadership research. In Part II, the *Handbook* takes up the personal traits of consequence to leadership, including activity level, authoritarianism, orientation to power, and Machiavellianism. Part II concludes with an examination of the values and ethics of leaders along with their feelings of self-esteem and well-being.

Part III deals with the externalities that affect the personal performance of a leader. These involve the leader's accorded status and power. How the power is distributed, how conflicts are resolved, and the leader's authority, accountability, and responsibility are considered. The leader's use of reinforcement in the instrumental exchange with followers and the follower's impact on the exchange conclude Part III.

Part IV reviews the alternative styles of leadership and their effects on individual, team, organizational, and societal performance.

Part V is about the "new leadership" of charisma and transformational leadership. Managerial work and executive and strategic leadership begin Part VI. Situational conditions that affect the manager and leader follow. They include the impact of the environment and organization, the immediate team, the task and technology, stress, physical distance and closeness, virtuality, substitutes for leadership, and the transfer of leadership and executive succession.

Part VII concentrates on women and minorities as leaders, as well as leadership across countries and cultures. Previous editions concentrated on African Americans, but the fourth edition has expanded to examine leadership among many other minorities, ranging from what has become the largest group, Hispanics, to another large group, Italian Americans, for whom less leadership literature exists.

Part VIII is concerned with development, training, and education of leaders and their assessment, appraisal, and selection.

Part IX concludes the *Handbook*, with extrapolation from the previous chapters of trends, likely environmental changes, and speculation about the future of leadership and leadership research.

I have used many secondary sources in my research. These include books, reviews, commentaries, technical reports, unpublished manuscripts, and theoretical papers. I also benefited from early drafts of prepublication manuscripts sent to me before a lot of the good ideas they contained were edited out in the publication process. I indicate in the references both the secondary sources and original publications from which the secondary sources are derived. Many of these references are presented in the footnotes, though they are by no means exhaustive. By 2008, there could be as many as 100 different citations of a popular research replication. I have tried to credit all the primary and secondary sources and have also included in the references some works which were not cited directly in the *Handbook*. The earlier seminal studies of 1950 to 1980 were not followed by numerous replication. Rather, I have tried to cover many of the meta-analyses of these replications, which continue to appear into the twentieth century.

I began collecting and reading for the fourth edition in 1989 and worked fairly steadily on the project. I never expected that it would take almost 20 years to complete. The first draft of the third edition was handwritten and took nine years to reach publication in 1990. It provided a substantial background and history of leadership research and practice, particularly from the 1940s onward; much of it is included in the fourth edition, along with additional work I found for the era. This material should help to defray the opinion that the only good leadership research is that which recently appeared. I have been privileged to contribute to the leadership literature dating back to 1946, and some of my early work is as valid and applicable today as it was then.

Bernard M. Bass

PART

I

Introduction

Concepts of Leadership

A definition is a sack of flour compressed into a thimble.

RÉMY DE GOURMONT (1858–1915)

The evidence is all around us. It is in our daily lives—in our schools, businesses, social groups, religious organizations, and public agencies. It is in our local community, in our more distant state government and national government, and on the international scene. Leadership makes the difference. Leadership can be good, as when your sales manager calls his department together to point out that last month's quotas have been met but that a new competitor is starting to make inroads. It can be better, as when a political party leader sums up what she and her team feel will be needed to win an election. It can be best, as when a community activist senses and articulates the community's pressing needs and mobilizes the community into effective action.

Leadership has been built into the human psyche because of the long period we need to be nurtured by parents for our survival. Early on, we learned to follow the leadership of parents and their proxies for satisfaction of our needs for food and comforting. Our mothers or their surrogates became our leaders in early childhood. They still are. Fathers came next when they were recognized. With socialization, as we grew, peers and other significant people gradually took the place of parental leadership. How we think and behave as leaders and followers when we reach adulthood is still likely to be affected by our earlier relations with our parents, as well as by our genetic makeup. So it is not surprising that leadership is a universal phenomenon. The importance of parenting for human development and survival makes leadership the world's oldest vocation. Parenthood makes for ready-made patterns of leadership.

During the period of hunting and gathering, leaders had to be independent and strong to defend the sovereignty of their group of followers against marauders and natural disasters (Lipman-Blumen, 1996). The study of leaders advanced with the rise of civilization. All societies have created myths to provide plausible and acceptable explanations for the dominance of leaders and the submission of subordinates (Paige, 1977). The greater the socioeconomic injustice in a society, the more distorted the realities of leadership—its powers, morality, and effectiveness—in the mythology.

The patterns of behavior that are regarded as acceptable in leaders differ from time to time and from one culture to another, although we will find some surprising commonalities. Citing various anthropological reports on primitive groups in Australia, Fiji, New Guinea, the Congo, and elsewhere, H. L. Smith and Krueger (1933) concluded that leadership occurs among all people, regardless of culture, be they isolated Indian villagers, nomads of the Eurasian steppes, or Polynesian fisherfolk. Lewis (1974) determined, from an anthropological review, that even when a society does not have institutionalized chiefs, rulers, or elected officials, there are always leaders who initiate action and play central roles in the group's decision making. No societies are known that do not have leadership in some aspects of their social life, although many may lack a single overall leader to make and enforce decisions. Such shared leadership is now representative of many scholarly and practical ideas about organizational life in the twenty-first century, the age of information, when no one member of a group has all the expertise and experience to help the group to reach its goals.

Myths, Legends, and Religious Texts

Myths and legends about great leaders were important in the development of civilized societies. According to Joseph Campbell, early myths about heroic leadership had much in common. The hero went forth and brought back something of great value. Prometheus brought back fire. Moses went up Mount Sinai and brought back God's Ten Commandments. Myths mature into legends. Legendary heroes figure prominently in the Hindu *Upanishads* and in the Greek and Latin classics. In the *Iliad*, higher transcendental goals were emphasized: "He serves me most, who serves his country best" (Book 10, line 201). The *Odyssey* advised leaders to maintain their social distance: "The leader, mingling with the vulgar host, is in the common mass of matter lost" (Book 3, line 297). Plato's ideal leader was the philosopher-king. Exploits of individual heroes were central to the Babylonian *Gilgamesh* and the Hindu *Ramayana*. Leadership was of much interest to Aśoka, Confucius, and Lao-tzu. Leadership was the focus of certain medieval classics of western literature such as *Beowulf*, the *Song of Roland*, and the Icelandic sagas. According to Gemmill and Oakley (1992), the social concept of leadership is a myth that maintains a belief in the need for hierarchies and organizational leaders in society. This myth results in alienated, intellectually and emotionally deskilled employees and the magical desire for an omnipotent leader.

Religions offer many accounts of leaders as prophets, priests, chiefs, and kings. Such leaders served as initiators, symbols, representatives, and examples to be followed. In the Old Testament, Moses led the Hebrews out of Egypt, and Joshua led them to the promised land. Leaders such as Abraham, Moses, David, Solomon, and the Macabees were singled out in the Old Testament for detailed expositions of their behavior and relations with God and their people. God was the supreme leader of his chosen people; he clarified, instructed, and directed what was to be done through the words of his prophets and arranged for rewards for compliance with and punishment for disobedience to the laws and rules he had handed down to Moses. The gospels of the New Testament are filled with stories about how Jesus led his small group of disciples as well as large audiences. Saint Paul was the initiator of a multinational organization of churches. To the leadership of Saint Peter is attributed the founding of the Roman Catholic Church. In Islam, religious law provided the basis for the leadership of the ideal caliphate (Rabi, 1967). The Koran still undergirds the legal systems of Islamic republics. Gautama Buddha led his movement by his precepts and example.

From Myths and Legends to Early Histories of Leaders

From its infancy, much of the study of history has been the study of leaders—what they did and why they did it. What would the first histories of Herodotus, Thucydides, or Xenophon, written before 400 B.C.E., have been like without discourses about leaders, leadership, and followers? Over the centuries, the effort to formulate principles of leadership spread from the study of history and philosophy to all the developing social sciences. In modern psychohistory, there is still a search for psychoanalytical generalizations about leadership, built on the in-depth analysis of the development, motivation, and competencies of prominent leaders, living and dead.

Early Principles of Leadership

Written principles of leadership go back nearly as far as the emergence of civilization, which shaped its leaders as much as it was shaped by them. Written principles of leadership can be found in Egypt in the *Instruction of Ptahhotep* (2300 B.C.E.). Confucius and Lao-tzu of the sixth century B.C.E. discussed the responsibilities of leaders and how leaders should conduct themselves. Like J. M. Burns (1978), Confucius said that leaders must set a moral example. Like Argyris (1983), Lao-tzu declared that leaders must participate in and share ownership of developments. In developing their ideas about imperialism and public service, leaders of the British Empire turned for inspiration to the classics, such as the works of Cicero and Marcus Aurelius. Roman and Greek authors such as Caesar, Cicero, Seneca, and Plutarch, to name just a few, wrote extensively on the subject of leadership and administration. For instance, in his *Parallel Lives* of around 100 C.E., Plutarch (1932) tried to show the moral similarities between 50 Greek and Roman leaders: for each Greek leader there was a Roman counterpart. The mythical founder of Athens, Theseus, was matched with the mythical founder of Rome, Romulus. The lawgiver of

Sparta, Lycurgus, was matched with the lawgiver of Rome, Numa Pompilius. Alexander the Great was matched with Julius Caesar.

The classical Greek and Roman writers had considerable influence during the medieval, Renaissance, and early modern periods, when many people looked back to the classics for guidance. The Greeks and Romans influenced Machiavelli in *The Prince* (1513), for instance, and Montesquieu in *The Spirit of Laws* (1748). In his *Two Treatises on Government* (1690), John Locke wrote that what we would now call leadership had to reach beyond institutional authority to create and maintain a liberal society (Weaver, 1991).

America's founding fathers were well versed in all these texts and were aware of how autocratic and democratic leadership had succeeded or failed in the Roman, Venetian, Dutch, and Swiss republics. Plato's *Republic* and Aristotle's *Politics* figured strongly in their deliberations at the Constitutional Convention in 1787. The constitutional checks and balances among executive, legislative, and judicial powers owe much to these writings.

Written Concepts and Principles of Leadership

Written concepts and principles of leadership emerged early. Figure 1.1 shows the Egyptian hieroglyphs for leadership (*seshemet*), leader (*seshemu*), and follower (*shemsu*), which were being written 5,000 years ago. In 2300 B.C.E., in the *Instruction of Ptahhotep*, three qualities were attributed to the pharaoh: "Authoritative utterance is in thy mouth, perception is in thy heart, and thy tongue is the shrine of justice" (Lichtheim, 1973).

Chinese classics written as early as the sixth century B.C.E. are filled with hortatory advice to leaders about their responsibilities to the people. Confucius urged leaders to set a moral example and to manipulate rewards and punishments for teaching what was right and good. Lao-tzu emphasized the need for a leader to work himself out of his job by making the people believe that success was due to their own efforts.

The Greeks' concepts of leadership were exemplified by the heroes in Homer's *Iliad*. Ajax symbolized inspirational leadership and law and order; Agamemnon, justice and judgment; Nestor, wisdom and counsel; Odysseus, shrewdness and cunning: and Achilles, valor and activism (Sarachek, 1968). Later, Greek philosophers, such as

Figure 1.1 Egyptian Hieroglyphs for Leadership, Leader, and Follower

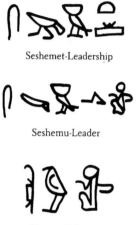

Seshemet-Leadership

Seshemu-Leader

Shemsu-Follower

SOURCE: Author

Plato, in the *Republic*, looked at the requirements for the ideal leader of the ideal state. Plato's philosopher-king was to be the most important element of good government, educated to rule with order and reason. In *Politics*, Aristotle was disturbed by a lack of virtue among those who wanted to be leaders. He emphasized the need to educate youths for such leadership. Plutarch, concerned with prosocial ideals about leadership, compared the traits and behavior of actual Greek and Roman leaders to support his point of view in *Parallel Lives* (Kellerman, 1987).

A famous Renaissance work was Machiavelli's (1513/1962) *The Prince*. Machiavelli's thesis that "there is nothing more difficult to take in hand, more perilous to conduct, or more uncertain in its success, than to take the lead in the introduction of a new order of things" is still a germane description of the risks of, and resistance to, leadership. Machiavelli was the ultimate pragmatist. He believed that leaders needed steadiness, firmness, and concern for the maintenance of authority, power, and order in government. It was best if these objectives could be accomplished by gaining the esteem of the populace; but if they could not, then craft, deceit, threats, treachery, and violence were required (Kellerman, 1987). Machiavelli is still widely quoted as a guide to an effective leadership of sorts, and he was the basis for a modern line of investigation using a "Mach scale" (Christie & Geis,

1970). In 1987, a survey of college presidents reported that they still found *The Prince* highly relevant.

Other famous works of the Renaissance include Shakespeare's plays, such as *Richard II*. As king of England, Richard made many mistakes in judgment, especially in his judgments of people, which alienated his nobles and ultimately led to his forced abdication and imprisonment (Payne, 2000).

Philosophy continued to contribute to principles of leadership. Thus a fundamental principle of leadership at West Point today can be traced back to Hegel's *Philosophy of Mind* (Hegel, 1830/1971), which argued that by first serving as a follower, a leader subsequently can best understand his followers. Hegel thought that this understanding was a paramount requirement for effective leadership.

The Modern Study of Leadership

Among the landmarks in the modern study of leadership are Terman's (1904) investigation of the psychology and development of leadership, Kohs and Irle's (1920) predictions of the promotion of U.S. Army officers, Freud's (1922) work dealing with group psychology, Weber's (1927/1947) introduction of charismatic leadership, Cox's (1926) analysis of the biographies of leaders, Moreno's (1934/1953) invention of sociometry, and Benne and Sheat's (1948) classification of roles in small groups. Leadership assessment centers began in 1923 in Germany (Ansbacher, 1951); they were initiated in Britain during World War II (Garforth, 1945) and by the Office of Strategic Services (1948) in the United States. By 1948, Stogdill (1948) was able to locate 128 studies of leadership, which he classified according to the traits of importance to leadership: capacity, achievement, responsibility, participation, and status. There were 124 articles, books, and abstracts on leadership published in English and four in German up to 1947 in the half-century preceding Stogdill's (1948) review of the literature (see chapter 4). In contrast, 188 articles on leadership appeared in just one journal, *Leadership Quarterly*, between 1990 and 1999.

In determining the leadership that emerged, Stogdill also found it necessary to consider the situation and the nature of the followers—their objectives and their need for leadership. After Stogdill, there was a paradigm shift away from research on the traits and personalities of leaders to an emphasis on the situation and context in which the leadership occurred. Stogdill himself maintained that the personal traits associated with leadership were still important, though their effects were modified by the needs of the situation. But most empirical researchers up to 1975 abandoned the search for traits and turned their attention to the situation. Another paradigm shift occurred in the late 1970s, with a rising interest in charismatic, visionary, and transformational leadership (Hunt, 1999) and a perspective that both personal traits and situations (including followers) were important in determining the emergence, success, and effectiveness of leadership. By the 1980s, traits had again become important for research, along with context.

Influence of Leadership Research on Popular Books and Management Techniques

Leadership is a widely discussed and popular topic. In mid-1999, 55,172 publications on leadership could be found in the Online Computer Library Center (OCLC). As of April 14, 2005, Amazon.com listed 18,299 books for sale on leadership in English, French, and Spanish. Google Scholar listed 16,800 books on leadership, 95,500 publications on leadership, and 386,000 citations related to leadership.

In the past, popular books on leadership consisted of hortatory advice to leaders based on a mixture of "armchair analysis" and unproven generalizations. The best seller *How to Win Friends and Influence People* by Dale Carnegie (1937) is illustrative, and is still used for confidence building, especially in workshops for public speaking and salesmanship. Dickson, BeShears, Borys, et al. (2003) selected 30 popular books on business leadership mainly written in the past 30 years such as *The One Minute Manager*, *The 7 Habits of Highly Effective People*, and *First, Break All the Rules*. Two reviewers prepared a summary of key points in each book. Much in common was found with the academic research literature on leadership. (This was confounded to some extent because some of the authors of the popular books were primarily academics.) Staw and Epstein (2000) looked at the effects during five annual periods on the largest 100 U.S. firms (in sales) of introducing three popular management programs: Teamwork, Total Quality Management (TQM), and Employee Empowerment. The firms' reputations were enhanced in news reports of the programs by the business press. The CEOs' salaries and bonuses also reflected the use of the three programs, but the firms' profitability remained unaffected.

Universality of Leadership

Leadership is a universal phenomenon in humans and is also observed in many species of animals, such as matriarchal elephants and patriarchal gorillas. Allee (1951) maintained that all vertebrates living in groups exhibit social organization and leadership. Koford (1963) observed that the relative dominance of two bands of monkeys encountering each other at an eating place was usually determined by the relative dominance of the leaders of the bands. Zajonc (1969) suggested that primate groups learn norms for the different status of members and their leadership. The norms are learned by group members, are stable but can be changed, and are complied with by the majority of members. Experimentation and observation in natural settings suggest that many groups of mammals learn strongly differentiated status hierarchies, which their members recognize and comply with. In primate groups, leaders obtain privileges that tend to bolster their dominance. Their presence is an advantage to the group in gaining possession of a desired territory and in expanding the area of free movement for the group. Whether these findings and similar results reported for packs of wolves and hyenas, elephant matriarchies, bands of gorillas, and pods of whales are relevant to understanding the human condition remains controversial.

Theory versus Problem Orientation

The earliest social science literature on leadership was concerned predominately with theoretical issues. Theorists sought to identify different types of leadership and to relate them to the functional demands of society. In addition, they sought to account for the emergence of leadership by examining either the qualities of the leader or the elements of the situation. Earlier theorists can be distinguished from more recent ones in that the former did not

consider interactions between individual and situational variables. Also, earlier theorists tended to develop more comprehensive theories than do their more recent counterparts. Between 1945 and 1960, students of leadership devoted more of their efforts to empirical research and, as a consequence, ignored various issues that earlier theorists regarded as important. But research on leadership became theory driven again from the 1970s on, although the theories involved tended to focus on a few phenomena and were less ambitious than those of the past. Empirical research increasingly tested hypotheses derived from a theoretical model. By the 1990s, advances in statistical analysis had made possible testing of multivariate models of leadership involving interactions contingent on leaders' and followers' traits and situational variables.

Empirical research on leadership in some segments of the population (students, military personnel, and business managers) was heavy, but sparse in other segments such as leaders of volunteer agencies, police officers, and health administrators. Because of growing employment in health, social services, and protection, there was an upsurge in studies of leadership among nurses, social workers, and the police. In the same way, the increase and upgrading of minorities in the U.S. labor force has resulted in an examination of leadership among women and minorities. Cross-cultural studies of leadership have burgeoned as well.

The emerging propositions about leadership maintain their validity over time in strong cultures. Nonetheless, they also are subject to change because of cultural changes. Thus, over 50% of more than 1,000 students from eight U.S. universities who were surveyed about their attraction to the television series, MASH, dealing with a medical unit in the Korean War, indicated that watching the program had modified their attitudes or behavior about organizational life. All but 5% considered MASH a realistic portrayal of organizational values and processes. The respondents felt an increased desire to work with superiors who treat subordinates with understanding and respect (Dyer & Dyer, 1984). Most of the coercive, tough, autocratic, bullying leaders in organizations of 1905 had been replaced by 2005 with leaders who may still be as highly concerned about getting the work done but also have concern for their followers. Much of the work itself has changed from unskilled labor to the application of knowledge, from repetitive tasks to more meaningful work, from individual work to team-work, from functional to project-based work, from single-skill to multiskill work. Coordination from above has decreased while coordination among peers has increased (Stein & Pinchot, 1995).

The Need for Leadership

Napoleon expressed his feeling about the importance of leadership in his quip that he would rather have an army of rabbits led by a lion than an army of lions led by a rabbit. Surveys of job satisfaction from the 1920s on illustrated the importance of leadership.[1] They uniformly reported that employees' favorable attitudes toward their supervisors contributed to the employees' satisfaction. In turn, employees' favorable attitudes toward their supervisors were usually found to be related to the productivity of the work group (see, for example, Lawshe & Nagle, 1953). Since then, countless surveys can be cited to support the contention that leaders make a difference in their subordinates' satisfaction and performance. For example, Becker (1992) found that compared with their commitment to the organization, employees' commitment to their supervisors and to top management was more highly related to their job satisfaction, their intention not to quit, and their prosocial behavior. Again, Becker, Billings, et al. (1996) showed that commitment by employees to their supervisors was more strongly associated with the employees' performance than was their commitment to the organization. Leaders also can make the difference in whether organizations succeed or fail. In the public sector, local government managers must be able to lead when angry, single-issue, negative minorities wish to take over public policy making about issues ranging from abortion rights to protective services (Abels, 1996).

Typically, efforts to estimate the number of leaders in the United States use census data on proprietors and officials. But Gardner (1986) noted that although owners, managers, and officials are in a position to do so, they do not necessarily act as leaders. Cleveland (1985) estimated the number of opinion leaders in the United States and how this number grew between 1955 and 1985. In 1955, he estimated that there were 555,000 opinion leaders; in

1971, he guessed that at least one million Americans could be classified as opinion leaders. He considered 7 out of 10 public executives to be opinion leaders—policy makers in public, philanthropic, voluntary, and large-scale private enterprises. By 1985, he estimated the number to have multiplied to one out of every 200 Americans. In the age of information—with the ever-present need for change to stay ahead of the competition, for learning from timely feedback, for teamwork, and for the introduction of new technology—the need for leadership at all organizational levels is apparent. On the basis of a field study of 12 large organizational reengineering attempts. Jaffe and Scott (1998) pointed out that without engaging the firm's leadership, efforts to reengineer, the operations will fail. Large-scale redesign requires leaders' and employees' commitment.

Need and Importance. It was the leadership of Robert E. Lee that enabled the Confederate forces to defeat the larger, better-equipped Union forces in many of the battles of the Civil War. It was the leadership of Henry V and longbow technology that produced the victory at Agincourt of 15,000 Englishmen over the 45,000 more heavily armored Frenchmen (Fiedler & Garcia, 1987). De Vries, Roe, et al. (1998) developed and validated a scale of "need for supervision" that can differentiate between conditions when employees need to be supervised and conditions when they do not. However, the effect of the need for leadership on the outcomes of leadership, though positive, is small (De Vries, Roe, and Taillieu, 2002). Supervisors do make a difference in employees' sense of equity in the workplace and are more important than issues of pay and long working hours (Porter, 1997). Leaders' vision, empowerment, and enabling of subordinates makes possible a highly adaptive, learning organization (Johnson, 1998). The Gallup Organization Workplace Audit, administered to 2 million employees in 61 countries, and supported by focus groups, identified five statistical factors associated with high-quality work environments. Two of these factors were one's immediate supervisor and the overall leadership in the firm (Gallup, 1995, 1998). Leadership was central to the success of Total Quality Management (TQM), which requires the support and commitment of top management (Shea and Howell, 1998). Some of the performance of football teams is beyond the control and ability of the coach's

---

[1] See also Viteles (1953).

leadership, but the coach can turn a consistently losing team into a consistently winning team—as Vince Lombardi did with the Green Bay Packers. Around the globe, leadership is widely required because of two antithetical forces: interdependence and diversity (economic, political, and social). But despite the importance of leadership, Conger (1999, p. 145) lamented, "A more competitive world forced many firms to reinvent themselves . . . (but) rarely did companies possess the courage to change management skills needed to orchestrate large-scale transformations. . . . The leadership talent necessary for such undertakings was . . . in short supply." Lipman-Blumen (1996) conceived a need for "connective" leaders who can bring divisive parties together by developing a sense of self-sacrifice, community, and common causes. Leadership is needed to change organizations. However, when De Vries, Roe, and Taillieu (2002) questioned 958 Dutch employees about how much they *individually* needed their supervisor to set goals, to decide what work should be done, etc., they found only modest effects on the relationship between the need for leadership and job satisfaction, commitment to the organization, stress of work, role conflict, and self-rated performance.

Caveat—Leadership is a Figment of the Imagination. Agency theorists (Meckling & Jensen, 1976) argued that an organization is a legal fiction that serves as the connection for contracts among parties. An organization is simply a network of individuals who exchange according to market conditions, rewards, resources, time, and skills. There is no distinction between leaders and followers. If there are no followers, there is no need for leadership (Arnott, 1995). Some critics have argued that all the effects of leadership are a romantic fiction, existing only in the eye of the beholder. Followers attribute to leadership effects that in fact are due to historical, economic, or social forces. Meindl, Ehrlich, and Dukerich (1985) presented five empirical studies of their concept of the "romance of leadership." In the first study, they demonstrated that among a total of 33,248 titles of articles in *The Wall Street Journal* between 1972 and 1982, 34 business firms in various industries, leadership was more likely to be emphasized in those years when the firms did well but not when they did poorly. Leadership also appeared much more often in the titles in the years that industries performed well rather than poorly. A sec-

ond study showed that the percentage of leadership topics between 1929 and 1983 in social science doctoral dissertations was greater after poor rather than good economic times. A third study found that the number of articles about leadership in business periodicals was also affected, but in the opposite way. The fourth and fifth studies demonstrated that students given various business scenarios were more likely to attribute large changes, up or down, to leadership rather than to alternative reasons for company success. Middling changes generated the least effect.

Other critics, such as Pandey (1976), have regarded the concept of leadership as useless for understanding social influence. Calder (1977) argued that the objective contributions of the "leader" to outcomes were possibly more interesting than true. Some critics attributed organizational outcomes primarily to other factors, but held that after the fact, leaders were credited with what happened. Organizational leaders who were perceived to be exerting leadership on organizational performance were merely the subjects of misperceptions. That is, organizational outcomes were objectively determined by environmental and organizational factors in which leadership, at best, could play only a minor role. For instance, M. C. Brown (1982, p. 1) concluded that "once other factors influencing effectiveness are accounted for, it is likely that leadership will have little bearing on organizational performance." Pfeffer (1977) took a similar but less extreme position: leadership is a sense-making heuristic to account for organizational performance and is important primarily for its symbolic role in organizations. Leaders are selected or self-selected to fulfill the fate of the organization and are highly constrained by organizational and external factors. Therefore, compared with external factors, they can have only a limited impact on organizational outcomes. Leaders are able only to react to contingencies, to facilitate the adjustment of the organization in its context, and to alter the environment to some limited extent. Also, they have no control over many factors that affect organizational performance. Typically, they have unilateral control over few resources.

Salancik and Pfeffer (1977) showed that the mayors of 30 U.S. cities had real influence on a just a few budgetary issues, such as libraries and parks, that were not in the domain of important special-interest groups, such as the police, firefighters, and highway maintenance personnel.

Seemingly influential leaders—political party officials, lobbyists, and contractors—often are followers, not leaders. Pfeffer concluded that since people want to feel they are in control of their environment, they find it useful to attribute their group and organizational performance to leaders rather than to the complex internal and external environmental forces that actually are most important. Meindl and Ehrlich (1987) showed that if performance outcomes of firms were attributed to the leadership of top management rather than to the employees, to market conditions, or to the government, evaluators gave better evaluations of the outcomes. Meindl and Ehrlich attributed this finding to the evaluators' assumption that leaders have a reliable and potent impact on outcomes. Even when the true causes of outcomes were logically not determinable, Meindl, Ehrlich, and Dukerich (1985) showed that there was a tendency to view leadership as the likely cause. This study and the one by Meindl and Ehrlich (1987) were thought to demonstrate that leadership is more of a romantic notion than a phenomenon that truly affects group and organizational outcomes. Support for the idea that leadership is a fiction was the evidence that would-be followers, subordinates, and groups of employees are so constrained by technology, rules, job requirements, and organizational policies that there is little discretionary room for a superior or leader to make much of a difference in how things get done (Katz & Kahn, 1966). Furthermore, subordinates may have much more effect on the behavior of their superiors than vice versa (Goodstadt & Kipnis, 1970).

Miner (1975, p. 200), a prominent scholar of leadership, was ready to abandon the concept of leadership, stating that "the concept of leadership itself has outlived its usefulness. Hence, I suggest that we abandon leadership in favor of some other, more fruitful way of cutting up the theoretic pie" (Hunt, 1999, p. 129). Miner (1982a) later recanted this statement but still maintained that the concept had limited usefulness because so much of the empirical research had been on emergent leadership in small groups rather than within more complex organizations. For Miner, the fragile, distressed leadership that arises in the small, temporary group to develop, maintain, and enforce the norms of the group may have little relevance for leadership in the impersonal "task system" of the traditional organization. Cronshaw and Lord (1987) found in a laboratory study that participants used simple cognitive rules of thumb to form their impressions of leadership. Bass (1949) showed that in an initially temporary, initially leaderless group discussion, ratings of members' leadership correlated as high as .90 with how much they talked in the discussion.

Leaders Do Make a Difference. Historians such as Arthur Schlesinger (1999) are mindful of how the course of history might have been changed by chance events in the lives of individual leaders. On a visit to New York in 1931, Winston Churchill was hit by an automobile while crossing Fifth Avenue. Suppose his injuries had been fatal. Would Britain have rallied in 1940 under Neville Chamberlain in the face of impending defeat by the Nazis? What if in 1932, an assassin's bullet intended for Franklin Roosevelt had killed him instead of Mayor Cermak of Chicago, who was beside him on the speakers' platform? Would his more conservative replacement, Vice President John Garner, have launched the New Deal? Would the country have shifted from isolationism to interventionism? Suppose Lenin had died of typhus when he was exiled to Siberia in 1897 or Hitler had been killed on the western front in 1916. Would the twentieth century have been the same?

Although there is some validity in Meindl's proposition that we wrongly attribute to leaders the success or failure of their groups, leaders do make a difference. It is not an all-or-none matter. An experienced expert group has less need for close leadership than a group of inexperienced novices. Posner and Kouzes (1996), after analyzing several thousand cases and surveys over a dozen years, found a consistent pattern of exemplary leadership practices. Leadership is not a "mystical or ethereal concept." Rather, leadership is an observable, learnable set of practices. Certainly leaders make a difference. There is no question about it. But, as noted by Henry Mintzberg, leaders often make a difference because they stimulate others (McCarthy, 2000).

The Role of Followers. Proponents of the follower theory of leadership of social and political movements, such as Rost (1993), argue that leaders find the parade of followers and get in front of it. These critics oversimplify. Social and political leaders discover what their followers need or should need, but the followers have not been able to articulate and mobilize for what they want. Leaders give voice and words to capture what is needed and mobilize others to follow. Despite skepticism about the reality and importance of leadership, all social and political movements require leaders to begin them. As Tucker (1981, p. 87) put it, "In the beginning is the leadership act. A 'leaderless movement' is naturally out of the question." This does not mean that *formal, institutionalized* leadership is required. Informal leaders can stir up a rioting mob. Organized slave revolts were initiated informally by leaders like Spartacus (70 B.C.E.) in Rome and Toussaint-Louverture (1792) in French Haiti. In fact, no leader in an institutional form appeared in the numerous peasant revolts from the sixteenth century to the nineteenth century in southern Germany. The same was true of journeymen's strikes during the eighteenth century. Leadership remained informal and egalitarian. Only in the middle of the nineteenth century did definite radical leaders like Ferdinand Lassalle emerge. Lassalle placed himself at the head of the German workers' movement and developed its explicit ideology along with the myth that he had founded the movement (Groh, 1986). This behavior is consistent with most cases of institutional development: Leaders determine the direction they will take. The early historical records of the British Royal Society in the seventeenth century illustrate that its secretaries were responsible for who joined the society and what kinds of science were sponsored (Mulligan & Mulligan, 1981).

Leadership May Be Critical to Organizational Success. Indeed, leadership is often regarded as the single most critical factor in the success of failure of institutions. For instance, T. H. Allen (1981) argued that the principal's leadership is the most important factor in determining a school's climate and the students' success. Sylvia and Hutchison (1985) concluded that the motivation of 167 teachers in Oklahoma depended considerably on their perception of the quality of their relationships with their superiors. And Smith, Carson, and Alexander (1984) found that among the 50 Methodist ministers they studied, some were more effective leaders than others. The effectiveness of these ministers was evidenced by the differential impact that their ministries had on church attendance, membership, property values, and contributions to the church.

In the business and industrial sector, leaders' effective-

ness is measured objectively by their organizational units' profit, profit margin, sales increase, market share, return on investment (ROI), unit productivity, cost per item produced, and cost relative to budgeted cost. Objective measures of effectiveness (and employees' satisfaction) also include safety records, absenteeism, voluntary turnover, grievances, complaints, requests for transfers, work slowdowns, and incidents of sabotage. Superiors', peers', subordinates', and customers' ratings and attitude surveys provide subjective measures of the effectiveness of unit leaders and their contribution to the units' processes. Product quality can be gauged by amount of required rework, number of rejects, and customers' complaints or subjective ratings (Yukl, 1998). Maccoby (1979, p. 313) concluded, from his observations of the manager as a game-playing politician, that the need of firms to survive and prosper in a world of increasing competition, technological advances, changing governmental regulations, and changing attitudes of workers requires "a higher level of leadership than ever before." Strong support for this proposition came in a study by Andersen Consulting's Institute for Strategic Change, which found that the stock price of firms seen as well-led increased 900% over a 10-year period. Stock prices of firms seen as poorly led increased only 74% (Bennis, 2000). When an organization must be changed to reflect changes in technology, the environment, and the completion of programs, its leadership is critical in orchestrating the process (Burke, Richley, & DeAngelis, 1985). Mintzberg and Waters (1982) examined the evolution of a retail firm over a 60-year period and found that a senior executive could successfully reorient the firm by intervening to change previous strategies and organizational structures. This finding was corroborated by Thomas (1988), whose data showed that over 60% of the sales and profits of British retail shops were due to changes in the top executive.

Leadership and Various Organizational Outcomes. Management and leadership do seem to have a substantial effect on some organizational outcomes. Thus when Lieberson and O'Connor (1972) examined the effects of top management on the success of 167 firms over a 20-year period, they found that these effects depended on which outcomes were considered. Senior managers had the greatest effect on profit margins but the least effect on sales; they also were of less consequence in capital-intensive industries. In the same way, Day and Lord (1986) noted that when confounding errors are controlled in studies of the effects of executive succession, differences in executive leaders can account for as much as 45% of their organizations' performance. Agreeing with Chandler (1962), they stated that historical analyses of changes of leadership over significant periods, demonstrated that leadership had a profound influence on an organization. Concurrent correlational analyses of a sample of executives and their organizations at the same point in time reach similar conclusions, although the effects are not as strong. Barrick, Day, et al. (1991) analyzed 15 years of data in 132 industrial organizations and found that high-performing executive leaders had a positive impact on their firms' new income, earnings per share, and return on equity. In a review of experiments in the United States on the productivity of workers between 1971 and 1981, Katzell and Guzzo (1983) concluded that supervisory methods seemed particularly effective in increasing output. In Sweden, Westerlund (1952a) observed that the high-quality performance of supervisors improved the attitudes and performance of telephone operators. Also in Sweden, Ekvall and Arvonen (1984) found that leadership styles accounted for 65% of the variance in organizational climate in the 25 units they studied. Virany and Tushman (1986) stated that the senior managers of better-performing minicomputer firms were systematically different from those of firms that performed poorly. The senior managers in the better firms had previous experience in the electronics industry and were more likely to include the founder of the firm, who still served as chief executive officer. Although most attention has been paid to industrial leaders as developers and builders, Hansen (1974) pointed out that the success with which a firm, such as the Ford Motor Company, closed a plant without much human dislocation depended on effective leadership.

Leadership has been considered a critical factor in military successes since records have been kept; that is, better-led forces repeatedly have been victorious over poorly led forces. Thus, not unexpectedly, morale and cohesion among Israeli and U.S. enlisted soldiers correlated with measures of the soldiers' confidence in their company, division, and battalion commanders (Gal & Manning, 1984).

Personnel of the Mississippi Cooperative Extension re-

ported that they felt less job stress if they saw their supervisors displaying more leadership in structuring the work to be done and showing concern for the subordinates' needs (Graham, 1982). In a study of 204 innovations in state programs, Cheek (1987) found that the governors came up with 55% of the innovations and the agencies with only 36%.

Effects of Presidential Performance. Studies by Tucker (1981), Hargrove and Nelson (1984), and Hargrove (1987) concluded that the style and performance of a U.S. president makes a big difference in what happens to legislation, policy, and programs. Successful presidents are more sensitive to the inherent politics of policy making. They define and publicize the policy dilemmas facing the country and earn widespread public and congressional support for their positions. They construct their policy agendas with the felt needs of the country in mind and create political support for their agendas; they also realize that timing is important (Tucker, 1981). But, like Jimmy Carter, they can fail if they push for what they deem to be right but what is not politically feasible and if they favor comprehensive integrated solutions, rather than incremental steps (Hargrove, 1987). Presidents can make decisions that are not implemented because they or their assistants do not follow them up. For example, as part of the agreement to resolve the Cuban missile crisis, President Kennedy ordered the removal of U.S. missiles from Turkey on the border of the Soviet Union. Six months later, he was astonished to learn that the missiles were still in place (Manchester, 1988). Although presidents spend relatively little time trying to make major reorientations in policy, they have an important impact on the smaller substantive decisions that affect larger overall strategies (Neustadt, 1980). History may be drastically altered by a sudden change in presidents. Before leaving Washington, D.C., for his fateful trip to Dallas, Texas, where he was assassinated in November 1963, Kennedy signed the first order for a phased withdrawal from Vietnam. On assuming office after Kennedy's assassination, Lyndon Johnson rescinded the order. The war continued for another decade.

According to Richard Nixon's "Silent Majority" speech in 1969, presidents may have to take an unpopular stand, but when they do, they can strengthen acceptance by explaining their reasons, soliciting support, and winning approval (Safire, 1975). Presidents also provide symbolic support for the development of norms, values, and beliefs that contribute to subsequent national and organizational development (Sayles, 1979). As Gardner (1988a) noted, for a society to function, its people must share beliefs and values regarding the standards of acceptable behavior. Bill Clinton, a popular president, was almost removed from office for violating standards of sexual propriety. Leaders can revitalize those shared beliefs and help keep the values fresh. "They have a role in creating the state of mind that is the society" (Gardner, 1988a, p. 18). They conceive and articulate goals that move people from their own interests to unite for higher ends.

Indirect Effects of Leadership. Often, the effects of leadership are indirect. For example, Katzell (1987) showed that although supervisors' direct influence on their subordinates was modest, they exerted indirect influence and improved the employees' morale by providing rewards, relating rewards to performance, and treating employees equitably. By increasing morale, these supervisors improved the employees' performance. Jongbloed and Frost (1985) modified Pfeffer's (1977) reasoning to argue that leaders still have an important general role to play. What leaders really manage in organizations is the employees' interpretation or understanding of what goes on in the organizations. The leaders manage meanings and, therefore, exert a strong impact on organizational outcomes. Jongbloed and Frost compared the laboratory director in one Canadian hospital with another director in a second hospital. The two had the same formal assignments, and neither of them had control over issues; but the first director successfully lobbied for the importance of pathology and persuaded the hospital administrators to allocate more funds for operations and budget than were allocated in the second hospital.

Relation to Development, Training, and Education. The importance of leadership is attested to by academics' and lay people's interest in leadership as a subject for development, training, and education (Campbell, 1977).[2] Although U.S. college presidents believe that our

educational institutions are reluctant to incorporate leadership education into their curricula (Cronin, 1984), the college landscape is not bleak. Quite the contrary. Gregory's (1986) survey of all known U.S. degree-granting institutions of higher learning found 53 that offered an academic course on leadership, 70 that made it possible to major or concentrate in the subject, and 181 that incorporated the study of leadership into an academic course or a student-affairs program.[3] These numbers increased during the 1990s. Undergraduate schools of leadership, such as the Jepson School, appeared—along with concentrations and certifications in leadership and research, such as those offered at Claremont McKenna College and Binghamton University. By the 1990s, leadership research and training centers such as the Center for Creative Leadership, the Center for Leadership Studies, the Kravis Institute, and the Drucker Foundation had appeared, as did journals such as the *Leadership Quarterly* and the *Journal of Leadership Studies*. The Alliance for Leadership Development promotes research on and the teaching of leadership and serves as a clearinghouse of information on leadership programs at universities and secondary schools, leadership development programs in the community, development programs for corporate executives, and continuing education programs for professionals.

Leadership as a Subject of Inquiry

The understanding of leadership has figured strongly in the quest for knowledge. Purposeful stories have been told through the generations about leaders' competencies, ambitions, and shortcomings; leaders' rights and privileges; leaders' roles, duties, and obligations; and leaders' successes and failures.

The importance of leadership is also demonstrated by its place in social science research. According to DeMeuse (1986), leadership has been a frequent subject of empirical research concentrating on the antecedents of

[2] Recognition of the importance to the notion of leadership and its development for all types of organizations is witnessed by the Alliance for Leadership Development, which includes the following members: American Leadership Forum of Houston; Association of American Colleges of Washington, D.C.; Association of Governing Boards of Universities and Colleges; Center for Creative Leadership of Greensboro, N.C.; Coro Foundation of St. Louis; International Leadership Center of Dallas, National Association of Secondary School Principals of Reston, Va.; and the National Executive Service Corps of New York. The Alliance's programs include the promotion of leadership-related conferences and publications.

[3] Details about these can be found in Clark, Freeman, and Britt (1987).

leaders' behavior and the factors that contribute to its effectiveness. Leadership is a featured topic in almost every textbook on organizational behavior (McFillen, 1977). Scholarly books on leadership and scholarly articles, reports, and essays form a considerable number of the total publications on leadership, as noted earlier.

Many schools of thought have existed, some simultaneously, since leadership first was studied. The early theorists explained leadership in terms of either the person or the environment. Later theorists viewed leadership as an aspect of role differentiation or as an outgrowth of social interaction processes. More recently, theories of leadership have focused on the mutual influence of leaders and followers. All this is as it should be. Theory and empirical research should move forward together, each stimulating, supporting, and modifying the other. Neither can stand alone. An elegant theory with no prospect of elegant data gathering is likely to be a sketchy theory. Early in a line of investigation, crude data and theory may be useful. Later, as understanding develops and practice improves, more stringent standards for theorizing are required (Bass, 1974).

The subject of inquiry has been changing over the years (Knights & Morgan, 1992). Small-group analysis of leadership has been giving way to organizational and strategic studies. Increasingly, empirical studies are about leaders and their strategies that create particular norms and values affecting organizational performance. The studies discussed in the chapters that follow are based on a wide variety of theoretical assumptions, methods, participants, and venues. Despite differences in the philosophies that guide them and the research methods used, there is considerable convergence of findings on many problems. This convergence, when it occurs, may be regarded as convincing evidence of the validity of the findings.

Caveat—Too Much Rehashing. An almost unanswerable question is the extent to which we pour old wine into new bottles when we propose "new" theories. For instance, Julius Caesar's descriptions of his leadership style in the Gallic wars in the first century B.C.E. are clear, succinct endorsements of the need for what Blake and Mouton (1964) conceived as 9, 9 style—a style that Fleishman (1953a) described in terms of strong initiation and consideration, and that some theorist will rename in the year 2050. When does a field advance? Are we beyond Caesar's understanding of how to lead infantry shock troops? In 1975, an unknown scholar of leadership declared, "Once I was active in the field. Then I left it for ten years. When I returned, it was as if I was gone only ten minutes" (Hunt, 1999, p. 129). Shortly after this pessimistic comment appeared, the new paradigms of neocharismatic and transformational leadership were introduced in the seminal publications of House (1977) and J. M. Burns (1978). They proved to be giant leaps forward for the study of leadership, as will be documented in chapters 21 and 22. Contrary to the criticism, according to House and Aditya (1997), the study of leadership has been truly cumulative.

Integration of Theories. The study of the dynamics of leadership was dominated by two broad themes. First, leadership was conceived as an exchange between the leader and the followers in which following the leader was rewarded and disciplinary action was avoided. Second, leadership was exerted through the leader's personality. Within this framework, emphasis was placed on traits, behaviors, and contexts. As we shall see, these have been integrated into many modern theories of leadership with practical applications to the assessment, development, and training of effective leaders, as will be described in Chapters 34 and 35.

My hope in this book is to catalog much of what is known about leadership and to suggest some of what we do not know and should try to find out. Although I agree with Burns (1978, p. 2) that "leadership is one of the most observed phenomena on earth," I disagree with Burn's statement that "it is one of the least understood." His position has probably become more optimistic since 1978, with the introduction into a good deal of leadership research of his original concept of transforming leadership.

More on the Meaning of Leadership. The word "leadership" refers to a sophisticated modern concept. In earlier times, words meaning head of state, military commander, princeps, proconsul, chief, or king were common in most societies; these words differentiated the ruler from other members of society. A preoccupation with leadership, as opposed to headship based on inheritance, usurpation, or appointment, occurred predominantly in countries with an Anglo-Saxon heritage.

Although the *Oxford English Dictionary* (1933) noted the appearance of the word "leader" in the English language as early as the year 1300, the word "leadership" did not appear until the first half of the nineteenth century, in writings about the political influence and control of the British Parliament. What was considered appropriate leadership changed as a consequence of the industrial revolution, first in the nineteenth century in England, and then in western Europe and America. Before the Industrial Revolution, shops were small and owner-managed, and relations were personal. The owners tended to be paternalistic authority figures. In the large factory system of the Industrial Revolution, the owner might be absent, the manager might be distant from the employees, and power over the employees rested in the shop foreman, who was likely to "rule his little kingdom as a tyrant, hiring, helping, firing and frustrating as he pleased. . . . The owners (and shareholders) were . . . impervious to the impact of factory life upon their workers, to the alienation and uncertainty, and degradation bred in these impersonal establishments" (Wiebe, 1967, p. 20). Economic rationality provided the rules of management and supervision, eventually softened by organized labor, progressive politics, and the Human Relations Movement. After the Industrial Revolution, in the age of information, concern for followers' interests by the leadership became mandatory in most establishments, large and small, in the developed world.

Defining Leadership

Different definitions and concepts of leadership have been presented in countless essays and discussions. Often, a two-day meeting to discuss leadership has started with a day of argument over the definition. Rost (1993) found 221 definitions of leadership in 587 publications he examined. Furthermore, the distinction between leadership and other processes of social influence such as coordination and control was blurred. Ciulla (2004) argued that Rost confused the issue further by conceiving theories about how leadership works as definitions. The many dimensions into which leadership was cast and their overlapping meanings added to the confusion. Representative of definitions of leadership in the 1920s was impressing the will of the leader on those led and inducing

obedience, respect, loyalty, and cooperation. In the 1930s, leadership was considered a process through which the many were organized to move in a specific direction by the leader. In the 1940s, leadership was the ability to persuade and direct beyond the effects of power, position, or circumstances. In the 1950s, it was what leaders did in groups and the authority accorded to leaders by the group members. In the 1960s, it was influence to move others in a shared direction. In the 1970s, the leader's influence was seen as discretionary and as varying from one member to another. In the 1980s, leadership was considered as inspiring others to take some purposeful action. In the 1990s, it was the influence of the leader *and* the followers who intended to make real changes that reflected their common purposes. In the first decade of the twenty-first century, the leader is seen as the person most responsible and accountable for the organization's actions. McFarland, Senn, and Childress (1993) considered six themes of leadership most appropriate for the twenty-first century: (1) Leadership is no longer the exclusive domain of the top boss. (2) Leadership facilitates excellence in others. (3) Leadership is not the same as management. (4) Leadership has a sensitive, humanistic dimension. (5) Leaders need to take a holistic approach, applying a variety of qualities, skills, and capabilities. (6) Leadership is the mastery of anticipating, initiating, and implementing change.

Hughes, Ginnett, and Curphy (1993) attributed the confusion over defining leadership to a lack of agreement about the major questions in the field of leadership and about the answers to them. There is a surfeit of definitions of leadership. Nonetheless, there is a useful body of knowledge about the subject, which can be applied (Church, 1998). Fleishman, Mumford, et al. (1991) identified 65 systems for classifying definitions of leadership, and there is sufficient similarity among definitions to permit such classification. The definitions most commonly used tend to concentrate on the leader as a person, on the behavior of the leader, on the effects of the leader, and on the interaction process between the leader and the led.

"Leadercentric" Definitions of Leaders and Leadership

"Leadercentric" definitions are about one-way effects due to the leader as a person. According to these definitions, the leader has the combination of traits necessary to induce others to accomplish a task (Tead, 1929).

The Leader as a Personality. The concept of personality appealed to several early theorists, who sought to explain why some persons are better able than others to exercise leadership. A. O. Bowden (1926) equated leadership with strength of personality: "Indeed, the amount of personality attributed to an individual may not be unfairly estimated by the degree of influence he can exert upon others." Bingham (1927) defined a leader as a person who possesses the greatest number of desirable traits of personality and character.

Leadership as an Attribution. Leadership may be conceived solely as a romantic figment of the imagination, used to explain why a group, organization, community, or nation has been successful. Or leadership may be conceived solely as the observable reason for outcomes that have occurred. The truth lies somewhere in between. André Maurois noted that the most important quality in a leader was to be acknowledged as a leader. Such acknowledgment is a matching of the traits and behaviors thought implicitly to be the characteristics of leaders (the prototype) and the traits and behaviors observed in the person acknowledged as a leader. Most people carry around in their heads implicit theories about what qualities leaders should have and what behaviors leaders should exhibit. When 378 undergraduates were asked what characteristics were needed for acceptance of a new leader by a group, topping the list were learning the group's goals, taking charge, and being a nice person (Kenney, Blascovich, & Shaver, 1994). For more than 15,000 respondents, the first four of 20 characteristics chosen to describe admired leaders were being honest, being forward-looking, being inspirational, and being competent (Kouzes & Posner, 2002).

Leaders as the Foci of Group Processes. Early on, definitions of leadership tended to view the leader as a focus of group change, activity, and process. Cooley (1902) maintained that the leader is always the nucleus of a tendency, and that any social movement, closely examined, will be found to have such a nucleus. E Mumford (1906–1907) observed that "leadership is the preeminence of one or a few individuals in a group in the process of control of societal phenomena." Blackmar

(1911) saw leadership as the "centralization of effort in one person as an expression of power in all." For M. Smith (1934), "the social group that expresses its unity in connected activity is always composed of but two essential portions: the center of focal activity, and the individuals who act with regard to the center." For Redl (1942), the leader was a central or focal person who integrated the group. As a nation develops, it needs a centralized locus for its operation, which can be achieved only by a single leader (Babikan, 1981). All important decisions and their implementation center on the cult of the leader, even when, as in parliamentary democracies, actual decision making is diffuse. The leader embodies the collective will. This single leader sorts out the essential problems, offers possible solutions, establishes priorities, and launches developmental operations.

J. F. Brown (1936) maintained that "the leader may not be separated from the group, but may be treated as a position of high potential in the field." Following in the same tradition, Krech and Crutchfield (1948) observed that the leader "by virtue of his special position in the group . . . serves as a primary agent for the determination of group structure, group atmosphere, group goals, group ideology, and group activities." For Knickerbocker (1948), "when conceived in terms of the dynamics of human social behavior, leadership is a function of needs existing within a given situation, and consists of a relationship between an individual and a group." In his book *If I'm in Charge Here, Why Is Everybody Laughing?* David Campbell (1992) suggested that no matter how competent and motivated a group is, it cannot be effective collectively without a central focal leader.

Chapin (1924b) viewed leadership as a point of polarization for group cooperation. According to L. L. Bernard (1927), leaders were influenced by the needs and wishes of the group members; in turn, they focused the attention and released the energies of group members in a desired direction. This emphasis on the leader as the center or focus of group activity directed attention to group structure and group processes in studies of leadership. On the one hand, some of the earliest theorists, such as Cooley and Mumford, were sophisticated in their concept of leadership. On the other hand, several of the definitions placed the leader in a particularly fortuitous, if not helpless, position, given the inexorable progress of the group. Leaders were thought to have to stay one step ahead of the group to avoid being run over. Centrality of location in the group could permit a person to control communications, and hence was likely to place him or her in a position of leadership, but centrality in itself is not leadership.

The Leader as a Symbol. Leaders serve a symbolic function and serve as representatives of their group to outsiders. They provide a way to simplify and find meaning in the group's external environment (Katz & Kahn, 1978). In doing so, leaders invoke symbols to reinforce the meaning of events and circumstances (Gronn, 1995).

Leadership as the Making of Meaning. Leaders provide understanding and meaning for situations that followers find confusing, ambiguous, unclear, vague, indistinct, or uncertain. They define reality for followers. Leaders provide credible explanations, interpretations, stories, parables, and accounts about what has happened, what is happening, and what will happen. They make sense of a situation for their followers. Leaders talk about values that are acceptable to the followers and that can guide their subsequent action (Gronn, 1995).

Leadership of Thought. This leadership is exerted through lectures, writing, or discovery by people like Darwin, Marx, and Einstein, whose original intellectual activities are profound and exciting (Clark & Clark, 1994).

Leadership as Purposive Behavior. One school of theorists preferred to define leadership in terms of activities or behaviors. These are the particular activities in which a leader engages in the course of directing and coordinating the work of group members. They may include acts such as structuring work relations, praising or criticizing group members, and showing consideration for members' welfare and feelings. For L. F. Carter (1953), "leadership behaviors are any behaviors the experimenter wishes to so designate or, more generally, any behaviors which experts in this area wish to consider as leadership behaviors." For Shartle (1956), a leadership act is "one which results in others acting or responding in a shared direction." Hemphill (1949a) suggested that "leadership may be defined as the behavior of an individual while he is involved in directing group activities." Fiedler (1967a) proposed a somewhat similar definition. For Heifitz (1994), leadership is adaptive work, the activity of mobilizing a social system to face challenges, clarify aspirations, and adapt challenges faced.

For Jacobs and Jaques (1987), leaders give purpose to others to expend and mobilize energy to try to compete. Outcomes are attributed more readily to the leader: thus when things go wrong, the leader is likely to be blamed and even removed (Hollander, 1986).

Leadership as Persuasive Behavior. Presidents Eisenhower and Truman emphasized the persuasive aspect of leadership. According to Truman (1958, p. 139), "a leader is a man who has the ability to get other people to do what needs to done and what they don't want to do, and like it." According to Eisenhower, "leadership is the ability to decide what is to be done, and then to get others to want to do it" (Larson, 1968, p. 21). And for Lippmann (1922), such persuasiveness is long-lasting: "The final test of a leader is that he leaves behind him in other men the conviction and the will to carry on."

Several theorists defined leadership as successful persuasion without coercion. Followers are convinced by the merits of the argument, not by the coercive power of the arguer. Neustadt (1960) concluded, from his study of U.S. presidents, that presidential leadership stems from the power to persuade. Schenk (1928) suggested that "leadership is the management of men by persuasion and inspiration rather than by the direct or implied threat of coercion." Merton (1969) regarded leadership as "an interpersonal relation in which others comply because they want to, not because they have to." According to Cleeton and Mason (1934), "leadership indicates the ability to influence men and secure results through emotional appeals rather than through the exercise of authority." Copeland (1942) maintained that leadership was the art of influencing a body of people by persuasion or example to follow a line of action. It was never to be confused with drivership—compelling a body of people by intimidation or force to follow a line of action. Odier (1948) differentiated between the value and the valence of a leader. Valence is the power of one person to strengthen or weaken the values of other persons—the influences exerted on others. Koontz and O'Donnell (1955) regarded leadership as "the activity of persuading people to cooperate in the achievement of a common objective."

Persuasion is one form of leadership. Much of what has been learned from studies of persuasion can be incorporated into an understanding of leadership. Persuasion is a powerful instrument for shaping expectations and beliefs—particularly in political, social, and religious affairs. The definition of leadership as a form of persuasion tended to be favored by students of politics and social movements and by military and industrial theorists who were opposed to authoritarian concepts. It was also the province of rhetoricians and communications theorists. Research on persuasion, persuasability, and communications paralleled research on leadership (W. Weiss, 1958).

Leadership as the Initiation of Structure. Several commentators viewed leadership not as passive occupancy of a position or as acquisition of a role but as a process of originating and maintaining the role structure—the pattern of role relationships. M. Smith (1935a) equated leadership with the management of social differentials through the process of providing stimuli that other people respond to integratively. Lapiere and Farnsworth (1936) observed that situations may be distinguished from one another by the extent to which they are organized by one member of the group. Such organizing is usually spoken of as leadership, with its nature and degree varying in different social situations.

Gouldner (1950) suggested that there is a difference in effect between a stimulus from a follower and one from a leader. A stimulus from a leader has a higher probability of structuring a group's behavior because the group believes that the leader is a legitimate source of such stimuli. Gouldner disagreed with C. A. Gibb (1947) regarding the notion that once the group's activity is dominated by an established and accepted organization, leadership tends to disappear. Thus Bavelas (1960) defined organizational leadership as the function of "maintaining the operational effectiveness of decision-making systems which comprise the management of the organization."

Homans (1950) identified the leader of a group as a member who "originates interaction." For Hemphill (1954), "to lead is to engage in an act that initiates a structure in interaction (pattern of relations) as part of the process of solving a mutual problem." And Stogdill (1959) defined leadership as "the initiation and maintenance of structure in expectation and interaction." Hemphill and Stogdill defined leadership in terms of the variables that give rise to the differentiation and maintenance of role structures in groups. Such a definition has greater theoretical utility than definitions that are more concrete and

descriptive to a layperson: it leads to the basic processes involved in the emergence of the leadership role. Again, what must be kept in mind is that leadership is more than just the initiation of structure. As Gouldner (1950) noted, we need room for acts of leadership in the completely structured group. Stogdill's (1959) inclusion of maintenance of structure is important. Furthermore, if structure is a consistent pattern of differentiated role relationships within a group, we must also be sure to consider persons, resources, and tasks within the differentiated roles. Much of chapter 20 is dedicated to initiation of structure.

Leadership as the Exercise of Influence. The concept of influence was a step in the direction of generality and abstraction in defining leadership. J. B. Nash (1929) suggested that "leadership implies influencing change in the conduct of people." Tead (1935) defined leadership as "the activity of influencing people to cooperate toward some goal which they come to find desirable." Stogdill (1950) described leadership as "the process of influencing the activities of an organized group in its efforts toward goal setting and goal achievement." The influence may be direct or indirect (Hunt, 1991). Shartle (1951a, b) proposed that the leader be considered an individual "who exercises positive–influence acts upon others" or "who exercises more important–influence acts than any other members of the group or organization." Similarly, Tannenbaum, Weschler, and Massarik (1961) defined leadership as "interpersonal influence, exercised in a situation and directed, through the communication process, toward the attainment of a specified goal or goals." This definition was expanded by Ferris and Rowland (1981), who conceived of the influence process in leadership as contextual influence that has an impact on subordinates' attitudes and performance through effects on their perceptions of their jobs.

The interactive aspect became apparent as leadership was linked by definition to influence processes. Haiman (1951) suggested that "direct leadership is an interaction process in which an individual, usually through the medium of speech, influences the behavior of others toward a particular end." According to Gerth and Mills (1953), "leadership . . . is a relation between leader and led in which the leader influences more than he is influenced: because of the leader, those who are led act or feel differently than they otherwise would." For Cartwright (1965), leadership was equated with the "domain of influence." Katz and Kahn (1966) considered "the essence of organizational leadership to be the influential increment over and above mechanical compliance with routine directions of the organization." They observed that although all supervisors at the same level of an organization have equal power, they do not use it with equal effectiveness to influence individuals and the organization. In the same way, Hollander and Julian (1969) suggested that "leadership in the broadest sense implies the presence of a particular influence relationship between two or more persons."

According to Hemphill (1949a), an individual's effort to change the behavior of others is "attempted" leadership. When the other members actually change, this outcome is "successful" leadership. If the others are reinforced or rewarded for changing their behavior, this evoked achievement is "effective" leadership. The distinctions between attempted, successful, and effective leadership are important because the dynamics of each are quite different. *Effective leadership* is *successful* influence by the leader that results in the attainment of goals by the influenced followers. Defining effective leadership in terms of attaining goals is especially useful because it permits the application of reinforcement theory to understand leader-follower behavior (Bass, 1960). "Emergent" leadership is a more widely used catch-all term for what occurs when leadership is attempted but may or may not be successful or effective.

The concept of influence recognizes the fact that individuals differ in the extent to which their behaviors affect the activities of a group. It implies a reciprocal relationship between the leader and the followers, but one that is not necessarily characterized by domination, control, or induction of compliance by the leader. It merely states that leadership, if successful, has a determining effect on the behaviors of group members and on activities of the group.

There is reciprocal influence between leaders and followers. In a dyad, if A influences B more than B influences A, A is leading B and B is following A (Bass, 1960). With regard to a larger group, Simonton (1994) suggests that the leader is the member whose influence on the group's attitudes, performance, or decision making greatly exceeds that of the average member. The definition of influence also recognizes that by their own example, lead-

ers can influence other members of a group. The Israeli lieutenant leads with the call, "Follow me." Leaders serve as models for the followers. As Gandhi suggested, "Clean examples have a curious method of multiplying themselves" (Paige, 1977, p. 65).

Leadership as Discretionary Influence. Numerous theorists have wanted to limit leadership to influence that is not mandated by the leader's role. As noted before, Katz and Kahn (1966) defined leadership as an influential increment over and above compliance with the routine directives of an organization. J. A. Miller (1973a) saw leaders as exerting influence "at the margin" to compensate for what was missing in a specified process and structure. Jacobs and Jaques (1987) conceived of and viewed leadership in complex organizations as "discretionary action directed toward dealing with unanticipated events that otherwise would influence outcomes of critical tasks at the actor's level." Osborn, Hunt, and Jauch (1980) focused attention on discretionary leadership as influence over and above what is typically invested in a role and typically required of a position. It is influence beyond what is due to formal procedures, rules, and regulations. Thus managers are leaders only when they take the opportunity to exert influence over activities beyond what has been prescribed as a requirement of their role.

Leadership as the Art of Inducing Compliance. Munson (1921) defined leadership as "the ability to handle men so as to achieve the most with the least friction and the greatest cooperation. . . . Leadership is the creative and directive force of morale." According to F. H. Ailport (1924), "leadership . . . is personal social control." B. V. Moore (1927) reported the results of a conference at which leadership was defined as "the ability to impress the will of the leader on those led and induce obedience, respect, loyalty, and cooperation." Similarly, Bundel (1930) regarded leadership as "the art of inducing others to do what one wants them to do." According to T. R. Phillips (1939), "leadership is the imposition, maintenance, and direction of moral unity to our ends." Warriner (1955) suggested that "leadership as a form of relationship between persons requires that one or several persons act in conformance with the request of another." For Bennis (1959), "leadership can be defined as the process by which an agent induces a subordinate to behave in a desired manner." According to Barker (1994), this definition is traceable to Machiavelli's ideas about leadership as a matter of controlling others.

The "compliance induction" theorists, perhaps even more than the personality theorists, tended to regard leadership as a unidirectional exertion of influence and as an instrument for molding the group to the leader's will. They expressed little recognition of the rights, desires, and necessities of group members or of a group's traditions and norms. This disregard for the followers and the group was rejected by various other theorists, who sought to remove, by definition, any possibility of legitimating an authoritarian concept of leadership. Yet, regardless of the sentiments of some behavioral scientists, one cannot ignore that much leadership is authoritarian, directive, and even coercive. Its effects are seen in public compliance but not necessarily in private acceptance. Nonetheless, compliance with the leader's point of view may be reinforced by identification with the leader and internalization of the perspective by the followers.

Defining Leadership as an Effect

The Leader as an Instrument of Goal Achievement. Numerous theorists have included the idea of goal achievement in their definitions. Several have defined leadership in terms of its instrumental value for accomplishing a group's goals and satisfying needs. According to Cowley (1928), "a leader is a person who has a program and is moving toward an objective with his group in a definite manner." Bellows (1959) defined leadership as "the process of arranging a situation so that various members of a group, including the leader, can achieve common goals with maximum economy and a minimum of time and work." For Knickerbocker (1948), "leadership exists when a leader is perceived by a group as controlling [the] means for the satisfaction of their needs."

Classical organizational theorists defined leadership in terms of achieving a group's objectives. R. C. Davis (1942) referred to leadership as "the principal dynamic force that motivates and coordinates the organization in the accomplishment of its objectives." Similarly, Urwick (1953) stated that the leader is "the personification of common purpose not only to all who work on the undertaking, but to everyone outside it." K. Davis (1962) defined leadership as "the human factor which binds a group together and motivates it toward goals." Cattell (1951) took the extreme position that leadership is whatever or whoever contributes to the group's performance. To measure each member's leadership, Cattell noted, remove him or her from the group, one at a time, and observe what happens to the group's performance. In a similar vein, as noted earlier, both Calder (1977) and Pfeffer (1977)[4] stated that leadership is mainly influence and is even attributed to participants after the fact. The attributions may be based on implicit theories of leadership (Rush, Thomas, & Lord, 1977). Implicit theories of leadership are what we expect leaders to say and do, the traits and behaviors we attribute to the stereotype of a leader. Offerman, Kennedy, and Wirtz (1994) reviewed the content, structure, and generalizability of implicit leadership theories.

For Burns (1978), Bennis (1983), Bass (1985a), and Tichy and Devanna (1986), leadership can transform followers, create visions of the goals that may be attained, and articulate for the followers the ways to attain those goals. Luis Muñoz Marin, former governor of Puerto Rico, said; "A political leader is a person with the ability to imagine non-existing states of affairs combined with the ability to influence other people to bring them about" (Paige, 1977, p. 65).

Envisioning goals involves intuition, fantasy, and dreaming, not just analytical, systematic, conscious thought processes. For Jack Sparks, the chief executive officer who transformed the Whirlpool Corporation, "the vision came after years of mulling over the kind of organization that Whirlpool could be, and after his constant interaction with people in other organizations and academics. The vision was his; and the strategic planning process became the vehicle for implementing that vision, not its source" (Tichy & Devanna, 1985, p. 138). Tucker (1981) observed that most current politicians must focus the attention of their constituents on short-term goals and programs. More statesmanlike opinion leaders are necessary to arouse and direct a democracy toward achieving longer-term goals, such as stabilization of the population, improvement of the environment, and arms control.

---

[4]Different definitions and conceptions of leadership have been reviewed briefly by Morris and Seeman (1950), Shartle (1951a, 1951b, 1956), L. F. Carter (1953), C. A. Gibb (1954, 1969a), Bass (1960), Stogdill (1975), and Schriesheim and Kerr (1977b).

Leadership as an Effect of Interaction. Several theorists have viewed leadership not as a cause or control but as an effect of group action. Bogardus (1929) stated that "as a social process, leadership is that social interstimulation which causes a number of people to set out toward an old goal with new zest or a new goal with hopeful courage—with different persons keeping different places." For Pigors (1935), "leadership is a process of mutual stimulation which, by the successful interplay of individual differences, controls human energy in the pursuit of a common cause." For H. H. Anderson (1940), "a true leader in the psychological sense is one who can make the most of individual differences, who can bring out the most differences in the group and therefore reveal to the group a sounder base for defining common purposes." The theorists in this group were important because they called attention to the fact that emergent leadership grows out of the interaction process itself. It can be observed that leadership truly exists only when it is acknowledged and conferred by other members of the group. Although these authors probably did not mean to imply it, their definitions suggested that this quality amounts to little more than passive acceptance of the importance of one's status. An individual often emerges as a leader in consequence of interactions within the group that arouse expectations that he or she, rather than someone else, can serve the group most usefully by helping it to attain its objectives.

Defining Leadership in Terms of the Interaction between the Leader and the Led

Leadership as a Process. This definition of leadership as a process is becoming increasingly popular. It concerns the cognitions, interpersonal behaviors, and attributions of both the leaders and the followers as they affect each others' pursuit of their mutual goals. For Northouse (2001), leadership is a process in which an individual influences a group of individuals to achieve a common goal. Leadership is not one-way but rather an interactive two-way process between a leader and a follower. Homans (1950) and Dansereau, Graen, et al. (1975) among many others, conceived the process as an exchange or transaction between the leader and the led. Such leadership can be enacted by any member of the group, not only the formally elected or appointed leader.

Leaders and followers can exchange roles during the process. Yukl (1994) defined leadership in organizations as influence processes that interpret events for followers, the choice of objectives for the group or organization, the organization of work to accomplish the objectives, the motivation of followers to achieve the objectives, the maintenance of cooperative relationships and teamwork, and the enlisting of outsiders to support and cooperate with the group or organization.

Leadership as a Power Relationship. Most political theorists, from Machiavelli through Marx to the academic political scientists of the twenty-first century, conceived of power as the basis of political leadership. For Machiavelli, leaders had to concentrate on what was under their control, not on what was controlled by others. Leadership was an effort to create and maintain power over others (Barker, 1996). The social psychologists J. R. P. French (1956) and Raven and French (1958a, b) defined leadership in terms of differential power relationships among members of a group. Power may be referent, expert, reward-based, coercive, or legitimate (see chapter 11). Power is "a resultant of the maximum force which A can induce on B minus the maximum resisting force which B can mobilize in the opposite direction." Similarly, Janda (1960) defined "leadership as a particular type of power relationship characterized by a group member's perception that another group member has the right to prescribe behavior patterns for the former regarding his or her activity as a member of a particular group."

M. Smith (1948) equated leadership with control of the interaction process. Thus, "the initiator of an interaction, A, stimulates a second participant, B. A asserts control by interfering with B's original course of action." The use of power is regarded as a form of influence relationship. Some leaders tend to transform any opportunity for leadership into an overt power relationship. In fact, the very frequency of this observation, combined with the often undesirable consequences for individuals and societies, induced many theorists to reject the notion of authoritarian leadership. Nevertheless, many of those, like Bennis (1970), who were most committed at one time to openness, participatory approaches, and building trust, faced the world as it is, not as they would like it to be, and came to acknowledge the importance of power relations in understanding leadership. The power relationship may be subtle or obscure: "a power relation . . . may be known to both leader and led, or unknown to either or both" (Gerth & Mills, 1953). Myths and symbols about the master-slave relationship may unconsciously influence superior-subordinate relationships in modern organizations (Denhardt, 1987).

Leadership as a Differentiated Role. According to role theory, each member of a society occupies a position in the community, as well as in various groups, organizations, and institutions. In each position, the individual is expected to play a more or less well-defined role. Different members occupying different positions play different roles. Birth and class may force the differentiation of roles. According to the leader of Ponape, Heinrich Iriarte, some Micronesians are born to rule while others are born to serve (Paige, 1977, p. 6R).

Leadership may be regarded as an aspect of role differentiation. H. H. Jennings (1944) observed that "leadership appears as a manner of interaction involving behavior by and toward the individual 'lifted' to a leadership role by other individuals." Similarly, C. A. Gibb (1954) regarded group leadership as a *position* emerging from the interaction process itself. For T. Gordon (1955), leadership was an interaction between a person and a group or, more accurately, between a person and the group members. Each participant in this interaction played a role. These roles differed from each other; the basis for their difference was a matter of influence—that is, one person, the leader, influenced; and the other persons responded.

Sherif and Sherif (1956) suggested that leadership is a role within the scheme of relations and is defined by reciprocal expectations between the leader and other members. The leadership role, like other roles, is defined by stabilized expectations (norms) that, in most matters and situations of consequence to the group, are more exacting and require greater obligations from the leader than do those for other members of the group. The recognition of leadership as an instrument of goal attainment, as a product of interaction processes, and as a differentiated role adds to the development of a coherent theory that fits most of the facts available to date. Leadership as a differentiated role is required to integrate the various other roles of the group and to maintain unity of action in the group's effort to achieve its goals. Newcomb, Turner, and

Converse (1965) observed that members of a group made different contributions to the achievement of goals. Insofar as any member's contributions were indispensable, they could be regarded as "leader-like"; and insofar as any member was recognized by others as a dependable source of such contributions, he or she was leader-like. To be so recognized was equivalent to having a role relationship to other members. Much of the research on the emergence and differentiation of roles pertains equally to leadership. As Sherif and Sherif (1956) indicated, roles are defined in terms of the expectations that group members develop in regard to themselves and other members. Thus the theory and research pertaining to the reinforcement, confirmation, and structuring of expectations applies also to leadership. Of all the available definitions, the concept of leadership as a role is most firmly buttressed by research.

Recognition of the Leader by the Led. Matching of the leadership prototype of traits and behaviors with face-to-face contact is required for a more controlled cognitive process. The matching is based on socially communicated processes (Lord & Maher, 1991). These implicit theories or social representations of leadership vary in different professional groups, as was shown when 257 French professionals were asked to define a person they thought best suited to lead a work group (Francois, 1993). Lord and Maher (1991) found a correlation of .83 between prototypes of leadership in business and finance but a correlation of only .18 between prototypes of leadership in business and sports. Similarly, they found a correlation of .80 between religious prototypes and educational prototypes but no correlation between religious prototypes and prototypes of leadership in the media.

Identification with the Leader. There is an emotional connection between the leader and the led. The leader provides an example to be imitated by followers. The aspirations of the leader become the followers' own aspirations (Shamir, 1991).

Leadership as a Combination of Elements. Naturally, some scholars combine several definitions of leadership to cover a larger set of meanings. Bogardus (1934) defined leadership as "personality in action under group conditions. . . . not only is leadership both a personality and a group phenomenon, it is also a social process involving a number of persons in mental contact in which one person assumes dominance over the others." Previously, Bogardus (1928) described leadership as the creation and setting forth of exceptional behavioral patterns in such a way that other persons respond to them. For Jago (1982), leadership is the exercise of noncoercive influence to coordinate the members of an organized group in accomplishing the group's objectives. Leadership is also a set of properties attributed to those who are perceived to use such influences successfully. Other definitions, such as Barrow (1977), have combined interpersonal influence and collective efforts to achieve goals into the definition of leadership. Dupuy and Dupuy (1959) added to this combination of definitions that leadership also involved obedience, confidence, respect, and loyal cooperation from followers. Still others defined leadership as a collection of roles that emerge from an interactional process. For Tichy and Devanna (1986), the combination of power with personality defined the transformational leader as a skilled, knowledgeable change agent with power, legitimacy, and energy. Such a leader was courageous, considerate, value-driven, and able to deal with ambiguity and complexity.

To summarize, the search for the one and only proper and true definition of leadership seems to be fruitless. Rather, the choice of an appropriate definition should depend on the methodological and substantive aspects of leadership in which one is interested. For instance, if one is to make extensive use of observation, then it would seem important to define leadership in terms of activities, behaviors, or roles played; its centrality to group processes; and its compliance with observed performance—rather than in terms of personality traits, perceived power relations, or perceived influence. But if an extensive examination of the impact of the authority of leadership is the focus of attention, then it would seem more important to define leadership in terms of perceived influence, control, and power relations. Nonetheless, 84 social scientists from 56 countries meeting in Calgary, Canada, in 1994 for the Globe Project (House, Hanges, Javidan, et al., 2004), despite their linguistic and cultural diversity, could agree on a combination of elements regarded as universal and elements more specific to cultures. They concluded that *leadership was the ability to influence, mo-* *tivate, and enable others to contribute to the effectiveness and success of the organizations of which they are members.*

Leadership, Headship, and Management

The concepts of leadership, headship, and management need to be distinguished from each other although the same person may be a department head and a leader of his or her department. The head or manager who is not a leader will plan but won't envisage an attractive future for the department. The head or manager who is not a leader will organize and structure the department, but won't enable its members to improve their performance. The head or manager will control what happens in the department but won't empower employees to make decisions. In 1950, a major complaint about leadership studies was that they concentrated on student leaders; in 2000, the complaint was that too many leadership studies focused on CEOs, managers, and administrators who were heads but might not be leaders.

Holloman (1986) conceived headship as being imposed on the group but leadership as being accorded by the group. C. A. Gibb (1969a, p. 213) distinguished leadership from headship as follows: (1) Headship is maintained through an organized system, not by group members' spontaneous recognition of an individual's contribution to group progress. (2) The group goal is chosen by the head person. (3) In headship, there is little sense of shared feeling in pursuit of the given goal. (4) In headship, there may be a wide social gap between the group members and the head. (5) The authority of the head derives from some power, external to the group, which he or she has over the members of the group. (6) The leader's authority is spontaneously accorded by fellow group members and particularly by followers.

Managers, executives, and agency officers must be both leaders and heads (Kochan, Schmidt, & de Cotus, 1975). In its conception, leadership can include headship. Defined more broadly, leadership includes the many ways it is exerted by leaders and heads and the various sources of power that make it work (Bass, 1960). With the broader definition, *heads* lead as a consequence of their status—the power of the position they occupy. Without such status, *leaders* can still gain a commitment to goals and can pursue arbitrary coercive paths with their power if their esteem—their accorded value to the group—is high. But then their esteem is likely to suffer. Status and esteem are not all-or-none qualities. In any group, members are likely to vary in both. Therefore, leadership may be distributed among them in similar fashion.[5] Although there is usually one head of a group, we cannot ordinarily attribute all leadership that occurs in a group to just its head.

An Evolving, Expanding Conceptualization of Leadership

It is not surprising that concepts and definitions of leadership have been evolving and expanding. In the first several decades of the twentieth century, leadership was considered a matter of impressing the will of the leader and inducing obedience. Currently, in the age of information, leadership is seen more as consulting and shared decision making. House (1995) noted a progressive broadening of the definition of leadership to include "contributing to social order, introducing major change, giving meaning and purpose to work and to organizations, empowering followers, and infusing organizations with values and ideology" (Clark & Clark, 1994, pp. 355–356).

Definitions can be used to serve a variety of purposes. The appropriate definition for a study of leadership depends on the purposes of the study (Bass, 1960). Yukl (1981, p. 2) concluded that "leadership research should be designed to provide information relevant to the entire range of definitions, so that over time it will be possible to compare the utility of different conceptualizations and arrive at some consensus on the matter." Either by explicit statement or by implication, various investigators have developed definitions to serve different purposes: (1) to identify the object to be observed, (2) to identify a form of practice, (3) to satisfy a particular value orientation, (4) to avoid a particular orientation or implication for a practice, and (5) to provide a basis for the development of theory. (The hope is that the definitions will provide critical new insights into the nature of leadership.)

The definitions indicate a progression of thought, although historically many trends have overlapped. The earlier definitions identified leadership as a focus of group process and movement—personality in action. The next definitions considered it the art of inducing compliance. The more recent definitions conceive of leadership in terms of influence relationships, power differentials, persuasion, influence on goal achievement, role differentiation, reinforcement, initiation of structure, and perceived attributions of behavior that are consistent with what the perceivers believe leadership to be. Leadership may involve all these things. Ciulla (1998, p. 11) noted that ". . . the problem of definition is not that scholars have radically different meanings of leadership. Leadership does not denote radically different things for different scholars. One can detect a family resemblance between the different definitions. All of them discuss leadership as some kind of process, act, or influence that in some way gets people to do something. A roomful of people, each holding one of these definitions of leadership, would understand each other. . . . The definitions differ . . . in their implications for the leader-follower relationship . . . [and] how leaders get people to do things . . . and how what is to be done is decided."

Applicability. Leadership research faces a dilemma. A definition that identifies something for the production supervisor or an agency director is not necessarily the most useful one for the development of a broad theory. Thus a definition that enables the researcher to identify a group leader—the person whose behavior exercises a determining effect on the behavior of other group members—may not provide much insight into the processes and structures involved in the emergence and maintenance of leadership in specific situations and conditions. But if the results of research are to be applied by the production supervisor, the agency director, or the military officer, then the definitions must be as close as possible to their ways of "wording the world" (Van de Vail & Bolas, 1980). A definition should do more than identify leaders and indicate the means by which they acquire their positions. It should also account for the maintenance and continuation of leadership. Thus few groups engage in interaction merely for the purpose of creating leaders and dropping them as soon as they emerge. For the purposes of this handbook, leadership must be defined broadly.

The introduction of the concepts of goal attainment and the solution of problems in certain definitions recog-

---

[5] More will be said later about defining the effects of leadership.

nizes the fact that leadership serves a continuing function in a group. But the definitions do not account for the continuation of leadership. The concepts of role, position, reinforcement of behavior, and structuring expectation serve better to account for the persistence of leadership. For the purposes of theory development, it would seem reasonable to include variables in the definition of leadership that account for the differentiation and maintenance of group roles. Finally, room is needed for a conception of leadership as an attribution that is consistent with the implicit theories about it that are held by the individuals and groups who are led.

Manz and Sims (1980, 1987) expanded the concept of leadership to "super-leadership" and "self-leadership." Super-leaders lead others to lead themselves. Teams are organized for production or service, and the former supervisors and technical staff serve as outside consultants to these teams. The teams decide what is to be done and how it is to be done. Leadership is shared among team members.

Finally, room is also needed for a concept of leadership as an attribution that is consistent with the implicit theories about it that are held by the individuals and groups who are led. As Ciulla (1991) suggests, definitions of leadership can be regarded as more like theories. Some of these, such as servant leadership, leadership as shared vision, and transformational leadership, will be introduced in the discussions of theories of leadership in later chapters.

As we will see, some principles of leadership are universal. They have been validated across different tasks, groups, organizations, and countries. Others depend on circumstances. A definition that is relevant for research on a broad theory may not be applicable to specific leadership—say, that required by a factory manager, prison warden, or priest.

Summary and Conclusions

The study of leaders and leadership is coterminous with the rise of civilization. Leadership is a universal phenomenon. It is not a figment of the imagination, although there are conditions in which the success or failure of groups and organizations will be incorrectly attributed to the leaders, rather than to environmental and organizational forces over which the leaders have no control. In industrial, educational, and military settings, and in social movements, leadership plays a critical, if not the most critical, role, and is therefore an important subject for study and research.

The years during and since World War II have seen increasing numbers of empirical studies of formal organizational leaders, in contrast to studies of informal leaders of small groups. Also, there has been less dependence on students as subjects. The period began with a primary focus on first-line supervisors. The focus then moved up to middle managers and administrators; and the twentieth century ended with substantially increased studies of senior executives. Again, as woman and minorities were increasingly appointed, elected, or self-selected to positions of leadership, studies of their performance as leaders increased, as did studies in health care, protective services, and other services in the past half century.

How to define leadership can generate long-drawn-out discussions, and such discussions have dominated the opening deliberations at many a scholarly meeting on the subject of leadership. Until an "academy of leadership" establishes an accepted standard definition, we must continue to live with both broad and narrow definitions, making sure we understand which kind is being used in any particular analysis.

Leadership is an interaction between two or more members of a group that often involves a structuring or restructuring of the situation and of the perceptions and expectations of the members. Leaders are agents of change, whose acts affect other people more than other people's acts affect them. Leadership occurs when one group member modifies the motivation or competencies of others in the group. Leadership can be conceived as directing the attention of other members to goals and the paths to achieve them. It should be clear that with this broad definition, any member of the group can exhibit some degree of leadership, and the members will vary in this regard.

There are many possible ways to define leadership. However, the definition of leadership should depend on the purposes to be served. Leadership has been conceived as the focus of group processes, as a personality attribute, as the art of inducing compliance, as an exercise of influence, as a particular kind of activity, as a form of persuasion, as a power relation, as an instrument in the attainment of goals, as an effect of interaction, as a differentiated role, and as the initiation of structure. Definitions can be broad, including many of these aspects; or they can be narrow.

A distinction may be made between headship and leadership. One complex definition that has evolved, particularly to help us understand a wide variety of research findings, delineates effective leadership as the interaction among members of a group that initiates and maintains improved expectations and the competence of the group to solve problems or to attain goals. Types of leaders can be differentiated according to some of these definitions, more often on the basis of role, function, or context.

2

Types and Taxonomies

A simple model of leadership may be a list of different types of leaders grouped according to one or more characteristics about them. Taxonomy classifies them according to their mutual relationships, similarities, and differences. The model or taxonomy describes but does not explain the relationships, as would a theory. U.S. presidents, state governors, and city mayors form a threefold taxonomy If the three categories are divided into Republican and Democratic, we obtain a more complex sixfold classification or taxonomy of Republican and Democratic presidents, governors, and mayors. This classification can be used to show how the different types of political leaders react, say, to pressures from their respective constituencies. A taxonomy is formed. Taxonomies are classifications in an ordered arrangement of types.

After defining leadership, earlier scholars usually developed a handy classification. This was either a simple typing of leaders or a multilayered taxonomy with formal rules for classifying the leaders by their roles, perceptions, cognitions, behaviors, traits, characteristics, qualities, and abilities. In *The Republic*, Plato offered three types of leaders of the polity: (1) the *philosopher-statesman*, to rule the republic with reason and justice; (2) the *military commander*, to defend the state and enforce its will; and (3) the *businessman*, to provide for citizens' material needs and to satisfy their lower appetites. This early taxonomy has been followed by a long line of taxonomies of leadership, some of which are probably being formulated at this moment by popularizers of the subject for sale in airport bookstores or for presentation in the popular press. A respite from new leadership typologies is unlikely in the foreseeable future, for although typologies lack rigor, they are appealing, convenient, and easy to discuss, comprehend, and remember.

One typology that continues to survive is formal versus informal leaders. *Formal* leaders are in positions that provide them with legitimacy and the power to lead. *Informal* leaders influence others as a consequence of their personal attributes and the esteem they are accorded. Compared with formal leaders, informal leaders are seen to be somewhat more communicative, relations-oriented, authentic, and self-confident (Pielstick, 2000). Informal leaders may emerge in newly formed small groups without structure—in street gangs, in small groups of friends, and in organizations independently of their positions (Bryman, 1992).

Different types of leaders have been studied. Many attempts have been made to extrapolate conclusions from one special type of leader and organization studied to leadership in general. The types of leaders studied have included task and team leaders as well as emergent, elected, or appointed small-group leaders. Early on, leaders of informal crowds and demonstrations were described. Some of the leaders studied in larger organizations have included college presidents, chief executive officers, military officers, school principals, student leaders, technical leaders, hospital and nursing administrators, and religious leaders—and have included leaders of revolutionaries, juvenile delinquents, criminals, and terrorists. Managers at all levels of business and industry, consumer-opinion leaders, work teams, minority leaders, women leaders, public officials, athletic leaders, child and adolescent leaders, leaders of social movements, political leaders, and administrators at all levels of various public agencies and private institutions have also been considered. Taxonomies have been created within and among these types.

Types of Leadership in Small Groups

Leaders of small groups have been classified in many ways, according to their different functions, roles, and behaviors. Pigors (1936) observed that leaders in group work tend to act either as masters or as educators. Cattell and Stice (1954) identified four types of leaders in experimental groups: (1) *persistent, momentary problem solvers*, who have a high rate of interaction; (2) *salient* leaders, who observers think exert the most powerful influence on the group; (3) *sociometric* leaders, who are nominated by their peers; and (4) *elected* leaders. Bales and Slater (1955) observed that the leader performs two essential functions; the first is associated with productivity, and the second is concerned with the socioemotional support of the group members.

Benne and Sheats (1948) proposed that group members who exert leadership play three types of functional roles: (1) group-task roles, such as *initiator, gatekeeper,* and *summarizer;* (2) group-building and group-maintenance roles, such as *harmonizer, supporter,* and *tension reducer;* and (3) individual roles, such as *blocker, pleader,* and *monopolizer.* Bales (1958a) noted that the first two roles are the major functions of leadership in small experimental groups. For Hemphill (1949a), the leader's behavior could be typed according to how much he or she set group goals with the members, helped them to reach the goals, coordinated their efforts, helped them fit into the group, expressed interest in the group, and showed humanness.

From another point of view, Roby (1961) developed a mathematical model of the functions of leadership that was based on response units and information load and developed the following classification of leadership functions: (1) to bring about congruence of goals among the members; (2) to balance the group's resources and capabilities with environmental demands; (3) to provide group structure that would focus information effectively on solving the problem; and (4) to make certain that all needed information is available at a decision center when required.

According to Schutz (1961b), the functions of leadership could be classified as follows: (1) to establish and recognize a hierarchy of group goals and values; (2) to recognize and integrate the various cognitive styles that exist in the group; (3) to maximize the utilization of group members' abilities; and (4) to help members resolve problems that involve adapting to external realities as well as the fulfillment of interpersonal needs.

S. Levine (1949) identified four types of leaders: (1) the *charismatic* leader, who helps the group rally around a common aim but tends to be dogmatically rigid; (2) the *organizational* leader, who emphasizes effective action and tends to drive people; (3) the *intellectual* leader, who usually lacks skill in attracting people; and (4) the *informal* leader, who tends to adapt his or her style of performance to the group's needs.

Clarke (1951) proposed three types of leaders applicable to small groups: (1) *popular* leaders, who wield influence because of their unique combination of personality traits or ability; (2) *group* leaders, who, through their understanding of personality, enable group members to achieve satisfying experiences; and (3) *indigenous* leaders, who arise in a specific situation when group members seek support and guidance.

Getzels and Guba (1957) offered three types of leadership, two of which are associated with separate dimensions of group activity: (1) *nomothetic* leadership, which is involved with the roles and expectations that define the normative dimensions of activity in groups; (2) *ideographic* leadership, which is associated with the individual needs and dispositions of members that define the personal dimensions of group activity; and (3) *synthetic* leadership, which reconciles the conflicting demands that arise from the two contrasting subgroups within a group. Bowers and Seashore (1967) maintained that the functions of leadership are support of members, facilitation of interaction and of work, and emphasis on goals. Cattell (1957) observed that the leader performs the following functions: maintaining the group, upholding roles and status satisfaction, maintaining task satisfaction, keeping ethical (norm) satisfaction, selecting and clarifying goals, and finding and clarifying means of attaining goals.

Using a factor analysis of behavioral ratings, Oliverson (1976) identified four types of leaders in 24 encounter groups: (1) *technical,* (2) *charismatic,* (3) *caring-interpersonal,* and (4) *peer-oriented.* The *technical leader* emphasizes a cognitive approach; the *charismatic* leader stresses his or her own impressive attributes; and types 3 and 4 accentuate the facilitation of interpersonal relations with caring and friendship.

After observing 16 group-therapy leaders of various theoretical persuasions, Lieberman, Yalom, and Miles (1973) formulated three types of group leaders: (1) *charismatic energizers,* who emphasize stimulation; (2) *providers,* who exhibit high levels of cognitive behavior and caring; and (3) *social engineers,* who stress management of the group as a social system for finding intellectual meaning. Three other styles—*impersonal, manager,* and *laissez-faire*—were variants of the initial three. Therapeutic change in participants was highest with providers and lowest with managers. Casualties were highest with energizers and impersonals and lowest with providers. Again from observations of therapy groups, Redl (1948) suggested that the leader may play the role of *patriarch, tyrant, ideal, scapegoat, organizer, seducer, hero,* and *bad* or *good influence.*

Komaki, Zlotnick, and Jensen (1986) provided a sophisticated and rigorous approach to classifying the behavior of leaders on the basis of a minute-by-minute time sampling of coded observations in a small-group setting. Their taxonomy, which was constructed to provide observers a way to categorize specific supervisory behaviors, includes seven categories. The first three categories are derived from operant-conditioning theory; they are related to effective supervision: (1) consequences of supervisees' performance, indicating knowledge of performance; (2) monitors of performance, involving collecting information; (3) performance antecedents, providing instructions for performance; (4) "own performance," referring to the supervisor's performance; (5) "work-related," referring to work but not performance; (6) "non-work-related," not pertaining to work; and (7) solitary, not interacting with others. The categories are linked, as shown in Figure 2.1.

Analyses of the behavior of leaders have also produced many other categorizations of such behavior in small groups (e.g., Reaser, Vaughan, & Kriner, 1974). Much of the leadership in small groups has relevance for groups within larger organizations and institutions.

Types of Leadership in Organizations and Institutions

Presentations of types of leaders in organizations and institutions coincided with the appearance of essays on effective management. J. H. Burns (1934) proposed the following types: the *intellectual,* the *business* type, the *adroit diplomat,* the leader of small groups, the mass leader, and the administrator.

Bogardus (1918) distinguished four types of organizational and institutional leaders: (1) the *autocratic* type, who rises to office in a powerful organization; (2) the

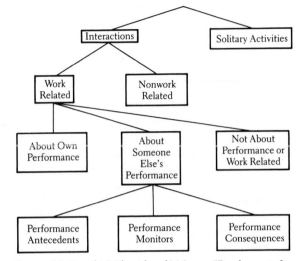

Figure 2.1 Operant Taxonomy of Supervisory Behavior

SOURCE: J. L. Komaki, S. Zlotnick, and M. Jensen, "Development of an Operant Based Taxonomy and Observational Index of Supervisory Behavior," *Journal of Applied Psychology,* 1986. Copyright 1986 by the American Psychological Association. Reprinted by permission of the publisher and author.

democratic type, who represents the interests of a group; (3) the *executive* type, who is granted leadership because he or she is able to get things done; and (4) the reflective-intellectual type, who may find it difficult to recruit a large following.

Sanderson and Nafe (1929) proposed four types of leaders: (1) the *static* leader is a professional or scientific person of distinction whose work influences the thoughts of others; (2) the *executive* leader exercises control through the authority and power of position; (3) the *professional* leader stimulates followers to develop and use their own abilities; (4) the *group* leader represents the interests of group members.

Chapin (1924a) differentiated *political-military* from *socialized* leaders. Political-military leaders imbue the masses with their personality; socialized leaders influence their followers to identify themselves with the common program or movement.

In Bartlett's (1926) threefold classification: (1) *institutional* leaders are established by virtue of the prestige of their position; (2) *dominative* types gain and maintain their position through the use of power and influence; and (3) *persuasive* types exercise influence through their ability to sway the sentiments of followers and to induce them to action.

In seminal German publications in 1921 and 1922, Weber (1947) delineated three types of legitimate authority in organizations and institutions, each associated with a specific type of leadership: (1) *bureaucratic* leaders operate with a staff of deputized officials and are supported by legal authority based on rational grounds. Their authority rests on belief in the legality of normative rules and in the right of those who are elevated to authority under such rules to issue commands; (2) *patrimonial* leaders operate with a staff of family relatives rather than officials. They are supported by traditional authority that rests on the sanctity of immemorial traditions and the legitimacy of status of those who exercise authority under them; (3) *charismatic* leaders operate with a staff of disciples, enthusiasts, and perhaps bodyguards. Such leaders tend to sponsor causes and revolutions and are supported by charismatic authority that rests on devotion to the sanctity, heroism, or inspirational character of the leaders and on the normative patterns revealed or ordained by them. House and Adidas (1995) equated *charismatic* with *transformational* leaders; but Bass (1985a) suggested that charismatic and inspirational leaders formed a single factor differentiated from the transformational factors of *intellectual stimulation* and *individualized consideration*. Jennings (1960) typed these charismatic and patrimonial leaders differently. The great men who break rules and value creativity are *supermen*; those who are dedicated to great and noble causes are *heroes*; and those who are motivated principally to dominate others are *princes*. Princes may maximize the use of their raw power, or they may be great manipulators. Heroes come in many varieties, including heroes of labor, consumption, and production; risk-taking heroes; and war heroes. Supermen may or may not seek power to dominate others.

Several commentators have noted that types of leadership are classifiable according to the model of organization in which the leadership occurs. Golembiewski (1967) proposed that the *collegial* model of organization permits leadership to pass from individual to individual at the same level in the organization. The *traditional* model implies that leadership is retained within the positions established by a hierarchy of authoritative relationships.

Influenced by Burns and Stalker (1961), Sedring (1969) suggested that political leaders in the adaptive, *or-ganismic* model of organization are characterized by interdependence, evolutionary change, and domination by factors that involve the whole organization of which their unit is a part.[1] In the rule-based *mechanistic* model of organization, leaders are classified by a lack of integration, by conflict in relationships, and by dominance by factors in their own units. Morrow and Stern (1988) typed managers according to their performance in assessment programs.[2] The *stars* were smart, sensitive, social, self-assured, sustained self-starters. The next best in assessments were the *adversaries*, who were able, analytic, argumentative, adamant, abrupt, and abrasive. The least adequate, according to their assessment, were the persevering, painstaking *producers* and the *phantoms* (polite, passive, and perturbed).

On the basis of John Dewey's philosophy and a search of the literature, Lippitt (1999) proposed six types of leaders of organizations, according to their priorities: (1) *inventor* (developing new ideas, products, and services); (2) *catalyst* (gaining market share and customers); (3) *developer* (creating systems for high performance); (4) *performer* (improving processes for effective use of resources; (5) *protector* (building a committed workforce and supporting values, identity, and culture); (6) *challenger* (identifying strategic options and positioning the organization for the future).

Maccoby (1979) posited three ideal types of leaders of business and industry in a longer view of production in the United States in the past 200 years: (1) *craftsman*, (2) *jungle fighter*, and (3) *gamesman*. These types matched the ideals of the prevailing social character of the time, which was linked to the mode of production then dominant and the leaders' functions in production and service. The independent craftsman was the prototypical social character in Jefferson's idealized democracy of farmers, craftsmen, and small businessmen. Leaders were independent lawyers, physicians, small businessmen, and farmers. They espoused egalitarian, autonomous, disciplined, and self-reliant virtues. After the Civil War, the paternalistic empire builder came to the fore, reflecting the rags-to-riches entrepreneurial spirit of Horatio Alger's stories. In this post-1865 social and economic environment, "ambitious boys had to find new fathers who had mastered the new chal-

---

[1] See glossary for definition of organismic.
[2] See Chapter 35.

lenges. The *paternalistic* leader . . . appealed to the immigrant . . . in need of a patron. . . . The still independent craftsmen . . . were forced into increasingly routinized factory jobs [and] struggled [by unionizing] against the paternalistic *jungle fighter*" (Maccoby, 1979, p. 308). The second ideal leader, the empire builder, the lionlike jungle fighter with patriarchal power, gave way to the third ideal, the *gamesman*. The gamesman emerged in the twentieth century when social character became more self-affirmative and the spirit more meritocratic. Adventurous and ambitious but fair and flexible leadership became the dominant ideal. "With a boyish, informal style, . . . [the gamesman] controls subordinates by persuasion, enthusiasm, and seduction rather than heavy and humiliating commands. Fair but detached, the gamesman has welcomed the era of rights and equal opportunity as both a fair and an efficient climate for moving the 'best' to the 'top' " (Maccoby, 1979, p. 309). The gamesman enjoys challenges and is daring, willing to innovate and to take risks (Maccoby, 1976). But the gamesman can become a liability to a firm when one person's gain can be another person's loss. Leadership is needed that values caring and the assurance that no one will be penalized for cooperation. Both sacrifice and reward need to be shared equitably (Maccoby, 1981).

In U.S. industry, *task-oriented* leaders dominated production in the 1940s, when everything that was produced could be easily sold. In the 1950s, these leaders gave way to *relations-oriented* leaders, who had to find markets for what was produced in an "other-oriented" nation of conformists. For a nation that next turned inward, *self-oriented* leaders emerged in the late 1960s and 1970s during the "me too" generation of drugs and flower children. Between 1980 and 2005, increased task-orientation was reflected in the start-ups in electronics and biotech firms coupled with increased relations-orientation to family and increased scandalous self-oriented, self-serving behavior in business and government, and then a turning inward toward spirituality and religiosity.

Executive Characteristics. Zaccaro (1996) used job analyses and psychological assessments to categorize required characteristics and skills for the executive position: *cognitive capacities and skills* (intelligence, analytical reasoning, ability to integrate complexities flexibly, verbal skills, writing skills, and creativity); *social capac-*

ities and skills (social reasoning, behavioral flexibilty, and skills in negotiation, persuasion, and conflict management); *personality traits* (openness, curiosity, self-discipline, flexibility, willingness to take risks, and inner locus of control); *motivation* (self-efficacy, need for achievement, need for socialized power); *expertise and knowledge,* and *metacognitive skills* (the ability to construct problems, encode information, specify categories, combine and reorganize best-fitting categories, evaluate ideas, implement, and monitor) were required. Also required was the need to know when to apply these skills (Mumford, Zaccaro, Harding, et al., 1993).

Leaders of Crowds. Leaders of mobs and crowds were the first to be given social psychological classification. LeBon (1897) described the crowd leader as a persuasive person of action whose intense faith and earnestness resist all reasoning and impel the mob to follow. Influenced by LeBon (1897), Conway (1915) observed three types of crowd leaders: (1) the "crowd-compeller" inflames followers with his or her point of view; (2) the "crowd-exponent" senses what the crowd desires and gives expression to it; and (3) the "crowd-representative" merely voices the already formed opinions of the crowd.

Since these early views about leadership of a crowd, spontaneous crowds have frequently been replaced by organized demonstrations complete with television reporters. In such demonstrations, the leader must add considerable administrative effort to this overall performance; usually, the leader here is Conway's third type—the crowd-representative—speaking to the already converted. Advanced planning as to time and place are important for the mobilization to be effective.

Student Leaders. As a result of observations and interviews, Spaulding (1934) classified elected student leaders into the following five types: (1) the social climber, (2) the intellectual success, (3) the good fellow, (4) the big athlete, and (5) the leader in student activities. From then on, the typing of student leaders as social, political, athletic, or intellectual became a common practice.

Educational Leaders. Typologies of educational leaders have included teachers, principals, and staff members in elementary, middle, and high schools. Likewise, studies have been completed of students, faculty members, department chairs, deans, presidents, and administrative leaders in colleges, universities, and technical schools. Harding (1949) distinguished 21 types of adult educational leaders: (1) autocrat, (2) cooperator, (3) elder statesman, (4) eager beaver, (5) pontifical type, (6) muddled person, (7) loyal staff person, (8) prophet, (9) scientist, (10) mystic, (11) dogmatist, (12) open-minded person, (13) philosopher, (14) business expert, (15) benevolent despot, (16) child protector, (17) laissez-faire type, (18) community-minded person, (19) cynic, (20) optimist, and (21) democrat.

Benezet, Katz, and Magnusson (1981) classified college presidents as founding presidents, explorers, take-charge presidents, standard-bearers, organization presidents, and moderators. A *founding* president fulfills many assignments until a regular staff has been assembled. The *explorer* brings on new programs and risky new plans; the *take-charge* president holds together an institution that is facing great difficulties; the *standard-bearer* leads an institution that has "arrived"; the *organization* president is a pragmatic administrator; and the *moderator* is an egalitarian administrator who consults with and delegates a great deal to faculty members and student leaders.[3]

Birnbaum (1988) typed college presidents as bureaucratic, collegial, political, or symbolic. They differed in their orientation toward their college's faculty, administrators, students, alumni, and finances. Looking to the future, Weber (1995) saw a need to replace the traditional bosses of command-structured organizations with leaders who were mentors, guides and cheerleaders.

Public Leaders: Statesmen, Politicians, and Influential People. Credit is due to Plato for the first taxonomy of political leaders. Plato classified such leaders as *timocratic*, ruling by pride and honor; *plutocratic*, ruling by wealth; *democratic*, ruling by popular consent on the basis of equality; and *tyrannical*, ruling by coercion (Shorey, 1933). This classification fits well with much of what will be analyzed in later chapters about the bases of influence and power. Plutocratic, democratic, and tyrannical leaders remain in the popular lexicon of political leadership.

Beckhard (1995) put public leaders into six commonly

[3] See also Astin and Scherrei (1980) for an empirical classification of college presidents based on factor analysis.

used categories: (1) *political* leaders, (2) leaders of *social change*, (3) leaders in *social science*, (4) leaders in *applied social thought*, (5) leaders of *business organizations*, and (6) leaders of *nongovernmental agencies*. What they all have in common is ego strength, strong convictions, and political astuteness. They need to use their power for efficiency and for the largest good.

Wills (1994) covered a much broader array of 16 representative archtypes of leaders, as well as their antitypes. The taxonomy mixed leadership roles, personality traits, cognition, styles, and behaviors. Many of the types overlapped considerably. These are common defects in many taxonomies, particularly those in popular books for the layperson. To illustrate, Wills's taxonomy comprised the democratically elected leader as the archtype versus the also-ran as the antitype, the radical leader versus the reactionary, the reform versus the conservative leader, the diplomatic versus the undiplomatic leader, the successful versus the unsuccessful military leader, the charismatic versus the bureaucratic leader, the effective versus the ineffective business leader, the revisionist of tradition versus the traditional leader, the constitutional versus the unconstitutional leader, the intellectual leader with consideration for others versus the intellectual without consideration, the church organizer versus the nonorganizer, the sports organizer with and without consideration for others, the artistic leader versus the exploiter, the rhetorical leader versus the nonuser of speeches, the opportunistic versus the inflexible leader, and the saintly versus the self-centered leader.

With respect to public leadership, Bell, Hill, and Wright (1961) identified *formal* leaders (who hold official positions, either appointed or elected), *reputational* leaders (who are believed to be influential in community or national affairs), *social* leaders (who are active participants in voluntary organizations), and *influential* leaders (who influence others in their daily contacts).

Haiman (1951) suggested that five types of leaders are needed in a democracy: (1) the executive, (2) the judge, (3) the advocate, (4) the expert, and (5) the discussion leader.

Hermann (1980) categorized political leaders, such as members of the politburo in the Soviet Union, according to whether they were generally sensitive to the political context and whether they wanted to control what happened or be an agent for the viewpoints of others.

Kaarbo and Hermann (1998) presented a taxonomy concerning political leaders' style of involvement in foreign policies according to their degree of interest and experience (high, moderate, low) and focus (developing policy or building support). Managing information was classified into those who interpret or filter sources of information (or do both). Additionally, managing conflict was categorized with the leader as advocate, consensus-builder, or arbitrator and as locus of decision (exclusive or inclusive, and balancer or bridge).

Prophets. For Kincheloe (1928), prophets were leaders without offices. Although prophets may arise in times of crisis, they create their own situation. Their real ability is to arouse their followers' interest so that the followers will accept prophetic goals and support these goals enthusiastically. Prophets become a symbol of the movement they have initiated, and their authoritative words tend to release inhibited impulses within their supporters. Kiernan (1975) clustered leadership patterns in African independent churches into two types: (1) preachers and prophets; and (2) chiefs, prophets, and messiahs.

Local Government Leaders. Parry (1999) coded respondents in interviews to study processes of social influence in local government authorities during times of turbulent change. Leadership strategies were seen as deliberate plans or emergent perspectives. Other categories of response included resolving uncertainty, clarifying roles, and enhancing adaptability.

Kotter and Lawrence (1974) subdivided city mayors into categories on the basis of the agendas set by the mayors, the networks they built, and the tasks they accomplished. *Ceremonial* mayors set short-run agendas of small scope; they were individualistic and had a personal appeal but no staffs. *Personality-individualistic* mayors also had no staff, but the scope of their agendas was greater and the time involved in them was longer. *Caretakers* set short-run agendas of large scope, had loyal staffs, and were moderately bureaucratic. *Executive* mayors set agendas of large scope and of longer range, had staffs, were bureaucratic, and had a mixed appeal. *Program entrepreneurs* set the agendas of the largest scope, had staff resources, and built extensive networks with mixed appeals.

World-Class Political Leaders. As an example of an empirical approach, Bass and Farrow (1977a) identified six types of world-class political leaders according to their leadership styles as revealed in an inverse factor analysis. Pairs of judges independently completed a 135-item questionnaire to describe the leaders on 31 scales after they had read considerable amounts of biographical literature written mainly by the immediate subordinates of the leaders. The 15 leaders were intercorrelated according to their scores on the 31 scales through use of the Bass and Valenzi systems model (Bass, 1976). An inverse factor analysis generated six clusters in relation to the behavior of leaders and subordinates, with the highest loadings for clustered figures as follows:

Autocratic-submissive: Adolf Hitler, Joseph Stalin, Nicholas II, Louis XIV.
Trustworthy subordinates: Hirohito, Alexander the Great, Franklin Delano Roosevelt.
Clear, orderly, relationships: Winston Churchill.
Structured, sensitivity to outside pressures: Fiorello La Guardia, John F. Kennedy, Franklin Delano Roosevelt.
Satisfying differential power: Lenin.
Egalitarian, analytic: Thomas Jefferson.

Revolutionary versus Loyalist Leaders. Rejai and Phillips (1988) discriminated between 50 well-known revolutionary leaders such as Fidel Castro, Thomas Jefferson, and Ho Chi Minh; and 50 who remained loyal to the existing government such as Fulgencio Batista, Thomas Hutchinson, and Nguyen Van Thieu. *Revolutionaries* were statistically more likely to abandon their religion and become atheists; they had fathers who had *not* been officials in government, the military, banking, or industry, or members of the landed gentry. They had an optimistic view of human nature but fluctuated in their attitudes toward their own country. By contrast, *loyalists* remained steadfast in their religious beliefs and had fathers who were more likely to be government officials or in the military, banking, and industry. They themselves were more likely to be in government service, and pessimistic about human nature but optimistic about their own country.

Legislative Leaders. J. M. Burns (1978) classified legislative leaders as ideologues, tribunes, careerists, parliamentarians, or brokers. *Ideologues* speak for doctrines (economic, religious, or political) that may be supported widely throughout their constituency but more typically are held by a small though highly articulate minority. *Tribunes* are discoverers or connoisseurs of popular needs; defenders of popular interests; or advocates for popular demands, aspirations, and governmental actions. *Careerists* see their legislative careers as a stepping-stone to higher office, provided they do a job that impresses their constituents and other observers. *Parliamentarians*, as political technicians, either expedite or obstruct legislation. They bolster the legislature as an institution of tradition, courtesy, mutual forbearance, and protection of fellow members. *Brokers* mediate among antagonistic legislators, balancing interests to create legislative unity and action.

Military Leaders. The military hierarchy is classified from general officer to private soldier. An example of a statistically sophisticated taxonomy of army leaders was created by Mumford, Zaccaro, Johnson et al. (2000). Their taxonomy of seven types of U.S. Army officers was based on matching profiles of abilities, personalities, and motivational characteristics with the requirements of their positions. A d^2 indexed the similarity of each profile to each officer's positional requirements. The officers were then clustered according to how well their profiles matched or failed to match the requirements for junior officer, either lieutenant or captain. Seven types of the 786 junior officers emerged; these types could also be applied to classifying 275 senior officers (captains to colonels) in the same way. The percentage of junior and senior officers of each type is shown below.

	Junior Officers	Senior Officers
Concrete Achievers	20%	11%
Motivated Communicators	17	40
Limited Defensives	15	12
Disengaged Introverts	10	16
Social Adapters	12	30
Struggling Misfits	13	3
Thoughtful Innovators	11	26

Stereotypes of Woman Leaders. Influential women have been classified in a number of ways, some fitting stereotypes about women in the workplace.[4] Women in a community have been classified as *fashion leaders* and *trendsetters*, in contrast to those who are content to *accept*, *ignore*, or *resist change*. For example, in determining opinion leadership among women in a community, Saunders, Davis, and Monsees (1974) found it useful to classify 587 women who attended a family planning clinic in Lima, Peru, as *early* or *late* adopters and as *pre-* or *postaccepters* of family planning.

Hammer (1978) described four stereotypes of women leaders in the workplace. The *earth mother* brings home-baked cookies to meetings and keeps the communal bottle of aspirin in her desk. The *manipulator* relies on feminine wiles to get her way. The *workaholic* cannot delegate responsibility. The *egalitarian* leader denies the power of her leadership and claims to relate to subordinates as a colleague. Similarly, Kanter (1976, 1977a, 1977b) discerned four stereotypes of women leaders who work primarily in a man's world: The *mother* provides solace, comfort, and aspirin. The *pet* is the little sister or mascot of the group. The *sex object* fails to establish herself as a professional. The *iron maiden* tries too hard to establish herself as a professional and is seen as more tyrannical than she actually is.

Sociopsychological Classifications

Nafe (1930) pioneered the classification of leaders according to social or psychological dynamics of leaders and subordinates. Nafe presented a perceptive analysis of the *dynamic-infusive* leader who directs and redirects followers' attention to the perceptual and ideational aspects of an issue until thought has been transferred into emotion and emotion into action. According to Nafe "the attitude of the leader toward the led and toward the project is found to be a problem in name only. The leader needs only to have the appearance of possessing the attitude desired by the followers." The real problem is the attitude of the led toward the leader. The attributes of leadership exist only in the minds of the led: "The leader may be this to one and that to another, but it is only by virtue of having a following that he or she is a leader." The *adhe-*

[4]See Chapter 31.

sive leader (who seems to share the followers' attitudes) is opposite in every respect to the infusive (inspiring and influential) type, according to Nafe, who added the following additional categories to his taxonomy: static versus dynamic, impressors versus expressors, volunteer versus drafted, general versus specialized, temporary versus permanent, conscious versus unconscious, professional versus amateur, and personal versus impersonal.

Using analogies with genetics, Krout (1942) identified the *social variant* leader, who arises out of the group's need to agree about its goals and what to do about its lagging forms of behavior. Krout also described *hybrid* leaders, who seek to change the social structure through discontinuous methods to achieve the group's goals; and *mutants*—innovators who redefine the cultural patterns of their group and may set new goals to achieve their objectives for the group.

Jones (1983) described the ranges of leadership in terms of the kinds of control leaders exert that affect a follower's reactions. The leader can control (1) the *process* or the *output*, and can be (2) *obtrusive* or *unobtrusive*, (3) *situational* or *personal*, and (4) *paternalistic* or *professional*. This taxonomy can be used to explain how groups can be both satisfied with their situation and yet unproductive.

Psychoanalytic Taxonomies. From a psychoanalytic perspective, Redl (1942) suggested that instinctual and emotional group processes take place around a member whose role may be patriarch, leader, tyrant, love object, object of aggression, organizer, seducer, hero, bad example, or good example. Continuing in the same vein, Zaleznik (1974) contrasted charismatic leaders with consensus leaders. *Charismatic* leaders are inner-directed and identify with objects, symbols, and ideals that are connected with introjection. They are father figures. *Consensus* leaders "appear" to be brothers or peers, rather than father figures.

Kets de Vries and Miller (1984b, 1986) presented a sixfold psychopathological classification of executives to account for their dysfunctional performance: (1) persecutory, (2) preoccupied, (3) helpless, (4) narcissistic, (5) compulsive, and (6) schizoid-detached.[5]

Narcissists, "resentfuls," and "highly likable low achiev-

[5]These will be discussed more fully in Chapter 8.

ers" were the three types of flawed managers described by Hogan, Raskin, and Fazzini (undated). The transference pattern of leaders' and followers' emotional relations were seen by Pauchant (1991) as depending on the self-development of the leader and follower.

Personality Types

Strengths and Signature Themes. These self-ratings fall into three domains of leadership: (1) relating, (2) striving, and (3) thinking. The eight themes of *relating* include the most effective ways to work with others individually and in groups: (1) arranging; (2) developing; (3) empathizing; (4) individualizing perception; (5) caring for people and building rapport with them; (6) accepting responsibility and ownership of projects with accountability, dependability, and ethics; (7) radiating enthusiasm and creating fun; and (8) enjoying working together with associates as a team. Types of *striving* are achieving, activating, competing by measuring oneself against others, increasing determination in the face of resistance and obstacles, maintaining discipline and establishing structure in one's own life and environment, and being focused and goal-oriented. The domain of *thinking* encompasses concepts, strategic thinking, constant measurement to improve perfomance, and a perception of how systems can improve performance (Clifton, 2000). At Gallup management seminars, participants are encouraged to focus on further improving their strengths and not to be as concerned about their weaknesses (Clifton & Nelson, 1992).

Character Types. According to Pitcher (1997), there is a continuing crisis in management and organizational leadership; this is due to managers' and leaders' technocratic mentality and character, in contrast to those managers and leaders who are artists or craftsmen. *Technocrats* lack emotion, imagination, good judgment, and vision. They are analytical, intense, methodological, and detail-oriented. They are put into power to try to ensure rationality in decision making. They drive out of the organization those whom they perceive as emotional. *Artists* are people-oriented, entrepreneurial, bold, intuitive, and imaginative. They are visionary leaders who talk in metaphors rather than specifics. *Craftsmen* are dedicated, reliable, realistic, and knowledgeable. They appreciate the past and near future in their thinking, They have a realistic strategic vision. They have "people skills" and generate loyalty from subordinates. Technocrats downgrade artists and craftsmen, whereas artists and craftsmen admire and cooperate with each other.

Lewis, Kuhnert, and Maginnis (1987) sorted military officers into three character types. *Operators* have a personal agenda that they pursue without concern for others; they lack empathy and cannot be trusted. *Team players* are highly sensitive to how others feel about them and value decisions according to what others will think or say, rather than according to the merits of the case. In contrast, *self-defining leaders* are personally committed to ideals and values and pursue what they regard as the right and most worthy solutions.

Myers-Briggs Types. Jung's (1971) psychoanalytic conceptualization was the basis of the popular Myers-Briggs fourfold classification of the thought processes of leaders and managers faced with decisions and problems. The Myers-Briggs Type Indicator (Myers & McCaulley, 1985) sorts leaders into four types and 16 subtypes based on their responses to the indicator. Leaders are: (1) *extroverted* or *introverted*, (2) *sensing* or *intuitive*, (3) *thinking* or *feeling*, and (4) *judging* or *perceiving*. The extrovert prefers the outer world of people, things, and activities, whereas the introvert prefers the inner world of ideas and concepts. The extrovert is gregarious and people-oriented; the introvert seeks accomplishment working with just a few key colleagues. The sensing type of leader is oriented toward facts, details, and reality; the intuitive leader is focused more on inferences, concepts, and possibilities. The thinking types prefer analysis, logical order, and rationality and are seen as "cold" by feeling types. The feeling types, who value feelings and harmony, are described as too "soft" by the thinking types. The judging types prefer to make decisions rapidly and move on to the next issue, but the perceiving types seek to delay decisions.

A sample of 875 U.S. managers who were tested by the Center for Creative Leadership (Osborn & Osborn, 1986) between 1979 and 1983 were distributed as follows: extroverts (50%), introverts (50%), sensors (52%), intuitives (48%), thinkers (82%), feelers (18%), judges (70%), and perceivers (30%).

The four Myers-Briggs types, as noted above, generate 16 subtypes of managers. The 875 managers were concentrated in four of the subtypes: ISTJ (introverted-sensing-thinking judges), ESTJ (extroverted-sensing-thinking judges), ENTJ (extroverted-intuitive-thinking judges), and INTJ (introverted-intuitive-thinking judges). Delunas (1983) showed that for 76 federal executives and managers from private industry, the Myers-Briggs types (sensors-perceivers, sensors-judges, intuitives-thinkers, and intuitives-feelers) were significantly linked with their most or least preferred administrative styles.

Data from almost 7,500 managers and administrators showed that the majority were types like judges who reached closure, rather than perceivers who missed nothing. They were more likely to be impersonal, logical, and analytical thinkers than to be more concerned with personal feeling and human priorities. The subtypes that were most likely to be concerned with enhancing human performance, the intuitive-feelers, were underrepresented except in human resources departments. Those who were involved in the production of tangible products or in following established procedures tended to be practical sensing types. Those who provided long-range vision tended to be imaginative, theoretical, intuitive types (McCaulley, 1989).

Other Examples of Personality Types. Other taxonomies of leadership based on personality have developed around scores that subjects obtain on various assessments of their personalities. For instance, using scales developed for the California Personality Inventory (CPI), Gough (1988) described four types of individuals who are found in diverse samples of students and adults: (1) *leaders*, (2) *innovators*, (3) *saints*, and (4) *artists*. Leaders and innovators are extroverts, but leaders are also ambitious, enterprising, and resolute, while innovators are adventurous, progressive, and versatile. Saints and artists are introverted, but the saints are steadfast, trustworthy, and unselfish whereas the artists are complex, imaginative, and sensitive. Leaders and saints accept norms; innovators and artists question norms. Although only 25% to 30% of the general population of students and adults were classified by the CPI as leaders, 66% of cadets at West Point were so typed. Leaders and innovators at West Point had a higher aptitude for military service than the saints or artists.

Taxonomies of Leaders According to Their Functions, Roles, Perceptions, and Behavior

Many attempts have been made to categorize organizational leaders and managers specifically according to the kinds of functions they perform, the roles they play, of the behaviors they display, and their cognitions and perceptions. Numerous classification schemes have appeared. Many of them prescribe functions for the ideal organizational leader. Others are derived from empirical job analyses or factored behavioral descriptions of the actual work performed by managers and administrators. For example, both approaches have concluded that the organizational leader may play the role of final arbitrator, the superordinate whose judgment settles disputes among followers. This function was often considered critical for the avoidance of anarchy in political units and societies. The maintenance and security of the state, it was believed, depended on the existence of a legitimate position at the top, to which all followers would acquiesce to avoid the continuation of conflict among them.

Functions

Classical theories of ideal management indicated that the primary functions of managers and executives could be neatly characterized as planning, organizing, and controlling. Although coordinating, supervising, motivating, and the like were added to the list, they were seen merely as variations managers' and executives' function of organizational control. On the other hand, behavioral descriptions of the functions of actual managers and executives included defining objectives, maintaining goal direction, providing means for attaining goals, providing and maintaining the group structure, facilitating action and interaction in the group, maintaining the cohesiveness of the group and the satisfaction of members, and facilitating the group's performance of tasks.

The functions identified by the behavioral descriptions grew out of research on basic group processes and on the emergence of the leadership role and its contribution to the performance, interaction, and satisfaction of members who are engaged in a group task. The classical functions of planning, organizing, and controlling were concerned with the rationalized processes of formal orga-

nizations. Although these functions are generalized and abstract, they are by no means unreal; however, they tend to ignore the human nature of members of the organization and the limited rationality with which the manager must operate. Yet organizations strive for rationality. Understanding the purposes of a leader in an organization requires a consideration of his or her planning, directing, and controlling. However, many more behaviors emerge in large-scale descriptive surveys and interviews with leaders.

Mooney and Reiley (1931) identified the three functional processes in any organization as being the same as in any governmental entity: legislative, executive, and judicial. Coffin (1944) suggested that the three functions of organizational leadership were formulation (planning), execution (organizing), and supervision (persuading). Barnard (1946b) identified the functions of organizational leadership as (1) determination of objectives, (2) manipulation of means, (3) instrumentation of action, and (4) stimulation of coordinated effort. Davis (1951) was in agreement with many others in declaring that the functions of the business leader are to plan, organize, and control an organization's activities. In a study of leadership in Samoa, Kessing and Kessing (1956) identified the following leadership functions: consultation, deliberation, negotiation, the formation of public opinion, and decision making. Gross (1961) proposed these functions: to define goals, clarify, and administer them; to choose appropriate means; assign and coordinate tasks; to motivate; create loyalty; represent the group; and spark the membership to action.

Selznick (1957) suggested that the functions of organizational leadership include: (1) definition of the institution's mission and goals; (2) creation of a structure to achieve the institution's purpose; (3) defense of institutional integrity; and (4) reevaluation of internal conflict.

Katz and Kahn (1966) advocated three functions for organizational leadership: (1) policy formation (the introduction of structural change); (2) the interpretation of structure (piecing out the incompleteness of the existing formal structure); and (3) administration (the use of a formal structure to keep the organization in motion and operating effectively).

Wofford (1967) proposed the following functions of management be selected: setting objectives, organizing, leading, and controlling. For Krech and Crutchfield

(1948), a leader could be an executive, planner, policy maker, expert, representative of the external group, controller of internal relationships, purveyor of rewards and punishments, arbitrator and mediator, exemplar, symbol of the group, surrogate for individual responsibility, ideologist, father figure, and scapegoat.

T. A. Mahoney (1955, 1961) and colleagues (Mahoney, Jerdee, & Carroll, 1965) typed managers according to their main functions. According to a survey of 452 managers in 13 firms, supervising was the main function of 51% of lower-level supervisors, 36% of middle managers, and 22% of top managers. Top managers were more likely than lower-level managers to be generalists and planners. Figure 2.2 shows how managers could be typed according to their main function. As can be seen, the type of manager depended on the organizational level.

Williams (1956) focused on dealing with knowledge, decision making, interaction with others, character, organization over person, policies, and records. Koontz, O'Donnell, and Weihrich (1958) wrote about planning, organizing, motivating, and controlling. McGrath's (1964) fourfold classification concerned monitoring, forecasting, taking direct action, and creating conditions. For Bennett (1971), the taxonomy included deciding, planning, analyzing, interacting with people, and using equipment. For Hemphill (1950a), who used factor analytical approaches of leaders, the functions of supervisors, managers, and executives were initiation, representation, fraternization organization, domination, recognition, production, integration, and communication down[6] and communication up (in the organization).[7] For Hemphill (1960), supervisors, managers, and executives dealt with the following: providing staff services; supervising work; controlling business, technical markets, and production; human, conducting community, and social affairs; engaging in long-range planning; exercising broad power and authority; maintaining one's business reputation; meeting personal demands; and preserving assets. For Fine (1977), who employed job analyses, the functions were analyzing, negotiating, consulting, instructing, and exchanging information. For Dowell and Wexley (1978), they included working with subordinates, organizing their work, planning and scheduling work, maintaining efficient and good-quality production, maintaining equipment, and compiling records and reports.

An outstanding example of a large-scale long-term analysis of management functions was Tornow and Pinto's (1976) taxonomy which involved long-range thinking and planning; the coordination of other organizational units and personnel; internal control; responsibility for products, services, finances, and board personnel; dealing with public and customer relations, complexity, and stress; advanced consulting; maintaining the autonomy of financial commitments; service to the staff; and supervision.[8]

The categorizations were fine-tuned and became more numerous. Winter (1978) generated 19 possible functional leadership competencies, ranging from conceptualizing to disciplining. They were expanded to 66 competencies by D. Campbell (1991). Metcalfe (1984) came up with 20 classes of leaders' behavior, ranging

Figure 2.2. Distribution of Assignments Among Job Types at Each Organizational Level

Low (N = 191)		Middle (N = 131)		High (N = 130)	
Planner	15%	Planner	18%		
Investigator	8%			Planner	28%
Coordinator	5%	Investigator	8%		
Evaluator	2%	Coordinator	7%	Investigator	6%
		Evaluator	2%	Coordinator	8%
				Evaluator	8%
Supervisor	51%	Supervisor	36%	Supervisor	22%
				Negotiator	3%
		Negotiator	8%	Multispecialist	5%
Negotiator	6%				
Multispecialist	6%	Multispecialist	8%	Generalist	20%
Generalist	9%	Generalist	10%		

(NOTE: *Totals do not add up to 100 percent because of rounding.*)
SOURCE: Mahoney, Jerdee, and Carroll (1965).

[6] Downward in the organization.
[7] Upward in the organization.
[8] More about this taxonomy will be discussed in Chapter 23.

from proposing procedures to shutting out other persons' efforts to participate. Van Fleet and Yukl (1986a) emerged with a detailed breakdown of 23 functions, ranging from showing consideration to monitoring reward contingencies. Subsequently these were combined by Yukl (1998) into 14 functions, reworked from a previous list of 15 functions (Yukl, 1989): (1) networking; (2) supporting; (3) managing conflict and team building; (4) motivating; (5) recognizing; (6) rewarding; (7) planning and organizing; (8) problem solving; (9) consulting; (10) delegating; (11) monitoring; (12) informing; (13) clarifying; (14) developing and mentoring.

Roles

On the basis of his observations of managers at work, Mintzberg (1973) created a taxonomy in which managers were seen to engage in three sets of roles: interpersonal, informational, and decisional. Within each of these sets, specific roles were conceived. The interpersonal set included the *figurehead*, *leader*, and *liaison*. Within the informational set were the *monitor*, *disseminator*, and *spokesman*. Within the decisional set were the *entrepreneur*, *disturbance handler*, *resource allocator*, and *negotiator*.

Javidan and Dastmalchian (1993) described five leadership roles: *mobilizer*, *ambassador*, *driver*, *auditor*, and *servant*.

Kraut, Pedigo, et al. (1989) delineated seven leadership roles: (1) managing individual performance, (2) instructing subordinates, (3) planning and allocating resources, (4) coordinating independent groups, (5) managing group performance, (6) monitoring the business environment, and (7) representing one's staff. Baehr (1992) proposed 16 leadership roles ranging from setting organizational objectives to handling outside contacts.

Wells (1997) proposed nine roles for organizational leaders driven by values: (1) *Sages* develop wisdom through gaining knowledge about the organization's history and future prospects, and can deal with complexities, ambiguities, and contradictions; (2) *Visionaries* push to go beyond what has been previously accomplished and stimulate others to share in pursuit of the vision; (3) *Magicians* coordinate change by balancing the organization's structures, systems, and processes; (4) *Globalists* build bridges across cultures and find common ground

on productive work can occur; (5) *Mentors* motivate others to advance their careers by helping people to learn and work to their potential and to find new perspectives and meaning in their jobs; (6) *Allies* build partnerships by seeking mutually beneficial collaborations that can improve performance; (7) *Sovereigns* take responsibility for the decisions they make and empower others with significant authority; (8) *Guides* use clearly stated principles to direct tasks toward goals important to the whole organization, are action-oriented, and are excited by the challenge of moving things forward; (9) *Artisans* are devoted to the mastery of a craft and the pursuit of excellence, concerned with the aesthetic as well as the practical to provide the customer with maximum value by continuous improvements. The same leader can perform a number of different roles.

Quinn's (1984) competing values framework is a taxonomy of management roles to indicate conditions under which enacting them would be most conducive to effectiveness. The patterns observed gave rise to seven types of managers. The same managers could play roles conceived to be opposite in value, and the roles could be placed at two ends of a continuum. The four bipolarities were: (1) mentor versus director; (2) facilitator versus producer; (3) coordinator versus innovator; and (4) monitor versus broker (Quinn, Dixit, & Faerman, 1987).

Mentors and facilitators are flexible and internally focused. Coordinators and monitors are internally focused and controlling. Directors and producers are externally focused and controlling. Innovators and brokers are flexible and externally focused. Mentors are particularly caring, empathetic, and concerned about individuals. Facilitators are interpersonally skilled and particularly concerned about group processes, cooperation, and cohesiveness. Producers are task-oriented, action-oriented, energetic, and specifically concerned about getting the work done. Coordinators are dependable, reliable, and concerned with maintaining continuity and equilibrium in the group. Innovators are clever, creative, conceptually skillful, and searching for better ways and opportunities. Monitors are well-prepared, well-informed, competent, and technically expert. Brokers are resource-oriented, politically astute, and especially concerned about influence, legitimacy, and acquiring resources. Effective leaders are typed as masters, conceptual producers, aggressive achievers, peaceful team builders, long-term intensives, and open adaptives. *Masters* are high in all eight opposing roles. *Conceptual producers* are almost like masters, except that they are lower in monitoring and coordinating. *Aggressive achievers* are high in monitoring, coordinating, directing, and producing but are lower in the other roles, particularly facilitating. *Peaceful team builders* are high in six of the roles but lower in the roles of broker and producer. *Long-term intensives* are high in the roles of innovator, producer, monitor, and facilitator and fall nearer the mean on the roles of mentor and director. *Open adaptives* are much less likely to monitor and coordinate. Ineffective managers were typed with the same kind of analysis of management roles into *chaotic adaptives, abrasive coordinators, drowning workaholics, extreme unproductives, obsessive monitors, permissive externals,* and *softhearted indecisives* (Hooijberg & Quinn, 1992). Hooijberg and Choi (2000) demonstrated that the effectiveness of managerial leadership was greater if the subordinate leaders saw themselves resembling their supervisors and managers in taking the effective roles of innovator, broker, monitor, mentor, producer, and facilitator.

Special Organizational Leadership Roles. According to Senge (1995), to lead learning organizations, organizations dedicated to continuous improvement and adaptation, three types of leaders are needed: (1) *executive leaders,* (2) *local line leaders,* and (3) *internal networkers or community leaders.*

Schein (1995) called for four kinds of leadership that were required in different stages of the development of an organization's culture: first, the *animator* was needed to build the culture; second came the *maintainer*; third came the *sustainer*; and fourth came the *change agent* to help promote necessary revisions.

As a strategic manager for General Electric and as a consultant, Rothschild (1993) developed a taxonomy of the types of strategic leader needed at different stages of an organization's life. As the organization starts up and grows rapidly, the strategic leader has to be a *risk taker.* When growth slows, a disciplined *caretaker* is needed to maintain stable long-term growth. If the organization must cope with significant declines, a *surgeon* leader is needed to act quickly. When there is no hope of turnaround, an *undertaker* leader is needed to dispose of the organization's assets compassionately and decisively.

Cognitions and Perceptions of Leaders

Compared with leaders' functions, roles and behaviors, their cognitions and perceptions have received much less research. Lord (1985) advanced the study of the structures underlying the cognitive categorization of leaders, which determined how they were perceived by others. The perceiver is seen as an active selector and organizer of stimulus information to provide cognitive economy. Categorizing information allows similar but nonidentical leaders to be seen as equivalent in a perceptual structure.

Hunt, Boal, et al. (1990) provided a fourfold categorization of leadership prototypes: (1) *Heroes* are leaders perceived as experts in both content and process. (2) *Technocrats* are perceived as experts in content but not process. (3) *Ringmasters* are perceived as experts in process but not content. (4) *Illegitimate leaders* are perceived as experts in neither content nor process.

Bimbaum (1988) organized a taxonomy of how college and university presidents differed in their frames of reference: bureaucratic, collegial, political, or symbolic. According to Bensimon (1990) *bureacratic* presidents control by being active in making decisions, resolving conflicts, solving problems, evaluating performance and outputs, and distributing rewards and penalties. They are likely to be authoritarian, decisive, and results-oriented. The *collegial* president views the members of the establishment as the most important resource. Collegial presidents favor goal achievement and define priorities through teamwork, collective action, building consensus, loyalty, and commitment. Presidents with a *political* frame of reference see their institution as consisting of formal and informal constituencies competing for power to control the college's processes and outcomes. Decisions are the result of bargaining and coalition building. The president serves as a mediator who must be persuasive, diplomatic, and able to deal with shifting power blocs. The president with a *symbolic* frame of reference focuses on his or her institution as a culture of shared meanings and beliefs. Rituals, symbols, and myths are sustained to provide a sense of the college's purpose and order by interpretation, elaboration, and reinforcement of its culture. The 32 college and university presidents who were interviewed by Bensimon (1990) described themselves as most symbolic in their frames of reference and least political. This was quite different from descriptions by their 80 trustees, deans, directors, and department heads, who described the presidents as most bureaucratic and least symbolic in their frames of reference. For presidents with a strong bureaucratic orientation, campus leaders saw little of the other types in the president.

Leaders' Styles and Patterns of Behavior

Leadership and management styles are alternative ways that leaders and managers pattern their interactive behavior with those they influence.

Transactional versus Transformational Leaders. As Buckley (1979) noted, the successful political leader is one who "crystallizes" what people desire, "illuminates" the rightness of that desire, and coordinates its achievement. Such leadership can be transactional or transformational. This distinction has become of considerable importance to the study of leadership since Burns's (1978) work (Bass, 1985a; Bennis & Nanus, 1985; Tichy & Devanna, 1986; Bryman, 1992; Curphy, 1992). In exchanging promises for votes, the transactional leader works within the framework of the self-interests of his or her constituency, whereas the transformational leader moves to change the framework. Forerunners of this distinction are to be found in Hook's (1943) differentiation of the *eventful* man and the *event-making* man. The eventful political leader is swept along by the tides of history; the event-making political leader initiates the actions that make history. President Lincoln's predecessor, Buchanan, was content to stand by and allow the Union to disintegrate slowly; Lincoln was determined to hold the Union together and to reverse what seemed at the time to be the inexorable course of southern secession.

Downton (1973) discussed the leadership of rebels in terms of this distinction between the transactional and the transformational leader. And Paige (1977) concluded that it would be useful to classify political leaders according to the changes they sought and achieved, as conservative, reformist, or revolutionary. *Conservative* leaders tend to maintain the existing political institutions and policies, *reformist* leaders promote moderate changes in institutions and policies, and *revolutionary* leaders (as well as *radical* leaders) strive for fundamental changes in existing institutions and policies. *Reactionaries* want to revert to institutions of the past.

For Burns (1978, p. 3), who provided a comprehensive theory to explain the differences between transactional and transformational political leaders, transactional leaders "approach followers with an eye to exchanging one thing for another: jobs for votes, or subsidies for campaign contributions. Such transactions comprise the bulk of the relationships among leaders and followers, especially in groups, legislatures, and parties." Burns noted that the transformational leader also recognizes the need for a potential follower, but he or she goes further, seeking to satisfy higher needs, in terms of Maslow's (1954) need hierarchy, to engage the full person of the follower. Transforming leadership results in mutual stimulation and elevation "that converts followers into leaders and may convert leaders into moral agents." If the follower's higher-level needs are authentic, more leadership occurs. Burns went on to classify transactional political leaders as *opinion leaders, bargainers or bureaucrats, party leaders, legislative leaders,* and *executive leaders.* Transformational leaders were categorized as *intellectual leaders, leaders of reform or revolution,* and *heroes* or *ideologues.*

Until the 1980s, most experimental research focused on transactional leadership (see, for example, Hollander, 1978), whereas the movers and shakers of the world are transformational leaders. Although both types of leaders sense the felt needs of their followers, it is the transformational leader who raises consciousness (about higher considerations) through articulation and role modeling. Through transformational leaders levels of aspiration are raised, legitimated, and turned into political demands.[9] The transformational/transactional classification has been used to study leaders in many sectors, including health care, the military, business, sports coaching, politics, government service, and nonprofit agencies (Bass & Riggio, 2005). Confirmatory factor analyses by Avolio, Bass, and Dong (1999) of 14 surveys that used the Multifactor Leadership Questionnaire concluded from the best-fitting model that *transformational* leaders are inspirational, intellectually stimulating and/or individually considerate; *transactional* leaders practice contingent reward and active management by exception (contingent negative feedback). On the basis of ratings of CEOs by

[9]Transformational leadership is discussed in detail in Chapter 22; transactional leadership in Chapters 15 and 16.

253 senior executives, and of middle managers by 208 supervisors, Pearce, Sims, Cox, et al. (2002) found that a four-factor model of leadership fit the data best in comparison with other models: *directive leadership* (instruction and command, assigned goals, contingent reprimand); *transactional leadership* (contingent material reward, contingent personal reward); *transformational leadership* (stimulation and inspiration, vision, idealism, challenge to the status quo); and *empowering leadership* (encouraging thinking in terms of opportunities, encouraging self-reward and self-leadership, setting goals participatively, and encouraging teamwork).

Relations-Oriented and Task-Oriented Leaders. Blake and Mouton (1964) studied the dimensions—from one (low) to nine (high)—of task- and relations-oriented leadership by using a grid. Five styles could be generated from the dimensions. These will be detailed in Chapter 19. Reddin (1977) advanced this popular taxonomy of management in relation to eight types, each of which is a consequence of being low or high in Blake and Mouton's two dimensions of relationships and task orientation and a third dimension—effectiveness. Managers are characterized as various combinations of this three-dimensional typology, as shown in the table here.

Managers Typed by their Leadership Styles

Type of Leadership	Relationship Orientation	Task Orientation	Effectiveness
Deserter	Low	Low	Low
Autocrat	Low	High	Low
Missionary	High	Low	Low
Compromiser	High	High	Low
Bureaucrat	Low	Low	High
Benevolent autocrat	Low	High	High
Developer	High	Low	High
Executive	High	High	High

An equally compelling typology of managerial styles was developed by Tannenbaum and Schmidt (1958), focusing on the issue of who shall decide—the leader or the follower. Their types were arranged along an authoritarian-democratic continuum: the leader who announces the decision, the leader who sells the decision, the leader who consults before deciding, the leader whose decisions are shared, and the leader who delegates decision making.[10] Hersey and Blanchard (1969a) made extensive use of this typology.

Bradford and Cohen (1984) categorized styles of managers: the manager as *technician*, the manager as *conductor*, and the manager as *developer*. The manager as technician relates information to subordinates who are committed to the leader because of the leader's technical competence and who depend on the leader for the answers to problems. The manager as conductor is a heroic figure "who orchestrates all the individual parts of the organization into one harmonious whole" (p. 45) with administrative systems for staffing and work flow. The manager as developer "works to develop management responsibility in subordinates and . . . the subordinates' abilities to share management of the unit's performance" (pp. 60–61).

Sorting managers in terms of their stylistic emphasis on rationality and quantitative analysis, Leavitt (1986) identified three types of mangers. *Pathfinders* are creative and visionary; they use instinct, wisdom, and imagination to meet their goals and know how to ask questions and search out problems. *Problem solvers* are analytic, quantitative, and oriented toward management controls. Implementers are political and stress consensus, teamwork, and good interpersonal relationships.

Cribbin (1981) classified effective managers into the following types: *entrepreneur* ("We do it my way and take risks"), *corporateur* ("I call the shots, but we all work together on my team"), *developer* ("People are our most important asset"), *craftsman* ("We do important work as perfectly as possible"), *integrator* ("We build consensus and commitment"), and *gamesman* ("We run together, but I must win more than you").

Har-Even (1992), developed four models of leaders: (1) *charismatic* ("Believe in me"); (2) authoritative ("We will act according to the laws and rules"); (3) *role model* ("Follow me, I have knowledge and personal experience"); and (4) *facilitator* ("Let's get together, and I will help to resolve our differences").

Fleishman, Mumford, Zaccaro, et al. (1991) reviewed 65 taxonomies of leaders' behavior published between 1944 and 1986. Three communalities were seen in these

---

[10]See Chapter 18.

65 taxonomies: (1) facilitating group social interaction and pursuing task accomplishment; (2) the occurrence of management and administrative functions; and (3) emphasis on leader-group interactions. Differences in taxonomies were due to the differences in the purposes of their creators; for instance, the purpose might be to focus on leaders' behavior or on leaders' effectiveness. The taxonomies also differed because of differences in methods, theoretical frameworks, and intended applications. Four dimensions emerged from the biographical review: (1) "information search and structuring" (acquiring, organizing, evaluating, feedback, and control of information); (2) "information use in problem solving" (identifying needs and requirements, planning, and coordinating and communicating information); (3) "managing personnel resources" (obtaining, developing, allocating, motivating, utilizing, and monitoring personnel resources); and (4) "managing material resources" (obtaining, allocating, maintaining, utilizing, and monitoring material resources).

Manz and Sims (1993) proposed four types of leaders, based on their different kinds of behavior: strong man, transactor, visionary hero, and super-leader. The *strong man* assigns goals, intimidates, and reprimands his followers. The *transactor* uses contingent reinforcement in interactive goal-setting to reward and reprimand followers. The *visionary hero* communicates his or her vision; emphasizes his or her values; and exhorts, inspires, and persuades followers. The *super-leader* models self-leadership and develops it in followers, creates positive thought patterns, develops self-leadership in followers through contingent rewards and reprimands, promotes self-leading teams, and facilitates a self-leadership culture. "Leaders become 'super'—that is, possess the strength of many persons—by helping to unleash the abilities of the 'followers' (self-leaders) that surround them."

Types of Strategic Leadership. Strategic leadership is behavior that depends on combining perceptions of threats, opportunities, cognitions, analyses, and risk preferences. Some strategies of leaders are emergent perspectives that evolve. Other strategies result from deliberate planning (Mintzberg & Jorgenson, 1987). These may be only implicit in the minds of the leaders (Lewis, Morkel, et al., 1993). To classify strategic leaders, Lord and Maher (1993) applied the same taxonomy of four organizational strategies posited by Miles and Snow (1978)—defenders, prospectors, analyzers, and reactors: *Defenders* stress efficiency and product stability; *prospectors* focus on product innovation and development; *analyzers* produce and market products developed by other organizations; *reactors* fall behind their industry in adopting new products. Organizations are more likely to be successful when their type of strategy matches the leaders' requisite personality; thus, for example, defender organizations are more successful if led by executives who stress efficiency and product stability.

Gupta and Govindarajan (1984) typed organizations as pursuing a *build* strategy of increasing market share rather than a *harvest* strategy of cash flow and short-term profits. For success, the *build* strategy requires risk-taking executives with a tolerance for ambiguity. The *harvest* strategy, by contrast, needs executives with little propensity for risk and little tolerance for ambiguity.

Using facet and smallest-space analysis of data from 27 business cases, Shrivastava and Nachman (1989) empirically established four patterns of strategic leadership behavior: *entrepreneurial* (a confident, charismatic chief executive singularly guides strategy and controls others with direct supervision); *bureaucratic* (strategy is based on rules and the way the bureaucracy interprets rules, policies, and procedures); *political* (coalitions of organizational managers with different functions, but in reciprocal interdependence, interact as colleagues to decide on strategies); and *professional* (small groups, dyads, or individuals control the requisite information in an open system and provide strategic direction with new rules).

On the basis of their experience as consultants, Farkas and De Backer (1996) enumerated five strategies that could be pursued by the chief executive to manage for success: (1) Act as the organization's top strategist, systematically envisioning the future and planning how to get there; (2) Concentrate on the organization's human assets—its policies, programs, and principles about people; (3) Champion specific expertise to focus the organization's human assets; (4) Create a "box" of rules, systems, procedures, and values to control behavior and outcomes within well-defined boundaries; (5) Act as a radical change agent to transform the organization from a bureaucracy into an adaptive organization that embraces what is new and different.

An important executive function is to remain alert to trends in one's own and other relevant industries, and one's own and other organizations, regarding the possibilities and expected utilities of insourcing and outsourcing. Parry (1999) conducted a qualitative study of local government administrators in New Zealand. From interviews with and responses of senior, middle, and operational leaders, it was possible to categorize their strategies. Social influence enhanced adaptability and resolved uncertainty. These leaders developed strategies to enhance their own and their followers' adaptability to the uncertainties of change.

Commonalties in Types and Taxonomies

Despite the plethora of diverse types and taxonomies of leadership, five common themes appear: (1) The leader helps set and clarify the missions and goals of the individual member, the group, or the organization; (2) The leader energizes and directs others to pursue the missions and goals; (3) The leader helps provide the structure, methods, tactics, and instruments for achieving the goals; (4) The leader helps resolve conflicting views about means and ends; (5) The leader evaluates the individual, group, or organizational contribution to the effort. Many of the taxonomies include certain styles: authoritative, dominating, directive, autocratic, and persuasive. Common types are democratic, participative, group-developing, supportive, and considerate. Other types include intellectual, expert, executive, bureaucrat, administrator, representative, spokesperson, and advocate.

It is possible to encapsulate many of these types into the dichotomy of autocratic versus democratic. The autocratic type correlates with the directive type, and the democratic type correlates with the participative or considerate type. The executive is not regarded as a separate type but is classified as either task-oriented (autocratic) or relations-oriented (democratic). The persuasive pattern of behavior is a subclass of task-oriented or initiating behavior. However, in many situations the representative (spokesperson's) pattern of behavior is independent of task orientation and relations orientation. The intellectual type, the expert, often ignored early on, was soon seen to be required for any comprehensive theory of leadership.[11] Yukl (2002) validated a hierarchical model of leaders' behavior as best fitting using *change* in addition to *task* and *relations* as second-order metacategories. *Change* included the first-order factors of visioning, intellectual stimulation, risk taking, and external monitoring. *Relations* encompassed developing, supporting, consulting, recognizing, and empowering. *Task* included the primary categories of clarifying, monitoring, and short-term planning. Goodness of fit and other tests of the model came from 275 questionnaire descriptions of the behavior of supervisors and middle managers by their immediate subordinates.

Yukl (1987a, 1989) found strong similarities across these types and taxonomies of the behavior of leaders, dealing with leadership in the small group and the large organization, as provided by other investigators including Bowers and Seashore (1966), House and Mitchell (1974), Luthans and Lockwood (1984), Mintzberg (1973), Morse and Wagner (1978), Page (1985), and Stogdill (1963). Yukl also demonstrated that the descriptive scales of his taxonomy when used by subordinates to describe their leaders were highly reliable and discriminated accurately among the supervisors being described (Yukl, 1987b).

An Integrated Model. Mumford, Fleishman, Levin, et al. (1988) summarized and integrated these efforts in a single taxonomic model. Their summary classification included: (1) the search for and structuring of information (acquisition, organization, evaluation, feedback, and control); (2) the use of information in problem solving (identifying requirements, planning, coordinating, and communicating); (3) managing personnel resources (acquisition, allocation, development, motivation, utilization, and monitoring); and (4) managing material resources (acquisition, maintenance, utilization, and monitoring). Information is acquired and then organized and evaluated to identify needs and requirements for planning and coordinating to obtain, allocate, and maintain material and personnel resources. For their utilization, personnel need development and motivation. Feedback and control loop back to the acquiring of information. Winter (1978, 1979b) created a similar model for tests and measures of leadership competencies that will be discussed in Chapter 23.[12]

[11] As detailed in Chapter 27.
[12] This taxonomy will be discussed in detail in Chapter 23.

Summary and Conclusions

Early in the scientific process, efforts were made to classify phenomena. Investigators have focused on classifications of leaders of crowds, institutions, industry, education, politics, legislative opinion, and communities. They have made an important distinction between transactional leaders, who concentrate on an exchange relation of what they and their followers want; and transformational leaders, who strive to arouse and satisfy the higher-level needs of their followers. Various sociopsychological classifications of small-group leaders are also available. Many of these classifications can be seen in terms of either a task orientation or a relations orientation.

Models and Theories of Leadership

Theories of leadership attempt to explain its emergence or its nature and its consequences. Theories of management focus on its governance and consequences. Models show the interplay among the variables that are perceived to be involved; they are replicas or reconstructions of reality. Both theories and models can be useful in defining research problems for the social and political scientist and in improving prediction and control in the development and application of leadership. In this chapter we will introduce briefly the most prominent theories of leadership, Many will be discussed in more detail in later chapters as appropriate.

Until the late 1940s, most theories of leadership focused on the personal traits of leaders. According to these theories, leadership depended on leaders' abilities and personality characteristics. Then, up to the late 1960s, personal styles of leadership rose in prominence. From the late 1960s to the early 1980s, leadership studies became contingent on a mix of leaders' and followers' traits and situations. Leadership theories of inspiration and transformation emerged in the early 1980s and became prominent in the 1990s and at the turn of the twenty-first century. Theories of management paralleled the rise of civilization, and management practice was exemplified in the rules of planning, organizing, and controlling. Theories of management became more sophisticated in the twentieth century and were strongly influenced by the advent of computerization, information science, and globalization.

Before 1970, there were many complaints about a lack of theory to provide hypotheses for empirical research to test. Since then, diverse theories and models have been abundant as a source of hypotheses. However, relatively few of these models and theories have dominated the research community, and many have been restatements of the obvious. On the other hand, progress has been made when the models and theories have been built on astute observations and on assumptions that are the result of insightful observations. Good theories are disciplined imagination (Weick, 1995). They are internally consistent and consistent with a more general body of propositions from the social sciences. For instance, theories about reinforcement leadership have been built from what is generally known about reinforcement theories. Transformational leadership theory has similarly benefited from motivational theory.

Good and Bad Theories

Diagrams, speculations, and hypotheses are not theories; nor are cited references, data, and variables that are used in place of theory (Sutton & Staw, 1995). Rather, good theories usually start from one idea or a small set of ideas. They make possible a logically detailed case characterized by simplicity and interconnectedness. Predictions are presented with underlying causal logic: "The process includes abstracting, generalizing, relating, selecting, explaining, synthesizing, and idealizing." Good theories explain how and why (Sutton & Staw, 1995, p. 389). DiMaggio (1995) adds that good theories provide "categories and . . . assumptions that . . . (clear) away conventional notions to make room for artful and exciting insights" (p. 391). Good theories emerge from various experiences. Observations and inferences from frequent contact with leaders and followers help. Connections are identified between observations and concepts that heretofore were not seen to be connected. There is a convergence of several interests and activities at the same time. Intuition and feelings supplement logical analysis. There is a desire to explain, understand, and find meaning in the real world. Ideas are confronted and confirmed or disconfirmed. Conventional wisdom may be revised or reversed. Research is restated in alternative ways. Established value judgments are challenged. Above all, to be good, theories need to be grounded in assumptions that fit the facts. Theorizing and modeling are now common-place in providing the rationale to justify and test empirical hypotheses. These will be discussed more fully as they become relevant to the topics of later chapters.

Nothing is supposed to be as practical as a good theory (Lewin, 1947), but nothing seems more impractical than a bad one (Bass, 1974). A theory is supposed to be a way of trying to explain the facts. Unfortunately, theories about leadership sometimes obscure the facts. Much effort then has to be expended in coping with the obscurity. Poor research derives from poor theory. Poor research is often expedient, quick, and convenient. Klimoski (2005) notes that bad theory is dangerous. And according to Ghoshal (2005), bad management theories are destroying good management practices. Examples are agency theory (Jensen & Meckling, 1976) and transaction costs theory (Williamson, 1975). *Agency theory* assumes that managers are bent on maximizing their own interests at the expense of all the other constituencies of the organization. *Transaction costs theory* assumes that managers are in deadly competition with each other. Monitoring and tight control of their opportunistic behavior are needed. They cannot be trusted. To gain a comparative advantage requires a company to compete not only with other companies but also with its own suppliers, customers, employees, and regulators (Porter, 1980). These "ideologically inspired" amoral theories are being preached in many business schools and management development programs. They free future organizational leaders from any sense of moral responsibility for their decisions. and encourage rather than inhibit their opportunistic behavior (Ghoshal & Moran, 1996). Scientism rather than science makes these bad theories appealing, for their derived propositions can be reproduced with mathematical models. They would be good theories if their assumptions about human behavior were correct. In fact, governance based on the assumption that managers are self-aggrandizing and cannot be trusted results in less trustworthy managers (Osterloh & Fry, 2003). Deductions from these economic theories that control of managers requires more independent boards of directors, and that corporate performance is improved if the positions of board chairman and CEO are separated, are not supported empirically (Dalton, Daily, Ellstrand, et al., 1998). But the same could be said about cognitive, behavioral, and social theories based on faulty assumptions about human and social behavior.

There was a long-held theory that efficiency increased if work was divided into parts so each worker could specialize; but the effects on the workers' motivation were ignored.

Ferraro, Pfeffer, and Sutton (2005) point to a further complication and effect of bad theory and practice. They cite evidence that corporate managers are less interested in first evaluating whether a new fad increases effectiveness and profitability, and more interested in showing that they have adopted the latest popular theory or practice without really finding out its effects. They treat the effects as self-fulfilling prophesies. And political leaders have done the same thing, according to Keynes (1936), with damaging long-term effects on the economy and society.

Sources of Current Models and Theories

With the growth of cognitive psychology we have seen cognitive theories and models of leadership added to the earlier behavioral and social theories. Zaccaro (1996) has combined cognitive, behavioral, and social approaches in a "Leaderplex Model" of executive leadership (see also Hooijberg, Hunt, & Dodge, 1997). Theories of leadership with extensive empirical support of effects on followers' effectiveness and satisfaction can be broadly classified as instrumental, inspirational, and informal. *Instrumental* theories focus on the leader's orientation to the task or to the person, on leaders' direction or followers' participation, on leaders' initiative or consideration of their followers', and on leaders' promises and rewards or threats and disciplinary action. *Inspirational* theories of leadership include charismatic, transformational, and visionary theories. These focus on emotional and ideological appeals, displaying exemplary behavior, confidence, symbolism, and concentrating on intrinsic motivation. *Informal* leadership theories deal with the emergence and service of effective leaders who lack formal positions and authority (House, 1995).

Cognitive Theories

Implicit Theories of Leadership (ILTs). Implicit theories of leadership (ILTs) are the concept of "leader" that different people have in mind. These implicit leadership theories about leaders and followers affect the relations between them. An ILT may be about instrumental, inspirational, or informal leadership. ILTs are beliefs about how leaders behave, in general, and what is expected of them (Eden & Levitan, 1975). Such theories are naive concepts of leadership, revealed (for instance) when people are asked to list a number of traits that come to mind when they think of the term "leader." Although respondents may be affected by individual, gender, social, organizational, and cultural differences, ordinarily their similarities outweigh their differences. Therefore, it is possible to determine a generalized image or "prototype" of the concept of a leader. We can then compare prototypes that may emerge from markedly different samples, such as Americans and Chinese. In the same way, different prototypes can be discriminated among the concepts of 11 types of leaders: business leaders, sports leaders, etc. (Lord, Foti, DeVader, 1984). There is little difference between the prototype of a "leader" and that of an "effective leader." However, the term "supervisor" receives somewhat less favorable trait ratings from college students than the terms "leader" and "effective" leader (Offerman, Kennedy, Wirtz, 1999).

For college students, T. Keller (1999) found ILTs for "leader" comparable to those of Offerman et al. (1999). In addition, she obtained modest correlations of selected ascribed traits of "leader," self-rated personality using the NEO five-factor personality inventory, and perceived parental traits. For instance, the extent to which respondents perceived *sensitivity* as a characteristic of a "leader" correlated significantly (.20) with the respondents' self-rated "openness." Dedication as a trait of a leader correlated .23 with their self-rated "conscientiousness" and .31 with their perceived "paternal dedication." A number of other such correlations were found, suggesting to Keller that individuals perceive a leader as mirroring traits of themselves and their fathers.

Another application of implicit leadership theory was a study to determine 378 undergraduates' idea of characteristics required for a new leader to be accepted by a group. The list of 16 expectations formed four abstract categories: (1) taking charge, (2) learning the group's goals, (3) being nervous, and (4) being a nice person (Kenny, Blascovich, & Shaver, 1994).

Increased interest in implicit leadership has paralleled a cognitive revolution in psychology and developments in information processing. Lord and Maher's (1991) book, *Leadership and Information Processing: Linking Perceptions and Performance*, is illustrative.

In organizations, these are—in contrast to implicit theories—concepts espoused in formal documents, memorandums, and executives' speeches. These state intentions, goals, objectives, and desired relationships of leaders and managers with their various constituencies. Or they may be *theories in practice*, theories actually guiding the behavior of members of the organization that can be observed, expressed, or inferred in interviews with members (Argyris, 1982).

Grounded Theory. Grounded theory is closely allied to implicit leadership theory. If a theory of leadership is to be used for diagnosis, training, and development, it must be grounded in the users' concepts, assumptions, language, and expressions. The users include emergent leaders and followers in informal organizations as well as managers, administrators, and officials in formal organizations (Glaser & Strauss, 1967; Strauss & Corbin, 1990). Qualitative research is often grounded. But such grounding requires conceptual rigor. There may be a loss of generality and less opportunity to apply standardized measurements. Grounded research generates rather than tests theory (Parry, 1998).

Biological-Genetic Theories

"He was born to lead." "She instinctively knew how to take charge." "The coach was a natural leader." Such comments assume that nature has been more important than nurture in the emergence of a particular leader. But until recently a majority of social scientists considered nurture more important than nature. Nonetheless, *leaders are both born and made*. The importance of health, physique, and energy in the emergence of leadership has long been recognized. Additionally, with advances in genetics and neuropsychology, as well as speculations about evolution and recognition of the biological differences between the sexes, has come an appreciation of inborn traits and the expression of genes.

As Spinoza said, "Man is a social animal." Lawrence (1997) has enumerated four built-in evolutionary survival factors in humans that affect their organizational life, and therefore leader-follower relations: (1) a need to acquire; (2) a need to bond; (3) a need to learn; and (4) an inborn reflexive mechanism to avoid pain. They involve strong emotions and a strong motivation toward goal-oriented behavior. The acquisitive needs of followers are helped by instrumental and transactional leadership. Social-bonding needs are fulfilled by considerate and charismatic leaders. Learning needs of followers are fulfilled when leaders clarify purposes. Followers' pain is avoided when coercive, ruthless leadership is avoided.

Great-Man Theories. Jennings (1960) reviewed the "great man" theory. For many commentators, history is shaped by the leadership of great men. Without Moses, according to these theorists, the Jews would have remained in Egypt; without Winston Churchill, the British would have given up in 1940; without Bill Gates, there would have been no firm like Microsoft.

The eighteenth-century rationalists felt that to determine the course of history, luck had to be added to the personal attributes of great men. The Russian Revolution would have taken a different course if Lenin had been hanged by the old regime instead of being exiled. For romantic philosophers such as Friedrich Nietzsche, a sudden decision by a great man (Thomas Jefferson's decision to purchase Louisiana, for example) could alter the course of history. William James (1880) believed that certain mutations of society were due to great men, who initiated movement and prevented others from leading society in another direction. According to James, the history of the world is the history of great men, who determined what the masses could accomplish. Carlyle's (1841) essay on heroes reinforced the concept of the leader as a person endowed with unique qualities that captured the imagination of the masses. The hero would contribute somehow, no matter where he was found. History was created by the acts of great leaders. Leaders molded the masses. (Despite the examples of Joan of Arc, Elizabeth I, and Catherine the Great, great women were ignored.) Dowd (1936) maintained that "there is no such thing as leadership by the masses. The individuals in every society possess different degrees of intelligence, energy, and moral force, and in whatever direction the masses may be influenced to go, they are always led by the superior few." Although one of many civil rights leaders, Martin Luther King, Jr., was considered the great man whose leadership inspired the civil rights movement. The great-man theory of leadership was espoused to show how faltering or threatened organizations could be turned around by business executives like Lee Iacocca,

military leaders like Douglas MacArthur, and political figures like Margaret Thatcher.

Influenced by Galton's (1869) study of the hereditary background of great men, several early theorists attempted to explain leadership on the basis of inheritance. Woods (1913) studied 14 nations over periods of five to ten centuries and found that the conditions of reign approximated the ruler's capability. The brothers of kings (as a result of natural endowment) also tended to become men of power and influence. Woods concluded that the man makes the nation and shapes it in accordance with his abilities. In line with the eugenics movement, Wiggam (1931) proposed that the survival of the fittest people and intermarriage among them produces an aristocratic class, which differs biologically from the lower classes. Thus an adequate supply of superior leaders depends on a proportionally high birthrate among the abler classes.

The Warrior Model of Leadership. This variant of the great-man theory appeared in several classics: Suntzu's *Art of War* (c. 400 B.C.), Aristotle's *Politics* (324 B.C.), Machiavelli's *The Prince* (1513), Gratian's *The Art of Worldly Wisdom* (1643), and Clausewitz's *On War* (1833). General George Patton exemplified the warrior model. Wars are won or lost, according to this theory, depending on the leadership of the opposing forces. Thus, Napoleon's and Julius Caesar's tactics often spelled the difference between victory and defeat in battle. President Lincoln had to replace the commanding general of his Union army numerous times before he found, in Ulysses Grant a commander who was able and willing to use his forces, superior in size and logistics, to take the initiative and accept the casualties needed to wear down Robert E. Lee's Confederate forces. Victorious warrior leaders win fame and power. They control flows of information. The means justify the ends for them, even if they must resort to deception, betrayal, violence, and other morally questionable acts. These acts may be delegated to subordinates so that the leaders are held blameless. Planning and preparation assume that the world is a dangerous place (Nice, 1998).

Trait Theories

The great-man theories drew attention to the specific qualities of leaders and their identification (Kohs and Irle, 1920). L. L. Bernard (1926), Bingham (1927), Tead

(1929), Page (1935), and Kilbourne (1935) all explained leadership in terms of traits of personality and character. Bird (1940) compiled a list of 79 relevant traits from 20 psychologically oriented studies. Similar reviews were done by Smith and Krueger (1933) for educators, and by W. O. Jenkins (1947) for military leaders.

Until the 1940s, much research about leaders and leadership focused on individual traits. Leaders were seen as different from nonleaders in various attributes and tested personality traits. Two questions were usually posed: (1) What traits distinguish leaders from other people?; (2) What is the extent of the differences? The pure trait theory eventually fell into disfavor. Stogdill's (1948) critique concluded that both person and situation had to be included to explain the emergence of leadership. But as will be seen in Chapter 5, traits are still considered of great importance in the study of leadership.

Charismatic-Transformational Leadership Theory.[1] Max Weber (1924/1947) introduced a religious concept—charisma—into the social sciences to describe leaders who are perceived as endowed with extraordinary abilities. Charismatic leaders are highly expressive, articulate, and emotionally appealing. They are self-confident, determined, active, and energetic. Their followers want to identify with them, have complete faith and confidence in them, and hold them in awe. Generally, charismatic leaders have strong positive effects on their followers. House (1977) presented a theory of charismatic leadership that specified the expected behavior of charismatic leaders and their followers, stimulating renewed interest in empirical studies of this subject.

According to Hunt (1999), for the empirical study of leadership, transformational leadership was a new paradigm (Kuhn, 1964)—a change of views, preferred methods, acceptable findings, interpretations of findings, and important areas to study. Transformational leadership was first mentioned by Downton (1973) and first formalized as a theory by Burns (1978). In contrast to transactional leaders, transformational leaders were said to motivate followers to go beyond their own self-interests for the good of the group, organization, or society. Followers' interests are raised by transformational leaders from concerns for security to concerns for achievement.

[1] More on theories about the charismatic leader will be found in Chapter 21.

Followers are encouraged to meet the challenges they face, to excel, and to self-actualize. Bass (1985a) presented models of the factors in transformational and transactional leadership. House and Aditya (1997) viewed transformational leadership as close in meaning to charismatic leadership. Bass (1985a) found that charismatic leadership was the largest factor in transformational leadership but only one of several other empirical factors with which it correlated, including inspirational leadership, intellectual stimulation, and individualized consideration. Transactional leadership encompassed contingent reward, management by exception, and passive or laissez-faire leadership. This was confirmed empirically by Avolio, Bass, and Jung (1999), among others.

By 1960, the dominant paradigm for the study of leadership had evolved from research on the traits and situations that affect leadership to something more dynamic. Leadership was now seen as contingent on traits and situations involving a *transaction* or exchange between the leader and the led (Hollander, 1986). In this view, leaders promise rewards and benefits to subordinates in exchange for the subordinates' fulfillment of agreements with the leader. Even the psychoanalysts conceived of followers as complying with the leader to obtain the leader's love. But Freud (1922) suggested that there was more to the concept of leadership than a mere exchange: the leader embodied ideals with which the follower identified. Barnard (1938) noted that personal loyalty was more powerful than "tangible inducements." But along with Downton (1973), Burns (1978) presented the new paradigm of the transformational as opposed to the transactional leader. The transformational leader asks followers to transcend their own self-interests for the good of the group, organization, or society; to consider their long-term need for self-development rather than their need of the moment; and to become more aware of what is really important. Hence, followers are converted into leaders. Among 90 transformational leaders who were interviewed, Bennis (1984) found evidence of competence to manage attention and meaning, to articulate visions of what was possible, and to empower the collective effect of their leadership.

Burns's conceptualization of leadership as either transforming or transactional was modified by Bass (1985a, 1985b), who proposed that transformational leadership augmented the effects of transactional leadership on the efforts, satisfaction, and effectiveness of followers. Many great transformational leaders, including Abraham Lincoln, Franklin Delano Roosevelt, and John F. Kennedy, did not shy away from being transactional as well as transformational. Lincoln, Roosevelt, and Kennedy were able to move the nation as well as play petty politics. Waldman and Bass's (1985) analysis of surveys of senior military officers and business managers confirmed the fidelity of the model. Tichy and Devanna (1986) described the hybrid nature of transformational leadership. According to them, transformational leadership is not due just to charisma. It is "a behavioral process capable of being learned and managed. It's a leadership process that is systematic, consisting of purposeful and organized search for changes, systematic analysis, and the capacity to move resources from areas of lesser to greater productivity . . . [to bring about] a strategic transformation" (p. viii).

On the basis of Kegan's (1982) theory of the evolving self, Kuhnert and Russell (1989) designed a four-stage model of how the transformational leader develops. Factor-analytic studies done by Bass (1985b) and confirmed by Avolio, Bass, and Jung (1999) have suggested that transformational leadership can be conceptually organized along four correlated dimensions: (1) charismatic leadership, (2) inspirational leadership, (3) intellectual stimulation, and (4) individualized consideration. For House (1977) and Conger (1999) all four components are contained within their concept of charismatic leadership (House & Shamir, 1993). Later chapters detail the antecedents and consequences of transformational and charismatic leadership. The components of *transactional* leadership are contingent reinforcement, expressed usually as contingent reinforcement and management by exception, which will be examined at length in Chapters 15 and 16.

According to a leader's subordinates, colleagues, and superiors, transformational-charismatic leadership correlates more highly with the leader's effectiveness than contingent-reward leadership does. Contingent reward, in turn, correlates more highly with the leader's effectiveness than reactive management by exception or contingent punishment do. Satisfaction with the leader follows a similar pattern (Bass & Avolio, 1989). Similar results can be obtained when different sources are used to describe the leader and to more objectively evaluate the outcomes of leadership in terms of effectiveness and sat-

isfaction (Lowe, Kroek, & Sivasubramaniam, 1996). In the same way, House and his associates (e.g., House, Spangler, & Woyke, 1991) have reported numerous studies showing positive correlations between charismatic and effective leadership. Conger and Kanungo (1998) along with Sashkin (1988) focused on the process effects of charisma on the followers and on the leader's need to articulate a vision to be accepted and followed.

Transformational leadership is closer to the "prototype" of leadership that people have in mind when they describe an ideal leader and is more likely to provide a role model with which subordinates want to identify (Bass & Avolio, 1988). In practice, this means that leaders develop in their subordinates an expectation of high performance rather than merely spend time praising or reprimanding them (Gilbert, 1985). For Bradford and Cohen (1984), the manager must be more than a hero of technical competence and organizing skills. He or she must become a developer of people and a builder of teams.

Servant Leadership. Less well researched but still prominent, servant leadership was formulated by Greenleaf (1977) and was based on his experiences as an executive. According to Greenleaf, ego spurs achievement, but leaders need to curb their own egos, convert their followers into leaders, and become the first among equals. The needs of others must be the leaders' highest priority. Power has to be shared by empowering followers. Leaders should think of themselves as servants building relationships with their followers that help their followers to grow (Buchen, 1998). Servant leaders must be oriented to the future as stewards of the human and physical resources for which they are responsible. Leaders who are stewards are similar to but not the same as servant leaders. Stewards try to balance the interests of all the different constituents of their organization: shareholders, owners, managers, peers, subordinates, customers, clients, and community (Bass, 1965; Donaldson, 1990). Servant leaders are especially concerned about constituencies with less power or more need for help. Servant leadership also shares much in common with transformational leadership: vision, influence, credibility, and trust (Farling, Gregory & Stone, 1999).

Closely aligned with servant leadership is a model of organizational leadership by Choi and Mai-Dalton

(1999): *self-sacrificial leaders* abandon or postpone their own interests, privileges, or welfare in the way they work with their followers. They give up or postpone rewards to which they are fairly or legitimately entitled. They voluntarily give up or refrain from using their positional or personal power. In one study that used scenarios about a self-sacrificing company president and a non-self-sacrificing president, university students and white-collar employees judged the self-sacrificing president as more charismatic and legitimate. These respondents stated that they would be more likely to reciprocate in self-sacrifice if the president was self-sacrificing.

Situational Theories

In direct opposition to trait theorists, situational theorists have argued that leadership is a matter of situational demands; that is, situational factors determine who will emerge as a leader. Particularly in the United States, situationalism was favored over the theory that leaders are born, not made. According to situationalism, the leader is a product of the situation and circumstances. not self-made and not a product of personality, drive, or ability (Stogdill, 1975).

The controversy over which is more important to leadership—situation or personality—is an ancient one. Plutarch's *Parallel Lives* (c. A.D. 100) described how for each type of leader who emerged in Greece, one emerged under parallel conditions in Rome. Alexander the Great, for instance, had his counterpart in Julius Caesar. The great-man theorists believed that it was all a matter of personality and personality development—that Alexanders and Caesars would surface no matter what conditions surrounded them. The situationalists thought otherwise: for example, they sought to identify conditions that gave rise to the emergence of the "man on the white horse," the dictator who appears following revolutionary upheaval, chaotic politics, social and economic distress, and a weakening of traditional institutions.

The situationalists advanced the view that the emergence of a great leader is a result of time, place, and circumstance. For Hegel, the great man was an expression of the needs of his times. What the great man did was automatically right, because he provided what was needed. The great man actually could not help what he did; he was directed and controlled by his historical environment. For example, the need for civil peace made it man-

datory for Octavian to make himself sole ruler of Rome, form the Roman Principate, and destroy republicanism. If Octavian had not appeared to carry out these changes, someone else would have done the same. Herbert Spencer believed that societies evolved in a uniform, gradual, progressive manner, and no great man could change the course of this development. Engels, Marx, and their successors believed that economic necessity made history. The American Civil War was, then, an inevitable clash caused by the conflicting economic interests of North and South. Economic determinists held that obstacles to expanding production had to be overcome. The greater the obstacles, the greater this need was and the more capable the required leader had to be. But who he turned out to be was irrelevant (Hook, 1943). Mumford (1909) agreed that who emerged as a leader depended on the abilities and skills required at a given time to solve the prevailing social problems. Although these abilities and skills were innate as well as acquired, leadership, as such, stemmed from the organized phases of the social process or the habitual ways in which people adapt to each other. Thus, according to the situationalists, the national condition determined the development and emergence of great military figures. For A. J. Murphy (1941), leadership did not reside in a person but was a function of the occasion. The situation called for certain types of action; the leader did not inject leadership but was the instrumental factor through which a problem was solved. For Person (1928), any particular situation played a large part in determining the leadership qualities and the leader for that situation. Moreover, the leadership required in that situation was a product of a succession of previous leadership situations that molded the leader.

J. Schneider (1937) noted that the number of great military leaders in England was proportional to the number of conflicts in which the nation engaged. Spiller (1929) concluded that a broad survey of the field of human progress would show that 95% of the advance was unconnected with great men. Rather, a great man like Martin Luther King, Jr., would appear at a critically important point of a socially valued cause, would devote himself to it, and would profit greatly from the work of many others. Thus, time itself was an important variable for the situationalists. The passage of time changed the situation and the people involved. Thierry, Den Hartog, Koopman, et al. (1997) viewed Dutch people's preferences for leadership as a matter of Dutch history and trends. Leadership was conceived as a relational process that unfolded over time. Time might be needed for trust to develop before an individual could emerge as a leader. Time made an important addition to models and theories of leadership. Repeated measurements over time are important to analyses of leaders' performance (Hollenbeck, Ilgen, & Sego, 1994). Bogardus (1918) presented the view that the type of leadership that developed in a group was determined by the nature of the group and the problems it had to solve. Hocking (1924) went even further, suggesting that leadership resided in the group and was granted to leaders only when they put forth a program that the group was willing to follow.

A *Rational-Deductive Model.* Vroom and Yetton (1974) rationally linked some of the accepted facts about directive and participative decision making as assumptions. From these, they created prescriptions for the leadership style that was most likely to succeed in a given situation. They posed ten questions that leaders should ask themselves in deciding whether to be directive or participative in making decisions with their subordinates and whether to do so primarily with individual subordinates or with the whole group at once. Essentially, the prescriptions were that supervisors ought to be directive when they were confident that they knew what needed to be done and when their subordinates did not have this knowledge. Furthermore, in this situation, the subordinates would accept the decision made by the supervisor. However, if the subordinates had more information than the supervisor, if the subordinates' acceptance and commitment were of paramount importance, and if the subordinates could be trusted to concern themselves with the organization's interests, the supervisor should be participative.

Vroom and Jago (1988) created an improved model. Instead of requiring yes-or-no answers to the questions, they provided a five-point scale of possible answers: (1) no, (2) probably no, (3) maybe, (4) probably yes, (5) yes. The older model used only two criteria for the decision rules: acceptance of the decision by followers, and the quality of the decision. The five-point scale made it possible for the leader to prioritize possible decisions, reducing the several feasible alternatives into a single decision.[2]

----

[2]Empirical research in support of the validity of the Vroom and Yetton model is presented in Chapter 18.

Person-Situation Theories

Although wars and other crises present opportunities for the acquisition of leadership by persons who would otherwise remain submerged in the daily round of routine activities, various theorists have maintained that the situation is not in itself sufficient to account for leadership. How many crises arise that do not produce a person who is equal to the occasion? A combination of personal and situational elements needs to be considered. James (1880) pointed out that the "great man" needs help. His talents need to fit with the situation. Ulysses Grant, for instance, was a failure in private life before his emergence as the Union's great military commander, and he failed again afterward as president. His rise to commanding general of the Army of the Potomac was delayed by the many political appointees who came before him and took turns displaying their ineptitude before an exasperated President Lincoln turned to him. Grant's leadership in the Vicksburg campaign brought victory, despite the orders of his superior, General Halleck, to fall back toward New Orleans. But it was Grant's persistence, and some help by congressmen, that overcame the inertia of the political appointment system; and the traits of persistence and confidence marked the style with which he hammered out his military victories (Williams, 1952).

The great man theorists and the situational theorists both attempt to explain leadership as an effect of a single set of forces, and both overlook the combined effects of individual and situational factors. In reaction, Westburgh (1931) suggested that the study of leadership must include the affective, intellectual, and action traits of the individual, as well as the specific conditions under which the individual operates. Case (1933) maintained that leadership is produced by a conjunction of three factors: (1) the personality traits of the leader, (2) the nature of the group and its members, and (3) the event confronting the group. J. F. Brown (1936) proposed five field-dynamic laws of leadership: leaders must (1) be identified as members of the group they are attempting to lead; (2) be of high interpersonal potential; (3) adapt themselves to the existing structure of relationships; (4) realize the long-term trends in the structure; (5) recognize that leadership increases in potency at the cost of reduced freedom of leadership.

Hook (1943) noted that there is some restriction in the range of traits that a given situation permits the emergent leader to have. Thus heroic action is decisive only when alternative courses of action are possible. Exiled to Elba, close to France, Napoleon had alternatives; exiled to Saint Helena, in the South Atlantic and more closely guarded, he had none.

Bass (1960) argued that controversy over the great man versus the situation was a pseudo problem. For any given case, some of the variance in what happens is due to the situation, some is due to the individual, and some is due to the combined effects of the individual and the situation. Mao Zedong played a critical role in the Chinese revolution, but without the chaotic state of Chinese affairs under the Kuomintang, his rise to power would not have been possible. Dansereau, Alutto, and Yammarino (1984) developed the multiple-levels analysis, to be described later. It provided a complete statistical formulation of models to examine the interplay of leader, individual follower, group, and organizational situation. Personal-situational theorists argue that theories of leadership cannot be constructed in a vacuum: they must contain elements of the person as well as elements of the situation. Any theory of leadership must take account of the interplay between the situation and the individual. Barnard (1938) and many others (C. A. Gibb, 1947; Jenkins, 1947; Lapiere, 1938; Murphy, 1941) attempted to resolve the controversy over situation versus personality by suggesting that leadership behavior is a less consistent attribute of individuals than such traits as nonsuggestibility, energy, and maturity, which are empirically associated and theoretically linked with overt leadership behavior. Leaders with a strong personal tendency to be consistent will display leadership across many situations.

Stogdill (1948) concluded that leaders' traits must bear some relevant relationship to the characteristics of the followers. An adequate analysis of leadership needs a study not only of leaders, but of the situation. Stogdill's position strongly influenced the theories that followed. According to Gerth and Mills (1952, pp. 405–406), "to understand leadership, attention must be paid to (1) the traits and motives of the leader as a man, (2) images that selected publics hold of him and their motives for following him, (3) the features of the role that he plays as a leader, and (4) the institutional context in which he and his followers may be involved." C. A. Gibb (1954, p. 914) suggested that "leadership is an interactional phenomenon arising when group formation takes place." A group

structure emerges. Each member of the group is assigned a relative position within the group depending on the nature of his or her relations with the other members. It is a general phenomenon and depends on the interrelation of individuals pursuing a common goal. Similarly, Stogdill and Shartle (1955) proposed that leadership needs to be studied in terms of the status, interactions, perceptions, and behavior of individuals in relation to other members of an organized group. Leadership should be regarded as a relationship between persons rather than as a characteristic of an isolated individual. Data for all the members of a group should be combined and interrelated to study leadership in terms of the structural and functional dimensions of the organized interrelationships.

Wofford (1981) presented an elaborate integration of concepts and research results from behavioral studies of ability, motivation, role perception, environmental constraints, determinants of the behavior of leaders, and environmental influences. This *leader-environment-follower interaction theory* conceived of the leader as a person who analyzes current deficiencies in the conditions that determine the performance of followers and takes corrective action. The theory appeared to concentrate on the practice of management by exception. Bennis (1961) concluded that theories explaining who emerged and succeeded as a leader in an organization had to take into account: (1) the impersonal bureaucracy, (2) the informal organization and interpersonal relations, (3) the benevolent autocracy that structures the relationship between superiors and subordinates, (4) the job design that permits individual self-actualization, and (5) the integration of individual and organizational goals.

The personal-situational approach has come to dominate the forecasting of leadership potential in prospective supervisors and managers. The effort builds on attempts to match individuals' personal history, competencies, and traits with the requirements of a job. Since the late 1970s, analyses of the inspirational, charismatic, transformational leader, and the servant leader have all looked at both the person and the situation. Crises are seen to lie behind the rise of charismatic leaders whose personal development and personality move them to succeed in taking charge. Transformational leaders are usually personally assertive. They react to their perceptions of what their followers need, but they also proactively influence what their followers want. Servant leaders are strongly service-oriented and are influenced by what their organization and followers need. A description that emerged from a conference about what was expected of senior managers illustrates the importance of both person and situation: "Leaders should be uncommon (yet congenial, vulnerable, and accessible); capable as almost to promote awe." A leader should be "a faultless reader of signals from the environment, a diagnostician capable of taking corrective action; . . . an architect who builds an enabling organization" (Wilson, 1994).

Increasingly, behavioral theories postulate leadership as an interaction among the leader, the situation, and the led (e.g., Popper, 2001). Yammarino (1991) reasoned that a full explanation of leadership and situation requires a multiple-level approach: leaders, leader-follower pairs, groups, and organizations. At the level of leaders, whether and how much the leaders differ are examined. At the level of the leader-follower pair (the dyad), analyzed is how much the leader relates differently to each follower. At the level of groups, the question is to what extent each leader's followers differ. At the level of organizations, the question is whether and how much differences in leadership depend on the organization—above and beyond any differences among the different groups and leaders. Many other analyses are possible across levels. These within-and-between analyses (WABAs) are appearing with increasing frequency.

Psychoanalytic Theories

Freud (1922), as well as many other psychoanalytically oriented writers such as Erikson (1964), Frank (1939), Fromm (1941), and H. Levinson (1970), addressed leadership at length, in terms of clinical studies. Favorite interpretations conceived of the leader as a source of love or fear, as the embodiment of the superego, and as an emotional outlet for followers' frustration and destructive aggression (Wolman, 1971). Freud (1913) proposed that the beginnings of civilization required a struggle with the leader (father) of the primitive clan. A primal horde of sons slew their father and formed a society of equals, but the need for leadership resulted in the rise of totemism and religion, in which gods substituted for the murdered father. According to Freud (1922), group behavior is emotional and irrational. Groups of followers are both

obedient to and intolerant of authority and require strength and forcefulness in their leaders. They are oppressed by, fearful of, and ruled by leaders. The group mind determines its cohesiveness. The followers' identification with the leader shapes their identification with each other. However, within their personalities, they remain in a state of tension. Their ego (rationality) is too weak to resolve the conflict with their id (instincts) and superego (social and moral imperatives). But leaders are without emotional attachment to anyone. They are narcissistic, independent, and self-confident.

Wolfenstein (1977) and Lasswell (1960) made extensive use of psychoanalytic theories to account for political and revolutionary leaders. Lasswell held that the personality of a political person compensates for feelings of inadaquacy and low esteem by displacement, by a continuing pursuit of power to maintain personal integrity. This personal need is rationalized as "in the public interest" (Lasswell, 1962). According to Wolfenstein, the personality of a revolutionary leader is an externalized revolt against a parent. It is the Oedipus complex projected against society. Much of this psychoanalytic theorizing about leadership attempted to explain leaders' political behavior by looking at their early childhood and families. Thus Freud and Bullitt (1932) said that Woodrow Wilson was obsessed with his articulate and impressive father. Wilson buried his resentment under an intense idealization of his father and publicly played out his private fantasies of Christlike greatness by attempting to become a new savior of the world.

For Freud, the father of the family defined the leader's psychological world: "He is everyone's own private leader, who mediates the transition . . . from inner to outer, from psychology to politics" (Strozier Offer, 1985, p. 43). Fenichel (1945) held that obedience to the father provided protection; the father could become a savior in a crisis (Bychowski, 1948). Mother figures could be as important as father figures. Strong mothers or absent fathers figured strongly in the careers of Franklin Delano Roosevelt, Douglas MacArthur, and many other world leaders (as will be noted in Chapter 34).

Psychohistory. Psychoanalysis was the theory of choice for psychohistorians attempting to understand political leaders in terms of childhood deprivation, cultural milieu, relationships with parental authority, and the psychodynamic needs of their followers. Illustrative of this approach are the psychoanalytic treatises written about Adolf Hitler (e.g., Waite, 1977). Other biographical subjects of psychoanalysts have been Abraham Lincoln, Martin Luther, and Mahatma Gandhi (Erikson, 1969). Psychohistory went beyond psychoanalysis by looking at the personality development and dynamics of leaders in their interactions with society and history. The personal conflicts of world leaders were linked to historical developments. For instance, Erikson (1968, 1969) concentrated on the importance of Martin Luther's adolescence and Mahatma Gandhi's adult life. Historical crises were explained in terms of personal traumas of a leader.

Kernberg (1979) focused on the *schizoid, obsessive, paranoid*, and *narcissistic* character of leaders. Kohut (1976, 1977) saw charismatic leaders as narcissists, who use their followers to maintain their self-esteem. The followers' shame, jealousy, and hate are buried by their idealization of the leader. The pathology of leadership was also explored by Kets de Vries (1980, 1984), among others. But although the psychoanalytic study of leadership has accentuated psychopathological issues, "it is . . . patently absurd to label all leaders as pathological" (Strozier & Offer, 1985, p. 6). There is an imbalance in the psychoanalytical attention given to the neurotic and psychotic aspects of leaders' behavior and the ignoring of what is healthy and creative in leaders. Therefore, the psychoanalytic view needs to be refocused to explain "that elusive fit between the *leader* and the *led* in the full richness of the unique moment of the past" (Strozier Offer, 1985, p. 7). For example, Alexander (1942) and Erikson (1964) considered mature leaders, in contrast to immature leaders, to have innate abilities to command attention, to be free from irrational conflicts, to be sensitive to the needs of others, and to be able and willing to relate emotionally to others.

Using the methods of psychohistory to delve deeper into questions concerning social insight, G. Davis (1975) explained how the psychodynamics of Theodore Roosevelt found expression in his affective insights as an adult leader. Personal recollections, published accounts, journalism, and biographies about Roosevelt as a child were meshed with an analysis of relevant cultural developments in the United States during his time. Davis concluded that Roosevelt's psyche resolved the childhood experiences of his generation.

Crises and Charisma. Psychoanalytical theory was also used by Kets de Vries (1980) and by Hummel (1975) to show how the interaction of the personalities of leaders and their situations is dramatized in times of crisis. Kets de Vries (1980) maintains that charismatic leaders arise during crises out of a sense of their own grandiosity and the group's sense of helpless dependency. Whether they serve well as leaders depends on whether they can test their "paranoid potential" and their sense of omnipotence against reality. In fragmented societies, such charisma may give rise to an integration of institutions and loyalties or it may spawn opposition movements (G. T. Stewart, 1974). For Hummel, "projection" by followers explains their intense love for a charismatic leader. Followers see the leader as a superhuman hero because they cannot become consciously aware of their unconscious projections. Zaleznik (1977) proposed that a true leader, in contrast to a manager, has resolved the conflicts of his id and superego and has developed strong ego ideals, embodied in his confidence and self-determination.

Cognitive-Experiential Self Theory. Freud's initial concept has been improved in the light of new clinical insights and experiments in cognition and the psychodynamic unconscious. Freud's single fundamental need to seek pleasure and avoid pain was replaced as a source of motivation by the need of a leader for a stable, coherent conceptual framework (Rogers, 1959) and the need to overcome feelings of inferiority (Adler, 1954), among many other alternatives of consequence to the leader-follower relationship. Particularly relevant was Epstein's (1994) integration of the cognitive and psychodynamic unconscious. Epstein assumed two interacting information processing systems — rational and emotional-experiential. Behavior is influenced by both. Four fundamental interacting needs are those (1) for pleasure, (2) to maintain coherence, (3) for relatedness, and (4) to enhance self-esteem. Both leaders and followers would be more likely to value emotional appeals based on hunches if they more often processed information on the basis of experience and emotions. Conversely, they would be moved by principles and deductions if they processed information more often by reasoning.

Group Dynamics. Psychoanalysis had much to say about the leader-follower development in the small group.[3] According to Freud (1922), group members act like siblings in developing their ego-identification. They form a common libidinal connection with their leader (father) by incorporating his image into their superego. According to Redl (1942), the central person in the group (not necessarily the group leader) becomes an object of the members' identification on the basis of love or fear, an object of aggression, and a support for their own egos. The central person can become a model to be admired—the members' *ego-ideal*. The followers may internalize the leader's standards of conduct or come to fear her or him as an aggressor. What had the most influence on the course of subsequent research on education and the practice of group dynamics was Bion's (1948, 1961) sorting of leader-member relations into four "cultures": (1) task-oriented, (2) dependent, (3) fight-flight, and (4) pairing.

Psychoanalysis also has much to say about leadership in therapeutic groups, although opinions differ on whether the group therapist is the group leader. For instance, Scheidlinger (1980) argued that the therapist's leadership is important to how the group will function, as well as how much the group can contribute to successful treatment by providing a climate of safety and support for the reenactment of family-child and parent-child encounters.

Political Theories of Leadership[4]

Political theorists, from Plato on, had explanations, either explicit or implicit, and prescriptions for leadership. Marxism-Leninism, with its focus on economic determination in history coupled with the dictatorship of the proletariat, laid out strong messages about who shall lead and what is expected of leaders. Mao Zedong's mass-line leadership was much more explicit. It incorporated operant conditioning, consciousness-raising in small groups, confession, self-criticism, and critical feedback. For Mao, the scattered and unsystematic ideas of the masses were to be studied to turn them into concentrated and systematic ideas that the leadership would take back and explain

to the masses. This was to continue until the masses became committed to the ideas and then implemented and tested them (Barlow, 1981).

Nazi ideology was centered on the *Führerprinzip*, which had figured strongly in German authoritarian ideology in the nineteenth century. As propounded by the Nazi movement, unquestioning obedience and loyalty to superiors produced order and prosperity, to be shared by those who were worthy by race (the Aryans) to participate in the "new order." The other races were to be relocated, enslaved, or exterminated (Evans, 2005). Worship in Japan and fascism in Spain, Italy, and elsewhere had a similar blend of feudalistic, authoritarian, and ethnocentric ideologies. Like kings with a divine right, like the emperor of China who pursued the "will of heaven," the national dictator could do no wrong, so each successive level of leadership below him was equally infallible. Superiors' decisions were to be obeyed, not questioned (Evans, 2005). In contrast, in the leadership espoused in the democratic world constitutionally elected representatives are responsible to their constituencies and follow laws based on the legislative vote of the majority, but the rights of the minority are constitutionally respected and protected.

According to J. M. Burns (1977), political leaders is "those processes and effects of political power in which a number of actors . . . spurred by aspirations, appeal to and respond to the needs . . . of would-be followers . . . for reciprocal betterment . . . or real change in the direction of 'higher' values. Political leadership is tested by the extent to which real and intended changes are achieved by leaders' interactions with followers through the use of their power bases. Political leadership is broadly intended "real change." It is "collectively purposeful causation" (p. 434). In established governments, "political power" refers to processes for the "authoritative allocation of values that are considered legitimate uses of power under existing . . . conventions, traditions, understandings, or constitutional processes. This legitimacy is usually linked to formal authority" (J. M. Burns, 1977, p. 434). Political theories of leadership explain the rise of conservative, reform, and rebel movements; the significance of historical events and forces; the mobilization of constituencies; and the importance of the leader's personality and power. They examine the leadership of presidents, ministers, cabinets, and legislatures in democratic, authoritarian,

---

[3]Psychoanalytic concepts of leadership and group dynamics have figured strongly in the work of Maslow (1965) and other humanistic theorists. Some of these will be considered further in Chapter 26.
[4]More will be said about these divergent political theories of leadership in Chapter 7.

and totalitarian states. Their focus ranges from the small community to the large urban center. They examine the results of public opinion polls and elections.

Leadership of Organizations

Chester Barnard had 40 years of experience with AT&T and eventually became president of New Jersey Bell. On the basis of his experience and observations, in his classic *Functions of the Executive* (1938), he concluded that *cooperation* was essential for an organization's survival. (At the time he wrote, command and control were regarded as more essential by management theorists.) Equally important were acceptance of purpose and the ability to communicate. The executive required the capacity for affirming decisions that provided quality and morality to the coordination of organized activities and to the "formulation of purpose." The purposes of cooperation were impossible without specialization, and the integration of the specializations demonstrated the cooperation needed for the organization to survive.

Barnard's ideas were modified by a focus on executive decision making (Simon, 1947; March & Simon, 1958), and more recently by other organizational theorists to fit with changes in society. Thus Guskin (1999) suggested that organizational instability may call for executive command and control until stable conditions are reestablished. Perloff (1999) argued that Barnard had left out the overriding importance of trust in the executive by his (or her) various constituencies (board members, managers, employees, customers, suppliers, government agents, and community). Fowler (1999) saw another factor as having been ignored: the importance to the executive of being allied with reliable advisers who tell what he needs to hear, not what he wants to hear. Among many others, Clifton (1999) added to Barnard's principles of purpose and the need for communication the psychological and humanistic need of the organization for a sense of shared mission, promoting employees' participation in decisions, matching employees' strengths and assignments, and offering incentives for measured superior performance.

Economic Theories of Organization. Economic theories are based on assumptions about the motivation of "economic man." For instance, according to Agency

Theory (Meckling & Jensen, 1976), owners of firms aim to maximize their profits. Nonowner managers are agents of the owners and cannot be trusted to have the same interests as the owners. They are likely to be interested in maximizing their own compensation and advancement. As economic persons, they are selfish, opportunistic, and individualistic, and they may ignore what is best for the organization in favor of what is best for themselves. They will need to be monitored closely by the owners. Williamson (1975) saw the firm as a marketplace in which all members are economically motivated in competition with one another. Bargaining replaces cooperation in getting things done. The interactions between leaders and followers are negotiations influenced by their differences in resources and power. Economic theories are in marked contrast to humanistic theories, which see people as basically cooperative, as having a strong sense of responsibility, and as willing to work toward common goals (Donaldson, 1990).

Social Psychological Theories. Social psychological leadership theories were influenced by the principles of American democracy and individual freedom. The human being is by nature a motivated organism. The organization is by nature structured and controlled. It is the function of leadership to modify the organization to provide freedom for individuals to realize their motivational potential for the fulfillment of their needs and to contribute to the accomplishment of organizational goals.

McGregor. One prominent analysis was McGregor's (1960, 1966) postulation of two types of organizational leadership—Theory X and Theory Y. Theory X assumed that people are passive: they resist organizational needs and attempts to direct and motivate them to fit these needs. Theory Y assumes that people already have motivation and a desire for responsibility: organizational conditions should be arranged to make it possible for people to fulfill their needs with efforts toward achieving organizational objectives.

Argyris. In his *maturity-immaturity* theory, Argyris (1957, 1962, 1964a) perceived a fundamental conflict between the organization and the individual. It is the nature of organizations to structure members' roles and to control their performance in the interest of achieving specified objectives. It is the individual's nature to be self-directive and to seek fulfillment through exercising initiative and responsibility. An organization will be most effective when its leadership provides the means whereby followers may make a creative contribution to it as a natural outgrowth of their own needs for growth, self-expression, and maturity. Most organizations pursue a one-way model of how people are supposed to relate to others. The model has a single loop or one-way link from the more powerful to the less powerful. In this model, there is preference for: (1) unilateral control; (2) a win-or-lose orientation toward others; (3) concealment of feelings; and (4) a rational censoring of information, freedom, and risk. In contrast, the model espoused by Argyris (1983) is double-looped in that it comprises: (1) a learning orientation; (2) a low-defensive, high-information environment; and (3) joint control by the more powerful and the less powerful. Choice is free and informed. This double-loop model ought to be more effective in the long run for both the individual and the organization.

Heavily influenced by Kurt Lewin (1947), Likert (1961a, 1961b, 1967) argued that leadership is a relative process because leaders must take into account the expectations, values, and interpersonal skills of those with whom they are interacting. Leaders must present behaviors and organizational processes that the followers perceive to be supportive of their efforts and of their sense of personal worth. Leaders will involve followers in making decisions that affect their welfare and work. They will use their influence to further the task performance and personal welfare of followers. Leaders will enhance the cohesiveness of the group and the members' motivation to be productive by providing followers with freedom for responsible decision making and the exercise of initiative.

Blake and Mouton. Blake and Mouton (1964, 1965) conceptualized leadership in terms of a managerial grid. Concern for people was represented by one axis of a two-dimensional grid; concern for production was represented by the other axis. Leaders may be high or low on both axes, or they may be high on one axis and low on the other. The leader who rates high on both axes develops followers who are committed to the accomplishment of work and have a sense of interdependence through a common stake in the organization's purposes. Relationships of trust and respect for the leader emerge as well.

Misumi and Peterson (1985) reviewed a line of theory and testing by Misumi and colleagues in Japan. Called Performance-Maintenance (PM) theory, it was similar to Blake and Mouton's concern for performance and concern for production. Optimum supervision occurred when both P and M were high rather than low.

Maslow. Maslow's theory of "eupsychian" management (1965) was derived from his observations of people at work in industry. Maslow stressed that it is important for managers to develop their subordinates' self-esteem and psychological health and emphasized the need for self-actualization so that everyone would have an opportunity to realize his or her own capacity. Eupsychian management distinguished between the person who was trying to be a democratic superior and one who was spontaneously democratic. According to this theory, the unconscious and the depths of personality had to be probed in the search for enlightened management. On the basis of such probes, different leaders would be chosen for different situations. The Blackfoot Indians were an example. The Blackfoots gave power to a leader only on an ad hoc basis for the situation in which it was warranted. Such leadership ought not to be left to self-seekers with a neurotic need for power, but should be given to those who are best suited to be leaders for the designated situation — those who can set things straight, who can do what needs to be done.

Hersey and Blanchard. Hersey and Blanchard's (1969a, 1972) life cycle theory of leadership synthesizes Blake and Mouton's (1964) managerial grid, Argyris's (1964a), maturity-immaturity theory and the Ohio State leadership study with regard to concepts of consideration and initiation of structure (Stogdill & Shartle, 1955). According to Hersey and Blanchard's situational leadership model, the leader's style of behavior should be related to the maturity of the subordinates As the subordinates mature, the leader should decrease emphasis on structuring tasks and increase emphasis on consideration. As the subordinates continue to mature, there could be an eventual decrease in consideration. Maturity is defined in terms of subordinates' experience, motivation to achieve, and willingness and ability to accept responsibility.

Rost. Rost's (1993) theory is at an extreme. Most theories of leadership focus on the leader. Rost argued for eliminating the distinction between leader and follower. Leadership is a process. Influenced by Maslow, Rost held that whoever had the information and motivation in a given set of informal relationships should be able to temporarily be the source of influence in the ideal group, a group without a formal distribution of power, authority, and responsibility.

Interaction and Social Learning Theories

Social psychology formed the basis of many other theories of leadership. Many other social interaction and social learning theories explain the leader-follower relationship as a consequence of the leader's interaction with the followers as well as with the circumstances involved. Interaction theories of leadership such as Gibb's (1958) study are characterized by a complex combination of the leader's personality; the followers' needs, values, attitudes, and personality; and the group's structure of interpersonal relations, character, task, and environmental setting. What happens also may be explained in terms of the leader's role and its attainment, reinforcement of change, paths to goals, and the effects of contingencies.

Leader-Role Theories. In *informal* groups, structure develops and roles are taken so as to permit one person or perhaps a few persons to emerge as leaders. According to leader-role theory, the characteristics of the individual member and the demands of the situation interact so that during the course of the members' interactions, groups become structured in terms of positions and roles. Leaders are expected to play a role that differs from the roles of other group members. Homans (1950) developed a theory of the leader's role based on action, interaction, and sentiments. He assumed that an increase in the frequency of interaction by group members and their participation in common activities was associated with an increase in their mutual liking and in the clarity of the group's norms. The higher the status of persons within the group, the more nearly their activities would conform to the group's norms, the wider their range of interactions would be, and the larger the number of group members with whom they would originate interactions would become.

In *formal* organizations, leaders behave according to what their colleagues expect of them and how—in their own perception—their roles are formally defined. The leaders' and colleagues' perceptions and expectations of their roles are further influenced by the organization's formal policies and procedures, by informal communications with colleagues, by past experience, and by their own needs and values (Kahn & Quinn, 1970). There is also an effect on the ratings of their performance as leaders, which depend on whose expectations are most salient for them in defining their roles (Tsui, 1995). The expectations will change as an organization changes. New and conflicting requirements will call for changes in roles (Eggleston & Bhagat, 1993). Managers ordinarily must cope with conflicts among different sources of information about their roles. Osborn & Hunt (1975a) argued that what the organization prescribes for the managers' routine activities is not leadership; rather, leadership involves only the discretionary activities that leaders perform when the prescriptions fail to tell them what to do. Hunt, Osborn, and Martin (1981, p. 3) presented a well-supported theory to explain why some leaders act efficiently in response "to specific opportunities and problems which the unit is not designed to handle."

Rules and procedures created by an organization can make the leadership role redundant. Kerr and Jermier (1978) pioneered the analysis of the *substitutes for leadership*. Nevertheless, a wrong inference can be drawn here—that more available regulations necessarily reduce the discretionary behavior of leaders. On the contrary, Hunt, Osborn, and Martin (1981) predicted and found that leaders in units with more rules, policies, and procedures were expected to respond with more discretionary use of those rules and procedures and actually did so. Jones (1983) analyzed the leader's role in terms of controls imposed by the organization. Jones argued that such controls of the work flow, of the way a task is structured, and of the way jobs are formalized may provide supervisors with as much influence over what goes on as does their power to discipline subordinates.

Theories on Attaining the Leadership Role. These theories attempt to explain who emerges as a leader of a group and why. Hemphill (1954) argues that leaders emerge in situations in which components of group tasks are interdependent and are related to the solution of a common problem among group members. Fundamental to his theory is the concept of *structure in interaction* or predictable interaction activity. The role structure of the group and the office of the leader are defined by institutionalized expectations with respect to *initiation* of structure in interaction. The probability that an attempted act of leadership will succeed is a function of the members' perceptions of their freedom to accept or reject the suggested structure in interaction. When such a structure leads to the solution of common problems, it acquires value and strengthens the expectation that all group members will conform to it. Thus initiation of structure in interaction is attempted leadership. Hollander and Julian (1969) hold that an emergent leader, instead of being just another undifferentiated member of the group, is the member who has built up *idiosyncrasy credit* with his or her followers by successive successful attempts to lead.

Role Expectations. According to Tsui (1984), superiors, peers, subordinates, and others indicate what they expect of the manager's role. The expectations of these various constituencies can be in conflict. Superiors may expect the manager's role to be that of a monitor; subordinates may see it as that of a coach. If the expectations are met, the leader gains reputational effectiveness. Consistent with Hemphill, Stogdill (1959) developed an *expectancy-reinforcement* theory of such role attainment. This theory attempted to explain the emergence and persistence of successful leadership in initially unstructured groups. It also tried to understand what leadership is and how it comes into existence. As group members interact and engage in shared tasks, they reinforce the expectation that their actions and interactions will continue in accord with their previous performance. Thus the members' roles are defined by confirmed expectations of the performances and interactions they will be permitted in order to contribute to the group. The potential of members to be successful leaders is the extent to which they initiate expectations and maintain structure in interaction. For Stein, Hoffman, Cooley, et al. (1979), emergent leaders are the group members who are most willing and able to perform those roles and functions that enable the group to accomplish its tasks. They guide and encourage others to contribute to the process. Such leadership will appear in phases that parallel Tuckman's (1965) stages of group development: orientation, conflict, and emergence. Some emergent leaders take charge early; others

move ahead with collaborators; and still others fail to maintain their initial success as leaders.

Path-Goal Theory.[5] The reinforcement of change in the subordinate by the leader is a prominent aspect of path-goal theory. Georgopoulos, Mahoney, and Jones (1957) and M. G. Evans (1970a) suggested that the successful leaders showed followers the rewards available to them. House (1971) maintained that the leader also showed the followers what paths (behaviors) to follow to obtain the rewards. The leader clarified the goals of the followers as well as the paths to reach those goals. This clarification enhanced the psychological state of the followers and aroused them to increase their efforts to perform well. Followers achieve satisfaction from the job to be done. The leaders enhanced satisfaction with the work itself and provided valued extrinsic rewards like recommendations for pay increases, contingent on the subordinates' performance. (The leader needed to be able to control the rewards that subordinates value.)

The situation determined which behavior by the leader could accomplish these path-goal purposes Two important situational aspects were how competent the subordinates were and how highly structured the task was (House & Dessler, 1974). To reconcile the theory with experimental results, House (1972) proposed that the effects of a leader's behavior were contingent on three kinds of "moderator variables": (1) task variables, such as role clarity, routine, and externally imposed controls; (2) environmental variables; and (3) individual differences in preferences, expectations, and personality.

Contingency Theories. Along with House's path-goal theory, Fiedler's contingency theory (1967a) dominated much of the research on leadership during the 1970s and 1980s. For Fiedler, the effectiveness of task-oriented and relations-oriented leaders was contingent on the demands imposed by the situation. Leaders were assessed as task oriented or relations oriented according to the way they judged their least preferred coworker. A situation was favorable to the leader if the leader was esteemed by the group; if the task was structured, clear, simple, and easy to solve; and if the leader had legitimacy and power by virtue of his or her position. The *task oriented* leader

[5] Empirical studies dealing with path-goal propositions will be discussed in detail in Chapter 27.

was most likely to be effective in situations that were most favorable or most unfavorable to him or her. The *relations oriented* leader was most likely to be effective in situations between the two extremes of favorable and unfavorable.

Most person-situation theorists focused on how the leader ought to be developed to adapt best to the needs of the situation. But Fiedler's research and theory emphasized that the leader ought to be placed in the situation for which he or she is best suited. Task oriented people should be selected to lead in situations that are very favorable or unfavorable to the leaders; relations-oriented people should be selected to lead in situations that are neither very high nor very low in favorability. Otherwise, leaders needed to learn how to change a situation to match their orientation. Therefore, Fiedler, Chemers, and Mahar (1976) developed a method to help a leader "match" his or her appropriate situation: the leader was helped to change the situation or to adjust better to its favorability or unfavorability. Fiedler, Chemers, and Mahar's (1976) leadership-training program consisted of first identifying the trainee's particular style—task or relations orientation—and then teaching the trainee how to analyze and classify leadership situations for their favorableness, or situational control. The next elements to be considered were the best fit of the situation and style and how to change one's style to suit the occasion or how to change the situation to fit one's style better. Fiedler's five decades of work involved a progression from empirical discoveries to the formation of the theory to the practical application of the theory and to validation of the applications.[6]

Situational contingencies. Many others have proposed that personal traits resulting in the emergence or success of a leader would be influenced by the task or goals, the followers' traits, and the organizational context of the situation (Bass, 1960).

Additional Theories and Models of Interactive Processes. Numerous additional elaborations have appeared to account for leadership and for leader-follower relations as an interactive process. For instance, Fulk and Wendler (1982) and Greene (1975) agreed that if subordinates

(followers) perform well, the leader displays more consideration, which then leads to increased satisfaction for the followers. If the followers do not perform well, the leader displays more structuring behavior and the followers' satisfaction does not increase.

Communication Theories. Communications and rhetoric provide another point of departure for theories about leader-follower interactions. For example, Sharf (1978) created a rhetorical framework based on a theory by Burke (1969) to analyze the relative success of emerging leaders in small groups in obtaining cooperation from the other members and in resolving the struggle for leadership status. When applied to recorded discussions of small, leaderless task groups, the analyses revealed the importance of going beyond symbolic divisions in the emergence of leadership.

Multiple-Linkage Model. Yukl (1971) agreed that the leader's initiation of structure enhances subordinates' ability to cope with a situation; the leader's consideration for the welfare of subordinates enhances the subordinates' satisfaction with the situation. Then Yukl (1981) greatly expanded the interaction framework with a multiple-linkage model suggesting that the subordinates' effort and skill in performing a task, the leader's role, the resources available, and the group's cohesiveness all moderate the effects of the leader's behavior on group outcomes. The model also differentiated between leadership required for short-term effectiveness and that required for long-term effectiveness. Yukl and Kanuk (1979) provided evidence that, in contrast to performance outcomes, subordinates' satisfaction resulted from different patterns of behavior by the leader and mediating conditions.

Multiple-Screen or Cognitive Resources Model. Another interaction approach to understanding the relations of the leader and the led is the multiple-screen model, which attempted to explain the relationship between the leader's intelligence and the group's performance. Fiedler and Leister (1977) suggested and provided empirical support for the proposal that intelligent leaders can generate effective groups if the leaders have good relations with their bosses. If relations are poor, then experienced rather than intelligent leaders bring about more productive groups. Experience is more important to effective leadership if leader-boss relations are poor.[7]

Exchange Theories

Exchange theories assume that group members make contributions at a cost to themselves and receive benefits at a cost to the group, the organization, or other members. As with Burns's (1978) transactional leadership, leaders exchange rewards or the avoidance of discipline for followers' satisfactory performance. Interaction continues because leader and followers find the social exchange rewarding. Blau (1964) began with the fact that most people consider it rewarding to be elevated to a position of high status. Also, it is rewarding for members to associate with their high-status leaders. But leaders tend to deplete their power when members have discharged their obligations to the leaders. The leaders than replenish their power by rendering valuable services to the group. They benefit as much as anyone else from following their good suggestions rather than somebody else's poorer ones. Followers' compliance constitutes a surplus profit that the leader earns.[8]

Vertical-Dyad Linkage (VDL) and Leader-Member Exchange (LMX) Theory. Graen's (1976) vertical-dyad linkage (subsequently called leader-member exchange) was one of many interaction theories that were based on the assumption that social interaction represents a form of exchange. The vertical dyad of leader and subordinate (VDL) is an interaction linkage of mutual influence. It emphasizes the relationship between the leader and each individual follower rather than between the leader and the group as a whole. In corresponding LMX theory, Graen (1976) assumed that the leader behaves differently toward each follower and that these differences must be analyzed separately. This theory is in opposition to most earlier theories, which assumed that the leader behaves in much the same way toward all group members and that behavioral descriptions from group members can be averaged to obtain an accurate description of the general behavior of the leader. According to Graen, leaders cate-

gorize followers as belonging to an in-group or an out-group, and the leader behaves differently toward members of these two groups. In-group members can be more independent of the leader and receive more attention from the leader, as well as more of the other rewards. As a consequence, in-group members perform better and are more satisfied than out-group members (Vecchio & Gobdel, 1984). Numerous, extensive empirical investigations by Graen and associates of vertical-dyad effects have been published and will be discussed more fully in Chapters 15 and 16.

Organizationally Defined Expectations. T. O. Jacobs (1970) formulated a social-exchange theory and buttressed it with a wide range of research findings. According to Jacobs, the group provides the leader with status and esteem in exchange for the leader's unique contributions to the attainment of the group's goals. Authority relationships in formal organizations define role expectations that enable group members to perform their tasks and to interact without the use of power. Leadership implies an equitable exchange relationship between the leader and the followers. When role obligations are mutually acknowledged, each party can satisfy the expectations of the other on an equitable basis.

Cue-Behavior-Reinforcement Theories

Aaronovich and Khotin (1929) reported using differentially cued reinforcements to alter the leadership behavior of monkeys in uncovering boxes of food. Mawhinney and Ford (1977) reinterpreted path-goal theory in terms of operant conditioning. W. E. Scott (1977) saw a need to replace the concept that leadership is due to influence or persuasion with an analysis of the observable behaviors of leaders that change the behavior of subordinates. All these behavioral theories emphasized reinforcement and making the receipt of rewards or the avoidance of punishment contingent on the subordinate's behaving as required. According to Davis and Luthans (1979, p. 239), "The leader's behavior is a cue to evoke the subordinate's task behavior. The subordinate's task behavior, in turn, can act as a consequence for the leader, which, in turn, reinforces, punishes, or extinguishes the leader's subsequent behavior. Similarly, the subordinate's behavior has its own consequences, which serve to reinforce, punish,

---

[7]Chapter 29 will discuss this model further.
[8]See also Gergen (1969), Homans (1958), March and Simon (1958), and Thibaut and Kelly (1959).

or extinguish this behavior. The consequences for the subordinate's behavior may be related to the leader's subsequent behavior [to] the work itself, and its outcomes, or [to] other organization members."

Supervisors do not directly cause subordinates' behavior; they merely set an occasion or provide a discriminative stimulus. The behavior of subordinates depends on its consequences. Environmental cues, discriminative stimuli, behaviors, and consequences form a behavioral contingency for analysis. Thus Sims (1977) conducted one of many investigations demonstrating that a leader's positive rewarding behavior will improve a subordinate's performance, particularly if the reward is contingent on the quality or quantity of the subordinate's performance.

Concentrating on the followers' reactions, Kerr and Abelson (1981) developed a model to represent extreme, rather than ordinary, leader-subordinate interactions. The day-to-day behavior of the leader may be relatively unimportant to the supervisor-subordinate relationship, compared with the leader's behavior when a subordinate experiences an intense demand or when the leader experiences a highly unexpected response. This model shows that subordinates can become so accustomed to frequent leadership activity that the effects of this activity are minimal and even dampening.

The importance of reinforcement in the leader-follower relationship will be examined in various contexts in many of the later chapters that deal with power relationships and exchange relationships. Reinforcement is central to the operant model of supervision as well as to path-goal theory.

Operant Model of Supervision. This model derives from Skinner's (1969) theories of behavioral conditioning. It describes what leaders should do "compellingly and consistently to motivate subordinates" (Komaki & Citera, 1990, p. 91). Three categories of behaviors are specified: (1) antecedents of subordinates' performance (instructions, rules, training, goals); (2) monitoring of performance (work sampling, subordinates' self-reporting, secondary sources) and; (3) consequences of performance (feedback, recognition, correcting). For an empirical example, more effective insurance managers spent more time than less effective insurance managers monitoring their agents (Komaki, 1986). Racing sailboat cap-

tains who monitored their crews hoisting their sails and provided feedback correlated (.51, .47) with the racing results (Komaki, Deselles, Bòwman, 1989).

Perceptual and Cognitive Theories

An early theoretical emphasis on the perceptual and cognitive aspects of leadership was provided by Goffman (1959), who analyzed social behavior as theater. That is, Goffman evaluated the roles, membership, and phenomena of groups in terms of actors, audience, front stage, and backstage. According to Goffman, social learning created disparities between the leader's intentions and the followers' understanding of what the leader was trying to do. As noted earlier, Quinn and Hall (1983) developed an integrated theory of leadership based on competing perceptual and cognitive dimensions such as leaders' flexibility versus their control, and leaders' internal versus external focus. Carrier (1984) constructed cognitive maps to locate traits of leadership in reference to these dimensions. For example, the trait of dominance was placed in a location that is high in both control and internal focus.

Perceptual and cognitive theories offer several advantages. They make use of advances in cognitive psychology and are immediately applicable in diagnosis and leadership education. They include theories about social and cognitive processes, attributions, integration with behavioral models, information processing, systems analysis, and rational-deductive decision trees.

Cognitive Processes. Before the late 1970s, empirical leadership research and theory paid little attention to leaders' behavior as a consequence of perceptions and thoughts about purposes, followers, or the task and situation. An exception was the use of *stimulated recall*, in which leaders and members of small groups were audiotaped, then listened to the tapes, and then indicated on a second tape recording what they had been thinking at the time of the original discussion (Bass, McGehee, & Hawkins, 1953). Conference videotaping would provide on a replication of the videotape sotto voce commentary by the participants about their thoughts concerning what was originally happening and what they were trying to do.

Leaders' and followers' perceptions and cognition rose in importance. Lord and Maher (1985) first showed how leadership could be best understood by attention to cognitive processes, the importance of implicit theories of leadership, and the "prototypes" or models of leadership that people form mentally. Concepts that have emerged in theories about cognitive processes include attention, encoding, attribution, memory storage, memory retrieval, evaluations, expectations, and attributions.

To appreciate a leader's behavior, we need to understand the leader's scripts and strategies. A *script* is a conceptual structure. It is held in the memory of events, objects, roles, feelings, and outcomes. There is a sequential pattern to the script's structure of familiar circumstances and tasks. According to Wofford (1998), if a leader uses a script to confront a familiar situation and finds in feedback no discrepancies between goal and outcome, he or she will continue to process the script. The process depends on recognition and is automatic. Otherwise, the process is inferential and is based on reflection of the recent past, integration of performance information, and causal attributions (Cronshaw & Lord, 1987). The leader is likely to include alternative paths to the goal in the script, so that if feedback indicates that the original path is blocked, an alternative will be tried. If no alternative path works, the leader changes strategy. A *strategy* is an original construction of a new script formulated in a pattern to deal with a specific situation for which available scripts have not worked. Or an alternative strategy may be retrieved from memory. Experienced and trained leaders should have a greater number of available scripts. Also, they will need to change strategies less often (Wofford, 1998).

Schemata

Another cognitive concept, the schema, is an organized knowledge structure. According to Lord Emerich (2001), it is necessary to consider the difference between an individual and a collective schema. An *individual* schema, as the term implies, is in the mind of an individual; it reflects perceived networks of implicit theories of leadership and categorizations of types of leaders into prototypes. A matched prototype is selected. A *collective* schema is "a socially constructed understanding of the world derived from social exchanges and interactions among multiple individuals in a group or organization" (p. 552). Central themes include organizational performance, "sense making," and transformations.

McCormick and Martinko (2005) have combined social cognitive theory with causal reasoning to provide an understanding of a group leader's thoughts and behavior and the group's performance. McCormick and Martinko assume that people regulate their own thoughts and can control their own actions. According to Locke and Latham (1990), people actively monitor the performance environment, develop functional task strategies, implement plans, and monitor results. McCormick and Martinko hold that leaders' and followers' self-regulation is guided by attention and attributions of the causal reasoning process as well as schemata about task-relevant knowledge, skills, abilities, personal goals, action plans, and beliefs in their own efficacy.

Self-efficacy is a cognitive concept in Bandura's (1985) social cognitive theory. It is the belief that one has the capability to handle prospective problem situations (Bandura, 1995). A leader's choice of goals and strategies will be affected by a belief in self-efficacy (Kane & Baltes, 1998). McCormick (2001) has built on Bandura to formulate a Social Cognitive Leadership Model. Engaged in self-regulation, the would-be leader, high in self-efficacy, is likely to generate attempts to lead and persist in persuasive efforts despite resistance (Savard & Rogers, 1992). If the leader's belief is valid, the leadership should be effective (Chemers, Watson, & May, 2000).

Propositions that follow include: (1) Leaders who are *not* self-serving and are objective in their perceptions of their environment generate more efficacious behavior. (2) Leaders have an implicit model or schema that influences how they perceive their causal relationships. (3) Leaders' task schema are influenced by their beliefs about causation in their environment. (4) Leaders' self-efficacy influences their goals, task strategies, and use of task schema. (5) Lofty goals are a result of perceptions of "resource-rich" task schemata and a strong belief in self-efficacy (McCormick & Martinko, 2005).

Attribution Theories. DeVries (1997) constructed a model of attribution that linked impression formation, categories, prototypes, perceptions of leadership ideals, and leadership success. Each leader and follower is perceived to have his or her own implicit theories of leadership. If we want to understand the behavior of individual leaders, we must begin by attempting to find out what they are thinking about the specific situation. Whether they are seen as acting like *leaders* depends on their own and their followers' implicit theories about leadership (Eden & Leviatan, 1975). We observe the behavior of leaders and infer that the causes of these behaviors are various personal traits or external constraints. If these causes match our naive assumptions about what leaders should do, then we use the term "leadership" to describe the persons who we observed. Thus Calder (1977) says that leadership changes from a scientific concept to a study of the social reality of group members and observers—a study in how the term is used and when it is used, and assumptions about the development and nature of leadership. For Calder, leadership is a perception of followers that caters to their perceptual needs. Attributions of leadership by observers and group members are biased by their individual social realities (Mitchell, Larson, & Green, 1977), which accounts for the low correlations that are often found between supervisors', peers', and subordinates' ratings of the same leaders (Bernardin & Alvares, 1975; Ilgen & Fugii, 1976; T. R. Mitchell, 1970a), as well as for the confounding of evaluations of the performance of subordinates and the behavior of leaders (Rush, Thomas, & Lord, 1977).

Green and Mitchell (1979) formulated a model to study such attributional processes in leaders. They explained that a leader's behavior is a consequence of his or her interpretation of the subordinates' performance. Thus a leader presented with an incident of a subordinate's poor performance (such as low productivity, lateness, a missed deadline, or disruptive behavior) will form an implicit theory about the subordinate and the situation, judging that the cause of the incident was the subordinate's own personality, ability, or effort, or an externality, such as lack of support, a difficult task, or insufficient information. Causality is attributed more to the subordinate than to the situation if the subordinate has had a history of poor performance and if the poor performance has severe outcomes (Mitchell & Wood, 1979). In such circumstances, the leader will focus remedial action on the subordinate, rather than on the situation, even if the situation was the cause of the problem. Meindl, Ehrlich, and Dukerich (1985), along with Pfeffer (1977) and Calder (1977), agreed that there is a tendency to attribute more

of the cause than is actually warranted to the subordinate rather than to the situational circumstances.[9]

The Romance of Leadership. Meindl, Ehrlich, and Dukerich (1985) argued that leadership is in the eye of the follower. It is a social construction in the followers' minds and is about their thoughts of how leaders are cognitively structured and represented. Followers place more emphasis on the image of the leader than on the actual behavior or effects of the leader. They are much less under the control and influence of the leader per se than under the control and influence of "the social forces that govern the social construction process itself" (Meindl, 1995, p. 330). The object of study is not the actual personality or behavior of the leader, but personality and behavior as constructed or imagined by the followers. Ordinarily, when correlations are found between the supposed leadership and the effectiveness of an organization, the traditional interpretation is that the effectiveness was the result of the leaders' performance. But interpreted as a romantic notion, leadership is imagined by the followers. Its purpose, as noted above, is to cater to the perceptual needs of the followers (Calder, 1977). Symbols and rituals reinforce the importance of the leader (Pfeffer, 1977). Meindl (1990, 1993) found empirical support for the romantic perspective. Nonetheless, a leader does have real effects on followers, although some effects may be imagined by them. Much additional evidence in this book will attest to the objective effectiveness of leadership when measured independently of followers' opinions. For instance, Smith, Carson, and Alexander (1984) found that leaders do moderately influence the performance of their organizations. Day and Lord (1988) demonstrated that the executive leadership of organizations can account for 45% of these organizations' effective performance. But the question remains in many studies: how much is real and how much is romance, and in what circumstances?

Integrated Cognitive and Behavioral Models and Theories. Although attributions by followers can strengthen explanations, any explanation needs to be based on behavior. Still, Lord and Maher (1993) assume that to be a leader one must be perceived as leader. Traits

[9]More will be discussed about attributional processes in Chapter 14.

are schemata, knowledge structures, and "sense makers." Perceptions of distant executive leaders depend mainly on attributions and *inferential processing* from events and outcomes. Prototypes, scripts, implicit theories, and categories grow out of experiences. They are stored in long-term memory and are activated automatically. *Controlled processing* is intentional information processing based on short-term memory. The distinction explains a loss of charisma as followers shift from inferential to controlled processing. To solve problems, experts use *automatic processing*; novices use controlled processing. Experts use meaningful categories. Diagnosis is implicit, intuitive, or both. Solutions and evaluations are scripts and heuristics available to the expert. Novices categorize the same problems by using surface or environmental features, and solutions evaluations.

Luthans (1977) left room for cognitive processes to enter the scenario "to assign concepts to behavior and to infer relationships between events." Luthan's functional analysis of the leader-subordinate dynamic used his S-O-B-C model, in which S is the antecedent stimulus, O is the organism's covert processes, B is the behavior, and C is the consequence. Chemers (1993) provided a behavioral model of leadership, which also took account of cognitive processes. The first of three dimensions of the model was relative to persons: it was the development of interpersonal relationships. The second dimension was resource utilization relevant to the task to be accomplished. The third dimension was the leader's image management, the effort of the leader to establish and maintain a specific image in the group, such as competence or conscientiousness. As already noted, Hoojberg, Hunt, and Dodge (1997) integrated cognitive, social, and behavioral complexity into a "Leaderplex" model to generate empirical leadership research on global organizations, team-based organizations, diversity, hierarchy, and charisma.

In a mixed model proposed by Bass (1960), leadership deals with the observed effort of one member in a group to change the motivation, understanding, or behavior of other members. Change will be observed in the followers if the leading member is successful in influencing the others. Motivation is increased by changing the followers' expectations of being rewarded or punished. Leaders acquire their position by virtue of their perceived ability to reinforce the behavior of group members by granting or denying rewards or punishments. Since the group's effectiveness is evaluated in terms of its ability to reward its members, leaders are valued when they enable a group to provide expected rewards. The congruence of a leader's perceived status (the value of the position held, and esteem) with the leader's ability and value as a person regardless of the position can account for the leader's success. Incongruence generates conflict and failure. This emphasis on congruence is also found in Halal's (1974) general theory. A particular style of leadership is congruent with specific technologies of tasks and specific motivations of subordinates. Adaptation occurs to achieve greater congruence.

Information Processing. Newell and Simon (1972) focused on the problem solver's "subjective problem space." This "space" contains encodings of goals, initial situations, intermediate states, rules, constraints, and other relevant aspects of the task environment. Lord (1976) saw the utility of studying the shared problem spaces of leaders and followers when they tackle a common task. For example, a leader was expected to devote more effort to developing an orientation and definition of the problem or the group when the actual task lacked structure.

Social cues and symbols take on more importance for an understanding of leadership if this information processing approach is employed. In addition to encoding, information processing involves selective attention, comprehension, storage, retention, retrieval, and judgment. According to both theory and evidence, perceptions of leaders are based largely on spontaneous recognition. Moreover, the cognitive category of leadership is hierarchically organized. Perceptions and expectations of the attributes and behavior of leaders are widely shared (Lord, 1976, 1985; Lord, Binning, Rush, et al., 1978). Recognition-based processes are dominated by automatic processing, categorizations, and implicit theories, ordinarily involved in face-to-face interactions at lower levels in the organization. Inferential processes are attributional, controlled, and inferred from events and outcomes ordinarily associated with distant executive leaders (Lord & Maher, 1991).

Open-Systems Theory

An open-systems point of view implies sensitivity to the larger environment and organization in which leaders and their subordinates are embedded. To convert inputs into outputs, flows of energy and of information must occur in the system. In open systems, the effects of the outputs on the environment are feedback and new inputs. The relations within the system grow and become more intricate with repeated input-output cycles. The cyclical conversion process can be increased in rate and intensity. Leaders or followers can import and introduce more information. Directive leaders do this alone; if followers are included, the process is participative. Energy can be increased by selecting as leaders and followers more highly motivated individuals or by increasing the reinforcements that accrue from outputs (Katz & Kahn, 1966). Agency theory (Meckling & Jensen, 1976) suggested that managers put their own interests ahead of those of owners and shareholders, as when they provide themselves with "golden parachutes." But open-systems theory sees the manager as a good steward (Donaldson, 1990), concerned with aligning as much as possible the interests of all the constituents of the organization: owners, shareholders, management, employees, and community. The worth of the organization depends on this alignment (Bass, 1952).

Bryson and Kelley (1978) created a systems model for understanding emergence, stability, and change in organizations in which formal leaders are elected, such as cooperatives, professional associations, and legislatures. They made a list of clusters of individual, procedural, structural, and environment variables that were likely to be of consequence to each other on the basis of earlier formulations by Peabody (1976) and Van de Ven (1976).

Change-Induction and Therapeutic Groups. Lieberman (1976a) explained change-induction groups, such as psychotherapy groups, encounter groups, self-help groups, and consciousness-raising groups, in terms of systems analysis. Five structural characteristics of the system were seen to affect the change-induction process: (1) the psychological distance between the participant and the leader; (2) felt causes, sources, and cures of psychological misery; (3) the extent to which the group is seen as a social microcosm; (4) the degree to which members stress differentiation rather than similarity; and (5) the relation-ship between the cognitive and expressive behavior of the leader.

Macro- and Microlevels. Many models and theories of leadership have been embedded in larger organizational models and theories. For example, Bowers and Seashore's (1966) four-factor theory of leadership is part of a larger systems theory of organizations. Osborn and Hunt (1975a, 1975b) formulated an adaptive-reactive model of leadership to incorporate environmental constraints and organizational demands as antecedents of the behavior of leaders. Likewise, Bass and Valenzi (1974) used systems theory to construct an open-systems model of leader-follower relationships. According to their model, the systems are open to the outside environment and are sensitive to the constraints imposed on them from outside. The system imports energy (power) and information from outside, converts it, and exports goods and services. The Bass-Valenzi model (Bass, 1976) proposes that whether leaders are directive, negotiative, consultative, participative, or delegative depends on their perceptions of the system's inputs and the relations within the system. The leader and his or her immediate work group form an open system of inputs (organizational, task, and work-group variables), relations within the system (power and information differentials), and outputs (productivity and satisfaction). For instance, the Bass-Valenzi model posits that leaders will be more *directive* if they perceive that they have more power and information than their subordinates. They will *consult* if they perceive that they have the power but that their subordinates have the necessary information to solve the group's problems. They will *delegate* when they perceive that their subordinates have both power and information. They will *negotiate* when they perceive that they have the information but not the power. A small-space analysis of empirical data by Shapira (1976) supported these propositions.[10]

Bass (1960) argued that the emergence of leadership success in influencing the group and its effectiveness (the group's actual achievement of its goals such as reward or the avoidance of punishment) depended on the *interaction potential* in the situation—the physical, psychological, and social proximity among the would-be leader and the followers. The likelihood that individuals would in-

---

[10] More will be said about these propositions in Chapters 18 and 19.

teract depends on the size of the group; the geographic and social proximity of the individuals; their opportunity for contact, intimacy, and familiarity; mutuality of esteem and attraction; and homogeneity of abilities and attitudes. Monge and Kirste (1975) extended the examination of proximity as a time-and-space opportunity, showing the positive association of proximity with the potential to interact as well as its contribution to satisfaction with the interaction.

Starting with open-systems theory and Jaques's (1978) general theory of bureaucratic organizations, Jacobs and Jaques (1987) formulated a theory to explain the requirements of leadership at successively higher echelons of large bureaucratic organizations such as the U.S. Department of Defense or General Motors. To operate successfully, these organizations must have an appropriate structure, which Jacobs and Jaques specified as no more than five operating echelons and two additional higher headquarters echelons. At each echelon, the complexity of the environment must be understood and clearly transmitted to the next echelon below to reduce uncertainty there. A reduction of uncertainty will add value to productivity at that echelon and define how it must adapt to remain competitive. At each echelon, the role of the leadership is to ensure the accuracy of the uncertainty reduction process and the availability of resources for the required adaptive changes. To accomplish this goal, leaders at successively higher echelons increasingly must have "the capacity to deal with more uncertain and more abstract concepts" and with longer time spans for accomplishment and evaluation.

At the lowest three echelons, leaders must focus on how they can contribute to the organization's productivity above and beyond the rules and policies that have been laid down for them by higher authority. At the next two echelons, leaders must concern themselves with how to maintain and improve their organizational arrangements. At the highest echelons, leadership involves strategic decision making in a "nearly unbounded" environment.

Multiple Levels Approach. It is possible to look at the same behavior at three levels of a system — individual, group, and organizational — although the operational character of a construct will change if we move from one level to another. For instance, *individualized consider-*ation, a component of transformational leadership, would be addressed at the individual level by a question such as, "Does the leader spend time with newcomers to help orient them to their jobs?" At the team or group level, the same issue would be addressed by, "Do the members of the team provide useful advice to newcomers?" At the organizational level, the question might be, "Are there special policies and programs for orienting newcomers?" (Avolio Bass, 1995). We need to specify at which level we are operating. For example, a leader may be described somewhat differently by each member of a team but uniformly by the team as a whole. Conger (1995) conceived a need to add a fourth level — the intrapsychic — within the leader's mentality. Data about a leader can form an additional level when they are collected during several different periods or phases. Markham, Yammarino, and Palanski (in press) found that the "leader-member exchange" had an effect on performance, which was greater in predicting performance for 25 manager's groups composed of their 110 subordinates when each leader-member dyad was taken into account, rather than each manager's group average of the exchange results.

Toward a Fuller Account

Cognitive, behavioral, and interactional explanations are likely to be needed to account fully for leader-follower relations and the outcomes of these relations. Gilmore, Beehr, and Richter (1979) instructed leaders in an experiment to display either a lot of or a little initiative and a lot of or a little consideration. Although the participants who were subjected to the leadership failed to perceive that their leaders' behavior actually differed, a lot of actual (but not perceived) initiation, coupled with a lot of actual (but not perceived) consideration by the leaders, resulted in better-quality work by the participants. The quality of the participants' work was lower when the leaders displayed a great deal of initiative but little consideration. Evidently, under certain conditions it is more profitable to make use of behavioral theories to understand the behavior of leaders. Under other circumstances, such as when leaders and subordinates must act on the basis of their interpretations of a situation, perceptual and cognitive theories are more useful. Some theories or aspects of theories may account better for the leadership that handles short-term disturbances; other theories may deal better with the leadership that corrects chronic deficiencies over the long term.

Winter (1978, 1979a) developed a complex model that combined aspects of the trait, reinforcement, behavioral, and cognitive approaches and the feedback loops of systems analysis. Winter's model was based on a battery of tests of skills and behavioral competence measures for over 1,000 naval personnel and their leaders. Figure 3.1 shows the emergent model that links various skills with particular performances. The model is based on empirical cluster analyses and subsequent regression analyses.

Greater optimization (assigning tasks to those subordinates who are most likely to do them well and making trade-offs between the requirements of the tasks and individual needs) and setting goals both contributed to more delegation by the leader. Increased monitoring by the leader resulted in more positive expectations, disciplining, advice, and counsel. It also contributed to more feedback, which in turn led to more disciplining and giving more advice and counsel.

Zand (1997) found that effective executives make use of knowledge, trust, and power. These three factors are needed to create an impelling vision and to direct a broad course of action. Working with their staff, the executives select a path, sharpen concepts, learn from mistakes, make adjustments, and refine their strategy and imple-

mentation as they go along, Johnston (1981) used many of the preceding theories to construct a model of a holistic leader-follower" grid. To represent the leader-follower interchange adequately, Johnston borrowed from Jung's (1968) psychoanalytic theory of life cycles, Berne's (1964) transactional analysis, McGregor's (1960) theory X and theory Y, Rogers's (1951) nondirective counseling, and Tannenbaum and Schmidt's (1958) model of decision making. Tomassini, Solomon, Romney, et al. (1982) also constructed a cognitive-behavioral model in which the leader's influence interacted with the subordinate's work behavior, and they identified situations that circumscribe what a leader can do.

Methods and Measurements

As noted in Chapter 4, Stogdill (1948) reviewed leadership studies between 1904 and 1947 and found that they employed one of six methods: (1) observation and time sampling of behavior in group situations; (2) choice of associates by voting, naming, ranking, or sociometrics; (3) nomination by qualified observers; (4) identification of persons occupying leadership positions; (5) analysis of biographical and case history data; and (6) listing of traits essential to leadership. Research on the traits of leaders

Figure 3.1 Flow Chart of Navy Leadership and Management Processes in Terms of the Cross-Validated Competencies

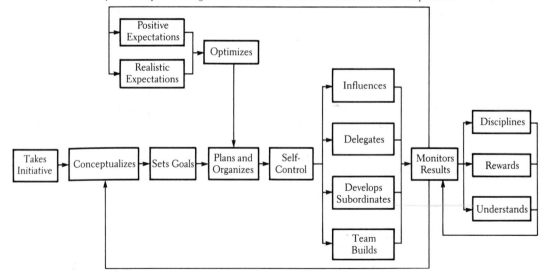

SOURCE: *Adapted from Winter (1978).*

tended to rely heavily on tests and questionnaires for the collection of data. With the development of interaction models and theories, it became important to know what was happening in the group. Expert or trained observers were used to keep a running record of the behavior of group members, and the leaders and followers also might be asked to report their feelings and observations. In some cases, observers merely reported what they saw; in other cases, they were provided with checklists of behaviors or processes to be reported. Bales (1950) developed a checklist for observations of a set of behavioral categories. Carter and associates (1951); Mann (1979); and Komaki, Zlotnick, and Jensen (1986), among others, also developed observational categories and procedures. Bass, Gaier, Farese, et al. (1957) relied on the changes in correlations among members' judgments from before to after group discussion to measure how influential each member had been.

Observational studies identified behaviors that the trait theorists did not anticipate. Whereas the trait theorists were interested in the leader's personality, the interaction experimenters were more concerned with observable interactional behaviors of leaders and their followers. The two approaches could produce moderately correlated results. Jacoby (1974) was able to demonstrate substantial construct validity based on agreement among three methods of assessing opinion leadership—(1) self-designating, (2) sociometric, and (3) key informant.

Laboratory experiments and field surveys have often been the method of choice in cognitive and behavioral investigations. Experiment and survey together provided more convincing evidence. By now, it is fair to say that almost every procedure known to social science has been applied specifically to the study of leadership. These procedures have included content analysis and thematic analysis of autobiographies, biographies, and case studies; verbal protocols; individual structured interviews face-to-face and by computer; panel interviews; interview boards; news and journal reports of historical events, stories, and anecdotes; historical accounts; memorandums; minutes of meetings; speeches; biodata; sociometry, using face-to-face and electronic communication patterns; autologs; cognitive maps; observers' logs of leaders' activities; and ratings by observers, superiors, peers, subordinates, and outsiders, such as clients, customers, and suppliers. Many analyses were based on leaders' self-

ratings; but to increase confidence, these increasingly were supported by investigations using two or more independent approaches. For example, Heller (1969a) first collected survey-questionnaire data from managers. After analyzing the results, he gathered the managers together in panels to interpret and confirm or refute the findings. Also, focused interviews of panels of voters provided the basic ideas for political media campaigns that were then followed up by public opinion polls of representative samples of voters (Kerman & Hadley, 1986).

For experiments, leaders were described in fictional sketches as being reacted to by readers as if they were followers. Leaders were self-selected, appointed, nominated, elected, emergent, or simulated. Methods were quantitative or purely qualitative. but there was increasing use of each method to buttress the other. The *historiometic* approach was the oldest method, beginning with Quetelet's (1835/1968) research on leading dramatists. Historiometric research on leadership was exemplified early on by Cox's (1913) study of the influence of monarchs, and more recently by O'Connor, Mumford, Clifton, et al. (1995) on famous and infamous world leaders. Simonton (1999) enumerated psychological studies of eminent persons such as famous sports stars, Nobel laureates, and chess grand masters. Quantitative methods are used to analyze historical sources of information. *Psychometric* research applied surveys, interviews, and psychological tests to study individual leaders. Modern *psychobiographical* research began with Freud's (1910/1964) psychoanalytic study of Leonardo da Vinci. An intensive study of a single individual, Roosevelt, *The Lion and the Fox* is illustrative (J. M. Burns, 1956). Psychobiographical research can also deal with multiple cases. It has usually been qualitative. Politicians and presidents are most often the subject of investigation. *Comparative* research looks at a small sample of leaders and contrasts them according to biographies, interviews, media accounts, and other sources of information and events. Among the many quantitative and qualitative methods, some of those used more in leadership are presented briefly below.

Quantitative Methods

Of the 188 articles published by the *Leadership Quarterly* between 1990 and 1999, descriptive statistics were provided by 87%, and simple inferential statistics by 69%.

From 25% to 32% of the articles made use of multivariate analyses. Less frequently employed were confirmatory factor analysis (14%), structural equation modeling (13%), and multiple-levels analyses (13%; Lowe & Gardner, 2001). The use of quantitative methods in social science such as Q sorting, confirmatory factor analysis, and structural equation modeling increased with the availability of computer analysis. Other quantitative methods in social science most applicable to studies of leadership were multiple-levels analysis, rotational designs, and designs for the avoidance of common error variance. Meta-analysis made possible valid statistical summaries of the results of replicated and similar studies using the same or comparable variables.

Q Sorting. Q sorts are measurements, usually rankings on a set of ratings or tests within each of the same individuals instead of the more common measurements between individuals on the same set. Individuals rather than measurements are correlated. When factor analysis is applied to the matrix of Q sorts, factor types with similar profiles usually emerge, instead of factors of measurements (Cattell, 1946). Q sorting was also applied to matching ratings in order of importance of job requirements with ratings of each candidate's profile of knowledge, skills, and abilities (O'Reilly, 1977). In a large consumer products company, the consistency of ratings of 60 statements of requirements for the position of production manager by 10 job experts was .96. The agreement among the rated manager, a peer, and the boss about the requirements was .81. The correlation of the person-job fit ranged from −.44. to .86. A high correlation meant a very good fit; a high negative correlation signified a very bad fit. The rank order of the fits correlated .98 with the rank order of performance of the managers rated by the human resources staff and superiors. Similar findings were reported in three further investigations (Caldwell & O'Reilly, undated).

Confirmatory Factor Analysis. Unlike the more traditional exploratory factor analysis, which extracts underlying factors from a matrix of correlations of individuals and variables, confirmatory factor analysis begins with a model of the assumed factors and provides several tests of the goodness of fit between the model and the factors. For instance, Avolio, Bass, and Jung (1999) determined that six factors of the "Full Range of Leadership" provided the best fit of 14 samples of data from scores on the Multifactor Leadership Questionnaire.

Structural Equation Modeling. This is a systematic analysis making use of partial and multiple regressions to explore or confirm causal relations between a set of predictors and a set of outcomes. The fit of the obtained model and the hypothesized model can be tested. The strengths of the relations between variables can be obtained from path coefficients similar to partial correlations. Computer programs like LISREL facilitate the analysis for exploration and confirmation.

Multiple-Levels Analyses

WABA: Within-and-Between Analysis. Dansereau, Alutto, and Yammarino (1984) began a continuing line of investigation of variant analyses which quantitatively shows how much of the ratings of the leader in a single study are due to different levels of analysis. The "person level" acknowledges the importance of consistent individual differences among leaders, followers, or both. The "dyad level" recognizes the importance of one-to-one relationships between a leader and each of the followers. The "group level" or "team level" takes cognizance of the face-to-face relations between a leader and a set of followers as a unit. For instance, the leader may treat the followers in the same set in the same way or different ways. The "collective level" or "organizational level" deals with hierarchically organized groups of groups, as when the same or different organizational policies apply to all groups (Yammarino, Dansereau, & Kennedy, 2001). The focus is between entities such as dyads or groups, not within them. Here, as in traditional analysis of variance, differences between entities are viewed as valid; differences within entities are viewed as random error. This is a between-units case in which the members of the unit are homogeneous and the whole unit is important. The "parts" view differs from the traditional analysis of variance in focusing within entities such as dyads or groups. Differences within entities are valid; differences between entities are considered random error. This is the within-units case in which members are heterogeneous; each member's position relative to others is important. Dyads can be viewed as parts of a group. In this case of dyads-within-groups, leaders differ from each other in the same group, and the same pattern is repeated in the other groups. Thus each leader may form a favored in-group of subordinates and a less favored out-group. Dyads may be completely independent of the groups to which they belong. Then they are viewed as whole dyads, independent and homogeneous entities. Analysis of variance (WABA I) as well as co-variance (WABA II) can be applied to quantitatively decompose a single survey of ratings of leaders and their correlated effectiveness.

Further breakdowns may test whether there is an equitable balance of leader and subordinate, whether relations between dyads are stronger in some groups than others, and whether consensus is the same in some dyads in some groups but not others. Cross-level effects from dyads to groups can also be specified (Yammarino, 1995; Dansereau, Yammarino, & Markham, 1995). In a study of insurance and retail salespersons' attitudes about factors controllable by management and supervisory ratings of the salespersons' performance, Yammarino and Dubinsky (1990) found differences between the groups of aggregated ratings as well as individual differences within the groups. Some groups of supervisors and subordinates were rated higher than others across the groups; some supervisors and subordinates in the same group were rated higher than others. Castro (2002) contrasted WABA with other multi-level methods of leadership research. These included intraclass correlation (r_{wg}), hierarchical linear modeling (HLM), and random group resampling (RGR).

Intraclass Correlation. The expression r_{wg} is the ratio of the difference in the variance of ratings between leaders' and followers' ratings of each of the same leaders, compared with the variance of ratings between leaders (suitably corrected for the number of leaders). This index provides the reliability of the ratings for the same and different leaders, the agreement among raters and whether aggregation of the ratings is justified (James, Demeree, & Wolf, 1984).

Hierarchical Linear Modeling (HLM) This is a two-level approach. First, the regression equations for the unaggregated ratings (the individual level) and outcomes are calculated. Then, the intercepts, slopes, error, and regressions become the data for the group level of a parallel analysis. The two levels of analysis permit tests of signifi-

cance of the individual ratings and the aggregated grouped ratings. HLM can be used to test moderator effects across levels and longitudinal changes, if not limited by the need to assume normality of the data, and if there are a sufficient number of cases (Bryk & Raudenbush, 1992).

Random Group Resampling (RGR). Based on Fischer's permutation test, proposed in 1930, RGR is related to the *bootstrap* and *jackknife* (Efron & Tibshirani, 1993). A pseudo group of the same size as the first actual group of the first followers' leadership ratings is created by sorting the data from lowest to highest and randomly forming a pseudo group without replacement. The remaining data are combined into a second pseudo group. The means of the two pseudo groups are calculated. Then, Monte Carlo techniques are applied to create a set of 1,000 pseudo groups and their distribution of differences in means. Finally, the mean group differences obtained from the actual data are tested as to whether they came from this distribution of differences of the pseudo groups and whether the average data at the group level or the individual differences in followers need to be considered. RGR can be used to test the significance of WABA II results for the co-variance between predictors and outcomes (Bliese Halverson, 2002).

Rotational Designs. To test for personal versus situational effects, the same individuals are rotated in a systematic way through a set of conditions. An individual is placed in different groups to examine the consistency of his or her emergent leadership in each group (Kenny & Hallmark, 1992). For instance, Zaccaro, Foti, and Kenny (1991) first tested participants on selected traits. Next, participants were systematically rotated through a set of group tasks in different groups. The investigators then were able to determine that the effects of the traits on the participants' emergent leadership in the different groups was much stronger than the differences from group to group, indicating that personality was much more important than the situation in determining who would lead.

Other Quantitative Issues

Increasing Response Rates to Survey Questionnaires. Responses to mail questionnaires can fall to 20% or lower.

One way to test whether the respondents are a valid or biased sample is to send out successive waves of the questionnaires to see if answers do not change as the numbers of respondents increase with each wave. Rogelberg and Luong (1998) listed techniques supported by research to increase the response rate: (1) Notify potential respondents in advance. (2) Follow nonrespondents with reminders. (3) Provide incentives. (4) Use appeals. (5) Keep surveys to a reasonable length. (6) Facilitate the returns by providing first-class-stamped envelopes. (7) Ask easy and interesting questions first and demographic questions last. (8) Tell who the sponsors of the research are. (9) Ensure respondents' anonymity. Telephone questioning can also increase response rates. Response rates can come close to 100% when questionnaires are handed out and completed in an assembly. According to a meta-analysis by Cycyota and Harrison (2002), response rates of executives can be increased by reaching them through their social networks such as associations, professional groups, and colleagues.

Rating Inaccuracies. Starbuck and Mezias (1996) reviewed 210 publications about misperceptions that are sources of inaccurate ratings by managers. These articles dealt with managerial perceptions of organizations and their internal and external environments. Ten other publications provided objective data for analysis. The authors concluded that perceptual data play an extremely important role in studies and theories about managerial behavior. Objective situations defined by perceptual data may not correlate with each other. Employees fail to agree about the properties of their organization. Perceptions may be very inaccurate. Needed in organizational and leadership research are studies to measure the errors and biases in perceptions and their determinants.

Anonymity. Anonymity eliminates the fear of reprisal, particularly when subordinates want to rate superiors unfavorably (Antonini, 1994). The extent to which subordinates' favorable or unfavorable ratings were reciprocated by superiors was examined in anonymous and nonanonymous conditions for 241 teams of female undergraduates in groups of six with an assigned leader. They conducted a discussion to reach decisions about the value of 15 items if they were stranded in a desert. Significant reciprocity of evaluations between the leader and the led occurred in the nonanonymous but not the anonymous condition (Haeggberg & Chen, 2000).

Avoiding Common or Same-Source Variance. Common methods variance is the overlap between two variables due to a common bias rather than to a relationship between the underlying constructs. For instance, a correlation between two measurements may be partially due to the fact that the measurements were obtained with the same method, at the same time, or by the same rater. Common or same-source error is greatest when two sets of data are collected at the same time, from the same respondent, on the same instrument, by the same method, and about the same trait. Campbell and Fiske (1959) suggested that each respondent be assessed on each of at least two different traits by at least two different methods to take common variance into account This *multitrait, multimethod* procedure is one of six ways proposed to eliminate or control error. None is foolproof, according to Podsakóff and Organ (1986), who suggested applying WABA analysis in which each rater is matched with a counterpart. The first rater rates one variable—say, leadership—and the second rates an outcome. (See Avolio, Yammarino, & Bass, 1991, for a more detailed exposition.)

Meta-Analyses. Meta-analysis is an effort to estimate the population or true effect of an analysis from results obtained from comparable samples. Three major types of meta-analysis have been developed by Rosenthal and Rubin (1988), Hedges and Olkin (1985), and Hunter and Schmidt (1990). The basic ideas go back to the early 1930s (Johnson, Muller, & Salas, 1995). Rosenthal and Rubin convert each sample of results into standardized scores (Z's) with one-tail probabilities for significance. *Effect sizes* derive from Fisher's conversion of correlations to Z's. Weighted means are generated for comparing the relevant dependent variables. Hedges and Olkin convert samples of results into standard deviation units (g's). These need correction because they overestimate the population effect size, especially with small samples. The results are combined, their consistency is tested, and their variability is explained by use of models with moderators. Hunter and Schmidt's approach is probably the best-known of the three approaches. It does not correct the biases in effect size or with moderators. Like the other approaches, it weights the means of each sample according to size. It corrects effect sizes for sampling error, attenuation due to restriction of range in each study, and the reliability of the variables used. By 2006, we were able to report numerous meta-analyses to support conclusions about many aspects of leadership and management and their effects.

Indexes of Change. To measure whether a change has occurred in the leader, the led, or the organization as a consequence of learning, three measures were proposed by Golembiewski, Billingsley, and Yeager (1976). *Alpha* change is a simple rise or fall in a measurement of the level of a state of affairs calibrated to reflect a one-to-one change in the concept assessed. *Beta* change is a rise or fall in the measurement where there is a recalibration to reflect systematic modification in relation to the concept assessed (see also Terborg, Howard, & Maxwell, 1960). *Gamma* change occurs if there is a change in any of these: perspective, frame of reference, or concept assessed. Factor analysis was applied to register changes in factor structures from before to after an intervention (Golembiewski et al., 1976; Schmitt, 1982).

Critique. MacCallum (1998) pointed to a need to correct interpretations drawn from quantitative methods in leadership and organizational research including structural equation modeling, factor analysis, analysis of variance, multiple levels of analysis, and basing measurement reliability on coefficient alpha. He also noted methodological problems in event history analysis. He favored making more use of archival data, using moderated regression, and comparing the goodness of fit of several models rather than depending for significance on the fit of a single model.

Increasingly, we are seeing efforts to use *triangulation* of quantitative and qualitative methods to reinforce conclusions from each. A quantitative survey is accompanied by a qualitative in-depth interview of selected respondents. The themes in a qualitative description of a case are categorized, counted, and content-analyzed.

Qualitative Methods

The 188 articles in the *Leadership Quarterly* in the 1990s used about half as many qualitative methods as quantitative methods. The most favored qualitative methods were content analyses (53%), case studies (45%), and grounded theory (24%; Lowe & Gardner, 2001). Results would have favored more qualitative methodology if the *Journal of Leadership Studies* or political science and sociological journals had been sampled instead of the psychology-oriented *Leadership Quarterly*.

Strauss and Corbin (1990) noted what was required to collect reliable and valuable observational data. Days and situations for observation need to be routine. Interviews need to be conducted with a cross-sectional sample representative of the population of subjects. Coding of data needs to be done through successive iterations from a smaller initial list to a more complex final list. These data need to be checked against recordings of the initial observations and interviews. From a background in cultural anthropology which depends heavily on qualitative research, Conger (1998) argued that qualitative methods, although time-intensive and complex, are the method of choice for capturing insights into contextual effects and longitudinal developments in the study of leadership. Running summaries are kept of the large amounts of the observations and data collected. General categories are refined as new data are gathered. Ideas, concepts, and theory emerge and evolve. We have already presented the qualitative endeavor of psychohistory. Psychoanalytic concepts are employed to infer the causes underlying the development and performance of individual leaders and their followers. Freud and Bullitt's (1932) interpretation of President Wilson's career is illustrative of an ideographic approach to psychohistory. Qualitative research may be idiographic or nomothetic. The *ideographic* approach is an intensive study of a single case; for example, Kofodimos, Kaplan, and Drath (1986) studied the character and development of a single manager. They included his work life and private life to try to understand why he behaved as he did. The *nomothetic* approach tries to draw inferences from a more limited exposure to a large number of cases. Most of the studies presented in this book are nomothetic.

Interviews. Some kind of structured or open-ended interviews begin many qualitative analyses. With a background like Conger's, Sayles (1964) applied the anthropologist's approach to interviewing. He sought to build a coherent, chronological account of problems, cases, and issues. His interviews focused on learning about events, transitions, and conflicts. Using triangulation, he would verify or reject new information about critical interactions. He learned how events were perceived by different managers in diverse roles and was able to "reconstruct the recurring social process underpinning the tough human challenges of the organization" (Sayles, 1999, p. 9). Sayles saw the challenges of leadership as the "heart" of management. Leaders' interventions had to be skillfully timed, sequenced, and executed.

Waldman, Lituchy, Gopalakrishnan, et al. (1998) conducted a qualitative analysis of managers. They drew themes and categorical schemes from interviews in a manufacturing plant, a hospital, and a police force engaged in quality-improvement programs. They uncovered two alternative paths of managerial commitment to the quality-improvement process. One path, following top management's vision and commitment, was characterised by continued commitment, planned adjustments, and a cultural shift favoring quality improvement. The other path, from top management leading down, was one of wavering commitment, knee-jerk reactions, and cynicism about organizational change. From the CNN broadcast *Pinnacle*, verbatim interviews with CEOs, videotapes of 30 of 80 interviewees were randomly selected by Piotrowski and Armstrong (1989) and rated on 25 personality-lifestyle dimensions by two raters. The two raters agreed that the CEOs exhibited clear values, tolerance of frustration, and egalitarian attitudes. They were also oriented toward tasks, people, results, and compulsivity. They were workaholics and needed more social recognition and family life.

Content Analysis. Content analysis is often employed in qualitative studies. After identifying the research question, the text to be examined, and the unit of analysis, an initial coding scheme is tried on a pilot text. The coding scheme is purified and the observational, interview, or written data are collected. The reliability of the trained coders is assessed. Modifications of the training and the coding may be required and tried out on a second pilot. The construct validity of the categorization is determined. If reliability and validity are satisfactory, the data are coded and analyzed. Insch, Moore, and Murphy (1997) provided examples of content analyses, methods of analysis, and their strengths and weaknesses.

Cognitive Mapping. Sims and Siew-Kim (1993) uncovered the tension involved in simultaneously being a woman, an Asian, and a manager by asking each of nine collaborating senior Singaporean woman managers to draw a cognitive map showing issues and experiences in becoming and being an Asian woman. Subsequently, each woman provided incidents about managing or being managed. The research was grounded in the women's own language, expressions, thought systems, beliefs, and concepts: the women explained what they thought was important and why. Nine themes emerged: (1) integrity, (2) coping with male insecurity, (3) western versus Taoist and Confucian values, (4) supporting friends and superiors, (5) female leadership, (6) fighting, (7) individual versus group rights, (8) not wishing to undermine others, and (9) high standards for oneself.

Repertory Grid. Although George Kelly (1955) originated this technique in the United States in the 1930s to use in counseling students, it gained more widespread use in management development and organizational research in Britain. It focused on people's implicit constructs, concepts, and theories; and the language they used to describe cognitions, perceptions, and behaviors. In its least structured form, interviewees are asked to identify the persons in a group who are most similar to each other. Next, they are asked to use words and phrases to tell in what ways these people are similar. Then interviewees are asked to identify the person in the group who is most different from the first two chosen persons and in what ways. The process is repeated for each member of the group. Content analysis of the responses follows. (For a more structured approach to the repertory grid, see Esterby-Smith, Thorpe, & Holman, 1996.)

Stories. Boje (1995) gained access to the Disney studio archives of audiotapes and videotapes of Walt Disney and other Disney leaders' speeches, work interactions, documentary interviews, and conversations. Also included were television shows, films, cartoon shorts, working meetings, and stockholders' meetings, as well as many public relations films. Boje was interested in stories about this storytelling organization and was able to infer from them that Walt Disney was a tyrant. Implications will be discussed in Chapter 17.

Spicochi and Tyran (2002) provided two examples of

the role of leaders as story tellers and how followers made sense of the stories. These stories were attempts to communicate a vision of transformation in the health care industry, where there is need for flexibility and responsiveness to a continually changing environment. The authors suggested a number of ways leaders can make their stories effective. First, in order to learn how their stories will be interpreted by employees, they should first learn about employees' reactions to past organizational change and how their attitudes have developed. Clarify the vision. Understand how employees will see the vision as affecting them. Believe in the vision. Minimize ambiguity. Appear in person to tell the story. Incorporate a range of stories from all levels of the organization to make sense for the leadership. Empathize with your audience and focus on their understanding. Finally, be ready to listen and to further clarify the meaning in the story.

Drawing from the Humanities and the Arts. According to Yammarino (2002), "Leadership is part art and part science. . . . An inclusive approach recognizes the complementary roles of the humanities, the arts, and the social sciences in the pursuit of leadership theory, research, and practice." History, drama, literature, and art are underutilized by students of leadership. Yet they could provide a stronger base for theory, building to avoid developing theories of leadership that are "academic amnesia" and "leadership *déjà vu*" (Hunt & Dodge, 2000). A good example of an historical source that has not been used for developing a modern theory of leadership is the *Anabasis* by Xenophon (c. 400 B.C.), whose account of the successful march of the 10,000 Greek soldiers through a hostile Persian empire illustrated the importance of cohesion, commitment, confidence, and leadership. Gordon (2002) notes that much of the emphasis on power in such historical sources and events has not been used to formulate testable concepts and theories of leadership.

Combining Quantitative and Qualitative Methods

McNamara's Fallacy. Camille Cavour and then Lord Curzon declared as early as the 1860s that if you can't measure something, you don't know what you are talking about. And so body counts were used invalidly to mea-

sure victory in battle in Vietnam. The need to qualify quantitative results was provided by a sophisticated view of quantitative data—"McNamara's Fallacy." This fallacy is named after Robert McNamara, who as U.S. Secretary of Defense tried to quantify military outcomes. The fallacy can be paraphrased as follows. First, measure what can easily be measured. *This is OK.* Second, disregard what can't be easily measured or give it an arbitrary quantitative value. *This is artificial and misleading.* Third, assume that what can't be easily measured is unimportant. *This is blindness.* Fourth, assume that what can't be easily measured really doesn't exist. *This is suicide.* The fallacy illustrated the need for qualitative methods to support quantitative analyses (Handy, 1994).

Among the valid methods combining quantitative and qualitative methods are the subjects of biographies assessed by personality tests and scales, triangulation, and data analyses about historical figures.

Biographies and Personality Tests. Biographies of political personages can become the basis for raters to complete personality tests about them. The tests are then scored to provide quantitative data about the political figures (Immelman, 1998).

Triangulation. Analogous to locating a target at the junction of two lines on a map, *triangulation* refers to combining results of a qualitative investigation with the results of a parallel quantitative investigation (Jick, 1979). For instance, Berson, Jung, and Tirmizi (1997) buttressed a quantitative analysis showing that light infantry platoon leaders, rated as transformational in their home station, subsequently led more effective platoons in near-combat. They also included a multi-level analysis in the process. The investigators found that the categorized responses of the observer-controllers to open-ended questions about the leaders and the platoons in action were predicted by the home station ratings, near-combat data, and U.S. Army leadership doctrine.

Modern historians with access to archival documents and data can use both to provide lessons for leaders and managers. Historians of southern history have made extensive use of data to show that slavery in the South was profitable to plantation owners. Apologists for slavery pointed to the humanitarianism of slave owners who bore the expense of caring for aged slaves who could no longer work. Mortality data show that most slaves did not live long enough to "retire."

Summary and Conclusions

Many of the most prominent theories and methods related to the study of leadership were reviewed briefly and will reappear in more detail in later chapters. The long history of reliance on great-man theories naturally led to a search for traits of leadership and theories of traits. Genetics has also increased in interest. In reaction, there arose an equally strong emphasis on environmental theories. Political, psychoanalytical, group dynamics, and humanistic theories appeared along with those built on communications and leaders' behavior, perception, cognition, and cognitive resources. Finally, syntheses were achieved in theories and methods of interacting persons and situations, built around exchanges, transformations, attributions, information processing, role attainment, reinforced change, paths to goals, contingencies of leader and situation, open-systems analysis, rational deduction, and multiple levels of analysis. Empirical research and modern theories of leadership began with studies of the personal factors that contributed to the emergence and success of a leader.

Personal Attributes of Leaders

II

Personal Attributes of Leaders

Traits of Leadership (1904–1970)

This chapter is partly a revision and expansion of a longer version of a seminal publication by Ralph Stogdill (1948) concluding that leaders differ consistently in personal dispositions or traits and are propelled into leadership position if warranted by the needs of the situation.[1] A review of research studies up to 1948, up to 1970, then up to 2005 will follow in this and the next chapter.

1904–1948

Up to the middle of the twentieth century, leadership research was dominated by the search for the traits of leadership. In Britain in the nineteenth century, personal traits such as height, weight, health, and education had been found to correlate with leadership. But as noted by Shackleton (2001), the powerful and wealthy were better fed, clothed, and housed than factory workers and farm laborers. They could pay for an education. Smith and Krueger (1933) surveyed the preceding studies on leadership to 1933. Developments in leadership methodology, as related especially to military situations, were reviewed by Jenkins (1947).

Stogdill (1948) reviewed 128 published studies that tried to determine the traits and characteristics of leaders. The results of the survey included those characteristics and traits that were studied by three or more investigators. When contradictory evidence occurred, those studies with positive, negative, and neutral results were pre-

sented. He concluded that to some degree the traits of leadership needed to match the needs of the situation. What follows first are shortened excerpts of Stogdill's 1948 review.

Chronological Age

Evidence of the relation of age to leadership in children was quite contradictory. Pigors (1933) observed that leadership did not appear in children before age two or three and then usually took the form of overt domination. Active leadership of a group seldom appeared before age nine or ten, at which age the formation of groups and gangs became a noticeable feature in the social development of children.

According to Pigors, four conditions were necessary for the appearance of leadership in children: (1) development of determination and self-control; (2) grasp of abstractions and social ideals; (3) awareness of personalities; (4) a sufficient memory span to pursue remote goals rather than immediate objectives. Arrington (1943), however, found no evidence from a survey of time-sampling experiments to support the proposition that leadership increases with age in preschool children.

Hunter and Jordan (1939) and Remmelin (1938) found leaders to be significantly younger than their followers. Bellingrath (1930) obtained results indicating that girl leaders were younger than nonleaders but boy leaders were older. However, leaders were found to be older than followers in 10 studies completed between 1915 and 1939 (Gowin, 1915; Zeleny, 1939). Correlations between age and leadership obtained in 13 studies ranged from −.32 to .72 with an average of .21.

Gowin (1918) established that on average, outstanding executives were 12.2 years older than lower-level executives. But Ackerson (1942) and Brown (1933) failed to find leaders and followers different in age.

According to Caldwell and Wellman (1926), the rela-

[1] The original review *Personal factors associated with leadership: A survey of the literature* appeared in the *Journal of Psychology*, 1948, 25, 35-71. It is excerpted by permission of *The Journal Press*, Provincetown, Massachusetts. This classic marked a turning point in the study of leadership. Prior to this work, the search for universal personal traits of leadership was emphasized. After it, situation-specific analyses took over and dominated the field. Much more emphasis was placed on the situation alone than was done in the publication. Both individual traits and situational assessments are important, as well as the interaction between them. That was Stogdill's main thesis. It was not until the 1980s that the importance of personal factors was restored.

tionship of age to leadership differed in various situations. Leaders in athletics were found to be close to the class average in age as were girl club leaders and student council and citizenship representatives. The correlation of chronological age with leadership appeared to depend on other variables. For instance, it was highly positive in an organization like the Roman Catholic church if policies dictated that rank was determined by age; but it was lower or negative in organizations that quickly promoted their "best and brightest" up through the ranks while their less endowed peers reached a plateau early.

Stature

Leaders were found to be taller in nine studies, shorter in two studies, and heavier in seven studies and lighter in two. No differences in height or weight were reported in four studies, and in two studies the results depended on the situation.

Height. Correlations between height and leadership ranged from $-.13$ to $.71$. The general trend of these studies was a low positive relationship between height and leadership. The average correlation was about .30. Nevertheless, Hunter and Jordan (1939) and Garrison (1933) found student leaders to be somewhat shorter than nonleaders. Baldwin (1932) and Reynolds (1944), could find no relation at all between height and leadership in students.

Weight. The correlations obtained suggested a low positive relationship between weight and leadership. The average correlation was about .23. But again, Hunter and Jordan (1939) found the reverse—that leaders were significantly lighter than nonleaders. Garrison (1933) and Moore (1935) also reported leaders to be somewhat lighter than followers. Since height and weight correlated positively, the same pattern of results was obtained for weight as for height.

Physique, Energy, Health

Physique was positively associated with leadership in five studies; athletic ability and physical prowess in seven; energy in five; and health in four. Moreover, health and physical condition were found to be a factor in four of the reviewed investigations.

Physique. Five studies between Webb (1915) and Bernard (1928) reported that superior physique was a characteristic of leaders. The correlations of .28, .18, .11, and .23 found by Kohs and Irle (1920), Nutting (1923), Sheldon (1927), and Webb (1915), respectively, suggested that this relationship was slight but reliable. But Bowden (1926) concluded from the results of his study of college students that leadership was not the result of a dominating physique, and Baldwin (1937) found that high school leaders did not differ from followers in freedom from physical defects.

Health. Leaders, according to Baldwin (1932), Bellingrath (1930), Reals (1938), and Stray (1934), appeared to have some advantage over nonleaders in possessing better health, although Ackerson (1942) and Hunter and Jordan (1939) failed to find that health was a differentiating factor.

Athletic Prowess. Athletic ability and physical prowess did appear to be associated with leadership status in boys' gangs and groups. Evidence to this effect was presented in seven studies between Puffer (1905) and Flemming (1935). Correlations of .38, .62, and .40 between athletic ability and leadership were reported by Flemming (1935), Patridge (1934), and Webb (1915), respectively.

Energy. According to Bellingrath (1930), Brown (1934), Cox (1926), Stray (1934), and Wetzel (1932), leaders were also characterized by high energy. But Cox (1926) found that various groups of great leaders differed markedly from each other in physique, energy, use, and athletic prowess; only military leaders were outstanding in these traits.

Appearance

Leaders presented a better appearance in 11 studies. They were better dressed in two others; but no relationship was found in one study, and appearance was negatively correlated with leadership in two studies. The results clearly depended on circumstances. Thus Dunkerley (1940) found that students who were chosen as leaders in social activities differed significantly from nonleaders in appearance and dress, but students chosen as leaders in intellectual and religious activities did not differ markedly from nonleaders in these respects. A correlation of .21 between attractive appearance and leadership in high school students was reported by Flemming (1935), but the correlation between leadership and being seen as beautiful was only .05. Yet Partridge (1934) found a correlation of .81 between ratings of appearance and leadership among adolescent boys. In Goodenough's (1930) study a negative correlation of −.20 was found between beauty and leadership in preschool children.

Tryon's (1939) analysis suggested that appearance is more closely associated with leadership in boys than in girls. Tryon reported correlations with leadership of .49 and .06, respectively, for 15-year-old boys and girls; the correlations for 12-year-old boys and girls were .31 and .08, respectively. Ackerson (1942) obtained correlations of .12 and −.06 between leadership and being seen as slovenly for boys and girls, respectively; a slovenly appearance and leading others into misconduct were correlated .32 and .31 for delinquent boys and girls.

Fluency of Speech

Speech was positively associated with leadership in all 12 studies that examined the relationship, although a few of the results were marginal.

Tone of Voice. Baldwin (1932) reported a definite trend for teachers to rate the tone of voice of leaders as confident and the tone of voice of nonleaders as lacking in confidence. Flemming's (1935) factor analysis of teachers' ratings of high school leaders revealed "pleasant voice" as one of the four factors found to be associated with leadership. The correlation between "pleasing voice" and leadership in high school students was .28. Partridge (1934) reported that boy leaders could be reliably distinguished from nonleaders when in the presence of strange boys but hidden from view, so that judgments had to be made on speech alone. However, Fay and Middleton (1943), in repeating this experiment under somewhat similar conditions, found a correlation of only .08 between leadership ratings and degree of leadership, as estimated by voice alone. Likewise, Eichler (1934) reported a correlation of only .11 between voice and leadership.

Talkativeness. Talkativeness and leadership were reported by Tryon (1939) to be correlated .41 and .31 for 12-year-old boys and girls, respectively; the correlations for 15-year-old boys and girls were .15 and .44, respectively. In Goodenough's (1930) study, a correlation of .61 between talkativeness and leadership was found. Thurstone (1944) did not find that highly paid administrators surpassed their lower-paid associates in scores on tests of word fluency, but he did find a significant difference in their scores on tests of linguistic ability. Simpson (1938) also reported that verbal ability was correlated .45 with the capacity to influence others.

Fluency. Chevaleva-Ianovskaia and Sylla (1929) noted that child leaders were characterized by longer durations of verbal excitation. Terman (1904) reported that leaders were more fluent in speech, and Leib (1928) observed that leaders excel in speaking ability. The same skills were reported in adult leaders by Bernard (1928) and Merriam (1926). Zeleny (1939) found a correlation of .59 between leadership ratings and total remarks made in class. Interesting conversation and leadership were correlated .28 in Flemming's (1935) study. Finally, Burks (1938) and Malloy (1936) found that vividness and originality of expression and facility of conversation were associated with successful social relationships. Considering the size of the experimental groups, the competence of the experimental methods employed, and the positive nature of the evidence presented, it was apparent that fluency of speech, if not tone of voice, was a factor to be considered in the study of leadership. It has long been recognized that effective leadership cannot be maintained in an organization without an adequate system of intercommunication. Thus it does not seem surprising that some of the most searching studies of leadership should reveal the capacity for ready communication as one of the skills associated with leadership.

Intelligence

All but 5 of 23 studies presented evidence that the average leader surpassed the average member of his or her group in intelligence. However, five of the studies suggested that too great a difference in the IQ of the leader and the average member will militate against leadership. Statistically reliable differences were reported, for example, by Hunter and Jordan (1939), Remmelin (1938), and Sward (1933). In most of these studies, there was considerable overlapping of the scores of leaders and nonleaders on intelligence tests, indicating that superior intelligence was not an absolute requirement for leadership. Nevertheless, the general trend of the findings suggested that leadership status was more often than not associated with superiority in intelligence. The correlations revealed a consistently positive relationship. The average of these coefficients was approximately .28.

Factorial studies demonstrated a number of points that may be of considerable significance for the study of leadership. Cattell (1946), for example, reported that the intelligence factor is heavily weighted with such elements of character as being wise, emotionally mature, persevering, mentally alert, vigorous, and conscientious. These items correspond fairly closely to the factors discussed later, which were found in the present survey to be supported by an excess of positive over negative evidence. For example, Thorndike (1936) reported a correlation of .60 for 305 male members of European royal families between their intellectual ability and their esteem (which, in turn, is related to leadership). Thus it appears that high intelligence may be associated with other characteristics that contribute to a person's value as a leader.

Limits. One of the most significant findings concerning the relation of intelligence to leadership is that extreme discrepancies between the intelligence of potential leaders and their followers militated against the exercise of leadership. Hollingworth (1926) found that among children with a mean IQ of 100, the IQ of the leader was likely to fall between 115 and 130. That is, the leader was likely to be more intelligent, but *not too much more intelligent than the average of the group led.* Observation further showed that a child with an IQ of 160 had little chance of being a popular leader in a group of children of average intelligence but might become a leader in a group of children with a mean IQ of 130. One of the difficulties in this connection seemed to be communication. The average child cannot comprehend a large part of the vocabulary used by a child of unusually superior intelligence to express exact meanings in relation to his

or her more mature and complicated interests. Differences in interests, goals, and activity patterns also act as barriers to joint participation, which is a necessary condition of group leadership.

Hollingworth's findings were confirmed by a number of investigations. Finch and Carroll (1932), studying groups of 66 gifted, 66 superior, and 66 average children, arrived at the conclusion that, "Given a superior group of children to lead, the leading will tend to be done by the gifted children," even though the leaders as a group tend to be younger than the group led. However, in an early study of the formation of boys' gangs, Warner (1923) found that leaders and followers differ much more in chronological age than in mental age. She observed that older boys who were mentally below normal tended to group with younger boys who had a mental age near their own and slightly higher, and that when groups of retarded delinquent boys contacted groups of brighter delinquents, the contacts were "so short and non-social that no noticeable event took place." Mailer (1925), studying cooperation and competition among children, found that homogeneity of intelligence, rather than level of intelligence, was important in cooperative behavior. McCuen (1929) studied leadership in 58 organizations of college students. He concluded that "the crowd seems to desire to be led by the average person. Evidently in a democratic society, the leader must not be too far detached from the group."

Two studies by Lehman (1937, 1942) are of interest in this connection. In the first study, Lehman determined the age intervals at which outstanding men in various professions made their best contributions. In the second study, he determined the optimal age intervals for eminent leadership. Chemists, for example, were found to make their best contributions during the age intervals 28–32 years, while the optimal ages for eminent leadership in chemistry were 45–49 years. Thus, it appears that even in science, individuals contributions and communications must be understood by, and in accord with the thinking of their contemporaries for them to rise to a position of leadership in their profession.

Scholarship

Leaders were reported to have better scholastic records in 22 studies and poorer records only once. No differences were obtained in four investigations. It is not surprising that leaders were found, with a high degree of uniformity, to have better average scholastic grades than did nonleaders, for, as was just noted, leaders had been found more intelligent than their followers. But the findings by Buttgereit (1932), Caldwell and Wellman (1926), and many others suggested that superior scholarship may not be a mere byproduct of superior intelligence, but may have direct importance for leadership when it is one aspect of a general ability to get things done. It was also suggested that superior accomplishment in areas valued by the group had prestige value, which may also contribute to leadership. At the same time, there was an abundance of evidence to indicate that a position of leadership was ordinarily not based on superior intelligence and accomplishment alone, since these two factors were present, to a high degree, in many persons who did not occupy positions of leadership. Thus, overall, the magnitude of the correlations suggests that intelligence and scholarship account for only a fraction of the total complex of factors associated with leadership.

Knowledge

The results of all 11 studies dealing with leadership and knowledge implied that persons who are chosen as leaders tended to know how to get things done. Of particular interest was Caldwell's (1920) experiment in which he asked 282 high school students to nominate boy and girl leaders for three different situations: (1) a trip to a wharf; (2) the production of a program and its presentation at a neighboring school; (3) the reorganization of a program for administering athletics in the school. The nominations revealed "a clear judgment on the part of these pupils as to the members of the group best fitted to lead them." The most important abilities ascribed to these leaders were intelligence and practical knowledge about the situations for which they were chosen as leaders.

In this connection, it seems worthwhile to consider the findings of Baldwin (1932) and Burks (1938) in relation to the association between leadership and the ability to make constructive and creative suggestions. Burks, for example, found that the ability to present constructive ideas for difficult situations was closely associated with successful social relationships.

The studies of Cox (1926), Drake (1944), Flemming

(1935), Stray (1934), and Thrasher (1927) found that constructive imagination was a characteristic of leaders. Additional evidence related to the ability to get things done was presented by Bellingrath (1930) and Dunkerley (1940). Cox (1926) and Peck (1931) reported that great leaders were characterized and differentiated from the average by a greater intensity of application and industry. In summary, the results of these various studies seemed to indicate that specialized knowledge, imagination, and the ability to get things done were factors that contributed to leadership.

Judgment and Decision

Soundness and finality of judgment were related to leadership in five studies; and speed and accuracy of thought and decision were related in four analyses. In view of the positive correlations found between intelligence and leadership, it was not surprising to find a similar relationship between judgment and leadership. Bellingrath (1932), Drake (1944), and Webb (1915) reported correlations ranging from .34 to .69 between common sense and leadership; Bellingrath (1930), Drake (1944), Flemming (1935), and Webb (1915) found correlations of 60, .34, .28, and .69, respectively, between judgment and leadership. Farsightedness and leadership were found to be correlated .55, .25, and .33 in the studies of Bellingrath, Drake, and Webb, respectively. Two of the factor-analytic studies—those of Cowley (1931) and Dunkerley (1940)—revealed that soundness and finality of judgment were common to leaders. In addition to judgment, Cowley (1931) also identified three factors that appeared to represent speed of decision. Hanawalt, Richardson, and Hamilton (1943) found that leaders used the "?", or "undecided," response on the Bernreuter Personality test significantly less frequently than nonleaders, and this tendency was especially noticeable on the most discriminating items. In spite of the small number of studies bearing on judgment and decision, the general competence of the methods lent confidence to the results obtained.

Insight

Leadership was found to be related to certain aspects of insight, as follows: "keenly alive to environment, alert" (six studies); ability to evaluate situations (five studies);

social insight (five studies); self-insight (two studies); and sympathetic understanding (seven studies). Traditionally, insight has been regarded as one aspect of general intelligence. However, Jennings (1943) and others suggested that insight may be socially conditioned to a high degree. Brown (1931), Buttgereit (1932), Caldwell and Wellman (1926), Cox (1926), Dunkerley (1940), and Fauquier and Gilchrist (1942) found that leaders were characterized by alertness and keen awareness of their environment. The ability to evaluate situations was found to be a factor in the studies by Bowden (1926), Buttgereit (1932), Chevaleva-Ianovskaia and Sylla (1929), Merriam and Gosnell (1929), and Thurstone (1944). Less clearly defined was social insight, reported as a factor associated with leadership in the studies by Bowden (1926), Hanfmann (1935), Jennings (1943), Pigors (1933), and Zeleny (1939). Brogden and Thomas (1943) and Guilford and Guilford (1939) found that a person who "studies the motives of others" was measured by Guilford's T factor of being thoughtful, and was viewed as offering a kind of intellectual leadership.

The results of these various studies suggested that alertness to one's surroundings and an understanding of situations were intimately associated with leadership ability, yet little was understood about the nature of these processes. No worker who is responsible for improving the social effectiveness of individuals can fail to be impressed by the persistent blindness of maladapted individuals to the social situations to which they are attempting to adjust. From the point of view of understanding personal qualifications for leadership, one issue that still needs thorough investigation is the fundamental nature of awareness and social insight.

Originality

Although only seven studies contained data on originality, the magnitude of the positive correlations use suggested that the relationship between originality and leadership was worthy of further investigation. The correlations reported by Bellingrath (1930), Drake (1944), Flemming (1935), and Webb (1915) ranged from .38 to .70 and were higher, on average, than those for any other trait except popularity. At the same time, Cox (1926) found that great leaders rated unusually high in originality.

Adaptability

The 10 studies involving adaptability and leadership suggested that ready adaptability to changing situations might be associated with leadership, although the correlations of .13 and .21 reported by Eichler (1934) and Flemming (1935) respectively were not impressive The ability to adjust to situations has also been regarded traditionally as an aspect of general intelligence but, as described in the investigations considered here, this factor appeared to have a large social component. This fact has long been recognized by clinical observers, who have repeatedly pointed out that persons of high intelligence may be rendered ineffectual in their vocational, social, and other adjustments through extreme self-preoccupation and inhibition to action. Such inhibition is negatively correlated with leadership.

Introversion-Extroversion

Leaders were found to be more extroverted in five studies and more introverted in three. No differences emerged in four studies. However, the only studies that reported a marked relationship between extroversion and leadership were those of Goodenough (1930) and Sward (1933). Goodenough reported a correlation of .46 between extroversion and leadership in children. Sward found that leaders scored reliably higher than nonleaders in extroversion on the Heidbreder scale. Richardson and Hanawalt (1943) observed that college leaders scored reliably lower in introversion than the Bernreuter norms and lower than nonleaders, although the difference between leaders and nonleaders was not significant. Hunter and Jordan (1939) and Remmelin (1938) also reported that introversion scores on the Bernreuter scale did not differentiate leaders from nonleaders. Middleton (1941) found that leaders scored low in extroversion. Bellingrath (1930) and Drake (1944) obtained no significant correlations between introversion-extroversion scores and leadership.

All the groups of great leaders except soldier-statesmen in Cox's (1926) study were rated as introverted, with soldier-fighters rating very high in introversion. Thurstone's (1944) study of administrators in Washington, D.C., revealed that successful administrators rated higher than less successful administrators in Guilford and Guilford's (1939) T factor, which is measured by such items as "introspective, analyzes himself"; "often in a meditative state"; "analyzes the motives of others"; and "not more interested in athletics than in intellectual pursuits." Brogden and Thomas (1943) added to this list such items as "he does not want anyone to be with him when he receives bad news"; "he does not try to find someone to cheer him up when in low spirits"; and "he prefers to make hurried decisions alone." These items are of interest when considered in relation to the findings on mood control. In view of the diversity of findings, it appears doubtful that leaders can be described with any degree of uniformity in terms of introversion-extroversion.

Self-Sufficiency

Much the same situation exists with regard to self-sufficiency. Hunter and Jordan (1939) and Richardson and Hanawalt (1944) found that leaders had high self-sufficiency scores on the Bernreuter test, but Dunkerley (1940), Remmelin (1938), and Richardson and Hanawalt (1943) obtained no such significant results.

Dominance

The evidence concerning the relationship of dominance to leadership is somewhat contradictory. Leaders were found to be more dominant and ascendant in 11 studies; potiential leaders were rejected if they were bossy and domineering in four studies; and no differences appeared in two studies.

Cox (1926) and Drake (1944) found "desire to impose will" to be associated with leadership, but Webb (1915) reported a zero-order correlation between those two factors. Ackerson (1942) reported a correlation of approximately .20 between bossiness and leadership in problem children. Leadership and bossiness were related, to some extent, in the children studied by Tryon (1939), who reported correlations of .28 and .29 between these two factors for 15-year-old boys and girls, respectively. Chapple and Donald (1946), Richardson and Hanawalt (1943, 1944), and Hunter and Jordan (1939) found leaders to be significantly more dominant than nonleaders. Small but positive differences in ascendance were reported by Bowden (1926) and Moore (1935). Eichler (1934), however, found that leaders and nonleaders did not differ in dominance. Still stronger contradictory evidence was presented by Broich (1929), Jennings (1943), and Hanfmann (1935), who concluded that bossy, domineering persons were rejected as leaders. Caldwell (1920) reported that high school pupils expressed preference for leaders who could keep order without being bossy. In all, these findings suggest that leadership cannot be defined in terms of personal dominance.

Initiative, Persistence, Ambition, and Industry

Initiative and a willingness to assume responsibility were related to leadership in 12 studies and persistence in the face of obstacles was related to leadership in 12 other inquiries. Ambition and desire to excel were of consequence to leadership in seven analyses, as were application and industry in six additional analyses.

Initiative and Assertiveness. All except one of the studies in which initiative was found to be a trait ascribed to leaders were investigations in which student leaders were nominated by their associates, and the traits that were thought to make them desirable as leaders were described. The study by Carlson and Harrel (1942) represented some departure from this method in that 53 Washington correspondents were asked to name the 10 ablest senators and the 10 ablest representatives in rank order and to rate them from 1 to 10 on integrity, intelligence, industry, and influence. A factor analysis of these ratings revealed Factor 1 to be heavily loaded with industry and influence and might also have been called push or assertiveness. Industriousness and leadership were correlated .55 and .16 in the studies of Bellingrath (1930) and Flemming (1935), Dunkerley's (1940) factor analysis also revealed a trait cluster, identified as initiative, which was descriptive of intellectual and social leaders but not of religious leaders. Finally, Drake (1944) and Sheldon (1927) respectively reported correlations of .56 and .52 between aggressiveness and leadership.

Persistence. Cox (1926) found that great face-to-face leaders were characterized, to an outstanding degree, by "persistence in the face of obstacles," "capacity to work with distant objects in view," "degree of strength of will or perseverance," and "tendency not to abandon tasks from mere changeability." Pigors (1933) observed that the development of determination and a sufficient memory span to pursue remote goals rather than immediate objectives were necessary conditions for the appearance of leadership in children. The remainder of the studies that presented evidence on this point represented a variety of points of view.

Pinard (1932), in an experimental study of perseverance in 194 "difficult" children ages 8–15, found that of 24 leaders, 17 belonging to the "moderate nonperseverator" group were rated as more reliable, self-controlled, persistent, and as the most constructive leaders. Drake (1944) and Webb (1915) obtained correlations of .13 and .59 between leadership and strength of will. Webb (1915) reported a correlation of .70 between leadership and "persistence in overcoming obstacles" and of .53 between leadership and persistence. In Bellingrath's (1930) study of high school students, persistence was correlated .68 with leadership. Eichler (1934) and Sheldon (1927) found correlations of .23 and .34 between leadership and persistence. An interesting sidelight was presented in Ackerson's (1942) study of problem children: stubbornness correlated .15 for boys and .12 for girls with leadership.

Ambition. Cox (1926) also presented evidence to indicate that great face-to-face leaders, such as soldiers, religious leaders, and statesmen, were characterized to an outstanding degree by a "desire to excel" at performance. Hanawalt, Hamilton, and Morris (1934), in a study of 20 college leaders and 20 nonleaders, found that the level of aspiration of leaders was significantly higher than that of nonleaders. Correlations of .47 .29 and .64 between leadership and desire to excel were reported by Webb (1915), Drake (1944), and Bellingrath (1930), respectively.

Application and Industry. That leadership is related to willingness to work rather than to passive status or position is suggested by the fact that a number of investigators found leaders to rate high in application and industry. Cox (1926) observed that great leaders ranked unusually high in this respect. The correlations reported by Bellingrath (1930), Flemming (1935), and Webb (1915) ranged from .16 to .55.

Responsibility

All 17 studies found responsibility to be related to leadership. Thus student leaders were seen to rate somewhat higher than followers on dependability, trustworthiness, and reliability in carrying out responsibilities in the studies by Baldwin (1932), Bellingrath (1930), Burks (1938), Caldwell (1920), Dunkerley (1940), Moore (1932), Nutting (1923), Pinard (1932), and Wetzel (1932). Trustworthiness and leadership were correlated .64 in Webb's (1915) study, .37 in Drake's (1944) study, and .10 in Flemming's (1935) study. Correlations of .42, .21, and .53 between conscientiousness and leadership were reported by Webb (1915), Drake (1944), and Bellingrath (1930), respectively. Partridge (1934) observed a correlation of .87 between dependability and leadership. Jennings (1943) observed that girls chosen as leaders tended to be those who inspired confidence. Cox (1926) found that all types of great face-to-face leaders rated high in trustworthiness and conscientiousness, with religious leaders rating outstandingly high in these traits. Additionally, Broich (1929), Jennings (1943), Leib (1928), Nutting (1923), and Pigors (1933) observed that leaders tend to be able to work for the group's welfare, and Buttgereit (1932) noted that a sense of social responsibility is characteristic of leaders.

Integrity and Conviction

Integrity and fortitude were related to leadership in six studies, and strength of convictions was related to it in another seven analyses.

Integrity. Intellectual fortitude and integrity of character represent traits that are apparently associated with eminent leadership in maturity. All but one of the studies that contributed evidence on this point were concerned with outstanding adult leaders. Middleton (1941) obtained supporting evidence in college students.

Michels (1915) reported that strength of convictions was a characteristic of successful political leaders. Cox (1926) found that the great face-to-face leader was characterized to an outstanding degree by "absence of readiness to accept the sentiments of his associates." This trait was especially conspicuous in revolutionary statesmen. Webb (1915) obtained a correlation of $-.32$ between leadership and acceptance of the sentiments of others. Caldwell and Wellman (1926) noted that one characteristic of high school leaders was insistence on the acceptance of their ideas and plans.

Conviction. Adult leaders in a community studied by Chapin (1945) appeared to hold opinions that were generally similar to those of the group, but they "expressed the trends of opinion of the rank and file more sharply, more decisively, and more consistently." Simpson (1938), in a study of those who influence and those who are influenced in discussions, found that influence scores correlated −.41 with influenceability scores. It appears that persons in various types of groups may be valued as leaders because they know what they want to accomplish and are not likely to be swayed from their convictions.

Liberalism or Conservatism

The evidence on liberalism or conservatism suggested that the attitudes regarded as acceptable in leaders are largely determined by the nature of the situation. Hunter and Jordan (1939) found college student leaders to be somewhat more liberal than nonleaders in attitudes toward social questions. Newcomb (1943) reported that in a college where liberalism is a tradition and an ideal, women students who had the most prestige were regarded as most liberal. But Middleton (1941) ascertained that campus leaders were low in radicalism. In Thurstone's (1944) study of Washington administrators, the Allport-Vernon Study of Values was found to be the most effective of a battery of 75 tests in differentiating higher-salaried from lower-salaried administrators. Successful administrators scored significantly higher in social and theoretical values and significantly lower in economic and religious values. Drake (1944) and Webb (1915) obtained low positive correlations between leadership and interest in religion.

Self-Confidence

Almost all authors reporting data on the relationship of self-confidence to leadership, were uniform in the positive direction of their findings. Self-assurance was associated with leadership in 11 studies; absence of modesty, in six studies. The general trend of these findings suggested that leaders rate higher than their followers in self-confidence and self-esteem and slightly lower in modesty. The following correlations were reported between self-confidence and leadership: .58 by Bellingrath (1930), .59 by Drake (1944), and, .12 by Webb (1915). Cowley (1931) found self-confidence to be one of six factors possessed in common by three widely different types of leaders. Cox (1926) noted that great leaders were characterized to an unusual degree by such traits as self-confidence, esteem of their special talents, and a tendency to rate their talents correctly. Buttgereit (1932), Moore (1932), and Zeleny (1939) also reported that leaders rated high in self-confidence. Tryon (1939) described student leaders as assured in class and as assured with adults. Richardson and Hanawalt (1943, 1944) found that college and adult leaders earned higher self-confidence scores on the Bernreuter test than nonleaders; but Hunter and Jordan (1939) and Remmelin (1938) failed to find that the self-confidence scores on the Bernreuter test differentiated between leaders and nonleaders.

Inferiority. Sward (1933) found that inferiority scores on the Heidbreder rating scale did not differentiate leaders from nonleaders, although women leaders rated themselves higher in inferiority attitudes than did their associates. But Ackerson (1942) reported correlations of only −.02 and .08 between feelings of inferiority and leadership in boys and girls.

Modesty. The findings here suggested that leaders tend not to be handicapped by excessive modesty. Cox (1926) reported that great military leaders and statesmen were characterized to a greater than average degree by eagerness for the admiration of the crowd and desire for the limelight, although they exhibited offensive manifestations of self-esteem to a lesser degree than the average. Middleton (1941) also found leaders to rate low in modesty. A correlation of .09 between leadership and modesty was reported by Flemming (1935). Eagerness for admiration was correlated .16 with leadership in Webb's (1915) study. Drake (1944) obtained a correlation of −.11 between conceit and leadership. Ackerson (1942) and Tryon (1939) found correlations between leadership and attention-getting and "showing off" ranging from .15 to .30.

Moods, Optimism, and Sense of Humor

In all six studies on the subject, leadership and a sense of humor were positively related. In four of six studies, leaders were controlled in mood and seldom gloomy; in two studies, leaders were happy and cheerful, but happiness was not a factor in two of the studies. The scarcity of evidence concerning the relation of mood control to leadership cannot be regarded as confirmation of its unimportance. The evidence suggests that mood control may be significantly related to effective leadership, and a sense of humor is certainly relevant. The topic appears to warrant thorough investigation.

Mood. Jennings (1943) stated that one characteristic of girl leaders in an institution was the ability to control their own moods so as not to impose their negative feelings, depression, and anxiety on others. Caldwell and Wellman (1926) and Malloy (1936) also found leaders to be constant in mood. Webb (1915) reported a correlation of $-.45$ between depression and leadership. Ackerson (1942) and Cox (1926), however, reported some association between leadership and moods of depression, although not to a significant degree, and the extent differed with different groups.

Drake (1944), Tryon (1939), and Webb (1915) found that a cheerful, happy disposition was associated with leadership. These authors reported correlations ranging from .29 to .60 between leadership and cheerfulness. However, Ackerson (1942) did not find cheerfulness to be a distinguishing factor in leadership. Unhappiness and leadership were correlated $-.03$ for boys and .06 for girls. Baldwin (1932) also found a lack of correlation.

Humor. Drake (1944), Flemming (1935), Tryon (1939), and Webb (1915) reported correlations ranging from .34 to .64 between leadership and sense of humor. Stray (1934) also found leaders to be characterized by a sense of humor. Goodenough's (1930) finding of a correlation of .53 between leadership and laughter was also relevant.

Emotional Control

Leaders were found to be more stable and emotionally controlled in 11 studies and less well controlled emotionally in five studies. No differences were found in three other studies.

Self-Control. A number of manuals that outline practical techniques for gaining friends and becoming a leader regard self-control as a very important prerequisite for attaining these goals. The evidence relating to this contention is divided. Eichler (1934) reported a correlation of .18 between leadership and self-control. Baldwin (1932), Pigors (1933), and Wetzel (1932) also found self-control to be a factor related to leadership. Bellingrath (1930) and Drake (1944) reported correlations of .70 to .38, respectively, between leadership and stability. Leaders were found by Middleton (1941) and Terman (1904) to rate low in emotionality. Bowden (1926) and Caldwell and Wellman (1926) found leaders to be well balanced and self-composed in comparison with their followers. Webb (1915) reported correlations of $-.25$ between irritability and leadership, and $-.36$ between readiness for anger and leadership.

Excitability. Despite the results above, Cox (1926) found that great face to-face leaders rated high in excitability. This trait was present to an unusual degree in revolutionary statesmen. In problem children, Ackerson (1942) reported correlations of .12 for boys and .36 for girls between irritability and leadership. A correlation of .16 between leadership and excitability was found by Sheldon (1927). Fauquier and Gilchrist (1942) also noted that leaders were more excitable than nonleaders. According to Chevaleva-Ianovskaia and Sylla (1929), leaders were characterized by a predominance of excitation over inhibition. But Zeleny (1939) could find no difference between leaders and nonleaders in degree of emotional control, and Drake (1944) and Flemming (1935) reported correlations close to zero between leadership and excitability.

Anger. The data on the relationship between leadership, anger, and fighting cast further light on this subject. Cox (1926) found that great face-to-face leaders, except statesmen, were characterized by a tendency to anger and "a tendency to flare up on slight provocation." Ackerson (1942) reported that in children "temper tantrums" and "leader" were positively correlated, but "temper tantrums" and "follower" were negatively correlated. Webb

(1915), however, found a correlation of $-.12$ between leadership and occasional extreme anger. Tryon (1939) obtained correlations of .59, .48, .25, and .40 between fighting and leadership for 12-year-old boys, 15-year-old boys, 12-year-old girls, and 15-year-old girls, respectively. Ackerson (1942) ascertained that fighting and leadership were correlated .13 for boys and $-.17$ for girls. Fighting and leading others into bad conduct were correlated .20 for boys and .36 for girls. Incorrigibility and defiance were also positively correlated with leadership, and to a still higher degree with leadership in misconduct, while these traits were correlated negatively among followers.

These studies did not lend convincing support to the view that leaders are necessarily characterized by a high degree of self-control or an incapacity for emotional expression.

Socioeconomic Status

In 15 studies the leaders came from higher socioeconomic backgrounds, but in two studies no differences were found. Baldwin (1932) and Goodenough (1930) reported negligible differences. The differences in the social and economic status of leaders and nonleaders were usually not extreme. Only Remmelin (1938) obtained differences that were large enough to be statistically reliable. Nonetheless, taken as a whole, the evidence presented in studies from a wide variety of leadership situations indicated that leaders tend to come from a socioeconomic background superior to that of the average of their followers.

Social Activity and Mobility

Leaders participated in more group activities in all 20 studies on the subject. They also exhibited a higher rate of social mobility in five additional studies.

Participation. Baldwin (1932), Brown (1933), Chapin (1945), Courtenay (1938), Richardson and Hanawalt (1943), Roslow (1940), Link (1944), Merriam and Gosnell (1929), Reals (1938), Smith and Nystrom (1937), Sorokin (1927), and Zeleny (1939) all found that leaders surpassed followers in the number, extent, and variety of group activities in which they participated. Zeleny (1939) reported correlations ranging from .17 to .68 between leadership and participation in extracurricular activities.

Leadership was defined by a number of authors as "occupying one or more positions of responsibility in group activities." On the other hand, social detachment appeared to be a factor in the formation of the boys' gangs studied by Thrasher (1927) and Warner (1923).

Mobility. Physical and social mobility were observed by Sorokin (1927), Sorokin and Zimmerman (1928), and Winston (1932) to be associated with adult leadership. Sorokin and Zimmerman reported that farmer leaders were characterized to a high degree by a tendency to shift from place to place and from one occupational or economic position to another. Winston (1937) observed the same tendency in inventors.

Sociophysical Activity. Sociophysical activities were related to leadership as follows: "active in games" (six studies); "active, restless" (nine studies); "daring, adventurous" (three studies).[2] Broich (1929), Brown (1931), Buttgereit (1932), and Reininger (1929) found that child leaders were more active in games than were nonleaders. In Tryon's (1939) study, leadership and "active in games" were correlated .52 to .74 for groups of 12- and 15-year-old boys and girls. Terman (1904), Thrasher (1927), and Tryon (1939) found leaders to be more daring and adventurous than followers. Correlations of .57 to .78 between daringness and leadership were reported by Tryon (1939). Cowley (1931) ascertained that motor impulsion was a factor common to different types of leaders. Liveliness was reported by Leib (1928) and Brown (1931) as characterizing leaders. Flemming (1935) found a correlation of .47 between leadership and liveliness. Goodenough (1930) reported a correlation of .29 between physical activity and leadership. Ackerson (1942) and Tryon (1939) obtained correlations close to .20 between "restlessness" and leadership. These findings suggested that physical activity, mobility, and sociophysical activity were associated with leadership.

---

[2] This list of traits of social activities is difficult to classify, since the behavior is clearly defined in few cases. The majority of investigators appeared to emphasis the social aspects of these behaviors, although some emphasized an underlying physical component of energy or vitality. This is merely one example of the difficulty mentioned by a number of investigators, of attempting to analyze human behavior by dividing it into distinct and separate traits.

Sociability. Sociability was associated with leadership in 13 of 14 studies, and diplomacy or tact was associated with leadership in 8 others. Fairly high positive correlations between sociability and leadership were reported by Bonney (1943), Drake (1944), Flemming (1935), Goodenough (1930), Sheldon (1927), Tryon (1939), and Webb (1915). Correlations ranged from .33 to .98. But the correlation found by Eichler (1934) between social intelligence and leadership was only .10. Burks (1938), Malloy (1936), Middleton (1941), and Prosh (1928) also found that student leaders rated higher than nonleaders in sociability. Ackerson (1942) observed that belonging to a gang was correlated .26 with being a leader and .21 with being a follower. Being a leader and being within an intimate circle were correlated .39 in Webb's (1915) study. Moore (1932) and Newcomb (1945) reported friendliness and social skills, respectively, as factors that distinguished leaders from followers. Cox (1926) also noted that, despite their higher introversion, great leaders were rated above average, but not to an outstanding degree, in fondness for companionship and social gatherings.

Tact. Courtesy, tact, and diplomacy were found by Bernard (1928), Wetzel (1932), Drake (1944), Flemming (1935), Hanfmann (1935), Parten (1933), Stray (1934), and Webb (1915) to be traits that distinguished leaders from nonleaders. Drake, Flemming, and Webb reported correlations of .08, .27, and .73, respectively, between tact and leadership. However, Flemming (1935) obtained a correlation of only −.03 between rudeness and leadership for boys and girls. But the correlations between rudeness and leading others into bad conduct were .24 and .40 for boys and girls, respectively. Ackerson determined that both bashfulness and seclusiveness were negatively correlated with leadership.

Misconduct. Ackerson (1942), Goodenough (1930), and Webb (1915) obtained correlations ranging from −.29 to .21 between offensive manifestations and leadership. Ackerson's (1942) findings suggested that misconduct is not necessarily a bar to leadership. Stealing, for example, was correlated .12 and .21 with leadership; stealing and leading others into misconduct were correlated .46 and .16 for boys and girls, respectively.

Popularity and Prestige

Evidence from 10 diverse studies indicated that leaders tend to be rated higher than average in popularity. Evidence presented by Ackerson (1942), Bellingrath (1930), Carlson and Harrell (1942), Cox (1926), Garrison (1933), Michels (1915), Miller and Dollard (1941), Nutting (1923), Tryon (1939), and Zeleny (1939) all indicated that popularity and prestige were rather closely associated with leadership status. The correlations, ranging from .23 and .80, suggested that the relationship between popularity and leadership was fairly high. However, Nutting (1923) pointed out that popularity cannot be regarded as synonymous with leadership.

Cooperation

Cooperativeness was related to leadership in 11 studies. Work for the group and corporate responsibility were related to leadership in eight others. The ability to enlist cooperation was related to leadership in seven additional analyses.

Leaders were found by Baldwin (1932), Dunkerley (1940), Fauquier and Gilchrist (1942), Newcomb (1943), and Wetzel (1932) to rate higher than followers in cooperativeness. Drake (1944) and Webb (1915) reported correlations of .44 and .69 between cooperativeness and leadership. The ability to enlist cooperation and to control others in a group enterprise were found by Baldwin (1932), Caldwell (1920), Hanfmann (1935), Merriam and Gosnell (1926), and Nutting (1923) to be characteristics associated with leadership ability. Webb (1915) reported a correlation of .69 between leadership and corporate spirit. Cox (1926) also reported that great leaders rate outstandingly high in a sense of corporate spirit.

Patterns of Leadership Traits Differ with the Situation

There was a preponderance of evidence from a wide variety of studies (19 in all) that indicated that patterns of leadership traits differed with the situation. Ackerson's (1942) study revealed marked differences in the conduct and personality patterns of children who were regarded as leaders in general and children who were regarded as leaders in misconduct. Boys and girls in these two groups also differed somewhat. Bellingrath (1930) found marked differences in the extent to which leaders in athletics, student government, publications, and clubs participated in extracurricular activities and were chosen as leaders under various circumstances. The investigation by Caldwell and Wellman (1926) revealed athletic leaders to be tallest among the leaders and to excel in physical achievements, while editors were younger and shorter than average but ranked higher in scholarship than the other groups of leaders who were studied. Cowley's (1928) study demonstrated large differences in the traits of criminal leaders, army leaders, and student leaders. The profiles of the average ratings of the traits of groups of great leaders studied by Cox (1926) differed markedly from one group to another, especially in physical and emotional traits, but much less so in traits that may be classified as intelligence, self-regard, and persistence. Dunkerley's (1940) factor analysis of the intercorrelations of 15 variables representing trait ratings of 167 women college students revealed a factor identified as social leadership and two factors identified as religious leadership.

Hanfmann (1935) observed three types of leaders among preschool children: (1) objective leaders who engage in constructive play and get what they want by saying why they need it; (2) social leaders, whose goal is to play with others rather than play for the sake of play itself; and (3) gangsters, who get their way by force and a complete disregard for others. Schuler (1935) concluded that although teachers may ascertain with increasing reliability the dominant-submissive behavior of older adolescent boys in one situation, such as the school, it becomes less possible to predict those tendencies in another environment, such as the home.

Sward (1933) found that superior socioeconomic status, as well as higher intelligence and scholastic attainment, differentiated 125 campus leaders from 125 followers. However a classification of the leaders into subgroups demonstrated the following distinguishing differences: (1) bright, relatively unmotivated, unsociable, self-confident campus editors; (2) rather insecure, intellectual, and very intelligent debaters; (3) strongly socialized and intellectually mediocre campus politicians; and (4) extroverted women leaders.

Terman (1904) found that children who were leaders in one experimental situation may not have been leaders when matched against different children in other situations. Children who were "automatons," or nonleaders,

in most situations might achieve leadership in some situations. Children who were leaders in most situations were said by their teachers to be characterized by intelligence, congeniality, liveliness, and goodness.

In Tryon's (1939) study, the clusters of traits that characterized boys and girls at age 12 differed from those found at age 15. This difference was especially noticeable for girls, who matured somewhat more rapidly than boys in social interests. The leadership cluster for 12-year-old boys was composed of the items: daring, leader, active in games, and friendly. The cluster for 15-year-old boys contained the items: daring, leader, active in games and fights. The leadership cluster for 12-year-old girls contained the items: daring, leader, and humor about jokes. The cluster for 15-year-old girls contained the following items: popular, friendly, enthusiastic, happy, humor about jokes, daring, leader. The total weight of the evidence presented in this group of studies suggests that if there were general traits that characterized leaders, nonetheless the patterns of such traits were likely to vary with the leadership requirements of different situations.

Transferability and Persistence of Leadership

Six follow-up studies, although yielding somewhat variable results, intimated a certain degree of persistence or transferability of leadership. Levi (1930) studied 230 leaders in elementary and junior high school, 206 of whom were studied again in senior high school. The correlation between leadership in elementary school and leadership in senior high school was .19; the correlation between leadership in junior high school and leadership in senior high school was .52. For athletic leadership there was a low negative correlation between elementary school and high school, but a correlation of .44 between junior high school and senior high school.

Kohs and Irle (1920) completed a follow-up study of the military careers of 116 college students. Three faculty members rated these students on various traits. Correlations between the U.S. Army rank attained and various ratings in college ranged from .11 to .39. The best assessments for predicting military success were found to be the raters' estimates of the assessees' potential value to the service and raters estimates of the assessees' intelligence. Assessments of leadership in college were correlated .11 with army rank attained, but scholarship was not predictive of army rank. Page (1935), studying cadets at West Point, found first-year leadership rank to be correlated .67 with fourth-year leadership rank. Rank in bearing and appearance was most highly correlated with rank in leadership, while the ranks in athletic activities, tactics, and academic standing were correlated with leadership rank to progressively lesser degrees.

Clem and Dodge (1933) conducted a comparative study of the success of 27 student leaders, 36 high-ranking student scholars, and 38 students selected at random after graduation from high school. High school student leaders ranked highest in subsequent outstanding achievements, number of honors received, and quantity of publications. The random group ranked highest in community leadership and the amount of money accumulated after graduation. In general, the student leaders tended to become more successful than the student scholars and the random group, although the differences were not impressive. Courtenay (1938) studied 100 women leaders and 100 nonleaders from 13 successive high school graduating classes. The two groups were matched in socioeconomic background, ethnic heritage, scholarship, and age at graduation. Courtenay found that 72 student leaders, but only 29 nonleaders, went to college and that twice as many high school leaders as nonleaders were engaged in professional work as adults. The average salary of the adults who had been high school leaders exceeded that of those who had been nonleaders. The high school leaders were more active as adults in community work. Shannon (1929) compared student leaders, scholars (honor-roll members), and a random group from five high school graduating classes. Although the honor graduates were little more successful than the random group, Shannon concluded that "whatever is required to excel in the extracurricular life of the high school seems to be the same thing that contributes most to success later."

These findings strongly suggested that leadership in school activities was somewhat predictive of later success. However, the extent to which leadership persisted and transferred was not clearly determined.

Conclusions as of 1948

1. The following conclusions were supported by uniformly positive evidence from 15 or more of the studies surveyed: (a) The average person who occupies a position of leadership exceeds the average member of his or her group in the following respects: intelligence, scholarship, dependability in exercising responsibility, activity and social participation, and socioeconomic status. (b) The qualities, characteristics, and skills required in a leader are determined, to a large extent, by the demands of the situation, in which he or she is to function as a leader.

2. The following conclusions were supported by uniformly positive evidence from ten or more of the studies surveyed: (a) The average person who occupied a position of leadership exceeded the average member of his or her group, to some degree, in the following respects: sociability, initiative, persistence, knowing how to get things done, self-confidence, alertness to and insight into situations, cooperativeness, popularity, adaptability, and verbal facility.

3. A number of factors were found to be specific to well-defined groups. For example, athletic ability and physical prowess were found to be characteristics of leaders of boys' gangs and play groups. Intellectual fortitude and integrity were found to be associated with eminent leadership in maturity.

4. The traits with the highest overall correlation with leadership were originality, popularity, sociability, judgment, assertiveness, desire to excel, humor, cooperativeness, liveliness, and athletic ability, in approximate order of magnitude of the average correlation.

5. Despite considerable negative evidence, the general trend of the results suggested a low positive correlation between leadership and such variables as chronological age, height, weight, physique, energy, appearance, dominance, and mood control. The evidence was about evenly divided concerning the relation to leadership of such traits as introversion-extroversion, self-sufficiency, and emotional control.

6. The evidence suggested that leadership exhibited

in various school situations may persist into college and later vocational and community life. However, knowledge of the facts related to the transferability of leadership remains meager and obscure.

7. For understanding leadership, the most fruitful studies were those in which the behavior of leaders was described and analyzed on the basis of direct observation or the analysis of biographical and case history data. The factors associated with leadership could all be classified under the following general headings: *Capacity* (intelligence, alertness, verbal facility, originality, and judgment); *Achievement* (scholarship, knowledge, and athletic accomplishments); *Responsibility* (dependability, initiative, persistence, aggressiveness, self-confidence, and the desire to excel); *Participation* (activity, sociability, cooperation, adaptability, and humor); *Status* (socioeconomic position and popularity); and *Situation* (mental level, status, skills, needs and interests of followers, objectives to be achieved, and so on).

It is primarily by participating in group activities and demonstrating a capacity for expediting the work of the group that a person becomes endowed as a leader. A number of investigators were careful to distinguish between the leader and the figurehead and to point out that leadership is always associated with the attainment of group objectives. Leadership implies activity, movement, and getting work done. The leader is a person who occupies a position of responsibility in coordinating the activities of the members of the group in their task of attaining a common goal. This definition leads to a consideration of another significant factor. A person does not become a leader by virtue of some combination of traits; but the pattern of personal characteristics of the leader must bear some relevant relationship to the characteristics, activities, and goals of the followers. Thus leadership must be conceived in terms of the interaction of variables that are in constant flux. The factor of change is especially characteristic of the situation, which may be radically altered by the addition or loss of members, changes in interpersonal relationships and in goals, the competition of external influences, and the like. The personal characteristics of the leader and of the followers are, in comparison, highly stable. The persistence of individual patterns of human behavior in the face of continual situational

change appears to be a primary obstacle not only to the practice of leaders but to their selection and placement. It is not especially difficult to find persons who are leaders. It is quite another matter to place these persons in different situations where they will be able to function as leaders. It becomes clear that an adequate analysis of leadership involves a study not only of leaders but also of situations.

The evidence suggests that leadership is a relationship between persons in a social situation and that persons who are leaders in one situation may not necessarily be leaders in other situations. Must it then be assumed that leadership is entirely incidental, haphazard, and unpredictable? Not at all. The very studies that provided the strongest arguments for the situational nature of leadership also supplied the strongest evidence to indicate that leadership patterns as well as nonleadership patterns of behavior were persistent and relatively stable. Jennings (1943, p. 210) observed that "the individual's choice behavior, in contrast to his social expansiveness, appears as an expression of needs which are, so to speak, so 'central' to his personality that he must fulfill them whether or not the possibility of fulfilling them is at hand or not." A somewhat similar observation was made by Newstetter, Feldstein, and Newcomb (1938, p. 92): "Being accepted or rejected is not determined by the cordiality or antagonism of the individual's treatment of his fellows, nor evidently, is the individual's treatment of his fellows much affected by the degree to which he is already being accepted or rejected by them. Their treatment of him is related to their acceptance or rejection of him. Their treatment of him is, of course, a reaction to some or all of his behaviors, but we have been completely unsuccessful in attempting to measure what these behaviors are."

The authors concluded that these findings provided "devastating evidence" against the concept of the operation of measurable traits in determining social interactions. Although these findings do not appear to provide direct evidence either for or against a theory of traits, they do indicate that the complex of factors that determines an individual's status in a group is most difficult to isolate and evaluate.

The findings of Jennings and Newsletter, Feldstein, and Newcomb suggested that *selecting* leaders should be much less difficult than *training* nonleaders to become leaders. The clinician or group worker who has observed the fruitless efforts of socially isolated individuals to gain acceptance or leadership status in a group is aware of the real nature of the phenomena just described. Some individuals are isolated in almost any group in which they find themselves, while others are readily accepted in most of their social contacts. A most pertinent observation on this point was made by Ackerson (1942, p. 45), who noted that "the correlations for 'leader' and 'follower' are not of opposite sign and similar magnitude as would be expected of traits supposed to be antithetical. These may not be the opposite poles of a single underlying trait." Ackerson went on: "It may be that the true antithesis of 'leader' is not 'follower,' but 'indifference,' i.e., the incapacity or unwillingness either to lead or to follow. Thus it may be that some individuals who under one situation are leaders may under other conditions take the role of follower, while the true 'opposite' is represented by the child who neither leads nor follows."

The findings suggest that leadership is not a matter of passive status or of the mere possession of some combination of traits. Rather, leadership appears to be a working relationship among members of a group, in which the leader acquires status through active participation and demonstration of his or her capacity to carry cooperative tasks to completion. Significant aspects of this capacity for organizing and expediting cooperative efforts appear to be intelligence, alertness to the needs and motives of others, and insight into situations, further reinforced by such habits as responsibility, initiative, persistence, and self-confidence.

But the studies surveyed offered little information as to the basic nature of these personal qualifications. Cattell's (1946) analysis suggested that these qualifications could be based, to some degree, on basic intelligence, but Cattell and others also implied that these personal qualifications were, to a high degree, socially conditioned. The problems requiring thorough investigation relate to factors that condition social participation, insight into situations, mood control, responsibility, and the transferability of leadership from one situation to another. Solutions to these problems seem basic not only to any adequate understanding of the personal qualifications of leaders, but to any effective training for leadership.

Traits of Leadership (1948–1970)

Improvements in Methods and Measurements

Many new methods and measurements were introduced into the study of leadership in the decades after 1948. Experiments involving one variable at a time gave way to factorial and multivariate designs in which the effects of various treatments could be analyzed in the same experiment. Theory began to guide much of the data collection. Questionnaire methodologists introduced a variety of techniques to reduce errors such as the halo effect, leniency, and social desirability, and to increase the relevance and reliability of results, although their efforts often met with limited success. The critical-incidents technique, forced-choice checklists, behaviorally-anchored rating scales, and semantic differentials were just a few of the specific new methods used. Factor analysis became the basic tool in the search for and verification of the existence of traits of consequence. Other multivariate regression procedures also became commonplace in efforts to establish the relative importance of different traits to successful leadership. Varieties of statistical tests increased, to support or reject findings.

The internationalization of efforts also became widespread. Whether the same traits of leadership were relevant to rural agricultural leaders in Chile and Mali or led to promotion to higher management in Norway, Italy, and Japan were among the subjects examined. In the United States, a topic of considerable interest was whether different leadership traits would emerge as important for women and for racial and ethnic-minority leaders. The human-potential movement sparked awareness of the need to deal with leadership at a level of socioemotional feeling that was deeper than surface intellectual perception. More studies focused such traits as self-exposure, empathy, energy level, intuition, and interpersonal competence. The whole field of small-group research expanded, with many investigations in the 1950s. At the same time, much more rigor was introduced into measurements of individual role taking and behavior in small-group interactions. In addition, experimenters became much more aware of the many threats to the validity of their findings.

As the era ended, situational leadership was the dominant theory used for management and leadership training, but some disquieting research that supported the primacy of individual differences in leaders appeared shortly afterward. There was a resurgence of interest in consistent individual differences across situations, braced with meta-analytic demonstrations of the validity and generalizability of a very limited battery of cognitive abilities tests for predicting successful performance in a wide variety of situations (Schmidt & Hunter, 1977). Reexamination of earlier data and meta-analytic theory itself suggested that situational variations frequently could and should be attributed not to substantive effects but to sampling error. Situational effects would have to be shown above and beyond what would be generated by the normal probability distribution of the means generated in the diverse situations. Strong inferences were drawn about personality and early developmental influences that had permanent effects on individuals and their behavior as leaders and followers.

Stogdill (1970) examined another 163 studies of the traits of leadership published between 1948 and 1970 and considered how findings could be meaningfully factor-analyzed and clustered. (These findings were first reported in full in Chapter 5 of the first edition of the *Handbook of Leadership* in 1974.) Stogdill summarized the physical characteristics, social background, intelligence and ability, personality, task-related characteristics, and social characteristics related to leadership. Between 1948 and 1970, the proportion of studies of adults in formal organizations increased and the proportion dealing with children and adolescents in informal groups decreased. In interpreting conclusions caution is urged on the basis of the published survey findings.[3]

[3] David Bakin pointed to the existence of a farcical but not necessarily fanciful prospect about positive and negative findings in social science. Suppose, he argued, that the difference between A and B is really zero. Thus in 95% of all studies of A and B, we would expect to reach a negative conclusion—a finding of no statistically significant difference between A and B at the 5% level of confidence. But 5% of all studies will reach a positive but erroneous conclusion—that there is a difference between A and B at the 5% level of confidence. Who publishes? Only those with positive findings! So if we depend on a count of publications of positive and negative findings, we will draw the wrong inference about the true difference between A and B.

Unfortunately, there is some truth in Bakin's burlesque: researchers and journal editors are reluctant to publish negative findings; hence, there is little question that positive findings are more likely to be published than negative ones. Let the reader beware. See for example, Borg and Tupes (1958), M. Coates and Pellegrin (1957), Ghiselli and Barthol (1956) and J. S. Guilford (1952).

Physical Characteristics

Measures of physical characteristics, such as activity, age, and appearance were of positive consequence to leadership. Appearance can affect first impressions, which in turn have significance for emergent leadership. Fewer than three studies were found for height and weight; nevertheless, height or weight above the average of the peer group is certainly not a disadvantage in achieving leadership status. (Many organizations like to be represented by impressive physical specimens. When faced with taller opponents in television debates, shorter presidential candidates such as Jimmy Carter and Michael Dukakis stood on raised platforms. Frederick the Great required that all his soldiers be tall; however, Napoleon is often cited as an example that a man of small stature can rise to a position of great power. Thus physical stature may complement a leader, or a leader may compensate for lack of physical stature. Yet there is a rational element involved when coercive leadership is needed. Robert Peel, who introduced the "bobbies" to London, made a highly effective police force without firearms by choosing only large men who could dominate scenes of social conflict. Conversely, it has been noted that smaller policemen are more likely to suffer attack and injury.)

Activity, Energy, Stamina. The 1970 survey found 25 studies[4] of these factors—many more than were found in the 1948 survey—which suggested that a leader tends to be endowed with an abundant reserve of energy, stamina, and ability to maintain a high rate of physical activity. Even when handicapped by physical disability or poor health, highly successful leaders tended to exhibit high energy.

Age. Age appeared in six studies reported between 1948 and 1970.[5] Age continued to be related to leadership in a complicated way, as noted before. A survey by Lehman (1953) on the relation of age to achievement in science, art, politics, and other fields found that great men tended to exhibit signs of outstanding accomplishment at a relatively early age. Many, but not all, had the

[4] The reader who is interested in the complete list of citations of these studies should consult Chapter 5 in the earlier editions of this handbook.
[5] See, for example, A. R. Bass (1964), Johnson Peterson, Kahler (1968), and Newcomer (1955).

advantage of specialized education or training because of the early recognition of their talent. However, it usually takes time to rise to the top in a corporate or governmental structure. Standard and Poor's (1967) reported that 74 percent of 66,336 American executives in its 1967 *Register of Corporations, Directors, and Executives* were over age 50. Only 168 executives were under age 30, while 8,085 were in the 71-to-80 age group. The two sets of findings indicate that the creative individual is likely to exhibit evidences of his or her ability at an early age; however, large organizations up to 1970 did not make much use of such creative gifts in administrative capacities. Rather, organizations tended to rely on administrative knowledge and demonstrations of success that come with experience and age.

Social Background

Social Status. Studies of the socioeconomic background of leaders continued to proliferate between 1948 and 1970; 19 studies were found for this period.[6] D. R. Mathews (1954) observed that from 1789 to 1934, 58 percent of the presidents, vice presidents, and cabinet members had fathers in the professional, proprietor, or official occupations; 38 percent had fathers who were farmers, but only 4 percent had fathers who were wage earners. It is apparent that high social status has provided an advantage in rising to high levels of political leadership. But Newcomer (1955) and *Scientific American* (1965) reported that, compared with 1900, more top executives in 1965 were beginning to come from the poorer and middle-income groups, rather than the wealthy strata of society. A. Porter (1965) found that the background of the father of an executive was significantly related to the executive's level in the organization and his authority for making policy. However, the father's background was not related to the size of the organization or to the executive's status in the business world or satisfaction with the progress of his career.

Miller and Dirksen (1965) reported that highly visible community leaders were differentiated from their less visible peers by being business oriented, Republican, members of the chamber of commerce, and named in the mass media. However, the hidden community leaders were characterized as holding administrative or professional jobs; they were not owners of large businesses, nor natives of the city, nor did they come from families in the city that were prominent. R. M. Powell's (1969) large-scale survey of the executive promotion process indicated that religious and ethnic background—usually linked with social status—were also important factors.

Studies of the social background of student leaders by Martin, Gross, and Darley (1952); Weinberg (1965); Krumboltz, Christal, and Ward (1959); and Kumar (1966) revealed few consistent relationships across samples, although Williamson (1948) found that fraternity members occupied a disproportionately large share of leadership positions on the college campus.

Mobility. Six studies dealt with the upward mobility of leaders.[7] Jennings's (1967a) study is illustrative of the work in this area; it presented an insightful analysis of the problems, stresses, and adaptations involved in rapid upward mobility in a large corporation. More specifically, Cussler (1958) found that once women executives reached middle management in an industrial organization, they found it difficult to rise higher. They hit the "glass ceiling."

Education. Fourteen studies showed the importance of education to leadership.[8] Reflecting a national rise in educational levels, senior managers with college degrees increased from 28.3 percent in 1900 to 74.3 percent in 1964 (*Scientific American*, 1965). In contrast, G. F. Lewis's (1960) review of several studies indicated that small businessmen have less education than top executives in large firms and more often start their careers as unskilled or semiskilled workers. Johnson, Peterson, and Kahler (1968) studied 496 first-line foremen in a company from 1940 to 1961. They found that the average age of these foremen increased from 31.2 years in 1940–1944 to 41.2 years in 1955–1959 and that their years of schooling increased from 10.8 to 11.2 during the same period.

The following conclusions were drawn from these studies of social background and education: (1) High so-

[6] See, for example, Ghiselli (1959), Hulin (1962), Lewis (1960), and Matthews (1954).
[7] See, for example, Hicks and Stone (1962, Powell (1969), and Roe (1956).
[8] See, for example, Feil (1950), Kumar (1966), Mandell (1949), and O'Donovan (1962).

cioeconomic status was an advantage in attaining leadership; (2) Leaders who rose to high positions in industry tended to come from a lower socioeconomic status than their counterparts of a half century earlier; (3) The leaders tended to be better educated than formerly. The rise in the general level of education of the population is common knowledge. Requirements for managerial and administrative positions increasingly demanded a graduate degree, such as an MBA. The trend toward reduced emphasis on social status and more emphasis on education was expected to accelerate as the effects of affirmative action manifest themselves. As firms and agencies aggressively promoted women, blacks, and other minorities, a considerable increase in the upward mobility of these groups was expected. For example, in 1960 hardly any women and blacks were observed in MBA on engineering programs.

Intelligence and Ability

Intelligence. In 1970, 25 reports of a positive relationship between leadership, intelligence, and ability were found to have been published between 1948 and 1970,[9] compared with 17 studies in the 1948 review correlating scores on intelligence tests with leadership status. The average correlation of .28 in the 1948 review was corroborated in the 1970 survey. However, five of the competent studies of 1948 ascertained that a large discrepancy between the intelligence of potential leaders and that of their followers militated against the exercise of leadership. Ghiselli (1963b, p. 898) reported supporting evidence. In a study of three groups of managers, he found that "the relationship between intelligence and managerial success is curvilinear with those individuals earning both low and very high scores being less likely to achieve success in management positions than those with scores at intermediate levels."

Thus leaders can be too able for those they lead. Persons with greater abilities may suffer from extreme self-preoccupation; their abilities may make it difficult for them to communicate with those they are attempting to lead; and their ideas may be too advanced to be accepted by their potential followers (pioneers are seldom outstanding leaders). The discrepancy in abilities is likely to

be paralleled by discrepancies in interests and goals. Also, Korman's (1968) extensive review on the prediction of managerial performance reported that "intelligence, as measured by verbal ability tests, is a fair predictor of first-line supervisory performance, but not of higher level managerial performance."[10] But one must also suppose that only those who already possess above-average intelligence are likely to have achieved top management positions in the organization. So there is a restriction in range, which makes it impossible for intelligence tests to discriminate the good from the bad performers at the top of the organization. Nevertheless, it should be clear that a high-level intelligence test that discriminates verbal intelligence among those at the upper end of the population's intelligence, such as the Miller Analogies (used for predicting success in graduate and professional schools), is also likely to be a valid predictor of the potential to rise in firms, agencies, and institutions.

Other Intellectual Abilities. Uniformly positive findings for studies completed between 1948 and 1970 were found, which indicated that leaders are characterized by superior judgment, decisiveness, or both (e.g., Roadman, 1964), knowledge (e.g., Colyer, 1951), and fluency of speech (e.g., Burnett, 1951b).

Personality

Up to 31 studies in the 1970 survey dealt with personality and leadership. Several differences were noted between the 1948 and 1970 surveys, which might have been due to changes in personality methods and theories, as well as the change in participants in the studies. Uniformly positive findings found in the 1970 survey were the traits of adjustment (e.g., Terrell & Shreffler, 1958), aggressiveness or assertiveness (e.g., Hobert & Dunnette, 1967), independence (e.g., Hornaday & Bunker, 1970), objectivity (e.g., Argyris, 1953), enthusiasm (e.g., Gibb, 1949), and tolerance of stress (e.g., Lange & Jacobs, 1960). Characteristics that appeared with positive findings in both 1948 and 1970 were alertness (e.g., Porter, 1959), originality (e.g., Randle, 1956), personal integrity (e.g., Stephen-

[9] See, for example, Ghiselli (1964), Rowland and Scott (1968), Rychalak (1963), and Thornton (1968).

[10] Later chapters show that higher levels of management call for a different kind of intelligence—fluid intelligence—which may be contrasted to the crystallized intelligence of import to lower levels of management.

son, 1959), self-confidence (e.g., Moment & Zaleznik, 1963), ascendance (e.g., Sanders, 1968), emotional balance (e.g., Harville, 1969), and extroversion (e.g., Harrell, 1966).

Task-Related Personality Characteristics. Both the 1948 review and the 1970 review produced uniformly positive results indicating that leaders are characterized by a need for achievement (e.g., Cummings & Scott, 1965) and a sense of responsibility (e.g., Gordon, 1952). Leaders tend to be task-oriented (e.g., Medow & Zander, 1965) and dependable in the pursuit of objectives (e.g., Powell & Nelson, 1969). They display enterprise and initiative (e.g., Helfrich & Schwirian, 1968) and are persistent in overcoming obstacles.

Social Personality Characteristics. The positive findings on social characteristics in both 1948 and 1970 suggested that leaders were active participants in various activities. They interacted easily with a wide range of personalities (e.g., Krumboltz, Christal, & Ward, 1959), and this interaction was valued by others. They not only were cooperative with others (e.g., J. S. Guilford, 1952) but were able to enlist cooperation (e.g., Bentz, 1964) and to execute (administer) projects (e.g., Kay, 1959). Interpersonal skills (e.g., D. S. Brown, 1964), including tact (e.g., Tarnapol, 1958), made them attractive to followers (e.g., Price, 1948). Leaders were valued by group members because they had characteristics such as nurturance (e.g., Roff, 1950) and popularity (e.g., Harrell & Lee, 1964) that fostered loyalty and cohesiveness in the group.

Factor Analyses of the Traits of Leadership

Stogdill's (1974) review of factorial studies of leadership published between 1945 and 1970 was based on 52 factorial studies, including surveys of a large number of military and industrial personnel, studies of leadership in military and industrial groups, and reports on experimental groups. It should be emphasized that the factors which emerged depended on the variables originally included in the battery of traits measured or ignored by the investigators. For instance, if an investigator included many measures of social distance, a common factor of social distance could emerge. If no measures of social distance

were included, no common factor of social distance could be extracted. Likewise, if only a single reliable measure of social distance was included, it would not appear in a separate common factor of social distance, as such. The most frequently occurring factors were descriptive of various skills of the leader.

They included social and interpersonal skills, technical skills, administrative skills, intellectual skills, leaders' effectiveness and achievement, social nearness, friendliness, supportiveness of the group task, and task motivation and application. These factors indicated that leaders differed from each other consistently in the effective use they made of interpersonal, administrative, technical, and intellectual skills. Some leaders could be described as highly task-motivated; others were most capable of maintaining close, friendly, personal relationships. The best leaders were able to do both. The next most frequent set of factors was concerned with how leaders relate to their groups. The behaviors included maintaining the cohesiveness of the group, coordination, task motivation, task performance, and high quality of output. A concern for the group's performance was softened by nurturant behavior and the use of informal controls. These factors were as follows: maintaining a cohesive work group, maintaining coordination and teamwork, maintaining standards of performance, maintaining informal control of the group (group freedom), and nurturant behavior. Next in frequency were factors concerned strictly with the personal characteristics of leaders. Leaders could be described in terms of emotional balance, willingness to assume responsibility, ethical conduct, ability to communicate readily, dominance, energy, experience, courage, and maturity.

In sum, successful leadership involves certain skills and capabilities—interpersonal, technical, administrative, and intellectual—that enable leaders to be of value to their group or organization. These skills allow leaders to maintain satisfactory levels of group cohesiveness, drive, and productivity. Leaders are further assisted in the execution of these functions if they possess a high degree of motivation to complete tasks, personal integrity, communicative ability, and the like. The 52 factorial studies as a whole seem to provide a well-balanced picture of the skills, functions, and personal characteristics of leaders in a wide variety of situations. The factors and the number of studies in which they emerged were as follows:

ascendance, dominance, decisiveness (11); willingness to assume responsibility (10); ethical conduct, personal integrity (10); maintaining a cohesive work group (9); maintaining coordination and teamwork (7); ability to communicate, articulativeness (6); physical energy (6); maintaining standards of performance (5); creative, independent (5); conforming (5); courageous, daring (4); experience and activity (4); nurturant behavior (4); maintaining informal control of the group (4); mature, cultivated (3); and aloof, distant (3).

Conclusions by 1970

The differences between 1948 and 1970 may be due primarily to the larger percentage of studies in the 1970 survey from the world of work rather than from children's, school, and social groups.[11] The similar results made it reasonable to conclude that many cognitive, social, and emotional traits differentiated leaders from followers, successful from unsuccessful leaders, and high-level from low-level leaders. One practical application of this conclusion was the assessment center for determining leadership potential among candidates for managerial positions (Bray, Campbell, & Grant, 1974; Bray & Grant, 1966). By the 1970s, over 1,000 such assessment centers were in operation. In these centers candidates are observed for two to three days in interviews, leaderless group activities, and other situational tests. They are also tested individually with personality and aptitude tests. The "in-basket," a sampling of managerial action requirements, is also often used. Observers meet to try to pool their results on the basis of inferences from the test results and their observations to yield a picture of the total personality of the candidate and his or her leadership potential in positions familiar to the observers. Much more will be presented about such assessment centers in Chapter 35.

The leader is characterized by a strong drive for responsibility and completion of tasks, vigor and persistence in the pursuit of goals, venturesomeness and originality in problem solving, a drive to exercise initia-

[11] Stogdill suspected that the absence of some particular positive findings in the 1970 survey were due, in part, to the decisions of his abstracters. We also must be cautious about the volume of results obtained for some traits and not for others. Researchers tend to pursue fads. Also, changes occur over the decades in the names that are used to label the same traits of behavior.

tive in social situations, self-confidence and a sense of personal identity, willingness to accept the consequences of his or her decisions and actions, readiness to absorb interpersonal stress, willingness to tolerate frustration and delay, ability to influence other people's behavior, and the capacity to structure social interaction systems to the purpose at hand. The clusters of characteristics discussed in this chapter differentiate leaders from followers, effective from ineffective leaders, and higher-echelon from lower-echelon leaders. In other words, different strata of leaders, and followers can be described in terms of the extent to which they exhibit some of the characteristics. Furthermore, research by Bass (1953), Moore and Smith (1953), and Tarnapol (1958) suggested that isolates and, to a lesser extent, followers and nonleaders can be described by the antonyms of trait names attributed to leaders. The characteristics generate personality dynamics that are advantageous to the person seeking the responsibilities of leadership.

The conclusion that traits are a factor in understanding leadership did not represent a return to the pure trait approach. It did represent a sensible modification of the extreme situationalist point of view. At first, the trait approach treated personality variables in an atomistic fashion, suggesting that each trait acts singly to determine the effects of leadership. Increasingly, models were tested describing how combinations of differentially weighted traits contributed to leadership. The wholly situationalist approach, on the other hand, denied the influences of individual differences, attributing all variance among persons to the demands of the environment. Again, it should be emphasized that some of the variance in who emerges as a leader and who is successful and effective is due to traits of consequence in the situation; some is due to situational effects; and some is due to the interaction of traits and situation. For example, suppose that candidates for management positions are tested in three situations: social service agencies, industrial firms, and military organizations. We are likely to find in the aggregate that individual interpersonal competence is predictive of successful performance. But it also may be more predictive in social service agencies and less predictive in military organizations. Considering the importance of competence to perform tasks and interpersonal competence at two stages in the careers of public accountants, engineers, and other technical specialists, one finds that both kinds of competence are important to performance. During a person's early years with a firm, technical competence is most strongly indicative of successful performance; but after two to five years, interpersonal competence becomes more important.

The element of chance would appear to play a part in the rise of individual leaders. A given leader may be able to rise to the top of the hierarchy in competition with one group of peers but may be unable to do so in another group of peers. An individual's upward mobility would seem to depend, to a considerable degree, on being in the right place at the right time. Finally, it should be noted that to some extent our conceptions of characteristics of leadership are culturally determined, as will be elucidated in Chapter 33. Situational contingencies will be examined more fully in chapters 25 through 29. These contingencies may be masked by consistent differences among individuals. This statement implies that there are regularities in individuals' abilities, interests, orientations, values, and personality that endure across time. Other differences of consequence may include age, sex, family background, physique, and so on. Since the begin-

ning of the study of leadership, the question has remained: how much do these individual differences account for the emergence of leadership and its effectiveness, and do the effects transcend situational circumstances? Some individuals will attempt to lead in most situations in which they find themselves, but others will avoid doing so whenever possible. Other individuals will attempt to be leaders only in certain situations, and their personal predispositions can be described. The same may be said about succeeding as a leader.

By 1970, there was plenty of evidence that particular patterns of traits were of consequence to leadership; these included determination, persistence, self-confidence, and ego strength. Additionally, the mass of research findings about the traits of leaders compared with nonleaders and of successful and effective leaders compared with unsuccessful and ineffective leaders included activity level, rate of talk, initiative, assertiveness, aggressiveness, dominance, ascendance, emotional balance, tolerance for stress, self-control, self-efficacy, enthusiasm, and extroversion. This was confirmed with qualification in studies in the years that followed.

Traits of Leadership (1970–2006)

$\mathbf{A}$ trait is a construct based on consistent individual differences between people. Personality is the organized pattern of distinctive traits of a specific person. Additional meanings may be added, such as the way personality traits are integrated. Simple to complex patterns may be formed. They may form hierarchies. For instance, the trait of agreeableness may consist of correlated subtraits: trustingness, altruism, compliance, and tendermindedness.

Traits and their expression may be captured as snapshots, but they are more enduring unlike momentary moods or states of being such as feeling angry or feeling happy. Roberts and DelVecchio (2000) demonstrated that traits were enduring and were not states like a person's mood, which can change in a short time. These investigators completed a meta-analysis of 152 longitudinal studies of 3,217 test-retest correlations of traits occurring during two age periods. The mean correlation between age periods was only .31 in childhood but rose to .54 in later life. Traits are not the same as motives. Thus the trait of extroversion brings about unconflicted social motive expression; the trait of introversion blocks social motive expression and the attainment of social goals (Winter, John, Stewart, et al., 1998).

When traits are requirements for doing something, they are called "competencies." Traits of leadership are competencies. They are needed if someone is to emerge, succeed, or be effective as a leader. Various kinds of traits are factors in leadership. *Cognitive* traits provide task competence and problem-solving abilities. These include intelligence, judgment, decisiveness, knowledge, fluency of speech, resourcefulness, technical abilities, intellectually stimulating qualities, vision, imagination, articulateness, diagnostic skills, originality, and creativity. *Social competency* traits include social intelligence, assertiveness, cooperativeness and the ability to enlist cooperation, attractiveness, affiliativeness, nurturance, sociability, interpersonal skills, social participation, tact,

diplomacy, empathy, social insight, and attributional accuracy. *Emotional competency* traits include emotional intelligence, emotional maturity, self-confidence, self-esteem, self-efficacy, hardiness, and optimism. Those traits with negative impact on leadership include arrogance, narcissism, depression, anxiety, rigidity, neuroticism, lack of self-confidence, lack of self-esteem, and lack of self-efficacy. *Biophysical* traits of consequence to leadership include physical fitness and stature. Traits of *character* include integrity, honesty, moral reasoning, resilience, and discipline. Eye color, walking stride, and uxoriousness are examples of traits which are not ordinarily competencies of consequence to leadership.

Situationalism

The quest for universal leadership traits for all situations was abandoned by most, but not all, researchers in the 1950s and 1960s. Reviews by Bird (1940), Jenkins (1947), and Stogdill (1948) were cited frequently (and incorrectly) after 1948 to support the view that leadership was entirely situational in origin and that particular personal characteristics could not accurately predict leadership. This view overemphasized the situational and underemphasized the significance of the individual leader's traits. For instance, Carter (1953), Gibb (1954), and Shartle (1956) inferred that stable relationships between traits and leadership pertained to specific situations only. The view that many are "born leaders" was rejected. Nevertheless, many scholars before and after 1970 still held that certain personal characteristics improved a leader's chances of success (Van Fleet & Yukl, 1986). The connection between traits and leadership remained true for a wide variety of situations. Nonetheless, evidence was amassed to indicate that different skills and traits were required for leadership in different situations. Many of the behaviors and traits that enable a mobster to gain and maintain control over a criminal gang are not the same as those that enable a television evangelist to gain and maintain a following. Yet these two leaders may share some important traits, such as persistence, cupidity, and self-monitoring.

The Contrary Evidence

It was noted in Chapter 4 that, as Stogdill (1948, 1974) concluded, certain general qualities—such as initiative and fortitude—have appeared repeatedly as characteristics of leaders. Stogdill found that particular traits contributed to a person's emergence as a leader in a wide variety of situations. This conclusion was supported in Mann's (1959) survey of research on the relation of personality to performance in small groups. Mann found positive relationships between personal traits (intelligence, adjustment, extroversion, dominance, masculinity, and sensitivity) and leadership in 71% to 80% of the studies he included in his review. As mentioned above, Roberts and Del Veccio (2000) did a meta-analysis of 152 studies showing the stability of an individual's traits, particularly among adults. They analyzed 3,217 test-retest correlations of personality tests with a controlled interval of 6.7 years between test and retest. Although the mean correlation was only .31 in childhood and .54 during college, it was .64 at age 30 and plateaued at .74 at ages from ages 50 to 70. Individual traits may be consistently important in a wide range of leadership situations.

Rotation Experiments

Barnlund (1962) rotated 25 participants in groups of six in different combinations but misinterpreted the results. He attributed most of the variance to differences in the composition and task situation of the group. Twenty-one years later, in reexamining Barnlund's data and conclusion, Kenny and Zaccaro (1983) noted that the average correlation in the leadership rank that individuals attained as members of the six composed and recomposed groups was .64. This correlation was substantial evidence of personal consistency in the emergence of leadership across the six situations. Kenny and Zaccaro concluded that Barnlund's results supported the contention that between 49% and 82% of the variance in leadership could be accounted for by a stable personality trait. They inferred that this trait was "the ability to perceive the needs

and goals of a constituency and to adjust one's personal approach to group action accordingly" (p. 678). Zaccaro, Foti, and Kenny (1991) rotated their participants through four different group tasks in groups of three so that no two participants worked with the same participant more than once. The emergent leadership of each participant was rated the others after every task. Every task required using a different style of leadership: persuasion, initiating structure, consideration, and emphasis on production. The investigators isolated the variance due to the raters, the ratees, and their interaction. They found that 59% of the variance was due to the participants' traits rather than to the different group task situations.

Heritability, Genes, and Biological Bases of Leadership Behavior

Leaders may be born as well as made, as we can see if we examine research of the past 30 years on genes, heritability, and leadership.

Leadership theory and research from 1975 to 2005 have turned us back again to considering the importance of traits. Research in cotwin studies and advances in microbiology and behavioral genetics have been helpful. Genetic factors have been shown to influence personality traits and their expression in different situations. At the same time, environmental experiences unique to individuals contribute to their development (Fulker & Cardon, 1993). Viken, Rose, et al. (1994) tested approximately 15,000 Finnish twins in extroversion and neuroticism, first at ages 18 to 53, and then six years later. Experience became more important with age, and no additional genetic effects appeared after age 30.

Methods of Genetic Leadership Analysis

Cotwin Studies. In cotwin studies, a strong genetic component has been found in many traits associated with leadership, such as intelligence and assertiveness (Rose, 1995). In a cotwin study, variance in agreement on a specific trait between monozygotic or identical twins (from one egg) is compared with the agreement between a comparable pair of dyzygotic or fraternal twins (from two eggs). The higher the ratio of agreement between identical twins compared with the agreement between fraternal twins in a sample, the stronger the genetic effect.

Ratios of .3 to .7 have been found for many traits associated with leadership. (A ratio of 1.0 would mean that 100 percent of the variance was genetic. A ratio approaching zero would mean there was no genetic effect.)

Molecular Biology Studies. At the level of molecular biology, traits and behaviors have been associated with multiple genes in a particular order in a chromosome (*Science,* 1995, pp. 4, 77; Cherney, 1998). But genes tend to work in a diffuse way (Hammer & Copeland, 1998). Neither a single gene nor the same genes in a different order may be of consequence. Identical twins share all their genes; fraternal twins share, on average, only half of their genes; nontwin brothers can share much less genetically. Thus, 33 out of 40 homosexual brothers had the same DNA variations in a region of the X chromosome, and half shared the same region of chromosome Xq28 (LeVay & Hamer, 1994). But heterosexual brothers inherited the opposite version of Xq28 (Hu, Pattatucci, et al., 1995).

Traits of Leadership Likely to Be Influenced by Genetics. Studies have found genetic effects of consequence to leadership for general intelligence (Bouchard & McGue, 1981), personality traits (Goldsmith, 1983), interests (Keller, 1992), and involvement in a job (Gilbert & Ones, 1998). Berenson (1997) suggested that strong effects based on cotwin studies and molecular biology demonstrate at least 30% heritability in traits related to leadership such as extroversion, shyness, sociability, self-confidence, cognitive abilities, verbal fluency, verbal comprehension, impulsivity, dominance, and aggression. Other traits subject to inheritance mentioned by investigators included achievement motivation, empathy, initiative, persistence, and speed of information processing (Dworkin, 1979; Ghodsian-Carpy & Baker, 1987; Horn, Plomin & Rosenman, 1976; Loehlin, 1992; Johnson, Vernon, & Harris, 2004; Mathews, Batson, et al., 1981; McCartney, Harris, & Bernieri, 1990; O'Connor, Foch, et al., 1980; Rose, 1995; Rushton, Fulker, et al., 1986; Tellegen, Lykken, et al., 1988). Estimates of the heritability of traits associated with leadership vary widely but converge on 30% to 50% of the total variance (Plomin, DeFries, & McClearn, 1990). For example, Loehlin (1992) found that 35% to 40% of the observed individual variation in extroversion attributed to genetics was correlated with leadership.

Mechanisms. The biological mechanisms linking genes and personality are beginning to be understood. For instance, "novelty seeking" is linked with variants of the gene for the dopamine molecule receptor in the brain. Dopamine is the brain's reward chemical; it makes one feel good. Parkinson's disease, caused by a degeneration of the dopamine-producing cells in the substantia nigra of the brain, significantly reduces novelty seeking (Hammer, 1997).

Direct Linkage of Genetics and Leadership

Not only are we able to present numerous studies showing the effects of genes on personality traits found to be predictive of leadership; there are also investigations that have directly connected genetics to leadership. Arvey, Rotundo, Johnson, et al. (2006) obtained data from the Minnesota Twin Registry to compare 238 identical twins (each pair genetically the same) with 188 fraternal twins (each pair with 50% in common in genetic background). They found that 30% of the variance in emergence as leaders was attributable to genetics. As part of a larger project by Vernon, McCarthy, et al. (undated) to study the effects of genetics on multiple dimensions of aggression, Johnson, Vernon, McCarthy, et al. (1998) surveyed 247 pairs of adult twins using mailed questionnaires: 183 pairs were monozygotic (MZ) and 64 pairs were dyzygotic (DZ). Forty-three of the pairs were men; 204 were women. The mean ages of the men and women were 42.8 and 44.5 years, respectively. They were recruited from a Canadian registry of twins or from the 3,000 pairs of twins from many countries who gather annually in Twinsburg, Ohio, for the Annual Twinsday Festival. Respondents completed self-report assessments of leadership, Cassel and Stancik's Leadership Ability Evaluation (LAE, 1982); Bass and Avolio's Multifactor Leadership Questionnaire (MLQ, 1991); and Gough and Heilbrun's Adjective Check List (ACL, 1983). Respondents also completed a "zygosity" questionnaire (Nichols & Bilbro, 1966) which had an accuracy of 93% when matched with blood-typing (Kasriel & Eaves, 1976).

For the LAE, the respondents are presented with 50 hypothetical situations and are asked to choose the style of leadership they would use to handle the situation: laissez-faire, democratic-cooperative, autocratic-submissive, or autocratic-aggressive. Additionally, nine transformational and transactional leadership scale scores were obtained from responses to the MLQ. From the ACL, a checklist of 300 adjectives, 49 were identified as descriptive of leader behavior.

Results were corrected for age and sex. All the leadership assessments except the transactional leadership scales showed genetic effects. That is, the correlation between MZ twins was significantly greater than that between DZ twins. For example, the correlation between the MZ twins' transformational leadership scales ranged from .47 to .50; the corresponding correlations for the DZ twins ranged from .13 to .20. However the correlations between MZ twins' transactional scales ranged from .25 to .31 and the corresponding scales for DZ twins ranged from .11 to .33. For ACL, the MZ twins correlated .50 with each other and the DZ twins correlated only .16. Correlations of the four LAE scores ranged from .31 to .45 for the MZ twins and from .09 to .29 for the DZ twins.

Plasticity of Gene Expression and Brain Functioning

Genes are inherited, but this does not mean their effects are entirely fixed. The expression of genes is often plastic. The brain can be changed through learning. For instance, in one study elderly inactive "couch potatoes" were engaged in a program of physical exercises for an extended period. Compared with a control sample who did not exercise, the experimental sample showed marked improvements in presumably genetically determined brain functions (Davidson, 2001).

Until recently, it was thought that we continue to lose brain cells and synapses (their connections) as we age. Evidence is accumulating from brain scan research that synaptic networks and the numbers of cells may be increased with specialized experiences. "Use it or lose it" implies that cognitive abilities do not decline with aging as much in professionals who continue to carry on their brain work as in unskilled workers who do not engage in as much cognitive activity as they age. The specific areas of the brain impacted by cognitive and physical activities are detected by brain scans.

Prenatal Environment

Monozygotic (MZ) twins may not show 100% concordance even though they share the same genes. This is because their prenatal environment may be different. Some MZ twins, for example, may not share the same placenta and chorion (membrane). Studies of MZ twins developing in the same or different placentas and chorions show that a shared prenatal environment plays a role in identical twins' concordant intelligence, cognition, and personality (Phelps, Davis, & Schwartz, 1997). Use of tobacco, alcohol, or drugs by the mother can have deleterious effects on the fetus, modifying the intelligence and personality after birth that would have been predicted from the genome of the fetus. Mothers' nutrition is thought to be of consequence in fetal development. But Stein, Susser, et al. (1975) found that test scores of 19-year-old Dutch males whose mothers had been exposed to three months of famine in the winter of 1944–1945, just before their sons were born, showed no evidence of depressed intelligence.

Personality Traits Correlated with Emergent and Effective Leadership

A meta-analysis by Judge, Bono, Ilies, et al. (2006) confirmed that personality variables are consistently correlated with the emergence and effectiveness of leadership. Some personality traits influence leaders' ability to cope with the external environment facing them and their followers. This is their task competence, involving a cluster of cognitive traits (such as intelligence) and abilities. A second cluster involves their socioemotional traits, interpersonal competence, personality, and character. We will follow up Chapter 4 by considering the findings about both clusters as they relate to emergent and effective leadership. Table 5.1 shows the cognitive and socioemotional traits as well as the physical and character traits found to be related to leadership since 1970.

Character traits are increasing in importance in the study of leadership. For instance, in 1999 a survey of 1,354 leaders in New Zealand ranging from supervisors to CEOs found a correlation of .61 between the perceived leaders' integrity and satisfaction with the leadership, .57 with leaders' effectiveness, and .56 with motivation (Parry & Proctor, 2000).

Table 5.1 Traits Found Related to Leadership 1970–2005

Characteristics	Number of Positive Findings		Number of Zero or Negative Findings
	1948 Survey	1970 Survey	1948 Survey Only
Physical Characteristics			
Activity, energy	5	24	
Age	10	6	8
Appearance, grooming	13	4	3
Height	9		4
Weight	7		4
Social Background			
Education	22	14	5
Social status	15	19	2
Mobility	5	6	
Intelligence and Ability			
Intelligence	23	25	10
Judgment, decisiveness	9	6	
Knowledge	11	12	
Fluency of speech	13	15	
Personality			
Adaptability	10		
Adjustment, normality		11	
Aggressiveness, assertiveness		12	
Alertness	6	4	
Ascendance, dominance	11	31	6
Emotional balance, control	11	14	8
Enthusiasm		3	
Extroversion	5	1	6
Independence, nonconformity		13	
Objectivity, tough-mindedness		7	
Originality, creativity	7	13	
Personal integrity, ethical conduct	6	9	
Resourcefulness		7	
Self-confidence	17	28	
Strength of conviction	7		
Tolerance of stress		9	
Task-related Characteristics			
Drive to achieve, desire to excel	7	21	
Drive for responsibility	12	17	
Enterprise, initiative		10	
Persistence against obstacles	12		
Responsibility in the pursuit of objectives	17	6	
Task orientation	6	13	
Social Characteristics			
Ability to enlist cooperation	7	3	
Administrative ability		16	

(Continued on next page)

Table 5.1 Traits Found Related to Leadership 1970–2005 (*Continued*)

	Number of Positive Findings		Number of Zero or Negative Findings
Characteristics	*1948 Survey*	*1970 Survey*	*1948 Survey Only*
Attractiveness		4	
Cooperativeness	11	5	
Nurturance		4	
Popularity, prestige	10	1	
Sociability, interpersonal skills	14	35	
Social participation	20	9	
Tact, diplomacy	8	4	

Task Competence

Competence, the capability that a person brings to a situation, may be a specific aptitude, ability, or knowledge relevant to meeting the requirements for successful performance in a particular setting (Boyatzis, 1982). It may invoke a person's more generalized intelligence, which is of consequence in a broad spectrum of situations. Or it may concern a person's understanding of how to realign an entire organizational culture (Tichy & Ulrich, 1983).

Those who consider themselves competent to deal with the tasks facing a group will be likely to attempt leadership. If the others agree with them about who has task competence, their attempts to lead will be successful. If these emergent leaders are actually task-competent, as they and others believe, their leadership will be effective—that is, the group will attain its objectives (Bass, 1960). But if the would-be leader's opinion of his or her competence is not shared by the prospective followers, the attempt to lead is unwise and will fail—or if the person does emerge as a leader, his or her leadership will be ineffective. Adlai Stevenson in 1952 and 1956, Michael Dukakis, and other also-rans have attempted to win the American presidency. Although they believed they had the competence to be president, the majority of the electorate disagreed with them and failed to support them.

This contribution of the leader's technical competence to the group's effectiveness has been given as one reason for Japan's rapid competitive success globally after World War II, in contrast to U.S. industry. For instance, although most tenth-grade Japanese students can solve and graph simultaneous equations, far fewer U.S. university students are capable of doing so. Also, Japanese executives are more likely to have engineering degrees, whereas U.S. executives are more likely to have degrees in law or accounting (Tsurumi, 1983b). On the other hand, the greater emphasis in U.S. education on initiative and discovery results in greater creativity in general and greater success of efforts to change.

The differences in the task competencies of such leaders as Robert F. Scott and Roald Amundsen go a long way toward explaining why Amundsen's team reached the South Pole first and returned in good order whereas Scott's team, although it managed with great fortitude to reach the pole, failed to survive the return trip. Amundsen knew, from his own experience in polar exploration and the experiences of others, that a small crew of men on skis, using sleds hauled by Greenland dog teams, offered the best chance of success. Scott, who had not profited from his own or Ernest Shackleton's past failures, tried to rely on Siberian ponies, motor sledges, and hauling by hand. Amundsen prepared for as many contingencies as he could; Scott, as on an earlier expedition, assumed the best and left little in reserve for emergencies (Huntford, 1984).

In distinguishing the transactional leader from the transformational leader, Downton (1973) noted that followers of a transactional leader are most willing to engage in "transacting goods" with the leader on the basis of their assessment that the leader can "grant them their most preferred choices." The leader's ability to do so requires task competence. As Downton (1973, p. 95) explained, "The greater a leader's competence as perceived by the follower, the greater the probability that the follower will transact goods with him. We should expect the leader's information, skills, and personal temperament to be important factors influencing the formation and maintenance of follower commitments. Competence to cope with the instrumental tasks of the group is an important criterion in selecting leaders, for it is through the leader's successful performance of his instrumental functions that rewards are accumulated by individual followers." Hambrick and Mason (1984) observed that when the senior managers of organizations have entrepreneurial experience, the firms will engage in more innovation of products and expansion of markets. Also, when senior managers are more educated, innovation is more likely (Becker, 1970; Kimberly & Evanisko, 1981). Analyses by Child (1974) and by Hart and Mellons (1970) found that the younger a corporation's managers were, the greater was the corporation's growth in sales and revenues. Profitability, however, was not affected. In a study of over 1,500 senior managers in 129 large firms in eight countries, Heller and Wilpert (1981) reported that the managers' competence, as seen in their experience, qualifications, and skills, influenced the extent to which participative and democratic behavior occurred at other levels in their organizations. Nevertheless, such managerial competence tended to be underutilized, according to Heller and Wilpert.

Competence and Leadership

The quantity of participation forecasts a person's emergence as a leader because it is correlated with quality. But continued incompetent talk will not be reinforced by others. As will be noted Chapter 6, Sorrentino and Boutillier (1975) and Gintner and Linkskold (1975) found that the "windbag" or compulsive talker who lacks interpersonal or task competence will ultimately fail in attempting to lead. Hollander (1960) found that when a group is given tasks, its leader is usually evaluated with respect to his or her competence. This acknowledged competence builds up the leader's credit, so the leader can subsequently depart from the group norms and move the group in novel ways, yet still be accepted by the group.

Task Competence versus Interpersonal or Socioemotional Competence

The most frequently obtained skill factors of leadership tended to involve task or socioemotional performance. Hollander (1978) observed that competent leadership included being a good facilitator, enabling others to make an effective contribution, having skill in handling the inner workings of the group, maintaining activities on a relatively smooth course, giving direction to activity, and acquainting followers with their roles in the main effort. The leader gives competent guidance to other group members concerning their jobs. He or she must be able to evaluate and discriminate between good and bad work.

Limerick (1976) offered a rigorous way to sort leadership in small groups into content or process that influenced performance. Similarly, Dunphy (1963), in a study of adolescent groups, identified two mutually supportive roles—*leader* and *sociocenter*. The leader was influential in group activities whereas the sociocenter relieved group tension. Again, using Bales's method of observational ratings of the behaviors of actual leaders, Bales and Slater (1955) and Slater (1955) offered two types of leadership behaviors: socioemotional and task-oriented. As one rises in an organization, the task competence that is required changes from technical prowess to cognitive complexity and abstract capabilities. The need for socioemotional and interpersonal competence remains much the same at all levels (Boyatzis, 1982). Baron (2000) concluded that competent entrepreneurs think differently from other people. They are less likely to engage in counterfactual thinking, but they are more likely to be overconfident in their judgments. At the same time, they are better social perceptiveness and at adapting to new social situations.

Task Competence Emergent and Effective Leadership

Evidence continues to mount that generalized intelligence or mental ability contributes to emergence as a leader and effectiveness as a manager. But the evidence also indicates variations in the strength of the association for different situations. For example, Mandell (1950a) reported the following correlations between tested mental ability and performance as a civil service administrator: housing agency executives, .30 and .64; Veterans Administration executives, .52; navy executives, .13. Traits that were checked on adjective checklists correlated, respectively, for 95 males and 98 females with their emergence as leaders in initially leaderless group discussions as follows: clear thinking .38 and .43; clever, .49 and .54; wise, .42 and .30 (Gough, 1988).

Intelligence and Leadership

As was seen in Chapter 4, intelligence generally is a positive indicator of competence. Much more specific information about its effects on leadership can be offered. For instance, its creative component becomes more important for leadership at higher levels of management.

General Intelligence. Schmidt and Hunter (1977) introduced theory and method to support the validity of the same particular ability or trait for predicting performance across a wide variety of situations. They argued that much of the variation observed from one situation to another requires correction for restriction in range and unreliability of the measurements. With this in mind, Cornwell (1983) and Lord, De Vader, and Alliger (1986) found from meta-analyses of the relationship that they could reach an even stronger conclusion than Stogdill (1948) or Mann (1959) about the importance of the personal trait—general intelligence—to leadership. Lord, De Vader, and Alliger used the data from 18 studies: those reviewed by Mann in 1959 and others published subsequently through 1977. Both Cornwell (1983) and Lord, De Vader, and Alliger concluded from their meta-analysis, after adjusting the studies for different sample sizes and errors of measurement, that the true mean correlation of general intelligence and being perceived as a leader was .50 across the different situations. These samples included male and female students in high school, college, and graduate school; management trainees and military cadets; and managers and salesmen.

In addition to cross-sectional studies, there is support from longitudinal predictions. Ball (1938) found that intelligence measures yielding an initial .50 correlation with leadership increased to .75 over a 10-year period. After a generation had passed, a follow-up of Terman's (1925) assessment of 1,000 gifted children reported that during their careers, the highly intelligent were far more likely than most to obtain leadership positions and to perform effectively in them, as indexed by such diverse criteria as being admitted to honorary societies and earning military medals. Howard and Bray (1988) noted the importance of initially tested intelligence in the success of managers at AT&T in eight-year and 20-year follow-ups of the assessments of their accomplishments.

Intelligence is a general factor of cognitive abilities such as verbal, spatial, numerical, and reasoning ability. These cognitive abilities are intercorrelated and predict effective performance in a wide variety of assignments including managerial and supervisory jobs. For example, executives, or their speechwriters, have to be able to articulate in appealing and simple language what followers want or should want to do but may not be able to state clearly. Still, specific tests of abilities add little to the prediction of successful leadership beyond what is found with general intelligence, which includes verbal ability (Hunter, 1986). Lord, Foti, and De Vader (1984) obtained a correlation of .52 between intelligence and emergent leadership. Morrow and Stem (1990) and Hogan, Raskin, and Fazzini (1990), among many others, likewise found significantly positive correlations between intelligence and emergent leadership, as did Smith and Foti (undated). Hater and Bass (1988) found that ratings of inspirational leadership of midlevel managers by management committees correlated .30 with managers' judgment scores and .23 with direct reports of ratings of their managers' intellectual stimulation.

If a group is to be effective, generally there should be a positive correlation between the intelligence of the leader and that of the members. Conflict and failure are likely if the correlation is zero or negative. Ordinarily, we are likely to see greater intelligence among those at higher organizational levels. Requirements are greater and more complex at these levels, as is discretionary opportunity and the need to plan ahead for longer periods of time. A first-level supervisor may have to plan ahead for three days—a CEO, for 10 years (Jaques, 2000).

Practical Intelligence. Sternberg (2002) suggested that intelligence as usually measured might be even more predictive of leadership if it were not primarily linked to academic performance. He conceived of practical intelligence relevant to successful adaptation, shaping, and choice in everyday life and based on *tacit knowledge* (Sternberg, Wagner, & Okagaki, 1993). Tacit knowledge is acquired on one's own; it is usually unspoken, implicit, procedural, and not readily articulated. It is directly related to valued practical goals. It is not at a matter of knowing formal rules. Tacit knowledge may be about managing oneself, others, and tasks. It may focus on short-term or long-term goals (Wagner & Sternberg, 1986). Generally, tests of tacit knowledge are situational-judgment inventories in which examinees choose among options for dealing with each situation (Wagner & Sternberg, 1991). Alternatively, answers may be obtained through interviews.

Tacit knowledge, like wisdom, increases with learning from experience. It is ordinarily uncorrelated with tests of multiple abilities and styles of personality and cognition. It can predict success on the job better than general intelligence tests do (Grigorenko, Gil, Jarvin, & Sternberg, 2000). Tacit knowledge correlates, .36 and .38 respectively, with the organizational level of managers in a high-tech firm and their compensation (Williams & Sternberg, 1996). Similar results have been obtained for bank managers (Wagner & Sternberg, 1985). The effectiveness of 368 platoon commanders and 163 company commanders as leaders was rated by superiors, peers, and subordinates. Additionally, 31 battalion commanders were rated by superiors and subordinates. Median correlations between practical intelligence scores and effective leadership ratings were highest (.42) for battalion commanders rated by their superiors and lowest (.17) for platoon commanders rated by their superiors (Hedlund, Forsythe, Horvath, et al., 1999).

Need for Pragmatic Intelligence. In a study of management students' ability to set appropriate priorities, Gill (1983) concluded that the very bright students spent too much time and put too much emphasis on the exclusive use of logic and rationality in making their decisions. Those who were a bit lower in intelligence were more pragmatic. They could accept the fact that there were costs and limits to the search for alternatives and to their efforts to achieve completely logical solutions. If the brightest students had been more experienced, they might have been more willing to use less reasoning and more intuition in setting priorities. Pondy (1983) and Weick (1983) considered such pragmatic thinking and action basic to the effectiveness of an executive. The ability to think and act incrementally characterizes successful executives, who must unite the intuitive and the rational and respond to behaviors, not intentions or preconceptions. These executives need to be ready to take action, rather than depend on moving ahead solely by thinking about requiring judgments about obvious consequences of matters. In taking action, they need to pay close attention to what is happening and to take correc-

tive steps as needed. They must be able to impose order and logic on situations in the absence of order and logic so as to consistently interpret what is happening.

Creative Intelligence. General intelligence has to do with how well one works with words, numbers, spatial orientation, and abstractions. There is also an independent factor—of creative intelligence—which can be measured by tests requiring judgments about obvious or remote consequences of actions and conditions, and which ask for the generation of unusual uses of objects (Guilford, 1967). Rusmore (1984) found that in comparison with general intelligence, creative intelligence is more predictive of success at higher levels of management than at lower levels (Rustmore, 1984). But although Dubinsky, Yammarino, and Jolson (1995) expected tranformational sales managers to be higher in abstact intelligence, they found just the opposite in a study of 140 sales subordinates' ratings of their 34 sales supervisors' abstract orientation—the ability to assess and evaluate critically ideas that seem vague or unformulated. Abstract orientation of the managers correlated between −.36 and −.42 with subordinates' ratings of their managers' transformational leadership.

Memory

Short-term and long-term storage of information are of considerable importance to the leader, especially the political leader. Willner (1968) found that most of the world-class leaders she studied projected "the image of unusual mental attainments." Gandhi and Lenin were "genuine intellectuals," but most of the others were primarily action-oriented. The majority displayed an ability to seize on information and ideas from many sources and to use their excellent memory to store information and retrieve it when they needed it. Franklin Delano Roosevelt could soak up facts and ideas and impress coal miners with the details of their situation or businesspeople with the complexity of their firms. He was constantly searching for information and storing it for use when he needed it. Likewise, Mussolini had a prodigious memory with which he could startle and impress others.

Repeatedly, general managers, senior officials, and chief executive officers are praised for practicing walk-around management, in which they can recognize individually a large number of their employees, call them by their first names, and remember small details about them and their families.

Knowledge, Skills, and Abilities

Knowledge, such as how to evaluate a subordinate's performance; skill, such as how to prepare clear instructions; and ability, such as how to program a computer, all may be involved in what a leader needs to help a group. In field studies with army combat squads performing a variety of field problems, Goodacre (1951); Greer, Galanter, and Nordlie (1954); and Havron and McGrath (1961) found that the characteristics of the squad leaders who were most highly associated with their units' effectiveness included overall ability, knowledge of their jobs, and knowledge of their men.

Knowledge, skills, and abilities that are of consequence to leadership can be more fully detailed, given the multiple functions that may be involved in specific situations, such as serving as a prime minister, a general manager, a school principal, or a naval officer. Specific situations call for specific task competencies in the leader. Leaders with the specific competencies result in more effective groups. For instance, leaders of guidance groups that are made up of members with different kinds of problems must include among their competencies a great deal of flexibility (Hollander, 1978). At the same time, certain specialties provide an impetus to move individuals into positions of leadership. At least half the members of the U.S. Congress are lawyers. In medical schools, leadership tends to be in the hands of physicians who specialize in internal medicine; 42% of deans of medical schools in 1977 were internists (Wilson & McLaughlin, 1984).

To determine what distinguished the competencies of superior and average naval officers, Spencer (undated) and Winter (1978) identified officers' activities according to the motivation and skills that were required to carry them out. This information could then be applied to selection and training. An analysis of approximately 800 incidents of leadership and management performance in a cross section of commissioned and noncommissioned naval officers identified 27 leadership and management competencies. The 27 competencies subsequently were grouped by factor analyses into five factors. Four of the five factors significantly predicted superior leadership

and management performance in a new sample. These four factors, which differentiated between superior and average leadership and management performance, were: (1) competence in achieving tasks; (2) skillful use of influence; (3) management control; and (4) competent advising and counseling.[1]

[1]It should be kept in mind that the factors which emerged from the analysis of intercorrelations of items describing leaders depended, to a large degree, on: (1) the kinds of items and variables for which descriptions were obtained; (2) the numbers of items and variables in different descriptive categories; (3) the nature of the population of leaders who were described. Few factorial studies of leadership were comparable when matched against these three criteria. As a result, few studies produced identical factors; however, certain factors with the same or similar names appeared with considerable frequency.

If factors with the same name appeared in two different studies, they did not necessarily contain loadings on identical items or variables. In other words, it could not be assumed that the factors described identical behaviors. A factor was identified or named on the basis of the nature of items or variables with the highest loadings on the factor. If several similar items or variables have high loadings, the element of the similarity of the item or variable is usually given heavy consideration in naming the factor.

The frequency with which a given factor appeared in the reports did not necessarily represent the frequency of its occurrence among leaders in general. An item or variable could not appear in a study unless measures were obtained on characteristics represented by the factor. Researchers, of course, differ in their ideas about what is important in the study of leadership. As a result, they tended to use different sets of items or variables in their efforts to measure leadership. Furthermore, it cannot be assumed that the listed factors constituted a complete catalog of the leader's qualities and abilities. One of the values of factor analysis is that it brings together in the same factor all items that act alike in describing the individuals in the samples. Thus, the resulting factor describes a generalized from of behavior, rather than the minute details of behavior.

It should also be kept in mind that factors can emerge only if leaders behave differently on different orthogonal dimensions. Thus, for initiation and consideration factors to emerge, there must be a low correlation between them. The same leaders who are high in initiation should vary in consideration from high to low. Those who are low in initiation should likewise vary from high to low in consideration. Conceptually, most leaders could be high in both and the factor could fail to appear, although the different behaviors could still be seen.

If the correlation is high between them, generally only a single factor will appear that contains items of both kinds. Nevertheless, the same leaders who are high in consultative behavior are also likely to participate in decision making. Only one factor, consideration, will appear. Consultation, in which the leader decides; and participation, in which decisions are consensual, are conceptually distinct, despite the fact that the same leaders who tend to use one of the approaches will also use the other approach. The distinctions are important both to theory and to practice. It may be particularly important for a leader to consult rather than participate in one circumstance but to share decision making with fully participating subordinates in another situation. Nevertheless, the generalized behaviors described by the 26 factors produce a more meaningful, logical picture of the leader than would be provided by a list of 100 haphazardly selected items or variables that were all correlated with

Kaplan (1986) reported results of the content analysis of interviews with 25 general managers and executives who were asked to provide examples of effective and ineffective general managers. The respondents thought that effective general managers did better in strategic long-term thinking than in short-time crisis management and in communicating well. They judged the general managers to have more vision, a greater knowledge of business, and an ability to establish priorities. Similarly, Bryson and Kelley (1978) found that congressional leadership depend on a variety of competencies. Personality, style, and skill, along with political savvy, were deemed crucial in determining who becomes a congressional leader and who stays a leader. Clearly, effective leaders need to be alert and sensitive to circumstances which suggest that a problem exists. Political leaders must be able to read signals of discontent, of the seriousness of natural disasters, and of dangerous international currents. With the aid of their staffs, they must be able to diagnose properly the conditions of a problem so that they can formulate appropriate policy responses (Tucker, 1981). This ability to diagnose the social and technical aspects of problems, to attribute causes accurately, and to identify the elements of consequence in a situation may depend, to a considerable degree, on intuition, which will be discussed below.

Education, Technical Knowledge, and Technical Competence

The level of management achieved after 20 years by college graduates and non–college men in the AT&T Management Progress Study showed clearly that college education made a difference (Howard & Bray, 1989). Eleven percent of 137 college graduates reached the fifth and sixth levels of management after 20 years of service, but none of 129 non–college graduates reached these two highest levels. Only 23% of college graduates were still at the two lowest levels after 20 years with the company while 68% of non–college graduates remained at the lowest rungs on the managerial ladder. Higher levels of education were expected in those appointed to posi-

tions of leadership. Twelve nursing directors, 86 head nurses, and 267 staff nurses in 12 Egyptian hospitals agreed in their expectation that head nurses should have advanced education beyond the baccalaureate degree in clinical nursing and administration (Essa, 1983).

Many surveys document the importance of technical competence in leaders' success and effectiveness. For instance, Penner, Malone, Coughlin, and Herz (1973) found that U.S. Army personnel were more satisfied with their officers and noncoms if they believed them to be technically competent. Farris (1971a) found that among 117 professionals at the National Aeronautics and Space Administration, including 20 supervisors, those who were identified as informal leaders in the informal organization were technically more competent and in more active contact with their colleagues. They were also more motivated by the technical aspects of their work, better rewarded, and more influential in their work.

Bass (1960) proposed that groups will be more effective if the hierarchy of influence in a group matches the members' abilities. Rohde (1954a, 1954b, 1954c) demonstrated this relationship in experimental groups in which members differed in their ability to perform a task. Rohde found that the group performed more effectively if the leader was qualified than if the leader was unqualified, regardless of the members' abilities and ideas. It was more difficult for an unqualified leader than for a qualified leader to retain control of the group, especially when the members were similar in ability.

The link between the technical competence of the leader and the effectiveness of the group was also seen by T. G. Walker (1976), who examined leadership in state supreme courts. Walker found that when leaders were selected on the basis of their merit instead of seniority, the courts generated less dissent with their rulings. Additional results reported by Jackson (1953b) and by Rock and Hay (1953) suggested that the emergence of leaders was not a matter of chance, unjust discrimination, or keeping good people down. Both leaders and members appeared to recognize the leader's potential for advancing the purpose of their groups. Also, groups were more effective if the leaders and members played the roles for which they were perceived to be best fitted.

Bugental (1964) found that participants who were trained in task-related skills emerged as leaders more often than untrained participants. G. J. Palmer (1962a,

---

leadership status and effectiveness. The results of the factorial studies indicate that an infinitely large number of variables are not needed to obtain a well-balanced description of a leader. A relatively few of the 26 factors can be the basis for organizing a fairly complete examination of leadership traits and behavior.

1962b) studied groups in which the members differed in their ability to perform tasks. "Task ability" was related to successful leadership (the successful influencing of the performance of others) and still more strongly to effective leadership (achieving the goals of tasks). Hollander (1966) varied the characteristics of group leaders, including whether they were task-competent or task-incompetent, and found that leaders who were perceived as task competent by members exerted significantly more influence than those who were perceived as task-incompetent. Julian and Hollander (1966) reported that the willingness of group members to accept a leader's attempts to influence them depended on the leader's competence. However, Hollander and Julian (1970) found that a less competent leader would continue to be tolerated if he or she was seen as highly motivated to perform the tasks of the group.

Hollander (1964) assigned an ambiguous task to groups. After a first trial, the groups were required to predict what would occur in the next trail. A confederate planted by the experimenter played the role of deviate from the group norms but was provided with the correct answers. The confederate's influence as a leader was measured by the number of trials in which his suggestion was accepted as the group's choice. Such influence increased as the trials progressed despite the confederate's violation of the group's norms. Thus the members' perceptions of the confederate's ability influenced his emergence as a leader. Similarly, Goldman and Fraas (1965) assembled 32 student groups of four members each to solve discussion problems. The groups worked under four types of leadership: (1) leader appointed because of ability; (2) leader appointed arbitrarily; (3) leader elected by group members; and (4) no leader. The groups worked best in situations in which they perceived the leader to have been correct in previous situations.

In surveys of 176 senior U.S. Army officers, 256 supervisors and managers, 23 educational administrators, and 45 professionals, Bass (1985a) found uniformly that subordinates who described their supervisor as intellectually stimulating also said they exerted extra effort, were more satisfied with their leader, and regarded him or her as more effective. The same findings appeared in data-feedback surveys in a variety of firms, such as IBM, Digital Equipment, General Electric, and Federal Express (Bass & Avolio, 1989). Superiors also thought that such

intellectually stimulating supervisors and managers had greater leadership potential (Hater & Bass, 1988).

In a study of 95 employees of a nonprofit organization, Podsakoff, Todor, and Schuler (1983) showed that the expertise attributed to the leader was critical to whether the leader's instrumental and supportive behavior reduced the employees' role ambiguities. That is, ordinarily such structuring of the paths of employees to their goals would have been expected to clarify what employees needed to do to carry out their role arrangements. But when the employees did not perceive the leader as having expertise, their sense of role ambiguity could not be reduced.

Kemp (1983) analyzed 94 questionnaires and 20 interviews of senior industrial and military executives who were concerned with the development of high technology. Kemp found that successful projects were led by project managers who, among other things, fully understood the technology and operational needs and could attract the support of professionally competent and experienced subordinates. Yukl (1998) suggested the same for lower-level supervisors: "Supervisors [of] the work of others need extensive knowledge of the techniques and equipment used by subordinates to perform the work. Technical knowledge of products and processes is necessary to plan and organize work operations, to direct and train subordinates with specialized activities, and to monitor and evaluate their performance" (Yukl, 1998).

Technical Competents Who Fail. Despite their technical competence, many supervisors and middle managers fail to rise in their organizations because of their socioemotional incompetence, according to interview research comparing those who succeed and those who fail. Failure was marked by discharge, transfer, or being "plateaued" until one quit or retired. Success was indicated by promotion to senior management. Failures exhibited neurotic traits: angry outbursts, moodiness, and inconsistency. They were defensive and blamed others for their mistakes or attempted to cover up their mistakes. They were self-aggrandizing and untrustworthy. They were abrasive, intimidating, arrogant, and insensitive. Those who succeeded were more flexible in shifting their focus as they rose in level and were more socially competent (McCall & Lombardo, 1983; Lombardo & McCauley, 1988). Nonetheless, on occasion one may be too competent. A candidate may be rejected as too educated or too intelligent or may be regarded as overqualified for a job.

Intuition

Intuition is the ability to know directly without reasoning. It is an insight, a hunch, on the experience of seeming to learn in one trial without much awareness of how we have learned something. Since it depends more on induction, intuition allows leaders to deal with complexity and irrationality in the face of uncertainties and contributes to their innovative and creative abilities (Goldberg, 1983).

Barnard (1938) first called attention to the rational and the intuitive components of effective executive decisions. This work was carried forward and qualified by Simon (1947). Simon (1987) explained unconscious intuitive decision making in contrast to conscious rational decision making as being a consequence of the decision maker's many earlier encounters with similar relevant circumstances. These earlier experiences built up relevant information that the decision maker could bring into play without awareness—leading to an instantaneous flash of insight, intuitive feeling, or assured judgment. In support, Simon called attention to Bhaskar's (1978) demonstration that although experienced businessmen and novice business students reached the same conclusions about a business policy case, the businessmen did so much more quickly and intuitively. The novices were slower, more conscious, and more deliberate in their analyses.

In addition to explaining intuition in terms of relevant experiences, Simon (1987) noted that some limitations on the rationality of managerial decision making can be explained as a favoring of intuition over reason. Instead of rationally choosing between the lesser of two evils, managers will intuitively choose neither and postpone making a decision. Unlike MBA students, experienced managers are likely to redefine problems on an "in-basket" test rather than accept them as presented (Merron, Fisher, & Torbert, 1987). But the intuitive ability to recognize and quickly diagnose situations calling for remedial action is seen as important to the effective decision making of managers. According to Litzinger and Schaefer (1986), effective managers achieve a balance between analytical reasoning, and their insight and spontaneity. CEOs use strategic planning to lay the foundation for convincing boards of directors and senior management that their intuitively sensed direction for their firms is the right way to go. Justification for the plans is provided by logic and reason.

Agor (1986a, 1986b) surveyed several thousand managers in the public and private sectors. In comparison with lower-level managers, top managers indicated that they were more likely to depend on intuition in making key decisions. But a follow-up of 200 of the most highly intuitive top managers reported that these managers mixed intuition with analytical reasoning in reaching key decisions. Intuition was most often brought into play in making decisions regarding uncertain situations when little precedence existed, when facts and time were limited, when relevant variables were less predicatable, and when several plausible possibilities could be entertained.

Burke and Miller (1999) conducted a thematic analysis of interviews with 60 experienced executives holding important positions in a variety of U.S. organizations. The interviewers asked, "What does it mean to make decisions using your intuition?" Five themes emerged: First, consistent with other studies emphasizing the importance of experience, 56% said they made decisions intuitively after looking though their "central processing" unit to base their decision on past experiences. Second, 40% based their decisions on feeling and emotions. "Sometimes, I had a strange feeling that 'something about the claim isn't quite right' and then I dug for more information and found the facts were not absolutely accurate as reported to me" (p. 92). Third, 23% mentioned applying congnitive skills, knowledge, and training in life and business school. Fourth, 11% said that subconscious mental processing led to an intuitively conscious decision to proceed without having available all the necessary information. Fifth, 10% said that the intuitive decision was a matter of ethics—personal or company values—a moral obligation that comes from within, without a book or manual to tell you what to do. Burke and Miller concluded that intuition may not be enigmatic or primarily the working of the subconscious mind.

Clemens and Mayer (1987) suggested that intuition may be the critical variable that separates the successful from the unsuccessful leader: "Those who 'listen' to their intuitive inner voice are far less likely than Othello to be manipulated by their Iagos' " (p. 120).

Intuition helps people anticipate the future—a trait that is important to successful leadership. In a study of 2,000 managers, top managers rated higher in intuition than managers at lower levels (Agor, 1984). All but one of 12 company presidents whose firms had doubled sales in the past four years scored high in a test of precognition, the intuitive ability to correctly sense what would happen next. Their counterparts with less impressive sales records scored lower in precognition (Rowan, 1986).

Bruce's (1986) in-depth interviews with chief executive officers (CEOs) of 11 large corporations established that the CEOs intuitively set the tone and direction for their firms. Although they had staffs, senior management, and consultants to provide advice, the CEOs had to be able to make the important final strategic decisions by themselves. These intuitive decisions are difficult to articulate; as Simon (1987) suggested, they are likely to be a consequence of the possession of a great deal of relevant information. The CEOs had a "tremendous reserve of knowledge about their companies" (p. 21). General George Patton replied to the accusation that he made snap decisions by declaring, "I've been studying the art of war for forty-odd years. . . . A surgeon who decides in the course of an operation to change its objective is not making a snap decision but one based on knowledge, experience and training. . . . So am I" (Puryear, 1971, p. 382).

Innovativeness, Imagination, and Vision

Closely allied to intuition are imagination, vision, and foresight. Imaginative ability has been seen as more important to Abraham Lincoln than intellectual brilliance (Hyman, 1954). Furthermore, imagination is shown, according to Woodrow Wilson, in a president's capacity to predict the course of events, in the problems to which he calls national attention, in his sense of timing, in his appreciation of the gravity of a problem, and in the urgency he creates when he proposes a solution to it. Imagination is also shown in the way safety nets are built against misfortune and old forms are stretched to cover new functions without arousing excitement about a change. According to the Kirton Adaption-Innovation Inventory (Kirton & DeCiantis, 1986), a leader with an innovative cognitive style thinks tangentially; questions assumptions; and challenges rules, tradition, and consensus. The innovative leader views the need to change as an opportu-

nity. He or she may be abrasive, but produce many ideas, some of which may be unsound and highly risky. Opposite to innovativeness is adaptivity. The adaptive leader is reliable, conforming, methodological, and prudent. He or she favors continuity, seldom challenges rules, and produces safe ideas for prompt implementation (Kirton, 1989).

Miller and Toulouse (1986) surveyed superiors (including the CEOs senior managers), peers, and subordinates of 97 firms in Quebec under 500 employees in size. The effectiveness of leadership was measured by these firms' organizational success. Innovative decentralization in the firms correlated .23 with profitability, .47 with sales growth, and .38 with net income growth. Comparable results were obtained for a large Italian health organization led by a strategic team and an operating team engaged in leading major organizational changes over a five-year period (Previde & Rotondi, 1996). More will be said about imagination and vision in later chapters discussing charismatic and intellectually stimulating leadership.

Optimal Competence

Optimal Intelligence. "A president or would-be president must be bright but not too bright, warm and accessible but not too folksy, down to earth but not pedestrian" (Cronin, 1980, p. 14). There is an optimal level for intelligence and competence. As was noted in Chapter 4, the leader cannot be too superior in intelligence to those to be led. The leader must be more able to solve the problems of the group, but not too much more able. In the same way, the previously cited work of Shaw and Penrod (1962) and M. E. Shaw (1963a) showed that prospective leaders could be given too much information as well as too little information for optimal performance.

A number of factors may militate against the "too superior" member becoming a leader. Communications and understanding may be made difficult by the intellectual disparity of the leader and followers. If a leader is vastly superior in competence the would be leader may no longer appreciate the group's problems or be concerned with helping to solve them. Rather than lead the group, he or she may withdraw from it. The ideas of the overly capable individual may call for too great a change in behavior by the group (Bass, 1960). Although the people who filled cabinet positions and other high governmental positions in the administration of John F. Kennedy were described as the "best and the brightest," Halberstam's (1983) study had to question why so many of their decisions and policies were later proved wrong. A lack of pragmatism in the very bright may be one reason.

Optimal Knowledge. Just as leaders may be too intelligent for the group, they can also have too much knowledge. When group members are overloaded with information, they can fail to lead effectively. Shaw and Penrod (1962) varied the amount of information provided to members of different groups. They found that the group's performance improved when moderate amounts of diverse information were given to individual members, but it did not improve when these individuals received large amounts of such information. With large amounts of information, the highly informed members' suggestions became implausible and unacceptable to the less-informed members. M. E. Shaw (1963a) obtained similar results in a comparison of groups in which one member was provided with either two units or six units of information. The specially informed member with two units of information entered the discussion earlier and initiated more task-oriented communication than the rest of the members of the group, but the situation was reversed for the member who received six units. The informed member was named more often as a leader in the two-unit group than in the six-unit group. Evidently, six units of information became an overload that impeded the informed member's ability to lead.

Wisdom: Combining Intelligence and Knowledge. Research on wisdom has been increasing but is still sparse, probably because, as Sternberg (1990) noted, wisdom is so elusive. Webster (2001) constructed a reliable and valid self-report questionnaire, the Self-Assessed Wisdom Scale. He found that those with higher scores were more likely to consider many factors when making social judgments, were more concerned about guiding and mentoring the coming generation, and were not afraid to form intimate relationships.

Moderators of the Effects of Task Competence

Task competence has its limitations. For example, Justis (1975) found that the competence of a leader had less impact on the performance of members when they were less dependent on the leader. The technical competence of a supervisor may be less important to the group's productivity if the supervisor consults with subordinates about decisions or allows them to share in decision making. Reeder (1981) found that for 78 clerks doing routine work and computer programmers doing nonroutine work for the U.S. Army in Germany, the supervisors' knowledge of the clerks' jobs was less causally related to the clerks' and the programmers' productivity than the supervisors' participative leadership.

Election or Appointment. Election increases the demand for competence in a leader (Hollander, 1978). Hollander and Julian (1970) conducted a set of experiments concerned with competence and the election or appointment of a leader. Six hundred college students served as participants in various group discussion tasks. In the first experiment, the members' perceptions of the leaders' competence were more important than how the leaders had gained office. In the second experiment, although only the leaders' competence was highly related to influence, the members tended to admit having been more influenced by elected than by appointed leaders. In the third experiment, the leaders were either elected or appointed to act as spokesmen for their groups. The elected incompetent leaders were rejected regardless of the group's success or failure in the task, whereas the group's success increased the endorsement of the elected competent leaders. The acceptance or rejection of appointed competent leaders was unrelated to the effects of their group's success or failure, but incompetence resulted in rejection of the appointed leaders. Carter, Haythorn, Shriver, and Lanzetta (1951) also compared the performance of appointed and emergent leaders. Emergent leaders were more active than appointed leaders and tended to dominate the situation. Presumably, unlike the appointed leaders, they had to struggle for status.

Relevance of Competencies. Fundamental to situational analyses of leadership is the realization that the ability to solve the group's problems is a relative matter. An ability relevant to solving problems of a group of farmers in Iowa may be irrelevant to solving the problems of a submarine crew, except to the extent that general intelligence may be important in both situations. As Bass (1960, pp. 174–175) noted, "A mathematician may be vastly superior to stevedores in the arithmetic of space, yet communication difficulties alone are likely to make it impossible for the math expert to supervise effectively the stevedores' loading of the hold of a ship. Similarly, the mathematician may successfully serve as a head of a mathematics department but remain inadequate to solve the problems of a department of agricultural statistics. Ability of a member to help a group must be considered in light of the group's problems. As J. F. Brown (1936) noted, the leader must be superior to other members in one or more characteristics relevant to the problems facing the group. And as Murphy (1941) concluded, the choice of leader is dictated by the needs of the group."

Dubno (1963) observed that groups requiring high-quality decisions did better with leaders who were slow to make decisions, while groups that were under pressure for speedy decisions were more effective with leaders who were fast decision makers. Similarly, Carter, Haythorn, Shriver, and Lanzetta (1951) found that the behavior of leaders differed according to the tasks of their groups. In groups that had a reasoning task, leaders asked for information or facts; in groups with a mechanical-assembly task, leaders asked that things be done; in a discussion task, leaders asked for the expression of feelings or opinions.

Following his review of military leadership, W. O. Jenkins (1947) concluded that military leaders in a given field were superior to other members in skills pertinent to that field. To lead and earn esteem from skilled followers, it helps to be a master of the craft. Thus in one of the early experiments on the relation of task ability to leadership, Carter and Nixon (1949a, 1949b) found that scores on mechanical tests were related to the emergence of a leader in groups performing mechanical tasks. However, scores on tests of word fluency and clerical aptitude were correlated with the emergence of leaders in groups performing clerical tasks. No test of ability was uniquely related to the emergence of a leader in groups performing intellectual tasks.

Stein and Heller (1978) and Heller and Stein (1978) reviewed studies in which group members' verbal interactions were categorized, through content analysis, according to the relevance of each of their statements to the ongoing group process. Emergent leaders were found to carry out a greater amount and variety of task-related behaviors than nonleaders. Leaders were found to be sig-nificantly more active than nonleaders in identifying problems; in proposing solutions to problems; in seeking information, opinions, or structure; in giving information or opinions; and in initiating procedures for the group's interaction or accomplishment of tasks.

Socioemotional and Interpersonal Competence

The traditional view of socioemotional and interpersonal competence emphasized the ability to socialize, to fit with group norms, to comply with authority, to avoid conflict, and to be polite and mannerly. A second view, propounded by the human relations movement, conceived of interpersonal competence as involving empathy, insight, heightened awareness, and the ability to give and receive feedback. Also included was openness to discussions about one's feelings, consensual solutions to conflict, and the development of commitment to actions (Argyris, 1962). Managers with interpersonal competence were considered less willing to depend on power than on trust and shared decision making (Zaleznlk, 1965b). It is the second meaning of interpersonal competence that will be accented here. A third meaning, implying the competence to manipulate others, will be looked at more fully in Chapter 7.

Interpersonal Skills

Everyday experience suggests that people differ in interpersonal competence. Yet beginning in 1920 with E. L. Thorndike (Thorndike & Stein, 1937), the effort to measure and investigate interpersonal competence empirically has been difficult. Earlier researchers found it hard to discriminate between *social intelligence* and general intelligence. Still, Erez (1980) was able to assess the social intelligence of 45 Israeli managers and to show how it related to their tendency to be employee-centered rather than job-oriented leaders.

Empathy has long been recognized as part of interpersonal competence, but as will be shown later in this chapter, efforts to measure empathy have been fraught with difficulty (Hogan, 1969). Virmani and Mathur (1984) conceived of "vivek," the ability to evaluate the implications of the attitudes, needs, desires, and intentions of others and oneself. Vivek, which is associated with effective leadership and management, is a fluid ability in that it can perceive complex relationships in human interactions in new environments.

The quality of one's verbal and nonverbal communication has been seen as contributing to overall interpersonal competence (Rosenthal, 1979b), along with the fear of negative evaluation (Watson & Friend, 1969) and apprehension about communication (McCroskey, 1977). Self-monitoring (Snyder, 1974) also involved basic social skills (Lennox & Wolfe, 1984).

With support from a factor analysis of a lengthy self-report by 339 male and female undergraduates, Riggio (1986) found seven basic socioemotional skills to be of consequence: (1) emotional expressivity ("I have been told that I have 'expressive' eyes); (2) emotional sensitivity ("It is nearly impossible for people to hide their true feelings from me"); (3) emotional control ("I am very good at maintaining a calm exterior, even when upset"); (4) social expressivity ("I usually take the initiative and introduce myself to strangers"); (5) social sensitivity ("While I was growing up, my parents were always stressing the importance of good manners"); (6) social control ("I find it very easy to play different roles at different times"); and (7) social manipulation ("If I really have to, I can 'use' other people to get what I want").

Interpersonal Competence and Leadership

Interpersonal competence is manifested in understanding of, caring for, and consideration for others. It is revealed in communicating easily and clearly and in fostering and maintaining good relations with others. It serves to increase harmony, reduce tension, and resolve conflict. Compared with interpersonally incompetent leaders, interpersonally competent leaders are influential but not dictatorial, good at dealing with people and at delegating. They are trustworthy and credible rather than overly political (Kaplan, 1986). They promote group decisions, not to keep their subordinates happy but to take full advantage of their followers' knowledge. They increase their subordinates' commitment to decisions (Lombardo, Ruderman, & McCauley, 1987). According to Hogan and Hogan (2002), everyone wants acceptance and status, and leaders are better at obtaining these. Hogan and Hogan see interpersonal competence as in-

cluding social skills—empathy, communications abilities, and social astuteness—essential to leadership.

Interpersonal competencies discriminated between effective and ineffective managers above and beyond situational effects (Boyatzis, 1982). J. Hogan and Holland (1998) found correlations of a CPI Empathy scale with five criteria of leadership between .45 and .73 for 25 managers at a large retail firm. Also, Baron (1989) ascertained that interpersonally competent members of small groups were more likely than other members to resolve conflicts and emerge as leaders.

Connelly, Gilbert, Zaccaro, et al. (2000) obtained open-ended responses to questions about problem scenarios in order to predict leaders' effectiveness. Ability measures of complex problem-solving skills, social judgment, and knowledge were obtained from ratings of the responses. These "constructed" responses added to the prediction of career achievement of a sample drawn from 1,807 U.S. Army officers at six grades in rank. This added validity was beyond that accounted for by measures of cognitive ability, motivation, and personality according to a series of hierarchical regression analyses.

Although a multinational sample of faster-climbing managers did not see as much value in being interpersonally competent as did managers whose advancement in their careers was slower, the faster climbers rated themselves higher than the slower climbers in "understanding why I do what I do" (Bass, Burger, et al., 1979). Hall and Donnell (1979) compared 1,884 managers who were either fast, medium, or slow in their career advancement; these researchers found that more rapid promotion was directly related to the self-rated ability to relate effectively with others. Similarly, Wolberg (1977) noted that the potential to be a group leader was directly linked to the ability to relate as a peer in role playing and to avoid immature "acting out" during training.

The Structure of Socioemotional and Interpersonal Traits of Leadership

Hogan and Hogan (2002) believe there is a general factor of sociopolitical intelligence, which is a generalized ability to take roles (Mead, 1934). It is at the core of social skill and of the ability to build and maintain a team. Hogan and Hogan cited research support from Conway (1999). Conway factor-analyzed 2,000 360-degree *benchmarks*—management appraisals of trainees at the Center for Creative Leadership (CCL)—and found that four of the five factors involved leadership and social skills. The fifth factor involved strategic thinking. By 1946, R. B. Cattell (1946) had applied factor analyses to responses to personality questionnaires. He generated 16 factors, many of which were found to be related to leadership in subsequent studies. Similarly, Guilford (1952) generated 10 factors—again, many of these were related to leadership. They included general activity, mood swings, ascendancy, sociability, emotional stability, thoughtfulness, and masculinity. Scholars, consultants, and leaders themselves produced many different lists of traits they felt were required for leadership. These were based on experience, published research, or both (Bray & Howard, 1983; Boal & Hooijberg, 2001; Atwater & Yammarino, 1993; Hogan, Curphy, & Hogan, 1994; O'Roark, 2000; Quinn, 1988). Warren Bennis (quoted in Norris, 1992) felt that in choosing managers, large organizations emphasize technical competence, "people skills," and conceptual skills. But additionally, they ought to focus more on judgment, taste, and character, along with sense of purpose, caring, constancy, competence, optimism, ambition, and integrity. After reviewing the literature on traits of leadership, Kirkpatrick and Locke (1991) listed drive involving achievement, ambition, energy, tenacity, and initiative—the personalized and socialized motivation to lead. Likewise, honesty, integrity, and self-confidence were listed as important. Also included were emotional stability, cognitive ability to marshal and interpret information, and knowledge of "the business" of the organization. Other traits, for which there was less support, included creativity, originality, and flexibility. By 1986, such lists could be replaced by a more rigorous and reliable analysis of accumulated evidence through the use of meta-analysis.

Meta-Analysis. This method pools the results of a number of separate research analyses. It provides statistical estimates of the average effects of variables from different research studies. The estimates are based on the much larger size of the pooled results and offer more confidence about the relationship in question—in this case, for instance, showing the likely average correlation between, say, managers' assessed friendliness and their effectiveness as leaders. The correlations are weighted ac-

cording to the number of cases contributing to them. They are also corrected for the reliability of the variables and their restrictions in range to obtain the true estimate, which is likely to be somewhat higher than the observed average. Confidence intervals of the true correlations are also provided to determine the probability that a correlation is not zero.

Meta-analyses of the Socioemotional Traits of Leadership. Lord, Devader, and Alliger (1986) conducted the first meta-analysis of traits of leadership. Their data were drawn from 18 studies about the emergence of leadership reviewed by Stogdill (1948) and Mann (1959).[2] Studies through 1977 were added. The traits of consequence included intelligence, dominance, masculinity, extroversion, and better adjustment. A number of other meta-analyses have followed. The most comprehensive, described later, were conducted by Judge, Bono, Ilias, et al. (2002) and Judge, Colbert, and Ilias (2004).

The Big Five Factor Structure of Personality

Although Tupes and Christal (1961) and Norman (1963) first found evidence for the validity of the "Big Five" factor structure, it did not become a hot research topic until the 1990s, when it was shown to be a reliable and valid model for describing the most important socioemotional aspects of personality. Each of the Big Five factors contains six traits or facets. By the end of the decade, the factor model had been validated for predicting various criteria such as job performance in eight meta-analyses (e.g., Barrick & Mount, 1991). McCrae and Costa (1992) developed the Revised NEO Personality Inventory (NEO-PI-R) as a standard for measuring the Big Five factored trait structure from a lengthy questionnaire. The five factors were: N, neuroticism versus emotional stability; E, extroversion or surgency versus introversion; O, openness to experience (called by others intellect, imagination, or culture); A, agreeableness versus antagonism; and C, conscientiousness or the will to achieve.

Neuroticism is the extent to which persons tend to

---

[2] Stogdill suspected that the absence of some particular positive findings in the 1970 survey were due, in part, to the decisions of his abstracters. We also must be cautious about the volume of results obtained for some traits and not for others. Researchers tend to pursue fads. Also, changes occur over the decades in the names that are used to label the same traits of behavior.

experience distress, emotionality, worry, nervousness, insecurity, and tension. Neurotics view the world, themselves, and others negatively (George, 1996). They are likely to be pessimists (Williams, 1997). Other names for this factor include "lack of emotional stability" and "negative affectivity." The traits of the intercorrelated subscales or facets of the neuroticism factor that can be scored separately include anxiety, hostility, depression, self-consciousness, impulsiveness, and vulnerability (Costa, 1994).

Extroversion is the extent to which persons tend to be assertive, gregarious, and enthusiastic (Barrick & Mount, 1993) and feel themselves to be efficacious. They are optimistic and tend to experience positive moods and emotions. They view others and the world favorably (George, 1996). Other terms for this factor are "social boldness" and "social presence." The six facets are warmth, gregariousness, assertiveness, activity, excitement-seeking, and positive emotions.

Openness to experience involves imagination, artistic sensibility, and intellect. Another name is "intellectance." Its six facets are fantasy, aesthetics, feelings, actions, ideas, and values (Costa, 1994).

Agreeableness is the extent to which a person is sympathetic, trusting, cooperative, warm, loving, affiliative, and good-natured. Its facets are trust, straightforwardness, altruism, compliance, tender-mindedness, and modesty (Costa, 1994). Highly modest self-presenters are favored by audiences if the presenters are female; moderately modest self-presenters are favored if they are male (Wosinska, Dabul, Whetson-Dion, et al., 1996).

Conscientiousness is the extent to which a person is dependable, responsible, hardworking, persevering, efficient, needing to achieve, prudent, ambitious, and organized (Barrrick & Mount, 1993). Facets include competence, order, dutifulness, striving for achievement, self-discipline, and deliberation (Costa, 1994). (For more about the NEOAC structure, see Digman, 1990; Eysenck, 1970; Goldberg, 1993; Guilford, 1975; Hough, 1992; McCrae & Costa, 1987; Peabody & Goldberg, 1989; and Tellegen, 1985.)

Goldberg (1993) developed a checklist of 100 adjectives, and Saucier (1994) reduced these to the Mini-Marker, a 40-item adjective checklist that when scored provides the same NEOAC factor results but with a little less reliability. Different labels may be attached to the factors. For example, adjustment may be substituted for emotional stability and lack of neuroticism; intellectance may be substituted for openness to experience. Facets are similar (Curphy, 2001).

Factorial validity was evidenced because each facet scale correlated much more highly with its appropriate factor than the other four factors. The NEOAC factorial structure displays considerable universality (MacCrae & Costa, 1997). As a demonstration of the construct validity of NEOAC, MacCrae, Zonderman, et al. (1996) compared the varimax-rotated factorial structures extracted from large adult and student samples in seven languages and cultures: American, German, Portuguese, Hebrew, Chinese, Korean, and Japanese. Orthogonal rotation using the normative American factorial structure generated average factor congruence coefficients across the other six cultures for N, E, O, A, and C ranging from .94 to .96. The Big Five factors tend to have low correlation with each other, demonstrating their *discriminant* validity (McCrae & Costa, 1990). The structure may have a biological basis (Eysenck, 1967). For many years, Eysenck advocated a two-factor theory of neuroticism and extroversion with a biological basis. *Convergent* validity was found when each factor scale correlated with relevant scales from other personality tests and inventories. *Discriminant* validity was seen in the expected greater correlation of a facet with its relevant measure on another test or inventory. For instance, the facet of assertiveness was correlated more highly with being forceful, enthusiastic, and confident on the Gough and Heilbrun Adjective Check List, compared with adjectives about other aspects of extroversion.

Supporting *consensual* and *construct* validation, coefficients of congruence of the Big Five factors were between .96 and .98 for a replication of the NEOAC with a sample of 211 people in sales, customer service, and lower, middle, and upper management. Additionally, performance evaluations of their successful interpersonal relations, their task orientation, and the adaptive capacity of their performance evaluated by their supervisors correlated significantly with their conscientious score. Their successful interpersonal relations and their adaptive capacity increased with conscientiousness and decreased with neuroticism. The facets of competence, striving for achievement, and self-discipline were the highest in correlation with the performance evaluations (Piedmont &

Weinstein, 1994). Numerous theoretically expected consistencies were found between the Adjective Check List and NEOAC (Piedmont & Weinstein, 1993).

The Big Five and Leadership. Judge, Bono, Ilies, et al. (2002) tested how well the Big Five model provided an adequate structure for the socioemotional traits of leadership, excluding intelligence and other capabilities. The criteria they predicted were emergent leadership, effective leadership, and transformational leadership. These investigators searched the PsychINFO database, 1887 to 1999, for articles on leadership and personality. They also searched for articles on personality, neuroticism, agreeableness, conscientiousness, extroversion, and openness to experience. Results were added from 48 additional traits mentioned in the third edition of this handbook (Bass, 1990), along with traits found in articles in *Leadership Quarterly* from the first to the tenth volume and the studies used by Lord, Devader, and Alliger (1986). A total of 1,200 abstracts were identified. Studies of opinion and fashion leadership were excluded, as were many others that did not provide correlations or sufficient data to calculate them. Extracted for analysis were 275 correlations from 79 studies and 15 doctoral dissertations. A wide variety of data on emergent and successful leadership were included, ranging from teachers' reports and peer ratings of student leadership to election of leaders in informal and formal groups. Studies using indexes of management such as salary level or organizational grade were excluded. Barrick and Mount's (1991) coding procedure was used to categorize traits with many different names into a coherent whole. For instance, as suggested by Hogan, Curphy, and Hogan (1994), the need for power was classified as a measure of extroversion. In addition to obtaining results for the broader Big Five, results were obtained for the more specific facets in the model, such as dominance and sociability. A study was included in the correlational analyses if it compared leaders and nonleaders in emergent, effective, or transformational leadership. Huffcutt, Roth, and McDaniel (1994) presented for each of the Big Five factors the number of correlations, the number of respondents, and the estimated true correlations, corrected for reliability, restriction in range, and the sharply skewed weightings of the 76 correlations based on the total numbers of cases contributing to each of the five factors, ranging from 8,314 to

18,830. The reliability of the Big Five personality factors ranged from .78 to .86.

The corrected average correlations between each of the Big Five personality factors and leadership were as follows: neuroticism, −.32; extroversion, .30; openness, .25; agreeableness, .10; conscientiousness, .19. Confidence intervals indicated a high probability that all five correlations were not zero. The multiple correlation was .47 for predicting leadership based on combining the optimally weighted five factors. Specific facets with substantial correlations with criteria of leadership included sociability, .38; dominance, .36; achievement, .36; and dependability, .32.

The criteria and samples of leadership analyzed made some difference. For government and military leaders, agreeableness correlated close to zero with the emergence of leadership, but .23 and .27, respectively, with leadership effectiveness and transformational leadership. Neuroticism correlated −.19, −.26, and −.21, respectively, with emerging, effective, and transformational leadership. Extroversion was most predictive (.34) of emerging leadership and somewhat less predictive of effectiveness (.23) and transformational leadership (.25). In other studies, Caliguri (2000) found that the conscientiousness scores of 94 supervisors of 280 expatriate employees correlated positively with 360-degree ratings of the supervisors' performance. McDaniel (1992) found that openness correlated .37 with the success of 162 change leaders. As rated by others, emotional stability correlated .32 with leaders' self-reports of success.

Martinsen (2000) calculated the stepwise multiple regressions of N, E, O, A, and C and their interactions on 360-degree ratings of entrepreneurial leadership orientation by 94 managers, 80 supervisors, 307 peers, and 426 subordinates. For example, N(−) + 0 + A(−), optimally weighted, accounted for 17.7% of the variance in the ratings of entrepreneurial orientation of the leaders. N + E + A plus the interactions N × E and E × A, optimally weighted, accounted for 19.3% of the 360-degree ratings of the task orientation of the leaders. N + E + O + A + C + N × A + O × C, optimally weighted, accounted for 33.4% in the variance of the leaders in dominance behavior.

Makiney, Marchioro, and Hall (1999) found some significant correlations between the 40-item Mini-Marker rendition of NEOAC and the self-reported Multifactor

Leadership Questionnaire (MLQ) for 69 undergraduates and other measures of leadership. N (−) emotional stability correlated .23 with transformational leadership. Extroversion correlated .40 with transformational leadership, −.31 with laissex-faire leadership, and .28 with students' self-schemata of social influence. 0, openness to experience, correlated .24 with the same self-schemata and .20 with leadership ranking in the class. A, agreeableness, correlated .32 with leadership ranking and the self-schemata of dedication. A, antagonism, correlated .25 with laissez-faire leadership. C, conscientiousness, correlated .20 with the leadership self-schemata of dedication.

Given the research interest in the Big Five, we will use its structure to present additional single and multiple personality studies since 1970 correlated with leadership. Many have appeared as facets of the Big Five.

Social Intelligence and Leadership

"Social intelligence" was a term in use before 1950 but then fell out of favor. However, Gardner (1985) defined social intelligence as the ability to distinguish other people's moods, temperaments, motivations, and intentions among others. It is the ability to understand others and act accordingly (Sternberg, 1985). It is also the wisdom to act at the appropriate time and in the appropriate way on the basis of this understanding (Boal & Hooijberg, 2001). For Zaccaro, Gilbert, Thor, et al. (1991), the social intelligence of successful leaders comprises social perceptiveness and behavioral flexibility. I will take the liberty of using social intelligence as the sum total of social competencies, including dominance, sociability, communicating styles, empathy, sensitivity, tact, and other interpersonal skills. Especially strong associations are found with communication styles and skills (Bass, 2002).

Dominance. Dominance tended to appear in lists of the traits of leadership drawn up in the 1970s and later (e.g., Hughes, Ginnet, & Curphy, 1993) but was less frequent as a subject of empirical investigations. This may have been due to an increased interest in democratic participation as opposed to autocratic directive leadership. One of the new empirical efforts was that of Stricker and Rock (1998). They developed a set of scales, including a dominance scale, from the biographical information sup-

plied by freshmen at the U.S. Naval Academy. The internally consistent and validated items on dominance included affirmative answers to such questions as these: "Your parents told you that you did not take 'no' for an answer." "You told classmates or friends that they did not stand up for their rights enough." "Classmates or friends told you that you were not interested in other people's ideas and opinions." The dominance scale correlated .57 with a biographical sociability scale and .39 with a similarly constructed emotional ability scale. The dominance scale correlated .82 with peer ratings of leadership. Lord, DeVader, and Alliger (1986) thought that Stogdill (1948) and Mann (1959) had both underestimated the correlation of the personal trait of extroversion and leadership. They conducted a meta-analysis of reports of different types of subjects and situations that related extroversion and leadership. This meta-analysis adjusted the grand mean of results for the sample sizes and various errors attenuating each of the obtained correlations. The researchers estimated that the true mean correlation between extroversion and leadership was .26 across the different samples of subjects and situations. The results for dominance and leadership were less supportive of the importance of the trait of dominance across situations, however; the estimate of the true mean correlation was .13.

Butt and Fiske (1968) recognized that dominance could be *socialized* or *aggressive*. Different personality scales of dominance emphasized one possibility or the other. Gough's (1957) dominance scale in the California Personality Inventory (CPI) assessed socialized dominance related to leadership in high school. Cattell, Saunders, and Stice's (1957) dominance scale in their Sixteen Personality Factors (16PF) assessed "an aggressive onslaught on the environment by a rather solemn, isolated, and egotistical person" (Butt & Fiske, 1968, p. 513). It would seem that if both scales were used to predict transformational and transactional leadership, the leadership would be true leadership when predicted by the CPI, and pseudo leadership when predicted by the 16PF.

Montagner, Arnaud, et al. (1973) observed differences in children. Socially dominant children were the center of attention, threatened only for short periods of time, and were conciliatory. They were more likely to exert leadership and to be imitated by other children. The aggressively dominant engaged in much physical violence.

They were highly self-oriented and spread fear in the other children with their threats. They were less likely to display leadership.

Socialized and Aggressive Dominance. Kalma, Visser, and Peters (1993) developed and validated factored scales of socialized and aggressive dominance, averaging results from seven Dutch samples ranging in size from 100 to 550. Statements such as "I have no problems talking in front of a group" loaded highest on socialized dominance (SD), and "I can look everybody in the eye, and lie with a straight face" loaded highest on a second factor, aggressive dominance (AD). In the first sample, students engaged in trios. They said they got their own way with simple statements if they scored high in socialized dominance ($r = .28$) but not aggressive dominance. ($r = .04$). Conversely, ADs were more likely than SDs to say that they got their way by being persistent, being persuasive, bargaining, threatening, being deceitful, being evasive, and using hints. The correlations of observers' ratings with AD factor scale scores ranged from .20 to .37. The correlations of observers with SD factor scale scores ranged from $-.15$ to .10. Observers noted that SDs (compared with ADs) looked more at the person to whom they were speaking ($r = .39$ versus $r = -16$), held a prolong gaze ($r = .29$ versus $r = .10$), and gesticulated ($r = .33$ versus $r = -.4$) ADs were more likely than SDs to interrupt others (.23 versus .13), raise their eyebrows (.28 versus .14), and express doubt (.30 versus .11). On self-reports, SDs were more likely than ADs to consider themselves and other people friendly ($r = .41, .40$ versus $r = -.19, -.14$). They were less likely than ADs to seek approval from others ($r = -.40$ versus $r = -.30$). SDs rated themselves higher than ADs did on task leadership ($r = .38$ versus $r = -.03$); ADs rated themselves lower on socioemotional leadership than did SDs ($-.23$ versus .17). Peers rated ADs higher on task leadership but lower on socioemotional leadership (.24 versus -24).

Socioemotional Competency Traits

Emotional Intelligence. The competency model is a recipe for a good leader, although there is a wide range of opinion on what should be included. Ashkanasy and Tse (2000) theorized that emotional intelligence correlated with transformational leadership and its factorial compo-

nents. George (2000) agreed that emotional intelligence correlated with effective leadership and its developing collective goals and encouraging flexibility. Cherniss and Goleman (2001) held that successful leaders model emotional intelligence. Caruso, Mayer, and Salovey (2002) qualified the relationship, suggesting that effective leadership could occur in the absence of emotional intelligence or that only some elements of emotional intelligence might be present. Church (1997) that in comparison with average-performing managers, highly effective managers' self-ratings were more in agreement with those of their subordinates. Dasborough, Ashkanasy, and Boyle (2002) theorized that emotionally intelligent followers could discriminate between the intentions of truly transformational leaders and self-oriented pseudo-transformational leaders who try to mislead their followers (Bass & Steidlemeier, 1999).

Salovey and Meyer (1990) introduced the concept of emotional intelligence as the ability to monitor the feelings and emotions of oneself and others to help guide one's own thinking and actions. Goleman (1995, 1998) popularized "emotional intelligence" as a term encompassing a limited number of socioemotional abilities and traits, including self-awareness; handling one's own feelings and impulses; motivating others; showing empathy; and remaining connected with others through optimism, enthusiasm, and energy. Emotional intelligence implies to think positively, understand relationships, and resolve conflicts.

The scope of the concept of emotional intelligence remains controversial. It may be seen as an *ability* to solve emotional problems as a *competency* mixes observed abilities, traits, and socioemotional behaviors. The ability model points to success in (1) perceiving and identifying emotions in the thoughts of oneself and others; (2) using emotions to think creatively and make decisions; (3) understanding and interpreting meaning in emotions, being open to feelings, avoiding defensiveness, and reflectively monitoring emotions.

The competency model points to: (1) self-awareness: emotional awareness and accurate self-assessment; (2) self-regulation: self-control, trustworthiness, conscientiousness, and innovativeness (Caruso, Mayer, & Salovey, 2002).

The ability model is favored because of its greater psychometric acceptability. The psychometric properties of the competency model are more problematic, since this model is often a collection of various self-ratings (Daus & Ashkanasy, 2003).

Sociability and Leadership. Sociability was included in the lists of traits of consequence to leadership drawn up by Kirkpatrick and Locke (1991), Hughes et al. (1993), and O'Roark (2000). It was a facet of extroversion in the NEOAC factor analyses, which figured even more strongly in leadership behavior (see Bass, 1998, on ascendancy). Stricker and Rock (1998) developed biographical information scales of emotional stability, need for achievement, self-confidence, and sociability. Sociability correlated highest with peer ratings of leadership (.28). Avolio and Bass (1994) obtained a correlation of .25 between the Gordon Personal Profile (GPP) sociability score of 188 leaders in a community and their followers' ratings of their charismatic leadership. Elsewhere, in a review of empirical investigations, Bass (1998, p. 125) found that sociability contributed to inspirational motivation, individualized consideration, and contingent rewarding by leaders.

Competence in Communicating. Communication competencies are basic to leadership (Barge & Hirokawa, 1989). The leader needs to be able to communicate to followers the framing and interpretation of experiences (Bowman & Deal, 1991). Comrey, High, and Wilson (1955b) found that "high-producing" supervisors in the aircraft industry communicated effectively. Alpander's (1974) survey of 217 corporations to determine which training needs were the highest priorities for currently employed managers found that oral communication abilities were rated highest. Mold (1952) reported that 490 industrial supervisors stated that they needed the most development in "how to sell ideas to my superior." And satisfaction with the effectiveness of officers and noncoms among over 30,000 U.S. Army personnel was strongly associated with their ability to communicate effectively with their subordinates, according to ratings by their superiors and subordinates (Penner, Malone, Coughlin, & Herz, 1973). The quality and style of a leader's communications to followers makes a difference in the success and effectiveness of the leadership.

Quality of Communications. Being active as a communicator is not enough. The quality of communicating with others is an important trait and competence of leaders. The quality of communication may be a matter of socioemotional competence as well as task competence, in which it is akin to oral and written fluency. Knowing something is not the same as being able to transfer the information to another individual or to transfer it to that person's satisfaction. Communicating goes beyond verbal fluency. A listener's acceptance of a message from an anchor on a televised news program is likely to depend considerably on how the anchor looks and how the message is delivered. President Reagan was known as the "great communicator" more for his perceived affability and the sincerity of his delivery than for his accuracy. President George W. Bush was known for mispronunciations and stumbling even when he was reading his speeches, yet he managed to remain popular during his first five years in office.[3]

Talking a lot in initially leaderless situations may result in the emergence of a leader, but the effectiveness of a leader will depend on the quality of the talk. Considerable evidence has been accumulated to demonstrate the connection between competence in *articulation* and effectiveness as a leader and manager. For instance, from 200 interviews with successful corporate leaders, Kanter (1983) found that the leaders had a number of communication skills in common. They were consistently able to expand their thinking by actively soliciting new ideas and feedback from others and were continually reaching out for new information. Also, they knew how to persuade others about the quality of their ideas and had the ability to communicate persuasively to others and to enlist their support by persistently working for it.

In a field setting, Klimoski and Hayes (1980) surveyed 231 editorial subordinates and their 15 assistant managers who abstracted current technical publications. Among the supervisory behaviors noted were *explicitness* in giving instructions and frequency of communication about job-related matters. The managers' explicitness correlated significantly with the subordinates' expectations of success and reward in their jobs, but frequency of com-

---

[3] See also: Hurwitz, Zander, and Hyrnovitch (1953); Riecken (1958); Kirscht, Lodahl, and Haire (1959); Regula (1967); Burroughs and Jaffee (1969) Jaffee and Lucas (1969); Regula and Julian (1973); and Gintner and Linkskold (1975).

munication did not. Explicitness correlated .57 with the subordinates' satisfaction with supervision, but frequency of communicating correlated only .19 with such satisfaction. The managers' explicitness correlated $-.44$ and $-.30$ with the subordinates' role ambiguity and role conflict. Frequency correlated .04 with each of these measures of problems in doing their jobs. The managers' explicitness contributed to the subordinates' self-rated effort; frequency did not.

Snyder and Morris (1984) were able to link the quality of supervisors' communications in 12 offices of a social service agency with the quality of services rendered by the agency and with lower costs of operations. Colleagues used a reliable four-item questionnaire that was based on previous work by Olmstead and Christensen to rate supervisors on the quality of their communications. The overall quality of the supervisor as a communicator contributed significantly to lower costs of operation, even after adjustments for the different numbers of clients served and the size of the different offices. Ward (1981) collected data from first-line supervisors in two manufacturing plants, three libraries, and two hospital nursing departments. The main concern was the supervisors' *rhetorical* sensitivity—their creative invention of effective discourse in writing and speaking. Ward found that the supervisors' rhetorical sensitivity correlated positively with the satisfaction of their subordinates.

Ability to Convey Meaning and to Enhance Retention. Getting across the meaning of a message is crucial and may require innovative approaches by the leader. The feelings as well as the ideas in the message need to be communicated effectively (Bennis & Nanus, 1985); also, the messages have to be remembered. According to survey studies, the messages sent by leaders that become memorable—are influential and are remembered for a long time—are brief oral injunctions such as, "Work smarter, not harder" or "No matter what the other girls are doing, act like a lady" (Knapp, Stohl, & Reardon, 1981). All 65 employees and managers of one firm interviewed by Stohl (1986) could recall such a memorable message. The messages were almost all single sentences and tended to be rules. The employees usually first heard the messages soon after joining the firm, and in a private one-to-one conversation. If an appropriate situation arose, the recipients said they would pass the message on in the

same way. A majority of messages in this organizational setting dealt with role behavior and were applicable to various situations. One such message was "If you're not helping, you're hindering." These pithy, memorable messages, usually from a sender of higher status to a recipient of lower status, provide "sense-making" structures and a guide to what behavior is appropriate in an organization. Memorable messages, content-analyzed, provide information about the norms, values, expectations, rules, requirement, and rationality of an organization's culture. Clearly, a manager who includes such memorable messages in his or her communications is likely to have a much greater impact on subsequent events in the organization.

Consistency of Statements. Inconsistency of contributions may not be as deleterious as one might expect. Contrary to their hypothesis, Goldberg and Iverson (1965) found that the influence wielded by high-status members depended on their status, rather than on the consistency of their statements. They did not lose influence if they changed their opinions several times during a discussion.

Timing. The timing of participation makes a difference in the influence of the participation on others. Leana (1985) and M. Smith (1935a) noted the importance of opportunity. Someone who succeeds as a leader may be but one of several in a group who might have been just as successful had they been present to attempt leadership first. Hollander (1978) concluded that to emerge as a leader, one needs to participate early. But M. E. Shaw (1961) found that the members of a group who stated their opinions either early or late were better able to have their opinions accepted than those who stated their opinion in the middle of a discussion. Bass (1967a) experimented with groups of male managers in which the heads of the groups revealed their opinions at the beginning or end of a session, or not at all. The other group members were able to influence each other most when the heads remained silent, but they exhibited greater coalescence around the heads when the heads revealed their opinions. Silent heads were most influenced by the other members and were most dissatisfied with their own final judgments.

Early presentation by a leader of his or her favorite alternatives to decisions followers' generation of additional alternatives (Maier & Sashkin, 1971). The search for alternatives is narrowed, and the quality of the decision may suffer (Brillhart & Jochem, 1964). When leaders were trained by Maier and McRay (1972) to delay presenting their preferences, their followers were more productive in proposing high-quality alternatives.

Style. Managers differ consistently in their style of communicating. Replicating earlier work, McCroskey and Young (1981) found that the communication style of senior managers and the immediate superiors of employees affected different aspects of their employees' satisfaction. In an information technology firm, a navy civilian agency, and a social service agency, Klauss and Bass (1982) conducted path analyses for the relationships among managers' communication styles, according to their supervisors, peers, and subordinates. Managers who were described as highly informative and trustworthy contributed considerably to their colleagues' role clarity, satisfaction with the managers, and evaluations of the effectiveness of the managers. *Trustworthiness* and credibility depended on being a careful listener, on being informal, and on being open in two-way conversations. For the Hanover Insurance Companies (1988), trust was a key to being open, one of their most central values supporting the goals of profitability, of giving customers "good value for their money," and of creating an environment that would help the individual and others to achieve their full potential. *Informativeness* in the Klauss and Bass path analysis depended on being seen as a careful transmitter of information and using frank, open, two-way communications. Similarly, St. John (1983) observed that the credibility of supervisors was enhanced by personal style, frankness, consistency, accessibility, keeping promises, accepting responsibility, and showing interest in others.

Luthans and Larsen (1986) directly observed the communication behavior of 120 managers from five organizational settings. They also gathered self-reports on how the managers communicated. Two dimensions emerged in analyses of the data. Consistent with the relationship between activity and leadership to be discussed in Chapter 6, the first dimension was the extent to which the manager actively communicated, rather than remaining a passive isolate who was drawn into communication activities only when these were necessary to manage con-

flicts. The second dimension involved the extent to which a manager was informal, spontaneous, and oriented toward development, rather than formal and communicative mainly when controlling others with regularly scheduled monitoring.

Competence with Linguistic Forms. It may not be what the leader says, but the way he or she says it. Drake and Moberg (1986) suggested that linguistic form may be more important than linguistic substance in affecting whether attempts to lead are accepted or rejected. Some forms can suppress the subordinates' tendency to calculate the costs and benefits of an exchange. For example, subordinate may be *sedated*. He or she may comply without thinking about the cost when told, "We've just got a last-minute rush order that needs to be filled before we leave tonight." The semantically direct "I want you to fill this rush order" might result in the employees' thinking about the cost of compliance and desiring an inducement for complying. Numerous other hints, prompts, teasing, and semantic indirectness can serve to sedate the subordinate. The leader can avoid responsibility for providing inducements for compliance: "You may find it worthwhile to fix the oil gauge." The leader's language can also be *palliative*. For example, a staff manager, with no way of rewarding line employees for information he requires, may get the information by *hedging*: "This won't take long, but would you locate some good estimates of the prices?"

Quality of Writing. The advent of electronic mail, through which every employee is in instant contact with every other employee's personal computer terminal, suggests that the quality of writing, although truncated, will regain the status for distance communication that it had before the invention of the telephone. The storage and retrieval of transmitted information will also be greatly improved. Nonetheless, oral communication is likely to remain highly important to leading.

Competence in Nonverbal Communication. Nonverbal communication is also important to leadership (Stein, 1975). In investigating the effects of nonverbal and verbal communications among 151 college students on their perceptions of leadership, Gitter, Black, and Fishman (1975) concluded that nonverbal communications could be even more important than verbal communication.

For example, Remland (1984) demonstrated that superiors in videotaped interactions with subordinates would be seen as more considerate (and therefore more satisfying as leaders) if they used nonverbal means to reduce the status differences between themselves and their subordinates. Elsewhere, Remland (1981) pointed out that when nonverbal messages contradicted verbal ones, the listener tended to trust the nonverbal messages more. Thus a manager who talked as if he wanted to share decision making with a subordinate, but looked bored whenever the subordinate spoke, would be regarded as manipulative and insincere. Baird (1977) examined eight categories of nonverbal behavior in 10 discussion groups of five students each. These categories were: (1) head-nodding agreement; (2) head-shaking disagreement; (3) eye contact; (4) facial agreement; (5) facial disagreement; (6) postural shift; (7) gesticulation with the shoulders or arms; and (8) gesticulation with the hands or fingers. A significant relationship was found, in particular, between emergence as a leader and the tendency to gesticulate with the shoulders or arms. Friedman and Riggio (1981) examined the extent to which individuals differed in their nonverbal expressiveness and indicated that those who were more nonverbally expressive were more likely to influence the mood of those who were less nonverbally expressive. Such nonverbal expressiveness was also found to contribute to patients' satisfaction with the interpersonal manners of their physicians (Freedman, DiMatteo, & Taranta, 1980).

Sense of Humor. Sense of humor is the ability to perceive, express, and enjoy what is amusing, laughable, or comical. There is more anecdotal evidence but less empirical research showing that leaders who use humor in communicating to their followers are more successful and effective than those who do not (Crawford, 1994). Some leaders have more of a sense of humor than others and make more use of it in their communications. Humorous communicating evokes a response by contrasting incongruent ideas, by engendering a feeling of superiority over others, by releasing tension, or by dealing with ambiguity in the environment (Hudson, 1979). Laughter is provoked by the unexpected punch line. *Clowning* wits are rated low in influence but high in popularity. *Sarcas-*

tic wits are rated higher in influence but lower in popularity (Gruner, 1965). Humor increases the favorableness of an audience toward the speaker, and makes a speech more interesting, persuasive, and memorable. Self-disparagement may be effective if it is witty, indirect, and based on clever wordplay rather than exaggerated personal defects. Put-downs of others need to be avoided if they offend the values of the listeners. (Munn & Gruner, 1981).

Humor and Effective Leadership. Southwest Airlines looks for a sense of humor in job applicants (Quick, 1993). Individuals with a greater sense of humor reveal traits associated with successful and effective leadership such as self-esteem, emotional stability, extroversion, and sociability (Kuiper & Martin, 1993). Use of humor by the leaders of work groups helps improve morale (Gruner, 1977), cohesiveness (Duncan, 1982), motivation, (Crawford, 1994), creativity and divergent thinking (Czikszentmihalyi, 1996), and productivity (Clouse & Spurgeon, 1995). Humor has alleviated intimidation and stress and encouraged communication (Vinton, 1989).

Kilinski-Depuis and Kottke (1999) correlated 80 subordinates' ratings of their supervisors. They were all employees of an international marketing firm. Their ratings of the sense of humor of their supervisors correlated .48 with their ratings of the supervisors' consideration. Sense of humor was measured by seven modified items drawn from the Situational Humor Response Questionnaire (Lefcourt & Martin, 1986), which assesses how much a person typically responds with mirth and laughter to a wide variety of life situations. Avolio, Howell, and Sosik (1999) tested, in a large financial insurance company, the impact of 115 leaders' use of humor on the productivity of their 322 subordinates. What was measured was the frequency of occurrence by rated subordinates of instances in which the leader "uses humor to take the edge off during stressful periods," "uses a funny story to turn an argument in his or her favor," "makes us laugh at ourselves when we are too serious," "uses amusing stories to defuse conflicts," and "uses wit to make friends of the opposition." Leadership was measured by the Multifactor Leadership Questionnaire (Bass & Avolio, 1997). The effectiveness of the leader was assessed by consolidated unit performance, the extent to which the leader's organizational unit achieved annual goals. Performance appraisals of the leaders also were available. Transformational leadership correlated .56 with a five-item "use of humor" scale. Contingent reward correlated .45 and laissez-faire leadership correlated −.50 with the use of humor. A partial least-squares analysis (PLS) showed that transformational leadership combined with the use of humor correlated highly with the leaders' appraised performance and the consolidated performance of the leaders' unit. But combining humor with contingent reward appeared ineffective.

Consideration. Consideration can be seen in prosocial behavior, such as helping, sharing, donating, cooperating, and volunteering. Such behavior aims to produce and maintain the well-being and integrity of others. Leaders will manifest it by showing leniency in personnel decisions, practicing a considerate style, sacrificing their own interests, and spending time and energy for the good of the group or organization or the individuals within it (Brief & Motowidlo, 1986). The leader who displays prosocial behavior serves as a role model for a good organizational citizen, who complies with the organization's requirements despite personal inconvenience, suggests improvements without personal benefit, and ignores hardships to carry on voluntarily (Smith, Organ, & Near, 1983). Thus probation officers will have little effect on recidivism if they show empathic, warm regard for parolees but fail to demonstrate prosocial values and socially acceptable ways of achieving goals and do not model, encourage, and reinforce noncriminal alternatives (Ross & Gendreau, 1980). A sample of 97 first-line supervisors reported spending an average of 2.5 hours a week discussing personal problems with their subordinates, such as difficulties with coworkers; opportunities for advancement; dissatisfaction with their jobs; and financial, physical, family, and emotional problems. Some supervisors also mentioned problems with sex, alcohol, and drugs. The most common strategies of the supervisors were to offer support, to listen, and to ask questions. In these discussions, the subordinates and supervisors generated solutions and shared personal experiences (Kaplan & Cowen, 1981). From structural and factor analyses of the descriptions of helping behavior by 58 first-line supervisors and their 355 subordinates, Konovsky (1986) found one factor in the helping behavior of supervisors that involved offering support and sympathy and a second factor

that involved assistance in solving problems. Although better-educated superiors were directly helpful, the supervisors' task competence and experience did not make any difference. Overall, the satisfaction of followers was enhanced when their leaders showed that they cared by demonstrating their consideration for the members of their group. Such consideration emerged early in factorial studies of the behavior of leaders (Fleishman, 1951) and has appeared repeatedly in subsequent analyses.

Individuation. Within the immediate group, the interpersonally competent leader can individualize his or her relationships, avoid treating all subordinates alike (Meyer 1980), and discriminate between the more competent and less competent members in the group (Fiedler, 1964). Diffusion of responsibility in group decisions is avoided unless the group decisions serve useful purposes, such as gaining commitment from peripherally involved members. Equity is favored rather than equality—each member may be given equal opportunities, but rewards will be contingent on each individual's contribution to the group's success. Group productivity is enhanced by such individuation (Ziller, 1964). Interpersonally competent leaders are oriented toward the individual development of their subordinates, as well as the development of their team. Morse and Wagner (1978) found that effective managerial behavior provided for the growth and development of both. Assignments are delegated to subordinates to provide such opportunities for development. Competent leaders take on responsibilities as mentors and coaches according to the differential needs of subordinates for guidance and counseling.

Bradford and Cohen (1984) say that the quintessence of "postheroic" transformational managers is their orientation toward developing their subordinates. These managers build teams that share responsibility and visions of the future, as well as support the continuous development of individual skills. In so doing, they enhance the motivation, commitment, and performance of their subordinates. Individualized consideration was one of the transformational leadership factors which emerged from descriptions of leaders by their colleagues and subordinates using the Multifactor Leadership Questionnaire (Bass & Avolio, 1989). Individualized consideration involved showing concern for each subordinate as an individual and attending to the subordinate's development.

This factor consistently correlated highly with subjective and objective measures of the leader's effectiveness (Bass, 1985a; Hater & Bass, 1988; Yammarino & Bass, 1989).

Social Insight, Empathy, and Leadership. Leadership of a group depends, to some extent, on the leader's ability and motivation to estimate accurately the group's attitudes, motives, and current level of effectiveness. As Bass (1960, pp. 167–168) indicated, "It is not enough for a leader to know how to get what followers want, or to tell them how to get what they want. The leader must be able to know what followers want, when they want it, and what prevents them from getting what they want. Empathic success should increase with increased motivation to attend to clues. It should also increase with information available about others' behavior. Two persons may display the same success in guessing the motives of some other members. One estimator may be more apt; the other estimator may be more interested in the question because of momentary situational demands or acquired motives. An alert teacher 'senses' from facial expressions, questions or lack of them, restlessness, and lack of response whether [he or] she is continuing to meet the needs of the student audience. An effective orator or actor requires similar skills."

Many others have offered similar propositions. Wittenberg (1951) emphasized the need-estimating aspect of leadership. That is, the leader of a group must know what the individual members need and then apply the group process so that the members will satisfy these needs. Coyle (1948) suggested that to work with young people, group leaders must understand the various motives that draw the group together, to "find the appropriate form to clothe their collective needs."

For political and organizational leadership, Titus (1950) and J. M. Bums (1978) noted that the leader must be able to choose the group's objectives wisely and forecast the cost of obtaining the objectives, the likelihood of doing so, and the degree to which goal attainment will be satisfying to the members. Lane (1985) suggested that organizational managers should examine their ability to be followers so that they can better understand the feelings and problems of their subordinates. Managers can do this by examining their own role as followers with different bosses.

Leaders should appreciate whether their subordinates

learn from them and whether their subordinates are comfortable sharing problems and confidences with them. They also need to know their subordinates' strengths and weaknesses. In the same vein, Haislip (1986) saw that a leader needs to be sensitive to those aspects of the work experience that illustrate how the organization values its employees' personal goals. Such sensitivity will keep the leader focused on helping to maintain the congruence of the goals of the employees and the organization and, thereby, the employees' commitment. Fielder, Warrington, and Blaisdell (1952) noted the importance of unconscious attitudes in sociometric choice. Deep probes are needed to test whether leaders are better able than nonleaders to diagnose social situations. Empathy is often emotional, intuitive, and unconscious. Projective techniques must be used to study it.

It is expected that leaders will be more insightful. Thus Shartle, Stogdill, and Campbell (1949) found that nominations for "popular leader" were correlated .47 with predictions of "who will be most accurate in estimating group opinion." In a study of 153 supervisors in seven organizations, E. J. Frank (1973) observed that leaders who perceived their roles as requiring sensitivity to others also perceived themselves as being sensitive. Along with this felt sensitivity, the leaders appeared to feel that they were openly accepted by the group and that the working environment was pleasant. Alertness to changing circumstances and shifts in needs was also considered important to leadership (Hollander, 1978).

In all, from the early studies on, it has been thought that insight and empathy give an individual the competence to gain, hold, and maintain the position of leader. In traditional Japan, the head of a group ostensibly made the group's decisions; and once the leader made a decision, it was regarded as the "will of the group" and accepted without challenge. But if one looked more carefully, one saw that the leader had the responsibility of sensing the will of the group in order to understand what was wanted, both intellectually and emotionally. He had to *hara de wakaru* or "understand with his belly" (Kerlinger, 1951). It appears that this is still required of the Japanese manager.

Insight, empathy, and accuracy about the other person appear to be particularly important in international negotiations. The ability to diagnose and understand the motives of others and to predict their subsequent actions accurately separates great statesmen from mediocre politicians. Because of the sentiment against war in Britain and France in 1938, the British prime minister Neville Chamberlain and the French premier Édouard Daladier wanted to believe that Adolf Hitler could be conciliated, regarding the local conflict over the Sudetenland, with goodwill and flexibility. In Winston Churchill's diagnosis, Hilter was using the local situation to destroy Czechoslovakia as a key bastion that was standing in the way of Hitler's plans to conquer Europe. At Munich, Chamberlain and Daladier completely misread Hitler's goals, values, and intentions; Churchill understood them accurately (Tucker, 1981). But the leadership and compliance displayed by all parties at Munich were strongly associated with the orientations of all the key figures to personal predilections, power, and politics.

Insight, Empathy, and Transactional and Transformational Leadership. Insight and empathic competence should be important if the leader is transactional and engages in an exchange relationship with followers. The leader needs to learn what the followers want so that he or she can make the right offers to them for their compliance. But the transformational leader also can build from a stronger base if he or she understands the current needs and concerns of prospective followers. The individually considerate transformational leader must have a sense of the followers' developmental needs and of how the followers' current wishes differ from one another. The inspirational leader has a sense of which appeals will be heard most readily by followers.

Problems with Insight and Empathy. Although insight and empathy have been regarded as important, empirical evidence of the association of these personal traits with leadership is often hard to establish. The data suggest that in comparison with others, leaders do not appear to exhibit a higher degree of generalized insight into the feelings or motivation of followers. Furthermore, various measurement problems complicate the conclusions, and many contingencies force the qualification of results. However, considerable positive evidence has been amassed about the insight of leaders into the feelings of their *immediate* followers and an understanding of the localized situation.

In the most general sense, "empathy" refers to awareness or appreciation, and "insight" refers to an understanding of what others are thinking and feeling about a matter. Empathy is "the ability to walk around in someone else's world" (Kilcourse, 1985, p. 23). President Bill Clinton impressed troubled supporters by saying, "I share your pain." Insight and empathy may be a matter of seeing others in relation to ourselves. But the linkages of empathic ability and social insight to leadership are complicated by the various definitions and ways of measuring empathy and insight.

Generalized Social Insight and Empathy. Empathy and insight can refer either to awareness and understanding of social phenomena at a general level (knowledge of cultural norms and social intelligence) or to understanding the most probable tendencies of prototypical others. History is replete with examples of political leaders whose success depended on their accurate sensing of the moods and desires of their constituencies. Many leaders depend on almost daily public opinion polling and focus groups. Others appear to attend to newspaper columnists, editorials, television anchors, and hosts of talk shows.

Various researchers have developed measures of social insight and empathy at this general level. These measures require participants to estimate the percentage of people in a designated population who will endorse the items on a test of personality, attitudes, or job satisfaction. The participants' accuracy is measured by how well their estimates match the actual endorsement by a sample of the population. Chowdhry and Newcomb (1952), Bell and Hall (1954), Nagle (1954), Trapp (1955), and Fleishman and Salter (1963) found that leaders were more accurate than nonleaders in estimating such responses in a general population. Kerr and Speroff (1951) and Van Zelst (1952) were able to forecast success as a salesman, union leader, and foreman with a brief test that purported to measure individual differences in empathic ability at the general level by the method just described. However, Sprunger (1949); Hites and Campbell (1950); Gage and Exline (1953); Talland (1954); Bugental and Lehner (1958); and Cohn, Fisher, and Brown (1961) did not find leaders to be significantly more accurate than nonleaders in such tested estimations. Along the same lines, Marchetti (1953) found no relation between grocery managers' ability to predict employees' responses on a test of attitudes in general and the managers' efficiency as rated by their superiors. Shartle, Stogdill, and Campbell (1949) reported a slight negative relation between naval officers' popularity as leaders and their tested ability to estimate group opinion in general. Thus decidedly mixed results have been found for the relationship between generalized social insight, generalized empathy, and leadership.

It is even questionable whether generalized empathy exists. Although Cline and Richards (1960, 1961) found low but significant correlations between a variety of different measures of ability to judge the behavior of other persons, Ausubel and Schiff (1955), Bender and Hastorf (1950), and Crow and Hammond (1957) found no support for the hypothesis that there is an ability to predict interpersonal responses in general. For one thing, education, experience, and general intelligence are likely to affect respondents' performance on measures of generalized empathy and insight.

Localized Social Insight and Empathy. Different from generalized insight and empathy are specific perceptual sensitivities at a local level—in a designated group working with specific other members. A considerable array of positive findings supports Stogdill's (1948) conclusion in Chapter 4 that "alertness to the surrounding environment and understanding of 'social' situations are intimately associated with leadership ability." The ability to size up situations differentiated leaders from followers in six pre-1948 studies. Carter, Haythorn, Shriver, and Lanzetta (1951) also found that leaders were able to evaluate situations. Insight into motives, thoughts, feelings, and actions of others was found to characterize leaders in seven pre-1948 studies. Reviews of the literature on localized social insight and empathy generally affirmed the connection between empathy and leadership, although they found that the effects were small and may have been nonexistent or negative in many cases. Thus, for example, after surveying 15 studies that reported 101 results concerning leadership and empathy, R. D. Mann (1959) noted that 74% of the results were positive, but researchers usually were unable to obtain statistically significant positive results in any single investigation.

To illustrate, Williams and Leavitt (1947a, 1947b); G. H. Green (1948); Greer, Galanter, and Nordlie (1954); and Lansing (1957) used sociometric nominations as a basis for studying insight. Group members were asked to nominate other members for leadership and to estimate the ranking that others would ascribe to them. Leaders were found to be more accurate than nonleaders in estimating their own sociometric rank (their esteem or value to the group in the eyes of the other members) or, in some studies, the rank of others. Gallo and McClintock (1962) also found that leaders were more accurate than nonleaders in perceiving their esteem in the group. Furthermore, Fiedler's (1967a) theory of leadership was first formulated around the linkage of empathy to leadership, and one's assumed similarity to others was the main measure of consequence. In studies of basketball teams and surveying teams, Fiedler (1953a, 1953b, 1954a) found that the teams were more effective if their esteemed members, who were likely to be the team leaders, perceived preferred members to differ from rejected members. Fiedler (1954b, 1955, 1959) obtained similar findings for B-29 bomber crews, tank crews, and groups in open-hearth steel shops. The groups were more effective if the crew leaders or supervisors discriminated more distinctly between members with whom they preferred to work and members whom they rejected.

Nagle (1954) reported high correlations between departmental productivity and the ability of departmental supervisors to estimate employees' attitudes. Anderhalter, Wilkins, and Rigby (1952) noted that candidates for the U.S. Marines Officers Candidate School who showed the highest ability to predict other candidates' future effectiveness were likely to make effective company officers themselves. Greer, Galanter, and Nordlie (1954) found leaders of infantry squads to be more accurate than other squad members in their perceptions of the esteem of other members. J. Hogan and Holland (1998) obtained correlations between .45 and .73 with the Hogan Personality Inventory Empathy scale and five criteria of leadership for 25 managers from a large retail firm.

Schrage (1965) reported that accurate perception and interpretation of the environment were more important than the motivation for power or the need for achievement in differentiating successful from unsuccessful entrepreneurs. Jennings (1952a) showed that supervisors who did not understand the behavior of their subordinates felt inadequate and insecure. As their frustration increased, they became less able to obtain cooperation and satisfactory performance from their subordinates. Studies of managers who fail to rise in their organizations find that these managers are unable to understand others' points of view. They are insensitive to others, unable to build a team, and unable to get work done when the work depends on the efforts of others (J. Hogan & R. Hogan, 2002).

Negative Results. On the basis of a survey of managers and their subordinates, Hatch (1962) concluded that the empathic accuracy of the managers had limited practical significance. He found no significant differences between the empathic accuracy of the managers and the superiors' description of the managers as good or poor in maintaining satisfactory relations with their subordinates. Similarly, Jerdee (1964) reported that supervisors' predictions of subordinates' morale were negatively related to the employees' actual morale scores. Andrews and Farris (1967) noted that subordinates' innovation was correlated negatively with their supervisors' effectiveness in planning if the supervisors were sensitive to individual differences, but the correlation was positive if the supervisors were insensitive to differences among people. Williams and Leavitt (1947a) observed that the more successful leaders they studied most underestimated the sociometric status accorded them by other group members. Finally, Shartle, Stogdill, and Campbell (1949) found that nominations for popular leaders were not correlated with errors in estimating group opinion. Likewise, such errors failed to correlate with predictions of who would be most accurate. Although popular leaders were not more accurate than unpopular leaders in estimating group opinion, other group members expected them to be. More often than not, positive or negative results have to be qualified by conditions. Only under particular localized circumstances was one likely to find that a leader was more insightful or empathic than a nonleader. Some of these variations in outcomes, of course, may be due to random error when subjected to a meta-analysis. Nevertheless, successful political leaders can sense what their constituencies want and articulate their needs even without public opinion polls.

Substance of Judgments. Foa (1960) found that workers' predictions of their supervisor's responses to a projective (picture) test were more accurate when the supervisor described the action in the ambiguous picture as positive and focused on the job rather than on interpersonal relations. Holmes (1969) compared leaders' esti-

mates of the frequency of interaction and duration of speech of group members with recordings of the groups' performance. Leaders evaluated the duration of behavior by followers more accurately than the frequency of the behavior.

Specific Relevance. Chowdhry and Newcomb (1952) found that leaders judged group opinion better than nonleaders or isolates, but the superiority of leaders over nonleaders was restricted mainly to issues that were relevant to their specific groups. When matters concerned groups in which they were not leaders, their superiority tended to disappear. Similarly, Northwood (1953) collected facts and opinions from a sample of residents in a housing project. Officeholders were found to be significantly more accurate than informal leaders and followers as judges of fact and opinion, but they were not superior judges of nonrelevant facts and opinion. Greer, Galanter, and Nordlie (1954) emphasized this type of contingent outcome. Hites and Campbell (1950) failed to obtain positive results, because they did not ask for estimations relevant to the members' goals.

Cohesiveness. Since cohesive groups usually involve considerable mutuality of choice among their high-status members, the leadership clique was expected to exhibit higher accuracy about others in the group than the members of lower status. Exline (1960) assigned members to high- or low-congeniality groups to discuss a task and measured the members' accuracy of knowledge of each other's task-relevant and person-relevant opinions. Exline found that only in cohesive groups were the leaders more accurate judges of person-relevant opinions, such as popularity. Lemann and Solomon (1952) also found that the accuracy of interpersonal perception was higher in cohesive than uncohesive groups.

Familiarity. Studies of newly formed groups obtained negative results when they correlated a member's first impressions of others with the member's initial success as a leader (C. B. Bell, 1951; H. E. Hall, 1953). Hatch (1962) found that only if managers felt that they were well acquainted with a subordinate were they able to predict the subordinate's attitudes beyond what would be predicted by chance.

The familiarity of members in a specific group related directly to the members' accuracy in judging each other's life goals. Filella (1971) asked 32 Indian college students in groups of eight members to individually rank their own life goals and then to rank the life goals of each of the other group members. The mean correlations between estimations by others and self-rankings systematically declined linearly with decreasing familiarity, from a correlation of .54 for the raters most familiar with the ratees to .12 for the raters least familiar with the ratees.

Lupfer (1965) recorded group members' interactions in a business game. At the end of each session, each subject indicated, on a questionnaire, a prediction of and a prescription for the behavior of every other member. As the sessions progressed, the members' role behavior tended to conform to prescriptive norms, and the prediction of behavior increased in accuracy. In a reversal of these findings, Browne and Shore (1956) noted that although second-level departmental managers were less close to operating employees than first-level supervisors were, the managers were somewhat more accurate than the supervisors in predicting the employees' attitudes.

Focused Attention. Lundy (1956) administered a scale of values to 52 students who later met in pairs to discuss a problem. Then each partner predicted the responses of the other, using the value scale, both with attention focused on the self and with attention focused on the partner. Lundy found that focusing attention on the partner increased accuracy in predicting the partner's responses.

Assumed and Actual Similarity. Localized social insight and empathy often present a multiple measurement problem. Bass, Burger, et al. (1979) used a model that was first formulated by Cronbach and Glaser (1953). The managers' ability to judge the life goals of specific other managers with whom they had been working in small exercise groups for several days was examined. The procedure was as follows. Participants ranked each of 11 life goals in order of importance to them. Then they ranked the goals in order of importance to each of the other members of their exercise group. Three correlational indexes were calculated. It was assumed that participants generally had an accurate appreciation of their own goals. The indexes were: (1) *Empathy* or accuracy in

judging others—the correlation between a participant's judgments about other members' life goals and the other members' self-judgments; (2) *Projection* or assumed similarity to others—the correlation between the ranking participants assigned to themselves and those they assigned to everyone else in the group; (3) *Homogeneity of the group* or *actual similarity to others*—the correlation of a participant's self-ratings with the self-ratings of each of the other members. In addition to the scoring biases pointed out by D. T Campbell (1955), studies of empathy at the local level are also likely to suffer from the generalized tendency of raters to assume that they are similar to others. Thus, for 1,026 managers in 12 countries, Bass, Burger, et al. found that assumed similarity among the raters averaged .50. But true similarity or homogeneity, evidenced by the average correlation of self-rating among all participants, was only .21. Likewise, Lazar (1953), after a review of eight studies, concluded that in judging the attitudes of groups, people err in the direction of their own beliefs or opinions.

The amount of actual similarity or homogeneity also affected what kinds of outcomes were obtained by Bass, Burger, et al. This finding was consistent with Octet and Silva's (1951) study, which found that the smaller the difference between actual self-descriptions and others' self-descriptions, the smaller the error when pairs of persons predicted each other's responses. Both rationally and empirically we are more accurate about others who happen to be like us because of the general tendency to assume that others are indeed like us. A leader's accuracy may be accounted for by the bias toward assumed similarity and the homogeneity of the leader and the group. In fact, to be a leader of a group, one must usually share many attitudes, values, and goals with the other members (Cartwright, 1951). By definition, the opinions of group members are more strongly influenced by the leaders of the group than by nonleaders. It follows that the forecasts of group opinion made by leaders will be more accurate than estimates made by nonleaders, since the opinions are close to those held by the leaders. Thus, when leadership was defined in terms of influence on a group decision, Talland (1954) demonstrated that leaders were better estimators of final group opinion because it was closer to their own initial opinion. But leaders are not more accurate in estimating opinion before interaction. These confoundings of measurements need to be kept in mind when one considers the correlations obtained between leadership and localized measures of empathy and insight.

Accuracy of Perceptions of Status and Importance of Organizational Position. E. L. Scott (1956) analyzed organizational charts drawn by 696 officers and men aboard 10 submarines in which the status structure was thought to be well defined. He found marked differences in the accuracy of status perceptions of the men on the various ships and among the men in various departments within the same ship. The most frequent type of error was to perceive superiors as peers, peers as subordinates, and persons outside one's department as subordinates in one's department. High-ranking personnel made fewer errors in their perception of superiors and peers, but not in total. The more widely superiors interacted with other persons, the greater was the perceptual error of their subordinates. The greater the disparity between an officer's rank and the level of his position aboard ship, the greater were the perceptual errors of his subordinates. At the same time, the subordinates were able to perceive status relationships more accurately when their superiors retained authority and delegated less. Scott's study pointed to some potent organizational factors that operate to determine the accuracy with which status is perceived in highly structured situations.

Summary and Conclusions

During the third quarter of the twentieth century, situational factors dominated the field. Individual traits and dispositions seemed unimportant. However, after correction, rotation experiments showed that traits were still important in accounting for leaders' behavior. In the last quarter of the century, we had to rethink whether leadership traits and leadership were a consequence of nature or nurture. Rapid advances in genetics, heritability research, and molecular biology suggested that we had to give a lot more attention to nature. Traits of leadership returned to center stage in the study of leadership. Situational effects remained important, but mainly as contingencies. Competence was seen as a matter of task accomplishment and interpersonal relations. Both were fundamental to successful and effective leadership. Task accomplishment involved traits like intelligence and knowledge. Interpersonal competence involved the ability to communicate and to demonstrate, caring, insight, and empathy. Effective leaders needed to sense the needs of their followers and point out ways to fulfill them.

The follow-up of the traits of leadership from before 1970 to after 1970 and into the twenty-first century generally showed renewed continuity and expansion. Competencies to deal with tasks and cognitive abilities were seen in more detail. Task competence results in attempts to lead that are more likely to yield success for the leader and effectiveness for the group. But competence is relative; this suggests that a complete understanding of leader-group relations requires an examination not only of individual differences in competencies, such as intelligence and experience, but of the relevance of the competencies for given situations. Intuition plays an important role in effective management; and leadership, particularly at higher organizational levels, appears to be a consequence of the possession of relevant information based on experience. The true correlation of intelligence with leadership is about .50 across a wide range of situations. Generally, more intelligent people are likely to be more task-competent and emerge as leaders, regardless of the situation. Other personal characteristics also contribute to task competence and leadership in different situations. On the other hand, since task requirements may vary from one situation to another, situational differences will also affect who emerges as a leader. Finally, other contingencies that moderate the relationship between competence and leadership need to be considered. Task competence is not enough. Many bright, able, and technically proficient individuals fail as leaders because they lack interpersonal competence.

Many socioemotional traits affect leadership. They will be discussed more fully in the next several chapters. Traits of character—conscientiousness, discipline, moral reasoning, integrity, and honesty—will be included in dealing with the ethics of leadership. The negative impact on leadership of neuroticism, arrogance, anxiety, depression, and narcissism, rigidity will also be examined. The biophysical traits of physical fitness, stature, hardiness, and energy level will resurface again, along with self-confidence, self-esteem, self-monitoring, self-regulating, and self-efficacy. We will turn next to when and whether active leadership emerges.

6

Activity Level

Active leaders and managers take the major responsibility for decision making when they are directive and consultative, whereas leaders and managers take little or no responsibility when they are inactive and laissez-faire. Various active leadership styles correlate between $-.30$ to $-.60$ with inactive, laissez-faire leadership (Bass & Avolio, 1997). The generally positive correlations between factorially and conceptually distinct styles of leadership will be detailed in chapters 17 through 22. That is, leaders who score high in direction, task orientation, change behavior, and initiation of structure also tend to score high in participation, relations orientation, and consideration. Thus for 112 managers, Jones, James, and Bruni (1975) found that the leaders' supportiveness correlated .64 with an emphasis on goals and .74 with facilitation of work. Likewise, facilitation of interaction correlated .58 with the emphasis on goals and .70 with facilitation of work. Schriesheim, House, and Kerr (1976) found a median correlation for 10 studies of .52 between "consideration" and "initiation of structure" on the Leader Behavior Description Questionnaire Form XII. Farrow, Valenzi, and Bass (1980) reported that the frequency of the leaders' *direction*, as described by over 1,200 subordinates, correlated .26 with the leaders' consultation and .13 with the leaders' *participation*.[1] Errors of leniency and halo effects may be involved in these descriptions. Even so, there is a tendency to describe leaders as being more active or less active on several conceptually distinct dimensions concurrently. This tendency may be due to the real behavior of leaders, as well as to subordinates' perceptual biases.

Leadership infused by a motivation to lead and to manage is opposite to that due to a leader's inclination to use the laissez-faire style. Active leadership is seen in much of McClelland's (1975) Leadership Motive Pattern, discussed in Chapter 7; and in Miner's "motivation to manage," detailed later in the present chapter. Miner (1982) theorized that managers actively engage in maintaining good relations with superiors, competing for advancement and recognition, acting as assertive father figures, exercising power over subordinates, being visibly different from subordinates, and accepting responsibility for administrative details.[2]

Antecedents of Active Leadership

As will be detailed in Chapter 7, McClelland found active leadership to be undergirded by a need for power and an absence of need for affiliation, coupled with an ability to inhibit the need for power. Miner and Smith (1982) inferred that a desire for control and power lay behind the motivation to manage. For Chan and Drasgow (2001), the motivation to lead involved cognitive abilities, values, personality, and attitudes that are augmented by social considerations such as affective identity and norms. According to Locke, one should lead actively for rational and selfish interests; according to Avolio, one should be motivated to lead actively for altruistic reasons (Avolio & Locke, 2002).

Effects of Active Leadership on Followers

Jongbloed and Frost (1985) attributed the differential budgetary growth and success of two Canadian hospital

---

[1] As defined in Chapter 18, *direction* refers only to giving orders with or without explanation. Direction (roman) includes ordering, persuading, and manipulating. *Participation* (italics) refers only to sharing in the decision process. Participation (roman) includes consulting, sharing, and delegating.

[2] Bartol, Anderson, and Schneier (1980) found that during the 1970s, there was an acute reversal of the decline in the motivation to manage of students at Syracuse University and the University of Maryland. They observed that the levels of motivation returned almost to those of 1960. However, the differences in trends in Oregon and Syracuse appear to be due to differences in the training of the scorers of the MSCS (Bartol, Schneier, & Anderson, 1985; Miner, Smith, & Ebrahimi, 1985).

laboratories to the motivation and activity of their directors. The desire of the director of the more successful laboratory "to achieve international recognition for outstanding research was apparent in the energy he devoted to lobbying hospital administrators and Ministry of Health Canada" (p. 102). The other laboratory director was not similarly motivated and did not engage in lobbying.

More activity by leaders, except when it is coercive, is usually associated with greater satisfaction and effectiveness among their followers. Conversely, more often than not, less activity in any of these active styles is negatively related to the performance and satisfaction of the followers. Thus, for instance, the structuring of expectations contributes positively to the productivity, cohesiveness, and satisfaction of the group. This pattern of behavior is the central factor in leadership when leadership is measured by initiation of structure, detailed in Chapter 20. The leader can accomplish these initiatives through *direction* or *participation*, inspiration or consultation, negotiation or delegation. Whatever the style, as long as it is not coercive and autocratic, it must involve the leader taking action. It is doubtful that leaders in most situations can be of positive value to the group's performance, satisfaction, and cohesiveness without this kind of active structuring unless all such structure has already been provided by other means such as self-management, culture, or organization.

Being active in direction, consultation, or both was better than being inactive in both. When data collected by Farrow, Valenzi, and Bass (1980) from 1,300 subordinates and their 340 managers describing the pooled frequency of the direction and consultation of the managers were correlated with the effectiveness of the groups, as seen by both the managers and the subordinates, the correlation with effectiveness (.41) was higher than that obtained for direction (.28) or consultation (.37) alone. Even more extreme, the combined direction-consultation index correlated .61 with satisfaction; consultation alone correlated .52. Bass, Valenzi, Farrow, and Solomon (1975) found overall correlations ranging from .30 to .60 between the behavior of leaders, as seen by their subordinates, and the judged effectiveness of the leaders' work units, regardless of whether the leaders were directive or participative. When *direction*, consultation, *participation*, and delegation were combined, their composite correlated .36

and .61 with effectiveness and satisfaction, respectively. Similarly, to predict increased effectiveness, System 4 participative management was combined with "high performance, no-nonsense goals, orderly systematic goal setting processes, and rigorous assessment of progress in achieving those goals" (R. Likert & J. Likert, 1976). Path analyses reported by R. Likert (1973) demonstrated that managerial leadership, whether task- or relations-oriented, contributed both directly and indirectly to the subordinates' satisfaction and productive efficiency. For large samples, the direct correlations between total leadership, subordinates' satisfaction, and total productive efficiency were .49 and .42, respectively. In addition, total managerial leadership correlated .42 with a good organizational climate, .23 with peer leadership, .27 with a good group process, and directly between .25 and .67 with subordinates' satisfaction and total productive efficiency.

Stogdill (1974) reviewed an array of surveys and experiments, mostly containing concurrent analyses of leader behavior and outcomes, more often than not in temporary, short-term groups and without reference to possible contingent conditions. He concluded that *both* the democratic leadership cluster (participation, relations orientation, and consideration) and the work-related cluster (direction, task orientation, structuring but not autocratic) were more likely to be positively than negatively related to the productivity, satisfaction, and cohesiveness of the group. Participative leadership behavior, as well as leadership behavior that structured followers' expectations, was consistently related to the group's cohesiveness.

As will be seen in Chapter 19, Blake and Mouton (1964) argued that the best leadership is achieved with a 9,9 style concerned both with production and with people. Hall and Donnell (1979) confirmed this contention, showing that the 190 out of 1,878 managers who were the fastest in their career advancement were likely to be high in both task orientation and relations orientation, according to their subordinates. And the 445 managers who advanced most slowly were clearly 1,1 and laissez-faire in style—that is, low in both task orientation and relations orientation. In an experiment with 80 undergraduates, Medcof and Evans (1986) demonstrated that plodders are the least desirable leaders in business—a finding that agreed with Blake and Mouton's argument. Misumi (1985) reported PM leadership, combining above-median performance in both performance and maintenance, was most efficacious in a wide variety of settings compared with below-median PM leadership.

Fleishman and Simmons (1970) concluded that leadership combining the factors of strong consideration and initiation of structure is most likely to optimize a number of criteria of effectiveness for a variety of supervisory jobs. In agreement, Karmel (1978) concluded that the combination of initiation and consideration—the total activity of leaders in contrast to their inactivity—may be the most important dimensions to investigate. A powerful general factor can be produced, if one so decides, by the selection of appropriate factor-analytical routines. It may be that pooling a diversity of decision-making styles for a new measure of generalized leadership activity will be useful.

Caveat: There are some obvious examples in which a group may do better with a less active leader. Leadership activity, as such, does not always guarantee the performance, satisfaction, or cohesion of a group. Highly active but coercive, monopolistic, autocratic leadership will contribute more to a group's dissatisfaction and lack of cohesiveness than to productivity. The qualities of the leadership activity must be taken into account. For the leader, doing something is usually, but not always, better than doing nothing. A calm, steady hand at the tiller may be required rather than an impulsive change of course. Moreover, as will be noted in Chapter 20, activity in two styles may add little more than activity in one style alone.[3]

Not all activity in interpersonal and organizational settings is conducive to successful leadership; nor is successful leadership associated with the generation of any and all activity in oneself and others. For instance, as will be noted in Chapter 7, McClelland's (1985) Leadership Motive Pattern (LMP) includes the tendency of individuals to tell stories about inhibiting activity on the Thematic Apperception Test (TAT). The more relevant question is whether activity will be influential and whether it will necessarily result in the increased performance, satisfaction, and cohesiveness of a group. The answer to this question appears to depend on whether the work-related leadership behavior is autocratic, directive, task oriented,

or structuring and whether the person-related leadership behavior is democratic, participative, relations oriented, or considerate. These determinants are in addition to the contingencies that also may have to be taken into account. The activist admonition—"Lead, follow, or get out of the way"—has to be qualified by adding "with forethought, responsibility, and care." The pressure for action may need to be inhibited. Many a general has been victorious by waiting patiently to be attacked by a more impulsive enemy.

McClelland's (1975) Leadership Motive Pattern (LMP) is high for individuals who score high on the projective Thematic Apperception Test (TAT) in their need for power but who score low in their need for affiliation and, as was just noted, who exhibit impulse control in their projected inhibition of the expression of power. (They are actually less active than they really are driven to be.) A high LMP index was seen to forecast success in management. Thus McClelland and Burnham (1976) scored the TAT responses of managers' needs for power, achievement, and affiliation. They found that successful managers (managers whose subordinates were higher in morale and productivity) wrote TAT stories with "need for power" scores that were above average and with "need for achievement" scores that were higher than the need for affiliation. The stories contained at least moderate levels of activity inhibition. In a follow-up study of 237 AT&T managers, McClelland and Boyatzis (1982) found that although a high need for achievement predicted the success of lower-level managers, the moderate to high need for power, the low need for affiliation, and high scores in activity inhibition predicted the success of most other managers. Progress over 16 years at AT&T correlated an estimated .33 with LMP (McClelland, 1980).

Cornelius and Lane (1984) collected LMP data for managers in a profit-making professionally oriented service organization. The service organization provided instruction in a second language to full-time students. The investigators failed to obtain positive correlations of McClelland's LMP profile of a high need for power and a low need for affiliation with measures of the performance of an administrative job or the subordinates' morale. In fact, they obtained a negative correlation of −.42 of LMP scores against an administrative efficiency index for the lower level of supervisors. Their analyses were weakened by their failure to include an expression for the activity

[3]See Larson, Hunt, and Osborn (1976); Nystrom (1978); and Schriesheim (1982).

inhibition of power in their measurement of LMR. Also, the service organization was a hierarchically arranged group of professionals. However, Cornelius and Lane did find that LMP scores predicted the assignment of managers to more prestigious work centers.

The Motivation to Manage

According to Miner (1965), people differ in their motivation to carry out the roles required of a manager and their success in doing so in a hierarchical organization. Miner used a projective approach—the Miner Sentence Completion Scale (MSCS), a sentence-completion test—in which examinees, without awareness, project their desires by completing incomplete sentences such as "Giving orders . . ."; "Athletic contests . . ."; and "My father . . ." He originated a theory of managerial role motivation, built on role theory, psychoanalytic theory, and the empirical results of Kahn (1956b) and Fleishman, Harris, and Burtt (1955). His theory was directed specifically toward role-taking propensities within the ideal large organization, formalized and rationalized to function bureaucratically. Miner argued that people who "repeatedly associate positive rather than negative emotion" with various managerial role prescriptions are more likely to meet the existing requirements for effectiveness.

Roles and Requisite Motivation

Six managerial role prescriptions were presented by Miner, along with the required motivation for success as a manager in a hierarchical organization: (1) Managers must behave in ways that do not provoke negative reactions from their superiors. To represent their group upward in the organization and to obtain support for their actions, managers should maintain good relationships with those above them. A generally positive attitude toward those holding positions of authority is required; (2) Since a strong competitive element is built into managerial work, managers must compete for the available rewards, both for themselves and for their groups. If they do not, they may lose ground as functions are relegated to lower their status. Without a willingness to complete, promotion is improbable. To meet this role requirement, managers should be favorably disposed toward engaging

in competition; (3) There is a parallel between managerial role requirements and the assertiveness that is traditionally demanded of the masculine role. Both a manager and a father are supposed to take charge, to make decisions, to take such disciplinary action as may be necessary, and to protect others. Even women managers will be expected to follow the essentially masculine pattern of behavior as traditionally defined.[4] A desire to meet the requirements of assertive masculinity will generally lead to success in meeting certain role prescriptions of the managerial job; (4) Managers must exercise power over subordinates and direct their behavior in a manner that is consistent with organizational and personal objectives. Managers must tell others what to do, when necessary, and enforce their words through the appropriate use of positive and negative sanctions. The person who finds such directive behavior difficult and emotionally disturbing will have difficulty meeting this managerial role prescription; (5) Managers must stand out from their groups and assume positions of high visibility. They cannot use the actions of their subordinates as a guide for their own behavior as managers. Rather, they must deviate from their immediate groups and do things that will inevitably invite attention, discussion, and perhaps criticism from those who report to them. When the idea of standing out from the group, of behaving in a different manner, and of being highly visible elicits unpleasant feelings, then behavior appropriate to the role will occur less often than is needed; (6) Managers must "get the work out" and keep on top of routine demands. Administrative requirements of this kind are found in all managerial work, although specific activities will vary somewhat from one situation to another. To meet these prescriptions, a manager must at least be willing to deal with routines and ideally gain some satisfaction from doing so.

Contradictions. As can be seen, Miner did not mince words. He argued that in a typical bureaucratic hierarchy, what is needed for leadership is an authority-accepting, upward-oriented, competitive, assertive, masculine, power-wielding, tough-minded person who will attend to details. In preparing his role prescriptions, he was selective about which facts about leadership he incorporated and which facts he ignored. A positive attitude to-

---

[4]More about this in Chapter 31.

ward authority may characterize authoritarian-submissive behavior. An organization of submissive managers would not seem to promise innovation and effectiveness. Competitive behavior presents many problems for an organization. Managers who are in competition with their peers hide necessary information from each other. They fail to consider the goals of subordinates. Competition means that managers negotiate with their peers instead of solving problems with them. Decisions are based on power, rather than on merit—again, a consequence that is not calculated to add to organizational effectiveness. It is true that visibility may help one's own advancement. However, the concern for such visibility may conflict with good team support from subordinates, who may feel exploited. The stern father image and the willingness and need to use sanctions seem to contradict most of the evidence about the costs of coercion and autocratic leadership. If attention to details means the inclusion of sanctions, and if the manager lacks a sense of priorities, this prescription can easily be overdone.

Despite these contradictions, considerable support for Miner's theory has been amassed for predicting the success of managers in a hierarchical organization. But, as shall be seen, the contradictions are stronger in a professional organization of colleagues in which innovation and creativity are priorities, and where cooperation, open communication, expert power, and helping relationships are paramount. For the professional type of organization, Miner laid out a different set of role prescriptions for leadership, accompanied by a different sentence-completion test (MSCS-Form P) than the one created for assessing managers in a hierarchical bureaucracy (MSCS-Form H).

Measuring the Motivation to Manage in Hierarchical Organizations

MSCS-Form H was used to measure managerial role motivation in bureaucratic organizations (Miner, 1965). It contains 40 items, 35 of which are scored. As was just mentioned, the scale is a projective measure in which examinees complete a list of incomplete sentences such as "Sitting behind a desk, I . . ." A majority of the incomplete sentences refer to situations that either are outside the work environment or are not specifically related to the managerial job. Ordinarily, examinees are unaware

of what is being measured, so they are unlikely to distort their responses to present themselves in a good light as managers. Subscales for the motivation to take each of the prescribed managerial roles can be obtained. For instance, completing the incomplete sentence "When playing cards . . ." with the response, "I always try to win" would contribute to one's score on the competitive games scale. The response "I usually become bored" would do the reverse. A multiple-choice version was developed by Steger, Kelley, Chouiniere, and Goldenbaum (1977), whose total score correlated .68, .38, .56, and .68 with the original MSCS-Form H in different samples. However, a considerable inflation of scores occurred when the multiple-choice format was used. Respondents did not choose the socially undesirable negative alternatives of the kind they ordinarily might produce in response to the open-ended incomplete sentences of the original projective test (Miner, 1977b).

Concurrent Validities. Berman and Miner (1985) obtained results indicating that 75 chief executive and operating officers, executive vice presidents, and group vice presidents who had worked their way upward most successfully through a bureaucratic hierarchy earned significantly higher MSCS scores than 65 lower-level managers of nearly the same age who had not risen as high in the hierarchy and 26 others, including the founder-entrepreneur and his relatives. Earlier, Miner (1965) found that the higher the total scores on MSCS-Form H, the higher the hierarchical level, the performance ratings, and the rated potentials of 81 to 100 managers of research and development (R & D) in a petrochemical firm. Furthermore, the total MSCS scores of 70 department store managers related significantly to the managers' grade levels and potential but not to their rated performance. Likewise, Gantz, Erickson, and Stephenson (1977a) reported that the total MSCS scores of 117 scientists and engineers in a government R & D laboratory related significantly to their peers' ratings of their supervisory potential. For 101 personnel and industrial managers, Miner and Miner (1977) established a significant relation between total MSCS scores and a composite measure of their success, compensation, and positional level. Miner (1977) obtained correlations of .20, .57, and .39, respectively, of MSCS with the performance ratings of 81 R & D managers, 61 oil company managers, and 81 administrators in a large school district. Similar correlations of MSCS scores with levels of position were found by Miner (1977a) for 142 personnel and industrial relation managers and for 395 managers from a variety of firms.

With 82 school administrators in a large city, Miner (1967) found that total MSCS scores were related significantly to their compensation, rated performance, and potential, but not to their hierarchical level. However, hierarchical level in the organization was significantly related to the total MSCS scores of 44 women department store managers (Miner, 1977a) and 50 and 37 textile managers, respectively (Southern, 1976). Two additional analyses reported by Miner (1982a) showed that MSCS scores were higher for those who were at a higher organizational level. The mean score for 22 personnel managers who were vice presidents was 5.7, but the mean score was only 2.4 for 79 personnel managers who were below the vice presidential level. The mean was 6.8 for 49 CEOs, presidents, and group vice presidents, but it was 0.9 for 49 matched managers at lower levels. Other concurrent significant differences that were in line with expectations for the scores on MSCS-Form H and the organizational level of managers were reported for hospital officers (Black, 1981). With samples of students, Miner and Crane (1977) obtained positive findings that related MSCS scores to the promotion of 47 MBA students to management, to the selection of a fraternity president from among 40 candidates (Steger, Kelley, Chouiniere, & Goldenbaum, 1977), and to the choice among 190 candidates for student offices. Miner, Rizzo, Harlow, and Hill (1974/1977) also reported positive findings for undergraduate students in a simulated bureaucratic organization. Finally, Miner and Crane (1981) found a correlation of .48 between the MSCS scores of 56 graduate students in management and the students' tendency to describe their present and planned work as more managerial in nature.

Predictive Validities. Total MSCS scores forecast the rise in organizational level and subsequent performance ratings of 49 to 81 R & D and marketing managers in a petrochemical firm (Miner, 1965). Lacey (1977) found that total MSCS scores were significantly able to predict the promotion to management of 95 scientists and engineers. Lardent (1977) likewise found that the total MSCS

scores of 251 candidates successfully forecast graduation from the U.S. Army Officer Candidate School at Fort Benning. Butler, Lardent, and Miner (1983) were able to do the same for 502 West Point cadets. But Bartol, Anderson, and Schneier (1980) failed to find concurrent differences in motivation to manage among classes of sophomores, juniors, and seniors in business schools; and Bartol and Martin (1982) were unable to find significant changes in the same MBA students in a longitudinal study in which the 232 students were assessed with the multiple-choice form of the MSCS at the beginning of their program and again after graduation. Moreover, unlike the military findings, no relation was found between the students' completion of the MBA program and their MSCS scores, although Bartol and Martin did report that the MSCS scores of 97 of the graduates were a significant predictor of these persons' salaries after graduation. Support for the construct validity of the MSCS as a motivational measure was also obtained, in that Bartol and Martin found correlations with MSCS scores of .26 and .34 respectively, with the students' desired managerial level and the level the students thought it was possible for them to attain.

Validity Contingent on Bureaucratic Hierarchy. Since the role prescriptions were applicable only to traditional bureaucratic hierarchies, Miner (1965) proposed and found that the total scores on MSCS-Form H were unrelated to the success of professionals outside such highly structured organizations. Miner (1977a) failed to find any significant relations between the scores on MSCS-Form H and various criteria of success of 24 to 51 managerial consultants, 49 faculty members at business schools, 36 to 57 school administrators in small and medium-size cities and consolidated districts, and 65 salesmen at an oil dealership (Miner, 1962a, 1962b). More convincing support for this argument was obtained by Miner, Rizzo, Harlow, and Hill (1977), who showed that in simulated low-structure situations, in which 89 students worked on various case projects in small teams of four to seven, scores on MSCS-Form H were unrelated to the students' emergence as leaders. However, in line with Miner's theory, in a high-structure situation in which students chose to work on current problems in assigned positions in a simulated organization with six divisional levels, the total scores on MSCS-Form H of higher-level leaders were highest and the scores of non-leaders and of those who opted to work outside the organization were lowest.

Motivation to Lead in Professional Organizations

Oliver (1982) created an inventory to discriminate reliably between hierarchical and professional organizations; and Miner (1982a) developed MSCS-Form P, another sentence-completion test, to measure professional motivation to deal with success in a professional, in contrast to a hierarchical, organization. The subscales of Form P concern the motivation to acquire knowledge, to act independently, to accept status, to provide help, and to be professionally committed. Motivation on Form P is more likely to correlate with the level and performance of professional leaders than hierarchical leaders. Miner reported correlations of .51, .55, .42, and .53, respectively, with the professional rank, professional compensation, number of journal articles published, and number of books published of 112 members of the Academy of Management. The correlations of such criteria of professional success with the corresponding scores for the motivation to manage on Form H were, respectively, .02, .08, .01, and .09.

Motivation for Entrepreneurial Leadership

The motivation to manage on MSCS-Form H failed to relate to the desire of 38 entrepreneurs in Oregon to expand. Consequently, Form T was constructed to assess the motivation for entrepreneurial leadership: the motivation to achieve, to take risks, to seek the results of performance, to innovate, to plan, and to set goals. On Form T, the mean for 23 entrepreneurs with faster-growing firms was 11.9; the mean was 0.5 for 28 entrepreneurs with slow-growth firms and 2.0 for nonentrepreneurs (Smith & Miner, 1984).

Critique. A number of difficulties emerge from Miner's work. Even restricting Miner's motivation to manage to traditional hierarchies fails to account for the contrast between his prescriptions for the managerial role and those, say, of most behavioral scientists who favor democratic, participative, relations-oriented, considerate leadership. Indeed, conspicuously absent from Miner's results are criteria for subordinates' satisfaction, produc-

tivity, cohesiveness, and growth. As was noted earlier, the satisfaction of subordinates may be strongly associated with considerate and relations-oriented leadership behavior, but the leaders' superiors may evaluate the leaders more favorably for their emphasis on production and their task orientation. As will be seen in Chapter 18, one leadership style—negotiation or manipulation—was related to the salary levels attained by managers (usually determined by their superiors) adjusted for age, seniority, education, function, and so on. Yet negotiative or manipulative behavior was the one leadership style that was likely to be negatively related to subordinates' satisfaction and subordinates' ratings of the effectiveness of work groups.

Thus individual managers may be most successful in hierarchical organizations if they pursue the role prescriptions set forth by Miner. However, in the absence of evidence, one can only guess, given R. Likert's (1977b) long-range studies (see Chapter 17), that their organizations are likely to suffer from the consequences of subordinates' grievances, absences, turnover, and dissatisfaction, as well as from vertical and lateral blockages and filtering of communication. Nevertheless, Miner may be performing an extremely important service in pointing out the fundamental conflict, noted by Argyris (1964a) and Culbert and McDonough (1980), among others, between the integration of the long-term objectives of the individual manager and those of the organization.

In the twenty-first century, to survive and prosper, even the largest of hierarchical organizations require flexibility in meeting the challenges of rapidly changing technologies and markets. Professional-like concerns for commitment, loyalty, and involvement have become increasingly important. Entrepreneurial (or intrapreneurial) attitudes and behavior are also important for the organization's members. It would seem that some complex combination of what is being measured by MSCS Forms H, P, and T would become increasingly relevant in the healthiest of organizations.

Inactive or Laissez-Faire Leadership

Bradford and Lippitt (1945) conceived of laissez-faire leadership as descriptive of leaders who avoid attempting to influence their subordinates and who shirk their supervisory duties. Such leaders are inactive and have no confidence in their ability to supervise. They bury themselves in paperwork and stay away from their subordinates. They may condone "license." They leave too much responsibility with subordinates, set no clear goals, and do not help the group to make decisions. They let things drift. Laissez-faire leaders are indifferent to what is happening. They avoid getting involved in making decisions and taking stands on issues. They divert attention from hard choices and abdicate responsibility. They "refuse to take sides in a dispute, are disorganized in dealing with priorities and talk about getting down to work, but never really do" (Bass, 1998). Fortunately, only a minority of elected or appointed leaders consistently abdicate their responsibilities. Although this inactivity is the least frequently observed by colleagues and subordinates (Bass & Avolio, 1989), many leaders still reveal it in varying amounts. Followers may replace such leaders in influence.

To some degree, the perception of leaders' passivity may be due to the motivation of their subordinates. For instance, Niebuhr, Bedeian, and Armenakis (1980) found that among 202 nursing personnel at a Veterans Administration hospital, those subordinates who were motivated toward self-goals of achievement, power, and independence perceived their leaders to be less active. Those with strong other-directed goals, such as a need for affiliation, saw their leaders as more active.

Presidential Examples. Ronald Reagan was one of the highest presidents and Lyndon Johnson was one of the lowest presidents in respect to inactivity. Jimmy Carter displayed such leadership only for some issues. Johnson and Carter immersed themselves in the details of what their administrations had to do. Yet although Carter ordinarily was greatly involved in detail, particularly in the creation of his programs, he was much less active in implementing voluntary wage and price guidelines, a macroeconomic strategy that a president can initiate by himself. Carter's lack of much leadership in this regard contrasted with Johnson's style: Johnson was much more willing to use his presidential powers of persuasion and bargaining with business and labor. Carter was more restricted in his efforts. Johnson would have earned a low rating as a laissez-faire leader on this issue, whereas Carter would have earned a higher one. On many matters, Ronald Reagan was much more inactive as president

than either Carter or Johnson. Reagan's subordinates usually had free rein to proceed as they thought best. The many scandals that surfaced during and after his administration could be attributed in part to his hands-off style and to poor choices by his subordinates. Still, in some matters he was highly active. He promoted activist interventions in economic policy such as cutting taxes and greatly increasing military spending. He strongly espoused less government intervention in domestic affairs. To take another example, whereas Theodore Roosevelt was a bundle of energetic activity, Calvin Coolidge slept 11 hours a day (Barber, 1985).

Differences from Other Leader Behavior

Inactive leadership should not be confused with empowering, delegation, management by exception, or granting autonomy to subordinates. Unlike a laissez-faire leader, an *empowering* leader sets boundaries within which subordinates are given discretion to act as they think best. The empowering leader follows up with resources, support, and caring. Delegation implies a leader's active direction of a subordinate to take responsibility for some role or task. The active *delegative* leader remains concerned and will follow up to see if the role has been enacted or the task has been successfully completed. The leader who practices *active management by exception* allows the subordinate to continue on paths that the subordinate and the leader have agreed on—until problems arise or standards are not met, at which time the leader intervenes to make corrections. In *passive management by exception*, the leader intervenes only if agreements are not kept or subordinates' performance falls below standards. This is less active leadership but still not laissez-faire.[5] More active leaders monitor their subordinates' performance, searching for discrepancies relative to accepted standards; more passive leaders wait for the discrepancies to be called to their attention (Hater & Bass, 1988). When *autonomy* is granted by a leader, subordinates are free to make many of the decisions affecting themselves and their assignments, but they work within

[5]Yammarino and Bass (1989) found that the correlations with laissez-faire leadership are negative when the manager actively searches for exceptions and are positive when the manager gets involved only when exceptions are called to his or her attention. Overall management by exception correlated .44 with passive leadership and .16 with active leadership (Bass, 1985a).

constraints set by the leader, the organization, and the environment.

Measuring Laissez-Faire Leadership

The Multifactor Leadership Questionnaire (MLQ 5X; Bass & Avolio, 1997)—one of several such instruments—contains a 10-item scale that directly assesses laissez-faire leadership. Examples of items on the laissez-faire scale include "Only tells me what I have to know to do my job"; "Avoids making decisions"; and "If we don't bother him/her, he/she doesn't bother us." Respondents indicate from 0 = "never" to 4 = "frequently, if not always" how often the focal leader displays each behavioral item. The scale total correlates .88 with a higher-order factor of passive leadership and −.11 with a higher-order factor of active leadership. A factor analysis of the 10 MLQ items disclosed that two factors rather than one factor were needed to account for the 10 items. Six of the items were laissez-faire, as expected, such as "Absent when needed." But the emergent second factor of three items dealt with empowering, e.g, "Avoids telling me how to perform my job." In a follow-up Italian sample of 1,053 MLQ managers rating their immediate superiors, the second empowering factor could again be extracted (Bass, 1998).

Correlates of Laissez-Faire Leadership

As expected, laissez-faire scores correlated negatively with various measures of transformational leadership. For 1,006 respondents' descriptions of their leaders on scales of transformational leadership, correlations were as follows: charisma, −.56; individualized consideration, −.55; intellectual stimulation, −.47; and inspirational leadership, −.49. Correlations are similarly negative with contingent reward and with active (but not passive) management by exception. Van Loan (1994) obtained similar findings from 585 MLQ ratings by the subordinates of 83 supervisors, managers, and executives in a large public telecommunications utility.

Antecedents of Laissez-Faire Leadership

Personal Predispositions. The tendency to be an inactive, absent, or avoidant leader was predictable from several personality traits. Makiney, Marchioro, and Hall

(1999) found for 69 undergraduates in 20 groups that MLQ laissez-faire scores were negatively correlated with "Big Five" agreeableness (−.25) and extroversion (−.31) as well as with self-schemata of dedication (−.31) and social influence (−.24). McCroskey (1977) conceived the notion of *communication apprehension* (CA) as a personality trait of fear and anxiety to describe stage fright, shyness, and reticence. CA inhibited verbal communication with others even when such communication was needed in responsible positions of authority. Verbal output was low (McCroskey & Richmond, 1979). A 20-item instrument was provided to assess CA by Scott, McCroskey, and Sheehan (1978). It was expected that some laissez-faire leaders would suffer from CA. In the same vein, Hogan and Hogan (2002) postulated an avoidant personality who fears failure and being criticized. The avoidant personality is cautious, detached, introverted, indecisive, conforming, and irrational. I would expect that an avoidant personality in a leadership role would be an inactive leader.

Situational Circumstances. A previously highly active manager can become inactive, avoiding taking any new initiatives, after learning that he or she is going to be transferred to another division or relocated in another country. Such leadership inactivity can be endemic in an organization with rigid boundaries between departments and individuals. Interdepartmental communications may be limited to infrequent e-mail and memos. Contacts may remain superficial and unimportant (Heuerman, 1999). Among 6,359 Roman Catholic priests, sisters, and brothers who responded to an MLQ survey, those in contemplative orders rated themselves highest (2.42) in laissez-faire leadership. Next highest (2.21) were those in mendicant orders. Lowest (2.08) were those in apostolic orders (Nygren & Ukeritus, 1993). Conversely, less inactivity would be expected among American managers compared with nationals from many other countries, because of the American cultural bias for action (Peters & Waterman, 1982). Van Loan (1994) found significant negative correlations in a public telecommunications utility company between MLQ (5X) laissez-faire scores of 83 executives, middle managers, and supervisors and organizational culture. The cultural variables had to do with humanism, achievement, affiliation, and self-actualizing. They were measured by Cooke and Lafferty's

Organizational Culture Inventory. Passive management by exception and laissez-faire leadership correlated positively with more dismissals of employees.

Effects of Inaction and Laissez-Faire Leadership

Research Beginnings. Democratic and autocratic leadership[6] were compared with the laissez-faire leadership of adults who were instructed how to lead boys' clubs (Lewin, Lippitt, & White, 1939; Lippitt, 1940a). Laissez-faire leaders gave group members complete freedom of action, provided them with materials, refrained from participating except to answer questions when asked, and did not make evaluative remarks. This behavior was in contrast to that of autocratic leaders, who displayed a much greater frequency of order giving, disrupting commands, praise and approval, and nonconstructive criticism. It also contrasted with the behavior of democratic leaders, who gave suggestions and stimulated the boys to guide each other. The groups were less well organized, less efficient, and less satisfying to the boys under laissez-faire conditions than under democratic conditions. The work was of poorer quality, less work was done, and there was more play, frustration, disorganization, discouragement, and aggression under laissez-faire leadership than under democratic leadership. When groups of boys were required to carry out various projects under highly laissez-faire leadership, they felt a lack of organization to get things done and did not know where they stood. When an autocratic leader was followed by a laissez-faire leader, the group exhibited an initial outburst of aggressive, uncontrolled behavior. This form of behavior subsided during the second and third meetings. Similar outbursts were not observed after the transition from laissez-faire to other forms of leadership. Although it did not stimulate as much aggression as the autocratic condition did, laissez-faire leadership was disliked because it was accompanied by less sense of accomplishment, less clarity about what to do, and less sense of group unity. The investigators (Lippitt & White, 1943; White & Lippitt, 1960) concluded that laissez-faire leadership resulted in less concentration on work and a poorer quality of work than did democratic and autocratic leadership. There was less general satisfaction with laissez-faire leadership

than with the democratic style, but somewhat more satisfaction with laissez-faire than with the autocratic style that was employed in this study. Subsequent research suggested that the satisfaction of followers will be lower under laissez-faire leadership than under autocratic leadership if the latter is nonpunitive, is appropriate for the followers' levels of competence, or is in keeping with the requirements of the situation.

Effects on Productivity, Satisfaction, and Effectiveness. Laissez-faire leadership has been consistently found to be the least satisfying and least effective management style. The original observations of Lewin, Lippitt, and White have been supported in a variety of survey and experimental investigations of the impact of laissez-faire leadership on subordinates' productivity and attitudes. Pelz (1956) reported that the laissez-faire pattern of leadership was negatively related to productivity in a research organization. In a study of railroad-section groups, Katz, Maccoby, Gurin, and Floor (1951) found that the work groups were unproductive if their supervisors avoided exercising the leadership role and relinquished it to members of the work group. These supervisors also did not differentiate their role from the role of worker. Like their subordinates, they engaged in production work rather than spend their time in supervisory functions. Berrien (1961) studied groups that differed in their adaptation to changes in work. Poorly adapted groups felt little pressure from their leaders and appeared to attribute their poor performance to lax discipline.

In an experiment by Murnighan and Leung (1976), undergraduate participants who were led by uninvolved leaders were less productive, in terms of the quality and quantity of the problems they solved, and less satisfied in comparison with participants who were led by involved leaders. Argyris (1954) conducted a case study in a bank in which the management recruited supervisors who were interested in security and predictability, disliked hostility and aggression, and wanted to be left alone. The bank's recruitment policy fostered in employees a norm of low work standards and unexpressed dissatisfaction.

Watson (1993) collected 47 evaluations of 10 radio stations and the MLQ laissez-faire scores of the station managers. The mean laissez-faire scores of the managers was 2.45 at the five poorer stations but 1.88 at the five better stations. The expected negative correlations of laissez-

[6]See Chapter 17.

faire leadership with the effectiveness of outcomes and subordinates' satisfaction with the leadership generalized across different kinds of leaders, across different kinds of situations, and for outcomes with both soft and hard data. Thus correlations ranging from −.29 to −.60 were reported by their subordinates for 49 division heads, 58 production managers, 75 project leaders, 28 religious ministers, 9 vice presidents, 38 midlevel managers, 186 junior naval officers, and 318 senior naval officers between the laissez-faire leadership of their leaders and the leaders' contribution to the effectiveness of their organizations (Bass & Avolio, 1989). Comparable negative correlations were found between laissez-faire leadership and superiors' appraisals of the performance and promotability of business managers (Hater & Bass, 1988) and naval officers (Yammarino & Bass, 1990), and with financial outcomes of simulated businesses (Avolio, Waldman, & Einstein, 1988). In the same way, Arvonnen (1995) established for Swedish workers in two plants that job satisfaction and sense of well-being were lower if their supervisors were rated by the workers as laissez-faire leaders. In the same way, Antonakis (2000) obtained the comparable negative correlations of the MLQ laissez-faire scores of 19 faculty members in 36 classrooms from ratings of 584 students at an international center in Switzerland, as follows: course evaluation, −.22 faculty member's skills, −.30, and faculty member's patience and accessibility, −.31.

Military Example. The negative effects of laissez-faire leadership are most pronounced in military commands. The Crimean War has been regarded as the most ill-managed in British history. The commander in chief, Lord Raglan, had no previous experience of command. Five of the seven members of his staff, known as the "nest of noodles," were his blood relatives. Raglan's incompetence was matched his by inactivity as a leader. His staff avoided troubling him with details and made light of possible difficulties. He was aloof and an extreme introvert who avoided direct contact with his men. (He must have had a bad case of oral communication apprehension.) "He could hardly bear to issue an order" (Dixon, 1976, p. 39). His one order before the successful battle of Alma was of little consequence, and the disaster of the charge of the Light Brigade into the Russian cannon batteries at Balaklava was partly due to his ambiguous order. He permitted his commander of cavalry, Lord Cardigan, to live separated from his troops every night on a private yacht and take up valuable Balaklava harbor space. Raglan was so confident that Sebastopol would be captured before the winter of 1854 that he made no plans to house and maintain his troops on high ground above the city. There was no issue of fuel or stores, and 35% of his army strength was lost over the winter due to exposure, malnutrition, and cholera. Raglan took no steps to ease the hardship of his troops, which he could have done if he had been concerned about their welfare and morale. After the first defeat in 1855 in the effort to scale the walls of the fortress at Redan, "Raglan's army had no illusions as to the incompetence of their general and his staff.... The plans . . . turned out to be so execrably bad that failure was inevitable. Others described the battle as mismanaged, botched, bungled and a disgracefully childish failure" (Dixon, 1976, pp. 48–49).

Other Effects. Before self-management (with shared leadership) was conceived in the 1970s, Arensberg and McGregor (1942) wrote a case study of an engineering department without supervisors. A management committee approved the department's plans and checked its progress. The management considered this arrangement to be ideal for creative work. The employees, however, felt insecure and constrained in this overly permissive environment. Farris (1972) demonstrated that the less-innovative of 21 scientific groups at the National Aeronautics and Space Administration had less peer and managerial leadership. In addition, the leadership of these less-innovative groups was less task or relations oriented and less consultative or participative. Baumgartel (1957) studied directive, laissez-faire, and participative patterns of leadership behavior. Group members under laissez-faire leadership reported more isolation from the leader and less participation in decision making than those under directive leadership. These results suggested that laissez-faire leadership lessened the cohesiveness of the group members. Makiney, Marchioro, and Hall (1999) noted that in 20 student task groups, less task-facilitation was reported if the leadership was rated laissez-faire. Without "leadership engagement"—that is, if the leader's involvement was limited and the leader lacked commitment—Jaffe and Scott (1998) felt that re-engineering programs were doomed to failure.

Kidd and Christy (1961) studied three patterns of behavior: laissez-faire, active monitoring, and participative leadership. They found that although the speed of processing work was greatest under laissez-faire leadership, there was much less avoidance of errors, particularly in comparison with active-monitoring leadership. Aspegren (1963) compared laissez-faire, directive, and participative patterns of leadership and found that laissez-faire leadership was associated with lower task motivation and lower satisfaction with superiors. Similarly, W. S. MacDonald's (1967a, 1967b) study of three styles of leadership (laissez-faire, dominant, and democratic) in the Job Corps found that laissez-faire leadership was associated with the highest rates of truancy and delinquency and with the slowest modifications in performance. Wehman, Goldstein, and Williams (1977) reported results from an experiment in which four leadership styles were varied to study their effects on 80 undergraduates' individual risk-taking behavior in group settings and the shift in risk-taking behavior when the responsibility for making decisions moved from the individuals to groups. They found that the shift in such behavior was more likely to occur in "laissez-faire-led" groups and "no-designated-leader" groups than in groups led by a democratic or autocratic leader.

Boss (1978) studied seven top-level administrative staffs from selected public agencies who engaged in a confrontation team-building program for six days. The only group that showed growth, according to subjective pre-post measures, was the group in which the chief executive officer (CEO) was present. The other six groups, in which no CEO was present, either retrogressed or did not change. This finding was consistent with the failures reported in organizational development efforts elsewhere, which were attributable to the lack of support from the CEO (Boss & McConkie, 1976) or the inability of the CEO to understand the objectives and processes of organizational development (Derr, 1972). This was consistent with 360 degree findings by Tsui, Ashford, St. Clair, et al. (1995) that ineffectiveness resulted when 410 managers failed to exert extra effort, failed to explain decisions, and avoided responsibilities.

Effects of Supervisory Lack of Concern for Performance and Maintenance

Misumi (1985) provided a great deal of indirect evidence that a leader's lack of active concern for subordinates' performance and for the maintenance of relations (combined pm leadership) was consistently worse for organizational outcomes than active PM leadership (that is,(P) (P)erformance-oriented or (M) (M)aintenance-oriented leadership, where p and m signify below median rating and P and M signify above median rating). For example, Misumi reported that the annual accident rate per 100 of Nishitetsu bus drivers for a three year period was 79.1 if the bus drivers were supervised by pm dispatchers; it was 44 to 52 per 100 if the dispatchers were P, M, or PM. Similarly, Misumi found that the job satisfaction of 2,257 employees in 186 Mitsubishi work groups was above average in 28% of the pm-led groups but above average in 37 to 73 percent of the P-, M-, or PM-led groups. A similar pattern emerged for the employees' satisfaction with the company.

Furthermore, the adequacy of communication was 14.7 under pm leadership and 16.0 to 17.5 under P, M, and PM leadership, respectively. The rated performance was high in only three of 92 squads in a bearing manufacturing firm led by pm supervision, but it was high in 10, 11, and 16 of P, M, and PM squads. Similar results with regard to productivity were obtained in surveys in other industrial companies (coal mining, shipbuilding, tire manufacturing, and automobile manufacturing). These surveys also found that regardless of the industry, pm leadership ranked last in relation to the productivity of groups, in comparison with P, M, and PM leadership. Only 6% of 883 pm engineering project managers were found to be successful, in contrast to 25, 16, and 52 percent of P, M, and PM project managers, respectively. Among 967 governmental employees, the measures of morale were uniformly lowest under the pm leadership of section chiefs than under the P, M, and PM leadership of such chiefs. The same pattern held for the leadership of Japanese schoolteachers, according to their pupils, and for children's reports about the consequences of their parents' pm, in contrast to P, M, and PM leadership for the children's understanding, compliance, pride, intimacy, and respect. Misumi (1985, pp. 251–259) also reported the results of a Japanese experiment in which for groups that were high in motivation to achieve, the highest productivity occurred with PM supervisors. When the motivation to achieve was low, P-type leadership alone generated the most productivity. But regardless of the group's motivation to achieve, productivity was lowest with PM supervisors.

Subordinates' Autonomy and Laissez-Faire Leadership

Subordinates favor autonomy. Laissez-faire leadership provides autonomy. Laissez-faire leadership is dissatisfying to subordinates. Is this a contradiction? Freedom is a mixed blessing. If it means anarchy—an absence of control of oneself or others; an absence of needed organizational sanctions; the concentration of organizational control at the bottom so that individual goals take precedence over organizational goals; and an unregulated, leaderless, competitive marketplace for resources within the organization in which all the members are trying to maximize their own self-interests—it is likely to generate organizational ineffectiveness (Miner, 1973; Price, 1968; Tannenbaum, 1968).

If freedom implies the lack of systematic processes in problem solving, it will also result in ineffectiveness of outcomes. Thus when Maier and Maier (1957) experimented with discussions under free and more systematic styles of leadership, they found that free discussion produced decisions of lower quality than systematic, controlled, step-by-step discussion. They also noted that freer approaches to problem solving were less effective and less satisfying and yielded less commitment from participants than did systematic problem solving. Thus, when Maier and Solem (1962) compared 50 free-discussion groups with 96 groups of four participants each who used problem solving in systematic steps, the quality of the solutions was likely to be lower in the free-discussion groups than in the systematic groups. Only 12% of the free-discussion groups created integrated solutions that met the criteria of success, whereas almost half the systematic groups did. Maier and Thurber (1969) reported similar results.

Nonetheless, evidence can be mustered to support the contention that employees who feel a great deal of freedom to do their work as they like tend to be more satisfied and productive. When Morse and Reimer (1956) arranged for the authority of operative employees in two departments to be increased to strengthen the employees' autonomy, they found that both satisfaction and productivity increased. O'Connell (1968) changed the responsibilities and behavioral patterns of first-level supervisors in an insurance company. Even though the supervisors became bogged down in paperwork to a greater extent than was expected, sales improved and insurance

lapse rates declined to some degree. Meltzer (1956) reported that scientists are most productive when they have freedom to control their research. Pelz and Andrews (1966a, 1966b) studied scientists and engineers in several laboratories. They found that the most effective scientists were self-directed and valued freedom, but that these scientists still welcomed coordination and guidance from other members of the organization. Similar results were reported by Weschler, Kahane, and Tannenbaum (1952) and by Tannenbaum, Weschler, and Massarik (1961) for two divisions of a research laboratory. Indik (1965b) studied 96 organizations of three types and found that workers' freedom to set their own pace of work was associated with productivity and satisfaction with their jobs. Trow (1957) reported that experimental groups with high degrees of autonomy provided greater satisfaction to members than groups in which members were dependent on a centralized structure. March (1955) analyzed patterns of interpersonal control in 15 primitive communities and found that productivity was related to the degree of the groups' autonomy. In A. K. Rice's (1953) study of a weaving shed in India, a type of reorganization that gave workers greater autonomy resulted in increased efficiency and decreased damage.

Effective Autonomy. Laissez-faire leadership does not imply effective autonomy for subordinates. Laissez-faire leadership is detrimental to the performance of subordinates, yet the autonomy of subordinates enhances the subordinates' performance. The reconciliation comes in considering what subordinates need to do their job well. If the subordinates are skilled, professional, or self-starting salespeople, they may need consultation, *participation*, or delegation, with the *directive* boundary conditions specified by the leader, the organization, or even the task itself. Within these boundaries, the leader should permit the already competent and motivated subordinates to complete their work in the manner they think best. This kind of leadership, paradoxically, requires that the leader exercise authority to permit such freedom of action (Bass, 1960). Active follow-up by the leader is also important because it provides evidence that the subordinates' performance is as expected and shows the subordinates that the leader cares about what they are doing. This type of leadership is not related in any way to laissez-faire leadership, in which the leader does nothing unless asked by colleagues and even then may procrastinate or fail to respond. The laissez-faire leader is inactive, rather than reactive or proactive. He or she does not provide clear boundary conditions; may work alongside subordinates; may withdraw into paperwork; and avoids, rather than shares, decision making. Under this type of leadership, subordinates do not feel free to carry out their jobs as they see fit; instead, they feel uncertain about their own authority, responsibilities, and duties. Results reported by Farris (1972) support this distinction between working under laissez-faire leadership and being provided with freedom. In a study of 21 research teams, Farris found that the provision of freedom to subordinates was highly related to innovation when the leaders preceded their decision making consult with their subordinates. But when supervisors made little use of consultation beforehand, their provision of freedom was uncorrelated with innovation by their subordinates.

Further indirect support comes from a review of leaderless groups by Desmond and Seligman (1977). In the 28 studies that were reviewed, groups with more intelligent participants obtained positive results and were likely to be more highly structured by specially prepared audiotapes, preprinted instruction, and instrumented feedback of group opinion, which substituted for the missing leaders. That is, the freedom of the leaderless group could result in productivity if the participants had the competence and information to deal with the situation and obtained the necessary instructions to clarify the boundary conditions within which they could carry on.

What About Delegation, Management by Exception, and Participation? The contrary consequences on the effectiveness of subordinates of the subordinates' freedom and autonomy on the one hand and the ineffectiveness of laissez-faire leadership on the other hand reside to some extent in the confusion of laissez-faire leadership with the practice of delegation, management by exception, and participative leadership. Although delegation and active management by exception are not as satisfying or effective as more active leadership, they nevertheless may contribute to the effectiveness of subordinates in some kinds of organizations, such as the military. This is unlike passive management by exception, which is more like laissez-faire leadership in its effects, and forms a factor of passive leadership with the latter (Bass & Avolio, 1997).

The inactive laissez-faire leader, unlike a leader who delegates, does not delineate the problem that needs to be solved or the requirements that must be met. The inactive laissez-faire leader, unlike a leader who practices management by exception, does not search for deviations from standards or intervene when deviations are found. The inactive laissez-faire leader, unlike a participative leader, does not engage in extended discussions with subordinates to achieve a consensual decision.

The inactivity of laissez-faire leaders—their inability or reluctance to accept responsibility, give directions, and provide support—has been consistently negatively related to productivity, satisfaction, and cohesiveness. Sheer energization, drive, motivation to succeed, and activity are likely to be correlated with successful leadership and influence.

Summary and Conclusions

This chapter began by looking at how some personality traits, such as energy level and assertiveness, contribute to one's attempts to lead, participate, interact, and emerge as a leader. In turn, the emergence of a leader is sustained by its positive consequences. Members of a group who possess information that enables them to contribute more than other members to the solution of the group's task tend to emerge as leaders. However, a would-be leader who is overloaded with information may become handicapped.

Observational studies have identified several patterns of leader behavior that were not anticipated by the trait theorists. Emergent leaders in experimental and in natural groups tend to be valued because their spontaneity is contagious and they stimulate spontaneity in others. They widen the field of participation for others and expand the area of the group's freedom to make decisions and to act. They protect the weak and underchosen, encourage participation by less capable members, are tolerant of those who deviate, and accept a wide range of personalities of members.

Leaders and managers need to empower themselves to shape their work environment. The simple fact that active, energetic, assertive people are more likely than the "silent majority" to influence the course of events around them makes it difficult to accept the notion that leadership is a phantom of our imagination. The data are compelling. Leaders and managers need to be active, not passive. But merely being active is only a small part of the total explanation of who emerges and succeeds as a leader. Managers' successful advancement depends on the motivation to manage, but it needs to be assessed differently in hierarchical and professional organizations. Theory and evidence were presented that contained the seeds of two propositions: (1) to emerge as a leader, one must be active in attempting to lead, and (2) to succeed and remain acceptable to others as a leader, the leader must exhibit competence. This chapter concentrated on the first proposition and indicated how it needs to be qualified.

Uniformly, laissez-faire leaders are downgraded by their subordinates. Productivity, cohesiveness, and satisfaction suffer under such leadership. But laissez-faire leadership should not be confused with delegation, empowerment, or granting autonomy to subordinates. Effective autonomy can enhance subordinates' performance. Freedom of action is usually conducive to innovation by subordinates. In contrast to laissez-faire leadership, active and responsible assertiveness among subordinates may be required. Whether leaders are active or passive may depend on the issues and circumstances, not just their own personal predilections. For example, a sharp increase in laissez-faire leadership may occur when leaders are notified that their positions are being eliminated or that they are to be transferred in the near future. These situational issues, as they affect leadership and management, will be addressed in Chapters 26 through 30. The antecedents and consequences of authoritarianism, Machiavellianism, and power orientation in the personality of the emergent leader will be considered next, in Chapter 7.

Authoritarianism, Power Orientation, Machiavellianism, and Leadership

Many seek power and depend on their use of power, rather than on their competence to lead (Jongbloed & Frost, 1985). It would seem reasonable to expect that those who strongly endorse the exercise of power and authority in dealing with subordinates would be motivated to lead. But the authoritarian personality, or syndrome, should not be confused with the overt exercise of authority (Christie & Cook, 1958). Similarly, the personal motivation to gain and hold power is not the same as having power to exercise. Nevertheless, Pinnell (1984) found that compared with leaders in positions that lack power and authority, leaders in positions of power and authority were more likely to perceive power as good. Thus when Pearson and Sanders (1981) conducted a survey of appointed career and political state executives in seven U.S. states using a questionnaire that contained six questions about authoritarianism, submissiveness, conventionality, power, and toughness, they found that the state executives, particularly the less-educated executives with more state service, supported authoritarianism to a greater degree than they opposed it. They also found that public safety executives were more authoritarian in attitude than social service executives.

Conformity is the acceptance of influence. *Conventionality* is the acceptance of impersonal standards. *Conservatism* is the acceptance of a social, economic, or political structure. *Ethnocentrism* is the acceptance of one's ethnic group and the rejection of others. *Dogmatism* is the acceptance of one system of thought and the rejection of other systems. *Acquiescence* is the acceptance rather than the rejection of ambiguous or unknown stimuli. *Religiosity* is the acceptance of a particular set of organized beliefs, rituals, and practices having to do with God, morality, the origins of life, and an afterlife. *Authoritarianism* correlates with conformity, conventionality, conservatism, ethnocentrism, dogmatism, acquiescence,

and religiosity, but is not the same as any of these. (Citizens of the Former Soviet Union who emigrated to Israel are an exception. Their lack of religiosity was unrelated to their authoritarianism, which was attributed to their socialization under Communism; Rubenstein, 2002).

The Authoritarian Personality

According to Samuelson (1986), Wilhelm Reich was the first to use authoritarianism in Marxist and Freudian terms to explain Hitler's rise to power in Germany in 1933. Erich Fromm (1941) expanded on the idea from an analysis of a survey of German workers. Also influential were the Frankfurt school of Critical Theory in the 1930s and the rise of the Nazis. The concept moved from politics and psychoanalysis into social psychology (Sanford, 1986). In their book *The Authoritarian Personality*, Adorno, Frenkel-Brunswik, Levinson, and Sanford (1950) postulated an authoritarian type of personality, characterized as politically and religiously conservative, emotionally cold, power seeking, hostile toward minority groups, resistant to change, and opposed to humanitarian values. To measure authoritarianism and assess the authoritarian personality, they presented the *F* Scale.

The F Scale as a Measure of Authoritarianism

Description of the F Scale. The statements in the *F* scale include such ideological right-wing clichés as: "People can be divided into two distinct classes, the weak and the strong"; "No weakness or difficulty can hold us back if we have enough willpower"; "What a youth needs most is strict discipline, rugged determination, and the will to work and fight for family and country"; and "Most of our social problems would be solved if we could somehow get rid of the immoral, crooked, and feebleminded people." The items dealt with conventionality, submissiveness, aggressiveness, superstition, toughness, cynicism, projection, preoccupation with sex, violation of sexual norms, and disapproval of emotionality and intellectuality. Correlations with the *F* Scale suggested that the authoritarian personality was unable to accept blame and favored using status and power over love and friendship (Sanford, 1956). A social and political reactionary was likely to earn a higher authoritarian score than a social and political liberal (Christie, 1954; Shils, 1954).

Critique. The *F* Scale was criticized for various reasons, including psychometric weaknesses. Some of its variance was due to the error of response set. For instance, all statements on the *F* Scale were couched in the same power-oriented terms. Endorsement of any statement implied support of an authoritarian ideological point of view. But it appeared applicable only to extreme conservatives. Rokeach (1960) argued that extreme radicals were just as authoritarian in their beliefs as extreme conservatives. He developed the Dogmatic (*D*) Scale which measured closed-mindedness without getting into political ideology and provided a psychometrically better instrument.

Bass (1955a) and Chapman and Campbell (1957b) completed research analyses suggesting that scores on the *F* Scale could be explained mainly by the response set of social acquiescence—the general tendency to agree rather than disagree, to say yes rather than no, to accept rather than reject statements. However, after an error in calculation was corrected, the percentage of variance due to social acquiescence was found to account for only about one-quarter of the variance in the scores on the *F* scale. Some of the responses to the *F* Scale could be attributed to social acquiescence, but for the most part the scores still provided a substantive measure of the authoritarian syndrome (Bass, 1970). Nonetheless, its relationship to social behavior did not appear consistently.

Factorial Validity. According to a factor analysis by Altemeyer (1981), some of the expected factors of authoritarianism emerged in the *F* scale; these included conventionality, submissiveness, and aggressiveness. However, in Bass and Valenzi's (1974) factor analysis, authoritarianism, as measured by the *F* Scale, was one of the four personality factors that appeared independent of assertiveness, sense of fairness, and introversion-extroversion.

Construct Validity. Evidence of the construct validity of the *F* Scale was obtained by Campbell and McCormack (1957), who found that the scores of U.S. Air Force cadets were more authoritarian than those of college students. But contrary to expectations, the cadets' scores on authoritarianism decreased with the time they were in the air force. According to Masling, Greer, and Gilmore (1955), authoritarians among 1,900 military personnel rated other group members less favorably than egalitarians did. In turn—as was consistent with earlier studies by Jones (1954) and Thibault and Riecken (1955a)—Wilkins and DeCharms (1962) reported that, as expected, authoritarians were influenced by external power cues in evaluating others and used fewer behavioral cues in describing others. Authoritarians were also more highly influenced by considerations of status in making evaluations. Many studies revealed that those with high *F* Scale scores were also ethnocentric and prejudiced toward minorities and foreigners (e.g., Linville & Jones, 1980). High *F*'s were conventionally religious and reactionary (Eckhardt, 1988) and scored high on scales of dogmatism and Machiavellianism (Eysenck & Wilson, 1978).

Low F Scores: Egalitarian Leaders. In an experiment and its replication, Haythorn, Couch, Haeffner, et al. (1956a,b) formed two groups, one with high ratings on the *F* Scale (authoritarian) and the other with low ratings on the *F* scale (egalitarian). The 32 participants viewed a film and met in their groups to compose dialogue for it. According to pairs of reliable observers, the egalitarian leaders were significantly more sensitive to others, contributed more toward moving the group closer to goals set by the group, showed greater effective intelligence, and were more submissive in their attitudes toward other group members than were the authoritarians.[1]

Since egalitarians are more likely to become leaders in their communities, Courtney, Greer, and Masling (1952) reported that the community leaders they studied were significantly more egalitarian than their followers. Greer

---

[1] Sensitivity to others is a potential contributor to effective leadership as noted in chapter 8.

(1953) interviewed 29 leaders in Philadelphia and found that the leaders' scores were significantly more egalitarian than those of nonleaders. Tarnapol (1958) obtained similar results. Leaders in highly conservative communities might be different. Egalitarian leaders tended to promote more participation. Thus in experiments by Haythorn, Couch, Haeffner, et al. (1956a, 1956b), followers tended to be able to exert more influence and to express more differences of opinion. Authoritarian leaders were described as being more autocratic, less democratic, and less concerned with the group's approval than the egalitarian leaders.

Rohde (1952) administered the F Scale to 176 members of an aircrew who were also rated by their crew commanders on three criteria: authoritarianism (high F scores) correlated −.33 with the commander's willingness to take the airmen into combat, −.46 with the commander's perception of the desirability of the airmen as friends, and −.11 with the commander's confidence in the airmen as members of the crew. Ley (1966) found a strong correlation of .76 between the turnover rate of industrial employees and the authoritarian scores of their supervisors. But contrary to hypothesis, a leader's authoritarianism was not related to several measures of the effectiveness and performance of his group. Likewise, Hamblin, Miller, and Wiggins (1961) failed to find a significant correlation between a leader's authoritarianism and measures of his group's morale and success. To obtain such effects from authoritarian leaders, contingent circumstances need to be taken into account.

Right-Wing Authoritarianism (RWA). Since both fascists and communists scored high on the F Scale, a Right Wing Authoritarianism (RWA) scale was developed and validated by Altemeyer (1981) as a motivational syndrome. It assesses submission to authority, aggressiveness sanctioned by established authorities, and adherence to conventions endorsed by authorities. Those with high RWA scores were more likely to: (1) accept illegal acts by government officials to harass and intimidate their opponents; (2) prefer right-wing political parties; (3) be less convinced that President Richard Nixon was engaged in a Watergate cover-up; (4) favor authoritarian leaders; (5) endorse punishment for disobedience without considering circumstances; (6) award longer prison sentences; (7) give more severe sentences to violent gay demonstrators compared to violent antigay demonstrators; (8) in experiments, administer supposedly stronger electric shocks to participants for failure to learn; and (9) be more ethnocentric.

Relation to Competence

On the basis of their reviews of the research literature, both Titus and Hollander (1957) and Christie and Cook (1958) concluded that authoritarianism, as measured by high scores on the F Scale, was negatively correlated with intelligence. Authoritarians tended to be not as bright as egalitarians and were also less educated. Courtney, Greer, and Masling (1952) administered the F Scale to a representative sample of residents of Philadelphia. Those who scored highest on authoritarianism were laborers and those with the least education. The lowest F scores were made by managers, officials, clericals, and salespeople. Professionals, semiprofessionals, and university students scored between these groups.

Newcomb (1961) observed that authoritarians were less able than egalitarians to determine which group members agreed with them, and their sociometric choices were determined accordingly. Authoritarians were also likely to be less popular with their peers. In studying 2,139 naval recruits, Masling (1953) found that authoritarianism was negatively related to popularity.

Authoritarianism appears to decline with experience. Thus Campbell and McCormack (1957) found that authoritarianism decreased with increasing military experience in various samples of military personnel, and Rohde (1952) discovered that authoritarianism was not highly valued by officers who attained the rank of aircrew commanders.

Authoritarianism and Leadership

Preferences in Leadership

Milton's (1952) data indicated that in 1952, authoritarian college students, as measured by their scores on the F Scale, supported Douglas MacArthur's nomination for president (MacArthur symbolized and emphasized power and authority in leadership). Students with low F scores supported the nomination of Adlai Stevenson, who was portrayed as a more consultative problem solver. Sanford

(1950) administered an authoritarian-egalitarian scale to 963 randomly selected adults in Philadelphia. Those who scored high on authoritarianism wanted a stern leader but one who was competent, understanding, and helpful. Those who scored low preferred a leader who was kind, friendly, and guided by the people. The strong leader who tells people what to do was accepted by the authoritarians but rejected by the egalitarians; the egalitarians wanted either to be told nothing by a leader or to be told what to do but not how to do it. The authoritarians tended to choose a leader for his or her personal magnetism and high status, whereas the egalitarians preferred a humanitarian leader who did things for people. Thus authoritarians favored being led by an autocratic, directive, structuring, task-oriented leader; egalitarians favored being led by a democratic, participative, considerate, relations-oriented leader.[2] Medalia (1955), who studied enlisted men in the U.S. Air Force, found that authoritarians expressed greater acceptance of formal leaders than egalitarians. Haythorn, Couch, Haefner, et al. (1956b) also found that authoritarians were more satisfied with appointed leaders and were less critical of their own group's performance.

Reactions to Leadership

Thibaut and Riecken (1955a) studied the effects on authoritarians and egalitarians of attempts to influence them by persons who were of different ranks in an organization. They found that the authoritarians were more sensitive than the egalitarians to the organizational rank of a leader. The results of E. E. Jones (1954) were similar. However, Jones found that compared with authoritarians, egalitarians viewed the *forceful-stimulus* person as more powerful and the *passive* leader as less powerful. The egalitarians were more highly sensitized to differences in personal power and to behavioral cues while the authoritarians tended to differentiate leaders according to the institutional status of the leaders.

Thibaut and Riecken (1955b) also studied group reactions to a leader's attempts to instigate aggressive behavior. They found that authoritarian participants became more submissive when they faced a high-status instigator but tended to reject the efforts of a low-status instigator.

[2]These leadership styles will be discussed in Chapter 17 through 20.

In overt communication, the authoritarian members were less intense in their rejection of the higher-status instigators than of the lower-status instigators. In a similar type of analysis, Lipetz and Ossorio (1967) found authoritarians less hostile toward high-status target persons than toward low-status targets whether or not these persons attempted to instigate aggression. To investigate a similar effect, Roberts and Jessor (1958) used projective tests to study the attitudes of authoritarians toward persons who were frustrating them. Compared with egalitarians, authoritarians tended to exhibit personal hostility toward low-status frustrators and to express hostility toward high-status frustrators only indirectly.

Reactions to Authority

According to Kelman and Hamilton (1989), persons of higher status and education were more likely to challenge and question authority. By contrast, rule-oriented followers tended to obey authority without question and to carry out orders without accepting personal responsibility. Rule-oriented followers obey out of a sense of powerlessness; role-oriented followers obey out of a sense of obligation to authority; value-oriented followers obey to fulfill a commitment to shared values.

Authoritarianism and the Attitudes and Behavior of Leaders

Dominating Behavior. Kalma, Visser, and Peters (1993) found that highly authoritarian personalities were much more likely to be aggressively dominant than sociably dominant. Aggressively dominant people had poorer interpersonal relationships than sociably dominant people and received lower ratings in task leadership.

Use of Punishment. Dustin and Davis (1967) asked participants to indicate whether they would use monetary rewards and penalties or evaluative communications to stimulate maximum performance in hypothetical followers. Compared with egalitarians, authoritarians used monetary penalties and negative evaluations more often. W. P. Smith (1967a) also found that authoritarians used punishment rather than reward as a method of inducing performance in others more than egalitarians. Authoritarian chief petty officers gave recruits more demerits

(Masling, 1953). According to a review by Smither (undated), authoritarian parents were more likely to punish their children for violations of a code of conduct. However, using a different scale to assess authoritarianism, Baker, DiMarco, and Scott (1975) failed to find that authoritarianism was correlated with the use of penalities.

Reactions to Unstructured Situations. Bass, McGehee, Hawkins, et al. (1953) demonstrated that authoritarian personalities, as measured by the *F* Scale, were less likely to attempt or exhibit successful leadership behavior in an initially leaderless discussion—a socially unstructured situation that calls for considerable flexibility if one wishes to emerge as a leader. This finding was consistent with results reported by Bass and Coates (1952), who found significant correlations of .32 and .33 between the tendency of ROTC cadets to display successful leadership in initially leaderless group discussions and their scores on two measures of perceptual flexibility. Similarly, Geier (1963) observed that overly rigid members tended to be eliminated as leaders in the early stages of group discussion. Consistent with these findings, Hollander (1954) obtained nominations for a student commander from 268 naval aviation cadets that correlated −.23 with the cadets' scores on authoritarianism.

Authoritarian Parental Leadership. According to research by Baumrind (1971), authoritarian parents try to teach their children to value obedience, respect for authority, tradition, order, and work. The parents believe that their children should accept their ideas about what is right and what is wrong without discussion. The children's reactions tend to be distrustful, withdrawn, and discontented. But *authoritarian* parenting is not the same as *authoritative* parenting. Authoritative or directive parents use their status, power, and reason to direct and control their children. Such parents are warm and positively encouraging, and develop children who are self-controlled, explorative, and satisfied.

Contingencies That Modify the Effects of a Leader's Authoritarianism

The effects of leader's authoritarianism tend to be moderated by their followers' authoritarianism or egalitarianism, as well as by various other personal and situational factors. Researchers have often focused on the impact of the *followers'* authoritarianism on the leadership process, because submissiveness and obedience to a higher authority are firmly entrenched in the authoritarian personality. Thus in a study of Israeli naval officers and crews, Foa (1957) concluded that authoritarian commanders should be in charge of subordinates with authoritarian expectations.

Match and Mismatch of Leaders and Followers: Effects on the Followers. Numerous attempts have been made to examine what happens when authoritarian and egalitarian leaders have to work with authoritarian and egalitarian subordinates. Systematic effects have been observed on both the followers and the leaders. Some effects depend on whether followers and leaders are matched or mismatched in personality. Thus Vroom (1959, 1960a) found that subordinates who were authoritarian (according to their scores on the *F* Scale) tended to be less satisfied with and less motivated by working under participative leaders than were egalitarian subordinates. In this study of a package delivery firm, Vroom found that the extent to which employees were satisfied and effective under participative supervision depended on their being egalitarian and highly in need of independence. Campion (1969) confirmed Vroom's findings in an experimental study. But another replication of Vroom's study by Tosi (1970), using the same survey method as Vroom with a different organization and different jobs, failed to corroborate Vroom's results. However, Tosi noted that his respondents were different from Vroom's in terms of values, interests, and gender.

Tosi (1973) tested a supervisory-subordinate congruency hypothesis: that a personality match between the supervisor and subordinate could result in greater satisfaction and morale and in less conflict than a mismatch. Data were collected from 488 managers of consumer loan offices. Four samples were formed, high-*F* and low-*F* samples of authoritarian and egalitarian employees that worked for bosses who rated either high or low in "tolerance for freedom" on the Leadership Behavior Description Questionnaire, Form XII.[3] The congruency hypothesis was partially supported: job satisfaction and degree of participation were highest for the authoritarian

---

[3] See Chapter 20.

subordinates who worked for bosses who lacked tolerance for freedom. But egalitarian subordinates working for bosses who had a high tolerance for freedom had the lowest levels of participation and satisfaction. These results suggest that some degree of structure or direction has to be present, whether in the boss or in the subordinate, to define the situation in which work is done.

Haythorn, Couch, Haefner, et al. (1956a, b) formed combinations of leaders and followers on the basis of high or low scores on the F Scale. They found that compared with egalitarian followers, authoritarian followers generally were rated by observers as less democratic and less sensitive to others, were more satisfied with their appointed leaders, and rated their groups higher in productivity and goal motivation. Unexpectedly, the authoritarian followers were not more submissive to the leaders than were the egalitarian followers, and they exercised more influence in their groups than did egalitarians. Observers rated the egalitarian followers lower than the authoritarian followers in productivity and goal orientation and higher in withdrawing from the field of activity.

Frey (1963) studied the disruptive behavior of differently composed groups under authoritarian and egalitarian leaders. The most disruption occurred in groups that were composed of both authoritarian leaders and followers; the least disruption occurred in groups that were composed of both egalitarian leaders and followers. The lowest performance occurred in groups that were composed of egalitarian leaders and authoritarian followers; the highest performance occurred in groups that were composed of both authoritarian leaders and followers.

Match and Mismatch of Leaders and Followers: Effects on the Leaders. Bass and Farrow (1977b), using path analysis, showed how the authoritarianism of leaders and followers affected a leader's style of leadership. They administered a short form of the F Scale to 77 managers and their 409 subordinates from industry and public agencies, and also asked subordinates to describe their managers' styles of leadership. Bass and Farrow found that authoritarian managers were not perceived to be wholly directive or participative. (Direction covers a variety of leadership styles including telling, ordering, and persuading; participation includes three styles: consulting, sharing decision making, and delegating.) Rather, authoritarian managers were seen as negotiative, manipulative, and opportunistic. Egalitarian managers were

seen as more fair minded and more likely to consult with their subordinates. Authoritarian subordinates viewed their managers as more negotiative, particularly if the managers' perspectives were short-term rather than long-term. Managers with authoritarian personalities were short-term maximizers.

Other Situational Contingencies. Harrell, Burnham, and Lee (1963) demonstrated that authoritarians were more likely to emerge as leaders in task-oriented groups and egalitarians to emerge as leaders in socioemotional groups. The size and structure of the group were also found to make a difference in the effects of the authoritarianism or egalitarianism of the leader. Authoritarian personalities appeared to do better as leaders when interaction among members was constrained by the large size of the group and by centralization of the organization's communications. In comparing large and small work groups Vroom and Mann (1960) found that supervisors who scored high on the F Scale were more readily accepted in large groups than in small groups and that egalitarian supervisors were better accepted in small groups. In large groups, employees described authoritarian supervisors as more participative, exerting less pressure on employees, and creating less tension between themselves and higher management. In small groups, they viewed authoritarian supervisors as less participative and as creating more tension between supervisors and subordinates. Vroom and Mann also examined the relationship between the authoritarianism of the supervisors and the satisfaction of their subordinates. Subordinates whose jobs were characterized by little interaction with their supervisors and little interdependence had more positive attitudes about authoritarian supervisors.

M. E. Shaw (1955) studied the effects of authoritarian and egalitarian leadership in different communication nets. He found that groups under authoritarian leaders were highly productive but had low morale. M. E. Shaw (1959a) further reported that, as expected, groups with leaders who scored high in authoritarianism performed better in centralized networks, whereas groups with egalitarian leaders performed better in less highly centralized networks.

Overall, the evidence suggests that the authoritarian personality syndrome in a leader or a follower systematically affects the performance of both and their satisfaction with each other. Yet by the 1980s, research interest in the leadership performance of the authoritarian personality had dissipated. In its place was a more sharply focused interest in those who most often seek and acquire power, how they use it, and with what effects.

Power Motivation

Individuals differ in their attitudes toward power; they also differ in their motivation and ability to seek and use it (P. J. Frost, 1986). Those with the motivation and willingness to use power in their dealings with others will use their interactions more consciously to get what they want and to gain control over situations. They will try to influence others directly by giving suggestions and opinions, by trying to change the opinions or actions of others, and by being forceful and argumentative. They may be seen by others as bossy and domineering, although if they have sufficient social skill, they may be perceived as inspirational (Stringer, 2001).

Those with skill in the use of power will embed that power in their communications with others and will use political tactics to influence what happens. Such tactical maneuvering or organizational politics embodies "the exercise of power [seen] . . . in the . . . tactics [members] use to get their way in the day-to-day, ongoing, present time functioning of [the] organization—it is power in action" (P. J. Frost, 1986, p. 22). According to a review by Dill and Pearson (1984), a model of such organizational politics better accounts for the effectiveness of managers of research and development projects than a rational model. Kotter (1979) adds that such dynamics of power contribute to an organization's functioning.

Stringer (2002) suggests that those who are power motivated prefer organizations that are highly structured and hierarchical, have formal systems and rules, provide a sense of boundaries, and have control and influence mechanisms. Gordon (2002) laments the insufficient research and development coverage of power, especially when it occurs at a "deep level."

Measurement of Power Motivation

Although need for power had been measured directly by questionnaires and personality inventories that assess manifest needs, power motivation and power needs have often been assessed by using respondents' answers to the Thematic Apperception Test (TAT). Scores on this test are based on how much power the examiners find in stories the respondents invent when shown ambiguous sketches such as one of a man seated at a desk. A "power response" to such an ambiguous sketch in the test would be: "He disapproved because he was determined to get his way." This response may be contrasted with a response that projects a need for achievement: "He was busy working and didn't hear the bell." It also may be contrasted with a response that projects the need for affiliation: "He kept looking at the photos of his family on his desk and wishing he was with them." The Miner Sentence Completion Scale is another projective technique in which examinees complete sentences beginning with such words as "I feel . . ." or "My job . . .", and the like. Power motivation can be estimated from the themes of the completed sentences.[4] Power orientation and motivation have also been measured indirectly but objectively by Harrell and Stahl (1981) by asking for preferences among alternative job assignments. Respondents indicated their relative preference for jobs having characteristics that appealed to different needs, including the need for power.

The Imperial Motive

Leaders need to have some degree of self-control and the ability to inhibit their own need for power. For instance, Jennings (1943) observed that leaders in girls' schools controlled their own moods and did not inflict their anxieties and depressed feelings on others. McClelland (1985) concluded that if power motivation is low leadership potential generally will be absent. If power motivation is high *and activity is uninhibited*, the individual behaves like a "conquistador." The tendency to inhibit activity is measured by obtaining the frequency with which the word "not" appears in stories written by an individual for the TAT. Activity inhibition is thought to reflect the restraint the individual feels about using power impulsively or using it to manipulate or coerce others. McClelland proposed that some successful leaders are high in power motivation, low in the need for affiliation, and high in the inhibition of activity. This is the imperial motive pattern and signifies highly efficient organizing that may sometimes be channeled into *selfless leadership* that is oriented toward doing good for others. Those who

---

[4] See Chapter 6.

score high in inhibition of activity reveal altruistic images of power. The good managers among McClelland and Burnham's (1976) imperials were motivated to serve their organizations. They generated among their subordinates team spirit, clarity of purpose, and a sense of responsibility for their work. House, Woycke, and Fodor (1986) found that six charismatic U.S. presidents—Jefferson, Jackson, Lincoln, the two Roosevelts, and Kennedy—revealed significantly more power and achievement motivation in their inaugural addresses, compared with the inaugural addresses of six noncharismatics: Presidents Tyler, Pierce, Buchanan, Arthur, Harding, and Coolidge.[5] (In Part V, charismatic imperials are seen as socialized transformational leaders.) Those who score low in inhibition of activity have thoughts of power that center much more on personal dominance and winning at someone else's expense. They are personalized, pseudo-transformational leaders. McClelland found that male imperials joined more organizations than did male conquistadors and argued more frequently. Women imperials were elected to more offices than women conquistadors and accepted more responsibility.

Since activity inhibition, based as it is on the number of "nots" in TAT protocols, has little theoretical support or empirical validation, Winter and Barenbaum (1985) extracted a measure of responsibility from the TAT protocols based on whether moral-legal standards, obligations, self-judgments, concern for others, and concern about consequences were expressed in the protocols.

Acquisition of Power

Some individuals strive to acquire and to use power. Others obtain it, sometimes reluctantly, by being in a position of authority to deal with uncertainty, to negotiate the allocation of resources, and to maintain collaborative efforts. Power seekers make use of the power they gain if they believe their attempts to lead through power will be successful (Kipnis, 1976). Mowday (1978) agreed. He found that managers who had revealed a high need for power employed it more frequently if they perceived it to be useful to do so. In general, such managers preferred assignments in which they could exert leadership and actively influence and exert control over others. They ob-

[5] Chapter 21 will look at length into the power-charisma leadership relationship.

tained emotional satisfaction from experiencing the effects of their use of power. Along with satisfaction, they experienced aggressive feelings and physiological reactions like the release of catecholamines, which is associated with emotional experiences.

While power can be wielded for personal aggrandizement, it can be used to benefit others. For instance, entrepreneurs (individuals who behave innovatively in large, complex organizations) are task-oriented personnel who use power whenever they can to ensure that their ideas, inventions, and innovations are accepted in their organizations (Pinchot, 1985). Such entrepreneurs regard power as instrumental for the accomplishment of tasks and as something they share with others, rather than as a basis for personal aggrandizement. Kanter (1983) described such individuals as "quiet entrepreneurs," who communicate in a collaborative-participative fashion. Although they could use their power to coerce others with threats and cajolery, they tended to be persuasive in their leadership style and to use many of the socially acceptable techniques of interpersonal competence—frequent staff meetings, frequent sharing of information, consulting with others, showing sensitivity to the interests of others, and a willingness to share rewards and recognition.

Power Motivation and Careers

The need for power was found important for success as a manager in a follow-up of 237 AT&T general managers in nontechnical areas (McClelland & Boyatzis, 1982). Power orientation, measured using the Miner Sentence Completion Scale, also contributed to predictions of the respondents' plans to work as managers, according to Miner and Crane (1981). Although scientists and engineers were found to prefer jobs that provide opportunities to satisfy their need for achievement, successful executives had a higher need for power (Harrell & Stahl, 1981). A sense of responsibility moderated the effects of power, as predicted. McClelland and Boyatzis (1982) examined the imperial power motive in the 422 managers in the original 1956 AT&T assessment study (Bray, Campbell, & Grant, 1974). Up to 77% of those revealing *responsible power* were at level 3 or higher at AT&T 16 years later. Only 56% with other motive patterns lacking in both power motivation and responsibility reached this level (Winter, undated).

Cummin (1967) and Wainer and Rubin (1969) found that high power motivation coupled with high achievement motivation was associated with the success of managers. Stahl (1983) corroborated these findings in a large nationwide sample of managers in which the rating of the managers' performance and the managers' rate of promotion were connected with a great need for power and for achievement, as measured by an objective test. In a study of elected politicians in two local settings, Browning and Jacob (1964) observed that strongly power-oriented and achievement-oriented men were more likely to occupy political offices with greater potential to achieve and to exercise power. Those with little need for power and for achievement did not hold such offices. Power-motivated individuals also pursue careers other than politics that allow them to exert influence over others, such as teaching, psychology, business, or journalism. Those with little power motivation choose careers with fewer opportunities to influence others.

Power Motivation and Leaders' Attitudes, Abilities, and Behavior

Power motivation makes for specific differences in leader behavior. For example, Fodor and Farrow (1979) found that leaders in an experiment who had a great need for power were partial toward followers who were ingratiating. Fodor (1984) reported that individuals who were strongly motivated for power became more active when supervising others than did those low in motivation for power. Active attempts to lead were highest when productivity was stressed and rewarded, but such attempts by participants with a high motivation for power to gain control of the situation and to increase productivity were thwarted.

McClelland (1985) noted that men with a high power motive displayed more instability in their interpersonal relations, had more arguments, were more impulsive, and engaged in more competitive sports. Furthermore, both men and women with a strong motivation for power reported holding more offices than those with a weak motivation for power (Winter, 1973). Similarly, Kureshi and Fatima (1984) found that highly power-motivated Indian Muslim students were activists, and showed concern for power in their everyday activities and in student elections.

Consistent with the effects of the personality traits of activity, dominance, and social boldness, those who are more oriented toward power would be expected to attempt to influence others. For instance, Veroff (1957) found that individuals who scored high on projective measures of power motivation also scored high on satisfaction with their status as leaders and were rated high in argumentation and attempts to convince others. However, Frantzve (1979) failed to find that power, measured by Stewart's social-maturity scale, predicted emergence as a leader in initially leaderless discussions among male and female students.[6]

Power, Leadership, and Cognitive Complexity. Along with personality traits like self-confidence, self-determination, and dominance, the acquisition and use of power to influence others is associated with the individual's cognitive complexity—the ability to differentiate and integrate abstract information. In a four-year study of employees of insurance companies, Sypher and Zorn (1986) found that the cognitive complexity of individuals contributed strongly to their persuasive ability. Such personnel were promoted more often within the organization than others were. House (1984) observed that cognitively complex individuals are better able to identify power relationships. As is true of leadership in general, communication skills are important in the wielding of power.

Power, Leadership, and Communication Ability. Communicative competence is required to articulate arguments, advocate positions, and persuade others—all useful for acquiring and using power (Parks, 1985). With such competence, many other strategies and tactics are available to exert influence by using one's power (Marwell & Schmitt, 1967; Wiseman & Schenek-Hamlin, 1981). These strategies are detailed later.

Power and Effectiveness of Leadership. Although individuals who base their leadership on power may create conditions that are unsatisfying to some or all of their subordinates, they may successfully influence the course of events, which results in the fulfillment of tasks and the attainment of goals by their group or organization. Thus

---

[6]More detail and compelling evidence about the relationship of power to attempted and successful leadership is presented in Chapter 11.

Shaw and Harkey (1976) found that groups in which the leaders displayed ascendant tendencies did better than groups in which nonascendant people were the leaders. O'Brien and Harary (1977) reported that those leaders whose power matched their desire for it were more effective as leaders. Batkins (1982) stated that among human service agency directors, those with a great need for power led more efficient agency operations than those with little need for power; the result for the need for affiliation was the opposite. Daily and Johnson (1997) found in a longitudinal study that a firm's successful financial performance enhanced the power of the CEO.

Fodor (1987) found that small, experimental groups of men in the ROTC who attempted to solve a subarctic survival problem did best if their leader had a strong need for power. However, Fodor and Smith (1982) obtained outcomes indicating that individuals with high power motivation tended to inhibit group discussions more than did those with low power motivation. The individuals with high motivation for power brought into the discussions fewer facts and proposals that were available to them exclusively. As a consequence, fewer alternatives were considered and the quality of decisions was lower for groups led by such individuals. Consistent with these findings, House and Singh (1987) concluded that power motivation is predictive of effective leadership only when the assertion of one's social influence is critical and technical expertise is not.

Machiavellianism

Organizational politics are intended and unintended preferences, policies, and practices. They can be constructive or destructive. In the popular mind, Machiavellianism stands for deceit, coercion, and using any means to reach desired ends. There is some truth in this view. Chang and Rosen 2003, in a meta-analysis involving between 2,865 and 11,753 respondents, found that all five criteria of an organization's well-being were adversely affected by the perception that more politics were present in the organization. The average correlations were as follows with the five criteria: job satisfaction, $-.49$; organizational commitment, $-.47$; performance, $-.11$; intention to quit and turnover, .36; stress, .44. But in fact Niccolò Machiavelli (1513/1962) himself did not ignore

the possibility of doing some good with power and manipulation.

The pursuit of power and its skillful use were seen as fundamental to successful leadership by Machiavelli and taken further into modern times by Lasswell (1948) and Lane (1961). Machiavelli's treatises *The Prince* (1513/1962) and *The Discourses* (1531/1950) are still widely read today by leaders, managers, and executives. Machiavelli served on diplomatic missions to such crafty rulers as Louis XII of France, the Holy Roman Emperor Maximilian, and Pope Julius II. The guile and political tricks Machiavelli observed firsthand were included in his advice to a prince, Cesare Borgia, a local dictator. Borgia was Machiavelli's model prince, who used all means at his disposal, both good and bad, including deviousness and coercion, to expand his power to achieve and maintain his political position.

Such power motivation and competence in the use of power contrast with the philosophy of the inherent goodness and perfectability of humankind espoused in the writings of Thomas Jefferson, Henry Thoreau, and Ralph Waldo Emerson and by modern socially oriented leadership theorists, such as Lewin (1939), Gibb (1964), Argyris (1962), and Bennis (1964), who reasoned that influence can and should be exerted on others when there is a need for it. For the good of oneself and others, they affirmed, one should be open, frank, and candid in communications; share decision making; and openly commit oneself to positions so that others will know where one stands. Further, they suggested, leaders ought to jointly select and identify mutually satisfying goals to work toward, develop and maintain mutual trust, and encourage group discussions including others above and below themselves in the organizational hierarchy.

Machiavelli's Advice

"It is impossible to satisfy the nobility by fair dealing . . . whereas it is very easy to satisfy the people. . . . From hostile nobles [the prince] has to fear not only desertion but their active opposition . . . in time to save themselves and with the one whom they expect will conquer. . . . The prince is able to make and unmake them at any time, and improve or deprive them of it. . . . [The nobles] that are bound to you and not rapacious, must be honored and loved. . . . But when they are not bound to you of set purpose, and for ambitious ends . . . they think more of themselves than of you. . . . From such men the prince must guard himself and look upon them as secret enemies" (Machiavelli, 1513/1962, pp. 71–72). "There is nothing more difficult to carry out, nor more doubtful of success, nor more dangerous to handle, than to initiate a new order of things. For the reformer has enemies in all those who profit by the old order, and only lukewarm defenders who would profit by the new order" (p. 55). Strong, ruthless, and cynical leadership is required of the prince because of his nobles' self serving. As a consequence, they will regularly subvert the state and reduce it to chaos. It is in their best interests for the prince and the people to do whatever he can in whatever way he can to prevent chaos from occurring. Religious and ethical criteria for justifying the leader's actions are irrelevant.

Political calculation is required to control events rather than be victimized by them. For "reasons of state," the ends always justify the means. The ends are the welfare of the state. Whatever the leader does to help strengthen and preserve the state is good; whatever tends to work against the state is bad. The leader must be pragmatic, not idealistic, in facing problems. He must always keep in mind the particular interests of his own state. In a sense, Machiavelli was an *early amoral behaviorist* who argued for studying what we do, rather than what we ought to do. He argued that "he who studies what might be done rather than what is done will learn the way to his downfall rather than to his preservation." Machiavelli was also an early situationalist, for instance, giving different advice to the prince about how to deal with acquired political states, depending on whether the states were culturally and politically similar or different from his own.

According to Machiavelli, the prince must be ready to imitate the behavior of the fox, who can "recognize traps," and the lion, who can "frighten wolves." He cannot place his trust in others. To obtain and maintain power, he needs a calculating attitude without any sense of guilt or shame. He should act in a way that conveys boldness, greatness, and strength. The prince should rely more on being feared than on being loved. If cruelty is required, it should be done all at once, not over an extended period. Although the prince does not need to have a moral character, he must seem to have one; he should appear to be merciful, faithful, humane, sincere, and religious, and avoid being despised. He must main-

tain an image of personal strength and confidence so that no one will try to mislead him. He must control his emotions. He has to uphold his dignity, "which must never be allowed to fail in anything whatever." He should not pay attention to advice unless he has asked for it. Machiavelli even had advice for the nobles around the prince. Anyone with cleverness and some power who helped the prince to gain his position must be careful because the prince cannot tolerate any competent, powerful people close to him.

Measuring Machiavellianism: The Mach Scale

Statements from *The Prince*, as well as from *The Discourses*, were used by Christie and Geis (1970) to form the Mach scale, which measures the extent to which respondents subscribe to Machiavelli's dictums about how the leader should act toward others to be most successful in obtaining and maintaining compliance with his interests. An original list of 71 statements dealt with tactics ("A white lie is a good thing"), views ("It is hard to get ahead without cutting corners"), and morality ("No one has the right to take his own life"). The Mach IV scale, consisting of 20 such items, had a split-half reliability of close to .80. Other versions of the Mach scale were devised to reduce the bias of social desirability that is inherent in the content. Obviously, to admit to being devious is usually not a socially desirable response. A high score on the Mach scale was seen as an indication of a predisposition to maximize self-interest using deceit and manipulation at the expense of others.

Influence Behavior of Machiavellians (High Machs). As well as being more authoritarian, Machiavellians are aggressively dominant but less socially dominant individuals, according to Kalma, Visser, and Peeters (1993). These researchers obtained a correlation of .35 between Machiavellianism and their scale of aggressive dominance and a correlation of only .13 with their scale of social dominance. Individuals who score high on the Mach scale (high Machs) resist social influences and are concerned with getting the job done rather than with emotional and moral considerations. They tend to initiate and control interactions with others. In contrast, low Machs—people who score low on the Mach scale—are more susceptible to social influence and are distracted by interpersonal concerns (Epstein, 1969). High Machs frequently practice deception, bluff, and other manipulative tactics in competitive situations and in contexts of uncertainty. They also exhibit a "cool" task-directed syndrome during face-to-face competition that allows for improvisation in both substance and timing of responses to the task or to other people (Shapiro, Lewicki, & Devine, 1995). High Machs are impervious to considerations that can interfere with manipulative behavior and effective bargaining (Christie & Geis, 1970). They are convincing liars (Lewicki, 1983), glib and emotionally detached, superficially charming and duplicitous, bordering on psychopathological (McKoskey, Worzel, & Szarto, 1998).

Drory and Gluskinos (1980) varied the leaders' power as perceived experts with authority and the task so it was more or less structured, to create situations that were more favorable or less favorable to the leaders. They found that as leaders, the high Machs generally gave more orders and reduced tension more than did the low Machs. However, the high Machs became less directive and requested more assistance when they had less power and the task had less structure than when they had more power and the task was highly structured. In respect to their flexibility of response as conditions changed, high Machs were like egalitarians (people with low F Scale scores) who had been found to do the same by Bass and Farrow (1977b). Low Machs were similar to high authoritarians in their inflexibility of response to changing situations.

Deluga (2001) agreed with Wilson, Near, and Miller (1996) that although Machiavellianism is generally socially unacceptable, some high Machs may be effective in stressful, competitive, unstructured face-to-face situations where their sense of timing, ability to improvise, persuasive ability, and ability to remain "cool" are assets to bargaining teams, to mock courtroom debates, and in leading temporary small teams (Huber & Neale, 1986). U.S. presidents who are high Machs (according to ratings of their profiles by three undergraduates) are more likely to get Congress to pass the legislation they support (Simonton, 1986). Among 39 presidents from Washington to Reagan, Deluga (2001) found that Machiavellianism was positively associated with their rated effectiveness according to Spangler and House (1991). Franklin Roosevelt, Martin Van Buren, and Richard Nixon were rated highest on the Mach scale; William McKinley, Ruther-

ford Hayes, and Zachary Taylor were rated lowest. In no way are Machiavellianism and charisma identical, but they share image-building behaviors, self-confidence, and effective emotional regulation.

The impact of a Machiavellian outlook seems to depend on how much a manager interacts with others in the organization. Coates (1984) obtained reports of the frequency of the contacts of 79 managers with their superiors and peers. The rated influence of managers who were high Machs was likely to be higher than that of low Machs if the managers had frequent contact with their superiors and peers.

Other Political Tactics

The number of politically astute, devious, deceptive, artful, and crafty tactics leaders can employ is much more extensive than Machiavelli described. Many other tactics were mentioned in Greek, Roman, and Chinese classics. However, Machiavellianism is a generic label for all such amoral political manipulativeness and deception, although Machievelli himself mentioned using politics to benefit the people—for instance, to protect them against nobles' efforts to exploit them. Moreover, organizational politics can be seen as functional (Boal & Deal, 1984), and as a constructive management of shared meanings. A political perspective can be applied with a social service rather than a self-serving orientation (Ammeter, Douglas, Gardner, et al., 2002). Lancaster (2002) sees using political tactics as essential for success in management. If you work in a corporation, he advises you to "promote yourself. You must pit your skills and competitiveness against ambitious colleagues, some who play fair and some who don't. You must learn to maneuver through the political thickets and often unjust realities of organizational life." Political tactics are used extensively by those of lower status to influence others with higher status. They employ self-serving impression management, ingratiation, intimidation, and supplication (Jones & Pittman, 1982). They can create an illusion of control (Alloy & Abramson, 1982).

Martin and Sims (1956), Jameson (1945), and Pfiffner (1951) described political tactics used in modern corporations which could be self-serving or beneficial to others. Politically oriented managers withhold the release of information or time its release for when it will do the most good. They bluff, acting confident even when they are unsure or lack relevant information. They make political alliances with those who have the power to protect their interests. They hide their real feelings about plans that are popular with others by starting to act on them but then retard and delay their implementation so that the plans are in process but never completed. They keep socially distant from subordinates and never become personally involved with them, always remaining the boss when interacting with them. They openly compromise, yet secretly divert or delay plans that involve compromise so that their aims will continue to be pursued despite public statements to the contrary. McCall (1978, p. 227) felt the same way about politically astute creative leaders. They tend to be "crafty, grouchy, dangerous, feisty, contrary, inconsistent, evangelistic, prejudiced, and spineless."

Political versus Social Approach. We advocate and invest less research on the Machiavellian way of establishing and maintaining leadership in contrast to the social approach. The very deviousness of Machiavellianism makes its widespread practice less visible. Overall, the social approach to interpersonal competence is more socially acceptable than the political approach. Bass (1968c, 1970b) found that only a minority of MBA students and middle managers responding to the Organizational Success Questionnaire (OSQ) espoused political tactics and rejected the Gibb-Bennis-Argyris social approach to effective interpersonal relations as the way "to get ahead in most large organizations." For the majority of the MBA students and managers, least endorsed were the tactics of diverting plans by retarding, delaying, and offering insincere compromises. However, published OSQ results for students in six countries and unpublished OSQ data gathered from samples of managers in over a dozen countries indicated that different nationalities differ widely in their endorsement of these political and social approaches (Bass & Franke, 1972).

Influence Tactics. Kipnis, Schmidt, and Wilkinson (1980) gathered data on what people say they do to influence others who work with them. They found that people used a mixture of both social and political approaches. In these researchers' first investigation, 165 lower-level managers wrote essays describing an incident in which they influenced their bosses, their coworkers, or their subordinates. A content analysis disclosed the use of 370 different influence tactics. The Machiavellian tactics that were identified included the following: lied to the target, acted in a pseudodemocratic manner, puffed up the importance of the job, manipulated information, made the target feel important, cajoled the target, pretended to understand the target's problem, became a nuisance, slowed down on the job, threatened to withdraw help, threatened to leave the job, blocked the target's actions, ignored the target, invoked past favors, waited until the target was in the right mood, was humble, showed dependence, invoked rules, obtained support informally from superiors, threatened to notify an outside agency, and made formal appeals to higher levels.

Ingratiation and Blocking. Kipnis and Schmidt extracted 58 tactics from the content analyses and then gave them to 754 graduate students who also worked full time. The students were asked how frequently they had used any of these tactics during the past six months to influence others with whom they worked. When the responses were factor-analyzed, two manipulative factors emerged: *ingratiation* and *blocking*. Ingratiating tactics were used more frequently to influence peers and subordinates than superiors. The primary reason the students gave for using the tactics to influence others was to get help on the job, to obtain benefits from these other persons, or to try to effect change. The ingratiating tactics included (1) making the target feel important ("Only you have the brains and talent to do this"); (2) acting very humble while making a request; (3) making the target feel good about the student before making a request; (4) inflating the importance of what needed to be done; (5) waiting until the target appeared in a receptive mood before asking; and (6) pretending they were letting the target decide to do what the student wanted done (acting in a pseudodemocratic fashion).

Blocking tactics were generally used less frequently than other tactics. These were efforts to get benefits and changes in decisions from the students' bosses. They included: (1) threatening to notify an outside agency if the boss did not give in to the request; (2) threatening to stop working with the boss until the matter was settled; (3) engaging in a slowdown of work until the boss did what the student wanted; (4) ignoring the boss, stopping being friendly, on both; and (5) lying about reasons the boss should do what the student wanted.

Along with ingatiation and blocking, political tactics are used to preserve and enhance one's self-esteem or to be esteemed by others (Kelley & Michela, 1980).[7] These tactics include; (1) engaging in *impression management*—doing or saying what it is should put one in a favorable light; (2) concealing some of the reasons for trying to be influential; (3) forming coalitions with others to exert the combined power of a group, rather than speaking in the lone voice of the individual; and (4) planning one's behavior—imagining or playing through situations to try—to time what one will do and to fit one's appeals to the expected outcomes (Nuttin, 1984).

Game Playing. P. J. Frost (1986) conceived tactical maneuvering to gain power and influence in terms of political "games" employees play in organizations:

> An organizational "game" involves social actors, payoffs, and a set of interpretive strategies . . . [that] specify the rules, data, and successful outcomes in the game. Given the social construction around power that is involved in such games there is a degree of elasticity in the way the game is constructed and played. Invention and adaptation enter into the development and enactment of game rules and meanings, because they come alive in the service of actors' strategic actions in the game (p. 527).

Members of organizations consciously play games to get their way for their own sake, for the sake of others, or for their organization. They use such games to disguise their political intentions, to mobilize support, and to quiet opposition. Power-seeking members play at empire building by following the rules to facilitate their upward mobility in their organizations (Pfeffer, 1981b).

The game of "making it" (moving up the ladder of success) goes along with impression management and esteem building. Mentoring and sponsorship can be seen as games to foster networks of supporters and as empire building (P. J. Frost, 1986). Through such games, players

seek justification for and meaning in their actions to allow them to increase their power and hence to participate in other organizational games. Games such as "lording" (Mintzberg, 1983) are played by actors with little power; who "lord it over" those who are subject to their influence. Those who play these games hold on to what little power they have by establishing a context in which they interpret the rules and routines of organizations literally and see that the rules are strictly enforced and the routines are rigidly implemented. They get their way and resist change by invoking the rule book—the bureaucracy—and by threatening to go to a higher authority for decisions (P. J. Frost, 1986). On occasion, they invent rules, expecting no challenge because of the large, complex book of rules that would have to be consulted to refute their argument. In these individual games, players manage impressions (Zerbe & Paulhus, 1985) and join and build networks and coalitions (Porter, Allen, & Angle, 1981).

Chameleon Behavior. Like chameleons, *high self-monitors* change in response to changes in situations. They also appear more ready to change careers, employers, or locations. Low self-monitors remain true to themselves and do not change as much; nor do they change careers, employers, or locations as much. Politically tactical moves by 67 high-monitoring MBA graduates followed up for 5 years paid off for them in accelerated promotions across organizations as well as in promotions within their organization if they did not leave. The 72 low self-monitors who did not change careers or organizations did not do as well.

Heresthetics. For Riker (1986), leadership as practiced by successful politicians is primarily political manipulation. According to this view, leadership is evident when a politician is able to change an issue in the minds of constituents and legislators so the minority support for the older framing of the issue swells to a majority because of the politician's new interpretation of the issue. The politician-leader achieves this goal by imparting to his or her description the exact twist to reality that will gain majority approval of the issue. It is a matter not of persuasive rhetoric but of a *heresthetic* argument that shows how the proposal will serve the best interests of the majority. In Riker's case studies, heresthetic leaders manipulated sup-

---

[7]These and still other tactics that those with lower status use to influence others with higher status will be examined in Chapter 16. Self-serving impression management, which uses some of these tactics including ingatiation, intimidation, and supplication—and which may create an illusion of control—will be considered more fully in Chapter 21.

port by setting and controlling agendas, calculating likely voting patterns, and then manipulating the values of importance. They made appeals to share organizational or societal purposes, but their private motives were paramount.

As Riker (1986, p. 64) noted, "the heresthetic neither creates preferences nor hypnotizes. . . . He probes until some new alternative, some new dimension [is found] that strikes a spark in the preferences of others." He manipulates private incentives even while remaining idealistic. To illustrate: because of isolationist sentiment in the United States in 1940, President Roosevelt could not gain approval from Congress to give 50 old American destroyers to Britain, which was being strangled by German submarines. But he did gain approval for "lend lease," in which the destroyers were exchanged for bases in Bermuda, the Bahamas, and elsewhere that could be viewed as a first-line offshore defense for the United States. He was able to persuade Congress to pass the Lend-Lease Act of 1941 by emphasizing the age and outmoded condition of the destroyers and the advantages of obtaining the bases.

Political Psychology and Leadership in Organizations

Political perspectives often are the basis for leadership in organizations. Political behavior in organizations is common and sometimes necessary. Thus impression management can be understood as a political maneuver (Ferris, Russ, & Fandt, 1989). Leadership in organizations can be conceived as a political process.

Harold D. Lasswell (1948) pioneered the study of the psychology of political leadership but did not have continuing impact on either political science or psychological leadership research. His major books and writings appeared between 1923 and 1948. Ascher and Hirschfelder-Ascher (2005) reminded us of his seminal publications, 10 of which have been republished since 1990. The decline in interest in Lasswell's psychodynamic approach to political leadership paralleled a decline in interest in psychoanalytic theory. Nevertheless, Lasswell's framework still provides an unexcelled agenda for the analysis of current policy and political issues (Ascher & Hirschfelder-Ascher, 2005). Lasswell showed:

(1) how emotions and beliefs were displaced from one target to another to shift blame; (2) how leaders could use political symbols and propaganda to be understood by appeals to the id, ego, and superego; (3) how democratic processes and civil liberties depend on democratic character, values, and expectations; and (4) how crisis erodes political self-restraint and brings on destructive behavior. Applying Lasswell's framework to the current interest in charismatic and transformational leadership (see Part V) suggests that such leadership brings risks to democratic accountability.

Negative Effects. Playing politics in organizations is often self-aggrandizing and of less benefit to others and to the organization. Politics in organizations is likely to cause job anxiety, stress, dissatisfaction, and withdrawal of followers (Cropanzano, Hawes, Grandby, et al., 1997; Valle & Perrewe, 2000). Politically astute, self-aggrandizing leaders are morally disengaged. Unethical violations committed by their subordinates are justified (Davis & Gardner, 2004). Davis and Gardner (2004) noted that in organizations, a leader who behaved politically resulted in subordinates who were cynical about the organization's sincerity, honesty, and integrity. Such leadership generally had negative effects on subordinates' job satisfaction, performance, morale, and turnover. Beu and Buckley (2004a, b) attributed corporate scandals to politically astute corporate leaders who created an environment where subordinates committed illegalities in obedience to their leaders. The leaders convinced their subordinates that the behavior was morally justified. The subordinates denied that they were the agents of the crime; they were convinced by the power and authority of the leaders and said that they were only obeying orders. (The same plea was made by Nazi war criminals.) According to a qualitative and quantitative study of nurses at a New Zealand hospital by Kan and Parry (2004), politics could offset the usually positive effects of transformational leadership. The leadership of the nurses was repressed, in their efforts to provide patient care, by the political realities of the greater power, status, and importance of the medical staff and the managers.

Positive Views. Spencer and Spencer (1993) argued that political skill is even more important for effective management than cognitive competence. Treadway,

Hochwarter, Ferris, et al. (2004) proposed that political skill involves the ability to comprehend social cues and build social networks and social capital (personal reputation and support from associates). The components formed two independent factors, which accounted for 16% and 32%, respectively, of work unit performance of an educational administrative staff (Douglas & Ammeter, 2004). Treadway, Hockwarter, Ferris, et al. (in press) modified the work of Ferris, Treadway, Kolodinsky, et al. (2005) to measure the *political skill* of supervisors as potentially positive in the eyes of their subordinates by: (1) trying to show a genuine interest in other people; (2) understanding people well; (3) building relationships with influential people at work; and (4) always instinctively knowing the right things to say to influence others. The investigators showed that politically oriented leaders in organizations could be seen favorably by their subordinates. They found that the supervisors' rated political skill correlated with their subordinates' ratings as follows: trust, .38; job satisfaction, .32; commitment, .41, and cynicism, $-.33$.

Summary and Conclusions

Leaders may be oriented toward the uses of power and political manipulation, rather than toward social approaches to influencing others. Authoritarianism, power motivation, and Machiavellianism are relevant aspects of their personalities. Measuring the authoritarianism of both leaders and followers has been helpful in understanding the preferences, performance, and satisfaction of these leaders, particularly as a function of the circumstances involved. They tend to be rejected in sociometric choice for leadership. But this tendency does not necessarily prevent authoritarians from performing as leaders in task-oriented, emergent groups, as well as in formal organizations.

The personalities of leaders and followers interact. Authoritarian followers tend to evaluate leaders in terms of status, power, and position, whereas egalitarians evaluate leaders as persons in terms of behavioral and personality cues. With directive leaders, egalitarian followers tend to feel more comfortable in large, structured groups. With directive leaders, egalitarians tend to react more favorably in small, less highly structured groups. Egalitarian followers are somewhat more hostile toward leaders in high-status positions. Thus the degree to which a leader is accepted and the degree of satisfaction that group members feel under authoritarian and egalitarian leaders generally are dependent on a matching of the leader's personality with the follower's personality, along with a congruent group structure.

Power-motivated leaders can be effective if they are task oriented rather then concerned about interpersonal relationships, and if they can inhibit their need for power. These imperialists can use their power for their own advancement or for the good of their organizations. Machiavellians are cool in their performance as leaders and are not distracted by interpersonal considerations or social influences in competitive situations. The use of Machiavellian tactics is probably more widespread than has been acknowledged. Yet the effects of politically astute leaders on their associates can have positive as well as negative effects on the organization, unit performance, and morale.

Many other personal values and beliefs about oneself are associated with the emergence of leadership.

Values, Self-Esteem, Well-Being, and Leadership

Leaders are multidimensional, complex personalities. Douglas MacArthur was, according to his biographer William Manchester (1978), "a great thundering paradox of a man, noble and ignoble, inspiring and outrageous, arrogant and shy, the best of men and the worst of men, the most protean, most ridiculous and most sublime." Manchester used traits, values, actions, orientations, motives, and self-concepts in his word painting of MacArthur's unique individuality. So far I have detailed how the intricacies of the personal factors of leadership involve a variety of traits including activism and orientation toward authority, power, and manipulativeness. This chapter examines how leaders regard themselves; Chapter 9 will discuss how others regard them. Presented are the leaders' self-ascribed personal values, valued activities, and identification; and how subconscious and conscious motives energize and direct leaders. Their risk taking, self-concept, physical fitness, and mental health are discussed. The attitudes of leaders toward their organization and their satisfaction with their roles as managers are also examined.

Values

A value is "an enduring belief that a specific mode of conduct or end-state of existence is personally or socially preferable to an opposite or converse mode of conduct or end-state" (Rokeach, 1973, p. 5). Objects and actions are valued if they are believed to be right, good, worthwhile, and important. A value may be *instrumental*, that is, a means to some desired end, or *terminal*, an end in itself. Ambition, honesty, and courage are instrumental values. A comfortable life, social recognition, and family security are terminal values. Rokeach (1973) provided 18 examples each of instrumental and terminal values. Values

may also be espoused or enacted. *Espoused* values are what people say they value. *Enacted* values are inferred from what people do. Enacted values resulted in greater organizational commitment of 135 assistant managers, according to a study by Furst, Cable, and Edwards (2001).

Leaders' Values

Personality is made up of cognitive and behavioral traits; *character* is made up of values. Piotrowski and Armstrong (1987) concluded that all 30 chief executive officers they interviewed had clear values. Values determine what is considered the right thing to do (Hughes, Ginnett, & Curphy, 1993). The leader who values courage will take unpopular stands on issues; the leader who values self-control will tend to remain aloof from a highly emotional follower. The leader who values being imaginative rather than logical will evaluate others depending whether they appear logical rather than imaginative. The leader who values obedience over independence will not question orders from higher authority. Bad values motivate bad behavior. The manager who scores high in vanity "does not share credit when we do something upper management really likes"; the greedy manager "is not calm when working under pressure" (Hogan, 2003).

Leaders and nonleaders value themselves differently. Peppers and Ryan (1986) found that when 79 individuals in positions of leadership were contrasted with 110 who were not, the leaders differed from the nonleaders in three general ways in traits and values. First, they saw themselves as more talkative, aggressive, intelligent, committed, and ambitious. Second, they aspired to be more sensitive, democratic, fair, committed, imaginative, confident, and self-assured. Third, there was more congruence between the leaders' aspirations and self-perceptions than the nonleaders'. Trow and Smith (1983) found that people who volunteered to serve on the boards of directors of agencies that planned and advocated social change systematically differed in their values from those in the same community who did not volunteer to serve. Those who volunteered were much more likely to value goodwill and the need to eradicate sin and were much less likely to endorse a hard line in dealing with social problems. Generally, leaders endorse the values of their social and political movements more strongly than do ordinary followers.

Importance of Values to Leaders. Baltzell (1980) illustrated how the careers that leaders pursued were influenced by the values they assimilated. He contrasted the values of upper-class Protestant Bostononians and upper-class Protestant Philadelphians. Puritan-influenced Bostonians viewed human beings as inherently sinful, in need of authoritative institutions headed by righteous leaders of superior education. Quaker-influenced Philadelphians viewed human beings as inherently good, individually perfectable, with no need of mediation by state or church, erudition, or professionalism. For Boston's Brahmins but not for Philadelphia's elite, public service became obligatory; Boston's Adamses, Cabots, and Lowells produced a good many eminent political leaders; Philadelphia's Biddles, Cadwaladers, and Whartons did not. Baltzell attributed the difference to the original Puritan and Quaker values inculcated in succeeding generations of family members. The Bostonians, who pursued political leadership, and the Philadelphians, who pursued leadership in business and finance, clearly differed in their attitudes and opinions about what was important to them and what interested them.

In a review of available research, Ghiselli (1968a) noted that managers' personal values correlated .25 to .30 with criteria of their effectiveness. U.S. Army officers and enlisted personnel are expected to live by the army's seven core values: (1) loyalty, (2) duty, (3) respect, (4) selfless service, (5) honor, (6) integrity, and (7) personal courage (Berenson, 1998). Violations could lead to disciplinary action.

Shared Values. "Leaders cannot function effectively without some base of shared values in their constituents or followers" (J. W. Gardner, 1988, p. 22). Shared values play an important role in Nel's (1993) value-centered leadership. Unity within diversity in an organization can be developed if its members and teams share a vision and values. Weiss (1978) found that leaders' success and competence were greater when the leaders and their subordinates held values in common. Job satisfaction was also greater (Murray, 1993). Nonetheless, leaders have to choose which values they should articulate (Beckhard, 1995). England and Lee (1974) offered six reasons for the influence on a leader's performance of the values that the leader regards as right, good, and important. These values affect: (1) a leader's perception of situations and problems to be faced; (2) a leader's decisions and solutions to problems; (3) the leader's view of other individuals and groups, and thus of interpersonal relationships; (4) the leader's perception of individual and organizational success, as well as how to achieve them; (5) the leader's determination of what is and what is not ethical behavior; and (6) the extent to which the leader accepts or resists organizational pressures and goals. The leader has to choose which values to articulate.

Values and Transformational Leadership. According to Burns (1978) and House, Howell, and Shamir (2002), values are central to the neocharismatic and transformational theories of leadership (see Chapters 21 and 22). In these theories, leaders are assumed to move their followers to transcend their own needs for the needs of their group, organization, or society. They foster the sharing of transcendental values with their followers. These values may include altruism, social welfare, supportiveness, service, spirituality, honesty, fairness, and aesthetics (Engelbrecht & Murray, 1995). Transformational leaders and their visions are also concerned with moral values and end values such as liberty, equality, and justice (Burns, 1976). Such leaders amplify, elevate, or idealize values of consequence to the followers (Conger & Kanungo, 1998). They are strongly convinced of the rightness of these values and imbue followers with the same feelings. Strongly held values underlie the commitments of both the neocharismatic leader and the led (House, 1977). For instance, to achieve a strong customer focus, an organization will need to promote the values of service, honesty, and integrity in its leadership, in its employees, and in itself (Snyder, Dowd, & Houghton, 1994).

For Drucker (1999, p. 73), "to work in an organization whose value system is unacceptable or incompatible with one's own values condemns a person both to frustration and to nonperformance." An organization may value a policy of hiring from the outside; a leader may value promoting from within. A leader may value developing subordinates but may be discouraged by the organization from spending time or resources to do so. A leader may value long-term results; organizational policies may emphasize short-term results.

Assessment of Values

Starting in the 1930s, the Allport-Vernon Study of Values (1931) became a widely used inventory for assessing Spranger's (1928) six-fold typology of values: (1) theoretical, (2) economic, (3) aesthetic, (4) social, (5) political, and (6) religious. Questionnaires asking respondents to rank Rokeach's 18 instrumental and 18 terminal values in order of preference became another common approach from the 1970s onward. The Allport-Vernon was criticized as too abstract and Rokeach's values were said to lack relevance in organizational and management contexts (Hambrick & Brandon, 1988). A more recent addition to the assessment of values, validated with working adults, is Hogan and Hogan's (1996) Motives, Values, Preferences Inventory (MVPI) with value scales such as aesthetic, affiliation, altruistic, commercial, hedonistic, power, recognition, scientific, and tradition. Each scale is reliable. Validated scale questions address respondents' valuing of lifestyles, beliefs, occupational preferences, aversions, and preferred associates.

Many methods other than questionnaires have been used to assess values. For instance, Hall (2000) and Benjamin Tonna ascertained that there are about 125 values embedded in written and spoken language that are basic to human behavior. Documents such as a presidential address can be analyzed using a thesaurus of more than 5,000 synonyms of the 125 values, to count their presence in the speech. The values can then be prioritized according to their frequency of appearance in the speech, in English and in translations into French, Spanish, or German. Bass (1975a) developed Exercise Objectives in which the performance of participants was a gauge of their pragmatism or idealism. In Exercise Objectives, five simulated budgeting decisions were required to deal with problems of safety, labor relations, the morale of managers, the quality of products, and environmental pollution. Bass's (1968c) study of 113 MBA students showed that an unwillingness to spend money to remedy any of the five problems was related to strong economic, rather than humanistic, values. Conversely, willingness to spend money to handle the problems was positively associated with a social orientation to trust others. It was negatively correlated with a political orientation to bluff and to maintain psychosocial distance (Bass, 1968c).

Determinants of Leaders' Values

Education. Systematic differences in the values of managers are associated with differences in their education. Esser and Strother (1962) found that managers with average amounts of education tended to be rule oriented. Those with the least education were least rule oriented, followed closely by those with the most education. And England (1967a) observed that managers with less education placed more value on organizational stability. Those with college majors in the humanities, the fine arts, and the social sciences stressed the importance of productivity and efficiency as organizational goals. The Indian civil service, mostly all British under the British raj, had been educated in public schools such as Eton and Harrow and universities such as Oxford and Cambridge. They had been bred and trained to feel and act superior. They despised altruism or sympathy for the Indians. Rather, they had been indoctrinated with ideals like fair and open justice, efficient administration, and the opportunity to make improvements. On this basis, the 1,200 members of the Indian civil service provided rule over hundreds of millions of Indians (Lapping, 1985).

Cognitive Style. Values are linked to differences in the way managers sense, think, judge, and feel, according to the Myers-Briggs Type Indicator (Myers, 1962). Mitroff and Kilmann (1976) showed in a content analysis of managers' stories about their ideal organization, that *sensory-thinkers* emphasized factual details, the physical features of work, impersonal organizational control, certainty, and specificity; *intuitive-thinkers* focused on broad, global issues built around theories of organization; and *intuitive-feelers* stressed personal and humanistic values in their ideal organization. Intuitive-feelers were also found to risk takers (Behling, Gifford, & Tolliver, 1980; Henderson & Nutt, 1980). The sensory-feelers described their ideal organization as one that focuses on facts and processes, with attention to human relationships and qualities.

Personal Considerations. A kind of discounting seems to occur on the basis of perceptions of abundance or scarcity. In a study of a hospital, Jensen and Morris (1960) found that supervisors valued leadership and executive ability more highly when these traits were less prevalent among them. And when the supervisors were socially adjusted and personable, they attached even less value to these qualities.

What leaders value as an activity for its own sake obviously depends on their vocation. Distinct patterns of interests demarcate the different professions (E. K. Strong, 1943). Among governmental leaders, one is likely to see leaders with strong political values; in the military, a strong interest in adventure; in business, a strong interest in computational matters; and in science, a strong preference for theoretical activities—understanding the "why" of things. Managers and executives tend to score highest among the professions in economic and political values, in contrast to scientific personnel who tend to value theory and understanding. Artists value creativity more highly; and people in the helping professions have stronger social or religious values.[1]

Student leaders, mostly from the middle class themselves, were more likely than followers or isolates to identify with middle-class values (Martin, Gross, & Darley, 1952). Some strongly valued academic and vocational activities and goals; others strongly valued socializing (Brainard & Dollar, 1971).

Status. As one rises on the organizational ladder, one usually finds shifts in values that cannot be attributed to age, education, or seniority. Status differences emerge, and commitment to the organization is generally more highly valued the higher one's level in the organization. Pfiffner and Wilson (1953) surveyed two levels of supervisors. Their results indicated that the higher-level supervisors felt at ease with superiors and were interested in duties involving management functions. The lower-level

supervisors identified with their work groups and were less critical of workers than were the higher-level supervisors. Rosen and Weaver (1960) found four levels of management in agreement regarding the importance of factors that affect the effectiveness of jobs (authority, knowledge of plans, consultation) as opposed to the importance of a role in policy making and communication with higher-ups. But first-line supervisors differed from higher levels of management in emphasizing the importance of consideration and fairness. Compared with workers, managers at all levels regarded themselves as upholders of group norms (Fruchter & Skinner, 1966). W. K. Graham (1969) factor-analyzed the intercorrelations among the job-attitude scores of personnel at three levels of organization in life insurance agencies. Higher-level managers differentiated managerial actions from the organizational climate, whereas supervisors and agents did not.

Meaning of the Job. Triandis (1960) factor-analyzed the meanings attached to job descriptions by managers and workers. Six factors were isolated, five of which were similar for managers and workers. However, in a study of meanings attached to words describing jobs and people, Triandis (1959a) found that upper-level managers stressed the importance of status, polish, and education; lower-level managers stressed power and position; and workers stressed money and dependability. In comparing the attitudes of Swedish managers, superiors, and workers, Lenneröf (1965b) discovered that workers value good personal relations to a greater extent than do supervisors, and supervisors value it more than do their superiors. Also, the supervisors and their workers felt more strongly than their superiors that the supervisor should strive to attain an independent and influential position. Nonetheless, when Schwartz, Jenusaitis, and Stark (1966) compared the values of U.S. supervisors and workers, they found that the two groups agreed in placing greater value on job security, wages, and working conditions than on interpersonal relations. Similarly, Friedlander (1966a) found few differences between the values of U.S. civil service employees at different levels of status. Top managers often espouse values in their top-down communications that may or may not be practiced. These values include openness, leanness, localizing initiatives, and decisions based on merit.

[1] Alport, Vernon, and Lindsey (1960); Bedrosian (1964); Nash (1965); and Tagiuri (1965).

Lifestyles. Bray, Campbell, and Grant (1974) reported on a comprehensive comparison of the assessed values of those who had advanced further in the Bell System with those who had not. Over the eight years of the survey, systematic changes occurred in the lives of 400 Bell System managers who were followed up after evaluations at an assessment center. Two contrasting lifestyles were identified—the *enlarger* and the *enfolder*. The enlarger's lifestyle stressed innovation, change, self-development, and movement away from traditional ways of thinking and doing things. The enfolder's lifestyle was oriented more toward tradition and maintaining the close family and friendship ties that the individual had gained during adolescence and college. Enfolders were less likely to leave their hometown area and were much less likely to engage in any self-improvement activities. More successful managers were enlargers; less successful managers were enfolders. Enlargers gained occupational interests and lost concern for parents and family; enfolders either suffered small losses in such concerns or remained the same. Enlargers sharply reduced their interest in recreational and social activities; enfolders showed only a slight loss in such interests.

Which is cause, and which is effect? As managers rise faster and higher, they may have less time for family ties and recreation. But they do obtain increasingly greater satisfaction from their job as they rise in rank. Less successful managers are likely to derive less satisfaction from their jobs and have more time for family and recreation. However, one cannot ignore the evidence that successful people are more likely to be career-oriented before they actually began to work, which suggests that they bring to their job at least some semblance of a lifestyle that will contribute to their success in the organization.

Societal Developments. Early on, the values of unfettered capitalism reflected societal and cultural trends. In developing industrial societies, a belief in social Darwinism (the social survival of the fittest) fit with the doctrine that an "invisible hand" made the unrestricted free market the best economic system. This belief also meshed with the Calvinist doctrine of predestination (of being chosen by God for success) and with the frontier value of individualism. All these beliefs and values combined to justify profit maximization (the bottom line) as the single objective of enterprise. Poverty, drudgery, and exploitative employment of the "unfit" (those not chosen) for the longest possible hours at the lowest possible wages were justified as the best means to achieve the highest profits to enrich the employer-owner and shareholders, who were blessed by God to prosper and were rightfully entitled to profits. Sharing the belief were the employer's agents—the managers. The constraints of governmental regulation and union movements were unnatural, uneconomic, unreligious, and immoral. In reaction to the excesses of unconstrained profit maximization came the voting public's and legislatures' more sophisticated views of the government's regulatory role, the acceptance of unionism, and more socially conscious religion. Equally if not even more important, these came some awareness by management that profit maximization was a chimera. There was a realization that instead of concentrating on the single objective function of maximizing profits, managers ought to concentrate on maintaining and improving the value of the systems for which they were responsible as stewards. Thus managers needed to integrate the needs and interests of the constituencies of the system—the owners and shareholders; the employees, including the managers themselves; the suppliers; the clients and customers; and the community. Instead of valuing the longest working hours at the lowest possible wages, managers ought to value the highest hourly productivity per employee at equitable and satisfying wages. Integration meant alignment of the employees' and the organization's interests in their mutual growth and development.

More often than not, managers need to view themselves as stewards. For example, in the technologically driven electronics industry, keeping abreast or ahead of competition in new products means maintaining a committed, loyal, and involved management, research and development, engineering, and manufacturing workforce; satisfied investors; cooperative suppliers; and confident consumers.

Pressures for Short-Term Results. Mergers, acquisitions, leveraged buyouts, and corporate raiding force managements to keep their eyes on short-term results, current earnings, and the price of their shares in relation to their assets. Nevertheless, attention to longer-term investment and outcomes must still be maintained if the firm is to remain healthy and viable (Freeman, 1984). At the same time, as reviewed by Laverty (1996), managers may still value short-term strategies for a variety of reasons. Intangible investments and qualitative payoffs may be ignored in formal quantitative techniques discounting the future (Hayes & Abernathy, 1980). A short-term strategy may be optimal for the manager who is planning to move out of the organization but suboptimal for the organization (Campbell & Marino, 1994; Rumelt, 1987). Investors and board directors may be impatient and want to see quick results (Jacobs, 1991); information about long-term prospects may be lacking (Thakor, 1990). And as said above, short-term maximizing of stock prices may be necessary when a hostile takeover by another corporation is possible (Drucker, 1986).

Short-term maximizing may be a matter of economic beliefs and ideals. Libertarians share a belief in unfettered free enterprise driven by self-interest. Everyone has a price. Everyone should try to maximize their own self-interests (Rand, 1959). Free-market consultants to Russia in the 1990s underestimated the effects of the human and cultural sides of enterprise. In 10 years, the new competitive economic policies had reduced the Russian economy by 50% and raised the poverty level disastrously (Lawrence, 2002).

Religious Faith. Toney and Oster (1998) presented the results of interviews and surveys of approximately 200 CEOs, of whom 65% were Protestant, 23% Catholic, and 12% Jewish. One specific question they were asked was how often they consciously applied the teachings of their religion to the daily decision process. Those who said they always did so were compared with those who said they never did so. The organizations led by CEOs who applied religious teachings earned 8% more net income than the organizations led by those who never did. In relation to their comparison group, these religious CEOs spent more time teaching and coaching and made more judgments on the basis of intuition and experience. They focused less on organizational and personal financial goals, were satisfied with a much smaller personal net worth, were more optimistic, gave twice as much to charity, more enjoyed being of service to others, and reported that their strong faith sustained them and made them more effective in coping with adversity.

Nationality. The value references in the annual reports for 1986–1990 of 53 American and 77 Australian organizations were content-analyzed and profiled in terms of nine values. Affiliation and leadership were espoused more frequently by the American organizations and authority and participation were espoused more frequently by the Australian organizations (Kabanoff & Daly, 2000). Presumably, the values espoused reflected the public views of the CEOs and managing directors. The GLOBE project (House, Hanges, Javidan, et al., 2004) assessed the leadership values of midlevel managers in 62 countries. The values of participative leadership were highest in the managers of the Anglo countries, Nordic Europe, and the Germanic cluster. These values were lowest in Eastern Europe, southern Asia, Confucian Asia (China, Taiwan, Korea), and the Middle East. Valuing team orientation was highest in Latin America and lowest in the Middle East. A humane orientation was most valued by managers in southern Asia, sub-Saharan Africa, and the Anglo countries and least valued in Latin and Nordic Europe. The value of self-protection was most important in the Middle East, southern Asia, Eastern Europe, and Confucian Asia and was least important in the Anglo, Germanic, and Nordic countries (see also Chapter 33).

Balancing Values

Some of the balanced, salient values are likely to remain the same in profit-making enterprises as in government, education, health, and social service organizations, although specific values that are consistent with the purposes of the organization obviously need to be substituted. Leaders of organizations providing environmental products and services value the environment more than do leaders of nonenvironmentally-oriented organizations whether or not the organizations are for profit or not for profit (Egri & Herman, 2000). In health organizations, concern for the care of patients is substituted for concern with the quality of products, but the steward in a health organization must keep alert to the employees' as well as the patients' interests. Maslow (1965, pp. 128, 131) captured an ideal set of balanced objectives for the management of any system:

[The leader in the work situation] is the one who . . . can help to organize things in such a fashion that the job gets done best. . . . [The good leader must also have the] ability to take pleasure in the growth and self-actualization of other people. . . . He must be strong, he must enjoy responsibility . . . ; he must be able to mete out discipline as necessary, to be stern as well as loving [like] a good father and a husband; . . . watching his children grow up well and . . . his wife . . . grow on toward greater maturity and self-actualization.

Competing Values. Quinn (1984) theorized that managers are faced with competing values that need to be kept under consideration. For example, they must make choices either for expansion and adaptation or for consolidation and continuity. They must choose between risk-taking inventiveness and conservative cautiousness, and sometimes between allocation of resources and information gathering and distribution.

Profit-maximizing values and balancing consituents' values may have to compete with a third set of values (Hay & Gray, 1974). For a minority of managers, quality of life, environmental protection, and other social and political values compete with constituent interests of the firm. For socially oriented managers, there can be no balanced compromise about the quality of a product, environmental pollution, or the safety of workers. Likewise, peace-minded investors avoid investing highly in the profitable military weapons industries, and public health advocates refuse to work for tobacco firms.

But it is not enough to say that some executives are profit maximizers, others are systems balancers, and still others have social concerns of consequence. There may be trade-offs between the three objectives that are not mutually exclusive. For instance, Osborn and Jackson (1988) presented data on the safety of 41 nuclear plants that suggested that the past experience of high profitability was associated with fewer major safety violations if the utility's total energy output was not committed to nuclear energy. However, if there was a relatively larger commitment to nuclear than to nonnuclear power, more major safety violations occurred with high profitability. Like riverboat gamblers, executives in the latter utilities appeared to be more willing to increase the risks of losing it all as profits increased. A survey of 6,000 business managers by Posner and Schmidt (1984) found that of 11 values, the 2 most important were effectiveness and productivity and the least important were value to the community and service to the public. In another study of 803 public officials at the federal GS-15 level, Schmidt and Posner (1986) reported that among the 11 values effectiveness and pro-

ductivity were first and third in importance, while service to the public and value to the community were seventh and eighth. The general public was tenth in ratings of the importance of constituents' interests; clients, bosses, self, technical personnel, managers, and coworkers were all more important. The evidence suggests that public and private administrators are less concerned about their obligations to society than about their obligations to their organization and its people.

A multiplicity of values involving personal and organizational considerations underlie the objectives of management. For managers to restrict themselves to a single objective function—profit maximization—is a fictional convenience for classical economists and some operational research specialists. For example, when Dent (1959) asked a representative sample of 145 U.S. chief executive officers or their deputies in confidential "off-the-record" interviews, "What are the aims of top management in your company?" only 36 percent mentioned as their first aim "to make money, profits, or a living." Three-fourths talked about multiple goals including growth, public service, the welfare of employees, and the quality of products. High-quality products and public service were mentioned more often by the executives in larger firms; the welfare of employees was cited more often in smaller nonunion and larger unionized companies. In firms with higher percentages of white-collar, professional, or supervisory employees, fewer executives spoke of profitability and more spoke of growth. In addition, the willingness of managers to pursue noneconomic objectives may be a matter of how much their own income depends on the profitability of the firm. Furthermore, if they have alternative sources of income, they may express a broader range of valued objectives for the company (Hambrick & Mason, 1984).

Factors in Organizational Values. Shartle (1956) conducted studies of the elements that executives in several kinds of organizations said they valued to various degrees. A factor analysis of item intercorrelations produced nine factors that described the value dimensions for business firms: (1) organizational magnitude, expansion, and structure; (2) internal consideration for welfare, health, and comfort; (3) the degree of competition, strategy, and shrewdness; (4) the degree of ethical and social responsibility; (5) the quality of the product or service; (6) the degree of change; (7) the degree of organization control over the identifications of members; (8) the degree of external political participation; and (9) the degree of equality and recognition of members.

In a survey of 1,576 first-time supervisors at Japanese National Railways, Furukawa (1981) isolated five valued objectives. Three were task related (to establish order, to increase motivation, and to accomplish goals), and two were interpersonally oriented (to establish and maintain dependable relationships and peaceful work units). To achieve the human relations objectives, the supervisors saw a need to be more considerate and less initiating. To achieve task-oriented objectives, the need was for more initiation of structure and less consideration.

Individual Differences in Values. Valuing nonprofitable activities such as social programs, community programs, and employee welfare programs seems rooted more in individual differences than in socialization processes within the organization. This idea was inferred by Sukel (1983), who found that status as a top, middle, or first-level manager in manufacturing, banking, or retailing made no difference to the valuing of such socially relevant activities. At the same time, senior management could be seen as self-serving rather than more broadly interested in the organization and its members. This was seen when the board of directors rejected the bid of its own senior management to buy control of the RJR-Nabisco conglomerate, although the bid matched an outsider's leveraged buyout offer. The board of directors openly said they did not trust the management to protect the rights of the employees or to maintain the integrity of the firms' operations (Sterngold, 1988).

Priority of Effectiveness and Productivity

While maintaining some sense of balance, most managers and business leaders, if given the choice, do tend to place a higher priority on organizational effectiveness and productivity, according to Posner and Schmidt (1984). For 803 senior federal officials, results were similar. Organizational effectiveness and productivity were rated first and third; value of service to the public and to the community were seventh and eighth (Schmidt & Posner, 1986). England (1967a, 1967b), who studied managers at nine hierarchical levels, found general agreement that the goals of organizational effectiveness and productivity

was more important than than social welfare goals. Community leaders of middle-size cities in the Midwest, most of whom were in business or banking, believed that economic development was the paramount goal of university extension services (Moss, 1974). A similar sample did not regard environmental concerns to be of much importance to their communities (Sofranko & Bridgeland, 1975). But community leaders in rural Georgia saw less need for economic exchange than for coordination, in contrast to rural heads of households with whom they were compared (Nix, Singh, & Cheatham, 1974). No doubt, concerns about the environment, climate change, and pollution have risen in importance in the past 30 years, along with concerns about health, education, and public affairs.

Using England's (1967a) Personal Values Questionnaire, England and Weber (1972) contrasted the extent to which U.S. managers regarded various issues as *successful*, as *right*, and as *pleasant*. From these judgments, managers were identifed as emphasizing either what is pragmatic, what is moral, or what is pleasurable. England and Lee (1974) then administered the Personal Values Questionnaire to almost 2,000 U.S., Australian, Indian, and Japanese managers. The success of these managers was measured by their income adjusted for their age. In all four countries, successful managers were more likely to hold pragmatic values emphasizing productivity, profitability, and achievement.

Fast-Track Managers' Priorities. From 46 to 77% of an international sample of 5,122 managers were willing to spend money for all five budgeting problems on Exercise Objectives described above; but faster-climbing managers tended to exhibit more pragmatism than idealism in that they were less willing to spend money to handle the requests for safety, to settle a strike, to deal with morale, to improve the quality of products, or to eradicate pollution in a stream. Although they did not want to risk wasting money, faster-climbing managers did value generosity and fair-mindedness. The faster-climbing managers wanted productive value for their expenditures (Bass, Burger, Doktor, et al., 1979).

What managers judge to be important and valuable for success as a manager is related to their own success. Managers who stressed the importance of inner-directed values such as imagination and self-confidence were rated more effective in their jobs than those who viewed their roles as demanding other-directed behavior such as co-operativeness and tactfulness (Lawler & Porter, 1967a, 1967b; Mitchell & Porter, 1967; Porter & Lawler, 1968). Bass, Burger, et al. (1979) found that for several thousand middle managers from 12 countries, fast-trackers considered the values of generosity, fair-mindedness, sharp-wittedness, and steadiness as more important for top management, whereas slower-climbing managers considered tolerance and adaptability more important. The values considered most important by fast-trackers for middle managers were generosity, sharp-wittedness, and reliability; for slow-trackers, tolerance, adaptability, and self-control were most important for middle managers. Fast-trackers thought that the most important values for first-line supervisors were generosity and reliability. In contrast, slow-trackers judged fair-mindedness, tolerance, and adaptability most important for first-line supervisors.

The Valuing of Pay. In response to the traditionalists' overemphasis on pay as a motivator, humanist scholars overreacted, attempting to minimize the importance of pay to managers and their subordinates. According to reviews of research on pay and managerial motivation, pay remained a strong motivator for managerial personnel.[2] Senior executives stressed the importance of pay slightly less than did managers at lower levels, but pay was highly significant for all. Pay may satisfy not only lower-order needs such as the need for safety and security, but also higher-order needs such as autonomy and self-actualization. Porter and Lawler (1986) found that managers who perceived that their pay depended to a great degree on their job performance tended to perform better on their jobs when both they and their superiors rated their performance. The relationship between the probability of higher pay and their likely effort was stronger for those who attached a high reward value to pay. Effective performance was related to the extent to which it was seen as instrumental to higher pay.

The Valuing of Technical Competence. Studies before 1965 indicated that first-line supervisors valued the technical aspects of their assignments more than their human relations responsibilities.[3] Their higher-level managers tended to agree with them (Rubenowitz, 1962). Increasingly, however, recognition of the importance of other attributes such as interpersonal competence has accompanied the valuing of technical competence in supervision. Such a shift in values (an increased subscription to pragmatism) occurred for managers in Western Australia in a period of 23 years. The change was attributed to changing Australian business conditions during the same period (Spillane, 1980). The valuing of technical competence was enhanced greatly by the information revolution.

Personal Priorities. Managers and leaders have their own personal priorities regarding what is important to them. In the aggregate, some personal goals—such as self-actualization, independence, and expertise—are more important than others such as duty, prestige, and wealth. There are wide individual differences among managers and leaders, depending on their organizational level, their nationality, whether they have job security, and so on. Hofstede (1978) found that in the responses of 65,000 supervisors, salesmen, and service personnel to a worldwide survey of IBM employees, these individual differences could be accounted for by two factors: (1) the valuing of personal assertiveness (leadership, independence, and self-realization), and (2) the valuing of personal comfort (pleasure, security, and affection). The Indian civil service, staffed mainly by 1,200 middle- and upper-class Britons educated at British public schools and universities, had contempt for moneymaking and the hustle and corruption accompanying it. They saw themselves as Plato's guardians and the "heaven born" (Lapping, 1985).

Bass, Burger, Doktor, et al. (1979) obtained results indicating that 3,082 managers in an international sample valued 11 life goals as follows (with 1.00 = most important, and 11.00 = least important): self-realization, 4.09; independence, 4.89; expertness, 5.17; affection, 5.21; leadership, 5.32; security, 5.50; service, 6.01; pleasure, 6.78; duty, 7.08; prestige, 7.65; and wealth to build a large estate, 8.27. But the standard deviations from 2.6 to 3.3 for each goal indicated that some managers rated the same goal first in importance whereas others ranked it

---

[2] More will be said about this in Chapter 15.

[3] Kelly (1964); Mandell and Duckworth (1955); Moore, Kennedy, and Castori (1946); and Sequeira (1962).

eleventh. Wide individual differences, particularly across the 12 countries studied, were the rule.

Belonging, Identification, and Loyalty

One value of importance that many leaders and managers gain from their membership in an organization is a feeling of belonging to and identification with it (Wald & Doty, 1954). For example, Mullen's (1954) survey of 140 clubs of supervisors in 32 states found that 88% of the supervisors wanted to feel identified with the company, and 71% reported being treated as if they were a part of management. D. D. Braun (1976) noted that identification with the community of Mankato, Minnesota, was strongly associated with community leadership rather than only with participation in community activities.

Orientation Toward Superiors or Subordinates

Some leaders tend to feel closer to the attitudes, beliefs, and values of the higher authorities in their organization; others tend to identify with those below themselves. The best leaders are able to do both. Furthermore, their performance will be affected by how much they identify with the organization's values. Their values are a key to understanding the relations between leaders and subordinates (Dienesch & Liden, 1986). D. T. Campbell and associates (1955, 1957, 1958, 1961) developed various methods of measuring orientation toward or identification with one's superiors and subordinates.

With these methods, Campbell and McCormack (1957) compared attitudes of air force and civilian personnel. The leader's location in the organization affected his or her orientation toward those above and those below. The researchers found that colonels were significantly less oriented toward their superiors than were majors or college men, and majors were less so than were air force cadets or their instructors. Air force majors and lieutenant colonels were significantly more subordinate-oriented than were the other groups tested. Orientation toward superiors or toward subordinates appeared to be independent of tested information about leadership (Campbell & Damarin, 1961); nor were self-reported orientation measures consistent with the observed orientation to superiors or subordinates in a role-playing exercise (Burwen & Campbell, 1957a). However, orientation to-

ward superiors did correlate with authoritarianism and with valuing discipline (Chapman & Campbell, 1957a).

Identification with the Values of Higher-Ups. The alignment of the individual manager's goals and those of the organization is central to the manager's sense of belonging to and identification with the organization (Culbertson & McDonough, 1980). Vroom (1960b) observed that the goals of a large firm are likely to be more accurately perceived by those executives who have more favorable attitudes toward the firm. Subordinates who resemble their superiors in the personality traits "sociable" and "stable" are better satisfied than those who do not closely resemble their superiors in this respect. Furthermore, subordinates who identify themselves with and express interests similar to their superiors are more satisfied than those who do not (Eran, 1966). Such identification also helps their careers. Top managers generally preferred and rated as more effective those subordinates whose attitudes and values were similar to their own (R. E. Miles, 1964a; V. F. Mitchell, 1968). Identification with management also contributed to the likelihood that an employee would be promoted to a management position (J. C. White, 1964).

Lawler, Porter, and Tannenbaum (1968) found that interactions with superiors were more favorably valued than were those with subordinates. Balma, Maloney, and Lawshe (1958a, 1958b) concluded that supervisors who identified with management were rated as having significantly more productive groups than were those who did not. But the employees' satisfaction with a supervisor was not related to the supervisor's orientation. R. S. Barrett (1963) also discovered that first-line supervisors who perceived that their approach to problems was similar to that of their immediate superiors tended to feel free to do things in their own way. Fleishman and Peters (1962) observed that the effectiveness of lower-level managers was identified with that of their immediate middle-level superiors. Read (1962) found that the successful upward mobility of managers was related to their problem-oriented communication with superiors. This tendency to communicate with superiors was associated with trust in their superiors and a perception of their superiors' influence.

Henry (1949) and others found that rapidly promoted executives tended to identify themselves with their superiors as a primary organization reference group. Campbell, Dunnette, Lawler, and Welck (1970) suggested that fast-trackers tended to identify with fast-trackers higher up in the organization and were less interested in their current group of subordinates. To get promoted, they might even work against the best interests of their immediate subordinates. But the extent to which they enhanced their subordinates' sense of belonging to the organization tended to pay off in their subordinates' better performance. Habbe (1947) demonstrated that insurance agents who thought they were fulfilling their managers' expectations sold more policies and experienced fewer lapses than did those who thought they were not meeting these expectations.

Identification with the Values of Subordinates. Some evidence also suggests that for many leaders, satisfaction and success are connected with identification with those who are below them in the organization. According to R. E. Miles (1964a), managers did not regard lower-level supervisors as being highly promotable when they identified only with the company. Similarly, Mann and Dent (1954b) found that supervisors and employees agreed that the promotable supervisor is one who will stand up for employees and their rights, train them for better jobs, and let them know where they stand on matters that concern them. Pelz's (1952) study of industrial work groups indicated that first-line supervisors who were oriented to subordinates tended to be evaluated positively by workers, but only of they were perceived to have sufficient influence with superiors so they could satisfy the workers' expectations.

Supervisors who valued belonging and identification did much to increase their subordinates' sense of "ownership" of activities (Habbe, 1947). Consistent with this finding was Anikeeff's finding (1957) that the greater the satisfaction of managers, the greater the similarity between the attitudes of managers and workers. Satisfied managers prevented a cleavage in attitudes between workers and management.

The favorable attitudes of leaders toward their subordinates are reciprocated. Obrochta (1960) reported that workers' attitudes toward supervisors were favorable only when the supervisors held favorable attitudes toward the workers. Murphy and Corenblum (1966) observed that loyalty to a superior was higher at all levels in an organization if the superior perceived his or her group of subordinates as a primary source of social support.

Leaders can provide a model of behavior and values (Borman & Motowidlo, 1993). They can set examples for their teams that result in the team's productivity (Podsakoff, MacKenzie & Ahearne, 1997). Lock and Thomas (1998) found that such leaders could influence team members in good group citizenship, voluntary behaviors, and suitable responses to the organization's vision that result in desired organizational outcomes. But team leaders who gave a high priority to making money were more likely to lead teams that were less responsive to customers' needs for changes. Also, leaders who valued fun and pleasure were less likely to have teams motivated to find technological solutions for their customers. Sosik (2005) reported that 945 subordinates with higher traditional, collectivistic, and self-enhancement values rated their 218 managers as more charismatic in leadership. In turn, charismatic leadership predicted greater performance, extra effort, and good organizational citizenship behavior.

Values and Political Leadership

One has to look to journalists, biographers, historians, and philosophers for the best understanding of the values that underlie the performance of political leaders. Rokeach (1973) suggested that two values—freedom and equality—were basic to systems of political philosophy. He analyzed four political leaders: Norman Thomas, Barry Goldwater, Vladimir Lenin, and Adolf Hitler. Each leader, revealed distinctively different patterns of reference to the values of "freedom" and "equality." For Thomas (a Socialist), the values of freedom and equality were both highly salient. Hitler (a Fascist), seldom referred to them. For Lenin (a Communist), equality was much more important than freedom. For the conservative Republican Goldwater, freedom was prized over equality (Rokeach, 1972).

Paige (1977) offered a number of hypotheses about the importance of values to the behavior of political leaders.

1. Terminal values (the worthwhileness of the end state) can be used by political leaders to justify contrary instrumental values (the worthwhileness of activities). Lenin argued that violence is justifiable

to destroy the state and achieve the peaceful communist society. Woodrow Wilson justified the United States' entry into World War I because this was to be the war to end all wars.

2. Values influence the scope of what is relevant. Political leaders who sincerely value "one world" look at the same conflicts between nations differently from the way ardent nationalists look at them and try to act accordingly—for instance, on the subject of nuclear proliferation.

3. Political leaders and followers very in the intensity of their value commitments. Both loyalty and treachery determine what happens to political movements in crises.

4. To achieve desired ends, political leaders may sacrifice the values of truth and honesty. "A good precinct captain [in Chicago] will always find a way to steal votes" (p. 124).

5. Values become salient to a political leader's behavior in reaction to circumstances and objectives. What a political leaders says to get elected may be the opposite of what he does after he is elected. In his campaign for the presidency in 1932, Franklin Delano Roosevelt argued for the popular economic value of a balanced federal budget. When elected, he moved rapidly into federal deficit spending to stimulate the economy to deal with the Great Depression.

To be politically successful in the United States a leader must emphasize the value of individualism. Since the two major U.S. political parties cross social boundaries to a considerable degree, personalized leadership, rather than social and economic policy issues, dominates elections. But economic values become salient in times of economic downturns, and foreign policy increases in importance in times of real or imagined threats to national security. Leaders differ in how much they value diplomacy over militancy and the support of international institutions to keep the peace. Fascist leaders value militarism and authoritarianism and are against welfare favored by democratic leaders (Eckhardt, 1965).

The U.S. Constitution was designed to check runaway leadership; nevertheless, individual leaders are seen as a panacea. Individual initiative and responsibility are

prized in the U.S. culture; the role of leader is similarly valued. During the long-drawn-out electoral process and then after gaining office, the president has to "showcase" and sell his (or her) own qualities as a person to obtain power and remain powerful and influential (Rockman, 1984).

Values of the Political Revolutionary. Certain values, including asceticism, appear to stand out among revolutionary leaders such as Oliver Cromwell, Maximilien Robespierre, Vladimir Lenin, and Mao Zedong (Mazlish, 1976). All 32 revolutionary leaders studied by Rejai and Phillips (1979) were driven by a sense of justice and injustice and a corresponding attempt to right wrongs. Nationalism and patriotism were also important. When Rejai and Phillips (1988) contrasted 50 revolutionary leaders who aimed to overthrow their governments and 50 loyalist leaders who aimed to preserve them, according to 96 scholars, values that were more apparent in the revolutionaries than in the loyalists were an optimistic view of their human nature but a fluctuating optimistic view of their countries. Revolutionaries tended to abandon religion and to become atheists.

Motives

Leaders vary in many motives, drives, desires, and needs that guide and energize them. These include curiosity, the desire for knowledge; order, the desire for structure; acquisition, the desire for saving and collecting; tranquillity, the desire for emotional calm; and eating, drinking, sex, romance, and physical activity (Reiss, 2000). How does a motive differ from a value or trait?

A *value* is a belief that an action or end state is preferable to its opposite. Leadership may be a value. A *trait* is a regular, consistent, and generalized cluster of intercorrelated behaviors. Extroversion is a trait. A *motive* can energize a variety of behaviors that may differ from each other but all create a similar inner affective state of goal satisfaction if consummated. A motive also provides direction or orientation to the energized behaviors. The need or desire to lead is a motive. Traits and motives interact with each other (Winter, John, Stewart, et al., 1998). For instance, in a study of 818 ROTC cadets, Thomas, Dickson and Bliese (2001) found that prediction of the cadets' assessed leadership in summer camp was completely mediated by the need for affiliation, and to a lesser extent by the need for power. Motives and needs may be conscious, implicit, or subconscious strivings toward our goals. If competing motives and obstacles do not interfere, we take action to satisfy our motives (Winter, 2002). The motives may be stable and generalizeable propensities that are *far from action*. Or they may be intentions and choices that are *close to action*—momentary and applicable to a specific situation (Locke & Latham, 1990).

The Achievement Motive (Subconscious)

Believing that we need not be completely aware of our motives to be able to accurately answer direct questions about them, McClelland (1961) and McClelland and Winter (1969) developed the Thematic Apperception Test (TAT). Winter (1969) provided strong initial evidence to support the proposition that the need for achievement is an important value for effective leaders, particularly successful entrepreneurs.[4] Their data were corroborated by numerous studies, both in the United States and abroad, that demonstrated that managerial and entrepreneurial success was predicted by the need for achievement.[5] Likewise, Cummin (1967) found that more successful executives had a higher need for achievement. Wainer and Rubin (1969) observed that the need for achievement of 51 technical entrepreneurs who founded and operated their own firms was related to the growth rate of their companies. The highest-performing companies were those whose owners had a strong need for achievement and a moderate need for power. Furthermore, data from over 1,000 managers gathered by Hall and Donnell (1979) found that the speed of these managers' career advancement was associated with their motivation to achieve. Mussen and Porter (1959) concluded that leaders who were more effective in group discussions scored significantly higher in the need for achievement and affiliation and in feelings of adequacy than those who were ineffective.

However, unlike most other investigators, Harrell and Harrell (1978) failed to find such a measured need for achievement in a forecast at Stanford University of the

subsequent success of trainees in small business. And Litwin and Stringer (1968) found that although participants in small-group experiments were more satisfied if their leaders had a high need for achievement, their groups experienced the same satisfaction if their leaders had a high need for affiliation. Nonetheless, the preponderance of many studies of the achievement motive suggest that those high in this motive try to outperform others. They are competitive. Winning makes them feel good. They get satisfaction from succeeding at tasks. They have self-imposed standards of excellence. Easy tasks may not be as interesting to achievers as challenging tasks on which they can succeed. Team success satisfies their high need for achievement only when each individual member's effort can be identified (Springer, 2001).

Power Motivation

This is concern with emotional impact for reputation, status, and strong actions affecting others. Achievement motivation and power, when each has been assessed alone, have been reasonably accurate in predicting the success of entrepreneurs and increases in their performance (McClelland & Winter, 1969). But each makes only a partial contribution to a full assessment of the motivation to manage. For a full assessment, as was noted in Chapter 7, one needs to return again to the imperial motive—i.e., how need for power combines with high achievement motivation and low need for affiliation to account for their behavior as leaders. (The affiliation motive is concerned with close social and emotional relations with others.) High inhibition also is important. As Browning and Jacob (1964) observed, whether the need for achievement and for power directs individuals toward leadership in the economic or political arena depends on which arena in the community is open and available to them. In the political arena, dynamic, activist, and effective presidents gave inaugural addresses high in both the need for achievement and the need for power. Inactive presidents, less highly regarded by posterity, gave inaugural addresses that were low in both needs (Winter & Stewart, 1977).

Vision statements were analyzed after being obtained from 111 supervisors in a government service organization and 269 CEOs heading mainly small manufacturing companies that produced and installed

[4] See also McClelland (1965a, 1965b, 1969).
[5] Andrews (1967); Hornaday and Aboud (1971); Meyer and Walker (1961); and Meyer, Walker, and Litwin (1961).

wood products. As hypothesized, the stronger appearance of the achievement motive in the vision statements was more important in manufacturing than in service. The affiliation motive was more important in service (Kirkpatrick, 1999).

Task Orientation (Conscious Motivation)

Defining Task Orientation. The achievement motive, far from action, as measured by projective techniques, reflects a deep-seated, subconscious fantasy about success and accomplishment (Winter, 2002). Task orientation is a self-reported, inventoried, conscious motive scored by the Orientation Inventory (ORI, Bass, 1962b). Although the projected need and the conscious orientation have low correlation with each other (Bass, 1967c), they both appear to contribute positively to the emergence and success of a leader. Successful accomplishment is rated highly as a value and personal goal by managers in diverse organizations and countries (Bass, Burger, et al., 1979; England, 1967a, 1967b). The desire to achieve and to complete tasks successfully is a motive associated with those who emerge and succeed as leaders. Bass (1960a, p. 149) conceived of task orientation as a characteristic of persons who in social settings "will [try] hardest to help obtain the group's goals, solve its problems, overcome barriers preventing the successful completion of the group's tasks, and who persist at . . . assignments." Task orientation is distinguished from interaction (relations) orientation (to have fun, work cooperatively, and be helpful) and from self-orientation (to be praised, recognized, respected, and have loyal associates). The ORI assessed orientation toward the task, toward relating to others, and toward the self (Beckhard, 1995).

According to a review of research by Bass (1967b), those who were in higher-status positions in organizations uniformly were more task oriented. Thus top managers scored higher on the ORI than middle managers; middle managers scored higher than supervisors; supervisors scored higher than nonsupervisory workers. In addition, the higher the task orientations revealed by college student leaders in sensitivity training groups, the more they were rated positively by their peers on behaviors that are relevant to leadership. The task-oriented student leaders were seen to help other group members express their ideas, help the groups stay on target, help get to the meat

of issues, give good suggestions on proceeding, provide good summaries, encourage high productivity, take the lead, work hard, and offer original ideas (Bass & Dunteman, 1963). Again, observers at an assessment center rated temporary supervisors who were under consideration for promotion as being more promotable if the supervisors were high in task orientation. Task orientation was higher among second-line supervisors whose superiors rated them "best" rather than "less than best." Likewise, it was higher among top- and middle-performing first-line supervisors than among those whose performance was low (Dunteman & Bass, 1963). Although tested intelligence correlated only .19 with task orientation, self-sufficiency and resourcefulness correlated .33 with task orientation. Other correlations with task orientaion found in various studies were as follows: .31, controlled willpower; .28, need for endurance, .28, sober-serious; and .27, tough-realistic (Bass; 1967b).

Other Measures of Conscious Task Motivation. Many self-reporting questionnaire inventories such as the California Personality Inventory contain scales of conscious task motivation. The Saville and Holdsworth Motivation Questionnaire (MQ) generated 18 factored primary scales based on 700 British respondents. Two of the four higher-order factors that emerged were (1) intrinsic motivation, dealing with desire for interesting work that allowed for flexiblity and autonomy; and (2) extrinsic motivation, from work which provided material rewards, career progress, and status. Status, in turn, systematically affected the strengths of the different motives. The MQ mean scores from 63 senior, 192 middle, and 231 junior managers revealed that the seniors were motivated most by the need to avoid failure. They would invest further energy in a project to ensure its success. Also, they had greater need for power and autonomy. At the same time, the junior managers were most concerned with their career progress. The middle managers fell in between these differences in motives. All the managers were similar in means on the other primary factor scales (Page & Baron, 1995).

Barbuto and Schell (1998) developed the reliable and valid Motivation Sources Inventory (MSI) to measure intrinsic, instumental, external, and internal motivation and goal internalization. The instrument was based on a typology by Leonard, Beauvais, and Scholl (1999).

Barbuto and Schell administered to 56 middle managers the MSI and Harrell and Stahl's (1981) Job Choice Decision-Making Exercise (JCE), a validated assessment of the needs for achievement, affiliation, and power. They also asked 217 raters to describe the managers' transformational leadership behavior using Bass and Avolio's (1991) Multifactor Leadership Questionnaire (MLQ) assessing the managers' idealized, inspirational, intellectually stimulating, and individually considerate leadership behaviors. Significant correlations were found between the MSI and the MLQ but not between the JCE and MLQ. Idealized influence correlated with internalized goals and instrumental motivation. Inspirational leadership was correlated with the managers' internalized goal motivation. Individualized consideration was correlated with instrumental motivation.

A variety of other indicators of conscious task motivation generally have been positively linked to attitudes and performance in work settings and their effects. For example, Rubenowitz (1962) found that superiors in an industrial situation tended to rate their subordinates higher in effectiveness when the subordinates were production-oriented rather than person-oriented. Tziner and Elizur (1985) created an assessment that was relevant to managers' motivation to achieve. It was unlike previous measures that were derived from projective approaches or self-reporting personality inventories. Their instrument consisted of 18 questions that asked 90 managers from a large Israeli corporation about how much they preferred to undertake difficult, problem-solving, high-responsibility tasks involving calculated risks, and how gratifying it was to do so if they were successful. The motivation to take calculated risks and solve problems correlated modestly with the rated performance of the managers, but no correlation was found between the motivation for responsible or difficult tasks and gratification for success with them.

Risk Taking

Some people enjoy taking risks, but others do not. Such preferences and behavior affect the leadership that emerges. Older leaders have been found to be generally more conservative and more likely to avoid taking risks (Alluto & Hrebiniak, 1975). They want more information and higher probabilities of success and may be content with lower payoffs as a consequence. The contrast between older and younger leaders was illustrated by two Roman consuls in 210 B.C.; Fabius who was older, was a delayer, whereas Maximus, who was younger, was eager to fight immediately to try to trap Hannibal's forces. Along with a higher than ordinary need to achieve (McClelland, 1965c) and an internal locus of control (Borland, 1974), entrepreneurs and the founder-leaders of organizations also, as would be expected, have higher risk-taking propensities than do managers, in general (Brockhaus, 1980). They also have a higher tolerance for ambiguity than do managers in general (Schere, 1981). Wallach, Kogan, and Bern (1962) found that high risk takers were more influential in discussions than low risk takers. Marquis (1962) and Collins and Guetzkow (1964) observed that high risk takers were more persuasive than more cautious members of a group.

For a random sample of 26 express-mail managers, Hater and Bass (1988) reported an average correlation of .47 between the extent to which each manager was described by three subordinates as a transformational leader (charismatic, individualizing, and intellectually stimulating) and the extent to which the same managers were judged by their bosses to be high in risk taking. But the correlation was .02 with risk taking judged by the boss if the manager was described by subordinates as transactional in leadership (practicing contingent reward and management by exception). Frost, Fiedler, and Anderson (1983) found that taking physical risks was also related to performance as a leader. In a questionnaire survey of 40 army leaders, they found that effective combat leaders engaged in more personally endangering acts than did ineffective combat leaders. Interviews with 19 fire-battalion chiefs and evaluations of 124 fire-service leaders again suggested that effective leaders exhibit more personal bravery than ineffective leaders. Such personal bravery is expected of combat leaders, as in the Israeli army, where policy dictates that they are expected to go first into danger, to be followed by their men.

Willingness to Take Risks and Achievement Motivation. Those high in need for achievment are calculating risk takers (Springer, 2001). Tasks with moderate risks are satisfying to those who have a great need to achieve. A risk-free task will lack challenge, and a highly risky task entails the likelihood of failure (Atkinson, 1964). However, a higher level of risk of failure will be entertained if a task is inherently interesting (Shapira, 1975). Leaders must take calculated risks using the limited information available to them. Thus Cleveland (1985) emphasized that an executive needs to be motivated to achieve and prepared to take risks if he or she is to take the lead in the "perilous, problematic and participatory climate for policy making of today's information-rich world."

Optimism. By definition, optimists are more willing to take risks. Leaders need to be optimists rather than pessimists. Successful leaders have revealed a more optimistic view of themselves and the world around them than have nonleaders and those leaders who have tried and failed. Content analyses of archival records by Zullow, Oettingen, Peterson, and Seligman (1988) found that 9 of the 10 losers of presidential elections between 1948 and 1984 tended in their speeches to see the pessimistic side of issues. Other analyses have found that bold leadership was predicted by optimistic styles. President George W. Bush is illustrative. Similarly, those individuals who have learned a sense of helplessness are much less likely to take the initiative in social situations (Abramson, Seligman, & Teasdale, 1978). Cleveland (1985) observed that the generalist executive in an information-rich world of work needs to be optimistic about what can be accomplished. Community leaders have more positive expectations about outcomes than do nonleaders.

Willingness to Trust

Closely associated with the willingness to take risks is the willingness to trust. Sgro et al. (1980) found that the leadership behavior of 41 cadet officers, as described by their 149 cadet subordinates, was associated with the officers' scores on a self-inventory of interpersonal trust. Interpersonal trust correlated significantly with their consideration and tolerance of freedom and their subordinates' satisfaction with them. According to Devine (1977), who conducted a survey of opinion leadership in three towns in Minnesota, both opinion leaders and opinion followers showed a willingness to trust others, but opinion isolates were less likely to trust. Rosenberg (1956) suggested that persons with low interpersonal trust would have difficulty establishing close friendships. As leaders, they would be less likely to permit freedom of action in their

subordinates. Willingness to trust others increases the likelihood of self-disclosure and the likelihood of obtaining valid feedback from them if the trust is mutual (Rusaw, 2000).

It may be that risk-taking, trusting leaders are able to maintain longer time spans for reaching decisions in contrast to those who press for quick solutions and immediate feedback (Frain & DuBrin, 1981). Clearly, willingness to risk and to trust others are required for meaningful delegation. More delegation should be seen in those leaders who are greater risk takers and are more willing to trust others. Conversely, the Machiavellian authoritarian, who expects others to share the same tendencies toward deception and surprise, is less likely to take chances on others.

Particularly salient in determining the proclivity to take risks is one's self-confidence. Both Clausen (1965) and Burnstein (1969) inferred that high risk takers tended to score high in self-confidence, which, in turn, led them to attempt and to succeed in influencing groups to follow their leadership. But many other aspects of one's self-concept enter into the emergence and success of a leader.

Concepts of the Self

"The leader's orientation toward self and others must be taken into account in order to understand fully the leadership dynamic" (Carey, 1992). How leaders think about themselves and what mental representations they form of their own roles and behaviors as leaders are underresearched (Murphy, 2002). Apart from what has been said so far, how people think, feel, and act about themselves affects their tendencies to lead. Thus, in contrast to others, *transformational* leaders value their capacity to learn from others and from their environment and believe they can learn more about themselves in doing so (Bennis & Nanus, 1985). Top business leaders, according to Levinson and Rosenthal (1984), have strong self-images and ego ideals. From a meta-analysis of the relationship of self-concepts to job satisfaction and performance, Judge and Bono (2001) concluded that these self-concepts (self-esteem, self-efficacy, and locus of control) were some of the best predictors of job satisfaction and job performance. Estimated true correlations ranged from .22 to

.45. Kark and Shamir (2002) noted that transformational leaders may appeal to their followers' *relational self* derived from the interpersonal connections between followers and individual others. Or the transformational leaders may appeal to their followers' *collective self* derived from larger work teams or organizations. The transformational leader's individualized consideration primes the interpersonal connections of the followers' relational self and self-identity. By linking the individual to the group's shared values and key role identities, the leader primes the collective self.

Self-Actualization

Maslow (1954) conceived of self-actualization—the desire to become what one is capable of becoming—as a higher level of maturity than the need for achievement. Compared with nonleaders, leaders tend to self-actualize more. They are more likely to perform up to their capacities and to develop themselves accordingly. This motivation was at the top of Maslow's (1954) needs hierarchy. Maslow (1965) believed that the attainment of self-actualization was revealed in characteristics of psychological health and well-being such as perceiving reality efficiently, accepting oneself, tolerating uncertainty, being problem-centered rather than self-centered, and identifying one's defenses with the courage to give them up. For Burns (1978), self-actualizers were potential transformational leaders because of their flexibility and their capacity for growth. Through their drive toward self-actualization, they could continually be one step ahead of their followers and help their followers rise as disciples behind them, as measured by their upward movement on Maslow's hierarchy of needs, from concern for safety and security toward concern for achievement and self-actualization.

Measurement. The Personal Orientation Inventory (POI) measures 12 interrelated aspects of self-actualization (Shostrom, 1974). POI assesses such self-concepts and values as self-directedness versus other-directedness, self-regard, self-acceptance, self-actualizing, responsiveness to one's own feelings and needs, capacity for intimate contact, and the extent to which one has a constructive view of humanity. In a survey of 58 executives in a high-technology firm, Gibbons (1986) found

many strong correlations between subordinates' descriptions of the transformational leadership behavior (charismatic, individually considerate, intellectually stimulating, and inspirational) of their superiors and the superiors' self-descriptions on the POI. Among these attributes, self-acceptance correlated .41 with being described as a charismatic and inspirational leader. The superiors' self-rated inner direction, self-regard, self-acceptance, and capacity for intimate contact all correlated above .40 with the subordinates' ratings of their superiors' individual consideration as a leader. Inner direction and self-acceptance also correlated above .40 with displaying contingent reward. Gaston (1983), too, found evidence that those managers who were identified in POI interviews and by their colleagues as self-actualized tended to perform well as leaders even in less than optimum organizational systems.

Some of Maslow's elements of self-actualization have to be reconsidered as contributions to the performance of leaders. For example, Gibbons (1986) found that spontaneity generally was closer to zero in correlation with various leadership factors. This finding seems to be consistent with McClelland's argument that the motivation to lead includes a need for inhibiting power; and, as will be discussed later, the emergence and success of a leader calls for a high degree of self-monitoring.

Ways of Achieving Self-Actualization. People differ in what they consider self-actualization to be. Politicians may see it as the attainment of power; business executives may see it as the attainment of organizational leadership; technologists, as the attainment of expertise; and entrepreneurs, as the attainment of wealth. Similarly, Maslow's social needs can be satisfied within the family and among friends through affection, on the job through service, and in the organization or community through duty. Wainer and Rubin's (1969) study of entrepreneurs who had started their own companies found that their strong need for achievement and their moderate need for power were associated with their companies' success. Ghiselli's (1986b) analysis of middle managers and hourly workers found that successful managers had less desire for security and financial rewards than did unsuccessful ones. However, Henderson (1977) failed to find support for expectations that self-actualization would influence choice of leadership style. Harrell and Alpert (1979) concluded that to maximize success and satisfaction, the need for autonomy should be strong among business entrepreneurs, moderate among tenured professors, and weak among bureaucrats. Appelbaum (1977) obtained data from 75 suburban supervisors in governments that strongly supported Harrell and Alpert's conclusion about bureaucrats.

Needs Satisfaction

Although rated as being most important in themselves, self-actualization and autonomy were the least satisfied managerial needs (L. W. Porter, 1961b).[6] Job security was less important and more readily satisfied (Centers, 1948).[7] This pattern changed in the 1980s with the increased concern for security. With the "downsizing" of management in the 1980s, and again during the recession of 2001, job security has become a more potent issue for lower and middle managers (McCormick & Powell, 1988).

Among 3,082 mostly middle managers from 12 countries, as noted before, Bass, Burger, et al. (1979) found that the managers had a clear set of preferences when they were asked to rank their life goals. The most important goals were self-realization (self-actualization) and independence (autonomy). Security was ranked much lower. Goals having to do with assertiveness and accomplishment were emphasized more often by fast-track managers, whereas goals associated with comfort tended to be favored by slow-track managers. Similarly, Hall and Donnell (1979) found that in comparing 190 slow-track, 442 average-track, and 32 fast-track managers, the fast advancers stressed the need for self-actualization, belonging, and esteem in motivating their subordinates. They paid only average attention to the need for safety and security. The slow-track managers emphasized mainly the need for safety and security. This was consistent with Porter and Lawler's (1968) finding that differences in successful managerial performance were more highly related to the need for self-actualization and autonomy than to the need for security, belonging, and esteem.

Self-Awareness

Self-awareness is assessed by comparing a leader's self-ratings of behavior and the ratings of behavior observed by superiors, peers, subordinates, or others (Atwater & Yammarino, 1992). Often the congruence is lower than expected. To improve their self-awareness, leaders need to be more introspective and to pay more attention to feedback from others (Ulmer, 1996).

Those leaders who underrate themselves receive higher performance appraisals. For instance, Wexley, Alexander, Greenawalt, et al. (1980) studied manager-subordinate dyads and obtained a significant correlation between a subordinate's satisfaction with supervision and the congruence between the manager's self-description and the subordinate's description of the manager.[8] Those who overrate themselves tend to be less effective leaders (Bass & Yammarino, 1991), possibly because they may be highly self-confident and ignore failures and criticism (Atwater & Yammarino, 1997). As Edwards and Parry (1993) and Edwards (2001) have noted, when a correlation is calculated between the criterion of performance (Y) and the difference between the self-rater (S) and the rater (R) score, not only is it the resulting difference between the simple correlation between r_{SY} and r_{RY}; it is dependent also on $S^2 + R^2 - 2RS$ and requires a quadratic correlation model. Accordingly, a richer examination of self-awareness was provided by Tekleab, Yun, Tesluk, et al. (2001) using polynomial regression analysis. It showed for 49 leaders and their 222 followers, effectiveness was highest for transformational leaders whose self-reports were congruent with those of their followers; underestimating leaders were next most effective; and overestimators of their transformational leadership were least effective. Leaders who were in agreement with their followers (accurate estimators) were more effective than leaders who were inaccurate estimators. Any change in accuracy from perfect agreement with followers was linked to a reduction in effectiveness. The decline was greater for overestimators than underestimators. Generally similar but not as clear-cut results occurred for the leaders with self-awareness of empowering leadership and its impact on followers' self-leadership. A leader's lack of self-awareness may reveal a lack of listening, a lack

[6]See also Haire, Ghiselli, and Porter (1963); Johnson and Marcrum (1968); and Porter (1962).
[7]See also Centers and Bugental (1966), Edel (1966), N. George (1958), and Raudsepp (1962).

[8]The importance of this congruence will be discussed again in later chapters.

of response to followers' demands, and a lack of attention to criticism and failures—a misdiagnosis of the leader's strengths and weaknesses (Tekleab, Yun, Tesluk, et al., 2001). Sosik and Megerian (1999) found that overestimators and underestimators were lower in transformational leadership, performance, and emotional intelligence than those who were more in agreement with their subordinates about their ratings. The results supported earlier findings by Atwater, Ostroff, Yammarino, et al. (1998).

Self-Understanding

"Know thyself," a favorite piece of wisdom to classical Greek philosophers, continues to be important advice for leaders today. In most surveys, leaders tend to give themselves an inflated evaluation in contrast to their colleagues' descriptions of their performance (Bass & Yammarino, 1989). They believe they have more important jobs than their superiors think they have. Modesty is not usually a trait of managers. But self-understanding is essential even for the most successful leaders. As was already noted, the interpersonally competent manager is open to receiving feedback, the approach most likely to promote and maintain a manager's accurate self-understanding. Supported by the Gallup Organization's worldwide individual survey feedback and consulting efforts, Clifton (1992) counseled that managers should find out what they do well and do more of it. They should also find out what they do poorly and stop doing it. "Focus on strengths and manage the weaknesses" (p. 18). Nonetheless,

> Executives need to be able to handle their own success. They can be derailed when . . . success goes to their heads. After being told how good they are for so long, some simply lose their humility and become cold and arrogant. . . . People no longer wish to work with them (or continue to provide feedback). (McCall & Lombardo, 1983, p. 11)

Concepts of the self can be at variance with the outside world and affect a leader's performance. For instance, Ziegenhagen (1964) subjected 15 world political leaders' autobiographies to content analysis and found that the leaders' ethnocentric behavior, conformity to in-group norms, and hostility to out-groups correlated highly with inconsistencies in the leaders' self-conceptions. These inconsistencies were assessed by a lack of agreement between the leaders' self-concept and the concept that the individual leaders thought others had of them. Interest has grown in helping managers to more accurately differentiate themselves from others, to recognize that they don't necessarily think like others, and to realize that they should not expect others to react in the same way as they do in situations (Chee, 2002).

Other self-concepts related to leadership that have been of particular interest include self-schemas, self-monitoring, locus of control, field independence, self-efficacy, self-confidence, and self-esteem.

Self-Schemas

Self-schema (also called self-schemata) are "cognitive generalizations about the self, derived from past experience, that organize and guide the processing of self-related information" (Markus, Smith & Moreland, 1977, p. 64). People with leadership self-schemas are likely to think about becoming leaders and to engage in leadership activities. Thus W. G. Smith, Brown, Lord, et al. (1996) found that high school students with leadership self-schemas were more likely to take leadership positions. They were also more likely to emerge as leaders in groups (Makiney, Marchioro & Hall, 1999).

Grosch, Salter, and Smith (2000) asked 74 managers in a manufacturing division of a multinational firm to complete a modified self-schema questionnaire developed by W. G. Smith, Brown, Lord, et al. (1996). Using five-point Likert scales to measure the self-schemas, the managers rated the self-descriptiveness and importance to their self-evaluation of each of 40 attributes. Twenty-four of the attributes were prototypical leadership traits according to Offerman, Kennedy, and Wirtz (1994). The reliability of the self-schemas was .94. As hypothesized, the leadership self-schemas correlated .50 with the managers' self-ratings of their own leadership ability. Such self-confidence was expected by Grosch, Salter, and Smith. Using shorter but similar measures of two leadership self-schemas, dedication, and social influence, along with the Multifactor Leadership Questionnaire (Bass & Avolio, 1991), Saucier's (1994) short version of the NEOAC "Big Five" Personality Inventory, and peer rankings and impressions, Makiney, Marchioro, and Hall (1999) found with 95 undergaduate students (75% female) that leadership self-schemas of dedication (goal-oriented, determined, organized) and social influence (persuasive, decisive, directing) both correlated .44 with transformational leadership in small groups as judged by peers over six time periods during a semester. The self-schema of dedication correlated .28 with agreeableness; the self-schema of social influence correlated .28 with extroversion and .24 with openness. Stepwise regression analysis showed that the schemas added to the MLQ and NEOAC in accounting for variance in peers' leadership rankings and peers' general impressions of the participants' leadership in the small groups.

Self-Monitoring and Self-Regulation

Self-Monitoring and Leadership. Snyder (1974, 1979) suggested that individuals differ in the extent to which they monitor and control presentations of themselves in social situations. As measured by a revised self-report inventory, self-monitoring involves at least two independent components: sensitivity to others' behavior and the ability to modify one's behavior accordingly (Lennox & Wolfe, 1984). Self-monitors are sensitive to cues about the appropriateness of various types of behavior (Snyder & Mason, 1975) and use these cues to guide their interpersonal behavior. Inhibition of activity is likely to be revealed in self-monitoring. Circumstances and their interpretation will determine whether high self-monitors display more or less leadership behavior than low self-monitors (Cader, Eby, Noble, et al., 1999).

Abilities associated with self-monitoring cut across the factors of sensitivity and control and contribute to a leader's effectiveness. Self-monitoring is concerned with social appropriateness, attention to social-comparison information, the ability to control and modify self-presentation, and the flexible use of this ability in particular situations (Snyder, 1974, p. 529). The elements of self-monitoring correlate with the ability to be a good actor and to give impromptu speeches (Briggs, Cheek, & Buss, 1980). Those who score low in self-monitoring are controlled by their own consistent attitudes and are not molded to the demands of the situation.

Snyder (1979) suggested that high self-monitoring individuals may be more likely to emerge as the leaders of groups because of their ability to regulate the interpersonal relationships in group interactions. Kenny and Zaccaro (1983) further proposed that experienced leaders became sensitive to differences in group situations and patterned their approaches accordingly. These leaders developed acuity in foreseeing the needs of their followers and altered their own behaviors to respond more effectively to those needs. Zaccaro, Foti, and Kenny (1991) demonstrated this in their experiment rotating participants through four tasks. Compared with low self-monitors, high self-monitors perceived the changes in task demands and showed somewhat more flexibility in their styles of leadership, according to their peers. Also contributing to the link between self-monitoring and leadership was the fact that high self-monitors present themselves in a socially desirable manner (Snyder, 1979) and construct an image of the ideal type of person for the situation they face. Using this ideal, the high self-monitors act according to the demands of this role (Snyder & Cantor, 1980).

When high self-monitors attempt to lead in a particular situation, they have several advantages over low self-monitors. Ickes and Barnes (1977) found that high self-monitors tend to speak first in an interaction and to initiate more conversational sequences than do low self-monitors. They also are perceived to be more friendly, outgoing, and extroverted than low self-monitors (Lippa, 1978). They are more successful as boundary spanners, a role that requires greater adaptability to situational requirements (Caldwell & O'Reilly, 1982).

Garland and Beard (1979) tested whether the effects of self-monitoring on emergent leadership would depend on the nature of the task confronting a group: a high self-monitor was expected to emerge as a leader when a task emphasized discussion and when task competence was difficult to assess. Such effects occurred in all-female groups but not in all-male groups. In an unpublished field study of natural groups, Mendenhall (1983) reported that high self-monitors were more likely to emerge as leaders of initially leaderless groups if they perceived themselves to be leaders rather than being perceived as leaders only by their peers. Nevertheless, peer-rated leadership of male students in semester-long mixed-sex study groups correlated .41 with the Lennox and Wolfe (1984) Revised Self-Monitoring scales, .26 with sensitivity to others' behavior, and .40 with the ability to modify one's behavior accordingly. But the correlations were lower for female participants, in reverse of Garland and Beard's (1979) results for all-male and all-female groups. A generation ago, females in mixed groups seemed more reluctant to assert leadership in the presence of males. This effect is likely to have disappeared since then.

Foti and Cohen (undated) involved three-person same-sex groups of students—one high, one moderate, and one low self-monitor—in a manufacturing exercise. The emergent leader was highly self-monitoring in 41 of the 58 groups, moderate in 11 of the groups, and low in self-monitoring in only 6 of the groups. High self-monitors, as expected, adapted their leadership style to the situation. They exhibited more initiation of structure when instructions emphasized the importance of the task rather than relationships, and more consideration when instructions emphasized developing good interpersonal relationships. Groups led by high self-monitors were somewhat more productive if the task was emphasized.

Self-Regulation. Self-regulation functions to enact and revise behavior as well as to change the environment. It involves how we set goals, how we plan or rehearse, and how we monitor progress toward goal attaiment (Murphy, 2002). The self-regulatory process begins with *self-awareness* of our thoughts and feelings. Then we estimate our *self-efficacy*—our judged capabilities (see below). Finally, with thoughts, motives, and feelings about what to do, we act accordingly (Bandura, 1986). Self-regulation is important to charismatic leaders (Murphy, 2002). Privately, charismatic leaders, compared with noncharismatic leaders, are more self-conscious, self-monitoring, and more purposeful in their behavior (Sosik & Dworakivsky, 1998). Along with self-schemas, self-esteem, and self-monitoring, they use a dramaturgical perspective to regulate the impressions of their identities they make on others (Gardner & Avolio, 1998).

Locus of Control

In his popular book *The Lonely Crowd*, Riesman (1950) suggested that the post–World War II generation, compared with its predecessors, was more outer-directed than inner-directed. Members of the postwar generation were controlled more by others and circumstances than by themselves. Locus of control (LOC), internal or external, was widely studied in the mid-1960s as a personal antecedent of consequence to a leader's behavior when the LOC measure of individual differences became available. Rotter (1966) developed and evaluated a self-report assessment instrument of LOC, the I-E Scale, which discriminates between persons who are controlled by internal forces (persons for whom outcomes are contingent on themselves) and persons who are controlled by outside influences (persons for whom outcomes are due to such forces as luck, fate, and powerful others whom they do not and cannot control). Respondents choose between pairs of statements such as "Without the right breaks, one cannot be an effective leader" or "Capable people who fail to become leaders have not taken advantage of their opportunities."

Carey (1992, p. 217) noted that "the leader's orientation toward self and others must be taken into account to understand fully the leadership dynamic." Nevertheless, DeBolt, Liska, and Weng (1976) concluded from a review of the literature that internal control, as measured by LOC, failed to relate consistently to the display of leadership in small groups of students. Also, Nystrom (1986) failed to detect much association between LOC and the performance of managers. Anderson and Schneier (1978) disagreed. It was differences in the approach to leadership that LOC predicted. Thus Durand and Nord (1976) found that the internal LOC of supervisors was linked to which their subordinates thought them to be considerate. In a simulated industrial setting, Goodstadt and Hielle (1973) found that supervisors with an external LOC were more likely to rely on persuasion and those with an internal LOC were more likely to rely on personal power. Mitchell, Smyser, and Weed (1975) obtained similar results. They noted that supervisors with an external LOC were more likely to use coercion and legitimate authority, whereas those with an internal LOC used rewards, respect, and expert power. Pryer and Distefano (1971) confirmed that nursing supervisors with an internal LOC were more considerate than those with an external LOC. In a study of 89 supervisors and their 345 subordinates, Johnson, Luthans, and Hennessey (1984) found that the leaders' LOC affected their influence on their subordinates' productivity and satisfaction with them as leaders. Supervisors who rated themselves as internally controlled were rated by their subordinates as significantly higher in persuasiveness and in their influence on higher authority.

Confounds. Some of the relationship between LOC and the performance of managers may be accounted for by the finding that internally controlled managers are more task oriented (Anderson, Hellriegel, & Slocum, 1977). This finding is consistent with those of several other studies, that found that managers with an internal LOC individually put forth more task-centered effort and performed better than did those with an external LOC (Anderson, 1977). There are other confounding elements. Managers with an internal LOC have higher activity levels than those with an external LOC (Brockhaus, 1975; Durand & Shea, 1974), appear more realistic about their aspirations (Phares, 1973), and perceive less stress under the same conditions (Anderson, 1977). The ambiguity of their roles did not seem to bother managers with a stronger internal LOC as much as it disturbed managers with a stronger external LOC (Abdel-Halim, 1980). Those with a higher internal LOC were less dogmatic, more trustful, and less suspicious of others (Joe, 1971). Not unexpectedly, Coates (1984) found a complex statistical interaction between the LOC and Mach scores of 79 managers, the number of contacts they reported with superiors and peers, and superiors' rating of their influence.[9]

Field Independence

A cognitive trait that is linked to inner directiveness and inner control is field independence. This trait is measured by Witkin's Rod and Frame Test, in which field-independent people judge that the field of a rod and frame is being reoriented, not that they themselves are. Paper-and-pencil correlates of field independence have also been found, for example, in people who can readily see incomplete figures as whole on the Group Embedded Figures Test. Field-independent Israeli managers with engineering backgrounds were more likely to be employee-centered than job-centered in their leadership styles (Erez, 1980). Results elsewhere have indicated that field-independent hospital managers preferred to use participative and delegative, rather than directive, leader-

ship styles, although more managers as a whole were field-dependent than were field-independent on the Group Embedded Figures Test.

Self-Efficacy

As noted elsewhere, individuals who see themselves as masters of their own fate, rather than at the mercy of luck, fate, or powerful other people, tend to cope better with stress, and generally make more effective and satisfying leaders. Such leaders are also likely to see themselves as more self-efficacious. Bandura (1982, p. 122) defined *self-efficacy* as a judgment of "how well one can execute courses of action required to deal with prospective situations." Self-efficacy is a broad set of expectations associated with beliefs about one's adaptability, ingenuity, and ability to work under stress, regardless of the case or the difficulty of the goals (Locke, Motowidlo, & Bobko, 1986). Expectations of efficacy change with new information and experiences of personal attainment, vicarious modeling, verbal persuasion, and emotional arousal (Gist & Mitchell, 1992). Those high in self-efficacy treat the same experiences differently from those low in self-efficacy. Although both see success as due to their abilities, self-efficacious people attribute failure to lack of effort or bad luck rather than to their lack of ability (Silver, Mitchell & Gist, 1991).

Bennis and Nanus (1985) saw the transforming leader as one who has a strong, positive self-regard and who employs the "Wallenda factor" (Wallenda is the name of the family of high-wire walkers)—that is, one who focuses on success with the risky task rather than being preoccupied with the possibility of failure. Self-efficacy "is critical to the leadership process" because it affects the motivation, development, and execution of a leader's strategies and goals (McCormack, 2001). Thus Savard and Rogers (1992) found that self-efficacy predicted a leader's persistence in trying to persuade others despite resistance. Wood and Bandura (1989) manipulated the belief in self-efficacy of business graduate students assigned to play roles in a simulated business. Beforehand, one set of students experienced a process that diminished their self-efficacy; the other set had an experience that increased their self-efficacy. The former set became increasingly discouraged as decision makers. Their analytical strategies declined in quality, as did their aspirations and suc-

[9]See also Andrisani and Nestel (1976); and Majumber, MacDonald, and Greever (1977).

cess in attaining organizational performance goals. The self-efficacious set created and met challenging goals for themselves and produced effective analytical strategies that yielded maximum performance. Self-efficacy is closely allied with self-confidence.

Self-Confidence

Self-confidence was positively associated with leadership in the reviews reported in Chapters 4 and 5. Bass (1985a) and Zaleznik (1977) found that it is particularly strong in transformational leaders. Mowday (1979) found that the leadership of 65 elementary school principals in dealing with four decisions was related to their self-confidence, and that the principals were more likely to be persuasive if they were self-confident. Conversely, Kipnis and Lane (1962) reported that supervisors who lacked confidence in their leadership ability were significantly less willing than self-confident supervisors to hold face-to-face discussions with subordinates. More often, they attempted to solve supervisory and development problems by using administrative rules or by referring the subordinates to a superior for a decision. According to Kaplan (1986), self-confidence weighed heavily in distinguishing between general managers who performed effectively and those who did not. The "effectives" were seen as personally secure, communicating their confidence and decisiveness to others; the "ineffectives" were characterized by incidents displaying their personal insecurity, their lack of "guts," and their unwillingness to make tough decisions or risk making enemies. The self-confidence of supervisors affected what they did to influence others. Those who felt confident in their ability to influence others were likely to use rewards and promises of rewards; those who lacked self-confidence were more likely to use coercion (Goodstadt & Kipnis, 1970; Kipnis & Lane, 1962).

Nonetheless, self-confidence can also result in an unrealistic, inflated evaluation of oneself. When such a self-evaluation is coupled with extremely low self-esteem, the performance of a leader is likely to be socially counterproductive (Reykowski, 1982). Self-confidence can also give rise to the stubbornness and obstinacy that Willner (1968, p. 65) described in charismatic world leaders "whose . . . determination . . . would not permit them to lose sight of their goals or swerve from a particular tactic they had decided upon, no matter how remote from achievement the goals may have appeared to others or how unwise the tactic." Moved by some intuition or an "inner voice," and undiscouraged by the obstacles that seemed insuperable to those around them, they pursued the course they had set themselves. Handy (1987) agreed that successful leaders have to believe in themselves in order to influence people and events. If they don't believe in themselves, neither will the others they seek to influence believe in them. At the same time, leaders must guard against arrogance and unwillingness to hear what others have to say.

Self-Esteem

Self-esteem differs from self-efficacy in that self-esteem deals with a generalized evaluation of the self and feelings of self-worth across most situations whereas self-efficacy is a belief in one's abilities to cope with specific situations — say, learning a new computer program (Gist & Mitchell, 1992). As was noted in Chapter 4, 17 pre-1948 studies found self-esteem to be higher in leaders than in their followers. Additional support came from subsequent investigations that found a positive relationship between self-esteem and leadership. Market research studies concluded that a majority of opinion leaders in fashion and personal grooming are high in self-esteem. Hemphill and Pepinsky (1955) found attempted leadership to be higher among participants who felt personally accepted or esteemed. Andrews (1984) found that among 64 undergraduates, those with high self-esteem were more likely to emerge as the leaders of their groups and were more likely to be rated as displaying such leadership behaviors as offering problem-relevant information, giving sound opinions, and making procedural suggestions. In Finland, Kalma, Visser, and Peeters (1993) found a correlation of .32 between self-esteem and social dominance.

Burns (1978) noted that the most potent sources of political leadership are unfulfilled needs for esteem and self-esteem. Erikson (1964) believed that great leaders become leaders because they have personally experienced, in a way that is representative of their people, the identity struggle for a particular niche in society compatible with their self-respect and expectations. But Barber (1965) thought that deciding to become a candidate for political office is indicative of either very high or very low self-esteem.

Bass (1960) postulated that those with high self-esteem would be more likely to attempt leadership. Bennis and Nanus (1985) concluded, from 90 interviews with top-level leaders, that such self-esteem was likely to be transferred to their subordinates. The leaders then could operate without having to resort to criticism or negative reinforcement. Higher performance expectations and confidence were generated in subordinates as a consequence. Defensiveness was lower if self-esteem was high. Self-esteem in leaders appears to be related to an ability to accept people as they are rather than as one would like them to be, to focus on the present rather than on the past, to be as courteous to close colleagues as to strangers, to trust others, and to do without constant approval and recognition.

According to Brandon (1998), self-esteem has become increasingly important in the information age because it takes self-esteem for information workers and leaders to initiate, innovate, and be self-reliant, trusting, and accepting of personal responsibility. Leaders need to create an environment that supports knowledge workers' self-esteem. The command and control system of the factory and office must be replaced by a system that promotes trust in the ability to think, to change, and to take on new ideas as new conditions arise. Intellectual capital is prized. Knowledge workers may know more about their work than their leaders do. But the leaders will need high self-esteem to inspire and support the workers. Leaders with low self-esteem will be insecure and likely to generate conflict with their subordinates.

Deployment of the Self

Bennis and Nanus (1985) suggested that the 90 leaders in their study were effective if they used their strengths as known to them and avoided using their weaknesses. They learned from and reflected on their own experiences. They were experimental, made comparisons with other leaders and organizations, and monitored the effects of environmental change on themselves. They asked their followers to do the same. According to Kets de Vries (1989), leaders gain influence through the transference and projection of the followers' hopes, desires, and fears onto the leader. The leaders fail if they are unable to live up to the followers' expectations of them. If leaders are narcissistic and have an inflated image of themselves, they become destructive.

Satisfaction with the Leadership Role

Status, Rank, Level, and Satisfaction

One of the most consistent findings in behavioral science is the positive correlation between one's status—the worth and importance of one's position in an organizational or social hierarchy—and one's satisfaction with it. Relying on early survey evidence, G. B. Watson (1942) was convinced that managers and supervisors were more satisfied with their work than were rank-and-file employees. Furthermore, top managers were generally more satisfied than managers at lower levels (Bass, 1960). The results of many studies supported the contention that the higher the level of individuals' positions in the organization, the greater was their job satisfaction. For instance, supervisors of municipal employees were much more satisfied with their jobs than were nonsupervisory employees. The supervisors also exhibited much less dissatisfaction (Jurkiewicz & Massey, 1997). And the reasons are not hard to find. Compensation is greater, and the need for self-actualization and autonomy is better satisfied at higher echelons of an organization (L. W. Porter, 1963a). Nevertheless, there are alternative or additional plausible explanations in some organizations in which status is unrelated to power and influence—for instance, organizations in which the top leaders are puppets or figureheads. Thus Ritchie and Miles (1970) studied 330 managers at five organizational levels. They found that satisfaction differed not as a consequence of the level of a position, but according to the amount of participation in decision making.

T. R. Mitchell (1970a, 1970b) studied line and staff officers of different military ranks and in different commands abroad. Not only did satisfaction rise with rank, but line officers of all ranks were better satisfied than were those in staff positions (staff positions are usually accorded less importance than line positions); however, this feeling varied greatly from one situation to another. Porter and Lawler (1965) confirmed these findings in a review of the empirical literature. Line managers were somewhat more satisfied than staff members and perceived more fulfillment of their need for self-actualization (Porter, 1963b). But satisfaction was unrelated to a manager's span of control.

In an experiment, Guetzkow (1954) found that key persons in a communication network saw themselves as most important and were more satisfied than members with less important positions. Bass, Pryer, Gaier, and Flint (1958) found that satisfaction was greater in a member who had been assigned more power, compared with four others with much less power. The attractiveness of a group was significantly lower for the average member when members were assigned control differentially, in contrast to groups in which all members were equal.

Clarity about Status and Role. It would seem obvious that a leader's satisfaction is strongly associated with the clarity of the position held and agreement about its importance, its power, and what is required for satisfactory performance. This idea was corroborated by Gross, Mason, and McEachern (1958), who conducted an extensive study of perceptions of role interactions between school board members and superintendents. The results indicated that the greater the consensus among board members, the higher the board members rated the superintendent, the higher he rated the board, and the greater the superintendent's job satisfaction. The board's rating of the superintendent was unrelated to his measured personality traits or to his agreement with the board. Within both samples, the degree of consensus in expectations of a position was related to the extent to which the role demands of the position had been formally or legally codified.

Status and Compensation. One obvious reason why those of higher status in an organization are more satisfied than their subordinates is that they ordinarily earn more pay. But this is not always true. Deans may earn less than professors, and supervisors may earn less than skilled subordinates. However, satisfaction with earnings is relative. One feels relatively deprived, depending on whom one compares oneself with. In a highly inflationary economy, dissatisfaction with pay is seen as being due primarily to inflation, governmental policy, and OPEC, not necessarily to one's employer. In a depression, relatively modest compensation may be highly satisfying. Furthermore, the greater the congruence between managers'

feeling about how pay should be determined and their perception of how it is determined, the greater their satisfaction with their pay (Lawler, 1966c, 1967b).

Penzer (1969) found that status-based expectations regarding external opportunities were major determinants of managers' satisfaction with their pay. Those who attended college brought different expectations with them than did those who did not attend college. Those expectations, when compared with external reference groups, partially determined their satisfaction with their compensation. Among the internal factors, commendations, rapid advancement, salary increases, and the like tended to inflate expectations. Thus managers' satisfaction with their pay is obviously related to how much they earn in an absolute sense, as well as to the correspondence between expected pay and actual pay. Managers prefer pay that is based on performance and merit, but they tend to define merit in terms of traits that they perceive themselves to possess.

More effective managers tend to feel more satisfied with their pay (Lawler & Porter, 1966; Porter & Lawler, 1968). Managers who score high in a preference for taking risks but not in achievement motivation prefer pay that is based on performance (Meyer & Walker, 1961). However, the more highly managers rate themselves in comparison with their peers on variables such as education, experience, productivity, effort, and skill, the more importance they attach to these variables as determinants of pay.

Further support was obtained by Klein and Maher (1966) for the relationship between the satisfaction of managers and the extent to which their level of pay corresponds with their status-based expectations for compensation. Middle managers overestimated the pay of subordinates and underestimated the pay of superiors. They believed that the difference between their pay and that of the persons above and below them was too small. The smaller the perceived difference between their pay and that of their subordinates, the less satisfied the managers were with their pay (Lawler, 1965, 1967b).

In a study of 919 low-to middle-level managers, Gorn and Kanungo (1980) isolated a job involvement factor ("For me, mornings at work really fly by; I'll stay overtime to finish a job even if I'm not paid for it"). Ninety-three managers were identified as motivated most by their extrinsic need for adequate salary and security, and 124 as motivated most by their intrinsic need for interesting work, responsibility, and independence. Status was not involved, but involvement was as high among the extrinsically motivated as among the intrinsically motivated, if their respective needs were being met.

Personal Factors Affecting Satisfaction

J. G. Mauer (1969) found that the job satisfaction of industrial supervisors was unrelated to their age, education, degree of involvement in work, or income, or to the size of their plant; but more often than not, these factors have been found by others to affect the satisfaction of managers.

Education and Managerial Satisfaction. Many studies have found that managers' satisfaction with their leadership role depends on their level of education. Higher pay may be expected but not necessarily forthcoming for those with more education. For example, Andrews and Henry (1963) and Klein and Maher (1966, 1968) reported that managers with more education felt less satisfied with their pay. However, Stogdill (1965b) and Lawler and Porter (1966) reported studies in which no relation was found between the education of managers and their satisfaction with their pay. Better-educated managers may be dissatisfied for other reasons. Stogdill (1965a) studied 442 managers and supervisors in six departments of an aircraft plant. He found that the better-educated managers were less satisfied with the company and with their freedom on the job; however, their level of education was not consistently related to their attitudes about their pay. According to Friedlander (1963), less-well-educated supervisors tended to derive satisfaction from the social and technical rather than the self-actualizing aspects of their work.

Age and Managerial Satisfaction. Saleh and Otis (1964) asked 80 managers, aged 60 to 65, to think back over their careers and indicate the age at which they had derived the most satisfaction from their work. These managers said that their satisfaction increased until age 59, then showed a sharp decrease. Another sample, aged 50 to 59, also reported an increase in satisfaction until age 59, but then anticipated a decrease in satisfaction after age 60. The authors interpreted the reduced enjoyment

after age 60 as due to a blockage of channels for further development and advancement.

Friedlander (1963) found that older supervisors tended to derive more satisfaction than younger supervisors from the social and technical aspects of their work, and less satisfaction from self-actualization. Results reported by England (1967a) indicated that older managers placed a higher value on social welfare and a lower value on organizational growth and leadership in the industry as goals of their organization. Gruenfeld (1962) found younger industrial supervisors to be more interested than older supervisors in high wages and fringe benefits. Older supervisors were more concerned about regular hours and freedom from stress.

Stogdill (1965a), in his study in an aircraft plant, found that with increasing age, managers tended to be more satisfied with the company but less satisfied with the recognition they received. But J. G. Mauer (1969) failed to find any relation between the age and the satisfaction of industrial supervisors. Some studies failed to find that managerial satisfaction was affected by the manager's age or other factors.

Tenure and Managerial Satisfaction. In Stogdill's (1965a) survey, the number of years a manager remained in the same position tended to contribute to all the aspects of dissatisfaction that were measured, but particularly to dissatisfaction with the failure to be promoted. However, Hall, Schneider, and Nygren (1970) reported that in the U.S. Forest Service, tenure, but not position, was related to identification with the organization and the satisfaction of needs.

Performance and Satisfaction

Consistently, the evidence points to the fact that better-satisfied managers perform better. Lawler and Porter (1967b) found that the degree to which an individual's needs are satisfied is related to his or her job performance, as evaluated by peers and superiors, and that this relationship is stronger for managers than for nonmanagers. Porter and Lawler (1968) reported that managers who were rated high in performance by themselves and their superiors expressed a higher degree of needs satisfaction than those who were rated low in performance. Managers who were rated high in effort also reported that they required a greater fulfillment of all their needs. Finally, Slocum, Miller, and Misshauk (1970) reported that high-producing supervisors were better satisfied than low-producing supervisors.

Health, Well-Being, and Leadership

"A grain of sand in a man's flesh, and empires totter and fall." So wrote Émile Zola (1902), referring to Napoleon III's incapacitation by stones in his bladder. A chronic disorder can have a continuing impact on a leader's performance, and acute disorders can alter specific situations. Interpersonal relations, concentration on necessary details, energy level, and availability all depend on a leader's physical stamina and mental health (L 'Etang, 1970). However, few controlled studies have been conducted to compare the performance of healthy and ill leaders. Quick, Gavin, Cooper, et al. (2000) defined executive health as including physical, mental, spiritual, and ethical well-being. Discussion of the last two of these aspects will be saved for Chapter 9. The researches attributed a leader's good or poor health to inherited and acquired conditions such as the loneliness of command, an overload of work, crises, and failures.

Physical Health

While they were in office, Adolph Hitler suffered from Parkinson's disease; François Mitterrand, the French premier, from prostate cancer; Lenin from renal disease; Woodrow Wilson from strokes; and the Japanese emperor Hirohito from pancreatic cancer (Accoce & Rentchnick, 1994 & 2003). The acute and chronic ailments of political and organizational leaders are common sources of concern, as are their health, diets, exercise regimens, medications, and lifestyles. Most important, their illnesses are likely to adversely affect their decisions. Prime Minister Neville Chamberlain was taking toxic analgesics for "blinding headaches" that affected his kidneys. Wilson's stroke of April 1919 brought about a sharp change in his personality and materially reduced his effectiveness in trying to win support for the League of Nations. A stroke on September 3, 1919, resulted in his complete incapacitation; thereafter, his wife, his physician, and Joseph Tumulty ran his office until March of 1920. None of his objectives that required persuading a majority in the Senate could be met. Franklin Delano Roosevelt's high blood pressure and other debilitating ailments made questionable his suitability for the presidency when he ran for his fourth term in 1944. His physician noted signs of hardening cerebral arteries before Roosevelt went to meet Churchill and Stalin at the fateful Yalta Conference in February 1945. Nikita Khrushchev also had to deal with high blood pressure. Illness dogged Dwight Eisenhower, limiting his activities at important international conferences. His weak heart caused acute problems at meetings in higher altitudes. John F. Kennedy's chronic back pain was well known to the public, but he was also a victim of Addison's disease, which was treated with cortisone. This disease and its treatment caused extreme mood swings and emotional instability at a time when Kennedy was dealing with the Bay of Pigs and the Cuban missile crisis. Ronald Reagan suffered from Alzheimer's disease, which began to show up beginning sometime during his second term. Benito Mussolini's judgment was impaired by syphilis. By 1938–1939, there was a noticeable deterioration in his intellectual capacity. In the four years before his downfall, he assisted Hitler at Munich, invaded Albania and Greece, and took Italy into a disasterous war with Britain. King George III's porphyria first appeared during the first year of his 60-year reign. This genetic disorder periodically made him mentally deranged, at a time when the British monarch not only reigned but ruled if he could manage Parliament. Intermittently, George III could do neither, and Britain lost its American colonies.

Park (1988) noted that in leaders, advanced age may be accompanied by a deterioration in judgment and temperament. Paul von Hindenburg, Germany's president, became decrepit during the last years of the Weimar Republic, making Hitler's rise to power much easier. During the same years, Ramsay MacDonald, the British prime minister, was a victim of Alzheimer's disease, which made his continued leadership of the Labour Party an embarrassment of ludicrous speeches and impaired judgment. Likewise, the premature aging of Poland's post–World War I leader Józef Pilsudski contributed to his delusions about his nation's military strength and status in its foreign relations with Germany and Russia. In the late 1980s and early 1990s, the political leaders exercising real power in the People's Republic of China were in their eighties (Fukuyama, 1997). Ronald Reagan's advanced age led to a lot of confusion in his thinking about events in his movie roles and in reality. Park suggested that governments set up independent disability commissions to make judgments and recommendations about removing seriously mentally disabled leaders from office.

Many historical questions remain about how physical health influenced the leadership of generals, politicians, statesmen, and emperors. Was it lead poisoning that resulted in a sudden change for the worse in Caligula (lead was used by the Romans to seal wine bottles and for piping water)? How was John Foster Dulles's last year in office as Secretary of State affected by his carcinoma of the bowel? What was the impact on the course of events of Prime Minister Anthony Eden's acute obstructive colitis, which caused him to have a high fever during the Suez crisis of 1956? Can effective leaders successfully mask or compensate for their debilitating illnesses? How are they affected by the medications they take to treat their conditions? How much of the success or failure of businesses can be traced to the ill health of top executives? Long working hours, lengthy meetings, and long travel time, as well as stressful responsibility for people and their performance, can reach debilitating levels. The impact of the sudden death of a chief executive officer will be discussed in Chapter 30.

Physical Fitness

Illnesses and early death can sometimes be avoided with suitable exercise and diet. Neck and Cooper (2000) recommended a program of optimum exercise and diet to offset the effects of heavy occupational demands. These authors compiled survey evidence reported by *Fortune*, *The Wall Street Journal*, and other business publications. Two-thirds of executives exercise at least three times a week, and 90% of these do aerobic exercises. Endurance, strength, and flexibility need to be developed and maintained.

Obesity, smoking, and alchohol addiction contribute to a variety of chronic diseases and early death. Neck and Cooper (2000) cite a survey of 3,000 executives who said they were careful about their diet. Only 10% of executives said they smoked, whereas almost a quarter of the U.S. population is still smoking. The need to reduce caloric intake as well as fat and cholesterol to recommended levels of nutritional standards is well-known. Vitamins,

minerals, and high-fiber foods are encouraged. Fruits, vegetables, and whole-grain products should form a large portion of the healthy diet. Antioxidants and calcium are also important.

Empirical surveys have supported the argument for maintaining physical fitness and a proper diet. For instance, stockbrokers who took part in an aerobics training program earned greater sales commissions than those who did not participate. A study of 10,000 men and 3,000 women found that in a given period the physically unfit had twice the mortality rate of the fit. Physical fitness also affects mental activities. A study of 56 physically active college professors found that they processed data faster and experienced a slower decline in information-processing speed as they aged. Physical fitness contributed to higher energy levels and feelings of well-being.

The Mentally Healthy Leader

A healthy self-concept contributes to a leader's effectiveness. What does it mean for leaders to be in good mental health? Effective, mentally healthy leaders retain a balanced view of themselves and how to deal with their work. They are at peace with themselves (Cleveland, 1985). They avoid maladaptive responses to the conflicts arising from their moving up the organizational ladder. They help themselves to understand their own motivations by establishing a firm sense of their identity, by maintaining continuity and predictability in their relations with their colleagues, by being selective in their activities and relationships, and by living appropriately with their own daily rhythms. They can face disappointments realistically and do not hide or deny their occurrence. They remain the masters of their fate and can tolerate their feelings of loss. They know when to withdraw and when to reexamine their emotional investments in people and activities (Zaleznik, 1963). If they had unsupportive parents and a disadvantaged childhood, they have been resiliant. Neurotic and disordered beliefs about oneself, by contrast, are most likely to result in leadership that is fraught with problems for colleagues and for the organization.

The Psychopathology of Leadership

Forms of mental maladjustment and ill health, including neuroses, psychoses, and personality disorders, are the opposite of emotional stability, self-efficacy, and mental well-being. Eysenck (1985) found neuroticism to be one of two dimensions of central importance in accounting for large amounts of variance in social and leadership behavior. The other was introversion-extroversion. In contrast to the general population, Eysenck noted, managers and administrators were likely to be low in neurotic tendencies and high in extroversion. This is consistent. Nevertheless, although pathological leaders are a minority, numerous links between pathological tendencies and leadership styles have been observed by clinical analysts. For example, Fernberg (1979) described frequently observed pathological character structures in administrators: schizoid, obsessive, narcissistic, and paranoid. Leonid Brezhnev, a leader of the Soviet Union, suffered from senile dementia. Habib Bourgiba, president of Tunisia, suffered from 25 years of depression. Kemal Atatürk, the founding leader of modern Turkey and George III of England, suffered from Korsakoff's psychosis, in which victims fill in gaps in their memory with imaginary events.

Anxiety. Heuerman and Olson (1999) postulated that anxiety "engulfs" some people in positions of leadership. They feel "lost, scared, confused, and panicked," in fear of obscure dangers. They repeatedly impose mindless "reorganizations, change programs, and superficial fixes." They are blindsided by their disappointments. "They work futilely to avoid pain, gain control, and find security." Nevertheless, they try to convey an impression of calm and confidence.

Feelings of Paranoid Persecution. Leaders may display additional neurotic or psychotic syndromes if their wishes are articulated in fantasies. The fantasies are "scenes in the private theatre of [the leader's] subjective world" (Kets de Vries and Miller, 1984a, p. 8). The syndromes that dominate are the bases for specific styles of leadership. They may, in turn, become shared fantasies that can permeate all levels in a centralized organization, creating a specific organizational culture and determining decision making, strategy, and structure. On the basis of clinical observations of executives in four firms, five pathological leadership constellations were observed to emerge. Kets de Vries and Miller (1984a, 1986) identified them and provided generalizations about their different effects on the organization and on the leaders'

colleagues. These five constellations were: (1) feelings of paranoid persecution, (2) feelings of helplessness, (3) narcissim, (4) compulsiveness, and (5) schizoid detachment.

The dominant fantasy of leaders suffering from paranoid persecution is that they cannot really trust anyone and that a menacing superior force is out to "get" them. Thus these leaders are quick to take offense and are always on guard. Along with their mistrust of others, they are suspicious, hypersensitive, and overconcerned with hidden motives and special meanings. They distort reality in an effort to confirm their suspicions. As Kets de Vries and Miller (1986, p. 269) stated:

> The boss may feel hostile to those who report to him [or her] and may want to harm or attack others as a defensive reaction to his/her own feelings of persecution and mistrust. . . . The leader sees . . . subordinates either as malingerers and incompetents, or as people who are deliberately out to raise his/her ire. As a consequence, he/she is likely to gravitate towards two extremes. He/she might try to exert a tremendous amount of control through intensive personal supervision, formal controls and rules, and harsh punishments. . . . The second, less common, reaction of the hostile leader toward . . . subordinates may be one of overt aggression. He/she may be reluctant to provide emotional or material rewards, striving always to come out on the winning side of any 'trades.' . . . Subordinates hold back their contributions and concentrate mostly on protecting themselves from exploitation.

In organizations that are dominated by paranoid leaders, emphasis is on management controls and continuous vigilance. Power is centralized, and decision making is top-down although information is sought from below. The organization is conservative and reacts to threats rather than being proactive with regard to opportunities. Risk taking is low. There is an increased need for control rather than constant goals, strategic plans, or unifying themes and traditions (Kets de Vries & Miller, 1984a).

Helplessness and Hopelessness. According to Kets de Vries and Miller (1986), the dominant fantasy here is that it is hopeless to change the course of events in life; one is just not good enough. This depressive neurosis gives rise to a lack of self-confidence and initiative, feelings of dependence, and low self-esteem (Jacobson,

1971). Feelings of guilt, worthlessness, and inadequacy are exhibited in self-depreciation and feelings of inferiority. Feelings of learned hopelessness develop; the manager believes that the malaise will last forever and that it will affect everything he or she does (Trotter, 1987). Kernberg (1979) noted that such depressive managers avoid responsibility, procrastinate about major decisions, and become passive and laissez-faire in their leadership style. Only routines get done; their groups stagnate, and goals are not clarified.

Narcissism. Of 32 revolutionary leaders, 23 were described as egotistical, narcissistic, and searching for personal fame and glory (Rejai, 1980). Narcissists are dominated by the fantasy of getting attention and impressing others dramatically. Some are histrionic, expressing emotions excessively and incessantly drawing attention to themselves. They are likely to be superficial and to exaggerate their evaluations of others (Kets de Vries & Miller, 1984a). Narcissists who reject the object-relations in their fantasy exhibit severe and frequent defensive reactions, are demanding taskmasters, and gather sycophant subordinates around themselves. Narcissists who deceive themselves are overly sensitive to criticism and privately harbor grudges against dissenters. As Kets de Vries and Miller (1985, pp. 16–17) stated:

Such leaders are hyperactive, impulsive, dramatically venturesome, and dangerously uninhibited. They live in a world of hunches and impressions rather than facts as they address a broad array of widely disparate projects, products, and markets in desultory fashion. The leaders' flair for the dramatic leads them to centralize power, allowing them to initiate bold ventures independently. . . . Instead of reacting to the environment (when at the top of the organization) the leader, often an entrepreneur, attempts to enact his own environment . . . [placing a] sizable proportion of the firm's capital . . . at risk. . . . Most of these . . . moves are made in the service of grandiosity. Unbridled growth is the goal. The organization's strategy is a function of its leader's considerable narcissistic needs—his desire for attention and visibility. . . . The top man wants to be at center stage, putting on a show. . . . He wants to finally "show the others over there" how great an executive he really is.

Some degree of self-concentration appears to be important for effective leadership. Charismatic leaders develop self-assuring internal images with which they have a dialogue and that form a basis for connections with their followers (Zaleznik, 1984). But concentration on the self may be a mixed blessing. Leaders may have highly inflated evaluations of themselves or severely negative self-images. As was noted earlier, in both instances of such self-concentration, prosocial leadership is unlikely to emerge (Reykowski, 1982).

Compulsiveness. This neurosis is fueled by the fantasy "I don't want to be at the mercy of events. I have to master and control all the things affecting me." The fantasy is articulated by behaving as a perfectionist. The compulsive person is preoccupied with trivial details and insists that others submit to his or her way of doing things. He or she sees relationships in terms of dominance and submission and is characterized by a lack of spontaneity, inability to relax, meticulousness, dogmatism, obstinacy, and a constant preoccupation with losing control. "Every last detail of operation is planned out in advance and carried on in a routinized and preprogrammed fashion. Thoroughness, completeness, and conformity with standard and established procedures are emphasized. . . . Surprises must be avoided" (Kets de Vries & Miller, 1984a, p. 14).

Schizoid Detachment. The fantasy here is that "the world of reality does not offer any satisfaction to me. All of my interactions with others will eventually fail and cause harm so it is safer to remain distant" (Kets de Vries & Miller, 1984a, p. 11). The manager with this problem is insecure, withdrawn, and noncommittal. He or she discourages interaction because of a fear of involvement. The world is an unhappy place, filled with frustrating colleagues. Most contacts will end painfully, this manager believes. To compensate for a lack of fulfillment, he or she daydreams. Again, the fantasy is articulated in ineffective, laissez-faire leadership.[10] The manager is detached and feels estranged from others. A cold, unemotional appearance is matched by an indifference to praise or reproof.

[10]The experimental and survey evidence on the counterproductive effects of laissez-faire leadership is detailed in Chapter 6.

Psychosomatic Syndromes—Type-A Personalities. The Type-A syndrome may include being hostile, driven, competitive, and time-conscious, Type-As may hurry the speech of others; become unduly irritated when forced to wait; exhibit explosive speech patterns or frequent use of obscenities; make a fetish of always being on time; have difficulty sitting and doing nothing; play nearly every game to win, even when playing with children; become impatient while watching others do things they think they can do better or faster. In addition to hard-driving competitiveness, these Type-A leaders' sense of urgency, may be accompanied by restlessness, multiple activities against deadlines, and impatience with delays and with others. These leaders may be self-centered and poor in interpersonal relationships.

In general, type-A managers seem to have an overwhelming need to assert control over whatever happens. Nonetheless, when they lose control, they overreact, with signs of helplessness. Their reaction is either "all or nothing." In the process, they waste energy and strain themselves needlessly. In a survey of 163 South African managers, type-A behavior was found to be correlated with a strong feeling of exhaustion, role conflict, absence of friendliness, and anxiety depression (reflecting joylessness). The behavior of these people as managers and leaders was affected accordingly, concomitant with effects on their hearts (Strumpfer, 1983).

Type-As are prone to heart disease, real and false (Friedman & Rosenman, 1974). False angina (pain in the left arm) and high blood pressure may not be organic in origin but due to frustration. False angina occurs not because Type-As are workaholics but because they are frustrated by feeling of being blocked from full accomplishment. Nevertheless, relationship between Type-A behavior and real heart disease was demonstrated in a large number of studies (Jenkins, 1976, 1978). Men who were in the highest third in Type-A scores on the Jenkins Activity Survey had 1.79 times the incidence of new coronary heart disease as men who were in the bottom third of the distribution. When men who had had a single heart attack were compared with men who had had second heart attacks, Jenkins, Zyzanski, and Rosenman (1976) demonstrated that the Type-A score was the strongest single predictor of recurrent coronary heart disease. However, there are three important qualifications. First, as Strumpfer (1983) noted, the majority of people with

Type-A behavior never develop heart disease. Second, it is difficult not to confound Type-A behavior with other risk factors such as smoking and obesity. Third, and most important, if it is a psychosomatic illness, the heart condition is a response to anger and frustration. The happy Type-A workaholic who enjoys his work and the challenges from it is not as likely to be at risk of heart disease. Also more likely to be free of heart disease may be Type-As who are emotionally expressive and genuinely confident in themselves, who laugh a lot, and who can be highly active (Hall, 1986). The entire Type-A syndrome of anger, impatience, aggravation, and irritation may not be the culprit but rather only one or more elements related to heart disease. For instance a cynical, mistrusting attitude or intense self-involvement may be the particular risk factor of consequence (Fischman, 1987).

Summary and Conclusions

Successful leaders share values with those they lead. What they and their followers regard as right, important, and good shapes their performance. These values depend on occupational and societal influences. But a majority are likely to see themselves as pragmatically balanced in outlook. Leaders differ in their values for many reasons, ranging from education to nationality. They may be selected by an organization because of their values or they may assimilate the organization's values after joining. Their profession and locale also make for obvious differences. Furthermore, their performance depends on their concepts about themselves, their pragmatism, their preference for taking risks, and their valuing of short-term maximization or long-term gain. Motives may be conscious like task orientation and subconscious like a need for achievement. Compensation is a strong motivator, but its effects are relative. Identification with the organization is also a strong motivator, as are commitment to the organization's goals and the managers' location in the organization. Leaders will be affected by whether they identify with superiors, peers, or subordinates. Satisfaction with the role of leader correlates with earnings and status and their accompanying power and control. Role clarity is particularly important. Although exceptions can be found, the higher one's status in an organization, the greater one's job satifaction. Managers' satisfaction with their role in the organization and with their compensation often depends on their education, age, and tenure and correlates with their effective performance.

Systematic differences in values separate radical from conservative political leaders and revolutionaries from loyalist leaders. Both the projected needs for achievement and task orientation contribute positively to the emergence of leaders. In turn, there is a link between such leadership and risk taking. Among the self-concepts that particularly affect the emergence and performance of leaders are: internal or external locus of control; a sense of self-efficacy, self-confidence, self-esteem; and valuing of self-actualization. Leadership research has been remiss in ignoring the importance of physical and mental health of leaders. Physical health can be essential to a leader's performance, and mental health problems are seen in leaders who feel persecuted, helpless, narcissistic, compulsive, or schizoid. Leaders' and managers' self-concepts, motives, values, and health move them to lead. How much others value them and accord them esteem and status affect the leaders' and managers' efforts to lead.

CHAPTER
9

Ethics and Leadership

Dame Anita Roddick of The Body Shop, James Burke of Johnson & Johnson, Sir Adrian Cadbury of Cadbury-Schweppes, Max De Pree of Herman Miller, and J. Irwin Miller of Cummins were business leaders whose careers exemplified ethical management (Murphy & Enderle, 1995). Anita Roddick (2000), founder of the worldwide retail cosmetics chain The Body Shop, suggested that companies should begin to focus on a new bottom line, making moral decisions. Thus when a new soap factory was needed, instead of being attached more conveniently to headquarters in a prosperous area of England, it was placed in an area of Scotland with 70% unemployment. Jobs were provided for 100 people who had been out of work for nine years, and 25% of the profits were plowed back into the community. An enthusiastic work force was created. Roddick also suggested that along with safe products, companies provide audits of their environmental performance.

Cyanide poison had been inserted into some Tylenol capsules after manufacturing. Although advised by FBI personnel that it would be an overreaction, James Burke, as CEO of Johnson & Johnson, advocating openness and candor, ordered a very costly recall. And when it was determined after a second poisoning incident that even tamperproof packaging could not be guaranteed to make the capsules safe for the consumer, the capsule form was abandoned permanently. For Burke, these actions were the right thing to do and consistent with his moral beliefs. Furthermore, the maintenance and enhancement of trust and goodwill was worth the cost of abandoning the highly profitable product.

Adrian Cadbury was an advocate of openness in dealing with ethical issues. Bribing prospective international purchasers was eliminated by demanding that bribes be shown on the purchase invoice. Openness also applied to gifts. Would a gift be an embarrassment if mentioned in the newspaper? For Cadbury, ethical actions were more important than ethical intentions. In making decisions,

one's personal rules of conduct had to be considered, followed by the interests of others who would be affected by the decision.

Max De Pree, as CEO of Herman Miller furniture (after consultation with Peter Drucker), arranged for the CEO's salary to be no more than 20 times the pay of the average factory worker. For De Pree, integrity—a fine sense of one's obligations—was the first requirement of leaders. In his speeches and writings, De Pree called for justice and the fair distribution of results. The leader had to be the steward of limited resources; had to exercise personal restraint; and had to keep in mind the common good of customers, managers, and employees. Also, there needed to be room for God, family, and others in one's life.

J. Irwin Miller of Cummins, Inc., a manufacturer of diesel engines, argued that business had a responsibility to help solve the nation's social problems. Leadership must be provided to help reduce discrimination, poverty, and pollution. Managers needed to set an example of commitment and trust before they could expect either from their employees. Employees learn the values of the organization from the example set by the top executives, not from the executives' sermons and espousals of corporate ethics. Furthermore, Miller advised business schools to add character and selflessness as bases for selecting students. Instructors needed to set an example of ethicality. The content of any course ought to take account of moral issues in decisions reached (Murphy & Enderle, 1995).

And yet, despite the many bright examples of ethical business leaders and honest political leaders, the news has continued to be filled with stories of corrupt and fraudulent executives. Ciulla (1998) could rightfully begin her book on the ethics of leadership by saying, "We live in a world where leaders are often morally disappointing" (p. 5). Self-aggrandizement among CEOs has increased. In 1965, for Fortune 500 CEOs, the ratio of their average compensation to that of a factory worker was 24 to one. In 2006, in the United States, the ratio was 262 to one (Anonymous, 2006).

According to Scott and Hart (1991), modern management arose with the promise that it would bring material affluence, material growth, and abundance. Its organizations were to be the engines of progress and prosperity. Professional managers who were skilled, competent, rational, and efficient replaced the idealized, wealthy, and powerful entrepreneurs of the nineteenth century. Professional managers were expected to be men with moral integrity. But by 1910, Woodrow Wilson was cautioning against the unrestrained power of some top corporate managers. In 1922, William Riply warned of their unregulated control over corporate assets. Adolph Berle and Gardner Means wrote in 1933 that society was in danger of becoming hostage to the professional managers' private cupidity. Burnum (1941) noted that the management elite was always able to get more than its fair share by using its power. But Barnard (1937) argued that unless managers had a strong sense of responsibility and were moral, cooperative, enlightened, and fair, they would be "winnowed out" because their organizations would perform poorly. Despite the importance of the ethics of management and leadership, it is only in the past several decades that this has become a major issue for empirical surveys and experimental research.

Philosophies of Ethical Leadership

There is much ancient and modern philosophical literature on ethical theories of leadership, and there are hortatory commentaries, but they contain little empirical evidence to confirm or refute derived hypotheses or propositions. The evidence is anecdotal, qualitative, and subjective rather than quantitative and objective. Nevertheless, ethics has been in the domain of philosophy for 2,500 years. Moral philosophies contain the principles and rules that leaders may use to determine right and wrong (Ferrell & Fraedrich, 1994).

Deontology treats ethics by considering the values inherent in the rules of human behavior or in the behavior itself. *Teleology* focuses on the consequences of rules or actions. *Virtues* are studied in theories about actions that fulfill good purposes or lead to right outcomes (Elliott & Engebretson, 1995).

[Its study] can be as rigorous [as social science research methods]. The philosophical study of ethics is not just a matter of opinion. Adequate treatment of any area of applied ethics involves sound argumentation, astute articulation of the relevant questions and a strong footing in the realities of the practice that is being analyzed. (Ciulla, 1994, p. 2)

Plato's republic was an ideal city-state of 5,000 inhabitants, to be led by an ethical philosopher-king. Plato recommended a formal program of education and development for the ruler and his guardians, supported by the working class. The ethical ruler needed to maintain justice and avoid self-interest and abuse of power. For Confucius, ethics was a matter of duty rigidly determined by tradition. The leader sought harmonious living in a well-ordered society. Harmony was derived when all people fulfilled their obligations to one another and to the rules of society. Particularly important were duties to parents and rulers. For Lao-tzu (sixth century B.C.E.), the best rulers behaved so that their people thought they had succeeded by themselves. The best leaders were not noticed. The worst were feared and reviled. Machiavelli (1469–1527) said in *The Prince* (as noted in Chapter 7) that rulers only needed to appear to be moral but did not actually have to be. A ruler had to be an authority who knew how to use his power to provide justice and order. Thomas Hobbes held that only through authority could an ethical order be established, because people were self-interested, naturally assertive, and power-seeking. Only anarchy could result if they were not ruled by firm authority (Ciulla, 2004).

According to Immanuel Kant, a deontologist, reason demands that moral duty transcends all other duties. Kant's *categorical imperative* was that we ought to believe that what is right for others is also right for us. It was a detailed version of the Golden Rule based on reason, not religion. It was the commanding influence of moral principles (Corsini, 1999). We have a moral duty to satisfy the legitimate needs of others as dictated by logic and reason. We ought to tell the truth because it is the right thing to do. Morality depends on the intention of doing good, not on outcomes. For Kant, morals were self-evident and derived from the natural order. Universal moral duties ought to direct one's conduct consistently and in all circumstances. Leaders must act on their strongly held beliefs even if not in their own self-interests (Ciulla, 1998).

David Hume, however, rejected reason as guide to morals in favor of emotions; and Baruch Spinoza emphasized the importance of the self. Utilitarians such as Jeremy Bentham (1823/1948) and John Stuart Mill argued for the greatest good for the greatest number (Elliot & Engretson, 1995). Friedrich Nietzsche envisioned a superman, a morally superior person who found the greatest power in self-control, art, and philosophy; his will to power made it possible to create the world, not accept it as it was. The superman was in control of his passions and was not motivated by self-interest. His virtues included sympathy, generosity, and honesty. John Dewey (1987) noted that societies change as a consequence of resolving conflict, a process in which leadership is essential. Rediscovered every several years in the psychological literature about the relationship between leaders and followers, and leaders and the situation is William James's (1882) observation of their influence on each other. Kierkegaard (1971) followed in the tradition of Kant but stressed the importance of religion to ethical thinking. Rawls (1985) provided a new philosophical view of justice and fairness. Kohlberg's (1969) six stages of moral development influenced the study of leadership ethics in psychology, education, and business management.

Are Moral Standards Universal or Relative?

Ethical standards are considerably different for traditionalists and nontraditionalists. Traditionalists are more Machiavellian: equity is more a matter of entitlement, and questionable ethics are justified in corporate settings if they benefit the organization rather than oneself (Mason & Mudrack, 1997). Militarists and pacifists differ on whether killing in wartime is ever justifiable. Circumstances may make a difference. A leader of a country declares a just war when the country fights to defend itself against an unprovoked attack, and even some pacifists may then change their minds. How much unintended collateral damage is morally acceptable?

Deering, Cavenagh, and Kelly (1994) surveyed individual and group differences in attitudes toward moral questions using Forsyth's Ethical Position Questionnaire (1980). They reported that 83% of the teachers and 66% of the business majors in the survey scored low in relativ-

ism and agreed that a universal set of moral principles ought to be followed. Although most ethical theorists, such as Kant and J. S. Mill, are absolutists, many liberal arts undergraduates accept few absolute moral principles as valid and water down their moral reasoning with a relativistic point of view. "An ethical absolutist . . . treats ethics like math. . . . There are right and wrong answers to moral questions. The answers are the same for all people, in all places and at all times. . . . Someone who thinks 5 + 7 = 13 is simply wrong" (Irvine, 2002, p. 43). For relativists, it all depends on who and what is involved. Lying is absolutely wrong, but the absolutist makes exceptions to moral rules for conditional claims. Lying is, therefore, permissible if it will save a life. Also, telling young children about Santa Claus or that they have done a good job or that their handiwork is beautiful is acceptable. Lying to fulfill a promise to keep a secret may be acceptable. A public official may prevaricate early in an emergency to prevent panic, at the expense of losing credibility and circulating false rumors. It is important, though, to get the truth out as soon as feasible. At times, we shade the truth to avoid seeming too harsh and critical. "An ethical relativist . . . [adds] relativistic clauses to . . . ethical judgments . . . [and] is disinclined to label an activity as right or wrong. . . . Rather the activity may be wrong for him (or her) but right for others. . . . The activity may be wrong for one culture but right for another culture" (p. 43).

Theories of Moral Leadership

Burns (1978) maintained that to be transformational, leadership had to have moral ends and had to raise the moral consciousness of followers. Rost (1991) held that to be leadership, the leader-follower process had to provide for ethical means—autonomy and the valuing of the individual leader and follower. Coercion, manipulation, and use of authority could not be leadership or ethical (Potts, 2001). Yet unethical leaders might use ethical means for immoral ends, unethical means for moral ends, or both.

Dimensions of Ethical Leadership. Northouse (2001) designed a questionnaire about six briefly stated ethical cases. The scores reflected how much a leader agreed with each of six ethical approaches for dealing with each case. (1) Egoistic: maximizes what is best for the leader (2) Utilitarian: promotes the greatest good for the greatest number; (3) Personally virtuous: the leader is good, worthy, and humane; (4) Distributing justice: each follower is treated fairly; (5) Dutiful: the leader's ethical duty is fulfilled; and (6) Caring: leaders nurture those with whom they have special relationships.

Importance of Leadership Ethics. Barnard (1938) introduced ethical considerations about leadership in his examination of the moral modes of administration. The administrator had to work with people who differed in their moral codes concerning right and wrong. The administrator's role in dealing with moral dilemmas was to adjudicate among alternative opinions and provide acceptable reasons for moral decisions. But not until the last few decades has the ethics of organizational leadership become a prominent subject of theory and research.

Offerman, Hanges, and Day (2001) noted that founders' often set the moral climates of their organizations and that a climate may remain long after the founder is gone. Shared perceptions of what is right and wrong behavior often stem from the personal values and motives of the founders and other early leaders of the organization (Dickson, Smith, Grojean, et al., 2001). Bloskie (1995) discussed the role that ethics, morality, principles, and values should play in leadership. Any works on the subject are likely to be a discourse on robust applied ethics and a superficial examination of leadership, or vice versa. Nonetheless, Kanungo and Mendonca (1996/1997) argued that without a consideration of ethics, understanding of leadership is incomplete: "Ethical values are always involved with leadership, regardless of whether or not leaders are explicitly aware of the fact." "The best leaders recognize their responsibilities as the chief custodian of the values of their group" (Knapp & Olson, 1996, pp. 84, 85). Leaders balance the fundamental values of the organization with the needs of its stakeholders, such as organizational survival and the bottom line (Grensing-Pophal, 1998). Included among the worst leaders who made *Fortune*'s list of the "greediest executives" (2002) were those who awarded themselves the generous amounts of stock and stock options approved by their boards of directors and who cashed out while their organizations were laying off workers, taking severe losses, and approaching bankruptcy. "The not-so-secret dirty secret of the crash [at the end of the 1990s] as [shareholders] were losing [70% to 100%] of their holdings, top officials of many companies that have crashed the hardest were getting immensely, extraordinarily, obscenely, wealthy" (Fortune, September 2000).

A firm's ethical reputation has practical importance. A survey by Duke University of 650 graduate business students from 11 top MBA programs found that ethical and political reasons (and possibly the future insecurity of the industries) affected their willingness to accept employment in particular industries. Almost 82% of the students said they would not work for tobacco companies, which had suppressed for 30 years the internal findings about the health risks of cigarette smoking. From 20 to 36% said they would not join firms with questionable environmental problems, liquor marketers, or defense contractors (Randall, 1994). The large and prestigious accounting firm of 40,000, Arthur Andersen, lost so many clients in 1992 in the wake of the Enron scandal due to the malfeasance of a few managing auditors, that it was forced into bankruptcy and dissolution.

Role of the Corporate Manager: Agent or Trustee? Theoretically, if the role of the manager is to act as an agent for the owners (shareholders) of the corporation, then morally the manager agrees to act under their direction on their behalf. The owners consent to accept the agent's actions in substitution for their own. The manager's duties are to do what the agent has proposed to do, to accept reasonable directions from the owners, and not to act contrary to the owner's interests, bearing in mind the interests of the other stakeholders of the organization. An ethical problem may arise when the manager is expert and the owners are not. Ordinarily, the individual shareholders have no institutional way to give routine instructions to the manager. They have to own a sizable percentage of shares to carry much weight. As a consequence, it makes more sense morally to regard the manager as a trustee of the organization. As a trustee, he or she ought to consider the rights of all the other stakeholders in the organization. A trustee has a moral duty to advance the shareholders' interests as well as the interests of the other stakeholders in the organization, such as the employees, customers, and community (McMahon, 1972). As a trustee, a manager and leader helps to lessen the gaps among others created by conflicting values and to adapt—in the face of competing perspectives and creative tension—to new approaches (Heifitz, 1994).

Ethical Principles of Leadership and Influence

Hodgeson (1994) viewed leadership as a moral activity. Leaders should respect the basic human dignity of followers and their rights and ability to make choices regarding their own affairs. To point to ethical principles of leadership implies that ethics and morality are absolute rather than relative. There are ethical imperatives—e.g., "thou shall not kill." But the absolute principle is conditional. Thou shall not kill except in self-defense or to save others' lives. To kill in war requires that it be a just war. Other exceptions, such as abortion and euthanasia, remain controversial. For Kant (1959/1985), it is a categorical imperative that humans be treated as ends, not means. Thus employees should be assigned to meaningful jobs and not treated impersonally as a means of production or service (Bowie, 1998). Irvine (2000–2001) argued that cultures tend to be far more similar in morals and ethics than different. It is circumstances that are different. The traditional Inuit left their elderly out in the cold to die, to avoid starvation of the whole family. The world leaders most admired by thousands of respondents—leaders such as Abraham Lincoln, Martin Luther King Jr., Jesus, Mahatma Gandhi, and Eleanor Roosevelt—all had strong beliefs about matters of principle. They were admired for their commitment and willingness to stand up for their beliefs (Kouzes & Posner, 2002).

The ethics of transformational leadership have been questioned. More often than not, these criticisms are about *pseudotransformational leadership* and *inauthenticity* (Bass, 2001)—discussed as vices of leadership later in this chapter. On the basis of his reading in philosophy and literature and his experiences on active duty and as a prisoner of war, Admiral James B. Stockdale (1981) drew up a list of universal ethical principles of leadership. In paraphrase, some of them are

1. If individual freedom is pushed to the limit, equality is lost. If you subordinate every social value to equality, freedom is sacrificed.
2. In a rigid hierarchical organization or a bloated bureaucracy in which people are trying to manipulate others, you need to avoid the temptation of thinking only about yourself. Sooner or later it becomes clear that the greatest good, the key for survival and self-respect, comes from solidarity with the others, not from taking credit for their good work or from superficial theatrics.
3. There is no moral economy in this world in which virtue is rewarded and evil is punished. The biblical Job lived a virtuous life and then with no reason or logic suffered the loss of all of his goods and reputation. Life is not fair. People need to be prepared for failure.
4. A good leader appreciates contrariness. You shouldn't force people to do what you think is good for them.
5. Goethe wrote that you should not appeal to what persons are but rather to what they might be. According to Aristotle, persuading people to reach their potential was a matter of reason (*logos*), emotion (*pathos*), and—most important—the leader's character.
6. A leader's moral responsibilities cannot be escaped. You cannot use your position as a shield against responsibility for your actions.

Cialdini (2001) has argued that although it is ethical to use expert advice and authority as a shortcut to deliberation and thoughtfulness in making good decisions, it is unethical to counterfeit or exaggerate consensus, social proof, expert authority, commitment, reciprocity, or scarcity as reasons for taking action. A controlled experiment demonstrated that 120 undergraduate college students could be taught to discriminate between honest authoritative advertisements and manipulative ones.

Ethical Pitfalls of Successful Leaders

The success of leaders may eventuate in unethical behavior. They may lose strategic focus and develop an inflated belief in their own ability to control outcomes. With privileged access to resources and enhanced status as a consequence of their successful leadership, they may be tempted into unethical acts for their own benefit at the expense of their exploited followers (Ciulla, 1998). The ordinarily ethical leader is corrupted by personal motivation, positional power, and success (Ludwig & Longenecker, 1993). Ethical norms may be violated when the well-meaning leader transforms individuals and their values to attain organizational goals but damages individual members (Stephens, D'Intino, & Victor, 1995). The righteous King David had an ethical lapse when he wanted to marry Bathsheba: he abused his acquired power to arrange the death of Uriah, her husband.

Ethics in Negotiations. The transactional leader may be highly successful at negotiating agreements with followers, but at the expense of maintaining ethical standards. The personally moral leader may lower standards in order to achieve settlements (Giampetro-Meyer, Brown, Browne, et al., 1998) or to achieve success by "cutting corners" or pressuring followers to produce (Fleming, 1999). Volkema (2001) presented data showing that among the tactics least offensive to moral sensibility were exaggerating an offer or demand, pretending not to be in a hurry, hiding one's bottom line, and making vacuous promises.

Tenbrunsel and Messick (2001) reviewed the temptations to be unethical in negotiating. Ethical transparency and full disclosure about preferences and alternatives could shift to shading the truth. Negotiators are prone to unethical misrepresentation, false threats, false promises, and falsely demeaning the opponent's best alternative to reaching an agreement. Some of these behaviors appear acceptable—such as making a high opening demand and pretending to be in no hurry to reach an agreement. Unethical behavior tends to escalate as a consequence of expectations about the ethics of the opposition. Differences in power also increase the unethical behavior of the negotiators.

Trade-Offs. Winston Churchill was supposed to have said that Lady Astor would not sleep with him for £10, but would for £10,000. Socially conscious investors are willing to accept lesser returns from mutual funds that invest only in firms that meet standards of social acceptability. Consumers may use a firm's services even though a competitor offers a lower price, because of the firms' ethical stance on the moral role of business in society. Conversely, consumers may boycott the products of a firm because they view the firm as engaged in unethical practices; for instance, Nestlé was accused of selling powdered infant formula in developing countries with unsanitary water supplies. A trade-off may cause an ordinarily moral leader without a strong enough character to ignore or engage in an unethical act because of its unusually beneficial effects for himself or herself or others. Ordinarily ethical leaders may fail to maintain standards so as to protect a family member. Moral actions may be sacrificed for opportunities and expediency (Dunfee, 2001). Ethical constraints are weakened by severe social, political, and economic conditions. Managers in the post-Communist nations of Eastern Europe used their new personal power to act abusively at the expense of their followers. This behavior was a legacy of the former Communist leadership and the socioeconomic conditions they left (Luthans, Peterson, & Ibrayeva, 1998).

Formal Ethical Education in Professional Schools. The Association of American Medical Colleges (AAMC) has listed altruism, knowledge, ability, skill, and duty as goals for graduating students. Compassion is given high priority for physicians; nevertheless, patients are likely to prefer a cold but knowledgeable and skilled physician to one who seemed warm but less expert (Gans, 2002). Rest (1988) concluded that deliberate educational interventions in the curricula in schools of law and medicine can effectively raise the moral reasoning of the students, as measured by Defining Issues Test (DIT) scores.

Business schools need to do more to teach business law and proper accounting practices. Many business schools have added ethics courses to their curricula. Taking into account the numerous corporate scandals and the amount of cheating in school, Sowell (2000) inferred that ethics courses in business schools have failed. Of approximately 2,000 MBA students entering one of 13 leading business schools, 68% agreed that maximizing shareholders' interest was the prime responsibility of corporate management. The figure rose to 82% at the end of the first year (Reiter, 2002). One reason may be the domination of many business schools by economists who believe that the sole purpose of business is to maximize shareholders' interests. Sowell's point of view is supported by Ponemon (1993). In a controlled experiment, he found that a semester course in auditing for 73 senior undergraduate and 53 graduate accounting majors did little to raise the students' level of moral reasoning. Etzioni (2002) suggested that part of the problem is what are acceptable lines of moral reasoning in business. Some people see business as a poker game in which bluffing and avoiding disclosure are permissible. Some argue that morality is relative and depends on who benefits from actions. Some suggest that customers may be gained by lying and cheating even though telling the truth may pay off in the long run.

On a more positive note, Williams and Dewett (2005) found empirical evidence to support the value of teaching ethics to enhance business students' moral development, ethical sensitivity to ethical issues, and appreciation and skill in dealing with complex ethical decisions. Penn and Collier (1985) found that business education promoted moral development. Compared with a control group of students in a marketing course, students in a business ethics course became more aware of and more sensitive to ethical issues, according to pre-post testing (Gautschi & Jones, 1990). Skepticism and relativistic attitudes changed to a better understanding of the scope of ethical issues and the complexity of making ethical decisions when students kept logs to reflect on ethical issues during a course in business ethics (MacFarlane, 2001). And students who took a business ethics course showed greater flexibility in reasoning afterward than they had shown before, as well as an increased ability to incorporate the complexities of circumstances. These students were dealing with a complicated case of CEO decision making (Carlson & Burke 1988).

Ethical Leader Behavior

The reputation of organizational leaders depends on their morality as persons and as managers and executives (Trevino, Hartman, & Brown, 2000). They may be moral in beliefs and ethical in behavior; they may be amoral in beliefs and neutral in ethical behavior; or they may be immoral in beliefs and unethical in behavior. Trevino, Brown, and Hartman (in press) conducted one-hour or longer interviews with 20 senior executives from different firms and 20 ethics officers from the same firms. The interviewees were asked to describe anonymously the ethical behavior of another executive. After answering in detail, they then were asked to describe an "ethically neutral" executive.

The ethical executives were more likely than the ethically neutrals to be perceived as people-oriented. The

neutrals were more likely to be seen as self-centered and uncaring about others. Compared with the neutrals, ethical leaders were more often seen as role models of ethical conduct who led by example and "walked the talk," who were more likely to do the right thing and were honest, trustworthy people of integrity. They were perceived as more likely to be good, open communicators and receptive listeners, as well as influential, inspirational, courageous, and strong. In short, they were more likely to be *transformational* leaders. Yet they were more likely to be *transactional* leaders as well (see Chapter 22). They set standards of conduct, reinforced ethical behavior, used rewards and punishments to hold people accountable for ethical standards, and did not tolerate ethical lapses. Ethical executives cared a great deal about the bottom line but were also concerned about multiple stakeholders, the common good, the community, and society. They were concerned also about the means of achieving business goals, not just the ends. Ethically neutral leaders differed from their ethical counterparts in being more short-term-oriented and financially oriented and being less aware of ethical issues.

Moral Exemplars

Organizational leaders can serve as moral exemplars:

> The moral impact of their leadership presence and behaviors [has] great power to shift the ethics mindfulness of organizational members . . . [They can] establish a social context . . . of positive self-regulation that becomes a clear and compelling organizational norm in which people act ethically . . . and corporate culture in which principled actions and ethics norms predominated (Thomas, Schermerhorn, & Dienhart, 2004, p. 56).

Excellent basketball coaches were identified as premier role models in interviews with nine of their peers. Not only were the coaches highly successful, competent teachers, committed to personal values and principles, but they also shaped the character of their players (Gerdes, 1994). Twenty-three living Americans were nominated as leading moral exemplary lives, because they: (1) integrated self-concepts and moral goals, did not compartmentalize morality apart from other motivating factors, and engaged in a broad range of commitments; (2) used moral concepts frequently in describing themselves; (3) denied that they had moral courage despite their history of moral courage; (4) behaved morally almost automatically and expressed certainty over doubt in their moral decision making; (5) converted seemingly depressing unfortunate occurrences into positive life-affirming events; and (6) exhibited high levels of religious faith and spirituality.

Measurement of Ethical Leadership Behavior

The Ethical Leadership Scale (ELS) was constructed, refined, and validated by Brown and Trevino (2002). Forty-eight brief statements were drawn from in-depth interviews with 20 ethics officers, 20 executives, and 20 MBA students. The statements were reduced to 21 items by means of an exploratory principal axis factor analysis with an oblique rotation of data from 154 MBAs from three large public universities and 127 employees from a large financial services organization. A confirmatory factor analysis followed using 184 employees from the same financial service. The analyses extracted and confirmed a single ethical leadership factor. The final instrument consisted of 10 items rated by subordinates about their supervisor, such as "When making decisions asks what is the right thing to do"; "Disciplines employees who violate ethical standards"; "Has the best interests of the employees in mind"; "Makes fair and balanced decisions"; and "Defines success not just by results but also [by] the way they are achieved." The ELS demonstrated convergent and discriminant validity for 571 employees from the same organization and 86 MBAs with correlations with MLQ transformational leadership ranging from .82 to .91 and correlations with LBDQ consideration (.72) and cognitive-based trust (.79).

Relation to Moral Reasoning. In this chapter, we describe the measurement of *moral reasoning* using the Defining Issues Test (DIT; Rest, 1979). People who reason ethically may not always act ethically. Managerialism was supposed to usher in material affluence and social harmony. According to Barnard (1938), the organizing principle of consensus and material growth was its moral authority. Organization required cooperation; organizations would fail if their leaders were immoral. Management was the steward of modernization, peace, and prosperity. Those in leadership positions must have impeccable moral integrity. In its absence, according to Gardner and Means (1933), the public interest would become hostage to private cupidity. For Drucker (1954), it was management's responsibility to make whatever is in the public good become the organization's self-interest. Progress depended on the technical rationality of management. For Simon (1947), management was responsible for the application of logical positivistic science and controlled experimentation for progress (Scott & Hart, 1991). But Scott and Hart (1991), writing about the business scandals of the 1980s, declared that the concept of managerial responsibility was put to shame by management frauds, abuses, and mismanagement. Nonetheless, a fundamental task of leadership may be to persuade people to go beyond a selfish agenda because left to their own devices, they will follow selfish rather than broader agendas (J. Hogan & R. Hogan, 2002).

Unethical Leader Behavior

We are at the end of a 300-year trend in decoupling the physical world of science, technology, and business from the moral landscape. The moral meltdown that leaves people working in an amoral context produces dissociation from the community. The profane earning of a living is disconnected from our sacred and spiritual cultural heritage (Reeves-Ellington, 1995). In a telephone survey of 1,500 respondents, one-third said they had seen unethical activities in their organization in the past year (Ethics Resource Center, 2001). J. Patterson and P. Kim (1991) conducted an anonymous survey of a random sample of 2,000 managers and workers. One-third judged the workers to be more ethical than the managers and only 9% to 13% saw the reverse. A majority judged the managers to be more greedy and willing to take credit for another's work; workers were judged much less so.

One cause is competitive pressure. Heggarty and Simms (1978) found that demands for performance resulted in unethical management decisions. Burnham (1941) argued that since management was in control of resources, it would use its power for self-interest. Selfless management was unlikely. Management controlled the organization's resources.

Management Corruption. The financial system exacerbates the pressure to concentrate on short-term interests, preventing managers from attending to social responsibilities (Korten, 1996). Supposedly serving the public and the shareholders, certified public accountants (CPAs) who audit the accounts of their clients are paid by the clients (Ruland, 1993). Bartol and Martin (1990) showed that managers awarded unjustifiably large raises to subordinates who threatened to use their connections with senior executives. According to Baucus and Near (1991), other environmental causes may include rapidly changing market conditions, patterns of wrongdoing in an industry, and lack of legal enforcement. Additionally, uncertainty, opportunities, and crises may be involved. Internal antecedents may include lax controls and a lack of standards. Important also are development, role models, education, work, early life, family experiences, and prior success and failures. Another factor is understanding one's duties and obligations in order to be able to fulfill them (Anonymous, 1997). Trust among members of a group or organization may be seen as an implicit moral duty. Although problematic, an explicit sense of, moral duty to trust one another could be effected and justified (Hosmer, 1995).

It is one thing to know what is right to do; it is another thing to do it (H. C. Smith, 1993). Good business may outweigh good ethics. Unethical behavior may be practiced contrary to one's moral beliefs. Other matters may override one's desire for a moral decision. Leaders may value political success and economic improvement over ethical behavior (Fritzsche & Becker, 1984). Opportunity may take precedence over ethics (Zey-Ferrell & Ferrell, 1982). A low risk of getting caught may tempt people to engage in illegal behavior (Fraedrich & Ferrell, 1992). Striving for goals over lengthy periods of time may generate unethical leadership behavior (Street, 1994). Leaders and managers may know right from wrong but convince themselves that ethically dubious enterprises are not only expedient but all right. We are more willing to harm others if we are pressured by authority (Milgrim 1974), if we are dealing with strangers rather than friends (Yamagishi & Sato, 1986), if we are at a distance from rather than close to those to be harmed, and if our self-efficacy is threatened (Bandura, 1989). But we are less likely to succumb to pressure to harm others, or to acquiesce in unethical commands if we are at Kohlberg's (1969) highest stages of moral reasoning (stage 5 or 6) and consider all people and universal ethical principles, rather than

at the lowest stages (1 and 2—the stages of self-interest and personal aspirations). In between (in stages 3 and 4), we are conventional; we obey the rules to avoid being punished, or we conform morally due to social pressure. Whereas 75% of people at the highest stages have refused to obey ethically dubious orders, only 13% at the lowest stages refused (Stewart & Sprinthall, 1994). Noted for his boastfulness about taking a hard line in cutting costs and for his ruthless layoffs that imperiled operations, "Chainsaw Al" Dunlap (1998)—at stage 1—was the epitome of the unethical CEO (Bennis, 1997). Dunlap severely harmed earnings at Sunbeam Corporation before he was fired. He bragged about his efforts to sharply downsize the firm (Dunlap & Andelman, 1996), efforts that subsequently resulted in a serious fall in sales and stock prices. Eventually, Sunbeam went bankrupt. Unethical accounting practices that inflated stock prices led to shareholder suits, personally costing Dunlap $15 million to settle an SEC investigation (Anonymous, 2002).

Daboub, Rasheed, Priem, et al. (1995) suggested that characteristics of a top management team, such as business education, seniority, and functional background, serve to enhance or neutralize illegal activity. The trustworthiness of banking executives was severely questioned and a number went to jail as a consequence of the savings and loan scandals of the 1980s. According to a *New York Times* CBS poll in 1985, 55% of the American public believed that the majority of corporate executives were dishonest and that executive white-collar crime was rampant. Of 671 executives surveyed in 1987, more than half said that they bent the rules in order to get ahead. A Prentice-Hall survey in 1990 revealed that 68% of employees believed that executives' unethical behavior resulted in the decline of business standards, productivity, and success. A majority of the employees justified their own malingering as a consequence of their perception of executives' unethical behavior (Gini, 1996). The Enron scandal of 2001 showed how widespread and devastating corruption could be, as it involved conspiracy and fraudulent behavior by the chief executives Ken Lay and Jeffery Skilling, and 16 chief executives in finance, accounting, and other units, all of whom pleaded guilty. Additionally, two other senior Enron executives in finance and accounting were convicted, as were three Merrill Lynch senior executives: a vice president and the heads of asset leasing and investment banking. Arrogance, recklessness, greed, buttressed by the size of the incentives, underlay the executives' wrongdoing. The corruption and criminality at Enron were paralleled at other giant firms, such as WorldCom, Adelphia, and HealthSouth (Eichenwald, 2006). The scandal resulted in the bankruptcy of Enron; the near destruction of one of the big-four auditing firms, Arthur Andersen; the loss of employment by thousands of Enron's employees, 4,000 in Houston alone; and the loss of employees' pensions and savings. Thousands of shareholders were left with worthless shares (Barrionuevo, 2006).

In a survey of a representative sampling of 747 human resources professionals, 53% reported they had observed misconduct occasionally (46%) or often (7%) within their organization during the past year; this misconduct violated the law or the organization's standards of ethical business. But 21% failed to report the misconduct, for fear that they would not be seen as team players; and 70% agreed that American business managers would choose profits over doing what is right. Almost all agreed that in the long run, good ethics makes good business sense; but 63% felt that ethical conduct was not rewarded. Only 69% said that their CEO was sufficiently committed to ethical business conduct; 68% felt that this was true of the rest of top management. However, more than four out of five human resources managers rated those closest to them—their direct supervisor and those they directly supervised—as sufficiently committed to ethical business behavior. The larger the organizations in size, the more likely they were to have a written code of ethical standards. Just over half of those with fewer than 100 employees, but 94% of those with over 5,000, had a code. Training in ethical standards of business was provided by 61% of these, and most employees (85%) said they occasionally or frequently used the principles they learned. Included in Martin Marietta's ethical code were: avoiding conflicts of interest; not accepting payments, gifts, or entertainment from suppliers and customers; maintaining complete and accurate books, records, and communications; preserving assets; cost-consciousness; compliance with securities, restrictive trade practices, and antitrust laws and regulations; not biasing or falsifying accounts; and avoiding political contributions, disciplinary actions for violating the code, supervisory failures, and retaliation for reporting violations.

Frauds and swindles such as making secret deals to profit insiders, securing loans with phony assets, selling assets that do not exist, trading of company stocks by insiders, and attempting to "corner" or manipulate a market seem to mount up in boom times and are discovered when the economic bust suddenly occurs. The scandals revealed in the first decade of the twenty-first century involved larger amounts of wealth and more major corporations and their senior executives than in the past, and more questionable business and auditing practices than usual. The wars in Afghanistan and Iraq produced a wave of shady deals and corruption by government contractors. The scandalous bankruptcies at Enron, Tyco International, Global Crossings, Adelphia, WorldCom, and other companies forced financial restructurings that were first brought to light in 2002. They resulted from the looting of these corporations by their top executives and no doubt led to negative feelings among employees and shareholders about corporate leadership. A few top executives, left uncontrolled by friendly, highly paid boards of directors and unchecked by unethical auditors, gave themselves as much as a fifth of a large firm's profits in the form of extraordinary perquisites, salaries, sweetheart deals, stock awards, and pensions, and ignored the corporation's investment needs and the rights of the other stakeholders—the lower-level managers, employees, and shareholders. The boundary between ethical and unethical compensation has become fuzzier. The fact that the CEO's compensation in 2005 averaged 262 times the pay of the average worker in the same firm made it difficult to maintain the rationale that the top executive's compensation was a reasonable practice, legal, and a matter of supply and demand. An ethical decision would be based on a more beneficial and equitable distribution of the firm's returns (Balcom & Brossy, 1997).

Example: Health Care As reported in the Minneapolis *Star Tribune* and by the attorney general of Minnesota, the not-for-profit Allina Health System of 16 hospitals, 47 clinics, and health care insurance units publicly espoused values such as wise use of resources, financial accountability, and earning the community's trust; but lavish expense accounts were provided. The hypocrisy was illustrated by eight Allina executives who attended an ethics seminar and charged Allina for a $1,500 dinner. A vice president of Medica, its subsidiary health insurance firm, was reimbursed $8,000 for his late fees at a golf club, to take care of his golf clubs, and to pay for his wife's use of the locker room. In 2001, Allina lost $71 million and its former subsidiary laid off 20% of its workforce (Heuerman, 2002).

Example: Labor Union The founders of labor unions and their successors fought hard to improve their constituents' welfare and working conditions. Nevertheless, corruption and exploitation of the rank and file crept into union movements, sometimes to counter employers' militancy, sometimes to take care of unscrupulous politicians, sometimes to deal with pressure from mobster's, and sometimes for the self-aggrandizement of the union leaders. Bouza (1996) noted that by 1995, 400 officials of the Teamsters Union had been charged with corruption and removed. In addition to the Teamsters, three other national unions were listed by the federal government as being controlled by organized crime.

Why? Unethical behavior by executives takes place in spite of ethical codes, laws, regulations, and ethics officers at large firms and agencies. So that "business ethics" does not become an oxymoron, reforms are needed. Marino (2002) noted that corporate officers need to be kept in the loop of information concerning executives' wrongdoing.

Ulmer (1996) suggested that senior executives fail to set an example by their personal behavior. Their misconduct provides a rationalization for everyone else to ignore ethical codes and considerations. They place unreasonable demands on those at lower levels, causing the latter to reveal incompetence and providing them with an excuse to cut corners. Borrowing from Aristotle and Kant, Jeannot (1989) argued that virtuous character is required of leaders. They need practical wisdom, autonomy, and a sense of responsibility. At the same time, business actions and accounting numbers need to be made more transparent. Taking personal responsibility for actions and ensuring a transparent supportive money trail could do the same for political ethics.

Enforceable laws and regulations may also be important. The scandals have resulted in a new federal law tightening accounting rules and toughening penalties for white-collar crime. The Sarbanes-Oxley Act made the CEO liable for the deliberate falsification of earnings in order to raise the price of the firms' shares (Lowenstein, 2002). The New York Stock Exchange began requiring all listed firms to provide a code of ethics. An ethical code is the norm for larger organizations. But scandals occur in firms despite their written codes of ethical conduct. According to an analysis of the codes of 75 Canadian firms and three American studies of corporate codes, their main purpose is to protect the firms against misconduct against them instead of promoting the firms' ethical responsibilities (Lefebvre & Singh, 1996).

Despite the laws, regulations, and codes and the punishments for violation, why do managers and executives engage in unethical and illegal behavior? Fraud in organizations commonly involves cooperation among otherwise ethical, upstanding members of the community. They justify corrupt acts. They have logic-tight compartments—dishonesty in business and loving care for the family at home. Newcomers to the organization are socialized into corruption (Anand, Ashforth, & Joshi, 2004). Bazerman, Bazerman, and Messick (1996) attributed the answer to psychological aspects of decision making. In weighing the desire for gain against possible punitive consequences, all but the one favored aspect of the decision will be ignored. Decision makers are confident that the risk of getting caught is overrestimated, or controllable, or can be ignored. Future events are perceived as more likely to be good than bad for the decision makers. They seek information only to confirm what they already believe. Unethical executives are further motivated by the rationalization that their gains are justified and are fair compensation for what they have contributed (Jenkins, 2002).

What motivates unethical behavior at lower levels in an organization? One's superiors may be an important factor. As a result of pressure from above to reach quarterly goals, sales teams at Global Crossings and Qwest engaged in dubious practices and suspicious deals. Higher-ups were able to overstate actual sales by approving network swaps.

Changed Norms. Ethical norms change. Ethical norms are broken. Physicians and lawyers at one time were not permitted to advertise. On the Internet prior to 1994, advertising was informally banned through self-regulation by its mostly educational, scholarly, and scientific early users. The costs were kept low. Management of the Internet was kept at a minimum. Then two lawyers advertised their services in news groups, and refused to quit. The dam was broken. The Internet was flooded with advertising, which led to congestion requiring a greater increase in Internet management. The World Wide Web that followed became even more congested with increased traffic and graphics (Fukuyama, 1995). With commercialization, both became targets of deceptive practices and fraud.

Bending the Rules. Of over 100 members of the executive advisory panel of the Academy of Management Executives, 87% said it was a common rationale to "bend the rules" to get the job done, and 77% said this was a common justification if performance standards were unfair and overly restrictive. Similar large majorities agreed that bending the rules was commonly justified in an emergency or if the rules were ambiguous or outdated. Most felt such rule-bending was appropriate behavior. But only between 19% and 27% felt it was appropriate to bend the rules under political or social pressure to do so, to pay back favors, or because "everyone does it." The five most important personal reasons they gave for not bending the rules were: (1) to avoid jeopardizing their jobs, (2) to avoid damage to their reputation, (3) to avoid being held responsible, (4) to avoid creating an unwanted precedent, and (5) their own code of ethics. Also, bending the rules might prove embarrassing and jeopardize the organization and others (Veiga, Golden, & Dechant, 2004).

Van Buren (2002) called for changing the contractual norms for employee-management relations to increase fairness. Employee consensus is usually lacking in the exchange agreements between them. "The goal of any movement for worker justice should be to restore the ability of workers to exercise rights of consent; that is to participate in meaningful ways in corporate governance processes with regard to employment policies and practices" (p. 2).

Ethics and Effectiveness

Ciulla (1998) suggested that leaders who do not look after the interests of their followers and other organizational stakeholders are not only unethical but also ineffective. Lee Iacocca made a moral gesture by cutting his yearly salary to one dollar, showing solidarity with his workforce when Congress bailed Chrysler out of bankruptcy. Ethics and business effectiveness also came together for Alan Weil, whose law firm's offices at the World Trade Center were destroyed by the terrorist attack of 9/11. He first checked to see if all his employees had escaped safely, then rented the necessary space in another building and arranged the same day by telephone for 800 desks and 300 computers to be delivered. The firm was open and ready for business the next day.

Ethical Imperatives. The ethical leader ought to be fair and truthful, avoid harm to others, and keep promises. But these absolutes must be conditional, depending on particular circumstances. Often supervisors are faced with dilemmas—two equally capable employees for instance, and room for only one promotion, so that only one or the other can be treated fairly. Should the supervisor tell the truth to a satisfied, valued employee—that her future in the firm is limited—increasing the likelihood that she will seek employment elsewhere? How much can we harm others by laying them off to save on expenses and at the same time support lavish bonuses for senior managers? It is more ethical as well as more effective to inform job applicants and new recruits about the rules and infractions as well as both the positives and the negatives in their prospective assignments. Recruits selected for employment are less likely to quit when the employment interviewer fairly presents to the job applicant both the positive and the negative aspects of the job rather than the good points alone. The subsequent orientation of newly hired employees with both positive and negative aspects of the job further reduces their propensity to quit. False expectations are avoided.

Ethical Reputation and Commitment. Simon Webley and Elisa More reported in a British study that companies with a clear commitment to ethical conduct outperform those with no such commitment. The ethical companies were more effective between 1997 and 2001, as gauged by return on capital and added economic and market value (E. Munson, 2004). Galvin (2000, p. 99) summed up the value of an ethical reputation to e-business, noting that "if four online retailers sell the same book at the same price, most people will purchase the book from the site they trust the most." According to

Panken (undated), in the ideal capitalist marketplace the most efficient organizations should survive and prosper. "The inefficient should sink in a sea of red ink" (p. 40). But ideally, capitalism should not mean minimizing expenses but rather optimizing benefits for all the stakeholders in the organization. Ideal socialism implies "To each according to his needs and from each according to his abilities." National political economies are now more or less regulated in differing proportions between the capitalistic ethics of efficiency and the socialistic ethics of need controlled by the market, politics, economic and social legislation, and "do-it-yourself" work. In all, ethically, there should be fairness of opportunity to earn a living in an atmosphere of respect.

Ethical Reputation, Product Quality, and Consumer Satisfaction. Galvin (2000) cited a number of reports attesting to the payoff to firms from ethical leadership and honesty and fairness in business. According to the Ethics Resources Center, "high standards in the way companies deal with their employees and customers translate into better product quality and assured customers" (p. 99). The ethical intentions of 144 insurance agents depended more on their moral obligation to disclose possibly unfavorable information to clients than to the compensation system. According to a 1999 Walker Report, "companies viewed as highly ethical by their employees were six times [more] likely to keep their staff members. On the other hand, 79% of employees who questioned their bosses' integrity said they felt trapped at work or were likely to leave their jobs soon" (p. 99). A Harris poll reported in 1988 that 89% of 1,200 workers and managers felt it was important for leaders to be honest, upright, and ethical, but only 41% said met these their current supervisor criteria (Hughes, Ginnett, & Curphy, 1993). The job satisfaction, commitment, and identification of 257 employees were positively correlated with their perceptions of the ethical behavior of management, but their perception of their organization's ethical climate was of less consequence (Spitzmueller, Gibby, & Stanton, 2003). Having a reputation for the virtues of forgiveness, optimism, compassion, trust, and integrity was found, in 75 interviews in a small hospital and an environmental consulting engineering firm, to contribute to subsequent success after the hospital and the firm downsized. A confirmatory survey of 804 respondents in 18 firms found that those with a reputation for integrity, trustworthiness, reliability, and dependability were more profitable after downsizing. Innovation was associated with optimism, trust, integrity, and forgiveness; customer retention was associated with a reputation for optimism and trust; employee was linked with a firm's reputation for trust and compassion (Cameron, Caza, & Bright, 2002).

Corporate Social Responsibility. Corporate social responsibility ought to be assessed by the extent to which all of the stakeholders' concerns are considered, including those of the community and the public. According to Black and Härtel (2002), firms that are *adaptive* in their orientation to social responsibility consider and value stakeholder interests in their operations. Firms *disengaged* in corporate responsibility are the opposite. They place little value on stakeholder' interests or ethical business conduct. The *missionary* type adopts any social cause not limited to its own business operations and sometimes may disturb some of its own stakeholders. The *economic* type acts only on matters it considers of instrumental value to the firm and its stakeholders. Community sponsorships, cause-related marketing, and strategic philanthropy are illustrative. Strategic corporate responsibility is shown when automobile companies invest in engines that use alternative, less polluting fuel. A network of firms oriented to corporate social responsibility would enhance the effort (Johnson & Brennan, 2002).

Socially Responsible and Irresponsible Accounting Statements. Pruzan and Thyssen (undated) suggested that accounting statements can be prepared that reflect a consensus among stakeholders' shared values and how the organization has lived up to them. Compared with a traditional accounting statement, such statements involve more values and more stakeholders. Operationalized, concrete verbal expressions in the statement can be applied to creating questionnaires to evaluate the organization's ethical performance. But short-term stock options for CEOs militate against ethically sound corporate governance. Sixty large firms that had to restate their accounts of 1999 or could not certify their 2001–2002 accounts because of corporate accounting irregularities were matched with 60 firms that did not have these problems. Compared with the CEOs of the "clean" firms, the CEOs of firms with irregularities were more likely to have short-term stock options and were judged to be "un-principled" agents of their corporations (O'Connor & Priem, 2003). Fraudulent accounting statements were also found by Troy, Smith, and Gordon (2003) in firms compared with matched firms when their CEOs were younger, did not have an MBA, and had more of their compensation based on stock options. The firms with fraudulent accounting engaged in riskier acquisition strategies, were more distressed financially, and lacked external audit oversight. When superiors turned a blind eye to fraudulent reports, subordinates were more likely to make such reports, especially if the subordinates were more generally accepting of social dominance (Smith-Crowe, Umphress, Brief, et al., 2003).

Ethical Climate. Individual character is a source of information about ethical climate (Anonymous, 1997). Over the long run, confidence in the leadership and its institutions depends on the character of the leader. The ethical climate of an organization often is a consequence of the character, motives, and values of its founders and early leaders (Dickson, Smith, Grojean, et al., 2001). It was also assumed that firms with an earned reputation for social responsibility were led by moral executives. In 95 studies, Margolis and Walsh (2001) carefully selected ethically exemplary and ethically notorious firms. For this, they reviewed a number of lists of firms according to the firms' perceived social responsibility. The firms' reputations on nine criteria including social responsibility were obtained by asking executives, outside directors, and corporate analysts. Also obtained were five additional measures of corporate social responsibility toward community, diversity, employee relations, the natural environment, and product safety and quality (pp. 9–10). Control variables were applied to the analysis of the "good" and "bad" firms. In 80 of the 95 studies, the data about corporate social performance preceded successful financial performance. Of these, 53% predicted financial performance. In 19 of the 80 studies, financial performance preceded social responsibility. Here the results were even more positive: 68% supported the argument that financially successful firms could afford to be socially responsible.

Bansal and Roth (2000) conducted interviews in Britain and Japan at 53 firms to ascertain what prompted their sense of ecological responsibility. It was seen as a matter of good business, for instance, to turn a waste product into something of value. This improved the firm's image, reputation, and legitimacy and avoided penalties and fines. It was the right thing to do and made the firm a good citizen, a morally better company, and a company that felt good about itself. However, managers' moral intentions—for example, those of 130 to 138 executives in the metal finishing industry regarding their firm's dealing with wastewater—were moderated by their moral intensity and the magnitude of the consequences. The executives' attitudes, norms, and sense of self-efficacy along with the financial costs and the ethical climate affected their ethical decisions (Flannery & May, 2000).

Ethical Constraints on Organizational Leaders' Influence. There are limits on what a superior can ask of subordinates and what the subordinates are permitted or expected to do. Superiors have a positive duty to avoid influence that violates ethical norms of society. They ought to use their influence to promote the common good of the organization and its members (Kelman, 2001). The values and decisions of subordinates should be respected. With justice and fairness, leaders ought to promote the welfare of subordinates and avoid harming them (Beauchamp, Faden, Wallace, et al., 1982). Ethical considerations ought to constrain leaders from being too coercive or directive in group decision processes (Peterson, 2001). Conversely, top managers' perspective on illegal corporate activities can make a difference to what leaders at all levels are tempted to do unethically (Daboub, Rasheed, Prien, et al., 1995). A corporation's code of ethics ought to be consistent with its incentive system, which should avoid shortcuts at the expense of the reputation and long-term survival of the corporation (Darley, 2001). Ethical congruence of the leader and the organization tends to increase the leader's job satisfaction, commitment to the organization, and intention to remain with the organization (Arnaud, Ambrose, & Schminke, 2002). Ethical considerations may cause an amoral leader to avoid giving a direct order to a subordinate to carry out an unethical act, but instead the leader will indirectly hint that the act be carried out. The subordinate can resist the suggestion or claim a misunderstanding if the ethical violation is discovered (Roloff & Paulson, 2001). Perreault (1997) reviewed how subordinates can make a difference in whether an ethical decision emerges in a situation. Often they are unaware of their potential impact. They ought not remain loyal to an unethical leader. Followers are ethical to the extent that they pursue the goals and practices of an ethical leader. Like leaders, they ought to be sensitive to ethical issues and to reason, decide, and act ethically.

Ethical Failures. Allinson (1995) attributed several disasters—the first Hubble space telescope, the Challenger space shuttle, the fire at the London Underground King's Cross Station, the ferry flooding at Zeebrugge in Belgium, and the aircraft tragedy at Mount Erebus in Antarctica—to the irresponsibility of management and its failure to be ethically centered. For instance, in the case of the flawed Hubble telescope, management actively discouraged quality control. Top management disowned responsibility for finding out and ensuring that the final product was problem-free and of the highest quality. They did not consider it their duty to inquire if there were any problems. They did not show respect for their employees by paying attention to suggestions and warnings. With regard to the need for independent testing, they ignored consultants. President Bill Clinton's dalliance with Monica Lewinski was a private affair, but once it became public knowledge, this unethical behavior and the attempts to cover it up with lies led to impeachment proceedings and loss of trust in the president.

Spiritual Leadership

Society is undergoing a spiritual revolution (Haasnoot, 2000) and a new awakening that cannot be ignored by organizational leaders (Judge, 1999). This awakening is moving people to a higher level of transcendence and morality, beyond Kohlberg's highest stage (stage 6). Some observers see spirituality as the "hottest new management theory," an opportunity to exploit religious language in service of organizational performance (Wallace, 2001). Southwest Airlines, Ben and Jerry's, and numerous other firms have taken on programs reflecting spiritual issues (Lewis, 2001). More than three-fourths of respondents in a Gallup poll in 1999 said they felt a need for spiritual growth (Moch & Bartunik, 2002). Mysticism is being introduced into management (Conlin, 1999). Spirituality

has been important to the leader-follower relationship in Taoism for over 2,500 years (Johnson, 2000).

Meaning. Spirituality is a mind-set that becomes a way of existing at all times and places. It is an approach to life that includes a transcendent being and a sense of oneness with the universe (Bruce & Plocha, 1999). It is a striving to integrate one's life and a desire for wholeness in the midst of fragmentation, for community in the face of isolation and loneliness, for meaning, and for enduring values (Pielstick, 2000). Václav Havel, former president of the Czech Republic and leader of the "velvet revolution," commented, "In my own life, I am reaching for something that goes far beyond me and the horizon of the world that I know. . . . In everything I do I touch eternity in a strange way" (Bolman & Deal, 1996, p. 530).

Concepts and Theory. Kanungo and Mendonca (1996) found a spiritual quality in the faith that many followers have in their charismatic leaders. Conger (1991) saw a spiritual union between charismatic leaders and their followers. Sanders, Hopkins, and Geroy (2002) maintained that the consciousness, moral character, and faith inherent in spirituality move transformational leadership into a higher *transcendental* leadership, applying consciousness, heart, and soul in the leader's daily accomplishments. According to Matusak (1997), *servant leadership* has deeply spiritual underpinnings. Greenleaf (1977), its originator, assumed that leaders exist primarily to serve their group of followers. The followers grant allegiance to the servant leader in order to achieve common goals. Servant leadership is deeply spiritual but has become a secular approach to promoting service to others, empowerment, shared decision making, participative management, and a holistic approach to work and to personal development (Lee & Zemke, 1993). May and Whittington (2003) describe *affirmative leadership* built on passages in the gospels of the New Testament that they compared with principles of servant and transformational leadership.

Relation to Religion. Religious tradition contains support and rules for spiritual seekers. Ethical principles often derive from religion, just as religion depends on spiritual experience. Such spiritual experience in a larger community of faith can lead to moral discourse and ethical behavior (Moch & Bartunik, 2002). Ordinarily, spirituality depends for collective discipline and knowledge on the stewardship of religion. But the relationship between spirituality and religiosity is complex. Conclusions drawn from reviews of evidence about religiosity and ethical behavior, ranging from cheating to criminal activity, are mixed. Religious role expectations, religious identity, and religious motivation may need to be considered as moderators (Weaver & Agle, 2002). Hicks (2002) argued that spirituality cannot be divorced from religious expression. Nevertheless, as noted by Roof (1999), among baby boomers at midlife, only 79% with a religious identity reported that they were spiritual and 54% without a religious identity said they were spiritual.

Relation to Leadership. Religious and philosophical teachings on morality and ethical behavior are being recast into research on spirituality and leadership. Bruce (2000) remarks that spiritual leadership pays special attention to the interconnections between God, humanity, and the world of nature; the immanence of the past and future in the present; issues of brotherhood and community; and the rejection of materialism. Emmons (1999) says that spirituality transcends the physical and the material. It provides an ability to experience heightened states of consciousness as well as to sanctify everyday experiences and solve problems. It involves the capacity to be virtuous (Cowan, 2002). Jesus, in his spiritual mission, was both transactional and transformational in his leadership (Ford, 1991). Whittington, Kageler, and Pitts (2002) found 10 principles of leadership in Saint Paul's first letter to the Thessalonians. But Hicks (2005) cautioned that organizational leaders should not promote a single spiritual framework. Rather, they ought to create a structure and organizational culture in which members can respectfully negotiate religious and spiritual diversity. A basic beginning is *respectful pluralism*, that welcomes fundamental aspects of each member's identity and dignity. Fry (2003) derived a causal theory of spiritual leadership from a model of motivation. Spiritual leadership is seen as creating vision and congruence of values that foster organizational commitment and productivity in individuals and teams. Fry distinguished between spirituality and religiosity but assumed a universal need for spirituality and a humanistic, theistic, or pantheistic higher power. Leaders need to get in touch with the core values

of their followers and communicate these values through vision and personal action to create a sense of spiritual survival.

Whereas the spirituality of religious fundamentalists is emotionally justified by a faith in a mythology of the past, the spirituality of religious liberals is more rationally oriented toward a future predicated on continued advances in science, technology, and human betterment (Armstrong, 2000). Both religious fundamentalists and religious liberals engage in leadership that is transformational. But more pseudotransformational leadership and more irrationality are likely to appear among fundamentalist religious leaders and followers.

Effects. Milliman and Neck (1994) suggested that spiritual-based values can increase commitment, teamwork, sense of service, and personal growth. Support was provided in a controlled longitudinal experiment by Fry and Malone (2003) using 223 elementary and middle school employees. A sense of spiritual survival, finding meaning in life, and the value of spiritual leadership were fostered that influenced a sense of well-being, commitment, and productivity.

Bolman and Deal (2001) present a parable about a manager who has found organizational life hollow and unfulfilling. His mentor helps the manager to put spirit and emotion into his leadership. The manager is awakened to his own inner world of feelings and soul. The mentor helps the manager to find spirit all around and to recognize the importance of working with others with the gifts of love, power, authorship, and significance. These gifts depend on timing for acceptance and value. The gift of love involves compassion, consideration, and caring. The gift of power is a sharing to bring about autonomy and empowerment. The gift of authorship provides a sense of accomplishment. The gift of significance uses ritual, celebration, and spontaneity to credit shared creativity at the workplace. It remains a challenge for organizational leaders to introduce more spiritual values in the workplace and to evaluate the effects on performance and satisfaction.

Moral Reasoning

Given a moral dilemma, moral reasoning entails why people make the ethical decision they make and what considerations are most important to the decision. But knowing and deciding what is right to do may not result in doing right. Leaders can have an important moral effect on those they lead. The leader may simply ask what is the right thing to do. The leader may direct or request more systematic deliberation on what is the right thing to do, to add confidence in the answer. Thus effective moral reasoning is needed by human resources executives if they are to satisfactorily balance the organization's fundamental values, employees' and other stakeholders' interests, and the firm's profitability (Grensing-Pophal (1998). The leaders' own values affect what they decide is right and wrong. Their moral decisions will depend on the importance they attach to terminal values such as inner harmony, social recognition, and family security, and to instrumental values such as being responsible, courageous, and imaginative (Hughes, Ginnett, & Curphy, 1993). It might be expected that moral reasoning correlates with moral action; that is, the more people are able to reason ethically, the more likely they are to behave ethically (Perreault, 1994), however the relationship is complex (Mudrack, 2002), as will be noted below

Measurement. Moral reasoning is most frequently measured by the P score on Rest's (1979, 1986) Defining Issues Test (DIT). The DIT has been used in over 500 studies and over 12,000 cases (Mudrock, 2000). For each dilemma presented, the respondent chooses the right action to be taken, rates the relative importance of 12 reasons in deciding, and ranks the four most important of these. The P score of a respondent is the proportion of reasons cited that respect rights, values, and universal principles (Kohlberg's post-conventional stages 5 and 6). The average P score for adults, in general, is 40.0. P scores increase with age and education. Available averages are those for junior high school students, 21.9; senior high school students, 31.8; college students, 42.3; graduate business students, 42.8; and advanced law students, 52.2. Delinquents have low P scores: 16-year-old delinquent boys, 18.9; prison inmates, 23.5. At the high end are seminarians (59.8) and moral philosophers and

theologians (65.2). Professionals score higher than adults in general: physicians, 49.5; staff nurses, 46.4 (Rest, 1993). Blasi (1980) failed to find significant correlations in only 18 of 75 studies of P scores and ethical behavior.

Nonetheless, knowing and choosing the reasons for the right thing to do is not the same as doing the right thing. Rule-bound leaders, those who are consistent in their choice of actions and the reasons they deem most important, earn high utilization (U) scores. The U score indicates whether people would act according to their reasoning. People who explain a decision by giving one important reason that is in conflict with another reason they regard as highly important earn low U scores (Thomas, 1985). Thus U scores are moderators that enhance the correlations of P scores with other expected measures of ethical behavior (Thomas, Rest, & Davison, 1991) and help to explain why moral decisions alone (P scores) failed to correlate with behavior in 18 of 75 studies (Blasi, 1980). Mudrack (2002) demonstrated that the negative correlations of P, U, and Machiavellianism (Christie & Geis, 1970) were high only when high U scores were added to P scores in a regression equation. Similar results were obtained by Mudrack (2002) with the multiple correlation of P added to U scores predicting right-wing authoritarianism (RWA; Altemeyer, 1998).

Principled Moral Reasoning. Traditionally, moral reasoning about the best solution to a moral dilemma was *principled moral reasoning*: applying general principles and rules relevant to the case to decide on the most just solution. Following Paine (1991), Reiter (2002) argued for a second approach: *character-based moral reasoning*. Here, the judgment is based on testing available actions against a rational theory that serves as a standard of what is right and good. But there is often a disconnect between the theoretically right thing to do and its actual application—between moral thinking and moral application. Furthermore, moral choice is supposedly impersonal and based on rationality. Broad general decision rules relevant to all similar cases are applied (Kupperman, 1991). However, competing moral claims may engender unresolvable conflicts that do not permit unique solutions. Using principled reasoning to decide on the right thing to do may result in more harm than good to all concerned. King Solomon threatened to give half of an infant to each of two women who were claiming to be its mother. The character of the decision maker supposedly has no effect on the moral decision. The social and historical context is ignored.

Principled participants who also believed strongly in a just world reasoned most ethically on the DIT. Morally principled leaders move their followers to higher ethical levels. Dukerich, Nichols, Elm, et al. (1990) found in a study of 21 four-person groups that if the emergent leaders were more principled in their reasoning, their group's moral reasoning achieved a higher level of ethical reasoning, as measured by the DIT. Similar results were obtained in a follow-up experiment in which members higher in DIT level were assigned as leaders of the groups. Nonetheless, after 118 business students completed the DIT, they engaged in a realistic competitive simulation calling for the sharing and use of common resources. During the competition, in comparison with their DIT scores, their scores on principled moral reasoning declined, as measured repeatedly by a "reasoning list" equivalent to the DIT (Reall, Bailey, & Stoll, 1994).

Character-Based Moral Reasoning. In real life, leaders do not use systems of rules to reach moral decisions. Rather, their moral deliberations are personal and contextual. To reason in this way, leaders need to (1) be ethically sensitive, to identify ethical issues; (2) be able to reason ethically;(3) conduct themselves ethically, with the ability to appreciate and empathize with another's situation; and(4) understand ethical leadership and how organizational factors affect the individual (Paine, 1991). Reiter (2002) suggested that the first two requirements are met by both principled and character-based moral deliberation, but the latter two call for character-based ethical conduct and ethical leadership as described extensively by Johnson (1993) and Senge (1990).

Reiter noted that one's "circle of concern" is a ring of actions and events one cares about. A leader's smaller circle includes the concerns that he or she can do something about proactively, to head off ethical problems early. Leaders should begin moral deliberation with the end in mind. In agreement with Burns (1978), Reiter pointed out that moral leaders should focus on clarifying values and achieving valued ends. They ought to facilitate interaction by converting disputes into win-win situations, seeking first to understand, and using empathic communication. Moral leaders ought to see problems

from other points of view and search for alternative solutions. They ought to continue to clarify what is important and continue to see current reality more clearly (Senge, 1990). *Moral imagination* is needed by leaders for character-based moral deliberation in order to explore various courses of action to harmonize conflicting values and conceptions of reason (Johnson, 1993).

Moral Decision Making. Covrig (2000) described how 11 school administrators coped with making decisions that forced them to violate one cherished value in order to satisfy another. Sometimes, these decisions were seen as challenges rather than dilemmas, or as dilemmas for which there were routine decisions. Various models of the moral decision-making process were proposed. For instance, Trevino (1986) emphasized the need for the moral dilemma to stimulate moral awareness in the decision maker. Sensitivity to the dilemma should be moderated by reinforcement, by the character of the work, and by the organizational culture. The decision maker's ego strength, locus of control, and field dependence should also be considered. As noted elsewhere, a leader's moral judgment comes after moral awareness and sensitivity indicate that a moral problem exists, a decision to act is made, and action is taken (Rest, 1986). Moderators such as timing, opportunity, and available sanctions occur. Jones (1991) proposed that the impetus to decide depends on the dilemma's social and critical consequences and on its closeness in time and space to the decision maker.

Rest (1984) saw a logical progression in moral reasoning. It begins with interpreting the situation involving possible ethical actions and the welfare of those affected by them, and then making and persevering in a moral choice. According to Langenderfer and Rockness (undated), the facts are identified, then the ethical issues and stakeholders. The norms, principles, and values are defined and the best course of action is chosen consistent with them and the consequences of alternatives. There is consultation with trusted others before the decision is made.

Leadership and Moral Development. John Gardner (1990) charged leaders with the task of revitalizing the values and beliefs they shared with their constituents—including moral values. Leaders "must conceive and articulate goals in ways that lift people out of their petty preoccupations and unite them toward higher ends" (p. 191). Galaz-Fontes, Hernando Morelos, et al. (1991) held that moving followers up in the stages of moral development depends on their leadership. Hollander (1995) said that ethical concerns of leaders and followers were essential to developing trust and loyalty between them. Hollander suggested that in their need for power and distance, self-serving leaders become detached from their followers' reactions. Poor leadership damages trust, loyalty, and teamwork and raises, in the followers, questions about the ethics of equity, responsibility, and accountability. Paine (1997) suggested that ethical leaders influence the development of morality of their group and organization by: (1) leading by example; (2) developing a framework of aspirations and standards of the behavior they expect of others in the organization; (3) aligning the organization with the framework of structures that maintain its ethicality; and (4) dealing with external challenges to its morality and integrity. Graham (1995) detailed the relations between leaders and followers' in ethical development according to Kohlberg's (1969) six stages of individual moral development. Leaders at stages 1 and 2 are most likely to foster transactional leadership and dependable task performance by followers. Managers at stages 3 and 4 focus on role and institutional relationships. Managers at stages 5 and 6 most likely are transformational. More managers, and adults in general, reason at stages 3 and 4, but those in larger organizations are more likely to reason at lower levels. Reasoning is also likely to be at a lower stage of morals when it concerns business rather than nonbusiness matters (Weber, 1990).

Williams (1994) suggested that transformational leaders had positive effects on followers' "organizational citizenship behavior" (OCB), but only if the leader was trusted. Turner and Barling (undated) asked 58 supervisors of nonfaculty personnel at a Canadian university to complete Rest's (1990) Defining Issues Test. On that basis supervisors were sorted into three categories of moral reasoning: (1) stages 1 and 2, preconventional moral reasoning; (2) stages 3 and 4, conventional moral reasoning; and (3) stages 5 and 6, post-conventional moral reasoning. The supervisors were rated by 173 subordinates using the Multifactor Leadership Questionnaire to assess the supervisors' transformational and transactional leadership scores. The transformational leadership scores increased linearly and significantly from preconventional through conventional to post-conventional moral reasoning. Conversely, the trend was reversed for transactional active management by exception. The less morally mature the supervisors, the more they were likely to practice management by exception (N. Turner, 1998).

Leader Styles, Moral Values, and Ethical Consequences. The coercive, autocratic leader values authoritarian rules and directions, to be obeyed uncritically. Such leadership is a cause of groupthink, pressure to conform, and biased stereotypes of out-groups (Sims, 1992). Behavior is less ethically developed than it is under democratic leadership. Rule-bound leadership found in bureaucracies and organizational hierarchies constrains moral reasoning and sense of moral responsibility. Mudrock (2002) found that the DIT P scores of 317 U.S. Coast Guard personnel were significantly lower than adult norms. But P scores rose with rank from seaman to captain, reflecting education and age.

The transactional leader attaches most importance to exchange agreements with instrumental compliance and enforceable contracts. The contract has to have moral legitimacy (Donaldson & Dunfee, 1994) that depends on telling the truth, keeping promises, and fair distribution of rewards and valid incentives. It recognizes the diversity of values and motivations (Rawls, 1971) and virtues in leaders and followers such as honesty, reliability, integrity, sensitivity, and a sense of reciprocity (Burns, 1978). In high-quality exchanges between leaders and members, role obligations are valued and met. (For full details about such exchanges, see Chapters 15 and 16.) The referent value is the personal relationship with the supervisor. For the institutional leader, cultural expectations about the fulfillment of social and organizational duties are deemed important.

Commentaries about ethical charismatic leaders (charismatic leadership is detailed in Chapter 21) and transformational leaders (Chapter 22) are consistent with each other. The ethical charismatic leader does what is morally right, goes beyond self-interest for others' benefit, and favors empowerment over control and followers' internalization of the leader's influence (Conger & Kanungo, 1998). Ethical charismatic leaders use their power to serve others rather than for personal gain. They align their vision with followers' needs. To deal with organizational and societal interests, they rely on internalized moral standards instead of convenient external moral standards that satisfy their own self-interest (Howell & Avolio, 1992). Transformational leaders' moral values take into account the costs and benefits to all stakeholders, the application of distributive justice, and universal moral principles (R. S. Peterson, 2001). In the Netherlands, 73 CEOs of small and medium-size profit and voluntary organizations were rated by their 125 direct reports. The MLQ survey and TAT testing examined how much they were charismatic and used their power motivation in a morally responsibility way. (The voluntary organizations focused on altruistic goals and morally responsible actions such as environmental protection, human rights, or animal welfare.) Overall, a sense of high moral responsibility was near the same mean level in for-profit and voluntary organizations; but in profit-making organizations the CEOs were more likely to be rated as highly charismatic even when they were not seen as morally responsible.

Rest's (1990) Defining Issues Test (DIT) was completed by 132 managers to measure their moral reasoning. Also, the Multifactor leadership Questionnaire (Bass & Avolio, 1995) was completed by their 407 subordinates to assess the managers' transformational and transactional leadership. Moral reasoning correlated significantly ($r = .26$) with transformational but not with transactional leadership. Again, transformational but not transactional leadership increased with successive stages of Kohlberg's moral maturity (Turner, Barling, Epitropaki, et al., 2002). Sixty-one senior executives higher in transformational leadership were lower in the Hall-Tonna (1944) values cycle 2 (Kohlberg's moral development stage of personal aspirations). They scored higher on values cycle 5 matching Kohlberg's higher moral stage of concern for others' rights (Goeglein, 1997). Such leaders provide examples of ethical behavior that should raise the moral standards and values of their followers (Stephens, D'Intino, & Victor, 1995). Brown and Travino (2003) found more trust and liking of their leaders among employees when the leaders were more transformational, but employees' unethical conduct was unaffected.

Accounts. Moral reasoning is not as strong might be expected among accountants, nor is it related to their success. The Arthur Anderson auditing firm's debacle of 2001 may be explained by the rather less-developed moral reasoning of accountants and auditors when their DIT scores are compared with those of other professionals. Seminarians, judges, and nurses score at the highest levels. At midlevel are CEOs, physicians, dentists, generals, and admirals. Below them are lawyers, college seniors, and staff and senior accountants. Still lower in DIT scores are college freshmen, accountant partners, and junior high school students. A representative U.S. sample of 650 CPAs drawn by mail with a response rate of 31% provided 57 senior CPAs, account managers, and accounting partners. Over a two-year period, those promoted had DIT scores of 36.1; those not promoted had scores of 41.2; those leaving their firm had scores of 48.3. Considerably more results from three studies also indicated that ethical socialization in the accounting firms' leaders resulted in *lower* ethical reasoning (Ponemon, 1992).

Personal and Moral Development. Torbert (1991) observed that the stages in personal development have a moral logic consistent with the historical development of moral philosophies from Hobbes in the seventeenth century to Rawls (1971) in the twentieth century. Later-stage leaders are capable of more nuanced ethical judgments (Lichtenstein, Smith, & Torbert, 1995). Torbert found that 24% of 37 first-line supervisors and 9% of 177 junior and middle managers were *diplomats* for whom what is right depends on social norms. Ethics were a matter of consent. Interpersonal conflict was to be avoided. A majority of first-line supervisors (68%), 43.5% to 47% of middle managers, 66 senior managers, and 104 executives were *technicians*. They were assertive, critical, legalistic, Kantian, and concerned about rights and duties. Only 8% of first-line supervisors were *achievers*, but from 33% to 40% of managers and executives were achievers. The system's success ruled their logic. They were organizers and directors. Like Rawls, they subscribed to a sense of fairness and justice and had internalized moral standards that balanced the ethics of Rousseau and Kant. Only 5% of junior and middle managers and hardly any senior managers were found by Torbert (1991) to be at the lowest stage, opportunism. *Opportunists* were governed by their own interests and giving tit for tat. They were Hobbsian and utilitarian in ethical philosophy and interpersonally manipulative and deceptive. As moral maturity develops from one stage to the next, there is an increase in: (1) ability to accept responsibility for one's actions, (2) empathy for others who hold different or conflicting worldviews, and (3) tolerance of stress and ambiguity (Bartunek, Gordon, & Weathersby, 1983).

Character

General Norman Schwarzkopf declared that managers and leaders are more likely to fail because of lack of character than lack of competence (Mason, 1992). Many CEOs see themselves as needing primarily to watch out warily for their near-term performance. Everything that can be quantified is quantified, and tighter controls are imposed. They avoid risk and long-term investment in research and development (Levinson, 1988). Legal suits, Securities and Exchange Commission regulations, and state and federal legislation emerge as reactions to questionable senior management practices. A 1989 New York State law required that the board of directors consider the costs to the community of accepting a takeover bid, as well as the benefits to the shareholders.

Morality is a set of values and social beliefs about right conduct. Moral behaviors are acceptable; immoral behaviors are unacceptable. *Ethicality* is concerned with implied standards such as fairness, justice, kindness, the differences between right and wrong, and morally acceptable conduct. The *character* of a leader involves his or her ethical and moral beliefs, intentions, and behavior. Various questions need to be asked about the character of leaders. Are there just a few bad apples in business leadership? A few rogue politicians in government? A few unethical health administrators? A few immoral religious pastors? A few unethical military and police officers? A few unethical educators? Are leaders using acceptable political means for their self-aggrandizement (Dalton, 1959), or are immorality and lack of ethics endemic among leaders of organizations and societies? Does power corrupt? We will try to examine these and related questions in this chapter.

The robber barons—entrepreneurs who dominated business leadership in the last half of the nineteenth century—brought on the regulatory reforms of the first half of the twentieth century. The latter part of the twentieth century saw history repeating itself. The many business scandals that continued into the twenty-first century reinforced the public's lack of confidence in the ethics of business executives. Fox (2000) noted that confidence in business leadership declined from a high of 70% in the late 1960s to about 15% in the late 1980s. By 1989, the costs of corporate crime—ranging from illegal dumping of waste to price fixing—had greatly exceeded the costs of street crime. Almost every day there were reports in the media about violations of ethical conduct by national and local leaders which Fineman (2006) described as "the fraying of America's moral fabric" (p. 31). A total of 110 senior officials during the eight years of the Reagan administration (1981–1989) were accused of illegal or unethical conduct (Thomas, 1988).

More statesmanship and less politics are needed from our political leaders. Statesmen are magnetized by the truth, unwilling to give up their good name, unable to put their interests ahead of the nation's. They avoid evasion, broken promises and lies for the sake of political victory. They are prepared for self-sacrifice (Halprin, 1998). But an untarnished hero is hard to find. Mother Teresa disclosed that she mistreated subordinates and took money from dictators. President Kennedy plotted to kill Fidel Castro and cavorted with call girls in the White House (Gibbon, 1997).

Ethical issues in communities and organizations increased greatly as a consequence of the increasing complexity and sensitivity of our society and the vast expansion of the mass media. It was difficult for enforceable laws to keep up with the ethical requirements of business and technological advances, property ownership, and political and military developments in the twentieth century. Unfair discrimination against minorities came to be treated as a violation of human and legal rights. Influence peddling became government-regulated lobbying. Many new governmental environmental constraints were imposed. Collective bargaining was legalized, and workers became stakeholders in corporations rather than just a means of production (Steidlmeier, 1989). The military was forced to reexamine its ethical guidelines, prompted by its warfighting emphasis in the last decade on precision engagement and protection of forces. How much collateral damage to civilians could be tolerated? The requirements for protecting forces have resulted in a dysfunctional aversion to casualties and eroded a core value: the possible need for self-sacrifice (Shaping American

Military Culture in the Twenty-First Century, 2000). The U.S. military response to terrorism and insurgency in the Middle East has resulted in unethical mistreatment of detainees and killing of innocent civilians.

Questions have always been raised about what is right and good or wrong and bad in work, trade, and political, social, and family life. These issues have accompanied the rise of humankind. Moral codes in primitive cultures accompanied the rise of civilization. The questions have been addressed in writing for more than 2,500 years by philosophers such as Plato in the West and Confucius in the East. However, only in the past several decades have they become a study in the behavioral sciences following commentaries on organizational life and moral concerns formulated much earlier in philosophy, sociology, political science, and social psychology.

Character Education

Ciulla (1996) suggested that to teach leaders to be ethical, you have to develop their moral imagination, critical thinking skills, and emotional strength to act on what is morally right. Secular and religious schools consider, in their curricula, honesty, democracy, acceptance of others from different races and of different ethnicity, caring for friends and group members, patriotism, moral courage, and the Golden Rule. Religious schools add spirituality, providence, and faith. Character education with a range of virtues has been introduced. Anecdotal reports of positive effects such as reduced conflict, reduced expulsions, and more orderly classrooms have appeared in places as disparate as Tyler, Texas and New York City. Liberals and conservatives seem able to agree about what values to focus on (Sharpe, 1994).

> Moral authority . . . and the idea of . . . ethical leadership emerged as . . . important themes in the secular educational leadership literature in the 1990s . . . [Included were] moral reasoning . . . and how a humanistic, person-centered articulation and embodiment of moral value provides the type of role model that inspires teachers and students. (Bess & Goldman, 2001, p. 432)

Character Traits

Character is the complex of moral, social, and religious traits. It is what we actually are, in contrast to our personality—what we appear to be (Corsini, 1999). Leadership is an expression of who we are, not just something we do. Therefore much of it must develop from the inside out through both conscious and subconscious beliefs. Leaders guided by their internal character rather than their external personality are more open to opportunities for learning, more meaningful purposes, adaptability, and maintenance of balance (Cashman, 1998). Thompson (2000) agrees that inner spirit is more important than outer strivings in the development of leaders. Posner (2002) has suggested that leaders need to go within to find "what grabs hold of them and won't let go. . . . Just what is it that I really care about?" (p. 3). "Authentic leadership comes from inside out" (p. 6).

Character integrates leaders' morals and ethical behavior with their personalities. It is grounded in core values, such as integrity, trust, truth, and human dignity, that shape the leaders' vision, ethics, moral literacy, and excellence. It empowers mentorship (Sankar, 2003). Its moral rectitude strengthens the position of political leaders who depend on public opinion (Mitchell, 1993). In the U.S. Army, doctrine gives primacy to the character of leaders and soldiers and their ethical behavior. Honor, courage, and commitment at the heart of the character expected in members of the U.S. Marine Corps (Lynch, 1995). Gal (1989) stressed the need for Israeli combat leaders to have strong moral commitment and conviction. Commitment to the profession rather than to one's career should motivate the office corps. Commitment rather than obedience should motivate compliance.

Good and Bad Character Traits. A leader with good character will have internalized the Platonic virtues of prudence, justice, temperance, and courage, as well as honesty, compassion, keeping promises, and dedication to the common good. A leader of bad character is motivated by vices such as greed, cruelty, indifference, and cowardice. Acts of leadership may be good or bad. *Deontics* relates to the effects of these actions, particularly on the well-being of others. The moral point of view of leaders depends on whether these effects benefit or harm the interests, rights, or duties of the affected parties. *Interests* may be self-interests, group interests, and interest in the greatest good. *Rights* may have to do with fair distribution and basic liberties. *Duties* may include fidelity to relations with others and the community (Goodpaster, No. 7). Ethical executives run firms with applied codes of ethics, have clear channels upward for whistle-blowers, reward integrity, and give the same training in ethics to executives, managers, and employees. All ought to know what to do, for example, if offered a bribe (Stern, 2002). George Washington was transformed from a military hero to the new republic's moral symbol as he refused, repeatedly, the powers and privileges of a king or dictator. His virtues were seen by the public as making him incorruptible (Schwartz, 1983).

Importance of Culture. Cultures clearly differ in what are seen as important traits of character. Whereas 79 American CEOs revealed more intuitive personalities, 87 Taiwanese CEOs were more reliant on sensing. The Americans valued honesty, self-esteem, and happiness more than the Taiwanese did; the Taiwanese attached more value to cheerfulness, competence, a comfortable life, a world of peace, and social recognition. The Americans were more spiritual than the Taiwanese. The Americans placed more of a premium on moral values and individualism; the Taiwanese on aesthetic values and collectivism (Judge, 2001). The many parallels in Chinese and Jewish cultural tradition, such as family-centeredness, valuing of education, rootedness in history, and survival despite continued hardships, are also seen in the character of the Chinese and Judiac ideal leaders: the Chinese *junzi* and the Jewish *zaddik*. Both were meritorious, elite, moral men. Their nobility was due to their character, not their birth. Nietzsche (1886) saw ethical concerns as an affliction of the weak character; but to support a moral position or to take an ethical stance in the face of an immoral climate, to be a whistle-blower, requires strength of character (see Singer, 1996). (The impact of culture on character traits will be greatly expanded in Chapter 32.)

Virtuous Traits, States, and Acts of Ethical Leadership

The Golden Rule is found in all the world's major religions and many of its minor ones. In Buddhism it appears as "Hurt not others in ways that you yourself would find hurtful;" in Brahmanism, "Do naught unto others which would cause you pain if done to you;" in Judaism, "What is hateful to you, do not to your fellowman;" in Christianity, "Whatsoever ye would that men should do to you, do ye even so to them;" in Islam, "A believer desires for his brother that which he desires for himself;" in Zoroastrianism, "Refrain from doing to another whatsoever is not good for (one) self;" in Confucianism, "Do not unto others that you would not have them do unto you;" and in pagan Wicca, "An it harm none, do as ye will" (Morgana's Observatory, 1997).

Virtues are positive character traits that are helpful to others in intention, such as fairness and integrity. The virtuous person recognizes and does the right thing. Among Aristotle's four virtues—prudence, justice, fortitude, and temperance—prudence is recognizing and making the right choice in specific contexts; fortitude is the courage to pursue the right path despite its risks; justice is fairness; and temperance is self-discipline and moderation of emotions and indulgences. "A person of good character . . . is someone who through repeated good acts achieves an appropriate balance of . . . virtues in his life" (Woodward, 1994, p. 39). Virtues cannot be instrumental. A virtue in search of a reward in not authentic (Cameron & Caza, 2002). Peterson and Seligman (2004) enumerated and described six virtues: (1) *Wisdom*—creativity, curiosity, open-mindedness; (2) *Courage*—bravery, persistence, integrity; (3) *Humanity*—love, kindness, social intelligence; (4) *Justice*—citizenship, fairness, leadership; (5) *Temperance*—forgiveness, humility, prudence; (6) *Transcendence*—gratitude, hope, humor. Socialized traits of leadership tend to be virtues; personalized traits of leadership tend to be vices. *Vices* are negative traits of character, such as lying and abusiveness, that are hurtful to others. (They will be discussed later as the dark side of leadership.) Moral values are virtues; immoral values are vices. The expression may be states, contingent on circumstances, or traits—that is, individual predilections.

O'Toole (1995) found the virtues of trust, integrity, listening, and respect for followers in the four American presidents (Washington, Jefferson, Lincoln, and Theodore Roosevelt) whose faces were carved on Mount Rushmore. Four CEOs—Max De Pree of Herman Miller, James Houghton of Corning Glass, Robert Galvin of Motorola, and Jan Carson of SAS—were identified as

"Rushmoreans" with the same virtues as the four presidents. Rushmoreans are able to lead change. They overcome the "ideology of comfort and the tyranny of custom." Bennett's *Book of Virtues* (1994) listed self-discipline, compassion, responsibility, friendship, work, courage, perseverance, honesty, loyalty, and faith. According to Bennett, Americans care about character as expressed in ideals of behavior. We need to educate youth in the importance of good character. Yet such a program of nostalgic moralism can turn into political fascism (Morrow, 1994). Integrity and selflessness are usually seen as prime virtues of leaders (Augustine, 1997). Kets de Vries (1995, p. 199) suggested that clinical observation was needed to unravel the knotty questions about the character of top executives. Their observed character traits needed to be understood as consequences of their thoughts and emotions: "Our internal theatre, in which the patterns that underlie our character come into play, influences our behavior throughout our lives and builds an essential role in molding of leaders." Kets de Vries mentioned Henry Ford's close relationship with his mother, who loved him unconditionally but died when Ford was 13. This experience was coupled with a difficult relationship with his father, whom Ford perceived as disapproving his career plans. These might be clues to why Ford was unable to retain executives and old friends. It might account for why he famously stuck to the model T for 19 years and "any color paint for the model as long as it was black" despite a big loss of market to competitors who produced more modernized cars in a variety of colors.

Integrity

The virtue of integrity is at the core of character and ethical leadership. Integrity was mentioned as important to leadership by almost all of 45 British chief executives (Cox & Cooper, 1989). Decrane (1996) declared that integrity of character is overriding for a leader in any field. Integrity is not synonymous with a wide range of virtues such as conscientiousness and honesty, but it is highly correlated with them. It is predicted with a multiple correlation of .20 by the "Big Five" traits: extroversion and agreeableness (Martinsen, 2001). Coherence of values, aims, and behaviors demonstrates a leader's integrity (Bloskie, 1995). It is the virtue of leaders who do what

they say they will do, who keep promises, admit their mistakes, and follow through on their commitments. Such leaders are almost universally esteemed and admired, according to a survey of over 15,000 respondents reported by Kouzes and Posner (1992). Integrity determines the credibility and trustworthiness of the leader. This leader behavior, consistent with the leader's espoused values, reflects the leader's integrity (Yukl, 1998). For Ayn Rand objectivists, integrity is loyalty to rational principles. It is practicing what one preaches regardless of emotional or social pressure. Irrational considerations are not allowed to overwhelm rational convictions. The values involved are morally justifiable (Becker, 1998). For Rand, egoism—pursuing one's own actual best interests—is good in that it is in one's best interests to be rational, to be realistic, to aim for being productive, to not sacrifice one's own convictions to the wishes of others, and to never seek what is unearned and undeserved. Along with Edwin A. Locke and Jaana Woiceshyn—disciples of the philosophy of Ayn Rand (1959)—many economists argue that the pursuit of one's self-interest in an open, free market achieves the greatest good for society. Nevertheless, in an experiment in which students were each given tokens that they could exchange personally for money or share with a group to exchange, 40% to 60% chose to share. The exceptions were graduate students in economics. They rejected sharing (Rhoad, 1985).

Leaders with the virtue of integrity are truthful rather than deceptive. They avoid making exaggerated claims. They are loyal and supportive of their deserving followers. They keep confidences about sensitive information. They set an example of what they expect from their followers and take responsibility for their own actions. In negotiations, leaders with a reputation for integrity can be trusted to keep agreements. They are trusted by their followers not to be exploitative or manipulative. They are perceived as dependable (Yukl, 1998). When McCall and Lombardo (1983) compared successful and "derailed" managers, they found that the successful managers were stronger in integrity. They were more attentive to their tasks and their subordinates. The derailed managers were less dependable and more concerned with impressing superiors or competing with rivals. They were seen as too ambitious and too ready to get ahead at the expense of others. They were more likely to break promises.

Measurement of Integrity. Craig and Gustafson (1998) developed the Perceived Leader Integrity Scale (PLIS) that includes several factors of integrity shown by a supervisor's lack of morals and ethics. They winnowed down 100 items originally gathered from undergraduates to 31 based on 299 university employees. Typical items that emerged as indicating a lack of integrity included "Would take credit for my ideas," "Would steal from the organization," and "Deliberately fuels conflict among employees." As a validation of PLIS, Parry and Proctor-Thompson (2002) found that among 6,025 managers throughout New Zealand, PLIS accounted for as much as 35% of the variance of the MLQ transformational leadership factors. The PLIS correlated .49 with satisfaction with leadership and .47 with the motivation of the followers. Brown and Figufe (2001) took a broader approach and included in the assessment both ethical and unethical aspects of leadership, such as various virtues and vices of character, decision making, uses of the reward system, and management symbolism. The survey was administered to 585 supervisors and their direct reports in a division of a large financial services organization. Four factors emerged: (1) Ethical interaction and decision making—"Fair and objective when making decisions"; (2) Ethical symbolic management—"Talks to employees about work-related ethical conduct"; (3) Unethical financial focus—"Is driven above all else by financial considerations"; (4) Unethical lack of integrity—"Acts unethically at work." Same-source errors were avoided in correlating the factors with leader personality and personnel data. Quite a few statistically significant relationships were obtained. The supervisors' assessed "Big Five" agreeableness predicted their direct reports' appraisals of ethical factors. Lack of agreeableness predicted unethical financial focus. Older supervisors were higher in ethical symbolic management and lower in both unethical factors. Ethical role models contributed to ethical symbolic management, and number of direct reports contributed to unethical lack of integrity.

Den Hartog (1997) found a positive integrity factor in role modeling containing such behavior as meeting obligations, setting a good example, being reliable, and doing what one says. A negative integrity factor included acting without considering others' feelings, holding others responsible for things that were not their fault, and behavior not consistent with expressed values. Den Hartog

found that perceived integrity correlated more highly with trust in management than inspirational factors did.

To help manage legal compliance, Trevino, Weaver, Toffler, et al. (1999) created a six-item scale to be completed by employees. This scale assessed integrity indirectly by asking the employees how much their supervisor cared about ethical behavior. Another indirect measurement of integrity was the Self-Reported Inappropriate Negotiation Strategies Scale (SINS). It listed 30 deceptive negotiation tactics, according to MBA students. Three of five factors that emerged were: (1) misrepresentation or lying, (2) deliberate misuse of information, and (3) false promises. Consistent with the tendency of women to be somewhat more transformational, women were more likely to avoid using these tactics. Self-rated competitive persons were more likely to use them (Robinson, Lewicki, & Donahue, 2000). The problem with direct measures of integrity is that the percentage of false positives is very high (Ronald & Zacharias, 2003). The direct tests are highly susceptible to faking and coaching, according to a research review by Alliger and Dwight (2000).

Authenticity

Authentic leaders are true to themselves and to others. Leaders may deceive others by not being true to themselves; they ignore Polonius's admonition to Laertes in Shakespeare's *Hamlet*, "This above all: to thine own self be true, and it must follow, as the night the day, thou canst not then be false to any man" (Clemens & Mayer, 1977). Herb Kelleher, the highly rated CEO of Southwest Airlines, declared that he didn't have a leadership style except being himself. Ruth Rothstein, chief of the Cook Country Bureau of Health Services in Chicago, described herself as very honest about herself; she never forgot that she had risen from being an organizer for the United Packing house union and a laboratory technician at Jackson Park Hospital in 1940 to head an agency with 12,000 employees and an annual budget of $650,000. She declared, "I don't delude myself. . . . I am willing to face up to [my weaknesses]. . . . I put a lot of emphasis on being truthful. If I say it, that is what I mean to do. . . . You don't have to love me, but you have to trust me. . . . I think you build trust by being authentic" (Heuerman & Olson, 1999).

Authentic leaders are trusted. They do what they say

they will do. They look at themselves honestly. They tell the truth. They have core values that are translated into actions congruent with their identity (Heuerman & Olson, 1998). Authentic transformational leaders align their interests with those of others and may sacrifice their own interests for the common good. Their communications can be trusted. They articulate their followers' real needs and envision an attainable future. They sound the alarm when real threats arise. They set examples to uplift the moral values of their followers. They are concerned for their followers' development and well-being.

Measurement of Authenticity. Henderson and Hoy (1982) defined *authenticity* as the extent to which a leader was viewed by others as exhibiting a salience of self over role. That is, the authentic leader did not rely on the narrow prescriptions of the role to justify personal actions. The authentic leader did not manipulate followers or treat them as objects. Such a leader accepted responsibility for her or his own personal and organizational actions. This description of authentic leadership was confirmed empirically for 42 elementary school principals, using a 32-item survey instrument (Henderson & Hoy, 1982). That instrument was subsequently refined by Henderson and Brookhart (1996) for more general use as the Organizational Leader Authenticity Scale (OLAS), with a form for a leader's staff (SAS). A typical positively scored item was, "My supervisor accepts and learns from mistakes." A typical negatively scored item was, "My su-

pervisor seems to talk at you and not with you." Data were collected from 63 educational leaders and their 835 staff members for OLAS and SAS along with other measures. According to path analyses, leader authenticity had a sizable impact on staff members authenticity ($r = .47$). The authenticity of both leader and staff contributed to organizational health and a positive organizational climate. Additionally, leader authenticity correlated .83 with the leader's supportive but not directive behavior (.04), initiation (.61), consideration (.81) and influence (.54).

Justice and Fairness

A virtue of leadership is being just and fair. Some leaders are more just and fair than others; this may be a consequence of the individual leader's character as well as conditional on circumstances. Being just and fair may be a matter of how the leader distributes reward and punishments, how others are treated and informed, and which procedures are used and when. Sometimes it is a matter of time. What may be ethical and fair in the short run may be unethical and unfair in the long run. Sufficient time is often needed to test whether a pharmaceutical drug is beneficial or harmful. Taking the drug DES reduced morning sickness in pregnant women but caused birth defects (Messick & Bazerman, 1996).

Forms of Justice. *Distributive* justice is the fairness with which rewards and resources are distributed to

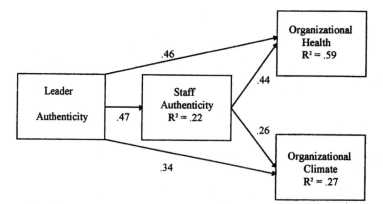

Figure 9.1 A Model of the Effects of Leader and Staff Authenticity on Organizational Health and Organizational Climate

NOTE: *All relationships are significant to the .01 level. N = 63.*
SOURCE: *Henderson and Brookhart, 1996, p. 97.*

members of a group or organization, consistent with their contributions, in comparison with others, or both. Even with the best of intentions, according to interviews with senior executives of an online division of a large parent firm, during the first 22 months it was difficult to maintain distributive justice in the new division because of complexity, ambiguities, and required speed (Brown & Gioia, 2002). Rawls (1985) examined the limits to fairness and the impossibility of completely eliminating disadvantageousness. There is inherent unfairness in the differences among us at birth: in our brains, beauty, inherited health and wealth, and the way we are parented. Society needs to provide equal opportunities within these constraints.

Justice comes in several forms of procedures or processes. *Procedural* justice follows along with other forms such as *interactional* justice (fairness of treatment) and *informational* justice (fairness of disseminated information). Procedural justice depends on high-quality information, well-informed opinions, consistency across different groups of employees, suppression of personal bias, and consideration of moral standards (Thibaut & Walker, 1975). Interactional justice involves the informational and interpersonal approaches to implementation that depend on the adequacy and timeliness of information about the procedures, and sensitivity to the quality of interpersonal relations (Konovsky & Folger, 1991). The various forms of justice tend to intercorrelate above .50 and are collectively referred to as *organizational* justice (Bell, 2001). Judgment of the fairness of the distribution of resources depends, in particular, on whether the procedures used to make the distribution are seen as just (Lind & Tyler, 1988). However, Turillo, Folger, Lavelle, and Umphress (2002) suggested that many leaders suffer from a *distributive bias*. They overestimate how much employees care about distributive outcomes and underestimate how much employees are concerned for procedural and interactional justice.

Distributive Justice. Although Rawls (1967) agreed that rewards and resources should be distributed for the "greatest good for the greatest number," he proposed that this required a fair distribution that can meet the expectations of the most privileged to the least privileged—from the wealthy entrepreneur to the poor unskilled worker. The social system affects their life prospects differently from before birth and according to their different natural attributes. But the system must allow liberty of the person, freedom of thought, and political equality. The differences in distribution are just if the greater expectations of the most advantaged, who play a role in the social system, improve the expectations of the least advantaged (Ciulla, 1998, 2004).

In international joint ventures in developing countries, local employees find it unfair that foreign expatriates are compensated more highly. However, Chen, Choi, and Chi (2002) found that Chinese locals' sense of unfairness was decreased if they were paid more than Chinese locals in other joint ventures, if they accepted the rationale for the discrepancy, and if the expatriates were more interpersonally sensitive toward the locals. As is usually the case, perceived distributive justice increased with satisfaction with compensation and with decreased intentions to quit.

Leventhal (1980) suggested six rules for just and fair processes: (1) Be consistent among people and across time; (2) Suppress the self-interests of authorities; (3) Use accurate information; (4) Maintain opportunities to make corrections; (5) Consider representative concerns; and (6) Maintain compatibility with social and moral values. Leaders can influence whether fair and just outcomes are achieved. They can determine who will be included in decision making. They can set the agenda. They can prioritize deliberations (Hoyt & Garrison, 1997). Leaders may also be able to convince others that they are fair in their procedures and distribution of information, when in fact they may not be (Greenberg, 1990).

Bell (2001) asked MBAs from one business school, in an e-mail survey, if they had ever received a performance evaluation "that was not as positive as they hoped or expected." Of 1,051 respondents, 130 had received such an appraisal. They completed the Colquitt Organizational Justice Scale (2000) to measure their perception of procedural, distributive, interpersonal, and informational justice as members of an organization. Procedural justice correlated highest with distributive justice (.69). Interpersonal justice correlated highest with informational justice (.71). The lowest correlation among the four types of justice was .47. One hundred ten participants also completed a retrospective "shame and guilt" scale adapted from Marschall and Tangney (1994). They answered questions about their loss of self-efficacy, the meaning of the organization to them personally, and their affective commitment to the organization. Regression analyses indicated that a perception of the organization as just and fair in all four types of justice *reduced* the participants' shame, guilt, loss of self-efficacy, and loss of identification with the organization.

These finding were consistent with other research showing that if a recipient considers negative feedback just and fair, the feedback is more likely to be accepted and less likely to have deleterious effects on the recipient (Lind & Tyler, 1988). In considering settling disputes with management, 301 employees of a large firm believed that among arrangements not requiring intervention by a law court, voluntary mediation provided the most justice and fairness, compared with mandatory mediation and binding arbitration (Richey, Garbi, & Bernardin, 2002). In one study, 143 employees who had a strong "exchange ideology" of fairness and justice, according to their supervisor, exhibited less affective commitment when they viewed their work environment as unfair. No such tendency was found in employees who were indifferent to a fair exchange (Witt, Kacmar, & Andrews, 2001).

Equity theory predicts a sense of being treated unfairly when we see others whom we consider similar to ourselves in effort, performance, status, experience, etc., being treated beneficially while we are not treated in the same way (Thibaut & Kelley, 1959; Mowday, 1987). Highly correlated measures of procedural, interactional, and distributive justice were rated by 265 students holding full-time jobs (31%) of part-time jobs (69%). Fairness was seen when leaders were judged to form higher-quality leader-member exchanges (LMXs) with employees who contributed more to their work group, and lower-quality LMXs with employees who seemed to have contributed less to the work group. In controlling for LMX quality satisfaction with supervision was higher if greater justice was perceived. At the same time, those employees higher in performance and organizational citizenship behavior were more negatively affected if they felt that the leaders were unfair in their differentiation (Erdogan, 2002).

Tyler (1984) found that perceived procedural justice depended on how much control employees had in presenting information to their supervisor on their trust in the supervisor, and on the supervisor's respect for them.

When procedural justice was perceived, high-quality LMXs were not as important in contributing to performance, commitment, or citizenship behavior (Sanchez, Bauer, & Trujillo, 2002). Nevertheless, Scandura and Tejeda (2003) reported that for 275 supervisor-subordinate dyads, job performance was better when LMX was of high quality and employees perceived that appraisals of their performance were fair. Bazerman, White, and Lowenstein (1995) concluded from a review of research that judgments of distributive justice are "remarkably nuanced, responding to a wide range of . . . situational and individual . . . factors." At the same time, "there are pervasive biases" in the way that fairness is judged, and "inconsistencies in the importance" placed "on fairness in different contexts" (p. 39).

Interactional and Informational Justice. Gratton and Zaleska (2002) analyzed over 300 semistructured interviews with employees to examine the roles played by line managers and human resources (HR) professionals in the enactment of justice. The context was eight large organizations in the United Kingdom, ranging from pharmaceutical and telecommunications firms to a hospital and a postal service. Interaction injustice was most frequently mentioned by interviewees—specifically, a lack of dissemination of information about promotions, rewards, and development:

> The greatest outrage [occurred] when employees felt that satisfactory explanations were not provided by the HR (Human Relations) function, and they were not given feedback about procedures, particularly [about] pay and reward decisions. . . . They blamed HR if they perceived the . . . procedures to be mute and secretive." (p. 11)

HR was expected to design and develop equitable processes. Line managers were expected to tailor policies to meet individual needs and suppress their own biases. When implementing policies, HR was expected to provide opportunities for employees to voice their opinions. Insensitive treatment from a line manager, rather than a sense that procedures were unfair, generated feelings of unfairness. The style of the line manager as well as the HR professional was important in determining whether justice or injustice was perceived. "A skilled HR professional or line manager with clear people-centered values and behaviors could have a positive effect on [employees'] perception of justice" (p. 16).

Altruism

There are leadership styles, such as servant leadership, that call for extreme altruism. Many other leadership styles also stress the importance of helping others or sacrificing for others (Kanungo & Conger, 1993). Altruism is the virtue of selflessness, reducing personal benefit for the sake of others (Margolis, 1982). But it is not usually associated with the world of business and utilitarian organizations. Supposedly, "the path to profits is not paved with caring concern but with Darwinian cleverness" (p. 37). Nevertheless—just as in our private lives when we devote time, energy, and money to charitable and public causes—altruism has a place in the management of our organizations. Even though a corporation is competing in the marketplace, the complexity of the market calls for more interdependence, attention to cooperation as well as competition, and consideration of all the corporation's stakeholders. Altruism may be utilitarian in the expectation of reciprocity for good deeds; it may be an act of impression management; and/or it may be genuine and morally right. Also, altruism has been found to correlate with self-esteem, perceived competence, internal locus of control, and decreased alienation (Caza, 2002). Altruism is the first factor in one widely used measurement, Organizational Citizenship Behavior (OCB; C. A. Smith, 1983).

In 1993, the Academy of Management Executives surveyed a panel of 40 executives, 24 human resource executives on a conference board council, and peers in their own firms on the question "In the past 20 years, do you think acts of corporate altruism have increased, decreased, or stayed the same?" Of the total, 52.5% said altruistic acts had increased, 31.7% said they had stayed the same, and 15.8% said they had decreased. Three corporate practices were seen by the vast majority (80% to 90%) as *utilitarian* ethics that benefit the company: (1) empowering management practices; (2) company-wide emphasis on cooperation; and (3) attention to work and family needs of employees through family-friendly policies. A majority noted three genuinely ethical practices that were the right thing to do and for which the company expected no payback (Anonymous, 1993,

p. 90): (1) a strong commitment to the disadvantaged in the community (64%); (2) recognizing people in the company and demonstrating concern and support for others (60%); and (3) having a well-understood and practiced set of corporate ethics (51%).

Martin-Marietta, now part of Lockheed-Martin, provided telephone and mail addresses of its ethics office, whose director reported directly to the president, the chairman of the five-member ethics committee. Its code of ethics gave examples of conflicts of interest, such as acceptance of gifts from those seeking to do business with the firm, placing business in a firm owned or controlled by an employee or employee's family, and acting as a consultant for a customer or supplier. Offering, giving, or soliciting bribes or kickbacks were forbidden. Financial statements, books, and records had to reflect accurately all transactions of the corporation. As a major government contractor, the corporation had to be especially sensitive to control of costs and had to follow rigorous procurement standards. It was every employee's duty to preserve the corporation's plants and equipment. In compliance with the Securities and Exchange Commission, antitrust regulations, and political campaign finance laws, the following were not permitted: "insider trading" of securities, restriction of trade that is harmful to consumers, and unapproved corporate political contributions. Disciplinary action would be taken against employees who participated in or authorized violations of the code, or who had deliberately failed to report a violation. Action would be taken against the violator's managerial superiors if the violation reflected their lack of diligence or supervision or if they retaliated against the employee who reported the violation.

Should Leaders Be Altruistic? In letters between E. A. Locke and B. J. Avolio, Locke, a disciple of the libertarian philosopher and novelist Ayn Rand (1964), argued that leaders should think and act in a rational way, with self-interest rather than altruism as the basis of action. By accomplishing their own interests, they will display their highest principles and achieve their highest performance. Implicit in the virtue of rationality are honesty that refuses to fake reality, integrity based on loyalty to one's rational judgments, independence in using one's own rational judgment to sustain one's own life, taking responsibility to be productive, judging others by a rational standard, and taking pride in being a self-made soul and seeking moral perfection. Leaders ought to listen to others but make their key decisions themselves. They ought not to pursue careers out of duty or obligation. They ought to seek to hire the best possible people and follow their best judgment as rationality dictates. Because it is the rational thing to do, they ought to treat clients and employees fairly; and they should not feel guilty if they succeed in becoming wealthy. Avolio countered that in many situations, competing interests could not be satisfied. The most effective leaders are those who transcend their own interests for the good of their group, organization, or society. Soldiers are called upon for self-sacrifice. Rationality itself may often be in the eye of the beholder (Avolio & Locke, 2002).

Other Virtues and Character Traits

The American Association of Medical Colleges called for medical students to be knowledgeable, skillful, and dutiful as well as altruistic. The order of importance is debatable, since most patients would prefer a "cold but smart doctor [to] a warm, dumb one" (Robinson, 2002). Other virtues of leadership include conscientiousness, wisdom, courage, dutifulness, compassion, and trustworthiness. The virtue of benevolence is also important to leadership. When the leader is benevolent, followers will display good organizational citizen behavior (Skarlicki & Dirks, 2002).

Conscientiousness. Conscientiousness tends to predict better job performance and good organizational citizens behavior. It correlates with fewer acts of delinquency such as stealing in work settings (Barrick, Mount, & Strauss, 1991). It also combines with supportive leadership to promote safe behavior at work (Griffin, Neal, & Burley, 2000). Although ability was expected to moderate the effects of conscientiousness on job performance, that was not found in three large samples of managers (Mount, Barrick, & Strauss, 1999). However, conscientiousness may be expected to impede performance when speed is more important than thoroughness, when rapid decisions are required but information is limited, and when rules stifle creativity (Collins, 1998). Sometimes conscientiousness may fail to predict effective management performance (Robertson, Baron, Gibbons, et al., 2000).

According to an examination by Moon (2001) of 360 decisions, when conscientiousness was associated with personal striving for achievement, commitment to making effective decisions escalated. But when conscientiousness was associated with an other-centered orientation, commitment de-escalated. Among the middle managers in 131 Fortune large global firms, conscientiousness mapped most distant from "entrepreneurial" as a desired trait—especially in the pharmaceutical industry as compared with the food industry (Chun, 2003). Conscientiousness and moral development begin early in life with bonding, cooperation, affection, and happy interactions. Parental influence and values are embraced (Kochanska, 2002).

Wisdom. This virtue allows the leader to activate bodies of factual and strategic knowledge simultaneously to address practical and uncertain aspects of life. It promotes understanding of what is true and right and guides effective rational and moral judgment. Requiring practical wisdom of the moral leader is consistent with Aristotle's virtuousness and Kant's moral leader as an autonomous individual (Jeannot, 1989; Baltes, 1999).

Courage. Courage is a mix of instant or longer emotional and cognitive states related to taking action in the face of vulnerability, risks, dangers, potential losses, and consequences to oneself. Courage and bravery occur as exceptional events outside the bounds of norms, routines, and expectations about how people should act in a specific context (Worline, 2002). Leaders or followers face uncertainties and dangers for the good of the group or organization in an exceptional event of potential danger to the collectivity. For Gal (1984), moral courage is the essence of leadership. In addition to remaining ethical, U.S. presidents need moral courageousness.

Compassion. Compassion is a central virtue in many religions. If authentic, it reflects a genuine empathic concern for others' pain (Batson, 1991). It is a virtue of benefit to individuals, organizations, and society (Wuthnow, 1991). It may involve an active regard for the other person's good aimed at alleviating the other's pain (Blum, 1980). It played a role in the politics of presidents Bill Clinton ("I feel your pain") and George W. Bush ("compassionate conservatism"). In the workplace, it can increase feelings of well-being and resilience and enhance productivity (Dutton, Frost, Worline, et al., 2000). Compassion and self-sacrifice were shown by Abraham Feuerman, owner of Malden Mills, whose mill burned down. Instead of laying off the workforce while rebuilding the mill, he continued to pay the workers their wages while the mill was being rebuilt. Unfortunately, however, because of overseas competition he was unable to repay the loans needed to continue.

Dutifulness. A *sense of duty* is a virtue expected of professionals. They need to avoid being self-serving. To the best of their ability, they ought to apply the principles of their profession. For instance, certified public accountants (CPAs) are accountable when auditing their clients' financial statements. The statements presented to the public need to be transparent and true (Piaker, 2002). In times of crisis, self-sacrificial leaders are looked at most favorably, according to a controlled experiment by Halverson, Holladay, Kazama, et al. (2004) involving 203 undergraduates. Israeli Colonel Eli Geva was self-sacrificial when he ended his military career in 1982 by refusing an order from his superior to move his troops into Beirut because he had grave reservations about the role of the Israeli military in Lebanon (Avolio, 1999).

Forgiveness. This is a virtue that abandons justified resentment, bitterness, and blame in response to harm or damage (Enright, Freedman, & Rique, 1998). The injustices, pain, and suffering inflicted on the nonwhite population of South Africa were met by Nelson Mandela, who spent 27 years in prison, with a plea for forgiveness and reconciliation. Desmond Tutu led the Truth and Reconciliation Commission to provide forgiveness from the testifying victims and amnesty for perpetrators of offenses including rape, torture, and murder during aparteid. To obtain forgiveness, the perpetrators had to confess voluntarily and in public. The wrongdoing had to be acknowledged. The offenses were due to political, government, or police policies. Civil war was averted (Cameron & Caza, 2002). Followers who forgive a leader's threats and punitive behavior are generally more agreeable and emotionally stable in personality. If they are more spiritual and religious, they believe that they are more forgiving. If they are more forgiving, they like and empathize more with

the leader and do not ruminate about the leader's actions (McCullough, 2001). Forgivers are physically ill less often and recover faster from illness. They feel more empowerment, hope, and self-esteem (McCullough, 2000).

Vices of Leadership

British treasury officials displayed inhumane vice when they explained as "natural causes" the reason for the starvation of the Irish peasantry during the potato famines of 1845 to 1849. Sir Charles Trevelyan, in charge of organizing relief, promulgated the following principles:

1. Starving men given government handouts would grow to depend on them rather than working for their bread. Therefore, food was to be provided only in county workhouses. (Useless work projects were set up for men too weak to work.)
2. Government intervention to lower the price of wheat and corn would injure traders and merchants.
3. When rent was not paid, the only remaining option for the tenant was emigration or dying. (The tenant's cottage was often burned.)

The population was reduced from 8 million to 3 million. Benjamin Jowett heard a political economist say that he feared the famine of 1848 would not kill more than a million people, and that this would scarcely do enough to do much good. Although not as extreme, such reactions can be found today in leaders and managers who justify unethical managerial behavior. A survey of 3,450 managers in three industries from 28 countries disclosed that managers were more inclined to justify vices in some countries than in others. Counter to some of the hypotheses of the investigators, Parboteah and Cullen (2002), those living in socialist countries—higher in religiosity, higher in social inequality, higher in access to education, but lower in industrialization—were more likely to justify unethical behavior such as buying stolen goods, cheating on taxes, lying in self-interest, and accepting bribes in the course of one's duties. Men were more likely than women, and younger employees were more likely than older employees, to justify unethical behavior.

Deceiving, Lying, and Cheating. These are common vices, seen in many of the traits and behaviors mentioned here. An exemplar of the vices of leadership was Sam Goldwyn, a founding father of the Hollywood movie industry. He was hard, ruthless, and arrogant. He was a chronic liar and compulsively rude. He cheated when he could. He quarreled continually with his partners. He was deceptive. People never knew how they stood with him. He had a dismal view of ethics in business (Berg, 1989). Like Goldwyn, many leaders have states and traits that may bring harm to their associates. They may be corrupt as well as incompetent (Kellerman, 2004). They may use their power and position to be abusive and unjust. They may hoard privileges, betray loyalties, or neglect responsibilities (C. E. Johnson, 2001). They are particularly insidious when they appear beneficial but are actually harmful. They lack authenticity and sincerity. Often they are hypocritical. There are those who may benefit some at the expense of others. Frank Lorenzo boldly persuaded financiers to provide the money for takeovers of businesses, like Eastern Airlines, that were in trouble. "By behaving with startling audacity at the edge of legality or beyond—violating past practice, lying, and employing hitherto unused legal devices, such as bankruptcy, to achieve his goals" (p. 251), he aroused hatred and fear in employees and managers at the companies he threatened, bankrupted, and stripped (Turner, 1993). For many politicians, selfish, personal private aggrandizement has been coupled with aggressive public preaching of altruism and social responsibility. Such has been the case with numerous dictators. Womanizing has been common among powerful reform politicians including Kemel Atatürk, Fidel Castro, John F. Kennedy, and Bill Clinton.

Moral identity of a negotiator appears to affect how much lying will occur. Aquino, Ray, and Reed (2003) engaged 224 students in simulated negotiations in a counterbalanced experiment. One student negotiator, who had access to privileged information (while the other negotiator did not), lied about it unless moral identity was important to the negotiator and lying was not rewarded.

Followers may also exhibit behaviors intended to harm their leaders and organizations. For instance. Skarlicki, Barclay, Patent, et al. (2002) showed that when laid off, untrustworthy employees (despite management efforts to explain the reasons) retaliated by such actions as destroying important documents and also considered getting even in other ways.

Self-Serving. When they can, self-serving leaders disregard the rights, values, and feelings of others. They reinterpret moral principles for their own benefit. They rely heavily on manipulation. They are unlikely to inhibit their use of power. They detach themselves from how they are perceived by their followers. They act in whatever ways will benefit themselves the most, ignoring the expense to others. Muttayya (1977) found that self-orientation in Indian leaders was associated with less commitment to principled public conduct. Fox (2000) has held that American political culture is dominated by self-serving, expediency, indifference, and opportunism. He questions how much progress we have made toward responsible government. Mitchell and Scott (1990) agreed that corruption, scandals, abuses of public and private trust, and the endemic lack of moral leadership are supported by an ethic of personal advantage and the value of short-run individualism. But a certain amount of this may be necessary. In order to win New Jersey's electoral votes in 1932, Franklin D. Roosevelt befriended Frank Hague, a known corrupt political boss, in order to gain his crucial support (Schoenbrun, 1984).

House and Howell (1992) called attention to the differences between *personalized*, self-serving, exploitative charismatic leaders and *socialized* charismatics. Whereas socialized charismatics were collectively oriented, egalitarian, and nonexploitative, personalized charismatics inhibited their need for power and were Machiavellian, authoritarian, and narcissistic. Roberts and Brindly (1955) saw the risk in training leaders to be charismatic: if these leaders were self-serving, they would practice deception and exploit their followers. Self-serving Machiavellian leaders try to maximize their self-interests. They are more likely to be egotistical and narcissistic. Like Napoleon, the self-aggrandizing "Chainsaw" Al Dunlap (Dunlap & Andelman, 1996) was proud to say how convinced he was of his own greatness (Nocera, 1996). O'Connor, Mumford, Clifton, et al. (1995) contrasted biographies about the rise to power of 38 personalized and 44 socialized world leaders as judged by five psychologists. The degree of self-serving of the leaders was seen in how much: (1) they felt they would not get what they desired because the world is uncertain; (2) they sought to subdue or convert others; (3) they viewed other people as instruments to achieve their own goals; (4) they were selfish, extremely self-interested, and overly concerned with self-satisfaction; and (5) they felt a strong need to protect themselves and to monitor their thoughts and actions in the presence of others. Personalized leadership—highly related to self-serving—correlated with harm to society, a failure to adhere to morality, and a lack of benefit to individuals. Such leadership was likely to be destructive rather than constructive. Kaiser Wilhelm II was partially responsible for inflicting World War I on humanity as a consequence of his preoccupation with emotional self-interest (Dietrich, 1981). Powerful, self-serving leaders use their power to satisfy their need for more status and esteem. They are rude and sexually exploitative. They collect symbols of prestige: offices, homes, and cars. They keep their subordinates weak and dependent. They centralize authority for making important decisions (McClelland & Burnham, 1976). Saddam Hussein may have seemed irrational, but he represented the extreme of self-serving and calculating craftiness. Anyone who did not support him was his enemy. Anyone within his control who opposed him was subject to severe punishment, including execution. Any movement that would threaten his power was met with force including poison gas. He was unconstrained by conscience. His murderous behavior was consistent with the culture of violence in which he grew up. He had messianic ambitions and dreams of glory as supreme leader of the Arab masses. In invading and looting Kuwait, then trying to destroy its rich oil fields, he defied the military power of the United Nations, led by the United States. He rose like a phoenix after Iraq's disastrous defeat in 1991, once more to challenge the United States and the United Nations for the following 12 years, again at the expense of Iraq's civilian economy and population. At the same time, during his three decades in power he built a modern secular state unlike most in other traditionally religious countries. His violent overthrow was followed by insurrection, civil war, and chaotic conditions bordering on anarchy despite a democratically elected government to replace him.

Most leaders are neither completely self-serving nor completely altruistic. Additionally, self-serving may do some good. Bolino (1999) suggests that leaders may display good organizational citizenship to impress others as a technique of impression management. Or it may be a matter of ingratiation or manipulative politicking. Ferris, Bhawak, Fedor, et al. (1995) noted that good organizational citizenship will be seen as prosocial if it is sincere, but as self-interested politics if it is insincere.

Greed is self-serving, seen in the compensation of too many U.S. CEOs and senior executives, relative to their employees. Conger (2005) noted that prior to 1930, professional managers—the agents of owners and shareholders—did not become millionaires like entrepreneurs and owners such as the Rockefellers. In 1929, Eugene Grace of Bethlehem Steel was the first professional chief executive to be awarded a bonus of $1.2 million. By 2000, Dennis Kozlowski, CEO of Tyco, obtained a compensation package of $137 million. According to Conger, there are seven reasons for greedy, unjustifiable compensation, a vice widespread in the United States despite monitoring and regulating by the Securities and Exchange Commission.

1. Corporate governance makes the CEO the leading corporation decision maker as the chairman of the board of directors. The directors vote on the compensation of the CEO and expect reciprocity. Many if not most of the directors are CEOs in other corporations and don't raise objections.

2. Outside compensation consultants who provide guidance and benchmark data depend on the CEO to buy other business services they provide.

3. For the media and the public, the CEO is a romantic hero who single-handedly triumphs over daunting challenges.

4. Corporations are conceived of as property of an owner rather than as a social institution accountable to the public.

5. Transparency is lacking in the compensation package.

6. Tax codes provide deductions for options and grants of restricted stock.

7. Too many senior business executives have narcissistic personalities.

Narcissism. Nietzsche's (1886) ego-enhancing, inner-directed, self-determined superman had many good qualities but also many elements of the narcissist. He had a sense of duty and responsibility to his unique self. He was free of the expected and was a point of contact with the future. Narcissism, as measured by the Narcissistic Personality Inventory (NPI), includes an inflated sense of self-importance and fantasies of success, superiority, power, beauty, and brilliance. Admiration is sought. Sometimes narcissism is a force for good; more often it is a vice. It is immoral when it leads to exploitation of others, expectations of undeserved special favors without reciprocation, indifference, and lack of empathy for others (Raskin & Hall, 1979). Narcissists "are capable of being extremely charming and manipulative and extremely cruel to others whenever it is in their self interest to do so. . . . Narcissists appear to experience little self-doubt . . . as a result of their behavior" (House & Howell, 1992, p. 98). Kets de Vries (1994) does not find it surprising that many narcissists, with their need for power and prestige, become leaders. They act out fantasies created by their followers, who become uncritical, submissive, and dependent. Self-loving leaders take advantage of their followers' loyalty by ignoring the followers' needs. Steyrer (2002) used a model to show how the grandiose self of the narcissistic, charismatic leader, when confirmed by attention received, is socially dramatized and results in fascinated, impressed, emotionally stimulated followers who may subsequently engage in destructive acts. Sankowsky (1995) added that such leaders are likely to abuse power. They share their belief system with their followers. Narcissistic leaders only want to hear advice that confirms their opinions; they reject anyone who challenges them. According to Hogan and Hogan (2002), unhealthy narcissistic leaders combine a grandiose sense of certainty with disdain for subordinates. They ingratiate themselves with those above them in the organization and brutalize those below them. Like Walter J. Connelly, Jr., who ruinously expanded the Bank of New England, they are good at self-promotion. Normal rules don't apply to them (Goleman, 1990). Narcissists have also been found by Helland and Blair (2005) to engage in unethical leadership behavior such as insensitivity to others, manipulative communication, and pseudotransformational behavior.

Hypocrisy. John Gardner (1990) notes that leaders must combat the hypocrisy that proclaims values and then proceeds to act in violation of them. Hypocritical leaders formulate moral standards that they refuse to apply to themselves. They do not accept the same consequences for ethical violations that they demand of others (Dyson, 2001). Smith and Craig (2002) saw insincerity in many CEOs who called for reforms in business and accounting practices to deal with unethical reporting. These CEOs were dissembling; they called for needed changes but weren't aggressive in carrying them out. Blalock (1996) found that the many executives valued self-respect but were ready to commit financial fraud.

Falseness or Inauthenticity. "Leaders sometimes behave immorally . . . because they are blinded by their own values" (Terry, 2003, p. 67). They may truly believe they are acting altruistically when in fact they are being self-serving. Concern for collective outcomes in the interests of altruism may harm opposing interests of individuals.

Inauthentic pseudotransformational leaders appear to support the common good, but their own self-interests have a higher priority. They ask to be trusted but cannot be. They create artificial and phantom needs in their followers. They manufacture artificial crises. They stretch the truth. They arouse fantasies and delusions in their followers. The example they set for their followers is inconsistent with or even the opposite of what they proclaim is right. At the extreme, they may be psychopaths who mask their antisocial traits, present a prosocial demeanor, and remain successful leaders (Babiak, 1995). They treat opposition as disloyalty. They "pass the buck" and blame others for their own mistakes. False expert authority in dishonest advertising can be more persuasive than true expert authority although it is possible to immunize students against such ads with brief training (Cialdina, Sagarin, & Rice, 2001).

True, authentic transformational and charismatic leaders respect the rights of others and may appeal for universal brotherhood; inauthentic leaders focus on "us" against "them" and demonize opponents. Authentics are open; inauthentics wear masks. True leaders tell followers what they need to hear; false leaders mislead, prevaricate, and tell followers what they want to hear. Authentics truly empower followers; false leaders appear to empower but actually create dependent followers. Authentics aim to develop their followers into leaders; inauthentics want to develop submissive disciples.

Authentic leaders, in general, are authentic and empathetic; inauthentic leaders shed crocodile tears. Authentic leaders build arguments on truth and evidence; inauthentics build arguments on ignorance, prejudice, and half-truths. Authentic leaders espouse fairness and human rights. Inauthentic leaders are ingratiating, patronizing, and condescending toward others; they talk about concern for the environment, humanity, and society but actually are interested in exploiting them (Bass & Steidlmeier, 1999).

Opinions among historians differ about whether Adolf Hitler actually believed he was doing the right thing. H. R. Trevor-Roper thought that Hitler was convinced of his own rectitude. Alan Bullock called him an actor who sometimes believed his role. Lucy Dawidowicz saw Hitler as a double-talking schemer (Gates, 1998). Hitler was the epitome of the pseudotransformational leader, frequently deceiving others and sometimes even deceiving himself (Evans, 2003).

Pseudotransformational Leadership. The behavior of pseudotransformational leaders is inauthentic although they may appear to be like transformational leaders. They are hypocritical politicians who preach the need for morality yet take bribes. They create the impression that they are doing the right thing, but secretly avoid doing so. They ask their followers and others to trust them, but they cannot be trusted. They make exceptions for themselves. Sometimes they may be blinded by their own values (Price, 2003) and come to believe they are doing the right thing by "killing with kindness" or saving a village by destroying it. The pseudotransformational leader's idealized influence produces a false messiah like Jim Jones who leads all his followers to destruction. The pseudotransformational leader highlights "we-they" differences. ("We have good values. They don't.") Such leaders seek power and status at the expense of their followers. They indulge in fantasies of power and success. They believe they know the right answers, which can be sold through impression management; but they may be deceiving themselves. Their visions are grandiose. They engage in self-displays to get attention for themselves. They may lack a sense of responsibility. The pseudotransformational leader's inspirational motivation appeals to unrealistic fantasies that make it difficult for followers to face reality. These are spiritual leaders who are false prophets, captains who sail under false colors. "They profess strong attachment to their organization and its people but privately are ready to sacrifice them. They downsize their organization [at the same time they] increase their own compensation, and weep crocodile tears for the employees who have lost their jobs" (Bass & Steidlmeier, 1999, p. 187).

Pseudotransformational leaders' intellectual stimulation uses false assumptions, overweighs authority, and underweighs reason (Sankowsky, 1995). These leaders feed on their followers' ignorance and willingness to accept ambiguity, which provides opportunities for the leaders' enhancement. They set and control the agenda to manipulate the values of importance to followers to reach decisions favorable to themselves. They argue that they are doing the right thing but actually do so only when their own interests are not threatened (Howell & Avolio, 1992). They substitute emotional arguments for rational discourse (Bass & Steidlmeier, 1999). Pseudotransformational leaders' individualized consideration creates dependent instead of empowered followers. The leaders expect blind obedience and loyalty. They maintain personal distance between their followers and themselves (Bass, 2001). The leaders exploit the feelings of their followers to maintain deference toward themselves (Sankowsky, 1995), and encourage fantasy and magic in visions of shared goals. They seek to maintain a parent-child relationship with their followers. They are publicly altruistic but privately self-serving. Privately, they are contemptuous of altruism (Howell & Avolio, 1992); privately, they are deceptive, domineering, and egotistical even when their public image is as holy savior. Television and radio preachers caught in ethical scandals are examples.

The esoteric leaders of extremist militias in the United States are pseudotransformationals. They manipulate their followers' fear of change by claiming that they can halt or reverse its impact. They offer simple explanations for complex changes in society. They pursue returning to a fictitious, glorified past. They advocate using violence against those whom they perceive as responsible for extreme changes in society and benefiting from such changes (Katner, 1996). The radio commentator Rush Limbaugh and the outspoken black political leader Louis Farrakhan are examples of popular pseudotransformationals. "Rush Limbaugh and Louis Farrakhan live well off ignorance . . . with great charisma. . . . [They] look like giants to people of minor intellect. . . . They exploit . . . frustrated people for personal gain in the name of doing good for the entire nation or race" (Lockman, 1995, p. 9a).

President George W. Bush was pseudotransformational in 2001 when he asked Congress for a resolution to take the country to war against Iraq in response to Al Qaeda's terrorist attacks of 9/11. He may have been misled by faulty intelligence about Iraq's nuclear weapons, but rationally he must have known that Saddam Hussein was a secularist dictator opposed to the Islamists, that at the time there were few terrorists hiding in Iraq, and that Saddam was an enemy of Al Qaeda and its leader, Osama bin Laden. Nevertheless, Bush eventually made a preemptive strike against Iraq to overthrow Saddam. Instead of thwarting terrorism and Iraq's nuclear activity, the effect of going to war in Iraq in 2003 was a great increase in the number of terrorists worldwide, a loss of international popularity for the United States, and the alienation of the Muslim world (Woodward, 2004). Pseudotransformationals dominate, exploit, manipulate, and self-aggrandize rather than seek consensus or foster trust (Connor, Mumford, Clifton, et al., 1995).

Kellerman (2000) ruled out Hitler as a leader because his influence was destructive and evil, even as he probably had a greater impact on the twentieth century than any other man. It seems more reasonable to say that he was a leader but, unfortunately for the world, a pseudotransformational one. In the same way, Potts (2001) conceives of leadership as inherently ethical, since its purpose is to do good (see Burns, 1978) or to use only good means (see Rost, 1991). According to Potts, any other influence in organizations or movements is manipulative management. Does this mean that management without leadership is inherently unethical? It makes more sense to regard leadership with harmful means and ends as false leadership, also keeping in mind that such leadership may be attempted, successful, or unsuccessful, and effective or ineffective whether or not it aims to do good (see Chapter 6).

Arrogance and Hubris. Kroll, Toombs, and Wright (2000) note that narcissism may generate *arrogance* and *hubris* when coupled with ignoring the rules, achieving many successes, and uncritically accepting many accolades. Such a pattern is seen in executives who pursue expansion for its own sake, make unwise and overpriced corporate acquisitions, take uncalculated risks, and knowingly violate moral and legal regulations. Hubris can be outspoken: "Chainsaw" Al Dunlap bragged that he could resurrect almost any dying business. Appointed CEO at Sunbeam in 1996, in 11 months he had eliminated 60% of its management and half its workforce—actions he said were difficult but should have been done by his predecessors (Turner, 1997). Dunlap was fired a year later. The firm subsequently went bankrupt.

Arrogant executives are excluded from the "humor network"—joking on the job (Duncan & Feisel, 1989). Likewise, the arrogance of military leaders has led them to underestimate the enemy, overestimate their own force and position, and ignore the advice of their staffs. Arrogant business and military leaders both rely on simplistic formulas for success and fail to pay attention to changing realities.

By 1812, except for some early, forgotten setbacks, Napoleon had lost very few of the 35 battles of which he himself had been in command and now had become the master of continental Europe and all its royal rulers. Russia and Tsar Alexander were the exception. They were of little threat to Napoleon's French Empire. But to satisfy his arrogant character, he assembled 150,000 French troops and 350,000 from other nationalities of Europe and set out to march the 800 miles to Moscow, where he expected that the Russians would formally surrender, submit to his authority, and acknowledge his supremacy over the continent. He had plenty of warnings of problems from his staff, which he confidently overlooked. The problems were to be handled by his will to succeed. He lost 50,000 at the Battle of Borodino and all but 20,000 of the remaining 450,000 because of his failure to consider his stretched supply lines, the Russian winter, Russian resilience, and guerrilla warfare. The defeat led to his downfall over the next three years.

Lack of Social Inhibition. Lack of social inhibition can be a vice. Socially uninhibited people are less effective as leaders despite their need for power and affiliation. They concentrate on dominating others and on winning at the expense of someone else (McClelland, 1985).

Abusiveness. Abusive leaders are arbitrary, condescending, and patronizing. They indulge in emotional outbursts (Ashforth, 1994) and use physical or verbal aggression. A leader's verbal aggression seeks to inflict pain on the self-concept of a subordinate. It is not mere impersonal argumentation (Marrs & Turban, 2002). Physical abuse by supervisors was more common in earlier industry, but nonphysical abuse continues, though it is more constrained by cultural and organizational sanctions. Abusiveness results in employee job dissatisfaction, role conflict, intentions to quit, and reduced organizational commitment (Tepper, 2000). Supervisor bullying, frightening, or threatening employees (Rayner, 1997) may be witnessed by 40% to 60% of employees, although it is likely to be confused with autocratic, directive, "no-nonsense" leadership (Sablynski, 2002). Abuse of power may be subtle when followers regard the leader as a parental figure (Sankowsky, 1995).

High Self-Monitoring. High self-monitors have the vice of overconcern about appearing unfavorably in what they say and do. They tend toward amorality. They avoid investing in emotional relationships. They are less committed to their current friends, current colleagues at work, and sexual partners. They are more ready to change employers. They are less constrained about pursuing opportunities wherever they may be found (Kilduff & Day, 1994). In a survey of members of a Canadian human resources professional organization, high self-monitors were more willing to behave unethically in eight scenarios in work and nonwork settings (Wahn, 2003).

Document Falsification. Into the early 1990s, as the principal financial institution for a number of Gulf sheikhdoms, arms traffickers, and terrorist organizations, and with branch banks worldwide, the Bank of Credit and Commerce International (BCCI) was ideal for moving funds among the sheikhdoms, arms traffickers, and terrorists because it was flexible in falsifying documents. Illegal and immoral transfers were kept from being transparent. The bank even arranged for princes in Abu Dhabi to pay the families of 16- to 20-year-old virgins and to pay for training them (London *Sunday Times*, 1992). Enron overreported $9 billion dollars in profits aided by Arthur Andersen auditors. This "cooking the books" cause of bankruptcies in a number of other large firms in 2002. Wessel (2002) listed 18 major corporations, from Adelphia to Xerox as following questionable practices. Adelphia, audited by Deloitte & Touche, failed to properly disclose $3.1 billion in loans and guarantees to its founder's family. Xerox, audited by KPMG, was fined $10 million but did not admit or deny that it inflated revenues and profits from 1997 to 2000 by including future payments on existing contracts.

Malevolence. This vice of destructive leaders brings harm, pain, and suffering to others (O'Connor, Mumford, Clifton, et al., 1995). If the vice is intentional and deliberate, the leaders are malevolent in personality. According to Goldberg (1995), they know what they are doing and understand the consequences of their actions. They choose doing evil over doing good in the hope of reducing their own shame and self-contempt, which they project onto others. They feel that they are superior to others and that they live by a higher morality. They become addicted to finding reasons for their cruel and insensitive behavior. They are unable, unwilling, and afraid to examine the dark, unknown side of themselves and believe they already know what needs to be known.

Masked Intentions. Dasborough and Ashkanasy (2002) theorized that depending on whether a leader was in a positive or negative mood, members' attributions about the leader's intentions would influence their evaluations and interpretations of his or her leadership and whether the attempted leadership was truly transformational or pseudotransformational. Leaders high in Machiavellianism can conceal their intentions and be evaluated by members as authentically transformational when they actually are pseudotransformational. When the members are in a negative mood, they will be more likely to view the leader as self-serving.

Toxic Leadership

Leaders with many of the vices listed above have been described as *toxic* by Lipman-Blumen (2005). She noted that such leaders are plentiful in all walks of life and display different vices at different times. Nevertheless, they are tolerated and sometimes admired. They survive despite their faults. Often, they achieve status as celebrities and are supported by the media's myopia about ethical considerations. Among other actions of toxic leaders, she noted that they: (1) do more harm than good to followers;

(2) violate the basic human rights of their own supporters; (3) consciously feed illusions to their followers that play on the followers' fears and needs; (4) mislead followers with lies; (5) stifle criticism of themselves; (6) engage in unethical, illegal, and criminal acts; (7) cling to power; (8) scapegoat others; and (9) ignore or promote incompetence, cronyism, and corruption.

Dealing with Ethical and Unethical Practices

Attitudes toward Corruption

Investigative journalism has, since its inception, put a spotlight on managerial and entrepreneurial corruption. Nonetheless, there has been a marked paucity of empirical research on managers' attitudes toward corruption and the ethics of their behavior. Pitt (1985) gave middle and senior managers in South Africa 15 scenarios involving ethical considerations and asked them to indicate whether they regarded the manager's behavior as wrong, how frequently such behavior had been observed, and what the company should do about it. Over 90% thought it was definitely wrong to accept a large bribe or to tell competitive bidders their rivals' offers for the manager's own material benefit. But 4 out of 10 thought it "understandable" for a firm that had just been awarded a contract by a project engineer to give the engineer a tip. Similar proportions thought it was all right for a geologist to use inside information about new developments to purchase company shares, and for a purchasing manager to accept an invitation from a supplier for a "night on the town" hosted by the supplier's secretary. Over 90% said they had observed colleagues and friends accepting a potential supplier's invitation to lunch and accepting a bottle of whisky as a Christmas gift from a supplier. Half or more said they had seen colleagues or friends accepting free trips and entertainment from suppliers, as well as conducting insider trading. Only 34% thought the company should take legal action in the case of large bribes, although 62% would fire the bribe taker. Similar reactions were registered for releasing information prematurely to rival bidders, but a plurality would only give such employees a warning for insider trading, accepting free trips, and filing false expense claims.

Although there is much divergence in ethical opinion among managers, a high set of standards can be described and appreciated. Six interviews were held with six leaders who were identified by well-informed observers as models of ethical leadership. These ethical leaders expressed a strong commitment to the mission of their organization, derived great satisfaction from progressing toward the mission, and empowered others to contribute to it. Furthermore, they cared for the various stakeholders in the organization, not only the owners and stockholders, and had a broad sense of community. They also remained informed about what was going on in their complex organizations. In all, they believed that bad means could not be justified to gain good ends (Shapiro, 1985).

Questionable Decisions

Three sets of questions need to be answered in determining whether one is making the right ethical decision:

1. Is it legal and legitimate? Will this decision violate laws or regulations? Will it violate organizational policies or standards or community norms? Will it violate agreements with unions, outside agencies, or other organizations?

2. Is it just and fair? Is everyone involved being treated equitably? Will some people be helped unfairly at the expense of others?

3. How will you feel after making the decision? How will you feel about yourself? Will you be proud of what you did? Would you be pleased to see the decision published in a newspaper and read by family and friends? (Anonymous, undated).

Nepotism. Favoring family members over others for selection, promotion, and organizational support may be embedded in constitutions, cultures, traditions, customs, and norms. Yet it may be unethical when a less qualified relative is chosen over someone more qualified. There are well-known family political dynasties such as the Bushes, Romneys, Longs, and Kennedys. In many countries widows and daughters are elected to replace their husbands and fathers. Brothers and sons are frequent successors to Muslim leaders. Sons may take over authoritarian governments after the death of their fathers. The great majority of American businesses are family-owned. Descendents of Henry Ford, the founder, have been chosen as succeeding CEOs of Ford Motors. Leadership in the crafts and service industries often passes from father to son. Numerous leaders in the movie and television industry owe their positions to their parents' careers in the industry. The father-son tradition continues in trade unions, the military, entertainment, the media, and religious institutions. Family name, connections, and wealth may be exploited; and it may not be regarded as wrong to give a qualified relative an opportunity in competition with an equally qualified stranger (Bellow, 2003). Affirmative action for family members has become an acceptable norm in the United States and in family-built and family-dominated businesses and in collectivistic cultures such as India, Singapore, and Taiwan. But there is a cost. People who are not family members feel that they have less of a future in the business.

Wrongful Behavior

The unethicality of 15 acts was analyzed by Pitt, Watson, and Nel (1990), who sent 500 questionnaires to purchasing managers in organizations over 500 in size. The managers rated how wrong the actions were and what punishment was justified, if any. Proposed punishments depended on the harm done to the organization by the wrongful actions. Two actions judged completely wrong were accepting bribes to award a large contract and giving a bidder on a contract information about all the rival bids. Perpetrators ought to be punished by dismissal and possibly legal action. Justifying only a warning but judged as almost equally wrong were siphoning fuel from a manager's company car to his wife's filing false expense claims, and keeping a trunk full of groceries discovered after returning from a supplier. At the other extreme, it was seen as understandable or not wrong to accept Christmas gifts, lunch from a supplier, or an invitation to a sporting event. In another study, using three scenarios of unethical behavior, 337 upperclass undergraduate students said that the perpetrator was morally wrong if they empathized with the victims of the possibly harmful actions (which involved selling autos or real estate). The likelihood that the harm would occur was irrelevant (Carlson, Kacmar, Wadsworth, et al., 2001).

Whistle-Blowing

In its December 19, 2002, issue, *Time* magazine named three whistle-blowers as "Persons of the Year," an honor ordinarily reserved for world leaders. Coleen Rowley, a middle manager, sent a letter to the director of the FBI about evidence of the 9/11 conspiracy that was ignored, and testified critically to the U.S. Senate that the agency was bogged down in bureaucracy and careerism; Cynthia Cooper, an internal auditor at WorldCom, alerted its board of directors to $3.8 billion in accounting irregularities; and Sherron Watkins, an Enron vice president, sent memos warning the CEO that improper accounting could cause the firm to collapse.

An ethical conscience, courage to act on one's ethical convictions, concern for others, ego strength, and inner locus of control are character traits of whistle-blowers in reacting to unethical authority (Perrault, 1997). They are willing to report the unethical behavior of higher-ups (Mumford, Gessner, Connelly, et al., 1993). Whistle-blowers also reveal character traits of spirituality and moral absolutism. Compared with pragmatists, idealists who strongly believe in a just world make the most mature ethical decisions about whistle-blowing. In an Australian study, Windsor, Trevino, Ashkanasy (2001) found that given the expectation in an "in-basket scenario" that management condoned unethical behavior by punishing rather than rewarding a whistle-blower, highly principled respondents—those who scored highest on Rest's (1993) Defining Interests Test (DIT)—responded most ethically. In contrast, pragmatic respondents—those scoring lowest on the DIT—were lowest in ethical responses.

Motivation to Intervene. For 398 employees in one study, willingness to intervene in the event of witnessing social-sexual behavior at work was affected by recognizing the behavior as a moral issue, by its moral intensity, and by the moral ideology of the witness (Bowes-Sperry & Powell, 1999). In the case of an office romance between an older married senior executive and a younger single employee, taking action was more likely if work was disrupted and the young person was believed to be motivated by job concerns. The desire to intervene was increased by group norms, and by the perceived reactions of the guilty parties (Barnett, Bass, & Brown, undated).

Whistle-blowers can be stimulated by leaders who give

immoral orders and suggest actions that are ambiguous so that blame for wrongdoing can be diverted from the leaders (Kelman & Hamilton, 1989). The whistle-blowers may delay or procrastinate until others confirm the seriousness of the unethical behavior. They will act to report the violation of organizational rules if preventive attention is urgent; if the violation is frequent or seriously harmful; if their relations with the violator are not close; if they feel responsible for doing so; if they are less concerned about the violator's reactions to the whistle-blowing; if fewer emotional, financial, time, and other personal resources may need to be committed by the whistle-blower; if the time and place are appropriate for a confrontation; and if it is likely that the whistle-blowing confrontation will end the violation (Newall & Stutman, 1991).

Deterrents to Whistle-Blowing. In the U.S. service academies, reporting on peers' unethical behavior, as called for by the honor system, was in conflict with the institutional norms of mutual support and teamwork. At the Naval Academy, the accepted slogan was, "Never bilge your classmates." Those who blew the whistle and disclosed mass cheating on an electrical engineering examination were expelled, while those who cheated but remained silent were not. For the midshipmen, the honor system was a joke that protected lying and cheating and punished those who blew the whistle (Caplan, 1994).

Impact of the Internet

Galvin (2000) saw 1999 as a banner year for lapses in business ethics, and anticipated the even bigger scandals to come in the years immediately following. The Internet has brought increased opportunities for cheating, lying, and stealing. It has also brought many additional problems, costs, and risks of unethical behavior by corporate leaders and the led, ranging from anonymous sexual harassment to improper contact with competitors by leaders to fix prices and by employees to reveal proprietary

information. Stock fraud, bogus business accounting, insurance scams, copyright violations, corporate espionage, and illicit data mining about unsuspecting customers have increased substantially with the increased use of the Internet. Over 60% of employees say they use their office e-mail for personal purposes on company time. Over 50% of firms say they monitor—without permission—their employees' e-mail; but 61% of employees surveyed said it was all right for the firm to do so. When seeking reasons to discharge an employee, firms find the monitored information a good source.

Summary and Conclusions

Many leaders serve as examples of ethical behavior and make moral decisions attributable to their character and professionalism. Others are amoral or immoral. Empirical research on leadership ethics was rare before 1975, although its philosophical underpinnings go back to ancient Greece and China. Spiritual leadership has taken ethical issues to a higher stage. Ethical and moral principles of leadership are well established but remain less well practiced. More attention needs to be paid to organizational and corporate social responsibility. Moral reasoning about what is right, good, and important is principle-based or character-based. Moral reasoning develops from self-interest to seeking the interests of others.

The character of a leader can be delineated in terms of virtues and vices. Among the virtuous traits of leaders are integrity, authenticity, and fairness. Justice may be distributive, interactional, or informational. Other virtues of leaders include altruism, conscientiousness, wisdom, courage, and compassion.

Unethical practices include nepotism, questionable decisions, wrongful behavior, and false accounting statements. The Internet has contributed to many new forms of wrongdoing. Whistle-blowers need a strong set of virtues and the willingness to confront those of much higher status than themselves.

Personal Attributes of Leadership

CHAPTER 10

Leadership and Accorded Status, Esteem, and Trust

People are valued by others because of the position they occupy in an informal or formal group, an organization, or society—this is their status. They may be valued as persons regardless of their position—this is their esteem. They may be valued as trustworthy by others who have confident, positive expectations about them. Blaise Pascal (1660/1950) described a great nobleman as being valued for the status he had in society that made it possible for him to be "the master of objects that men covet," and for these objects deference was paid to him. But he was not esteemed by Pascal as a person. In contrast, Pascal mentioned "M. N. [who] is a greater geometrician than I . . . [and whom] I esteem for his enlightenment of mind, virtue, health and strength" (Bass, 1960, p. 277). Pascal's nobleman was of worth to others because of his noble status, the lofty hierarchical position he held in society. The nobleman's position gave him wealth, control, power, and influence. A poor nobleman position would still be accorded some status and influence. Even without control of wealth to distribute, a nobleman's position could still be of more importance than a commoner's. Pascal's mathematician was esteemed for his technical competence and personal qualities. Many noblemen of high status lacked such personal qualities and were held in low esteem by those who knew them personally or by reputation. Many ordinary folks who lacked status could be esteemed by others for their personal value.

Status

The value that others accord members for their position—informally or in a group, organization, or society—is the members' *status*. Status contributes to the members' emergence as leaders. The same is true of the members' *esteem*, the value accorded them by others for their personal qualities (Bass, 1960). Conflicts abound and ineffectiveness increases in the group, organization, or society when the esteem and status of the members are not correlated. A group will be in conflict and ineffective when its high-status members are low in esteem; it will also be in conflict and ineffective when its highly esteemed members are relegated to positions that accord them low status.

Warner, Meeker, and Eells (1949) observed that all societies and social groups of any size or complexity have status systems. Status structure and differentiation of functions are necessary for the coordination of efforts. Even collectives that are designed to minimize functional specialization and the differential distribution of rewards develop well-defined status structures (E. Rosenfeld, 1951). In traditional societies, age was an important determinant of status. However, the details concerning what was expected of members of different ages—infants, boys, girls, young men, young women, old men, and old women—differed from one society to another (Linton, 1945).

Occupants of various positions are provided with cues to make it easy to identify their status. Status differences in military organizations are clearly visible. In many societies, the adolescent often is easily discriminated by dress from the preadolescent, as is the married woman from the unmarried woman. Until modern times, each profession had its own identifiable costume. And the signs and symbols of differential status in the modern business organization are familiar. The top managers and administrators have extralarge corner offices on the top floor, custom-made desks, large leather desk chairs, carpeting, coffee tables, couches, and special parking spaces for their cars; first-line supervisors have small offices in the basement with wooden desks and chairs, and park in the lot wherever they can (Barnard, 1952).

Status differences affect how members group with each other. In a mixed social gathering, high-level officials will cluster, as will those who are lower in status. At a cocktail party, men often stay together in one corner of the room and women in another corner. In organizations, members tend to maintain some degree of physical distance between themselves and other members who differ from them in status. Status also determines how people communicate with others who are working at a distance. Thus members of organizations send memos to those above or below them in status but telephone those who are at their same level (Klauss & Bass, 1981). E-mail may substitute for both the telephone and written memos for senders several echelons above, below, or at the same organizational level.

Concomitants of Status

Some positions provide occupants with direct control over what is rewarding to others; occupants of such positions have greater status in the organization (Barnard, 1951). In turn, such status-derived power makes it possible for the possessors to exert leadership and influence over others. Some roles make it possible for the role players to have access to information and the ability to solve the group's problems.

Sherif, White, and Harvey (1955) found that the higher the importance of a member's position, the greater was his or her competence as judged by other members. This finding fits with the facts of everyday life. Studies of the status hierarchy in social organizations show that positions accord their occupants more status if occupants of those positions either acquire more knowledge once they occupy the position or are selected for the position only if they have the knowledge. The occupations with the highest societal status (that is, value or importance to society), according to college students, are physician, lawyer, banker, engineer, and school administrator—all require a great deal of education and specialized knowledge. Low-status occupations include truck driver, coal miner, janitor, and ditchdigger—all of which necessitate little or no education. The status of occupations is remarkably stable. For 25 occupations, the correlations in status in 1925, 1946, and 1967 were all above .09 (Hakel, Hollman, & Dunnette, 1968) and were likely to be as high in 2000. Furthermore, miners' and laborers' perceptions of

occupational status were similar to those of the college students (Cattell, 1942). But a strikingly different occupational hierarchy appeared when researchers asked a random sample of 2,000 Americans to rate the extent to which they valued the honesty and integrity of different occupational groups. The highest 10 occupations were firemen, paramedics, farmers, grade school teachers, college professors, dentists, U.S. military officers, plumbers, college athletes, and advertising executives. The lowest 10 were drug dealers, organized crime bosses, television evangelists, prostitutes, street peddlers, local politicians, congressmen, car salesmen, rock and roll stars, and insurance salesmen (Patterson & Kim, 1991). Evidently, trustworthiness did not coincide with high status.

In primitive societies, the high status of the medicine man and tribal elders was partly due to the knowledge held by anyone occupying such positions. In a world that had to depend on the memory of events and procedures (since no books were available), and in which life expectancy was short, age was highly prized. Because wisdom required age and experience, age, status, and leadership were strongly linked. Conversely, the lower status of women and children in patriarchal societies was often partly due to their ignorance of magic, ritual, and tribal history, which were known by the men only. The reverse was true in matriarchal societies, in which women were accorded much higher status.

Value and Importance of Positions. Zaccaro (1996) compared the executive performance requirements found in interviews with generals and lieutenant generals by Harris and Lucas (1991), major generals and brigadier generals by Lucas and Markessini (1993), and colonels by Steinberg and Leaman (1999a). Systematic differences could be seen in the importance of positional requirements at successively lower organizational ranks. Generals had longer work-time spans than did lieutenant generals and more boundary-spanning responsibilities. Shorter planning-time spans were available for major generals and brigadier generals, who also had less boundary spanning to do. Colonels were more likely than those below them in rank to be involved in goal setting, planning, and policy making.

People are appointed to positions by higher authority, or they may be elected. Their status is established by appointment if it is legitimate. If they are legitimately elected, their esteem is also likely to be higher. Status may also accrue from inherited positions or from volunteering for the position.

A price can be set on one's status in an organization or society. Job evaluation establishes the worth of each position to the organization. One's pay, then, depends on the established value and importance of a position, regardless of who occupies it. To control inflation, in 301 C.E. the Roman emperor Diocletian decreed fixed ceilings on prices and wages with penalties—exile or death—for exceeding the maximum allowed. A brace of chickens was to cost no more than 60 denarii, and first-quality boots no more than 120 denarii. Daily wages with maintenance were to be limited as follows: 20 denarii for shepherds; 25 for farm laborers; 50 for carpenters; 150 for picture painters. Monthly wages were to be no more than 50 denarii per pupil for elementary teachers; 75 for teachers of arithmetic; 200 for teachers of Latin or Greek; and 250 for teachers of rhetoric. For jurists or advocates pleading a case, the maximum allowed was 1,000 denarii (Lewis & Meyer, 1955). Similarly, one's status and value to family, clan, or social organization were clearly fixed in Anglo-Saxon law. The *wergild*, or "man price," varied with a person's status in society. If the person was murdered or killed by accident, it was to be paid by the culprit to the victim's relatives as retribution. The various social strata were valued by their respective prices. The church placed its own members on the wergild scale. It equated a priest with a thane. The price of a king was from 6 to 15 times that of a thane (Whitelock, 1950). Today, the executive who is incapacitated owing to the fault of another person still sues for a far greater estimated loss of income than does the manual laborer. The estimates are based on the expected future earnings of executives and laborers in the same general circumstances.

Striving for Increased Status. The desire for upward mobility is associated with attaining a more important and valued position to increase one's influence. Those with lower status in a group are more likely to be concerned about raising their status than those who already have attained important leadership roles. In three industrial plants, M. Dalton (1950) observed that the lower-status executives tried to get more personnel to supervise and tried to transfer from staff positions (less influential) to line positions (more influential). The line executives,

on the other hand, did not seek staff jobs and were more concerned about moving higher on the line and entering the management "eating circle." Similarly, Bentz (undated) observed that members of college faculties who accorded themselves lower status tended to report more concern within their department about rank, status, and influence.

Aspirations for Upward Mobility. Upward striving for status may be reflected in a desire to identify with those of higher status or to accumulate the signs and symbols of higher status. Beshers (1962) called this striving "one-way status mirrors" when he observed the behavior of poor people of lower-class status aspiring to join the middle class.

Expectations of higher status are conducive to greater satisfaction. Kipnis (1964) reported that those who expect to move up are generally more satisfied with their work. Vroom (1966) studied students working for a master's degree in a business school before and after they accepted positions and found that they rated organizations as attractive when they perceived that these organizations were instrumental to the attainment of their personal goals. H. H. Kelley (1951) found that high-status members with no possibility of promotion were least attracted to a group. Conversely, in another laboratory study, Spector (1953) reported that participants in an experiment who were placed in a pseudomilitary hierarchy and were promoted were the most satisfied. In the U.S. Air Force, Borgatta (1955b) noted that personnel who saw adequate opportunities for advancement to officer positions were less critical of the rewards and punishments possible. However, those who were actually striving for advancement in status were more critical than those who did not seek promotion.

In addition to seeking higher status, most of us, within limits, enjoy associating with groups of somewhat higher status, since these groups are likely to have more power and influence. J. W. Mann (1961) found that members of a group, especially low-status members, preferred to associate with groups of similar or higher status. Their desire tended to focus on the group that was next highest in status relative to their own group.

This striving for status—usually provided by a position of leadership—often involves the desire to achieve congruence in status among the various positions one holds.

Dissatisfaction with one's status in one organization may be due to one's status in another. Benoit-Smullyan (1944) hypothesized that individuals with different status in different groups would attempt to equalize their stature in the various groups. Thus a business leader may endow an art institute to gain status in cultural circles. Fenchel, Monderer, and Hartley (1951) found that subjects' striving for status in five groups to which they belonged was higher in those groups in which their current status was low.

Rejection of Higher Status. Although the desire for upward movement in an organization may be the norm, it may nevertheless require changes in residence, associates, and patterns of living. Upward mobility also may require a change in relationships with friends, associates, and former coworkers in the organization. In addition, a higher-status position involves changes in responsibility and accountability for results. It may even mean lower pay for some workers, who, if promoted to supervisor, will no longer be paid for overtime. Not all members of an organization welcome such upward mobility. For example, Springer (1956) found that 13 percent of 10,533 workers who were recommended for promotion to leadman, assistant foreman, or foreman refused the promotion.

A significant factor in the emotional breakdown of medical officers during World War II was their promotion to a higher-level position of responsibility and status, according to Reider (1944). The young officer who depended on a superior for support not only lost it when he became a status peer of the senior officer but was also expected to provide support for his subordinates.

Losing Status. Although Olmsted (1957) found that members of a group can drop from a position of leadership to the status of participant without reducing their activities or losing their liking for their group, most people in important positions will be concerned about losing status. E. L. Thorndike (1940) noted that for many—perhaps most—people, political power is a habit-forming psychological drug. Abdications are rare. It is one's general status that is involved, not the specific position. A president of the Teamsters Union is tenacious about maintaining his union office because it is inconceivable for him to return to driving a truck after a term

in such a high-status position. Yet a cabinet secretary or the president of the American Association of University Professors can return to a high-status position in business or in academia after serving a term in office and so usually is not as reluctant to relinquish office (Selznick, 1943).

Lowered Status, Dissatisfaction, and Performance. Lowered status is likely to result in dissatisfaction and a decline in performance. H. H. Kelley (1951) studied, experimentally, the written communications of group members in high-status and low-status positions, with and without the possibility of status mobility, and found that low status was associated with relative dislike for the group task. Low-status members communicated their dissatisfaction to other low-status members. Furthermore, the high-status members who could lose their status made fewer positive comments than did those whose status was secure, and the low-status members with the possibility of upward mobility made fewer negative comments than did those who had no such opportunity.

Burnstein and Zajonc (1965a) observed that the performance of group members tended to suffer when their status was decreased and tended to improve when their status was increased. Loss of status was likely to generate hostility. Lindzey and Kalnins (1958) asked students to compare themselves and other persons with figures in a picture test of projective attitudes. The students tended to identify themselves with heroic figures, but identified other persons more often with nonheroic figures. In the students' projections, changes in status after frustration revealed increased aggression by the hero against others and by others against the hero. Consistent with these findings, Worchel (1961) showed that one's expressions of hostility against others were reduced by restoring one's lost status.

Status and Leadership

Substantial evidence and everyday experience support a strong connection between status and leadership. Many people confuse and merge the two concepts. The worth or value of a manager's position in the organizational hierarchy increases as he or she moves to higher echelons. Greater responsibility and authority accrue along with higher status. So does the manager's leadership behavior.

Thus, according to D. T. Campbell (1956), descriptions of the behavior of leaders and nominations for leadership of submarine officers were highly correlated with the officers' rank and the organizational level of their positions.

A rise in status and status differentiation were reflected in effective leadership. In one Mexican village, economic development resulted in the emergence of a cohesive and wealthier class. These wealthier members led the initiation of projects, the mobilization of community support, and the successful completion of the projects. In a second village, without such economic and class developments, little change was possible. Only the first village could deal effectively with outside influences that sought to control local decision making (Krejci, 1976).

Increased Requirements. Systematic differences are observed in the requirements for leadership as one's status increases. Routine production is of concern at the lowest organizational levels; systems and the external environment are of concern at the highest levels. Compared with the position of the lowest-level manager, the position of the top manager requires more innovativeness, vision, persuasiveness, and long-term orientation. It requires less modesty and participativeness.

Coercive Leadership. Bass (1960) deduced that the power accruing from members' high status makes it possible for them to become *coercive* leaders—giving orders, demanding, deciding without explanation. This power, coupled with information and the ability to help the group that stem from their high-status positions, also allows them to persuade others or to permit participation by others in decision making. Although coerciveness is still possible, it has been much more constrained in the past century by changes in attitudes against it of both superiors and subordinates, by legislation, and by societal changes in the democratized world. Much of the research of 50 years ago on coercion is less applicable today, although the many current harassment cases in civilian and military life attest to its continuing occurrence.

Schell (1951) suggested that higher-status people may offer security, protection, and opportunity to their subordinates in return for obedience and zeal. Roethlisberger (1945, p. 287) remarked, "Personal dependence upon the judgments and decisions of his superiors, so charac-teristic of the subordinate-superior relation . . . makes the foreman . . . feel a constant need to adjust himself to demands of his superior and to seek approval of his superior." Gerard (1957) found in an experiment that participants with high status tended to be *controlling* in their behavior, whether their role relationships was clear or unclear. But low-status participants required a clearly defined set of role expectations to be effective. Without group goals, high-status participants assumed broader prerogatives, whereas low-status participants seemed bewildered. High-status participants also perceived themselves to have more freedom of action than did low-status participants.

Attempted and Successful Leadership. Attempts to lead were more likely to be successful when the members differed in accorded status and when they were highly motivated than under the opposite conditions (Bass, 1963). A correlation of .88 was obtained between the organizational level of 131 supervisors in an oil refinery and their success in initially leaderless group discussions for which no one was appointed leader (Bass & Wurster, 1953b). If the problem concerned company matters, the correlation was even higher (Bass & Wurster, 1953a). A correlation of .51 was found between the rank of 264 ROTC cadets and their tendency to lead discussions among associates. When 180 cadets were retested in a new discussion among their associates a year after an initial discussion, those who had risen in rank from cadet noncommissioned officer to first lieutenant or higher during that year gained significantly more in observed success as leaders on the retest than did those who received a lesser promotion to cadet second lieutenant (Bass, 1964).

Status and Influence

The power of the higher-status manager to influence his or her lower-status subordinates has been observed in numerous empirical studies. For instance, Jacobson, Charters, and Lieberman (1951) found that subordinate supervisors conformed to what they thought their bosses expected of them. Supervisors who said their bosses expected them to be considerate tended to describe themselves as more considerate leaders and were so described by their subordinates (Fleishman, 1953b). Similarly,

F. C. Mann (1951) observed that supervisors who changed more as a consequence of training in leadership received more encouragement from their superiors and felt more secure in their relations with their superiors. Bass (1960) reported finding that the higher a salesman's rank in a sales organization, the more likely was he to be nominated by the others as influential.

J. C. Moore (1968) ascertained that when dyads worked on an ambiguous task, partners of lower status in the same experimental condition tended to defer to the choices made by their partners of higher status. Subsequently, J. C. Moore (1969) found that agreement among partners eroded their expectations of differential performance that were activated by the differences in their status. O. J. Harvey (1953) found that members of a group expected more of their high-status members and overestimated the performance of the high-status members.

The influence of the leader's status may contribute to better performance among subordinates. Thus Doyle (1971) showed how the processes and productivity of schoolteachers were linked systematically to the status attained by their principals. And Tang, Tollison, and Whiteside (1988) reported that among 47 quality circles (QCs), the attendance rate by others was higher over a three-year period when the meetings were attended frequently by senior managers than when these managers seldom attended them. The QCs with a high level of attendance by middle management attempted more projects and had greater cost savings. But the effect of attendance by lower management on QC effectiveness was not significant.

Reasons for the Status-Influence Relationship. Influence accrues from high status because more attention is paid to high-status persons and because the behavior of persons with high status is more acceptable. Pedestrians at a traffic signal committed significantly more violations when they witnessed violations committed by a confederate of the experimenter who was dressed to represent a person of high social status, than when the confederate was less well dressed (Lefkowitz, Blake, & Mouton, 1955). Vrugt (undated) found that when a confederate who was introduced as a higher-status graduate student of psychology violated nonverbal rules in an experiment, it was more acceptable, since the behavior was considered to be intentional. But when a supposedly lower-status undergraduate did the same thing, it was attributed

to an inability to behave suitably. In the same way, it has been found that group members address more remarks to high-status than to low-status members (Katz, Goldston, & Benjamin, 1958; H. H. Kelley, 1951). Sabath (1964) presented a confederate as a new member of either high or low status to groups who were performing discussion and construction tasks. During the construction task, the new member exhibited disruptive behavior, followed by actions that enhanced or impeded the group's performance of the task. The high-status disruptive member was seen in a generally favorable manner whereas the low-status disruptive member was viewed favorably only when that person's performance enhanced the group's functioning. Consistent with these results, Pepitone (1958) concluded from a research review that the higher the status of group members, the greater was the attribution of good intentions and justification to their positive and negative acts. Persons accorded high status were more acceptable as authority figures, and their idiosyncratic behavior received greater acceptance (Hollander, 1961a).

Incorrect Attributions of Status. Leadership can be incorrectly attributed to high status. The romantic theory of leadership suggests that effective leadership is often attributed to individuals because they have been in high-status positions when the business organization has been effective, when in fact external or internal factors such as market conditions, governmental regulations, or highly qualified employees were responsible for the effectiveness (Meindl, Ehrlich, & Dukerich, 1985).

Effects of Self-Accorded Status. When it mirrors status accorded by others, self-accorded status correlates with attempts to lead and to be successful as a leader. Guetzkow (1954) showed that key persons' ratings of their own importance to communication networks correlated with their influential behavior in the networks. If there was a mismatch between self-accorded and accorded status, the attempts were likely to misfire.

A common but not well recognized phenomenon, and a source of potential conflict, is the belief by all people in a hierarchy that they have bigger and more important jobs than their bosses think they have (Haas, Porat, & Vaughan, 1969; Volkerding & Grasha, 1988). Gold (1951–1952) described how interactions between tenants and the janitor in a multiple dwelling changed when the janitor's concept of his status changed as he adopted "professional standards" and began earning a higher salary than some of the tenants. The stage was set for conflict with those tenants who did not appreciate the janitor's changed concept of the importance of his job.

Socioeconomic Status

Effects of Socioeconomic Status. Chapter 4 noted 15 studies through 1947 indicating that leaders were likely to come from a socioeconomic background according them higher status. For instance, C. A. Smith (1937) found that the leaders of an industrial town in Connecticut came from wealthy families with "connections." Many additional works followed in support. Hollingshead (1949) observed that Elmstown's young people displayed leadership behavior as a function of the social class of their family. Baltzell (1958) noted that the descendants of colonial merchants and statesmen, pioneering businessmen, and mining and railroad tycoons of Philadelphia all went to school with one another, lived in fashionable neighborhoods, were Episcopalian, joined the same clubs, intermarried, and eventually entered the elite class. They became the community leaders.

J. A. Davis (1929) found that only 19% of 163 Russian Communist leaders had peasant fathers, and only 29% had working-class fathers.[1] Taussig and Joslyn (1932) observed that 70% of the fathers of 7,371 American business executives were businessmen, although businessmen constituted only 10% of the workforce. Even labor leaders tended to be the sons of professionals and businessmen (Sorokin, 1927b).

Numerous studies of opinion leaders attest to the strong link between socioeconomic status and leadership. Switzer (1975) found that peasant leaders in a progressive industrial-agrarian department of Colombia were better-educated, were more economically secure, and had a clearer land title than peasant leaders in a rural, conservative department. Farmers in Orissa, India, were more effective in motivating other farmers to apply improved agricultural techniques if they were higher in socioeconomic status (Rath & Sahoo, 1974). In addition, Roy, Jaiswal, and Shankar (1974) reported that sociometrically identified leaders in four villages in Bihar, India,

tended to be higher in caste and had greater landholdings than their followers. But Chesterfield and Ruddle (1976) warned that extension agents did not pay enough attention to the less-visible opinion leaders in rural Venezuela, such as relatives, symbolic kin, and older community members. The middle class in Muslim countries, not the peasants, supplied the leaders of Al Qaeda.

Changes in Socioeconomic Status. Systematic changes have occurred, both in the United States and abroad. In the United States, status increases with money, education, and marriage into a higher class. Starting in 1944, the GI Bill made it possible for many working-class war veterans to attend college. Before this, a college education had been possible mainly for middle- and upper-class students. As a consequence of the GI Bill, a large number of working-class veterans moved up in class by meeting and marrying women who came from the middle and upper classes. The reverse occurred in the communist world. After a decade of socialism, 96% of managers in Poland reported that they came from the working class or lower middle class (McClelland, 1961).

In the United States, the Air Force Command passed in the 1980s to officers whose background was quite different from those who had engaged in World War II. According to Margiotta (1976), because of broader social recruitment in the 1950s and 1960s, U.S. Air Force leaders in the 1980s became more representative of the U.S. population in terms of socioeconomic origin, regional affiliation, size of their hometown, and religion. As with the military, U.S. political, business, and educational leaders in the 1980s, 1990s, and the early twenty-first century have been drawn less often from the mainstream. Affirmative action, a broadening of the right to vote, and a liberalization of attitudes about race, ethnicity, and religion greatly raised the educational level, status, and leadership opportunities of disadvantaged minorities. However, leadership opportunities still remain somewhat less for those not of European ancestry and for ethnic and religious minorities outside the mainstream (Korman, 1988).

Confounds. Ability and status are likely to be confounded. For example, early studies (Davis, 1929; Sward, 1933; Taussig & Joslyn, 1932) found that intelligence, skill, and educational level tended to be higher among those who were higher in socioeconomic status. Middle-

---

[1] After generations of communism, leaders were likely to emerge from the new privileged classes of party members, intellectuals, military officers, and managers.

class adolescents may become school leaders more often because they are somewhat higher in verbal aptitude than working-class students. Regardless of the cause, most psychological studies indicate the existence of class differences in verbal aptitude. For example, among 140 college women, a significant correlation of .21 was obtained between verbal aptitude (as measured by the American Council on Education linguistic score) and socioeconomic status as measured by father's occupation, parents' education, and religious affiliation (Bass, Wurster, Doll, et al., 1953). The relationship between leadership and socioeconomic status is also confounded with the tendency of higher socioeconomic status to be correlated with greater education and opportunity. The collateral interrelations were apparent to Jencks, Bartlett, Corcoran, et al. (1979), who looked at 13 demographic variables having to do with fathers and sons and concluded that a father's occupation, family background, education, and intelligence are the best predictors of a son's occupational success. Although credentials, demonstrated by degrees in engineering, law, or business administration, provide avenues to success in business leadership, it also helps to marry the boss's daughter. Middle-class students can pursue more extracurricular leadership opportunities; working-class students frequently have to put their time into part-time jobs. Celebrity, wealth, marriage, and education can also move one's status and influence upward. In the information age, education and knowledge have increased considerably in importance relative to the other variables.

The concordance of status and leadership is also confounded by the relationship of both status and leadership to how much time people spend with each other. Stogdill and Koehler (1952) found that the extent to which persons in lower organizational echelons mentioned an individual as one with whom they spent the most time correlated .82 with the mentioned person's level in the organization. However, these mentions of frequency of contact also correlated .31, .33, and .23 with being preferred as a leader. Time spent with persons in other units also correlated highly with the other person's level in the organization ($r = .69$). Similarly, Browne (1949) found that an executive who was mentioned frequently as one with whom others spent time was also an officeholder who described himself as being higher in authority and who was in a higher echelon in the organization. An-

other confound with status was noted by Jackson and Fuller (1966), who discovered that lower-class pupils liked middle-class teachers better. They seemed to the pupils to be less authoritarian.

Symbolic Value of Status

Did Pascal overstate the case in suggesting that the nobleman would lose all his influence if he lost the power to control what lesser men wanted? The symbols, signs, and privileges would still make the poor nobleman's position valuable in the eyes of others—a continued source of envy, deference, and respect. The rich commoner might still be willing to exchange places with the poor nobleman or to pay handsomely to have him as a son-in-law. Others' perception of the legitimacy and value of the nobleman's privileged position in the societal hierarchy would still give him some influence apart from his personal qualities. Thus the poor nobleman's position would still provide *referent* power, and the rich commoner might still want to identify with the nobleman, regardless of the nobleman's impoverishment. Nevertheless, Pascal was right to some degree, for the absence of any real power attached to one's position generally results in the reduced ability to lead. Viteles (1953) talked about the first-level foreman as the "forgotten man," since the foreman was left with only some of the symbols of status but little control over his subordinates. In a study of an electric utility company, Pelz (1951) found that supervisors who attempted leadership behavior failed to obtain changes in their subordinates if the supervisors lacked influence with higher-ups, if they had no voice in decisions made by their superiors, if they lacked freedom from superiors' orders, and if their salary was low. Supervisors who were in positions that had more value and importance and had influence with higher authority were more successful when they made the same attempts at leadership. Influential supervisors were seen by their subordinates as being more able to obtain rewards and provide punishments for their subordinates. Supervisors who were unable to grant or deny rewards, despite their title and position, had the signs of status but were unsuccessful in leading their subordinates.

Status of Celebrities. Popular icons are famous, or sometimes infamous, personages. They are well-known figures but not necessarily heroes or charismatic leaders. As long as they remain highly visible, celebrities are extremely high in status and highly paid in relation to the general population. Their position as superstars— sports stars, rock music stars, movie stars, playboys, or aristocrats—is of much greater importance and value than their personal qualities because of the public image of their position that publicity agents and media hype create for them. That is, their image, rather than their talent, makes them influential. As long as they remain visible in their celebrated positions, the public will react toward them as if they were truly heroic or charismatic and will want to identify with them (that is, will want to be in their position as media stars). All or segments of the public will be ready to accept the testimonials of celebrities regarding products and politics. With some exceptions, celebrity status generally tends to be ephemeral, declining with a decline in publicity. Popular television anchors who remain at their posts can maintain their celebrity status over a long career, but movie and sports stars tend to fade if their public careers are short.

Esteem

Esteem is the value of each member of a formal or informal collectivity as a person, regardless of his or her position in the collectivity. It is each member's perceived potential to help the group, the organization, or society to attain goals, *independent of the position the member occupies.* Esteem is the person's *reputation* in the eyes of others. Recognition of differences in esteem among members is established during the history of a natural group (Sherif, 1967) and increases in discrimination with the age of the group (Lippitt, Thelen, & Leff, undated). Such evaluations of the adequacy of group members are found among children eight years of age or even younger (Campbell & Radke-Yarrow, 1956). Heroes and heroines are highly esteemed. They serve as examples. They have the ability to persevere and overcome the obstacles that impede others. They may become legends through their sacrifice for the benefit of others. They may be real or fictitious.

> While . . . [heroic] greatness appears almost magical, it is indeed most human. . . . Because of that human-

ness . . . individuals attain heroic stature. They are of us, but are clearly different. . . . We look to heroes and heroines for inspiration. Through their achievements, we see humankind more positively. They make us feel good . . . and feel proud. They may become definite role models, and our lives follow a different direction. . . . By learning about their lives, our lives become enriched. Denenberg, 1997, p. 23

Those with more personal ability, regardless of their position, will be more esteemed, since they can be helpful to others through their ability to solve others' problems. They can help the group, organization, or society to attain its goals. In the same way, those with personal power, regardless of their position, will be more esteemed, since they can directly give or deny love, friendship, security, and other interpersonal rewards. It is possible for them to coerce others by manipulating such rewards, but they are likely to lose esteem if they do. People with esteem that is due primarily to their personal ability will be more successful in persuading others when they attempt to do so (Mowday, 1979). If their esteem depends on both personal ability and personal power, they can emerge as leaders (Bass, 1960). For children, the real heroes of the past such as George Washington have been replaced by cartoon characters such as Mickey Mouse; for adolescents, by the unreal world of 50 Cent; for adults by the hype of Tom Cruise. The picture of George Washington in one classroom was replaced by a cartoon of Snoopy (Dennenberg, 1997).

Need for Esteem. Maslow (1954) called attention to the need for esteem. Just as we would like to occupy valued positions, most of us also desire to be valued as persons, particularly by those we value (Wurster, Bass, & Alcock, 1961). Lippitt, Thelen, and Leff (undated) hypothesized that we are more concerned about being criticized personally than about being criticized for the social role we play. This concern with one's value was implicit in Festinger's (1954) theory of social-comparison processes. It results in the practical advice to supervisors that if they need to correct a subordinate's poor performance, they should focus on the performance, not the subordinate's personal motives, attitudes, or value.

We are more satisfied with situations and groups that provide us with esteem. For instance, Van Zelst (1951) indicated that highly esteemed workers were more satisfied with their jobs and with their firm. Heyns (1950) noted that participants who felt they were accepted were more satisfied with the decisions of a conference. But Flint, Bass, and Pryer (1957a) failed to find any relation between esteem of members and their attraction to problem-solving groups.

Correlates of Esteem

The value, importance, or worth of a person as a person, regardless of the person's status, is in the eye of the beholder. *Pocketbook* voters will esteem a president according to their perception of his effect on their personal economic life; *sociotropic* voters will evaluate a president on what he does for the national economy (Kinder, 1981). Extensive evidence points to the ease with which members share perceptions of each other's esteem. Potential differences in esteem are quickly recognized by other members of a group (Gronlund, 1955a) as well as by trained observers (Stein, 1971).

Importance of First Impressions. Gronlund (1955a) observed that group members agree about as well on their relative esteem at the beginning of their interaction as after extended acquaintance. In experiments with dyads, Levinger (1959) found that although later behavior influenced a partner's behavior more than first impressions did, the first impressions tended to determine behavior throughout the experiment. Likewise, Barker (1942) found that after a few moments of getting acquainted, a group of strangers exhibited a high degree of agreement in choosing members for seatmates. Vielhaber and Gottheil (1965) studied 117 cadets who were rated by four judges after only 20 to 35 seconds of observation. The judges' ratings correlated .45 with the upperclassmen's evaluations after four weeks of observation and correlated .31 with composite evaluations of aptitude for service made 14 weeks later. According to Hall and Lord (1996), these effects of first impressions are due to rapid cognitive processing of likes and dislikes.

Experimentally, it was possible to raise or lower the esteem of a neutral stranger merely by providing some false cues about the stranger. The results depended on others' attitudes toward those cues (Asch, 1946). H. H. Kelley (1950) introduced two persons to an audience, one as "warm," the other as "cold." The audience's perceptions of the personality of the two was altered by the adjective used in introducing them. The "warm" person became more esteemed than the "cold" person.

Esteem and Self-Esteem. As with comparisons of self-ratings and ratings received from others, in most situations—unless we are depressed, lack need for control, or are overly modest due to cultural inhibitions or a self-deprecating personality—our self-ratings of esteem tend to be more favorable to us than ratings of esteem accorded us by others. We overestimate our self-esteem. According to Thompson (1999), we have an illusion of control, and therefore of our personal influence if the situation is familiar to us, if we are personally involved, if we have foreknowledge about the desired outcome, and if we are focused on success. Even in circumstances with chance outcomes, we think we personally can influence the outcome. Gilovich and Savitsky (1999) offer a different explanation. When making judgments about ourselves, we anchor them in our own experiences. The *spotlight* effect biases our estimate. We overestimate the attention others pay to our behavior and appearance. We also overestimate the extent to which our unexpressed contributions to the group are discerned by the other members.

Agreement is not high between ratings of our self-esteem and the esteem that others accord us. Gronlund (1955b) correlated each individual's rank according to the others in a group with the individual's ranking of the other group members. The median rank order correlation was only .40 for 104 graduate students. Blake, Mouton, and Fruchter (1954) studied 10 trios in a discussion task. There was limited agreement between the individuals' ratings of themselves and the observers' ratings of them. Generally, 360-degree ratings of merit, leadership, and other personal appraisals highly related to esteem by superiors, peers, and subordinates have only low to zero correlations with self-ratings.

Chapter 8 detailed the importance to leadership of self-confidence and self-esteem. As was noted, Bass (1955b) found a correlation of .38 between self-esteem and emergence as a leader in initially leaderless groups, but the correlations between self-esteem and objective success as a leader were only .17 and .18 for a total of 95 participants. Moreover, self-esteem may be quite different from the esteem accorded by another person. For instance, one would expect that those with extremely low or extremely high self-esteem would be too preoccupied with their own concerns to be highly esteemed by others (Reykowski, 1982). Nonetheless, one would ordinarily expect some correlation between self-esteem and esteem. Shapiro and Klein (1975) found such a correlation in encounter groups, but only after two days of meetings and only for a composite profile of the leaders as seen by themselves and by the nonleaders. Similarly, Willerman and Swanson (1953) found that members' evaluations of themselves were only modestly related to other members' evaluations of them.

Accuracy of Leaders. Leaders tend to be more accurate about their own esteem than are other members. But this tendency is not surprising, since everyone in the group can make more accurate judgments about the leader than about other members. The leader's behavior is more visible, more frequent, and more observable than the behavior of most other members (Bass, 1949). According to H. H. Jennings's (1943) sociometric analyses in a girls' school, a comparison of self-estimates with estimates by others showed that the "overchosen" (the stars) appraised themselves most accurately on having good ideas and making others feel benefited, whereas the "underchosen" (the rejectees and isolates) estimated themselves most accurately in expressing discouragement and being easily hurt.

Agreement among Others. Pairs of observers completed final ratings of esteem achieved in initially leaderless group discussions among members of similar status. Correlations between the pairs of observers ranged from .51 to .83. Similar results were obtained for ratings of cadet leaders. A reliability of .68 was obtained as an index of agreement among ratings by 2 to 17 ROTC cadets rating a total of 307 fellow cadets (Bass & Wurster, 1953a, 1953b). Prien and Culler (1964) found, however, that observers agreed better about those who participated a little than about those who participated a lot.

The sociometric ratings among very young children were inconsistent from one period to the next (Lazar, 1953). But according to Newsletter, Feldstein, and Newcomb (1938), as the age of campers increased, the stability of their sociometric ratings increased as well. Northway

(1946) reported rate-rerate correlations of .8 to .9 when summer campers rerated each other a week after a first rating. Bjerstedt (1956) reported correlations of .82 between ratings and reratings four months apart among 867 Swedish schoolchildren aged nine and older; even after 13 months, the rate-rerate correlation was .73. McGuire, Lammon, and White (1953) found a similar consistency among adolescents from one year to the next. Even when half the children in a group, aged 6 to 12, are replaced with new members, the remaining children's ratings of esteem were consistent, to some extent, with earlier ratings (E. Campbell, undated).

Popularity and Respect. People desire to be respected, admire those whom they esteem, and want to be esteemed by those they esteem (Wurster, Bass, & Alcock, 1963). The acceptance of a stranger is related to his or her esteem and prestige (Byrne, Griffitt, & Golightly, 1966). Santee and Vanderpol (1976) found a correlation of .83 between being liked and being respected and a correlation of .78 between being liked and being seen to be of value to the organization. In Bass's analysis (1960) of five sociometric ratings of 203 salesmen by their associates, being liked correlated .60 with being seen as of value to the firm and .49 with being seen as capable. Graves and Powell (1988) found that 398 college recruiters rated applicants' subjective qualifications for being hired substantially higher if they personally liked the applicants.

Perceived Similarity. We esteem those whom we regard as most similar to us in attitudes, interests, and abilities. We tend to reject those whom we regard as different or unlike us. Thus Graves and Powell (1988) found that recruiters gave more favorable ratings to applicants if the recruiters considered themselves similar to the applicants. Also, we tend to choose as friends those who are similar to us or only slightly higher than us in socioeconomic status (A. Ellis, 1956).

Many investigators have demonstrated that similarity in attitudes is a significant factor in sociometric choice.[2] Byrne (1965) found that acceptance of a stranger was related to similarity of attitudes. A stranger who was perceived to have attitudes similar to those of the raters was

---

[2] See, for example, Byrne and Clore (1966); Davitz (1955); Fensterheim and Tressel (1953); Fielder, Warrington, and Blaisdell (1952); and A. J. Smith (1957).

adjudged more intelligent, more moral, and better in-formed (Byrne, 1961). Furthermore, we particularly like others who are similar to us on socially desirable dimen-sions (Hendrick & Brown, 1971; Palmer & Byrne, 1970). We prefer those who share our group's norms and values (Stein, 1982b).

In numerous studies,[3] perceived similarity in personal-ity characteristics is also significantly related to interper-sonal choices. A review by Berscheid and Walster (1969) suggested that similarity of attitudes and personality was associated with mutual attractiveness and therefore with valuing of each other.

Mutual Attractiveness. People tend to like those who like them (Newcomb, 1956). Furthermore, the extent to which people are attracted to each other and the extent to which they actually interact are enhanced by their per-ceived similarity in attitudes and personality and even more by the degree to which they like each other (Aron-son & Worchel, 1966; Byrne & Griffitt, 1966a, 1966b). For instance, the expectation of being liked by a partici-pant in an experimental task was significantly related to interpersonal attraction (Backman & Secord, 1959; Dar-ley & Berscheid, 1967). Similarity in competence also makes a difference in personal attractiveness. Thus Zander and Havelin (1960) found that members of ex-perimental groups tended to be attracted to others whose competence was closest to their own.

Competence. M. A. Price (1948) studied esteem among 223 women in a junior college. Women who were esteemed by their schoolmates were mentioned on an 11-item "guess who" test as most similar to the person who has good ideas, expresses joy and satisfaction, keeps the central idea in mind, appeals for group loyalty, and makes others feel that they will benefit by following her suggestions. Women who were rejected were more fre-quently mentioned as being most similar to the person who expresses fear and worry and embarrasses others.

Bass and Coates (1953) found positive correlations be-tween scores on intelligence tests and peers' ratings of es-teem in the ROTC. The "ability" items that were listed

on a peer-evaluation scale for assessing esteem among Marine cadets at Officer Candidate School (OCS) in-cluded "well trained," "experienced," "performs well be-fore the group," "has sound judgment," "thinks quickly," "exhibits imagination," "is well educated," and "is a fine athlete" (Hoffman & Rohrer, 1954). Likewise, H. H. Jen-nings (1943) noted that institutionalized girls who were "overchosen" (those who were more desired as associates) exhibited more ingenuity, planning, and organization. The more esteemed members of Whyte's (1943) street-corner society were known for their resourcefulness and the past success of their ideas. In the same way, Zeleny (1946–1947) found that cadets with exceptional ability in flying were more likely to be chosen as flying partners. Similarly, Feinberg (1953) noted that regardless of eco-nomic background, esteemed adolescent boys were higher in athletic and scholastic proficiency than were those who were rejected by their peers. But in choosing friends, Riley and Flowerman (1951) suggested, we tend to select those who are "smart, but not too smart; pretty, but not too pretty."

Demonstrated competence increases one's esteem. Gilchrist (1952) found that people who consistently suc-ceeded on assigned tasks became more attractive to oth-ers. Lippitt, Polansky, Redl, et al. (1952) reported that at a summer camp, boys with a history of success were most liked. Zander and Havelin (1960) found that those who were highly competent in experimental groups were pre-ferred over those who lacked competence. And Jackson (1953a) noted that when members of a formal organiza-tion judged other members of the work group, they valued most those whom they perceived as having con-tributed to the achievement of the group's goals and hav-ing conformed to the group's standards.

An individual's ability to help the group can be in-creased, of course. R. E. Andrews (1955) suggested that supervisors should be given as much information about policies and decisions as possible to enhance their stand-ing with their subordinates. Whyte (1943) noted that leaders can increase or maintain their perceived value to their group by making sure the group engages in activi-ties at which the leaders are most proficient.

"Unearned" Esteem. Yet it must be clear that one can be esteemed for a variety of reasons that have little or nothing to do with one's ability to help the group. People

[3] Hoffman (1958); Izard (1960); Lindzey and Urdan (1954); Lundy, Kat-kovsky, Cromwell, and Shoemaker (1955); Secord and Backman (1964); and Steiner and Dodge (1957).

may gain esteem merely because of their similarity to stereotypes or popular conceptions of esteemed or popular figures. For instance, youthful looks, gray hair, and a handsome face are strong political assets in television campaigning; immature facial characteristics (associated with infantile helplessness) will reduce a would-be leader's expected value (Berry & McArthur, 1986). Also, one's family name may carry great weight. The meteoric rise of George W. Bush to the office of governor of Texas and then the presidency is illustrative.

Esteem, Conformity, and Deviations. Before new individuals can be accepted by the other members of an established group and rise in esteem, they usually must demonstrate that they will abide by the rules of the group and share its ways of behaving and its goals (N. Anderson, 1923).[4] Thus Bonney and Powell (1953) found that the highly esteemed children in sociometric analyses were more cooperative. Likewise, Marwell (1966) found that experimental subjects chose those who had been cooperative on a first task assignment as partners for a second task assignment. Christie (1952) found that if a new army recruit increased his acceptance of the prevailing authoritarian attitudes, he was more likely to be esteemed by his peers after six weeks in service. Similarly, Havighurst and Taba (1949) noted that adolescents who conformed best to the middle-class standards of a school were most likely to be esteemed by their middle-class peers. Following a survey of the literature, Northway, Frankel, and Potashin (1947) concluded that esteem was highest in children who were not extremely shy nor so aggressive as to interfere with the group's activities. However, Stein (1982b) theorized that highly esteemed members of a group only appear to conform to the group's norms, since they actually exemplify them. They do not have to move from their own points of view to be seen as conforming to the group's normative values and attitudes.

Numerous exceptions have been reported. Mumford (1959) found more deviation among highly esteemed canteen workers. Blau (1960) reported that when cases were unimportant, caseworkers deviated more from the norms about gossiping. Conformity to the ideals of one's reference group may be more important than conformity to the opinions of a temporary group or a particular local group (Sherif & Sherif, 1964). What is most important, as Hollander's (1978) theory and research demonstrated, is that the member with esteem who first conforms to the group builds up *idiosyncrasy* credit that permits him or her to deviate and to emerge as a group leader.

Meeting Expectations. We like and value those who behave according to our expectations. Thus Sharpe (1956) reported that the evaluation of principals' effectiveness by teachers and staff was highly related to the principals' conformity to the expectations of the teachers and staff. Jackson (1953) found that foremen were evaluated by subordinates according to the match between the foremen's behavior and the subordinates' expectations. Baumgartel (1956) reported the same kinds of results for the staff's evaluations of the directors of a medical research center. Foa (1956) asked Israeli factory workers what they thought was the best way for a foreman to handle difficult situations involving workers, and how their foremen usually dealt with such incidents. Favorable evaluations of their foremen increased as the discrepancies decreased in how the workers thought the foremen should behave and how the foremen usually behaved. Tsui (1982) found that in a sample of 217 middle managers, the managers' reputation for effectiveness correlated with their bosses', subordinates', and peers' expectations about the managers' role.

Santee and Vanderpol (1976) correlated the degree to which professors conformed to students' expectations. One group of students rated their satisfaction with different professorial behaviors; another group of students indicated which behaviors were typical of their professors and rated the professors' esteem. The professors' conformity to the students' expectations correlated .56 with the students' ratings of respect and .61 with the students' ratings of the professors' value to the university. Fulfilling campaign promises with legislation approved by Congress has been used as an index of public satisfaction with a president's performance. Reelected presidents from Wilson to Nixon fulfilled 75% of their pledges. Jimmy Carter, who fulfilled 60% of his campaign promises, failed to win reelection. The failure was also attributed to the importance of his failed pledge to reduce unemployment and inflation (Krukones, 1985). Because he had been able to fulfill so many of his campaign promises, Bill Clinton was reelected in 1996 and ended his second term in of-

[4]See also Merei (1949), Pellegrin (1953), Thrasher (1927), and Whyte (1943).

fice with high approval ratings despite the scandals that had marred his presidency.

Esteem and Leadership

Interviews with 11 chief executive officers led Bruce (1986) to conclude that the CEO's status and the power accruing from their top position in the firm were not enough to ensure their success in office. Their first task was to gain acceptance and to get a lot of people in the organization to know and trust them personally. They had to see the company and to be seen. The CEOs took control in such a way that their firms began to take on their personal character.

Esteem and Successful Influence. Bird (1940) concluded that leadership reflects the esteem in which the member is held. Similarly, Homans (1950) proposed that those of "higher social rank" in a group initiated the interactions with others. Lazarsfeld, Berelson, and Gaudet (1948) suggested that the influence on opinion of personal contact depended on trust in esteemed persons. Sims and Manz (1981) noted that esteemed leaders attract more attention to themselves and, therefore, could serve as models in organizational life. Rosenthal and Frank (1956) reasoned that the efficacy of psychotherapy depended on the patient's confidence in the therapist.

Brim (1954) discovered that mothers were more willing to adopt recommended child-rearing practices if they esteemed the physician who suggested the new methods. But esteem of the physician was not enough to sustain the new behavior. To sustain the new behavior, approval and support from their husbands was also required. Lanzetta and Haythorn (1954) observed that the more students esteemed their instructors, the more their opinions would coalesce with those of the instructors.

Garrison (1933) obtained a correlation of .82 between the tendency of high school seniors to be admired and their tendency to be chosen as leaders. Page (1984) showed that U.S. presidents from the 1930s to the 1970s could move public opinion on such issues as inflation, energy, foreign policy, and civil rights only if their performance in office was approved by the public. If their performance was disapproved, they either had no effect or actually pushed people farther from their positions.

Sociometric Evidence. In sociometric studies, members of a group nominate the person or persons in the group with whom they spend the most time or with whom they prefer to work, to play, and so on. "Stars" receive many nominations; "isolates" receive few or none. As more attractive persons, stars are higher in esteem than isolates. In his seminal sociometric studies, Moreno (1934/1953) observed that the higher the esteem of group members, the more nominations they received and the greater was the volume of words expected and accepted from them by other members. The esteemed member was more frequently permitted to assume the initiative and to terminate activities. In the same way, H. H. Jennings (1947) found that the sociometrically "overchosen" in a girls' institution exhibited four times as much behavior described as "making new events happen" or "enlarging the extent of activities" as the "average chosen." When the girls were free to choose a leader, H. H. Jennings (1943) observed, they tended to select someone who displayed spontaneity and enlarged the field of action for others. C. A. Gibb (1950) and Borgatta (1954) indicated that ratings of the effectiveness of leaders were highly related to the leaders' ratings as desired work partners but were unrelated to their ratings as persons desired as friends. The member who showed a great deal of initiative and participation attracted a large portion of the positive emotional responses of the other group members. Similarly, Newsletter, Feldstein, and Newcomb (1938) found that an individual's leadership in a group was determined largely by the cordiality received from others rather than by the leader's cordiality toward others.

Peer and Buddy Nominations. The highly chosen tend to be successful leaders in future settings. This tendency has resulted in the use of nominations by peers and buddies to forecast the subsequent success of leaders in the military. From World War II onward, peer ratings of esteem by cadets in Officer Candidate School or the military service academies have been found to be one of the best single predictors of subsequent success as a regular U.S. Army officer (Haggerty, Johnson, & King, 1954). Thus, a correlation of .51 was obtained between esteem among peers at West Point and rated success as an infantry officer 18 months later. A correlation of .42 was obtained between esteem among fellow trainees in Officer

Candidate School and combat performance as a U.S. Army officer (Baier, 1947). Similar results were reported by the U.S. Air Force (1952) and the U.S. Marine Corps (Wilkins, 1953; Williams & Leavitt, 1947b).

Evidence from Leaderless Group Discussions (LGDs). A strong case can be made for the personal factor from studies using an initially leaderless group discussion (LGD) to assess esteem and leadership during the discussion and again in real life as much as two years later. In these small-group discussions, in which no member is appointed leader, high correlations were found between ratings by observers or peers of the value and contribution of members to the group and their influence and emergence as leaders of the group (Bass, 1954a). Moreover, those members who were esteemed most highly by their peers had the most influence on the other members and on the group's decision, according to objective measurements of changes in opinion (Bass, 1955a). Elsewhere, Bass (1961c) reported that attempts to lead were more successful among able and esteemed leaders, especially when the congruence between the leaders' esteem and self-esteem was great. Wurster, Bass, and Alcock (1961) obtained results with 95 LGD participants indicating that they felt more responsive toward the suggestions and opinions of persons whom they esteemed than toward those of people in general. Thus the highly esteemed person had an advantage in opportunities to influence others because the others tended to feel responsive toward his or her behavior. Bass (1954a) reported a median adjusted correlation of .51 for 17 studies of emergence as leader in LGD and subsequent appraisals of meritorious leadership performance from one week to two years later. The criteria included rated merit as a U.S. Army cadet and officer (Weislogel, 1953), nominations for positions of leadership in a sorority or fraternity (Bass & White, 1951), rated potential and general merit as a civil service administrator (Arbous & Maree, 1951), rated adequacy as a foreman (Mandell, 1950a; Wurster & Bass, 1953), and rated suitability for the foreign service of South Africa (Vernon, 1950). Similar findings were reported for British supervisors (Handyside & Duncan, 1954), Finnish foremen (Rainio, 1955), and military trainees (Gleason, 1957).[5]

[5]As will be noted in Chapter 35, the LGD is now a routine part of management assessment centers.

Leadership and Perceived Helpfulness. Leaders will be successful to the degree that they are seen as having the potential to be helpful. In 72 business and governmental conferences, Crockett (1955) noted that emergent leaders were rated as members who were most needed by the group. In another study of industry, N. A. Rosen (1969) obtained ratings of workers' preference for eight foremen. Foremen who were high and low in preference then changed places. The findings suggested that the new foremen were evaluated in terms of their ability to help the group. The greater the consensus among the workers in weeks 1 to 10 that the new foreman "is our leader," the greater was the increase in productivity and cohesiveness in weeks 11 to 16. Also, S. Rosen, Levinger, and Lippitt (1961) found that schoolchildren and college students rated helpfulness and fairness as the most important traits that enable individuals to influence others; and that adults rated fairness first and helpfulness second in importance. Kelman (1970), Olsen (1968), and Sells (1968) placed particular importance on the confidence and trust that followers had in their leaders. In turn, such confidence and trust in the leader were linked to the competence of the leader. In a report on 72 men in the Antarctic for a year, P. D. Nelson (1964b) concluded that what differentiated leaders from nonleaders in maintaining their esteem was their stronger motivational commitment to the group.

Feelings about the helpfulness of leaders are multidimensional. R. D. Mann, Gibbard, and Hartman (1967) obtained college students' expressions of feeling toward different leaders as well as descriptions of the followers' responses. The data were factor-analyzed. Among the factors that emerged were feelings about the leader as an analyst, as an authority figure, and as committed to the leader-member relationship. The investigators found that the leaders were esteemed for supporting the members' independence, identification, and social closeness. But M. G. Evans (1973) and Lawler and Hall (1970) noted that such perceived esteem in leaders can be induced in subordinates by their own needs and desires for particular behaviors by leaders. The distortion becomes great in the charismatic leader who may be perceived by followers as a savior. Leaders of therapy groups were seen as more helpful if they were evaluated as higher in self-disclosure and as more mentally healthy (May & Thompson, 1973). Bolman (1973) reported on the extent to which therapeutic improvement occurred according to individuals' and peers' ratings of the members of therapy groups. A favorable characterization of the therapist helped, but Bolman failed to replicate previous findings in which liking the therapist as a person contributed to improvement in the members. Though how well one is liked may increase one's emergence as a leader (Schubert et al., 1974), being liked is not necessarily a substitute for esteem in contributing to the leader's performance.

Visibility, Likeability, Esteem, and Leadership. Numerous commentators have pointed out that it is important for aspiring managers to make themselves visible to those with higher authority in order to increase their prospects for promotion. Tagiuri and Kogan (1957) found that self-confidence enhanced an individual's visibility in a group. Although visibility made some contribution to a person's emergence as a leader, it did not make as much of a contribution as did the person's perceived value to the group.

Being liked, popular, and chosen as a friend tend to make some contribution to emergent leadership, but not as much as esteem does. Numerous investigators have found nominations received for leader and for friend to be positively correlated.[6] Duncan (1984) observed that managers who were first seen as friends by employees could then be admitted to the employee's "humor network." Perceived friends could become initiators and foci of work-related jokes. However, friendship tended to correlate less with leadership than did other variables, such as nominations for followership and amount of participation (Lana, Vaughan, & McGinnies, 1960).

Bass (1960) found that influence is more strongly associated with one's sociometrically rated value and ability than one's sociometrically determined popularity and visibility. Table 10.1 shows the results of such a sociometric study of 203 salesmen. In each of their sales units, the salesmen nominated seven others as "liked as a coworker" and rejected seven. They repeated these nominations for "value to the company," "ability to solve the company's problems," and "influence." Each salesman's score was the number of his nominations less the number of rejections by others on each criterion. His visibility was the percentage of all salesmen in his division who knew him.

[6]See, for example, Borgatta (1954), Burnett (1951a, 1951b), Hollander and Webb (1955), and M. A. Price (1948).

Being of value and ability correlated .68 and .74 with influence; being visible correlated only .29 with influence; and being liked or popular correlated .50 with influence. Visibility and popularity were unrelated; but as Riedesel (1974) noted popularity and likeability systematically confound sociometric studies of the esteem-leadership relationship. In all, it would appear that being liked and being visible may still be of some importance to one's influence, but in general, perceived competence and values are of much more importance to leadership. Nevertheless, being visible to higher-ups remains important in moving up the career ladder. Organizations and cultures differ in what is found estimable, so it is expected that in an organizational culture in which only the "bottom line" is valued and the well-being of its constituents is disregarded, esteem will accrue to the hard-driving, ruthless leader who brings victory over competition. Polls conducted in Russia early in the twenty-first century indicate that despite the killing, imprisonment, and starvation of millions of innocent victims, and despite his authoritarian mismanagement, Stalin is still esteemed by 20% of the Russian public for successfully building the Communist Soviet Union and for defeating Nazi Germany.

Status and Esteem

It is often difficult to sort out whether members' value and contribution to the group, organization, or society is due to the information, control, and importance of their position or to their personal qualities. In fact, since more qualified people are ordinarily promoted and occupy higher-status positions in an organization, a positive correlation is expected between members' status and their esteem. This was found in experimental groups (Flint, Bass, & Pryer, 1957b). Additionally, status is often gained through personal ability and effort. Persons who are likely to be esteemed because of their personal characteristics are also likely to be promoted to positions of greater worth in formal hierarchical organizations. Thus esteem often leads to the achievement of a higher status (Pellegrin, 1952). Promotion to a higher status in industrial and military organizations often depends on superiors' ratings of one's worth to the organization, although, of course, upward mobility in status can also be due to chance, tradition, or favoritism—unrelated to one's esteem.

According to Sherif and Sherif (1953), those in posi-

Table 10.1 Median Intercorrelations among Five Sociometric Ratings of 203 Salesmen by Their Associates

Visibility	Popularity	Value	Ability	Influence
Visibility	−.05	.39	.38	.29
Popularity		.60	.49	.50
Value			.73	.68
Ability				.74

SOURCE: Adapted from Bass (1960, p. 282).

tions of control (high status) are perceived by others to be endowed with superior personal traits. Perlmutter (1954) confirmed that the greater the perceived capacity of individuals to influence the perceiver, the more traits will be assigned to them and the more desirable the traits will be. In the same way, Courtney, Greer, Masling, and Orlans (1953) noted that military recruits who were given positions with the most responsibility and authority were most esteemed. Barnard (1951) agreed that abilities would be imputed to persons of higher status even when the abilities could not be recognized. This, he suggested, was a way that low-status followers maintained their own self-esteem. The followers rationalized that they were being *persuaded* by the most capable members of the organization, rather than *coerced* only because of differences in status.

Esteem was found to be higher for individuals with the status of owners and professionals in agricultural communities (Hooker, 1928). Likewise, among three canteen work groups, those living at higher socioeconomic levels were more esteemed (Mumford, 1959). Prestige and popularity were observed to be higher for persons who were heads of organizations in their communities (J. E. White, 1950). D. T. Campbell (1953) noted that among the crews of 7 out of 10 submarines, the commanding officer was most esteemed. He received the most nominations as the person others wanted to see in command. Merit ratings (esteem) of military officers tended to be higher if their military rank was higher (Robins, Willemin, & Brueckel, 1954). A review of efficiency ratings from 1922 to 1945 revealed a positive correlation between the rank of officers and their merit ratings. In Korea, those at higher grades in the service received more favorable ratings of their performance in combat (U.S. Army, 1952). In a study of 1,900 military personnel, Masling, Greer, and Gilmore (1955) found that the higher individuals

ranked in the military organization, the greater the number of favorable sociometric mentions they tended to receive in regard to both military and personal matters.

The fact that status and esteem are correlated may be a valid assessment of the value of both the positions and the personal qualities of the people involved. When status and esteem are truly mismatched, the lack of correlation may reflect the overevaluation of esteem associated with an accurate appraisal of status. Thus almost all high-ranking military officers are usually appraised as excellent or superior in performance. An appraisal may also reflect the overevaluation of a position because of the high esteem earned by the occupant. For example, although paraprofessionals have lower status than registered nurses, the importance of the paraprofessionals' position may be raised significantly in the eyes of patients if the patients think their well-being depends more on the performance of the paraprofessionals than on that of the nurses.

Maintaining Esteem and Status. Subordinates value and esteem leaders who are considerate of their needs and who avoid being domineering (D. T. Campbell, 1953). Leaders will lose their esteem if they fail a group or if, as was mentioned earlier, they use their esteem to coerce members into accepting their influence and if they threaten to withdraw support and affection. Conversely, the esteem of leaders will be enhanced if they effectively contribute to their groups' success (Bass, 1960). More important positions and higher status will be assigned to those who are seen to contribute or who have the potential to contribute to the well-being of others or the success of the organization.

Trust

Americans' trust of business, government, organized religion, and one another has been declining rapidly in the past four decades. In 1996, 55% of those polled said they had confidence in big corporations, big government, and organized religion. By the early twenty-first century, such trust was down to 23%. Since 1960, trust in other people had declined from 50% to 30%. The many business scandals and stock and accounting frauds accelerated the mistrust of business corporations. There was a marked decline in trust in companies of 19% between 2002 and 2006. The attacks of 9/11 and the war on terror caused a turnaround in trust of government. Americans' trust in their fellow citizens rose to 65% (compared with 3% in Brazil). Nevertheless, the increasing disparity in the incomes and wealth of the rich and the poor in the United States and the economic segregation of the rich and poor in urban neighborhoods and suburbs increased mistrust among the poor (Purdy, 2004). A similar decline in trust occurred in many other countries. In December 2005, a poll in France found only 1% of voters saying they would support President Chirac's reelection in 2007. Declines in the public's trust in business ranged from 11% to 36% in Germany, Turkey, Canada, and Spain in polls in 2004 and 2005. Trust in business fell from 5% to 9% during those same years in Mexico, China, Indonesia, India, Britain, and Brazil (Kingsbury, 2006).

Meaning. Trust in a person has been defined as "reliance on the . . . authenticity of a person . . . in the absence of absolute knowledge or proof of . . . the truth. . . . Trust represents our best guess that [the person] is as he or she is purported to be" (Fairholm, 1995, p. 11). Trust in a leader is a follower's belief and willingness to act on the basis of the leader's words, actions, and decisions (McAllister, 1995). In trusting the leader, the follower increases vulnerability to the leader (Deutsch, 1962). Blind trust with no realistic knowledge of the leader, or with no assurance of the truth about the leader, is fraught with risk (Fairholm, 1995).

Importance to Leadership. Trust in the leader has become a particularly prominent issue in the study of leadership. Brinkly (1994) argued that the erosion in public

confidence in our politicians is due to lack of trust in their leadership. For Butler and Cantrell (1984), interpersonal trust is a determinant of the amount of cooperation to be expected between subordinate and superior. Podsakoff et al. (1990) found that it was the important intervening variable in a factor-analytic investigation of transformational leadership. Jung and Avolio (2000) conducted a controlled brainstorming experiment with 194 undergraduate business upperclassmen in groups led by two confederates who were trained in either transformational or transactional leadership. The task was to recommend ideas for improving education. Path analyses showed that trust in the leaders and value congruence with them mediated the extent to which the quality of the ideas (long-term orientation and innovativeness) was significantly augmented by transformational but not transactional leadership. There were both direct and indirect effects on the participants' subjective satisfaction with the leadership.

"There is scarcely any form of economic activity, from running a dry-cleaning business to fabricating large-scale integrated circuits, that does not require social collaboration" (Fukuyama, 1997, p. 6). Unless it can be tightly controlled by habit, contract, law, rules, norms, and regulations, such collaboration requires trusting relationships to be effective. *Mutual trust* is an important outgrowth of the exchange between a leader and a member of a group. As leader-member exchanges (LMXs) continue, the leader and the member evaluate each other's ability, benevolence, and integrity. If the evaluations are positive, trust is built between them (Brower, Schoorman, & Tan, 2000).

Correlates of Trust in the Leader. Ordinarily, trust in the leader is likely to be correlated with the leader's esteem. It involves confident positive expectations by the follower of the leader's motives regarding the follower in circumstances that are risky for the follower (Boon & Holmes, 1991). The leader's status also makes a difference. Those who were higher in status, as indexed by their position in the organizational hierarchy of a large Australian mining firm, were more trusting of their superiors. They perceived themselves to be more influential than did those supervisors and employees of lower status (Savery & Waters, 1989). Transformational leaders appeared to generate more trust. Den Hartog (1997) found that among 1,289 subordinates in six Dutch organizations, trust in management was greater with charismatic, inspirational, and individualized considerate leadership than with transactional leadership. Jung and Avolio (2000) obtained a correlation of .56 between experimentally created transformational leadership and rated trust in the leader. Blackburn (1992) reported that trust in a leader was increased by participation of subordinates in decision making, and by clear and open communications (Blackburn, 1992). Leaders who explained decisions, delegated, shared control, and showed concern also contributed to trust (Whitener, Brodt, Korsgaard, et al., 1998). But in South Africa, Engelbrecht and Cloete (2000) did not find (as they expected) that how long the supervisor and subordinate had worked together moderated the effects of the supervisor's integrity and benevolence on the trust in the supervisor.

Antecedents to trust in quality LMX relationships have included credibility (Butler, 1991), congruence of values (Sitkin & Roth, 1993), and previous positive outcomes (Gabarro, 1979). Brockner, Siegel, Daly, et al. (1997) conducted telephone interviews with 354 employees. The investigators found that subordinates trusted management if procedures were fair ($r = .64$); the outcomes of their supervisor's decisions were favorable to them ($r = .63$); and they supported their supervisor ($r = .70$).

Unconditional trust was expected to be based on mutual respect and shared values (Jones & George, 1998). Hua (2003) argued that the subordinate's reaction to uncertainty and vulnerability serves as a frame for evaluation of management behavior, generally, which in turn affects trust in the supervisor. Supportive evidence was collected in China and the United States. Kouzes & Posner (1993, p. 108) summed it up: "To be trusted . . . we [leaders] have to extend ourselves by being available, by sharing . . . personal experiences, and by making connections with the experiences and aspirations of our constituents."

Personality and Trust in the Leader. Leaders differ consistently from each other in personal traits associated with how much they can be trusted by their subordinates. Subordinates' trust in their supervisors was linked to the supervisors' integrity and benevolence (Mayer, Davis, & Schoorman, 1995) and to the leader's integrity and ability (Boies & Corbett, 2005). Along with integrity and

benevolence, supervisors' competence appears linked—though to a lesser extent—with the tendency to be trusted (Engelbrecht & Cloete, 2000). Other personality traits of consequence to being trusted include loyalty, respect, openness, receptivity, discreetness, fairness, honesty, judgment, and consistency. It remains controversial whether or not the traits also apply to supervisors' trust in their subordinates (Schindler & Thomas, 1993). Behaviors and expressed attitudes that increase a leader's trustworthiness in the eyes of followers include caring, helping, moral character, and willingness to serve others.

Stages in the Trust Relationship. According to Lewicki, Stevenson, and Bunker (1997), trust between people is dynamic and develops over time. In the leader-follower relationship, early on a follower's trust in the leader is a matter of calculation. The follower learns under which circumstances the leader rewards performance and under which circumstances the leader imposes discipline and penalties. In the second stage of the development of trust, the follower learns about the leader's attitudes and behavior in different contexts and the leader's reactions in different situations. In this second stage of trust development, inconsistencies in the leader's reactions can be forgiven if they are understood by the follower. In the third stage of trust in the leader, the follower identifies with the leader's wants and intentions. The follower appreciates and understands the leader's needs and can effectively act for the leader. The leader can be confident that his or her interests will be protected—for the leader's development of trust in the follower will parallel the three stages of the follower's development. At first, the leader's trust in the follower will not be high and will also be a matter of calculation. The leader will monitor, reward, or take corrective action based on the follower's performance. Trust becomes information-based in the second stage, as the leader learns that the follower can be depended on to do the right things and to do them well. In the third stage—identification—the leader can confidently expect that the follower will be cooperative and can share their common goals. According to Lewicki, Stevenson, and Bunker's (1997) factor analyses of ratings of trust in others by 482 undergraduates, the three stages could be determined by a single general factor. The two ratings of trust with the highest factor loadings were: "This person and I really stand for the same basic things" (.88) and "This person and I share the same basic values" (.87).

Authenticity and Trust. Authenticity and trust have been stressed frequently in theory and research on leadership. I have already noted the repeated appearance of trust as an important aspect of interpersonal communications. In one of many such studies, Sgro, Worchel, Pence, and Orban (1980) obtained significant positive correlations between Rotter's Interpersonal Trust Orientation Scale for 41 cadet leaders and how satisfied their subordinates were with the leaders. The trust scores of their subordinates were related to positive evaluations of them on various dimensions of behavior, such as consideration, tolerance for freedom, persuasion, and initiation of structure. A leader caught in insincerity, duplicity, deceit, and double-dealing would be hard to trust. A trustworthy leader would be seen as expressing genuine feelings and thoughts.

Smircich and Chesser (1981) constructed and evaluated a highly reliable standardized questionnaire for subordinates to use in describing the authenticity of their superiors. Convergent validity was demonstrated. The measure of authenticity dealt with existential aspects of the superior-subordinate relationship, for example, "My relationship with my superior is open and direct." It had sociological elements ("My superior shows flexibility in carrying out the role of supervisor"), empathic aspects ("My superior could step into my shoes and know how I feel"), and social-psychological issues ("When we talk, I know my superior really listens to me"). However, authenticity did not necessarily mean mutual understanding between superiors and subordinates. The authenticity attributed to the superiors was of no consequence for 141 subordinates and 58 superiors whose respective ratings of the subordinates' performance did not agree.

Building Trust

Hackman and Johnson (1991) suggested five nonverbal ways for the leader to build trust and confidence: (1) Maintain eye contact when talking to others and avoid shifting the eyes, looking away, and downcast eyes. (2) Use spontaneous gestures to emphasize points to convey emotional intensity, and avoid too many pauses or speaking too rapidly. (3) Maintain an open, relaxed pos-

ture and avoid keeping hands and arms crossed and close to the body. (4) Maintain a conversational speaking tone with a varied rate, pitch, and volume. (5) Avoid wearing dark glasses, which convey a stereotype of untrustworthiness. Six other suggestions they made are: (1) Be consistent by knowing your own values and clarifying to yourself what you believe; (2) Appreciate the followers and what they believe. (3) Affirm shared values. (4) Help followers to develop. (5) Create a sense of direction. (6) Sustain hope.

Trust in leaders is enhanced by the way they explain their decisions (Whitener, Brodt, Korsgaard, et al., 1998). If subordinates judge the explanation for the decision procedure and the process to be adequate, the decision maker will be rated as more trustworthy than if the explanation and process are judged inadequate (Shapiro, 1991). Adequacy requires more information about the logic and fairness of the decision (Bies, Shapiro, & Cummings, 1988). Lee Kuan Yew was reelected to office by overwhelming majorities for 30 years and was of prime importance in Singapore's rapid economic development, cultural maturity, and political stability as a "guided" democracy. Despite its lack of natural resources, the small former British colony rose in the 30 years to a modern postindustrial state with one of the world's highest per capita incomes. An important factor was the trust placed in Lee by the electorate; this trust was built by his words and deeds. Twenty-six of his annual National Day Rally speeches were content-analyzed by M. D. Barr (2000–2002). His rhetoric appealed to tradition and the desirability of continuity to connect present and future goals to the past. He noted past successes and the need to overcome threats to future successes. He expressed confidence that constituents would meet present and future challenges. He also expressed self-confidence, though indirectly—modesty is a requirement of Chinese culture. Similarities between Lee and his constituents, rather than their differences, were emphasized, as was the collective identity of the three largest ethnic groups: Chinese, Muslims, and Tamils. "We swim or sink together." Lee pointed to adherence to a specific set of values and principles to gain the electorate's trust.

Elsbach and Elofson (2000) conducted an experiment comparing explanations for decisions that were hard or easy to understand and were or were not legitimated. In contrast to technical explanations, which were hard to understand, trust was much higher when the explanation was in simple language and easy to understand, with cues about the motives and character of the decision maker rather the logic of the decision. Legitimation was of consequence only when the decisions were hard to understand. The authors suggest that the decision maker may not be trusted if decisions are explained only in technical language that is hard to understand or dependent on expert systems. To build long-term trust, leaders need to spend time preparing explanations of their decisions and need to consider the language and labeling of the explanations.

More on Effects of Trust

To paraphrase Kouzes and Posner (1996, p. 5), the credibility of a leader's message rests on trust in the messenger. Such trust depends on belief in the messenger as honest, forward-looking, inspiring, and competent. One cannot lead successfully without trust. Considerable evidence bolsters the expectation that effective teamwork hinges on mutual trust between team members and the team leader (Day, 2001). The level of trust between school principals and teachers correlated with the teachers' agreement about teacher certification policy regardless of their principal's position on the issue (Steele & Pinto, 2005).

Martin (1996) examined the effect on 22,000 subordinates' ratings of 4,454 executives when the executives exhibited more trust-directed behaviors, and the effect on subordinates' favorable attitudes. Trust-directed behaviors of the executives were strongly correlated with subordinates' favorable attitudes; this correlation was stronger even than correlations of rated "executive vision" behaviors with subordinates' attitudes. However, trust combined with vision yielded the most favorable attitudes. Martin pointed to the value of executives' establishing an organizational environment in which trust is pervasive and essential to successful leadership.

Dirks (2000) examined trust in the coach among 355 basketball players in a men's college conference. He found that it correlated .57 with future performance and .60 with past performance of the teams. The teams' talent and experience added to the prediction of performance, but trust in the leader was an antecedent as well as a consequence of successful performance by these teams. A meta-analysis of 106 findings based on 847 to 10,631 cases was conducted by Dirks and Ferrin (2002). They examined antecedents and consequences of trust in the leader. Antecedents that were predictive of trust in the leader included transformational leadership (.72), transactional leadership (.59), and participative leadership (.46). Perceived distributive, procedural, and interactional justice, respectively, predicted trust with correlations of .50, .61, and .65, but length of relationship did not predict it ($r = .01$). Unmet expectations correlated $-.40$ with trust. In turn, trust predicted outcomes including job satisfaction, .51; job performance, .16; and various organizational citizenship behaviors. Intention to quit correlated $-.40$ with trust. In another study, of 1,686 employees, when decisions were made by higher authority with outcomes perceived as unfavorable to the employees, such as relocating work facilities or ordering job layoffs, the establishment of trust in supervision overcame what would have been adverse employee reactions to the decisions (Brockner, Siegel, Daly, et al., 1997).

Trust in management and in the immediate supervisor also goes along with commitment to the leadership and the organization, according to many studies. An ethical trusting relationship between subordinate and superior is established if the subordinate is able to align personal with organizational values, to disclose thoughts and feelings, to seek and learn from constructive feedback, to think and behave independently, to move beyond self-interests, and to work in a warm, friendly, open, and cooperative environment (Rusaw, 2000).

Summary and Conclusions

The value of a person's position in a group or organization is the person's *status*; the value of the person to others—to the group or organization—is the person's *esteem*. Consensus about status and esteem is usually established quickly. More knowledge is usually associated with those in higher-status occupations and positions. Throughout history, differences in the value of positions and differences in the value of occupations have been recognized. In 2002, the average compensation of a CEO was 200 times that of the lowest-paid employee. The rate doubled by 2005. Upward mobility in status is sought and downward mobility is dissatisfying. Individual members of a group or organization can be more coercive if their accorded status depends on their personal control of what is desired by others in the group. Such members will attempt more leadership. However, continued direction, particularly if it is coercive, may lead to resentment and loss of esteem. High-status people can also be more influential because others pay more attention to them and tend to judge their behavior as more acceptable. High-status people can break the rules more easily ("The king can do no wrong"). Conflict arises if accorded status is mismatched with self-accorded status, but the status accorded to figureheads without real power will still give them some influence.

Individuals tend to choose friends whose social status is similar to their own. Group members, however, tend to prefer highly esteemed and high-status persons for positions of leadership. Members interact more frequently with these highly esteemed and high-status persons than they do with low-status members without esteem; they also accept high-status, highly esteemed people more readily as authority figures, justify their actions on behalf of the group more readily, and exhibit more tolerance of their deviant behavior. The highly esteemed members with high status are permitted to suggest innovations in the group, but they are not expected to interrupt or otherwise to behave inconsiderately toward low-status members with less esteem.

Members of a group quickly size up the leadership potential of a new member. Status evaluations that are made on first acquaintance are rather highly correlated with evaluations made several weeks later. Group members tend to choose other members, as well as leaders, whose values, interests, and personalities are similar to their own. They tend to regard leaders as more attractive than members of lower status, and to consider both the positive and the negative actions of high-status members as legitimate.

We tend to evaluate ourselves in terms of the reactions of others. The more attractive the group, the greater its impact on the members' evaluations of themselves. For this reason, a loss of status is damaging to the members' self-respect, particularly if the downward mobility is interpreted as evidence of decreased liking by other group members. A loss of status may be accompanied by a decline in performance, reduced liking for the task and the group, and feelings of hostility. However, ordinary members may reject the opportunity to rise in status if doing so involves radical changes in responsibility and style of living that are in conflict with their self-concept and system of values. Thus those who become leaders appear more willing to accept the responsibilities that accompany the rewards of high status.

The concomitants of esteem include respect, admiration, being liked as a person, and being judged as competent. But esteem may also be earned for irrelevant reasons. Furthermore, esteem may be misjudged as status, and vice versa. Members can be more persuasive if their esteem depends on their being perceived as able to solve the group's problems. To gain esteem, they first need to conform to the rules, but thereafter they can begin to innovate and deviate without losing their esteem. Assumed similarity of beliefs, attitudes, and values contributes to being esteemed and attractive to others. We lose esteem by violating others' expectations of us.

Considerable evidence from sociometric research—use of the LGD, and studies of students, salesmen, managers, school principals, military officers, and therapists—demonstrates the contributions of esteem and perceived helpfulness to success as a leader above and beyond considerations of visibility and likeability. The esteemed leader may achieve charisma in the eyes of others.

Trust of followers in the leader is linked to the leader's esteem. Strongly related to trust in the leader is the follower's perception of the leader's competence, caring, integrity, and willingness to serve others. Also important are the leader's accuracy and consistency in communications that explain decisions in simple, easily understood language. Perceived authenticity is likely to make a difference as well.

11

Power and Leadership

Power as an engine of influence and leadership has been of concern to priests, philosophers, and kings since the beginnings of civilization and to chiefs and medicine men before that. Who can influence whom clearly depends on who is more powerful and who is less so. Only with God on his side could Moses persuade the pharaoh to let his people go. Shakespeare's plays are filled with concern about power and innocence, failing power, and personality and power (Hill, 1985). "To say a leader is preoccupied with power is like saying that a tennis player is preoccupied with making shots his opponent cannot return" (Gardner, 1986a, p. 5). This chapter explores the meaning of social power, the bases of power, and how power contributes to leadership in societies, communities, formal organizations, and small groups.[1]

Definitions of Social Power

Power is the force that can be applied to work. It is the rate at which energy can be absorbed. Social power is the ability to take actions and to initiate interactions. It is a force underlying social exchanges in which the dependent person in the exchange relationship has less power and the person with more power is able to obtain compliance with his or her wishes. Compliance implies acceptance of the more powerful person's influence. It can be assent given enthusiastically or reluctantly. The compliant person depends on the more powerful person for desired outcomes that cannot be obtained from other sources (Emerson, 1964).

Power as Force

Power has been defined as the production of intended effects (Russell, 1938); the ability to apply force (Bierstedt, 1950); the right to prescribe behavioral patterns for others (Janda, 1960); and the intended, successful control of others (Wrong, 1968). But, as Gardner (1986a, p. 5) observed, "power does not need to be exercised to have its effect—as any hold-up man can tell you." Most behavioral theorists maintain that power can be exerted without intention. Cartwright (1965) conceived of power in terms of controlling information and personal affection. Bierstedt (1950) focused on prestige.

Simon (1957) saw power as a manifestation of an asymmetry in the relationship between A and B. For J. R. P. French (1956), as well as Cartwright (1959a, 1959b), the power of A over B equals the maximum force that A can induce on B minus the maximum resisting force that B can mobilize in the opposing direction. For Dahl (1957), "A has power over B to the extent that A can get B to do something that B would not otherwise do." For Pfeffer (1981a), power is A's ability to change the course of action of B from what B would otherwise have done. A can overcome B's resistance or reluctance to act. For Presthus (1960), power was a matter of A's and B's rapport with each other. Emerson (1964) emphasized the dependency relationship between A and B. If B is more dependent on A than vice versa, B has less power than A. B's dependence on A can be due to A's control of resources that B cannot obtain elsewhere. It can be due to A's ability to reduce uncertainties for B, or to A's ability to cope with critical contingencies in the attainment of organizational goals based on the organization's strategy, environment, or technology (Daft, 1983). A can obtain B's compliance with A's wishes. Thus Bagozzi and Phillips (1982) calculated that 64% of the power that suppliers have over wholesale distributors can be accounted for by the inability of the distributors to find other suppliers, the critical value of the resources controlled by the suppliers, the

[1] Power and its effects on leadership were the subject of comprehensive reviews by Cartwright (1959a, 1959b, 1965), House (1984, 1988), Podsakoff and Schriesheim (1985a), and Yukl (1981), among others.

countervailing power of the distributors, and how much business is involved. According to Bennis and Nanus (1985, p. 17), power is "the basic energy needed to initiate and sustain action . . . the capacity to translate intention into reality and sustain it." For Burns (1978), power can be wielded nakedly, as when people are treated as things; or it can be relational, collective, and purposeful.

Power as Social Exchange

Thibaut and Kelley (1959) regarded power as an exchange relationship in which one member has control over another's behavior or fate. As Gardner (1986a, p. 5) said,

> It is possible to think of the exercise of power as a kind of exchange. You want something from me and you have the power to produce in return certain outcomes that I want—or want to avoid. You can give me an A or flunk me. You can promote me to supervisor or reduce me to clerk. You can raise my salary or lower it. You can give or withhold love.

Individuals tend to maintain a balance in the exchange of social values (Homans, 1958). The differentiation of social roles that results in organizations is based initially on such exchange relations (Gouldner, 1960).

Blau (1964) and Adams and Romney (1959) saw power as negative in A's use of deprivation, aversive stimulation, and sanctions to control B's behavior. Harsanyi (1962a, 1962b) took a broader view and weighed social benefits against social costs in defining power relations. Bass (1960) defined the power of A and B as A's control of what B needs and values. If B is satiated or uninterested in what A controls, A loses power over B. Burns (1978) agreed. Cartwright (1965) emphasized the importance of ecological control: power can be exercised by controlling resources or necessities, by occupying space, or by avoiding or boycotting a location. Thus a leader's power is reflected in the ability to impose standards, limits, and boundaries on a group and to indicate what is expected of members to obtain rewards or avoid harm. It also hinges on the ability to enforce such rules. The boundaries are likely to be areas of increasing threat and impenetrability. This situation requires judgment by those who are being controlled about how far they can deviate without punishment (Timasheff, 1938). One way lack of power manifests itself is in hesitant speech: hedges like "I guess;" tag questions such as "Isn't it?" at the end of an affirmative sentence; and disclaimers such as "Don't get me wrong but . . .". Powerlessness also shows itself in excuses and justifications for doing the wrong thing (Hackman & Johnson, 1991, p. 99)

The social exchange can be seen in the exchange relationship between the Roman patron and his freedmen clients and between the ward boss and his neighborhood constituents. The clients' and constituents' votes and obedience provided the bases of power for the patron and the ward boss, in return for which the followers received protection, security, and material support. Lobbyists can exert power over state and federal legislators through financial support of their political campaigns. The political leader in the United States disperses tangible divisible rewards, favors, contracts and services to his or her constituents. For example, Borowiec's (1975) study of 83 Polish-American leaders in Buffalo indicated that they provided constituents with special information and personal assistance in dealing with public agencies. Privatization of government agency functions has meant billions of dollars in no-bid contracts for private firms in exchange for political support.

The exchange calculus may be complex; leaders of more powerful constituents are likely to be more powerful than leaders of less powerful followers. The leaders can mobilize the power of their followers and can be granted or deprived of power by their constituents. In combination with their constituents, they can collectively acquire more power (Burns, 1978). This mutuality in the power relation is seen when constituents must complete their assignments if they and the leader are to be rewarded. The slowdown, inattention, or corruption of constituents can result in a loss of benefits for the leader.

Power Is Not Synonymous with Influence

House (1984) operationalized the measurement of power by its effects. Power was equated with "the capacity to produce effects on others. These effects are achieved by the exercise of authority, expertise, political influence and charisma . . . each having a different base or source and each having different effects" (p. 26). But it is useful to maintain the distinction between power and influence, although the boundaries between power and influence remain unclear (Faucheux, 1984). Unfortunately, "power" is often used synonymously with "influence." Tautologies have been endemic. We observe that A influences B; therefore, we conclude that A has more power than B. Inferences about power and its effects must begin with measures of power that are completely independent of observed relations between A and B. The observed relations are a product of the power differences between A and B, not the behavior observed. Leadership can be conceived of as the exercise of power (Berlew & Heller, 1983). Thus Milewicz (1983) concluded, after interviews with purchasing agents about their relations with their many suppliers, that the tendency of the agents to exert leadership in dealing with suppliers was a consequence of the agents' self-perceived power. The agents had such power because they could, for example, control the length of the order cycle. Whether they fully used this power to exert leadership depended on their personal desire to be influential.

Leadership and influence obviously are a function of power. Power is the potential to influence. It is the probable rate and amount of influence of a person or the occupant of a position. Thus, for instance, Barber (1966) inferred that the power relations among members of a legislative committee could be accounted for by such factors as the rate of success in getting suggestions accepted and the rate of agreement received. Although Lord (1977) found that for 144 undergraduates, perceived leadership and social power were related, the unexplained variance required maintaining separate conceptual distinctions between them. Follett (1983) constructed a 20-item scale to measure the power of a manager. The scores obtained were related to the structuring leadership of the manager and to subordinates' compliance with requests, but were clearly distinguishable from the scale of power.

We need to separate the holding of power because of: (1) one's person, (2) one's office, (3) the willingness to exercise it, and (4) the tendency actually to do so. Studies tend to confuse all four causes and sometimes even fail to distinguish between power and influence.

Moderators of the Effects of Power

Status, gender, personality, and subordinates' power moderate the effects of a leader's power.

Status. How leaders use power will depend on their status. A leader higher in the organizational hierarchy uses more aspects of power to influence (Koslowsky & Schwarzwald, 1993). Vecchio and Sussman (1989) argued that the leader's status altered the effect of his or her power on subordinate compliance. According to Fitness (2000), the status of a leader markedly altered reactions to a situation that provoked anger. Structured interviews were conducted with 175 participants about a work-related incident with a superior, peer, or subordinate that made the respondent angry. Angry superiors were more likely to vent their anger and consider the incident closed; angry subordinates were more likely to suppress their anger and consider the incident unresolved.

Gender. When men's satisfaction with a heterosexual relationship decreases, they tend to become more coercive and unfeeling toward their partner; when women's satisfaction with the relationship declines, they tend to fall back on their *referent* power based on being liked or identified with in the relationship (Schwartzwald, 1993).

Personality. Thomas, Dickson, and Bliese (2001) found that ROTC cadets' extroversion partially mediated the relationship between the power of the cadets and their effectiveness as leaders. For 818 cadets, the *direct*-path correlation between their power and their leadership was only an insignificant .07. The *indirect*-path correlation from power to extroversion was .35; from extroversion to effective leadership it was .11.

Power of Subordinates. Power is not an absolute amount. As was already noted, it depends on the power of those to be influenced, both positively and negatively. The power of those who are influenced adds to the total power available in the situation and can be increased by the synergistic action of the leader and the followers. The leader's power may be diminished to the extent that it can be offset by the power of individual followers or of the group led. Self-managing teams clearly reduce the power of a leader (Manz & Simms, 1980).

Bass and Valenzi (1973) developed one set of five-point scales to assess a boss's power and another set of five-point scales to assess a subordinate's power. The subordinate and boss each described how frequently the boss could override or veto any decisions made by the subordinate, grant or deny promotion or salary increases to the subordinate, reverse the subordinate's priorities, control the size of the subordinate's budget, and get support from a higher authority for what he or she wanted to do. In turn, the superior and subordinate each described how frequently the subordinate could bring outside pressure to support what he or she wanted; do the opposite of what the boss wanted him or her to do; maintain final control over his or her plans, assignments, and targets, regardless of what the boss thought about them; ignore the boss and submit requests to a higher authority; and nominate or vote for who would be the boss. The differences in the power of superiors and subordinates then became the metric of importance in predicting the superiors' styles of leading the subordinates through, direction, consultation, negotiation, or the delegation of decision making (Chitayat & Venezia, 1984; Shapira, 1976).

Gardner (1986a, p. 16) pointed to the reversals that can occur between hierarchical rank in an organization and the power accompanying it: "Every experienced observer knows of cases in which such second and third level leadership is formidable—capable, for example, of paralyzing a newly appointed top executive." Gardner concluded that the efforts to reform high school curricula in the 1960s failed because of the power of rank-and-file teachers whose support was not enlisted in the attempted improvements. The power of subordinates over their superiors is widespread when the skills and knowledge of the subordinates are hard to replace. On the one hand, superiors need to guard against becoming overly dependent on subordinates with power; on the other hand, the superiors need to maintain good interpersonal relations, trust, and openness of communications with them (Kotter, 1985a).

Numerous other factors reduce subordinates' willingness to comply with the attempted influence of the power figure. For example, 240 Israeli subordinates of 40 police captains said they were less likely to comply with their captains if the captains coupled their power with acts of transactional instead of transformational leadership (Schwarzwald & Koslowsky, 1998).

Personal versus Positional Power

Personal Power

As noted before, power can derive from one's person or one's position. Although it may seem otherwise, the evidence to date suggests that prospective followers tend to consider the personal power of a highly esteemed expert more important than the legitimacy and power to reward and punish that may derive from appointment to a position of leadership. Those with personal power can grant affection, consideration, sympathy, and recognition, and can secure relationships and attachments to others (Bass, 1960). For example, Rosen, Levinger, and Lippitt (1961) asked teachers and emotionally disturbed boys to rank in order of importance six items related to power. The two groups basically agreed on the relative importance of physical strength, sociability, expertness, fairness, fearlessness, and helpfulness as sources of power. But those with personal power were seen also as able to punish others by becoming more distant, formal, cold, and businesslike.

Bass, Wurster, and Alcock (1961) demonstrated that we want to be valued and esteemed mainly by those we value and esteem. We endow these people with personal power. Hurwitz, Zander, and Hymovitch (1953) showed that we seek the affection and support of those we hold to be personally powerful. Professional personnel were continually reshuffled to form 32 sextets. The power to influence and the extent to which each member was liked after the first half hour of interaction were assessed. Those with low esteem wanted most to be liked by those with high esteem. According to Yukl and Falbe (1991), personal power is based on expertise, referent power, esteem, persuasiveness, and charisma. Transformational leaders have more personal power and accordingly generate more compliance from subordinates than do leaders lacking in personal power (Atwater & Yammarino, 1996).

Identification and Personal Power. As will be described in Chapter 21, the charismatic leader can serve as the focus of positive emotional feelings, as the ideal object for psychoanalytic transference and identification (Kelman, 1958). The transference of coping with problems to parental figures provides followers with an escape from responsibility and making decisions—let the leader do it (Fromm, 1941). Followers identify with their successful superiors. Business executives see successful superiors as symbols of achievement (Henry 1949). Leaders of gangs of delinquents become the superego of the members. By submitting to the leader, members are relieved of all personal responsibility for their antisocial activities (Deutschberger, 1947).

The charismatic leader is the ultimate in personal power. Such a leader is personally endowed by followers with infallibility, wisdom, omniscience, virtue, and supernatural powers. Personal power is manifested in the emotional bonding between the leader and followers and in the followers' dependence on the parental figure. They may have deep-seated affection for the leader. Charismatics such as the Reverend Jim Jones and Osama bin Laden have had the power to induce extremes of behavior—suicide and martyrdom—in their followers. Understanding such personal power requires an examination of strong emotional fixations that go beyond the ordinary considerations of social exchange, cognitions, rewards, and punishments.

Positional Power

The status associated with one's position gives one power to influence those who are lower in status. Custom, tradition, rules, and regulations assign power to incumbents of positions. Some superiors can be the "purveyors of rewards and punishments" to their subordinates (Krech & Crutchfield, 1948). Leaders with positional power can recommend punishments and rewards, instruct group members on what to do, and correct each member's job performance (Fiedler & Chemers, 1974). Such power can be wielded crudely or with subtlety. It may be obtrusive or unobtrusive and overt or covert (Ford, 1980). Overtly, a superior may have the power to recommend or deny pay increases to subordinates. Less obviously, a first-line supervisor, for example, may have power because of his or her influence with more powerful leaders who are higher up in the organization (Pelz, 1951). This power, in turn, may be due to the higher-ups' attitudes about the role of supervisors who are lower in the organization, as well as to the personal attributes and merit of specific supervisors. Pelz found that only those supervisors who had influence with higher-ups exhibited behavior that made

a difference in their subordinates' satisfaction. Supervisors without influence "upstairs"—although they tried—were much less likely to have effects on their subordinates. Supervisors who had influence with higher-ups were much more likely to be able to obtain rewards for their employees. Their power was greater and, therefore, what they did in their own group made more of a difference to their subordinates.

Supervisors' position in a hierarchy provides them with various sources of power. Supervisors command resources that are not ordinarily available to subordinates. They have discretion in assigning dirty and boring or interesting and challenging tasks. They can open or close doors to opportunities for the subordinates' growth and advancement. They have power to reduce uncertainty or to prolong anxiety in subordinates by providing or withholding hard information. They can act as a buffer to keep their subordinates from becoming too vulnerable to an unstable external environment and thus sustain their subordinates' optimism and hope (Hollander, 1978). According to Fiedler and Chemers (1974), leaders' positional power combines with their esteem and orientation—task or relationship—to determine whether they will be effective in designated situations. According to Yukl and Falbe (1991), the power derived from one's position is based on legitimacy, the power to reward or coerce, and access to and control of information. The use of positional power is more frequent among transactional than transformational leaders (Atwater & Yammarino, 1996).

Executives' power over decisions depends on their functionally specialized roles. Accounting executives have more power over budgeting decisions; marketing executives have more power over decisions about advertising and distributing products. Extra power also accrues to those executives involved in activities critical to the firms' strategic success, that is, to those who scan critical information and the environment for threats and opportunities (Hambrick, 1981). Similarly, although clinical interdisciplinary teams of health professionals are supposed to meet as equals, physicians dominate decisions about treatment, according to a survey of 137 team members' descriptions of 19 meetings (Fiorelli, 1988).

One's position in an organization can provide power because occupancy of the position gives control of important organizational resources and information. Control over resources such as the size of the staff, budgetary expenditures, and evaluation procedures may be involved (Gomez-Mejla, Page, & Tornow, 1982). A manager who controls such resources may be able to maintain a good working relationship with subordinates even if they have little trust in him or her (Novak & Graen, 1985). Power also accrues to positions that control critical contingencies originating in the environment or technology of the organization. This hinges on the extent to which the position makes it possible to cope with critical demands that the organization is facing (House, 1988b). The importance of positional power was illustrated when Geissler (1984) compared 131 women heads of university nursing programs with 108 women heads of other university departments. The heads of nursing felt significantly more powerful in their preferred roles than did the women who led other university departments. Position upgrades in a department were more likely to be recommended in job evaluations for those with more positional power (Welbourne & Trevor, 2000).

Socialization Processes. Members of organizations need to know how to use increases in their positional power (Taylor, 1986). Gouldner (1960) maintained that power is based on socializing norms, role differentiation, and organization that binds people together in the same social system. Gilman (1962) agreed that a power relationship is authoritative anywhere within the boundaries of a social system that gives it consensual support.

In many cultures, business transactions are conducted without written contracts because norms of obligation are regarded as binding (Macaulay, 1963). Similarly, politicians wield considerable power based on IOUs through which they can expect that favors they granted to other politicians in the past will be reciprocated when they call in their unwritten "chits" for services rendered.

Power Begets Power. House (1984) pointed out that individuals who are in positions of power not only can assert it successfully, but also can maintain and increase their level of power. Thus power-oriented individuals who gain positions of power will strive to retain and increase their power, since they are in a favored position to ensure that their power continues. Unless there are limits, incumbents of political offices tend to be reelected. (Over 99% of the members of the U.S. House of Representatives are reelected every two years.) On the basis of

interview data from a study of the administrations of California governors Ronald Reagan and Jerry Brown, Biggart and Hamilton (1987) added the corollary that for people to sustain their power in an organizational setting, they must self-consciously exercise their power to signal those working for them to be aware of obligations to carry out assignments as expected.

Varied Uses of Power

Leaders may exercise both *competitive* and *collective* power. In a survey of 350 business and university managers, Roberts (1986) observed the widespread use of power to compete with bosses, peers, and subordinates, as well as the use of collective power to collaborate with others. McClelland (1975) saw the competitive exercise of power in the exertion of personal dominance or the search for victory over adversaries. This use of power was in contrast in cooperative settings with joining with others to form shared goals to instill in the collective a sense of power to pursue such goals. Undergraduates acting as managers in a simulated organization used their control of useful information to influence those acting as subordinates only if they saw themselves as being in a cooperative situation with their "subordinates" rather than as being in a competitive or individualistic situation (Tjosvold, 1985a).

The power of supervisors could be used in four ways, according to Jones (1983). (1) Power could be *obtrusive* or *unobtrusive*; (2) it could be *situation-based* or *personal*; (3) it could be *professional* or *paternalistic*; and (4) it could be exercised over *process* or *output*. Ford (1980) agreed on the utility of looking at covert power and showed experimentally that dependent participants in peripheral positions in a network will suppress decisions, particularly if they are uncertain about the preferences of the person in the central location in the network[2] who has covert positional power.

Power and Emergence as a Leader

Power over others depends on one's control of resources to give or deny and control of rewards and punishments

---

[2]More will be said in Chapter 29 about the power and importance of central and peripheral positions in a network.

to distribute. Power manifests itself in influence over others (Bass, 1960). The labeling of positions may induce a sense of control of leaders over subordinates. Power may be sought for its own sake or for social reasons. The *personalized* leader is motivated to use power to dominate others; the *socialized* leader is motivated to use power to achieve mutually desired goals with others (McClelland, 1975).

Control and Power

Bass, Gaier, and Flint (1956) studied experimental male ROTC groups in which members varied in the amount of control they could exercise over each other's avoidance of punishment—extra marching—because of demerits. Each member drew a card that specified whether he could exercise one, two, three, or four units of control to reduce the required marching. Members with four units of control attempted twice as much leadership as those with one unit of control under high motivation, but there was no difference in unmotivated groups with no demerits requiring the extra marching. Attempted leadership increased with the amount of control a member obtained in the lottery. But the amount of control ceased to have import when what was being controlled was unimportant to the member. Thus members attempted more leadership acts when they had a lot of control and when what was controlled was desired. Members had power to influence when they had control over what was desired (Bass, Pryer, Gaier, & Flint, 1958). Members' attempts to lead increased with increases in their control and power, even if the control and power accrued from a lottery.

Power and Influence

Influence is correlated with power but is not the same. Power is the ability to exert some amount of control over others. It correlates with authority and may be coercive in its effects. Influence is more likely to depend on persuasion, with followers having more latitude to accept or reject the leader. Since "the unfettered use of power can be highly dysfunctional in creating numerous points of resistance and lingering negative feelings" (Hollander, 1985, p. 489), leaders tend to prefer persuasion rather than coercion. Nonetheless, some members of a group tend to be more influential than others if they perceive themselves as having more power. Moreover, they tend to be more satisfied than members who have little power. They are also better liked, and their attempts to influence are better accepted. Lippitt, Polansky, Redl, and Rosen (1952) found that children at a summer camp who had more power attributed to them by other children were better liked, made more attempts to influence others, and scored higher in the initiation of behavioral contagion (imitation by others without intent or awareness). The camper's perceptions of their own power were highly correlated with the power that others attributed to them. Consistent with these results, Levinger (1959) demonstrated that members of experimental groups, informed that they had more power than other members, tended to perceive themselves as actually having more power, became more assertive, and made more attempts to influence others.

Yukl (1998) noted that power has a variety of effects on influence. Power makes it possible for a leader to choose which influence tactics to use. For instance, the leader needs power to be able to make an exchange of benefits with a follower. A leader's power may enhance or diminish the effectiveness of an influence tactic. For example, a leader with considerable power will influence decisions about relevant operations more than a leader without such power. Wolman (1956) found a strong relationship between a leader's power and the leader's acceptability to members as seen by observers and in peer ratings. Ziller (1955) showed that group opinion was influenced more strongly by a high-power figure than by a low-power figure. Similarly, Levinger (1959) found that the perceived relative power of a group member correlated .55 with number of attempts to influence others, .51 with range of assertiveness, and .48 with degree of assertiveness. A change in attempts to influence tended to change along with a change in perceived power as the group continued with the problem. Dahl, March, and Nastair (1957) observed the power of some U.S. senators whose announced roll-call votes influenced other senators in making their final decisions. According to Krupp (1986), the power of school principals provided them with the influence "to develop staff to high levels of productivity and enthusiasm" (p. 100).

Michener and Burt (1975a) examined determinants of leaders' success in inducing compliance. They found that compliance was greater when leaders had reward power (i.e., justified their demands as being good for the group), had coercive power (i.e., could punish those who did not do as they had asked), and had a legitimate right to make demands on subordinates. However, neither the success nor failure of the groups, nor the approval of the leaders by their subordinates affected the leader's ability to be influential. Consistent with this, Gainson (1968) suggested that leaders would shift toward coercion of subordinates if they felt they lacked the subordinates' approval but had legitimate authority to ask for compliance, although such coercive power is often counterproductive.

Power can be counterproductive, undermining one's efforts to be a leader, because it can be threatening, particularly in unstructured situations. A. R. Cohen (1953, 1959) found that in the face of powerful leaders, followers felt more threatened in unstructured than in structured groups. Followers whose self-esteem was low also tended to feel more threatened in the presence of power, and this feeling was intensified in unstructured situations.

Motivation for Power

McNeese-Smith (1999) conducted a study of 19 nurse managers, 221 staff nurses, and 299 patients. The managers' motivation for power was negatively correlated with their leadership behaviors, as was the staff nurses' job satisfaction. Nevertheless, the nurse managers' power motivation contributed positively to patients' satisfaction. According to a study by Kirchmeyer (1990) of 225 managers of both sexes, women, but not men, who were higher in need for power were more active in office politics. Men who played office politics were high self-monitors who felt that they worked in a difficult world. Matusak (1997) suggested that in many organizations, people strive to posses and guard their power, which they see as a valuable personal possession limited to a few. But in a trusting workplace, sharing power is seen positively and is unlimited, as will be discussed in Chapter 12 when empowering others is considered.

The Bases of Power

Etzioni (1961) conceived of power as physical, material, or symbolic. He defined these three forms of power as follows, giving the bases of each:

Coercive power rests on the application or . . . threat of . . . physical sanctions . . . ; generation of frustration, . . . or controlling through force the satisfaction of needs. . . . *Remunerative* power is based on control over material resources and rewards. . . . *Normative* power rests on the allocation and manipulation of symbolic rewards and deprivations.

Parsons (1951) held that normative power could be based on esteem, prestige, and ritualistic symbols or on acceptance. Etzioni also pointed out that it would be wasteful for a leader to emphasize remunerative power if the followers were already committed to the leader's choice of action, since only normative symbolic rewards would be appropriate for such followers. Highly alienated followers would be inclined to disobey, despite material sanctions. Followers would be more likely to consider normative power legitimate and least likely to accept coercive power as legitimate.

French and Raven Model

French and Raven (1959) identified five kinds of power that quickly became popular among investigators as a way to type variations among the bases of power. Their five bases were as follows:

1. *Expert* power is based on B's perception of A's competence.
2. *Referent* power is based on B's liking or identification with A.
3. *Reward* power depends on A's ability to provide rewards for B.
4. *Coercive* power is based on B's perception that A can impose penalties for noncompliance.
5. *Legitimate* power is based on the internalization of common norms or values.

Measurement. Several earlier survey questionnaires (e.g., Hinkin & Schriesheim, 1989) preceded the Interpersonal Power Inventory (Raven, Schwarzwald, & Koslowsky, 1998). Rahim (1988) developed a "leader power" questionnaire from the answers of 1,256 respondents. The final inventory contained five factorially independent scales to measure each of the bases of power. Subsequent validations were completed with a national random sample of 476 executives and a sample of 297 employed college students.

Problems with the Five-Base Model. The French and Raven model had a number of problems. First, the five bases are not conceptually distinct. For example, expertise is valued highly, so that sources of personal power in bases of expert power and referent power are likely to be correlated empirically, that is, lodged in the same people. In the same way, the position holder with the power to reward is also likely to have the power to punish. The position will give some degree of legitimacy as well. By definition, formal hierarchies are structures of legitimate, reward, and coercive power relationships.

Further conceptual difficulties were noted by Patchen (1974), who suggested that French and Raven's classification was inadequate because the various bases of power were not conceptually parallel. Thus reward power and coercive power were defined in terms of resources that the influencer could apply. Referent and legitimate power were defined in terms of the characteristics and motives of the target person. Expert power depended on the characteristics of the influencers and on the information resources they personally possessed.

It was not surprising, therefore, to find that the five bases of power are empirically correlated. Rahim (1986) obtained, in a national random sample of 477 executives, a correlation of .58 between the expert and referent power the executives attributed to their superiors. The superiors' control of rewards and coercive punishments correlated similarly with their legitimate power according to their subordinates. For 280 employees in 45 organizations rating the power of their 118 supervisors, Atwater and Yammarino (1996) reported correlations ranging from .33 to .55 among referent, expert, legitimate, and reward power. Coercive power correlated .51 with legitimate power and .41 with reward power.

Student (1968) regarded referent power and expert power as *individually derived* but thought that reward power, legitimate power, and coercive power were *organizationally derived*. He found that supervisors' scores on incremental influence, referent power, and expert power were positively and significantly related to the quality of the group's performance and to a reduction in costs. But average earnings declined with the reward power of the supervisor, and the maintenance costs of the group rose with coercion.

Podsakoff and Schriesheim's (1985) review found expert and referent power positively correlated with each other as well as with employee performance, attendance, retention, and satisfaction with supervision. Legitimate, reward, and coercive power were intercorrelated and less effective. The empirical correlations between the bases of power make sense because power begets power. Power from one base can generate power in another. For example, individuals whose power is based on the legitimacy of their positions can acquire additional power by controlling the rewards that accompany the legitimacy of the positions. In the same way, people tend to defer to those they perceive to be experts. Perceived expertness, in turn, tends to legitimate the leadership role (Goodstadt & Kipnis, 1970). Although we may be able to sort out conceptually the different bases of power, in nature they are likely to be intertwined.

Added Sources and Bases of Power

Filley and Grimes (1967) emerged with a finer set of distinctions. They studied 44 full-time professional employees in a nonprofit organization who reported to a director and to an associate director. The employees were interviewed about hypothetical incidents that might require them to seek a decision from the director or the associate director. The respondents were asked to whom they should go for a decision, to whom they would like to go, and to whom they would in fact go, and why. Answers to the "why" questions were classified according to the bases of power to which the organizational members appear to have responded. Twelve different bases were discerned. For example, instead of one category for legitimate power, several emerged. Legitimate power could be based on formal authority, on responsibility, on control of resources, on bureaucratic rules, or on traditional rules. Raven (1993) added equity, reciprocity, and dependence as bases for power. If A could control the equitable distribution of rewards to B, then A had power above and beyond reward power. If A could exchange one good for another with B, then A had the power of reciprocation. And if B depended on A, then A had power over B. An old adage is "Knowledge is power," and in the information age it is not surprising to suggest that if A has knowledge personally or from his or her position that is desirable or useful to B, then A has informational power over B. Ordinarily, A is a leader and B is a follower, but the roles can be reversed.

Yukl and Falbe (1991) looked at the differences between *lateral* and *downward* power. In interviews with the peers of 49 middle and lower managers, *persuasiveness* was an important additional power. Persuasiveness, legitimate power, and expert power were the most important reasons mentioned by employees for their compliance with supervisor and peer requests. Rahim (1989) showed that expert and referent power were associated with compliance and satisfaction, while legitimate power was positively correlated with compliance but negatively correlated with satisfaction.

Hinken and Schriesheim (1989) made sharper distinctions in the French and Raven model:

Expert power is the ability to administer to another person information, knowledge, or expertise.

Referent power is the ability to administer to another person feelings of personal acceptance or approval.

Reward power is the ability to administer to another person things he or she desires or to remove or decrease things he or she does not desire.

Coercive power is the ability to administer to another person things he or she does not desire or to remove or decrease things he or she does desire.

Legitimate power is the ability to administer to another person feelings of obligation or responsibility.

Table 11.1 is a list of statements that emerged in factor analyses of the extent to which respondents agreed that the statements described their supervisors. The three samples of over 500 respondents were part-time employees enrolled in undergraduate business courses, full-time employees at psychiatric hospitals, and full-time employees taking MBA courses.

Table 11.1 Final Scale Items Responding to the Statement "My Supervisor Can ..."

1. *Expert Power*
   Give me good technical suggestions.
   Share with me his/her considerable experience and/or training.
   Provide me with sound job-related advice.
   Provide me with needed technical knowledge.
2. *Referent Power*
   Make me feel valued.
   Make me feel like he/she approves of me.
   Make me feel personally accepted.
   Make me feel important.
3. *Reward Power*
   Increase my pay level.
   Influence my getting a pay raise.
   Provide me with special benefits.
   Influence my getting a promotion.
4. *Coercive Power*
   Give me undesirable job assignments.
   Make my work difficult for me.
   Make things unpleasant here.
   Make being at work distasteful.
5. *Legitimate Power*
   Make me feel that I have commitments to meet.
   Make me feel like I should satisfy my job requirements.
   Give me the feeling I have responsibilities to fulfill.
   Make me recognize that I have tasks to accomplish.

SOURCE: Adapted from Hinkin and Schriesheim (1989, table 1).

Antecedents and Consequences
of the Bases of Power

Expert Power

In 1597, Sir Francis Bacon declared that "knowledge is power." Expert power, perhaps unseen, can lie behind effective leadership. Gardner (1986a, p. 12) quoted Lyndon Johnson as saying, "When the press talks about my successes as Senate majority leader they always emphasize my capacity to persuade, to wheel and deal. Hardly anyone ever mentions that I usually had more and better information than my colleagues."

Expert power may be manifest in information, knowledge, and wisdom; in good decisions; in sound judgment; and in accurate perceptions of reality (Watts, 1986). An item that is highly loaded (.78) on a factor of expert power is, "Has considerable professional experience to draw from in helping me do my work" (Rahim, 1986). In comparison with other bases, expert power appears to be most acceptable to and most effective with followers. It most readily gains their compliance and is least likely to provoke their resistance (Podsakoff & Schriesheim, 1985a).

The power of revolutionary or reform leaders often begins with their perceived power as experts, which they use to define prevailing problems and to develop innovative solutions. Followers are persuaded that the leaders have the right answers to their problems and are organized to provide support (Gjestland, 1982).

In the physician-patient relationship, the physician wields expert power and the patient plays a distinctly subordinate role, particularly if the patient is also lower in socioeconomic status (Fisher, 1982). But whether the patient complies with the physician's expert advice will depend on what that advice entails as well as the physician's referent power. Members of a group who have relevant information about a task will attempt to lead the group (Hemphill, Pepinsky, Shevitz, et al., 1954). Such attempts are likely to be successful if the members are perceived to be expert, and effective if they really have the expertise. Groups tend to defer to the actual and the perceived expert. They are likely to be persuaded by the perceived expert, to accept the expert's opinion both publicly and privately (Bass, 1960).

H. T. Moore (1921) obtained experimental support for the idea that we readily accept the influence of those whom we accept as experts. Moore observed that students shifted their judgments (about linguistic, ethical, and musical matters) toward what the experimenter led them to believe was the opinion of experts. When Mausner (1953) introduced one student as an art student and another as an art expert, the group's opinion was more strongly influenced by the art expert than by the art student. Knight and Weiss (1980) arranged for leaders of task groups to be seen as "expert" or "nonexpert" on the basis of how they were chosen. Those who were chosen as experts were better able to influence the group than were those who were chosen as nonexperts. The selection of leaders from inside or from outside the group made no difference.

In another experiment, Mausner (1954b) demonstrated that subjects tended to agree more often with a partner whom they observed to succeed than with one whom they observed to fail. Luchins and Luchins (1961) demonstrated that an expert's opinion was more influential than the majority opinion of the group in determining the group's response to a judgmental task. Torrance (1952) and M. A. Levi (1954) both obtained greater improvement on survival problems when groups were fed back expert information after an initial training period.

Evan and Zelditch (1961) studied experimental groups with supervisors who differed in their knowledge of the task. Differences in the supervisors' knowledge did not affect the group's productivity; however, group members exhibited more covert disobedience and resistance to the least informed supervisor than to the moderately or well-informed supervisor. This effect was attributed to changes in the followers' attitudes toward the right of the poorly informed supervisor to occupy a position of leadership. Similar results were reported by G. M. Mahoney (1953), who found that workers were much more satisfied with a wage-incentive system when they thought the supervisor did a good job of explaining the reasons for changes in the system. A survey of more than 200 graduate students found that faculty members with a large amount of expert power were more likely to be acceptable to the students as thesis advisers, coinvestigators in research, and coauthors of conference papers. This was in contrast to potential faculty advisers who were perceived as coercive (Aguinis, Nesler, Quigley, et al., 1996).

Caveats. The impact of expert power has its limits, as was noted in Chapter 4: would-be leaders must be able, but not too much more able than their followers. Many examples can be cited of experiments in which experts failed to be influential. C. B. Smith (1984) observed that apparent technical and administrative expertise in a contrived short-term employment situation did not increase the experimental subjects' output as coders or their compliance with directives. Collaros and Anderson (1969) studied groups with one expert, all experts, and no experts. Groups in which all members were told that they were experts were more inhibited in their performance.

Although individuals can become more influential by acquiring more knowledge and expertise, the technological revolution in the spread of knowledge, and the ease with which information can be transmitted, can quickly alter who is expert about the available information and thus alter the resulting patterns of influence. Under some circumstances, then, a clerk with access to a computer program may become more expert and influential than a PhD without access to the program. Cleveland (1985) noted that information is expandable, compressible, substitutable, transportable, diffusable, and shareable. It is not necessarily a scarce resource. Expert power is more fluid than fixed in a position or a person. It can be found in a computerized database, a computer software program, or in a search engine such as Google. Custom-made expert programs can substitute for human expertise. Increasingly, research focuses on information power, which may differ from expert power as such.

Some further qualifications are in order. The stronger status-leadership relationship can override expert power. Torrance (1955a) concluded that the high status of a team member contributed more to influencing other members to accept the correct answer to a problem than did knowing the correct answer. Paradoxically, two supposed experts may generate less confidence than one alone. Torrance and Aliotti (1965) studied groups involved in information seeking with one or two randomly selected students in the role of expert. They found that groups with two "experts" obtained more accurate information than did those with one "expert," but the groups with two "experts" were less certain of their judgment.

Referent Power

Liked, respected, and esteemed leaders have referent power. Followers want to identify with leaders who have referent power and be accepted by them. The evidence is primarily indirect about the extent to which referent power contributes to influence and leadership. Like expert power, referent power is correlated with the tendency to use rational tactics (Hinkin & Schriesheim, 1990). Referent power has become more important with the downward shift of power to lower organizational levels and the increasing importance of personal values and convictions in the influence process (Behr, 1998). Being esteemed and valued by followers is highly related to leaders' referent power. Yukl, Kim, and Falbe (1996) asked 195 full-time-employed MBA night students to describe three critical incidents in their organizations. In these incidents, leaders who had more referent power were also likely to generate more commitment. They were less likely to use pressure tactics. Hinkin and Schriesheim (1990) reported similar findings, as well as a substantial direct relation-ship between referent (and expert) power and the use of rationality as an influence tactic.

We need to consider indirect evidence of referent power due to ingratiation and the desire for acceptance by followers. For much of this indirect evidence, referent power is assumed from friendship or popularity. Thus Rahim (1986) found factor loadings for referent power of .81 and .85 for such items as, "I like the personal qualities of my superior" and "My superior is the type of person I enjoy working with." Studies of referent power need to capture its essence in the desire of the less powerful to identify with those who have referent power (Podsakoff & Schriesheim, 1985a). For example, referent power is clearly seen when a charismatic relationship exists between the leader and the follower, since what binds the follower to the leader is the desire to identify with the leader.

Esteemed individuals are more likely to emerge as leaders. In 17 studies of executives in various organizations, esteem—as estimated by merit ratings received from superiors—was highly related to "real-life" success as a leader (Bass, 1960). The same has been found in controlled experimental settings, but with qualifications based on selected experimental manipulations of referent power. French and Snyder (1959) found that more highly accepted leaders in experimental groups attempted to exercise more influence, and had more effective groups, than did those who were less well accepted. Followers also attempted to use more influence when they were accepted by their leader. In a review, Podsakoff and Schriesheim (1985a) found that the use of referent power by leaders usually contributed to better performance, greater satisfaction, greater role clarity, and fewer excused absences among their subordinates.

Acceptance, Popularity, and Power. Zander (1953) and Zander and Cohen (1955) introduced two strangers to groups. The one introduced as high in prestige felt better accepted and more at ease than the one introduced as in a low-prestige role. Hurwitz, Zander, and Hymovitch (1953) combined and recombined members of six-person discussion groups. Each individual rated the others on the degree of liking and perceived power and participation. Members with a high degree of power were better liked and participated more often than those with a low degree of power.

Ingratiation. As mentioned earlier, Bass, Wurster, and Alcock (1961) demonstrated that we want to be esteemed by those we esteem. We are more concerned with being liked and accepted by those we respect and accept— those with referent power. This concern, in turn, may lead to ingratiation—the striving by followers to be valued and rewarded by those they esteem or see as more powerful. A line of investigation by Jones and Jones (1964) indicated that followers who want to be liked by high-power figures employ subtle ingratiation tactics, such as flattery, in an effort to gain acceptance. Jones, Gergen, Gumpert, et al. (1965) showed that participants in an experiment who faced the prospect of poor task performance attempted to ingratiate themselves with the experimental supervisor by presenting themselves as strong and competent, but only if the supervisor was open to influence. L. Wheeler (1964) demonstrated that low-power subjects remembered more autobiographical statements made by the high-power figure. Wheeler did not find that participants who were highly dependent on their task leader sought information as a means of ingratiation or to increase their own power. But A. R. Cohen (1958) demonstrated that low-status members who could increase their status in the group tended to communicate in

friendly, ingratiating ways. These tactics were designed to protect and enhance their relations with those who controlled the upward-mobility process. But those members with little perceived opportunity to increase their status made relatively few such attempts. There may be a rational payoff in ingratiating behavior by followers. Thus Kipnis and Vanderveer (1971) observed that leaders tend to reward their ingratiating followers.

Referent power can become coercive. Moreno (1934/1953) postulated that if A highly valued B, B could injure A. And Bass (1960, p. 289) described how referent power could be subverted:

> [If] you can give me affection, self-esteem through association with you and vicarious satisfaction by identification . . . although I may not privately accept what you say, I will publicly agree with you so that you will grant me what I want from you . . . (And such referent power may be lost as a consequence) . . . because if I must continue to inhibit my own opinions . . . I will begin to value you less, to dislike you and eventually reject you.

Reward Power

Reward power implies an ability to facilitate the attainment of desired outcomes by others. An item highly loaded on a factor of reward power is, "Can recommend a promotion for me if my performance is consistently above average" (Rahim, 1986). Marak (1964) studied some groups who were rewarded for a correct decision and others who were not. The results indicated that the ability to provide rewards was related to leadership, as measured by sociometric, interaction, and influence scores. The more valuable reward a member could provide, the more closely this ability was related to leadership. Evidence for the emergence of a leadership structure was suggested by the finding that attempted leadership, actual influence, and rewards for initiating leadership increased as the sessions progressed. Similarly, Herold (1977) showed that the behavior of subordinates in 32 trios depended on the manipulation of monetary rewards by the trio leaders. In a leader-subordinate experimental simulation, Dustin and Davis (1967) observed that when given a choice, leaders used monetary rewards twice as much as they used praise. Kipnis (1972) also found that economic incentives were favored over other ways of improving subordinates' performance. As before, Hinton and Barrow (1975) found that when subordinates performed at high levels, supervisors tended to make more use of economic reinforcements than of praise. However, when subordinates performed poorly, leaders tended to make more use of reproof.

Many of the critical behaviors that separate successful from unsuccessful noncommissioned officers in situational tests were found by Flanagan, Levy, et al. (1952) to be due to the differential reinforcements provided by these officers. Successful officers more often encouraged their men to follow rules and regulations, gave pep talks when the men were tired, and constantly checked the behavior of their men. However, S. Kerr (1975) noted that in their desire to achieve one kind of behavior, leaders as well as organizations sometimes unintentionally reward another kind.

Greene (1976a, 1976b) conducted the first longitudinal study of the effects of rewarding behavior by leaders and concluded that it could result in improved performance by the subordinates. Sims (1977), Sims and Szilagyi (1978), and Szilagyi (1980b) also found a causal relationship between such reward behavior and follower performance in a series of longitudinal studies.

Justis (1975) examined effective leadership as a function of the extent to which followers' rewards depended on the leader's competence and performance. The leader's effectiveness and influence were greater the more the leader was seen to be competent and the more the followers' rewards depended on the leader's performance. Expert power interacted with reward power.[3]

Interdependence Effects. Berkowitz (1957b) experimented with pairs of participants, one or both of whom could earn a reward. The perception of interdependence increased the members' motivation when both were eligible for valued rewards. Participants were also motivated to work toward a partner's reward even when they were not eligible. Berkowitz and Daniels (1963) demonstrated that participants worked harder for a "supervisor" whose success was dependent on their performance than when no such interdependence existed. Berkowitz and Connor (1966) varied both success and dependence for pairs who

[3]Chapter 15 will review the use of rewards and punishment by leaders in much more detail.

could win rewards. Participants who experienced failure expressed stronger dislike for their partner the greater their feeling of responsibility toward the partner. Successful participants, however, worked harder for their dependent partner than did the control participants.

The leader may also have to share the power to reward with other authorities, especially in matrix organizations where a subordinate reports to a functional leader and a project leader. In such a case, Hinton and Barrow (1975) found that leaders were more likely to use their reward power if they had to share its use than if they operated alone.

Distributing Rewards. A norm that is often common to students and workers in the same small-group settings is "Share and share alike." Thus Morgan and Sawyer (1967) found that pairs of boys, when permitted to earn equal or unequal rewards, preferred equal rewards whether their partners were friends or strangers. But their perception of the other's expectation played an important part in determining their preference. Even ingratiating subordinates who disparaged the competence of their student supervisors failed to modify the allocation of rewards by the supervisor (Fodor, 1974). And when Shriver (1952) gave leaders of discussion groups checks of various amounts with which they were required to reward the contributions of other members, some leaders solved the problem by drawing lots; others, after delay and emotional upset, passed out the checks quickly and departed. Shriver interpreted these results as indicating that there are limits to the reward power that an emergent leader can exercise with comfort. Nevertheless, W. P. Smith (1967b) found that participants with a highly valued outcome liked their partners less than those with less highly valued outcomes. Those with little power valued their outcome more highly and used their power more positively than did those with much power.

Yet considerations of equity and loyalty do have an impact on the situation. Thibaut and Faucheux (1965) varied equity and loyalty to one's group in bargaining for individual gain. Partners who were told that they had greater power tended to use it; other partners tended to acquiesce. Lower-power members appealed for "a fair share" when the high-power members could manipulate rewards, but they appealed to "loyalty" when rewards were manipulated by an outsider. Thibaut and Cruder

(1969) found that participants tended to form contractual agreements when they discovered that an agreement restricted the power of each to prevent their joint attainment of maximum outcomes. P. Murdoch (1967) observed that members tended to develop contractual norms when the divider of rewards was presented as being likely to withdraw from the relationship. Butler and Miller (1965) and McMartin (1970) determined that participants tended to distribute rewards in proportion to the difference in the average rewards received from others. Swingle (1970a) demonstrated that cooperative participants were exploited more when they were powerful than when they were weak, even when exploitation resulted in reduced rewards for the exploiter.

Power affects promises to cooperate for mutual benefit. Tedeschi, Lindskold, Horai, et al. (1969) studied reactions to participants who repeatedly promised to cooperate but who varied in credibility (their degree of cooperation following their promises). Powerful teammates ignored the promises and failed to cooperate. Participants equal in power were most cooperative with the willing member. Participants weak in power became more exploitative as the credibility of promises increased. L. Solomon (1960) demonstrated that unconditional offers of cooperation by one member equal in power to a partner was exploited by the partner who became less liked. However, if the offers to cooperate were conditional, more cooperation and more liking of the partner were elicited. If the partners were unequal in power, the results were reversed.

Antecedents to Usage and Effects. Hinton and Barrow (1976) showed that reward behavior was most frequently used by responsible, confident, and enthusiastic leaders. Barrow (1976) and Herold (1977) found that leaders rewarded good performers and were more punitive toward poor performers. Hunt and Schuler (1976), Oldham (1976), and Sims (1980) obtained similar results. But Greenberg and Leventhal (1976) reported that leaders offered financial bonuses to poor performers to motivate them when that was the only motivator available.

Bennis, Berkowitz, Affinito, and Malone (1958) studied reward power in hospitals. They found that supervisors at hospitals where the rewards that were given were congruent with those hoped for by the subordinates exercised more influence than did supervisors at hospitals where the rewards were not congruent with the subordinates' hopes. Furthermore, the hospitals that gave congruent rewards were more effective. But supervisors exhibited little awareness of the subordinates' preferences for rewards. A participative style of leadership (see Chapter 18) was reported by Singh-Gupta (1997) among Indian managers correlated with their use of expert and reward power.

To appreciate fully the effects of reward power, one must consider how it is used. On the one hand, many studies have demonstrated the utility of rewarding by supervisors in exchange for compliance by subordinates. Supervisors' recommendations for rewards that are contingent on the subordinates' performance have been widely found to contribute to productivity and to effective operations. However, such rewards may be resented by subordinates and may actually be coercive. In such cases, compliance will be public only, not private, especially when subordinates see the supervisors' use of rewards as capricious, arbitrary, and unfair, rather than reasonable, predictable, and fair.

Coercive Power

Epictetus declared:

> . . . no one is afraid of Caesar himself, but he is afraid of death, loss of property, prison, and disenfranchisement. Nor does anyone love Caesar himself unless in some way Caesar is a person of great merit; but we love wealth, a tribuneship, a praetorship, a consulship. When we love and hate and fear these things, it needs must be that those who control them are masters over us. . . . That is how at a meeting of the Senate a man does not say what he thinks, while within his breast his judgment shouts loudly. Starr, 1954, p. 144

The leader who uses coercive power controls the granting or denying of valued rewards or feared penalties; subordinates' private opinions and feelings remain hidden, but there is pressure on them to express publicly what they really feel. In hierarchical settings, coercion is manifest when the subordinate "holds in abeyance his own critical faculties for choosing between alternatives and uses the formal criterion of the receipt of a command or signal as his basis for choice" (Simon, 1947, p. 126). Extremes in coercive power were seen in Shaka, the Zulu king, who was known to have summarily executed his courtiers for a breach of etiquette, a smile at the wrong time, disagreeing with him over a minor point, or one of many other slight causes of his displeasure (Morris, 1966). As Matusak (1997) noted, "Power without caring, commitment, and empathy can become a selfish tyranny."

Tannenbaum (1950) listed ways in which executives may use their power to restrict or inhibit subordinates' behavior. The executives may arbitrarily identify the organization's goals, set up criteria for evaluating alternative paths to the goals, rule out alternatives, limit the general activities in which subordinates are permitted to engage, identify the positions with control and power, give or withhold information, and set deadlines to be met to avoid punishment or earn rewards.

Among Indian managers (as well as elsewhere), authoritarian leadership is associated with the use of coercive power (Singh-Gupta, 1997). Coercive power implies the ability to impose penalties for noncompliance. Rahim (1986) found that endorsement of the statement "My superior can fire me if I neglect my duties" correlated .82 with a factor of coercive power. French and Raven (1959) reported that conformity by followers (public acceptance but private rejection) was a direct function of earlier threats of punishment for noncompliance. Although coercion most commonly involves punishment or its threat, more subtle uses of power to coerce may involve promising rewards for compliance. One will comply publicly but perhaps not privately as a consequence of such promises and one's concern about failing to obtain promised rewards in the absence of compliance. Thus A has power over B if A can control whether B is rewarded or punished and B seeks rewards and wants to avoid punishment. A is coercive if B behaves publicly according to A's demands, although B privately rejects A (Bass, 1960). A clear demonstration of coercion that results from power was reported by French, Morrison, and Levinger (1960). In laboratory assignments, participants serving as subordinates exhibited a much greater discrepancy between their public and private reactions when supervisors could assess monetary fines than when no fines were established.

Militant leaders of social and political movements apply coercive pressure on officials who are vulnerable to their attacks, such as "high-minded" university presidents, elected politicians, or executives whose business may suffer. These militant leaders gain visibility and mobilize their supporters to support their coercive efforts, which are directed at changing the actions of their targets before changing the targets' attitudes. Such leaders harass, threaten, cajole, disrupt, provoke, and intimidate in speeches, dress, manners, gestures, slogans, rituals, and violent confrontations (Simons, 1970).

Usage. The use of coercive power is less popular with leaders and subordinates alike. Leaders tend to use this form of power to deal with unacceptable performance by a subordinate when they do not have the power to reward the subordinate for acceptable performance (Kipnis, 1976) or do not have other bases of power. But even in this instance, there is reluctance to use coercive power. McFillen and New (1979) demonstrated that leaders were less willing to exercise monetary sanctions for poor performance when they had only the power to punish. They were more willing to use monetary rewards for good performance when they had only the power to reward their subordinates. Leaders were more inclined to use their coercive power when they were under pressure to maintain high-productivity schedules and had lost their power to reward good performance (Greene & Podsakoff, 1981). Nonetheless, Simon (1947) argued that the use of coercive power is hard to avoid in any formal hierarchy, for five reasons: (1) subordinates develop expectations for obedience to symbols of higher status; (2) the superior can satisfy the subordinates' personal need for security from a substitute father or mother; (3) the subordinates may share the same goals as the superior and perceive that blind obedience provides a means to obtain the goals; (4) the subordinates are freed from the responsibility for making difficult decisions, and the superior bears the burden of these decisions for them; and (5) most simply, the superior may be able to reward or punish the subordinates materially.

Subordinates in a business organization are coerced by others besides their immediate superiors. They may have to accept publicly, yet reject privately, the dictates of buyers of the organization's products; contractual agreements with labor unions or industrial cartels; and the demands of government, custom, and tradition (Bass, 1960). More often than not, coercion in a hierarchical setting is subtle. Subordinates may not even be aware that they are being coerced (Timasheff, 1938) and may repress any private feelings that are at odds with their public statements. For example, an executive may be reminded by the CEO of the costs in lost stock options if the executive quits. Or a young executive with new ideas may be coerced by a superior who keeps emphasizing the possibility of failure (Kets de Vries, 1980).

Although it may not be very subtle, pure political influence can be coercive when it displaces the rational and legitimate use of power with Machiavellian deception, divisiveness, defensiveness, or emotional appeals. Even an offer of rewards for political favors can be seen as coercive and may require a strong countervailing conscience to resist. Power can be wielded by political manipulations, such as covertly denying, delaying, or distorting information that is sent to another member of the organization so that the latter's choices are restricted (House, 1984).

Indirect Coercion. Observing vicariously how penalties are tied to the performance of one's colleagues may be more effective than direct threats in maintaining performance in the short term. Schnake (1986) studied the effects of punishment on the attitudes and behavior of coworkers who observed a peer receiving punishment. Students hired for temporary clerical employment observed a coworker receiving a reduction in pay, a coworker receiving a threat of a reduction in pay, or a coworker who was not penalized. Those who observed the coworker receiving a reduction in pay produced significantly more output than those who observed the coworker being threatened with a reduction in pay or not being penalized. Job satisfaction was not affected, and the effects held for at least a week.

"It's Not What You Say, But the Way You Say It." Compliance can actually be due to coercion even if the person who complies does not feel coerced, as a consequence of the language used in the attempt at influence. Drake and Moberg (1986) detailed how both public and private compliance can result from the language used by A to obtain B's compliance when ordinarily B would see A's request as exploitative and coercive. For instance, A can use sedating language, which suppresses B's tendency to analyze whether B will gain or lose by complying. Or A can be indirect ("Something needs to be done about the trash"), rather than direct ("Take out the

trash"); in this case, A becomes the observer, not the leader. Also, A's observation of the existence of a problem and related hints, prompts, and teases can substitute for a direct order. A can first determine B's availability and willingness to comply before assigning new responsibilities to B. (But if A behaves this way routinely, B may interpret A's effort as a characteristically annoying ploy and hence may lose trust in A.)

Giving orders or making requests without explanation is likely to produce less compliance and more sense of being coerced than giving logical reasons. However, more compliance will occur and less coerciveness will be felt even if the reasons do not really make any sense. Such reasons can be substituted because cognitive processing is limited when decisions are made to follow orders in many seemingly legitimate situations. For example, Langer, Blank, and Chanowitz (1978) showed that personnel who were using a copying machine would allow a usurper to take over the machine for an irrelevant reason ("I have to make copies") but they would comply less often if no reason was given.

Power is legitimated in the language used. Hence, A increases power over B by using rich, rather than redundant, vocabulary and by expressing less uncertainty in appeals (Berger & Braduc, 1982).

Another approach to offset the potential coerciveness of a direct order is to precede it with *disclaimers.* As quoted by Drake and Moberg (1986, p. 578), Hewitt and Stokes (1975) outlined five forms of disclaimers:

Hedging (I'm not really committed): "I haven't given this much thought but . . ."

Credentialing (I'm not prejudiced): "Some of my best friends are . . ."

Sin licensing (I'm not a rule breaker): "I know this is against the rules but . . ."

Cognitive disclaimers (I'm not confused): "This may seem strange but . . ."

Appeals to suspend judgment (Don't get offended): "Don't get me wrong but . . ."

Excuses and justifications may also be used to palliate feelings of exploitation and to increase compliance. Compliance can be increased by avoiding messages of powerlessness. O'Barr (1982) reported that more convincing witnesses in court trials avoided using power-less language—intensifiers (e.g., "very") and hedges (e.g., "sort of").

Conditions That Increase the Use of Coercive Power. Coercive power dominated supervisory-subordinate relations in a factory where workers were marginal, handicapped, without skills, and unable to get jobs elsewhere (Goode & Fowler, 1949). Kipnis and Cosentino (1969) compared corrective actions used by military and industrial executives. Industrial supervisors tended to reprimand and to transfer offending employees, whereas military supervisors more often used instruction, reassignment, extra work, and reduced privileges as corrective measures.

Boise (1965) studied attitudes of supervisors in a city's police, street, and water departments toward correcting subordinates' peformance. All but authoritarian supervisors (those with high F scores) and police supervisors agreed with the concept of a uniform penalty for unacceptable performance. Coercive power is most likely to be used to deal with noncompliance. Katz, Maccoby, Gurin, and Floor (1951) found that the foremen of low-producing railroad section gangs were more punitive. A longitudinal study by Greene (1976b) concluded that supervisors are punitive in reaction to their subordinates' poor performance. Szilagyi (1980b) established that higher levels of punishment tended to follow higher levels of absenteeism by employees. Bankart and Lanzetta (1970), Barrow (1976), and Hinton and Barrow (1975) also reported the tendency of supervisors to become coercive as a consequence of subordinates' inadequate performance. Situational variables, such as difficulty of the task and prospects for failure, increase a leader's tendency to employ coercion (Michener, Fleishman, Elliot, et al., 1976). That is, leaders who face failure will tend to become more coercive (Kipnis, 1976). T. R. Mitchell (1979) further showed that more coercion was practiced if the supervisor attributed poor performance to a lack of motivation rather than to a lack of ability, or to policy changes or bad luck.

Goodstadt and Kipnis (1970) studied student work groups under different types of supervisory power. Student supervisors tended to use coercive power to solve disciplinary problems, but they used expert power to solve problems arising from ineptness. Sims (1980) concluded

from a review of both longitudinal field studies and laboratory studies that punishment tends to be more a result than a cause of employees' behavior. More specifically, managers tend to increase punishment in response to the poor performance of employees. Illustrating the use of punishment in reaction to other events, including the loss of other bases of power, Greene and Podsakoff (1979) found that after a contingent (positive reinforcement) pay plan at two paper plants had been abandoned, supervisors began to use rewards less and punishment more. Fodor (1976) found that leaders were more authoritarian and coercive with disparaging and disruptive subordinates. The leaders rated such subordinates lower and gave them less pay than they gave to other subordinates. In the same study, Fodor noted that supervisors who were subjected to group stress also tended to become more coercive and less rewarding.[4]

Support for Coercive Power. Legitimacy coupled with coercion will increase public and private acceptance of coercive demands. In a study of experimental groups, Levinger, Morrison, and French (1957) found that the threat of punisment induced conforming behavior in group members before punishment but not after punishment. Most to the point was the fact that the group members' perceptions of the legitimacy of the punishment reduced their resistance to conform. Particularly important is the support of the status structure. When Iverson (1964) presented taped speeches by people who were identified as high or low in status, those who listened to speakers who made punitive remarks formed more favorable impressions of the personalities of the high-status speakers than they did of the low-status speakers. The coercive demands of an attractive esteemed leader are more likely to be accepted, although continued use of coercive power will reduce such attractiveness and esteem. Another support for ready obedience to coercive power is the immaturity of participants. Kipnis and Wagner (1967) found that immature participants performed better than did mature participants under a leader whose decisions to administer punishment were backed up by superior authority. Brass and Oldham (1976) examined the reactions of first-line supervisors to an "in-

---

[4]Chapter 15 will detail further conditions under which leadership will be punitive. Chapter 28 will examine the effects of stress on leadership.

basket" simulation.[5] Overall, the supervisors punished more often than they rewarded their subordinates. The more active supervisors, those who used both more reward and more coercive powers, were rated as more effective.

Leaders use coercion more easily when they rationalize that they are only following orders from higher authority without questioning the legitimacy of those orders. They are more coercive if they attribute the coercion to their position, rather than to themselves as persons, and if they can maintain sociopsychological distance by thinking of those they are coercing as enemies, inferiors, and troublemakers. Adolf Hitler made coercion acceptable to the Germans by consolidating the attention of the German people as the "master race" against a single adversary and then lumping different opponents together in the single category of those who were antithetical to the master race (Paige, 1977).

Resistance to Coercive Power. When Milgram (1965b) instructed students to activate a device that supposedly administered electric shock to subjects who made errors in a learning experiment, the students were willing to administer "dangerous" degrees of shock on command. The students had a strong tendency to obey authority and to accept being coerced by it. But when students who were administering the electric shock were permitted to observe two other individuals who refused to do so, the number of refusals was significantly increased. Stotland (1959) found that when participants were required to work with a domineering supervisor, they tended to identify with the supervisor. However, when they were able to interact with a peer from another group, they would exert more independence from the power figure, show more hostility toward him, and exhibit greater motivation to reach the goal despite the supervisor's hindrance. French, Morrison, and Levinger (1960) observed that the greater the threat of punishment, the less the resistance to compliance, but the resistance increased after the threat disappeared.

A form of "group compensation" may arise, according to Stotland (1959), in resistance to attempts to be coerced

if the opportunity to do so is made available. In Stotland's study, individuals used models to design a city and were subject to the veto power of a "supervisor," who interrupted their work twice. Some of the participants were given the opportunity to meet privately in the absence of the "supervisor;" others were not. Those who met privately became much more aggressive and hostile toward the supervisor, whereas those who did not continued to accept the supervisor publicly. Private assembly permitted the formation of an informal organization to present a unified front against the "supervisor's" continued attempts to coerce the participants. In sum, group members were better able to resist coercive power when they had an opportunity to interact with peers in the absence of the supervisor or to observe other members who disobeyed orders. Resistance would be higher if the orders were judged to be illegitimate and the leader was personally unattractive.

Resisting attempts by superiors to exercise their coercive power may be productive. In an experiment by Horwitz, Goldman, and Lee (1955), students were frustrated by the arbitrary refusal of their teacher to repeat instructions. However, they shifted to more favorable attitudes toward the teacher, were less annoyed, and regarded the teacher as less coercive when the teacher read their opinions and agreed to repeat the instructions. These more favorable attitudes occurred less often when the teacher was informed by a "higher authority" that the instructions should be repeated. The students solved problems and learned best when they could take direct action to "reform" the coercive teacher; problem solving and learning were somewhat less efficient when the students could only state their grievances, and were poorest when the students were led to believe that all the other students accepted the coercive teacher's refusal to repeat the instructions.

Unintended Consequences of Coercion. Those with coercive power will readily fall back on it when necessary. They are tempted to exploit their power by demanding a greater share of available resources and rewards. The process is reinforced by colleagues' development of mistrust of the coercive power holder and by the power holder's counterreaction of suspiciousness about the colleagues' intentions, which results in his or her greater reliance on coerciveness (Kipnis, 1976). Coercive power

---

[5]A standard sample of memos, notes, letters, and bulletins requiring actions and decisions likely to be found in a supervisor's in-basket. The adequacy with which the problems in the correspondence are handled can be scored. Chapter 35 will provide more details.

can turn a mutually benevolent relationship into one of mutual hostility (Deutsch & Krauss, 1960). The costs of depending on coercive power in formal organizations are well known. For instance, satisfaction with supervision is almost uniformly lower. Thus whereas the satisfaction of life insurance agents was related positively to their manager's use of referent and expert power, it was related negatively to their perceptions of the degree of reward, coercive, and legitimate power that the manager exercised (Bachman, Smith, & Slesinger, 1966). Weschler, Kahane, and Tannenbaum (1952) observed that a research laboratory headed by a coercive leader was more productive but less satisfying to its members than a laboratory that was under less coercive leadership. Zander and Curtis (1962) indicated that participants in a coercive situation found each other less attractive, less well accepted, and less motivated than they were in a referent situation. Weiss and Fine (undated) found that participants who had experienced insult and failure were receptive to arguments to be hostile and punitive, whereas comparable participants who had satisfying experiences were more ready to accept communications asking them to be lenient. Hostility toward power figures who can coerce other members was also found by Stotland (1959). Participants may withdraw from the problems at hand to avoid being coerced. Riecken (1952) attributed such withdrawal to the frustrations of coercion. Oldham (1976) related punishment by leaders to evaluations of their subordinates' effectiveness. Generally, punishment was correlated not with subordinates' performance, but with their lack of "motivational effectiveness." Punitive leadership was found by Sims and Szilagyi (1975) and Sims (1977) to be uncorrelated with the subordinate performance of professionals and technical personnel, but it had a significant inverse correlation with the satisfactory performance of administrative and service personnel as subordinates.

A line of investigation beginning with Janis and Feshbach (1953) generally supported the contention that strong threats are less productive than moderate or mild threats. In the prototype experiment by Janis and Feshbach, conditions of strong, mild, and minimal fear were included in propaganda about dental hygiene, and resistance to counterpropaganda was measured. The arousal of minimal fear seemed to provide the most persistent influence, whereas the arousal of strong fear resulted in the ignoring or avoiding of attempts to influence (a form of withdrawal) or the development of conflicting tendencies to minimize the importance of the threatening propaganda. On the basis of similar findings, Kelman (1953) argued that when coercion is too great, interfering responses and hostility toward the coercer made participants less prone to accept the coercer's attempts to influence them. Yet the crushing of the prodemocracy movement at Tiananmen Square in 1989 in China illustrates that credible strong threats followed by application of overpowering force and punishment can be a powerful deterrent. Nevertheless, subjugation to continued coercion is likely to contribute to dysfunctional outcomes such as learned helplessness, feelings of powerlessness, alienation, and depression. When possible, it can generate verbal and interpersonal aggression and provoke sabotage in those who are being coerced (Spector, 1975). In a study of 216 nurses and nurses' aides, Sheridan and Vredenburgh (1978a) found that the use of coercive power contributed to heightened tension.

Caveat. Most of the research on coercive power was completed before 1980. Since then, the use of coercion has probably declined or become more subtle, owing to societal enlightenment, threats of lawsuits, liberalization of education, and public condemnation of glaring examples of abusiveness. Coercion is still more acceptable in authoritarian societies than in western democracies. But terrorism and military force remain strong as efforts to use coercive power to influence.

Legitimate Power

Legitimate power is based on norms and expectations regarding behaviors that are appropriate in a given role or position. The legitimatization of a role is derived from such norms and expectations. Members are more likely to accept the position of the leader and his or her influence as legitimate when the leader holds attitudes that conform to the norms of the group or organization. Read (1974) argues that the legitimacy of leaders involves a complex set of attitudes toward them and their source of authority; the leaders' actual behavior contributes to their continuing legitimacy. Bleda, Gitter, and d'Agostino (1977) observed that the satisfaction of enlisted personnel with army life was related more to the leadership of those they saw as the originators, rather than as the relayers, of their daily orders.

French and Raven (1959) suggested three sources of legitimate power: (1) cultural values that endow some persons with the right to exercise power; (2) occupancy of a position organized to confer authority; and (3) appointment or designation by a legitimizing agent. An item that Rahim (1986) found to be highly correlated (.74) with a factor of legitimate power was, "My superior has the right to expect me to carry out her (his) instructions."

According to Hollander (1993), "influence and power flow from legitimacy" (p. 29). By legitimatizing leadership, followers affect their leaders' influence and behavior and the performance of the group. The legitimacy of leaders depends fundamentally on their standing with their followers.

In goal-setting experiments, students and workers usually try to do what they are asked (Latham & Lee, 1986); they generally regard the requests from experimenters in laboratories and supervisors in work settings to be legitimate. The experiment is a "demand situation." In the workplace, employees think it is legitimate for their supervisor to tell them what to do—that this is inherent in the employment contract (Locke, Latham, & Erez, 1987). The legitimacy of supervisors' orders was significantly related to the subordinates' intention to work hard for an assigned goal in Oldham's experiment (1975).

A survey of 1,155 soldiers who had completed basic training to prepare them for action in the Korean War showed that the soldiers had a stronger "fighter spirit" to the degree that they perceived their leader had legitimacy (R. B. Smith, 1983). According to Michener and Burt (1975a, 1975b), studies of college students indicated that recognition of the authority of the leader's office was more important to their compliance than was endorsement of the leader's personal right to exercise power.

House (1984) provided a rationale for the fact that although people accept leadership based on legitimate power, they do not do so with any special enthusiasm or as readily as they accept leadership based on expert power. When influenced by legitimate direction, followers are being responsive to the source, not the content, of the attempted leadership (Wrong, 1980). They tend to attribute the consequences of their compliance to external factors, not to themselves (Litman-Adizes, Raven, & Fontaine, 1978). They are less personally involved and can take less credit for and less satisfaction from success due to their compliance. They do what is expected of them but not more than may occur in response to leadership based on referent or expert power.

Legitimacy Through Appointment, Election, or Emergence. How the legitimacy of a position is established makes a difference. Appointment or election to a position tends to legitimate the leadership role to a greater extent than does emergence in the role through interaction or capture of the role by force. Thus in an experiment with 82 groups of three to five male undergraduates, Burke (1971) found that the basis on which leadership was legitimated by election, emergence, or counterelection was more important to the role differentiation that occurred within the groups than whether the goal was or was not established by consensus and whether pay was distributed equally or differentially. Huertas and Powell (1986) found an increase of ingratiation and conforming statements among members if a leader was not appointed but was allowed to emerge.

Legitimacy was manipulated in an experiment by Goldman and Fraas (1965). Leaders of groups playing "twenty questions" were either elected, appointed by reason of their competence, or randomly appointed. Control groups had no formal leader. The groups' performance, as measured by the time required and the number of questions needed to reach the solution, was poorer if the leaders were randomly appointed or if no leader was put in place than if leaders were legitimated by election or appointment because of their competence.

Hollander and Julian (1969) and Firestone, Lichtman, and Colamosea (1975) demonstrated that leaders are in the best possible position to get things done if they first emerged informally as leaders in the group and then were elected by the members. Ben-Yoav, Hollander, and Carnevale (1983) similarly observed that elected leaders were more likely than are appointed leaders to contribute to the group's discussion and to receive greater responsiveness and support subsequently from other members. Group members regard elected leaders as more competent, more responsive to the members' needs, and more interested in the group's task. Election gives followers a greater sense of responsibility for leadership and heightens their expectations for the leader's performance (Hollander, 1978).

Legitimacy will allow leaders more latitude when representing their group in negotiations with higher authority or with other groups. In turn, legitimate leaders will expect to receive more support from the group they are representing (Boyd, 1972). If elected leaders are also self-confident, they are likely to use their legitimate power and persuasion instead of punishment to correct their subordinates' poor performance (Goodstadt & Kipnis, 1970). Hollander, Fallon, and Edwards (1977) found that elected leaders had greater influence than appointed leaders on small experimental groups that were perceived by their members to be failing, although the greater influence of a newly elected leader in a group that continued to fail was soon lost.

Winning the election establishes a much higher degree of legitimate acceptance of the U.S. president as the embodiment of the nation and as the head of state, head of government, head of political party, and commander in chief of the military than would be expected from the president's initial support from the voters. Usually, only about half of the eligible U.S. electorate votes in presidential elections. Often, the difference between the votes for the winner and the votes for the loser is so close that the president, with his enormous powers, is legitimated by only about 25% of the eligible voters. In 2000, the Republican candidate, George W. Bush, received 500,000 fewer popular votes than his Democratic opponent, Al Gore; but the Republican-appointed majority of justices of the U.S. Supreme Court decided 5–4 to award the contested 25 electoral votes of Florida to Bush to give him a majority of the electoral vote and thus legitimacy as president. Although for a while many Democrats continued to question Bush's legitimacy, it was helped by Gore's quickly announced concession of defeat.

Other experiments have shown that legitimacy is enhanced when an office is permanent rather than temporary and when it is filled by appointment by a higher authority rather than by election. As mentioned earlier, leaders' negotiations with higher authorities will have more legitimacy in the eyes of group members if the leaders are elected by the groups rather than fortuitously appointed (Julian, Hollander, & Regula, 1969), but arbitrarily appointed leaders can increase their legitimacy by consulting with the members (Lamm, 1973).

Appointed leaders in a hierarchical setting also are likely to have legitimate power. The amount of power they have is a direct reflection of the power and status of the legitimatizing authority. For example, the commissions of U.S. Army officers confer powerful legitimacy;

the appointment of a university chancellor by a board of trustees does likewise. However, when the legitimator is seen as incompetent and lacking in authority, the appointee's power and ability will be questioned (Knight & Weiss, 1980). In Torrance's (1954) study of decision making in established and newly formed groups, the members' influence on decision making depended on their position in the power structure of the group and was stronger in permanent than in transitory groups. Furthermore, although Raven and French's (1958a) examination of groups with elected and emergent leaders concluded that "the very occupation of a key position in a structure lends legitimacy to the occupant," the authors also noted that elected leaders were better liked than emergent leaders and their influence was better accepted. Anderson, Karuza, and Blanchard (1977) observed that individuals who were elected to an undesirable leadership position had greater social power than those elected to a desirable position, but that appointment to either position made no difference. Julian, Hollander, and Regula (1969) found that the appointed leaders in experimental groups had a source of authority that was perceived to give them stability in their position. But election made the leaders more vulnerable to censure if they later proved inadequate. Members were most willing for the leaders to continue in their positions when the leaders were competent at the task, interested in the group members, and involved in the group's activities.

Inner Circle versus Outer Circle. Vecchio (1979) showed that the leader's legitimate power was particularly important to the performance of those subordinates who were not part of the leader's "inner circle" of confidants and trusted assistants. At the same time, the subordinates in the inner circle did best when their superior did not possess power that was due to his or her formal position. The inner circle was most optimistic about its leader when the outer circle treated their leader in a friendly manner (Koulack, 1977).

Enhancement of Legitimate Power. Leaders can increase their legitimate power by becoming the accepted "makers of meaning," definers of reality and the situation (Conger, 1991). In a formal organization, legitimate power becomes equivalent to the authority vested in a position. Illustrating the importance of such legitimate power, Klimoski, Friedman, and Weldon (1980) set up a laboratory simulation of an assessment center[6] that required the assessors in a group meeting to integrate their assessments. The chairpersons of these integrative panel discussions either were or were not granted formal voting rights. If they were granted such rights, they were able to exert more influence on the panel and in the final evaluations of the candidates that emerged.

Subordinates' trust of legitimate authority makes a difference in the authority's power. Earley (1986b) reported that British tire workers who were assigned goals accepted them more when the reasoning for the goals was explained by their union steward, in whom they presumably felt more trust, than when the explanation was offered by their supervisors, whom they viewed as members of management—the untrustworthy opposition. The loss of such trust and confidence is particularly damaging to legitimate power.

Reduction in Legitimate Power. In Chapter 10, we noted the sharp fall in public trust in our business, government, and other institutions between 1945 and 2005 (Kingsbury, 2006). Mitchell and Scott (1987) examined the dramatic decline in the American public's confidence in the legitimate leaders of various institutions. In the late 1970s, President Jimmy Carter saw it as a "crisis of confidence." According to public opinion polls, trust in government declined from about 80% in the 1950s to 33% in 1976 (just after the Watergate scandal). From the late 1960s to the late 1970s, the American public's confidence in business leaders fell equally dramatically. It was the leaders of government and business who were seen as particularly untrustworthy, not necessarily the institutions. In the 1980s, over 100 political appointees of the Reagan administration were forced to resign in a cloud of scandals and indictments. The "sleaze factor" in the Reagan administration did not help to restore confidence in governmental leaders; nor did the Wall Street scandals, the Iran-Contra affair, the many plant closings, or the stock market crash of 1987. Confidence in Ronald Reagan appeared to have been maintained during his administration because he conveyed the impression of a personable, likeable, strong, and decisive leader.

New and different scandals emerged during the presidencies of Bill Clinton and George W. Bush. Business leadership again suffered a crisis of confidence in the 1990s and the early twenty-first century from scandals, bankruptcies, the collapse of the boom in technology stocks, the huge expansion of the federal deficit, the continuing overseas migration of jobs, the decline in real income of the working class, the increasing gap between the rich and the poor, the lack of one-seventh of the population of health insurance, and the unpopular war in Iraq. Lipset (1985) found that a "great deal of confidence in the people running the various institutions" was expressed in 1966, but by 1984 it had declined, as follows: physicians, from 72% to 43%; educators, 61% to 40%; military leaders, 62% to 45%; religious leaders, 41% to 24%; members of the Supreme Court, 50% to 35%; CEOs of major companies, 55% to 19%; leaders of labor unions, 22% to 12%; members of Congress, 42% to 28%; and journalists, 29% to 18%. These figures continued to fall into the twenty-first century (Kingsbury, 2006).

The legitimacy of these institutional leaders is founded on the public's belief in their special expertise, in their serving as stewards with legal and moral responsibility for the management of their institutions in the best interests of their constituencies, and in their ability to innovate and to inspire progress. Mitchell and Scott (1987) suggested that the decline in confidence was due to the loss of belief that institutional leaders had the expertise and motives that were once attributed to them. Rather than serving as stewards, the leaders had become self-serving. With the decline in confidence has come the loss of legitimacy. The competence of the leaders in government is increasingly questioned, particularly because of continued mishandling of terrorism and natural disasters. Progressive taxation has been bent out of shape, with the heaviest relative burden falling on the poor and working classes and increasingly favored treatment of the wealthiest. Leaders appear to be more self-aggrandizing. Their prospective innovations are increasingly constrained by the felt need to protect others from them. The decline in their legitimacy results in a public that feels much less "obligation or responsibility to believe in what their leaders tell them or to do what their leaders ask of them" (Mitchell & Scott, 1987, p. 449).

Countervailing power can also reduce legitimacy. Caplow (1968) observed that a majority coalition formed in opposition to leaders may not only undermine the

[6] See Chapter 14.

legitimacy of their position but may take over the leadership. For instance, Worthy, Wright, and Shaw (1964) created groups in which a confederate accused a naïve teammate of losing a game. When the accusation was legitimate, other members of the team were less willing to interact with the accused member. When the accusation was not legitimate, they were less willing to interact with either the accused or the accuser.

Those with legitimate power may also be ready to give it up or to avoid exercising it. This tendency is more common in young low-level managers. In a survey of 569 managers, Veiga (1986) identified various causes for giving up control:

1. The manager, especially the young low-level manager, may think the group lacks direction, commitment, or a belief that it can do well.
2. The manager personally feels no commitment to or responsibility for the outcome and has nothing to gain from it.
3. The manager feels unwilling or unable to make a meaningful contribution to the decision.
4. The group's task may seem ill-defined or too difficult.
5. The manager may believe that someone else in the group has more conviction, experience, ability, and willingness to take responsibility.
6. Someone else's idea may be seen as similar to the manager's.
7. The manager may feel intimidated by an attack or by higher authority.
8. The manager may wish to avoid damaging a relationship.

When Legitimacy Is Counterproductive. Kaplan, Drath, and Kofodimos (1985) noted that legitimate power may be counterproductive if the superior's demeanor, isolation, and autonomy impede the flow of criticism from the subordinates to the superior. The subordinates' performance may suffer if the leader's legitimacy results in an aura of power, in a tendency to monopolize discussions, or in an abrasive style. The use of power in this way may increase social distance between the superior and the subordinates, further restricting communication. If subordinates perceive that the superior's power is an em-

bodiment of the organization, they may interpret criticism of the superior as disloyalty to the organization.

Legitimacy will be counterproductive if powerful superiors appoint only subordinates who agree with them or if the subordinates exempt themselves from the formal appraisals that others who are less powerful must undergo. But knowingly or unknowingly, supervisors may give up some of their legitimate power to their subordinates as a way of increasing overall satisfaction and responsibility. Blake and Mouton (1961a) asked a supervisor and a subordinate to rank lists of items in order of importance. The level of satisfaction and responsibility of both supervisors and subordinates combined was higher when they alternated in exercising power.[7]

Additional Aspects of the Bases of Power

Yukl and Falbe (1991) added to or replaced the five bases of power with charisma, persuasiveness, and information. Information is a particularly important base of power for political leaders. It gives political, congressional, and parliamentary leaders important knowledge about the rules of their legislatures, the predilections of key members, and their constituents' needs and attitudes. Yasir Arafat's continued presidency of the Palestinian Authority was based partly on his encyclopedic knowledge of the tribes and factions from the many towns, cities, and refugee camps whose diverse interests he had to reconcile if he was to maintain internal harmony (*Dallas Morning News*, 1997). For business leaders, accurate information about the informal networks in an organization of friends, potential advisors, and central figures can also be an important base of power (Krackhart, 1990).

Comparisons of the Bases of Power

Relative Importance. In 13 studies reviewed by Podsakoff and Schriesheim (1985a), large samples of respondents ranked French and Raven's five bases of power according to their importance in the superior-subordinate relationship. Agreement was high among the respondents, regardless of whether they were salespeople, members of a liberal arts faculty, insurance agents, or factory workers. For each sample as a whole, expert and legiti-

---

[7] Voluntary power sharing will be discussed in Chapters 18, 25, and 26.

mate power always ranked first or second in importance. Mean ranks were tied at 1.6. The other bases were seen as far less important. Means were: referent, 3.3; reward, 4.1; coercive, 4.6. However, Podsakoff and Schriesheim urged caution in interpreting these findings on their face value.

Relative Willingness to Use Power. Effective principals establish higher standards for their school by using their power to enlist the support of the teachers to improve standards. They use their power to support the teachers' career development during early adulthood to midlife and to help teachers find fulfillment in their work (Krupp, 1986). Leaders differ in their willingness to use power that derives from one base rather than another. Lord (1977) identified 12 functions that are typically performed by a leader, such as developing plans, proposing solutions, and providing resources. He watched to see how often each leader in a sample displayed the 12 functions. He also determined which of French and Raven's (1959) five bases of power the leaders used in attempts to exert their power. Lord then correlated the occurrence of each leadership function with the basis of power the leader used. He found that task-relevant behavior to complete the work of the group correlated with the type of power used, but the leaders' efforts to establish socioemotional relations did not. For example, the extent to which leaders relied on themselves as task experts correlated with the extent to which they proposed solutions. However, the extent to which the leaders tried to use referent power in their socioemotional efforts did not increase their being liked.

Coercion is more likely to be used by leaders who lack self-confidence and who have coercive power. In a laboratory experiment, Instone, Major, and Bunker (1983) found that, compared with those whose self-confidence was high, those who lacked self-confidence tended to use coercion rather than expert power. House (1984) listed other personal attributes that contribute to a leader's tendency to use coercive power, including the leader's power orientation, Machiavellianism, and dogmatism. In another laboratory study, Goodstadt and Hjelle (1973) reported that individuals who perceived themselves to be externally controlled by their environment used punishment to maintain their influence much more frequently than those who saw themselves as internally

self-controlling. "Self-controlling internals" attempted to lead through their expert power rather than coercively.

Raven and Kruglanski (1970) suggested that those with power anticipate the consequences of using the various kinds of power they may have and avoid using powers that are believed to be least effective. Thus coercive power will be avoided unless the power holders expect resistance—in which case they will be tempted to employ more coercive power if they are capable of doing so (Kipnis, 1976). Support for this contention was found for managers in state agencies, industry, and the military (Kipnis & Cosentino, 1969), as well as in laboratory experiments (Goodstadt & Kipnis, 1970). In the Kipnis studies, supervisors were asked to describe an incident in which they had to correct the behavior of a subordinate. Which type of power was brought to bear in this situation depended on the supervisors' diagnosis of the subordinate's problem, the subsequent and most likely reactions of the subordinate, and what was likely to be best for the continuing relationship with the subordinate.

Culture, tradition, hierarchical relations, and organizational norms will also determine what type of power may be applied in a given situation. For instance, tradition may give those with seniority and age power that can be used and accepted by those who are younger and have less seniority. Age itself may make a difference. When I asked Japanese managers meeting with each other for the first time at a workshop to form informal groups with group leaders, the groups selected their leaders by asking members who was oldest. More authoritarian, coercive uses of power will come into greater use and acceptability during times of stress. Managers can use more reward and legitimate power with subordinates than with peers (Yukl, Kim, & Falbe, 1996).

Legitimacy will be stressed by those who believe in "rules of law rather than rules of men." House (1984) suggested that legitimate power will be favored over arbitrariness and political influence because legitimate power provides more orderliness and predictability. Legitimacy has more clear-cut limitations; unbounded arbitrary power generates excess costs and inefficiencies. Legitimate power can be exerted impersonally without a buildup of allegations of political exchanges. Legitimate power is ordinarily more acceptable to the subordinate and more supported by the larger group than power based on the personal arbitrary predilections of the superior.

House (1984) obtained considerable support for the greater acceptability of legitimacy in studies in which employees were asked why they complied with manager's requests, suggestions, or directions.

Willingness to use one type of power rather than another was observed by Rosenberg and Pearlin (1962) in a study of the attitudes of 1,138 hospital nurses toward power. The percentages of nurses who stated that they would use each form of power were as follows: persuasion, 54%; benevolent manipulation, 38%; legitimate authority, 5%; coercive power, 2%; contractual power, 1%. Kappelman (1981) reported that male school principals were more likely than their female counterparts to use reward and coercive power, although women principals were likely to be described as more active leaders.

Since the bases of power are interrelated, changes in one will have effects on the others. For example, Greene and Podsakoff (1981) found that when the reward power of 37 supervisors in a paper mill was lowered by abandoning an incentive pay plan in which the supervisors' evaluation of the performance of 392 subordinates had figured strongly, not only did the supervisors' reward power decline, but their referent, legitimate, and organizationally sanctioned power declined as well, while the subordinates' perceptions of the supervisors' coerciveness increased significantly. No such changes in the bases of supervisory power were found in a second comparable paper mill that did not change its pay policy. Consistent with this, Garrison (1968) concluded that when leaders' efforts to succeed through legitimacy failed, they resorted to coercive power.

Effects of Different Bases of Power

The compliance caused by different bases of power is perceived differently. Rodrigues and Lloyd (1998) concluded from five studies using a total of 570 participants that compliance induced by reward, informational, and referent power was more internalized and controllable than compliance induced by expert, legitimate, and coercive power. Rubin, Lewicki, and Dunn (1973) found that cooperativeness, benevolence, friendliness, and generosity were attributed to those in power who used rewards rather than penalties. The reverse attributions were made about those who used authority or political persuasion.

Table 11.2 shows correlations between the perceived power base of first-line supervisors and their *initiating* be-

havior and *consideration* as leaders.[8] Martin and Hunt (1980) found these results for 289 professional personnel in a construction bureau and 118 in a design bureau of a midwestern state highway department who responded to a mailed survey. As can be seen, of all the bases of power, expert power made the most important contribution to leadership. The effect was not always beneficial; design professionals who complied with their supervisor because of the latter's expert power signaled a greater intention to quit.

Ivancevich (1970) reported that the satisfaction of life insurance agents correlated .35 with the agency manager's use of referent power, expert power, and reward power, but satisfaction correlated −.28 with the use of coercive power and .14 with the use of legitimate power. Bachman (1968) found that faculty members at colleges were better satisfied under powerful deans with control over college affairs whose influence was based on expert and referent power than under deans who relied on reward, legitimate, or coercive power. However, in a study of salesmen's perceptions of branch managers' power, Ivancevich and Donnelly (1970a) found that coercive and legitimate powers were not related to productivity. Only the expert and referent powers of the branch managers were positively related to the salesmen's performance.

Caveat. Podsakoff and Schriesheim's (1985a) review of these and other field studies of the relationship of the five sources of power of supervisors and the outcomes for subordinates concluded that unlike studies of the *actual* reward behavior of supervisors that usually generates positive outcomes, the supervisors' *power to reward* was unrelated or even negatively related to such outcomes. But Podsakoff and Schriesheim attributed the difference in findings to the way these field studies measured power. Often the measure consisted only of respondents' rank ordering of the bases of power as defined. The power to reward was confounded with a sense of illegitimacy used in exchange for reluctant compliance rather than for performance. Coerciveness was seen to be confounded with the potentially illegitimate use of punishment. The actual narrow content of the scales of legitimate power failed to match French and Raven's broader conceptualization, and the desired identification of the subordinate

---

[8]See Chapter 20 for detailed definitions of initiation and consideration.

Table 11.2 Correlations between the Perceived Basis of Power and Ratings of the Initiation of Structure and Consideration by First-Line Supervisors

Basis of Power	Initiation of Structure*		Consideration*	
	Construction Bureau	Design Bureau	Construction Bureau	Design Bureau
Expert	.44	.41	.50	.48
Referent	.23	.16	.15	.10
Reward	.24	.06	.11	.02
Coercive	.10	.01	−.10	.01
Legitimate	.04	.11	−.03	.00

* See Chapter 20 for detailed definitions of initiation and consideration.
SOURCE: Adapted from Martin and Hunt (1980).

with the superior was not included in measures of referent power, which often seemed no more than assessments of friendship.

Hinkin and Schriesheim's (1989) surveys of three samples of students who described their part-time or full-time supervisors found that although coercive power correlated with legitimate power to some extent, it was likely to be independent of the other bases of power. The other bases—expert, referent, and reward—correlated with legitimate power as a base as well as with each other as bases.

Despite these shortcomings, seven of the field studies[9] in Podsakoff and Schriesheim's (1985a) review emerged consistently with positive associations between supervisors' expert and referent power and subordinates' satisfaction and performance. The results were uniformly negative or reversed for coercive power and mixed for legitimate and reward power. Negative correlations were found between the supervisors' expert and referent power and the excused absences of production workers (Student, 1968), but no power measure was related to unexcused absences or turnover. However, Busch (1980) found that the expert power of supervisors contributed to the subordinates' intentions to remain in the three companies studied. Less consistent findings emerged for referent and legitimate power. A similar pattern was noted by Gemmill and Thamhain (1974) in the outcomes of support by supervisors and the commitment of subordinates to the work associated with supervisory powers. Only expert power was consistently positively correlated with

[9]Bachman (1968); Bachman, Bowers, and Marcus (1968); Bachman, Smith, and Slesinger (1966); Burke and Wilcox (1971); Busch (1980); Hinken and Schriesheim (1989); and Slocum (1970).

such outcomes and with the clarity of the subordinates' role. Also, such role clarity appeared to be enhanced if the superiors had referent power.

Yukl and Taber (1983) agreed with Podsakoff and Schriesheim (1985a) that the use of expert and referent power is most efficacious. Nevertheless, the skill of application and appropriateness of power must be considered. Leaders need to exercise authority with courtesy and clarity and to verify compliance. Reward power should be used to reinforce desirable behaviors after they occur. Coercive power should be used only when absolutely necessary, for example, to deter behavior that is detrimental to the individual, group, or organization. Leaders accumulate and foster expert and referent power over time by showing that they are confident, decisive, considerate, and protective of subordinates' interests. In the same vein, Watts (1986, p. 286) suggested that "using too much power can express the need to control, the flip side of which is the fear of being out of control. Using too little power can express a tremendous need to be liked, to avoid conflict." Furthermore, leaders need to avoid promising more (on the basis of their reward power) than they can deliver, and they need to avoid being corrupted by their power.

Power and Corruption

In the 1840s, Count Cavour, a future cofounding statesman of modern Italy, wrote that "absolute power inevitably corrupts," a remark which Lord Acton later made famous as "Power tends to corrupt; absolute power corrupts absolutely" (D. M. Smith, 1985, p. 26). The process was elucidated by Kipnis (1976). First, the desire for power becomes an end in itself. Next, access to power tempts the officeholder to use institutional resources for illegitimate self-aggrandizement. Self-aggrandizement is followed by false feedback from others, which elevates the leader's self-esteem, devalues the worth of others, and distances the leader from them.

Gardner (1986a) listed four ways to help mitigate the corruption of power in government. First, the rule of law and the accountability of leaders to abide within explicit and universally applicable constraints must be accepted. Second, power needs to be dispersed, as in the U.S. system of checks and balances of executive, legislative, and judicial powers. Third, a strong private sector must be maintained. Fourth, an alert citizenry is essential.

So far, analyses of power and corruption have been left to investigative journalists and the legal profession. Controlled surveys and experiments are needed to increase our understanding of the interrelation of power-corruption relationship, its antecedents and its consequences for business, governmental, and other institutions. How do various factors—the fear of being caught; public humiliation; regulatory control; a sense of duty, obligation, patriotism, and loyalty; and internalized ethical and professional standards—inhibit the corruptive influence of holding power over others? Chapter 9, on the ethics of leadership, has already dealt with some aspects of the corrupt use of power.

Importance of Content

Organizational formalization, rules, and norms can substitute for the expert power of leaders and their influence. On the other hand, if the *expert* power of leaders is seen to improve the functioning of their subordinates or to be applied usefully, their perceived influence will be enhanced (Podsakoff & Schriesheim, 1985). A leader's *referent* power was found by Yukl and Falbe (1991) to be most important to compliance by followers; a leader's *legitimate* and *coercive* power were most important for employee compliance in routine operations. If the holder of power is working on a task in an experiment with another person requiring cooperation, power will be used for their joint benefit. If they are in competition, power will be used to benefit its holder at the expense of the other. The amount of power used will not differ. The perceived competence

of the power holder will affect the use of power in the cooperative context, but not in the competitive context (van Kippenberg, van Kippenberg, & Wilke, 2001).

Summary and Conclusions

Power is a force giving one person the potential to influence others. Power can be personal (expert and referent) and positional (reward, coercive, and legitimate). It contributes to leadership and influence but is not synonymous with them. Information is among many other sources of power. It makes power expandable. Status and esteem provide power, influence, and leadership. Followers react differently to leaders whose power derives from different sources. The followers seek to be liked by those with referent and reward power. Although the threat of punishment tends to induce compliance, followers find leaders who use coercive power less attractive than those who use other forms of power. Furthermore, followers respond to reward power either by developing contractual agreements or by forming coalitions that tend to equalize the bargaining positions of participants in the power structure. Appointment or election to a position tends to legitimate it to a greater degree than does acquisition of a position by force or by the emergence of a leader in interactions.

Leaders draw consciously or unconsciously on multiple sources of power. Reward and coercive power are controlled most easily. Leaders have less control over referent power—the extent to which group members like them and are attracted to them. Self-confidence, self-esteem, and knowledge of the task enable subordinates to resist the effects of power. Interacting with peers and gaining support from reference groups strengthen the followers' resistance to coercion. The influence of a leader can be weakened if the followers form coalitions with countervailing power. Followers can reduce their subjection to influence by asking and receiving a clear definition of the situation. The power of a leader is weakened by the presence of members whose values and goals are in opposition to those of the leader and the organization and who challenge the legitimacy of the leadership role. Ingratiation may also be a means of private resistance. Power can corrupt both leaders and their followers. It can be shared and distributed for personal or organizational reasons.

CHAPTER 12

Leadership and the Distribution of Power

The distribution of power and the leadership associated with it have been a main theme in both political history and the history of management-worker relations. Autocracies and oligarchies have represented concentrations of power; democracies have represented a wider distribution of power. In the former, the individual autocrat with a patronizing staff of subordinates dictated to a relatively powerless membership. In the latter, power was dispersed voluntarily or as legally mandated. The past century has witnessed in the developed world a substantial reduction in the range between the powerful and the powerless. The differences in power between women and men, parents and children, teachers and students, and supervisors and supervisees have all been reduced. Apart from some Asian, African, and Latin American countries, autocracies, dictatorships, feudalistic, and tribal societies have been replaced by more democratic forms of government, business, and other institutions. Nevertheless, in many organizations, communities, and countries, large differences in political, economic, and social power are the rule rather than the exception. In informal groups, power differences are likely to evolve. In initially leaderless groups, power accrues to the active and more knowledgeable members.

Importance of Differences in Power

Mulder (1976) focused attention on such differences in power in organizations and the tendency of those who are striving for more power to reduce them. Hofstede (1980, 1997) unearthed a "power distance" factor in a large-scale survey of employees' attitudes in 50 countries. A large power distance was indicated, for example, in countries in which employees expressed fear of disagreeing with their supervisors.

Power and Leadership Style. Hofstede suggested that with a large power distance between leaders and followers, or supervisors and employees, the followers and employees became either dependent or counterdependent. When differences in power are great, more autocratic leadership and more coercion are likely. Large differences within a group, organization, or society—particularly in coercive power, and to a lesser extent in personal, reward, and legitimate power—may guarantee public success and acceptance of the leadership. But resistance, at least private resistance, will bring about unintended consequences, such as resentment and apathy. On the other hand, the maintenance by leaders and supervisors of a small power distance between themselves and their followers and employees encourages consultation and participation. Many behavioral science theorists[1] have observed that the sharing, leveling, and equalization of power among members of a group increases the members' participation and results in their full commitment and their acceptance, both public and private, of the leader.

Elitism versus Populism. Even within a society's democratic order, there are wide differences in power. Populism competes with elitism. Populists believe that all citizens share equally in the opportunity to exert influence through political activity. Elitists believe that power should be delegated to those who are committed to the rules of decision making and are highly knowledgeable and skilled in analysis, negotiation, persuasion, and manipulation. Populism calls for a high degree of citizen participation; elitism calls for a relatively passive, uninvolved citizenry, who, from time to time, "in a single elemental choice," elect active officials who will be re-

[1] See, for instance, Argyris (1957), Lawler (1986), R. Likert (1961a), Lippitt (1942), and McGregor (1960).

sponsible for the stability, efficiency, and authority of the state (Summers, 1987). Populism within the work organization translates into shop-floor democracy, in which all employees share consultation and decision making with their immediate superiors. Elitism within the organization translates into the election of experienced and knowledgeable union officials and council representatives, or heavy dependence on informal leaders from within the workforce.

Distribution of Power in the Small Group or Team

Populism within the small group or team translates into shared decision making by the group members; elitism translates into elected heads whose power to decide is unchallenged by the members, who remain passive following the election. In elitist groups, most of the power resides in the leader; in populist groups, it is widely shared and equalized among the members and the leader. With such equalization of power, the members become as influential as the leader, and their effects on each other become important to the process of interpersonal influence. Thelen (1954) noted the power and control of the group over its members. Group agreements "have teeth in them." The determination of what is possible and at what cost or with what reward is under the control of the group. Leadership occurs in changing the agreements and working out new ones to fit the continual diagnosis of realities in the group problem situation.

According to Tannenbaum and Massarik (1950), shared decision making increases the likelihood that workers will accept the goals desired by the management. This results in their greater satisfaction and increased efforts to move toward the selected goals. Likewise, McGregor (1944) argued that the effectiveness of workers will be increased when they are given opportunities to participate in finding solutions to problems, to discuss actions that affect them, and to assume responsibilities when they are ready to do so. If members of a group participate in setting goals, they will be more motivated to achieve the goals. If they have the capabilities, they can be delegated more responsibility or freedom to act without a review by a higher authority (Learned, Ulrich, & Booz, 1951).

When all members are equal in status and power, more communication of feelings will occur (Bovard,

1952). Differences in status and power in a group result in the inhibition of the ventilation of feelings by members who are lower in the status and power hierarchy. Such inhibition can be detrimental to the group's functioning. Thibaut and Coules (1952) found that the communication of hostility toward instigators will reduce the residual hostility toward them. Again, power differences can offset the influencing effects of participation. Bass, Flint, and Pryer (1957b) and Bass (1963) ascertained that for individuals to influence a group's decisions, they had to participate and to attempt to lead. Nonetheless, such active participation did not necessarily influence the group's decision when the members of a small group varied widely in power.

Caveats. This does not mean that all communications are easier and all outcomes are better when members are equal in status and power. Although some believe that power sharing and participation are a universal panacea for promoting change, productivity, and satisfaction, experimental researchers such as Locke, Latham, and Erez (1987) have pointed out that considerable qualification is needed. For instance, if the leader is clear and supportive, the members' acceptance of hard group goals can be obtained without the power sharing implied in group discussions and decision making. More competition from members and persistence by the leader in the face of rejection are likely to be required of the would-be leader of a group in which all members are equal in status and power. Thus Bovard (1951a) observed that in groups where there is little status differentiation among members and all have similar power to influence each other, verbal interaction is higher and more influencing is attempted than when a single person of higher status directs the activities. It may be that although communication seems easier when members are equal in power, it really is more difficult. Shepherd and Weschler (1955) studied work groups that differed in internal status stratification. The members of these groups felt they had fewer communication difficulties, but they actually experienced more such difficulties.

Formation of Coalitions. The distribution of power in a small group is dynamic. Two or more members can combine their power to increase their joint power and influence the course of events. Lawler (1975) found that expectations of support from others were an important cognitive determinant of the formation of a coalition against inequitable and threatening leaders. How reward power is distributed in the triad has been the focus of experiments regarding the bargaining process. Mills (1953) assembled triads in which one member was given high reward power; one, medium reward power; and one, low reward power. A strong tendency was found for two of the members to form a coalition that acted in opposition to the third member. Vinacke and Arkoff (1957) confirmed hypotheses advanced by Caplow (1956) that: (1) when all members of a triad are equal in power, all possible combinations will be formed; (2) when two equal members who are stronger than the third member combine, they will form a coalition in opposition to the third member; (3) when one member is weaker than the two equal members, he or she will form a coalition with one of them; and (4) when one member is stronger than the other two combined, no coalition will ensue. Turk and Turk (1962) confirmed the fourth of these hypotheses. But Kelley and Arrowood (1960) found that the results reported by Vinacke and Arkoff depended on the clarity of the game and on whether a player was assured of a certain return whether or not he or she joined a coalition.[2]

Coalitions are also organized as a tactic to increase one's upward influence. Kipnis and Schmidt reported that respondents exerted more upward influence on their boss by obtaining the support of their coworkers and subordinates to back up their request, or they arranged a formal meeting with the boss at which they made their request. Such coalitions were used at about the same frequency to influence coworkers, subordinates, and the boss.

Stability in Small Groups

The stability of the distribution of power begins early. In an observational study of kindergarten children, Hanfmann (1935) noted a stable power structure that was similar to a pecking order. The same child would continue to give orders to the same second child, who did the same to the same third child. Gellert's (1961) observations of pairs of preschool children during three play periods found that in a significant proportion of these dyads, the same child maintained the same position of dominance or submission during the three periods. This again suggests that a pecking order was at work.

Structuralism versus Human Relations

There are two opposing arguments about how power should be distributed in organizations. In the *structuralist* view, organizations are mechanistic rather than organic (T. Burns & Stalker, 1961). It is inherent in the nature of organizations with systems of command and control that power is distributed unevenly. As organizations develop, power accrues in varying amounts among the units and supervisors. Some units (and, therefore, their supervisors) obtain more power than others in influencing the allocation of the organization's scarce resources (Pfeffer & Salancik, 1978). The units and supervisors with more power have control over strategic contingencies and the activities of other departments that are critical to their functioning; this makes it less likely that there will be any way of substituting for the more powerful units' and supervisors' activities. Also, information is provided to the less powerful units and supervisors to decrease uncertainties. Thus more powerful units and supervisors are in the center rather than at the periphery of information and work flow (Hickson, Hinings, et al., 1971). Support for these propositions was found in 20 subunits of five breweries by Hinings, Hickson, Pennings, et al. (1974). Similar results were obtained for 62 vice presidents, deans, and directors of six universities (Saunders & Scamell, 1982).

Power holders want to retain their power, so the power distribution in mechanistic organizations remains stable over time unless there are shifts in technological and environmental demands or the power holders are replaced (House, 1991). But temporary downward shifts in power become necessary as leaders' positions enlarge. Increasingly, leaders need to rely on subordinate staff as intermediaries, deputies, and surrogates. Kings had to share their power in distant colonies with viceroys. Whyte (1953) and Simon (1957) argued for structure, power differences, and status differentiation. They contended that hierarchical organization is the natural, biological, and sociological solution for ensuring a group's survival. R. B. Cattell (1953) hypothesized that status differentiation

---

[2] See Caplow (1968) for a detailed analysis of power relations in the triad.

and the accompanying power differences promote speed in decision making and the faster attainment of goals.

Human Relations Perspective. The opposing *human relations* perspective sets forth that increasing the equalization of power in organizations was essential to the organization's health. Reducing power differences was a basic tenet of modern organizational development theory and practice (Bennis, 1965) and the human potential movement (Maslow, 1965). The organic organization was favored. It had its roots in those aspects of democratic and egalitarian values that stress the importance of informal trusting relationships rather than a formal structure in which relationships depend on the authority of position and role requirements. Practical applications include unstructured leadership, job enlargement, leadership sharing, participative management, consultative supervision, joint consultation, workers' councils, and other forms of industrial democracy. Patchen (1970) administered questionnaires to 90 employees in plants operated by the Tennessee Valley Authority and found that the degree of control workers had over their jobs was significantly correlated with their general interest in their jobs, concern with innovations in their work, and pride in their work. These findings were supported by communication-net studies (McCurdy & Eber, 1953).

Argyris (1957) and McGregor (1960) were convinced that individuals, motivated by their basic desire for autonomy and self-actualization, were frustrated by organizational structure, specialization of work, and philosophies of management that assumed that workers would remain complacent and unproductive unless they were subjected to controls hampering unwanted initiatives from them. When workers were less encumbered by controls, their first-line supervisors also benefited. Atwater (1996) found that in organic organizations, more power was bestowed on first-line supervisors relative to the power at higher levels of management, as reported by 280 employees from 45 traditional or organic organizations.

Stability in Organizations. House (1984) deduced that the distribution of power in organizations would tend to become stable over time and would change only if there were major shifts in environmental or technological demands on the organization. But even here, changes in the power distribution would come slowly because

those in power are reluctant to part with any of it. In fact, given the tendency of the powerful to gain more power, demands for change in the organization may bring about a greater concentration of power rather than equalization.

Implications for Organizational Design. The two views have been the basis of opposing prescriptions for how organizations should be designed. *Structuralism* emphasizes designing organizations with power differences; *humanism* emphasizes designing organizations with more power equalization. Legitimate differences in power are manifested in an organization in how much the positions of members are structured—that is, prescribed and bound by rules and regulations or the dictates and policies of a higher authority. An infantry squad is highly structured; an initially leaderless discussion group is not. In the infantry squad, there is a clear legitimate hierarchy of power from the squad leader down to the new private; there is no such legitimate hierarchy in the leaderless discussion group. Equalization of power is fostered by humanism in its support for informality, trust, learning, and the sharing of information.

Structuralism as enunciated by such classical management theorists as Taylor (1911), Fayol (1916), Follett (1918), and Davis (1942) depends on external constraints to gain the compliance and commitment of followers. The human relations viewpoint, through the equalization of power, expected to gain even more commitment as well as compliance through the individual's awareness of and insight into effective interpersonal relations and trust.

Structuralism called for someone to be responsible for supervising all essential activities. The hierarchical pyramid of supervisor-subordinate relationships was mandated. Power sharing proposed that any team member could take on leadership responsibilities when he or she saw the need to do so. The autonomous team with no formally appointed leader was the extreme example.

Structuralism avoids the duplication or overlapping of responsibilities. However, overlapping, cross-training, rotation, and other forms of sharing responsibilities to increase the reliability of the system are encouraged by human relationists when informal relationships are developed among workers who are committed to see that their group prospers. The simplification of jobs is fundamental to a structuralist approach. According to this perspective, no individual should be responsible for a wide assortment of unrelated acts. In contrast, human relations theorists call for the enlargement and enrichment of jobs; they believe that subordinates who receive bigger jobs with greater responsibilities become closer in power to superiors.

The structuralist position calls for subordinates to receive clear, written job specifications and role assignments. The human relations position calls for making goals clear and allowing subordinates, commensurate with their training and experience, to decide how to reach the goals. Both structuralists and human relationists agree that authority should be delegated so that decisions take place as close as possible to the action. For structuralists, the decision maker is the superior in the situation; for human relationists, the decision is shared or delegated to the subordinates as much as possible.

Structuralists emphasize the chain of command. Human relationists argue that organizations require much communicating, reporting, proposing, influencing, complying, and deciding in complex vertical, diagonal, and horizontal paths that are not shown on the formal organizational charts. Again, participants need some sense of the equalization of power for this flow to occur effectively.

Neither the structuralists nor the human relationists have a monopoly on the most effective design (Bass & Ryterband, 1979). Situational elements and personal preferences affect which approach pays off. Young professional workers, compared with older unskilled employees, are likely to call for less structure and more equalization of power. Small-business managers, secure in their personal relations with their parents and attachment to their spouses, will be more comfortable in decentralized organizations with less structure; less secure counterparts who prefer distance in their personal relationships will want centralization of power (Johnston, 2000). Some pupils thrive in schools with a great deal of freedom to choose what and how to learn, but others do best in a highly structured environment. Juvenile delinquents who adjust most readily to institutionalization may have more difficulty avoiding antisocial, criminal behavior once they are back on the streets. The optimum differentiation of power is likely to lie between the extreme structuralist and extreme human relations posi-

tions, depending on the situation. In a pluralistic society, the only thing one can safely say is that wide differences in performance, attitudes, and response to hierarchy are likely to depend on task, time, place, immediate needs, and such.

Distribution of Power in Communities and Organizations

The distribution of power provides the potential for leadership and influence over events and people. It shows itself and its effects in how it is distributed in communities, in formal organizations, and in smaller groups. In small communities, citizens may have the power to directly participate in decisions, such as at town meetings. In cities, they may have the power to participate indirectly through attendance at civic meetings, consultation with officials, and keeping themselves informed. They may reveal their power in elections, formal petitions, protests, initiatives, and referenda. Or they may be powerless and manipulable (Couto, 1992). Central to civic improvement in many U.S. metropolitan areas has been citizens' power to directly participate in decisions regarding innovation and change. In Portland, Oregon, citizen participation became expected as mayors, governors, and legislators introduced land laws, new parklands, light rail, and a revived active downtown to provide a high quality of life. In San Antonio, civic organizations pushed their elected officials into major changes, such as on the riverfront. In many cities such as Denver, business and government leaders shared power and responsibilities in turning the economy around. Catholics were mobilized by a bishop in Cleveland to deal with urban sprawl and its effects on the poor of the inner city. Neighborhood associations, commonplace in cities and suburban communities, deal with local as well as communitywide issues (Pierce & Johnson, 1997).

Community Power Structures

The earliest research on power was concerned with identifying individuals who had the power to influence their local communities. Lynd and Lynd (1929) pointed the way in their study *Middletown*. F. Hunter (1953) used interviews in a large city to obtain a list of 175 persons who were mentioned as wielding influence in the community, with reasons for the belief that they had such power to influence. A panel of experts reduced the list to 40 persons who were regarded as constituting a monolithic power structure in the city. However, Dahl (1961) maintained that the nominating technique hid important details that could be uncovered by a study of community issues. He concentrated on identifying those individuals who had played key roles in promoting or blocking issues. His analysis of the data suggested that there was a pluralist power structure in the city. Using both Hunter's and Dahl's methods, Freeman, Fararo, Bloomberg, and Sunshine (1963) and Presthus (1964) found that the two methods identified a common core of power figures and that Dahl's method revealed additional subgroups of individuals who could influence different issues.

The status and power structures of many communities were studied.[3] Consistently, people who were identified as having power also tended to rate high in social and economic status. Educational level, as such, was less important (Alford & Scoble, 1968). However, the acceleration of the importance of new technology in everyday life has given professionals increased power in their communities. That is, as problems of health, economics, safety, and so on come to the fore, the expert power of professionals takes on increasing importance in the community.

When Hunter and Fritz (1985) studied the power structures in four Chicago suburbs, they found that the smaller communities contained less complex structures. This finding fit with V. Williams's (1965) conclusion that smaller communities may be able to function effectively without the differentiation of roles and individuals in specialization, power, and authority. Similarly, Nix, Dressel, and Bates (1977) described the dispersion of power in small rural communities, drawing on 189 interviews and the reconstructed history of a country in the southeastern United States since 1900. They noted that the initial bossism was replaced by informal cliques, organized pluralism, bifactionalism, multifactionalism, and amorphous leadership. In the Chicago suburbs studied by Hunter and Fritz, the informal status structures were less complex in the richer suburbs than in the poorer ones.

[3] See Blumberg (1955), Bonjean (1963, 1964), Clelland and Form (1964), Fanelli (1956), Form and Sauer (1963), Lowry (1968), Olmsted (1954), Schulze (1958), and Wildavsky (1964), among others.

Equal status and equal power are more commonly found when familiarity, homogeneity, and the potential to interact are high. Caplow and Forman (1950) observed that when neighborhoods contained families who were homogeneous in duration of their residence, their interests, and their type of dwelling, no status differentiation occurred. Form (1945) reported similar findings for Greenbelt, Maryland, when it was a newly established community for federal white-collar employees of similar occupations, age, nativity, and housing. Similarly, Munch (1945) found that the homogeneous inhabitants of isolated Tristan da Cunha in the South Atlantic maintained their community without status differentiation or institutionalized government.

Interlocking Office Holding. Perrucci and Pilisak (1970) compiled a list of 434 organizations in a community with a population of 50,000. Of 1,677 executives in these organizations, 1,368 held a position in only one organization. Twenty-six executives who occupied positions in four or more organizations were compared with 26 executives who occupied a position in only one organization. The multiorganizational leaders were regarded by both groups as being more powerful and as having more influence on actual and theoretical issues. These leaders were named more often as social and business friends and were found to constitute a powerful network of influence relationships. The concentration of power was seen in the city boss, studied in detail by Banfield and Wilson (1963), Moos and Koslin (1951), and Zink (1930). Mayor Richard Daley of Chicago epitomized the use of social exchange relationships with other bloc leaders and centers of community power to build the powerful political machine that claimed to "make Chicago work." His son, as mayor, continued the tradition of relationships.

Power Systems

Power reveals itself in formal organizations in the extent to which it is associated with status and authority—the formal authority system—and in the beliefs shared by the members in the organization's system of ideology. An organization's *system of authority* involves the way legitimate power is distributed and enacted in goals, rewards, sanctions, and the division of labor. It is based on the legitimate power of the different roles and positions, and the status and authority of the position holders. The organization's *system of expertise* is the way information and knowledge are distributed among its positions and position holders. It is more informally applied to solving the complex problems of the organization (Mintzberg, 1983). The interlocking of systems was illustrated by Majchrzak (1987), who found that rates of unauthorized absences in units in 20 Marine Corps companies were significantly reduced, in contrast to 20 control companies, if policies were clarified and communicated effectively to all levels involved and there was a hierarchical consistency in agreement and understanding of the policies and requirements at the different levels.

The systems offset each other. Although the authority system would dictate otherwise, the system of expertise may result in managers being less influential than their subordinate staff experts. B. Walter (1966) traced the transmission of influence in two municipal organizations. Superiors generally were found no more influential than their staff subordinates in making decisions; in fact, the subordinates were more influential when making novel decisions.

The *political system* operates outside the system of formal authority to benefit some constituents at the expense of others or at the expense of the organization (Mintzberg, 1983). Although the political system is likely to conflict with the other systems, it can also serve to mobilize power when needed for the acceptance and implementation of new strategies. The interacting systems of power can be observed in community settings as well.

Status and Power. One of the most consistent findings in social science is the general tendency for those higher in status in an organization to wield more power to influence those who are lower in status. Thus, at Walt Disney World leaders are expected to encourage their staffs of "cast members" to connect with visitors emotionally by "owning" their roles and monitoring their performances and the visitors' reactions. Among many studies of the relationship, Blankenship and Miles (1968) found hierarchical position to be a more important determinant of managers' decision-making behavior than the size of a company or the number of subordinates that the manager supervised. Bass (1960) argued that by creating greater differences in power and status between the

leader and followers, one can increase the proportion of success in acts of leadership. This outcome was observed by Hemphill, Seigel, and Westie (1951) in a study of 100 groups that varied in status differentiation. Such leadership was also likely to be more dominating, directive, and coercive and more likely to define and structure the work for the membership. Again, as was expected, a related study of 212 aircrews by Rush (undated) found that commanders were much less considerate of their subordinates when the crews were highly stratified in status.

House (1988a) concluded that when social stratification (status differentiation) exists and the holders of authority feel strongly about their status, they will have fewer inhibitions against being coercive. The greater the social stratification, the more likely they are to be coercive in order to obtain compliance from those at lower levels. Nevertheless, high-status powerful persons may fail to be successful leaders over the powerless. They may become distrusted (Tenbrunsel & Messick, 2001), particularly if they usurp power or are coercive.

Effects of the Total Amount of an Organization's Power and Control. A. S. Tannenbaum (1956a, 1956b, 1968) proposed that the total power and control in an organization varies rather than remaining fixed. Power and control can be expanded by increasing authority— legitimate power—at one or two levels or at all levels of the organization. An organization tends to gain most in the total amount of its control of its members when authority is expanded all the way down the line particularly to the lowest levels. In studies of two industrial plants (1956a) and four labor unions (1956b), Tannenbaum found that organizations of the same type could differ in the amount of authority exercised by executives at different levels and in the total amount of organizational control.

Smith and Tannenbaum (1963) studied 200 units of large firms. They found that the total amount of organizational control was positively and significantly related to the members' loyalty, morale, and judged effectiveness but not to objective measures of effectiveness. Nevertheless, leader-member agreement on the ideal amount of control and the actual total amount of control over members was related to rates of effectiveness. On the other hand, when Smith and Tannenbaum (1965) examined the effects of the total amount of control by the members of women's organizations, the total amount of control failed to increase the coordination of leadership, although such leadership contributed to the group's effectiveness.

In a study of insurance agencies, Bowers (1964b) reported that total organizational control was related to the members' satisfaction and performance but not to the volume of business, the growth of business, or the turnover of personnel. Furthermore, the amount of power at different levels of an organization was not associated with effectiveness. Smith and Ari (1964) observed that a consensus among members of work groups and among superiors and subordinates was related to the total amount of organizational control but not to the amount of control of individuals at the work level.

Ivancevich (1970) studied the effects of the total amount of organizational control and members' satisfaction in insurance agencies. The agents' satisfaction with status, autonomy, and growth was correlated about .30 with the manager's control over the agency, the agents' control over the agency, and the total amount of organizational control. Ivancevich found that agents were equally satisfied whether they or the manager exercised control. In another study of insurance agencies, Bachman, Smith, and Slesinger (1966) found that the agents' satisfaction was highly related to the total amount of control, control by the manager, and control by the agents.

In addition to the effect of differences in the total amount of control exercised by members, the total amount of control is higher when exercised by members in all echelons of the hierarchy rather than at just one or two levels. The total amount of control, but not control in the various echelons, is related to productivity and to members' satisfaction. Furthermore, in some organizations members tend to feel more satisfied when the top-level leader is charismatic and exercises strong control over organizational activities (House, 1988).

Although this point has not been examined, the reason why high total control increases satisfaction and productivity may be that goals and expectations are much clearer for members and conflict is much lower than when organizational anarchy exists. Nonetheless, many of the older studies of satisfaction with control need replication, because organizations have become flatter and workers and managers expect more from participation and democratic leadership.

Measurement of the Distribution of Power

The distribution of power is ordinarily inferred from observing variance among members of a group or organization in the success of their efforts to influence each other. This inference leads to a tautology. Observed differences in influence indicate the distribution of power; differential power begets differential influence. The equalization of power is seen in shared leadership. Power differences are also inferred from differences in status and esteem. The general has more legitimate power than the colonel. The admired parent will have more referent power in the family than an estranged one.

Measuring the responsibility, authority, and delegation associated with a position is a more direct way to understand an incumbent's power.[4] To obtain a direct measure of power differentiation independent of observed influence and status, Bass and Valenzi (1974) asked subordinates and managers to describe the power that managers had over manager-subordinate relations and the power the subordinates had over these relations. Questionnaire items dealing with the managers' power included the extent to which the managers had the power to override or veto any decisions the subordinates made; grant or deny promotion or salary increases to subordinates; reverse the priorities of subordinates; control the size of subordinates' budgets; and get the support of a higher authority for what the managers wanted to do. The subordinates' power included bringing outside pressure to support what they want; doing the opposite of what the manager wants done; maintaining final control over their own plans, assignments, and targets; ignoring the manager and submitting their own requests to a higher authority; and nominating or electing the manager. Bass and Valenzi obtained alpha coefficients of .60 for the reliability of both management's and subordinates' power. They found that on scores ranging from one to nine, superiors' power was typically above six whereas the subordinates' score was below four.

Dependency. Kotter (1978) took a different route to study power differences in organizations. His interviews focused on whom the incumbent in a particular management position felt dependent. Kotter also assessed the in-

---

[4]See Chapter 14.

cumbent's efforts to obtain cooperation, compliance, and deference from others in the system. Integrating these concerns about power and dependence with a concern for the organization's goals was seen as the key to effective performance and was consistent, as was noted in Chapter 7, with McClelland and Burnham's (1976) demonstration that effective managers have a strong need for power but are oriented toward organizational goals rather than self-aggrandizement.

Power of Departments. For their study of the distribution of power among departments at universities, Saunders and Scamell (1982) modeled their assessments after Hinings, Hickson, Pennings, and Schneck (1974). They were able to obtain valid measures of three determinants of how departments differed in power. From data obtained in interviews and questionnaires, they indexed the department's centrality in the flow of work and information, the difficulty of substituting an alternative department for the department's activities, and how much ability the department had to cope with uncertainties. Using small-space analysis, Shapira (1976) showed that the differences between the power of managers and subordinates, when combined with the information that each had, could predict, as theoretically expected, which style of leadership would be most often displayed by the managers. Managers with more power and information than their subordinates were most *directive*; managers with more power but less information were most *consultative*; managers with more information but less power were most *negotiative*; managers with less power and information were most *delegative*.

Autonomy. The distribution of power can be measured indirectly by how much is delegated to the less powerful and by how much autonomy and freedom they have to choose how to operate in the work setting. Objective characteristics of the situation may constrain autonomy. It also is a subjective experience, such as being one's own boss. Sinha and Viswesvaran (1998) conducted a meta-analysis of 99 samples of autonomy from 56 published studies. The variety of scales and measurements registered a mean reliability of .69 for the managers' perceived autonomy and .73 for nonmanagers. Meanings of autonomy included being allowed to try and fail without fear of reprisals; freedom from constant evaluation; free-

dom from close supervision; sense of ownership of the work; discretion in scheduling the work; determination of what needed to be done; freedom to make decisions without checking with a supervisor; taking part in decisions affecting the work situation; exercising personal judgment; having an opportunity to express ideas, and being treated as an equal by the supervisor.

The Power of the Group

Power sharing with all members of a group does not necessarily mean increased initiative and freedom for members. On the contrary, powerful groups can constrain and influence their members more strongly than any individual leader with power can. Mere membership in a group makes a difference. Deutsch and Gerard (1954) found that individuals in a group were more influenced by observed standards than were those who were not in a group. Katz and Lazarsfeld (1955) concluded that people are more likely to change their opinions if their relatives or friends are undergoing a similar change. The changes are also more likely to persist if supported by such group affiliations. In the same way, individuals are more influenced by the mass media when they are listening in groups than when they are alone.

Socialization processes in organizations are a familiar phenomenon. For example, after liberal students enter the world of work, they tend to adopt more conservative attitudes involving the norms of the firms they join. S. Lieberman (1954) found that workers who were promoted to foremen tended to shift their attitudes in favor of the management as they became members of management. Workers with the same attitudes as those who became foremen but who subsequently were elected as union shop stewards, shifted their attitudes in the union's direction after 12 months as stewards.

The Tendency to Conform

Many early investigators demonstrated the tendency of members of a group to shift toward the attitudes and behavior of the group.[5] Subsequently, Bass (1957b), Hare

[5] See Bechterew and Lange (1924/1931); Conradi (1905); Hilgard, Sait, and Magaret (1940); Marple (1933); H. T. Moore (1921); Thorndike (1938); and Wheeler and Jordan (1929).

(1953), and McKeachie (1954) found in various experiments that group discussions were more effective than reading or listening to arguments in increasing group members' agreement with one another, both publicly and privately. Generally, such group discussion leads to improvement in the members' understanding, commitment, and decision making. But the reverse is also true. Janis (1972) saw groupthink as the reason why highly competent members made extremely poor collective decisions, such as in the Bay of Pigs fiasco shortly after Fidel Castro seized power in Cuba. Highly cohesive, highly intelligent top officials of the Kennedy administration assumed a unanimous view when it did not exist. Conformity occurred out of a sense of loyalty to the group.

The signs of conformity in workers' performance as a consequence of the work group's power over its members were well known when pay-for-performance was commonly established by the number of pieces a worker produced in an hour or day. The fear of "rate busting" and that management would lower the price per piece paid to workers resulted in distributions of outputs of workers that peaked at an arbitrary limit set by the group. The variance in output was not a normal probability distribution; the distribution was truncated at the upper end.[6]

Subtle Influences. In a series of well-known experiments, Asch (1952) showed that conformity to the opinion of a simulated group can be induced even when the group decision defies the senses. A fair proportion of duped participants will agree that the clearly shorter of two lines is longer if they see all the other persons (all confederates) in the same situation stating that the shorter line is the longer one. Subtler influences of group power were measured by A. L. Hoffman (1956) and Horwitz (1954). Hoffman confronted participants with group norms that alternately agreed and disagreed with the participants' responses. The psychogalvanic skin responses of participants suggested that tension was reduced when they believed they had conformed to the group instead of being in disagreement with others. Horwitz (1954) found that individual members were under the greatest tension according to their greater recall of interrupted tasks (Zeigarnik effect), when they voted not to continue a task that the group had voted to continue.

[6]Rothe (1946, 1947, 1949, 1960, 1961) and Rothe and Nye (1958, 1959).

The effects of conformity persist even after the group disbands. When partners are separated after experiencing a judging situation together, they continue to influence each other's judgments when asked to judge alone (E. Cohen, 1956). Bovard (1948) found that the tendency to be affected in this way persisted for at least 28 days.

Power Sharing to Promote Change

Speaking to government employees, Robert Reich, the secretary of labor, declared:

> To provide quality service is through fundamentally changing the relationship between management and labor, by pushing responsibility downward and giving people on the front line the power they need to do their jobs. . . . It's not giving up authority. It's joining in partnership to give everybody more authority (including me). Reich & Copening, 1994, pp. 35, 36.

Group Discussion. The use of discussion in groups is an approach to increasing power sharing in the decision-making process and to increasing the influence of the group decision on individual members. K. Lewin (1943) conducted a seminal experiment to demonstrate how group discussion influenced housewives' choice of meats for their families' meals. Group discussion will produce more change in members than will the arguments of individuals; it has been found superior to lecture techniques in reducing biases in the merit-rating tendencies of supervisors, prejudice, hostile attitudes, alcoholism, and emotional disturbances in children. Group discussion has also proved superior to lectures in reaching solutions to community problems and modifying food habits (Lichtenberg & Deutsch, 1954). In addition, Radke and Klisurich (1947) observed that new mothers who engaged in discussions under the leadership of a dietitian much more readily adopted desired behavioral patterns that coincided with the usual recommended procedures than did a control group who received individual instruction. Similarly, Levine and Butler (1952) significantly reduced the halo effect in merit ratings by foremen by permitting them to discuss and make decisions regarding more realistic evaluations. Torrance and staff (1955) found that B-29 aircrews were more likely to reach a state of efficiency that enabled them to go into combat if they had been observed to participate in decision making earlier in survival school.

Coch and French (1948), J. R. P. French (1950), and French and Zander (1949) reported the results of an experiment in a clothing manufacturing plant. The factory had experienced a considerable turnover of labor after each change in operating methods. The experimenters studied four groups of employees. For the control group, a change was merely announced. For the three experimental groups, the workers were given an opportunity to discuss the change, to offer suggestions, and to agree on the necessity for the change. Productivity increased and turnover of personnel decreased in the experimental groups but not in the control group.

The same plant studied by Coch and French and a second plant were studied in 1962, 1964, and 1969 by Seashore and Bowers (1963, 1970) and by Marrow, Bowers, and Seashore (1968). Managers and workers were given group training in joint problem solving. Although the employees' satisfaction did not change to a marked degree, their commitment to the task improved, productivity norms were raised, and productivity increased. Ronken and Lawrence (1952) studied a firm that was experiencing difficulties in communication. When small groups and committees were formed to discuss and analyze the problem and to suggest solutions, communications became freer and operations were conducted more smoothly.

Additional Evidence of Group Power

Lawrence and Smith (1955) compared groups of workers who set their own production goals with other groups who merely discussed production problems. Groups who set their own goals showed significantly greater increases in productivity. Lawler and Hackman (1969) reported experimental results using group power to develop a pay-incentive plan for maintenance crews. Three groups developed their own pay-incentive plans to reward good attendance on the job. The plans were then imposed on two other groups. One type of control group was given a lecture about job attendance and the other received no experimental treatment. Only those in the groups who developed their own plans increased their attendance.

Sharma (1955) surveyed 568 teachers in 20 school systems and found that their satisfaction was related to the extent to which they reported that they were involved in decision making as individuals or as groups.

Zander and Gyr (1955) examined employees' attitudes toward a merit rating system. They found that a significant change in attitudes required monthly feedback, and that consultation and discussion were somewhat more effective than mere explanations of the system. In addition, under both conditions, changes in attitudes occurred only when subordinates described the supervisor as sincere, when the supervisor knew the plan and the issues, when the supervisor's and the subordinates' opinions were in agreement, and when the supervisor was skilled as a chairperson.[7]

Increasing Group Power and Its Effects

The more power the work group has over its members, the fewer differences will be seen in the members' output. Thus Seashore (1954) found less variance in productivity among different members of the more cohesive of 228 factory groups. The more members expect to be rewarded and to avoid punishment through membership in the group, the more they value the group and—as in Asch's experiments described above—the more the group will have the power to produce conformity (Deutsch & Gerard, 1954). Gerard (1954) noted that the greater the attraction of the members to a group, the more their opinions coalesced. Gorden (1952) observed more conformity in members who were identified most with the group. Similarly, Newcomb (1943) observed that the extent to which Bennington College students wanted to "belong" on campus determined the extent to which they shifted their social attitudes in the direction of the liberal attitudes prevailing on campus. Rasmussen and Zander (1954) found that teachers' levels of aspiration conformed more to the ideal of their group the more they were at-

[7] For more on the sharing and redistribution of power to effect planned change, the reader may wish to examine Bennis, Benne, and Chin (1962); French, Bell, and Zawacki (1978); and Zollschan and Hirsch (1964)—all edited collections of readings on the theory and techniques of planned change—and theoretical and technical reviews such as those by Bavelas (1948); Bennis (1963, 1965, 1966a); Burns and Stalker (1961); Cartwright (1951); Ginzberg and Reilley (1957); Kanter (1983); Lippitt, Watson, and Westley (1958); Low (1948); McMurry (1947); Patchen (1964); Schein and Bennis (1965); Sofer (1955); Spicer (1952); Tannenbaum and Massarik (1950); Tichy and Devanna (1986); Winn (1966); and Zander (1949, 1950).

tracted to the group—that is, the more they saw the group as potentially rewarding.

Visibility and Salience of the Group. Groups will exert more power over their members when the members' behavior is visible than when it is unobservable (Deutsch & Gerard, 1954). The effects of conformity can be increased by giving the group more power and by making it more important to its members. For example, Dickinson (1937) observed that the effectiveness of a group's wage incentives depended on mutual policing. Members who work for group rewards are more likely to keep up with each other in groups that are sufficiently small to permit effective mutual observation. Grossack (1954b) found that members of such groups, rewarded as groups, demanded more uniformity from each other than did individuals who were competing with others for rewards.

A significant factor in a group's power over its members is whether the members are clear about the modal or majority opinion of the other members. The clearer the members are about what they must conform to, the more likely they are to conform. In judging intelligence from photographs, participants tended to shift their judgments toward the group decision if they obtained knowledge of it (S. C. Goldberg, 1954). Gorden (1952) observed that when expressing their public opinion, members of a cooperative living project tended to be influenced by what they perceived to be the group's opinion. Bennett (1955) found more compliance with a request for volunteers among those who perceived most others complying. Pennington, Haravey, and Bass (1958) obtained the greatest objective increase in agreement among members in groups in which members made their initial opinions public in discussions or when a group decision was announced rather than kept secret; agreement was less when either group decision or group discussion was absent, and it was least when both were absent. Similarly, in studies of autokinetic judgment, N. Walter (undated) found that agreement among participants decreased when they were no longer given information that was ostensibly based on the judgments of typical students at a prestigious school.

Power, Leadership, and Structure

As was noted earlier, differences in power are established in formal organizational structures. Some positions and roles are assigned more power than others, and power increases as people move from the bottom to the top of the organization. Management-worker hierarchies and political bureaucracies replace traditional power structures based on family, class, tribe, wealth, strength, and age. Even in a country with long-standing democratic traditions, preferences for formal power structures vary. Some citizens prefer highly structured settings, and others prefer highly unstructured ones.

Preferences for More Structure or Less Structure

In some situations, everyone wants total structuring. Automobile drivers on through streets want assurance that drivers coming from side streets will halt at stop signs and red lights, and that oncoming drivers will stay on their side of the white dividing lines. Conversely, the hostess at a social gathering may be faulted for trying to structure interactions. In work and educational settings, there is much divergence of opinion about structure. Thus Heron (1942) observed that if employees do not have access to information about rules and procedures and must learn by trial and error, they are dissatisfied and afraid to take the initiative because of possible infractions and penalties. Seeman (1950) found that a majority of schoolteachers preferred a group-oriented style of leadership yet also exhibited a substantial preference for a type of leadership that called for the differentiation of power.

Bradshaw (1970) obtained ratings of the ideal as well as the actual behavior of leaders in a professional organization. The rank order of the means for both observed and desired behavior was as follows: (1) structuring of expectations, (2) tolerance of freedom, (3) consideration, and (4) emphasis on production. The observed tolerance of freedom was close to ideal, but more structure was desired than was provided by supervisors. More autonomy and self-actualization were desired than realized. Bradshaw concluded that deficiencies in structure were associated with failure to satisfy higher-order needs.

Wispe and Lloyd (1955) found that low producers preferred a more structured group whereas high producers favored a less structured group. The high producers perceived their superiors as less threatening than did low producers. Lowin and Craig (1968) studied supervisors in experimental groups and found that supervisors advocated more structure and closer supervision of subordinates who were incompetent. This was consistent with what has been noted earlier about the effect of subordinates' incompetence on their supervisor's punitiveness.

Structure and Effectiveness

If any sizable group is to reach a common objective, some degree of structure in its internal role relations is required. Individuals need to be able to predict each other's behavior. Unless informal means are possible, the reliability of individual performances will be obtained only by distributing authority, power, and responsibility to holders of the various positions in the group through some structure. Otherwise, the group is likely to remain highly ineffective. Lucas (1965), who studied the effects of feedback on problem solving in groups, found that a group's effectiveness was related to the degree of its structure. Gerard (1957) observed that leaders tend to perform more effectively when they have a wider scope of freedom but that followers are more effective in a somewhat more highly structured situation. Gross, Martin, and Darley (1953) found that groups with strong formal leaders were more productive and more cohesive than groups with weak informal leaders. Sexton (1967) studied 170 line workers in jobs whose structure varied widely, according to both the supervisors and the workers, and reported that the degree of job structure was positively and significantly related to the employees' satisfaction of needs. Hickson, Pugh, and Pheysey (1969) studied a variety of organizations in England and found that the structuring of activities, role specialization, and functional specialization were positively and significantly related to the size and productivity of the groups. Similarly, in a study of manufacturing firms, Pheysey, Payne, and Pugh (1971) noted that formality and an orientation toward rules were related to the employees' satisfaction with their promotions and with fellow workers, and to greater involvement by the managers with the group. Bass and Valenzi (1974) also obtained a positive association between the perceived effectiveness of work groups and the

extent to which relations between managers and subordinates in such groups were structured.

Hobhouse, Wheeler, and Ginsberg (1930) rated the level and complexity of development of some 200 societies. They found that efficient government, which resulted from a strong and stable leadership position or council of leaders, was positively correlated with high cultural achievement. Two opposing factors were found to reduce the power of the leader. In less well-developed societies, the frequent lack of a permanent government deprived the leaders of any effective structure for exercising power except in sporadic undertakings. In more highly developed societies, the presence of a stable governing council limited the powers of the primary leader.

Fox, Lorge, et al. (1953) compared the effectiveness of six-to-eight-man discussions by U.S. Air Force officers with groups of 12 or 13. Although smaller groups ordinarily would be more effective, here the larger groups yielded higher-quality decisions. The larger groups overcame their disadvantage by organizing themselves to solve the problem so as to make maximum use of the larger number of participants. F. L. Bates (1953) observed that the performance of four medium-size bomber wings was better when there was a greater use of authority and a greater frequency of production plans, orders, and instructions sanctioned by authority. Again, if additional members are not redundant in contributing to a group's decision and if efficient computerization can be arranged to process, establish priorities, distribute, and pool their individual contributions, groups of 35 with computers may be able to become as effective in utilizing the informational resources of their individual members as can groups of six lacking computerization and information-processing technology (see Chapter 29).

Bureaucracy and the Distribution of Power. The theory of bureaucracy is concerned with problems involved in the structure of power relations in formal organizations. Weber (1924/1947) observed that bureaucracy is characterized by the continuous organization of official functions bound by rules, specified spheres of competence, the hierarchical ordering of authority relations, and impersonality. Responsibility and authority reside in the office, rather than in the person. Bureaucratic structure does not necessarily limit all autonomy for the organization's managers, although as expected, Engel (1970) found that managers' autonomy was greater in organizations with moderate bureaucratic structures than in those with extreme ones. Numerous case studies[8] have suggested that when organizations become overly concerned with rules and formalities, they tend to lose touch with the external demands made on them and to become insensitive to the internal problems that they generate. (These defects are not confined only to bureaucracies.) Dissatisfaction and ineffectiveness are unintended effects. Although it is the rational purpose of a bureaucracy to use specialized talent effectively, bureaucratic organizations and institutions often emphasize formalisms and legalisms to such a degree that the perpetuation of the system takes precedence over whatever function it was intended to perform. In agreement, Burns (1978, pp. 295–296) declared:

> Bureaucracy is the world of explicitly formulated goals, rules, procedures, . . . specialization, and expertise, with the roles of individuals minutely specified and differentiated . . . organized by purpose, process, clientele, or place. [It] prizes consistency, predictability, stability, and efficiency . . . more than creativity and principle. Roles and duties are prescribed less by superiors . . . than by tradition, formal examinations, and technical qualifications. Careers and job security are protected by tenure, pensions, union rules, professional standards, and appeal procedures. The structure . . . approaches the . . . elimination of personalized relationships and . . . reciprocity, response to wants, needs, and values. . . .
>
> Through its methodical allotment of tasks, its mediating and harmonizing and "adjustment" procedures, its stress on organizational ethos, goals, and authority, bureaucracy assumes consensus, discounts and discredits clash and controversy, which are seen as threats to organizational stability. Bureaucracy discourages the kind of power that is generated by the tapping of motivational bases among employees and the marshaling of personal—as opposed to organizational—resources. Bureaucracy pursues goals that may as easily become separated from a hierarchy of original purposes and values as from human needs. And bureaucracy, far from directing social change or serving as a

factor in historical causation, consciously or not helps buttress the status quo.

Thus the status and power differentiation of a bureaucracy, initially organized to meet objectives expeditiously and efficiently, often experiences hardening of the arteries when it fails to adapt to changes in outside conditions and its own personnel.

But a complete lack of power differentiation generates problems that are equally damaging to the group's and organization's performance. To illustrate, Kingsley (1967) described a group of therapists that fell apart and disbanded after the collapse of its structured power relations when the discussion leader left. Members were unable to maintain interactive relationships in the absence of the power structure provided by the leader. Similarly, over a period of one year, L. M. Smith (1967) observed an experimental elementary school whose administration, scheduling, curriculum, teaching, and discipline were highly unstructured and in which authority resided in the pupils. The teachers engaged in a ceaseless struggle for power, and there were continuous confusion, delay, noise, and frustration. All but two of the teachers decided to leave at the end of the year. J. W. Gardner (1998, p. 13) summed up the utility to organizations of sharing power to maintain their vitality. There needs to be

> the willingness of many people scattered throughout the organization to take the initiative [in] identifying problems and solving them. Without that, the organization becomes another of those sodden, inert, nonadaptive bureaucracies that are the bane of corporate and governmental life—rigid, unimaginative, and totally unequipped to deal with a swiftly changing environment.

Empowerment

The past century saw the rise and acceleration of a movement to change the distribution of power by delegating decision making to lower levels of organizational managers and employees closer to the need for action (Kanter, 1977, 1993). Power sharing took on a life of its own as empowerment at all organizational levels became a popular strategy in the 1980s (Block, 1986; Burke, 1986). Empowerment gave organizational members the respon-

---

[8] See, for example, Bennis (1970); Merton, Gray, Hockey, and Selvin (1952); and Peabody and Rourke (1964).

sibility and authority to carry out their jobs so that psychologically they felt they "owned" their jobs. It aligned their personal mission to the organization as a whole (Potter, 1994). It was adopted by service industry firms such as American Airlines, Marriot, American Express, and Federal Express. It meant encouraging frontline employees to exercise initiative and imagination. It also implied giving overall direction with considerable autonomy to employees, and latitude to carry out their assignments. It could be limited to deciding on the best way to complete an assigned task. It could involve identifying and solving problems and dealing with larger organizational issues (Ford & Fottler, 1995). It also came to mean empowering individuals at all levels in the organization, although in a study of hospital personnel perceived empowerment was higher among those higher in rank and tenure (Koberg, Boss, Senjem, et al., 1999). "Organizations must move away from policies that encourage employees to 'leave their brains at the door' to those that nurture, develop, and more directly reward employees' intellectual capital" (Avolio, 1997, p. 2). But Wall, Cordery, and Clegg (2002) opined that empowerment was not a universal panacea—its effectiveness was contingent on the extent of operational uncertainty. In discussing new product development projects, Forrester (2002) agreed that management should yield power to the development team when uncertainty is highest, as when a radical innovation is being sought. When there is less uncertainty about the product—as when a change is to be just an incremental improvement—empowering the team is less important. Also, Shamir and Howell (1999) suggested that followers can empower leaders by cooperating and showing respect and admiration. They can also provide the leader with resources.

Empowerment is similar to but not the same as delegation. It is a more exacting kind of involvement. It implies "the freedom and ability to make decisions and commitments, not just to suggest them or [only] be a part of making them" (Forrester, 2000, p. 67). Organizational structures are changed. In many cases, middle managers are eliminated. Their decisions are now made by the empowered first-line supervisor and shared with the workers or work team. For Lawler (1986), this was an important aspect of *high-involvement* management. Team members were granted more autonomy, more self-direction, and more control over how they accomplished

their tasks. As a consequence, they had more positive attitudes about their responsibilities and more positive feelings about their work. For instance, at Ericsson General Electric, suggestions from gainsharing programs were reviewed by employee teams, not managers. These teams could accept suggestions, put them into action, and authorize limited expenditures (Filipczak, 1993). Conger and Kanungo (1988) linked a sense of empowerment to a sense of self-efficacy. When leaders were supportive and empowered by higher authority, Parker and Price (1994) found that subordinates were more likely to perceive that they had control over decisions affecting themselves. Keller and Dansereau (1995) reported that for 92 superior-subordinate dyads, empowerment gave subordinates more control and a perception of more fairness in their superiors. Among 194 employees in a human service organization, self-efficacy and intrinsic motivation were enhanced by fostering their autonomy (Seltzer & Miller, 1990).

Empowerment can be structural or psychological. *Structural empowerment* accrues from occupying a position that is visible and central to the organization's goals and allows the occupant flexibility (Kanter, 1993). An employee or manager is also empowered by structures that give access to information, support, access to resources, and opportunities to learn and develop. *Psychological empowerment* is intrinsically task-motivating by providing meaning to one's role in the organization, a sense of competence, a sense of self-determination, and awareness of the impact of what one is doing (Thomas & Velthouse, 1990). Spreitzer (1995) extracted and validated as dimensions of psychological empowerment: *meaning* (for example, "The work I do is very important to me"); *competence* ("I am confident about my ability to do my job"); *self-determination* ("I have significant autonomy in determining how I do my job"); and *impact* ("I have a great deal of control over what happens in my department"). Shea and Howell (1992) combined structural and psychological empowerment in their model, understanding of the relationship between actions and desired outcomes. However, although structural empowerment enhanced job satisfaction for 185 staff nurses, psychological empowerment had no effect on job satisfaction after structural empowerment was taken into account (Laschinger, Finegan, Shamian, et al., 2002).

Herrenkohl, Judson, Thomas, et al. (1999) validated

three additional dimensions that discriminated between those with more and less empowerment, fairness in the recognition system, fairness in decision processes, and clarity of company goals for 28 work groups. Felt empowerment was higher among middle managers if there was little role ambiguity in their work unit and if the unit had access to information, strong support, and a participative climate. Leaders learned empowerment roles from models provided by higher-ups in their organization. Compared with 561 male counterparts, 351 women leaders in 25 organizations were likely to be more empowering, according to their 912 direct reports (Howard & Wellins, 1994). Empowered managers worked for a superior with a wide span of control. Empowering management recognizes that reducing organizational controls can increase the individual's shift toward personal control and outcomes. Management arranges conditions to facilitate the shift. The empowered individuals are induced to engage not only in "role behaviors" but also in discretionary behaviors that go beyond their roles and beyond minimum job requirements. Empowered persons expect to have favorable effects on outcomes if they take action (Spreitzer, 1996).

Benefits of Empowerment

Empowerment is seen to be of benefit to the empowering leaders, their followers, and their organization. The leaders are relieved of routine work and are more committed to their organization, according to a survey by Howard and Wellins (1994) of 32 senior managers, 29 middle managers, and 323 supervisors from 25 organizations. The 948 nonleadership employees reporting to these leaders felt more positive about the work and the organization and experienced less work-related stress. The organization also benefited from an improved customer focus and improved quality. Pfeffer (1995) suggested that the organization also benefits by gaining a comparative advantage over traditionally organized rivals, and in the greater commitment, satisfaction, and involvement of its employees and managers.

Moreover, the organization benefits from making it possible for every member to be a source of ideas, initiatives, and influence. Benefits increase over time. Empowered people feel that they have a greater impact on their work and are more satisfied with it (Thomas &

Tyman, 1994). They feel that they have a greater impact on the organization (Brossoit, 2001). This also contributes to greater satisfaction with their work (Ashforth, 1989). For instance, among 612 technically skilled professionals and managerial hospital employees those who felt more empowered reported greater job satisfaction, work productivity, and intent to stay (Koberg, Boss, Senjem, et al., 1999).

Democratic organizational flexibility replaces hierarchical rigidity. The controlling manager becomes the enabling leader (Cook, 1994). Nonetheless, the expected effects of empowerment on effectiveness, work satisfaction, and job-related strain vary with how much each of the components of psychological empowerment—meaning, competence, self-determination, and impact—is involved (Spreitzer, Kizilos, & Nason, 1997).

Contingent Effects. In some studies, empowerment was found to only indirectly affect beneficial outcomes. Niehoff, Moorman, Blakely, et al. (2001) observed that empowerment indirectly increased the loyalty of 203 employees as a consequence of enriching their jobs. In 128 leader-employee exchange dyads, managerial trust contributed to empowerment, but only when the exchange relationship was good for both the management and the employees (Gomez & Rosen, 2001).

Effects of Operator Control of Machinery. In manufacturing operations, empowerment meant giving operators the power to control loading, unloading, and monitoring their machinery. They also took responsibility for maintaining their equipment and for programming changes and corrections that formerly had been the province of staff specialists. Operators developed into their own staff specialists. A survey of 584 machining manufacturing plants in 1987 showed that plants where the machine operators routinely wrote and edited their own programs were 30% more efficient than plants where the operators were not so empowered (Ralls, 1994).

Operator empowerment in a British electronics manufacturer resulted in a saving of 10 hours of production time per week in the operations of seven numerically controlled insertion machines. The operators reported increased intrinsic satisfaction with their work and less job pressure. The former staff specialists were freed to work on other projects (Jackson & Wall, 1991). Over time, machine reliability was increased as the operators developed more skill in preventing problems. Downtime was reduced by 20% and eventually by over 70% (Wall, Corbett, Clegg, et al., 1990).

Empowering industrial employees by involving them in management decisions—according to a survey of human resources managers at 30 U.S. mini steel mills—reduced scrap rates, reduced employee turnover, and reduced the number of labor hours to make one ton of steel (Arthur, 1994).

Problems with Empowerment

A British laundry and work wear business, in dealing with small problems, generally found improvements from empowerment; yet some workers did not want to be empowered—nor did some managers want to change their practices to accommodate empowering their workers (Seath & Clark, 1993). Forrester (2000) enumerated several reasons why empowerment might cause problems and might fail to improve performance and satisfaction:

1. Empowerment may be introduced precipitately without adequate preparation of the people who are to be empowered. At the lowest levels, work has been enriched—i.e., increased—by administrative duties, decision making, and coordination requirements, but the workers have been given no additional time and no training to carry out functions that were previously done full-time by better-paid persons. The hasty changes take away power from supervisors and managers, who now suddenly must supervise differently, also without adequate time to train and prepare.

2. While increasing intrinsic task motivation matters, other motivations need to be considered, such as individual differences in preferences regarding autonomy, structure, money, competitiveness, desire to help others, and being accountable for results.

3. Accountability and responsibility for results may be confused and distorted.

4. Managers and supervisors may not be willing or ready to accept their loss of control, their reduced sense of achievement, and their reduced recognition.

Managers may have a problem with being accountable without control. They may feel that their job security is threatened—as indeed it may be, with the flattening of the organization (Stewart & Manz, 1995).

Additionally, managers of technology may have been negatively indoctrinated about empowerment by their engineering education. Fewer than half of 100 engineering textbooks and equipment design books made any mention of the operators' or workers' roles in production. Where people were mentioned, they were always subordinate to technology (Ralls, 1994).

A survey of 282 MBA students revealed another possible reason for resistance to empowering subordinates. These students felt that the quality of work would be better if workers were supervised than if they were unsupervised. They thought the supervisor would be more personally involved than subordinates in the quality of the product (Pfeffer, Cialdini, Hanna, et al., 1998).

Successful Empowerment

For successful empowerment of others, Burdett (1991) suggested that leaders need to manage the context, not the individuals. A common vision is required. Organization values have to be enunciated, and leaders have to facilitate opportunities for action. According to Payne, Cangemi, Fuqua, et al. (1997), an environment of support and decentralized decision making must be created, and certain values must be communicated: high quality, good service, and excellence. For Randolph (1995), the most important factors in successful empowerment were sharing information about the organization, promoting understanding about it, building trust through the sharing of sensitive information, and replacing hierarchy with teams. Paradoxically, forceful leadership must be used, and power must be used effectively to give it to others, with limits—letting go of controls but remaining ready to help when necessary (PriceWaterhouse Change Integration Team, 1996). Forrester (2000) suggested that empowerment needs to proceed top-down, cascading from higher to lower levels in the organization as each level becomes knowledgeable, familiar, comfortable, and successful with it. Those with power must have enough control to share it. There is a need to develop members at each lower level in knowledge, skills, and information as well as to provide more access to important people. At each level, initially, low-risk decisions should be delegated. Censoring mistakes should be avoided. Rather, mistakes should be corrected and treated as learning experiences. Roberts and Thorsheim (1987) suggested that in interaction with employees, leaders need to express their own doubts, concerns, and uncertainties; ask and listen; reflect feelings; identify common experiences; paraphrase and summarize; and acknowledge and use others' ideas. Howard and Wellins (1994) noted in their large-scale multiechelon survey that the empowerment strategies used most frequently were reengineering, training, pushing down decision making to lower levels, reducing layers of management, and using high-quality problem-solving teams. Support was provided by satisfying, high-involvement leadership but with no special financial rewards.

Feelings of empowerment among 531 individuals in 53 organizations were positively related to the rated transformational behavior of their leaders (Masi, 1994). Among a randomized sample of 327 managers in Fortune 100 firms, Brossoit (2001) found that transformational leaders provided their empowered employees with a sense of meaning in their jobs, a perception of choice, a sense of progress toward goals, and the belief that they were influencing the system. However, while transformational leadership resulted in a sense of empowerment at 76 Israeli banks, according to their 932 employees, as expected, it also increased the sense of dependence on the managers (Kark, 2000). A converse effect has also been reported. If managers feel they are empowered, they are more likely to be transformational but not transactional, according to a survey of 314 diverse middle managers of Fortune 50 firms rated by themselves and their subordinates (Spreitzer & Janasz, 1994).

Unsuccessful Empowerment

Cook (1994) suggested that empowerment suffers if senior management endorses it but does not set a positive example; fails to communicate the reasons for empowerment and how it will help the organization; fails to explain the leader's role as more than getting rid of work; and fails to provide training and a support network. According to Howard and Wellins's (1994) survey of 948 employees, 323 supervisors, and 61 higher-ups in 39 business units of 25 organizations, some leaders might dis-

courage empowering their subordinates by failing to get higher management to act on subordinates' suggestions or by failing to praise success publicly. Leaders often failed to match empowering their direct reports with the readiness of the direct reports to handle more responsibility. The leaders couldn't let go. Faulty implementation of empowerment could be also due to other reasons, such as failure to provide sufficient direction and training to accompany the empowerment. Chakravarthy and Gargiulo (1998) noted that in the restructuring of a hierarchy, trust and the legitimacy of leadership may be lost. Dover (1999) mentioned two other reasons for failure: being impatient, and expecting that giving power would provide self-reliance, competence, and commitment. Empowerment might be the objective, but its opposite might appear, as learned helplessness (Campbell & Martinko, 1998) or as *bogus empowerment* (Ciulla, 1998), in which subordinates feel they are free to make decisions as long as the decisions are ones their boss wants; or when subordinates are given responsibility they did not expect nor want nor request (Stayer, 1990).

Other Perspectives

Burns (1996) argued that empowerment comes about from collective leadership, which occurs in a "web of relationships" in which different people take on roles of influence as needed. Some initiate action; some join with others to take action. Different reactions occur: some follow the initiator; some oppose or ignore the initiative. Mutual empowerment is seen when team members influence one another both positively and negatively. An opponent may consider alternatives to an initiative.

Political scientists view empowerment of minority voters as evidenced by increased political participation and success in elections (Bobo & Gilliam, 1990). For educational administration, empowerment is pushing decision making from the district office to the local school, and from the board and superintendent to the principals, teachers, parents, and students (Glickman, 1990).

One of the best examples of empowerment—long before the term came into vogue—is what happened during the Normandy landings on D-Day, June 6, 1944. The U.S. Army suffered more casualties on that one day than in any 12 months in Vietnam. Omaha Beach turned into a killing zone.

But what happened in the face of this was truly a decentralized empowered event. . . . For the most part, the beach assault was an unorganized mass of intermixed units with little or no functioning chain of command. . . . Individuals moved forward, took initiative, took risks, and displayed awesome courage. *Ad hoc* teams formed on the beaches and . . . inland where paratroopers had been scattered over the landscape miles away from their planned drop zones. Ulmer, 1994, p. 8.

Self-Empowerment

Since the settling of America, groups, movements, and organizations have arisen—and continue to arise—who are self-empowered or empowered by local, state, and federal governments in communities to organize action to meet needs and satisfy common purposes not adequately addressed by other formal institutions (Bachrach & Botwinnick, 1992). Critics viewed them as bureaucratic self-defense, co-optation of government agencies, and surrogates for public policy (Couto, 1992). But much citizen action now depends on the empowerment of such voluntary assemblages, ranging from neighborhood to environmental organizations.

Measurement of Empowerment

Two of the more prominent questionnaires about empowerment serve different purposes. The Leader Empowering Behavior Questionnaire (LEBQ), developed by Konczak, Stelly, and Trusty (1996), contains 22 statements to be rated from 1 (strongly disagree) to 7 (strongly agree), which assess leader behaviors that empower followers. The Empowering Instrument (EI), developed by Chiles and Zorn (1995), assesses the extent to which followers feel empowered. Its six statements are rated using the same seven-point scale of agreement as the LEBQ.

Leader Empowering Behavior

In the Howard and Wellins (1994) survey, modeling trust and facilitation were, on average, the most important leadership empowering behaviors (6.2 on a 7-point scale of importance). Many other behaviors were cited as of considerable importance (5.8); these included support-

ing, coaching, partnering, envisioning, inspiring, team building, and championing. Ensuring compliance (5.4) was the only transactional behavior seen as important. Other transactional behaviors—such as controlling the way work is done (3.9) and pointing out failures (3.1)—were seen as not important to empowerment. Heslin (1999), along with many others, called attention to the need for empowering leaders to raise the self-efficacy of subordinates through mentoring, coaching, stimulating, demonstrating, and providing satisfying outcomes. Empowering leaders, willing to relinquish control and authority, did so on the basis of reasoned planning and actions, according to a study of 502 external team leaders from 64 Australian organizations (Wu, Cordery, & Morrison, 2001). Stewart and Manz (1995) ascertained that supervisors with positive attitudes about empowerment, according to their subordinates, helped subordinates' empowerment. Arad, Arnold, Rhoades, et al. (1995) obtained the best-fitting model of the behaviors of the empowered team leaders of 95 customer service representatives and 110 building products supplier employees. The five correlated factors were: (1) leading by example, (2) coaching, (3) practicing participative leadership, (4) informing, and (5) interacting frequently. A similar analysis by Konczak, Stelly, and Trusty (1996) based on 424 managers and their 1,309 direct reports yielded a best-fitting model of empowering with six factors: (1) delegation of authority, (2) accountability, (3) encouragement of self-directed decisions, (4) information sharing, (5) skill development, and (6) coaching for innovative performance. Ford and Fottier (1995) agreed that empowerment involved shared responsibility and sharing of information. For Manz and Sims (1990), empowering members of self-managed groups involved encouraging self-set goals, positive thinking, personal initiative, and self-directed problem solving. Leaders lead the members to be self-leaders.

Discrepancy between Leader and Follower Perceptions. Larmore and Ayman (1998) administered the LEBQ, the EI, and the 20 transformational leadership items from the Multifactor Leadership Questionnaire (MLQ) to 52 CEOs and their 217 direct reports. The CEOs rated their own empowering and leadership behaviors. The direct reports rated the empowering and transformational leadership behaviors of their own CEO.

The direct reports also rated their own feelings of empowerment. Correlational and variant analyses indicated that although the CEOs as a whole did not overrate the extent to which they empowered their direct reports, results suggested considerable disagreement between particular CEOs and their teams of direct reports. When some CEOs thought they were empowering their direct reports, the direct reports felt otherwise. Nonetheless, a correlation of .56 was obtained between the individual direct reports' ratings of their own CEO's empowering behaviors (LEBQ) and ratings of their own felt empowerment (EI). Direct reports' sense of empowerment correlated .49 with their ratings of their CEOs' transformational leadership. The transformational leadership was found to have mediated the relationship, among the teams of direct reports, between their feeling of empowerment and their perceptions of the empowering behaviors of their CEOs. These findings were more a matter of team differences than individual differences. Keiser and Shen (2000) found that leaders believed they were empowering subordinates more than the subordinates felt they had been empowered. When 9,098 school principals and their 47,105 teachers were queried, the principals reported that they gave teachers more power than the teachers felt they had to evaluate teachers, hire new teachers, decide on expenditures, establish curricula, determine the content of in-service programs, and set disciplinary policy. Howard and Wellins (1994) reported similar discrepancies between leaders at various organizational levels and their direct reports.

Differences in Empowering, Laissez-Faire, and Delegating Leadership. Empowering, laissez-faire, and delegating leadership behaviors are similar but not the same. When the 10 laissez-faire items of the Multifactor Leadership Questionnaire (Bass & Avolio, 1991) were factored by themselves for diverse samples of leaders rated by their followers, two distinct factors emerged. Six of the items were, as intended, measures of laissez-faire leadership (e.g., "Likely to be absent when needed," "Avoids making decisions," and "Fails to follow up requests for assistance"). Two items on a second factor were closer in meaning to empowering leadership: "Avoids telling me how to do my job," and "Resists expressing views on important issues" (Bass, 1994). *Delegation* is assignment by the leader to a subordinate of activities and responsibilities. Leaders pass on to others tasks or specific aspects of their own jobs. They delegate to free their time to do other things, to develop the subordinates, or for other reasons. The leaders need to provide necessary direction and power for subordinates to effectively carry out the assignments (Shackleton, 1990). Adequate and inadequate delegation discriminated between innovative and uninnovative groups of Dutch teachers in 10 schools, according to keyword analyses of interview statements about the groups (Geijsel, Sleegers, & van den Berg, 1999). The innovative capacities of the primary schools (Geijsel, van den Berg, & Sleegers, 1999) and secondary schools (van den Berg & Sleegers, 1996) were also calculated. For leaders in their schools to effectively delegate and to sort out "the failures that are the price of delegation," clear statements of purpose and secure, strong leaders and followers were needed. Babbitt (1987) suggested that these are also needed in bureaucracies.

Industrial Democracy

Power may be formally redistributed by assigning worker-representatives to management boards and committees. The redistribution may be voluntary on the part of management, as in the United States, or mandated by legislation, as in Germany. Although some attempts had been made earlier in the United States, and elsewhere, representative industrial democracy appears to have been initiated in Sweden about 1938. It arose from the deliberations of national representations of employees and workers in response to labor unrest that was more common to Sweden in the 1920s and 1930s than in most other countries. The occupying military authorities in Germany after World War II, interested in ensuring that resurgent German industry could not again be exploited for military purposes or for the subversion of democratic government, passed a law prescribing *Mitbestimmung*—the representation of workers on a firm's supervisory board. The *Betriebsverfassungsgesetz* (Works Constitution Act) was also formally prescribed by law somewhat later, to provide for the participation of employees in a wide range of matters. To signal Yugoslavia's break with Soviet state centralism in 1950, Marshal Tito introduced self-management, another early method to use legislation to guarantee employees representative participation in the management of production and administration (Stymne, 1986). In the United States, along with a century of trade unionism came efforts, especially in the 1920s, to establish representative democracy in industry. However, it has been within the past 30 years that legislated tax advantages have contributed to the growth of employee stock ownership plans (ESOPs), through which employees begin to share in the company's ownership. By 1986, 7,000 U.S. firms had ESOPs (Meek, 1987). Also, representatives of employees and consumers have been elected to serve on the boards of directors of corporations. Finally, groups of employees, such as those of United Airlines, began to purchase control of their own firms, and employees began to elect the directors who are responsible for the firm's management and policies. Thus, quite a few businesses became partly or fully employee-owned. But attempts to share profits or gains in productivity such as Scanlon Plans, ESOPs, suggestion schemes, and productivity bonuses may founder on conflicts of interest and power differences between management and labor (Collins, 1995).

Difficulties with Industrial Democracy and Worker Representation

Efforts to create power-sharing institutions may be only a semblance of worker participation that may not yield the same degree of commitment, motivation, or productivity. Workers may have sat on boards of directors in the former Yugoslavia, but in fact party members, financial experts, and technocrats held most of the power, initiative, and influence (Obradovic, 1975). In some countries, unionism has declined. In the United States, for example, it declined to 11% of employees in 2005 since its peak in the 1930s and appears to remain strong only in the public sector. In Europe, it has remained stronger and better aligned with government, often controlling major political parties.

Representative democracy at the workplace is different from empowerment of employees. In workplace empowerment, workers participate directly with their immediate supervisor in decisions that are of consequence to their own work and working situation. Industrial cooperatives, such as Mondragon in Spain, became community- and-employee-owned holding companies for subsidiary plants. In the United States, ESOPs gave employees voting privileges and sometimes control over management. In reaction to threatened plant closings, on occasion, employees purchased the ownership of their plants. Trade unions, such as Histadrut in Israel, became holding companies for large conglomerates of business and industrial establishments. But none of these formal developments necessarily means that a participative climate in superior-subordinate relations will develop as a consequence; nor do such developments necessarily produce a real equalization of power. For example, who owns the company may not be as important to a new employee entering the firm at a low level as to an older employee with an important position in the company.

Nonetheless, empowerment of employees can result in increased democratization of union-management relations. In the 1960s, Ed Dulworth, an engineer working for General Foods, discovered how much he could enhance a Gaines Pet Food plant by designing into it all the elements that subsequently became known as employee empowerment. Output rose 50% in four years, but the successful redistribution of power became a threat to General Foods' top management and to managers in other plants, and Dulworth had to move on. After arriving in Scranton, Pennsylvania, he organized a labor-management council to spread the word about what he had learned. By 1983, 15 in-plant labor-management committees had been established in the area (Osborne, 1988).

One purpose of equalizing power is to increase the commitment of those who initially have little power, despite their desire for more. However, Styskal (1980) failed to find the expected increased commitment in three federally sponsored temporary educational organizations in New York City when subunits were given more decision-making authority over the curriculum, program, employees, budgets, and work assignments. Many other problems can be cited. Discussing efforts by U.S. corporations to introduce voluntary and obligatory participation, Kanter (1982b) noted such problems as the paternalistic imposition of democracy; the need that results of participation be visible; concern by both management and the union about losing power; the time required; the lack of relevant knowledge by many employees; the limiting of participation to more abstract decisions that are remote from the employees' concerns at the workplace; tension between innovation and democracy; the constraints of previous decisions; the need for leadership; the resistance to change of various interest groups; tension between social, emotional, and business needs; and excessive expectations about gains that may accrue from participation. Management may resist sharing power, not only from a fear of losing its prerogatives but also because of a disinclination to learn new leadership styles involved in consensus building. Unions may not only fear a loss of power but may remain suspicious of the management's motives. And employees may be satisfied with their current inefficiencies in getting the work done (Alexander, 1984).

Dixon (1984) proposed that some interrelated elements are necessary for any participatory program to succeed. First, an information system is required to provide feedback on the organization's performance. Ownership of the information must reside with the group, feedback must be timely, and results must be visible to all employees. Second, employees at all levels need to be represented. Representation calls for groups of competent employees to identify and solve problems, to have the power to act on their decisions, and to agree on a common vision. Finally, the organization's leadership needs to believe in the creativity and responsibility of the employees.

Early Examples of Voluntary Programs

Selekman (1924) reported the results of a management sharing plan in a chemical firm. For management to gain a better understanding of the workers' point of view, two boards were created. The board of operatives was composed of elected workers, and was responsible for working conditions, grievances, recreation, training, company housing, and the like. The board of management, which was composed of a representation of executives and stockholders, was responsible for production, wages, farm equipment, hours, and financial policies. Although the board of operatives was slow to accept responsibilities, it gradually participated in planning and decision making. Effects attributed to the experiment included a reduction in the turnover of personnel and greater cooperation to improve production. Given (1949), a company president, experimented with a "bottom-up management" plan, in which he delegated authority down the line to employees and encouraged the employees to use their initiative and to assume responsibility. Results were good. Another

company president worked directly with employees to stimulate their responsibility and initiative at the workplace. His activities placed foremen under great conflict and stress, but he worked with them until they accepted his philosophy of participation. He concluded that his organization became more informal and his workers more responsible and involved (Richard, 1959). W. M. Blumenthal (1956) described the management of steel plants in Germany. Each plant was managed by a board of three men, one a union representative. The general trend was for the two management representatives to assume responsibility for production while the union representative assumed responsibility for personnel, wages, and grievances.

Joint Consultation. Wyndham and White (1952) found that workers in an Australian refinery tended to regard the elected representative to worker-management committees as an alternative to their foremen. The foremen then regarded their positions as threatened, even though they were members of the joint consultation committees. H. Campbell (1953) concluded that for joint consultation to be effective, the foreman had to be involved in the process as an active participant.

A study by W. H. Scott (1952) of joint consultation in three British industrial firms also indicated that the procedure was subject to strains in different segments and levels of the organization. Although workers' representatives were generally well accepted in their discussions with management, both the workers and their representatives reported that little was accomplished because only trivial issues were discussed. The workers felt that they were neither consulted nor kept informed by the representatives. The foremen reported that they were bypassed in communications between management and workers' representatives. The workers and their representatives complained that the foremen failed to take action on many matters that could have been handled more effectively on the spot rather than being referred to joint consultation. Although the majority of workers' representatives were also union stewards, the union members complained that they were not adequately represented. Scott concluded that joint consultation resulted in few advantages that could not be produced as well as by responsible leadership.

Jaques (1952) completed an intensive case study of a

single British factory that formed works councils and work committees to participate in management. The workers tended to feel dissatisfied with the performance of their elected representatives. The representatives were under heavy stress because of their different, conflicting demands; because they had little authority for making decisions; and because of their increasing separation from the workers. Other, similar problems were also revealed, but the study threw greater light on details of the consultative procedure. Jaques's findings suggested that the difficulties encountered resulted not so much from the unwillingness of either management or employees to make the system work, as from their confusion about their respective responsibilities. Management tended to feel that it should not trespass on the responsibilities of workers' representatives on the works council, particularly in matters involving social relationships; hence, the managers tended to take passive roles. The workers' representatives tended to regard operative problems and policies as the responsibility of management and adopted passive attitudes toward those matters. When the general manager of the factory accepted the idea that he was responsible for all aspects of organizational life and activity, and that giving orders is not necessarily autocratic or unethical, he was able to "assume more fully his leadership mantle." In turn, his subordinates accepted theirs. With their responsibilities more clearly focused, they were able to initiate building a works council more broadly representative of the factory. Jaques's study suggested that members cannot act effectively in their own interests or in behalf of the group unless the leader exercises the functions of his or her role and takes the initiative in clarifying the definitions of roles throughout the system.

Power Sharing Cost-Reduction Plans. The Scanlon Plan is a means for sharing reductions in unit costs that are under the control of labor. Such reductions are determined first by establishing a normal labor cost for a factory. This labor cost may be arrived at by a joint worker-management agreement. Whenever labor costs fall below the norm, the workers receive from 50% to 100% of the amount. A second element of the Scanlon Plan is a suggestion system in which benefits that accrue from the reduction in labor costs are shared with all workers in the plant. Reports indicate that as many as 80% of the suggestions submitted in a Scanlon Plan plant

are accepted, whereas plants with individual suggestion plans commonly accept only 25%. Furthermore, with the Scanlon Plan there is no reason for the workers to withhold suggestions that will increase productivity; the result is lower labor costs and consequently a bonus for everyone (Lesieur, 1958).

To determine the effects of the Scanlon Plan, Puckett (1958) surveyed 9 firms with 11 plants that made many different products, and whose workers' skills ranged from manual labor to highly technical. In the 11 plants that were followed over a two-year period, the gain in productivity varied from 17% to 49%, with a mean gain of 23%. Bonuses averaged 17% of gross pay and were based on splitting the savings in labor costs, with 75% going to the workers and 25% to the company. Besides the direct benefits from increased production and higher profits, there were also better service to the customers, higher-quality products, an improved competitive position, and no decline in employment.

Many other power sharing cost-reduction practices now in evidence can be mentioned, some of which, such as suggestion systems, were first introduced by the Yale Manufacturing Company in 1892. The upward communication provided by quality circles and survey feedback systems are other examples.

Employee Stock Ownership Plans (ESOPs)

Rosen, Klein, and Young (1986) completed a survey of 2,804 employee stock owners at 37 firms with ESOPs. A majority of the respondents reported that stock ownership increased their interest in their company's financial performance, their personal identification with the company, and their desire to stay with the firm. However, the ESOP arrangement was seen as having less of an effect on their job satisfaction and their influence at the workplace or over company policy. Nor did it result in managers treating them more like equals.

French and Rosenstein (1984) conducted a survey in a prosperous plumbing installation and services firm that began an employee stock ownership plan in 1958. Its managerial employees held 76% of the shares, which have substantially increased in value. For 461 respondents, the amount of their equity in the firm correlated with their desire to be of influence in it. However, the extent to which they identified with the firm depended more on their status and perceived influence in the firm than on the amount of stock they held. Also the amount of their equity was unrelated to their job satisfaction, which correlated only with their perceived influence. But their interest in financial information about the firm did depend on their equity position and their white-collar status.

Mandated Programs

Legislation in the United States has been directed toward establishing fairness in collective bargaining of employees and management and in employment practices. Elsewhere, power sharing through the representation of employees on supervisory and directors' boards was legislatively mandated. Countries have tended to concentrate on one or two types of power-sharing legislation (Walker, 1975). Figures 12.1 and 12.2 show the degree of legal support for individual workers and representative bodies in 12 European countries. For each country, the figures show the average right to participate in 16 specified decisions, ranging from such daily routine decisions as the assignment of tasks to workers, to such long-range decisions as major capital investments. Each of the decisions was rated from "no right" to "final say," based on assessment of laws and collective bargaining agreements and on interviews with labor and legal experts, and employers about company policies. Then they were averaged (In-

Figure 12.1 Workers' Legal Rights in 1976

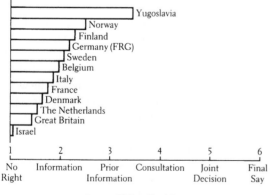

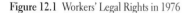

Average Right to Participate

Figure 12.2 Legal Rights of Representative Bodies of Workers in 1976

Figure 14.2. Legal Rights of Representative Bodies of Workers in 1976

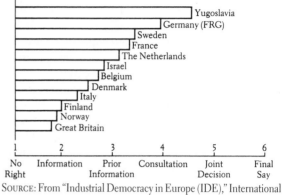

dustrial Democracy in Europe, International Research Group, 1981).

Effectiveness and Acceptance. Evaluations of the operations and effectiveness of workers' councils have been reported for the former West Germany (Hartmann, 1970; Wilpert, 1975), Norway (Thorsrud & Emery, 1970), Great Britain (K. Walker, 1974), the former Yugoslavia (Obradovic, 1970, 1975; Rus, 1970), Sweden (Link, 1971), and socialist countries (Sturmthal, 1961, 1964). Derber (1970) suggested that although effective power sharing implied in industrial democracy was considerable, it tends to be moderated by a number of factors. First, as managers become more professional, their professionalism imposes a barrier to involving employees in decision making. Second, the majority of employees are not strongly motivated to assume managerial responsibilities as long as their financial and other personal needs are satisfied. Third, when union officials and employee representatives become involved in management decision making, they stir up political and factional conflicts that weaken their influence with workers. Last, joint decision making involves too much of management's time for operations to run efficiently.

A number of other studies pointed to differences among managers in their acceptance of industrial democracy and power sharing. In agreement with Derber, Norrgren (1981a) found that Swedish managers who were young, had little seniority but much formal education, and were high in the hierarchy had positive beliefs and intentions about participation. Managers who were involved in white-collar union activities had positive beliefs and intentions and evaluated participative activities highly. Managers from several Canadian companies expressed more willingness to share power with employees if the managers felt they had more job security and influence and if they regarded their employees as competent (Long, 1982). Bass and Shackleton (1979) called attention to the exclusion of the lower- and middle-management levels from the participatory process when representatives of workers meet with top management. These lower-level managers, often ignored and eliminated from the mechanisms of industrial democracy, disassociate themselves from the participatory process and undermine its potential effectiveness.

After a carefully planned observational study of worker-management council meetings in the former Yugoslavia, Obradovic (1975) concluded that initiatives came mainly from the engineers, financial experts, and members of the Communist Party, not from the rank-and-file employees serving as council representatives. The few attempts of ordinary workers to lead were unlikely to be successful. Consistent with this finding, Rubenowitz and Norrgren (1980) used survey questionnaires and interviews to study the effects of different forms of participation in 10 Swedish plants that varied in size from 40 to 830 employees. The actual participation of employees was of much more perceived consequence when formal agreements for power sharing included acceptance of a policy to promote decision making by employees in their daily work. Much less participation was perceived if it involved only formal participation by representatives of the employees. Rosenstein (1977) observed that just because a powerful trade union with a strong social mission is the entrepreneur and owner of industries, as is the case with the Israeli Histadrut, this does not necessarily mean that participation by employees will be encouraged. Actually, the various power centers of the Histadrut—the managers, the trade union officials, the ideologists, and the politicians—have had to be persuaded and educated about the nature of the joint management program that is in effect. As of 1977, Histadrut had established such joint management in 30 of its plants. Success depends on the continuing support of both top management and em-

ployees. Nevertheless, a 12-country longitudinal survey revealed extensive behavioral changes in organizational relationships that were derived from mandatory programs of industrial democracy (Industrial Democracy in Europe, International Research Group, 1979).

Selective Power Sharing. Bass and Rosenstein (1977) and Bass and Shackleton (1979) proposed that industrial democracy is most likely to work well for some issues, such as dealing with pay and benefits, career development, working conditions, and job security, but not for others, such as financial planning or marketing strategies. The 12-country consortium study (Industrial Democracy in Europe, International Research Group, 1981) revealed in detail the extent to which these arguments were valid. In the same way, a total of 103 top Scottish managers and shop stewards who were interviewed by Dickson (1980) tended to favor the direct participation of employees on safety committees and briefing groups, and in dealing with the job enrichment of groups. The managers were less enthusiastic about the employees' participation through representatives on company boards, works councils, and plantwide committees. However, shop stewards felt a bit more positive than the managers about the value of such representative participation. The managers saw the direct involvement of employees as a way to enhance communication and the acceptance of decisions. The shop stewards thought that both direct and representative participation were a moral right and that both contributed to the employees' morale if they were acknowledged by management.

A random sample of 7,832 employees from a total of 134 European firms in metal engineering, banking, and insurance were asked how much they were involved in the 16 decisions for which they had legal rights (refer back to Figures 12.1 and 12.2). Their legally mandated involvement was more important in determining power sharing about long-term decisions. For workers in the 134 firms, the laws and regulations accounted for 24% of the variance in their involvement in short-term decisions; 50%, in medium-range decisions; and 58% in long-term decisions. The legal right of unions and other representative bodies to participate collectively short-term in such decisions had a negative effect on the actual involvement of individual workers. For the involvement of workers in medium- and long-term decisions, the right of both workers and their representatives to participate had a positive effect. The degree of power sharing that could be explained by legal norms was much higher than what could be explained by the firm's technology, its organizational structure, or market conditions. It was concluded that the actual participation of employees depends on "an intricate interrelation of internal management practices and externally promoted support systems based on formal laws or collective bargaining agreements" (Industrial Democracy in Europe, International Research Group, 1981, p. 292).

The success of introducing industrial democracy in different countries was mixed. Straus & Rosenstein (1970) found that most plans in India had died. Israel's plant council and Norway's work council did not survive. In England, shop floor bargaining between union stewards and workers replaced joint consultative committees. In France, important welfare and shop floor bargaining functions survived, although joint consultative activities were hampered by interunion rivalries and union-management conflicts. Industrial democracy was most successful in the former Yugoslavia, in Sweden, in the German iron and steel industry, and in some American Scanlon Plan companies. Industrial democracy gave labor a sense of having won something. It broadened the scope of bargaining and strengthened management to the extent that the leaders of unions and workers were co-opted to advocate common goals. It provided channels of communication and opportunities for training prospective new managers. In 2006, a central issue in the United States was how to share rising employee health insurance costs, which, unlike in many other industrial nations where health insurance is covered by single-payer government programs, are becoming such a burden that 16% of the population are uninsured.

Power Sharing in Planning Change

Roethlisberger (1941) observed that any technological change by management may affect not only the physical but also the social location of an individual in the organization. The possibility of social dislocation within the organization constitutes a severe threat to many members. Individuals in leadership positions tend to feel more tolerant of change and stress than do those in follower posi-

tions. In addition to being more receptive, members in leadership positions usually have access to information that enables them to predict some consequences of change. The member in a follower position has less access to such information unless it is provided by the management. Rumor, imagination, and speculation often lead to grossly inaccurate evaluations of the effects of an announced change. Participation in planning change provides at least a minimum base of information on which a member may evaluate some possible effects of a given change on his or her work, status, and relationship to the organization. Workers will feel more receptive to change if they are involved in planning it. Reducing the power differences between superior and subordinate at the shop floor level in the work group is a main theme of behavioral theorists and practitioners' interventions. "Every employee a manager" sums up M. S. Myers's (1968) changeover of supervisor relations. Formerly, the powerful supervisor fully planned for and controlled the performance of the powerless operator, whose only responsibility was to carry out orders. Now, as much as possible, the operator becomes self-planning, self-directing, and self-controlling.

Legally mandated democracy is not a substitute for participation in decisions. The correlation between legally mandated democracy and participation in decisions that affect daily work was only .10 in the 12-country survey mentioned above (Industrial Democracy in Europe, International Research Group, 1981). The workers' satisfaction with the firm was also unrelated to legally mandated democracy, which suggests that mandated democracy is not a substitute for participative management and democratic leadership. The Swedish Codetermination Act gave legal rights for employees to be consulted by their supervisors at the workplace. White- and blue-collar workers reported an increase in their own influence five years after the Swedish Codetermination Act was passed, but managers did not report increased power sharing with their bosses as a consequence of the act (Stymne, 1986).

Sharing the Power to Plan Change. Shifting the distribution of power results in a sharing of planning and control that has positive effects on the commitment, understanding, satisfaction, and productivity of workers. Structure still remains, but it is based not on differences in power but on a structural design to which the workers have contributed. The utility of such self-planning was reaffirmed in a series of experiments by Bass (1970a, 1977) and Bass and Leavitt (1963).

In a first simulation, Bass and Leavitt (1963) demonstrated the importance of self-planning, both to productivity and to satisfaction. Several simple exercises were devised. In each, trios of managers in training developed a plan for themselves and then exchanged plans with another trio. A counterbalanced order was used so that half the teams executed their own plan first and half executed the other team's plan first. Then they executed both plans. The result was that managers were more productive and more satisfied with operating their own plan.

In a similar simulation, 1,416 managers in training settings completed Exercise Organization (Bass, 1975h). As expected, the objective output and efficiency were significantly greater when they executed their own plans. Moreover, self-planning resulted in greater felt responsibility, job satisfaction, and satisfaction with the plan. However, the payoff was much greater when participants with practice, experience, and knowledge made their own plans than when those without the advantage of practice did so.

The importance of maintaining some special elements that the supervisor can bring to the planning process, such as support, experience, and knowledge, was illustrated by Schlacter (1969), who studied six highway maintenance crews over 25 weeks. In two crews, the foremen assisted their supervisor in planning and reported results back to their crews. Two other crews assisted their superiors in planning. The third pair of crews assumed full responsibility for planning. The first two crews maintained stable job satisfaction scores and production records throughout the 25 weeks. The third pair of crews gained significantly in job satisfaction, but lost significantly in productivity. Similarly, Latham and Saari (1979) showed experimentally that supportive leadership resulted in higher goals being set by student participants than did nonsupportive leadership.

Rationale. Reasons given by participants for the utility of reducing differences in power for the purposes of planning included: (1) it increases the sense of accomplishment when carrying out the plan; (2) it generates more efforts to confirm the validity of the plan by executing it successfully and generates more confidence to see

that it can be done; (3) it may increase commitment to see that the plan works well; (4) it may increase flexibility, room for modification, and initiative to make improvements; (5) it is likely to generate a greater understanding of the plan; (6) it may allow for better use of human resources; (7) it may reduce communication problems and the consequent errors and distortions in following instructions; and (8) it may avoid competitive feelings among planners and those who must execute the plans (Bass, 1970a).

Utility of Self-Managed Teams. Increasingly, project teams are being formed with informal leadership in which no one member is appointed as leader. Rather, power is fully shared in planning, operations, and control. Manz and Sims's (1980, 1984, 1986) research investigated the utility of such self-managed teams (Cohen, Chang, & Ledford, 1997). More will be said about these teams in Chapter 26.

The Redistribution of Power

Copeland and McLaughlin (2000) called for redistributing power and authority in schools from the principals to staff and teachers, to meet shared responsibilities and shared purposes. "The capacity for leadership lies in the larger school community . . . originating from many peoples' personal resources, and flowing through networks of roles" (p. 2). The authors reported on the success of the redistribution over a five-year period in 86 schools in the San Francisco Bay Area. The principals found increases in teacher leadership (90%), teacher voice in school decisions (69%), staff discussion of teaching and learning (95%), and parent voice in school decisions (70%). A survey of the teachers in 27 of the same schools disclosed some agreement that there had been increases in shared leadership and the development of leadership capacities.

In countries with large power differences, power is redistributed usually by a peaceful or violent coup d'état in which those in power are replaced. Where differences in power are smaller, redistribution is a matter of election (Hofstede, 1997). Redistribution of power in a country may also be due to changes in the rules and in political control. The power of women in Afghanistan increased with the fall of the Taliban and with women's suffrage. In Kuwait, women were given the right to vote in 2005, and in the 2006 election for legislators, about 78% did so. Expectations were that corruption would be reduced and economic development and women's rights would improve as a consequence (*New York Times*, June 30, 2006).

House (1988) suggested that increased power sharing may come about through major shifts in environmental or technological demands that require the lodging of greater power with lower-status but expert employees. Power sharing may also come about through the replacement of managers and employees; by a deliberate redesign of the organization's structures and systems, so that critical information is broadly disseminated throughout the organization; by creating multiple centers of control; and by decoupling parts of the organization with different interests and unconnected requirements. However, the voluntary redistribution of power is likely to come about slowly and only after prolonged debate and conflict. Thus Dalton, Barnes, and Zaleznik (1968) intervened to shift power downward from managers to scientists in departments of a research and development organization. The scientists at the different levels gained in functional power and favored acceleration in the downward shift. But at the same time, the managers at various levels experienced a reduction of their hierarchical power and consequently favored slowing the downward distribution of power. The privileged, dominant coalitions in an organization will be reluctant to surrender power. They may shift technologies or move the organization into different environments to maintain their own competence-enhancing power.

By the 1990s, the downward shift in power had become commonplace to meet the organizational needs for flexibility and innovation. Structural changes in hierarchical relations had shifted to more collaborative relations across divisions and organizations. More channels had developed for influencing and taking actions. Peer networks were becoming more important than chains of command. Higher-ups increasingly had to face redistributed power that required them to use new ways of motivating their subordinates (Kanter, 1989).

Summary and Conclusions

How power is distributed in groups, organizations, and societies determines relations between leaders and followers. Power distribution depends on the structure of role relations. The human relations point of view about the distribution of power calls for its equalization among members. Structuralists favor strengthening it. Personal and situational contingencies need to be taken into account in determining whether differences in power and structure need to be reduced or increased to promote effective operations and relationships. Different distributions of power are likely to exist side by side, and deal with the legitimacy, politics, expertise, and identification processes. The total power of a group, which can be increased or decreased, strongly affects the conformity of members, their persistence, and their changes in attitudes and behavior. Research about the power of the group to induce conformity among its members peaked between 1950 and 1970. Structure is necessary under conditions of stress, threat, and the pressure of tasks. Group and organizational members are more satisfied under moderate degrees of structure than under overly structured or totally unstructured conditions. Sharing power under normal conditions has many benefits. Opportunities to consider a proposed change facilitate the acceptance of the change by members who will be affected by it. Participation in planning and decision making regarding the change induces a still higher degree of acceptance. As a consequence, power-sharing programs and restructuring, both voluntary and legally mandated, have become common. Their acceptance depends on the nature of the problems and decisions to be reached, as well as on whether the power sharing is voluntary or legally mandated, direct or through representatives. The practice of industrial democracy has been increasingly institutionalized by legislation in western Europe since World War II. Industrial democracy in the United States has been more likely to take the form of voluntary power sharing and collective bargaining. Increases in legislation to promote the fairness of collective bargaining and to equalize the power of employers and employees came in the 1930s. But how power is distributed can be a major source of conflict.

CHAPTER
13

Resolution of Conflict

Dealing with conflict has been recognized as of particular importance in leadership. In organizational life, the typical manager may spend 25% of his time dealing with conflicts (Thomas & Schmidt, 1976). A common conflict occurs between the manager's boss, whose paramount concern is for productivity, and the manager's subordinates, whose paramount concern is for consideration.

The leader's personality affects his or her rational and emotional feelings about conflict and what to do about it. One president, Lyndon Johnson, wanted every American to love him; another president, Harry Truman, concluded that, "If you can't stand the heat, stay out of the kitchen." National leaders must settle for less than universal affection. They must be willing to be unloved and they must deal with conflict (J. M. Burns, 1978). And so must most other leaders, for conflict often attends the leadership role. No leaders can be successful if they are not prepared to be rejected (T. O. Jacobs, 1970). Nonetheless, Levinson (1984, p. 133) pointed out that executives go to great lengths to avoid conflict because of their discomfort with feelings of anger. He observed that "much of the irrational in management practices arises because of people's efforts to cope with their own anger and to avoid the anger of others. . . . But the very fact that they have angry feelings, when they often feel it is wrong to be angry, leaves them feeling guilty." To contend with these feelings of anger and guilt, they make irrational decisions to deny their anger and to appease their conscience. Or they may avoid making or announcing the decision to avoid the conflict implied. Many leaders are like President Nixon, who had to rely on subordinates to relay the bad news to someone whom he wanted to fire or whose actions had been displeasing to him.

Sources of Conflict

Appointed leaders with appropriate competencies and styles may still find their attempts to lead stymied because of numerous possible conflicts with their subordinates. The appointed leader may be resented as a representative of higher authority (Seaman, 1981), or subordinates may favor the appointment of someone else. The leader and the subordinates may have different opinions about the means and ends of their efforts, as well as other ideas. For example, college presidents and vice presidents may disagree about their institutions' goals, although they generally are more likely to agree about means (Birnbaum, 1987a). A superior's and a subordinate's differences of opinion about the difficulty of achieving competence in the superior's job may be another source of conflict. In an eight-country sample of 1,600 managers, the average time that senior executives thought it would take their subordinates to learn the senior executive's job was 18 months; their subordinates estimated it would take them less than six months (Heller & Wilpert, 1981).

Cognitive versus Emotional Conflict

A conflict is mainly cognitive in nature when, say, executives disagree about the legality of an action and then call on the legal department to inform them about the law or regulation involved. A conflict is mainly emotional if, say, executives disagree on whether or not they have been disparaged and ignored by the CEO and should or should not tell him so. According to an analysis of conflict among 72 supervisor-subordinate dyads, cognitive and emotional conflict form a two-factor structure. One factor is purely emotional; the second factor is a combination of emotional and task conflict (Xin & Pelled, 2003). Generally, if a conflict is mainly cognitive, the outcome could lead to better understanding, affective acceptance, and a higher-quality decision, but more often does not. Making conflict constructive will be discussed later in the chapter. If a conflict is mainly emotional, the outcome will be less well understood and will result in a less emotionally acceptable decision. The resulting decision will be poorer (Amason, 1996). Xin and Pelled's (2003) data revealed that both emotional, and a mix of emotional and task conflicts, were negatively related to supervisory leadership behavior—more strongly in the case of emotional conflict. In agreement, Carsten and Weingart (2002) conducted a meta-analysis, which showed that in studies of task conflicts the average correlation was −.27 with individual satisfaction (12 studies) and −.26 with team performance (25 studies). The corresponding correlations in studies of socioemotional conflicts were −.48 (14 studies) and −.22 (24 studies). From 1,048 to 1,808 individuals were involved.

Role Conflict

Sources of role conflict for leaders include the ambiguity of a role, personal inadequacy to meet the demands of a role, incompatibility among several roles, conflicting demands, mixed costs and benefits associated with playing a role, and discrepancies between actual and self-accorded status. Role ambiguity occurs when leaders' roles are not clearly defined and the leaders cannot determine what they are expected to do (Kahn, Wolfe, Quinn, et al., 1964). Also, leaders may not be able to meet the demands of a task or the interpersonal demands of their role (D. J. Levinson, 1959). An incongruence occurs when, for instance, old, experienced workers are assigned to young, inexperienced supervisors. The workers are likely to perceive a discrepancy between their seniority and their rank in the status hierarchy (S. Adams, 1953). *Interrole incompatibility* occurs when an individual plays two or more roles in a group and the demands of these roles may be incompatible. For example, the role of group representative may be incompatible with the role of enforcer of discipline (Stouffer, 1949). Or there may be *within-role conflict*. That is, when different followers make conflicting demands on a given leadership role, the occupant of the role will find it difficult to take any course of action that will satisfy the various sets of expectations (Merton, 1940).

Conflict can occur if one would lose power, esteem, autonomy, or self-determination by joining or forming another group. For example, group members may reject an opportunity to join suggested coalitions with others in three-way bargaining situations even if that would be otherwise rewarding, because joining would cause loss of esteem in relation to the other members (Hoffman, Festinger, & Lawrence, 1954). Holt (1952a, 1952b) inferred from analyses of French cabinets and college interfraternity councils that otherwise mutually rewarding coalitions were rejected because a loss of autonomy or self-determination was involved.

Conflicts and disagreements may arise in the legitimatization process—in the right to function as a leader. Thus, when kingdoms were reconstituted in the nineteenth century in such countries as Belgium, Bulgaria, Greece, and Sweden, outsiders from Germany and France were legitimated as kings to avoid internal dissent. Selection of a presumably impartial outsider as constitutional monarch is consistent with the tendency for a leader of an organization to be acknowledged as the one organizational member with the legitimate power to play the role of final arbitrator, the superordinate whose judgment can settle disputes among political factions. This function was often believed to be critical for the avoidance of anarchy. The maintenance and security of the state depended on the existence of a legitimate position at the top whose occupant could arbitrate conflicts among all followers. Daum (1975) looked at the impact of internal promotion versus bringing in an outsider to lead the group. The results were as expected. The selection of a leader from within the group tended to cause the remaining members to express lower overall satisfaction and to reduce their voluntary participation following the change.

If members can agree on the leadership structure, they are more likely to be satisfied with the group, according to results obtained by Shelley (1960b). Similarly, Bass and Flint (1958a) found that early agreement about who shall lead increases a group's effectiveness. Heslin and Dunphy (1964) noted that the satisfaction of members was high when the degree of consensus about one another's status was also high.

Location in the Organizational Hierarchy

Role Ambiguity. One's location in an organizational hierarchy will make a difference in how much role ambiguity one experiences. Culbert and McDonough

(1985) suggested that much of the conflict observed in organizations starts at the top with excessive competition among senior executives with special interests vying for power. Without their awareness, a domino effect is created; the competitive conflicts at the top set off conflicts at each echelon below. Culbert and McDonough (1985) attributed much of the conflict in industry to the failure of those who are in conflict to recognize that they actually have compatible interests. Sometimes they did not acknowledge one individual's contributions to another or to the organization, and sometimes they did not achieve "a common frame of reference so that each could see that the other's efforts made organizational sense."

More role ambiguity occurs among lower-level managers. The responsibilities and authority of first-line supervisors and middle managers are less clearly defined than those of top management. Uncertain about what they are allowed and expected to do, they experience more tension than the top managers and feel less satisfied with their jobs. Thus D. C. Miller and Schull (1962) reported that middle managers registered more role stress than top managers and more frequently stated that they were unclear about the scope of their responsibilities and what their colleagues expected of them. Likewise, Brinker (1955) reported that first-line supervisors in industry worked under constant frustration because they were not given enough authority to believe they were part of management or to solve the problems presented by their subordinates. Supervisors of 140 management clubs wanted to be more closely identified with higher management because most of them felt that they did not know the company policy on many important matters and, as a result, they had to work in the dark (Mullen, 1954). Moore and Smith (1953) found that in the military, non-commissioned officers rather than higher-ups felt constant pressure because of their inadequate authority, a lack of distinction between supervisors and technicians, and conflicts among the leadership philosophies of different levels of organization. Consistent with all these findings, Wispe and Thayer (1957) found less consensus about the functions of the assistant manager than about those of the manager. The assistant manager's role was ambiguous in that neither the manager nor the assistant manager knew whether certain functions were obligatory or optional. Strain and tension were higher for the assistant manager in the more ambiguous role.

Different Assignments. Conflict arises between managers and professionals; between people in *boundary-spanning* activities that link activities outside and inside an organization, such as marketing, and people in internal operations such as manufacturing. Interviews have established that boundary spanners had interpersonal and cooperative orientations, whereas line managers emphasized authority, power, and rationality (Anonymous, undated). Conflict arises between staff and line workers and between individuals, in general, who work in different parts of the same organization. For example, there is continual tension between university administrators and faculty members and between hospital administrators and community physicians. Much of this tension is due to their differences in perception (Browne & Golembiewski, 1974), attribution (Sonnenfeld, 1981), and cognitive orientation (Kochan, Cummings, & Huber, 1976). Nystrom (1986) found systematic significant differences in the work-related beliefs of middle managers who were responsible for the supervision of line personnel and those in the same manufacturing organization who were responsible for designing the work processes and specifying outputs and controls. Middle-line managers believed more strongly in the desirability of structuring people's work activities than the technical design managers, who had a stronger belief in internal rather than external loci of control. The middle managers also were more motivated to manage than the technical design managers.

Different Perspectives. A mail survey of 155 organizations indicated that divided or unclear support by senior management for employees' involvement resulted in resistance by middle management to such involvement. The expected benefits to the firms of employees' involvement failed to appear when management was in conflict about the practice (Fenton-O'Creevey, 1998). Those at the bottom and top of their union hierarchy may have unflattering opinions about each other. S. M. Peck (1966) found that union stewards saw corruption in their top union officials but justified the unethical activities of the top officials on the grounds that strong methods were required to cope with existing conditions and that corruption was endemic. Miles and Ritchie (1968) reported that high-ranking union officials "agreed" that shop stewards and rank-and-file members should be encouraged to participate more in decision making and that such participation would result in improved morale, better decisions, and willingness to accept the goals of bargaining. Nonetheless, they were uncertain whether stewards and rank-and-file members would set reasonable goals for themselves if given the opportunity.

Control of Resources

Another source of continuing conflict is the limited control that managers have over the resources they need to get their work done (Pfeffer, 1981a). In a study of laboratory directors at hospitals, Jongbloed and Frost (1985) found that the laboratory directors were constrained by numerous individuals and groups outside the laboratories, including the physicians who were responsible for ordering the laboratory's tests; by the hospital's higher administration; and by the head of the department of pathology, as well as accreditation councils, labor unions, and professional societies. One laboratory director coped satisfactorily with this conflict; another did not. The successful laboratory director devoted a lot of energy to lobbying for increased resources and gained more needed funding. The unsuccessful director concentrated on the technical aspects of the laboratory operations and was forced to continue with a less adequate budget.

Pfeffer and Salancik (1978) examined the amount of discretion mayors had in determining items for their cities' budgets. They found that mayors who dealt with powerful organized interest groups, such as businesses, professional societies, and labor unions, had less discretion over the budgets than mayors whose cities had a higher proportion of nonwhites, governmental employees, and construction workers, and a lower median income.

Conflict Between Family and Work

Conflicts between work and family—particularly conflicts over child care and home care—have become major issues since the movement of large numbers of women into the workforce (Lerner, 1994). Imbalance between work and life has become a major source of stress at the workplace and in the family (Kozek 1998). Fisher-McAuley, Stanton, Jolton, et al. (2003) calculated the path analysis for 603 physical fitness professionals (89% female, mean age close to 41). Their opportunity to balance their work and life revealed a path coefficient of .50

with their job satisfaction, which in turn correlated $-.61$ with their intention to quit.

Relation of Conflict to Leaders' Performance and Satisfaction

To some extent, role conflict and its effects are in the eye of the beholder. Maier and Hoffman's (1965) study of role-playing groups found that some discussion leaders perceived interpersonal conflict as a source of lower-quality decisions. Other leaders saw disagreement as a source of innovation and new ideas. But more often, role ambiguity and role conflict tend to be deleterious to leaders' performance and satisfaction. Uncertainty about whether one's performance is adequate is a symptom of role ambiguity and a source of ineffectiveness, according to Pepinsky, Pepinsky, Minor, et al. (1959), who studied experimental groups working on a construction problem. The leaders of half the groups were required to work with a superior officer whose approval or disapproval of transactions could be predicted. The leaders of the other groups were required to deal with a superior whose behavior could not be predicted. The researchers found that the productivity of the team was higher under conditions of high predictability than under conditions of low predictability.

Rizzo, House, and Lirtzman (1970) found that with more perceived role ambiguity and conflict, less overall leadership behavior and less job satisfaction were reported in two industrial firms. Tosi (1971) also obtained results indicating that role conflict was negatively related to job satisfaction but not necessarily to the effectiveness of the group. Supervisors seemed able to tolerate role conflict better if they did not have to interact much with their own immediate bosses. In a study of seven companies, supplemented by a national survey, R. L. Kahn, Wolfe, Quinn, et al. (1964) found that role conflict increased as the ambiguity of the situation increased and the rate of communication with one's superiors was high. Job satisfaction decreased under these same conditions. They inferred that the source of most role conflicts is in interactions with one's immediate superiors. Subsequent studies corroborated this, reporting that as much as 88% of all role conflict was with one's boss.

In all, anyone in an organizational hierarchy needs to act both cooperatively and competitively. Roberts (1986) surveyed 350 managers from three levels of management in two business firms and two universities. In all four organizations, managers reported using both cooperative and competitive styles in their relations with their bosses, peers, and subordinates. This is likely to be one reason why successful performance in an initially leaderless group discussion is a valid predictor of success in management positions (Bass, 1954a): both situations call for cooperating and competing with others.

Incongruities in Status, Esteem, and Roles, and Other Mismatches

Conflicts within and between individuals arise when there are incongruities or mismatches among their levels of status and esteem, their rules, roles, influence, competence, personality, and expectations.

Status-Status Incongruence. Ordinarily, people have multiple roles and positions and are accorded status for each. Each status may be matched in value with the other statuses, or it may be incongruent. In organizations that are a mix of bureaucracies and collegial entities, conflict arises because the same individuals must play roles with various degrees of status and importance, depending on the decisions involved. For example, in a university hospital, the university president, the vice president for health sciences, and the medical school faculty will have more influence than the hospital's governing board over the selection of the dean of medicine, the hospital director, and the chief of the medical staff; but the reverse will be true of issues related to the financial integrity of the hospital. Among 26 such decision-making issues, Wilson and McLaughlin (1984) found that with regard to influence there was little correlation between the medical school department head, the dean, and the hospital director. The influence of the incumbent of a particular position in the hospital depended mainly on the issue.

Conflict results if there is an incongruity between one's status in one situation and in another. For example, military enlisted personnel who had high-status civilian positions were more dissatisfied with their officers than were enlisted personnel who came from civilian jobs of lower status. Former engineers were more critical of their officers than former truck drivers were (Stouffer, Suchman,

De Vinney, et al., 1949). Conflict is less and performance more effective when there is congruence between two sources of a leader's status. Knapp and Knapp (1966) studied elected officers and nonofficers who served as group leaders in a verbal conditioning experiment. Groups led by officers exhibited a higher rate of response and conditioned more readily than groups led by nonofficers. The official status of the leaders facilitated the groups' learning.

Search for Congruence. People tend to try to increase status-status congruence. In class-conscious Britain, 156 first-line supervisors varied in the social class to which they felt they belonged. Those who perceived themselves as higher in social class more readily identified with their senior managers. And the more they thought that their role as supervisor was lower in status than the status of their social class, the more they identified with the senior managers (Child, Pearce, & King, 1980). Jaques (1952) observed much anxiety and confusion when a British worker (low status) was assigned to chair (high status) a conference with management. Relief and satisfaction came only after the managing director took the chair. Trow and Herschdorfer (1965) found that groups with *incongruent* status structures that were free to change did so, whereas those with equal freedom but with *congruent* structures did not change. Furthermore, groups with high degrees of status incongruency were rated low in the performance of tasks and in the satisfaction of their members. Similarly, in a study of 50 workers in one department of a firm, Zaleznik, Christensen, and Roethlisberger (1958) found that members with high status congruence were most likely to meet the productivity standards of management. Likewise, S. Adams (1953) demonstrated that group members were better satisfied when leadership and other high-level positions were occupied by persons who ranked high in age, education, experience, and prestige. The group's productivity tended to suffer when the high-status positions were occupied by persons who ranked low in other aspects of status (age, education, experience, and social position). Yet Singer (1966) found that although status incongruence in groups was associated with tension, disorganization, and hostile communications, it did not result in lower productivity by the group or in the dissatisfaction of the group members.

Two Leaders. Two consuls were appointed each year to lead the Roman republic to avoid the possibility of dictatorship by one. Groups with two appointed, elected, or emergent leaders are inherently likely to generate conflict. Osborn, Hunt, and Skaret (1977) looked at potential conflicts between two leaders whose duties overlapped—the fraternity chapter adviser and the elected president—in each of 33 local chapters of a national business fraternity. The authors concluded that organizational effectiveness would be enhanced if only one leader played an active role in influencing subordinates and exchanges with other units. Similar conclusions about the inherent conflict in the overlapping roles of two leaders were reached by Whyte (1943), who examined two-leader configurations in mental institutions.[1] When coleaders are appointed as joint heads of social work training groups, conflicts between the leaders will block the groups' development. But if the two leaders can work together and resolve their potential disagreements, advantages will accrue in the greater opportunities to vary their roles, the wider perspectives for solving problems, and better management of and support and reinforcement for the group (Galinsky & Schopler, 1980). Such duality is built into German firms, which are led by a technical director and a commercial director and—unlike U.S. firms—have no single president. Again, although conflicting loyalties may be created, the benefits of this organizational design include equal attention to the quality of the products and to commercial success. Co-directors and co-presidents of organizations can conflict, and this will block an organization from successfully functioning.

Formal-Informal Incongruence. Mismatched formal and informal structures in any organization may be a threat to the organization (Selznick, 1948). Moreno (1934/1953) noted that the formal groupings which a higher authority superimposes on informal, spontaneous groupings are a chronic source of conflict. Roethlisberger and Dickson (1947) associated workers' dissatisfaction with discrepancies between the formal and informal organizations in an industrial plant.

Cause and effect may be reversed. Inadequacy of and dissatisfaction with the formal organization may give rise to an unrelated informal organization that is at variance

with the formal one. The informal organization emerges as a means to resist the coercive demands of high-status members of the formal organization (Shartle, 1949b). Such an informal organization may arise if the formal organization cannot provide the members with rewards like recognition or opportunity (Pfiffner, 1951), and may bypass incompetent, high-status members in order to achieve the goals of the formal organization (Lichtenberg & Deutsch, 1954). When the formal and informal structures are remerged, however, conflict is lower and the group's performance is better. Stouffer, Suchman, DeVinney, et al. (1949) observed that discussions were more satisfying to the participants when the informal leaders were given higher status by being placed in the position of discussion leaders. Haythorn (1954a) reported that the performance and cohesiveness of bomber crews were highly related to the extent to which the aircraft commander (the formal leader) performed the informal leadership roles usually expected of the formal group leader.

Role-Role Incongruence. Playing a variety of roles is not necessarily stressful. The average individual learns to play the role of child, sibling, parent, subordinate, peer, and superior without apparent effort. However, some individuals play only dependent roles well, and others are content only when they play the role of superior. Professionals tend to assume the role of authoritative, independent agents. Professional actors seem to enjoy enacting a great variety of roles but can experience personal conflict in separating their real selves from the parts they play: that is, in separating their private life from their public image. Although we may not be accomplished actors, we can play a variety of roles without apparent stress if the different roles are compatible. Nevertheless, we may find different roles incompatible with each other and, therefore, a source of conflict for us. Thus Getzels (1963) found that schoolteachers were expected to maintain a socioeconomic role that was higher than their salaries could sustain. On the one hand, in their role as citizens, they were often expected to be more active in church affairs and less active in political affairs than the average citizen; on the other hand, in their professional roles, they were expected to be certified as experts in various fields of knowledge, but they could be challenged by any parent or taxpayer. Thus teachers were subject to several

---

[1] See also reviews by Hunt, Hill, and Reaser (1973); Kerr, Schriesheim, Murphy, and Stogdill (1974); and Nealy and Fiedler (1968).

sources of conflict in each of several incompatible roles. Getzels and Guba (1954) also studied individuals with two or more roles that were subject to contradictory or mutually exclusive expectations. They found that such role conflict tended to increase when one of the individual's roles was perceived as illegitimate. Moonlighting workers would be an example if their daytime bosses frowned on their workers taking a second job or if taking a second job was illegal.

Status-Authority Incongruence. Evan and Simmons (1969) studied students who were hired to work as proofreaders. In the first experiment, their pay (supposedly an indicator of the worth and importance of their position) was inconsistent with their acknowledged level of competence. In the second experiment, their pay was inconsistent with their level of authority. Incongruity, particularly the underpayment of students in relation to their authority, resulted in a reduction in the quality of work and in conformity to the organization's rules.

Status-Esteem Incongruence. Conflict ensues and a group's performance is adversely affected when the group members who are in positions of importance (high status) are not esteemed (Bass, 1960). J. G. Jenkins's (1948) study of two naval air squadrons—one with high morale and one with low morale—found that in the high-morale group, the squadron commander and executive officer were most often nominated as individuals with whom others would want to fly (that is, they were esteemed as well as high in status); but in the low-morale squadron, the commander or executive officer was not the most esteemed member. Palmer and Myers (1955) found a correlation of .38 between the effectiveness with which 40 antiaircraft radar crews maintained their equipment and the extent to which they esteemed their key noncommissioned officers. Similarly, Bass, Flint, and Pryer (1957b) obtained a correlation of .25 between the extent to which status was correlated with esteem in an experimental group and the subsequent effectiveness of the group. Gottheil and Vielhaber (1966) also observed that groups performed more effectively when their leaders were esteemed. Using interview studies, Shils and Janowitz (1948) concluded that German enlisted soldiers' high morale and motivation to resist surrender during World War II seemed primarily due to their esteem for their officers. It continues to be true that German workers esteem their supervisors (Fukuyama, 1997). Among those Israeli soldiers in Lebanon in 1982 who believed the incursion to be immoral, morale remained high only if they highly esteemed their officers (Gal, 1987).

Firestone, Lichtman, and Colamosca (1975) had college students elect their own group leader after participating in an initially leaderless group discussion. The groups that were subsequently most effective in an emergency were those led by the elected member with the highest ratings for performance in the leaderless group discussion. Those that were worst in the emergency were led by the person they believed had the lowest ratings for performance in the preceding leaderless group discussion.

Status-Influence Incongruence. Ordinarily, those who are higher in status more frequently emerge and succeed as leaders. It becomes a source of conflict if a person of low status attempts to lead. Watson (1982) coded the taped interactions of 16 leader-subordinate dyads in a goal-setting discussion to discern their specific effects on each other. The dyads were made up of an elected leader of a student team and one randomly chosen subordinate team member. When the elected leaders attempted to dominate by abruptly changing the topic, by challenging a previous comment, or by making an ideational or personal challenge, the subordinates were most likely to respond with deference and a willingness to relinquish some but not all behavioral options. When the subordinates tried to dominate, however, the leaders resisted and competed for control of the situation. Thus when persons of higher status, the elected leaders, acted in congruence with their status, the subordinates complemented and completed the interaction with deference and simple agreement; but when the subordinates with lower status tried to dominate, the leaders resisted.

Inversions can occur in which those who are lower in status are able to be more influential than those who are higher in status. Such inversions can be a source of continuing resentment and hidden conflict when the high-status figures grudgingly acquiesce to those who are lower in status. Obviously, subordinates can be more influential over leaders who abdicate their role. Pettigrew (1973) gave examples of situations in which subordinates or those who are otherwise lower in status have influence over those who are higher in status. Generally, in these situations, higher-status superiors became dependent on their subordinates (Mechanic, 1962). Physicians can become so dependent on attendants in hospital wards that the attendants can block reforms. Prison guards can become dependent on the inmates for the inmates' good behavior. Although guards can report prisoners for disobedience, too many such reports from the same guards create the impression among their superiors that they are ineffective. As a consequence, guards agree to let certain violations by prisoners go unreported in exchange for the prisoners' cooperation in other matters. Experts can keep their superiors dependent on them for information, particularly about risky innovations, and thereby maintain power over their superiors (Crozier, 1984). Subordinates in the Soviet Union held their superiors hostage with their knowledge of illegal acts the superiors committed in order for the group to meet its production quotas (Granick, 1962).

Status-Competence Incongruence. If those with high status are incompetent for their role assignments, the group will be less productive, less successful, and less satisfied; and more conflict will be generated within the group. But strong positive associations between competence and effective leadership have been found in surveys and experiments. Woods (1913) related the judged ability (strong, mediocre, or weak) of 386 European sovereigns to their states' performance from the eleventh century to 1789. A correlation of .60 was found between judged ability of a sovereign and ratings of the political, material, and economic progress of the state the sovereign headed. Similarly, Rohde (1954c) reported correlations up to .63 between the success of groups learning to go through a maze and the adequacy of the pretest performance of the person in charge of each of the groups. Furthermore, in a comparison of nine orientation discussion groups, Stouffer, Suchman, DeVinney, et al. (1949) observed that members were much more likely to say they "got a lot out of the discussion" when the member of the group who was chosen to lead the discussion was better educated. Bass (1961c) found that successful leadership was more highly related to ability in effective groups than in ineffective groups.

The choice of a competent leader is a major determinant of the effectiveness of a team and stimulates effective mutual influence among team members (Borg,

1956). Thus after analyzing a large number of small-group studies, Heslin and Dunphy (1964) concluded that group members are most likely to achieve consensus on the status structure of the group when: (1) the leader is perceived to be highly competent; (2) a leader emerges who is high in both group-task and group-maintenance functions; or (3) two mutually supportive leaders emerge, one specializing in task functions and the other in group-maintenance functions. (But two leaders of a single group may present problems, as was noted earlier.)

The mismatching of status and competence in a group is likely to result in the downgrading of the group leader. Thus Ghiselli and Lodahl (1958a) found that a supervisor was likely to be poorly regarded by higher management if he led a group containing a worker whose supervisory ability was superior to his. Goldman and Fraas (1965) noted the importance of matching competence and status in their comparison of groups whose leaders were elected, appointed for competence, or appointed randomly. They found that groups with leaders who were appointed for competence did best; groups with elected leaders did next best; and groups without leaders or whose leaders had been appointed randomly did the worst.

Effects of Loyalty. Ordinarily, we would expect that competent groups would produce higher-quality decisions. But Dooley and Fryxell (1999), in a study of 86 strategic decision teams in hospitals, found that the quality of these teams' decisions was higher—according to independent judges—only when the members were seen as more loyal (they did not try to take advantage of each other) and expressed many differing opinions. The quality of decisions suffered when the team members expressed many different opinions but were low in loyalty (tried to mislead each other). For high-quality decisions and commitment, both competence and willingness to disagree were necessary.

Incongruence of Competence and Power. Exline and Ziller (1959) assembled groups in which members held positions that were incongruent in competence and power, and other groups in which competence and power were congruent. The participants rated the congruent groups as significantly more congenial, as exhibiting stronger agreement between members, and as involving less overlap of activities.

Incongruence of Personality Traits and Roles. As might be expected, effectiveness is reduced by incongruities between the organization or group members' personality traits and the roles required of them. Smelser (1961) selected students who scored either high or low on a personality test of dominance. The least productive dyads were composed of pairs in which the partner assessed as submissive was assigned to a role that required dominance and the partner assessed as dominant was given a role that required submissiveness. The most productive dyads were those in which role assignments were consistent with personality assessments.

Requisite personality may be a matter of expectations. Violated expectations generate conflict. Lipham (1960) tested the hypothesis that personality traits compatible with expectations about a leadership role will be related to the leader's effectiveness. In a study of school principals, Lipham found that those who scored high on expected characteristics, such as drive, emotional control, and sociability, were rated more effective than those who scored high on unexpected characteristics such as submissiveness and abasement. In a study of insurance agencies, Wispe (1955, 1957) found that successful agents were characterized by a strong drive for success. But the same attitude toward success, when exhibited by the agency manager, was at variance with the agents' expectation of a more humane, considerate orientation toward their problems. Thus the characteristic that was perceived to contribute to successful selling was not necessarily expected to contribute to effective supervision.

Overt conflict was avoided (at a price) when those of lower status hid their abilities from those of higher status. Before the social revolution of the 1960s, college women often used to "play dumb" on dates, just as black subordinates did in dealing with white superiors. Ordinarily, a better way for an organization to avoid conflict and to enhance satisfaction and performance is to develop suitable promotional policies that match the competence of employees with their status (Bass, 1960).

Within-Role Conflicts

The failure of individuals to align their own needs for personal meaning, identity, and success with what they believe the organization needs to receive from those in their roles is at the heart of individual members' conflicts within an organization (Culbert & McDonough, 1980). Organizational and personal needs must be fused to allow both the individual and the organization to reach high levels of achievement and satisfaction (Lester, 1981).

Within-Role Expectations. The negative effect of within-role expectations in groups, organizations, and society is largely attributable to discrepancies between what the members expect they should do and what others expect them to do. They experience conflicts when others make contradictory demands on their roles in the group, organization, or society that cannot be satisfied by any compatible course of action (Brandon, 1965). The man or woman in the middle is a well-known example.

The Man or Woman in the Middle. This is a common dilemma. Like everyone else at each successive level in an organizational hierarchy, the supervisor is a man or woman in the middle. Such persons face conflicting role demands from at least two sources: their superiors and their subordinates. Although the person in the middle is likely to be subjected to competing demands from numerous other sources—peers, higher authority, rules, suppliers, and customers—most attention has been paid to the conflicting demands on supervisors from superiors and subordinates (Gardner & Whyte, 1945; Smith, 1948). Superiors expect results, initiative, planning, firmness, and structure. Subordinates expect recognition, opportunity, consideration, approachability, encouragement, and representation (Brooks, 1955). Thus Pfeffer and Salancik (1975) demonstrated that superiors expected more task behavior from first-line supervisors whereas subordinates expected more socializing from them. Likewise, Snoek (1966) found that supervisors "in the middle" experienced more conflict than operatives "at the bottom." Supervisors had a wider diversity of interactions than the operating personnel, and the conflicting demands placed on them led them to experience more role strain.

In military organizations, officers above and enlisted personnel below disagree on what characterizes the good noncommissioned officer in between them (U.S. Air Force, 1952). Factor-analytic studies by J. V. Moore (1953) showed, for example, that subordinates wanted noncoms to be less strict whereas superiors emphasized noncoms' military bearing and ability. Halpin (1957b) found that commanders of aircrews who highly emphasized consideration were most highly rated by their subordinates, whereas those who most often initiated structure were more likely to be rated effective leaders by their superiors. Similarly, Zenter (1951) noted that 87% of the officers studied thought that a good noncommissioned officer follows orders while only 44% of the enlisted men accepted this idea. At the same time, 49% of enlisted men believed that a good noncommissioned officer has to gain popularity, but only 7% of officers agreed. One discordant note in these findings was that Graen, Dansereau, and Minami (1972b) failed to find the expected discrepancy between subordinates' and superiors' role expectations of executives in the middle.

Nonetheless, Lawler, Porter, and Tannenbaum (1968) found that interactions with superiors were more valued than those with subordinates. In addition, the managers reacted more favorably to interactions that their superiors initiated than to those initiated by others. Porter and Kaufman (1959) devised a scale for determining the extent to which supervisors described themselves as similar to top managers. Self-perceptions that were similar to those of top managers were associated with patterns of interaction that peers perceived to be similar to those of managers in high-level positions.

Subordinates whose attitudes and role perceptions were similar to those of their superiors were preferred by their superiors (Miles, 1964a) and rated by them as more effective (V. F. Mitchell, 1968). In turn, subordinates who resembled their superiors in the personality traits "sociable" and "stable" were better satisfied than those who resembled their superiors less closely. Henry (1949) and others found that rapidly promoted executives particularly tended to identify themselves with their superiors. On the other hand, Pelz (1952) found that first-line supervisors who were subordinate oriented tended to be evaluated positively by their workers, but only if they were perceived to have sufficient influence with superiors to satisfy the workers' expectations.

Balma, Maloney, and Lawshe (1958a, 1958b) studied more than 1,000 foremen in 19 plants. They found that foremen who identified themselves with management were rated as having significantly more productive groups than those who did not identify with their superiors. However, the employees' satisfaction with a foreman was not related to the foreman's orientation. R. S. Barrett (1963) discovered that foremen who perceived that their approach to problems was similar to the approach of their immediate superiors tended to feel free to do things their own way. Fleishman and Peters (1962) observed that top-level managers tended to connect the effectiveness of lower-level managers with that of these managers' immediate middle-level superiors.

Customers and Management. Employees who are in contact with customers face competing expectations from customers and management. Management expects these employees to follow the rules while providing high-quality service. The customers may have requests that require bending the rules. Customers may exacerbate the situation by rewarding the contact employees with tips. Such employees need to balance the competing expectations of customers and managers (Eddleston, Kidder, & Litzky, 2002).

Conflicts between Organizational Levels. Neuberger (1983) viewed the supervisor as the focus of multilateral expectations that could be ambiguous, conflicting, and contradictory. Rules, regulations, and structure do not necessarily provide solutions to such conflicts, which can result in political behavior and unstable leadership behavior. Conflict may arise because there are decided differences in what members at different levels of the organization expect is appropriate behavior for them. L. W. Porter (1959) reported that first-level supervisors viewed themselves as careful and controlled in their approach to the job and to other people. Their second-level managers, in contrast, described themselves as enterprising, original, and bold. First-level supervisors differed from line workers as much as they differed from higher-level managers; they perceived themselves to be significantly more careful and controlled than the workers saw themselves. The first-level supervisory role imposed demands for behavioral patterns that differed from those of superiors and subordinates. A form of conflict that has long been recognized (Coser, 1956) is superior-subordinate conflict involving viewpoints, opinions, and ideas about the task being performed and, on the other hand, tension, animosity, and annoyances—socioemotional, interpersonal incompatibilities (Jehn, 1995). D. E. Frost (1983) reported that for 121 first-level supervisors, perceived conflict in their own role correlated .27 with their boss's emphasis on production and

.35 with conflict with their boss. Consistent with the multiple-screen model of Fiedler, Potter, Zais, et al. (1979), *experienced* first-level supervisors' performance was greater if conflict was high with their bosses and declined when conflict was low. The reverse was true of the relationship between the first-level supervisors' *intelligence* and their performance.

The conflicts of middle management were reflected in an opinion research poll of 1982, which found that over half the respondents had "lost confidence in their superiors"; 69% saw too many decisions being made (and made poorly) at the top by persons who were unfamiliar with the particular problems (Fowler, 1982). Adding to the middle managers' malaise was job insecurity, brought on by drastic reductions in middle-management positions in the 1980s (Clutterbuck, 1982a)—a development predicted 30 years earlier by Leavitt and Whisler (1958), who foresaw that dramatic improvements in information processing would substitute for this level of management. The trend continued into the early twenty-first century, when many plants and offices closed because of foreign competition and the movement of companies offshore.

Conflicts with the Boss. Kahn, Wolfe, Quinn, et al. (1964) found that 88% of all organizational role conflict involves pressure from above. D. E. Frost (1983) discovered that the boss's behavior created most of the role conflict and ambiguity for first- and second-level leaders in an urban fire department. Managers were the overriding reason for the role ambiguity and conflict experienced by 123 salaried employees of a metal fabricating firm who were surveyed by Deluga (1986). Jambor (1954) found that when supervisors' perception of their role differed from their superiors' perception of it, the supervisors experienced more anxiety than when their role perception differed from their subordinates' perception of it. Fiedler (1984) amassed considerable evidence to show that when *experienced* leaders are in conflict with their boss, they tend to be able to maintain productive groups. But *intelligent* leaders without such experience are handicapped by conflicts with their boss. Experience, not intelligence, helps leaders deal with the stress engendered by conflicts with their own superiors.

Conflicts with Subordinates. Using clinical observation and psychoanalytical theory, Zaleznik (1965a) conceived of four types of malfunctioning subordinates, each representing a type of personality that is in conflict with the demands of a higher authority:

(1) *Impulsive* subordinates rebel and strive to overthrow authority and its symbols; unconscious motives may be to displace parental authority or to deal with painful loneliness;

(2) *Compulsive* subordinates also want to dominate the struggle with authority, but they do so passively. Their behavior is rigid, and they avoid making decisions. Underneath, there are doubts, rapid shifts in feelings about interpersonal encounters, hidden aggression, and denial of responsibility, coupled with a power conscience and strong guilt feelings;

(3) Immature early development results in *masochists*, illustrated by accident-prone employees who evoke sympathy when hurt. Their performance is inadequate and invites criticism and shame. Their identity is with the oppressed, helpless, and weak;

(4) *Withdrawn* subordinates turn their interests inward and passively submit to a perceived malevolent world and untrustworthy superiors. Although they may handle routine tasks well, they make little effort to be innovative.

Zaleznik's advice for supervising these four types of subordinates is to avoid being trapped into their dynamics—for example, by reinforcing the doubts of compulsive subordinates or losing control to the impulsive, rebellious subordinates. Conflict with such subordinates needs to be objectified, and conflicting issues need to be broken into their components. Realities need to be recognized.

Discordant Expectations. Discrepancies between people's expectations about assignments, jobs, or positions and the expectations of their subordinates, peers, superiors, and clients about these assignments, jobs, or positions have been studied extensively as fundamental sources of conflict. Similarly, conflicts arise as a consequence of discrepancies between what is done by people and what ought to be done. Thus Colmen, Fiedler, and Boulger (1954) reported little agreement among 45 leaders in the U.S. Air Force in evaluating their own duties.

Further confusion resulted from a discrepancy between what potential leaders thought they ought to do and what they actually did. Halpin (1957b) found little relationship between how aircraft commanders and school superintendents said they might behave and how their subordinates said they actually behaved.

Stogdill, Scott, and Jaynes (1956) asked officers at various levels of a large naval organization to describe what they did and what they ought to do. In addition, their direct reports described what the immediate superiors did and ought to do. The subordinates' self-expectations were much more highly related to their expectations for their superiors than were their self-descriptions to their descriptions of their superiors. Subordinates entertained similar expectations for themselves and for their superiors, but their descriptions of their own and their superiors' behavior were not as similar. Except for handling paperwork and other forms of individual effort, they did not perceive that their own behavior resembled that of their superiors. Discrepancies between superiors' self-descriptions and self-expectations were highly related to their level of responsibility.[2] Superiors who obtained high scores from their subordinates on level of responsibility perceived themselves as having too much responsibility and as acting as representatives of their followers more extensively than they should. They also reported spending too little time inspecting the organization and too much time on paperwork and engaging in all forms of leadership behavior. Discrepancies between subordinates' self-descriptions and self-expectations were greater at higher organizational levels where their superiors were recipients of frequent interactions. Under these conditions, the subordinates perceived themselves to be doing more than they should in attending conferences, interviewing personnel, handling paperwork, and representing their own subordinates. When a superior delegated a great deal, the subordinates thought that they had been given too much responsibility, and spent less time than they should on coordination and professional activities.

Along similar lines, Triandis (1959a) found that the smaller the discrepancy between workers' ideal supervisor behavior and actual descriptions of their supervisors' behavior, the better the supervisor was liked by the workers. Results obtained by Holden (1954) indicated that the more a leader's behavior conformed to the group members' expectations, the more productive the group was. Havron and McGrath (1961) suggested that the leaders of highly effective groups either behave as expected or are successful in inducing group members to form ideals that are similar to the leaders' actual behavior. Thus Foa (1956), who studied supervisors and workers in Israeli factories, found that these supervisors and workers agreed on the ideal behavior for a supervisor, but that they did not agree on what the supervisor actually did. The more agreement there was between the ideal and perceived behavior of the supervisor, the better satisfied the workers were with their supervisor. Workers who identified with their supervisor tended to attribute to the supervisor the ideals that they held. Ambivalent workers attempted to conform to the ideal attributed to their supervisor but were aware of the supervisor's deviation from it. Indifferent workers felt less inclined to accept the ideal of the supervisor in their own behavior and were also less likely to notice discrepancies between the supervisor's ideal and real behavior. However, F. J. Davis (1954) failed to corroborate these effects among U.S. Air Force officers: in his study the successful adjustment of the followers did not depend on their agreement with the leader about the leader's role.

Other Sources of Within-Role Conflict. Differences in perceived needs, values, interests, and goals are structural sources of conflict among managers at different hierarchical levels as well as between leaders and followers in the community. For example, Fiedler, Fiedler, and Camp (1971) found that whereas community leaders thought poor government, neighborhood disunity, and the failure of public services were the concerns of consequence, householders believed that crime, immorality, traffic, and unemployment were the issues that needed attention. Managers and union leaders both generally overemphasize the importance of pay as a source of dissatisfaction of employees and underemphasize the importance of such concerns as security, job satisfaction, and opportunity (Bass & Ryterband, 1979).

Contradictory demands may stem from discrepancies between one's immediate work group and one's reference group. At some colleges, professors may be caught between the demands of their cosmopolitan, professional, research-oriented reference groups and the role demands

[2] See Chapter 14.

of their local campus for high-quality teaching and good relations with students. Industrial scientists may be caught between their professional reference groups' demand that they get their work published and their business firms' demand for secrecy. These conflicts are a source of dissatisfaction, as was illustrated in an industrial study by Browne and Neitzel (1952), who found that workers' satisfaction declined as the disagreement between what their leaders demanded of them and what was wanted by their reference groups increased. Jacobson (1951) and Jacobson, Charters, and Lieberman (1951) studied foremen, union stewards, and workers. The foremen expected the stewards to play a passive role in the organization, whereas the stewards and the workers expected the stewards to play an active role on behalf of employees and the union. Foremen and stewards whose expectations deviated from the norm of their reference group got along more easily with each other.

Supervisors in training are often caught in a conflict when their managers are opposed to what the supervisors are being taught by their trainers. Furthermore, trainers are more likely to succeed in modifying the supervisors' behavior if their bosses show interest in the training program, participate in its development, and take the training course first (W. Mahler, 1952). Politicians must continually cope with conflict between what they must do and what they would prefer to do. They must choose between what they find expedient and what they know is right. Personal integrity has to be sacrificed to unholy alliances. Henry IV of France, a Protestant Huguenot, converted to Catholicism because "Paris is well worth a mass." For Adolf Hitler and Joseph Stalin, making a deal with each other in 1939 bought them time. For President Dwight D. Eisenhower, keeping silent in the face of Senator Joseph McCarthy's virulent attacks on George Marshall, Eisenhower's close friend, was justified as a means of maintaining the Republican coalition. Presidents Ronald Reagan and George H. W. Bush both embraced the agenda of the far right while campaigning for election but tended to give a lower priority to many of the right wing's demands once they were elected.

Habitual Sources of Conflict

Punctuality. Some celebrities, such as Madonna and Elizabeth Taylor, have been noted for being chronically late for appointments. Politicians such as Bill Clinton and Jesse Jackson were likewise known for showing up late for meetings. According to Janine Braier, "Being late is a statement; if you are chronically late . . . it's a way of saying 'you need me but I don't need you.' . . . I never want to have the experience of needing someone. I always want them to want me." People who are habitually late usually are overloaded with tasks and somehow schedule impossibilities into their workdays. They deny the reality that by being late they are delaying others. They feel omnipotent and in complete control. Being late may be a way of deliberately manipulating time to emphasize one's own importance and others' dependence (Jennings, 1999, p. 18).

Identification. Racial, ethnic, and national identification is well known as a source of conflict. Conflict may then be exacerbated by divergent beliefs based on historical memories, "we-they" polarization, religious intolerance, and economic, social, and political privileges (Rouhana & Bar-Tel, 1998). But Kelman (1999), in discussing the continuing Israeli-Palestinian confrontation and each side's negative identification with the other, is realistic, also noting positive interdependence (Palestinians are a source of labor for Israel; Israelis are a source of jobs for Palestine). The leaders of both sides must work to change the beliefs of their own people that they are the victims and the other side are the aggressors.

Identification with superiors or subordinates appears to be a key to understanding the man or woman in the middle. Potential conflicts with supervisors and subordinates depend on with whom identification and similarity are sought. Thus Pfeffer and Salancik (1978) observed that when leaders were more responsive to their subordinates' demands, the leaders' characteristics and activities were more like those of their subordinates. The leaders were more responsive to their bosses' pressure to produce when the leaders' activities were more like those of their own superiors. A second study found that supervisors who were required to engage in a great deal of peer-oriented interdepartmental coordination were less likely to be responsive to their subordinates.

D. T. Campbell and his associates developed various methods of measuring identification with superiors and subordinates. Of the variety of independent subscales that emerged (Campbell, Burwen, & Chapman,

1955), the most promising were identification with discipline, superior-subordinate orientation, and eagerness for responsibility and advancement. Identification with superiors rather than subordinates correlated .21 with authoritarianism, .25 with identification with discipline, and −.20 with cooperation (Chapman & Campbell, 1957a). Paradoxically, those of higher rank appear to be less concerned about their superiors and more concerned about their subordinates. Campbell and McCormack (1957) found that colonels in the U.S. Air Force were significantly less oriented toward superiors than were Air Force majors or college men, and majors were less so than Air Force cadets or their instructors. Furthermore, Air Force majors and lieutenant colonels were significantly more subordinate-oriented than the other groups tested.

Generational Conflict. A generational conflict resulting in a lack of identification with senior leadership was suggested as a cause of an expected 13% attrition of U.S. Army captains in just one year, 2001. The captains were members of the cohort called Generation X, who were born between 1960 and 1980. Above them in rank from major to general was the baby-boomer generation, whose members were born between 1943 and 1960. The Generation Xers tended to have more divorced, two-career parents, more disruptive families, and less idyllic childhoods than the baby boomers, whose families were more stable, with parents in more traditional roles. Compared with Generation Xers, baby boomers value work and promotion as more important. Baby boomers are more likely to be workaholics. In contrast, Generation Xers value having more free time, more friendships, and a better family life (Wong, 2000).

Conditions That Resolve or Reduce Conflicts

Both the leader and the led determine whether conflicts can be readily reduced or resolved. Among the six factors that identified the effective manager, Morse and Wagner (1978) found one that involved the ability to deal with conflict among colleagues and associates and to avoid continuing conflicts that got in the way of completing assignments. Walton (1972) noted that effectiveness as a leader was associated with the ability to convert conflicts of interests among subordinates and colleagues into ac-

commodation, conciliation, compromise, and, better yet, consensual agreement. Effective leaders did not run away from conflict or try to deal with it arbitrarily.

In contrast with transactional leaders, transformational leaders seem to have more ability to deal with conflict. They are less readily disturbed by it, possibly because they are "more at peace with themselves." Gibbons (1986) reached this conclusion on the basis of in-depth interviews with 16 senior executives in a high-technology firm identified as transformational or transactional by peer nominations and by subordinates' descriptions of them on the Multifactor Leadership Questionnaire (Bass & Avolio, 1989).

In organizational mergers, a source of considerable conflict, the acquired employees are more satisfied with the merger when their leaders are transformational (Covin, Kolenko, Sightler, et al., 1997). Followers also make a difference. Lien, Kottke, and Agars (2003) found that emotional conflicts among 84 employees of public organizations in southern California were lessened by collectivistic rather than individualistic attitudes and by tolerance for multicultural diversity.

Dual Loyalties

Conflicts may be resolved or lessened if the leaders and the led have *dual loyalties*. They may be loyal both to the management and to the union in conflict. They may have interests in both the organization and its members. They may want to remain concerned about the feelings of both their superiors and associates who may be in conflict.

Conflicting interests may be overriden by multiple identifications and allegiances. Potential conflicts may be reduced, avoided, and even resolved because people who are members of two groups or organizations with conflicting interests may consider themselves loyal to both. For example, Stagner (1954) obtained a correlation of .33 between the favorableness of workers' attitudes toward their company and toward the union. Purcell (1954) found that although more workers identified with the company than with the union, 73% of the men and women surveyed expressed loyalty to both. Supervisors and stewards each identified with the organization that they represented officially, but both supervisors (57%) and stewards (88%) generally felt favorable toward the others' organization. In a case study of 18 supervisors at a British shoe factory, Armstrong (1983) was chagrined (because of his Marxist orientation) to find that despite the supervisors' resentment about their deteriorating income and status relative to the workforce, they remained loyal to the senior management. For Armstrong, this continuing loyalty to senior management meant that the supervisors failed to recognize their interests as members of the working class who were exploited by the capitalist senior management.

Obrochta (1960) obtained results indicating that supervisors and workers were most similar regarding their attitudes toward the company and least similar regarding their attitudes toward union leaders. The supervisors' attitudes toward both the union leaders and the company were more favorable than those of the hourly workers, and the attitudes of the hourly workers toward the union were more favorable than the supervisors'. Obrochta also found that the workers' attitudes toward their foreman were somewhat more favorable than the supervisor's attitude toward them. Further evidence on reciprocity or the lack of it was gathered by Derber, Chalmers, Edelman, et al. (1965) in a study of 37 industrial plants. The results indicated that managers' attitudes toward the union and union leaders' attitudes toward the management were positively and significantly correlated; each group was moderately favorable in its attitude toward the other. Obviously, there are variations and exceptions. For instance, Stagner, Chalmers, and Derber (1958), using separate scales for measuring attitudes toward the company and the union, found no relation between the management's attitudes toward the union and the union's attitudes toward the management. Yet in many firms, managers and union officials regard each other in generally favorable terms, despite the conflict between them about substantive issues, particularly issues involving their respective powers. Investigating managers in a southern city, Alsikafi, Jokinen, Spray, et al. (1968) suggested that unfavorable managerial attitudes toward the union tended to be connected with the inclusion in labor contracts of union security clauses that the managers perceived as challenging their authority to manage. Spillane (1980) noted that in contrast to a survey done in 1959, a survey done in 1978 found that the gap between the attitudes of Australian union leaders and Australian business executives had narrowed substantially. Both groups in the later survey strongly supported arbitration as a way of resolving industrial disputes. On the other hand, Edwards and Heery (1985) noted that when the interests of shop floor democracy in 35 British collieries came into conflict with the interests of union officials or national interests the local leaders upheld the concern for shop floor democracy.

In a plant of 3,400 employees, in which top management and union leaders espoused cooperation and mutual confidence, one-fourth of the shop stewards did not share information with the shop supervisors, and half of the supervisors held back from sharing information with the stewards. Yet in a survey of 263 U.S. firms, information exchange was reported as the most frequent form of union-management cooperation.

As elected officers appealing to their constituents, union leaders need to publicly enunciate more extreme points of view than their counterparts in management (Bass, 1965). To study perceptual distortions between 76 union officers in a central labor council and 108 human resources executives, Haire (1948) showed photographs of two middle-aged men to half of a sample: one photo was identified as secretary-treasurer of a union, the other as the local manager of a small plant. The identifications were switched for the other half of the sample. The union officials used a checklist to describe the photo identified as a union secretary-treasurer as that of a man who was conscientious, honest, trustworthy, responsible, considerate, cooperative, fair, and impartial. The human resources executives were even more complimentary in describing the same photo as that of a plant manager.

Differences in communication behavior show up when union stewards are compared with counterparts who are plant supervisors. Nonetheless, dual allegiance to the union and the company is the rule rather than the exception. This was seen in interviews with 202 employees in the garment, construction, trucking, grain processing, and metalworking industries. If the employees had favorable attitudes to either the union or the company, they had favorable attitudes toward the other as well. Dual allegiance was found in 73% of packinghouse employees, 88% of union stewards, and 57% of company supervisors (Purcell, 1953).

Multiple Orientations

Three of every four first-line supervisors who were rated as promotable by their superiors were described by their subordinates as pulling for both the employees and the company. Only 40% of those seen as less worthy of promotion were so described (Mann & Dent, 1954b). Simultaneous upward and downward orientation and sensitivity are required of the effective supervisor, as a person in the middle. Sarbin and Jones (1955) reported that a successful supervisor not only is competent in the eyes of superiors but fulfills the expectations of subordinates. According to Wray (1949), this is not an easy task, since superiors and subordinates present conflicting expectations that are difficult to reconcile. Nonetheless, in his study of an industrial plant, H. Rosen (1961a, 1961b) found that managers could have an upward orientation toward the demands of their superiors while remaining sensitive to the demands of their subordinates. The experience of supervisors in their subordinates' jobs has been found to be of consequence. Maier, Hoffman, and Read (1963) compared managers who had previously held the jobs of their subordinates with peers who had not held these jobs. Subordinates trusted mutual agreements about their current problems only when the agreements were made with managers who had previously been in the subordinates' jobs, although a manager's previous assignment to a subordinate's job did not facilitate effective communication.

Perspective-Taking

Conflict has a tendency to escalate and to be exacerbated by *mirror imaging*—attributing opposite qualities to the opposition in a conflict. Thus, "we" are honest, just, rational, and benevolent; "they" are dishonest, unjust, emotional, and malevolent. Leaders of groups, organizations, and nations tend to exploit and exaggerate these opposing attributions, as was seen among Americans who exhibited mirror imaging of Iranians soon after the American hostages were seized in Tehran in 1979 (Conover, Mingst, & Sigelman, 1980). However, McPherson-Frantz and Janoff-Bulman (2000) found in an experiment with college students about parent-adolescent conflict that partisanship could be ameliorated to the extent that partisans liked the opposing party. Instructions to be fair and unbiased resulted in reducing attention to arguments from both sides but also bolstered original partisan perspectives.

Union-Management Relations

The marked decline in union membership in the United States in the past half century has been paralleled by a decline in studies of union-management relations. Furthermore, there has been a shift in unionization from industrial business to governmental agencies. Despite mirror imaging, K. F. Walker (1962) found that managers and union leaders were accurate in predicting each other's attitudes, but both perceived more conflict than actually existed. Supervisors and shop stewards who wanted the company and union to coexist amicably experienced more stress than normal and tended to hold favorable attitudes toward each other (Purcell, 1954). However, the underlying bases for evaluating the management and the union differed. Stagner, Derber, and Chalmers (1959) surveyed the attitudes of two labor leaders and two managers in each of 41 establishments. When they computed a composite score for each establishment for each of 35 attitude and satisfaction variables, they found that the management's evaluation of the union emerged as a single general factor but that the union's evaluations were denoted by two factors, one involving union-management relations and the other concerned with the union's achievements (1949). Miller and Remmers (1950) examined the attitudes of managers and labor leaders toward human relations–oriented supervision. Managers tended to overestimate labor leaders' scores, whereas labor leaders underestimated managers' scores. In a comparative study of managers and union officials, Weaver (1958) found, as expected, that union officials exhibited strong prolabor attitudes. But not as obviously, managers were neutral about grievances, arbitration, the labor movement, and working during a strike.

Schwartz and Levine (1965) compared the interests of managers and union officials in the same companies. The managers scored higher on interest in supervisory initiative and production, and the union officials scored higher on interest in seeking power and in propaganda, bargaining, arbitration, and disputation. Similarly, Bogard (1960) compared the values of management trainees and labor leader trainees and found that management trainees scored higher in aggressiveness and lower in altruistic values than the union trainees.

Managing Conflict

The management of conflict is an important component of most leadership roles. Thomas and Schmidt (1976) reported that middle managers spent more than 25% of their time dealing with conflict with their colleagues. The figure was even higher for first-line supervisors. Often, managing a conflict may involve gaining the acceptance of a resolution by persuading the conflicting employees, groups, or organizations that the proposed settlement will bring more benefits and less cost to both parties than continuing the dispute.

Leaders can manage conflict with supportive, friendly, obliging, compromising, and integrative efforts to move the parties from a competitive to a cooperative stance (Musser & Martin, 1988). The conflict between the felt security of employees in the old ways of doing things and changes required by new demands can be managed by a leader who instills pride in the past coupled with a need to meet the challenges of the future (Tichy & Devanna, 1986). According to Oscar Arias, a former president of Costa Rica, reelected in 2006, who has frequently been involved in international negotiation of conflicts, the negotiator needs patience but not passivity, perseverance but not inflexibility, commitment and respect for others' viewpoints, skills in building trust, and the ability to compromise in good faith.

Diagnosis and Remediation

Diagnosis of the causes of a conflict is a rational way to begin to manage it. For example, if a conflict is due to a failure to match status and esteem, it can be reduced by incorporating the results of subordinates' evaluations of esteem into promotional policies or building up the esteem of those with high status. If conflict is anticipated because of a rise in status of one member at the expense of the others, it can be avoided by bringing in an outsider to lead the group (Bass, 1960). Kabanoff (1985a) proposed a typology of conflict situations. Each type suggested a relevant rationale for its management. For

instance, if a diagnosis showed that the team members' esteem was lower than their actual ability and expertise, public praise could be used to increase their esteem. In addition, counseling could help peers increase their acceptance of expert but unesteemed members.

Conflict-Management Tactics and Strategies

Kabanoff (1985a, 1985b) provided a list of diagnosed *intrapersonal* conflicts, such as conflict between one's status and esteem, with implied or self-explanatory strategies for handling them. In addition, tactics were suggested for dealing with conflicts of status and esteem, when conflicts arose between low esteem and high-needed ability, low commitment and high centrality, low popularity and high status, incompatability and required collaboration, low ability and required-high ability, low ability and high status, and low ability and a highly critical task.

Kindler (1996) focused on resolving *interpersonal* conflicts by suggesting ways a person such as a leader could deal with a conflict, depending on the diagnosis of the circumstances. The ways of dealing with such conflicts included direction, resistance, adapting, accommodating, and yielding. They also depended on a diagnosis of the intention to be firm or flexible, and on how involved a party in the conflict wanted to be in the resolution. According to Kindler, *domination* pressures the opposition to comply. This is a costly, inflexible alternative because of its potentially negative effects, but it may be necessary when speed is vital, when confidentiality prevents disclosing all the relevant facts, or when a stalemate cannot be ended. *Smoothing* is another inflexible tactic; it accentuates the information that supports the benefits of one's position and steers the conversation away from alternatives that would intensify the opposition. *Maintenance* is a firm but interim tactic to deal with conflict when time is needed to collect information, calm emotions, enlist allies, take care of higher priorities, or allow nature to take its course—as when an obstinate opponent is expected to retire soon. *Bargaining* works when each side wants something that the other controls. Offers and counteroffers lead to a compromise agreement if both parties can gain from it. *Coexisting* is an agreement for the parties to follow separate paths until after additional testing, when an agreement on a single path can be made. *Deciding by rule*—such as by seniority, arbitration, or coin-flipping—may be appropriate when any alternative solution is better than none and decisive action is needed. *Collaboration* requires time, trust, and interpersonal competence with attentive listening and the probing of underlying assumptions in the search for creative solutions. Each side must be flexible and open about what it wants to see in the solution. *Releasing* allows the decision to be made by the other party, as when a flexible supervisor delegates the matter to the subordinate to handle after limitations on what is possible have been set. *Yielding* occurs when a flexible supervisor expresses a difference of opinion with a subordinate but agrees to go along with what the subordinate wants to do. It is useful in dealing with an issue that may be more important to the subordinate than to the supervisor.

Another approach to diagnosis of the conflict situation, leading to the use of political skills, was offered by Block (1987). *Allies* are those with whom you share a high level of trust; *opponents* can be trusted but are in disagreement with you over issues; *bedfellows* are in agreement but can't be trusted; *fence sitters* can be trusted, but you don't know their positions; and *adversaries* are those with whom trust and agreement are low. Like Kabanoff's and Kindler's models, solutions depending on the diagnosis are implied and need empirical testing.

Influence Tactics. The extent to which threats or promises were used for dealing with interpersonal, intergroup, and international conflicts was studied by Betz and Fry (1995). Promises were seen as more likely to be used in interpersonal conflicts, and threats as more likely to be used in intergroup and international conflicts. It was more important to use strength and force to resolve international conflicts. Filella (1971) queried 27 Spanish managers who formed the top three levels of their banking organization about how they dealt with disagreements with each other. In terms of the influence tactics described by Kipnis, Schmidt, and Wilkinson (1980), the bankers used reasoning most often, followed, in order, by the formation of coalitions, friendliness, assertiveness, bargaining, and appeals to a higher authority. Subordinates used all these tactics—except reasoning—more often than their superiors in trying to resolve disagreements with them. Rational justification appears to be particularly useful to superiors in heading off potential conflict and dissatisfaction when managers are faced with

maintaining the status quo or with trying to promote change. Bies and Shapiro (1986) asked 137 evening MBA students who had full-time jobs during the day to recount an incident in which their current manager had rejected their proposal or request. The managers could reject the proposal or request without losing their subordinates' respect, trust, and esteem if the subordinates judged that the managers provided good and sufficient justifications for their decision. Such justification was either that the issue was not in the manager's control or that the request did not fit with goals and priorities. Managers who are facing the need to make changes likewise must be prepared to give their subordinates good and sufficient justification. According to Deluga (1986), the ambiguity of the employees' role was unrelated to the influence tactics they used in dealing with their bosses. However, those who experienced more role conflict were more likely to use reason and assertiveness with their bosses than try to bargain with them. If a manager continued to resist their efforts to influence, the subordinates who felt more role conflict then tried ingratiation, impression management, flattery, the creation of goodwill, and gaining the support of the higher authority and their coworkers.

Although resistance to change is a problem in all social settings, it is both endemic and fraught with increasing penalties in productive and service enterprises that must deal with rapidly changing markets and technologies. Tichy and Devanna (1986) suggested that senior managers can assuage middle managers' tension about the need for stability and change by creating organizations that "embrace paradox." Such organizations can provide a balance between the need for adaptation and the need for stability and between the denial and acceptance of reality. (For example, "We're not number one yet, but we will be.") The old forms can be abandoned, and the new can be better.

Tichy and Devanna noted that senior managers must deal with *technical* reasons for resistance to change, such as habit, inertia, fear of the unknown, loss of organizational predictability, and sunk costs (the organization's investment of resources in the old ways). Senior managers must also deal with *political* reasons for resistance to change, including the threat to currently powerful coalitions of vested interests, win-lose decision making about scarce resources, and fault found with their own previous decisions. They must likewise deal with *cultural* reasons for resistance to change, such as the extent to which the organizational culture has highlighted old values and methods that now must be abandoned. Or, they must handle the felt security in regressing to the "good old days." The organization may lack a climate for change. There may be demands for conformity to the old ways, and a lack of receptivity to new ideas.

In managing the *rational* and *socioemotional* conflicts associated with resistance to change in industrial firms, senior managers must summarize the past and eulogize its value, emphasize the continuities of the past with the future, and justify the changes. To counter the political and socioemotional reasons, they must mobilize coalitions of support for the changes (Tichy & Devanna, 1986). Thus Kanter (1983) mentioned 200 *change-masters*—executives who could successfully bring about new developments in their organizations. They knew how to build coalitions to get the funds, staff, and authorization to move ahead to carry out their innovations.[3]

Palliation. Student participants in an experiment, whose anger and aggression had been aroused, could be induced to collaborate with an accomplice by palliating their anger and aggression. Baron (1984) arranged for undergraduate subjects to play the role of executives who discussed important issues with an accomplice of the experimenter. The accomplice disagreed strongly with the students in an arrogant and condescending manner that angered them. But subsequently, the accomplice palliated the situation by offering a token gift of candy (a Life Saver), by generating sympathy with justification for his earlier aggressive behavior, or by asking for help with a humorous task. These palliative efforts increased the likeability of the accomplice. In contrast to the subjects in a control condition, in which such palliative efforts were not made, the subjects in the experimental condition indicated that they would be more likely to collaborate with the accomplice and be less likely to avoid him if conflict with him arose in the future.

Force and Avoidance. Dutch studies of a test for handling conflict found satisfactory agreement among self-reports, opponents' reports, and observers' ratings of

[3] Bass (1983b), Janis and Mann (1977), and Levi and Benjamin (1977), among others, also reviewed behavioral approaches that leaders can use to manage conflict.

forcing and *yielding*, but not *avoiding* (De Dreu, Evers, Beersma, et al., 2001) The use of force by superiors and avoidance by subordinates to manage the conflicts between them appears to be a matter of individual differences, for conflict is in the eye of the beholder. In some circumstances, some people see conflict with others but the others see none. To illustrate, in a study of one supervisor and one subordinate each from 113 agencies for parks and recreation, Howat and London (1980) found that the supervisors and subordinates who perceived more frequent conflicts were likely to be rated unfavorably and tended to see each other as more likely to use force as a way of dealing with conflict. Supervisors who perceived more conflicts were also viewed by their subordinates as likely to withdraw from conflict; subordinates who perceived more conflicts were viewed by their supervisors as likely to avoid confrontation and compromise. Sometimes avoiding the use of force turns a conflict into a tragedy. In 1995, a Dutch peacekeeping force stood by when Serbs took prisoner 8,000 Muslim men and boys in Srbrenicia, Bosnia, and subsequently massacred them.

Identification. Halpin and Winer (1957) listed four ways for an airplane commander to manage conflicts with his superiors and subordinates: (1) he could identify completely with the higher authority and disparage the need to be considerate of the welfare of his subordinates; (2) he could reduce intimacy with his subordinates to minimize any guilty feelings he might have about having been inconsiderate of them; (3) he could be inconsiderate to his subordinates on the job but "pal around with them" off the job; (4) he could focus completely on satisfying the needs of his subordinates. Evidence in support of these findings accrued from a factor analysis by Hites (1953) of the results of a survey of aircrews. Hites noted that leaders varied in their loyalty and deference to superiors and also varied in their loyalty to their subordinates. That is, some commanders were loyal to their superiors, some were loyal to their subordinates, some were loyal to both, and some were loyal to neither. Halpin's (1953) follow-up study of 89 commanders of B-29 aircraft found that the commanders were likely to be highly rated by their superiors and their subordinates if they exhibited consideration, friendliness, and warmth toward their subordinates and initiated clear patterns of organization and ways of accomplishing missions.

Pelz (1952) and Likert (1961a, 1961b) observed that managers in the middle can perceive themselves as members of overlapping subgroups. Effective leaders can see themselves as members of two groups: one composed of their superior and their peers, the other composed of their subordinates and themselves. They have sufficient influence with their superior (as members of their peer and superior group) to represent their subordinates' interests effectively; they are well enough identified with their subordinates to be supported by them (as members, themselves, of their subordinates' group). Thus, they are both good followers and good leaders, able to satisfy the expectations of both their subordinates and their superior.

Summarizing the results of organizational surveys, Kahn and Katz (1953, 1960) inferred that effective leaders differ from ineffective leaders in making it clear that their role differs from that of their subordinates. They do so by avoiding performing the subordinates' functions; by spending time on supervision but not closely supervising subordinates; and by concerning themselves with their subordinates' needs, rather than with rules. A chain effect was observed by Bowers (1963, 1964a), who studied management-supervisor-worker relations in an industrial firm. The more supportively the supervisor's superior behaved toward him, the higher was the supervisor's self-esteem. The higher the supervisor's self-esteem, the less often he discussed his problems with subordinates and the better he perceived their attitudes toward him. The better the attitudes that the supervisor perceived his boss and subordinates sharing about him, the more he felt friendly toward his subordinates. The more friendly he felt, the more supportively he behaved toward his subordinates. Bowers concluded that the supervisor's self-esteem converted the behavior of his boss into a mandate for the supervisor's actions. A study of nursing supervisors by Kamano, Powell, and Martin (1966) provided corroborative evidence. These authors reported that supervisors who were evaluated more favorably by higher-level administrators likewise tended to rate their own subordinates more favorably.

Organizational Politics. The competing self-interests of people in an organization give rise to organizational politics. In this situation, the members vie for control in a struggle to obtain cooperation. Their different beliefs about desired actions and outcomes are complicated by their uncertainties over the link between means and ends. The win-lose possibilities of political activity are threatening to the members' self-interests and are likely to arouse resistance if the politicking is open rather than concealed (Frost & Hayes, 1979).

Organizational politics may be seen in the performance of *intrapreneurs*, who break the organization's rules to pursue new products and ideas in which they are personally interested (Pinchot, 1985). According to P. J. Frost (1986), politicking can be seen in the intentional building of frameworks of the rules and meanings of communication for systems of influence. Although the exertion of influence on the surface activities of the organization is primarily a matter of the appropriate open use of ability, power, and control of resources, organizational politics may be required, particularly if the deeper organizational structure calls for *reshaping*. Reshaping is necessary when the organization can no longer function with the old arrangements for balancing members' self-interests. New alignments are needed to accomplish objectives in the face of likely resistance. Such legitimate politics can be seen in whistle-blowing (dissent based on principles) and bargaining. Conflicts can be reshaped by enlistment of critics, as when a legislative majority vote can come about only with the help of members of the opposition. Channels of communication need to remain open. The CEO must avoid letting the "palace guard" block the view from below or from organizational outsiders (Block, 1987).

Politicking is overtly rational, but much of the time it covertly caters to the self-interests of the political actor. It aims to confront others and gain their compliance by manipulative actions. At deeper organizational levels, it becomes an effort to shape conscious and unconscious organizational values, beliefs, and practices. Resistance from others is reduced by concealment of the true self-interests of the political actor. Machiavellian tactics are applied.

Machiavellian Tactics. Although it would seem that people in the middle use open compromise to manage the contradictory demands placed on them, they may employ more subtle or sometimes devious ways of momentarily reducing but not resolving conflict. First, all the conflicting parties may be told what they want to hear. For example, when he addressed liberal audiences, President Lyndon B. Johnson would emphasize how much he admired Franklin Delano Roosevelt's liberal policies. When he met with his conservative financial backers, however, he would say how much he was against the liberal policies (Caro, 1982). Chairman Yasir Arafat of the Palestinian Authority talked about peace when addressing international and Israeli audiences in English. But when addressing Arab audiences in Arabic, he talked about driving Israel into the sea.

Persons in the middle may withhold information from superiors or subordinates and mask their feelings. Thus W. H. Read (1962) found that managers who communicated to their superiors with less than complete accuracy were more upwardly mobile. The relationship was conditioned by the extent to which managers trusted their superiors and perceived them to have influence with higher management. Walker, Guest, and Turner (1956) studied the problems of supervisors on an assembly line where the workers were under constant pressure because of their inability to control the speed of their work. The most effective supervisors were found to absorb the pressures and criticisms from higher management without communicating their frustrations and tensions to the workers.

In her survey of 350 managers, Roberts (1986) noted that managers in the middle said they were more inclined to try to impress their boss, somewhat less likely to try to impress their peers, and least likely to try to impress their subordinates. A negotiated solution was more often sought with the boss or peers than with the subordinates. Jambor (1954) suggested that persons in the middle of conflicts, between those above and those below them in the hierarchy, often yielded to their more powerful superiors and rationalized their position with their less powerful subordinates. Jablin (1981) observed the same pattern but thought that such political behavior might result in a loss of support from the subordinates. Subordinates who perceived their supervisors as highly political were less open in their communications with these supervisors and less satisfied with them than they were with other supervisors whom they saw as less political. This same effect was also noted by Roff (1950). Political behavior by combat officers led their immediate subordinates to rate them as less sincere, less impartial, and more concerned with personal advantage. Wickert (1947) found that an officer

had to appear sincere and consistent to be rated as a successful leader of a combat crew. Elected officials are caught in a cauldron of conflicting demands from their various constituencies. Followers have difficulty checking on the authenticity of their leaders, who often can maintain office indefinitely without much need for sincerity and consistency. One person's hypocrisy is another's tactfulness. According to Titus (1950), hypocrisy may be necessary in dealing with followers, but minimal use should be made of it. Jameson (1945) noted that leaders need to "wear masks" to disguise their own feelings and to live up to expectations, despite conflicting demands made on them. Political leaders contrive both conflict and its resolution. For instance, the Nazis set fire to the Reichstag in 1933 and pinned the guilt on the communists, setting them up as criminal plotters against the government. In 1934, Joseph Stalin secretly arranged for the assassination of a party leader in Leningrad, then dramatized it as a plot against the state, providing a rationale for the terroristic purge that followed. In 1964, the Johnson administration contrived to magnify the Gulf of Tonkin incident into a major assault on the U.S. Navy so as to gain congressional support for escalation of the U.S. response in Vietnam. In 2003, George W. Bush took the United States to war in Iraq on the basis of intelligence that Iraq had weapons of mass destruction, but this intelligence had been discredited a year earlier.

"Divide and conquer" is a classic strategy that Machiavellians use to gain and maintain their power over subordinates. Dissension within the opposition weakens it and keeps it from mobilizing effectively against those in control. Lawler (1983) examined how this strategy by an imaginary leader affected two female subordinates in a triad who were working under inequitable rates of pay. Conflicts of interest were increased between the subordinates, but co-optation—a promise of advancement—was more effective than threats in preventing their rebellion. The subordinate who was promised advancement was less susceptible to pressure from the other two subordinates to rebel against the imaginary leader. (For more on Machievellian tactics, see Chapter 7.)

Ignoring Dissonance. Political leaders may also avoid immediate conflict by ignoring the facts about the circumstances and relying on their own strongly held beliefs, needs, and wishes. When Hitler broke the Treaty of

Versailles of 1919, he promised to keep the Treaty of Locarno of 1925. He broke the Treaty of Locarno, but he promised no further territorial aggression when his troops marched into the Saar in 1936. When he entered Austria by force in 1938, his government promised no interference in Czechoslovakia. Later in the year, at the time of the Munich crisis in 1938, when the British prime minister Neville Chamberlain and the French premier Édouard Daladier were confronted with such interference and more territorial demands, they ignored all of Hitler's previous broken promises. For the sake of peace at any price, and because of their image of Hitler as a "bulwark against Bolshevism," Chamberlain and Daladier engaged in wishful thinking. They appeased Hitler and relied again on his good faith. His troops occupied Czechoslovakia and attacked Poland in 1939.

Reserving Judgment. Barnard (1938) described the "fine art of executive decision" and noted that superiors' demands for conflict-laden decisions by the executive must be met, but responsibility for them can be delegated. Subordinates' demands for such decisions need be met only when the decisions are important, and they cannot be delegated. The tactful executive can avoid conflict-laden decisions on questions that are not pertinent, as well as premature decisions, impossible solutions, and decisions that others should make.

Effective Leadership. Shartle (1956) noted that efficacious organizational leaders are able to switch from one goal to another. This can be done if the leaders have a balanced, flexible set of identifications with various organizational projects and plans. If they find themselves blocked in one line of activity, they can shift to another, thus avoiding a sense of frustration and failure. J. M. Burns (1978, p. 39) saw conflict as an opportunity to display leadership. Leaders (in contrast to status quo administrators) convert the demands, values, and goals of conflicting constituencies into workable programs: "Leaders, whatever their professions of harmony, do not shun conflict; they confront it, exploit it, ultimately embody it. Standing at the points of contact among latent conflict groups, they can take various roles, sometimes acting directly for their followers, sometimes bargaining with others, sometimes overriding certain motives of followers and summoning others into play."

Feyerheim (1994) observed influence patterns for a year in two groups that were formulating governmental regulations regarding pollution. Diverse interests were represented in these groups, but shared frameworks had to be developed so as to create solutions. Several individuals took the lead. The leadership that was most successful in shifting the frameworks highlighted assumptions, created new possibilities, and initiated collective actions.

Eisenstat (1954) found leadership to be ineffective when followers were apathetic toward an issue that required integrative action, when the leaders' broader orientation did not correspond with the practical issues faced by the followers, when the leaders had no authority to deal with broader issues, and when the leaders were in conflict with other leaders.

Conflict Management Styles. Lehnen, Ayman, and Korabik (1995) used the Rahim Organizational Inventory (ROCI—Form B) to obtain descriptions of conflict management styles according to the subordinates of 120 Canadian vice principals of schools and managers from an accounting firm, a bank, and a manufacturer. Five styles are assessed by the ROCI: (1) integrating, (2) obliging, (3) compromising, (4) dominating, and (5) avoiding. Consistent with earlier investigations by Rahim and Buntzman (1989) and Witteman (1991), Lehnen, Ayman, and Korabik found that the *integrative* style (solving problems and listening considerately to subordinates) was most positively related to subordinates' satisfaction with supervision. The *avoiding* style was most negatively related to subordinates' satisfaction. What is required here is a belief that discussions of conflict can be constructive and that conflicting parties can be trusted to work toward effective outcomes if communications between them are open. According to Culbert and McDonough (1980), awareness of every member's self-interests and the need to deal with them is essential to organizational and individual effectiveness. Subordinates need to confront their superiors about their needs. Out of this confrontation can come an alignment of the subordinates' needs and the organization's needs. The conflict between downward and upward demands can be best resolved through such open confrontation and discussion.

But evidence is mixed in support of this contention. On the one hand, according to a survey of 350 managers by Roberts (1986), a search for consensus was the most

popular way for the managers to deal with their superiors, peers, and subordinates. Likewise, Friedlander and
Margulies (1969) found that the task motivation and involvement of research personnel were maximized by
their trust in management. Wilcox and Burke (1969)
concluded that openness between workers and supervisors resulted in greater job satisfaction for both. Similarly,
Klauss and Bass (1982) reported that colleagues were
more satisfied with focal persons perceived as more open
in their communications. In 147 established managerial
work groups, Crouch (1986) found that managers were
more willing to encourage the open expression of conflicting views and that they, as well as their subordinates,
had little need to dominate. Strong dominant personalities were likely to suppress such conflict. Crouch also
found that the work groups' performance was enhanced
to the extent the managers legitimized such open expression of conflicts in points of view.

However, Rubin and Goldman (1968) found no difference in the openness of communication of effective and
ineffective managers. Crouch and Yetton (1987) suggested that the benefits of open group discussions depend
on the leader's skills in managing conflict. Willits (1967),
who studied 20 small manufacturing firms, found that although the measures of their success were positively related to the president's openness in communicating his
ideas, as was expected, the ideas were negatively related
to the open communication of his *feelings*. Furthermore,
open communication by the other executives did not coincide with a company's success.

Conflict Management by Political Appointees and Career Civil Servants.

Even if they have strong political
or professional credentials, new political appointees to
senior management positions in public bureaucracies
move into a situation that is inherently full of conflict.
They must confront long-established rules and regulations, entrenched cliques, and deception from career
civil servants who become defensive, passively obstruct
new policies, and withhold or delay providing information to and from the appointees (House & Covello,
1984). For their part, the career governmental executives
often must keep an agency operating while they await a
new political appointee as its new head. Potential conflicts between incoming, newly appointed agency heads
and permanent civil servants are likely to be minimized
by a mutual understanding that is established before the
appointee takes office, or is developed later. "Civil servants have some ideas of the thinking and requirements
of their [newly appointed heads], and [the agency heads]
acquire knowledge of the dispositions of their civil servants. A civil servant who gives advice is likely to frame it
on the basis of his understanding of the needs of [the
agency head], and [the head] is likely to modify his policy
preferences on the basis of his knowledge of what
is . . . feasible" (Page, 1987, p. 133).

To reduce potential conflicts with the incoming political head of the agency, Schmidt (1985) suggested that
while awaiting the new head, the career executive should
continue to make normal decisions about filling vacan-
cies and about policies to be implemented or postponed,
emphasize greater cooperation among antagonistic organizations, hold informational meetings, avoid the usurpation of power by bureaucratic processes, and try to keep
rivalries about turf to a minimum. Newly appointed incompetent political heads and replacements of many experienced civil servants can quickly change an efficient
agency of competent civil servants into an incompetent
organization—as was seen in the disastrous handling by
the Federal Emergency Management Agency of hurricane Katrina in 2005.

Converting Conflict to Problem Solving.

Walton and
McKersie (1965, 1966) and Likert and Likert (1978)
thought that conflict can be managed best when it is converted from win-lose negotiations to a problem-solving
situation from which both parties can emerge as winners.
Furthermore, Likert and Likert noted that it is particularly important for conflicting parties to avoid becoming
adversaries who debate solutions to a conflict before they
have reached agreement on what outcomes they deem
essential and desirable. This position is consistent with
Bass's (1966b) finding that negotiators who began with
committed solutions were much more likely to reach a
deadlock than those who entered negotiations without
firm solutions in mind. It also fitted with Maier's (1967,
1970b) results, which indicated that an early focus on
ready-made solutions causes groups to avoid trying to find
more creative ways to deal with their problems. Adversarial groups cling to their favorite solutions as they proceed
with negotiations. Brams (1990) demonstrated how it was
possible to use mathematical game theory to reach an

overall greater gain for each side if both sides were disputing the weighted importance of the various divisive issues.

Changing Win-Lose to Win-Win. Conflict between union and management over costs and benefits may be resolved by working out arrangements to increase the returns both to management and to employees. Management can invite joint decision making and profit sharing and support the importance of seniority, security, and pension benefits. The union can support the redesign of jobs, the introduction of cost-reduction techniques, and the retraining of employees. The management and the unions can collaborate on safety programs. Win-lose bargaining is converted into win-win problem solving. At the level of the individual union and management representative, Rosen, Greenhalgh, and Anderson (undated) pointed out that studies have found that union stewards may spend an average of 11 hours per week on socioemotional leadership functions, as do their counterparts in management in dealing with the absenteeism, insecurities, and grievances of employees.

Druckman (1994) conducted a meta-analysis of 82 experimental studies of negotiating to reach compromises and the time required in 28 of them to reach a compromise. Compromises were more difficult to negotiate when: (1) the negotiators were representing constituents and did not expect to have any further interaction with the opponents in the future; (2) the negotiators prepared strategies in cohesive groups beforehand; (3) bureacratic superiors introduced competitive orientations and new strategies; (4) negotiations took place with an audience and under face-saving pressures; (5) long-held social attitudes and contrasting ideologies were involved; (6) a tough exploitative opponent was faced.

Institutionalizing Collaboration. A mature, collaborative approach substitutes a mutually acceptable culture and a common philosophy for minutely detailed agreements that cover all possible contingencies. Fixed periodic negotiations are replaced by joint study groups and more open discussions. A reward system is determined, but the levels of reward are not (Lawler & Mohrman, 1987). According to Long's (1988) survey of two Canadian firms, managers were most likely to favor such a collaborative approach if they were dissatisfied

with the behavioral and attitudinal conditions in the firm and if they thought that increasing the workers' influence on policy decisions would improve these conditions. In 1987, General Motors and the United Auto Workers agreed to establish continuous joint methods for addressing specific issues at each plant. The objective was to design solutions that would improve the efficiency of each plant and the quality of its products. Johnson (1988) thought that such continuous joint processes worked well if the local manager was adept at mobilizing the skills and energies of the workers and providing them with sound direction. Continuous joint process emphasizes mutual listening and the sharing of information and ideas. But managers need to have more than just labor's interests in mind; they are also custodians of the interests of the shareholders and various other constituencies of the corporation, and they are concerned with its need to remain competitive in the international marketplace.

Promoting Congruence of the Formal and Informal Organization. A leader can avoid or reduce conflict by fostering congruence of status, esteem, and competence within the group and its activities, and congruence between the informal and the formal organization. For example, formal-informal incongruencies were seen within technical units of the U.S. Air Force. On the one hand, the formal and informal organizations agreed that cooperation and pride in the formal organization were desirable and that the most competent personnel were most valuable. On the other hand, the formal and informal organizations had conflicting attitudes about punishment for laxity and the need for high standards of performance (Anonymous, 1945–1946). Leadership increased the congruence in attitudes. According to Whyte and Gardner (1945), leaders of the formal organization foster such congruence by becoming aware of the informal organization, discovering the informal leader, and obtaining his or her cooperation and agreement to work toward common goals. Formal leaders use the informal organization constructively to convey attitudes, to locate grievances, and to maintain social stability (K. Davis, 1951). They identify the differences and values that buttress the informal organization relative to the formal organization.

Legitimatization and Conflict

"Legitimatization" of a role refers to others' perception of an individual's right to function in a given position. An individual's appointment to a given position legitimates his or her status and performance of the role, at least for those who do the appointing. Likewise, in democracies, election to an office legitimates the role of the office-holders in the eyes of those who voted for them as well as in the eyes of most others. In traditional societies, legitimacy can be provided by inherited status and rank as well as election or appointment. For instance, Vengroff (1974) noted that it made no difference in community participation in the development of 31 villages in Botswana whether the leaders were elected councilors or were traditional tribal chiefs. But conflict would arise when what was regarded as legitimate for one member in one situation was viewed as illegitimate for others in the same situation or different situations. Although legitimacy might be lost if an individual fails to perform as expected, the legitimacy of an appointment has to be sharply separated from competence or perceived competence to perform the role. C. B. Smith's (1984) experiment showed that the presence or absence of competence in appointed supervisors did not affect the legitimacy of their authority or the conformity of subordinates to organizational directives.

The Meaning Attached to Legitimacy

Legitimacy is affected by the culture in which an appointment is embedded. It is not just a matter of agreeing on a list of uniformly interpretable regulations about appropriate behavior in the organization. Indeed, it is a fundamental source of conflict in that what is legitimate depends on both written and unwritten rules whose creation and interpretation are a developing process of shared meanings. In analyzing the relationship between the CEO and vice presidents of a Bell Telephone operating company, Feldman (1986) noted that the meaning attached to the positions held by the executives was often overlooked. The meaning is provided by the cultural system of the bureaucracy. In turn, it restricts the courses of action that are open to position holders. Neilsen and Rao (1987) agreed that the meaning of legitimacy that

emerges about a position is a dynamic process, which develops as new ideas and understandings are accepted within the organization. The meaning is enhanced when it is given more credence from demonstrations of trustworthiness as hidden agendas surface. Additionally, the language that reinforces the legitimacy of a leader's actions is multilayered. At the institutional level, shared meanings evolve from history and habit. For instance, many business leaders may be legitimately consumer-oriented rather than technology-oriented because their business has been driven by customers' loyalty and interests. At another level, such meanings may be supported by stories and myths. A customer-oriented engineer may convince a new client about the product with a humorous demonstration. At a third level, theories are articulated that legitimately guide action. Changing market conditions add more response to clients' needs. Finally, "symbolic universes of meaning" buttress legitimacy. Modern professional management is more market-oriented than traditional management was.

Legitimatization and Conflict in Different Settings

As was already noted, discrepancies between what others expect and one's own expectations will be a source of role conflict. A group's failure to achieve consensus in its expectations about requirements likewise causes conflict. Conversely, agreement about role requirements and conformity to normative expectations about what is legitimate action for the role generally contribute to effectiveness in organizational life.

Many research analysts point to similarities and differences in opinions about what constitutes departures from legitimacy and the effects of such departures in political, educational, military, and industrial settings. For example, Schein and Ott (1962) studied the attitudes of managers, union leaders, and college students toward the legitimacy of influencing various kinds of behavior. The three groups and a sample of U.S. Air Force personnel (F. J. Davis, 1954) agreed about the legitimacy of influencing job-related behaviors. The groups considered it legitimate for a supervisor to try to influence the job performance and work environment of employees. However, they differed about the legitimacy of a supervisor's trying to influence behavior that was not job-related.

Public and Community Settings. Substantive conflicts over the legitimatization of the leader's rights can best be cataloged in the context of their social settings. Numerous examples have been reported of a loss or lack of legitimacy due to incongruities, discordant expectations, and within-role and between-role conflict. These incongruities resulted in dissatisfaction and ineffectiveness. Homemakers are faced with the same pressures to deal with new technologies and ambiguous standards of quality as professionals and managers are. However, because homemakers are not accorded the social legitimacy that professionals and managers receive, they experience an unusual conflict (Chafetz & Dworkin, 1984). For instance, homemakers are likely to see themselves as lacking the power and resources to confront a manufacturer of a shoddy product. Conflict may be sharper in public bureaucracies because of their legal obligations to respond to clients who can exert pressure on them. Conflict within public bureaucracies is exacerbated when the external political climate restricts objective goal setting and evenhanded decision making (J. M. Burns, 1978). Those who are at the outer boundaries of a bureaucracy are much more likely to face such politically based conflict than those who are deep inside the organization (Katz & Kahn, 1966).

Each of several resettlement communities in Israel that Eisenstadt (1954) studied had developed specific norms. At the same time, the communities had also incorporated the norms of the surrounding culture. The norms prescribed proper behavior for given roles and role situations. To some extent, reference group norms served as general standards by which various patterns of behavior were evaluated. Because of their wider range of reference groups, the leaders served as a medium for consolidating the subgroups and integrating them into an effective larger group.

Business and Industry. In a study of managers' attitudes, Schein and Lippitt (1966) found that managers whose roles involved close supervision and centralization of responsibility regarded it as legitimate to influence subordinates in more areas than did other managers. Contrary to the hypothesis, managers whose subordinates had more visible roles and interacted more frequently with outsiders did not exercise more influence than those whose subordinates had less visible roles.

Both superiors and subordinates expected communication, development, delegation, understanding, know-how, and teamwork from supervisors (Brooks, 1955). But for the supervisors, their own autonomy was more critical to them than their legitimacy. In a study of first-line supervisors, Klein and Maher (1970) found that the supervisors' lack of autonomy was related to role conflict, but neither the perceived legitimacy of autonomy nor the discrepancy between legitimate and actual autonomy was related to it. However, Ulrich, Booz, and Lawrence (1950) observed that superiors made legitimate but conflicting demands on managers.

Conflict was latent in Freeman and Taylor's (1950) survey of 100 top executives. These executives said they looked for aggressive, energetic applicants for management positions in the company, even though they personally wanted "tactful subordinates." The executives attributed their own success to "brains and character," but they preferred "emotionally controlled and balanced" rather than overly bright or highly ethical subordinates. Conflict was illustrated most clearly when the executives' self-perceptions were compared with those of 170 middle managers. Whereas the executives emphasized their self-determination, enterprise, and dignity, the middle managers emphasized their discreetness, modesty, practicality, patience, deliberateness, and planfulness. Whereas the top executives disavowed stinginess, shyness, and a lack of ambition, the middle managers avoided describing themselves as reckless, disorderly, aggressive, and outspoken (Porter & Ghiselli, 1957). However, Bass, Waldman, Avolio, et al. (1987) generally found positive correlations between what subordinates in New Zealand said they required in the leadership of their supervisors and what the supervisors, in turn, required of their bosses. This domino effect suggested that, in reality, there tend to be more positive than negative associations in what is legitimated for supervisory roles at each successive level in the organization, although some strong bosses may prefer to keep their subordinates weak in power and autonomy.

Wernimont (1971) found that workers tended to make contradictory demands on their supervisors. On the one hand, they expressed a desire for clear instructions and goals. On the other hand, they wanted considerable freedom to work in their own way. Similarly, Foa (1956) compared ideal and actual descriptions of the behavior of first-level supervisors and workers in Israeli factories. He found that the workers complained most frequently about their supervisors' ineffective social relations but were more critical of their own conduct than of their supervisors' conduct. But the supervisors complained little about work behavior. The smaller the discrepancy between the workers' ideal for the supervisors and their descriptions of a supervisors' actual behavior, the better satisfied the workers were with the supervisor. When the workers identified with their supervisors, they attributed their own ideals to the supervisor.

There seems to be a fundamental difference in the ideals of managers' roles and how managers are actually required to enact the roles. Hortatory admonitions, managerial ideals, popular literature, and normative expectations all counsel the need for system and deliberation at every level. As McCall (1977) noted, the assumption is that managers are likely to be engaged in just a few events and will have enough time to ponder over how they should behave in response to these events. In reality, however, the demands on a typical manager make such deliberation impossible. For example, Guest (1956) found that supervisors were involved in 200 to 583 activities in a single day. S. Carlson (1951) reported that Swedish top executives were undisturbed for only an average of 23 minutes during a day. Mintzberg (1973) found that half the activities of the five top executives he observed lasted nine minutes or less and concluded that the executives' activities were fragmented, brief, and varied and that the executives had little control over them. Also, 93% of the executives' contacts were arranged ad hoc, and the executives initiated only 32% of them.[4]

Educational Settings. Generally, students are prepared to accept direction from instructors who are behaving legitimately. Torrance (1959) studied groups that were under different degrees of pressure from instructors to accept a new food. He found that group members expected instructors to exercise influence and that they did not perceive such influence as pressure. In Lee, Horwitz, and Goldman's (1954) experiment, each of three instructors of classes of ROTC cadets was given more authority or less authority to decide whether certain instructions should be repeated. Most students voted to repeat the instructions, but in each class, the instructor arbitrarily decided not to repeat the assignment. The instructor met the greatest resentment and hostility when the students believed he had little authority to make a decision. The rejection was even greater when the instructor acted as if he had a great deal of authority but did not have it. If the students believed the instructor had the authority, he could act in this manner and was less resented by the students for doing so.

M. V. Campbell (1958) reported that when teachers' needs and role behavior were close to the principal's expectations for them, the teachers tended to feel better satisfied, were more confident in the principal's leadership, and were rated by the principal as more effective. Seeman (1953, 1960) found among principals and teachers in 26 communities that although the teachers expected their principal to attend to matters within the school, the principal's success in improving the school situation depended on devoting time to public relations outside the school. When principal and teachers disagreed about the principal's role, the principal reported less indecision than the teachers, because the principal was required to take action more often than the teachers were.

Gross, Mason, and McEachern (1958) and Gross, McEachern, and Mason (1966) studied role conflict in school superintendents. They found that the superintendents differed in their perceptions of the legitimacy of the various expectations that others held for them. In particular, the superintendents differed about the severity of sanctions that might be applied if they did not comply with what they thought was expected of them. Those superintendents with a moralistic orientation tended to conform to what they regarded as legitimate expectations but rejected expectations they regarded as illegitimate, regardless of the sanctions that might be involved. Those with an expedient orientation tended to conform to the expectations that were attended by the strongest sanctions for noncompliance, or to compromise between what they actually would do and what they expected to do to minimize possible sanctions. A third type of superintendent gave equal weight to legitimacy and possible sanctions.

Gross, Mason, and McEachern (1958) also studied reference group identifications and consensus among superintendents and members of school boards. The superintendents were more strongly identified than the

[4]See more about this in Chapter 23.

school board members with external professional reference groups. In the division of responsibilities, both the superintendents and the members of the school boards assigned more tasks to themselves and expressed great approval for bypassing each other. Superintendents rated the school boards more highly and were better satisfied with them when there was consensus among the board members. In turn, the greater the consensus on the board, the higher was its rating of the superintendent.

Military Settings. Numerous military studies have examined the effects of role sanctions, legitimacy, and conflict. For instance, Greer (1954) reported finding that in six hours of simulated combat, only among the more effective of 26 infantry rifle squads did appointed leaders act more closely to what was desired and expected of them by the rest of the squad. Failure to live up to subordinates' expectations resulted in conflict and the squads' ineffectiveness.

Stouffer, Suchman, DeVinney, et al. (1949) found that U.S. officers and enlisted personnel disagreed markedly during World War II on whether officers should maintain social distance from enlisted personnel. Although 82% of the enlisted personnel agreed that "an officer will have the respect of his men if he pals around with them off duty," only 27% of the captains, 39% of the first lieutenants, and 54% of the second lieutenants agreed. Similarly, E. L. Scott (1956) found that enlisted personnel on small ships perceived the organization's status structure more accurately when superiors interacted less extensively throughout the organization, retained authority, and delegated less freely. Merton and Kitt (1950) discovered that enlisted personnel who expressed attitudes in conformity with the norms of the U.S. Army were promoted more rapidly. If the enlisted personnel accepted the status structure of the army as legitimate, they were more readily identified with others at their own level or those of the next highest status level.

The effects of more legitimacy or less legitimacy were examined by Levy (1954), who contrasted aircrews led in periodic discussions by their own commanders with aircrews whose discussions were led by clinical psychologists. Members of the groups led by their commanders had more favorable attitudes toward their groups and a greater sense of well-being than members of groups led by the clinical psychologists.

In the military, the most extreme conflicts between subordinates and higher authority are likely to arise when acts of collective insubordination occur, despite fears of reprisal. In the Israeli defense forces, these acts seem to be due to unresolved grievances about impersonal conditions, such as slow demobilization, poor food, unacceptable discipline, or unfair discrimination, rather than individual resentment (Gal, 1985). Personal conflict over goals and commitments (Rose, 1982), such as occurred among American servicemen in Vietnam and Israeli soldiers in Lebanon in 1982, produced withdrawal or protest rather than group revolt. Gal (1985) saw a need for legitimacy in military decision making to deal with such personal conflicts. Decisions must serve proper goals, must be made through appropriate processes, and must be in accord with a common value system with which the individual soldier identifies.

Conditions Affecting Legitimacy and Conflict

Various conditions can be enumerated that enhance or reduce legitimacy and, therefore, affect the amount of conflict and inefficiency that occurs. For instance, legitimacy depends on clear, accepted group norms. B. R. Clark (1956) found that high-status members of a group could not be fully legitimate if the group norms were not clearly defined and were not well accepted by the members. Legitimate power can enhance the positive impact of a leader's effectiveness. Knapp and Knapp (1966) studied elected officers and nonofficers who served as group leaders in a verbal conditioning experiment. Groups led by officers had a higher rate of response and conditioned more readily than groups led by nonofficers. Official status of the leaders facilitated the groups' learning. The importance of legitimate power was illustrated in a Dutch experiment by Mulder, Van Dijk, Stirwagen, et al. (1966). The power distance between leaders and followers was varied by permitting leaders to distribute rewards of different amounts. The legitimate leader was elected by the group. The illegitimate leader (a confederate of the experimenter) forced his way into the experimental control booth and took over the leadership function. Under conditions of great power distance, the followers resisted the illegitimate leader more than they did the legitimate leader. P. B. Read (1974) demonstrated how conflict arose among jurors in mock trials if their differences of opinion were legitimate. Paradoxically, organizations with excessive levels of hierarchy and excessive dependence on the differentiation of power are hotbeds of politics and conflict (Culbert & McDonough, 1985). For communications to move through the excessive layers requires an illegitimate bypassing of channels. For timely decisions to be made, illegitimate actions may be needed. For work to get done, the pursuit of creative ad hoc alternatives may be required, rather than conformity to the rules.

Election versus Appointment. Experimentation offers an opportunity to compare the legitimatization of the leadership role by election and by appointment. When N. A. Rosen (1969), in an industrial field experiment, used the preference of work group employees to reassign those who became their supervisors, all seven groups showed initial increases in productivity. Similarly, Ben-Yoav, Hollander, and Carnevale (1983) gave a decision-making task to 21 groups of four college students each and compared leaders who were appointed or elected. Elected leaders were considered more responsive to the followers' needs, more interested in the group task, and more competent than those who were appointed. Dellva, McElroy, and Schrader (1987) compared 64 formally appointed leaders with leaders who emerged in student groups at the U.S. Army Command and General Staff College. Over time, the formally appointed leaders tended to lose influence, whereas the emergent leaders gained influence. Raven and French (1957) instructed experimental groups to elect one of their members as supervisor and subsequently replaced the supervisors of half the groups with appointed leaders. These researchers found that in contrast to the appointed leaders, the elected leaders became more personally attractive to the other members and their suggestions were more likely to be accepted by the groups. In the same vein, Hollander and Julian (1970) found that members of problem-solving groups were more willing to accept a selfish action by an elected leader than the same action by an appointed leader. In another experiment by Hollander and Julian (1970), team members ranked the relative importance of several items, and the leaders could accept each ranking or reverse it. Elected leaders deviated from their groups more than appointed leaders. Both types of leaders deviated more if they had strong rather than weak support

from group members. The authors concluded that more is expected of elected than appointed leaders. Elected leaders are given greater latitude to deviate and act on behalf of the group's goals; but to profit from this advantage, they must be aware of it.

When spokespersons for a group were elected rather than appointed, their legitimacy was greater, but they were more likely than appointed spokespersons to be rejected if they were seen as incompetent or as unable to produce results. Nonetheless, the appointed spokespersons also had to be competent or successful in order to satisfy the group members (Julian, Hollander, & Regula, 1969). According to Hollander (1978), election created greater demands by group members for their spokesperson's performance. The elected spokespersons showed greater firmness than the appointed spokespersons, who were as firm only if they could consult their members (Hollander, Fallon, & Edwards, 1977). Elected spokespersons also felt freer to yield (Boyd, 1972) and to accept or reject the decisions of the group they were representing (Hollander & Julian, 1970). This is consistent with the finding that elected leaders evaluated their followers more highly than appointed leaders did (Elgie, Hollander, & Rice, 1988). But appointed leaders, when representing their own groups, could achieve agreement with each other about the solutions to problems more easily and with less conflict than elected leaders in the same circumstances (Manheim, 1960).

The Struggle for Status and Legitimacy. When all members of a community, a work unit, or an experimental setting are initially equal in status (the value of their initial positions in their groups), a struggle for status will result. In an informal discussion, no one initially has the "right to lead." Gaining the right to lead and obtaining the status of leader will depend on individual initiative, assertiveness, competence, and esteem. To the degree that individuals strive for status, a struggle for status is likely to occur unless a leader has been elected or appointed in advance. Many factors will affect this struggle, including each contestant's self-esteem and credibility. Furthermore, leaders seem more concerned than followers about maintaining their status. Gallo and McClintock (1962) studied leaders and nonleaders in sessions where three accomplices were present. The accomplices supported the participants in the first session but withdrew their support in the second session. The researchers found that leaders initiated more task-oriented behaviors than followers, especially when their positions were threatened during the second session. The leaders also exhibited more hostility and antagonism when their status was threatened. Gartner and Iverson (1967) informed experimental groups that one member would be selected for a superior position in another group. This chance for upward mobility in status interfered with the task performance in well-established groups but reduced the members' morale rather than their productivity in newly formed groups.

The struggle for status is most likely among a group of strangers. But if the abilities and past performance records of members are made clear to all, and if their esteem is made more visible, the conflict about who will lead is reduced. Bradford and French (1948) emphasized that the productivity of group thinking depended on the ability of group members to clearly perceive each other's roles. Drucker (1946) observed that despite the informality of relations among executives in the different divisions of General Motors, the executives worked together with relatively little conflict. The absence of conflict was attributed to objective measures of the performance of the divisions that made the effectiveness of the executives visible to each other.

Overestimated Self-Accorded Status. The struggle for status is augmented by a general tendency of members of organizations and groups to overestimate their own status and power (Bass, 1960; Bass & Flint, 1958a). They believe that their positions are more important than others do. In this situation, role conflict is inevitable. People at a designated organizational level think that all those below them have "smaller" jobs than the job holders themselves think they have; and all those above the person at the designated level perceive that the occupants' jobs are "smaller" than the occupants perceive these jobs to be (Haas, Porat, & Vaughan, 1969). This bias is quite general. J. D. Campbell (1952) found that 250 residents of Boston tended to rate the value of their own jobs higher than they rated jobs similar to their own. Conflict results when people who interact or work together overestimate the importance of their own positions and underestimate the importance of others with whom they interact. For example, a janitor of an apartment house may adopt "pro-

fessional standards" and accord himself more status than his tenants grant that he has (Gold, 1951–1952). When supervisors accord themselves more status and authority than their unionized subordinates grant them, their attempts to lead their subordinates will be rebuffed (Wray, 1949).

Bass and Flint (1958a) showed with 51 groups of ROTC cadets that although members with greater power attempted more leadership and were seen by others as having exhibited more success, they actually were no more successful. Moreover, high-control[5] members significantly overestimated their esteem compared with low-control members. The control and power differences that were arbitrarily assigned to some of these participants were likely to have aroused hostility and resentment among those without control. Although low-control members perceived themselves as submitting to the powerful members, a greater proportion of them actually rejected the attempts to lead by the arbitrarily more powerful members.

Self-Authorization. Morrison and Phelps (1999) surveyed 275 white-collar employees to ascertain what made some of them authorize themselves to take charge despite a lack of status that made their efforts questionable. Factor and regression analyses established that three factors contributed most to such self-authorizing behavior: (1) felt responsibility, (2) self-efficacy, and (3) top management's openness. These factors explained 27% of the variance in self-authorization.

Credibility. Legitimatization involves gaining credibility for being trustworthy and informative. Klauss and Bass (1982) found strong positive correlations in social service agencies, military organizations, and industrial firms between subordinates' ratings of managers' credibility and the managers' success as leaders. One establishes one's trustworthiness by gaining "membership character," by being seen as loyal to the group, by conforming to the prevailing norms, and by establishing that one is motivated to belong to and identify with the group (Hollander, 1958).

---

[5] "Control" refers to the extent to which one member can provide possible incentives for another member. If the other member values the incentives, control becomes power.

Stability of Legitimacy and Leadership. The stability of legitimate power and the tendency of leaders to hold on to their offices are fostered by at least five factors: (1) the validators, (2) continuing redefinitions, (3) acquisition of relevant information, (4) controlling the resources that are needed for change and thwarting the restructuring of the situation, (5) maintaining favorable conditions. In regard to the first factor, *validation*, Hollander (1978) pointed out that leaders have validators of their positions who can support the leader's legitimacy or withdraw support. The validators uphold the leader's right to office even when a leader's performance may be inadequate. Unable to admit their errors, because they have an investment in and a sense of responsibility for the leader, they continue to support a failing leader (Hollander, Fallon, & Edwards, 1977). The second factor, *redefinition*, was demonstrated by A. R. Cohen (1958). Cohen found that leaders who are threatened with losing their status can redefine their groups' boundaries to isolate themselves from the very members whose support they need. High-status members, faced with the loss of status, communicated less with low-status members than did high-status members who were not facing a loss of status. The third factor, *acquisition of knowledge*, is illustrated by an incumbent political leader who amasses knowledge of rules and regulations; develops the required organizational constituents, contacts, and contracts; acquires the trappings of power; and is more visible than rival candidates for the office. The fourth factor, *control of change*, involves high-status members blocking the restructuring of a situation if a new structure would cause them to lose their status (Burnstein & Zajonc, 1965b). Those with high status control the machinery for change. In authoritarian states, dictators coerce the opposition; in democratic states, elected officials use their legitimate power to reject electoral reforms in financing, redistricting, limited terms of office, and so on that would threaten their reelection. Party officials in the former Soviet Union were most reluctant to relinquish their power, privileges, and perquisites. Over 99% of members in the U.S. House of Representatives sought reelection and were reelected to office in 1988 (Rosenbaum, 1988). *Maintaining conditions* favorable to the leader is the fifth factor. Katz, Blau, Brown, and Strodtbeck (1957) studied four-member groups who first engaged in a discussion about possible tasks. The members then chose a task for the next session, in which half of all the groups performed the chosen task and the other half were required to complete tasks imposed on them. The chance that a member would remain a leader from the first discussion to the completion of the chosen or imposed task depended on whether the task was chosen by the group or imposed by the experimenter. If the group's choice of task was guided by the leader, the imposition of a different task threatened his leadership. However, his position was strengthened if he did not enforce the imposed task that the group rejected. In addition, the more the leader stirred up controversy about the choice of tasks during the first discussion, the less likely he was to remain a leader during the task-completion phase. If the leader experienced little initial opposition to his choice of task and his choice was supported by the group, he was more likely to retain his leadership than if a different task was arbitrarily imposed on the group by the experimenter.

Changes in the Behavior of Leaders. Only after the struggle for status has ended and a stable hierarchy has been organized can those who achieved the high status reduce their level of activity (Heinicke & Bales, 1953; Whyte, 1953). Once a person is fully recognized by the other members as the leader and has won the struggle for status, he or she needs to attempt less leadership in order to exhibit the same amount of successful leadership. Thus, Bass, Gaier, and Flint (1956) found that when all members of a group of ROTC cadets had equal control over each other, any member had to attempt more than the average amount of leadership to exhibit more than the average amount of observable leadership. But when the members of a group differed initially in their control over each other, the successful leader did not require as many attempts to lead.

Usurpation. When the legitimate leader continues to be inadequate in meeting the needs of the group, the role may be usurped. However, the usurper may not do as well in the leadership role as the legitimate leader. According to Crockett (1955), who studied conference leadership, emergent leaders tended to take control when the designated chairperson failed to set enough goals, seek enough information, and propose enough problems and solutions. Usurpation also occurred when cliques with divergent goals were present. Similarly, Lowin and Craig

(1968) found that members initiated more structure in work groups when their superiors were incompetent. Katz, Maccoby, Gurin, et al. (1951) found the same usurpation of leadership in groups of men who were engaged in railroad maintenance work. Heyns (1948) observed that if the appointed leader of a group fails to perform his or her duties satisfactorily, the attempts by other group members to assume leadership are more readily accepted than they would be if the leader were adequate. P. J. Burke (1966a, 1966b) noted that disruptive behavior in experimental groups was significantly related to the leader's failure to establish an authority structure. Stogdill (1965a) found that in metal shops in which the work was precise and a piece could be ruined by interference and horseplay, the workers applied pressure on deviant group members when the supervisor failed to provide structure. In textile mills, women operators of high-speed sewing machines who were paid on an output basis applied pressure on deviant members if their supervisors were inexperienced or failed to keep order. Many other investigators have concluded that members initiate needed actions in a group if the leader fails to do so.[6]

Replacement of Leaders. In addition to the democratically required replacement of term-limited heads of state, governmental, ministerial, and agency leaders are deposed as a consequence of their failure to serve their constituencies, or they are replaced when their validators or higher authorities lose confidence in their competence (Hollander, 1978). Also, they may fall out of favor politically. In business and industry, for the years 1988 to 1992, Ward, Bishop, and Sonnenfeld (1999) compared voluntary exits by the CEOs of 1,000 corporations with exits forced by the boards of directors because of poor performance, personal mismanagement, illegal improper behavior, strategic disagreement, personality clashes, takeovers, and single issues such as the failure of a pet project. The replacement process was costly to the initiators of the replacement and to those deposed. The boards that forced out a CEO underwent much more involuntary change themselves afterward than after a CEO voluntarily retired or exited amicably.

Personality Differences in Reactions to Conflict. People vary in their willingness to subject themselves to con-

flict and to serve in marginal roles. Those who are higher in task orientation and lower in interpersonal orientation, as measured by the Orientation Inventory (Bass, 1963), have shown that they are more ready to engage in conflict in small-group discussions (Bass, 1967c) and are more likely to accept marginal roles. Marginal roles exist between groups with conflicting norms, values, and goals (Stonequist, 1937). Individuals who prefer such marginal roles have lower social needs (Ziller, 1973), are less extroverted (Wonder & Cotton, 1980), and reveal a higher task orientation and a lower interpersonal orientation (Cotton & Cotton, 1982).

Other personality differences make some leaders more prone than others to generate conflict with their subordinates, with consequential losses in effectiveness. Tjosvold, Andrews, and Jones (1983) asked 310 medical technicians to describe the cooperative, competitive, and individualistic orientations of their immediate superiors. The technicians' satisfaction, desire to perform well, and willingness to remain in their jobs were reduced substantially if they reported that their leaders were competitive and individualistic rather than cooperative. Kohn (1986) came to similar conclusions after a review of other survey and experimental investigations. Even among business leaders, there seems to be more interpersonal payoff from a cooperative than from a competitive outlook.

These personality differences in competitiveness and cooperativeness manifest themselves in feelings about conflict and reactions to it. They can be understood through a model created by Blake and Mouton (1964) and Thomas (1976). As Figure 13.1 shows, individuals differ in their concern for themselves and for others as well as in their assertiveness. Self-concern and assertiveness give rise to competitiveness; self-concern and a lack of assertiveness produce avoidance and withdrawal; assertiveness and a concern for others yield collaboration; and a lack of assertiveness and a concern for others generate accommodation. Compromise is literally an in-between result. According to Blake and Mouton (1964), ideal leaders are both assertive and concerned about others. They deal with conflict by integrating conflicting ideas through collaborative problem solving.

Kabanoff (1985a) validated Blake and Mouton's model of conflict by asking 104 MBA students to describe their feelings, reactions, and preferred ways of dealing with various overt or covert conflicts described in scenarios. Four of the five ways of coping emerged as expected. The

---

[6] See Carlson (1960), Hamblin (1958b), Helmreich and Collins (1967), Mulder and Stemerding (1963), and Polis (1964).

Figure 13.1 Reactions to Conflict

	Self		Others
Assertive	Competition or Countervailing Power		Collaboration
		Compromise	
Unassertive	Avoidance or Withdrawal		Accommodation

Concerned for Self or Others

SOURCE: Adapted from Blake and Mouton (1964) and Thomas (1976).

exception was a finding that accommodation was equally acceptable to the unassertive respondent whether he or she was self-concerned or concerned about others. A factor analysis by Rahim (1983) of the self-descriptions of a national sample of 1,219 executives on how they deal with conflict substantiated the a priori conceptualization of the five independent styles of coping with conflict. A factor analysis by Kipnis, Castell, Gergen, et al. (1976) resulted in a modified version of Blake and Mouton's model for how husbands and wives resolve their disagreements. Using the model, Rim (1981) found that the spouses' values affected how they resolved conflicts with each other. For example, they were more likely to be accommodating if both valued broadmindedness, independence, loving, and true friendship but not self-control. An empirical personality assessment by Kilmann and Thomas (1975) provided further indirect support for Blake and Mouton's model. For example, introverts avoided conflict, and extroverts collaborated. Terhune (1970) and Jones and Melcher (1982) found that those who had a high need for affiliation were more likely to accommodate than to compete. Chanin and Schneer (1984) reported more of a tendency to compromise or accommodate than to compete or collaborate among undergraduate seniors who were higher in feeling than in sensing, according to their scores on the Myers-Briggs Type Indicator.

Constructive Conflict

Conflict and disagreement can be constructive, and when they are, they should be encouraged. Paraphrasing Caudron (1998, p. 48), "Instead of pulling out the weeds of conflict, leaders should nurture them. From the roots of conflict come the fruits of innovation." Heifitz (1994) suggested that leaders need to confront followers with quandaries needing examination, clarification, and solution. The movement toward team efforts has generated the possibility of constructive disagreement with old ways of doing things instead of conformity to whatever was thought to be wanted by management. Out of the conflict have come new and better ways of doing things (Burke, 1970). Constructive leadership can attempt to find the reasons for a conflict, clarify the differences in a team, and indicate how much they are valued. It can convert a win-lose conflict to a win-win solution, encourage positive changes in attitudes to improve communications among team members, and focus attention on mutual goals.

Summary and Conclusions

Leaders face many conflicts. There are many sources of conflict that need the leaders' attention. Role ambiguity and lack of a clear definition of a task are conducive to less job satisfaction and to reluctance to initiate action. Location in an organization predisposes leaders to engage in some conflicts more than others. Incongruities, discrepancies, and imbalances between roles, status, esteem, and competencies give rise to many of these conflicts. Emotional conflicts are harder to resolve than rational conflicts. The leadership role is subject to a variety of conflicting expectations, which may result in an inability to fulfill these expectations and may diminish the effects of the leader's authority and responsibility in the formal organization. Conflicts arise within discordant roles, norms, and expectations. Within their roles, managers are faced with contradictory demands from superiors, peers, subordinates, and others. Multiple identifications by the managers are a way of coping with the resulting conflicts. Conflicts are also reduced or resolved by rational cause-effect analyses, by open discussion of the conflicts to convert negotiations into problem solving, or by more devious means.

Middle managers and first-line supervisors experience more role ambiguity than top managers. Workers are better satisfied and more productive when their supervisors are able to predict the reactions of their superiors. The failure of a superior to support supervisors decreases the supervisors' self-esteem and also reduces their subordinates' esteem of them. Disagreement between supervisors and their superiors about the roles of the supervisors results in greater anxiety and disagreement between the supervisors and their subordinates. Conflict can be constructive, but an important function of leaders is to reduce or resolve destructive conflict.

Conflict has been observed in business, industry, education, the military, and the public sector when a leader's legitimacy is questioned. Legitimacy may be an outcome of a struggle for status or a matter of election or appointment. The basis of legitimacy will affect its acceptance by followers. Effective management and resolution of conflict can be brought about when authority, responsibility, and accountability are aligned.

Authority, Responsibility, Accountability, and Leadership

In ancient Egypt, the *Instruction of Ptahhotep* (c. 2300 B.C.) declared, "To resist him that is put in authority is evil" (Lichtheim, 1973). Pericles, in Athens during the fifth century B.C., said that a spirit of reverence and respect for authority and the laws constrained public acts and inhibited wrongdoing (Thucydides, 404 B.C./1910). In the sixth century, Saint Benedict's rule for the authority and responsibilities of the abbots, priors, deacons, and monks were essential to the survival of the monasteries he founded (Chittister, 1992). John Locke (1960), writing at the end of the seventeenth century, held that authority was needed to make a liberal society work and survive. He noted that for the creation, maintenance, and progress of a liberal society, authority that would be more than leadership had to be established (Weaver, 1991). Edmund Burke (1790/1967) believed that those appointed to exercise authority were assigned a holy function. Recognized authority gives rise to power, and power brings responsibility. Thus Friedrich Nietzsche (1888/1935) declared that responsibility increases toward the summit. Abraham Lincoln, in his second annual message to Congress, observed that those who have the power to save the Union also bore the responsibility to do so.

The legitimate power of individuals in groups, organizations, and societies derives from their authority and responsibility. Whether they are viziers, company presidents, military officers, school principals, or first-line supervisors, their responsibility should be commensurate with their authority so as to minimize their role conflict. Often, it is not. Variations in and mismatchings of authority and responsibility have been reported for people who hold the same kinds of positions. Surveys by Bass and Valenzi (1974) discovered many managers who thought that they were delegated responsibility without the necessary authority to go along with it. Interviews with 32 college presidents by Birnbaum (1988a) disclosed that

responsibility without authority made the presidents' leadership role most difficult. The presidents coped by accepting the ambiguities of their situation, by incrementally pursuing limited objectives, and by practicing management by exception.

A study by Munson (1981) of social work supervisors and their subordinates revealed differences between preferred and actual authority and in the structure of relations that were relevant to supervisory practices and control. Aiken and Bacharach (1985) studied 44 local governmental administrative agencies in Belgium and found considerable discrepancy between subordinates' self-reported authority to make decisions and the authority their superiors said these subordinates had. The discrepancy was increased if the local government was controlled by a coalition, the organization was open to outside influences, and the structure of control was fragmented.

The allocation of responsibility and authority to managers should reflect what is required to meet organizational objectives. However, responsibility and authority may, in fact, be allocated as rewards or punishments, as political symbols, or as political gestures to imply that improvements are occurring in the organization (Benze, 1985). The managers' accountability implies their acceptance of the responsibilities of their leadership position, the expectation that they will be linked publicly to their words and actions, and the expectation that they may be called on to explain them (Wood & Winston, 2005).

Authority

Meaning of Authority

Formally, authority is the legitimate right to exercise power. According to Freud (1939), the need for authority figures develops during childhood from the yearning for a father. Zander, Cohen, and Stotland (1957) observed that the felt possession and exercise of authority and the exercise of authority are highly correlated. Traditionally, legitimacy comes from norms dealing with society, organizations, and membership within them (House, 1991). It includes the right to command and to induce compliance as well as the ability to control subordinates and to make decisions by oneself (Katzenbach & Smith, 1992). Authority is a central feature of the structure of formal organizations. It prescribes "expectations that certain individuals should exert control and direction over others within defined areas of competence." Authority is derived from implicit or explicit contracts concerning the individual's position or knowledge. The potential conflicts arising from incongruities between authority and responsibilities and between authority and knowledge are the same as those for imbalances in status and competence. Loss of authority because of a restructuring of the organization will be reflected in feelings of deprivation (C. S. George, 1972).

Both traditional and behavioral definitions are phrased in terms of value judgments in support of two conflicting moralities or ideologies (Wells, 1963). Peabody (1962) found that executives in a city welfare agency emphasized legitimacy and position as the basis of authority, whereas policemen in the same city stressed knowledge and competence as the basis. In a later study, Peabody (1964) observed that supervisors in a police department, a welfare agency, and a public school thought of authority in terms of internal (superior-subordinate) relations, whereas the people supervised thought of it in terms of external (worker-client) relations. Supervisors in the police department unquestioningly accepted authoritative instructions that produced conflict more frequently than did those in the welfare agency or the school. The unacceptable use of authority was more common in the welfare agency than in the police department or the school.

Scope of Authority

Influenced by Barnard (1938), behaviorists maintained that leaders have authority only to the extent that followers are willing to accept their commands. Authority was defined operationally in terms of the areas in which members of an organization are to carry out their respon-

sibilities (Petersen, Plowman, & Trickett, 1962). Authority in an organization specifies a member's perceived area of freedom of action and interaction, along with the formally delegated or informally recognized right to initiate action. Members act in accordance with their perception of: (1) the degree of freedom that is allowed to them, and (2) the initiative that they feel they can safely exercise. Their perception may or may not coincide with the expectations of their supervisors, peers, or subordinates. Authority is also connected with the affirmation of certain values, as illustrated by the inaugural oath of the president of the United States to preserve, protect, and defend the Constitution (Paige, 1977).

In general, group leaders perceive themselves as having a higher degree of authority than do the leaders of subgroups; and leaders of subgroups, in turn, perceive their authority to be higher than the perceived authority of individual members of the subgroups who are responsible for performing individual tasks. Authority gives legitimate power, which depends on the norms and expectations held by a group that are appropriate to a given role—the accorded rights, duties, and privileges that go along with appointment or election to a position.

Authority as Dependent on Superiors and Subordinates

Authority depends on the relationship between leaders and followers. Leaders can restrict the authority of subordinates by withholding their rights to act and decide. They can increase their subordinates' authority by delegating to them the right to act. Followers can reduce the leader's authority by failing or refusing to accept the leader's decisions. They can increase their leader's authority by referring matters to the leader for decision. The authority of leaders and followers also depends on other sources of power. The authority of professionals, for instance, stems from a wide variety of sources, such as their exclusive information, their control of resources, and their assigned responsibilities (Filley & Grimes, 1967).

Conflict results if colleagues think that leaders have misperceived or exceeded the limits of their authority (Pondy, 1967). For example, U.S. workers would find it unacceptable if their supervisors gave them orders about where they should live. According to Haas, Porat, and Vaughan (1969), an almost universal source of conflict is the tendency of individuals at any designated level to see themselves as having more authority and responsibility than their superiors believe they have. Lennerlöf (1965a) also noted a tendency for supervisors to rate themselves as having more authority than their superiors reported delegating to them. George W. Bush has argued that as president during wartime he has the authority to ignore congressional statutes and the Constitution, as did Abraham Lincoln during the Civil War.

Legitimacy for actions may be accorded by higher officials, but it still depends on an acceptance by subordinates. Followers give a form of consent to legitimacy, which they can grant or withhold, sometimes at considerable cost (Hollander, 1978). According to Barnard (1938), this means that authority is delegated upward and is granted by one's subordinates. Furthermore, the perception that a superior has the right to give orders must be widely held and shared by other subordinates. Nor does one gain such support of one's authority from subordinates passively. Bendix (1974) thought that the compliance of subordinates with authority depends on the leader's active cultivation of the legitimacy of authority. Whitson (1980) suggested that there is a tense equilibrium between authority and the confidence followers have in the authority structure. Ironically, as confidence wanes, more formal authority and more coercion are applied, escalating the loss of confidence. Presumably, renewed confidence, accompanied by less coercion, is required before authority can be restored.

Zones of Indifference and Acceptance. Barnard expanded his argument about the extent to which authority derives from subordinates' acceptance of orders by noting conditions that increase or decrease such compliance. Orders will be complied with to the extent that they are understood, are consistent with the purpose of the organization, and are compatible with the personal interests of the subordinate. Also, orders will be followed to the extent that the subordinate is physically and mentally able to comply with them. Each subordinate has a "zone of indifference" within which orders are acceptable with no conscious questioning of authority. These zones of indifference are maintained by the interests of the group. In bureaucracies, they give the higher authority some latitude and autonomy in its dealings with organizational members (Downs, 1967).

A leader's authority, legitimated by his or her position, can bring about a wide or narrow zone of acceptance in subordinates by instilling in them the belief that the benefits of compliance will exceed the costs involved in remaining members in good standing in the organization. Using the Professional Zone of Acceptance Inventory (Hoy, Tarter, & Forsyth, 1978), Johnston (undated, b) surveyed 490 teachers in 55 elementary and secondary schools. In the 26 secondary schools, the teachers' zones of acceptance correlated .71 with their loyalty to the principals. However, the more authoritarian the principal, the lower was the teacher's zone of acceptance. The more the principal enforced the rules rationally and legitimately in the eyes of the teacher, the larger was the teacher's zone of acceptance. This finding was consistent with Gouldner's (1954) observation that according to the factory workers he interviewed, rational discipline was necessary for efficient functioning of the work process. Rational discipline maintained workers' loyalty to their supervisor. Workers thought that it required being lenient and "not too strict" (p. 46): "[When] there's work to be done they expect you to do it. . . . Otherwise they leave you alone" (p. 47). However, with professionals, Johnston found that the zone of acceptance was increased more by the extent to which the principals granted the teachers professional autonomy than by rational discipline and rule enforcement.

Authority and Power

Authority is not power. "No amount of legal authority over the grizzly bears of British Columbia would enable you to get yourself obeyed by them out in the woods" (National Research Council, 1943). In supervisor-subordinate relationships, coercive and reward power, as well as legitimate power, are expected in the supervisor's position in addition to authority, but subordinates have learned to associate reward and punishment with the supervisory position and its symbols of status and authority. An analysis of authority and power requires an examination of attitudes and expectations about authority figures and symbols, as well as of the rules and regulations that describe what should be expected of holders of positions of authority (Bass, 1960).

Authority is power that is legitimatized by tradition, law, agreements, religion, and the rights of succession; it is distinguished from force and coercion (J. M. Burns,

1978). In bureaucracies, superiors in the hierarchy have authority over subordinates. This provides formal organizational coordination of members' behavior based on officially defined structure. In traditional societies, authority is the legitimate support for the father, the priest, and the noble. It comes from God, the will of heaven, or nature. In modern societies, formal authority derives from man-made constitutions, compacts, charters, legislation, judges' rulings, and due process. The state has the authority to charter the board. The board has the authority to appoint the organization's president. The president has the authority to hire a staff, and so on. Decisions can be reversed in the same way. Those who appoint the leaders to a given position usually have the authority to revoke functions previously assigned, to remove units of the organization from the leaders' jurisdiction, and to dismiss leaders from office. Even when supported by their superiors, appointed leaders may find themselves frustrated and powerless if subordinates (like grizzly bears) refuse to obey their commands. In volunteer organizations, nongovernmental organizations (NGOs), and political protest groups, formerly powerful elected or appointed leaders may find that they no longer have influence after their followers and subordinates withdraw support or give it to opponents. Thus the concept of role legitimatization calls attention to the fact that the power and influence of leaders are dependent on the acknowledgment of their authority by followers and, in some circumstances, by superiors or peers. Needless to say, the acceptance and exercise of authority will also depend on the interpretation by the individuals in authority of their rights, duties, obligations, privileges, and powers. Thus, for instance, "President Eisenhower simply did not believe that he should be leading crusades of a moral, humanitarian, or civil rights nature. He believed that his job was to operate exclusively within the governmental powers of his office" (Larson, 1968, p. 21).

Centralized or Distributed Authority

Some people argue that authority and the concomitant differentiation of power are essential for cooperative efforts in organizations; others advocate equalization, leveling, and power sharing. At one extreme, Carney (1982) saw authority as the organization's universal panacea for keeping power in the hands of a few. The absence of such

authority made improbable the spontaneous and comprehensive cooperation of the organization's members to work together toward common goals. Authority provided managers with the right to control rewards and punishments; to maintain discipline, order, and security; and to avoid confusion and frustration. However, at the other extreme, Baker (1982) noted that when members of an organization are committed to equality in the distribution of power, as was seen in a radical feminist community, the maintenance of an encrusted bureaucracy was prevented, and a shifting cadre of leaders could emerge, both informally and formally, to generate policy and cooperation. Authority could be shared.

School principals were seen as administering rules in three ways. In 31 secondary and 39 elementary schools, Johnston (undated) observed that when some principals enforced the rules with explanations and understanding, compliance by the staff was high. When some other principals enforced rules with discipline and punishment, the staff complied grudgingly. When still other principals did not enforce the rules, the teachers did not obey the rules. The principal's influence and the felt loyalty of the teachers to their principal correlated .39 and .51, respectively, when the principal used explanation and understanding to enforce the rules. The correlations when punishment was used to maintain the rules were .01 and −.03. The correlations with influence and loyalty were negative (−.31 and −.20) when the rules were neither enforced by the principal nor obeyed by the teachers. Venable (1983) corroborated the finding that the principals' exercise of nonpunitive legitimate authority (use of "rule-administration behavior") correlated with the teachers' loyalty to the principals.

Strength and Ubiquity of Authority

Authority is pervasive in its effects, often accounting for unquestioned influence. Thus in Milgram's (1965b) famous experiment, participants accepted without much consideration an experimenter's authority and delivered supposedly dangerous shocks to other student participants. Scheffler and Winslow (1950) found that people in low-status positions did not reject authority any more than did those in high-status positions. W. E. Scott's (1965) study of the attitudes of workers in a professional organization that allowed little autonomy on the job found that workers tended to accept the system of restrictive supervision. However, those who were professionally (externally) oriented were more critical of the authority structure than were those who identified themselves as internally oriented. Self-confidence about one's interpersonal relationships also appeared to make a difference in one's responsiveness to authority. Thus Berkowitz and Lundy (1957) observed that individuals strong in interpersonal confidence tended to be influenced more readily by authority figures than by peers, whereas the reverse was true for persons weak in interpersonal confidence.

Authority is not confined to the leadership structure. All members of an organization possess or believe they possess some degree of authority to perform their respective jobs. In a study of more than 1,700 individuals in formal organizations, Stogdill (1957a) found that only about 1 in 500 checked the statement, "I have no authority whatsoever." Unskilled mechanical workers rated themselves as having more than zero responsibility and authority.

Motivational Effects on Acceptance of Authority. Control over what others want establishes power over them (Bass, 1960). For leaders, such power, rather than empty formal authority, depends on the extent to which they can activate the needs and motives of their subordinates (J. M. Burns, 1978). The stronger the motivational base the leader can tap, the more authority, power, and control he or she can exercise. Thus Hollander and Bair (1954) reported that compared with members whose motivation was low, highly motivated members of a group identified more strongly with authority figures. According to the German field marshal Erwin Rommel, "The commander must try, above all, to establish personal and comradely contact with his men, but without giving away an inch of his authority" (as quoted in Mack & Konetzni, 1982, p. 3). Taylor (1983) suggested that leader-subordinate relationships in the U.S. Army were systematically undermined during the 1960s and the 1970s by the decrease in personal contact because of the introduction of information technology. More detached, self-centered subordinates and institutional policies also contributed. Lower-level commanders were given more responsibility but less authority. An effort to restore personal contact and authority at each level was initiated in 1979. In the same vein, H. I. Bowman (1964) revealed

that school principals who described their superiors as high in consideration on the Leader Behavior Description Questionnaire tended to rate themselves as high in responsibility and authority. In Shakespeare's plays *Richard III*, *Macbeth*, and *Coriolanus*, fear was used to maintain authority, and ultimately loyalty to the leaders was lost (Corrigan, 1999).

Effects of the Scope of Authority. Scope of authority depends on the influence needed to accomplish legitimate and recognized role requirements and organizational objectives (Barnard, 1952). Even though the scope may be expressed in writing, the boundaries may be blurred, and conflicts in understanding and actions may result (Reitz, 1977). Bachand (1981) contrasted Canadian crown corporations headed by government-appointed boards of directors with Canadian private-sector corporations headed by boards of directors who were elected by stockholders. The boards differed in their scope of authority, which affected their actions and those of the executives who reported to them. The members of the crown boards of directors, compared with those of the boards of directors of private corporations, believed they had the authority to do more than just give advice and counsel. The members of the crown boards faced more potential for direct conflict between political and economic objectives and had to be more active than members of the private-sector boards. As appointees of the government, the members of the crown boards of directors believed themselves to be more independent than did the members of the private-sector boards. In turn, the chief executives of the crown corporations sought their support for specific policies and decisions more often than the chief executives of private-sector corporations sought the support of their boards.

D. E. Tannenbaum (1959) observed that boards of directors in five agencies enlarged or restricted the chief executives' role by their willingness or refusal to delegate authority to the executives to act and decide. S. Epstein (1956) studied the effects of this enlargement or restriction on supervisors in experimental groups who were given different degrees of freedom of action. Severe restriction induced the supervisors to restrict the behavior of their subordinates, to supervise them more closely, and to supervise in a management-oriented manner. The absence of such restrictions induced the supervisors to give their subordinates more freedom and to supervise them less closely.

Dalton, Barnes, and Zaleznik (1968) studied the effects of changes in the authority structure of some departments of a research organization when other departments were left unchanged. In those departments where authority was transferred from department heads to scientists and engineers, the scientists and engineers favored the change, but the department heads did not. In the unchanged departments, expectations were heightened by the shifts in authority in the changed departments. Subordinates in the unchanged departments became dissatisfied with their superiors, and there was a greater tendency of those whose authority remained unchanged to seek positions elsewhere.

Parallel Authority Structures. Throughout the former Soviet Union, the scope of authority of the formal organizational leadership was limited by a parallel Communist Party structure. The dualism was seen in the parallel state and party organizational structures, factory management and party representatives, military commanders and political commissars. The recognition of the costliness of this dualism resulted in its elimination in the military (Mack & Konetzni, 1982) and industry (Gorbachev, 1988). Heifitz (1994) clarified the role of authority relative to leadership by considering the physician-patient relationship. In a type 1 situation, when faced with a purely definable technical problem with a clear solution about which the physician is expert and the patient lacks any knowledge, the physician should use his or her authority to recommend the appropriate course of action. In a type 2 situation, the problem is definable but the solution is not clear. Here, adaptive work is needed. The physician and patient need to pursue the solution together. In a type 3 situation, the problem is not clearly definable and there are no recognizable technical solutions. Again, adaptive work must be done in which leadership is required to promote learning to understand the problem and create solutions.

Discretionary and Nondiscretionary Leadership

Traditionally, leadership was fully determined by authority (Barker, 1994). But Hunt, Osborn, and Schuler (1978) conceptualized leadership as consisting of a discretionary and a nondiscretionary component. According to this concept, discretionary leadership is under the control of the leader, and nondiscretionary leadership is invoked by the organizational setting in which the leader operates. With civilian control and with concern about avoiding incidents that might provoke war, U.S. military officers, in particular, are limited in their discretionary activities. Although they are fully accountable and responsible for the actions of their subordinates, they are held on a tight leash by the higher command (Mack & Konetzni, 1982). Interviews with 32 college presidents revealed that their discretionary opportunities to lead are increasingly being constrained by governmental intervention, demographic trends, fiscal constraints, unrealistic public expectations, divergent interest groups on campus, and confusing patterns of authority. Beyond the presidents' nondiscretionary responsibility to balance their budgets, they still have discretion in how much they try to locate new sources of support (Birnbaum, 1988b).

One way of measuring discretionary and nondiscretionary leadership is to use subordinates' responses to the Leader Behavior Description Questionnaire (LBDQ), asking them on selected items if their supervisor "can and does," "could but doesn't," "can't and doesn't," or "can't but tries anyway" (Martin & Hunt, 1981). Van de Ven and Ferry (1980) asked supervisors and employees to judge the amount of authority they had in making decisions in four areas of their jobs: (1) determining what tasks the employee will do; (2) setting quotas; (3) establishing rules and procedures; (4) determining how exceptions to the usual work were to be handled. In a large engineering division of a public utility, Hunt, Osborn, and Schuler (1978) derived a leader's nondiscretionary score from the results of a leadership survey. Nondiscretionary leadership was that portion of the original score predicted by organizational practices. The discretionary score was equal to the difference between predicted and original scores. Table 14.1 shows the relative extent to which each of four original behaviors by leaders toward subordinates (approval, consideration, disapproval, and ego deflation) were accounted for as discretionary and nondiscretionary. It can be seen that in the public utility, the rewarding leadership behavior of managers had more of a nondiscretionary component than did disapproval or ego deflation.

Table 14.1 Percentage of Variance That Accounts for the Discretionary and Nondiscretionary Leadership Components of a Manager's Behavior

	Manager's Leader Behavior			
	Approval	*Consideration*	*Disapproval*	*Ego Deflation*
Discretionary	77	77	90	81
Nondiscretionary	20	22	9	1
Error	3	1	1	18

SOURCE: Adapted from Hunt, Osborn, and Schuler (1978).

Effective leaders in order to clarify what is required of their subordinates use discretionary leadership (Gast, 1984), but the subordinates may also display discretionary leadership behavior. Goodacre (1953) studied the performance of good and poor combat units on simulated problems. There was a greater tendency in good units than in poorly performing units for the men without authority to take the initiative in giving orders during the problem and to be better satisfied with their leaders' management of the problem. Hambrick and Abrahamson (1995) obtained academics' and security analysts' ratings of managerial discretion in selected industries. Discretion was rated highest in R & D–intensive industries such as computers, motion picture production, and scientific instruments; discretion was rated lowest in steel mills, petroleum and natural gas production, and gold and silver mining.

Changing Patterns of Authority

Heller (1985, p. 488) summed up the decline in authority in Britain and elsewhere during the past several decades, at the macro level and the microlevel, as the basis of relationships between the subordinate and the superior: "The loss of authority is . . . evidenced by a decline in public confidence in institutions and institutional leaders, a loss of loyalty and commitment of organizational members, and a trend toward identification with multiple organizations. . . . The loss is [also] evidenced in a decline in willingness to be bossed as well as a loss of desire to be the boss, and in a trend toward rating oneself as 'better than' the boss on desirable traits." However, Heller noted that the loss of authority, brings on a challenge for new bases for inducing compliance. One possibility is a return to strong, personal, charismatic leaders. Other alternatives include industrial democracy, power sharing, participa-

tive management, and the development of commitment to common goals. The social network may be another substitute for authority. Personal initiative may also substitute for authority. One night, when the outpost of guards responsible for patrolling for North Korean submarine infiltrators refused to take action because an incident was outside their area, a Korean taxi driver took it on himself to arouse a sleeping South Korean army garrison and lead the soldiers to a group of suspicious men he had noticed. They turned out to be North Korean infiltrators from an offshore submarine (Kristoff, 1996).

In addition to cultural changes that have diminished authority as a basis for successful leadership, Zaleznik (1980) presented a number of cases of executives whose neuroses got in the way of their obtaining compliance from subordinates. Sometimes, for example, the superior isolated himself, became tyrannical, and caused a palace revolution against his authority. In other cases, executives could not exert their authority because of their obsessive fear of hurting their subordinates. Generally, managers are becoming less dependent on their authority for their leadership and influence. Peter Drucker sees a marked change from the command and control structure where rank provides authority. This was copied from the Prussian army in the 1870s by the emerging big businesses system. "We are now evolving toward structures in which rank means responsibility but not authority . . . and in which your job is not to command but to persuade" (Cohen, 1996, p. 16). Boccialetti (1996) argued that a more reciprocal approach to authority is needed, particularly in times of change in internal and external organizational conditions. Those lower in the organizational hierarchy need to become more proactive in their relations with higher-ups, stay better informed about big issues, and accept more responsibility.

Responsibility

Meaning of Responsibility

Organizational leaders are given *responsibility* to carry out an assignment and are held *accountable* for it. They are expected to carry out their responsibilities in conformance with the norms and rules of the organization. The leaders should have the *authority* (legitimate power, right, or permission) to do so. Authority in organizations is meant to be used to fulfill assigned responsibilities (Hollander, 1978). The responsibilities are the members' perceptions of expectations by the organization that they will perform on its behalf. Generally, leaders perceive their responsibilities to be broader and more far-reaching than other group members perceive their own responsibilities. Leaders consider it their responsibility to make policies and to initiate action for themselves and for those members for whom they are responsible. The other members perceive themselves to be responsible for initiating action in specific subgroups or for executing individual assignments. In any event, neither leaders nor followers can learn to assume responsibilities until they are given them (Deci, 1972). Supervisors in naval organizations who are more conscious of their active leadership are perceived to be more responsible naval officers by their subordinates (Stogdill, Scott, & Jaynes, 1956). In Senge's (1990) learning organization, mind-sets are shifted so that members assume responsibility for actions connected to outcomes. Negative outcomes may result in rejection of responsibility. Thus failure of group decisions may result in a diffusion of individuals' sense of responsibility (Whyte, 1991). Sense of responsibility may be a matter of: (1) moral and legal standards of right and wrong, or legal and illegal; (2) obligation or sense of duty; and (3) concern for the consequences (Winter, 1991). Alternatively, having a sense of responsibility may be a matter of how one evaluates one's own character.

Interdependence

Like authority, responsibility also depends on leader-follower relations. The leader can reduce the responsibility of other group members by failing or refusing to relinquish duties that others could perform, by overly close supervision, and by requiring consultation before others can perform. Other group members can reduce the leader's responsibility by performing tasks that the leader would be expected to perform. They can increase the leader's responsibility by failing to carry out assigned and expected duties. Even when responsibilities are closely defined, the actions of their leaders tend to condition the perceived responsibilities of the subordinates, and the performance of the subordinates tends to condition the responsibilities of the leader. To be effective, anyone desiring influence in an organization needs to accept responsibility for knowing about values, strengths, performance, and communications with other members (Drucker, 1999).

Relation of Responsibility to Effective Leadership

H. H. Meyer (1959) found that supervisors and their bosses did not differ significantly on 77 items in their evaluations of the amount of the supervisors' responsibilities. However, more effective supervisors rated themselves significantly higher in responsibility than ineffective supervisors did. In a later study in 21 plants, Meyer (1970b) found that the most effective supervisors assumed that they had full responsibility when there was any ambiguity about who was in charge. Ziller (1959) studied group leaders' decision making regarding a difficult problem that risked the safety of their group. The leaders could base their actions on a throw of dice or by making a rational decision. Leaders who accepted responsibility for their group's action tended to be nonconformists. They possessed personal resources that enabled them to take risks without undue stress and strain.

Accountability

Meaning of Accountability

Accountability of an organizational leader may be defined as: (1) acceptance of responsibility for one's own and associates' behavior and effects; (2) answerability—providing explanation and justification of actions, commitments, decisions, and opinions; and (3) liability for them (Dubnick, 2003). In the governance of public and private institutions, accountability is a formal means of feedback and control common in bureaucracies (Gruber, 1987). Wood and Winston (2005) expanded the definition so that accountability implied: (4) willingness to accept the responsibility to serve the well-being of the organization; (5) the expectation that position holders would be linked to their actions or words; and (6) the expectation that they would be called on to explain their beliefs, decisions, commitments, and actions to their constituents.

Along with a leader's authority and responsibility must come accountability. The leader is held answerable for using authority legally and meeting responsibilities (Brooks, 1995). Leaders are more likely than others to be held accountable. A leader cannot evade the consequences of having more influence over others; more control over events; greater visibility and recognition; and greater responsibility for failures, misplaced efforts, or inaction in the face of an evident threat to the group's well-being (Hollander, 1978). Mack and Konetzni (1982, p. 5) noted: "In navies in general, and in the United States Navy in particular, strict accountability is an integral part of command. Not even the profession of medicine embraces the absolute relationship found at sea. A doctor may lose a patient under trying circumstances and continue to practice; but a naval officer seldom has the opportunity to hazard a second ship." More safeguards are imposed as a leader's reputation for trustworthiness declines (Hall, Blass, Ferris, et al., 2004).

In democracies, leaders need power to get things done. But accountability must go along with that power. Many others, such as bureaucrats, elected officials, educators, military leaders, land developers, marketers, and bankers, are granted powers that have important consequences to the public and need to be held accountable for their actions (Gardner, 2003). Formal accountability mechanisms are placed on leaders in the public and private sectors as safeguards against violations of the public trust. Fry, Scott, and Mitchell (1987) obtained survey results about accountability of deans, chairpersons, and faculty members at 369 business schools. Sources of information were the president, the dean, and two department heads. Faculty members were much more likely than deans to be evaluated formally and more frequently by multiple raters from below. Deans and department heads were more likely to be evaluated informally from above, and less frequently.

Purposes of Accountability

Accountability builds and sustains a climate of trust and credibility in leadership. The accountability of leaders to their group has important effects when they represent their group in negotiations (Lamm, 1973). Studies have found that being held accountable increases resolution of ethical issues (Brief, Dukerich, & Doran, 1991) and leads to more thoughtful decision processes (McAllister, Mitchell, & Beach, 1979). Also, making corporate boards, executives, and managers more accountable for their decisions and actions reduces illegal behavior, reduces lawsuits (T. M. Jones, 1986), and reduces the use of unapproved influence tactics (Baucus & Near, 1991). In a study of 210 respondents from a variety of occupations, Hall, Hochwarter, Ferris, et al. (2003) reported, as expected, that increases in accountability were correlated with increased "organizational citizenship." But an unexpected finding was that for respondents high in job efficacy (their ability to perform their jobs), political behavior increased with accountability, whereas for those low in job efficacy the ability decreased.

Demands for accountability have increased with increased reports about violated trust and scandals in the clergy, business, politics, and government. Accountability reminds leaders of their need to comply with prevailing norms (Wood & Winston, 2005). However, leaders may try to avoid accountability or displace blame by resorting to collective responsibility vested in a committee, a board, or shared authority.

Sensed Accountability

A leader's feelings of accountability depend on perceptions of the applicability and enforcement of external laws, rules, and regulations to which organizations add their own norms, standards, and constraints on actions and outcomes for which managers should feel accountable. Accountability will also be a matter of what we think others expect of us and how they will treat us for our actions (Tetlock, 1985). In the Fry, Scott, Mitchell study, accountability appeared to be greater with the use of multiple evaluators, frequency and formality of evaluation, and accessibility of results. We may feel accountable as individuals. Also, we may be socialized into feeling accountable if we and others in a group are interdependent (Roberts, 2001). Accenture and Williams (2000) surveyed 104 respondents from a midwestern marketing firm and found that they felt personally accountable for their own development to the degree that that: they could do their work well ($r = .47$); they were high in need for achievement (r = .34); they were in a supportive work situation (r = .25); they had a supportive supervisor (r = .55); they intended to engage and actually engaged in developmental behavior (r = .80). Their time and resources for development mediated how much they participated.

Time Span. As a measure of responsibility, Jaques (1956) introduced the time span of responsibility—the length of time during which a manager or employee can be held accountable for decisions. Time span was found to correlate between .86 and .92 with the compensation that the job occupant judged to be fair (Richardson, 1971). It also was a good index of the location of a position in an organizational hierarchy. Thus a supervisor may have a time span of one month; a department head, one year; a general manager, three years; and a chief executive officer of a corporation, 20 years. Similarly, in an army, the company commander may have a time span of three months; the battalion commander, one year; the brigade commander, two years; and a full general, up to 20 years.

Ethical Accountability. Berman and Van Wart (1999) suggested holding managers, particularly public service administrators, ethically accountable to the public. Cost efficiency and profitability are relatively less important to evaluate than effectiveness of services. Public service managers may be held accountable for providing services working with partners in the private sector that are timely, responsive, reliable, accurate, error-free, customer-friendly, and convenient.

Ensuring Accountability

Formally, in a hierarchy in the private sector, accountability is ensured when a leader's mandated actions and decisions are evaluated by his or her higher authority, with consequential reward or punishment (Kearns, 1996). For administrators in the public sector, authority is vested in the elected president and his appointees, the legislature, and the judiciary. Elected officials are held accountable through the election process, rules, regulations, and traditions. But leaders create arrangements to protect their positions and avoid openness, transparency, and accountability. As evidenced by numerous financial

scandals, the CEO is often not held accountable by the corporate board of directors—a signal flaw in corporate governance in the private sector and NGOs. Monitoring systems are required. In the private sector, these include effective legal regulation and uncorrupted accountants, dedicated lawyers, investigative media, and protected whistle-blowers. In the public sector, they include a free press, citizen advocacy groups, open political parties, rule of law, minimum secrecy in agencies, and an uncorrupted electoral process and judiciary (Gardner, 1988). Unfortunately, T. R. Mitchell (1993) found no assured accountability in either the public or the private sector. Neither government administrators nor business managers can be recalled by democratic voting procedures. More often than not, administrators and managers are protected by a concentration of economic and governmental power and by immunity from criminal and civil liability. Unconstrained power affects accountability by biasing appraisals of one's own and others' performance (Kipnis, 1987). Nevertheless, "The requirement that one be answerable for one's decisions and actions is an implicit, if not explicit, assumption of organizational systems. Accountability is an integral part . . . of understanding . . . organizational theory" (T. R. Mitchell, 1993, pp. 116–117).

Delegation

Delegation implies that one has been empowered by one's superior to take responsibility for certain activities. The degree of delegation is associated with the trust the superior has for the subordinate to whom responsibilities have been delegated.[1] When a group is the repository of authority and power, it likewise may delegate responsibilities to its individual members.

The delegation of responsibilities should not be confused with laissez-faire leadership[2] or abdication. A leader who delegates is still responsible for following up whether the delegation has been accepted and the requisite activities have been carried out. The leader remains accountable (Anonymous, 1989).

The delegation of decision making implies that the decision is lowered to a hierarchical level that is closer to

---

[1] The relationship between a leader's trust in subordinates and the tendency to delegate will be discussed more fully in Chapter 18.
[2] See Chapter 6.

where it will be implemented. Such delegation is consistent with the encouragement of self-planning, self-direction, and self-control.

Why Delegate?

Yukl (1998) suggests several reasons why leaders delegate: (1) the task can be done better by a subordinate; (2) the task is low-priority and not urgent; (3) the task is a career development experience; (4) the task is not central to the leader's role. Furthermore, the leader can use the time for other necessary activities. The leader's capabilities and influence can be multiplied. Better use can be made of the subordinate's time and abilities. The leader can demonstrate trust in the subordinate. Delegation can develop a greater sense of challenge, initiative, responsibility, authority, and autonomy in the subordinate (Avolio & Bass, 1991).[3]

Kuhnert (1994) offered several reasons why leaders may avoid delegating. A transactional leader cannot suspend an agenda or coordinate an agenda with others. A transformational leader may place too much weight on current role expectations and may be unable to make difficult decisions that might entail possible loss of respect.

Reponsibility, Authority, Delegation— Approximating Accountability

Stogdill and Shartle (1948, 1955, 1975) developed the RAD scales to measure organizational responsibility (R), authority (A), and delegation (D). Responsibility and authority, when combined, were said to approximate accountability. The self-rated responses by individuals describing their own jobs formed scales that had high reliability. Correlational results were obtained in 10 organizations engaged in the production of chemicals, the manufacturing of metal products, and governmental work. As expected, the responsibility and authority of job occupants were correlated positively, ranging from .13 to .63 with a mean of .45. But the relationship of delegation to authority and responsibility was not as high. Delegation averaged .17 in correlation with responsibility in the 10 organizations, with a range from −.27 to .38. Delegation averaged only .23 with authority, with a range from

[3] Delegation will be discussed as an aspect of managerial style in Chapter 18.

organization to organization from −.42 to .49. (These surveys are over half a century old and would be worth replicating in the twenty-first century.)

A complaint of managers is that they are often delegated a great deal of responsibility by their superiors without the associated authority. This is a commonplace occurrence where leaders are delegated to lead teams of professionals (McKenna & Maister, 2002). The leaders need to depend on their personal expertise, esteem, and persuasiveness. Yet satisfaction and productivity are greater when delegation, responsibility, and authority are matched. In one of the 10 organizations that Stogdill and Shartle studied, there was a correlation of .42 between the managers' self-rated delegation and their actual authority. Dissatisfaction and ineffectiveness were rampant. In the eight organizations in which delegation correlated highly, authority, satisfaction, and effectiveness were much higher than in the two organizations in which delegation and authority were mismatched. Similar inferences could be suggested about the wide range of correlations, from .13 to .63 obtained between responsibility and authority. In the organization in which responsibility and authority correlated .63, operations went much more smoothly than in the organization in which the correlation was only .13.

Age, Rank, and R, A, and D. Some other patterns of interest emerged in Stogdill and Shartle data that were a useful way to describe likely differences among organizations in leadership and management. For instance, age and seniority varied from one organization to another in their relation to responsibility, authority, and delegation. In one organization, authority was invested in older members, but in another organization it was invested in younger ones. The correlation between age and authority within the organizations ranged from −.26 to .45. It does not take much imagination to contrast the organization in which self-estimated authority correlated .45 with age and the one in which the correlation was −.26. The organization with the negative correlation was a rapidly expanding technology firm; the organization with the high positive correlation was a stable agency where age and promotion were in lockstep. More often than not, the educational level of an organization's managers correlated positively with their responsibilities and authority. The managers' own perceived responsibility and authority were unrelated to their subordinates' job satisfaction, but a mean correlation of .19 for the 10 organizations was found between the managers' perceived authority and the extent to which their superiors were seen as considerate in leadership behavior. Evidently, the higher members rise in authority in an organization, the more they are treated with consideration by their superiors. H. J. Bowman (1964) found, similarly, that school principals who rated themselves higher in responsibility, authority, and delegation described their superiors as being more considerate of them.

Rank, Salary, and R, A, and D. Kenan (1948) used the RAD scales to study large governmental organizations and found, as expected, that executives in higher-level positions described themselves as being higher in responsibility and authority than did those in lower-level positions. Correspondingly, Browne (1949) noted that executives' salaries related positively to self-estimates of responsibility and authority. D. T. Campbell (1956) reported that authority and delegation but not responsibility were positively and significantly related to one's level in various organizations, military rank, time in the position, and recognition for being in a position of leadership. Strong positive correlations should be expected between Jaques's (1956) time span of accountability and authority and responsibility as measured by the RAD scales.

Hierarchical Effects. In four large naval organizations, Stogdill and Scott (1957) found that the higher the responsibility and authority of their superiors, the less the subordinates tended to delegate. Yet, as might be expected, those superiors who delegated the most had subordinates who rated themselves highest in responsibility, authority, and delegation.

When superiors rated themselves as having a high level of responsibility, their subordinates rated themselves as having high levels of responsibility and authority, but these subordinates' self-ratings were unrelated to the authority of their superiors.

Stogdill and Scott (1957) analyzed the responsibility, authority, and delegation scores of commanding officers and executive officers and the average RAD scores of their junior officers on submarines and on landing ships. The executive officers tended to delegate more freely to those below them on both types of ships when the command-

ing officers exercised a wider scope of responsibility and authority and delegated more freely. But the relationship between commanding officers and executive officers on the submarines and landing ships differed substantially. Executive officers reported more responsibility and authority when their commanding officers were high in responsibility, authority, and delegation on the submarines, but the reverse was true on the landing ships.

The RAD scores of the junior officers were systematically related to the RAD scores of their executive officers and to those of their commanding officers. As the authority of their executive officer increased, junior officers' RAD scores tended to decrease. When their commanding officer delegated more freely, the junior officers reported an increase in responsibility on landing ships but a decrease in responsibility on submarines. Stogdill and Scott concluded that the commanding officers could increase or decrease the workloads and freedom of action of their executive officers. In the same way, junior officers tended to tighten their controls as superiors increased their own sense of responsibility and freedom of action. However, responsibility and authority did not flow without interruption down the chain of command. The responsibility, authority, and delegation of subordinates were more highly influenced by the subordinates' immediate supervisors than by their higher-level commanding officers and executive officers.

According to Stogdill, Scott, and Jaynes (1956), when U.S. Navy supervisors were perceived as delegating freely, their subordinates not only rated themselves higher in responsibility and authority but thought that they should have a high degree of responsibility and authority. However, the subordinates believed that they themselves spent too much time on inspections, preparing procedures, training, and consulting peers and not enough time on coordination and interpretation.

The responsibility of subordinates appeared to be more highly related than their authority to the responsibility and authority of their superiors. An increase in the responsibility of superiors had the effect of increasing the responsibility of their subordinates, but it did not necessarily increase the subordinates' authority. This was a latent cause of dissatisfaction. An increase in the superiors' responsibility, authority, and delegation also appeared to require that the subordinates increase their coordination activities.

Summary and Conclusions

Authority, responsibility, delegation, and accountability have been subjects of commentary and research in leadership and management since early in the twentieth century. Authority is the legitimate right to exercise power, but it depends on the willingness of others to accept it. It is less often the main source of leadership than it used to be. Authority is both allocated from above and acknowledged from below before it converts into power and leadership and becomes strong in its effects on leadership and wide in scope. Leaders are assigned responsibility and held accountable for using it commensurately with their authority. This situation can provide a check on leaders. Discretionary leadership is needed beyond that required by authority and responsibility, particularly as a consequence of changing patterns of authority. Authority and responsibility are correlated, and both contribute to accountability. Leaders' responsibilities are broader than those of their subordinates but are dependent on their subordinates. Responsibilities but not accountability can be delegated. Delegation should be to levels in the organization closest to the decisions that need to be made.

Supervisors with more responsibility generate more responsibility among their subordinates, but the same is not true for the downward flow of authority. The responsibilities of superiors tend to influence the performance of subordinates, but their authority has a stronger impact on the subordinates' expectations. When superiors have a great deal of responsibility and authority, their subordinates believe that the demands made on them for coordination increase. However, when superiors delegate a great deal to their subordinates, the subordinates report that they are overburdened with responsibilities and need more authority than they possess. Subordinates do not view delegation as an unmixed blessing when they have critical or burdensome duties to perform.

Organizational effectiveness depends on the congruence of responsibility, authority, and delegation and their interrelationships at different levels of the organization. Their combination provides a gauge of their accountability. The link between the authority and responsibility of superiors and subordinates is embedded in the larger framework of superior-subordinate interdependence and mutual reinforcements.

CHAPTER
15

Reinforcement and Instrumental Leadership

Contingent reinforcement occurs when leaders arrange for followers to be praised, commended, or rewarded materially for successfully carrying out agreed-upon assignments—or to be reproved, reprimanded, or disciplined for failure to do so. Responsiveness by followers to a leader is heightened by their expectation that satisfactory performance will be rewarded and unsatisfactory performance will be punished materially, socially, or symbolically. According to Sims and Lorenzi (1992), effective leadership reinforces desired followers' behavior and eliminates undesired follower behavior through providing or denying social, symbolic, and material rewards and punishments. According to Sims (1977), a leader is a manager of reinforcement contingencies. Connelly, Gaddis, and Helton-Fauth (2002) have suggested that leaders arouse positive emotions in followers by consistently applying contingent reinforcements and generating mutual liking. Negative emotions are aroused when leaders display a negative demeanor during punitive incidents.

The *Iliad* is filled with stories of contingent reinforcement. The heroes of the *Iliad* often engaged in contingent reward or punishment with men and the gods to gain compliance with their wishes. Achilles refused to fight further and went off to sulk over the arbitrary confiscation of Briseis, a girl captured from Achilles by the king, Agamemnon. Briseis was taken from Achilles to compensate Agamemnon for the loss of his own prize, Chryseis. To assuage the wrath of Apollo, public pressure was brought on Agamemnon to return Chryseis to her father, a priest of Apollo. Without Achilles, the Achaeans faced defeat. Agamemnon sent Odysseus and Ajax to lure Achilles back to take charge of the Achaean forces with promises by Agamemnon that Achilles would receive booty, land, and women if he achieved victory over the Trojans (*Iliad*, 1720/1943, Book IX).

For effective leadership, leaders need to let followers know what rewards are available and what behavior will be rewarded. They need to make clear what behavior will be rewarded—for example, quality rather than speed; lasting solutions not quick fixes; and creativity, not conformity. Reprimands should be directed against specific behaviors, not the person. They are given privately. They should be low-key, prompt, and unemotional. The leader should take responsibility for the reprimand. It should be accompanied by information about what behavior would be desirable (Howell & Costley, 2001, 2006).

Leadership as a Social Exchange

Transformational leadership may transcend the satisfaction of self-interests; nevertheless, the dynamics of leadership-followership have most often been explained as a social exchange. The exchange is established and maintained if the benefits to both the leader and the followers outweigh the costs (Homans, 1958, 1961). This exchange is fair if "the leader gives things of value to followers such as a sense of direction, values, and recognition, and receives other things in return such as esteem and responsiveness" (Hollander, 1987, p. 16). Followers expect that the leader will enable them to achieve a favorable outcome, and they believe the exchange to be fair if the rewards are distributed equitably. However, they perceive the leader's failure in this regard as unjust, particularly if the leader has not made an effort or is self-serving. "Fundamentally, there is a *psychological contract* between the leader and followers, which depends upon a variety of expectations and actions on both sides" (Hollander, 1987, p. 16).

The exchange or transaction cycle contains the following phases. The leader and the followers perceive each other as being potentially instrumental to the fulfillment

Table 15.1 The Task-Cycle Model

| A Generic Task | Executives | Leaders | Managers | Personnel | |
				Service	Sales
The Goal What do I do?	The Goal Clarify and direct mission achievement	The Goal Envision and initiate change for future	The Goal Clarify and communicate today's goals	The Goal Give service, keep one's own goals clearly in mind	The Goal Meet the client's needs, earn revenues
The Plan How do I do it?	The Plan Develop and communicate strategies	The Plan Solve novel problems resourcefully	The Plan Plan and solve problems that are encountered	The Plan Solve the client's problems as an adviser	The Plan Give service, be professional, analyze needs
Resources How do I carry out the plan?	Resources Develop a supportive culture	Resources Modeling, mentoring, and challenging	Resources Facilitate by coaching and training	Resources Professional/technical skills	Resources Knowledge of the product, empathy, probing skills
Feedback How do I know I am performing?	Feedback Track and share information	Feedback Develop an awareness of the impact of the task	Feedback Obtain and give feedback on the subordinate's performance	Feedback Inquire about and follow up on the impact	Feedback Ask and identify questions and resistances
Adjustments How do I fix my mistakes?	Adjustments Direct/oversee other managers	Adjustments Use persuasion to gain and maintain commitment	Adjustments Correct the time and details to meet the goal	Adjustments Self-control to meet commitments to service	Adjustments Answer objections, ask for order
Reinforcement Satisfaction from achievement of the task	Reinforcement Share rewards for the organization's success	Reinforcement Share rewards for supporting the change	Reinforcement Recognize and reinforce the subordinate's performance	Reinforcement Recognize and reinforce cooperation	Reinforcement Express appreciation to clients
Result Task achieved	Result Mission accomplished	Result Change for the better	Result Today's goals achieved	Result Service rendered	Result A sale

Source: Adapted from Wilson, O'Hare, and Shipper (1989), p. 2.

of each other's needs, say, for the completion of a task. If necessary, the leader clarifies what the followers must do (usually, they must successfully complete the task) to fulfill the transaction to obtain the material or psychic reward, or to satisfy their needs.[1] The followers' failure to comply may move the leader to take corrective action. The followers' receipt of a reward or avoidance of punishment is contingent on their successful compliance with and completion of the task. Satisfaction of the leader's

need accrues from the followers' success. Wilson, O'Hare, and Shipper (1989) expanded the description of the task cycle for the tasks performed by service and sales personnel (Table 15.1).

Blanchard and Johnson (1982) set out the following rules for contingent reinforcement in the "one-minute manager's game plan": First, obtain the subordinate's agreement with the goal, including the appropriate behavior for achieving it. Check the subordinate's behavior to see whether it matches the agreed-on goal. Second, if the goal is achieved, provide praise (contingent reward)

---

[1] As will be seen in Chapter 27, if the task is already highly structured, then little or no clarification by the leader will be needed.

as soon as possible that is specific to what the subordinate did right. Indicate how the subordinate's action helps others and the organization. Third, if the subordinate's performance fails to match expectations, deliver a reprimand (contingent punishment) as soon as possible after the failure. Despite the reprimand, it must be added, you should continue to think well of the subordinate, though not of this specific performance. Fourth, the subordinate's success may call for setting a new goal; the subordinate's failure may require a review and clarification of the old goal.

Reinforcement (Instrumental) Leadership and Followership

It takes at least two people for leadership to occur. Someone has to act, and someone else has to react. Whether the actions and reactions take place will depend on who the "someones" are and what their needs, competencies, and goals are. If one is perceived as instrumental to the other's attainment of the goal, because of greater competence or power, the stage is set for an interaction and leadership to occur. *Reinforcement* leadership is often referred to as *instrumental* leadership.

In this transactional process, leaders are agents of reinforcement for the followers. At the same time, the followers' compliance or noncompliance makes them agents for reinforcement of the leaders. "Leader and subordinate accept interconnected roles and responsibilities to reach designated goals. Directly or indirectly, leaders can provide rewards for progress toward such goals or for reaching them. Or, they can impose penalties for failure ranging from negative feedback to dismissal. . . . Contingent-positive reinforcement, reward if agreed-upon performance is achieved, reinforces the effort to maintain the desired . . . employee performance. Contingent-aversive reinforcement . . . signals the need to halt the decline in speed or accuracy of the employee's performance, to modify or change the employee's behavior. It signals the need for a reclarification of what needs to be done and how" (Bass, 1985a, pp. 121–122).

Adams, Instone, Prince, and Rice (1981) collected West Point cadets' narratives about incidents of good or bad leadership that occurred during summer training. High on the list of good incidents was contingent-

rewarding behavior. High on the list of bad incidents was punishing subordinates with or without provocation.

Utility of Reinforcement Leadership

Rewarding by leaders, whether contingent on followers' performance or noncontingent, was seen by 84 college students as exemplifying the good leader. Noncontingent punishment, but not contingent punishment, biased the students in the opposite direction (Korukonda & Hunt, 1989). Atwater, Dionne, Avolio, and Camobreco (1996) obtained 1,109 critical incidents along with leadership ratings for 286 cadet leaders at Virginia Military Institute (VMI), each rated by five subordinates. Of the four transactional reinforcers, only contingent reward was related to the effectiveness of leadership. Noncontingent reward was irrelevant. At VMI, noncontingent punishment such as reprimands, extra physical exercise, and assignment of extra duties was counterproductive (Arvey, Davis, & Nelson, 1984). Similar findings were obtained about the effects of noncontingent punishment on cohesiveness at the U.S. Naval Academy (Roush, 1991) and the U.S. Coast Guard Academy (Blake & Rotter, et al, 1993).

According to Peters and Waterman (1982, p. 123), the managers of the excellent companies they examined exerted a good deal of effort to provide positive reinforcement for the successful completion of tasks. They made a conscious effort to reinforce any action that was valuable to the organization. Subordinates' satisfaction was increased the most, according to a field study by Reitz (1971), when their supervisors praised and rewarded them for acceptable performance (but reproved them for unacceptable work). For 231 subordinates surveyed by Klimoski and Hayes (1980), particularly strong associations were found between their satisfaction with their supervisors and the supervisors' explicitness in giving instructions on what was required, support for efforts to perform effectively, and consistency toward the subordinates. The supervisors' explicitness and consistency also had moderate effects on reducing role ambiguity and role conflict. The supervisors' consistency contributed to some extent to the subordinates' performance and knowledge of the job, although these appeared to be enhanced by the subordinates' involvement in determining standards. The leaders' behavior in the contingent-reward path-goal processes contributed to the subordinates' efforts and performance by clarifying the subordinates' expectations that a payoff would accrue to them as a consequence of their efforts. To a lesser extent, some of the contingent rewarding behaviors also contributed directly to the subordinates' improved performance and satisfaction with supervision by reducing role ambiguities and role conflicts.

Effects on Satisfaction. Podsakoff and Schriesheim (1985) completed a comprehensive review of field studies of the effects on subordinates of supervisors' contingent and noncontingent reinforcement.[2] Among the general conclusions they reached was that subordinates were more satisfied with their situation if their leaders provided them with rewards (positive feedback) contingent on their performance.

Such satisfaction was not present if rewards were not contingent on their performance. "I feel well treated by my supervisor no matter what I do. In other words, it makes no difference how I perform; my supervisor will always arrange for me to be rewarded." This noncontingent reward by the supervisor was not as satisfying as earning rewards for the subordinates' good performance. Particularly dissatisfying to subordinates was noncontingent negative feedback—that is, not really being able to link reprimands with the behaviors that elicited them. This condition is likely to promote learned helplessness.

Field studies involved 17 large samples, with a median size of 275 cases, of financial managers, paramedics, engineers, white-collar employees of public utilities, registered nurses and nurses' aides, administrators of nonprofit organizations, city and state government employees, hospital pharmacists, and mental health employees. For the 17 samples, a mean positive concurrent correlation close to .50 was found between the subordinates' satisfaction with supervision and the extent to which the supervisors practiced contingent reward. The corresponding mean correlation was near zero between satisfaction with supervision and the practice of contingent punishment. Noncontingent reward had little relation to satisfaction with supervision. At the same time, noncontingent pun-

ishment was negatively correlated with satisfaction with supervision in these samples. The mean correlation here was −.32 for 11 of the samples in which the measures were available. Even after the same single source of variance was removed by removing the general factor of each individual's responses to all questions (the subordinate raters described the leaders' as well as their own satisfaction and performance), Podsakoff and Todor (1985) still found a positive association between contingent reinforcement leadership and a group's cohesiveness, drive, and productivity. But Brown and Moshavi (2002) did not find that contingent rewarding of 440 faculty members by chairpersons in 70 academic departments enhanced the faculty members' job satisfaction, expenditure of extra effort, or organizational effectiveness.

Effects on Performance. Considerable evidence from laboratory experiments and field studies has indicated that reinforcement leadership contributes to the effectiveness of subordinates and collegial groups. Spector and Suttell (1957) contrasted reinforcement leadership with authoritarian and democratic leadership of teams in producing correct plans in a controlled, laboratory setting. The reinforcing leader was encouraging and expressed approval of good solutions to problems every time the teams reached them. When incorrect planning occurred, the reinforcement leader suggested how it could be improved. The authoritarian leader made the groups' decisions and did their planning. Under the democratic leader, the leader and the teams shared the responsibility for planning and decision making. The teams that received reinforcement leadership were the most productive, and members with little ability appeared to profit most from it. According to a survey of 526 subordinates and 543 peers describing the downward influence tactics of their 128 managers, least effective leadership involved using demands, threats, and persistent reminders; seeking the aid of others to persuade teams; and claiming the authority to legitimate requests. Moderate results were achieved with getting teams to think favorably of the leader before making a request, or making promises of later reward or reciprocating the favor later on. Most effective were rational persuasion and inspirational appeals to values, ideals, and aspirations.

For 11 of the samples in the Podsakoff and Schriesheim (1985) review, the mean concurrent correlation was .32

[2]The studies included those of Bateman, Strasser, and Dailey (1982); Bigoness, Ryan, and Hamner (1981); Hunt and Schuler (1976); Keller and Szilagyi (1976); Podsakoff and Todor (1983a, 1983b); Podsakoff, Todor, Grover, and Huber (1984); Podsakoff, Todor, and Skov (1982); Reitz (1971); and Sims and Szilagyi (1975).

between contingent rewarding supervision and the effectiveness of the performance of subordinates and work groups. For 10 samples, the mean correlation was close to zero between contingent punishment by the leader and subordinates' performance. Luthans and Kreitner (1975) did find that contingent penalization for unacceptable actions improved performance, but only when it was coupled with contingent reward for acceptable performance. The mean correlation was also close to zero between performance and noncontingent reward for eight samples and $-.12$ between noncontingent punishment and performance.

Material versus Nonmaterial Rewards. Pay for performance still remains a popular contingent reward in the United States, Britain, and elsewhere, with schedules set by the human resources staff. Supervisors may recommend pay raises in their performance reports of subordinates, but nonmaterial rewarding may be more important in motivating and maintaining performance. Although pay motivates people to seek and accept employment for better wages and salaries, leaders are likely to have even more discretionary effects on their subordinates in their use of nonmaterial positive feedback of praise and recognition for work well done (Kohn, 1993).

Contingent Reward and Other Leadership Behavior

Generally, contingent rewarding correlated almost as highly as transformational leadership with outcomes in effectiveness and satisfaction. Among 19 female managers rated in transformational leadership by 38 subordinates, transformational leadership did not further account for performance of the subordinates rated by the managers beyond what was accounted for by contingent reward (Dionne, Yammarino, Comer, et al., 1996). *Behavioral management*, which included providing rewards contingent on performance, proved more effective at increasing productivity than did *participative management*, according to an experiment in a Russian textile factory by Welsh, Luthans, and Sommer (1993). According to a survey of 125 managers by Howell, Neufeld, and Avolio (2005), contingent rewarding was correlated with better communication—frankness (.41), two-way communications (.45), and careful transmitting (.22). Generally, creative performance and divergent thinking were increased

by promises of reward contingent on performance (Eisenberger, Armeli, & Pretz, 1998). On the basis of his own experience in the Israeli Army, and after reviewing the literature, Berson (undated) noted that rewarding soldiers for the adequacy of their performance was especially relevant for their motivation.

In cross-lagged causal analyses of 206 employees, Greene (1976a) demonstrated that contingent rewarding by supervisors resulted in the improved *subsequent* performance and satisfaction of subordinates. The correlation was .48. The effect had some permanency. In a six-month longitudinal field study of 61 working MBA students, Sims (1977) corroborated Greene's conclusion about how much contingent rewarding by supervisors contributed to the respondents' subsequent performance. The correlation was .50. Szilagyi (1980b), in a three-month longitudinal study of 128 employees in a controller's department, obtained a comparable coefficient of .48.

Contingent Punishment

Szilagi's (1980b) results were reversed or nil $(-.23, -.12, -.07)$ for the effects of earlier contingent punishment by supervisors on the future performance of subordinates in Greene's, Sims's, and Szilagyi's studies. Future punitive supervision appeared to be more a consequence of past poor performance of subordinates: the correlations for the three studies were $-.40, -.04,$ and $-.59$. But future contingent reward was not consistently a consequence of subordinates' earlier good performance: the correlations for the three studies were $.26, .09, -.17$.

Laboratory and field studies have indicated that although contingent reward leads to improved performance by subordinates, contingent punishment has less consistent effects. The performance of subordinates may be improved by a supervisor's correction and by other forms of negative feedback (Arvey & Ivancevich, 1980). Sims and Szilagyi (1975) suggested that negative sanctions may improve performance by reducing role ambiguity. According to Podsakoff (1982), high-performing leaders use both contingent-positive and contingent-aversive reinforcement. O'Reilly and Weitz (1980) found that managers of high-performing units used negative reinforcers more quickly. Franke and Kaul (1978) reinterpreted the statistical inferences that could be drawn from the Hawthorne experiments (Roethlisberger, 1941) and concluded that managers' tightening of discipline was an important reason for the increased productivity of workers—a change that was ignored by the original investigators. O'Reilly and Puffer (1983) asked 142 sales representatives to describe critical incidents of good and poor performance with and without supervisory reinforcement. They found that effort, satisfaction, and a sense of equity were enhanced as well by formal or informal reprimands for poor performance as by favorable recognition for good performance.

Reasons for Disciplinary Action. Contingent punishment is more likely to occur if the manager's authority is challenged, or if the manager is inconvenienced by a trained and experienced subordinate's failure to live up to expectations. For example, a subordinate might deviate from the norms, production might fall below agreed-on standards, or the quality of the product might become unacceptable (Rollinson, Hook, Foot, et al., 1996). The leader may call attention to the deviation. Being told of one's failure to meet standards may be sufficient to provide aversive reinforcement for what was done wrong. Being told why can be particularly helpful to an inexperienced subordinate, especially if the message includes further clarification of the desired performance. The leader may administer penalties, such as fines or suspensions without pay. The leader may withdraw support, or the employee may be discharged.

Effects of Disciplinary Actions. Following initial interviews with a random sample of 100 hourly refinery employees, Arvey, Davis, and Nelson (1984) surveyed 526 hourly employees. The employees were asked to describe their perceptions of their immediate supervisors' disciplinary behavior, as well as the factors that supervisors take into account when applying discipline. Of the employees, 20% reported that they had experienced disciplinary actions. The employees' evaluation of the supervisors differed strongly, depending on how much and in what ways the supervisors used punishment. The more the supervisors used formal punishment ("Write you up for an infraction") or informal punishment ("Yell at you"), the less satisfied their subordinates were with them. The employees' satisfaction with their supervisors correlated −.46 with overly harsh discipline and −.50

with discipline lacking a clear explanation. On the other hand, satisfaction with the supervisors correlated .31 with the supervisors' tendency to discipline people immediately after an infraction of the rules occurred, .60 with the tendency to maintain close and friendly relations with employees they had disciplined, and .32 with consistency in disciplining employees from person to person and situation to situation.

Justifications for Punishment. Future-oriented punishment aims to reduce or eliminate undesirable behaviors such as unsafe behavior. By itself, it does not reinforce the correct way to act, but it can avoid costly errors. Past-oriented punishment, by contrast, is retribution for past misdeeds, and it may only assuage the administrating leader and increase the emotional reactions of the follower. According to qualitative interviews with 77 managers from diverse organizations by Butterfield, Trevino, and Ball (1996), the interviewed managers generally were uncomfortable with punishing subordinates for poor performance and sought to avoid it. Many managers felt pressure against it from the subordinates as well as from the organization and work groups. These managers were aware that the emotional effects could spread much beyond what was intended. Nonetheless, the investigators concluded that punishment could be instrumental in improving subordinates' behavior, attitudes, respect, and vicarious organizational learning. Many of the managers engaged in impression management when punishing, using justifications and excuses in acknowledgment of past mistakes. They considered the subordinates' expectations, reactions, and acceptance, and their own past relations with the subordinates. To many of the managers, fairness and timeliness were less important than consistency, privacy, and the poor performance of the subordinates. Judging from the reactions of 421 graduate business students to scenarios, Fukami and Hopkins (1990) concluded that the severity of punishment meted out depended on the subordinates' past performance and the amount of property damage and personal injury, not on whether the offending employee was a man or a woman.

Incorrect behavior may be only temporarily suppressed by disciplinary punishment alone, but when disciplinary punishment is coupled with advice on correct behavior, it is more likely to suppress the undesired behavior permanently (Arvey & Ivancevich, 1980). In a simulation experiment in which 182 undergraduates played roles as managers and poorly performing workers, the "managers' " advice added to corrective action increased the "workers" sense of interactional justice.

Content analyses by Atwater, Waldman, Carey, et al. (2001) of interviews with 123 disciplined persons and 46 observers disclosed some positive effects of the discipline. But respect for the discipliner was lost and negative attitudes developed toward the organization. The discipline was seen as unfair, particularly when it was applied for violations of informal rather than formal rules. Ball and Trevino (1990) asked 65 managers from different organizations and different kinds of positions to indicate whether they had been pleased or discouraged by a disciplinary event they had reported and whether justice had been served. As expected, the perception of justice depended on the appropriateness of the severity of the punishment ($r = .31$), the closeness of the punishment to the violation ($r = .22$) and the constructiveness of the punishment ($r = .54$). Managers were less discouraged when the punishment was perceived as just ($r = -.21$), when it was given in private ($r = -.26$), and when the manager perceived the relationship with the disciplined employee as remaining good ($r = -.29$).

Management by Exception. When leaders take corrective actions and intervene only when subordinates' failures and deviations occur, they are practicing management by exception (MBE). In practicing MBE, some managers *actively* search for deviations and shortfalls. They set up standards and regularly monitor subordinates' performance to see if the standards are being met. Other managers are more *passive*, asking no more than what is essential to get the work done (Hater & Bass, 1988). Leaders who practice MBE intervene only when something goes wrong. If a subordinate's performance falls below some threshold, the leader feeds back information to the subordinate, at the emotionally mildest level, that the threshold has been crossed. The negative feedback may be accompanied by a contingent reward from the leader, in the form of reclarification and encouragement, At the other extreme, it may be accompanied by disapproval, a reprimand, a formal citation, suspension, or discharge. MBE is consistent with the cybernetics of negative feedback—feedback that signals the

system to move back toward its steady-state base. The manager is alert for deviations and provides the negative feedback as needed.

A simulation of management control strategies used 182 students acting as managers and poorly performing employees. Punitive corrective actions and verbal reprimands were used repeatedly; but over time, the "managers" experimented in the search for effective management control (Gavin, Green, & Fairhurst, 1995) and the "employees' " sense of justice was affected. In most surveys of descriptions of industrial leaders by their colleagues and subordinates, MBE—especially if it is passive—does not contribute to positive appraisals of the leaders' effectiveness or to satisfaction with the leaders (Bass, 1985a). However, it correlated .23 and .25 with the rated effectiveness of officers in the U.S. Army and U.S. Air Force and .29 and .31 with subordinates' satisfaction with the officers' leadership (Colby & Zak, 1988).

Particularly important to the effectiveness of leadership is whether MBE is active or passive. A leader who arranges to monitor errors and deviance that need to be corrected is said to be *actively* engaged in management by exception. A leader who waits to be informed about errors and deviance before taking action is said to be practicing *passive* management by exception. The correlations for 186 junior naval officers described by their subordinates as actively managing by exception were .50 and .54 with the subordinates' evaluation of the effectiveness of the officers and satisfaction with them, and .28 and .22 with fitness reports and recommendations for early promotions from their superiors. The same correlations with passively managing by exception were, respectively, .11, .19, −.04, and −.05 (Yammarino & Bass, 1988).

Personal and Situational Modifiers. In interviews with 474 managers about their use of discipline, Beyer (1981) found that both personal and situational factors could account for the extent to which supervisors took disciplinary actions with problem employees. For example, managers who personally endorsed humane pragmatism—concern for both the employees' welfare and the company's productivity—were more likely to be constructive and confrontational with problem drinkers and less likely to take disciplinary action against these employees. At the same time, the judged seriousness of the drinking problem was the strongest determinant of whether disciplinary action, including issuing warnings in writing or ordering a suspension or discharge, would be taken. Union and management policies had systematic effects, as did the managers' expectations that their constructive or disciplinary efforts would or would not please their higher authority. Unfortunately, the results were often different when the managers dealt with problem employees other than those who had drinking problems. Commentaries suggest that less serious disciplinary cases are handled personally by supervisors with a prescriptive autocratic style. More serious threats to the organization result in stronger disciplinary action. Additionally, whether the supervisor takes any disciplinary action depends on the subordinate's length of service and on how much the subordinate's violation inconveniences the supervisor, is a threat to the organization, and challenges authority. Also important are the supervisor's training and the subordinate's length of service (Hook, Rollinson, Foot, et al., 1996; Rollinson, Hook, Foot, et al., 1996). Observing coworkers who are being threatened or punished by supervisors can also provide vicarious reinforcement that promotes the productivity of the onlookers. Schnake (1986) hired students at $5 an hour ostensibly to perform clerical work, along with a confederate of the experimenter who made sure to perform more poorly than the student subjects. Threats to reduce the confederate's wage to $3.50 and actually cutting the confederate's pay resulted in significant increases in the output of the student subjects.

Applying Contingent Reinforcement

According to Zaleznik (1967), contingent reinforcement with an emphasis on the exchange should be practiced by managers who are interested in efficient processes rather than substantive ideas. It will be facilitated by the managers' flexibility in using their powers to reward or punish to maintain or improve processes and organizational arrangements. Blanchard and Johnson (1982) advised that inexperienced subordinates may need to be told by their superior what they did right and how their superior feels about their work, and encouraged to continue. Experienced subordinates may need to be told what they did wrong without diminishing their self-esteem. Further-

more, a reprimand will work if it is timely and specific to the behavior involved, not to the person. It should focus on what was done wrong, how the supervisor feels about it, and the expectation that the subordinate's performance is going to improve. The subordinate's failure to appreciate what is expected calls for a clarification of requirements, rather than punitive actions. Failure that is due to a lack of knowledge calls for information, training, or transfer. Failure that is a result of insufficient challenge calls for enlarging the task, transfer, increased extrinsic incentives, or acceptance of reality by the subordinate. A lack of commitment requires that the employee's involvement in the planning or control process be increased. An overload of goals necessitates the establishment of priorities.

Operant Reinforcement

According to Scott and Podsakoff (1982), if leadership and followership can be conceived of as behaviors, then the principles of operant reinforcement can be used to modify these behaviors. Leaders need to learn what reinforcers work with what kinds of followers. They also must be able to identify and specify the types of behavior by subordinates that will maximize the group's performance. If this is not possible, they need to identify and specify the desired results and to keep up with changes that are required. Over time, a shift of control by the leader to self-control by the followers is salutary.

If extrinsic reinforcers are used, leaders must be able to link the reinforcement to the subordinates' performance. Leaders need to be consistent in their administration of reinforcements. Punishment must be delivered quickly, and with reasons, in order to stamp out undesirable responses. Environmental events that sustain the dysfunctional behavior need to be eliminated. McElroy (1985) also argued that reinforcement is not received mindlessly. Rather, when reinforced, a subordinate will develop a reason for the reinforcement that may be the same as or different from the reason given by the leader. It is likely that the subordinate will attribute rewards for successful performance to his or her personal efforts but attribute penalties for failure to external causes. It is presumed that because of this attribution, penalties will have less effect on the subordinate's subsequent behavior. Schedules of reinforcement will systematically affect causal attributes.

For example, if one is rewarded only some of the time for good performance, one will tend to attribute the reward to effort or luck, rather than to ability.

Caveats. Caution is required in applying reinforcement theory that is based on animal research to human leader-subordinate relations. If animals are faced with choices X and Y and are reinforced 90% of the time for choosing X and 10% of the time for choosing Y, they will choose X 90% of the time. However, humans will make a cognitive leap, deducing that they will maximize their reward by choosing X 100% of the time. Animals will earn rewards only 81% of the time; humans will earn rewards 90% of the time (Mawhinney, 1982).

Using contingent reward or punishment is a tricky business. A 100% schedule of praise for every success will probably satiate the subordinates, lead them to discount the supervisor, and cause them to perceive the superior's behavior as ingratiating. Continued praise in front of associates may create considerable feelings of discomfort and defensive feelings. Too infrequent a schedule of contingent praise may raise questions about the superior's motivation. The subordinate's expectation of an extrinsic reward that is contingent on his or her performance may reduce the intrinsic motivation to continue that performance (Deci, 1972). Thus in a field study of 48 health care technicians caring for handicapped and mentally retarded children, Jordan (1986) found that the intrinsic motivation of those whose rewards were contingent on performance decreased 21 or 22 months after the extrinsic incentive program started. The technicians' intrinsic motivation increased if the rewards of the incentive program were not contingent on performance. Their satisfaction with the extrinsic reward of pay was not affected, however.

Mild punishment in private, in the form of suggested corrections by the superior of the subordinate's behavior, may be salutary. Severe punishment, in the form of a suspension, may provoke hostility, resentment, and anxiety. Frequent contingent punishment may increase anxiety to the point where it interferes with the subordinate's performance. Contingent punishment that is too infrequent may allow incorrect habits to become so entrenched that they are difficult to eliminate.

In a nationwide survey of 5,000 employees, almost half the respondents said that the managers at their firm were too lenient with poor performers (Anonymous, 1988a). Nonetheless, according to Veiga (1988), a majority of executives are in favor of candor in dealing with problem subordinates. Unwanted behaviors and outcomes need to be clarified. Both the leader and the subordinate need to acknowledge their responsibilities for the situation. Clear-cut expectations about what will be changed need to be established, and positive support for making a small new change needs to be given.

On the basis of theory and research, Arvey and Ivancevich (1980) offered a set of propositions that outline the conditions under which punishment is likely to be effective in organizational settings. They stated that punishment should be delivered as close as possible to the time of the subordinate's undesired behavior, should be given by an otherwise close and friendly supervisor, and should be moderate in intensity. Furthermore, punishment should be accompanied by explanation. Alternatives to the undesired behavior should be available.

Contingent motivation remains a reality at the macro level. It was possible to eliminate the draft and change to an all-volunteer military. Opportunities for education, training, and advancement became important inducements to influence volunteers to enlist in the U.S. Armed Forces, Reserve, and National Guard. But at the time of this writing, as the insurrection in Iraq had heated up and threats to safety and security had increased, enlistment rates had fallen.

A Model for Contingent Reinforcement

Bass (1985a, pp. 147, 149) presented a model of the most important linkages between contingent-positive and -aversive reinforcement by leaders and the resultant effort of their followers to comply and carry out the transaction:

> Leaders . . . reward followers to encourage the followers' acceptance of their work roles. Followers comply with the leaders' directions . . . to gain the rewards promised by the leaders for such compliance. If the followers succeed, they earn material rewards, . . . satisfaction and enhanced self-esteem. . . . [In maintaining their] role behavior and . . . [in] renewing their efforts . . . [to] comply with what is expected of them . . . the leaders also clarify such expectations.

Such clarification promotes followers' understanding of their roles and builds followers' confidence, further contributing to their compliance.

If the followers fail to comply and the failure is attributed by the leaders [to a lack of] follower clarity and understanding, then the leaders will renew their clarification of what they expect. If the leaders attribute the failure of their followers to lack of motivation [and they wish to be positively reinforcing] the leaders will renew their promises of reward and confidence in the followers.... [Or if the leaders wish to use] aversive reinforcement such as reprimand, they [run the risk] of followers' anxiety and withdrawal.

Leaders practicing contingent aversive reinforcement ... will foster followers' efforts to comply with the clarified standards to avoid negative consequences for failure. If followers succeed in complying, they avoid being aversively reinforced and may increase in self-esteem and self-reinforcement. If they fail and leaders attribute the failure to lack of clarity, ability, and understanding, the leaders will renew clarification and attempt to improve followers' ability through training, thus increasing the likelihood of ultimate successful performance by followers. On the other hand, if aversively reinforcing leaders attribute followers' failure to comply to [a] lack of follower motivation, they are likely to reprimand or threaten, possibly generating the unintended effects on followers of hostility, apathy, anxiety, and loss of self-esteem. In turn, there will be a reduction in self-reinforced effort and interference with the efforts of followers to comply.

Specific Behaviors and Measures of Contingent Reward and Punishment

Contingent Reward Behaviors. Klimoski and Hayes (1980) found four of six behaviors of supervisors that 231 surveyed subordinates thought were ways their supervisors provided contingent reward: (1) being explicit when giving instructions, (2) allowing the subordinates to be involved in determining standards of performance, (3) giving support for efforts to perform effectively, and (4) being consistent toward subordinates. When a supervisor behaved in these four ways, subordinates expected that their effort would lead to successful performance and that their successful performance would generate commensurate rewards. Two other seemingly relevant behaviors of supervisors—frequency of communications and frequency of reviews—were irrelevant to these subordinates' expectations.

Yukl (1981) used content analysis to derive a category of "structuring reward contingencies"—the extent to which a leader rewards a subordinate's effective performance with tangible benefits, such as a pay increase, promotion, more desirable assignments, a better work schedule, or more time off. Examples of contingent reward structuring included: "My supervisor established a new policy that any subordinate who brought in a new client would earn 10 percent of the contracted fee" and "My supervisor recommended a promotion for a subordinate with the best performance record in the group" (p. 122).

Leaders who give contingent rewards establish "contracts" with subordinates to set goals for each important aspect of a subordinate's job, measure the subordinate's progress toward reaching the goals, and provide concrete feedback. Yukl (1981, p. 123) cited these examples: "The supervisor held a meeting to discuss the sales quota for next month" and "My supervisor met with me for two hours to establish performance goals for the coming year and to develop action plans"

Using factor analyses of survey results, Sims (1977) found that contingent reward took two main forms: (1) praise for work well done; and (2) recommendations for pay increases, bonuses, and promotions. Also, there may be commendations for meritorious effort and honors for outstanding service. The first positive-reward behavior factor explained 37% of the variance among the supervisors. Items most highly correlated with this first factor included: "Your supervisor would show a great deal of interest if you suggested a new and better way of doing things." "Your supervisor would give you special recognition if you suggested a new and better way of doing things." "Your supervisor would give you special recognition if your work performance was especially good." "Your supervisor would personally pay you a compliment if you did outstanding work" (p. 126). The second factor, which accounted for 18% of the variance, dealt with recommendations for promotion and advancement. Items highly correlated with the second factor included: "Your supervisor would see that you will eventually go as far as you would like to go in this organization, if your work is consistently above average." "Your supervisor would recommend that you be promoted if your work was better than others who were otherwise equally qualified." "Your supervisor would help you get a transfer if you asked for one" (p. 126). Bass and Avolio (1989) validated a scale of 10 items within the Multifactor Leadership Questionnaire (MLQ) to measure contingent reward in an exchange context that contained items such as: "Tells me what to do if I want to be rewarded for my efforts" and "There is close agreement between what I am expected to put into the group effort and what I can get out of it."

Management by Exception and Contingent Punishment. Yukl and Van Fleet (1982) found numerous critical incidents of management by exception and contingent punitiveness among officers in Korea, such as: "Checks to see that tasks are accomplished satisfactorily." "Shows concern about the appearance of cadets." "Expresses disappointment that the unit did not perform better." "Explains to a person why he is being disciplined." Sims (1977) uncovered a factor of supervisory behavior that dealt with contingent punishment. The items include: "Your supervisor would get on you if your work was not as good as the work of others in your department" and "Your supervisor would give you a reprimand [written or verbal] if your work was consistently below acceptable standards." As was noted earlier, a contingent-aversive or -punitive factor is involved in the practice of management by exception. Hater and Bass (1988) and Yammarino and Bass (1988) created factored scales of active and passive management by exception within the MLQ. The active practice of management by exception (MBEA) dealt with monitoring and searching for subordinates' deviations from standards and making suitable corrections ("Checks to see if things are going along all right"). The passive practice of management by exception (MBEP) involved reacting only when deviations were brought to the manager's attention ("Endorses the adage, 'If it ain't broke, don't fix it' "). Compared with other ways of measuring leadership performance, these behavioral scales of contingent reinforcement by leaders tend to be relatively free of the usual biases of respondents to rate according to the social desirability of the behaviors (Podsakoff, Todor, Grover, & Huber, 1984) or the raters' implicit theories of leadership (Bass & Avolio, 1988). MBEA tends to correlate with contingent rewarding whereas MBEP tends to correlate with laissez-faire leadership (Bass, Avolio, & Jung, 1999).

Scales of Contingent Reinforcement. The Contingency Questionnaire (Johnson, 1970; Reitz, 1971) assessed the extent to which subordinates perceive contingencies between their performance and how the organization responds to it. Three factors emerged: (1) supportive instrumentality—the contingency between the subordinate's behaviors and a supportive or rewarding organizational response; (2) punitive instrumentality—the contingency between the subordinate's undesirable behaviors and the administration of punitive events by the organization or the withdrawal of rewards; and (3) advancement instrumentality—the contingency between the subordinate's behavior and the subordinate's advancement in the organization. The three factors accounted for approximately 50% of the common variance in the scale of 20 items. House and Dessler (1974) developed four-item scales to measure leader-contingent approval behavior and leader-contingent disapproval behavior. Scales to assess noncontingent reward and noncontingent sanctioning were also added. Hunt and Schuler (1976); Fulk and Wendler (1982); and Podsakoff, Todor, and Skov (1982) likewise developed and evaluated the Leader Reward and Punishment Questionnaire, which had a total of 23 items to measure both contingent and noncontingent reinforcement by the leader. In typical items from the most recent report, supervisors were described in paraphrase as follows: *Contingent reward*—personally compliments me when I do outstanding work; *Noncontingent reward*—Praises me when I do poorly as when I do well; *Contingent punishment*—would reprimand me if my work was below standard; *Noncontingent punishment*—holds me accountable for things over which I have no control. Schriesheim, Hinken, and Tetrault (1988) corroborated the factorial validity of the four dimensions of contingent reward, noncontingent reward, contingent punishment, and noncontingent punishment with the responses of 176 aircraft controllers and 375 employees of a psychiatric hospital to a questionnaire in which they were asked to describe their supervisors.

Reinforcement and the Emergence of Leaders

In addition to the use by leaders of contingent reinforcement to develop and maintain effective follower compliance, contingent reinforcement processes also can explain who emerges as a leader. A variety of experiments have been conducted to show how reinforcement can increase individual members' attempts to lead and their processes in leadership.

Who attempts and continues to lead and who attempts and continues to follow in newly formed groups without appointed leaders can be explained by the differential reinforcement experiences of the various members of the groups. To be successful in influencing others, one must attempt to lead. Such attempts to lead are increased by the positive reinforcement of success as a leader and are decreased by failure and aversive reinforcement. If one member's attempts at leadership are inhibited by failure, the leadership attempts of others may increase. The positive reinforcement of one member can result in "crowding out" the other members. Contrived reward has been applied in experiments to test its efficacy in reinforcing attempts to lead the interaction process, as well as its efficacy in reinforcing the probability of successfully leading others.

Reinforcing Attempts to Lead

Bavelas, Hastorf, Gross, and Kite (1965) assessed the amount of activity of each participant in initial discussions without an appointed leader. In a second session, only one particular member of each discussion group was reinforced for participation, by the flashing of a green light. Additionally, in some of these groups the participation of the remaining members was inhibited by the flashing of a red light. When other members were not inhibited by a red flashing light, those who were positively reinforced with the green flashing light significantly increased their talking (which is highly correlated with attempts to lead in initially leaderless discussions). But it was necessary to use positive reinforcement (the green flashing light) with the initially least active talker and to inhibit (with the red flashing light) the initially most active talker in order to increase the amount of talking by the originally least active talker. The least active talker's gain was mostly at the expense of the originally most active talker.

Jaffee (1968) and Jaffee and Skaja (1968) reinforced the leadership acts of one member of pairs of experimental partners. The number of leadership attempts by the members who were reinforced by the appearance of a light significantly exceeded attempts by the nonreinforced and control participants. The effects lasted over a test period of one week and were found to generalize to a different experimental situation. Zdep and Oakes (1967) likewise demonstrated that reinforcement of a group member's leadership acts resulted in an increase in talking and leadership. In the same way, Binder, Wolin, and Terebinski (1965, 1966) and Wolin and Terebinski (1965) controlled the proportion of decisions as a leader for which each member of a group was reinforced. The resulting emergence as a leader fit a Markov mathematical model. Increases in leadership behavior were found to be responsive to changes in such rates of reinforcement.

Aiken (1965a) rewarded a group member in a second session who had talked the least in a preceding session. The other three members were punished for speaking in the second session. The rewarded member's verbal output significantly increased in comparison with the output of unrewarded control group members, but punishment did not significantly decrease output. After the second session, the three unrewarded members of the experimental group rated the rewarded member higher than members of the control group rated each other in leadership, participation, and self-confidence.

Reinforcing Successful Leadership

In these experiments, mainly with school pupils and college students, group members whose leadership was reinforced with success rather than failure were more likely to increase their influence over the other members. Mausner (1954a) gave participants either positive, negative, or no reinforcement when they were working alone on a judgmental task. When combined in pairs, the nonreinforced partners had a significant tendency to shift their judgments to comply with those of their reinforced partners, whereas the reinforced participants did not change. The participants who had received positive reinforcement were significantly less influenced by their partners than were those who had received negative reinforcement. Thus Mausner demonstrated that the participants' perception of the success of their partners gave them prestige and reinforced their expectation of future success. The participants who worked with previously successful partners were significantly more influenced by them than were those who worked with previously unsuccessful partners in a judgmental task. Banta and Nelson (1964) showed that for positively reinforced participants, the probability of having their suggestions adopted increased over 60 trials, whereas for negatively reinforced participants, the probability decreased. Kanareff and Lanzetta (1960) also found that the tendency to be imitated by others was related to the rate at which the imitated participant was positively reinforced. McClintock (1966) used paid accomplices who either supported, shifted their support of, or did not support the leaders of discussion groups. It was found that leaders evidenced more release of tension, more positive affect, and more task-oriented responses when they were supported than when they were not supported.

Cohen and Lindsley (1964) gave pairs of subjects a monetary reward for social responses or punished them, by blacking out the room, for individual (nonsocial) responses. They rewarded acts of leadership by opening a panel that permitted subjects to see each other briefly. Differential leadership responses were established by the differential reinforcement procedures. James and Lott (1964) rewarded some members of an experimental task group with six nickels, rewarded others with three nickels, and did not reward still others. Those who were rewarded with six nickels chose each other significantly more often than did those who were rewarded with three nickels or those who were not rewarded. G. Gardner (1956) studied groups of boys who were assigned fictitious scores for success in operating switches that activated various combinations of lights. The scores correlated .93 with their nomination as team captain. Observations of success appeared to reinforce the group's perception of a member's suitability for the leadership role. Katz, Blau, Brown, and Strodtbeck (1957) found that the greater the extent to which the leader's suggestions were reinforced by the follower's acceptance and support in the first session of a discussion task, the more the leadership was retained in later sessions. Likewise, York (1969) and Hastorf (1965) demonstrated that reinforcement of member's behavior in a group significantly increased their leadership.

Hamblin, Miller, and Wiggins (1961) studied the effects on a group's morale of the leader's competence, reinforcement of the leader, and conflicting suggestions by group members. Reinforcement rate, perceptions of the leader's competence, manipulation of the leader's success, and the group's morale were all highly and significantly intercorrelated. The members' opposition to the leaders' suggestions was reduced by reinforcement of the leader, the leader's success and competence, and the group's morale. Mausner and Bloch (1957) found that reinforcement of a partner and the partner's prestige interacted in a judgmental task. That is, both the partner's prestige and earlier reinforcement contributed to the partner's influence in a condition of success but not when failure was contrived. Reinforcement did not overcome the effect of a partner's failure to make correct judgments in a previous situation.

Caveats. Some qualifying considerations are in order. Reinforcements may have unintended and unwanted effects on attempted and successful leadership. Zdep (1969) assembled groups of four members in which one member scored either high or low in self-reported leadership (the Leadership Scale of the California Psychological Inventory). Under the experimenter's reinforcement, the participation rate increased for high scorers but not for low scorers. As the high scorers' rate of participation rose, the subsequent leadership ratings by the other members increased. But the experimenter's reinforcement of one member built up expectations about that member among the others. Low scorers who failed to respond when given the reinforcement were rated as poorer leaders than low scorers who were not so reinforced. Aiken (1965b) also found that the use of reinforcement for operant conditioning of specific behaviors, such as giving suggestions and asking for contributions, resulted in marked changes in leadership style but produced a tense, anxious leader. This finding suggested that simple reinforcement technology, by itself, may be inadequate for leadership training. The shaping of one member's responses must take into consideration the larger context of the interaction with other active participants.[3]

The Dynamics of the Exchange Relationship

The superior-subordinate relationship has been conceived of as a social exchange or negotiated transaction. This conception led to a fully developed theory to explain

[3] More about this will follow in Chapter 16, which examines limitations of and constraints on the use of contingent reinforcement to shape subordinates' and leaders' behavior.

the effects of leadership on the compliance of subordinates. Leader-member exchange implied an informally developed role—one that was negotiated between each individual group member and the leader (Graen, 1976).[4] Coworkers may get involved in the role definition, but the leader, in particular, has a vested interest in the member's role. The definition of a member's role indicates what the member and the leader will expect the member to do. This was found with 62 new nonacademic employees on a college campus by Graen, Dansereau, Minami, and Cashman (1973). Given the leader's control of reinforcements, the interpersonal exchange relationship of the member and leader is particularly important in shaping the member's performance.

The leader-follower transactional exchange is the essence of the dynamics of leadership, according to Hollander (1958, 1978). Hollander concluded that the leader and the follower enter into an exchange that begins with negotiation to establish what is being exchanged and whether it is satisfactory. The exchange results in the follower's compliance for the leader's assistance in pointing the way toward the attainment of mutual goals.

Idiosyncrasy Credit

In real life, there is no experimenter to reinforce the attempts of one member rather than another to lead. On a playing field with similar personalities and a common situation, what, then, makes one member a leader and another a follower? According to Hollander, it is a matter of how much *idiosyncrasy credit* each member has previously earned. The interplay that determines who will lead and who will follow builds up idiosyncrasy credit for the emerging leader relative to the follower. Competence in the group's task and conformity to the group's norms earn idiosyncrasy credit for a member and, as a consequence, emergence as leader or success as an appointed leader. A buildup of such credit makes subsequent initiatives even more likely to be accepted and strengthens the

[4]First known as vertical-dyad linkage theory (Dansereau, Cashman, & Graen, 1973), the theory of leader-member exchange implies that there is a different exchange relationship between each individual member and the leader. An analysis of the leader's relationship with the average member or the group cannot account for the differences in these exchanges. Leader-member exchange is likely to be coded as LMX in the literature, to contrast it with theory and analysis based on the average group member's relation with the leader (ALS).

member's status as a leader. With idiosyncrasy credit, the emerging leader can deviate from the group's norms in a way that is not permitted to those without such credit. Newcomers, for instance, are unlikely to have the necessary credit, although some may bring derivative credit with them from another group as a consequence of their reputation in that group. There is a complex interplay between the requisite competence and the requisite conformity in maintaining idiosyncrasy credit. Alvarez (1968) observed that a leader's greater deviance from the norms was tolerated when it was accompanied by the group's success. In a study of a simulated organization, Alvarez found that the leader lost credit at a slower rate than did the followers, but only in successful organizations. In unsuccessful organizations, the leader lost credit at a faster rate than the followers.

Consistent with the concept of idiosyncrasy credit, Zierden (1980) suggested that leading through the followers' points of view is the way to achieve success and effectiveness as a leader. Litzinger and Schaefer (1982, p. 139) saw the fundamental conformity of leaders to their followers' norms and values as being manifested in the way the Pope John Paul II called himself "The Servant of the Servants of God" and in Hegel's conception of leadership: "Leadership is possible . . . not only on the condition that followership has been learned, but on the more radical condition that the leader has known . . . the travail of the follower; he must here and now incorporate within himself all that the follower is. The school for leadership is indeed followership, a followership that is fully preserved within leadership, but transformed for having moved beyond itself." Litzinger and Schaefer also saw the idea that good followership precedes good leadership in the West Point faculty doctrine that leadership is developed by cadets first learning how to be good followers. Prior to gaining powerful office, many world leaders, such as Otto von Bismarck and George H. W. Bush, were seen as "faithful takers of orders." To be elected, the first President Bush strongly espoused the norms of the majority of the electorate about law enforcement, the flag, taxes, education, and the environment. Once he was elected, his actions could deviate to some extent from these espousals without alienating too much of his majority constituency. President Bill Clinton consulted public opinion polls daily. President George W. Bush spoke of the political capital he earned by winning reelection in 2004, which would make it possible for him to launch new programs. But he failed to recognize that he could rapidly lose his credit with increasingly unpopular policies such as "staying the course" in Iraq. By February 2006, according to a Zogby-LeMoyne (2006) poll, only 23% of 944 American soldiers serving in Iraq supported staying as long as necessary. They agreed with polls of previous civilian majorities that the policy was wrong. But President George W. Bush said that to be successful, all he had to do was continue to ignore his critics and please the majority of voters who had elected him. By 2008, it was clear that a majority of citizens had no desire for an open-ended war in Iraq and wished for an exit strategy to be developed.

Limitations on Idiosyncrasy Credit. With idiosyncrasy credit, the leader can step out from the rest of the pack and suggest innovations that will bring about changes in the group. Nevertheless, although the leader is able to deviate from the group's norm, he or she must continue to pay attention to the group's norms, values, and standards in order to remain successful in influencing others. Holders of idiosyncrasy credit have other limitations on the deviance that they are permitted. For example, they have less latitude to deviate from particular role obligations (Hollander, 1961a, 1961b), although they may deviate from norms with less cost than other members. In effect, the leader's freedom to deviate from general norms is exchanged for conforming more closely to the expectation others have about the requirements of the leader's role.

A leader will lose much of his or her idiosyncrasy credit by an outrageous violation of the members' expectations. In 2006 President George W. Bush got into trouble with his supporters as well as his critics and lost a lot of credit when, after five years of creating a climate of fear by maintaining that terrorism was the greatest continuing threat to national security and well-being, he gave immediate and strong support for a firm owned by an Arab country to take over the management of six U.S. seaports (Krugman, 2006). Ironically, the port deal was innocuous. Still, his policy of "staying the course" in Iraq became increasingly unpopular and resulted, in June 2006, in his accepting a plan for a phased withdrawal of American troops.

There is experimental evidence about possible limits of deviation from norms. Hollander (1961a) conducted an experiment in which the participants were given brief descriptions of persons who were to be ranked from high to low in accorded status. The participants were then given lists of behaviors that might be exhibited by the persons whom they had ranked. As the perceived status of those who were ranked increased, the participants expressed progressively less disapproval for "suggesting changes from group plans" and "discussing group concerns with outsiders." However, "interrupting others to make comments" was increasingly disapproved for persons with increasing status. High-status members were permitted to innovate group changes but were not expected to interrupt low-status members.

Looking at the same issue, Michener and Lawler (1975) found that group members were more likely to endorse the continuance of leaders in their positions when the groups were positively reinforced by success in their efforts, when the members got more rewards than the leader, or when the leaders were not permanently fixed in the office. But the members were less enthusiastic about endorsing the continuance of leaders in office if the leaders were inconsistent in their competence or fairness. Polansky, Lippitt, and Redl (1950a) and Grosser, Polansky, and Lippitt (1951) showed that those group members who attempted to be more influential and those who were more successful in this attempt were more susceptible to contagious influence from other members. Compared with members who tried but failed to exert influence on the group, they were more likely to act in reference to the demands of the group situation than in terms of their own needs. Although they were able to react spontaneously to others and to initiate spontaneity in others, they also felt secure enough to resist direct attempts by others to influence them. They could maintain conformity to the steady state as well as enlarge the other members' freedom to act.

Negotiation of Equity

In the social exchange, followers may exert influence and make demands on the leader. Negotiation may be required about what will be done and by whom. The negotiation may consider the distribution of effort and rewards between the leader and the followers, including need, justice, merit, equity, and fairness. Dyer, Lambert, and

Tracy (1953) observed that in the more effective of two bomber wings (the wing in which the most successful leadership was likely), there were more favorable attitudes toward the method of allocating rewards and punishments. A satisfactory interchange between the leader and followers has been found to be enhanced by mutual trust (Deutsch, 1973), a sense of fairness and equity, mutual support, involvement, and wider latitudes of acceptance (Dansereau & Dumas, 1977; Graen, 1976). But the interdependence of the followers affected how important equity was the satisfactory exchange. According to Miller and Hamblin (1963), differential rewarding for relative achievement decreased a group's productivity when the members were highly interdependent but not when they were less interdependent.

True equity would require that rewards be commensurate with contributions. But equity is relative. Members judge the equity of their costs and benefits in comparison with the costs and benefits of others whom they regard as similar to them (J. S. Adams, 1963). Negotiations may be between the leader and the group or between the leader and each individual member. Graen and Cashman (1975) suggested that such individualized exchanges will be closer to the parties involved than an exchange between the leader and the group would be. Such closeness will increase acceptance of more responsible tasks by the individual members and also increase the leader's assistance of the members. There will also be more support, sensitivity, and trust in the closer relationship.

Limits to Contingent Reinforcement

How much can a leader depend on using contingent reinforcement? What limits it? What moderates its use and its impact on subordinates? Like most other concepts and practices in social science, contingent reinforcement is neither a universal panacea nor of trivial importance. Rather, the limitations to its use and effectiveness need to be detailed. For instance, subordinates may take shortcuts to complete the exchange of reward for compliance. Quality may be sacrificed to obtain rewards for quantity of output. Complicated piece-rate, reward, and bonus systems generate ambiguity and are likely to induce game playing and a fear of rate busting. Subordinates may react defensively. Reaction formation, withdrawal, or hostility

may ensue. Also, the schedule of reinforcements—their timeliness, variability, and consistency—will have considerable effect on the inducements (Bass, 1985a).

Perceptions of injustice may outweigh cost-benefit considerations. Tyler, Rasinski, and McGraw (1985) found that the changes in the governmental benefits that 584 undergraduates and 300 Chicago residents personally received were less important to them than more abstract judgments of injustice when they endorsed their leaders. In the same way, federal managers regarded merit-based pay as inequitable and as undermining their agencies' effectiveness. However, they believed that performance appraisal and performance standards contributed to supervisor-subordinate communications and to the planning of work, particularly if the appraisals and standards focused on the subordinates' development (Gaertner & Gaertner, 1985). Silverman (1983) argued that the merit-pay contingent reward system in the federal government failed for numerous political, economic, and psychological reasons, including open-ended regulations, drifting implementation policies, overcomplication, inconsistent treatment of employees, the compression of managers' pay, and simultaneous budget reductions. To this list could be added administrative blunders and unintended statutory provisions. Pearce, Stevenson, and Perry (1985) collected data two years before and two years after the introduction of a merit-pay program in the Social Security Administration and found no improvement in organizational performance.

Pay and Performance

As was already noted, contingent rewards for compliance may entail recommended increases in pay or advancement. If it is possible to make pay fully contingent on performance, such as by placing employees on a straight piece-rate or straight commission basis, productivity may rise as much as 30%, according to some studies. But in practice, for most work, there is likely to be little linkage between pay and performance, despite revealed wisdom to the contrary. Often when workers are placed on a piece-rate or straight commission basis, the work group exerts strong pressure to restrict all its members to conform to the same standard output so that all earn the same pay (Rothe, 1960, 1961). At the executive level, Barkema and Gomez-Mejia (1998) have argued for linking pay to performance, but within a larger framework of a long-term orientation and relative to a designated level of compensation. They recognize that in addition to performance, compensation should reflect market conditions, peer compensation, personal and positional factors, and the size of operations. Miscellaneous other factors need to be considered, such as the tax system, industry regulation, and the ownership structure.

In Japan, a familiar practice is to link pay and promotion primarily to age and seniority, not meritorious performance. In the United States, according to an interview study of a representative sample of 845 U.S. workers by Yankelovich and Immerwahr (1983), only 22% said there was a direct relationship between how hard they worked and how much they were paid. A similar representative national survey of 5,000 U.S. employees found that only 28% saw a correlation between the salaries and performance of workers (Anonymous, 1988b). In the first survey, 61 percent said they preferred a closer link between performance and pay.[5] In the second survey, almost half the respondents said that managers at their firms were too lenient with underperformers and continued to reward them despite their continuing poor performance. Even when rewards have been found to be distributed according to merit, the link is modest. Lawler (1966c) surveyed 600 middle- and lower-level managers in several organizations and discovered only a small correlation between their pay and their performance ratings. In examining salary ranges at a single corporation, Patten (1968b) found no statistically significant evidence that employees whose performance was rated more highly were also paid better. Heneman (1973) reported one instance of a high correlation between performance and reward: .65 for a sample of 51 managers. In line with these contradictory findings, Kopelman and Reinharth (1982) found much variation in the correlation between performance and reward among 10 branches of a large financial organization.

Contingent Recommendations

In contracts, the compensation of chief executive officers (CEOs) is usually related to industry norms and comparable firms and depends not only on a CEO's performance but also on the size and scope of the organization

---

(Deckop, 1987). Firms going into bankruptcy may award the CEO a multimillion-dollar compensation because of contractual obligations, not the CEO's performance. However, Gomez-Mejia, Tosi, and Hinkin (1987) found that the compensation of CEOs was linked to their performance if the firms were owner-controlled.

In simulations, recommended pay increases by 4,255 managers in an international survey correlated with meritorious performance, although they were modified extensively outside North America for other reasons, such as family considerations and personal circumstances (Bass, Burger, et al., 1979). Nonetheless, awarding more pay or less pay to subordinates seems to be a matter of the recommenders' values. Bass (1968a) reported that students' value orientations were related to their generosity in recommending pay increases for fictitious engineers. Students who were lower in intelligence and ability and those who scored high in social and service values, as opposed to theoretical and economic values, were more generous in recommending salary increases. In the international survey, Bass, Burger, et al. (1979) found that more successful managers recommended significantly greater salary increases for a fictitious average meritorious engineer, but they were no different from their slower-climbing counterparts in their salary recommendations for engineers on other grounds. In another simulation, Martin (1987) showed that recommendations increased for both meritorious performance and specialized expertise needed in particular circumstances.

Moderating Conditions

Time and events can modify the influence of the same behavior by leaders that was effective earlier, and subordinates' reactions to it. Similar behavior by the leader can be ineffective (Sleeth & Showalter, 2000). This is a case of negative transfer of an old response to a new stimulus. A breakdown can occur. A leader can lose control of a situation by ignoring the changes caused by an event. For example, suppose that a leader is accustomed to loosely monitoring an operation, but a new employee who needs close supervision enters the scene. The same leadership is now inadequate. A breakdown can occur in the operation.

In managerial in-basket experiments by Martin and Harder (1988), students' use of simulated financial-

---

[5] Many other empirical studies support this finding. See, for instance, F. S. Hills (1979), W. J. Kearny (1979), and H. H. Meyer (1975).

related rewards, such as profit sharing, office space, and company cars, was contingent on satisfactory performance; but simulated interpersonal rewards, such as help or friendliness, were distributed according to subordinates' needs.

Managers may lack the necessary reward power required to deliver recommendations for pay increases. Those who can fulfill the self-interested expectations of their subordinates gain and maintain the reputation of being able to deliver pay, promotions, and recognition. Those who fail to deliver lose that reputation in the eyes of their subordinates and, therefore, no longer can be seriously seen as effective contingent reward leaders (Tsui, 1982). Worse yet, they may be seen as having become more punitive, and their legitimacy and influence will be reduced (Greene & Podsakoff, 1979, 1981). Subordinates' resistance will increase according to Tepper, Schriesheim, et al. (1998), who asked a sample of 389 respondents to recall an instance within the last month in which they resisted and avoided doing something their supervisor asked them to do. Thirty-two scale items were extracted from the responses. These items formed two factors: (1) passive resistance ("I procrastinate, hoping that my supervisor will forget about it"; "I say OK but don't get to it"; "I don't do it in a timely manner") and (2) active resistance ("I explain that the request will not yield the expected results"; "I explain that it should be done differently"; "I present logical reasons for doing the task differently or at a different time"). In multiple regression analyses for 133 subordinates of 50 managers in a mental health rehabilitation organization, scores for passive resistance were higher if they worked for abusive supervisors and were less conscientious on the NEOAC Personality Inventory. Active resistance was higher if they worked for higher-status managers and were more open and less agreeable on the personality inventory.

Yukl (1981) enumerated the conditions that made it possible for managers to engage profitably in the contingent rewarding of their employees. As was already indicated, the managers needed substantial authority and discretion to administer tangible rewards to their subordinates. Their subordinates had to be dependent on them for access to the valued rewards. It was necessary for performance outcomes to be determined primarily by the subordinates' efforts and skills, rather than by events be-

yond the subordinates' control. It was also necessary to be able to measure the subordinates' performance accurately. Finally, contingent reward was likely to have more impact if the work was "repetitive, boring, and tedious, rather than varied, interesting, and meaningful" (p. 141).

Positive versus Negative Reinforcement

In the Soviet Union, workers were fined for failing to meet production quotas. Workers everywhere face suspensions for infractions of rules. A sufficient cause for dismissal may be simply displeasing a domineering boss. Feedback can be negative as well as positive. As indicated in earlier chapters, such contingent penalization, in general, is less effective than contingent reward. After observing 126 incidents of feedback, Balcazar, Hopkins, and Suarez (1985–1986) noted that feedback does not uniformly improve performance. In a survey by Ilgen, Fisher, and Taylor (1979), the role ambiguity of 527 Australian employees was reduced much more by positive rather than negative feedback about their performance. Although the effect of positive feedback is to reinforce behavior already displayed and hence to generate more of the same, for negative feedback to be effective, changes are required in performance as a consequence of changes in perception, motivation, or learning. Also, negative feedback may fail to work because of its unfavorable motivational impact on the subordinate's self-image.[6]

Disciplinary actions may cause emotional reactions and a deterioration of supervisory-subordinate relations instead of their intended correctional effects, according to a survey of 177 firefighters in eight cities (Greer & Labig, 1987). The unintended results will occur if the administration of the actions is unpleasant, if poor relations already exist, and if the supervisor is judged to be inaccurate in his diagnosis and fails to represent adequate reasons for the disciplinary action.

Despite its potential to contribute to conflict and its relatively lower contributions to the improvement of subordinates, negative reinforcement is often used. There are many reasons for "accenting the negative," despite the greater utility of emphasizing the positive and despite the decreased contribution of such leadership to the performance of subordinates. For instance, a supervisor may

[6]It will make a difference if the negative feedback is sought by the recipient.

have a large span of control; as a consequence, the supervisor's time may be fully occupied with monitoring deviations from the standard. Failure to pay attention to the deviations may invite disaster. A preoccupation with prospective failures will inhibit attention to the positive, particularly in the absence of clear goals, clear policies, and long-term objectives. Managers may lack the power to provide or recommend rewards. Faced with continuing demands for productivity, they will increase their tendency to use punishment, especially since managers report less difficulty identifying poor performance than good performance (Podsakoff, 1982).

Performance of subordinates that is below standard is more salient for a supervisor than performance that exceeds the standard (Larson, 1980). Thus subjects who were acting as supervisors were found, in a laboratory experiment by Fisher (1979), to require a smaller sample of work to evaluate a subordinate who was performing below average than to evaluate one who was performing above average. Larson (1980, p. 199) offered the following reasons for the greater sensitivity of supervisors to the failure rather than to the success of subordinates: "The criteria for minimally acceptable . . . performance are frequently more clearly defined than are the criteria for superior performance; poor performance often has a more significant impact upon the work group's functioning than does superior performance." Supervisors are likely to be more sensitive to their subordinates' failure if how well the supervisors do their job depends on how well the subordinates have completed assignments and if, as was noted earlier, the supervisors' pay, recognition, or promotion depends on the subordinates' performance (Larson, 1980).

Other Problems

Contingent reinforcement may fail because there is no clear differentiation of reinforcements for functionally adequate and functionally inadequate performance. Praise alone, without other accompanying rewards, may not work. Feedback may lack impact because goals have not been clearly set. In addition, to understand the effects of reinforcement leadership, according to Fedor, Buckley, and Eder (1990), the impact on a subordinate's behavior of a supervisor's attempts at differential reinforcement of the subordinate will depend on the subordinate's perception of the supervisor's intentions: "Does the supervisor want to dominate me, to focus my attention on unit standards, to support me, or to urge me to increase my productivity?" Many of the 220 subordinates in this study believed it was most likely that their supervisor wanted to dominate them rather than to support or assist them in achieving higher performance levels. This belief may be due, in part, to the tendency of subordinates to attribute their poor performance to situational causes like bad luck or difficulties with the problem, equipment, or supplies. As the observers of the subordinates' behavior, the supervisors, especially if they are unfamiliar with the specific tasks involved, are more likely to attribute the poor performance to the subordinates' lack of ability or a lack of effort. Mitchell and Kalb (1982) showed that if the supervisor had no experience with the subordinate's job, he or she was less likely to accept situational reasons for the subordinate's performance. Whether a supervisor likes or dislikes a subordinate also makes a difference. According to an experiment and field study by Dobbins and Russell (1986), although leaders may attribute the same reason for the poor performance of subordinates they like and subordinates they dislike, they will tend to act more punitively toward the subordinates they dislike and will be less inclined to punish the subordinates they like.

A Jackass Theory? Many scholars, consultants, and practitioners find contingent reinforcement a full and sufficient driving force for predicting, controlling, and understanding leader-follower relations. Many others are considerably less confident. Still others find that faults and failures override its successful applications. Levinson (1980) termed contingent reinforcement the "jackass theory" of leadership: When you, as a subordinate, are between a carrot and a stick, tempted by the carrot or threatened with the stick, it makes you feel like a jackass. Your self-esteem as a mature, conscientious, worthy individual is diminished. Furthermore, when you are between a carrot and a stick, you may see yourself in a contest that requires agility to reach the carrot or to avoid the stick. Or you may be immobilized by uncertainty, not knowing whether the benefits of the carrot are outweighed by the costs of being beaten by the stick. Feelings of being manipulated may outweigh responsiveness to the contingent rewards. Drawing from Dostoyevsky, Vice Admiral J. B. Stockdale (1981, p. 15) argued that people do not like to feel they are being programmed: "You cannot persuade [people] to act in their own self-interest all of the time. A good leader appreciates contrariness. . . . Some men all of the time and all men some of the time knowingly will do what is clearly to their disadvantage if only because they do not like to be suffocated by carrot-and-stick coercion. I will not be a piano key; I will not bow to the tyranny of reason."

As Maccoby (1988) noted, with increasing technology and its servicing, employees are expected to work and think as mature persons. They are expected to make judgments; to solve problems; to develop good working relationships with colleagues, clients, and customers; and to be committed to and understand what they are doing. These expectations require a broader view of what motivates people to work. About half the sample studied by Maccoby regarded themselves as experts who got much of their reward from doing the work itself. Being helpful to others and maintaining good relationships are important to many employees. Although about a fifth of the sample were interested in material rewards, their self-development of a full career and personal life was more important to them.

Simple carrot-and-stick supervisory reinforcement clearly has considerable limitations. It will not work well in the absence of a trusting relationship between superiors and subordinates. Subordinates need to trust that their leaders can fulfill their promises. Leaders must be able to trust that their subordinates will comply as expected rather than take shortcuts or superficial actions to achieve promised rewards (Dwivedi, 1983). Many other forces constrain the superiors' intentions when they use reinforcement to deal with their subordinates' performance. These forces include information requirements, conflicting interests, biased perceptions, differential use of reward and punishment, and individual differences in reaction to contingent rewards.

Conflicts. Contingent reinforcement may fail to achieve the compliance of subordinates because intrapersonal or interpersonal conflicts may be involved. For instance, the leader may establish dyadic contingent reinforcement with each member of a group, although the members need to reach decisions in a highly coordinated fashion. The members may suffer from *pluralistic ignorance*, each subordinate not knowing every other member's views (Schanck, 1932). Or the members may find the costs greater than the promised benefits and, wishing to avoid confrontation with the leader, they may withdraw into anomie, apathy, or alienation. Followers may also rationalize, concluding that the leader's demands on them are excessive or that the leader is incompetent. Ansbacher (1948) interviewed German prisoners of war during World War II, providing extensive evidence that although many continued to esteem Adolf Hitler and maintain confidence in him, they personally disagreed with him on many significant issues and interpreted his directions to suit their own needs. For example, Hitler demanded that Germany should never capitulate. But a majority of those who had confidence in him decided that he did not really want unnecessary bloodshed; therefore, they thought he would consider it his duty to end a lost war. And so, despite the fact that Hitler issued explicit orders that soldiers were to fight to the end, his supporters rationalized that it was all right to surrender.

Ephemeral or Negative Effects. Contingent reinforcement may succeed only in the short run, or sometimes not at all. In some circumstances, feedback about one's job performance actually may be counterproductive and yield negative results, as Kiggundu (1983) reported for 138 employees at a head office. Greene's (1979a) longitudinal study of new employees during their first nine months of work found that the subordinates' performance, compliance, and satisfaction improved because of contingent rewards by the leader. Satisfaction accompanied the leader's rewarding of subordinates for their good performance, and dissatisfaction emerged from the leader's punishment of the subordinates for their poor performance. But the effects mainly occurred earlier in the subordinates' employment. Contingent reinforcement may generate conflicting deleterious side effects that contribute to long-term failure. For example, subordinates may continue to accept the top managers' direction but displace their aggression onto less powerful targets. Purcell (1953) found that packinghouse employees were more ready to blame their lower-status supervisors than their top managers for difficulties entailed in trying to comply with directions.

Biased Perceptions. Despite Peterson's (1985b) conclusion that, in general, rewards for good performance tend to be effective, many errors are likely to be made in the application of contingent reward. Leaders' performance evaluations are likely to be biased. Subordinates are likely to overestimate their own performance and that of their peers. Also, biased judgments may work both ways. Subordinates may inflate the attractiveness of an order to justify their compliance with it (Campbell, Dunnette, Lawler, & Weick, 1970). Furthermore, subordinates' attributions of the reasons for the leader's behavior will affect their satisfaction with it. And a leader whom subordinates judge to be willing but incompetent may be more forgivable than a leader who is judged to be competent but unwilling (Bass, 1982). The same leadership behavior—say, initiation of structure—has been seen more favorably by managers than by graduate students, although a more punitive emphasis on pushing for production was seen more unfavorably by both managers and students (Butterfield & Bartol, 1977).

Contingent Reinforcement May Be Avoided or Ignored. The use of contingent reinforcement is not essential for effective leadership or for a productive organization. Jacoby, Mazursky, Troutman, and Kuss (1984) found considerable avoidance of opportunities for obtaining feedback or ignoring it if it was given. In their simulation, they had 17 security analysts decide which common stocks represent a good purchase. During a sequence of four periods, the analysts were able to request feedback about their performance. The feedback provided results that could have predictive or explanatory value for the analysts. Some analysts did not request or consider any feedback, and other analysts were not consistent about doing so. The researchers found that the better-performing analysts were more likely than the poorer-performing analysts to ignore feedback that had no predictive or explanatory value.

Communes. When selected individuals and groups have a strong feeling of community, they have been able to maintain the high productivity that is associated with a strong work ethic without using reinforcement as the basis of their motivation to work. Communes depend even more strongly on trusting relationships than organizations where motivation to work is based on contingent reinforcement. In the Israeli kibbutz, "The underlying philosophy of the kibbutz insists that there must be no

linkage between what a particular individual is able to contribute through his efforts and . . . what rewards he is entitled to. . . . In the kibbutz, everyone is entitled—as a human being and as a member of the community—to the comprehensive satisfaction of his needs . . . subject to limitations due to the economic capacity of the particular kibbutz. . . . This right is no way infringed if, because of health or for any other reason, he is unable to contribute to the kibbutz anything at all. In this respect the kibbutz constitutes a full-scale insurance system for every member. . . . [Although there may be some slackers] the large majority of kibbutz members generally perform at their best, and the prevailing differences in efficiency are the result of individual differences in ability, rhythm, [and] energy, . . . rather than of deficient motivation" (Tsur, 1983, pp. 24, 26). The young people who leave the kibbutz to work elsewhere tend to be highly praised by their employers because of the strong self-reinforcing work ethic of the kibbutz they continue to maintain.

Group Rather Than Individual Reward. There may be much more of this group effect in the U.S. industrial sector than one ordinarily supposes, which again points to the lesser importance of contingent reinforcement to the individual employee. For example, for the 71 managers and professionals of a manufacturing facility, Markham (1988) reported a correlation of $-.03$ between their rated performance and their merit raises within their own units, but .45 between the performance ratings of all the members of a unit and the merit raises they received. In this facility, group, not individual, performance was being rewarded.

The Augmentation Effect. Bass (1985a) theorized that contingent reward can be catalyzed by transformational leadership. Empirical support came from Waldman, Bass, and Einstein (1987) and Waldman, Bass, and Yammarino (1988) and indirectly from Schriesheim, Castro, Zhou, et al. (2006). The leadership of Ernest Shackleton, whose men overcame formidable obstacles in the Antarctic—or the leadership of Joan of Arc, Martin Luther King, Jr., Mahatma Gandhi, or Winston Churchill—can be perceived as leadership that added to any cost-benefit exchange a transformation of the followers' needs from those at lower levels to higher-level concerns for achievement, glory, humanity, fortune, country, faith, or family, demanding excessive costs relative to tangible benefits. Self-interest was transcended; cost-benefit calculations were abandoned. It is difficult to conceive of the emotional response to the Ayatollah Khomeini in the rush to martyrdom during the Iranian-Iraqi war by the Iranian masses or the terrorist suicide bombers since then, merely as a social cost-benefit exchange between a leader and followers. On the positive side of reinforcement, appeals to self-interests alone will not result ultimately in leadership that is able to reward followers as much as they want. Continued attention to followers' self-interests alone will not permit a group, organization, or society to operate optimally. A culture of cooperation is needed, as is trust in the benefit of optimal organizational outcomes. A prosocial charismatic leader who appeals to interests that transcend the individual member will be more likely to create such a culture than a leader who is limited to contingent reinforcement and the use of individual incentives (Miller, 1987). In the public sector, political leadership must appeal to both self-interests and shared values (Meier, 1988). In the early twenty-first century moral issues have become as important as bread-and-butter issues to American voters. The shared environment has become as powerful a political issue as self-interested economic gains. A 50-cent increase in the federal gasoline tax (from 18 cents) was supported by 70% of the American public as a response to automobile pollution and global warming.

Individual Differences. Contingent reinforcement may also be irrelevant if the subordinate attaches no importance or value to the reinforcement—if the subordinate is not interested in the rewards, promises of reward, or avoidance of punishment (Ilgen, Fisher, & Taylor, 1979). Subordinates' indifference may be due to low expectations that satisfactory levels can be attained to merit the rewards or that the promises of reward will be kept (Larson, 1984).

Beyond the specialized circumstance of communal living or group reinforcement, one finds that individuals differ in their preference for external or self-reinforcement. In a survey of 339 utility company managers, Parsons, Herold, and Turlington (1981) found that the managers varied in their preference for external feedback—that is, in their agreement with the statement, "Even though I may think I have done a good job, I feel a lot more

confident of it after someone else tells me so." They also differed in their ability and tendency to reinforce themselves—that is, in agreeing that "If I have done something well, I know it without other people telling me so" and "As long as I think that I have done something well, I am not too concerned about how other people think I have done." Bass (1967c) concluded that task-oriented subordinates and experienced subordinates are more likely to be self-reinforcing, whereas relations-oriented and self-oriented subordinates are more likely to be sensitive to both positive and negative reinforcement from others.

One is likely to see personally counterdependent followers working in opposition to what the leader intended with contingent rewards. Much of this reverse twist may also be seen in personally independent and even dependent followers. Among five styles of leadership—(1) directive, (2) manipulative, (3) consultative, (4) participative, and (5) delegative—displayed by large samples of managers, Bass, Valenzi, Farrow, and Solomon (1975) found manipulative leadership least satisfying to subordinates and least effective with them. But the managers' superiors may not find fault with the manipulative potential of the managers in practicing contingent reinforcement. In fact, manipulative managers are more successful with higher-ups in that they earn salaries, after adjustment for their seniority, function, education, sex, and organization, that are higher than average (Farrow, Valenzi, & Bass, 1981).

Constraints on the Use and Impact of Feedback

Feedback is not always effective (Fedor, Buckley, & Eder, 1990). In fact, according to a meta-analysis by DiNisi & Kluger (2000), among 131 studies of feedback, 38% were ineffective in outcomes. Overall, the improvement in performance from feedback was less than half a standard deviation. Numerous factors constrain the use and impact of downward feedback, in which supervisory contingent reward is delivered. These factors include problems with the performance appraisal interviews, coping with unintentional consequences, and a reluctance to give feedback. For instance, among 508 air force personnel, lack of feedback was one of the highest concerns of leadership and management (Kunich & Lester, 1996). Even when given, it is not very helpful if it is insufficiently frequent, if it comes too late, if it is not based on evidence, if it is a one-way discourse instead of a dialogue, or if it is unclear or inaccurate. Rather, feedback should be timely, flexible, direct, specific, and descriptive (Hughes, Ginnet, & Curphy, 1993); and it should be about the subordinate's performance, not the subordinate as a person: "Your report came in too late to be used," not "You're too slow" (Kluger & DiNisi, 1996). DiNisi and Kluger's meta-analysis indicated that for improvement in performance, feedback must focus on the recipients' performance, not on their self-concept. Furthermore, the recipient's ego must not be threatened. Information on how to improve should be included; the performance of specific others should be excluded.

Reluctance to Give Positive Feedback

Contingent reinforcement may be constrained by the reluctance of some supervisors to give positive feedback. Komaki (1981) offered numerous reasons for this reluctance: time pressure, poor appraisal methods, doubts about the efficacy of positive reinforcement, lack of skill, and discomfort to the leader and the subordinate. Feldman (1986, p. 39) offered a number of reasons why some supervisors may avoid giving positive feedback: "Who among us has not found, much to our chagrin, that our praise, rewards, and favors often go unnoticed and unthanked? . . . Consider the colleague who responds to subordinates' efforts above and beyond the call of duty with no comment, as if those efforts were simply his due. Consider the supervisor who compliments a subordinate for a job well done, and receives in return a comment like 'No thanks to you.' "

Subordinates may interpret feedback as a signal that the superior expects them to continue to perform at a high level. In such a case, the subordinates will regard the positive reinforcement as pressure to keep performing at the top of their capacity. Particularly when positive reinforcement is rare, subordinates may be ambivalent about receiving it for fear of becoming emotionally dependent on the good opinion of the supervisor, a good opinion that may easily be lost. Subordinates with low self-esteem will be jarred by the contrasting praise given to them and will evaluate it as only a momentary departure from their generally poor performance. Furthermore, the positive feedback that is given is often actually trivial and meaningless, or it may be interpreted as such. The supervisor who gives it frequently may be seen as politically motivated, manipulative, ingratiating, and insincere. Feldman (1986) agreed that positive feedback will be less favorably received when it is given frequently and for trivialities than when it is given only for unusually good performance.

Subordinates who are in conflict with their supervisors may react defensively to positive feedback and even interpret it as negative feedback or a precursor of negative feedback. "When receiving praise, some people may be waiting, like Pavlov's dog, for the anticipated punishment to follow" (Feldman, 1986, p. 40).

Feedback May Not Work

Even if positive feedback is given, it may not provide the expected reinforcement. Subordinates may not believe that positive feedback from a supervisor is a consequence of their performance. Rather, they may perceive that the supervisor praises when he or she feels like doing so, not when the performance is good. Subordinates may also believe that positive reinforcement is too small or inequitable, which makes the subordinate angry because the subordinate believes that more of a reward should have been given for the performance. Finally, subordinates may feel a need to reciprocate and give unjustified, unwarranted positive feedback to the supervisor, and they will resent feeling pressured to do so.

Gaddis, Connelly, and Mumford (2004) set up an experiment to study the effects of a leader's feedback that a subordinate had failed. Negative affect of the leader accompanying the feedback (as compared with positive affect) reduced the leader's perceived effectiveness and lowered the quality of performance.

Reluctance to Give Negative Feedback

Supervisory negative feedback may be delayed, distorted, or avoided following poor subordinate performance whether or not the poor performance is attributed to lack of effort or failure of mastery of what needs to be done (Moss & Martinko, 1998).

Attitudes about Discipline, Reprimands, and Punishment. Although some supervisors and subordinates may find even positive feedback discomforting, many more are reluctant to give and receive negative feedback (Larson, 1986; Sims & Manz, 1984). An experiment by C. D. Fisher (1979) with 168 college students indicated that "supervisors" gave feedback sooner when the "subordinates'" performance was poor than when it was good; but Fisher believed that the results would be reversed in any long-term field study, since supervisors in real life are more likely to be reluctant to give negative feedback. It is one thing to say something negative to a stranger in a transient experience than to say it to someone with whom one will remain in close contact. Managers often are reluctant to discipline an employee because it is an unpleasant task for most of them. Discipline and friendship are difficult to maintain side by side (Harrison, 1982). Nevertheless, numerous factors contribute to supervisors' willingness to use punishment. These factors include positive attitudes about punishment (O'Reilly & Weitz, 1980), supervisors' independence of their subordinates' performance (Ilgen, Mitchell, & Fredrickson, 1981), subordinates' poor performance relative to coworkers' (Ivancevich, 1983), and supervisors' lack of reward power (Greene & Podsakoff, 1979/1981).

Salience of Poor Performance. It may take a considerable worsening of a subordinate's performance for a supervisor to overcome his or her reluctance to give negative feedback (Larson, 1986) although, as was mentioned earlier, subordinates' poor performance is more salient to supervisors than their subordinates' good performance. The salience of the poor performance must outweigh how much the supervisor personally admires a subordinate. A supervisor may avoid giving negative feedback for poor performance to avoid risking a deterioration in personal relationships with subordinates. The supervisor may also be less likely to attribute poor performance to subordinates if relations with the subordinates are good (Bass, 1985a).

Use of Distortion. When supervisors are faced with poor performance that they attribute to the subordinates' lack of ability, they tend to pull their punches. They distort their feedback and make it more positive than it should be (Fisher, 1979; Ilgen & Knowlton, 1980). Programmatic efforts to change the supervisor's feedback behavior were not successful (Frank & Hackman, 1975; French, Kay, & Meyer, 1966). Some of this distortion may be due to the effort of the supervisor to act prosocially, to be more concerned with the subordinate's feelings than with the supervisor's or the organization's best interests. To avoid causing distress to the subordinate, the supervisor may remain lenient and avoid giving needed negative feedback.

The reluctance to give negative feedback is abetted by supervisors' tendency to search for excuses and justifications for the poor performance of subordinates. Gioia and Sims (1986) arranged for 24 experienced managers to handle a simulated performance appraisal interview. During the interviews, the managers tended to probe for excuses to justify the subordinates' performance. After the interviews, the managers reduced their blame of the poorly performing subordinates.

Other Reasons. Various other reasons may also make the supervisor reluctant to use negative feedback. The supervisor may be highly dependent on the subordinate to attain their mutual objectives (Tjosvold, 1985) or may have limited authority to bring about a punishment (Beyer & Trice, 1984). Since negative reinforcement may cause the employee to quit (Parsons, Herold, & Leatherwood, 1985), the supervisor's reluctance may be based on that concern. Political considerations may deter a supervisor from giving negative feedback for fear of the employee's retaliation. An admonished employee may file a grievance for unfair discrimination or may complain to powerful friends in the organization. The supervisor's ability and motivation to correct a problem employee are also decreased if the performance of most of the workforce is poor (Crawford, Thomas, & Fink, 1980).

Nevertheless, despite their reluctance, managers will become punitive with continuing poor performers and problem employees after asking questions and trying to solve the problems they believe are causing the poor performance (Fairhurst, Green, & Snavely, 1984). In the case of problem drinkers, for example, discipline by supervisors is widespread when the work context supports its use (Beyer & Trice, 1984). O'Reilly and Weitz (1980) found that supervisors who used informal warnings, formal warnings, and discharges led groups that performed better; but Kipnis (1976) concluded, from research evidence, that supervisors were most likely to use such sanctions when they did not expect to be successful in using their influence to improve their subordinates' performance.

Improving the Positive Effects of Negative Feedback. Salespeople said they worked harder if they had a performance orientation but said they worked harder and smarter if they had a learning orientation (Sujan, Weitz, & Kumar, 1994). A review by Ilgen and Davis (2000) concluded that feedback was more likely to be effective if the recipients believed they had control and influence regarding the performance in question, if they were oriented toward a learning rather than a performance goal, and if they were self-efficacious. If they had a learning goal, failure was legitimate. If they had a performance goal, negative feedback, if not too harsh, could generate specific alternative ways of doing the task more effectively. "Mastery goals facilitate positive . . . strategies in the face of performance decrements" (Ilgen & Davis, 2000, p. 560).

Subordinates as Moderators of Supervisors' Feedback Efforts

Fedor, Buckley, and Eder (1990) found that subordinates perceived four possible intentions for supervisors to give them feedback: (1) to build relationships, (2) to provide self-evaluation, (3) to facilitate productivity, and (4) to serve the interests of the supervisor. The subordinates' perceptions of a supervisor's intentions may have an effect on their interpretation and acceptance of feedback. By expressing dissatisfaction with the process, subordinates, the intended receivers of feedback, may also add to the reluctance of supervisors to give it (Greller, 1978). They may discourage the supervisor from efforts to provide it by frequent rejections of the supervisor, displays of hostility, and displacement of the blame onto others. Many subordinates are likely to take personal responsibility for their successes but to attribute failures to external or situational causes, such as the difficulty of a task, bad luck, or a lack of cooperation and assistance from others (Greenwald, 1980; Sims & Gioia, 1984).

Interpretation and Acceptance. The contingency between performance and outcome may be more apparent

to the subordinates when they are successful. Subordinates may expect success and tend to validate their expectations by reinterpreting as an actual success a failure that their supervisor sees. They may base their judgments of their performance on the desirability of the outcome to them personally, rather than on the explicit link between performance and outcome (Miller & Ross, 1975).

Negative feedback may be interpreted as helpful and therefore may be regarded as a contingent reward, rather than as a contingent punishment. It all depends on how the feedback is presented, how much it is embedded in sedating and palliating language, and how open the subordinates are to it. The subordinates may fail to "hear" negative feedback because they convert it into what they want to hear. Subordinates accept positive feedback more readily and recall negative feedback less accurately (Ilgen, Peterson, Martin, & Boeschen, 1981). Considerable discrepancy is found between the extent to which supervisors say they give feedback to their subordinates and the extent to which the subordinates say they receive such feedback. For example, in a survey of 178 managers and their subordinates by Mann and Dent (1954b), 82% of the managers said they gave "pats on the back" to their subordinates often, but only 13% of their subordinates agreed with them. Eighty percent of the managers said they gave subordinates sincere and thorough praise often, but only 14 percent of their subordinates agreed with them.

Context. Subordinates may ignore supervisors' feedback because it is not backed up with evidence, because it is not consistent with feedback they have received from coworkers, because they judge it to be unimportant, or because they regard self-reinforcement as more relevant. Different working situations and levels of experience of the recipients of the feedback will determine which source of feedback the subordinates think is most useful and important (DeNisi, Randolph, & Blencoe, 1983). Greller and Herold (1975) obtained results indicating that a heterogeneous sample of working people attached more importance to feedback from a higher authority than from their peers; but Pavett (1983) noted that in a hospital, feedback from patients and coworkers had a greater impact than feedback from supervisors on nurses' perceptions of the connection between delivering high-quality care and valued outcomes. In a different work setting, Ivancevich and McMahon (1982) reported that self-generated feedback about the attainment of goals did more than feedback from supervisors to improve the subordinates' performance, intrinsic job satisfaction, and commitment to the organization. And according to Greller (1980), who surveyed 26 supervisors and 63 of their subordinates in the maintenance department of a metropolitan transit agency, the subordinates attached more importance than the supervisors to the feedback from the task itself, to their own comparisons with the work of others, and to coworkers' comments about their work.

Insurance salespeople have fewer contacts with each other than do metropolitan transit employees, for whom feedback from coworkers is important. Brief and Hollenbeck (1985) found that among the 62 insurance salespeople they interviewed, the greatest amount of feedback on performance came from the supervisor and themselves, not from coworkers. Despite the general observation that we attribute our successes to ourselves and our failures to others and to external conditions, most of the contingent self-reinforcement of the insurance employees was negative, in the form of self-criticism; and it had detrimental effects on their performance.

Views about the Supervisor. Subordinates may rationalize feedback as being due to a supervisor's need to complain, the supervisor's failure to understand the situation, or the supervisor's boss's malevolence. According to Coy (1982), who conducted a laboratory experiment with undergraduates, "subordinates" were readier to accept feedback from a leader they perceived as competent rather than incompetent, particularly if the leader had a strong need for achievement. If they perceived the leader as incompetent, they would seek alternative sources of task-relevant information.

Self-Esteem. Subordinates' self-esteem will moderate their request for feedback and their acceptance of it. Those with high self-esteem set higher goals, perform at a higher level, and experience more positive affect when performing well than subordinates with low self-esteem (Taylor & Slania, 1981). Those with high self-esteem seek less information from others in making decisions and forming judgments. They are more self-reinforcing. Those with low self-esteem tend to be more dependent on social and environmental feedback (Weiss, 1977) and

are more responsive to it. Inexperienced personnel prefer to receive feedback from their superiors, but experienced personnel prefer to be more self-reinforcing (Hillery & Wexley, 1974). However, in contrast to reinforcement only from the supervisor, a combination of both self-feedback and supervisory feedback, in which the subordinate first prepares a self-appraisal and then meets to compare it with the superior's feedback, appears to reduce the subordinate's defensiveness and to bring about greater subsequent improvement in the subordinate's performance (Bassett & Meyer, 1968). Whether the subordinate seeks feedback will also be affected by his or her role ambiguity and tolerance of ambiguity (Ashford & Cummings, 1981). Whether a subordinate will improve in performance after receiving negative feedback from the supervisor will depend on the subordinate's self-esteem as well as the supervisor's sources of power (Fedor, Davis, Maslyn, et al., 2001).

Feedback Characteristics as Moderators

Problems inherent in the feedback itself may cause it to fail to work as intended. In place of the summary ratings many supervisors use, Deets and Tyler (1986) introduced detailed feedback about the specific initiation and consideration behaviors[7] of supervisors at Xerox, along with interim evaluations of the supervisors' progress toward specific personal and professional goals that were given closer to the events involved. They found a marked improvement in attitudes toward the appraisal system and toward teamwork.

The accuracy, amount, distinctiveness, consistency, and method of giving feedback (oral, written, or face-to-face) may also matter (Duncan & Bruwelheide, 1985–1986). But in a study of 360 pairs of managers and subordinates from more than 50 organizations in three countries, Larson, Glynn, Fleenor, and Scontrino (1986) found it impossible to single out the specificity of feedback from other positive features of good-quality feedback, such as its timeliness, frequency, and sensitivity. However, Quaglieri and Carnazza (1985) found that most subordinates paid attention to multiple aspects of feedback, including its accuracy, timeliness, attractiveness, and specificity, as well as to the trustworthiness, ex-

---

[7] Detailed more fully in Chapter 20.

pertise, and power of the source. Furthermore, these and other features of feedback could be experimentally manipulated. Earley (1986a) completed a field experiment in which 60 subjects believed they were in a working situation processing subscriptions. Positive feedback increased their expectations of successful performance more than did negative feedback, as expected. The subjects' performance was better than anticipated if the feedback was specific rather than general. In turn, specific feedback resulted in more planning by the subordinates, which contributed to the subordinates' better performance. However, the supervisors had less of an impact on the subordinates' performance than self-generated feedback retrieved from computer storage, particularly if the positive or negative feedback was general. Only when the supervisors' feedback was specific and negative did its effect match that of self-generated feedback. Mediating these effects was the extent to which the subordinates trusted the computer feedback more than they trusted the supervisors' feedback.

The credibility of the source of feedback is important. Feedback will be more effective if the leader is respected and trusted, if the subordinate regards the feedback as useful, and if it is delivered with consideration, tact, and support Another important consideration is whether feedback from one source is discordant with feedback from other sources (Liden & Mitchell, 1985). When one colleague finds fault with a member's behavior, the impact is much less if other colleagues do not agree.

Coping with Unintended Consequences. Contingent negative feedback may have unintended consequences. Reprimands may serve not only to increase clarity about what is undesirable behavior and to correct it (Reitz, 1971), but they can also generate unproductive anxiety. In turn, this anxiety can result in a variety of dysfunctional behaviors, such as reaction formation, guilt, and hostility, particularly in highly motivated subordinates who are already overloaded or under stress and who may interpret well-intentioned negative feedback as a personal attack (Bass, 1985a).

Komaki (1982) and Sims and Gioia (1984) suggested ways to cope with the unintended consequences and potential shortcomings of feedback processes and make better use of them. According to 60 professionals interviewed by Komaki, to increase the effective utilization of feed-

back the long-term benefits of reinforcement need to be emphasized. More positive feedback should be used, but it should not be limited just to delivering praise; it should include connections to the performance involved. Reinforcement schedules have to be adapted to fit busy schedules. Standards of performance and of performance appraisals need to be clarified.

To reduce self-serving bias among subordinates and to increase the subordinates' acceptance of negative feedback, Sims and Gioia proposed that the supervisor needs to recognize and expect the biased reaction to negative feedback for poor performance. The subordinate's acceptance of negative feedback should be positively reinforced, and efforts to cover up mistakes should be rejected. Emphasis should be placed on determining the causes of and remedies for the poor performance.

Constraints on the Performance Appraisal Interview

Problems and Possibilities

Contingent reinforcement may occur at the time the supervisor observes the subordinate's good or poor performance or in a performance appraisal interview. An annual appraisal review seems to be the norm in the United States. However, more frequent appraisal interviews are suggested for poor performers (Kay, Meyer, & French, 1965) and for subordinates in nonroutine jobs in which goals are set, progress is evaluated, and then goals are reset (Cummings & Schwab, 1973, 1978; McConkie, 1979). Numerous problems can impair the efficacy of the feedback in this interview. Reinforcement theory suggests that the feedback will be most reinforcing if it is given as soon as possible after the occurrence of the subordinate's good or poor performance. Yet the delay caused by waiting to provide the feedback in a formal interview increases the reliability of the evidence to be discussed by the supervisor and the subordinate. Such a discussion can also take into account broader systematic issues and longer-range goals and plans than could feedback given immediately after an incident. Since the supervisor and subordinate can both be better organized to give and receive the feedback, a more orderly, calm, and thoughtful exchange is possible than in the heat of the immediate operations. Of course, nothing precludes both timely feedback and feedback for an extensive period given during an appraisal interview in which the subordinates' performance during the six months or year preceding the interview is reviewed. In this formal meeting of the superior and the subordinate, the subordinate's performance during a preceding period is reviewed, evaluations are made, and suggestions for improvement are advanced. The meeting can involve the superior's and subordinate's sharing of information or it can be directed by the supervisor. The interview can be structured in a variety of ways around goals and their attainment or around traits and behavior.

Although it is an organized effort to provide positive reinforcement for good performance and negative feedback for poor performance, the performance appraisal interview may fail to improve the subordinate's subsequent performance, for numerous reasons. First, the formal feedback process tends to be constrained in use and impact by, for example, the supervisor's lack of familiarity with the subordinate's job. Second, the superior may not encourage the subordinate's participation and two-way communication in the interview (Cederblom, 1982). Other reasons for ineffective feedback during a performance appraisal include a lack of supervisory support, a lack of goals, an unfocused discussion, and a failure to separate administrative and developmental feedback (Ivancevich, 1982). The performance appraisal interview may also fail to have an impact if no reward is linked to it (Burke, Weitzel, & Weir, 1978).

The lack of connection between performance appraisals and performance may be due to a variety of other goals that managers have in mind when they evaluate their subordinates (Longnecker, Sims, & Gioia, 1987). Supervisors may avoid discouraging subordinates or confronting them with their inadequacies, may seek favors from the subordinates, or may discourage a top-performing employee from demanding a commensurate increase in salary. Thus appraisals may be unrelated to performance even in the face of available objective evidence about the performance. For example, Leana (1984) discovered that the periodic evaluations of 98 claims adjustors by their 44 supervisors were not correlated with such objective measures of performance as the settlement ratio and the average cost of the claims that were settled.

Supervisors' and Subordinates' Evaluations of the Process

Lawler, Mohrman, and Resnick (1984) conducted a survey of over 300 supervisor-subordinate dyads regarding the extent to which the performance appraisal interviews fulfilled their purposes. They found that although 82% of the supervisors said that all important matters had been discussed, most subordinates thought there had been less than a full discussion of their development, work, planning, or pay. Furthermore, they thought that not enough attention was being paid to documenting their performance. On the other hand, supervisors in general were unenthusiastic about discussing decisions about pay or documenting subordinates' performance in these interviews. Presumably, both these matters would be extremely important for leaders to cover as means of contingent reinforcement (Mohrman & Lawler, 1983). Consistent with these findings was the survey by Greller (1980), which showed that supervisors actually overestimated the importance of the feedback they provided to subordinates and underestimated the value their subordinates place on feedback from sources under their own control such as the task and comparisons with the work of colleagues.

Avoidance

Many supervisors avoid conducting appraisal interviews. When forced by organizational policy, they often hold perfunctory general discussions with subordinates, which the subordinates do not consider to be the formal feedback of a performance appraisal interview (Meyer, Kay, & French, 1965). The failure to conduct high-quality performance appraisal interviews with optimal frequency may militate against these interviews' serving to provide effective contingent reinforcement. Most employees seek more such feedback opportunities than they receive (Ashford & Cummings, 1983).

Other Aspects of the Process

Frequent appraisals, however, particularly negative appraisals, may generate more resistance and defensiveness in subordinates (Burke, Weitzel, & Weir, 1978). If the feedback is not what the subordinate expected, it may arouse resistance (Bernstein & Lecomte, 1979), or the subordinate may consider it less accurate (Taylor, 1981). If the feedback is not as positive as expected, it may reduce the subordinate's commitment to the organization (Pearce & Porter, 1986). Decreased commitment is likely to be common, since subordinates ordinarily give themselves higher evaluations than their superiors do (Bradley, 1978). Furthermore, subordinates' reactions to the performance appraisal interview will depend on their opinions about the supervisor's credibility, knowledge, and trustworthiness, which parallel their reactions to informal feedback from their supervisor, as was mentioned earlier. Ilgen, Fisher, and Taylor (1979) noted that subordinates' judgments of their supervisors' credibility as an appraiser will influence how the subordinates react in performance appraisal interviews. If the subordinates think their supervisor is knowledgeable about their job and performance, they will regard the interview as fair and accurate, but those who judge their supervisor to be less knowledgeable will think the interview is unfair and inaccurate (Landy, Barnes, & Murphy, 1978). And, as Ilgen, Peterson, Martin, and Boeschen (1981) observed, subordinates who trust their supervisor will be more satisfied with the appraisal interview process than subordinates who do not trust their supervisor.

Herold and Greller (1977) added a number of other characteristics of feedback that recipients can discern in the performance appraisal interview, such as whether the feedback is helpful or unhelpful, clear or ambiguous, important or unimportant, and formal or informal. The utility of the feedback appeared to be most strongly related to its frequency, helpfulness, and importance. In the interviews, ratings and discussions that focus on the past performance of the subordinates appear to be the most satisfactory to both superiors and subordinates (Fletcher & Williams, 1976; Mount, 1984). The subordinates' participation in the development of the rating forms also seems to help (Landy & Farr, 1980). Agreement on the meaning of scores and terms, such as "good" and "satisfactory," will help as well (Taylor, Fisher, & Ilgen, 1984). Supervisors who begin the interviews with positive feedback before giving negative feedback are seen as more accurate by the subordinates than supervisors who begin with the negatives before presenting the positive aspects of the subordinates' performance (Stone, Gueutal, & MacIntosh, 1984).

An Ideal System

Fox (1987–1988) enumerated guidelines for an improved performance appraisal system. First, credit should be given for good form. Second, emphasis should be on work-relevant behaviors that are known to be desirable and productive, rather than on outcomes that are often beyond the employee's total control. These behaviors should be determined from critical-incidents surveys of the occurrence of highly effective and highly ineffective job events. Third, the appraisals should be from multiple sources, not just from the boss. Fourth, ratings should be accompanied by evidence. According to Fox, improvement in an employee's performance would stem from an ongoing defining of behaviors that need to be changed, setting goals for change, and administering feedback and other reinforcements on appropriate schedules.

Following a comprehensive review of the literature, Biddle and Fisher (1987) described an ideal procedure for promoting such contingent reinforcement from performance appraisal interviews. First, there would be a preperformance meeting in which the supervisor and subordinate reached an understanding of exactly how the subordinate's future performance was to be assessed. If rating scales were to be used, the meaning of each dimension and anchor point would be clarified. A performance monitoring system would be set up to ensure that good data were available for the appraisal. The sources of feedback would be considered, and the supervisor would arrange to collect data, as needed, from these sources, such as peers and clients, as well as to gather his or her own data. The subordinate would also keep track of his or her performance and accomplishments through self-monitoring. Between interviews, the supervisor would give more frequent informal feedback and coaching, so that the formal performance appraisal interview would not bring up much that was unexpected for the subordinate. The timeliness of the frequent informal feedback would allow the subordinate to learn from and correct his or her errors immediately. It also would afford opportunities to clear up differences in attributions for the same specific incidents of performance. In sum, the actual performance appraisal interview would begin with a self-appraisal, followed by the supervisor's sharing of his or her feedback with the subordinate as well as feedback collected from the other sources. Discussion should then center on how the subordinate might be able to do things differently and what additional support the superior might provide. Finally, new goals for the upcoming period would be discussed and established.

Implicit Theories of Leadership as Moderators of LMX

The perceived and actual descriptions of the quality of the exchange, the causes of the exchange, and the consequences of the exchange may be obscured or magnified by the implicit theories of leadership that are held by the leaders and subordinates who are involved in the relationship.

Meaning of Implicit Theories of Leadership

Implicit Theories of Leadership as Cognitive Frameworks. The implicit theories we hold about leadership and its antecedents and consequences join with our explicitly expressed attitudes, beliefs, values, and ideologies about leadership[8] to color our judgments of specific leaders we describe or evaluate. Implicit theories are cognitive frameworks or categorization systems that are in use during information processing to encode, process, and recall specific events and behavior. An implicit theory can also be conceived of as the personalized factor structure we use for information processing.

Both the leader and the led are affected in their exchange relationship by the implicit theories of leadership they carry around in their heads. If they both believe that leadership is mainly a matter of striking a deal for the payment for services rendered and monitoring the arrangements, then they are likely to judge that contingent reinforcement explains the motivation and performance of the leader and the subordinate. But if they believe that leadership is mainly an inspirational process, then they will judge contingent reinforcement as being of little or no consequence. Thus Eden and Leviatan (1975) noted that people have preconceptions about what constitutes appropriate behavior by leaders. Subordinates have expectations regarding the kind and amount of leadership behavior that is proper for given situations (L. R. Ander-

son, 1966b), as do the leaders themselves (Yukl, 1971). These preconceptions are important, according to Pfeffer and Salancik (1975), who obtained results showing that the leadership behavior of focal supervisors was affected by the expectations of both their superiors and their subordinates. In addition, subordinates attach their own individual specific value-laden meanings to the actions of their superiors (McConkie, 1984), whereas leaders may regard their performance as leaders to be a matter of their traits, their power, or the way they act.

Birnbaum (1987c) collected the definitions of leadership provided in interviews with 32 college and university presidents. Almost all of the presidents thought that leadership involved power, influence, and ways of behaving. About a quarter talked as well about traits of consequence, situational determinants, or the symbolism of leadership. Content analyses of the interviews suggested that about a third of the presidents believed that the goals of leadership stemmed from the mission of the institution; a few thought that the goals came from followers; and the rest thought that the goals came from the leaders themselves. Presidents saw themselves as either: (1) the heads of a bureaucracy; (2) collegial in their relations with the staff, faculty, and students; (3) political manipulators; or (4) occupants of a highly symbolic office. Some of the presidents had a single frame of reference about leadership, and about a quarter had multiple frames of reference (Bensimon, 1987). According to Bolman and Deal (1984), those with multiple frames of reference were better equipped to deal with the complexities of the modern college community.

Effects on Raters of Leadership. Implicit theories of leadership facilitate the assimilation of specific events and behaviors into a collective interpretation. They help raters to categorize their stimulus environment into less complex classifications. Implicit theories make it possible to simplify complex information by enabling raters to process that information automatically, as well as to add missing details not observed in the actual behavior of the leader (Lord, Foti, & DeVader, 1984). The raters' application of their own implicit theory to observed events affects the truth of their observations. The result is that their responses to the survey questions are closer to their own implicit theories than to the actual events they observed. The impact of these implicit theories is greatest

[8]Enumerated by Bass and Barrett (1981).

when raters are asked to recall the behavior and events they observed sometime in the past.

Lord, Binning, Rush, and Thomas (1978) estimated that up to 40% of the variance in ratings of leadership can be accounted for by implicit theories. Thus instead of describing the actual behavior of the individual leader who is being judged, we respond in a way that is highly biased by our preconceptions about how leaders in general are supposed to behave. Support for this proposition first emerged when Eden and Leviatan (1975) applied D. J. Schneider's (1973) Implicit Personality theory to the study of leadership. Staw and Ross (1980) and McElroy (1982) provided additional support for the idea that the implicit conceptions we use in attributing what we observe to leadership seriously alter our attributions. Thus an exchange may take place between a supervisor and a subordinate. The subordinate is actually complying with the supervisor's request to gain a recommendation for promotion from the supervisor. But the subordinate has an implicit theory that says leaders are inspiring. The subordinate reports she is complying as a consequence of the way the supervisor inspired her to work with him. Thus an actual transactional exchange is reported as a transformational event. Or the reverse may occur. A subordinate is actually inspired to transcend her own interests. However, she holds an implicit theory that you get what you give, so she interprets her appraisal by the supervisor as compliance because she wants to be recommended by him for a promotion.

Effects on Leaders' Behavior. Supervisors are also clearly affected by the implicit theories of leadership they hold. Neubauer (1982) found, in a sample of 90 German supervisors, that implicit leadership theories are characterized by a belief in participative management and acceptance of informal leader-member relations for workers who live up to the supervisors' expectations. But for workers who fail to live up to expectations, not very helpful implicit theories emphasize the limiting of such workers to simple activities, the need for supervisory control, and the prevention of the development of informal leader-member relations.

Managing the Effects of Implicit Theories

Implicit theories of leadership can be manipulated in advance to get raters to assess the same observed leadership behavior differently. If we are told that a leader is effective and believe the leader to be effective in carrying out his or her assignment, this will influence how much and what type of leadership we judge to exist in the subsequent performance we observe. In a laboratory study by Gioia and Sims (1985), subjects viewed videotapes of contingently reinforcing leadership behavior by managers in action. When managers were presented to the subjects as effective leaders before the subjects saw the tapes, the subjects described the managers subsequently as being significantly higher in initiating structure than the managers who were presented to the subjects as ineffective before the same tapes were viewed. Similar results were reported by Rush, Thomas, and Lord (1977).

Other conditions can be arranged to increase the effect of implicit theories of leadership. Thus the more ambiguous a leader's actual behavior, the more implicit theories will affect how we describe or evaluate it (DeNisi & Pritchard, 1978). Also, implicit theories of leadership will have more of an impact in less structured situations (Gioia & Sims, 1985). *Halo* effects can also be connected with implicit theories (Nathan & Alexander, 1985). In addition, subordinates are likely to fall back on their implicit theories of leadership when they lack information about a situation (Schriesheim & DeNisi, 1978).

Implicit theories of leadership need to take into account the causal expectations that leaders have about themselves and their followers, as well as the complementary theories held by the followers. The extent to which leaders will modify their reactions to the good and poor performance of subordinates, depending on whether they attribute the performance to the subordinates' competence or motivation, to external causes, or to luck, has already been addressed. The leaders are also likely to respond according to their own beliefs about the value of promises of reward for compliance or threats of punishment for noncompliance. As a consequence, one supervisor may praise a subordinate for an effort to reach desired standards that failed because of uncontrollable obstacles, and another supervisor may reprove the same subordinate for the failure despite the obstacles.

Larson (1980) suggested that supervisors vary in the

implicit theories they have about feedback in general, as well as their theories about the consequences of feedback to specific subordinates. Some supervisors may think that reprimands invite retaliation and that praise lacks credibility. Disapproval is more likely if rationality, objectivity, and certainty are regarded as more important than adaptability; if security is valued as more important than affiliation; and if the leaders see themselves as aiming for homogeneity, regularity, standardization, safety, or consolidation (Quinn & Hall, 1983). Subordinates will use various tactics to try to influence their leaders, according to the subordinates' beliefs about the likely effects on the leader of reason, ingratiation, excuses, and coalitions, as well as the implications for the subordinate's self-image involving his or her integrity and self-esteem. The organizational role the subordinate believes he or she expected to play is also important.

The Prototypical Leader

Phillips and Lord (1981) concluded that implicit theories of leadership could best be understood in terms of cognitive categorization processes. ("In my head, Joe comes across as a dynamic leader. Dynamic leaders are a category containing 'such and such attributes.' Therefore, Joe has these attributes.") The researchers demonstrated this experimentally by using 128 undergraduates to view one or another of two videotapes of a four-person problem-solving group in which the leader's salience and the group's performance were manipulated. Furthermore, Lord, Foti, and Phillips (1982) argued that implicit theories reflect the cognitive categories used to distinguish leaders from nonleaders. Such categories can be applied to explaining which information is connected to designated labels of leadership (Cronshaw & Lord, 1987; Lord, Foti, & Phillips, 1982).

For most people from the same culture, a common set of categories fits the image of what the typical leader is like. These categories describe the "prototypical" leader. A prototypical leader is *actively participating*; an "anti-prototypical" leader *remains withdrawn*. Perceiving someone as a leader involves a relatively simple categorization of the stimulus person as a leader or a nonleader. Such a categorical judgment, according to Rosch (1975), is made on the basis of the similarity between the stimulus person and the "prototype" of the category. The proto-type (in this definition) is an abstract representation of the most representative features of members of the category.

Foti, Fraser, and Lord (1982) asked students to rate the extent to which phrases like "bright" or "sides with the average citizen" (taken from a Gallup poll) fit their image of a leader, a political leader, an effective leader, or an effective political leader. The students' different prototypical categorizations helped considerably to account for changes in Gallup poll results of public support for President Jimmy Carter at different times during his administration. If Jimmy Carter acted more like the students' prototype of an effective political leader, he received more support from the public. The mere social desirability of the categorizations was not as predictive.

People simplify rather than describe or evaluate their leaders in terms of many specifications. People form mental images of categories of leaders. As was noted before, they rapidly judge whether their leader falls into these categories according to their beliefs about the leader and how they see the leader acting (Phillips & Lord, 1981, 1982). Lord, Foti, and DeVader (1984) conducted three studies that used 263 undergraduates to specify the internal structure of these leadership categories and how they relate to prototypicality. These studies showed how properties of the categories can be used to facilitate information processing, such as recalling information about a leader, and to explain simplified perceptions about leadership.

In the first study, different students were each given five minutes to generate attributes of a particular type of leader or nonleader in 11 different situations: (1) business, (2) education, (3) finance, (4) labor, (5) politics, (6) the mass media, (7) the military, (8) minorities, (9) religion, (10) sports, and (11) at the world level. Master lists of attributes of the frequency of mentions of specific clusters of traits were then assembled. *Intelligence* was seen as highest in "family resemblance," that is, attributed generally to leaders in almost all of the 11 situations. Other categories with relatively high family resemblance for leaders included *honesty, outgoing, understanding, verbal skills, aggressiveness, determined*, and *industrious*. Most of the other 59 attributes, such as *caring, authoritarian*, and *decisive*, were limited to just one or two types of leaders.

In the second study, a different set of students judged

how much these attributes were "prototypical" for leadership. The students rated the categories according to how well they "fit my image of a leader or a nonleader." Attributes "fitting the image of leader" included *intelligence, honesty, verbal skills, determined, informed, strong character, believable, concerned, goal-oriented*, and *disciplined*. The family resemblance of these attributes correlated .40 with the attributes of the prototypical leader. A correlation of .42 was found between the speed of reaction in judging these attributes and their fitting the image of the prototypical leader. Such attributes of prototypicality were thus linked to implicit theories as reactions "off the top of the head."

In the third study, Lord, Foti, and DeVader presented vignettes about a district store manager. One vignette ascribed to the manager four or five attributes of the prototypical leader, such as "provides information" and "talks frequently." Another vignette ascribed to the manager neutral attributes, such as "seeks information" or "explains actions." Still another vignette ascribed to the manager "antiprototypical" attributes, such as "admits mistakes" and "withholds rewards." Those who read the vignette containing the prototypical, rather than the neutral or antiprototypical, attributes perceived that the manager displayed more leadership and made much more of a contribution to the store's effectiveness and to the successful merchandising of a new product. The investigators inferred that attributes of causes and responsibility were a retrospective rationalization of events in which "leadership" was the central construct stimulated by the few prototypical attributes embedded in the vignette. However, Lord and Alliger (1985) did not find that prototypicality weightings of the 12 functional leadership behaviors of members of small task groups had much impact on the frequent correlation between the sheer frequency of activity of group members and the leadership ratings they received.

Prototypicality and Contingent Reinforcement. Bass and Avolio (1988) asked 87 part-time MBA students to describe their full-time supervisors' transactional and transformational leadership behavior with the Multifactor Leadership Questionnaire. They also had the students complete the prototypicality ratings developed by Lord and his associates about the attributes that "fit my image of a leader." They found that contingent reinforcement

was less highly correlated with the prototypicality of the leader than was charismatic leadership, individualized consideration, or intellectual stimulation. When the prototypicality ratings were statistically controlled by partial correlation, only charismatic leadership remained correlated significantly with effectiveness of operations (.34) and continued satisfaction with the leadership (.68). The partial correlation with contingent reinforcement was reduced to close to zero. Bass and Avolio concluded that the positive contribution that contingent rewarding by a leader is often seen to make to perceived effectiveness may be accounted for by the image of leadership held by the raters. The same may be true for the transformational effects of intellectual stimulation and individualized consideration. However, the charismatic effect cannot be accounted for in this way. Complicating these results may be the extent to which the followers' motivation affects their image of the ideal leader.

Imagined Ideal Leader and the Followers' Needs. Singer and Singer (1986) reported that among male undergraduates in New Zealand, the extent to which contingent-reinforcement leadership was desired in an imagined ideal leader did not depend on the men's motivation. But those who had a higher need for affiliation were more likely to prefer transforming, charismatic, and considerate leaders. Nonconformists were more likely to prefer transforming intellectually stimulating leaders.

Summary and Conclusions

Leadership can be understood as a transaction or exchange of material, social, and psychological benefits. In a fair and profitable exchange, the benefits to both the leader and the follower exceed their costs. In the transactional process, leaders and followers reinforce each other's behavior with either reward or punishment—preferably reward, and preferably reward that is contingent on fulfilling the transacted role arrangements. But the exchange may be less rewarding; it can involve management by exception or punitive discipline. In the dynamics of the exchange relationship, competence and early acceptance of the group's norms are important, as a follower builds the idiosyncrasy credit of a member, making it more likely that his or her attempts to lead will be successful. With enough idiosyncrasy credit, one can begin to stand out in the group and be successful in introducing new ideas. But those with credit need to avoid violating the norms and expectations of the group.

Leaders' rewarding and punishing may be contingent or noncontingent, depending on followers' performance. Management by exception may be active or passive. Leaders may treat each follower differently or in the same way. Within-group and between-group analyses can show how much leaders vary in these respects.

Reinforcement can be manipulated in experiments to determine who emerges as a leader. Reinforcement can be used to increase different members' attempts to lead and to affect whether their attempts will be successful in influencing other members. To understand many individual and organizational outcomes of leadership, it is necessary to focus attention on the dyadic leader-member exchange, for the same leader is likely to have different expectations and reactions about his or her different subordinates. These different perceptions and behaviors of leaders result in different levels of performance by subordinates—who are working for the same leader—that cannot be captured by looking only at leader-group relationships. However, this is not an either-or matter.

The combination of dyadic and group effects can be teased out.

Contingent reward may be effective for leaders in many situations, but it has limitations. Rewards for performance and disciplinary actions for failures may not work as expected, for numerous reasons ranging from the leader's lack of control over what the followers are seeking to the overriding impact of group norms. The carrot-or-stick approach may make the subordinate feel denigrated and less than an adult person. What can be accomplished with feedback depends on its timeliness, accuracy, attractiveness, and judged importance, as well as the trustworthiness, expertise, and authority of the source. Negative feedback is often distorted by both the leader who sends it and the subordinate who receives it. Many other factors related to superiors and subordinates will moderate its effects and generate unintended consequences. Systematically affecting the meaning, interpretation, and understanding of the leader's efforts to provide contingent reinforcement will be the leader's and followers' implicit theories about leadership. Important here are the prototypical leaders that fit the followers' images of what leaders are like. Leaders and followers have been likened to two sides of the same coin. The behavior of each can serve to reinforce the other.

Followers and Mutual Influence on Leadership

[After making profuse apologies for disturbing the Minister, . . . the civil servant] indicated that some urgent matters has arisen as a result of the day's business in the House, and the Minister must take certain decisions which would then be implemented in time for the question hour the next day. The civil servant . . . had brought the file so the Minister could study the questions, before [deciding]. But . . . all the Minister said was: 'Where do I sign?' A pen was produced by the civil servant, the places for signature were indicated, and with [deference and more apologies, he] . . . backed out of the room. Bailey, 1969, p. 73

Successful leaders influence their followers and bring about changes in their followers' attitudes and behavior. In the same way, by accepting, modifying, or rejecting the influence, followers influence the leader's subsequent behavior and attitudes. Sometimes, subordinates lead and superiors follow.

Leaders and followers matter to each other, as do the quality of relations between them. "Governments and laws cannot work without people in authority, and those in authority are powerless without support, cooperation, and obedience from the people they govern" (Sarsar & Stunkel, 1994). Leaders and followers are similar in many ways. The antitheses of leaders are not followers, but alienated, apathetic isolates and rejectees. Like good leaders, good followers are transformational, committed to principles and purposes beyond themselves. Like leaders, followers use both hard and soft tactics. Hegel suggested that to be a good leader, one needed to be a good follower. "The school for leadership is indeed followership, a followership that is fully preserved within leadership, but transformed for having moved beyond itself" (Litzinger & Schaefer, 1982). Nevertheless, the study of

followers has always played second fiddle to the study of leaders.

According to critical incidents obtained from 81 respondents, good leadership is distinguished from bad leadership by the quality of the leaders' relations with the followers (Hollander & Kelly, 1990). Leaders need to be helped by their followers to understand the tasks and challenges they face. Followers need to learn to challenge their leaders while respecting the leaders' authority (Hirschhorn, 1990). Leaders need to engage followers in satisfactory mutual pursuits. Followers give or withdraw support of their leaders (Hollander, 1997). The exchanges vary considerably in nature and amount. Different leaders have different relations with their followers; likewise, followers have different relations with their leaders. According to a survey in three British companies, the organizational culture affects what types of leaders are dominant, and the leaders in turn affect what types of followers are dominant (Brown & Thornborrow, 1996). Leaders command more attention, but followers affect and constrain what the leaders can do (Hollander, 1992). "Leadership is not what the leader does but what the leaders and collaborators do together to change organizations" (Rost, 1993, p. 92). Bennis (1999) agrees, stating that effective change in organizations requires an alliance between the leaders and the led.

This chapter examines the roles of both the leader and the led in the exchange that takes place between them. Specifically, it looks at the antecedents and consequences of the leader's downward influence on the subordinate, the subordinate's upward influence, and their mutual influence.

The Leader's Influence

Leaders can be found who exert little discretionary influence on their followers. These leaders are the rule-governed, fully programmed administrator; the paper-pushing absentee supervisor; and the token officeholder without power. They are glorified doormen, whose behavior is almost fully determined by others. Other leaders use a lot of discretionary influence as disciplinarians, rule makers, active monitors, and instrumental purveyors of praise, reward, or penalties. They also use discretionary influence to be considerate, stimulating, informative, and inspirational. As a consequence of their influence, their followers can perform better and be more fully informed. These followers can avoid mistakes. Their interests may be enlarged. Their expectations may be developed, their preference for taking risks may be altered, and their satisfaction with their roles may be enhanced. The emphasis that followers believe their leaders place on self-guiding performance determines whether or not the followers persist at working on unsolvable problems (Brown, 2000). But followers fail to benefit from leaders' successful influence when it is not effective in achieving goals of consequence.

In the formal organization, the performance of individual subordinates or groups depends on their energy, direction, competence, and motivation. They perform what is required to reach the objectives of their positions in the system. The leader may contribute to the adequacy of their performance by: (1) clarifying what is expected of the subordinates, particularly the purposes and objectives of their performance; (2) explaining how to meet such expectations; (3) spelling out the criteria for the evaluation of effective performance; (4) providing feedback on whether the individual subordinate or group is meeting the objectives; and (5) allocating rewards that are contingent on their meeting the objectives.

Effective leadership develops understanding and agreement about the leader's and subordinate's roles in this process. For instance, if the leader engages in management by objectives, leadership may take the form of periodic discussions between the leader and the subordinate. A review of past performance and obstacles to effectiveness is the basis for setting mutually acceptable objectives for the next period. Legitimacy for the roles of both the leader and the led is provided by organizational policies that declare and support the roles.

The Downward Influence Tactics of Leaders

Influence tactics are behaviors designed to change another person's values, attitudes, beliefs, or behaviors (Hughes, Ginnett, & Curphy, 1993). Yukl and Falbe (1990) used the Influence Behavior Questionnaire (IBQ) to measure nine tactics of influence upward, laterally, or downward, conceptually originated by Kipnis and Schmidt (1982) and assessed with the Profile of Organizational Influence Strategies (POIS).

The transactional leader may introduce a proposal with: (1) the tactic of *ingratiation*: "Mary, I know you can do this job;" (2) An *exchange* may be offered: "George, you can leave early if you get this work done;" (3) Another tactic is a *personal appeal* from the leader: "Bill, I need your help;" (4) Another influence tactic is *pressure*: "Jenny, if you want to stay out of trouble, you had better finish this now;" (5) A *legitimating* tactic is: "Carl, I am an attorney here to represent you;" (6) A *coalition* tactic is: "Eleanor, let's join forces to confront the opposition."

A transformational[1] leader may use intellectual stimulation for *rational persuasion*: "Martha, considering the alternatives, it is the treatment with the least risk." *Inspirational appeal* is another transformational tactic: "We must give until it hurts!" A tactic of considerate leadership is *consultation*: "Ann, before the decision, I need to know what you think about it."

Although ingratiation, exchange, and personal appeal yielded task commitment from subordinates and pressure reduced it, the tactics that were actually effective were the transformational ones, according to a survey of 128 managers and their 526 subordinates from five companies in diverse industries (Yukl & Tracey, 1992). When "critical influence" incidents were gathered by 215 night MBA students, Yukl, Kim, and Falbe (1996) found that managers with lack of referent power used more pressure tactics ($r = -.33$), which tended to damage their relations with subordinates and peers. Managers with more referent power were less likely to use pressure tactics. Multiple regression analyses indicated that strong rational persuasion, inspirational appeal, and consultation

[1] See Chapter 22.

were more likely to result in desired outcomes. Followers accord more discretionary opportunities to leaders who are seen as more competent, legitimate, and expert in solving problems (Lord & Maher, 1991). In a study of 78 leaders and their 156 subordinates, Tepper (1990) showed that less controlling downward influence tactics were displayed by follower-oriented than self-oriented leaders.

Hard tactics such as pressure and legitimizing are used when the user is powerful and resistance is expected; *soft* tactics such as ingratiation or personal appeal are used if the user lacks power or will personally benefit from a successful attempt (Hughes, Ginnett, & Curphy, 1993).

Leaders as a Source of Feedback

Feedback about a subordinate's performance is the most common contingent reinforcement provided by a leader. Supervisory feedback often is required to improve the subordinate's performance and can affect either the subordinate's ability or his or her motivation to do the job (Locke, Latham, Saari, & Shaw, 1981; Payne & Hauty, 1955). Cook (1968) found that improvement in the attitudes and performance of managers who participated in a business simulation game was directly related to the frequency with which reports of their performance were fed back to them.

Rewarding when positive, feedback can be highly punitive when negative. However, negative feedback may quickly come to be interpreted as rewarding if it is seen as intended to be helpful and if it actually results in improved performance. Subordinates will see negative feedback about their failures as fair and accurate if the causes are attributed to bad luck or external circumstances rather than to their lack of ability or motivation, and if the feedback is about the task, not about them (Liden, Ferris, & Dienesch, 1988). Nevertheless, when subordinates suspect that they are doing poorly, they will seek feedback to short-circuit the buildup of negative feedback in order to uphold their self-esteem. They can arrange how and when feedback is given, and they can mitigate blame (Larson, 1989). Feedback can also be neutral and non-reinforcing, as when the superior merely acknowledges, without evaluating it, he or she has seen a subordinate's behavior or has heard a subordinate's statement.

According to a survey of 360 supervisor-subordinate dyads by Glynn, Larson, Fleenor, et al. (1985), supervi-sors differ from each other in the timeliness, specificity, frequency, and sensitivity of their feedback. But these four dimensions are highly intercorrelated. Furthermore, negative feedback that is prefaced by the Drake-Moberg (1986) sedative or palliative statements will be accepted by subordinates with less sense that they are being negatively reinforced ("It's probably not necessary to say this, but . . ." or "I know it's hard, but . . .").

Types of Feedback. Supervisory feedback can range from a formal annual appraisal interview (see Chapter 35) to a grunt of acknowledgment of a message received or a pat on the back for a job well done. The grunt or pat has the advantage of occurring soon after the behavior about which the feedback is being given. The appraisal interview has the advantage of being systematic and of couching the feedback in the context of goals, needs, and plans for future action.

Impact of Feedback. It is important that subordinates accept and agree with the performance feedback their supervisors believe they are giving them (Ilgen, Fisher, & Taylor, 1979). Naturally, agreement and acceptance are more likely if the feedback is positive (Jacobs, Jacobs, Feldman, & Cavior, 1973). Agreement and acceptance are also more likely if the feedback is clear, convincing, credible, and frequent.[2] The credibility of the superior's feedback is likely to be enhanced if the subordinate believes the superior is highly knowledgeable about the subordinate's job and has had sufficient opportunities to observe the subordinate's performance.[3] The context in which feedback is delivered will affect whether subordinates interpret it as positive or negative. For example, if feedback is solicited, it may be received more positively than if it is volunteered unexpectedly.

Pavett (1983) illustrated the positive effects of feedback on the performance of 203 staff nurses. Komaki, Collins, and Penn (1982) found feedback to have a positive impact beyond giving instructions. They monitored the safety performance of 200 employees over 46 weeks. After a baseline was established, safety rules were clarified at meetings in which considerable supervisory-subordinate

[2]Halperin, Snyder, Shenkel, & Houston, 1976; Shaw & Fisher, 1986; Tuckman & Oliver, 1968.
[3]Landy, Barnes, & Murphy, 1978; Stone, Gueutal, & MacIntosh, 1984.

interaction occurred. In contrast to the baseline record of performance, modest improvements occurred in two of four departments as a consequence of the clarification efforts. Then safety performance feedback graphs were introduced. It was this feedback that produced significant improvements in safety over the baseline. Whether the feedback was delivered once a week or twice a week did not seem to matter. According to a similarly designed investigation by Chhokar and Wallin (1984), similar effects of feedback on improvements in safety occurred among 58 employees over a 10-month period.

Leaders as Communicators

In addition to giving feedback, the leaders' words and actions convey meaning. Their communications distinguish leaders who are successful and effective from those who are not. "Understanding and consensus . . . at an operational level are indispensable . . . to gain success [in] global competition" (Testa, 1998, p. 32). As was noted in earlier chapters, emergent leaders contribute strongly to the interactions in their groups. They initiate more ideas, express more opinions, and ask more questions than members who do not emerge as leaders (Bass, 1954a; Morris & Hackman, 1969). Elected and appointed leaders would be expected to do likewise in discussions with their groups, as well as in separate dyadic interactions with each of their team members (Watson, 1982).

In a survey, chief executive officers (CEOs) of large businesses ranked face-to-face communication as the most important source of their effectiveness (Anonymous, 1978). An intensive study of nine senior executives by S. Carlson (1951) over a four-week period noted that they spent approximately 80% of their time talking with others. A detailed study of four departmental-level managers also found that more than 80% of their time was spent in conversation. Zelko and Dance (1965) stated that when managers were asked how much of their workday was spent in communicating, their replies ranged from about 88% to 99%, with most saying that it was above 90%.[4]

According to Baird (1980), the credibility of managers' communications depends on their competence, esteem, personality, dynamism, character, and perceived inten-

tions. Empirically, Klauss and Bass (1982) established strong positive linkages between the trustworthiness and informativeness of supervisors and their careful communications to subordinates; their two-way rather than one-way communications; and their attentive listening. In turn, the trustworthiness, informativeness, and care of supervisors contributed to their subordinates' role clarity, satisfaction with their supervision, and to the effectiveness of their groups.

Hain (1972) reported that in four General Motors plants, productivity and profitability increased most in the plant that also showed the greatest improvement in communications. Similar parallel improvements in other General Motors plants were reported by Widgery and Tubbs (1975) and Tubbs and Widgery (1978). Hain and Tubbs (1974) found greater efficiency, fewer grievances, and lower absenteeism to be associated with employees' ratings of the effectiveness of their supervisors' communication. The effectiveness of supervisors' communication was the best predictor of low grievance activity in still another General Motors automotive assembly plant (Tubbs & Porter, 1978). Such effective communication included agreement that supervisors were friendly, were easy to talk to, listened with interest, paid attention to what others said, were willing to listen to others' problems, were receptive to ideas and suggestions, and showed how performance could be improved. These various communication behaviors are usually included in measures of leadership. It is not surprising that Klauss and Bass (1981) found correlations as high as .65 between the various communication styles of supervisors and the supervisors' leadership styles as described by their subordinates.

Leaders as Models for Their Subordinates

Porter and Kaufman (1959) devised a scale for determining the extent to which supervisors described themselves as similar to top managers. Self-perceptions similar to those of top managers were associated with patterns of interaction that peers of the supervisors perceived to be similar to the interaction patterns of managers in top-level positions. Katz, Maccoby, and Morse (1950) noted that supervisors in an insurance firm tended to model their tendency to be coercive or participative on whether their bosses were coercive or permissive. Likewise, R. Cooper (1966) showed that workers tended to pattern their own

---

[4]Similar results were reported by Lawler, Porter, and Tannenbaum (1968); Mintzberg (1973); and P. A. Stewart (1967).

task behavior after that of their supervisors. Task-oriented leaders supervised groups in which workers made fewer errors in their work and had lower rates of absenteeism and tardiness than was true of groups whose leaders did not have a task orientation. According to a study by Kern and Bahr (1974) of approximately 100 staff personnel in the Washington State Division of Parole, parole officers who interacted a lot with their supervisors used their superiors as models for the way they supervised their parolees. But such modeling did not occur when the parole officers interacted less frequently with their supervisors. H. M. Weiss (1977) studied 141 superior-subordinate pairs of leaders, obtaining from each member of the dyad a self-description of his or her supervisory behavior, along with the subordinate's evaluation of the superior's competence and success. These items were then correlated with the degree of similarity found in the self-descriptions of the superior-subordinate dyads. Weiss found that subordinates tended to choose for role models those superiors they saw as more competent and successful. Although transformational leaders are more likely to serve as models for subordinates who identify with them, transactional leaders may also serve as models

Adler (1982) found that the characteristics of superiors whom subordinates chose as models depended on the subordinates' self-esteem. Among the subordinates of 66 Israeli heads of bank departments, those with high self-esteem were more likely to model themselves on the heads whom they perceived to have reward and coercive power; those subordinates with low self-esteem were more inclined to model themselves on heads whom they perceived to have referent power. Regardless of the subordinates' self-esteem, modeling was also more apparent of heads who displayed more initiation and consideration in their leadership behavior. Behavioral contagion is less obvious modeling. A crude boss can spawn crude subordinates. The subordinates unconsciously adopt the boss's spoken expressions, intonations, and peculiar nonverbal mannerisms.

Leaders as Cues. Followers may come to depend on their leader's view of reality as their prime source of information and expectations. Beyond followers' modeling of their leader's behavior, Graen and Cashman (1975) noted that followers also enlarged their interests to match those of their leader more closely. Followers attempt to increase their esteem in the eyes of their leader to ingratiate themselves with the leader (E. E. Jones, 1964). Friedlander (1966b) asked members of a research and development organization to describe various aspects of members' interaction and the group's performance. The effectiveness of the group was associated with open discussion and with the leader's suggestion of new approaches to problems. At the same time, a member's influence on other members was associated with his or her influence on the leader. Members accepted the leader's influence when policies were clear-cut and group tensions were low. The members tended to play their expected roles and discuss divergent ideas when the leader was oriented toward productivity and efficiency.

Daniels and Berkowitz (1963) experimentally varied supervisor-worker dependence for the attainment of goals, the degree of liking, and the time required for a supervisor to learn of a worker's performance. They found that workers tried hardest under independent conditions when they believed that the supervisor would learn about their performance quickly. They also worked hardest when they had to depend on a supervisor whom they liked. Similarly, Katzell (1987) showed, from the results of a survey, how complex is the impact on the morale, involvement, and performance of employees of the extent to which supervisors help employees achieve intrinsic and extrinsic rewards. The extent to which they do so is linked to the extent to which they cue the employees by setting goals for them, maintaining normative standards, and preserving equity.

Falling Dominoes: Modeling or Alternating? Do strong leaders at one hierarchical level alternate with weak leaders at the level below them? Or does the style of leadership cascade from one management level to another through modeling and other processes? Do subordinates at each descending level below the boss imitate their boss, or do they complement their boss's leadership with compliance to fit it? If A kicks B, will B kick C or will B become solicitous of C after being kicked by A? Do modeling and matching one's superior make a difference, or is alteration from one level of supervision to the next more likely to be productive? The modeling of transactional leadership behavior is supported in a number of ways. When a manager's boss rewards the manager for performance or allocates requested resources to him or her, some of these rewards and resources make it easier for the manager, in turn, to reward his or her subordinates for their performance. Discipline applied by the boss usually will require similar disciplinary action by the manager. Subordinates will be safer targets of the manager's displaced hostility, which is sparked by the hostility of the boss toward the manager. The boss's clarification of goals for the manager provides the means by which the manager clarifies goals for his or her subordinates. On the other hand, the threatening boss may create a manager who is attentive to rewarding subordinates in exchange for their support against the threatening boss. The inefficiencies of the boss who practices noncontingent reinforcement with the manager may result in the manager rejecting the boss's style in favor of contingently reinforcing his or her subordinates. In the case of transformational leaders, J. M. Burns (1978) argued for the former point of view, but Tichy and Ulrich (1984) argued for the latter position. According to Burns, dedication, caring, and participation are multiplied outward from the leaders through their disciples; the leaders become the models to be imitated by successive expanding layers of followers. Tichy and Ulrich (1984) suggested that organizational changes envisioned by top management require lower-level managers to adopt leadership behavior supporting the practical implementation of their superiors' vision.

Most evidence supports modeling rather than alternating. Bowers and Seashore (1966) found that leadership behavior patterns exhibited by executives in insurance agencies were reflected in similar behavioral patterns by the supervisors below them. The supervisors' emphasis on the facilitation of goals and interaction with their subordinates was related to the extent to which the executives did the same. Similarly, Stogdill (1955) obtained data to indicate that participatory leadership at lower levels in an organization was dependent on its being practiced at higher levels. Ouchi and Maguire (1975) found that subordinates tended to use the same methods of control as their superiors in dealing with their own subordinates. Summarizing his studies of Japanese managers from the 1960s onward, Misumi (1985) reported that the supervisory style of a manager, with emphasis on either performance or maintenance, tended to be similar to the style found above and below the manager in the organizational hierarchy.

Bass, Waldman, Avolio, and Bebb (1987) collected self-rated and subordinate-rated leadership descriptions of second-line managers, their first-line supervisors, and their subordinates in New Zealand. A cascading effect of leadership behavior emerged. The amount of transformational and transactional leadership behavior observed at one level of management tended to be seen at the next lower level as well. The leadership patterns of subordinate-superior dyads tended to match each other. The correlation of the actual leadership observed among the levels was highest ($r = .51$) for the transactional exchange involved in providing contingent rewards.

To examine whether modeling of one's superior made a difference in the performance of one's group, Misumi (1985) calculated the capital growth rate in two Japanese banks with 25 and 54 branches, respectively. Pairs of high-producing and low-producing branches with similar socioeconomic characteristics were compared. First-level and second-level superiors were identified as being low or high in performance (P) and in maintenance (M) orientation. In one bank, 38% of the first- and second-level superiors matched each other in orientation in both the more productive and less productive branches; but in the second bank, 77% of the first- and second-level superiors in the less productive branches matched each other's orientation and 33% did so in the productive branches. The probability of matching on a chance basis was 25%. If the matching was high in P and M at both levels, effects were salutary; but if the matching was low in P and M, effects were counterproductive.

The alternating approach was observed indirectly when the same performance by commanding officers of ships and their executive officers appeared to produce opposite effects. In a study of shipboard organizations, D. T. Campbell (1956) found that although the leadership scores and sociometric interaction scores of the commanding officers were positively correlated with measures of shipboard efficiency and morale, the leadership and sociometric interaction scores of the executive officers, the commanders' closest aides, were negatively correlated with shipboard efficiency and morale.

Superleaders: Leading Followers to Lead Themselves

Manz and Sims (1987) first studied self-leading and discussed its theory, constraints, and effectiveness (Manz

& Sims, 1990). It could replace the leaders' providing orders, promises, or objectives about what needed to be done. Power was to be shared with followers. Followers would provide more direction for themselves. Their commitment would be higher because they "owned" how they proceeded. The superleaders would model self-leadership for the followers, create positive thought patterns, and use contingent reinforcement of the self-leading individuals, teams, and cultures (Manz & Sims, 1991). Manz, Keating, and Donellon (1990) discussed the transition from traditional supervisor to superleadership of teams of self-leaders. Self-led teams and self-management have become popular practices and are discussed further in Chapter 26, with regard to what conditions further the success or failure of self-leadership and self-management.

Complementary Linkages

The leader's relations with followers can depend on his or her relations with others, such as superiors and peers. In many organizations, the CEO and the chairman of the board work closely together to make corporate decisions. Gronn (1999) presented the case of close coupling, for over 10 years, of the founder, J. R. Darling, and the first head, E. H. Montgomery, in leading Timbertop, an Australian school. Another prominent leadership couple is the platoon leader and the platoon sergeant. The platoon leader is usually a commissioned officer and the platoon sergeant, a noncom. The officer is in charge, but the sergeant often is more experienced. Together, they provide the leadership of the platoon. According to a study of 72 light infantry platoons in near-combat testing for 11 missions, when the relations between the leaders and sergeants were good rather than poor, the platoons were rated much higher in effectiveness by pairs of independent observers of the platoons in action (Bass, Avolio, Jung, & Berson, 1999).

Importance of Supervisors' Influence with Higher-Ups. Pelz (1949, 1951, 1952) noted that when supervisors who had influence with their superiors took the side of their subordinates, the subordinates tended to feel more satisfied. But when a supervisor without such influence identified with the subordinates' interests, the subordinates tended to be more dissatisfied. Closeness to

subordinates and taking their side increased the subordinates' job satisfaction only when the supervisors had enough influence with their superiors to provide conditions that could result in the fulfillment of the subordinates' expectations. Jablin's (1980) results concurred with Pelz's findings, particularly for supportive supervisors with upward influence rather than nonsupportive supervisors with upward influence. Nahabetian (1969) found that in general, group members were better satisfied under leaders who had influence with their superiors than under leaders without such influence. Influential leaders were seen to facilitate the group's task, whereas those without influence higher up were seen as hindering it. Ronken and Lawrence (1952) reported similar findings. Anderson, Tolson, Fields, et al. (1990) demonstrated the Pelz effect in a study of 195 nurses and 201 clerical employees who were more satisfied with their jobs and felt more upward control if they perceived that their superiors had more influence with higher authority.

Combined Effects of Multiple Hierarchical Levels. Misumi (1985) showed the combined effects of two layers of supervision on the performance of banking subordinates. Hill and Hunt (1970) observed that although the leadership behavior of supervisors one level removed from the employees was not related to the employees' satisfaction, the combined behavior of first- and second-level supervisors did affect their satisfaction. Much initiative by both first- and second-level supervisors was significantly related to the employees' satisfaction with their own esteem and autonomy. George (1995) found that the contingent reward behavior of leaders was correlated at successive levels of sales management.

As evidence of the systematic connections between subordinates, supervisors, and their superiors, Stogdill and Goode (1957) concluded that when supervisors interacted frequently with their superiors, their subordinates thought the leaders should spend more time than they did in interviewing personnel and in coordination. According to Stogdill and Haase (1957), more impersonal performance by superiors, such as inspection, kept subordinates away from superiors. When superiors spent little time in preparing procedures and much time in technical performance, their subordinates tended to interact with peers; but when superiors spent more than an average amount of time in supervision, subordinates tended to interact with them. A high rate of communicating and integrating behavior by superiors enlarged the total number of interactions initiated and received by their subordinates, increased reciprocated interactions within the subgroups, and decreased interactions with members outside the subgroups.

Stogdill (1955) studied the effects of interactions among three hierarchical levels of organization members—subordinates, supervisors, and the superiors of the supervisors. The supervisors tended to interact more with their own subordinates when their superiors interacted more with them. The interactions of these supervisors with members outside their own subgroups were affected by whether their superiors were the initiators or the recipients of interactions within their own subgroups of supervisors. If their superiors were initiators rather than recipients of interaction with the subgroup of supervisors, the supervisors tended to interact less frequently with members outside their own subgroups. When their superiors interacted frequently with members outside the subgroups of supervisors, the supervisors also interacted with members outside this unit, but the supervisors interacted less often with their superiors.

When superiors interacted with the supervisors' peers, the supervisors tended to initiate more interactions with their superiors but received fewer interactions in return. In general, the superiors' interactions with the supervisors induced similar patterns of interaction between the supervisors and their subordinates. The supervisors' interactions with their superiors exerted the strongest effects in restricting the area of interaction of their subordinates.

In the previously mentioned study of three hierarchical levels of organization members (Bass, Waldman, Avolio, & Bebb, 1987), lower-level leaders who were seen by their subordinates as more charismatic, in turn, required less, not more charisma, in their superiors. It appears that charismatic leaders would rather not have a charismatic superior with whom they may have to compete.

Other Combinatory Effects. Stogdill and Goode (1957) observed also that leaders who interacted frequently with peers had subordinates who believed that their leaders had too little responsibility, were less active than they ought to be in representing their subordinates,

and spent too much time in planning. When leaders interacted extensively with people outside their own units, their subordinates reported having to delegate and represent their groups too much. These followers also thought they ought to spend more time than they did in inspection, planning, and preparation. In a study of a large naval organization, Stogdill and Haase (1957) found that the more time superiors actually spent in highly personal interactions with others, such as interviewing personnel, the less their subordinates actually interacted with their peers and initiated interactions with members of other subgroups with whom their interactions were reciprocated. On the other hand, Greenberg and Barling (1999) reported that the more supervisors monitored subordinates, the more hostility and aggression were found among 136 full-time employees, particularly when the monitoring was seen as unfair workplace surveillance. In a survey of 116 employees, Fedor, Davis, Maslyn, et al. (2001) found that the sources of a supervisor's power and the recipient's self-esteem made a difference in how much negative feedback affected subordinate performance.

Explanations. The multilevel and falling-dominoes effects may be due to differential selection as well as modeling. Lower-level supervisors can be either self-selected, selected by their second-level manager, or selected by the organization. It is not a matter of chance that they may be stylistically compatible with their superior. It is also possible that certain leadership behaviors are reinforced by the norms of organizational subunits; therefore, the cascade effects may be due to the subculture of norms, beliefs, and values within which the leaders operate. In the same way, the environmental and technical demands in one subunit may generate common job requirements and therefore dictate the differential leadership observed and required at the different levels of the subunit. Thus Smith, Moscow, Berger, and Cooper (1969) found weak support for the hypothesis that under conditions of slow organizational change, good interpersonal relations between managers and superiors were associated with good relations between managers and subordinates. But strong support was found for the hypothesis that under rapid organizational change, good relations between managers and their superiors changed into poor relations between the managers and their subordinates. The greater need for rapid change put pressure on the managers to push their subordinates for better performance and faster response. Superiors encouraged the managers in this regard; subordinates were disturbed by it.

Followers' Impact on Leaders

According to regression analysis, in eight organizations social distance and demographic divergence were important influences on 213 followers' relations with their leader (Boccialetti, 1995). Followers come in three types, according to Boccialetti. *Helpers* show deference and comply with the leadership; *independents* distance themselves from the leadership and show less compliance; and *rebels* show divergence from the leader and are least compliant. Among other types of followers, moderate in compliance, are *diplomats*, *partisans*, and *counselors*. The types differ in how they put up with their leaders as authority figures, accept responsibility, seize initiatives, and stay informed. Barbuto (2000) formulated a framework for predicting follower compliance from the leader's bases of power, the self-concept of the follower, the follower's intrinsic and extrinsic motivation, and the follower's zones of resistance to requests.

Heller and Van Til (1982, p. 405) argued that "leadership and followership are linked concepts; neither can be comprehended without understanding the other." The compliance of followers is the mirror image of successful leadership. Just as successful leadership may be seen to influence the completion of tasks and socioemotional relations, so the compliance of followers can be seen as instrumental to the completion of tasks and both public and private socioemotional acceptance of the leadership effort. It also seems obvious that by their performance, subordinates control the nature of feedback from their superior (Jablin, 1980). In the same way, just as the leader can influence subordinates by initiatives and information, the subordinates can complete the process and influence their leaders by giving feedback to them. Hegarty (undated) demonstrated that feedback of subordinates' ratings to supervisors resulted in positive changes in the supervisors' behavior. The employees of the 58 supervisors in the experimental and control groups completed an information opinion survey. The survey results were used to prepare feedback reports for the experimental supervisors but not for the control supervisors. A second survey was conducted 10 weeks later to measure change. After adjusting for the initial scores, Hegarty found that all 17 measures of change shifted more in the expected direction in the experimental than the control supervisors, six significantly so. Such feedback has become common in many organizations as a means for improving the effectiveness of leaders and their operations.[5]

Followership and Leadership

In the political arena, both immediate followers and grassroots citizens make a difference to what a leader can accomplish. Karl Rove, President George W. Bush's close advisor, influenced the president as much as or more than the president has influenced Rove. President Bill Clinton's Universal Health Plan of 1994 was defeated in Congress because of failure to gain public understanding and grassroots support. Active followers matter, as does their relationship to their leaders (Hollander, 1996). Followers increase their respect for a good leader and lose their respect for a bad one. A supportive, clearly communicating, and rewarding leader develops and strengthens the relationship with the follower and enhances the follower's satisfaction and performance. Unsupportive, harsh, and demeaning leaders create poor relations with followers, who then withhold information, become passive, withdrawn, and discouraged, and consider quitting (Hollander, 1996).

Followers' expectations affect the performance of their leaders. Followers' perceptions of their leaders' motives and actions constrain what their leaders can succeed in doing (Stewart, 1982b). Followers allow more discretionary opportunities for leaders who are seen to be more competent, legitimate, and expert in solving problems (Lord & Maher, 1991). From an analysis of a representative sample of 100 Swedish managers and their subordinates, Norrgren (1981a) found that the subordinates' levels of education and aspirations affected the managers' beliefs, intentions, and evaluations, particularly those of the younger managers. Furthermore, although older subordinates and subordinates with high aspirations and substantial seniority were most specifically favorable to-

---

[5] See, for instance, Bass (1976), Bowers and Franklin (1975), Carnmann and Nadler (1976), and Likert (1967).

ward managers who had beliefs and intentions to allow the subordinates to participate in decisions, it was the younger subordinates who reacted most negatively to managers with beliefs and intentions that were opposed to such participation (Norrgren, 1981b).

The compliance of subordinates is not automatic; it depends on the active cultivation of the leader's legitimacy. A leader's management style is affected by how the subordinates respond to it. The subordinates can actively work to undermine it, or they can work hard to support it because it serves their own interests or the "greater good." Self-interest, according to Biggart (1981), may have accounted for the strong loyalty of most of Ronald Reagan's subordinates, despite his hands-off management style when he served as governor of California and later as president of the United States. Cabinet officers resign when they can no longer support the policies of a prime minister. As will be noted below, good followers go beyond their self-interests for the good of their group, organization, or society.

The follower's influence on the leader also means that, contrary to popular notions, followership and leadership are highly similar, as are followers and leaders. Hollander and Webb (1955) showed that the same peers who are nominated as most desired leaders are also nominated as most desired followers. Nelson (1964a) found that among 72 men on a U.S. Antarctic expedition, the characteristics that made the men liked were about the same for the leaders as for the followers.

There are no sharp boundaries between the roles of leader and follower (J. M. Burns, 1978). Both roles always must be played in any group. Leaders cannot exist without followers; nor can followers exist without leaders. Moreover, leaders and followers exchange roles over time and in different settings. Many persons are leaders and followers at the same time. But the interaction between the leader and the follower is not symmetrical. K. M. Watson (1982) coded the antecedent acts of dyadic interactions of subordinates and leaders. When the leaders attempted to initiate structure, the subordinates were most likely to comply with deference. However, when the subordinates attempted to initiate structure, the most common reaction of the leaders was to resist by responding with efforts to try to structure the situation differently rather than to comply with the subordinates' initiative (Boccialetti, 1996).

The Good Follower. James (1995) argued that we need to pay more attention to the good follower. Kelley (1988) enumerated many elements that go into being a good follower. These elements are similar in many respects to what makes a good leader. The differences between the effective leader and the effective follower are mainly in the different roles they play. Good followers are active, independent, critical thinkers who can manage themselves. They are committed to the organization and to persons, principles, or purposes beyond themselves. Their personal and organizational goals are aligned. They are competent and avoid obsolescence by pursuing continuing education and development. They disagree agreeably. They build credibility. They can move easily into the leadership role and return again to the role of follower. Campbell (2000) adds that the follower who is proactive is not only competent, interpersonally effective, and organizationally oriented but also has integrity and is enterprising. Such followers are good "organizational citizens" who willingly contribute to the firm's effective functioning. They volunteer for assignments and put forth extra effort. They take the initiative to expand their role and take on new tasks. Albino (1999), a college president, agreed with Kelley (1992) that good followers are essential in higher education. Good followership is a discipline that requires going beyond self-interests. Effective leadership requires good followership. Effective leaders know how and when to follow. Lao-tzu suggested that to lead people, one must walk behind them. The effective leader follows the lead of the group (Rinne & Karl, 1990). According to 37 supervisors at retail stores and 58 bank supervisors, satisfactory subordinates (among a total of 274) helped to get things done.

One example is the turnaround in IBM in 1994 from a complacent manufacturer of mainframe computers and PCs that had been recognized by *Fortune* as a "most admired" company in the mid-1980s. In the three years preceding 1994 it had accumulated $15 billion in losses. David Grossman, a midlevel IBM programmer, was one of the first people to download the Mosaic browser and experience the Web. IBM was the highly advertised technology sponsor of the 1994 Winter Olympics, providing raw results on television. But when Grossman surfed the Web, he found that newcomer Sun Microsystems presented the results as a Sun contribution. Grossman drove to IBM headquarters with the necessary equipment to show the Internet to John Patrick, a senior marketing executive manager on IBM's strategic task force. Grossman and an associate built a primitive intranet for IBM, and Patrick published a document extolling uses of the Web, from replacing paper communication to e-commerce, and giving every employee an e-mail address. The new CEO was highly supportive. By 1996, IBM's Web site was able to earn $5 million from its e-commerce and launch into an effective changeover, becoming a consulting business (Hamel & Schonfeld, 2000).

The Susceptible Follower. According to Shamir and Howell (1999), followers who are more susceptible to the influence of a leader, particularly a directive and charismatic one, are likely to be unstable, uncertain, and inconsistent about their own self-concept. They do not have a clear, consistent self-concept that could guide their behavior. Furthermore, susceptible followers' values and identities are congruent with those of their leader. They will also be more readily influenced by a leader who seemingly has the support of majority opinion.

Antitheses of Leaders. If not the followers, then who are the opposites of leaders? They are those barred from the process (for instance, the underage, who cannot vote). They are the isolates, the rejectees, and the anomic. They are those who exclude themselves from participation—the apathetic and the alienated. The apathetic may be too busy with other affairs or too busy just surviving. The alienated may reject and resist participation; they believe that the power to lead is in the hands of others, for the benefit of others. The anomic feel powerless, normless, and aimless, and see leaders indifferent to their needs (J. M. Burns, 1978). These nonleaders-nonfollowers, by their lack of involvement, can have a negative impact on their groups, organizations, and societies. Quoting deJouvenal ("A society of sheep must in time beget a government of wolves"), Gardner (1987b) noted that those who fail to follow but remain the antithesis of leadership invite the leader's abuse of power.

Upward Influence

Despite the asymmetry of the relationship, followers exert considerable upward influence on their leaders (Gabarro & Kotter, 1980). Followers can actively affect leaders in

many important ways (Hollander, 1992). Upward feedback was provided by subordinates to their managers in a quasi-experimental Australian study. Compared with the managers' initial performance and a control group, managerial performance was improved considerably six months later, particularly if the managers had an orientation toward the goal of learning (Heslin & Latham, 2004). Farmer and Maslyn (1999) confirmed three styles of upward influence first typed by Kipnis and Schmidt (1988): *bystander, tactician,* and *shotgun.*

Acts of moral courage by elected political leaders can be strongly pressured by constituencies, economic blocs, and organized letter writers (Paige, 1977). Reed (1996) argued that civic followers are actually leaders as they monitor the affairs of society and react accordingly. On tour, President Woodrow Wilson was first shocked, then braced, by hearing a voice from the crowd shout, "Attaboy, Woody" (Davies, 1963). After they have been elected, U.S. presidents may try to ignore their own campaign rhetoric or reinterpret it to fit their preferred policies. But when public opinion is sufficiently aroused, the presidents become responsive and usually adopt the opinion of the strong public majority as their own. In 1983, public opinion polls indicated that the public did not find much reason for placing U.S. Marines at risk in Lebanon in the exercise of a presidential policy that had been in effect for at least a year. Despite the continuing lack of public approval, days before the terrorist bombing of the Marine barracks President Reagan publicly expressed his opinion that we would never "cut and run." Days after the bombing and the loss of life, which greatly aroused public opinion against the policy, the Marines were "redeployed offshore" (Gwertzman, 1983). President Clinton was sensitive to the results of daily public opinion polling. But like Reagan, President George W. Bush was less responsive to adverse domestic or foreign public opinion about American military forces and kept accusing the Democrats of wanting to "cut and run" from Iraq. Still, suddenly, in June 2006, Bush accepted a plan for a staged withdrawal from Iraq, which subsequently did not occur.

Upward influence is seen as an important contribution to organizational effectiveness (Gabarro, 1979) and a key to understanding organizational politics (Porter, Allen, & Angle, 1981). Subordinates have the responsibility to exert upward influence on their bosses for their mutual benefit and the benefit of the organization as a whole. Subordinates should challenge their superiors' proposals and help them avoid mistakes, but subordinates can do so only if they have contributed to building trust between their superiors and themselves. The subordinates must provide adequate information and account for their performance in carrying out delegated assignments. Effective subordinates will actively invite review, support, and feedback from their superiors (Crockett, 1981).

The Tactics of Upward Influence. Upward influence tactics used by subordinates were identified and scaled by Kipnis, Schmidt, and Wilkinson (1980) as: assertiveness; reasoning; bargaining about the exchange of benefits; appealing to a higher authority; forming coalitions; or trying friendliness, ingratiation, and flattery.[6] The list of items was refined and the subscales confirmed by Schriesheim and Hinkin (1988). For Schilit and Locke (1982), upward influence tactics included logical or rational presentation of ideas; informal exchange not related to performance, such as ingratiation or praising the superior; promising rewards or threatening sanctions; adhering to rules; manipulating matters so that the superior is unaware of being influenced; mobilizing coalitions of support among coworkers and higher-ups; and being persistent or assertive.

Supervisor-focused upward influence tactics by subordinates such as ingratiation and impression management aim to increase being liked by the supervisor. They result in receiving higher performance ratings from the supervisor (Wayne & Liden, 1995). Job-focused upward influence tactics are self-promoting and self-serving distortions to increase the appearance of competence (Dulebohn & Ferris, 1999).

Hard, Soft, or Persuasive? Like leaders, followers may use tactics of upward influence that are hard (assertiveness), soft (friendliness, ingratiation), and rational (persuasive). In a national sample of 225 mainly women employees of 60 branches of a nonprofit health and advocacy organization, Fedor, Goodman, and Maslyn (1992) found that hard tactics of upward influence were used

more frequently by respondents higher in Machiavellianism; soft tactics were used by those higher in internal locus of control and self-monitoring. Followers were also more likely to use soft tactics with leaders perceived to have more control of rewards and punishments. Rational tactics were used more by followers if their leaders were valued and esteemed with referent power. Deluga (1991a) found that 102 bank employees high in self-monitoring used all three kinds of tactics for upward influence, particularly if they also were high in deceiving others. According to another survey by Deluga (1988), soft upward influence tactics such as reason and friendliness were used more frequently by 70 managers and employees from various departments when they rated their leaders as transformational. In still another survey by Deluga (1991b), 82 hospital personnel were shown to contribute to their managers' felt interpersonal stress by using hard upward influence tactics ($r = .72$) and reduced such stress by using rational influence tactics ($r = .52$). Assertiveness, coalition, and bargaining were used less frequently. Epitropaki and Martin (2001) found that "to get their way with their manager" 271 employees in one service company and six manufacturing companies said they were more likely to use soft and rational tactics with a transformational manager and less likely to use hard tactics. They were also less likely to use hard or rational tactics with transactional leaders. According to Deluga and Souza (1991), 117 police officers reviewing scenarios were more likely to choose rational upward influence as more appropriate if the supervisor were transformational rather than transactional. Elsewhere, Deluga (1988) noted that when leaders were rated as transactional, fewer if any upward influence tactics were tried.

Impression Management. Followers practice impression management with defensive tactics such as trying to justify inadequate performance with excuses and apologies, or with proactive tactics such as self-promotion to appear competent and dependable so as to attract their boss's attention or to obtain authorization for changes. They may also do personal favors for the boss and ingratiate themselves with the boss in other ways (Wayne & Ferris, 1990; Yukl, 1998). From 67 manager-subordinate pairs, Rao, Schmidt, and Murray (1995) obtained the managers' appraisals of the subordinates and the subordinates' styles of influence. Coalitions resulted in favorable

---

[6]Hinkin and Schriesheim (1986) and Schriesheim and Hinkin (1989) reworked the original upward influence measures of Kipnis, Schmidt, and Wilkinson, which resulted in improving their factorial structure and content validity with a shorter set of 27 questionnaire items.

impressions and appraisals of the subordinates, but subordinate ingratiation and assertiveness did not. Wayne and Liden (1995), in a study of 111 supervisor-subordinate dyads, found path coefficients of .40 and .33 between the subordinates' supervisor-focused impression management and the supervisors' liking of and perceived similarity to the subordinate. This in turn yielded a path coefficient of .21 for appraised subordinate performance when demographic similarity was taken into account.

Usages. All 123 salaried employees in a metal fabricating firm surveyed by Deluga (1986) used ingratiation, flattery, reason, and assertiveness much more frequently when trying to influence their superiors than they used bargaining and appeals to coworkers or to a higher authority. Deluga (1988) reported that when their first efforts to influence their transactional but not their transformational superiors did not work, 117 managers and employees of a northeastern manufacturing firm subsequently displayed significantly less friendliness and assertiveness toward their superiors and appealed less to a higher authority. According to Schmidt and Kipnis (1984), staff managers were more likely than line managers to attempt more upward influence to achieve individual goals.

Purposes. Subordinates' goals will determine which tactics they use. To affect policy, subordinates will be more likely to use reasoning and the rational presentation of ideas (Kipnis, Schmidt, & Wilkinson, 1980; Schmidt & Kipnis, 1984). Mowday (1978) found that elementary school principals who were power motivated were more likely to attempt upward influence. In a study in India, the need for power determined the particular power strategies that 96 managers from the public sector said they used to influence their superiors. Most of the strategies they used were "soft and subtle" (Singh, Kumari, & Singh, 1988). To promote self-interests, to attain personal goals, and to obtain benefits, the Indian administrators were more likely to try ingratiation and promises for a satisfactory exchange with their superior based on their evaluation of the superior's preferences. In looking at the specific reasons why subordinates attempt to ingratiate themselves with their bosses, Ralston (1985) argued that ingratiation was more likely to be used by Machiavellian subordinates with autocratic superiors in an ambiguous setting. In an experiment in India, Pandey

and Bohra (1984) confirmed that subjects who acted as subordinates were likely to endorse ingratiating tactics with executives who liked to have admirers around them; who preferred employees who supported their views, praised their ideas, and conformed to their policies uncritically; who used subjective criteria in making decisions about employees' requests for benefits; and who rewarded those whose behavior flattered and pleased them. In contrast, ingratiation was less likely to be suggested as a viable tactic if one was working for an executive who had the opposite tendencies.

Successful Upward Influence. Schilit and Locke (1982) asked employees and supervisors about more and less successful ways for subordinates to influence their superiors. Both subordinates and supervisors agreed that subordinates used logical presentations more than any other tactic in attempts at upward influence and agreed that the substance of the effort determined its success. But they disagreed on what caused attempts at upward influence to fail. Although the supervisors attributed failure to the substance of the attempt, subordinates attributed failure to the closed-mindedness of the supervisors. In an analysis of the diaries of 60 middle-level managers over a two-month period, Schilit (1987) found that the managers high in tested need for power thought they had more upward influence on strategic decisions. Such felt upward influence coincided with a high need for achievement, self-control, and experience with their superiors. As a whole, the managers tended to believe themselves to be successful in their attempts at upward influence, particularly in attempts involving less risky strategic decisions. Rice (1986) offered suggestions on how to cope with a difficult boss: subordinates should observe how others succeed in getting along with the boss; they should offer to be helpful; they need to keep track of their boss's mood swings, discussing his or her mistreatment of them in private, when the boss is calm; subordinates should avoid seeking the boss's approval when it is not required, but they should not dispute the boss's legitimate authority even if they disagree with his or her judgments.

The Subordinate as a Source of Feedback. Considerable upward influence may occur in the course of the subordinate's feedback to the superior. For effective superior-subordinate relations, feedback must flow both ways; a loop must be maintained. In their attitudes and behavior, leaders can hinder the flow or help close the loop from the subordinates back to them (Kaplan, Drath, & Kofodimos, 1985). Hegarty (1974) showed that subordinate ratings of supervisors could improve supervisors' behavior. Reliability and validity of upward appraisals was likely to be higher than appraisal from a single boss, since multiple subordinates are available to rate each supervisor (Harris & Schaubroeck, 1988). Improvements in managerial performance were found over a five-year period for 252 managers who received feedback from their direct reports and discussed their previous year's feedback, compared with managers who did not (Walker & Smither, 1999). Subordinate upward appraisals were found to be among the best predictors of managerial performance (McEvoy & Beatty, 1989).

Facilitators and Inhibitors. The willingness of 153 employees in a university affairs office to provide feedback to their supervisors was greater if they felt it was beneficial ($r = .52$), if they did not fear retaliation ($r = .39$), if they perceived organizational support ($r = .39$), if they felt it was appropriate to their role ($r = .26$), if they were knowledgeable about upward feedback ($r = .23$), and if they sought feedback themselves ($r = .22$; Smith, Kudisch, & Thibodeaux, 2000). At a research university, 411 of 1,135 faculty members who participated in anonymous upward appraisals were more confident about the accuracy of the ratings, felt they did not have to bias ratings, felt more secure in rating superiors, and perceived that more effects would accrue from the process (Westerman & Rosse, 1997).

Superiors prevent their subordinates' criticism from reaching them by monopolizing conversations, by developing an abrasive style, by emphasizing their own power and status, and by "adopting the mantle of their office when interacting with lower level managers" (Bruce, 1986). Leaders who receive positive feedback do not seem to evaluate subordinates differently, but they do evaluate less active subordinates less favorably if the feedback is negative (Elgie, Hollander, & Rice, 1988). They avoid discussing issues until they are ready to make a decision. They distance themselves from subordinates and become isolated and insulated from feedback from below by selecting subordinates to bolster their own thoughts and feelings.

Channels of communication dry up as one moves upward in an organization. Information is increasingly filtered, as it must flow through more levels. To promote the upward flow of information, superiors need to reduce perceived differences in power, make themselves more accessible, and open informal channels (Bruce, 1986). They need to reward—not punish—messengers who bring bad news or disturbing opinions. They need to be aware that despite the greater pressure to communicate upward than downward, their subordinates are quite reluctant to risk their displeasure by being seen as critics of the current state of affairs or as bearers of unpleasant messages. Superiors can encourage systematic surveys of subordinates' attitudes that are a formal medium for upward feedback. They can institute a policy, as did the British Army in World War II, that each commander must pay frequent visits to all the unit commanders at the level immediately below. They can practice "walk-around" management, in which managers visit employees' work stations. This policy can promote upward feedback informally if the employees recognize that their superiors, particularly those at high levels in the organization, may feel out of touch with those at the lower levels and would appreciate receiving positive, supportive feedback as well as constructive criticism. The higher-level receivers must make it clear that they are open to accept feedback; the lower-level senders must be ready to provide feedback that is free of the distortion commonly observed in upward messages in which subordinates tell the superiors what they believe the superiors want to hear (Jablin, 1980).

In addition to such motivated distortion, there is cognitive distortion because of the different meanings that superiors and subordinates attach to the same words and their different perceptions and broader views about the same issues (Smircich & Chesser, 1981). When upward feedback was provided to supervising officers in a police agency, the extent to which they reacted positively and took steps to improve depended on their organizational cynicism (Atwater, Waldman, Atwater, et al., 2000). When subordinate feedback is given as part of a 360-degree appraisal program, the upward feedback is perceived as useful if there is organizational support for it (Facteau, Facteau, Schoel, et al., 1998).

Maturity of Followers

An axiom of learning theory and counseling is that a learner needs more guidance early in training and less guidance later in training. In the same way, the novice subordinate requires more direction and the mature subordinate requires less. Less can be delegated to the novice; more can be delegated to the mature subordinate. The subordinates' readiness and competence determine how much and what kind of leadership can be efficacious.[7]

Readiness and Maturity. Followers strongly affect the likelihood of a leader's success in influencing them as a consequence of whether they are ready for the leader. J. M. Burns (1978) suggested that followers could be ripe for mobilization by a leader or, on the contrary, imprisoned by fixed beliefs that would make it impossible to lead them. In the same vein, Heller (1969a) pointed out that some level of agreement about procedures, interests, and norms among followers is necessary for effective participatory leadership. Nie, Powell, and Prewitt (1969) found five sets of attitudes that were of consequence to such readiness among political followers in Germany, Italy, Mexico, the United States, and Britain: (1) a sense of duty; (2) information about politics; (3) a stake in political outcomes; (4) a sense of political efficiency; and (5) attentiveness to politics. According to L. L. Moore (1976), fully effective leadership tends to depend on mature followership. Moore developed a maturity index based on observations of verbal and nonverbal behavior of followers in task groups. Dimensions of maturity were perspective, position, awareness, activity level, dependence, motivation to achieve, ability and willingness to take responsibility, task-relevant education or experience, and variety of behavioral interests. The leader's knowledge of the followers' maturity can facilitate and modify the followers' and the leader's behavior.

One's readiness to accept the suggestions of leaders will depend on one's immediately preceding experiences. For instance, negative arguments that were introduced before an attempt to persuade students to volunteer for civil defense work were found more likely to reduce the success of the positive arguments than were the negative arguments that came later (Feierabend & Janis, 1954). Another antecedent to determining the readiness of subordinates for a subsequent attempt to lead them is the extent to which the attempted leadership fits with previous experiences. Weiss and Fine (undated) found that groups who were first subjected to failure and insult were more influenced by suggestions to be punitive; groups first subjected to rewarding experiences were more likely to respond to suggestions to be lenient. Also important is the followers' sense of security—whether the followers have a general trust of others and are comfortable with others. The insecure are anxious and avoid attachments (Hazen & Shaver, 1987). Among 127 undergraduate management students who ranked themselves as followers in their small class groups, Berson and Yammarino (1998) found that on scales of implicit leadership, the secure students ranked their ideal leader high if the leader was charismatic and considerate. They ranked low a leader who tried to initiate structure but did not lead. Insecure students ranked their ideal leader as a nonleader low in consideration. Lord, Brown, and Frieberg (1999) suggested that the working self-concepts of followers are changed by the leader through the development of schemas and are influenced by the leader's self-schema.

Effects on the Leader of the Follower's Interest and Competence. What subordinates seek in their jobs affects what their supervisor can and will do (Maier, 1965). Jones, James, and Bruni (1975) showed that the degree to which trust and confidence of 112 engineering employees correlated with the behavior of their supervisors was affected by whether the employees were involved in their work. If the subordinates preferred to avoid risk, if they did not wish to become involved in the task, if they were uninterested in the task, and if their interest was of no relevance to getting the job done, leaders became directive. But if subordinates wanted to be involved and were interested in what happened, more supervisory leadership occurred to engage them. Thus when the British managers who were surveyed by Heller (1969a) saw a decision as being important to subordinates but not to the company, they used a high degree of power sharing. Conversely, when a decision was a matter of concern to the company but not to subordinates, they preferred the centralization of power.

If the time required for subordinates to participate in

[7]Hersey and Blanchard's Life Cycle Theory of Leadership is built on this premise and will be discussed in detail in Chapter 19.

decision making is more expensive than the value of their contribution, effective supervisors will be more directive than participative (Tannenbaum & Massarik, 1950; Lowin, 1968). On the other hand, if the supervisors value the competence of their subordinates, they will be more participative (Likert, 1959). Thus Hsu and Newton (1974) found that supervisors of unskilled employees in a manufacturing plant were more directive than were supervisors of skilled employees in the same plant. Similar results were obtained experimentally by Lowin and Craig (1968) with students who thought themselves to be in part-time jobs. When the students thought they lacked competence for the tasks to be done, they were more appreciative of close, directive supervision than when they considered themselves competent. Likewise, Heller (1969a) reported that whenever managers considered their technical ability, decisiveness, and intelligence much greater than those of their subordinates, they were more likely to use autocratic decision methods. But when the subordinates were valued for their expertise, they were more likely to be invited to share in the decision process with their supervisors.

Ashour and England (1971) found, in experimental teams of supervisors and secretaries, that the perceived competence of followers was the major determinant in assignment of discretionary tasks. Supervisors allowed competent secretaries more discretion than they permitted incompetent secretaries. Another effect of the competence of subordinates on superiors was seen by Kim and Organ (1982) using an in-basket simulation. "Supervisors" were more likely to initiate noncontractual social exchanges with competent "subordinates." Scandura, Graen, and Novak (1986) showed, in this regard, that supervisors were more willing to involve competent subordinates in nontrivial decisions, particularly subordinates with whom they had good relations. However, the competence of followers could produce resistance. Thus Mausner (1954a) showed that participants with a past history of positive reinforcement in a given type of judgment were less influenced by their partners in a group-judgment situation than were participants with a history of negative reinforcement. Nevertheless, effective followers are those who, despite their own competence, can avoid being overly resistant to influence from others because of the followers' capacity and willingness to learn from others. They listen, discriminate, and are guided by

others without feeling threatened or fearing loss of status (J. M. Burns, 1978).

The competence of followers affects how they view their leaders' initiation and consideration. Cashman and Snyder (1980) reported systematic differences in the factor structure of 475 descriptions of supervisors by more competent and less competent subordinates. Snyder and Bruning (1985) found that the competence of 815 employees of federally funded social service organizations correlated .24 with their evaluations of the quality of the dyadic linkage with their superiors. The same correlation was obtained by Bass (undated) for 220 manufacturing employees who were sorted by their supervisors into "best" and "less than best" and the employees' satisfaction with their supervision.

Subordinates' competence may affect their ability to comply. Numerous studies have shown, as seems obvious, that the compliance of subordinates affects their superiors' attitudes and behavior toward them. In a laboratory experiment, Price and Garland (1981) demonstrated that when the group members were low in competence, they were much more willing to comply with their leader's suggestions. Nevertheless, in some situations, compliance can suffer because the member is unable to comply, rather than unwilling. Kessler (1968) hypothesized that highly rated subordinates in a governmental agency would be highly motivated to act in accord with their superiors' expectations; instead, Kessler found that these subordinates were most independent. Consistent with this, Simmons (1968) observed that in a business game, students who were rated as very low, low, or average in performance complied more closely with the managers' expectations than did those who were rated high in performance. Evidently, the competent, highly valued subordinates felt greater freedom than did the less highly valued subordinates to deviate from managers' expectations.

Performance of Followers

Effects of Followers' Good or Poor Performance. The quality of the subordinates' performance—good or poor—has obvious effects on whether their leaders will be supportive or punitive toward them (Podsakoff & Schriesheim, 1958a, b). The evidence in this regard is overwhelming. Barrow (1976) and Herold (1977) found that leaders rewarded good performers and behaved more punitively toward poor performers. Farris and Lim (1969) agreed. They divided 200 male graduate management students into 50 groups to play a business discussion game. Some leaders, appointed at random, were told that they had high-producing groups, and other leaders were told they had low-producing groups. Leaders who were told that their groups were high producers were significantly more likely to be seen by their groups as sensitive, nonpunitive, maintaining high standards, exerting less pressure to produce, allowing freedom, and emphasizing teamwork than were leaders who were told their groups were low producers. The subordinates in the high-performance condition were better satisfied, felt they had more influence, and described their groups as more cohesive.

In a laboratory study, Lowin and Craig (1968) artificially established the level of subordinates' performance as either high or low. "Poor" performing subordinates tended to elicit from their appointed leader close supervision with frequent directions and checking. The ideas of the "poor" subordinates were ignored. These subordinates were held closely to prescribed procedures, viewed by their leader as irresponsible, and treated with less consideration. The laboratory "supervisors" of the "poorly" performing subordinates criticized them more for their work and for taking unauthorized breaks, ordered them to return to work, and showed them less support than did supervisors of "high-producing" subordinates. In studying the behavior of 82 coaches of boys' baseball teams, Curtis, Smith, and Smoll (1979) found that compared with the behavior of winning coaches, proportionally more of the behaviors of coaches on losing teams were reactions to players' mistakes and misbehaviors. (Of course, players on losing teams usually make more mistakes.) But more important, players perceived the coaches of losing teams to be more punitive and less supportive than winning coaches. With teams of older boys, such perceptions by team members became more significant to their continuing performance as winners or losers.

Lanzetta and Hannah (1969) found that trainers were rewarding when trainees responded correctly, but the trainers were punitive when the trainees responded incorrectly. Bankart and Lanzetta (1970) found that reward and punishment were systematically related to observed performance; rewards were given for good performance

and punishments for poor performance. Kipnis and Vanderveer (1971) concluded that "managers" in a simulated work setting rewarded superior performers more than average performers and average performers more than poor performers. Fodor (1973a) also reported that superior performers were given more rewards than average workers. Chow and Grusky (1980), in a laboratory study, observed that supervision was less close for productive workers than for unproductive workers. Sims and Manz (1984) studied laboratory subjects who served as the appointed supervisors of "subordinates" who actually were confederates of the experimenters. The subjects tended to provide positive verbal rewards for the "subordinates'" good performance and punitive and goal-setting verbal comments when the "subordinates'" performance was poor. More of the subjects' supervisory activity dealt with clarifying how the task could be accomplished than with evaluations of the subordinates' efforts.

Continued punishment may lead to a downward spiral in performance. Moreover, *learned helplessness* can occur. A particular area of poor performance will be dealt with even more punitively than usual if a subordinate is generally viewed as a poor performer (James & White, 1983). Overall performance will deteriorate further (Peterson, 1985a). However, there is some buffering against the downward spiral. Rothbart (1968) found that when the use of rewards in a prior trial in an experiment produced improved performance, the administrator had a strong tendency to use reward again. But if punishment on a previous trial led to increased performance, it was unlikely to be used in the next trial.

Effects of the Causes Supervisors Attribute to Subordinates' Performance. Calder (1977) and Green and Mitchell (1979) proposed that to understand how a subordinate's performance affects a supervisor's reactions requires a determination of the cause of the subordinate's good or poor performance as identified by the supervisor.[8] Four causes were seen as possibilities: competence, effort, luck, and external causes within or outside the subordinate's control. Competence and effort were causes internal to the subordinate; luck and uncontrollable causes were external. Knowlton and Mitchell (1980) demonstrated, with 40 undergraduates who were ostensi-

[8]This comprehensive line of investigation grew from earlier theorization by Kelley (1973) and by Weiner, Frieze, Kukla, et al. (1971).

bly supervising confederates of the experimenter, that if supervisors attributed the good performance of their subordinates to the subordinates' efforts, they evaluated the subordinates more highly than ordinarily. But this did not happen if the good performance was attributed to the subordinates' competence. Ilgen and Knowlton (1980) reached similar conclusions. Mitchell (1981) and Brown and Mitchell (1986) found that supervisors were more likely to blame subordinates for a poor performance and its consequences than for external causes. In doing so, the supervisors gave more weight to information about the subordinates' lack of effort than to the subordinates' lack of ability.

For supervisors in a role-playing simulation conducted by Liden and Green (1980), the poor performance of subordinates in missing a deadline was described as being due either to their taking an overextended lunch break (an internal cause) or to a delay in receiving materials (an external cause). The supervisors attributed taking too much time for lunch to the subordinates' personal character and failure to take responsibility for their action. Supervisors were more intense in their punitive reactions to the subordinates who missed the deadline because they took a long lunch. The supervisors thought they should do something more punitive than just talking to the subordinate about the matter, but the subordinates thought that such a discussion was sufficient. The supervisors were less likely to carry out stated corrective policies when the failure was due to an external cause—the delay in receiving materials.

In similar studies, supervisors generally were found to be more punitive when they attributed poor performance to internal causes—subordinate ability or effort—rather than to external causes. If lack of effort was the diagnosed cause, punitive action was more likely than if lack of ability was seen as the cause. If lack of ability was regarded as the cause of the subordinate's poor performance, then training or replacement of the subordinate was indicated (Mitchell & Wood, 1980; Wood & Mitchell, 1981). Employees who were described as succeeding because of their ability were seen to have more potential for top management positions than those who were thought to be successful because of their efforts, external conditions, or good luck (Heilman & Guzzo, 1978).

Brown and Mitchell (1986) reported that attributions of internal causes increased if poor performance was de-

tected in just one of several employees. The employees did not have to be working on interdependent tasks for this to happen. However, in a laboratory experiment with undergraduates, Offerman, Schroyer, and Green (1986) showed that leaders advocated reward or punishment for actual success or failure rather than for the reasons they attributed for the subordinates' performance. The leaders also increased their talking to subordinates whose success they attributed to luck, as well as to subordinates whose poor performance was attributed to a lack of effort. Attributions by leaders of the causes of followers' failures also affected their talking and negative comments (Offerman, Schroyer, & Green, 1998). Heneman, Greenberger, et al. (1989) found that the reported quality of leader-subordinate exchanges by 188 supervisors in 37 organizations was increased by how much they attributed competence and effort to their subordinates' performance, but not by how much they attributed the performance to luck or other external causes.

Effect of Supervisory Experience. In a laboratory experiment and in a field study with military officers, Mitchell and Kalb (1982) found that the superiors' experience made a difference. Experienced supervisors were more likely to emphasize external causes than internal causes as the reason for the subordinates' poor performance. Liden (1981) obtained similar findings for bank managers' explanations of the poor performance of subordinates; again, more experience resulted in more external attributions. On the other hand, Mitchell and Kalb argued that if the subordinate had performed poorly on the same task before, if the subordinate also performed poorly on other tasks, and if coworkers were performing well on the task, supervisors would be expected to attribute the subordinate's poor performance to the subordinate rather than to external causes, and to act accordingly. Gioia and Sims (1986) demonstrated with 24 experienced managers, each interacting with four different subordinates in simulated performance appraisal interviews, that the interviews resulted in a more lenient appraisal of the subordinates afterward. The managers attached less blame to their subordinates for failure and more credit for success after the meeting than before it.

Effects of Subordinates' Accounts. If subordinates apologize or provide an explanation of the external causes for their poor performance, they can affect their supervisor's interpretation and reaction. In an experiment with 109 nursing supervisors, Wood and Mitchell (1981) showed that although both tactics may work to reduce the supervisor's blame of the subordinate, explanations were much more effective than were apologies. In another study, Mitchell and Liden (1982) established that a supervisor's punitive action for a subordinate's poor performance might be moderated by the subordinate's social skills and popularity. Lenient reactions of supervisors, according to a study in Israel by Bizman and Fox (1984), may result because supervisors see good acts by subordinates—such as avoiding waste; not squandering resources; performing duties with precision and thoroughness; and making efficient and practical use of information—as being more stable in occurrence than bad acts by subordinates, such as setting up difficulties in planning and organizing work, creating unpleasantness, and not following supervisors' instructions.

Martinko and Gardner (1987) traced different likely outcomes from the combined attributions of leaders and subordinates about the subordinates' failure to perform adequately. If both the leader and the subordinate consider that the subordinate's failure was due to bad luck, the leader will take no action and the subordinate will not change. If the leader attributes the subordinate's failure to a lack of effort, if the subordinate does likewise, and if the leader reprimands the subordinate, the subordinate will increase his or her effort. However, if subordinates continue to perform poorly or if the leader continues to punish them, they will attribute the continued failure to external conditions, including the leader's punitiveness.

Followers' Compliance

Effects on Leaders of Compliance or Noncompliance. It is evident from the previous section that leaders tend to react to their subordinates' compliance or noncompliance. As expected, Hinton and Barrow (1975) found that supervisors rewarded subordinates for compliance with the supervisors' requests and were punitive when subordinates did not comply. Fodor (1974) demonstrated, also as expected, that leaders became more authoritarian when faced with a disparaging and disruptive subordinate. Naturally, they rated such a subordinate lower and gave the subordinate less pay than they did

subordinates who did not engage in such behavior. In an experiment by Crowe, Bochner, and Clark (1972), male management students were asked to play the role of a leader. Each was confronted with accomplices of the experimenters who served as subordinates and acted either *democratically* or *submissively*. "Democratic" subordinates showed initiative by putting forth ideas and trying to set their own goals. "Submissive" subordinates avoided taking any initiative and asked for detailed instructions, which they followed without question. The student subjects' leader behavior was affected accordingly. For example, the students were more autocratic with the submissive subordinates and more democratic with the democratic ones. Chow and Grusky (1980) found that in laboratory-simulated organizational settings, subordinates' compliance generated employee-oriented supervision, whereas subordinate's aggressiveness resulted in punitive supervision.

In a longitudinal field survey, Greene (1979a) reported that the subordinate's compliance exerted considerable subsequent influence on the supervisor. If the subordinate was more compliant and performed better early on, the supervisor in the following three months displayed more considerate, supportive, and participative leadership. However, if the subordinate's performance was poor early on, the supervisor initiated more structure and role clarification later. Poor subordinate performance, particularly noncompliance, generated the leader's greater use of punishment three or six months later.

Better supervisors in real life tend to look for and to reward independent action in subordinates, whereas less effective supervisors tend to reward conformity and group action. The better supervisors are also less lenient (Kirchner, 1961; Kirchner & Reisberg, 1962).

Effects of Contrasting Subordinates. A supervisor's reactions to a subordinate's compliance appears to depend on the failure of other subordinates to comply. In a field study of the performance of clerical workers, Grey and Kipnis (1976) found that the supervisors' evaluations of compliant workers were higher in work groups with more noncompliant workers. Evaluations of noncompliant workers tended to be lower in work groups with more compliant workers. Goodstadt and Kipnis (1970) and Kipnis and Vanderveer (1971) found that in the presence of a poorly performing subordinate with a bad attitude, subjects allocated nearly twice as many pay raises to compliant workers as they did when the poorly performing subordinate was seen as simply inept, rather than disparaging.

Leader-Member Exchange (LMX)

Inner Circle versus Outer Circle

The concept of leader-member exchange (LMX) originated with the phenomenon that leaders of a group or work unit tend to perceive each member as *in-group* or *out-group*. The leaders pay more attention to the inner core and maintain different relations with the "inners" and "outers." They "incorporate some members into the inner life of an organization but exclude others" (Sparrowe & Liden, 1997). Leaders' relations (LMXs) with the inner and outer circles differ. They evaluate members of the inner circle less critically (Duarte, Goodson, & Klich, 1994). According to LMX theory, the development of the members' roles will be differentially reinforced because the leader does not have the time to give all members equal attention. Furthermore, the leader differentially values subordinates and fosters the success of those he or she values most (Chassie, 1984). The leader also initiates more exchanges with highly competent subordinates (Kim & Organ, 1982) and establishes a close relationship with only a few key members—the inner group. Subordinates who are similar to their leader in the leader's perceived use of power, and in the subordinates' use of negotiation, choose to enhance their closeness to the leader. Those not in the inner circle use distancing tactics with leaders seen as dissimilar, according to an analysis of 230 supervisor-subordinate dyads by Townsend and Jones (2000). For dealing with the outer group, the leader relies on formal authority (Graen, 1976). Hollander (1978), among others, observed that it is commonplace in groups and organizations for an inner clique to form with whom the leader has closer relations than with the rest of the group. The inner clique gets more attention and more approval and possibly more status but is expected to be more loyal and committed to the leader and the group. The envy of members of the outer circle is likely to be aroused, and the inner clique must share more blame for the leader's failures. According to Mayfield and Mayfield (1998), the performance of members of the inner group is about 20% higher than that of members of the outer group.

Differences in Influence. Dansereau, Graen, and Haga (1975) interviewed 60 leaders and their individual subordinates four times over nine months. For members of the inner group, the leader-subordinate dyadic exchange was seen as a partnership that was characterized by reciprocal influence; extracontractual behavior; mutual trust, respect, and liking; and a sense of a common fate. For the members of the outer group, the exchange was characterized by downward influence, role-defined relations, and a sense of loosely coupled fates. The leader was seen as an overseer. The higher quality of the vertical-dyad linkage for the inner group than for the outer group was correlated with the leader's greater attention to the inner group. The energy and effort of the inner group were greater; they had fewer job problems. Duchon, Green, and Tabor (1986) found that members of the inner group were more compatible with the leader and had better relations with the leader than did members of the outer group, although outer-group members were not necessarily less satisfied with their leader or with their influence. Graen and Schiemann (1978) obtained results indicating that leader-member dyads in the inner group agreed more on the meaning of shared experiences than did leader-member dyads of the outer circle. In a study of first-level supervisors and their immediate superiors by Liden and Graen (1980), the outer-group members reported spending less time in decision making and were less likely to volunteer for special assignments and extra work.

Effects. Where outcomes have been based on criteria other than self-reports of the leaders and the members, the findings about membership in the inner and outer circles have been mixed. For instance, when the performance of the inner and outer circles was measured objectively, the expected differences were not found among bank tellers or for enlisted airmen completing small-group tasks. Nor was there a significant correlation between the quality of the leader-subordinate relationship and the turnover of the bank tellers (Vecchio, 1982, 1985). Rosse and Kraut (1983) studied 433 managerial dyads and found that the exchange that gave subordinates considerable latitude in negotiations was positively correlated with the subordinates' job satisfaction and was negatively related to their having job problems. But these researchers failed to confirm other predictions about job performance.

The quality of LMXs and productivity did improve as expected with special training among 106 governmental form-processing employees (Graen, Novak, & Sommerkamp, 1982). Also, for 45 supervisor-subordinate dyads in a business organization, Vecchio and Gobdel (1984) found that leader-member dyadic exchanges in the inner circle were of a higher quality and were associated with the members' higher performance ratings, better actual job performance, lower tendency to quit, and greater satisfaction with supervision. Inner-group members become trusted lieutenants. For a sample of 83 administrators in a large midwestern hospital, Mael (1986) showed that such lieutenants had more latitude in negotiations in their dyadic exchange relationship with their leader and were more satisfied than were others with their job and their leader's performance.

Life-Cycle Model for LMX Development

Graen and Scandura (1987) proposed a life-cycle model for a high-quality relationship of superior and subordinate. First, leader and member of a group or work unit test the attitudes and resources each has to offer the other and what to expect from each other. Then mutual trust, respect, and loyalty are developed. Finally, the relationship matures into mutual commitment. The relationship begins with the self-interest of transactional leadership and matures into the transcending self-interest of transformational leadership Although the relations may be different with each subordinate, the leader can maintain mutual trust and loyalty with all of them. The leader develops a different partnership with each subordinate. The dyadic relations grow into an organizational system (Graen & Uhl-Bien, 1991). Leadership becomes less important than dyadic relationships to the system (Graen & Uhl-Bien, 1995). Schriesheim, Castro, and Cogliser (1997) found 182 journal publications, dissertations, and other research reports on LMX between 1972 and 1997, beginning with Graen, Dansereau, and Minami (1972).

Measures of the Exchange

To quantify the quality of the exchange, the leader rates the quality of the relationship with each member on a set of items. Each member does the same for the relationship with the leader. (See Scandura, Graen, & Novak,

1986, for an example.) Unfortunately, over the three decades of research and application of LMX, the number of items that have been the basis of LMX scores has ranged from 1 to 40, and the items have involved at least six kinds of content: liking, mutual support, trust, latitude, attention, and loyalty (Schriesheim, Castro, & Cogliser, 1997). In all, at least 16 different versions of LMX measurement have been used in reported studies. However, in 36 of 86 studies meta-analyzed by Gerstner and Day (1997), seven items were used. This version is increasingly the favorite. Although Scandura, Graen, and Novak (1986) found only a correlation of .24 between the LMX ratings of leaders and their subordinates, Deinisch and Liden (1986) noted that three dimensions were needed to account for LMX: contribution, loyalty, and affection. Graen and Wakabayashi (1992) obtained a different three-dimensional factor structure to describe the necessary content of LMX: respect, trust, and obligation. Liden & Maslyn (1998) created a multidimensional measurement of four factors (LMX-MDM): affect, loyalty, contribution, and professional respect. The average relationship for the leader (ALX) ordinarily is not as informative as LMX, nor predictive of various outcomes, since the leaders have different relations with different subordinates. Some relations are mainly role-defined and downward in influence; others involve reciprocal influence with mutual respect and trust. There may be less agreement than desired between a supervisor and a subordinate about the quality of their relationship, but according to a survey of 166 newly hired university employees and their direct supervisors, LMX appears to be reasonably stable. Employee LMX ratings made at the end of two weeks and six weeks, respectively, correlated .66 and .47 with their LMX ratings at the end of six months. For supervisors, the comparable correlations were .65 and .38 (Liden, Wayne, & Stilwell, 1993).

There is a need to obtain LMX from the point of view of the leader as well as the subordinate. Gerstner and Day (1997) found an average uncorrected correlation of .29 based on the leader as the only source of information about LMX and the subordinate as the only source of information. According to analyses of 422 matched supervisor-subordinate dyads by Ford and Greguras (2001), incremental validities were obtained beyond using only those from supervisor or from subordinate in predicting such criteria as subordinate job involvement by using both supervisor and subordinate ratings of LMX.

Quality of the Exchange

The "quality" of the leader-member exchange—the satisfaction of either or both parties with it—should be a determinant of subsequent outcomes. A high-quality LMX is a social exchange based on high trust, respect, support, mutual obligation, and latitude. A low-quality LMX is a social exchange that depends on a formal contract providing service for reward or avoidance of punishment (Dienesch & Liden, 1986). For 41 LMX dyads studied by Liden and Graen (1980), members with higher-quality relationships with the leader assumed more responsibility for their jobs, contributed more to their units, and were rated higher in performance than their colleagues who reported lower-quality relationships with their leader. According to Dienesch and Liden (1986), the quality of the exchange may be affected by the mutual trust of the leader and the member, mutual loyalty, their influence on each other, the competence of one or the other, the perceived equity of the exchange, and the interpersonal attraction of the leader and member.

Dimensions of Quality. Dienesch and Liden (1986) suggested three theoretically and methodologically appropriate dimensions that should be considered:

(a) Perceived contribution to the exchange—perception of the amount, direction, and quality of work-oriented activity each member puts forth toward the mutual goals (explicit or implicit) of the dyad; (b) Loyalty—the expression of public support for the goals and the personal character of the other member of the [leader-member exchange] dyad; . . . (c) Affect—the mutual affection members of the dyad have for each other based primarily on interpersonal attraction rather than work or professional values. (pp. 624–625)

Liden and Maslyn (1998) obtained three factors—contribution, loyalty, and affect—in validation studies of LMX with 302 working students and 249 employees, along with a fourth factor, professional respect. The three dimensions also appeared to be conceptually distinct, according to judges, but were empirically correlated (Dienesch, 1985). Each of the three dimensions would

be expected to have a different impact. Mutually perceived contributions should result in the undertaking of more challenging assignments and joint efforts. Mutual loyalty should be reflected in more shared confidences. Interpersonal attraction should generate greater warmth in the workplace and emotional support for nonwork problems.

Following Sparrowe and Liden's (1997) suggestion, Uhl-Bien and Maslyn (2000) identified positive and negative reciprocal relationships in 36 work groups with 29 managers and 280 subordinates in a sample from 1,100 employees in a division of an international firm. These relationships included immediacy (time for reciprocating in an exchange between manager and subordinate), equivalence (elements of equal value are exchanged), and motive (the exchange involves self-interests, mutual interests, and other interests). *Negative reciprocity* is characterized by extreme equivalence, extreme immediacy, and self-interest; *balanced reciprocity* by high equivalence, high immediacy, and mutual interest; and *generalized reciprocity* by low equivalence and low immediacy and concern for others (Sparrowe & Liden, 1997). The reciprocity of "strangers" ordinarily needs immediate equivalency and self-interest. The reciprocity of partners needs mutual interests and tolerates lengthy delays and only in-kind equivalence (Uhl-Bien & Maslyn, 2000).

Effects of the Quality of LMX. The quality of the leader-member exchange and the satisfaction of either or both parties with it should be determinants of subsequent outcomes of joint efforts. For example, for 41 such leader-member dyads studied by Liden and Graen (1980), members with higher-quality relationships with the leader assumed more responsiblity for their jobs, contributed more to their units, and were rated higher in performance than were their colleagues who reported lower-quality relationships with their leader. In a large firm when the leaders and subordinates were high rather than low in self-efficacy, LMX was found to be higher in quality among 56 leader-subordinate dyads. Performance was also better (Murphy and Ensher, 1999).

Gerstner and Day (1997) concluded from their meta-analysis that LMX quality was related to better job performance, higher overall satisfaction, more commitment, less role conflict, more role clarity, competence of leaders and followers, and less intention to quit.

Compared with low-quality LMX, high-quality LMX was often found, along with better task performance (Dansereau, Graen, & Haga, 1975), conducive to subordinate innovation (Basu, 1991). Murray and Markham (undated) obtained results with 25 managers paired with their 110 subordinates showing that high-quality LMX was related to performance effectiveness when there was agreement about this quality within each manager-subordinate dyad. Tierney, Farmer, and Graen (1999) found that among 191 nonclerical employees in R & D, those with higher LMX scores earned higher ratings for creativity from their supervisors, submitted more high-quality "invention-disclosures," and did more research reports. (Results were moderated by the employees' cognitive styles.) Deluga (1991) showed that among 376 managers, professionals, and white- and blue-collar personnel, higher LMX correlated with more leader effectiveness and greater satisfaction with the leadership. The Gerstner and Day (1997) meta-analysis reported a mean corrected correlation of .41 for 17 studies of LMX scores and organizational commitment, as did Green, Anderson, and Shivers (1996). Gerstner and Day also reported a mean corrected correlation of −.35 for 10 studies of LMX and role conflict, .34 for 14 studies of LMX and role clarity, and only −.13 for LMX and turnover. But mixed and insignificant results were found for LMX and turnover by Vecchio & Norris (1996).

Individual Differences. Kinicki and Vecchio (1994) reported a correlation of .32 between LMX and members' locus of control. They also found a correlation of .48 of LMX with felt time pressure. Murphy and Ensher (1999) observed that among women supervisors, self-efficacy correlated with subordinates' LMX. House and Aditya (1997) suggested that LMX would probably be lower among members with a low need for growth and authoritarianism, and with a desire for autonomy. Basu and Green (1995) found that good "organizational citizen" behavior was correlated with high-quality LMX. However, the meta-analysis by Gerstner and Day (1997) noted a lack of correlation between antecedents such as age, education, and sex and quality ratings of LMX. Member competence correlated only .12 with high-quality LMX in 13 studies. As might be expected, mutual liking by members was highly predictive of LMX (Engle & Lord, 1997).

Expectations and Effort. Liden, Wayne, and Stilwell (1993) demonstrated for 166 supervisor-subordinate dyads that mutual expectations of competence and future achievement correlated with high-quality LMX. Maslyn and Uhl-Bien (2001) showed with 232 manager-subordinate dyads that higher-quality LMX was reported by subordinates when the judged effort of the leader correlated with the subordinate's own effort. But according to the leader, if LMX was high in quality as seen by the leader, and leader effort correlated with subordinate effort, leader effort could be lower with higher LMX. If one's effort to develop quality relations with a partner was high, and the partner's was low, the quality of the relationship would be low. In a Dutch firm, 170 employees with an orientation of mastery displayed higher job performance, innovation, and job satisfaction. In contrast, those employees with a performance orientation were the same or lower in these outcomes (Janssen & Yperen, 2004).

Communications. A total of 537 students viewed videotapes of the facial expressions of leaders giving simulated performance appraisal feedback to subordinates. The participant rated the likely LMX quality of the consequences of positive and negative communications and coordinated actors' facial expressions. Positive performance evaluations and "message-congruent" facial expression yielded ratings of higher-quality LMX (Ashkanasy & Newcombe, 2000). Kacmar, Witt, and Zivnuska (2001) conducted three experiments showing that subordinates in a high-LMX relationship who communicated frequently with their supervisor received higher performance ratings. Subordinates in low-LMX relationships interacted less frequently with their supervisor. Those with high LMX scores also were more likely to communicate by telephone and face-to-face than by memos and e-mail. When LMX relationships were poor according to the supervisors, the subordinates made more use of memos and e-mail than telephone and face-to-face communications with the supervisors. Communications between leader and subordinate increase in frequency and quality if LMX is high rather than low (Crouch & Yetton, 1988).

Tactics. The quality of the exchange relation between a leader and followers (LMX) affected the upward tactics used by the followers. In a sample of 376 employees, when the exchange relation with their leader was lower in quality, they were more likely to use hard tactics: assertiveness, cultivation of relations with higher authority, and coalition with colleagues (Deluga & Perry, 1991). Upward influence tactics such as ingratiation and impression management by subordinates added to the positive contribution of LMX to performance and commitment in an analysis of 150 manager-subordinate dyads of 75 managers. Each manager was coupled with one highly performing and one poorly performing subordinate (Schriesheim, Castro, & Yammarino, 1994).

Similarity. Similarity of attitudes and education of supervisor and subordinate correlated with LMX among dyads composed from 223 subordinates and their 58 supervisors (Basu & Green, 1995). Similarity of cognitive style correlated with LMX for 142 pairs of managers and their subordinates in two British manufacturing organizations (Allison, Armstrong, & Hayes, 2001). Likewise, similarity of ratings about supervisors' power and subordinates' negotiation in 230 supervisor-subordinate dyads correlated .77 with LMX according to the subordinates and .23 with LMX according to the supervisors (Townsend & Jones, 2000). Ashkanasy and O'Connor (1997) obtained similar findings for 160 members of 30 Australian work groups between LMX and the congruence of five personal values. For 42 dyads of different racial or ethnic background and 67 of mixed gender, LMX correlated .71 with perceived similarity of subordinates' and leaders' values and attitudes, .31 with speed of forming the relationship, and .33 with the similarity in age of the leader and member The same investigators obtained a correlation between LMX and speed in forming the relationship among dyads of 83 sales representatives and their 13 managers (Hepperlen & Reiter-Palmon, 2000, 2001). In all, in their meta-analysis, Gerstner and Day (1997) reported that for 28 studies, LMX correlated .34 with agreement by the leader and member.

Person-Organization Fit. To assess how closely schoolteachers' personal attitudes fit those of their school, Erdogan, Kraimer, and Liden (2002) calculated the correlation of the individual culture profiles of 524 teachers with the organizational profiles of their 30 schools. The fits were uncorrelated with LMX of teacher and supervi-

sor. However, when LMX was low, job and career satisfaction remained high if the fit between teacher and school was good. When LMX was high, job and career satisfaction could remain high even if the fit between teacher and school profile was low: LMX could make up for the lack of fit in personal attitudes with the school norms.

Health. For 312 retail and health care managers and professionals, Rose and Nelson (1998) found that LMX correlated positively with job satisfaction (.63) and negatively with job burnout (−.39), medical problems, personal impatience and irritability (−.24).

"Organizational Citizenship" Behavior. Manogran and Conlon (1993) and many others have found that high-quality LMX is correlated with organizational citizenship behavior (OCB). A meta-analysis by Hackett, Farh, and Song (2003) found an average correlation of .29 between LMX and OCB. High-quality LMX was also associated with more rapid movement up the corporate ladder (Wakabayashi, Graen, Graen, et al. 1988) and with more favorable perceptions of the organizational climate (Kozlowski & Doherty, 1989). But contrary to expectations, felt empowerment did not mediate the correlations of LMX and organizational commitment and other such outcomes, according to a survey of 337 employees and their immediate superiors (Liden, Wayne, & Sparrowe, 2000). The meta-analysis by Gerstner and Day (1997) reported for 10 and 30 studies, respectively, a mean corrected correlation of .37 of LMX and performance ratings according to leaders and .29 according to members. Mean satisfaction with supervision correlated .74 with LMX in 25 studies. Effects last and remain strong (Crouch & Yetton, 1988; Mayfield & Mayfield, 1998).

Leadership Style. The quality of LMX was higher if there was a match between leaders' and subordinates' styles of implicit leadership (Engle & Lord, 1997). Kuhnert and Lewis (1987) contrasted the quality of leader-member relationships in terms of three levels of the leader's perspective—how meaning is made from the regularities of social interactions. At the lowest level, leaders are transactional and self-interested. At the middle level, they focus on mutual rewarding, looking out for both their own and their subordinates' interests; there is positively reinforcing interaction between leaders and subordinates. The highest level is transformational: the interaction goes beyond the self-interests of both parties. Howell and Hall-Merenda (1999) reported positive correlations of LMX with both transformational and contingent reward leadership but not management by exception. Transformational, especially charismatic and individually considerate leaders, had higher-quality exchanges (Deluga, 1991; Deluga & Perry, 1991). Deluga (1992) found that LMX correlated with *individualized consideration*, a component of transformational leadership. Schriesheim, Neider, and Scandura (1998) found that when LMX was higher in 106 dyads, delegation by leaders was higher, as was subordinate satisfaction and performance. They also showed, for 183 dyads of managers, that rated performance, promotion, and salary progress were greater with higher LMX scores—independent of mentoring, which also contributed to the criteria of managerial success. In India, Aryee, Tan, and Budhwar (2002) obtained results for 161 subordinates and their 40 supervisors indicating that if LMX was of high quality, the correlation with willingness to initiate actions was higher (.36), particularly when subordinates felt a sense of autonomy.

Critique of LMX

Given the continuing problems with the meaning of LMX, the variations in the content of its measurements, the variations in its effectiveness outcomes, biased design flaws, the need to control for individual differences, and the need to consider individual differences and numerous mediating variables, many questions about LMX still require answering, although methods and measurements are converging. House and Aditya (1997) concluded that LMX and performance outcomes may reflect common biases. The results depend as much on the characteristics and behavior of the subordinates as of the leaders. Thus LMX may be a better explanation of the development of superior-subordinate relationships than of the effects of the leaders on their subordinates. Also, LMX theory may be about dyadic relationships and their subjective consequences rather than about leadership effects on followers. The positive relations of LMX and organizational citizenship behavior may be over-

stated. One question not fully answered concerns the level of analysis.

Group or Dyadic Analysis?

The Case for Group Analysis. Some investigators remain unconvinced that much is added by substituting dyadic relationships for the group's average relationship with the leader. For example, Fujii (1977) found that analyses of leader-subordinate relations in an experimental setting based on dyads did not differ greatly from analyses based on mean group results. Proponents of *leader-group exchange* argue that most measures remain reliable and valid even though they are couched in terms of leader-group rather than leader-member relationships (for example, "He shows the group what to do," not "He shows me what to do"; Schriesheim, 1979a). Variations among members within a group are merely individual differences in describing the same leadership behavior (Nachman, Dansereau, & Naughton, 1985). In a study of public utility employees, Schriesheim (1979a) found little difference in the correlations of descriptions of leader-member relations and outcomes, compared with correlations of leader-group descriptions and these same variables. Schriesheim concluded that distinguishing between leader-member and leader-group measurements, although theoretically meaningful, may have little practical utility; however, he favored continuing to use available leader-member descriptions rather than leader-group descriptions for theoretical purposes.

The Case for Dyadic Analysis. Graen (1978) and Graen and Cashman (1975), among others, provided evidence to support the importance of studying the dyadic exchange relationship (LMX) instead of the average exchange (ALX). Graen, Liden, and Hoel (1982) showed that a group analysis alone might fail to detect important outcomes. For example, in an information systems department, although the average way a leader related to the group did not predict the turnover of group members, the quality of the dyadic leader-member exchange did predict the tendency of 20 out of 48 individual members to quit. Ferris (1985) replicated this finding and showed again that the differences of the dyadic-exchange quality scores of the individual members within the groups predicted turnover. But the quality of the average exchange relationships of the groups and the leaders did not.

Graen, Orris, and Johnson (1973) found that supervisors established effective dyadic exchange relationships with some newly hired employees and established ineffective relationships with others. Early on, the supervisors thought they could predict which newcomers would stay and which would leave within a few months, and they fulfilled their prophecy by acting on it. They invested most of their time and energy in the development of those who they thought would stay. The newcomers who were expected to leave early remained unclear about what their supervisors expected of them, whereas those who worked for the same supervisors but were expected to remain were quite clear after the first week of employment. These results could not have been captured by analyzing only the supervisor's relation to the group of newly hired employees. Crouch and Yetton (1988) looked at 323 manager-subordinate dyads in Australia in which 78 managers were involved. The same manager maintained a different relationship with subordinates, depending on the subordinates' performance. High-performing subordinates whose experience with the managers was friendly had more task contact with the managers; low performers had less contact and experienced less friendliness.

In the previously mentioned nine-month study of a management hierarchy by Dansereau, Graen, and Haga (1975), most of the dyadic relationships were new at the beginning of the study. The same manager developed different dyadic relations with different subordinates. These relations ranged from mentor-protégé to overseer-peon. The quality of each dyadic exchange relationship remained stable from the first month onward and could forecast career outcomes. Graen and Cashman (1975) showed over a nine-month period of study that the different quality of the dyadic relationship of different subordinates with the same superior determined the role assignments of the subordinates. Subordinates who had a high-quality relationship with the manager carried out less routine activities. They had more responsible administrative discretionary opportunities. They also had more resources at their disposal. The dyadic exchange was not just in the perceptions of the superior and subordinate who were directly involved. Peer observers tended to agree with the particular superior and subordinate about the quality of that relationship.

This is not an either-or question. Both analyses are needed. Dyads can be examined within groups. They may be viewed as independent of the group of which they are a part. Most supervisors have learned to praise subordinates in public and to reprove them in private. We should expect that the extent to which a leader praises subordinates will be seen in the same way by the subordinates (whichever description is used), since praise is likely to be a public affair. In this case, the average member of the group of employees will provide a description of the leader that is equal in accuracy to the description provided member by member. But to describe the leader's contingent punishment, dyadic analysis should prove more fruitful, since such contingent punishment is more likely to be a private one-on-one exchange. In some circumstances, the effects on the group are likely to be more important; in others, individual exchanges will be more important. Much more multiplex examinations are required to take into account both possibilities as well as their statistical interaction (Dansereau, Alutto, Markham, & Dumas, 1982).

In an effort to examine both group and individual effects, Dansereau, Alutto, and Yammarino (1984) created a theory and methodology for analyzing variance in leadership along with covariance in leadership outcomes of leader-member relations and their effects for the dyad, the group, and higher organizational levels of analysis. Dansereau, Alutto, and Yammarino's DETECT computer program facilitated an examination of what had heretofore not been fully analyzed—variances and covariances within the same group and in a set of groups as opposed to variance and covariances among these groups. Dansereau, Alutto, and Yammarino's strategy and analysis program determined whether the relationships were a function of: (1) different styles of leaders described by their average differences in perceptions by their subordinates; (2) leadership processes that occur only within groups; or (3) individualized differences in perceptions of the same leader's behavior.

Along with demonstrating that inner and outer circles of subordinates are likely to be working for the same superior, researchers have built a case for focusing on LMX, in contrast to the average exchange relationship between the leader and the group (Graen, 1978; Graen & Cashman, 1975).

Graen, Cashman, Ginsburgh, and Schiemann (1977) showed that managers who developed higher-quality dyadic linkages with their bosses produced greater resources for their subordinates than did those managers who developed lower-quality linkages. Liden and Graen (1980) obtained the same results with first-level supervisors. Some supervisors appeared to collaborate with their bosses on unstructured tasks and to receive appropriate resources in return; others who were led by the same bosses did not collaborate or obtain desired resources.

Theory of Variance

Katerberg and Hom (1981) correlated the satisfaction and role perceptions of 672 National Guardsmen and their leadership descriptions of their first sergeants and unit commanders. Between-units leadership effects were based on the usual correlations between scores averaged for each unit. Within-unit effects were obtained by means of a hierarchical regression analysis in which unit means were entered as the first step and the remainder were then regarded as being due to within-group effects. Considerable increases in explanatory covariance emerged when the within-group component was added to the leadership-satisfaction outcomes, despite the fact that the instrument used to assess leadership, the Leadership Behavior Description Questionnaire, was couched in terms of group, not individual members. This preliminary effort was followed shortly by the work, mentioned on page 427, of Dansereau, Alutto, and Yammarino (1984).

Members' ratings of their leader or of outcomes within a group may be similar but differ from the ratings of the average members of other groups about their own leaders and outcomes. These *whole-group* differences lie between and not within groups. There are *intergroup* differences in responses, coupled with the *homogeneity* of responses within the groups. This condition fits with the average-member-exchange approach to studying leadership based on the average member of each group. For instance, the reinforcing style used by a leader with all the group members correlated with the leader's sense of security and personality (Hinton & Barrow, 1976).

Another possibility is that in a *group-parts* condition, individuals' responses differ from one another within a group, but their average does not differ from the average responses provided by the members of other groups. Differences lie within groups, not between groups. There are *intragroup* differences, and there is *heterogeneity* among the members within the groups. The LMX approach is necessary to study the leadership and outcomes.

A third alternative is that the reports of the individuals may differ reliably and consistently both within or between the groups. This condition is *equivocal*, for the ratings are *codeterminable* from both sources. Individual implicit theories may dominate an equivocal condition.

A fourth possibility is that members may respond not as a group but only independently; thus their identity as a member of a particular group or the set of groups under analysis may be irrelevant. Here the results of interest are *inexplicable*, accounted for neither by systematic differences among individual member differences nor by the groups. There are no reliable differences among individuals within or between groups, and thus a null case is demonstrated.

Dyadic and Group Possibilities. Yammarino (1995) pointed out four types of supervisor-subordinate dyads: (1) *Dyads within groups* can be examined to see if they are different in a group, if the same differences in supervisor-subordinate relations appear in other groups but aggregated, and if the supervisors show up the same across the groups. (2) *Independent dyads* are not influenced by which group they are in. The supervisor-subordinate relationships differ from each other without reference to their group association. (3) *Independence within dyads* occur if the supervisors and subordinates differ from each other regardless of their group membership. (4) *Cross-level dyads* occur when each leader and subordinate in a dyad are in agreement but dyads within groups differ from each other. Independent dyads become dyads within groups.

Some WABA Results. Variance theory is tested empirically by within-and-between analysis (WABA) of variance and covariance. Yammarino and Naughton (1987) completed within-and-between analyses of the variances in LBDQ initiation and consideration scores (WABA I) of 70 members of a law enforcement organization on a university campus. Each member of the different hierarchically arranged units described his or her own immediate superiors. The investigators also completed corresponding analyses of within-and-between analyses of the covariances in the leadership-outcomes descriptions (WABA II). Outcomes included satisfaction with supervision, satisfaction with rewards, supervisory control, adequacy of communications, efforts of subordinates, and stress on subordinates. The results for the WABA I analyses of variance indicated the existence of an equivocal or codeterminable condition. There was significant variance both within and between groups; also, consistent individual differences in perceptions were at work here, rather than just differences between leaders. On the other hand, the WABA II analyses of covariance generally supported the conclusion for 10 of the 28 relationships that leader-outcome differences between whole groups dominated. This supported the acceptance of the average leadership style or *whole-group* approach. For example, members' satisfaction with rewards and the leader's initiation of structure correlated .67 among groups led by the different leaders and only .09 for members within groups led by the same leader. It did not matter if the descriptions were correlated in *group* terms ("The leader rewards the group if . . .") or in *individual* terms ("The leader rewards me if . . ."). In the case of six variables, an equivocal condition was seen. For example, satisfaction with supervision emerged as codeterminable; there were covarying differences between leaders and outcomes as well as among members' descriptions of their leader within the groups. The correlations between initiation and consideration were particularly likely to emerge as equivocal in interpretation. Finally, in the case of 12 variables, such as leadership and communications, the results were inexplicable. There was no statistically significant between-or-within covariance.

Table 16.1 illustrates the importance of both a dyadic and group account of leader-outcome relationships based on members' descriptions. We need to ask the same questions about such relationships in two ways, dyadic and group. We need to examine both within-and-between covariances. As is seen in Table 16.1, satisfaction is correlated modestly with rewards and with considerate leadership (.26 to .42), regardless of the analytic component (between or within leaders) or type of description (leader-group or leader-member). Differences between leaders in initiation correlate with the average members' satisfaction with rewards. The same results apply for all the members, regardless of their group. However, the leaders' perceived use of initiation correlates with satisfaction only between the leaders' groups, not within the leaders' groups.

In the replication of the Graen, Liden, and Hoel (1982) study, it was concluded that the group effect was also of consequence when 81 registered nurses who quit or remained described their supervisors, although the dyadic effect on turnover was still the stronger (Ferris, 1985). However, Yammarino, Spangler, and Dubinsky (1998) analyzed individual, dyadic, and group results for 111 subordinates and their 34 superiors in a sales organization, who formed 111 dyads in 34 groups. The Multifactor Leadership Questionnaire (MLQ) was used by the respondents to measure transformational leadership and contingent reward along with satisfaction with job and leadership. WABA I and WABA II results were of consequence for the MLQ and satisfaction, but only at the individual level, not the dyadic or group levels. In a sample of 285 employees of a county library system, work-unit size, cohesiveness, organizational climate, and leader power all predicted the quality of leader-member exchanges (LMX), but WABA also found individual

Table 16.1 Correlations between Leader-Members and Leader-Group Satisfaction and Rewards

Members' Satisfaction with Rewards	Initiation		Consideration	
	Leader-Group Relation Described	Leader-Member Relation Described	Leader-Group Relation Described	Leader-Member Relation Described
Between Leaders	.67	.57	.42	.30
Within the Same Leaders	.09	.03	.27	.26

SOURCE: Yammarino and Naughton (1987).

differences—that is, effects at the level of the individual employee (Cogliser & Schriesheim, 2000). A sample of 83 sales personnel and their supervisors in a chain of retail stores rated their relationships. According to WABA, in comparison with effects at the group and individual levels, differences between the 83 dyads were most significant. But for a second sample of 116 dyads composed of insurance sales personnel and their supervisors in 37 organizations, the most significant differences were at the level of individuals (Yammarino & Dubinsky, 1992).

Although the group, dyadic, or individual approach may be appropriate in some instances, only analyses that take all the possibilities into account are likely to explain more fully what is happening. Schriesheim, Castro, and Yammarino (2000) examined the quality of LMX ratings of 75 managers, each paired with a high-performing and a low-performing subordinate. Generally, individual differences appeared more important than the group or dyadic effects implied by the span of supervision, efforts at upward influence, and commitment of the managers or subordinates.

Behavioral Interdependence of Dyads

The preceding research examined the processes through which leaders affect their followers or the processes through which followers affect their leaders. In fact, of course, both processes are occurring simultaneously and may be discussed as two-way dynamics. For example, Graen (1976) examined the dyadic relation between the leader and each member of the group. He noted that the dyads formed a behavioral interdependence between the respective roles. This interdependence included the dyadic "partnership" engaged in reciprocal influence, its extracontractual behavioral exchanges, its role-defined relations, and its loosely coupled fates (Dansereau, Graen, & Haga, 1975). Graen and Schiemann (1978) observed that the manager's and subordinate's agreement about the relationship was higher if the quality of their behavioral interdependencies was high. Such interdependence of the manager and the subordinate is necessary for the leader to give and the subordinate to receive opportunities for growth on the job (Graen & Scandura, 1986). Subordinates with high need for growth are more likely to collaborate in a closer and better-quality relationship with superiors on tasks that provide opportunities for growth.

But behavioral interdependence has its dark side. A superior and subordinate can share a delusion—a folie à deux—when both have a strong need to be dependent and are in an isolated position, say, on a space exploration mission. The delusion is likely to occur in more everyday settings if mutual trust and closeness are lacking. The subordinate may have the need to depend on the superior, but this need is frustrated if he or she cannot depend on the superior. In turn, the superior may want to depend on the subordinate but feels it unwise to do so. The world becomes dangerous, and the danger is compounded by the superior's and subordinate's lack of trust in each other. Each can trust only a few people, but not each other. The superior and subordinate can elaborate their mistrust of each other into a common fantasy about an organizational betrayal of both of them. Thus they become trapped by their shared delusion (Kets de Vries, 1984).

The Reciprocal Relationship

Individualized Leadership

Chapters 17 through 20 will present consistent styles of leadership that describe how leaders relate in the same way to all their followers. But according to Dansereau (1995), when previously the variations in a leader's behavior toward different individuals in a group were treated as statistical error, WABA theory and WABA allowed for a leader to regard each subordinate as an independent, unique individual. To be successful, the leadership efforts must vary within *and* between work groups (Dansereau, Yammarino, Markham, et al., 1998). Perceptions of the same leader differ from one subordinate to another. Nevertheless, if the leader supports the individual subordinate in exchange for satisfactory performance, the leader will reinforce the subordinate's sense of self-worth The knowledge, skills, and abilities of both the supervisor and the subordinate set the stage for *individualized leadership*. Individualized leadership is expected to correlate positively with LMX (Yammarino & Dansereau, 2002). This result was found by Paul, Scheyns, and Rigotti (2001).

Psychological Contracts

Psychological contracts are the expectations and obligations of the leaders and the led toward each other, their unit, and the organization (Argyris, 1960; Schein, 1965). The concept was accepted but little empirical work on it was completed until the 1990s.

Building on a 13-nation survey of psychological contracts by Rousseau (1995) and Rousseau and Schalk (2000), Van den Brande, Janssens, et al. (2002) analyzed survey data from structured interviews with 1,106 Belgian employees from public, private, for-profit, and nonprofit agencies. Formal written legal contracts and statutes also covered their employment. The employees' expected entitlements generated five factors: long-term involvement; tangibility, clarity, and transparency of obligations and rights; treatment as a person, not an economic resource; carefulness about arrangements; and equal treatment of all employees. The employees' expected obligations factored into: loyalty; open attitude; high personal investment; flexibility and tolerance for internal organizational changes; and respect for authority. On the basis of their high and low entitlement and obligation factor scores, employees formed the following six clusters of types of contracts:

1. Contractual loyalty—high long-term involvement, equal treatment, loyalty, and low personal investment. The employee perceives loyalty in his or her contract. He or she is a poorly educated, low-paid blue-collar employee or civil servant in a large organization with a personal investment and flexibility but lower expectations about the operational job.

2. Contractual instrumentality—high expectations but low obligations. The employee is a poorly educated, low-paid white-collar or blue-collar employee in a medium-size organization with reasonable job opportunities elsewhere.

3. Contractual investing—higher employee. The psychological contract is as perceived by a highly paid executive in senior management in a small company.

4. Contract strength—high on all dimensions. The psychological contract is that of a young, highly educated, highly paid white-collar employee or executive, holding a professional or senior management position in a small or medium-size organization and readily marketable.

5. Contract weakness—low scores on all dimensions of expected entitlements and obligations. Reasonably employable elsewhere with an average education and jobs at all hierarchical levels. The employee perceives a weak contract and is average in pay for his or her level in the hierarchy.

6. Contractual lack of attachment—low scores on all dimensions, particularly involvement and loyalty. These psychological contracts were typical of young, highly educated, highly paid executives or white-collar employees in professional or senior management jobs in small or medium-size organizations.

Rousseau (1995) suggested that psychological contracts may appear as: (1) *Transactional*: Short-term, economically focused, specific and clear about expected performance and rewards, as in seasonal work; (2) *Transitional*: Short-term, uncertain, and ambiguous with unspecified mutual obligations, rewards, and performance expectations, as in jobs in radical reorganizations, mergers, and takeovers; (3) *Balanced*: Long-term, economically focused, with clear and specific terms, as among structured work team members. Psychological contracts may be also said to be in balance when the obligations of employees and employers are at relatively the same level (Shore & Barksdale, 1998); or (4) *Relational*: Long-term, ambiguous, and lacking tangibility, as in a family business.

As might be expected, personality affects the type of psychological contracts formed. For example, individuals with high self-esteem would be expected to form balanced psychological contracts; individuals with low self-esteem, transitional psychological contracts (Raja, Ntalianis, & Johns, 2002). Among 210 graduate business students with two years of work experience, varying in attachment style, those who were avoidant were less likely than those secure or anxious in attachment to ask others for contractual information. The secure seek more information about various aspects of their psychological contract than do others and are most likely to believe their employers will fulfill their obligations. The insecure, avoidant, and anxious are most pessimistic about the probability that employers will fulfill obligations. If violations occur, those with a secure attachment style are most likely to speak out against contractual violations by higher authority. Again, the insecure are less likely to do so (Bendapudi, Bendapudi, & Ballam, 2002).

Models of Mutual Influence

Crouch (1987) and Zahn and Wolfe (1981) started with different assumptions and used different methods to construct different models to describe how mutual influence develops between superiors and subordinates. Crouch (1987) assumed that manager-subordinate relationships stem from the influence that the subordinates can exert in solving unstructured problems that they and the manager face. Over time, the model predicts the emergence of stable relationships. Either high- or low-performing groups will be developed to deal with outside demands on the groups. Zahn and Wolf (1981) provided Markov mathematical states-events models to deduce the continuing interplay of the superior and the subordinate, showing how their emerging task and interactional relationships can predict future outcomes. Unexpected results appeared. Contrary to Crouch, the model predicted long-term behavior to be highly variable and versatile, rather than stable. The mutual biases of the superior and the subordinate were most salient in effect; both were likely to contribute to the cyclical maintenance of their relationships.

Two-Way Impact

Considerable empirical evidence is available to provide a cross-sectional picture of the two-way impact—the combined effects of the leader's and the follower's competence and compatibility, the interplay of the leader's style and the follower's personality and motivation, and the combined effects of the leader's and follower's concerns for the task and for their relationship with each other. Pratt and Liambalvo (1982) showed that an understanding of the leadership of accounting auditors in working with their auditing assistants required consideration of aspects of the auditor, the assistants, and their interplay. Outcomes depended on the personal dominance of the auditors, the intolerance of ambiguity by the assistants, and the match between the perceived complexity of the task for the auditor and the assistants and the assistants' job experience.

Rao (1982) conducted an experiment in which the leader could reward the subordinate. In one setting, the leader was to receive a bonus based on the subordinate's performance. The results were the leader's increased rewarding of the subordinate, large improvements in the subordinate's performance, and greater stability and cooperativeness between the leader and the subordinate. These results were different from those in the situation in which the leader was not offered any bonus for the subordinate's good performance.

The two-way nature of leadership and followership was investigated by Herold (1974), who carried out a double-substitution laboratory experiment in which both leaders' and subordinates' actual behaviors were intercepted and substituted with fully programmed supervisory and subordinate behaviors. Thirty-two groups of three persons each, consisting of one leader and two subordinates, were balanced in treatment so that the subordinates were powerful in half the groups and the leaders were powerful in the other half. The experimental task consisted of proofreading manuscripts and finding errors. The leader of each group received a "good product" from one of the subordinates and a "bad product" from the other. Within each group, one subordinate received a punitive communication following the performance, while the other received a supportive communication. Herold found strong mutual effects on the attitudes of the leaders and followers toward each other and toward the situation. Whether the leader received a good or bad product from a subordinate strongly affected what the leader did, but whether the subordinate received a punitive or a supportive communication from the leader had somewhat less of an impact on the subordinate. The leader's power was important in its effects on subordinates, but the subordinates' power was not significant in affecting the leader's behavior.

This lack of symmetry was also seen by G. J. Palmer (1962a, 1962b), who studied leaders and followers in a difficult task situation. Palmer concluded that followership in such a situation is explained largely by the lack of ability. Leadership, on the other hand, requires a more complex explanation involving both individual and situational variables. For instance, the joint competence of the leader and the subordinate has to be considered. This conclusion was confirmed by Rohde (1958), who observed different combinations of qualified and unqualified leaders and followers under four conditions of reward and punishment. The leader's ability to perform the task was found to be more highly related to the group's performance than to the group's motivation. Not unexpectedly, the poorest performance was exhibited by groups with both unqualified leaders and unqualified followers. Almost equally poor were groups with qualified leaders and two unqualified followers.

Blades (1976) studied the joint effects of leaders' and subordinates' competence on their group's performance in servicing U.S. Army mess halls. Ratings of the group's performance by inspectors were correlated with ratings by 102 mess hall personnel of the intelligence, ability, and behavior of the leader. Blades found that the subordinates' intelligence, ability to perform the task, and motivation correlated positively with their performance only under participative management and when the subordinates were highly motivated. The leader's intelligence correlated positively with the group's performance only under directive management with highly motivated leaders and subordinates. The leader's ability to perform the task and the leader's motivation correlated positively with the group's performance only with directive supervision of highly motivated subordinates. Blades concluded that competent, motivated subordinates can be led best if they are allowed to participate in the decision-making process, and that competent, motivated leaders do best with a directive style if their subordinates' competence is limited.

The Leader-Follower Exchange

The leader and the follower depend on each other because each stimulates and reinforces the other's behavior. The leader initiates, questions, or proposes; the follower complies, resists, or ignores. Leadership and followership are mutual activities of influence and counterinfluence. Leaders and followers both give and both receive benefits. The relationship is maintained by this social exchange and this mutual influence (Hollander, 1978). As Hollander and Julian (1969) noted, when leaders are effective, they give something and get something in return. This transactional approach to leadership involves trading of benefits. The leader provides a benefit by directing the group toward desirable results. In return, the followers provide the leader with status and the privileges of authority, influence, and prestige. However, the leader may demand from the followers what they regard as an excessive expenditure of energy. The followers' compliance may be tempered if desired outcomes do not match the perceived effort required. As members become less involved in the group's success, they complain less about obstacles to such success but more about demands for expending their time and energy (Willerman, 1954). Bass, Gaier, and Flint (1956) observed that ROTC cadets who were strongly motivated to enter advanced training complained about the difficulty of the test used to screen applicants, whereas those whose motivation was low complained about having to take the test rather than about its difficulty.

Intermember Expectations. Much of the differentiation of members' roles and the emergence of leadership in an informal group comes about as a result of the mutual reinforcement of intermember expectations. Because of their initiative, interaction, and contributions to the group's task, some members reinforce the expectation that they will be more likely than other members to establish conditions that promote progress in the task, members' freedom and acceptance, and the group's cohesiveness. Other members, by compliance, reinforce the expectation that whoever has started and succeeded with it should continue in the leadership role; that is, "Don't change horses in midstream." Similarly, members build up expectations regarding the contributions that they are to make. The reactions of other members confirm the expectation that they are (or are not) to continue in the same role. The role system and the status structure of a group are determined by a set of such mutually reinforced intermember expectations. Thus in a verbal learning experiment, Bachrach, Candland, and Gibson (1961) observed that the members of the group differentially reinforced the behavior of other members. Such differential reinforcement accounts, in large part, for individual differences in role specialization and conformity to norms.

Seeking Feedback. Some people seek feedback; others shy away from it; still others ignore it when it is given to them. Subordinates have been found more likely to seek feedback if their leaders were perceived to be supportive, esteemed, expert, and transformational (Steelman, Williams, & Levy, 1996; Williams, Miller, Steelman, et al., 1999). Also, they were more likely to seek feedback from supervisors who were thought to be accessible, who clarified roles, and who had constructive intentions (Vancouver & Morrison, 1995; Levy, Miller, & Cobar, 2000). In addition to confirming many of these effects, Thibodeaux and Kudisch (2000) showed that feedback was more likely to be sought if the quality of LMX was high. But Dunford and Williams (1999) found that nurse supervisors were less likely to ask for feedback from the nurses in 200 nurse-supervisor pairs when there was stronger agreement between the nurses' and the supervisors' ratings of the nurses.

In the United States, information exchange is more direct and explicit. In East Asian cultures, it is more indirect and implicit, with more nonverbal nuances and symbolism (Hall, 1976). More cost in seeking feedback was seen by 167 Taiwanese university students than by 76 American counterparts; the Taiwanese noted greater effort and loss of face (Kung & Steelman, 2003). The norm is unlikely to encourage the Asian student to seek feedback (Ashford & Northcraft, 1992). Ashford and Tsui (1991) conducted a study of the feedback-seeking behavior of 387 managers from their superiors, peers, and subordinates. Some of the managers regulated their own performance by seeking negative feedback ("Tell me what I did wrong") and tended to increase the accuracy of their understanding of how their work was evaluated by the three sources. In turn, the three sources formed better opinions of the effectiveness of these negative feedback–seeking managers. But the sources tended to downgrade managers who sought positive feedback.

Differing Leader Treatment of Subordinates. Leaders do not deal with each of their subordinates in the same way. Leaders give more directions to followers who are performing poorly and monitor them more closely. The leaders are more considerate, cooperative, and tolerant when dealing with able subordinates (Podsakoff & Schriesheim, 1985). Leader-follower interaction and mutual support are seen among political leaders and their followers. The leaders activate and mobilize support for their objectives, control the communications media, and make use of intermediary opinion leaders. The followers may be actively interested and ready to be motivated to engage in political activity. Multilayered networks of leaders and followers are formed. Those below yield an aggregate of public opinion to support the aims of those at the top. The importance of such followers' support for leaders was seen by Pepinsky, Hemphill, and Shevitz (1958), who studied experimental groups working on construction problems. When the leaders were made to believe that they were accepted by the members, the groups were more productive and exhibited high degrees of satisfaction and participation. When the leaders were made to feel that they were rejected, the groups made fewer and poorer decisions and exhibited less participation and satisfaction.

Key Interactions. Komaki and Citera (1990) conducted an experiment with 60 "manager-subordinate" pairs consisting of 160 female undergraduate students. Managers either were only monitors of subordinates' performance or only directed the subordinates. Afterward, in comparison with the "directing manager" condition, managers who monitored spent much more time talking about the consequences rather than their own performance. Their subordinates spent more time talking about their own performance. The same interaction was stimulated in the next trial.

Effects of Language. More than direct cost-benefit calculations may lie behind an interaction between the leader and the followers. Drake and Moberg (1986) suggested that two adjustments in language can be made to change the cost-benefit calculations by a follower who is considering an attempt by a leader to influence him or her into compliance. First, *sedating* language, such as semantic indirectness, can be used in the leader's attempt to keep the follower from considering the costs of compliance. For example, instead of giving a direct order, the leader can hint at the need for action or prompt the follower by saying, "It is getting warm in here" instead of, "Please turn down the heat." Other sedative language includes teases and questioning: "I wonder what that's all about?"

Second, the linguistic form may *palliate* the follower to protect him or her from loss of respect that might occur if a more straightforward order is used to correct a follower or to reverse a decision. Numerous positive polite strategies may be used as palliatives, such as expressing admiration, claiming common viewpoints, displaying concern for the follower, and desiring cooperation. With palliatives, the attempt to influence may be accompanied by efforts to reduce the difference in power between the leader and the follower. Instead of the direct order, "Check the switch again," the leader suggests "You may want to try to check the switch again." Other palliation includes disclaimers, hedging, appeals to suspend judgment, excuses, and justifications.

Mutual Effects of the Task and Clarity of the Goal

Under some circumstances, clarification of what needs to be done may depend on the subordinates' participation with the leader in agreeing on the tasks and setting of the group's goals. Critical experiments described by Locke, Latham, and Erez (1987) suggested that such participation by subordinates in setting goals is important to their understanding, commitment, and productivity if the leader is curt and unsupportive. The subordinates' participation in goal setting is not necessary if the leader assigns goals in a friendly and supportive manner. This may explain why Dossett, Cella, Greenberg, and Adrian (1983) found in a laboratory study with 40 undergraduates that although, as was expected, productivity on a clerical task was highest when a supervisor set high, clear, standards for them and gave them friendly support, the subordinates' participation in setting the goals did not contribute to their productivity by itself.

The failure of participation in setting goals to make a difference also may be explained by the character of the participation. Neider (1980) demonstrated, in a study of performance in retail stores, that positive outcomes were obtained from such participation only when the participation process clarified the linkage of effort and performance, and only when the rewards given for high performance were valued. The effects of clarification also depend on the competence of the leader. Podsakoff, Todor, and Schuler (1983) found that expert leaders who work at setting and clarifying goals did decrease their subordinates' sense of role ambiguity. But the reverse was true for leaders who were inept; their efforts resulted in increasing their subordinates' sense of role ambiguity.

In the previously mentioned longitudinal survey by Greene (1979b) of the mutual effects of leaders and subordinates, 60 subordinates from five manufacturing organizations, were queried. These subordinates had joined the management of their firms within the past three months and had never before worked for their immediate superiors. Greene assumed that because these subordinates were newly appointed, their expectations were unclear and they were not yet fully compliant. The subordinates described their leaders' behavior and indicated their own expectations, compliance, performance, and satisfaction. The data were gathered three times at three-month intervals to permit path analyses. Consistent with path-goal theory (see Chapter 27), early role clarification by a leader directly resulted in greater satisfaction of and compliance by the subordinates three and six months later. Role clarification by the leader also was seen to enhance the subordinates' expectations that their greater effort would produce better performance.

Compatibility. It seems obvious that if leaders and their subordinates, individually or in groups, share the same approaches, values, and attitudes, they will be more satisfied with their relationship and experience less conflict and more mutual support. Such positive associations between the compatibility of the values of superiors and subordinates and satisfaction with their relationships were obtained by Duchon, Green, and Tabor (1986) in a field study of 49 Junior Achievement companies. Avolio and Howell (1993) showed in regression analysis of 76 senior executives and their 237 immediate direct reports that a match in personality (locus of control, innovation, and risk taking) contributed to the performance of their units.

Fuji (1977) conducted an experiment in which the independent variables were manipulated by simulating a division of a greeting card company. Eighty paid male volunteers participated as work-group leaders or workers in this unit. The followers' performance, based on merit ratings by the leaders but not on objective performance, was positively related to greater interpersonal compatibility between the leaders and the followers. Extrinsic satisfaction increased with leader-member compatibility. The relationship between leader-member compatibility and intrinsic and overall satisfaction was moderated by the amount of cooperation required by the task and the amount of experience with the task. Compatibility was positively related to relations-oriented leadership behavior, but less so to task-oriented leadership behavior.

McLachlan (1974) reported a study of group therapy with 94 alcoholic inpatients in which patients and therapists were matched for conceptual compatibility on the basis of Hunt's Paragraph Completion Test. Matched pairs of patients and therapists were positively associated with outcomes as evaluated by staff ratings 12 to 16 months later. Beutler, Jobe, and Elkins (1974) also investigated the effects of patient-therapist matching on attitudes. Matched attitudes were associated with self-rated improvement (although some dissimilarity of attitudes resulted in more attitudinal changes in patients). Similarly, Steiner and Dobbins (undated) conducted a laboratory study of 111 management students and their ostensible subordinates in which high and low intrinsic and extrinsic work-related values were the manipulated bases of matched and mismatched "superiors" and "subordinates." When superiors and subordinates matched each other in high extrinsic or high intrinsic work values, the superiors were more likely to attribute the subordinates' past good performance to internal rather than external causes.

Pulakos and Wexley (1983) examined 171 manager-subordinate dyads composed of the same and opposite sexes. Sex as such was not as important as perceived compatibility. The managers' leadership, particularly their facilitation and support of the work, was appraised higher by their subordinates when both the managers and the subordinates felt they were "similar kinds of people." Subordinates also were rated more favorably by their managers if they were perceived as similar. Conversely, lower performance appraisals occurred when the managers and subordinates were mutually perceived as dissimilar. When the subordinates saw themselves as similar to their managers, the managers gave higher dependability ratings to their female than to their male subordinates. When subordinates said they were dissimilar to their managers, managers rated both males and females uniformly lower.

Actual Similarity. The actual similarity between managers and their subordinates tends to correlate with the managers' appraisals of their subordinates' performance (Miles, 1964a; Senger, 1971); with the subordinates' evaluations of their managers; and with the subordinates' satisfaction with their managers (Weiss, 1977). Subordinates who perceive their superiors' attitudes toward work more accurately are rated more highly by their superiors and are more satisfied with their superiors (Greene, 1972; Howard, 1968; Labovitz, 1972).

Subordinates are more satisfied in general if their descriptions of their manager's attitudes more accurately match the manager's self-description. In turn, subordinates receive higher evaluations from their manager if the manager's description of the subordinates' attitudes matches the subordinates' self-descriptions (Wexley, Alexander, Greenawalt, & Couch, 1980). As noted above, Avolio and Howell (1993) found that unit performance and satisfaction were higher when Canadian senior executives were matched rather than mismatched in locus of control, innovation, and risk taking.

Interplay of Leaders' Style and Subordinates' Motivation and Personality

Using Exercise Supervise (Bass, 1975c), approximately 3,500 managers in training workshops in 12 countries enacted one of three supervisory roles—authoritarian, persuasive, or participative—or one of three subordinate roles: highly involved, moderately involved, or uninvolved. Meetings took place between dyads composed of one supervisor and one subordinate. The three tasks were to decide which of 25 traits are most and least characteristic of lower, middle, and top managers. A Latin-Square design was completed so that data about all nine supervisory-subordinate combinations of role play emerged. As might be expected, the uninvolved, apathetic subordinate was least preferred by supervisors as a whole, and the participative supervisor was most preferred by subordinates as a whole. The fastest and most easily completed interactions took place between the authoritarian supervisors and the uninvolved, apathetic subordinates. Dissatisfaction of subordinates and supervisors tended to be greatest for highly involved subordinates meeting with authoritarian supervisors; satisfaction tended to be greatest for highly involved subordinates meeting with participative supervisors. The interaction effects of persuasive supervision and subordinates at the three different levels of involvement fell in between in satisfaction and speed of decision (Bass, Burger, et al., 1979; Thiagarajan & Deep, 1970).

Sales, Levanoni, and Saleh (1984) contrasted the reactions of 226 intrinsically and extrinsically motivated clerical, technical, and professional employees to two types of supervision. *General* supervision provided broad specifications of goals and gave subordinates the means of achieving them. *Close* supervision involved giving detailed instructions at each stage in the process of completing a task and checking to see that instructions were carried out. The investigators found that intrinsically oriented employees expressed more satisfaction with their supervisors under general supervision than under close supervision; extrinsically oriented employees indicated the opposite. Steiner and Dobbins (undated) experimented with the extrinsic and intrinsic work values of the subordinates of management students who were acting as their supervisors. Subordinates with high intrinsic work values were given more autonomy and more challenging assignments by their "supervisors" than were the other subordinates. W. W. Burke (1965) studied student leaders in 24 groups participating in an interfraternity contest. Each group performed a clerical and organizational task, as well as a decision-making task. Regardless of the task, followers with high need-achievement scores, working with relations-oriented leaders, reported more tension than followers with high need-achievement scores working with task-oriented leaders. Those with low need-achievement scores, working with task-oriented leaders, reported more tension than those working with relations-oriented leaders. The more relaxed situation occurred when the leader's personality met the needs of the group of followers. Misumi and Seki (1971) showed that Japanese subjects with low need for achievement demonstrated relatively high performance but low satisfaction with a task-oriented leader in experimental tasks. Subjects with high need for achievement were most productive and most satisfied under leaders with high task and relations orientation and performed worst under leaders whose task and relations orientations were low. Misumi (1985) also noted that high-anxiety subjects did better under a relations-oriented leader than under a task-oriented leader.

Superiors were viewed as less active and directive by hospital employees who were more concerned with power, achievement, and independence (Niebuhr, Bedeian, & Armenakis, 1980). Engineering personnel with high self-esteem who were in dyads with superiors of long duration saw more initiation and consideration in their superiors' leadership behavior (Niebuhr & Davis, 1984).

Greer (1960–1961) reported that authoritarian infantrymen and airmen worked better under authoritarian leaders whereas egalitarian men did better when led by egalitarians. A group's performance was positively related to followers' perceptions of the leader as a problem solver and the extent to which the leader met the followers' expectations. Weed, Mitchell, and Moffitt (1976) concluded, from a laboratory study, that supervision that was structuring generated higher performance by subordinates if the subordinates were higher in dogmatism. Considerate supervision generated higher performance in subordinates who were lower in dogmatism.

Concerns for Task or Relationships. Back (1948) analyzed the interactions of leaders and followers in two discussion groups—work-centered and "emotionally toned." When the leaders emphasized work performance more than did the followers in the first period, the followers increased their work responses in the next period. When the leaders emphasized friendliness more than did the followers in the first period, the followers exhibited more friendly responses in the next period. The emotionally toned group devoted more time in the first period to establishing stable intermember relations and a group structure. The work-oriented group spent more time in strengthening goal-directed activities. In the next period, the emotionally toned group spent more time maintaining participation among members and with leaders. In the work-oriented group, the leader tended to lose importance, whereas interactions between members were strengthened. Bass and Dunteman (1963) studied sensitivity training groups that were composed of participants who were homogeneous in relations (interaction) orientation, task orientation, and self-orientation. Relations-oriented groups tended to be most satisfied with their highly relations-oriented leaders. The leaders who emerged in task-oriented groups tended to be even more highly task-oriented than the average member. However, the emergent leaders of the self-oriented groups were relatively low in self-orientation. Stimpson and Bass (1964) found that compared with task-oriented and self-oriented participants, relations-oriented participants in problem-solving groups made it more difficult for their work partners to attempt and succeed as leaders, to reach agreement, and to feel responsible.

Bass (1967c) observed task-oriented and relations-oriented followers under coercive and persuasive styles of leadership. He found that task-oriented followers produced greater quantities of work under persuasive leadership and that relations-oriented followers produced more work under coercive leadership. The followers' satisfaction with the task was significantly higher under a directive relations-oriented leader than under a participative relations-oriented leader. Conversely, their satisfaction was lower under a directive than under a persuasive task-oriented leader.

Summary and Conclusions

In their interaction with followers, leaders show what needs to be done, provide feedback to subordinates on how well it is done, communicate needed information, and act as models for their subordinates. They mediate between and connect their followers to their superiors. They are a source of feedback and serve as models for their subordinates. They need to have influence with those above them as well as those below them in the hierarchical organization.

Leadership and followership are reciprocal. Followers have an impact on their leaders. To be a good leader, one needs to be a good follower. Isolates, not followers, are the opposite of leaders. Followers are an important source of feedback to leaders. Followers' readiness, maturity, interests, competence, and compliance affect their leaders'

performance. Followers' effects on leaders also depend on the leaders' and followers' explanations for the followers' dispositions and performance. Among the interactions of importance to performance are the leader's style and the followers' motivation and personality. Another important effect is due to the interaction of the task and relations orientations of the leaders and their followers. Groups operate more successfully when the task, the leader's personality, and the follower's personality are compatible. For example, groups with task-oriented leaders perform better than do those with person-oriented leaders when followers are also task-oriented. Followers whose task orientation is low experience less tension under person-oriented leaders.

Leaders may treat each follower in a group the same or differently, depending on whether followers are members of the inner or outer circle. It is important to examine the quality of the dyadic leader-member exchange (LMX) as well as the leader-group exchange. Analysis of variance within groups may be as important as analysis of variance between groups.

Followers affect, to a considerable extent, what their leaders may do and can do. The exertion of this upward influence involves many different tactics ranging from ingratiation to establishing coalitions of influence. Important feedback can flow upward.

Still to be determined is whether the exchange relationship between the leader and subordinates becomes stable or remains variable in the long term.

Styles of Leadership

CHAPTER 17

Autocratic versus Democratic Leadership

The duality of autocratic and democratic leadership has been seen throughout history. How should people be led? How should people be governed? How should people be guided? Two views prevailed, based on opposing doctrines about human nature. For centuries, theologians and philosophers argued that human nature was cursed by original sin or that human nature was blessed with the inherent ability to find salvation. The former proponents of original sin advised that people were essentially bad; they had to be controlled, directed, and uplifted by authority. The proponents of inherent salvation set forth that people were essentially good and they must be given freedom in which to act, learn, grow, and overcome. Adam Smith, a moral philosopher as well as a political economist, saw both sides of human nature. He agreed with David Hume that self-interest required a distrust of human intentions and motives, but at the same time he also believed in the innate goodness of humankind and the power of education to enlighten and liberate (Herman, 2001).

The framers of the U.S. Constitution recognized the benefits and the costs of an independent executive with authority and a democratic legislative body. They handled the dilemma posed by balancing the powers of the executive against those of a bicameral legislature: two senators from each of the 13 sovereign states and population-based representatives of each state's male, white, property-qualified electorate. This arrangement recognized the contribution of the democratic majority vote of statewide and electoral district representatives to the commitment, interests, and satisfaction of the various constituencies. At the same time, an indirectly elected president could provide the need for order and for the execution and maintenance of federal laws, foreign affairs, and national defense. Much authority and power for direction and control were given to the president, but with safeguards. The president was commander in chief of the armed forces, but he had to face reelection and could be removed from office by the legislature. He could veto the legislative decisions of the representatives, but the veto could be overridden by the legislature.

The same dilemma confronts organizational leaders today. They must balance the advantages of a more democratic approach, which ordinarily contributes to the commitment, loyalty, involvement, and satisfaction of followers, with a more autocratic approach, which contributes to order, consistency, and the resolution of conflict. Whitty and Butts (1989) argue that authoritarian and elitist leadership sets the rules and has the power to control behavior. But more culturally accepted principles encourage democratic sharing of influence to obtain higher productivity, friendly interpersonal relations, and group cohesiveness.

The Two Opposing Approaches

Leaders and managers vary in how they deal with the dilemma of autocratic leadership at one extreme and democratic leadership at the other. These dichotomies are simplifications. Sweeney, Fiechtner, and Samores (1975) conducted a factor analysis of the leadership focus of 103 male employed part-time college students that corroborated the high degree of complexity to be found in examining autocratic and democratic leadership. The factors were: (1) authoritarian role preference, (2) authoritarian role pressure, (3) egalitarian role preference, (4) egalitarian role pressure, (5) balanced manager, (6) people-oriented manager, (7) assumed similarity between opposites, (8) contemptuous indulgence, (9) supportive values, (10) tolerance of people; and (11) organizational tolerance. Nevertheless, the same persons who engage in one type of autocratic behavior when, say, initiating structure, are also likely to be seen as facilitating work and persuading. The same persons who engage in one type of democratic behavior are likely to be seen as supportive, considerate, and people-oriented as well, but the empirical correlations are far from perfect (Edwards & Rode, 1986).

The Autocratic-Authoritarian Leadership Cluster

The autocratic-authoritarian cluster encompasses being arbitrary, controlling, power-oriented, coercive, punitive, and closed-minded. The cluster has often been described in pejorative terms. Stripped of negatives (emphasized by so many social scientists), it means taking full and sole responsibility for decisions and control of followers' performance. Autocrats stress obedience, loyalty, and strict adherence to roles. They make and enforce the rules. They see that decisions are carried out (Smither, 1991). Powerful autocratic leaders throughout history have often been praised for their ability to develop reliable and devoted followers and to act as the principal authority figures in establishing and maintaining order.

Authoritarian sports coaches may be disliked by their players. But this dislike may evolve into respect, appreciation, and fondness. Players may hate autocratic coaches but play well under them (Bernath, 1991). A list of the toughest bosses in America is compiled regularly by *Fortune* magazine. They are described as merciless with people who tell them less than the truth. They are intensely persistent, imperious, unwilling to entertain ideas that don't fit with their own. They get the job done, but the cost to themselves and others may be high (Flax, 1984).

The dark side of autocratic behavior is abusiveness, creating fear and distrust, using arbitrary and unconditional punishment, ignoring subordinates' information and inputs to decisions, and relying exclusively on one's own judgment (Smither, 1991). Henry Ford II was described by Lee Iacocca (1984), who worked directly under him, as the consummate autocrat in control of Ford Motor Company. Ford was bigoted and hypocritical. He would fire people without reason or for trivial reasons such as not wearing the right clothes. But autocrats can also be considerate. Pope John Paul II was called a spiritual dictator; he declared autocratically, "The

Church is not a democracy and no one from below can decide the truth" (November 20, 1998). Yet repeatedly, he could show personal concern and sympathy for others whether or not they liked or agreed with him (Bane, 2005).

Abusive leaders engage in hostile verbal and nonverbal behaviors (Tepper, 2000). Lyndon Johnson, exemplifying the autocratic taskmaster, abused and exhausted his staff. He paid them the lowest salaries and worked them the longest hours. He played favorites and publicly humiliated his loyal aides (Reedy, 1982). He was terrorizing (though he could be tender at times), ruthless, impatient, petty, bullying, devious, brutal, suspicious, and crafty. Yet he could sometimes also be caring, patient, devoted to family and friends, compassionate, and generous (Valenti, 1975). Another autocratic leader was a terminated former president of Kellogg Foods, who was abrasive, abrupt, unwilling to listen, and inclined to manage without being questioned (Manz & Sims, 1991). In a review of the literature, Smither (1991) conceived of authoritarian managers in work organizations as taking full responsibility for decisions and subordinate performance. They believe their assignment is to make decisions and see that the decisions are carried out. They do not share power. They may be exploitative or benevolent in their relations with others (R. Likert, 1961a). Wallechinsky (2003) listed as the 10 worst living political dictators those who suppressed freedom and human rights taken for granted in democracies, executed or jailed political opponents, tortured prisoners, caused their citizens to starve, and used violence domestically and to interfere in other countries. Joseph Stalin was a model adopted by Saddam Hussein (Montefiore, 2004).

Although investigations use many terms whose meanings do not entirely overlap, correlations generally will be high among descriptions of various authoritarian ways of organizing to get things done. That is, the same leaders who are described as autocratic or authoritarian (Lewin & Lippitt, 1938) will also be described as directive (Bass & Barrett, 1981; Heller, 1969a), coercive and persuasive (Bass, 1960), concerned with production (Blake & Mouton, 1964), lone decision makers (Vroom & Yetton, 1974), initiators of structure (Fleishman, 1953c), production-centered (R. Likert, 1961a), goal emphasizers and work facilitators (Bowers & Seashore, 1966), task-oriented (Fiedler, 1967a), and concerned about performance

(Misumi, 1985). Howard and Wellins (1994) listed five types of autocratic leader behavior in work settings: (1) The *controller* enforces a prescribed way of working. (2) The *commander* tells what to do and expects obedience. (3) The *ruler* considers decision making a privilege of management. (4) The *judge* evaluates subordinate performance and metes out rewards and punishments. (5) The *guard* protects turf and hoards resources.

The "bulls of the woods"—the early-twentieth-century shop foremen, exploitative autocrats, and punitive task-directed leaders—made the decisions for their groups and told workers what to do. They used physical force when necessary to cow their workers (Muszyk & Reimann, 1987). Such leaders discouraged subordinates from contributing to the decision process. They paid little or no attention to their subordinates' needs. More modern and less punitive autocratic leaders still reserve decisions for themselves and remain more concerned about getting the job done than about the needs of their subordinates.

Autocratic leaders tend to initiate structure, provide information, determine what is to be done, issue the rules, promise rewards for compliance, and threaten punishments for disobedience. They use their power to obtain compliance with what they have decided. They depend on their knowledge of policies and regulations and their official rank to regulate the behavior of their subordinates. They use their technical knowledge to solve problems to gain their subordinates' respect and willing compliance with their orders (Nelson, 1950). They are more often charismatic than consensual (Zaleznik, 1974). Autocratic leaders are ideologues who believe that people are basically lazy and must be driven and controlled by external rewards and punishments.

The Warrior Model of Leader. Nice (undated) has enumerated the characteristics of a subcategory of authoritarian leader. This model is of leadership related to conflict and to triumph over opposition. The flow of information is controlled. Results are more important than the methods used to achieve them. The warrior leader knows friend and foe. Battles are selected carefully and unnecessary fighting is avoided. Plans and preparations are made for future contingencies in a world seen as dangerous and hostile, in which few people can be trusted.

The Democratic Leadership Cluster

The democratic or egalitarian leadership cluster reflects concern about the followers in many different ways. Leadership is considerate (Fleishman, 1953c), democratic (Lewin & Lippitt, 1938), consultative and participative (Bass, 1976), consensual (Zaleznik, 1974), employee-centered (R. Likert, 1961a), concerned with people (Blake & Mouton, 1964), concerned with the maintenance of good working relations (Misumi, 1985), supportive and oriented toward facilitating interaction (Bowers & Seashore, 1966), relations-oriented (Fiedler, 1967a), oriented toward joint decision making (Heller, 1969a), and oriented toward group decision making (Vroom & Yetton, 1974). Democratic leaders are Theory Y ideologues (McGregor, 1960). They solicit advice, opinions, and information from their followers and share decision making with their followers. Democratic leaders use their power to set the constraints within which followers are encouraged to join in deciding what is to be done. Democratic leaders depend on their followers' skills, as well as on their own interpersonal ability and knowledge of their followers' individual needs, interests, and capabilities (Nelson, 1950). Democratic leaders believe that workers are internally motivated to do well, and seek autonomy and the opportunity to prove their worth. These leaders move decision making in organization hierarchies to lower levels, encourage questioning and ideas from below about better ways of doing things, are open to criticism, treat subordinates' mistakes as learning opportunities, celebrate subordinates' accomplishments, and promote subordinates' ideas to higher authority (Howard & Wellins, 1994). But democratic leaders often need to do more to involve their followers in decision processes. Concerned with the corruption and shortcomings of democratic governance, Rost (1996) would reform it by changing the many passive followers in an organization or community into active collaborators who help their leaders to set the major policies of governance. According to Gill (1996), five principles govern all democratic societies: (1) personal responsibility, (2) empowering others to become leaders, (3) inclusiveness, (4) equality, and (5) full deliberation. Democratic leadership has internal conflicts and is often messy. It is not to be confused with laissez-faire leadership (discussed in Chapter 6), in which the leader abstains, withdraws, or abdicates responsibility and shows none of the concern seen in the authoritarian or democratic cluster.

Illustrating the meaningfulness of the clusters, Stanton (1960) reported higher scores for consideration and for a human relations orientation among managers of clerical employees of one firm that was known for more democratic supervision, compared with another firm that was known for more autocratic supervision. Conversely, the amount of initiation of structure was much higher in the autocratic firm than in the democratic firm.

Latent or Underlying Structure

Edwards and Rode (1986) asked 100 students, mainly in ROTC, to complete four different ways of measuring authoritarian and democratic leadership preferences. The Leader Behavior Opinion Questionnaire[1] assessed how frequently they should initiate structure as leaders and how considerate they should be. Blake and Mouton's (1978) Managerial Grid was used to describe a concern for people and a concern for production. Hersey and Blanchard's (1973) LEAD-Self questionnaire (Leadership Effectiveness and Adaptability Description) generated authoritative telling and selling scores and democratic, participating, and delegating scores. Fiedler's (1967a) Least Preferred Coworker (LPC) score was used to assess task and relations orientation.[2] The intercorrelations among the authoritarian task measures were positive but rather low. The same was true for the democratic measures. However, a path model of the intercorrelations, adjusted for measurement errors by Jöreskog and Sorbos (1978), indicated that the latent structure underlying the observed correlations was a continuum stretching from authoritative behavior at one end to democratic behavior at the other.

Distinctions among Styles of Leadership

This chapter and Chapters 18, 19, and 20 will look at concepts of the differences in leadership styles or patterns of leadership behavior and their effects: the overarching

---

[1] See Chapter 20 and Fleishman (1960) for an extended discussion of the concepts and measurement of consideration and initiation of structure.
[2] For a discussion of the Managerial Grid, the LEAD-Self questionnaire, and the LPC score, see Chapter 19.

concept of and evidence about autocratic versus democratic leadership (this chapter), participative versus directive decision making (Chapter 18), relations versus task orientation (Chapter 19), and consideration versus initiation (Chapter 20). Laissez-faire leadership versus motivation to manage was discussed in Chapter 6. Autocratic-authoritarian versus democratic-egalitarian leadership is the most multifaceted issue. It refers to the way power is distributed, whose needs are met, and how decisions are made. Participative versus directive leadership refers primarily to how decisions are made. Relations- versus task-oriented leadership focuses on whose needs are met. Consideration versus initiation of structure is a behaviorally factor-derived dichotomy. Consideration and initiation refer to how decisions are made and to the structuring of tasks, goals, and role relationships. Laissez-faire leadership and motivation to manage refer to the extent to which leadership is either avoided or attempted. It should be kept in mind that styles of leadership are distinguished not only by behavioral differences but also by differences in cognition and intentions. To the degree that leaders are consistent in what they think they ought to do, they will have a consistent style of leadership (Wofford & Goodwin, 1998).

Authoritarian and Democratic Leadership

Why do we emerge with just two overarching clusters of leadership styles? Possibly because there are only two ways to change a follower's behavior (apart from using drugs or physical force). The leader alters either the follower's information, understanding, and ability to cope with the task at hand, or the follower's motivation to deal with the task. When the leader has more relevant knowledge than the follower, authoritarian, task-focused direction can transfer the information quickly. Powerful leaders can arouse follower motivation. But in many situations, followers have at least as much information as the leader. Power may be shared. Follower motivation can be enhanced by involving them in decisions about handling the task, their concerns about the task and themselves.

Misumi (1985) argued that two fundamental dimensions—the performance leadership function (P) and the maintenance leadership function (M)—underlie all the others in the clusters. Thus, for instance, participative and democratic leadership are situationally specific manifestations of the underlying maintenance function, whose aim is to promote social integration and group stability. The manifestation of the maintenance function may appear as consideration if it is directed primarily toward satisfying subordinates' needs.

Use of Power and Ability

MacIver (1947) and Bass (1960) noted that authoritarian leaders may depend on their power to coerce and their ability to persuade. An able leader successfully persuades others to follow him or her because they expect that following the leader's suggestions will result in solving the problems the group faces. A powerful person successfully coerces others to follow him or her because the power of the leader's position or the power of the leader as a person makes others expect that the leader will reward them for compliance or punish them for noncompliance. An able leader can indirectly reinforce the behavior of others. Such a leader can provide the cues that help them attain their goals. A powerful leader can directly reinforce the behavior of others by granting or denying them rewards or punishments (Bass, 1960).

These types of authoritarian leadership were described by F. C. Bartlett (1926). He observed that leaders in any complex social group maintain their success either because of the social prestige of their position and their personal capacity to impress and dominate or by virtue of their personal capacity to persuade their followers. Blau and Scott (1962) described the authoritarian supervisor as one who, among other things, uses power to be strict rather than lenient, to supervise closely, and to ensure adherence to procedures. Using one-minute sampling to observe the spontaneous play of children in nursery school, Parten (1932) found two types of leadership possible in the situation: persuasive leadership, which uses diplomatic, "artful" suggestion; and leadership through personal power, which uses brute force to dominate others. Zillig (1933) observed the same two types of leadership in the German classroom—leaders who dominate and leaders who direct and guide.

Colin Powell (1995, p. 332) described how he used his power and ability when he was a senior official in the Department of the Army to make Policy Review Group meetings more effective. He was delegated responsibility by his boss, Frank Carlucci, to chair the interagency discussions. Frustrated by "endless, pointless, time-wasters," he used his legitimate power and perspicacity to structure the meetings highly. Everyone could contribute in advance to the agenda, but Powell controlled the final listing. No one else could change it. The meeting was to last only one hour. In the first 5 to 10 minutes, Powell reviewed its purposes and what had to be decided. Participants could present their positions without interruption for the next 20 minutes, followed by open discussion until the last 15 minutes, when Powell spent 5 minutes summarizing everyone's positions, allowing the participants one minute each to critique the summary and reserving the last few minutes for himself to present the conclusions. Participants' objections could be taken up with their superiors and referred by them to Carlucci.

The processes of democratic leadership usually require maturity and some education. Some leaders may be identified as democratic on the basis of their use of parliamentary procedures and majority decision making. Others may consult; strive for consensus; and pursue an open, trusting, follower-oriented relationship. Such consensus leadership has deep roots in the American national character (Cooley, 1956). According to Zaleznik (1974), the idealized image of the leader in America is that of brother rather than father. The leaders are first among equals whose sense of timing may be more important than their expertise. Leaders may be more dependent on the followers than the followers are on the leaders. Compromise, caring, and a sense of responsibility and attachment to followers characterize the consensus leader.

Effects of Autocratic and Democratic Leadership

Ideal Types

In the first experiments—using instructed camp counselors leading preadolescent boys and girls—to contrast the authoritarian and the democratic leader, the authoritarian leader dictated what was to be done and was unconcerned about the group members' needs for autonomy and development. The democratic leader shared the decision making with followers and was concerned about their need to contribute to deciding what was to be done.

The authoritarian leader was personal in praise or reproof of each follower; the democratic leader was factual and rational. The authoritarian leader emphasized his or her social distance from the followers; the democratic leader deemphasized social distance.

Following the earlier experiments with authoritarian and democratic leadership, subsequent studies tended to concentrate on one of four aspects of the distinction between authoritarian and democratic leadership: (1) whether the leader shared decision making, (2) whether the followers were of primary concern to the leader, (3) whether social distance was maintained, and (4) whether punishment and coercion were used.

It must be stressed that these are ideal types of authoritarian and democratic leadership. In practice, one is likely to find much variation and overlap. For instance, benevolent autocrats, although they are likely to be dictatorial, may also be considerably concerned about the needs of their followers. The democratic manager may encourage group decision making but may also emphasize getting the job done, as well as the needs of the group. The charismatic leader may rely on personal power and the followers' desire for identification, but also may choose to support democratic efforts and the attainment of prosocial goals. Some researchers have taken greater care than others to define and "purify" the patterns of leadership behavior to be studied. But often it is difficult to determine whether the pattern of leadership behavior examined was democratic, participative, considerate, relations-oriented, or some combination of these characteristics.

The Prototype Experiments

Consistent with Kurt Lewin's ideas (1939) about the behavioral dynamics in groups, two seminal experiments were conducted (Lewin & Lippitt, 1938; Lippitt, 1940a) to explore the effects of democratic and authoritarian atmospheres upon the behavior of group members. These studies were preceded by a report by Mowrer (1938) on how infractions of rules were reduced at the New Haven Children's Center in 1937 when a democratic approach was offered to the children (aged 4 to 12) to deal with problems, in contrast to the authoritarian staff control that had been in place before.[3] Reporting on the two ex-

periments, Lippitt (1940) defined democratic and authoritarian leader behavior. By means of careful coaching and practice, the authoritarian leader was trained to (1) determine all policy for group members, (2) dictate the methods and stages of goal attainment one step at a time, (3) direct the actions and interactions of group members, and (4) praise the members in a personal manner. The democratic leader was trained to (1) encourage group members to determine their own policies, (2) give them perspective by explaining in advance the steps toward attaining the goals, (3) award them freedom to initiate their own tasks and interactions, and (4) praise them in an objective manner. The leaders were adult counselors. The group members were 10-year-old boys and girls, closely matched on several control variables. Two groups of five members each worked on hobby projects. The behavior of leaders and members was recorded by trained observers.

Both the leaders and the group members initiated more actions in the authoritarian-led group. Members of the authoritarian-led group had more submissive reactions to the leader, however, and treated him less as an equal than was the case in the democratic-led group. In the authoritarian-led group, members became progressively more submissive to the leader. Although they tended to respond to the leader rather than to initiate interaction with each other, they hesitated to approach him because to do so might further reduce their personal power and freedom of movement. The democratic form of leadership, on the other hand, tended to increase the freedom of action of group members. The members of the democratically led group exhibited less tension and hostility, and their subgroups were more cohesive and enduring than was the case for the authoritarian-led group.[4] Curfman (1939) replicated (1940a) Lippitt's first experiment with two clubs of fifth- and sixth-graders, with similar results.[5]

Implications and Contrary Points of View

Research and development by Rensis Likert (1961a, 1967, 1977b) flowed from a direct inference from the prototype experiments that the democratic approach was

---

[3] Mentioned in Fox (1954).

[4] Laissez-faire leadership was introduced as a third leadership style by Lippitt (1940a) in his expansion of the experimental investigation. Its effects were discussed in Chapter 6.
[5] Mentioned in Fox (1954).

to be advocated in organizations to foster effectiveness and satisfaction. In this, Likert was joined by the entire human relations movement (see, for example, Argyris, 1957; McGregor, 1960). In counteraction, joining with the classical "scientific managers," Miner (1968), among others, argued for an emphasis on the manager-leader as a task-oriented authority figure. Blake and Mouton (1964) pioneered the point of view that the best leaders and managers were highly concerned with both production and people and could integrate the two approaches. A fourth group of advocates, such as Fiedler (1967a), Vroom and Yetton (1974), and Hersey and Blanchard (1977), argued that which style was best depended on the situation.

As we shall see in this and succeeding chapters, there is some truth in all these positions. Evidence has accumulated that in specified circumstances, authoritarian direction may, in fact, result in heightened productivity, particularly in the short term; but overall, the democratic approach is likely to be more effective, particularly in the long run. And in general, under most conditions, working for a democratic supervisor will be more satisfying. This last conclusion is simplest to document.

Over 30 empirical laboratory experiments and 10 field studies on the subject were conducted between 1940 and 1975. Under democratic leadership, members' satisfaction with the leaders was the rule rather than the exception. On the other hand, more positive correlations were found between the authoritative leadership style and productivity in the laboratory experiments. Fortunately, a more rigorous meta-analysis, including some of these findings as well as more recent reports, provided a greater opportunity to be more specific about these effects on productivity. In field studies, it could be concluded that a democratic style worked better. In the laboratory, the autocratic style resulted in more productivity.

Miller and Monge (1986) first conducted such a meta-analysis of short-term laboratory experiments of the effects on productivity and satisfaction of "employees" of contrived autocratic versus participative "supervisors" by Ivancevich (1974); Katzell, Miller, Rotter, and Venet (1970); McCurdy and Lambert (1952); and Shaw (1955). In these experiments, productivity was greater when the leader in the laboratory manipulation was more authoritarian than democratic. For the four short-term laboratory experiments in which the "supervisor" was trained to act autocratically or democratically, productivity was greater with authoritarian, directive supervision. The mean correlation between productivity and authoritarianism was .33.

However, Miller and Monge (1986) also completed a meta-analysis for 10 longer-term field studies. Consistent with what will be reviewed next, they found strong support in reports from 41 analyses. In such real-life settings, the mean correlation was .27 between democratic supervision and the productivity of the persons or groups supervised. The researchers also concluded that the more democratic supervisory styles correlated with the satisfaction of subordinates. The mean correlation was .34. Consistent with this conclusion is the massive survey evidence accumulated by R. Likert (1977b) and his colleagues. Despite the fact that in the short run, in brief laboratory experiments, authoritarian supervision pays off in more productivity than does democratic supervision, in the long run democratic approaches tend to generate bigger improvements in an organization's productivity as well as in the satisfaction of its employees.

When It Pays to Be an Autocratic Leader. Jack Welch, CEO of General Electric, headed the 1984 *Fortune* list of the 10 toughest bosses in America (Flax, 1984). Yet he moved General Electric to the top of the list in earnings and successfully changed its line of products and competitive performance. Muczyk and Steel (1998) cite successful turnarounds by business executives. During organizational crises, despite the aversion to autocratic leadership, when organizations need to be turned around quickly, autocratic and directive leadership is needed. Sometimes unpopular decisions are required along with legitimate and reasonable goals and fair and respectful treatment of subordinates. Teachers, coaches, and religious leaders exert powerful influence over many followers who learn from them by being told what they should do (Smither, 1991). Not unexpectedly, the military tends to value the use of authority more favorably. In a survey of 30,735 U.S. Army superiors, peers, and subordinates of commissioned and noncommissioned officers, Penner, Malone, Coughlin, and Herz (1973) found that leaders who established a high level of discipline were likely to be rated much higher in their overall performance by their superiors. Consistent with this, Torrance (1959) reported that U.S. Air Force aircrews who were given feedback by highly authoritarian methods improved their performance more than those who were given feedback by less highly structured methods.

Supportive evidence was also found elsewhere. Hise (1968), studying simulated business groups, found that productivity was positively related to close rather than general supervision. M. E. Shaw (1955) obtained results indicating that the speed and accuracy of a group's performance in a highly structured communications network were significantly higher under autocratic than under democratic leadership. In a study of groups in a formal organization, Shepherd and Weschler (1955) found that psychosocial distance between the leader and the followers was associated with fewer communication difficulties. Working closely together was related to greater difficulty in communication. Bergum and Lehr (1963) studied subordinates' monitoring performance under different conditions of supervision. They found that the vigilance of subordinates could be maintained at fairly high levels under authoritarian conditions.

Whether authoritarian leadership pays off will depend on the extent to which the leader has more knowledge about what needs to be done as well as control of the necessary resources. This payoff can be routinely demonstrated in leadership training exercises. Authoritarian leadership can be productive if the trainee who is assigned the role of autocratic leader happens, by chance, to know more about the problem to be solved than does the person who is playing the role of subordinate (Shackleton, Bass, & Allison, 1975). When autocratic leaders know the correct answer in such exercises, they can ensure highly accurate group outcomes better than can democratic leaders. But authoritative leaders with misinformation can lead their groups farther astray than can democratic leaders with the same degree of misinformation (Cammalleri, Hendrick, Pittman, et al., 1973). An increase in rules constraining managerial behavior was found salutary in Malaysia (Mansor & Ali, 1998).

When Autocratic Leadership Is Worse. The American public was led to believe that 11,500 unionized air controllers went on strike in August 1981 for unreasonable economic demands and because of peer pressure. However, a U.S. Department of Transportation task force discovered that they had struck because they wanted improvements in working conditions to alleviate job stress and because their managers put autocratic values and be-

liefs into practice (Bowers, 1983). In 1989, the newly formed union of air controllers made the same claim that morale was low because of autocratic management (Cushman, 1989). Ziller (1957) found group members to be least satisfied under autocratic leadership. In a study of personnel turnover, Ley (1966) found that the supervisor's authoritarian behavior was the factor most frequently associated with subordinates quitting their jobs.

More deleterious effects are likely when autocratic leadership takes the form of abusive, punitive, and disciplinary actions. The only U.S. Navy captain to be relieved of duty "for cause" as commander of a nuclear submarine was relieved for abusive treatment of the crew, resulting in their "despondency" and low morale (Ricks, 1997). Richman, Flaherty, Rospenda, et al. (1992) found that abusive supervision of medical students and medical residents was related to their sense of distress and dissatisfaction. Ashforth (1997) reported that belittling of subordinates and noncontingent punishment by their supervisors were correlated with subordinates' feelings of frustration, alienation, and helplessness. Tepper (2000) conducted follow-up surveys of 390 home telephone interviews of full-time employees of service, retail, manufacturing, and small-business organizations about their experience with abusive supervision. Abuse was infrequent on 15 items of behavior such as "Ridicules me" and "Puts me down in front of others" (1 = never uses this behavior; 5 = uses this behavior very often). The mean obtained was 1.38. Abusiveness correlated negatively with job satisfaction ($-.35$), organizational commitment ($-.24$, $-.27$), and positively with respondents' emotional exhaustion.

Cultural norms dampen enthusiasm for using autocratic leadership. In earlier chapters, we observed that supervisors tend to avoid disciplinary, punitive action even when confronted with poor performance by subordinates. Thus, for instance, Maier and Danielson (1956) reported that even when disciplinary rules call for punishment, supervisors tend to avoid it. They perceive that punishment will reduce productivity, even when it is used to control the violation of rules. In fact, Keller and Szilagyi (1976) found that punitive leadership, rather than improving performance, primarily increased role ambiguity. Day and Hamblin (1964) found punitive and close supervision to be connected with reductions in productivity and group harmony. They studied 24 quartets who had to follow elaborate blueprints to assemble models of molecules using pegs, springs, and colored balls. In this complex task, the members were subjected to either punitive or nonpunitive supervision, as well as to close or general supervision. Punitive and close supervision, in contrast to nonpunitive and general supervision, tended to increase the subjects' feelings of aggression toward their coworkers, as well as toward their supervisor, which significantly lowered their productivity.

Numerous other experiments point to the deleterious main and side effects of punitive supervision. French (1957) examined the effects of the "supervisor" who obtained compliance by using the power to fine paid participants who were working at a simple task—sorting IBM punch cards according to the total number of holes the cards contained. The assignment was supposedly part of a research project. Participants were fined for failure to maintain the standard of speed and accuracy. In comparison with participants who were rewarded with extra pay when they reached and maintained the standard, participants who were punished by fines for failure were more likely to show signs of resistance to maintaining production. After four working periods, punishment for failure became detrimental to speed and accuracy. The participants had a greater desire to leave the work and were more likely to want to do something else and to make suggestions for changing the work situation. Furthermore, they showed greater feelings of aggression, liked their supervisor less, and were less likely to accept the supervisor as competent to evaluate their work. In a similar experiment, Raven and French (1958b) levied fines when participants failed to conform to the demands of "supervisors." These fines led the participants to resist by overconforming to the suggestions of their supervisors. That is, metaphorically, if participants were ordered against their will to "polish the silverware," they rubbed so hard that they rubbed off all the silver.

Experiments by deCharms and Hamblin (1960) yielded similar results finding that punitive supervision resulted in increased tension in "employees" and lowered their productivity. These studies of the effects of punitive supervision are consistent with the general psychological findings that severe punishment tends to be disruptive and anxiety producing. Mild punishment, however, may provide, under certain circumstances, more appropriate attention to the failure to comply with authority and serve as a way to eliminate undesired acts. Thus Georgopoulos (1965) observed higher productivity to be associated with a pattern of supervisors' disciplinary behavior that employees regarded as "just right" and "not too strict." Mild aversive reinforcements and negative feedback have their uses.

When It Pays to Be a Democratic Leader. Smither (1991) listed four conditions in which democratic leadership works best in organizations: (1) it is visibly supported by higher authority; (2) members are well-educated and support the organization's goals; (3) leaders have the skills to conduct meetings with the members; and (4) time can be afforded for trust to develop. Comrey, Pfiffner, and Beem (1952) studied employees at six levels of organization in the U.S. Forest Survey. Supervisors of more effective departments were described as sympathetic, democratic, social, and willing to share information. Similarly, Comrey, High, and Wilson (1955a, 1955b) studied supervisors and workers in an aircraft factory. Supervisors of effective groups were characterized by adequate authority, communication downward, and sympathy; these supervisors were not arbitrary, and their attitude toward employees was not hypercritical. Argyle, Gardner, and Ciofi (1958) also reported higher rates of productivity, reduced personnel turnover, and reduced absenteeism under democratic, nonpunitive supervision in work groups in seven British factories. Zweig (1966) found that democratic supervisors were rated by higher management as being more effective than supervisors exhibiting less democratic styles of behavior. Similarly, Hall and Donnell (1979) reported that the managers whose career advancement was the fastest, compared with those who advanced more slowly, were less likely to subscribe to Theory X beliefs[6] that workers are lazy and immature, and need to be carefully monitored and controlled. Levy-Leboyer and Pineau (1981) obtained interview data from 151 French laboratory supervisors. The success of their laboratories was appraised subjectively and from research publication records. Leaders of more successful laboratories supervised less strictly, allowed for participation by technicians in decision making, and held more frequent meetings and evaluations.

[6]McGregor (1960) formulated Theory X (autocratic beliefs about how workers needed to be led) and Theory Y (democratic beliefs about how workers needed to be led).

In a federal agency, J. C. White (1972) observed that both the effective county office managers and the effective managers at headquarters used a more democratic style. The effectiveness of business supervisors and purchasing managers was also seen by H. C. White (1971a, 1972) to be associated with the extent to which they were more democratic and less autocratic. Hollman (1973) and Tanimoto (1977) found that the effectiveness of management by objectives, as seen by subordinates, was greater when practiced by a more democratic manager than by a more autocratic manager. Other studies have shown that democratic approaches in organizations have a favorable effect on the physical and mental health of the members (Caplan, Cobb, French, et al., 1975).

Ordinarily, satisfaction and morale are likely to be lower with autocratic supervision and higher with democratic supervision. Under autocratic leadership greater resentment, less loyalty, less commitment, less involvement, and less satisfaction are commonly found (Gouldner, 1954). Such subjective reactions to the supervisors and poorer relations with them affect the willing compliance of subordinates with their supervisors' initiatives (Barnard, 1938). In both the short term and the long term, subordinates generally will be more satisfied with democratic leaders.

Beam (1975) showed that enlisted personnel in the U.S. Navy had a strong desire to be treated democratically, regardless of the level of technology or physical activity in which they were involved. Mohr (1971) obtained similar results in 144 works groups from 13 local health departments, as did Pennings (1975) in 40 branch offices of a large U.S. brokerage firm. The subordinates' satisfaction was strongly associated with democratic supervision in these as well as in many other large-scale field studies.

Baumgartel (1957) studied attitudes and motivations of scientists in governmental research-and-development labs under three leadership conditions (democratic, authoritarian, and laissez-faire). He found that scientists who worked under the democratic leadership held the most favorable attitudes and had a greater job motivation, whereas the least favorable attitudes were found among those who worked under the authoritarian leadership. Harnquist (1956) observed that group members tended to feel more satisfied under democratic than under autocratic leadership. Mullen (1965, 1966b) reported that the satisfaction of employees was associated with democratic

supervision but saw no relationship between supervisory style and employees' requests for transfers.

Mandell and Duckworth (1955) reported that the overall morale of 64 trade employees in civil service was high if the employees said that their "supervisor lets them know how they are doing." In a series of surveys, R. Likert (1961a) found that employees of public utilities revealed higher job satisfaction when their supervisors were more "personal" than "institutional" in their dealings and more "downward" or employee-oriented, and when the supervisors trained the subordinates for better jobs. Supervisors of high-morale groups differed from supervisors of low-morale groups in that they reviewed their subordinates' work more frequently, welcomed the discussion of mutual problems with subordinates, carried on group discussions, and kept subordinates posted on new information.

D'Angelo (1973) found that sales managers who believed themselves to be practicing a democratic, human relations style brought about more change in their subordinates in an organizational development program than did those who believed they were practicing either authoritarian or "human resources" leadership. H. H. Meyer (1968) studied two plants, one managed according to Theory Y and the other managed according to Theory X.[7] Workers under the more democratic type of management (Theory Y) reported higher felt responsibility, risk, reward, warmth, and identity. Beehr and Gupta (1987) compared two manufacturing firms—one, formally democratic; the other, more traditional—that were similar in size and technology. They found that employees' perceptions, attitudes, and behavior were more favorable in the democratic firm.

Hendrix and McNichols's (1982) survey of 4,786 military and civilian personnel in the U.S. Air Force showed that managers who were described as self-enhancing, outspoken, and demanding and who used their authority as their primary means of influencing their subordinates were seen as contributing to a much less attractive organizational climate, to much less job satisfaction, and to much less perceived productivity than were other more democratic managers who tended to show concern for their subordinates and for group processes. Results were the same for three different work settings involving cus-

_____

[7] See McGregor (1960).

tomer service, routine jobs, and unique jobs with a lot of autonomy.

Brollier (1984) surveyed 93 directors of departments of occupational therapy and 348 staff therapists. The directors' democratic leadership had much more of a positive effect on the staff's satisfaction than on the staff's performance. A survey by Field (1984) of 295 human services professionals indicated that democratic leadership tended to promote greater job satisfaction among the staff, particularly satisfaction with salaries and career advancement.

When Democratic Leadership Is Worse or When Alternative Styles of Leadership Are Better. Studebaker went out of business in 1964, after competing against other auto manufacturers that practiced less industrial democracy and less committee management (Clemens & Meyer, 1987). Contingent reinforcement and transformational leadership may be more effective than the emphasis on either authority or democracy (Bass, 1998). Ziller (1957) observed greater problems among members who were led democratically. Neither autocratic nor democratic leadership was as effective as a type of *reinforcement* leadership that consistently approved the correct performance of members and made suggestions for improvements. Spector and Suttell (1956) demonstrated that this type of leader brought about better achievement by the group than did an authoritarian type who made decisions for the group or a democratic type who permitted maximum participation by members. D'Angelo (1973) reported that a *human resources* style, which involves "striving to continually expand the areas over which the manager's subordinates have self-direction and self-control," was associated with more effective work groups before and after an organizational development program for 103 sales managers and their 360 salesmen subordinates. Autocratic or human relations styles were less effective. Howell (1985) showed that in contrast to task-structuring and considerate leaders, actors who were trained as *charismatic* leaders were most effective in enhancing productivity in the face of normative resistance among subordinates.

Anticipating future interest in transformational leadership, Litwin and Stringer (1966) organized 45 business students into three "firms." The firms competed in the construction and marketing of "radar equipment" manufactured from Erector set materials. Three different business climates were created: (1) an *authoritarian-structured* business, with a strong emphasis on the careful definition of duties and the exercise of formal authority; (2) a *democratic-friendly* business, in which cooperative behavior, group loyalty, teamwork, freedom from punishment, and a loose informal structure were emphasized; and (3) an *achieving (transformational)* business, in which innovation was encouraged, competitive feedback was given, pride in the organization was fostered, a certain amount of risk taking was deemed desirable, and high personal goals were encouraged. The "president" of each company was a member of the research staff who adopted an authoritarian, democratic, or achieving leadership style. The achieving (transforming) style resulted in the greatest dollar volume, the most new products, and the most cost-saving innovations. The authoritarian style did succeed in producing the finished goods with the highest quality, primarily by never deviating from the specifications. Consistent with most other findings, students who were working with a democratic president were more satisfied with their jobs than were the students in the two other firms.

When There Are No Differences. Some studies have failed to find that democratic or autocratic supervision had any significant effect on satisfaction or productivity. Thus, with experimental groups of students, Hamblin, Miller, and Wiggins (1961) reported no relationship between authoritarian leadership and group morale. J. D. White (1963) examined whether the morale of boards of directors was affected by how they were led. Although the power of members was found to be higher on boards with democratic leaders than with autocratic leaders, morale was not related to the different styles of leadership. In the case of sports coaches, Browne and Mahoney (1984) concluded that it sometimes appears best for the coach to act in an authoritarian manner. At other times, it is best for the coach to be more democratic by talking to players with individualized consideration and by allowing them to participate in goal setting. Still other investigators found no significant differences in productivity between democratically and autocratically led groups. Thus Lyle (1961) and Spector and Suttell (1956) found no differences in the performance of groups under democratic and autocratic leadership. However, Lyle (1961) observed a tendency for democratic groups to work faster under restricted communication, whereas authoritarian groups worked faster under open communication. Results obtained by S. Adams (1952) indicated that bomber crews performed more effectively under medium than under high or low degrees of democratic leadership. Sales (1964) obtained no significant difference in the performance scores of groups with democratic and autocratic leaders. Johnson and Smith (1953) studied classes taught traditionally and under democratic leadership. They found no significant differences in achievement gains or in the students' evaluations.

Mullen (1965, 1966b) also failed to find that group productivity was related to supervisory style. Likewise, T. A. Mahoney (1967) obtained no relationship between democratic supervision and measures of organizational effectiveness in a study of industrial organizations. Similarly, Swartz (1973) found that whether football coaches were autocratic, democratic, or laissez-faire was unrelated to their success in winning games. G. H. Graham (1969) conducted one class democratically according to Theory Y and another autocratically according to Theory X.[8] The two groups did not differ in examination scores. The top quartile of students did better when led by the democratic instructor, but the lower 75% of students got better grades under the autocratic instructor.

Antecedent Conditions That Moderate the Effects of Autocratic and Democratic Leadership

Chapter 7 noted that authoritarian leadership works better with authoritarian followers and in authoritarian cultures. Other potential personal and interpersonal modifiers were also discussed. Chapters 25 through 29 will look at how situational conditions may affect the leader's style, and Chapters 31 to 33 will examine how race, sex, and culture make a difference. Some of the findings will be introduced here that have demonstrated that the effects of authoritarian and democratic leadership depend on these antecedent conditions.

Taylor (1980) pointed out that immature, dependent, inexperienced subordinates are more likely to expect and accept authoritarian direction and that democratic lead-

ership is likely to result in their more rapid development. Nisbett (1986) suggested that a more democratic leadership is desirable as the workforce becomes more educated and seeks greater participation, as business becomes more complex and requires a team of experts to deal with its problems, and as the use of high technology increases. The symphony conductor Daniel Barenboim (2001) felt that one could learn to live in a democratic society through experience in a symphony orchestra: "For when you do so, you know when to lead and when to follow. You leave space for others and at the same time you have no inhibitions about claiming a place for yourself." The fall of communism in Eastern Europe gave Luthans and Riolli (1997) the opportunity to compare managers in Albania at a fully privatized company starting over, a company slowly converting to privatization, and a large old-line state-owned enterprise. Most managers in the privatized company preferred and practiced a democratic style of getting everyone involved in decisions. Most in the slowly converting company preferred and practiced a consulting style, getting input from others. Most in the state enterprise practiced benevolent autocracy, explaining their decisions, but preferred a more consultative style.

Effects of Followers' Expectations, Orientation, and Competence

In examining the effects of followers' expectations about leadership, we need to take into account cultural changes that have occurred in the past 60 years. Earlier studies are likely to show willingness to accept autocratic leadership by many followers; later studies are less likely to show this. Nevertheless, Smither (1989) noted that in the right context authoritarian leadership can be effective in accomplishing organizational goals. Tough leaders can be effective, according to anecdotal evidence. Autocratic leadership may be what is required if employees are poorly educated and are uninterested in responsibility or in the organization's mission. Immediate productivity may be more important than employee satisfaction. Employees may have strong emotional ties to the leader and may not resent tough leadership.

According to French, Morrison, and Levinger (1960), autocratic leadership is likely to generate dissatisfaction and hostility in subordinates unless they see it as a legitimate part of the supervisor's role. Thus Foa's (1957) study

[8] See McGregor (1960).

of groups of Israeli workers under democratic and autocratic leadership found that groups with authoritarian and democratic expectations were about equally well satisfied with democratic leaders. But when leaders were autocratic, crews with authoritarian expectations were better satisfied than those with democratic expectations. Hemphill (1949b) noted that arbitrary inconsistency and reversal of opinion by the leader are more readily tolerated in groups that lack well-established rules and regulations, well-defined goal direction, and strong cohesiveness among the members. Vroom and Mann (1960) studied industrial work groups that varied in size and in style of supervision. In the small work groups, high rates of interaction occurred between workers and supervisors, and egalitarian leaders were preferred. In the large work groups, members interacted less frequently with each other and with their leaders and exhibited more positive attitudes toward authoritarian leaders.

Tepper, Duffy, and Shaw (2001) found that constructive resistance to abusive supervision was greater if subordinates were conscientious. But resistance was dysfunctional if the subordinates were also agreeable. Tepper, Duffy, and Hoobler (2002) reported that for 176 employees, abusive supervision made a difference in how their coworkers' organizational citizenship behavior (OCB) affected these employees' job satisfaction. When abusive supervision was low, coworker OCB contributed to employee job satisfaction. When abusive supervision was high, coworker OCB had a negative impact on employee satisfaction.

Calvin, Hoffmann, and Harden (1957) constructed experimental groups that differed according to their members' scores on intelligence tests and the authoritarianism or egalitarianism of the leaders. The performance of groups composed of bright members did not differ under authoritarian and egalitarian leadership. But dull members in authoritarian-led groups were more effective than were dull members in egalitarian-led groups. McCurdy and Eber (1953) arranged for leaders to be coached in democratic and autocratic patterns of behavior. Authoritarian participants solved problems somewhat less speedily under democratic than under autocratic leadership.

Circularity. Kruglanski (1969) reported that managers tended to supervise less closely those subordinates whom they trusted. However, a circularity occurs. In an experiment, Strickland (1967) found that laboratory "supervisors" came to mistrust "subordinates" whom they were directed to monitor closely and increased their trust of "subordinates" whom they were not instructed to watch closely. In the same way, McFillen (1978) and McFillen and New (1978) failed to find any significant relationship between supervisory rewards or punishment and subordinates' performance, but subordinates' performance caused a difference in closeness of supervision. Low-performing subordinates were more closely supervised. McFillen and New (1979) demonstrated experimentally that not only is mistrust increased under close supervision, but the supervisor attributes more success to the closely supervised subordinate who succeeds than to the generally supervised subordinate who succeeds, and more failure to the closely supervised subordinate who fails.

Immediate Task Demands

Which leadership style works best depends on the task of the leader and the led. As Plato observed, there may be no time for a democratic vote on a ship in a storm. Sailors may not know as much about what to do as the captain. The captain's individual judgment may be better than the sailors' consensus. When the democratic management of Steve Jobs, which had promoted the creativity and innovation that launched Apple Computer, was no longer effective in competing with IBM's entry into the personal computer market, Jobs was replaced by the tough John Scully, a top-down decision maker (Clemens & Meyer, 1987).

According to Rudin (1964), a punitive style of supervision leads to good performance on simple tasks and to poor performance on complex tasks. Becker and Baloff (1969) suggested that the optimum style of leadership is likely to depend on whether the task involves information processing or the generation of ideas. In a laboratory experiment involving complex mechanical tasks under close or general supervision and punitive or nonpunitive styles, Day and Hamblin (1964) found that close supervision produced a large increase in aggressive feelings toward the supervisor. Close supervision did not affect satisfaction with the task, but production was significantly lower. The punitive style also resulted in increased aggressive feelings toward the supervisor, but again without any effect on satisfaction with the task. As with close supervision, punitive supervision led to a decrease in production. However, Patchen (1962) obtained a positive relationship between close supervision and better performance in manual work when there was strong group cohesiveness and when the supervisor was seen as rewarding rather than punitive. Thus although close supervision is usually considered part of a more autocratic style, its effects may depend more on whether it also includes a punitive component. (A benevolent autocrat would be more rewarding and less punitive.)

The phase in the task also makes a difference. R. C. Anderson's (1959) survey of leadership in experimental groups disclosed that groups under authoritarian leaders required less time in the planning phases but were less efficient in the task-solution phases. Consistent with what was said earlier, democratic leadership resulted in greater satisfaction for members in both phases of problem solving. Subsequently, Doyle (1971) ascertained that egalitarian leadership was most effective in the analysis phase of group problem solving, but in the final synthesizing phase that required coordination, groups with powerful leaders were particularly effective.

Falling Dominoes Again

As was seen in Chapter 16, managers' behavior toward subordinates depends on how the managers' superiors act toward the managers. Thus D. Katz (1951) found that highly productive groups had less close supervision from their supervisors, who in turn were less closely supervised by their superiors. Hunt, Osborn, and Larson (1975) observed that whether or not upper-level management was autocratic had an impact on what leadership style was most effective at lower levels. Morse (1953) studied employees and supervisors in an office situation. General supervision and delegation of authority facilitated the workers' satisfaction with the work group. Job satisfaction or satisfaction with the company was not fostered unless the supervisors' orientation toward employees was reinforced by higher management.

Large-Scale, Long-Term Comparisons of Autocratic and Democratic Systems

Bowers (1997) argued that top-down hierarchical command of business is out of date—that decision making is needed at all levels of a firm. At all levels, leaders and subordinates need to work out decisions together, and a democratic model should replace command and control systems. The outstanding application of democratic as opposed to autocratic processes in organizations was an extensive effort at the University of Michigan. Strong evidence was accumulated from over 500 studies completed between 1950 and 1977 that in the long run, democratic leadership pays off in both higher productivity and greater satisfaction for employees. Katz, Maccoby, and Morse (1950) began the line of investigation in the home office of a large insurance company. Twenty-four work groups were studied; half were high and half were low in productivity. Each highly productive unit was matched with another unit that was low in productivity. Differences in supervisory behavior between the high- and low-productivity units were assessed by means of interviews with supervisors and their subordinates. Highly productive supervisors were more frequently employee-centered rather than production-centered. They were more likely to exercise general rather than close supervision, and they were more likely to differentiate their roles from those of their subordinates in terms of the duties they performed.

Next, Katz, Maccoby, Gurin, and Floor (1951) studied railroad maintenance-of-way workers. Again, the more productive supervisors were found to be more employee centered and to exercise more general supervision than those whose units were less productive. However, no difference in role differentiation was found. The line of investigation was continued by Morse and Reimer (1956). They showed that although authoritarian methods contributed more to increased productivity in an insurance firm during the first year of an experimental effort to change, a sizable drop in performance followed in subsequent years because of the adverse impact of the authoritarian approach on human factors.

These studies led to the formulation of a rationale for organizational improvement. This rationale relied partly on democratizing the leadership patterns in the organization, predicated on the efficacy of democratic over autocratic processes.

Rationale

Borrowing heavily from the original experimental concepts and results of Lewin and Lippitt (1938), R. Likert

(1961a) conceived of four systems of interpersonal relationships in large organizations: (1) exploitative autocratic, (2) benevolent autocratic, (3) consultative, and (4) democratic. These systems varied as System 1 to System 4 on a number of criteria. Likert proposed and demonstrated that moving organizations away from Systems 1 and 2 and toward Systems 3 and 4 would result, given sufficient time for effects to take place, in increases in both the productivity and satisfaction of employees.

Method

The Profile of Organizational Characteristics (POC) was constructed using 18 survey questions such as: "How much confidence and trust is shown in subordinates?" "How free do subordinates feel to talk to superiors about the job?" and "How often are subordinates' ideas sought and used constructively?" An assessment was generated to indicate where the organization lay between System 1 and System 4. The correlations among the 18 scales of leader, peer, subordinate, and organizational behaviors ranged between .40 and .80. These correlations indicated that there was considerable consistency among the various questions. For leadership and influence in the autocratic Systems 1 and 2, the *exploitative autocrat* of System 1 emphasizes threats, fear, and punishment with some promise of reward. The *benevolent autocrat* of System 2 emphasizes more positive and less negative reinforcement. Top-down communication is stressed. Subordinates have little influence on goals and methods. Decisions and controls are centralized and are made person to person. The leadership and influence processes in the *consultative* System 3 and the *democratic* System 4 are such that supervisors and subordinates trust each other; and the supervisors are very supportive, very easy to talk to, and virtually always get subordinates' ideas to try to make constructive use of them. There is an emphasis on economic and achievement motivation as well as on personal worth. The subordinates' participation in goal setting is encouraged, along with bottom-up communication. Subordinates are influential in determining goals, tasks, and methods. Decisions and controls are decentralized. Virtually no confidence is shown by supervisors to subordinates in System 1 and a great deal of such confidence is shown in System 4.

R. Likert (1967) applied Bowers and Seashore's (1966) four dimensions of leadership behavior to distinguish among autocratic and democratic leaders. He found that System 4 leaders were highest and System 1 leaders were lowest on the four dimensions of a leader's behavior: (1) support—friendly, pays attention to what one is saying, listens to subordinates' problems; (2) team building—encourages subordinates to work as a team and encourages the exchange of opinions and ideas; (3) goal emphasis—encourages best efforts and maintains high standards; and (4) helps with work—shows ways to do a better job; helps subordinates plan, organize, and schedule; and offers new ideas and solutions to problems.

Overall Results

Correlations of the respondents' mean scores on the POC with the quality and quantity of organizational performance ranged from .30 to .60 (R. Likert, 1977a). In other words, in the more than 500 studies completed by 1997, positive associations generally were found between measures of the organizations' performance. The modal system was System 3. Surveys before and after shifts upward from more autocratic to more democratic systems were reflected in improvements in organizational performance. For example, R. Likert (1975) reported that the shift from System 1 to System 4 between 1969 and 1970 at a General Motors plant resulted in substantial increases in direct labor efficiency in 1971 and 1972. Although indirect labor efficiency declined between 1970 and 1971, it increased sharply between 1971 and 1972. Particular effects cannot be attributed exclusively to changes in leadership style. However, given the pattern of large-scale, long-term changes reported by R. Likert (1977b), associated with changes in both leadership and other aspects of organizational development, it seems plausible to attribute many of these effects to the changes in leadership. By 1997, more than 500 studies had been completed in petroleum, automotive, pharmaceuticals, investment banking, insurance, delivery service, publishing, utilities, textiles, office equipment, packaging, paper making, and railroad companies. Research also had been conducted in governmental organizations, hospitals, schools, colleges, correctional institutions, military organizations, and voluntary organizations. Data were obtained from more than 20,000 managers at all hierarchical levels, and from more than 200,000 nonsupervisory employees.

Immediate versus Long-Term Effects

These results need to be understood in terms of the differential impact of authoritarian and democratic systems on immediate, compared with long-term, labor costs. When belt-tightening was autocratically imposed in three continuous-processing plants, it produced an immediate reduction in costs in one organization of 600. However, this reduction occurred at the expense of the employees' deteriorating motivation, dissatisfaction with company policy, and dissatisfaction with the leadership and was reflected in lowered quality and increased grievances, turnover, work stoppages, and failures to meet delivery dates. In one study, it took three or more years for these effects to show up clearly.[9] The immediate savings of $250,000 actually produced losses of $450,000 in the longer term, owing to the fact that employees became more hostile, less motivated, and less individually productive as a result of the autocratic imposition (R. Likert, 1977b). Consistent with this finding, Dunnington, Sirota, and Klein (1963) noted that when engineered work standards were imposed on managers and supervisors at an IBM manufacturing plant, the employees resented the pressure, and the same adverse trends occurred in the measurements of the human consequences. Yet Dunnington, Sirota, and Klein did find exceptions. When particular supervisors were more democratic, employees showed much less resentment of the engineered work standards than did employees whose supervisors were more autocratic. The employees who worked for democratic supervisors felt less resentful because the democratic supervisors were more likely to try to do something if an employee complained that the work standard was unreasonable.

Contingency research, to be discussed in Chapter 25, supports the need for different organizational structures in different industries (see Lawrence & Lorsch, 1967a, 1967b; Woodward, 1965). Assembly plants (mass and batch production) have different organizational structures from oil refineries (continuous-processing). Nevertheless, Likert (1977b) noted that regardless of industry, the better-performing plant or department was likely to be closer to System 4 in its leadership processes, and the poorer-performing plant or department was likely to be closer to System 1 in its management system.[10]

Effects on Business Organizations. Results from 30 studies in 35 business firms involving some 260 sections, departments, or similar organizational units containing more than 50,000 employees were reported by R. Likert (1961a), Likert (1967), Likert and Likert (1976), and Likert and Fisher (1977). They demonstrated the efficacy of democratic as opposed to autocratic systems of management.

Nineteen of the studies, as summarized by Likert (1977b), were comparisons of more democratic organizations that were closer to System 4 in their leadership and management with organizations that were closer to the autocratic System 1. The differences in productivity and earnings favoring System 3 or 4 over System 1 or 2 ranged from 14% to 75%. In "before-after" studies, in which management shifted toward System 3, productivity and earnings improved from 15% to 40% one or two years after the shift. In two comparisons in which control groups were available, no such improvements were obtained for the control groups.

These improvements continued if the democratic shift was maintained. In departments of fewer than 200 employees, the improvement usually resulted in annual savings of $50,000 to $100,000. In a large plant of 6,000 employees, the annual saving was more than $5 million. Guest (1962a) observed similar results for productivity, quality, and safety when a new manager of the poorest-performing of six plants shifted the organization toward democratic Theory Y leadership.

For 15 business firms, Taylor and Bowers (1972) reported the relations between the measures obtained from the POC and various organizational outcomes 6 months prior to the survey to 18 months afterward. Correlations between having a democratic climate and efficiency reached as high as .80. But correlations were somewhat lower with reductions in absenteeism, minor injuries, ill health, and grievances.

Effects on Governmental Agencies. Heslin (1966) found that the high-producing units in a federal govern-

---

[9]There are many such examples of harmful effects on attitudes and performance—effects that linger long after an autocratic leader has left the organization. These effects of coercion often do not surface until the autocratic leader has departed, since one of his or her techniques may include using threats to repress dissent (see R. H. Solomon, 1976).

[10]Such results have been reported by R. Likert (1967); R. Likert and J. Likert (1976); Marrow, Bowers, and Seashore (1968); McCullough (1975); Mohr (1971); Roberts, Miles, and Blankenship (1968); and Toronto (1972).

ment agency engaged in automatic data processing were closer to Likert's System 4 than to System 1 in their management, as seen by the employees, than were the low-producing units. Operational bureaus of the Department of State were seen as providing better budgeting, space, travel, and personnel services if their management (according to their own subordinates) was closer to System 4 than to System 1 (Warwick, 1975). Similarly, Likert (1977b) reported that city managers, when asked to compare the highest-producing unit with a matched lowest-producing unit they knew well, described the highest unit as between Systems 3 and 4 and the lowest unit as pursuing benevolent autocratic (System 2) management. Bruns and Shuman (1988) administered the POC to 298 Arizona police sergeants and 67 police lieutenants. The modal leadership system in departments of large and medium size was System 2, benevolent-autocratic. The modal leadership system in smaller departments was consultative, System 3.

Effects on Military Organizations. In data from 20 ships and 18 shore stations of the U.S. Navy, Bowers (1975) found a strong relationship between an individual's intention to reenlist (which is a good predictor of actual reenlistment) and the extent to which the ship or station was closer to System 4 and farther from System 1. Likert (1977b) reported that among 14 U.S. Navy crews, the absence of mishaps and operational failures was associated with supervisory facilitation of work and team development. D. E. Johnson (1969) found that of 93 U.S. Air Force ROTC units, those that were judged by higher authority to be operating closer to System 4 than to System 1 were also evaluated as better-performing units.

Effects on Educational Institutions. Summarizing 40 studies in school systems, R. Likert (1977b) concluded—from school POC surveys of members of boards of education, superintendents, central staff, principals, department heads, teachers, students, and parents—that school systems closer to System 4, compared with those closer to System 1, exhibited better communications, cooperation, and coordination (Lepkowski, 1970). They were more flexible and innovative (Broman, 1974)[11] and more effective overall (Ferris, 1965; Riedel, 1974). Their

personnel felt a greater sense of self-actualization and satisfaction from their work (Wagstaff, 1970).[12] Furthermore, they were judged as achieving superior educational results. They had better board-employee relations (R. C. Key, 1974) and union-management relations (Bernhardt, 1972; Haynes, 1972). Their students were more highly motivated and attained higher educational achievement for given IQ and socioeconomic levels (Belasco, 1973; A. K. Gibson, 1974). Their students had more favorable attitudes and were less likely to engage in disruptive behavior or acts of aggression against the schools (Cullers, Hughes, & McGreal, 1973; Morall, 1974).

For 12 studies of higher education, Likert (1977b) concluded that institutions whose administrations were closer to System 4 than to System 1 experienced more favorable outcomes. The faculty members were more satisfied with administrative decision making (A. B. Smith, 1971).[13] There was less need for collective bargaining (Cline, 1974), more innovativeness (Bowers, 1976; Hanna, 1973) and commitment to college objectives (T. G. Fox, 1973; Laughlin, 1973), and more favorable student outcomes (Bowers, 1976; Gilbert, 1972).

Effects in Health Care Organizations. On the basis of data from 351 nurses in 55 patient teams in eight hospitals, Munson (reported by Likert, 1977b) found that the closer the head nurse was to System 4, the more generally satisfied the nurses were. H. C. White (1971b, 1971c, 1971d) obtained similar results for peers who described effective and ineffective supervisors they had known. System 4 was seen to be more effective than System 1 in three outpatient clinics (National Tuberculosis and Respiratory Disease Association, unpublished) and by Ketchel (1972), who studied the effectiveness of volunteer health planning in 17 Ohio counties.

Effects in Other Nonprofit Organizations. In three community-based reintegration centers for ex-convicts in Ohio, McGruder (1976) concluded that in comparison with the most autocratic center on Likert's POC, the most democratic center was most effective, as measured by graduation rates and low rates of recidivism and rein-

---

[11]See also Gehrman (1970), Ladouceur (1973), and Naumann-Etienne (1975).

[12]See also Brindisi (1976), Byrnes (1973), Carr (1971), Chung (1970), Feitler and Blumberg (1971), Morall (1974), Prieto (1975), C. E. Shaw (1976), Smallridge (1972), A. C. Smith (1975), and D. E. Thompson (1971).
[13]See also Gardner (1971), Javier (1972), and Lasher (1975).

carceration. Similarly, Marchant (1976) obtained data on Likert's POC from the staffs of 22 research-oriented university libraries. The closer the libraries were to System 4 and the farther they were from System 1, staffs were more satisfied, and faculty evaluations of service were higher. Haggard (as reported by Likert, 1977b) found that as management of a YMCA shifted away from System 2 toward System 4, the number of people served by the YMCA increased from 11,064 to 23,794, and the budget increased (from $173,000 to $303,000.

Critique

Methodology. Despite the amount of support attesting to the efficacy of democratic leadership in the long term, disquieting ambiguities remain. Thus among the reasons why Miller and Monge (1986) excluded the results of 15 journal articles from their meta-analysis was their determination that the democratic approach had not been clearly measured or experimentally manipulated. They found additional methodological problems in seven other studies.

Differing Outcome Measures. Other difficulties arise, reducing confidence in the reported conclusions, owing to the extent to which differences occur from one study to the next in the definition and measurement of the satisfaction of followers and the productivity of groups. Some studies measure global satisfaction, whereas others measure satisfaction with leadership, the job, the group, or the organization. Some researchers count units of output or rates of performance as measures of productivity. Others use ratings of quantity or quality of output as productivity measures.

Circumstances. Leadership style may be a product of circumstances rather than of personal preferences. Scully, Sims, Olian, et al. (1994) found in 56 high-tech business firms that when financial performance was poor rather than better, the CEOs tended to be tougher, more directive, and more punitive toward their top managers. Southern Baptist preachers become more authoritarian in response to ambiguity in their role definition. Ingraham (1981) suggested that the ambiguity of the pastor's role in Southern Baptist churches results in the development of an authoritarian self-image among pastors. When the pastors are unsuccessful in influencing their congre-

gations, they either withdraw from their attempts to lead or try to become manipulative authority figures.

Effects on the Leader. The leadership style that is adopted may affect the leader as well as the follower. Kipnis, Schmidt, Price, and Stitt (1981) randomly assigned 113 business students to act as authoritarian or democratic leaders of five-person work groups that manufactured model airplanes. They found that those who acted as democratic leaders perceived their group members to be more internally motivated to work effectively than did those who acted as authoritarian leaders. As a consequence, the democratic leaders gave the members more favorable evaluations, although their productivity was not necessarily higher.

Confounding of Cause and Effect. Chapter 16 noted that followers condition a leader's behavior; that is, the leader of a productive group can afford to be more considerate to his or her subordinates than can the leader of a poorly performing group. In addition, Mitchell, Larson, and Green (1977) showed that subordinates' descriptions of a leader's initiation and consideration are erroneously confounded with the perceived quality of his or her group's success and morale. The error is compounded because the same source of information about the leader's behavior provides the indicators of perceived group success and morale. Under these conditions, the correlations between democratic leadership on the one hand, and group success and morale on the other, are inflated above the true correlations.

In interpreting the findings, which comes first, the chicken or the egg? A concurrent study of leadership and its consequences may in reality be a study of leadership and its antecedent conditions. Leaders may be authoritarian because their groups are unproductive, or can afford to be democratic because their groups are productive. The longitudinal studies are few; the concurrent studies are many. Even the efforts to move organizations in a democratic direction suggest that results may not be immediately apparent. One or two years may elapse before a change in leadership style has measurable effects on organizational performance.

Reflection of Implicit Theories in Results. The issue of cause and effect is complicated by the extent to which correlations reflect the raters' implicit theories of leadership. That is, a rater may assume that subordinates will be more productive under a particular pattern of supervision. They may make their report about the supervisor's style of behavior as a consequence of how they see the group performing (Rush, Thomas, & Lord, 1977). In Mitchell, Larson, and Green's (1977) study, knowledge that a group performed well caused increases in the rated consideration and initiating of structure of that group's supervisor, whereas knowledge that a group performed poorly caused large decreases in the supervisor's rated consideration and initiating of structure. These distortions in leadership ratings because of the knowledge of performance also occurred when raters of high- and low-performing leaders were exposed to identical and highly salient leadership behaviors (Lord, Binning, Rush, & Thomas, 1978).

Summary and Conclusions

A large cluster of styles can be included in democratic leadership and member-related behaviors: employee-oriented, considerate, concerned with the satisfaction of needs, maintenance-oriented, rewarding and nonpunitive, supportive, relations-oriented, open, close, informal, warm, System 3 or System 4, and people-centered. Included in autocratic leadership or work-related behaviors are opposites of those just mentioned: job-centered,

structuring, task-oriented, punitive, closed, distant, formal, cold, System 1 or System 2, and work-centered.

The positive effects of democratic approaches are most apparent if based on the results of large-scale field surveys and lagged productivity measurements rather than on small-group laboratory experiments with immediate, concurrent effects. Generally, the patterns of behavior included in democratic leadership are more satisfying than those associated with autocratic leadership. But in the short term, productivity may be enhanced more by autocratic leadership than by democratic leadership. This is especially so when the democratic leadership ignores concern for the task and production goals. Nevertheless, in the long term, the positive effects of democratic leadership are evident, especially if the employees' development, commitment, loyalty, and involvement are important to productivity. But numerous conditions, such as the authoritarianism of subordinates or the nature of the task, increase the utility of autocratic methods, particularly in the short run.

Looking at their components provides a fuller appreciation of the autocratic and democratic styles of leadership behavior. Leaning toward the autocratic are direction, task orientation, and initiation of structure. Leaning toward the democratic are participation, relations orientation, and consideration for followers. These components are covered in the chapters that immediately follow.

CHAPTER
18

Directive versus
Participative Leadership

In Ayn Rand's (1957) novel *Atlas Shrugged*, E. Locke found the prescription for heroic business leaders like Jack, who formulated rule for business leaders: face reality as it is, not as it was or as you wish it to be (Tichy & Sherman, 1993). Although the many current business scandals would suggest otherwise, honesty and candor are needed to avoid self-deception and unethical behavior. Failing executives refuse to face reality. Characteristics of business heroes, according to Rand and Locke, are independence, self-confidence, an active mind, vision, and competence. They also need sufficient intelligence to understand their markets and causal connections of consequence and the ability to accurately generalize from what they have observed. They need to have passion in their work. As was already noted in Chapter 17 about autocratic leaders, these tough-minded, directive, task-oriented CEOs are best known for their success and effectiveness in turning around large, previously successful businesses that were encrusted with strong bureaucracies which failed to adapt to changes in their markets. Examples of business leaders illustrate that some whose style is directive and task-oriented may be successful and effective in reaching their goals and satisfying their constituencies. Other examples can be found of business leaders who were successful and effective by being more consultative, participative, and relations-oriented. Generally, they need to be both directive and participative as well as concerned about tasks and relationships.

The more directive leaders, such as Lou Gerstner at IBM and Jack Welch at General Electric, were likely to ask a lot of direct questions; they made some subordinates feel that a meeting was an inquisition rather than a consultation. They made shareholders happier but some employees unhappier. Lou Gerstner was described as tough, ferocious, and driven, yet respected by associates. At the same time, he contributed a great deal to philanthropies and worked hard to invigorate educational systems in many locations. He was a demanding boss, was highly disciplined, stayed focused, set very high standards, and could go beyond less important matters to get at key issues. He had earned a degree in engineering *magna cum laude* and had previously been a successful top executive at American Express and RJR Nabisco. He envisioned that giant IBM, as a smaller firm with fewer hierarchical levels, would be better able to adapt and compete in the world marketplace. He consolidated operations, closed plants, sold subsidiaries, and laid off many managers and a large number of employees. He wanted to take advantage of IBM's potential to offer consulting and a full range of services to provide an integrated information system for its business customers. He brought in 60 new executives and took the firm from bleeding losses back to profitability again (Waga, 1997). His legacy continued after he retired: IBM continued to divest itself of much of its computer manufacturing business and reduced its barriers to integrating its efforts with non-IBM programs and products.

Jack Welch of General Electric projected himself in his 1997 annual letter in which he said that grade A leaders have

a vision and the ability to articulate that vision so vividly and powerfully to the team that it also becomes their vision. . . . [These leaders have] enormous personal energy . . . and the ability to energize others . . . [The leaders] have the . . . courage to make the tough calls. . . . [In engineering], they relish the rapid change in technology and continually re-educate themselves. In manufacturing, they consider inventory an embarrassment. . . . In sales . . . they emphasize the enormous customer value of the Six Sigma quality program that differentiates GE from the competition. In finance, "A" talents transcend traditional controllership. The bigger role is full-fledged participation in driving the business to win. (Henry, 1998, p. 7a)

Welch made sure his frank and honest opinions on management and operations were known and were a guide to GE's future. Welch demonstrated his ability to change a large firm with strong historical institutions. He remained personally involved in everyday matters. He charted clear, specific directions for GE, emphasizing its core businesses and venturing into new businesses. He made GE fast and flexible. He invested heavily in R & D to ensure GE's future, reduced its top-heavy hierarchy, and reduced the number of its employees. In his first three years in office, he reduced GE's employees by 18%. Welch insisted on consolidating GE's 150 businesses into 15 lines, and these lines reduced to three circles: services, industrial automation and high tech, and manufacturing. Executives were under orders to make every business they ran either first or second in market share. Businesses without the potential to grow were divested and plants closed. They were replaced with others judged as having more potential. Many of the acquisitions were made in Europe and Asia. Under Welch, decisions were made more rapidly. He made it possible in 20 years for GE to become one of the largest and most successful multinational conglomerates (Lueck, 1985; Wall Street Transcript, 1985; Forbes, 1985).

Other examples of directive leaders are Jeffrey Immelt and Michael Armstrong. Jeffrey Immelt was appointed CEO of Welch's successfully restructured GE. Immelt took charge following the many financial scandals exposed among top corporate managers at WorldCom, Enron, Tyco, and elsewhere. With concern for ethical standards of top management, he reformed the board of directors by increasing the number of independent outsiders, strengthening its auditing committee, and removing directors with conflicts of interest. Directors were asked to visit two GE businesses each year, without HQ management, to have frank discussions with operating managers. Immelt emphasized consensual management and teamwork in his directiveness (Hymowitz, 2003). Michael Armstrong accepted the CEO position at Hughes Aircraft, informing the current top management team that he admired them but they should either accept his vision for restructuring Hughes or resign. Hughes

then had a strong culture focused on product development. A need for restructuring had been recognized but not implemented. Armstrong successfully directed reorganization toward market needs and increased revenue growth (Cole, 1993).

Making Decisions

Who decides? The leader? The led? Both? On what does the answer depend? What are the consequences? Should leaders give directions and tell followers how to do the work, or should they share with followers the need for solving problems or handling situations and involve them in working out what is to be done and how? Is there one best way? Eleanor Roosevelt (April 16, 1945) noted that international peace required both: "a leader may . . . point out the road to lasting peace, but . . . many peoples must do the building." Numerous humanistic researchers and writers support the need for participative leadership—in which the leader and the led jointly make the decision. The conventional wisdom is that participative leadership is preferred to directive leadership, and that participative leadership is more satisfying and effective than directive leadership. A survey of 485 upper-level managers from 59 industrial firms agreed, but did not install participative systems (Collins, Ross, & Ross, 1989). As Wagner (1994) noted, in 11 meta-analytic reviews of studies, participation does have positive effects on performance and satisfaction, but the average size of these effects is small enough to raise questions about their practical significance. In many contexts, leader direction may still be of consequence. Depending on circumstances, leader direction may be effective (Hogan, Curphy, & Hogan, 1994). Furthermore, the same leader who is participative at times may also be directive at other times, with equal effectiveness. Their frequency is positively correlated rather than independent of each other.

The Continuum

Most leaders, managers, and supervisors are both directive and participative, depending on the circumstances, but in different amounts. Tannenbaum and Schmidt (1958) suggested that direction and participation are two parts of a continuum, with many gradations possible in between. At one extreme of the continuum, *directive* leaders decide and announce the decision to their followers. They give directions and orders to followers without explaining why. These leaders expect unquestioning compliance; participation in the decision by followers is minimized. At the next gradation, leaders *sell* the decision. They accompany their orders with detailed explanations to persuade followers and manipulate or bargain with them. At the third gradation, (in between directive and participative leadership), leaders consult with followers before deciding what is to be done. They present ideas and problems and invite questions. At the fourth gradation, *participation* by both leaders and followers occurs. Leaders define limits and ask for a consensual decision. Followers join in deciding what is to be done. At the fifth gradation, leaders delegate to the followers what is to be done, and the leader's participation is minimized. At this gradation, within the established limits and constraints, the followers decide what to do; the leaders need to review what was delegated. At this extreme of the continuum, some leaders may completely abdicate their responsibilities.[1] Similar continua were advanced by many others (Hersey & Blanchard, 1969a, 1969b; Heller & Yukl, 1969: Sadler & Hofstede, 1972; Bass & Valenzi, 1974; Vroom & Yetton, 1974; Drenth & Koopman, 1984; and Scandura, Graen, & Novak, 1986). Scores could be generated to describe points on the continuum.

Directive Leadership

Directive leadership implies that leaders play the active role in problem solving and decision making, and expect followers to be guided by their decisions. There are two types of directive leadership. In one type, the leader makes the decisions for the followers often without an explanation and without consulting or informing them until he directs them to carry out his decisions. This type will be italicized (*directive*) when referred to. Other directive leaders play a more active role and try to persuade their followers to accept them. They gain acceptance of their proposals by using reason and logic (Berlew & Heller, 1983). They may assert an expectation or need and offer rewards, or they may coerce, threaten, and exert

pressure to gain acceptance. They may generate charismatic identification to motivate and build commitment. They may try partial disengagement by backing away from time-consuming issues with a lower priority and by concentrating colleagues' attention on more important issues. Unlike participative leaders, directive leaders do not ask their followers to get involved in making decisions. They direct followers' activities and give permission to their followers to carry out duties as the leaders see fit to do (Muszyk & Reimann, 1987). If in a position of authority, the directive leader may make decisions for him- or herself and others. Directive leaders may be persuasive as they attempt to raise their followers' efficacy beliefs. Such persuasion will depend on the leader's rationale, the followers' confidence in the leader, and the leader's emotional, verbal and nonverbal expression (El Haddad, 2001). Directive leaders may decide, announce their decisions, and give orders without consulting followers and colleagues beforehand or after consulting with them.

Participation

Participation, when italicized (*participation*), refers only to sharing in the decision process. There are different types of participative leaders who may draw followers out, listen actively and carefully, and gain acceptance through engaging colleagues in the planning or decision-making process (Berlew & Heller, 1983). Participation may refer to a particular way of leader-subordinate decision making in which the leader equalizes power and shares the final decision making with the subordinates. Consensus is sought. Participative leadership aims to involve followers in decision processes—in generating alternatives, planning, and evaluation. Such involvement is expected to enhance satisfaction and performance (Stewart & Gregersen, 1997), but such expectations do not always materialize. Wilson-Evered, Hartel, & Neale (2001) found participative decision making highly correlated with supportive leadership of 277 Australian hospital employees for their ideas and objectives.

Roberts and Thorsheim (1987) note that participative leaders express their doubts, concerns, and uncertainties; verbalize their problem-solving processes; ask questions of followers and listen to the answers; reflect feelings; and paraphrase, summarize, acknowledge, and use followers'

---

[1] This has been discussed in Chapter 6 as laissez-faire leadership.

ideas. Participative leaders use group processes to promote follower inclusion, ownership, involvement, consensus, mutual help, cooperative orientation, and free and informed choice. These leaders try to avoid unilateral control, hidden agendas, and inhibition of expression of feelings and relevant information. Additionally, according to West (1990), the leaders provide safety for followers by creating a nonthreatening environment in which the participants can be involved in decisions that affect them.

"Participative leadership" suggests that the leader makes group members feel free to participate actively in discussions, problem solving, and decision making. It implies increased autonomy for followers, power sharing, information sharing, and due process (Lawler, 1986). Participation implies that followers have a "voice" and influence in deliberations (Wright, Philo, & Pritchard, 2003). But freedom and safety to participate do not mean license. In *participative* decision making, the leader remains an active member among equals. The belief that it is safe to speak up depends not only on one's immediate supervisor but also on senior leaders higher in the hierarchy (Detert, 2003). In Europe, employee participation is seen as depending on the acceptance of varying rules of industrial democracy developed for middle management (Jaeger & Pekruhl, 1998).

Specific differences can be seen in the way directive and participative leaders communicate with their subordinates (Sargent & Miller, 1971). For instance, different uses would be made of palliatives and sedatives. The brisk directive leader is likely to say, "I want you to . . ." The more sophisticated directive leader is likely to ask, "Would you be kind enough to . . . ?" The participative leader would ask, "Would it be a good idea if we . . . ?"

Example: An Effective Leader Who Was Directive and Participative. Horatio Nelson was both directive and participative. Clearly, Nelson made the decision how his fleet was to be positioned for the battle of the Nile, but prior to making the decision, he called all his captains aboard his flagship to obtain their opinions about the best way to station the ships of the line. He did not take a vote nor ask for consensus. The decision was his alone. Paramount was his vision of the overwhelming need to find and destroy the French fleet, even at the cost of many British lives, in order to cut off Napoléon and his

troops, just landed in Egypt. As usual, Nelson's disposition of his ships was innovative. His fleet had been brought to a high state of readiness by his attention to continuous training and his own practice (unusual for the era) of "walking the talk"—conversing one-on-one with officers, seamen, and marines, and cultivating his own image of courage and bravery. Part of Nelson's orders delegated to each ship's captain the responsibility for making decisions when his ship had to engage in a general melée (Walder, 1978).

Delegation

When participation takes the form of delegation, it does not mean that the leader abdicates his or her responsibilities. The leader may follow up delegation by reclarifying what needs to be done, giving support and encouragement, and making periodic requests for progress reports, as well as by giving praise and rewards for subordinates' successful efforts (Bass, 1985a). Delegation should not be confused with laissez-faire leadership. A leader who delegates still remains responsible for follow-up to see whether the delegation has been accepted and whether the requisite activities have been carried out.

Schriesheim and Neider (1988) distinguished among three types of delegation: advisory, informational, and extreme. In advisory delegation, subordinates share problems with their supervisor, asking their supervisor for his or her opinions regarding solutions; however, the subordinates make the final decisions by themselves. In informational delegation, the subordinates ask the supervisor for information, then make the decisions by themselves. Extreme delegation occurs when subordinates make decisions by themselves without any input from their supervisor. A factor analysis of a survey of 196 nurses and 281 executive MBA students disclosed the independence of these three kinds of delegation. That is, leaders who used one kind of delegation did not necessarily use the other kinds.

Delegation implies that a subordinate has been empowered by a superior to take responsibility for certain activities. The degree of delegation is associated with the trust the superior has for the subordinate. When a group is the repository of authority and power, it likewise may delegate responsibilities to individual members.

Delegation of decision making implies that the decision making is lowered to a hierarchical level closer to where the decision will be implemented. Such delegation is consistent with self-planning (see Chapter 12). Delegation is a simple way for a leader who is faced with a heavy workload to reduce time-consuming chores, and it provides subordinates with learning opportunities and multiplies the executive's accomplishments (Anonymous, 1978). It also increases latitude and freedom for subordinates (Strasser, 1983). The act of delegation is often directive, but it can be based on a prior participative decision. Nevertheless, Leana (1984) called attention to a need to avoid confusing the "power relinquishment" of delegation with the power sharing of participation. In agreement with Strauss (1963), Heller (1976), and Locke and Schweiger (1979), Leana (1987) also noted that delegation, compared with participation, is more concerned about subordinates' autonomy and individual development. According to 118 managers who were asked how to handle eight situations involving the assignment of a task to a subordinate engineer, some managers are willing to delegate regardless of the circumstances. But other managers are unwilling to delegate because of any one of three considerations: (1) Some do not delegate because they do not feel confident in the capabilities of their subordinates. (2) Some avoid delegating because they think the task is too important to be left to the subordinates. (3) Some are unwilling to delegate because of the technical difficulty of the task (Dewhirst, Metts, & Ladd, 1987).

Aspects of Direction and Participation

Token Participation and Misuse of Participation

When executives call meetings ostensibly to reach shared decisions but actually to announce their own decision to subordinates (Guetzkow, 1951), they are practicing token participation. They are also practicing this when they invite the wrong people to participate, knowing in advance that these people lack genuine interest or have conforming tendencies. Halpern and Osofsky (1990) criticize management by objectives (Drucker, 1954)—which purports to be participative—as unrealistic; they say that it fails to protect employees against managers' manipulation, arbitrariness, and retaliation for speaking out about problems. Furthermore, employees may lack incentives and the necessary expertise to evaluate issues.

Holding frequent group meetings does not necessarily imply participative leadership. Guetzkow and Kriesberg (1950) found that leaders may use meetings to sell and gain acceptance of their own solutions, as well as to explain their own preferences. These executives see meetings as a way to transmit information and to make announcements, rather than as an opportunity to share information and opinions or to reach decisions. According to Rosenfeld and Smith (1967), subordinates recognize this phony participation and respond negatively to it.

If one can assume that followers in formal organizations appreciate autonomy, one should expect that leaders who say they delegate freely will be described as considerate. Employee satisfaction should also be highly related to delegation. But the effects obtained by Stogdill and Shartle (1955) were marginal. Subordinates often feel that their superiors do not really delegate to them the authority to accompany the responsibilities they are given. Subordinates feel that superiors delegate work they don't want to do themselves. Superiors may believe they are delegating, but their subordinates may see this as abdication—a most unsatisfying state of affairs for subordinates.

Some leaders risk participative decision making (consultation, *participation*, or delegation) only when a high-quality solution is not needed. Other leaders push for participation regardless of the need for it and despite the extra time it takes (Wright, 1984–1985). Participation has become an ethical imperative for some of its advocates, but Locke, Schweiger, and Latham (1986) argued that it should be seen as a managerial procedure which is appropriate in only some situations, because its effects—although possibly satisfying to followers—may fail to contribute to productivity. In some circumstances, directive leadership may result in both higher productivity and greater satisfaction. Participation is usually thought to enhance subordinates' compliance with decisions to change (Carson, 1985; Kanter, 1983); however, direction may be better for envisioning what needs to be changed. Some studies have reported that neither directive nor participative leadership made much difference in outcomes. McCurdy and Eber (1953) observed that groups in which free communication and decision making were practiced did not perform more effectively than groups in which the leader made all the decisions. Similarly, neither Spector and Suttell (1956) nor Tomekovic (1962) found differences in productivity between participative and nonparticipative groups.

In a study of 20 small shoe-manufacturing firms, Willits (1967) found that neither the degree of delegation by the president nor the extent of participation by executives in decision making was related to measures of the companies' success. Heyns (1948) and W. M. Fox (1957) also found no differences of consequence.

Contextual Aspects of Participation

Lawler (1986) argued that participation is a way for U.S. business to offset foreign competition and to deal with increasingly specialized work and the higher labor costs associated with some of it. But clearer goals and directions could also help. The pressure for more participation in the workplace and involvement in decisions about work has been fostered in the United States by workers' greater expectations for upward mobility and their desire for more interesting work, but Lawler (1985) pointed out that education has not equipped many to participate effectively at work. Participative management requires an appropriate organizational design, as well as a design that is relevant to the employees' backgrounds, motivation, and abilities. Employees with more education are more concerned about participating in decisions that affect their work (Wright & Hamilton, 1979). In the shift of the management of libraries from direction to participation, Sager (1982) noted that the roles of management and staff at all levels needed to be shifted, along with essential changes in regulations and policies.

Conceptual Distinctions and Empirical Overlaps

Tannenbaum and Schmidt (1958) thought that participation and direction were based on how much authority the superior used, relative to how much freedom the subordinates were permitted. Bass (1960) noted that participative leadership required leaders with power who were willing to share it. With their power, such leaders set the boundaries within which the subordinates' participation or consultation was welcomed. In contrast, with the powerless leader, as in the leaderless group, a struggle for status occurred among group members.

Graves (1983) noted that two of the three categories of concepts used by students to cluster 23 supervisory behaviors indicated their implicit theories of leadership.

They dealt first with task direction ("Sets goals for employee performance") and second with participation ("Asks employees for opinions and suggestions"). The third category of concepts dealt with reward ("Praises those who perform well"). Although conceptually independent, the dimensions of task direction and participation correlated .53 for the students' implicit theories of leadership.

Similarly, Bass, Valenzi, Farrow, and Solomon (1975) found that according to subordinates' descriptions of their superiors, *direction* and persuasive negotiation were positively correlated. Even more highly intercorrelated were democratic consultation, *participation*, and delegation. However, 46 judges, using response-allocation procedures, could readily and reliably discriminate among the specific behaviors involved in (1) *direction* and (2) negotiation, as well as among the behaviors involved in (3) consultation, (4) *participation*, and (5) delegation. The five styles were found to be conceptually independent, although they were correlated empirically. For instance, the judges clearly saw consultation as a different pattern of behavior from, say, delegation; nevertheless, the same managers who were most likely to consult were also more likely to delegate, according to their subordinates' descriptions (Bass, Valenzi, Farrow, & Solomon, 1975). Similar results were reported by Filella (1971) for 77 Spanish managers, as well as in Saville and Holdsworth's OPQ manual (Anonymous, 1985) for 527 British professionals and managers.

Nevertheless, three styles—consultation, *participation*, and delegation—are distinct and may, to some degree, have different antecedents and consequences. Factorial independence of each of the styles would make research with them easier; however, maintaining conceptually distinct but correlated styles remains viable and useful. (In the same way, analyses of body height and body weight continue to be separated, although height and weight are also empirically correlated. In general, tall people are heavier than short people, but it remains useful to talk about how people differ in height and how they differ in weight, as well as how they differ in stature or body mass, the combination of height and weight.)

Vertical versus Shared Leadership

With growing use of teamwork and empowerment of team members has come leadership behavior by the formal head of the team and shared leadership by team members. The team leaders do considerably more than members to empower the members and are more directive than the members themselves. Leaders and members appear otherwise to display similar participation in aversive, transactional, and transformational leadership behavior (Pearce & Sims, 2002).

Empirical Interrelations among Styles

Additional evidence that the same managers empirically exhibit many of the conceptually different styles of decision making is obtained from examining the intercorrelations in style found in survey studies. Consultation, *participation*, and delegation are highly intercorrelated. That is, consultative managers also tend to be highly *participative* and delegative. The intercorrelations were above .60 for a sample of 343 to 396 respondents who described their organizational superiors. Even the extent to which managers are *directive* tends to correlate positively with the extent to which they are manipulative or negotiative, .25; consultative, .31; *participative*, .28; and delegative, .13. Consultation, the most popular style observed among 142 assistant school superintendents in Missouri, correlated highly with *participation* (.64) and delegation (.47). Actually, all five styles have active leadership in common, and all are the opposite of inactivity and laissez-faire leadership.

Despite these intercorrelations, Wilcox (1982), using the Bass-Valenzi Management Styles Survey, reported systematic differences for the independent contributions of direction, consultation, and delegation to satisfaction with and the effectiveness of leadership, even after the effects of many other organizational and personal variables of the leader and the led were removed. Chitayat and Venezia (1984) conducted a smallest-space analysis for 224 Israeli managers and executives from business and nonbusiness organizations and attained patterns for the Bass-Valenzi survey measures showing that direction and negotiation (persuasion and manipulation) were closer together but distant from delegation, *participation*, and consultation—which, in turn, were closer to each other in usage by the respondents. Consistent with the reports of Bass, Valenzi, Farrow, and Solomon (1975) and Wilcox (1982) about subordinates' descriptions of their superiors' styles, intercorrelations of .41, .33, and .51

were found among delegation, *participation*, and consultation, and .23 was found between direction and negotiation for the Israeli managers. The correlations between decision styles within the two clusters were close to zero.

Some leaders and managers may lean toward inactivity. Whereas any of the preceding styles require activity, laissez-faire leadership—or abdication of responsibility and avoidance of leadership—does not. Laissez-faire leadership calls for doing little or nothing with subordinates, remaining passive, or withdrawing, as was discussed in Chapter 6. Such passivity correlates with passive managing by exception, in which the leader waits for problems to arise before taking any corrective action. This is in contrast to active managing by exception, in which the leader monitors follower performance and makes corrections as needed (Bass & Avolio, 1991).

Related Leadership Behavior

Negotiative Leadership. The leader bargains with the follower who has a different interest or point of view. Differences are settled with persuasive arguments and agreements.

Manipulative Leadership. The leaders act shrewdly or deviously to enhance their own advantage and gain, and to exploit the followers. Manipulation can shade into falsification (see Chapter 7).

Close Supervision. Directive leadership is more likely to be exhibited by the same leaders who are also close supervisors, who do a lot of structuring, and who are manipulative and persuasive. This persuasive, manipulative emphasis has been seen in political tactics: withholding information, bluffing, making alliances, publicly supporting but privately opposing particular views, compromising, and using delaying and diversionary tactics.[2] Participation is likely to be seen with general, rather than close, supervision; with the equalization of power; and with nondirective leadership.

Considerate Leadership. Participative decision-making leadership includes many elements. One of these, consideration, calls on the leader to ask subordi-

[2] See Bass (1968c), Jameson (1945), and Martin and Sims (1956), as well as Chapter 7.

nates for their suggestions before going ahead, get the approval of subordinates on important matters, treat subordinates as equals, make subordinates feel at ease when talking with them, put subordinates' suggestions into operation, and remain easily approachable. Graves (undated) found that implicit task direction correlated .61 with the factor of initiating structure, and implicit participation correlated .81 with consideration, one of the two important dimensions of the Leader Behavior Description Questionnaire (LBDQ). Many elements of direction are to be found on the LBDQ scale of the initiation of structure, such as making attitudes clear, assigning subordinates to particular tasks, and deciding in detail what shall be done and how.[3]

Social Factors. Bass (1968c) contrasted MBA students' and managers' beliefs about how to succeed in business. Two social factors emerged: sharing decision making and emphasizing candor, openness, and trust. The factors involved making open and complete commitments, establishing mutual goals, and organizing group discussions. The factors coincided with ideal participative decision making as proposed by Argyris (1962) and Bennis (1964).

Transformational and Transactional Leadership. As noted in Chapter 22, contrary to many misconceptions about transformational and transactional leadership, such leadership can be directive and participative. The intellectually stimulating leader can issue instructions and participatively arouse curiosity. The inspiring directive leader can state that conditions are improving greatly. The inspiring participative leader can ask for all to merge their aspirations and work together for the good of the group (Bass, 1998).

Warrior Leadership. Related to directive leadership, the *warrior style*—as already discussed in Chapter 17—is most likely to emerge when conflict and opposition are present, the world is seen as dangerous and hostile, people cannot be trusted, and direction is needed. Flows of information are controlled. Results are more important than the methods used to achieve them. There is an em-

[3] See Chapter 23.

phasis on knowing the people that the leader is seeking to defeat or lead. Battles are selected carefully, and unnecessary fighting is avoided. There is planning and preparation for future militant contingencies (Nice, undated).

Persuasive Rhetoric. Directive leadership through persuasive rhetoric was a theme of Aristotle and much of classical instruction in general. Orators from Martin Luther to Martin Luther King Jr. have followed Aristotle's prescription for persuasion: identify the discontent among audiences, name the enemy, and provide the needed response. Give the restless a voice, a motive, and legitimacy (Monty, 2004).

Forcing, Coercing, and Controlling. These forms of directive influence involve pressure or persuasion by a leader to induce follower compliance and avoid undesired outcomes. Ordinarily, continued use of force by a leader is likely to generate ill feelings and resistance. However, Emans, Munduate, Klaver, et al. (2003) showed that 145 police officers complied effectively with supervisory orders if forcing influence was interspersed over time with non-forcing influence. Hard tactics of persuasive direction are employed, such as giving orders without explanation, threatening unsatisfactory performance evaluations, and getting the backup of higher authority, when the persuader has the power to do so, when resistance is expected, or when the subordinate is violating norms. Soft tactics of persuasion are employed, such as acknowledgment of the subordinate's goodwill and ability, when the influencer is at a disadvantage. Rational tactics of persuasion are employed if power is balanced, if no resistance is anticipated, and benefits for compliance will be mutual (Kipnis & Schmidt, 1985). *Tight or loose controls* are likely to coincide with the leadership styles of direction and participation. As Avolio (1999) noted, leaders will maintain tight controls if they don't trust their subordinates. There are reciprocal effects. When employees are allowed to participate more fully in decisions, they are likely to feel that they are more trusted by their leaders. They may confirm this by showing better organizational citizenship behavior (OCB). Van Yperen, van den Berg, and Willering (1999) demonstrated in a study of employees from 10 departments in a Dutch company that employee participation in decision making fostered better employee OCB.

Frequency of Usage

A popular stereotype of the ideal leader is the decisive, directive, heroic order giver. The prototypical supervisor in the workplace of MBA students with full-time jobs had these directive transformational characteristics (Bass & Avolio, 1989). Yet in the behavioral science literature, participative decision making is most commonly advocated. And managers themselves are most likely to favor a consultative style. Actually, Heller and Yukl (1969) and Bass and Valenzi (1974) have shown that neither extreme direction nor extreme participation is reported most frequently by subordinates in describing their superior. Rather, subordinates most often see their superior as consulting with them. Thus on a scale of frequency ranging from 1 (never) to 5 (always), according to over 400 subordinates from a variety of organizations, the average frequency with which superiors were observed to exhibit each of the styles on many items of supervisory decision-making behavior was as follows: consultation, 3.10; participation, 2.65; delegation, 2.46; direction with reasons, 1.97; direction without reasons, 1.90; and manipulation, 1.88 (Bass & Valenzi, 1974). In agreement, H. R. Gillespie (1980) concluded, from self-reports of 48 manufacturing executives, that participation, particularly consultation, was more frequent, especially among executives at the top level. Kraitem (1981) likewise found that consultative leadership was favored in the self-reports of top executives in financial institutions and that there had been a shift away from more directive approaches.

Manipulation and negotiation were reported to occur least frequently, perhaps because of the greater subtlety of manipulative behavior, which is more difficult to discern when it happens. The most artful manipulative behavior is that which is misperceived as participative. There is less reliability in judgment about manipulation than in judgment about other decision-making styles. Subordinates feel they are being manipulated when they think managers know in advance what they will decide and what they want the subordinates to do. These managers strike bargains and play favorites. Such manipulative behavior tends to be exhibited by directive managers but not by managers who generally tend to be participative (Bass, Valenzi, Farrow, & Solomon, 1975).

Multiplicity of Styles

For followers, a leader who is a consistently autocratic or consistently laissez-faire leader in all situations is likely to be least satisfactory and least effective. Generally, followers will favor participative leadership over directive leadership. Nonetheless, subordinates may agree with their superior that supervisory *direction* is called for in a crisis and that consultation is indicated when subordinates are knowledgeable, experienced, and expert. Followers are likely to applaud their superior's flexibility in being directive in the first situation and consultative in the second. In fact, few leaders use only a single style; most use a variety of styles, ranging from extreme direction to extreme participation. Among 124 middle- and first-level supervisors, W. A. Hill (1973) found that only 14% of the supervisors were seen as likely to use the same one of four styles in four different hypothetical situations.

Bass and Valenzi (1974) obtained sharper results with 124 subordinates who described how frequently their superiors actually used six styles, ranging from deciding without explanation to delegating decisions to subordinates. A manager was classified as exhibiting a *single* style if the subordinate indicated that only one of these styles was displayed by the manager "very often" or "always," and the remaining styles "never" or "seldom." Managers were classified as exhibiting a *dual* approach if they were described by their subordinates as displaying two styles "very often" or "always," and the other styles "never" or "seldom." Managers were classified as exhibiting a *multistyle* approach if they were described as displaying three or more of the six styles "sometimes," "fairly often," "very often," or "always." Of 124 subordinates, less than 4% indicated that their superior exhibited a single style or a dual approach; 117, or almost 95%, indicated that their boss exhibited a multistyle approach.[4] Consistent with Bass and Valenzi's findings, Hollander (1978) noted that although political leaders, in particular, often try to project a consistent image to a wide audience, based on a particular style that is uniform across situations, most change their style after they are elected; they also change their style from one constituency to another.[5] History is replete with examples illustrating that the most powerful dictators may also be strong advocates of consultation.

[4] Less than 3% were unclassifiable.
[5] President George H. W. Bush was extreme in this regard.

Lenin, according to his biographers, frequently consulted his immediate subordinates (Bass & Farrow, 1977a). Mao Zedong urged party leaders to be consultative and instructed them carefully on how to carry out a doctrine stressing consultation: "We should never pretend to know what we don't know, we should not feel ashamed to ask and learn from people below, and we should listen carefully to the views of the cadres at the lower levels. Be a pupil before you become a teacher; learn from the cadres at the lower levels before you issue orders" (Burns, 1978, p. 238). But in his later years, Mao could also be ruthless as a leader, unleashing his Cultural Revolution on the Chinese population.

Differences in Problems. The overwhelming tendency for managers to use multiple decision-making styles is seen most clearly in studies of how the same managers use different styles depending on the nature of the problem. Thus McDonnell (1974) found that when 226 respondents were asked whether they would be autocratic, consultative, *participative*, or laissez-faire, each chose a different style depending on which of 12 problem situations was presented for consideration. Heller and Yukl (1969) and Heller (1972a) demonstrated that a senior manager varies his or her style according to the nature of the required decisions. For example, prior consultation was the modal style for decisions that were critical to individual staff members but not to the organization. Participation in all three forms was most frequent for decisions of importance to subordinates and least frequent for decisions of importance to the company. Supervisory delegation and supervisory decision making without explanation were most frequent for decisions that were unimportant to both the leader and the subordinates. Using a different method (to be detailed later in this chapter), Vroom and Yetton (1973) came up with similar results. Several thousand managers indicated the decision-making style they would employ if confronted with different kinds of cases requiring or not requiring high-quality solutions and subordinates' acceptance. Only about 10% of the variance in response could be attributed to the personal tendencies of the managers to be more directive or more participative; 30% of their responses depended on whether high-quality solutions and subordinate acceptance were required. Hill and Schmitt (1977) tested a shortened version of Vroom and Yetton's method and found that 37% of the variance in the leaders' decision-making style was due to ease-requirement effects and only 8% was due to the effects of the respondents' individual dispositional differences. These results tended to be relatively insensitive to the hierarchical levels dealt with in the cases presented to the managers (Jago, 1978a). This was so despite the fact that, as was noted in Chapter 14, both the authority to be directive and the authority to be delegative increase as one rises in the organizational hierarchy (Stogdill & Shartle, 1955). Such increased authority makes it possible for superiors to delegate more responsibilities to subordinates. But it also allows the superiors to be more participative.

Discrepancies between Self-Descriptions and Others' Descriptions

In Wilcox's (1982) dissertation, agreement was quite close between the school superintendent's self-descriptions of their directiveness, participation, and delegation and the descriptions provided by their subordinates. But the superintendents believed they were more consultative and less negotiative than their subordinates thought they were. Generally, when managers' self-rated styles are contrasted with descriptions provided by their subordinates, one is likely to find many more managers who see themselves as favoring their subordinates' participation than subordinates who see such participation occurring. Also, many authoritarian leaders would be surprised to learn that their subordinates say they are far more directive than they believe themselves to be. Harrison (1985) studied 30 supervisors and their 234 college-educated subordinates in a large social service organization. There was little correspondence between the subordinates' feelings of participation in decision making and the supervisors' tendency to see themselves as participative. For the superiors, participation meant interacting with subordinates; but for the subordinates, it also meant that the subordinates could both send and receive information related to their own desires. Moreover, the subordinates' judgments of the extent to which their superior was participative correlated .61 with the interpersonal support they received from the superior, .59 with the team-building activities led by the superior, and .30 with the accuracy of the information they felt they received from the superior. The superior generally failed to recognize that any of these actions was connected to being participative.

A Harris (1987) poll revealed still another aspect of the discrepancy between managers and white-collar workers. Although 77% of the workers considered it very important to be allowed to participate in decisions that controlled their working conditions, only 41% of their superiors agreed with them. Some samples of leaders subscribed to direction rather than participation. None of 450 interviewed Australian managers rated their executive superiors as collaborative in organizational development. They regarded the high and medium performers as more tough and directive in style when it came to making organizational changes. The lower performers were viewed as careful, timid fine-tuners (Heller, 1994).

Antecedents of Direction and Participation

As was already noted, different studies using a variety of methods showed that leaders in organized settings said they preferred to be consultative and were most often seen by their subordinates as consultative. Such consultation involved their subordinates to some extent in the decision process, but the supervisors reserved the final decision for themselves. At the same time, a given leader was seen to use the whole range, from *direction* to delegation, in varying amounts. However, different patterns of usage were revealed—some leaders were more directive on the whole, whereas others were more participative. Both deductive and inductive research point to a variety of factors that predispose leaders to pursue one style rather than another. These antecedent conditions include the attributes of the leader and of the subordinates; their preferences, goals, tasks, and assignments; and the organizational and external environment.

Personality or Situation?

Some argue that direction or participation will depend on the nature of the situation; others state that it depends on the leader's judgment of the situation (Hersey & Blanchard, 1977; Vroom & Yetton, 1973). Still others find that the predispositions of the leader are most significant (Fiedler, 1967a).

Situations have an obvious impact. On the one hand,

crisis conditions may make any leader directive. On the other hand, a leader of a project team that is composed of experts from different fields will most likely benefit the project by being participative. Nevertheless, it may be that personality has more of an effect on a leader's being directive, but the situation has more of an effect on the leader's being participative (Farrow & Bass, 1977). Both the contingency and the noncontingency theorists may be right. Frequency of directiveness may be mainly a matter of personality; frequency of participation may hinge mainly on contingent factors. Farrow and Bass (1977) found, for 77 managers who were described by their 407 subordinates, that situational factors, as seen by the managers or by the subordinates, were irrelevant in determining whether a manager would be *directive*. Path analyses indicated that managers who were most frequently *directive*, according to their subordinates, were highly assertive and regarded people as fundamentally unfair. Such managers were highly satisfied with their own jobs. If the managers had short-term rather than long-term objectives, their subordinates saw them to be manipulative and negotiative. These results went beyond various organizational, intrapersonal, and personal attributes of the subordinates. However, the amount of participation seen by subordinates depended on the extent to which the manager perceived that the subordinates had discretionary opportunities and highly interdependent tasks.

Personal Antecedents:
Effects of the Leaders Themselves

Self-confidence and a personal sense of security were likely to have a strong effect on a leader's tendencies to be directive or participative (Bass & Barrett, 1981). Vroom (1960a) found that managers with authoritarian personalities, as measured by the *F* Scale of Adorno, Frenkel-Brunswik, Levinson, and Sanford (1950), were more directive. The lower the managers' need for independence and the higher their degree of authoritarianism, the higher was their directiveness. Belief in the legitimacy of the manager's prerogative to plan, direct, and control had similar effects. Managers who characterized themselves on personality inventories as unwilling to believe that people are fair-minded were more likely to be *directive*, according to their subordinates. This finding was consistent with the proposition that managers will be directive because they believe in Theory X: that employees cannot be trusted (McGregor, 1960). Conversely, those who felt people were fair-minded tended to be participative (Farrow & Bass, 1977). Among 122 undergraduates, dominance correlated with effectiveness as directive leaders. Dominance and supportiveness correlated with effectiveness as participative leaders (Sorenson & Savage, 1989).

Educational background also made a difference. Bass, Valenzi, and Farrow (1977) found a correlation of .37 between the educational level of 76 managers and their tendency to be participative. If leaders were women, more participative leadership was expected of them (Pelletier, 1999).

Myers-Briggs Types. There is a consistent linkage between one's thought processes and the tendency to be directive or participative. For example, according to a study of 55 managers and executives by O'Roark (1986), who correlated scores on the Myers-Briggs Type Indicator with the Bass-Valenzi preferred management styles, *thinking* types were most directive and feeling types were least directive; *sensing* types were least negotiating and *intuitive* types were more consulting. Schweiger and Jago (1982) reported that among 62 graduate business students, Myers-Briggs intuitive types tended to choose fewer participative solutions to the problem set of Vroom and Yetton (1974), whereas *sensing* types tended to choose more such participative solutions. Overall, personality seemed less important than situational determinants in the choices that were made.

Risk Preferences and Propensities. Whether managers delegate certain duties to subordinates may depend on whether the managers enjoy doing the tasks themselves, as well as on their willingness to take risks and wait for others to succeed (Matthews, 1980). Managers also need to feel secure and confident in themselves and in their subordinates (Hollingsworth & Al-Jafary, 1983). The riskiness of a decision to a supervisor is decreased if it is to be implemented on a trial basis. In a simulation with 143 bank employees under such conditions, Rosen and Jerdee (1978) found the leaders to be more willing to engage in participation when decisions were to be implemented on a trial basis than when decisions implied permanent solutions. The risk of decisions is increased for top managers who face intense competition from the marketplace. In such situations, the top manager tends to be more *directive* and highly controlling in some decisions—say, about production, purchasing, and cost control—and more *participative* in others, such as those dealing with raising capital, research and development, policy changes, and marketing strategies (Khandwalla, 1973).

Power. Leaders with power can be more directive. Leaders who are esteemed and valued by subordinates, who are acknowledged as experts, and who are seen by subordinates to control rewards (that the leaders can allocate among the subordinates) have the power to be directive (Mulder, 1971; Raven, 1965b). In addition to the effects of expert, reward, and referent power on being directive, there are also effects of coercive and legitimate power. If the power of leaders is suddenly increased in an experiment, the amount the leaders can be directive is also increased, and in fact the leaders do tend to increase their directiveness (Shiflett, 1973). But, paradoxically, leadership power is required to create participative circumstances. Whether power results in direction or participation depends on other factors. The results are decidedly mixed. Chitayat and Venezia (1984) noted that in Israeli business organizations, leaders' self-reported power contributed to their being *directive*, but the reverse occurred in the Israeli armed forces and governmental agencies. In such bureaucratic organizations, powerful leaders were more participative because the rules and procedures required directiveness, and only executives with more power could be participative if they chose to be. However, Hord, Hall, and Stiegelbauer (1984) found that more powerful school principals were more directive than were their less powerful assistant principals, teachers, or curriculum coordinators.

Experience. Heller and Yukl (1969) reported, in a study of 203 British managers at all hierarchical levels in 16 organizations, that despite their greater power and status, senior managers, particularly those who had been in their positions for a considerable time, were more likely than junior managers to share in decision making with their subordinates. Seversky (1982) found that more delegation was practiced by school superintendents who had more experience in their jobs. Likewise, Pinder, Pinto, and England (1973) found that older managers tended to be more participative, whereas younger managers tended to be more directive. Age, however, was unrelated to participativeness in a study of 48 manufacturing executives (H.R. Gillespie, 1980).

Ideological Beliefs. Locke and Schweiger (1979) provided academic and management advocacy for the moral reasons for participative leadership. The humanist movement argued that participative leadership was right and good. Directive leadership was questionable (Maslow, 1965). Likewise, participative leadership was regarded by some leaders as morally correct in a democratic society. Some extremists, such as Rost (1993), suggested that engaging followers (relabeled "collaborators") as participants in decisions is *always* the right thing to do. For Rost, the old paradigm to be discarded was doing what the leader wishes. The new paradigm to replace it was doing what both the leader and the collaborators wished to do. Nonetheless, Sagie (1997) pointed out that although a directive, tell-and-sell strategy of assigning goals could be as productive in performance and the quality of decision making (Sagie, 1994), and that assigning goals could be as effective as participation in goal setting (Locke & Latham, 1990), the continuing arguments for participation were based on ideological reasons (Dickson, 1982) rather than empirical evidence.

Effects of the Superiors of the Leaders

As was noted in Chapter 14, there is a clear linkage between what a U.S. Navy executive officer of a ship can and does do and the responsibility, authority, and delegation of his immediate superior—the commanding officer. Stogdill and Scott (1957) correlated the responsibility (R), authority (A), and delegation (D) scores (RAD scores; see Chapter 14) of commanding officers and executive officers with the average RAD scores of their junior officers on submarines and landing ships. The executive officers tended to delegate more freely to their subordinates on both types of ships when their commanding officers exercised wider scopes of responsibility and authority and delegated more freely. Commanding officers could increase or decrease their executive officers' workload and freedom of action. Subordinates tended to tighten their

controls as superiors increased their own responsibility and freedom of action. However, responsibility and authority did not flow without interruption down the chain of command. The responsibility, authority, and delegation of subordinates were more highly influenced by the subordinates' immediate supervisors than by the subordinates' higher-level officers.

Effects of the Followers

Some degree of agreement between the leader and the led about procedures, interests, and norms is necessary before effective participation can take place (Heller, 1969). In addition, they must concur that participation is relevant. Yukl and Yu (1999) reported that participative leadership with subordinates—like consultation and delegation—depended on the competence of the follower, task objectives shared with the leader, status of the follower as a supervisor, and favorable relations between the leader and the follower.

Relevance of Participation. Subordinates or followers vary in how much they would like to participate in decisions. As was noted earlier, Heller (1972a, 1976) found, in a number of samples in several countries, that managers used participation more frequently when decisions were more important to their subordinates than to the firm. In an overall review of the literature, Hespe and Wall (1976) demonstrated that although workers wanted to participate more than they actually were given the opportunity to do, they expressed the greatest interest in participating in decisions that were related directly to the performance of their jobs, followed by matters concerning their immediate work units. They expressed little interest in participating in general policy decisions. This finding was corroborated by Long (1979), who asked workers in a Canadian trucking company that had become wholly owned by its employees about their participation in company affairs after the employee takeover. According to Maier (1965), subordinates will prefer participation rather than direction if they are seeking personal growth, if they are striving to be more creative, and if they are highly interested in the objectives of the task. On the other hand, they may prefer a great deal of direction, guidance, and attention from their supervisor until they have mastered the job, particularly if the job does not involve much creativity but requires only attention to routine details that must be learned (Bennis, 1966c).

Followers' Personality. Abdel-Halim (1983a), Abdel-Halim and Rowland (1976), and Vroom (1960a), among others, found that the personality traits of subordinates are of consequence to the participatory process. Just as authoritarian leaders wanted to be directive with their subordinates, so their authoritarian subordinates wanted to be directed by authoritarian leaders. Followers with authoritarian attitudes were likely to reject participative leadership. Highly authoritarian personalities wanted powerful, prestigious leaders who would strongly direct them.[6]

Followers' Competence. Raudsepp (1981) suggested that managers need a comprehensive inventory of subordinates' capabilities before deciding what duties they can delegate to subordinates and in which areas subordinates need further experience. Managers will consider participative approaches too risky when they have reservations about the competence and commitment of their lower-level employees (Rosen & Jerdee, 1977). Lowin (1968) showed that subordinates who perceived that they were not competent in the tasks to be completed were more appreciative of directive supervision than were those who thought of themselves as competent. Similarly, Heller (1969a) found that whenever managers reported a big difference in skills between themselves and their subordinates, they were more likely to use *direction*. The differentials in skills that were of particular importance were technical ability, decisiveness, and intelligence. Managers were more likely to engage in participation when they esteemed the subordinates for their expertise and personal qualities. Heller (1976) also found that participative leadership was favored at senior organizational levels when the competence of subordinates was high. Similarly, on the basis of a study of members of 144 work groups in 13 local health agencies, Mohr (1977) concluded that supervisors favored participation when their subordinates had more training and were at higher technical and professional levels. Sinha and Chowdhry (1981) found, in a survey of 135 Indian executives, that the executives tended to be participative if they believed

their subordinates were better prepared but were more directive with subordinates who they felt were less well prepared. Locke and Schweiger (1979) also concluded that leaders are more likely to be participative when they believe their subordinates have the necessary information to contribute to the quality of decisions. In a mass role-playing experiment, Maier and Hoffman (1965) observed experimentally that the "foreman" who regarded his "subordinates" as men with ideas was more likely to lead his crew toward an integrated solution to their problem on the basis of their participation in making the decision. However, if the "foreman" thought he was dealing with difficult employees, he was more likely to direct them toward a solution he favored than to involve them extensively in the decision-making process.

In their prescriptive model, Vroom and Yetton (1973) deduced that leaders need to consider being more participative if they think they lack information that their subordinates are likely to have. The Hersey and Blanchard (1977) model assumed that the subordinates' competence is the most important determinant of whether and when a manager should be directive or participative (see Chapter 19). Leana (1987) reported a correlation of .42 between the willingness of insurance supervisors to delegate responsibilities to their 122 subordinate claims adjusters and their judgment of the capabilities of these subordinates. Tendencies to delegate correlated .27 with the subordinates' appraised trustworthiness. As was mentioned before, Dewhirst, Metts, and Ladd (1987–1988) found strong indications that managers were less willing to delegate if the subordinates were incompetent or the tasks were difficult and highly technical.

Superior-Subordinate Relations

The interplay of the superior and the subordinate contributes to the superior's tendency to be directive or participative. Thus in an Israeli study, Somech and Drach-Zahavy (2003) reported that demographic similarity in age, tenure, education, and sex and the quality of the leader-member exchange (LMX; Chapter 16) were conducive to participative leadership.

Differences in Power and Information. Bass and Valenzi (1974) proposed that the frequency with which a particular leadership style is used could be accounted for

---

[6]See Chapter 27.

by the differences in power between the manager and the subordinates and by the differences in their competence or the information available to them. Shapira (1976) confirmed, through smallest-space analysis, the validity of Bass and Valenzi's deductions. Given the managers' power (P_m), the subordinates' power (P_s), the managers' information (I_m), and the subordinate's information (I_s), then *direction* is more likely if $P_m > P_s$ and $I_m > I_s$. Manipulation or negotiation is more likely if $P_m < P_s$ and $I_m > I_s$. Consultation is more likely if $P_m > P_s$ and $I_m < I_s$. Delegation is more likely if $P_m < P_s$ and $I_m < I_s$.

Effects of the Quality of the Exchange Relationship.

An analysis of 58 superior-subordinate paired questionnaires by Scandura, Graen, and Novak (1986) revealed that the quality of LMX further complicates matters. Regardless of their competence, as rated by their superiors, subordinates who perceive they are in a more satisfying exchange relationship with their superiors also believe that their superiors allow them to participate much more in decision making. But subordinates who think they are in a dissatisfying relationship will perceive such participation only if their performance has been rated highly by their superiors. If the relationship with superiors is poor and the subordinates' performance has been rated low, the superiors will be seen as much more directive. Superiors agree with this description of the exchange relationship and its effects.

Situational Antecedents: Constraints and Objectives

Policies, goals, task requirements, and functions constrain how directive or participative a leader can be. They also furnish objectives that the leader will see as being met more satisfactorily by either direction or participation. Both the leader and the subordinates may be constrained by rules, regulations, and schedules, demands on their time, and fixed requirements for methods and solutions over which they have no control. The requirements of a decision may be highly programmed. Greater acceptance and change by the group may be desired or required. The manager may consider the objectives to be long-range rather than a quick payoff—that is, the development of subordinates or the creation of a capable and effective operation for the long run may be more important than immediate profitability. According to Vroom

(1976a), it "seems unlikely" that the same leadership style would be appropriate when the objective was to save time than when the objective was the long-term development of subordinates. If the cost of the time required of subordinates is more expensive than the value of the outcomes of their participation, directive approaches are more likely (Tannenbaum & Massarik, 1950).

Muscyk and Steele (1998) reviewed the characteristics of "turnaround" executives. When organizations are faced with crises, such executives are brought in to prevent the organization from failing. Directive leadership is required. Unpopular decisions have to be made. Subordinate autonomy and participation may have to be reined in.

Organizational Function.

Chitayat and Venezia (1984) found, in their previously cited investigation of 224 Israeli executives, that differences in the frequency of use of leadership styles were associated with differences in organizational norms, climate, and structure.

Since marketing is usually under shorter time constraints than research, a directive style may be appropriate more often in work units in marketing than in research (Lawrence & Lorsch, 1967a, 1967b). Heller and Yukl (1969) found that production and finance managers tended to use directive decision making, whereas general and personnel managers were more participative.

In a study of 155 managers of police (Kuykendall and Unsinger, 1982), the managers stated that they would avoid delegating, regardless of the problem faced. Like managers in accounting, finance, and production, managers of police supervise more standardized, programmed types of jobs that permit less freedom, less flexibility, and less meaningful participation by subordinates. Nevertheless, when faced with unprogrammed personnel decisions, they could be more participative. Similar findings appeared for accountants. A study of 212 chief accountants (McKenna, undated) found that although they were generally more likely to be directive than participative, they were more likely to use consultation and *participation* than *direction* or delegation when they had to make unprogrammed rather than programmed decisions. This was also true when they had to make decisions dealing with personnel rather than with tasks. Similarly, as noted above, the police managers were more likely to be participative than directive when faced with such decisions.

Service managers thought that they generally faced more unprogrammed decisions. Child and Ellis (1973) found, in a study of 787 managers in service organizations, that these managers saw their roles as less formal, less well defined, and less routine than did managers in manufacturing organizations, Miner (1973) concluded that participative management was most likely to be found in organizations of professionals. Miller (1986) advocated participativeness with R & D professionals whose work was less programmed.

Woodward (1965) studied the impact of technology on decision-making processes in 100 British firms. She concluded that in companies involved in mass or batch production, decision making was more likely to be directive but usually did not set precedents. However, in continuous-processing industries such as petroleum refining, decisions were more likely to be made by committees with considerable participation by subordinates, and these decisions had long-term implications.

Organizational Level. Stogdill and Shartle (1955) reported correlations between the tendency to delegate and the self-rated authority and responsibility of managers on the RAD scales in 10 organizations (Stogdill & Shartle, 1948). On the average, delegation correlated .17 with responsibility and .23 with authority. Since greater authority and responsibility naturally went with higher-level positions, it was not surprising to find that delegation was also higher among managers in those positions. Moreover, delegation must be practiced at higher levels because organizations cannot afford to pay high-level executives to spend their time carrying out activities that could be performed by the lower-paid staff (Major, 1984). Using the RAD scales (Chapter 14) to study large governmental organizations, Kenan (1948) also found, as expected, that executives in higher-level positions described themselves as having a greater tendency to delegate than those in lower-level positions. Browne (1949) noted that executives' salaries related positively to their estimates of how much they delegated. D. T. Campbell (1956) reported that delegation was positively and significantly related to one's level in various types of organizations, as well as to one's military rank, time in one's position, and regard for being in a position of leadership.

Blankenship and Miles (1968) observed that the level of one's position was more important than the span of control or size of the organization in determining delegation by managers. Compared with managers at lower levels, upper-level managers not only reported greater freedom from their superiors with regard to decisions but tended to involve their subordinates more in decisions. H. R. Gillespie (1980) agreed, finding that among 48 manufacturing executives, those at the top level were more participative than were those at the next two levels below them.

A higher organizational level brings with it many of the conditions that promote greater participation, and lower organizational levels do the reverse. Senior executives are concerned with longer-range problems and policies, norms, and values. They are dealing directly with more creative, more educated, higher-status subordinates, who expect more opportunities to participate and have a greater interest in long-term commitments and in their own development. Directive practices are more prevalent at lower levels, since managers are dealing with more routine types of work, more clearly defined objectives, and less well-educated subordinates of lower status who have fewer expectations about participating in the decision-making process (Selznick, 1957). Thus in their intensive study of workers on the assembly line, Walker and Guest (1952) emphasized that supervision was likely to be more directive, particularly if the tasks were routine.

Tasks. The nature of the work may determine whether the leader will need to be more directive or participative. If the tasks are simple, direction may be more acceptable than when tasks are complex. Although Ford (1983) argued that there must be some way to measure the outcomes of tasks if tasks are to be delegated, Mohr (1971) found that the degree of "task manageability" did not increase a manager's participatory style, but the task interdependence of the manager's subordinates did. Understandably, Leana (1986) reported that supervisors with heavier workloads were more likely than supervisors with lighter loads to delegate work to their insurance claims adjusters.

Phase. The phase in the work or decision process will affect whether leadership should be directive or participative. Wilson-Evered, Dall, and Neale (2001) noted that direction from the top may facilitate the initiation of innovative tasks; participation may generate more support for new ideas, their diffusion, and their implementation. Heifitz (1994) used the example of the physician-patient relationship in the diagnostic-treatment process to illustrate when direction or participation should dominate. In the first phase of diagnosis and treatment, the work is technical and the physician is primarily responsible for the work. When the patient is under stress, the flow of diagnostic and prognostic information to him or her may need to be paced and sequenced. The second phase, implementation, is technical but also requires the patient to learn and adapt. Here responsibility needs to be shared between physician and patient. In the third phase, as the relationship continues, the patient needs to learn to take on more responsibility than the physician. Heller, Drenth, Koopman, et al. (1988) studied the phases in 56 decisions in three Dutch organizations. Management dominated the first (start-up) phase and the third (finalization) stage. Professional staffs and middle management were most influential in the second (developmental) phase. Participation by lower organizational levels was limited to the fourth (implementation) phase. Richard Nixon saw participation as limited to the first phase of decision making and direction as mandatory in its finalization. "I would not think of making a decision by going around the table. Of course, I like to hear everyone, but then I go off alone and then decide. The decisions that are important must be made alone" (Schecter, 1982, pp. 18, 19).

Perceived Importance of Outside Environmental Influences. Managers differ in what aspects of the outside environment they regard as most important to their work, and as a consequence they behave differently inside the organization. Bass, Valenzi, and Farrow (1977) asked 76 managers to describe the importance of economic, political, social, and legal influences on the work of their 277 immediate subordinates. These subordinates, in turn, described the frequency with which their own manager displayed *direction*, negotiation, consultation, *participation*, and delegation. Managers who tended to see economic events, such as inflation and taxes, as having strong effects on their work situation were more likely to be *directive* or negotiative. Managers who tended to see political, social, or legal issues as more important were more likely to be consultative or *participative*.

Higher Authority. If rules and regulations that are set by a higher authority or the central administration restrict subordinates' decisions, then supervisors dominate the group and make the decisions (Hemphill, Seigel, & Westie, 1951). A higher authority can indirectly prevent subordinates' participation in decisions by demanding immediate answers from supervisors and allowing the supervisors no time or opportunity to consult their subordinates. In addition, whether supervisors can be participative with their subordinates depends on the extent to which the higher authority requires the employees to be secretive about products, techniques, and business strategies. If people in the organization are supposed to know only "what they need to know," employees cannot be consulted about some decisions because much of the information required to discuss and consider such decisions cannot be revealed to them (Tannenbaum & Massarik, 1950).

The number of hierarchical levels at which participation is encouraged by policy will increase the tendency of supervisors to be participative throughout the system. The acceptance and promotion of the participative ideology by the sponsors of the organization and its top management are particularly important (Marrow, Bowers, & Seashore, 1968).[7] The efforts of chief executive officers (CEOs) at General Motors, National Intergroup, and W. L. Gore & Associates demonstrated that participative leadership could be increased throughout their systems through the transformational leadership of their CEOs. The CEOs articulated a corporate mission and philosophy to encourage participation. They worked to gain acceptance of the approach by other key top executives, then the acceptance of those at lower levels. Participation at all levels was encouraged by changing the corporate culture, developing trust at all levels, and building the necessary skills for effective participation. These actions of top management resulted in increased employee commitment, job satisfaction, and role clarity (Niehoff, Enz, & Grover, 1989). If top management is transformational, there will be more support for participation at lower levels, according to the survey of 485 upper-level managers by Collins and Ross (1989). Board and top management pressure to promote from within may also increase the need for and importance of delegation at all levels in the

[7] See also Maccoby (1981), O'Toole (1985), and Tichy and Devanna (1986).

organization to develop personnel for higher-level positions. The effectiveness of such delegation depends on setting early expectations about the results that are desired.

L. B. Ward's (1965) large-scale survey of top management in the United States suggested strongly that (at the time) the religious affiliation of the top managers in a firm affected the firm's personnel policies. Leadership at lower levels was more likely to be participative when the top management was not restricted to members of one religious group. When the top management was restricted to one religion, participation was most likely in all-Jewish-led firms and least likely in all-Catholic-led firms. These findings need replication in the early twenty-first century.

Organizational Size. Blankenship and Miles (1968), McKenna (undated), and Wofford (1971) reported systematic trends between the size of the organization and the leadership style observed in it. On the whole, managers in larger firms exhibited more participation and less directiveness. However, a third variable may have been responsible, such as more education among managers of larger firms, differences in policies, and so forth.

The results for small naval vessels differed markedly from those obtained for larger ships (Stogdill & Scott, 1957), particularly for delegation. The effects of delegation continued unbroken down the chain of command in the large organizations of the bigger vessels. On the small ships, the delegation process was broken or reversed in the third echelon down from the top. Characterized by a high rate of face-to-face interaction, the personnel of the small ships were subject to greater interpersonal stresses and strains than were crews of the large ships. The formalized interactions in highly stratified larger organizations appeared to reduce some of the tension found in the smaller organizations, where personal interaction is conducted less formally. A formalized interaction structure had the effect of enlarging members' area of freedom of action, whereas the context inherent in face-to-face interaction tended to restrict freedom of action for some group members.[8]

[8] These findings are in accord with those reported by Cattell, Saunders, and Stice (1953); Shepherd and Weschler (1955); and others.

General Effects on Benefits and Costs of Directive and Participative Leadership

So far, this chapter has identified the attributes of the leader and the led, as well as the constraints and objectives of the task and surrounding conditions, that influence whether a leader will be directive or participative. This section examines the effects of direction or participation on follower acceptance of leadership, their satisfaction and morale, their involvement and commitment, the quality of decisions reached, and innovation and productivity.

The evidence does not automatically favor one leadership style over the other. Even the leadership that emerges in self-managed work groups, according to observations and group interviews by Manz and Sims (1984), needs to balance a hands-off with a directive style if it is to be effective. When asked about what managers do to appear fair, group members saw both direction with explanations and participative decision making as important. A survey of 815 managers by Greenberg (1988) found that to be seen as fair, 81% of the managers thought they needed to announce all pay raises and promotions; 76% thought they should explain how raises are determined; 43% thought they should explain why work assignments are made; and 55% said that subordinates should be allowed to participate in decisions. Yukl (1998, p. 126)) concluded from 40 years of research evidence that "participative leadership sometimes results in higher satisfaction, effort, and performance, and at other times it does not."

A meta-analysis by Spector (1986) found the following average correlations of employee outcomes with amount of participative leadership: involvement, .65; job satisfaction, .44; motivation, −.43; commitment, −.43; intention to quit, −.20; role ambiguity, −.54. Average correlations of the amount of participativeness with employee performance was .23; with turnover, −.38; and with role conflict, −.42. Despite this evidence, a variety of contingencies must be taken into consideration with regard to the benefits and costs of participation. Early on, Miner (1973, p. 348) suggested that the costs of participation may outweigh the benefits in many circumstances:

> The change in value[s] . . . required to implement participation on a large scale can be costly. . . . Many

managers must be retrained to the participative leadership style; many others will find change difficult and end by seeking other employment. Among these latter may be individuals with considerable talent in aspects of the management process . . . such as planning, coordinating, and controlling. . . . Individuals whose opinions are rejected . . . can become alienated. . . . [P]articipation may yield a sense of closeness and belonging . . . that is mobilized behind objectives not in the best interest of the organization. . . . [P]articipative decision making is a slow process which may not be adequately responsive to rapid changes in an organization's environment.

Lawler (1986) strongly advocated participation as a means of decreasing workers' resistance to changes in procedures and increasing the flexibility of assignments. Nonetheless, he expected that salary and training costs would increase, as would resistance by some staff personnel and line managers to participative decision making. A sampling of evidence on the general effects of directive and participative leadership follows. Then evidence about contingencies that moderate the effects will be presented.

Effects on Acceptance and Agreement

In general, the available evidence supports the contention that participative leadership promotes the acceptance of decisions and agreement to a greater extent than does directive leadership. When participative leadership is practiced in a group, R. Likert (1961a, 1961b) found that each member has the opportunity to gain recognition and a sense of self-worth. This type of leadership also creates conditions that allow each subordinate to observe how everyone else in the group feels about a matter under consideration. Such conditions reduce the individual's resistance to suggestions and changes of opinion. Thus Bennett (1955) obtained results indicating that students were much more likely to volunteer as experimental subjects if they perceived that almost all other members of their class had volunteered. Observing near-consensus and the opportunity to make public decisions increased volunteering more than did the opportunity for discussion. In a more tightly controlled experiment, Pennington, Haravey, and Bass (1958) showed that the followers'

acceptance and change were greatest when both discussion and group decision were permitted; less when only group discussion or announcements of group opinion were allowed; and least when only secret balloting was used.

In a seminal experiment, "participatory leaders" were instructed primarily to inhibit hasty decisions and domination of the group by any one member. They were contrasted by Preston and Heintz (1949) with "supervisory leaders," who were instructed to keep the group on the task. With more shared participation under participatory leaders, members as a whole showed more agreement with each other than did members without the opportunity to interact as much. The latter were more likely to be coerced, in that they showed less acceptance of decisions privately than publicly. Pennington, Haravey, and Bass (1958) found that experimental groups under participative leadership achieved greater coalescence and changes in opinion than did groups who were denied the opportunity to discuss and decide. Bovard (1951a, 1951b) observed that group-centered teams shifted their perceptions toward a common group norm more readily than did leader-centered teams. Hare (1953) found that although both participative and supervisory (directive) styles of leadership produced significant changes in the amount of agreement among group members, participative leaders were more in agreement with the group's rankings than were directive leaders. Likewise, Levine and Butler (1952) found participative leadership and group decisions to be more successful in producing behavioral change than did a lecture or control condition.

T. P. Wilson (1968) reported that prisoners make a better cooperative adaptation to prison life under participative rather than under bureaucratic management. Similarly, French, Kay, and Meyer (1966) observed that lower-level managers' participation in an appraisal system facilitated their acceptance of the goal, the group's cohesiveness, and favorable attitudes toward the appraisal procedures. Jacobson, Charters, and Lieberman (1951) showed that workers who were involved in decision making by their foremen but not by their shop stewards tended to share the values and goals of management, whereas workers who were involved in decisions by their stewards but not by their foremen tended to share the goals and standards of the union.

In a demonstration of how to change housewives'

meat-buying behavior (from steaks and chops to kidneys and liver) during World War II, Lewin (1947b) pointed the way toward the use of participative leadership to overcome resistance to change. Coch and French (1948) illustrated how a combination of participation in goal setting and the redesign of jobs resulted in increased productivity of three groups of garment workers with no such change obtained for a control group. Participation remains a key tool for those who cope with resistance to change (Lawler, 1986).

Effect of Opinionated Leaders

In an experiment with 47 executives, Bass (1967a) reported that the simulated advisory staff of a department head shifted and coalesced more if the department head announced his opinion, particularly if he did so at the beginning of the problem-solving meeting. Anderson and Balzer (1988) showed for 19 teams in a university residence hall who were dealing with various problems, that if the leaders immediately stated their opinions instead of withholding them until later in the discussion, fewer alternatives were proposed. Presumably, this was indicative of greater acceptance of the leader's point of view. However, T. A. Hill (1973) found that in student groups, consensus was more likely to be achieved when the leader was least opinionated. More will be said about the effects of directiveness on acceptance in the discussion of how contingencies modify the effects of participation and direction.

Effects on Satisfaction and Morale

Participation in all its forms has generally been found to increase subordinate satisfaction. However, evidence has been gathered that direction and persuasion can also be satisfying to followers, although to a lesser extent. And examples can be cited for situations in which participation fails to be satisfying to subordinates.

Preston and Heintz's (1949) previously mentioned study revealed the greater satisfaction of subordinates under participatory than under supervisory (directive) leaders. Similarly, Bass, Burger, et al. (1979) found that for an international sample of 1,641 managers who were engaged as subordinates in a training simulation, 51.7%

preferred working again with a *participative* rather than with either of two kinds of directive supervisors (the choice by chance was 33.3%). Zimet and Fine (1955) contrasted the results of lectures given to 15 chief school administrators with those of group-centered participative discussions. Although the administrators were initially more defensive in the discussions, subsequent sessions reduced their hostility and yielded increased warm, friendly behavior and more favorable attitudes toward themselves and others outside the meeting. Likewise, Ziller (1954) found that aircrews were more satisfied with decisions concerning simulated problems if they discussed the problem and their participative leader stated his opinion after the discussion. They were less satisfied when the decision was made authoritatively by a more directive leader. According to Aspegren (1963), participatory leadership produced higher levels of satisfaction and task motivation among group members than either directive or laissez-faire leadership. Storey's (1954) study of groups with participative leaders and groups with directive leaders found that members of participative groups were better satisfied with the group procedures, the decisions reached, and intermember acceptance, although no significant differences were found in satisfaction with the leadership.

Effects of the Opportunity to Participate. A. S. Tannenbaum (1963) reported greater satisfaction among 200 clerks as a consequence of their increased opportunity to participate. Morse, Reimer, and Tannenbaum (1951) noted increased satisfaction with a new organizational arrangement that promoted more self-determination and group decision making by lowering by one echelon the authority to make and execute various decisions. What the supervisor had previously decided was now delegated to subordinates. Mann and Baumgartel (1952) found that employees who felt free to discuss job-related and personal problems with their supervisors were better satisfied with the company, exhibited less absenteeism, and enjoyed membership in more cohesive work groups. Baumgartel (1956, 1957) obtained results showing that scientists in research laboratories exhibited higher degrees of task motivation and job satisfaction under participatory than under directive supervisors. In a large metropolitan social service agency, Harrison (1985) found correlations of .42 and .47, respectively, between the extent to which the 30 superiors used participative decision making and the 233 subordinates' desire to continue interacting with their leaders. Likewise, Mann, Indik, and Vroom (1963) reported that workers' satisfaction was highly related to their participation in decision making; their satisfaction and task motivation were especially low under directive supervision. Absences of white-collar workers were related to how free they said they felt to discuss their job with their supervisor. Of the employees who were absent four or more times during a six-month period, only 29% said they felt very free to talk with their boss; 57% to 69% of those who were absent less often said they felt very free to hold such discussions (R. Likert, 1961a).

In a Dutch study, Drenth and Koopman (1984) obtained correlations for 175 municipal transport employees, 154 railway employees, and 153 steelworkers of .44, .57, and .35, respectively, between the employees' participation in decision processes and the employees' satisfaction with the processes. Early participation in the decision process was particularly important to satisfaction. In Australia, Wilson-Evered, Dall, and Neale (2001), found that for 277 employees, participative leadership correlated with their morale and their support for team objectives. Weschler, Kahane, and Tannenbaum (1952) found that a research group led by a directive leader was less satisfied with its job. Alutto and Belasco (1972) reported that dissatisfaction and job tension were associated with "decision making deprivation."

Effects of Directive Leadership on Satisfaction. Direction may also be satisfying. Farrow, Valenzi, and Bass's (1980) analyses of approximately 1,400 subordinates' descriptions of their 350 managers in the Bass-Valenzi Management Styles Survey found that the managers' *direction* was positively correlated with satisfaction (.17 and .18). For the same sample, consultation correlated .34 with the subordinates' satisfaction with their jobs and .53 with the subordinates' satisfaction with their supervisors. The managers' *participation*, as seen by the subordinates, correlated .25 with their job satisfaction and .41 with their satisfaction with the leader. Comparable correlations of delegation with satisfaction were .32 and .46. Only negotiation or manipulation was negatively related to job satisfaction (−.16) and satisfaction with the leader (−.16). Using the same Bass-Valenzi instrument with 147 assistant school superintendents' descriptions of their super-

intendents, Wilcox (1982) obtained similar results. The rated superintendents' frequency of *direction* by the assistants correlated .50 with their satisfaction with the superintendents' leadership, although only .25 with their job satisfaction. The superintendents' frequency of *participation*, according to their assistant superintendents, correlated .37 with the assistants' job satisfaction and .41 with their satisfaction with the superintendents' leadership. In both Farrow, Bass, and Valenzi's study and Wilcox's study, consultation (in which the leader seeks advice from subordinates but makes the final decision) and delegation (in which the decision is left to the subordinates) were seen as more satisfying leadership styles than was *participation* (in which the decision is shared between the leader and the subordinates). Thus Wilcox obtained a correlation of .58 between consultation and satisfaction with the superintendents' leadership and .43 between delegation and such satisfaction. *Participation* and satisfaction correlated somewhat lower. A similar pattern of correlations with the same instrument translated into Turkish was obtained by Ergun and Onaran (1981) for 107 subordinates' descriptions of their supervisors in the Turkish Electrical Authority.

Berkowitz (1953b) observed decision-making groups in business and governmental organizations and found that group cohesiveness and the members' satisfaction decreased with participative leadership and increased with directive leadership. Although one would expect to find that leaders who say they delegate a great deal generate greater satisfaction among their subordinates, often the subordinates fail to appreciate the delegation (Stogdill & Shartle, 1948). The subordinates may not appreciate it because they believe they lack the authority to go along with the responsibilities that have been delegated to them. Also, superiors may believe they are delegating, but their subordinates may see the same behavior as dumping undesirable assignments on them. Or, they may think the delegation is marred by overly close monitoring; the resources necessary to carry out the delegated task may not be provided; or the leader's instructions may be ambiguous. Conditions that contribute to the failure of participation to be satisfying to subordinates can be a consequence of contingencies such as whether the participation is for the short or long term. For instance, Cotton, Vollrath, Froggatt, et al. (1988) showed that short-term participation failed to contribute to either employee satisfaction or productivity. Participation required more time to be effective.

Compared with a nondirective leader, a directive leader is more satisfying. Page and McGinnies (1959) showed a motion picture to groups of subjects who discussed the film under two styles of leadership—directive and nondirective. The directive leader was rated by the members as significantly more interesting, satisfying, purposeful, frank, industrious, and persuasive than the nondirective leader. Levy (1954a, 1954b) also found that the satisfaction of members was higher under directive than under nondirective leadership.

Effects on Involvement, Commitment, and Loyalty

According to D. Katz (1951), workers tend to enter groups or withdraw psychologically from groups as a function of their ability to make decisions in those groups. Many commentators (see, for example, Tichy & Devanna, 1986) have noted that the participation of employees is critical for the reorganization of a firm or agency and its successful implementation.

Kahn and Tannenbaum (1957) and Tannenbaum and Smith (1964) surveyed organized workers and members of women's clubs. The members' participation was facilitated by leaders who encouraged consultation and participation in activities. The members' loyalty to the organization was also strengthened by participation in activities. Likewise, in a study of technicians and laboratory testers at the Tennessee Valley Authority, Patchen (1970) found that participative management led to increased individual integration into the organization. Individuals became more involved in the work project when they were engaged in participative decision making. Siegel and Ruh (1973) reported similar results in a study of manufacturing employees; participative leadership was positively related to the employees' involvement in their jobs.

The opportunity to participate can be a mixed blessing. According to a nationwide survey by Gurin, Veroff, and Feld (1960), participation in the decision-making process increases both one's involvement in one's job and one's frustration with it. A. S. Tannenbaum (1963) studied 200 clerks who were given greater responsibility to make decisions. Despite their general increase in satisfaction, the clerks felt less sense of accomplishment at the end of the workday and were less satisfied with their present level in the organization. In acquiring an increased feeling of responsibility for the work, the clerks developed standards of achievement that were harder to satisfy.

Locke (1968) began a long line of investigation by questioning whether the mere directive assignment of hard goals to people was sufficient to generate heightened commitment and productivity; the people did not have to participate in the decision to set the hard goals. Considerable experimental support was obtained in U.S. studies (Latham & Baldes, 1975). Likewise, feedback appeared more important than participation in a study of the safety practices of 150 U.S. workers by Fellner and Sulzer-Azaroff (1985). But in Israel, Erez and Arad (1986) noted that involvement and commitment were required for the heightened productivity to occur, and such involvement and commitment could be obtained only if the experimental subjects participated in setting the goals. These differences between the United States and Israel appear to have been resolved (Locke, Latham, & Erez, 1987) when it was discovered that participation was unnecessary in the United States for the required commitment to be achieved, because the commitment seemed to have been gained by the friendly, supportive behavior of the experimenter in assigning the goals. In Israel, the experimenter who assigned the goals was curt and abrupt. Here, only with participation in goal setting, was it possible to obtain the expected commitment and subsequent heightened performance. Thus relations-oriented leadership, a subject of Chapter 19, may substitute (as in the U.S. experiments) for actual participation in gaining the commitment of subordinates.

Effect on Task Performance

Generally, both participation and direction can affect subordinates' task performance and task outcomes. For example, Nutt (1986) examined 84 cases from service organizations, such as hospitals, governmental agencies, charities, and professional societies, in which managers had sponsored efforts to implement planned changes. In 16 cases, the directive managers first acquired the necessary authority and then demonstrated or justified the changes with appropriate information; their implementation efforts were successful in 100% of these 16 cases. In another 14 cases, the participative managers first stipulated the needs, opportunities, and objectives and then set up task forces to develop recommendations; overall success occurred in 84% of these 14 cases. In 35 cases, managers used persuasion to sell the planned changes after the changes had been formulated by the staff or consultants; here the success rate was 73%. In the remaining 19 cases, implementation was by management edict and least success was found. Here, the sponsor of the change used positional and personal power to issue directives ordering the changes; this approach achieved a success rate of 71%.

Bass (2000) suggested that directive supervision was more effective when supervising novices working on routine tasks, especially if the supervisor was experienced, knowledgeable, and esteemed. According to Portin and Shen (1998, p. 96), "the school principal remains the singular individual at the nexus of leadership in the school . . . [with] a mandatory responsibility [to deal with] the increasing complexity of schools and school administration." Smither (1991) argued that, to be effective, managers may need to be authoritarian and directive. Tetrick (1989) provided supportive evidence with data from 422 naval personnel and their immediate supervisors. Informative and controlling supervisors enhanced their subordinates' role clarity, motivation, and felt influence. P. J. Burke (1966a, 1966b), as well as Katzell, Miller, Rotter, et al. (1970), found that directive leadership could enhance group cohesiveness. Thiagarajan and Deep (1970) studied groups in which supervisors played three roles: *directive*, persuasive, and *participative*. The *directive* leader was more influential on coalescing agreement of follower and leader than the persuasive leader, and the persuasive leader was more influential than the *participative* one. Several meta-analytic reviews found that directive leadership could be as effective as participative leadership in increasing worker productivity (e.g., Sagie, 1994). Sagie (1997) offered three explanations:

1. As Muczyk and Reimann (1987–1989) suggested, participation is called for in making an effective decision; direction is concerned with executing the decision effectively once it has been made.
2. Since the superior is more knowledgeable about strategic issues, and the subordinates are more knowledgeable about tactical operations, direction

should be used for strategic decisions and participation for tactical decisions.
3. For effectiveness, a coupling is needed between participatory goal setting and directive leadership that sets the framework for action, structures the interaction, and urges subordinates to contribute.

Sagie (1996) demonstrated that the third explanation was most accurate for 183 experimental team members required to solve problems in the least amount of time.

Effects on the Quality of Decisions

Experiments generally show that group decisions are superior to decisions reached by the average member of a group, although it is also true that the group decision may not be as good as that of the best member of the group. But how often is the supervisor the best? If it could be guaranteed that the supervisor was always the best, then the quality of the decision might be better when decisions were made by the supervisor alone (Bass, 1960).

When 66 U.S. Air Force officers wrote decisions before a discussion and then met as an ad hoc staff to write the decisions, the decisions written by the staff were superior to the average quality of the decisions written by individuals without a discussion. But the quality was the same after the discussion, whether the decision was written by the staff or by the commander who had listened to the staff's discussion. Group discussions contributed to better decision making whether the final decision was written by the group or by the person leading the group (Lorge, Fox, Davitz, & Brenner, 1958). Many others have also studied the improved quality of decisions made by discussion groups.[9]

The quality of the decision was higher under participation than under a directive style of leadership that discouraged discussion. Lanzetta and Roby (1960) found that both time and error scores were better under participative than under directive leadership.

Leana (1983) engaged 208 undergraduate students in a role-play of a business problem. In the four-person groups, if the "vice president of operations" (the formal

[9]These investigators included Blake and Mouton (1962b); Hoffman, Burke, and Maier (1965); Hoffman, Harburg, and Maier (1962); Hoffman and Maier (1967); Maier (1950); Maier and Solem (1952); and Solem (1953).

leader of the group) was participative rather than directive, the group generated and discussed significantly more alternative solutions. Directive leaders tended to produce premature closure of the search for solutions, which presumably reduced the quality of the final decision. These effects were independent of the groups' cohesiveness. Watson and Michaelsen (1984) demonstrated that participative leadership in a role-playing setting with 35 four-person student groups generated more effective problem solving than did directive leadership.

However, numerous other studies can be cited in support of directive leadership. Katzell, Miller, Rotter, and Venet (1970) studied small problem-solving groups. More directiveness by leaders was positively associated with the groups' greater effectiveness. Kidd and Christy (1961) found that avoidance of errors was greatest under directive leadership. Schumer (1962) obtained evidence indicating that both the quality and quantity of results were enhanced by a directive form of leadership. Torrance (1952) contrasted five types of critiques following 16 minutes of problem-solving activity by air crews in survival school to see which resulted in the greatest improvement in the ability to solve subsequent problems. The largest gains were made when an expert directed the critique; the next largest gains with guided discussion (participative leadership); and the least gain with free discussion (laissez-faire leadership) in which no control was exerted.

Schlesinger, Jackson, and Butman (1960) found that committees are more effective in solving problems under directive than under nondirective leadership. Stagner (1969), who studied a large sample of corporation executives by questionnaire, observed that corporate profits were associated with more formality, more centralization of decision making, and less personalized management.

Effects on Productivity

If one searches for universal answers about the immediate effects of participation and direction on productivity, almost every possible alternative emerges. From a review of the results of laboratory, correlational, and univariate field studies of the effects of leadership style on productivity, Locke and Schweiger (1979) concluded that they could find no overall trend favoring participative or directive leadership. As for field studies with multiple anteced-

ent conditions and outcomes, they thought that other factors, such as training and reward systems, often could account for effects on productivity that were attributed to participation. Likewise, Erez and Arad (1986) demonstrated that appropriate information and involvement in goal setting were needed for a participative group discussion to generate higher-quality performance. Nonetheless, Miller and Monge's (1986) meta-analysis confirmed the significance of participative leadership to productivity. In a seminal experiment (detailed in Chapter 12), Coch and French (1948) demonstrated that the participation of pajama-manufacturing workers in decision making generated higher productivity and a lower turnover of personnel than did nonparticipation by a control group. A subsequent replication yielded comparable results (Marrow, Bowers, & Seashore, 1968). With groups of employees of a large supplier of aerospace electronics, Hinrichs (1978) obtained production increases of 20% to 30% and reductions in errors of 30% to 50% in 27 of 40 employee groups who were encouraged to participate over a four-year period.

R. Likert (1977b), aiming toward long-range effects, involved various business and industrial groups in management by group objectives (MBGO), which generates the participative sharing of data and the setting of a group's goals. A 27% increase in profits over the previous year was reported from a retail sales division. Such participation by teams of foremen resulted in a rise in productivity of 15% and a decrease in scrap of 7% to 14% in an auto assembly plant. In an early study reported by the Survey Research Center (1948), work groups were more productive among those first-level supervisors in an insurance company who encouraged their workers to participate in decisions. Indik, Georgopoulos, and Seashore (1961) showed that among 975 deliverymen at 27 parcel delivery stations, the ease and freedom they felt in communicating with their superiors at a station correlated between .39 and .48 with the average deliveries the men completed daily in relation to the standard time allotted for completion.

R. J. Solomon (1976) demonstrated the greater effectiveness of participative library directors. The immediate subordinates of these directors evaluated the effectiveness of the services supplied by other departments. For instance, personnel in the acquisition departments evaluated the effectiveness of the circulation departments.

Directors who were consultative and participative were the most conducive to high ratings of effective departments under them, and directors who were manipulative were the least conducive. Similarly, Reeder (1981) employed path analysis to show that participative leadership by supervisors of U.S. Army clerks and programmers was more causally related to the subordinates' productivity than to the supervisors' knowledge of their subordinates' work. Programs of management by objectives (MBO) imply participative setting of goals. Gains in productivity occurred in 68 of 70 studies, but the average gain was 56% when top management was committed to the program and only 6% when it was not committed, according to a meta-analysis by Rodgers and Hunter (1991).

In still other studies, participation and direction were seen to have similar effects on task performance. According to Weschler, Kahane, and Tannenbaum (1952), a research group with a directive leader perceived itself to be less productive than one with a participative leader. However, the leaders' boss thought the group led by the directive leader was more productive. Lange and Jacobs (1960) and Lange, Campbell, Katter, and Shanley (1958) found that directive patterns of leadership and encouraging participation were positively and significantly related to the performance ratings of groups. Similarly, Farrow, Valenzi, and Bass (1980) found that effectiveness correlated positively with the amount of *direction* (.23) by about 250 managers, as seen by 1,400 subordinates. Effectiveness also correlated positively with various participatory approaches: consultation (.23), *participation* (.23), and delegation (.22). Only negotiation or manipulation by managers was negatively related to effectiveness (−.25).

Effects on the Manager's Rate of Advancement

Hall and Donnell (1979) calculated the rate at which managers had been promoted by comparing their organizational level with their age. Over 2,000 subordinates indicated the extent to which the 731 managers allowed and encouraged them to participate in making and influencing work-related decisions. Although slowly and moderately advancing managers were seen to permit or encourage very little participation, faster-advancing managers did a lot of it. But Farrow, Valenzi, and Bass (1981) determined, for more than 1,200 managers and their sub-

ordinates, that the managers whose salaries were higher than would have been predicted from their function, their organization, their sex, and their seniority were seen by their subordinates to be persuasive, manipulative, and negotiative. Such managers were downgraded in effectiveness by their subordinates but evidently were pleasing to their bosses, who awarded them higher-than-expected salaries. Managers who were favored by their subordinates for their frequent consultation, *participation*, delegation, and *direction* were not similarly awarded salaries above the norms.

Models in Support of Participation

Support for participative leadership can be built into cognitive, affective, and contingent models (Miller & Menge, 1986). *Cognitive* models propose that participation contributes to subordinates' satisfaction and productivity because it improves the interchange of important information in the organization. For example, Anthony (1978) argued that workers have more knowledge than do their managers and that their participation increases the information needed for high-quality decision making. Furthermore, as Melcher (1976) noted, people will work better under the requirements for implementing decisions if they have participated in the decision-making process. In a study of 12 high-technology R & D projects, McDonough and Kinnunen (1984) found that in the more successful projects, there was more discussion among the different levels of management about the projects' goals and more constant distribution of information about progress.

The satisfaction of employees is a side effect of such participation (Ritchie & Miles, 1970). Since the distribution of information is the crucial aspect of participation, Miller and Monge (1986) deduced that stronger effects should occur with the participation of employees in decisions about the design of a job than in companywide policy decisions. Satisfaction should occur only after the feedback of information about the consequences of participation. Participation should not necessarily pay off in greater satisfaction merely for working in a participative climate or for a participative leader. It should pay off only when the exchange of knowledge is relevant to the decisions.

The *affective* model, strongly endorsed by the human

relations school of thought (see, for example, Maslow, 1965; McGregor, 1960), posits that participation generates the satisfaction of higher-order needs in subordinates, which, in turn, increase the subordinates' motivation, satisfaction, and quality and quantity of performance.

The third or *contingency* model stresses the importance of the perception of participation. Another contingency is the felt opportunity to participate. Still another contingency is the number of issues involved. From all 41 weighted and adjusted estimates of the relation between the amount of participative leadership and the satisfaction of subordinates, Miller and Monge (1986) obtained a mean correlation of .34 in their meta-analysis. The results were similar for students and organizational respondents. The correlation rose to .48 when the respondents *perceived* themselves to be participating on a multiplicity of issues (see, for example, Obradovic, 1970). It dropped to .21 if only a single specific issue was involved (see, for instance, Alutto & Acito, 1974). The correlation was only .16 between actual participation and satisfaction. What makes participative leadership satisfying for subordinates is not so much their actual participation in the decision-making process as their feeling that they genuinely have the opportunity to participate if they want to contribute to making a decision. Only about 50% of the American electorate actually votes in presidential elections; the rest are satisfied to remain on the sidelines. Yet if they were denied the ballot, strong protests, cries of dictatorship, and a great increase in dissatisfaction with the system would ensue.

From 25 studies, the Miller-Monge meta-analysis yielded a mean of .15 between participative leadership and the productivity of subordinates. The mean rose to .27 for field studies (in contrast to laboratory settings). As was reported earlier, in the laboratory studies in which participants were subject to participative or directive leadership, the mean correlation was −.33 (productivity was higher with direction). When a friendly supervisor subjected the participants to arbitrarily assigned goals or to participation in setting the goals, the mean correlation with productivity was −.01. It made no difference in these temporary conditions with a friendly experimenter whether arbitrary direction or participation was used.

Miller and Monge did not find a change in these mean results for managers compared to lower-level employees, or in different kinds of organizations; nor could they test

the effects of personality. They concluded that with reference to such contingencies, they had found more support for the affective model than for the cognitive or contingent models. They reasoned in favor of the affective model because (1) they had found stronger effects between participation and satisfaction than between participation and productivity and (2) they had found stronger effects of a participative climate on the satisfaction of subordinates who were involved in multiple issues rather than in a single issue.

With reference to another contingency, they obtained mean correlations of −.33 versus .27 between participation and productivity in the laboratory versus the field studies. They inferred that directive leadership contributed to productivity in the laboratory because laboratory tasks tend to be simpler and to have clear objectives and outcomes. They thought that participation yielded more productivity in the field because tasks in the real-life work setting are likely to be more complex and to have unclear objectives and outcomes.

Wagner and Gooding (1987) uncovered another contingency. If single-source bias is present, in that the same respondent provides the data on participation and outcomes, mean correlations range from .34 to .42. But if one source provides the measure of participation and another source provides the data on outcomes, the range of correlations lowers to between .09 and .21. Overall, the impact of participation per se on performance and satisfaction is evident.

Additional support for the contingent model stems from the fact that, as was noted earlier, a majority of managers actually are directive or participative, depending on the nature of the decision to be made. With this fact in mind, Hambleton and Gumpert (1982) found that for 65 managers, their 189 subordinates, and their 56 supervisors, the adaptable, flexible manager who made a greater use of the variety of styles appropriate to different situations, according to the Hersey-Blanchard model (1977),[10] emerged with significant and practical gains in the subordinates' performance.

Integration of Models. Lawler (1986) integrated the models, suggesting that the effective participative process requires a multiplicative combination of the adequate

---

[10]To be detailed in Chapter 19.

flow of information, the requisite knowledge by employees of what needs to be done, shared power to decide, and satisfactory rewards for implementation. If any one of these elements is missing, the process will fail.

Additional Contingent Effects of Directive and Participative Leadership

R. Likert (1977a) argued that if long-term measures of effectiveness are the criteria of consequence, then a democratic approach, including shared participative decision making, is universally more effective as long as the leader is task oriented. There are few contingencies for Likert. Blake and Mouton (1964) presented similar arguments for an integrated task- and relations-oriented approach. On the other hand, Bass and Barrett (1981) noted in reviewing the literature that participative leadership is contraindicated in situations with short-term perspectives when interaction is restricted by the task, when the higher authority disapproves, when maximum output is demanded, when subordinates do not expect to participate, when leaders are unready for participation, and when emergencies occur. Many comparable theories have been advanced on the basis of the postulate that effective leaders use participation or directive leadership styles to fit the situation. (See, for example, Austin's [1981] style-flex model.) And countless commentaries and the inspirational management literature of the 1980s repeated the virtues of the life-cycle theory (Hersey & Blanchard, 1969a) that the key situational factor for leaders to consider is the maturity of their subordinates (Carbone, 1981).

The evidence so far is that although the meta-analytic effects are not as large as some commentators expect, generally participative leadership enhances performance, the quality of decisions, and satisfaction, but in the short run, at least, it may be less conducive to productivity than is directive leadership. Various contingencies have already been mentioned, which must be taken into account to predict and understand more fully the impact of direction and participation. What follows further elaborates on the effects of contingencies such as the differences between leaders and their followers and the constraints under which they must operate.

Three bases for understanding exist. First, one can draw empirical inferences from surveys in which correlations have been run between the style of the leader and outcomes under different contingencies. Second, one can draw further inferences from experiments in which each leadership style has been introduced under each contingency. Third, beginning with several acceptable assumptions that are consistent with what was said earlier about the impact of participation on outcomes, it becomes possible to prescribe which style of leadership is likely to be more effective. Empirical data supporting or refuting the propositions derived from the models can also be presented.

Effects of Superior Subordinate Competence, Motivation, and Personality

Ability and Motivation. Whether direction or participation is more effective as a leadership style has been found in a number of investigations to depend on the competence, motivation, and personality of the leaders and their subordinates. Probably the single most emphasized modifier in determining whether participative or directive leadership will be more effective is the competence of the subordinate relative to the leader, and the information each possesses (Hersey & Blanchard, 1977). Mulder (1971) and Miner (1973) pointed out that it may be counterproductive for leaders to be participative in style if they are much more expert than their subordinates on the matters to be decided. What is important to whether direction or participation will work better is how much training and information the leader and the subordinate have (Filley, House, & Kerr, 1979; Locke & Schweiger, 1979).

Blades and Fiedler (1976) and Fiedler and Garcia (1987) demonstrated that whether directive leaders are more effective depends on the leaders' task ability and their subordinates' support and motivation. The followers' performance is better if the leaders are expert and intelligent and the followers are supportive and motivated. If the followers are more intelligent and motivated, then nondirective leadership is more effective. Thus Bons and Fiedler (1976) found that among 138 U.S. Army squad leaders, the leaders' intelligence correlated .44 with their squads' performance of tasks. Yet the correlation fell to .04 when the squad leaders failed to be directive. Similar results were obtained by Fiedler, O'Brien, and Ilgen

(1969) in a study of 41 small public health teams in Honduras. When the leaders' direction was high, their intelligence correlated .48 with community developments. When the leaders' direction was low, the correlation fell to −.20. More intelligent, informed, technically competent leaders—both when contrasted with the competence of their followers and when contrasted with less competent leaders—are more effective if they are directive rather than nondirective and if their subordinates are already highly motivated and supportive of their efforts (Fiedler, 1982; Murphy, Blyth, & Fiedler, 1992).

Latham and Baldes (1975) provided the strongest evidence to support the contention that both the ability and motivation of the leader, combined with the ability and motivation of the subordinates, determine what style of leadership will prove more effective. Latham and Baldes studied 49 groups of U.S. Army enlisted cooks. The cooks operated mess halls, each of which was led by a mess steward who was either directive or nondirective, according to behavioral descriptions of the steward by the group on such items as, "The mess steward decides what shall be done and how it shall be done." The tendency of the steward to enforce standards was measured by such items as, "The mess steward maintains definite standards of performance." Motivation was measured by responses to such questions as, "How hard do you work and do as good a job as possible?" The ability of the stewards and cooks was obtained from a 50-item test. Measures of the quality of mess hall services were obtained from weekly inspections made by food service officers. Nondirective participative leadership worked better when the cooks were higher in both ability and motivation. However, directive leadership resulted in a much more effective food service when the stewards were higher in ability and the cooks were highly motivated. Such directive leadership resulted in lower inspection ratings if the steward was lower in ability and the cooks were lower in motivation. Enforcement of standards by the steward generated the best food inspection ratings when the cooks were either high in both ability and motivation or low in both ability and motivation. Particularly deleterious was the enforcement of standards when the cooks were high in ability but low in motivation.

The steward's tested intelligence contributed to the effectiveness of the mess halls, but only when the steward was directive and the cooks were highly motivated. Furthermore, with highly motivated cooks, nondirective leadership resulted in a correlation of .56 between the cooks' level of ability as cooks and the effectiveness of operations. But here, directive leadership generated an opposite correlation of −.48 between the cooks' ability and effectiveness. With nondirective leadership, if the cooks' motivation was low, the cooks' ability correlated −.45 with the effectiveness of the mess halls; with directive leadership, the correlation was −.20. Parallel results were obtained when the tested intelligence of the cooks was used as an indicator of their ability.

Effects of Training

Blyth (1987) randomly assigned leaders to four conditions: the leaders were either trained or untrained in the use of survival gear and were instructed to be either directive or participative with their groups. Only the directive leaders who had been trained to use the survival gear had groups that performed well; participative leaders with the training performed no better than did those without training. When Blyth trained the group members but not the leaders to use the gear and then instructed the leaders to be directive or participative, the groups with participative leaders performed better than those with directive leaders.

Effects of Centrality

Communication network experiments reported in Chapter 29 demonstrated that if leaders are at the center of a network, they are likely to be most informed, since they are in two-way contact with all the people at the periphery. Their network will be more effective if they are directive. On the other hand, if the leaders occupy peripheral positions, their network will be most effective if they are more participative (Shaw, 1954a).

Effects of Task Relevance

Bass and Ryterband (1979) reported a study in which 18 wives of managers were asked to meet individually with a male manager (not their own spouse) to reach decisions about either company affairs or household affairs. The managers were instructed to be either directive or participative as the leaders in a counterbalanced design. The women felt responsibility for the household discussion regardless of the leader's style, but felt responsibility for the discussion about the company only with the participative leader—not with the directive leader. The wives reported considerable hostility toward the directive leader in the discussions of household affairs, and such meetings were the least satisfying experience for them. In contrast, the wives did not react negatively when leaders directed the decision-making process if the problem concerned company issues.

Effects of Personality

Mitchell, Smyser, and Weed (1975) showed that for workers, locus of control determined whether a directive or participative supervisor was more satisfactory as a leader. For workers with an external locus of control, satisfaction with work was higher with directive supervisors and lower with participative supervisors. Conversely, for those with an internal locus, satisfaction was higher with participative leaders and lower with directive leaders.

In Vroom's (1959) study of 108 supervisors in a retail parcel-delivery service, productivity was found to correlate with felt influence on decisions among egalitarians much more than among authoritarians. Satisfaction on the job was increased by participation, but only for subordinates with egalitarian attitudes. A. S. Tannenbaum (1958) noted that followers who were predisposed to participation tended to be satisfied under conditions of increased involvement. Those who were predisposed to dependence, however, reacted adversely to increased participation. Runyon (1973) and Mitchell, Smyser, and Weed (1975) found that, as might be expected, internally controlled subordinates were more satisfied with participative supervisor, but externally controlled subordinates were more satisfied with directive supervisors.

Passive followers favored a more directive leader in Page and McGinnies's (1959) comparison of discussion groups led by directive and participative leaders. Likewise, in simulations (Bass, Burger, et al., 1979), apathetic subordinates were found to be relatively more comfortable with *directive* supervisors.

Saville (1984) proposed that supervisors who favored some form of direction or participation could be matched with subordinates who complemented them to maximize supervisor-subordinate compatibility and to minimize the development of serious problems between them. Receptive, dependent subordinates should be matched with *directive* supervisors; more reciprocating types of subordinates complement negotiative supervisors; more innovative, critical subordinates should be assigned to consultative supervisors; more affiliative, democratic subordinates should be matched with *participative* supervisors; and more self-reliant subordinates will fit best with delegative supervisors.

Bass, Valenzi, and Farrow (1977) found that for 244 managers and their 992 subordinates, judged effectiveness by both managers and subordinates correlated positively with delegative supervision (as seen by the subordinates) if the managers tended to regard the world as fair minded and if the subordinates were introspective but not assertive. The same was true for the effectiveness of *participative* leadership. In addition, it helped if the manager had an assertive personality. Consultation was more effective with introspective, unassertive subordinates and assertive managers. Manipulation and negotiation were more effective with introspective managers and subordinates. The personalities of the managers or the subordinates were of no consequence to the effectiveness of *direction*. In a consumer finance firm, Tosi (1970) failed to find that the subordinates' personalities made any difference.

Effects of Organizational and Interpersonal Relations

Commitment by top business management played a crucial role in the effectiveness of participative leadership at hierarchical levels below them (Rodgers & Hunter, 1991). Renn (1998) showed that while task performance was not directly enhanced by the participation of 200 employees in a goal-setting program, it was enhanced by goal acceptance, which was a direct consequence of participation. In a related experiment, Li and Butler (2004) found that persuasive rationales for goals were particularly important to effective outcomes and sense of procedural justice when goals were assigned rather than set by means of participation. In a military setting (Virginia Military Institute), Atwater, Lau, Bass, et al. (1994) found that subordinates' effectiveness rankings of their cadet leaders correlated .33 with the frequency of *direction* of the leaders and .19 with the frequency of their persuasion but only .09 with their frequency of *participation* and .12 with frequency of consultation. Colquist, Noe, and Janz (1998) surveyed 230 employees from 27 work teams in information systems departments of Fortune 500 firms in six industries. When the employees strongly identified as team members, felt interdependent, were satisfied with their jobs, and were in small teams, there was less need for participative leadership to generate cooperation among them. There was more need for participative leadership when the reverse conditions prevailed. Bass, Valenzi, and Farrow (1977) developed discriminant functions for 244 managers and 992 subordinates in work groups who were above and below the median in effectiveness who had responded to a questionnaire about the system of inputs, relations, and outputs under which they perceived themselves to operate. They found that the effectiveness of operations was higher if harmony and trust were higher. A greater amount of harmony made consultative leadership even more conducive to effective operations, and a greater amount of trust in the organization contributed more to the impact on effectiveness of the leader's participation.

Power. Kipnis (1958) studied groups of children under different conditions of leadership, reward, and threat. Both reward and threat produced more public compliance than did the control condition. Participative leadership induced more children to change their beliefs when leadership was associated with the power to reward. When the children were threatened with punishment for noncompliance, significantly fewer of them changed their beliefs under participative leadership than under lecture conditions. The participative leader was better liked than the lecturer if he did not threaten. Similarly, Patchen (1962) found that directive supervision resulted in a group's high output only if the group was also cohesive and directed by a supervisor who was seen to be a rewarding figure.

Ergun and Onaran (1981) found that Turkish supervisors who were more active in either direction or participation were judged more effective when both the managers and the subordinates lacked power. Activity appeared to be a substitute for power.

Pelz (1951) observed that participative leadership by Detroit Edison managers generated satisfaction among employees only when the managers had influence "up-

stairs." But House, Filley, and Gujarati (1971) failed to replicate this finding for R & D managers in another firm.

Falling Dominoes Effects. The effectiveness of participatory leadership at lower levels in an organization will depend on the practice of such leadership at higher levels, as well as in adjacent departments. Otherwise, conflict emerges (Lowin, 1968). Such conflict may be avoided if R. Likert's (1967) organization of overlapping groups is used. Here, every manager is a linchpin that connects the participatory group of the manager and his or her subordinates with the participatory group of the manager's boss, the manager's peers, and the manager.

Constraints and Goals. Hemphill (1949b) found that directive behavior by leaders is most readily accepted in groups with a closely restricted membership, a stratified status structure, and members who are dependent on the group. But Murnighan and Leung (1976) obtained results indicating that participation helped performance only when subordinates thought the task was important. According to Ergun and Onaran (1981), the effectiveness of the unit, organization, and supervisor increased, particularly if the leader used direction when constraints were low, goals were clear, and the interdependence of tasks was high. Participation correlated more highly with effectiveness for interdependent work teams that had clear objectives and considerable discretionary opportunities.

Task Requirements. Shaw and Blum (1966) found that directive leadership was more effective in structured task situations, whereas nondirective leadership was more effective in less structured conditions. Roby, Nicol, and Farrell (1963) obtained indications that problems requiring a reaction to environmental changes were more quickly solved under participative conditions, but that problems necessitating coordinated action were solved more efficiently under directive leadership.

The leadership decision-making style in an organization is influenced by whether the organization must deal with a stable or turbulent market. Firms that operate in turbulent markets are more effective if they encourage participation and decision making at the lowest possible levels (Emery & Trist, 1965). Burns and Stalker (1961) contrasted the relatively stable environment of a rayon mill with the more unstable conditions faced by firms in the electronics industry. For the mill, in its stable environment, a "mechanistic" system with directive supervision was most effective. In the electronics industry, with its rapidly changing environment, a more participative, "organic" system seemed most effective.

Similar conclusions were reached by Lawrence and Lorsch (1967a, 1967b). For a container firm with a stable environment, effective decision-making processes within the firm were likely to be directive; in a plastics firm facing a more turbulent environment, effective decision-making processes were more likely to be participative. Nonetheless, Wagner and Gooding's (1987) meta-analysis of 118 correlational analyses on the extent to which the interdependence and complexity of tasks and performance standards moderate the effects of participation on employees' performance, motivation, satisfaction with decisions, and acceptance of decisions revealed few differences in the effects of participation on outcomes if the task was complex rather than simple, if the task involved independence or interdependence, and if performance standards were present or absent.

Objectives. Korten (1968) observed that if the final product of a task was practical, more directive supervision was in order; but if the outcome was theoretical, participation was more useful. However, participative leadership needs to have a focus if it is to affect productivity. Lawrence and Smith (1955) studied checkers and mail openers over a five-week period. Groups of each type of employee held participative discussions either about their work or to set the group's goals. Only the goal-setting groups showed increased productivity, although both types of meetings were equally satisfying to the participants.

The increased productivity of the goal-setting groups was probably connected to the importance attached to the meeting in which the participative leadership occurred. Thus Cosier and Aplin (1980) concluded, from an experiment with 84 undergraduate business students, that having the freedom to choose objectives about a task of prediction was important to them, but having the freedom to schedule the procedure to be used was not. Delegation to them of the choice of objectives yielded a much better performance than assignment of the objectives, but delegation or assignment of the schedule to be

followed made no difference to them. Similarly, Drenth and Koopman (1984) reported that among 56 Dutch employees, satisfaction with decisions was enhanced most by opportunities to participate for those employees who were unclear about their goals. For these same employees, however, satisfaction with the outcomes and implementation of the decisions correlated between .26 and .40 if the decisions were about tactical matters of consequence to them. But the parallel correlations ranged from −.11 to .13 if the decisions were about organizational strategies that the employees did not think were of direct consequence to them. This finding lent confidence to arguments by Bass and Shackleton (1979) that participative management should be restricted to decisions that are of direct concern to employees. Consultation with production employees about financial and marketing decisions may make little sense, in contrast to consultations about overtime policies.

When leaders overstep their authority by forcing an arbitrary decision on their groups, the expected resistance and hostility may fail to materialize if the leaders' behavior actually facilitates the achievement of the groups' goals. Whether leaders reach their objectives depends on whether the style of leadership they choose meets the needs of their subordinates to attain their goals and whether it clarifies for the subordinates the paths to achieve the goals (House & Mitchell, 1974). Participation may meet subordinates' needs but may fail to clarify goals without some direction from the leaders.

Time Perspective. If the supervisors' time perspective is short—that is, if they have some immediate objectives to attain—they are likely to find it most effective to be directive. Alternatively, if an important objective is the long-term efficiency of their groups, participation is more likely to pay off (Hahn & Trittipoe, 1961).

Other Contingent Effects

The passage of time itself may make a difference in the efficacy of early participation. Ivancevich (1976) demonstrated that over time, the positive effects of involvement in goal setting may dissipate. Employees may become immersed in the job itself and forget their earlier involvement in decisions. It is possible that some individuals in a group may be satisfied with a participative leader and some with a directive leader, although the group as a whole may be more satisfied with participation. Yammarino and Naughton (1992) conducted a Within-and-Between Groups Analysis (WABA) of the responses of 70 officers in a law enforcement agency about the outcomes of their participation in decisions. Included were the director and his lieutenants as well as investigators, patrol officers, and dispatchers. Both the groups and the individuals who reported high levels of participative decision making were those who felt that they had respect and status and were satisfied with their work. But commitment was not affected.

Although research on virtual team leadership is in its infancy, direction or participation may be favored for the same contingent reasons as with face-to-face leadership. For example, directive decisions will be more effective when the leader is expert and the followers are novices. Participation will result in more effective outcomes when the followers are sources of information, knowledge, and experience.

Followers may get bored, weary, and frustrated with continuing participation. The amount of participation by subordinates seems to reach an optimum. If actual participation is greater than expected, R. Likert (1959) noted that dissatisfaction will result. Ivancevich (1979) found that there could be too much as well as too little participation. Performance suffered when participation was above or below optimum. However, e-leadership may benefit from participative leadership. Yukl (1998) pointed out that quantitative studies in which measures of leadership and effective performance were obtained from the same source tended to favor participative leadership as more effective. Evidence is much more modest when different sources are used about the leaders and about their effects. Case studies of participation also tend to be favorable, but plenty of successful, tough, directive leaders who are effective are cited in the popular press.

Deduced Models for Achieving Decision Quality or Subordinate Acceptance

Among the prescriptive models that indicate when leaders should be directive and when they should be participative, two have been particularly popular—that by Hersey and Blanchard (1977) and that by Vroom and Yetton (1974). Each model details the situations in which practicing managers should be directive and those in which they should be participative to maximize satisfaction and effectiveness. The former model is derived from empirical studies, the latter from more rigorous deduction. The former is supported mainly by observation and commentaries of users and is seen as fuzzy in its prescription and application; the latter is supported (and sometimes refuted) by controlled empirical surveys and experiments. Nevertheless, early on, the Vroom-Yetton model was criticized for its lack of parsimony and its inapplicability to management (Filley, House, & Kerr, 1976). Yet unlike the Hersey-Blanchard model, the Vroom-Yetton model was more intellectually rigorous and lent itself more readily to empirical testing of its validity, although, as shall be seen, it is not without serious flaws. The Vroom-Yetton model is examined in detail here; the Hersey-Blanchard model is discussed extensively in Chapter 19.

Description of the Vroom-Yetton Model

The leadership decision style that is most conducive to effectiveness in the Vroom-Yetton model depends on the demand characteristics of the situation. Particularly important is whether the leader is aiming for a high-quality decision or for the subordinates' acceptance of the decision. Efforts have been made to show an adequate correspondence between deductions derived from the model and what can be induced empirically from managers' preferred and actual styles in dealing with problems containing various combinations of the demand characteristics.

The Direction-Participation Continuum. Vroom and Yetton (1973, p. 13) laid out the direction-participation continuum as follows:

AI: You solve problem or make decision yourself using information available to you.

AII: You obtain necessary information from subordinates, then decide on the solution to the problem yourself. Subordinates are not asked to generate or evaluate alternative solutions.

CI: You share the problem with relevant subordinates *individually*, getting their ideas and suggestions.

Then you make the decision, which may or may not reflect your subordinates' influence.

CII: You share the problem with your subordinates *as a group*, collectively obtaining their ideas and suggestions. Then you make the decision, which may or may not reflect your subordinates' influence.

GI: You share the problem with relevant subordinates *individually*. Together you generate and evaluate alternatives and attempt to reach a solution. You do not try to influence the subordinate to adopt "your" solution and you are willing to implement any solution reached.

GII: You share the problem with your subordinates *as a group*. Together you generate and evaluate alternatives and attempt to reach a solution. You do not try to influence the group to adopt "your" solution, and you are willing to accept and implement any solution which has the support of the entire group.

Thus CI and CII are consultative leadership either with each subordinate alone or all together. Similarly, GI and GII are *participative* either with each subordinate alone or all together. Subsequently, Vroom and Jago (1974, p. 745) added another choice:

DI: You delegate the problem to one of your subordinates, providing him with any relevant information that you possess, but giving him responsibility for solving the problem by himself. Any solution which the person reaches will receive your support.

The choice of AI is *directive*. AII is also directive and CI and CII are consultative. GI and GII are *participative* and DI is delegative.

The Situational Demands. The situational-demand characteristics and the requirements of the problem for the leader depend on whether the answers to the following seven questions are "yes" or "no":

A. Is there a quality requirement such that one solution is better than another?

B. Does the leader have sufficient information to make a high-quality decision?

C. Is the problem structured?

D. Is the subordinates' acceptance of the decision critical to effective implementation?

E. If the leader were to make the decision by himself or herself, is it reasonably certain that the decision would be accepted by the subordinates?

F. Do subordinates share the organizational goals to be obtained in solving this problem?

G. Is conflict among subordinates likely in preferred solutions?

The Feasible Sets. Seven rules are imposed to limit various styles of leadership to those feasible sets that can be deduced to protect the quality of the solution and acceptance of the decision: (1) AI is eliminated as a possible choice for the leader when the quality of the solution is important and the leader lacks information; (2) CII is eliminated from the feasible set of leadership styles if quality is important and subordinates do not share organizational goals; (3) AI, AII, and CI are eliminated when quality is important, the leader lacks information, and the problem is unstructured; (4) AI and AII are eliminated from the feasible set if the subordinates' acceptance of the solution is critical; (5) AI, AII, and CI are eliminated (a group approach is necessary to resolve conflicts) if the subordinates' acceptance is critical and subordinates are likely to disagree about the solution; (6) AI, AII, CI, and CII are eliminated if acceptance but not quality is critical; and (7) AI, AII, CI, and CII are eliminated if acceptance is critical and subordinates share the organization's goals. Shared *participation*, GII, is deduced to be the only suitable leadership style.

Figure 18.1 shows the decision tree that must be followed, given the situational characteristics and the rules for eliminating choices of leadership styles. For example, in this flowchart, if the leader's answer to question A is that the problem does not require a high-quality decision, the leader's next decision is about whether the subordinates' acceptance is important (question D). If a directive decision is seen to be unacceptable (question E), the appropriate style for the leader to choose is GII, *participation* of the leader and all subordinates together in making the decision.

Figure 18.1 Decision Process Flowchart (Feasible Set)

A. Does the problem possess a quality requirement?
B. Do I have sufficient information to make a high-quality decision?
C. Is the problem structured?
D. Is acceptance of the decision by subordinates important for effective implementation?
E. If I were to make the decision by myself, am I reasonably certain that it would be accepted by my subordinates?
F. Do subordinates share the organizational goals to be attained in solving this problem?
G. Is conflict among subordinates likely in preferred solutions?

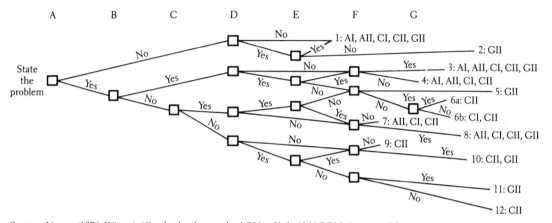

SOURCE: Vroom (1976, Winter), "Can leaders learn to lead?" New York: AMACOM, American Management Association.

Development of the Diagnostic Procedure

An initial roster of managers were asked to describe, in writing, a recent problem that they had to solve in carrying out their leadership role. The managers then specified the style (AI, AII, CI, CII, or GII) that came closest to the one they had actually used in dealing with that problem. They described the problem in terms of its quality and its situational-demand characteristics. The diagnosis of the situation determined what styles the leaders used. There was considerable correspondence between what the managers said they had done and what was prescribed by the decision tree (Vroom, 1976) based on Vroom and Yetton's (1973) model.

The problems disclosed by these managers were used to prepare 30 to 54 standardized cases that were then given to several thousand managers to diagnose in terms of the seven questions and to decide which style they would use. Most of the differences in the styles used depended on case differences rather than individual differences among the managers. Vroom and Yetton (1973)

concluded that, on the average, managers said they would (or did) use exactly the same decision style as the decision-tree model in about 40% of the situations. In two-thirds of the situations, the managers' behavior was consistent with the feasible set of styles proposed in the model. In other words, in only about one-third of the situations did their behavior violate at least one of the seven rules underlying the model.

Nevertheless, Vroom and Yetton also noted that the model called for more variance in style than the average manager recalled or proposed. Thus if managers used the model as the basis for choosing their leadership styles, all would become both more directive and more participative. They would use direction more frequently in situations in which their subordinates were unaffected by the decision. They would use participative approaches more frequently when their subordinates' cooperation and support were critical or their subordinates' information and expertise were required.

Table 18.1   Mean Freqency of the Choice Process for Dealing with Group and Individual Problems (N = 98)

Tannenbaum and Schmidt (1958)	Hersey and Blanchard (1969a, 1969b)	Sadler and Hofstede (1972)	Heller and Yukl (1969)	Bass and Valenzi (1974)	Vroom and Yetton (1974)
The leader decides and announces the decision.	The leader tells	The leader tells	The leader uses own decision with no explanation	The leader is directive	The leader uses AI, AII
"sells" the decision.	sells	sells	own decision with an explanation	persuasive— manipulative	
presents ideas and invites questions.		consults	consultation	consultative	
presents tentative decisions that are subject to modification.		consults	consultation	consultative	
presents problems, gets suggestions, makes decisions.		consults	consultation	consultative	CI, CII
defines limits and asks for a consensual decision.	participates	joins	joint decision	participative	GI, GII
permits followers to function within limits.	delegates		delegation	delegative	DI

SOURCE: Vroom and Jago (1978).

Individual versus Group Problems. The frequency of the choice of process reflects strongly whether the problem concerned the group or its individual members. Table 18.1 shows how 98 managers, military officers, and heads of research departments dealt differently with individual and group problems they faced. With group problems, managers more frequently chose CII and GII; with individual problems, they more frequently chose AI, CI, GI, and DI (Vroom & Jago, 1974). Consistent with the survey research summarized earlier in the chapter (Bass & Valenzi, 1974), the consulting styles CI and CII were the most popular solutions to the various problems presented. But a clear need was evident to distinguish between consulting with one's group or with individual members, depending on whether the problems concerned the group as a whole or particular members.

Vroom (1998) reported that over a 25-year period, there has been a rising choice among managers for the participative processes.

Evidence of Validity

Evidence to support or refute the validity of the model has been gathered in the field from numerous studies based on self-reports[11] and in the laboratory by Field (1982).

In Vroom and Jago's (1978) study of 96 managers from a variety of organizations who were unaware of the decision-tree model, the managers described 181 situations and their leadership behavior in these situations. The model was then used to predict the ratings of the technical quality, the subordinates' acceptance, and the overall effectiveness of the final leadership styles chosen by the managers. The managers noted the extent to which their chosen leadership style in the situation they described had resulted in a high-quality solution and the subordinates' acceptance. The logical Vroom-Yetton (1973) model and decision tree (Vroom, 1976) came up with prescribed leadership styles that matched what the managers reported they actually did in 117 (65%) of the

[11] See, for example, Margerison and Globe (1979), Pate and Heiman (1981), Vroom and Jago (1978), and Vroom and Yetton (1973).

181 situations. Among these 117 situations, 80 (68%) were judged to be effective in the situation and 37 (32%) were judged to be ineffective. In 64 instances, the chosen leadership style was outside Vroom and Yetton's feasible sets for the situation described. In those cases, only 14 (22%) were seen by the managers to be effective leadership behavior and 50 (78%) were seen as ineffective. The more often Vroom and Yetton's seven rules were violated, the solution was regarded as less effective, particularly when the subordinates' acceptance was involved.

Pate and Heiman (1981) reported the results of a survey of 530 mostly female supervisors, middle managers, and top administrators from seven hospitals. Three specially developed problem cases that were generated by the nurses and personnel directors were likely to call for autocratic (A), consultative (C), and delegative styles (D). When the respondents employed the Vroom-Yetton model and decision tree, 71% of their choices were within the model and 29% were outside it. These results were close to those of Vroom and Jago (1978) and Vroom and Yetton (1973).

A field validation was provided by Paul and Ebadi (1989) based on a survey of the job satisfaction and performance of 216 sales employees in a service organization. The leaders who used decision-making styles that agreed with the Vroom-Yetton model had more productive subordinates, and these subordinates were more satisfied with their coworkers.

Experimental Support. Field (1979) thought there was a need to examine the validity of the Vroom-Yetton model in circumstances that did not depend on the self-reports of managers. He conducted an experimental test in which 276 business students in four-person groups solved five decision-making problems. However, the students also were instructed to use different decision processes of the model for each problem. This forced more solutions that diverged from the Vroom-Yetton feasible set. Field found that decisions fitting with the Vroom-Yetton feasible set were significantly more effective than decisions outside the feasible set. Of the 105 decisions in which the leader's behavior agreed with the feasible set, 51 (49%) were effective, whereas only 31 of 87 decisions (36%) outside the feasible set were effective. One of three quality rules and three of four acceptance rules had effects as predicted. Pace, Hartley, and Davenport (1992)

validated the standardized cases in the Vroom-Jago (1988) scenarios in three laboratory studies. Both leaders and subordinates were aware of the need for situation-specific behaviors. Subordinate evaluations of leader effectiveness were most favorable when leaders made correct use of participative methods.

Scaling of Participation. According to Vroom and Yetton's (1973) model, the leadership decision styles could be judgmentally scaled according to the greater opportunities for subordinates to participate and to influence outcomes. The scale that emerged was roughly as follows: AI = 0; AII = 1; CI = 5; CII = 8; GII = 10. Jago (1978a) scored the amount of participativeness by leaders from 0 to 10 in choices of leaders' responses to 72 problems. He found that, as expected, subjects who used a variant of the model displayed less participativeness (4.1) when the leader in a stated problem had all the information required to make a high-quality decision than when he did not (5.9). More participativeness occurred (7.6) when the subordinates' acceptance was required and was not likely to result from an autocratic decision. Less participativeness occurred if such acceptance was likely to result from an autocratic decision (5.0) or when such acceptance was irrelevant (3.3). Also, more participativeness occurred when subordinates expected to share organizational goals (5.8) than when such goal congruence was not expected (4.9).

Caveat. Mixed support for the model came from Clement (1983), who found that only the sixth rule—the subordinates' acceptance is more critical than the quality of the decision—contributed significantly to the model's validity. Clement also found that the seventh rule—subordinates share organizational goals—undermined the validity of the model in matching its prescribed leadership behavior with responses chosen by financial executives and managers of nonprofit organizations.

Although Field acknowledged the possibility that subordinates may accept autocratic leadership in dealing with some of the Vroom-Yetton problems, experimental evidence gathered by Heilman, Cage, Hornstein, and Herschlag (1984) suggested that this may not occur. The latter researchers conducted two experiments in which a leader's reported actions were either correct or incorrect according to the Vroom-Yetton model. Nevertheless, no matter what the circumstances, subjects who took the subordinate's point of view favored a participative solution even when the model prescribed an autocratic one. This finding is consistent with Sinha and Chowdhry's (1981) study, which found that although the Vroom-Yetton and Hersey-Blanchard models prescribe that leaders be more directive with less well-prepared subordinates, such autocratic leadership was detrimental to the group's efficiency and the subordinates' satisfaction.

Alternative Models

Model of Randomness. Pate and Heiman (1981, pp. 8–9) suggested that the level of matching of the model prescriptives with outcomes could have been due to random responding. They advised that

> By selecting a style at random it is possible to trace the style backwards through the model and compute the probability that a style will be "within" the model . . . When this is done, the following probabilities result: .563 (A1 & A2), .680 (C1), .813 (C2), .750 (D), and .711 (any style). Thus, if a group of people chose any style and answered the decision rule questions blindfolded, 71.1% of their responses would be "within the model."

Wedley and Field (1982) examined the feasible-set choices of 102 undergraduates and 51 managers. However, the different branching that occurred to reach the various options was by no means random. In fact, the students and managers tended to prefer, to a high degree, the same particular branching of the decision tree leading to GII (participation with all subordinates together). This was only one branching among the 23 they could have followed.

Constructive Controversy. Tjosvold, Wedley, and Field (1986) proposed that a single concept, *constructive controversy*, could account for the greater effectiveness of the decision making. Constructive controversy encompasses cooperation ("We seek a solution that is good and acceptable to all"), controversy ("Persons express their own views fully"), confirmation ("Persons feel understood and accepted by each other"), collaboration ("We all influence each other"), and differentiation ("All ideas are expressed before we began to evaluate them"). The

investigators completed a study of 58 managers who retrospectively examined two previous problems. One decision was decidedly successful; the other was a failure. The managers applied the Vroom-Yetton model and described, on a 15-item questionnaire, how much constructive controversy had occurred in dealing with each of the two problems. Constructive-controversy scores accounted for 45% of the tendency to achieve a successful rather than a failing decision. Only 5% was attributable to the Vroom-Yetton model.

Model B. The original model, referred to here as Model A, is "time-driven" (Vroom, 1998). It is predicated on the short-term objective of minimizing the time of the leader and the subordinates. A somewhat different model, Model B, is required if long-term objectives for the subordinates' development are involved. Vroom (1998) now refers to the model as "development-driven." A sample situation in which Model A or B is used is illustrated below with a problem case (paraphrased).

> You manage a region for an international consulting firm with a staff of six consultants. One of them is the subject of complaints from several clients that the consultant is not doing an effective job, although the clients are not explicit about what is wrong. For his first four or five years, the consultant's performance was superb. Now he has a "chip on his shoulder" and has lost identification with the firm and its objectives. You need to deal with the problem quickly to retain the client who most recently complained. What should you do?

The decision tree analysis is as follows:

A. (Quality?) = Yes
B. (Leader's information?) = No
C. (Structured?) = No
D. (Acceptance?) = Yes
E. (Prior Probability of Acceptance?) = No
F. (Goal Congruence?) = No

Given the fact that the problem is about an individual, not the group, the synthesized model A and model B solutions are these.

Feasible Set   CI, GI
Model A Behavior   CI (Individual Consulta-
                                tion)
Model B Behavior   GI (Individual *Participa-
                                tion*)

Maier's and Field's Models. Field (1979) suggested returning to an earlier, simpler fourfold model, developed by Maier (1970b) on the basis of earlier creativity and problem-solving experiments.[12] According to the model, a Type I problem has a quality requirement, acceptance is likely to be obtained easily, and the decision should be made by the leader. Type II problems do not have a quality requirement, but acceptance is critical; therefore, these problems should be resolved by group decision. Type III problems do not have quality or acceptance requirements and should be decided by tossing a coin; participative approaches with this type of problem generate unnecessary conflicts. Type IV problems require both quality and acceptance and are solved by using persuasion or, better yet, by group discussion. Field also noted that in Figure 18.1, the decision CII is in the feasible set for 19 of the 23 situations included in the four types of problems. But in the four situations in which CII is not in the feasible set, GII is in the feasible set. A more parsimonious rule that Field (p. 256) proposed to protect the quality of the decision and the acceptance of subordinates is this: "If acceptance of the decision by subordinates is critical to effective implementation and it is not reasonably certain that subordinates would accept an autocratic decision, but they share organizational goals (or decision quality is not important), use GII; otherwise, use CII." This simple model uses only four situation-demand characteristics instead of seven, and only two leadership styles, CII or GII, instead of the five in the Vroom-Yetton model. Also, this simple model offers a balance between the short-term time-efficient Model A and the long-term group-development model B. Field concluded that what needs to be prescribed is either consultation with the group of subordinates or shared participatory leadership with the group, unless it is certain that a directive decision would be acceptable to subordinates.

Jago and Vroom (1980) ran a comparative test of the

[12] Maier (1960), Maier (1963), Maier and Danielson (1956), Maier and Hoffman (1960a, 1964), Maier and Maier (1957), and Maier and Solem (1962).

Vroom-Yetton prescriptions with those of Field (1979) as well as those of Maier (1970b). For each prescription, the actual reported behavior of 96 managers dealing with 181 cases was collected. Sixty-five percent conformed to the Vroom-Yetton model, 79% conformed to Maier's prescriptions, but only 33% conformed to Field's. Of the 117 decisions that conformed to the Vroom-Yetton model, 80% fit Maier's model and 50% fit Field's. Furthermore, the Vroom-Yetton model provided more predictive power of effectiveness, quality, and acceptance of the decision by subordinates beyond what Maier's and Field's prescriptions did. Jago and Vroom (p. 354) concluded that although Field's

formulation guarantees conformity to the Vroom-Yetton prescriptions, yet his rules presumably are easier to learn and apply because they involve fewer situational variables and fewer normative contingencies. However, the apparent attractiveness may be misleading. The behavior of untrained managers violates Field's prescriptions substantially more often than such behavior violates the prescriptions of either Maier's model or the Vroom/Yetton model. Because its highly participative prescriptions represent a large departure from the decision-making style of most managers, implementing Field's model would require some rather dramatic behavioral changes that may meet with some resistance. Although its prescriptions are indeed easy to learn, Field's model may be quite difficult for some managers to internalize and practice. On the other hand, the Vroom/Yetton model may be more difficult to learn initially but more easily internalized and implemented.

Individual versus Situational Differences

Another issue that has been looked at extensively is how much the Vroom-Yetton situational requirements determine which choices of leadership style will be made and how much individual differences arise. For instance, will authoritarians be autocratic in choosing a response to any Vroom-Yetton problem, regardless of the prescriptive rules and the nature of the problem? Vroom and Yetton (1973), Hill and Schmitt (1977), and Clement (1983) all demonstrated that situational main effects accounted for almost half the variance in choices, whereas individual differences were likely to account for less than 15% of the results. In dealing with problems about groups, 35% of the decisions were determined by the situation and 12% were due to individual differences in the preferences of the managers. In dealing with problems about individuals, 44% were due to situational elements and 9% to consistent individual differences among the managers (Vroom & Jago, 1974). Vroom and Yetton thought that these results suggested the need to talk more about autocratic and participative situations, rather than autocratic and participative persons. However, Jago (1978b) concluded, from an analysis of differences among managers in the rules they used, that there was a need to focus on autocratic versus participative decision-making rules. Furthermore, Jago's results indicated that the decision maker cannot be fully represented as a linear processor who handles the rules in a simple additive fashion. Rather, the decision maker's choices interact, to some degree, so that a more complex configuration may provide a better portrait.

Vroom-Jago Model. Vroom (1984) summed up some of the strengths and weaknesses of the model's fit with actualities. Generally, the model was supported by consistencies between decision-making styles and superiors' and subordinates' perceptions of decision-making requirements based on characteristics of the decision process. Nevertheless, he pointed to several deficiencies for practical application, owing to the simplicity in defining the variables that influence the decision-making process. Along with developing a differentiation for the group and individual problems faced by a manager (Vroom & Jago, 1974) and to take account of the failure of the original model to consider the importance of subordinates' knowledge, external influences outside the immediate work group, and the matter of time constraints, Vroom and Jago (1984) added the following questions to a determination of the feasible sets.

H. Do subordinates have sufficient information to make a high-quality decision?
I. Does a severe time constraint limit your ability to involve subordinates?
J. Are the costs involved in bringing together geographically dispersed subordinates prohibitive?

According to a simulational analysis by Vroom and Jago (1984), the subordinates' knowledge, lack of time constraints, or lack of geographic dispersion greatly increased the expanded model's prescription for participative rather than directive leadership.

Vroom and Jago (1988) created a new model with considerably greater validity than the original Vroom-Yetton model by adding a number of objectives, such as cost reduction, that could be sought by the leader. Further, five-point ratings were substituted for the yes/no responses. Multiple regression replaced deductions of the feasible sets. Effectiveness and commitment were introduced as alternative outcomes that might be sought by the leader. Also, they created conditions to encourage reflection on past decisions.

Summary and Conclusions

Decisions are made by the superior, the subordinate, or both. Conceptual distinctions can be clearly maintained between *direction*, negotiation, *participation*, and delegation. But empirically, most leaders exhibit all these modes with different patterns of frequency. Many antecedent conditions add to the variance found in these patterns. Participative leadership works best when the subordinates' acceptance, satisfaction, and commitment are important and when subordinates have the required information. But directive leadership can also be effective, especially when structure is needed, when the leader (but not the followers) has the necessary information, and when the quality of the decision is more important than the commitment of the followers. Leaders will increase their delegative tendencies if they have confidence in their subordinates' competence. Empirical and rational models are available for specifying the conditions under which either more direction or more participation is appropriate. Direction may often work as well as or better than participation in short-term laboratory studies, but greater payoff from participative leadership appears in the field for longer-term relations and outcomes, although the effects are small when subjected to meta-analyses. Whether the leader, the led, or both will decide is affected by the importance of the relations among them and by what needs to be done, as will be seen next.

CHAPTER 19

Task versus Relations Orientation

Most executives who make it to the top of their organizations are highly task-oriented. But many are also inclined to be concerned with their relationships. Ten CEOs and managing directors of divisions in a large, multinational firm were identified by a group of senior executives at the firm's headquarters. Vansina (1982) carried out a qualitative description of the 10 leaders using semistructured taped interviews that were subsequently content-analyzed. The 10 leaders were selected for their consistently "excellent performance in different business situations in different parts of the world" (p. 2). Vansina inferred that the leaders worked through people for whom they cared. They wanted to create an operating climate in which employees at every level in their organization knew what they were working for and what tasks needed to be done. Concerns about tasks and relationships were to be met by providing members with the appropriate means, authority, knowledge, and resources. The leaders had a keen interest in spotting and developing young talent and a low tolerance for poor performers. To establish organizational commitment, they saw their need to develop personal and professional relationships and collaboration through personal example, consultation, and removal of obstructions and incompetent people. They kept actions simple and followed them up to monitor progress. They carefully managed the linkages between headquarters and key persons, and between business objectives and social responsibilities. They were self-confident, responsible, and open-minded. They learned the local language and had direct contact with employees.

Concern for task and relations was illustrated by Andrew Grove, CEO of Intel, known for his innovation in the design and manufacture of computer chips. His egalitarianism came from his escape from Hungary during the Nazi occupation. For him, America was symbolized by respect for intellect and for others as human beings.

The culture of Intel he initiated combined informality in relationships, high standards, and hard work (Tolkoff, 1998). Also equally concerned about tasks and relationships, Robert E. Wood changed Sears from solely a mail-order business into a chain of retail stores with a strategy of meeting customer needs, buying to specification, building good relations with suppliers, and creating an image of each store as local rather than as part of a chain. He instituted a radically different hierarchy for a large organization. There were only five echelons between the salesclerk and the CEO. His belief in decentralization was buttressed by the need for employees and managers to grow and learn from their mistakes (Worthy, 1984).

Task, Relations, and Change Orientation

Leaders differ from each other in their focus of attention. Some focus more on the task to be accomplished, others more on the quality of their relations with others (Blank, Weitzel, & Green, 1990), and still others more on change. Bergan (1986) observed leaders concentrating on their group's working methods or on mutual trust building. Ekvall and Arvonen (1991) added that leaders may also concentrate on making changes. Effective leaders do any of these things, or all three. For instance, when Berkowitz (1953a) asked members of air crews to describe their commander with a behavioral description inventory, a factor analysis of the results revealed factors concerned with both task and relationships, including maintaining standards of performance, acting on an awareness of situational needs, maintaining coordination and teamwork, and behaving in a nurturant manner. The conceptualizations may be universal. Thus Shenkar, Ronen, Shefy, et al. (1998) reported that the Chinese manager's role could be partly accounted for by attention to task-related and relations-oriented activities.

Task-Oriented Leadership

Task-oriented leaders differ in their concern for their groups' goals and the means to achieve the goals. They engage more in task roles (Bass, 1967b; Fiedler, 1967a). They are more concerned with production (Blake & Mouton, 1964) and need for achievement (McClelland, 1961; Wofford, 1970). They are identified as achievement oriented (Indvik, 1986b), production oriented (Katz, Maccoby, & Morse, 1950), production-emphasizing (Fleishman, 1957a), goal achieving (Cartwright & Zander, 1960), work facilitative, goal emphasizing (Bowers & Seashore, 1966), performance planning and performance pressuring (Misumi, 1985; Peterson, Smith, & Tayeb, 1993). The leaders' assumptions about their roles, purposes, and behavior reflect their interest in completing assignments and getting the work done. A high task orientation underlies selected types of leaders, such as Birnbrauer and Tyson's (1984) hard driver and persuader or Reddin's (1977) autocrat. Purely task-oriented leaders are likely to keep their distance psychologically from their followers and to be more cold and aloof (Blau & Scott, 1962). When coupled with an inability to trust subordinates, their concern for production is likely to manifest itself in close, controlling supervision (McGregor, 1960). Successful task-oriented leaders are instrumental in contributing to their groups' effectiveness by setting goals, allocating labor, and enforcing sanctions (Bales, 1958a). They initiate structure for their followers (Hemphill, 1950a), define the roles of others, explain what to do and why, establish well-defined patterns of organization and channels of communication, and determine how to accomplish assignments (Hersey & Blanchard, 1981). Chapter 18 provided illustrations of executives—Jack Welch and Lou Gerstner—who were highly task-oriented and less concerned about interpersonal relationships.

Conceptions. Task-oriented leadership can be a source of expert advice and challenging motivation for subordinates. Misumi (1985) conceived of task-oriented leadership behavior as performance leadership—behavior that prompts and motivates the group's achievement of goals. For example, when deadlines are necessary, the leader clearly specifies them and has a good grasp of how work is progressing. According to Cleveland (1980), such a focus on the task is seen in strategic thinking, in projecting patterns of collective behavior, and in considering the whole situation. It is also seen in the leader's manifest curiosity about issues and methods and the system that can connect people and things to achieve objectives. Akin and Hopelain (1986) described a "culture of productivity" in three highly productive organizations. Immediate supervision, combined with management as a whole, can foster a shared image of a highly productive work setting in which supervisors, managers, and workers alike focus on the work being done and how to maintain successful operations.

Purposes. Yukl (1994) proposed five purposes of task-oriented leader behavior: (1) to propose an objective, introduce a procedure, present an agenda, and redirect attention to the task; (2) to stimulate communication, seek specific information, or encourage the introduction of new ideas; (3) to clarify communication, reduce confusion, ask for interpretations, and show how different ideas are related; (4) to summarize accomplishments, to review or ask for reviews; and (5) to test for consensus about objectives, interpretations, evaluations, and readiness for decisions.

Caveat. Although the various conceptualizations of task orientation have similar-sounding labels, their intercorrelations are not necessarily high. In fact, they may point to different attributes of an individual. Thus the direct assessment of the task orientation of 81 Polish industrial personnel—using the Orientation Inventory (ORI), which directly asks examinees for their preferred activities—correlated only 32 with the need for achievement as measured by the Thematic Apperception Test, an assessment of the projected fantasies of the same examinees (Dobruszek, 1967). Similarly, Fiedler's (1967a) determination of task orientation, based on the leaders' rejection of the coworker with whom they found it most difficult to work, did not correlate as highly with other approaches to measuring task orientation. (In fact, the least preferred coworker, or LPC, measure seems so unlike any other that it will be treated separately in this chapter.) Thus it is necessary to review results in the light of variations that are due to how task orientation and relations orientation are measured.

Relations-Oriented Leadership

Concept. Relations-oriented leadership is expressing concern for others, attempting to reduce emotional conflicts, harmonizing relations among others, and regulating participation (Yukl, 1994). Relations-oriented leadership is likely to contribute to the development of followers and to more mature relationships.

Leaders differ in the extent to which they pursue a human relations approach and try to maintain friendly, supportive relations with their followers. They are identified as relations-oriented (Katz, Maccoby, & Morse, 1950), concerned for maintenance (Misumi, 1985) or group maintenance (Cartwright & Zander, 1960; Wofford, 1970), concerned for people (Blake & Mouton, 1964), people centered (D. R. Anderson, 1974), interaction facilitative and supportive (Bowers & Seashore, 1966), interaction oriented (Bass, 1967b), employee emphasizing (Fleishman, 1957a), and in need for affiliation (McClelland, 1961). Such leaders are expressive and tend to establish social and emotional ties (Bales, 1958a). Dansereau and Yammarino (2002) have used the term *individualized leadership* to describe relations among leaders and subordinates that reflect an exchange of leader support for subordinates' feelings of self-worth and the subordinates' satisfactory performance. The relationship is revealed in the extent the leaders relate similarly or differently to each of their subordinates in the component of individual differences in WABA analysis. Dasborough and Ashkanasy (2003) suggest that leaders can shape affective events by positive uplifts or negative hassles. The negative hassles are more likely to be recalled by subordinates. Usually associated with a positive relations orientation are the leader's sense of trust in subordinates, less felt need to control them, and more general rather than close supervision of them (McGregor, 1960).

A strong relations orientation is the basis of Reddin's (1977) "missionary" and "developer" types of leader. Relations-oriented leadership is associated with consideration for the welfare of subordinates (Hemphill, 1950a). For Hersey and Blanchard (1982a, b), it is linked to relationship behavior: maintaining personal relationships, opening channels of communication, and delegating to give subordinates opportunities to use their potential. It is characterized by involved support, friendship, and mutual trust. It is leadership that is likely to be more democratic and employee-oriented rather than autocratic and production-oriented. Misumi (1985, p. 11) saw it as maintenance-oriented leadership behavior "directed toward dispelling excessive tensions that arise in interpersonal relations within a group or organization, promoting the resolution of conflict and strife, giving encouragement and support, providing an opportunity for minority opinions to be expressed, inspiring personal need fulfillment and promoting an acceptance of interdependence among group members."

Relations-oriented supervision is seen in the communication patterns of supervisors and subordinates. Kirmeyer and Lin (1987) arranged for observers to record an average of 107 face-to-face interactions with the supervisors of 60 randomly chosen police radio dispatchers. Communications with the dispatchers' supervisors were facilitated if the dispatchers felt they were receiving social support from their superiors. Felt support correlated .33 with the dispatchers' communications about work to their superior and .48 with communications to their superiors about other matters. It correlated .55 and .26 with observed face-to-face communications from the superiors to the dispatchers about work and nonwork matters.

Quality of Relations. Kottke and Sharafinski (1988) and Hutchison (1997) defined the quality of the relations of employees with their immediate supervisor according to how much the employees felt that their supervisors supported and cared about them. It was correlated with the quality of leader-member exchange (LMX) but could be distinguished from LMX, and from perceived organizational support. However, a Belgian-French study of 293 university alumni respondents found a correlation of .55 between perceived supervisory and perceived organizational support (Stinglhamber & Vandenberghe, 2001). A similar positive correlation was found between enacted supervisory and environmental support by Slack, Etchegary, Jones, et al. (2002). A high quality of relations might be found in self-sacrificing leadership (Choi & Mai-Dalton, 1999).

Organizational Systems. The concern for relations is manifest in different ways with different organizational systems. Such concern and effort are involved in shifting organizations from autocratic systems 1 and 2 to democratic systems 3 and 4 (Likert, 1977b) and in contributing to industrial democracy and participative management.[1] The concern for relations is central to humanistic management (Daley, 1986), which is dedicated to promoting the personal significance of work, the autonomy of employees, and fairness in appraisals. In Taiwan, it is seen as a matter of doing favors. It is seen in Britain with Theory P, a deemphasis of traditional management-employee relationships in favor of management's increased awareness of employees' needs, increased involvement in the community, and increased use of consultation (Jaap, 1982). It is seen in Japanese management and Theory Z, with its emphasis on long-term employment, unhurried evaluation and promotion processes, wide-ranging career opportunities, and consensual decision making. Theory Z leadership beliefs represent a mix of task direction and relations orientation; generating commitment, loyalty, and involvement in the organization; and treating followers as members of a family (Ouchi, 1981).

Examples: Relations-Oriented Executives. Herb Kelleher was credited by Wall Street analysts as the major reason for Southwest's continuing profitability after the first two years of business. Southwest often generated larger earnings than any of its competitors, which as of 2005 had registered increasing losses or gone bankrupt. Kelleher was a cofounder of the airline in 1971 and introduced low-priced, frequent point-to-point service instead of the hub-and-spoke service of the major airlines. He used a fleet of one type of aircraft, the Boeing 737, instead of the many types found among his competitors. His cost per available seat mile, employees per aircraft, and employees per passenger were as low as 50% to 75% of his competitors'. But he also ensured employees' and customers' satisfaction. In addition to providing employees with 15% of the net profits and matching up to 100% of individual employee contributions to their 401(k) retirement plans, his unusually good labor-management relations and his unusually friendly personality resulted in strong loyalty to the company. Employees were willing to do whatever was needed. (I was surprised, at a stop on my first trip on Southwest, to see the flight attendants cleaning up the aircraft cabin.) Pilots might help out as ticket agents, and ticket agents as baggage carriers. Individualized consideration, kindness, and spirit

were nurtured. Recruits were selected for their sense of humor. "Employees are our most important resource" may be a cliché, but it is a major principle at Southwest. Kelleher is like the very funny father of a family and the center of formal and informal festivities (Labich, 1994).

Ben Cohen and Jerry Greenfield, founders of successful Ben and Jerry's, were extremely egalitarian and focused on the human side of the enterprise, with a strong sense of social responsibility. Before selling their homemade ice cream company, they ran it like a human service agency. They practiced walk-around management and had fun with their employees and at their annual meetings. They formed a committee to put more joy into employees' work and decrease stress. They created an organizational culture of charity, goodwill, and respect for the community and kept their top salaries to five times the lowest employee base pay (Levine, 1988; Severance, 1988).

Other CEOs have showed that they cared about their employees in a variety of ways. Jack Stack of Springfield ReManufacturing emphasized teaching employees the financial aspects of the business. Patricia Gallup of PC Connection nurtured her more than 800 employees and interacted directly with them by e-mail. Mary Kay Ash of Mary Kay, Inc. felt she had compassion for her people and viewed them as more important than the bottom line.

The Need for Both Task and Relations Orientation

Blake and Mouton (1964), Cleveland (1980), and many others have strongly advocated leadership that integrates both task orientation and relations orientation. Leaders have to be strong and decisive, yet sensitive to people (Calloway, 1985). Blake and Mouton (1964) argued that maximum leadership effectiveness occurs only when the leader is highly concerned for both production and for people and integrates the human and task requirements of the job. The exclusively task-oriented manager is seen to treat employees as machines, to the detriment of their commitment, growth, and morale. The exclusively people-oriented manager is viewed as running a "country club," to the detriment of productivity.[2]

---

[1] See Chapters 15 and 21.

[2] Kahn and Katz (1953), R. Likert (1977a), and Oaklander and Heishman (1964), among many others, came to similar conclusions.

Leaders exhibit both task and relations orientation. Kaiser and Kaplan (2001) reported that although 46% of managers they sampled in their consulting work were highly task oriented and 19% were highly relations oriented, 6% were versatile in that they displayed just the right amount of both task and relations orientation. The remaining 30% were disengaged (laissez-faire). Further complicating matters are the "switch-hitters." The autocratic leader is likely to be directive and caught up with getting the work done and the democratic leader is likely to be participative and concerned about maintaining relationships; nevertheless, some benevolent autocrats, who pursue a patronizing leadership style, are still likely to be concerned about their relationships and the needs of their followers. Likewise, highly task-oriented democratic leaders may encourage participation in decision making for the sake of reaching high-quality decisions. Presumably, they would be characterized as R. Likert's (1977b) System 4 leaders.

Change-Oriented Leadership

Given the increased efforts required to keep up with rapid technological, societal, and market changes, Mintzberg and James (1985) suggested that leaders needed to have an "umbrella" strategy, concerned with getting new ideas accepted and implemented. Morgan (1986) proposed that it was important to focus on challenging constraints. Ekvall (1988) in Sweden and Lindell (1989) in Finland revealed an orientation toward change that they found factorially independent of task and relations orientation (Ekvall & Arvonen, 1989). The change-oriented leader was interested in innovation, creativity, new ways to accomplish old tasks, and new ways to relate to others. The change-oriented leader engaged in Argyris's (1982) double-loop learning and attention to feedback. In a Swedish factor study of 502 respondents in four manufacturing and five service firms, Lindell and Rosenqvist (undated) were able to confirm a three-factor model for 502 respondents to a 36-item questionnaire about their superiors' behavior and orientation to task, relations, and change. In a sample of 711 mainly middle managers attending management training centers in Sweden, Finland, and the United States who each described their boss, Ekvall and Arvonen (1991) extracted three orthogonal factors: change-centered, employee-centered, and

production-centered. (Nationality was inconsequential.) The change-centered boss was rated as a promoter of change and growth (pushes for growth; initiates new projects), had a creative attitude (saw possibilities rather than problems, offered ideas, encouraged thinking about new and creative ways and tried them), was a risk taker and was particularly willing to take risks in decisions, made quick decisions when necessary, and was visionary—engendering thoughts and plans about the future.

Relationship of Change Orientation to Concern for Task and Relation. As noted earlier, leaders may emphasize both task and relationships or neither. Observers can accurately discriminate among the ratings for emerging task and socioemotional leadership earned by interacting members of experimental task groups (Stein, Geis, & Damarin, 1973). Hermigar and Taylor (1980) found that the assessed receptivity to change of 80 middle-management administrators of public schools was high if the administrators were either highly concerned for people or highly concerned for productivity. But a lack of concern for either was connected with a lack of openness to change. Experience in leading change affected orientation. Tullett (1995) noted that 133 managers in charge of change projects in Britain were more likely to be innovative in their score on the Kirton Adaptation-Innovation Inventory than managers in general.

Antecedents of Task-, Relations-, and Change-Oriented Leadership

As with the tendencies toward and preferences for direction or participation, task, relations, and change orientation tend to depend on the leader's personal characteristics as well as situational contingencies. These contingencies include the characteristics of the follower, the organization, the task, the goals, and the constraints.

Personal Antecedents

Along with Bales (1958a) and Etzioni (1965), Downton (1973) surmised that *instrumental* (task-oriented) and *expressive* (relations-oriented) modes of leadership are assumed by individuals with different temperaments. Instrumental leaders are seen to be more aggressive, more able to tolerate hostility, and more anxious to be respected. Expressive leaders are more accommodating, less able to tolerate hostility, and more anxious to be loved. A variety of surveys and experiments demonstrated this linkage of personality to leadership orientation. For instance, Klebanoff (1976) used observers' and peers' rankings of the task- or relations-oriented behavior displayed by 160 participants in 40 small groups working on various tasks. Task-oriented leaders were more likely to have been firstborn children; they felt more personal autonomy and tended to be more actively involved. Menon (2003) found that among 370 managers, those who were more task-focused, goal-oriented, and persistent despite difficulties or distractions were more satisfied with their jobs. Task-focused students were more conscientious and emotionally stable and less hesitant and preoccupied. Konovsky (1986) analyzed the extent to which supervisors of 484 hospital subordinates were seen by their subordinates as providing emotional support and as helping to solve the subordinates' problems. Supervisors offering such support and assistance also scored higher in personal competence, sociability, emotionality, and altruism.

Helmich and Erzen (1975) surveyed 108 corporation presidents and found that task-oriented leaders lacked fulfillment as presidents. The needs of relations-oriented presidents were better met by their assignment. According to a study of 194 employees in a human service organization, persistence at tasks was greater if the employees perceived themselves to be self-efficacious (Seltzer & Miller, 1990). Bolino, Turnley, and Bloodgood (2002) argued that employees' favorable attitudes toward organizational citizenship provided organizations with social capital that contributed to better relationships and better performance.

The Orientation Inventory (ORI). Preferences of highly task-oriented examinees on the ORI (Bass, 1962c) included to be wise; to have the feeling of a job well done; to have bright, interesting friends; and to be a leader who gets things done. For interaction-oriented (relations-oriented) examinees, preferences included to have fun with friends, to have helpful friends, to work cooperatively, to make more friends, and to be a leader who was easy to talk to. According to scores on various personality inventories, personal factors significantly correlated with task orientation, as assessed by the ORI, included being more highly self-sufficient, resourceful, controlled in willpower, aloof, not sociable, sober-serious, tough-realistic, and aggressive-competitive (Bass & Dunteman, 1963). Task-oriented leaders were more likely to show more restraint, ascendance, masculinity, objectivity, thoughtfulness, endurance, need for achievement, and heterosexuality (Bass, 1967b).

Task orientation as assessed by the ORI was higher among men than among women and among those with greater maturity, education, status, and technical training. Task-oriented students were more likely to volunteer and to persist at tasks voluntarily until the tasks were completed (Frye & Spruill, 1965). They were self-reinforcers (Marston, 1964) and more likely to be seen as helpful to others in sensitivity training groups (Bass & Dunteman, 1963). In a Polish study, task orientation on the ORI was found to correlate positively as high as .41 with intelligence, as measured by a Polish version of the Army General Classification Test. Interaction (relations) orientation correlated negatively as low as −.32 with tested intelligence (Dobruszek, 1967). Relations orientation was higher among examinees who, according to various personality inventories, were warm, sociable, in need of affiliation, and dependent on the group (Bass & Dunteman, 1963). Relations orientation was also correlated with wanting to be controlled by others, to be close to others, to receive affection from others, to include others, and to be included with others (Bass, 1967b).

Immutable Conditions? These personal factors, seldom mentioned in the prescriptive literature of the past two decades, call attention to Fiedler's (1967a) argument that one often needs to find or change the situations to fit the leader's personality. These personal factors make managers and administrators skeptical about the possibilities of training and developing leaders to be both relations and task oriented and about those who say they already are. Nevertheless, the correlations of task and relations orientation with personality and intelligence are modest. Much can be changed in leadership orientation and behavior through learning, role modeling, and experience, reinforced by socialization processes and organizational culture.[3]

_____

[3] See Chapter 34.

Situational Antecedents

Leaders will be more concerned about the task when their superiors want them to remain focused on it. Managers who are under the gun to produce immediate results are more likely to be task oriented and less likely to devote time and energy to their relationships. Brady and Helmich (1982) found, in a survey of chief executive officers (CEOs) and their boards of directors, that the CEOs were more task oriented than relations oriented if their boards were made up of outsiders. The reverse was true if the boards were composed of insiders. Relations-oriented leaders are likely to emerge when leaders are more attentive to pleasing their followers than their superiors and, by definition, when they are more concerned about the needs of their followers.

In utilitarian hierarchies, organizational level makes a difference in orientation. For 6,434 subordinates in 13 countries describing their superiors, change orientation was most prevalent at the top and production orientation was most common at the bottom; relations orientation was about the same at both echelons (Arvonen, 1992). Nevertheless, senior managers seriously underestimate how much they are distrusted by lower-level employees (Howard & Wellins, 1994). Relations orientation is to be expected in communal organizations, such as the Israeli kibbutzim, whose espoused beliefs emphasize providing for members according to their needs. Socioeconomic differences between communities of workers are also likely to be of consequence. Thus Blood and Hulin (1967) reported that workers in communities in which one would expect adherence to middle-class norms (for example, small suburban communities) tended to favor a human relations style of supervision. Strong organizational policies supporting either a relations or a task orientation (or both) particularly coincide with a top management that provides role models for lower management and engenders task, relations, or change orientations among the individual managers and supervisors. Also, the leaders' orientation is likely to be affected by those below them.

Subordinates and Their Performance. Earlier chapters noted that poor performance by subordinates appears to cause much of the observed punitiveness of leaders. But good performance by subordinates appears to increase leaders' tendency to be relations oriented. In a study of routine clerical workers and their supervisors at a life insurance company, Katz, Maccoby, and Morse (1950) found that supervisors of high-producing sections were significantly more likely to be employee oriented than production-oriented. Barrow (1975) showed that increasing the performance of subordinates in a laboratory setting resulted in the leader becoming significantly more supportive. Decreasing the subordinates' performance caused the leader to become more task-oriented. This finding is consistent with Bass, Binder, and Breed's (1967) findings about the performance of a simulated organization (discussed below).

Farris and Lim (1969) showed that if the performance of groups was good in the past, the groups' leaders subsequently tended to be more relations-oriented. The leaders were more sensitive to the needs and feelings of the members and had more trust and confidence in the members. These leaders allowed members more freedom and autonomy in their work. Members were encouraged to speak out and were listened to with respect. The leaders gave recognition for good work, communicated clearly, stressed pride in the group, and emphasized teamwork. The leaders of high-performing groups were also more task oriented than were the leaders of low-performing groups, in that they maintained high performance standards without being punitive. They were less likely than the leaders of low-performing groups to be critical of their groups' performance and less likely to exert unreasonable pressure for better performance.

Jones, James, and Bruni (1975) could not separate cause and effect in a study of 112 engineering employees. But the results suggest the followers' influence on their leader's orientation and behavior, although the reverse possibility is also tenable.[4] Jones, James, and Bruni obtained correlations of from .41 to .55 between employees' confidence and trust in their supervisors and the extent to which their supervisors were seen as high in support, emphasis on goals, facilitation of work, and facilitation of interaction. As was noted in Chapter 7, Sanford (1951) found, in a survey of Philadelphia residents, that egalitarians wanted leaders who were warm and generally supportive, but authoritarians preferred leaders who would serve their special interests. Indirectly, one

---

[4]See Katz, Maccoby, and Morse (1950), whose results are mentioned later.

may infer that more relations-oriented leadership would be demanded by highly self-oriented followers, by followers with personal problems, by followers in need of nurturance, and by followers seeking affection. As will be detailed later, the "psychological and job maturity" of subordinates dominates the Hersey-Blanchard (1977, 1981) prescriptions for determining whether leaders should be relations or task oriented or both in their behavior toward subordinates.

Prior Effectiveness of the Organization. Commonly observed as well as deplored (see, for instance, R. Likert, 1977b) is the extent to which human relations concerns are abandoned when an enterprise's profits are seriously eroded. In such situations, akin to a stress response, task orientation is increased at the expense of relations orientation. Bass, Binder, and Breed (1967) demonstrated this phenomenon in a simulated budgeting exercise. The concern of decision makers for the satisfaction and well-being of employees and their willingness to accept more employee-centered solutions to problems in the areas of safety, labor relations, and management development were strongly influenced by whether the company had just finished a profitable year. In this exercise, MBA students were given one of three firms' year-end profit-and-loss statements. One firm showed a net loss of $86,000; the second firm's statement showed that moderate profits had been earned; the third firm reported large profits. Three-quarters of the students in the profitable circumstances recommended buying safety equipment. Only half of the students in the moderately profitable enterprise and only 25% of those in the firm that lost money were willing to spend the required funds to settle a strike quickly. The goals emphasized in the most profitable situation were the welfare, goodwill, and satisfactory operations of employees. The goals stressed in the firm that had experienced a loss were meeting competition and raising profits.

General Consequences of Relations-Oriented, Task-Oriented, and Change-Oriented Leadership

Three kinds of evidence are available: (1) the extent to which relations-oriented and task-oriented leaders are

seen to be more or less meritorious by others; (2) the differential impact of these orientations on the satisfaction of subordinates; and (3) the differential effects of these orientations on the performance of groups. Care must be maintained about the validity of the evidence. Consistently, one sees managers who describe themselves as both more task oriented and more relations oriented than their subordinates perceive them to be (see, for example, Rees & O'Karma, 1980).

Evaluations as a Leader

Reports on correlations of evaluations as a leader and relations or task orientation have generally found both orientations to be of positive importance. Followers' values affected the extent to which they favored leaders of one kind or another. Ehrhart and Klein (2001) reported that employees who were more interested in extrinsic rewards for performance favored more relations-oriented supervisors whereas employees who preferred more structure and security in their work favored more task-oriented supervisors. Mathieu (1990) found that among 298 ROTC cadets, those high in need for achievement preferred instrumental (task-oriented) leadership; those low in need for achievement preferred relations-oriented leadership.

Relations Orientation. Shartle (1934) used interviews and questionnaires in a comparative study of supervisors who were rated as either effective or ineffective. Effective supervisors did not differ from their ineffective peers in technical skills, but they were found to excel in their ability to interact effectively and in their interest in people. Similarly, Katzell, Barrett, Vann, and Hogan (1968) found that executives whose roles emphasized administrative, rather than technical, performance received higher performance ratings from their superiors.

Mann and Dent (1954b) studied supervisors who were rated for promotability by higher-level managers. Highly promotable supervisors were described by their employees as being good at handling people; approachable; willing to go to bat for employees; letting the employees know where they stand; pulling for both the company and the workers, rather than just for one or the other; and using general, rather than close, supervision. In turn, the highly promotable supervisors saw their own superiors as being good at handling people, letting the supervisors know where they stood, and permitting the supervisors the freedom to make decisions.

H. H. Meyer (1951) observed that effective supervisors regarded others as individuals with motives, feelings, and goals of their own and did not avoid interactional stress. Similarly, Kay and Meyer (1962), using both questionnaire and observational methods, found that higher-rated foremen were less production oriented and gave general, rather than close, supervision. Likewise, Walker, Guest, and Turner (1956) observed that effective supervisors established personal relationships with employees, stuck up for them, and absorbed pressure from higher levels of authority. A. N. Turner (1954) reported that workers regarded supervisors as good if the supervisors did not pressure their subordinates unnecessarily; were fair, friendly, and understanding; and did not tell subordinates to quit if they did not like the conditions.

Among the 17 Americans on the 1963 Mount Everest expedition, all of whom were highly task oriented, those who were most interaction oriented and highest on FIRO-B (Fundamental Interpersonal Relations Orientation-Behavior) expressed inclusion were rated highest in leadership. Lester (1965, p. 45) noted,

> The results pointed to the importance . . . of being emotionally responsive, affectionate and warm, inviting in manner, or placing primary value on the emotional give-and-take in face-to-face relations. The men reacted negatively to emotional constriction, to too much emphasis on method, efficiency, productivity, and the imposition of high impersonal standards.

However, when interaction-orientation scores are high at the expense of task-orientation scores—as when *ipsative scoring*[5] is used—task orientation, rather than interaction or relations orientation, is likely to correlate with merit as a leader.

Task Orientation. Rubenowitz (1962) reported that job-oriented supervisors were regarded by higher management as more effective than person-oriented supervisors. Shortly afterward, Kelly (1964) found that the technical features of executives' behavior outweighed the effects of personal style.

According to Dunteman (1966), task orientation, as measured by the ORI, correlated with promotability ratings based on three days of assessment of 96 supervisors (but correlations were negative among the younger, temporary supervisors and the journeymen who were so assessed). For both 66 first-level and 27 second-level supervisors, task orientation significantly contributed to their high on-the-job performance ratings by their supervisors (Dunteman & Bass, 1963). Rutherford (1984) reviewed studies of the success of elementary school principals. In attempts to implement new programs or to improve the schools, the successful principals appeared highly task-oriented. They made strong instructional efforts; set clear, high expectations for teachers and students; and monitored performance. They actively intervened when intervention was needed. The successful principals also paid attention to relationships, remaining in close contact with the teachers.

Many other studies, enumerated in Chapter 27, have found that leaders who are concerned about the task in situations in which such a concern is relevant are likely to be evaluated highly by others. Furthermore, the plethora of studies of the need for achievement[6] provide additional evidence of the positive association of task orientation and success as a leader.

Impact on Subordinates' Satisfaction

Supervisors' attention to relationships was seen early in several investigations focused on the impact on subordinates' satisfaction of psychological and social closeness or distance, a component of relations orientation. Julian (1964) found that job satisfaction was higher when there was psychological closeness between the leader and the led. However, Blau and Scott (1962) and E. R. Shaw (1965) reported that the cohesiveness of the group was strengthened by the social distance between the leader and the followers, and Sample and Wilson (1965) found cohesiveness to be unrelated to social distance. Still, the majority of reports from both field studies and laboratory experiments have indicated that subordinates' satisfaction with their leaders was linked to the leaders' relations-oriented attitudes and behavior. Particularly important for follower satisfaction, performance, and willingness

---

[5]In ipsative scoring, the task score and relations score sum to a fixed total—say, 100. If the task score is 65, then the relations score must be 35.

[6]See Chapter 8.

to follow the leader is the extent to which the leader evinces support for the followers' feelings of self-worth (Dansereau, Yammarino, Markham, et al., 1995). A supportive change-oriented supervisory attitude also lies behind subordinates' efforts to innovate (Delbecq & Mills, 1985) and to be creative (Langley & Jones, 1988).

Field Studies. Hoppock's (1935) analysis of the early literature on job satisfaction indicated that workers tended to feel more satisfied when supervisors understood their problems and helped them as needed. In a survey of more than 10,000 managerial, supervisory, and hourly personnel, Ronan (1970) obtained similar results, as did Roberts, Blankenship, and Miles (1968). Stagner, Flebbe, and Wood (1952) found that railroad workers were better satisfied when their supervisors were good at handling grievances and communicating with employees. Likewise, Bose (1955) observed that workers under employee-centered supervisors had more pride in their groups than those under work-centered supervisors. Mann and Hoffman (1960) found that in two plants— one automated, the other not—employees were more satisfied with supervisors who were considerate of their feelings, recognized good work, were reasonable in their expectations, and stood up for the subordinates.

Stampolis (1958) showed that the more employees rated their supervisor as fair, able to handle people, giving credit, ready to discuss problems, and keeping employees informed, the less the employees expressed a desire for their company to be unionized. Bass and Mitchell (1976) reported similar results for professional and scientific workers. The United Auto Workers had difficulty organizing the highly relations-oriented Japanese-owned automobile plants in the United States (Gladstone, 1989).

Wager (1965) found that a supportive style of leadership assisted the supervisor in fulfilling and satisfying the employees' role expectations. In an aircraft factory, where team leaders devoted much of their time to facilitating the work of the teams and attending to the members' personal problems, indicators of dissatisfaction, such as absenteeism and turnover, were lower (Mayo & Lombard, 1944).

York and Hastings (1985–1986) asked 172 employees working in North Carolina social services to complete the Survey of Organizations (D. G. Bowers, 1976). At all

levels of the assessed maturity of workers, facilitative and supportive performance of supervisors was associated with the subordinates' satisfaction and motivation to work. A review of nursing studies by Maloney (1979) concluded that people-oriented leaders generally were more satisfying to their employees. In addition, employees' grievances and turnover were lower when the leaders were seen as relations oriented.

When the socioemotional and task-oriented leadership of residence hall leaders were measured separately by MacDonald (1969), both were linked to the satisfaction of students. However, the effects of task orientation on subordinates' satisfaction have usually been found to be somewhat less consistent. Task-relevant behavioral measures, which contain elements of the leaders' punitiveness, will generate dissatisfaction, grievances, and turnover (Schriesheim & Kerr, 1974). In a survey of several thousand employees, R. Likert (1955) found that job satisfaction decreased as the supervisors' pressure for production increased. However, it is not uncommon to find positive correlations for both the task- and relations-oriented behavior of supervisors and the satisfaction of their subordinates. Generally, for nurse supervisors, for example, a strong task orientation that is not coupled with a high relations orientation results in less satisfied subordinates (Maloney, 1979). Gruenfeld and Kassum (1973) showed that nurses were satisfied with highly task-oriented supervisors, but only if the supervisors' people orientation was high as well. The strong task orientation of supervisors was dissatisfying when coupled with a medium or low orientation to people. But Arvonen (1995) found, in Swedish forest-product manufacturing, that supervisor task orientation—as revealed in their structuring, clarification, and ordering of work—did not produce dissatisfaction among blue-collar employees, as it did among white-collar employees and managers.

In a very large undertaking of over two decades, Misumi (1985) conducted studies of over 150,000 Japanese employees working in banks, post offices, coal mines, shipyards, transportation, utilities, and manufacturing, under supervisors with different performance (P) and maintenance (M) orientations. The supervisors were classified as P-type (above the median in performance alone), M-type (above the median in maintenance alone), neither type (pm), or both types (PM). The subordinates of a PM supervisor had a more favorable attitude toward their supervisor than did the subordinates of an M-type or P-type supervisor. The least satisfying supervisors were those who were pm types. In a bank that had branches in Okinawa, Misumi and Mannari (1982) surveyed an average of 1,325 subordinates who described their 303 superiors' leadership. The P and M leadership orientations of the supervisors, as well as the subordinates' morale (interest in work and satisfaction with supervision), were collected five times at 15-month intervals. The supervisors were changed in 287 groups but not in 159 groups. There was less change in morale from interval to interval if the supervisor did not change. However, the morale of the subordinates rose if the P and M leadership orientation of the supervisor's successor was higher than that of the former supervisor. The previous morale of the subordinates had less of an effect on the incoming supervisor's leadership than vice versa.

Along with relations and task orientation ($r = -.33$), change orientation also appears to contribute to satisfaction. Arvonen (1995) collected survey data from 781 employees in two production plants of a Swedish forest-products firm. Dissatisfaction and lack of well-being were less if supervisors were structure-oriented ($r = -.27$), relations-oriented ($r = -.33$), and change-oriented ($r = -.25$).

Laboratory Experiments. Experiments may provide additional convincing evidence of the relationship between a leader's relations orientation and subordinates' satisfaction. As with the field studies, most experimental studies have concluded that satisfaction of subordinates was positively associated with the leader's relations-oriented behavior. Wischmeier (1955) found that group-centered, rather than task-centered, discussions resulted in a warm, friendly group atmosphere. T. Gordon (1955) found that group-centered discussion was associated with members' sense of belonging, respect for others, ability to listen to and understand others, and loss of self-defensiveness. Similarly, Thelen and Whitehall (1949) and Schwartz and Cekoski (1960) reported that follower-oriented leadership enhanced satisfaction. Maier and Danielson (1956) reported that an employee-oriented solution to a disciplinary problem produced greater satisfaction in groups of problem solvers than a solution bound by legalistic restrictions.

Heyns (1948) coached one set of leaders to play a positive, supportive role that emphasized agreement, mutual liking, and cooperation. Leaders in another set were coached to play a negative role in which they overtly displayed a misunderstanding of the members and made no effort to develop their groups' cohesiveness. Although the two styles produced no significant difference in the quality of the groups' decision or the members' satisfaction, the groups with positive leaders exhibited evidence of greater cohesiveness. W. M. Fox (1954) used scenarios to coach leaders in a positive relations approach or a "biased, diplomatic, persuasive" role. Groups with positively supportive leaders exhibited higher degrees of cohesiveness and members' satisfaction but were slower in solving problems. With a different group of participants, W. M. Fox (1957) also found that supportive leadership was associated with the members' satisfaction and the groups' cohesiveness.

Impact on the Group's and Members' Performance

Zaleznik (1997) lamented the extent that attention to the task has suffered from too much concern for relationships. He attributed this to the increased complexity of the organization, in which managers and executives have to play many roles; and to the success of the human relations movement. This movement emphasized the need for cooperation and workplace harmony and had "an unhealthy preoccupation with process at the expense of productivity" (p. 7). The substantive hard work of business was displaced by psychopolitics; by "smoothing over conflict, greasing the wheels of human interaction" (p. 7); and by driving out the necessary "real" work of cutting costs and creating products. However, generally, we shall see that effectiveness is greatest when leaders attend to both task and relationships.

It may be difficult to separate the impact of the leader's orientation on the members' satisfaction from its impact on the members' and the group's effectiveness. For example, Medalia and Miller (1955) observed that human relations leadership and employees' satisfaction interact to influence the group's effectiveness. And although a leader's relations orientation and task orientation are both generally found to be positively associated with the group's productivity, the group's attainment of goals, and followers' performance, there are exceptions. Some situations may call for more relations-oriented leadership and others for more task-oriented leadership. However, it may be that in a vast majority of circumstances, strong doses of both types of leadership orientation are optimal.

When positive associations are found, it is usually inferred that the relations orientation or task orientation of the leader resulted in the improved performance of subordinates. But the reverse may be equally true. Few of the findings have been causal. That is, the previous performance of subordinates is as likely to affect the orientation of the leader as the leader's orientation is likely to influence the subsequent performance of the subordinates (Bass, 1965c). Farris and Lim (1969), as was previously mentioned, showed that the past good or poor performance of groups determined, to a considerable degree, the task and relations orientation of their leaders.

Relations-Oriented Leadership and Follower Performance. Pandey (1976) reported that groups with relations-oriented leaders generated more ideas than groups with task-oriented leaders. Katz, Maccoby, and Morse (1950) and Roberts, Miles, and Blankenship (1968) found that the performance of groups was higher under an employee-oriented style than under a more disinterested style of supervision. Philipsen (1965a, 1965b) also found that human relations leadership correlated positively with group effectiveness. But in a study of skilled tradesmen, Wison, Beem, and Comrey (1953) established that supervisors of both high- and low-performing shops were described as more helpful, sympathetic, consistent, and self-reliant than were those in medium-performing shops. Slack, Etchegaray, Jones, et al. (2002) reported that supervisory-espoused support was linked to enacted support. Enacted supervisory support was linked to employee performance because the employees perceived a supportive environment. Bliese, Bienvenu, Castro, et al. (2002) found that a supportive leadership climate played an important role in determining whether the stress of the work overload of soldiers on assignment in Kosovo could be buffered by job control. Abdel-Halim (1982) showed how much of subordinates' role conflict and role ambiguity—which affected their intrinsic satisfaction with, involvement in, and anxiety about their jobs—were moderated by the support they received from their supervisor. In the report by Konovsky (1986), supervisors who were judged by their 484 subordinates as helpful and emotionally supportive contributed to the subordinates' commitment to their hospital organization and to the supervisors' judged interpersonal effectiveness. Riegel (1955) found that employees' interest in their company's success increased when their supervisor was seen to help them with their difficulties, to give necessary training and explanations, and to "take an interest in us and our ideas."

Indik, Georgopoulos, and Seashore (1961) studied the employees of a transportation company. Their results indicated that high levels of group performance were associated with satisfaction with the supervisors' supportiveness, open communication, mutual understanding, and workers' autonomy on the job. As documented in Chapter 17, R. Likert (1967a, 1967, 1977b) concluded, from many surveys, that supportive attitudes toward employees, combined with the group's loyalty toward management, were associated with increased productivity and a desire for responsibility by the employees. With the introduction of a human relations approach to management, as well as high performance goals, long-term gains in productivity were achieved. Similarly, Daley (1986) surveyed 340 employees of Iowa public agencies and obtained uniformly positive associations between their perceptions of relations-oriented, humanistic management practices and their evaluations of the effectiveness and responsiveness of their organizations to the public. Stinglhamber and Vandenberghe (2001) obtained correlations of .44 and .38 between perceived supervisory supportive relations and employee satisfaction with job conditions.

Supportive leadership increases the likelihood that organizations can police and correct themselves. Near and Miceli (1986) found that the felt support from their leaders was the most important factor in protecting employees from retaliation for calling attention to observed wrongdoing. Conversely, in a random sample of 8,600 federal employees the perceived likelihood of retaliation for whistle-blowing correlated with the lack of support from their supervisors and higher management. This perception was realistic. Honest whistle-blowers were actually more likely to be punished than their corrupt senior managers in the Department of Housing and Urban Development under Samuel Pierce from 1981 to 1988.

Ramus and Steger (2000) surveyed 353 employees in 12 countries in large environmentally-proactive companies with headquarters in Europe. The survey disclosed that employees who perceived management support were willing to promote self-described environmental initiatives. Without such perceived support, they were unlikely to do so.

Deluga (1988) noted that faculty members in a school of higher education, when negotiating a second time, reduced their bargaining and use of authority as influence strategies if the leadership was perceived as relations-centered.

Correlations of Task-Oriented Leadership with Performance. In contrast to the above in Deluga's study of influence strategies, faculty member bargaining, assertiveness, coalition formation, and reference to higher authority emerged if the leadership was perceived as task centered. R. Likert (1955) reported that a survey of several thousand workers indicated a tendency for productivity to be higher in the presence of higher pressure by supervisors for production. Similarly, Litwin (1968) noted that experimental groups whose leaders had a strong need for achievement were much more productive than groups whose leaders had a great need for affiliation or power. Dunteman and Bass (1963) studied foremen who had an interaction orientation or a task orientation. Groups who worked under task-oriented leaders were more productive than those under interaction-oriented leaders. Mann, Indik, and Vroom (1963) showed that the productivity of workers was associated with the supervisor's task orientation. R. Cooper (1966) also reported that first-level supervisors whose bosses judged them to be higher in "task relevance" tended to have more productive and more task-motivated subordinates.

For 14 U.S. Navy airplane-maintenance groups, R. Likert (1977a) reported a strong association between the extent to which supervisors facilitated the work by helping with advanced scheduling and offering new ideas to solve problems in the job, and the extent to which airplanes serviced by the groups were not involved in accidents or disasters because of operational failures.

Effects of Change/Development Orientation. Lindell and Rosenqvist (undated) reported results for change and development styles for 502 Swedish cases from four manufacturing and five service companies. Management change correlated .67 with managerial competence, .73 with comfort with the manager, and .17 with comfort with the employees' own tasks. The comparable correlations for managerial development were .67, .53, and .24. For task orientation, the correlations were .59, .52, and .26. LaPolice and Costanza (undated) found that a three-factor model, which included change-related leadership along with task and relations orientation, was the best predictor of the behavior of 16,795 employees from 16 government agencies Analyses were based on the Office of Personnel Management's Organizational Assessment Survey.

Effects of a Combined Task and Relations Orientation. There is considerable theoretical and empirical support for the idea that regardless of circumstances, the effectiveness of leadership is greatest when the leaders are both task oriented and relations oriented in attitudes and behavior. Thus Patchen (1962) reported that the leader who maintained high performance norms, encouraged efficiency, and attempted to obtain rewards for followers was likely to have a high-performing group. However, the maintenance of high performance standards alone and attempting to obtain rewards for followers alone each had a negative effect on productivity. These two patterns of behavior had to be combined to have a positive impact on productivity.

Numerous other studies and lines of investigation have supported the utility of a combined high task- and relations-oriented approach to leadership. Tjosvold (1984b) demonstrated, in an experiment with 56 college students, that the students were most productive in completing a subsequent task if they had experienced beforehand a leader who nonverbally conveyed warmth and who was directive about what was to be done. The experience of the warm leader, along with the absence of direction, was satisfying but was least conducive to subsequent productivity. Similarly, Klimoski and Hayes (1980) found that the effort, performance, and satisfaction of 241 assistants in the production department of a large information-processing firm were enhanced if the supervising editors were task centered in being explicit in their expectations and consistent in their demands, as well as supportive of their employees. Daniel (1985) found that subordinates perceived that they were working in a more productive organization if their managers were concerned both about tasks and about people. Hall and Donnell (1979) conducted a survey study of 2,024 subordinates who described their managers' attention to the demands of the task and concern for the quality of manager-subordinate relationships. The managers who were high in both earned high "career achievement quotients." (The quotient reflected the speed with which they had climbed their organizational ladder.) They were also the most collaborative in their leadership style. These results were consistent with findings by Blake and Mouton (1964) and J. Hall (1976) for large samples. The moderately successful managers had a low relations orientation but a high task orientation, while those whose career success was lowest were low in both task and relations orientation.

Erez and Kanfer (1983) argued that the relations orientation implied in allowing subjects to participate in goal setting enhanced the task-oriented impetus for more goal setting than did assigning goals to subjects without permitting them to participate in setting the goals. Erez, Earley, and Hulin (1985) obtained experimental evidence to show that such participation increased acceptance of the goals and hence increased productivity. However, Erez (1986) found that the organizational culture from which the participants were drawn affected the need for such participation: subjects from the Israeli private sector did better with assigned goals; subjects from the kibbutz sector did better with group participation in setting goals.

As described earlier in discussing the utility of participation, Locke, Latham, and Erez's (1987) critical experiment tried to understand why, in their respective investigative efforts and using the same standardized experimental conditions, assigning goals to subjects generated more productivity in the United States (Latham & Steele, 1983), while allowing the subjects to participate in goal setting generated more productivity in Israel (Erez & Arad, 1986). The one difference that turned out to account for the highly significant difference in productivity was that the Israeli experimenter was curt and unsupportive in giving instructions, but the U.S. experimenter was friendly and supportive. The friendly, supportive experimenter's instructions facilitated the subjects' acceptance of the assigned goal without their having participated in setting it.

Misumi (1985), and Misumi and Peterson (1985), consistently found, in the previously mentioned studies of 150,000 Japanese employees in business and industry,

greater productivity by employees under PM supervision than under pm supervision—that is, under managers who were above rather than below the median in both performance orientation and maintenance orientation. In one of these studies, P and M were systematically manipulated for coordinated first-level and second-level supervision in an experiment with 15 postal trainees working in trios. The PM-type first-level supervision generated more productivity than did either P or M alone. Second-level supervision, present only in the form of written instructions to the subjects from the second level, had the same effects, although with less statistical significance. For 215 of 500 groups of coal miners, when the second-level supervisor was actually present, the PM pattern at both the first and second level of supervision was most typical for the high-producing groups. For 186 working groups of about 10 employees each, involving a total of 2,257 workers in a Mitsubishi shipyard, evaluations of group meetings were most positive under PM-type leaders (evaluation mean = 17.5), followed by M-type (mean = 16.4), P-type (mean = 15.3), and pm-type (mean = 14.5) leaders.

The rated performance of 92 squads in a bearing manufacturing firm was most often high under PM leadership and least often high under pm leadership. The results for ratings above the median for P alone or above the median for M alone were in between. The same pattern emerged in a tire-manufacturing firm, where the success or failure rate of 889 project managers was strongly associated with their style of leadership: PM, P, M, or pm. The success rate was highest (52%) and the failure rate was lowest (5%) with the combined PM style.

Peterson (1988) concluded that introducing PM theory and practice in China and the West may need modification. For instance, more attention may need to be paid to merging self-interests with working hard. Peterson, Smith, and Tayeb (1993), in a British and in a U.S. plant, found results consistent for M but unlike those in Japan. "Pressuring" leadership was negatively related to interpersonal cooperation. This was confirmed when Royal Australian Air Force service personnel and blue- and white-collar employees were questioned about how much they liked or disliked supervisory pressure statements such as, "Hurry up, you have to work harder" and "There are a number of tasks I want you to complete today" (p. 263). As will be noted in Chapter 20, such pressuring for production had to be eliminated from the "initiation of structure" factor assessment in the Leadership Behavior Questionnaire to improve its prediction of subordinates' satisfaction and performance (Fleishman, 1973). In order to be palatable to Australian subordinates, such statements had to be preceded by socioemotional supportive statements such as, "You have been doing a good job" and "I appreciate the extra effort you have been making" (p. 263).

Negative Evidence. A number of additional exceptions to the positive effects of task or relations orientation on productivity have been reported, particularly in short-range analyses. Andrews and Farris (1967) found no evidence that innovation was higher when supervisors of scientific personnel were high in both task and human relations functions. Human relations skills had little moderating effect on the generally positive relationships between the leader's carrying out task functions and innovation. The most innovation occurred under supervisors who were neither high nor low in their attention to human relations, regardless of the task functions that were completed.

Lundquist's (1957) results indicated that regardless of whether supervisors were worker-oriented, the sheer frequency of their interaction with workers increased their effectiveness. Weitz and Nuckols (1953) found that supervisors' scores on a test measuring human relations orientation were not related to the productivity of the group or to the turnover of personnel. MacKinney, Kavanagh, Wolins, and Rapparlie (1970) found that both production-oriented and employee-oriented management were unrelated to the satisfaction of employees. Carp, Vitola, and McLanathan (1963) showed that supervisors of effective postal teams maintained their social distance from subordinates, an attitude that reduced the surfacing of emotional problems. Fernandez and Vecchio (1997) found little descriptive utility in the Hersey-Blanchard predictions of the performance of university employees. However, they did find that supervisory monitoring had a positive impact on lower-level employee performance, and supervisory consideration had a positive impact on higher-level employee performance.

In a study of simulated management groups, Kaczka and Kirk (1967) established that the profitability of teams was associated with relations-oriented leadership. But

this type of leadership also resulted in less pressure to accomplish tasks and less cohesiveness in the groups. C. A. Dawson (1969), studying the achievement of schoolchildren, observed that the children performed equally well under "cold" or "warm" leadership.

Blake and Mouton's Grid Theory

Among the models of task and relations orientation of the past 40 years with the power to survive into the twenty-first century are Blake and Mouton's (1964) Grid, Hersey and Blanchard's (1969 a, b) Situational Leadership, and Fiedler's (1964a, 1967) Contingency Model. Fiedler and Hersey and Blanchard emphasized that what the leader should do to be effective depended on diverse circumstances. But Blake and Mouton (1964) prescribed the integration of task and relations orientations as the one best way to achieve effective leadership. Their managerial grid (see Figure 19.1) is based on the concept that managers and leaders vary from 1 to 9 in their concern for people (the vertical axis of the grid) and from 1 to 9 in their concern for production (the horizontal axis). The measurement of these concerns is based on a manager's endorsement of statements about management assumptions and beliefs. But these concerns are interactive rather than independent. They are manifested in the five styles shown on the grid as published in 1985 (Blake & Mouton, 1985) and "softened" in a later version by Blake and McCanse (1991), with concern for production replaced with concern for results.

The revised grid and its expected effects are shown in Figure 19.1. Further elaboration was provided by Blake and McKee (1993).

9,1: *Authority-Compliance Management.* Efficiency in operations results from arranging conditions of work so that human elements interfere to a minimum degree. Expected effects: Productive, but quality suffers. Strong conflict, resentment, antiorganizational creativity, and efforts to "beat the system" are high.

1,9: *"Country Club" Management.* Thoughtful attention to the needs of people for satisfying relationships leads to a comfortable, friendly organizational atmosphere and work tempo. Ex-

Figure 19.1 Managerial Grid

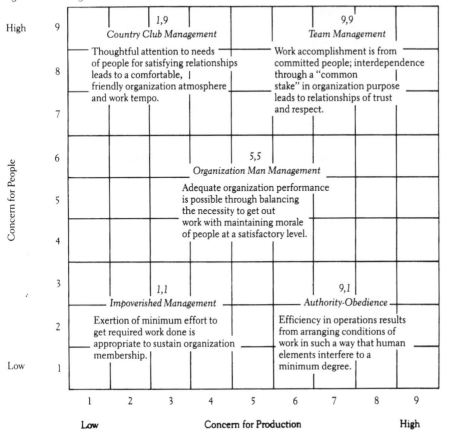

SOURCE: Blake and Mouton, *Managerial Grid III: The Key to Leadership Excellence.* Houston, TX: Gulf Publishing, 1985.

pected effects: Low productivity, indifferent quality, low conflict, easygoing and pleasant atmosphere.

1,1 *Impoverished Management.* Exertion of minimum effort to get required work done as appropriate to sustain organization membership. Expected effects: Low productivity and quality, poor creativity, low conflict, low involvement.

5,5: *Middle-of-the-Road Management.* Adequate organizational performance is possible through balancing the necessity to get out work with maintaining morale at a satisfactory level. Expected effects: Acceptable performance based on the status quo, moderate quality, good team players who go along to get along, low creativity.

9,9: *Team Management.* Work accomplishment from

committed people; interdependence through a "common stake" in organization, purpose leads to relationships of trust and respect. Expected effects: High productivity, quality, and creativity stimulated by internalized goals and objectives; commitment to goals, resulting in a high degree of interdependent cooperation; conflict is productive confrontation. 9,9 can take the form of paternalism if the leader fails to integrate the concerns for people and results—that is, if the two are kept in logic-tight compartments. The leader cares as father or mother for dependent subordinates, from whom unconditional loyalty is expected.

Opportunistic leaders use several styles interchangeably, depending on the persons with whom they are dealing. Sometimes leaders masquerade as 9,9s when they really are paternalists or opportunists hiding behind facades.

The leader's dominant style is likely to be backed up by other styles. Thus, for instance, the 1,9 leader may begin a meeting in a casual, friendly way but quickly become a tough, no-nonsense 9,1, which is his or her dominant style (Blake & Mouton, 1985c).

Team leadership (9,9) is prescribed. It is attained by behavioral science principles that involve participation, openness, trust, respect, involvement, commitment, open confrontation to resolve conflicts, consensus, synergistic utilization of the human resources represented by the leader and followers, mutually determined management by objectives, mutual support, and change and development through feedback (Blake & Mouton, 1981a).

According to a study reported by Blake and Mouton (1985c), prior to a seminar on the subject, 68% of the managers saw themselves as 9,9; 10% as 9,1; 19% as 5,5; and 2 to 3% as 1,9 or 1,1. After the seminar, a modal 41% admitted to being 5,5 and another 36% saw themselves as 9,1. Only 16% now believed they were 9,9. Blake and Mouton thought that these changes in results indicated the self-deception that occurs if understanding is impaired and feedback is not provided.

According to Blake and Mouton (1978), a 9,9 orientation has consistently proved to contribute positively to a variety of performance criteria in organizational development studies. In one of these studies, two matched subsidiaries of the same company were involved in a pre-post comparison over 10 years. One subsidiary engaged in an extensive organizational development program that stressed 9,9 management; the other was not involved in any comparable program. The experimental subsidiary increased its profitability by 400% over the matched control.

In a study of 716 managers from a single firm, Blake and Mouton (1964) found (after correcting for age differences) that 9,9-oriented managers were more likely than those with other dominant styles to advance further in their careers. J. Hall (1976) replicated these findings with an independent sample for 731 managers from a variety of companies.

Blake and Mouton (1985b) determined that the 9,9 style of team-management orientation characterized the leadership of the twentieth-century U.S. presidents who had performed with greatness, in contrast to those who had not. This style was inferred from contemporary writings about the presidents' different ways of decision making, exercising initiatives, analyzing problems, taking advocacy roles, dealing with conflicts between themselves and their subordinates, and using critiques to increase their effectiveness in achieving results with and through subordinates.

Situational Contingencies Affecting Outcomes

Blake and Mouton did not leave much room for exceptions. Nevertheless, in a substantial number of investigations of the impact of task and relations orientation the findings have been mixed or negative. Explanations have been sought in situational contingencies. These situational contingencies need to be examined for their moderating effects on the impact of relations- and task-oriented leadership on the satisfaction and productivity of followers. For instance, Miner (1982a, 1982b) suggested that high-task, high-relations leadership orientation is most likely to be effective when organizations are a mix of systems of hierarchies and groups. The task orientation fits the hierarchies; the relations orientation fits the groups.

One example of a moderated result was the upward influence tactics used by subordinates who were subjected to task- or people-centered leadership in Deluga's (1987b) study of 48 faculty members at a school of higher education. Deluga found that in the faculty members' first attempt to influence their superiors, only the superiors' relations orientation was of consequence. The faculty members said they were less likely to bargain or appeal to a higher authority if their superiors were more people centered. But if their first attempt failed to influence their superiors, the task orientation of the leaders became important in the second attempt. Here, the faculty members said that the more they thought their superior was task-centered, the more likely they would be to try friendliness, bargaining, assertiveness, appeals to a higher authority, and forming coalitions.

The Subordinate as a Moderator

Although relations-oriented leadership was expected to generate more satisfaction among subordinates, moderating effects were seen in a number of investigations. In a study of community hospitals, F. C. Mann (1965) observed that the satisfaction of the nurses was related to the human relations skills of their supervisors, but the satisfaction of the nursing supervisors was related to the administrative skills of their superiors. The satisfaction of the hospital technicians was related to their supervisors' technical and human relations skills. Tannenbaum and Allport (1956) studied two departments of women workers. One department was given more responsibility and authority for work and for decisions about the work, and the second department emphasized top-down line authority. A personality test was administered initially and scored as to the suitability of the workers' personality to the situation in which they worked. One year later, an attitude test was administered. The results of the test revealed that significantly more suited than unsuited workers in the situation with more authority and responsibility wanted the situation to continue. However, suited and unsuited workers did not differ in their attitudes toward the program if they had not been given authority and responsibility. In another large-scale field study, Seashore (1954) found that supportive leadership with cohesive work groups paid off in higher productivity. However, the same group cohesiveness also resulted in lower productivity when the groups' supervisors were unsupportive.

A number of investigators saw the followers' need for achievement as making a difference in the way the followers reacted to particular styles of leadership. W. W. Burke (1965) discovered that followers with a high need to achieve who had socially close leaders rated their situation as more tense than did those with a high need to achieve who were under socially distant leaders. Followers with a low need to achieve who had socially close leaders rated their situation as more tense than did followers with a high need to achieve who had socially distant leaders. Followers with a high need to achieve rated socially close leaders high in authoritarianism; those with a low need to achieve did the same for socially distant leaders. Misumi and Seki (1971) also studied the effects of leadership style on the performance of students with a high or low need to achieve. Those who were achieve-

ment oriented performed best under a PM leader. In groups whose members had a low need to achieve, performance was best under a P-type leader.

Constraints and Goals as Moderators

Several studies obtained results suggesting that the style of supervision interacted with situational variables to influence productivity and satisfaction with the job. For example, Lundquist (1957) reported that foremen who are worker oriented produce better results in small groups than in large groups. In an Indian study of officers in central government departments, Srivastava and Kumar (1984) demonstrated that high task and high relationship styles of leadership both contributed to the effectiveness and adaptability of the middle-level officers; however, they did not do so for the junior-level officers. Nealey and Blood (1968) showed that among nurses in a Veterans Administration hospital, task-oriented first-level supervisors received higher performance appraisals, but it was the people-oriented second-level supervisors who received such higher performance appraisals. Although the subordinates' job satisfaction was correlated significantly at both levels with the supervisors' people orientation, task orientation contributed to the nurses' job satisfaction at the first but not at the second level of supervision.

The Task as a Moderator

W. W. Burke (1965) found that a group's performance of a coding task was completed more effectively under a production-oriented leader, but the completion of a decision task was carried out more effectively under a relations-oriented leader. Weed, Mitchell, and Moffitt (1976), among others, found that it was necessary to take the tasks into account to uncover the moderating of the linkage between a leader's relations orientation and the subordinates' satisfaction as a consequence of the subordinates' personality and orientation. Overall, they studied the effects of task versus relations orientation on a group's performance and satisfaction with supervision as a function of the subordinates' personality and orientation. They compared leaders who scored high in human relations orientation and high in task orientation, low in human relations orientation and low in task orientation, low in human relations orientation and high in task orientation, and high in human relations orientation and low in task orientation. Each leader worked with subordinates high or low in dogmatism. Subordinates varied in their task and relations orientations as well. Regardless of their personality and orientations, the subordinates were significantly more satisfied with leadership behavior that was high in human relations orientation. But Weed, Mitchell, and Moffitt had also varied the ambiguity and difficulty of the tasks. The interacting effects of the leadership style—relations or task oriented—and the subordinates' relations or task orientation were strongest on difficult and ambiguous tasks than on clear and easy tasks. That is, the compatibility of the leader's and follower's personality made a difference only if the task was difficult and ambiguous.

Wofford (1971) obtained results indicating that a relations-oriented manager is likely to be more effective in terms of the productivity and morale of the group in simple, centralized, structured operations. Shaskin, Festinger, Willerman, and Hyman (1961) generated somewhat different and more convincing evidence in an experiment with work groups matched in age, productivity, seniority, and disciplinary records. For three weeks, managers were friendly and helpful to the favored group, which they praised. To the unfavored group, they were threatening, reproving, and deliberately annoying in their demands. The favorable and unfavorable relations ceased at the end of three weeks, when minor changes in work were instituted. Table 19.1 shows the percentage of assembled units requiring repair during each phase of the experiment. When the employees continued to work on old, familiar tasks, the unfavorable supervision had only slight effects on their performance. But when a changeover occurred that required work on new, unfamiliar tasks, the repair rates of the unfavored group jumped much higher than those of the favored group. Equally important, although the favored group rapidly returned to its normal repair record by the end of the third week after the changeover, the unfavored group continued to exhibit a repair rate that was three times worse than its normal record before the onset of the unfavorable supervisory relations. Unlike the results of surveys, this experiment demonstrated that unfavorable supervisory human relations cause decrements in performance primarily when new learning is required, not when accustomed tasks are performed.

Management Functions as Moderators

Woodward (1958) reported that friendly supervisors were rated as more effective in service departments but less effective in production departments. Consistent with this finding, B. Schneider (1973) noted that in social service agencies, supervisors set examples of how they expected their subordinates to relate to clients. Satisfied clients coincided with friendly, concerned, supervisory relations with subordinates. Schneider also found that good customer relations at a bank reflected good relations between the bank tellers and their superiors. Relations-oriented supervision thus would seem to be particularly indicated in service operations.

The manager and the coach of English football teams differ greatly in function. The manager has little continuous contact with the players, whereas the coach main-

Table 19.1 Quality of Work Done Before and After the Changeover of Work Groups That Were Subjected to Favored and Unfavored Supervisory Treatment

Phase of the Experiment	Percentage of Assembled Units Requiring Repair	
	Favored Group	Unfavored Group
During the first week of contrived disturbance	10.6	11.8
During the second two weeks of contrived disturbance	11.7	14.7
The first week after the changeover	21.1	31.4
The second week after the changeover	13.8	28.0
The third and fourth weeks after the changeover	11.6	29.0

SOURCE: Schachter, Festinger, Willerman, and Hyman (1961), p. 206.

tains a high degree of contact. Cooper and Payne (1967) found a correlation of .72 between the task orientation of the team coach and the success of the teams in winning games, but the correlation was close to zero for managers.

Interrelations with Other Leadership Behaviors as Moderators

The effects of other types of behavior by the leader moderate the impact of the leader's task or relations orientation. Thus Larkin (1975) showed that task-oriented elementary school teachers created high morale among pupils, regardless of how much they also resorted to power. But teachers whose task-oriented behavior was low and who used power generated rebellious pupils. Among supervisors of technical personnel, participative approaches (the provision of freedom) resulted in the most innovation if the supervisors were low in task or human relations orientation (Andrews & Farris, 1967). In an experiment with small groups of ROTC students, Anderson and Fiedler (1964) found that those under task-oriented leaders were most productive and satisfied when the leaders were participative, but the students' satisfaction was greater when relations-oriented leaders were directive. Similarly, Pandey (1976) showed that the behavior and effectiveness of relations- and task-oriented leaders of discussion groups depended on whether the leaders were appointed, elected, or rotated: the elected and rotated leaders tended to be more participative than the appointed leaders.

A number of models of situational or contingent leadership have been constructed to provide advice to leaders on when they should be task-oriented and hence directive and when they should be relations oriented and hence participative. The Hersey-Blanchard situational leadership model has been widely applied but has received less research support than the Fiedler contingency model, which has been more widely researched than applied.

The Hersey-Blanchard Situational Leadership Theory (SLT)

Basis

The Hersey and Blanchard (1969a) situational leadership model was built on propositions that were based on Hersey and Blanchard's understanding of prior empirical research:

1. Leadership styles vary considerably from leader to leader (Stogdill & Coons, 1957).

2. Some leaders' behavior primarily involves initiating structure to accomplish tasks; other leaders behave to build and maintain good personal relationships; and still others do both or do neither (Halpin, 1956a).

3. The most effective behavioral style of leaders is one that varies with the situation (Fiedler, 1967a; Korman, 1966).

4. The best attitudinal style is a high task orientation and a high relations orientation (Blake & Mouton, 1964; Reddin, 1967).

5. The job maturity and psychological maturity of the followers are most crucial in determining which behavioral style of leaders will result in the most effectiveness (Argyris, 1962).

6. Maturity relates to the stage in a group's life cycle or to the previous education and training of the followers. Just as parental leadership of offspring must change to reflect the life cycle (infancy, adolescence, and adulthood), so must leading groups reflect the life cycle of followers from novices and newcomers to experts and people with experience.

Prescriptions

According to Hersey and Blanchard (1969a, 1969b, 1977, 1982a), as shown in Figure 19.2, depending on the maturity of subordinates, a manager should be task oriented and tell or sell subordinates regarding what to do; or a manager should be relations oriented and *participate*[7]

---

[7]As defined in chapter 18, *participation* (italicized) refers only to sharing in the decision process. Participation (roman) includes consulting, sharing, and delegating. *Direction* (italicized) refers only to giving orders

Figure 19.2 Hersey-Blanchard Model of the Relationship between Leader Style and Maturity of Followers

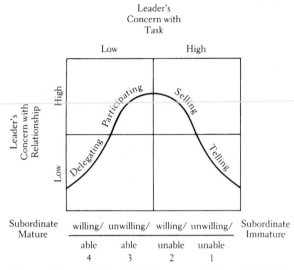

Leader's
Concern with
Task

SOURCE: Hersey and Blanchard, *Management of Organizational Behavior: Utilizing Human Behavior*, Copyright 1977, p. 170. Adapted by permission of Prentice Hall, Inc., Englewood Cliffs, New Jersey, 1977.

with subordinates in joint decision making; or the decision should be delegated to them. What to do should depend on the subordinates' task-relevant job maturity (capacity, ability, education, and experience) and their psychological maturity (motivation, self-esteem, confidence, and willingness to do a good job). The maturity manifests itself in the subordinates' performance of their jobs. Newly appointed, inexperienced employees seek task-oriented direction from their superiors; they should be told what to do. As their life cycle on the job continues and their experience increases, they have to be sold to continue their performance. Later, with the subordinates' further development, relations orientation and *participation* become most efficacious in order to engage both their knowledge and their maturation. Finally, fully mature subordinates work best when the leaders delegate what needs to be done. The most effective leadership is conceived of as depending on whether the leader's task-oriented or relations-oriented behavior matches the subordinate's maturity.

LASI or LEAD. The Leader Adaptability and Style Inventory (LASI)—later renamed the Leadership Effectiveness and Adaptability Description (LEAD)—provides brief vignettes of 12 situations, each with four alternatives (Hersey & Blanchard, 1974). Maturity of the subordinates is at one of four levels in the situations. Each level involves a different combination of attention to relations and task.

For example, in one of the situations, you supervise a group with a fine record of accomplishment whose members respect the need for change. You indicate from among four choices what supervisory action you would take to deal with the problem. One alternative, under answer C, is to delegate by allowing the group to work out the solution itself. This delegation is leadership behavior that is low in task orientation and low in relations orientation. The response adds 2 points to your self-rated delegation score. It also adds to your flexibility score, for it best matches the requirements of the particular situation according to the model. The next best answer is A—to be *participative*, to allow the group to be involved in the change, and is scored +1 for flexibility. It is a moderately adaptive leadership response, low in task orientation and high in relations orientation. The next best answer, D—to be persuasive by directing the change but incorporating the group's recommendations—is scored −1 for flexibility; it is a response that is high in task orientation and high in relations orientation. Finally, the worst and least flexible answer is B—announce the changes and implement them with close supervision. This is a highly *directive*, high-task–low-relations response; it is scored −2 for flexibility. Subordinates and colleagues can also complete the form, indicating what they believe the focal manager would do. Their responses can provide useful feedback to the focal leader (Hersey & Blanchard, 1981).

A curvilinear relationship between a leader's task and relations orientation and the subordinates' maturity was postulated by Hersey and Blanchard (1977), as displayed in Figure 19.2. Unwilling and unable subordinates should be told what to do; willing but unable subordinates should be sold; unwilling but able subordinates should participate; and willing and able subordinates should be delegated assignments.

---

with or without explanation. Direction (roman) includes ordering, persuading (selling), and manipulating.

Positive Evidence

Despite problems with the model, some supportive empirical evidence has emerged for it along with contrary findings. Hersey, Angelim, and Carakushansky (1982) obtained support for the model as an approach to improve learning. The participants in their study were 60 managers who attended a management-training seminar. The experimental groups were trained in four stages; a control group was not trained. Early on, the instructor engaged in a great deal of *direction*. The instructor next did some selling and then *participated* with the trainees in the learning process. Finally, the instructor delegated the responsibility for learning to the trainees but remained available to support them. Thus as the maturity of the trainees increased, the instructor decreased the task-oriented direction. The final examination at the end of training showed that the experimental group learned significantly more than did the control group.

Jacobsen (1984) found that LASI ratings by colleagues of the appropriate flexibility of the style of 338 managers correlated significantly with the progress of the managers' careers, as well as with selected performance criteria. Although the maturity level of their subordinates was found to moderate between the managers' behavior and effectiveness, it was less important than other situational variables. For 209 supervisors and managers from five organizations, Haley (1983) obtained positive correlations between the subordinates' LASI assessments of the adaptability of their superiors' styles and the subordinates' ratings of the effectiveness of their own work groups. Hambleton and Gumpert (1982) found a statistically significant and practical gain in the job performance of 189 subordinates when their 56 supervisors applied the Hersey-Blanchard model correctly. High-performing managers rated higher than low performers on the effectiveness of their leadership and the flexibility of their style, both in their self-reports and in the appraisals by their subordinates and superiors. They also showed greater knowledge and use of the model of situational leadership.

Kohut (1983) found that the flexibility of 281 women managers, as measured by LEAD, was related to their effectiveness and sex-role identity. Vecchio (1987) surveyed 303 teachers from 14 high schools with the less controversial Leader Behavior Description Questionnaire

(LBDQ), to be discussed in Chapter 20. Consistent with the Hersey-Blanchard model, Vecchio concluded that recently hired teachers, compared with those with more experience, may need and appreciate more initiation of structure from their supervisors. A replication with seven supervisors and 91 nurses reached similar conclusions (Norris & Vecchio, 1992); but another replication with 332 university employees and 32 supervisors (Fernandez & Vecchio, 1997) failed to find support for Situational Leadership Theory (SLT). Stirling (1998) obtained support for SLT by examining leadership in condominium and homeowner associations. Highly active members serve on committees and volunteer their time. Moderately active members participate in elections and occasionally attend meetings. Apathetic members expect a maintenance-free life and efficient management of the association. Stirling anticipated finding that apathetic members would be more satisfied with communication and decision making if the annually elected leader was task-oriented, telling, and a one-way communicator. Moderately active members were expected to favor selling and participative leadership. Highly active members were expected to want the leader to encourage participation and delegate responsibilities. Satisfaction of members was somewhat higher the more the leader adopted an appropriate style to match the perceived activity level of the member.

Negative Evidence

Consistent with other studies using other instruments, such as leaders' self-ratings on the LBDQ (Weissenberg & Kavanagh, 1972), Haley (1983) found response bias, low reliability, and lack of correlation between self-ratings and others' LASI ratings of the focal managers. Narayanan, Venkatachalam, and Bharathiar (1982) could find no relation between the LEAD self-reports of 30 owners of small Indian hosiery-knitting units and their employees' descriptions of the owners' styles. Nor could these researchers find any connection with the productivity of the units.

Goodson, McGee, and Cashman (1989) tested the Hersey-Blanchard propositions about effective leadership using 459 employees from 100 stores in a retail chain. The effectiveness of the style of leader behavior was unrelated to follower maturity; nor was the ranking of usefulness of the four styles from delegation to telling relevant to employee outcomes in commitment, satisfaction with the supervisor, or effectiveness in the different situations. York and Hastings (1985–1986) surveyed 172 employees in three North Carolina social service departments to ascertain the effects of the supervisors' behavior on their subordinates' performance in the context of the subordinates' level of maturity. They found that regardless of the level of the subordinates' maturity, supervisors' supportive and work-facilitation behavior, as measured in the Survey of Organization, contributed in the same way to the subordinates' performance.

Blank, Weitzel, and Green (1990) examined the situational leadership performance of 27 directors of residence halls (full-time professionals) who were responsible for 353 resident advisers (part-time paraprofessional students) in two large midwestern universities. A psychological maturity index was developed for the advisers, starting with 40 items about independence, the ability to take responsibility, and the motivation to achieve. Several factor analyses resulted in a refined single-factor scale of 11 items, such as "Acts conscientiously on the job," "Follows through on job tasks," "Takes care to do the job right," and "Works hard on the job." Peer ratings using the items were obtained from other advisers to measure the psychological maturity of the advisers (the subordinates of the directors). Satisfaction with their work and supervision were obtained from the advisers, along with ratings of their performance by their directors. The psychological maturity of the advisers correlated .40 with the directors' ratings of their job performance. As predicted by the model, for those low in psychological maturity, work satisfaction increased linearly with the task-oriented, directive, and persuasive behavior of their directors. However, work satisfaction was much higher in advisers whose psychological maturity was high, regardless of the leadership behavior of their directors. The investigators concluded that their analyses as a whole lent little particular support for the Hersey-Blanchard model, although they agreed that further exploration of the relationship between the maturity of subordinates and the behavior of leaders would be useful.

Critique

The curvilinear model (Figure 19.2) has been roundly criticized because of the lack of internal consistency of its measures (Aldag & Brief, 1981), its conceptual contradictions, and its conceptual ambiguities (Graeff, 1983). The model appears to have no theoretical or logical justification (Graeff, 1983); nevertheless, the model has intuitive appeal. As was already noted, Blake and Mouton (1981a) argued that although situational leadership as such may be interesting, a preponderance of the empirical evidence supports their one best way: leadership that integrates both task and relations orientation. For example, in the research by Blank, Weitzel, and Green, the advisers' satisfaction with their supervision correlated .41 and .54, respectively, with the task and relations behavior of their directors, regardless of the advisers' maturity. To this, Hersey and Blanchard (1982b) replied that Blake and Mouton deal with attitudinal models, while they deal with a behavioral model. Conflict occurs only when behavioral assumptions are drawn from the analysis of attitudinal models. Blake and Mouton (1981a, 1981b) countered with other difficulties of the Hersey-Blanchard model. They noted the extent to which task and relations orientation and behavior tend to be interdependent rather than uncorrelated with each other. Merely adding high task concerns to high relations concerns makes for benevolent paternalism, not teamwork. Qualitative differences at different ends of the continua in orientation and behavior need to be taken into account. For example, a high relations orientation that achieves high productivity (9,9) is characterized by openness, trust, respect, understanding, and mutual commitment. A high relations orientation that results in low productivity (1,9) is warm, friendly, and harmonious. To demonstrate this issue, Blake and Mouton (1981a, 1981b, 1982a) revised each of the 12 LEAD situations by adding fifth choices that reflected their 9,9 style. In paraphrase, the first Hersey-Blanchard situation was as follows:

A group is not responding favorably to our friendly conversation and concern for their welfare. Their performance is going down quite quickly.

The prescribed Hersey-Blanchard answer is a high task–low relations orientation, with the leader behaving according to response A. The least desirable choice is response D.

(A) Stress and apply uniform procedures and the need for accomplishing the task.
(B) Keep yourself on hand for discussion, but don't pressure subordinates to involve you.
(C) Set goals for subordinates after talking with them.
(D) Demonstrate your intentions by not interfering.

For this situation, Blake and Mouton thought the 9,9 style was the most efficacious: initiate a critique session with the entire group to diagnose the underlying problems responsible for this rapidly declining production and to decide what to do about it. From Blake and Mouton's point of view, the prescribed Hersey-Blanchard answer, A, is 9,1 behavior: telling subordinates what to do and pushing for production (Blake & Mouton, 1982a, 1982b).

One hundred experienced managers from 41 organizations completed the revised form without prior knowledge of the controversy. They ranked the choices for each of the 12 problems from most effective to least effective. The managers chose the fifth alternative, which reflects Blake-Mouton's 9,9 behavior (integration of the task and relations orientations) between 72% and 90% of the time to handle each of the 12 situations. The managers chose the 9,9 alternative for situations at the four levels of the maturity of followers, from lowest to highest, 79%, 86%, 76%, and 78% of the time, respectively. They chose the appropriate alternative presented by Hersey-Blanchard to reflect the followers' maturity only 9%, 7%, 11%, and 5% of the time, respectively. Similar results were obtained with 36 mental health professionals.

In line with these results, Slocum (1984) suggested that the emphasis on the maturity of subordinates to determine when direction or participation is appropriate is of minor importance, in contrast to a number of other variables: the subordinates' tasks, the technology employed, the information required, the managerial control and coordination systems in place, the amount of self-control that is possible, and the extent to which the decision is operational and complex. Norris and Vecchio (1992) attributed to chance effects the occasional theoretically correct matches of leader style and subordinate readiness.

Efforts to Improve the Hersey-Blanchard Model and Its Measures

Nicholls (1985) suggested correcting the model's logical flaws by requiring a smooth progression of the leader from the *parent* style of high task orientation–high relations orientation to the *developer* style of low task–high relations. In this developmental progression, the leader will maintain a balanced emphasis on both the task and relationships as long as the ability and willingness of the group are developing symmetrically. If ability and willingness develop asymmetrically, the leader may find it more appropriate to act highly task-oriented, like a *coach* or a *driver*.

Boone (1981) improved the LEAD by modifying its scoring. The reliability of the LEAD self-report was increased by changing it from forced-choice scoring to scoring that captures the intensity of the endorsement of each alternative. In this way, a study of 249 managers from South Africa and the United States obtained more satisfactory test-retest reliabilities, ranging from .66 to .79.

Leader Behavior Analysis (LBA). Blanchard, Hambleton, Zigarmi, et al. (1982) developed a revised instrument, Leader Behavior Analysis (LBA), with 20 incidents, to improve on the 12-incident LASI or LEAD. The LBA was constructed recognizing that effective task orientation and effective relations orientation were not independent of each other. Three of the four principal leadership styles were relabled in 1985. *Telling* became *directing*; *selling* was seen as manipulative and became *coaching*; and *participating* became *supporting* for purposes of clarification and retention (Blanchard, Zigarmi, & Zigarmi, 1985). *Readiness* and *maturity* were also relabeled, as *development level*, to change the implication from age and status to mastery of necessary skills for task accomplishment and competence. The lowest developmental level of followers was changed from being *unwilling and unable* to being *committed but unable*. At the second level of development, followers were conceived to be low in commitment but somewhat competent. An *effectiveness* score could be calculated from the extent to which the chosen responses to the 20 incidents matched what was required according to the revised Situational Leadership model.

Evidence of the Effectiveness of the Revised Model. Using the LBA, Wilkinson (1990) compared 116 high- and low-scoring leaders in a government agency. Compared with low scorers, high scorers were rated by their subordinates as significantly more satisfying as supervisors. Stoner-Zemel (1988) obtained significant positive correlations between LBA effectiveness of supervisors according to others and the perceptions by 293 employees of their high productivity ($r = .25$), alignment ($r = .28$), and feelings of empowerment ($r = .34$). Duke (1988) also reported a positive correlation for nurses between LBA effectiveness scores of supervisors and subordinates' sense of empowerment. Zigarmi, Edeburn, and Blanchard (1993) compiled results for 552 employees for whom morale was higher, tension was lower, and felt opportunities for growth were higher if the employees' LBA descriptions of their manager generated high rather than low effectiveness scores. Price (1993) found positive correlations between effectiveness scores and various managerial competencies as found in the Boyatzis' (1982) model.

Should Leaders Be Consistent or Flexible?

Measurement. A *flexibility* score can be calculated based on the extent to which the leader or rater reported use of varying styles to handle the 20 LBA incidents. The most inflexible score would describe a leader who used the same single style to deal with all 20 incidents. Use of the LBA and the flexibility score could further understanding of the importance of leadership constancy and flexibility.

Effects. If leaders recognize that different circumstances call for different actions on their part, do they risk being downgraded for being inconsistent and unpredictable? Do they cause subordinates to feel unsure about what is expected? The evidence is mixed. Bruce (1986) reported that CEOs placed a premium on being consistent and predictable in word and action. Staw and Ross (1980) asked 95 practicing managers and 127 undergraduates to read one of several case descriptions of administrators who were consistent or flexible and ultimately successful or unsuccessful in their actions. Although both sets of respondents assigned the highest ratings to administrators who were consistent, particularly those who also

were successful, the practicing managers valued consistency more than did the undergraduates. Block and Kennedy (1986) asked 133 employees to rate leaders who were described as consistently autocratic or participative rather than flexible and varying in their style depending on the circumstances. The employees opted most often for the consistently participative manager than for the more flexible one. Graves (1985) obtained similar results for 141 undergraduate leaders. Those who persisted in one particular way were evaluated more favorably than were those who varied in their responses, despite the different levels of complexity with which they had to cope. Also supporting the utility of consistency, Aldag and Brief (1977) obtained strong negative correlations between an index of the variability of leaders' behavior and measures of subordinates' satisfaction, involvement with their jobs, organizational commitment, and experienced meaningfulness of the work. Thus Blake and Mouton's (1982a) arguments for a consistent 9,9 leadership style have more empirical support than do Hersey and Blanchard's notions about how leaders must vary their style according to the situation.

Some exceptions need to be noted. James and White (1983) showed that 377 U.S. Navy managers were in favor of flexibility and varied their leadership behavior toward their subordinates depending on their perceptions of what specifically caused these subordinates to perform inadequately. When 159 undergraduates judged systematically differing leadership descriptions, Knight (1984) found that the perceived competence among managers was more important in evaluating them than whether they were consistent or flexible.

One factor that seemed to account for the differences in support for consistency or flexibility was whether the evaluators were the superiors or subordinates of the leaders. According to a simulation used by Heilman, Hornstein, Cage, and Herschlag (1984), appropriate flexible responses were more likely to be favored if the evaluator was a superior of the leader; consistent participativeness was more likely to be favored if the evaluator was a subordinate. In addition, it seems that flexible leadership will be judged favorably if the shifts in a leader's style or behavior are meaningful and explainable to those who are evaluating the leader as shifts to accommodate the requirements of the circumstances. If no such change in requirements is perceived, consistency will be prized in a leader because it is predictable and fits with colleagues' expectations.

Why Is the Hersey-Blanchard Model So Popular?

The Hersey-Blanchard model has had remarkably widespread intuitive appeal to practicing managers and to leaders of management-training programs. An understanding of its popularity with management may require an analysis of the sociology of knowledge, not of the model's theoretical or empirical validity.

Situationalism may be popular because it provides freedom from principles ("You can do your own thing as you see fit"). Principles are more complex to learn and practice. Situationalism allows a leader to keep all options open (Blake & Mouton, 1982b). Although LEAD lacks the desired level of reliability, and its validity remains in doubt, its situations and choices seem to provide interesting discussion material for training. The simplicity of this instrument makes it possible to retain its prescriptions on a single small card. This simplicity may also give managers a sense of quick mastery of a complex problem. For the personally authoritarian manager, the model calls attention to the need for a flexible response. To the personally democratic manager, it gives legitimacy to being directive at times.

Fiedler's Contingency Model of Leadership

Fiedler's contingency model (1967a) avoids the problem of a leader's consistency in the face of situations with different requirements. Leaders are conceived to have a personally consistent style of task or relations orientation. Either different types of leaders need to be chosen for various situations, or leaders need to change the situations to suit their particular personal style. According to the heavily researched contingency model of leadership, leaders with high "least preferred coworker" (LPC) scores do best in situations moderately favorable to them; low-scoring leaders do best in situations extremely favorable or extremely unfavorable to them. This model is presented here as part of the discussion of relations- and task-oriented leadership. Nevertheless, controversy continues about whether Fiedler's LPC questionnaire measures task orientation or something else. The controversy, in turn, affects our ability to understand LPC's contribution to effectiveness in different situations. On the surface, LPC measures how much each of 16 to 18 attributes reflect respondents' feelings about a person with whom they can work least effectively.

Development of the LPC Measurement

Starting in the early 1950s, Fiedler (1953a, 1953b, 1953c) began studying the success of psychological therapists as a function of their accuracy and assumed similarity to their patients. This research was then extended to leaders and the effectiveness of their groups (Fiedler, 1954a, 1954b, 1955, 1956). A measure of Assumed Similarity between opposites (ASo) was developed. ASo scores were obtained by computing the difference between two sets of semantic differential ratings. One set was the leader's description of his or her least preferred coworker (LPC). The other set consisted of ratings of the leader's most preferred coworker. ASo scores were viewed as indicators of leadership style, and were correlated with the performance of groups. Success in accurately predicting performance of outcomes from ASo scores was mixed.

Eventually, the most preferred coworker was abandoned as an assessment, and attention was focused on LPC. In its standard version, the examinee is asked to think of everyone with whom he or she has ever worked and then to describe the one person with whom he or she could work least well. This description of one's LPC is made by marking 16 items, as shown in Table 19.2. The favorable pole of each scale is scored as 8 and the unfavorable pole is scored as 1 (Fiedler, Chemers, & Mahar, 1976). The sum of the scale scores of items constitutes the individual's LPC score. A relatively high LPC score (favoring the LPC) was most generally conceived by Fiedler (1967a, 1970b) to indicate a relations-motivated person, whereas a low LPC score (rejecting the LPC) was conceived to indicate a task-motivated person.

Measurement Properties of LPC

A good deal of evidence is available concerning the internal consistency and stability of the LPC, but its validity remains a complex question.

Table 19.2 Least Preferred Coworker Scale

> Think of the person with whom you can work *least* well. This person may be someone you work with now or someone you knew in the past. This person does not have to be the person you like least well, but should be the person with whom you had the most difficulty in getting a job done.
>
> Please describe this person as he or she appears to you by putting an "X" in the appropriate space on the following scales.

Pleasant	:___:___:___:___:___:___:___:	Unpleasant
Friendly	:___:___:___:___:___:___:___:	Unfriendly
Rejecting	:___:___:___:___:___:___:___:	Accepting
Helpful	:___:___:___:___:___:___:___:	Frustrating
Unenthusiastic	:___:___:___:___:___:___:___:	Enthusiastic
Tense	:___:___:___:___:___:___:___:	Relaxed
Distant	:___:___:___:___:___:___:___:	Close
Cold	:___:___:___:___:___:___:___:	Warm
Cooperative	:___:___:___:___:___:___:___:	Uncooperative
Supportive	:___:___:___:___:___:___:___:	Hostile
Boring	:___:___:___:___:___:___:___:	Interesting
Quarrelsome	:___:___:___:___:___:___:___:	Harmonious
Self-Assured	:___:___:___:___:___:___:___:	Hesitant
Efficient	:___:___:___:___:___:___:___:	Inefficient
Gloomy	:___:___:___:___:___:___:___:	Cheerful
Open	:___:___:___:___:___:___:___:	Guarded

SOURCE: Fiedler (1967), p. 41.

Internal Consistency. Do the same people respond in the same way to the different items of the LPC scale? For earlier versions of LPC, Rice (1978a) obtained a mean split-half reliability of .88 for a variety of investigations. Fox, Hill, and Guertin (1973); Shiflett (1974); and Yukl (1970) discovered separate interpersonal and task factors in these earlier LPC scales, but the secondarily scored task factor was seen to be relatively unimportant. Therefore, a newer 18-item scale was designed to minimize task-factor items and, as a consequence, was somewhat higher in internal consistency (Fiedler, 1978). In five studies with the newer 18-item version, shown in Table 19.2, Rice (1979) reported coefficient alphas of .90, .91, .79, .84, and .89.

Stability. Do people's LPC scores remain the same over time? Rice (1978a) found 23 reports of test-retest reliability ranging from .01 to .91, with a median of .67. Stability indexed by high test-retest correlations was obtained by Chemers and Skrzypek (1972)[8] when the test and retest were separated by at least several weeks. However, the time between the test and retest did not affect

stability (as might have been expected), according to an analysis of studies in which the intervals between the test and the retest ranged from several days to over two years (Rice, 1978a). Hence, stability can be maintained over extended intervals of time. Bons (1974) obtained a test-retest reliability of .72 for 45 higher-level army leaders over a five-month period, and Prothero and Fiedler (1974) obtained a test-retest correlation of .67 for 18 faculty members at a school of nursing over a 16- to 24-month period. However, Fox (1976) found a decline in reliability when the retest was obtained nine weeks instead of four weeks after the test. With intervals of three to five weeks, test-retest reliabilities ranged from .73 to .85. With intervals of eight to nine weeks, they ranged from .23 to .68. When the interval was 130 weeks, the test-retest reliability was only .45. Fox (1976) found that stability was reduced if the same LPC was not described in the test and in the retest.

Thus, LPC is not necessarily as invariant an attribute of an individual as is a personality trait, such as sociability. Offerman (1984) and other investigators[9] obtained results suggesting that the LPC is more like a transitory

---

[8]It was also obtained by Fiedler, O'Brien, and Ilgen (1969); Hardy (1971, 1975); Hardy and Bohren (1975); and Hardy, Sack, and Harpine (1973).

[9]Fishbein, Landy, and Hatch (1969a); E. J. Frank (1973); and Stinson and Tracy (1974).

attitude. For example, in a comparative experiment with male and female undergraduates who led opposite, mixed, or same-sex groups, Offerman (1984) found significant differences among the leaders as a consequence of the sex composition of the groups. The LPC scores of females who had just led male groups were most task-oriented; the LPC scores of males who had just led female groups were most relations-oriented.

Temporary shifts also can be induced by unsatisfactory work experiences in laboratory experiments. When instability has been found in such experiments, it has been attributed to "implicit instructions" of training interventions as to how one should adapt toward poor coworkers (Rice, 1978a). The LPC also appears sensitive to major life changes, such as being subjected to stressful contact assignments (Bons, Bass, & Komorita, 1970). In spite of the satisfactory median test-retest results, Schriesheim, Bannister, and Money (1979) remained unconvinced of the stability of LPC because of the wide variation in test-retest results within the various reported analyses. For instance, Schriesheim and Kerr (1977a) noted that a significant proportion of persons also changed category from high to low LPCs, or vice versa.

Parallel-Form Reliability. Do LPC scores remain the same if different attributes are included in the items? For instance, in one form, the choice may be between dull and bright. In the parallel form, the choice may be between stupid and smart. Rice (1978a) reported one study in which scales whose items had different content and different formats were fairly well correlated with each other. Different versions of the LPC have contained various numbers of task-oriented items, which may reduce their parallel-form reliability. This difference may account for some of the variations in correlations of the LPC version used with other tests and measures of the effectiveness of groups in attempts to determine the meaning of LPC (Schriesheim, Bannister, & Money, 1979). But Rice (1979) argued that since correlations of .79, .78, and .66 were obtained when items and formats to assess LPC had been changed, correlated parallel forms could be constructed successfully.

Content Validity. Are the items of the LPC scale biased? If LPC is a measure of the degree to which task-oriented individuals are negative about those with whom they cannot work—an attitude reflected by ascribing

negative values to the LPCs on such attributes as pleasant-unpleasant, which are not necessarily related directly to their work—then task-oriented items, such as bright-dull, reduce the content validity of the LPC, since brightness and dullness are directly related to getting the work done (Schriesheim, Bannister, & Money, 1979). An 18-item version that omits such clearly task-relevant items is now operative. As was noted earlier, Shiflett (1974) and Yukl (1970), among others, demonstrated that the earlier versions of the LPC contained two factors, one associated with interpersonal relations items, the other with task-oriented items. Studies by Fiedler (1967a) and Schriesheim (1979b) have found LPC scores to be relatively free of social desirability, unlike so many other personality measures.

Construct Validity. What is really being measured by the LPC? How does the LPC logically and empirically link with other known entities? Fiedler and Chemers (1974, p. 74) observed that "For nearly 20 years, we have been attempting to correlate [LPC] with every conceivable personality trait and every conceivable behavior observation score. By and large these analyses have been uniformly fruitless."

But Rice (1978b), who sampled 66 out of 114 studies involving over 2,000 empirical relationships between the LPC and other variables, thought he could lay out the nomological network of empirical relationships of the LPC and other measures. He concluded more optimistically that although it remains unclear whether the LPC is a measure of social distance, personal need, cognitive complexity, or motivational hierarchy (as will be discussed later), the LPC score as a measure of interpersonal relations versus task orientation is not in doubt.

The inconsistent results can be seen if one examines the correlations of LPC with biographical data and then compares what Bass (1967b) reported about the correlations of direct measures of relations orientation and task orientation. In agreement with Bass's review, a low LPC score (task orientation) was higher with increasing age (Fiedler & Hoffman, 1962) and with experience (Bons, Bass, & Komorita, 1970). But opposed to Bass's conclusions, a high LPC score (relations orientation) was positively correlated with managerial level (Alpander, 1974) and with Protestant rather than Catholic affiliation (Fiedler & Hoffman, 1962). Above and beyond these results, no significant relations of biodata and LPC were found by Eagly (1970) or numerous other investigators.[10]

Schriesheim and Kerr (1974) have critically noted, as new evidence has emerged, that the LPC has been redefined as an orientation toward work, as an attitude, as a cognitive complexity measure (E. J. Frank, 1973), as the ability to differentiate conceptually (Foa, Mitchell, & Fiedler, 1971), or as an index of a hierarchy of goals (Fiedler, 1972a). However, this redefinition could be a virtue rather than a fault. (Theoretical constructs, like ether, should wither away, leaving behind empirical facts, like the electrical discharge in lightning.) But critics fail to see that the new data justify the new interpretations (Hosking, 1978). For example, Evans and Dermer (1974) correlated the LPC scores for 112 business students, managers, and systems analysts with two measures of cognitive differentiation and cognitive complexity and found that low LPC scores were associated with cognitive simplicity. Nevertheless, high LPC scores were not unequivocally related to cognitive complexity.

LPC as a Measure of Relations and Task Orientation. A number of studies have supported the contention that a high LPC score is connected with relations orientation and a low LPC score is connected with task orientation.

Fiedler (1964, 1967a) proposed that high-LPC people have a strong need to attain and maintain successful interpersonal relationships, whereas low-LPC people have a strong need for successful task performance. Four sets of data generally gave some support for this interpretation (although many reversals were noted). The behavior of low-LPC leaders tended to be task oriented, and the behavior of high-LPC leaders was generally relations oriented. Members of groups with high- and low-LPC leaders tended to exhibit task-oriented and relations-oriented leadership. Higher levels of satisfaction and lower levels of anxiety were found among groups with high-LPC leaders. Finally, data suggested that low-LPC people gained self-esteem and satisfaction from the successful performance of tasks and high-LPC people gained self-esteem and satisfaction from successful interpersonal relations.

Fiedler (1978) inferred that for an individual who describes his or her LPC in negative, rejecting terms, the completion of the task is of such overriding importance that it completely colors the perception of all other personality traits attributed to the LPC score. Fiedler's interpretation was as follows: "If I cannot work with you, if you frustrate my need to get the job done, then you can't be any good in other respects. You are unfriendly, unpleasant, tense, and distant, etc."

The relationship-motivated individual who sees his or her LPC in more positive terms says, "Getting a job done is not everything. Therefore, even though I can't work with you, you may still be friendly, relaxed, interesting, etc. — in other words, someone with whom I could get along quite well on a personal basis." Thus a high-LPC person looks at his or her least LPC in a more differentiated manner and is more interested in the personality of the individual than merely in whether this is or is not someone with whom one can get a job done (p. 61). But Hare, Hare, and Blumberg (1998) found among 20 groups of managers that leaders who were both relations- and task-oriented were prone to give lower ratings to their LPCs.

LPC and Other Relevant Measures of Orientation. Vroom and Yetton (1973) and Sashkin, Taylor, and Tripathi (1974) reported that high LPC scores related to the preference for participation in resolving conflict. Nebeker and Hansson (1972) found that high LPC scores correlated with support of giving children the freedom to use facilities. Alpander (1974) obtained results indicating a positive relationship between high LPC scores and the judged importance of people-oriented management functions. Similarly, Ayman and Chemers (1986) found that high-LPC Mexican managers described the ideal leader as a "people person" and low-LPC managers described the ideal leader as a taskmaster; low-LPC managers were also more self-monitoring. However, Singh (1983) failed to find support, in experiments with 53 Indian engineering students, that high-LPC students would place greater importance on the equity of the distribution of rewards whereas low-LPC students would emphasize performance. Contrary to expectations, Steiner and McDiarmid (1957) found that a high LPC score coincided with authoritarian beliefs, and Evans and Dermer (1974) and others[11] found LPC to be unrelated significantly to authoritarianism or dogmatism.

---

[10] See, for example, A. R. Bass, Fiedler, and Krueger (1964); Lawrence and Lorsch (1967a); Nealey and Blood (1968); Posthuma (1970); and Shiflett (1974).

[11] See also A. R. Bass, Fiedler, and Krueger (1964); Fishbein, Landy, and Hatch (1969a); and Sashkin, Taylor, and Tripathi (1974).

LPC and Observed Leader Behavior. Observers and other group members found that a low LPC score coincided, as expected, with initiating structure and task-oriented leadership behavior, and a high LPC score coincided with relations-oriented behavior in a number of studies.[12] But complete reversals (Nealey & Blood, 1968) and negative results were also reported.[13] Interactions with situations had to be considered.[14]

LPC scores did not relate much to decision-making styles. McKenna (undated) obtained correlations between LPC and style of decision making of 22 chief accountants, as follows: directive without explanation, $-.12$; *directive* with explanation, $-.01$; consultative, .06; *participative*, .03; delegative, .13.

Mitchell (1970a) found that, as expected, high-LPC leaders gave more weight to interpersonal relations. Gottheil and Lauterbach (1969) studied military cadets and squads who were competing in field exercises and found that a leader's low LPC score was associated with a group's performance, whereas leader's high LPC score was associated with a group's morale. But contrary to expectations, LPC scores were higher for leaders working in the short term than in the long term (Miller, 1970).

Such complete reversals of results and the weakness of LPC scores as indicators of leadership behavior led Vroom (1976b) to suggest caution in characterizing leadership style on the basis of LPC score alone. According to Fiedler (1967a), leadership style depends on combining LPC scores with measures of the situation in which high- or low-LPC people find themselves. A high LPC score, Fiedler (1978) noted, does not always predict that a leader will behave according to a relations orientation. Nor will a low LPC score always predict that the leader will push for production, for completion of the task, or for more structuring. At any rate, although LPC may prove to discriminate among leaders in ways that are of consequence to their effectiveness in different contingencies, LPC is

not directly symptomatic of the other styles of leadership behavior discussed earlier or yet to be discussed. Hence the results with LPC must stand alone. In fact, some question remains about whether LPC is measuring task and relations orientation or something else.

Alternative Meanings of LPC

LPC has gone through a series of reinterpretations based on empirical studies of its characteristics. It has been conceived as a measure of social distance, cognitive complexity, motivational priorities, and a value attitude.

LPC as a Measure of Social Distance. At first, Fiedler (1957, 1958) interpreted LPC—then called ASo, an index almost perfectly correlated with LPC—as a generalized index of psychological closeness. Low-LPC people were conceived to be more socially or psychologically distant from other group members than were high-LPC persons. The assumed similarity data were drawn from person-perception research conducted in therapeutic settings. Fiedler (1953a, 1953b) inferred that respondents showed greater assumed similarity between themselves and group members they liked than between themselves and members they disliked. Analyses suggested that LPC was a measure of emotional and psychological distance, since high-LPC people conformed more in the face of social pressure and were more closely involved with other group members. But following a review of studies of the reactions of others to high- and low-LPC persons, Rice (1978b) concluded that the data were contradictory.

LPC as a Measure of Cognitive Complexity. Foa, Mitchell, and Fiedler (1971) and Hill (1969a) argued that compared with low-LPC people, high-LPC people are more cognitively complex, favoring the abstract over the concrete and using less broad categorizations. These researchers based their proposal on positive correlations they found between LPC and several measures of cognitive complexity. In addition, the intercorrelations among the factor scores of the LPC scale were lower for high-LPC persons; and greater responsiveness to interpersonal factors was observed in the judgments and behavior of high-LPC persons.

Although LPC was found to be correlated significantly with intelligence in only 1 to 14 analyses, in several of 11

[12] See Blades and Fiedler (1973); Chemers and Skrzypek (1972); Green, Nebeker, and Boni (1974); Gruenfeld, Rance, and Weissenberg (1969); Meuwese and Fiedler (1965); Sample and Wilson (1965); Sashkin (1972); and Yukl (1970).
[13] See L. R. Anderson (1964); Evans (1973); Fiedler (1967a); Fiedler, O'Brien, and Ilgen (1969); Fox (1974); Graen, Orris, and Alvares (1971); and Stinson (1972).
[14] W. W. Burke (1965), Chemers (1969), Fiedler (1967a, 1971b, 1971c, 1971d, 1972a), W. K. Graham (1970/1973), Green and Nebeker (1974), Nealy and Blood (1968), Rice and Chemers (1975), Shiflett and Nealy (1972), Shima (1968), and Yukl (1970).

other analyses LPC was related to specific cognitive tendencies. Thus Mitchell (1970a, 1970b) found that high-LPC leaders gave more weight to power and structure in making discriminations, whereas low-LPC leaders gave more weight to interpersonal relations. Foa, Mitchell, and Fiedler (1970) observed that the high-LPC leader performed better in situations that presented difficulties in either interpersonal or task relations and thus that required a high degree of cognitive differentiation between them. Jacoby (1968) found positive correlations between LPC and scores on the Remote Associates Test, a test of creativity. Similarly, Triandis, Mikesell, and Ewen (1962) reported a possibly positive correlation between LPC and the judged creativity of two written passages. Singh (1983) also obtained data to support LPC as a measure of cognitive complexity by demonstrating that high-LPC engineering students did better than low-LPC students in obeying the precise prescriptions of a model for the equitable distribution of rewards.

The findings for cognitive complexity dealing with field independence-dependence, as measured by the Embedded Figures Test, were less consistent (Gruenfeld & Arbuthnot, 1968; Weissenberg & Gruenfeld, 1966). Furthermore, a number of other studies[15] found no evidence to support LPC as a measure of cognitive complexity.

LPC as a Measure of a Motivational Hierarchy. To account for so much variation in results, Fiedler (1972a) saw the need for a "hierarchical" conceptualization of LPC. Since, according to Fiedler, the high-LPC person needs to be related and socially connected to others, he or she will show concern for good interpersonal relations when the situation is tense and anxiety arousing and when relations with coworkers seem tenuous. But when the goals of being related are secure, the relationship-motivated high-LPC person will then seek the self-oriented admiration of others and the attainment of prominence. In work groups, such goals can be attained by showing concern for the task-relevant aspects of the groups' interaction. The major objectives of the low-LPC person are to accomplish a task and to earn self-esteem by doing a good job (D. W. Bishop, 1964). But when the

completion of a task presents no problem, the low-LPC person will seek friendly, good interpersonal relations with coworkers, partly because he or she believes that good interpersonal relations are conducive to accomplishing the task (Fiedler, 1971b).

Nevertheless, this interpretation, like previous interpretations, remains controversial. Green and Nebeker (1977) presented data to support it. But evidence by Rice and Chemers (1975) failed to confirm predictions based on a motivational hierarchy. Rather, LPC as a measure of cognitive complexity better fit their results. Kunezik (1976a, 1976b) found no support for the motivational hierarchy in studies of the relationship of ASo to various personality measures among 1,590 German army recruits and 148 group leaders. Schriesheim and Kerr (1977b) concluded that neither sufficient theoretical nor empirical support had emerged for this interpretation of LPC.

LPC as a Measure of a Value Attitude. On the basis of a review of available evidence, Rice (1978b) agreed that the data did not support the shift in orientation required by the motivational hierarchy concept of LPC. According to Rice, the data fit better with a simpler conceptualization of LPC as a value and an attitude, for LPC was more consistently and strongly related to attitudes and judgments than to behavioral manifestations. Therefore, LPC was seen as an attitude that reflects differences toward interpersonal relations and the accomplishment of tasks. One can make some general statements about the behavior of high- and low-LPC leaders, but situational variables have a strong influence.

How can Fiedler and Chemers's (1974) beliefs in the uniqueness of LPC be reconciled with Rice's conclusion that LPC is a value-attitude assessment? One problem was Rice's strategy of building his summary around published relationships that were statistically significant at the 5% level. As David Bakan quipped in a private communication, significant relationships are more likely to be published than nonsignificant ones. The total universe of studies is probably far greater than what Rice compiled. And with so many studies in the significant pool at the margin of significance, with no attention paid to the strength of the relationships that were found, it is difficult to accept Rice's evidence as compelling. However, Rice (1978b) concluded, as a consequence of his analysis of 313 reported relationships, that LPC was more

[15]See Fiedler (1954a, 1954b); Fishbein, Landy, and Hatch (1969b); Nealey and Blood (1968); Shiflett (1974); Shima (1968); and Larson and Rowland (1974).

strongly linked (that is, significant results at the 5% level were obtained) with values and attitudes. But even here, only 27% of the 313 relationships were significant. Yet even among these, certain expected and reasonable inferences could be made with some conviction. Thus, as would be expected from relations-oriented individuals, high-LPC people were found to make more favorable judgments of other group members—the leader, coworkers, and followers in general[16]—than low-LPC persons did in 18 of 20 analyses. Low-LPC people tended to be more favorable than high-LPC people in judgments of their best friends, more preferred coworkers, and loyal subordinates.[17] But negative results were also reported.[18]

Rice (1978b) concluded from these studies that low-LPC persons discriminated more sharply than high-LPC persons among other group members on task competence. Also, LPC was related to judgments about oneself; low-LPC persons judged themselves significantly more favorably than did high-LPC persons in 34 of 102 analyses, particularly in direct evaluations (88% of the relationships were statistically significant).[19] A complete reversal (not necessarily unexpected) occurred in a Japanese study (Shima, 1968), and negative results were reported by others.[20]

Evidence that low-LPC persons value the successful completion of tasks was seen in the defensiveness of their attributions about the cause of the failure of a task and their evaluation of the task-relevant ability of the group. In addition, low-LPC persons were found to be more optimistic about succeeding in a task and about earning important rewards as a consequence. High-LPC persons were more optimistic about succeeding at interpersonal relationships and expected that such success would lead to important outcomes (Fiedler, 1967a, 1972a).

Taking everything into account, Rice (1978b), on the basis of these mixed results, agreed with Fiedler that low-LPC persons value being successful in tasks and high-LPC persons value interpersonal success. But Fiedler concluded that any interpretation of the meaning of LPC must take into account situational considerations in determining how LPC will manifest itself in effective leadership. That is, Fiedler (1978) believed that the main effects of LPC on a leader's behavior are weak, in comparison with the effects of the interaction of LPC with the favorableness of the situation to the leader.

Situational Favorability for the Leader

In Fiedler's (1967a, 1978) exposition of his model, low-LPC (task-oriented) leaders performed better and led more effective groups when the quality of leader-member relationships, the degree of task structure, and the positional power of the leader are either altogether highly favorable or altogether highly unfavorable to the leader. High-LPC (relations-oriented) leaders are most effective when favorability is neither high nor low; that is, high-LPC leaders are expected to be most effective in moderately favorable circumstances. Fiedler envisaged eight situations (octants I through VIII), one for each combination of poor or good relations with group members, low or high structure of the group, and weak or strong power of the leader. The extremes of octants I and VIII are clearly determined by their location at the ends of the dimension of situational favorability. In octant I, leader-member relations are good, the task is highly structured, and the leader's positional power is strong. In octant VIII, leader-member relations are poor, the task is unstructured, and the leader's positional power is weak. But octants II and III, for instance, would exchange places on the dimension of favorability if the leader's position power was considered the second horizontal dimension and structure was considered the third horizontal dimension. The eight octants of the situational favorability dimension are shown along the horizontal axis of Figure 19.3.

Weighting. The relative importance of the three situational factors to the leader's situational favorability was

[16] See, for example, Alpander (1974); Cronbach, Hartmann, and Ehat (1953); Godfrey, Fiedler, and Hall (1959); Hunt (1971); Wearing and Bishop (1976); and Wood and Sobel (1970).

[17] See A. R. Bass, Fiedler, and Krueger (1964); Bons, A. R. Bass, and Komorita (1970); Fiedler (1958, 1962, 1964, 1967a); Godfrey, Fiedler and Hall (1959); Gottheil and Vielhaber (1966); Jones and Johnson (1971); and Shiflett (1974).

[18] See Bishop (1967), Chemers (1969), Gottheil and Lauterbach (1969), Hutchins and Fiedler (1960), and Steiner and Peters (1958).

[19] See, for example, D. R. Anderson (1964); Ayer (1968); A. R. Bass, Fiedler, and Krueger (1964); Bons, A. R. Bass, and Komorita (1970); W. W. Burke (1965); Fiedler (1972a); W. M. Fox (1974); and Shiflett (1974).

[20] Bishop (1967); Fiedler (1967a); Golb and Fiedler (1955); Gottheil and Lauterbach (1969); Gottheil and Vielhaber (1966); Gruenfeld and Arbuthnot (1968); Sashkin, Taylor, and Tripathi (1974); Steiner and McDiarmid (1957); and Strickland (1967).

Figure 19.3 The Contingency Model of Leadership Effectiveness Based on Original Studies

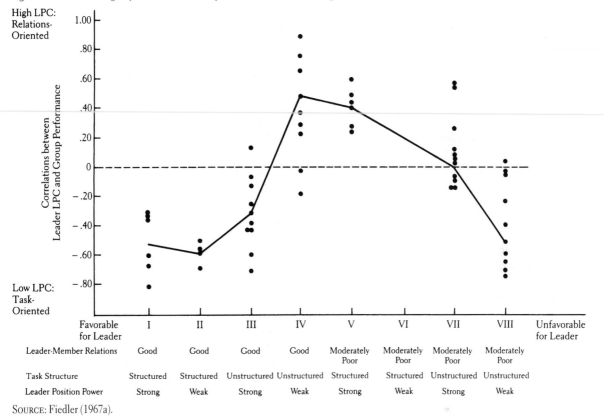

	I	II	III	IV	V	VI	VII	VIII	
Favorable for Leader									Unfavorable for Leader
Leader-Member Relations	Good	Good	Good	Good	Moderately Poor	Moderately Poor	Moderately Poor	Moderately Poor	
Task Structure	Structured	Structured	Unstructured	Unstructured	Structured	Structured	Unstructured	Unstructured	
Leader Position Power	Strong	Weak	Strong	Weak	Strong	Weak	Strong	Weak	

SOURCE: Fiedler (1967a).

reflected in a continuous scale constructed by Nebeker (1975). Nebeker's scale weighted standardized scores for each of the three situational variables so that the leader's situational favorability = 4 (leader-member relations) + 2 (task structure) + (positional power).

The theoretical combinations required by Fiedler for octant analysis fit the empirical multiple regression analyses conducted by Nebeker (1975). Beach and Beach (1978) also reported findings that supported an independent, additive view of the three variables of leader-member relations, task structure, and leader's positional power. Beach and Beach (1978) asked students to estimate the probability of success and the situational favorability of a series of hypothetical leadership situations. These situations were presented as involving either good or poor leader-member relations, high or low task structure, and the leader's high or low positional power. A correlation of .89 was obtained between the estimated

probability of the leader's success and the degree of situational favorability. A multiple correlation was then compared with situational favorableness as the criterion and the three situational favorability subscales as predictors. The beta weights obtained were .45 for leader-member relations, .33 for task structure, and .11 for positional power, comparable to the Nebeker formula of 4:2:1.

Earlier, situational favorability had been defined in terms of how much control the leader had in the situation. Support for the linkage of situational favorability and situational control came from a study by Mai-Dalton (1975) in which participants were asked to complete a leader's in-basket test. The study found that high-LPC leaders tended to be most effective and were most likely to ask for additional information in moderate-control situations, whereas low-LPC persons engaged in the most information-searching behavior in high-control situations.

Determination of Situational Characteristics. In Fiedler's original studies, the quality of interpersonal relations was measured by sociometric choices and related measures of liking. Open-hearth steel crews were judged to be highly structured and boards of directors or transient student groups were judged to be highly unstructured. The leader's power was judged to be high for managers of gasoline stations and to be low for the informal leaders of basketball teams. Subsequently, Fiedler developed specific scales to provide measurements of the three situational variables for any leader-group situation. Other situational variables that have been assumed to determine the leader's situational control included stress, cultural and linguistic heterogeneity, and the amount of experience.[21]

To measure leader-member relations, an eight-item group-atmosphere scale was developed that correlated .88 with earlier methods of estimating these relations. Respondents rated how much the situation was friendly or unfriendly, accepting or rejecting, satisfying or frustrating, etc. To measure task structure, a scale was created to obtain judgments about whether the goal was clearly stated, whether there was only one way to accomplish the task, whether there was one correct answer, and whether results were easy to check for correctness. To measure a leader's positional power, a scale asked whether the leader could evaluate subordinates and recommend rewards, punishments, promotions, and demotions (Fiedler, Chemers, & Mahar, 1976). Schriesheim (1979a) found the group-atmosphere scale to be free of social desirability, but the positional-power scale correlated .42 with social desirability.

Meaning of Situational Favorability. For Fiedler (1978), situational favorability implied that leaders were certain that their decisions and actions would have predictable results, would achieve the desired goals, and would satisfy the leaders. At the favorable extreme and the unfavorable extreme, the leaders know where they stand in relation to their groups. In between, relations are more cloudy for the leaders.

Schriesheim and Hosking (1978) found a number of problems with the measurement of situational favorability. The three variables were assumed to interact in a rela-

tively simple way to determine the amount of influence the leader had over the group, an assumption subsequently supported by Beach and Beach's (1978) results. However, although Fiedler (1978) acknowledged the importance of other variables, he relied on just the aforementioned three among the many possible variables of consequence (Filley, House, & Kerr, 1976).

Situational Favorability and LPC

Between 1953 and 1964, Fiedler and his associates studied the effectiveness of leadership in a variety of groups and tested a contingency hypothesis from the results of those studies. Fiedler (1964) plotted the correlations and their medians between LPC scores (actually ASo) and group performance for the different octants—the different levels of situational favorability. Each plotted point in Figure 19.3 represented an obtained correlation between the leaders in a particular study in a designated octant of situational favorability for the leaders and the effectiveness of their groups. A positive correlation indicated that high-LPC (relations-oriented) leaders coincided with more effective groups. A negative correlation showed that low-LPC (task-oriented) leaders ran more effective groups. A positive median correlation for all analyses completed in a designated octant denoted the extent to which high-LPC leaders performed more effectively than low-LPC leaders. A negative median correlation disclosed that the low-LPC leaders were superior for a designated octant. Fiedler theorized that the curvilinear relation (as seen in Figure 19.3) was an indication that low-LPC leaders were more effective than high-LPC leaders in very favorable and very unfavorable situations (e.g., octants I and VIII), whereas high-LPC leaders were more effective in situations of intermediate favorability (e.g., octants IV and V).

Validity of the Model

Early on, Fiedler (1971b, 1978) was able to review efforts to validate the contingency model.[22] The empirical investigations included field studies, field experiments, laboratory experiments, and octant analyses. Many more reviews followed (among them Ayman, 2002).

---

[21]Ayer (1968); Fiedler (1966); Fiedler, Meuwese, and Oonk (1961); Fiedler, O'Brien, and Ilgen (1969); and Meuwese and Fiedler (1965).

[22]Other such reviews were completed by Fiedler and Chemers (1974); and Mitchell, Biglan, Oncken, and Fiedler (1970).

Field Studies. Field tests validating the model were completed with basketball teams, student surveying teams, bomber crews, tank crews, open-hearth shops, farm-supply cooperatives, training groups, departments of a large physical science research laboratory, a chain of supermarkets, and a plant that manufactured heavy machinery. W. A. Hill (1969a) reported analyses in a large electronics firm with assembly-line instructors. Fiedler, O'Brien, and Ilgen (1969) worked with public health volunteer groups in Honduras. Shima (1968) studied Japanese student groups; Mitchell (1970b), participants in a church-leadership workshop; and Fiedler (1971c), trainees in an executive development program.

An example of the operational support of applied findings was Loyer and O'Reilly's (1985) study of Ontario community health supervisors. In favorable situations on the group-atmosphere scale, units led by low-LPC (task-oriented) supervisors were more effective (according to nursing directors' evaluations of the units) than were groups led by high-LPC supervisors. As predicted by the model, groups led by high-LPC (relations-oriented) supervisors, compared with those led by low-LPC (task-oriented) supervisors, were more effective in situations that were moderately favorable to the supervisors. A similar confirmatory pattern was reported by Wearing and Bishop (1974) for the LPC scores of leaders of U.S. Army combat-engineer training squads.

Kennedy (1982) reanalyzed data from 697 fire and military personnel in 13 studies. As the contingency theory postulated, low-LPC leaders did best, according to supervisors' and observers' evaluations, in very favorable and very unfavorable situations, and high-LPC leaders did best in the moderately favorable situations. However, Kennedy also observed that leaders whose LPC scores were intermediate were generally more effective than those whose LPC scores were high or low; and their effectiveness was relatively unaffected by the favorability of the situation.

Conclusions supporting the validity of the contingency model were most likely to be reached if the criterion measure of effectiveness was limited to superiors' evaluations of the performance of high- and low-LPC persons in carrying out their tasks as leaders. Rice (1978b) reviewed the relevant correlations by octants and found that almost all predictions fit the model. Table 19.3 presents Rice's results. However, Giffort and Ayman (1988) found that the contingency model was also supported when they used subordinates' satisfaction with coworkers as a criterion of effective leadership. The outcomes were dependent on situational favorability, as expected, but two other measures of subordinates' satisfaction (with the job and with supervision) failed to be sensitive in the same way.

Field Experiments. A number of experiments and controlled field studies also tested the model. Fiedler (1966) studied 96 experimentally assembled groups of Belgian sailors, half of which were led by petty officers and half by recruits. Half the groups began with structured tasks (routing a ship convoy through 10 and then 12 ports); the other half began with unstructured tasks (writing a recruitment letter). The results were consistent with the contingency model. In a controlled experiment conducted by Chemers and Skrzypek (1972) at West Point, leaders were chosen on the basis of sociometric choices by the members to determine in advance whom the members would choose as a leader. Then half the groups were assembled with preferred leaders and half

Table 19.3 Extent to Which the Contingency Model Fits Obtained Correlations of LPC and Superiors' Appraisals as a Function of Situational Favorability in Eight Octants

Predicted Direction:	I Negative	II Negative	III Negative	IV Positive	V Positive	VI Positive	VII Positive	VIII Negative
Empirical Analyses:								
Correlation of superior's appraisal and LPC in the direction predicted by the model	14	1	18	—	12	0	2	16
Total number of analyses	17	1	18	—	12	1	2	16

SOURCE: Rice (1978b).

Figure 19.4 Median Correlations between Leader's Performance and Group Performance for the Original Studies, Validation Studies, and the Chemers and Skrzypek (1972) Study

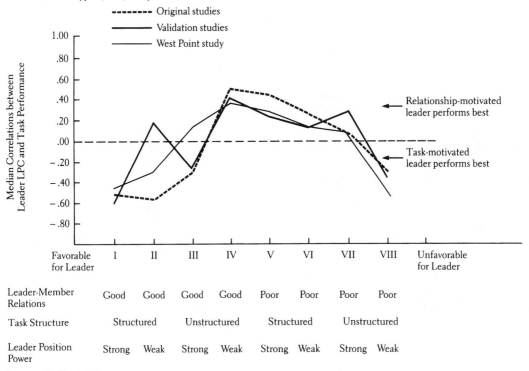

SOURCE: Fiedler (1997b).

with nonpreferred leaders. This study, with carefully preselected leaders, replicated the predicted median correlations. The generally supportive results are displayed in Figure 19.4. Fiedler (1978) concluded that the results of field research on work groups almost uniformly supported the model but that the results of experimental group research were somewhat less supportive

Laboratory Experiments. Gruenfeld, Rance, and Weissenberg (1969) studied leaders under high, medium, or low support in experimental groups. They found that low-LPC leaders behaved in a more dominant manner than did high-LPC leaders, regardless of the level of group support, but especially under medium support.

Exceptions to the predicted relations were found in octant II (good leader-member relations and structured, weak power of the leader), where the correlations between LPC and group effectiveness in the laboratory studies were positive, rather than negative as predicted. The same results occurred in laboratory experiments

by Hardy (1971, 1975) and Hardy, Sack, and Harpine (1973), who obtained LPC scores one or two weeks before their experiment. In two of these studies, leader-member relations were experimentally manipulated by assigning subjects to groups on the basis of preassessed sociometric scores. Rice, Bender, and Vitters (1980) conducted a laboratory study of 72 four-person temporary groups of West Point cadets using female and male leaders. The LPC scores related significantly to the groups' performance of tasks, according to the contingency model, in several cases, although the investigators qualified their findings because they lacked direct measures of situational favorableness.

Singh, Bohra, and Dalal (1979) conducted four experiments with male Indian engineering students and demonstrated that a much better fit with the contingency model could be obtained if the situational favorability of the octants was placed on the horizontal axis according to how much the ratings of the quality of leader-member relations, task structure, and position actually contributed to situational favorability. They discovered that ratings of the power relations declined in importance to situational favorability, and ratings of leader-member relations increased in importance to situational favorability. They attributed the changes in the importance of the components of situational favorability to India's return to democracy after the emergency rule by Indira Gandhi, which coincided with the repeated data collection. These shifts called into question Nebeker's (1975) 4:2:1 fixed scheme for weighting the three variables that contribute to situational favorability.

Comparisons of the Octants. As shown in Table 19.3, a large number of studies have assessed the hypothesized relationships for designated octants. In these studies, usually efforts were made to select or create and compare two of the eight octants and to note the LPC of the leader in relation to the group's effectiveness. Thirty-eight of these studies have been generally supportive of the contingency model.[23]

Supportive analyses of selected octants include dissertation studies of 122 child-study teams and their chairpersons in public schools (Jacobs, 1976), 64 groups of secondary-school juniors (Smith, 1974), and 40 task-oriented three-person experimental groups (Maher, 1976). Beebe (1975) manipulated the leader's positional power by instruction, structure, and task assignments. Only good leader-member relations were involved to determine the effectiveness of 37 three-person groups for octants II and IV. The correlation of LPC and group productivity was .01 in octant II and .40 in octant IV, both nonsignificant. Nevertheless, the result for octant IV was near the usual results obtained in many other studies.

Unsupportive Results. Along with the field, laboratory, and octant studies that support the validity of the contingency model, there are a number of studies that

[23]W. W. Burke (1965); Chemers and Skrzypek (1912); Cleven and Fiedler (1956); Csoka (1974, 1975); Cummins (1970); Eagly (1970); Fiedler (1954a, 1955, 1966, 1967a, 1972a); Fiedler and Meuwese (1963); Fiedler, Meuwese, and Oonk (1961); Fiedler, O'Brien, and Ilgen (1969); Green and Nebeker (1977); Hardy (1971); Hawkins (1962); W. Hill (1969); Hovey (1974); Hunt (1967, 1971); Hutchins and Fiedler (1960); Ilgen and O'Brien (1974); Julian (1964); Kunczik (1976a, 1976b); L. K. Michaelson (1973); Miller (1970); Nealey and Blood (1968); Reavis and Derlega (1976); Rice and Chemers (1973, 1975); Sample and Wilson (1965); Sashkin (1972); Schneier (1978); and Ziller (1963).

have failed to find support for it. Lanaghan's (1972) analyses of the effectiveness of 59 Illinois elementary schools and their principals and of the satisfaction of the teachers as a function of the behavior of the principals provided support for Fiedler's contingency-model predictions in only six of the 80 situations analyzed (at the 5% level of confidence). In seven other situations, results for relations and task orientation were opposite to what would have been predicted by the model. Shiflett and Nealey (1972) compared the performance of three-man college groups with very high intellectual ability and with moderate ability in creative tasks in octants III and IV (weak and strong positional power). The results of the moderate-ability groups supported the prediction of the model, but those of the very-high-ability groups were contradictory and nonsignificant.

Two laboratory experiments by Graen, Orris, and Alvares (1971) and a field study by Fox (1982) of tax examiners in the Internal Revenue Service also failed to find the expected outcomes. But Fiedler (1971a) and Chemers and Skrzypek (1972) attributed these failures to methodological manipulations that were inadequate to test the model. The results obtained by Utecht and Heier (1976) and Vecchio (1977) also failed to support the model, but Fiedler (1978) found that Vecchio's assignment of leaders to mixes of classmates whom the leaders ranked favorably and unfavorably was an invalid manipulation of good and poor relations. Isenberg (1981) found no support for the model in a study of communications. When the LPC scores of 62 Indian woolen mills supervisors were combined with task-structure and positional-power ratings of situational favorableness by Upmanyu and Singh (1981), they suggested that there was a need to reclassify the octants. A review by Rice (1981) concluded that followers were more satisfied when there were low-LPC (task-oriented) leaders in favorable situations and high-LPC (relations-oriented) leaders in unfavorable situations. Furthermore, contrary to the usual expectation that homogeneity of the leader and followers would be more satisfying to the followers, Rice noted that the followers' satisfaction was highest when they and the leader had dissimilar LPC scores.

Some unsupportive studies only indirectly tested the contingency model. Fiedler (1977b) pointed out that much research designed to test the model failed to use favorable and unfavorable situations sufficiently different from each other to provide a valid test.

Criticisms of the Contingency Model and Rejoinders

In studies that used only an approximate classification of situations—favorable, intermediate, or unfavorable to the leader—26 of 35 correlations of LPC and group effectiveness were as predicted by the model (Fiedler, 1971b). But critics faulted these conclusions. Some correlation coefficients were based on subsamples in the same study in which one subsample may have had good and the other may have had poor leader-member relations (Ashour, 1973a, 1973b; Graen, Alvares, Orris, & Martella, 1970).

A more general criticism was that most of the validations were based on concurrent measurements of LPC, leader-member relations, and group performance scores. Measures of leader-member relations and even LPC scores might be affected by the group's performance (Vroom, 1976b). This cause-effect criticism could be leveled at a considerable percentage of research on leadership, not just at studies that have tested Fiedler's model (Kerr & Schriesheim, 1974), but Katz and Farris (1976) actually found specific evidence that group performance could cause variations in leaders' LPC scores.

Among 140 significant relations reported in the literature, Rice (1976) could find only one clear significant pattern relating the leader's LPC score to the group's effectiveness. When the leader described leader-member relations favorably, low-LPC leaders were clearly more effective; 23 of 26 significant effects (88%) under such conditions showed low-LPC leaders to be more effective than high-LPC leaders. When leaders described leader-member relations as poor, there was no clear pattern. This finding could be considered evidence that the group's performance affected the leader's judgment of the quality of relations with members. But a longitudinal study by Konar-Coldband, Rice, and Monkarsh (1979) of eight intramural basketball teams over a nine-week season concluded that previously assessed LPC scores of the leaders and the groups' initial atmosphere did predict the groups' subsequent performance according to the contingency model. Increments in effective performance beyond the initial levels were most likely for groups with low-LPC leaders and a good group atmosphere. An additional 7% of the variance in effective performance was accounted for by the interaction of the groups' previous atmosphere and leaders' LPC scores. The investigators also found that 10% of the increment in the groups' atmosphere beyond the initial levels was accounted for by LPC interacting with the groups' initial performance. They concluded that a systems approach that allows cause and effects to flow in both directions is required.

Differences in Octants. As was noted earlier, octant II, in toto, yielded mixed and widely diverging results. However, Fiedler (1978) argued that octant II, which requires a structured task with a powerless leader, may be created experimentally but is unlikely to exist in the field. Fiedler (1978) suggested that leaders who are placed in such circumstances will find the situation unmanageable. This suggestion, of course, fails to explain what is causing the varying results of octant II. A more important question is this: why is octant II, for example, less favorable to a leader than is octant III, since in both octants two of three variables favor the leader? What is required is differential weighting of the variables. The difference in task structure between octant II and octant III must be given more weight toward favorability than the leader's positional power as weak or strong. This weighting was provided by Nebeker (1975) and Beach and Beach (1978). However, except for permitting the graphics to remain the same, a rationale and evidence are needed to support the logic that task structure is twice as important to a leader's situational favorability as the power of the leader's position. The same problem exists between octants IV and V, for which leader-member relations must be given more weight than task structure (as has been done).

Variations in Results. Empirically troublesome to some critics is the wide divergence of individual correlation coefficients in each octant, as can be seen in Figures 19.3 and 19.4. The median correlation for octant IV, for instance, may be .40, but the results that contribute to the median may range from .00 to .71. Another problem for which explanations are offered, but not necessarily accepted, is how to interpret some of the sudden shifts—say, from octant III to octant IV of the median correlation of −.29 to the median correlation of .40. Hosking (1978) believed that the most supportable inference about all octants except octant I is that the median correlations are random departures from a true correlation of zero. Schriesheim and Kerr (1977b) agreed, in a review of additional studies. Schriesheim and Hosking (1978, p. 500) concluded:

When the relevant studies are critically examined, and a distinction [is] drawn between those that constitute adequate tests of the model and those that do not, the results are far from encouraging. Examining both the size and direction of the correlations in each of the eight octants of the situational favorableness dimension, reveals that Fiedler's model really has little empirical support.

However, Strube and Garcia (1981), using R. Rosenthal's (1978, 1979a) meta-analyses of the contingency model, thought that all but octants III and VII in Fiedler's original validation were supportable, but they ignored octant VI. Strube and Garcia identified 33 analyses from which the model was built and 145 subsequent tests of the validity of the model. A meta-analysis of these data strongly supported the model's validity. Vecchio (1983) believed that Strube and Garcia had used a biased sample of studies and suggested a need to qualify the conclusions they had reached, but Strube and Garcia (1983) rejected Vecchio's criticisms. Then, a less extensive meta-analysis by Peters, Hartke, and Pohlmann (1985) provided additional but somewhat less strong support for the validity of the model than Strube and Garcia obtained. Finally, after including almost twice as many validation correlations as had been listed by Strube and Garcia (1981) and Peters, Hartke, and Pohlmann (1985), Nathan, Haas, and Nathan (1986) rejected the earlier supportive conclusions of both previous meta-analyses. Nathan, Haas, and Nathan based their rejection on the fact that the set of validity coeficients within each octant varied much too much. They stated:

The confidence intervals are too broad to allow any one to expect, as the theory predicts, that low LPC leaders would be effective when situational favorability was good and high LPC leaders would be effective when situational favorability was moderately poor. Worse, the fairly stable finding in Octant II, that when situational favorability is very good, high rather than low LPC leaders will be effective is directly opposite to what the theory predicts. At best, one can conclude that over half the time, correlations are above and below zero as predicted. (p. 10)

Fiedler (1971a, 1971b, 1973, 1978) systematically dealt with many of the earlier criticisms of his methodology. These included the statistical strength of evidence, of the conceptual meaning of the three variables defining situational favorability, and of the construct assessed by the LPC scales. He even anticipated many of the criticisms (Mitchell, Biglan, Oncken, & Fiedler, 1970). As T. R. Mitchell (1972) noted, if the validity of the hypothesized curvilinear relationship is to be tested, all eight octants must be assessed in a given study. Despite the difficulty of obtaining sufficient participants when the group, rather than the individual, is the unit of analysis, research designs must have adequate sample sizes and resulting statistical power (T. R. Mitchell, 1972).

Although the contingency model may still appear to be supported by a wide array of studies, the meaning of LPC remains unclear and controversial, and no adequate theoretical explanation of its effects has been presented. Moreover, the variability of the findings and the reverse results with octant II continue to undermine confidence in it. Yet analytically, the model compares favorably with alternative models.

Comparison with Alternative Contingency Models. Schriesheim, Tepper, and Tetrault (1988) compared two alternative contingency models with Fiedler's contingency model. In the declining-octant model (Shiflett, 1973), the performance of both high- and low-LPC leaders should decline systematically from octant I to octant VIII as the situation becomes less favorable to the leader. In the declining-zone model, octants I, II, and III are most situationally favorable; octants IV, V, VI, and VII are the next most favorable; and octant VIII is the least favorable to the leader.

Fiedler's contingency model predicts that high-LPC leaders will be more effective in octant IV than in octant I, II, III, or octant VIII. Four tests of the significance of the difference can be made to compare octant I with each of these other octants (II, III, and VIII). Four such tests can also be made for octants V against octants I, II, III, and VIII. Also, four such tests can be made for octant VI and four more for octant VII. A comparable number of tests across pairs of octants can be made for low-LPC leaders who are predicted by the contingency model to be more effective in octants I, II, III, and VIII and less effective in octants IV, V, VI, and VII. Similar tests can be made for the rival models. In the declining-octant model, effectiveness is expected to decline from octant I to octant VIII. Since octant I is the most favorable situation, it should coincide with the leader's being more effective than in each of the other octants; octant II should yield better performance than each of the remaining octants; and so on.

Each octant was compared individually with each other relevant octant by Schriesheim, Tepper, and Tetrault (1988) using meta-analytical procedures. The data came from a variety of published investigations. Of 245 tests of the differences between pairs of octants, 62% fit the contingency model; of 281 tests, 54% fit the declining-octant model; and of 274 tests, 51% fit the declining-zone model. The investigators concluded that, overall, these results supported the greater validity of Fiedler's contingency model than of the proposed alternatives.

Other Moderating and Mediating Variables

In a cross-cultural situation, Chemers (1969) trained leaders in the culture of their followers or in the geography of the country. Low-LPC leaders were more supportive and developed a more enjoyable group atmosphere in the culture training situation than high-LPC leaders did in the geography-training situation. These findings agreed with Fiedler's model in that in favorable situations, high-LPC leaders should tend to be concerned with the task whereas low-LPC leaders should tend to behave in a relationship-oriented manner. In unfavorable situations, the high-LPC leaders should be concerned with relations and the low-LPC leaders with tasks (Cummins, 1970).

Arrangements. Whether members of groups were coacting (performing side by side) or interacting did not seem to influence the findings of Hunt (1967) or W. Hill (1969a), which were generally supportive but nonsignificant.

Verbal Behavior. The behavior, as well as the effectiveness of followers, depends on the favorability of the situation and the leader's LPC. Fiedler (1967a) found that group members made more task-related comments in favorable situations and fewer such comments in unfa-

vorable situations under a high-LPC leader. The reverse was true for group members under the low-LPC leader. Furthermore, the group made more person-related comments in the unfavorable situation and fewer such comments in the favorable situation under the high-LPC leader.

Followers' LPCs. The followers' LPCs also may make a difference. Schuster and Clark (1970) studied first- and second-level supervisors in post offices. Under high-LPC second-level supervision, high-LPC first-level supervisors were better satisfied than their low-LPC peers. With low-LPC second-level supervisors, the satisfaction of high- and low-LPC first-level supervisors did not differ.

Hunt (1971) assembled groups—each with a manager, two supervisors, and two workers—to play a business game. Although the effects of manager-supervisor interaction did not account for variance in the teams' performance, the effects of the manager and supervisor alone were each significantly related to the performance of the workers. Low-LPC managers and high-LPC supervisors had the best-performing groups; high-LPC managers and low-LPC supervisors had the poorest-performing groups. The two-level interaction effect also predicted the satisfaction of workers better than did either LPC effect alone.

Leaders' Self-Monitoring. Ayman and Chemers (1991) found that among 83 Mexican middle-level managers, the predictions of the contingency model were valid only if the managers were low in self-monitoring. The managers rated their self-monitoring behavior. Their 184 subordinates rated satisfaction with the supervisors, coworkers, and the work. The predictions from the model failed to work when the managers rated themselves high in self-monitoring, but the results did conform to the contingency model when managers rated themselves low in self-monitoring.

Leaders' Experience. The leaders' experience with leadership changes the situational favorability (Bons & Fiedler, 1976). With continued experience, tasks become more routine and leaders get to know their subordinates and usually can work better with them. In addition, the leaders learn the expectations of the higher authority.

Although the effectiveness of leaders, as a whole, does not necessarily improve with experience (Fiedler, 1970a, 1972a), the contingency model predicts that leadership experience will have different effects on the performance of high- and low-LPC leaders. In a study of infantry squads by Fiedler, Bons, and Hastings (1975), 28 sergeants who served as squad leaders were evaluated at the time the units were formed and after they had five months of experience. The sergeants' judgments about their situational favorability increased over the five months, as expected. The high-LPC leaders performed better at first when they had little experience and situational favorability than they did five months later. As predicted by the model, the low-LPC leaders performed relatively better after they had five months' experience and gained situational favorability. Similar results were found by Godfrey, Fiedler, and Hall (1959) for the general managers of 32 consumer cooperatives; by McNamara (1968) for Canadian elementary and secondary school principals; and by Hardy and Bohren (1975) for college teachers. Furthermore, the training of leaders based on the contingency model generates similar dynamics and results (Chemers, Rice, Sundstrom, & Butler, 1975; Fiedler, 1972a).[24]

Organizational Shifting. Changes in organization can have similar effects on situational favorability, as can increased experience. Bons and Fiedler (1976) tested the contingency model using experienced leaders of army squads who were given new subordinates, new bosses, or new jobs.

In the stable condition of continuing with the same bosses, subordinates, and jobs, the experienced leaders who were low in LPC were unaffected, but the performance of experienced high-LPC leaders declined. When a change of boss, subordinates, or job moved leaders from moderate situational favorability to low situational favorability, the low-LPC leaders again did relatively better.

Implications

Fiedler's Contingency Model offers a remedial plan for increasing the effectiveness of leaders that is different from all other theories of leadership. Blake and Mouton

[24]This issue will be discussed in Chapter 34.

(1964), Hersey and Blanchard (1969b), R. Likert (1977a), and Vroom and Yetton (1974) would see a need to educate leaders to improve their styles. For Blake and Mouton, improvement would be toward the one best style: 9,9. For Hersey and Blanchard, it would depend on the stage in the group's life cycle and the followers' maturity. For Likert, it would be toward a democratic style. For Vroom and Yetton, the decision process to use would depend on the problem situation. But Fiedler (1978) suggested an entirely different course of action. Because a leader's LPC is what matters, and because LPC is not very changeable, either one must identify and select leaders of high or low LPC to fit given situations, or leaders need to know their LPC scores and in what situations they are most effective—then they can try to change the situation, rather than themselves. Fiedler argued that changing leader-member relations, the structure of the task, or a leader's positional power is easier than changing a leader's personality. Leader Match (Fiedler, Chemers, & Mahar, 1976), a training program that tries to do so, is discussed in Chapter 34. The contingency model also has implications for leadership under stressful conditions, which is examined in Chapter 28.

Summary and Conclusions

In general, the leader who is more highly rated by superiors and peers, who is most satisfying to subordinates, and whose approach results in the good performance of the group is likely to be both relations-oriented and task-oriented in an integrated fashion. Blake and Mouton's theory is the strongest endorsement of this conclusion.

However, many situational contingencies have been found to moderate the effects. These contingencies include the makeup of the subordinates and the organizational constraints, tasks, goals, and functions in the situation. The popular but underresearched and controversial Hersey-Blanchard model has focused on the followers' psychological maturity and job experience as the most important contingencies affecting the leader's need to be task-oriented or relations-oriented.

According to Fiedler's widely researched contingency model, (1) task orientation (as measured by LPC) works best in situations which are either extremely favorable or extremely unfavorable to the leader, or in which the leader has very high or very low control; and (2) relations orientation works best in situations that are moderately favorable to the leader or in which the leader has moderate control. Despite a vast array of publications on the reliability, validity, and meaning of LPC and situational favorableness, and despite tests supportive of the model, the validity of the model continues to be disputed. Less controversial are the equally widely researched concepts and behavioral measures of the leaders' consideration of their subordinates and the leaders' initiation of structure for their subordinates, the subject of Chapter 20.

Initiation versus Consideration

In 1945, C. L. Shartle (1950b) launched the Ohio State Leadership Studies. He was influenced by his work on gathering occupational information to describe tasks, jobs, and occupational requirements in all echelons of industry, government, and the military. He focused on defining and classifying work done in each of the 30,000 occupations that had appeared originally in the 1939 *Dictionary of Occupational Titles* and in the *U.S. Military Occupational Specialties*. He and his colleagues now applied this background to the study of leaders. This was different from the emphasis in previous leadership research, which had sought to identify the traits of leaders. Reviews by Bird (1940), W. O. Jenkins (1947), and Stogdill (1948) had concluded that the personality-traits approach had reached a dead-end, for several reasons: (1) attempts to select leaders in terms of traits had had little success; (2) numerous traits differentiated leaders from followers; (3) the traits demanded of a leader varied from one situation to another; and (4) the traits approach ignored the interaction between the leader and his or her group. Attention was shifted to what leaders did.

Needed were descriptions of individuals' actions when they acted as leaders of groups or organizations. Hemphill (1949a) had already initiated such work at the University of Maryland. After joining the Ohio State Leadership Studies, Hemphill and his associates developed a list of approximately 1,800 statements that described different aspects of the behavior of leaders, such as "He insists on meeting deadlines." Most statements were assigned to several subscales. However, staff members agreed on 150 statements that could each be assigned to only one subscale. These statements were used to develop the first form of the Leader Behavior Description Questionnaire, or LBDQ (Hemphill, 1950a; Hemphill & Coons, 1957). On the LBDQ, respondents rated a leader by using one of five alternatives to indicate the frequency or amount of a particular behavior that was descriptive of the leader being rated. Responses to items were simply scored and added in combinations to form subscales on the basis of the similarity of their content. These subscale totals were then intercorrelated and factor-analyzed (Fleishman, 1951, 1953c; Halpin & Winer, 1957). "Consideration" and "initiation of structure" were primary factors identified by Halpin and Winer (1957) with regard to Air Force officers, and by Fleishman (1951, 1953c, 1957) with regard to industrial supervisors. They emerged in successive factor studies (Fleishman, 1973) as the two most prominent factors that described leaders according to questionnaires completed by themselves and others.

Descriptive Factors

Consideration

This first factor describes the extent to which a leader exhibits concern for the welfare of the other members of the group. The *considerate* leader expresses appreciation for good work, stresses the importance of job satisfaction, maintains and strengthens the self-esteem of subordinates by treating them as equals, makes special efforts to help subordinates feel at ease, is easy to approach, puts subordinates' suggestions into operation, and obtains subordinates' approval on important matters before going ahead. Considerate leaders provide support that is oriented toward relationships, friendship, mutual trust, and interpersonal warmth. Participation and the maintenance of the group accompany such support (Atwater, 1988). In contrast, the *inconsiderate* leader criticizes subordinates in public, treats them without considering their feelings, threatens their security, and refuses to accept their suggestions or to explain his or her actions.

Initiation of Structure

This second factor shows the extent to which a leader initiates activity in the group, organizes it, and defines the way work is to be done. Initiation of structure includes such leadership behavior as insisting on maintaining standards and meeting deadlines and deciding in detail what will be done and how it should be done. Clear channels of communication and clear patterns of work organization are established. Orientation is toward the task. The leader acts directively without consulting the group. Particularly relevant are defining and structuring the leader's own role and the roles of subordinates in attaining goals. The leader whose factor score in initiating structure is low is described as hesitant about taking initiatives in the group. He or she fails to take necessary actions, makes suggestions only when members ask for it, and lets members do the work the way they think best.

Psychometric Properties

Three Leader Behavior Description Questionnaires

The LBDQ, consisting of 40 statements, was designed to measure the two factors of consideration and initiation (Hemphill & Coons, 1957). An industrial version, the Supervisory Behavior Description Questionnaire (SBDQ), followed (Fleishman, 1972), as did LBDQ—Form XII, hereafter referred to as LBDQ-XII (Stogdill, 1963a). Each of the LBDQs had instructions such as these:

The following . . . are items that may be used to describe the behavior of your leader or supervisor. Each item describes a specific kind of behavior, but does not ask you to judge whether the behavior is desirable or undesirable. This is not a test of ability. It simply asks you to describe, as accurately as you can, the behavior of your supervisor or leader. *Group* refers to an organization or to a department, division, or other unit of organization that is supervised by the person being described. . . . *Members* refer to all the people in the unit of organization that is supervised by the person being described.

THINK about how frequently the leader engages in the behavior described by the item.

DECIDE whether he (A) *always*, (B) *often*, (C) oc-

casionally, (D) *seldom*, or (E) *never* acts as described by the item.

Typical items were: "He lets group members know what is expected of them." "He is friendly and approachable."

The intentions of the developers of the LBDQs and the SBDQ, particularly with regard to initiating structure, differed somewhat in the construction of the different versions. The LBDQ contained a subset of 15 items that asked subordinates to describe the actual structuring behavior of their leader. This structuring behavior was the leader's behavior in delineating relationships with subordinates, in establishing well-defined patterns of communication, and in detailing ways to get a job done (Halpin, 1957b). The Supervisory Behavior Description Questionnaire (SBDQ) consisted of 20 items that included asking subordinates about their leader's actual structuring behavior. Initiating structure, as measured by the SBDQ, was intended to reflect the extent to which the leader organizes and defines interactions among group members, establishes ways to get the job done, schedules, criticizes, and so on (Fleishman, 1972). The SBDQ items for the factor of initiation of structure included a wider variety of structuring behaviors drawn from the loadings on this factor. Several were close to Misumi's (1985) *Production Pressure*. Items on the LBDQ came mostly from original conceptualizations about communication and organization (Schriesheim, House, & Kerr, 1976). The revised LBDQ-XII had 10 items that measured initiation of structure in terms of the actions of leaders who clearly define their own role and let followers know what is expected of them (Stogdill, 1963a).

Reliability and Validity

As noted, ratings of the consideration and initiation of structure by leaders are highly stable and consistent from one situation to another (Taylor, Crook, & Dropkin, 1961; and Philipsen, 1965a). According to Schriesheim and Kerr's (1974) review of the psychometric properties of the LBDQ and SBDQ, the descriptions maintain the high internal consistency that was the basis for their construction. That is, items on the "consideration behavior" in each instrument correlate highly with all the other consideration items and do not correlate with items on the "initiation behavior" factor. Conversely, items on the "initiating structure" factor are independent of the "consideration" items and are highly intercorrelated with all the other structuring items. Using a sample of 308 public utilities employees, Schriesheim (1979a) found that consideration and initiation were so psychometrically robust that it did not make much difference in a supervisor's scores whether one asked a subordinate to describe how the supervisor behaved toward him or her personally (the dyadic approach) or how the supervisor behaved toward the whole work group (the standard approach).

Nonetheless, the factor scores left a lot to be desired. They suffered from halo effects and were plagued by a variety of other response errors, such as leniency and social desirability, as well as a response set to agree rather than to disagree (Schriesheim, Kinicki, & Schriesheim, 1979). It was not known whether they were valid measures of true consideration and initiation of structure. Most important, as research with the original LBDQ and SBDQ instruments continued, it became apparent that some of what leaders do had been missed. A great deal of the behavior of leaders was being lost in the emphasis on just two factors to account for all the common variance among items describing this behavior. Therefore, for LBDQ-XII, various additional factored scales were constructed, possibly lacking complete independence from structuring and consideration, yet likely to include much of the missing information of consequence.

Comparison of the Three Forms. All three versions—LBDQ, SBDQ, and LBDQ-Form XII—have been used extensively, and each has been subjected to additional factor analyses (Bish & Schriesheim, 1974; Szilagyi & Sims, 1974a; Tscheulin, 1973). A direct comparison of all three became possible after a survey and factor-analytic study of 242 hourly employees by Schriesheim and Stogdill (1975). This comparison study was necessary, since, as Korman (1966) and others had noted, the content of the scales varied, which caused differences in outcomes. The original LBDQ and particularly the SBDQ contained several items such as "Needles subordinates for greater effort" and "Prods subordinates for production" that measured punitive, arbitrary, coercive, and dominating behaviors and that affected the scores for initiation of structure. The LBDQ-XII was considered to be most nearly free of such autocratic items (Schriesheim &

Kerr, 1974). As has usually been found, internal consistency reliabilities were high for scores on both factors that were derived from the items drawn according to their use in the LBDQ, SBDQ, or LBDQ-XII. For consideration and initiation, reliabilities were .93 and .81 for the LBDQ, .81 and .68 for the SBDQ, and .90 and .78 for the LBDQ-XII. (The reliability of .68 for initiation of structure on the SBDQ was raised to .78 when three SBDQ punitive items were removed from the scoring of the scale.) The primary factors that were extracted indicated that all three versions contained some degree of arbitrary punitive performance ("The leader demands more than we can do"). But, as expected, the pattern was most marked in the SBDQ. A hierarchical factor analysis disclosed the existence of a higher-order factor of rater bias, which appeared in all three questionnaires.

According to Schriesheim and Kerr, the items loading highest on the SBDQ in initiating structure were: "He insists that he be informed on decisions made by people under him" (.60), "He insists that people under him follow standard ways of doing things in every detail" (.65), and "He stresses being ahead of competing work groups" (.64). In fact, Atwater (1988) found that two items—"Demands a great deal from his workers" and "Pushes his workers to work harder"—correlated highest with the SBDQ factor she obtained and labeled *demanding behavior*. But on the LBDQ, the two items loading highest on initiating structure were: "He maintains definite standards of performance" (.59) and "He lets members know what is expected of them" (.54).

Matters further were complicated because many researchers deleted items or modified the wording of items for use in a particular study, as Podsakoff and Schriesheim (1985) found in their review of studies that used the LBDQ. Also, many researchers failed to specify which version of the LBDQ they had used or how they had modified the scales (Hunt, Osborn, & Schriesheim, 1978).

Other Psychometric Issues

The items ask how the leader acts toward the work group rather than toward specific individuals. Critics, such as Graen and Schiemann (1978), assume that there are large variations in the leader's behavior toward different individual members of a work group, and therefore that the wording of items should allow for this. Individual differences among raters also underlie the ratings. Although WABA analysis could handle this, it was not introduced until 1984 (see Chapter 16). The previously cited findings of Schriesheim (1979a) suggested, however, that the matter may be overblown. D. M. Lee (1976) asked 80 students to judge the initiation and consideration of their English professors over an eight-week period. The results indicated that the individual students differed widely in the cues they used as the basis of their ratings of the same professors. The questionnaires fail to weight the timing, appropriateness, importance, and specificity or generality of responses. They may assess the circumstantial requirements of the job, rather than the leader as a person with discretionary opportunities to behave in the manner indicated.

Leniency Effects. Seeman (1957) reported that the LBDQ scales suffered from halo effects. Even making items more detailed was of no help in reducing the halo. Schriesheim, Kinicki, and Schriesheim (1979) completed five studies of the extent to which consideration and initiation of structure were biased by leniency effects. They inferred from the results that leniency response bias—the tendency to describe others in favorable but probably untrue terms—did not particularly affect descriptions of initiation of structure. But even though consideration and leniency are conceptually distinct, they concluded that (1) consideration items were not socially neutral and were susceptible to leniency, (2) consideration reflected an underlying leniency factor when applied in a field setting, and (3) leniency explained much or most of the variance in consideration. Leniency may explain why consideration tends to correlate higher with other evaluative variables than does initiation of structure (Fleishman, 1973).

Implicit Theories. D. J. Schneider (1973), among others, suggested that respondents express their own implicit theories about and stereotypes of leaders and leaders' behavior, rather than the behavior of the specific leader they are supposed to be describing with the LBDQ. That is, respondents describe their idealized prototype of a leader, rather than the actual leader they should be describing (Rush, Thomas, & Lord, 1977). Eden and Leviatan (1975) noted that leader-behavior de-

scriptions of a fictitious manager using the Survey of Organizations resulted in a factor structure highly similar to that obtained from descriptions of real managers reported by Taylor and Bowers (1972).[1] Rush, Thomas, and Lord (1977) found a high degree of congruence between factor structures obtained from descriptions of a fictitious supervisor using LBDQ-XII and descriptions of real leaders from a field study by Schriesheim and Stogdill (1975). In both studies, the authors concluded that since practically identical factor structures emerged for fictitious and specific real leaders, the actual behavior of a leader is relatively unimportant for behavioral descriptions, because descriptions are based mainly on implicit theories or stereotypes.

One might suggest that this tendency to project or to use implicit theories tells more about the subordinate than about the leader. But the tendency is a consequence of ambiguity and of a lack of specific information about the leader to be rated. Schriesheim and DeNisi (1978) studied 110 bank employees and 205 workers in a manufacturing plant who used the LBDQ-XII to describe supervisors in general after first describing their own supervisors. The investigators, as expected, found comparable factors emerging from the general and specific descriptions when each was analyzed separately. However, separate real and imaginary factors emerged when the combined data were subjected to an analysis that provided an opportunity for statistical differentiation. As before, in both real and imaginary descriptions, initiation of structure and consideration was correlated above .50, with reliabilities ranging from .84 to .87.

Schriesheim and DeNisi discovered that although satisfaction with one's real supervisor correlated between .51 and .75 with descriptions of the actual consideration and initiation of the real supervisors, it correlated only .23 and −.03 with scores for initiating structure and consideration for the stereotypes of supervisors. This was a particularly important finding.

Subsequent experimentation by Schriesheim and DeNisi (1978) with 360 undergraduates strongly supported the contention that as more specific information became available to them, the respondents' LBDQ responses became more accurate and were less likely to depend on implicit theories. These results are consistent with those

---

[1] See Chapter 17 for a discussion of the Survey of Organizations.

of Bass, Valenzi, Farrow, and Solomon (1975), who found that subordinates describing the same real leader were in much more significant agreement with each other than with subordinates who described other leaders.

Self-Ratings Unrelated to Subordinates' Ratings. As many researchers reported for self-rated directive versus participative leadership, for autocratic versus democratic leadership, and for task- versus relations-oriented leadership,[2] little relation was obtained between leaders' self-descriptions of their own initiation and consideration and their subordinates' descriptions on the LBDQ. Similarly, there was only a weak relation between what leaders say they should do, according to scores on the Leadership Opinion Questionnaire, and what they actually do, according to their subordinates' descriptions of them on the LBDQ (Schriesheim & Kerr, 1974).

Relationship between Consideration and Initiation of Structure

Theoretically, given the original orthogonal factor structure, consideration and initiation of structure should be independent, but this is not the case. Schriesheim, House, and Kerr (1976) reexamined Weissenberg and Kavanagh's (1972) review of the data, along with work published subsequently. In 11 of 13 studies using the LBDQ, a positive correlation was reported. The median correlation for the 13 analyses was .45. Likewise, for the LBDQ-XII for 10 studies, the median correlation was .52 between consideration and initiation of structure. The correlation was even higher in situations where job pressure was strong. In addition, the correlations between consideration and initiation were positive both when group-by-group values were correlated and when the scores for individuals within the groups were correlated (Katerberg & Hom, 1981). Of the 16 studies that used the SBDQ, which includes some "autocratic" items, 11 studies yielded some significant negative correlations between consideration and initiation. However, the median correlation was −.05. Without the punitive items, consideration and initiation on the LBDQ tend to correlate more positively. A comprehensive review (Fleishman, 1989a), which included 32 studies with the SBDQ, found

[2] Bass (1957a), Besco and Lawshe (1959), D. T. Campbell (1956), Graham and Gleno (1970), Solomon (1976), and T. R. Mitchell (1970a).

a median correlation of −.02 between the score for consideration and the score for structure.

Alternative and Additional Scales

Industrial Examples

Oldham (1976), among others, developed alternative and additional scales to provide a more detailed profile of leader behavior. The scales included behaviors such as these: personally rewarding, personally punishing, setting goals, designing feedback systems, placing personnel, and designing job systems. These scales were higher in relation to effectiveness than were measures of consideration and the initiation of structure. Seltzer and Bass (1987) found that the transformational leadership factors of charisma, individualized consideration, and intellectual stimulation added substantially to the effects of consideration on subordinates' satisfaction and effectiveness. Seltzer and Bass conceived of consideration and initiation of structure as primarily transactional.

Halpin and Croft (1962) also were not convinced that the behavior of leaders could be adequately described with just two factors. Using items containing additional content about school principals, as well as items from the LBDQ, they extracted four factors to account for the common variance in the obtained descriptions of school principals' behavior: (1) aloofness, formality, and social distance; (2) Production emphasis—pushing for results; (3) Thrust—personal hard work and task structure; and (4) Consideration—concern for the comfort and welfare of followers. These factored scales for describing the behavior of school principals were supplemented by the following four scales used to describe the behavior of teachers: (1) Disengagement—clique formation, withdrawal, (2) Hindrance—frustration from routine and overwork, (3) Esprit—high morale, enthusiasm, and (4) Intimacy, mutual liking, and teamwork.

When Halpin and Croft classified 71 schools into six categories according to climate, they found that an open school climate was associated with the esprit of teachers under a principal who was high in thrust. An autonomous climate produced intimacy in teachers under an aloof principal. A controlled climate resulted in hindrance in teachers under a principal who pushed for production. A familiar climate was associated with the disengagement of teachers under a considerate principal. A climate with potential but with the disengagement of teachers resulted in a principal who exhibited consideration, along with an emphasis on production. A closed climate, also with the disengagement of teachers, was associated with an aloof principal. These results yielded considerably more insight into the dynamic interplay among the climate of schools, the behavior of leaders, and the response of teachers than could be produced by the use of just two factors to describe the behavior of leaders.

Leadership Behavior Description Questionnaire— Form XII

The most direct expansion from consideration and initiation of structure to a broader array of leader-behavior dimensions was the development of LBDQ-XII.

On the basis of a theoretical analysis of the differentiation of roles in groups, Stogdill (1959) proposed 10 additional patterns of behavior involved in leadership, conceptually independent of consideration and initiation of structure, to be included in the LBDQ-XII along with consideration and initiation of structure. These patterns were: (1) Representation—speaks and acts as the representative of the group; (2) Reconciliation—reconciles conflicting organizational demands and reduces disorder in the system; (3) Tolerance of uncertainty—is able to tolerate uncertainty and postponement without anxiety or upset; (4) Persuasiveness—uses persuasion and argument effectively; exhibits strong convictions; (5) Tolerance of freedom—allows followers scope for initiative, decisions, and action; (6) Role retention—actively exercises the leadership role, rather than surrendering leadership to others; (7) "Production emphasis"—applies pressure for productive output; (8) Predictive accuracy—exhibits foresight and the ability to predict outcomes accurately; (9) Integration—maintains a close-knit organization and resolves intermember conflicts; and (10) Influence with supervisors—maintains cordial relations with superiors; has influence with them; strives for higher status. Subsequently, these patterns became the 10 scored factors of LBDQ-XII. The conception of the persuasiveness pattern anticipated the more recent focus on the measurement of charismatic and inspirational leadership.

Interdescriber Agreement. In a study of a governmental organization by Day (1968), high-ranking administrators were each described by two male and two female subordinates. Correlations were computed to determine the extent to which pairs of subordinates agreed with each other in their descriptions of their immediate superiors. The greatest agreement was shown by pairs of female subordinates describing their female superiors. Their correlations ranged from .39 (integration) to .73 (retention of the leadership role). The least agreement was shown by pairs of male subordinates describing their female superiors. Their correlations ranged from −.02 (tolerance of freedom) to .53 (retention of the leadership role). Pairs of female subordinates tended to exhibit higher degrees of agreement than male subordinates in descriptions of male superiors on 8 of the 12 scales. The four exceptions occurred for representation, production emphasis, integration, and influence with superiors. The scales with the highest degrees of interdescriber agreement across groups of raters, male or female, were demand reconciliation, tolerance of uncertainty, persuasiveness, role retention, predictive accuracy, and influence with superiors. The scales with the lowest degrees of agreement across samples were representation, tolerance of freedom, and integration.

Divergent Validities. To test the divergent validities of several scales of the LBDQ-XII, Stogdill (1969), with the assistance of a playwright, wrote a scenario for each of six scales (consideration, structure, representation, tolerance of freedom, production emphasis, and superior orientation). The items in each scale were used as a basis for writing the scenario for that pattern of behavior. Experienced actors played the roles of supervisor and workers. Each role was played by two actors, and each actor played two different roles. Motion pictures were made of the performances. Observers used LBDQ-XII to describe the "supervisor's" behavior. No significant differences were found between two actors playing the same role. Still, the actors playing a given role were described as behaving significantly more like that role than the other roles. Stogdill concluded that the scales measured what they purported to measure.

Factor Validation of LBDQ-XII.[3] Data collected by Stogdill, Goode, and Day (1963a, 1963b, 1964, 1965) used nine of the LBDQ-XII scales to obtain descriptions of the leadership behavior of U.S. senators, corporation presidents, presidents of international labor unions, and presidents of colleges and universities. For leaders in each setting, the scores for the scales were intercorrelated and factor-analyzed. In general, the results suggested that each factor was strongly dominated by a single appropriate scale. For example, in all four analyses the representation factor emerged with only the representation scale correlated highly with it. The representation scale correlated, respectively, with the representation factor, .80, .94, .92, and .92, in the four locales. Similarly, the role retention subscale correlated only with its own role retention factor, .89, .93, .81, and .92. However, production emphasis tended to load highly on initiation of structuring as well as on production emphasis.

"Reconciliation of conflicting demands" failed to emerge as a factor differentiating college presidents, presumably because they all were described similarly highly in this behavior. "Orientation to superiors," of course, did not fit with the role of senators; nor did union presidents differ from each other in orientation to a higher authority. The differences in predictive accuracy generated the factor "predictive accuracy" for only the corporate and union leaders, not the senators or college presidents.

Slightly different results emerged when all the items of the LBDQ-Form XII were intercorrelated and factor-analyzed for three additional locales. Eight factors emerged: (1) General persuasive leadership; (2) tolerance of uncertainty; (3) tolerance of followers' freedom of action; (4) representation of the group; (5) influence with superiors; (6) production emphasis; (7) structuring expectations; (8) retention of the leadership role. In addition, two distinct factors of consideration were extracted.

The most numerous and most highly loaded items on general persuasive leadership, aside from measures of persuasiveness, were scales with items about the reconciliation of conflicting demands, structuring expectations, retention of the leadership role, influence with superiors, consideration, and production emphasis. These items represented the followers' general impression of the leaders. In fulfilling these functions, leaders were seen

[3] The glossary provides definitions of the factor-analytical terms used in this and subsequent sections.

as considerate of their followers' welfare. Each of the remaining factors tended to be composed of items from a single scale, but some contained stray items from other scales. Consideration broke down into two separate factors, to be discussed later in connection with J. A. Miller's (1973b) hierarchical factor analysis.

The first nine factors showed similar loadings for senators, union leaders and college presidents. But "retention of the leadership role" appeared as a separate factor only in the ratings of the state senators. All scales except those dealing with tolerance of uncertainty, tolerance of freedom, and representation contributed some items to the general factor. However, all scales except persuasiveness and the reconciliation of conflicting demands emerged in separate factors differentiated from each other. These findings indicated that the behavior of leaders is indeed complex in structure and that followers are able to differentiate among different aspects of behavior. The general persuasion factor provided valuable additional insight into the nature of leadership, strongly suggesting that this general factor may be particularly useful given what was said in Chapter 6 about its opposite, laissez-faire leadership.

Initiation and Consideration as Higher-Order Dimensions. A. F. Brown (1967) used the LBDQ-XII to obtain scores on each of the 12 factors for 170 principals described by 1,551 teachers in Canadian schools. He found that two higher-order factors accounted for 76% of the total factor variance for the 12 primary factors. When the loadings for the two factors were plotted against each other, "production emphasis," "structuring expectations," and "representation of the group" clustered about an axis of "initiation of structure" and "tolerance of uncertainty." "Tolerance of freedom" and "consideration" clustered about an axis of "consideration." The loadings for the remaining factors fell between the clusters at the extremes of these two orthogonal axes. A plot of factor loadings obtained for descriptions of university presidents on the LBDQ-XII (Stogdill, Goode, & Day, 1965) produced similar results. "Representation," "structuring expectations," "emphasis," and "persuasiveness" clustered around the first axis and "freedom," "uncertainty," and "consideration" clustered around the second axis. Marder (1960) obtained a somewhat different pattern of loadings when military rather than educational leaders were studied. The data consisted of 235 descriptions of U.S. Army officers by enlisted men. "Productivity emphasis" and "initiation of structure" centered on one axis and "tolerance for freedom" and "tolerance for uncertainty" clustered around the other. "Consideration" was displaced toward the central cluster of items.

Psychometric Outcomes as Dependent on Factor Theory

There are different schools of thought regarding the use of factor analysis. One school maintains that as much of the total factor variance as possible should be explained in terms of a general factor. Another school holds that rotational procedures, such as the *varimax* that reduces the magnitude of the general factor, are legitimate. The former school, while admitting that systems of events in the real world may involve a variety of factors, maintains that human perception contains a large element of bias and halo that should be removed in the general factor before any attempt to determine the structure of measurements representing the real world. The second school argues that the apparent halo in the general factor has its equivalent in the opacity of the real world and that the purpose of research is to reduce this opacity by making full use of all the structure differentiated by human perception. The structure that is perceived should not be permitted to remain hidden in the general factor.

If one prefers a two-factor theory of leadership behavior, initiation of structure, production emphasis, or persuasiveness can define one of the factors; consideration, tolerance of freedom, and tolerance of uncertainty can define the other. A two-factor solution, which leaves a considerable amount of the total variance unexplained, can always be obtained in the analyses of descriptions of leaders' behavior. However, a multifactor solution should not be rejected until its consequences have been thoroughly explored and it has been proved untenable. Furthermore, the dilemma can be reconciled, as J. A. Miller (1973b) and Schriesheim and Stogdill (1975) showed, by recourse to hierarchical factor analysis. The former used rotation and differentiation; the latter, the general evaluative bias factor. Finally, the positive association routinely found (as noted earlier) between consideration and initiation of structure, as measured by LBDQ-XII, suggests that a single, general factor solution may be warranted. Nevertheless, with reference to the contents of the

LBDQs, the two-factor framework for describing leadership behavior—consideration and the initiation of structure—emerges consistently from factor analyses when no additional constraints are placed on the analyses, such as first requiring the isolation of a general factor that, no doubt, has strong connections with the respondents' prototypes of leaders.

Refining Initiation and Consideration

Consideration and initiating structure can be finely factored in a number of ways by adding detailed behaviors, other than those found on the LBDQ-XII, and pursuing reconceptualizations about consideration and initiation. As was just noted, Stogdill (1963a) added new content dealing with different domains of leadership behavior to obtain the 10 additional scales for LBDQ-XII. More detail about initiation and consideration can also intensify the analysis of the basic content of initiation and consideration and related measures. Yukl (1971) demonstrated the feasibility of a three-factor approach (consideration, initiation of structure, and centralization of decisions). Saris (1969) offered "responsibility reference" and Karmel (1978) offered "active engagement" as a third factor. Another three-factor approach—initiating structure, participation, and decision making—was pursued by R. H. Johnson (1973). Wofford (1971) expanded the framework of leadership behavior to five factors: (1) group achievement and order, (2) personal enhancement, (3) personal interaction, (4) dynamic achievement, and (5) security and maintenance.

Using several thousand members of a nationwide business fraternity, who described their leaders on both a new instrument (FFTQ) and the comparable scales of the LBDQ-XII, Yukl and Hunt (1976) demonstrated some degree of communality between factors and scales purporting to deal with similar dimensions; yet overall, unfortunately, the scales were not equivalent.

Hierarchical Factor Analysis. Because of earlier reported findings that the LBDQ and supposedly similar instruments were not equivalent,[4] J. A. Miller (1973b) assembled 160 items from nine frequently cited standard

---

[4]See Korman (1966), Lowin (1968), House (1972), and Yukl (1971).

instruments used in published research concerning leadership behavior described in this and preceding chapters. The objective was to gain a better understanding of similarities and differences in the measures of consideration and initiation of structure. The original pool included items from the following: the LBDQ (Halpin & Winer, 1957), Survey of Organizations (Taylor & Bowers, 1972), interaction process analysis (Bales, 1950), the Job Descriptive Index (Smith, Kendall, & Hulin, 1969), the Orientation Inventory (Bass, 1963), scale anchors use to describe a "continuum of leadership behavior" (Tannenbaum & Schmidt, 1958), six categorical statements describing a continuum of decision-making styles (Vroom & Yetton, 1974), five bases of social power (French & Raven, 1959), and adjectives used by Fiedler (1967a) for measuring the least preferred coworker (LPC). Miller drew 73 nonduplicative items from the pool of 160 that were most specific and that were descriptive, rather than evaluative, and then collected data from 200 respondents from 10 organizations, including social agencies, industrial firms, and military organizations.

The first step in the hierarchical solution was a factor analysis stipulating a two-factor solution. Then the process was repeated with a stipulated three-factor solution, then a four-factor solution, and so on (Zavala, 1971). Miller then successively rotated all 12 principal components, using the varimax (orthogonal) rotation algorithm. At each level, interpretable solutions reflecting familiar leader-behavior factors emerged. The two-factor solution clearly paralleled consideration and initiation of structure. Other clearly identifiable factors that had been discovered in previous research emerged when an additional factor in each successive level of analysis was called for. Production, goal emphasis, and close supervision split apart as subfactors of initiation of structure in the four-factor solution. Participation emerged at level 6, information sharing at level 7, and supporting (the narrowly interpersonal interpretation of consideration) at level 8. Enforcing rules and procedures emerged as a subfactor of close supervision at level 9, and so forth. The emergence of the factors and the hierarchical linkages are shown in Figure 20.1. Here, the two-factor solution appears at level 2, the three factor solution at level 3, and so on. A subsequent higher-order factor analysis, based on an oblique solution, obtained a higher-order factor of consideration and another of initiation of structure.

It can be seen from Figure 20.1 that consideration includes behavior ordinarily regarded as concern for the welfare of subordinates, such as supportive behavior and sharing information, but it also appears linked to participative group decision making, to abdication, and to delegation.

Behavioral Descriptions of the Ideal Leader

Ideal Form—What a Leader Should Do

Hemphill, Seigel, and Westie (1951) developed and Halpin (1957c) revised an ideal form of the LBDQ that asks respondents to describe how their leader *should* behave—not, as on the LBDQ, how they see their leader actually behaving. For example, in a study of 50 principals, J. E. Hunt (1968) found that teachers described principals as lower in actual consideration and structure than the teachers believed to be ideal. Such discrepancies between subordinates' descriptions of what their leaders should do and what the leaders actually do are more highly related to various measures of group performance than are desired or observed leadership behavior alone. Such discrepancies are measures of dissatisfaction with the leaders' performance and, as a consequence, are more strongly related to various group outcomes.

Stogdill, Scott, and Jaynes (1956) studied a large military research organization in which executives and their subordinates described themselves—and subordinates described their superiors—on the real and ideal forms of the LBDQ. When superiors were really high in initiation of structure, according to their subordinates, the subordinates described these superiors on the ideal forms as having less responsibility than they should, as delegating more than they should, and as devoting more time than they should to teaching. When superiors were really high in consideration on the LBDQ, according to their subordinates, the subordinates said on the ideal form that they expected the superiors to assume more responsibility than they perceived the superiors to assume, devote more time than necessary to scheduling, and devote less time to teaching and mathematical computation. When superiors were really high in initiating structure, as seen by their subordinates, the superiors perceived themselves to be devoting more time than they should to evaluation, consulting peers, and teaching and not enough time to

Figure 20.1 The Hierarchical Structure of Leadership Behaviors

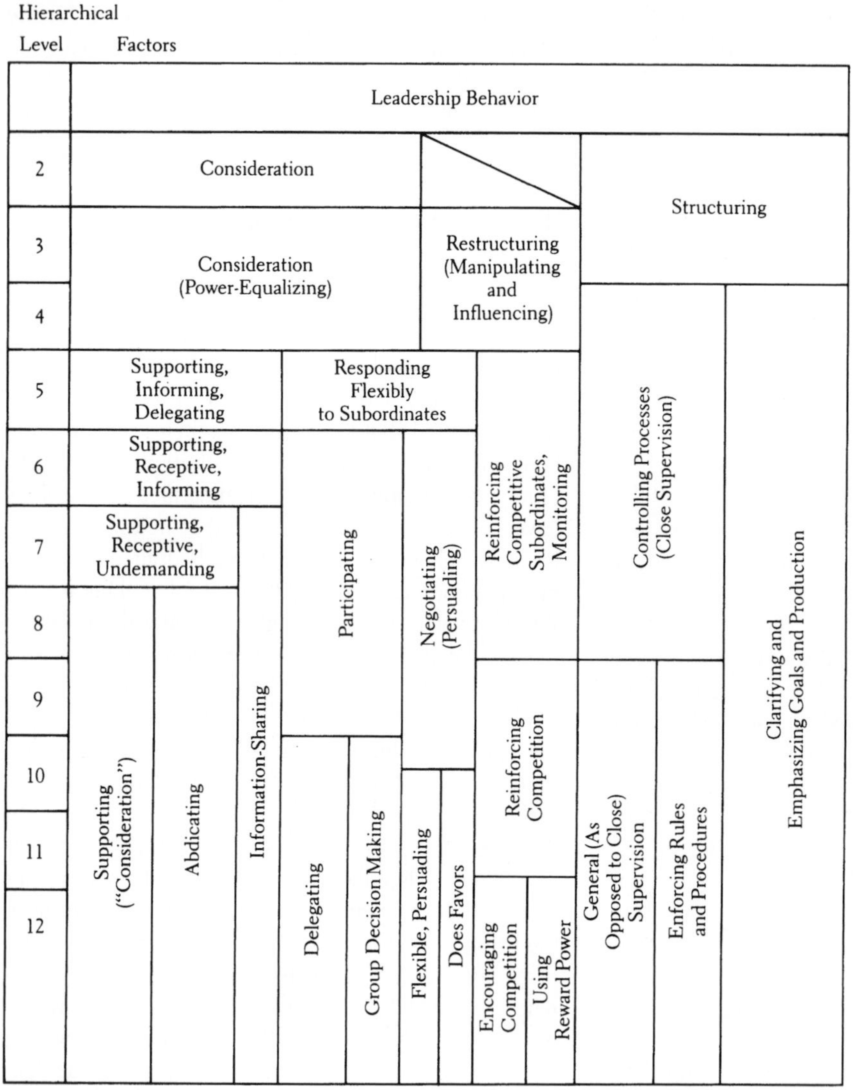

SOURCE: J. A. Miller (1973b).

professional consultation. When superiors were described as actually high in consideration, subordinates perceived themselves as having more responsibility than they should. The subordinates also reported that the superiors ought to devote more time to coordination, professional consultation, and writing reports but less time to preparing charts. The leaders' initiation of structure was more highly related to subordinates' actual work performance. The leaders' consideration, by contrast, was more highly related to subordinates' idealization of their own work performance.

In a similar type of study, Bledsoe, Brown, and Dalton (1980) showed that the actual behavior of school business managers, as described by 132 school superintendents, principals, and school board members, tended to differ considerably from the ideal for initiation and consideration. Board members tended to describe the ideal school business managers as actually more considerate than did the school principals. Ogbuehi (1981) surveyed 270 Nigerian managers' and administrators' self-descriptions of their ideal behavior using the LBDQ-XII. The results were consistent with their superiors' judgments of their effectiveness.

Vecchio and Boatwright (2002) examined the preferences of 1,137 employees in three organizations regarding leaders' structuring and consideration. More highly educated and tenured employees preferred less structuring in their leaders; women preferred more consideration.

Leadership Opinion Questionnaire (LOQ)

Fleishman's (1989a) LOQ differs from the ideal forms of Hemphill, Seigel, and Westie (1951). It asks the leaders themselves to choose the alternative that most nearly expresses their opinion on how frequently they should do what is described by each item on the questionnaire, and what they, as a supervisor or manager, sincerely believe to be the desirable way to act. The LOQ also differs from the ideal form in that the LOQ scale for initiation of structure contains several items that Stogdill, Goode, and Day (1962) later found to measure production emphasis. Production emphasis correlates with initiating structure but is not identical with it.

Following a review, Schriesheim and Kerr (1974) concluded that the test-retest reliability of the LOQ had been adequately demonstrated over a one- to three-month period. Internal consistency reliabilities are also high (Fleishman, 1960, 1989b). In 60 studies, the median correlation between consideration and structure on the LOQ was −.06, with 57 of these correlations below .19 and only 9 above .20 found significant (Fleishman, 1989). According to a review of 20 LOQ validation studies (Fleishman, 1989b), a number of studies showed that supervisors higher in both consideration and structure were more likely to be higher on criteria of effectiveness, such as performance ratings, staff satisfaction, low stress, and less burnout of subordinates.

Antecedents and Correlates of Consideration and Initiation of Structure

The internal consistency and test-retest reliability of the various scales of leader-behavior descriptions may be satisfactory, but to understand their effects, differences in content make it mandatory to distinguish whether the measures were based on the LBDQ, SBDQ, LOQ, or LBDQ-XII. This is essential in reviewing the antecedent conditions that influence the extent to which a particular behavior is exhibited and concurrent conditions are associated with such behavior.

Interpreting Concurrent Analyses. Most of the available research consists of surveys in which leadership behavior and other variables in the leader or the situation were measured concurrently. However, it seems reasonable to infer that a relatively invariant attribute such as the intelligence of the leader is an antecedent to the leader's display of consideration or initiation as rated by their colleagues. The national origin of the leader's organization is antecedent to the leader's behavior; but the average leader's behavior in the organization cannot affect its origin. Likewise, the leader's educational level is obviously antecedent to his or her behavior, but that behavior cannot cause a change in the leader's educational level. Similar inferences can be made about situational influences on the leader's behavior with less confidence, because the leader often can influence the situation, just as the situation is influencing the leader. If an association is found between company policy and the behavior of first-line supervisors, it seems reasonable to infer that the policy has influenced the supervisors, but the policy may also reflect the continuing behavior of the supervisors and may be a reaction to it. If an association is found between the leader's behavior and conflict in the work group, it is likely that the leader is a source of the conflict; but the continuing conflict is likely to be influencing the leader's behavior as well.

Suppose that a positive association is found between a leader's consideration and an absence of conflict within a group. The most plausible hypothesis is probably that the leader's behavior contributes to the absence of conflict; but the harmony within the group makes it possible for the leader to be more considerate. Therefore, in examining concurrent results, the reader will have to decide what meaning to draw from the reported associations. Such criteria of effectiveness as the subordinates' productivity, satisfaction, cohesion, and role clarity can be seen to be a consequence of the leader's behavior, yet they may influence the leader's behavior as well.

Personal Attributes Related to Initiation and Consideration

In a study of ROTC cadets, Fleishman (1957a) found that their attitudes toward consideration and initiation on the LOQ were not related to their intelligence or to their level of aspiration. But among school principals described by 726 teachers, Rooker (1968) found that principals with a strong need for achievement were described as high in tolerance of freedom and reconciliation of conflicting demands on the LBDQ-XII. However, Tronc and Enns (1969) found that promotion-oriented executives tended to emphasize initiation of structure over consideration to a greater degree than executives who were less highly oriented toward promotion. And Lindemuth (1969) reported that for college deans, consideration was related to their scholarship, propriety, and practicality.

Experience and sex have been correlated with LBDQ scores. For 124 managers of state rehabilitation agencies who were described by their 118 subordinates, Latta and Emener (1983) found that initiation of structure on the LBDQ increased directly with experience. Serafini and Pearson (1984) reported that at a university initiation of structure was higher only among the 208 male nonadministrative supervisors and managers. For the female leaders, consideration was higher. This is consistent with the expectation that females are likely to be more relations-oriented.

Personality, Values, and Interests. Although one might expect authoritarianism to coincide with initiation of structure, this does not appear to occur. For example, Fleishman (1957a) observed that the leader's endorsement of authoritarian attitudes was negatively related to initiation of structure on the LOQ, but it was unrelated to consideration. Stanton (1960) also found no relation between consideration and authoritarianism. Flocco (1969), who studied 1,200 school administrators, showed that consideration and initiation of structure, as indicated

by subordinates' responses to the LBDQ, were unrelated to the administrators' scores for dogmatism on a personality test.

Fleishman (1957b) also found that supervisors who favored consideration tended to have high scores on a personality scale of benevolence, whereas those favoring initiation of structure were more meticulous and sociable. Also, Fleishman and Peters (1962) obtained results for supervisors indicating that the trait of independence was correlated negatively with both initiation of structure and consideration, and the trait of benevolence was positively correlated with initiation of structure and consideration. Consideration was more highly related than initiation to ratings of social adjustment and charm (Marks & Jenkins, 1965). Litzinger (1965) reported that managers who favored consideration tended to value support (being treated with understanding and encouragement), whereas those who favored initiation of structure tended to place a low value on independence. Atwater and White (1985) reported that certain personal characteristics significantly correlated with demanding (SBDQ structuring) behavior by first-line supervisors; these included being inflexible, aggressive, uncooperative, harsh, strict, tense, ambitious, and unforgiving.

Newport (1962) studied 48 cadet flight leaders, each described on the LBDQ by seven flight members. Leaders who were rated high in both consideration and initiation of structure differed from those who were rated weak in desire for individual freedom of expression, resistance to social pressure, desire for power, cooperativeness, and aggressive attitudes.

In line with expectations, R. M. Anderson (1964) found, in a study of nursing supervisors, that those who preferred nursing-care activities were described as high in consideration but those who preferred coordinating activities were described as high in initiation. According to analyses by Stromberg (1967), school principals with emergent value systems were perceived by teachers as high in initiating structure, whereas those with traditional value orientations were perceived as high in consideration. Durand and Nord (1976) noted that 45 managers in a midwestern textile and plastics firm were rated by their subordinates as higher in both consideration and initiation of structure if the managers were externally, rather than internally, controlled—that is, if the managers believed that personal outcomes were due to forces outside their control rather than to their own actions.

Fleishman and Salter (1963) measured empathy in terms of supervisors' ability to guess how their subordinates would fill out a self-description questionnaire. They found that empathy was significantly related to employees' descriptions of their supervisors' consideration but not their initiation of structure. L. V. Gordon (1963a) showed that personal ascendancy was positively related to initiating structure but negatively related to consideration. Neither score was related to responsibility or emotional stability, although sociability was correlated with initiating structure (but not with consideration). Rowland and Scott (1968) failed to find any relation between consideration on the LOQ and the social sensitivity of supervisors. Pierson (1984) failed to find any significant relations between the Myers-Briggs Indicator of perceptual and judgmental tendencies and consideration or initiation. Numerous other investigators[5] also failed to find LBDQ and LOQ scores related to any of the personality measures they used. Situational factors, to be discussed later, may override or eliminate the effects of personality on initiation and consideration.

Cognitive Complexity. A number of studies of the influence of cognitive complexity on leadership behavior have obtained positive findings, particularly when the additional LBDQ-Form XII factors have been used. W. R. Kelley (1968) reported that school superintendents who were high in cognitive complexity were also described as high in predictive accuracy and in reconciliation of conflicting demands. Streufert, Streufert, and Castore (1968) found significant differences between emergent leaders whose scores on perceptual complexity varied in a negotiations game. Leaders who were lower in cognitive complexity scored higher on initiating structure, production emphasis, and reconciliation. Leaders who were higher in cognitive complexity scored higher on tolerance of uncertainty, retaining the leadership role, consideration, and predictive accuracy. Results obtained by Weissenberg and Gruenfeld (1966) indicated that supervisors who scored high in field independence endorsed less consideration than those who scored high in field dependence. But Erez (1979) found that the self-described

consideration of 45 Israeli managers with engineering backgrounds was positively related to field independence and to social intelligence, whereas initiating structure was negatively related to these two factors.

Preferences for Taking Risks. Rim (1965) studied risky decision making by supervisors and reported that male supervisors who scored high on both consideration and initiating structure and head nurses who scored high on initiation of structure tended to make riskier decisions. Men and women who scored high on both tended to be more influential in their groups and to lead the groups toward riskier decisions. However, Trimble (1968) found that for a sample of teachers who described their principals as being higher in consideration than in initiating structure, neither of the principals' scores was related to the principals' perceptions of their own decision-making behavior.

Personal Satisfaction. Initiation and consideration are greater among more satisfied leaders, whose tendencies to make decisions and attempts to lead are also related. To some degree, these tendencies may be consequences rather than antecedents of initiation and consideration. Managers who are more satisfied with their circumstances tend to have higher LBDQ scores, according to Siegel (1969). Similarly, A. F. Brown (1966) reported that better-satisfied school principals were described as higher than dissatisfied principals on all subscales except tolerance of uncertainty.

Relationship of Initiation and Consideration to Other Leadership Styles

Democratic versus autocratic, participative versus directive, and relations-oriented, task-oriented, transactional, and transformational leadership styles are discussed in Chapters 17, 18 and 19. It should come as no surprise that consideration and initiation are related to these other leadership styles. Miner (1973) noted that concepts used in other studies—such as providing support, an orientation toward employees, human relations skills, providing for the direct satisfaction of needs, and group-maintenance skills—are akin to consideration. Concepts similar to initiating structure include facilitation of work, production orientation, enabling the achievement of

[5]See, for example, Bell (1969), Greenwood and McNamara (1969), and J. P. Siegel (1969).

goals, differentiation of the supervisory role, and the utilization of technical skills. Miner further pointed out that with its emphasis on organizing, planning, coordinating, and controlling, initiating structure has much in common with the ideas of classical management.

Democratic and Autocratic Styles. Although factorially independent, the various scales of consideration and initiation contain the conceptually mixed bag of authoritarian and democratic leadership behaviors. Each scale contains a variety of authoritarian or democratic elements. Although empirically these elements cluster on one side or the other of authoritarian or democratic leadership, they are conceptually distinct. The industrial version, SBDQ, added strongly directive behaviors ("He rules with an iron hand") to its factor of initiating structure (House & Filley, 1971).

Yukl and Hunt (1976) correlated Bowers and Seashore's (1966) four leadership styles of support, the facilitation of interaction, emphasis on goals, and the facilitation of work with the LBDQ for 74 presidents of business fraternities. Support correlated .66 with consideration and .61 with initiation of structure. On the other hand, the emphasis on goals correlated .64 with consideration and .76 with initiation. Facilitation of work correlated .56 with consideration and .64 with initiation of structure. Clearly, a large general factor of leadership permeates all these measures, and leadership generally is or is not actively displayed. Karmel (1978) drew attention to the ubiquity of initiation and consideration in the study of leadership and in efforts to theorize about it. What she primarily added was the importance of the total amount of both kinds of activity by leaders, in contrast to inactivity.

This general factor becomes most apparent when the LBDQ rather than the LOQ is used. Weissenberg and Kavanagh (1972) concluded from a review that although managers think they should behave as if consideration and initiating structure are independent, in 13 of 22 industrial studies and in eight of nine military studies, a significant positive correlation was found between these two factors of leadership behavior on the LBDQ as completed by subordinates. This was especially so when LBDQ-XII was the version used in the survey (Schriesheim & Kerr, 1974). Seeman (1957) noted that a school principal's overall leadership performance was seen to be a matter of

how much consideration and initiation of structure were exhibited. When Capelle (1967) asked 50 student leaders and 50 nonleaders to fill out the LOQ, he found that leaders scored significantly higher than did nonleaders on both consideration and initiation of structure. However, G. W. Bryant (1968) did not find that appointed and sociometrically chosen leaders (college students in ROTC) differed significantly in their conceptions of the ideal leader on the LOQ. These results fit with the general contention that, *conceptually*, initiation of structure is readily distinguishable from consideration, just as autocratic and democratic or relations-oriented and task-oriented leadership can be conceptually discriminated. But *empirically*, the same leaders who are high on one factor are often high on the other as well.

Task and Relations Orientation. Initiation of structure emphasized concern with tasks ("Insists on maintaining standards," "Sees that subordinates work to their full capacity," "Emphasizes the meeting of deadlines"), as well as directiveness ("Makes attitudes clear," "Decides in detail what should be done and how it should be done"). Consideration emphasized the leader's orientation to followers ("Stresses the importance of people and their satisfaction at work," "Sees that subordinates are rewarded for a job well done," "Makes subordinates feel at ease when talking with them"), as well as participative decision making ("Puts subordinates' suggestions into operation," "Gets approval of subordinates on important matters before going ahead"). Social distance was also minimized for considerate leaders ("Treats subordinates as equals," "Is easy to approach"). Conceptually opposite to initiation of structure is destructuring behavior (J. A. Miller, 1973a)—that is, reducing the request for consistent patterns of relations within the group. The lack of initiation of structure implies allowing conditions to continue without structure, avoiding giving directions, and avoiding being task-oriented. Conceptually opposite to consideration is leadership behavior that is exploitative, unsupportive, and uncaring (Bernardin, 1976).

Among 55 corporation presidents according to ratings by a staff member, a correlation of .55 was found between task-oriented production emphasis and initiating structure. Similarly, these presidents' consideration correlated .49 with the relations-oriented representation of their subordinates' interests and .41 with toleration of freedom of action for their subordinates (Stogdill, Goode, & Day, 1963a). W. K. Graham (1968) found, as predicted, that high-LPC (relations-oriented) leaders were described as higher in consideration and initiating structure than low-LPC (task-oriented) leaders. Yukl (1968) also noted that low-LPC leaders tended to be described as high in initiation and low in consideration. However, Meuwese and Fiedler (1965) reported that leaders who were high and low on LPC tended to differ significantly only on specific items of the LBDQ, not in the total scores for consideration and initiating structure. Yukl (1971) and Kavanagh (1975) concluded that task-oriented behavior is implicit in initiating structure, but subordinates can still influence their superior's decisions. Misumi's Production and Maintenance (PM) style of leadership uses maintenance items that correlate highly with consideration. Production has two components: pressure and planning. Pressure correlates highly with initiation of structure when measured by the original SBDQ, which contained items such as "Prods for production" but is less correlated with initiation of structure as measured by the LPDQ without such autocratic items (Peterson, Smith, & Tayeb, 1993).

Power, Authority, and Responsibility of the Leader. Martin and Hunt (1980) obtained LBDQ evaluations by 407 professionals and quasi-professionals of their first-line supervisors in the construction and design units of 10 state highway department districts. Related data on morale were also collected. The expert power of the supervisors correlated .44 and .41 with their initiating structure and .48 and .51 with their consideration; but the other sources of power—referent, reward, coercive, and legitimate—correlated close to zero with the leadership measures. Foote (1970) found that members of the managerial staffs of television stations who tended to describe themselves on the RAD scales[6] as high in responsibility and authority also tended to be described on the LBDQ-XII as high in tolerance of freedom. Those who delegated most freely were described as high in production emphasis and low in representation orientation toward superiors.

Attempts to lead, manifest in one's emergence as a leader in a leaderless group discussion, were negatively

related to consideration and positively related to initiation of structure (Fleishman, 1957a).

Transactional and Transformational Leadership. Cheng (1994) suggested that transformational school-teachers could be innovative and could demand clear rules in managing the classroom (structuring) as well as provide support to the students (consideration). Seltzer and Bass (1987) found that for 294 MBAs with full-time jobs who described their immediate supervisors' Initiation of Structure on the LBDQ-XII correlated .53, .55, and .59, respectively, with charisma, individualized consideration, and intellectual stimulation on the Multifactor Leadership Questionnaire (MLQ); and .48 and .06, respectively, with the transactional measures of contingent reward and management by exception on the MLQ. However, consideration on the LBDQ-XII correlated .78, .78, and .65, respectively, with the same MLQ transformational leadership measures and .64 and −.23, respectively, with the same MLQ transactional leadership measures. Evidently, active leadership is common to initiation, consideration, and transformational and transactional leadership behavior, and there are particularly strong associations between transformational leadership and consideration. Miliffe, Piccolo, and Judge (2005) reported correlations of .46 and .27, respectively, of transformational leadership with consideration and initiation. Furthermore, adding the transformational scales to initiation and consideration increased substantially the prediction of outcomes of the rated effectiveness of leaders and satisfaction with leadership. Similar results were reported for 138 subordinates and 55 managers (Seltzer & Bass, 1990).

Peterson, Phillips, and Duran (1989) found that the MLQ scale of charismatic leadership correlated higher with measures of consideration than measures of initiation in a study of 264 retail chain-store employees describing their supervisors. Thus charismatic leadership correlated .48 with maintenance orientation and .74 with support but only .16 with pressure for production and .22 with assigning work.

Epitome of Consideration: The Servant Leader

Greenleaf (1977, 1991), an AT&T executive, conceived the idea of the servant leader from Herman Hesse's *Jour-*

[6]See Chapter 14.

ney to the East. Leo, the servant to a band of men on a mythical journey, does their menial chores but also sustains them with his spirit and song. Leo disappears. The group falls apart and the journey is abandoned. It turns out later that Leo is the titular head of the order that sponsored the journey. For Greenleaf, as for Hesse, the leader is the servant, first. The leader ensures that the highest priorities of followers are met. He first listens and questions before suggesting initiatives. Instead of coercion and manipulation, the servant leader depends on awareness, empathy, and foresight. To illustrate:

> John Woolman visited Quaker communities for 30 years asking Quaker slaveholders about what . . . slave-owning did to them morally. . . . What were they passing on to their children? Non-judgmental persuasion followed. The Quakers became the first religious group in America to denounce and forbid slavery among its members. (Greenleaf, 1991, p. 21)

Servant leaders encourage skill and moral development in followers. They are sensitive to the needs of organizational stakeholders and hold themselves accountable for their actions (Graham, 1991). Servant leadership can be a model for higher education. Faculty members need to curtail and redirect their ego and image. Power needs to be shared with students. They become collaborators in an ethic of collective study. "The faculty member who has never learned from his students is a failure" (Buchen, 1998, p. 130). In Block's (1993) replacement of leadership with stewardship, service is chosen over self-interest. As noted by Heuerman (2002), caring about others, seen in servant leaders, underlies considerate leadership behavior. Followers are regarded as real people, not machines or expense categories. For leaders who care, service is an obligation, not a burden. At the extreme of the leader as servant, leaders sacrifice themselves for the perceived good of the group. In experiments with 357 students and 157 industrial personnel, Choi and Mai-Dalton (1998) found that self-sacrificing leaders were seen as more charismatic and legitimate, and generated intentions to reciprocate. Self-sacrificing leaders were also judged as more competent by the students. Block (1993) argued that self-interest, dependency, and control of others should be replaced by organizational stewards with service, responsibility, and accountability.

The self-sacrificing servant leader has to be a good steward. Abraham Feuerman was praised for continuing to pay full wages to his employees at Malden Mills from reserves and insurance during the period it was out of operation after it burned down. He might have been expected to use the money to rebuild overseas to make use of cheaper labor, as other textile companies had done. Instead, he continued to pay his employees, who were able to return with high morale to a beautiful new plant, for which he became extensively indebted. Unfortunately, his competitors used the time to catch and pass Malden Mills and gain some of its customers. Product leadership was lost. Bankruptcy ensued. In attending to the needs of his people, the servant CEO had not fully taken care of his organization's financial future.

Situational Factors in Initiation and Consideration

The organization, the immediate group that is led, and the task requirements affect the extent to which a leader initiates structure, is considerate, or both. For instance, when faced with a complex task and need for planning, a leader is likely to be more structuring in a group of low diversity. Structuring and the leader's planning skills contribute to the quality and originality of the plans, according to a study of 195 participants working in 55 groups (Daniels, Leritz, & Mumford, 2003).

Organizational Policies. A clear example of the impact of the organizational context on the behavior of individual leaders within it was provided by Stanton (1960), who described two medium-size firms. In one company, which was interested only in profits, authoritarian policies were dominant, and subordinates had to understand what was expected of them. The personal qualities of leadership were emphasized, and all information in the company was restricted to the managers except when the information clearly applied to an employee's job. The second firm, which had democratic policies, stressed participation as a matter of policy and was concerned about the employees' well-being as well as about profits. This firm made a maximum effort to inform the employees about company matters. Supervisors in the firm with democratic policies favored more consideration, whereas supervisors in the firm with authoritarian policies favored more initiation.

The importance of the higher authority represented by

the organization and its policies also can be inferred indirectly from results obtained in a progressive petrochemical refinery and in a national food-processing firm, where the extent to which supervisors felt they should be considerate was positively correlated with how highly they were rated by their superiors (Bass, 1956, 1958). Yet in other companies no such correlation was found (Rambo, 1958). Supervisors' perceptions of their superiors' and subordinates' expectations affect their leadership behavior. That is, supervisors will be more supportive or more demanding, depending on what they perceive their superiors and subordinates expect of them (Atwater, 1988).

Organizational Size. Vienneau (1982) examined the LBDQ scores of 33 presidents of amateur sports organizations, obtained from the responses of 85 members of their executive committees. Although the presidents' sex or language was of no consequence, both consideration and initiation were higher in the larger of the amateur organizations. The presidents agreed on what was required of their ideal leader on the Ideal Leader Behavior Questionnaire regardless of other organizational differences.

Functional Differences. D. R. Day (1961) found that upper-level marketing executives were described on the LBDQ-XII as high in tolerance of freedom and low in structuring, but upper-level engineering executives were described as low in tolerance of freedom and high in initiation. In the same firm, manufacturing executives were rated high and personnel executives were rated low in tolerance of uncertainty.

Military versus Civilian Supervisors. Holloman (1967) studied military and civilian personnel in a large U.S. Air Force organization and found that superiors did not perceive military and civilian supervisors to be different in observed consideration or initiation of structure, although they expected military supervisors to rank higher than civilian supervisors in initiation of structure and lower in showing consideration. Unexpectedly, Holloman found that subordinates—both military and civilian—perceived the military supervisors to be higher in consideration as well as in initiating structure than they did the civilian supervisors. Thus in comparison with civilian supervisors, military supervisors were seen to display more leadership by both their civilian and their military subordinates.

Halpin (1955b) administered the *ideal* form of the LBDQ to educational administrators and aircraft commanders. Subordinates described their leaders on the *real* form of the LBDQ. The educators exhibited more consideration and less initiation of structure than did the aircraft commanders, both in observed behavior and in ideal behavior. But in both samples, the leaders' ideals of how they should behave were not highly related to their actual behavior as described by their subordinates.

Attributes of Subordinates. Atwater and White (1985) and Atwater (1988) found that supportive (considerate) behavior by supervisors correlated highly with the subordinates' loyalty and trust. Kerr, Schriesheim, Murphy, and Stogdill (1974) concluded, from a review of LBDQ studies, that if the subordinates' interest in the task and need for information are high, less consideration by the leader is necessary and more initiation of structure is acceptable to them. Consistent with this conclusion, Hsu and Newton (1974) showed that supervisors of unskilled employees were able to initiate more structure than were supervisors of skilled employees in the same manufacturing plant. In a large sample survey of employees, Vecchio (2000) found that less mature employees were more inclined to favor structuring by leaders.

Chacko (1990) noted in data from 144 department heads in institutions of higher education that subordinates were more likely to be assertive and appeal to higher authority when their supervisors were low in structuring and in consideration. Gemmill and Heisler (1972) and Lester and Genz (1978) analyzed the impact of subordinates' locus of control—internal or external—on their perceptions of their supervisors' leadership and their satisfaction with it. Internally controlled subordinates tended to see significantly more consideration and initiation in their supervisors' behavior (Evans, 1974). Although internally controlled subordinates in a textile and plastics firm tended to see their supervisors as initiating more structure, they also felt that their supervisors were less considerate (Duran & Nord, 1976). But Blank, Weitzel, and Green (1987) found correlations close to zero between the psychological and job maturity of 353 advisers of residence halls and the initiation and consideration, respectively, of their 27 residence-hall directors.

General Effects on Productivity, Satisfaction, and Other Criteria

Except for a few cross-lagged analyses and experiments, most of the results reported here come from concurrent surveys of leadership behavior and criteria such as subordinates' satisfaction and productivity. For instance, Brooks (1955) found that all the items measuring consideration and initiation of structure differentiated managers rated as excellent from those rated as average or below average in effectiveness. Although one tends to infer that productivity and satisfaction are a consequence of leadership behavior, the effective outcomes modify the leader's behavior to some extent as well. Greene and Schriesheim's (1977) longitudinal study suggested that more consideration early on by a leader can contribute to good group relations, which in turn may later result in higher group productivity. In any event, Fisher and Edwards (1988), in a series of meta-analyses, established that subordinates were more satisfied with work and supervision if their supervisors were high in consideration.

Using an early version of the LBDQ scales, Hemphill, Seigel, and Westie (1951) found that leaders' organizing behavior (initiating structure) and membership behavior (consideration) were both significantly related to the cohesiveness of the group. Likewise, Christner and Hemphill (1955) noted that subordinates' ratings of the leaders' consideration and initiation were positively related to ratings of the effectiveness of their units, but leaders' self-descriptions of consideration and initiation were not.

A sample of 256 MBA students who were working full-time in many different organizations described the initiation and consideration of their immediate supervisors at work. They also completed a "burnout" questionnaire. Although their leaders' initiation correlated only $-.15$ with the respondents' feeling of being burned out, the leaders' consideration correlated $-.55$ with this feeling. Thus considerate supervision appears to reduce substantially the sense of burnout in subordinates (Seltzer & Numerof, 1988). Considerate supervision also promotes creativity, according to Oldham and Cummings (1996). They found that supportive and noncontrolling supervision of 171 employees in two manufacturing plants correlated with subordinates' pattern disclosures, contributions to suggestion programs, and rated creativity. But

Williams (2001) reported that the amount of structure supervisors initiated reduced the divergent thinking of their subordinates.

In an extensive analysis of 27 organizations involving more than 1,300 supervisors and 3,700 employees, Stogdill (1965a) ascertained that supervisors' consideration was related to the employees' satisfaction with the companies and to measures of the cohesiveness of the groups and the organizations. But as with authoritarian and democratic leadership, neither the supervisors' consideration nor their initiation of structure was consistently related to group productivity. Organizational differences had to be considered. The contribution to effectiveness of initiation and consideration appears quite variable and hence requires further examination of the context in which the data are collected.

Business Studies

Leader Behavior. Fleishman (1989a) reviewed more than 20 validity studies of the SBDQ. Fleishman, Harris, and Burt (1955) found that production foremen rated higher in performance by their managers were higher in initiation of structure and lower in consideration. But absenteeism and turnover were greater in work groups that had foremen with this pattern. Many other studies with the SBDQ have confirmed this strong relation between leader consideration and worker job satisfaction in industry (Badin, 1974; Fleishman & Simmons, 1970; Skinner, 1969), hospitals (Szabo, 1981; Oaklander & Fleishman, 1964), educational settings (Petty & Lee, 1975), and government organizations (Miles & Petty, 1977).

The relationship between initiation of structure, as measured by the SBDQ, and performance criteria tended to vary with situations. Thus both initiation of structure and consideration were positively related to proficiency ratings in nonproduction departments (Fleishman & Harris, 1955). Using the SBDQ, Hammer and Dachler (1973) showed that the leader's consideration was positively related to the subordinates' perceptions that their job performance was instrumental in obtaining the desired outcomes. However, the leader's initiation of structure was negatively related to such perceptions. Likewise, Gekoski (1952) found that supervisors' initiation of structure, but not their consideration, was related positively to group-productivity measures in a clerical situation.

Lawshe and Nagle (1953) obtained a high positive correlation, for a small sample of work groups, between group productivity and employees' perceptions of how considerate their supervisor was. In a study of the leadership of foremen, Besco and Lawshe (1959) found that superiors' descriptions of a foreman's consideration and initiation of structure were both related positively to ratings of the effectiveness of the foreman's unit. However, subordinates' descriptions of foremen's consideration, but not initiation of structure, were positively related to such effectiveness.

In later studies, the LBDQ or LBDQ-XII was more likely to be used. Trieb and Marion (1969) studied two chains of retail grocery stores. They found that the supervisors' consideration, as described by the workers, was positively related to productivity, cohesiveness, and satisfaction in both chains. The supervisors' initiation of structure was related positively to the productivity of subordinates and to cohesiveness in one chain, but not in the other. In a study of two companies, House and Filley (1971) found that the supervisors' consideration in both companies related significantly to the subordinates' satisfaction with the company and with their jobs as well as to their freedom of action. In both companies, initiating structure was also related significantly to the subordinates' satisfaction with the company and their jobs, along with favorable family attitudes toward the company and their jobs. Fleishman and Simmons (1970) showed that the effectiveness of Israeli supervisors was positively related to their initiation of structure and consideration.

M. G. Evans (1968) reported that supervisors' consideration and initiation of structure were positively related to the importance of the goal to workers and to their job satisfaction. Under high supervisory consideration, a strong positive relationship existed between the supervisor's initiation of structure and the group's performance. In a later study, M. G. Evans (1970a) found that the supervisors' consideration and initiation were related to the workers' perception of opportunities to satisfy their need for security but not to their actual satisfaction with their job security. Weiss (1977) demonstrated that subordinates tended to be more likely to share values with their supervisors if the supervisors displayed considerate behavior toward them. Marks and Jenkins (1965) reported that initiation of structure was more highly related than was consideration to global ratings of effectiveness. However,

supervisors' initiation of structure and consideration were unrelated to the satisfaction of subordinates' needs for social esteem, autonomy, and self-actualization.

In a study of insurance sales supervisors, W. K. Graham (1970/1973) found that supervisory consideration was positively associated with group performance. In a similar setting in seven retail discount department stores, Hodge (1976) obtained results for 21 second-level managers as reported on the LBDQ by 188 first-line managers. Satisfaction of subordinates' needs was positively associated with the higher-level managers' initiation of structure. But there was an unexpected negative correlation with consideration. These results were similar to what Patchen (1962) found for the supervision of manual workers, but contrary to what was reported by Fleishman and Harris (1962) for similar types of workers.

The source of the criteria makes some difference. Kofman (1966) reviewed research in which industrial supervisors' scores for consideration and initiating structure were related to various criteria of the supervisors' effectiveness and the work groups' performance. Generally, he found that the peer ratings of the groups' performance were unrelated to the peer ratings of the supervisors' consideration and initiation of structure. However, evaluations of the supervisors' effectiveness by superiors and subordinates, as well as evaluations based on objective criteria, tended to relate positively to the supervisors' initiation and consideration as described by subordinates.

A number of industrial studies were completed using the additional scales of LBDQ-XII. D. R. Day (1961) obtained 165 ratings of executives in an aircraft manufacturing firm. The effectiveness of leaders correlated with a general factor, as well as with the predictive accuracy of LBDQ-XII, persuasiveness, role enactment, and the reconciliation of conflicting demands. According to R. E. Hastings (1964), leaders who were rated high in initiating structure and production emphasis supervised research teams that were rated high in the volume of work they completed. If the leaders were rated high in orientation to superiors, their groups were rated low in harmony. Leaders who were rated high in representation and role retention tended to supervise teams that were rated high in enthusiastic effort. Leaders who were high in persuasiveness supervised teams whose quality of work was rated as high. Even after the effects of many other morale variables were removed, freedom and consideration by supervisors on LBDQ-XII were important contributors to the amount of innovative behavior displayed by 309 federal R & D aerospace scientists and engineers (Dalessio & Davis, 1986).

M. Beer (1964) used the LBDQ-XII to test McGregor's (1960) hypothesis that employees become motivated and are enabled to satisfy their higher-order needs (for autonomy, esteem, and self-actualization) only when supervisors allow them freedom from organizational structure and pressure. He found support in that the employees' satisfaction of the need for autonomy, esteem, and self-actualization was positively related to the supervisors' consideration and tolerance of freedom. However, contrary to his hypothesis, the leaders' considerate behaviors that resulted in the satisfaction of higher-order needs were not the ones that led to employees' strong striving for the needs. Rather, the leaders' initiation of structure was the leaders' behavior associated with such striving.

Leaders' Opinions and Attitudes. As with the effects of leaders' behavior on effective and satisfying outcome, findings about the effects of leaders' attitudes were also mixed. Bass (1956) found that the effectiveness ratings by superiors of 53 supervisors were significantly related to their opinion scores on consideration but not on initiation expressed two years previously on the Leadership Opinion Questionnaire (LOQ). In a replication, a significant correlation of .32 was found between sales supervisors' attitudes toward consideration and effectiveness ratings by superiors three years later (Bass, 1958). But Bass (1957a) also reported that neither attitudes toward consideration nor attitudes toward initiation of structure were related to peer ratings of sales supervisors on criteria such as popularity, problem-solving ability, and value to the company. Fleishman and Peters (1962) found no relation between LOQ measures of supervisors' attitudes toward leadership and their rated effectiveness as supervisors. Rowland and Scott (1968) also noted that LOQ measures of supervisory consideration were unrelated to employees' satisfaction. According to T. C. Parker (1963), 1,760 employees of a wholesale pharmaceutical company in 80 decentralized warehouses were more satisfied with their supervision, their recognition, and their job security when their supervisors felt that consideration and initiation were important, as measured by the LOQ. The correlations of subordinates' satisfaction and supervisors'

attitudes were .51 with supervisory consideration and .22 with supervisory initiation. Although there was no relation of the supervisors' attitudes to such objective measures of group performance as productivity and errors in filling orders, the supervisor's favoring of initiating structure correlated .23 with pricing errors of the unit being supervised. Spitzer and McNamara (1964) also reported that managers' attitudes toward consideration and initiation were not related to salary as a criterion of the managers' success; nor were such attitudes related to superiors' ratings of the managers' success. However, Weissenberg and Gruenfeld (1966) found that supervisors who had favorable attitudes toward consideration and initiation were also more favorably inclined toward the personal development of their subordinates. Generally, satisfactory supervisors reveal this "hi-hi" pattern (Fleishman, 1989b), and it has been found to be related to low stress and low burnout among subordinates (Duxbury, Armstrong, Drew, & Henly, 1984).

Military Studies

In the first extensive use of the LBDQ with U.S. Air Force personnel, Christner and Hemphill (1955) found that changes in the attitudes of crew members toward each other over time were related to the leadership behavior of the crew commander. When crew members rated their commander as high in consideration, they increased their ratings of each other's friendliness, mutual confidence, conversation on duty, and willingness to engage in combat. Crews that described their commander as high in initiation of structure increased their ratings of each other's friendship and confidence. But Halpin (1954) found that superiors tended to evaluate positively those aircrew commanders they rated high in initiating structure and to evaluate negatively those rated high in consideration. In training, the satisfaction of crew members was positively related to rated commanders' consideration ($r = .48$) and negatively related to commanders' initiating structure ($r = -.17$). In combat, however, commanders' consideration ($r = .64$) and initiating structure ($r = .35$) were positively related to the same crew members' satisfaction. In a later study, Halpin (1957a) found that superiors' ratings of the commanders' effectiveness in combat were unrelated to crew members' descriptions of their commander's consideration. However, superiors' ratings, as before, were positively and significantly related to the commander's initiation of structure. Significantly, crew members' ratings of their commander on confidence and proficiency, friendship and cooperation, and morale and satisfaction were positively related to both consideration and the initiation of structure by their commander.

Fleishman (1957a) found that the consideration and initiation scores of ROTC leaders were positively and significantly related to peers' ratings of the leaders' value to their groups, but superiors' ratings were not related to either pattern of behavior. In a study of trainee leaders in the military, Hood (1963) ascertained that the trainees reported more affiliation and less communication when their superiors were higher in initiating structure and consideration. Enlisted personnel attained higher scores on a pencil-paper test of military leadership when their leaders structured the situation and pushed for production. However, such higher attainment by the enlisted personnel was not related to their leaders' consideration.

Hooper (1968/1969) obtained results with the LOQ indicating that the attitudes of U.S. Air Force cadets toward consideration and initiation were not significantly related to their effectiveness ratings. However, the two factors differentiated significantly between those scoring high and those scoring low on a composite leadership criterion.

Group Effects. C. H. Rush (1957) reported the effects of leadership behavior on other dimensions of the performance of 212 aircrews. Crew members described the leadership behavior of the crew leaders and conditions in the crews on Hemphill and Westie's (1950) Group Dimension Descriptions. The leaders' consideration was associated with more intimacy and harmony and less control and stratification in the crews. The leaders' high rating on the initiation of structure was related to greater harmony and procedural clarity and to less stratification in the crews.

In examining the satisfaction and the initiation and consideration of their leaders, according to 672 U.S. Army National Guardsmen in the study by Katerberg and Hom (1981), it was necessary to account statistically for both the group effects and the individual dyadic effects of LBDQ ratings of the first sergeants and the company commanders on the guardsmen's satisfaction with the sergeants and commanders. First sergeants and commanders who earned high mean LBDQ scores on initiation and consideration from their collective unit of subordinates also had units with higher mean satisfaction. But beyond this, within the groups, individual subordinates were more satisfied if they saw their leader exhibiting more initiation and consideration. The adjusted correlations between satisfaction and the initiation and consideration scores on the LBDQ were .37 and .47 for the group-by-group analyses for the first sergeants and commanders, respectively. The individual-within-group analyses added substantially to the correlations between leadership and satisfaction. Although there were problems with Katerberg and Hom's failure to separate the group and dyadic effects completely (Dansereau, Alutto, & Yammarino, 1984), the strong associations with satisfaction found for both initiation and consideration in the military were supported by similar LBDQ evidence obtained for 30,000 U.S. Army personnel in 63 national and overseas installations (Marsh & Atherton, 1981–1982).

Educational Studies

Various investigations of the leadership behavior of college administrators, school administrators, school principals, and classroom teachers have been conducted. Hemphill (1955) used the LBDQ to study the leadership of heads of academic departments in a university. The department head's reputation for administrative competence correlated .36 with consideration and .48 with initiation of structure. But Lindemuth (1969) failed to establish any relationship between a college dean's initiation of structure and various measures of organizational climate. Superintendents who were rated as effective leaders by both their staff and school board members were described as high in both consideration and initiation of structure (Halpin, 1956a). H. J. Bowman (1964) asked school principals to describe the leadership behavior of higher-level school executives and themselves. Principals perceived themselves as exercising high degrees of responsibility and authority and as delegating extensively when they described their own superiors as being high in consideration but not in initiation. Among the school administrators studied by Flocco (1969), those described by subordinates as higher in consideration and initiation of structure were rated more effective. Those administrators who described themselves as being higher in consideration and initiation than their staff subordinates described them were rated ineffective.

School Principals. A. F. Brown (1967) and Greenfield (1968) concluded from reviews of Canadian studies that the performance of pupils was associated with the principals' LBDQ scores. Keeler and Andrews (1963) studied the relation of principals' leadership to the performance of pupils and the cohesiveness of staffs in Canadian public schools. Both consideration and initiation of structure by principals, as described by teachers, were significantly and positively related to the pupils' examination scores on a province-wide examination. Initiation of structure by the principals was positively related to the cohesiveness of their staffs, but consideration was not. Nevertheless, A. F. Brown (1966) reported that effective principals generally scored higher on the LBDQ-XII scales. Seeman (1957) found performance evaluations of the school principals' leadership positively related to consideration, initiation of structure, communication, and willingness to change, and negatively related to domination and social distance. According to Fast (1964), consideration and initiation of structure by principals, as described by teachers, were positively related to the teachers' satisfaction, although expected behavior was not. Stromberg (1967) obtained a significant relation between teachers' morale and the attitudes of their principals toward consideration and initiation of structure.

C. C. Wall (1970) studied four effective and four ineffective principals in terms of their dialogue, decision making, and action. Effective principals were described by their teachers as higher than ineffective principals in consideration and tolerance of freedom on the LBDQ-XII. Ineffective principals were scored high in production emphasis. Teachers in seven of the eight schools studied believed that the principals ought to initiate more than they were perceived to do. Teachers in the ineffective schools believed that the principals should exhibit more persuasion and demand more reconciliation and more integration of the group than they were perceived to do. Mansour (1969) found that these discrepancies between the expected and actual behavior of principals were negatively relative to teachers' job satisfaction and participation. Fast (1964) also obtained results indicating that the greater the discrepancy between the teachers' ex-

pectations and observations of principals' behavior, the lower the teachers' satisfaction.

Among different schools, Punch (1967) found that the principals' initiation of structure was positively related and the principals' consideration was negatively related to a measure of bureaucracy in the school. Mathews (1963) reported that principals' initiation of structure and consideration were significantly related to Hemphill and Westie's (1950) measures of their staff's stratification, control, homogeneity, cohesiveness, hedonic tone, and participation.

Hills (1963) obtained descriptions by 872 teachers of 53 principals. Both consideration and initiating structure were highly correlated with two representative functions of the principals: (1) representing the teachers' interests to higher levels of the organization and (2) representing the teachers' interests to pupils and their parents. Hills concluded that consideration and initiation of structure were not solely concerned with internal leadership but were reflected in how the principals, as leaders, dealt with outsiders and higher levels of authority.

However, Rasmussen (1976) failed to establish any significant relationship between the success of 25 elementary schools, the satisfaction of teachers, and the behavior of principals described on the LBDQ. Bailey (1966) studied four principals who were described by their superintendents and four teachers as higher in consideration than in initiating structure and four other principals who were described as being higher in initiating structure than in consideration. Each principal and four teachers played a decision-making game. Although the principals' consideration was found to be significantly related to the teachers' satisfaction with the decision and support of it, neither the principals' consideration scores nor their initiating structure scores were significantly related to the ability of a group to arrive at a decision or to perceptions that teachers had helped make the decisions.

Classroom Teachers. Using the appraisal of the performance of their classroom teachers by 2,084 business students, Baba and Ace (1989) extracted stable initiation factors as well as factors of evaluation and effort. Class size and course level made no difference. In another large-scale Canadian study, Greenfield and Andrews (1961) obtained results indicating that consideration and initiation of structure by classroom teachers were positively and significantly related to the scores of their pupils on achievement tests. Cheng (1994) found that teachers high in initiating structure and consideration were more influential as a consequence of their greater expertise and attractiveness. Their classrooms had a more positive social climate.

Health Organization Studies

In a study of nurses and their supervisors, Nealey and Blood (1968) found that the satisfaction of subordinates was related to the consideration scores of both their first- and second-level supervisors. The supervisors' initiation of structure contributed to the subordinates' job satisfaction at the first, but not at the second, level of supervision. Oaklander and Fleishman (1964) observed that when hospital administrators endorsed both high consideration and high initiation of structure on the LOQ, stress was lower in the units they supervised.

A path analysis by Sheridan and Vredenburgh (1979) for the descriptions by 372 nurses, practical nurses, and nursing aides of the behavior of their head nurses disclosed a positive effect of the head nurses' initiation of structure on the subordinates' group relations. But these group relations did not affect the subordinates' performance or turnover rates. Good group relations also reduced the subordinates' felt job tension. However, such job tension had only a slight positive association with job performance or turnover rates. Yet the head nurses' consideration had a direct positive effect, as well as an indirect effect, on the subordinates' performance. It also reduced the subordinates' felt job tension. This result fits with Weed, Mitchell, and Moffitt's (1976) laboratory finding that the leader's consideration makes for a pleasant working situation, although it may not necessarily contribute to the group's productivity.

The critical importance of the leader's initiation and consideration to the performance of subordinates in health organizations was confirmed by Dagirmanjian (1981), Blaihed (1982), and Denton (1976). On the basis of a data analysis, Dagirmanjian (1981) concluded that the supervisors' initiation of structure and consideration were the central links between the organizational structure in mental health services and the staffs. Blaihed (1982) obtained the LBDQ-XII scores of chief executive officers (CEOs) and staffs of hospitals in Los Angeles and related the results to criteria of hospital performance furnished by the California Health Facilities Commission. Initiation of structure by the CEOs and staffs contributed to the efficiency of the hospitals and the quality of care they provided, as did a number of the other scale scores of the LBDQ. Similarly, for 80 professional mental health workers and their directors, Denton (1976) found significant, direct relationships between supervisors' consideration and initiation of structure, on the one hand, and the workers' job satisfaction and satisfactory relations with clients on the other. Conversely, Duxbury, Armstrong, Drew, and Henly (1984) found that head nurses with low consideration and high initiation scores on the LOQ had the lowest staff satisfaction and highest staff burnout.

Studies in Other Not-for-Profit Organizations

Bernardin (1976) found that for 501 police officers in a metropolitan department, consideration by supervisors was positively and linearly related to the police officers' satisfaction but not to their performance or absenteeism. To account for the results more adequately, additional descriptive data about the supervisors were required, such as the supervisors' specific reward orientation and punitiveness.

Stogdill (1965a) studied 10 regional organizations in a department of a state government. He noted that throughout the 10 organizations, executives who described their superiors as high in representation on the LBDQ-XII tended to manage groups that were rated high in support of the organization, and their subordinates tended to be satisfied with their pay. Tolerance of uncertainty by their superiors was related to harmony in the groups. Superiors who were rated high in initiating structure had subordinates who were satisfied with the organization. When the state employees described their first-line supervisors, Stogdill found that those first-line supervisors who were rated high in initiation of structure, consideration, and "influence upstairs" tended to have subordinates who were satisfied with the organization and groups that were rated strong in drive. Employees who described their supervisors as tolerant of freedom expressed satisfaction with their own freedom on the job. Klepinger (1980) collected LBDQ and outcome data from a stratified sample of 35 executive directors of social service departments who were rated by their 227 employees. Directors who scored high in initiation and consideration were also seen as highly effective managers, but their leadership behavior did not influence their employees' job satisfaction.

Hood (1963) found that business trainees reported more affiliation and less communication when their leaders were rated high both in initiating structure and in consideration. Furthermore, the trainees attained higher scores on a paper-and-pencil test of performance when their leaders structured the situation and pushed for production. But such increased attainment was not related to the leaders' consideration. Cunningham (1964) observed that the most effective agricultural agents and 4-H club agents were above the median in both consideration and initiation of structure on the LBDQ. Similarly, Osborn and Hunt (1975a, 1975b) obtained data indicating that most aspects of the satisfaction of members in 60 chapters of a business fraternity were positively associated with their presidents' initiation and consideration. But Yukl and Hunt (1976) reported that in 74 chapters the correlations between LBDQ assessments of the chapter presidents' initiation and consideration and the chapters' efficiency in fulfilling specified requirements were only .12 and .10, respectively.

Meta-Analyses

Fisher and Edwards (1988) completed a meta-analysis of studies in the computer abstracts of *Psychological Abstracts*. These studies presumably were published mainly after 1968. As can be seen in Table 20.1, after the mean

findings were corrected for sample size, restriction in range, and unreliability, the adjusted mean correlation of leader consideration on the LBDQ with job performance ranged from .27 to .45. The adjusted correlations of employee job performance with LBDQ initiation of structure were similar, but this was not true of the SBDQ measure of initiation with its punitive elements.

Except for the SBDQ measure of leaders' initiation, considerably higher adjusted correlations were obtained, as expected, between leaders' initiation, consideration, and outcomes in job satisfaction, and satisfaction with supervision, as shown in Tables 20.2 and 20.3.

The patterns of results lent support to Larson, Hunt, and Osborn (1976), who concluded after examining 14 samples of first-line supervisors involving 2,474 respondents that the multiple regression additive or interactive combining of initiation and consideration was unwarranted, since it did not add sufficiently to the prediction of outcomes beyond what each measure could do alone. Part of this lack of augmentation of one measure by the other was due to the mean intercorrelation of .52 between them found for 10 samples on the LBDQ-XII by Schriesheim, House, and Kerr (1976). For four samples, Schriesheim (1982) obtained results indicating that consideration alone accounted for most of the effects on the satisfaction of subordinates. For samples of 230 hourly employees, 178 college seniors and graduate students with employment experience, 96 middle managers, and 258 clerks and middle managers who described their supervisors' leadership behavior by means of the LBDQ

Table 20.1 Mean Correlations of Leader Consideration and the Initiation of Structure with Job Performance

Leadership Measure	Number of Respondents	Number of Correlations	Mean Correlation	
			Unadjusted	Adjusted
Consideration				
LBDQ	1,486	19	.19	.45
SBDQ	1,953	21	.19	.46
LBDQ-XII	1,424	11	.13	.27
Initiation of Structure				
LBDQ	1,486	19	.20	.47
SBDQ	1,953	21	−.02	−.06
LBDQ-XII	1,424	11	.09	.22

SOURCE: Adapted from Fisher and Edwards (1988), p. 202.

Table 20.2 Mean Correlations of Leader Consideration and Initiation of Structure with Overall Job Satisfaction

Leadership Measure	Number of Respondents	Number of Correlations	Mean Correlation	
			Unadjusted	Adjusted
Consideration				
LBDQ	2,517	21	.34	.65
SBDQ	1,134	8	.47	.83
LBDQ-XII	4,347	25	.38	.70
Initiation of Structure				
LBDQ	2,517	21	.26	.51
SBDQ	1,134	8	−.02	−.04
LBDQ-XII	4,347	25	.23	.46

SOURCE: Adapted from Fisher and Edwards (1988), p. 202.

and the SBDQ, Schreisheim found that the supervisors' consideration alone correlated between .62 and .77 with satisfaction with the respondents' jobs and with their supervisors. The results for the supervisors' initiation of structure, in multiple regression analysis, added only from 2% to 4% to the consideration effects in accounting for satisfaction. However, while Nystrom (1978) reached the same conclusion about consideration and the satisfaction of subordinates' needs, with a sample of 100 junior and senior managers, he noted that managers who were high in initiating structure and in consideration had relatively lower salary levels and progressed more slowly in their careers. Low initiation of structure, rather than high consideration, contributed the most to higher sala-

ries and career advancement. Nystrom's results may say much about the culture and policies in the firm from which the 100 managers were drawn. Contingent factors need to be considered.

Judge, Piccolo, and Remus (undated) conducted three meta-analyses involving over 20,000 cases of 209 correlations from 154 samples in 103 publications and dissertations; 203 correlations from 151 samples in 99 studies; and 181 correlations from 166 samples in 78 studies. The SBDQ, LBDQ, LBDQ-XII, LOQ, and other measures of initiation and consideration were included. The estimated true score correlation was .48 between consideration and measures of follower satisfaction with job, motivation, leader, and leader effectiveness. The highest

Table 20.3 Mean Correlations of Leaders Consideration and Initiation of Structure with Satisfaction with Supervision

Leadership Measure	Number of Respondents	Number of Correlations	Mean Correlation	
			Unadjusted	Adjusted
Consideration				
LBDQ	632	7	.63	.99
SBDQ	1,048	10	.79	.99
LBDQ-XII	3,455	19	.57	.95
Initiation of Structure				
LBDQ	632	7	.29	.57
SBDQ	1,048	10	−.15	−.30
LBDQ-XII	3,455	19	.39	.73

SOURCE: Adapted from Fisher and Edwards (1988), p. 203.

correlation was with satisfaction with the leader ($r = .78$). The somewhat lower estimated true score correlation was .24 for initiation of structure with follower performance. The comparable estimated correlation between consideration and initiation of structure was .17, supporting their factorial independence. Although there was variability, the results were generalizable across many conditions. These were negligible for SBDQ, lower at supervisory than middle or upper hierarchical levels, and lower for cross-sectional compared with longitudinal studies. The consideration estimated correlations were higher for studies in the public sector and colleges ($r = .56, r = .53$) and lower in business and the military ($r = .43, r = .40$). The initiation estimates were higher in the military studies ($r = .46$) and lower elsewhere ($r = .29, .28, .25$).

Contingencies in the Effects of Consideration and Initiation

Generally, the consideration of supervisors seems to be associated with subordinates' satisfaction with the supervisors, fewer absences, and less likelihood of quitting. But, as we have just seen, the correlations between a leader's initiation of structure and the satisfaction and productivity of subordinates vary, in outcome, depending on the instruments used to measure them. The constraints and goals in the situation also make a difference. The personnel involved may be particularly important. Followers in a wide variety of groups consider it legitimate for the leader to exercise influence on matters related to the performance of tasks and the work environment (Fleishman & Peters, 1962). At higher executive levels, initiation of structure is seen in planning, innovation, and coordination; at lower levels, it is seen in the push for production (Brooks, 1955).

Although too much initiation often increases the likelihood of grievances, absenteeism, and turnover (Fleishman & Harris, 1962), a certain amount of pointing out the "paths to successful effort" (Bass, 1965c) is characteristic of the effective supervisor. This yields the greatest effectiveness and satisfaction in the work group—especially when workers are untrained, unmotivated, or both, for example, or when the group lacks cohesiveness. Untrained personnel need more help; trained people prefer less help.

The variety of mixed results noted in reviews[7] of the effects of consideration and initiation suggests that to gain a better understanding of these effects, researchers need to specify the measures used and the conditions involved (House, 1971; Kerr, Schriesheim, Murphy, & Stogdill, 1974). For example, initiation of structure usually has been found to be associated with subordinates' role clarity, but somewhat less frequently with subordinates' performance. The correlation with subordinates' satisfaction varies considerably from study to study (Fleishman, 1973). The leadership climate under which the supervisors work has been found to be related to the supervisors' own consideration and initiating structure behavior and attitudes (Fleishman, 1953b).

Instrumentation

As noted earlier, variations in results depend to some degree on whether the LBDQ, the SBDQ, the LBDQ-XII, or the LOQ has been used.

Schriesheim, House, and Kerr (1976) did a masterful detective job in reconciling the mixed results obtained with the various versions of the LBDQ and SBDQ in measuring initiation of structure. First, they pointed out that the LBDQ of Halpin (1957b) contained 15 items asking subordinates to describe the actual initiating structure behavior of their leader to establish well-defined patterns of communication and to set up ways to get the job done. But the revised LBDQ-XII (Stogdill, 1963a) contained 10 items for measuring initiation of structure that dealt with the actions of the leaders in clearly defining their own roles and informing followers about what was expected of them. Even more substantial differences were found in the leadership behavior tapped by the SBDQ and the LBDQ in a comprehensive item-by-item analysis of 242 employees' descriptions of their supervisors. In addition to role clarification by the leader, as was noted earlier, the SBDQ included a cluster of items measuring punitive, autocratic, and production-oriented behaviors, such as "He rules with an iron hand" and "He needles those under him for greater effort." Thus the three questionnaires—SBDQ and the earlier and later versions of the LBDQ—differed markedly in content. The initiation items of the LBDQ versions largely re-

[7] See L. R. Anderson (1966a); Campbell, Dunnette, Lawler, and Weick (1970); and Korman (1966).

flected communication and organization elements; the SBDQ initiating structure, however, contained domination and production pressure items.

An essential component of initiation of structure in all the instruments involved role-clarification behaviors. A specific aspect of role clarification—establishing methods to get the work done—is mentioned in the LBDQs, but other aspects, such as scheduling and criticizing, are found only in the SBDQ. Schriesheim, House, and Kerr (1976, p. 301) concluded:

> When measured by the SBDQ, leader Initiation of Structure is generally positively related to performance ratings by superiors of manufacturing first-level supervisors' subordinates.[8] This generalization also holds with regard to noncommissioned . . . infantry officers and air force officers[9] . . . with Initiating Structure being measured in these studies by a form containing items similar to the autocratic behavior items of the SBDQ. A similar although much weaker pattern of relationships has been found concerning non-manufacturing supervisors of clerical workers doing routine tasks . . . using selected items from the SBDQ in a laboratory experiment.[10] When the revised LBDQ Initiating Structure scale is used to measure leader behavior of first-line supervisors of non-manufacturing employees performing routine tasks, correlations with subordinate satisfaction are positive, although generally [lower] . . . using a very modified version of the revised LBDQ.[11]

Meheut and Siegel (1973) demonstrated the differences by dividing the items on initiation of structure in the SBDQ into those concerned with role clarification and those concerned with the autocratic behavior of leaders. They obtained a correlation of .26 between leaders' role clarification and subordinates' satisfaction, but a correlation of −.21 between leaders' autocratic behavior and subordinates' satisfaction.

Another source of error that accounts for variations in results with the SBDQ, according to Schriesheim, House, and Kerr, is the SBDQ's failure to provide opportunity for

[8]Fleishman and Harris (1962); Fleishman, Harris, and Burtt (1955); Harris and Fleishman (1955); and Skinner (1969).
[9]Moore (1953), Moore and Smith (1956), and Stouffer (1949).
[10]Fleishman, Harris, and Burtt (1955); and Lowin, Hrapehak, and Kavanagh (1969).
[11]Beer (1966); Dessler (1973); Hunt and Hill (1971); Hunt, Hill, and Reaser (1971); and Hunt and Liebscher (1973).

respondents to describe the timing or appropriateness of the structuring of the particular task or of the context in which respondents work, even though empirical evidence indicates that timing may be more important than the frequency of specific leadership behaviors (see, for example, W. K. Graham, 1968; Sample & Wilson, 1965). In addition, leaders who have adequate knowledge of the demands of their subordinates' tasks may vary the amount of initiation of structure and the kind and timing of the structure they provide. Some tasks require more structure during the goal-setting (goal-clarification) stage, whereas others require more path clarification and feedback on performance. Furthermore, some subordinates need more administrative structure to relate their work to other employees. Other subordinates could benefit more from technical guidance. Leaders may have no control over standards. Their initiation of structure may depend on circumstances outside their purview. "He decides what shall be done and how it shall be done" may be physically impossible for leaders in some situations. Other items on initiation of structure, such as "He tries out his ideas in the group," are less likely to be affected by circumstances.

Some items deal with specific behavior, and others deal with general tendencies. Such initiation of structure items as "He schedules the work to be done" refer to specific actions; items like "He encourages overtime work" relate to general practices. Even farther removed from specific behaviors and more concerned with the skills, traits, and personality attributed to the leader are such items as "He makes accurate decisions" and "He is a very persuasive talker."

Organizational Contingencies

The impact of a leader's initiation and consideration will depend on the organization in which they occur. House, Filley, and Gujarati (1971) found that both the leader's consideration and the leader's initiation of structure moderated the employees' satisfaction with freedom on the job, job security, and family attitudes in one firm, but not in another. Similarly, Larson, Hunt, and Osborn (1974) found that in one state mental health institution, the leaders' consideration was related to the performance of different groups of personnel, but that in another institution, initiating structure was more highly related to overall groups' performance. The report by Marsh and Atherton (1981–1982) of the results of a study of 30,000 U.S. Army personnel concluded that whether a military unit was *mechanistic* or *organic* moderated the extent to which the leader's initiation or consideration was related to the subordinates' satisfaction.

Differences in Function and Task. Fleishman, Harris, and Burtt (1955) noted that the leader's greater initiation of structure contributed to absences and grievances of subordinates in manufacturing departments and to heightened rates of turnover in nonmanufacturing departments. At the same time, Fleishman, Harris, and Burtt found that supervisors in manufacturing departments or in other departments that were working under time constraints were likely to receive higher merit ratings from their own supervisors if they tended to exhibit more initiation of structure, whereas the reverse was true for supervisors in service departments. In addition, in the nonmanufacturing service departments, the more considerate supervisors were seen as more proficient. "Pressure for production" was the moderator.

In Cunningham's (1964) study of county agricultural agents and 4-H club agents cited earlier, the agricultural agents' consideration was significantly related to effectiveness, but initiation of structure was not. In contrast, initiating structure was significantly related to the effectiveness of 4-H club agents, but consideration was not. However, as was noted earlier, the most effective agents in both organizations were those who were described as above the median in both consideration and initiation. Mannheim, Rim, and Grinberg (1967) reported that manual workers tolerated more initiation of structure by their supervisors than did clerical workers. Only clerical workers tended to reject the high-structuring supervisor when they expected the initiation of structure to be low. When high consideration was expected, both groups chose the leader who conformed to their expectations.

Hunt and Liebscher (1973) showed that leaders' consideration was more strongly associated with subordinates' satisfaction in a construction bureau than in a bureau of design of a state highway department; the leaders' initiation of structure did not vary as much in its effects on satisfaction. Dagirmanjian's (1981) study of 126 mental health service personnel showed that when organizational differentiation was in force, the leaders'

consideration generated employee satisfaction with supervision, but when organizational integration was involved, the leaders' initiation of structure generated such satisfaction.

Leaders in the Middle. Although Rambo (1958) failed to find any significant differences in the initiation and consideration of executives in different echelons of the hierarchical structure, Halpin (1956a) saw such hierarchical differences when he examined the reactions of organizational members at different levels to the leader in between them in level. Halpin studied the leadership of school superintendents described by staff members, school board members, and themselves on both the real and ideal forms of the LBDQ. He found that the board members agreed among themselves and the staff members agreed among themselves in their descriptions of the superintendents' behavior, but the two groups differed significantly in their perceptions. Staff members saw the superintendents as less considerate than the superintendents saw themselves or the board members saw the superintendents. The board members described the superintendents as being higher in initiating structure than did the staff members or the superintendents. The staff members and the board members differed significantly regarding how considerate the superintendents should be, but they did not differ significantly about the extent to which superintendents should initiate structure. The board members expected the superintendents to act in a more considerate manner than the staff members considered ideal. There was a nonsignificant tendency for board members to expect more initiation of structure than either the staff members or the superintendents considered ideal.

Other studies in educational institutions by raters of a leader in the middle were conducted by Sharpe (1956), Carson and Schultz (1964), and Luckie (1963). Sharpe studied the leadership of principals as described by teachers, staff members, and the principals themselves. The three groups held similar ideals of leadership behavior, but the teachers and staff members perceived the principals as deviating less from the ideal norms than did the principals themselves. Occupants of high-status positions perceived the principals as deviating more from the ideal norms than did those in lower-status positions. Carson and Schultz (1964) obtained descriptions of junior college deans by college presidents, department heads, student leaders, and the deans themselves. The greatest discrepancies were found between the presidents' and student leaders' perceptions and expectations of the dean's behavior. The evidence suggested that the greatest source of role conflict for the deans was the discrepant expectations of their behavior. Luckie (1963) obtained 434 descriptions of 53 directors of instruction by superintendents, staff members, and the directors themselves. The results indicated that the instructional directors actually behaved at a lower level of consideration than superintendents, the directors themselves, and the staff members rated as ideal. The superintendents and the staff members expected the directors to exhibit higher degrees of initiating structure than the directors considered ideal.

The conflict of the leader in the middle seems to reside in the question of how considerate to be, not how much structure to provide. Graen, Dansereau, and Minarm (1972b) obtained data indicating that at lower organizational levels, both superiors and subordinates evaluated the leader in between them more highly if the leader initiated more structure. But the leader's consideration had more of an impact on subordinates than on superiors.

Lawrie (1966) used real and ideal consideration and initiation in a study of superiors' and subordinates' expectations of foremen in two departments. The convergence between real and expected behavior, as described by subordinates, was not related to ratings of the foremen's effectiveness. However, in one of the two departments, the foremen's ability to predict the superiors' expectations and the congruence between the foremen's and the superiors' expectations were related to ratings of the foremen's effectiveness.

Influence "Upstairs." Leaders' influence with higher authority has been found to affect the impact of their initiation of structure and consideration on their subordinates' satisfaction and performance. Consideration often involves promises of tangible rewards, and leaders may need influence "upstairs" to deliver on their promises. Initiation of structure involves setting forth goals and plans; influence "upstairs" adds to the leaders' ability to do so with authority and credibility. In one of two companies studied, House, Filley, and Gujarati (1971) found the expected strong positive relation between a supervi-

sor's influence with a higher authority and an increase in the correlation of the supervisor's consideration with the subordinates' satisfaction. As Wager (1965) found earlier, in both the companies studied, the greater a supervisor's influence with higher authority, the greater was the supervisor's tendency to be considerate. Presumably, the influential leader could offer support and rewards with more certainty of providing them. The more influential supervisor exhibited more initiation of structure in only one of the firms studied, but, generally, employees were more satisfied with most aspects of their jobs if their supervisors were more influential with higher authority.

Falling Dominoes Again. The falling dominoes effect, discussed at length in earlier chapters, was observed by Hunt, Hill, and Reaser (1973) for results with the LBDQ-XII. In a school for the mentally retarded, an increase was found in the association of considerate supervision and the performance of aides when the LBDQ scores of the second-level and first-level supervisors were combined. Hunt, Osborn, and Larson (1975), with data from three mental institutions, showed that leaders' consideration had more of a positive impact on their groups' performance if the leaders' superiors were high in authoritarianism. However, group performance was higher if the leaders' initiation of structure was low, whether the leaders' superiors were authoritarian or egalitarian.

In his first study with the LOQ, Fleishman (1953a) found that the higher the supervisors' positions in the hierarchy of a plant, the less considerate the supervisors thought they should be and the more structure they thought should be initiated. These attitudes had an impact on those below them. Foremen whose superiors expected them to lead with less consideration and with more structuring revealed high grievance rates among their subordinates.

Size of Group Led. Ordinarily, one would expect that when a group is enlarged, a leader would have to display more initiation of structure to be as effective as before the unit was enlarged (Bass, 1960). It would be expected that the leader would find it increasingly difficult to maintain the same level of consideration for the concerns of all subordinates as the group enlarged. Corollary results that are consistent with this expectation were found by Badin (1974), who showed that in the smaller of 42 work groups of 489 manufacturing employees, the initiation of structure by the leader correlated negatively with productivity, but that the amount of a supervisor's initiation of Structure was unrelated to productivity in the larger groups.

Osborn and Hunt (1975b), in their previously cited study of presidents of chapters of a business fraternity, found that the size of a chapter moderated the positive effects of initiation and consideration on the members' satisfaction. However, Sheridan and Vredenburgh (1979) failed to find any relation between the size of units led and the head nurses' leadership behavior, although size correlated with perceived job tension, which, in turn, was related to the subordinates' performance.

Structure of the Work Group. J. A. Miller (1973a) deduced that more initiation of structure would be contraindicated in a highly structured setting. Thus for a supervisor to tell skilled crafts personnel how to do their job was expected to be detrimental to their performance. Consistent with this expectation, Badin (1974) found that when first-line supervisors initiated structure a great deal in the previously mentioned 42 work groups at the manufacturing firm, effectiveness was reduced in the groups that were already most structured. In these highly structured groups, the correlation of group effectiveness and the supervisors' initiation of structure was −.56. But in the less structured work groups, the effectiveness of the groups was correlated .20 with the extent to which their first-line supervisors initiated structure.

Also consistent with Miller's argument, Jurma (1978) demonstrated, in an experimental comparison, that workers in 20 discussion groups were more satisfied when leaders provided discussants with task-related information, gave guiding suggestions, helped groups to budget their time, and established group goals. This was especially true when the workers were faced with a debatable, ambiguous discussion task rather than one with clear choices for making a decision.

Dyadic versus Group Relationships. By the late 1970s, considerable research had concentrated on the dyadic leader-subordinate relationship (Graen & Schiemann, 1978), instead of on the leader and the primary work group (Hunt, Osborn, & Schriesheim, 1978). Substantive differences in results from standard leader-group

investigations have failed often to emerge. Thus, for example, in the case of the LBDQ, for 308 managerial and clerical employees in 43 work groups in a public utility, C. A. Schriesheim (1979a) found correlations of .77 and .89 between dyadic and group LBDQ descriptions of supervisors for initiation and consideration, respectively. Nevertheless, Yammarino (1990) collected LBDQ-Form XII data in 13 groups from 54 members of a campus police department at various hierarchical levels from patrol officers and dispatchers to lieutenants and directors. Each group reported to a single superior. Yammarino found for that for initiation of structure, individual member and group correlations of supervisory control and satisfaction with rewards were due to differences between the groups but not within them. Individual supervisors were the reason. The same was true for the correlations between consideration and role ambiguity and effort. But the correlations of the LBDQ assessments with satisfaction with supervision were a matter of individual differences.

Cohesion. Among 308 low- and middle-level managerial and clerical employees, J. F. Schriesheim (1980) used a modification of the LBDQ-XII. She asked subordinates to indicate how their superiors acted toward them as individuals rather than toward the group as a whole. In line with her expectations, she showed that when the cohesion of the work group was low, the leader's initiation of structure was positively related to the subordinates' satisfaction with supervision, role clarity, and self-rated performance. But when cohesiveness was high in the work group, the leader's consideration was positively related to the measures of satisfaction, clarity, and performance.

Alignment with Objectives. The contribution of initiation and consideration to productivity will depend on the extent to which the group of subordinates is supportive of the objectives of the productivity. In Howell's (1985) experiment, detailed in Chapter 21, the leader who initiated structure generated more than average actual productivity in the experimental subject if the confederate fellow worker established high norms for productivity. The experimental subject produced much less if the confederate induced low norms for productivity. The leader's consideration had the same effect, but to a lesser extent. Similar results occurred for the effect of initiating structure on satisfaction and freedom from role conflict, but here the effects of consideration were not moderated by productivity norms set by the confederates of the experimenter.

Hernandez and Kaluzny (1982) studied the leadership and performance of 20 work groups of public health nurses. They found that the supervisors' initiation of structure had a strong positive relationship to productivity but that consideration did not. Likewise, satisfaction was enhanced by the supervisors' and peers' initiation of structure. Instead of the amount of communication flow and group processing correlating positively with the groups' productivity and satisfaction, the reverse occurred. The explanation of these results lay in the lack of support by the nurses for the appropriateness of the services they offered.

Group Conflicts. Various kinds of conflict between the group and external agents, as well as within groups, moderate the extent to which consideration and initiation will be effective. R. Katz (1977) found that considerate leadership was most effective when the group faced external conflicts but that initiation of structure by the leader was most effective in dealing with internal interpersonal conflicts.

Stumpf (undated) completed a path analysis for questionnaire data from 144 professionals in a government R & D organization. Leadership behavior was not directly related to the subordinates' job satisfaction or performance, but it was related through two moderating or intervening variables that linked the leader's consideration and initiation to subordinates' job satisfaction and performance. The leader's initiation of structure correlated with the subordinates' skill-role compatibility, which in turn correlated with the subordinates' job satisfaction. Thus the R & D professionals' satisfaction with their jobs depended on the extent to which their skills were not in conflict with the demands of their roles, which in turn depended on the structuring of the situation by their supervisors.

Curvilinear Effects. Skinner (1969) obtained results indicating that supervisors who scored high in consideration experienced lower than average grievance and turnover rates among their subordinates. As did Fleishman and Harris (1962), Skinner concluded that the consideration of supervisors bears a curvilinear relationship to turnover and grievances of employees. As consideration increases, grievances decrease to a point and then level off. Supervisory initiation also had a curvilinear relationship to grievances.

Interaction of Effects. The interacting effects of consideration and initiation of structure were observed to vary, depending on the situation. Thus considerate foremen could initiate structure without increasing turnover or grievances (Cummins, 1971). Fleishman and Harris (1962) found in using the SBDQ that consideration and initiation of structure by foremen interacted to affect the grievances and turnover of employees. Medium and high degrees of consideration, along with low degrees of initiation of structure by foremen, were associated with the lowest rates of turnover and grievances of employees. Graen, Dansereau, and Minami (1972a) found, among 660 managers of a large corporation, that for those managers who saw their leader as either extremely high or extremely low in initiating structure, the relationship between the leader's consideration behavior and the managers' performance evaluation was positive. But for those managers who saw their leader as intermediate in initiating structure, the relationship between the leader's consideration and the managers' performance was near zero.

But other studies failed to establish any interaction effects of initiation and consideration on outcomes. Filley, House, and Kerr (1976) studied three companies to test Fleishman and Harris's (1962) hypothesis that the leader's initiation of structure acts as a mediator of the relationship between the leader's consideration and employees' job satisfaction. Initiating structure was positively and significantly related to satisfaction with the company in all three organizations. Consideration was significantly related to satisfaction with the company and freedom of action in all three organizations. The data failed to support the mediating hypothesis. Similarly, as will be examined more fully in Chapter 27, M. G. Evans (1970a) tested the path-goal hypothesis in two organizations. He found that consideration and initiation of structure did not interact in path-goal facilitation but, rather, that consideration and initiation of structure each acted separately to enhance path-goal instrumentality. The mixed findings suggest that the occurrence of the interaction effect depends on particular circumstances.

Contingent Aspects of the Subordinates. As might have been expected from what has been presented regarding the effects of autocratic leader behavior compounded with authoritarian subordinates, Weed, Mitchell, and Moffitt (1976) found that leaders who initiated structure more with dogmatic subordinates were likely to achieve higher levels of performance; leaders who exhibited more consideration yielded greater performance among less dogmatic subordinates. In the path analysis by Sheridan and Vredenburgh (1979), greater job experience of the nursing personnel was found to be related to less considerate leadership from the head nurses, which, in turn, increased the subordinates' tension and had mixed effects on their performance.

M. Beer's (1964) industrial study of the effects of leadership behavior on subordinates' fulfillment of needs disclosed that subordinates whose need for self-actualization, esteem, autonomy, production emphasis, and consideration was high were positively motivated by the leader's initiation of structure, contrary to the hypothesis that the leader's consideration would be more effective in motivating subordinates. Abdel-Halim (1981) collected data from 89 lower- and middle-level manufacturing managers and demonstrated that the subordinates' locus of control moderated the effects of the ambiguity and complexity of tasks on the effectiveness of initiation and consideration.

Contingent Aspects of the Leaders. The effects of initiation or consideration appear to depend on whether the leader has a strong need for achievement. Leaders with a high need for achievement who initiated structure obtained a better performance from their subordinates than did leaders with a low need for achievement who also initiated structure (T. Mayes, 1979). Another illustration of a contingent effect that is due to the leader was provided by Miklos (1963), who observed that the longer the tenure of school principals who were high in the initiation of structure, the greater the consensus among teachers in their role expectations for teachers and the greater the agreement between teachers and principals. Agreement between teachers and principals was highest when principals were rated high in both consideration and initiation of structure.

The expert power of the leader also moderated the effects of initiation and consideration. Path analyses by

Martin and Hunt (1980) that initiation and consideration, when combined directly or indirectly with expert power, linearly enhanced the group's cohesiveness, job satisfaction, and intentions to remain on the job. Podsakoff, Todor, and Schuler (1983) helped to explain this effect of expert power and leadership. They collected data from 101 employees of a large nonprofit organization who used modified LBDQ scales to describe their supervisors. As the supervisors' initiation of structure increased, if the supervisors were highly expert, the role ambiguity of the subordinates decreased. However, if the leaders who were high in initiation were low in expert power, the reverse occurred—the role ambiguity of the subordinates increased. A similar though less extreme pattern emerged with the increasing consideration of the leaders. Expert considerate leaders generated less role ambiguity in their subordinates, whereas inexpert considerate leaders generated more role ambiguity.

Causal Effects

Cross-Lagged Analyses

The limitations of the results of LBDQ surveys in ascertaining whether the described leadership is a cause, a consequence, or a coincidence of group effectiveness, satisfaction, or other valued outcomes has already been noted. Do considerate and structuring leaders promote the satisfaction and productivity of subordinates, or do leaders of satisfied and productive subordinates show them more consideration and tend to initiate less structure? Cross-lagged analyses suggest that the causality is reciprocal. Leaders affect subsequent outcomes, and outcomes affect the leaders' subsequent behavior (Greene, 1973, 1974, 1975, 1979a).

Greene (1975) asked first-level managers in insurance, marketing, finance, and research and engineering to describe their own consideration and initiation of structure on the LBDQ. Two subordinates of each of the managers rated their own work satisfaction. Peers of these subordinates rated the subordinates' productivity. The measures were picked up on successive occasions one month apart. Cross-lagged comparisons were made of the leaders' behavior at time 1 correlated with the subordinates' satisfaction or productivity at time 2 and contrasted with the subordinates' satisfaction or performance at time 1 correlated with the leaders' behavior at time 2. The results strongly suggested that considerate leadership resulted subsequently in the increased satisfaction of subordinates. At the same time, the subordinates' productivity resulted subsequently in their managers' increased consideration for them. Finally, the subordinates' productivity subsequently resulted in a reduction in the managers' initiation of structure.

Experimental Effects

Even greater confidence about the cause and effects of initiation and consideration comes from the rare experiment in which the leader's initiation or consideration (or both) is arbitrarily manipulated experimentally and measurements are taken of the subsequent effects on subordinates. Some results were obtained to support the argument that initiation or consideration causes the subsequent improved performance or increased satisfaction of subordinates. Dawson, Messé, and Phillips (1972) arranged for teachers to increase their initiation of structure deliberately. They found that their students' work group productivity improved as a consequence. When the teachers subsequently increased their consideration deliberately, the students' work-group productivity again increased as a consequence. In a laboratory experiment by Gilmore, Beehr, and Richter (1979), 48 participants were subjected to either low or high consideration and low or high structure by specially coached student supervisors who were working with groups of four members each. The LBDQ completed by the members failed to discriminate the behavior of the four types of supervisors, even though the leadership behavior itself had differential effects on the quality of the participants' performance. The quality of the participants' performance was highest with leaders who were high in initiation of structure but low in consideration. But neither the amount of initiation nor the amount of consideration was related to various measures of satisfaction of the participants. Finally, as mentioned before, Howell's (1985) experiment demonstrated that if group norms were supportive of high productivity, the leaders' initiation and consideration resulted in a rise in productivity and satisfaction.

Summary and Conclusions

Hundreds of statements about leaders' behavior formed two factors—consideration and initiation of structure—but it was recognized that some important elements in leadership might still be left out. Twelve factors were found to exhaust the list. To initiation and consideration were added representing, reconciling, tolerating uncertainty, persuasiveness, tolerating (followers') freedom, role retention, production emphasis, predictive accuracy, integrating (of organization), and influence with supervisors. Although factorially and conceptually independent, the leader's consideration and initiation of structure factors were ordinarily found to correlate moderately with each other in their revised measurement with LBDQ-Form XII scales.

The two factors are systematically affected by many personal and situational variables. Initiation of structure becomes more important when the group is not already highly structured. Psychometric reviews of results using the original and revised LBDQ and the SBDQ indicate that the generally negative associations between task-oriented initiation of structure, as measured by the SBDQ, and satisfaction and morale become positive when the coercive elements are removed. But leniency is likely to continue to bias the results, along with halo effects when single sources of variance are used to evaluate both leadership and outcomes. Self-ratings seem unlikely to indicate what leaders do according to their subordinates. Moreover, many contingencies can be cited as moderators of the relationships. A variety of expanded and alternative factor structures are available for a more detailed study of leadership behavior with the LBDQ-XII.

Causal analyses by cross-lagged surveys and experimentation suggest that consideration both increases the satisfaction of subordinates and is increased by it. Initiation of structure by the leader (if structure is low) improves the subordinates' performance, which in turn increases the leader's subsequent consideration and reduces the leader's initiation of structure.

Several components that are variously involved in the different versions of scales that measure the leader's initiation of structure must be taken into account for a full appreciation of their antecedents and their effects on the subordinates' performance. The elements of role and task clarification are likely to have positive effects on satisfaction and productivity; the autocratic elements in the earlier LBDQs may have negative effects, especially on satisfaction. Consideration, likewise, may contribute differently in different situations to satisfaction and effectiveness as a consequence of its several components, including participatory and consultative decision making and concern for the welfare of subordinates. As we shall see next, together initiation and consideration can account for the transactional exchange between the leader and the led, but much more is involved when the leadership is transformational.

The "New" Leadership: Charismatic and Transformational Leadership

chapter 21

Charismatic Leadership

In trying to understand the rise of the Prussian bureaucracy early in the twentieth century, the German sociologist Max Weber (1924/1947) introduced the formerly religious concept of *charisma* to the study of leadership and organizations. Coordination in organizations required authority, either rational-legal, traditional, or charismatic. This became of interest in the sociological study of social and political movements as well as in psychoanalytical interpretations of historical leadership. Sociologists such as Parsons (1937) suggested that there is usually some charismatic leadership preceding the development of traditional and legal authority. Early on, psychoanalysts including Sigmund Freud (1922/1939) and Eric Fromm (1941), began explorations of individual charismatic leaders and their impact on followers. But into the 1970s, charismatic leadership still had not become a subject for much survey, experimental, or behavioral research (Stark, 1977).

Concepts of Charismatic Leadership

Weber's Concept of Charisma. Weber's concept of charisma was an adaptation of the theological concept, which involves endowment with the gift of divine grace. Weber's (1922/1963) charismatic leader was a mystical, narcissistic, and personally magnetic savior with extraordinary capabilities and a doctrine to promote. Such a leader arose in times of crisis.

Weber (1924/1947) applied the concept of charisma to explain the development and maintenance of complex organizations in which the gift of extraordinariness as a person was now bestowed by colleagues and subordinates instead of by God. According to Weber, charismatic leaders inspired the development of organizations, which subsequently came to be traditionally or bureaucratically managed. Charismatic offices, such as pope, king, or hereditary chief, could arise and then become traditional.

Routinization would finally occur and managerial bureaucrats would take charge. The charismatics formulated the basic purposes and principles for bureaucratic administrators to live by.

Trice and Beyer (1986) summed up Weber's conceptualization as having five components: (1) a person with extraordinary gifts, (2) a crisis, (3) a radical solution to the crisis, (4) followers who are attracted to the exceptional person because they believe that they are linked through him to transcendent powers, and (5) validation of the person's gifts and transcendence in repeated experiences of success. According to Beyer (1999), leaving out any of these components was a "taming" of charisma.

Post-Weberian Charisma. For some writers, charismatic leadership implied radical innovation (Stark, 1969); for others, it implied pathology (Davies, 1954). Its conversion from an extremely unusual character was "tamed" (Beyer, 1999) by House (1977), Bass (1985) and Conger and Kanungo (1988) and became accessible for leadership research in everyday life. House (1977) theorized that leaders deserved to be called charismatic if they exerted various effects and influences on their followers such as followers' trust in the leader's beliefs, unquestioning obedience and acceptance of the leader, identification with the leader, emotional involvement with the mission, elevated goals, self-efficacy, and collective efficacy. Bass held that charisma was a component of transformational leadership (see Chapter 22). Conger and Kanungo held that charisma was a set of behaviors and attributions such as being unconventional, visionary, and willing to take risks. DiThomaso (1993) faulted these neo-Weberian conceptions as ignoring the tensions involved in the emergence and development of the charismatic leader.

Closest to Weber is the continued conception of charisma as an institutional phenomenon. It deals with how social changes are introduced by charismatic leaders and formalized into organizational arrangements, routiniza-tion, and the leadership succession (Bryman, 1993). The post-Weberian charismatic leader was conceived by House (1977) in terms of particular behaviors and attri-butes.

Another conception was psychoanalytical, concerned mainly with the predispositions of dependent followers and charismatic leaders. Charismatics exude confidence, dominance, a sense of purpose, and the ability to articu-late the goals and ideas for which followers are already prepared psychologically (Fromm, 1941). The response of followers is likewise extreme. It is both cognitive and emotional as well as devoted and unquestioning. Charis-matic leaders have extraordinary influence over their fol-lowers, who become imbued with moral inspiration and purpose. The followers experience a magnetic attraction that transcends their usual experience. They become dis-ciples and zealots.

Charisma also may be viewed as a reciprocally interde-pendent but asymmetric relationship of a powerful leader and dependent followers (Bryman, 1992). Other post-Weberian conceptions include finding charismatic lead-ership in some everyday situations; at all organizational levels; in the complex interaction between leader, follow-ers, and situation; and in a mission bonding leader and followers (Jermier, 1993).

Although most attention had been paid to charismatic leaders in the religious, political, and societal arenas, such leaders are also studied increasingly in business, ed-ucational, and military settings (Handy, 1976). On the basis of his observations of such successful leaders, Lawler (1982) concluded that their leadership occurs "through a combination of factors" that can be captured by words like "vision," "communication," "symbols," and "cha-risma." Such leaders are more concerned with doing the right thing than with doing things right. Charismatic leaders often emerge in times of crises as prospective sav-iors who by their magical endowments will fulfill the unmet emotional needs of their completely trusting, overly dependent, and submissive followers. If successful, charismatic leaders can bring about radical transforma-tions in their groups, organizations, or societies.

Weber's Legacy. Although contradictions were seen in Weber's conceptualization (Downton, 1973), charisma has continued to figure strongly as an explanatory con-cept in sociology, political science, and psychoanalysis, and more recently in organizational psychology and management studies. Weber's original concept has been modified, expounded on, and extended in numerous so-ciological, political science, and psychoanalytic treatis-es.[1] Charisma plays a major role, conceptually, in the psychoanalytical offshoot of psychohistorical analysis (Demause, 1982). Weber's lead was also followed by a number of organizational theorists, who found charisma among some officeholders in complex organizations, particularly at higher levels.[2] Such charismatics were likely to be at the center of institutional structures and have the power to radicalize them (Berger, 1963).

The revisers of Weber's concept have seen a need to account for Weber's conception of the charismatic leader's break with continuity, as well as his or her deal-ing with the aftermath. They have also questioned the relative importance and meaning of charisma to demo-cratic politics (Schiffer, 1973). According to Weber (1924/1947), the charismatic leader is obeyed because of the moral authority with which he is endowed, not be-cause of democratic consent.

Some commentators take a severely restricted view of charisma. Friedrich (1961) would limit charisma to in-spirational leadership characterized by the charismatic having a call from God for his or her mission. Trice and Beyer (1986) wanted to see all five Weberian components present before a condition was accepted as charismatic. They rejected labeling any leadership as charismatic merely because it was inspiring or dynamic. Berlew (1979) had identified three characteristics of charismatic leadership: confidence building, shared vision, and cre-ating valued opportunities. But Trice and Beyer argued that these were "rather incomplete and pale in compari-son to Weber's conception of charisma" (p. 122). They also dismissed Solomon's (1977) discussion, which they said was about personalized, autocratic leadership, not charisma. And although George Washington has often been considered charismatic because he embodied the values of his society (Schwartz, 1983), they concluded that he was not charismatic, because he and his situation lacked some of the other Weberian features.

Other extremists, such as Bradley (1984), have argued

[1] See, for example, Schiffer (1973), Schweitzer (1984), and Willner (1968).
[2] Blau and Scott (1962), Etzioni (1961), and Friedland (1964).

that intense cohesiveness of the group would result in endowing leaders with charismatic qualities. By contrast, Dow (1969a) emphasized, almost exclusively, the exceptional individual and his ideas rather than the social or political scene. Willner (1984) saw charisma as a consequence of both context and individual personality. Likewise, Erickson (1958) thought that people would seek a charismatic leader when they were faced with cultural shock, fears, anxieties, and identity crises.

Toward a Pragmatic Concept of Charisma

As with definitions of leadership, absolutists have insisted that their definition of charisma is the only proper one. In fact, however, definitions should be formulated for their operational and explanatory utility (Bass, 1960). Nor does the meaning of charisma have to remain fixed with Weber and his interpreters. Some of the variance in the phenomenon of charisma is due to the exceptional individual, some to the exceptional situation, and some to the interaction of the exceptional individual and the exceptional situation.

There have been and continue to be a considerable number of exceptional people. For example, it is likely that there were many other charismatic reformist preachers who were contemporaries of the more famous ones from Martin Luther to Martin Luther King Jr. Although these others were less publicized, each had dedicated followers, radical solutions, a mission, and self-confidence. In all walks of life and at all organizational levels, we are likely to encounter charisma and charismatic interactions between confident, gifted leaders with seemingly radical solutions to critical problems and followers who are unquestioningly and magnetically attracted to these leaders (Smith, 1982). Such leadership is not merely inspiring or dynamic; it involves unusual reactions by the followers. For purists, we may need to talk about the charismalike behavior of leaders or the charismalike devotion of followers. For the purposes in this chapter, the Weberian requirements and those of some revisionists will be regarded as sufficient, but not all are necessarily essential in each instance. In the hi-tech industry, strong substantive arguments may be characteristic of charismatic leaders and their immediate technical subordinates, who never accept these leaders unquestioningly. Continued unquestioning acceptance of the leader is not

an absolutely essential consequence of charismatic leadership. As Tucker (1970, p. 4) noted:

> Followers can be under the spell of a leader and can accept him as supremely authoritative without necessarily agreeing with him on all occasions or refraining from argument with him. In the highly argumentative atmosphere of a modern radical party, for example, a leader can be both charismatic and contested on specific points, as Lenin often was by his close followers. Indeed, he can even manifest some of his charisma in the inspired way in which he conquers dissent by the sheer power of his political discourse. Immense persuasiveness in argument may, in other words, be one of the extraordinary qualities by virtue of which a leader acquires charisma in his followers' eyes.

The charismatic relationship can appear in the absence of a crisis. For instance, dynamic leaders of financial investing have devoted, unquestioning followers. The leaders provide these followers with an exhilarating mission—to grasp an opportunity for improving the followers' portfolios (even though the followers are often already wealthy). The followers show every indication of wanting to identify with the leaders and their ideas. Does the fact that there is no crisis mean that these leaders must be something other than charismatic? Boal and Bryson (1987, 1988) agree that visionary charismatics need no crisis.

What do we call charismatic leaders who have all the Weberian attributes except success? Early in their careers, Mao Zedong and Yasir Arafat suffered one defeat after another. Perhaps it was their successful escapes that were emphasized. What about the charismatic leader who is incompetent? Schiffer (1973) suggests it is easier for many followers to identify with a charismatic leader who lacks talent, just as they do.

As the concept of charisma spread from sociology and political science to psychoanalysis and psychology, increasing attention was paid to the followers' need to identify with the leader and to the endurance of the charismatic leader, rather than to the routinization of the organization that was to follow, according to Weber. It also has been observed that the charismatic leader inspires opposition and hatred in those who strongly favor the old order (Tucker, 1970). This view argues strongly for dyadic, rather than group, analyses of charismatic leader-follower relationships. One can see the subordinates of a single charismatic supervisor divided in the extent to which they love, fear, or hate him or her. The very behaviors and qualities that transport supporters of the charismatic into extremes of love, veneration, and admiration may send opponents into extremes of hatred, animosity, and detestation (Bass, 1985a). President George W. Bush generated such contrasting reactions between his socially conservative political supporters and his liberal opponents.

Charismatic leaders vary greatly in pragmatism, flexibility, and opportunism, and adopt different styles to achieve their impact. Charles de Gaulle, for instance, was always more concerned about being right than achieving immediate results and spoke of his "contempt for contingencies." Generally, his attitude was unbending (Hoffman & Hoffman, 1970). He became pragmatic only when forced to do so in order to resolve the Algerian crisis. Other inflexible charismatics of our time have included Muammar al-Qaddafi of Libya and the Ayatollah Khomeini of Iran. In contrast, John F. Kennedy and Franklin Delano Roosevelt avoided speaking out, to sidestep political battles that they thought they might lose. Lenin also was a practical activist and a pragmatic organizer ready to reverse course when necessary (Tucker, 1970).

Another reason to look at the charismatic leader as exemplifying some but not all of the Weberian characteristics is that the move toward routinization of leader-follower relations may have been initiated by charismatic leaders rather than by their successors. Marshal Tito of Yugoslavia is a case in point, as are Augustus, Joseph Stalin, and Jawaharlal Nehru, who, respectively, continued the routinization begun by the charismatic Julius Caesar, Lenin, and Mahatma Gandhi, and who had many, if not all, the charismatic qualities of their predecessors. Were not the successors as charismatic as the founders, even though cumbersome bureaucracies emerged under them?

Types of Charismatics

Personalized versus Socialized Charismatic Leaders. Howell (1988) distinguished between ideal types of *personalized* and *socialized* charismatic leaders. Charismatics can foster antisocial or prosocial behavior. Personalized charismatic leaders are dominant, self-interested,

and authoritarian. Freud similarly (1922) distinguished between *totemic* leaders, who could be worshipped as idols to satisfy the fantasies of their followers; and *true* charismatics, who directed their followers toward more worthy transcendental purposes. Personalized charismatic leaders use their powers of persuasion to obtain their followers' obedience and submission (McClelland, 1975). Such leaders are self-aggrandizing and maintain psychological distance from their followers; this distance increases their magical, supernatural, charismatic image. In contrast, socialized charismatic leaders are oriented toward serving others. They develop shared goals with their followers and inspire the attainment of these goals. Psychological distance between socialized leaders and followers is reduced, enhancing the followers' expectation of an equalization of power and mutual stimulation.

Socialized charismatic leaders are socially constructive, are egalitarian, and serve collective interests. They perpetuate their influence by the continued relevance of their ideas and their mission to the followers' intrinsic satisfaction. That is, followers accept the influence of socialized leaders' ideas because these ideas are intrinsically rewarding (Howell, 1988). Socialized leaders are similar to Lipman-Blumen's (1996) "third stage" connective leaders, who use the right gestures and perfect symbols and rituals to underscore their messages. Like a magnet, their dramatics attract followers to their cause. "Untainted by a self-serving addiction to power, their leadership is dedicated to the well-being of the group" (p. 230). To some degree, socialized charismatic leadership—with its emphasis on the mutuality of goals and contribution to the greater good, rather than on the followers' unquestioned identification with the leader—fits with what will be discussed later in this chapter as inspirational leadership. Their Leadership Motive Patterns (LMP) of high power need coupled with *high* activity inhibition is directed toward using social influence in socially desirable ways and for collective benefit rather than for self-aggrandizement (House & Howell, 1992).

Followers accept the influence of *personalized* charismatic leaders in order to identify with them. Following is intrinsically rewarding (Kelman, 1958). Howell deduced that to continue to remain influential, personalized charismatic leaders must maintain a physical or psychological presence and a satisfying relationship with their followers. On the basis of extensive research by McClelland (1985) on the LMP, House and Howell (1992) inferred that personalized leaders were likely to have a high *need for power* combined with *low activity inhibition*. Such leaders responded to the Thematic Apperception Test (TAT) by telling stories that concentrated on dominating and winning at someone else's expense. House and Howell also expected personalized charismatic leaders to score high in Machiavellianism (Christie & Geis 1970), narcissism (Raskin & Hall, 1979), and authoritarianism (Altemeyer, 1981).

The "Office Charismatic" and the Personal Charismatic. Etzioni (1961) and Hollander (1978) noted that charismalike leadership could be a property of one's position as well as one's person. An American president has luster, some of which he loses after he leaves office. "Office charismatics" attain high status by virtue of the strong public image they have as holders of a valued role. Personal charismatics like Betty Friedan or Simone de Beauvoir, prominent figures in the women's movement, gained high esteem through their writings and speeches. Their followers had faith in them as persons. Furthermore, personal charismatics may be in high- or low-status positions. A personal charismatic can occupy the highly valued office of president, but a charismatic like Saint Francis or a Hindu *sadhu* can attract people because of their sacrificial renunciation of all worldly power and possessions.

Etzioni (1961) suggested that although charismatic office frequently has to be achieved, "office charisma" is ascribed. Regardless of their ability or performance, incumbents obtain it with the office. Charisma can attach to any high social status, achieved or inherited, as is seen in the public reactions to a visit, marriage, or divorce of the Prince of Wales. The charisma as well as celebrity status goes with the role.

Celebrities. One cannot ignore the vicarious effects on a mass audience of the superstar who can be only an image and a name to identify with. For example, enlistment rates can go up substantially after a popular star appears in a war movie. Psychological projection and identification play important roles in the process of charismatic influence at a distance. As Schiffer (1983, p. 9) noted:

To most people . . . political figures . . . are just like box-office attractions in the field of entertainment despite the fact that many politicians are often bearers of ideals and ideologies. . . . We embrace the images . . . [of] popular actors, actresses, and musicians who, above and beyond their talents, have been given charismatic status despite—or perhaps because of certain flaws in their character or theatrical skills.

Weber believed that the personal charismatic creates a charismatic office to be filled by an uncharismatic successor. However, Etzioni (1961) pointed out that personal charisma may be revealed more forcefully when the holder of the office is an incumbent who follows uncharismatic predecessors in the same office—as was the case with Franklin Delano Roosevelt, who followed Warren Harding, Calvin Coolidge, and Herbert Hoover. Also, nothing seems to preclude one charismatic succeeding another.

Publicly celebrated charismatics may have little charisma in their private lives. As Etzioni (1961, p. 316) put it, "Top executives, heads of state, and kings, who have charisma in the eyes of the public . . . may have little or [none] in the eyes of [their] private secretaries, valets, and cabinet ministers."

Close and Distant Charismatic Leaders. Shamir (1995) called attention to the fact that some charismatic relationships were close, directly connected, usually face-to-face: supervisor and subordinate, teacher and student, physician and patient. Other relationships involved, for example, CEOs, presidents, prime ministers, mass movement leaders, generals, and church leaders, who were socially distant from their followers. Followers connected only indirectly to distant leaders, through the media or through layers of intermediaries. The followers could observe and interact personally only with the close leaders. The closest they could come to the distant leader was on television or at a public meeting. Katz and Kahn (1978) suggested that for the leader to be viewed as charismatic, some distance was required between the leader and the led. Shamir disagreed: he found that close as well as distant leaders could be identified as charismatic by 320 Israeli students. Although both types of charismatic leaders were described by these students as self-confident, dominant, willing to sacrifice, and willing to set personal examples, the traits and behaviors attributed to the leaders were somewhat different. For instance, the close charismatics were identified as sociable, open, and considerate; the distant charismatics had rhetorical skills. Also, different effects were attributed to close and distant charismatic leaders. Task-related motivation was more frequently attributed to the close leader; substantive achievements were more frequently attributed to the distant leader. A follow-up by Yagil (1998) with 554 Israeli combat soldiers found that although they described close charismatic platoon commanders and distant charismatic battalion commanders as having extraordinary traits, only the close platoon commanders were seen as having confidence in individual and exemplary behavior.

Individualized and Group-Assessed Charisma. To the extent that charismatic leadership is an attribution based on questionnaire ratings, the individual followers' ratings can be averaged regardless of whether they report to the same or different leaders; or we can average the results for each group of ratings for each leader. Avolio and Yammarino (1990) collected data from the Multifactor Leadership Questionnaire (MLQ): the charismatic leadership behavior scores of 111 line and staff managers based on ratings by their 375 subordinates. Within-and-between groups analysis (WABA) suggested that for practical purposes individual differences among subordinates, regardless of their group, gave a more valid assessment of the leaders than did the group averages. Charisma was in the eye of the individual beholder, not in the eyes of a group of beholders. However, Klein and House (1995) argued that a full explanation of the emergence of charisma required looking at the interaction of the individual leader, each group of followers, and the situation.

Absolute, Normative, Executive, and Policy Charismatics. Zablock (1980) was able to order four kinds of charismatic leadership in communes according to the completeness of the issues covered by the leadership.[3] *Absolute* charismatic leadership was commonly found in selected religious communes. These communes concen-

[3] Descriptions of the communes could be Guttman-scaled with a reproducibility of the hierarchy of 93. (A Guttman scale is a set of statements that can be ordered so that endorsement of a particular statment will predict endorsement of all those higher in the ordering of the statements and rejection of all those lower in the ordering. A perfect ordering has a reproducibility of 1.00.)

trated authority about meanings, goals, strategies, norms, and alternatives. *Normative* charismatic leadership occurred in other religious communes that were similar except that authority about alternatives was missing. *Executive* charismatic leadership was found in some psychological, counterculture, and political communes in which one or several leaders concentrated authority about meanings, goals, and strategies, but not about norms or alternatives. *Policy* charismatic leadership was particularly salient in counterculture and political communes in which authority was concentrated only about meanings or only meanings and goals.

Alternative Concepts Similar to Charismatic Leadership

Inspirational Leadership. Charismatic leadership? Inspirational leadership? What's the difference? According to Downton (1973), the difference is in the way followers accept and comply with the leader's initiatives. If there are no dynamics for the followers' identification with the leader, and if the followers are drawn to the leader's goals and purposes but not to the leader per se, then the leader is inspirational but not charismatic. Followers believe that they share a social philosophy with the inspirational leader. If the followers feel that they are more powerful as a consequence of the leader's exhortations because the leader has pointed out desirable goals and how to achieve them—not because the powerful leader is their model—then the leader is inspirational, not necessarily charismatic (McClelland, 1975). Followers impute God-given powers to charismatic leaders and are incapable of criticizing such leaders. But although followers may regard inspirational leaders as symbols of beliefs and shared problems, they can also roundly criticize them more than those whom they regard as charismatic leaders (Downtown, 1973).

Heroic Leadership. Burns (1978) preferred to speak about *heroic* leadership, believing that the term "charisma" had been overworked. The highly esteemed individual is a hero. There is

a belief in [heroic] leaders because of their personage alone, aside from their tested capacities, experience, or stand on issues; faith in the leaders' capacity to overcome obstacles and crises; readiness to grant to leaders the powers to handle crises; mass support for such leaders expressed directly—through votes, applause, letters, shaking hands—rather than through intermediaries or institutions. Heroic leadership is not simply a quality or entity possessed by someone; it is a type of relationship between leader and led. A crucial aspect of this relationship is the absence of conflict. (p. 244)

The heroic, transcending leader excites and transforms previously dormant followers into active ones. For example, leaders of an exodus heighten the followers' motivation, purposes, and missionary zeal. Followers become proselytizers, who, in turn, act as leaders as a consequence of their exalted awareness.

Visionary Leadership. Envisioning an attractive future is often seen as a component of charisma but it is not limited to charismatics. Sashkin (1988) suggested that visionary leadership does require dealing with change, ideal goals, and working together. (This will be elaborated in Chapter 22.)

Value-Based Leadership and Idealized Influence. House (1997a) introduced this concept to replace charismatic leadership as a relationship between a leader and followers based on internalized ideological values espoused by the leader. Bass and Avolio (1994) substituted the term "idealized influence," with the same meaning as charismatic leadership. In both cases, the authors wanted to abandon the term "charisma" because of its popular connotations of celebrity and popularity and its widespread usage. As Bensman and Givant (1975) noted, charisma is the name of a perfume, a shirt brand, a pop tune, and a laundry, an attribute of any popular politician.

Outstanding Leadership. Outstanding leaders achieve outstanding results, compared with ordinary leaders. Their behaviors are a compilation of all those associated with charismatic, visionary, heroic, transformational, and inspirational leadership, all of which tend to be highly correlated (House & Podsakoff, 1994).

Maximum Leadership. Zaleznick and Kets de Vries (1975) conceived of *maximum* leaders who were charis-

matic, creative institution builders as a consequence of their personalities and early childhood development. They were highly self-confident. They led with strength and vision. In contrast, *minimum* managers were more concerned about the opinions of their peers and followers, and followed such opinions instead of leading.

Transformational Leadership. Leaders motivate their followers by raising their followers' concerns from security and belonging to achievement and self-actualization, and by moving them beyond self-interest to concerns for their group, organization, or society (Burns, 1978). Components are charisma or idealized influence, inspirational leadership, intellectual stimulation, and individualized consideration (Bass, 1985a). Chapter 22 is about transformational leadership.

Charismatic/Transformational Leadership. House (1995), Hunt (1999), and others believe that charismatic and transformational leadership are one and the same and prefer to use the term "charismatic/transformational leadership." So do Behling and McFillan (1996), who created a synthesis of the two concepts in which the leader's words and actions both demonstrate empathy, empower followers, project self-assurance, dramatize the mission, and affirm collective efficacy.

The Charismatic Relationship Theories

Post-Weberian explanations of the charismatic relationship abound. There is reciprocity, in that the leader's vision tends to be congruent with the followers' values and identities, and the followers tend to support a leader who shares their beliefs (Yukl, 1998). Explanations differ in their emphases on motivation, antecedents, and the mechanisms they postulate. They also differ in their dependence on attributions, self-concepts, symbolism, and psychoanalysis (Shamir, 1991).

Historical essays, surveys and several experiments have examined the charismatic relationship, as have psychoanalytical accounts (Zaleznik, 1990). Behavioral models and theories also emerged to explain charismatic leadership (House, 1977). For example, Behling and McFillan (1996) proposed operationalizing a *syncretic* model combining the effects of the leader's empathy, mission, and assurance and the followers' awe, inspiration, and empowerment.

Behavioral Theories and Findings. As noted above, House (1977) launched a theory to account for what the charismatic leader did to motivate the observable behaviors of followers. It was an effort to take some of the mystery out of charismatic effects. The theory was subsequently revised by House, Shamir, and Smith (1992) and Shamir, House, and Arthur (1993) to better fit findings. The charismatic leader connects the followers' self-concepts to the collective mission and makes it valued as an aspect of the followers' self-concepts. The leader engages the followers' motivation for self-expression, self-esteem, self-worth, and self-consistency. The charismatic leader changes followers' perceptions of what the group needs to do, proposes an appealing vision of the future, strengthens collective identity and frame alignment, and increases individual and collective efficacy. The specific messages of the charismatic leader, compared with those of the noncharismatic leader, make more references to values, moral justifications, history, distal rather than proximal goals, more positive references about the followers' worth, and more expressions of high expectations for self and followers. Jacobsen and House (2001) matched 16 sets of data about six "clearly charismatic" leaders to verify a six-stage model of the charismatic relationship: (1) identification with the leader, (2) arousal of follower activity, (3) commitment, (4) disenchantment, (5) depersonalization, and (6) alienation. The model accounted for 76.7% of the variance in the data.

Shamir, Zakay, Breinein, et al. (1998) obtained generally supportive findings in data collected in 50 Israeli army companies. The charismatic leader's ideology, emphasis on collective identity, and display of exemplary behavior resulted in the followers' trust and identification with the leader. Also enhanced were the followers' identification, intrinsic motivation, efficacy with the task, willingness to sacrifice in performing the task, and attachment to their group.

Conger and Kanungo (1988) listed behaviors of the charismatic leader as: radical, unconventional, risk taking, visionary, entrepreneurial, and exemplary. Of the elements associated with the charismatic relationship, two appeared essential. The first was the pattern of abilities, interests, and personal traits that is common to most char-

ismatic leaders. The second was the strong desire by followers to identify with the leader. Charismatic leaders have strong referent power. Often, but not always, leaders present concise and radical solutions to crises. The followers' belief in the solutions comes as a consequence of their faith in the charismatic leader. If the effect of the emotion-driven charismatic relationship is to endure, it must therefore give way to a more rationally driven routinization. Conger and Kanungo (1998) theorized that the charismatic relationship develops in three stages. First, the leader critically evaluates the followers' inclinations and the existing situation. Second, when the time is right, the leader formulates and articulates a vision (an idealized goal) that makes her or him worthy of identification. Third, the leader demonstrates how the goal can be achieved by setting a personal example, taking risks, and applying unconventional expertise. The leader who impresses followers with total dedication, commitment, exemplary acts, and personal investment earns the attribution of charismatic leader.

Characteristics of Charismatic Leaders

Requisite Abilities

Although followers endow a leader with charisma to fulfill their situational needs, they do not endow just anybody. The person who is so endowed must have abilities that are relevant to the situation. Thus according to historians, charismatic presidents, compared with noncharismatic presidents, were more highly esteemed by their contemporaries and were able to accomplish more during their administrations (Maranell, 1970). Pitman (1993) found that 245 white-collar workers' ratings of their supervisors in charismatic leadership on the Multifactor Leadership Questionnaire (MLQ)[4] correlated .36 with their supervisors' rational and technical competence. The correlation was .27 with verbal dominance. The equivalent correlation between the Conger-Kanungo overall scale of charismatic leadership and these abilities were .37 and .32.

At Federal Express, the superiors of 54 managers rated the managers significantly higher in judgment, quality of

---

[4]This questionnaire was developed to measure the factors in transformational and transactional leadership, one of which was charismatic leadership. The scale of charismatic leadership is described later in this chapter.

Table 21.1 Correlations between Ratings of Transformational and Transactional Leadership Factors and of Specific Performance as a Manager, According to Superiors for 54 Managers Rated on the Multifactor Leadership Questionnaire by 306 Subordinates[a]

Subordinates' Description	Superior's Appraisal				
	Judgment and Decision Making	Financial Management	Communication	Persuasion	Risk Taking
Charismatic Leadership	.33**[a]	.36**	.32*	.33*	.45**
Intellectual Stimulation	.23	.35**	.29*	.24	.18
Contingent Reward	−.08	−.07	.18	.08	.01

*$p < .05$.
**$p < .01$.
[a]These data are from a sample of high performers and from a random sample drawn from a larger population. Differences between the samples have been removed by a partial correlation analysis.

SOURCE: Adapted from Hater and Bass (1988).

decision making, financial management, communication, persuasion, and risk taking if the managers were described by their 306 subordinates as more charismatic. No such significant correlations were found when the managers were described by their subordinates as practicing transactional contingent reward (Hater & Bass, 1988). Similar results were reported by Yammarino and Bass (1988) in a representative sample of junior officers in the surface navy.

Personal Traits

Several empirical studies of charismatic and noncharismatic leaders revealed patterns of systematic differences consistent with the profile of the charismatic that has emerged from historical and sociological analyses. Hall (1983) conducted a study of 10 leaders in the Atlanta area who were nominated for their charisma; in particular, these leaders described themselves as less accepting of authority than did 99% of a normative population. Labak (1973) asked 9,609 students to rate the charisma of the faculty at the University of Northern Colorado on a standardized questionnaire; 26 teachers, identified as charismatic, were matched with noncharismatic teachers. On standardized self-report inventories, the charismatic teachers described themselves as more enthusiastic, self-actualized, and tolerant of ambiguity, and less defensive. Wilson (1975) reported that charismatic heroes were high in self-esteem, self-possession, generosity, openness, honesty, and concern for others. Conger and Kanungo (1988, 1994) suggested that above and beyond their task

orientation and relations orientation, leaders described as charismatic were also rated as highly sensitive to the needs of followers, strongly articulate, willing to take personal risks, agents of radical change, and idealistic in their vision of the future. Levit (1992) noted that charismatic leaders had a strong purpose in life. Sosik and Dworakivsky (1998) found that manager's self-monitoring correlated with the charisma attributed to them by their subordinates, but only when they had a strong purpose in life. Crant and Bateman (2000) showed that among 156 managers, self-rated *proactive personality* added to the prediction of their charismatic leadership as rated by their immediate supervisors. This was above and beyond that accounted for by the five NEOAC personality factors. In a Dutch study, De Hoogh, Den Hartog, Koopman, et al. (2005) coded interviews with 73 CEOs and found that the *power motive* correlated positively with 125 subordinates' ratings of the CEOs' charismatic leadership. Charismatic leadership also contributed to the subordinates' positive attitudes toward their work.

Charismatic leaders are likely to display high levels of emotional expressiveness, self-confidence, self-determination, freedom from internal conflict, and are likely to have a strong conviction of the moral righteousness of their beliefs (House, 1977). Biographies, case studies, anecdotal material, and quantitative research provide evidence of these characteristics. One example is Anita Roddick, founder and head of The Body Shop International, who was a champion of human rights, animal rights, and recycling of refuse. The Body Shop comprises more than 2,100 stores in 55 countries selling cosmetics.

The chain actively champions environmental quality; human, civil, and animal rights; AIDS awareness; and other causes. Much of the success of The Body Shop has been attributed to Roddick. An article about her in the popular press said that she exuded "intelligence, energy, humor, spontaneity, impatience, and [passion] . . . [She was] uncompromising when it [came] to her core values" (Gaines, 1993, p. 348). Roddick was seen as exceptional by her followers, had a mission that attracted followers, and inspired commitment in them (Bryman, 1993).

Charismatics can be on the bright side of charismatic leadership without being personally lovable. At the Diet before the Holy Roman Emperor, Martin Luther, charged with heretical writings and rejection of the authority of popes and church councils, recanted nothing, concluding with, "Here I stand, I can do no other." Then he walked out alone unsure about how much protection he might receive from the German electors. In addition to possessing determination, he was willful, intolerant, contemptuous of art and learning, and driven by his own vision of a pure Christianity (Manchester, 1992).

Expressive Behavior. Friedman, Prince, Riggio, and DiMatteo (1980) suggested that charismatic leadership manifests itself in nonverbal emotional expressiveness. Expressive people can use verbal and nonverbal cues "to move, inspire, or captivate others" (p. 133). Such expressiveness can be assessed with the self-reporting Affective Communication Test. Items on the validated test include: "I often touch friends during conversations," "I can easily express emotion over the telephone," "I [don't] usually have a neutral facial expression," and "I am [good] at pantomime in games like charades." Expressiveness is related to dramatic flair and experience in acting and in politics. Females score higher in emotional expressiveness, just as they tend to be seen as more charismatic than comparable males (Avolio & Bass, 1989). Emotional expressiveness correlates .60 with the need for exhibition and .45 with the need for dominance—personality attributes of the charismatic leader.

Bensman and Givant (1975) and Willner (1968) describe charismatic leaders as projecting a powerful, confident, dynamic presence. The leaders' tone of voice is

Table 21.2 Correlations of Subordinates' Ratings of Leadership Behavior and Superiors' Ratings of Successful Performance for 186 U.S. Navy Lieutenants and Lieutenants, Junior Grade[a]

Subordinates' Ratings of Officers' Leadership Behavior	Superiors' Ratings of Performance	
	Cumulative Fitness-Report Evaluations	Cumulative Recommendation for Early Promotion
Transformational		
Charisma	.38**	.37**
Intellectual stimulation	.31**	.34**
Inspirational leadership	.25**	.28**
Individualized consideration	.21**	.24**
Transactional		
Contingent rewards (promises)	.17*	.17*
Contingent rewards (rewards)	.20**	.24**
Management-by-exception (active)	.22**	.28**
Management-by-exception (passive)	−.05	−.04
Nonleadership		
Laissez-faire	−.31**	−.31**

*p ≤ .05; r ≥ .19.
**p ≤ .01.
[a]N = 186; r ≥ .14.
SOURCE: Adapted from Yammarino and Bass (1988).

engaging and captivating, and their facial expressions are animated, yet they remain relaxed (Friedman & Riggio, 1981). Not only do they maintain direct eye contact, but their eyes have a magnetic attraction (Wilner, 1968). Riggio (2002) showed that extroverted and charismatic females were facially expressive; as a result, they were evaluated more favorably than their nonexpressive counterparts. Spontaneously expressive females received more positive evaluations from judges, but similarly expressive males did not; the judges viewed the *emotional control* of males in a more favorable light. Expressive cues included fluid, outward-directed cues, such as rate and fluency of speech, outward-directed gestural fluency, and smiles; and of body emphasis, contact with the body, and inward directed gestures. Appealing rhetoric is characteristic of charismatics.

Self-Confidence. Charismatic leaders display complete confidence in the correctness of their positions and in their capabilities (Hoffman & Hoffman, 1970), and they make this confidence a clear aspect of their public image. Even when personally discouraged and facing failure, they are unlikely to make such feelings public (Tucker, 1968). Such elevated self-esteem helps charismatics to avoid defensiveness in conflicting interpersonal situations and to maintain the confidence that their subordinates have in them (Hill, 1976). Charismatics tend to project onto like-minded loyal followers their continuing confident opinion of themselves (Bass, 1985a). They are great actors—always onstage, projecting to their followers their extreme self-confidence and convictions, so they become larger than life. They must be able to present themselves as miracle workers who are likely to succeed when others would fail (House, 1977).

Self-Determination. Weber (1924/1947) considered charisma as first a personal attribute of some leaders whose purposes, powers, and extraordinary determination set them apart from ordinary people. Friedrich Nietzsche's (1883/1974) superman had some of the same characteristics: inner direction, originality, self-determination, sense of duty, and responsibility for the unique self. Nietzsche said that ordinary men conformed to the expectations of others, but the superman could free himself from the expected. He was a point of contact with the future, and created new values and goals. He was also a

highly self-oriented narcissist. Weber's charismatic could also be a mystical ascetic, concerned with himself rather than involved with others, and interested in promoting ideas for their own sake rather than for material gain. According to Weber, the determined charismatic leader would set aside normal political life.

But self-determination can also imply obstinacy. Instead of being open to new ideas, some charismatic leaders may become closed-minded, dogmatic, and rigid. They may announce that they have provided the only true way to enlightenment. They think that their continued development is unnecessary, and regard differences of opinion as heretical (Stark, 1969).

Insight. The charismatic leader can arouse, as well as articulate, feelings of need among followers and find radical solutions to their problems. Gorbachev's glasnost (openness) and perestroika (restructuring) were radical solutions aimed at removing the problems of secrecy, censorship, and rigidity in the Soviet Union's planned economy. Charismatics have insight into the needs, values, and hopes of followers (McClelland, 1975) and the ability to build on them through dramatic and persuasive words and actions. According to Gardner (1961), they are able to "conceive and articulate goals that lift people out of their petty preoccupations." Such leaders can unite people to seek objectives that are "worthy of their best efforts." According to Yukl (1981), charismatics can say things publicly that followers feel privately but cannot express. Charismatic leaders move the change process by first breaking frames (interpretive schemes) through negation; next, by including in the frames' referents like "we" instead of "I"; and finally, endorsing and affirming the changes (Fiol, Harris, & House, 1999).

Freedom from Internal Conflict. Charismatic leaders maintain their confidence and determination, despite serious setbacks and defeats, through a self-assurance that is "at one with their inner images" (Kets de Vries, 1984, p. 117). The confidence and determination of charismatic leaders stem from their greater freedom from the internal conflict that ordinary mortals are more likely to experience between their emotions, impressions, and feelings (Freud's id) and their controlling conscience (superego). Freedom from the id-superego conflict makes for strong ego ideals and assuredness about what the leader values as good, right, and important. Convinced of the goodness, rightness, and importance of their own point of view, charismatic leaders are likely to be more forthright and candid in reprimanding subordinates and can maintain a clear conscience if they feel they must replace a subordinate (Keichel, 1983). (Ronald Reagan was an exception in this respect. Like Richard Nixon, he avoided such confrontations.) By contrast, ordinary managers are victimized by self-doubt and personal trauma in such circumstances, regardless of the extent or success of their careers (Levinson, Darrow, Klein, et al., 1978).

Eloquence and Rhetoric. Martin Luther King Jr.'s powerful oratory made him larger than life and an even more charismatic leader of the black movement than he really was. Carson (1987) noted that the "great man" mythology exaggerated King's importance to the civil rights movement and distorted his considerable contributions to the effort. His moral and intellectual oratory was an inspiration for many activists, but King did not receive unquestioning obedience from them. He was seen by them as outstanding among many prominent ideologues, strategists, and institutional leaders. His strategy of nonviolence was never fully accepted by the masses in the movement and was at odds with their beliefs. Many of the most important initiatives in the movement, such as the Montgomery bus boycott and the student sit-ins, were started and guided by local leaders. Many ideas first surfaced among the grassroots followers. King was a great conciliator among the activists, and he mobilized supporters through continuous involvement in the network of black churches and other black institutions. He certainly was a charismatic leader, although he was not the superhuman he became in retrospect.

Because we are now in an era of speechwriters, we can no longer readily attribute the emotional flair for expressive language to the leaders who use it. But the highly charismatic Mario Cuomo did write his own colorful, incisive, inspiring speeches, such as the famous one he gave at the 1984 Democratic convention. Cuomo could respond extemporaneously to telephone questions in the same dynamic way. This facile use of language helped him win a record landslide vote in 1986, when he was reelected as governor of New York.

The *content* of charismatic messages is simple, focuses on the collective identity of the speaker and the audience, and evokes a response from the audience (Bord, 1975). In addition, charismatic speeches allude to the individual worth of the followers, their collective efficacy, their collective history, the continuity of the past, present, and distant future, and the similarities of the followers and the leader. The speeches provide moral justifications, long-term goals, and the importance of faith and hope (Shamir, Arthur, & House, 1994).

The *delivery* of political charismatic leaders (Willner, 1984) and organizational charismatic leaders (Conger, 1989) make heavy use of metaphors, rhythm, and alliteration. The language they use is modified to fit the nature of their audience. Charismatic leaders attract and sustain audiences with arousing, novel rhetoric, and remote associations in unusual combinations. They use high-action verbs, short pauses between phrases and sentences, and reiteration in their speeches. Compared with noncharismatics, they favor words and ideas that are image-based rather than abstract. For example, they use words such as "root" instead of "source," "rock" instead of "dependable" and "path" instead of "alternative" (Emrich, Brower, Feldman, et al, 2001). Often, nonverbal gestures and cues reinforce the emotional appeals (Den Hartog & Verburg, 1997). Awamleh and Gardner (1999) presented to 304 undergraduates a videotape of one of six supposed speeches by a CEO of a software company: visionary or nonvisionary, with good or poor organizational performance, and with strong or weak delivery. The students attributed charismatic leadership to the CEO mostly as a consequence of strong rather than weak delivery, and much less as a consequence of the speech's vision or lack of vision, or of good rather than poor organizational performance. Likewise, two experiments by Holladay and Coombs (1993, 1994) showed that strong delivery of a speech was more important than the content in managing the impression of a leader as charismatic. Greater vocal fluency, natural body gestures, and extensive eye contact made for a stronger delivery and the attribution of charisma. Although content was less significant than delivery, visionary speech did produce more attributions of a charismatic leader than nonvisionary speech.

Howell, Neufeld, and Avolio (undated) found in a survey of 343 employees that among 125 managers, those who scored high in charismatic leadership on the MLQ were more likely to use communication styles (Klaus &

Bass, 1982) that were open two-way, carefully transmitted, and frank. While openness and care contributed to business unit performance, frankness was contraindicated. This was mainly true for managers at a physical distance from, rather than close to, their listeners.

Activity and Energy Levels. Leaders tend to be more active than followers, and charismatic leaders are even more so. Grant and Bateman (2000) showed that for 156 managers, those who scored themselves as more *proactive* were also rated by their supervisors as more charismatic. The relationship was greater than could be accounted for by the "Big Five" personality variables, social desirability, or in-role performance. According to a three-year survey by the Group for the Advancement of Psychiatry (1974), the charismatic qualities needed by candidates for 100 vacant medical school psychiatry chairs were a high energy level, optimism, fatherliness, and a capacity to inspire loyalty. Previously collected opinions of political historians demonstrated that charismatic presidents were more active and took significantly stronger actions than did noncharismatic presidents (Maranell, 1970).

Self-Sacrificial Disposition. Sacrifices may involve voluntary giving up of power, privileges, or personal resources; or going into harm's way for the benefit of other individuals or the group, organization, or society. House and Shamir (1993) expected that charismatic leaders might make sacrifices to build trust and show loyalty. Javidan (1992) suggested that charismatic leaders might make sacrifices to encourage followers to do the same to reduce followers' fears of an uncertain future, and to gain followers' acceptance of the leader's vision. Yorges, Weiss, and Strickland (1999) demonstrated that if leaders were willing to endure hardships for the expression of their beliefs, they would be more likely to be perceived as charismatic and more influential than if they personally benefited from their actions. In two experiments with 157 industrial participants and 457 students, Choi and Mai-Dalton (1998) found that followers were more likely to attribute charisma to a self-sacrificial leader described in different scenarios, especially if the leader was described as competent rather than incompetent. Unexpectedly, the outcomes were unaffected by whether or not the organization's future was uncertain.

Envisioning and Charismatic Leadership

The vision charismatic leaders articulate contains an idealized perspective shared with their followers. It calls for radical change yet is within the latitude of acceptance. To achieve the vision, charismatics express a willingness to go beyond their self-interests, to make personal sacrifices, and to take high risks. Charismatic leaders search for and envision opportunities and threats to their organization or movement. They use the vision to frame the alignment of the members and to implement actions to try to make the vision come true (Conger & Kanungo, 1998). Transformational leaders are motivated to accomplish the vision and to persuade others to agree with it. They act according to a vision specifying a better future state; communicate with references to the vision; articulate the vision and the accomplishments needed to attain the vision. They influence followers to make decisions in line with the vision and role model the values implied by the vision. However, unlike the ideologue, the authentic transformational leader will change the vision to better fit with the needs of followers (Mumford & Strange, 2002). The charismatic's vision and effects differ from the ideologue's in other ways. According to a biographical analysis of 60 notable leaders by Mumford and Mowry (undated), the charismatic's or transformational's vision is broad; the ideologue's is narrow. Ideologues are more likely than charismatics to direct punitive influence tactics toward followers who diverge from their vision.

Characteristics of Followers

So far, we have concentrated on the leader as the source of the charismatic relationship. But increasingly detailed attention has been paid to followers in their relationship with charismatic leaders (e.g., Weierter, 1997). Tritten (1995, p. 85) declared, "The fundamental determinate of a 'charismatic leader' is the perception of 'charisma' and the response of followers." Uncertainties and anxieties upset followers' sense of mastery and efficacy, and they look to a hero or charismatic leader to guide them (Lipman-Blumen, 1996). They will see leaders as the cause of events even if the events were due to other reasons. Shamir (1992) found that respondents high on Meindl and Erlich's (1987) Romance of

Leadership Scale were more likely to regard leaders as charismatic. The novelty to the follower of the leader's message will increase the follower's attention to it. The follower's uncertainty in the current situation will also increase attention to the leader's message (Avolio & Bass, 1988).

Such followers want to identify with the charismatic leader and mission. They place their trust in him to lead them to the promised land. Followers differ in their preferences for charismatic leaders. In reviewing scenarios of district managers, those who preferred to work with charismatic managers described the managers as encouraging, inclusive, success-oriented, goal- and team-oriented, creative, adaptive, committed, and energized. Those low in preference for charismatic managers felt that such managers were ambitious, zealous, arrogant, overbearing, too pushy, too enthusiastic, overconfident, all-talk, narrow-minded, and forceful (Ehrhart & Klein, 2001). Conger, Kanungo, and Menon (2000) found that 252 managers gave higher ratings of charismatic leadership on the Conger-Kanungo questionnaire if they strongly revered the leader they were rating. Follower reverence mediated their trust in and satisfaction with the leader.

Followers' Susceptibility to Charismatic Leaders

Shamir and Howell (2005) suggested reasons why some followers are more susceptible than others to the influence of charismatic leaders. Followers in distress and with low self-esteem and an unclear self-concept are more susceptible. They do not have a well-defined negative view of themselves but rather an uncertain, unstable, inconsistent self-concept (Campbell, Trapnell, Heine, et al., 1996). Freemesser and Kaplan (1976) found that young people who joined a charismatic cult were lower in self-esteem than a comparison sample; these young people's self-esteem was raised in 6 to 12 months by membership in the cult. Still, followers of charismatic entrepreneurs who may be highly self-confident and who accept calculated risks for large potential gains also may readily accept the influence of a charismatic leader (Conger, 1993). Galanter (1982) suggests that managers with low self-esteem would be unlikely to be promoted into senior executive positions led by a charismatic chief. To reach such a position they would need a reasonable

amount of self-confidence and self-esteem. Least likely to accept the charismatic leader are those followers who are independent-minded or counterdependent.

Shamir and Howell (1999) note that followers are more ready to comply with the charismatic leader if they have a *collectivistic* rather than an *individualistic* orientation, if they have an expressive rather than an instrumental orientation to work and life, if they have a *principled* rather than *pragmatic* orientation toward the leader, and if the leader appeals to the susceptible follower's values and identity. Charismatic leaders increase the importance of specific values already held by those who can be influenced and for whom the values can be connected to what is to be done. Charismatic leaders appeal to followers with matching ideological goals and those seeking intrinsic satisfaction. Such followers internalize the charismatic influences (Shamir, House, & Arthur, 1993).

In a study using Boccialetti's (1995) inventory of follower-authority relations and the Conger-Kanungo scale of charisma, Arsenault (1998) compared the perceived charismatic leadership in six small organizations ranging from 17 to 55 members (a family-owned business, a microbrewery, an adoption agency, a sports team, a mayor's office, and an inner-city church). Of 209 respondents, 66% were typed as accommodating, 26% as adversarial, and 8% as autonomous. Followers perceived more charisma if they felt closer in social and physical distance to the leader ($r = .52; .28$). They were more likely to agree with their leader about goals and achieving them ($r = .20$) and to agree that their organization was transformational ($r = .27$). Preference for a charismatic leader was significantly higher for 261 to 267 university students if they valued participative leadership ($r = .23$), achievement ($r = .16$) and self-esteem ($r = .16$; Ehrhart, 2001).

Followers' Desire to Identify with the Charismatic Leader

Weber (1924/1947, p. 328) wrote about the followers' "devotion to the specific and exceptional sanctity, heroism or exemplary character of an individual charismatic person, and of the normative patterns or order revealed or ordained by him." Willner (1968) saw followers as having an intense emotional and cognitive attraction to charismatic leaders above and beyond ordinary esteem, affection, admiration, and trust; this attraction involves "devotion, awe, reverence, and blind faith" (p. 6). Followers have an unqualified belief in the "man and his mission about what is, what should be, and what should be done" (p. 9). Nonetheless, more important than what charismatics do or say is what their prospective followers feel about them. The same words or actions by a would-be leader can seem charismatic and extremely influential to ardent disciples but humbug to others. According to Madsen and Snow (1983), charismatic leadership depends as much on the "magnetizability" of the followers as on the magnetism of the leader. Those who are in psychological distress are prone to join a charismatic leader's coterie, according to Galanter's (1982) review of clinical evidence. For example, although Charles Manson had been in prison for two decades, this magnetic murderer still could maintain a devoted following of misfit personalities on California's Russian River. Similarly, the "Moonies," ardently devoted to their charismatic leader the Reverend Sun Myung Moon, showed more feelings of helplessness, cynicism, and distrust of political action and less confidence in their own sexual identity, their own values, and the future than did a sample of college students (Lodahl, 1982). Charismatic gurus and leaders of sects attract insecure and lonely people, who join other followers and relinquish their right to make decisions in exchange for strict, protective boundaries and security. The magnetism of the gurus often has a strong sexual component (Newman, 1983). Freemesser and Kaplan (1976) observed in interviews that those who joined a charismatic religious cult had lower self-esteem than a comparable sample.

Corsino (1982) argued that the charismatic leadership of Malcolm X was due to his personality traits and to the intellectual, moral, and emotional predispositions of his followers, who could identify with his experiences and who projected their own frustrations with white society onto him. After a content analysis of statements that followers made about Adlai Stevenson and Dwight D. Eisenhower during the 1952 presidential election campaign, Davies (1954) concluded that compared with other voters, those who attributed special qualities to their leader had a higher intolerance for indecision and crisis, applied rigid categories of good and evil, and felt that other people were more in agreement with them than was actually the case.

Personal versus Social Identification. Followers who may personally identify with a charismatic leader do so for personal reasons. Such followers have low self-esteem, a weak self-concept, weak self-identity, and a strong need to depend on authority figures.

Social identification is based on seeing oneself as a member of a group, organization, or society. Values, ideologies and role identities are shared with other members, and the charismatic leader reinforces them with symbols, rituals, ceremonies, and by calling attention to the successes of the past (Shamir, House, & Arthur, 1993).

The Identification Process. Shamir, House, and Arthur (1993) emphasized that charismatic leadership changes the self-concept of followers. The followers find in the charismatic leader an affirmation of their sense of identity, and changes in their perceptions about the future and about what is to be done. A stronger shared and collective identity and efficacy emerge (Shamir, 1991). Their self-concept is tied by the charismatic leader to the goals and collective experiences of their missions "so that they become valued aspects of the followers' self-concept" (Conger, 1999, p. 155).

According to Freud (1922), the follower's identification with and commitment to the charismatic leader are ways for the follower to resolve ego-superego conflicts. Downton (1973) agreed, seeing that we resolve the conflict between our self-image and what we want and think it should be by making the leader the embodiment of our ego ideal. By accepting a leader with transcendental objectives, followers can fulfill their desires to go beyond their own self-interests and to become more noble and worthy. The leader is idealized and becomes the model of behavior to be emulated—the embodiment of the follower's aspirations. Commitment is directed to the person of the charismatic leader (whether the leader's goals are self-aggrandizing or prosocial). Through the leader, the follower can achieve the strongly desired ideal self (Marcus, 1961). Obedience to new attitudes and goals develops from the effort to emulate the leader's example and adopt the leader's mission. At the same time, the follower's capacity to criticize the leader is impaired (Weber, 1924/1947).

Erikson (1968) conceived *identity confusion* as deriving from a failure to mature in adolescence and young adulthood and a failure to develop a strong ego ideal because of oppressive, weak, or absent parents. The lack of an ego ideal to guide one's behavior and interpersonal relationships arouses uneasiness and a sense of drift (and more susceptibility to the blandishments of the charismatic leader). Downton (1973) held that identifying with the charismatic leader was a way of coping with such identity confusion, as well as with the conflict between the ego and the ego ideal. As a consequence, the charismatic leader benefits the follower by providing him or her with new goals and a positive identity, and by enhancing the follower's self-esteem. The charismatic leader gives the follower a second chance to attain maturity. Young women's identification with Mother Teresa, who devoted herself to the poorest of the poor, can give them an enhanced self-image and make them agents of contribution to a worthy cause. Identification with the maniacal murderer Charles Manson can also enhance a follower's self-image, but in this case the contribution would be to a most unworthy cause.

Charisma, as an endowment of spiritual grace from God, was converted by social science into an endowment of leaders by their followers with a high degree of esteem and referent power. The value, popularity, and celebrity that others attribute to a leader engenders in followers strong emotional responses of affection and the leader's generalized influence beyond the immediate situation and beyond the ordinary exchange of compliance for promises of reward or threats of punishment. The vicarious satisfaction obtained from basking in the glory of the charismatic may be as sufficient a reward for the star-struck as doing God's work is for the pious. Admiration of the charismatic leader and the desire to identify with and emulate him or her are powerful influences on followers. Charisma is in the eye of the beholder and, therefore, is relative to the beholder. Nevertheless, the charismatic leader actively shapes and enlarges his or her audience through energy, self-confidence, assertiveness, ambition, and seized opportunities (Bass, 1985a).

The Dynamics of the Charismatic Leader-Follower Relationship

House (1977) described the dynamic process involved as follows: confident of their own competence, convinced of their own beliefs and ideals, and strong in the need for power, charismatic leaders are highly motivated to influence their followers. Their self-confidence and strong convictions increase their followers' trust in leaders' judgments. Charismatics engage in impression management to bolster their image of competence, increasing their subordinates' compliance and faith in them. They relate the work and mission of their group to the strongly held values, ideals, and aspirations that are part of their organization's culture. In organizational settings, they vividly portray for their subordinates an attractive vision of what the outcomes of their efforts could be. This portrayal provides subordinates with more meaning for their work and arouses their enthusiasm, excitement, emotional involvement, and commitment to the group's objectives. Roles are defined in ideological terms that appeal to the subordinates. What makes this process more than just inspirational is that charismatic leaders use themselves as examples for subordinates to follow. Thus cadets at the U.S. Air Force Academy said they most wanted to emulate those squadron commanders whom they had described as highly charismatic on the MLQ (Clover, 1989).

In some instances, their very lack of talent may make popular but untalented charismatic figures easier for their uncritical followers to identify with; such followers gain vicarious satisfaction from their own frustrated ambitions (Schiffer, 1973). Unlike Freud's (1922) Moses-like charismatic leader, who orients followers toward personal and moral growth and transcendental purpose and mission, pseudocharismatic *totemic* leaders are idols who are easy to identify with at a superficial level because they cater to the whims and fantasies of the followers. Token identity and perfunctory rituals satisfy the followers' need to belong (Faucheux, 1984). Logic-tight compartments in the followers separate what is not wanted in the leader from what is wanted—they repress the former and enhance the latter. Charisma depends on a regression to imagery. The childlike image of the faultless leader replaces a realistic appraisal (Schiffer, 1973). Even when the leader's faults are recognized, as was the case with Ronald Reagan and George W. Bush, supporters see them as illustrations of greater humanity and find it easier to forgive them their shortcomings. This leniency connects with the fact that in evaluating their superiors, subordinates often do not rate them as they have been asked to do; rather, they rate their own mental prototypes of a generalized leader.

Followers tend to perceive charismatic leaders as ideal leaders. Bass and Avolio (1987) obtained a correlation of .83 between subordinates' behavioral descriptions of the charismatic leadership of their superiors on the MLQ and the subordinates' ratings of the prototypical leader using the Lord, Foti, and Phillips (1982) prototypically scale. Correlations of prototypicality with other leadership styles were much lower; prototypicality correlations fell to .61 with practicing contingent reward and .38 with practicing management by exception.

At the crux of the phenomenon of charisma is the emotional response of the follower. Schiffer (1973, p. 3) describes the charismatic rally:

> Commonly . . . some specific . . . unique personality is supposedly the true source of the process. . . . TV cameras and commentators . . . lend luster and dimension to the whole happening; a strange hypnoid state begins to infiltrate the most vulnerable minds.
>
> . . . The social scientist looks for economic and cultural factors . . . to explain the new "miracle"; the intelligentsia dissect the personal mystique of the hero.

Charismatic leaders reduce the followers' resistance to change by arousing emotional rather than rational responses. The cost of such emotional responding may be impaired judgment and uncritical acceptance of the leaders.

The Mystique. The magical and the fantasy aspects of charisma and their costs need to be considered more fully. The dependence generated by charismatic leadership is evident when the loss of an inspiring, charismatic leader is accompanied by demoralization and disruption among the followers (Hays & Thomas, 1967). Charismatics are not merely self-confident, determined, and convinced of their own beliefs. They may believe they have supernatural missions and purposes. Martin Luther King Jr. really had a waking dream of what he was to accomplish. Downton (1973, p. 230) noted that "the charismatic relationship can be a two-way exchange in which the leader comes to see himself as charismatic and lives from day to day on the deferential treatment he sees as rightfully his."

Followers do not merely have favorable perceptions of the leader; for them, the charismatic leader may be larger than life, with eyes that seem to mesmerize. The leader may be a superhuman hero to followers, someone to be worshipped as a spiritual guide. Furthermore, followers can act as if they have been mesmerized, suspending their ability to make critical judgments. If we cannot have the loved object, we may try to imitate and emulate it to gain its approval and to meet its standards and expectations (Kets de Vries, 1984, 1988).

The sense of reality of both the charismatic leader and the followers can be distorted by psychodynamic mechanisms, such as projection, transference, regression, and disassociation. For instance, the followers can project their processes and needs onto the charismatic leader, who may become the catalyst for the followers' rationalizations. President John F. Kennedy is a case in point:

> John F. Kennedy ushered in a new Camelot complete with his Queen Guinevere and knights ready to do battle in Cuba, Berlin and Vietnam with the villainous foes of freedom, the Cuban devils and Soviet dragons. The depth of the public depression resulting from Kennedy's assassination can only be explained by the strong, emotional idolization of the image of Kennedy as dragon slayer, savior, and creator of a new life on earth for the disadvantaged. In reality, he was an astute politician who changed a fictitious Soviet superiority in missiles—the so-called missile gap—into the beginning of a new arms race led by the United States. . . . His statesman-like qualities grew with his experience in office. But for the mass of the U.S. public, his image was that of the youthful world leader who was lifting the U.S. out of the stodgy Eisenhower years with the focus of a future of U.S. leadership among the nations of the world and in space. (Bass, 1985a, pp. 56–57)

The Transformation of Followers

The charismatic (as well as inspirational) leader concretizes a vision that the follower views as worthy of effort, thereby raising the follower's excitement and effort. However, people who seek to identify with the leader but who are distant from him or her may become only passingly aroused and committed, and may not take action to conform to the leader's initiatives. Nevertheless, if they are free to act and are not constrained by other commitments or the lack of opportunity, they will actually become committed to leaders even at a distance. Presaging Burns

(1978), Downton (1973, p. 230) described this process as *transformational* rather than *transactional*, noting its greater likelihood of taking effect:

> In the formation of a charismatic commitment, the opportunity for action is apt to be greater than strictly transactional relationships because the follower who identifies with a leader can transform his behavioral pattern without necessarily exchanging tangible goods with the leader. For example, the follower . . . can act when the leader initiates a new moral code that can be put immediately into practice, no matter how distant the leader and the opportunities for organizational activity.

Tension is reduced in the follower who strongly identifies with the charismatic leader. Since the leader has come to substitute for the follower's ego ideal, continuing and uncritical acceptance of the leader's initiatives is a way of bringing the ego into line with the ego ideal. In the case of identity confusion, when the follower has been unable to "find himself" and to decide who he is and what he wants to be, the follower's intolerance of criticism of the leader counteracts the problems of identity. The follower protects the idealized identity of the leader as a defense. Such criticism is a challenge to the person who is defending the image, since it is by identifying with that image that the person develops a sense of who he is and what he wants to become.

Behavioral Contagion. The nonverbal expressive behavior of 84 college students in a simulated campaign speech where charisma was introduced—with more smiling, more intense smiling, and longer and more frequent attention to the audience by the speaker—resulted in more of the same expressive behaviors in the audience. In a second study, audiences were shown videos of a 1992 pre-election presidential debate between the more emotionally expressive, charismatic Bill Clinton and the less emotional George H. W. Bush. The audience exposed to Clinton showed more emotionally expressive reactions than the audience exposed to Bush (Cherulnik, Donley, Tay, et al., 2001).

The Emergence of Charisma

Crises and Their Solutions

Some explanations of the charismatic relationship have emphasized that social crisis is the root cause of its emergence. According to this viewpoint, the charismatic appears in times of great societal distress to save society. This salvation from distress engenders "special emotional intensity of the charismatic response. . . . followers respond to the charismatic leader with passionate loyalty because the [promise of] salvation . . . that he appears to embody represents the fulfillment of urgently felt needs" (Tucker, 1970, p. 81).

In work in organizations, threat, distress, and crises contribute to the emergence of the importance of charismatic leadership (Pillai & Meindl, 1991). Pillai (1995) found, in a survey of 101 units of a health organization, that the more charismatic the 454 workers in the units rated their supervisor as charismatic, the less they felt stressed by their job ($r = -.27$) or in crisis in the past three months ($r = -.24$) Crisis was measured by responses to five items: response uncertainty, time pressure, surprise, frequency, and resolution.

Among the five sociopolitical factors that accounted for half the variance in the degree to which charismatic leadership was attributed to twentieth-century heads of state, Cell (1974) isolated such factors as a national social crisis and disruptive youth. Not only acute crisis brings out the charismatic leader. Charismatic leadership also arises when the crisis is chronic, as when the ultimate values of a culture are being devalued and radical social change is occurring (Hummel, 1973). Charisma carries with it a challenge to the old order; a break with continuity; a risky adventure; and continual movement, ferment, and change (Bass, 1985b). The empowered leaders can continue to influence these feelings to maintain their position, but they need to provide new, usually radical, solutions to the crisis or to relate it "to a higher purpose that has intrinsic validity" for the followers (Boal & Bryson, 1987). The charismatic leader can also promote unlearning and a search for new actions. In highly ambiguous situations, such new solutions may be chosen precipitately (Hedberg, 1981). Earlier, I noted the development of the revolutionary, reform, and counterrevolutionary leaders as well as charismatic leaders, which leaders of sociopolitical movements tend to be. In democracies, radical leaders, usually leftists, push for more active citizen participation, equality, and community involvement (Alinsky, 1971). Radical rightists argue for less government intervention for libertarianism, and for a return to earlier practices, privileges, and values. The initiators of the movement provide rational and emotional arguments for discrediting opposing beliefs and replacing them with new ones. Zealots and dogmatists join the cause and become the leaders of action (Hoffer, 1951).

Individuals who feel that they have lost control over their environment are more ready to accept the authority of a charismatic leader (Devereux, 1955). People become "charisma hungry" owing to the decline of old values and rituals; shocks to the culture; and growing fears, anxieties, and identity crises. For example, Mahatma Gandhi satisfied such "hunger" in Indians by giving them a new collective identity and new rituals (Erikson, 1969). Adolf Hitler arose as the savior of Germany in response to the disappointments of military defeat and social, political, and economic distress. Despite Italy's final victory in World War I, the rise of Benito Mussolini to power in 1922 illustrated the same theme of distress (Fermi, 1966). Martin Luther King Jr. and Jesse Jackson stirred disadvantaged blacks to believe that their personal efforts, combined with collective action, could reshape American society to advance their place in it, ultimately for the benefit of all Americans.

When organizational cultures are in transition, charismatic leaders appear. They arise when traditional authority and legal, rational, and bureaucratic means cannot meet the organization's or society's need for leadership. Old, highly structured, successful organizations are unlikely to need such leadership. Charismatic leaders are more likely to appear in failing organizations or newly emerging ones that are struggling to survive. In such organizations, charismatic leaders can radicalize from within, rather than in response to a challenge from outside (Berger, 1963). They create new cultures for their supporters by creating new meanings and beliefs for them.

In the absence of threats and any need for new strategies or reorientation, toward the existing order and organizational culture can be maintained by institutional processes and by symbolic acts of the leaders' reaffirmation of the organization's values and standards. But when the organization must change to survive, its reorientation requires substantive changes in the distribution of power, interruption of previously established commitments and beliefs, and management of the development of a new set of values, norms, beliefs, and rationalizations (Romanelli & Tushman, 1983). During the 1980s, many colleges were faced with declining enrollments and declining resources, coupled with increasing competition for available public and private funds. Charismatic presidents were needed. Delson's (1986) analysis of interviews in and news clippings from five schools suggested, among other things, that such presidents had to have a sense of purpose and had to recognize the need to build for the future. They had to choose strong deputies, gain the active involvement of public officials, and seize opportunities that arose.

Rapid changes in the nature of work and organizations may give rise to new types of charismatic labor leaders, although such leaders may have particular difficulty institutionalizing changes in their unions (Spector, 1987). Charismatic political leaders create crises. Serbian leader Slobodan Milošević started the breakup of Yugoslavia in 1989, and wars with Croatia, Bosnia, and the Albanians in Kosovo. Hitler's rise to power was marked by one crisis after another, which he created. Whether spurred by a crisis or an ideology, the charismatic leaders' solutions can take opposite directions. The dedicated follower of one charismatic can be uplifted and moved to a new and better life; the dedicated follower of another can be moved to murder or suicide. Thus charismatic leadership can be beneficial or deleterious to society and to organizational life, depending on whether the followers' needs are authentic or contrived and whether the leader has prosocial or antisocial goals.

Experimentation with Crises. Crises are relatively rare. Experimental studies and simulations provide an opportunity to study causality in these situations and to reveal the most effective leadership approaches (D. J. Brown & Lord, 1999). Pillai and Meindl (1991a) had 125 undergraduate management students read one of four contrived scenarios about the 10-year performance of a fast-food company. Then they rated the mean charismatic score of the supposed CEO using the scale from the Multifactor Leadership Questionnaire (MLQ; Bass & Avolio, 1989). The mean charismatic leadership score for the CEO with each of the company's performance scenarios exhibited a significant linear trend from a crisis followed by decline, no crisis but a steady decline, no crisis but a steady growth, and a crisis followed by a turnaround to steady growth. As predicted by the Romance of Leadership theory (Meindl, 1990), the "CEO" received higher leadership ratings if perceived to be heading a firm that successfully turned around from a crisis, with steady growth rather than steady decline. The same investigators, Pillai and Meindl (1991b), manipulated crisis or no-crisis conditions for 96 undergraduates in 16 sextets by extremely positive or extremely negative feedback of their task performance as individuals and groups. The feedback, particularly the negative feedback, was ostensibly to contribute substantially to their grades. Members chose their leaders and afterward rated them using the MLQ. Again, charismatic leadership was significantly higher in the crisis condition than the noncrisis condition. Path analyses indicated that there was no direct path from crisis to satisfaction and effectiveness of the leader. Rather, crisis generated a path coefficient of .27 with the emergence of charismatic leadership, which in turn generated a path coefficient of .79 with rated satisfaction and effectiveness of the leader. But elsewhere, Pillai (1993) reported that a crisis was not always necessary for charismatic leadership to emerge. Hunt, Boal, and Dodge (1999) conducted an experiment in which 191 upper undergraduate students (juniors or seniors) were in a contest to cut costs and enhance revenue to improve a university's standing. The participants were or were not subjected to serious time and task load pressures introduced unexpectedly to simulate a crisis. Scripted leaders (confederates) used one of three styles: visionary, exchange (transactional), or unexpressive (laissez-faire). The visionaries began as such: the crisis-responsive leaders began unexpressively and started to behave as visionaries only after the crisis was introduced. Three weeks later, all participants worked on a counterbalanced equivalent task under unexpressive leadership. Manipulation checks confirmed that the crisis and noncrisis conditions were perceived by the participants as intended, as were the three styles of leadership. Both visionary leaders and crisis-responsive leaders received similar attributions from the participants: that they were charismatic and performing beyond expectations. However, after the crisis abated, the effects of crisis-responsive leadership as a source of charismatic leadership lingered.

Cultural Expectations. Charismatics appear in societies with traditions of support for them and expectations about their emergence. Thus charismatic prophets and messiahs could arise in ancient Israel because they fit with a long prophetic tradition. They were being awaited. The intense spiritual relationship of the charismatic leader and his followers is distinctive in modern Islam, which flowed out of the Judeo-Christian tradition. The prophet is an extraordinary personality who emerges in a social crisis, carrying a messianic message that becomes legitimated and routinized (Dekmejian & Wyszomirski, 1972). In the absence of such tradition in ancient and modern China, the emergence of such charismatics is somewhat less frequent. Mao Zedong was an exception. In determining leader-follower relations in China, hierarchy continues to be more important than the possibility that charismatic leaders will arise. For the charismatic leader to resort to particular psychological mechanisms in his appeals, the followers must have shared norms. Since sinfulness is a shared norm in the Judeo-Christian world, the western charismatic leader can stimulate guilt among followers. The importance of "face" is a shared norm in the Orient; the Oriental charismatic leader has to focus on shame (Hummel, 1972).

According to Tsurumi (1982), an important aspect of the introduction of quality-control circles in Japan was the American consultant Charles Protzman's emphasis on the need for a charismalike manager to "secure the faith and respect of those under him by his being an example of high purpose, courage, honor and independence." This focus conformed with the Japanese tradition of leaders as men of exemplary moral courage and self-sacrifice. In India, charismatic status can come from practicing asceticism, passive meditation, and physical austerity, which may or may not translate into leadership and does not depend on a crisis (Singer, 1969).

Organizational Level. Executives at the top of the organization are expected to be concerned with its ultimate purposes. Such leaders must reflect on long-term issues and be sensitive about keeping their organization in tune with the external environment (Watson, 1988). A correlation of .23 was found for 45 New Zealand professionals on the MLQ between subordinates' descriptions of the charisma of their leader and the leader's level in the organizational hierarchy (Bass, 1985a). Bass, Waldman,

Avolio, et al. (1987) reported similar results for the mean charismatic behavior described and required by subordinates of their leaders at two successive levels of the organization. However, such differences in the MLQ failed to be found when junior and senior officers in the U.S. Navy were compared (Yammarino & Bass, 1988) and when majors were compared with colonels in the U.S., Canadian, and German armies (Boyd, 1989a).

Charisma without Crisis. Charismatic effects can emerge not only in crises, but as a consequence of the charismatic's vision and its articulation, which create a sense of need for action by the followers. The *visionary* charismatic begins with ideological fervor and moves to action, unlike the *crisis* charismatic who begins with solutions to a crisis and then develops ideological justifications for them (Boal & Bryson, 1987). In a study of charismatic business entrepreneurs, Conger (1989) observed that they were stimulated into action as a consequence of opportunity and optimism rather than a distressful situation. Change can be driven by opportunity as well as threat. The business opportunities present in changing market demands and technological developments can bring forth calculated risk taking and charismatic leadership of consequence, and can result in necessary organizational changes. Charismatic leaders identify trends and assess resources and constraints in dealing with needed changes (Howell, 1997). An alienated organizational membership may be led by a charismatic leader who creates a compelling new vision for them of a more attractive future better attuned to fulfilling their values and purposes (Boal & Bryson, 1988).

Charismatic leaders may emerge in the absence of crisis if the organization is organic rather than mechanical (Bass, 1985a), and if it is flexible and innovative (Koopman, 1991). Charismatic leaders may arise if the tasks are unstructured and collective, and if goals are ambiguous (House, Spangler, & Woyke, 1991). Since different threats and opportunities exist at every organizational level, it is not surprising that charismatic leadership can be revealed at any level without crisis conditions. Charisma without crisis deteriorated faster compared to continuous visionary leadership with or without crisis conditions.

Whether spurred by a crisis or an ideology, the charismatic leaders' solutions can take opposite directions. The dedicated follower of one charismatic can be uplifted and moved to a new and better life; the dedicated follower of another can be moved to murder or suicide. Thus, charismatic leadership can be beneficial or deleterious to society and to organizational life, depending on whether the leaders are authentic leaders have prosocial or antisocial goals.

Routinization

History is replete with charismatic leaders whose revolutionary changes endured. As Bass (1985a, p. 41) noted:

> The world from the Danube to the Indus was remade socially, culturally and politically by Alexander the Great in his own brief career. Simon Bolivar's efforts had lasting political effects on much of Latin America. Mohammed's lasting effects transformed societies stretching from Morocco to Indonesia and left lasting effects on cultures from Spain to the Philippines.

What makes for the lasting effects of charismatic leaders? Weber (1924/1947) attributed them to routinization. Focused on the expressive and the emotional, the relationship between the charismatic leader and the led is basically unstable, Weber thought; it must be routinized by the development of organizational rules and arrangements to achieve stability. The charismatic leader's mission can be routinized in several ways. For example, unless the leader is replaced by an equally charismatic successor, an administrative apparatus is created, along with rites and ceremonies, to provide continuity of the message and mission. Or oral and written traditions emerge to enable the charismatic's effects to endure. The charismatic revolutionary hero Napoléon Bonaparte became the Emperor Napoleon, with a new court, new legal codes, a new educational system, and a new administration. Mao Zedong, the "permanent revolutionary," was succeeded by Deng Xiaoping, the administrator, who sought to maintain most of the bureaucratic political system created by Mao, but not as much of Mao's economic system. The charismatic founder of Mothers Against Drunk Driving, Candy Lightner, succeeded in arousing the public with her moral expressiveness and moral mission and was able to obtain funding for a national organization. But conflict within the organization between the functionaries required to run a rational administration and the charismatic Lightner resulted in her replacement as leader (Weed, 1993).

The charismatic leader is a hard act to follow. Institutional practices and the cultural imperatives built by the charismatic leader must replace him after he is gone. Marshal Tito of Yugoslavia planned carefully for the succession after his death but was not optimistic that any associate could accumulate the personal authority that his charisma had given him (Drachkovitch, 1964). For a while, the structures that the Croat Tito had created remained in place in Yugoslavia. These generally favored the Serbs; but the ethnic divisions, aided and abetted by a new aggrandizing dictatorial leader, the Serbian President Milošević, caused the Yugoslav republics to fly apart after three wars between Serbia and Croatia, the Bosnian war, and the war in Kosovo.

Continuity is also provided by key groups of believers and by distinctive practices and imagery in the form of visual art, ceremonies, and stories. In the survival and growth of Alcoholics Anonymous and the National Council on Alcoholism, founded by charismatic leaders in 1935 and 1946, respectively, Trice and Beyer (1986) noted: (1) the development of an administrative apparatus that puts the charismatic's program into practice; (2) the transfer of charisma to others in the organization by rites and ceremonies; (3) the incorporation of the charismatic's message and mission into the organization's traditions; and (4) the selection of a successor who resembles the charismatic founder and has the esteem to achieve the charismatic's personal influence.

Government bureaucracies are highly routinized. Charismatic leadership is seldom seen. Impersonal rules provide standardization. There is little latitude for "creative administration." Nonetheless, at times creative administrators do manage to decide which rules to apply and how to interpret them in order to accomplish their objectives legally and without censorship. Reforms do occur in response to clients and political pressures (Kamensky, 1996). Politically well-connected agency directors with experience know how to use or go around the rules for their own ends.

Charisma May Emerge from Routinization. The office may make the leader. Apart from "office charisma," the demands of the office may greatly elevate the esteem of the officeholder. For instance, in Shakespeare's play, the profligate Prince Hal develops into the charismatic Henry V in response to the demands of kingship.

Charisma grows from administrative routine. This interesting reverse effect was demonstrated by Scott (1978). Rather than supporting Weber's thesis that charismatic authority eventually results in routinization, Scott found that routinization, as evidenced by years of tenure in a bureaucratic office, contributed to one's charismatic authority. In a random sample of Kentucky school superintendents, Scott found a correlation of .52 between their years in office and their charismatic authority. Not until the thirteenth year of their tenure was the superintendents' charismatic authority rated consistently high. A peak of charismatic authority was reached after 13 years of tenure and continued through the twenty-first year of tenure before declining slightly, just before the superintendents' retirement.

Using Mao Zedong as an example, Chang (1982) argued that the emergence of a charismatic leader is a long-term process of interaction between the leader and followers and their collective ability to accumulate political power. Mao's charismatic leadership was legitimated, reinforced, and maintained through institutional efforts. After Mao, a powerful political bureaucracy maintained itself, but the bureaucratic hold on the Chinese economy was relaxed. We need to allow for various possible relations between charismatic leaders, their immediate colleagues, and the environment that may result in a more personalized leadership, rather than routinization of the leadership over time.

Loss of the Charismatic Relationship

Since the relationship depends on followers and conditions as well as the leader, leaders may lose their charisma in the eyes of their followers if changes occur in the followers and conditions. Yukl (1999) argued that charismatic leadership theory and research provided little insight about how and why charisma is lost. He suggested that the attribution of charisma might fall away if the crisis conditions disappear, if followers become more competent, if the leader fails or betrays the followers, or if rivals appear who are more credible and more attractive. Paradoxically, charismatic leaders may be victims of their own success in founding and building organizations. The charismatic founders may be replaced as the organization becomes more professional and bureaucratic, because their expertise is no longer unique and their emotionally appealing, unconventional behavior is no longer functional.

The Charismatic Leader in Complex Organizations: A Conceptual Examination

The concept of the charismatic relationship is now used to understand leaders and leadership in a wide variety of organizations and political, social, and religious movements. Numerous theorists have used the concept to account for organizational members' emotional responses to work-related stimuli, for their trust and confidence in their leader, and for their adoption of the leader's values, which results in their heightened motivation to perform.

Widespread Distribution

Charismatic leader-follower relationships are widely found in political life, social movements, and complex organizations. They appear not only "in extravagant forms and fleeting moments, but in an abiding, if combustible, aspect of social life that occasionally bursts into open flame" (Geertz, 1977, p. 151). Charismatic relationships have been reported in such diverse organizations as suburban school systems, communes, utopian communities, colleges, Alcoholics Anonymous, the National Council on Alcoholism, the Chippewa Nation, a maternity home, a British manufacturing firm, and Tanzanian labor unions (Trice & Beyer, 1984). Some of the most prominent charismatic leaders in the United States have been leaders of labor movements and labor unions, such as Bill Haywood of the Industrial Workers of the World (IWW), Rose Schneiderman of the Women's Trade Union League (WTUL), A. Philip Randolph of the Brotherhood of Sleeping Car Porters (BSCP), Cesar Chavez of the United Farm Workers (UFW), and John L. Lewis of the United Mine Workers (UMW), cofounder of the Congress of Industrial Organizations (CIO). They tended to be dedicated, visionary, determined, mission-oriented, magnetic, inspirational, and articulate (Dubofsky & Van Tine, 1987).

As Shils (1965), Dow (1969a), and Oberg (1972) had observed earlier, Bass (1985a, pp. 56–57) found in empirical surveys that charisma is widely distributed as an interpersonal relationship and is not limited only to world leaders or to founders of movements or heads of organizations:

[Charisma] shows up with . . . Lee Iacocca at Chrysler convincing workers, suppliers, Congressmen, and customers that Chrysler could be turned around and doing it; the young Robert Hutchins recasting the prestigious University of Chicago in his own image; Hyman Rickover, taking on the whole Navy Department with an idea, the nuclear submarine, whose time had come. . . . [Much] of what the Iacoccas, Hutchinses and Rickovers can do from the top of the organization, can occur in varying amounts and degrees all through complex organizations. Such charismatic effects can be studied and found or developed in supervisors at all levels of the complex organization.

Charisma, in turn, is a component—the most general and important component—of the larger concept of transformational leadership. In this regard, it is to be found, to a considerable degree, in industrial, educational, government, and military leaders at all organizational levels. In questionnaire surveys, many followers described their military or industrial superiors as persons who made everyone enthusiastic about assignments, who inspired loyalty to the organization, who commanded respect from everyone, who had a special gift of seeing what was really important, who had a sense of mission, and who excited subordinates. Some of these subordinates had complete faith in the leaders with charisma and felt good to be near them. They were proud to be associated with the charismatic leaders and trusted the leaders' capacity to overcome any obstacle. The charismatic leaders served as a symbol of success and accomplishment for their followers (Bass, 1985a).

Charismatics may be more likely to appear in political and religious movements than in business or industry (Katz & Kahn, 1978), but they also appear at various levels in the complex organizations of business executives, educational administrators, military officers, and industrial managers. According to Zaleznik (1983), charisma distinguishes the ordinary manager from the true leader in organizational settings. The true leader attracts intense feelings of love (and sometimes hate) from his or her subordinates, who want to identify with him or her. Feelings about ordinary managers are bland, but relations are smoother and steadier. However, like most intimate relationships, the relations between the charismatic leader and his or her followers tend to be turbulent. Such "commando leaders" emerge to accomplish challenging and exhilarating tasks that need to be undertaken in an organization. Although they are highly effective, they may be "glamorous nuisances" (Handy, 1976).

Katz and Kahn (1978) argued that the charismatic relationship is strengthened to the degree that leaders distance themselves from their followers. This idea fits with Hollander's (1978) inference that charismatic leadership is less likely to emerge in complex organizations because of the close contact of superiors and subordinates, which prevents the maintenance of the magical properties of charisma. But many charismatic leaders, such as Vladimir Lenin and Lyndon Johnson, had close, immediate, lifelong subordinates who worshiped them with intense devotion. Social distance between leaders and followers is not essential for the maintenance of the charismatic relationship. In fact, Howell (1988) argued that socialized charismatics do not maintain such a distance.

Yukl (1981) attributed the presumed scarcity of charismatic leaders in business and industry to the lack of managers with the necessary skills. Berlew (1974) thought that many managers have the skills but do not recognize the opportunities. Bass (1985a) suggested that such managers may be less willing to risk standing out among their peers in organizations when they believe that conformity may be more important for success. Nevertheless, House (1977) proposed that charismatics may be found throughout complex organizations. Evidence of their effects on their followers includes the followers' trust in the correctness of the leader's beliefs, followers' beliefs that are similar to the leader's, unquestioning acceptance of the leader, affection for the leader, willingness to obey the leader, emotional involvement in the mission of the organization, heightened goals for performance, and belief by the followers that they are able to contribute to the success of the organization's mission.

Utility of Charismatic Leadership in Organizations

Weber (1946) noted that charismatic leadership is a way to provide order and direction in complex organizations that were not bureaucratized or operated according to traditions. To meet the challenges of a rapidly changing workforce, markets, and technologies in the past few de-

cades, productive organizations increased their efforts to avoid bureaucratic and traditional rigidity by using ad hoc groups, temporary systems, and organicity (Robbins, 1983). Elaborate formal coordination and planning were replaced with teamwork and devoted, intense efforts by members. Increasingly, leader-subordinate relationships displayed more charismatic characteristics (Quinn & Cameron, 1983).

Shamir, House, and Arthur (1993) suggested that charismatic leaders generate more effort in their subordinates in a number of ways. These leaders enhance, for their subordinates, the intrinsic worth of the goals and of the activities required to reach the goals; instill in them faith in the future and the belief that the goals are beyond ordinary, rational purposes; and, in the process, raise subordinates' self-esteem.

The charismatic prophet's antiestablishment preaching can be destructive, but it also may contribute to organizational renewal. Etzioni (1961) suggested that more charismalike leadership is needed in organizations to induce subordinates to accept guidance in expressive matters, in value judgments, and in decisions about purpose. Less charisma is needed to achieve agreement about instrumental means that usually are based on facts and rationales. More charisma is also needed if compliance depends on moral involvement; less is needed if it depends on material rewards or the avoidance of penalties. According to Etzioni, personnel in the lower ranks are instrumental performers, decisions about means are relegated to personnel in the middle levels, and charismatic concerns for the ends should be restricted to the top levels. Thus lower-level charismatic leadership would be dysfunctional in service and production bureaucracies: "Development of charisma on levels other than the top is not only unnecessary but is likely to undermine the rational processes required to maximize organizational effectiveness" (p. 317).

Nevertheless, Etzioni saw that when decisions about ends remain important—as they do for priests, shop stewards, and junior military combat officers and noncoms who are lower in the hierarchy of their organizations—charismatic leadership still has utility. Greater amounts of charismatic leadership were seen by the surveyed subordinates of U.S. Army combat officers than among combat-support officers (Bass, 1985a). Etzioni's argument that decisions about values, objectives, goals, and missions should be limited to the top organizational levels can be countered by the argument that participation in aspects of such decisions should be encouraged among leaders at all levels. Subordinates in lower organizational ranks who describe their immediate supervisors as charismatic also think their units and their organization are more productive. And opinions about the effectiveness of lower- and middle-level charismatic leaders are shared by their superiors (Hater & Bass, 1988; Yammarino & Bass, 1988).

Negative Utility. Nadler and Tushman (1990) pointed out possible negative effects of the charismatic leader. Expectations may be created that are unrealistic or unattainable. Everyone else will avoid taking the initiative and will remain dependent on the leader. Next-lower levels of management may be unable to exert any leadership. They will be reluctant to disagree with the charismatic leader's suggestions. When things fail to go as planned, followers may feel betrayed. The charismatic leader's magic may wear off, and he or she may take foolish steps to try to regain the loyalty of followers.

Differences in the Behavior and Accomplishments of Charismatics

Weber did not pay much attention to individual differences in the personalities of charismatic leaders but saw only that routinization would follow from the development of the charismatic's religious, political, or organizational authority. However, some charismatic leaders' sense of omnipotent personal power may prevent the institutionalization of charismatic authority into procedures and routines to be managed by subordinates and successors (Mitscherlich, 1967). This situation seems to have occurred with Kwame Nkrumah of Ghana but not with Jomo Kenyatta of Kenya. Both leaders were charismatic, but only Kenyatta could accept political opposition (Dow, 1969b). Thus charismatic leaders may differ considerably from each other in what they do and what they can accomplish.

Charismatic mentors will guide and support the personal growth of their disciples. Equally charismatic patrons will exchange support, protection and security for loyalty and service, keeping their clients in the same

continued state of dependency. Charismatic teachers will provide intellectual stimulation; charismatic celebrities who lack the intellect will not. Charismatic junior army officers with their cry of "follow me," will . . . [stimulate soldiers] to take action; charismatic ascetics or mystics will foster [followers'] escapism and lethargy. (Bass, 1985a, p. 52)

When Charismatic Leaders Fail. The situation may cause the charismatic leader to fail. For example, charismatic conductors of symphony orchestras will be seriously constrained by the unionization of the musicians they direct, as well as by the evaluation and control of employers, patrons, critics, business managers, and audiences (Kamerman, 1981). But more often, their personal weaknesses may lie behind their failure.

Despite their self-confidence, self-determination, and freedom from inner conflicts, some charismatics will fail . . . as a consequence of particular deficiencies or exaggerated tendencies. Sometimes they may fail due to the overwhelming constraints they face and how they try to cope with them. Thus, how leaders with a sense of mission, self-confidence, ambition and other attributes of charisma handle the organizational constraints that frustrate their aims also makes a difference in whether they succeed in transforming organization managements, or fail in a dissatisfying standoff between what they want to see done and what can be done. (Bass, 1985a, pp. 50–51)

What McCall and Lombardo (1983) discovered in "derailed" promising young executives is illustrative. Unpredictability, insensitivity to others, the betrayal of trust, the failure to delegate to staff effectively, and the failure to build a team halted these executives' move up the organizational ladder. A political leader who operates at a distance from colleagues and constituents may get away with cronyism and extreme ambitiousness; but for industrial executives, too many such flaws create strong antipathy to their subsequent promotion among their more powerful colleagues.

Charismatic leaders tend to generate both love and hate in followers. Brown and Keeping (1999) observed that leaders obtaining higher scores on the MLQ were liked better than those earning lower scores. It may be that some charismatic leaders fail because they are more disliked than liked by their diverse followers. In a study of fire department personnel, Bramwell (1991) demonstrated that teams dealing with a first simulated task that was familiar were more effective if led by unseen charismatic leaders. Compared to suitable controls, the teams did worse on an unfamiliar second simulated task when they could see the nonverbal behavior of the charismatic leaders. If strong identification with a charismatic leader produces dependent, immature followers, rather than providing a model and inspiring support for self-actualizing followers (Musser, 1987), early successes nourish unrealistic expectations on the part of both the leader and the followers. If the problems become too great, the group's expectations may eventually surpass the leader's presumed magical powers, causing the leader's downfall (Heifetz & Sinder, 1987).

According to McGill and Slocum (1998), many organizations now expect and encourage their managers to behave more like charismatic leaders, yet most managers do not have the personal requisites and will fail in this attempt. The authors suggest instead that the managers know their job, act in alignment with their organization's vision and values, and encourage listening and choice.

Empirical Studies of Charismatic Leadership

The earlier case studies, retrospective analyses, and commentaries about the impact of charismatic leaders on their followers have been augmented, beginning in the mid-1980s, by laboratory experiments and questionnaire and interview surveys of the military, health organizations, business firms, NGOs (nongovernmental organizations), and educational organizations. Trice and Beyer (1986) were able to list nine sociological and anthropological field studies of charisma as of 1977 that they regarded as relevant, but House (1977) was unable to unearth any controlled empirical efforts to investigate the phenomenon at that time. The paucity of studies may explain why charisma was not indexed in *Psychological Abstracts* as of 1969 (Stark, 1970). At least two reasons may underlie the paucity of such laboratory and field experiments and surveys until recently. First, many if not most scholars, such as Beyer (1998), assumed charisma to be a rare attribute, limited to a few extraordinary leaders. Second, they thought it was impossible to bring charisma

into the laboratory or to measure it with adequate validity. Both assumptions proved to be unwarranted.

Laboratory Experiments on Charisma

Brown and Lord (1999) pointed out the advantages of using experiments to study charisma. Experiments can avoid the effects of perceptual and cognitive errors in memory, nonverbal leadership, and unconscious influences that distort perceptions and beliefs in surveys and interviews. Howell (1985) succeeded in bringing the phenomenon of charisma into the laboratory. In the first such laboratory experiment, she compared the effects on subordinates of three types of leaders: charismatic, structuring, and considerate. The leaders' roles were played by two actresses, both of whom were trained for 30 hours. The actresses' training consisted of in-depth descriptions of their roles and a demonstration of the behaviors, emotional states, body language, facial expressions, and paralinguistic cues that they were to use in the experiment. The actresses viewed videotapes of actual managers who portrayed the different styles of leadership, and they rehearsed extensively. Videotapes of the actresses enacting the three styles after training were rated by 203 judges; this manipulation check attested to the validity of the actresses' performance. When playing the charismatic, structuring, and considerate roles:

> The [charismatic] leader articulated an overarching goal, communicated high performance expectations, exhibited confidence in participants' ability to meet these expectations, and empathized with the needs of participants. . . . The highly charismatic leader also projected a powerful, confident, and dynamic presence and had a captivating, engaging voice tone. . . . Nonverbally, the charismatic leader alternated between pacing and sitting on the edge of her desk, leaned toward the participant, maintained direct eye contact, and had a relaxed posture and animated facial expressions. . . .
>
> The structuring leader . . . explained the nature of the task, provided detailed directions, emphasized the quantity of work to be accomplished within the specified time period, maintained definite standards of work performance, and answered any task related questions. . . . Nonverbally, the structuring leader sat on

the edge of her desk, maintained intermittent eye contact, and had neutral facial expressions and a moderate level of speech intonation. . . .

The considerate . . . leader engaged in participative two-way conversations, emphasized the comfort, well-being, and satisfaction of participants, and reassured and relaxed participants. The highly considerate leader was also friendly and approachable and had a warm voice tone. Nonverbally, the considerate leader sat on the edge of her desk, leaned toward participants, maintained direct eye contact and had a relaxed posture and friendly facial expressions. (Howell, 1985, p. 8)

The laboratory task was an in-basket exercise requiring the completion of 15 memos in 45 minutes, followed by an optional task of five memos to be completed in an additional 15 minutes; most participants actually completed the optional task. Two coworkers who were confederates of the experimenter, plus a participant subject, made up the task group. The confederate coworkers (also trained) either encouraged the participant (high-productivity norming) or discouraged the participant (low-productivity norming). A total of 144 undergraduates were allocated to the six experimental treatments, 24 participants per treatment, so that each type of leadership was combined with the contrived high- or low-productivity norm. The most important finding was that only the charismatic leader was able to generate high productivity when confederate coworkers tried to discourage the participant. The leader who initiated structure did almost as well, but only if the coworkers encouraged high productivity. The structuring leader generated even less productivity than the considerate leader when coworkers were discouraging and set a low-productivity norm. In addition, in contrast to participants who worked under the leaders who initiated structure or were considerate, participants who worked under a charismatic leader had higher task performance, suggested more courses of action, had greater satisfaction with the task, felt less role conflict, and were more satisfied with the leader. Also, the qualitative task performance of individuals with a charismatic leader was better than that of individuals with a considerate leader.

Bramwell (undated) arranged for female participants to receive instructions from a female leader about completing an essay, to see how people reacted physiologically to the task. The leader acted like a charismatic for 32 of the participants and noncharismatic for 30. The subjects wore a blood pressure cuff and completed questionnaires during the course of the experiment. Systolic blood pressure rose from means of 107 to 110 for those with the charismatic leader but remained almost unchanged for those instructed by the noncharismatic leader. Those experiencing the charismatic leader thought their performance was higher (although it was not) and reported a more positive mood than those instructed by the noncharismatic leader.

Shea and Howell (1999) conducted an experiment with a 2 × 3 design. The situation involved confederates acting as charismatic leaders on noncharismatic leaders, and internal, external, or no feedback. There were four trials of the task for the 99 participating graduate students, which was to manufacture real electrical wiring harnesses as directed by the leader. The performance of the participants instructed by the noncharismatic leader without feedback deteriorated substantially, but those working under the charismatic leadership did as well with or without feedback, perhaps sustained by their heightened motivation. Results indicated that the presence of feedback reduced the self-efficacy effects of charismatic leadership on performance.

Hunt, Boal, and Dodge (1999) conducted an experiment to compare the effects of charismatic visionary leadership and charismatic leadership brought on by a crisis and after the crisis disappeared. Awamleh and Gardner (1999) compared the impact of charismatic leadership on perceptions of the contents of a message and its delivery with nonverbal gesturing and facial expression. The delivery accounted for 58% of the variance in attributed charisma.

Surveys and Interviews

Based on House's (1977) theory of charismatic leadership, Smith (1982) identified, by nominations, a sample of 30 charismatic and 30 noncharismatic leaders, who represented a broad sample of formal work organizations in the business, industrial, and governmental sectors. Smith administered 38 scales to subordinates to describe their superiors' attitudes and behavior. A discriminant analysis and cross-validation revealed that 7 of 18 emergent dimensions formed from the 38 scales significantly differentiated the charismatic from the noncharismatic leaders. The charismatic leaders were seen to be dynamic (emphatic, active, fast, aggressive, bold, extroverted, energetic, and frank). Subordinates who worked for charismatic leaders developed more self-assurance than did those who worked for noncharismatic leaders. They said they experienced more meaningfulness if their leader had been nominated earlier as charismatic. In addition, they worked longer hours per week, which suggests that their motivation was heightened. Compared with subordinates of the noncharismatic leaders, they revealed a higher level of trust and acceptance of the charismatic leader in their ratings of "self-disclosure" to the leader.

O'Reilly (1984) found, in a survey of employees of Silicon Valley electronic firms that the credibility of top managers, as judged by their dynamism, trustworthiness, and expertise, was significantly enhanced if the CEOs were regarded as charismatic. The employees' commitment was similarly elevated.

Applying a revised scale of charisma developed by Podsakoff, MacKensie, Moorman, et al. (1990), Agle (1994) showed that 250 CEOs rated as more charismatic (dynamic, exemplary, etc.) by their top management team were more effective in terms of their organization's independently obtained performance record. Deluga (1995) found that 63 subordinates in an engineering division of a manufacturing firm who attributed more charismatic leadership on the Conger-Kanungo (CK) questionnaire to their 29 supervisors were also more likely to display organizational citizen behaviors (OCBs): conscientiousness, sportsmanship, civic virtue, courtesy, and altruism. Pitman (1993) obtained correlations between overall commitment of 245 white-collar workers in six firms of .24 and .23, respectively, with their MLQ charisma and CK ratings of their supervisors.

Shamir, Zakay, Breinen, et al. (1998) derived and tested several hypotheses about the effects of charisma. The hypotheses were derived from Shamir, House, and Arthur's (1993) Theory of Charismatic Leadership and its extension. The leadership of each of 50 company officers from the Israeli Defense Forces (infantry, tank, and engineering) were rated by superiors, peers, and subordinates A total of 135 officers, 218 noncoms, and 1,197 soldiers participated. Respondents (11 or 12 per company) answered questions about either the company commanders or the companies. Four factors were extracted from the data about the company commanders: (1) Support-

ive behaviors (e.g., talks to soldiers like a friend of theirs); (2) Exemplary (e.g., full of energy and very active), (3) Ideological emphasis (e.g., often refers to national history); (4) Emphasizes collective identity (e.g., emphasizes the differences between the company and other companies). Stepwise analyses of the leaders' support regressed on the subordinates' attitudes toward their companies indicated that leader support was more important than the leaders' emphasis on collective identity. The leaders' exemplary behaviors were unrelated to any of the unit appraisals. An unanticipated finding was that the leaders' emphasis on ideology was *negatively* related to predicting soldiers' self-efficacy, identification with their unit, and attachment to their unit. The investigators concluded that the soldiers had become somewhat alienated from the mandatory military service—they viewed the highly dedicated company leaders as representatives of the interests of the larger system rather than their own interests. The leaders' ideological comments were seen as an effort to pressure them to perform.

Meta-Analytical Findings. DeGroot, Kiker, and Cross (2000) conducted 16 meta-analyses of studies of the correlations between leader charisma and effectiveness, as well as between leader charisma and subordinate effectiveness, effort, and satisfaction. For 23 analyses involving 5,577 respondents, charismatic leadership correlated on the average .74 (when corrected) with leadership effectiveness. But the mean correlation dropped to .50 for five studies when same-source variance was controlled. When 467 groups were used as the basis for analysis, the corrected mean correlation was .49, compared with .76 when the analysis was at the level of 5,110 individuals for 18 studies. The corrected mean correlation between the leaders' charisma and their subordinates' effectiveness was .31.

Multifactor Leadership Questionnaire (MLQ) Scale of Charismatic Leadership. Bass (1985c) developed a charismatic leadership scale of 10 items of the MLQ (Bass & Avolio, 1988) dealing with both the leader's behavior and the follower's reactions. He began with Burns's (1978) definition of a transformational leader who raises the followers' level of consciousness about the importance and value of designated outcomes and ways of reaching them; gets the followers to transcend their own self-interests for the sake of the team, organization, or larger polity; and raises their level of need on Maslow's (1954) hierarchy from lower-level concerns for safety and security to higher-level needs for achievement and self-actualization.

Seventy senior South African executives (all male) were able to describe at least one such transformational leader they had known during their careers. Their descriptive statements, along with others about transactional leadership that featured an exchange of rewards for the follower's compliance with the leader, were sorted by 11 graduate students into transformational and transactional. The 73 statements on which the judges could agree were administered to 177 senior U.S. Army officers who were asked to describe their most recent superior, using a 5-point scale of frequency, from 0 = the behavior is displayed not at all to 4 = the behavior is displayed frequently, if not always. The first factor that emerged was labeled charismatic leadership because it seemed to contain most of the components of such leadership. Highest item factor loadings on the first factor were:

.87, I have complete faith in him.

.86, Is a model for me to follow.

.85; Makes me proud to be associated with him.

Sixty-six percent of the variances of the 73 items could be accounted for by this first factor of charismatic leadership (Bass, 1985a). An even larger percentage was accounted for in a comparable sample of U.S. Air Force officers (Colby & Zak, 1988). Hater and Bass (1988) achieved similar results when they refactored the 70-item questionnaire that subordinates completed to describe their immediate management superiors. Onnen (1987) obtained similar findings from 454 parishioners who described their Methodist ministers. A 10-item scale of these charisma items was included in the Revised MLQ-5X. Reliabilities of .85 and above were routinely reported for descriptions of superiors by large samples of subordinates in military and industrial settings (Bass & Avolio, 1991). Hater and Bass found that 28 managers in an express package shipping firm who were identified by their superiors as "top performers" earned a significantly higher charismatic leadership score from their subordinates than did a random sample of 26 ordinary performers.

Relationship to Effective Leadership. For the samples of officers in the U.S. Army and U.S. Air Force, the MLQ charisma scale correlated .85 and .90 with the rated effectiveness of the officers and .91 and .95 with satisfaction with their performance as leaders. For a sample of Indian managers in an engineering firm and an American sample from high-tech companies, Waldman, Bass, and Einstein (1985) reported correlations of .72 and .81 between subordinates' ratings of the charisma of their leaders and the effectiveness of their leadership. This finding was in contrast to the correlations between rated effectiveness and how much contingent rewarding and management by exception the managers practiced. The average correlation between contingent reward and effectiveness was only .48. The correlation between ratings of the leaders' activity in practicing management by exception and the leaders' effectiveness was .06.

Gibbons (1986) obtained similar results in a computer firm; Bass (1985a) for New Zealand educational administrators and professional personnel. Yokochi Bryce (1989) for managers from 14 Japanese firms, and Boyd (1989b) for U.S., Canadian, and German NATO field grade officers. Similarly, Hoover (1987) reported correlations of .69 and .66 between the charisma on the MLQ of headmasters of private schools and their effectiveness and satisfied subordinates.

Seltzer and Bass (1987) obtained a correlation of .81 between charismatic leadership and effectiveness, according to 875 part-time MBA students who described their current boss, and according to the subordinates of 98 currently enrolled part-time MBA students. The correlation with satisfaction with the leader was .86. This correlation was considerably higher than the correlations of effectiveness and satisfaction with other measures of leadership behavior, such as consideration and the initiation of structure. A similar pattern emerged in determining how much stress and burnout was avoided in the subordinates of charismatic leaders (Seltzer, Numerof, & Bass, 1989). Among 264 retail chain-store employees, Peterson, Phillips, and Duran (1989) found that the MLQ charismatic leadership ratings they gave their supervisors contributed more to the predictions of organizational commitment of the employees and their perceptions of the store's effectiveness than did any of the other leadership measures employed in the study—which included performance (P) and maintenance (M) leadership and initiation and consideration. Leaders with high charisma scores on the MLQ encouraged self-actualization among subordinates. Correlations between charisma and measures of subordinate self-actualization ranged from .43 to .65 (Seltzer & Bass, 1987).

Caveat. Much of the foregoing correlational evidence was from the same source, the leaders' subordinates. Avolio, Bass, and Yammarino (1988) showed that although the charisma-effectiveness connection was inflated, coming as it did from the same source, when one subordinate of the same leader provided the assessment of leadership and another the assessment of effectiveness, the connection remained, but to a lesser extent. Nor was the connection affected by a generalized feeling of satisfaction. Only about 10% of the measure of charisma could be accounted for by the bias of leniency (Bass & Avolio, 1988). In addition, superiors agreed that charismatics, as described by subordinates, were more effective (Hater & Bass, 1988). As was seen in Table 21.1, superiors gave higher ratings of performance to managers whom subordinates had described as charismatic on MLQ-R, Form 5. As is shown in Table 21.2, Yammarino and Bass (1989) found that better fitness reports and recommendations for early promotion from their superiors were earned by 186 naval officers whose subordinates had described the officers on MLQ, Form II as charismatic leaders. The subordinates' descriptions of the charismatic leadership of these officers, all graduates of the U.S. Naval Academy, were also predicted by the grades for overall military performance that the officers had earned at the academy.

In addition, subordinates' identification of charismatic leaders on the MLQ predicted independent objective criteria of the leaders' effectiveness. Onnen (1987) reported a substantial correlation between the parishioners' descriptions of charismatic Methodist ministers on the MLQ and the parishioners' Sunday church attendance. The charismatic leadership scores also correlated with the growth in church membership.[5]

Simulated Business Competition. The pattern of correlations was the same when the MLQ, Form 5 questionnaire was used by MBA students in a simulation to rate

[5] Further evidence about the predictions of objective leader effectiveness from MLQ charisma scores will be presented in Chapter 22 on transformational leadership.

the presidents of 27 fictional companies. Each firm was composed of nine MBA students who were competing in a semester-long complex business game with students representing two other such firms. Although the business game ran for 12 weeks, it simulated eight quarters of business performance. Leadership ratings of each team's president were collected at the end of the eighth quarter. The success of the presidents and their firms was announced at the end of each of the first eight quarters. Although each company began with equivalent assets, companies led by presidents rated highly in charismatic leadership also performed significantly better on objective indexes of success such as returns on investment, stock prices, and share of the market. The results were the same when independent raters viewed videotapes of the company meetings to complete the MLQ to describe the presidents. The judgments of the raters of the videotapes were in agreement with those of the students who acted as colleagues of the company presidents (Avolio, Waldman, & Einstein, 1988).

Conger-Kanungo Charismatic Leadership Questionnaire (CK). To examine the behavioral and attributional components of their model of charismatic leadership to describe a leader, Conger and Kanungo (1994) distributed a refined questionnaire to 488 U.S. and Canadian managers in four organizations. Examples of the 25 items (Conger & Kanungo, 1988) with responses ranging from 6 = Very characteristic to 1 = Very uncharacteristic were: "Often incurs high personal costs for the good of the organization;" "Exciting public speaker;" "Uses untraditional means to achieve organizational goals." The researchers demonstrated their scale's convergent and divergent validities. Factor analysis exposed their elements of charisma: vision and articulation, sensitivity to environment and member needs, personal risk, unconventional behavior, and avoiding the status quo. The CK overall charisma scale has been found to be correlated 0.85 with the attributed charisma scale of the MLQ.

Some Other Charismatic Leadership Scales. Kouzes and Posner (1987) organized scales labeled challenging the process; inspiring a shared vision; enabling others to act; modeling the way; and encouraging the heart. House (1997a) substituted *value-based* for charisma scales: articulation of a vision; communication of high performance expectation; displaying self-confidence; role modeling; showing confidence in and challenging followers; integrity; and intellectual stimulation. Behling and McFillen (1996) developed charismalike scales for displaying empathy, dramatizing the mission, projecting self-assurance to enhance image, assuring competency, and providing opportunities to experience success.

A Dynamic Model of the Charismatic Process of the Leader, the Followers, and Their Social Interaction

Jacobsen and House selected six highly documented charismatic leaders (J. F. Kennedy, Theodore Herzl, O. C. Wingate, Lee Iacocca, Adolf Hitler, and Mary Baker Eddy) to develop a dynamic model (Forrester, 1961) to reproduce a time series of data for each of them so as to determine how well the data matched a theoretical integration of the charismatic process. The process involved integrating the leader, the led, and their interaction. The computer simulation began with the percentage of the followers who accepted the status quo, identified with the leader, were active, or were dedicated. Next to be entered were the time and the percentage who recognized the leader. This was followed by times and percentages of people aroused, then committed, disenchanted, and defected. Finally entered were the times and percentages of followers who developed resentment and alienation as a consequence of bureaucratic regimentation. After the necessary estimates of parameters were included, 16 sets of data were successfully reproduced from the theoretical integration. The theoretical numbers accounted for 76.7% of the empirical data.

Criticisms of Charismatic Theory

As a religious concept that was adopted by Weber, charismatic leadership was explained by divine inspiration. Turner (1993) argued that the secularization of charisma by Weber (1922/1947) failed to explain the secular power of charismatics on the followers' expectations and internalization of changes in attitudes and behavior. Turner suggested that the charismatic offers a new vision of opportunities with risks and "provides through his or her

own conduct evidence of the realizability of this vision through submission" (p. 235). Beyer (1999) argued that the neo-Weberian theories downgraded the power of the truly Weberian charismatic leader. She felt that the concept was a tamed version of charisma "diluted in its richness and distinctiveness" (p. 308). As noted earlier, she reiterated that five elements must be present for charismatic leadership to be seen: an extraordinary gifted person, a social crisis, a radical solution, transcendent powers, and repeated success. House (1999) agreed with Beyer that too much emphasis is placed on the effects of charismatic leaders on individual followers, compared with their effects on collectives or organizational performance. More attention needs to be paid to charismatic effects on radical change, specific follower behaviors, and different follower preferences in different situations. According to DiTomaso (1993), the post-1990 theories of charismatic leadership have "insufficiently used" the insights of Weber and Etzioni, for whom charisma is about wisdom. Furthermore, insufficient attention has been paid to the tension in the emergence and development of charisma. Calas (1993) faulted neo-Weberian theorists for omitting Weber's text on routinization of charisma and for upholding the wildest aspects of charisma. Hummel (1975) argued that charismatic leadership was not applicable to East Asian cultures. Shamir and Howell (1999) agreed with Bass (1997) and House, Wright, and Aditya (1997) that charismatic leadership can be found universally, to some degree, across cultures and countries. However, in many situations, the context may be particularly important to its emergence and continuance.

Yukl (1999) saw ambiguity in the concept because of the differences in how charisma is defined and measured. Conger and Kanungo (1998) regard charisma as an attribution; Shamir, House, and Arthur (1993) viewed charisma in terms of the behavior of the charismatic leader and how the leader profoundly influences the followers. Bass and Avolio (1991) conceived of charisma as behavior and as an attribution in the MLQ scales of idealized influence (charisma). Charismatic theory placed too much emphasis on the dyadic leader-follower relationship and not enough on the leader-group relationship. Theorists of charisma looked more often at socially acceptable behaviors and avoided manipulative and political behaviors such as staging events and indoctrinating new members. They did not pay enough attention to how charisma is lost. Although the dark side of charismatic leadership is acknowledged (Howell, 1988), Yukl (1999) suggests there is a need for further clarification of conditions in which a charismatic leader is not desirable. For instance, the need for a charismatic leader may be contraindicated in a self-managed team. Moreover, due to insufficient research, we don't know how charisma is lost. How is charisma affected by the end of a crisis, or by the leaders' obvious failures and betrayals? What leads to hate, resentment, and alienation in the love-hate relation of followers with charismatic leaders?

Inspirational Leadership

Differences from Charismatic Leadership. Although inspirational leadership is highly correlated with charismatic leadership, inspirational leadership does not necessarily imply that inspired followers resolve their intrapsychic tensions by identifying with the leader, forming a strong commitment to the leader with uncritical and unquestioning obedience, or attributing supernatural powers to the leader. The inspirational leader can symbolize or represent the follower's ego; the charismatic leader can substitute for the follower's ego ideal (Bass, 1988).

Followers perceive an inspiring leader to be knowledgeable, enlightened, and sensitive to the problems at hand, and from these perceptions, their confidence in the leader grows. Their trust in the inspiring leader arises from the meaning the leader can give to their needs and actions. Followers share with the leader common beliefs about what is wrong, beliefs the leader articulates publicly for them. Unlike the charismatic leader, who substitutes for the followers' ego ideal, the inspirational leader provides symbols for it. Inspirational leaders help followers feel more powerful by setting forth desirable goals and providing the means to achieve them (McClelland, 1975). Also, inspiring leaders may serve well as spokespersons or representatives of their group. Winter (1967) showed business students a film of President John F. Kennedy presenting his inaugural address. The stories that the students were asked to write after seeing the film were contrasted with those written by other students who saw a film about modern architecture. Kennedy inspired an uplifting of spirit and an elevation in the students' sense of power, not the usual responses to charisma—obedience, loyalty, and submission.

Charismatic leaders are more likely than inspirational leaders to be regarded with awe and a sense of mystery, and to be considered infallible. But Tepper and Percy (1994) factored a 24-item version of the MLQ and concluded along with Bass (1985a) that charisma and inspirational leadership form a single construct. A serious problem in meaning for the followers creates the possibility that an inspirational leader will emerge.

Although conceptual distinctions between charismatic and inspirational leadership can be made, they may be difficult to establish empirically. In military and industrial surveys of subordinates' descriptions of their superiors on questionnaires, Bass (1985a) was unable to obtain a consistent inspirational factor that was separate from a factor of charismatic leadership. According to Fromm (1941, p. 65), the charismatic leader not only embodies a more extreme and clearly defined personality for those who identify with him but is able to "arrive at a clearer . . . outspoken formulation of . . . ideas for which his followers are already prepared psychologically."

In reality, charismatic leaders tend to be highly inspirational, although inspirational leaders may not be charismatic. Inspirational leaders who are effective would be *outstanding* leaders as defined by House (1999) and Fromm (1941, p. 65). In contrast to typical leaders, outstanding leaders can articulate the mission of their followers, have the capacity to act efficiently, have conceptual and analytic skills, and are self-confident (Nygren & Ukeritis, 1993).

Behavior of Inspirational Leaders

As with charismatic leaders, the behavior of an inspirational leader may be perceived as inspirational by one person and as hokum by another. What is challenging for one follower is easy and dull for another. The inspirational leader needs to have insight into what will be challenging to followers, and why. Inspirational leaders set challenging objectives; align followers with a sense of mission; use symbols and images cleverly to get ideas across; mold followers' expectations; provide meaning for proposed actions; point out reasons why followers will succeed; remain calm in crises; appeal to feelings; call for meaningful action; emphasize beating the competition and cooperating with collaborators; envision an attractive, attainable future; and articulate how to achieve that future. They provide and manage meanings, build confidence in followers, encourage sharing of goals, instill pride, take calculated risks, and are positive. They focus on "the bright side of things" (Avolio & Bass, 1991). Inspirational leaders in a situation requiring teamwork and cohesion selectively try to arouse followers' need for affiliation; in a situation requiring followers to persuade others, the leaders try to arouse the power motive in their followers (House & Podsakoff, 1994).

Inspirational leader express goals that their followers want to attain (McClelland, 1975). But the leaders need to express vivid goals that strengthen and uplift the followers (DeCharms, 1968). Such leaders "conceive and articulate goals that lift people out of their petty preoccupations, carry them above the conflicts that tear a society apart, and unite them in the pursuit of objectives worthy of their best efforts" (Gardner, 1965b, p. 98). According to Yukl and Van Fleet (1982, p. 90), inspirational leadership "stimulates enthusiasm among subordinates for the work of the group and says things to build their confidence in their ability to successfully perform assignments and attain group objectives." Inspirational leaders encourage followers' self-expression and enhance their self-efficacy with positive feedback and expressed expectations about their performance. Group efficacy is also encouraged in the same way.

Inspirational leadership was mentioned frequently in 1,511 critical incidents collected by Yukl and Van Fleet about the behavior of effective leaders in the ROTC, and in 129 such incidents about U.S. Air Force officers during the Korean War. The inspirational behavior of leaders included instilling pride in individuals and units, using pep talks, setting examples of what is expected with their own behavior, and building confidence and enthusiasm. In these critical incidents, inspirational leadership behavior correlated with objective measures of effectiveness as a leader.

High levels of activity, coupled with strong self-confidence, determination, ego ideals and a sense of mission, were seen to lie behind the inspiring success of CEOs in turning around their organizations. Peters (1980) reported on 20 companies that had "executed major shifts in directions with notable skill and efficiency.

Their CEOs chose a single theme and almost unfailingly . . . never miss[ed] an opportunity to hammer it home." They consistently supported the theme, usually over a period of years. In this way, they orchestrated a shift of attention throughout management. According to 413 management students, a good president of the United States exhibits the same kinds of inspirational qualities as a good CEO. Such good leaders share high levels of energy, active involvement, and articulateness (Butterfield & Powell, 1985). Similarly, Fahey and Harris (1987) reported on the inspirational aspects of effective leadership in the U.S. Navy. Nearly 30 naval commands were nominated for their excellence by 300 naval officers. A total of 600 interviews were then held with the officers and enlisted personnel. Among other things, the leaders of these excellent commands were described as "passionate about their mission," and the message they gave to their commands was that everyone could be a winner. High standards were to be maintained. Like the CEOs, they had points of focus such as safety and cleanliness when they made face-to-face contact throughout their commands.

Vaill (1978, p.110) found that members in high-performing systems could relate "peak experiences in connection with their participation. They were enthused and communicated joy and exultation." When elated by inspiring leaders, euphoric subordinates would accept increased risks.

> [Familiar are] . . . the stirring preachers of evangelism, the lectern-pounding political orators, and the rousing after-dinner speakers. . . . Much of this arousal has been institutionalized in anonymous media messages. Social and political movements . . . depend heavily on transforming a passive, inactive constituency into an aroused, excited, active one. (Bass, 1985a, p. 66)

Listening to audiotaped inspirational speeches, such as Winston Churchill's speech about Dunkirk, Thomas Jefferson's first inaugural address, and Henry V's St. Crispin's Day speech at Agincourt in Shakespeare's play, generated more activation among subjects (according to their responses to an adjective checklist and their urinary epinephrine level—a physiological indicator of activation) than did listening to audiotaped travel lectures. However, the inspirational speeches also increased the subjects' need for power, which was reflected subsequently in their stories on the Thematic Apperception Test, or TAT (Steele, 1973, 1977; Stewart & Winter, 1976).

Inspiring leaders have the ability to influence subordinates to exert themselves beyond their own expectations and self-interests. That extra effort is inspired by the persuasive appeal of the leaders' language, symbols, images, and vision of a better state of affairs. It is stimulated by the subordinates' perceptions that they and the leader have common purposes. It is reinforced by various ritualistic institutional practices and by peer pressure.

As Conger (1991) noted, the vision has to be framed in words that amplify values, beliefs, and the importance of the mission. Would-be inspiring leaders have to communicate the vision powerfully. They must use rhetoric that can energize through the words chosen. They use metaphors, analogies, and stories to convey the message. Alliteration, cadence, and repetition strengthen what is sensed. The main overlapping components of inspirational leadership behavior can be seen to include managing meaning, molding followers' expectations, envisioning, and intellectually stimulating followers.

The Management of Meaning

Den Hartog (1997) suggested that inspirational leadership infuses work with values and increases the enthusiasm and commitment of followers by making the work more meaningful. Thus goals are presented in terms of their values. This makes accomplishment of the goals more meaningful to followers. Increased meaningfulness increases their willingness to expend effort to achieve those goals.

Heifetz and Sinder (1987) found a high degree of agreement among several hundred elected, appointed, and career officials at the local, state, and federal levels of the U.S. government, foreign government officials, military officers, and managers in the private sector when these respondents were asked what their constituents expected of them. Many answered that their constituents expected inspiration, hope, consistency, direction, and order. What the leaders felt was most often expected of them was that they would provide their constituents with meaning, security, and solutions to problems. This ability to manage meaning was seen by Smircich and Morgan (1982, p. 261) to be particularly important to a leader:

Leadership works by influencing the relationship between figure and ground, and hence the meaning and definition of the context as a whole. The actions and utterances of leaders guide the attention of those involved in a situation in ways that are conciously or unconsciously designed to shape the meaning of the situation. They . . . draw attention to particular aspects of the overall flow of experience, transforming what may be complex and ambiguous into something more discrete and vested with a specific pattern of meaning. . . . They . . . frame and shape [and "punctuate"] the context of action in such a way that the members of that context are able to use the meaning thus created as a point of reference for their own action and understanding of the situation.

The leader must be able to deal with the equivocalities of many interactive situations and the intepretive schemes of those involved. The leader must then "embody through use of appropriate language, rituals, and other forms of symbolic discourse, the meanings and values conducive to desired modes of organized action" (Smircich & Morgan, 1982, p. 269). Levinson and Rosenthal (1984, p. 284) agreed: "The fundamental communication [by leaders] is that of the meaning of the organization." The meaning is found in the image of the organization, its place in the environment, and its collective purpose.

Inspirational leaders compare their groups with various referents such as: (1) competitors—"we can do better than all of our competitors;" (2) ideals—"we can achieve our best performance;" (3) goals—"we can attain whatever we set our minds to do;" (4) the past—"we can do better than we've done before;" (5) traits—"this is what we should look like;" and (6) stakeholders—"we can make our employees our strongest advocates." New meaning can be provided by unfreezing old interpretations and creating new ones. New languages, new jargons, new lexicons, and new arrangements can be introduced to provide the new meanings (Cameron & Ulrich, 1986). All these efforts of the inspirational leader serve to increase the *frame alignment* of followers and leaders, linking their interpretive orientations (House & Podsakoff, 1994).

Inspirational leadership has also been equated with demagoguery, manipulation, exploitation, and mob psychology, for it tends to involve an emphasis on persuasive appeals and emotional acceptance. Riker's (1986) switching tactics may come into play. Meaning may become convoluted in the leader's efforts to resolve the rhetorical problems facing his or her followers. Simons (1970) listed the ways in which leaders of social movements may resolve rhetorically the problems a social movement has in attracting and maintaining followers, securing the adoption of its program by the larger society, and dealing with resistance from the larger entity. The radical goal images the leaders depict may be crossed with the conservative ways they propose to attain them. Or the leaders may disavow the radical program they seek to achieve to gain a more widespread, diverse following. Insistence on maintaining the movement's values may require abandoning the tactics that would implement its program. Ethics give way to rationalized expediency.

Ideology built on logic gains intellectual respectability, but mass followings may find more meaning in oversimplified, magical beliefs about solutions to problems. Folk arguments, myths, and deceptions replace logical exposition.

Use of Symbols

Inspirational leaders make extensive use of symbols—representations of chunks of information. Symbols are signs that represent sets of cognitions. The cognitions are linked by overlapping functional associations (Eoyang, 1983). But as Tierney (1987) noted, symbols are more than objectifications of meaning. They are strategies for understanding, for making sense, consciously or unconsciously, of the organization or the environment. Leaders justify their existence and actions by their insignia, formalities, stories, ceremonies, conferences, and appurtenances. The symbols mark them as the center of attention and influence (Geertz, 1983). Inspiring leaders select relevant gestures and symbols to convey their message. They also use paradoxical and counterintuitive symbols to communicate their vision for the future (Lipman-Blumen, 1996).

Tierney (1987) collected interview data from 32 college presidents to focus attention on their symbolic purposes and performance. The presidents talked about themselves as metaphors. For example, they said that they provided "the glue so that their organization stuck together." They would give a personal computer to every faculty member as a physical symbol that teaching was going to be changed at the institution. The personal computer could become as much of a physical symbol as the school tie. Presidential concern was symbolized by the practice of walking-around management, knowing every faculty member by his or her first name, or meeting students "on their own turf." Structural innovations, such as the creation of task forces, symbolized the prospect of a new broom for sweeping the organization clean. The president was a personal symbol of the campus when speaking to the community. He or she converted ideas about the institution's values into images that could be symbolized; thus, the diploma mill was changed to the seat of learning.

Symbols provide a greatly simplified message that can have inspirational meaning. For instance, the cross symbolizes Christianity, as well as its emphasis on suffering, sacrifice, and redemption. Gandhi's spinning wheel symbolized Indian self-reliance, the value of cottage industries, the rejection of the British raj, and the demand for India's independence. Confusing, contradictory, or ill-understood ideas can be made into a coherent whole through symbols. Inspirational leaders substitute symbols, as well as slogans and simple images, for complex ideas. The metaphor of a row of falling dominoes substituted for the complexities of the Cold War. The slogan "Never again!" conveys 2,000 years of Jewish history, the Holocaust, and the rebirth of Israel. "Inshallah" conveys the Muslim's fatalistic submission to God's will. The conservative dress code for IBM employees, instituted by Thomas J. Watson, Sr., was intended to impress customers and employees alike. The code symbolized dedication to service, uniformly high quality, and seriousness of purpose. Social and organizational realities are created from such codes and symbols (Stech, 1983).

The replacement of old symbols by new ones helps people recall new ideas and beliefs with new emotional values. For example, the Iranian revolutionaries who marched with flowers sticking out of their rifle barrels to signify a new era of peace and brotherhood marched again against Iraq with headbands to signify their readiness for martyrdom and war to the death. Symbols can stand for inspirational solutions to problems. In communist societies, the hammer and sickle signify the worker and peasant. The 50 stars and 13 stripes in the American flag signal the federation of the original 13 sovereign states and the current 50 states. Inspirational leaders use symbols to draw attention to their leadership. The "crowns and coronations, limousines and ideas come together with leading institutions. The important events within the arena are seen by followers as what "translates intentions into reality" (Bennis, 1982, p. 56).

Management of Information

Impression management is aided by the fact that people are willing to draw inferences about the personal characteristics of others with only limited information (Schneider, Hastorf, & Ellsworth, 1979) about their physical appearance, expectations from the role or status, or expressive behavior, such as facial expressions (Goffman, 1959) and vocal intensity (Allport & Vernon, 1933).

Television has both helped and complicated the building and maintenance of images. Thus a short presidential candidate may have to avoid being seen with a tall opponent in a television debate, and may arrange to stand on a higher platform to make his height equal to that of taller candidates. The brevity and selective editing capabilities of television can be used to protect the leader's image, but the live camera is also a force for bringing reality into the living room. Events that are favorable to the person's image can be staged, but events that are unfavorable to the image can also dramatically show up, as if the leader were face-to-face with supporters. Impression management is effective up to a point; it then can backfire or have a boomerang effect (Jones & Wortman, 1973). According to a field survey of direct observations by Gardner and Martinko (1988), high school principals who flattered people more often were less adequate in their performance than were those who talked more about the organization.

Gardner and Martinko agreed with Schneider (1981) that the management of impressions is achieved through "the manipulation of information about the self by the actor," but it also can be achieved by manipulating information about the organization that the impression manager leads. The presentation can be verbal, nonverbal, or in the form of artifactual displays such as dress and office decor. The preferred targets of the principals' verbal presentations about themselves were their superiors. The principals were more apologetic to familiar than to unfamiliar listeners, and used descriptions of their organiza-

tions and of themselves more frequently in dyadic than in group settings and in interactions with those outside their organization than those inside it.

The annual reports of CEOs to stockholders are often efforts to impress the stockholders with the quality of the firms' performance and future. Salancik and Meindl (1984) examined the annual reports of 18 U.S. corporations over an 18-year period and concluded that those CEOs whose firms operated in unstable environments and who therefore lacked real control over the organization's annual focus emphasized how much they were in control over organizational outcomes. For instance, they announced executive changes to imply that management was dealing with the organization's unstable environment. But these impressional explanations had a positive impact on the future performance of the firms that used these tactics. A similar effect was achieved by a bogus professor who delivered a nonsensical lecture on the application of mathematical game theory to the education of physicians. The bogus professor (a trained actor) was introduced to his audience as having degrees and publications (all of which were phony). The lecture consisted of double-talk, contradictory statements, seductive gestures, humor, and meaningless references to unrelated topics. The "professor" earned high ratings from the 55 students, none of whom detected the hoax. However, when videotapes of a similarly seductive lecture included valid content, students actually learned more of the content from the seductive lecturer (Scully, 1973).

Kerman and Hadley (1986) described in detail how the images of political candidates are created by media consultants. The consultants begin with analyses of the current image. For example, Jay Rockefeller, a West Virginia gubernatorial candidate in 1980, began as an individual whom the public saw as unforceful, ineffective, and a stranger—neither as a leader nor a friend. As a member of the Rockefeller family, he was judged to be cold, elitist, uncaring, and manipulative. The media consultants carefully planned what Rockefeller would say, how he would say it, and when. They determined the exact language and terminology he would use in his speeches, press releases, and television commercials; the specific issues and subject matter that he would communicate to the voters; and his physical appearance, including his haircut and style of clothing. At the end of the campaign, the image of Jay Rockefeller was that of a casual, down-to-earth, warm, open, and friendly person. Even as a member of the Rockefeller family, he was not seen as powerful, forceful, effective, or influential. A Democrat, he won the election decisively, despite the Republican landslide everywhere else, in the wake of President Reagan's election in 1980.

Much of the successful political career of George W. Bush, twice elected governor of Texas and twice elected U.S. president, was attributable to the astute media manipulations directed by his advisor Karl Rove.

Molding Followers' Expectations

Livingston (1969) called attention to the effects in management of interpersonal expectancies. According to Edwards (1973), the most effective supervisors are those who can create high expectations for performance for subordinates to fulfill. Less effective supervisors fail to develop such expectations. And the more ambiguous the criteria for evaluating the group's performance, the greater is the leader's influence in defining expectations about the situation. Arvey and Neel (1974) showed that the performance level of 130 engineers was a function of their expectation that their effective performance of their jobs would be rewarded and that their supervisor was concerned about their performance. Likert (1961a) also emphasized the importance for superiors to communicate their high expectations to their subordinates.

As molders of expectations, inspirational leaders can redirect their organizations with clear agendas of what needs to be done. They know enough not to be satisfied with easy cures or apparent panaceas. They also are able to avoid letting their enthusiasm trap them into creating unreasonable expectations in their subordinates and uninvited acceptance of their ideas (Tichy & Devanna, 1986). Harold Geneen, the former CEO who built IT&T, saw himself as setting high expectations in a number of ways. He considered himself a leader who established hard, challenging goals for the organization and who served as a model of hard work and long working hours for his subordinates (Geneen & Moscow, 1984). Kanter (1983) reported on 200 "change-masters" (leaders who successfully changed their groups). They led their teams to expect to share in the credit for the results of the changes. After the changes, they continued to inspire, encourage, and stimulate the teams who worked with them.

Closely allied to the preceding expectation setting is Vaill's (1982) concept of *purposing*, a continuous stream of actions by inspiring leaders in complex organizations that induces clarity, consensus, and commitment regarding the organization's basic purposes. Leaders of a high-performing system define and maintain a sense of purpose among all members of the system. Purposing is seen when the members can develop and express deep feelings about the system, its aims, its people, its history, and its future, and therefore can focus on the issues and variables in the system that make a difference in its performance.

Enabling and Empowering. Followers' expectations about what they may accomplish can be increased if their leader obtains or shows them how to obtain the resources that will enable them to reach their higher goals. Or the leader may reduce or remove constraints or show the followers how to do so. For instance, the leader can focus attention on the technical, political, and cultural resistance to change and can work with followers to overcome such resistance. Threats can be turned into opportunities. The expectations of followers can also be raised by the leader's nonverbal behavior toward them. When in discussion with followers, leaders can avoid keeping the followers waiting, avoid using furniture as a barrier, make frequent direct eye contact, sit or stand close, nod their head rather than tilt it backward when the follower is speaking, smile frequently, and avoid sounding bored and uninterested (Baird & Weiting, 1979).

Followers can be empowered by increasing their autonomy and discretionary opportunities and getting support from higher authority for their efforts. Leaders can arrange for key employees and higher authorities to signal their public commitment to new goals. Encouragement and involvement can be stressed at all levels. Structure and systems can be modified to enable and empower subordinates to stretch to achieve greater accomplishments (Cameron & Ulrich, 1986).

Leaders can promote enabling by stressing that everyone can be a winner through constant learning and improvement. Risks can be taken, and mistakes can be tolerated. Performance can be steadily improved by incremental demands on subordinates. For starters, a half-mile run can be achieved by everyone. Then a mile run can be accomplished. Ultimately, everyone can run seven or eight miles (Harris, 1987). Enabling and encouraging others to act, and showing the way, requires inspiring a shared vision (Kouzes & Posner, 1987).

The Pygmalion and Galatea Effects. The Cyprian king Pygmalion fell in love with the beautiful statue he had carved. Aphrodite turned the statue into a real woman, Galatea. Pygmalion's fantasy about Galatea became a living reality.

The Pygmalion and Galatea effects have been seen at school and work. What teachers expect of their pupils and what managers expect of their subordinates influences the pupils' and subordinates' performance and progress. In turn, pupils and subordinates tend to do what they believe is expected of them (Livingstone, 1969). These effects were first demonstrated in experiments by Rosenthal and Jacobson (1968) in relation to schoolteachers' expectations about their pupils and their pupils' intellectual gain in test scores over a period of eight months. King (1971) showed that, compared with controls, employees fictitiously identified to their supervisors as of high aptitude achieved higher appraisals, higher retention and peer ratings, and lower absenteeism. Chapman and McCaulley (1993) looked for the Pygmalion and Galatea effects in a large-scale study with unobtrusive measures and without needing any interventions or manipulation. For 3,234 students, they found that those who received National Science Foundation fellowships, compared with those who did not receive them, were much more likely to graduate four or more years later. Both their own and their professors' expectations were raised. An uncontrolled factor was how the NSF award provided financial freedom and greater access to departmental support.

McNatt (1997) conducted a meta-analysis of 19 studies with 7,542 subjects in management or organizational settings supporting Pygmalion effects, which accounted for 2% to 6% of the differences in outcomes. In 11 military studies, the Pygmalion effect accounted for 5% of the differences between experimental and control groups. In eight nonmilitary studies, the comparable figure was 2%. Eden (1988b) suggested that the mediating variable is self-efficacy. Positive expectations increase self-efficacy, which leads to improvement.

Rosenthal (1994) noted that by 1994, 464 experiments had been completed examining Pygmalion effects. The interpersonal expectancy effects have been found influential when experimental treatments have been compared with controls in many other diverse settings. Subjects included judges who believed the defendant was guilty when they instructed juries, and for nursing home caregivers ameliorating depression in patients.

Groups can increase their effectiveness by harnessing the Pygmalion and Galatea effects (Eden, 1984). Leaders who have confidence in their subordinates set difficult goals and arouse the subordinates' expectations about achieving these goals (Eden, 1988). Doing so encourages the self-fulfilling prophecy among the subordinates that they will succeed and, as a consequence, actually increases the likelihood that they will attain the goals (Livingstone, 1969). Eden and Shani (1982) found that the performance of leadership trainees in a field experiment in the Israeli Defense Forces was improved by building up their instructors' positive expectations about them. The 105 trainees were assigned at random to one of three conditions: high, regular, or unknown "command potential." The instructors and assistants were led to believe that each trainee had one of the three levels of command potential. The *expectancy induction* accounted for 73% of the variance in the trainees' objective achievement scores. Similar effects occurred for the trainees' attitudes. Those in the "high-potential" condition reported greater satisfaction with the course and more motivation to go on to the next course The instructors' expectations about the performance of the trainees appeared to transfer to the trainees' self-expectations. This is the Galatea effect When 20 sales supervisors of 259 salaried sales employees were told which of their employees were supposedly "exceptional" (actually a random designation), the Pygmalion effect emerged in the employees' sales performance over the next three months as well as in higher evaluations of their performance and in higher self-expectations (Sutton & Woodman, 1989). Atwater (1988) showed that supervisors' social and supportive leadership behaviors were correlated .48 and .38, respectively, with what the supervisors felt their bosses expected of them. Eden (1988a) suggested that Pygmalion induction can be used with supervisors of new hires, as was done for an assembling and packaging unit in an Israeli production plant. The plant manager told the production manager that he had personally selected the new hires, and that they were all excellent workers who should give the supervisor no problems and should attain standard production levels quickly. Actually, these workers were chosen at random, as were the workers in the control group. The experimental group reached standard production before the controls and went on to exceed it.

To test the Galatea effect, Eden and Ravid (1982) had a psychologist inform trainees in advance that they had "high, regular, or unknown" command potential. Then the psychologist withdrew. Instructors were not preconditioned. Trainees who were given the most positive messages about their "command potential" did better. Ignoring the sex differences, Eden (1984) concluded, as had Locke, Latham, Saari, et al. (1981), that managers need to be shown the utility of encouraging their subordinates with hard goals and high expectations.

Findings were only modest for seven field training experiments by Eden, Geller, Gerwitz, et al. (2000). Managers were trained in the "Pygmalion leadership style" to convey high performance expectations to subordinates, create a supportive climate, and attribute subordinate success to stable internal causes. The mean effect size with 61 effects of the training for leaders and followers was only .13.

Some of the earlier Pygmalion results were questioned because of inadequate methods. For instance, expectancy manipulations were weak and unchecked. Other results were found to be due mainly to moderator variables, as when only those of low achievement were influenced and nonverbal effects were uncontrolled (McNatt, 1997). Rosenthal (1974) observed that teachers of high-expectancy children provided a more supportive climate, harder materials to be learned, verbal and nonverbal cues, more time, and more feedback.

Metharme Effect. Metharme was Pygmalion and Galatea's daughter, the result of a self-fulfilling prophesy. Field (1989) proposed that leaders' prophesies could be self-fulfilling or self-defeating, depending upon the leader's optimism or pessimism about the follower and the follower's positive or negative reactions to the leader. If the leader's prophesy was optimistic and the follower reacted positively, the Pygmalion effect would emerge. But if the leader was pessimistic and the follower was *counterdependent*, a positive outcome was also possible. The prophesy could also be self-defeating despite the leader's optimism if the follower reacted negatively and the anticipated outcome was suppressed. If the leader was pessimistic and the follower negative, outcome failure would be confirmed by the prophecy.

Golem Effect. The golem was a legendary automaton—an inadequate person created by a cabalist rabbi. The leaders of inadequate persons, known underachievers, expect less of them, and the underachievers perform accordingly. However, greater effects for improvement can occur with underachievers than others if there are upper limits of performance and if the leaders' and underachievers' expectations are raised. This golem effect was demonstrated by Babad, Inbar, and Rosenthal (1982). In McNatt's (2000) meta-analysis for 1106 cases from eight studies, the golem effect accounted for 15% of the differences between experimental treatments and controls.

Female trainers of 20 squads totaling 225 soldiers in a special program for disadvantaged 18-year-old women (with limited schooling and substandard or borderline qualifications, from disadvantaged families, and of low socioeconomic status) who enlisted in the Israeli Defense Force were divided into an experimental group and a control group. Davidson and Eden (1997) observed the golem effect in the 10 squads who served as the control group. The low outcomes achieved by the controls were explained by the trainers' low expectations of the special program recruits. But the squad trainers who were led to believe that the underprivileged women had high potential avoided the golem effect. The trainers' expectations were much higher and the trainees' expectations, motivation, and performance were significantly higher than those of the controls.

Impression Management

Self-presentation is a natural part of social interaction (Goffman, 1959). Impression management involves what we do in social interactions to create and maintain desired impressions of ourselves in others (Schlenker, 1980). It is the attempt to control the image others have of us (Rosenfeld, Giacalone, & Riordan, 1995). It may be an honest self-presentation or it may be deceptive (Gardner & Avolio, 1997). Such impressions will affect how much we are esteemed by others and, therefore, how much we can be successful in influencing them.

Wayne and Ferris (1988) arranged for 96 undergraduates to serve, in turn, as the supervisor of a confederate of the experimenters. The confederate acted as a subordinate in a simulated work setting in which mail orders were processed for a catalog firm. Compared with a control, the supposed subordinate impressed each of the 96 student subjects with self-enhancing communications, flattery, conformity, and doing favors for the supervisor. The subordinate's use of impression management substantially increased the supervisor's liking and appraised performance of the subordinate, as well as satisfaction with the exchange relationship. The same kind of impression management by bank employees was reported in a survey of how much these subordinates reported they praised their supervisor and did personal favors for him or her. According to the 23 supervisors of the 84 bank employees, those employees who practiced impression management were better liked by the supervisors. Being better liked, in turn, resulted in higher performance appraisals for the subordinates and more satisfying exchange relations. Impression management may also involve creating and maintaining desired impressions about organizations to promote the loyalty and commitment of others to the organizations.

The ability to impress others is affected by physical distance, demographic dissimilarity, and reduced network centrality. Barness, Diekmann, and Seidel (2002) obtained results indicating that—contrary to their expectations—among 98 subordinates and their 29 supervisors, the more the pairs of subordinates and supervisors worked in different physical locations as members of an Internet firm, the more the subordinates used impression management in their communications. If subordinates differed in age, they were less likely to try to ingratiate themselves with their supervisors; but if subordinates differed in sex, they were more likely to try to impress their supervisors. These relationships were affected by the familiarity of the subordinates with the other members of the firm.

Although some of the political leaders Willner (1968) studied were primarily men of action and not of a scholarly bent, Willner wrote of "their capacity to project the image of unusual mental attainments." These leaders could seize on information and ideas from many sources and, with their excellent memory, they would convey the impression of possessing a powerful mind and a wide range of knowledge. Franklin Delano Roosevelt and Ben-

ito Mussolini, for instance, used their prodigious memories to impress listeners. Horatio Nelson was a master of impression management and "took care to foster his own legend." He arranged for his after-action dispatches to be leaked immediately to the press and for his image to appear on souvenirs. At the same time, Nelson was extremely competent, and developed new strategies that were employed by the British Navy for a hundred years following his death at the Battle of Trafalgar in 1805. He reinforced the confidence of the fleet's personnel when he signaled his fleet that "England expects every man to do his duty" (Adair, 1989).

It is a leader's *perceived* competence that determines whether his or her attempts to influence will be accepted by followers. Impression management is an important requirement for building followers' confidence in leaders (Adams & Yoder, 1985). To some degree, one's success as an inspiring (as well as charismatic) leader may be due to how one presents oneself to the other members of the group (Goffman, 1959). For example, if would-be leaders give the impression that they have had previous experience (even if they have not) with the group's task, their views are more likely to be accepted. Of course, they have to be credible. In the same way, by paying attention to their own dress and speech, by an appropriate amount of name-dropping, by being seen with the "right" people, and so on, leaders can raise their esteem in the eyes of their fellow members, which will contribute to their followers' confidence in them. Political leaders, in contrast to statesmen, stand or fall at election time on how well they and their staffs manage the public's impressions of them. For example, President Gerald Ford actually was successful in bringing inflation down and reducing unemployment. However, he failed to win a full term in office after his appointment to a first term following Nixon's resignation. This was partly because he lacked communication skills, and the voting majority in 1976 perceived him to be the cause of a recession he actually had inherited (Sloan, 1984).

The president's wife is another illustration of the management of impressions. Her loyalty, discipline, and circumspection are all dramatically, and continually, presented to the public. (Caesar's wife must be above reproach.) The wife's visible presence alongside the president in rituals of public leadership assures the viewer symbolically of the morality and trustworthiness of the president (J. B. Gillespie, 1980). The damage done to Bill Clinton's popularity by his sexual peccadilloes was offset to a considerable degree by his wife, Hillary Rodham Clinton, who continued to stand by him. Such damage control to protect the public impression of political leaders is often the work of "spinmasters" who quickly offer alternative explanations for the leader's misbehaviors.

Gardner and Avolio (1997) note that just as leaders may want to impress followers, so followers may want to impress their leaders. Leaders more often use tactics such as exemplification and self-promotion; followers use ingratiation and supplication more often (Jones & Pittman, 1982). Exemplification was most frequently used by charismatic world leaders, according to a biographical study of them (Gardner & Cleavenger, 1996). Gardiner and Martinko (1988) suggested that followers were most likely to use ingratiation. Ronald Reagan exemplified traditional American values; Nelson Mandela exemplified the victim of oppression who could forgive and forget.

Leaders often engage in self-promotion so that followers can attribute to them expertise, esteem, and power. In turn, leaders seek to project their power as well as to be seen by followers as influential, innovative, and unconventional. Followers may cue leaders about their uncomfortable uncertainty about a situation; leaders may respond by impressing followers with their knowledge about how to handle the situation and their self-confidence in doing so. But such self-promotion may be overdone, and the leaders' attributed good qualities may be diminished. Charismatic leaders are particularly skillful in deflecting threats to their reputation. Ronald Reagan was labeled the Teflon president because numerous scandals in his administration could not stick to him (Gardner & Avolio, 1997).

Leary and Kowalski (1990) conceived of two separate processes to describe impression management: the motivation to impress others and the impression the leader (or follower) tries to construct. The motivation depends on the goals sought by impressing others, the value of the outcomes sought, and the discrepancy between current and desired impressions held by others. The construction of the image depends on the leader's (or follower's) self-concept, the desired images of their identity, role constraints, the others' values, and their current social image. Indirect managing of impressions was connected by An-

drews and Kacmar (2001) with factored scales of boasting, blurring, blaring, and burying. Bratton, Carlson, Witt, et al. (2003) reported that impression management influenced performance appraisals in highly political environments, but not in nonpolitical environments.

Nguyen and McDaniel (2001) conducted a meta-analysis of the impact of various tactics used to impress others. They accumulated 20 studies in work settings in which they found, for 220 to 3,870 employees, mean correlations between the effects of impressing others and various outcomes. Interviewers were most affected by job applicants' impression management ($r = .50$). The use of ingratiation by applicants correlated .43 and the use of self-promotion correlated .59, on average with interviewer ratings. Being liked by peers and appraisals of promotability were unaffected. Modest effects were found for employees being liked by supervisors ($r = .29$) and performance appraisals from their supervisors ($r = .22$). When various tactics used to impress others were combined for 19 correlations and 2,072 employees, a mean corrected effect of .22 was obtained. With 18 available correlations for 918 employees, a mean corrected effect of the use by subordinates of ingratiation on their supervisors' performance appraisals of them was .27.

Image Building. Impression management reaches its peak in image building. This was seen by House (1997) as an important behavior of the charismatic leader. Gardner and Avolio (1997) also regarded image building as critical to charismatic leaders to build and maintain their reputation in the eyes of their followers. When contact with political leaders is mainly through interviews on television and the leader's image is systematically modified to suit the feedback obtained from public opinion polls, the voting public responds to the image created for that purpose. The 1988 Bush-Dukakis presidential election campaign clearly showed the manufacturing of images of leadership that were unrelated to reality. George H. W. Bush, the conservative "wimp," was converted overnight into the strong, decisive, patriotic, religious, forceful law-and-order candidate, who stood for mainstream American values of family, patriotism, and support of education and the environment. Michael Dukakis, the low-key pragmatist, was converted into a liberal ideologue by the same myth makers. Dukakis was pictured as a "card-carrying" member of the American

Civil Liberties Union who furloughed murderers to repeat their crimes, would take away citizens' rights to own guns, and opposed the recital of the Pledge of Allegiance in public schools. Continued polling and the election itself reflected the extent to which voters chose one image over the other, rather than one person over the other.

Envisioning

Envisioning a desired future state and showing followers how to get to it are basic components of the inspirational process. They require not only technical competence but artistry and creativity. Despite the thoroughness of the data and the complexities of the problem, the capable inspiring leader can reduce matters to a few key issues before asking others to consider what is to be done. Doing so does not necessarily mean advocating simple solutions; rather, it means that complex problems are organized into a few central themes for examination (Tichy & Devanna, 1986). Envisioning is particularly important when the group or organization is facing ill-structured problems (Mitroff, 1978). Planful opportunism in leaders "can turn unpredictable events into building blocks of change" (Tichy & Devanna, 1986, p. 94). Inspiring leaders look ahead optimistically despite the current uncertainties of internal and external threats to, and opportunities for, the organizations. Yet Bruce (1986, p. 20) noted:

> In the minds of CEOs . . . the vision is never clear, only a foggy haze and a multitude of conflicting signals. We see the future darkly, while ignorant armies of experts shout across a smoky field at one another.

Envisioning is the creating of an image of a desired future organizational state that can serve as a guide for interim strategies, decisions, and behavior. It is an important function in the public as well as private sectors (Berger, 1997). It is fundamental to effective executive leadership. Without the ability to define a desired future state, the executive would be "rudderless in a sea of conflicting demands, contradictory data, and environmental uncertainty" (Sashkin, 1986, p. 2). Envisioning integrates what is possible and what can be realized. It provides goals for others to pursue and drives and guides an organization's development (Srivastva, 1983). Bennis and Nanus (1985) concluded, from in-depth interviews with 90 top directors and executives, that envisioning requires translating intentions into realities by communicating the vision to others to gain their support. Envisioning is the basis for empowering others, for providing them with the "social architecture" that will move them toward the envisioned state. It involves paying close attention to those with whom one is communicating, zooming in on the key issues with clarity and a sense of priorities. Risks are accepted, but only after a careful analysis of success or failure. However, it should be noted that envisioning focuses more on success than failure and more on action than on procrastination. Baum, Locke, and Kirkpatrck (1998) used a longitudinal design to collect data from 183 CEO entrepreneurs and selected employees. Structural modeling confirmed that the attributes and contents of visions expressed orally or in writing led directly to future growth in ventures.

Counterintuitive Initiatives. Some leaders, such as Mahatma Gandhi and Mikhail Gorbachev, introduced inspiring ideologies and actions that are the opposite of what was expected. In return for violence against their supporters, Gandhi and Martin Luther King Jr. preached nonviolence. For the 70-year-old, closed, highly structured, authoritarian Soviet society, Mikhail Gorbachev introduced perestroika and glasnost—restructuring and openness—in an effort to reform the system (Lipman-Blumen, 1996). After four decades of continued belligerency between Israel and Egypt, President Anwar Sadat went to Jerusalem to address the Israeli Knesset. The peace treaty that was eventually signed has lasted for almost 30 years. When Nelson Mandela visited the United States and was strongly criticized for his support for opponents of U.S. policy—Yasir Arafat, Fidel Castro, and Muammar al-Qaddafi—he said he welcomed their endorsement of his antiapartheid movement but declined to comment further about them (Greenfield, 1990).

Intellectual Stimulation

I was unable to consistently separate an inspirational from a charismatic leadership factor in factor analyses of U.S. Army officers' MLQ descriptions of their superiors. But I did obtain a separate factor of intellectual stimulation (Bass, 1985a). Hater and Bass (1988) replicated this finding with a sample of industrial managers. Items of this factor included such statements as "Provides reasons to change my way of thinking about problems," "Stresses the use of intelligence to overcome obstacles," and "Makes me think through what is involved before taking actions."

Subordinates in military, industrial, and educational organizations who described their superiors as frequently engaging in intellectual stimulation tended to view the superiors as highly effective and satisfying. Avolio, Bass, and Yammarino (1988) found correlations of .54 and .73 between intellectual stimulation and effectiveness for two samples of managers. Comparable correlations of the relation of the leadership to subordinate satisfaction were .48 and .67. Bass (1985a) and Seltzer and Bass (1987) reported correlations in the same range. As was seen earlier in Table 21.1, Hater and Bass (1988) found positive correlations between superior's evaluations of managers and the extent to which the managers were described as intellectually stimulating. Avolio, Waldman, and Einstein (1988) obtained correlations between the extent to which the supposed presidents of 27 complex business-gaming teams were intellectually stimulating and the teams' market share (.56), debt-to-equity ratio ($-.56$), returns on assets (.46), stock prices (.47), and earnings per share (.37).

Keller (1989) correlated the MLQ intellectual stimulation of 66 R & D project team leaders according to the team members with superiors' evaluations of the teams' effectiveness and the number of patents produced by the teams. Intellectual stimulation of the team leaders correlated .36 with the supervisors' evaluations of the team performance and .25 with patents produced by the teams. The effect was more specifically pinpointed in the case of patents produced when the results were subdivided for the 30 teams engaged in research projects and the 36 teams engaged in developmental projects. Intellectual stimulation of the leaders correlated .57 with patents produced by the research teams but only .01 for those engaged in more routine developmental activities. However, along with the benefits to teams and organizations of intellectually stimulating leadership, elsewhere a cost of intellectual stimulation may have been revealed as well.

Summary and Conclusions

Since its conception by Weber in the early twentieth century, charismatic leadership has undergone considerable development, although until the 1980s there was much commentary but little empirical research about it. Charismatic leaders may be personalized or socialized, due to their positions or personalities, and close or distant. By 2006, charisma had become a frequent topic of empirical research. Two attributes are seen to be essential for the charismatic relationship: charismatic leaders must be persons of strong convictions, determined, self-confident, and emotionally expressive; and their followers must want to identify with the leaders as persons, whether they are or are not in a crisis. Whether charismatic leaders are self-aggrandizing or prosocial, they generate extraordinary performance in the followers. Followers are more susceptible to charismatic leadership in their readiness to identify with it and accept its mystique.

Crises may or may not be the underlying cause for the emergence of charismatic leaders. Generally, charismatic leaders are more effective than noncharismatic leaders, but effectiveness and routinization may or may not automatically follow in their successors.

Inspirational leadership does not necessarily depend on charismatic personal identification processes. Rather, the mutual goals of leaders and followers are identified and encouraged by the leader. Inspirational leadership stems from the management of meaning and impression management. Inspirational leaders build their followers' expectations by envisioning describable futures and articulating how to attain them. Charismatic leadership and inspirational leadership are major components of transformational leadership, discussed in Chapter 22.

Transformational Leadership

A leader is *transactional* when the follower is rewarded with a carrot for meeting agreements and standards or beaten with a stick for failing in what was supposed to be done. If the leader is limited to such behavior, the follower will feel like a jackass (Levinson, 1980b). Leaders must also address the follower's sense of self-worth, one of the things that *transformational* leaders do. Transformational leaders motivate their followers to do more than the followers originally intended and thought possible. The leader sets challenging expectations and achieves higher standards of performance. Transformational leadership looks to higher purposes. Transformational leaders are expected to cope better with adversity (Parry, 2005). Parameshwar (2003) noted that 10 global leaders of social change developed transcendental higher purposes and went beyond the ordinary by: (1) exposing unresolved, disturbing human rights problems; (2) untangling false interpretations of the world; (3) breaking out of conventional solutions; and (4) making use of transcendental metaphors. Many leaders of world religions, such as Jesus, Mohammed, and Buddha, were transforming. They created visions, shaped values, and empowered change (Leighton Ford, 1981). Both transactional and transformational leadership were demonstrated by the Greek leaders of the *Anabasis* (Xenophon, c. 400 B.C.E.) marching the mercenary Greek army safely through 1,000 miles of hostile Persian territory (Humphries, 2002).

Transactional leadership emphasizes the exchange that occurs between a leader and followers. This exchange involves direction from the leader or mutual discussion with the followers about requirements to reach desired objectives. Reaching objectives will appear psychologically or materially rewarding. If not overlooked or forgiven, failure will bring disappointment, excuses, dissatisfaction, and psychological or material punishment. If the transaction occurs and needs of leader and follower are met, and if the leader has the formal or informal power to do so, he or she reinforces the successful performance.

Up to the late 1970s, leadership theory and empirical work were concentrated almost exclusively on the equivalent of transactional leadership. The exceptions were political, sociological, and psychoanalytical discussions of charisma. Today both transformational and transactional leadership have a wide range of applications, ranging from teaching and nursing to police work and personal selling (Jolson, Dubinsky, & Yammarino et al. 1993).

Freud (1922) recognized that leadership was more than a transactional exchange. The leader embodied ideals with which the follower could identify. Bernard (1938) noted in his examination of corporate executives that tangible inducements were less powerful than personal loyalties. Hook's (1943) heroes in history made events as well as waiting for them to happen. Political leaders could be reactionary, conservative, reforming, radical, or revolutionary agents of change (Dvir, 1998).

Transformational leadership was first mentioned, as such, by Downton (1973) as different from transactional leadership. Soon after, House (1977) presented a theory of charismatic leadership with testable hypotheses. But with perspectives from Maslow's needs hierarchy and from writing biographical studies of Presidents Roosevelt and John F. Kennedy, in a book entitled *Leadership*, James MacGregor Burns (1978) opened wide the impetus for research to contrast transformational leadership to transactional leadership as its opposite. This was followed by Bass (1985a), who demonstrated that empirically transformational and transactional leadership were two positively correlated dimensions. Furthermore, transformational added to transactional leadership effects.

Empirical leadership research up to the late 1970s attended mainly to observable, short-term, leader-follower relations in small groups on the micro level of organizations. There was much less empirical research about senior executives and heads of organizations at the macro level or leaders of societies at the meta-level, although much had been written about leadership at the higher levels. In the mid-1970s, the survival of the field of leadership study was seriously questioned. In 1975, a commentator was reported to have quipped, "Once I was active in the leadership field, Then I left it for about 10 years. When I returned, it was if I had been gone only 10 minutes" (Hunt, 1999, p. 130). In 1975, John Miner argued that "the concept of leadership itself has outlived its usefulness" (Hunt & Larson, 1975, p. 200). Some theorists and practitioners thought the concept of leadership might whither away. They suggested that what was attributed to effective leadership could better be explained by social, organizational, and environmental effects (Pfeffer, 1977). Leadership was thought to be a fiction of the imagination, overemphasized in the highly individualistic United States (Hosking & Hunt, 1982). According to Hunt (1999, p. 130),

> the study of charismatic and transformational leadership came in to save the day. . . . [A] major contribution, if not *the* major contribution of transformational and charismatic leadership has been its transformation of the field. This transformation involves a field that had been rigorous, boring and static . . . examining more and more inconsequential questions and providing little added [by] the plethora of published studies.

Transformational leadership represented a seminal shift in the field of leadership (Bass, 1993).

The New Leadership. Bryman (1992) labeled as the "new leadership" the introduction of transformational leadership and related concepts such as charismatic, visionary, inspirational, values-oriented, and change-oriented leadership. House and Aditya (1997) referred to these concepts as *neocharismatic*. The new leadership represents a paradigm shift that moved the field out of its doldrums (Hunt, 1999). Along with reinforcing the importance of transformational leadership, Burns (2003) agreed with Thomas Jefferson about the importance of leadership in the pursuit of happiness. Evidence of the transactional and transformational behavior of leaders in a wide variety of circumstances, political, business, education, family, sports, and law enforcement (Bass & Riggio, 2006) is well documented. Less well known is street-level transformational leadership of social caseworkers with their disabled or welfare clients (Dicke, 2004)

Components of Transformational Leadership

Burns (1978) defined a *transforming* leader as one who: (1) raises the followers' level of consciousness about the importance and value of designated outcomes and ways of reaching them; (2) gets the followers to transcend their own self-interests for the sake of the team, organization, or larger polity; and (3) raises the followers' level of need on Maslow's (1954) hierarchy from lower-level concerns for safety and security to higher-level needs for achievement and self-actualization. Transforming leadership elevates the follower's level of maturity, ideals, and concerns for the well-being of others, the organization, and society. The content of transformational leaders tends to be optimistic (Berson, Shamir, Avolio, et al. (1998). Transforming leaders point to mutual interests with followers. They engage followers closely without using power, using moral leadership. They transform individuals, groups, organizations, and societies. Between 1980 and 1985, Bass (1985a) formulated a multidimensional theory of transformational and transactional leadership and verified it with military and civilians describing their respective leaders. Burns agreed that transformational and transactional leadership were not opposite ends of a single dimension but multidimensional.

Measurement. Seventy senior South African executives (all male, one black) described how one such leader they had known in their careers had influenced them. Their descriptive statements were sorted by 11 graduate students into transformational and transactional. Seventy-three of the 143 statements on which the judges could agree were administered to 104 senior U.S. Army officers (almost all male). The officers were asked to describe their most recent superior, using a five-point scale of frequency, from 0 = the behavior is displayed not at all to 4 = the behavior is displayed frequently, if not always.

A first factor analysis of the 73 items was completed (Bass, 1985c) The factors described the behavior and attitudes of transformational and transactional leaders in three correlated transformational leadership factors:

(1) charisma, (2) intellectual stimulation, and (3) individualized consideration. Later a cluster of three items was identified as inspirational motivation. Also, two transactional factors emerged that reflected positive and negative reinforcement, respectively: (4) contingent reward and (5) management by exception. They were uncorrelated with each other. Subsequently, Bass and Avolio (1990) relabeled the charismatic factor idealized influence because of the popular meaning of charisma in the public mind as being celebrated, flamboyant, exciting, and arousing. It was often a highly publicized creation of media hype. It was also associated pejoratively with Hitler's effects on the German people.

Charismatic Leadership (CH) or Idealized Influence (II)

Charisma was the subject of Chapter 21. As Bass (1985a) and others noted, it could not be separated factorially from inspirational leadership (Hinken & Tracey, 1999). Nevertheless, the charismatic leader is likely to be transformational, but it is possible—although unlikely—to be transformational without being charismatic. A highly intellectually stimulating teacher, for instance, may transform students without their regarding the teacher as charismatic.

Inspirational Motivation (IM)

Although inspirational motivation could not be separated factorially from charisma because of the conceptual differences between charisma and inspiration discussed in the previous chapter, a 10-item scale of inspirational motivation was maintained in the Multifactor Leadership Questionnaire-Form 5X along with the other factor scales (Bass, 1985c).

Intellectual Stimulation (IS)

This is probably the least recognized of the transformational factors. Avolio (1999) pointed out that a majority of managers and employees believe that their intellect is underutilized, yet in the postindustrial world an organization's intellectual capital may be more important than its physical capital. Worldwide, at least 40 idea generation methods are known, but often they remain misun-

derstood and mistrusted by skeptics. Some, using intuitive association, such as brainstorming, are well known; others, involving systematic variation and idea structuring, less so (Geschka, von Reibnitz, & Storvik, undated). It is an intellectually stimulating challenge to persuade a group to use any one of these methods and to teach it how to do so.

Bass (1985a) obtained a factor of intellectual stimulation in U.S. Army officers' MLQ descriptions of their superiors. Many subsequent factor analyses replicated this finding with a variety of samples of military, industrial, and educational managers and leaders (Avolio, Bass, & Dong, 1999; Antonakis, 2000). Items of this factor included such statements as "Provides reasons to change my way of thinking about problems," "Stresses the use of intelligence to overcome obstacles," and "Makes me think through what is involved before taking actions."

Personal Creativity versus the Intellectual Stimulation of Others.

There is a difference between possessing competence, knowledge, skill, ability, aptitude, and intelligence and being able to translate these qualities into action as intellectual inspiration and the stimulation of others. Presidents Jimmy Carter and Herbert Hoover exemplified technically competent leaders who failed to inspire. John F. Kennedy and Franklin Delano Roosevelt are illustrations of presidents who were not as intellectually astute as Carter and Hoover but were far superior in their ability to stimulate others intellectually, to imagine, to articulate, and to gain acceptance of and commitment to their ideas. The proposals and ideas of Daniel Patrick Moynihan, the liberal Democratic senator from New York, were repeatedly ahead of his time. He introduced original and provocative ideas that often stimulated liberal opposition rather than support. His 1965 report suggested that the black family was falling apart and social legislation was needed. He was roundly attacked by blacks and liberals. It was only in the 1980s that adverse black family statistics revealed Moynihan as a visionary. In 1970, he supported a guaranteed annual income for the impoverished. It was shot down by the Welfare Rights Organization with right-wing assistance. Welfare reform had to wait until 1988, when he supported the beginnings of workfare legislation. "No politician is as good as Moynihan at generating good ideas . . . (but not) getting things done" (Lemann, 1990, p. 4).

Intellectual stimulation is much more than a matter of broadcasting good ideas. For instance, in the public sector, Roberts (1988) demonstrated that the intellectual generation of ideas and framing of problems were not enough. Makers of politically innovative policies have to serve as catalysts by: (1) mobilizing and building support for their ideas; (2) circulating their ideas through various media available to them; (3) collaborating with other highly visible and reputable groups and organizations; (4) creating demonstration projects; (5) sponsoring reforms in the legislature; (6) positioning and developing supporters in the government; (7) enlisting champions to introduce their proposed legislation; (8) influencing and creating public interest groups and associations; and (9) monitoring and evaluating the extent to which the legislation that is passed conforms to the policies that were promoted.

What Leaders Do To Be Intellectually Stimulating.

Intellectually stimulating leaders help to make their followers more innovative and creative. They question assumptions, reframe problems, and look at old problems in new ways. Public criticism of followers and their mistakes is avoided. New ideas are sought from followers. They are encouraged to "think out of the box," to address problems, and to consider alternative solutions (Bass, 1998). Intellectually stimulating leaders see themselves as part of an interactive creative process (Brown, 1987). Not bound by current solutions, they create images of other possibilities. Orientations are shifted and awareness of the tensions between visions and realities is increased.

Intellectually stimulating leaders are often empowering (Spreitzer & Janasz, 1998). They move subordinates to focus on some things and ignore others. A pattern is imposed on a flow of events to simplify their complexity and diversity. The real world is made easier to understand (Bailey, 1983). Intellectual stimulation can move subordinates out of their conceptual ruts by reformulating the problem that needs to be solved. Wicker (1985) provided numerous examples of what can be done to move followers to "think out of the box." Ideas can be played with by applying metaphors and similes (e.g., interpersonal attractiveness is like a magnetic field). The scale can be changed (e.g., a sandbar can be likened to a galaxy of stars). The absurd or fantasy can be considered (e.g., suppose water floated on oil). Alternative states can be imag-

ined, such as particles becoming a wave. Nouns can be changed into verbs. The figure and ground can be transposed (e.g., to concentrate on the space around the object instead of the object). Contexts can be enlarged or subdivided. Hidden assumptions can be uncovered (e.g., failures may be due to poor planning, not to lack of ability). Infante and Gordon (1985) noted that it was more satisfying to subordinates if their supervisors argued for their own formulations and refuted other points of view, but it was more dissatisfying if the supervisors attacked subordinates' self-concepts. Unfortunately, some people mistake argumentation for hostility. The former is favored in leaders; the latter is not.

Quinn and Hall (1983) proposed that leaders intellectually stimulate followers in one of four ways: rational, existential, empirical, and ideological. *Rationally oriented leaders* emphasize ability, independence, and hard work. They try to convince colleagues to use logic and reason to deal with the group's or organization's problems. *Existentially oriented leaders* try to move others toward a creative synthesis by first generating various possible solutions in informal interactions with others and their common problems. *Empirically oriented leaders* promote attention to externally generated data and the search for one best answer from a great deal of information. *Idealists* encourage speedy decisions; they foster the use of internally generated intuition. They gather only a minimum amount of data before reaching a conclusion (Quinn & Hall, 1983).

Intellectually stimulating leaders see themselves as part of an interactive creative process (Brown, 1987). Not bound by current solutions, they create images of other possibilities. Orientations are shifted, awareness is increased of the tensions between visions and realities, and experiments are encouraged (Fritz, 1986). Intellectual stimulation contributes to the independence and autonomy of subordinates and prevents *habituated followership*, characterized by the unquestioning trust and obedience of charismatic leader-follower relations (Graham, 1987). Intellectual stimulation is much more than a matter of broadcasting good ideas.

Chaffee (1985) suggested that three strategies are pursued in finding solutions to the organization's problems: linear, adaptive, and interpretive. If *linear* data are gathered and analyzed, alternative actions are formulated with expected outcomes if a particular action is taken. If an *adaptive* strategy is pursued, the effort will be to adjust the organization to environmental threats and opportunities by being particularly cognizant of the revenues and resources needed from the environment. If an *interpretive* strategy is pursued, reality is less important than are perceptions and feelings about it. Values, symbols, emotions, and meanings need to be addressed. Neumann's (1987) interview study of 32 college presidents found that with experience, the presidents tended to move toward more interpretive strategies if they had not initially emphasized them. The shift of experienced presidents away from purely adaptive strategies was most evident.

Military and political planners need to be encouraged to engage in *second-curve thinking*. They need to develop alternative possible scenarios of what is likely to happen after the victory they have planned for. In the same way, planners for organizations need to consider looking at alternative scenarios of how the organization and its environment is likely to be affected by the success of their *first-curve* plans. Royal Dutch Shell executives draw up such possibilities and distribute them widely to keep its executives thinking ahead to avoid being surprised (Handy, 1994). There was insufficient and inadequate second-curve thinking by the U.S. administration about what would happen in Iraq after the initial success of its first-curve plan to bring down Saddam Hussein's regime (Woodward, 2004).

Central versus Peripheral Routing. Intellectual stimulation takes people on what Petty and Cacioppo (1980) conceived of as the *central* route to being persuaded, which occurs when people are ready and able to think about an issue. It may be contrasted to persuasion via the *peripheral* route, which occurs when people lack either motivation or ability. Persuasion through the central route produces enduring effects; persuasion via the peripheral route lasts only if it is bolstered by supportive cognitive arguments. If persuasion is by the peripheral route, it is necessary only for the source of the persuasion to be liked. The distinction between central and peripheral processing has much in common with the distinctions between deep versus shallow processing, controlled versus automatic processing, systematic versus heuristic processing, and thoughtful versus mindless or scripted processing (Cialdini, Petty, & Cacioppo, 1981).

Individualized Consideration (IC)

Individually considerate leaders pay special attention to each follower's needs for achievement and growth. New learning opportunities are created, along with a supportive climate. Individual differences in needs are recognized. The leaders serve as coaches and mentors for their followers. They attend to the individual followers' differential needs for growth and achievement. Followers are helped to reach successively higher levels of development. New learning opportunities are created in a supportive environment. "Walking-around management" is practiced. The individually considerate leader personalizes relations, remembering names and previous conversations. Two-way communication is encouraged. Tasks are delegated to provide experience and to develop followers. The individually considerate leader is an effective listener (Bass, 1998) and more delegative in management style (Gill, 1997).

Bracey, Rosenbaum, Sanford, et al. (1990) stated that leaders need to be caring by telling the truth with compassion, looking for others' loving intentions, disagreeing with others without making them feel wrong, avoiding suspiciousness, and recognizing the qualities in each individual regardless of cultural differences. Greenleaf's (1979) servant leadership heavily emphasizes individualized consideration.

When faced with changed processes making employees redundant or the need to cut costs, individually considerate management restructures the organization responsibly (Cascio, 1995). Whenever possible, employees are retrained and redeployed to avoid layoffs. Merck even arranged for temporary transfers of employees to other firms. Actually, it may be less profitable for firms to downsize to cut costs because of the expense of separations and rehiring when business turns around (McKinley, Sanchez, & Scheck, 1995).

A Combining of Transformational Factors

Although they are conceptually different and form independent clusters of items, the component factors of transformational leadership uncovered by Bass (1985a) are intercorrelated. Sixty-six percent of the covariance of all the items in transformational leadership could be accounted for by the first factor of charismatic leadership

(Bass, 1985c). An even larger amount was accounted for in a comparable sample of U.S. Air Force officers (Colby & Zak, 1988). Hater and Bass (1988) achieved similar results when they refactored the 70-item questionnaire that subordinates completed to describe their immediate management superiors. Onnen (1987) obtained similar findings from 454 parishioners who described their Methodist ministers. A single transformational leadership score can be meaningfully calculated for selected studies and analyses. The antecedents and effects of this transformational score have been compared with the effects of transactional leadership that is composed of the factors of contingent reward and management by exception. The results of extensive surveys of more than 1,500 general managers, leaders of technical teams, government and educational administrators, upper middle managers, and senior U.S. Army officers that were discussed earlier for charismatic leadership are also relevant for transformational leadership. Subordinates of these leaders, who described their managers on the MLQ-Form 5 as being more transformational, were also more likely to say that the organizations they led were highly effective. Such transformational leaders were judged to have better relations with higher-ups and to make more of a contribution to the organization than were those who were described only as transactional. Subordinates said they also exerted a lot of extra effort for such transformational leaders. If leaders were only transactional, the organizations were seen as less effective, particularly if most of the leaders practiced passive, reactive management by exception intervening only when standards were not met.

Components of Transactional Leadership

According to Burns (1978), transactional leadership is the exchange relationship between leader and followers aimed at satisfying their own self-interests. Its factors in Bass (1985c) were contingent reward and management by exception. The latter factor was subsequently divided into active management by exception and part of passive leadership and laissez-faire, the avoidance of leadership, delineated in Chapter 6. Contingent reward and management by exception are ways of looking at *reinforcement leadership*, discussed in Chapter 15. With active management by exception, the leader attends to each fol-

lower's performance and takes corrective action if the follower fails to meet standards. With passive management by exception, the leader waits for problems to arise in the follower's performance before taking corrective action in the belief that "If it ain't broke, don't fix it" (Bass & Avolio, 1990). "The transactional leader closely resembles the traditional definition of the manager" (Kouzes & Posner, 1995, p. 321).

Ten-item scales of transactional leadership were included with MLQ 5-R. High reliabilities (.85 and above) were routinely reported for descriptions of superiors by large samples of subordinates in military and industrial settings (Bass & Avolio, 1989). The 10 items of each scale were reduced to four in a short form (MLQ-5X) with some loss of reliabilities, as expected (Bass & Avolio, 1990).

Contingent Reward (CR)

This is a *constructive* transaction. The leader assigns a task or obtains agreement from the follower on what needs to be done and arranges for psychological or material rewards of followers in exchange for satisfactorily carrying out the assignment (Bass, 1998). For 207 British managers, Gill (1997) found that the managers who were *directive* practiced more contingent rewarding ($r = .24$). The psychological rewards may include positive feedback, praise, and approval. The material rewards may include a raise in salary, an award, or citation for merit.

Originally conceived as a transactional reinforcement, contingent reward correlates more with transformational than with transactional leadership. Explanations were found by Silins (1994) and by Goodwin, Wofford, and Whittington (2001). Contingent reward has two aspects. Silins found that contingent rewarding with external material rewards such as a raise in pay was transactional; contingent rewarding involving internal psychological processes such as praise was transformational. For Goodwin et al., the transactional factor was explicit reward, such as a commendation for good performance; the transformational factor was implicit, such as expressing admiration of the follower for good performance. Goodwin, Wofford, and Whittington (2001) completed a factor analysis of 154 employees describing their supervisors with the MLQ and a confirmation with MLQ data from an additional 209 employees describing their supervisors.

Two CR factors were found and confirmed: explicit contingent rewarding and implicit psychological contracting. Consistent with these findings, higher-order factors unearthed in large sample factor analyses by Avolio & Bass (1999), Antonakis (2001), and others also showed that contingent reward could be both transformational and transactional. CR was transformational when the rewards were psychological, like supervisory recognition and praise for a follower's good work. CR was transactional when the rewards were material, like increased pay.

Management by Exception (MBE)

This is a corrective transaction. If active, the leader monitors the deviances, mistakes, and errors in the performance of the followers and takes corrective action accordingly. If passive, the leader takes no corrective action before a problem comes to his or her attention that indicates unsatisfactory follower performance (Bass, 1998). The corrective action may be negative feedback, reproof, disapproval, or disciplinary action. Denston and Gray (1998) completed both qualitative and quantitative studies of MBE showing that MBE behavior fell into three categories: autocratic (directive), maintaining the status quo, and overregulation. As noted above, Gill also found that the more directive the leaders, the more they practiced MBE. Generally, MBE is lower in reliability than the other MLQ factors.

The Model of the Full Range of Leadership

Transformational and transactional factors were conceived by Avolio and Bass (1991) as continua in leadership activity and effectiveness. Added was laissez-faire or nonleadership to the bottom of the continua in activity and effectiveness. By definition, transformational leadership was more active than transactional leadership, which was more active than laissez-faire leadership. Empirically, transformational leadership was more effective than transactional leadership, which was more effective than nonleadership. Avolio and Bass (1999) used 14 samples involving 3,786 MLQ survey participants describing their leaders to test nine factorial structures to determine the best fitting models. The best fitting models contained six

lower-order factors: charisma (CH + IN), intellectual stimulation (IS), individualized consideration (IC), contingent reward (CR), active management by exception (MBEA), and passive avoidance (PA). Three higher-order factors emerged: transformational leadership and contingent reward, developmental exchange (IC + CR), and corrective avoidance (PA + MBEA). Antonakis (2001) and Antonakis and House (2002) found that the model of the full range of leadership remained valid, although they could point to a variety of moderators that affected results. These included the sex of leaders and followers, the risk and stability of conditions, and the leaders' hierarchical level.

Other Concepts and Methods Relevant to Transformational and Transactional Leadership

Qualitative Approaches

The pattern of factors that Bass (1985c) extracted provided a portrait of the transformational leader that Zaleznik (1977) had independently drawn from clinical evidence. Zaleznik's leaders attracted strong feelings of identity and intense feelings about the leader (charisma). They sent clear messages of purpose and mission (inspirational leadership), generated excitement at work, and heightened expectations through images and meanings (inspirational leadership). They cultivated intensive one-on-one relationships and empathy for individuals (individualized consideration) and were more interested in ideas than in processes (intellectual stimulation). Tichy and Devanna (1986) concluded from interviews with 12 executives that transformational leadership is broader than charisma. They reported that transformational leaders were intuitive, cautious to avoid unrealistic expectations, empowering, and envisioning with clarity. Bennis and Nanus (1985, 1988) interviewed 90 public and private CEOs who said they made special efforts to inspire followers to greater productivity. Their followers said the executives raised their consciousness and provided a radiant but realistic vision of the future.

Marion and Uhl-Bien (2001) introduced *complexity leadership*, that enlarges transformational leadership to include catalyzing organizations from the bottom up through fostering the microdynamics of interaction among ensembles, coordinates the behavior among the ensembles. It allows for random effects and futures dependent on networks, structure, and relationships. It is based on complexity theory, borrowed by the social sciences from the physical sciences (Marion, 1999). Anderson (2000) suggested five leadership skills of increasing complexity needed by leaders to be transformational: (1) personal mastery to provide for clarity of beliefs and purpose of life; (2) interpersonal communications to build interpersonal relationships; (3) counseling on how to manage problems; (4) consulting about team and organizational development; and (5) versatility in styles, roles, and skills.

Quantitative Approaches

Podsakoff, MacKenzie, Moorman, et al. (1990) validated six transformational factors for the Transformational Leadership Inventory (TLI): (1) articulating a vision, (2) providing an appropriate model, (3) fostering the acceptance of group goals, (4) high performance expectations, (5) providing individualized support, and (6) individualized consideration. Podsakoff, MacKenzie, and Bommer (1996) showed that transformational leadership was generally independent of most contextual substitutes for leadership. Alimo-Metcalfe and Alban-Metcalfe (2000) used Kelly's Repertory Grid Technique to elicit constructs from 48 female and 44 male middle, senior, and top managers about the similarities and differences of managers with whom they had worked in the British Health Service or local government. To form constructs, the managers were asked to chose the most and least alike leaders who had "had a powerful effect on their motivation, self-confidence, self-efficacy and performance." The 1,464 responses were factor analyzed to yield reliable factors that generally appeared close to the transformational components of leadership described above: (1) inspirational networker and promoter; (2) encourages critical and strategic thinking; (3) empowers, develops potential; (4) genuine concern for others; (5) accessible, approachable. Other factors described the personality of the transformational leader: (6) decisiveness determination and self-confidence and (7) integrity (trustworthiness, honesty, and openness). Two transactional factors surfaced, one concerned with (8) political sensitivity and skills (in local government) and (9) clarifying bound-

aries. This last factor also included involving others in decisions. The nine factors were formed into the Transformational Leadership Questionnaire (TLQ).

Kouzes and Posner (1987) extracted a profile of transformational leadership from interviews asking leaders to describe their personal best leadership experience. Subsequently, they used the interview information to develop the Leadership Practices Inventory (LPI) for followers to complete. They noted that transformational leaders (1) challenge the process, constantly searching for new opportunities, ready to experiment and take risks, and remaining open to new ideas; (2) inspire a shared vision, articulating direction, ideals, and the special nature of the organization; (3) enable others to act by promoting collaboration and cooperative goals and establishing trust and empowerment; (4) model the way by behavior that is consistent with the vision and instills values supporting the vision; and (5) encourage the heart with high expectations, supporting persistence, rewarding others for success, and celebrating achievements. Carless (1999) administered the LPI and MLQ to 777 subordinates of 695 branch managers in an international bank in Australia. The LPI scales and the MLQ transformational scales were highly correlated.

Yukl (1987) initiated the Managerial Practices Survey (MPS) (Yukl, Wall, & Lepsinger, 1990) by first organizing a taxonomy of leadership and management practices based on factor analyses, expert groups, and prior theory. In the MPS scales that resulted, transformational leadership could be seen conceptually in motivating and inspiring, intellectually stimulating, problem solving, coaching, and supporting and mentoring. Transactional leadership could be seen in recognition, rewards, informing, clarifying roles, and monitoring operations. Tracy and Hinken (1998) found correlations ranging from .67 to .82 between the MLQ components and four selected MPS scales: clarifying roles, inspiring, supporting and team building. House (1997a) substituted value-based for charisma scales. Included were articulation of a vision, communication of high performance expectation, displaying self-confidence, role modeling, showing confidence in and challenging followers, integrity, and intellectual stimulation. Behling and McFillen (1996) developed scales for rating leaders on displaying empathy, dramatizing the mission, and projecting self-assurance to enhance image, to ensure competency and to provide opportunities to experience success. Jackson, Duehr, and Bono (2005) reported on the utility of using a questionnaire to measure empowerment along with a questionnaire to measure transformational leadership to predict performance, job satisfaction, and commitment. Jaussi and Dionne (2004) showed that an assessment of a leader's unconventional behavior (e.g., standing on furniture or hanging ideas on clotheslines) added in regression analysis beyond transformational leadership to the prediction of followers' satisfaction and perceived leader's effectiveness.

The Neocharismatic Leadership Paradigm (NLP)

According to House and Aditya (1997), the theories of NLP include various theories of charismatic leadership (House, 1977; Conger & Kanungo, 1987; Shamir, House, & Arthur, 1993), theories of transformational leadership (Burns, 1978; Bass, 1985a), and visionary theories (Bennis & Nanus, 1985; Sashkin, 1988; Nanus, 1992). House, and Shamir (1993) provided a chart of the behaviors to be found in these theories cited by their authors (Table 22.1)

As currently defined by theorists and empiricists such as House (1999) and House and Shamir (1993), no distinction is made between charismatic and transformational leadership. They prefer to merge the two concepts as charismatic/transformational leadership. They see the same common motivational elements in charisma and transformational leadership (excluding individualized consideration). They connect the merged concept to followers' self-concepts, internalized values, and cherished identities. The concept correlates with increasing collective efficacy and high expectations. Goals and values are linked to a sense of mission and to an ideal vision of a better future. But Bass (1998) argues that although the same leaders tend to be inspirational, intellectually stimulating, and individually considerate as charismatics, it is useful to keep the concepts separate, for they involve different behaviors and development. Although inspirational motivation and charismatic leadership are highly correlated and charismatic leaders are inspirational, inspirational leaders may not necessarily be charismatic: General Omar Bradley is an example. Napoleon and Alexander the Great were charismatic, inspirational, and intellectually stimulating but not particularly individually considerate as they grew in power and success. Hora-

tio Nelson, the British admiral, was a transformational leader in the truest sense. He was charismatic and idealized by the English, he inspired his seamen and officers, and he revolutionized war at sea. He was also individually considerate and tried to meet the needs of his officers and seamen (Adair, 1989).

More rather than less differentiation is needed between charisma and transformational leadership, according to Hunt and Conger (1999). Conger (1999) and Yukl (1999) further discussed the need to maintain the distinction. Beyer (1999) asked how a charismatic leader transformed an organization.

Leader-Member Exchange (LMX)

LMX focuses on the rated quality of the dyadic relationship between superior and subordinate (Graen & Scandura, 1986). Since it can be a motivating exchange between two parties, it was assumed to be transactional (1989). Nevertheless, Graen and Uhl-Bien (1991) examined how quality LMX develops over time. LMX is a transactional exchange early in the process and later may correlate positively with transformational leadership. Tejeda and Scandura (1994) found a positive common correlation between supervisors' transformational leadership and the quality of LMX between supervisors and subordinates in a health care organization. Furthermore, Dansereau (1995) argued that the quality of LMX depended on the leader supporting subordinates' self-worth and showing confidence in the subordinate's integrity, motivation, and ability, as well as being concerned for subordinates' needs. Greenleaf's (1977) servant leadership and Block's (1993) leader as steward come to mind.

Servant Leadership

Smith, Montagno, and Kuzmenko (2004) compared transformational leadership with servant leadership. While transformational leaders share and align their followers' interests, servant leaders put the interests of their followers before their own. Both emphasize personal development and empowerment of the followers. Both facilitate the achievement of followers.

Transformational leadership may be more relevant in a dynamic, changing environment; servant leadership may be more applicable in a stable environment.

Table 22.1 Behaviors Specified in Charismatic, Transformational, and Visionary Theories of Leadership

	Weber, 1947	House, 1977	Burns, 1978	Bass, 1985	Bennis and Nanus, 1985	Conger and Kanungo, 1987	Sashkin, 1988	Shamir et al., 1991
Visionary	X	X	X	X	X	X	X	X
Frame alignment								X
Empowering								
Showing confidence in and respect for followers		X	X	X	X	X	X	X
Setting challenging expectations	X							X
Role modeling								
Setting personal example	X	X		X		X	X	X
Showing self-confidence	X	X		X			X	X
Image building								
Establishing trustworthiness		X				X	X	X
Displaying competence	X	X				X	X	X
Behaving exceptionally	X				X	X	X	X
Taking risks	X					X	X	X
Supporting								
Showing consideration and/or concern				X			X	
Adapting								
Showing versatility							X	
Environmentally sensitive						X	X	
Intellectually stimulating				X				X

Source: Adapted from "Toward the integration of transformational, charismatic, and visionary theories," by R. J. House and B. Shamir, in *Leadership theory and research: Perspectives and directions* (p. 85), by M. M. Chemers and R. Ayman, 1993. San Diego, CA: Academic Press. Copyright 1993 by Academic Press. Reprinted by permission of Academic Press, Inc.

Deming's Quality Improvement

Leadership was an important aspect of W. Edwards Deming's 14 points for Total Quality Management. Sosik and Dionne (1994) selected five of Deming's points for improving quality—change agency, teamwork, trust building, short-term goal eradication, and continuous improvement—and their likely linkage to the Full Range of Leadership. They proposed that in line with Deming, transformational leaders are agents of change, encourage teamwork, promote continuous improvement, build trust, and eradicate short-term goals.

Directive and Participative Leadership

Transformational leaders can be *directive* or *participative*. Charismatic leaders may direct their dependents out of crises; inspirational leaders direct their followers with slogans like "Never again." Intellectually stimulating leaders direct their followers how to think through problems. Individually considerate leaders decide that only some followers need help. Critics see transformational leaders as elitist and autocratic. Nonetheless, charismatic leaders can be participative, for instance, by sharing in the building of visions. Inspirational leaders may listen to their followers before asking for a consensus about simplifying their ideas. Intellectually stimulating leaders may help followers to reexamine their assumptions. Individually considerate leaders may encourage followers to give one another support when they need it (Bass, 1998). After spending 27 years imprisoned by the white South African government, Nelson Mandela was directive and transformational when he declared, "Forget the past," and showed his strong support for reconciliation. Gill (1995) reported a correlation of .29 between inspirational and participative leadership.

In the same way, the transactional leader can be *directive* or *participative*. The directive leader, practicing contingent reward, may decide to reward followers for their good performance. The *directive* leader can practice management by exception by taking disciplinary action for an observed violation of the rules by followers. Gill (1995) found correlations with *directive* leadership of .25 with contingent reward and .20 with management by exception. The *participative* leader may practice contingent reward by asking followers what needs to be done to achieve common goals. The participative leader can practice management by exception by asking how observed mistakes could be corrected. Nelson Mandela was *participative* and transactional when he campaigned for his successor as president and promised voters better housing. Gill (1995) reported a correlation of .35 between *participative* leadership and contingent reward but −.18 with management by exception.

LBDQ Consideration

Individualized consideration, as measured by the MLQ, is empirically correlated .69 with consideration of the Leader Behavior Description Questionnaire, yet they are somewhat distinct in concept (Seltzer & Bass, 1990). Consideration involves the leader's friendliness, approachability, and participative decision making. Individualized consideration involves the leader's concerns for each follower as an individual and with the follower's development. It includes knowing the individual follower's needs, raising followers to higher levels of maturity, delegating opportunities for follower self-actualization, and helping followers to attain higher moral standards. Individually considerate leadership is closely associated with quality orientation and good behavioral relations with individual subordinates, less so with relations with all the subordinates as a group. Leaders high on both scores may be either directive or participative (Bass & Avolio, 1993a).

Connective Leadership and Social Processes of Leadership

Lipman-Blumen (1996) conceived of *connective* leadership as a contrast to *instrumental* leadership. Connective leaders intuitively focus on the interconnections among people, processes, and institutions. They make use of ethical social and political strategies to join their vision with the dreams of others. They strive to overcome mutual problems. They create a sense of community in which diverse groups can be valued members and enjoy a sense of belonging. They bring together others to encourage the assumption of responsibilities by active participants. They nurture potential leaders and successors. They build democratic institutions instead of creating dynasties and oligarchies. They dedicate themselves to

goals beyond their own and demand sacrifices from others only after they have made sacrifices themselves. Connective leaders can also be instrumental. They will try to use others as well as themselves as instruments to achieve their common goals. Readers will recognize similar elements in connective leadership and transformational, charismatic, and servant leadership. Examples of connective leaders are leaders of voluntary organizations who attract dedicated workers by providing opportunities for ennobling action. They combine collaboration, nurturance, and altruism with the use of power and instrumental action. They assemble temporary creative teams of professionals for each new organizational project. They rally multiple short-term political coalitions to address diverse problems. They are dedicated activists, sacrificing careers, well-being, or even their lives for their community (Lipman-Blumen, 1996). Akin to constructive leadership, Parry (2002) validated a scale, Social Processes of Leadership (SPL). SPL was about influence, processes, relationships, interactions, and position in organized society. Parry found the scale highly correlated with various measures of transformational leadership.

A Hierarchy of Leader Effectiveness. Ordinarily, a hierarchy of effectiveness was found. Transformational leadership was more effective than contingent reward; contingent reward was more effective than active management by exception; and active management by exception might be positive or negative in effect on subordinates' performance but was more effective than passive management by exception. Laissez-faire leadership was correlated moderately to highly negatively in effectiveness. Similar results were found for managers, project leaders, and staff professionals in a wide variety of firms and agencies (Bass, 1998) and in many developed and developing countries on five continents (Bass, 1997).

Envisioning

Vision arose as a leadership concept in the 1980s as a response to the need for firms to adapt rapidly to advancing technology and domestic and global competition (Conger, 2000). The concept of vision spread rapidly to nonprofit agencies and had always been of consequence to politicians and statesmen. Sashkin (1986, 1988) detailed and assessed the visionary leader. Vision is a notable correlate of the transformational process (Brown, 1993) and the transformational components of charismatic, inspirational, and intellectually stimulating leadership. As noted in Table 22.1, envisioning is included in most theories of charismatic and transformational leadership. The vision of the charismatic leader has both a stimulating and unifying effect on the follower (Berlew, 1992). Visionary leaders have a sense of identity, direction, and strategy for implementation (Nygren & Ukeritis, 1993). The vision is often a collaborative effort of a leader and colleagues and ties together a variety of issues and problems. To maintain their emotional appeal, it is better for a vision to be presented visually rather than only be posted or in writing (Hughes et al. 1993).

Purposes. Visions are goals that are forward-looking and meaningful to followers. They involve accurately interpreting trends or articulating future-oriented organizational goals. They provide a road map to the future with emotional appeal to followers. They help followers know how they fit into the organization (Bryman, 1992). They evolve in one or more of four ways from: (1) a leader with foresight who is sensitive to emerging opportunities; (2) networks of insightful organizational members; (3) the accidental stumbling onto opportunities and recognizing them; and (4) a process of trial and error with many experiences. They may be value and mission statements. According to Sashkin (1988), the cognitive skills required for envisioning are: expressing and sharing the vision with managers and employees in order to detail, revise, and review policies and programs, and to monitor their effects. Most people can envisage near futures up to one year, but few can think 10 to 20 years ahead, as might be required in a vision of the head of a large firm, political movement, or military organization.

A vision serves as a guide for interim strategies, decisions, and behavior. "Vision provides the direction and sustenance for change . . . and help us navigate through crises" (M. Hunt, 1999, p. 12). It is an important function in the public as well as private sectors (Berger, 1997). It is fundamental to effective executive leadership. Without the ability to define a desired future state, the executive would be "rudderless in a sea of conflicting demands, contradictory data, and environmental uncertainty" (Sashkin, 1986, p. 2). A vision integrates what is possible and what can be realized. It provides goals for others to pursue and drives and guides an organization's development (Srivastva, 1983). Vision is a mental model of a future state of the organization (Nanus, 1992), an ideal image of the future (Kouzes & Posner, 1995). It connects beliefs about what can be done in the future (Thoms & Greenberger, 1995). Mikhail Gorbachev, in the 1980s, envisioned a unified Europe stretching to the Urals. By 2002, a step in this direction had been taken by Russia in accepting a seat as a limited partner in NATO.

Bennis (1982) called attention to the importance of vision to leaders. It was a major contributor to the success of 90 executives interviewed by Bennis and Nanus (1985). Likewise, Martin (1996) found that visionary leadership contributed to followers' supportive attitudes. Envisioning is particularly important when the organization is facing ill-structured problems (Mitroff, 1978). Conger (1999) viewed what distinguished charismatic leaders at higher organizational levels from others as the strategic decisions they formulated and articulated. The more the vision was out of the ordinary, the more it became challenging and a force for change (Conger, 1999). But for Harari (1997), "Vision must be pragmatically bifocal," i.e., expected to encompass both current and future best opportunities. And Bruce (1986, p. 20) noted, "In the minds of CEOs . . . the vision is never clear, only a foggy haze and a multitude of conflicting signals. We see the future darkly, while ignorant armies of experts shout across a smoky field at one another."

Example: J. Robert Oppenheimer. The primary source of the attractiveness of a vision to followers is their perception of the qualities of the leadership (Conger, 2000). This was illustrated by the case of J. Robert Oppenheimer, who in 1943 was appointed director of the newly founded Los Alamos National Laboratory to develop the atom bomb. I. I. Rabi (1969) said that based on his experience and personality, it was difficult to imagine a *less* likely choice. Oppenheimer had no administrative experience other than building the theoretical physics department at Berkeley. He was unknown to the government leaders who initiated and championed the project. He was seen as arrogant and nasty and at times made others feel foolish and inferior. It was expected that the director would be an expert in experimental, not theoretical, physics. Nonetheless, Oppenheimer succeeded brilliantly, first because he had a clear vision of the mission of the laboratory and was able to communicate that vision to organization members at every level, and second, because he was technically brilliant and outstanding in his intellectual stimulation, which helped colleagues think through problems. According to such scientists as Hans Bethe, Joseph Hirschfelder, Emilio Segre, and Edward Teller, he was "a genius in finding other people's mistakes," was a remarkably fast thinker, had an "iron memory," and understood everything that was done in the lab, whether it was chemistry, physics, or machining, and then could coordinate the activities. He supported the vision by creating a laboratory environment of commitment and involvement of several thousand members, making each of them feel that he could contribute to the project. He overcame demands from higher authority for secrecy between laboratory divisions by organizing interdivisional meetings and sharing of problems and progress. Trust in him was high because of his integrity (Ringer, 2002).

Vision Statements. An organization's *mission* statement describes the activities to be performed for its clients, constituents, or customers (Yukl, 1998). It is not the same as vision. The core of a vision for the organization is its mission, but it adds meaning and purpose for the activities, arouses emotions, and is inspirational and intellectually stimulating. The vision should present an optimistic view of the future. It should express complex ideas in simple words and be a clear and credible statement of the future (Bass & Avolio, 1990). The vision should convey an image of what can be achieved, why it is worthwhile, and how it can be done (Yukl, 1998, p. 443). In a workshop for various sectors of a community, Berson, Shamir, Avolio, et al. (2001) sorted the vision statements of 141 participating leaders into 12 categories. They rated the "inspirational strength" of each vision and obtained four orthogonal factors. The first factor, optimism and confidence of the vision, accounted for 53.7% of the variance among the 12 categories. The factors were correlated with the MLQ assessments obtained prior to the workshop from the participants' subordinates back at work. The factor of optimism and confidence correlated significantly .28, with charisma; .20 with inspirational motivation; .21 with intellectual stimulation; .15 with individualized consideration; and .15 with contingent reward. Specificity and direction of the vision correlated

.15 with intellectual stimulation. McClelland and Winter's motive imagery provided reliable and relevant measures of visionary statements. The effects of the statements were related to the expectations of government agency managers and managers in entrepreneural businesses. Their individual and unit performance in the government agencies were significantly affected by affiliative motive imagery. Power motive imagery in the vision statements correlated significantly with venture business growth in sales and profits in entrepreneurial firms (Kirkpatrick, Wofford, & Baum, 2002). Different factors emerged when a total of 672 vision statements were factored for 194 Singaporean respondents into (1) expertise, (2) strategic thinking, and (3) unconventionality (Khatri, Ng, & Lee, 2001).

The organizational culture plays a significant role. Visionary leaders turn their cultural ideals into organizational realities. In the process, they promote a philosophy that will be enacted by the vision's policies and programs (Sashkin, 1988). Followers react positively when the vision reflects their values and provides information to direct their future behavior. The vision serves as a metagoal for the leader to pursue (Thoms & Govekar, 1997).

Vision Requirements. A new vision guides the leader in maintaining or changing the organization's culture to redirect it into different missions (Bryman, 1992). For this, the vision needs to be properly communicated.

> This can be achieved through leaders themselves acting as personifications of their visions and by proper attention to the rhetorical strategies by which the vision is communicated. . . . Equally, the leaders need to establish an organizational framework which will facilitate the accomplishment of the vision. . . . Leaders must constantly reiterate the vision and its desirability. (Bryman, 1992, pp. 137, 175)

The propagation of a vision is an important requirement of the CEO and top management. The CEO needs to align the TMT around the vision to effectively transmit it to the organization. The CEO needs to be the chief sense maker and sense giver. Although there may be negotiation, reformulation, and realignment, as the vision moves through the organization, the CEO remains responsible for its maintenance (Williams & Zukin, 1997).

Bennis and Nanus (1985) concluded, from in-depth

interviews with 90 top directors and executives, that envisioning requires translating intentions into realities by communicating that vision to others to gain their support. Envisioning is the basis for empowering others, for providing them with the social architecture that will move them toward the envisioned state. It involves paying close attention to those with whom one is communicating, zooming in on the key issues with clarity and a sense of priorities. Risks are accepted, but only after a careful analysis of success or failure. Judge and Bono (2002) confirmed in surveys of 115 supervisors rated by 319 direct reports that transformational leadership was associated with vision content of higher-than-average quality.

Measurement and Correlates. Envisioning focuses more on success than on failure and more on action than on procrastination (Brown, 1993). Sashkin (1986, 1988) detailed the requirements to assess the visionary leader. The Leader Behavior Questionnaire (LBQ), developed by Sashkin and Fulmer (1985), a self-report of visionary leadership, included scales of focused attention, long-term goals, clarity of expression, caring, propensity to take risks, and empowerment. Stoner-Zemel (1988) found that visionary leadership, as measured by the LBQ, correlated with employees' perceptions of the quality of their work lives. Ray (1989) showed that LBQ-assessed visionary leadership was related to a factory culture of organizational excellence. And Major (1988) obtained LBQ assessments in 60 high schools that linked the visionary leadership behavior of their principals with whether the schools performed high or low on various objective criteria.

Visionary leaders have a sense of identity, direction, and strategy for implementation (Nygren & Ukeritis, 1993). A 12-item Vision Ability Scale was validated by Thoms and Blasko (1999). For samples of a total of 891 college leaders attending the same national program in various locations, the scale correlated significantly .37, with self-rated MLQ inspirational motivation and .42 with the combined MLQ transformational leadership scores. Likewise, vision ability correlated .38 with LPI inspiring a shared vision. Significant positive correlations were also found with measures of optimism, positive outlook, and future time perspective. Baum, Locke, and Kirkpatrck (1998) used a longitudinal design to collect data from 183 CEO entrepreneurs and selected employ-

ees. Structural modeling confirmed that the attributes and contents of visions expressed verbally or in writing directly led to future venture growth.

Vision and the Transformation of Followers. The transformational leader concretizes a vision that the followers view as worthy of their effort, thereby raising their arousal and effort levels. However, people who seek to identify with the leader but who are distant from him or her may become only partially aroused and committed and may not take action to conform to the leader's initiatives. Nevertheless, if they are free to act and are not constrained by other commitments or the lack of opportunity, they will actually become committed to leaders even at a distance. This was confirmed by Judge and Bono (2002) in surveys of 130 leaders' visions, each described by their supervisor and three direct reports, that transformational leaders articulate and use visions more than do transactional leaders. Followers are more confident in the visions of transformational leaders and more committed to the visions. Downton (1973, p. 230) described this process as *transformational* rather than *transactional*, noting its greater likelihood of taking effect:

> The opportunity for action is apt to be greater than strictly transactional relationships because the follower who identifies with a leader can transform his behavioral pattern without necessarily exchanging tangible goods with the leader . . . a new moral code . . . can be put immediately into practice, no matter how distant the leader and the opportunities for organizational activity.

Visions of Reformers, Revolutionaries, and Radicals. *Reformers* of political movements and governments such as Vicente Fox of Mexico, are able to convey to others a vision of what the society would be like, how it would look, if its ideals were supported. They espouse myths that sustain the political community and its professed ideal cultural patterns. Practices that depart from the ideals must be changed or eliminated in the desired future state. *Revolutionary leaders* such as Fidel Castro, on the other hand, envisage a future in which the sustaining myths and current cultural patterns have been rejected and society has been fundamentally reconstituted (Paige, 1977). The future the revolutionaries envisage in their rhetoric of the new regime is surprisingly devoid of details or mentions of justice, despite their focus on the injustices of the regime they intend to overthrow by force (Martin, Scully, & Levitt, 1988). *Radicals* of both the political Right and the political Left are likely to be ideologues, inflexible in their vision with everything black or white, never gray, extreme in their views, and intolerant of those who don't share their vision (Mumford & Strange, 2002). Nevertheless, radical dissenters may contribute to transformations by disrupting fundamental assumptions and beliefs of the mainstream majority (Elmes & Smith, 1991).

Rational and Emotional Elements. Cameron and Ulrich (1986) pointed to the rational and emotional elements of envisioning. The rational element articulates a vision in which questions about purpose, problems, missing information, and available resources are answered. The emotional element articulates a vision of a holistic picture that is intuitive, imaginative, and insightful. It uses symbols and language that evoke meaning and commitment.

Strategic Planning. Other aspects of envisioning that are relevant in different ways at different levels of management in the complex organization include the formulation of strategies based on the contingencies of the threats and opportunities of the organization, its resources, and the interests of its constituencies. Leaders must be able to formulate and evaluate appropriate organizational responses and arrange for their implementation in operations and policies (Wortman, 1982). Leaders will be more effective in doing so if they are proficient in gathering and evaluating ideas, storing information, thinking logically, and learning from their mistakes (Srivastva, 1983). As they rise in their organizations, the abilities that are required of them will shift from dealing with concrete matters that have short-term consequences and for which all the parameters are known to more abstract issues with greater amounts of uncertainty and longer-term consequences (Jacobs & Jaques, 1987).

Vision and Consciousness Raising. Long-range visions need to be detailed. The leader must understand the key elements of the vision and consider the "spill-over" effects of their future development. Furthermore, the leader must be able to communicate his or her vision in ways that are compelling, make people committed to it, and help make it happen. As Bennis (1982, 1983) concluded after his interviews with 90 innovative organizational leaders, the leaders could communicate their vision to clarify it and induce the commitment of their multiple constituencies to maintaining the organization's course. These leaders also revealed the self-determination and persistence of charismatic leaders, especially when the going got rough. Yet they emphasized their and their organizations' adaptability to new conditions and to new problems. They concentrated on the purposes of their organizations and on "paradigms of action." They made extensive use of metaphors, symbolism, ceremonials, and insignias as ways of concretizing and transmitting their visions of what could be. They pictured what was right, good, and important for their organization and thus contributed considerably to their organization's culture of shared norms and values.

This arousal of consciousness and awareness in followers of what is right, good, and important, which new directions must be taken, and why, is the most important aspects of intellectual stimulation. The "mass line" leadership of Mao Zedong illustrated its application to social and political movements. The scattered and unsystematic ideas of the Chinese masses about marriage, land, and the written language were converted by the Communist Party leadership into a set of coherent, concentrated, and systematic ideas for reform, which were fed back to the masses until they embraced them as their own. Mao even seemed to practice this strategy in his one-on-one discussions with others (Barlow, 1981).

Intuitive Aspects. For Pondy (1983), envisioning begins with intuitive interpretations of events and data that give meaning to new images of the world that ultimately can be clarified into strategies for an organization. Symbols and phrases are invented to focus attention on the strategic questions that are needed to get others involved in the process. As Jim Renier, the CEO of Honeywell, suggested, although the vision that emerges may be that of the single-minded chief, it often evolves, in larger organizations in particular, out of the chief's give-and-take with many others during repeated reviews of the possibilities of the desired future state. Renier (as quoted in Tichy

& Devanna, 1986, p. 128) put it this way: "What you've got to do is constantly engage in iterating what you say [about the vision] and what they say is possible. And over a couple of years the different visions come together."

With their ability to provide images of the future state, inspiring leaders provide direction. A commonly used metaphoric vision, a cliché favored by political leaders, is the path, road, or journey that must be taken that gives direction to the followers (Tucker, 1981). But metaphoric visions can boomerang into apocryphal anecdotes and reverse in meaning. For example, King Canute wanted to convey his limitations to his courtiers and used his lack of control over the ocean tides to illustrate his point. History converted the metaphor into an illustration of the king's foolish pomposity in trying to command the sea not to roll up the beach.

Can Envisioning Be Developed? Mendell and Gerjuoy (1984) accepted the conventional wisdom that visionary leadership cannot be effectively taught. Unless the talent is there already, managers can only be prepared to anticipate possibilities. If this were true, then only recruiting and selection would ensure an adequate number of capable inspiring leaders with vision. But is it possible for managers to develop their ability to envision and to be more inspirational leaders, in general?

Exercises provide practice that engages trainees in envisioning their organization's future. In such exercises, executives are asked to talk about how they expect to spend their day at some future date—say, three years hence—or what they expect their organization to look like. Or they may be asked to write a business article about their organization's future. These comments are then evaluated with feedback. From these visions, leaders and managers can draw up mission statements and the specifications that must be met by such an organization (Tichy & Devanna, 1986).[1]

Caveat. Visions may be too abstract, too complex, unrealistic, unreachable, or impractical. They may also be too inspirational. Fulfilling a vision may become an end in itself or a distraction rather than paving the way to a valued goal (Langeleler, 1992). Meindl (1998) regarded visionary leadership as a "vague and mysterious concept."

[1] Such educational activities will be discussed further in Chapter 34.

He cited Collins and Porras (1994), who declared that the best companies have not relied on visionary leadership to sustain their competitive advantage. Additionally, Meindl (1998) argued that much of the salutary reporting about the positive effects of visionary leadership on organizational performance may be a myth, a product of the "Romance of Leadership" (Meindl, 1995). Successful organizations often attribute the outcome, incorrectly, to effective leadership. Meindl (1998) suggested that there may be more significant leadership tasks than envisioning: "We too often rely on overblown, highly romanticized images of great visionary leaders with special cognitions of the future" (p. 22). Nevertheless, at the same time, Meindl agreed that organizational members could be guided by a shared vision of a desired future state and that a leader with the necessary skills can shape and foster that vision.

Antecedents of Transformational and Transactional Leadership

What predisposes individual leaders to transformational or transactional leadership? The answers include individual differences in personality and differences in cognitive, social, and emotional competencies. Much evidence has accumulated that age, education, and experience are likely to correlate with the transformational leadership and transactional leadership of both the rated leaders and the followers. Additionally, leaders' inventoried or tested traits and beliefs have been found to be correlated with their leadership ratings by their followers, peers, and/or superiors. In turn, these ratings have been found to be dependent on the traits of the followers.[2]

Personality

Personality predictors of transformational leadership have been found in a wide variety of sites, ranging from busi-

[2] A trait may be an antecedent or predisposition that relates to the appraised leadership performance. Yet in many cases, the correlation between the trait and obtained leadership can be due to a third variable, such as likability. Same-source bias is present when the same raters provide the data for both the trait and the leader's performance. Some measures, such as age and experience, are clearly antecedents of the current leadership and can arguably be regarded as cause and effect if not accounted for by their mutual correlations with a third variable

ness and industry to community leaders' programs. According to Popper and Mayseless (2002), the internal world of the transformational leader is characterized by the motivation to lead, self-efficacy, and the capacity to relate to others in a prosocial way. The transformational leader is optimistic and open to new experiences and others' points of view. There is a disposition for social dominance, the capacity to serve as a role model, and a belief in the ability to influence others. As noted in Chapter 5, the Big 5 structure of personality with its five factors, each with several facets, has provided a widely accepted way to structure the study of personality as a predictor of performance. For example, Judge and Bono (2001) collected 14 samples of community leaders' Big 5 NEOAC scores and their facets using the Costa and McCrae (1992) 240-item NEO Personality Inventory. Also, the 261 leaders were each MLQ-rated by one or two subordinates. The simple correlations of charisma, inspirational leadership, intellectual stimulation, and individualized consideration correlated with extraversion, openness, and agreeableness, respectively, as follows: extraversion, .22, .24, .14, and .23; openness, .18, .22, .10, and .21; and agreeableness, .28, .21, .24, and .23. Neuroticism and conscientiousness did not correlate with any of the transformational leadership factors. The MLQ transactional factor of contingent reward was negatively correlated −.20 with agreeableness. Passive management by exception correlated −.15 with agreeableness and −.18 with conscientiousness

Lim and Ployhart (2000) correlated the five NEOAC factors with the transformational leadership scores of the leaders of 39 Singaporean combat teams. The 202 team followers used the MLQ to rate their respective team leaders. Correlations of transformational leadership of the leaders with the five personality factors NEOAC, measured by the International Personality Item Pool (IPIP) were as follows: neuroticism, −.39; extraversion, .31, openness, −.08; agreeableness, −.29; and conscientiousness, −.09. Among the 79 studies classified in terms of the Big-Five factors in the meta-analysis by Judge, Bono, Iies, et al. (2000), reviewed in Chapter 5, 11 to 15 correlations between each of the NEOAC categories and judgments of transformational leadership were significant, as follows: neuroticism, −.21; extraversion, .25; openness, .30; agreeableness, .27; and conscientiousness, .19. In line with predictions, Bommer, Rubin, and Bald-

win (2004) found that cynicism about change among 2,247 subordinates correlated −.29 with the transformational leadership of their focal leaders. This was offset by the correlation of .45 when transformational peer leadership of the 227 managers was present. Van Eron and Burke (1992) completed a survey of 128 senior executives and their 615 subordinates from a global firm and showed that the executives who described themselves as sensing rather than intuitive on the MBTI were more inspirational on the MLQ. Also, they were more judging than perceiving, according to their subordinates (r = .44; .30). They also were more likely to regard work as a strong sense of mission (r = .34; .23).

Military Studies. Clover (1988) compared on selected personality traits U.S. Air Force Academy commissioned officers who scored higher in charisma, intellectual stimulation, and individualized consideration on the MLQ with those who scored lower. Clover concluded that the transformational leaders were more likely to be more flexible, more compassionate, more pragmatic, and less tough. Ross and Offerman (1997) replicated the study with 40 Air Force Academy officers who completed the Adjective Checklist (ACL) (Gough & Heilbrun, 1983) and 4,400 cadets who completed a shortened form of the MLQ on the officer who commanded their squadron. Four cadets also completed the ACL on their squadron commander. The officers' self-ratings on the ACL were combined with the four cadets' ACL ratings to provide the personality trait measures. Transformational officers were more self-confident, more pragmatic, more nurturant, less critical, and less aggressive.

Avolio, Bass, Atwater, et al. (1994) examined the tested personality traits of junior-year cadet officers at Virginia Military Institute (VMI). MLQ ratings were provided by their subordinates. Hardiness (Kobasi, Maddi, & Puccelli, 1982) and physical fitness correlated with the cadet officers' transformational leadership. Atwater and Yammarino (1993) correlated Cattell's (1950) 16 PF Inventory personality assessments with MLQ ratings of 107 Annapolis midshipmen who served as summer squad leaders of 1,235 plebes. MLQ-rated transformational leadership, as appraised by the plebes' superiors, correlated .24 with 16 PF self-discipline and .26 with 16 PF conformity. Additionally, Atwater and Yammarino (1989) found that the Annapolis midshipmen squad leaders appraised by their plebe subordinates as transformational described themselves as more likely to react emotionally and with feeling.

Community Leaders. Avolio and Bass (1994) correlated the Gordon (1963) Personal Profile (GPP), a forced-choice inventory, with MLQ ratings by subordinates of 118 leaders in their various public and private agencies and business firms in one middle-sized city in the United States. GPP ascendancy and sociability scores correlated .21 and .23 with charisma and inspirational motivation, respectively. Bass and Avolio also administered a sense of humor scale, which correlated positively but not significantly with all four components of transformational leadership. The MLQ component scores of the community leaders were also correlated with the Myers-Briggs Type Indicator (MBTI). Charisma and individualized consideration were predicted, respectively, by more MBTI feeling and less thinking ($r = .25, .22$). Inspirational motivation was predicted by intuition ($r = .20$) and not sensing ($r = .19$). The transactional factor of passive management by exception correlated with more sensing ($r = .23$) and less intuition ($r = .28$).

A meta-analysis by Lowe, Kroek, and Sivasubrahmanian (1996) compared public with private organizations and showed that leaders from public organizations were higher in mean factor scores than leaders from private ones in transformational leadership: charisma, 2.61 versus 2.33; individualized consideration, 2.58 versus 2.33; and intellectual stimulation, 2.52 versus 2.40. They also differed in transactional management by exception, 2.41 versus 2.16, and contingent reward, 1.85 versus 1.75. The meta-analysis also compared military with civilian organizations. Military leaders were higher than civilians in the factor mean scores for transformational leadership and for management by exception.

Competence

Cognitive, social, emotional, and other competencies have been found to be significant antecedents of transformational and transactional leadership, especially social and emotional competence (Bass, 2002). Older and more experienced Dutch managers, usually at higher organizational levels, saw a greater need for inspirational leadership, cognitive, and social competence. Younger Dutch respondents viewed their leaders as more transactional, especially if they were in sales or marketing (Taillieu, Schruijer, & van Dijck, undated).

Cognitive Competence. According to Wofford and Goodwin (1994), cognitive ability is what distinguishes transformational from transactional leaders. Subordinates' MLQ ratings of the charisma and inspirational motivation of 782 managers correlated .13 and .16, respectively, with the Owens Biographical Questionnaire scale of intelligence (Southwick, 1998). Subordinate ratings of charisma, inspirational motivation, and intellectual stimulation correlated .33, .33, and .23 respectively, with management commitee evaluations of middle managers' good judgment (Hater & Bass, 1988). Cattell's (1950) 16 PF Inventory intelligence score correlated .20 with midshipmen's transformational leadership. However, the Scholastic Aptitude Test (SAT) failed as a significant predictor of transformational leadership among midshipmen (Atwater & Yammarino, 1993) and military cadets (Avolio, Bass, Lau, et al., 1994).

Social Competence. The use of humor was found by Avolio, Howell, and Sosik (1999) to correlate .56 with the transformational leadership behavior of 115 Canadian managers and executives and .45 with their practice of contingent reward.

Eloquence is one of the most important competencies for transformational leaders. Persuasiveness and social sensitivity, as obtained from Owens's biodata, correlated between .14 and .22 with charisma and inspiration (Southwick, 1998). For Hater and Bass, the correlations with the transformational leadership factors were .32, .33, and .33 with the quality of the managers' communications. According to their 968 subordinates, Israeli industrial managers who were more transformational leaders were more open, informal, frank, careful listeners and careful transmitters on the Klauss & Bass Communications Style Inventory (1982). Correlations ranged from .30 to .64 (Berson, 1999). Social sensitivity in biodata correlated .14 and .18 with charisma and inspirational motivation and .15 with individualized consideration (Southwick, 1998). Sociability and ascendance on the Gordon Personal Profile correlated between .21 and .25 with the charisma and inspirational motivation of community leaders (Avolio & Bass, 1994).

Emotional Competence. Transformational leaders were higher in their internal locus of control (Rotter, 1966). Internal locus of control, as measured by the Personality Orientation Inventory (Shostrum, 1974), correlated higher (between .33 and .46) with the four transformational components as obtained from the subordinates of Digital Equipment executives (Gibbons, 1986). Internal locus of control of 78 senior executives in a Canadian financial institution correlated significantly with a short version of the MLQ rated by an average of four followers, as follows: charisma, .18, .25, and individualized consideration, .33. (Howell & Avolio, 1993). Similarly, inner direction on the Personal Orientation Inventory (Shostrom, 1974) of 20 Digital Equipment executives correlated .37, .33, and .44 respectively, with the three transformational factors of charisma, inspirational motivation, and individualized consideration, as MLQ-rated by their subordinates.

Other emotional competency (or emotional intelligence) assessments that were antecedents of transformational leaders included self-acceptance, .43 to .46 (Gibbons, 1986) and significant biodata antecedents such as self-esteem, self confidence, being energetic, having a strong work ethic and sense of responsibility, setting difficult self-goals, and being comfortable in new situations (Southwick, 1998). In an experiment by Newcombe and Ashkanasy (2002), when 537 participants evaluated videotaped leaders, they rated leaders more favorably if the leader's positive or negative emotional facial expressions were congruent with the emotional content of their verbal messages. According to a study by McColl-Kennedy and Anderson (2002), frustration had a negative mediating effect on the impact of transformational leadership. The emotion of optimism had a bolstering effect.

Emotional competencies that significantly predicted transformational leadership were hardiness (Kobasa, Maddi, & Kahn, 1982), optimism, positive thinking, behavioral coping, feeling over thinking (Atwater & Yammarino, 1993); risk taking (Hater & Bass, 1988); personal adjustment and nurturance (Ross & Offerman, 1997). The optimism and positive thinking of transformational leaders was confirmed by Speitzer and Quinn (1996). Ashkanasy and Tse (2000) inferred that transformational leaders have a positively biased schema for processing information. They constructed a model that, among other things, showed that transformational leaders were in touch with their own emotions, could regulate their own emotions, and were emotionally stable and less stressed. Transformational leaders could control their own and others' emotions. They had emotional intelligence (Dasborough, 2002). Pastor and Nebeker (2002) reported that among 170 executives, managers, and supervisors and 380 to 450 subordinates, emotional reasoning correlated .33 with contingent reward but understanding emotions was negatively correlated with active and passive management by exception ($r = -.29; -.28$).

Organizational Levels

A study of how the organizational level of leaders' positions affects their transformational and transactional performance was completed by Bullis, Kane, and Tremble (1997). They reported on three levels of U.S. Army officers. At the highest level studied were approximately 295 battalion commanders (lieutenant colonels); at the second level were approximately 440 company commanders (captains); and lowest were approximately 3,170 platoon leaders (lieutenants). Officers at each level were MLQ-rated by members one level below them. Table 22.2 shows the generally increasing scores at each level. Gottlieb (1990) found the same trend when she compared each of the transformational factor scores of 76 Veterans Administration hospital chief nurses and 545 associate chief nurses, except that management by exception was the same at both organizational levels she studied. The chief nurses were MLQ-rated by their immediate subordinates, the associate chief nurses, who, in turn, were MLQ-rated by their 1,532 immediate subordinates.

Organizational Characteristics

Bass (1985c) proposed that transformational leadership would be more likely to appear in *organic* organizations, as described by Burns & Stalker (1961), and transactional leaders would be more common in *mechanistic* organizations. In a comparison of 511 employees in a manufacturing environment with 539 employees in an R & D environment, Berson and Linton (undated) found that transformational leadership related more to quality climate perceptions and satisfaction with projects than with processes or manufacturing settings. Koopman (1991) expected that transformational leadership was more effective in innovative organizations and transactional leadership in bureaucratic organizations. For Quinn (1988), the orientation of organic organizations was supportive, innovative, and flexible (i.e., transformational). The orientation of mechanical organizations was toward rules, goals, and control (i.e., transactional). Den Hartog, Van Muijen, and Koopman (1996) randomly split the 330 employees in 28 departments in different Dutch organizations in business, social service, health care, and local government. One of the subsamples used the MLQ (8Y) to rate the transformational and transactional leadership of its supervisors; the other subsample completed the Focus-Culture Questionnaire about its departmental culture. The results were as predicted: transformational leadership correlated .72 with cultural support and .69 with innovativeness; transactional leadership correlated .52 with cultural support and .48 with innovativeness. On the other hand, transactional leadership was more prevalent than transformational leadership in departments with more rules and goals orientation. Transactional leadership correlated .54 with rules and goals in departmental cultures.

Both similarities and differences were present in the occurrence and effects of transformational leadership from one country culture to another (Bass, 1997). This was subsequently documented in the Globe Study (House,

Hanges, & Javidan, 2004) involving more than 15,000 managers in the same three industries in 62 countries. Considerable amounts of both universality and specificity were found in the data from the different organizations and countries (see Chapter 33).

Follower Characteristics

The findings were mixed. The followers' locus of control made a difference. A thesis by Pastor and Mayo (1996) showed that for 180 college students MLQ-rating their classroom professors, internal locus of control correlated significantly with inspirational, individually considerate, and contingent rewarding teachers. Among 54 Israeli military groups, the followers' level of development predicted their leaders' transformational leadership (Dvir & Shamir, 2003). In the 1996 presidential election, those affiliated with the Democratic Party saw Bill Clinton, the Democratic candidate, as more transformational ($r = .31$) and the Republican candidate, Bob Dole, as less transformational ($r = -.36$).(Pillai & Williams, undated).

Ehrlhart and Klein (2001) created a scenario of a transformational district manager who communicates high performance expectations, exhibits confidence in followers' abilities, takes calculated risks against the status quo,

Table 22.2 U.S. Army Organizational Levels as Antecedents of the Mean Multifactor Leadership (MLQ) Means of Platoon Leaders (Lieutenants), Company Commanders (Captains), and Battalion Commanders (Lt. Colonels)

	Platoon Leaders	Company Commanders	Battalion Commanders
	Lieutenants	Captains	Lt. Colonels
Attributed Charisma	3.08	3.83	4.02
Behavioral Charisma	2.99	3.77	4.03
Inspirational Leadership	3.10	3.79	3.99
Intellectual Stimulation	2.83	3.45	3.56
Individualized Consideration	2.82	3.66	3.57
Contingent Reward	2.59	2.86	2.87
Active Mgmt by Exception	2.92	3.01	2.90
Passive Mgmt by Exception	2.61	2.20	2.14
Number of Leaders Rated	442	213	53
Nunber of Subordinate Raters	3170	440	295

SOURCE: Bullis, Kane, and Tremble (1997).

and articulates a value-based vision and collective identity. Scenarios of relations-oriented and task-oriented district managers were also created. A total of 267 University of Maryland students (62% female) of diverse ethnicities, almost all with work experience, were asked to rate their preferences to work for each of the three district managers. The students chose to work with the transformational manager if the students had participative work values ($r = .23$) and high self-esteem ($r = .16$). In addition to showing the expected positive effect on 502 service employees on their identification with the organization when their leaders were transformational, Epitropaki and Martin (2005) also found that the effect was greater when the employees were low in positive emotionality and high in negative emotionality. Harland, Harrison, Jones, et al. demonstrated that resilience was stronger among subordinates of transformational leaders (2005). But Bono and Judge (2000) found few significant effects on transformational leadership of various follower personality characteristics for more than 1,200 followers rating their more than 300 leaders. And contrary to expectations, Dockery (1993) failed to find that subordinates who were low in independence would respond more favorably to transformational leaders.

Effects of Transformational and Transactional Leadership

Numerous scholars expected that transformational leadership was a key to organizational and follower success. Bryant (2003) proposed that transformational leaders may be more effective in creating and sharing knowledge individually and in small groups but transactional leaders may be more effective in exploiting knowledge at the organizational level. Underlying the effects of the transformational leader on follower performance is its enhancing personal identification with the leader through bolstering the self-worth of the follower in contributing to what needs to be done and the social identification of the follower with the organization (Kark & Shamir, 2002). These scholarly expectations were supported by biographies of world-class industrial, military, and political leaders (Bass, Avolio, & Goodheim, 1987). The results of the extensive surveys of over 1,500 managers, leaders of technical teams, government and educational admin-

istrators, upper middle managers, and senior U.S. Army officers that were discussed in Chapter 21 for charismatic leadership are also relevant for transformational leadership. Subordinates of these leaders who described their managers on the MLQ—Form 5 as more transformational were also more likely to say that the leaders and the organizations they led were highly effective. Such transformational leaders were judged to have better relations with higher-ups and to make more of a contribution to the organization than were those who were described only as transactional. Subordinates said they also exerted a lot of extra effort for the transformational leaders. If leaders were only transactional, the organizations were seen as less effective, particularly if most of the leaders practiced reactive passive management by exception (intervening only when standards were not being met). Subordinates said they exerted much less effort for such leaders (Bass & Avolio, 1989). Subordinates and followers set higher purposes in their work for transformational leaders (Sparks & Schenk, 2001); performed beyond social expectations (Berson, undated); expended more effort and were more committed and involved (Harvey, Royal, & Stout, undated).

However, Vera and Crossan (2004) noted that strategic leaders can promote using both transactional and transformational leadership. Bono and Judge (2003) showed in two studies with diverse samples that followers of transformational leaders felt their work was more important and more in accord with their motives, values, and self-concepts. Dumdum, Lowe, and Avolio (2002) extended the meta-analysis of Lowe, Kroeck, and Sivasubramaniam (1996), validating the effects on followers' effort, performance, and job satisfaction.

The commentary and empirical results of political leaders, educators, military leaders, and business leaders indicated that transformational leadership was more effective in military than civilian studies. Also, management by exception was less effective in civilian than military studies (Coleman, Patterson, Fuller, et al., 1995; Lowe, Kroeck, & Sivasubramaniam, 1996).

Political Leaders, Public Service, and Other Nonprofit Leaders

When faced with political chaos and an angry public, with policy making taken over by radical minorities and legislatures elected on the basis of single negative issues, Abels (1996) suggested that political leaders must compete by being more transformational. Rosenbach and Mueller (1988) used an abbreviated version of the MLQ to survey the descriptions of 110 fire chiefs by their 732 subordinates and again showed that the transformational leader components were more highly correlated with the subordinates' perceptions of effectiveness and satisfaction than were the components of transactional leadership.

Police officers of various ranks were asked to take the role of subordinates negotiating with transformational or transactional superiors described to them in scenarios. Officers whose "superiors" were described as transformational were significantly more likely to attempt to influence their superiors upwardly than were those officers whose superiors were supposedly transactional. Officers with transformational superiors were significantly more likely to employ rational tactics of upward influence rather than try to be ingratiating or use direct requests and strong emotion (Deluga & Sousa, 1990). South African cricket union chief executive officers rated their teams as more effective on the Effectiveness Survey for Cricket Administration if the executives were more transformational in their MLQ scores, according to ratings by their subordinates (Ristow, Amos, & Staude, 1999). Onnen (1986) demonstrated that Methodist ministers who were transformational generated more growth in their church membership, budgets, and attendance at Sunday services.

Many historical examples can be cited about the effects of transformational and transactional leaders on international relations. Henry Kissinger's (1994) description of U.S. diplomacy was transformational when it emphasized ideals of democracy, freedom, and individualism and the United States was a haven for the oppressed of Europe. Vision drove the American dream of a continentwide country. The purchases of the Louisiana Territory and of Alaska were due to the visionary leadership of President Thomas Jefferson in 1803 and Secretary of State John Seward in 1867. On the other hand, diplomats negotiate deals between countries in which much transactional leadership is exerted to exchange resources for agreements and promises. Threats and counterthreats are used to try to forestall actions of competing parties.

Educators

C. Patterson (1995) suggested that college faculty needed to be transformational leaders in order to inspire their students to become more active, enthusiastic learners. Sergiovanni (1990) posited that when transformative leadership results in moral authority that goes beyond bureaucratic direction and unites followers in pursuit of higher-level goals, commitment and performance far exceed expectations. Leaders' vision, individualized consideration, and intellectual stimulation lie behind improved teachers' practices, according to a large-scale qualitative study of innovation in the Netherlands (Geijsel, Sleegers, & van den Berg, 1999). Similar conclusions were reached about the positive correlations obtained between effectiveness and the factors of transformational leadership for vocational education administrators (Daughtry, 1997), chairpersons of university academic departments (Brown & Moshavi, 2002), public school principals (Kirby, Paradise, & King, 1992; Leithwood, 1994), private school principals, and principals of private schools (Hoover, 1987) and similarly for chairpersons of academic university departments. Among 440 university faculty in 70 departments, faculty satisfaction was positively correlated with the transformational leadership of their department heads (Brown & Moshavi, 2002). When 120 liberal arts undergraduates rated each one of their instructors in the arts and sciences as higher in transformational leadership, they also indicated that the instructor was more respected, trusted, and involving, as well as more satisfying and effective (Harvey, Royal, & Stout, 2003).

Using enrollment growth as an indicator of institutional effectiveness, Cowen (1990) found it to be correlated with transformational leadership on the part of 153 university presidents. Vistro (1999) obtained a positive relationship between the performance of Filipino Teacher Licensure exams and the transformational leadership of the deans and chairpersons of the private teacher education institutions the teachers had attended. Again in the Philippines, if schoolteachers rated their principal as transformational leaders, student learning was better (Catanyag, 1995). Philbin (1997) found that teacher satisfaction, perceived school effectiveness, and effort were higher if the high school principal was transformational. Students' learning, as measured by Indiana's annual achievement test, was greater, but only if the students were higher in cognitive ability and socioeconomic status. Students lower in cognitive ability and socioeconomic status did not benefit from the principal's style of leadership. Major (1988) reported that pupils demonstrated better performance in schools led by principals who were high rather than low in transformational leadership. Following a review of six qualitative and 15 quantitative studies of the effects of transformational leadership in schools by Leithwood, Tomlinson, and Genge (1995), Leithwood (1995) concluded that the effects of transformational leadership included: (1) identification of goals, development of a schoolwide vision, and its inspirational dissemination, along with high expectations for the functioning of teachers and students; (2) involvement of staff, teachers, parents, and students; (3) development of structures from the bottom up; and (4) development of a collaborative culture. Effectiveness was seen in the professional development of the teachers and the expansion of their problem-solving capacity. Leithwood and Steinbach (1991) noted that the transformational leadership of effective school principals would show up in their expert everyday problem solving. They can articulate interpretations of problems for others and share with others their strong concerns about problems. They demonstrate respect for others and strong appreciation of professional and human values. Major (1988) obtained LBQ assessments in 60 high schools that linked the visionary leadership behavior of school principals with how well the schools performed on various objective criteria.

Military and Naval Leaders

As noted in the preceding chapter, Yammarino and Bass (1988, 1989) collected subordinates' MLQ ratings of a 5% representative sample of the junior commissioned officers serving in the U.S. surface fleet. Also obtained from the superiors for the 186 officers were their cumulative fitness reports and recommendations for early promotion. The component factors of transformational leadership correlated as follows with fitness and promotion recommendations, respectively: (1) charisma, .38, .37; (2) inspirational motivation, .25, .28; (3) intellectual stimulation, .31, .34; and (4) individualized consideration, .21, .24. The transactional factors describing the subordinates correlated with their superiors' appraisals as follows: (5) contingent reward, .20, .24; (6) active man-

agement by exception, .22, .28; (7) passive management by exception, −.05, −.04; and (8) laissez-faire leadership, −.31, −.31. Similarly, transformational leadership of focal officers in Marine Corps transport squadrons in terms of MLQ ratings from their supervisor, peers, and subordinates had a strong relationship with the effectiveness of the focal officers and unit cohesion and morale (Salter, 1989). Findings were the same for correlations obtained in ratings by subordinates of U.S., Canadian, and German field-grade officers serving in NATO (Boyd, 1988). Masi and Cooke (2000) found that the MLQ transformational leadership of 78 company commanders accounted for 36% of the variance in motivation of their 145 army recruiting station managers. Positive correlations were routinely found between transformational leadership and satisfaction with military leaders and with the unit led by the leader (Lowe, Kroeck, and Sivasubramanian, 1996). For instance, the 4,400 Air Force Academy cadets who MLQ-rated the commissioned officers in charge of their squadron yielded significant MLQ correlations with satisfaction with their squadrons as follows: charisma, .43; individualized consideration, .38; and intellectual stimulation, .23.

Clover (1989) used an abbreviated version of the MLQ to correlate the descriptions of 3,500 subordinates at the U.S. Air Force Academy of their commissioned officer squadron commanders and various measures of their squadrons' performance. Commanders who received higher ratings in transformational leadership led better-performing squadrons and were more likely to be seen as preferred role models by the cadets. On the other hand, open-ended questions in interviews with cadets revealed that *transactional* squadron leaders were perceived as selfish, lacking in empathy, social skills, and trust. They made rash decisions and caused frustration, reduced morale, and created disunity in the group (Clover, 1990). At the U.S. Military Academy (West Point), 437 junior year cadets MLQ-rated their 250 senior-year cadet leaders. The transformational leadership scores of the cadet leaders significantly correlated .20 with their military performance grades as seniors. Their corresponding transactional scores correlated .01 with their military performance grades (Bartone & Dardis, 2001). On the other hand, Ross and Offerman (1994) failed to find that the academic, athletic, or military performance of Air Force Academy cadets was predicted by the transformational leadership of their commissioned officers. They did find that contingent reward correlated .34 with satisfaction.

Business and Industrial Managers

If widely practiced in a firm, transformational leadership ought to earn the firm a corporate image as a good company to work for and to do business with (Bass, 1990). It should help recruiting and improve organizational and individual development. Many studies have found positive correlations between subordinate ratings of the transformational leadership of managers and professionals and their effectiveness as leaders. Posner and Kouzes (1990) found that scores based on their five transformational leadership practices as a whole accounted for 55% of the variance in subordinates' appraisals of the effectiveness of their leaders. Shea and Howell (1998) proposed that transformational leadership enhanced followers' self-efficacy and outcome expectancies.

National Findings. Williams, Turner, and Parker (2000) reported that those of 211 Australian manufacturing technicians who rated their team supervisors as transformational were more likely to comply with safety regulations and were more likely to take safety initiatives. Zhu, Chew, and Spangler (2005) demonstrated that CEOs' transformational leadership, mediated with a committed and capable workforce, produced superior organizational outcomes. Singer (1985) showed that employees in New Zealand preferred working with leaders who were more transformational than transactional. In the United States, at Federal Express, transformational leaders were found to assume a focal role in innovation by creating a learning orientation that promoted organizational learning (Hult, 1995). In Canada, Howell and Avolio (1993) obtained strong positive results showing that the consolidated business units of a Canadian insurance company were significantly more likely to reach targeted quotas a year later if the 78 senior managers had been MLQ-rated as transformational a year before. (The reverse was true for transactional managers.) In a study of 267 employees in three Dutch organizations, Den Hartog (2000) found that if 267 employees in three Dutch organizations rated their supervisors as more inspirational, the employees were more emotionally committed to their line of work, but Den Hartog failed to find

that the rated inspirational leadership of the supervisors predicted employee self-efficacy. In 24 German firms, positive and significant regressions were found between the transformational leader behavior of supervisors and innovation among 161 R & D, marketing, and HR employees. Task performance was predicted to the same extent, but active management by exception by the supervisors was contraindicated (Rank, Nelson, & Xu, 2003). In Austria, the MLQ transformational leadership scores of 120 branch bank managers predicted long-term market share and customer satisfaction (Geyer & Steyner, 1998). On North Sea oil rig platforms off the coast of Scotland, supervisors rated more transformational by their subordinates were more effective (Carnegie, 1995). Transformational middle and top managers in a large Israeli telecommunications firm were more effective communicators, according to their immediate subordinates. They conveyed strategic organization goals better. Their subordinates were more familiar with the goals of the organization (Berson & Avolio, 2004). In a Chinese state enterprise, transformational managers, as rated by their subordinates, were judged to be more effective (Davis, 1997). Shin and Zhou (2003) demonstrated that creativity was greater among 290 employees in 46 Korean companies if their supervision was transformational. At three Japanese nuclear power stations, both transformational supervisors and their subordinates received better performance ratings by 566 maintenance employees than did their transactional counterparts (Bettin, Hunt, Macauley, et al., 1992).

Labor Leadership. The transformational leadership of union stewards predicted greater participation of members in union activities and loyalty to the union (Kelloway & Barling, 1993). Many labor union presidents transformed the everyday lives of working men and women. They were shapers of a new order and movers, shakers, and servants of the labor movement (Dubinsky & Van Tine, 1992).

Other Findings. Zorn (1988) observed that the transformational leaders among 73 pairs of small-business owners and their employees were more person-centered and more complex interpersonally. Sridhar, Valecha, and Sridhar (1994) obtained positive relations between transformational leadership and follower empowerment: Bass

(1990, 1998, 1999) reported that subordinates indicated that they exerted extra effort and were more satisfied with supervisors whom they rated highly in transformational leadership. In a medical technology firm, the frequency and quality of the content of information sought from their supervisor depended on how much 75 employees rated their supervisor as transformational (Madzar, 2001). Salespersons assessed as more transformational also performed better in sales (Garcia, 1995).

In six organizations, transformational leadership of supervisors correlated with commitment to their organizations of white-collar employees (Pitman, 1993). The commitment of 862 insurance employees was enhanced by the inspirational leadership of senior management (Niehoff, Eng, & Grover, 1990). In an experiment with 194 business students, Waldman, Bass, and Einstein (1987) showed that the performance appraisals of subordinates were higher if their leaders were described as transformational on the MLQ. Federal Express superiors of 54 managers rated the managers significantly higher in judgment, quality of decision making, financial management, communication, persuasion, and risk taking if the managers were described by their 306 subordinates as more charismatic or intellectually stimulating. No such significant correlations were found when the managers were described by their subordinates as practicing transactional leadership (Hater & Bass, 1988). Tepper (1993) reported finding that among 95 lower-level managers from a large financial institution, transformational managers were more likely to use legitimating tactics and to foster more identification and internalization in their subordinates, but transactional managers (as would be expected) were more likely to use exchange and pressure tactics.

Findings in Simulations. Similar results were obtained in simulations. Avolio, Waldman, and Einstein (1988) found that transformational "presidents" of simulated business firms generated more profitability, a greater share of the market, and better debt-to-equity ratios (Avolio, Waldman, & Einstein, 1988) than did the transactional "presidents." Ahead of their time, Litwin and Stringer (1966) demonstrated that transformation-like leadership resulted in more productivity at lower costs than did authoritarian or democratic styles imposed on simulated business firms. Jung (2000–2001) found

that the fluency and flexibility of divergent thinking in brainstorming in simulated business exercises was greater under transformational than transactional leadership.

Stress and Burnout. Selzer, Numeroff, and Bass (1989) found, as expected, for 875 part-time MBAs MLQ-rating their work supervisors that charisma, intellectual stimulation, and individualized consideration correlated $-.52$, $-.36$, and $-.46$, respectively, with the Gillespie and Numeroff Burnout Inventory (sample item: "I'm fed up with my job.") (Gillespie & Numeroff, 1984). Management by exception correlated .22 with burnout. Leadership style and symptoms of stress correlated significantly but to a lesser extent. However, the part of intellectual stimulation that required backing opinions with reason correlated *positively* with burnout and symptoms of stress when charisma and individualized consideration were held constant.

Health Care Directors and Personnel

Among Pennsylvania hospital nurse executives, 37% of the variance in effectiveness, 63% of the variance in the job satisfaction, and 89% of the extra effort their staff nurses made were accounted for by the transformational leadership model (Altieri, 1995). Gottlieb (1990) found that older Veterans Administration chief nurses and associate chief nurses were rated by their immediate subordinates higher in all MLQ factors of transformational but not transactional leadership. In 87 Spanish health care centers and 88 drug treatment centers, the family doctors, pediatricians, nurses, and clerks MLQ-rated the center coordinators. If they rated the coordinators as more transformational, they were more likely to regard them as legitimate in organizing, managing, controlling, and evaluating each team member. There were fewer role conflicts better interpersonal relations, and a greater sense of autonomy if the coordinators were rated as more transformational (Morales & Molero, 1994, 1995).

Caveat

Some of the preceding findings on effectiveness of leadership behavior were based on ratings by the same person of *both* the leadership and the outcomes. Nonetheless, there is considerable evidence from meta-analyses that factors of transformational leadership correlate moderately positive or higher with effectiveness even when such results are eliminated from consideration. At least two meta-analyses of the correlations of *subjective* percept-percept ratings where the same rater provided both leadership ratings and outcomes were compared with correlations of transformational leadership ratings with *objective* measures of effectiveness free of same-source bias. The subjective mean correlations results were higher with same-source outcomes and lower with objective outcomes. For example, Coleman, Patterson, Fuller, et al. (1995) analyzing 16 studies involving 4,034 cases using rated subjective effectiveness and 11 studies totaling 577 cases using objective effectiveness, found that the factors of transformational leadership varied in mean correlation with subjective effectiveness from .45 to .48. The comparable figures for objective effectiveness varied from .28 to .36.

The possibilities of same-source bias were eliminated in a study of 90 U.S. Army light infantry platoons. On their home base, half the 30-odd riflemen in each platoon MLQ-rated the leaders of their platoon. The other half provided measurements, using a Team MLQ, of platoon or company effectiveness (potency, cohesiveness, etc.). Peers and company commanders also MLQ-rated the platoons' leaders. The platoons then underwent 11 near-combat missions in a Joint Readiness Training Center (JRTC) accompanied by 2 of 38 trained observer-controllers (O/Cs) who evaluated the effectiveness of each of the leaders and the platoons after the first and last missions and 1 in between. There were significant positive correlations among the home base MLQ leadership ratings and the independently obtained measurements of home base platoon potency, cohesiveness, and effectiveness. The home base MLQ data significantly predicted the performance of the leaders and the platoons in the JRTC near-combat missions as evaluated by the O/Cs.

A structural model showed that direct and indirect home base MLQ and Team MLQ scores assessing the platoons, lieutenants, and platoon sergeants had significant path correlations with MLQ predictions from home base that could account for 14% of the variance in platoon effective performance at the JRTC. The indirect effects were mediated by potency and cohesion. The home base transformational leadership of the lieutenants and sergeants correlated .33 and .35 with potency and .27 and

.46 with cohesion, respectively, which in turn correlated .17 and .26 with JRTC performance. Transactional leadership was negatively correlated with the mediators and often not significantly.

Another of the examples validating the effectiveness of transformational leadership free of same-source bias was obtained for Singaporean combat team leaders. They were rated in efficiency and quality at the end of their training by five supervisors each. They were also appraised in military combat efficiency and quality by an independent assessor following a one-day assessment as the trained teams dealt with six military tasks. The 202 team followers completed the MLQ on their leaders. Transformational leadership, as rated by the followers, correlated .41 with efficiency plus quality as rated by the supervisors and .43 as rated by the assessor (Bass, Avolio, Jung, & Berson, 2003).

Other Related Concepts and Propositions

Champions of Innovation

Radical military innovations require champions, committed, persistent, and courageous, in advocating the innovation (Schon, 1963). Brigadier General Billy Mitchell, the commander of the Allied Expeditionary Forces' air force in World War I, championed airpower over battleships, and Admiral Hyman Rickover championed nuclear over conventional submarines. The same entrepreneurial supporters are required for the success of new business ventures, according to Collins, Moore, and Unwalla's (1970) psychological profile of 150 entrepreneurs. Champions keep product innovations alive (Dougherty & Hardy, 1996). The same is true for the success of environmental issues. According to L. R. Anderson's (1996) dissertation on 132 environmental champions, success depended on selling behaviors opportunistically, framing dimensions distinctive to the issue, packaging the matter as a business issue, and avoiding drama, emotion, and proenvironmental rhetoric. Action was inspired by an educational and intellectually stimulating approach. Howell, Shea, and Higgins (1998) completed a factor analysis of the acts of champions. Three factors were extracted: (1) demonstrating confidence in the innovation, (2) gathering support and involvement, and (3) persisting under adversity.

In comparison to matched leaders of established businesses, organizational champions were found by Ippoliti (1989) to score significantly higher on the combined four transformational MLQ scale scores provided by their subordinates. Champions also scored higher than average on the scales of charisma (3.15 versus 2.48), individualized consideration (2.83 versus 2.35), intellectual stimulation (2.75 versus 2.44), and inspirational motivation (2.49 versus 1.87).

Comparisons of Champions and Nonchampions. Twenty-five champions of innovation in information technology in 25 different companies and 25 nonchampions were matched by Howell and Higgins (1990) by company, age, salary, job, function, and education. They were identified from 153 interviews with colleagues and peer nominations. Themes drawn from content analysis of interviews with the champions and nonchampions were accurately classified 82% by discriminant analysis as champions or nonchampions. Champions were more likely to reveal ideological goals, confidence in self and others, and unconventional and environmentally sensitive behaviors. A factor of champion leadership behavior discriminated champions from nonchampions with 84% accuracy. Factor loadings on this factor were high for charisma .48; inspirational leadership, .77; intellectual stimulation, .36; and individualized consideration, .27. Other discriminating behaviors were risk taking, achievement, innovativeness, social adroitness, and endurance. Still another comparison of interviews of 19 pairs of matched champions and nonchampions of innovations by Howell and Boies (2004) revealed that the champions showed more enthusiastic support for new ideas, connected the innovation to positive organizational outcomes, and made use of more informal selling.

Transformational Leadership Augments Transactional Leadership

Burns (1978) originally argued that transformational leadership and transactional leadership are at opposite ends of a continuum. However, Bass (1985a) suggested that transformational leadership augmented the effects of transactional leadership. To specify the effects more clearly, Waldman, Bass, and Einstein (1985) computed a hierarchical regression analysis of transactional and trans-

formational leadership on self-reported measures of effort and performance for two samples of U.S. Army officers and one sample of industrial managers. They first entered the two transactional leadership scores for contingent reward and management by exception into the regression equation. When they followed with the entry of the interrelated transformational leadership scales of charisma (containing inspirational elements), intellectual stimulation, and individualized consideration, they demonstrated that transformational leadership had an incremental effect over and above transactional leadership. The incremental increases ranged from 9% to 48% for the different samples and outcomes predicted. For both outcomes and in all three samples, transformational leadership had a highly significant incremental effect, over and above transactional leadership. Seltzer and Bass (1987) obtained similar results for part-time MBA students' descriptions of their full-time superiors on the transactional scales of initiation and consideration and the augmenting transformational scales. Waldman and Bass (1989) found the augmentation effect of transformational charisma on transactional contingent reward when predicting the fitness reports obtained by U.S. Navy officers. The same augmentation in leaders' effectiveness was obtained when the transformational MLQ scale ratings of U.S. Army platoon lieutenants, company commanders, and battalion commanders of 3,216 soldiers were added in regression to transactional LBDQ initiation of structure.

The augmentation effects of transformational leadership on effectiveness and satisfaction were reported by King (1989) for high school and higher educational administrators and by Koh, Terborg, and Steers (1991) and Terborg (1995) for Singapore high school principals. Kessler (1993) reported an augmentation effect of transformational leadership on transactional leadership on employee job satisfaction in a research work environment. Howell and Avolio (1989) obtained results of an even more complex model of the role of transformational leadership among 76 Canadian insurance managers in their contributing to their organizations' effectiveness. They combined the managers' inner directiveness, their transactional and transformational leadership (MLQ-10), and their managers' perceptions of the organizational culture. Accounted for was 36% of the variance in the sales targets that units met a year later, according to a hierarchical regression analysis. Transformational leadership alone accounted for one third of the accuracy of the multiple predictions from augmented transactional leadership in predicting sales performance.

Integration of Transformational, Charismatic, Visionary, and Related Theories

Based on Shamir's (1992) ideas about the importance of the followers' self-concept, House and Shamir (1993) integrated theories of the new leadership. They centered the theories around how the charismatic leader increases the value and salience of followers' efforts by connecting them to valued aspects of the followers' self-concept. In this way, the new leadership theories "harness the motivational forces of self-expression, self-consistency, self-esteem, and self-worth" (p. 90). Charismatics have, in common with transformational, visionary, and other new-style leaders, role modeling, risk taking, image building, trust building and establishing competence. The leaders are intellectually stimulating but not necessarily individually considerate or adaptive. In their Neocharismatic Leadership Theory, House and Aditya (1997) emphasized four common characteristics of the various new-style leadership theories. They all attempt to explain: (1) how followers are led into attaining outstanding accomplishments; (2) how leaders achieve high degrees of motivation, commitment, loyalty, admiration, respect, and trust; (3) the importance of leaders' symbolic, emotionally appealing, supportive, and intellectually stimulating behaviors; and (4) the leader's effects on follower satisfaction, performance, self-esteem, and identification with the leader's vision and values and the collective.

A Syncretic Model of Charismatic/Transformational Leadership. Behling and McFillen (1996) applied what they regarded as six attributes of leader behavior drawn from the literature on charismatic and transformational leadership. They developed an inventory of internally consistent and leader behavior scales: (1) displays empathy, dramatizes the mission; (2) projects self-assurance; (3) enhances the leader's image, assures followers of the followers' competency; and (4) provides followers with opportunities for success. Another section of the inventory of ratings dealt with followers' beliefs in their leaders. The beliefs formed three distinct factors: (1) inspirational

leadership, (2) awe of the leader, and (3) sense of empowerment. Additionally, the three belief factors correlated .63, .28, and .38, respectively, with ratings of how much the meaningfulness of work was experienced. The leader's empathy and dramatization of the mission were inspiring. The leader's self-confidence and image enhancement generated awe. Finally, the leader assured followers of their competency to provide them with a sense of empowerment and opportunities for success.

Criticisms and Problems

Northouse (1995) believed that transformational leadership had a strong intuitive appeal, emphasized the importance of followers in the leadership process, went beyond the traditional exchange models of leadership, broadened the concept of leadership to include the growth of followers, and placed emphasis on morals and values. However, he saw, as weaknesses, lack of conceptual clarity and implications that transformational leadership is a personal trait. Furthermore, he felt, it was elitist and undemocratic. Hoffman, Blair, and Helland (2005) could not find the expected agreement between subordinates' ratings of transformational leaders and observers' ratings. Gronn (1997) viewed transformational leadership as of little use in fostering organizational learning in the Anglo-American world.

Yammarino, Spangler, and Dubinsky (1998) completed a WABA analysis for the MLQ-rated transformational, contingent reward, and satisfaction of 111 salespeople and their 34 superiors embedded in 34 work groups. Only individuals made a difference. Dyadic and group relations were of no consequence.

The Taming of Charisma. Beyer (1999) argued that the current concept of charismatic/transformational leadership was a watered-down version dealing with ordinary rather than exceptional leadership, but Beyer contradicted herself by arguing that charismatic/transformational leadership presented a heroic portrayal of leadership. House (1999) agreed with her that too much emphasis was being placed on the effects of leaders on individual followers instead of group and organizational performance. There was a failure to relate specific follower behaviors to leader visions. Charisma was tamed by its dilution. Beyer added that Weber's (1924/1947) concept of *radical* change by the charismatic/transformational leader was ignored. Ignored also was the importance of contextual and cross-cultural differences. But House faulted Beyer for ignoring the evidence, and refused to accept her other criticisms: confusing behavior and outcomes, recognizing charisma as transient, failing to account for powerful charismatic attraction, and failing to focus exclusively on truly exceptional and extraordinary leaders and leadership.

Change in Concept

Couto (1993) decried the falling away in Bass (1985c) from the humanistic concept of transforming leadership that Burns (1978) had introduced. *Transforming* leadership was focused on leadership of political and social movements and social change; Bass's *transformational* leadership emphasized its precursors and effects in formal organizations and agencies but did not exclude political leaders. Couto explained that, for Burns, the transforming leader changes followers into disciples whom, in time, others may follow. The leader is a moral agent who moves followers to be aware of how strongly they feel about their needs and to define their values so meaningfully that they can proceed with purpose. Transforming leaders are invested with power to use their principles to move followers to change others and themselves into persons who share both modal and end values.

The concept of heroic leadership is substituted for charismatic leadership. Followers place their confidence in heroes because of their reputation. Heroes are idealized, but they are not transforming since they lack the deeply held motives and goals shared by transforming leaders and followers. Nor are executives in formal organizations and institutions transforming leaders, since they do not ordinarily achieve social change. Couto concluded with the reasons for maintaining the differences between transforming and transformational leadership and their relevance to different contexts with an analogy:

> Bass has done for transforming leadership what David Lilienthal did for the concept of "grassroots democracy" within the Tennessee Valley Authority (TVA). He has placed a radically transforming concept in the service of institutional practice. Bass, like Lilienthal,

changed . . . radical transformation from social change to . . . achievement of institutional goals. (Couto, 1993, p. 6)

Psychometric Problems

There are several problems with the Multifactor Leadership Questionnaire. Management by exception is lower in internal consistency than the other factored scales. Different factor structures emerge in some studies. A single factor could account for transformational leadership based respectively on a Dutch version of inspirational leadership (Den Hartog, Van Muijen, & Koopman, 1997), the transformational components of the MLQ (Tepper & Percy, 1994), or the five transformational components of the LPI (Fields & Herold, 1997). Carless (1999) reported the same results for MLQ data and suggested that the underlying common element might be a general impression of liking the leader. Vandenberghe, Stordeur, D'hoore, et al. (2001) proposed in a factor study of 1,059 nurses in Belgium that the single factor of active leadership could encompass all of transformational leadership and contingent reward. On the other hand, Antonakis (2001) obtained results indicating that the MLQ components were structurally all distinctly different factors. Similarly, Bass (1985c), Antonakis (2001), Tejeda and Scandura (1997), and Avolio, Bass, and Jung (1999), among others, were able to discriminate three or four transformational factors from among scales of behavioral charisma, attributed charisma, inspirational motivation, intellectual stimulation, and individualized consideration. Second-order factors were extracted to facilitate the unbundling of the correlated transformational leadership scales.

Level of Analysis. Much transformational leadership research has examined the relation of the leadership to group and organizational outcomes. However, Yammarino and Dubinsky (1994) completed a WABA study for 105 drug firm salespersons (detail persons who call on physicians, dentists, and other health professionals). The analysis showed that the leader-subordinate relations could be accounted for by the individual differences among the raters of each supervisor of the detail persons. Each supervisor viewed each subordinate uniquely; each subordinate rated each supervisor uniquely. But it was also possible that each dyad of subordinate and supervisor was meaningfully different within the same group supervised. Some dyads might involve in-group members; others, out-group members. In any case, there was little or no explanatory variance left in the leader and whole group, as such (Dansereau, 1995; Yammarino, 2002; Yammarino, Dionne, & Chun, 2002). The relation of the leader to his or her entire group is usually the basis of leadership research, but these studies suggested that leaders did not differ from one another as much as a given leader differed in relation from one subordinate to another.

Lack of Ethnographic Studies. Gronn (1999) decried the lack of ethnographic studies of transformational leadership. These should be studies by trained observers over time of the dynamics of the leaders in action. Instead, he noted, "The bulk of transformational leadership research is confined either to orthodox, tick-a-box or circle-a-number respondent surveys of superiors or structured interviews with diverse informant samples" (p. 16).

Other Possible Biases. Ratings of transformational leaders may be strongly affected by the leaders' celebrity status as well as by their popularity. How much salespersons were perceived as influential correlated .74 with their perceived ability, .68 with their perceived value, and .50 with their popularity, according to sociometric ratings of 202 salespersons (Bass, 1960). It is likely that the perceived ability, value, and popularity of leaders would correlate with the extent they exerted transformational leadership. In the same way, transformational behavior is usually seen as more desirable than transactional behavior and is reflected in MLQ items. When a forced choice version of the MLQ (Form 8X) was compared with a regular listing of items (Form 8Y), the transformational mean scores were deflated. Again, correction for social desirability of the items is needed.

Contingent Reward: Both Transactional and Transformational. Among the transactional factors, as noted earlier, contingent reward empirically forms two factors. It is partly transformational when it concerns psychological reward and is intrinsically valued by the follower.

Contingent reward is transactional when it is material in nature and extrinsically valued. The pruning of management by exception by the shortening of its original 10 items to create active and passive factors (Hater & Bass, 1987) was psychometrically acceptable in the six-factor models of Tejeda and Scandura (1997) and Avolio, Bass, and Dong (1999). Nevertheless, the scales need enlarging for practical purposes.

Need for More Experimentation. Brown and Lord (1999) argue that the study of the new leadership has been too dependent on survey and field studies. There has not been a comparable amount of study invested in experimental studies. For instance, we are often not cognizant of nonverbal behaviors, as they are processed too quickly. Brown and Lord cited a study by Awamleh and Gardner (1999), noted before, in which it was concluded, on the basis of a controlled experiment, that only 3% of the perceived charisma of a visionary message was due to its content and 40% to 58% was due to its style of delivery. Brown and Lord also argued that since transformational leadership involves followers' strong emotional attachment, its antecedents may occur too rapidly and outside of conscious awareness to be reported in a survey. To reliably capture the effect requires controlled experiments.

Summary and Conclusions

Transformational leadership builds on transactional leadership. Leaders have a profile of how frequently they are transformational and how frequently they are transactional. Many active leaders may be high in both. Others may be high in one and low in the other. Less active leaders may be low in both. Considerable evidence has accumulated on the greater effectiveness of transformational leadership of political leaders, public officials, nonprofit agency leaders, religious leaders, educators, military officers, business managers, and health care directors.

Inspirational leadership does not depend on personal identification processes. Rather, the mutual goals of leaders and followers are identified and encouraged by the leader. Inspirational leadership stems from the management of meaning and impression management. The inspirational leader builds followers' expectations by envisioning a mutually describable future and articulating how to attain it. Leaders can use many intellectually stimulating ways to move followers out of their conceptual ruts. Intellectual stimulation, charismatic leadership, and inspirational leadership are major components of transformational leadership, which adds to transactional leadership in generating positive outcomes in the groups and organizations led. But above and beyond this, understanding the effects of such leadership requires examining the situation further.

Management and Organizations

Managerial Work

What roles in organizations do leaders and managers play? What organizational functions do they serve? How does the hierarchical level of the organizational leader and manager affect these activities? Are their roles changing? What makes their activities more or less effective?

From the top to the bottom echelons of the formal organization, except for the lowest level, all members report directly to a higher authority and lead followers at the levels below them. They are leaders *inside* organizations as well as leaders *of* organizations. The operating employee reports to a supervisor, the supervisor to a manager, the manager to an executive, the executive to the chief executive, and the chief executive to a board of directors, which is responsible to a constituency of shareholders or a public body.

Functions of Management and Leadership in Formal Organizations

As was noted in Chapter 2, for classical management theorists like R. C. Davis (1942), Urwick (1952), and Fayol (1916), orderly planning, organizing, and controlling were the functions of supervisors, managers, and executives in formal organizations of hierarchically arranged groups and individuals. Planning, organizing, and controlling were regarded as completely rational processes. For some, such as K. Davis (1951), the prescription for business leaders was the same as for managers—to plan, organize, and control an organization's activities. Little attention was paid to the human nature of the members constituting the organization. Although organizations strive for rationality, observation suggests that such rationality is limited (March & Simon, 1958). Nevertheless, understanding the purpose of the manager requires consideration of the planning, organizing, and controlling functions of the manager, for whom supervision and leadership may often be the most important but not the

only aspect of his or her responsibilities. Thus an empirical factored survey, completed by Wofford (1967) (one among many), could reveal factors to describe managers' functions as setting objectives, planning, organizing, leading, and controlling. Managers in organizations do perform the functions of planning, organizing, and controlling. But limiting the analysis to such general functions inhibits a more searching type of inquiry into the nature of managerial performance—about what administrators, managers, and executives actually do. Leadership remains an important component to the degree that management means getting work done with and through others. The overlapping needs of the organization, task, team, and individual must be addressed. Thus Coffin (1944) modified the classical functions of management as follows: formulation (planning), execution (organizing), and supervision (persuading). Adair (1973) conceived the functions as planning, initiating, controlling, supporting, informing, and evaluating.

Cognitive, Behavioral, and Socioemotional Components. Organizational leadership has both interpersonal and strategic components (Lohmann, 1992). Barnard (1938) was most influential in introducing the need to include more behavioral, intuitive, social, and emotional components in the functional analyses of organizational leadership. Numerous other scholars incorporated behavioral, social, and political elements in their analyses of the functions of organizational leadership. Barnard (1946b) identified the functions of organizational leadership as: (1) the determination of objectives; (2) the manipulation of means; (3) the instrumentation of action; (4) the stimulation of coordinated effort. In this light, E. Gross (1961) elaborated on the functions of organizational leadership to define goals, clarify and administer them, choose appropriate means, assign and coordinate tasks, motivate, create loyalty, represent the group, and spark the membership to action. Similarly, Selznick

(1957) suggested the following functions of organizational leadership: (1) definition of the institution's mission and goals; (2) creation of a structure for accomplishing the purpose; (3) defense of institutional integrity; (4) reevaluation of internal conflict. In a study of leadership in Samoa, Kessing and Kessing (1956) identified as leadership functions consultation, deliberation, negotiation, formation of public opinion, and decision making. Katz and Kahn (1966) proposed three functions of leadership in terms of the organization's actual formal structure: (1) the introduction of structural change (policy formation); (2) the interpretation of structure (piercing out the incompleteness of the existing formal structure); (3) the use of structure that is formally provided to keep the organization in effective motion, operation, and administration. Organizational leaders and leaders within organizations need to deal with both *intellectual* and *social* complexity. Intellectually, they must be able to assimilate complex information, work with cognitive complexities and conflicting points of view, and integrate diverse organizational stimuli. Social complexity arises, as leaders must deal with diverse individuals and units with conflicting demands, agendas, and goals. The complexity of roles increases with increasing organizational levels in both military and civilian hierarchies (Jacobs & Jaques, 1987). Self-monitoring, social intelligence, social perceptiveness, and behavioral flexibility become important with an increasing hierarchical level (Zaccaro, Gilbert, Janelle, et al., 1991). Zaccaro, Marks, O'Connor-Boes, et al. (1995) found that skills in solving complex problems increased with rank when 101 lieutenants, majors, and colonels were compared. Dean and Sharfman (1996) analyzed 52 decisions made by the top executives of 24 firms. The decisions were more effective when the executives collected relevant information and used analytical techniques. On the other hand, decisions were less effective when the executives made use of power or hidden agendas. Drucker (2000) suggested that organizational leaders need to self-assess their ethics, engage in constant self-development, be flexible in mentality, and know when to lead and when to follow. A 1992 manual of functions for operations manager, team leader, and supervisor (Anonymous, 1992) included planning, controlling, problem solving, continuous improvement, providing performance feedback, coaching, counseling, and training, creating and maintaining a motivated work environment, and representing the organization.

Overlap between Managing and Leading. This overlap is seen most clearly when one considers the human factor and the interpersonal activities involved in managing and leading. Skill as a leader and in relating to others is a most important requirement at all levels of management. It is clearly recognized at the first level of supervision; it is not as well recognized at the top of the organization. Nonetheless, interviews with 71 corporate executives by Glickman, Hahn, Fleishman, and Baxter (1969) revealed that at the top of a corporation, the group of consequence is relatively small. The group's members have highly personal relationships. They interact with one another as in a small group. A high proportion of group involvement is usual. Informal procedures supplant formal ones. Consistent with these findings, when Richards and Inskeep (1974) questioned 87 business school deans, 58 business executives, and 40 executives in trade associations about what kind of continuing education middle managers need most, these executives gave top priority to improving human relations skills. They considered improving quantitative and technical skills to be of secondary importance. Similarly, Mahoney, Jerdee, and Carroll (1965) found that the single most important function of first-level managers is to supervise others. The authors recognized eight important managerial functions: planning, investigating, coordinating, evaluating, supervising, staffing, negotiating, and representing. Their questionnaire survey of 452 managers from 13 companies in a variety of industries varying in size from 100 to over 400 employees revealed that more time was spent on supervision than on any other function (28.4%). Supervising, along with the four other functions of planning, investigating, coordinating, and evaluating, accounted for almost 90% of the time that the 452 managers spent at work.

Solem, Onachilla, and Heller (1961) lent further weight to the importance of the human factor by asking 211 supervisors in 26 discussion groups to post and select problems for discussion. In all, 58.8% of the first-level supervisors and 35.3% of the middle managers wanted to talk about subordinates' motivation to follow instructions, meet deadlines, or maintain the quality of production. Over 40% of the staff supervisors were concerned about dealing with resistance to change, as were 36.4% of the middle managers and 22.7% of the first-line supervisors. The first-line supervisors were most concerned about disciplinary problems and problems of promoting, rating, and classifying employees, while the middle managers were most interested in talking about problems of selecting, orienting, and training employees.

What Leaders and Managers Do

Gilmore (1982) saw leadership as being centrally concerned with the management of boundaries. Managing at the top organizational levels, the leader protects the organization from the risk of subversion by outsiders' values and practices. At the same time, the leader manages the importation into the organization of opportunities for learning. At the interpersonal level, the leader manages the boundary between maintaining the role requirements of self and others and making decisions based on personal considerations.

Managers as Linchpins

Rensis Likert (1961a, 1967) emphasized the linchpin function of managers. As linchpin, the manager connects a group that is composed of the manager's superior and his or her peers with a group that is composed of the manager and his or her subordinates. For Dagirmanjian (1981), leaders serve as managers by linking the whole organization with their subordinates. The leadership function in nursing was seen by Bernhard and Walsh (1981) to involve coordinating similar activities in two groups: those who seek care and those who give it.

Leaders or Managers?

There is a line of reasoning that draws a sharp distinction between leadership and management. It considers leadership to be the discretionary activities and processes that are beyond the manager's role requirements as mandated by rules, regulations, and procedures. Leadership is whatever discretionary actions are needed to solve the problems a group faces that are embedded in the large system (Osborn, Hunt, & Jauch, 1980). Leadership fits with an *organismic* view of organizations; management, with a *mechanistic* view (Terry, 1995). The environment of leaders is more hectic; the environment of managers is more static and stable (Bhatia, 1995). Leaders are more transformational; managers are more transactional. Leaders do the more correct things; managers do things correctly (Parry, 1996). However, Grove (1986) roundly rejected the distinction, stating that the effective manager must have the clarity of purpose and motivation of the effective leader. J. W. Gardner (1986b, p. 7) agreed: "Every time I encounter an utterly first-class manager, he turns out to have quite a lot of leader in him . . . even the most visionary leader will be faced on occasion with decisions that every manager faces: when to take a short-term loss to achieve a long-term gain, how to allocate scarce resources among important goals, whom to trust with a delicate assignment." For Gardner (1993), the required distinction is between the *leader-manager* and the routine manager. Gardner's leader-manager, in contrast to the routine manager, thinks long-term, can look beyond the unit he or she heads to see its relation to the larger system, and can reach and influence others outside his or her unit. The leader-manager emphasizes vision, values, motivation, and renewal and can cope with conflict. Gardner summed up leader-managers' tasks as: envisioning the group's goals; affirming the group's values, motivating its members; managing; achieving workable unity among the members; explaining what needs to be done; serving as a symbol; representing the group; and renewing the group. Leaders must be able to resolve conflicts, mediate, compromise, and build coalitions and trust. For this they need political skills as well as task and socioemotional competencies (J. W. Gardner, 1988).

Gardner (1990) also noted that senior leader-managers took advantage of the informal network to get information and used their centrality to set agendas, make strategic moves, and mobilize support from allies and from lower-level leaders. According to Zaccaro (2002), senior leader-managers also engage in goal setting, boundary spanning, planning, strategizing, and envisioning. At lower levels, they are responsible for operations and maintenance within their unit. At higher levels, they face more informational and social complexity. They need to search their environment for opportunities and threats. Nonetheless, Krantz and Gilmore (1990) suggested that management and leadership are completely different. Management is idealized as the technique for achieving an organization's objectives. Leadership is idealized as heroic, visionary, and mission-oriented. The modern leader-manager is more like a team coach who expects a 100% team effort, scouts for talent, and motivates individual initiative and imagination (Conway, 1993). Parry (1996) also listed additional differences between leaders and managers. He cited Australian Prime Minister Bob Hawke as an example of a person who was a transactional manager when meeting with his cabinet and a transformational leader when addressing the Australian public on television.

Leaders manage and managers lead, but the two activities are not synonymous. Leaders facilitate interpersonal interaction and positive working relations; they promote structuring of the task and the work to be accomplished. (E. C. Mann, 1965). All the management functions of planning, coordinating, staffing, and so on can potentially provide leadership; all the leadership activities can contribute to managing. But if trust is a key to leadership, and competence in making decisions is essential to building trust, trust and competence are important in managing resource allocations (Ulmer, 1996). Nevertheless, some managers do not lead, and some leaders do not manage (Zaleznik, 1977). Some leaders are authentic, others are not. In the past century, there has been a decided change in both leadership and management. The autocratic "bridge to engine room management" no longer works (Conway, 1993).

For the military, the leader-manager controversy continues about the importance of leading soldiers rather than managing bureaucratic technological systems. Advancement to senior levels may be due to technological proficiency instead of leadership potential, when the reverse may be needed. As Sarkesian (1985) noted, low-intensity warfare against terrorism and insurgencies calls for leadership and management of fewer large divisions and more smaller brigades and special operations units. Meyer (1983) saw the solution as the development and maintenance of unit-based organizations that make strong, continuing leader-follower relationships possible.

Leadership is path-finding; management is path-following. Leaders do the right things; managers do things right (Bennis & Nanus, 1985). Leaders develop; managers maintain. Leaders ask what and why; managers ask how and when. Leaders originate; managers imitate. Leaders challenge the status quo; managers accept

it (Bennis, 1985, 1989). Leaders function in a higher domain of cognitive analysis, synthesis, and evaluation; managers function in a lower cognitive domain of knowledge, comprehension, and application (Capozzoli, 1995). Leadership is concerned with constructive or adaptive change, establishing and changing direction, aligning people, and inspiring and motivating people (Kotter, 1990). Leaders' behaviors arouse followers' motives. They are relations-oriented. They set the direction for organizations. They articulate a collective vision. They infuse values and set examples. They sacrifice and take risks to further the vision. They appeal to the self-concepts of their followers. They inspire followers by exhibiting self-confidence, persistence, and determination. They influence their followers through the esteem attributed to them by their followers. They show how much they value their group. They speak for their group. Followers internalize the leader's expressed values, identify with the group, and can continue without the leader (House, 1995).

Managers plan, organize, and arrange systems of administration and control. They hold positions of formal authority. Their position provides them with reward, disciplinary, or coercive power to influence and obtain compliance from subordinates. The subordinates follow directions from the manager and accept the manager's authority as long as the manager has the legitimate power to maintain compliance—or the subordinates follow out of habit or deference to other powers of the leader (House, 1995). Management is concerned with consistency and order, details, timetables, and the marshaling of resources to achieve results. It plans, budgets, and allocates staffs to fulfill plans (Kotter, 1990).

The psychoanalyst Zaleznik (1977) stated that leaders and managers differ in how they relate to their roles and their subordinates. Leaders but not managers tend to be more charismalike. Leaders attract strong feelings of wanting to be identified with them. They maintain intense interpersonal relations. Leaders send out clear signals of their purpose and mission; managers tend to be more ambiguous or silent about their purpose. Leaders, but not managers, generate excitement at work. Managers are more likely to see themselves as playing a role; leaders behave as themselves. Leaders are more concerned about ideas to be articulated and projected into images; managers are more concerned about process.

Leaders, for Zaleznik, are more likely to be transformational than are managers. On the other hand, managers more readily practice contingent-reward and management by exception; they want to maintain a controlled, rational, equitable system. While managers tolerate the mundane, leaders react to it "as to an affliction." Managers who combine intuition with rationality as well as the personal characteristics of a leader make the most successful general managers (Kotter, 1982a), middle managers (Kotter, 1985), and senior and lowest-level managers (Kotter, 1988). Based on 900 questionnaires and interviews with executives from 150 organizations, Kotter (1988) concluded that successful managerial leadership requires sophisticated recruiting, early identification of development needs and planning for them, an attractive working environment, challenging opportunities, and support of line management without short-term pressure.

A Leader-Management Model. MacKenzie (1969) illustrated the great variety of activities that a typical manager may perform. Some of them, such as forecasting and budgeting, have relatively less to do with leadership as such (unless the latter is defined most broadly); and some have relatively less to do with management. People, ideas, and things are at the core of the different elements, tasks, functions, and activities that may be part of the manager's job. These are the basic components of every organization with which the manager must work. According to MacKenzie, ideas create the need for conceptual thinking; things, for administration; people, for leadership. Three functions—the analysis of problems, decision making, and communication—are important at all times and in all aspects of the jobs held by managers. These three functions permeate the entire work process. Also, at all times, managers must sense the pulse of their organization. Other functions occur ideally (but not necessarily in actual practice) in a predictable sequence of planning, organizing, staffing, directing, and controlling. How much managers are involved in these sequential functions depends on their position and the stage of completion of the projects with which they are most concerned. We may quarrel with the idea of limiting leadership to the people element; but, as will be noted later, the administrative and conceptual thinking required are so interlocked with the influence processes that the distinction

is of academic rather than practical consequence. However, the sheer diversity of activities and their linkages to the functions and tasks of management are important. This diversity shows the inadequacy of any simple approach to capture what is involved in the managerial and leadership processes. The diversity in how managers and organizational leaders spend their time, with whom they spend it, and what they do has been corroborated by numerous investigators. For example, Stewart (1967) confirmed the diversity of managerial activities when she asked 160 managers to record all job behavior incidents longer than five minutes in duration that occurred for them.

Alignment. Leaders and managers align the objectives of their subordinates and themselves with the goals of the organization to manage innovations, manage resources, lead change, lead learning, and manage the diverse interests of stakeholders. Both leaders and managers make mistakes, but the good ones learn from their mistakes, accept responsibility for them, and try not to make the same mistake twice. They ask the right questions, anticipate crises, and do not allow short-term objectives to interfere with longer-term goals (J. Reynolds, 1994). Gustafson (1999) suggests that an individual-organizational "balanced scorecard" needs to be used by leaders and managers in evaluations. Individual performance appraisals need to reflect what the organization wants to accomplish. Outcome measures can help align operations with strategic goals. Three to five cycles of application are needed for adequate testing and revision of the appraisal framework.

Innovation. Innovations are stimulated by unexpected occurrences, incongruities, process needs, and changes in industries and markets (Drucker, 1991) Leaders need to be alert to these occurrences (Kotter, 1991). Bennis (1991) listed six ways for leaders and managers to foster and support innovation: (1) create a compelling vision; (2) create a climate of trust; (3) create an environment that reminds people about what is important; (4) encourage learning from mistakes; (5) create an empowering environment; (6) create a flat, flexible, adaptive, decentralized organization. Organizational leaders need constancy. They need to practice empowerment and to encourage flatter, adaptive, flexible, decentralized organizations.

Resources. The benefits and costs of resources need to be weighed. Equitable distribution of resources needs to be maintained. Knowledge is an essential resource for leaders and managers. Where technology is important, engineering and science may be necessary. Likewise, in health care administration, medicine or nursing is of consequence. In financial services, accounting, finance, and business law are of equal consequence. Knowledge of marketing, salesmanship, and consumer behavior is needed in the mass retailing and consumer service industries.

Change. Leadership is central to the organizational change process. Sometimes it is managed from the top with little feedback from followers. Other times it may begin with suggestions from supervisors or middle management and their subordinates and work its way up. Envisioning, energizing, and enabling characterize leaders of the change process (Dodge, 1998). An action learning procedure, Organizational Fitness Profiling, can be introduced to provide a guided process for organizational change (Beer, 1997). Changing corporate culture and members' behavior takes three to ten years. Changes in the culture's values may enhance the behavior. Change usually begins with corporate strategy set by top management. To implement change, the vision, strategies, and values to be changed are communicated downward. Upward initiatives, feedback modifications, and other inputs are sought from below, from the board of directors, and from relevant outsiders. Needs, required learning, and learning opportunities are assessed, modeled, and rewarded to fit the strategies. The changes are constantly reinforced (Wilhelm, 1992). Beer, Eisenstat, and Spector (1990) proposed a six-step change process: (1) Mobilize commitment to change through joint diagnosis of problems; (2) Develop a shared vision of how to organize and manage; (3) Foster consensus for the new vision and competence in how to begin and continue the change; (4) Begin with the units most ready for change; (5) Spread the change to the other units; (6) Monitor and adjust the process to handle problems that arise in the change effort. Top management must practice what it preaches. Attention to needed change can both create economic value for shareholders in the short term as well as develop an open, trusting culture in the long term (Beer & Nohria, 2000).

To illustrate Weick's (1988, 1995) theory of how leaders make change meaningful to others and bring about change, Kurke and Brindle (1999) used what Alexander the Great did to enact change in his brief but highly successful conquest of much of the known world. Alexander *reframed the problems he faced.* For instance, at the time, Tyre was on an island with a strong fleet. Alexander took nine months to build a causeway from the mainland to the island so his soldiers could walk to the island. He used *symbolism.* It was predicted that whoever untied the Gordian Knot would conquer the world. Alexander cut the knot with his sword. Wherever possible, he made *strategic alliances.* When he crossed into India and defeated Porus, instead of killing him he made him an ally. He strengthened his identity as ruler of the former Persian Empire rather than the conquering Greek general by adopting Persian garb and ritual and marrying his Macedonian soldiers (and himself) to Persian women. Kirke and Stein (1986) made the case that Alexander's successful strategies made him great.

Learning. Leading and managing learning include mentoring, modeling, and monitoring the learning of followers. Leaders take a personal interest in the learning of others. They reflect on their experiences, and, where applicable, they define problems using solutions they have already learned. They find time for self-renewal and for serving as catalysts. In learning organizations, leaders continually attend to the learning agenda and institutionalize the commitment to the learning process. They establish routines to receive undistorted feedback. They learn from mistakes and encourage others to do the same (McGill & Slocum, 1994).

Stakeholders. Stakeholders include all those who have an interest in the actions of the organization and the ability to influence it. Stakeholders benefit from leaders and managers who can balance the relative satisfaction of stakeholders' interests in the corporation: owners, shareholders, management, employees, suppliers, customers, families, community, state, and nation. Leaders and managers need to achieve a consensus from their stakeholders about what and how to do so (Savage, Nix, Whitehead, et al., 1991). Charismatic-transformational leaders and managers can induce change among immediate followers and those at a distance. But transactional leaders can use contingent reward to do the same.

Public Service and Nonprofit Leaders and Managers

Law Enforcement and Police Officers. These leaders are faced with problems equivalent to those of other public service and not-for-profit managers of the same hierarchical rank. According to Ceballos (1999), they have to deal, in order, with five issues: budgets and funding, developing leaders and managers, advances in technology, community policing, and ethics. Finances depend on how much federal, state, and local governments are involved and how much support can be obtained for developing police managers and executives. New technology, such as DNA testing, is helping investigative police work. Changes in community policies on policing can have dramatic effects on local crime rates. The use of force, accountability, and responsibility are affected by ethical conduct. These same characteristics are relevant to the role of prison warden. The warden is likened to a military commander with lieutenants and sergeants. Wardens learn their roles for this "most arduous occupation" (Bryans & Wilson, p. 191) by word of mouth and by copying role models. They receive little training for the role. There has been little research on their behavior and the relation of their behavior to success and effectiveness in prisons in the United States, and even less in Britain. The Federal Bureau of Prisons' Institutional Character Profiling, available since 1990, provides a way of assessing institutional stability, the staff's quality of work life, inmates' working and living conditions, and relations among the correctional officers. Written tests and simulations are also available for candidate selection (Bryans & Wilson, 2000). In his review of *A View from the Trenches: A Manual for Wardens and by Wardens* (NAAWS, 1999), Morganbesser (1999) quotes a former warden (Bronson, 1997), who called the warden's job impossible. The warden's discretionary authority was likely to be challenged and the warden suffer from burnout. Nevertheless, Cullen et al. (1993) found that wardens had a high level of job satisfaction. According to Morganbesser, considerable efforts are beginning to occur in training for wardens and correctional officers at the National Academy of Corrections and the Federal Bureau of Prisons. These include peer-oriented training, mentoring, and other management development programs. As would be expected of free workers, Gillis, Getkate, Robinson, et al. (1995) found that inmates of a correctional institution who rated their supervisors as transformational had more motivation to work; supervisors rated as laissez-faire leaders correlated with less motivation by inmates to work.

College Presidents. These executives have to engage in many of the same activities as leader-administrators and CEOs. Nonetheless, few are like Father Theodore Hesburgh of Notre Dame in performance and strategy. Over a 35-year period in office, Father Hesburgh's actions raised Notre Dame's endowment fund from less than $10 million to more than $300 million. At the same time, he greatly increased Notre Dame's scholarly mission at the expense of moving football (ordinarily a prime reason for alumni giving) from its preeminent niche to a more appropriate place in the university (Anonymous, 1987).

Finances are seen to be the main issue confronting college presidents (*The New York Times*, 2005). For Cohen and March (1974), college presidents face a great deal of ambiguity. Their organizations have problematic goals and operate with inconsistent and ill-defined preferences. Their technology is unclear. They use trial and error to operate. The participation of its members varies. The organizational boundaries are uncertain. The presidents must exert leadership on issues of high inertia and low salience for most members in an "organized anarchy." Bensimon (1988, pp. 3–7) obtained suggestions from interviews with 35 new and experienced presidents about what new presidents should do. They need to: (1) make several visits to their new campus before taking office; (2) get to know and become known to the significant players; (3) read as much as possible about the institution's operations, procedures, and history and pay attention to them; (4) listen to constituents and observe processes before launching a search for problems; (5) get involved in the budgetary process; (6) accumulate credit for consulting others and being willing to listen before launching change efforts. In a study of 32 institutions of higher education, Birnbaum (1990) found that 75% of newly appointed presidents had faculty support that fell to 25% for presidents who had been in office for a longer time. Those who were able to maintain faculty support throughout their tenure were more likely to seek faculty input. They supported governance structures and an action orientation. They remained totally involved but did not micromanage. Long-term presidents who lost faculty support as well as support from other constituencies, such as the students, the board, and the community, were authoritarian and saw leadership as top down. They outraged the faculty when they took precipitous action without consultation. In evaluating a president, board members and administrators are more favorable in their evaluation compared to other campus leaders; faculty leaders are least favorable (Fujita, 1990).

Nine effective state university presidents and their institutions of higher learning were nominated by experts and compared to 16 representative state university presidents and institutions. The 25 universities had undergone the stress of five successive annual budget cuts. The presidents displayed more transformational leadership based on the Fisher-Tack Effective Leadership Inventory and were more likely to survive (Fisher, Tack, & Wheeler, 1988). Cowen (1990) failed to find that the style of leadership displayed by 153 presidents of four-year public colleges and universities improved student enrollments over a five-year period. However, enrollments did show improvement when the presidents were rated more favorably by their constituents and had been on campus longer.

School Principals. Repeatedly, studies of school effectiveness have shown that the principal's leadership and management are the keys to a school's effectiveness (Austin & Reynolds, 1990) and the initiation of improvement and change (Fullan, 1991). Effective school principals must contend with multiple demands placed on them daily. They must be instructional leaders, administrators, head teachers, moral leaders, role models, community workers, social service providers, and even fund-raisers. Time for reflection on needed systematic changes in the school is hard to find (Tewel, 1986). As instructional leader, the principal must be knowledgeable about effective instruction and able to evaluate it (Schlechty, 1990). Allen (1981) formulated a model for the school principal's performance that showed how successful outcomes for a school depend on the principal's selection of appropriate roles to enact for a given situation. Support for the model was obtained from panels of experts. The roles played by principals are similar to those of middle managers. They encompass managing resources, ensuring a safe school environment, and maintaining good relations with parents and community (Austin & Reynolds, 1990). Like most managers, they are subject to constant interruptions, lack of time to plan, fragmentation of activities, and the need to comply with rules and regulations that are often statutory (Richardson, Short, Prickett, et al., 1991). In Ontario, principals at all levels of effectiveness cited difficulties with their boards and students. But only the ineffective principals added difficulties with their role and with their community (Leithwood & Montgomery, 1984).

By 1990, principals' roles were changing, according to 76% to 91% of a survey of 840 mostly principals or assistant principals in Washington State. Increasing were decentralization, diversity requirements, interaction with parents, special education, school community relations, and efforts to monitor truancy (Austin & Reynolds, 1990). According to Lake and Martinko (1982) and Martinko and Gardner (1984a, 1984b), who observed and coded the activities of highly effective and moderately effective school principals, the moderately effective principals spent more time with students and parents but less time with other outsiders than did the highly effective principals. The highly effective principals initiated 64% of the contacts; the moderates, 54%. While 47% of the moderates' contacts were judged to be human relations–oriented, only 30% of the highly effective principals' contacts were so judged. Conversely, 66% of the highly effective principals' contacts were task-oriented; 51% of the moderately effective principals' contacts were so designated.

Assistant principals serve schools in several ways. According to a study of the work of eight assistant principals in three large comprehensive public secondary schools in Southern California, they: (1) implement state requirements for the curriculum, its master schedule, and the schools' organizational regularity; (2) prepare the annual extracurricular activity calendar, which involves the values of the local community and the school. In completing this work, their supervisory duties require monitoring, supporting, and remediating (Reed & Himmler, 1985).

"Grassroots" Community Leaders. "Grassroots" leaders are ordinarily involved in a community issue but

are less often in the mainstream of institutional leadership. They tend to use unconventional techniques and are motivated more by passion than money, by personal commitment to service, social change, and social justice. Their leadership efforts are often initiated by a struggle. They may be involved because of religious or spiritual beliefs. They are more enthusiastic about shared leadership than about hierarchical leadership (Anonymous, 1999). "Grass roots" leaders can now be mobilized very quickly through the Internet and have become a political force as lobbyists in local, state, and national affairs.

Methods and Dimensions for Studying What Managers Do

Chapters 4 and 5 described many of the methods that are available for studying leaders as persons. Most of these methods are paralleled by procedures for studying the positions of managers and executives. They include checklists, logs, diaries, and retrospective accounts from interviews, panel discussions, observations, and questionnaire surveys of focal managers and their colleagues. Positions are analyzed, as well as functions, activities, and completed work. The characteristics of the process in which the manager works are another way of analyzing what the manager does. Stewart (1967, 1982b) analyzed the duration of specific activities, the mode of communications used, and the particular persons contacted to detail the characteristics that distinguish among managers' positions.

Recording of Activities

Managers' behaviors may be recorded by observers in a log or by the managers themselves in a diary or rated in response by interviewers. Based on diaries, observations, and interviews, Stewart (1982) proposed that three dimensions could describe any manager's job: (1) *demands*—the role expectations set by superiors, rules, policies, deadlines, and situational conditions requiring conformity for survival in the role; (2) *constraints*—organizational, technological, or environmental conditions limiting the manager's role and choices; (3) opportunities and activities the manager can freely choose and prioritize. Manag-

ers need to reduce the demands and constraints in order to be freer to determine strategies. This may call for interpersonal skills and cognitive competencies. Economic downturns, increased competition, government regulations, and labor unions are some of the sources of external constraints on top management. Their discretion may also be restricted by internal sources such as the legacy of the organization's founder, the influence of the dominant owner, lack of membership in a family-owned corporation, and the strength of the board of directors (Hambrick & Finkelstein, 1987).

S. Carlson (1951) analyzed self- and assistants' recordings of the activities of 10 mainly Swedish executives for four weeks. For each action, the recordings noted the site, the person who was contacted, how the communications were conducted (face-to-face or otherwise), the issues involved, and the actions taken. Employing similar records, T. Burns (1957) collected three to five weeks of the diary entries of 76 British top managers. Dubin and Spray (1964) depended on the self-descriptions by eight executives of all "job behavior episodes" over a two-week period, For each episode, they indicated its behavioral content, when it began and ended, who initiated it, with whom the interaction occurred, and how it was conducted. Home and Lupton (1965) made use of checklist records of the activities of 66 managers for a one-week period.

Carlson and James (1971) asked 88 insurance agency managers and 252 supervisors to record their work activities over five weeks and again six months later. Correlations between the first and second measures ranged from .78 to .96, indicating a rather high degree of stability in reported work performance over time. Kelly (1964) used activity sampling in a study of manufacturing executives. His results showed that managers who performed identical functions exhibited similar activity profiles. Likewise, Stogdill and Shartle (1955) asked U.S. Navy officers to keep a minute-by-minute log of their activities for a period of three days. After the logs were collected, the officers were asked to estimate the percentage of time they had spent in different activities during the period. The correlations between logged time and estimated time were computed. The results indicated a fairly high correspondence between logged time and estimated time for objectively observable performances such as talking with other persons, reading and answering mail, reading and writing reports, and operating machines. Less objective, less readily observable forms of behavior, such as planning and reflection, failed to yield estimates that corresponded highly with logged time. Nor was there a high correlation between logged and estimated behavior for infrequent activities such as teaching and research. Carroll and Taylor (1968, 1969) collected brief self-reports from 21 managers on what they were doing at a randomly selected minute during each half hour of a period of investigation. The same information for the 21 managers was provided as the time estimates and other observational methods used by an outside observer. Komaki, Zlotnick, and Jensen (1986) introduced further sophistication into observational procedures by using microanalytical coding procedures that were again based on careful time sampling.

Content Analysis of Biographies of Organizational Leaders.

Van Fleet and Peterson (1995) created the Career Description Analysis, a procedure for content analysis of biographies and autobiographies of organizational leaders. For instance, of 10 military leaders, Generals Omar Bradley (14%) and Dwight Eisenhower (11%) were considerably higher in their percentages of frequency of clarifying work roles and objectives than were Marine General Alexander Vandergrift (5%) and General George Patton (4%). Most frequently *inspiring* of 14 business leaders were Mary Kay Ash (12%) and Thomas Watson, Sr. (11%), compared to John DeLorean (3%) and Alfred P. Sloan (2%).

Case Studies.

Qualitative studies of individual or multiple cases that might include quantitative data were popularized as the method of choice for professional education by the Harvard Business School. It was influenced by the use of legal cases for setting precedents and educating lawyers and judges. Hunt and Ropo (1995) demonstrated that with a suitable conceptual framework, a case could generate testable propositions. For example, in the case of Roger Smith's tenure as CEO from 1981 to 1990 at General Motors, they proposed that the availability of vast amounts of resources tends to encourage bold but not necessarily wise decisions. Other propositions concerned Smith's limited behavioral complexity, critical tasks, and organizational culture.

Critique.

Despite the face validity of observational approaches, Martinko and Gardner (1985) found a number of shortcomings in them. First, because sample sizes are usually small, the result is the questionable generalizability of conclusions. Second, such approaches often lack adequate reliability checks. Observers need to take account of the multiple purposes of a single action, whose coding is often unreliable. Third, observational reporting is usually simplistic, mechanistic, and narrow in perspective and tends to ignore variations among positions and their situational circumstances. Fourth, such approaches fail to remain consistent in using an ideographic, longitudinal, or case-by-case orientation or a nomothetic approach that aggregates and averages observations across individual positions and situations.

Self-reporters and observers are likely to miss many fleeting, transient actions. Usually, observers can only infer the manager's purposes and the intentions of a manager's observable action. Moreover, much of a manager's behavior is cognitive and unobservable (Stewart, 1965). Observational studies need to be buttressed by interviews and questionnaires using larger samples.

Questionnaires, Interviews, and Panel Discussions

Extensive interviews precede the development of custom-made questionnaires if suitable questionnaires are not already available. A sample of senior managers might be interviewed for developing questionnaires about work done. A cross-sectional sample of the hierarchical levels and functional areas would be needed for developing a questionnaire about the work done by supervisors, managers, and executives. The questions may be structured, with alternative possible answers provided, or with an open-ended section, with respondents free to answer in their own words. Then managers or their associates can be asked to complete the structured questionnaires organized by clusters, factors, or dimensions of activities in which ratings are made of how much time the managers spend on the different functions, tasks, and activities; with whom they spend their time; and in what ways. Illustrative are investigations by Allen (1981), Korotkin and Yarkin-Levin (1985), and Sperry (1985). Allen collected self-rated questionnaire descriptions from 1,476 New York City government managers about their tasks. Korotkin and Yarkin-Levin used both interviews and questionnaires to generate lists of tasks describing the required activities of U.S. Army commissioned and non-commissioned officers. Sperry held a series of discussions with senior federal career managers to obtain information about their role orientation and job problems.

Questionnaires for describing positions have been used extensively. Hemphill (1960) used the Executive Position Description Questionnaire (EPDQ) to examine the positions of 93 business executives located in five companies. The positions represented three levels of organization and five specialties (research and development, sales, manufacturing, general administration, and industrial relations). Data were obtained on 575 items that were classified as: (1) position activities, (2) position responsibilities, (3) position demands and restrictions, (4) position characteristics. Correlations were computed between positions: (1) within each organization, (2) within each level of the organization, and (3) within each specialty. Again, systematic differences were associated with differences in the hierarchical levels in which the positions were located. The results indicated a greater degree of similarity between positions in the same specialty but were different at different levels. Hemphill also factor-analyzed the correlations among the 575 items. Ten factors emerged: (1) providing a staff service for a nonoperational area; (2) supervising work; (3) business control; (4) technical (markets and product); (5) human, community, and social affairs; (6) long-range planning; (7) exercise of broad power and authority; (8) business reputation; (9) personal demands; and (10) preservation of assets.

With a heavier emphasis on the functional responsibilities of different managerial positions, Tornow and Pinto (1976) developed the Management Position Description Questionnaire (MPDQ) to provide a similar analysis for higher-level managers. Thirteen functions and associated work done for executives could be differentiated and evaluated. These were (1) product, marketing, and financial strategy planning—long-range thinking and planning; (2) coordination of other organization units and personnel—coordinating the efforts of others over whom one exercises no direct control; (3) internal business control—reviewing and controlling the allocation of personnel and other resources, cost reduction, performance goals, budgets, and employee relations practices; (4) products and services responsibility—

planning, scheduling, and monitoring products and the delivery of services; (5) public and customer relations—promoting the company's products and services, the goodwill of the company, and general public relations; (6) advanced consulting—application of technical expertise to special problems, issues, questions, or policies; (7) autonomy of action—discretion in the handling of the job, making decisions that are most often not subject to review; (8) approval of financial commitments—authority to obligate the company; (9) staff service fact gathering—the acquisition and compilation of data and record keeping for a higher authority; (10) supervision—getting work done efficiently through the effective use of people; (11) complexity and stress—handling information under time pressure to meet deadlines, frequently taking risks, interfering with personal or family life; (12) advanced financial responsibility—preservation of assets, making investment decisions and large-scale financial decisions that affect the company's performance; (13) broad personnel responsibility—management of human resources and the policies affecting it. Tornow and his colleagues continued this line of investigation for 11 years in different industries, for different organizational levels, and in upward of 20 countries involving more than 10,000 managers. The instrument they validated, the MPDQ, contains about 250 items of required activities, contacts, skills, knowledge, and abilities. In rating each item to describe the management position, the job analyst weighed the importance, the criticality, and the frequency of occurrence of the item. Managers indicated that 85% of their jobs were adequately described by the items of the MPDQ, according to managers in both the United States and foreign countries (Page, 1985, 1987).

Profiles of Managerial Positions. Managerial positions can be usefully profiled on factors and compared with norms for the different levels of management. Seven large-scale studies that searched for factor analytic solutions were carried out in a variety of industries, including banking, manufacturing, and retailing. Seven types of these factors consistently emerged across these studies: (1) planning, (2) controlling, (3) monitoring business indicators, (4) supervising, (5) coordinating, (6) sales/marketing, and (7) public relations and consulting (Page & Tornow, 1987). In the profiles of the factor scores for the positions of 108 executives, 125 managers, and 196 supervisors, executive positions stood out in their planning, controlling, and monitoring business indicators and in their public relations activities. Supervisors' positions differed the most from those of the managers and executives in supervisory activities and their relatively low scores in comparison to the others on most of the other factors. The managers' position tended to come closer to those of the executives in planning, controlling, coordinating, and consulting and closer to the supervisors in public relations.

Consistent with these findings, a factor analysis reported by Dunnette (1986) of 65 managerial tasks yielded factors, including: (1) monitoring the business environment; (2) planning and allocating resources; (3) managing individuals' performance; (4) instructing subordinates; (5) managing the performance of groups; (6) representing the groups. Comparisons among 574 first-level, 466 middle-level, and 165 executive-level managers indicated that as the hierarchical level increased, so did the managers' functions of monitoring the business environment and coordinating groups. At the same time, the instruction of subordinates and the management of individual performance decreased.

Yukl, Wall, and Lepsinger (1988) reported on the development and validation of the Managerial Practices Survey (MPS). The survey focused on managerial behavior, i.e., "answers requests, invites participation, determines how to reach objectives, assigns tasks, praises, facilitates the resolution of conflicts, and develops contacts." Colleagues and job incumbents rated the importance and relevance of each behavior to carrying out the manager's responsibilities effectively. The 1988 version (Yukl, 1988, 1989, 2002) was grouped into 11 scales. The scales were developed using factor analysis and judges' categorizations of the items. The 11 scales assessed the following behavioral dimensions: informing, clarifying, monitoring, problem solving, planning and organizing, consulting/delegating, motivating, recognizing/rewarding, supporting, networking/interfacing, and conflict management/team building.

Managerial Role Activities. Empirically obtained managerial roles by Hales (1986) and Page and Tornow (1987) included disturbance handling, innovating, sales/marketing, public relations, and labor relations. Morse and Wagner (1978) used a modified list of nine of Mintzberg's (1973)[1] managerial roles (see below) to classify managerial activities in a descriptive questionnaire. After several refinements by means of factor analysis, they constructed a list of 51 activities that could be used by managers to evaluate the effectiveness of another manager with whom they worked closely. By rating a manager on each activity, a colleague could evaluate the manager's behavior. Six extracted factors covered the original nine role activities: (1) managing the organization's environment and its resources (effective managers are proactive and stay ahead of changes in their environment; basing plans and actions pertaining to the organization's resources on clear, up-to-date, accurate knowledge of the objectives of the company), (2) organizing and coordinating (effective managers fit the amount of formal rules and regulations in their organizations to the tasks to be done and to the abilities and personalities of the people doing them; these managers are not difficult to get along with or to coordinate with), (3) information handling (effective managers make sure that information entering the organization is processed by formal reports, memos, and word of mouth on a timely basis so it is usable and current and provides rapid feedback; they make sure that the person who has to use the information clearly understands it), (4) providing for growth and development (effective managers ensure, through career counseling and careful observation and recording, that their subordinates grow and develop in their ability to perform their work; they guide subordinates by commending the subordinates' good performance); (5) motivating and conflict handling (effective managers transmit their own enthusiasm for attaining organizational goals to others; they are not plagued by recurring conflicts of a similar nature that get in the way of associates' efforts to perform their jobs), (6) strategic problem solving (effective managers periodically schedule strategy and review sessions involving the design of projects to improve organizational performance and to solve organizational problems; they spend considerable amounts of time looking at their organization for problem situations and for opportunities to improve their subordinates' performance).

Managers are often required to allocate or recover re-

[1] See, e.g., Kmetz and Willower (1982), Kurke and Aldrich (1979), Martin and Willower (1981), O'Dempsey (1976), Snyder and Clue (1980), and Sproull (1981).

sources. They need to understand the rules involved. Allocators generally favor giving and taking back resources based on needs. Equality is favored particularly when resources are to be recovered. Generally, recovery decisions are harder to make than allocations. Monetary and facilitative resources tend to be most difficult to allocate (Parks, Conlon, Ang, et al., 1999). Evaluations of 231 managers by colleagues were higher for better-performing managers on all six dimensions in three of six offices, according to objective criteria such as net profit, data budgeting, and the volume of customer billing. The evaluations were correlated between .41 and .65 with superiors' rankings of how well the managers were performing. Multiple regression analyses indicated that the managerial activities that were of most consequence to the end results were, first, managing the organization's environment and resources; and, second, motivation and conflict handling. But the consequences depended on the organization's objectives. Thus, according to multiple regressions, in contrast to other kinds of firms, in a data processing firm, accounting and handling financial records for clients, information handling, and strategic problem solving by the managers contributed the most to the appraised performance of the managers by their superiors. A similar line of investigation was completed using the Management Practices Survey (MPS). Yukl and Kanuk (1979) showed that for 151 employees of beauty salons who described their salon managers, the average monthly profit margins of the salons correlated .47 and .49, respectively, with the extent to which managers were seen to engage in clarifying and motivating activities.

Numerous other examples can be provided. Thus cadet sergeants' clarifying and motivating correlated .26 and .30, respectively, with the performance of the ROTC units for which they were responsible (Yukl & Van Fleet, 1982). Problem solving and recognizing/rewarding correlated .39 and .42, respectively, with the behavior of managers when the managers were responsible for the performance of insurance salespersons in retail department store outlets (Yukl & Carrier, 1986). For 24 school principals studied by Martinko and Gardner (1984b), whose managerial behavior was described by their schoolteachers, again problem solving, clarifying, monitoring, and motivating correlated with effectiveness (between .36 and .49), as did networking/interfacing (.47). Miles (1985) found that these and the other 13 scales of activi-

ties of the MPS by 48 directors of home economics programs correlated between .21 and .42 with the quality of the county programs they administered. Similar results were found for department heads.

A Behavioral Checklist Analysis. Tsui (1984) pointed out that a manager's reputation for effectiveness depends on satisfying at least three constituencies: superiors, peers, and subordinates. The performance appraisals earned by a manager, merit pay increases, rate of promotion, and career advancement were highest when the manager's reputation for effectiveness was high among all three constituencies. Such threefold reputational effectiveness correlated with behavioral checklists of roles taken by a sample of managers. Mean correlations for the threefold reputational effectiveness of managers and the extent to which the managers engaged in each of six Mintzberg roles were as follows: leader (.45), liaison (.23), entrepreneur (.37), environmental monitor (.34), resource allocator (.37), and spokesperson (.35). Multiple regression analyses indicated that almost 30% of the reputational effectiveness could be accounted for alone by the extent to which managers engaged in the roles of leader and entrepreneur. Expected differences emerged, however, among the constituencies in what role activities were important for reputational effectiveness. In a subsequent study, Tsui and Ohlott (1986) found that the various constituencies had similar models of the elements of managerial effectiveness but differed on the relative importance to attach to each. The roles of leader and entrepreneur (planner, controller, implementer of change) were most salient for managerial effectiveness in their models of what was important in the role repertoire of the focal manager they described.

A Three-Stage Model of Effective Leader-Managers. Neider and Schriesheim (1988) developed a three-stage model that is presented in Figure 23.1. The three stages deal with precursor conditions, maintenance functions, and reassessment and monitoring. Precursor conditions are the organizational functions and tasks that take place to set the stage for effective leadership and management. They include a thorough job analysis, detailed compensation analysis, good selection strategies, and sound orientation training of the subordinates. In the first stage, effective leaders pay attention to the data necessary to

Figure 23.1 A Diagnostic Model of Effective Leadership

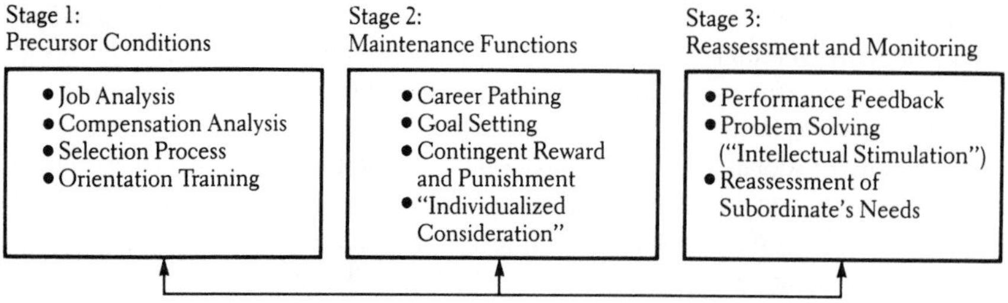

SOURCE: Neider and Schriesheim (1988).

clarify fully for subordinates how their efforts will result in the attainment of the objectives of the job. Equity and desired rewards that are contingent on performance are key considerations. Effective leaders ensure that the subordinate's knowledge, skills, and abilities match the requirements of the job. The second stage involves career pathing for the subordinate, goal setting, and performance-contingent and individualized consideration focused on the development of the subordinate through suitable delegation. Both the subordinate's self-esteem and the organization's attractiveness to the subordinate are thus enhanced. In the third stage, the effective leader provides feedback and meetings at which the alignment of the subordinate's needs and performance with the organization are reassessed and misperceptions are corrected. Here, intellectually stimulating leadership helps solve the subordinate's problems.

Critical Incidents. Flanagan (1951) originated the *critical incidents* technique. Respondents describe incidents of effective and ineffective job performance they have observed or in which they have been involved. The technique was applied to a study of the jobs of U.S. Air Force officers and research executives. It was possible to classify the incidents under the following major headings: supervision, planning and direction, handling of administrative details, exercise of responsibility, exercise of personal responsibility, and proficiency in a given specialty. In the same way, Wallace and Gallagher (1952) analyzed the job activities and behaviors of 171 production supervisors in five plants. They collected and classified 3,765 behavioral incidents by the topic involved, location of the incident, person contacted, and nature of the foreman's behavior during the incident. Along simi-

lar lines, Williams (1956) and Kay (1959), among others, were able to describe managerial jobs in terms of critical requirements. Williams collected more than 3,500 incidents from a representative sample of 742 executives who were distributed proportionally by industry, company size, and geographic location. Kay collected 691 critical incidents of foremen's behavior from managers and rank-and-file employees.

Biases in Time and Work Methods of Study

According to a review by Carlson and James (1971) of the various methods employed to study what managers do, how they spend their time, and what functions they perform, adequate reliabilities and validities have been obtained.[2] Nonetheless, systematic biases can be seen.

Substantive Problems. An obvious error occurs if the description is more about a particular job incumbent than about the position as it is and should be performed by the average or typical incumbent. Another bias is due to the fact that managers in a hierarchy think they have a bigger job than their immediate superiors think they have. At the same time, managers think their subordinates have smaller jobs than the subordinates think they have (Haas, Porat, & Vaughan, 1969). The importance of the position and its duties depends on who is describing them. Several investigations corroborated this fact.

Brooks (1955) asked 96 executives, their superiors,

[2] See also Anderson and Nilsson (1964); Carroll and Taylor (1968); Flanagan (1951, 1954); Hemphill (1959); Kay and Meyer (1962); Lau, Newman, and Broedling (1980); Lau and Pavett (1980); O'Neill and Kubany (1957); McCall, Morrison, and Hanman (1978); Pavett and Lau (1983); Shartle (1956); and P. A. Stewart (1967).

and their subordinates to rate the work performed by the executives as indicated by 150 functional items. The executives rated themselves higher than they were rated by their subordinates in such activities as defining authority, delegating, planning, and showing how jobs related to the whole picture. Again, supervisors and subordinates differed in the requirements they saw for other aspects of the supervisor's job. According to Sequeira (1964), supervisors perceived that they were required to perform duties that did not legitimately belong to their jobs. Among these duties were: training new workers on the job, arranging wage agreements, and checking supplies. Workers expected their supervisors to do more than the supervisors required of themselves in settling personnel problems and grievances, clarifying work difficulties, and improving work methods and conditions. A study by Yoga (1964) of 11 plants in India in three industries (textiles, processing, and engineering) yielded similar results.

Methodological Problems. According to McCall, Morrison, and Hanman (1978), managers' behavior is usually described in global dimensions, such as planning and controlling, instead of actual observable behaviors because so many studies depend on interviews or questionnaires of the managers themselves. The results are then summarized with factor analyses. The responses of the managers provide only indirect information about what the managers do. This is in contrast to observations of what they actually do. The self-reports deviate considerably from observations and records of their behavior (Horne & Lupton, 1965; Kelly, 1964)—although as noted before, Navy officers could accurately estimate the logged time they spent on observable activities. Diaries, as self-reports, are also likely to deviate from summary estimates as well as from independent observers' descriptions (T. Burns, 1954). "Managers are poor estimators of their own activities" (Mintzberg, 1973, p. 222). Thus, as Lewis and Dahl (1976) point out, although 12 university administrators estimated in a summary judgment that they had spent 47% of their time in meetings, their diaries for five weeks indicated that they had spent 69% of their time in such meetings (Lewis & Dahl, 1976).

The discrepancy between what managers say they do in response to questionnaires and what they actually do is to be expected. Managers do not consciously plan ahead to summarize all their activities in a retrospective survey. "Managerial work activities are fragmented, brief, diverse, fast-paced and primarily oral, [and] the sheer volume and nature of activities seriously hinder a manager's efforts to conscientiously observe and purposively memorize activities for accurate reporting on a future survey" (McCall, Morrison, & Hanman, 1978, p. 27). Furthermore, regardless of the self-reporting method used, social desirability is likely to inflate results (Weiss, Davis, England, & Lofquist, 1961). As with many other methodological problems, for confidence in the conclusions reached, the solution usually lies in using multiple methods that combine self-colleagues', and observers' reports with a mix of logs or diaries and interviews or questionnaires.

Personal Preferences. Different managers can occupy a position with the same requirements yet display considerable differences in how they fulfill their responsibilities. Stewart (1976b) observed that the activities of incumbents in management positions with the same function and at the same level varied considerably because managerial jobs have a certain amount of choice beyond the basic demands of the job. To a considerable degree, managers can work on tasks of their choosing and when they want to. Stogdill and Shartle (1955) pointed out that regardless of the different requirements of the new position to which they were transferred, naval officers spent the same amount of time on some activities in both positions. In the same way, Castaldi (1982) found that seven of ten CEOs who headed companies of the same size in the same industry (small furniture manufacturing) agreed about the importance they attached to operational activities. The seven attached more importance to strategic activities only. The majority's emphasis on strategic activities was seen to be a consequence of the static technology of the furniture industry, the strong competitiveness among firms, and the long tenure of the CEOs.

Time Spent and Work Done by Managers

Use of Time

Most studies have focused on how managers spend their time, what work they do, and what roles they play. The frequency, importance, and criticality of these factors have been the usual gauges of consequence. Clearly, according to diaries and observational studies, managers work long hours, ranging from 50 to 90 hours per week, some of which may be carried on outside the office. Senior managers work longer than do lower-level managers but on fewer activities. Those with well-defined functions, such as accounting managers, can work fewer hours (McCall, Morrison, & Hanman, 1978). Shipping supervisors differ systematically from production supervisors in the time they spend in planning and scheduling work and in maintaining equipment and machinery (Dowell & Wexley, 1978).

With his background as a former director of research on job and occupational information, Shartle (1934, 1949b) suggested that executive work could most meaningfully be quantified in terms of the amount of time devoted to various activities. Stogdill and Shartle (1955) compared the time use profiles of 470 U.S. Navy officers and 66 business executives. They found that both groups spent more time (about 34%) with subordinates than with superiors or peers. Furthermore, both groups devoted about 15% to 20% of their time to inspections, examining reports, and writing reports, and spent somewhat more time in planning than in other major administrative functions. The profiles suggested a high degree of similarity in administrative work between military and business organizations. Similarly, Jaynes (1956) analyzed variations in the performance of 24 officers in four submarines and 24 officers who occupied identical positions in four landing ships. He reported that variance in performance was more closely related to the type of position than to the type of organization in which the position was located.

In the previously cited study of executives in Sweden, S. Carlson (1951) found that they spent about 20% of their time in internal and external inspections and almost 40% of their time acquiring information. The remainder of their time was divided about equally among advising and explaining, making decisions, and giving orders. Most of the executives felt overworked, complaining that they had little time for family or friends. According to Horne and Lupton's (1965) study of 66 managers, a large percentage of a manager's time is spent in discussions with others—44% informally, 10% in formal meetings, and 9% on the telephone. In contrast, only 2% is spent in reflecting, 10% in reading, and 14% on paperwork. At least half these activities occur in the manager's own office. The most frequent purposes are to transmit information (42%), discuss explanations (15%), review plans (11%), discuss instructions (9%), review decisions (8%), or give and receive advice (6%). Mowll (1989) found in a study of more than 1,200 health care patient account managers that they spent more than 30% of their typical day supervising their departmental staff. Their effectiveness depended on how well they allocated their time and motivated their staff. As will be discussed in Chapter 29, by the 1990s, these percentages had to be adjusted due to the fact that managers were spending an increasing amount of their time on e-mail, the Internet, and their organizations' intranet.

Time Spent on Activity by Position. Stogdill, Shartle, Wherry, and Jaynes (1955) studied 470 U.S. Navy officers in 45 different positions or job categories. The officers were located in 47 different organizations. Data were obtained from all officers on the percentage of their working time that was devoted to the performance of 35 tasks, including personal contacts, individual efforts, and handling other major responsibilities. The results were related to the officers' level in the organization, military rank, scope or responsibility, scope of authority, and leadership behavior. Stogdill, Wherry, and Jaynes (1953) factor-analyzed these naval officers' profiles to cluster the positions of officers doing similar work, such as public relations directors, coordinators, and consultants. Then, they correlated the scores for the specialties with how occupants spent their time. Eight factors emerged from the analysis: (1) high-level policy making, (2) administrative coordination, (3) methods planning, (4) representation of members' interests, (5) personnel service, (6) professional consultation, (7) maintenance services, and (8) inspection. The officers clustered in terms of how their assignments and activities made use of their time. The clusters were (1) technical supervisors (teaching, supervising, using machines, and computing); (2) planners such as operations officers (scheduling, preparing, procedures, reading technical publications, interviewing personnel, and consulting peers); (3) maintenance administrators (interpreting, consulting, attending meetings, and engaging in technical performances); (4) commanders and directors (representing, inspecting, and preparing reports); (5) coordinators, such as executive or staff officers (consulting juniors, supervising, scheduling, examining reports, and interviewing personnel); (6) public relations officers (writing for publication, consulting outsiders, reflecting, and representing); (7) legal or accounting officers (consulting juniors, professional consulting, interpreting); and (8) personnel administration officers (attending meetings, planning, and interviewing personnel).

T. A. Mahoney (1955) plotted the time usage profiles of 50 company presidents against those of 66 business executives reported by Stogdill and Shartle (1956). The two profiles were almost identical. T. A. Mahoney (1961) next analyzed the performance of 348 business executives in terms of eight functions. The performances with the percentage of time devoted to them were as follows: supervision (39%), planning (18%), generalist (14%), investigation (8%), coordination (6%), negotiation (5%), evaluation (4%), and miscellaneous (7%). Similar patterns of time usage were reported by Mahoney, Jerdee, and Carroll (1965) for a sample of 452 managers drawn from all organizational levels. A minimum amount of time was spent on each of these functions, although the percentage varied as a function of hierarchical level. For example, at lower hierarchical levels, more time was spent in supervision. At higher levels, more time was spent in planning. Replicated by Penfield (1975), these results were consistent with Stogdill, Shartle, Wherry, and Jaynes's (1955) findings for naval officers, and Haas, Porat, and Vaughan's (1969) findings for bank officials. Fleishman (1956) used the same kinds of data to analyze the differences between administrators in military and industrial organizations. He observed that differences *between* the patterns of administrative performance in industrial and naval organizations were generally no greater than differences *within* the two types of organizations. Taken together, all these studies indicated that time profiles of managerial positions tend to shift systematically with the hierarchical level of positions and the functional role of the positions in the organization. The patterns of time spent tend to be similar for positions that are comparable in level and function in different types of organizations.

Yukl (1998) concluded that managers need to understand the demands and constraints on their time. They need to know what others expect of their time. They need to appreciate what priorities in the use of their time are expected of them by subordinates, colleagues, and their superior. But they also need to be proactive in taking a broader perspective on how to spend their time aligned with organizational strategies. They need to make time for reflection, planning, daily and weekly activities, and avoiding procrastination.

Work Done

Contrary to both popular and classical images of management, much more managerial work involves handling information than making decisions. McCall, Morrison, and Hanman (1978) reached this conclusion from diaries and observational studies by Brewer and Tomlinson (1964) and Horne and Lupton (1965). As Carroll and Gillen (1987) noted, the simple classical view of the manager as one who gets work done through prescribed and orderly planning, organizing, and controlling has given way to a more complex romantic view, stimulated by the work of Mintzberg (1973), which is detailed below. Instead of the prescribed best ways to fulfill the managerial role, what we now have is a picture of harried executives putting out fires on demand, rather than systematically carrying out their prescribed functions in an orderly fashion. Both Guest (1956) and Ponder (1958) reached similar conclusions earlier from observational studies of production supervisors who had to handle a variety of problems quickly. One problem followed another with less than a minute for each on the average. More than 50% of the supervisor's time was spent in face-to-face interactions, more often with subordinates than with outsiders, although the supervisors had more total contacts with the latter. Landsberger (1961) also noted at the middle-management level the same pattern of brief, varied, and fragmented activities with much lateral interpersonal interaction.

Numerous other empirical investigations revealed a great variety in the functions describing what managers actually did. Managers do not behave according to textbook requirements for orderliness, planning, optimum decisions, and maximum efficiency. Rather, managerial processes, according to Mintzberg's (1973) in-depth study of five executives, are characterized by brevity, variety, and discontinuity. Managers rely on judgment and intuition, rather than on formal analysis, which makes it difficult to observe clearly their decision making processes.

Kurke and Aldrich (1983) supported Mintzberg's conclusions in a complete replication with four CEOs for one week. Yet Snyder and Glueck (1977), in a replication of Mintzberg's (1973) study, found managers to be more careful planners. But brevity in any one activity, interruptions of that activity, and discontinuity from one activity to the next were characteristic of what was gleaned from managers' diaries, recordings, and observations (Mintzberg, 1973). Although planning was regarded as a key element in the classical view of management, managers at all levels, according to diaries and observation, actually spent less time at it because of interruptions and demands on their time for other activities (McCall, Morrison, & Hanman, 1978). Mintzberg concluded that managers were oriented toward action, not reflection.

There is a certain amount of ritualistic and regular duties in managerial work. Since personal communication is favored over written documents, managers spent a good deal of time on the telephone or in meetings. Klauss and Bass (1981) found that this tendency increased when managers dealt with peers. If the peers are at a distance, contact was by telephone; if they were close, the contact was face-to-face. But if the communication was with persons who were higher or lower in the organizational hierarchy, it was usually done through memos. E-mail now substitutes considerably for memos, telephone, and meetings, as will be discussed in Chapter 29.

Effects of Hierarchical Level. Barnard (1938) considered how the functions of the executive varied according to the location of the executive's position in the organizational hierarchy. Political considerations also affected what could be done at different levels of the hierarchy. Nicholls (1990) noted that managers at lower levels engaged in *micro* managerial leadership with jobs and tasks and short-term performance goals. At upper levels of management—*macro* managerial leadership was concerned about organizations and long-term performance goals. T. V. Mumford (2003) agreed that the skill requirements for managerial leadership were different at different organizational levels, although some basic management skills were needed at all levels. This model was supported by evidence from close to a thousand lower-level military officers. The scope of activities, the need for more conceptualization, and complexity of relations increased with increases in hierarchical level. For Zac-

caro (1996), managerial leadership of single units is direct; problems are concrete and have a short time frame. At higher levels, multiple units are managed, and managerial leadership is more indirect.

In the U.S. Army, majors, captains, and lieutenants are like middle managers; sergeants and corporals are the equivalent of civilian supervisors and technical specialists. Job analytic studies were completed by Stogdill, Scott, and Jaynes (1956), who asked U.S. Navy officers to use Work Analysis Forms (Stogdill & Shartle, 1958) to indicate "what I do" and "what I ought to do." Junior officers also indicated their perception of what their senior officer did and ought to do. Senior officers expected and were expected by the junior officers to engage more often than junior officers in such activities as attending conferences, consulting superiors, examining reports, planning, and coordination. Seniors expected and were expected by juniors to do less than junior officers in writing reports, reading technical publications, scheduling and routing, research, and engaging in technical and professional operations. Both junior and senior military officers reported that, compared with what they *actually* did, they *should* do more inspecting, research, planning, public relations, reflection, reading of technical periodicals, and writing for publication. Both senior and junior officers reported that they should do less consulting with assistants and superiors, interviewing personnel, reading and answering mail, preparing charts, supervising, interpreting, and scheduling. Sherif (1969) used the Work Analysis Forms in a comparative study of three levels of managers in six diverse organizations. As would be expected, top managers consulted more with subordinates, while managers at the bottom consulted more with superiors and peers. Middle managers fell between the other two groups in contacts with superiors, peers, and subordinates. In regard to individual effort, examining reports and thinking increased with the level of the position, while writing reports, computation, and use of machines decreased. With respect to major functions, preparing procedures, coordinating, and evaluating increased with the level of the position, and supervision and personnel activities decreased. Haas, Porat, and Vaughan (1969) also used an adaptation of the Work Analysis Forms in a comparative study of three levels of organization. Planning and coordination were done most in top-level positions; negotiating, in middle-level positions; and supervising, at lower levels. All levels combined did more investigating but less planning than they thought ideal.

The First-Level Supervisor.

In a survey of 10,392 supervisors, Richardson, Bellows, and Henry (RBH) noted the five most important of supervisory role requirements of 25 listed. These were: (1) to work with others; (2) to get others to do what needs to be done; (3) to adapt quickly in emergency or problem situations; (4) to pass on and explain instructions to others; (5) to plan ahead. No contribution to strategic thinking was included among the 25. Observational studies of the work done compared effective and ineffective production supervisors. The better supervisors were compared with the poorer ones by performance appraisals and the productivity of their groups. The better supervisors spent less time on purely production matters, gave more general work orders, initiated interpersonal contacts more frequently, and spent more time with staff and service personnel outside their work group (Pondey, 1958).

Specialized questionnaires were developed for the study of the position of first-level supervisor. Following Hemphill's (1960) work on the dimensions of managerial jobs, Prien (1963) constructed the Supervisor Position Description Questionnaire with items written by job analysts who were guided by an outline of general supervisory functions. Thirty supervisors indicated the extent to which each of the items was descriptive of their work. Prien extracted seven factors: (1) employee supervision; (2) employee contact and communication; (3) union-management relations; (4) manpower coordination and administration; (5) work organization, planning, and preparation; (6) manufacturing process supervision; (7) manufacturing process administration. Using a similar methodology, Dowell and Wexley (1978) factor-analyzed the responses of 251 supervisors regarding the importance of 89 work activities of first-line supervisors. The factor structure obtained from the intercorrelations among ratings of importance was highly congruent with the factor structure obtained from the intercorrelations among the ratings of the amount of time spent in an activity. The seven dimensions along which the positions of first-level supervisors could be ordered were: (1) working with subordinates (informing them of the performance expected, instructing them in safe working habits, seeing that safety equipment is used, instructing them in the proper use of materials and equipment, observing their work activities, listening to their ideals and problems, and settling disciplinary problems or potential grievances); (2) organizing the work of subordinates (talking with supervisors in other departments about production, scheduling overtime, shifting people to other jobs, establishing priorities on "down" equipment, and assigning employees to specific jobs); (3) work planning and scheduling (consulting with the departing supervisor about conditions on the shift, reading records of previous shifts' activities, planning production for the shift, and completing reports on conditions at the end of the shift); (4) maintaining efficient and high-quality production (checking the quality of production; finding the causes of low production or poor quality; determining production levels, the quality of the production, and the kinds and causes of waste; and soliciting suggestions from subordinates regarding improvements in work methods); (5) maintaining safe, clean work areas (communicating Occupational Safety and Health Act regulations to workers, checking that walkways and fire exits are clear, completing maintenance records, and inspecting work areas for cleanliness); (6) maintaining equipment and machinery (diagnosing problems with machines, adjusting machines, checking maintenance work when completed, inspecting machines for proper working order, and setting up machines); (7) compiling records and reports (compiling miscellaneous reports, distributing tools or equipment, keeping personal records of job incidents, performing routine checks of safety devices, and notifying people of changes in schedules).

Dynamic Models.

Wofford (1967, 1970, 1971) reached a somewhat simpler set of more psychologically defined dynamic factors to describe a manager's behavior: (1) neatness and accuracy in planning, organizing, and controlling; (2) use of power and pressure to achieve employees' compliance; (3) maintenance of interpersonal relationships (personal interaction as a leader); (4) security and maintenance (reactions to or the avoidance of feelings of insecurity); and (5) dynamic and achievement orientation (setting specific goals). Mumford, Fleishman, et al. (1988) started with a list of 156 tasks and 69 possible job performance dimensions to describe the positions of U.S. Army officers. A total of 96 officers judged the importance, time spent, and freedom to decide on how, when, and where each of 13 job performance dimensions was relevant. The most important dimension was setting an example for others to follow. The dynamic model the authors were able to organize linked the job performance dimensions into a coherent design.

Networking and Boundary Management. Mumford, Fleishman, et al. (1988) modeled the leader-subordinate relation without much reference to persons outside the group except as imported information. However, McCall, Morrison, and Hanman (1978) concluded, from diary and observational studies,[3] that although lower-level managers spend most of their time within their own departments and organizations, senior managers have much more contact with those outside the organization. Luthans (1986), among others, paid special attention to the relations of the managers to others, outside their immediate subordinates or immediate superior. He concluded from observing more than 300 managers that although three clusters[4] of inside activities could be described, the most important was the fourth cluster of "networking," socializing, and "politicking" with those other than one's immediate colleagues. Such networking appeared to be most important among the four clusters of activities. Luthans, Rosenkrantz, and Hennessey (1985) inferred, from participant observers' records of 52 managers in a state department of revenue, a manufacturing plant, and a campus police department, that success in the organization was enhanced by networking with such outsiders, socializing, and playing politics. Gardner (1988) noted that "politics" can make a positive contribution within organizations or can be regarded pejoratively. As a positive contribution, the leader-manager may reconcile conflicting parties by intervening in a dispute or mobilizing the group to agree to common goals. Or playing politics may mean manipulation, mistrust, self-promotion, favoritism, and hidden alliances.

Successful managers engaged more than did the less successful managers in conflict management, planning, coordinating, and decision making. An in-depth study of

15 successful general managers by Kotter (1982a) again emphasized the importance of time spent with outsiders as well as with others in their own organization. Kotter considered many of these contacts to be network building. A manager's agenda could be more readily implemented if he or she had developed a high-quality network. Sayles (1964) also focused particular attention on the manager's lateral networking. The networks included relationships dealing with: the work flow, trading, service, giving or receiving advice, evaluating other groups or responding to the requests of those evaluating one's group, limiting or controlling decisions made by other managers, and engaging in innovations. McHenry (1986) generated two factors involving the importance attached to a manager's lateral activities for a sample of 400 managers: (1) coordinating interdependent groups and (2) representing one's work group. In the same way, after general managers set agendas to establish loosely connected goals and plans for short-, medium-, and long-term responsibilities, they develop a cooperative relationship networking with those individuals needed to satisfy the agendas. They get the networks to implement the agendas (Kotter, 1982a).

Mintzberg's Managerial Roles

Mintzberg (1973) presented a model of 10 management roles that was dynamic and included activities both inside and outside the organization. It generated a great deal of interest and subsequent use. A former journalist, he intensively studied five CEOs and their organizations, along with a calendar of their scheduled appointments for a month. Additional data collected during a week of structured observations included anecdotal data about specific activities, chronological records of activity patterns, a record of incoming and outgoing mail, and a record of the executive's verbal contacts with others. The CEOs were found to work at an unrelenting pace on a wide variety of tasks. They were subject to frequent interruptions. They preferred specific, well-defined activities of current importance over work on general functions of less certainty and less immediate relevance. In addition, they preferred verbal contact with others to written contact.[5]

---

[3] See also T. Burns (1954), Horne and Lupton (1965), Mintzberg (1970), and Stewart (1967).

[4] The three clusters were: (1) routine communication associated with processing paperwork and exchanging routine information; (2) planning, decision making, and controlling; (3) human resource management activities, such as motivating, positively reinforcing, disciplining, punishing, managing conflict, staffing, and training and developing.

[5] Many previously cited, large-scale management surveys of communication patterns, time spent, and work done corroborated the tendency for interpersonal interaction among managers in large organizations to

Ten Integrated Roles

On the basis of these data, Mintzberg divided managerial activities into interpersonal, informational, and decisional roles. The interpersonal category contained three specific roles: (1) the *figurehead* role, (2) the *leader* role, and (3) the *liaison* role. In the figurehead role, managers perform symbolic duties as heads of the organization. In the leader role, managers establish the work atmosphere and motivate subordinates to achieve organizational goals. In the liaison role, managers develop and maintain webs of contacts outside the organization to obtain favors and information. The informational category also included three roles: (1) the *monitor* role, (2) the *disseminator* role, and (3) the *spokesman* role. In the monitor role, managers act as collectors of all information that is relevant to the organization. In the disseminator role, managers transmit information from the outside to members in the organization. In the spokesman role, managers transmit information from inside the organization to outsiders. Last, there were four specific decisional roles: (1) *entrepreneur*, (2) *disturbance handler*, (3) *resource allocator*, and (4) *negotiator*. Managers adopt the entrepreneurial role when they initiate controlled change in their organization to adapt to the changing conditions in the environment. In the disturbance handler role, they are forced to deal with unexpected changes. In the resource allocator role, they make decisions concerning the use of organizational resources. In the negotiator role, they deal with other organizations or individuals. The 10 roles are an integrated set. Formal authority supports the three interpersonal roles, which in turn result in three informational roles. The authority and informational roles enable the CEO and senior executive to play the four decisional roles. Fewer of the roles are relevant at the middle-management and supervisory levels.

To measure the extent to which managers had to be engaged in Mintzberg's roles, Pavett and Lau (1983) asked 48 manufacturing managers to indicate the importance of 69 activities in carrying out their duties and the approximate amount of time they spent on each activity. The roles of leader and entrepreneur were deemed most important and were those on which the most time was spent. Time spent on a role correlated with its importance between .63 and .85.

Although McCall and Segrist (1980) found that managers' performance in six of the roles correlated with the managers' rate of promotion, they obtained too much overlap in the activities among the roles that were supposed to be distinct. Snyder and Wheelen (1981) reported difficulty in assigning specific activities to specific roles. One activity appeared relevant to several roles, and the roles were not mutually exclusive. For instance, when one of the subordinates of a school superintendent attended a United Way campaign fund-raising meeting, she did so as the formal representative of the school system. The superintendent, if present at the meeting, attended as a figurehead. The superintendent took the opportunity to chat with an influential outsider about a problem to obtain advice. In this case, he was acting as liaison, monitor, and spokesperson. As many others found, particularly at executive levels, as Mintzberg had emphasized, relatively little time was spent on any one role. There was much shifting from one role to another (Aldrich, 1983).

Role Clusters. Shapira and Dunbar (1978) simulated the CEO's job as head of a firm of 6,000 employees with an in-basket test completed by 54 MBA students at Hebrew University in Jerusalem, Israel. Each "CEO" could exercise each of the 10 managerial roles in dealing with the 16 memos in the in-basket and with the agenda he or she had prepared. A small space analysis indicated that the 10 roles could be described meaningfully with two clusters. The first cluster was made up of the liaison, disseminator, spokesman, and figurehead roles. These roles were concerned primarily with the generation and transmission of information. The cluster corresponded with Mintzberg's (1975) notion of the executive as the general nerve center of the organizational unit. The second cluster of roles—entrepreneur, negotiator, leader, disturbance handler, monitor, and resource allocator—was concerned primarily with the active formulation and execution of decisions.

Role Factors. A number of investigators, such as Morse and Wagner (1978), Lau, Newman, and Broedling (1980), and Tsui (1984), used Mintzberg's set of roles to generate and factor specific leadership and management role activities that could then be used for checklists of observed behaviors and questionnaire surveys. These could then be self-rated or completed by superiors, peers, or

---

be primarily verbal rather than written. This was changed by the advent of e-communications.

subordinates. Lau, Newman, and Broedling (1980) extracted four factors from a questionnaire survey of the behavior of 210 governmental managers: (1) leadership and supervision, (2) information gathering and dissemination, (3) technical problem solving and executive decision making, (4) allocating resources. On the basis of ratings by 1,080 personnel in the division of a large corporation of self, superiors, peers, or subordinates using survey questionnaires, Tsui (1984) extracted six factors: (1) leader (evaluates subordinates, resolves conflicts, facilitates development, and alerts subordinates to problems); (2) spokesperson (serves as expert, represents unit); (3) resource allocator (distributes resources, decides on programs to be supported); (4) entrepreneur (plans, implements, controls change); (5) environmental monitor (gathers information about market, customers, and competition); (6) liaison (attends meetings in other units and social functions).

Managerial Activities

Managers in the same positions may be required to engage in somewhat different activities, or they may do so as a matter of personal competence or preference. They may be more effective or less effective depending on the extent to which they emphasize certain activities and processes at the expense of other work they might do. Campbell, Dunnette, Lawler, and Weick (1970) proposed a *person-process-product model* of managerial effectiveness. The *person* in the model refers to the managers' competencies, such as those discussed in Chapter 5. The *product* is an organizational result, such as productivity. The *process* is the manager's on-the-job activities. All three components—person, process, and product—need to be understood in evaluating the manager's effectiveness in identifying and judging the observable actions and roles resulting in the accomplishment of organizational objectives (Porter, Lawler, & Hackman, 1975).

Differences in Activity

Effective leaders tend to be more active than ineffective leaders, although the contrary was found for first-level supervisors dealing with production in less well conducted investigations in the 1950s. These supervisors of well-run

work groups may have had more free time to plan and think ahead. They may have been more efficient in getting done what needed to be done or they were better at delegating. Or they may have had more competent subordinates. Martinko and Gardner (1985) suggested that the earlier findings about supervisors' activity rates were too fraught with statistical problems to be accepted with any confidence. A much stricter study by Komaki, Zlotnick, and Jensen (1986) supported the more general conclusions that effective leaders are more active than ineffective ones are. They observed 24 managers in a medical insurance firm up to 20 times over the interval of the study, using a rigorous set of observational procedures. They classified observations and activities according to operant theory: performance antecedents, performance monitoring, performance consequences, own performance, work-related, non-work-related, and solitary. Sets of observers were trained to achieve high interobserver agreement of 90% or better. Of the 24 managers, 12 were identified by their superiors as effective, and 12 as marginal. Significantly more time was spent by the effective than the marginal managers in collecting information on employees' performance. The effective managers were more likely to observe employees in action than to depend on self-reports or secondary sources. They more often sampled the employees' work, but they did not provide any more positive, neutral, or negative consequences. Komaki inferred that given their greater monitoring behavior, the effective managers were more likely to provide contingent reinforcement of the subordinates. Similar observational analyses were completed on the behavior of 19 sailboat racing captains by Komaki, Desselles, and Bowman (1989). The correlation of the order in which the boats finished the race (from first to last) was $-.53$ with the amount of monitoring by their captains and $-.59$ with the amount they fed back consequences. Their coaches' ratings of the captains' effective handling of their crews were related in the same way to their observed monitoring and consequences.

Amount and Quality of Planning

The activities of managers are supposed to be organized and orderly, but, as Mintzberg (1973) noted, they may be just the opposite. An executive commented, "My day consists in running from one meeting to the next, fielding questions from my internal staff and outsiders, trying to respond to telephone messages, trying to smooth over an argument between a couple of people, and keeping my ever-higher in-basket from toppling down on me" (p. 26). Setting a daily, weekly, and longer-term work agenda with intentions and priorities about time, tasks, and goals can help to increase the organization and order in the activities (Barry, Cramton, & Carroll, 1997). Many managers do find time for short-term and long-term planning. Despite the lack of time for reflection and planning, how much time is spent on planning seems to differentiate effective from ineffective managers at the top as well as the bottom of the hierarchy. Stagner (1969) found that the time that 109 CEOs spent in organizational planning was related to the firm's profitability. Similarly, General Electric (1957) supervisors with better production records were seen to spend more time in long-range planning and organizing than were supervisors with poorer production records. E. Williams (1968) compared the activity patterns and preferences of 30 effective and 30 ineffective executives. The effective executives scored significantly higher in planning as well as in responsibility, human relations, decision making, and problem solving. Although the two samples differed in the time devoted to organizing and controlling, the ineffective executives spent less time in planning and rated organizing and controlling significantly higher in importance than did the effective executives. Apparently, the comparative deficiency in planning among the ineffective executives was accompanied by a perceived need for higher degrees of control.

The quality of planning has been assessed based on the demonstrated skills of the planners. Bray, Campbell, and Grant (1974) showed that skill in planning, as measured in AT&T assessment center exercises, was one of the best predictors of subsequent managerial success. Boyatzis (1982) also found competence in planning to be related to managerial effectiveness. Gillen and Carroll (1985) reported a correlation between planning skill and unit production of .34 in manufacturing firms and .43 in aerospace firms for a total sample of 103 unit managers in 10 firms.

Functional Differences Related to Managerial Effectiveness. In addition to differences in planning, other functional differences were found by Heizer (1969) in managers assigned to the same line and staff positions. The differences correlated with their effectiveness. Heizer asked 200 managers to write about incidents of effective and ineffective managerial behavior. Effective managers differed significantly from ineffective managers in planning, coordination, delegation, and staffing. In the same way, Kavanagh, MacKinney, and Wolins (1970) reported that the extent to which the department head fulfilled the functions of planning, investigating, coordinating, evaluating, supervising, and representing was related to the job satisfaction of the supervisors below the department head. Effective managers differed from ineffective ones in what they did to contribute to the surrounding organization. In a study of 345 R & D employees in a large chemical laboratory, Allen, Lee, and Tushman (1980) discovered that the overall performance of technical service projects was better if the project manager planned to link the project with other parts of the organization. Ghiselli and Barthol (1956) found that successful supervisors differed from unsuccessful ones in perceiving themselves as full of plans, loyal to the company and to subordinates, and as having the responsibility of working with people to achieve organizational goals. Unsuccessful supervisors saw themselves as good fellows, well liked, and responsible for production. The unsuccessful managers relied on their ingenuity and resourcefulness to get the job done, rather than on their planning. Successful supervisors identified with their work group and its members, whereas unsuccessful supervisors were more interested in making a living. Levi and Mainstone (1992) examined the effects of the breadth and focus of priorities planned for by 165 business students participating in 20 top management positions for a day in the Looking-Glass, a high-fidelity simulation of the organization of a glass company. The participants concentrated more on crises than on problems and opportunities. The quality of their decisions was greater if they kept a broader focus.

Same Role Requirements but Different Processes. The same role requirements may be met by managers in different ways with different processes. For instance, Strauss (1962) found considerable differences in interpersonal patterns of contact and in oral versus written communications among purchasing agents with similar job descriptions. Similarly, Whitely (1985) demonstrated, with 70 managers studied for seven consecutive days during two weeks, that managerial positions with similar behavioral content still allow incumbents considerable latitude in how they choose to enact their roles. For instance, managers in accounting, management analysis, and reimbursements, engaged in the function of internal business control, differed significantly in the frequency of their scheduled activities, activities lasting 60 minutes or more, and contacts with their boss and peers. As Stewart (1982a) emphasized, there is a need to distinguish between the demands placed on an incumbent to a job, the constraints within functions that must be carried out, and the choices that can be made in carrying them out.

The characteristics of the process in which the manager engages are another way of analyzing what the manager does. R. Stewart (1967, 1982b) analyzed the duration of specific activities, the mode of communications used, and the particular persons contacted to detail the characteristics that distinguish among managers' positions. Thirteen reliably discriminable categories of characteristics of the managerial process were obtained by Whitely in his study of 70 managers: (1) scheduled activities, (2) activities of fewer than five minutes' duration, (3) activities of more than 60 minutes' duration, (4) face-to-face contacts, (5) self-initiated activities, (6) activities carried out alone, (7) contacts with two or more persons, (8) percentage of contacts with the boss, (9) contacts with peers, (10) contacts with subordinates, (11) contacts with external persons, (12) information-seeking activities, (13) decision-making activities.

Moderators of the Manager's Work, Function, and Roles

Considerable evidence has been amassed to show how management positions differ depending on their area of responsibility in the organization, their hierarchical level in the organization, changes within organizations, and differences among organizations.

Function of the Manager's Position

Managers' areas of responsibility make a considerable difference in how they spend their time, on what activi-ties they work on, and which are most critical and important to their success. For instance, supervising is more significant to merchandising managers than to data processing or finance managers. Thus, Alexander (1979b) found that informational roles, as expected, were much more salient in staff positions while interpersonal roles were more important in sales positions. Among the 225 managers studied in production, marketing, and accounting, Alexander noted, that compared to production managers, marketing and accounting managers reported themselves as facing more requirements to enact the informational roles of monitor, disseminator, and spokesperson. Fewer differences were seen in the requirements of other roles. Pavett and Lau (1983) reported on the self-ratings of 180 top, middle, and lower managers in Southern California, on 54 items concerning the importance to their success of enacting Mintzberg's 10 roles plus an eleventh role of technical expert. The roles of leader and monitor were perceived to be highest in importance to sales and marketing; spokesperson and resource allocator to accounting and finance; and technical expert to research and development. For general managers, human and conceptual skills were seen as most important. In accounting and finance, the greatest importance was attached to technical skills, and in sales and marketing it was apportioned most to political skills.

In an in-depth report on 20 project managers, Spitz (1982) pointed out that the pattern of demands on a project manager may change over time as the project develops. That is, the particular skills required for the project manager's integrative efforts will shift with the changing project. Vaughan (1981) concurred. Using structured interviews, she found that for expatriate matrix project managers in a large multinational firm, there were important shifts in roles owing to the matrix in which they worked and as a consequence of changes in the phases of the project. The project managers could best be described as boundary-spanning experts and focal managers of a developmental process.

The Importance of Functional Area of Experience

In a survey of 700 managers, Shapira (2000) found that each manager's personal experience and perceptions had a strong influence on the willingness to make risky decisions. In the same way, Waller, Huber, and Glick's (1995) interviews with executives—31 in manufacturing, 17 in health care service, and 15 in other kinds of service—revealed that their different functional area experience resulted in their differing perceptions about their own organizations' effectiveness. However, unexpectedly, their perceptions of their organizational environments did not differ.

The Importance of Hierarchical Level on Role Requirements

For Hunt (1991), leaders perform the functions appropriate to their task requirements. To develop leaders for higher levels requires developing their ability to handle complexity. Barnard (1938) noted that top management is concerned with broad policies, objectives, and plans. These purposes and objectives become more specific as they filter down to lower levels, where the work is actually done. In addition, according to W. A. Scott (1967), unlike middle and lower managers, top managers are both the ultimate teachers and the judges of subordinates. They must be sensitive to the interactions among people below them and to their material resources. They must be more than just subject matter experts in their thinking. They need to look at a broad scope of information, while the expert analyzes a narrow scope in depth. They need to adopt multiple perspectives, while the expert fixes on a single perspective. They need to consider long-range consequences, while the expert deals with short-term problems. They manage group interactions, while experts participate as members of the group. They need to integrate multiple inputs, while the expert provides the inputs of knowledge. They focus on process, while the expert attends to content (Laskey, Leddo, & Bresnick, 1990). At lower levels in the organizational hierarchy, Whyte (1956) observed that the primary function is to perceive one's task accurately and to conform to it. Technology and controls are most important. Nevertheless, if the broad objectives and policies set at the top are to be operationalized and successfully carried out, managers at lower levels must exhibit considerable initiative (Fiedler & Nealey, 1966). Innovative breakthroughs or discontinuous innovation require continuing senior management support of R & D efforts (Morone, 1997). Senior management must provide a safe place where incubation of innovations can occur, old practices can be questioned, and new ideas can be encouraged and communicated upward for a fair evaluation. Control can be relaxed by using self-managed teams of creative people who can think "outside the box" (Nutt, 1999).

On the one hand, Argyris (1964a) observed that the objectives of the job and interpersonal factors play more important roles in influencing the effectiveness of managers higher in the hierarchy. On the other hand, Pfiffner and Sherwood (1960) noted that, in particular, first-level supervisors work under considerable time pressure and have frequent and direct personal contact with the work. Nealey and Fiedler (1968) added more specifically that the typical functions of first-line supervisors are production, maintenance, on-the-job training, and control of materials and supplies. Second-level managers deal with cost control, setting standards, selection and placement, coordination of work units, and formal training. The second-level manager needs less technical expertise about specific production processes than does the first-level supervisor, for the second-level manager may supervise several departments involving different technical processes.

A survey of 1,476 New York City managers revealed that those at higher levels reported having a considerably greater variety of activities to perform than did those at lower levels (Allen, 1981). Dubin and Spray (1964) analyzed the logs kept by executives over a two-week period. Lower-level managers were more likely than those at higher levels to concentrate their time on a single activity. At the same time, the sheer number of incidents per day in which a manager is involved is highest for first-line supervisors and declines with increasing levels of management. For example, Thomason (1967) reported the average number of activities for different levels of management as follows: first-level supervisor, 413; superintendent, 309; area superintendent, 274; general manager, 91.

Pfiffner and Sherwood (1960) noted other differences in activity and function between first-level and middle managers. First-level supervisors work under more time pressure and have more direct and frequent contact with subordinates with the work. T. Burns (1954) found that middle managers spend more time with their superiors than first-level supervisors do and use formal communications in their work to a greater extent than do first-level supervisors.

Effect on Roles Enacted. Paolillo (1981b) found that among 352 managers, the importance and time spent on 7 of the 10 roles identified by Mintzberg depended on the managers' level in the organizational hierarchy. Similarly, Klauss, Flanders, Fisher, and Carlson (1981b) asked 753 senior and 847 midlevel federal managers to indicate how important Mintzberg's roles were and how much time was spent on each of them. Seniors attached more importance than did midlevel managers to all the roles except leader, disseminator, and negotiator. Senior managers were particularly likely to spend more time acting as figureheads and spokespersons than were the midlevel managers.

In agreement with L. D. Alexander (1979a) and Paolillo (1981b), Pavett and Lau (1983) reported that hierarchical levels made a difference in the importance attached to the different roles. All three studies found that the roles of disseminator, figurehead, negotiator, liaison, and spokesperson were deemed more important at the higher managerial levels than at the lower levels. Consistent with these results, Hall, Bowen, Lewicki, and Hall (1975) reported that among the 10 roles carried out by 103 middle managers in manufacturing, the role of leader was most important and consumed the most time. Being a figurehead was least important and least time-consuming. The amount of time spent in leading declined with increasing echelons in the hierarchy (Pavett & Lau, 1983).

P. Allen (1981) examined the task dimensions of 1,476 managers working for New York City. The *analytical-evaluative task* dimension required managers to analyze and evaluate laws, problems, programs, work procedures, processes, and reports. The task was more important for senior-level managers than for managers at either the entry or the middle level. However, *monitoring* required managers to develop and use mechanisms to ensure adequate progress toward goals, to maintain appropriate records, and to inspect ongoing activities. This task was less important for the senior level than for the middle or lower level. In L. D. Alexander's (1979a) previously cited study, hierarchical level made a considerable difference in 7 of Mintzberg's 10 role requirements. With increasing hierarchical level, there were increasing requirements for the roles of figurehead, liaison, monitor, disseminator, spokesperson, and entrepreneur. The negotiator role was seen as being required most by middle managers.

Level and Time Spent. T. A. Mahoney (1961) concluded from several studies (e.g., L. Strong, 1956; *Fortune*, 1946), that the higher the level of managers' positions, the more hours per week they devoted to their job and the more time they spent in planning and organizing, rather than in the technical work of the organization. This finding was corroborated by Mahoney, Jerdee, and Carroll (1965). Whereas supervising was the main activity of 51% of the lower-level supervisors, it was the main function of only 36% of the middle managers and 22% of the senior managers. On the other hand, executives were more likely to be generalists and planners than lower-level managers were.

Second-level managers appear to be more oriented toward their superiors, and first-level managers toward their subordinates (Pfiffner & Sherwood, 1960). Berkowitz and Bennis (1961), Guest (1956), and Piersol (1958) concluded that first-level supervisors spent more time interacting with their subordinates than with their superiors. Although face-to-face communication was the most frequent form of interaction for managers at all levels, senior executives more often initiate than receive contacts, according to the logs they kept for two weeks (Dubin & Spray, 1964).

Time Lag between Decisions and Consequences. Jaques (1956) advanced the hypothesis that high-level administrative work is characterized by long time lags between the time a decision is made and the impact of the decision on the organization. If so, high-level managers would personally exhibit comparatively high degrees of future orientation and tolerance for delayed outcomes in their time perspectives. Jaques's proposition was supported by an investigation of four levels of supervisors and managers from the shift supervisor at the bottom to works managers at the top in the same British factory. Almost all decisions of a shift supervisor were about matters that occurred within a two-week period. On the other hand, only 3.3% of the decisions of the works manager involved questions of short duration; 50% of the decisions of the works manager involved policies with time perspectives of a year or longer. No one at lower levels was involved in decisions involving such periods of time (Martin, 1959). However, in a study of 141 managers at six levels of a plant, Goodman (1967) failed to find that future orientation and preference for delayed gratification were highly related to the level of an executive's position.

Despite Goodman's (1961) negative results, most other observers agreed with Jaques. The time perspective of managers at higher levels requires them to live with more uncertainty and lack of feedback. They need to consider longer-range goals. They need to go without evaluating the effects of their decisions for long periods. Decisions at the highest levels involve especially high uncertainty and risk. Thus W. A. Scott (1967) observed that "top management must have the ability to detach itself from the internal imperatives of coordination and to reflect on the general purposes and objectives of the company in its industry and society." Because of the nature of their role, top managers are often detached from outside judgment or objective criteria against which they can appraise their approach to problems to their decisions, and to their philosophy. The lower-level manager can be appraised against the tangible output and the department's performance. The long time span of the decision and the subjectivity of the job of the top manager make appraisals more difficult.

According to detailed interviews with 31 senior federal executives in six different government agencies, Klauss (1981) concluded that senior federal executives need a systems view, a strategic focus, and a proactive stance. They need the ability and willingness to: (1) maintain a network of formal and informal contacts; (2) support and encourage staff personnel; (3) manage diverse interests; (4) market and persuade; (5) take risks; (6) maintain integrity and credibility. They must be concerned for broad-based sources of information. Persistence, persuasiveness, flexibility, open-mindedness, and self-confidence are also important.

Jacobs and Jaques (1987) argued that different critical tasks with different time lags between decisions and their consequences are required of leaders at different organizational levels. As leaders rise in the hierarchical level, the nature of their tasks changes systematically in the direction of requiring greater conceptual effort and the capacity to deal with more uncertain and more abstract constructs. Effectiveness at any given level thus depends on the capacity to learn the role behaviors demanded by the tasks at that level. As Rusmore (1984) demonstrated, *fluid intelligence* or creativity becomes more predictive of success at higher organizational levels; *crystallized intelligence* is more predictive of success at lower levels. Jacobs and Jaques (1987) spelled out the different types of activities performed by leaders in the lower, middle, and top echelons of a large corporation. Leadership at each level has discrete tasks to perform that add value to each other level. The time spans of the tasks increase with increasing levels.

Effect on Implicit Requirements. Den Hartog, Koopman, and Van Muijen (1997) used the Internet to query a Dutch telepanel of 2,161 respondents (1,198 men, 963 women) about 22 characteristics for being a good or outstanding top manager, and again for being a good or outstanding department manager or supervisor. As might be expected, traits identified as more important for top managers were "charismatic," "inspirational," "visionary," "innovative," and "persuasive." Characteristics seen as more important for lower level managers were "supportive," "compassionate," "people-oriented," "participative," "leading," and "concerned for subordinates' interests." Women raters considered dominance as less desirable for leaders and attached more importance to people orientation, long-term orientation, and diplomacy; men placed more importance on being inspirational, rational, and persuasive.

Peters (1979) noted the peculiar difficulties involved in carrying out the role of CEO or senior executive and the remedies for each of these difficulties. For example, according to Peters, senior managers are given only one option, usually in accord with their preferences. However, over time, they can shape each option presented by subordinates in their review and contextual evaluation. Time is fragmented, but the senior manager can use the fragments as a succession of opportunities "to tackle bits of the issue stream." The fragments also provide a rich variety of information. Although major choices take months or years to emerge, the time provides opportunities to build a strong consensus and requirements for implementation. Peters concluded that top management's most important role is that of shaping the organization's values to provide coherence "in an untidy world, where goal setting, option selection, and policy implementation hopelessly fuzz together." Although CEOs are supposed to formulate strategy for subordinate executives and middle managers to implement, the CEOs actually spend more of their time on implementation than formulation. They are more action-oriented than reflective (Zaccaro, 1996) This conclusion was illustrated in Kotter and Lawrence's (1974) study of the activities of city mayors. Effective mayors built consensus among key stakeholders in favor of a few new directions. Ineffective mayors tended to make major commitments before they had developed the support for them.

Effects of Level by Function. Using Hemphill's (1959) EPDQ, other investigators have generally corroborated the influence of hierarchical level and function on a manager's activities.[6] For positions within the functional areas of data processing, finance, and merchandising, McHenry (1986) reported mainly positive correlations between the pay grade of 343 first-level and middle-level managers in a large retail organization and their activities, but pay also depended on their functions. For instance, the activity of supervising appears much more strongly linked with the hierarchical level of a position in merchandising than with positions in data processing and finance. On the other hand, long-range planning is related more to the hierarchical level of a position in finance and merchandising. Generally, the effect of hierarchical level is less strong in data processing. At each level, the manager's constituents and interests are different. At the top, managers are concerned with sponsors, clients, and the community, as well as with their own subordinates. At the bottom, the first-level supervisors are concerned with the interests of their superiors, their peers, and their subordinates, as well as with the interests of others, such as union stewards and outside inspectors. In all, managers spend relatively little of their time with their superiors, according to Brewer and Tomlinson (1963–1964), and, as was noted, much time may be spent with a wide variety of other parties, not just subordinates (M. W. McCall, 1974, 1977).

Importance of Differences among Organizations

Earlier, it was noted that, generally speaking, a manager in one organization will exhibit the same time profile and pattern of work as counterparts in other organizations with the same type of job. Nevertheless, the characteristics of an organization can make an obvious difference in the manager's activities. For instance, executives in public utilities must spend more time dealing with com-

[6] See Liem and Slivinski (1975), Meyer (1961), and Rusmore (1961).

munity relations than do their counterparts in manufacturing. Katzell, Barrett, Vann, and Hogan (1968) studied the relationship between nine executive role patterns and their organizations' characteristics. The data were provided by 194 middle-management personnel working for the U.S. Army. The organizational dimensions that were most highly related to the roles performed depended on the level and mission of the organization within the army. The roles most affected were controlling, staffing, and time spent with other persons. Schneider and Mitchel (1980) used a mailed questionnaire to survey 1,282 field agency managers working in one of 40 different life insurance companies. The investigators were able to identify six factors that could be used to describe the activities of the agency managers: (1) general management, (2) training and evaluation, (3) supervising, (4) goal setting, (5) serving clients' needs, and (6) enhancing agency visibility and capability. Schneider and Mitchel obtained modest correlations between the frequency at which the agency managers engaged in the six factored activities and the characteristics of the agencies studied. General management activity and the enhancement of visibility were more frequent in agencies with a larger number of agents and supervisors. The managers' client service activities depended on whether the agency was a branch or was independent. Differences in company policies and practices also made a difference in the managers' activities.

Effects on the General Manager. Interviews with senior executives of 24 Canadian companies and the executives' responses to questionnaires showed that general managers engaged in different activities, depending on their companies' particular strategies. If the companies were trying to develop themselves by expanding their markets, personnel, and investments, the functions and activities that were most important to their general managers were marketing, finance, and research and development (R & D). If the companies were trying to stabilize themselves by lowering costs and improving products, productivity, and investments, the functions of consequence to their general managers were production engineering, finance, and R & D. If the companies were trying to reverse their declining markets and cash flows, along with paying special attention to finance and production, general managers needed to be flexible and able to deal with uncertainties and crises. Yet, regardless of the company's strategy, the general manager had to be an effective leader. Leadership played an important integrative role in whatever other roles were assigned to the manager (Herbert & Deresky, 1987).

Promoting Individual Relationships in the Large Organization

Although interpersonal skills are important at every level of management in an organization, Jacobs and Jaques (1987) deduced different components of such skills that are required at different levels. At the lower production levels of the organization, managers must provide interpersonal feedback, try to create a supportive work atmosphere, "map" the interpersonal relations within the small work group and among work groups, and maintain equity within the workforce. They must also counsel and evaluate individuals and orient new personnel. At the upper middle-management levels, interpersonal skills are required to build and maintain a consensus on objectives within the organization, develop the capabilities of subordinates, and begin the development of information networks that are essential for effectiveness. Organizational communication must be facilitated, along with a supportive environment. Personal problems of colleagues may need to be handled. At the top of the organization, systems managers need to be competent in their relations with outside agents, agencies, and the community. Again, they need to foster a climate that is supportive and motivating. Many top executives are able and willing to open and maintain interpersonal contacts all through their system. They practice management by "walking around" to meet employees—whatever their level in the organization—as they perform their tasks. Such one-on-one communications contribute substantially to the effectiveness of the organization and the satisfaction of employees (Peters & Austin, 1985).

Another tactic of top executives is to communicate directly with every employee in brief, attention-grabbing notes. Admiral Elmo Zumwalt did so with his famous Z-grams to the various units under his command. Electronic mail, which instantly links every member of the organization with every other member, provides a ready opportunity for such contact between the top and the bottom levels of an organization. However, whether such one-on-one contact enhances relationships depends on whether overloading is avoided and the quality and interest of the messages remain high.

Klauss's (1981) study of 31 senior executives in government service found that a cluster of competencies, which involved sensitivity to individual and interpersonal dynamics, contributed to their effectiveness. When the effective executives spoke of critical incidents, they added to the technical or political aspects by clarifying information about the personalities involved and the human dynamics that influenced the situation. What was important to them was an understanding of the key actors involved—their general predispositions, biases, and orientations to given issues. The executives conveyed a sensitivity to the personal reactions and feelings of key officials who could be affected by or who could influence a course of action. Not only were they acutely aware of the personal and interpersonal factors that were important to each situation, they maintained informal networks to obtain insights into the predispositions and views of key higher-level officials.

Effects of Changes in Organization, Technology, and Society. Changes in the managers' organization will result in considerable changes in their activities. In a study of first-level production supervisors in four plants, Wikstrom (1967) initially found that the supervisors tended to make decisions the way individual workers do, without reference to larger organizational considerations. Then numerous specialists were introduced into the organization who influenced production in various ways. After the specialists were introduced, the supervisors were required to coordinate and sequence the manufacturing processes. Since the supervisors had to coordinate the impact of the various specialists, they had to assume managerial functions and decision making responsibilities. K. W. Harris (1968) surveyed 23 school superintendents, each with more than 25 years of tenure in the same position. The superintendents reported spending much less time on curriculum and pupil personnel problems than they had done a quarter century earlier and much more time on problems involving buildings, finance, and school-community relations. Clearly, the activities of the superintendents had changed within the same school districts with the changes in societal requirements.

Baliga and Hunt (1988) detailed the finer tuning of requirements for leadership as the organization goes through its life cycle of gestation, birth, growth, maturity, and revitalization or death. For gestation and birth, effective leadership at the top calls for developing a viable strategy and acquiring the resources to translate the strategy into an organizational reality. The representation of ideas and transformational leadership among external stakeholders are most salient here. Likewise, recruitment and commitment from key personnel are critical. For lower-level managers, the socialization of subordinates is of primary importance, along with the selection of appropriate technologies and the design of information, control, and evaluation systems. During the growth stage, Baliga and Hunt noted that although senior managers need to maintain transformational leadership with external stockholders, their transactional activities are of more consequence with subordinates. For lower-level managers, initiation, consideration, and task- and relations-oriented leadership become most important. At maturity, senior managers are required to pay more attention to subordinates, compared to their earlier emphasis on relations with external stakeholders. Ideally, junior managers should be able to handle all problems that occur at levels below them. With decline and revitalization, more transformational attention by senior management is again needed with external stakeholders as well as with subordinates. Lower-level managers have to assist the seniors in this regard.

Computerization. Much of the research discussed in this chapter predated the computer and electronic revolutions. As will be detailed in Chapter 29, much of the management decision making in firms is computer-assisted or even fully programmed. The computer at the manager's desk may provide instant electronic contact with every other manager or professional in the firm, as well as with voluminous information banks. Clearly, new descriptions of the way managers spend their time and the activities in which they engage are essential. Leavitt and Whisler (1958) and Uris (1958) anticipated that in the 1980s changes in the content and scope of the manager's role would occur because of the computer. They noted that the ranks of middle managers would be reduced and that top managers would communicate directly with lower-level managers through their computers. The "downsizing" of management in many U.S. firms in the 1980s through layoffs, "outplacements," and early retirement (McCormick & Powell, 1988) are a validation of these earlier prophecies about the decline of middle management. And the activities as well as the number of first-level supervisors have changed. Kerr, Hill, and Broedling (1986) called for using self-managed, autonomous work groups in which leadership is shared or informally provided by a team leader. Managers of such groups remain external to the groups. Leadership facilitates self-observation, self-evaluation, and self-reinforcement (Manz & Sims, 1987). Vanderslice (1988) went further to propose flat, "leaderless organizational structures." Self-managed teams have become prominent in the twenty-first century, as has teamwork in general (see Chapter 26).

Computer-driven automation and information management continue to increase at the workplace of first-level supervisors and their work groups; likewise, technology and required technical knowledge advances for the supervisor have increased. Specialized staff units continue to grow in size and importance, adding to the prospects of increasing conflicts between supervisors and staff experts. The particular activities and characteristics of the management process of first-level supervisors continue to change. First-level supervisors now spend more time with outside staff consultants who are involved with management information systems, new technologies, retraining workers, equal employment opportunities, and legal issues. They also spend more time serving as participative leaders of their work groups.

Pedigo (1986) completed a survey of the impact of the computer on the manager's role. First-level managers were the heaviest computer users. However, over time, as these first-level supervisors are promoted, usage increases at higher levels. Pedigo may be underestimating upper management's usage in that even though such managers may not use computers directly, they may be dependent on computer-generated information obtained from staff assistants. Again, as high school and college graduates of the 1980s and 1990s, who have had "hands-on" experience with personal computers, move into middle- and senior-management ranks, they are likely to replace pencils, written memos, and telephone with online personal computers and pocket PCs. The typical executive now travels with a wireless cell phone and a laptop or pocket computer.

Summary and Conclusions

Managers must both lead and manage (Hosmer, 1982). Leaders manage and managers lead, but there is considerable correlation in what both do. Much depends on the level and function of the manager. Diaries and observational studies compete with interviews and questionnaire surveys in helping us understand how leaders and managers spend their time and the work they do. Attention was directed toward the frequency, importance, and criticality to the organization of the manager's various activities, functions, and roles, as well as to the knowledge, skills, and ability required for the position. The informants could be observers, colleagues, or managers themselves, who responded in structured interviews or surveys. These descriptions could be augmented by prescriptions about what managers ought to do. What managers ought to do could be sought empirically by comparing the work done by effective and ineffective managers. There is much more to management than planning, directing, controlling, and supervising subordinates. However, the manager's effectiveness depends, to a considerable degree, on getting work done through others and networks of others. Activities are brief, fragmented, and discontinuous, rather than deliberate and reflective. Key activities include monitoring the environment, coordinating and representing others, and handling information and its sources. Interpersonal skills are needed at all hierarchical levels.

A manager's hierarchical level affects the time during which decisions are to be made and the lag in feedback about the effects. Work overload is a common experience at all organizational levels, as are systematic differences in the effective and ineffective performance of managers.

Earlier chapters delineated how leaders and managers differ in competencies, attitudes, values, and styles of behavior. This chapter showed how their activities and roles have been described and prescribed and how organizational leaders and managers in the same position may differ in their models of what is required and how they will actually perform in the position. Senior managers also need to be adept at strategic thinking.

Strategic and Executive Leadership

Executive strategic thinking may be premised on a serious flaw. Michael Porter (1980) convinced academia and management alike that the most important criterion for success of a business in the global marketplace was getting and staying ahead of its competitors. Market share was logically expected to correlate with profitability. This placed the emphasis of strategic leadership on beating the competition. Beliefs remain strong that a firm should do better than its competition. Just doing the best it can is not enough (Armstrong & Collopy, 1996). But empirical evidence suggests otherwise. Armstrong and Collopy (1996) showed that 40% of 1,016 participants in a laboratory experiment were willing to sacrifice profits in their pricing decisions in order to beat or harm their competition. Additionally, in a field study, they found that firms with competition-oriented strategy of enlarging market share were less profitable than those that were directly oriented to profits. Again, using the results of 48 studies and 276 effects, Szymanski, Bharadwaj, and Varadarajan (1993) completed a meta-analysis of the relationship between market share and lagged return on investment (ROI). They discovered that the relationship disappeared when other variables were controlled. Armstrong and Green (2005) reported that over five successive seven-year periods between 1938 and 1983, for 20 of the largest U.S. corporations, correlations between competitive orientation and ROI ranged from .37 to .54. Pursuing market share for its own sake was actually harmful to ROI! A replication with additional criteria of profitability from 1955 to 1997 of real return on equity and percentage of after-tax returns on sales again revealed that all correlations were negative, ranging from −.28 to −.73. Furthermore, the objectives of strategic thinking of leaders in for-profit firms must encompass more than profitability alone. The leaders of nonprofit organizations and government agencies must also look at the benefits generated by their expenditures.

Upper–Level Management Theory

Increasingly referred to as *upper-level management theory*, strategies are a product of the interaction of the individual leader and the organization's internal and external environment. Systems thinking is required that aims to produce the synergies that are more than the sum of the individual parts of the organization. Complexity is the rule rather than the exception. The complexity is illustrated by two organizations jointly supporting basic research but competing in the same market.

Agency Theory

This theory builds on the delegation by the sponsors, owners, and shareholders of for-profit organizations to managers as agents of authority and responsibility. It assumes that corporate owners and their agents are individualistic, self-serving, and opportunistic and that chief and senior executives, as agents of the owners and shareholders, are motivated primarily to increase their own rewards and secondarily to please the owners, shareholders, and boards of directors. For profit-making organizations, financial success is the criterion of organizational success (Jensen & Meckling, 1976). For Porter (2001), it is the single goal for business strategizing. Satisfaction of employees, customers, and other constituents is relegated to being the *means* to the objective of financial success. Clearly, to stay in business, firms have to make money or be continually subsidized by parent companies or government. Inside the organization, Williamson (1975) conceived the business organization as a marketplace for resources and rewards among competing departments, managers, and employees. But for those concerned with the human side of enterprise, along with achieving financial goals, chief and senior executives need to balance the needs and interests of their various stakeholders in the corporation—the owners, shareholders, managers, employees, customers, and community. This has to occur in the framework of local, state, national, and international agency regulations, as well as be reflected in the satisfactory treatment of the corporation's physical and social environment (Bass, 1952; Davis, Schoorman, & Donaldson, 1997). As Simon (1979) argued, to improve the performance of organizations, optimal decision making requires considering *both* economic and better utilization of human resources (Franke & Miller 2005).

Interplay between Strategy and Executive Leadership

Eddie Rickenbacker was president of Eastern Airlines from 1934 to 1959 and then CEO until 1963. His strategy and leadership style, which made Eastern the largest and most profitable U.S. airline, also led to its bankruptcy. A World War I hero, he was personally adventurous, but when it came to business, he was extremely cost-conscious and was last to invest in new models of planes and equipment. He let other airlines learn how to deal with the problems of the new aircraft. Maintenance costs were kept low. Before 1978, the federal government highly regulated the airline industry and allowed no competition on Eastern's lucrative New York–Miami route. Eastern had a monopoly on flights from the Northeast to Florida and promoted summer vacations in Florida to provide year-round business. But then the external environment changed in three ways: (1) Instead of carriers being limited to one for each route, another one or more were added to Eastern's routes; (2) Piston engine planes with propellers were replaced by jets; (3) The federal regulators did not allow Eastern to fly to the Pacific coast as all of its competitors did. Rickenbacker's strategies subsequently resulted in his continuing to purchase propeller planes such as the Lockheed Electra while his competitors purchased jets. In 1955, he ordered 26 jets but cut back orders to 16, foreseeing an oversupply of jet seats. This allowed Delta to obtain a competitive advantage by purchasing the planes. To minimizing costs with tight scheduling, Rickenbacker approved heavy use of his fleet, the arrangement of first-class seats five to a row (instead of four), overbooking, and reduced attention to passenger services—and lost many customers. When he

tried to attract more passengers by scheduling more flights on the same routes, the result was a lot of empty seats. Eastern never recovered its preeminence in the industry and finally went bankrupt.

Personally, "Captain Eddie" dominated the company. He was a stickler for detail. When he found problems or inconsistencies, he was immediately on the phone to the offending unit head. He challenged, heckled, and threatened his managers and executives when they presented performance appraisals of their units to him. But instead of hurting morale, his actions built a sense of camaraderie. Though he was feared, he was also respected. He knew all his pilots by name. He was a benevolent autocrat in that he saw that employees who originated good ideas were rewarded, and he gave many managers a lot of responsibility. Eastern employees felt like members of one big family with a patriarch at its head. Unfortunately for Eastern, Captain Eddie couldn't change his ways (Spencer & Carte, 1991).

Since Eastern folded, other airlines such as Pan Am have also terminated or changed. In spite of mismatched airline fleets, problems with pilots' seniority, and unions, as of April 2008 Delta Airlines and Northwest Airlines were moving toward a merger to create the world's largest airline. Only short-term benefits are expected for stockholders and executives; smaller airports may suffer and more efficient management may not materialize. Information about the merger has appeared in major newspapers.

Executive Leadership

Professionalization of the CEO

Keiser (2004) found, among 70 CEOs from 247 firms, systematic increases in the criteria of professionalization for some but not all between 1960 and 1990. By 2000, most organizations had adopted the title CEO; none had used it in 1960. During the same period, the CEOs' intellectual capital increased. In the early 1960s, about 40% had graduate degrees; by the late 1980s, the same was true for 80%. MBAs increased from 7% in 1960–1964 to 34% in 1985–1989. Only 3% were selected from the outside in 1960–1964; 28% were outsiders in 1985–1989. Many more entered the firm at higher echelons in 1985–1990 than in prior years. But they lacked other aspects of professionals that physicians, lawyers, engineers, and accountants had, such as licensing and a code of ethics. When CEOs subscribe to agency theory and attempt to maximize satisfaction of their own interests, they are unlike professionals, who are more likely to have a service orientation.

The Top-Management Team (TMT)

The senior executives in the upper echelons of an organization may be a loose collection, each running a different unit and seldom meeting or working with their counterparts. They lack the behavioral integration of a team. The members of a top-management team (TMT) synthesize their knowledge and expertise. They interact to discuss and make decisions and recommendations based on their varying expertise and knowledge (Hambrick, 1994). Thirty-eight top-management Australian teams were more likely to share tacit knowledge when they felt they had supportive leadership (Rowe, Christie, & Martin, 2003). Mooney (2003) studied 42 groups of senior executives and found that whether or not they formed real teams depended on the size of the firm, its strategy, the amount of organizational slack, and the executives' homogeneity. According to Quinn (1996), TMTs need to overcome the divisiveness of individual self-interest, insecurity, distrust, and political posturing. High-level cooperation and enthusiasm can come about only among competent people with clearly defined roles who work cohesively in trusting relationships, exercise personal discipline, and are willing to work for the good of the team.

Long-tenured top-management teams' strategic decisions about investing in R & D are tempered by the oversight of the board of directors and individual investors. This is especially so when the outside directors are prominent members of the board and the senior executives are long-tenured and diverse in their functions in the organization (Kor, 2002). The tenure of senior executive teams in 100 chemical, computer, and natural gas distribution firms affected their strategies and performance, according to a study by Finkelstein and Hambrick (1990). If they long had had tenure, they followed more persistent strategies and conformed closer to the average in their industry in strategy and performance. The more discretion they had, the more successful their strategies were.

Diversity within TMTs. Results on the effects of diversity of backgrounds of TMT members on outcomes have been mixed. Fishman (2003) reported that pharmaceutical patent citations and technological boundary spanning of TMT members in 52 firms were predicted by heterogeneity in their functional backgrounds. Roure and Keeley (1990) found that functional heterogeneity of the backgrounds of TMT members had positive effects on financial performance of their firms, but West and Schwenk (1996) did not. Barsade, Ward, Turner, et al. (2000) obtained evidence that if the 36 TMTs of profit and nonprofit organizations, named by their CEOs as members of the CEO's TMT, were diverse in their functional backgrounds, the organizations exhibited significantly greater market-adjusted returns on investment for the years the TMTs worked together. However, diversity of affect of the team members failed to significantly relate to TMT performance.

Knight, Pearce, Smith, Smith, Olian, et al. (1999) found that educational diversity contributed to financial success, but diversity of experience did the reverse. Certo, Lester, Daily, et al. (2003) presented a meta-analysis of the financial performance of firms and their TMTs' demographic characteristics. The functional heterogeneity of the TMT members accounted for 16.5% of the variance in sales growth and 7.5% of the rate of return on investment. Sales growth was also significantly greater when TMTs were larger ($R^2 = .079$). But diversity of organizational tenure, executive tenure, and education had little or no effect. The functional heterogeneity of a 20% survey sample of 450 hospital TMTs by Michie, Dooley, and Fryxell (2003) found that greater functional heterogeneity contributed to greater cooperation and greater decision quality mainly when there was greater consensus about goals. Where goals consensus was low, functional heterogeneity was contraindicated. But for the effect to occur, the diversity of backgrounds had to be related to the tasks that needed to be done (Simons, Pelled, & Smith, 1999).

Consistent with the above findings about the impact of TMTs' diversity on organizational strategic effectiveness, the same results appeared for diversity of power and for cognitive conflict in attitudes, beliefs, and opinions in interaction about strategy. For example, greater *distribution of power* among the most important members of their TMTs contributed to the effective performance of 51 hospitals. Power was defined for the peer raters as the ability to influence strategic agendas (A. Smith, Pitcher, Houghton, et al. 2003). Similar results were obtained in computer firms by Haleblian and Finkelstein (1993). Again, Ensley and Pearce (2001) used structural equation modeling to predict the performance of 158 new venture firms in 1994 and 1995. The path coefficient between diversity of opinions—cognitive conflict—and new venture growth in 1994 was .32. In 1995, the path coefficients of cognitive conflict were −.63 with new venture revenues and 0.77 with new venture profit. In both years, *emotional* conflict was negatively related to profit and revenues (−.34, −.38).

Variety of Executives' Roles. The roles of CEOs and senior organizational leaders vary to some extent depending on the nature of the organization. Providing strategic leadership is an important role for the CEO and may be the most important role for many (Farkus & De Backer, 1996; Korn-Ferry, 1988). However, CEOs and senior executives are likely to spend more time on implementing strategies than formulating them. But over time, successive organizational leaders play an important role in strategy formulation (Leavey, 1996).

The knowledge requirements of an ad agency business director, for example, differ from those of the head of an automobile manufacturing business. But they also have much in common (Levinson, 1981; Jaques & Clement, 1991). They need to understand balance sheets, the health of their markets, the products and services that can serve those markets advantageously, and the availability of capital. They need to know how to optimize the interests of the organization's various constituencies, how to manage change in good times and bad times, how to use authority and accountability, and how to assemble an effective management team of diverse competencies and interests (Ball, 1999). Not to be ignored is the less visible role of supporting or failing to support an organizational project. For instance, an organizational development project was run for two years without the cooperation or interest of the CEO of a hospital. The CEO was pressured into accepting the project. A new CEO in the next two years was enthusiastic about the project. Interviews with 150 employees and questionnaires with 650 employees found negative results for the project conducted for the first two years with the uncooperative CEO and pos-

itive results during the second two years with the cooperative CEO (Boss & Golembiewski, 1995).

Roles Differ from Those of Lower-Level Managers. Zaccaro (1996) distinguished executives from lower-level leaders in their (1) planning and creating policy within a larger time horizon; (2) interacting more frequently with external organizational constituencies; (3) engaging in more network development and consensus building; (4) developing a more comprehensive cognitive map of the organization and its environment. Executives contribute to organizational effectiveness by their long-term planning, boundary-spanning activities, network development, consensus building, and high-quality cognitive map of the organization and its environment. Although the myth continues that executives spend most of their time in *formulating* strategies, the facts are otherwise: they spend much more of their time in *implementing* strategies. Executives are action-oriented rather than reflective (Zaccaro, 1996). According to a job analysis by Baehr (1992) involving 1,358 managers, executives concentrate on setting objectives, making decisions, developing the workforce, and dealing with outside contacts and the community. Previous successful financial performance of the CEO's firm increases the CEO's power to influence the board of directors, the shareholders, and the employees. In turn, powerful CEOs induce better financial performance in the future (Daily & Johnson, 1997).

Relationship of the CEO to the Board of Directors. Rational economic models such as agency theory assume that the CEO will try to maximize his or her own preferences at the expense of the shareholders. Board governance should protect the shareholders against the self-aggrandizement of the CEO. Shareholders prefer to make CEO compensation dependent on corporate performance. The effective performance of 504 Fortune 500 firms related more highly to specific, guaranteed CEO salaries than to uncertain stock options whose value depended on stock performance. Sanders (1995, p. 268) concluded that "Agency theory has little explanatory power regarding the structure of CEO compensation." More helpful in explaining results were behavioral models, as with whom the CEO was being compared and the distribution of power. A behavioral model assumes that ideal CEOs are selected and rewarded by boards as stewards who have satisfied the interests of diverse stakeholders. A political model assumes that the selection and evaluation of the CEO by the board may depend on whether family members, friends, insiders, social acquaintances or prominent politicians are on the board. Xie, O'Neill, and Cardinal (2003) looked at how the composition of 41 boards affected the R & D performance of their respective firms. The intensity of R & D was lower if the board contained more directors from outside who were more diverse in functional backgrounds. Also, R & D performance was lower if the board members had more outside commitments.

The application of the board's controls will diminish as the CEO learns the role, increases in decision-making competence, learns how to work with the board and top management, and learns who are the most important stakeholders (Shen, 2003). CEOs can exert influence on boards when selecting new members and serving as outside board members of other organizations. They can help or hinder work in the boardroom (Rankin & Golden, 2002). Until recently, boards have been reluctant to exert their power to force the resignation of the chief executive, but increasingly they have ousted CEOs for the poor performance of their organizations, for failure to meet expectations, for scandalous behavior, for causing too much internal friction by being too autocratic, or for failure to keep up with the competition. In one month alone in 2005, a record number of company heads (103) were changed (Barrionuevo, 2005).

Relationship of the CEO to Stakeholders and Shareholders. Ackermann and Eden (2003) noted the importance of the CEO and top management to identifying the most powerful stakeholders inside and outside their organization, particularly how they notice and react to intended strategies and whether or not they are supportive. During times of change there is an increase in communications, usually letters, from the CEO to the shareholders to supplement quarterly reports and annual meetings. Between 1980 and 1999, General Electric sent out letters to try to reassure shareholders of the value of its radical reorganization and to reduce their uncertainties about its effects. The letters were more supportive than operational. They included warnings, actions, explanations, achievements, and predictions (Palmer & King, 2003).

CEOs differ in the priorities they set for paying attention to the different stakeholders. Agle, Mitchell, and Sonnenfeld (1999) examined, for 80 CEOs, how important to them were the various stakeholders of their corporation and the extent to which the various stakeholders had power, legitimacy, urgency, and salience for the CEOs, and high priority from top management. According to regression analyses, the percentage of the combined covariance of stakeholder power plus legitimacy plus urgency plus salience in the eyes of the 80 CEOs was 52% for customers, 48% for community, 30% for shareholders, 23% for government, and 17% for employees. When top management had values more oriented to others than to self, it gave higher priority to employees, government, and community. Top management also paid more attention to ethical and corporate social responsibility and was attentive to all the stakeholders. But according to Cannella and Monroe (1997), the economic and social models are limited. A more realistic view of how top managers strategize needs to include technology, markets, personality, transformational leadership, and executive envisioning. For instance, high-technology companies need to rapidly develop and implement strategies for short product life cycles that make it possible to integrate technology with market opportunity (Hughes, 1990).

Requisites for Executive Effectiveness. By 1840, the need of the emerging railroad industry to deal with organizing personnel and equipment over a broad geographic area sparked the growth of traditional rational organizational theory (Fox, 1994). Many theories of organization became prominent in the years that followed in the industrialized world, like those of Taylor (1911), Fayol (1916), Diemer (1925), and Cornell (1928). R. C. Davis (1951) built his functions of the executive around planning, direction, and control, a strategy that today is regarded as the traditional approach to executive management. But according to Fox (1994), Davis also took into account behavioral considerations, such as the motivating value of goals and their multiplicity and modification over time. Also included by Davis was the importance of coordination, status, evaluation apprehension, the utility of participation, pattern recognition, and feedback.

A corporation's *reputational capital* is another intangible value that contributes to its effectiveness and gives it greater competitive advantage. Reputation is enhanced by executive leadership, oversight, a reputational audit, and publicized awards and rankings for excellence (Petrick, Scherer, Brodzinski, et al., 1999).

In *systems theory*, the functions of executives are divided into exploratory functions and decisions about *inputs* of personnel, equipment, materials, accounting, and information; *throughputs* of production and processing; and *outputs* such as sales, marketing, growth opportunities, and again information (Hambrick & Mason, 1984). Rather than maintaining a compartmentalized silo mentality, executives need to draw their expertise from a wide range of experiences to contribute to innovative decision making (Hoffman & Hegarty, 1993). Zaccaro (1996) listed traits that were likely to assist executives in carrying out their functions. Some of them included career experience, relevant education, and functional background. Effective executives are able to deal with cognitive complexity, ready to take risks, and self-efficacious, and want to achieve. From a study of 27 government executives, Markessini, Lucas, Chandler, et al. (1994) added that effective executives required envisioning, multinational knowledge, consensus building, and an understanding of their whole organizational system. From a review of studies, Zaccaro (1996) concluded that organizations were more effective when their executives engaged in long-range planning and boundary spanning along with consensus building and network development. Javidan (1992) described a survey of the effectiveness of more than 500 middle, upper-middle, and senior executives by their immediate subordinates. Effective senior executives were viewed as dedicated and tenacious visionaries who could mobilize their subordinates. They were concerned coaches and remained in touch with their employees. They recognized accomplishments and served as good representatives outside the organization. According to Kennedy (1995), they avoided making political mistakes when newly promoted into senior management. They took care to understand top management's agenda and did not try to micromanage the successors to their previous positions.

Agency theory accounts for the behavior of self-interested CEOs. They are agents of the owners and shareholders. As their compensation often tends to depend more on the size rather than their organization's profitability, they need to have bonuses and other incentives to share their stockholders' interests in returns on investments (Jensen & Meckling, 1976). However, a more effective, mature, transformational CEO goes beyond self-interest and balances the competing demands of the marketplace with the demands of the organization's managers, employees, and other stakeholders. The opposing demands on senior executives are for flexibility versus stability, process versus outcome, and focus inside versus outside the organization (Hart & Quinn, 1993). The effective executive can deal with these competing requirements (Quinn, 1988). The less self-oriented, narcissistic CEO becomes a steward or custodian of the organization and its constituencies and takes satisfaction from building and maintaining a healthy organization. The steward may actually generate better returns on investment. Such a CEO may gain more support from the organization's stakeholders and enhance their motivation to excel.

Executive Effectiveness in the Nonprofit Organization. From a review of the literature, Mary S. Hall (1994) extracted 70 requirements for executive effectiveness in nonprofit organizations. Many requirements that she found were the same for executives in the nonprofit sector as for those in for-profit organizations. But particularly essential for the nonprofit executive are: (1) a deep commitment to the organization and projection of devotion to achieving its goals; (2) understanding and communicating the unique tradition and role of the nonprofit sector; (3) commitment to the common good and practicing what is preached; (4) knowing what and how to make quantitative and qualitative evaluations of the organization's performance; (5) building an organization that cares about the people and the clients it serves; (6) understanding clients' needs and serving as an advocate for them; (7) building the knowledge, commitment, and skills of the board; (8) recruiting, managing, and developing dedicated volunteers with recognition and rewards; (9) understanding public policy-making processes; (10) building community relations to facilitate cooperation with other public and private organizations; (11) mastering the use of media and practicing good public relations; (12) knowing the fund-raising process and negotiating effectively with funding sources.

Military Executive Effectiveness. U.S. Army lieutenant generals and full four-star generals are the equivalent of civilian CEOs in terms of the size of the organizations they lead and their level in the hierarchy. The brigadiers, major generals, and colonels below them also have executive functions. Leadership is seen as an important function of military service. Four-star generals report more boundary spanning and longer time spans of work than do lieutenant generals (Harris & Lucas, 1991). Both ranks of top generals engage in development of networks and more spanning of boundaries than do major and brigadier generals, but the lower-level generals need to know more details about the Army system (Lucas & Markessini, 1993). Colonels are more involved in setting goals and policies planning, and other executive functions than are officers below them (Steinberg & Leaman, 1990).

Competencies of Effective CEOs and Senior Executives

Zaccaro (1996) summarized studies that had compared the abilities of executives with those of lower-level managers and supervisors. Executives exceeded those lower in the organization in intelligence, creative potential, creative thinking, intuition, intuitive thinking, problem-management skills, toleration of ambiguity, and dealing with anxiety. Hurley and Sonnenfeld (1995) compared 683 top managers with a matched sample of middle managers, finding that the breadth, length, and nature of experience were significantly higher in the top-management sample. Jacobs and Jaques (1987) pointed out that executives develop a framework of understanding that provides meaning for organizational members' efforts toward collective action. According to Zaccaro (1996) *conceptual capacity* is required in executives as they deal with issues of *cognitive complexity*, that is, novel, unstructured, and ill-defined problems (Davidson, Deuser, & Sternberg, 1994). Executives must be able to display *behavioral complexity*—the ability to enact different and sometimes opposing roles. They must attend to *social complexities* when proposing actions. Senior executives are likely to be boundary spanners and need to deal with subordinates from different cooperating and competing groups, managers, employees, and functions (Zaccaro, 1996). In-depth interviews with 18 business leaders by Tait (1996) revealed that requisite qualities for their success included the ability to make sense of complicated patterns of events and extract clear goals for the organization. They also needed to be able to take independent and unpopular courses of action when necessary. As strategic leaders,

CEOs and senior executives must know how to harness the brainpower within their organizations, according to Percy Barnevik of ABB. In a similar vein, Jack Welch at General Electric would ask GE managers what their ideas were, with whom they had shared; and who had adopted them (Bennis, 1999). A high level of conceptual development is needed by senior executives. Their cognitive capacity should enable them to construct a perspective on a broad, complex understanding of events both inside and outside the organization and to handle highly complex managerial work (Lewis & Jacobs, 1992). They must deal with cognitive complexity (Hunt, 1991). Sashkin (1990) added to the need for cognitive capacity, self-efficacy, and the power motive as personal requirements for competence in strategic leadership.

Foresight. Farkas and De Backer (1996) also noted that entrepreneurial leaders should be as intuitive about what customers want next as the next maneuver of a competitor. Nevertheless, cognitive capacity is involved in the goal of adding value to the organization, with systematic and structured analysis of the state of the organization now and in the future. Strategically oriented CEOs focus on what comes next and try to make it happen. In 1995, Coca-Cola's senior management concentrated on reinventing the brand to make it new and relevant. Dell Computer CEO Michael Dell aimed to position the Dell personal computer for the future. Bob Galvin of Motorola (1991) argued that organizational leaders must be better anticipators and committers. Tom Sternberg, the CEO of Staples, carefully studied purchasing patterns and competitors. He questioned customers about what his chain of stores could do better. Jack Welch reinvented General Electric by selling the companies that were not profitable and keeping only those that dominated their markets and fit with a strategy to move into high technology and services.

Social Skills and Self-Monitoring. Connelly, Gilbert, and Zaccaro (2000) found that executives' social skills and knowledge contributed to quality solutions and achievement. For Mumford, Zaccaro, Harding, et al. (2000), executives' effectiveness depended on their ability to solve the complex social problems of organizations. K. L. Scott (2003) argued that self-monitoring would affect CEOs' strategic leadership practices. She hypothesized that high self-monitoring CEOs would be more effective at exploiting and maintaining the organization's core competencies, developing human capital, sustaining the organizational culture, and balancing organizational controls. Low self-monitors would be more effective at emphasizing ethical practices and communicating visions and plans. For new product ventures, S. M. Jensen (2003) proposed that entrepreneurs must have sufficient influence and confidence, involving self-efficacy, optimism, resiliency, and hope, to exert leadership in order to collaborate with others.

Korn/Ferry International (1988) and Columbia University conducted a survey in 1988 and then again in 2000 of 1,500 chief executives in the United States, Western Europe, Latin America, and Japan about the requirements of their positions. Strategy formulation was ranked first among the 10 most important areas of competence required both times by 75% to 80% of the respondents. There was general agreement about the importance of the required expertise, although strategic formulation was rated slightly lower in Latin America. Seen as important by 45% to 50%, competence in marketing and sales ranked second in 1988 and third in 2000. Human resource management changed places with marketing and sales, ranking third in 1988 and second in 2000, with the percentage of endorsement ranging from 40% to 50% (with western Europe lower than the other regions). Negotiation and conflict resolution ranked fourth and accounting and finance fifth in both years, with lower percentages of endorsement (under 30% with Japan being much lower than the other regions). Lower still in ranking were media skills, international economics and politics, production and operations, science, technology, and R & D. In 2000, computer literacy replaced foreign languages in tenth place. Implementation of strategies was probably included in strategic formulation or left to subordinate senior executives to do.

Charismatic Leaders. Charismatic leaders are expected to increase the effectiveness of those they lead both closely and at a distance (Waldman & Yammarino, 1999). They earn premium compensation for their charismatic personalities. Nevertheless, sometimes they may do more harm than good for their organizations (Vara, 2002). Khurana (2002) discovered that charisma was one of the criteria used by boards of directors in their search for and selection of 40 CEOs. For 59 very large firms, CEOs' charisma contributed to shareholder returns only during perceived uncertainties in the firms' markets. In these same firms, charismatic CEOs were paid a premium when there was high uncertainty or crisis in the market, such as instability in countries where business was conducted. However, their salaries and bonuses were lower than average when there was perceived high political uncertainty, such as unpredictability of government agencies (Tosi, Misangyi, Fanelli, et al. 2004).

Agle (1993) factor-analyzed a survey of 1,540 members of 258 top management teams who rated the charismatic leadership of their 250 CEOs using scales adapted from Podsakoff, Mackenzie, Moorman, et al. (1990). In the best regression model, five factors emerged. Three correlated significantly with CEO accomplishment, organizational effectiveness, and better stock performance. The correlations were as follows: (1) dynamic leadership (−.39, −.33, −.29), (2) exemplary leadership (−.52, −.36, −.19), (3) leader high performance expectations (−.21, −.23, −.04). For an analysis reported by Wolfe, Lucius, and Sonnenfeld (1998), 66 of these top-management teams also reported that their influence over their organizations was greater and the teams experienced less conflict if they and their own CEO served as trusted examples and exhibited personal dynamism.

When CEOs and Senior Executives Fail. The turnover of CEOs increased by 53% between 1995 and 2001. Average tenure declined from 9.5 to 7.3 years and has continued to decline since then. Poor financial performance of the firms led by a CEO increased 130% and was the reason for the CEOs' discharge or resignation (Pasternak, 2002). Based on a survey of 91 chief executives and seven interviews, Judge (1999) concluded that executives failed for several reasons: they did not provide a vision of the needed strategic path, did not understand the different interests of their important constituencies, did not prioritize goals, and failed to exemplify trust and integrity for their organization. Charan, Rosen, and Abarbanel (1991) described cases where the easier-to-do top management's strategic formulation failed in the harder-to-do strategic implementation. One CEO discovered that top-management team members delayed high-priority strategic divestitures with which they disagreed. A critical computer system conversion had not started when its expected time for implementation was already half over. Internal pricing disagreements were holding back sales efforts and reaching strategic goals.

Levinson (1988) argued that many executives fail because they have focused on short-term results and are insensitive to the feelings of employees and customers. They run a tight, highly controlled organization that is inflexible and unadaptive when faced with the need to change. Nutt (1999, 2002) pointed out that the self-interest that causes executives to fail can take many forms: they keep secret their plans of action for fear that openness will reduce the success of the plan; they pursue a plan and want to keep secret their self-interest in the plan; they make quick decisions without considering alternatives; they ignore ethical considerations and carry out deceptions to protect themselves; they skip or limit search; they make premature commitments and misuse resources; they blunder by making poor decisions, premature commitments, and misusing resources. Examples include the decisions by Quaker Oats' executives to acquire Snapple and Disney's executives to open Euro Disney.

Executives fail when they become too involved in their personal interests and not enough in their constituent's and organization's interests. Senior executives fail when their strategic vision of the future direction blocks out important opportunities, distorts market realities; fails to recognize a changed environment (Conger, 1990). Executives fail when they stretch the organization's resources beyond limits (Ulmer, 1998). They fail when they confuse a good, well-communicated strategy to their organizational implementation of the strategy. They fail when their strategy for change is "narrow, unsystematic, and programmatic [and] does not address root causes" (Beer & Eisenstat, 2000). They fail when they allow narcissism to dominate strategic thinking. They fail when they create illogical organizational structures and compensation plans (Levinson, 1994). Like Levinson, Kets De Vries (1989) attributes executives' failure to internal personal considerations. Executives who isolate themselves from reality self-destruct by becoming divorced from it, as do those who fear success. According to Hitt, Hoskisson, and Harrison (1991), misdirected attention and effort cause executives' failure; they put too much emphasis on mergers and acquisitions, diversify too much, and ignore their human capital. They fail because

of lack of attention to productivity, quality, innovation, and the need for a global strategy. Bennis (1999) attributes the failure of chief executives of public institutions to institutional and societal forces: (1) public institutions and agencies are easily politicized, (2) Politicized institutions are pulled in many directions at the same time and lose sight of their reason for existing, (3) Society overloads the institution with problems.

Executive Derailment. Lombardo and Eichinger (1989) followed up McCall and Lombardo's (1983) analysis of managerial derailment with an examination of why senior executives are derailed. Derailed executives are those who have been plateaued, demoted or fired, accepted early retirement, or have seen their responsibilities reduced. In comparison to those who made it to the top, those who were derailed treated others poorly due to overambition, overindependence, isolation, abrasiveness, lack of caring, and/or volatility under pressure. They had difficulty in building a team due to poor selection, and/or they were dictatorial, overcontrolling, unable to resolve conflicts, and delegated poorly. They were unable to deal with complexity and ambiguity and collapsed under the pressure of a new situation. They were disorganized and attended to detail poorly. They failed to follow through and/or were untrustworthy. Or they were overly dependent on one strength, relied on others to shield their weaknesses, and/or were sheltered too long under the same boss or mentor. They had poor relations with senior management, in their inability to persuade or adapt to a boss with a different style. They had disagreements about strategy and/or were unable to influence across functions. They were insensitive to others, were arrogant, and ignored advice. Although such insensitivity was tolerated at lower levels of management, particularly if the managers were technical experts, it was the most common reason for derailment (Lombardo & Eichinger, 1989). The pattern of derailment was somewhat different in Britain. Compared on the 16 PF personality questionnaire with employed managers, 204 *redundant* executives were more socially bold, forthright, uninhibited, imaginative, and unconventional but less self-critical and politically skilled (Tyson et al., 1986). Again in Britain, 676 managers who had been derailed were extroverted, innovative, change-oriented, and independent. These traits might have resulted in more success in the United

States. However, like derailed executives in the United States, the British managers, were less warm (Brindle, 1992).

Van Velsor and Leslie (1995) extracted four themes in a review of research reports between 1983 and 1994 of derailed executives and managers: (1) problems with interpersonal relationships, (2) failure to meet business objectives, (3) inability to build and lead a team, and (4) inability to develop and adapt. They also found increasing sources of failure in lack of business experience, preparation for promotion, and broad functional orientation. Of less importance was overdependency on an advocate or mentor. Sometimes the competent CEO was dismissed as a scapegoat for trusting the wrong people on the board or in the organization or for similar reasons (Boeker, 1992). This may be one of the reasons that for 400 firms in 21 industries between 1987 and 1996, CEOs who had chief operating officers (COO) under them as second-in-command generated $10 million less in returns on assets (1%) than did those without such subordinates (Hambrick, 1989).

Brockman, Hoffman, and Fornaciari (2003) analyzed 194 large organizations that had filed for Chapter 11 bankruptcy protection from their creditors. If their CEOs had more formal power, the businesses were more likely to survive and return to normality in a shorter time than those with less formally powerful CEOs. Recovery took longer and survival was more problematic for organizations led by CEOs with more informal power or prestige.

Examples of CEOs Who Failed. Don Burr founded PEOPLExpress in the early 1980s with an emphasis on good working relationships among the employees. Leadership was shared, and employees had multiple job assignments For instance, pilots might help at the ticket counter. The commitment, cohesion, satisfaction, and motivation of employees were high. The airline grew rapidly by offering no-frills, low-cost service that competed favorably with the industry giants like United, American, and TWA. High-performing teams were developed. But Burr failed to pay attention to what his competitors were doing. They were modernizing their information, scheduling, ticketing, and pricing systems in the newly deregulated airline industry. With much better financial and information resources, they could immediately undercut PEOPLExpress's prices. Scanning for competitive threats was missing, as was keeping up with available technology.

In comparison, Braniff Airways self-destructed rather than succumbed to more aggressive competition. Its management failed to train and reward its employees in order to compete effectively. It developed a reputation for disgruntled employees, delays, and poor relationships with passengers, particularly in Dallas, its home airport. Shortsighted and uninformed top management had poor relations with the federal agencies, creating angry regulators. CEO Harding Lawrence, among other Braniff senior executives, was seen as pushy, arrogant, and domineering. When Braniff got into financial trouble, the regulators went out of their way to aggravate conditions for the airline. Safety and maintenance problems were usually handled quietly by the Federal Aviation Agency. News about Braniff was spread to the metropolitan media and resulted in a major loss of customers. In dealing with its financial difficulties, top management got its employees to accept a 10% pay cut, but the news made travel agents wary about using Braniff for future bookings. Reducing unprofitable routes to reduce costs resulted in continuous schedule changes, which confused travel agents, the airline's own reservation agents, and travelers, particularly business travelers. The self-destruction was further mismanaged by poor communications. The last CEO, Howard Putnam, further exacerbated the loss of travelers by guaranteeing only one day at a time that Braniff would stay in business (Nance, 1984).

Dale Sundby, founder of PowerAgent was a good salesman but an ineffective CEO. He sold his investors on his business plan to revolutionize online advertising. Customers were to register online to receive ads in exchange for points to discount the cost of purchases. The highly persuasive CEO organized a board of directors, backers for the necessary capital, and 60 employees. But he was highly self-oriented and could not see beyond his own vision, which dominated his thinking, and his expectation that everyone would agree with him. He ignored market research. He spent lavishly on himself and associates. Without a product or production staff, he budgeted over half his capital on advertising. He expected to outsource software coding. This delayed the Internet process. He invested heavily in a marketing management team. He didn't listen when told that many prospects were being lost because registration was too long. Also, prospects wanted daily tips, not daily ads. Because he did not tell anyone else in the organization what was happening, morale and support disappeared. The board split on his spending and business plan. Refinancing that he expected because of his persuasiveness did not materialize. In 20 months, he burned through $20 million and 60 employees (*New Business*, 1998).

Executive Compensation

Barkema and Gomez-Mejia (1998) presented a general framework for variables that determined executive compensation; these variables included market, organization size, executives' roles, and peers' compensation. Compensation was also determined by the governance structure, such as ownership, and the board of directors, and by contigencies such as strategy, national culture, and tax system. Effects on compensation depended on whether compensation was linked to performance, short- or long-term. A meta-analysis by Tosi, Werner, Katz et al. (2000) of 187 CEO compensation studies found that firm size in assets, market value, and revenues accounted for half the variance in CEOs' compensation. Khan, Dharwadkar, Brandes, et al. showed that CEOs' salaries alone correlated negatively with the rate of return on investment (ROI) of 106 firms in 71 industries but positively in 45 with the number of institutional owners of the firms (banks, insurance companies, investment advisors, and investment companies). Although 570 CEOs' contracts in the largest corporations called for incentive plans to compensate CEOs for increasing the value of the firm, the plans tended to be ignored and were more symbolic than substantive, especially in firms with poor prior performance and strong CEOs (Westphal & Zajac, 1994). The relationship between stock returns and CEO tenure weakened, according to analyses by Hill and Phan (1991), as the longer-tenured CEO increased influence over the board. However, compensation based on performance correlated positively when the CEO faced moderate risks and had greater control of performance outcomes (Miller, Wiseman, & Gomez-Mejia, 2002). In the same way, pay contingent on performance was more likely in firms that were owner-controlled (an owner or institution owned more than 5% of the shares of the firm) than where the managers were in control. In the latter firms,

size was more important (Tosi & Werner, 1995). Salaries tended to be linked to sales in highly regulated industries such as railroads and banks and tended to be linked to total profits in less regulated industries, according to a survey of 1,200 corporations by Kokkelenberg (1988).

CEOs' compensation increased by 600% between 1990 and 1999, far more than increases in inflation and employee wages (Reingold & Jesperson, 2000). CEOs may exit a firm with 20% or more of the recent annual profit of a firm, leaving 80% or less for all the other shareholders. After 18 months of service, a recent Disney CEO departed legally with a termination package of $140 million! Halock (2004) compared for-profit firms with nonprofits in the same deciles of their respective distributions of CEO compensation. For managing the same relative level of assets, the for-profit executives earned more than as much annually as the nonprofit executives. Only under conditions of uncertainty was there a correlation between executive compensation and financial effectiveness in 48 Fortune 500 firms (Waldman, Ramirez, House, et al., 2001). Compensation was higher in times of crisis but lower in times of political uncertainty (Tosi, Misangyi, Fanelli, et al., 2004). However, under conditions of uncertainty, a correlation was found with financial effectiveness in 48 Fortune 500 firms (Waldman, Ramirez, House, et al., 2001). For a sample of 848 Fortune 1000 firms, CEOs' compensation was more accurately predicted by comparisons with CEOs in other firms by institutional and social comparison theory than by agency theory (Gilley, Coombs, Parayitam, et al., 2003). CEOs' compensation in 112 of Fortune 1000 firms was also found to be contingent on the percentage of outsiders on the board of directors (Olson, 2003). But in 90 high-technology firms agency theory did help account for the relationships between short-term compensation of CEOs and innovations as assessed by the number of patents obtained and the amount spent on R & D (Balkin, Markin, & Gomez-Mejia, 2000). The form of compensation—stock or stock options—had different motivating effects on the executives' tendencies to make acquisitions or divestitures. The form of compensation also influenced whether CEOs preferred taking risks with options or avoiding risks with stock (Sanders, 2001). Jaques (2001) noted that the compensation at the highest level of the managerial hierarchy (responsible for a time span of 20 years of control) was felt to be fair by the job occupant at

51 times the lowest management level (responsible for a time span of one day). Felt-fair compensation correlated .86 with time span of control. The same average ratios for these levels and all those in between have been universally endorsed for the past 50 years. However, there is much variation in CEOs' compensation among firms skewed to overpayment from the mean. The compensation and severance packages in excess of industry norms that CEOs and key executives, supported by their boards, have been awarded have raise questions about whether they are justified. While 50 years ago CEOs averaged 40 times the annual compensation of the average worker, by 2005 the figure had increased to more than 400 times. Combs and Skill (2003) found that for 77 firms whose founders had just died, the successors' compensation was higher than expected when the support of the executive, the board, and the nominating committee for a successor was stronger. Other variables, such as firm size, were controlled. Executives' performance was less important than their executive entrenchment.

Executives' Accountability. To link executives' accountability and discretion to their compensation, Grossman and Hoskisson (1998) suggested a need to identify the organization's strategies and what can provide it with competitive advantages. If cash flow and operating efficiency are keys to corporate success, accounting measures should be used to link executives' competence to their compensation. If innovation is a key factor, compensation should be tied to measures of marketing success. If short-term success is emphasized, annual bonuses can be awarded. If long-term success is more important, restricted shares, stock options, or other forms of delayed compensation should be linked to performance.

The strategy of voluntary disclosures in 28 different firms appeared dependent on whether their CEOs were compensated by long-term incentives, owned a smaller percentage of shares in the company, and were in later stages of their careers (Natarajan & Rasheed, 2003). For Streufort and Swezey (1986), executives of firms in stable environments needed to be ready, willing, and able to engage in long-term planning. Conversely, Miller and Friesen (1980) suggested that CEOs in office for a long time are resistant to change and this rigidity is often a cause for strategic failure (see also Kets de Vries & Miller, 1984.) In 97 randomly selected small, mainly Franco-phone firms in a variety of industries in Quebec, Miller and Toulouse (1986) found that the CEOs' years in office correlated $-.33$ with return on investment (ROI). On the other hand, net income growth correlated .36 with the strategy to spend on R & D and commercialization of products. Net income growth correlated .47 with a strategy of delegating authority.

Setting Policies and Strategies

Masoud Ardekani–Yasai (in press) obtained evidence from 101 small manufacturing firms that the firms exhibited superior performance when their management's functional experience was congruent with the requirements of their strategies. CEOs and top management set policies and strategies for acquiring and integrating resources for the organization. Among their goals are to reduce uncertainty, increase stability, increase resources, and reduce competition. They strive to create favorable public images and opinions of the organization and its products and services. They oversee conformance with government policies, regulations, taxes, and trade. Indirectly, they influence government through personal influence, support of lobbyists, trade associations, and political campaigns. Ideally, top-level business leaders choose markets based on strategic planning and location of their facilities. They manage the management, production, and services systems. Their evaluations, coordination, and policies influence the organization's subsystems of finance, capital, and personnel (Day & Lord, 1988). James Webb, long-term director of the National Aeronautics and Space Administration, exemplified the effective chief administrator of a federal agency. According to Sayles (1979), NASA was superbly managed. In less than 10 years, the agency went from no knowledge of man in space to an operational space program. It was a tremendous accomplishment in organizational leadership. The required strategic thinking and implementation occurred in the face of many risks, uncertainties, and unknowns.

There is an interplay between the corporate strategy formulated by CEOs and what is required of the organization. If a CEO pursues a human assets strategy for the organization instead of one based on a bureaucratic box of rules, management will need to be ready to be more participative, consultative, and considerate in its leadership. Interpersonal skills will be seen as the sine qua non of the effective top executive (Sessa, 1999). The more the strategy is to take account of uncertainty and ambiguity in the organizational environment, the more top management will need to be adaptable, flexible, and open (Zaccaro, Gilbert, Thor, et al., 1991). They will need to determine *strategic inflection points* when major changes take place in their business, such as the introduction of a new technology, a change in the regulatory environment, or a change in what their customers want. The inflection point is a sudden drastic change from a steady state or gradual expansion or contraction of supplies, demands, or organizational performance. At such a point, a fundamental change in business strategy is called for (Grove, 1999).

For Toney (1996), a firm's profitability depends on the CEO's actions. CEOs whose firms are consistently profitable maintain their focus on the bottom line. They pursue a corporate strategy and structure with profitability as a goal, as do their subordinates. Accounting and finance are stressed in an analysis of their daily decisions. It is unclear whether this approach is optimal for the various stakeholders and the long-term health of the organization. The successful implementation of strategies formulated by the CEO and top management will depend on their leadership and the qualities of their relations with managers and employees (Cannella & Monroe, 1997).

Finkelstein (1992) completed several studies of the powers of the CEO and the dominant coalition of senior executives. Four factors were extracted and validated from a survey of 1,763 executives. The highest-loaded item on each factor was (1) structural power (compensation, .86); (2) ownership power (family shares, .86); (3) expert power (critical functional experience, .85); and (4) prestige power (membership on nonprofit boards, .75). Evidence was found that diversification strategies and acquisitions in 102 firms were influenced in particular by the financial backgrounds and powers of their dominant coalitions of executives. Finkelstein concluded that to understand the strategic decision making in an organization, one must include the distribution of power in the dominant coalition of senior executives as well as the CEO's power and functional background. Song (1982) also found that firms tended to diversify by acquisitions if their senior executives had backgrounds in law, account-

ing, and finance rather than production or marketing. Acquisitions could be beneficial to the degree that, as Bergh (2001) argued, the acquiring firm attempted to hold on to the managers from the acquisition who had the highest rank and longest longevity in that firm. Bergh examined the success of 104 acquisitions retained or resold in five years. He reasoned that long-tenured top executives possess specific knowledge about the firm and demonstrate long-term commitment to the firm and its stakeholders. They are a source of continuity during the turmoil that follows an acquisition.

Strategic Challenges

The challenges of globalization have been accompanied by climate change, nanotechnology, Internet piracy, new societal norms, terrorist disruptions, the aging population, alternative measures of performance, and manmade environmental degradation (Grant, 2005). At the personal level, newly installed CEOs and top managers may miss the close peers and counsel they had before. Along with the oft-cited "loneliness at the top" syndrome, there is tension between attention to the present and attention to the future: "If you do not satisfy the present, there will be no future" (Bruce, 1986, p. 19). A survey of executives reported by Hughes (1998) suggested that the most important challenges facing their organizations were dealing with change; thinking strategically; dealing with business issues; and achieving focus, consensus, and vision. Well known is the extent to which domestic firms increasingly face competitive challenges from abroad. Many products and services first produced in the advanced industrial countries are now produced in China, India, and the developing countries. A huge annual trade deficit has been created in the United States even though its consumers benefit from lower prices. But higher-paying manufacturing employment in the United States is being replaced by lower-paying employment in services industries. Competing firms are a challenge in the United States, connected to a number of strategic factors that senior executives may be able to control. But as foreign competitiveness increases for various reasons, such as lower labor costs, the challenge may be met with increased innovation and productivity, greater investment in capital, and more attention to human resources, quality, productivity, and innovation. Also needed is a better long-term global strategy. Better use of capital investment and human resources can contribute more to corporate profitability and economic growth than increased capital investment alone, according to empirical analyses by Franke and Miller (2005).

How many people should be employed by an organization is a question that cannot be answered by expanding immediately when the demand for the organization's products or services increases, and contracting immediately when they decrease. Strategically planned *rightsizing* is needed, taking into account the costs of cutting the labor force, laying off employees, and early retirements. With downsizing, there is a loss of teamwork, long-term corporate identity, and core competencies. The better employees may retire early. There may be a costly lowering of morale, negative effects on families and community, and the need to rebuild the staff when there is a turnaround. The alternative strategy is rightsizing; restructuring; transferring and retraining redundant employees; sharing jobs; cutting average working hours; providing temporary reassignments; and protecting teamwork and core competencies (Cascio, 1995; Hitt, Keats, Harback, et al., 1994).

History judges a CEO on the strategic conceptualizations that contribute to future success, not on a maintenance of the present situation. But the present imposes strong demands on the CEO's time, with its numerous review committees, preparations for board meetings and annual meetings, critical regulatory responses to governmental requests, and exorbitantly time-consuming internal and external ceremonial duties. Top corporate managers have to free themselves from these day-to-day operations and short-term goal orientations to focus more attention on long-term threats and opportunities and to provide long-term leadership on strategic issues and their analysis, the formulation of implementation, interpretation, and evaluation (Wortman, 1982). The strategies reflect the CEO's inclination and leadership (Staw & Sutton, 1993). Large organizations establish a chief of organizational operations (COO) to relieve the CEO of day-to-day burdens. According to Hambrick (1991), in general, the CEO's tenure in office may undergo five phases that determine the CEO's attention, behavior, and organizational performance: (1) response to the mandate to lead, (2) experimentation, (3) selection of an enduring theme, (4) convergence, and (5) dysfunction.

Larger strategic changes are made earlier in the chief executive's time in office (Gabarro, 1987). As might be expected, CEOs remain in office longer in stable rather than turbulent industries (Norburn & Burley, 1988).

Hambrick, Finklestein, and Mooney (2005) have proposed as hypotheses that executives challenged by greater demands of their jobs, compared to their less challenged counterparts, will tend to (1) imitate the strategic actions of other firms and (2) display more extreme strategic behavior and vacillation. Different organizational strategies are needed to meet the different challenges to a firm and its management, depending on the rate of technological change in their industry and the maturity of the firm. For instance, in a growing company in a fast-changing industry, a *pioneering* strategy is needed for development of new products, licensing of larger firms, fast innovations, movement into markets, and speed of expansion. In a mature firm in a slowly changing industry, a *consolidation* strategy is needed, with wide product lines for broad markets, long-term supplier relations, and standardized products (Lei & Slocum, 2005).

Dual CEOs. Occasionally when two giant corporations, such as Citicorp and Travelers Group, merge, instead of a single CEO taking charge, co-CEOs are appointed to work as partners. The strategy is based on it being impossible for one CEO to oversee the challenging diversity and geographic spread. Other examples of organizations whose size led to a strategy of dual CEOs include ABC, Capital Cities, Unilever, and Goldman Sachs (Troiano, 1999).

Strategic Change. To make strategic changes, the organization needs to rethink its current values and reorient itself (Fitzgerald, 1988). Struckman and Yammarino (2003, p. 234) noted that a key difficulty in handling strategic change is "keeping an organization focused on delivering quality and timely products and services while dealing with various change initiatives. . . . Everywhere managers turn, another change activity kicks off." Furthermore, if leaders want to carry out a long-term strategic change, they will need to be inspirational so that the concurrence of constituent stakeholders is internalized. To obtain quicker support for a short-term strategic change, executives will find that transactional leadership may work as well.

For O'Toole (1995), effective strategic leaders promote organizational alignment and adaptability, which are "powerful predictors of long-term organizational excellence" (p. 82). "*Alignment* is observable when everyone down the line in the organization knows and understands corporate objectives, is motivated to pursue them, and knows what they must do to contribute to meeting overall corporate goals. . . . *Adaptability* . . . allows the organization to innovate, avoid threats, and seize new opportunities" (pp. 92, 94). Perceived awareness of the alignment of the strategy with its conception and what is being realized begins to fall off rapidly at the second level of managers from the top and declines further with movement down the line. There is a need to remind the organization about the actual strategy that has been formulated, its connection to behavior (Hambrick, 1981), and how the organization is going to become distinctive and continue to improve on its ability to deliver to its stakeholders. Continuity of strategy as well as continual improvement needs to be maintained. Continuity and change support each other. The more explicit the strategy and goals, the more new opportunities can be recognized. Choice, trade-off, and fit are required for strategic change (Porter, 2001). Strategic change is more likely to occur when a new CEO is brought into the firm with a mandate for change from the board of directors based on tentative agreements between the CEO and the board. If the mandate is for continuing the old policies, little change can be expected. According to a study of 40 cases by Tishman, Newman, and Romanelli (1986), less change in strategy may be expected with a long-tenured CEO or if the CEO retires and is replaced by an insider without the board's mandate for change (Hambrick & Fukutomi, 1991). When first appointed, CEOs, even before they move into their offices, may visit plants and shops, ask questions of personnel at various levels, talk with key people, and examine reports and other information sources to develop an understanding of operations and needed improvements. Initial changes are usually made in functional areas in which the CEO has had previous experience to demonstrate and evaluate success early on (Gabarro, 1985). If the CEO is hired during a crisis, the change will be for immediate relief in the short term to find time for longer-term solutions. Over time, commitment to a chosen strategy will increase, barring new alternatives. The relatively brief tenure of CEOs,

currently averaging five years or less, may be due to the tasks becoming more routine, the CEOs' increasing power, and CEOs becoming less responsive to associates and the rapidly changing business environment. Dramatic leadership successions, particularly of new CEOs from the outside, can bring on a change in a familiar corporate name to reflect the new leadership, new strategies, and reorganizations (Glynn & Slepian, 1992).

Janson (undated) suggested an eight-step strategy for a new CEO wanting to make an organizationwide change: (1) Ask the most powerful people in the organization what they regard as the organization's strengths and weaknesses and what they would change if they had the opportunity; (2) Complete a diagnosis with the help of many others on what needs changing and the receptivity and obstacles to the changes, and identify people who can lead the change efforts; (3) Envision the changed organization; (4) Identify the gaps between the current organization and the envisioned organization; (5) Encourage total involvement of significant others in the change effort; (6) Tailor the change effort to the nature of the organization; (7) Enlist the relevant department heads and a transition manager to provide needed network communication and recognition of project coordinators and team leaders about what has been happening; (8) Measure how well objectives of the change efforts have been met. The survival of Sears for well over a century may be attributed to the strategic changes initiated by its new incoming chairmen that fit Sears' changing internal and external environment. Julius Rosenwald, as new CEO, overhauled Sears' cost and control mail-order systems to achieve greater efficiency. As retail stores gradually supported and replaced the mail-order business, Robert Wood came along as CEO to radically alter the business to fit the changing environment, from rural to urban marketplace (Stryker, 1961). It's still too early to tell how Sears' institutionalized values of customer service and product quality will be affected by its merger with Kmart, which has focused on competing with lower prices.

The financial services industry has gone through two strategic transitions guided by strategic considerations. At first, in the typical insurance office, a few people handled the business. The same person might sell, underwrite, and process claims, Jobs were whole, customer service was personalized, the organization was flat, there was little overhead, and costs were acceptable. As business expanded, the industrial office was created, adapting the then-prominent rules for the factory of "scientific management." Work was fragmented, direct contact with customers was abandoned, production lines were created, and people were organized to fit the system. Costly tangential jobs and multiple levels of management were created, and errors increased. Growth and work simplification were accompanied by a loss of service orientation and eventually diminishing effectiveness. The successful service organization pursues a new strategy for quality service, including: (1) a vision of customer service that focuses the organization's values, beliefs, and norms on customer service; (2) a structure that is designed around some aspect of the customer, such as market segment or geographical location, rather than around the work process; (3) assigning responsibility for satisfying a particular set of clients; (4) moving accountability and decision making to the lowest possible level in the organization; (5) creating systems of customer feedback; (6) using computer technology to provide instant access by the service employee to the complete customer file (Janson, 1989).

Strategic Leadership. The founder's personality has an impact on the culture of the organization and its subsequent strategies. If the founder is autocratic and controlling, like Harold Geneen of ITT, the organization will pursue a top-down strategy of leadership. If the founder is, like Bill Gore, team-oriented and participative, the strategy of leadership will reflect these values, as happened at Gore-Tex (Nahavandi & Malekzadeh, 1993). Top management's leadership is required if a total quality program is to succeed. For instance, Choi and Behling (1997) noted that the attitudes and commitment of top executives were critical to the success or failure of total quality management (TQM) programs. During the 1990s, many were tried and abandoned. Success, continuation of TQM programs, and annual introduction of new TQM practices were much more likely when top management had a *developmental* orientation than when they had a *defensive* orientation—preoccupation with past problems, customers being seen as threatening, and unrealistic expectations. Management's commitment to programs is critical. A meta-analysis of 18 studies of the impact on organizations of management by objectives (MBO) found that the gain in job satisfaction from the

installation of MBO occurred only in organizations with highly committed top management. There was little gain in employees' job satisfaction in firms where top management was less committed to implementing the MBO program (Rodgers, Hunter, & Rogers, 1993).

A new CEO is often chosen to match the organization's current strategy. (Nahavandi & Malekzadeh, 1993), resulting in better implementation of the strategy (Michel & Hambrick, 1992). Strategic requirements provide the CEO with a cognitive map of the organization and its environment (Calori, Johnson, & Sarnin, 1994). However, the typical strategically oriented leader looks forward to setting directions for the organization (Arnott, 1995). The executive's power is increased when the critical sectors of the environment can be scanned and scoped (Hambrick, 1981). Strategic leaders make and communicate decisions for their organization's future (Zaccaro, 1996). They: (1) formulate or modify the organization's goals and strategies; (2) develop structures, processes, controls, and core competencies for the organization; (3) manage multiple constituencies; (4) choose key executives; (5) groom the next generation of executives and personnel; (6) provide direction with respect to organizational policies; (7) maintain an effective organizational culture; (8) sustain a system of ethical values; (9) serve as the representative of the organization to government and other organizations and constituencies as well as negotiate with them. Such strategic leadership must be able to deal with ambiguity, complexity, and information overload. Adaptability and a sense of timing are required (House & Aditya, 1997; Boal & Hooijberg, 2001).

The organization's strategy reflects its top management and its internal and external environments. According to Nutt (1986), managers with different styles of leadership are likely to see a different amount of risk in a situation and to choose different strategies. Those who are more judgmental will choose strategies oriented toward action and capital expansion. Those who are more systematic will choose strategies that avoid taking immediate action. Innovations are most likely to be pursued by managements classified according to their strategies as *prospectors* rather than as *defenders* of the status quo; *analyzers*, who try to maximize profits by minimizing risks; or *reactors*, who are inconsistent in dealing with their environment (Miles & Snow, 1978). Prospectors look to discover and work with innovative products even though risks are high. Their firms are flexible in administration and technology. Their organizations invest in human resources and favor decentralization, organicity, and decentralization (Heller, 1994). The top managements of prospectors are most likely to be former outsiders (Chaganti & Sambhara, 1987). They prospect for strategies that others have already proved successful and therefore enter second into a market. This appears more advantageous to them than pioneering an innovation and entering the market first (Schnaars, 1994).

Strategic leadership requires creating meaning and purpose for the organization, with a powerful vision and mission that create a future for the organization (Ireland & Hitt, 1999). Sosik, Jung, Berson, et al. (2001, 2004) agree and call envisioning the heart of strategic leadership. In many organizations, the CEO and top management formulate and implement their strategies. Inputs from lower levels of management and employee networks contribute in a collaborative effort (Senge, 1997), particularly in the implementation of strategies (Cogliser, 2002). *Strategic maneuvering* is required when a firm is challenged by hypercompetitiveness in price, service, and quality, timing and knowledge, and strongly held markets and products. Hypercompetitiveness is illustrated by the airline-pricing fare wars. By the beginning of 2005, two discount airlines, Southwest and JetBlue, with lower costs, simpler fare structures, and lower prices than the main carriers, had captured 30% of the U.S. market. A major carrier, Delta Air Lines, cut its prices and fare rules drastically to match those of Southwest and JetBlue. Then other main carriers, American Airlines, Northwest, and US Airways followed suit, even though they could not afford the potential loss of revenues, in their effort to meet the competition. US Airways did not have the necessary "deep pockets," it was already bankrupt, as was another main carrier, United Airlines.

A firm's seizing the initiative with hypercompetitiveness disrupts the status quo and may create a series of temporary competitive advantages with speed, surprise, and accurate forecasting (D' Aveni, 1994). Structural equation modeling for 76 executives and 528 colleagues who rated them showed that positive interpersonal relations and confident speech were antecedents of strategic leadership. In turn, the executives' strategic leadership contributed to their rated effectiveness, potential, and the

performance of the unit they supervised (Gist & Gerson, c. 1998?) As might be expected, in a survey of more than 100 small and medium-sized businesses in Britain, transformational leaders engaged in significantly more strategic planning than did transactional leaders to achieve financial results, avoid problem areas, innovate, and improve short- and long-term organizational performance (O'Regan & Ghobadian, 2003).

Strategic Decisions. Like most organizational decisions, strategic decisions should proceed in an orderly fashion, beginning with anticipation and scanning for information (Bass, 1982). Both U.S. and Indian entrepreneurs and managers increase their scanning when they perceive increases in environmental changes and the importance and accessibility of information (Stewart, May, & Arvind, 2003). Ordinarily, this leads to the discovery of problems; diagnosis; a search for solutions; innovation; evaluation of and choice among alternative solutions; authorization; and implementation. Each phase may call for a return to an earlier one before going forward. Some phases are ignored more than others for rational or emotional reasons. For instance, a favorite alternative is seized on without considering other possibilities. Most of the phases may be implicit when the decision is based on intuition (Bass, 1982).

Such decisions coordinate diverse divisions in the organization, analyze contradictory and ambiguous information, and interpret events. Sometimes they need a long-term perspective (as much as 20 years ahead in the military or government and industries), requiring heavy capital investments. Weiner and Mahoney (1981) sampled the performance of 193 manufacturing corporations. They concluded that what the top leadership decided to do had a strong influence on the corporations' profitability. Niehoff, Enz, and Grover (1990) reached similar conclusions about the effects on the commitment and satisfaction of 862 employees if their top management teams encouraged innovation, supported employees' efforts, and shared a vision and participation in decisions. But Crosby (1990) argued that creating the vision and the organization's direction was to be accomplished by the chief executive and implemented by his subordinates.

Farkas and De Backer (1998) formulated five approaches that CEOs headquartered in the United States, western Europe, and Japan say they pursue. They can all be considered as based on different strategic decisions about the best way to manage: (1) *strategic*, envisioning the future and planning how to get there (e.g., Coca-Cola, Newmont Mining, Staples, and Deutsche Bank); (2) *human assets*: managing people, policies, programs, and principles (e.g., Southwest Airlines, PepsiCo, Philips, and Massachusetts General Hospital; (3) *expertise*: championing specific proprietary expertise and using it to focus the organization (e.g., AngloAmerican, Ogilvy & Mather, Motorola, and Saint-Gobain); (4) *box*: creating, rules, systems, procedures, and values to control behavior and outcomes within well-defined boundaries (e.g., British Airways, HSBC, and Nintendo); (5) *change agent*: CEO acts as an agent of radical change from bureaucracies to new and different organizations (e.g., Goldman Sachs, Tenneco, and Mitsui). Each of the approaches may fail. For instance, at ITT the box approach was too rigid; Digital Equipment focused on its expertise approach, when actually it needed to change. All the interviewees saw the strategic approach as one of their roles, but only 20% saw it as their *defining* role.

Use of Intuition. Sadler-Smith and Sheffy (2004) suggested that rational and intuitive decision making should be seen as reinforcing rather than opposing each other, since much cognition occurs automatically and is intuitive. Intuition is the interplay of knowing based on expertise and sensing based on feeling. Understanding can be gained directly from intuition without rational thought or logical inference. Executives make considerable use of intuition. It increases with seniority, since it depends on experience. It is likely to develop from implicit, incidental, and unplanned learning experience and feedback. Also important are emotional memories and a "library of expertise" built up over the years. Intuitive understanding is gained from gut feeling and by attending to experiences that seemed to work even when they were contraindicated (Simon, 1987). According to Miller (2002) and Miller and Ireland (2005), much prior learning has been stored in memory with less than complete awareness and rationale. Intuition is conceived of as *automated expertise* or as a *holistic hunch*. Automated expertise is brought to the surface of awareness. Years of experience and learning are packed together into an instantaneous insight. A holistic hunch is a subconscious

synthesis of diverse experiences, novel combinations of information, and strong feelings of "being right." The error rate of decisions based on automated expertise and hunches is high and unpredictable compared to the slower decision-making process of scanning, generation, and consideration of alternatives. Nevertheless, sometimes going ahead on a hunch cautiously with scrutiny, checking, and the use of explicit decision tools may pay off.

For David Myers, intuition may involve subliminal priming, implicit memory, emotional processing, and nonverbal communication. He pointed out that, actually, rapid cognition is the basis for many frequent small decisions we make without much awareness. We need accurate feedback when we make good decisions. To avoid bad intuitive decisions, we need to recognize when our reactions are being controlled by our rapid cognitions and subconscious biases. Intuition, for Seymour Epstein, is what we have learned without realizing it. It can be useful or maladaptive (Hogarth, 2001; Winerman, 2003). Greer (2003) noted that intuition helps us to make connections between events. But sometimes the connections don't exist. Intuition may interfere with sound decision making.

Strategic Formulation. Based on interviews of 75 executives, Sosik, Jung, Berson, et al. (2004) conceived strategy formulation as a weaving by leaders of inputs from people, technology, ideas, and opportunities into a system of social, technological, and intellectual resources, to produce organizational success. From an empirical analysis of 27 business cases, Shevastava and Nachman (1989) developed a fourfold taxonomy of how and by whom business strategies are formulated. Strategies were formulated by: (1) a confident, dominant, aggressive, strong-willed, knowledgeable entrepreneurial type of executive with direct control and influence. The executive makes roles for others and controls their efforts; (2) a bureaucracy bounded by rules and structure that is guided by standard operating rules, procedures, and policies in shaping the strategy. Members take preassigned roles. The bureaucracy specifies the kind of information analysis, the criteria for choosing alternatives, and the procedures for ratification and authorization in the decision making; (3) a dominant coalition of executives, each with authority over an area. They shape strategy through negotiations; and decisions reflect their differing interests; (4) a professional individual or small group of professionals with control over information. The professionals are open, expert, autonomous, committed, and collegial. New rules are devised when needed.

In the 1988 and 2000 Korn/Ferry International surveys of 1,500 interviews with executives in the United States, Latin America, western Europe, and Japan, almost all agreed that in strategy formulation, it was very important for the CEO to convey a vision of the organization's future and to link compensation to performance. Almost all the North and Latin American and at least 75% of the European and Japanese chief executives agreed that ethics, frequent communications from the CEO to the employees, and promoting training and development were very important. Still seen by a majority of respondents as very important for the CEO to do in implementing formulation were frequent visits by the CEO to plants and offices and participation in community affairs. Pluralities varying from one region to another saw it as very important for the CEO to reward loyalty and tenure and to use outside consultants. Few, except in Japan (where the leader announces a decision after full consultation), required the CEO to make all the decisions.

Management Awareness and Contributions to Strategy.
As the organization's strategy is formulated from the top down, perceived awareness of the alignment of the strategy with its realized strategy and the chief executive's conception begins to fall off rapidly at the second level of executives from the top and declines further with movement down the line. The CEO needs to be consulted to define the actual strategy that was formulated to connect strategy and organizational behavior. Executives and managers need to be queried (Hambrick, 1981).

Corporations are made up of many business units. Watson and Wooldridge (2001) surveyed, by mail, 82 business unit managers and executives in Britain below the CEO; they indicated that there was also an upward influence in the formulation of their corporations' strategies. Upward influence was relatively greatest from those managers and executives (1) who reported directly to the CEO; (2) from each corporation's largest business units; (3) from business units related to each corporation's core business; (4) from the most effective business units in each corporation, measured objectively.

Components of Effective Strategic Leadership

Top management sets the strategic purpose and direction of the firm by articulating and communicating a desired vision of the organization's future. Effective strategy is needed for an organization to achieve optimum performance or comparative advantage. It is also needed to keep up with competition in changes in technology and markets (Rowe, 2001). According to Beer and Eisenstat (2000), required for formulating and implementing an effective strategy are: (1) top-down direction that accepts upward influence; (2) clear strategies and priorities; (3) an effective top-management team with a general management orientation; (4) open vertical communication; (5) effective coordination; (6) allocation of clear accountability and authority to middle management. According to Ireland and Hitt (1999), effective strategic leadership practices also include: (1) focusing attention on outcomes and processes; (2) seeking to acquire and leverage knowledge; (3) fostering learning and creativity; (4) improving work flows by attention to relationships; (5) anticipating internal and external environmental changes; (6) maintaining a global mind-set; (7) meeting the diversity of the interests of the multiple stakeholders; (8) building for the long term while meeting short-term needs; (9) developing human capital. These and other effective practices can give the organization advantages in a competitive environment (Ireland & Hitt, 1999). Competitive advantages in a global economy can also be gained from a strategy that depends on the leaders' global leadership skills as well as the reputation of the organization (Petrick, 1999). Raising the cognitive limits of the CEO and top management can result in strategic decisions such as restructuring, becoming larger by making acquisitions, and entering new markets (Mowday & Sutton, 1993).

The involvement of executive management in strategic planning is furthered by the presence in the organization of a salient strategic vision, according to a sample of 226 upper level executives in a Fortune 100 corporation undertaking a major strategic change (Oswald, Mossholder, & Harris, 1997). Additionally, CEOs and top management need to be able to channel and support the champions of innovation and adaptation and the incubation of new ideas in a safe space without higher-ups who prematurely criticize new, undeveloped ideas. Controls need to be minimized and innovators need to feel free to speculate (Nutt, 1999).

Personal Predilections. In their strategizing, executives are faced with many alternatives, conflicting demands by constituencies, and information overload. Their decisions depend on their values, experiences, knowledge, and preferences (Finkelstein & Hambrick, 1996; Hambrick & Mason, 1984) and sometimes on whimsy. W. R. Grace stopped for breakfast at Coco's, a coffee shop, and liked it so much, he bought the company that owned the chain. In the same way, Victor Kiam liked the Remington razor so much that as the ads said; he acquired the company (Hall, 1984). IBM President Thomas Watson, Jr., chose a small prairie town, Rochester, Minnesota, as a site for a new plant because of a World War II army air force buddy who came from there.

Elenkov and Judge (2002) collected MLQ—Form 6S questionnaires from 490 presidents, CEOs, managing directors, and 371 other top-management team members in the United States, United Kingdom, Germany, Austria, Russia, and Ukraine. These executives were all involved in strategic decisions. Their transformational leadership scores accounted for 52% of the variance in product market innovations and 55% of their administrative innovations.

Effective Strategic Decision Making. Effective strategies depend on effective decision making. While snap judgments based on intuition may sometimes work out well, effective decisions ordinarily require an order in the process. Opportunities, threats, variance from expectations, or disturbances are observed. The problem is diagnosed, usually calling for more information and a search for solutions; development of innovations occurs, evaluation and choice among alternatives takes place, and the selected alternative is authorized and implemented. Whenever a phase cannot be completed successfully, there is a return to an earlier phase (Bass, 1983). Murnighan and Mowen (2002) add more in the process to the importance of feeling and intuition. The search phase is for detecting signals of threats and opportunities, followed by finding the causes. Blind spots need to be eliminated. The risks and rewards of alternative solutions are estimated, with choice based on avoiding a missed opportunity or a needless blunder. Whether or not to implement the choice should be based on a calculation of the *risk ratio*, the maximum estimated risk, compared with the probability estimate—the probability of success. This rational approach must be balanced with intuition (wisdom based on many reinforced experiences), particularly at top-management levels, even though rationality outperforms intuition in experimental studies (Nutt, 2002).

Ineffective Strategies. Cognitive shortcomings explain poor strategic decisions, such as paying too much for an unneeded acquisition. This seems to occur more often than not. Irrational and overconfident bidders do not know they are bidding against other bidders who are similarly overconfident (Zajac & Bazerman, 1991). Overall, as a consequence of the self-confidence and hubris of its CEO, a premium is paid by an acquiring firm beyond the worth of the acquisition. *Firms that acquire other firms tend to decline in long-term profitability* (Valle, 1998). A number of critics agree that CEOs take self-serving positions in their strategic thinking. They attribute good performance to their organization and poor performance to the external environment (Mowday & Sutton, 1993). However, D'Aveni and MacMillen (1990) found evidence to the contrary. They compared the letters written by the leaders of 57 banks that declared bankruptcy with a matched sample of letters by solvent bank leaders. The letters were written during the five years before the declaration of bankruptcy. The strategies of the future bankrupt firms tended to ignore or deny their external environment, such as the lack of demand for their products and services. They focused internally on their debt, their creditors' demands, and changing their organization.

Greenwald (1985) pointed to three cognitive biases in strategic decision making: (1) Strategists look at events primarily in relation to themselves, (2) They see themselves as responsible for desired but not undesired outcomes, (3) They stick to their initial and favorite alternatives even when the supporting evidence is disconfirming. Other cognitive sources of error are that attention is directed away from goal direction by frequent disruptions, erroneous causal attributions are made; and people hold implicit, readily available, and strong but erroneous beliefs (Peterson & Sorenson, 1990). To avoid failure, strategic leaders need to avoid being enticed by the reputed and popular strategies for success in the new economy. Greco, Caggiano, and Ballon (1999) provide examples of how false assumptions and failure to qualify good ideas result in pursuing strategies that die or fail to grow.

Middle Management's Role in Organizational Strategies. Often, middle managers are responsible for implementing strategic decisions made by senior executives. Separating planning from implementation creates special problems (Bass, 1970a). As noted by Floyd and Wooldridge (1992), senior executives complain that middle managers fail to take the necessary steps to implement strategies. The commitment to and understanding of what needs to be done may be poor. Middle managers don't articulate the same goals as do senior executives. If middle managers disagree with the strategic initiatives, they frequently work against implementation. To promote commitment, rewards systems and structures need to be aligned to fit the intended strategy. Middle management and supervisors' understanding of the strategy will be fostered by increased discussions with senior managers about the strategy and their criteria for success. Consensus is needed on how to implement the strategy. Strategically useful ideas can come from anywhere in the organization.

Supervisors' Role in Organizational Strategies. At the lowest leadership levels of the organization are department heads, supervisors, and team leaders. They may make suggestions upward that have implications for company strategy but generally are responsible for maintaining the work flow, morale, equipment, and safety of their subordinates. Sales supervisors and salespersons can bring home to the organization important ideas about competing products and organizational practices. They can serve as early warning signals. Production supervisors and their employees can contribute significant ideas about needed changes in internal organizational processes.

Political Leadership

The Scottish philosopher David Hume (1741–1742) presented the first modern concept of political leadership. Political leaders share the values of the people and in a democracy formulate policies that a majority favor. Successful leaders are responsible for appointing judges, passing legislation, and providing political stability. Leaders with less support from the electorate form a loyal opposition. But this is no guarantee that the leader chosen will be effective. In a stable a democratic system, leadership takes place in an environment of political trust, social tolerance, recognition of political liberties, and popular support for equality of the sexes. This is in contrast to the pseudodemocratic system common to many developing countries, where political and civil rights are ignored, emotionality trumps rationality, and religious zealotry is pervasive.

Even in true democracies, voters are highly biased in favor of one candidate over another for irrational reasons. They attribute favorable personality traits to leaders who share their political beliefs. For example, right-wing Israeli voters evaluate right-wing leaders as more friendly and task-oriented than left-wing leaders. Left-wing voters attribute friendliness and task orientation more to left-wing leaders than right-wing leaders. Both groups see the leaders on their side of political issues as closer to their ideal leader (Ellis, Nadler, & Rabin, 1996). Shamir (1994) found that the perceived charisma of candidates combined with Israeli voters' ideological positions to predict their voting preferences.

"Political leadership is one of the most widely noted and reported and least understood phenomena in modern politics." This was a comment in the 1976 presidential address by James MacGregor Burns to the American Political Science Association. He argued that lacking a general theory of political leadership, of necessity research fell back on a more specific study of the numerous political leaders. For Adel Safty (2000), political leadership is needed globally to promote peace, democracy, and human development within and between states. World War II was a consequence of the collective failure of the League of Nations and its political leadership.

There is much revisionism in what may be written about a political figure after 50 years. When seeking and retaining office, the politician must usually face pluralistic pressures. "The actions that endear the leader to one constituency may anger another . . . the leader must show different faces to different constituencies or one enigmatic face to all." (Leaders have to consider the needs of their constituencies, the demands of powerful lobbies, and hopefully use their own best judgment.) "But all too often their judgment, befuddled by conflicting pressures, or their character, eroded by sell-outs, fails the test" (Gardner, 1993, p. 151).

Mikhail Gorbachev was unusual as a world-class leader in an authoritarian society. He openly called attention to what he did not know and invited help. He was crucial in changing the Soviet system (Khoubesserian, 1987). Was his career a success or a failure? Although he proceeded with caution to try to modernize the system, he was ousted from power and the Soviet Union crumbled as Ukraine and other Soviet republics seceded from the USSR. Innovation is difficult for political leaders who attempt to democratize an authoritarian regime. The new way must be initiated, legitimated, and sustained (Edinger, 1993). The political innovators Mahatma Gandhi and Jawaharlal Nehru captured, sustained, and adapted the British structure of government for India (Sheffer, 1993). In 1986, the CIA was perplexed by photos of Mikhail Gorbachev's facial expressions during conversation, which mirrored the facial features of the other leader, Ronald Reagan, with whom he was talking. Was this a sign of intense concentration? Empathy?

Burns (1978) introduced his theory of transformational and transactional leadership, to be presented in the next chapter, which advances the understanding of political leaders. The importance of charisma to political leaders was discussed in Chapter 22. In his address, Burns pointed out that political leaders are expected to inspire and elevate the public and to show moral leadership. In a democracy, political leaders are expected to focus on the public's authentic needs. They turn threats into opportunities. In 1940, France was completely defeated by the German blitzkrieg. Charles de Gaulle took on the role of hero, seized the opportunity to mobilize Free French forces outside France, and did not succumb to irrational fears. In 1945, at the end of World War II, when Winston Churchill was asked by a woman, "During this terrible war, what was your darkest hour?," he replied, "Frankly my dear, I enjoyed every minute of it!"

Influence of Public Leaders

The influence of public leaders is felt when they bring together important figures from industry, government, education, health care, and community activist organiza-

tions to collaborate on issues of mutual interest. They provide visions, initiate structure, and clarify what needs to be done (Berger, 1997). The credibility of public managers is critical when they try to introduce reforms in public agencies for their improvement (Gabris & Ihrke, 2003).

Avant (1994) regards most politicians as inauthentic. They are self-interested strategists. They try to ensure that they remain in power. They pursue goals based on whether they will help them stay in power. They try to control the bureaucracy to maintain their political advantage.

American Presidents as Leaders

The American presidents since George Washington's two terms in office have formed an important field of leadership study for political scientists, historians, biographers, psychologists, psychoanalysts, and sociologists. Each president redefines his role as national leader, chief executive of the government, and commander in chief of the military. The president has a "bully pulpit" from which he can exert strong influence on the public and Congress. His rhetoric is important in articulating the concerns and aspirations as he sees them. He tries to form a sense of national purpose and identification (Fields, 1994). This is especially true if his rhetoric is *image-based* rather than *concept-based*. Image-based words include sweat, hand, root, heart, explore, rock, grow, path, journey, sweet, dream, listen, and see. Concept words include work, help, source, commitment, inquire, dependable, produce, endeavor, limit, alternative, request, moderate, idea, think, consider, and understand (Martindale, 1975). Emrich, Brower, Feldman, et al. (2001) calculated the relative frequencies compared to the total length of image-based and concept-based words in presidential inaugural addresses from George Washington to Jimmy Carter. A correlation of .50 was found of image-based indices with Murray and Blessing's (1983) list of the charisma of the 32 presidents. The correlation with charisma for concept-based rhetoric was −.27. There were no significant comparable correlations of concept-based indices with the list of greatness.

If members of the president's own party in Congress who supported his election found themselves opposed to one of his proposals, they would often change to supporting it. Nonetheless, Zeidentstein (1983) could find no consistent pattern of the relationship between presidents' popularity, from Dwight Eisenhower to Jimmy Carter, and their legislative success, although it appeared that Reagan's popularity helped his success in passing legislation through Congress. Some found that most important for a president's popularity was his perceived effect on the national economy or the economic well-being of voters (Kinder, 1981). Barber (1977) found that a president's success depended on how active the president was and whether or not he enjoyed power. The speeches of some presidents, like John Kennedy's, tended to be *positive* rather than *disapproving*, like Richard Nixon's. Two-term president George W. Bush's addresses were *simplified* solutions to problems in black or white. He was not a *complexifyer* like Jimmy Carter—defeated for reelection—for whom possible alternatives had various shades of gray (Mazlich & Diamond, 1979). A relatively *inactive* one-term president, William Howard Taft, sandwiched between the *active* Theodore Roosevelt and *active* Woodrow Wilson, served as a transition between them in the regulation of corporations. Unlike Roosevelt, who viewed the president as a steward of the country and its constituencies, Taft was a constitutional literalist who emphasized the separation of powers of president, Congress, and the courts. He was concerned with controlling radical majorities (Anderson, 1982).

Presidential Power

With the tyranny of the British King George III in mind, the framers of the U.S. Constitution were wary of placing much power in the executive branch. Yet they also saw the ineffectiveness of the Articles of Confederation, which lacked a strong executive. But they assumed that the first president would be George Washington, who had the unreserved trust of the people and had to be persuaded to take the office by Alexander Hamilton. The powers of the president have been expanded ever since by strong presidents such as Jefferson, Jackson, Polk, Lincoln, Wilson, and the two Roosevelts (McDonald, 1994). Between 2001 and 2006, George W. Bush wielded extraordinary powers by decree in the war against terrorism, through executive orders. Additionally, he wrote signing statements on whether or not his administration would

enforce new legislation enacted by Congress. This presidential behavior was never envisioned by the framers of the Constitution. Bush's popularity dropped from 90% to 30%.

Presidents' Management Style

Presidents differ in their management styles. Franklin D. Roosevelt kept his subordinates in competition with one another over decisions. He did not give them sufficient authority to act on their own, so he could maintain his power over decisions. He could be tricky and tough, but his objective was the emancipation of humanity. John F. Kennedy and Bill Clinton also kept their subordinates guessing about decisions. This was a way of keeping administrators in charge of large bureaucracies from tying up actions that the presidents wanted to see implemented. The three also had trusted informal advisers: Eleanor Roosevelt and Harry Hopkins for FDR, Robert Kennedy for JFK, Hillary Clinton for Bill Clinton, and Karl Rove for George W. Bush. Dwight Eisenhower, Gerald Ford, Ronald Reagan, and George H. W. Bush took a very different tack: they pursued an orderly process in which decisions were delegated to their subordinates in charge of the agencies and departments of the federal government. Jimmy Carter was known for his inability to delegate and impose orderliness to stop the feuds among federal agencies. Richard Nixon was highly controlling and secretive and kept information close to his vest. Lyndon Johnson worked closely and directly with Congress (Haass, 1995). Kennedy was open to communication, took responsibility for his administration's mistakes, and arranged to be the center of a network that included his subordinates, advisers, and consultants. Modern presidents have differed in their regard for public opinion polls. Some, like Truman, disliked and ignored them; some, like Clinton, consulted them almost daily. Nonetheless, there was a strong association between the presidents' annual positive approval ratings in Gallup Polls for each year in office of Eisenhower, Kennedy, Johnson, Nixon, Ford, Carter, and Reagan, and their legislative success on issues where the president took a position Rockman (1984, p. 118). These presidents' leadership and management styles were classified by Rockman as *drivers* or *coasters*. Drivers, like Johnson and Nixon, were entrepreneurial chief operating officers; coasters, like

Eisenhower and Ford, were chief executive officers. Drivers pushed expansive policies; coasters were more incremental. Drivers were centrists and interventionist, using informal channels and uncertain jurisdictions; coasters favored decentralization and used formal channels and jurisdictions. Drivers were hierarchical and delegative. Critics branded Johnson as a micromanager and Nixon as ruthless and isolated. Some critics branded Eisenhower as an inefficient manager but, in reality, in his two terms in office, he gave the government a sense of direction and purpose with the support of public opinion (McInerney, 1981).

Ronald Reagan (1986) and his recruiters put a lot of effort into choosing his political appointees so he could delegate authority to them with the expectation that his policies would be pursued without his involvement in details. He insisted on mutual loyalty, which resulted in a relatively large number of scandals. Most of his carefully vetted aides were self-made millionaires and shared his probusiness attitudes (Nathan, 1983). It was easy for him to encourage free and open discussion among his aides because of their shared attitudes. When conflicts arose, he would reduce tension with a joke from his extensive repertoire of jokes. He had a high tolerance for listening to hotly contested issues. His agenda and priorities were simple and clear. The most memorable lines in his speeches were his own when he rewrote his speechwriters' efforts. He focused on big issues and avoided spending time on less important ones. He enabled the introduction into his administration of many private business practices, such as like new systems of credit management and cash management and the use of private collection agencies. He changed the federal budgeting process; instead of agencies submitting proposals to meet their anticipated needs, which then would be reviewed and sent to Congress for approval, Reagan introduced a top down budgetary process to reflect his plans to cut taxes and shift priorities. The White House set goals and priorities and the agencies had to fit their requests to the president's plan. He organized committees of cabinet members to propose ways he should deal with suggested policies; they could work out the differences among their various agencies. When they could reach consensus, he accepted their decisions as if they were a board of directors (Fishel, 1985). When they could not agree, he made a decision and stuck to it, even when it was likely to be unpopular with the public. Reagan handled disasters such as the terrorist bombing of a Marine barracks in Lebanon by going public quickly with a full account, taking the blame as if he were at fault, and defusing the crisis (Dowd, 1986). He could be highly directive, as in the case where he declared that it was illegal for aircraft controllers, as federal employees, to strike and ordered the FAA to fire and replace them.

President's Personality

Winter (1987) used previous findings to form a composite of presidents' performance: consensus of greatness, avoidance of war, entry into war, and great decisions. The composite measure of greatness was correlated with the extent to which the presidents' inaugural addresses projected the needs for power, achievement, and affiliation. Need for affiliation was negatively related to greatness; presidents who were overly concerned with close relations with their friends, advisors, and subordinates correlated .53 with scandals in their administrations (Winter & Stewart, 1977). House, Spangler, and Woyke (1991) showed that performance based on Simonton's (1987, 1988) list of 31 presidents from Washington to Carter was related positively, according to path analysis, to a need for power (.52) and negatively to a need for affiliation (−.37). For 39 presidents ranked by Simonton (from Washington to Reagan) on their tendency to take direct action, ranking is related significantly to a need for power (.62), and a need for affiliation (−.21). A need for power correlated .36 with international relations performance, .19 with economic performance, and .51 with social performance. Other significant path coefficients were negative between the performance measures need for achievement and need for affiliation. The power motive was stronger than the achievement motive in F. D. Roosevelt, Truman, Kennedy, and Reagan. These presidents found ways to deal with subordinates whom they had not appointed but could not fully trust or get rid of. Roosevelt assigned the same task to several different such appointees and let them compete for his favoring of one decision over the others. The achievement motive was higher than the power motive in Presidents Wilson, Hoover, L. B. Johnson, Nixon, and Carter. (Need for achievement correlated .51 with idealism.) These presidents were unable to fully implement their idealistic goals (Winter, 2002).

Rubenzer, Fashingbauer, and Ones (2000) arranged for up to 13 students to score 41 presidents on the five-factor personality questionnaire NEO-PI-R. The presidents' mean factor scores were more extroverted, less open to experience, and less agreeable than American norms. They had high average facet scores on achievement striving, assertiveness, and openness to feelings; they had low average facet scores on openness to values, straightforwardness, and modesty. As an example, Washington showed an unusually high factor score for conscientiousness, but his scores were lower than the present American norms on openness, extraversion, and agreeableness. His facet scores were high in achievement striving, competence, assertiveness, discipline, and deliberation. Other facet scores compared to current American norms revealed him to be low in vulnerability (he was able to tolerate adversity and stress), low in openness to values (he was traditional in morality), and low in tender-mindedness (he was less concerned about the unfortunate). Conscientiousness correlated .17 with presidential characters listed by Ridings and McIver (1997). Lower in conscientiousness than other presidents were Andrew Jackson, Kennedy, and FDR. T. Roosevelt was high in the facet of achievement striving, setting ambitious goals, and trying to meet them. (achievement striving correlated .32 to .39 with presidential greatness). Grant and Harding were not high in achievement striving. The facet of assertiveness correlated with greatness from .34 to .44. T. Roosevelt, Jackson, and Harding were highest in assertiveness, and Harding and Coolidge were lowest. Competence correlated with greatness ($r =$ .30, .39).

Lyndon Johnson grew up in the hardscrabble country of Texas with a knowledge of the history of the political careers of his forebears and father. Early on, he developed a strong need to dominate his peers whatever the cost. He conducted a single-minded pursuit of power, which he achieved by striking alliances with Texas moneyed interests and powerful congressmen such as Sam Rayburn, speaker of the House of Representatives (Caro, 1987).

Bill Clinton, highly intelligent, well educated, ambitious, and interpersonally competent, overcame his childhood in a troubled family from a small town, but effects on his personality remained. He compartmentalized his public and private lives. He could deny reality at times, block out problems, try to overcome almost any obstacle, and feel a continuing need for affirmation. He could remain optimistic in the face of serious problems and readily recover from setbacks. (Optimists do not ignore adverse information but use it to change their strategy.) Like many powerful leaders and presidents before him, such as JFK and Lyndon Johnson, he had a strong need for sex. Clinton was easily tempted by women attracted to powerful figures (Maraniss, 1998). He was regularly condemned for inconsistency and indecisiveness. Sometimes this stood him in good stead, such as when he announced that he had no further options but a military invasion of Haiti and then, the next day, sent peace negotiators (Sonnenfeld, 1994). In the 1996 presidential election, voters who rated Bill Clinton as charismatic-transformational and identified with the Democratic Party voted for Clinton; Republican voters did the same for Bob Dole (Pillai & Williams, 1998). Elsewhere, diagnostic profiles (Millon, 1990) of Clinton suggested that he was highly assertive/self-promoting, outgoing/gregarious and charismatic/extraverted, while Dole was highly controlling/dominant, conforming/dutiful, and deliberative/conscientious but low on interpersonality/agreeableness (Immelman, 1998).

Avolio (1999) extracted from Simonton's (1988) list the best and worst twentieth-century presidents in selected leadership styles. Ford scored highest in interpersonal style, which contributed to his success with Congress. Wilson and Nixon were lowest. A weakness in all these findings is that politicians, in particular, have different public and private personae. Truman's public image of irascibility and feistiness, for instance, was very different from his behavior with his staff and friends (McCullough, 1992). Consistent with what we noted earlier, Franklin Delano Roosevelt was highest in charisma and Coolidge lowest. McKinley and Kennedy were most deliberative, Truman least so. The two Roosevelts were most creative, Taft least so. Lyndon Johnson scored highest in neuroticism and Ronald Reagan lowest. Caprera and Zimbardo (2004) found a great deal of empirical support for the hypothesis that people vote for presidential candidates whose personality traits fit with the ideology of their preferred political party. Voters tend to elect presidents whose publicly expressed traits and values are congruent with voters' self-reported traits and values. Thus George W. Bush remains in favor with right-wing fundamentalist Christians despite the many failings of his administration.

Charisma of American Presidents and Canadian Prime Ministers

George Washington, because of his highly principled conduct as a military leader, was a great moral symbol in the new republic. The populace was suspicious of all forms of power. For it, virtue was the cure for corruption. His refusal to accept the role of monarch or dictator made him the opposite of a personalized charismatic but a hero with socialized charisma and tremendous idealized influence. He was worshiped by his individualistic, republican countrymen. Writing on the death of the charismatic president Franklin D. Roosevelt, Walter Lippmann (1945) noted that the final test of such a leader is the conviction and will left behind for others to carry on. FDR's New Deal left a lasting legacy of liberal reforms. House (1985) content-analyzed the inaugural addresses, speeches, and writings of 10 charismatic and nine noncharismatic U.S. presidents along with four charismatic Canadian prime ministers. Judgments of charisma were based on how much the content referred: (1) values and moral justifications rather than tangible outcomes; (2) the collective identity rather than individual self-interests; (3) distant rather than close goals; (4) history; (5) positive worth and efficacy of followers; (6) high expectations of followers; (7) self-confidence. Charismatic presidents were more likely to be seen as effective by their cabinets (House, Woyke, & Fodor, 1988). Charisma was correlated with the overall performance, both economic and social, of 39 presidents (House, Spangler, and Woyke, 1989, 1991). According to content analyses of the writings of cabinet members, the judgments of presidential charisma for 31 presidents had path analysis coefficients of .51 with presidential direct action, .56 with personal use of power, .46 with domestic economic performance, and .46 with domestic social performance (House, Howell, Shamir, et al. 1994). John F. Kennedy was a highly charismatic president. His inaugural address set the tone for his administration: "The torch has been passed to a new generation." He emphasized contributions to the public good rather than private gain: "Ask not what your country can do for you, ask what you can do for your country." Kennedy's addresses were direct, factual, specific, and spellbinding with his visions of the future, such as putting a man on the moon in nine years to provide assurance that the Soviets would not remain ahead in the space race. Although in office less than three years before he was assassinated, he made many effective crucial decisions, except for the Bay of Pigs fiasco, which the previous administration had planned but for which he took responsibility. He was well prepared in advance to force the steel companies to rescind a 30% price hike after government mediation resulted in removing the need for large wage concessions to labor. Although he endorsed and sympathized with the Civil Rights movement, he introduced little legislation on the subject but paved the way for his successor, Lyndon Johnson, to do so in 1965. In 1962, he avoided a possible nuclear war with the Soviets after learning that the Soviets had installed a base in Cuba that could launch missiles to most parts of the United States. After thorough deliberation, based on photointelligence as evidence, he warned Nikita Khrushchev that he would embargo Soviet ships bringing missiles to Cuba and told the American public and the Soviets what Soviet actions would and would not be permitted. U.S. missiles in Turkey, on the Soviet Union's southern border, were subsequently withdrawn (Manchester, 1967). The crisis ended with a peaceful settlement. In 1963, Kennedy was planning to reverse the course of the U.S. commitment in Vietnam and American intervention, which eventually ended in 1975 in failure and the loss of 55,000 American and an estimated million Vietnamese lives (Sorensen, 1965). He was a strong supporter of the arts, sciences, and literature, and the White House, metaphorically, became "Camelot." His weaknesses were glossed over by the public in the reality and myth of his greatness (Lasky, 1966).

Among the 39 presidents through Reagan, Deluga (2001) found that charismatic presidents were also Machiavellian, according to prepared profiles of their behavior, which were then rated by 117 undergraduates. The presidents could and would engage in political expediency and duplicity. Highly Machiavellian presidents, as measured on the Mach Scale (Christie & Geis, 1970), were high in their levels of expressive activity, self-confidence, emotional regulation, and desire to be influential. For them, the ends justified the means. They could be deceptive. They exhibited both personalized and socialized charisma. They were opportunists. They built favorable images of themselves. Their public pronouncements were often at odds with their private opinions. When President Kennedy was told that black African ambassadors to the United Nation and the United States got into trouble driving though segregated Maryland to reach Washington, D.C., his response was "Tell them to fly." In the struggle for civil rights, both blacks and whites thought he was supporting their opposing sides. President Eisenhower was personally opposed to the 1954 *Brown v. Board of Education of Topeka* Supreme Court decision, which declared school segregation unconstitutional, but publicly he did not voice his opinion (Reeves, 1995).

According to Rubenzer, Faschingbauer, and Ones (2000), great presidents earned lower scores on the facet of Straightforwardness on the NEO Personality Inventory, according to judgments of their biographies. When necessary, both Lyndon Johnson and Franklin Roosevelt tricked, cajoled, bullied, or lied. The correlation between Machiavellianism and charisma was .32. (Deluga, 2001). After the terrorist attacks of September 11, 2001, George W. Bush became more charismatic, according to content analyses of his speeches before and after the attack (Bligh, Kohles, & Meindl, 2004). Like many charismatic leaders, he was both loved and hated. In 2000, he lost the popular vote by more than 500,000 votes but won the disputed electoral count by four electors: The Supreme Court had stopped the Florida recount when Bush was ahead of Al Gore by 300 votes. As his father, President George H. W. Bush, had done, George W. Bush surrounded himself with top management team members who, except for his secretary of state, Colin Powell, thought alike. Long before the war with Iraq began in 2003, he ordered military planning for it in 2002, despite his public pronouncements that he had been reluctant to begin it (Woodward, 1994). George W. Bush lost many opportunities to improve the domestic economy because his chief of staff felt nothing needed to be done, his OMB director blocked ideas not his own, and his advisors kept telling him that more studies of the issues were needed. His vice president, Richard Cheney, was the secretive "power behind the throne." Adding to the lack of action were the stifling of debate within the team and the atmosphere of purposelessness in the presidential office (Kolb, 1993).

Twelve presidents were included in a student survey of biographies of world-class leaders by Bass, Avolio,

and Goodheim (1987). After reading one or more biographies, students completed the Multifactor Leadership Questionnaire on one of the 12 presidents. On the transformational scales, of the 12 presidents, Kennedy, Theodore Roosevelt, Franklin D. Roosevelt, and Ronald Reagan were rated highest in charismatic leadership. Truman, Theodore Roosevelt, and Eisenhower were rated most individually considerate. Kennedy, Theodore Roosevelt, John Adams, Eisenhower, and Reagan were rated the most intellectually stimulating. On the transactional scales, John Adams and Theodore Roosevelt most practiced contingent reward; Gerald Ford most practiced management by exception. A more rigorous and extensive study of all 39 presidents was completed by Simonton (1986, 1988). Descriptive profiles were prepared from abstracts of standard biographical sources and presidential fact books. Individual biographies were omitted as sources of abstracts due to possible author biases. Seven students independently assessed each presidential profile using the Gough Adjective Check List (1985). Five factors were extracted: interpersonal, deliberative, neurotic, charismatic, and creative. Simonton's list correlated highly with previous lists and was used as the basis of other studies of greatness and effectiveness.

House (1985) asked eight historians to classify U.S. presidents and Canadian prime ministers as charismatic or noncharismatic. Seven of the eight historians were in complete agreement. The historians identified Thomas Jefferson, Andrew Jackson, Abraham Lincoln, Theodore Roosevelt, Franklin Delano Roosevelt, and John F. Kennedy as charismatic presidents and Calvin Coolidge, Warren Harding, Chester A. Arthur, James Buchanan, Franklin Pierce, and John Tyler as noncharismatic presidents. They also listed the following charismatic Canadian prime ministers: Ramsey MacDonald, Sir Wilfred Laurier, John George Diefenbaker, and Pierre Elliott Trudeau. Biographies of these presidents, prime ministers, and their cabinet members were content-analyzed to compare the effects of the charismatics and the noncharismatics on the cabinet members. To measure the presidents' behavior, House coded passages that indicated the leaders' display of self-confidence and their expression of expected high performance by their followers, confidence in their followers' ability and performance, strong ideological goals, and individualized consideration for their followers. The presidents' inaugural addresses were similarly content-analyzed to assess the presidents' achievement, power, and affiliation motives. The cabinet members of charismatic presidents and prime ministers attributed more positive affect to them than did the cabinet members of noncharismatic presidents. The need for achievement and the need for power were higher among the charismatics than among the noncharismatics. The charismatic leaders were more likely than the noncharismatics to be seen as great and as effective (House, Woycke, & Fodor, 1988). In another analysis, charisma, combined with power and other needs, accounted for 37% of the variance in the overall performance of 39 presidents, 41% of the economic performance of their administrations, and 45% of their domestic social performance (House, Spangler, & Woycke, 1989).

Pillai, Williams, Lowe et al. (2003) replicated Pillai and Williams' (1998) study of what prompted 342 matched preelection and postelection choices of candidates in the 1996 presidential election. Again, the investigators found that attributions of charisma and transformational leadership were associated with their choices beyond party affiliation. Trust was an important mediating variable.

Presidents' Effectiveness

Franke and New (1984) showed that presidents' effectiveness from William McKinley to Ronald Reagan, as measured by policies that led to more efficient use of resources and increased employment and capacity utilization, was correlated with active presidents like T. Roosevelt rather than passive presidents like Calvin "Silent Cal" Coolidge. People were frustrated when they tried to get Coolidge to talk. He was elected vice president and assumed the presidency on Harding's death. He was elected for another term, having made neither enemies nor friends. He seldom solicited advice but showed concern for the workingman even though he was conservative. He practiced a laissez-faire style, intervening only when absolutely necessary. He believed that the chief business of America was business and government should not interfere with it (McCoy, 1967). He was neither aggressive nor self-confident and did not anticipate any future but the continued prosperity of the "Roaring Twenties" (Fuess, 1940).

Pritchard (1983) measured each president's effectiveness by the extent to which the senators and representatives of both parties voted for his proposals. Hargrove (1987) indicated that presidents' effectiveness depended on their manipulative skills in: (1) creating bargaining coalitions, (2) establishing authority over subordinates, (3) keeping prospective opponents off balance, (4) maintaining alternate sources of information and advice, (5) using power to leverage available institutional forces to influence other powerful figures, (6) remaining sensitive to the politics of policy making. Equally important for effectiveness were the abilities to (1) define the policy questions of consequence to the nation in terms of their historical emergence and felt necessities of the time; (2) suggest solutions and a policy agenda; (3) gain widespread support for the solutions. Timing was crucial. According to Adam Yarmolinsky, Lyndon Johnson never decided where he wanted to go until he could figure out how to get there. Jimmy Carter was seen as unsuccessful because he mostly ignored playing politics and tried to know and do what was right. He waited for his staff to provide information and failed to mobilize the political strength needed to take action. He failed to win a second term in office. While the average for the success of presidents from Wilson to Nixon in fulfilling their campaign promises was 75%, Carter was successful in fulfilling only 60% of his promises (Krukones, 1985).

Tourigny (2002) obtained the effectiveness ratings on the American Presidential Management Inventory by surveying 98 scholars in political science and American history. Each rated one president. She uncovered six higher-order factors that accounted for the variance in presidential effectiveness: (1) principle-guided actions (wisdom, judgment, impartiality) (44.8%), (2) vision (inclusive, responsive to constituents, and individually considerate of congressmen's needs and interests) (10.5%), (3) acknowledgment of differences (recognized ideologies, minorities, and protection of constitutional rights), (4) consultative and participative style (fostered collaboration between cabinet and Congress and collaborative decision making with subordinates) (5.2%), (5) moving Congress forward (clear guidance and monitoring of subordinates' efforts) (4.4%), (6) nondeceptive means to achieve objectives (did not bypass the cabinet or use subordinates for personal benefit) (3.9%).

Franklin Delano Roosevelt is high on every presidential ranking for effectiveness. He led the United States into war when the country was isolationist. The country did not see the need to become involved in what was regarded as a war that the western hemisphere could stay out of. Roosevelt saw that if totalitarian forces prevailed in Europe and Asia, the United States would inevitably suffer the same fate. Using political credit, deception, manipulation, cajolery, coercion, haranguing, and enticing, he led Congress to pass needed legislation to help Britain against Germany, such as the Lend-Lease Act of 1940, which transferred 50 aged destroyers to Britain in exchange for granting bases in British possessions to the United States. He said, with tongue in cheek, "We'll take the ships back after the war." Gradually he increased support for Britain and its empire, which in mid-1940 were fighting almost alone against Germany and Italy. In 1941, he embargoed shipments of American oil to Japan and got the Dutch in the Dutch East Indies to do the same. Without oil, the Japanese economy and military machine would have collapsed. Japan's response was the attack on Pearl Harbor and the invasion of the Dutch East Indies. He provoked Adolf Hitler with taunts that led Hitler and subsequently Benito Mussolini to declare war on the United States, ensuring the demise of totalitarianism in Italy in 1943 and in Japan and Germany by 1945. Roosevelt allowed the different ideologies, identified problems, and solutions of his staff to compete with one another until a practical solution appeared. He said a leader should not get too far ahead of his followers; otherwise, when he looked around, nobody would be there.

Bill Clinton lacked discipline in his daily routine. He procrastinated after lengthy meetings and would return to the same question again at the next meeting with his advisors. He might delay necessary decisions for months, which drove his advisors to despair. He was knowledgeable and highly educated and conceived many alternative answers to a question. His public speaking made members of big audiences feel as though they were being addressed personally. He was a political centrist, sought conciliation and consensus, and employed military force sparingly despite many international provocations. He was hated by a large right-wing minority and was close to being impeached and convicted for lying about his sexual peccadilloes. Nevertheless, his policies made him an effective president. His 1993 spending cuts and tax increases set into motion economic prosperity to the end of the century. His welfare reform legislation in 1996, counter to the philosophy of his political allies, was effective in moving many welfare recipients to seek training and work. His military and diplomatic interventions in Bosnia, Kosovo, and Serbia brought peace to the Balkans after 10 years and war criminals to trial (Harris, 2005).

Ronald Reagan was a highly popular president and an extremely effective communicator. He had an informal style of delivery that made him attractive and successful at winning elections and getting most of the legislation his administration endorsed accepted by Congress. He cut inflation, taxes, and regulations but greatly increased the deficit and the national debt. Critics accused him of playing the role of president, during his two terms in office, from outlines prepared for him (Slansky, 1989). Liberal evaluators questioned whether his administration's probusiness, antienvironmental, and military goals were in the best interests of the country. He hired many business friends and delegated too much. He was unable to discharge people. He was controlled too much by his staff, wife, and friends. He was easily influenced when he was unconcerned about an issue yet stubbornly held to his position on issues about which he lacked knowledge but felt strongly (G. Winter, 1987). He was outspoken and made many gaffes in expressing himself, both in his words and in his behavior (Gates, 1989). He failed to control his subordinates adequately and was too impulsive. He committed faux pas ranging from confusing events in movies with real events to falling asleep in an audience with the pope. One of many Reaganisms referred to the Nicaraguan contras, whom he illegally tried to support against the Sandinista government, as "the moral equal of our Founding Fathers." Nevertheless, he was labeled "the Teflon president," as none of these mistakes in policy and speech stuck to him. His popularity remained high during his two terms in office.

Given the negative impact of laissez-faire leadership detailed in Chapter 25, how does one explain the effects of President Ronald Reagan's generally laissez-faire leadership style, which was based on his stated belief that he was properly delegating when he sat back and let his subordinates proceed as they thought best? Reagan was able to leave office in 1988 with one of the highest popularity ratings (64% to 68%) of any U.S. president in a public opinion poll. One explanation may be his choice of subordinates. With subordinates, such as David Stockman, who were highly competent, great achievements were possible. With sleazy or incompetent subordinates, like

Edwin Meese, the results were disastrous. The disaster was compounded when a subordinate cabinet officer, such as Samuel Pierce of the Department of Housing and Urban Development, was an extremely laissez-faire executive himself (Waldman, Cohn, & Thomas, 1989). The astute management of the news by his staff helped make it possible to credit Reagan with the successes of his subordinates and to distance him from their failures. He remained the "Teflon president," immune to the many scandals that marred his administration. Furthermore, although Reagan exemplified the laissez-faire leader in much of his behavior, he was also a mass of contradictions in his orientation and style. He did a lot of homework after hours; nevertheless, he was described as the "least informed of the presidents I have known," by former Speaker of the House Tip O'Neill. He remained highly charismatic. He derided the plight of the disadvantaged as a group yet often exhibited compassion for an unfortunate individual.

Although it is obviously impossible to evaluate Reagan's overall success and effectiveness as a president at the time of this writing, from this vantage point, his presidency appears to have been a highly mixed bag. The end of the cold war and the Soviet Union was attributed partly to Reagan's policies and speeches. Popular tax reform was matched with a mounting gap in the distribution of income between the rich and the poor. Diplomatic victories were matched by the transformation of the United States from the world's largest creditor nation to its largest debtor nation. The perceptions of Reagan's building of U.S. military strength and power were matched by the country's relative economic decline related to Japan and western Europe. Although Reagan's administration exerted leadership in developing improved relations with and solutions to problems in Canada, Angola, and the Middle East, it followed, rather than led, the way to improved outcomes in the Philippines, Latin America, and the Soviet Union, for which the administration was quick to take credit. The subsequent breakup of the Soviet Union was credited to his policies, leaving the United States without a rival world superpower. An archproponent of a balanced budget, Reagan nevertheless instituted policies that resulted in a budget deficit that was larger than the deficits created by all his predecessors combined. The good feelings the American majority had for him when he left office were coupled with the worsening problems of land despoilation, drugs, child care, care of

the elderly, homelessness, health costs and insurance, education, acid rain, of savings and loan bankruptcies, and nuclear waste. Many of these problems were left to be addressed seriously by his successors. To conclude, Ronald Reagan's laissez-faire style did not seem to hurt his overall popularity, but it no doubt resulted in considerable ineffectiveness, especially when he had to depend on irresponsible, incompetent, or laissez-faire subordinates and when he made statements or deals without consulting with more knowledgeable colleagues.

Presidents' Greatness

Arthur Schlesinger, Sr. (1948), asked 55 experts, mostly historians, to use their own criteria to judge the greatness of the presidents from Washington to F. D. Roosevelt. He repeated the effort in 1962 using an additional 20 experts, mainly political scientists. In both polls, the top five presidents in greatness were Abraham Lincoln, George Washington, Franklin D. Roosevelt, Woodrow Wilson, and Thomas Jefferson. At the bottom of the list were Ulyssess. Grant and Warren Harding. Thomas Bailey, in 1962, created 43 tests of greatness to apply to each president. His list of presidents was close to Schlesinger's: Lincoln, Washington, and Roosevelt came out as greatest. A similar consensus of greatness was obtained by Maranell (1970) and the American Historical Society in 1977. The society asked 100 history department heads to name the ten greatest presidents. Lincoln, Washington, and Roosevelt topped the list. In 1982, the *Chicago Tribune* asked 49 leading historians and political scientists the same thing. The same three presidents were at the top (Neal, 1982). With similar findings, D. Porter (1981, unpublished) also asked 41 American historians for the presidents with the lowest ratings. Those named were Nixon, Buchanan, and Harding. Murray and Blessing (1983) provided some of the preceding information and also conducted a poll of their own. They sent 1,997 questionnaires to PhDs in history with the rank of assistant professor or higher. They received 953 completed returns. From the mean ratings, four presidents were considered by the investigators to be great: Lincoln, F. D. Roosevelt, Washington, and Jefferson. Considered near great were Theodore Roosevelt, Wilson, Jackson, and Truman. Above average were John Adams, Lyndon Johnson, Eisenhower, Polk, Kennedy, Madison, Monroe, John Quincy Adams, and Cleveland. At the bottom of the list were Andrew Johnson, Buchanan, Nixon, Grant, and Harding.

Revisions in Reputation

Often it takes years following a president's time in office to judge the effectiveness of his policies while in office. President Eisenhower was regarded as mediocre during his time in office, with an image of caring more for playing golf than leading the country. Although he delegated much work to his subordinates, he was actually active and successful and set a high standard for integrity and trust in domestic politics. He reached a truce with North Korea in 1953 that has lasted more than half a century and in 1955 began the Interstate Highway System, which revolutionized suburbia and intercity travel. He had the foresight to warn against the military-industrial complex. Judgments of his effectiveness have been revised upward considerably (Hoxie, 1983). Among presidents from Truman to Reagan, Eisenhower was rated highest (and Nixon lowest) in 2000, in effective servant leadership decision making by a sample of Canadian and American scholars (Tourigny, 2000). As a former military commander, Eisenhower understood the limits of power in international affairs and considered the use of overt military force as a last resort (Saunders, 1985). The same was true of Harry Truman, who, when he took office in 1945 after the death of FDR, was seen as a failed haberdasher. Without experience and without knowledge of FDR's plans and commitments, Truman was seen as totally unprepared for the office. A strict party man, he was perceived as beholden to big-city political bosses. His popularity plunged further when he dismissed Douglas MacArthur as commanding general of U.N. forces in the Korean War for failing to bring peace. Nevertheless, although his responsiveness to public concerns decreased (K. Smith, 1983), Truman's reputation was revised upward by his performance as a statesman and for the many tough decisions he made, such as using the atom bomb on Hiroshima and Nagasaki in 1945 to bring World War II to a speedy end, avoiding a predicted million American casualties from invading Japan. He was behind the Marshall Plan, which set a prostrate Western Europe back on its feet. He promulgated the Truman Doctrine in 1948 to halt the Communist takeover in Greece. This was an early example of support for containing Soviet expansion, which was U.S. foreign policy until the breakup of the Soviet Union in 1991 (Coffey, 1985). He racially integrated the military forces in 1948, a time when segregation was in force in the South and de facto in much of the rest of the country. He also took decisive action to deal with a national coal strike that threatened a large percentage of industrial operations and home heating. He was equally forceful in avoiding long, injurious national steel and railroad strikes (Gardner, 1987; McCullough, 1992). Also, among presidents from Truman to Reagan, he was almost the highest in his relations with Congress as a servant leader in principle-guided action, moral empowerment, and universal, constitutional, and humanitarian values, according to a sample of Canadian and American scholars (Tourigny, 2000).

While in office, Gerald Ford was seen as a nice guy, a plodder, whose public speaking style was unanimated, who stumbled when walking downstairs, who was appointed, not elected, and who pardoned Richard Nixon after he had resigned, to avoid Nixon's impeachment over the Watergate scandal. But Ford was the right man to take over the office, as required by the Constitution, for the 30 months he served. His pardon of Nixon, the amnesty program for 50,000 Vietnam War draft evaders, and healing some of the other wounds of the Vietnam War moved public attention away from these virulent media issues and redirected public attention to the future. Ford picked qualified people for his cabinet and as advisers. For instance, he chose Edward Levi, dean of the Law School at the University of Chicago, to be his attorney general, and Henry Kissinger to head the State Department. He was a manager without much vision, but he got his cabinet to work by encouraging expressions of differing views and vigorous debate. He defined realistic objectives, established principles to reach the objectives, determined the path to the goals, and as the former speaker of the House was flexible in his negotiations with Congress. He inherited and turned around an economy that was suffering rampant double-digit inflation when he came into office. To some degree, he went beyond political expediency (Hersey, 1975; Casserly, 1977; Nessen, 1978; Hartmann, 1980).

Why Presidents Fail

Many of the presidents' failures could be attributed to their tendency to ignore warnings from their many sources of information. The federal government had a large early warning system to watch the oil industry but the Nixon administration failed to take early action that could have mitigated the 40-fold increase in prices engineered by OPEC. Instead, Nixon and Secretary of State Kissinger suggested that the shah of Iran, a member of OPEC, should raise oil prices to pay for armaments to be used to defend the oil-rich Persian Gulf region. Continued warnings of the public unrest in Iran went unnoticed. Carter did not pay attention to his State Department Iranian experts, who warned him in advance of the Iranian attack on the U.S. Embassy in Tehran, after which Americans were held hostage for 444 days. The CIA issued five advance warnings that Fidel Castro was planning to ship Cuban criminals and mental patients to Florida from Cuba, which Carter could have prevented. Carter was taken by surprise by the Soviet invasion of Afghanistan. He had made the mistake of believing Leonid Brezhnev, who lied to him. With intelligence reports about the plans of Argentine generals, Reagan might have prevented the Argentinian invasion of the Falklands by disabusing the generals of their impression that the United States supported their invasion. Reagan wanted policy memos and alternative proposals reduced to a single page. Top advisors showed their loyalty by telling him what they thought he wanted to hear. He took the wrong steps in dealing with the civil war in Lebanon. In the Iran-contra scandal, cash was obtained by Reagan administration staff by secretly and illegally providing Iran with missiles. Then the money was used illegally to support the Nicaraguan contras fighting the Sandinista government forces. Reagan apologized, admitted failure and took personal responsibility. He acknowleged that that mistakes had been made and appealed for America to move on (J. Anderson, 1983).

Reagan favored reducing federal regulations and relying more on free markets to allocate resources, giving freer rein to business. He cut the budget for environmental protection and weakened enforcement. States and localities were to be more responsible for the environment. Ideology and loyalty determined his appointments. Policy planning was centralized in the White House (Kraft & Vig, 1984).

Ulysses S. Grant was a victim of pressures from Republican Party bosses to avoid taking a stand against robber barons' raids on railroad property. William Howard Taft had been T. Roosevelt's efficient assistant. He was the charismatic Roosevelt's successor as president in 1908,

and Roosevelt expected him to carry on with his plans and policies, which he did not do. Taft came in a distant third when seeking reelection in 1912. Roosevelt formed the Bull Moose Party to run against him, allowing Woodrow Wilson, a Democrat, to win the election. Taft would not engage in political bargaining and scheming. He would not play party politics but remained concerned for the public good. He was honest and friendly but unfortunately surrounded himself with Roosevelt's enemies. He did succeed in enacting legislation that was highly beneficial to the country (Cotton, 1932).

Warren Harding is at the bottom of most lists of presidential accomplishment, prestige, activity, and strength of action. His failings included his loyalty to corrupt friends (Trani & Wilson, 1977), his poor cabinet appointments, his lack of education, and his political ineptness (Murray, 1969). Herbert Hoover had the misfortune to take office 10 months before the stock market crash of 1929 and the onset of the Great Depression. The unemployment rate was 25% when the time came for him to seek reelection. As a conservative Republican, his attitude toward government intervention was that the economy would recover by itself. But the economy kept getting worse during his administration. Hoover failed because he was extremely introverted, sensitive, and proud of his integrity, which led him to try to work for the best interests of the country as he saw it. He lacked the kind of persona to speak out with confidence that FDR, his successful successor in 1932, demonstrated extremely well. Hoover blamed his Quaker background for his desire for privacy, which led him to prefer to work as much as possible behind the scenes of administration, which he did very well. He was a mining engineer who gained his fame by effectively organizing and administering Belgian war relief. He raised the necessary funds and arranged for the transportation of millions of tons of concentrated food for four years at the end of World War I. He preferred to credit his subordinates and newspapers for the success rather than himself (Burner, 1979; Hoff, 1975). But he did little to ameliorate the Great Depression or its effects, which began soon after he took office. He was opposed to government intervention and believed the business cycle would take care of itself.

Richard Nixon's Quaker background had a different effect. Like Hoover, he distanced himself interpersonally. Although Nixon had won reelection in 1972, was highly intelligent like Hoover, and was the statesman who established relations with China, at the time of his resignation, Nixon was the least loved modern president. It was a relief when he resigned in 1974. He was seen as a self-aggrandizing exploiter without principle. He was secretive, manipulative, self-righteous, hypocritical, insecure, untrusting, and self-righteous. He used innuendo, trickery, fraud, and ruthless single-mindedness in winning elections. He was determined to succeed at all costs. But he was unable to make close friends. He was uncomfortable making social conversation and being onstage. He often supported both sides of an issue (Ambrose, 1987). He was in constant conflict emotionally between his extreme ambition and what he felt he needed to do socially as a politician (Abramsen, 1977). He never seemed able to run a clean election campaign. The Watergate break-in was not the only Nixon scandal. Incidents of sabotage, extortion, forgery, and slander were reported in his earlier campaigns for Congress. In office, he was autocratic and controlling (Mankiewicz, 1973).

Jimmy Carter was a puzzle as president. He attempted to be a transformational leader, with lofty ideals and principles of ethics and the common good that were not understood by transactional politicians, for whom trading favors was more important. He avoided the dramatic, rhetorical style of his predecessors, played down his own importance, and did not show up on television as a powerful leader (Meyrowitz, 1980). He was seen by his critics as indecisive, rigid, and unable to be practical and accept compromise in order to take necessary actions (Mollenhoff, 1980). According to interviews by Mazlich and Diamond (1979) with those close to Carter, he was tied down by self-imposed constraints, such as a concern for human rights. From his mother came a strong social consciousness. From his father came a strong competitiveness. After success in business, he turned to politics, where he could satisfy both drives. Coming late to a political career, he was always an outsider in Washington. He was close only to his family. He was emotionally conflicted between his southern heritage and his moral and rational support for African Americans' civil rights. He was a populist who believed that people were inherently good; they would know and do what was right without his needing to explain his intentions to them. But Congress was another matter. He read all the details of every legislative bill that came to his office before signing or vetoing it. Believed to have a photographic memory, he stored a lot of data in his head. As a former nuclear engineer and naval officer, he used systematic problem solving, weighing the alternatives, to choose the best solution to a problem. However, he saw each problem in isolation from other issues. He was modest about his abilities but was expected to find the answers to the nation's problems. Despite his highly orderly, disciplined, and hardworking character, and despite his empathy for the less fortunate, he lost the confidence of the public by making forceful speeches about matters he could do little about. Like George W. Bush, another "born-again" Christian, he tried to appeal to moral and religious values, but, unlike Bush, he failed to be reelected (Mazlich & Diamond, 1979). Although Carter espoused democracy in the abstract, he was actually a highly directive leader. His failures to consult with his staff and Congress led to many mistakes. His model for leadership was the highly directive and controlling perfectionist Admiral Hyman Rickover, who was known for not providing subordinates with feedback unless it was negative (Glad, 1980). Carter was seen by his subordinates as the sole decision maker. He was a demanding boss and retained tight control. When he had to delegate minor projects, his delegation was done poorly because he failed to provide sufficient information about what was needed (Jordan, 1982) Critics saw this as evidence of administrative disorganization despite Carter's retaining tight control. According to a survey of 212 career civil service executives in his administration, he lacked the political and personal skills to convince them of his legitimacy as a manager (Benze, 1981). Carter used his advisors to teach and facilitate, but not to provide answers. Despite his failure in office, he became one of America's best *ex-presidents*. He began this next career while he was still president by mediating a peace agreement between Israel and Egypt that has lasted since 1977. Since then he has served as a successful mediator of many international conflicts in other countries, such as that between Indonesia and East Timor.

George H. W. Bush neglected domestic economics and in the 1992 campaign for reelection failed to judge the public mood. One of George W. Bush's failings was his unwillingness to admit mistakes. Genovese (1996) suggested that presidents' failure could be avoided if the traits of many presidents could be combined in one person: Kennedy's vision, Johnson's political skill, Nixon's insights, Ford's integrity, Carter's trustworthiness, Reagan's personality, G. H. W. Bush's experience, and Clinton's interpersonal skills. Aside from Clinton's private missteps, which cost him dearly, Clinton tried to maintain moderation in his decisions and policies but failed to arouse legislative support from his strong stands on positions (Burns & Sorenson, 2000). Always wanting to be liked, he responded almost daily to public opinion polls in determining his actions. George W. Bush sunk to the lowest public approval ratings of 30% for a president since Nixon, he even lost the confidence of many among his Republican congressional majority. Despite the continued optimistic spin on his many domestic and foreign policy failures, the realities of mishandling, incompetence, and arrogance of his administration set in. But conservative commentators disagree about whether he continues to be successful or is starting to fail (Kakutani, 2006).

Prime Ministers and Chancellors as Leaders

Several dilemmas face prime ministers in parliamentary forms of government. How should they maintain control over policy while other members of their cabinet are delegated authority? How much can they shape the policy agenda when problems and opportunities can be posed by other members of the government? (Karbo & Hermann, 1998). They may pursue a leadership style of relating to constituents and other leaders and management strategies that is reinforced by their first and subsequent political successes (Barber, 1977). They may consult with their cabinet as a whole, a smaller committee of cabinet members, or individual members. They may impose or advocate a position, bargain, or be participative. A hundred press conferences and parliamentary question period news reports were content-analyzed by Karbo and Hermann (1998) for British Prime Ministers Margaret Thatcher and John Major and again for German Chancellors Konrad Adenauer and Helmut Kohl. The leaders' responses were scored for responsiveness to political constraints, openness to information, motivational orientation, and expansionist or opportunistic political orientation. Thatcher and Adenauer challenged political constraints; Major and Kohl respected them. John Major was more open to information than were the other three leaders. Thatcher and Adenauer were more concerned about tasks and problems; Major and Kohl were more oriented to relationships. Thatcher and Adenauer had an expansionist political orientation. They wanted to increase their control over people and resources. Major was most opportunistic, and Kohl was most politically oriented toward being influential. Tony Blair stands out as a prime minister who was truly transformational. Neither extremely conservative nor extremely liberal, he was able to take a middle position that transformed the Labor Party and enabled his domination of politics in Britain for 12 years as prime minister. Seen as the giant of his age in Britain, he has appeared as extremely earnest and ambitious rather than cynical. He willingly took on unpopular causes such as the war in Iraq. He advanced a morally idealistic, communitarian vision with the family as the most important institution in society. His political style was to reconcile opposites: fiscal discipline with social spending, tough anticrime and antiterrorism policies with compassionate welfare assistance, free-market policies with government activism.

Summary and Conclusions

Providing strategic leadership is an important role for CEOs and senior executives. They are challenged by the need to honor the past and present while considering the future of the organization and its environment. They need to support both continuity and change. By scanning their organizations and the surrounding environment, strategic leaders formulate the goals and directions of the organization and communicate them. Using consultation, intuition, and a long-term perspective, they make strategic decisions that affect corporate profitability and the success of nonprofit organizations. Strategies can follow a variety of approaches ranging from purely economic considerations to emphasis on good human and customer relations. Modern strategies will need to fit the environment and organizations to which the leaders belong.

Environment and Organizational Effects

As recognized by Jenkins (1947) and Stogdill (1948), the traits required in a leader are related to the demands of the situation (Jenkins, 1947; Stogdill, 1948), In a review of situational aspects of charismatic leadership, Shamir and Howell (1999, p. 258) took the more qualified view that the principles and processes of charismatic leadership "—apply across a wide variety of situations; however, there are situations in which they apply more than in others.... [Leadership] emergence and effectiveness ... may be facilitated by some contexts and inhibited by others." Individuals differ in their motivation to lead, but their motivation will depend on whether they are in a hierarchical, professional, or entrepreneurial organization (Smith & Miner, 1984). U.S. presidents are more likely to be successful if they introduce administrative actions and proposals for legislation as early as possible in their terms (Barber, 1985). Sayles (1958, 1979) and Osborne (1999) focused attention on the interaction between managers' roles, organizational designs, and organizational environments. Nebekcr and Mitchell (1974) found that differences in leaders' behavior could be explained by the leader's expectations that a certain style of leadership would be effective in a particular kind of situation. For example, the success of the careers of 310 British and U.S. managers in 28 different companies corresponded to the extent to which the managers' achievement orientation matched their companies' support of risk taking. The managers' success was evidenced by the progress of their salaries compared to their age. On the other hand, other matches of orientation and the company situation that were expected to make a difference in the managers' advancement failed to do so (Ansari, Baumgartel, & Sullivan, 1982).

The preceding chapters have examined the personal and situational aspects that account for leadership. In these chapters, we have put more emphasis on general effects across situations and on personal predispositions. Now we will accent situations and contexts, keeping generalities and personal predispositions in mind. Contingencies of situation and predispositions of leaders and followers can give rise to hypotheses about the emergence of successful transformational leadership. For instance, inspirational leadership is likely to arise if the leaders are articulate, the followers are inexperienced, and they are faced with ambiguous tasks, goals, and reinforcements. Considerate leadership is more likely with caring, empathic leaders and inexperienced subordinates with unmet needs. Intellectual stimulation will more likely be generated by a rational and unconventional leader with inexperienced subordinates. Contingent reinforcement will appear if a materialistic leader is in control of material reinforcements and materialist subordinates. Active management by exception will be more likely to appear with a task-oriented leader and inexperienced subordinates working in a context of objective, measureable performance. Passive and laissez-faire leadership are more likely to emerge where tasks, goals, and reinforcements are unimportant, where the leader is neither task- nor relations-oriented, and the subordinates are experienced.

O'Connor and Farrow (1979) illustrated the significance of fitting leaders' behavior to the situation. They demonstrated the personal satisfaction that accrued from matching the amount of structure required by managers in research and production and the managers' preferences for such structure. Similarly, managers reported that they needed to engage in political and manipulative behavior most often in organizations that lacked structure, where there was much continuing ambiguity about goals and processes and a great many technological uncertainties (Allen, Panian, & Lotz, 1979; Madison, Allen, Porter, et al., 1980). While transformational leadership of department managers predicted business unit performance a year later, the effect was moderated by support provided for innovation (Howell & Avolio, 1993). Yet, based on 37 years of observation and membership in the U.S. Army and large civilian organizations, Ulmer (1997, p. 78) declared, "Good leaders in our Army look very much like good leaders elsewhere." Such leaders show flexibility in responding to different situational requirements. Quinn (1988) provided a competing values framework that set forth that leaders need to focus on predictability and order in situations requiring centralization and integration. But they need to value spontaneity and flexibility if situations call for decentralization and differentiation. Hunt and Phillips (1991) were able to apply Quinn's model to illustrate the various attitudes, values, and behaviors needed by military commanders for successful leadership in garrison and in combat.

Trait Approach versus Situation

As was noted in Chapter 4, the trait approach is not enough for understanding leadership. Above and beyond personal attributes of consequence, the situation can make a difference. Whereas some types of leadership are reported or expected of leaders in all situations, other types are more specific to particular types of situations (Hemphill, 1952). For instance, according to a survey by Hemphill, Seigel, and Westie (1951), when a group has a high degree of control over its members, the leader is expected to dominate and actually does so. In groups whose members participate to a high degree, however, these expectations and reports of leader domination do not occur.

What is required for leadership in a stressful situation is likely to differ from what is needed in calm and steady circumstances. For a given leader in one situation or the other, some subordinates are likely to be more experienced, more motivated, or better adjusted to their situation. The leader may need to deal differently with various kinds of subordinates. Some leadership behavior is a function of individual differences, but other leadership behavior appears to depend mainly on situational differences or on the interaction of the individual and the situation. Any full account requires the "within-and-between" analysis (WABA) advocated by Dansereau, Alutto, and Yammarino (1984). WABA allocates the percentage of variance in leadership behavior and the percentage of the effects of the leadership on performance and satisfaction to the leaders across situations, across the groups led, and to the individual leader-follower relationships within the groups led. Thus for 116 insurance agents in 31 work groups, Yammarino, Dubinsky, and Hartley (1987) showed that 28 percent of the average correlation of subordinates and supervisors about the subordinates' performance was attributed to the differences among the work groups and their leaders. Fourteen percent was attributed to differences among the subordinates within the work groups led by the same supervisor. The remaining variance was attributed to fluctuations of the followers' relations with some leaders but not with others. For a sample of 83 retail sales associates in 26 work groups, only 14% could be attributable to differences among the supervisors, while 7% was due to supervisor-subordinate relations within the groups.

Stogdill's (1951b) study of transferred naval officers suggested that some behaviors of the transferee in the new situations were characteristic of the transferee himself rather than of the position. Such behaviors included a tendency to delegate authority; to spend time in public relations; to evaluate, read, and answer mail; to read technical publications; and to spend time with outsiders. But other behavior, such as the amount of personal contact time; time spent with superiors; and time spent in supervision, coordination, and writing reports, was more a matter of demands of the situation. Barnlund (1962) rotated 25 participants in differing combinations in differing groups dealing with differing tasks and erroneously concluded that the individual participants were less important than the situations involved in the emergence of the leaders of the groups. Kenny and Zaccaro (1983) recalculated Barnlund's statistics and showed that 49% to 82% of the variance in who emerged as leader was due to some stable aspect of the individual leader. Again, Zaccaro, Foti, and Kenny (1991) conducted a similar experiment using 108 undergraduate students who rotated through four different group tasks. Fifty-nine percent of the variance in the leadership that emerged was due to the individual students across the four group task situations. The students' self-monitoring was of consequence.

Patterning

W. O. Jenkins (1947) reviewed a large number of military studies that indicated that the traits required in a leader are related to the demands of the situation. Stogdill's (1948) review of 124 studies from a broader array of situations suggested that although there may be general traits associated with leadership, the patterns of those traits required for leadership differ with the situation.[1] Subsequently, DuBrin (1963) found that a leadership inventory, consisting of both trait and situational items, correlated significantly with a leadership criterion, whereas neither set of items alone was significantly related to the criterion. Again, O. L. Campbell (1961) reported significant differences among leaders in eight different situations when described on the Consideration and Initiating Structure scales of the Leader Behavior Description questionnaire (LBDQ).[2]

Leadership Styles

Chapter 19 examined the premium placed on the maturity of subordinates by the Hersey-Blanchard (1977) situational leadership model in determining what style of leadership is appropriate. Even Blake and Mouton (1964) would agree that how the 9,9 style—integrated, highly task- and relations-oriented leadership—properly manifested itself in a leader's behavior depended on a subordinate's maturity. Vecchio (1981), among many others, concluded, from an analysis of LBDQ data from 107 subordinates' descriptions of their supervisors, that a matching of the leader's style to the needs of subordinates and the work setting yielded the maximum satisfaction of subordinates with the leadership. Such matching was seen as the reason that when each of four CEOs displayed a different pattern of traits, all four emerged as effective leaders in their four different organizational cultures (Free, 1983). Again, in Fiedler's (1967a) contingency model detailed in Chapter 19, relations-oriented leadership is optimal when the situation is neither highly favorable nor highly unfavorable to the leader in terms of his or her esteem and power and the situation's structure. Task-oriented leadership is optimal when the situation is either highly favorable or highly unfavorable to the leader.

[1] See Chapter 4.
[2] See Chapter 20.

Situations Alter Leadership Styles. Much has been learned about how the demands of a task and the characteristics of immediate group members modify the type of leadership that occurs. The *external environment*, the *organization* in which the tasks are to be accomplished, and the *leader's group* may exert important effects on the leader's behavior. Modern theories of leadership style take note of how the leader's behavior is systematically changed by changes in situational conditions (Evans, 1974). Changes in the complex organization and its external environment will ordinarily bring on changes in its leadership. As organizations mature, the charismatic founders of social movements usually give way to bureaucratic successors.

In the case of the union movement in the United States, unions had to struggle first for recognition, then to become established institutions. Now many are struggling for survival. In each stage, the requirements for leadership differed. The low-paid, lower-skilled immigrants with limited English who made up the members of the United Steel Workers changed to a new generation of highly paid, skilled, English-speaking, better-educated members. Leading them required new approaches. Patronage had to give way to persuasion. Newer issues involving the match between the leader and the situation emerged. These issues reflect societal changes, the sharp increase in political and legislative intervention into the world of work, and the changed relations between employers and employees. Further changes in the leadership of the steel union were necessary to deal with the impact of foreign competition and new technologies.

Again, doing business successfully in the competitive and rapidly changing global market and its rules required leadership that was visionary and dedicated with "a balanced scorecard, corporate accountability, (creation of) dynamic capabilities, (and) effective management of intangible resources and assets." (Zahra, 1999, p. 36). The importance of the situation was illustrated in the case of a successful and effective transformational Minnesota school superintendent who greatly improved her distressed district. She became less successful as a leader when she was appointed a state commissioner in a bureaucratic agency, larger and more complex than her district, that provided her with less freedom to take initiatives and display her transformational qualities (Roberts & Bradley, 1988).

Leaders Change Situations. In all this, one must keep in mind that leaders are not merely reactive to situations; often they can change the situation to suit their own proclivities (Yukl, 1971; Fiedler, Chemers, & Maher, 1976; Wofford, 1982). Graen and Uhl-Bien (1995) advised that leaders could improve the quality of their group's performance by developing better relations with all of the members. In 1917, the German leaders sent the exiled Lenin from Zurich to Saint Petersburg, enabling him to initiate the Bolshevik Revolution and achieve a peace treaty with Germany. Many of the world's most eminent leaders could not be deflected from their pursuits by environmental, organizational, or collegial considerations.[3] Thus, Singh (1982) argued that Indian managers must avoid allowing the situation to dominate them to such an extent that normlessness results. Fiedler advocated training the leader to make the situation better fit the leader's LPC orientation. What leaders do can predict long-term organizational alignment, adaptability, and excellence (O'Toole, 1995). Dan Wiens (Dyck, 1994), the Canadian farm movement ecodevelopment leader, envisaged changing the agrifood system to fit environmental and democratic values and principles. He set an example by building his leadership on participative involvement and empowering collaboration. The organizational climate and financial performance of 50 Dutch supermarkets were improved if their store managers were charismatic and considerate in their leadership (Koene, Vogelaar, & Soeters, 2002).

Theories, Models, and Prescriptions

Increasing attention has been devoted to providing rationales for understanding the connections between personal and situational effects. Katz and Kahn's (1966) introduction of systems theory to the study of leadership and social interaction is illustrative. Most efforts to develop theories, models, and prescriptions for directly fitting the leader's behavior to the situational requirements appear somewhat like Ashby's (1957, 1960) Law of Requisite Variety that the functions evolving within a brain or created within a computer must be differentiated to match the different elements in the outside environment

with which they must deal. The variety of the leader's behaviors must coincide with the situational demands that parallel them. Or the explanations take the form of tautologies. The appropriate leadership is that which serves to fix, or get five others to fix, whatever is malfunctioning or less than optimal in the system.

One also has to remain alert to the possibilities of coincidental correlations between leadership attributes or behavior and situations, since theories may inadvertently be built on them. One needs to see the link of direct or indirect causation of the situation on the leader or the leader on the situation. An organization's size itself may correlate with a more directive leadership style but cannot account for it. Mediating organizational and psychological processes that are connected with both size and leadership are needed to confirm and understand the relationship (Indik, 1965b).

Kerr, Schriesheim, Murphy, and Stogdill (1974) reviewed how situational elements determined whether consideration or initiation of structure was more effective.[4] Among the situational variables found to determine whether initiation of structure or consideration yielded satisfaction and productivity were the subordinates' need for information, job level, expectations of the leaders' behavior, and perceived organizational independence. Also important were how similar the leaders' attitudes and behavior were to the managerial style of higher management and the leaders' upward influence. In addition, the effects of the task, including whether there were pressures to produce and provisions for intrinsic satisfaction, were significant.

Yukl (1981) specified the situations in which 19 leadership behaviors would be most essential. For task-oriented behaviors, for instance, Yukl put forward that the leaders' emphasis on performance is needed more when subordinates' errors and deficiencies in the quality of products are costly and difficult to correct or would endanger the health and lives of people. Leaders can structure reward contingencies better when it is possible to measure the subordinates' performance accurately. More role clarification is desirable when the organization has elaborate rules and regulations and subordinates are not familiar with them. Goal setting by leaders is more effective when the outcomes of performance are highly dependent on

[3] See Chapter 21.

[4] See Chapter 20.

the subordinates' efforts and are not strongly affected by fluctuating conditions that are beyond the control of subordinates. The dissemination of information by the leaders is most important when the work of subordinates is strongly affected by developments in other parts of the organization and subordinates are dependent on the leaders to keep them informed about the developments. The facilitation of work by leaders is required more when shortages of inputs or inadequate support services would result in the serious and immediate disruption of the work.

Yukl also prescribed a number of relations-oriented leadership behaviors for particular situations. The need for more consideration by the leader occurs, according to Yukl, when the leader works in close proximity to subordinates or must interact frequently with them owing to the nature of the task. Praise and recognition by the leader become more important when subordinates are not able to get much direct feedback about their performance from the work itself or from clients, customers, or coworkers. The facilitation of interaction by the leader is essential when the organizational unit is large and contains competing groups or factions.

Leadership, Organization, and the External Environment

Conger (1999) noted some of the variables of the external environment that are likely to affect the organization's and leader's behavior. The effect of crisis conditions on the emergence of charismatic leadership is well documented. Closer proximity to followers may make more relationship building possible. The external environment may provide a variety of opportunities for entrepreneural leadership to appear. Environmental uncertainties will bring out demands in leadership that restores order.

Stable, Turbulent, and Dynamic Environments

Systems theory postulates that what takes place outside a system is likely to affect what takes place inside it. External environmental forces interact with the organization and continuously modify what is going on inside it. Thus, if a business operates in a stable environment, it is likely to have more consistent leadership and stable organiza-

tional policies and departments that are similar in structure. If an environment is unstable, policies are less uniform and greater differences emerge among the various divisions of the firm (Lawrence & Lorsch, 1967b). Leadership is likely to be less consistent over time and place. Shamir and Howell (1999, p. 265) hypothesized that "charismatic leadership is more likely to emerge and be effective in dynamic organizational environments that require and enable the introduction of new strategies, markets, products and technologies."

The failure of organizational structures to change in response to changing environmental processing requirements led J. A. Miller (1974), who studied leadership behavior in 10 organizations, to propose and find support for the argument that the optimal degree of initiation of structure by the leader depends on how much the processes demand such structure when the organization has not already provided it. Osborn, Hunt, and Bussom (1977), like Miller, proposed to extend Ashby's (1957, 1960) Law of Requisite Variety to understand the relationship between environmental demands on the organization and the organization's structure. The organization must possess as much required variety as the variety that can be expected from the environment. Internal variety of organizational structure should correspond to the environmental variety of demand on the organization. Organizations in environments with numerous disturbances should, therefore, contain an equally sophisticated capability to vary important internal characteristics. Similarly, leaders in environments that vary should show more varied behavior than leaders in stable environments. Osborn, Hunt, and Bussom (1977) tested whether the consistency of the matching of the leader's behavior with environmental conditions was more valid than an alternative model indicating that the leader's behavior offsets and compensates (as Miller argued) for the environmental demands. In 60 chapters of a business fraternity, within-chapter variations across selected environmental dimensions gave a measure of environmental variety. Five leadership dimensions from the LBDQ-XII[5] for each leader of a fraternity chapter yielded a measure of leadership variety. The overall performance of the fraternity was best when environmental variety was low and was mismatched with high leadership variety. However,

[5] See Chapter 20.

leadership variety that matched high environmental variety was associated with better performance by the fraternity, but the effects were much smaller.

An attribute of the outside environment that is likely to influence the behavior of leaders inside an organization is the stability of the market in which a firm or agency operates. If the firm operates in a stable marketplace, less total leadership is needed and more substitutes for leadership can be employed. Matters can be programmed; policies can be set; and leadership, when needed, can be directive.[6] In a turbulent market, more leadership, particularly consultation, will be needed on a continuing basis.

Entrepreneureal leaders of new ventures need to adapt to the stability or turbulance of their environments. The success of 66 new ventures, according to Ensley, Hmielesky, and Pearce (2006), was greater if the leaders were transactional in stable environments and transformational in dynamic environments. Again, according to Wu, Levitas, and Priem (2005), the number of successful patents filed by 97 pharmaceutical firms from 1992 to 1995 was greater if their technological environment was dynamic rather than stable and their CEOs held shorter tenures of office. Burns and Stalker (1961) found that executives in a sales engineering company were required to deal repeatedly with the same customers, suppliers, and regulatory bodies. The demand for direct interaction with the environment was greater for the sales engineering executives than for those in a clothing company where interaction with outsiders was accomplished indirectly, mainly in written form. Executives had less autonomy in an environment when there was less differentiation of customers, greater feedback, and indirect communication with the environment. The executives in the clothing company spent less time in decision making and more time dealing with routine tasks. Their autonomy was more restricted, both horizontally and vertically, than that of the sales engineering executives (Burns & Stalker, 1961).

Firms that had to operate in turbulent fields were more likely to share the power of decision making inside their organization (Emery & Trist, 1965). In agreement, Lawrence and Lorsch (1967a) compared decision making in the stable container industry with decision making in the more turbulent plastics industry. Again, in a stable environment, the decision-making processes within the container firm were likely to be directive; in the more turbulent environment of the plastics firm, decision-making processes were more likely to be consultative.

Mechanistic versus Organic Organizations

Conceiving organizations as machines or as organisms goes back to the nineteenth century. *Mechanistic* organizations appear to work better in a stable environment; *organic* organizations, in a turbulent environment. Burns and Stalker (1961) interviewed key people in 20 organizations in a variety of industries. They classified the management methods as either *mechanistic* or *organic*. The mechanistic organization was characterized by rule-based, vertical communication patterns, with decision and influence centered at the top levels. Cooperation depended on understanding, conforming to, and agreeing with the rules. Organic forms featured lateral communication, adaptability based on learning, and less rigidly defined jobs. Cooperation depended on understanding, alignment, and acceptance of the organization's goals. The mechanistic style was more appropriate for dealing with stable environments, whereas the organic style was more suited to turbulent environments. The effective firms in relatively stable environments were mechanistic in their concentration of decision making and influence at the top level of management. Lower-level managers in such stable environments and mechanistic organizations found satisfaction from being able to get a quick decision from those at higher levels. The organic organization was more satisfying as it provided more autonomy, more discretionary opportunities, and appropriate involvement in relevant decisions. The effective firms in a rapidly changing, complex environment were more organic. They involved their lower-level managers in joint departmental decisions. Managers who possessed the competence and knowledge to deal with the environment had more decision-making influence than did those who did not.

Dickson (1998) considered mechanistic–organic as a continuum and extracted six items from the Globe Organizational Policies and Practices questionnaire (House,

---

[6]As defined in Chapter 18, *direction* (italic) refers to giving orders with or without explanation; direction (roman) includes ordering, persuading, and manipulating. *Participation* (italic) refers to sharing in the decision process; participation (roman) includes consulting, sharing, and delegating.

Hanges, Dickson, et al., 1996–1998) and the responses of 9,527 persons from 225 organizations and 42 countries. He demonstrated that the continuum was reliable and generalizable across organizations and that agreement about their organization was higher among members of mechanistic than organic organizations. Howell (1997) suggested that exchange/transactional leadership was more likely to emerge in mechanistic organizations; charismatic/transformational leadership, in organic organizations. Pillai and Meindl (1998) found that for 596 personnel from 101 work units, compared to generation by crisis conditions, the emergence of charismatic leadership was favored by an organic unit organization and a collectivistic orientation. A study of 45 manager-subordinate dyads in two plants, one organic, the other mechanistic, showed that consultation was most practiced in the plant with an organic organization; a directive style of communication was the most common form of interaction in the plant that was mechanistic (Courtright, Fairhurst, & Rogers, 1989).

Strong versus Weak Organizational Cultures. Organizations with *strong* and *weak* cultures were differentiated by Deal and Kennedy (1982). The values of what is right, good, and important are more fixed and fully shared by members in a strong culture, and norms are more fully crystallized. According to Tosi (1991, 1992), mechanistic organizations, with their authority structures and elaborated control systems, are strong in situational effects, for they allow less leeway for individual differences and preferences. In comparison, structurally weaker organic organizations permit individual personalities, competencies, beliefs, and preferences to have more effect. Organic organizations are structurally weaker, as they impose fewer constraints on members and offer less specific mandatory direction on how to deal with problems. They encourage the individual expression of solutions by leaders and followers. O'Regan and Ghobadian (2003) surveyed a sample of 194 small and medium-sized British enterprises and showed that the firms in the upper 25%—in strength of their cultures of external and internal orientation, departmental cooperation, and empowerment—compared with the lowest 25%, were more likely to meet performance objectives, avoid problems, and be more innovative. The same was true for the effects of strong leadership styles.

Economic, Ecological, Political, Social, and Legal Influences

Studies of legislative leadership by Peabody (1976) and Rosenthal (1974) suggested that a variety of environmental forces strongly affects the stability of political leadership. The same variables can be seen to operate even more intensively in the private sector, where market forces and technological changes often dramatically affect the stability and succession of leadership (Bryson & Kelley, 1978). Performance reviews, in the form of annual elections for the board of directors, periodic audits, and stockholders' meetings by outsiders, can influence the actions of the leadership and the stability of the dominant coalition inside the organization (M. P. Allen, 1974). A change in the law, in resources, or in competing organizations also may force changes in leadership (Pfeffer, 1972b). Groups of clients, unions, professional associations, and regulatory agencies affect how and what will be discussed and decided, both in legislatures and in private organizations, especially with regard to visible and emotional questions. Feature stories, publicity, and exposures can be used to support or destroy the leadership in both locations (Ilchman & Uphoff, 1969).

Using factored questionnaires, Bass, Valenzi, and Farrow (1977) asked 76 managers to rate the extent to which economic, political, social, and legal forces outside their organization influenced them and their immediate subordinates. Each of the 277 subordinates described the leadership behavior of the managers. Production, accounting, and finance managers saw economic forces as most important; service, sales, marketing, and personnel managers saw economic forces as least important compared to political, social, or legal forces. But even after separating out the effects of the managers' personality, background characteristics, and managerial function, Bass, Valenzi, and Farrow found that managers who perceived external economic forces as important to their supervisor-subordinate relations tended to be more *directive* and manipulative, according to their subordinates. On the other hand, managers who felt that external political, social, and legal forces were more important tended to be more consultative, according to their subordinates.

In a follow-up analysis, Farrow, Valenzi, and Bass (1980) examined 250 managers in profit-making organizations and 95 in nonprofit organizations. In the nonprofit firms, the leaders' styles, as seen by the subordinates, were affected more by the managers' perceptions of outside environmental influences. Their perceptions of strong economic influences were correlated $-.30$, $-.25$, and $-.21$ with consultation, *participation*, and delegation, respectively, in the nonprofit organizations. The parallel correlations in the profit-making organizations were $-.05$, $-.11$, and $-.02$. Egri and Herman (2000) interviewed and surveyed 73 leaders in ecological products and services in for-profit and nonprofit organizations. Transformational leadership was more likely to appear in nonprofit than for-profit organizations engaged in ecological activities. Compared to the for-profit environmental industry leaders, the nonprofit leaders also attached significantly more importance to the values of self-transcendence, benevolence, and universalism and less importance to power. Again, the case of the Safety-Kleen Corporation (Flannery & May, 1994) revealed how moral norms, values, environmental attitudes, constituent influence, and behavioral controls influence environmental leadership and strategy.

Community leaders differed in their thoughts about which influences affected the developmental needs of their communities, depending on their regional location. Although those in the Southwest believed that local businesses determined their communities' needs, far fewer leaders from the Northeast did believed this. At the same time, leaders from the Northeast thought that nonlocal governments and nonlocal businesses exerted more influence on developmental needs (Olien, Tichenor, & Donohue, 1987). These regional findings, no doubt, have been affected by the expansion of business and industry from the Northeast and the Midwest to the South and West and overseas in the twenty-first century, and by the change in the U.S. business structure in the previous decades.

Economic Conditions. A commonly observed reaction of management to economic recession, loss of markets, and reduced sales and profits is to cut programs that contribute to the improvement of leadership and interpersonal relations within the organization. Training and development are seen as overhead that can be sacrificed to assist the firm's economic balance. During these times, security needs rise, among both workers and managers,

that affect their relationships and problems that must be addressed, such as layoffs, retraining, early retirement, and reductions in compensation and benefits. Franke and Kaul (1978) stirred up controversy over the Hawthorne studies (Roethlisberger, 1947). The heightened productivity of the Western Electric personnel at the Hawthorne Works had been attributed by Roethlisberger to the increased attention by supervisors to human relations and the concerns of the workers. Franke and Kaul, in contrast, accounted statistically for the results by an economic downturn in the late 1920s that resulted in an increase in closer supervision and workers' fearing that they might lose their jobs.

In the 1980s and the 1990s, there was an escalation of mergers, acquisitions, and leveraged buyouts, aided by favorable investor attitudes and increased tax advantages for company debt over equity,[7] which some economists applauded for shaking up complacent managements. But others saw mainly predatory business practices that benefited entrepreneurs and management at the expense of other constituents of the organization. Commitment, loyalty, and involvement suffered. Long-term investment for research and development had to be sacrificed in favor of marshaling resources to maintain short-term strength and elevated stock prices. Confusion and anxiety permeated the members of organizations, threatened by the loss of their jobs, policy changes, plant closings, and general uncertainty.

The Sociopolitical Ethos. In an interview survey by Bruce (1986), CEOs noted that the political environment was important to what they could accomplish. Mergers in the preceding 25 years could not have been possible in the antitrust environment of the 1960s. Maccoby (1983) pointed out the need to consider the continual change in societal attitudes toward the ethics of work. He identified four ethics in earlier U.S. history, each of which was replaced when its ideals could no longer meet society's social and economic needs. The four dominant ethics were: (1) the Protestant or Puritan ethic, (2) the craft ethic, (3) the entrepreneurial ethic, and (4) the ca-

---

[7] High-risk, high-interest junk bonds were floated to provide the leverage for purchases of an acquisition. Such interest was fully tax-deductible as a business expense. The bonds were to be paid from the earnings and sales of assets of the acquisition, whose reduced profits, due to the payments and sales of its assets, would result in lower tax liabilities.

reer ethic. Each ethic generated different predominant styles of leadership, respectively: work orientation, expert orientation, risky competitiveness, and careerism. Likewise, Bass (1960) saw leadership styles affected by the dominance of task orientation in the United States before 1950 giving way to concern in the 1950s for getting along with others, followed by an increasing self-orientation, which began in the 1960s. The same cycle repeated itself between 1975 and 2000. Each, in turn, had different effects on the practice of leadership in U.S. organizations. Production and the heroes of production are paramount in a task-oriented society. Marketing, conformity, and interpersonal relationships became the predominant issues of the 1950s, followed by the predicted self-oriented focus of the "me-too" outlook from the late 1960s onward, in which issues ranging from individual alienation to careerism surfaced. At the same time, concern for human relations in management and leadership grew. By the turn of the century, we saw a generation of working adults concentrating on family relations and security.

A longer psychohistorical focus of societal effects on leadership was proposed by Demause (1982). Demause noted that the common practice of infanticide and infant abandonment in classical and medieval times promoted the survivors' view that their parents and the leaders who displaced the parents were their saviors. The ambivalence toward children that followed in the next centuries fostered the model of parents and leaders as benevolent autocrats. Between 1800 and 1950, the prevailing practice of treating children as subjects for training and socialization created the model of the leader as the source of contingent reinforcement. Finally, the post-1950 Dr. Spock generation created a model of parents and leaders as helpers.

Regulatory Agencies. Ungson, James, and Spicer (1985) surveyed 89 firms in two industries—wood products and high technology—about the effects of regulatory agencies on their planning and goal setting and the need to adjust their organizations to the regulatory agencies' actions. In both industries, managers saw governmental regulatory agencies as more unpredictable and uncontrollable than they did their suppliers of raw material, competitors, customers, and labor. Generally, in the wood products industry, adjustments in personnel were most likely to occur because of governmental regulatory

agencies and least likely to occur because of competitors or investors. But in the high-technology industry, none of the outside factors was as important in affecting the adjustments of personnel.

Legal actions often determine an organization's future. In 1984, after 10 years of work by the antitrust division of the Justice Department, AT&T was ordered by a federal court to break up into competitive sectors. It met the court order by divesting "Ma Bell" from the seven "Baby Bells," the regional local exchanges, leaving long-distance and global activities to AT&T. The new CEOs emphasized competition between the units and their personnel, shutting down the former free-flowing communications among units. They placed a premium on competing for customers rather than continuing concern for service and cooperation. To improve finances, they acquired many new firms to enter the highly competitive computer business and similarly entered the highly competitive cable business. By 2005, AT&T had lost most of its experienced managers. The regulated monopoly shrank from a million personnel in 1984 to a prospective subsidiary of one of its former divisions. The former "widows and orphans" secure AT&T shares were hitting rock bottom, and the remnants of the firm expected to be acquired by one of its own Baby Bells.

Ownership. Agency theory (Meckling & Jensen, 1976) argues that managers are agents of the owners and shareholders and therefore have divergent economic interests. In 2005, CEOs were taking in compensation equal to as much as a fifth of the annual corporate profits after expenses, allowing the owners and shareholders just four fifths. By 2005, the average CEO in the United States was earning more than 450 times more than the average employee in the firm. These extreme results could be dampened only by concerns for social justice, continuing transparency, and stronger regulation by the SEC, and by boards of directors and their audit committees. The treatment of executives by a higher authority in 71 large manufacturing firms depended, according to Gomez-Mejia, Tosi, and Hinkin (1987), on whether the firm had dominant outside shareholders. Conyon and Peck (1998) reached the same conclusion for Britain. Outside shareholders are owners who view the firms primarily as financial investments. They use their power to compensate hired CEOs according to the economic performance of the firms. Firms without such dominant shareholders are controlled more by the management itself. Here, the compensation awarded to CEOs depends more on the size of the firm's operations than on its performance. In the scandals of 2002, the compensation of some senior executives was increased substantially even as the firms were moving toward declarations of bankruptcy! There was some semblance of rationality found by Finkelstein and Boyd (1998), who reported that the performance of firms was higher when the CEO's pay was congruent with the CEO's latitude of action. Balkin, Markman, and Gomez-Mejia (2000) found, in 90 high-tech firms, that CEOs' short-term compensation was related to innovation as measured by the firm's number of patents and spending for R & D. No such relationship of compensation with innovation was found for long-term CEO compensation, nor was there any linkage, long or short term, of CEOs' compensation with innovation in 74 low-tech firms. Nonetheless, as is usually found, compensation depended on the size of the organization and its operations.

Socioeconomic Status of the Community. Chapter 10 detailed the general contribution of accorded status to leadership. Osborn and Hunt (1979) created an index of the socioeconomic level of a community and showed it correlated with the leadership among college students. A community's status was based on its median income per family, mean educational level of its residents, the tendency of residents to vote, and other socioeconomic conditions. For the 60 chapters of a national business fraternity mentioned earlier, the investigators obtained a correlation of .40 between the socioeconomic community status of the college chapter leaders and their initiation of structure, and .68 with their consideration, as measured by the LBDQ. Again, secondary school students were affected by the socioeconomic status of their communities. Philbin (1997) reported that secondary school students' learning increased if the principal was transformational, but only if the students came from the highest socioeconomic levels. However, the transformational leadership of principals was satisfying to teachers in schools of both high and low socioeconomic status.

Religious Affiliation. L. B. Ward (1965) completed a large-scale survey of top managements in the United States that suggested that the religious affiliation of the top managers in a firm affected the personnel policies promoted within the firm. Personnel practices were more likely to be liberal when the top management was not restricted to members of one religious group. Policies were more likely to be liberal if the top management was exclusively Jewish than if it was exclusively Protestant. The most conservative managements were exclusively Catholic.

Reference Groups

Other environmental influences on leaders and members of any organization are their reference groups—those people with whom they compare themselves. Hyman (1942) asked subjects to estimate their status along several dimensions: social, economic, intellectual, physical, and the like. He found that individuals estimated some aspects of their status in relation to family members, others in relation to friends or peers at work, and still others in relation to people in general. Small reference groups were usually more important than were people in general in determining the subjects' satisfaction with their status. Satisfaction with their income was highly dependent on the reference group with which the individuals compared themselves.

Local versus Cosmopolitan. Merton (1949/1957) showed that the identification with different reference groups was associated with variations in patterns of leadership behavior. In a community study, 86 informants identified 379 individuals as persons of some influence. The 30 most influential members of the community were interviewed. Of these 30, 16 were classified as *locals* and 14 as *cosmopolitans* in their reference group identifications. The two groups differed in attitudes and behavior that were of consequence to their serving as leaders or followers. Locals were reared locally. They were reluctant to leave the community. They focused on their community interests and fellow members of local fraternal and business groups. They wanted to know many people. Their influence rested on a complex network of personal relationships. They wanted to understand their community. Cosmopolitans were mostly newcomers, willing to leave the community, interested in the world at large, and members of national professional societies. They were selective in their choice of organizations, and their influence derived from their prestige and professional position. They wanted to understand their job.

Multiple Reference Groups. If asked, "What are you?" people usually see themselves as members of several reference groups. In Texas, a Texan may say first that he is an American. Outside Texas, the Texan may first say Texan, then American, businessman, father, and Episcopalian. Each is a reference group, and the effects are complex. Thus, when Festinger (1949) brought Catholic and Jewish girls together in a small club and asked them to elect officers before the girls' religion was identified, both groups voted as much for nonmembers as for members of their own religion. In a control situation, in which religious identities were publicly disclosed, 64 percent of the Catholics voted for Catholic girls, but the Jewish girls continued to vote equally as often for members of either religion. However, in a large group in which the voters were only privately identified by religious affiliation, Jewish girls showed the same tendency to vote for members of their own religion as did Catholic girls. The same effects were observed when confederates were identified alternately as Catholics and Jews for the benefit of different groups of voters to rule out any influences of the individual nominee on the outcomes.

To understand and predict a person's interpersonal behavior in a designated social situation, one has to determine his or her various reference groups. For example, if two people collide in a crowded street, they may ignore the collision, they may beg each other's pardon, or one may shove the other. What each person does will depend, to some extent, on whether the interacting persons are male or female; white or black; and upper, middle, or lower class; and whether the situation occurs in North America or Zambia.[8]

Real Outside Networks of Relationships

Leaders usually belong to more groups than do followers. They integrate the various subgroups of a larger group and mediate between the membership groups and the wider community. J. B. Marks (1959) found that leaders maintained significantly more extraclique friendship links than did followers and tended to mediate between their groups and the surrounding social environment. Schiffman and Gaccione (1974) found that the opinion

leaders in the nursing home industry were administrators who interacted more often with administrators from other nursing homes. However, the leaders who identified with the norms of the in-house group were more strongly supported by members than were the leaders who identified with the norms of the external groups.

The effects of leaders' outside connections are well known. Interlocking company directorates can take considerable advantage of such linkages for the good of their organizations, even though doing so has the potential for corruption. When the boards of social service organizations were composed of high-status (business leaders) rather than middle-status (middle management and professional) members, the organizations were found to be more effective, better financed, and able to provide a higher quality of service (Zald, 1967). Pettigrew (1973) observed that developing and maintaining a network of contacts outside as well as inside the organization is the means by which many leaders help their subordinates reach their desired objectives. Xoulack (1977) involved 44 undergraduates in simulated bargaining situations. Leaders who did all the bargaining were treated by outgroup members either with friendliness or with hostility. The leaders who were treated in a friendly manner by the out-group members were rated as more effective by the in-group members.

Organizations and Leadership

Xenophon's *Anabasis* told how 13,000 Greek mercenaries were stranded in Mesopotamia in 401 B.C.E., when the Persian prince who had recruited them was killed and their Greek military leaders were treacherously slain. Nevertheless, their military organization and training and their common Greek culture made it possible for them to march 1,000 miles through hostile territory to safety despite the enemy's efforts to stop them (Aupperlie, 1996).

Influenced by David Hume and other eighteenth-century fellow Scots philosophers (Herman, 2001), Adam Smith (1776) in his famous *Wealth of Nations*, observed that civilizing social improvement and merchants, bankers, engineers, and industrial and business organizations developed out of subsistence farmers, fisherman, and miners as a result of the division of labor. Specialization

---

[8]Chapters 31 to 33 examine the effects of these affiliations of sex, race, ethnicity, and national identity on the emergence and success of leaders and managers.

arose from enlightened self-interest and the need for co-operation. Order and good government were required, along with individual liberty and security.

Leadership in an organization is determined by the organization's legitimating principles and cultural norms and by the social structure within which it occurs. Pawar and Eastman (1997) posited four organizational considerations that influence its leadership: (1) the organization's structures, (2) the organization's governance, (3) an emphasis on adaptation or efficiency, and (4) dominance of the organization's technical core or its boundary-spanning units. They suggested that charismatic/transformational leadership was more likely to succeed in an ad hoc structure of temporary task groups or if the structure was simple and governed by a single entrepreneurial leader rather than by a complex bureaucracy. In the adaptive organization, leadership had to overcome resistance to change and to align the organization's members to new goals and values. If the emphasis was on efficiency, goal stability would be sought and more transactional leadership would be required. Transactional leadership was more prevalent when the technical core emphasized stability, standardization, and routinization. More transformational leadership is likely if the focus is on boundary spanning and keeping ahead of the external environment.

As the organization matures, so will the strategies of its leadership change (Biggart & Hamilton, 1987). Pellegrin (1953), Weinberg (1965), and Philipsen and Cassee (1965) observed that institutional requirements determine the characteristics of members who are accepted as leaders. It is apparent that the kind of leader who emerges in an organization and the individual who is successful as a leader and is evaluated as effective as a leader depends on the philosophy of the larger organization in which the leader's group is embedded. The philosophy influences the organization's directors. In turn, its effects move down to successively lower levels of management and contribute to the constraints that are imposed, the structures that are created, and the ways in which people are mobilized, resources are allocated, and performance is evaluated. These, in turn, affect the patterns of leader-member relations in the organization.

Organizational Philosophy

The organization's philosophy includes its assumptions, values, foci of attention, priorities, goals, and the techniques it promulgates to implement its efforts. Clearly, its philosophy and culture overlap and reinforce each other in determining what is the right thing to do and what is important and good. McGill and Slocum (1993) labeled the *knowing* organization as believing in the one best way to organize, to manage, and to get the job done; the *understanding* organization as making only those changes compatible with the organization's core values and culture; the *thinking* organization as identifying, analyzing, and fixing problems as they occur; and the *learning* organization as creating and fostering experimentation, open communication, constructive dialogue, and processing of experience.

Nonprofit Organizations. Carl and Stokes (1991) listed seven elements of value to the nonprofit organization: (1) workshops and formal educational experiences; (2) two-way feedback; (3) teamwork; (4) psychological recognition and rewards in the absence of unaffordable high salaries and bonuses; (5) high standards; (6) a well-functioning board of directors; and (7) high levels of collaboration with the private sector. Without the measure of profitability, nonprofits need to adopt indicators of success in their mission, service, and efficiency. Their accomplishments may be indicated by prevention and control of negative incidents, compliance with standards, timely delivery of services, fairness to access of services, public satisfaction with agency and service, and management of available resources (Gustafson, 1999).

For-Profit Organizations. Some firms concentrate their attention on their financial or physical resources in the search for long-run success. They may adopt Williamson's (1975) view of organizations as internal markets in which members are opportunistic and self-interested rather than trusting. Conflicts are resolved by fiat or costly bargaining. Some firms may concentrate on their intellectual capital and its exploitation at strategic and operational levels. They take advantage of the extent that knowledge grows exponentially. They can leverage their intellectual capital with a few top professionals who can multiply applications and development of knowledge at lower levels. They can foster intellectual challenges (Quinn, Anderson, & Finkelstein, 1996). Still other firms try managing meaning for their members to arouse their existential needs for satisfying self, family, and life. Attention is on aligning individual members' and the organization's goals (Sievers, 1986). The corporation of the twenty-first century may still be seen as legitimate, although scandals are eroding its social legitimacy. Many still vest it with more authority and influence than political party, church, or community. Corporations create, control, and distribute much of society's wealth (Ghoshal & Bartlett, 1997).

Scientific Management and Its Alternative. Frederick W. Taylor's (1911) *Scientific Management* described how production was to be accomplished in the organization. Work on the shop floor was to be subdivided into the smallest and simplest task units possible. Workers were to follow instructions as they were told by their supervisors, who similarly were given little discretion and were expected to be motivated by higher wages. Favored by Taylor were job specialization, short training requirements, and little autonomy. But the lesser-known Ernst Abbe (1900), at the Zeiss optical instruments company in Germany, formulated principles that involved employees in how work was to be done. Knowledge, legitimacy, and intrinsic motivation were emphasized, which better suited the firm's objectives of making the highest-quality instruments and developing new applications of science. To enable long-term growth of the firm, employees' skills were to be enhanced. Management decision making was to be rationalized. Progressive labor relations and enlightened social policies were stressed (Buenstorf & Murmann, 2003).

Social Capital. Social capital means different things to different writers (Santos, 2003). It may be the organization's resources, based on any of the following: reputation, entrepreneurship, exchange opportunities, networking, strategic alliances, public-private connections, performance-based trust, career opportunities, compensation plans, and favorable attitudes of its suppliers, clients, consumers, shareholders, managers, employees, and their families. It may refer to the quality of its human resources. The democratic practices of

McGregor's (1960) Theory Y have increased, but some firms are still ruled with an iron hand. Theory X is still in evidence.

Then there are Theory Z firms. Ouchi (1981) described Theory Z as the basis for Japanese management and recognized a number of U.S. firms, such as Procter & Gamble, IBM, and Hewlett-Packard, for following Theory Z in their own systems. These firms at the time were characterized by long-term employment, intensive socialization, and clear statements of objectives and values emphasizing cooperation and teamwork. Management policies to implement these approaches included slow promotion from within, the rotation of jobs, the creation of generalists rather than specialists, complex appraisal systems, emphasis on work groups rather than individuals, open communication, consultative decision making, and a relations-oriented concern for employees. In comparison to top-down, Theory X (authoritarian) organizations, Theory Z organizations are more decentralized and have flatter structures—fewer levels of management. When Roberts (1986) compared the reports of 97 managers in a Type Z business firm with those of 147 managers in a Type X organization, she found, not unexpectedly, that subordinates exercised more upward influence in dealing with their bosses in the Type Z than in the Type X organization.

According to Robbins (1983), although Theory Z gives the impression of greater equalization of power and control and "bottom-up" management, in fact, it actually has mixed effects on top management's power and control and, for the most part, increases rather than decreases its top managers' power and control. The decentralization and team decision making of Theory Z increase the equalization of power, but employee-organization lifelong commitments may increase employees' tolerance for what ordinarily might be subjects of complaints. The emphasis on good human relations may reduce constructive confrontation; generalist career development may reduce the ability to move to another company; and the flatter Theory Z organizations eliminate middle managers, who, in taller structured bureaucracies, for example, filter and control what information gets to top management. Interest in Theory Z and its practice declined with the 15-year recession of the Japanese domestic industries, which in 2006 appeared to be close to ending by 2007. Its export industries did not experience the same decline.

Differing Views of Organization. House (1991) presented a theory to explain how the distribution of power in a complex organization depends on the organization's environment, form, and the personal characteristics of its members. Organizations may be viewed as *rational-structural systems*. Metaphorically, in such a view, they are machines composed of interdependent parts, and leadership is a matter of specifying who does what for whom and why. A second view is that organizations are *extended families* with networks of relations and obligations. In this view, leadership is more concerned with relations, with the socialization and development of subordinates. A third view is that organizations are a *political system*, a jungle of coalitions and conflicts of interests. According to this view, leadership is based on power and the allocation of scarce resources. A fourth view of organizations is *symbolic*. It sees organizations as theaters, with members continually trying to play roles that communicate meaning to others about what is happening. In such a view, the leaders are artists and actors (Bolman, 1986).

Variations in 1,200 managers' and subordinates' perceptions of their organizations had systematic effects on the organizations' leadership styles. A factor analysis by Farrow (undated) of managers' and subordinates' descriptions of their organizations using the Bass-Valenzi Management Styles Survey found that the views could be factored as follows: (1) well managed (harmonious, clearly organized, orderly, clear task objectives, warm, and trusting), (2) amount of management (management activity, importance of external influences, commitment of members, interdependence of members and units, complexity of operations), (3) mechanistic (many organizational constraints, strong organizational structure, much routine work), (4) bottom-up (subordinate power, discretionary opportunities, independence of members, absence of routine work); (5) top-down (superior's power, superior's information). The frequency with which different styles of leadership appeared was related to the factored descriptions. For example, more consultative leadership was seen in well-managed firms, more directive leadership in top-down firms, and more participative leadership in bottom-up firms.

Effects of Stated Policies. The effects of stated organizational policies on a supervisor's use of reward and pun-

ishment were examined experimentally by Greenberg (1978) and Leventhal and Whiteside (1973), who found that experimental subjects rewarded low performers more when they were instructed to encourage high future performance than when they were instructed to reward on the basis of past performance.[9] Leventhal, Michaels, and Sanford (1972) found that experimental subjects who were given the policy of minimizing conflict allocated more rewards to low performers than did those subjects who were advised to ignore conflict. Landau and Leventhal (1976) reported that subjects who were required to retain only the best performers, compared to those who had to try to retain all workers, gave fewer rewards to low performers.

Moderation of Organizational Policies. Complicating matters was Liden and Graen's (1980) finding that the relationship between organizational policies and supervisors' behavior may be moderated by the severity of the policy and the supervisor's attributions of the causes of the subordinate's behavior. An experiment was set up so that subjects had to deal with a "subordinate" who had missed a production deadline. The failure to make the deadline was due to the subordinate in one experimental treatment and was outside the subordinate's control in the other treatment. Company policy was mild in one case and severe in the other. The mild policy required the supervisor to issue a verbal warning that the subordinate's pay would be docked if the deadline was missed again. The severe policy was to dock the subordinate for one day's pay. The results demonstrated that the subjects who acted as supervisors were more likely to follow the policy when the cause of missing the deadline was attributed to the subordinate than when it was attributed to a cause outside the subordinate's control and when the stated company policy was mild rather than severe.

In a field study, Hammer and Turk (1985) showed that when the management philosophy resulted in intentional pressure on 160 first-line supervisors by higher-ups to supervise strictly, there was a significant unique, negative correlation with the supervisors' attention to the maintenance of the work group. The supervisors' percep-

[9]As will be seen in Chapter 33, this use of rewards to energize future efforts appears to be more common in developing countries, such as Colombia and India, than in developed countries, such as the United States and Sweden (Ryterband & Thiagarajan, 1968).

tions of their authority to fire subordinates were also significantly affected.

Organizations' Phases and Life Cycles. Baliga and Hunt (1988) reviewed the literature on organizations' life cycles. Like organic organisms, they transit from one stage to another—from gestation to birth to growth to maturity and finally to revitalization or death. Each stage creates its own demands for constraints on, and choices in, the leaders' and managers' roles (Stewart, 1982). For instance, in the birthing phase, the demand is to establish the organization. Choices include selecting the needed resources, and constraints arise in obtaining them. The most effective leaders and managers fulfill demands with the least amount of resources and constraints. They create future favorable demands and the most future organizational slack. Decisions are cost-effective. A viable strategy is developed. Stakeholder confidence is maintained. Key personnel are recruited and committed to the organizational vision and objectives. Lower-level managers socialize their subordinates to the organization's goals and objectives and design information, control, and appraisal systems. They identify needed technology. Shamir and Howell (1999) suggested that charismatic leadership is most likely to emerge in the early stages in the organization's life cycle of birth and growth and again in the late stage of renewal.

Organizational Objectives and Functions. The values, beliefs, and rationales that make up an organization's philosophy affect and are affected by the organization's mission—its purposes and objectives and the functions it performs to accomplish its mission. In turn, the purposes and functions of an organization affect and are affected by its leadership. Systematic differences have been seen among departments of larger organizations, such as those concerned with manufacturing, personnel, finance, marketing, and R & D. Much has also been written about the different types of leadership that are required for different types of organizations and institutions to meet their systematically different purposes, functions, and membership. For instance, Shamir and Howell (1999) inferred that charismatic leadership is most likely to emerge and be effective when an organization's members face challenging and complex tasks. Such tasks require initiative, responsibility, creativity, and intense effort if the or-

ganization's goals are ambiguous and extrinsic rewards cannot be linked to performance. A number of person-situation examples have been observed in universities, schools, libraries, cooperatives, unions, and the military. Attention needs to be paid to the local organizational scene and what it requires for leadership.

Goals Differ by Functions. Goals depend on a manager's functions. C. G. Browne (1950a, 1950b, 1950c) and Dearborn and Simon (1958) found that top-ranking executives of a business firm tended to perceive organizational goals in terms of the functions of their own departments. Manufacturing managers believed that the quality of a product and keeping the costs of production low were goals that were important to the firm; sales and marketing managers saw effective advertising, customer service, and keeping the price of the product low as more important goals.

In a survey of British managers, Heller (1969a) found that those in personnel and general management functions typically used less directive procedures than did their colleagues in finance and production. Managers who led groups in purchasing, stores, and sales tended to be in between. This finding was consistent with earlier work by Fleishman, Harris, and Burtt (1955). They noted that supervisors in manufacturing departments or other departments that worked under time constraints were likely to receive higher merit ratings if they tended to initiate structure more often, while the reverse was true for supervisors in service departments. In addition, in non-manufacturing service departments with fewer time constraints, considerate supervisors were seen as more proficient. More supervisory initiation contributed to greater absenteeism and grievances mainly in manufacturing departments and to turnover in service departments.

Forbes (1985) divided a sample of 246 British and American managers according to their functional areas. He ranked the functional areas according to the presumed degree of uncertainty in the work as follows: personnel and training, R & D, sales and marketing, production, and finance and accounting. The more uncertainty in the function, the more managers reported concern for rules, use of authority, search for learning opportunities, and breadth of focus. An international sample of managers' interpersonal orientation was recorded in a data bank of results of simulated training exercises (Bass, Burger, et al., 1979). It involved human relations concerns, the ability to listen, trust in others, willingness to discuss feelings, tolerance of conflict, and acceptance of affection and feedback. Interpersonal orientation was higher for 123 managers in sales, marketing, personnel, and training—functional areas with more "people content" in the work to be done. It was lower for the 123 managers in the functional areas of finance, accounting, production, and R & D, where jobs were lower in people content.

Manufacturing versus Service. Manufacturing usually demands more routinization and coordination than do service functions. In a study of 787 managers, Child and Ellis (1973) found that managers in manufacturing organizations saw their roles as more formal, better defined, and more routine than did managers in service organizations. Consistent with this, Solomon (1986) found that Israeli firms that engaged in production, public or private, were more oriented toward performance-based rewards and to contingent rewarding than were public or private firms engaged in services.

Utilitarian versus Voluntary Organizations. Etzioni (1961) suggested that different dynamics of leadership would be at play in *utilitarian* organizations that produce goods or services than in normative organizations such as *voluntary* professional societies. Activity may be personally costly, and the rewards are different for office holding in voluntary organizations. Relations are likely to be more personal and informal in voluntary organizations (Walker, 1982). But the expected greater power differentials of the leaders and the led in utilitarian as compared to voluntary organizations did not surface in an interview and questionnaire survey by Pearce (1983). Pearce (1982) compared four volunteer organizations (newspaper, poverty relief, family planning, and fire department) with four counterpart organizations staffed by regular employees. Interviews with random samples in each organization concluded that the workers in the volunteer organizations were much more variable in their performance than were the employees of the utilitarian organizations. In the volunteer organizations, workers were much more likely to ignore their leaders and to work when they wanted and in the way they wanted. Paid employees of utilitarian organizations were more likely to work within the constraints of organizational policies and leaders' directives.

Leaders of voluntary organizations differed systematically from those in utilitarian organizations. In voluntary organizations, authority was invested in the membership as a whole. Their leaders were the representatives of the membership who could assume some of its authority. It was a bottom-up process. Volunteer followers reported having significantly more personal influence than did utilitarian employee followers. In the utilitarian organizations, employers had the authority to direct top-down to the leaders in the organization. Leaders in the voluntary organizations depended much more on their subordinates than did the leaders in the utilitarian organizations.

Leaders in voluntary organizations are likely to be reluctant to be too directive or controlling for fear of losing volunteers (LaCour, 1977). This reluctance results in their tendency to be relations-oriented (Rawls, Ulrich, & Nelson, 1973). But Kellogg and White (1987) suggested that matters are more complex. Volunteers exchange their time and service for social and psychic rewards such as recognition, worthwhile work, sense of belonging, socializing, and personal growth. The directiveness of volunteer leaders to facilitate the achievement of goals and the satisfaction of the volunteers' needs may be quite appropriate. Many volunteers are intrinsically motivated by their organizations' accomplishment of worthwhile purposes. In a survey study of 127 volunteers in 10 voluntary organizations, Kellogg and White (1987) found that, as expected, the leaders' relations orientation, in the form of support, contributed to the volunteers' satisfaction. But at the same time, directive role clarification by the leaders enhanced the volunteers' satisfaction with their work, more so if they originally were lower in intrinsic motivation. Presumably, such leaders gave more meaning and purpose to the work for those who were not particularly motivated by it initially. But specifying the work to be done did combine with high intrinsic motivation to promote the volunteers' satisfaction.

Some Illustrative Public Institutions

Governments, universities, schools, and libraries provide evidence of the extent to which organizational policies, purposes, and functions systematically relate to the leadership required.

Governments and Government Agencies. As with most long-standing institutions, governments have a history and sphere of operation of their own, apart from the constituencies they represent. Government institutions maintain ideals, values, and expert capacities across time. Although their constituencies can influence what the government does, the government may also affect the politics of its constituents and how they are represented (Hargrove, 1988).

Even more than in utilitarian organizations, leaders of government institutions, as well as their agencies and departments, are likely to be much more than rational actors pursuing calculated self-interest, knowing their preferences, and how to achieve them. Rather, they are strongly influenced by institutional norms, symbols, and rules that have developed historically. Activities may be carried out as a duty or obligation as well as for self-interest. Helping to maintain the institution may be seen as more important than helping to implement a particular policy. Leaders may have solutions that are looking for problems just as much as problems that are searching for solutions (March & Olsen, 1984). Civil servants, with expert and legitimate power, working within their own professional and institutional norms, may shape policies that depart considerably from a simple balancing of the interests of a diverse constituency (Heclo, 1974).

The leader, manager, or administrator in a government agency begins with a different overall mission than his or her counterpart in a private for-profit firm. The public agency survives as a function of its services in serving the public, legislatures, elected officials, and political power blocs. The private firm survives (if it is not subsidized by public money) by producing wanted goals, services, and profits that satisfy its owners, managers, employees, and community.

The public sector firm or agency differs from the private firm in its lack of dependence on its market, immunity from bankruptcy but not from deficit budgets, different legal and formal constraints, greater exposure to political influences, stronger relations with political authorities, greater exposure to public scrutiny, and greater accountability (Lachman, 1985). Also, executives of public organizations operate with more formalization and less autonomy in hiring, firing, and rewarding than do executives in the private sector (Rainey, 1983). But in an interview of 141 Israeli chief executive officers (40 public, 91 private), all engaged in production, the expected differences about political and market influences did not appear. Likewise, according to Kaminitz (1977) and Palgi (1984), differences in workers' participation in public versus private industries in Israel also failed to appear. As expected, however, satisfaction was lower for public sector than private sector leaders. An unexpected finding was that the CEOs of public firms had longer time spans of discretion. According to still another comparison of Israeli public and private businesses and industries, managers from private industries were more likely to consult coworkers when they needed help on their own jobs than were managers in government-owned firms (Erez & Rim, 1982). Solomon's (1986) survey of 240 top Israeli executives, half from the public and half from the private sector, found that the differences in perceptions and satisfaction were in line with expectations. There was much greater emphasis on contingent rewards in the private sector. Also, in the private sector, executives were more likely to promote efficient work methods, task clarification, and task autonomy.

Guyot (1962) compared 100 business managers with 147 public administrators. Contrary to expectations, the public administrators were higher in need for achievement and lower in need for affiliation than the business managers. They were equal in need for power. U.S. managers, like Israeli managers, have generally been more satisfied in the private sector. For example, managers in business organizations were seen to be better satisfied than those in military or governmental organizations (Porter & Mitchell, 1967).[10] Rainey (1979) found that, compared to business managers, governmental managers: (1) express weaker expectations of extrinsic reward for performance; (2) are lower on measures of satisfaction; (3) perceive rules about personnel and civil service regulations as constraints on incentives; (4) show no difference in role perceptions and motivation.

Farrow, Valenzi, and Bass (1980) compared the perceptions of managers in 250 profit-making and 95 nonprofit U.S. firms and agencies about their environment, organization, task, work group, and leadership styles. As

[10]See also Buchanan (1974); Paine, Carroll, and Leete (1966); Rainey (1983); and Rhinehart, Barrell, DeWolfe, et al. (1969).

noted earlier, those in the private sector reported significantly more economic and less political social influence on leader-subordinate relations than those in the public sector, but the same amount of legal influence. The felt constraints, and amount of order and structure were significantly higher in the public sector. The managers in the private sector reported more discretionary opportunities, more complex tasks, and more managerial activities. The managers in the public sector reported more routine work. The power of subordinates was seen to be higher in the public sector. Private sector managers, in comparison to public sector managers, saw themselves as more active as leaders. They perceived themselves to be more *directive*, negotiative, consultative, and delegative. These results differed from those of an Israeli survey by Chitayat and Venezia (1984), who reported that senior executives in business organizations displayed less direction and more participation than their counterparts in the public sector. As in all earlier studies, the U.S. managers were more satisfied with their own jobs and with their supervisors.

The Israeli kibbutz organization is a mix of service and production-oriented purposes and of utilitarian and normative character. Kibbutzim have strong social and political components. In a simulation study of the work performance of 135 first-level Israeli supervisors from the public and private sectors and from kibbutzim, the kibbutzim leaders, compared to those in the private sector, were most effective when they used direct group participation. Private sector leaders were most effective when they assigned goals; public sector leaders did best with participation from representatives (Erez, 1986).

Educational Institutions: American Universities. Universities contrast greatly with mainline utilitarian organizations and have been described as organized anarchies. According to Cohen and March (1974), who interviewed 42 university presidents, universities are likely to have problematic goals, unclear technologies, and fluid participation in decision making. Inertia is high. Most issues are of little consequence to the members as a whole. Decisions depend on who happens to be involved at the time they have to be made. There is a weak base of information available. Effective decision making in universities requires overcoming inertia by: (1) managing unobtrusively, (2) providing arenas for discussing a wide variety of problems, (3) facilitating the participation of opposing points of view, (4) persisting in attempts to accomplish objectives.

It makes a considerable difference to the leadership of a U.S. university if it is a rich private one or a less well-endowed public university. Roberts (1986) reported that the charismatic, inspirational style of leadership was more likely to be seen in 45 administrators in a rich private university than in 61 administrators in a counterpart public university that operated with fewer resources and had to be mainly transactional rather than transformational in leadership.

The leadership styles of administrators in university settings appear to differ from those of managers in business organizations. Roberts (1986) also compared 106 administrators from two universities with 244 managers from two businesses. She found that the administrators in the universities, in contrast to the business managers, reported using much more competitive impression management to create favorable impressions on others. This was done by working effectively behind the scenes by taking action without the relevant others' awareness.

Educational Institutions: European Universities. Drenth (1986) noted that European colleges and universities can be structured to provide more organization and less anarchy. The different structures impose different demands on the leadership. Before 1968, the European university was a collegial organization that tended to be run by a fraternity of scholars organized into autonomous departments. Decentralization, informality, and a low level of programming and standardization were intended to provide self-fulfillment and the achievement of personal objectives, particularly the objectives of the departmental chairpersons. The rector fulfilled primarily a ceremonial role, representing the university, chairing traditional sessions, and presiding at other ritual formalities. The rare central decision making was generally based on consensus. Trust, seniority, acceptability, and respect were more effective than managerial direction and task-oriented leadership.

After the student revolution of 1968, the European university emerged as a political organization in which the power of the individual autonomous chair holder was replaced by that of departmental boards with substantial representation by all layers of participants. The forming of coalitions and alliances and use of bargaining, delaying tactics, resistance, and procedural manipulation became normal parts of organizational decision making. Leadership required participation, negotiating, and conflict management, along with inventiveness and initiative.

Some European universities operate as traditional bureaucracies with standardized and formalized work processes, rules, and prescriptions. The influence of the technostructure is strong, with planning and regulation, forms and records, registration and control. The role of the leader involves timing the bureaucratic machinery and using the control systems available from the standardization of processes, output, and skills. Emphasis is placed on regulations and the routine handling of problems.

Almost opposite in organization are those universities, often newly created, whose structure remains simple. These universities emphasize the centralization of decision making and pay relatively little attention to the formalization and standardization of procedures. There is a sense of mission, an identification with common objectives, dependence on one person, and instability. The rector is often a dynamic, powerful, task-oriented individual with charismatic features.

Educational Institutions: Public Schools. Many studies of school principals and superintendents have been cited in the context of other leadership issues. This section summarizes what is known about the particular elements in the school principal's personality and situation that are of consequence to his or her leadership and administration and their effectiveness. Anecdotes and cases imply that "strong" leadership of a school enhances the effectiveness of the school, but there is no consensus on what is meant by either strong leadership or an effective school (Firestone & Wilson, 1985; Hoy & Ferguson, 1985). Dwyer (1984) interviewed and observed 42 "successful" principals but found no single factor that could account for the success of those principals. According to Goldberg (1984), however, as with transformational leaders in general, successful school leaders establish challenging expectations that force students and teachers alike to work harder to support a vision that they collectively adopt and whose implementation they share. For instance, in a case study of nine New York City elementary schools, Sweeney (1982) found a strong association

between the high expectations of the principal and staff and positive school outcomes.

Manasse (1984) reported that in effective school systems, principals build and shape their vision. Simultaneously, they involve the staff and students in the development and implementation of that vision and the expectations to support it. Morphet, Johns, and Reller (1982) argued further that by increasing followers' involvement and responsibility in the administration of the school, the principal can adopt a more positive, proactive role as a change agent. Less effective principals react to the demands and constraints in their school systems but do not create them (Firestone & Wilson, 1985). Effective principals indicate to their staffs and students the important and valuable goals for the school. They recognize individual differences not only in *what* individuals can learn but in *how* they learn (Cole, 1984). J. S. Brown (1970) compared 84 public school administrators with 63 business managers. The school administrators made choices in a simulation with lower payoff coupled with lower risk. They were lower in assessed initiative and achievement orientation but were no different from the business managers in decisiveness and self-assurance.

Libraries. Libraries are more circumscribed educational institutions with distinctive patterns of the emergent and successful leadership by their directors and departmental supervisors. Although service should be the main goal of libraries, the goal is in conflict with a sense of elitism and self-serving preservation (Sager, 1982). New information technologies to enhance the quality-of-service conflict with budgetary constraints, acquisitions of books, and political considerations. In addition, conflicts may arise between the libraries' two levels of employees, professional and clerical, whose interests may differ.

Dragon (1979) surveyed administrators in three large public libraries with the LBDQ and concluded that the directors and supervisors tended to be higher in initiating structure and lower in consideration than were their counterparts in many other types of organizations. Sparks (1976) found that library administrators, like most other leaders, saw themselves on the LBDQ as more considerate than their subordinates thought them to be. Consistent with this finding, Hall (1979) noted that students who were graduating from library school preferred consultation to more directive styles of leadership. In the same way, R. J. Solomon (1976) demonstrated that the directors of university library departments who earned higher leadership scores (according to their subordinates) led library departments that were more effective in serving other departments, according to the directors of the other library departments. On the basis of the results of administering the Jackson Personality Inventory and the Ghiselli Self-Description Inventory to library directors, Moore (1983) described several traits that are essential for success as an academic library director: flexibility and adaptability, willingness to accept change, a stable and equable temperament, emotional balance, and endurance.

Other Institutions

Other kinds of institutions have their own special effects on leadership. For instance, in hospitals and health clinics, in competition with the inside supervisors, outside physicians with expert power exert a strong influence on in-house administrators, nurses, and paraprofessionals, In prisons, the role of guards increases their authoritarian tendencies, tempered by the special exchange relationships that guards develop with inmates. In the military, technical readiness for combat competes with the maintenance of high-quality relationships for career advancement in a bureaucracy. Ulmer (1993) notes that army officers spend at least twice as much time in their career in training and education as their civilian counterparts. Promotion is always from within. Character is more important than expertise.

Many other organizations in both the public and private sectors, such as recreational cruise ships, circuses, extended families, clans, and friendship groups are subjects for leadership study. Some, like voluntary community organizations, require members who can establish relations across organizational boundaries and networks of unity in diversity. Values need to be shared, and a sense of mutual trust and obligation must be developed, along with a sense of responsibility for the community (J. W. Gardner, 1997).

Criminal Organizations. Much still needs to be known about the leadership of terrorist organizations such as the Islamic Al Qaeda. It is quite different in the way its leadership is organized: It does not need to maintain a specific organizational structure. Members appear and disappear. Any member with assets can find volunteers, support, prospects, and purposes. There is no command or control center, no set agenda. Small transient groups of zealots meet fairly openly in mosques and schoolrooms. Continuing aid may be provided from many divergent sources, ranging from governments to individuals. Founded by Osama bin Laden and still a powerful influence, it was more a "field of potential" rather than a tangible single structure of cells and agents. It became more like the nineteenth-century anarchist movement. It still had the potential to generate operational organizations such as schools, secret militias, and illicit financial institutions. Brutal suppression was required to deal with it (J. B. Bell, 2002). By 2006, efforts to suppress and splinter Al Qaeda further made it more of a philosophical, militant, Islamic movement and less of an active operational terrorist network although it can regenerate its most violent component at any time, in either the main body or in splinter groups.

Criminal organizations such as the Mafia, the Columbian drug gangs, the Japanese Yakuza, and the Crips and Bloods street gangs are widely publicized but are less often the study of formal leadership research. Developing better understanding of their nature may emerge from the principles of leadership extracted by Himsel (2004) about the fictitious Sopranos, the television Mafia family, and its leader, Joe Soprano.

Athletic Teams. Leadership by athletic coaches and managers has become an important subject for research in its own right (Maby & Brady, 1996). Coaching practices have been seen as dehumanizing and coaches as autocratic and insensitive (Hendry, 1974). Ogivie and Tutko (1966) found that more successful basketball, football, baseball, and track coaches rated themselves as aggressive, dominant, and inflexible as well as sociable, conscientious, open, trusting, and emotionally stable. Based on House's Path Goal Theory, Vos Strache (1979) showed that the leadership behavior of losing coaches failed to identify the path to success for team members. Chelladurai and Carron's (1978) multidimensional theory of sports leadership noted the need to distinguish between the coaching of players of individual and team sports. It suggested that the more the coach's behavior matched players' preferences, the better was their performance and satisfaction. The Leadership Scale for Sports was developed to test the theory (Chelladurai & Saleh,

1980). The contribution of the coach's leadership behavior to task and social cohesion of teams was demonstrated, along with the effect of the team on the coach's behavior (Westre & Weiss, 1991).

Labor Unions. Leadership research has tended to ignore labor and professional unions and important union leaders. The unions they led had major impact on our economic, political, and social environment as well as private organizations and public agencies. Their leadership shaped politics, modern industrial relations, the lives of their constituents, business, industry and public institutions. Among the most prominent of these leaders were Samuel Gompers, founder of the American Federation of Labor (AFL); Eugene V. Debs, U.S. Socialist Party candidate in five elections for U.S. president; William D. Haywood of the militant Industrial Workers of the World; John L. Lewis, cofounder of the Congress of Industrial Organizations (CIO); Sidney Hillman, cofounder and president of the Amalgamated Clothing Workers of America; César Chávez of the United Farm Workers; Philip Murray of the United Mine Workers; A. Philip Randolph of the Brotherhood of Sleeping Car Porters; Walter Reuther of the United Automobile Workers; and George Meany of the AFL-CIO (Dubofsky & Van Tine, 1987). While membership has declined a great deal in postindustrial United States, labor unions have been replaced to some extent by unions of government employees, schoolteachers, and agricultural workers.

Leadership and the Organization's Internal Environment

Leadership in organizations is affected by the organization's philosophy, size, structure, objectives, functions, complexity, and institutional characteristics. Additionally, some aspects of leadership in business, military, educational, and religious organizations may stem from the nature of the leader's organization.

Size of an Organization

The size of an organization was recognized early on as a variable that is of consequence to its leadership. The CEO of a hundred-person organization can get to know each member individually and act accordingly, but this is impossible in a thousand-person organization. Nevertheless, based on his experience leading both an army corps of 120,000 soldiers and a complex civilian organization of 120 professionals, Ulmer (1997) felt that both organizations required from him the same amount of energy to fulfill the role of leader.

The size of an organization can be gauged from the number of its members, the amount of its assets, and its output of product or services. Ordinarily, larger organizations require more structure to constrain the geometrically expanding possibilities of connections and interactions among the growing number of units and members.

CEOs' compensation is likely to be determined by the size of their operations, not by their profitability, particularly if their boards of directors are mainly members of the organization's management and shares in the firm are widely held by the public. Leading an infantry squad has different requirements from leading an infantry division. Emergent and appointed leadership within these respective organizations are likely to be systematically different. Erez and Rim (1982) found that compared to managers in smaller Israeli firms, those in firms with more than 600 workers turned more frequently to their coworkers for assistance on their own jobs. In firms with 600 to 4,000 workers, in contrast to larger or smaller firms, managers were most concerned with getting coworkers to do the jobs to which the coworkers were assigned. In firms with 4,000 to 6,000 workers, managers most often sought the assistance of their own bosses than did managers in the larger or smaller firms. And managers in firms with up to 600 employees were least likely to use rational tactics with their bosses compared with those in larger organizations.

L. W. Porter (1963a) reported that the overall satisfaction of managers was greater in large companies than in small ones. However, lower levels of management were better satisfied in small companies than in large ones. Higher levels of management were better satisfied in large companies than in small ones. But ElSalmi and Cummings (1968) found that small companies fulfilled the needs of top managers more than did large ones. For middle and lower managers, the reverse was true. Nonetheless, size was not the critical factor. Cummings and ElSalmi (1970) reported that the diversity of roles and the level of the position were more highly related to managers' satisfaction of their needs than was the size of the department or company.

Confounds. Size itself does not really make the difference. What matters is what size brings with it. Larger organizational size is ordinarily accompanied by a greater need for structural complexity, more filtered and delayed information, geometric increases in the number of dyadic and group relationships, greater social distance, and additional constraints on change. Although many correlations between organizational size and leadership can be singled out for attention, ordinarily they are discussed in the context of other related mediating variables. For example, Koene, Vogelaar, and Soeters (2002) examined the positive effect of charismatic, considerate, and structuring leadership of managers of 50 stores of a Dutch retail chain varying in size from 16 to 120 full-time "personnel equivalents." Managers' initiation of structure had little effect on store performance. In the larger stores, it was neutralized by the availability of structures, procedures and systems. Compared to the smaller stores, overall, larger stores showed better results and better organizational climate than smaller stores. Managers in small stores tended to display more leadership in the aggregate. Controllable costs were reduced by charismatic and considerate leadership mainly in the smaller stores. Organizational climate was particularly better under considerate leadership in the smaller stores. In the smaller stores, the manager was the center of communication and had one-to-one contact with employees. In the larger stores, the managers' charismatic and considerate leadership could influence only the organization's climate. In the same way, Friesen (1983) needed a combination of organizational size, organizational structure, and organizational auspices to account for subordinates' descriptions of leaders' behavior in 23 public and private mental health agencies. The Dover Corporation was divided into many small independent autonomous corporations to provide flexible response to customers, a fair system of compensation, fast decisions, more satisfied managers and employees, and the elimination of corporate politics (G. D. Smith & Sobel, 1989)

Downsizing. It seems logical that when revenues slacken, shrinking the size of the firm will reduce its costs.

The payrolls of managers and their staffs can be reduced if the organizational hierarchy is flattened or delayered. But Cascio (1995, 2003) has demonstrated that such involuntary shrinkage may be more costly in many ways, compared to available alternatives. The immediate savings in wages and salaries are offset directly by the increased costs of severance pay and bonuses, accrued vacation and sick pay, pension and benefit payoffs, and administrative processing costs. Indirect costs are the lowered morale, loss of commitment, increased insecurity, and reduced productivity of the remaining workforce, increased employment tax rates, and potential discrimination suits. Additionally, there is the cost to families and the community. When a turnaround in the economy or market occurs, new costs are incurred in recruiting, employing, and training new hires. A lot of experience and knowledge will have been lost. Employee turnover cost 1.5 to 2.5 times an employee's annual salary at Merck, a pharmaceutical company (J. Solomon, 1988). At the same time, in 25 large companies over a seven-year period, the expected improvements in financial performance failed to materialize from downsizing (Cascio & Morris, 1994). On the other hand, firms that dealt with declines in demand by instituting *responsible restructuring* instead of downsizing illustrated that financial as well as social benefits accrue from avoiding downsizing. For instance, faced with a seasonal decline, instead of laying off employees, Brooks Beverage Management maintained their benefits and arranged for their transfer to Haworth, a nearby furniture manufacture. In the 1990s, Ford Motor Co. delayered and flattened its organizational hierarchy without layoffs by realigning its worldwide automotive processes and management as well as by instituting early retirement plans. But in 2006 as SUVs fell out of favor, Ford had to plan to close plants with a total of 30,000 employees by 2009. Chase Manhattan Bank changed its organizational culture to increase its efficiency and use of its resources through teamwork across departmental boundaries. The Eaton manufacturing corporation, instead of downsizing, introduced continuous improvement, involving its employees in cost control. IBM arranged, with other firms, buyouts of whole plants and their labor force that no longer fit IBM's business strategy to other firms and management groups. Employment continued under new managements. The United Steelworkers helped firms reduce immediate labor costs without downsizing by agreeing to contracts with significant wage reductions in exchange for employee stock ownership plans (ESOPs). Intel was able to redeploy employees rather than lay them off, using development centers, self-assessment tools, career counseling, temporary assignments, and skill training. Employees were thus enabled to transfer within Intel from manufacturing to sales and from obsolete technology divisions to new centers. Outplacement services were also provided when internal transfer was not feasible. Between 1991 and 1994, Intel placed 90% of its employees through internal redeployment. Finally, in times of sales declines, days worked per month can be reduced and unpaid voluntary leaves of absence (with state unemployment benefits) can be encouraged to reduce costs temporarily. This was done by the Reflexite Corporation (Cascio, 1995).

Structure and Formalization

Many more obvious differences in leadership patterns occur in organizations that differ substantially in size. One striking difference is how much relationships have to become more structured and formalized in larger organizations. As Robbins (1983, pp. 70–71) noted, "Decision making is different for an organization (of) ninety thousand employees than . . . ninety . . . As size increases, so does departmentalization, job specialization, the height of the structure, the number of horizontal units, and the number of rules and regulations."

On the basis of empirical factor studies, Pugh, Hickson, Hinings, and Turner (1968) developed the Aston model. The model included two major organizational factors: structuring of activities (prescribed work roles) and centralization of decision making (limits on discretion). These factors represented the two principal strategies of administrative control. Both usually increase as an organization enlarges.

Along with increasing size, the routineness of operations also leads to greater standardization and structuring of relations. Convenience food restaurants represent the ultimate in routine service, accompanied by a high degree of standardization and structure. In addition, as was noted earlier, stable, predictable environments permit organizations to formalize and structure themselves to a higher degree than those in unstable or uncertain environments.

Chapin and Tsouderos (1955) concluded from the case histories of 91 organizations that as organizations increase in size and differentiation, rank-and-file members become more passive and farther removed from the policy-making centers. Likewise, the executives become farther removed from the activities they plan and initiate. The long lines of command impose problems in communication. Robbins (1983) noted that structure also reflects the needs of the top leaders of the large organization to maintain maximum control over it. As a consequence, a bureaucratic structure is favored, with specialized jobs, standardization, rules and regulations, and centralized decision making. But as was mentioned before, even when the top managers favor a more humanistic organizational philosophy, such as with Theory Z, they may do so because they can still maintain their desired power and control. Compliance can be maintained through commitment at the lower levels rather than through sanctions. Middle managers do not have to be dominated; they can be eliminated.

Katz and Allen (1985) illustrated the importance of structure in a study of the 86 R & D teams embedded in matrix managements in nine firms. The performance of these teams was best when their project manager had more organizational influence and their functional boss had more influence over the technical details of their work. Their performance was also better when the team members perceived that the project manager and the functional manager had equal influence over their salaries and promotions. Lanzetta and Roby (1955) contrasted antiaircraft crews of three men, each performing all functions, with the crews arranged in a hierarchical structure. They found that the performance of crews improved with the structure in place, particularly when the workload was heavy. Results also depended on how relations are structured within a group. Naylor and Dickinson (1969) observed that arranging the way the task was to be carried out, but not distributing the work components among the group members, was positively related to the effectiveness of the group.

Organizational Design. In designing an organization, a balance needs to be struck among three variables: centralized control, decentralized autonomy, and cooperation and teamwork. Control and cooperation need to be balanced between consistency and flexibility. Cooperation and autonomy need to be balanced between synergy and accountability. Autonomy and control need to be balanced between distant and local perspectives (Keidel, 1990).

Utilitarian organizations are usually designed according to functions and products, or a mix of the two. In a functionally designed production organization, people are grouped into units such as marketing, manufacturing, R & D, human resources, finance, and accounting. A functional service agency is similar. Client relations and consulting are substituted for manufacturing. The functional organization is expected to make efficient use of scarce resources, to better develop its personnel, and to centralize decision making. Its disadvantage is the creation of logic-tight silos of thinking, slower responses to change, and too much top-down direction. Units are grouped by products (or services) in product design, e.g., men's wear, women's wear, and children's wear. Coordination is better across necessary functional skills but not as good across product units. Organizational rather than functional goals are stressed. Control over diverse products or services is better. However, there is duplication of resources.

In a mixed design, such as the *matrix* organization, the manager of the product must obtain necessary resources from functional specialties. But there is better utilization of the needed specialists. On the other hand, the specialist needs to satisfy two bosses at the same time: the product manager and the specialties manager (Hughes, Ginnett, & Curphy, 1993).

Hierarchical Level. Efforts to change organizations are expected to flow through hierarchical levels (Griffin & Mathieu, 1997), usually from the top down but sometimes starting with initiatives from the bottom or the middle. A leader high in the hierarchy and at a social distance from followers needs to be visionary to be seen as charismatic, but a leader lower in the hierarchy and closer to followers needs to be considerate to be seen as charismatic (Shamir, 1995). At higher organizational levels, charismatic leaders rely on image building, strategic envisioning, rhetorical skills, and symbolic activities to influence followers; at lower levels, role modeling and building confidence and a collective identity become salient (Shamir & Howell, 1999). Along with transformational leadership, information technology firms also have need of transactional leadership at higher and middle levels to create structures and systems to deal with knowledge (Stross, 1998).

Pence and Dilts (2003) compared the survey responses of 32 project managers and their 24 senior executives about decisions to terminate a project. The *sunk cost bias* (the tendency to want to continue a project once an initial investment of money and effort has been made) of the 32 project managers was driven by their own personal efforts. The executives, who heavily weighed their initial expectations, revealed more of a *hindsight bias* (the tendency to distort a previous judgment in the direction of new information).

Structural Clarity. An important role for leaders is to provide structural clarity for their followers. E. E. Smith (1957) studied experimental groups in which both productivity and satisfaction were found to be related to the degree of role clarity of the members. Similarly, Lenski (1956) noted that group members with low degrees of *status crystallization* tended to experience difficulty in establishing effective, satisfying patterns of interaction with others. Dyer and Lambert (1953) observed that bomber wings were more efficient when members had a clear recognition of the status structure. In a study conducted by the Life Insurance Agency Management Association (1964a), it was found that agents who reported that the job was accurately described before they were hired were less likely to quit than those who had been less clearly informed. Similarly, Wanous (1973) showed that newly recruited telephone operators who were told both the good and the bad about the job were less likely to quit than those who were told only about the good aspects. After a study in two companies, Trieb and Marion (1969) agreed that the extent to which new employees had been fully oriented to their jobs was highly related to the employees' subsequent job satisfaction and loyalty to their companies.

Timing and Need for Structure. Kinder and Kolmann (1976) found that self-actualization gained from sensitivity training groups[11] was greatest when leaders' and members' roles were highly structured at first and less structured later on. Similarly, Bridges, Doyle, and Mahan (1968) found that hierarchically undifferentiated groups were more effective than differentiated groups in the analysis of problems but not in the synthetic phases of problem solving. Ambrose and Schminke (2003) ob-

[11] See Chapter 34.

tained the responses of 506 individuals from 98 departments in 64 organizations. They indicated the extent, on a seven-item survey of Khandwalla (1976–1977), to which their organization was *mechanistic* or *organic*. As expected, effects were somewhat stronger in mechanistic than organic organizations; perceived organizational support correlated .52 and .53 respectively, with perceived procedural and distributive justice.

Individual Differences. Some leaders work better in unstructured situations, while others work better in structured ones. According to Maas (1950), leaders who projected blame on others exhibited a desirable behavioral change when they led relatively informal, unstructured groups. On the other hand, leaders who absorbed blame showed the desirable change when they led formal, structured groups. When placed in reversed situations, both types of leaders exhibited anxiety and signs of stress. Overall, highly structured organizations, both public and private, were expected to determine the types of individuals to work within them. Individuals who choose to join such bureaucracies are also particular types of individuals. Most important, highly structured organizations socialize those who work within them.

Bureaucratic Leadership. In line with Weber's arguments about bureaucracies (1924/1947), Merton (1940) suggested that bureaucrats are likely to be inflexible. They are likely to overemphasize the importance of goals for those whose attainment the rules were established. The goals will be displaced by attention to outmoded rules. When bureaucratic leaders are inflexible, actions will continue to be bound by inapplicable rules. The career orientation of bureaucrats makes them cautious, conservative, and protective of an entrenched position. They are unwilling to be innovative or to take risks. They are impersonal in their thinking and ignore the concerns of clients and their individuals needs. Their formal authority breeds arrogance. Furthermore, the selection and socialization processes induce a bureaucratic personality without a sense of personal identity. There is little intrinsic interest in work and uncompromising adherence to rules (Bensman & Rosenberg, 1960).

While the above descriptions of bureaucrats fit the conventional wisdom about them, Goodsell (1983) marshaled considerable evidence to support a contrary argu-

ment: bureaucrats are human, too. In fact, citing Kohn's (1971) structured interview study of 3,101 men working in public and private bureaucratic organizations, men who worked in bureaucratic firms and public agencies were more, not less, self-directed than those who worked in nonbureaucratic firms and agencies. They were more open-minded, had more personally responsible standards of morality, were more receptive to change, and showed greater flexibility in dealing with problems. In explaining why Weber's, Merton's, and Bensman and Rosenberg's expectations about the bureaucratic mind were unsupported, Kohn suggested that bureaucratic organizations tend to select better-educated personnel, who are challenged to a great degree by their assignments and whose education makes for greater intellectual flexibility. Also, within the bureaucracy, they are freer from arbitrary actions by their superiors.

Structural Complexity. The more an organization increases in age, size, and structural differentiation, the more complex it becomes. More specialization develops within it. Special staffs that often have different interests arise. More political behavior becomes necessary, requiring more compromise and accommodation. Decision making and implementation processes also become more complicated (Thompson, 1967). As the complexity of the organization increases, the dynamics within it must change. For example, the number of possible coalitions increases. The greater an organization's complexity, the more leadership positions are required. The positions will be arranged hierarchically, with carefully delineated roles and responsibilities. Additional power is attached to each position that is higher in the heirarchy (Bryson & Kelley, 1978).

The complexity of the organization will affect the pattern of succession.[12] The greater the complexity, the more levels any candidate needs to climb to reach the top of the hierarchy. Complexity probably also has an effect on the nature of accession to office. As complexity increases, so does factionalism (Tichy, 1973; Tushman, 1977). A structurally complex organization, such as a major corporation, gives rise to officials who are oriented more toward Theory X in their outlook and who are more concerned than usual about their need for safety and less

---

[12] See Chapter 30.

concerned about ego and self-actualizing needs (Applebaum, 1977).

Hunt, Osborn, and Martin (1979, 1981) completed a line of investigation of that part of a leader's behavior that is required—that is, determined by the structured relationships imposed by the organization—and that part which is discretionary. In a study of 68 army telecommunication units, they found that greater complexity in the structure of the unit coincided with more discretionary leadership to improve role clarity and provide support. However, such discretionary leadership did not deal with work assignments or with rules and procedures. In addition, the amount of discretionary leadership correlated with both performance and satisfaction. At the same time, the role clarity required from the leadership correlated .25 with the subordinates' involvement in their jobs and $-.24$ with subordinates' intentions to quit (Osborn & Hunt, 1979)

Tall versus Flat Structures. Flat-structured organizations have few hierarchical levels and many members or units at each level; tall-structured organizations have many more levels but fewer members or units at each level. Findings are mixed about the relative effects of tall and flat structures. Worthy (1950) maintained that flat-structured organizations resulted in greater satisfaction of employees than did tall-structured organizations. Richardson and Walker (1948) studied a company (IBM) when the number of vertical levels of organization was reduced and concluded that the reduction of social distance between the management and workers resulted in improved satisfaction and teamwork. Ghiselli and Johnson (1970) obtained some support for Worthy's contention by showing that satisfaction of the needs for esteem, autonomy, and self-actualization was higher in the flat than in the tall organizations they studied. However, satisfaction of the needs for security and social relationships did not differ in the two types of organizations. At the same time, ElSalmi and Cummings (1968) found that at the top levels, tall structures produced less fulfillment than did flat or intermediate structures. For lower levels, tall structures resulted in greater fulfillment.

In an analysis of experimental organizations with tall and flat structures, Carzo and Yanouzas (1969) found that tall structures required more time to process decisions, but flat structures required more time to coordinate

efforts and resolve conflicts. However, tall organizations were superior in profits and rate of return. Porter and Lawler (1964) and Porter and Siegel (1965) surveyed managers in tall or flat organizations that varied in size. In small organizations, the satisfaction of managers was greater in flat than in tall structures, but the findings were reversed for large companies (with more than 5,000 employees). Generally, tall organizations yielded greater satisfaction of security and social needs, while flat organizations gave greater satisfaction of self-actualization. But structure was not at all related to satisfaction of the needs for esteem and autonomy. Esser and Strother (1962) found no relationship between the orientation toward rules by managers and the size or flatness of their organization.

Span of Control. Another way of looking at the effects of tall and flat structures is by examining the effects of the average number of subordinates supervised by each manager. Each manager must supervise many more subordinates in a flat structure than in a tall structure.[13] For example, Kipnis and Cosentino (1969) found that as the supervisory span of control of 131 supervisors from five manufacturing firms increased, the number of official warnings the supervisors used to correct employees' undesirable attitudes and behavior also increased. Goodstadt and Kipnis (1970) experimentally manipulated the leaders' span of control so that subjects were led to believe they were supervising either three or eight subordinates. The subjects who believed they were supervising eight subordinates spent significantly less time talking to problem workers and threatened to fire them on earlier trials than did subjects who believed they had only three subordinates. Likewise, Ford (1981) found that when supervisors had larger departments to manage, subordinates felt they were shown less consideration by their supervisors. These results are all consistent with the expectation that when faced with a larger number of subordinates who are reporting directly to them, supervisors will be forced to reduce the amount of time they can spend individually with each subordinate. Although it may be possible to remedy the situation with more group meetings, delegation, and the granting of more autonomy, as was seen in the three just-cited studies, management by ex-

[13] See Van Heet (1983) for a further discussion of span-of-control research.

ception often emerges. With a large span of control, the supervisor tends to concentrate on deviations from standards in efforts to remedy the situation.

Leavitt and Whisler (1956) first recognized that organizational hierarchies would be flattened into shorter structures with wider spans of control as a consequence of the introduction of computers. They forecast that middle management was likely to shrink, as in fact it did in the next half century. A national survey of Australian employers by Littler, Hede, Bramble, et al. (1995) found that 44% of firms had cut out layers of managers, particularly middle managers. One CEO remarked that "Middle managers'... main effect is to stuff up the business" (p. 2). The flattening organizations were seen to make careers "shorter, sharper and harder." Career laddering was less prevalent. There was less long-term security in a one company career. Flattened organizations represent a particular challenge to first-line supervisors. For instance, they may have more difficulty dealing with an ethical question, as they are faced with less guidance from a distant impersonal senior management (Sims, Veres, Jackson, et al. 2001).

New Organizational Configurations. Quinn-Mills (1991) proposed a self-managing workforce that could use available technologies of production and service to replace the usual organizational hierarchy, even if flattened. They suggested introducing a flexible, adaptive, semipermanent, residual hierarchy and clusters of 30 to 50 employees from different disciplines working in subclusters of five to seven without direct reporting relationships. Leadership would be rotated depending on competence. Members would be responsible and accountable to their cluster or subcluster linked through employee contacts and with the firm through the residual hierarchy. As with Bennis's (1959) *adhocracy,* Gerstein and Shaw (1992) agreed on the need for fluid, transitory organizations that form teams of participants to meet the requirements of different situations with freedom and authority to optimize their work processes. Furthermore, Doloff (1999) argued that rather than depending on job titles and the formal hierarchy of formal channels and protracted process, one must attend to the informal network to determine who is really making the decisions and advancing the work to be done. And Ellerman (1999) advised that much more than codified

knowledge transmitted top-down is needed in the new circumstances. More implicit knowledge must be transferred horizontally.

Centralization versus Decentralization

Centralization implies that more leadership accrues in the headquarters, nucleus, or central authority of the organization and fewer decisions are possible in the peripheral units. Centralization promotes greater coordination of efforts and activities among the units, and more uniform policies with respect to the common goals of the larger organization. It makes possible a more rapid, concerted reaction of the whole organization. Centralization or decentralization may be a consequence rather than a cause. Blau (1968) investigated 250 government agencies and found that decentralization was most prevalent in agencies that employed a large number of highly qualified personnel. On the other hand, the presence of automation and poorly qualified personnel in large agencies was accompanied by more vertical levels of organization and tighter managerial control. Centralization of legislative leadership was seen by Bryson and Kelley (1978) as being likely to give greater enforcement power to the leadership and more stability. But more conflicts are also likely because of reduced consultation and a lack of information sharing. (A. Rosenthal, 1974). Consensual decision making becomes less frequent with centralization (Mechanic, 1962; Pettigrew, 1972). Adversarial relationships are greater (R. A. Gordon, 1961), unless statesmen appear at the top of the centralized leadership (Selznick, 1951). Centralization promotes coups (S. Kahn, 1970).

Baker and France (1954) examined the personnel and industrial relations departments of a sample of firms. They observed that top managers tended to prefer the decentralization of industrial relations functions so that local problems arising in a specific plant could be solved as they arose. Union officials, on the other hand, preferred the centralization of industrial relations functions as an aid in industrywide bargaining. M. Whitehill (1968) surveyed companies in the meatpacking industry and found that union negotiations with centralized structures by means of contacts with the main office resulted in more benefits for employees than did negotiations with decentralized structures involving contacts with local plants.

Decentralization usually brings with it more opportunity for its leaders to react quickly and flexibly to opportunities and threats to the organization. Less filtering of information can occur that is of consequence to the decisions made by the decentralized units. The decentralized organization is more likely to adopt an open learning philosophy and recognize the need to invent local adaptations of best practices. It can experiment with new ideas more readily than can the centralized organization (Ellerman, 1999). More "ownership," sense of responsibility, and commitment are expected for the decentralized-designed organization.

But there are costs to decentralization. Kanter (1982a) described decentralized units that were so concerned about operating issues that their definition of "long range" was the next quarter. T. A. Mahoney (1967) surveyed 283 organizations, obtaining managers' perceptions on 114 variables. Decentralization was found to be correlated negatively with most criteria of organizational effectiveness. In a survey of 217 executives in 109 firms, Stagner (1969) found that the decentralization of business enterprises was not related to profitability from sales. However, profitability from capital was significantly higher in centralized than in decentralized firms. Nevertheless, Newman and Summer (1961) outlined a set of guides for determining the degree of decentralization that is desirable for an organization, and W. T. Morris (1967) formulated 40 propositions, along with a set of mathematical models, for evaluating the factors involved in the consequences of decentralization.

Dispersion of Authority and Power. Dispersion of authority and power and empowerment to the lowest possible hierarchical levels is made possible with suitable selection and training of personnel (Conger & Kanungo, 1988). To further the possibilities and potential of empowerment, organizational policies can promote emphasis on self-determination, collaboration, and high performance standards (House, 1988). Furthermore, empowering organizations provide loosely committed resources at operational levels, opportunities for networking, and open communication systems (Kanter, 1983). But such policy is not necessarily dependent on decentralization, although it is more easily facilitated by senior managers when they work through the fewer layers of authority of the decentralized organization (Cordiner, 1952; Newman & Logan, 1965; Zald, 1964). Thus, decentralization has been advocated as a method for reducing the concentration of authority in high-level positions and for filtering it down to employees (Kline & Martin, 1958; Kruisinga, 1954). However, the major reason that managers are motivated to decentralize is that they are concerned about coordination problems. As organizations become larger, with many geographically dispersed subunits involving numerous products, the problems of coordination and response to local changes induce a tendency toward decentralization (Chandler, 1956, 1962). Globalization of organizations has probably increased their decentralization, although information technology has made more centralization possible. Mergers and acquisitions have also probably increased decentralization in the enlarged corporations.

Legitimate power is usually disseminated outward when an organization decentralizes. The effects were seen by Baum (1961), who studied the U.S. Civil Service Commission and eight other dependent federal agencies. The commission formulates and enforces policies that must be applied by the agencies in hiring and promoting personnel. Baum found that the decentralization of hiring and promotion were handled effectively only when the agencies accepted and attempted to comply with the policies of the controlling commission. Executives in the more successful agencies regarded decentralization as providing them with the authority they deserve, but the executives in the less successful agencies saw the decentralized function as more work for them. In Baum's study, decentralization was accompanied by an increase in the decision-making authority of those in the higher levels of administration. Likewise, M. W. Meyer's (1968) survey of 254 city, county, and state departments of finance found that with the size of the organizations held constant, the number of organizational subunits decreased, but the number of levels of supervision within the subunits increased with the decentralization of decision making. Most important, decentralization was associated with more rules for the evaluation of decisions.

Stable versus Dynamic and Changing Organizations

The importance of organizational stability was seen to vary according to the size of organizations. England (1976b) reported that managers of middle-sized companies rated organizational stability generally higher in importance than did managers of small companies. Stability was of least importance to managers of large firms.

Using data from 215 governmental departments, M. W. Meyer (1975) found that the stability of an organization's structure was lower when the leaders had changed a great deal in the past, when leaders were dependent on a higher authority, and when the leaders maintained close contact with their superiors. The top managements of stable firms were found by T. Burns (1957) to differ from those of firms that were growing. Burns (1957) collected diaries for three to five weeks from 76 British top managers in medium-sized companies. Top managers in expanding firms spent relatively more time in discussions with one another. There was less flow of information up and down the hierarchical structures in the growing than in the stable firms. Again, Kerr (1985) demonstrated, in 89 interviews about the managerial compensation systems of 20 large industrial firms, that compensation was hierarchically based in the stable, steady-state firms that were committed to existing products and markets. On the other hand, compensation was more likely to be performance-based in less stable "evolutionary" firms that were involved in acquisitions, mergers, and joint ventures, sometimes in unfamiliar external markets and technologies.

House (1995) noted that employee commitment to unstable organizations in environments of uncertainty was higher when the organizations were led by charismatic leaders. Again, Bass (1998) reported that transformational leadership ratings were higher in dynamic, changing organizational environments than in stable organizations. But Hinken and Tracy (1999) concluded from a modeling analysis of the Multifactor Leadership Questionnaire that while the transformational leadership factors of inspirational motivation, intellectual stimulation, and individualized consideration are generally relevant for organizational performance improvement, the factor idealized influence (charismatic leadership) may be limited in relevance to unstable organizations, if at all. They were in agreement with Bennis and Nanus (1985), who did not find in interviews that otherwise transformational leaders were charismatic.

Leaders' Latitude and Constraint in Organizations

Managers have considerable supportive latitude to act within boundaries and rules but must also operate under many organizational constraints that will systematically affect their styles of behavior, performance, and satisfaction. The various task-related, interpersonal, and policy barriers to getting work done are also constraints that affect supervisors' style, performance, and satisfaction. Also constraining are the extent to which organizations require secrecy, restrict employees from bypassing the chain of command, and are scarce in resources. Latitude and constraint often create conflict. Managers must keep both broad and specific objectives in mind; plan, but be flexible; centralize some activities and decentralize others; and provide subordinates with autonomy. Collaboration and maintaining control is expected, yet delegation is to be practiced.

Organizational Support. Approximately 370 recent graduates of a Belgian university responded to a mail survey. If the organization in which they were working was supportive, they were more likely to see their supervisor as representing their organization (Sucharski, 2002). Among 263 manufacturing supervisors and employees working in a Fortune 100 Best Company, perceived organizational support contributed to job dedication and interpersonal communications. The effects were mediated by job satisfaction and affective commitment (Muse & Stamper, 2003). Among 185 pharmaceutical sales representatives, perceived organizational support mediated the effects of situational factors on affective commitment to the organization. The factors included procedural and distributive justice, and satisfaction with communication and supervision and the labor-management climate. (Moideenkutty, Blau, Kumar, et al., 2001).

Organizational Constraints. Hare (1957) observed that self-oriented and group-oriented leaders among groups of boys did not differ in aggression at an adult-supervised playground at school, but self-oriented leaders were significantly more aggressive in unsupervised neighborhood play conditions. There were more differences between the situations than between the leadership styles. Disagreement was higher in both styles on the supervised playground, while tension and antagonism were higher in the unsupervised neighborhood play conditions. Similarly, Farrow, Valenzi, and Bass (1980) found that the leadership styles of direction and consultation were greater when more organization, order, and imposed constraints were present. But less manipulation by leaders was observed under these conditions if goals were clear and levels of trust among the members were high.

Leadership and patterns of social interaction in an organization will be affected by how difficult or easy it is for its members to identify with the organization and its purposes and what outsiders believe about it (Dutton, Dukerich, & Harquail, 1994). According to Fukuyama (1997, p. 156), "managers . . . instill a . . . sense of pride in their employees, [and that] they are part of something larger than themselves. People feel . . . motivated to do their share if . . . their company's purpose is . . . to push back the frontiers of knowledge rather than . . . to maximize their stockholders' return on equity."

Peters and O'Connor (1980) identified a number of situational variables likely to interfere with supervisors' accomplishment of tasks, such as lack of ready availability of materials and supplies. Laboratory studies confirmed the importance of this factor to job satisfaction and getting the work done (Peters, Fisher, & O'Connor, 1982). Field studies yielded more complex results. From an open-ended questionnaire, completed by 300 national managers of a chain of convenience stores, O'Connor, Peters, Pooyan, et al. (1984) identified 22 organizational constraints on the managers' work. Some of these constraints included: (1) shortage of help; (2) lack of authority to enforce company standards; (3) bypassed authority; (4) insufficient training; (5) inadequate equipment; (6) inadequate help; (7) frequent, long, and inappropriate meetings; (8) excessive paperwork; (9) unscheduled activities; (10) ignorance of company policies and procedures; (11) an inadequate amount of merchandise; (12) lack of job-related information; (13) inadequate response time and budgetary support; (14) inappropriate work space; (15) unkept appointments; (16) excessive or wrong inventory; (17) insufficient materials and supplies; (18) theft by customers and by employees; (19) work overload; (20) wrong inventory. For a sample of 1,450 first-, second-, and third-level managers of the chain of convenience stores, the investigators obtained a correlation of −.40 between the managers' satisfaction with supervision and the extent to which they perceived overall

that these constraints were operating in their work settings. These relations held for all three levels of management, although, as expected, satisfaction with supervision was greater at each successive level of management. In the same way, Mathieu, Tannenbaum, and Salas (1992) developed a 10-item instrument that measured the situational constraints perceived by the leader, such as the leader's need to correct others' mistakes, which correlated −.33 with sales performance and −.36 with the quality of leader-member relations (LMX). Nevertheless, Shamir and Howell (1999) hypothesized that charismatic leadership was more likely to emerge when the technology in a situation was difficult to analyze.

Along with institutional constraints, an important constraint on a mental health care staff was the lack of collegial support (Corrigan, Kwartarini, & Pramana, 1992). Situational constraints may place managers under a double handicap. In addition to making their assignments more difficult, the managers may also be appraised as performing less adequately than is justified by the objective evidence. Steel and Mento (1986) investigated the impact of situational constraints (job-induced obstacles, interpersonal obstacles, environmental policy, and procedural constraints) on objective performance. Also obtained were supervisors' appraisals and self-ratings of 438 branch managers of a finance company. The constraints were highly intercorrelated and formed a single factor scale. The district manager's supervisory appraisals of the branch managers correlated −.36 with the situational constraints faced by the managers. That is, the more constraints faced by the branch managers, the lower the appraisals they earned. But the constraints had little actual effect on the objective performance of the managers except possibly on their ability to control past due accounts.

Requirements of Secrecy. Required secrecy has impaired communications within and between government agencies in the struggle against terror and crime. A constraint that limits whether managers can be participative with their subordinates is the extent to which the organization requires secrecy concerning products, techniques, and business strategies. Employees cannot be asked to participate in decisions if much of the information required to discuss such decisions cannot be revealed to them (Tannenbaum & Massarik, 1950). Pay secrecy is justified by privacy concerns, by the potential reduction of labor mobility, and by a desire to avoid conflict. But that secrecy may be at the expense of an unwarranted sense of injustice and impaired performance (Colella, Zardkoohi, Paetzold, et al. 2003). Also, some evidence is available to suggest that "open-book" management may be more efficacious than maintaining secrecy. When a campus newspaper of a public university listed the salaries of all its professors (which was actually available for the asking), overall the effect was positive on faculty and students in providing a realistic picture rather than an exaggerated one. Goitein (2004) described the positive effects of open-book management practiced by the employee-owned Springfield ReManufacturing Corporation. Employees were educated about the financial requirements for success and the operational variables critical to meeting the financial requirements. Progress in doing so was shared. For firms with publicly traded securities, regulations of the Securities and Exchange Commission govern disclosures.

Chain of Command. The ability or lack of ability to bypass formal organizational lines of communication appears to affect leaders' evaluations of their subordinates. On the basis of the responses to a questionnaire, of 395 white-collar employees and managers of the engineering division of a public utility, Hunt, Osborn, and Schuler (1978) concluded that a manager's approval of subordinates was predicted by the adequacy of the organization's general communication and planning and how frequently the manager received orders out of the chain of command. The manager's disapproval of subordinates was also affected by these out-of-the-chain-of-command orders, over which the manager had no control.

Unionization. Labor and professional unions provide alternate channels of influence, both upward and downward. Although leader-subordinate relations within an organization would seem to be mediated by whether the subordinates belonged to a strong or weak union or to none at all, few empirical comparisons have been made. One would expect, for example, that arbitrary, capricious, coercive management would be highly constrained if workers had a second route to upward influence via a strong, effective union. It is more likely that such management would result in unionization that, in turn, would

reinforce management's rule-bound leadership in place of arbitrariness. A rare empirical study of the effect of unionization on supervisory-subordinate relations within a firm was completed by Hammer and Turk (1985), who collected data from 160 first-line supervisors in 12 sections of a factory with an employee union. The percentage of workers who belonged to the union varied from 0% to 82%, depending on the section they were in. Regression analyses showed that the "density" of union members in a section contributed uniquely to the section supervisor's emphasis on performance, "going by the book," and sense of a clear authority to discipline. This last result could be explained by the union contract. The supervisors' use of discipline and penalties against subordinates was regulated. It was power granted to the supervisor through negotiations between management and labor, specified in the union contract. Supervisors, abiding by the contract, knew the rights they had both to reward and to punish; so did their unionized subordinates. Union stewards, as well, according to E. L. Miller (1966), need to remain mindful of the employees' rights and interests.

Leadership and Organizational Culture

Intertwined with the philosophy, purposes, functions, and structure of the organization is its culture. Pericles identified the four aspects of the culture of Athens as an organized polity for its citizens that made it so valuable to them. First, it was open, democratic, and optimistic about its citizens' individual capabilities. Job assignments and promotions were based on merit, and the individual's dignity was upheld. Everyone was equal before the law. Second, its culture promoted beauty, good taste, and personal satisfaction in home, work, and play. Third, it was a culture of innovation; it provided the models for others to follow. Fourth, it encouraged an alignment of the interests of the individual citizen with those of the state (Clemens & Mayer, 1987).

Organizational Culture Defined

For Schein (1992), an organizational culture is the language, stories, customs, traditions, and rites shared or held in common by its members. It also includes its norms and implicit standards. The culture contains the organization's espoused values, formal philosophy, and implicit rules for getting along in the organization. To the meaning of culture, Trice (1984) adds its myths, sagas, legends, gestures, and the artifacts it creates to express activities. For Schein, also involved is the organizational climate—the way members feel about how they interact with one another as well as with outsiders. Further included are the knowledge, skills, and habits of thinking that are displayed in getting things done. The integrating symbols, ideas, feelings, and images that characterize the organization are another factor. They become consciously or unconsciously embedded in the organization's offices, sales rooms, plants, and products.

For Weick (1979), the primary function of organizations is *sense making*. An organization's members develop a set of mutually acceptable ideas and beliefs about what is real, what is important, and how to respond. The members learn shared patterns of behavior that are transmitted from one generation to the next (Deal & Kennedy, 1982). Along with the values that are shared by the members are the heroes who exemplify the organization's values, the rituals that inculcate the expressive bonding of members, and the stories that transmit the culture's values and ideas.

Martin, Feldman, Hatch, and Sitkin (1983) collected three types of stories that members told to assert the distinctiveness of their own impact on how the organizational culture communicates what is expected from its leadership. The stories described: (1) whether the boss was human and, when presented with an opportunity to perform a status-equalizing act, did or did not perform it; (2) rule-breaking (for instance, a senior manager broke a rule and was confronted by a junior person); (3) how the boss reacted to mistakes. Rosen (1985) completed an ethnographic study of an advertising agency that demonstrated how senior management manipulated the language, gestures, and context of a breakfast ritual to ensure acceptance of the goals and practices of the company. This ritual reinforced and reaffirmed the bureaucratic structure of the organization and its capitalistic values.

Jung's (1971) psychological classification provides a useful fourfold view of widely divergent organizational cultures. These four cultures are: bureaucracies, with *sense-thinking* managers; matrix organizations, with *intuitive-thinking* leaders; organic organizations, with *intuitive-feeling* leaders; and familiar cultures, with *sensing-feeling* members (Mitroff, 1983). Schein (1985, 1990) provided a fuller set of dimensions along which organizational cultures differ: (1) Relation to its environment—dominant or submissive, harmonizing, searching for a niche? (2) Nature of human activity—proactive, harmonizing, or passive? (3) Determination of truth and reality—pragmatic, relying on wisdom or social consensus? (4) Nature of time—orientation to the past, present, and/or future? (5) Human nature—good, neutral, or evil; fixed or perfectible? (6) Human relationships—competitive or cooperative, favoring individualism or groups, autocracy and paternalism, or collegiality and participation? (7) Homogeneity or diversity—encouragement of similarities or differences; conformity or innovation?

Assumptions. Basic assumptions about the nature of reality, time, space, human nature, and the environment are taken for granted at a preconscious level by those who are embedded in an organization's culture. There is a greater level of awareness about the interrelated values. The art, technology, and behavior that emerge are visible but not necessarily decipherable. It often takes an outsider to understand the cultural connections of the observable products and behavior to the underlying values and preconscious assumptions. Early in its development, an organization's culture is the glue that holds the organization together as a source of identity and distinctive competence. But in an organization's decline, its culture can become a constraint on innovation, since it is focused on the organization's past glories (Schein, 1985). Hatch's (1993) model of cultural dynamics is a framework involving processes of manifestation, realization, symbolism, and interpretation. What members of the organization assume to be true influences their values. Their values affect their assumptions and are realized in their artifacts. Symbols and interpretations follow. A visionary culture is able to align its core values and their preservation, "to reinforce its purposes, and to stimulate progress towards its aspirations" (Collins, 1996, p. 19).

Describing Different Organizational Cultures. Ethnographic and case studies have provided the most common means of depicting organizations. To describe a particular organization's culture, Kilmann and Saxton (1983) listed eight questions that the organizational culture answers: (1) What makes sense; what can be talked about? (2) Who am I; where do I belong? (3) Who rules; how, why, and by what means? (4) What are the unwritten rules of the game for what really counts; how do I stay out of trouble? (5) Why are we here, and for what purposes? (6) What are our history, geography, and the structure we build? (7) What are the stories about ourselves and others? (8) What are our morality and ethics? Are people basically good or evil? As a quantitative survey, the Kilmann-Saxton (1983) cultural gap survey asked organizational members to assess the strength of their organization's norms. The norms dealt with task support, task innovation, social relationships, and autonomy of individual members, all of which are expected to contribute to an organization's performance and satisfaction. Low scores reflected gaps in the organization's culture required for better performance and satisfaction. Cooke and Lafferty (1983) constructed the Organizational Culture Inventory (OCI), asking what was the extent an employee was expected to fit into the organization, such as "Be a good listener," "Look for mistakes," and "Keep on top of everything." Twelve variables could be generated describing the organization's values culture. They could be factor-analyzed into three types: (1) constructive (humanistic, achieving, affiliative, and self-actualizing), (2) passive/defensive (conventional, approval-seeking, and dependent), (3) aggressive/defensive (power-oriented, competitive, and perfectionistic) (Cooke & Szumal, 1992). Anthony (1994) obtained 585 raters, including 83 managers from first-line to executive. They used the OCI to describe the culture of their 11,000-person telecommunications firm and the Multifactor Leadership Questionnaire (MLQ) to rate the transformational and transactional leadership of their immediate superior. The four constructive culture variables correlated between .42 and .55 with the four MLQ transformational leadership scores, between −.03 and .05 with MLQ transactional active management by exception, and between −.41 and −.39 with passive management by exception. O'Reilly, Chatman, and Caldwell (1991) developed the Organizational Culture Profile (OCP) to provide a measure of the extent which there was a match between individual organizational members' preferences for 26 cultural norms that characterized their organizations. The factors that emerged were: (1) innovation, (2) attention to detail, (3) outcome orientation, (4) aggressiveness, (5) supportive-

ness, (6) emphasis on rewards, (7) team orientation, and (8) decisiveness. A year later, the fit of personal preferences and organization norms correlated .28 with commitment, .36 with job satisfaction, and with greater retention after two years.

To assess the aspects of a corporate culture that contribute to organizational excellence more specifically, Sashkin (1986, 1988) extracted seven explicit and three implicit core values or beliefs from Peters and Waterman (1982). Included were task-relevant values, such as being the best at what the company does, attending to details in doing a job, importance of superior quality, service, economic growth, profits, and managers as "hands-on doers," not just planners and administrators. Other values were more concerned with relationships: people, as individuals, are important; people in the organization should be innovators and should be able to take risks without feeling that they will be punished if they fail; informality is important, as is improving the flow of communication throughout the organization; and people should have fun doing their work. All these values need to be made explicit in a recognized organizational philosophy that is developed and supported by those at the top. Sashkin constructed the Organizational Beliefs Questionnaire to measure respondents' estimations of whether others in their organization subscribed to such beliefs as "people in this organization believe in being the very best at what we do." Construct validation was obtained by showing greater variance among rather than within 46 organizations. A total score reflecting the endorsement of values that promote excellence was found to be higher in more effective organizations.

Transformational Cultures. Bass and Avolio (1993) applied the transformational/transactional paradigm to portray organizational cultures. A *transformational* culture emphasized such concepts as: "we trust each other to do what's right," people go out of their way for the good of the department or organization," and "new ideas are greeted with enthusiasm." In a *transactional* culture, the concepts were: "rules and procedures limit discretionary behavior," "decisions often require several levels of authorization," and "we negotiate with each other for resources." Cultures can be typed according to their transformational and transactional scores on the Organization Description Questionnaire (ODQ), as was done for 69 organizations, ranging from hospitals and police departments to civil service agencies and manufacturing firms. In a high-transformational–high-transactional *contrast* culture, there is much leadership and constructive conflict about the best ways to proceed. In a high-transformational–low-transactional organizational culture, there is much talk about purpose, vision, values, and fulfillment, without much need for formal agreements. Trust has been internalized, and expressiveness and creativity are high. Leaders emphasize confidence and improvement. *Bureaucracies* are opposite in type: low-transformational–high-transactional. A *coasting* organization is a mix of moderate-transformational and moderate-transactional values and behaviors. The leadership fails to make full use of the organization's resources and opportunities. The *garbage can* organizational culture is neither transformational nor transactional. Leadership, consensus, and cooperation are absent. The organization is anarchic, without clear purposes or rules to control activities. The *pedestrian* organizational culture, with moderate-transactional rules and regulations but no transformational qualities manages to stagger along as a consequence of formal arrangements but with few improvements and risks (Bass & Avolio, 1993b). Not surprisingly, there is a strong linkage between the ODQ and the MLQ. As expected, leaders earn higher MLQ transformational leadership ratings from their followers in organizations assessed as transformational in culture on the ODQ. They earn higher transactional ratings in bureaucracies. Such high correlations were reported by Corrigan, Lickey, McCracken, et al. (2001) for 118 staff members in four Illinois mental health outpatient service agencies.

The Leader as Culture Builder

An organization's culture derives from its antecedent leadership. Anecdotal evidence and discourse abound in considering how an organization's leadership influences its culture. For Sayles and Wright (1985), the CEO's behavior is the most important determinant of the organization's culture. For Schein (1985), leadership is critical to the creation and maintenance of culture. One is likely to see a constant interplay between culture and leadership. Leaders create the mechanisms for cultural embedding and cultural reinforcement. Cultural norms arise and change because of what leaders attend to, their reactions to crises, their role modeling, and their recruitment strategies. For Schein, the organizational culture is taught by its leadership.

Bass (1988) observed that charismatic leaders create new cultures for their followers by creating new meanings for them. The process is advanced by *frame alignment*, or shared interpretive orientations of leader and followers (Snow, Rochford, Worden, et al., 1986). While transactional leaders work within their organizational culture, transformational leaders change them (Bass, 1998). Tichy and Ulrich (1984) thought that the tranformational leader needs to understand and realign the organization's culture as a way of providing meaning, by making sense of symbols and events. The transformational director of Food for the Hungry/Kenya, an NGO, has been its servant leader as well and has built an organizational culture of shared responsibilities and leadership roles, a strong organizational identity, and a healthy sense of community (Kroll & Vandenberg, 1996).

Hickman and Silva (1984) argued that the two bases of effective organizational performance are strategic thinking and culture building by the leaders. Strategic thinking creates the vision of a firm's future. The vision becomes a reality when the leaders build a culture that is dedicated to the vision. In contrast to transactional leadership, the leaders here are visionary executives who integrate creative insight and sensitivity to "forge the strategy-culture alloy." These leaders combine versatility, focus, and patience to maintain the organization's highly effective performance over the long term. According to Kiefer and Senge (1984), such leadership pushes for a "metanoic" organization, building on such assumptions as those that say that people are inherently good, honest, trustworthy, and purposeful; everyone has a unique contribution to make; and complex problems require local solutions. Leaders who build such cultures need to have personalities with a deep sense of vision and purposefulness. They are aligned around that vision and can balance reason and intuition, as well as empower others (Kiefer, 1986; Senge, 1980). Such leaders display much individualized consideration (Bass, 1985a). They facilitate and teach. They create rather than maintain and are personally involved with the development of key managers (Senge, 1984, 1986). Quinn (1988) applied his competing values model to set forth four alternate ways a leader orients an organization's climate or culture. A climate or culture with a *supportive* orientation arises if the leader focuses on flexibility rather than control in the internal organization's environment; an *innovative* orientation is built for the external environment with the same flexibility. On the other hand, if the leader is more concerned about control than flexibility, the internal environment will be rules-oriented and the external environment will be goal-oriented. Den Hartog, Muijen, and Koopman (1996) found, for 330 Dutch employees in 28 departments from five different organizations, that rules and goals orientations correlated more highly with transactional leadership ($-.54$, .61) than with transformational leadership (.42, .54). An innovative and supportive orientation correlated more highly with transformational leadership ($-.72$, $-.69$) than with transactional leadership (.52, .48). But emphasizing cultural rather than individual issues did not add to the impact of transformational leadership. In a survey of 4,454 executives rated by approximately 40,000 subordinates, Colvin (1996) reported that transformational leadership had the same positive effects on subordinates whether the executives focused on cultural issues such as setting visions and shaping values or on individual issues such as coaching and empowering. Organizational cultures can also create the negative effects of resistance to change and rejection of innovation and implementation.

The Leader as Cultural Transmitter. Kouzes and Posner (1987) emphasized the importance of the leader in transmitting the organization's culture and values. An organization contains a network of "priests," who maintain and bless the values; "storytellers," who watch over the values; and "gossips," who are key transmitters of the culture (Deal & Kennedy, 1982). Kotter and Heskett (1992, p. 84) argued that "the single most visible factor that distinguishes major cultural changes that succeed from those that fail is competent leadership at the top." Leaders act as effective role models, articulate ideologies, and inspire commitment to both old and new values. They use cultural forms to communicate new values and help to institute cultural change (Trice & Beyer, 1991).

Leadership and Organizational Climate. As noted earlier, an important feature of an organization's culture is its *climate*—the subjective feelings about the organiza-

tion among those who work within it. Leaders influence the organizational climate through their behavior and decisions (Van Muijen, Koopman, et al., 1992). The climate directly affects how organizational members relate to one another and the culture within which they work (Den Hartog, Van Muijen, & Koopman, 1996). As might be expected, Kozlowski and Doherty (1989) showed that the quality of leader-subordinate relations was directly related to the satisfaction felt about the organization's climate. Halpin and Croft (1962) found systematic connections among scales measuring different aspects of a school's organizational climate and leadership and the response of teachers. Sheridan and Vredenburgh (1978a) showed that head nurses' consideration and initiation of structure in a hospital could be explained partly by the turnover among staff members and the administrative climate, as measured by an instrument developed by Pritchard and Karasick (1973). J. L. Franklin (1975) examined similar relations in a broader organizational context. Particularly important to an organization's climate is how clear its leaders make the organization's goals to the members and convey a sense that the climate is one in which there is a high degree of trust.

For 78 executives described by 407 subordinates, Bass, Valenzi, Farrow, and Solomon (1975) used stepwise regression to determine that in organizations described as more trusting, more participative leadership behavior was observed. In organizations where the subordinates perceived clear goals, the managers were described as more directive, more likely to consult with their subordinates, and more likely to share decision making with the subordinates. In a follow-up, with descriptions by more than 1,200 subordinates of their superiors' leadership behavior and aspects of the organization, Farrow, Valenzi, and Bass (1980) found that consultation was most frequent when an organization's goals were clear and levels of trust were high. Similarly, according to Hunt, Osborn, and Schuler (1978), an organization with overall practices that promoted the clarity of jobs and clear standards increased the leaders' supportive behavior toward their subordinates. Child and Ellis (1973) concluded that more delegation by the superior was seen if work roles were clear and much discretion was perceived in the organization's climate.

In a survey study of 440 Indian managers from seven organizations, Ansari (1988) found that whether the climate was favorable or unfavorable affected the managers' efforts to influence. If the climate was favorable, participative managers said they were more individually considerate to their subordinates and less likely to try to block or defy their bosses; task-oriented managers said they increased the use of their expertise and reasoning with both their bosses and their subordinates; and bureaucrats said they were more likely to challenge their subordinates and be ingratiating toward their boss. If the climate was unfavorable, participative managers said they were more likely to use coalition tactics, to manipulate their subordinates, and be more ingratiating with their bosses. The task-oriented managers said they were less defiant toward their bosses, and the bureaucrats said they were more assertive with their subordinates and more transactional and diplomatic with their bosses.

Founders of Organizational Cultures

The creation of much of organizational culture is attributed to companies' entrepreneurial founders (Pettigrew, 1973, 1979). Schein (1983) noted that a founder creates a culture from a preconceived *cultural paradigm* in his or her head. Then the founder's and successor's leadership shapes the culture and the mechanisms to restrain it. Schein and others assumed that a monolithic culture of shared values emerges that is guided and controlled by the founder. Martin, Sitkin, and Boehm's (1985) detailed interview study with 700 employees of a young and growing electronics manufacturing firm in Silicon Valley, California, implied that the founders' values may conflict to some extent with those of various constituencies in the firm. In this case, although 72% of the employees' explanations of the company's origins, quality control, and turnover agreed with the founders' interpretations, 19% did not.

Some founders, such as Steven Jobs of Apple Computer, who do not have previous leadership and management experience or much formal education, form companies and originate corporate cultures that they then must leave to others to manage. Jobs subsequently returned to further continue Apple's unique culture. Among the CEOs of the fastest-growing companies in the United States, three fourths were founders of their companies, and 83% like Walt Disney of Disney Productions and Ray Kroc of McDonald's, never made

plans to retire. They were not just inspired originators; they also had the credentials for long-term tenure. Most were highly educated. All but 19% were college graduates; 46% held graduate degrees, mostly in engineering. Bill Gates of Microsoft, a dropout from Harvard, was an exception. Half had managerial experience in a Fortune 500 company before founding their own company (Nicholson, 1983).

Founders of Countercultures

John DeLorean and Hyman Rickover are examples of founders of countercultures. Martin and Siehl (1983) described DeLorean's counterculture, built within General Motors (GM) in reaction to GM's dominant cultural values of deference to authority, invisibility, and loyalty. GM's division heads, despite some degree of autonomy, were expected to conform closely to GM's dominant values. Deference to authority was expressed, for instance, in the way subordinates were expected to meet their superiors from out of town at the airport, carry their bags, pay their hotel and meal bills, and chauffeur them around day and night. The higher the status of the superior, the more people would accompany him on the flight and the larger the retinue that would await him at the airport (p. 57).

DeLorean enraged his boss by failing to meet him at the airport, and thereby signaling disrespect for his boss's authority. He also created and recounted stories about the foolish extravagances of subordinates who catered to the whims of visiting VIPs. In the GM culture, invisibility was expressed in such ways as maintaining standardized offices; eating together in the executive dining room; and adopting a uniform dress code of dark suit, white shirt, and blue or black tie. Again, DeLorean violated these rules—for example, in requesting a brighter, more modern and attractive office decor and dressing in a more fashionable but still conservative continental mode. Loyalty in the GM culture was expressed by not voicing criticisms in front of the corporate management. DeLorean invented stories to interpret the costs to GM of "groupthink" and conformity.

DeLorean's counterculture was an attempt to support the value of productivity instead of deference, of objective measures of performance instead of subjective indicators of conformity, and of independence instead of blind loyalty. But his deviance remained within tolerable limits until he left to found his own company, which had notorious consequences. It remained for Roger Smith, a new CEO, to reshape GM's dominant culture. Ultimately, GM's inflexibilities in management, marketing, and labor contracts forced radical reductions in size in 2006 to keep up with its competitors.

Hyman Rickover almost singlehandedly constructed a powerful naval counterestablishment in the Nuclear Reactors Branch of the U.S. Navy (Polmar & Allen, 1982). This branch became a separate elite nuclear establishment in de facto control, by 1980, of one third of the U.S. naval fleet! Rickover formed this counterestablishment for his self-satisfaction and to coincide with his personal views of what was wrong with the U.S. Navy's values and practices, in general, and the U.S. Naval Academy at Annapolis, in particular. His manufactured culture included horrendous stress interviews that were of questionable validity for applicants, generally favoring graduates of NROTC rather than of the academy. Discipline was extreme, focused on overlearning and dedication. There was an intense emphasis on both detailed directive leadership and the practice of management by exception, which involved the bypassing of channels and weekly reports written personally to Rickover, There was an unrelenting pressure to work and study. Rickover, himself, set the workaholic pace in a spartan office with spartan lunches. He was almost always in civilian dress. Expertise took precedence over rank and specialization over general management.

As civilian chief of the Naval Reactors Branch of the Atomic Energy Commission and later, of the Department of Energy, then as the U.S. Navy's chief for nuclear propulsion, Rickover was the nuclear organization's network center. For two decades after he would have been retired by the U.S. Navy, he maintained his power, authority, and budget, bypassing the Navy and going directly to Congress. Although experiments with nuclear reactors for propulsion preceded him, he made himself the mythological originator. He rejected cost considerations in the decisions as to whether to build nuclear or conventional fleets. Only nuclear submarines and surface vessels were valued. The result of all this was a large, first-rate nuclear navy, built at the expense of a larger, possibly more nationally useful conventional fleet. A higher price was paid in financial and human costs than

was necessary. The human costs were ultimately evidenced in the failure to maintain a sufficient number of volunteers for the nuclear submarine fleet (Polmar & Allen, 1982).

Promoting Changes in the Dominant Culture

One does not have to construct a counterculture to improve the existing culture. The issue to which top management is particularly sensitive is the leadership required for managing organizational change in its culture. Such change is necessitated by new marketing requirements, new technologies, and new kinds of personnel (Bass, 1985a; Bennis & Nanus, 1985).

Leavitt (1986) and Tichy and Devanna (1986), among others, provided book-length advice, consistent with research results about transformational leaders, on how to accomplish the needed changes in the organizational culture. It is essential for top management to articulate the change that is required. The message may be of a vision that entails *directive* and persuasive leadership; it may permit modifications and contributions from others. Changes, consistent with the message, are introduced in the structure, processes, and practices. Sufficient participation is encouraged to generate commitment, loyalty, and involvement, accompanied by full, two-way communication with adequate feedback loops. Desired role and behavioral models of leadership begin at the top and are encouraged at each successive level below. Furthermore, leaders who are concerned about organizational renewal will seek to foster organizational cultures and climates that are hospitable and conducive to creativity, problem solving, risk taking, and experimentation. To foster cultural changes in an organization, say to shift it from a service to a market orientation (as with AT&T), leaders should first honor the past, returning to it for inspiration and instruction and identifying past objectives, principles, and still-successful approaches that will be maintained (Wilkins & Bristow, 1987). Kane (1984) described how the General Electric culture was changed in this way by the transformational leadership of Jack Welch. First, there was articulation of the changes that were desired. Next, the necessary changes in structure, processes, and practices were made and were widely communicated. Finally, new role and behavioral models were established. "Leaders must understand the interweaving of continuity and change . . . in long-term purposes and values." Promotions should be made to ensure that these older values can survive despite the oncoming changes. Ceremonial events are needed to mourn the loss of the cherished past. Finally, changes should be organic, developing out of new ways that are already desired and providing reinforcement for new incremental efforts that are attempted and successful (J. W. Gardner, 1988b, p. 6).

Organizational Culture and Manipulation by Management. Mitchell (1985) contrasted the values explicit in two empirical studies of successful enterprises. One was Peters and Waterman's (1982) *In Search of Excellence*, which identified 62 firms that had a history of growth, economic success, and innovativeness over a 25-year period.[14] The other was Levering, Moskowitz, and Katz's (1984) *The 100 Best Companies to Work for in America*. These were the 100 companies that employees most said they liked to work for. Only 21 of the 100 best-liked firms showed up among the 62 excellently managed companies mentioned by Peters and Waterman (1982). (There was considerable change in the lists between 1982 and 2006.) Management of the task-effective culture appeared to be manipulative. That is, in such a culture, people are valued not for themselves but as being instrumental to productivity. Employees' values are shaped to increase their commitment to productivity, the institution, and the maintenance of the work ethic. The manipulation is done not through conviction but through myths, fables, and fairy tales about values that the management itself does not necessarily believe in.

The effort to manage meaning is a case in point. Charismatic leaders give meaning to employees' efforts and goals by linking them to the employees' values (Shamir & Howell, 1999). Although finding meaning in one's work is intrinsically satisfying, an existential view of organizations and the importance of meaning in understanding organizational life has led to efforts to manage meaning at the cost of individual members' authenticity (Maddi, 1989). A manager of meaning "is concerned with the tricks of the pedagogue, the mentor, the linguist,

the more successfully to become the value shaper, the exemplar, the making of meanings" (Peters & Waterman, 1982, p. 82). In contrast, many of the 100 best companies to work for, according to their employees, stressed more truly relations-oriented values, such as making employees feel they were part of a team or family, encouraging open communication, encouraging suggestions, promoting from within, enabling people to feel pride in their products or services, sharing profits, reducing social distance, making the workplace as pleasant as possible, encouraging the employees' participation in community service, matching employees' savings funds, avoiding layoffs whenever possible, showing concern for employees' health, and providing training and reimbursement of tuition.

Specific policy statements about these values were found among many of the 100 best-liked firms. For instance, Apple Computer stated that employees should be able to trust the motives and integrity of their supervisors. Armstrong declared that management should respect the dignity and inherent rights of the individual, maintain high moral and ethical standards, and reflect honesty, integrity, reliability, and forthrightness. According to the policy statements of Doyle Dane Bernbach, employees and the firm may refuse to work on advertising accounts for ethical reasons or on accounts that may have negative effects on the public. Other firms, such as Rolm, focused on honesty; Moog, on statements about the need for mutual trust and respect; and Celestial Seasonings, on dignity, fairness, kindness, and the professional treatment of all individuals and organizations with whom it works. Mitchell (1985) concluded that what seems to be the best-managed firms may be different from those for whom employees most like to work. The best-managed firms create a culture, with symbols and myths, to get employees to work harder and better; managements of the best-liked firms seem genuinely to care about the quality of the experience of everyone in the firm. In the former, management may practice consideration but really believe in exploitation; in the latter, a truer concern for others is seen in their employees' evaluations. Showing the influence of positive psychology, Luthans (in press) concluded that management should focus on the strengths and capabilities of its people instead of trying to fix what is wrong with them. Singled out for attention would be an organizational culture that encourages self-efficacy,

---

[14]Excellently managed firms actually do not appear to provide greater returns on investment to shareholders than do their less well managed counterparts. However, they do seem to be less risky investments in that the price of their stocks is less variable (Simpson & Ireland, 1987).

hope, optimism, subjective well-being, and emotional intelligence.

The Effects of the Organization's Culture on the Leader

Schein (1985) suggested that culture manages management more than management manages culture. For instance, a strong organizational culture, with values and internal guidelines for more autonomy at lower levels, can prevent top management from increasing its personal power at the expense of middle management (Rubin & Berlew, 1984). Osborn and Ashforth (1990) concluded that the culture of complex high-technology organizations laden with high-risk liability, such as nuclear energy plants, affects its managers as well as its workers with myths and institutionalized structures that the leaders use to focus the attention of their subordinates. Trice and Beyer (1984, p. 666) noted that "managers need to learn to . . . assess not only the technical consequences of any activities and programs, but also . . . they need to learn . . . effective ceremonial skills. Some flair for the dramatic and the ability to be expressive in speech, writing, and gestures could be an asset in meeting . . . ceremonial requirements."

Adaptive organizational cultures emphasize innovation, risk taking, open communications, teamwork, and enthusiasm. *Nonadaptive* cultures stress order, efficiency, and aversion to innovation and change. It follows that transformational leadership is more likely in adaptive organizational cultures and transactional leadership in nonadaptive cultures (Kotter & Heskett, 1992). In addition to individual cognitive processes, organizational culture affects the tendency of managers to "throw good money after bad" and continue failing courses of action. Rathbun, Miller, and Aniolek (2003) hypothesize that failing actions are often escalated as a consequence of cultural norms such as dishonest reporting, the valuing of impression management, and ambivalence about ethical considerations. Escalation is limited if the cultural norms diffuse blame for failure and stimulate generation of alternatives Managers particularly need to attend to the conservativeness, reflected in rites and ceremonials, that can hinder efforts to change the organization. They need to modify the rites and ceremonials, when it is possible to do so, to fit with the desired new directions for the organization. They can invent new rites to replace the old, some of which symbolize the value of change itself (Hedberg, Nystrom, & Starbuck, 1976). One example is the ceremonial introduction of a new product or process to replace an older one.

Lombardo (1983) described three corporations, each of whose different cultures (highly task-oriented, highly pragmatic, and highly considerate of others) resulted in the development of parallel differences among their respective managers. In the same way, Roberts's (1986) survey described earlier, of the styles used by 350 business managers and university administrators with their subordinates, peers, and bosses found that managers in Type Z organizations (Japanese-style organizations) were less likely to be directive than were their counterparts in Type A (authoritarian, top-down organizations). Shamir, Zackay, and Popper (1998) asked soldiers in 50 field companies of the Israel Defense Forces to what extent their company had special slogans, special songs, special nicknames, special rituals, special jargon, and internal jokes. These provided a measure of each company's culture. This soldier-rated company culture correlated .31 with the staff's ratings of the company leader's *supportive* leadership behavior (openness, friendliness, sensitivity toward their needs and feelings, giving them autonomy, and deemphasis on social and power distance from followers). Organizational culture also correlated .30 with the leader's emphasis on *collective identity* using symbols and emphasis on differences from other companies. But culture did not correlate with exemplary leadership or with the leader's emphasis on ideology.

Effects of Clan and Market Cultures. Kerr and Slocum (1987) identified two types of corporate reward systems that give rise to two different cultures—clan and market—and characteristically different leadership experiences. The clan is fraternal. Commitments are long-term; interests are mutual. There is stress on teamwork and pressure to conform. Socialization takes a long time, superiors are agents of socialization, and the culture governs a wide range of behaviors. The marketing culture is contractual, commitment is short-term, and self-interests dominate. There is less socialization, superiors are distant, and the cultural norms govern few behaviors. In the *clan* culture, one's superior defines and evaluates, usually subjectively, one's managerial performance. There is promotion from within, often connected with one's need for further development. People are expected to do more than just what is agreed in contracts. Loyalty to the organization is exchanged for commitment to it. A contrasting *market* culture develops from a performance-based contingent reward system. One's role is specifically defined and evaluated by objective financial outcomes. There is much less need for superior-subordinate interaction or concern for subordinates' socialization and development. Presumably, the clan culture provides more potential for transformational leadership and the market culture, for more transactional leadership.

Effects of Kibbutz Ownership. The effects of the culture of kibbutzim on their top officials' leadership of firms that the kibbutzim owned as cooperatives was contrasted to the leadership of counterpart publicly and privately owned Israeli business firms. Among a sample of 224 Israeli senior executives, the business executives were more *directive*, negotiative, and delegative and less *participative* than were the general managers of firms owned by the kibbutzim. They also had relatively greater power and were more assertive, but they did not differ from the executives of the kibbutzim-owned firms in the amount of consultation they did or how well informed they were (Chitayat & Venezia, 1984).

Instrumentality and Expressiveness in the Culture. Santner (1986) used the High School Characteristics Index to describe two schools, one with a low-instrumental–low-expressive school climate and the other with a high-instrumental–high-expressive school climate,[15] to show the different effects of the two climates on the character of those who emerged as student leaders in the two situations. In the low-instrumental–

[15]A highly instrumental climate is one in which rewards are contingent on the appropriate performance of subordinates and means are more important than ends. In an expressive climate, there is more spontaneity, more actions based on sentiments and feelings rather than on carefully thought out means to ends.

low-expressive school, personality-tested dominance and friendliness discriminated the formal leaders of official school groups as well as the informal leaders whom their peers distinguished from the nonleaders. In addition, in this low-instrumental–low-expressive school, highly achievement-oriented girls were most likely to be the formal leaders and lower-achievement-oriented boys were more likely to be the informal leaders. But in the high-instrumental–high-expressive school, tested dominance was the only significant factor that differentiated the leaders from the nonleaders.

Summary and Conclusions

Situational contingencies that influence the behavior of leaders and followers are emphasized in this chapter. Leader-subordinate relations within a group depend on societal influences, real outside relationships, and reference groups in the minds of both. Leaders who see economic externalities as most important tend to be more directive, whereas leaders who believe social or political influences from the outside to be more important tend to be more participative. The surrounding organization and its policies, size, structure, and culture are of special consequence to leader-subordinate interactions. Although an organization and its culture influence what is expected of the leaders and what they will do, the leaders in turn, shape their organizations and culture to fit their needs. Environmental factors external to the organization and cultural factors, both external and internal, influence leader-subordinate relations inside the organization. Small-group, task, and other situational factors of consequence will be examined further separately in the following chapters. The leader's discretionary and non-discretionary behavior depend on organizational and environmental considerations. But equally important is the immediate group in which the leadership occurs—the subject that is discussed next.

Leadership in Groups and Teams

I commented to an Egyptologist at the Temple of Luxor how remarkable it was to see four fellahin with only ropes skillfully maneuvering a ten-ton stone block. "Oh," he replied, "they have been doing that kind of teamwork for the past five thousand years!" (Bass, 1995). The team or small group may be permanent or temporary. Contact is usually face-to-face but increasingly may take place through e-mail and conference television. Regardless of whether they arise spontaneously or are elected or appointed, the members who emerge as leaders perform two essential functions: (1) they deal with the groups and the member's performance, and (2) they provide socioemotional support to the group members (Bales, 1958a; Bales & Slater, 1955).

Roles of the Leader

Any or all members can emerge as leaders, depending on how much of the functional roles they enact—the particular patterns of behavior they display in relation to the performance of the group or its socioemotional development. Leaders enact these task-relevant and socioemotional group-building and maintenance roles. Nonleaders are more likely to enact individual roles. These are less functional for the group's development and maintenance. As formulated by Benne and Sheats (1948), task roles include those of initiator of the activity, information seeker, information giver, opinion giver, elaborator, coordinator, summarizer, feasibility tester, evaluator, and diagnostician. Group-building and maintenance roles include patterns of behavior such as encouraging, gatekeeping (limiting monopolistic talkers, returning the group to the agenda, and keeping the group on course), standard setting, expressing group feelings, consensus taking (sending up "trial balloons"), harmonizing, reducing tension (joking, "pouring oil on troubled waters"), and following. (This last role is consistent with what was said in earlier chapters about the positive correlation of leadership and followership.) Nonfunctional individual, self-concerned roles involve patterns of behavior such as aggression, blocking, self-confessing, competing, seeking sympathy, special pleading, disrupting, seeking recognition, and withdrawing.

Functions of the Leader

Roby (1961) developed a mathematical model of leadership functions based on response units and information load. According to Roby, the functions of leadership are to: (1) bring about a congruence of goals among members; (2) balance the group's resources and capabilities with environmental demands; (3) provide a group structure that is necessary to focus information effectively on solving the problem; (4) make certain that needed information is available at a decision center when required. Consistent with this view, Stogdill (1959) suggested that it is the function of the leader to maintain the group's structure and goal direction and to reconcile conflicting demands that arise within and outside the group. For Stogdill, the functions of leadership also included defining objectives, providing means for attaining goals, facilitating action and interaction in the group, maintaining the group's cohesiveness and the members' satisfaction, and facilitating the group's performance of the task. According to Schutz (1961b), the leader has the functions of: (1) establishing and recognizing a hierarchy of group goals and values; (2) recognizing and integrating the various cognitive styles that exist in the group; (3) maximizing the use of group members' abilities; (4) helping members resolve problems involved in adapting to external realities, as well as those involving interpersonal needs. Bowers and Seashore (1967) maintained that the functions of leadership are the support of members, the facilitation of interaction, the emphasis on goals, and the facilitation of work. For Cattell (1957), the leader maintains the group, upholds role and status satisfactions, maintains task satisfaction, keeps ethical (norm) satisfaction, selects and clarifies goals, and finds and clarifies the means of attaining goals. For Hollander (1978), goal setting was a particularly important function of the leader. And P. J. Burke (1966a, 1966b) showed that antagonism, tension, and absenteeism occurred when the leader failed in this function. According to Hollander, the leader also provides direction and defines reality, two more functions that are necessary for the group's effectiveness. If successful, such direction by the leader is a valued resource. As a definer of reality, the leader communicates relevant information about progress and provides needed redirection to followers.

Earlier chapters explored the interacting nature of leader-follower relations. This chapter concentrates on the effects of the followers as a group or team on its leadership and the effects of the leadership on the group or team. It concludes with sharing of leadership of the team. What the leadership does depends on the nature of the team. In the same way, the team depends on the nature of the leadership. Its leadership often makes the difference in the success or failure of the team's efforts (Katzenbach, 1997). In the last century, there were several revolutionary changes in how work and service were to be done. The job of an individual became less a single bundle of tasks and more a varying set of tasks in coordination with other members of a team. Increasingly, work is done in teams. Even when individuals still have much work to do by themselves, they must still join *parallel* teams to complete it or for other reasons, such as to contribute to quality improvement, committees, and task forces. A single person may be a member of many parallel teams while still responsible for individual assignments (Campion, Pappar, & Medsker, 1996). Lawler and Cohen (1992) estimated that 85% of Fortune 100 firms used parallel teams.

Teams versus Groups

A *group* is a collection of people with common boundaries, sometimes with broad objectives. A *team* is a group that is focused on a task with a narrow set of objectives (Hackman & Johnson, 1993). A group may have a task,

such as to follow directions or to find answers to problems. But a group is less likely to be focused like a team primarily on specific tasks. Before 1990 many studies of groups were actually studies of teams. Both groups and teams exhibited mutual and reciprocal influence among members. But usually there is a stronger sense of identification by members of a team than a group. Team members share common goals and tasks; group members may belong to the group for personal reasons that are in conflict with the group's objectives. Task members usually work interdependently; group members may work independently. Team members have more specialized and differentiated roles, although they are likely to play a single primary role; group members more often play a variety of roles (Hughes, Ginnett, & Curphy, 1993). Teamwork more often requires monitoring performance of self and other members, self-correcting errors, providing task and motivation reinforcement, adapting to unpredictable occurrences, closing communication loops, and predicting other team members' behavior. Mental models need to be shared (Salas, 1993). Much of the leadership in teams may be provided by the members themselves.

In the third edition of *Handbook of Leadership*, this chapter focused on leadership of small groups. In the fourth edition, the chapter reflects the rapid growth in interest from the 1980s onward in organizing teams, teamwork, and team leadership and the declining research interest in leading informal, transient small groups (Ilgen, 1999). However, much of what was learned about small groups remains relevant to teams and team leadership. Research about work and leadership in groups is now more likely to be called work in teams. Among other things, to be an effective *team*, members in their interdependence must pursue shared and valued objectives. They must pay more attention to processes and their shared roles and responsibilities must be more clearly defined (Dyer, 1984).

From Division of Labor to Teamwork

The use of teams by utilitarian organizations has increased since the 1990s (Lawler, 1998). Authority has been decentralized. Traditional chains of command have been replaced by empowered teams (Ray & Bronstein, 1995). We are in the midst of a changeover from dividing the tasks of labor into their simplest components, as advocated by theorists ranging from Adam Smith (1776) to Frederick Taylor (1912). Work has been reengineered from production in assembly lines to teamwork in policy-making decisions, therapeutic efforts, family assistance, and education (McGrath, 1997). The reason is that teams ordinarily achieve more than pooling the individual efforts of the members working alone (Bass, 1965). "The growing interdependence of human functioning is placing a premium on the exercise of collective agency through shared beliefs in the power to produce effects by collective action" (Bandura, 2000, p. 75).

Early Interest in Group Effort. There were early instances of the changeover in interest from individual to group effort. De Toqueville (1832/1966) commented on how American settlers formed voluntary, temporary teams to get work done. LeBon (1897) explained what happens when people are in groups rather than alone. People in groups were found by H. Clark (1916) more suggestive than when isolated. Bechterew and Lange (1924) completed numerous experiments on the influence of the group, a topic of considerable political interest in a Soviet society aiming to develop collectivism in the workplace. Elton Mayo's familiar Hawthorne studies begun in 1924 to show the importance of good lighting in the workplace, publicized the importance of interpersonal relations between supervisor and workers (Roethlisberger & Dixon, 1947). Burtt (1929) made explicit the case for working in groups rather than alone: "We are essentially social animals and most of us find it more agreeable to do things in company than to do them alone" (p. 193). Moreno (1934/1953) introduced sociometry to show the influence on group performance of choice of partners. Lewin's (1939) theory of group dynamics was seminal in demonstrating the value of participation and team goals.

Trist and Bamforth (1951) described the teamwork in long-wall coal mining. Bamforth had been a miner and came from a village of coal miners. He won a scholarship to work with Trist. Assigned by Trist, he returned to the same mine in which he had originally worked to find that its individually assigned jobs had been replaced by working in teams. Productivity and satisfaction had increased. Bamforth told Trist that work in the mine had returned to the way the miners' fathers had worked before "rationalization" had introduced inflexible individ-

ual assignments (Fox, 1990)! Our earlier chapters noted developments from the mid–twentieth century onward, exemplified by military leadership research ranging from army squads to air force aircrews, and Coch and French's (1948) study of the effects of goal setting and participative practices. By the 1960s, Nonlinear Systems, a small California electronics firm, had eliminated its assembly line in favor of an organization of teams, and Volvo's automobile engine assembly was changed from assembly lines to teamwork (Bass, 1965). Teamwork was encouraged by System 4 of Likert's concept (1961a) of organized overlapping groups from one echelon to the next in decision-making hierarchies. Each leader of a group participated in a decision-making group of his peers at the next higher organizational level (see Chapter 17).

Prevalence. Teams have been employed in Japan since the days of the Samurai. Small-group research in the mid–twentieth century attested to the greater effectiveness of team over individual work. Lawler, Lawler, Mohrman, and Ledford (1995) estimated that as many as 85% of large Western firms were using some form of teams, many self-managed. Team decision making is more effective than the decisions of its individual members. Among 222 project teams solving problems, the decision based on the group process was better that that of the team's most proficient member in 97% of the cases. Only 40% of the superior decisions could be explained by the average member's decision (Michaelson, Watson, & Black, 1989).

Teams permit each member to take on larger tasks. With cross-training and reengineering of tasks, members can substitute for one another. They are better motivated when given wider latitude than operating on a traditional assembly line. The greater productivity in the United States with fewer employees is usually attributed in the popular press to technological advances, but some of it may be due to the switch from assembly lines to teamwork. The attitudes and activities of the group transcend those of its individual members. Group and team norms can survive even if all the members are changed. Members behave differently when they are isolated from one another than when they are all together. The leader's dyadic relations with each of his or her subordinates may not reflect the leader's relations with the same subordinates as a team. The team's relationship to the leader may be more important than the individual employee's relationship to the leader (Bramel & Friend, 1987). The team approach has had to be extensively modified from its application in collectivistic Japan to individualistic North America. In Japan, harmony is of singular importance. In the United States, dissent has to be endorsed and valued, allowing for productive controversy and constructive thinking. Team structure has to be fluid, incorporating core members with part-timers. Teams have to be encouraged and enabled to make decisions for themselves (Nahavandi & Aranda, 1994).

The team's drive, cohesion, collective efficacy, potency, selection, alignment, and attainment of goals are likely to be influenced by its leadership. Its leadership is likely to be influenced by the team's drive, cohesion, collective efficacy, selection, and attainment of objectives. The overall evidence points to greater accomplishment in teams with greater collective drive, cohesion, efficacy, and potency. For example, a group's beliefs in its collective efficacy have been shown in banking to make an important contribution to continuing effort and performance accomplishment (Lewis & Gibson, 1998). Comparable results have appeared in both experimental teams and natural groups in business, athletics, military combat, and urban neighborhoods (Bandura, 2000). A meta-analysis by Gully, Beaubien, Incalcaterra, et al. (1998) found a strong relationship between collective capability and team performance. These results go beyond the performance of the individual members and generalize across tasks and cultures (Gibson, 1999).

Deindividuation. The group effect becomes especially strong if *deindividuation* occurs, that is, if the group members lose their identity as individuals and merge themselves into the group. In such a case, the members lose many of their inhibitions and behave uncharacteristically (LeBon, 1897). The *disinhibition of deindividuation* makes it easier for team members to discuss intimate problems with a stranger whom they expect never to see again than with friends or relatives. Festinger, Pepitone, and Newcomb (1952) studied groups of students who were required to discuss personal family matters. They confirmed that the students experienced less restraint in doing so under a condition of deindividuation. They minimized the attention they paid to one another as individuals. When it was present, deindividuation was a satisfying state of group affairs associated with increased group attractiveness. In the same way, Rosenbaum (1959) and Leipold (1963) found that participants preferred to maintain a greater psychosocial distance between themselves and their partners when potentially unfavorable evaluations might be fed back to them than when no such information was anticipated. The disinhibition of deindividuation may help explain how members of special operations teams can take on extremely dangerous, life-threatening missions.

Individual identity is ordinarily stressed if rewards are anticipated; deindividuation is more likely to occur if punishment is expected. Furthermore, deindividuation increases with anonymity, the level of emotional arousal, and the novelty of the situation. The loss of inhibition is reflected in less compliance with outside authority and more conforming to the demands of the group or team. Responses are more immediate, and there is less self-awareness and premeditation. The collective mission is stressed over the individual's needs. Disinhibition and the loss of self-identity unleash the energy to accomplish great feats if they have constructive direction. They also facilitate the rabble-rouser. We become disinhibited from ordinary social constraints when we lose ourselves in a crowd. A riot-inciting leader can generate mindless mob violence.

Emotional contagion occurs even in a two-person conversation. People automatically mimic and synchronize their own movements with the facial expressions, postures, vocal utterances, and behaviors of other people. Subjective feelings are induced in the same way (Hatfield, Cacioppo, & Rapson, 1993).

Overt and Covert Effects. Particularly in collectivist societies such as China, Japan, and Korea, the group is likely to have a strong influence on its leader. Thus, Furukawa (1981) showed, in a survey of 1,576 Japanese managers, that managers establish their primary management objective from among a set of possibilities after judging how well it fits with their work team's interests and favorability to them.

Leader-member relations are also affected less overtly by the team or group. Some of the assumptions that determine an organizational culture are fantasies that are shared by members of a group that is embedded in the larger organization (Kets de Vries & Miller, 1984a). Idealization or devaluation of the leader and dependence on him or her is one such shared fantasy. One group, as a group, in the same larger organization will be dependent on whoever is assigned the job of group leader. Another group, without the same assumptions, will displays more independence or counterdependence, regardless of who is appointed leader. A leader of a group with a clique who behaves the same way as the leader of another team without a clique will be evaluated differently by the two groups. E. R. Carlson (1960) showed that groups that contain cliques are less satisfied with their leaders than are groups that are free from such cliques.

Team-Member Exchange Effects. Team effects appear to augment the leader's impact on the satisfaction of individual members. Thus Seers (undated) extended Graen's (1976) concept of the quality of the dyadic leader-member exchange to the quality of the team-member exchange. Items that correlated most highly with the factor of the quality of the team-member exchange among 178 hourly employees who worked in one of 19 teams included "how often I volunteer extra help to the team" and "how often others on the team help me to learn better work methods." Eighteen percent of a team member's work satisfaction was accounted for by the favorable quality of the member's exchange relationship with the team leader. An additional 4% was due to the quality of the exchange relationship with the team. The comparable figures for a member's satisfaction with co-workers were 11% owing to the quality of the leader-member exchange and 27% owing to the quality of the team-member exchange.

Characteristics of the Group's Members. The means and variances in the attributes of individual members make a difference to the leadership of the group and its patterns of influence. Thus, Dyson, Godwin, and Hazelwood (1976) were able to link members' consensus to the influence of decisions in homogeneous but not in heterogeneous groups. D. G. Bowers (1969) found that the leaders' importance is greater for teams composed of particular kinds of employees. Among 1,700 work groups from 22 organizations, Bowers observed that groups made up of longer-service, older, and less educated members attached greater importance to the supervisor and his or her direct influence on their behavior. The

effects were especially relevant in administrative, staff, production, and marketing groups. In better-educated, shorter-service, younger groups, especially those whose members were primarily female, such as clerical and service groups, less importance was given to the role of the supervisor and greater importance was given to the behavior of peer members of the group.

Caveat. The return for effort needs to be an equitable exchange for the team members (Naylor, Pritchard, & Ilgen, 1980) and must also meet social and transformational objectives (Sivasubrahmaniam, Murray, & Avolio, 2002). Group efforts are superior to the average individual operating alone. However, there are notable exceptions. A survey of 15% of 4,500 teams in 500 organizations mentioned inadequate conflict management and group problem solving as barriers to team effectiveness. And 80% noted as shortcomings of team organization instances where rewards, appraisals, and compensation were based on individual, not team performance. Also, group effectiveness was limited by individuals' competitiveness (Koze & Masciale, 1993). Carless, Mann, and Wearing (1995) reported that team cohesion was even more highly correlated with team performance than transformational leadership. But Erwin (1995) failed to find that team cohesion predicted team performance.

Leadership and Team Performance. The team narrows the range of possible leader–individual subordinate interactions in the interests of equity and time and because of the team's expectations about its leadership. The leadership is evaluated on the basis of the team's quantity and quality of productivity, service, and costs, the team's ability to work together, the team members' satisfaction and development (Hackman, 1990), and the performance of the teams rather than on the performance of their individual members (Schriesheim, Mowday, & Stogdill, 1979). The leader's contribution to the team's productivity is likely to be reduced by faulty group interaction processes (Steiner, 1972) or enhanced by "assembly bonus effects" (Collins & Guetzkow, 1964), which occur mainly with difficult tasks (Shaw & Ashton, 1976). That is, above and beyond individual members' capabilities to deal with the task they face, faulty leader-team interactions may result in performance that is worse than if the members had been free to work alone and to remain uninfluenced by the leader. Nonetheless, when members work in a well-led team, their performance is likely to be better than what might have been expected from a simple pooling of their individual capabilities as members (Bass, 1980).

Measuring Team Attributes

By the late 1940s, Hemphill (1949b) and Hemphill and Westie (1950) had published reliable and valid measures of group dimensions, such as status differentiation, group potency, and cohesion. Fleishman and his colleagues completed a program of investigations about team performance involving refined measures of human abilities, tasks, and contexts (Fleishman & Quaintance, 1984). Seven dimensions of team performance and refined ways to measure them were developed: (1) orientation, assignments, and exchange of information; (2) distribution of resources to match tasks; (3) timing and pacing; (4) response coordination; (5) development and acceptance of team performance norms, reinforcements, conflict resolution, and balanced competition and cooperation; (6) monitoring system and individual adjustment to errors; (7) monitoring individual and team level procedures and adjusting to nonstandard activities (Fleishman & Zaccaro, 1992). Two among the many team survey inventories that have been created since then are the Bass and Avolio (1993) Team Multifactor Leadership Questionnaire (TMLQ), and the Elliott (1997) Linking Skills Index (LSI). The TMLQ deals with the shared transactional and transformational leadership behavior within the team as a whole. Team variables such as collective efficacy, team trust, team potency, and team cohesiveness have been added. The LSI measures 11 dimensions, including the extent to which the team displays quality standards, setting objectives, participative decision making, delegation, active listening, and satisfactory work allocation. At a more microanalytical level Coovert, Campbell, Cannon-Bowers, et al. (1995) applied graph theoretical *petrinets* (Reisig, 1992) to quantitative analysis of effective and ineffective laboratory team coordination. Petrinets made it possible to describe moment-to-moment interactions among team members and to distinguish between effective and ineffective processes, strategies, and behaviors (Salas, Dickenson, Converse, et al., 1992).

Team Development

Stages in the Development of Groups into Teams. The consistency and importance of the phases in a group's development were noted and observed by many investigators. Leaders have to learn to respect these phases. Thus, Terborg, Caetore, and DeNinno (1975) demonstrated that groups must work together for some time before they can begin to behave as a team. The early period is crucial. Eriksen (2003) compared high- and low-performing teams. The high-performing teams, early on, started off well and progressed well until completion of their projects. The low-performing teams faltered in getting started and never fully recovered.

In one of the early studies of group development, Bales (1950) observed that small groups consistently exhibit phases in their problem-solving behavior. Bales and Strodtbeck (1951)[1] demonstrated that after an introductory polite stage, the second phase in the development of small groups tends to involve a great deal of tension because of the members' competition for leadership and the stabilization of the status structure. Thus, Heinicke and Bales (1953) observed that emergent leaders tended to be rated high in initiating suggestions and opinions in the first session and at the beginning of the second session, but during the second session, they began to engage in an active struggle for status. After consolidating their position in the second session, they became less active in the third and fourth sessions, permitting other members to play more active roles. But the leaders' opinions and suggestions were still accepted. The leaders did not have to make as much effort to win their points.

In a detailed study of the first two stages of unstructured small experimental teams, Geier (1967) instructed some participants in a team task. Members entered their teams without an assigned role. The leader was the member whom the members perceived by consensus as having made the most successful attempt to influence the team. Stage 1 involved the rapid and painless elimination of contenders with negative characteristics. The second stage involved an intense struggle for leadership and the further elimination of competitors. Only 2 of 80 members in the various teams studied made no effort to gain leadership. Those who were uninformed, unpartici-

[1] See also Borgatta and Bales (1953b), Heinicke and Bales (1953), and Philip and Dunphy (1959).

pative, and rigid and hindered the attainment of goals were eliminated first. Attempts to recruit lieutenants and to gain the members' support were most obvious in Stage 2. The roles of lieutenant developed in 11 of 16 teams. Of the 11 lieutenants, 7 had been contenders for leadership in Stage 1.

Tuckman (1965) reviewed some 60 studies involving experimental, training, and therapeutic groups. An analysis of these studies suggested two additional stages of development through which the groups had to go to reach full group maturity. The first two stages of *forming* and *storming* were like stages of politeness followed by conflict. Forming was characterized by testing and orientation; storming was characterized by intragroup conflict, status differentiation, and emotional response. The third stage was norming, characterized by the development of group cohesion, norms, and intermember exchange; and the fourth stage was performing as a team, marked by functional role interrelations and the effective performance of tasks. These stages of forming, storming, norming, and performing could overlap in some groups and alternate in others (Heinen & Jacobsen, 1976). The emergence and success of the different kinds of leadership that were needed could clearly be connected to each of these phases. For example, Erwin (1995) suggested that during the stages of norming and storming, compared to any external leadership, the internal team leadership was more important to the team's effective development. Nevertheless, Pearce and Rode (2001) showed that for 71 teams in a program of change, the amount of *enablement* by higher-level management (providing needed resources, training, and support) correlated from −.28 to −.35 with the teams' prosocial behavior, commitment, effectiveness, and absence of social loafing.

Re-forming. The development of teams continues into further stages (Gersick, 1985). About halfway through the life cycle of problem solving as groups and teams (which presumably have reached the fourth, performing, stage), the teams re-form themselves. During this re-formation, groups reevaluate their progress to date, reach agreement on final goals, revise their plans for completing their assigned task, and refocus their effort toward completing the task. Following this re-formation, they concentrate more of their efforts on the critical as-

pects of performing the task and focus on accomplishing their task to meet the stated requirements. Near the completion of the task, efforts are made to shape the team product so it will fit environmental demands. Work is finalized, consistent with the requirements of the situation.

Structure and Purpose. Avolio and Bass (1994) conceived the stages in group development as going from unstructured *groups* to highly structured *teams* based on sharing of purposes, commitments, trust, drive, and expectations. In unstructured groups, there is no clear agenda or assignments; members are confused or conflicted about responsibilities and perspectives. Direction may be irrelevant to the group's reason for existence. In highly structured teams, there is close monitoring by the members of one another for any deviations, which are then addressed. Rules are strictly enforced. Members are unwilling to take risks.

A team begins as a group without a necessarily shared purpose, commitment, trust, or drive. It becomes structured into a team and becomes fully developed when it reaches a high degree of shared purpose, commitment, trust, and drive (Avolio & Bass, 1994). The mental stage of the team as a team is important to the emergence of leaders and the effects of leadership. For example, different leaders emerged in successive stages of therapy in a psychiatric ward (S. Parker, 1958). Likewise, Sterling and Rosenthal (1950) reported that leaders and followers changed with different phases of the group process; the same leaders recur when the same phases return. Kinder and Kolmarm (1976) found that in 23-hour *marathon groups* (night-and-day-long sensitivity training groups), gains in self-actualization were greatest when initially highly structured leadership roles were maintained early in the groups' development and switched to low-structured leadership roles later in the groups' development. Okanes and Stinson (1974) concluded that more Machiavellian persons were chosen as informal leaders early in the development when groups could still improvise; once the groups became more highly structured teams, however, Machiavellian persons were less likely to be chosen as leaders. Vecchio (1987) concluded that the one aspect of the Hersey-Blanchard model (1977) that had validity was the utility of using directive leadership early in the group's development and then em-

Figure 26.1 Model Linking Leadership to Group Outcomes

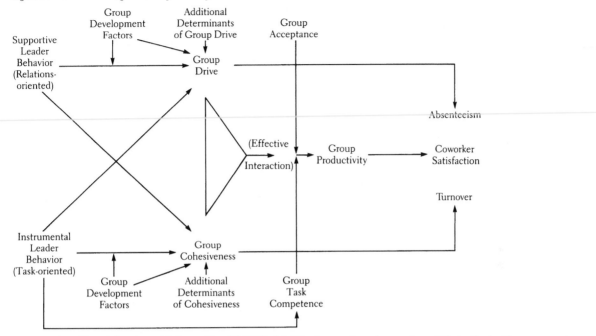

SOURCE: Adapted from Schriesheim, Moday, and Stogdill (1979). (Modifications are shown in parentheses. Effects of leadership on group outcomes are not shown.)

ploying more participative leadership for the group as it matured.

On the basis of a review of the literature, Stogdill (1959, 1972) identified three possible main effects of the leader on organized groups: productivity, drive, and cohesiveness. The rational model (Figure 26.1) created by Schriesheim, Mowday, and Stogdill (1979) proposed that a group's drive and cohesiveness interact with each other to generate a group's productivity. In the model, supportive or relations-oriented leadership behavior interacts with instrumental or task-oriented leadership behavior to promote a group's drive and cohesiveness. All this occurs in the context of the group's development, which also contributes to the group's drive and cohesiveness and results in more effective interaction among its members. Then, if the group as a team has the competence to complete the task and accepts the responsibility for doing so, its productivity increases; the satisfaction of members with one another is greater; and the members' tendency to be frequently absent or to quit is reduced. According to a meta-analysis by Salas, Mullen, Rozell, et al. (1997),

role clarification and structuring relationships were keys to successfully developing teams and their performance.

Leaders Make a Difference in Team Structure. Leaders differ in how much they affect the extent to which the intended structure of relations within a team and its input and outputs is actually the enacted structure. In a study of 39 work groups in three organizations, Inderrieden (1984) found that, along with the uncertainty of the task, the leaders' need for power and self-actualization were the strongest predictors of the actual structure of the work groups.

Effective leadership allows groups to move systematically through the necessary developmental stages. Groups that are unable to develop a differentiated leader-follower role structure will be unable to engage in the effective performance of tasks (Borgatta & Bales, 1953b). Conversely, groups with a high degree of consensus about their leadership will be more effective and better satisfied than will those that do not reach such a consensus. De Souza and Klein (1995) conducted an experiment using

468 college students in initially leaderless quartets of four with tasks and goals. Groups with emergent leaders outperformed groups without such leadership. The emergent leaders had greater ability for the task and commitment to the group goal. The clarity of leadership in 170 health care teams was related to clear team objectives, high levels of participation, commitment to excellence, and support for innovation (West, Borrill, Dawson, et al. (2003).

Stages and Outcomes. Avolio, Jung, Murray, et al. (1996) studied the shared team leadership of 188 undergraduates in teams of five to seven members early and late in the semester. They used the Team MLQ. The expected correlations with outcomes in extra effort, effectiveness, and satisfaction declined from the early phase to the late phase, but inspirational motivation increased in correlation with collective efficacy from .33 to .63 and with potency from .49 to .66. For contingent reward, increases were recorded from .11 to .63 with collective efficacy and .18 to .63 with potency. Passive and active management by exception showed little change.

Stogdill (1972) suggested that the cohesiveness, drive, and productivity of a team are closely related to its developmental stage and what is required of the team leader. The team's drive appears in every stage, but the arousal and tensions of the second stage of storming most closely reflect the amount of that drive. The specific tasks that the team is motivated to perform, however, may differ across the stages. Thus, for instance, in the second stage, the team's drive is directed toward evolving a structure for the team. In the third stage, it operates to develop greater cohesiveness. In the third stage (norming), roles have finally been accepted and communication has improved; team cohesiveness emerges. In the fourth and final stage, effective performance of the task, team productivity is seen.

The functions of the leader depend on the stage of a group's development. For instance, relations-oriented leadership behavior will contribute to the team's need to develop cohesiveness in the third stage (norming), and task-oriented leadership behavior will facilitate the team's accomplishment of the task in the fourth stage (performing).

Stages and Role Boundaries. The team's development can be seen in the stabilization of the role boundaries of the individual members, including those of the leader. The role boundary set of any member encompasses the acts that the other group members will accept. Boundaries are established by fairly stable role expectations that are often conveyed by the leader. In group experiments by Gibb (1961), one leader with a permissive leadership style was followed by another with a restrictive style, and vice versa. In other groups, one leader was followed by another with the same style. Group members accepted and responded more readily to leaders who followed other leaders with the same style of either latitude or restriction in the members' prescribed range of behaviors. The members were also less defensive and more productive in problem solving. Expectations were built quickly, with minimum cues, and survived over long periods. Esteemed and influential members—those frequently nominated as such in sociometric tests—tended to stay within the realistic boundaries prescribed by the group. Individuals who were less frequently chosen were those more likely to violate the boundary specifications. (Perhaps those who were chosen more often had a wider range of behaviors and more role space in which to move.) The members responded to an individual member's role actions outside the role's boundaries by pretending not to see or hear the behavior, ignoring it, engaging subtle fighting or open rebellion, isolating the member, or forcing his or her withdrawal.

Given the power of norms, groups tended to select goals and perform activities that were commensurate with the norms. To exert influence, the behavior and goals of the leader had to be consonant with the group's goals. But high levels of defensiveness in the group prevented the effective exercise of such influence. The leadership also needs to take into account whether members conform to avoid criticism, to serve their own interests, to fulfill obligations, or to fit with the member's values and principles.

Groups undergo an orderly reduction in defensiveness as they mature, according to J. R. Gibb (1964). While a group is forming, its members remain superficial and polite to each other and trust is low. After members have learned to trust one another (presumably after some storming), they learn how to make effective decisions and gain greater control over the choice of goals in the norming phase. With these better goals, they can make better use of the group's resources.

Leadership and a Stable Structure

A stable structure of relations must be developed for a group or team to become cohesive (Heinen & Jacobsen, 1976; Sherwood & Walker, 1960; Tuckman, 1965). A leader has important effects on a group's development of a stable structure (Heslin & Dunphy, 1964). Recognizing this fact, Bion (1961) found that if the discussion leader of a therapy group failed to provide structure, the members, striving to arrive at a structure, sought a leader among themselves. As was discussed in previous chapters, during the early stages of a group's development, members may want and accept more direction. At this time, leaders may exert a greater influence on the stabilization of a group's role structures and thus have a greater impact on the group's cohesiveness.

In a study of Japanese nursery school children, Toki (1935) observed that early separation of an emergent leader from the group resulted in a disintegration of the structure of the group. The structure was more likely to hold up when the emergent leader left late in the group's development. When an adult leader was introduced, the structure built around the child leader collapsed.

Effects of Groups and Teams on Their Leaders

Differences among groups that are likely to affect what the leader can and will do include the group's drive, cohesiveness, size, compatibility, norms, and status. Earlier chapters looked at some of these effects from a variety of different perspectives.

Effects of Drive

Grant, Graham, and Hebeling (2001) noted from 32 case study reports about team projects that when the team members dedicated all of their time to the project and the project was of singular importance to the leader, the leader had to dedicate a great deal of time to the careful selection of skilled, compatible, and collaborative members. Bass, Flint, and Pryer (1957b) demonstrated that the motivation of all the members of a team affected the success of the leader. When all members are initially equal in status, an individual is more likely to become influential as a team leader if he or she attempts more leadership than others do. However, among highly motivated members, such attempted leadership was found to exert little effect on who emerged as a leader to influence the team's decision. In the same way, Hemphill, Pepinsky, Shevitz, et al. (1954) showed that team members attempted to lead more frequently when the rewards for solving a problem were relatively high and they had a reasonable expectation that efforts to lead would contribute to the accomplishment of the task. Durand and Nord (1976) observed subordinates in a textile and plastics firm who felt that their success or failure was in the hands of forces outside their control. (Presumably they were lower in team motivation. They tended to see their supervisors as initiating more structure and showing less consideration.)

A team's drive is likely to be high when members are highly committed. Members are more likely to want to expend energy for such teams. Gustafson (1968) manipulated members' commitment to their student discussion teams by varying the extent to which grades for a course depended on the team's performance. Less role differentiation into leaders, task specialists, and social-emotional specialists was perceived by members with either a strong commitment or a weak commitment; that is, the three functions were not differentiated, but the teams showed less social-emotional behavior when their members were highly committed. In an analysis of 1,200 to 1,400 subordinates' descriptions of their teams, Farrow, Valenzi, and Bass (1980) found that directive leadership and delegative leadership were seen more frequently when the subordinates' commitment to the teams was high.

Effects of Cohesiveness

Group cohesiveness has been defined in many different ways. It has been defined as the average member's attraction to the group (Bass, 1960) and as all the forces acting on members to remain in the group (Festinger, 1950). It has been conceived of as the level of the group's morale (C. E. Shaw, 1976), the individual needs satisfied from group membership (Cartwright, 1965), and the extent to which members reinforce one anothers' expectations about the value of maintaining the identity of the group (Stogdill, 1972). It has been identified by highly correlated variables such as the members' commitment to the group, the presence of peer pressure, the felt support from the group, and the absence of role conflict in the group. For some, it has meant valued group activities, group solidarity, willingness to be identified as a member of the group, and agreement about norms, structure, and roles.

Podsakoff, Todor, Grover, et al. (1984) collected data from 1,116 mainly male employees working in a variety of city and state government agencies. Cohesiveness significantly increased the employees' satisfaction with supervisors who practiced a good deal of contingent rewarding. It significantly decreased satisfaction with supervisors who engaged in a lot of noncontingent punishment. Cohesion had no significant effect on satisfaction with supervisors who were contingent punishers or noncontingent rewarders. According to Dobbins and Zaccaro (1986), cohesiveness moderated the effects of leaders' consideration and initiation of structure on subordinates' satisfaction among 203 military cadets. Leaders' consideration and initiation of structure was correlated more highly with subordinates' satisfaction in cohesive compared to uncohesive groups.

Drive and Cohesiveness. The motivation of a group includes its drive along with its cohesiveness. The drive of a group refers to its level of directed energization; the cohesiveness of the group is the level of attachment of the members to the group and its purposes. Clearly, the two are related in that both increase with the extent to which the group and its activities are valued by the members. Nevertheless, many investigations have focused on one or the other. The drive and cohesiveness have been merged by focusing on the members' loyalty, involvement, and commitment to the group (Furukawa, 1981). Stogdill (1972) conceived group drive to be the arousal, freedom, enthusiasm, or esprit of the group and the intensity with which members invest their expectations and energy on behalf of the group. Steiner (1972) defined group motivation similarly as the willingness of members to contribute their resources to the collective effort. Zander (1971) found such motivation to depend on the members' desires to achieve success and avoid failure, as well as their previous history of success (Zander, 1968) and pressures for high performance (Zander, Mcdow, & Dustin, 1964).

Although drive and cohesiveness ordinarily are corre-lated, Stogdill (1972) concluded, from a review of 60 studies, that under certain circumstances, the level of group drive (or team drive) conditions the relationship between productivity and cohesiveness. Under routine operating conditions and low drive, team productivity and cohesiveness tend to be negatively related, while under high drive, they tend to be positively related. The seemingly paradoxical findings are readily explained when group drive is studied along with productivity and cohesiveness. When the team's drive is high, members' energies are directed toward its goal. If the team is also cohesive, the members will work collectively and productively toward that goal. On the other hand, if the group's drive is low, the members' energies will be directed elsewhere. If the team also remains cohesive, the members will reinforce one another's tendencies to ignore the team's productive goals and seek satisfaction from nonproductive activities.

Expectations, Solidarity, and Identification. Avolio and Bass (1994) observed that the expectations of unstructured, uncohesive groups were lower than those of more structured, cohesive teams and that expectations were exceeded in high-performance, highly cohesive teams. Borgatta, Cottrell, and Wilker (1959) studied groups that differed in the members' expectations about the value of group activities. The higher the initial expectation, the higher the final level of satisfaction for groups as a whole. Leaders of low-expectation groups changed their assessments more than leaders of high-expectation groups did.

The ease of the flow of influence between the leader and followers was expected to be associated with cohesive social relations (Turk, Hartley, & Shaw, 1962). Theodorson (1957) found that the roles of task leader and social leader were combined in cohesive groups but were separated in poorly integrated groups. Weak group cohesiveness provided a condition under which those who scored high in sociability attempted to develop cooperation through increased interaction, while those who scored low in sociability tended to remain passive (Armilla, 1967).

Gergen and Taylor (1969) demonstrated that high-status participants, when presented to a group in a *solidarity setting*, tended to meet the group's expectations but failed to meet expectations when they were presented in a *productivity setting*. Low-status participants in the productivity context presented themselves more positively; in the solidarity condition, they became more self-demeaning.

Acceptance of a group's leaders is linked to identification with the in-group. Bulgarian or Yemenite immigrants to Israel identified themselves first as Jewish, then second as Bulgarians or Yemenites. As a consequence, they could more easily support and follow Israeli leaders. On the other hand, Israeli immigrants who identified themselves first as Germans, Americans, or Moroccans were more likely to accept the Israeli leaders only if their self-evaluation was not rooted in the old country (Eisenstadt, 1952).

Implications for Structuring. Arguing that norms, structure, and roles are clearer in cohesive groups, J. F. Schriesheim (1980) proposed that initiation of structure by the leader is redundant in cohesive groups. But more initiation by the leader is likely in groups in which cohesiveness is low, groups that have less of a normative influence on members, and groups in which the members are more likely to be dependent on the leader than on the group. An analysis of data from 43 work groups in a public utility supported Schriesheim's proposition by showing that satisfaction with supervision, role clarity, and self-rated performance correlated much more highly with initiation of structure by the leader if the groups were low rather than high in cohesiveness. Schriesheim also expected that the leaders' consideration would contribute to the subordinates' role clarity only in groups whose cohesiveness was high. Again, her supposition was borne out. She found a correlation of .31 between the leaders' consideration and the subordinates' role clarity in highly cohesive groups but corresponding correlations of −.05 and −.04 in groups in which cohesiveness was medium or low. Schriesheim inferred from these results that highly cohesive groups provide members with clear roles and that clarity is reinforced by supportive, considerate leaders. Such groups have little need for additional initiation from their leaders. Leaders need to structure such groups less tightly (House & Dessler, 1974). Again, consultative leadership will yield more subordinates' satisfaction if the leaders feel that members are highly committed to the group and its goals (Farrow, Valenzi, & Bass, 1980).

Effects of the Group's Agreement about a Leader. The leadership process is affected by whether the immediate group is in agreement on who will lead it. Agreement among the members about who should lead was found to be correlated with greater group cohesiveness (Shelley, 1960a) and with more frequent attempts to lead (Banta & Nelson, 1964). Bales and Slater (1955) obtained results showing that three different roles of members tended to emerge in groups that did not reach a consensus on who should lead: an active role, a task specialist role, and a best-liked-person role. In groups that had attained such a consensus, less role differentiation occurred; the active and task specialist roles were performed by the same member. Harrell and Gustafson (1966) reported that in groups lacking consensus, an active task specialist role emerged along with a best-liked-member role. Role differentiation occurred less in both their high- and low-consensus groups than in Bales and Slater's study. In addition, attractive groups and those with the most interesting tasks tended to exhibit the least role differentiation.

Harmony and Cooperativeness. Consultation by the group leader was more frequent in work groups that were described by their members as harmonious and free of conflict (Bass, Valenzi, Farrow, & Solomon, 1975). Groups with cooperative members, compared with groups with competitive members, were more likely to develop leaders, evaluate fellow members more favorably, show less hostility, and solve their problems as a group more rapidly (Raven & Eachus, 1963). This finding is consistent with the conventional wisdom that suggests that it usually benefits the organization to encourage competition among groups with independent tasks but that competition should be discouraged within the groups.

Compatible Members. Groups composed of compatible rather than incompatible members are better able to elect competent leaders. They are also better able to use the resources and abilities of their members, since they are more likely to elect leaders who allow the highly competent members enough freedom to express themselves and to influence the groups' performance (W. C. Schutz, 1955). Lester (1965) found that the emergent leader among the highly task-oriented members of an American

Mount Everest climbing expedition was able to be more relations-oriented.

Thelen et al. (1954) factor analyzed the self- and group descriptions made by members of a discussion group. Five clusters of members were identified. Cluster A, composed of members who rejected fighting and pairing, made significantly more leadership attempts than did any other cluster. It preferred structure and cohesiveness, which prevent undue domination and intimacy. Cluster B, with ego needs for intimate relationships, showed little interest in differences in status. Cluster C, which preferred to avoid power struggles or responsibility, rejected competition for leadership. Cluster AC, which rejected fighting, supported and looked to the leader to support their status needs. Cluster BC, which accepted fighting, supported the leader and attempted to mediate conflicts to maintain the group's cohesion.

Effects of the Group's Size

Increased size affects a group's leadership. It brings with it reduced opportunities to lead, more responsibilities and demands on the leader, and a possible widening of the span of control.[2] As the size of the group increases, the number of interactional relationships among members increases at an extremely rapid rate. Graicunas (1937) deduced that a leader with two subordinates can interact with them both singly and in combination. The contacts can be initiated by the leader or by the subordinates, so that six relationships are possible. With four subordinates, the number of possible relationships is 44. With six subordinates, the number of possible relationships is 222. Graicunas concluded that executives should not have more than four or five subordinates reporting to them directly; because of the time required for personal contacts. Nevertheless, surveys of industrial executives[3] indicated that corporation presidents may have from 1 to 25 assistants reporting to them. The average in the several surveys ranged from five to nine immediate assistants. But the evidence accumulated over the years indicates that five to seven is an optimum size for most groups, with the task determining whether smaller or larger size

is most efficient (Bass, 1981). Data collected between 1993 and 1995 for 74 software product teams were found by Carmel and Bird (1997) to have a median membership size of five. The researchers accounted for the effectiveness that results from keeping team size small. It makes possible close communication and participation of all members in decisions.

Opportunities to Lead. The size of the group affects the emergence of a leader. Bass and Norton (1951) reported that the opportunity of any single member to take on the functions of leadership in a group decreased as the number of members increased.[4] In agreement, Hare (1962) reviewed several studies that suggested that as the size of the group increases, individual members have less opportunity to talk and to attempt to lead. Fewer members can initiate leadership acts. Again, Warner and Hilander's (1964) study of 191 voluntary organizations in a community found that the involvement and participation of members decreased as the size of the organization increased. To the contrary, J. H. Healy (1956) found that for chief executives of corporations, subordinates' involvement in policy making was greater as the number of immediate subordinates increased.

As the size of a group increases, more differences appear in the members' tendency to be talkative and in their attempts to be influential (Bales & Slater, 1955). In groups that ranged from 2 to 12 members, Bass and Norton (1951) reported that such differences increased directly with the increase in the size of the groups, and reached the maximum in groups of six members. But contrary to most researchers, Kidd (1958) found no relation between the size of a group and increases in the differences among members' influence in groups of two, four, or six members. Blankenship and Miles (1968) also noted that the size of the units they led was less important to the decision-making behavior of executives than was their organizational level.

Changes in Leadership Style and Effects. Hemphill (1950b) studied groups with leaders whom the group members considered to be superior. He found that as the size of the groups increased, the members made greater

---

[2]For a detailed review of the effects of span of control in relation to the size of the group, see House and Miner (1969).
[3]See Dale (1952), Entwisle and Walton (1961), J. H. Healy (1956), and F. W. Mahler (1961).

[4]Evidence that the opportunity for leadership tends to decrease as the size of the group increases was also provided by Bales, Strodtbeck, Mills, and Roseborough (1951); Dawe (1934); and Stephan (1952).

demands on the leaders. Larger groups made significantly stronger demands on the leaders' strength, reliability, predictability, coordination, impartial enforcement of rules, and competence to do the job. At the same time, larger groups required less consideration from the leaders for individual members.

Pelz (1951) observed that small groups were better satisfied with leaders who took their part than with those who sided with the organization. Larger groups (10 or more members) were better satisfied with leaders who supported the organization. Medalia's (1954) results indicated that as the size of the work unit increased, workers' perception of their leaders as "human relations–minded" decreased. Goodstadt and Kipnis (1970) found that as the size of the groups increased, supervisors tended to spend less time with poor workers and to give fewer pay raises to good workers. In 100 randomly selected chapters of the League of Women Voters, J. Likert (1958) found that officers engaged in more activities as the chapters increased in size, but the chapter presidents exhibited less interest in individual members' ideas. Consistent with all these findings, Schriesheim and Murphy (1976) found that the leaders' initiation of structure was related to satisfaction of members in larger work groups and that the leaders' consideration was related to the satisfaction of members in smaller groups. However, Greene and Schriesheim (1980) showed that instrumented leadership was actually most influential in affecting drive and cohesiveness in larger work groups, while supportive leadership was most influential in smaller work groups.

A meta-analysis by Wagner and Gooding (1987) of 7 to 19 studies of the effects of participative leadership on various outcomes found that the positive correlation of perceived participative leadership with perceived satisfaction of subordinates remained at .44 and .42, respectively, in small and large groups, but the correlation between participative leadership as perceived by members and their acceptance of decisions fell from .44 in small groups to .31 in large groups. When independent sources of leadership and outcome data that were free of single-source bias were correlated, the results again fell for the acceptance of decisions, from .27 to .20, and for satisfaction from .25 to .03. Thus overall, participatory leadership practices generally had more salutary effects in smaller than in larger groups.

Kipnis, Schmidt, and Wilkinson (1980) reported that

when trying to be influential, supervisors of large groups were likely to choose impersonal tactics such as assertiveness and appeals to a higher authority instead of more personal influence tactics such as ingratiation and bargaining. In small groups, relatively more personal and fewer impersonal tactics were employed by the same supervisors. This finding may explain why a small span of control does not produce close supervision (Bell, 1967; Udell, 1967).

Changes in Requirements. Thomas and Fink (1963) reviewed several studies that concluded that as groups enlarged, the leaders had to deal with more role differentiation, more role specialization, and more cliques. Slater (1958) noted that the stabilization of a group's role structure became increasingly difficult with increasing size of the group.

Hare (1952) studied boys in groups ranging from 5 to 12 members. Leaders were found to exert more influence on decisions in the smaller groups, but the leaders' level of skill was not related to influence. The larger groups demanded more skill from their leaders. In large groups, the leaders' skill was positively correlated with the increased movement of members toward group consensus. Yet, in a comprehensive summary of personal factors found to be associated with leadership in natural and experimental groups, R. D. Mann (1959) noted that in groups of seven or smaller, intelligence seemed a little more important to leadership than adjustment; but in larger groups, adjustment increased slightly and intelligence decreased slightly in correlation with leadership.

Antecedents. Guion (1953) and G. D. Bell (1967) found that first-level supervisors tended to supervise fewer subordinates as the complexity of the job increased. The number of subordinates of chief executives tended to increase with the growth of the size of firms, according to J. H. Healy (1956). His results suggested that individuals differ in their ability to interact and that many who become leaders of very large organizations are able to interact with 12 to 15 or more assistants without feeling overburdened or pressured for time. Indik (1964) surveyed 116 organizations that ranged in size from 15 to 3,000 members and found that as organizations increase in size, they take on more operating members before they add new supervisors.

Confounds. Indik (1963, 1965a) cautioned that most generalizations about the effects of size are confounded by other factors. Two of these factors are the greater cohesiveness to be found in the smaller group, and the optimum size for the group's task. In a survey of 5,871 workers from 228 factory groups that ranged from 5 to 50 members, Seashore (1954) found that the smaller groups were also more cohesive. The same was true for the conference groups studied by N. E. Miller (1950).

As was noted, demands on a leader's initiatives increase along with the group's size, and the potential of the leader or members to interact individually with one another decreases as the group enlarges. If additional members are superfluous and unnecessary as far as the completion of a team's task is concerned, effectiveness and satisfaction are likely to suffer with an increase in the number of members. For any given task, there is an optimum-size team. Two people or even one person may be adequate and optimal for many tasks; five or six appear to be optimal for discussion groups (Bass, 1960). A larger number of different kinds of experts are likely to be needed for complex tasks whose completion requires skills and knowledge from many disciplines. The leader may need to deal with teams that are suboptimal in size or too large for the team's task. When the team is too large for the task, the leader may need to initiate more structure so members do not get in each other's way. When the team is too small for the task, the leader may need to provide for more time and resources or reduce the team's goals.

Effects of the Status and Esteem of the Group or Team

Some groups in a large organization are seen as more valuable and critical to the organization's success than are other groups. For example, line groups are likely to be considered more important than staff teams. Prestige also may vary. Thus the biology department may be perceived as more prestigious than the agriculture department at a university. Groups of skilled craftsmen may be thought of as more prestigious than groups of assembly line operatives. The reputations of groups of the same type may vary as well. For instance, one biology department may be viewed as ossified, while another is seen as being at the forefront of the field. Similarly, one group of skilled craftsmen may be seen as quarrelsome, recalcitrant, and hard to please, whereas another group may be considered highly efficient, competent, and dependable. Fried (1988) showed that within organizations like hospitals, the relative power of the nurses group, administrative staff, and physicians' group were seen, particularly by the nurses, to depend on the centrality, nonsubstitutability, and coping with uncertainty of their respective roles.

Leadership within these different groups is likely to be affected in several ways. It will be easier to attract and hold members in the groups that have higher status and esteem. Members of these more highly valued groups will have relatively more influence with their leaders. In turn, their leaders will have more influence when they represent their groups in dealings with higher authority and with representatives of other groups at the same organizational level.

Functionally Diverse, Cross-Functional, and Multifunctional Teams.

Functionally Diverse, Cross-Functional, and Multifunctional Teams. Leading a faculty group from different departments and disciplines is described as akin to herding cats. Yet diversity of education, profession, interest, knowledge, abilities, and departmental location in organizations is commonplace. Such functional diversity is witnessed in bringing together, on a regular or ad hoc basis, the vice presidents from the different divisions of the organization to generate policy suggestions; the scientists, engineers, and production heads to staff a functionally diverse team to innovate a new product; or the psychologist, social worker, psychiatrist, and nurse to discuss treatment of a mental health patient. Functionally diverse teams are expected to make better, more informed decisions but have a harder time reaching consensus. They help the leadership by facilitating organizational processes (Bantel & Jackson, 1989). They can help the top management interpret environmental ambiguities and reduce uncertainty (Zaccaro, Rittman, & Marks, 2001). As expert teams, they contribute to surveillance of the outside environment for the leadership and provide boundary spanning (Ancona & Caldwell, 1988). The leaders of cross-functional teams need to be technically competent and particularly skillful politically and interpersonally. They need to understand how the different functions are relevant to the success of the team (Yukl, 1998). Additionally, Jassawalla and Sashittal (1999) suggest, cross-functional team leaders should emphasize informal, intense meetings and exchanges of information.

Forums should be provided for airing of issues and clarifications. Every member's response to decisions should be treated as important. Members should be replaced if they are unable to overcome protecting their own turf or show mistrust of others or lack of commitment to collective intentions. Constructive conflict and delays should be tolerated.

Waldman (1994) noted some problems of multifunctional teams. At Honda, they generated procrastination and divisiveness (where harmony is prized). Leaders had to intervene to avoid costly delays. Waldman mentions seven roles of these leaders: (1) careful staffing; (2) coordinating and facilitating rather than directing; (3) encouraging members to form links with one another and the team's clients; (4) establishing group-based evaluation and incentives; (5) anticipating and tolerating mistakes; (6) eliminating impediments to team performance; (7) aligning individual members' and team goals. The leaders also need to maintain the vision, to be inspiring, to question assumptions, and to carry on in many other transformational ways.

Effects of the Group's Norms

The group's norms (its definition of tasks, goals, the paths to the goals, and the appropriate relationships among members) strongly affect what a leader can accomplish in the group as well as who will emerge as the leader. In turn, the leader often has an impact on group outcomes by influencing the group's norms.

Frame of Reference. Sherif's conception of the social norm exerted a marked influence on research on leadership. In an autokinetic experience, Sherif (1936) seated a subject in a darkened room and asked the person to observe a spot of light projected on a screen. The subject reported the distance that the light appeared to move. The average distance for several trials was recorded as the subject's individual norm. When the subject was later placed with a confederate of the experimenter who uniformly reported a distance that varied markedly from that reported by the participant, the subject tended to change his or her estimates to conform to the group norm. Asch (1952) obtained similar results when a subject was asked to judge the length of lines after six confederates of the experimenter had rendered judgments that defied

the senses. The confederates uniformly declared that the shorter of two lines was longer. It was the norm of the confederates, not any single emergent leader, that influenced many of the subjects.

Other demonstrations of the effect of group norms showed how these norms moderate whether actual leadership behavior will be perceived as such. Thus, in an experimental comparison, Lord and Alliger (1985) found that the correlation of group members' perceptions of emergent leadership with actually observed leadership behaviors was greater when norms were established for members to be systematic rather than remaining spontaneous. Likewise, Phillips and Lord (1981) demonstrated that if a group was described as effective but members were led to believe that the group's success could be explained by other factors than the leader, the group's performance had less of an effect on the members' ratings of the leader.

The Group's History of Successes or Failures. Some groups and organizations have histories of success and high performance that contribute to their esteem, while others have histories of failure and low performance. For instance, different United Fund agencies were found by Zander, Forward, and Albert (1969) to be consistently successful or consistently unsuccessful in meeting the goals of their fund drives. In the same way, Denison (1984) reported consistencies in the rate of return on investments by companies over a five-year period. Some companies tend to do well continually; others always do poorly. Histories of success give rise to norms of success and high performance, while histories of failure give rise to norms of failure and low performance. Thus, Farris and Lim (1969) found that high-performance groups had higher expectations of their future success as groups than did low-performance groups. Leaders whose accession to office coincides with a failure when the groups have been accustomed to success will no doubt earn more blame than ordinarily. Conversely, leaders whose accession coincides with the success of previously failing groups will gain an unusual amount of credit, which may not be justified. According to experimental results obtained by Howell (1985), a role conflict condition will arise for members when performance norms are low but the leader is high in the initiation of structure, particularly in the pressure to produce.

Conformity and Deviation. Ordinarily, when a discrepancy exists between the opinion of one member and the rest of the group, the deviating member tends to move closer to the group norm. But if an extreme deviate refuses to yield, he or she will be rejected by the other members (Festinger, 1950, 1954; Schachter, 1951). Gerard (1953) and Berkowitz and Howard (1959) obtained results to indicate that leaders directed most of their communications to such deviates. If a deviate was unreceptive to accepting the majority point of view, the group tended to expel the deviate from the group psychologically. Raven's (1959a) report of the results of an experiment noted that deviates would shift toward the norm if they could express their opinions both privately and in public. Presumably, the leader could make a difference by encouraging such expression by the deviates.

Conformity to Norms and the Leader. Scioli, Dyson, and Fleitas (1974) found that when conformity was demanded by college groups, the most dominant members became the groups' instrumental (task-oriented) leaders. Thibaut and Strickland (1956) obtained results indicating that as the group's pressure to conform increased (often pushed by the leader), more members increased in conformity under a *group set*, while more decreased in conformity under a *task set*.[5] At the same time, McKeachie (1954) reported that the members' conformity to the norms of their groups and liking for the groups were greater in leader-oriented than in group-oriented classes.

Newcomb (1943) conducted a study of social values on a college campus. He found that the most influential members represented the dominant values of the campus. Those who conformed in conduct but not in attitude possessed social skills but maintained close ties to their families. Those who conformed in attitude but not in conduct tended to lack social skills but regarded conformity of attitudes to be a mark of community acceptance and superior intelligence. Similarly, Sharma (1974) found that Indian students who were activists and prominent as leaders of demonstrations were concerned primarily with student issues, not with social change. The attitudes of these student activists tended to reflect the traditional values of their communities regarding religion, caste, marriage, and family. Likewise, in a study of modernization in India that sampled 606 heads of households engaged in agriculture, Trivedi (1974) found that although opinion leaders may have accepted innovations in agriculture, they, like Sharma's (1974) student activists, adhered to traditional religious beliefs and convictions. They differentiated agricultural from religious activities more fully in the process. (But in the United States in the late 1960s and early 1970s and in France in 1968, as in China in 1919 and 1989, the norms of student activists placed them in the vanguard of reform and revolutionary change.)

In a Hungarian study, Merei (1949) formed groups that were composed of submissive nursery school children. When placed in separate rooms, each group developed its own role structure, rules for play, and routine of activities. After these had become stabilized, a child with strong propensities to lead in play activities was introduced into each group. Although the new members were widely successful in gaining leadership positions, they were not able to change the norms and procedural rules of the groups. The groups had more of an impact on the leaders than the leaders had on the groups. Consistent with this finding, Bates (1952) showed that the closer that the behavior of individuals comes to realizing the norms of the group, the higher these individuals' likely position as leaders in the group. However, many other investigators found that group leaders ranked higher in the assimilation of group norms because they were highly influential in the formation of the norms.[6] Although leaders may be influential in establishing group norms, once the norms are adopted, they are expected to observe the norms (Hare, 1962).

O. J. Harvey (1960) found that formal leaders conformed more to group norms than did informal (sociometrically identified) leaders or other group members, especially under conditions of uncertainty. Mulder (1960) also found that the judgment of leaders was most influenced by other members when they, the leaders, were appointed in an ambiguous situation. But the emergent, informal leaders were the least influenced in the ambiguous situation without established norms.

---

[5] Under a task set, subjects were instructed to focus their attention on the task; under a group set, they were to concentrate on the group.

[6] See Borgatta (1955b); Jones, Gergen, and Jones (1963); Kates and Mahony (1958); Katz, Libby, and Strodtbeck (1964); E. M. Mumford (1959); Tannenbaum and Bachman (1966); and Turk (1961).

When the Leader Can Deviate. The fact that leaders tend to be prime exemplars of their groups' value systems is not to suggest that they are slaves to the groups' norms (Rittenhouse, 1966). In fact, they may deviate considerably from the norms in various aspects of their conduct. In a study of sociometric cliques among teachers, Rasmussen and Zander (1954) found that leaders were less threatened than were followers by deviation from their subgroup's norms. Leaders appeared secure enough to feel they could depart from the norms without jeopardizing their status. Similarly, Harvey and Consalvi (1960) found that the member who was second highest in status as a leader of a group was significantly more conforming than was the member who was at the top or bottom of the status hierarchy. The leader conformed the least, but not significantly less than the lowest-status member. Likewise, Hughes (1946) observed that members of industrial work groups let *rate busters* know in forceful terms that their violation of group norms would not be tolerated. However, the leaders of the work groups were allowed more freedom to deviate from certain group norms than were other members whose positions were less secure.

The Leader's Need for Early Conformity. As was detailed in previous chapters, Hollander (1958, 1960, 1964) suggested that the early conformity of leaders to the norms of their groups gains for them *idiosyncrasy credits* that enable them to deviate from the norms at later dates without their groups' disapproval (Hollander, 1964). The lesson for would-be leaders who wish to bring about changes in groups is that they must usually first accept the groups' current norms to be accepted. Practical politicians often can bring about more change by first identifying with a country's current norms and then moving the country ahead with statesmanship that takes the country where it would not have gone without the politician's direction. Franklin Delano Roosevelt's leadership of the isolationist United States into World War II is an illustration.

Acceptance and the Leader's Freedom to Deviate. In a study of personnel in the U.S. Air Force, Biddle, French, and Moore (1953) found that the closer the attitudes of crew chiefs were to the policies of the U.S. Air Force, the stronger were their attempts to lead. Chiefs who accepted their role as supervisors used their influence to further the institutional goals and purposes. But the amount of such attempted leadership was not related to the extent to which the chiefs were accepted by the crew members. However, crew chiefs who were accepted by their groups deviated further from the norms and policies than those who were not accepted.

Effects of the Group's Goals. Without doubt, the group's purposes, objectives, or goals are predominant as norms of the group. Studies of experimental groups indicate that members readily accept or commit themselves to the defined task and seem to develop other norms in support of the norms of the task. Once the members understand and agree on the group's goal, the goal operates as a norm against which the members evaluate one another's potential for leadership. Goode and Fowler (1949) observed, in a small industrial plant, that the informal groups supported the company's production goals despite the workers' low satisfaction with their jobs. The authors attributed this outcome to leadership that provided clear statements of the groups' goals; clear definitions of the members' roles; and strong, congruent group pressures toward conformity from within and outside the informal group.

Members differ in their commitment to the goals of a group. The greater a member's responsibility for attaining a goal, the stronger his or her commitment to the goal. Ordinarily, leaders exhibit more concern than do followers for the group's attainment of its goals. The attainment of goals is used by members as a criterion for evaluating the group's performance. Once members agree on their expectations for a group, these expectations operate as a norm that induces pressure for compliance. This makes routine leadership easier. The expectations also make leadership that attempts to move the group away from its chosen paths more difficult.

Stability of the Group

The group's stability affects its leadership. B. D. Fine (1970) studied 151 members of an unstable pool of workers and 582 workers who were assigned to stable groups in a refinery. The groups did not differ significantly in coordination, communication, participation, decision making, satisfaction, or mental health. The unstable groups were higher than were the stable groups in motivation and the resolution of conflict. Leaders of stable groups were significantly stronger in facilitating interaction but not in support, the emphasis on goals, or the facilitation of work. Leaders of unstable groups exercised less control, and the workers in these groups expressed less need for freedom.

Other Group Effects

The group variables affecting leadership that have been discussed so far should be considered suggestive rather than exhaustive. For example, the source of information makes a difference. On the one hand, Woods (1984) observed more participative leadership in quality circles than in other group activities in manufacturing firms. Likewise, significantly more quality circles than other types of groups perceived their leaders to be highly participative. Nevertheless, the leaders themselves perceived no differences in their own behavior in the two situations. How the members are the same or different in attributes makes a decided difference in group outcomes. For instance, according to a meta-analysis by Bowers, Pharmer, and Salas (2000) the effectiveness of team heterogeneity depends not only on the nature of the task but also upon which variables the team members vary.

Experience in another group affects the attitudes toward leadership of those who subsequently become leaders. It also presumably affects their performance as leaders. Akhtar and Haleem (1980) showed that newly promoted superiors in an Indian hydroelectric power station exhibited the same attitudes toward initiation and consideration as the attitudes that had been the norm in the groups of employees from which they had come.

Bushe (1987) studied 415 managers' attitudes toward quality-of-work-life (QWL) projects. Those who were involved in *permanent* problem-solving groups were most favorable, and those in *temporary* groups were least favorable toward such projects in comparison to those with no experience in problem solving in QWL groups. The quality of the team leader's *linchpin* relationship linking each team project member with his or her superior was shown by McComb, Green, and Compton (2003) to correlate positively with the team project's efficiency, members' abilities, upper-management support, leader continuity, and team size.

The Effects of Leaders on the Group or Team

Just as characteristics of the group or team affect their leadership, the leadership of the team, whether from a single individual or shared among individuals, makes a difference in the team's development. Leadership sets and achieves team goals, drive, cohesiveness, and the way the members work together and interact with each other. According to a meta-analysis of 50 empirical studies by Burke, Stagl, Klein, et al. (2006), task-focused leaders' behavior-averaged (size-corrected) correlations of .36 with rated team effectiveness and .20 with team productivity. Person-focused leader behavior correlated .36 with team effectiveness, .28 with team productivity, and .56 with team learning. A detailed book of suggestions by D. Tjosvold and M. Tjosvold (2000) indicates the many and varied ways in which leaders can help their teams to become more effective.

Team Effectiveness

Leadership. The preceding chapters were replete with illustrations of the impact of the leader's competence, personality, and style on the outcomes of the group. Leadership makes a difference in the team's effectiveness, drive, and cohesiveness and on closely allied variables like the team's collective efficacy and potency. For example, based on 32 cases, Grant, Graham, and Heberling (2001) concluded that where project managers lead a number of projects that compete for their attention, the credibility of the managers may suffer, there may be more competition for leadership among the team members, and the member's commitment may falter. To further illustrate, Remdisch (1995) concluded from a German interview and survey study at an Opel automobile manufacturing plant of 86 shop floor leaders and 360 workers that the leaders played an important role in implementing group work. The *meisters*, the traditional supervisors, already had a history of good relations, trust, mutual regard, and respect from the individual workers, like that occurring between the noncom and the soldier in the *Wehrmacht* (Fukuyama, 1997). Nonetheless, those leading teams rather than individuals spent more time on cooperation, communication, and making decisions with workers. They needed less time to control line jobs, coordination, work performance, and quality. Again, the transformational leadership and contingent reward by platoon leaders and platoon sergeants significantly predicted observer-rated potency, cohesion and unit performance in 11 days of "on the ground" near-combat exercises of 72 U.S. Army light infantry rifle platoons (Bass, Avolio, Jung, & Berson, 2003).

Importance of Network Connections. According to a meta-analysis by Balkundi and Harrison (2006) of 37 teams in natural settings, team leaders are central in the network of relations among members within the teams that are effective. Their teams are central in the networks they share with other teams. A team's effectiveness is affected by its social network structures. Teams with "densely configured" interpersonal ties are more effective and more committed. Team performance and viability are greater. Strong networks facilitate the timing of required sequences of members' performance and members' familiarity with them.

Obstacles to Avoid and Actions to Take for Effective Team Leadership. Team leaders need to avoid faulty decisions. They need to watch out for *collective traps*, where individuals, but not the teams, are rewarded and to avoid *collective fences*, where individual members ignore one another and fail to share information. The leaders need to deal with *social loafing* and *free riders*. They need to avoid *groupthink* (Janis, 1972). They need to suppress their own egos and go beyond their self-interests for the good of the team. They need to encourage the team members to do the same.

McGrath (1962) proposed that team leaders define the team's goals and structure the team to enable maintenance and task activities to proceed (McGrath, 1962). For Kinlaw (1991), team leaders must manage with the teams' norms and values in mind. They need to initiate actions, set examples, and join efforts. Team leaders need to champion the teams and be directive or participative as circumstances require (Bassin, unpublished). According to Zaccaro, Rittman, and Marks (2001), team leaders are responsible for making judicious choices in solving the problems facing the team. The leaders need to search for, organize, and evaluate information for use by the team in problem solving. They need to translate their mission into a plan and communicate it to the team.

They have to acquire and utilize their personnel and material resources, ideally matching individual abilities and selected resources with team requirements (Hackman & Walters, 1986; Fleishman, Mumford, Zaccaro, et al., 1991) They have to help their members share a mental model of a team that gives, and make sense about the team and its mission (Zaccaro, Rittman, & Marks, 2001).

As Tannenbaum, Smith-Jentsch, and Behson (1998) found for team effectiveness, the group dynamics technologies developed in the 1950s need to be applied by team leaders. Leaders of effective teams facilitate their members' discussions about teamwork, their critiques, and their feedback to each other. Giles and Mann (2003) showed that among 56 teams of 350 employees, boundary spanning was best done by the team leaders, not the teams. Morgeson (2000) found that the assistance of 34 leaders was needed by their 293 team members when disruptive, critical, urgent, and long-enduring team events, occurred such as a deficiency in resources, task-performance failures, missed deadlines, accidents, and conflicts. Leaders were more effective when they were proactive and assessed potential problems. In semiautonomous teams with external leaders (see below), event criticality and urgency were more disruptive and required the external leader to spend more time intervening (Morgeson & DeRue, 2006).

Leader Coordination. Leaders also contribute indirectly to team effectiveness by influencing team coordination that facilitates team effectiveness. First, they identify, plan, and integrate the team members' prospective contributions that are likely to contribute to team effectiveness (Fleishman, Mumford, Zaccaro, et al., 1991). Then the team leaders develop, regulate, standardize, and monitor the necessary patterns of interaction among the members for team effectiveness (Zaccaro, Rittman, & Marks, 2001). Leaders' briefings and team interaction training produced mental models, in 237 undergraduates in three-member simulated tank teams, that enhanced performance, especially in novel versus routine situations (Marks, Zaccaro, & Mathieu, 2000).

Integrating Athletic Cooperation and Competition. Sports team leaders are more effective and their teams are more successful if they: (1) integrate cooperation and competition among the team members—the team members are encouraged to help one another as well as strive to outdo each other; (2) try for early success, such as scoring the first goal in a hockey game; (3) avoid sustaining downward spirals of failure based on attributions of stable uncontrollability—the coach needs to influence the team members to consider a more optimistic outlook; (4) make practices opportunities for experimentation and innovation and accept that it is okay to try but fail; (5) use rest intervals such as half-times to review the preceding performance and decide on what might be improved in the remainder of the game; (6) keep the team membership stable so that teammates can learn to work together and combine their efforts—for all teams in the National Basketball Association between 1980 and 1994, those most stable were most likely to win games; (7) arrange for the team to study the videos of each game to provide different ways of analyzing what happened.

Effectively Organizing. The 149 British Iron and Steel Trades Confederation workplace representatives who indicated, compared to their peers, that their management introduced teamworking by delayering management, creating flexible job descriptions, and maintaining fewer pay grades, achieved greater product quality, more customer satisfaction, and greater market competitiveness (Bacon & Blyton, 2000). The extraordinarily gifted leader J. Robert Oppenheimer, led the Los Alamos laboratory team in the creation of the atom bomb. The highly effective team combined highly talented experts into an expert team. Invariably, the leaders of such "great groups," according to Bennis (1997), call attention to what is important and why the group's work makes a difference. They promote trust of the group in itself and the processes of turbulence. They favor curiosity and risk taking. They convey hope in tangible and symbolic ways that the group and team can overcome the obstacles to success. The leaders make more effective use of the team by assigning subparts of the task to individuals whose competencies best match the requirements of the subparts (Bass, 1960). They can also prevent premature closure in the team's evaluation of alternatives (E. R. Alexander, 1979).

Cross-Training. More of the positive effects of working in teams and groups can be obtained by arranging for the cross-training of members so that one can fill another's

shoes in case of absence. Regularly scheduled meetings will ordinarily help (Dyer & Lambert, 1953), as will other ways of improving communications among the members. But many changeovers from individuals to teams are failures. They tend to lack quality leadership and management support. They are difficult to integrate into the management hierarchy. Many employees may feel that teams are a waste of time. They are unable to deal appropriately with freeloaders. The best workers may feel their performance goes unrewarded (Nahavandi & Aranda, 1994).

Leader Intervention. A leader's questioning set can help members evaluate alternatives systematically. What current resource could be substituted, modified, combined, omitted, or reversed? (Osborn, 1953). The "rush to judgment" that often occurs can be avoided. Frequently, a single solution gets most of the group's attention. Leaders can encourage more even participation by giving inactive members confidence and discouraging monopolizers. On the other hand, the leadership can achieve a more effective group outcome by recognizing differences in the competencies of the members. To some degree, the leader may have to encourage participation by the more competent members and discourage participation by the less competent members. Leaders can clarify the group's goals and ensure agreement about them and an understanding of them. Leaders can help get the group to view its problem in such a way that the problem can be reorganized to increase efficiency. Even when the group feels satisfied with its solution, its return to the same problem a second time is likely to generate an even better solution (Maier & Hoffman, 1960b).

Optimizing Efficiency of Meetings. Leaders can make the difference in whether a team meeting optimizes its time, effort, and achievements. Leaders may be efficient or inefficient in their uses of group meetings. In discussing how he made interagency meetings more efficient, Colin Powell (1995, p. 332) remarked that when he was given the authority to chair functionally diverse meetings, after suffering "through endless, pointless, mindless, time-wasters for years," he set rules for increasing the efficiency of interagency meetings he chaired: "Everyone could recommend items for the agenda, but I controlled the final agenda, which I distributed before the meeting. Once the meeting started, no one was allowed to switch the agenda." The meeting was to last exactly one hour. In the first five minutes, Powell reviewed the purposes of the meeting and the decisions that had to be reached. In the next 20 minutes, participants presented their positions without interruption, followed by free discussion until the last 10 minutes, in which Powell summarized conclusions and decisions for five minutes and participants could state one-minute disagreements. Those remaining in disagreement could complain to their bosses. The meetings were certainly more efficient than the usual uncontrolled, rambling affairs, but were effectiveness and satisfaction sacrificed?

Leaders need to actively monitor whether meetings are on the right course and make corrective changes as needed. They need to pay attention to foot-dragging, signs of boredom, convoluted ways of getting things done, frustrations about individual roles, pessimistic attitudes about ability to carry out assignments, too much or too little structure, poor external relations, and lack of organizational support (Kanaga & Browning, 2003). Hackman and Johnson (1993) suggest that meetings should be called when necessary for clarifying, sharing objectives, and reaching consensus, but not if alternative communications that can achieve the same results are available or personal matters can be better handled individually. They agree with Powell about the need for clear agendas on which the meeting is focused and for the leader's active, attentive listening. The advantages and disadvantages of virtual rather than face-to-face meetings will be detailed in Chapter 29.

Impact of Leadership on the Group's Drive and Motivation

The preceding chapters were replete with illustrations of the impact of the leader's competence, personality, and style on the outcomes of the group. Here I wish to call attention to the effects of leadership, in general, on the group's effectiveness, drive, and cohesiveness and the variables that are closely allied with them, such as the group's collective efficacy and potency.

As discussed earlier, charismatic and inspirational leadership has strong effects on the drive of a group since it correlates highly with individual members' reports of extra efforts. Team leaders persuade their members to work hard for their own or the team's benefit (Bass, 1985) and raise the collective sense that the team is capable of achieving its goals (Zaccaro, Blair, Peterson, et al., 1995). The leaders' persuasiveness is aided by their nonverbal expressiveness and their emotional state (El Haddad, undated). Collective efficacy beliefs underlie the team's drive. The beliefs derive from prior success experiences, observation of team performance, and the influences of leaders and members (Bandura, 1982). Leaders use the beliefs to build confidence (Kozlowski, Gully, Salas, et al., 1996). Drive is increased further by the leader encouraging the exchange of ideas and mutual support (Zacarro, Rittman, & Marks, 2001). Jung, Butler, and Baik (1998) demonstrated that for 47 groups of 217 employees of a large South Korean firm, transformational leadership correlated .36 with collective efficacy, which in turn correlated .66 with perceived group performance.

Cross-Lagged Effects. Greene and Schriesheim (1977, 1980) examined leadership behavior and group drive using a longitudinal design with 123 work groups. Using cross-lagged correlational, cross-lagged path, and corrected dynamic correlational analyses, they found that both instrumental (task-oriented) and supportive (relations-oriented) leadership behavior were causally antecedent to the groups' drive.

Location. Medow and Zander (1956) found that group members who were in positions of centrality—and therefore more likely to exert leadership—exhibited more concern for the group's goals than did members in peripheral positions.[7] Central members selected goals in terms of the group's probability of success, were more insistent that the group be correct, exhibited a stronger desire for the group's success, and perceived themselves as having more influence than other members perceived them having.

Leader Presence. The presence of a leader can help team members remain interested in the goal of a task. Zander and Curtis (1965) reported that team members whose task performance was poorer than they expected tended to lower their aspirations. But they did not down-

---

[7] See Chapter 29 for more about the effects of central and peripheral positions on leadership.

grade or reject the task as much when a leader was present.

Those who exert leadership tend to feel more responsible for the outcomes of their groups. E. Pepitone (1952) found that the more responsible a member's role, the greater his or her concern for the success of the group. E. J. Thomas (1957) reported that when members were highly dependent on each other for the performance of a task, those who were able to facilitate the performance of other members worked harder for the group.

Zander (1971) showed that the leader's feedback about the group's performance and the leader's reward practices had a positive impact on the group's desire to achieve success. The absence of a leader to clarify the requirements of the task and the goals of the group resulted in the group's spending considerable time in clarification and the quest for orderliness. Members of unorganized groups (J. R. P. French, 1941) and members of groups under a laissez-faire type of leadership (Lippitt, 1940a) frequently expressed a desire to get things organized, to buckle down to work, and to stick to the job that was supposed to be done.

Leaders' Intentions. In a large-scale Swedish study, Norrgren (1981a) observed that the positive behavioral intentions of managers exerted considerable influence on the quality of the relations among the members of their work groups. The positive intentions also motivated subordinates to perform and increased how much challenge and stimulation the subordinates felt that they received from their jobs. J. Likert's (1958) previously cited study of the chapters of the League of Women Voters showed that members were more active when the presidents were interested in their ideas (as in the smaller chapters). The members were also more active when the officers of the chapter believed that the members should have more influence on policies and activities. The members participated less actively in chapter activities when they felt pressure from the president but participated more actively under peer pressure and pressure from the leaders of their project discussion groups.

Transactional and Transformational Leadership. Transactional leadership can enhance team members' drive and motivation in three ways. First, leaders make members aware that their contributions are necessary if the team is to reach its goals. Second, leaders arrange to reward individual members' contributions to the team reaching its goal. Third, leaders arrange for the benefits to outweigh the costs. Free riding and social loafing are discouraged (Shepperd, 1995). Transformational leaders animate team members by highlighting the values of the team's efforts to the members and to others, and the importance of the team's success to the organization, community, or society.

Impact of the Leadership on the Group's Cohesiveness

Leadership Style. Democratic, participative, and relations-oriented leadership behavior was found to contribute to the cohesiveness of groups in a number of studies.[8] Smith (1948) obtained a positive correlation between group cohesion and supportive leadership in area management teams in English social agencies but not among local social work groups in these agencies. Similarly, task-oriented, directive leadership behavior was seen to increase cohesiveness according to many other investigations.[9] Both types of leadership behavior were ascertained to contribute to the cohesiveness of groups in still other studies.[10] In the Korean study noted above, Jung, Butler, and Baik (1998) found that transformational leadership correlated .65 with group cohesiveness, which in turn correlated .36 with collective efficacy. Linear regression programs for 72 U.S. Army platoons and their platoon leaders and sergeants showed that in addition to the strong direct effects of transformational leadership on the readiness of the platoons and the rated performance of the leaders and sergeants in simulated combat, platoon cohesion added indirectly to the effects on the platoons' effective performance (Bass, Avolio, & Berson, 2002).

Regard for Mission and Leaders. According to a review of military leadership, Manning (1991) concluded that leadership promoted unit cohesion by providing

[8] The studies were by Lewin (1939), R. Likert (1961a, 1967), Lippitt (1940a, 1940b), and Mann and Baumgartel (1952), among others. See also Part IV.
[9] The studies were by Berkowitz (1953a); P. J. Burke (1966a, 1966b); Katzell, Miller, Rotter, and Venet (1970); Keeler and Andrews (1963); and Stogdill (1965a).
[10] See Christner and Hemphill (1955); Greene and Schriesheim (1977, 1980); Hemphill, Seigel, and Westie (1951); and Trieb and Marion (1969).

clear and meaningful group missions. The missions and the risks undertaken needed to be seen by the unit soldiers as worthwhile. The unit cohesiveness of soldiers of the German Wermacht in the face of defeat in World War II was due not to the sharing of ideology but to the mutual regard and respect of the soldiers, noncoms, and officers. The cohesiveness supplied a sense of power, regulated relations with authority, and minimized self-concerns in battle (Shils & Janowitz, 1948). To promote cohesion in other military settings, units have been rotated as units so as to maintain bonding among the members, commitment to the unit, and mission accomplishment despite combat or mission stress (Meyer, 1982). In Vietnam, the U.S. military ignored the importance of unit cohesiveness; as a result, unit effectiveness deteriorated because of the rotations in and out of combat soldiers and their replacements. The lesson was learned, and now whole brigades are rotated simultaneously into and out of Iraq.

Cohesion of Leaders. Mael and Alderks (1993) found the importance of the cohesion of squad and platoon leaders in 60 platoons as they engaged in simulated combat. The 49 platoon sergeants, 54 platoon leaders (usually lieutenants), and 166 squad leaders were rated by the squad members of their platoon on whether "the leaders in this platoon work well together as a team," "really care about each other," and "pull together to get the job done." This leader cohesion was rated somewhat higher by those higher in rank in the platoon. For the 1,012 squad members' ratings, leader cohesion correlations of .48 were obtained with platoon-simulated combat effectiveness, .47 with job involvement and motivation, and .43 with identification with the army. The findings were consistent with the results for the ratings by the leaders and specially trained observer-controllers.

Integrated Concerns of Leaders. A leader of a work group who combines high concerns for the task with high concerns for relations, such as Misumi's high-performance (P) and high-maintenance (M) leader, was expected to establish shared attitudes favoring a high level of performance. Indeed, such performance norms were the highest under Japanese high-performance and -maintenance leaders—PM types (mean = 17.3), followed by M-type leaders (mean = 16.5), P-type lead-ers (mean = 16.3), and low-performance maintenance—pm-type leaders (mean = 15.8). Using Jackson's (1960) return-potential model of norms, Sasaki and Yamaguchi (1971) obtained results that were parallel to Misumi's for 160 second-year Japanese junior high school students in 32 groups—16 groups of boys and 16 groups of girls. The point of maximum return (the point maximally approved by the group members) varied as follows: PM, 25.0; P, 20.0; M, 16.3; and pm, 18.8. The degree of agreement among members about a behavioral norm differed with the styles of their leaders as follows: PM, 3.02; P, 1.71; M, 1.63; and pm, 1.99.

Impact of Leadership on Collective Efficacy and Potency

An experiment with 268 undergraduates assigned to one of 59 teams showed that collective efficacy was enhanced when the leaders and members had confidence that they could fulfill the role requirements. The teams with the best performance had the highest collective efficacy (Taggar & Seijts, 2003). A transformational leader directly influences a team's potency by raising its confidence of success (Guzzo, Yost, Campbell, et al., 1993). As noted above, the potency of 72 platoons in joint readiness simulated combat was raised if their platoon leaders were transformational (Bass, Avolio, Jung, & Berson, 2003).

Impact of the Leadership on Team Conflict and Emotions

Leaders may generate cognitive conflict with and among members over ideas and information. Such conflict can be constructive and help the group reach its objectives, but the leaders need to help the team reduce or eliminate affective and emotional conflicts that involve personal arguments, incompatibilities, and attacks (Zaccaro, Rittman, & Marks, 2001). Amason (1986) surveyed 48 top management teams and found that cognitive conflict, usually task-oriented, and matters of differences in opinion and judgment about how the team should achieve its objectives contributed to the team's quality, understanding, and satisfaction with decisions. Emotional conflict had the opposite effect, as noted earlier by Katz (1977). Pirola-Merlo, Hartel, Mann, et al. (2002) demonstrated that transformational and facilitative leadership mainly had an indirect effect on the performance of 54 Australian R & D teams in the face of negative events and obstacles preventing team success. In the face of such frustrating obstacles, the path coefficient between leadership and team climate for excellence and safety was .52, and the path coefficient between team climate and team performance was .71, while the direct prediction from leadership to team performance was only an insignificant .09.

Team Satisfaction. Although the team leader makes the final decision, when members can make suggestions to the team leader, they are more satisfied if the decision reflects their recommendation. Such teams perform better, according to a controlled experiment by Phillips (2001) using 76 confederate-led teams of four undergraduates each assigned to a computer task.

Impact of Leadership on Team Climate. A survey of the weekly team climate of 187 Australian participants in 19 teams stationed at one of four permanent Antarctic stations between 1996 and 2001 found that effective leadership was the most important variable affecting weekly team climate, according to team results. Age, sex, and other individual variables were of little consequence (Schmidt, Wood, & Lugg, 2003). Wilson-Evered, Hartel, and Neale (2001) showed in a longitudinal study of hospital teams that the climate of morale mediated the effect of transformational leadership. Pirola-Merlo, Hartel, Mann, et al. (2002) completed a complex analysis of the mediation of team climate on the effects of transformational leadership (instilling a sense of vision and pride) and facilitative leadership (building working relations among the members) on the reactions to obstacles to performance of 54 R & D teams with a total of 313 team members. Obstacles included technical problems, staff availability, member relationships, and funding shortages. For 34 teams, climate for excellence correlated directly (r = .49) with team effectiveness. Leadership did not correlate directly with team performance (r = .09), but most of the positive effect of leadership (r = .32) was due to team climate. Leadership appeared to serve to suppress the negative impact of obstacles on team climate.

Other Mediators of the Impact of the Leadership

How a leader's behavior affects the group's drive and cohesiveness depends, to some extent, on the characteristics of the group. The same leadership that may contribute to motivated and cohesive subordinates in one kind of group may fail to do so in another. Greene and Schriesheim's (1980) analysis of 123 work groups revealed that instrumental leadership had strong effects on drive and cohesiveness, particularly in large and new groups. The reverse was true for supportive leadership, which exerted the most influence on drive and cohesiveness in small and recently established groups.

Leana (1983) manipulated the same variables in an experiment on how the style of leadership and cohesiveness affected *groupthink*. Groupthink is the extreme seeking of concurrence in decision-making groups (Janis, 1972). Concurrence seeking overrides the realistic appraisal of alternative courses of action and vigilant information processing (Janis & Mann, 1977). It results in faulty decision making. Janis (1982) hypothesized that concurrence seeking or groupthink would occur more readily in cohesive groups with directive leaders. Other conditions that would generate groupthink included stress and pressure for a solution, insulation of the group from outside sources of information, and lack of adequate procedures for finding and evaluating information. Leana (1982) created experimental conditions for groupthink but varied whether the leader was directive or participative and whether the four-member groups that were drawn from a total of 208 college students were high or low in cohesiveness. In contrast to participative leadership, directive leadership produced more groupthink, which was reflected in incomplete canvassing of alternatives, failure to discuss alternatives, and decisions that were strongly based on the leader's preferences. Unexpectedly, high cohesiveness did not result in more groupthink than did low cohesiveness. In fact, high cohesiveness actually widened the search for information. The effects of style of leadership and cohesiveness were independent of each other. Bunderson (2003) found that *power centralization*, based on work flow within teams, served to moderate effects on 44 business unit managers' teams in a large consumer products firm. He examined how much team members' expertise and the similarity of their functional backgrounds determined the influence of their involvement in decisions. When decentralization was high, expertise became of increasing importance to involvement in decisions. The reverse was true for highly centralized teams. With decentralization, functional background similarity decreased in importance to member involvement in decisions, while with centralization, it increased.

Team-Member Exchange (TMX). Analogous to Leader-Member Exchange (LMX) is Team-Member Exchange (TMX), the quality of the relations between the individual team member. According to Seers (1989), among 123 blue-collar employees TMX was better when their teams were given more autonomy by management. The leaders can make more efficient use of the team by assigning subparts of the task to those individuals whose competencies best match the requirements of the subparts (Bass, 1960). The leaders can also prevent premature closure in the team's evaluation of alternatives (E. R. Alexander, 1979).

The leader can pursue a questioning set, which helps members evaluate alternatives systematically. What current resource could be substituted, modified, combined, omitted, or reversed? (Osborn, 1953). The "rush to judgment" that often occurs can thus be avoided. Frequently, only one solution gets most of the group's attention. The leader can encourage a more even distribution of participation by encouraging inactive members and discouraging monopolizers. On the other hand, the leader can make for a more effective group outcome by recognizing differences in the competencies of members. To some degree, leaders may have to encourage the participation of the more competent members and discourage the participation of the less competent members. The leaders can clarify the teams' goals, ensuring understanding and agreement about them. The leaders can help get the teams to view their problems in such a way that the problems can be reorganized for more efficient handling. Even when the teams feel satisfied with their solutions, their return to the same problem a second time is likely to generate even better solutions (Maier & Hoffman, 1960b).

Team leaders can obtain more of the benefits of working together by arranging for the cross-training of team members. One member can fill another's shoes in case of absence. Regularly scheduled meetings will usually help

(Dyer & Lambert, 1953), as will other ways of improving communications among the members.[11]

Self-Managed Teams

In addition to the shift from individual work to teamwork (Lawler, Mohrman, & Ledford, 1995), there has been a shift to some extent away from supervision by a formally appointed leader one level up in the hierarchy from the team members supervised. Instead, appointed leaders may remain team members, or the members share some or all of the leadership among themselves (see below) in self-managed, self-directed, or autonomous teams. A leader, external to the team, serves as a coach, advisor, and liaison with the organization and may be responsible for several self-managed teams. Team members are linked together by process, not function. A self-managed consumer products innovation team is made up of an engineer, a product designer, a technical specialist, and a marketer (Benson, 1992). The teams may have autonomy in some tasks but not others. However, as of 1997, in the automobile industry, Murakami (1997) noted that in 13 plants owned by U.S., European, and Japanese automakers, while autonomy was present for several of nine tasks, there were no *fully* autonomous teams to be found. As early as 1924, Mary Parker Follett proposed that leadership in a group should come from the person with the most knowledge of the situation. Bales and Slater (1955) observed that although the formal task functions of an appointed leader were carried out by a single person, several group members could provide socioemotional leadership. Bowers and Seashore (1966) recognized that leadership could emerge from individual team members as well as the appointed leader. Manz and Sims (1980) introduced their pioneering line of investigation about *self-managing* work teams. They devised a 21-item questionnaire to measure leadership in self-managed teams (Manz & Sims, 1987). Shared leadership is a group process. As detailed below, it is distributed among the team members and derives from them (Pearce & Sims, 2002). Position power and status are less important than esteem to the informal, plural leadership that emerges. Leaders arise by being perceived as prototypical team members (Hogg, 2001). The teams have a great deal of autonomy

[11] See Chapter 29.

and fit-flattened organizational structures. Vertical hierarchies of leaders and the led are replaced by networks of relationships (Seers, 2002). The teams are considered the fundamental units of the organization's work, supplementing or replacing the vertical structure (DeSanctis & Poole, 1997). Barry (1991) has enumerated the functions that can be carried out by cross-functional teams. Self-management and self-leadership are correlated concepts, but Manz and Sims (1986) distinguish between their theoretical underpinnings. *Self-management* is concerned with externally generated standards about how the team ought to be working. *Self-leadership* is part of self-management but is also concerned about the direction of efforts as well as how to achieve them (Manz, 1992). Akin to the effects of participative leadership, the increased level of decision making is expected to enhance satisfaction and performance. Members become "masters of their own fate."

Internal Leaders. Self-managed team members lead themselves. They meet as a team to make collective decisions. One or more team members may be emergent, elected, appointed, or automatically rotated to serve as internal team leaders in a highly equitable team structure. They can represent the team in meetings with other team leaders. Their appointments may be temporary (Manz & Sims, 1987). They become *superleaders* (see below) when they maximize the contributions to the team of other members and bring out the talents of other members (Manz & Sims, 1989). According to a review by Gummer (1988), the most important components of self-managed team leadership are encouragement of self-reinforcement and self-evaluation by team members. Basu, Simmons, and Kumar (1997) examined data from 238 self-managed work teams in seven subsidiaries of a Fortune 500 organization. Teams rated by their members as high in self-direction were higher than average in performance. Yukl (1998) listed other conditions in self-led teams that can be facilitated by their leadership: adequate socialization of the members, appropriate task design, adequate information distribution, appropriate rewards and recognition, adequate human and material resources, clarification of team goals, alignment of team goals with the organization's objectives, and a gain in support from top management.

The internal leaders that emerge in self-managed teams and their effectiveness depend on individual members' personalities. Humphrey, Hollenbeck, Meyer, et al. (2003) administered the Five-Factor Model personality inventory to 198 MBA students formed in self-led teams of five or six who worked and studied together for two semesters. The academic performance, including group coursework grades and GPAs of the originally matched teams, was better if, within the teams, there was more variance among the members in extroversion, and the extroverted members were high-scoring rather than low-scoring on conscientiousness. More leadership emerged, resulting in better performance, when the extroverts were also high in agreeableness. Wolff, Pescosolido, and Druskat (2002) found that among 382 MBA students in 48 self-managing teams working on a project for an academic year, those somewhat higher in empathy, support for developing of others, perspective taking, and pattern recognition were more likely to engage in team task coordination. They were also more likely to emerge as team leaders.

External Leaders. The organization usually appoints a former supervisor, manager, or specialist as an external leader who serves as a facilitator, coach, advisor, or consultant, usually for several self-directed teams. The external leader is the primary catalyst for the sharing of team activities within the teams (Conger & Pearce, 2002). The external leader's most important function is to facilitate the team's own observations, evaluations, and reinforcements. But the roles and status of external leaders are often unclear (Manz & Sims, 1984). External leaders may be criticized by teams for controlling too much, and by their bosses for controlling too little (Walton, 1982). Prodded by their bosses, external leaders will increase their control over the team (Klein, 1984). External managers may maintain responsibilities, such as allocating resources. The team may make the final decision, but the external leader can still indicate how much can be afforded. Nevertheless, the hardest part of changing to self-managing teams may be changing the external leader's role from manager to coach. Constant learning is required (Benson, 1992).

Druskat and Wheeler (2001, 2003) completed a study of the behavior of 19 external advisers responsible for external leadership of five to eight of 300 self-managed teams in a Fortune 500 durable goods manufacturing plant. Superior-performing external leaders of high-performance teams were compared with average-performing leaders of average performing teams. Interviews and focus groups with 119 members of the organization provided the data. Compared to average external leaders, superior external leaders were more aware socially and politically. Superior leaders paid more attention to building team trust and caring for team members. They did more scouting for information from managers, peers, and specialists. They investigated problems systematically. They did more to obtain external support for their teams and to influence the teams. They also did more coaching and delegating of authority and were more flexible about team decisions.

Empowerment of Teams. Teams and individual members may be empowered to do their own planning and organizing. Control comes from commitment and social pressure to conform. Wellins, Byam, and Wilson (1991) suggest that teams should be empowered in stages. First they can be assigned to take care of their own housekeeping, training one another, and scheduling production. Managing suppliers and external customer contact can come later. Finally, when the team is fully mature, it can handle its own performance appraisals, disciplinary processes, and compensation decisions. Burpitt and Bigoness (1997) found in 20 firms that team-level innovation among 60 project teams was enhanced by leader-empowering behavior. Barker (1993) noted that in a small manufacturing company, the self-managed teams applied social pressure on any member who violated the standards they had collectively set for themselves.

Shared Leadership. Arguments for sharing leadership come from a variety of theories, such as those dealing with group cohesion, influence tactics, social exchange, and social networks (Seibert & Sparrowe, 2002). Innovation is greater in project innovation teams when members share a vision of what is required (Pearce & Ensley, 2003). The dynamics, moderators, appropriateness, contingencies, and implementation of shared leadership have been presented by Pearce and Conger (2002). Following principles enunciated in the group dynamics movement, team members play many of the task and relations roles of leadership listed by Back (1948). Leadership is shared in that any member who sees a need by the team for a lead-

ership role to be played, and believes she or he is competent to do so, calls attention to the problem and attempts to enact the leadership role or encourages other members with more knowledge and expertise to do so. The leadership function is transferred to take advantage of the different team members' competencies, perspectives, attitudes, contacts, and available time (Burke, Fiore, & Salas, 2002). Australian case studies compared six hotel units with plural leaders who were successfully implementing quality service programs, with six that were not satisfactorily doing so. The successful units benefited from plural leaders who were either task-oriented or relations-oriented (Waldersee, Simmons, & Eagleson, 1995).

Ensley, Hmielseski, and Pearce (2006) compared 220 top management teams in new venture start-up firms that were vertically organized, with appointed leaders and teams that shared leadership. Both kinds of teams performed well, as measured by employee and revenue growth. However, aspects of the teams that shared leadership contributed more to better performance. Again, Mehra, Smith, Dixon, et al. (2006) failed to find that shared leadership generally contributed to team performance, but some kinds of decentralization arrangements were better for performance than others.

Unlike leaderless groups, in which members compete in attempts to lead the group, *shared leadership* is a cooperative endeavor in which different members take initiatives that they see are needed for self-directed team success (Ray & Bronstein, 1995). Much training and coaching of team members and leaders is essential for shared leadership. Incentive programs and regular measurements are needed as self-directed teams with shared leadership become accountable for discipline, human resources, and setting and meeting goals. The team needs to avoid wandering off course (Benson, 1992).

Superleadership. Manz and Sims (1989, 2001) created the concept of *superleadership* to describe the facilitation of the self-leadership of other team members. Members can be helped to lead themselves effectively. Other team members need to achieve self-motivation and self-management. They need to observe themselves, set goals for themselves, manage cues, reward themselves, and rehearse in the context of teamwork. The superleader serves to reinforce such self-leadership and gets the team members to be the best self-leaders they can be. The authors assume that all team members want to be leaders and are free of traits that would inhibit them.

Effectiveness of Self-Managed Teams. In self-managed teams, compared with traditional work groups, there is a more constructive challenge to the status quo with the intention to improve the situation rather than to merely criticize (LePine & Van Dyne, 1998). Cohen and Ledford (1994) completed a quasiexperimental analysis to evaluate the effectiveness of self-management teams in a telecommunications firm. The teams came from various locations and included technical support, customer service, administrative support, and management involving 1,044 employees, 142 supervisors, 136 managers, and 15 union presidents. Self-managing teams were found to be more effective compared with traditionally managed teams performing the same kind of work in that: (1) output at Honeywell increased by 2809; (2) processing of lease applications at AT&T Credit doubled; (3) turnaround time at Carrier was reduced from two weeks to two days; (4) the defect rate at Corning Glass was reduced from 1,800 parts to 9 parts per million; (5) package losses and incorrect bills at Federal Express were reduced by 13%; (6) productivity at Xerox increased by 30%; (7) case-handling time at Shenandoah Life Insurance was reduced from 27 to two days (Benson, 1992; Dumaine, 1990; Fisher, 1993). *Semipermanent* management teams in a large automobile manufacturing firm, unlike temporary task forces, were expected to initiate and contribute new ideas on an ongoing basis for improving product quality, productivity, and quality of work life. Although not completely self-managing, the 71 teams were sufficiently empowered, with considerable autonomy. They were expected to identify opportunities for positive change as well as to implement them. The shared leadership had a stronger effect than hierarchical leadership on their success (Pearce & Sims, 2002).

Shared leadership is not the same as multiple leadership, for it implies common purposes. Neubert (1999) did not find that performance was better in 21 self-directed manufacturing teams if the appointed leader was supplemented by member-identified informal leaders. Several studies found that team performance and satisfaction were higher in self-directed teams (see, e.g., Wall, Kemp, Jackson, et al., 1991). Absenteeism and turnover were also higher rather than lower than among counter-part groups, but there were other differences between the self-managed and traditional groups that might explain the effects on absenteeism and turnover (Basu, Simmons, & Kumar, 1997)

Mixed and Negative Effects. Cordery, Mueller, and Smith (1991) reported that, consistent with previous studies, as noted above, members of autonomous work groups were more satisfied than those working in traditional groups but at the same time the members were higher in absenteeism and turnover. Additionally, Allender (1993) argued that the costs of implementing the changeover to self-managed teams outweigh the benefits. Narrowly skilled employees have to be trained in a much wider set of skills. Implementation takes two to five years.

Summary and Conclusions

Team-leader effects go beyond effects of individual members interacting with the leader. There may be an assembly bonus effect for the team so that the team does better than the sum of its members. Or faulty processes may result in the team doing worse. The leader makes a difference in which outcome occurs. In turn, the leader is affected in many ways by the group. Thus, leadership systematically depends on the phase of the group's development in which the leadership is occurring, as well as on the group's history. As newly formed groups progress, they find it necessary to resolve contests for influence and to develop role structure and cohesiveness before they can engage in the effective performance of tasks. Leaders are expected to provide role structure, maintain goal direction, and resolve interpersonal problems. If leaders fail to fulfill their expected roles, new leaders tend to emerge.

Group drive and group cohesiveness make considerable differences in what is required of the leader and what the leader is able to do. Likewise, the size of the group affects the leadership. The larger the group, the more difficult it becomes for any member to acquire leadership. Large groups make greater demands on their leaders than do small ones.

Groups develop norms that define the appropriate conduct of the members. Once a norm has become stabilized, in the mutual expectations of members, members bring strong pressures to bear on any individual who deviates from the norm. The greater the extent to which members assimilate a group's norms and values, the greater the probability of their emergence as leaders. As leaders, they tend to act as strong exponents of these group norms and tend to conform to them. However, once leaders have consolidated their position, they are likely to be granted considerable latitude in departing from the same norms. The goals of a group operate as group norms in terms of how the members evaluate the group's performance. Leaders exhibit a stronger concern for and commitment to their groups' goals and work harder for their groups' success than do followers. Other aspects of the group, that affect the requirements for a leader's success include the group's stability, the group's status and esteem, the group's frame of reference, and the group's past history. Many other attributes of groups, are likely to influence the results with their leaders and managers: the sources of information; the age of the groups; the leaders' and members' earlier experiences elsewhere; whether the groups are part of a larger organization, are temporary or permanent, and are easy or difficult to enter;

and whether the membership is homogeneous or heterogeneous. Each of these attributes is likely to influence what is required of the persons who emerge as the leaders and what leadership behavior is most likely to be effective.

Leaders have systematic effects on the drive of their groups, although little attention has been paid to this aspect of charismatic and inspirational leadership. Both directive and participative leadership can contribute to group cohesiveness, as can the interest and concern the leader shows for the group. Inspirational leadership would be expected to increase the group's cohesiveness. The leader can make more effective use of the group by assigning subparts of the task to individuals whose competencies best match the requirements of the subparts (Bass, 1960). He or she can also prevent premature closure in the group's evaluation of alternatives (E. R. Alexander, 1979).

We now turn from attending to the team and its members to a concentration on the effects of the tasks faced by the team.

Effects of Task and Technology

Effective leadership is influenced by the requirements of the tasks faced. But the same individuals tend to emerge as leaders as the tasks change. There seems to be a generalized competence for task leadership. Nevertheless, the competence needed for effective leadership differs from one task to another. The tasks faced by the group, the organization, and its individual members affect and are affected by the leadership. The leadership roles required by the tasks have consequences for the outcomes of the members' satisfaction, the group's productivity, and the organization's performance. In the same way, the leadership involved in the tasks to be accomplished is linked to the technology used. Doing business is shifting from making and distributing products to providing services. Work is being redefined, calling for "constant learning, more higher-order thinking, and less 'nine-to-five'" limits on concerns about the tasks to be accomplished (Bedone, 1993, p. 39).

Singled out for special attention has been the extent to which the task is structured or unstructured and the members' roles to accomplish the task are clear. This, in turn, is expected to moderate the leader's directive or participative style and its effects on outcomes. By 1986, at least 48 reasonably rigorous laboratory and survey efforts to verify this *path-goal theory* had been reported (Indvik, 1986b). However, before I conclude this chapter with a review of path-goal theory and its validity, I will first examine the more general issues of the extent to which various requirements of tasks and technologies have been linked with leadership and its effects. Ordinarily, technology facilitates improvements. The ability to make such improvements in products and services are important in determining whether firms remain competitive (Bedone, 1993) and government administrations and NGOs remain effective.

Leadership in a Technology-Enabled Working Environment

Life and work have been transformed in the postindustrial world by advances in technology. For instance, the telecommunications industry has swung full circle. Early in the twentieth century, AT&T's CEO Henry Vail set the company's major goal as a regulated monopoly to provide customer service. Cost was secondary. Profits were regulated. With its breakup in 1984 into Baby Bells and the advent of the Internet, the telecommunication business became driven by the competitive marketplace and technology. Now quality and convenient customer service are not only seen as a good in their own right but provide important, if not most important, competitive advantages as a shrunken AT&T now competes with its former subsidiaries.

The Associated Press reported in mid-April 2008 that AT&T, the nation's largest telecommunications provider, planned to cut about 4,600 jobs, or 1.5 percent of its work force. Most of the layoffs will be among managers, particularly in wire-line operations, including local service for large corporate customers. The company also reported its shares for the first quarter of 2008 had fallen.

Optimum Reengineering

A Wake-up Call. In 1956, Leavitt and Whisler predicted that by the 1980s technology would replace middle-management decision making. Middle management has indeed shrunk in numbers. In successfully coping with the change in the past several decades, the telecom firms must have adaptable cultures. Firms that were slow to adapt in the 1980s were Texaco, Coors, and General Motors. Texaco was seduced by its dominant position in the market and its prior successful growth and profits. Coors did not place enough value on its customers, shareholders, and employees. General Motors did not promote managers who showed too much leadership. On the other hand, firms with adaptable cultures such as those of Wal-Mart, PepsiCo, and Hewlett-Packard more quickly made the transition into the competitive 1990s. They conceived of leadership as an engine of change. They stressed the value of addressing constituents' needs. They introduced adaptable new systems and favored adaptable managers.

Optimal Use of Technology. Simply regarding technology as a black box to replace personnel does not provide for optimization. Full automation is not usually the answer. What is to be sought is optimization of the human-technological interface. Sometimes there is too much human intervention with automated systems, as in the case of the automated thermostatic controls on the German cruiser *Prinz Eugen* being taken in 1945 to Kwajalein as an H-bomb target. Fearful of blowing up the boilers, one of two U.S. Navy cardinal sins, the American captain assigned one seaman to monitor the thermostat and a second seaman to monitor the first seaman. This resulted in continuing overcorrection.

Also suboptimal is the introduction of overengineered information systems without sufficient regard for the human user. For example, fully automated telemarketing and teleinterviewing may generate a lot of annoyed customers and poorer survey response rates than do human callers. Nonetheless, the efficiency of the human callers can be enhanced with automatic dialing, automatic recording, keyboard tallying, prompting, and so on. On occasion, Luddites may have had the right idea about technological advances for the wrong reasons. The costs of technological advancement may be greater than the anticipated gains. This is particularly so if we look for the hidden costs and unintended consequences of technological advances. Automation brings many other problems with it. For example, *automation complacency* may set in. A systems operator responsible for monitoring automated equipment as well as manual tracking will focus attention continuously on the tracking display and "look at but not see" the automated displays, like an inattentive listener at a dull lecture with blank stares on their faces.

Intellectual Stimulation and Dealing with Resistance to Change Needed. Some, but fewer, middle managers sufficiently educated in information technology (IT) are in place to implement systems of service that optimize the human and IT capabilities. The required mix of human and IT differs in each situation. Some, such as in the case of calling card dialing, may work best with full automation; others, such as handling an irate customer, may require a fully sympathetic human counselor. In two ways middle managers are challenged by the need for effective use of IT and human resources. First, they can solve the problems of optimization of IT and personnel by being intellectually stimulating as transformational leaders. Second, they can systematically review with their team and colleagues the obstacles and resistances to change and how to overcome them. They can prepare their colleagues to be ready for continuing new applications and improvements in IT.

To intellectually stimulate their direct reports, leaders and managers can reformulate the specific problem; turn to metaphors or analogies; imagine alternative states; widen, shrink, or split context; or uncover and challenge hidden, deeply rooted opinions and assumptions. They can work with direct reports to avoid premature conclusions, match competencies with subparts of the problem, and play devil's advocate. They can do much the same with colleagues and supervisors. To deal with resistance to change, they can answer such questions as: Is the need to change perceived, and by whom? Who is the sponsor? How ready is the person, unit, or organization for change? What motives underlie resistance? How will change be implemented, supported, and maintained? Are leaders and managers engaged in continuous learning to prepare to deal with the technological imperatives they face? What needs to be done to shape the vision of a business's future state? How much have middle managers and others bought into the new technology? How will career interests be aligned with the organization's vision of its future state? (Bass, 1999).

The Leader's Competence and the Requirements of Tasks

The requirements of tasks affect whether a leader is needed, who emerges as a leader, how the leader behaves, and what kinds of leadership behavior result in the better performance and greater satisfaction of the followers. Early on, the evidence was mixed about how requirements of the task situation determined the traits that distinguish those who are chosen to lead. Some of the earliest research on leadership in small groups was carried out in the Soviet Union by Chevaleva-Ianovskaia and Sylla (1929), who observed that no leadership arose in spontaneous preschool groups unless special problems occurred. Caldwell and Wellman (1926) showed that the basis of choice varied according to the activities for which leaders were picked by their junior high school classmates. For example, physical abilities determined the selection of athletic leaders. Nevertheless, among the students who were studied before 1950, scholarship was high among chosen leaders in all designated situations. Dunkerley (1940) found that college women who were selected as intellectual leaders were superior in judgment, initiative, and intellectual ability and those who were picked as social leaders were superior in dress and appearance. Those who were chosen as religious leaders were least neurotic, while those who were chosen as social leaders were most neurotic. Again, some consistency was found in a leader's performance in different situations, but there was also systematic change in what happens when a leader is transferred to new assignments and tasks.

Influence of Task Assignment on Leader

Stogdill, Shartle, Scott, et al. (1956) studied 20 naval officers who were to be transferred to new positions and the 20 officers whom they were to replace. After several months in their new positions, the transferred officers were found to have shifted their patterns of work performance, but not their interpersonal behavior, to resemble the patterns of the officers they had replaced. In other words, the officers tended to transfer their patterns of interpersonal behavior from one assignment to another but changed their patterns of work performance in response to the task requirements of the new assignments. In a similar way, the individual who emerged as the leader in one group tended to become a leader when placed in other groups, particularly if the different groups were performing similar tasks. Boyatis (1982) conceived such individuals as having the *competencies* to lead others—

the necessary abilities, motives, drives, and behaviors. A change in task may permit new leaders to emerge.

Rotation Experiments. Barnlund (1962) rotated group members through a set of different tasks and through groups with changing memberships. The highest degree of leadership transferability occurred between literary and construction tasks and the lowest degree between coordination and mathematical tasks. Barnlund attached too much importance to changes in both task and group membership as to who emerged as leader; as Kenny and Zaccaro (1983) reported when they reanalyzed Barnlund's data, 49% to 82% of the variance was attributable to individual consistencies and not as much to changes in tasks and group members. The correlation was .64 in the ranking in leadership across the different situations. Borg and Tupes (1958) and Blake, Mouton, and Fruchter (1954) also reported consistency of behavior in the same leader performing in different groups with varying tasks. Evidently, leaders tend to change certain aspects of their behavior in response to changes in the demands of the group's task.[1]

Relevance of Ability to Task. One can think of some competencies such as effective listening linked to leadership in decision making (Johnson & Bechler, 1998), which would correlate with leadership in many different situations. And so, while we find the same individuals emerging as undergraduate leaders in different task situations, we also find that the emergence of leadership is correlated with how much the emergent leader's abilities are relevant to the tasks the group faces. Different tasks call for different abilities, and the leaders who emerge have different competencies that are relevant to the requirements of the different tasks. Thus, Carter and Nixon (1949a) performed a complicated experiment in which the leadership performance of 100 high school boys was measured by teachers' ratings, nominations by students, school activity records, and observers' ratings in three group tasks. A seven-hour battery of tests was also administered. It was found that the boys' scores on the mechanical ability test coincided with leadership in mechanical tasks on all criteria. Scores on the numerical test and for

---

[1] A further examination of how the change in the requirements of a task from one situation to another affects the transfer of leadership appears in Chapter 30.

persuasiveness were correlated with leadership in intellectual tasks, while the scores on the work fluency and clerical tests predicted leadership in clerical tasks on all criteria. Scores on the reasoning test were positively related to leadership in all tasks on all criteria, while the scores on the musical interest test were negatively related.

Clifford and Cohn (1964) described how different attributes of group members, according to colleagues, correlated with nine different leadership positions. Nominations for the role of planner were significantly related to having ideas and being smart, friendly, liked, empathic, and a good influence. Nominations for swimming captain were significantly correlated with being good at swimming and being a good influence. A different pattern of characteristics was associated with each role, but none of the attributes was significantly related to being chosen for the role of banquet chairman.

Effects of Different Tasks. Different tasks had different effects. Hemphill, Pepinsky, Shevitz, et al. (1956) observed the effects of task ability on leadership processes by providing different amounts of advance information to different members of a group. Outcomes were different with different types of tasks. Individuals who were given task-relevant information before an experiment scored higher in attempted leadership in assembly and construction tasks but not in strategic and discussion tasks. Kellett, Humphrey, and Sleeth (2002) noted that some individuals are recognized as leaders because of their mental abilities and competence in dealing with complex tasks. Others are recognized as leaders because of their empathic ability, their emotional intelligence as observed in their socioemotional competence to deal successfully with problems of relationships among people. Still others are recognized as leaders for their competence in both tasks and relationships (see Chapter 19).

Competence Relative to Subordinates' Abilities. The competence of the leader for the task and how the leader behaves as a consequence are moderated by the subordinates' ability to handle the task. If supervisors believe their subordinates have the requisite skills, the supervisors are more likely to be consultative, *participative*,[2] or

delegative (Heller, 1969a), and so they should be (Hersey & Blanchard, 1977). It seems equally true that if subordinates do have the skills and interest for the particular tasks of consequence, their productivity and satisfaction will be greater if supervisors permit them to participate partially or fully in the decision-making process. Full participation will be less than optimum when subordinates do not have the requisite skills and interest.

The Leader's Personality and the Requirements of Tasks

Not only do group tasks affect which abilities are important for leadership, they are also linked to personality factors that seem to promote the choice of leaders. Wardlow and Greene (1952) reported that adolescent girls with high scores on tests measuring their adjustment to school and home and health problems were preferred by peers who were working with them on an intellectual task. Megargee, Bogart, and Anderson (1966) asked pairs of participants, one with a high score and one with a low score on a dominance test, to perform two different tasks. When the instructions emphasized the task, the dominant participants did not emerge as leaders significantly more often than did their partners. However, when leadership was emphasized in the instructions, the dominant members emerged as leaders in 90% of the pairs.

Effects of Task Structure. B. B. Roberts (1969) administered a battery of personality tests to leaders and followers who were studied under different conditions. Concrete and practical-thinking persons were chosen as leaders in structured tasks by all group members, but they were chosen only by the practical and concrete choosers for unstructured tasks. The theoretically oriented members were chosen as leaders in unstructured tasks by abstract, theoretical followers. Although more frequent leader initiation and direction may actually be seen in structured task situations (Stech, 1981; Wolcott, 1984), they also may be superfluous when task structure is already sufficient. More leader task orienting and objective setting may be necessary for effectiveness when

---

[2] As defined in Chapter 18, *participation* (italic) refers only to sharing in the decision process; participation (roman) includes consulting, sharing, and delegating. *Direction* (italic) refers only to giving orders with or without explanation; direction (roman) includes ordering, persuading, and manipulating.

tasks are ill defined (Taggar, 2001; Bain, Mann, & Pirola-Merlo, 2001). But when innovation and creativity are sought and tasks are ill defined, overcontrolling leaders with too much initiation may stifle the autonomy conducive to creativity (Trevelyan, 2001). There is some optimum direction and participation for maximizing performance with ill-defined problems and problems calling for creative thinking (Mumford, Scott, Gaddis, et al. 2002).

Effects of Different Task Requirements. W. W. Burke (1965) found that followers who worked under a socially distant leader rated their groups as more satisfying and productive in a decision-making task than on a code-solving task. Dubno (1963) obtained results indicating that the effectiveness of groups was higher when quality rather than the speed of performing a task was emphasized by their leaders and when the leaders reached decisions more quickly than did the other members. But Hoyt and Stoner (1968) failed to confirm that the risky decisions made by groups were due to the leadership of risk-prone members. With leadership effects held constant, group discussions still produced group decisions that were riskier than the mean of the individual decisions of members. Nevertheless, as will be detailed later, the risk behavior of the leader is likely to depend on his or her speed in reaching decisions, on the organization's stage of development, and on whether the group is at an early or late phase in problem solving. The task requirements of newly formed groups and organizations are different from those of mature groups and organizations, and what is required of their leaders at different stages is also likely to be different. Furthermore, just as the patterns of interpersonal behavior do not change substantially but the patterns of work performance do change when leaders are transferred, the leader's initiation of structure and directive leadership are more likely to shift with the changing demands of tasks than are the leader's consideration and relations orientation (Ford, 1981).

Effects of Followers' Personality and Task Preferences

Indvik (1986b) surveyed 467 nonacademic staff at a university and found that followers' perceptions of their ability and preference for structure systematically affected what kinds of leadership behavior, under various task

circumstances, generated elevated expectations, satisfaction, and meritorious performance. For followers who preferred structure, participative leadership messages were most effective when formalization of the organization was low and the importance of the work group was high. For followers who did not prefer structure, participative leadership messages enhanced their satisfaction when the task was highly structured, the importance of the work group was low, and the formalization of the organization was high. (More will be said later about leading creative followers.) Again, Keller (1992) found among 462 personnel in three R & D departments led by charismatic and intellectually stimulating project leaders that project quality was higher for research projects than for developmental projects.

Cynicism. Reichers, Wanous, and Austin (1997) conducted interviews, surveys, and follow-ups with approximately 2,000 unionized workers and their managers. Forty-three percent of the hourly workers and 23% of the managers were classified as cynical about change. (Many previous change efforts had been unsuccessful.) The results pointed to the detrimental effects of followers' cynicism about leaders' efforts to make changes in the organization. The cynics were likely to be pessimistic about the success of changes and accused those responsible for the change efforts to be lazy and incompetent. The cynics felt that they lacked information about the changes, respect from supervisors and union representatives, and opportunities to participate in decisions making. They had experienced failures in previous change efforts and were personally disposed to be cynical. They lacked commitment, satisfaction, and motivation to make the changes.

Followers' Competence. There is an obvious correlation between followers' competence and their effectiveness unless they are in conflict with one another about objectives, have contrasting values, and are poorly led and poorly motivated. However, an extremely competent follower may usurp the leadership, "take control and then begin to undermine the influence of others. The work climate is poisoned, and morale declines. Cooperation turns to competition, then ill-will, and then into subtle forms of sabotage" (Quinn, 1996, p. 116).

Important Dimensions of Tasks

Task interdependence has been found to be an important determinant of whether leaders should be appointed or elected. Basik, Gershenoff, and Foti (1999) reported that when members' tasks were highly interdependent, team performance was high if team leaders were elected, but when members' tasks were low in interdependence, the teams did better with assigned leaders. Valenzi, Miller, Eldridge, et al. (1972) reviewed previous research on the impact of leaders' behavior on task requirements. They concluded that task interdependence, structure, routineness, complexity, and intellectual (but not manipulative) requirements systematically alter the amount and kind of leadership that is most effective. On the basis of this review, a survey was conducted. Using stepwise regression analyses, Bass, Valenzi, Farrow, and Solomon (1975) found, for 78 managers described by their 407 subordinates, that tasks with clear objectives were seen to result in more *direction* and consultation by the managers. Routine tasks were associated with less *participative* leadership. More complex tasks correlated with negotiative leadership and more frequent delegation. Delegation was also reported to be more frequent among executives if their subordinate managers had to engage in planning, coordination, and other managerial activities. I confirmed more frequent leader *direction* in an unpublished follow-up of the effect of structure on 340 managers and 1,300 subordinates. As noted just below, more frequent direction may occur with strong structure, when actually direction is less needed.

Structure

Leaders of groups and individuals with structured, as opposed to unstructured, tasks have been considered in a great many studies.[3] For instance, Hill and Hughes (1974) reported that leaders displayed more socioemotional behaviors, both positive and negative, when subordinates performed unstructured as opposed to structured tasks. Widely used to examine the effects of structure is House and Dessler's (1974) measure of task structure, a ten-item questionnaire on which respondents describe

[3]See, e.g., Fiedler (1964), Hunt (1967), Shaw and Blum (1966), and Wofford (1971).

the extent to which their tasks are simple, repetitive, and unambiguous.

Task structure varies in how much is specified, is certain, and has to be done. For example, Lawrence and Lorsch (1967b) assumed that task structure went from the lowest to the highest as one moved from fundamental research to applied research, to sales, and finally to production. In six organizations, they found that production personnel (whose work was most specified and certain) and fundamental research personnel (whose tasks were least specified and certain) both preferred task-oriented leaders. Members in the sales subsystem (which had moderately specified and certain work) preferred more interpersonal, socially oriented leaders. Structure may be strong or weak, tightly or loosely arranged, clear or ambiguous (Mischel, 1977). When it is strong, tight, and clear, everyone sees the situation in the same way. It induces uniform expectations and provides clear incentives for appropriate responses. Less guidance and directive leadership are needed. When structure is weak, loose, and ambiguous, there is more acceptance of guidance, direction, and charismatic leadership (Shamir & Howell, 1999).

Fiedler's Task Structure. A tenet of Fiedler's (1967a) contingency model was based on the effect of task structure. For Fiedler, task structure creates a more favorable situation for the leader. A task-oriented leader will be more effective when there is either a great deal of task structure or very little task structure. A relations-oriented leader will be more effective if task structure is moderate. Although the conclusions remain controversial (see, e.g., Graen, Alvares, Orris, & Martella, 1970; Graen, Orris, & Alvares, 1971), considerable empirical support for this proposition was presented in Chapter 19. However, the effects of task structure may be much weaker than other contingent situational elements that favor the leader (W. Hill, 1969a).

Some Effects on Leadership Behavior and Outcomes. Wofford (1971) observed that unstructured tasks elicited more achievement-oriented and organizing managerial behavior than did structured tasks. Lord (1975) found that the degree of task structure in a situation was negatively related to the occurrence of facilitative leadership behavior. An unexpected curvilinear effect emerged. Instrumental (task-directed) leadership was most effective with tasks that were moderate in structure. Shaw and Blum (1966) found that structured problems were better served by directive supervision. Thus, when the problem on which five-person groups were working was highly structured so that clear procedures could be followed, directive supervision led to quick results. Yet when leaders initiated structure a great deal, as was seen in a study by Badin (1974) of 42 work groups in a manufacturing firm, their effectiveness was reduced if the groups were already highly structured. The correlation of effectiveness and Initiating Structure was $-.56$. But in the less structured of the 42 groups, the effectiveness of the groups correlated .20 with the extent to which the first-line supervisors initiated structure.

Filley, House, and Kerr (1979) found that task structure moderated the relationship between participation and performance and between participation and the attitudes of subordinates. Participative leadership had no effect or was contraindicated when tasks were machine-paced, mechanized, and highly structured in other ways. But when tasks were unstructured, the effects of participative leadership on both the attitudes and productivity of subordinates were consistently positive. Hanaway (1985) examined the effects of the uncertainty of tasks on the initiating and search behavior of 18 upper-level and 32 lower-level administrators of school districts. The lower-level administrators were observed to be more reticent to take actions when conditions were uncertain, but the results for the upper-level administrators were less clear.

Role Clarity. Generally, people, particularly those with a great need for structure, prefer to work in clear task settings. Valenzi and Dessler (1978) showed that among 284 employees in two electronics firms, satisfaction was uniformly high when role clarity was high. The leaders' consideration promoted even more satisfaction. In addition, Benson, Kemery, Sauser, and Tankesley (1985) found that a high need for clarity was related to low job satisfaction among 370 university employees above and beyond the effects of their role ambiguity on the employees' dissatisfaction.

The determination of perceived role ambiguity or perceived role clarity is a way to discern how much structure exists in a group. Kinicki and Schriesheim (1978) studied the role clarity of 173 freshmen in 16 classes. Role clarity

was measured by Rizzo, House, and Lirtzman's (1970) scale dealing with clear objectives, responsibilities, expectations, and explanations about what has to be done. They found that students were more satisfied with relations-oriented teachers, particularly when role clarity in the situation was low. But the students were more productive with directive teachers when role clarity was low, not when it was high. As Siegall and Cummings (1986) demonstrated, satisfaction with supervision is enhanced if a subordinate's role is initially ambiguous and if the supervisor contributes to clarifying the role by issuing instructions and directions. Fulk and Wendler (1982) found, among 308 clerical and managerial employees, that role clarity was associated with nonpunitive, task-oriented leadership and contingent reward. Such leadership was satisfying. But role clarity could also emerge as a consequence of arbitrary and punitive leadership behavior that was dissatisfying. However, Schriesheim and Murphy (1976) failed to find that role clarity moderated the relationship between any kind of leadership behavior and the satisfaction and performance of subordinates. To help further in the understanding of the above evidence, later in this chapter, when the path-goal theory and the specific tests to validate it are reviewed, more will be said about the extent to which structure and role clarity affect the impact of leadership on performance and satisfaction.

Clarity of Objectives. Nagata (1965) observed that groups with goal-relevant tasks enabled leaders to exercise more influence on the members than on members in groups in which the tasks were not relevant to the goal. To some extent, clear objectives may substitute for structured relationships or clear role relationships in getting a job done, particularly if little coordination is required. Multiple regression analyses by Bass, Farrow, and Valenzi (1977) for 250 managers and their 924 subordinates suggested that the effectiveness of work groups was significantly greater if the mangers had clear objectives. Furthermore, when these organizational members were competent and motivated to attain their objectives and could operate independently or in cooperation with one another, the effectiveness of their performance was strongly associated with the clarity of their objectives and the adequacy of their resources.

Error criticality is the extent to which mistakes at

work produce negative outcomes. In health care, error criticality is high for those in nursing and pharmacy departments, for their mistakes can lead to patient injury or death. Their motivation to perform well is not increased or decreased by the quality of their supervision or by job design (autonomy and variety). On the other hand, error critically is generally low for those in hospital administrative units. Compared to nursing or the pharmacy, mistakes in administrative work ordinarily are not life-threatening. Administrative employees' motivation to work is more strongly affected by the quality of their supervision, by their morale, by their job autonomy, and the job variety in their jobs, according to a study by Morgeson (2005) of 189 hospital employees.

Autonomy and Discretionary Opportunities

One's felt autonomy and discretion to do one's job appear to be complex perceptions that are affected by various factors, such as the organization's technology and the frames of reference shared with coworkers, as well as the style of leadership employed. Presumably, leaders who initiate a great deal of structure by definition, reduce their subordinates' autonomy. But leaders' consideration should enhance subordinates' feelings of autonomy. Ferris and Rowland (1981) suggested that the leaders' initiating structure and consideration systematically affect the subordinates' perceptions of autonomy in this way, which, in turn, may or may not contribute to the subordinates' performance.

The same leadership will have different effects depending on whether subordinates' autonomy is high or low. Johns (1978) found a correlation of .29 between leaders' initiation of structure and subordinates' job satisfaction when 232 union employees reported that their autonomy was high, and a correlation of .01 when they indicated that their autonomy was low. The leaders' consideration and the subordinates' job satisfaction correlated only .20 when the subordinates' autonomy was high but .52 when it was low. More than 1,300 subordinates' descriptions of 340 managers indicated that if managers were viewed as delegative and negotiative, their subordinates felt in possession of more discretionary opportunities (Bass & Valenzi, 1974). Managers were also less likely to be seen as directive under such conditions (Bass, Valenzi, Farrow, & Solomon, 1975).

Innovation and Creativity. Discretionary opportunities enhance innovation and creativity. Such opportunities are likely when leaders and subordinates have good relations with each other. Scott and Bruce (1994), Scott and Bruce (1998), and Tierney, Farmer, and Graen (1999) reported positive correlations between the quality of leader-member exchange (LMX), task innovation, and creativity of managers, scientists, and engineers. Amabile and Gryskiewicz (1987) interviewed 120 R & D scientists to elicit two critical incidents from each of them, one to illustrate the occurrence of high creativity, the other to provide an instance of low creativity. Consistent with what has been said about participative leadership and creativity, in describing the incidents of high creativity, more than 74% of the interviewees mentioned freedom to decide what to do and how to do one's work, a sense of control over one's work and ideas, freedom from contraints, and an open atmosphere. This finding agrees with conclusions reached by Andrews and Farris (1967) and others, although Amabile and Gryskiewicz hastened to add that there is a limit to the amount of such freedom, for it must be bounded by the team supervisor's coordination of the team's overall efforts (Pelz & Andrews, 1966b). In presenting these incidents of high creativity, one-third to one-half the 120 scientists revealed that their leaders' enthusiasm, interest, and commitment to new ideas and challenges encouraged their creativity.[4] Supportive leadership was seen in the willingness to take risks, provide recognition for success, and clarify what was needed. The leaders accepted failure without destructive criticism and avoided excessive evaluations. Such leaders did not dwell on the status quo. Keller (1989) reported that the productivity of 30 project *research* teams correlated .57 with the intellectual stimulation of their leaders but close to zero with the same leadership in 36 project *development* teams. According to Allen, Katz, Grady, et al. (1988), the performance of 181 project teams was greater when their leaders kept them current in the science and knowledge they needed to know. Frischer (1993) found that when 38 managers of new product development empowered and gave a sense of responsibility to their subordinates, the subordinates perceived a greater innovative climate. In agreement, Judge, Gryxell, and Dooley (1997) noted

---

[4]Here there is consistency with the effects of the transformational leadership factors of inspirational leadership, intellectual stimulation, and individualized consideration.

that R & D managers enhanced innovation by giving their subordinates operational autonomy, personal recognition, cohesiveness, and a continuity of slack resources.

Routineness versus Variations in Tasks

Jobs can require that employees carry out the same few tasks in a repetitive cycle or may involve a greater variety of tasks that are more variable in sequence. Optimal performance by leaders depends on whether the work involves uniform, recurring, repetitive tasks or considerable variability (Valenzi, Miller, Eldridge, et al., 1972). In their classic study of workers on the assembly line, Walker and Guest (1952) emphasized the extent to which supervision was likely to be more directive when the tasks to be performed were extremely routine. Likewise, Bass, Valenzi, Farrow, and Solomon (1975) reported more directive leadership as well as less supervisory delegation in work groups that were carrying out routine tasks. Similarly, Ford (1981) showed that in 35 departments in a book-publishing firm, a bank, and a university, the routineness of work uniquely correlated .36 with the extent to which the departmental manager initiated structure but only .05 with his or her consideration as a leader.

In a study involving 16 departments in 10 organizations, R. H. Hall (1962) distinguished between uniform, easily routinized, standardized activities and nonuniform, difficult-to-routinize, creative activities. He found that departments and hierarchical levels whose activities were more nonroutine were also less bureaucratic than were those departments and levels that were oriented toward routine activities. In nonroutine situations, the atmosphere was more personal, had less hierarchical emphasis, and required fewer procedures and regulations. Consistent with all these findings, Heller and Yukl (1969) found that production and finance managers (who supervised more routinized work) tended to use centralized decision making, while general and personnel managers (who supervised less routinized work) were more participative.

The linkage of routineness to the greater initiation of structure by leaders is consistent with the hypothesis, verified by Kipnis (1984) for several levels of managers in Australia and the United States, that employees who work on routine tasks are likely to be undervalued by their supervisors. Despite this finding, Jiambalvo and Pratt (1982)

reported that in four large accounting firms, considerate leadership behavior by senior accountants increased the involvement in tasks among staff assistants who performed relatively simple tasks more than it did among those who performed relatively complex tasks.

Variety. Hackman and Oldham's (1975) Job Diagnostic Survey included job variety as an important variable that was likely to relate to the motivation to work. Using ratings based on the survey, Johns (1978) showed that with job variety, the leaders' initiating structure generated greater job satisfaction and fewer intentions to quit among subordinates. Without such variety, the leaders' initiation was unrelated to the subordinates' satisfaction and increased their intentions to quit. However, the leaders' consideration was strongly associated with satisfaction, regardless of whether the job was varied or routine. Yet only when variety was absent was the leaders' lack of consideration associated with the subordinates' intentions to quit. In contrast, Brief, Aldag, Russell, and Rude (1981) found, in an investigation of police officers, relatively little of the expected effects of the variety of job skills on the favorability of police officers' attitudes toward the citizenry.

In a study that distinguished working on uniform and nonuniform tasks, Pelz (cited in Litwak, 1961) found a higher correlation between the motivation to work and productivity when those engaged in nonuniform tasks were permitted by their supervisors to make their own job decisions. But for those involved with uniform tasks, there was a higher correlation between motivation and productivity when freedom to make decisions was restricted. Nonetheless, Katz, Maccoby, and Morse (1950) found that supervisors of high-producing sections were significantly more likely to provide general rather than close supervision, even though they were supervising routine clerical work in a life insurance company. However, in a subsequent study of less routine railroad work (Katz, Maccoby, Gurin, & Floor, 1951), little difference was found between the closeness of supervision by supervisors of high- and low-producing sections. In these and the many other related studies that followed,[5] R. Likert could find no diminution in the utility of participative (System 4) leadership in routine jobs as compared to

[5] See Chapter 17.

those with more variety. But Griffin (1980) suggested otherwise. He contrasted the leadership-outcome relations among employees who had "high-scope" tasks (varied, involving, and autonomous) and those who had "low-scope" tasks (simple, routine). In his first survey of 129 employees, the scope of the employees' tasks did not correlate with the leadership style of their supervisors. However, for a subset of employees with high-scope jobs *but a low need for personal growth*, directive supervision subsequently resulted in greater satisfaction. On the other hand, employees with low-scope jobs were more satisfied with their subsequent supervision if their supervisors were more supportive and practiced more management by exception. Such supervisors were described by such statements as "My supervisor doesn't bother me as long as I do a good job" and "My supervisor leaves me alone and lets me work."

Low-Scope Tasks and Passive Leadership. Although passive management by exception has generally been downgraded by subordinates as a satisfying style of supervision,[6] the results suggest that employees in low-scope jobs prefer and feel better when their supervisors practice management by exception. This suggestion was confirmed in a survey of 195 full-time employees by Algattan (1985). When the scope of the tasks that subordinates performed was low and the subordinates had little need for growth, leaders' maintenance of the status quo was more positively related to outcomes than was more active directive, participative, or task-oriented leadership.

Complexity of Tasks and Technologies

Technologies are simple if they can readily be understood and communicated between experts. Complex technologies cannot. As they move from simple to complex technologies, leaders need to shift from gatekeepers of information to facilitating and insulating information networks. These networks have to create knowledge, not just transfer information and knowledge (Kash & Rycroft, 1996, 1997). Bell (1967) viewed the complexity of tasks in terms of the degree of predictability of the demands of the work, the amount of discretion exercised,

the extent of responsibility, and the number of different tasks performed. When informal groups face complex tasks, leaders emerge who have the cognitive abilities to handle the tasks and to help others to do so. They may also have the socioemotional skills to deal with the others facing the complex tasks (Kellet, Humphey & Sleeth, 2002). Among supervisors in a hospital, Bell (1967) found that the more complex the subordinates' tasks or the supervisor's job, the narrower the supervisor's span of control. But the complexity of tasks did not influence how closely the subordinates were supervised. Barrow's (1976) study indicated that leaders exhibited more task orientation when faced with more complex tasks, but the complexity of the tasks did not affect their tendency to be punitive. However, Cuthbertson (1982), in a survey of 175 subordinates and their 25 supervisors in a central office of a school district, found more directive leadership than she expected in relation to the complexity of the tasks involved. Among 61 to 68 telecommunications units, Osborn and Hunt (1979) obtained contrasting patterns of correlations with leadership, the structural complexity of the units led, and the difficulty of the units' tasks. They found that the leadership that was required was unrelated to the complexity of the units led or the difficulty of the tasks. However, the actual amount of support and role clarification by the leaders, as expected, correlated between .24 and .31 with structural complexity of the units but unexpectedly between $-.30$ and $-.42$ with the difficulty of the task.

Barrow (1976) observed, in a simulation using 120 male college students as leaders, that more initiation of structure was caused by increasing the complexity of the task but autocratic behavior was generated more by workers' poor performance than by increasing the complexity of the task. Considerate leadership was evoked by improvements in the workers' performance. Relevant to these results, Wofford (1971) found that a personal interaction (relations-oriented) manager was more effective for complex operations. A self-oriented, autocratic manager was more suited to situations with simple work schedules. Hammer and Turk (1985) showed that supervisors were less likely to perform group maintenance activities if they supervised employees who worked with *intensive technology*, as in a repair shop or an R & D laboratory where tasks were complex and nonroutinized. On the other hand, supervisors of workers who were engaged

---

[6] See Chapter 15.

in *long-linked technologies*, such as mass production assembly lines, and whose tasks were interdependent were more likely to engage in network activities. In addition, supervisors in the intensive-technology situation felt, to a greater extent, that they had the authority to reward subordinates, whereas supervisors in the long-linked technology settings felt they had more authority to discharge employees and, in turn, were less likely to be seen as experts.

The effects of the increasing complexity of tasks on requirements for leadership are illustrated by the changing military scene. Those who are now being selected to serve as military leaders in the next several decades will have to operate under conditions for which there is less public consensus than existed during World War II. They will be expected to know how to use minimal force in unconventional conflicts in which they will be trying to keep the peace. Fighting, as it continues in Iraq, is intense, lethal, and destructive. For this type of fighting, an understanding of the local values of what is right, good, and important, along with intellectual sensitivity, is particularly important. Officers are required to respond thoughtfully to increasingly ambiguous circumstances. They need to inspire subordinates with a vision of the future that strengthens the subordinates' loyalty and commitment rather than merely fosters the subordinates' grudging obedience. Gal's (1986) forecasts fairly accurately described the task and technology requirements for coalition forces in the Persian Gulf War in 1991 and the wars in Afghanistan and Iraq and their continuing insurgent aftermaths.

Difficulty of Tasks. A factor analysis of 104 different experimental tasks by M. E. Shaw (1963b) disclosed three factors that contribute to the effects of the complexity of tasks: (1) the difficulty of a task (the number of operations, skills, and knowledge required to complete the task); (2) the multiplicity of correct solutions; and (3) the requirements for cooperation (integrated efforts). C. G. Morris (1966a, 1966b) found that as the difficulty of the tasks increased for groups, there was a concomitant increase in leaders' and members' attempts to structure answers, propose solutions, and seek evaluations. However, tasks of intermediate difficulty generated the highest frequency of attempts to structure the problem, followed by tasks that were the most difficult. Easy tasks produced the

most irrelevant interactions. At the same time, Nagata (1966) found that groups with easy tasks exhibited more role differentiation and permitted leaders to exercise more influence than did groups with difficult tasks. Nevertheless, Bass, Pryer, Gaier, and Flint (1958) observed fewer attempts to lead in groups with easy problems. But it is important to recognize that the difficulty of a task is in the eye of the beholder. Manz, Adsit, Campbell, and Mathison-Hance (1988) surveyed 3,580 managers in a large firm about the hindrances to their performance. Better-performing managers paid more attention to external hindrances, such as inadequate appraisal systems and the absence of opportunities for promotion. Poorer performers focused more on deficiencies in skills, such as the lack of interpersonal or technical abilities.

When it was arranged for students to instruct others on easy and hard tasks in a laboratory setting, the "instructors" used less punishment when trainees performed difficult tasks than when they performed easy ones. A meta-analysis by Tubbs (1986) of 87 studies tested Locke's (1968) hypotheses on how the difficulty and specificity of goals enhance the speed and quantity of work that subordinates perform. Motivating leaders (in this case the experimenters) were more structuring with specific, difficult goals than were leaders who told subordinates just to do their best or did not tell them anything about the goals. Difficult goals resulted in higher motivation and performance of participants in short-term laboratory studies, but according to the meta-analysis, such results were somewhat less likely to materialize in survey studies of workers in longer-term assignments, perhaps because sometimes assignments might be too difficult, as noted next.

Fast pace, time pressure, and the need to meet deadlines contribute to the difficulty of tasks. For research scientists and engineers, Hall and Lawler (1971) found that the pressure to do high-quality work and to help their company attain its financial goals contributed to the successful performance of their research laboratories. Andrews and Farris (1972) also reported that time pressures experienced by scientists and engineers correlated positively with their subsequent performance. However, pressure that was perceived as unreasonable or excessive resulted in poor or decreased performance. Such excessive pressure could result in the setting of unrealistically high goals (Forward & Zander, 1971). Excessive pressure by a supervisor is likely to be contraindicated when tasks become more difficult with multitasking by operators who are novices and when the pace is conducive to errors because of its speed. Nonetheless, Shamir and Howell (1999) argued that a charismatic leader could emerge and be effective if the followers faced challenging and complex tasks, required intense efforts, and if performance goals were ambiguous and extrinsic rewards could not be linked to performance.

Temporal Complexity. Halbesleben, Novicevic, Harvey, et al. (2003) called attention to the importance of time and timing to giving organizations competitive advantage. Awareness of the dimensions of temporal complexity is an important competency for leading in creativity and innovation. Leaders need to be aware of the *time frame* of a task, such as the deadline for completing it. They need to pay attention to the timing of required activities. They need to be aware of the limited time spans of processes and events within the *time scope* of the task. They need to be aware of individual differences in pauses and gaps in the work and to support the simultaneity, sequence, and synchronization of operators, events, and processes. Leaders need to appreciate *timelessness,* losing one's sense of time while engaged in creative thinking, which contributes to optimal *flow* (Csikszentmihalyi, 1997) for creativity and innovation (Sosik, Kahai, & Avolio, 1999).

Uncertainty of Tasks. Wilson and Rhodes (1997) found in a set of experiments that coordination among followers facing uncertainty depended on particular kinds of leadership. According to De Mayer, Loch, and Pich (2002), there are four kinds of uncertainty and the leadership required as a consequence: (1) *Variation.* A task may vary, causing uncertainty, for example, about the time needed for completion. Here the leader needs to monitor deviations, set limits, or take corrective action, and arrange for buffers at critical points. (2) *Foreseen uncertainty.* A few known factors may influence carrying out the task in unpredictable ways. The leadership needs to plan for contingencies and alternate ways of completing the task. (3) *Unforeseen uncertainty.* Some factors influencing the task cannot be predicted. The leadership needs to plan for foreseen uncertainty but also scan for and recognize unexpected influences and arrange new contingent actions accordingly. (4) *Chaos.* Unforeseen

events completely invalidate previous plans and efforts. The leadership needs to reexamine its assumptions, redefine the task, and do contingent planning based on incremental learning, constant feedback, and continual iterations, to gradually select the final approach.

Multiplicity of Solutions. Shaw and Blum (1966) noted that directive supervision was more effective if the problem called for agreement on a single solution, whereas participative leadership paid off when multiple, divergent solutions were needed. Experimental groups of five members each performed three tasks that required different types of solutions. Directive supervision was more effective when the problem called for a single final decision or involved the convergence of judgments into some final product. On the other hand, when the problem required multiple, divergent final solutions, participative approaches were more effective.

Participative leadership is suggested by the *assembly bonus effect*—groups achieve better solutions to problems with multiple alternative possibilities than does their average member working alone (Bass, 1960; Steiner, 1972). (The group decision may, however, not be as good as the decision achieved by the best member working alone.) This assembly bonus effect occurs unless individual members already have the requisite information to solve the problem alone, for instance, when every member is a professional expert who is highly trained to deal with the same standard types of problems in the same way. There will be less of an assembly bonus if the addition of members produces interference rather than nonredundant information. According to Heller (1969a), the primary reason managers in 15 firms reported using participative leadership was to improve the technical quality of complex decisions. In fact, some form of consultation is mandatory in highly technically oriented organizations, for the available technical expertise does not fully reside with supervisors but is distributed, to some degree, among subordinates.

Required Cooperation and Interdependence of Tasks. Adam Smith, in *The Theory of Moral Sentiments,* called attention to the paradox he had noted in *The Wealth of Nations* that the economy was driven by self-interest, yet people also recognized that the pursuit of self-interest required cooperation from others. Conflicting evidence has emerged here. To emerge as a leader in an initially leaderless group, one needs to both compete with and cooperate with the other members of the group (Bass, 1954). Cooperation and the interdependence of task performance among subordinates have been found to be promoted by participative leadership in some research studies. Other investigations have failed to find any effects, and evidence from still other laboratory and survey studies suggests that when subordinates engage in interdependent tasks, directive leadership and initiation of structure by the leader are more efficacious.

O'Brien (1969b) theorized that the equalization of power and participative leadership would be appropriate for tasks that require a great deal of cooperation. A power differential between the superior and the subordinates would be more effective in situations in which subordinates carry out tasks independently of one another. Vroom and Mann's (1960) results were illustrative. Vroom and Mann studied drivers and positioners in a package delivery company. The positioner's job required a high degree of interdependence and considerable interaction with coworkers and with the supervisor. The driver's job involved little interpersonal interaction and considerable independence in work activity. In line with expectations, the positioners favored democratic leaders and the drivers preferred authoritarian leaders.

Bass, Valenzi, Farrow, and Solomon (1975) failed to find statistically significant correlations between leadership styles and the interdependence of tasks of work group members. But larger-scale follow-up analysis by Bass and Valenzi (1974) indicated that more *directive* leadership and consultative leadership were associated with the interdependence of tasks. Nevertheless, negotiative leadership was greater when members worked independently of one another.

In a survey of 25 departmental managers and their 445 departmental associates, Ford (1981) did not find that the amount of interdependence in the workflow within the departments did not account for initiation of structure or consideration by the managers beyond that already explained by the routineness or uncertainty of departmental tasks. On the other hand, Lord and Rowzee's (1979) laboratory experiment with four-person teams showed that when tasks required a high degree of interdependence among the subjects, more frequent directive leadership behaviors emerged to develop orientation, plans,

and coordination. Consistent with these results, Fry, Kerr, and Lee (1986) found that among 22 high school and college teams in eight sports, winning coaches of highly interdependent sports teams (like basketball) were described by their players as displaying more initiation of structure and less consideration than were winning coaches of sports teams, such as golf, that required little or no interdependence. Coaches of winning teams that were highly interdependent also displayed more initiation and less consideration than did coaches of losing teams that were highly interdependent.

To adequately explain these results requires attention to another variable: the competence of the team members. Directive leadership to clarify roles may be needed more when team members must work in collaboration but the team members are novices. Participative leadership that is focused on commitment becomes more important for high-quality collaborative efforts when the members are already trained and experienced.

Required Interdependencies among Members. Thompson (1967) distinguished among three kinds of interdependencies: pooled, sequential, and reciprocal. In the *pooled* circumstance, each individual, such as a baseball player at bat, performs alone, but the results have collective effects. In the *sequential* effect, one person, such as a running quarterback in a football play for whom others will block the opposition, depends on others earlier in a sequence. *Reciprocal* interdependence occurs when each person must interact with others, such as in basketball. Leadership and management in conditions of pooled interdependence require continuing attention to tactical judgments and the development of individual performers, but cohesiveness may not be as important. In sequential performance, leadership and management must attend more to planning and the preparation of the team. The requirements for performance are tighter and more highly specified and scheduled. Cohesiveness is more important. In reciprocal interdependence, satisfactory mutual adjustments are of the greatest importance and necessitate that the most attention be paid to relationships and continuing cooperation (Keidel, 1984).

Kabanoff and O'Brien (1979) studied leadership when members of a team either had to *coordinate* their efforts (work on subtasks arranged in an order of precedence) or *collaborate* (work simultaneously with one another on every subtask). Teams that had to coordinate their efforts were more productive, especially when the leaders were more task-competent. But the leaders' task competence was irrelevant to productivity in the collaborative task situation. This finding may be explained by a suggestion by Hill and Hughes (1974) that there is a greater emphasis on the leaders' socioemotional function than on their task function in the collaborative situation. As a consequence, their task competence is relatively less important when collaboration is required.

Socioemotional versus Task Requirements

As was just observed, a distinction that is important for understanding what type of competence will be demanded of a leader is whether socioemotional or task requirements will be emphasized for leadership. This is the most frequent role differentiation that occurs in discussion groups. In groups, when the demands of the task are high, being liked does not contribute much to leadership and socioemotional skills are not highly valued (Slater, 1955). On the other hand, in social and personal development groups, such as therapy groups, sensitivity training groups, social clubs, and gangs, the socioemotional function is emphasized. As was concluded in Chapter 19, in most kinds of groups, both types of leadership usually need to be present. A. S. Miles (1970) reported that student leaders who rated high on both task ability and socioemotional ability were considered most influential. Empirically, the differentiation between the two types of abilities often is not found. For instance, Gustafson and Harrell (1970) observed relatively little differentiation between task and socioemotional roles in experimental groups. Similarly, V. Williams (1965) noted that some types of group structures were able to operate effectively without differentiating task specialists from socioemotional specialists. Kellet, Humphrey, and Sleeth (2002) noted that either or both could be identified as a leader.

To sort out the effects, Olmsted (1954) gave one set of groups instructions that were designed to induce socioemotional concerns for group processes and the satisfaction of members. The directions given to the second set of groups emphasized the accomplishment of tasks and maintenance of impersonal relationships among members. The most talkative members in the task-directed

groups talked longer than did their counterparts in the socioemotional groups, perhaps as the result of a group norm related to the intensity of participation. Task-directed groups tended to develop stable leadership status structures. Members of socioemotional groups continued to jockey for position for a longer time. Olmsted (1955) later found that the amount of agreement among members in discussion groups moderated the effects. In groups that achieved a high degree of consensus on solutions to problems. The highest participator (who was more likely to be a leader than a follower) usually received the highest rating for helping the group meet the requirements of its task. In low-consensus groups, the highest participator was not rated high.

Sociotechnical Systems

Adam Smith (1775) noted that civilization arose with the division of labor. Instead of the same primitive humans both farming and fishing, one farmed and another fished. Such specialization of energies made for more efficiency. A merchant trader specialty emerged when the farmer bartered or sold his corn to the fisherman through the merchant trader. With the advent of the Industrial Revolution, instead of one craftsman making an entire pin, efficiency was increased by dividing the work in the pin factory into various simpler subtasks, each carried out by a different worker (Herman, 2001). Unfortunately, *job simplification*, as opposed to crafting a whole product, also brought with it boredom and dissatisfaction, which leaders had to deal with until it was widely recognized in the mid–twentieth century that making the same worker responsible for a whole, more meaningful task, product or process, a sociotechnical design of work, was likely to be more satisfying and efficient. There was less need for coordinating leadership among subtasks carried out by different workers. There has been an increasing interest in designing tasks and work to take account of both the task and the socioemotional requirements.

Sociotechnical Designs

When technical and social systems are integrated, joint optimization is needed. Bamforth observed that long-wall coal miners became much more productive and satisfied when they were able to return to the earlier, traditional premechanization methods of working as a team instead of on individual assignments as directed by a supervisor (Trist & Bamforth, 1951). Along with Fred Emery (1959, 1967), Trist (1971, 1981) set out the principles of sociotechnical systems design. They were consistent with Lewin's (1939) theories and experiments in group dynamics (Fox, 1995).

The critical dimensions, methods, and principles of socioeconomic systems concern control and coordination and who was mainly responsible for them—managers or workers. The principle was that decisions should be made at the lowest organizational level possible. Instead of specialists, engineers, or supervisors making the decisions for corrections and changes in the production process or production line, the operators themselves, suitably trained, make the corrections and recalibrations and perform preventive maintenance. Operators are empowered to load, unload, and monitor machinery as well as to program them. In Britain, this change from specialist to operator control in an electronics company resulted in reducing downtime in computerized equipment that saved 10 hours of production time. In time, it became a 70% reduction as workers became more skilled and increased their intrinsic job satisfaction. Machine reliability was increased (Wall, Corbett, & Clegg, 1990; Jackson & Wall, 1991). In Japan, this was seen as "giving wisdom to the machine" (Ralls, 1994, p. 36). In 1987, a survey of 584 machine-manufacturing plants found that plants where machine operators routinely programmed the machines were 30% more efficient than plants where they did not. Such worker control in the more efficient plants depended on providing workers with technical training (Kelly, 1995).

According to Salzman (1992), the introduction of operator control met with a lot of resistance. Of 200 engineering design and engineering textbooks published between 1938 and 1989, only 42 mentioned worker roles in production and technology. The roles were mainly subservient to the machinery. Illustrative of the prevailing orientation in engineering design was the admonition that "the operator should not read an (*ohm*) meter. She should not be told what an *ohm* is. She should not be asked to make borderline judgments—Any adjusting may upset (her) . . . any slight gain in efficiency will be lost in retraining time" (Gibson, 1968). Nevertheless, as computers and technology have become more user-friendly, operators have become able to maintain, modify, and program their own equipment and machinery. This allows computer specialists and engineers to serve as coaches and to do more specialized work (Ralls, 1994).

Considerable consultation with the workers is seen as fundamental to establishing the bases for meeting both the requirements of the task and the workers' socioemotional needs. Participative leadership becomes mandatory in the actual operations and is built into the design. For instance, *minimal critical specification* is a principle of sociotechnical design. According to this principle, the design process should identify what is essential to be accomplished in a task, and no more should be specified than what is essential. For example, although the design process may be precise about what needs to be done, it should leave maximum latitude about the method the employee may use to accomplish the task. Again, the *multifunctional* principle of sociotechnical design proposes that for an organization to be sufficiently adaptive to meet environmental demands, it is necessary for its members to be willing and able to perform more than one function or to perform the same function in a variety of ways to meet changing circumstances. Clearly, both task-oriented and relations-oriented leadership are needed to obtain the requisite employee performance and the commitment of employees to such fluid arrangements (Bass & Barrett, 1981).

Sociotechical principles are consistent with E. E. Lawler's (1986) high-involvement management practices that promote more effective uses of technology and the introduction of new technologies. With suitable training, operators are enabled to make relevant decisions about maintaining and improving their technology-assisted work. Their involvement and alignment with organizational productivity goals are fostered by gain sharing, skill-based pay, teamwork, flexible assignments, reduced status differentiation between operators and supervisors, and engagement in problem solving. Such practices are key to successful implementing of technology in the work place (Klein & Ralls, 1994). At first, sociotechnical designs were applied only to routine, linear work. But by 1995, they had been found useful for improving services and noncontinuous processes, processing transactions, and nonroutine and professional work (Fox, 1995).

Leadership and Phases in Group Problem Solving

The requirements of the task change as a group progresses in its solution of a problem. Given these changing requirements during the course of group problem solving, Valenzi, Miller, Eldridge, et al. (1972) concluded that effective leadership for one phase of problem solving may be different than it is for another phase. Early on, the group usually engages in the divergent generation of alternatives. In this phase, broad participation is needed. As a consequence, Doyle (1971) considered democratic leaders to be most effective. But in the convergent, final, synthesizing phase, when coordination becomes more important, groups with leaders of high status were particularly effective. Becker and Baloff (1969) also suggested that optimal leader-subordinate relations may depend on whether the group's immediate task involves information processing, the generation of alternatives, or decision making.

Ghiselli (1966a) observed experimental groups at various stages of problem solving. The presence of a strongly self-confident decision maker, along with highly intelligent, confident, and cohesive followers, was associated with the better performance of the group in the later stages of the group's development. Nonetheless, initial performance was poor in its early, storming phase. Presumably, such confidence, competence, and motivation generated many conflicting alternatives that later formed the basis of high-quality decisions. Sample and Wilson (1965) also studied groups in different phases of problem solving. They found that task-oriented leaders quickly structured the group procedures during the planning phase and were then able to play a more relaxed role in the operational phase. Relations-oriented leaders, on the other hand, tended to hold group discussions during the planning stage, and the work did not get organized. As a result, these leaders had to try to organize procedures during the operational stage, with only partial success. In such circumstances, groups under task-oriented leaders performed more effectively.

Effects of Type of Task

Korten (1968) advised that if the final product of a task was practical, more directive supervision was in order. If the outcome was theoretical, participative leadership was likely to be more useful. Carter and Nixon (1949b) found that different participants emerged as leaders, depending on whether intellectual, clerical, or mechanical assembly tasks were involved. Carter, Haythorn, and Howell (1950) studied the effects of six types of tasks (reasoning, intellectual construction, clerical, discussion, motor cooperation, and mechanical assembly) on leadership in initially leaderless groups. Although there was some generality of leadership performance across all tasks, two clusters of tasks made a difference in who emerged as a leader. The leaders of the intellectual tasks were different from the leaders of the tasks involving doing things with one's hands. As was mentioned earlier, C. G. Morris (1966a, 1966b) varied the type of task and the difficulty of the task for 108 groups. The variance in the leaders' behavior was related more to the type of task than to the difficulty of the task. Discussion tasks elicited significantly more structuring of problems and more explanatory and defensive comments by leaders. Production tasks resulted in more structuring of proposed solutions, disagreement, and procedural comments. Problem-solving tasks were similar to discussion tasks but led to more irrelevant activity and less structuring of problems.

Creative and Innovative Work

Among others, Mumford and Gustafeson (1988) saw an upsurge in organizations of an interest in stimulating creativity, generation of new ideas, and their conversion into action. Traditionally, such creativity had usually been seen as the product of a lone individual with a flash of insight about gravity as he observed an apple falling from a tree. Nonetheless, the research of Pelz (1963) and Pelz and Andrews (1966a, b) recognized early on the importance of the leadership of laboratory directors and leaders at the National Institutes of Health to the productivity of their scientists. Suggestion systems had been around since the end of the nineteenth century, but the interest in leaders who fostered creativity and innovation among their followers as a core purpose was sparked by rapid advances in technology, the information revolution, and global competition (Dess & Pickens, 2000). Tierney and Farmer (2003) developed a reliable and valid Creativity Leadership Index using five samples to assess the leadership of creativity. The data were based on responses from 1,219 employees.

The importance of autonomy and discretion was mentioned earlier in promoting innovation and creativity. Supervisory support was important to the generating of patents by 171 design and manufacturing engineers, design drafters, tool makers, and technicians in two manufacturing plants (Oldham & Cummings, 1996). On the other hand, when their group leader's supervisory control was tight and the introduction of new ideas was discouraged among 200 scientists, the scientists' creativity was squelched (Andrews, 1967). Mumford, Scott, Gaddis, et al. (2002) noted dilemmas facing the leader of creative people. Creative tasks are ill defined. To opimize creativity, the leader needs to avoid imposing too much or too little structure. Followers' goals need to be aligned with the organization's. Furthermore, the leader must evaluate the proposed work but not be overrestrictive in what is to be done.

Slusher, Van Dyke, and Rose (1972) found in a small sample study of nine engineering design groups that it was more important to group productivity for group leaders to initiate structure and be considerate than to be technically proficient. However, in most subsequent studies, it was seen as more important for creative group leaders to be technically proficient as well as expert problem solvers. Additionally, they needed to have general planning skills (Mumford, 2000). Glassman (1989) suggested that leaders of creative workers need to be able to negotiate disagreements and to listen nonevaluatively. Leading R&D activities requires the ability to communicate clearly with colleagues and top management. The R&D leader must appreciate the values and intrinsic motivation of professionals and the importance to them of challenging work and freedom to explore promising lines of inquiry.

According to Strohmeier (1998), technical leaders and senior scientists are specialized experts. They keep abreast of the literature in their field, value being recognized for patents, publications, and conference presentations, and are highly task-oriented and less concerned with relationships. Technical leaders need broad techni-

cal competence to maintain credibility with their technical followers. Yet they need to depend on their followers for additional specialized knowledge. Jaussi and Dionne (2003) showed experimentally, with 364 undergraduates in 79 groups, that leaders who were unconventional in their behavior tended to contribute indirectly to the creativity of their groups. Mumford, Scott, Gaddis, et al. (2002) provided more details about satisfying and effective leading of creative and innovative people.

Tasks at Different Organizational Levels. Systematic changes in the type of tasks that are performed occur as leaders move up the organizational ladder.[7] Different types of tasks call for different kinds of leadership. At the production and operations levels, the processes are direct and concrete. Work and service are with tangible materials and methods that are accomplished by people, tools, and machines. At these levels, leaders deal with issues of routines, pacing, meeting deadlines, and balancing the need for immediate production or service with the need for the development of individual subordinates and the need to prepare subordinates for future operations. Trust is based on personal contact and knowledge. Leadership involves face-to-face interaction and interpersonal skills. At higher organizational levels, leadership deals much more with buffering the rational production and service at lower levels from the turbulence of the external environment. At these levels, the subordinates' operations are monitored indirectly, and the coordination and integration of efforts with the market and the external environment become the tasks of consequence (Jaques, 1978). Not unexpectedly, Bass, Valenzi, Farrow, and Solomon (1975) found that the more subordinates' work involved planning, coordination, evaluation, and other managerial activities, the more frequently their superior was likely to delegate decision making to them. However, follow-up analyses on a larger scale added that such subordinates were also given more direction.

Changes in the Organization's Tasks. As the organization matures, its tasks change. Consequently, the type of leadership that is needed also changes, especially at higher organizational levels. Brenner (1972) and Lavoie and Culbert (1978), among others, described the com-

[7] See Chapter 23.

monly observed progression of organizations through development, maturity, and decline as different tasks arise. Different stages of an organization's development call for the emergence of different styles of executive leadership in the different phases. Early on, the tasks of a business enterprise, for example, are to develop products, processes, and procedures; create a demand for them; build loyalty to a brand; find a significant niche in the market; attract financing; develop personnel and new technology. Later, the tasks may require more attention to cost containment, divestment, maintaining the share of the market, and integrating new product lines with older ones. The founders who conceive and originate organizations that grow and thrive, for example, are more prone to take calculated risks than are their counterparts who must deal with old, declining organizations.[8] Leadership that is predictable and that works within the established rules and procedures and under greater formal constraints is more characteristic of mature organizations than of those in the early stages of their development.

In the established organization in a stable environment, the executive must be able to serve as a transactional leader who works within the institutionalized values and systems. The executive leader serves as a steward, balancing out the strongly developed interests of the different constituencies that may be in conflict with each other. Much political compromise and accommodation are needed. During periods of gestation, birth, development, resolution, re-formation, and renewal, the executive's tasks require more transformational leadership, greater persistence and effort, and greater inspirational and charismaticlike behavior.[9] New strategies and commitments to new values and new systems are required. The cycle of development, maturity, and decline is not inevitable. Rather, intervention by transformational managers can provide for the renewal of an organization through reform or revolution (Normann, 1977).

Computerized Work. By 1990, more than 80% of office workers were using computers. In the developed world in 2006, it would have been difficult to find office workers operating without them. Office supervisors need to be familiar with computers and the complexities of computer systems. The same is true for workers and blue-

[8] See Chapter 25.
[9] See Chapter 21.

collar supervisors as automation continues to increase in factories, mills, and warehouses. Public agencies are now among the biggest users for documentation and dissemination of information. In addition to the rapid expansion of technological capabilities are the concomitant changes in organizational arrangements and leadership. In the U.S. military, online instant communication makes it possible to link the U.S. president with the local combat commander on the battle site, bypassing many organizational echelons. Likewise, fax and e-mail make for instant communication and potential control across continents, oceans, and organizational levels. Increasingly, the centralization of decision making or overcontrol of the local commander is the result. Similarly, tighter reins by higher-level civilian executives are made possible by computer systems. Although the greatest emphasis has been placed on the impact of automation on stable, repetitive, processing systems, computer-assisted creative designing and engineering are now commonplace for production and service processes. Computerized planning and control models are also available for real-time planning and control. Word processing and office automation increase the productivity of individual typists. Nevertheless, supposedly to take advantage of the automation, the individualized dyadic relationship of the manager and the typist may be severed and replaced with an anonymous pool of typists or by eliminating most of the pool by having each manager using his own personal computer. First-line supervisors become more like area supervisors when advanced manufacturing computer technology or computer integrated manufacturing is put in place. Area supervisors are shop floor experts or engineering trained personnel with some shop experience who serve as consultants and coaches to the operators. Minimally, the new technology brings about changes in the roles of first-line supervisor and middle managers (Ettle, 1986).

Supervisory Relations. According to Kraemer and Danziger (1984), computerization at the workplace increases the closeness of the supervisor with those at the bottom of the hierarchy. The supervisors lose some of their potential for upward influence, while those who are higher up feel a greater sense of control. The pressure of time and the importance of deadlines increase. These changes enhance the possibilities of bureaucratic management. But the effects may be counterproductive. Applebaum (1982) noted that computer programming applied to the construction industry resulted in the reliance on authoritarian and mechanistic procedures. For a while, the outcome was inefficient and irrational; control of the work process was decreased instead of increased.

However, Kerr, Hill, and Broedling (1986) offered a more balanced perspective. They suggested that automation should have its biggest effects on workers whose work had been labor-intensive and closely supervised and required little discretion and judgment. Obviously, the supervisors of such workers would be responsible for more sophisticated equipment. Nevertheless, computerized systems directly give upper management detailed information on the individual worker, such as his or her error rate and missed deadlines. Upper-level managers can bypass the first-level supervisor to obtain such information. The supervisor will then be expected to explain the reasons for the worker's deviation from the production plans. Further conflicts of interest arise for the first-level supervisor, who now faces demands from a specialized staff of systems analysts and programmers, along with those from the traditional line superiors, subordinates, and staff personnel: "first-line supervisors will have to be more technically proficient, as well as more highly skilled in human relations than their predecessors" (p. 114).

Other Changes in Supervising. Computerization shortcuts the need for management controls, for it can provide direct feedback from work performed on the task without any supervisory intervention. The self-managed employee can be provided by computer with continued feedback about his or her performance along with the information needed to improve it. In contrast to the findings of Kraemer and Danzinger (1984), Kerr, Hill, and Broedling (1986) inferred that first-line supervisors have moved farther from their subordinates and closer to middle managers. They reasoned that computerization reduces the time that supervisors need to spend in planning and scheduling work; documenting records and reports; engaging in coordination and control; organizing subordinates' work; and maintaining quality and efficiency, safety and cleanliness, and machinery and equipment. Presumably, spans of control can be increased. Nonetheless, the first-line supervisor's role does not seem to be diminished, for computerization facilitates his or her service as a boundary spanner; a maintainer of relations with other units; or a selector, trainer, and motivator of subordinates. Computerization makes it possible for first-line supervisors to operate more like middle managers, relative to the total organization, rather than remain oriented toward dealing mainly with subordinates (Hill & Kerr, 1984). Chapter 29 will detail how computerized networks have replaced human real ones.

Shift from Power to Achievement. The increasing technology and computerization of tasks suggests that in more technologically advanced organizations, the power motive may become less important than the need for achievement as a predictor of success in advancement to higher levels of management. As was noted in Chapter 8, McClelland (1975) demonstrated that individuals who scored high on the Thematic Apperception Test in the need for power and the inhibition of power tended to emerge as more successful leaders in a variety of situations. However, when McClelland and Boyatzis (1982) examined whether the leadership motive pattern was predictive of the long-term managerial success of technical and nontechnical managers at AT&T, the power motive pattern was related to significantly higher levels of advancement after 8 to 16 years with the company only by nontechnical managers. For technically trained and experienced managers, the need for achievement, rather than the power motive, predicted advancement into the next several echelons of the firm.

Path-Goal Theory: The Explanation of Task Effects on Leadership

Beginning with Georgopolous, Mahoney, and Jones (1957) and delineated by M. G. Evans (1970a) and House (1971), path-goal theory stimulated the search for an explanation of how the nature of the group's task systematically affects whether leader consideration, initiation of structure, or interplay makes a contribution to the group's satisfaction and effectiveness. Rightfully, the theory has been modified on a continuing basis by experimental failures. According to T. R. Mitchell (1979), path-goal theory calls for the leader to provide subordinates with coaching, guidance, and the rewards necessary for satisfaction and effective performance necessitated by the subordinates' abilities to meet the particular task requirements and attain the designated goals. Focus is on ways for the leader to influence subordinates' perceptions of the clarity of the paths to goals and the desirability of the goals themselves. Leadership behavior that is best suited for increasing motivation depends on the subordinates' personal characteristics and the demands of the task. Valued rewards should be awarded contingently on effective performance.[10]

Path-Goal: An Exchange Theory of Leadership

Path-goal theory is an exchange theory of leadership. It attempts to explain why contingent reward works and how it influences the motivation and satisfaction of subordinates. In its earliest version by Georgopolous, Mahoney, and Jones (1957), it focused on the need for leaders to "point out the paths to successful effort" (Bass, 1965, p. 150). Leaders do so by "increasing personal payoffs to subordinates for workgoal attainment, and making the path to these payoffs easier to travel, by clarifying it, reducing roadblocks and pitfalls, and increasing the opportunities for personal satisfaction en route" (House, 1971, p. 324).

Path instrumentalities are the subordinate's subjective estimates that his or her performance will lead to the accomplishment of the goal. Achievement of the goal will result in ends desired by the subordinate. The leader enhances the subordinate's motivation, performance, and satisfaction by clarifying and enhancing path instrumentalities (Van Fleet & Yukl, 1986). This cognitive-perceptual explanation of path-goal theory can be matched in terms of operant behavior and reinforcement theory (Mawhinney & Ford, 1977).

The Leader's Role. Leaders can affect a subordinate's efforts in several ways in the path-goal process. They can clarify the subordinate's role, that is, state what they expect the subordinate to do. They can make the rewards to the subordinate more dependent on his or her satisfactory performance. They can increase the size and value of the rewards (M. G. Evans, 1970a). Specific leadership behaviors can contribute to their followers' attainment of the goal by coaching, providing direction, and support

to followers, alleviating their boredom and frustration with work, and fostering their expectations that their efforts will result in the successful completion of the task (Fiedler & House, 1988).

But early on, House and Mitchell (1974) recognized that path-goal leadership, as such, was needed and useful only in certain circumstances. The leader needs to complement only what is missing in a situation to enhance the followers' motivation, satisfaction, and performance. What is missing is determined by the environment, the task, and the competence and motivation of the followers (Fiedler & House, 1988). Thus, the followers' productivity is enhanced if the leader provides needed structure to clarify means and ends if they are missing or unclear to the followers. This contribution of the leader is particularly apparent in jazz ensembles. A deviation-counteracting loop is observed in jazz that involves the leader's interpretation, criticism, and adjustments of the ensemble. The need for such correction is increased by the variety of selections the ensemble plays, the availability to them of new musical numbers, the difficulty of the numbers played, and the lack of rehearsal time (Voyer & Faulkner, 1986).

Given clear tasks and roles, the supervisor contributes to continued productivity by consideration, support, and attention to the followers' personal and interpersonal needs for satisfying relationships (Fiedler & House, 1988). If what is missing can be supplied in other ways by the organization through policies, regulations, improved communications, channels of information, contingent reward schemes, and counseling services, such substitutes for the leadership[11] may result in the same outcomes that would have been expected from the appropriate leadership.

The Path-Goal Linkage. The exchange involved in path-goal theory is seen when subordinates perceive high productivity to be an easy "path" to attain personal goals and, as a consequence, the subordinates are productive. Directive leadership increases the promise of reward to the followers for their performance and makes the paths to their goals clearer and easier. Accordingly, such directive leadership is needed only if the task is complex, difficult, or ambiguous and its goals are unclear. Whether the

---

[10]See Chapter 15.

[11]See Chapter 29.

followers are self-reinforcing and have a great need for autonomy, growth, achievement, or affection will also make a difference. On the other hand, if subordinates are faced with simple but boring tasks, a leader may do better by being supportive and considerate rather than directive. Too much motivation among followers, evidenced by a state of high anxiety, may call for calming support from the leader rather than any talk about contingent (uncertain) rewards, which will increase such anxiety. Supportive confidence building may be required rather than more drive (Yukl, 1981).

Efforts to Test the Theory

Translated into experiments, considerate leadership behavior or supportive relations-oriented leadership was expected to correlate more highly with satisfaction and productivity in structured than in unstructured situations. The leader's initiation of structure was expected to correlate more highly with satisfaction and productivity in unstructured than in structured situations. These expectations fit with the conventional wisdom that "chaos is the midwife of dictatorship" (Durant, 1957).

Supportive Results. Reviews of the empirical literature by House and Mitchell (1974) and Schriesheim and Kerr (1974) tended to confirm the theory, as did a meta-analysis by Indvik (1986a) involving 87 empirical tests. In addition, House and Dessler (1974) demonstrated that, as predicted, the available task structure generally determined whether the initiating structure and consideration by the leader would contribute to the followers' satisfaction, positive expectations, and role clarity. Earlier, House (1971) found support a posteriori in several studies cited in earlier chapters.[12] In specific a priori tests of the theory, House found, as expected, that the satisfaction of followers was associated with the extent to which the leader's initiating structure reduced role ambiguity. Likewise, Meheut and Siegel (1973) observed that the leader's initiation that was role clarifying was positively related to the followers' satisfaction with management by objectives. A more complicated finding was that the

more autonomous the followers, the more the leader's initiation of structure correlated with followers' satisfaction but the less the leader's initiation correlated with the followers' performance. At the same time, as the scope of the subordinates' task decreased, the leader's consideration correlated more with the followers' satisfaction and performance. Also supportive were direct tests of the theory by Dessler (1973), who found that with the leader's consideration held constant, the leader's initiation of structure correlated less with the followers' satisfaction and role clarity as the ambiguity of the task decreased.

Schriesheim and DeNisi (1981) studied how the variety of tasks in a job, feedback, and dealing with others moderated the impact of the initiation of structure on satisfaction with supervision among 110 employees who were working in a medium-size plant and among 205 employees of a medium-size manufacturer. The variety of tasks was expected to require more initiation of structure for employees' satisfaction with supervision. Such initiation would be redundant with routine jobs (House & Dessler, 1974) and when feedback was already structured and followers dealt with others a lot. The results confirmed the moderating effect of all three task variables.

Mixed and Nonsupportive Results. Szilagyi and Sims (1974) obtained data from 53 administrative, 240 professional, 117 technical, and 231 service personnel at multiple levels of occupational skills in a hospital. Although the results supported path-goal propositions concerning the demands of the task and the relationship between the leader's initiating structure and the followers' satisfaction, they failed to do so for the relationship between the leader's initiation and the followers' performance. Similarly, Stinson and Johnson (1975) tested hypotheses derived from the path-goal theory of leadership that the correlations between the leader's initiating structure and satisfaction and role clarity are more positive under conditions of low task structure, low task repetitiveness, and high task autonomy than under high task structure, high task repetitiveness, and low task autonomy. The leader's consideration and the subordinates' satisfaction and role clarity were expected to be more positively related under structured, repetitive, dependent conditions than under unstructured, unrepetitive, autonomous conditions. The

---

[12]The studies were by Fleishman, Harris, and Burtt (1955); Halpin (1954); Mulder, van Eck, and de Jong (1971); Mulder and Sternerding (1963); Rush (1957); and Sales (1972).

subjects were military officers, civil service personnel, and project engineers. The results were consistent with path-goal theory with respect to consideration but tended to be contrary to the theory regarding the initiation of structure.

Contrary to path-goal theory, the leader's consideration was still generally found to result in the higher satisfaction of followers, regardless of the characteristics of the task (Johns, 1978; Miles & Petty, 1977). Thus, J. F. Schriesheim and C. A. Schriesheim (1980) surveyed 290 managerial and clinical employees in nine different jobs at five levels in the operations divisions of a large public utility. Contrary to path-goal theory, they found that regardless of the task structure, organizational level, or type of job, supportive (considerate) leadership explained 63% of the variance in the followers' satisfaction with their supervisors after instrumental leadership (initiation) was partialled out. But, as predicted, instrumental leadership (after supportive leadership was partialed out) contributed 17% to accounting for the variance in role clarity. However, again this covariance was unmoderated by the task structure, organizational level, or type of job. Likewise, Seers and Graen (1984) found that without reference to leadership, performance and satisfaction outcomes directly depended on the characteristics of the task, as well as on the followers' need for growth. In the same way, the satisfactory quality of the leader-followers relationship independently added to the prediction of the outcomes of performance and satisfaction without reference to the task and the followers' needs, which were also related to the outcomes.

Wolcott (1984) tested path-goal predictions for library supervisors and the performance of their reference librarians and catalogers. Contrary to path-goal predictions, the initiation of more structure contributed to better performance when the task structure was already high than when it was low. The librarians' high educational level and low need for independence were seen to be possible explanations for the results.

More initiation of structure is likely to be seen when the group task is already structured (Bass, Valenzi, Farrow, & Solomon, 1975). It may be that a leader's initiation may be easier to accomplish if subordinates' tasks are already structured but actually may be useful when tasks are unstructured. Generally, initiating structure still frequently increases tensions, especially when consideration is low (Miles & Petty, 1977; Schriesheim & Murphy, 1976) and when the initiation of structure measure continues to contain coercive, threatening items, along with direction and order giving. In turn, this linkage of direction and coercion is a consequence of dependence on empirical rather than conceptual analyses for developing measurements. Although autocrats tend to want to structure situations, conceptually one can give orders without being a threatening autocrat. For more than 1,300 subordinates of their 340 managers, the correlation between being coercive and being directive was only .38 (Farrow, Valenzi, and Bass, 1980).

In a first study, Greene (1979a) showed that, as expected, instrumental (structuring) leadership behavior was correlated positively with the satisfaction and performance of 119 engineers, scientists, or technicians if they faced tasks with little structure. But such instrumental leadership was negatively correlated with satisfaction and minimally with performance when the tasks were more structured. Considerate or supportive leadership, as expected from the theory, increased the correlation with intrinsic satisfaction (but not with performance or extrinsic satisfaction) as the task structure increased. In a second study, Greene (1979b) tested several assumptions about causation that underlie the theory. The findings supported the theory, except, again, for the hypotheses concerning the followers' performance. Downey, Sheridan, and Slocum (1975) found only partial support for the path-goal predictions, and J. P. Siegel (1973) and Szilagyi and Sims (1974b) found none. Dessler and Valenzi (1977) failed to find moderator effects across supervisory levels. T. R. Mitchell (1979) concluded that the findings were stronger for the consideration hypothesis than for the structuring hypothesis and stronger for satisfaction as a criterion than for performance.

Indvik (1985, 1986a) completed a meta-analysis of 48 path-goal studies involving 11,862 respondents. Task structure, as such, was measured directly in some of the studies. In the rest of the studies, low job level was accepted as an indicator of high task structure, as was large organizational size. As predicted, when structure was absent from the work environment, directive, structuring leadership behavior contributed to the intrinsic motivation of followers, their satisfaction with the leader, and their overall satisfaction, but, surprisingly, it failed to add to role clarity, as such. However, contrary to predictions, directive, structuring leadership contributed to the subordinates' performance when the structure was high but not when the structure was low.

Considerate, supportive leadership behavior in a highly structured work setting did enhance motivation, satisfaction, performance, and role clarity, as predicted. In a related meta-analytic report, Indvik (1986b) concluded that participative leadership provided the most overall satisfaction to subordinates who preferred and experienced a low task structure. Furthermore, when the task structure was high, achievement-oriented leadership behavior was related to increased intrinsic satisfaction among subordinates but decreased extrinsic satisfaction and performance for those subordinates with a high need for achievement.

Efforts to Reconcile Path-Goal Theory with the Mixed Results

Johns (1978) suggested that much more is "missing" that the leader may supply efficaciously than just task structure, as measured by House and Dessler's (1974) scale about the extent to which tasks are simple, repetitive, and unambiguous. Johns (1978) argued for using a broader measurement of the scope of a job for determining what could be missing from it. Such a measurement would be Hackman and Oldham's (1975) index based on variety, autonomy, the significance of the job, feedback from the job, and the identity that the job provides to its occupant. Johns (1978) found that Sims, Szilagyi, and Keller's (1976) Job Characteristics Inventory, which measures the scope of a job, provided a measure to moderate more consistently the relationships between leadership behavior and the satisfaction of subordinates than task structure alone could do.

Coercive versus Noncoercive Initiation of Structure.
The measures of leadership behavior are obtained most often from the Leader Behavior Description Questionnaire — Form XII (LBDQ-XII) and less from the Supervisory Behavior Description Questionnaire (SBDQ).[13] Schriesheim and Von Glinow (1977) first noted that path-goal predictions of job satisfaction were less likely to be supported when a more coercive measure, such

as the SBDQ initiation of structure, had been used.[14] Schriesheim and Von Glinow then demonstrated, with 230 maintenance workers, that if a coercion-loaded scale was used, reverse results were obtained for the path-goal predictions for job satisfaction. But when coercion-free scales (the LBDQ and the LBDQ-XII) or items from them were employed, path-goal predictions were confirmed if task structure and role clarity were used to moderate the relationship between the leader's consideration and initiation of structure and the followers' job satisfaction.

Conditions Affect What Leaders Can Do.
A second source of contradictory findings results from the fact, as noted above, that leaders tend to be more directive when it is easier for them to do so, such as when roles are clear, conditions are structured, and jobs are routine (Bass, Valenzi, Farrow, & Solomon, 1975). But such structuring would seem to be redundant for subordinates' productivity when conditions are already structured. Rather, it would seem that such direction is needed more when conditions are unstructured, for in such unstructured situations, it might be argued that the group wants some direction from the leader, not just the leader's sympathy. Nevertheless, Indvik's (1985, 1986a) previously mentioned meta-analysis proved otherwise: directive, structuring leadership contributed to followers' performance when structure was high, not when it was low.

Attributes of Leaders and Subordinates.
The leader's personality also needs to be taken into account in the structured situation, given Farrow and Bass's (1977) finding that highly *directive* leaders tend primarily to be satisfied authoritarians. In addition, the subordinates' personalities need to be considered. Griffin (1979) proposed a set of prescriptions combining path-goal theory and the subordinates' need for achievement and self-actualization. Griffin called for achievement-oriented, consultative leadership for self-actualizing followers with "big" jobs. But for self-actualizers in routine jobs of little scope, supportive leadership (consideration without consultation) was required. For "big" jobs performed by occupants who are uninterested in self-actualization, di-

---

[13] See Chapter 20, which discusses the coercive elements in the SBDQ that are absent from the LBDQ.

[14] See, e.g., Downey, Sheridan, and Slocum (1975, 1976); and J. P. Siegel (1973).

rective leadership (structuring without threat) was seen as most needed. For occupants of routine jobs who have no need for self-actualization, maintenance leadership behavior (management by exception) was suggested.

Schriesheim and Schriesheim (1980) added other subordinate variables that are likely to act as path-goal moderators of the leader-outcome relationships. These variables included the followers' authoritarianism, ability, training, need for affiliation, and experience relative to the demands of the task and their internalization of professional norms and standards. Similarly, Abdel-Halim (1981) found that the subordinates' locus of control (internal or external) had important effects on the path-goal leader-outcome relationships associated with the ambiguity of the role and the complexity of the job.

Algattan (1985) examined the extent to which the scope of the followers' task, strength of the need for growth, and locus of control moderated leader-outcome relationships for two periods, two months apart. At each time period, if the subordinates' locus of control was external, the scope of their tasks and the strength of their need for growth increased the extent to which both participative and directive leadership contributed to their satisfaction and performance. But if the subordinates' locus of control was internal, task-oriented leadership, as such, was of more importance to their satisfaction and performance. However, a cross-lagged analysis of the correlations for the two time periods failed to support the existence of casuality in the relationships.

Craig (1983) attempted to show the importance of subordinates' self-esteem to path-goal leader-outcome relationships but failed to find the expected interactions. Wolcott (1984) found no effect on the relationships from differences in the subordinates' need for independence. Keller (1987) argued that the discomfort of role ambiguity may differ from one follower to another. Some people who may want to clarify and structure their roles themselves are unlikely to be enthusiastic about a leader who initiates structure even if the task is unstructured or ambiguous. Followers with high levels of education, such as R & D professionals, who may have internalized professional norms that provide them with role clarity, may not need or want the leader to initiate structure. Some followers may actually enjoy the unstructured nature of a task; they may have a low need for clarity and prefer to create their own structure. For Keller, compared to task structure, the followers' need or lack of need for clarity was seen to be a more important moderator of the correlations between the leader's initiation of structure and the subordinates' satisfaction and performance.

In a survey of 477 professionals employed in four R & D organizations, Keller (1988) employed Rizzo, House, and Lirtzman's (1970) role ambiguity scale to measure the subordinate's perceived task clarity, as well as Ivancevich and Donnelly's (1974) scale to measure the subordinate's felt need for clarity on the job. He found that the need for clarity had a moderating effect on the initiation of structure-satisfaction relationship for both concurrent data and data gathered one year later. The higher a subordinate's felt need for clarity, the stronger was the relationship between the leader's initiation of structure and the subordinate's job satisfaction. The subordinate's need for clarity was similarly found to moderate the initiation-performance relationship in the largest of the R & D organizations. But, as proposed, the actual clarity of the task for the subordinates, as such, failed to serve as a moderator for these leader-outcome relationships. In the same way, Kroll and Pringle (1985) failed to find the expected effects of the leader's directiveness on the satisfaction of 43 middle managers in marketing. Kroll and Pringle explained the results by noting that managers rated the ambiguous situation as a positive experience, particularly if they judged the amount of direction they received to be the amount they actually desired.

A Comprehensive Study. Using data from a survey of 467 nonacademic staff at a university, Indvik (1988) completed tests of 17 hypotheses that involved directive, supportive, participative, and achievement-oriented leadership behavior, plus the expectancies that increased effort would improve performance and that improved performance would yield valued outcomes. Also measured were intrinsic satisfaction with work, extrinsic satisfaction with pay and promotion, and satisfaction with one's superior. The subordinates' performance was appraised by their superiors. Indvik examined the task structure, norms of the work group, and organizational formalization as situational moderators of the relations between superiors' leadership behavior and subordinate outcomes. Personal subordinate moderators included the need for achievement and preference for environmental structure. Hierarchical stepwise regression analyses[15] provided support for seven of the 17 hypotheses tested. Moderators that had significant effects included the subordinates' preference for structure and need for achievement. However, Indvik concluded that generally, because of its low reliability, the subordinates' preference for structure had a weak moderating effect on the relations of leadership behavior to subordinate outcomes. Directive and achievement-oriented leadership behaviors were too highly correlated with each other to be distinguishable. Indvik recommended that future studies should measure transformational leadership behavior instead of the transactional leadership behavior on which path-goal research has concentrated, for it is likely that transformational leadership behavior is more sensitive to task structure and the characteristics of subordinates.

Integration of Findings. Neider and Schriesheim (1988) constructed a comprehensive path-goal model, shown in Figure 27.1, that attempts to incorporate many of the consistent findings about the process and the variables of consequence.

In the model, the manager stimulates the subordinate's

[15] In a stepwise regression analysis, predictors are added according to their contribution to the overall prediction of outcomes. In a hierarchical regression, they are added in a predetermined order. The order used was based on path-goal propositions.

effort by offering valued rewards and linking them to the subordinate's effort and performance. How much the effort yields high performance depends on the subordinate's knowledge, skills, and abilities, as well as on the absence of hurdles to performing the job. The rewards received by the subordinate, if valued and equitable, create satisfaction and encourage the subordinate to remain on the job.

By 1993, Wofford and Liska had located 120 studies that tested aspects of path-goal theory, not counting reviews and expositions. Jermier (1996) explained the continuing popularity of the theory as being that it rejected a single best way to lead and focused attention on situational contingencies. It placed more emphasis on the effects on leaders and followers of dyadic than group relationships. Although in some instances its derived propositions were sometimes invalidated, they remained interesting and stimulating to scholarly research. Raw empirical publication in leadership was no longer acceptable or convincing without guidance from theory and hypothesis testing. Path-goal theory provided a more sophisticated way to examine leadership processes.

Caveat. Despite a considerable amount of general empirical support for it, path-goal theory is complex, which makes it difficult to test the theory's deduced relationships. Furthermore, too much rigor may be required

Figure 27.1 An Integrated Path-Goal Perspective of Motivation and Leadership

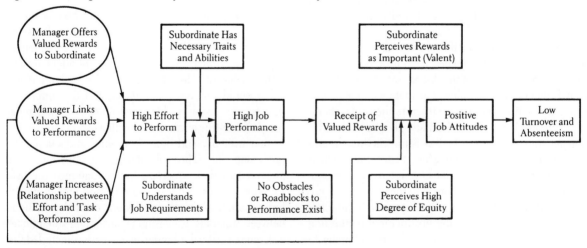

SOURCE: Neider and Schriesheim (1988).

of such tests, and sampling and measurements may be inadequate to meet the requirements (Yukl & Van Fleet, 1986). It is not surprising that a wide array of empirical results, sometimes contradictory, have emerged from the surveys and experiments that tested various propositions derived from path-goal theory.

Summary and Conclusions

The leader's and subordinates' competence, personality, and autonomy and the requirements of the task systematically moderate how different leadership behaviors affect what happens in the group. The characteristics of the task that make a difference include its structure, clarity, provisions for the subordinate's autonomy and use of discretion, routineness, variety, complexity, difficulty, interdependencies, automation, multiplicity of solutions to problems, and task requirements for cooperation. As the task is different at different phases in a group's development and at different organizational levels, so is the requisite leadership. Socioemotional and task requirements call for sociotechnical designs of the workplace.

Path-goal theory has been widely tested and modified to account for the impact of the task on optimum leader-subordinate relations. Currently, it suggests that to obtain subordinates' effective performance and satisfaction, the leader must provide structure if it is missing and must supply rewards that are contingent on the adequate performance of the subordinates. To do so, leaders must clarify the desirability of the goals for the subordinates, a role seemingly suited for transformational leaders. But their efficacy in doing so will depend on such personal characteristics as the subordinates' need for clarity. However, the lack of clarity and ambiguity of the situation may also be sources of stress—to be examined next.

Stress Effects

Individuals, groups, and organizations confronted with threats to their well-being will experience stress. Rowney and Cahoon (1988) noted that the burnout scores among individuals who work in the same unit are more similar than those of individuals who work in different units doing similar kinds of work. In many instances, the available leadership makes the difference in the prevention or occurrence of stress and burnout. Leadership can be the source of increased stress, negative emotions, and negative outcomes. But leadership can provide for avoiding stress or coping with it. Thus Graham (1982) found that with professional employees of a county extension service, job stress was lower when the leaders of their district program were described as higher on the Leader Behavior Description Questionnaire (LBDQ)[1] in both initiation of structure and consideration. Leadership can also be the source of positive emotions; when, threats are converted to opportunities, stress may yield positive outcomes (Folkman & Moskowitz, 2000).

The Nature of Stress

Signs of Stress

Rodney Lowman advised that signs of stress in the workplace that need to be recognized by the leader include: (1) absenteeism, whether due to illness or other reasons; (2) workers who have become more irritable and hard to get along with; (3) more confusion is appearing and mistakes are more frequent on tasks that usually are performed well; (4) stress is felt by the leaders and felt and expressed by the workers (Perry, 1999).

Stress symptoms include increased emotional arousal, frustration, defensiveness, faulty decision making, and physiological symptoms like sweating, heavier breathing, and increased heartbeat. A state of anxiety is a percep-

tual manifestation of such objective conditions of stress (Spielberger, 1972). Well known is the extent to which stress is generated in subordinates by hostile, abusive superiors (Roberto, 2002). The hostile, abusive leader who uses power to bully, humiliate, intimidate, and threaten subordinates is a major source of stress (Aquino, 2000; Tepper, 2000). Deadlines are set that are impossible to meet. There are inordinate pressures to produce and constant unnecessary disruptions of work by the supervisor. The stress shows itself in subordinate dissatisfaction, negative emotional reactions, moods, and feelings, and psychosomatic and physical symptoms, particularly if quitting is not possible. Anxiety, anger, depression, negativity, and loss in self-esteem may be further consequences of the continuing stress.

Assessments. Among many assessments of stress and anxiety, the anxiety state was measured on the job by Schriesheim and Murphy (1976) with the 20-item State Anxiety subscale of the State-Trait Anxiety Inventory (Spielberger, Gorsuch, & Lushene, 1970). The Job Stress Survey (Spielberger, 1994) was applied by Spielberger and Reheiser (1994) to measure job stress in business, university, and military organizations. The Maslach Burnout Inventory (1986) assessed stress and burnout in MBAs, professionals, and employees.

Faulty Decision Making. Decision making under stress becomes faulty. Instead of careful analysis and calculation or the effective use of the intuition of the expert based on learning and experience, stressed decision makers fall back on nonproductive intuitive reactions that satisfy their immediate personal emotional needs rather than the objective requirements of the situation. As Simon (1987, p. 62) noted, "Lying, for example, is much more often the result of panic than of Machiavellian scheming." When Sorokin (1943) examined reports of

[1] See Chapter 20.

the reactions of groups and communities to the calamities of famine, war, and revolution, he found that a calamity tended to intensify emotional arousal, distort cognitive processes, focus attention on the dangers and away from other features of the environment, hasten disintegration of the self, and decrease the rationality of decision making. The erroneous decision that resulted in the shooting down by the U.S. Navy ship *Vincennes* in the Persian Gulf of an Iranian commercial jet liner was attributed to the stressed personnel misreading and misinterpreting their radar displays as a descending attacking aircraft instead of a plane taking off on a routine commercial trip between Iran and Saudi Arabia.

The ordinary healthy reaction of an individual, group, or organization to dissatisfaction with the current state of affairs is to examine fully what prevents the attainment of the more desired state, then to consider various alternative courses of action, and finally to take appropriate steps to achieve the goal. But if motivation is high, if obstacles are severe, or if remaining in the current state is threatening to one's welfare or survival, malfunctions in the coping process occur. There may be no time to deliberate about choices among actions. There may be communication outages or severe information overloads. The mobilization of autonomic energy occurs with the felt emotional arousal and related symptoms of stress. Such arousal narrows perceptions and limits the ability to think creatively (Lazarus, 1966). Memory and cognitive functions become impaired (Weschler, 1955). Stress is an evolution-based reaction that prepares the individual for fight or flight in the face of danger and threat. When one is unable to cope with the threat, the autonomic symptoms appear. A year after the Katrina disaster of 2005, more than 100,000 residents who fled have been unable to rebuild because of the severity of the flooding or lack of personal resources. They have not returned to New Orleans. Those still in temporary shelters remain depressed.

Stress may generate positive emotional arousal. With personal control, prolonged distress may be reduced when those affected can focus on the good in the situation by reappraising it or finding humor in it; by viewing the situation as a problem to be solved; or by taking a time-out to concentrate on some positive emotional arousal or finding humor in it to provide relief from the stress (Moskowitz, Folkman, Colette, et al., 1996).

Frequency of Felt Stress among Managers. In response to 17 questions, such as how much in the last month they had felt nervous and stressed (0 = never to 4 = very often a problem), several hundred each of Japanese managers registered an overall mean of 1.59; Indian managers, a mean of 1.37; and American managers, a mean of 1.33. The average manager in the three countries experienced a stressful experience at least once a month (Ivancevich, Schweiger, & Ragan, 1986). The figures for U.S. managers were much lower in response to questions about their experiencing stress daily, somatic symptoms, anxiety, and social dysfunctioning and much higher for their reports of job-induced stress ("I am not sure exactly what is expected of me") and the discharge of job tension off the job (Matteson & Ivancevich, 1982). The use of tobacco, alcohol, tranquilizers, sedatives, and other drugs is commonly an effort by managers and professionals to cope with job stress, as are physical exercise, socializing with friends, and recreational activities (Latack, 1986). In an Indian study, workers were found to be subjected to significantly more stress (boredom, frustration, bereavement, and physical stress) than their supervisors and managers (Biswas, 1998).

Causes of Stress. Stress occurs to individuals, groups, and organizations when their situation is overly complex, ambiguous, unclear, and demanding in relation to the competence, resources, or structural adequacy available to deal with the demands. Compared to Europeans, U.S. workers work longer hours to maintain higher output than elsewhere. Higher productivity due to technological advances is accompanied by the insecurities of layoffs and unemployment. The same insecurities accompany the movement of factories and offices to regions with lower labor costs, less taxation, fewer environmental controls, cheaper energy, and government subsidies. In order to remain competitive, management pushes for faster and more efficient production. Currently the shibboleth is *continuous improvement*.

Continuous improvement means continuous change. Organizational change is stressful. In a Swedish survey, Arvonen (1995) found psychosomatic reactions of stress in employees under supervisors who were change-oriented if the employees lacked commitment. As Stuart (1996, p. 11) surmised, "having one's department reorganized, one's responsibilities outsourced, and several tiers of one's peer managers taken out . . . would stress a manager in the same way as a natural or man-made catastrophe." The threat of downsizing and actually being laid off is an important source of insecurity and its accompanying fears and anxieties. Additionally, the survivors of an organizational downsizing, although perhaps relieved for the moment, are also likely to reveal feelings of fear, anxiety, and distrust. Less well known are the effects of denial of their feelings of guilt and the depression that denial can cause (Noer, 1993). A sudden unexpected promotion might be stressful in a positive way. Roskies and Lewis-Guerin (1990) found that 1,291 Canadian managers who were insecure in their jobs reported poor health. Their health was worse depending on their level of insecurity. They mainly were anxious about the long-term threat to their jobs and the deterioration of their positions. According to Judge, Boudreau, and Bretz (1994), among 1,309 executives using a search firm for possible opportunities to change jobs, job stress correlated $-.21$ with life satisfaction, $-.29$ with job satisfaction, $-.26$ with family matters that caused conflicts at work, and $-.44$ with job conditions that caused conflicts in the family.

The need to make changes in themselves and their work is often a source of stress to managers as well as their employees. They may be stressed by feeling that they increasingly need to face unfamiliar products, services, and situations and that they will increasingly need more skills (Rago, 1973; Frew, 1977). The pressure for change correlated .46 with stress for 88 Tennessee state government supervisors (Rohricht & Rush, 1977).

The most commonly reported sources of stress in the working environment are lack of good relations and lack of support from supervision, according to a Job Stress Survey of 209 managers reported by O'Roark (1995). (Arvonen (1995) reported the same effect.) The results were the same for all personalities as assessed by the Myers-Briggs Type Indicator (MBTI). Conversely, Crawford (1995) noted that the socially supportive leader mediated the effects of stress. O'Roark also found that for executives in a regional medical center, the difficulties that generated the most stress for them were meeting deadlines, frequent interruptions, dealing with crises, and having to make on-the-spot decisions. Among 781 Swedish personnel, creative leaders were found by blue-collar workers to generate more stress (Arvonen, 1995).

This was consistent with Seltzer, Numerof, and Bass (1987), who observed that burnout among employees was higher when their leaders were more intellectually stimulating. The Swedish managers and white-collar workers felt more stressed if they described their immediate managers as bureaucrats. This fitted with Crawford's (1995) opinion that stress among their followers was likely to be generated by transactional leaders.

Workplace violence, such as shooting incidents in the U.S. Postal Service, is an extreme case of the effects of stress resulting from the confluence of stressed-out employees, autocratic and punitive leadership, and a high degree of tension in the environment. Simple, repetitive tasks have often been replaced by complex job demands, yet employees remain under a high degree of control. The perpetrators felt a sense of injustice and had low self-esteem and paranoid tendencies. They came from unstable families, had few outlets for rage, called for help many times but did not receive any, and felt poorly treated by their supervisors. Most unfortunately, they were fascinated by guns and the military (DeAngelis, 1993). The symptoms of aggression begin early. Garcia and Shaw et al. (2000) observed aggression in two-year-old boys engaged in a clean-up task with mothers whose parenting style was rejecting, critical, hostile, and physically punitive.

Stress Is Multifaceted

A variety of different antecedent conditions may give rise to stress in groups. To some degree, the observed and appropriate leadership behavior will depend on the particular antecedents that were involved. Bass, Hurder, and Ellis (1954) identified four emotionally arousing stress experiences with different antecedents: (1) *frustration* is likely to be felt when highly prized positive goals are unattainable because of inability or difficulties in the path to the goals; (2) *fear* occurs when escape from noxious conditions is threatened by obstacles in the path; (3) *anxiety* is aroused when these paths, obstacles, and goals become unclear (fear and frustration turn to anxiety with increasing uncertainty); and (4) *conflict* arises when one faces incompatible choices of goals. Potentially high risks and costs compete with the anticipated benefits of a course of action.

After examining the physiological reactions and the

cognitive and psychomotor performance of 200 college men under experimentally induced frustration, fear, anxiety, and conflict, Bass, Hurder, and Ellis (1954) concluded that performance under these various stress conditions would decrease or increase in contrast to a stress-free condition depending on which tasks and skills were involved, which type of stress was imposed, and the initial level of arousal of the participants. Differences among the men were also large.

Individual Differences

Leader-subordinate dyadic analysis would seem particularly important in understanding leadership in threatening situations. What one subordinate may see as an invigorating challenge, another may perceive as a stress-laden threat. It is all in the eye of the beholder. As McCauley (1987, p. 1) put it, "A challenging, rewarding task for one person may be flooded with stress and anxiety for others. How one appraises self and situation makes all the difference."

According to Bunker (1986), less stress in the same threatening conditions are felt by those who are generally optimistic, who believe that such conditions are matters of their own fate and not controlled by external forces, who can tolerate ambiguity and uncertainty, and who feel they can improve their own abilities. In agreement, Spector, Cooper, and Aguilar-Vafaie (in press) found that among both Iranian and U.S. managers, those with higher locus of control reported less strain from job pressures. Such confidence is enhanced with experience. The effects of stress and anxiety are reduced as experience is gained with the same threats (Benner, 1984). The effect of experience is similar to the effects of preparation, overlearning, and overtraining. Smith (1994) notes that managers and business leaders are most often thinking-judging (TJ) personality types on the Myers-Briggs Type Inventory (Myers & McCaully, 1985). TJs are likely to be more comfortable in a structured and organized environment. But those who are not TJs—artists who emphasize feeling-sensing, for instance—are more likely to be stressed by the manager's role.

Stress can also vary from one individual to another as a consequence of deep-seated feelings of inadequacy that surface in aggression or overdependence when real or imagined threats occur. People differ from each other in

this intrapsychic tension.[2] Levinson (1980) conceived of stress as a consequence of such intrapsychic tension—the increased gap between one's ego ideal (the partly conscious image of oneself at one's future best) and one's current self-image. Among both U.S. and Iranian managers, those who had a greater internal locus of control showed less feelings of strain due to the pressures of their roles, work-family conflict, constraints, and lack of support (Spector, Cooper, & Aguilar-Vafaie, in press).

To some extent, the loss of 5 of a party of 23 climbers on Mount Everest in 1996 could be attributed to the overconfidence of the leader, expectations of continuing good weather, lack of cooperation, failure to observe the rule to turn around before reaching the top if it was 1 or 2 P.M. to avoid being caught descending to camp in the dark. But a sudden storm came up, changing the situation.

Resilience. People differ in their ability to restore their equilibrium after an event or period of stressful adversity. They learn to grow out of their adversity (Bonanno, 2005). Many handicapped and disadvantaged children overcome their handicaps and disadvantages to become successful and effective adults. Eleanor Roosevelt, for example, was treated as an "ugly duckling" by her family. She overcame her shyness and thin voice to become a world-class leader.

Situational Differences

The study of leadership under stressful conditions has often treated stress as a homogeneous situation. Yet the same stressful experience can stem from a variety of precipitating conditions, and the variety of possible reactions to it may depend on the different precipitating conditions. Thus, research on disasters has found systematic differences in community reactions to warnings of tornadoes and warnings of floods. Communities react much more quickly to threats of tornadoes than to threats of floods.

Other Situational Stressors. The pace of work can become a source of stress, particularly if the operators are inexperienced novices. Workplace relocations can be dis-

---

[2] See Chapter 21.

ruptive and stressful, as shown when supermarket personnel were transferred from one store to another (Moyle & Parkes, 1999). Downsizing is stressful not only to the employees who lose their jobs but also to the survivors. About half of the survivors after downsizing, according to Cascio (1995), reported feelings of anxiety and insecurity. The volatility and instability of family incomes have increased substantially since the 1970s. Instability was five times greater in the 1990s than the 1970s. Stability peaked in 1972. The spread between the rich and the poor increased. Lower-paid workforce income failed to keep up with inflation. Many families faced a new level of insecurity and stress as they became two-earner households to maintain the same standard of living as was once possible with just the single wage earner (Lind, 2004).

Frequent business and government travelers reveal emotional upset, physical strains, irritability, and impaired performance before, during, and after trips (De-Frank, Konopaske, & Ivancevich, 2000). Many face an overstimulating lifestyle. Before the trip there are the distractions of planning the trip, making suitable work and family arrangements, and preparing to visit different cultures and climates. Almost 75% of married people and 50% of travelers on business say it is difficult to be away from home for extended periods. Fifty percent say they worry about what is happening at home and in the office (Fisher, 1998). Particularly stressful are airline delays and cancellations, needing to visit numerous locations in one or two days in a single city with heavy traffic, a lack of opportunity for healthy exercise, sleep deprivation, and eating too much or too little while on the road.

Reactions to changing time zones and jet lag are often discomforting aspects during and after travel. On returning home, travelers have to make up for what they missed. On returning to their office, they are faced with an overloaded in-box, finding out what happened during absence, catching up with changes, and completing expense account reports (DeFrank, Konopaske, & Ivancevich, 2000).

Role Stress

Kahn, Wolfe, Quinn, et al. (1964) showed that two distinct sources of stress could be identified in organizations: role conflict and role ambiguity. Each has different antecedents and consequences. *Role conflict* involves contra-

dictory requirements, competing demands for one's time, and inadequate resources. *Role ambiguity* involves lack of clarity about tasks and goals and uncertainty about the requirements of one's job.[3] Latack (1986, p. 380) noted how managers and professionals tried either to control role ambiguity, role conflict, and role overload or to escape from them. To control role ambiguity, they "try to see the situation as an opportunity to learn and develop new skills" (p. 380). To escape from role ambiguity, they "try to do their best to get out of the situation gracefully." To control role conflict, they "work on changing policies which caused this situation." To escape from role conflict, they "separate themselves as much as possible from the people who created this situation." Deluga (1989) found that 106 to 109 employees in a metal-fabricating firm who experienced role conflict in the demands their jobs placed on them used upward influence tactics on their supervisors to alleviate the stress. Specifically, as the role conflict increased they first tried to influence their supervisors to change the conflicting demands on their jobs with friendliness, bargaining, reasoning, assertiveness, appeals to higher authority, and coalitions with other employees. When the attempted influence failed, they resorted a second time to assertiveness, friendliness, and coalition efforts.

Role Overload. To role conflict and ambiguity, Latack (1986) added *role overload* as a source of stress. To control role overload, managers and professionals "try to be very organized so they can keep on top of things." To escape from role overload, they "set their own priorities based on what they like to do." When the Job-Related Tension Index of Kahn, Wolfe, Quinn, et al. (1964) was completed by 113 Canadian managers for R. E. Rogers (1977), four factors were extracted from the results. These factors were (1) too heavy a work load, (2) self-doubts, (3) sense of insufficient authority and influence upstairs, and (4) need to make unpopular decisions against their better judgment.

Shaw and Weekley (1985) also found actual qualitative overload to be stressful. Nonetheless, other investigators did not conclude that work overload was necessarily stressful to managers. S. Carlson (1951) found that it was

---

[3] House and Rizzo (1972a, 1972b) and Rizzo, House, and Lirtzman (1970) also conceived of role conflict and role ambiguity as critically distinct phenomena.

normal for most Swedish executives to report being overloaded and having little time for family or friends.[4] A business management survey of 179 company presidents and board chairmen obtained results indicating that the average executive worked approximately 63 hours per week but did not feel overworked, although more than 70% thought they did not have enough time for thinking and planning (Anonymous, 1968). But W. E. Moore (1970) observed that detailed chores involving problems in communication and operations interfered with the managers' effective use of their time. Yet Jaques (1966) noted that hard work and long hours were not sufficient conditions for producing stress symptoms in executives. Rather, stress conditions are generated from within the manager as responses to impossible standards of achievement or tasks that are perceived as overly difficult.

The conclusions about work overload are seen in the extent to which some harried executives are aggressively involved in achieving more in less time. As discussed in Chapter 8, such executives habitually have a sense of urgency (Friedman & Rosenman, 1974). They are labeled Type A personalities; many are highly stressed, as is evidenced by their proneness to heart disease. Nevertheless, many other harried Type As are not under such stress. The difference is that those Type As who are subject to heart disease are also depressed, tense, and generally prone to illness. They are not generally healthy, talkative, self-confident, and in control of their situations (Friedman, Hall, & Harris, 1985).

Combat Conditions. Military combat is illustrative of both the situational and personal elements that are of consequence to the generation of stress and the reactions to it. The actions and coping of soldiers in conditions of combat stress are responses to a situational and personal complex of antecedent and mediating variables. Whether soldiers and their leaders actively carry out their duties, become passive, or collapse will depend on the amount of surprise and uncertainty in the battle; the weather and terrain; and particularly whether the operations are mobile and offensive or static and defensive. Stress is likely to be higher in the enforced passivity of the static or defensive condition, which generates a feeling of helplessness (Gal & Lazarus, 1975). Again, individual differences

in personality, family problems, and prior exposure to combat will be of importance. Active "fighters" are more intelligent and masculine and have more leadership potential (Egbert, Meeland, Cline, et al., 1957). Winners of medals are more persevering, decisive, and devoted to duty (Gal, 1983).

One's role in combat makes a difference. The higher physiological responses of Israeli officers compared with those of enlisted men are coupled with fewer somatic complaints and breakdowns among the officers. Leaders are more emotionally aroused but appear to suffer much less decrement in their performance during combat than do enlisted men, although in general, as in the Israeli-Arab confrontations, the officers were much more at risk than were the enlisted personnel. Gal and Jones (1985) suggest that one's perceived role as a leader provides a sense of mastery and control and causes one to concentrate on tasks that distract attention from the realistic dangers.

Stress and Motivation

As already noted, stress occurs when the group's drive is too high for the demands of the task. When members are blocked from obtaining a goal or from escaping from a noxious condition, their stress increases with their increasing motivation to obtain the goal or escape the situation. Tjosvold (1985b) found that although executives made effective decisions under moderate levels of motivation, when faced with a crisis, their performance deteriorated and quick solutions requiring the least effort were chosen instead of high-quality ones.

Since cohesiveness and commitment imply heightened motivation to attain goals, more stress should be seen in cohesive than in noncohesive groups. When J. R. P. French (1941) frustrated groups of cohesive teammates and groups of strangers who were lower in cohesiveness, the more cohesive teams experienced greater fear and frustration. Similarly, Festinger (1949) reported that more complaints that were suggestive of stress appeared among more cohesive groups. Also, M. E. Wright (1943) found that more cohesive pairs of friends exhibited more aggression when frustrated than did pairs whose cohesiveness was lower.

Given a high degree of group drive, the group members' sensed inability to obtain the group's goals or to escape from danger increases the likelihood of stress.

[4]See Chapter 14.

Groups that are unable to interact easily or that do not have the formal or informal structure that enables quick reactions are likely to experience stress (Bass, 1960). Panic ensues when members of a group lack superordinate goals—goals that transcend the self-interests of each participant. Mintz (1951) found that when members of an experimental group in a crisis sought uncoordinated individual reward (or the avoidance of individual punishment), panic was likely to ensue. If the group was organized and perceived a single goal for all, such panic did not materialize. Similarly, in an analysis of anxiety in aerial combat, D. G. Wright (1946) concluded that an aircrew could cope with stress when a common threat was perceived and when a common goal and action toward it were maintained under an apparent plan of action. Clearly, the leader who can transform a group of members with different self-interests into a group with goals that transcend their own self-interests will make it possible for the group to cope more effectively with potentially stressing circumstances.

Stress and Structure

An individual is stressed when he or she is highly motivated to escape threat or to obtain highly valued goals but is unable to respond adequately, unready to react, untrained, and inexperienced. Increased preparedness and overlearning are ways of helping the individual to cope with anticipated stressful situations. At the group or organizational level, the reliability and predictability of the group's response become essential. Everyone needs to know what everyone else is likely to do. Roles must be clear and free of conflict and ambiguity. Structure, through an informal or formal organization, becomes important. Thus, Isenberg (1981) demonstrated, in an experiment with four-person groups who were making decisions under the stress of the pressure of time, that the structure of relations increased and leadership became more salient. Differences in how much time the members were able to speak increased. Again, Gladstein and Reilly (1985) found that when stress was induced in a business simulation by introducing threats and time pressure, decision making became centralized. A small number of members had much more influence than did others in the group than when time pressure and threatening events were absent.

When a group does not have the necessary structure to meet emergencies and threats, the initiation of such a structure by a strong leader is seen as needed and useful to the group. Path-goal formulations[5] examine such requisite leadership behavior when the roles of workers are unclear. When subordinates have clear perceptions of their work roles, the leader's initiation of structure is redundant. However, the leader's initiation of structure should help highly motivated subordinates with less clear role perceptions to perform their jobs and thus increase their satisfaction and performance. Schriesheim and Murphy (1976) found that job stress, like the lack of structure, moderated the initiation of structure–job satisfaction relationship, as expected. In J. R. P. French's (1941) previously cited investigation, eight organized groups (with elected leaders) and eight unorganized groups were studied. Frustration was produced by requiring the groups to work on unsolvable problems. Unorganized groups showed a greater tendency to split into opposing factions, whereas the previously organized group exhibited greater social freedom, cohesiveness, and motivation. The greater the differentiation of function that occurred with organization, the greater was the interdependence of members and unity of the group as a whole.

The need for structure at the macro level, as well as at the individual level, was seen by Sorokin (1943). In times of disaster, ideal human conduct depends on a well-integrated system of values. The values conform to the ethics of the larger society. There is little discrepancy between values and conduct. But individuals who engage in antisocial and delinquent behavior (murder, assault, robbery, looting, and the like) tend to be guided by self-centered, materialistic, disillusioned ideologies. They are not integrated into a larger organized effort. The wanton massacre of inmates of a penitentiary in New Mexico in early 1980 by berserk fellow prisoners was partly attributable to the lack of organization in the prisoners' rebellion and the sudden complete availability of drugs (Hollie, 1980).

Gal and Jones (1985) noted that a strong informal structure within a military unit helped reduce the perceived stress of combat. Elite units, with strong bonds between comrades and leaders, were found to suffer less

---

[5] See Chapter 27.

stress, as evidenced by much lower psychiatric casualty rates, despite greater exposure than ordinary units to the risks of high-intensity battle.

A Model of Group Responses to Stress

Janis and Mann (1977) looked at responses under stress that were induced by conflict in the face of an impending threat and the risks and costs of taking action to avoid stress. They argued that the completely rational approach to an authentic warning of impending danger would be a thorough examination of objectives, values, and alternative courses of action. Costs and risks would be weighed. A final choice would be based on a cost-benefit analysis. Included in the effective process would be development, careful implementation, and contingency planning. But such vigilance, thorough search, appraisal, and contigency planning are likely to be short-circuited as a consequence of emotional arousal and the socio-emotional phenomena generated by the impending threat. Various defective reactions to the warnings of danger are likely to occur. These reactions include adherence to the status quo, too-hasty change, defensive avoidance, and panic.

Unconflicted Adherence to the Steady State

One inadequate reaction is the hasty decision that dealing with the threat involves more serious costs and risks than doing nothing. The threat is disbelieved and disregarded. People remain in their homes despite slowly rising floodwaters and warnings to evacuate. An inadequate analysis, in which appropriate information is ignored, sees the costs of evacuation as greater than the risks of remaining. This response is less likely in the case of sudden threats, such as tornado warnings. Analogously, the energy crises of 1973 and 1979 had built up for 20 years in the face of inertia to cope with them adequately. The threats to the environment of the depletion of the ozone layer, acid rain, and the greenhouse effect likewise failed in the 1980s to mobilize the necessary public support for a political effort to deal with the threats. But in 1941, full national commitment and mobilization to deal with the Japanese threat, signaled by the attack on Pearl Harbor, was instantaneous.

Staw, Sandelands, and Dutton (1981) pointed to the increased rigidity in organizations when they are threatened. Consistent with this, Gladstein and Reilly (1985) engaged 128 MBA students in a full six-day business simulation to show that threatening events and the pressure of time each systematically constrain decision-making processes by reducing the amount of information used by the groups before they reach their decisions.

Hasty Change

If the costs and risks of taking action to deal with a perceived threat are thought to be low, a new course of action is adopted, often too hastily, without an adequate examination of the threat, risks, and long-term implications. People who experience a high degree of tension from an intense structural strain in the social or political fabric become susceptible to the influence of rebel leaders who promise to restructure the situation quickly, particularly if the established leadership fails to do so (Downtown, 1973). A field investigation by Torrance and staff (1955) reported that air crews who were "forced down" and faced simulated difficulties of surviving in "enemy" territory tended to turn to immediate but ineffective solutions to their problems and to concede more to comfort as their stress level increased. For example, as the hardships increased, they chose to travel on roads in "enemy" territory instead of traveling over routes where they were less likely to be seen.

Rapid, decisive leadership is valued highly under conditions of perceived threat to the group. Executives and politicians incrementally "put out one fire after another," drifting into a new policy to cope with each successive threat, rather than formulating a new policy based on a thorough search, appraisal, and plan (Lindbloom, 1959).

Defensive Avoidance

When the risks of change are seen to be high and the current course of action is maintained because of fatalism and a sense that no better course can be found, the various Freudian mechanisms, such as rationalization, displacement, fantasy, and denial, provide psychological defenses to avoid the threat, rather than to cope rationally with the danger. Particularly common to managers in large organizations, according to Janis (1972), are procrastination, shifting responsibility (buck passing), and bolstering—providing social support for quickly seizing on the least objectionable choice. These are defective ways of dealing with a threat.

Hypervigilance (Panic)

If the threat contains time pressures and deadlines and if individual motivation to escape the threat is high, hypervigilance (panic) may set in. Defective search is illustrated by the failure to take the time to choose a satisfactory escape route from a fire. Instead, a person in panic, in a highly suggestible state, simply starts imitating what everybody else is doing, failing to anticipate the consequences of blocking common exits. According to a review by A. L. Strauss (1944), the major factors in panic are: (1) conditions that weaken individuals physically; (2) reduced mental ability and lessened capacity to act rationally; (3) heightened emotionality, tension, and imagination, which facilitate impulsive action; (4) heightened suggestibility and contagion, which may precipitate flight; and (5) loss of contact with previous leaders and a predisposition to follow those at hand.

When disaster strikes, panic is not most people's first reaction. Acute fear and attempts to flee the disaster occur only when immediate danger is perceived and individuals see their escape routes blocked (Quarantelli, 1954). Exasperating the panic reaction is a strong sense of isolation. For some, the unadaptive reaction is to freeze in place or to become blinded to the events occurring around them. (When the atomic bomb was dropped on Hiroshima, many people ceased to feel [Lifton, 1967].) Nevertheless, despite their sense of panic, some people do begin trying to cope with the disaster if they receive no formal directions from authorities.

Leadership under Stress

Informal leadership and temporary groups may emerge if the formal authorities and emergency services cannot deal with the crisis (Mileti, Drabek, & Haas, 1975). The direct removal of the threats and obstacles that are the source of stress may be facilitated. Drive and anxiety may be reduced by providing informal and formal leadership support and an increasing sense of security. Individuals,

groups, and organizations that are frozen into inertia and disbelief when they are seriously threatened may be aroused and alerted. Faced with hasty, poorly thought-out decisions, leaders may delay the premature disclosure of options and call for a reconsideration of proposals. When their followers are engaged in defensive avoidance, leaders may bring them back to reality. Panic can be reduced or avoided by strong leadership that points the way to safety.

Thus, leaders can help their groups to cope with stress in many ways. Nonetheless, they also can cause more of it. Yet, as shall be seen, in general, groups with leaders are likely to cope better with stress than are those without leaders. Groups and organizations that are under stress expect and desire more directiveness from leaders. Moreover, whoever takes the role of leader during times of social stress will be expected to revise goals, define common objectives, restructure situations, and suggest solutions to deal with the sources of stress and conflict (Downtown, 1973). But, as shall also be seen, although directive leadership is most expected, desired, and successful when stress is high, it may not always be the most effective style.

The personality-leader linkage will be affected by stress. Under conditions with short, unpredictable time pressures in which unusual physical and emotional exertion is required, such as in military combat, more charismatic leadership will be seen, in contrast to military leadership in noncombat operations (Bass, 1985a). Personal assertiveness may be a stronger determinant of emergence as a leader under stress. It may be less important in determining emergence as a leader in unstressed circumstances.

Leadership May Contribute to Stress

Unfortunately, as noted above with abusive leaders, leadership may be the cause, rather than the amelioration, of stressful conditions that result in emotionally driven actions by the followers and poorer long-term outcomes. And the leaders who emerge are likely to be different from those in unstressed situations. They may actually contribute to the stress. Political leaders manufacture crises to enhance their own power, to divert public attention from the real problems, and to gain public support for their arbitrary actions.

Those who are elected to office may be more prone to stress themselves. Sanders and Malkis (1982) manipulated the importance and difficulty of a problem and external incentives involving recognition of esteem and success. They found that Type A (stress-prone) personalities were nominated more often as leaders than were Type B personalities. However, the fewer Type Bs who were chosen as leaders tended to be more effective as individuals in the assigned task than were the Type As (Bass, 1982, p. 135).

Many studies have reported that for subordinates, their immediate supervisor is the most stressful aspect of their work (e.g., Herzberg, 1966). The tyrannical boss is the most frequently mentioned source of stress (McCormick & Powell, 1988). Shipper and Wilson (1992) obtained a correlation of .49 in supervisory goal pressure behavior and perceived tension, according to their 85 hospital employees. Supervisory controlling of details and time emphasis also contributed to tension. Numerof, Seltzer, and Bass (1989) unexpectedly found that when other transformational factors[6] were held constant, intellectually stimulating leaders increased the felt stress and job "burnout" of their subordinates. Misumi (1985) reported the results of a series of experiments that showed that production-prodding leaders giving instructions such as "Work more quickly," "Work accurately," "You could do more," and "Hurry up, we haven't much time left" generated detectable physiological symptoms of stress. The systolic and diastolic blood pressure of experimental subjects increased, as did their galvanic skin responses. In similar laboratory experiments, such production-prodding leaders caused feelings of hostility and anxiety about the experiment.

In a sample of police officers, half of their "harmful stressors" were the administrative styles of their superiors (Griggs, 1985). Stressful conditions affect what is expected of a leader, who attempts to lead, and who emerges as a leader. In stressful conditions, leaders differ in the extent to which they promote the attainment of goals, the satisfaction of members, and the survival of their groups.

Nystrom and Starbuck (1984) suggested that top managers can guide organizations into crises and intensify the crises by blindness, rigidity, and the inability to unlearn their inadequate old ways of doing things. In the same way, Sutton, Eisenhardt, and Jucker (1986) thought that the Atari Corporation's decline and imminent collapse was due to its management's rigidity in continuing to market products that no longer were selling and their failure to develop new products.

Sometimes the decrement in leadership performance may be a consequence of the external imposition of handicaps on the leaders. Thus, loss of support from a higher authority may weaken the leaders' influence, control of needed resources, and continued attention to the organization's purposes. During the early years of the Reagan administration, under James Watt, a director who emphasized deregulation and showed a lack of sympathy for environmental concerns, the Environmental Protection Agency (EPA), came under both clear and unclear threats to its mission from its own leadership, coupled with serious staff and budget cuts. A survey of 181 EPA managers and staff showed a consequential deterioration in their optimism, satisfaction, and identification with the organization and in the quality of supervisor-subordinate relations (Morganthau & Hager, 1981). Again starting in 2001 under the George W. Bush administration, the EPA once again suffered a loss of much of its experienced staff and performance effectiveness.

Effects of Prolonged Stress

Prolonged stress from internal or external challenges that are too great for the group to deal with can result in the group's demise. What leads to the death of some groups and the survival of others over a long period of time? Survival of a group, organization, or community under prolonged stress is closely dependent on leadership that is able to maintain the group or organization's integrity, drive, and goal direction. Such leadership needs to work with increasing the cohesion and dealing with the reduced performance of tasks by groups that are under continued threat.[7] But instead of helping to stave off decline and death, ineffective leaders contribute to the prolonged stress of the group, organization, or community and to its eventual demise.

F. E. Parker (1923, 1927) sent questionnaires to some 3,000 consumer cooperative societies. Among those that

---

[6]See Chapter 21.

[7]See Lanzetta (1955); Lanzetta, Haefner, Langharn, and Axelrod (1954); and Torrance (1961).

had failed, the most frequent reasons were: (1) inefficient leadership and management; (2) declining interest and cooperative spirit among the members; (3) factional disputes among the members; and (4) members' interference with the management. Blumenthal (1932) attributed the decline of social and fraternal groups in small towns to the departure of young people (the towns' best leadership potential) for the cities.

Munro's (1930) study of community service organizations found that ineffective organizations that were less likely to survive were characterized by ineffective leadership, lack of political sagacity, unwise policies and tactics, spasmodic work, and overorganized and duplicated services. Kolb (1933) and Sorokin (1943) observed that without religious purposes and a commitment to an integrative ideology of religion, such as were fostered by leadership, rural communities were less likely to survive disasters. In reviewing the decline and fall of special-interest groups in rural communities, Kolb and Wileden (1927) pointed to factional competition for leadership and irreconcilable differences between leaders and followers.

Most communes cannot survive for any considerable period without strong leadership to maintain discipline and control (Gide, 1930; May & Doob, 1937). Conversely, a whole commune can commit suicide when led to it by a highly charismatic, paranoid leader, as was the case in Jonestown, Guyana, in 1978. The same situation almost occurred in Germany in 1945, when Hitler pleaded for a Götterdämmerung for all Germany, turning in frustration from his fantasy of being Odin the Savior to becoming Odin the Destroyer.

Successful but Not Necessarily Effective Leadership

In Chapter 21, we noted that charismatic leaders emerge in times of crisis. They successfully influence their followers but may lead them astray. The leadership that succeeds in influencing followers may not be most effective in stressful situations, particularly in the long run. It may result in faulty decisions made too hastily or defensive reactions, although it is likely to contribute to escape from panic situations. In crises, political leaders and politically adept executives often win the plaudits of their constitu-

ents in the short run, but their decisions may turn out to be ineffective and unsatisfying in the long run:

> succeeding in . . . managing stressful organizational environment is . . . partially due to the exceptionally good political skills possessed by many executives . . . manifested in social astuteness and . . . behaviors (foster in followers) feelings of confidence, trust and sincerity. . . . Executives with political skills . . . (allow) . . . followers to interpret the stressors in less aversive ways. (Perrewé, Ferris, Frink, et al., 2000, p. 115)

Stress, Hasty Decision Making, and Directive Leadership

Crisis provokes a centralization of authority (Hermann, 1963). Berkowitz (1953b) found that both governmental and industrial groups were more likely to accept leadership when the problem was urgent. When followers are under stress, they are likely to accept readily the speedy decisions of directive, task-oriented, structuring leaders. However, Goldstein and Hoffman (1995) suggested that followers in crises who see themselves as efficacious may not accept directive leadership as readily. Additionally, speedy decisions do not necessarily provide the best solutions to the problems facing the followers.

It is not the speed of the decision or the leader's directiveness that may result in inadequate solutions to the stressful circumstances. It is rapid decision making without the opportunity for careful structuring and support in advance. For, as shall be seen, rapid decision making is generally sought in crises and disasters but is effective if the decisions are not hastily made at the last minute but are based on advance warning, preparation, and organization, along with commitment and support.

As Janis and Mann (1977) noted, when a threat is finally perceived, it generates the desire for prompt, decisive action. Leadership becomes centered in one or a few persons, who gain increased power to decide for the group. The price of the rapid, arbitrary dictation is abuse, corruption, and the loss of freedom when power is placed in the hands of the dictator. Hertzler (1940) examined 35 historical dictatorships and concluded that they arose during crises and when sudden change was desired. In addition, Downton (1973) suggested that followers who are stressed by ambiguity become easily influenced by aggressive, powerful leaders who promise to reduce the ambiguity and restructure the situation.

Alwon (1980) argued that administrators of social agencies must adopt a strong, directive style (even if it means changing their leadership style) during times of crisis to avoid dangers and to seize opportunities. In emergencies, when danger threatens, subordinates want to be told what to do and to be told in a hurry. They perceive that they have no time to consider alternatives. Rapid, decisive leadership is demanded (Hemphill, 1950b). Five hundred groups were described on questionnaires by members on a variety of dimensions formulated by Hemphill. The adequacy of various leadership behaviors was correlated with the groups' characteristics. Hemphill concluded that in frequently changing and emerging groups, leaders who failed to make decisions quickly would be judged inadequate.

Considerable evidence is available to support the contention that leaders speed up their decision making as a consequence of stress. Their failure to do so leads to their rejection as leaders (Korten, 1962; Sherif & Sherif, 1953). Acceptance of their rapid, arbitrary decisions without consultation, negotiation, or *participation*[8] is also increased. A leader who can react quickly in emergencies will be judged as better by followers than one who cannot.

Flanagan, Levy, et al. (1952) found that, according to respondents, "taking prompt action in emergency situations" was a critical behavior that differentiated those who were judged to be better military officers from those whose performance was judged to be worse. Large-scale surveys by Stouffer, Suchman, DeVinney, et al. (1949) of American soldiers during World War II confirmed that particularly at lower levels in the organization, the military stressed rapidity of response to orders from a higher authority despite the fact that a unit actually operated under battlefield conditions relatively infrequently.

When rapid decisions are needed, executives are likely to become more directive than participative (Lowin, 1968). Consistent with this finding, the more organiza-

tions wish to be prepared for emergency action, the more they are likely to stress a high degree of structure, attention to orders, and authoritarian direction. Fodor (1976, 1978) demonstrated that industrial supervisors who were exposed to the stress of simulated, disturbing subordinates became more autocratic in dealing with the situation. College students did likewise (Fodor, 1973b). Half to two-thirds of 181 airmen, when asked for their opinions about missile teams, rescue teams, scientific teams, or other small crews facing emergencies, strongly agreed that they should respond to the orders of the commander with less question than under normal conditions. In an emergency, the commander was expected to "check more closely to see that everyone is carrying out his responsibility." A majority felt that "the commander should not be 'just one of the boys' " (Torrance, 1956–1957).

In a survey of Dutch naval officers' performance by Mulder, de Jong, Koppelaar, and Verhage (1986), the officers were more favorably evaluated by their superiors if they were seen to make more use of their formal power in crisis situations than in noncrisis situations. In crisis conditions, both the superiors and the subordinates of the officers looked for more authoritative direction from the officers. At the same time, the officers were evaluated more favorably by their subordinates if they were seen to be more openly consultative in noncrisis situations than in crisis situations. Moreover, the referent power of the officers in the eyes of the subordinates correlated .55 with their consultativeness under noncrisis conditions, but the corresponding correlation was .10 in crisis conditions. The officers relied more on formal and expert power in crisis conditions than in noncrisis conditions, according to their subordinates.

Similarly, militant, decisive, aggressive leadership is demanded during the unstable period of a labor union's organization as it goes from one emergency to the next. Under stress, strength and activity take on more importance for leadership. After the struggle for survival is over and the union is recognized, the leadership is required to change. Now it must exhibit more willingness to compromise and to cooperate (Selekman, 1947). Confrontation must change to consultation.

Individuals who are more predisposed toward direction and the initiation of structure are more likely to try to take charge when their groups are stressed. They will preempt the leadership role from members who would

[8]As defined in Chapter 18, *direction* (italic) refers only to giving orders with or without explanation; direction (roman) includes ordering, persuading, and manipulating. *Participation* (italic) refers only to sharing in the decision process; participation (roman) includes consulting, sharing, and delegating.

consult with others before taking action. Given the authoritarian-submissive syndrome, authoritarians who are assigned to the roles of subordinates will be more ready to submit unquestioningly to the dictates of whoever has been assigned the role of leader. Lanzetta (1953) found that aggressive members were more likely to emerge as successful leaders when laboratory groups were stressed by harassment, space, and time restrictions than when no stress was induced. Along similar lines, Ziller (1954) concluded that leaders who accepted responsibility for their groups' action under conditions of uncertainty and risk were also relatively unconcerned about what the groups thought about the issues.

The same results appeared in still a different context. Firestone, Lichtman, and Colamosca (1975) showed that initially leaderless groups with assertive leaders responded more frequently and more rapidly to a confederate member's "diabetic reaction" than did groups whose leaders were less assertive. In such emergencies, unassertive leaders tended to be replaced. The holding of the American embassy staff in Teheran in 1979–1980 is a classic example of how an external threat dramatically increased the followers' (in this case, the American public's) support for strong leadership to deal with the threats. Ranks were closed, dissension was muted, and rapid decision making was sought from President Jimmy Carter with little examination of the causes, intensity, and risks of the threats or of the costs of taking actions to deal with them. If anything, President Carter failed to come on as strongly and decisively as demanded, although he was effective in ultimately obtaining the release of the hostages. In the face of crises, nations condemn the vacillating, indecisive leader and applaud the would-be hero-savior (Hook, 1943). President Ronald Reagan was much more popular for being seen as bold and decisive in dealing with the Lebanese crisis in 1983, yet his actions were disastrous. Again, George W. Bush's boldness and decisiveness after the World Trade Center calamity of September 11, 2001, gave him soaring popularity, with more than 90% public support. But when, in the five years that followed, his reactions led to the quagmire in Iraq, his popularity plummeted to only 30%.

When calamity threatens, followers want immediate action to escape. The leader's attempts to influence them will be accepted and complied with more readily than when such stress is absent. Although a participative discussion may make for better solutions, holding one to generate a high-quality decision to which the group is committed may be unacceptable. The commitment will come from the followers' restriction of the options they think they have. The leader who shows initiative, inventiveness, and decisiveness is valued most (Barnard, 1948). Helmreich and Collins (1967) observed that participants who faced a fearful experimental situation showed less of a preference for the company of peers and favored being in a leader-dominated group. Polis (1964) also found that under stress, individuals tended to manifest a need for strong leadership and to continue their association with the group. Again, Wispe and Lloyd (1955) concluded that of 43 sales agents, those who generally were less secure and more anxious were also more in favor of their superiors making decisions for them.

One reversal of the call for rapid-decision leadership in crisis conditions was found by Streib, Folts, and LaGreca (1985) in 36 retirement communities. Most residents were ordinarily satisfied to let others make decisions for them, but they wanted the chance to be involved in decision making if crises arose or the stability of the community was threatened. Another contingency was demonstrated in an experiment by Goldstein (1995). When followers had high self-efficacy, they desired less directive leadership no matter how they perceived the leaders' efficacy. But if the followers were low in self-efficacy, they sought mainly a directive leader when they perceived that the efficacy of the leader was high.

Directive Leadership and Prolonged Stress

When stress is chronic or prolonged, the same tendencies toward directive leadership and acceptance of it are observed. During World War II, Japanese-American residents of California were interned and subjected to isolation, loss of subsistence, threats to loved ones, enforced idleness, and physiological stress. As a consequence, the internees were apathetic and blindly obedient to influence (Leighton, 1945). Similarly, Fisher and Rubinstein (1956) reported that experimental participants who were deprived of sleep for 48 to 54 hours showed significantly greater shifts in autokinetic judgments, which indicated that they were more susceptible than normal to the social influence of their partners.

Hall and Mansfield (1971) studied the longer-term effects of stress and the response to it in three research and development organizations. The stress was caused by a sudden drop in available research funds, which resulted in strong internal pressures for reduced spending and an increased search for new funds. As would be expected, the response to the threat was to increase the control and direction by the top management and to reduce consultation with the researchers. Subsequently, the effect on the researchers over two years was to decrease their satisfaction and identification with the organization. However, their research performance was unaffected.

To conclude, directive leadership is preferred and will be successful in influencing followers under stress. But such leadership may be counterproductive in the long run.

Leadership and Defensive Avoidance

As was already noted, often it is the political leadership that contrives the threats, crises, and ambiguities. For centuries, political leaders have used real or imagined threat to increase the cohesiveness among their followers and to gain unquestioning support for their own dictates. The common scenario begins with economic weakness and dislocation, followed by international complications, revolution and sometimes civil war, and finally a breakdown of political institutions. The dictator organizes ready-made immediate solutions that soothe, flatter, and exalt the public but do not promote its well-being. Blame is directed elsewhere.

When business and governmental leaders are seen to consult and share decisions with subordinates in times of crises (Berkowitz, 1953b), it is often because they seek bolstering from their subordinates about the wisdom of their already-chosen solutions. Also, they would like to spread the responsibility for the decision from themselves to their group.

We-They Relations. "We-they" discrimination is encouraged by leaders of groups that are in competition and conflict with each other. In-group and out-group differences are magnified. The power of the leaders of the groups is strengthened. Deviants are not tolerated. Thus, Mulder and Sternerding (1963) found, as expected, that when individuals feel threatened from outside, they tend to depend on strong leaders. The leaders, in turn, pro-mote a variety of defense mechanisms as pseudosolutions to the stressful problems facing their constituents, Scapegoats are found to account for the social malaise and economic failures. Fanciful promises of a bountiful future are put forth and accepted. Real social, economic, and political issues are avoided and imagined dragons are slain.

Avoidance can be accomplished by physical self-segregation. This was observed by Hayashida (1976) in the in-group and out-group relations of leaders in organizations under the stress of conflicting ideas with outsiders. The leaders of 146 students in an evangelical Christian organization, whose stated beliefs diverged from the cosmopolitan culture of the campus, isolated themselves formally and informally from the rest of the campus. They coped with intergroup conflict by avoiding it.

Leadership and Panic

The ready acceptance of leadership, which may encourage maladaptive hasty decision making and defensiveness, is also seen in panic conditions. But here, leadership generally seems to offset maladaptive reactions to the panic. Kugihara, Misumi, Sato, and Shigeoka (1982) simulated a panic situation of 672 undergraduates in groups of six. In each group, one student was elected leader. Successful escape from the panic was more likely when the leader was in the same room as the other members than when the leader was placed in another room and was unable to determine the disposition of the members. Conceding to others was higher, and less jamming and aggression occurred, when the leader was present. Other Japanese experiments with simulated panic demonstrated that the greater the ratio of trained leaders to followers, the faster was the escape and the less the jamming and aggression (Misumi & Peterson, 1987).

Hamblin (1958b) found that followers were more willing to accept the influence of leaders during crises than during noncrisis periods. They gave leaders more responsibility and were seen as more competent in coping with the panic that had been induced experimentally. In the same way, A. L. Klein (1976) observed, in an experimental study of panic conditions of too many people trying to escape through the same door, that the stress group preferred a strong leader rather than a leader who was elected under low stress and was more highly acceptable. Acceptance and election, which gave the accepted legitimate leader control of the group's fate under conditions of low stress, was replaced under conditions of high stress by the group's choice of a less legitimate but stronger leader, whom the members thought was more competent.

Stress and Effective Leaders

Leadership that is effective in coping with stress implies leadership that results in rationally defensible, high-quality decisions; the appropriate use of available information, skills, and resources; and the enhanced performance of followers in reaching their goals, despite the threats and obstacles to doing so. Reducing stress in the workplace increases productivity (Perry, 1999). House and Rizzo (1972b) and Gillespie and Cohen (1984), among others, showed the importance of leaders in helping their groups cope effectively with conflict and stress. In this respect, individual differences among managers are apparent. Lyness and Moses (1989) were able to separate 258 high-potential AT&T managers by the managers' comfort in ambiguous environments. According to Moses and Lyness (1988), adaptive managers cope far better with stress in assessment centers than those who are overwhelmed by ambiguity. They have a broad perspective, are sensitive to feedback, and use both intuition and logic to deal effectively with ambiguity. They are comfortable in doing so. Managers who are inflexible in their approach also react to ambiguity but are uncomfortable and ineffective in dealing with it. Still other managers ignore or are overwhelmed by ambiguity.

Among the many ways the leader can effectively reduce stress among followers are: (1) identifying sources of stress and encouraging followers to speak up; (2) encouraging positive language and making affirmative thinking contagious among them; (3) organizing flexibility in the followers' schedules and arranging for them to maintain control of what they do; (4) organizing the followers in high-risk groups such as nuclear plant operators, hospital trauma teams, and aircraft carrier flight deck crews into high-reliability teams whose members engage in "heedful interaction," share responsibilities for each other's safety, cross-monitor each other's performance, and track each other's focus of attention (Weick

& Roberts, 1993; Weick, Sutcliffe, & Obstfeld, 1999; Xiao, 2002). Among hospital employees using Wilson's Survey of Management Practices to rate their 85 managers, Shipper and Wilson (1992) found that their tension was significantly lower when there was upward communication and participation ($r = -.54$), orderly work planning ($r = -.55$); control of details ($r = -.24$) and emphasis on time ($r = .31$); when the manager was expert ($r = -.64$), delegative ($r = -.48$), and facilitative ($r = -.59$); and when the manager provided feedback ($r = -.59$), recognized for good performance ($r = -.58$), and made goals clear and important. On the other hand, tension was rated significantly higher with goal pressure ($r = .49$). Some of these results may have been attributable to the hospital setting. Decreased tension among 46 employees a year later was associated with highly committed managers who practiced instrumental leadership.

Constent with what we have already noted, Burgess, Riddle, Hall, et al. (1992) concluded from a review of 13 articles on the subject of leadership and stress that increased workload, increased time pressure, and increasing task difficulty degrade team performance, communications, team spirit, coordination, and cooperation. But effective team leaders offset these effects with acceptance of input from other members; collecting performance information; and planning, coordinating, facilitating, and structuring the team to work together. Also, the leaders are approachable and unintimidating. They justify and explain their decisions and actions. They use strategic communication to prepare for crises. They justify and explain their actions. The converse was found for ineffective leaders with stressed teams.

Summing up earlier research, Zaccaro, Rittman, and Marks (2001, p. 471) declared that "team members are likely to display less emotional reactions to stressors if leaders provide clear team goals, clear specifications of member roles, . . . unambiguous performance strategies . . . and foster a climate where disagreements about team strategies can be aired constructively."

Requirements Vary with Different Stressful Conditions

Leadership that deals effectively with stress cannot be summed up in one simple proposition. For instance, anxious groups and groups that are in conflict call for different types of responses from the leader. For anxious personnel, the leader needs to direct attention to the specifies of their problems. For groups that are facing severe conflicts, the leaders must make possible a full analysis of the costs and benefits of pursuing one goal rather than another. Although active, directive, structuring, and transformational leadership are needed, the nature of conflict—socioemotional, interpersonal, or task-related—may make some difference in the extent to which initiation of structure by the leader will contribute to effectiveness (Guetzkow & Gyr, 1954; R. Likert & J. Likert, 1976). But if the leader has the ability and authority and if the situation generates stress, pressure, and tension to achieve success, directive leadership is still the most likely to be effective (Rosenbaum & Rosenbaum, 1971).

In dealing with inertia or defensive avoidance among followers, the leader must challenge outworn decisions and stimulate the followers to rise beyond their own self-serving rationalizations. Followers need to be made aware of their rationalizations and defense mechanisms that conflict with their true values and interests (Reed & Janis, 1974; Rokeach, 1971). Radical speakers attempt to do so by confronting audiences with the contradictions and inconsistencies of popular, accepted points of view.

In dealing with layoffs, managers can help deal with the stress by fair, equitable treatment, employees' participation, advance notification, and taking care of the employees to be laid off with severance pay and outplacement programs. The survivors may also be helped by their leaders through empowering, listening, and coaching (Noer, 1993).

Tsur (2003) demonstrated in a content analysis of 202 speeches that the six Israeli prime ministers between 1949 and 1992 used *anesthetic* rhetoric in Knesset speeches to calm the public in times of Arab-Israeli crises. They pointed out that the causes of the stress were under control and that the leader knew best how to handle the situation. They tended to use only carefully examined, selective information. During such crises, the rhetoric was likely to be less *informational* about past or future events, *mobilizing* of support for actions and policies, *motivating* for future action, *apologetic* to explain mistakes, or *ceremonial* to influence identification with common values.

The Nature of the Task

The task makes a difference in the effects of leadership in groups under the pressure to reach decisions quickly. Dubno (1968) assembled experimental groups, some with fast-decision-making leaders and others with slow-decision-making leaders. Congruent groups were those with fast-decision-making leaders and tasks that required speed and quick decision making. Incongruent groups were those with slow-decision-making leaders but with tasks that still required speedy performance and quick decisions. With appointed leaders, the most effective groups were those with slow-decision-making leaders who urged the members to arrive at high-quality solutions under the pressure of speed. For groups with emergent leaders, the most effective were those with fast-decision-making leaders who emphasized the high quality of the members' performance.

Butler and Jones (1979) also saw that the task made a difference for 776 U.S. Navy ship personnel. They found that when the risks of accidents were high and hazards from equipment were evident (as among engineering personnel), leadership was unrelated to the occurrence of accidents (presumably, structure was already very high). But in the work setting of deck personnel, in which environmental hazards were less evident and personnel were less experienced and hence less clear and competent about tasks, hazards, and goals, the occurrence of accidents was lower when leaders emphasized goals and facilitated interaction. More of any kind of leadership (support, emphasis on goals, and the facilitation of work and interaction) seemed to reduce multiple accidents for deck personnel but was irrelevant to the accident rates of engineering personnel.

Dealing with Conflict

Among 84 randomly selected faculty members from 20 departments of two universities, R. Katz (1977) found that the amount of affective and substantive conflict in departments contributed to the felt tension (.49 and .47) and the department's perceived lack of effectiveness (−.28 and −.29). At the same time, for departments that were in conflict, the leader's initiation of structure correlated more highly with the department's effectiveness than when such conflict was absent. The correlation between the leader's initiation of structure in a department and its effectiveness was .63 when affective conflict was high and only .29 when affective conflict was low. The correlation between initiation of structure and effectiveness was .51 when substantive conflict was high and .38 when substantive conflict was low. In an experiment to confirm these findings, participants were hired to perform routine tasks. For a routine coding task, initiation of structure correlated .46 with productivity when conflict was high and −.62 when conflict was absent. Less clear results materialized with a cross-checking task. Consistent with these findings, Katz, Phillips, and Cheston (1976) demonstrated that more directive, structured, peremptory forcing can often be more effective in resolving interpersonal conflicts than more leisurely problem solving.

Task- and Relations-Oriented Leadership

Although many studies have found that task-oriented leadership is most likely to be effective under stressful conditions, more often, both task-oriented and relations-oriented performance make for effective leadership under stress. Thus, Numerof and Seltzer (1986) showed that having a superior who scored high on the LBDQ in both initiation of structure and consideration was associated with lower felt stress and burnout among subordinates. And as will be seen, leaders who were high in both task- and relations-orientation were most effective in coping with stress conditions in a series of Japanese experiments. At the same time, task-oriented leaders, those who scored low on Fiedler's Least Preferred Coworker (LPC) Questionnaire, were found by Kim and Organ (1982) to be more sensitive to choosing competent subordinates when stressed by the pressure for effective task outcomes. Sample and Wilson (1965) also found that groups with task-oriented leaders performed better than those with person-oriented leaders under conditions of stress but not under routine conditions. Long-term psychosomatic stress reactions among workers were found in Arvonen's (1995) Swedish survey when immediate supervisors lacked a relations orientation. However, reversed results were obtained by Fiedler, O'Brien, and Ilgen (1969), in a study of American volunteers in Honduras, who found that low-LPC, task-oriented leaders were more effective in relatively stress-free villages, whereas high-LPC,

relations-oriented leaders exerted a more therapeutic effect in villages that were under more stress. The reversal may be a function of how task orientation was measured. It may be that in both stressed and nonstressed situations, although relations-oriented, supportive, considerate leadership generally contributes to adaptive performance and satisfaction in the groups and organizations that are led, task-oriented, instrumental, structuring leadership becomes essential, especially when stress and conflict are high. Such task structuring may still contribute to performance in the nonstressed condition, but it may be less essential.

Bliese, Ritzer, and Thomas (2001) pointed out that the reason that evidence is mixed about the importance of leader behavior such as leader support as a buffer against stress among followers is due to: (1) the lack of statistical power in the studies using too few subjects, (2) the lack of connection between the support and the specific source of stress, and (3) the need for WABA analysis to tease out the individual personalities of the stressed raters. They obtained ratings of both commissioned officer and noncom support from 2,403 U.S. Army personnel from 31 companies in two brigades. The assessed stress perceived was interpersonal conflict.

Soldiers in units with a high degrees of leadership support had high continuance commitment to the army even when they perceived a high degree of stress in their work. Cummins (1990) showed that the job stress in their workplace of 96 business students was buffered by supportive (high-LPC) supervisors.

The Intelligence and Experience of the Leader

In coping with conflict with their own superior officer, subordinate leaders' experience and intelligence appear to have opposite effects (Fiedler, Potter, Zais, & Knowlton, 1979; Potter & Fiedler, 1993).[9] Among 158 infantry squad leaders who perceived a very high degree of stress in their relations with their immediate superiors, the squad leaders' experience, but not their tested intelligence, correlated with their rated performance as leaders (Fiedler & Leister, 1977b). When perceived stress was low, experience correlated between −.20 and .00 with rated performance. When perceived stress was high, ex-

---

[9] See Chapter 27.

perience correlated between .39 and .66 with rated performance. For 45 first sergeants in the U.S. Army who were studied by Knowlton (1979), correlations between their rated performance and their intelligence were between .51 and .78 when they perceived little conflict between themselves and their superiors. The correlations ranged from −.04 to .24 when such perceived conflict was high. Similar findings were obtained by Zais (1979) for line and staff officers in nine army battalions; by Frost (1983) for 123 first-level and second-level superiors in an urban fire department; by Potter (1978) for 103 Coast Guard officers; and by Borden (1980), who collected data from 45 company commanders, 37 company executive officers, 106 platoon leaders, 42 first sergeants, and 163 platoon sergeants in a combat infantry division. Here, the leaders' intelligence correlated .44 with their performance when their conflict with their own superior was low; .31, when the conflict was moderate; and −.02, when the conflict was high.

Given the importance of preparedness in coping with stress, the positive impact of experience in dealing with conflict is not unexpected, but the reverse effects for intelligence are yet to be explained. In a bureaucracy, the highly intelligent subordinate leader may be a threat to his or her superiors, who, in turn, downgrade the subordinate's performance. Conflict with superiors appears to be more disturbing to the potentially creative, intelligent, subordinate leader. The leader who is in conflict with higher authority is likely to have less "influence upstairs," which reduces the leader's likely effectiveness and ability to use his or her intelligence.

Fiedler's (1982) cognitive resource theory is an effort to explain the findings. Fiedler assumed that the intelligent leader's contributions to the group's effectiveness depend on his or her direction of plans, decisions, and ideas. But under stressful conditions, the quality of such plans, decisions, and ideas is associated more highly with the leader's experience than with his or her intelligence. The highly intelligent leader will focus on problems that are not directly relevant to the task and will rely on intellectual solutions to tasks, when the tasks may not be amenable to intellectual solutions. A nondirective intelligent leader will make even less of a contribution to groups under stress, primarily because he or she will prolong the decision-making process, be inactive, or perform poorly.

The cognitive resource interpretation was supported by data about the effectiveness of staff leaders of U.S. Army mess halls, U.S. Army squad leaders, and leaders of public health teams (Fiedler, 1986). Cognitive resource theory explained why leaders with fluid intelligence (the ability to solve new and unusual problems) contributed to high-quality decisions and effective analyses of problems when stress was low but leaders with crystallized intelligence (the ability to solve problems on the basis of previous learning and experience) did better when stress was high (Fiedler & McGuire, 1987). An in-basket simulation, completed by 34 ROTC cadets either in a threatening military atmosphere or under relaxed conditions, found that the contribution of the cadets' crystallized intelligence to the effectiveness of their leadership remained the same under high or low stress. However, the contribution of their fluid intelligence (analysis of problems, decisiveness, and planning and organizing) to their effectiveness was significantly lower under the high stress (McGuire, 1987).

In a study of 130 Coast Guard officers, Potter and Fiedler (1981) found that the contribution of intelligence to performance was not related to conflict with one's boss in carrying out routine staff work, but it was negatively correlated with the effectiveness of decision making for those officers who engaged in policy making when conflict with their own boss was high. Fiedler, Potter, and McGuire (1988) concluded that the stress of conflict with one's superiors may interfere with the leader's ability to develop plans and make sound judgments, to communicate these plans to the group, and to supervise and monitor their implementation. However, they noted that the available evidence suggests that such conflict primarily interfere with the leader's ability to analyze the problem and make sound judgments and decisions rather than with the communication or implementation of decisions, plans, and strategies.

Dealing with Losses

If a sales crisis hits, business crumbles, and a large number of employees have to be laid off, management can do much to alleviate the resulting distress. Managers can set realistic expectations, keep employees informed, and implement even-handed layoff policies. They can allow employees to leave with dignity, help displaced employees find new jobs, and provide ceremonies to reduce frustration and anger. In handling the reduced demand for products and plant closings, the management of IBM in the 1980s tried to maintain the employees' felt and actual job security by redeploying displaced employees elsewhere, encouraging early retirement, and discontinuing overtime. They found temporary employment with others and contracted out work to subcontractors in times of temporary surplus loads (Greenhalgh, McKersie, & Gilkey, 1986). This is the model that larger and better-known Japanese firms pursued before the economic downturn of the 1990s.

Mergers

Schweiger, Ivancevich, and Power (1987) noted that when one firm is acquired by another, the employees in the firm that was taken over are stressed by the loss of identity, purpose, and ego ideal. Shock, anger, disbelief, depression, and helplessness are frequent responses, as is anxiety because of the lack of information. The employees see the resignations and forced departure of others as a loss of talent as well as a threat to their own security. Survival in the reorganization becomes an obsession. Transformational leadership is needed to deal with the merger of the acquired firm's culture and that of the firm that is taking over. It may contribute to creating a new culture in the acquired firm or to a new one that transcends both firms. The contingent reward system for the future needs to be clearly communicated as well as feedback on how it is working. Again, support, consideration, and commitment at each level of supervision in the acquired firm are essential to cope with subordinates' stress. It is particularly important, if it is possible to do so, for those with leadership responsibilities in the acquired firm to "get information about the acquiring firm for their subordinates; identify counterparts in the other firm and make contact and help subordinates to understand that their counterparts in the acquiring firm are not the bad guys and, in many cases, are in a situation similar to their own." (Schweiger, Ivancevich, & Power, 1987, p. 135).

At all levels in the firm, transformational leadership can help subordinates and colleagues end their previous attachments to the scene before the takeover. It can help reduce the tensions of disengagement accompanied by the disidentification with the old situation and disenchantment with the new that may produce disorientation

without anchors to the past or the future. Leaders can help colleagues and subordinates work through their denial and anger and move toward acceptance of the new situation (Tichy & Devanna, 1986). Assistance with outplacement may buffer the losses experienced by those squeezed out of the organization by the merger.

Change of Leaders

Lanzetta (1953) found that different leaders emerged in the same groups as more stressful conditions were imposed. Groups, organizations, and communities under stressful conditions may remedy the inadequacies of their leadership by changing either the group or the leaders. Hamblin (1958b) observed that members of experimental groups, when facing genuine crisis situations, tended to replace their old leaders with new ones if the old leaders were unable to cope with the crises.

Combat

High morale and less stress are found in soldiers in combat who have confidence in their commanders (Gal & Jones, 1985). This confidence is seen in the judged professional competence of the commander, the belief in his credibility, and the perception that he cares about his troops. But under continuing combat stress, professional competence becomes particularly important, according to Kalay's (1983) study of Israeli soldiers in combat in Lebanon in 1982.

According to an initial draft of a special edition of U.S. Army Field Manual FS-100 (1997), leaders are responsible for protecting their subordinates from the stress of battle fatigue by ensuring that their subordinates know what they are capable of doing. Training must be realistic, tough, and demanding. Exaggeration of the enemy's capabilities should be avoided. The leaders should conduct after-action mission reviews after every mission to keep subordinates informed and involved. They should also help their subordinates to talk through personal and mission problems. Both leaders and subordinates need plans for sleep, rest, and standing down to an area of lower risk. The leaders' superiors need to be advised of the needs. Replacements of casualties need to be welcomed and integrated quickly. Above all, the leaders need to look and be calm and in control. They must handle subordinates' anxiety by keeping them informed (pp. 8–17, 18). They also need to be authentically authoritative (Gal, 1985).

Dealing with Panic

Strauss (1944) observed six elements that reduce panic. These elements were (1) calm, intelligent leadership; (2) group discipline and morale; (3) rational action according to a plan; (4) prior training; (5) sound physical health; and (6) attention directed toward a realistic appraisal of conditions and alternatives.

The effect of clear, unambiguous direction can be seen in Japanese experiments by Sugiman, Misumi, and Sako (1983) and by Sugiman and Misumi (1984). These experiments demonstrated that in an emergency, a speedier evacuation from a simulated underground shopping arcade of a railroad station by city employees was obtained when the leader told one of the subjects, "Follow me," and led the way to the exit. Evacuation was slower when the leader gave instructions to the subject, indicating the exit in a loud voice and with large gestures. The investigators suggested that the "follow me" method using one subject worked because small groups tend to congregate around leaders. However, the "follow me" method worked better when one leader was involved with four other persons rather than eight others (Sugiman & Misumi, 1988).

The most effective leaders in helping groups to escape from panic conditions display high performance maintenance (PM) leadership. In the previously mentioned study by Kugihara, Misumi, Sato, and Shigeoka (1982) in which a panic situation was simulated in six-person groups, aggressiveness, the percentage of successful escaping, and the degree of jamming were measured. Four styles of leadership were compared. The percentage of successful escaping was highest and aggression was lowest in the PM condition, in which leaders focused on both performance planning and the maintenance of relationships, rather than on only one or the other or neither. PM leadership behavior was seen as most appropriate by the subjects. In addition, Misumi and Sako (1982) found that it was important first to provide the support and encouragement and then to concentrate on the requirements of performance, rather than vice versa.

Kugihara and Misumi (1984) compared subjects who dealt with a maze under fearful and unfearful conditions. Consistent with the previously cited Japanese experiments of reaction to simulated panic, they found that PM leadership generated the least fear, the largest amount of planning, and the least unreasonable felt pressure from the leader compared with P leadership or M leadership alone or the absence of both.

Dealing with Disasters

A body of observation, commentary, and research on coping with disasters points to the critical contributions of leaders and public managers who are well organized, well prepared, and well trained to provide both the needed instrumental and supportive leadership (Harman, 1984). At the mass populace and community levels, this translates into leadership that provides credible warning systems and advanced preparation for when disasters actually strike. The absence of such effective leadership and management is marked by maladaptive coping, defensiveness on the part of the public, and exacerbation of panic reactions. At the organizational level, Mitroff, Shrivastava, and Udwadia (1987) advocated both technical and behavioral preparation for crisis by organizations. Management needs early warning systems, high-quality control, and crisis command centers. Among other things, employees need training in security and detection, as well as emotional preparation for emergencies. Weinberg (1978) reviewed 30 cases of the behavior of groups during disasters: earthquakes, blizzards, accidents, and hurricanes. Trained judges examined each case history. Weinberg found that breakdown occurs in situations of high stress when there is an absence of appropriate leadership. Effective coping occurs with leadership that provides the needed support, structure, and preparations. For example, according to Hammerschlag and Astrachan (1971), in the Kennedy Airport "snow-in" of February 1969, the assembled people became passive, compliant, helpless, and without initiative and indigenous leadership. Salvation was predicted on the arrival of some technical authority who could ensure their deliverance—a "leader," the "omnipotent one," who would clear runways, facilitate their departure, feed the hungry, and make everyone happy. The persons in the snow-in never became collaborating groups. There was no task that could have unified them. They developed a sense of abandonment, which was internalized as a retribution for some fantasized wrongdoing. Food swindling and hoarding began to occur. The people did not see the need to initiate planning and coordinating with others.

Initiating and Maintaining Structure. Tests of the Lawrence-Douglas County, Kansas, emergency preparedness system demonstrated that the structure needs to be ready for future disasters and that there must be a strong chain of command. Resources must be well organized and the staff highly trained (Watson, 1984). Citywide drills for ambulance drivers were seen to have paid off in the handling of the Hyatt Regency disaster in Kansas City (Ross, 1982). Similar conclusions about preparation for emergencies were reached in Alexandria, Virginia's, dealing with a disastrous flood (Harman, 1984).

The need for structure and prepared response is the reason why local public service agencies, such as police, fire, ambulance services and public works departments, are the critical human resources whose effective utilization is paramount in times of crisis (Dynes, 1970; Kartez, 1984). Furthermore, the available leadership of these resources makes a difference in the effectiveness of the organized response to disasters. The most effective organizations maintain their own identity and do not depend on outside help from volunteers. The least effective organizations have an amorphous structure, and their leadership is elected or composed of quasi-professional persons who operate with volunteers who are not subject to discipline (Form & Nosow, 1958). In metropolitan Dade County, Florida, emergencies are dealth with by stripped-down administrative processes, rapid decision making, and emergency powers to mobilize resources when needed, as occurred in handling the Mariel boat lift and the influx of Haitians (Stierheim, 1984). Informal social networks can serve as the needed structure, according to an experiment using computer simulation of linkages of friends (Harvey, Kelloway, & Duncan-Leiper, undated). The delay and inadequate response of the Federal Emergency Management Agency to Hurricane Katrina, which devastated New Orleans and much of the Gulf Coast in August 2005, could be attributed in part to severe budgetary cuts and loss of much of FEMA's experienced personnel, its becoming part of the larger Homeland Security Agency, and the political replacement of its effective director with a director without credentials for the position. Both effective leadership and structure were missing.

Planning for Contingencies. Crises can be prevented or their stressful effects mitigated by effective political leaders who plan ahead (Yarmolinsky, 1987). Effective transactional leaders set up early warning mechanisms to avoid surprises that arise from hasty, ill-conceived responses. Active practice of management by exception can result in the rational recognition of potential crises. By planning ahead, anticipating potential crises, and preparing the group for crises, leaders will be more effective than if they deal only with immediate problems. Studies of leadership behavior in a public utility company, an insurance office, an automobile plant, and heavy industry found that supervisors of groups with better production records more often engaged in longer-range planning and anticipated future problems instead of limiting themselves to day-to-day operations (D. Katz, 1951).

Failure to plan ahead for contingencies such as loss of access to the disaster site, as occurred in the Flixborough, England, disaster in 1974 with the explosion at and destruction of a chemical plant, resulted in chaotic evacuation and impeded the arrival of emergency services (Bodycombe, 1982). Yet a preset structure and roles can be vulnerable to destruction and may prove too rigid for appropriate responses to disasters, such as earthquakes (Lanzara, 1983). Contingent planning, which sets response priorities on the basis of past experiences and future expectations of natural and man-made calamities, is necessary (Spencer, 1981). Minor crises, such as the shortage of supplies, that disrupt work can be the subject of similar planning (Bensahel, 1981).

Establishing and Maintaining Communication Plans. Planning for emergencies calls for planning communication strategies. The news media overreact at first. The available information is likely to be sketchy or incorrect, and the location and timing of an emergency are likely to be inconvenient. Communication plans are essential for the effective management of a crisis (Clark, 1986). Potentially destructive rumors need to be squelched (McSweeney, 1976). A center can be set up to provide frequent news about the disaster to the public (Kemp, 1984), along with an emergency resource catalog of suppliers of services and equipment (Ross, 1982).

A survey of 1,500 companies to find who was responsible for getting crisis information to employees indicated that 55% of the corporations had such a plan to alert personnel and deal with emergencies (Anonymous, 1984).

Communication plans should be prepared for the worst possibilities. They should be formulated especially in developing countries, where information is distributed mainly by word of mouth (Hall, 1985).

Using Past Experience. Recurrent disasters can be the source of learning and improvement of responses to them. Personnel managers learned how to handle pay for employees who are trapped by a snowstorm and what kinds of nonperishable supplies should be stored (Garlitz, 1983). In reviewing the Mount St. Helens volcanic disaster, Kartez (1984) suggested that responses to emergencies can be more effective when recurring individual and organizational patterns have been recognized and institutional plans are developed with these patterns in mind.

The importance of learning is also demonstrated by the fact that the most highly organized preparation exists in communities that have had repeated and recent experiences with similar types of disasters (Mileti, Drabek, & Haas, 1975). Furthermore, organizations that deal with predictable kinds of disaster, such as recurrent floods, are likely to be more effective than are those that attempt to cope with unfamiliar or erratic calamities, such as volcanic eruptions or once-in-a-lifetime earthquakes (Cuny, 1983). But learning may also have negative consequences. Community leaders will increase their delay in communicating warnings depending on the amount of prior experience they have had with such warnings. Previous experiences with a disaster may condition a false sense of security ("We had our 'once-in-a-hundred-years flood' last year") (Mileti, Drabek, & Haas, 1975).

Dealing with Prolonged Stress

The survival of a group under conditions of extreme hardship depends on the competent exercise of the leadership role and the maintenance of the group's unity, goal direction, and communications. Under conditions of extreme hardship and stress, a group's chances of survival are enhanced when it has a leader who maintains its integrity, keeps it realistically informed of the situation confronting it, fulfills members' expectations, is willing to act outside the bounds of stated authority, maintains its commitment and goal direction, and is able to transform members' personal concerns into concerns for achieving the group's goals. Evidence of the importance of this type of leadership is contained in Stockdale's (1987) autobiographical account of how, as the senior ranking American officer in an extremely stressful Vietnamese prisoner-of-war camp, he provided a purposeful and meaningful structure for the prisoners, establishing priorities and rules, stressing the need to resist early, and determining the conditions under which to take torture. He emphasized cohesion with the rule that all were to go home together.

To illustrate both the task-oriented and supportive actions that leaders can take to help subordinates who are reacting maladaptively to continued stress, Figure 28.1 shows an actual packet guide, *Stress in Battle*, prepared by the British Army's Personnel Research Establishment for noncommissioned officers and junior commanders to carry into combat. Note that some stress reaction is considered normal and requires no remediation. Note also the importance of leaders' being both supportive and attentive to keep stressed soldiers assigned to specific tasks or to help with small jobs.

The detrimental effect of the inadequate performance of leaders of groups that are under stress—that is, their failure to provide the needed support and structure—was observed by Torrance (1961). Torrance conducted an extensive, outstanding program of research on military groups that were undergoing training for survival. The following leadership behaviors and group conditions were found to produce an adverse effect on the survival of a group: (1) conflict between various echelons of leadership; (2) failure of the formal leader to accept the informal leadership structure; (3) formation of cliques, some with resources and others without; (4) the leader's isolation from the remainder of the group; (5) reduction of the power of the group, with the resulting hostility toward the leader; (6) the leader's abdication of customarily performed leadership roles or functions; (7) unwillingness of the designated leader to act outside authority; (8) the group's attempt to function without a designated leader; (9) the leader's failure to fulfill the group's expectations; and (10) the leader's failure to resolve the members' feelings of isolation and loneliness. Stress resulting from differences in values among members or between

Figure 28.1 Combat Stress and Treatment

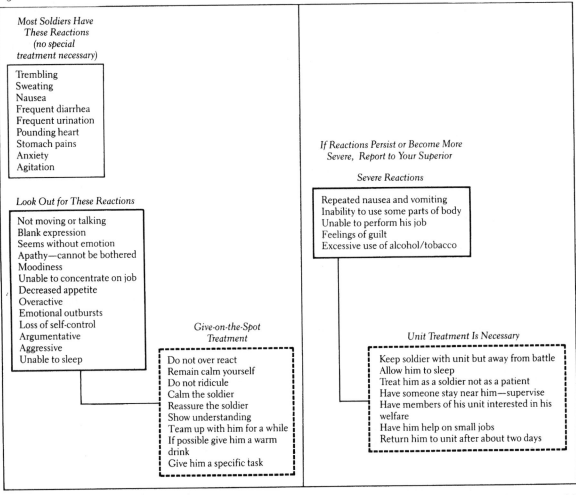

*Most Soldiers Have
These Reactions
(no special
treatment necessary)*

Trembling
Sweating
Nausea
Frequent diarrhea
Frequent urination
Pounding heart
Stomach pains
Anxiety
Agitation

Look Out for These Reactions

Not moving or talking
Blank expression
Seems without emotion
Apathy—cannot be bothered
Moodiness
Unable to concentrate on job
Decreased appetite
Overactive
Emotional outbursts
Loss of self-control
Argumentative
Aggressive
Unable to sleep

*Give-on-the-Spot
Treatment*

Do not over react
Remain calm yourself
Do not ridicule
Calm the soldier
Reassure the soldier
Show understanding
Team up with him for a while
If possible give him a warm drink
Give him a specific task

*If Reactions Persist or Become More
Severe, Report to Your Superior*

Severe Reactions

Repeated nausea and vomiting
Inability to use some parts of body
Unable to perform his job
Feelings of guilt
Excessive use of alcohol/tobacco

Unit Treatment Is Necessary

Keep soldier with unit but away from battle
Allow him to sleep
Treat him as a soldier not as a patient
Have someone stay near him—supervise
Have members of his unit interested in his welfare
Have him help on small jobs
Return him to unit after about two days

SOURCE: Adapted from "Part 1: Combat Stress and Treatment," in *Stress and Battle: A Guide for NCO's and Junior Commanders* (courtesy of the Army Personnel Research Establishment, United Kingdom).

the leader and the members, the failure of members to give realistic information to others about what they were doing, and the members' failure to give mutual support and to sacrifice their personal goals for the group's goals also tended to jeopardize survival.

Dealing with Role Stress

LaRocco and Jones (1978) concluded that for 3,725 U.S. Navy enlisted personnel, supportive leadership and facilitation of interaction contributed to job satisfaction and satisfaction with the U.S. Navy. Nonetheless, more initiation of structure was needed to alleviate the effects of stress, such as by structuring work and emphasizing goals, increasing role clarity, and reducing role ambiguity. Consistent with these results, 54 subordinates of 19 unit heads in a national black social services organization, who revealed little on-the-job anxiety, generated a correlation of $-.45$ between their unit head's initiation of structure and a 17-item measure of their unit's performance (Schriesheim & Murphy, 1976). But the corresponding correlation was .15 for subordinates with strong job anxiety. For the leader's consideration, the figures were reversed: .41 between consideration and performance when anxiety was low and −.24 when anxiety was high.

In a hospital emergency room, problems must be diagnosed correctly and dealt with as quickly as possible to alleviate role stress among ER personnel (Auerbach, 2002). Ziegart (2002) conducted a 15-month observational study of a trauma resuscitation team at an urban shock trauma center. The team was a medical staff of attending surgeons, surgical fellows, anesthesiologists, residents, and students, as well as consultants, nurses, and specialists. The leader might be the attending surgeon or another staff member. Outcomes depended on the team's success in coordinating their abilities and efforts. Computer displays or visual display boards were set up to coordinate personnel by keeping them up to date with incoming surgery patients and changes needed in immediate staffing (Xiao, Lasome, Moss, et al., 2001). According to Ziegart, problem solving, strategizing, teaching, monitoring, and providing contingent reward were seen by members as leader behavior that contributed to team effectiveness. But motivational and inspirational leader behaviors were rare and had no impact on the performance of the team. Murphy (2002) demonstrated that leaders who are socially and emotionally intelligent cope with their roles in such stressful conditions by exhibiting self-regulation and efficacy.

Dealing with Burnout

As assessed by the Maslach Burnout Inventory (1986), prolonged stress manifests itself in *burnout*, the feeling of being exhausted by one's work, the development of depersonalization (impersonal responding to service), and indifference to personal accomplishment. Among 90 Japanese airline employees, *exhaustion* and *depersonalization* were moderated by supervisory support (Tourigny, Baba, & Lituchy, 2005).

Transactional and Transformational Leadership

Denston and Sarros (1995) reported that 12% less emotional exhaustion and 3% less burnout on the Maslach inventory among 480 Australian law enforcement officers was accounted for by their ratings of their superiors' trans-formational idealized influence and transactional contingent rewarding. Intellectual stimulation accounted for 4% of the variance in depersonalization. Burnout was greater among junior-ranking officers, in larger departments, and among those with less supportive families. Seltzer, Numerof, and Bass (1989) asked 277 part-time MBA students to complete the Personal Stress Symptoms Assessment (Numerof, Cramer, & Shachar-Hendin, 1984) to indicate how often they experienced headaches, fatigue, irritability, loss of appetite, insomnia, and inability to relax. They also completed the Gillespie-Numerof Burnout Inventory, responding to such items as "I'm fed up with my job" and "My job has me at the end of my rope." Felt stress and burnout correlated .58. The 277 respondents described their immediate superiors on the Multifactor Leadership Questionnaire (Bass, 1985c). Table 28.1 shows the first-order correlations of the MLQ scores for the transformational and transactional leadership of the superiors and the felt stress and burnout of their subordinates. Seltzer, Numerof, and Bass concluded that 14% of the variance in the symptoms of stress and 34% of the variance in feelings of burnout could be attributed to the lack of transformational leadership. But intellectual stimulation increased burnout when other transformational factor scores were held constant.

In regard to transactional leadership, contingent rewarding was modestly associated with less stress and management by exception with more stress. The pattern was the same for feelings of burnout, but the relations with transformational leadership was much stronger (Bass, 1988d). In addition to ameliorating the effects of stress and burnout, transformational leaders tend to keep their "cool" when faced with threats to their lives. Mahatma Gandhi, Franklin Delano Roosevelt, Kemal Atatürk, Benito Mussolini, Kwame Nkrumah, and Ronald Reagan displayed composure and presence of mind when faced with attempts to assassinate them. They were not easily frightened, disconcerted, or thrown off balance but remained calm and maintained their sense of humor in the face of danger or crisis (Willner, 1968). They were like medal-winning heroes of military combat. According to Gal's (1985a) analysis of 77 Israeli medal winners in the Yom Kippur War compared with ordinary soldiers, the medal winners exhibited more leadership, perseverance under stress, decisiveness, devotion to duty, and emotional stability.

Table 28.1 First-Order Correlations of Transactional and Transformational Leadership of Superiors and the Stress and Burnout Felt by Their Subordinates

Leadership	Symptoms of Stress (N = 285)	Felt Burnout (N = 296)
Transformational		
Charisma	−.17**	−.53**
Individualized consideration	−.18**	−.47**
Intellectual stimulation	−.11*	−.36**
Transactional		
Contingent rewards	−.09*	−.43**
Management by exception	.11*	.22**

**$p < .01$, $r = .14$.
 *$p < .05$, $r = .10$.

SOURCE: Adapted from Numerof, Seltzer, and Bass (1987).

While transactional leadership can provide for structure and reward, transformational leadership adds to it by helping the followers transcend their own immediate self-interest, increase their awareness of larger issues, and shift their goals away from personal safety toward the safety of the group. Transformational leaders may convert crises into developmental challenges. They may provide intellectual stimulation to promote subordinates' thoughtful, creative, adaptive solutions to stressful conditions, to replace hasty, defensive, maladaptive ones. The transformational leader may have the charisma[10] to satisfy the followers' frustrated need for identity and feeling of the lack of social support. In a study of 57 communes over a four-year period, Bradley (1987) showed that the presence or absence of charisma in the commune's leader contributed to the commune's likelihood of survival. Communes were least likely to survive if their members were strongly seeking charismatic leadership that was not provided. Those with charismatic leaders were most likely to survive, as were those that did not seek such leadership.

Transactional Leadership. Transactional leaders can also be influential in groups that are under stress. They can supply solutions for the immediate needs that members perceive they have. They can set up rapid reaction systems of active management by exception to deal with

emergencies, disasters, panic, and combat conditions. They can employ contingent reward to coordinate reactions to threat. Such leadership will provide perceived efficacy but may not be effective in the long term. What may be required is a transformational leader who can evoke higher-level needs, such as for the common good, and who can move the group into a fully vigilant search for long-term solutions. Mulder, Ritsema van Eck, and de Jong (1971) studied leadership patterns in a Dutch navy flotilla on active duty. The usual interpersonal and task-oriented factors emerged, but what distinguished crisis from noncrisis leadership was that in crises, the leadership was intense, powerful, and self-confident (leadership that characterizes the transformational leader[11]). In noncrisis situations, it took the form of the "mild" person-leader relationship.

As noted in Chapter 22, the best leaders are both transformational and transactional. They deal with stressful conditions by transforming crises into challenges, enhancing the group identity of their followers, providing social support for them, helping to meet material and psychological needs, transcending the immediate circumstances, and planning ahead.

Transforming Crises into Challenges. According to Reilly (1990), crises are harmful and disruptive for organizations. She confirmed this conception of crises in

[10]Transformational leadership includes the factors of charisma, inspirational leadership, intellectual stimulation, and individualized consideration (Bass, 1985a). See Chapter 22.

[11]See Chapter 21.

interviews and surveys with 71 bank executives and 87 industry experts, plus archival data from 35 banking organizations. Crises are sudden, acute, and of great magnitude, and demand a timely response. They are outside the organization's typical operations, but they place extreme demands on the organization, especially on managers' time and attention. To ready itself to meet crises, an organization must have suitably prepared people and technology beyond that required for routine operations. The response to the crisis and its effective implementation are crucial. For this, timely availability and flow of information are essential, and in the aftermath, the strategic implications must be considered by the leadership.

Effective transformational leaders can halt crises by disclosing opportunities, arousing courage, and stimulating enthusiasm. The key here, according to Nystrom and Starbuck (1984), is the need for the leaders to be intellectually stimulating, to foster unlearning, and to eliminate the fixation on old ways of doing things. When the lacing of Tylenol with cyanide struck Johnson & Johnson in 1982, the public relations department had no plans for dealing with such a crisis. The CEO rejected any halfway steps to gloss over the disaster and converted the marketing disaster into an opportunity to gain credit for good citizenship. The firm regained its market share by introducing a more tamper-proof Tylenol package at a time of great public consciousness and publicity about the problem (Snyder, 1983).

Pines (1980) summarized the ways leaders can provide support to make subordinates "hardier" and maintain their high-quality performance and decision making despite the presence of stressful conditions. Dramatic changes can be presented as challenges, not as disturbances. Stress can become challenging if the leaders select subordinates for the stressful conditions who prefer a vigorous, fast-paced lifestyle and have the knowledge, intelligence, and preparation to cope adequately with the stress. Subordinates' sense that they control their fate can be enhanced and their sense of powerlessness can be lessened. Subordinates' involvement and commitment can offset their focus on the deleterious effects of the stress. For example, rather than paying attention to the dangerous exposure that he or she sees when looking up or down a vertical cliff face, a climber should focus on the holds and grips that are available immediately in front of him or her.

McCauley (1987) pointed to a number of transforma-

tional and transactional ways leaders can enhance subordinates' performance by converting a potentially stressful situation into a challenging one. The leader needs to ensure that there will be positive outcomes and that the subordinates know what they are. Although it may be difficult, goals can be set that are clear and attainable. Interim rewards for progress can be given. More generally, taxing conditions can be converted into problems to be solved. Self-confidence can be increased, as can the tolerance for ambiguity, uncertainty, and working in new and unfamiliar conditions. Situations that are beyond one's control can be faced with the recognition that one may be unable to change an undesired state of affairs. The situation may need to be redefined, goals may need to be changed, and patience may be needed (seemingly insurmountable problems sometimes disappear when they are ignored).

Aside from their better effects on subordinates, leaders who view situations as challenges, rather than crises, tend to be more open to ideas and suggestions from their subordinates, which enables them to make more effective decisions. This tendency was shown by Tjosvold (1984a), who conducted an experiment in which the focal "managers" led confederates of the experimenter in dealing with an issue of the rotation of jobs, which was a crisis condition, a challenging condition, or of minor consequence. The "managers" who thought they were in a crisis situation were most closed-minded. Not only did they feel that they disagreed most with their subordinates, but they were the least interested in hearing more from their subordinates, demonstrated less knowledge of their subordinates' arguments, and were least likely to change from their original position. In contrast, the managers who thought they were in a challenging situation were most likely to explore and incorporate subordinates' views (even opposing ones) into their own. They were most likely to indicate the desire to hear more arguments. They most incorporated specific information from subordinates to make a complex integrated decision that would likely promote both the simulated company's profits and the employees' satisfaction.

Consistent with Tjosvold's results, Blake and Mouton (1985a) observed that flight captains were able to respond to a crisis situation more effectively if they readily received information and feedback from their flight crews and were receptive to the information. Similar results were obtained for supervisors of fighters of forest fires. To deal with crises effectively, subordinates need to be ready and willing to provide their leaders with information and feedback and the leaders need to be ready and willing to consider it.

Transcending the Immediate Circumstances

Instead of autocratic, rapid decisions to make a stressed group ready to accept a leader's demands, effective leadership in stressful situations organizes group efforts of followers in ways that promote vigilance, thorough search, thorough appraisal, and contingency planning to avoid defective coping with a threat. Bolstering can be minimized by encouraging devil's advocates. Heterogeneity, rather than homogeneity, can be pursued by selecting members for the group who will promote harder-to-attain creativity rather than quick and easy decision making. Considering the distinctions between frustration, fear, anxiety, and conflict, the leader must be transformational to be effective under stress—able to rise above what the group sees as its immediate needs and appropriate reactions. The leader must arouse an inert group about the significance of threats and the group's lack of preparedness. The leader must alter the inert group's willingness to live with frustration rather than make efforts to deal more adequately with obstacles in its path to positive goals. To be effective, instead of catering to the group's immediate needs and fears, the leader may need to calm the demands for hasty change. An effective leader may need to be transformational in identifying and publicizing the inadequacy of defensive pseudosolutions. The effective leader is transformational in providing superordinate goals that transcend the self-interests of the hypervigilant group in a state of panic. Clear, confident direction is important for effective leadership when panic is imminent. But transactional leadership may also be important in planning ahead.

Enhancing Identification and Social Support

Felt stress is likely to be reduced if individuals can be made to feel part of a larger entity. The insecurity of feeling isolated is replaced by the security of a sense of belonging. Transformational leaders can create a sense of identity with a social network of support. Pines (1980) cited research that demonstrated that people with the social support of close friends, relatives, and group associations have lower mortality rates than do those without such social support.

During prolonged bombardments, the social support of children in kibbutzim made them less anxious than urban Israeli children. Loss of such social ties, ostracism, and isolation can be deadly among primitive peoples. Ganster, Fusilier, and Mayes (1986) reported that for 326 employees of a large contracting firm, social support from their supervisors, coworkers, family members, and friends moderately buffered the experience of strain. The strains included somatic complaints, depression, role ambiguity, role conflict, and frustration about the underutilization of skills. Nelson's (1978) surveyed the experiences of 30 child care workers in dealing with child care crises. Nelson found that crises were dealt with most effectively when the leader was supportive, respectful, and calm; had confidence; clarified the situation; and prepared for future crises. On the other hand, crises were dealt with ineffectively by leaders who displayed authoritarian attitudes and behavior, lack of support, loss of control, and poor communication.

As was seen in Chapter 21, followers may be under their own intrapsychic tensions, feeling personally inadequate because of the gap between their self-perceived images of what they are and what they ideally should and would like to be. Their stress will be increased if they feel they cannot reduce the gap. The frustration may result in aggression and feelings of dependence. To help followers cope with their frustration, self-aggrandizing leaders make themselves the object of identification for the followers (Downtown, 1973). Socially concerned leaders show individualized consideration by providing opportunities for their followers to develop themselves (Levinson, 1980).

Information about threats to safety and well-being can be instituted without hasty defensiveness. Transformational leaders can sound the alarm, articulate the need for early caution, and mobilize the organization to avoid the threat or prepare for it (Tichy & Devanna, 1986). Such leaders devise strategies to avoid or defuse the crisis. They persuade immediate subordinates and peers to accept the proposed strategies and mobilize support for them. In this regard, transformational political leaders take on an important teaching function (Yarmolinsky, 1987).

Summary and Conclusions

Leaders may have to deal with teams and groups that are frustrated by unattainable goals. Leaders can help to reduce the stress caused by fear of impending dangers. They may be needed to relieve the anxiety of groups caused by unclear and ambiguous demands. They may help teams in conflict over competing demands or with other groups. Leaders can arouse groups from a state of inertia where they perceive inaction as less risky and costly than an active response to warnings of danger. They can help groups avoid responding impulsively, defensively, or in panic. These groups may be facing stress caused by threats to survival that are internal or external, substantive or interpersonal.

It is not necessarily the speed of decision making nor the directiveness of leadership that is sought or commonly found during crises that makes a decision maladaptive. Rather, the inadequacy of the decision is due to the hastiness with which it is formulated and evaluated and to the lack of preparation for and commitment to it. Such hasty directive leadership will also be sought when followers must endure prolonged stress. In the same way, real or imagined threat will result in the acceptance of leaders who encourage defensive avoidance. Likewise, panic will heighten the followers' susceptibility to be influenced by decisions that will be maladaptive.

The emergent leader will do what is immediately required to provide the group with ways of coping with the stress. Rapid direction, initiation of structure, and task-oriented leadership will make the leader more likely to successfully influence the group to succeed. At the same time, the group will be more susceptible to such influence.

Both demagogues and statesmen can be influential but not necessarily effective in times of crisis, as can transactional and transformational leaders. The transactional demagogue can assure inactive followers that warnings are unimportant and persuade impulsive followers that simple solutions are acceptable. He or she can convince defensive followers by bolstering them and shifting responsibility for the crisis, and he or she can sway panicking followers with otherworldly solutions. The demagogue can successfully lead the popular, easier search for internal subversion when complex external problems are paramount.

The effective leader (who, of course, must also successfully influence followers) is a transforming statesman who addresses the inert followers by shaking them out of their torpor in the face of impending dangers or by rousing them to work toward what, at first, may seem to be unobtainable goals. The transforming statesman shows followers the inadequacies of simple solutions and defensive avoidance. Superordinate goals are provided for the hypervigilant, and motivation and initiation of structure are provided for the adequate search, appraisal of alternatives, and contingency plans.

The survival of a group is dependent on a type of leadership that is able to keep members and subgroups working together toward a common purpose, to maintain productivity at a level that is sufficient to sustain the group or to justify its existence, and to satisfy members' expectations of the leader and the group. Competent leadership is especially needed in times of crisis to unite the efforts of members and to strengthen the group's cohesiveness around a common purpose. A group that desires to survive will prevent leaders of contending factions from destroying its legitimacy.

Different types of stress call for different types of leadership behavior. More task-oriented structuring may be required in many stressful circumstances; the creation of supportive groups will be important to the leader's effectiveness in other situations. Ordinarily, both are important. Stress can also arise from dysfunctional structuring of work and interpersonal space.

CHAPTER 29

Effects of Space, Virtuality, and Substitutes for Leadership

Leadership depends on interaction. Interaction depends on physical proximity, social and organizational propinquity, and networks of open channels of communications. And so, not surprisingly, the emergence and success of leadership depend to some degree on physical and social arrangements. Such arrangements may also be substitutes for leadership.

Interaction Potential

Interaction potential is the likelihood that any two individuals will interact with each other. The more the individuals interact, the more one is likely to influence or lead the other. Although the purpose of interaction with another person may often be to give or receive information, to play, or to do other things that are unrelated to attempts to lead, many interactions are attempts to influence and to lead. Whatever increases the potential for interaction is also likely to increase attempts to lead. Successful leadership requires such attempts and thus is likely also to be correlated with interaction potential.

Physical proximity and the availability of channels of communication increase interaction potential. Thus, in reviewing studies of the effect of the spatial arrangement of participants in a small group, C. D. Ward (1968) concluded that the distance between participants was the most important single factor that influenced interaction. It was even more important than friendship. But friendship, familiarity, similarity, and other social factors also increase the potential to interact (Bass, 1960). Furthermore, the interaction of individuals may be a consequence of their freedom and autonomy from a higher authority. Some jobs permit more autonomy from a superior. This greater autonomy, in turn, increases the time that individuals spend communicating with others (Yammarino & Naughton, 1988).

Organizational proximity of members also increases their potential to interact and to communicate. With *ecco analysis*, members of an organization report whether they received a particular message and, if they received it, the time of receipt and the immediate source of the message. Using ecco analysis, Davis (1968b) showed that organizational proximity makes a difference in the extent to which informal communications for a particular oral message will be received. Thus the percentage of higher-level supervisors and managers who reported receiving information about parking or layoffs originated by those at the top of the organization was more than was reported by assistant foremen and foremen at lower levels. As messages moved downward through the system, the time of receipt increased along with delays and blockages.

Physical barriers would be expected to decrease the interaction between those with such barriers between them. But the opposite seems to be true, according to 99 employees in two high-tech firms surveyed by Hatch (1987). Interaction appeared to increase with the height of partitions between offices and the use of a secretary and a door between the offices. The only negative effect on interaction (which would be expected, according to Stech, 1981) was when a desk was positioned away from the office entrance. Nonetheless, fences and walls have been built to protect property, to control the borders of countries, to protect cities from attackers, to cut off the free flow of aliens illegally into the United States, to provide privacy of homeowners from neighbors, and to block uncontrolled movement from the West Bank into Israel.

Leadership and Physical Space

The *spatial proximity* of the leader to the led systematically enhances the influence process and the quality of the exchange between them. Conversely, the distance between them reduces the possibilities of influence and the quality of their exchange. It is not surprising that the traditional Inuit culture was highly individualistic rather than cooperative or competitive (Mead, Mirsky, Landes, et al., 1937). The low population density of the Arctic meant that the opportunity for contact among people was low. And without such an opportunity, the amount of influence and leadership was severely limited. Worthy (undated) noted that the rise of organized civilizations required the development of management that could occur only with denser settlements. Stable agriculture, animal husbandry, and fishing were needed to support the requisite density of population in which such organizing leadership was possible, as well as for civilization to emerge. Density was particularly important to agriculture, which needed irrigation works to support it.

Leadership and Physical Proximity

Schrag (1954) found physical proximity to be an important determinant of leadership among prison inmates. Toki (1935) studied the effects on groups of children of the introduction of physical distance to separate them from their adult leaders. The early separation and distancing of the leaders had much more deleterious effects on the groups that were early in their development than did such separation later on. Podsakoff, Todor, Grover, and Huber (1984) analyzed[1] 1,946 employees' descriptions of the reinforcement behavior of their superiors. The greater the spatial distance between the superior and the subordinates, significantly more likely was the superior to practice noncontingent punishment and less likely was the superior to practice either contingent or noncontingent reward. Other direct and indirect effects of the leader's physical proximity to followers were observed in territorial behavior, choice of friends, communication patterns, and physical arrangements. When followers

[1] Detailed in Chapter 15.

were more physically distant than close, charismatic leaders were seen to be more ideological in their visions and opinions. If closer, they were seen to be more open, considerate, and task-motivating (Shamir, 1995). Also, distant charismatic bank leaders demonstrated greater effects on financial performance than did closer charismatics (Howell, Neufeld, & Avolio, 1998).

Leadership and Territoriality. Territoriality implies ownership of physically closer space and has similar effects on efforts to influence and the processes of influencing. Our interaction is higher with those who are within the boundaries of what we consider to be our territory. Our interaction and potential for leadership expand if we can stretch those boundaries. Leadership will contract if the boundaries are contracted. Territoriality is one of the major phenomena of interest to students of animal behavior. One of the primary functions of leadership in animal societies appears to be the location and protection of territory (Allee, 1945, 1951; Allee, Emerson, Park, et al., 1949). It has its counterpart in the attitudes of delinquent gangs about their own "turf" and domestic firms about foreign imports.

Proximity and Friendship. The potential to influence others is seen indirectly in the effects of proximity and distance on choice and acceptance. Willerman and Swanson (1952) found that sorority girls who lived in the same house chose each other as friends significantly more often than did girls who lived in more scattered locations in town. Proximity contributed to mutual choice. Maisonneuve (1952) and Priest and Sawyer (1967) also found proximity to be a factor in interpersonal choice. Gullahorn (1952) examined the interactions of female clerks seated in rows separated by filing cabinets. Interaction within rows was greater than that across rows. Within rows, the clerks related more with those near them than with those seated at a distance. When distance did not operate as a factor, friendship was the next most important influence on the clerks' choice of others with whom to interact.

Proximity of distance between persons may also be a consequence, rather than a cause, of the relations between those who are engaged in interactions. Willis (1966) observed that individuals stand closer to one another when talking to friends and assume a greater distance when talking to strangers or persons of high status. It may be a matter of custom and habit. Latin Americans stand closer to each other than do Anglo Americans. Again, Little (1965) observed pairs of individuals in various situations. The distance between pairs of individuals in interaction was found to increase as their relationship changed from that of friend to acquaintance to stranger. Distance between pairs increased as the impersonality of the situation increased from living room to office to street corner. Streufert (1965) indicated that attitudes toward a member who deviates from group norms become more unfavorable as the distance between the member and the respondent increases. In the same way, attitudes toward a conforming member become more favorable as the member's proximity to the respondent increases.

Effect of Distance on Communication. Indirect evidence of the effects of distance on influence processes is also seen in studies of communication. Gullahorn (1952) observed that greater distance between the work locations of clerical personnel led to less communication among them. Allen and Gerstberger (1973) discovered that communication among product engineers was significantly higher with an open, nonterritorial office layout than with the traditional arrangements of office walls and assigned permanent workplaces. To the contrary, Hage (1974) found that the more the departments of an organization were physically dispersed, the more intensive were committee and departmental meetings and unscheduled communications. Also, there were fewer interactions *within* physically dispersed departments and more frequent interactions *between* physically dispersed departments. In explanation, Klauss and Bass (1982) concluded that physical distance among organizational entities increases the physical need for coordination, as shown by the increased volume of communication between distant organizational units. Although physical distance may initially hamper interpersonal communication, over time social structure compensates for physical distance and barriers (Barnlund & Harland, 1963). Similarly, modern technology provides alternative modes of communication to help overcome the factors of distance. Conrath (1973a) noted that when authority was involved in an interaction, communications were in writing; when task issues were involved, the telephone was used instead. The impact of information technology on eliminating the effects of distance will be discussed later.

Bass, Klauss, and DeMarco (1977) found that as physical distance increases among members of an organization at the same organizational level, there is a direct increase in the use of the telephone instead of face-to-face meetings for interacting with colleagues. But as the hierarchical distance in the number of organizational levels between a manager and a colleague increased along with physical distance, agreeing with Conrath's (1973) findings, Bass, Klauss, and DeMarco, found an increase in the use of memos instead of face-to-face contact or the telephone. The introduction of electronic mail moderated these effects of physical distance as such on collegial efforts to influence one another.

Leadership and Physical Location. The respective physical locations of individuals make a difference. The group discussant who grabs the chalk and controls the blackboard at a meeting can influence what ideas are singled out for attention. A. M. Rose (1968) identified job occupants who, because of their physical locations, take on "ecologically influential" roles of leadership. Their leadership is not based on personal, social, or psychological traits. These persons may be somewhat influential because they occupy a position that permits them to mediate ideas among several societal groups. Beauticians, barbers, bartenders, and traveling salespeople are examples of such leaders. In the same way, those who settled at the crossroads of several communities before the advent of the telephone were more likely to emerge as leaders. As will be noted later, those at the center of a network are more likely to lead those at the periphery.

As was noted in the last chapter, the physical presence of formal leaders helped their groups to cope better with a panic situation. Likewise, Ronan, Latham, and Kinne (1973) demonstrated that when supervisors of timber workers stayed on the job with the workers after assigning goals, they generated more output from their crews than did supervisors who assigned goals but did not stay on the job. Supervisors who remained on the job could effectively emphasize the importance of reaching or exceeding the goal and serve as reminders and monitors.

Seating Arrangements. Seating arrangements are not as trivial a matter as they might seem. A major difficulty in beginning serious peace negotiations among the United States, the Viet Cong, the South Vietnamese, and the North Vietnamese was disagreement over the shape of the table, round or square. A considerable amount of research has been completed on the extent to which one's influence in a small discussion group is dependent on the location of one's seat in relation to the rest of the group. Traditionally, the appointed leader took his or her place at the head of the table and those who were near in status to the appointed leader were grouped around him or her. Low-status people, as in feudal times, gathered "below the salt." This pattern is still maintained in informal groups, according to several studies. Leaders in small discussion groups tend to gravitate toward the head of the table (Sommer, 1959).[2] In simulated juries, Strodtbeck and Hook (1961) found that those who sat at the end of the table were more likely to be elected jury foreman. For U-shaped arrangements, those with higher status outside the group gravitate toward the apex (Bass & Klubeck, 1952). When the leader does not occupy the head position, other members tend to sit opposite, rather than alongside, him or her. When more than one leader or person of high status is present, these persons tend to seat themselves symmetrically around one end of the table (Sommer, 1961). Members as a whole tend to seat themselves closer to peers in status than to members who are higher or lower than themselves in status (Lott & Sommer, 1967). In a study of 88 supervisors and their managers, Bass and Wurster (1953b) found that the first-level supervisors seated themselves on one side of a long table while their second-level superiors sat down on the other side of the table. More dominant members of a group were observed by Hare and Bales (1963) to choose central seats and to do most of the talking. Group members sitting at end positions of a rectangular arrangement participate more and were rated as wielding more influence than are those seated at the sides (Strodtbeck & Hook, 1961). Lecuyer (1976) found, with French undergraduates, that the leader's position at the end of a rectangular table enhanced the leader's ability to direct the group.

H. Harris (1949) suggested that a semicircular or U arrangement, such as for a panel discussion, isolates those at the ends and spotlights those at the center. But Bass and Klubeck (1952) failed to find any such differences when the status of participants outside the group was taken into account. Howells and Becker (1962) seated two group members on one side of a table and three members on the opposite side. A greater number of leaders than would be expected by chance emerged on the side with two seats. C. D. Ward (1968) studied groups of strangers seated in a circle with several empty seats. The individuals facing the largest number of other members were most likely to be judged as leaders by other group members.

Are you more likely to interact with and influence someone sitting next to you or across the table from you? The evidence is mixed. Steinzor (1950) noted that when members of a discussion group were seated in a circle, an individual seated opposite a member who had just stopped talking, rather than one alongside the member, tended to speak next. Similarly, Festinger, Schachter, and Back (1950) showed that individuals who were positioned opposite each other interacted more than did those who were side by side. However, Sommer (1959) found that persons in neighboring seats interacted more than did persons in distant locations. Those in corner positions interacted more than did those who sat side by side or opposite each other. Felipe (1966) also found that such spatial arrangements similarly affected the rates of interaction. It may be that one is more likely to speak to the group after someone else across the table has just finished but to respond privately to those adjacent.

Seating arrangements are also a consequence of the purposes of meetings. Sommer (1965) reported that casual groups prefer corner seating, cooperating groups sit side by side, coacting groups sit at a distance, and competing groups sit opposite each other.[3] Stech (1983) suggested that managers who preferred relations-oriented leadership or task-oriented leadership could affect their success by choosing various layouts for their offices that determine the seating arrangements of themselves and those who visit their offices. Some of his differentiations are shown in Table 29.1

Leadership and Psychosocial Space

The impact of psychosocial space on leadership is mapped by sociometry. The choice of friends, work partners, and leaders can be displayed in two or three dimen-

---

[2] See also, Lécuyer (1976), Lott and Sommer (1967), and Sommer (1961).

[3] For more on the effects of propinquity and location, see the reviews by Barker (1968), Dogan and Rokkan (1969), Klopfer (1969), Mehrabian (1968a), M. Patterson (1968), and Sommer (1967, 1969).

Table 29.1   Office Layout to Enhance a Manager's Relations Orientation or Task Orientation

Relations-Oriented Layout	*Task-Oriented Layout*
1. The desk is placed against the wall. The manager turns away from the desk to talk with visitors.	1. The desk is placed so the visitors are seated across from the manager.
2. An informal conversation area is used. For example, the manager and visitor can sit side by side at a coffee table.	2. Most of the space for visitors consists of large, formal furniture.
3. All participants in a conversation are seated on the same level.	3. The manager's chair elevates him or her to a physically higher level than that of others.
4. The office door is open.	4. The office door is closed, and a secretary acts as a buffer.
5. The office space is relatively small and the seats are fairly close together.	5. The office space is large, and furniture is placed so that there are large distances between persons.

Source: Stech (1981, pp. 73–74).

sions of space and the correlated networks and linkages can be seen. Moreno (1934/1953) invented this approach to examine patterns of interaction. He asked each member of a group to choose among the others according to some criterion such as whom he or she liked best. Usually, the large share of choices was garnered by just a few individual members. Figure 29.1 presents a sociometric diagram for a group of eight members. Only the first and second choices are shown. Member A, who received five choices, is the most highly preferred member of the group. Members B and E, who did not receive any choices, are isolates.

Here are some of the kinds of questions asked members of groups and organizations from which interaction and the influence process can be discerned and mapped: With whom do you spend your work time? Whom do you contact in your organization if you have a particular

Figure 29.1   Sociometric Diagram

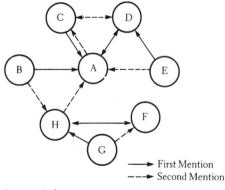

First Mention
Second Mention

Source: Author

problem? Whom do you avoid? We are more likely to contact and to spend more time with those we esteem, those we regard as important, those with whom we are more familiar, those whom we regard as friends, and those whom we think are more like us than different from us. Those who are esteemed, competent, knowledgeable, familiar, friends, or similar to us have more potential to interact with us than do those who are unesteemed, incompetent, strangers, and different from us. The latter have less potential to interact with us and, therefore, are less likely to be able to influence us. This conclusion is supported by considerable evidence.

Effects of Psychological, Structural, and Functional Distance

Psychological distance between leaders and followers is due to differences between them in status, power, demography, and perceived dissimilarity. *Structural* distance is physical or organizational. *Functional* distance is a matter of the distance of leaders and followers in working relationships (Antonakis & Atwater, 2002). The authors offered 17 propositions about the effects of such distances on leader-follower relations. For instance, they expected that power distance between leader and followers would correlate with their distance in social status. Leaders with strong need for power would maintain greater social distance from their followers than leaders low in need for power. Leaders with strong need for affiliation would do the opposite, while leaders with strong need for achievement would be expected to interact more with followers about their tasks.

Status Differences. Differences in status can be either emphasized or minimized in the search for organizational effectiveness. Status differences can be accentuated by the physical characteristics of one's office, dress, and privileges, as well as more subtle social calibrations, such as the use of "Sir" or "Madam" by a younger person addressing an older one. Status differences can be minimized by uniform offices, dress, and privileges, as well as by casual speech, familiar address, self-disclosure, and humor. Claims of common views, common leadership, cooperativeness, sympathy, and understanding also reduce the perceived differences in status (Drake & Moberg, 1986). (For more details about accorded status, see Chapter 10.)

Seeman (1960) studied teachers' and principals' perceptions of the differences in their status in 27 public school systems and found that teachers who perceived wide differences between their status and that of the principal tended to describe the principal as being more changeable in leadership but less dominating. Principals were identified who rated themselves high in status. They saw sharp differences between their status and that of their teachers. Such principals were described by their teachers as communicative, changeable in behavior, and effective as leaders. In an earlier study, Seeman (1950) found that teachers who favored wide differences in status in society and in organizations tended to prefer a directive rather than a group-oriented style of leadership. The number of teachers with these preferences was considerably greater than expected.[4] Rettig, Despres, and Pasamanick (1960) obtained results indicating that persons in professional positions who perceived wide differences in status among various occupations tended to attach greater importance to personal freedom than did those who perceived narrow differences in status.

Differences in status can give rise to physical, psychological, and social distancing. McKenzie and Strongman (1981) compared the way British police superintendents, inspectors, and constables placed figurines to indicate how each of them would be positioned for an ordinary conversation between them. The figurines were placed at a greater distance for conversations with those of higher status (the superintendents). The superintendents then

[4]This number has fallen substantially since 1950, as evidenced by the increasing demand of teachers to participate in the design of curricula and the governance of schools.

set up figurine placements with larger distances between themselves and those of lower status.

Utility of Psychosocial Distance. Psychosocial distance in sentiment appears to increase for high-status persons who have coercive power over low-status persons and decrease for low-status persons. Prison guards distance themselves from prisoners (Zimbardo, 1973), but prisoners and hostages, in time, come closer in sentiment to their terrorist captors (Eckholm, 1985)—the "Stockholm Syndrome." Controversy continues about whether such distance is necessary or desirable for leadership and organizational effectiveness. Social and behavioral theorists like J. R. Gibb (1964) and Argyris (1962) and many others in the Human Relations Movement saw greater costs to leaders and organizations when psychosocial distance was maintained. More virtue was seen in reducing the psychosocial distance among organizational members and in maintaining close, personal relations among those of different status and at various levels in the organization. On the other hand, Martin and Sims (1956), Jameson (1945), and Pfiffner (1951) argued strongly for maintaining such psychosocial distance to promote organizational effectiveness.

In a questionnaire on what respondents thought was required to succeed in business, administered to 107 MBA students, Bass (1968c) found a factor endorsing the maintenance of social distance and prerogatives. This factor was correlated with the students' perceptions of the importance of personal gain as a motivator to students with strong economic values and to students with less human or social concerns, as revealed in simulated budgeting decisions. Working managers saw somewhat less utility in maintaining such psychosocial distance than did the MBA students. Also less supportive of maintaining social distance were managers with human relations training (Bass, 1970b).

Proponents of the maintenance of psychosocial distance from followers suggest that by doing so leaders enhance their power and effectiveness. To maintain distance, leaders limit access to themselves and accent the difference between their status, esteem, ability, and power and those of their followers. They avoid personal self-disclosures and intimacy with their followers and employ various symbolic separations. (Emperors, sultans, and kings raised the height of their thrones above their audience chambers so they could literally talk down to their subjects from "on high.") Such social distance may either promote the legitimacy of the leader and follower roles or be a consequence of it.[5] By maintaining psychosocial distance, a leader can remain impartial, task-directed, and free of emotional concern for individual followers. A general can order individual groups of soldiers to a high risk of death for the sake of expected victory. A manager who would have difficulty discharging an incompetent personal secretary might find it easier to lay off a hundred employees several levels below in the hierarchy.

Barnard (1946a) suggested that the maintenance of psychosocial distance in an organization serves several other functions. It may help coordination, protects members from the need to compete for leadership, and acknowledges the importance of each individual's special contribution. It also protects the integrity of the individual in that it acknowledges certain rights, privileges, and obligations that pertain to his or her position. Furthermore, it obviates the necessity of unfavorable comparisons between individuals who differ in training and ability.

Social distance can reduce the amount of extraneous talking between employees that may interfere with their productivity. Such extraneous talking may, on occasion, replace work and thus have distracting and deleterious effects on the productive efforts of individual members. Thus, Ingham, Levinger, Graves, and Peckham (1974) observed that individuals did not work quite as hard when they were paired with one or two others than when they worked alone.

Costs of Maintaining Distance

The costs of psychosocial distancing can be high. They can include more defensive behavior by followers, loss of contact, poorer quality of communications, poorer selection of goals, less commitment to the group's goals, incipient revolt, and organizational rigidity. Barnard (1946a) observed that psychosocial distance can limit the adaptability of the organization, distort the system of distributive justice, and exalt the symbolic function at the expense of efficient performance. In the same vein,

[5] See Chapter 13. Conversely, when presidents walk down the street in their inaugural parades or move into a crowd to chat, they are ceremoniously reducing social as well as physical distance.

Reykowski (1982) inferred that the more socially distant from us are other persons, the less is our tendency to maintain equal exchange relationships with them. One may dehumanize psychosocially distant persons and show less concern for justice in dealing with them.

Variations in Preferences and Effects. The optimal social distance between the leader and the follower appears to vary from one leader-follower relationship to another. Differences in preferences occur for both leaders and followers. The effects of psychosocial distance depend on such personal factors as the leader's and followers' motivation to achieve and their degree of friendship. The effects of distance also depend on situational factors such as the favorableness of the situation to the leader.

There seems to be some optimal psychosocial distance between the leader and his or her subordinates. Carp, Vitola, and McLanathan (1963) found that effective leaders have a perceptual set that enables them to maintain optimal psychological distance from subordinates—neither so close that they are hampered by emotional ties nor so distant that they lose emotional contact. Consistent with this finding, in writing about what it takes to be a successful captain of a ship in the U.S. Navy, Mack and Konetzni (1982, p. 3) described this optimum: "The successful commanding officer . . . must learn to become as one with his wardroom and his crew; yet, at the same time, he must remain above and apart. . . . It is a skill that must be mastered in turn by each commander if he is to carry out his task with success." To reduce the social distance between a senior executive and operating employees, to move it closer to the optimum, the executive practices *walk-around* management. General Joseph Stilwell went much further to reduce the psychosocial distance between himself and his enlisted personnel. He was known for his tendency to wear an unmarked private's uniform, lead infantry marches on foot, and eat in the enlisted men's mess (Tuchman, 1971).

Effects of Follower Motivation to Achieve. W. W. Burke (1965) studied different combinations of leaders and followers, each combination differentiated by social distance and the need to achieve. In a group situation that varied in tenseness, followers with a strong need to achieve rated the situation as more tense under a socially close leader than did followers with a strong need to achieve who were under a socially distant leader. Followers with a weak need to achieve rated the situation as less tense under a socially close leader than under a socially distant leader. Followers with a strong need to achieve rated socially close leaders as more autocratic than they did socially distant leaders. Followers with a weak need to achieve rated socially distant leaders as more autocratic. At the same time, regardless of the followers' needs for achievement, socially distant leaders were rated more effective in a coding task and socially close leaders were rated more effective in a human relations task. Overall, followers with a socially distant leader considered their groups to be less productive and less satisfying than did those with a socially close leader.

Sociometrics of Leadership

Sociograms are sensitive to interaction potential because they show the choices members make about other members of the group. Some members are overchosen; others are underchosen. The patterns of choice point to interpersonal attractiveness and familiarity among members and help to identify the leaders. Different uses have been made of sociometry in the study of leadership. H. H. Jennings (1943) used sociometry to distinguish the choice of leaders from the choice of others. She found that group members are much more selective in choosing leaders than they are in choosing friends or roommates. R. L. French (1951) studied the choice patterns of companies of naval recruits. The frequency of sick bay attendance was negatively related to sociometric choice by peers; leadership ratings were positively related to being chosen. In a study of bomber crews, Roby (1953) found that the sociometric choices of members were unrelated to ratings of the effectiveness of the crews. Nevertheless, as with the preponderance of military studies, Levi, Torrance, and Pletts (1954) observed that the effectiveness of aircrews was enhanced when the officially designated leader was also the sociometrically chosen leader of the crew. The formal and informal structures were congruent.[6] (see figure 29.1)

Massarik, Tannenbaum, Kahane, and Weschler (1953)

[6]This congruence, as noted in Chapter 13, is likely to minimize conflicts between status and esteem. Chapter 35 provides a detailed review of the utility of peer nominations, or "buddy ratings," for forecasting success as a military officer.

used five sociometric indexes in studying an organization. The indexes were (1) relations prescribed by the organizational chart, (2) perceived relations, (3) reported interactions, (4) preferred interactions, and (5) rejected interactions. Preferred interactions were more highly related to members' satisfaction than were prescribed or reported interactions. The members related more freely and were better satisfied under participative than under more directive leadership.

College Presidents' Relationships. The leadership role of college presidents can be more fully appreciated by examining with whom they spend their time, according to interviews with 44 presidents. The average university president is fairly isolated. Most of his contacts center on his inner circle of staff and vice presidents. The isolation is broken mainly by contacts with students. Only 11% of the 44 presidents reported daily contacts with faculty members, while 18% to 21% reported daily contact with visitors and students. A factor analysis of these data uncovered four types of college presidents: bureaucrats, intellectuals, egalitarians, and counselors. The *bureaucrats* spent more of their time with their academic and fiscal vice presidents and their staffs. They tended to communicate to others indirectly, through their staffs. These presidents were perceived by faculty members and other administrators as remote, ineffective, and closed. The *intellectuals* spent relatively more of their time with faculty members and other administrators whom they perceived as intellectuals. *Egalitarians* and *counselors* spent more time with students and faculty, respectively, and those individuals involved in student and faculty affairs. They tended to be more highly rated by both faculty and students (Astin & Scherrei, 1980).

Communal Relationships. Bradley (1987) found that different sociometric patterns emerged in communes with different types of leaders. Sociograms were constructed of the responses to the questions of whether the relations with each other member in a communal network were loving, optimistic, and exciting. Systematic differences in sociograms were found when the commune's charismatic leader lived in the commune or was an absent and distant leader. They showed when it was possible for charismatic leadership to emerge. Charismatic leadership, particularly when the leader is in residence, coincided with many more members' being in affectionate connection with each other. Other relations were more loving and exciting when the charismatic leader was charismatic. The least communal linkages were seen in a commune without the potential for the emergence of a charismatic leader.

Effects of Interpersonal Attractiveness. Sociometric analyses and other interpersonal assessment procedures make possible the study of interpersonal attractiveness and its effects. Variables of consequence here include esteem, popularity, likeability, and perceived friendliness. Each of these variables has been found to increase interaction potential and therefore attempts to lead and successful leadership. Frequency of contact may increase esteem and less often may decrease such admiration. Some interaction between individuals is usually necessary before they can increase or decrease their evaluation of each other. If the interaction or its effects are unrewarding, mutual esteem between the individuals is likely to lessen.

Individuals are more likely to interact the more they value each other and the more they value the interaction among them (Bass, 1960). Thus, Blau (1954a) found that the more esteemed members of a law enforcement agency were contacted by the rest of the group more frequently. Conversely, Festinger and Hutte (1954) reported that people tended to talk least with those toward whom they felt indifferent.

Mutual esteem, familiarity, contact, and influence are interdependent. When 140 sorority women chose the seven most and seven least valued members of their sorority, correlations of .48 to .58 emerged between the tendency to be mentioned at all and to be selected as a competent leader (Bass, Wurster, Doll, & Clair, 1953). Similar results were obtained with salesmen.[7] The tendency to be mentioned (visibility) correlated positively with sociometrically rated value, ability, and influence as a salesman (Bass, 1960). Bovard (1951b) reported that more pleasant interactions yielded greater attraction among members. But Festinger and Kelley (1951) found that unpleasant interactions resulted in no change in mutual attraction. However, according to Seashore (1954), a longer duration of shared group friendship yielded

greater cohesiveness among 228 factory groups. Similarly, a mean increase in "likeability" among dramatics participants over an 11-week rehearsal period was found by Timmons (1944). If mutual esteem increases interaction, it should also increase effectiveness, and such was found by Van Zelst (1952a). Carpenters and bricklayers were paired either arbitrarily or with work partners they chose sociometrically. Sociometrically assembled pairs were considerably more productive than were pairs who were assembled arbitrarily.

Kelley (1950) presented information to some college students that a visiting instructor would be warm but told other students that the visiting instructor would be cold. The students asked more questions of the "warm" instructor than of the "cold" one. They formed more positive impressions of the "warm" instructor and more negative impressions of the "cold," instructor even though the visiting instructor behaved in the same way in both conditions.

Generally, physically attractive persons tend to make more favorable impressions on others and to be contacted more frequently and for longer periods (Berscheid & Walster, 1969). But the converse has also been seen. Subjects tend to terminate interactions with physically handicapped persons more quickly (Kleck, Ono, & Hastorf, 1966). Similarly, subjects working with supposedly mentally ill persons talk less, initiate less conversation, and express opinions that are less representative of their beliefs (Farina, Allen, & Saul, 1966).

Hierarchical Effects. T. Burns (1954) reported that middle managers spent more time with superiors than with subordinates, while the reverse was true for first-level supervisors. Likewise, Guest (1956) and Piersol (1958) reported that first-level supervisors spent more time with their subordinates than with their superiors. Zajonc and Wolfe (1966) found that managers in high-level positions and those performing staff functions maintained the widest range of formal contacts within the organization, but these informal contacts did not seem to follow a distinct pattern associated with hierarchical level or function.

Effects of Familiarity. The potential to interact with another particular member increases as the group becomes smaller. Open network connections among members also increase the likelihood of interaction. In

[7] See Chapter 10.

addition, familiarity, as such, breeds interaction, and interaction breeds familiarity. (Neither necessarily breeds contempt.) The more intimate or familiar we are with one another, the more likely we are to interact. The more we interact, the more intimate we become (Bass, 1960). Thelen (1954) noted that subgroups that are composed of friends are likely to have more energy to spend in participation with each other than are subgroups composed of strangers.

Intimacy and familiarity are not identical. Caplow and Forman (1950) found that the length of residence in a college community merely increased the number of one's acquaintances rather than the intensity of relationships with one's neighbors. We can be familiar without being intimate, although they are likely to be correlated. According to Klauss and Bass (1982), data from a large governmental agency indicated that the familiarity of a colleague with a focal person was associated directly with the frequency of their contact during any given week, as well as with the length of their acquaintanceship. Likewise, intimacy among 75 college students was a function of the frequency and amount of hours of contact among the students (Fischer, 1953).

In studying a rumor's origin and spread, Festinger, Cartwright, Barber, et al. (1947) observed that people were less restrained in talking about such rumors to close friends than to mere acquaintances. Similarly, Hare and Hare (1948) noted a positive correlation between the amount of social activity and the number of family friends among 70 families in a veterans' housing project. Increased congeniality of members was observed by Curtis and Gibbard (1955) with the members' increased experience with one another in both voluntary and compulsory college groups. Likewise, Seashore (1954) found that members' attraction for each other was greater in factory groups in which the members were friends for longer periods of time. Finally, Faunce and Beegle (1948) found that cliques at a teenage farmers' camp gradually developed on the basis of newly emerged familiarities, although they were initially formed around homogeneity of age, sex, and country of origin. Bass (1960) advanced two reasons for interaction among members of groups as their familiarity and intimacy increased: (1) members feel more secure in interacting with friends than with strangers and (2) since they can predict each other's actions, they can interact with less difficulty.

Morgan and Sawyer (1967) found that schoolboys prefer strict equality in the distribution of rewards, both with friends and with others. (We see this preference repeatedly when conducting experimental gaming with students.) Nevertheless, although they prefer equality, friends are willing to accept inequality if one friend thinks that the other friend may want it. But ordinarily friends are less willing to accept inequality. Familiarity with what the other expects facilitates the ability to reach agreement about how rewards should be distributed.

Effectiveness in the form of goal attainment tends to be associated with increased interaction. If so, it should also be associated with increased familiarity and/or intimacy. Husband (1940) found that pairs of close friends took less time than pairs of strangers to solve problems in code, puzzles, and arithmetic. Similarly, Goodacre (1953) reported that the members of the most effective of 26 infantry squads in handling field problems had a greater tendency to socialize together after hours. However, Horsfall and Arensberg (1949), in a study of a shoe factory, failed to find any relationship between productivity and the tendency of its supervisors to interact frequently.

Klauss and Bass (1982) reported that colleagues of 577 governmental professionals thought that the more familiar focal colleagues were more trustworthy, informative, and dynamic than were the less familiar focal ones. Colleagues also felt more satisfied in their relations with the more familiar focal persons. A correlation of .27 emerged between familiarity and perceived effectiveness of relations. But the length of acquaintanceship between the colleagues and the focal persons was unrelated to measures of effective communication. A higher frequency of interaction between colleagues and focal persons, however, correlated with satisfaction and effectiveness but not with the colleagues' judgments of the trustworthiness and informativeness of the focal persons.

Effects of Similarity. Individuals interact more with those who are like them than those who are unlike them (Bass, 1960). The effect can be seen in student cafeterias, where students are attracted to eat at tables according to sex, race, ethnicity, class, age, and status. Pfiffner (1951) observed that employees of the same age, physical attractiveness, marital status, education, and race tended to group together. Strangers associate first on the basis of their homogeneity of sex, age, and place of origin, according to Faunce and Beegle's (1948) study of campers. Likewise, Caplow and Forman (1950) found that interaction among neighbors in a university community was greater if families were homogeneous in occupation, number of children in the family, length of residence, and type of housing. Similarly, in the more turbulent neighborhoods of Chicago, leaders of 181 public and private human service organizations who had similar racial or educational backgrounds were more likely to establish cooperative relations with one another than were those from different backgrounds (Galaskiewicz & Shatin, 1981).

Formal versus Informal Organization. Stogdill (1949) asked members of organizations to estimate the amount of time they actually spent with other members. Sociometric charts of these working relationships were superimposed on the formal organizational chart to determine the correspondence between the formally specified and actual working relationships. Such a determination would make it possible to diagnose communication and interactional problems within the organization. Such a chart is shown in Figure 29.2. It should be noted that in this figure, the vice president, rather than the president, is the focus of working interactions. Department heads A and B also tend to be foci of interactions. Department

head C is bypassed by his subordinates, who do not interact much with each other, which suggests that the department head is not an effective leader of his group. With such a pattern of interactions, it is apparent that coordination is effected either by the vice president or by the cross-departmental contacts among section heads. The dominant trend of contact here is upward rather than downward. This trend is consistent with the commonly observed latent pressure to communicate upward more than downward. Such efforts to initiate interactions with superiors may serve more to reduce anxiety and to increase feelings of security and less to communicate about issues of work (A. Kadushin, 1968; Schwartzbaum & Gruenfeld, 1969).

Stogdill (1951a) plotted the number of times each of 22 officers in a small U.S. Navy organization was mentioned as a work partner by his peers. Officers who occupied high-level positions tended to mention subordinates and outsiders more frequently and superiors less frequently than did officers in lower-level positions. The same trend was observed in the number of mentions received. High levels of responsibility were related to more total mentions given and received and to more mentions received from members inside one's own unit and from superiors. Scope of authority was not significantly related to any sociometric scores. Those who delegated most freely tended to be mentioned most frequently as work partners by members inside their own units.

Networks

Social distance and status differences can be increased or decreased by the network available or imposed. A network is a set of people connected by friendship, influence, work, or communications.[8] Networks are composed of people or stations and links between them. Within organizations, it is a reciprocating set of relationships that stabilizes the manager's world and gives it predictability (Sayles, 1964). As shown in Figure 29.3, a manager's network is likely to include vertical, horizontal, and diagonal segments, with mutual contacts with his or her boss, his or her subordinates and their subordinates, and many other colleagues at the same level or at higher and lower

Figure 29.2 Sociometric Diagram Superimposed on Organization

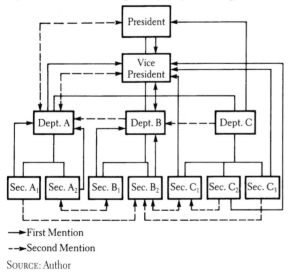

→ First Mention

-→ Second Mention

[8]Networks can obviously be mapped in sociograms produced by sociometry.

Figure 29.3 Organizational Network

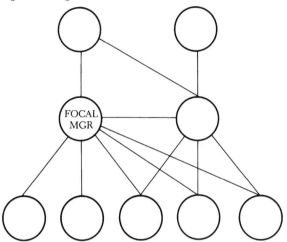

SOURCE: Adapted from Graen and Scandura (1987, p. 203) by permission of JAI Press Inc., Greenwich, CT.

levels. It is also likely to include individuals outside the organization, such as consultants, clients, and suppliers. Network analysis is the study of the links that bind such people and their positions.

Networks can be formed in a variety of ways and for a variety of purposes. Clearinghouses of information can serve as the centers of networks of influence. The insurance industry encourages social responsibility and community leadership by its individual member companies in this manner (Karson, 1979). Brown and Detterman's (1987) longitudinal study of the community networks of leaders in a large metropolitan center found that a formal leadership program increased contacts among the white but not among the black participants. New networks emerged and old ones were strengthened for addressing community problems. Underlying the networks were the social establishment, political leaders, business leaders, and community activists.

The vertical, diagonal, and lateral dyads, each of which may be formal or informal, make up the organizational network shown in Figure 29.3. The dyadic relations particularly important to the focal manager are displayed. It can be seen here that relations between other members of the organization may be important to a third member. For instance, the dyadic relations between a director and his associate director may have consequences for a staff scientist, who has no direct connection with either per-

son. A more powerful analysis of networks may be provided by triadic analysis (Holland & Leinhardt, 1976). An analysis of three members might show, for instance, two members linked to a third, but the third member not reciprocating. Bradley (1987) reported systematic differences in which the type of triads appearing in communes was a function of whether the charismatic leader of the commune was in residence or was an absentee leader.

The typical supervisor's communications network is composed of links to his or her subordinates, to one or more peers and superiors, and to outsiders, as well as to libraries, databases, and computers. The links may be oral, written, and electronic. Unless replaced by e-mail, at least one-third of the supervisor's time is spent mainly in face-to-face contact with subordinates (Jablin, 1985), but these links may not be seen as being as important and challenging as those with outsiders (Whitely, 1984).

Importance of Networks

Ordinarily, a manager's network operates on a transactional exchange relationship: managers receive information, services, and resources in exchange for promises, returned favors, support, and recognition (Kaplan & Mazique, 1983). Nonetheless, networks are important to both transformational and transactional leaders. For instance, in a changing organization, old networks are broken up and new ones are established. The transformational leader manages "to foster a new set of social networks with new flows and ties" (Tichy & Devanna, 1986, p. 193). Managers also develop networks of lateral reciprocal exchanges with their peers. Such trading connections enable them to get their own department's work done (Kaplan & Mazique, 1983).

Networking supports one's image in the organization. Managers earn esteem by linking themselves to winning causes (Kotter, 1979), and such alliances promote their advancement. Few managers can function without the linkage of their networks (McCall, Morrison, & Hanman, 1978). With the exponential increase in knowledge and the knowledge worker, communication networks have taken on an ever-increasing role of importance in the success or failure of organizations (Cleveland, 1985). Networks connecting managers in separate organizations play an important role in the hiring of members for top management teams (Williamson & Cable, 2003).

In the absence of finding much research about managerial and professional networking, Hall-Merenda and Howell (undated) proposed that the networks are a form of socialized exchanges. Networkers concentrate their boundary spanning to identify useful ties for projects. They find gaps in the organizational structure in which to establish ties. An exchange at first is based on a formal agreement; subsequent exchanges can be based on trust. Successful completion of projects increases trust and the retention of partners and creates wider opportunities for partnering. Yukl (1998, p. 39) concluded that best practices for networkers are to seek opportunities to make contacts, to do unconditional favors, to become a valuable trading partner, and to keep in touch with network members.

Effects of Network Centrality on Leadership

Leaders' performance and effects depend on their centrality in networks, their domain of influence, and their contacts and connections in the networks (McElroy & Schrader, 1987). In an analysis of 140 full-time nonsupervisory employees of a newspaper publishing company, Brass (1984) showed that perceived influence and promotion to a supervisory position depended on one's location in the networks of work flow, communication, and friendship. Contacts beyond the normal work requirements were important in the acquisition of influence, particularly by technical core employees. Also important to perceived influence were the critical importance of one's position to operations and one's centrality in the networks. The leadership potential of professional members of a Russian high-tech consulting firm, as assessed by their superiors, was significantly related to their centrality in advice and friendship networks based on sociometric nominations (Korotov & Onyemah, 2003).

Insko, Thibaut, Moehle, et al. (1980) showed that when 432 students were organized into trading groups, the group through which all trades had to be channeled made the most money and emerged as the leading group. Such functional centrality was also seen to be important to leadership by Tropp and Landers (1979), who examined the relationship of emergent leadership to the frequency of passing to field hockey teammates. *Spatial* centrality was not as important as *functional* centrality to effective plays. As hypothesized for 308 executives in 32

firms by Liang, Ndofor, & Picken (2003), network centrality in their communication patterns was more effective if it fit with the uncertainty of their environment. And although the leader of a jazz ensemble is its central figure, the role is tempered by the number of criticisms received and disagreements on interpretations that affect the quality of the performance (Voyer & Faulkner, 1986).

Open and Closed Channels. The mutual influence of leaders and followers depends on how open or closed the channels of communication are between them. Thus, those who have access to the political leaders and decision makers in a community are more likely to be influential in the community (Bockman & Gayk, 1977). Group members can also influence each other more readily if they are in open communication with each other.

The openness of a channel between superior and subordinate must be two-way. That is, both must be perceived as being ready both to communicate and to listen (Redding, 1972). Both verbal and nonverbal behavior (such as eye gaze, posture, tone of voice, and facial expressions) can signal such readiness or lack of it (Tjosvold, 1984b). Subordinates' satisfaction with their work and with their superiors is strongly related to their perception of the possibilities of open communication with their superior (Pincus, 1986).

The direction of the flow of information in a channel between the superior and the subordinate and the superior's style of relating to the subordinate will depend on who initially has more information that is relevant to their joint task. Shapira (1976) confirmed that if the superior initially possesses more information than the subordinate about what needs to be done, the superior will be more *directive* with the subordinate. If the superior initially possesses less information about what needs to be done, he or she will be more consultative or *participative.*[9]

The use of a channel appears to depend more on its openness and accessibility than on the perceived quality

[9]As defined in Chapter 18, *direction* (italic) refers only to giving orders with or without explanation; direction (roman) includes ordering, persuading, and manipulating. *Participation* (italic) refers only to sharing in the decision process; participation (roman) includes consulting, sharing, and delegating.

of the information that can be obtained from it (Allen, 1966) or the ease of its use (Gerstberger & Allen, 1968). Thus, neighborhood leaders who have common membership in different organizations tend to have more open cooperative relations with one another (Galaskiewicz & Shatin, 1981). More upward communication channels will be used in hierarchical organizations if trust is present and aspirations for mobility are high (Level & Johnson, 1978; O'Reilly & Roberts, 1974). Horizontal flows of unsolicited information will be increased by reductions in organizational constraints (Albaum, 1964) and increases in the organization's technological certainty (Randolph & Finch, 1977).

Network Preferences. To accommodate their own influence and work preferences, U.S. presidents differed in the networks of staff assistants they constructed. Dwight D. Eisenhower's immediate staff reported to him indirectly through his chief of staff, Sherman Adams. John F. Kennedy was the center of a network of his immediate staff. Lyndon B. Johnson used the telephone extensively to extend his network of direct contacts. Jimmy Carter created groups of staff assistants, each of whom dealt comprehensively and independently with a single different source, and he related directly to each group. Ronald Reagan, like Eisenhower, depended heavily on a chief of staff to screen and funnel the staff's recommendations.

The self-interests of the senders and receivers of information will contribute to distorting or shutting down channels by tactics of overloading, circumventing, or reinterpreting the organization's policies and regulations (P. J. Frost, 1986). Leaders can expand their networks informally to increase their own influence. For instance, Admiral Hyman Rickover greatly increased his control and influence by building a large network of his nuclear-trained officers, all of whom reported directly to him each week, bypassing the official channels (Polmar & Allen, 1981).

Effects of Group or Organizational Task

Networks of communication in an organization can result from the demands of authority, the demands for information, the demands of particular tasks, the bonds of friendship, or the more formal status characteristics of organizations. The purpose served by a network affects how information is transmitted within it. For example, communication in an authority network is typically more formalized than is communication in a friendship network (Bass & Ryterband, 1979). Heise and Miller (1951) concluded that the task faced by the network is a determinant of the leadership and the group behavior that are likely to occur. The uniqueness of the solution, the number of decisions to be made, and the amount of previous structure are all involved. For example, G. B. Cohen (1969) studied groups who performed an information-processing task and found that centrality facilitated their performance most when the tasks were highly interdependent.

Effective Network Communications

Systematic effects on the leadership effectiveness of those led emerge as a consequence of the communication pattern fostered by the leader, policy, motivation, and training.

Leadership and Styles of Communication. An important aspect of a manager's leadership style is the way he or she communicates with colleagues and subordinates. Thus, under authoritarian managers, networks with restricted communications take less time to plan than do groups led with less direction and structure. However, the results of the planning are likely to be less efficient in accomplishing the required tasks (Snadowsky, 1972).

Table 29.2 shows the correlations between leadership and communication styles that Klauss and Bass (1982) obtained when 71 subordinates described the leadership and communication styles of their 28 focal managers. It can be seen that participative leadership styles[10] correlated highly with the leader's being seen as an informal, frank, open, two-way communicator, careful transmitter, and careful listener. Trustworthiness and informativeness, but not dynamism, were also highly correlated with participative styles of leadership. *Directive* leadership was less highly correlated with careful transmission, being open and frank and a careful listener, but not at all with being informal and a careful listener. Dynamism was highly correlated with *directiveness* but at the expense of trustworthiness. Being negotiative and manipulative was unrelated to the style of communication.

---

[10]Consulting, participating, and delegating.

Table 29.2 Correlations between Communication Styles, Credibility, and Leadership Styles as Seen by 71 Subordinates of 28 Focal Managers

Communication Style and Credibility	Directive	Negotiative	Style of Leadership Consultative	Participative	Delegative
Communication style					
Careful transmitter	.37	.08	.63	.59	.64
Open and two-way	.36	.06	.70	.65	.61
Frank	.42	.04	.50	.45	.36
Careful listener	.15	−.08	.51	.55	.59
Informal	.18	−.01	.53	.55	.55
Credibility					
Trustworthy	.19	−.03	.57	.54	.57
Informative	.31	−.05	.59	.58	.63
Dynamic	.49	−.08	.38	.25	.14

[a]Underlined values are significant at $p < .01$.

SOURCE: Adapted from Klauss and Bass (1982).

Posner and Kouzes (1988b) obtained even stronger linkages between transformational leadership and the communication styles of 146 senior managers, according to their 998 subordinates. Transformational leadership was measured by the Leadership Practices Inventory (Kouzes & Posner, 1987). The five factors (challenging the proces, inspiring a shared vision, enabling others to act, modeling the way, and encouraging the heart) correlated between .40 and .68 with the trustworthiness, informativeness, and dynamism of the leaders' communication styles, as measured by Klauss and Bass (1982). For instance, inspirational envisioning correlated .56 with trustworthiness, .58 with informativeness, and .68 with dynamism.

Ordinarily, open, easy, ready communications contribute to the extent the leader and the group can influence each other and to the extent to which they will be effective. On the basis of research with B-29 aircrews, Roby and Forgays (1953) noted that crews who could send information faster to decision stations could solve problems faster. In a report on maintenance in four medium bomber wings, Bates (1953) inferred that in the two better-performing maintenance systems, there was more contact among subgroups. The system's leaders were usually involved in such contacts. Torrance (1954b) ascertained that plane crews in simulated survival exercises were most likely to "survive" if communications were resumed quickly among scattered crew members, leading to a clarification of the situation. Again, such resumption of communication was usually connected to the initiatives of the formal or emerging leadership.

The leadership is often responsible for the ease with which members of a group can communicate with one another. Thus, O'Reilly (1977) found that decision making by subordinates was improved if they could readily make use of their supervisors as sources of information. Such easy communication correlated highly with the described effectiveness of 500 work groups (Bass, 1954b) and teams engaged in naval ordnance testing (Weschler & Shepard, 1954). Leaders who scheduled regular meetings with their groups made for more effective group operations. Dyer and Lambert (1953) found that in two medium bomber wings, regular personnel meetings were scheduled in the wing with a better record of performance and effectiveness but not in the less effective wing. In addition, the executive officer of the superior wing was a more active communicator of information to others in the wing. Likewise, Habbe (1952) noted that in an individual plant with regularly scheduled meetings of work groups, workers felt freer to talk about their problems with the supervisor and favored such meetings more than did workers of a plant without such regular meetings.

Generally, the imposition of a complex hierarchical structure tends to impede the flow of information, particularly the flow upward. The formal channels may need to be bypassed to reduce the difficulties of communication (Wilensky, 1967). The formal authority structure supposedly enables the necessary flow of technical information, but an informal structure may be needed to increase the ease of the flow, according to a study of an R & D organization by Allen and Cohen (1969). Upward communication that must be relayed through intermediate levels often suffers greatly from filtering by officials at these intermediate levels. The problem is particularly severe for U.S. presidents. The advice and judgment of foreign-area experts at the working level, for example, are blocked or filtered by intermediates to give the president more of what the intermediates believe is consistent with the presidents' beliefs and stated policies than with the realistic facts about pending crises (L. R. Anderson, 1983). Much of the faulty U.S. decisions about Iraq's intentions and capabilities leading to war in 2003 and its aftermath could be attributed to blockages and filtering of intelligence in its upward flow from field agents, analysts, and policy experts to the White House political staff and the president.

Communication and Successful Performance. The successful performance of social service professionals, industrial managers, and military officers[11] was found by Klauss and Bass (1982) to relate to aspects of the way they were seen to communicate. However, the results depended on whether the questionnaire descriptions were obtained from their subordinates, peers, or supervisors. The more successful social service professionals were seen as more open and two-way communicators by their subordinates and peers but less trustworthy by their supervisors. The more successful industrial managers were described by their supervisors as more careful transmitters, more frank, and more informative. The more successful military officers were described by their subordinates as more careful listeners and more open and two-way in their communications. They were less careful transmitters, according to their peers.

Successful leadership hinges on access to information. Leaders who successfully influenced community opinion about public affairs, education, and family planning in

450 households in a South African black township were found by Heath and Bekker (1986) to have greater exposure to newspapers and television than were those who were not influential. In comparison with the nonleaders, the leaders were more active in interpersonal communication. The network opinion leaders also had more contact with white change agents.

Media of Communication

Networks may be built on consistent patterns of oral, written, or electronic contacts or combinations thereof. The medium will make a difference in what happens and how. Channels of oral communication are favored over channels based on written messages. Face-to-face meetings are favored over telephone conversations (Lee & Lee, 1956). Oral communication is promoted by the cultural norms of information sharing in the organization. Written communications are substituted in the absense of such norms (Dewhirst, 1971b). Crucial information can be communicated orally through successive channels more readily than can routine information, which is better transmitted in writing. Thus, Davis (1968b) found that routine information on parking was poorly communicated orally down the managerial hierarchy, while information on a production-oriented layoff was very well communicated orally. Nevertheless, in a survey of 72 business supervisors, Level (1972) found that in dealing with each of 10 problems at the workplace, the supervisors thought that oral communication followed by written communication was likely to be most effective. E-communication has become a favored and effective addition to networking.

Electronic Communication Networking

The mass application of electronic networking to work and life came along with more than a half century of computer and Internet development, greatly accelerated by the availability of the personal computer and the World Wide Web. The first teleworker was a Boston bank manager who installed a telephone in his home in 1876. In 1966, I forecast that in the year 2000, employees working at home would be supervised by telecommunications; supervisors in the business office and supervisees at home would be connected by cable networks (Bass, 1966). By

[11] Success was measured by the extent to which their salaries were greater than predicted by their age, sex, education, and years of service, and by the size of the operations for which they were responsible.

1996, in fact, 10% of the U.S workforce was doing some telecommuting. Two of three employees and almost all managers of Fortune 500 companies were teleworking to some degree by 2000, 137 million worldwide (Rivenbark, 2000) and by 2004, more than 30 million in the United States alone (Gibson, Blackwell, Dominicis, et al., 2002). In 2005, an estimated 400,000 U.S. federal tax returns were processed for the IRS in India. A hamburger order at a McDonald's drive-through window off of a Missouri highway goes to a Colorado call center and is ready in a few minutes at the pickup window in Missouri. A call center operator in Bangalore may service your airline reservation request for a ticket from Dallas to Atlanta (Friedman, 2005).

Teleworking

We are familiar with the extent to which work can be supervised at a distance. E-communication makes possible continued instant interaction and networking between home and office, between distant shops, between distant speaker and audience, and between diagnostician and patient. With e-communication, the network of the individual organizational member is greatly expanded. Boundaries of time, geography, and organization disappear. Time and distance to information about resources, customers, markets, remote operations, and personnel are eliminated (Mohrman, 1998). When the oral and written channels of networks are joined by e-communication and information systems, the network of the individual organizational member is greatly expanded. The time spans between interchanges are greatly decreased, and overload of information becomes a much greater problem than does underload. Although the concern for privacy and security is heightened, some of the problems that are due to organizational distance decrease. With the filtering and transmission of information by e-mail, delays are eliminated. What originates at a high managerial level in the organization can quickly reach those at the lowest managerial level. Likewise, e-mail provides instant contact between physically distant employees at the same organization level (Bass, 2005). A physically networked organization can be replaced by a virtual one using desktop videoconferencing, collaborative software, and the Internet, as well as the intranet within the virtual organization (Townsend, DeMarie, & Hendrickson,

1998). Global organizations whose units are located in many different time zones can carry on work by moving developing information from zone to zone as each unit becomes available for work. Firms can integrate organizational functions in different time zones to fit organizational purposes. Radiologists in Stockholm can give diagnosticians in Montreal second opinions about X-ray results in a few hours. Work by Trend Micro on a computer antivirus program can begin in New York, to be ready for application when an office opens in California three hours later. Wipro Technologies has 17,000 of its 20,000 engineers and consultants in India—at one fifth the labor costs of those in Silicon Valley—connected to its executives in the United States, where most of its customers are located (Hamm, 2003).

Jobs Best Suited for Teleworking. The jobs best suited for teleworking are dynamic and service-oriented, like those in management, sales, marketing, consulting, design, and project engineering (Cascio, 2000a). According to a survey of 350 executives by Lee, Hecht, Harrison, Inc. (1999), 90% of the executives used e-mail, 88% used voice mail, 81% used fax, and 53% used the Internet. When Hewlett-Packard transferred its sales force to virtual workplaces, revenue doubled (O'Connell, 1996). Teleworking at US West improved productivity by as much as 40% (Matthes, 1992). Firms like Ford and Delta Air Lines have given personnel computers for home use (Cascio, 2000a).

Telecommuting from Home. The need for business office space is reduced and home-to-office commuting time and personal and environmental costs are eliminated when workers telecommute from home. More time can be spent by home-based sales personnel visiting with customers face to face. Some members of the sales and customer relations department of Florida Power & Light operate out of their homes (Parks, 1998).

A better *work–family life balance* can be achieved with teleworking from home. When 212 teleworkers were compared with 922 nonteleworkers in telephone interviews, the teleworkers were more satisfied with their jobs and more committed to their organization. Those who worked at home had greater autonomy and were most satisfied with their jobs (Davis & Polonko, 2003). When 157 IBM office teleworkers were compared with 89 traditional workers, productivity, flexibility and work–life balance were significantly better for the teleworkers with home offices, according to a quantitative multivariate analysis (Hill, Miller, Weiner, & Colihan, 1998). While only 9% of 769 managers surveyed worked regularly from their homes, four of five in a survey of 769 managers said they would telecommute from home if they had the option (Lee, Hecht, Harrison, Inc., 1999).

All-Channel Linkage. James Barksdale, CEO of Netscape, noted that with all its personnel linked, every Netscape manager and employee could be informed directly and immediately about another major organization's announcement that might have a large impact on Netscape's business. In the past, he would have called a meeting of the top executive team for consultation about the competitive development. Then meetings would be called at lower levels until everyone in the organization had been consulted. Barksdale was now able to get a message to every Netscape employee in the world in a few minutes.

Disadvantages of Teleworking. Costs include setup and maintenance of the equipment, loss of socializing, and feared loss of visibility when it comes to personal advancement (Cascio, 2001). Other costs are information overload, duplication of effort, message ambiguities causing conflict, frustration by the loss of face-to-face (FTF) communication, and not knowing the effect on the receiver of an e-mail message. A survey of 350 executives reported that a majority felt that they are bombarded with more information than they can handle. They see much duplication of effort and unnecessary actions. They suffer from information overload and the intrusion of e-communications into their personal lives. E-communications can lack clarity and cause unnecessary conflicts. Customers are frustrated by machine responses to their telephone inquiries. Executives can be frustrated by being unable to discuss matters FTF with their subordinates. The loss of socialization is expected to be offset as people become more comfortable with the Internet, e-mail, pagers, chat rooms, instant messaging, blog information, instant exchanges about daily life, and an enlarging set of e-mail acquaintances (Abernathy, 1999).

E-Mail and Its Effects

Electronic mail provides a communication channel through which people communicate more equally. Early in its use, electronic mail was more likely to be originated by those with keyboard skills. Social and business status differences are minimized as is the ability to judge others by visual clues. When rating others by e-mail, there is less bias due to liking the other person (Weisband & Atwater, 1999). E-mail was more likely to be sent to known users and its use was encouraged by company policy.

By 1989, R&D supervisors were being E-rated more than nonsupervisors. The ratings were also having more impact on the supervisors (Fulk, Schmitz, Ryn & Steinfeld, 1989). A successful experience with one application like income tax preparation was conducive to adapting other applications (Martins & Kambil, 1999). When electronic and paper surveys were compared, little difference was found in rate of response, but response time is shorter and more comments are produced in Web-based surveys.

Absence of Nonverbal Cues. Eye contact, dress, facial expression, voice modulation, and physical gestures that are available in face-to-face (FTF) interactions are missing in E-mail without video. What are likely to be affected when FTF interactions and their nonverbal cues are absent are the clarification of the transmitted information and contextual embellishments (Birdwhistell, 1970). With E-mail, senders may be less inhibited because their feelings can be disguised more readily. This adds to the need for supervisors to provide more empowerment and trust in their subordinates (Ahuja, Robert, & Chudoba, 2003), more trust of their superiors by subordinates (Speitzer & Mishra, 1999), and peer colleagues trust in each other. Identification with their organization needs to be strengthened. But, Hallowell (1998) argues that voice mail and e-mail cannot substitute for the *human moment* of FTF interaction to allay the anxieties caused by voice mail and e-mail which often can raise uncertainties to brood over. When possible, an FTF meeting should precede the initiation of an electronic network.

E-mail and teleconferencing both eliminate many of the nonverbal cues that help clarify the information transmitted and the support for continued interaction among senders and receivers.

Effects on Influence and Leadership. Siegel, Dubrovsky, Kiesler, et al. (1986) compared the efficiency of communication, participation, and interpersonal behavior of 144 undergraduates in trios who discussed their career choices in one of three ways: FTF, by computer mail, or mediated by computer. When the trio members were linked by computer, they made fewer remarks than they did face-to-face and took longer to make their group decisions. The amount of participation in the discussion was more evenly distributed, and the members' behavior was more uninhibited (the members felt freer to use strong and inflammatory expressions). More overall influence appeared to occur in the computer-mediated condition. The group decisions shifted farther away from the members' initial individual choices than did the decisions that followed FTF discussions.

Teleconferencing and Videoconferencing

As just noted, computer-supported collaboration can be provided for FTF or physically distant individuals. Rawlins (1983) found that with audio-only teleconferencing by 20 four-person groups, the assigned leaders did not retain as much of their leadership roles as they did in FTF meetings. Rather, the leadership roles were more widely shared if the groups had a teleconference without an FTF meeting. U.S. and German engineers could avoid numerous transatlantic trips using audio and videoconferencing, although FTF meetings were required for some technical exchanges (Hart & Kamath, 1996). Craig and Jull (1974) and Rawlins (1983) all reported that FTF problem solving took longer than did problem solving by means of audio telecommunications.

Teleconferencing can be organized into different kinds of more restricted or less restricted channels of communication. For example, Pagery and Chapanis (1983) compared problem solving by closed-circuit television when central switching made it possible for only one participant to talk at a time and participants at each station were freer to intervene. Although members in the groups under the central-switching arrangement took longer to solve problems and used fewer and longer messages than did those in the less controlled condition, there was little difference in the effects of the two arrangements on the leadership processes. Integrated Voice Response (IVR), telephone touch-tone keypad inputs, and replies with voice, fax, callback, e-mail and other media can still be frustrating when you can't talk to humans except after a long delay.

Videoconferencing comes much closer to FTF communication in its ability to supply the nonverbal cues that Mehrabian (1968a) found important. Mehrabian concluded that facial expression ordinarily accounts for half of what is communicated. When eye contact is low or absent, individuals come across as less positive, warm, and friendly (Kleck & Nuessle, 1968). Short (1973), Craig and Jull (1974), and Rawlins (1983) all reported that FTF problem solving took longer than did problem solving by means of audio telecommunications.

Although videoconferencing makes more of the visual nonverbal cues possible, there are still differences between it and FTF meetings as media for linking members in problem-solving tasks. Teleconferencing is less likely to provide the same amount of opportunities for social feedback, the sociopsychological distance among members is likely to be greater, and the ability of individual members to control the flow of communication is limited. But the evidence of the differential effects of FTF meetings and teleconferencing is mixed. Strickland, Guild, Barefoot, and Paterson (1978) found that when members of a problem-solving group are linked by closed-circuit television networks, rather than by FTF meetings, they are less likely to agree on a leader. However, Nicol (1983) reported that a clearer task-leadership hierarchy emerged for 20 groups that held closed-circuit television conferences than for 13 groups who met FTF to solve a problem. No differences were seen in the extent to which socioemotional leaders clearly emerged in the two media. Teleconferencing comes still closer to an FTF meeting with the use of whiteboards and fax for the instantaneous exchange of documents.

Group Decision Support Systems (GDSS)

Bass, Gaier, Farese, et al. (1957) constructed and ran experiments on a rudimentary group decision analog computer, made possible by the newly available transistor. We correlated the responses of five participants with their group decisions and the correct answers before and after discussion. The leadership of a member was assumed to be higher if others moved closer in agreement to the member from before to after the discussion and the group decision was closer to the members'. These correlations provided an index of leadership for each of the five participants. By 1990, a highly sophisticated group decision support system (GDSS) was commercially available from the Ventana Corporation, based on continuing research (Avolio, Kahai, & Dodge, 2001). Each participant had a keyboard and monitor linked to all other member stations and the central station for an administrator. The basic software toolbox of GDSS makes possible electronic brainstorming in which participants rapidly submit comments to a question or issue to a central file and to each other. They can reorganize, evaluate, and modify ideas, proposals, and policies. Meeting Manager is the control panel of the network, which allows the administrator to prepare agendas, save session information, and edit and generate reports. Advanced software can be used to examine and quantify the relations between two sets of ideas in a matrix. The software can provide a test of the praticality of a plan. Participants identify the plan's assumptions and their importance to stakeholders, and consensus is graphed. Other software facilitates creation of outline structures, editorial processes by the group, and agreements about terminology. Groups up to 20 or more in size can be accommodated. (Basecamp is one of several similar, more current products available from 37 signals.)

Anonymity. In an experiment with 36 four- or five-person undergraduate student groups, GDSS responses either remained anonymous or were identified. The groups were treated to either *transformational* or *transactional* comments by an administrator. The transformational leadership comments were observed to encourage more fluency, flexibility, and elaboration. Inspirational leadership comments and perceptions of transactional goals contributed to creativity, but intellectual stimulation and individualized consideration comments correlated negatively with creativity. Anonymity amplified the effects of transformational leadership on group potency and group effectiveness (Sosik, Avolio, & Kahai, 1997). By itself, anonymity was less important, although in general, leadership effects were stronger under anonymity (Sosik, 1997; Sosik, Avolio, & Kahai, 1998). From a literature review, Kahai, Avolio, and Sosik (1998) concluded that the effects of anonymity on participation and satisfaction depended on the kind and degree of anonymity

and whether the virtual team members initially differed in their opinions.

Style of Leadership. Kahai, Sosik, and Avolio (1997) reported that both *directive* and *participative* leadership improved group performance in the GDSS meeting environment. Consultative comments by the administrator fostered support. Directive leadership promoted more proposals for fairly structured problems; participative leadership promoted more proposals for structured problems.

Influences of GDSS on Effectiveness. Similar experiments established that compared to FTF meetings, GDSS produced better decisions (Steeb & Johnston, 1981; Lewis, 1981; Gallupe, DeSanctis, & Dickson, 1988). However, no differences in decision quality were found in favor of GDSS by others (e.g., Ruble, 1984). Hiltz, Johnson, and Turoff (1991) used GDSS with 24 groups of professionals and managers with and without an elected leader and with and without statistical feedback. Decisions were better with a leader but not with statistical feedback. George, Eastman, Nunamaker, et al. (1990) studied assigned leadership and anonymity in GDSS in comparison to manual discussion groups. Assigned leaders in GDSS groups resulted in unequal participation rates among members. Such leaders had strong influences on outcomes in a study in Singapore (Lim, Raman, & Wei, 1994). In another study in Singapore, Ho and Raman (1991) found with 240 undergraduates that in a preference task, GDSS groups with consensus before decisions exhibited more equality of influence but members were willing to let one member dominate the final solution.

In larger groups, GDSS was found to reduce the process losses in traditional brainstorming due to production blocking, evaluation apprehension, and free riding. However, when GDSS was used in 12-member brainstorming groups, more ideas were generated than in nominal groups. However, there were no differences in productivity in six-member brainstorming groups. Small nominal groups where individuals work by themselves were more productive than members trying to produce ideas together (Dennis & Valacich, 1993).

E-Leadership

Computer and telecommunication technology make possible *e-leaders* who can exert influence on linked individuals. One or several leaders may be linked with one or several teleworkers at a distance to form virtual teams (Cascio & Shurygailo, 2002). Virtual teams make for flat organizational structures (Townsend, DeMarie, & Hendrickson, 1998). What does it take to be a successful and effective leader in the electronic environment? Much is the same as for leadership in nonelectronic circumstances. The focus is still on people (Avolio & Kahai, 2003), but particular aspects of e-networking must be considered.

The E-Environment

In the electronic environment, real-time information is available. There is greater opportunity for sharing knowledge with organizational members and outsiders. Relationships can be customized. More pressure is put on leaders from inside and outside the organization (Avolio & Kahai, 2003). With e-technology, social and technical systems are more interdependent than postulated by Trist's (1993) sociotechnical systems theory. The e-environment and the organization's structure are built and changed in coordination with each other (Orlikowsi, 1992).

Temporal Coordination. Some types of e-communication are *synchronous*. Telephone conversations, desktop networks, real-time audio and videoconferencing, electronic meeting system, and electronic displays are synchronous between leaders and followers. Other types of e-communication—for example, telephone messaging, e-mail, group schedules and calendars, e–bulletin boards, workflow applications, and non-real-time database sharing—are *asynchronous*. Replies and answers to comments and questions are not immediately forthcoming (Duarte & Snyder, 1999). When communications are across many time zones, the problems are exacerbated. Nevertheless, temporal coordination for 35 experimental virtual teams was found to moderate the negative effects of such problems (Montoya-Weiss, Massey, & Song, 2001). As noted earlier, temporal coordination makes possible continuous teleworking as teams in time zones such as Britain, India, Japan, and the United States pass on the work near the end of their respective work spells (Kimball & Eunice, 1999).

E-communications are intermittent. Instant messaging comes closest to spontaneous conversation. Ordinarily, only a "snapshot" is sent between sender and receiver. Spontaneous interaction and nonverbals are missing (Thompson, 2000; Cooper & Kurland, 2002). The social status and diversity of senders and receivers are less apparent. Personality cues are absent (Bekson & Eveland, 2000). Without full video, there is *behavioral invisibility*. Traditional forms of control and monitoring are absent (Wilson, 2001). Collegial and subordinate efforts cannot be observed. Participants can cheat, neglect team interests, and fail to anticipate others' actions (Sheppard & Sherman, 1998). Maynard (2003) suggests that ethicality may be helped by increasing trust, team tenure, and transformational leadership and by reducing team size.

Evaluation. Subordinates are evaluated less favorably in electronic than in FTF environments. Evaluations must depend on results rather than perceived effort (Perlow, 1997). Friendships formed FTF are weakened in computer-mediated environments, according to a Japanese study of a 25-person network (Fujishima & Murata, 1998).

Needs and Limitations. Leaders and their virtual teams need well-indexed, automated central data files accessible from remote locations, and a way to track teleworkers if they are mobile (Cascio, 1998). Some Internet companies, such as eBay, can be mainly online, with no particular physical identity. Brown and Gioia (2002) tracked and interviewed the top managements of a prototypical online division of a Fortune 500 firm over the first 22 months of the launch of a business venture. The investigators concluded that the online business environment was characterized by extraordinary speed, complexity, and ambiguity, requiring the leadership to become a learning organization and to deal with the tensions of image and identity with the offline parent organization. In their review of 10 kinds of e-communications, Duarte and Snyder (1999) concluded that no online was as effective as FTF communications for resolving interpersonal conflict, especially when issues were highly ambiguous and emotional. Knowledge networks, such as in research institutions, are sources of potential conflict among virtual workers. They may compete instead of cooperating if rewarded for knowledge generation, and identifying sources of ideas becomes murky (Jarvenpaa & Tanriverdi, 2002).

Required Competencies for E-Leadership

E-leaders need specific competencies to deal with the challenges of e-networks. Systematic differences in knowledge, skills, and attitudes emerged when 41 successful e-leaders were compared with 50 traditional leaders (Higgins, Jones, & Paddock, 2002). E-leaders must be role models for using e-communications. They must be comfortable in working with and through e-networking (Spreitzer, 2003). The *telepresence* of the leader needs to be felt by means of the vividness of a rich telecommunications environment and the influence effects of interactivity with team members (Steuer, 1993). E-leaders must understand what key stakeholders expect of their teams. They need to understand receivers' agendas, priorities, and motives (Cohen & Gibson, 2000). E-leaders need to be able to diagnose what is happening quickly. They need to be particularly sensitive to differences as they network across cultures and organizations. They must be more directive in leading some individuals and groups and more participative in leading others. At times, they must sense whether more direction or participation is needed with the same individuals. They must have a clear vision of what needs to done (Thompsen, 2000). In global networks, they must consider time zones, national holidays, cultural differences, and the immediate local needs and pressures as opposed to world-wide global concerns (Kerber & Buono, 2003). E-leaders must know how to use e-technology, but they also need to know how to stimulate their networks into using it.

The use of Lotus Notes increased collaboration among office workers only if the workers had previously collaborated without the software (Vandenbosch & Ginzberg, 1997). Leadership was needed. E-leaders need to know how to avoid or resolve the conflicts that arise in knowledge networks about responsibilities and credit for knowledge creation (Jarvenpaa & Tanriverdi, 2002).

Most e-leaders continue to have FTF relations with some of their nearby associates as well as from mutual visiting with distant ones. They need to know how to balance their concerns and time between close and distant followers. Those depending on e-communications need to be made to feel they can carry as much weight as those engaged in FTF. E-leaders need to remain alert for miscommunications and misinterpretations. They need to communicate their intentions (Avolio & Kahai, 2003a). Until they receive reassuring replies, they have to live with uncertainties created by their initiations, suggestions, and advice. Cascio (2000) summed up five requirements for e-leaders: (1) an open, positive attitude focused on solutions to issues; (2) the ability to lead in the absence of structure and control; (3) a results-oriented management style; (4) effective formal and informal communication skills; and (5) the ability to delegate and follow up effectively.

Other Necessary Factors in Effective E-Leadership

To expedite teleconferencing, Solomon (1998) suggested that for conference effectiveness, a rotating leader be chosen by the group and written agendas be distributed before the meeting, including the length of time allotted to it. The leader should recap the discussion goals at the beginning of the meeting and encourage everyone to participate. Notes on the main points of the conference should be distributed afterward.

Although interpersonal trust among managers and employees in 631 groups was found to be even more important in FTF groups than virtual teams, *cognitive* trust (as distinct from *affective* trust) in the e-leader was of particular consequence. E-leaders promote cognitive trust by demonstrating their competence, responsibility, and professionalism to their virtual team members (Staples, 1999). Nevertheless, affective trust is also important. Jarvenpaa, Knoll, and Leidner (1998) compared the trust in 29 global virtual teams that communicated solely by e-mail. Compared to the low-trust teams, the higher-trust teams began by introducing themselves and providing information about their personal backgrounds. They were led to set clear roles for one another.

E-leaders need to establish norms that emphasize the appropriateness of sharing perspectives and the acceptance of task-based conflict. Personality conflict is to be avoided. E-leaders need to help deal with adversity and provide substitutes for the social support available in FTF teams (Zaccaro & Bader, 2002). They also need to make sure that communications are secure. They need to provide training time for their subordinates to learn e-networking (Thompsen, 2000). They need to confirm what they understand in communications they receive (Cooper & Kurland, 2002). Meetings of all connected members and leaders are important and should begin with a roll call of all members announcing themselves. Senders always need to identify themselves and know how to ensure needed follow-up communications (Cascio, 2002).

As with initially FTF leaderless groups, in a longitudinal study of six virtual project teams, there were early struggles for leadership (Furst, Rosen, & Blackburn, 2003). Appointed or elected e-leaders need to begin a virtual team by learning more about its purpose and its individual members. E-leaders need to try to select internally motivated self-starters for the virtual team. If possible, they should first meet FTF (Cascio, 2000; McDonough, Barczak, et al., 2000). Early on, E-leaders need to clarify whether decisions will be by consensus or otherwise and whether all will share responsibility for implementing the final decision (Cascio, 2000). They especially need to work with virtual teams to reduce the members' feelings of isolation by creating a shared mental model (Kurland & Bailey, 1999) and shared expectations (Maznevski & Chudoba, 2000). They need to ensure that the team members jointly define and commit to the team's identity, goals, and routines. Both familiar and new technologies need to be implemented (Kerber & Buono, 2003). E-leaders need to cope with the self-limiting behaviors of some members that inhibit their participation due to pressures to conform or lack of self-confidence. They should do less supervising of work content and more supervising of overall performance (Cascio, 2000). E-leaders need to monitor progress toward the fulfillment of each expectation and to publicly recognize success. They also need to negotiate with partner groups and organizations for resources and support for their team (Cohen & Gibson, 2000). (For additional detailed suggestions on effectively managing virtual teams, see Cascio, 2002; Zigurs, 2003.)

Leaders' Relations

Hart and McLeod (2003) studied seven virtual teams of professionals, national and global. The investigators examined e-mails, diaries, interviews, audioconference transcripts, and rated strength of relations with others. They inferred that in virtual teams, close personal relations were developed one message at a time. But most messaging was task-related and not about relationships. Personal content had little to do with developing strong personal relations. This suggested that virtual team-building activities should follow, not precede, work on tasks. Those linked with strong rather than weak relationships communicated frequently, with short messages. Those in weaker relations used longer messages, as they needed to add opinions, reasons, and explanations. Leaders needed to encourage communications among the members to work together on tasks and problem solving. Relations were strengthened by working together to solve problems. Leaders assumed fewer roles in teleconferences than in FTF meetings (Rawlins, 1989). E-leaders of projects in six high-tech firms had to change from their FTF roles. They had to give up some of their technical work and take on more negotiating to help different virtual teams work together.

Shared Leadership. The rated potency, social integration, problem solving, and effectiveness of *elected* leadership in approximately seven-member virtual teams were compared with *informally shared* leadership. The participants were 206 social workers developing community revitalization plans. The social workers were linked by e-mail, groupware, fax, and telephone for 10 weeks. The informally shared leadership had a positive effect. According to hierarchical regression analyses, the shared leadership of the virtual team members did add significantly to the four outcomes ($\Delta R^2 = .43, .46, .36, .15$) (Pearce, Yoo, & Alavi, 2004). Avolio and Maritz (2000) concluded that the models of e-leadership to deal with virtual interactions need to be based on the fundamental principles of effective leadership. With e-leadership, command and control leadership will need to give way to more sharing of leadership and shared mental models by leaders and followers of how they can collaborate and what they need to accomplish.

Organizational Actions. At the organizational level, many e-leader actions are needed. E-leaders of global networks have to provide strategic direction and focus. They need to set organizational goals and align them with strategies. They need to provide virtual teams with organizational support. They need to ensure early experiences with new technologies. Transformational leadership is an effective style for e-leaders. Passive, laissez-faire leadership is contraindicated (Davis & Bryant, 2003).

Leadership in Experimental Communication Networks

Communication networks circumscribe who can communicate with whom, thereby affecting interactions, the group's performance, and the potential leadership process. The control of the channels of communication among members of a group has been used widely to examine systematically the effects on performance and leadership of the network of arrangements provided. Bavelas (1950) originated a laboratory experiment to study the effects of systematic changes in who among five participants could communicate directly with each of the other participants. Bavelas dealt poker hands to the five members of a group. The members could communicate with each other only by written messages. The object was to select the one best poker hand from the combined cards of all the members. The groups differed in communication channels, as shown in Figure 29.4. In the circle arrangement, the members had an equal opportunity to send messages to and receive messages from

the member in the position to their left and the member in the position to their right. In the chain, members in peripheral positions could send messages through intermediaries toward the position in the center. In the wheel, four of the members had equal opportunities to send messages to the person in the center and could also communicate with adjacent members. In the Y, three members could send messages to a fourth person in the central position, but the fifth member was required to communicate with the member in the center through another member. In the star, all communications had to flow through the central position. The kite added an open channel between two of the peripheral positions. These networks contrasted with the all-channel network, in which any member could send messages to any other member.

The Standard Design

Subsequently, Leavitt (1951) developed a standardized task that was free of the potential bias that could occur from differences among members who knew how to play poker. At the beginning of each trial, each of five participants was given a card on which five of six symbols were printed; one symbol was missing from each card, and each card lacked a different symbol. The problem each time was to have the group discover and record the one symbol that everyone had in common. The participants were seated around a circular table and were separated from one another by five vertical partitions. They passed messages to one another through open interconnecting slots—the only way of communicating. Leavitt analyzed the pattern of messages that developed and the speed with which the problem was solved when a particular network of channels was open for use.[12]

Centrality. Organizational centrality was greatest in the wheel and decreased in the following order: Y, chain, and circle. The star network was more centralized than the kite network. The greater the inequalities in the opportunities for different members of the network to communicate, the more the members differed in centrality. The star and Y networks are most centralized because

Figure 29.4 Communication Networks and Other Networks

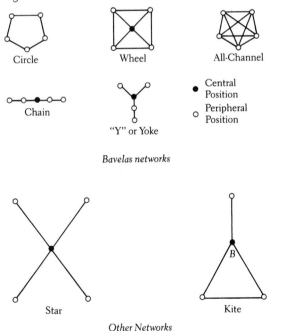

Circle   Wheel   All-Channel

Chain

"Y" or Yoke

● Central Position
○ Peripheral Position

Bavelas networks

Star   Kite

Other Networks

SOURCE: R. Dubin, Stability of human organizations. In M. Haire (ed.), *Modern Organizational Theory.* (New York: Wiley, 1959, 1962)

[12]Reviews of the method and outcomes of research can be found in Cartwright and Zander (1960), Glanzer and Glaser (1961), and Mulder (1963).

one member has a central position and all the others occupy peripheral positions. The circle and all-channel
networks are least centralized, since all members have
equal opportunities to communicate. Individual member
centrality exists in three ways: a person in a network is
more spatially central, more central in the exchange of
information in the network, or more central in the decisions of the network. Ordinarily, central positions and
those who occupy them have greater position power
because of their greater access to information and the
control of its distribution. This power makes those in central positions more influential with those who occupy peripheral positions in the Bavelas-Leavitt networks—a
finding that was confirmed in numerous studies.[13] The
network member who occupies a position of centrality is
most likely to emerge as the network leader. However,
Abrahamson (1969) removed the partitions that prevented group members from seeing one another. In the
FTF situation, central members emerged as leaders only
when no dominance owing to personality was present.
Abrahamson concluded that an individual's centrality
contributes to his or her emergence as a leader only when
physical isolation prevents personality factors from having an impact.

Effects of Network Centralization. Centralization of
a network has important effects on the network's performance. Bales (1953) observed that since the group member who was able to control the communication network
was most likely to emerge as the leader, the emergence of
leadership was more frequent in the star network, with its
one central position, than in other networks (see also
Shaw & Rothschild, 1956).

Leavitt (1951) found that speed in solving problems,
agreement on who is the leader, satisfaction with the
group, and development of an organization were highly
correlated with the organization centrality of the network.
That is, it took the least time to solve problems and to
agree on leadership when there was one clear central position, such as in the Y network. It took more time in the
chain and the most time in the circle, in which there was
no central position. The circle network experienced difficulty in developing a stable structure for problem solving. However, Burgess (1969) showed that differences in

[13] See, for example, Cohen, Bennis, and Wolkon (1961); M. L. Goldberg (1955); and Shaw, Rothschild, and Strickland (1957).

the performance of the various networks tended to disappear once groups had worked under a given arrangement
for a time and had attained a steady state—particularly if
contingent reinforcement was used to influence member
performance.

Development of Centralization. Consistent informal
roles emerged within the restrictions of the formal networks, more in some networks, less in others. Little informality was possible in the wheel network. The highly
restricted wheel network rapidly developed a stable hierarchy that conformed to the formal demands of the
system. In that network, the central person sent out information to all participants once he or she had received information from all. In contrast, all-channel groups could
display much more variety in the informal organizations
they built, particularly in distributing answers. Some
evolved a system in which each person sent answers to
every other member, while others developed patterns
identical to the wheel or to the chain. The groups that
were formally restricted to the circle network had the
greatest difficulty developing and maintaining a single
formal pattern of communications. Over many trials,
they tended to fluctuate in the particular patterns of communication they used, especially in exchanging answers
(Guetzkow & Simon, 1955).

Usually, a network that began with a central position or
informally developed a centralizing procedure was able
to complete the task faster, with fewer errors (Mulder,
1960). Thus, Cohen, Robinson, and Edwards (1969),
who studied groups that were required to solve experimental problems of organization, found that centralized
problem-solving systems were developed by 211 subgroups in both the wheel and the all-channel networks.
However, such centralization was likely to give rise to less
satisfying peripheral jobs. There was less opportunity for
members as a whole to modify their own organization, to
learn about how the organization operated, to be flexible,
and to be creative when new challenges were imposed
on the group (Bass & Ryterband, 1979). More will be said
about this later.

Roles and Role Structures. Participants who occupy
peripheral positions carry out different tasks from those
who occupy central positions. For example, those in
peripheral positions spend more of their time receiving

information (Guetzkow & Simon, 1955). Only the participant in the central position spends a great deal of time compiling data, forming solutions, and transmitting answers.

Using 76 five-member groups with Leavitt designs, Guetzkow (1960, 1961) found that three types of roles and role structures tended to emerge. The central participant tended to receive information, formulate answers, and send answers. The peripheral participant sent his or her own missing information and received answers. The relayer passed on his or her and other information and relayed answers. The wheel and all-channel networks tended to develop two-level structures consisting of a central person and four peripheral members. One-third of the circle groups developed three-level structures consisting of a central person and four peripheral participants. One-third of the circle groups developed three-level structures consisting of a central participant, two relayers, and two peripheral participants. Two-thirds of the circle groups did not develop organized structures of mutually supporting roles. Groups with differentiated role structures solved the problem faster than did those that remained undifferentiated. The central participants and the relayers perceived the structure more accurately than did the peripheral participants in all except the all-channel groups. The central participants also sent more messages containing proposals for the organization and nominated themselves more often as leaders.

Stability of Leadership. A. M. Cohen (1962) observed greater continuity of leadership in communication networks when members could elect their leaders. Cohen and Bennis (1961) studied groups with changing structures. They found that groups that had changed from a wheel to a circle network tended to organize themselves into a more efficient chain system, but with different leaders than had been present in the wheel network. Also, networks with elected leaders retained the same leaders longer than did those that were not permitted to elect leaders.

Central versus Peripheral Involvement. Zander and Forward (1968) found that participants who were in central positions developed a stronger desire for their groups' success than did participants in peripheral positions. Participants whose need to avoid personal failure exceeded their need for personal success tended to become more concerned about their group's performance than participants whose need for personal success was greater than their need to avoid failure.

Centrality and Satisfaction. Centralized groups typically have one member at their hub, who is likely to be the most satisfied. In routine tasks, the more centralized the structure, the more efficiently members solve problems, but those in the more numerous peripheral positions may remain less satisfied (Cohen, 1964). Shaw and Rothschild (1956) found that the occupant of the central position in a star design was more satisfied; otherwise, the other participants' dissatisfaction did not differ in the various network structures. Using the same designs, Shaw, Rothschild, and Strickland (1957) determined that the satisfaction of participants was a joint function of centrality and the amount of support the participants received. Central members, more than peripheral members, tried to change the opinion of those who disagreed. However, if the central members failed, their satisfaction changed more than did that of the peripheral members. Cohen, Robinson, and Edwards (1969), like many others, found that the satisfaction of members differed with their position in the system. Also, it was somewhat higher in decentralized networks. Vannoy and Morrissette (1969) obtained results suggesting that although satisfaction with a role in the network was related to its centrality, satisfaction with one's group was related to the effectiveness of the group's network operations.

In an experimental effort to detect the underlying elements that were of consequence, Trow (1957) studied groups of participants who were matched according to their scores on the need for autonomy. Some members were led to believe that they occupied positions of centrality, and others were led to believe that they occupied positions of dependence. The autonomous situation provided greater satisfaction than the dependent situation. The effect of centrality on satisfaction was positive but not significant.

Access to Information and Its Distribution. Trow (1957) analyzed the interacting effects of providing the occupant of a position in a communications network with access to information and with access to communication channels with others. Perceived status was more a matter of access to the communication channels than to knowledge. On the other hand, Guetzkow (1954) found that persons in central positions had better knowledge and understanding of the network than did persons in peripheral positions. Changing the information available to members had an effect similar to that of changing the centrality of their position or the channels available to their position (M. E. Shaw, 1954a). In a follow-up of this earlier finding, M. E. Shaw (1963a) studied the influence of the availability of information in various networks. Compared to group members with no previous information about the problem, members with an informational advantage were found to enter the discussion earlier, to initiate more task-oriented communications, to find their suggestions accepted more frequently, and to be rated by others as contributing more to the group's task. Likewise, Gilchrist, Shaw, and Walker (1954) varied the information available to the four members of a wheel network. They found that the centrality of a position rather than available knowledge of the problem generated the emergence of the leadership and the satisfaction.

Other Contingent Factors. Planning opportunities made a difference. Members were more likely to learn how to use their own position to the best advantage of the group when the group was given the opportunity to plan between trials, particularly if members were connected with each other by open channels (Guetzkow & Dill, 1957). The members were also likely to develop different patterns of communication, depending on the amount and type of previous experience they had with alternative networks (A. R. Cohen, 1964).

The placement of persons of lower or higher status or esteem in key positions could alter the outcomes of communication networks. For G. B. Cohen (1969), the presence of high-status members in positions of centrality facilitated the networks' performance. Nevertheless, low-status members became more effective in positions of centrality. Cohen concluded that in a pluricentral social system, the various centers of influence should have easy access to communication with all parts of the organization. Consistent with this conclusion, Mohanna and Argyle (1960) assigned sociometrically popular and unpopular participants to wheel and circle networks. They found that wheel groups with esteemed central members

learned faster than did the other groups and required less time and fewer messages to solve the problem.[14]

Networks and Effective Leadership Style

M. E. Shaw (1955) compared democratic and authoritarian (order-giving) leaders of the different communication networks and found that the type of network made less of a difference than did leadership style. Speed and accuracy of performance were greater under authoritarian than under democratic leadership, but the members' satisfaction with and nominations for leadership were greater under a democratic style of leadership. Nevertheless, the type of communication network imposed on the group also determined which kind of leadership would be most effective. The central member of the wheel or yoke network and a designated member in the all-channel network were instructed to be coercive (to use the power of their position to require compliance) or to be persuasive by convincing with logic and information. Fewer errors in information were made in all three types of networks. However, the relative superiority of coercion over persuasion was greatest in the wheel network, was less great in the yoke network, and was least apparent in the all-channel network. But under all three conditions, as might be expected, members were less satisfied with coercion than with persuasion. In the all-channel and yoke networks, the same or similar amounts of decision-making errors occurred with persuasive and coercive leadership. Only in the wheel network were there fewer decision-making errors under coercive than under persuasive leadership (Shaw & Blum, 1966; Shepard, 1956).

Influence of Personal Factors

The placement of individuals with particular personal attributes in central positions or the use of participants who have some strong personal characteristics may systematically affect the outcomes of a communication network. However, M. E. Shaw (1960) failed to find that the homogeneity of members of a network in such attributes as intelligence, acceptance of authority, and individual

[14]As was noted in Chapter 13, efficiency is increased and conflict is reduced in organizations when one's self-esteem is congruent with the importance of the position to which one is assigned.

prominence changed depending on whether centralized or decentralized structures resulted in more satisfaction and efficiency. But Trow (1957) observed that the stronger the participants' desire for autonomy, the higher was the correlation between the participants' satisfaction and the extent to which they believed they occupied positions of centrality.

Cohen and Foerst (1968) studied groups composed of *repressors* (members who repress or deny anxiety) and *sensitizers* (members who react to anxiety and worry). They found that leadership was significantly more continuous in the groups of repressors than in the groups of sensitizers. The groups of repressors developed centralized systems earlier than did the groups of sensitizers. Nevertheless, when given the opportunity, both types of groups rejected the all-channel network in favor of the centralized structure.

The centralized networks produced the fastest solutions with the fewest errors in the simplest kind of problem-solving situation, such as finding the common symbol. But the superiority of the centralized star, wheel, or yoke disappeared when the problem was made more complex by adding "noise" to the communications. For instance, when participants had to solve anagram problems for which they might or might not need information from one another, noise and irrelevant information in the communication system resulted in differences in the efficiency of the various networks. The effectiveness of a communication network depended on the characteristics of the task. No one type of network was always best (Glanzer & Glaser, 1961).

Implications for Organizational Leadership

Organizations are composed of networks that contain one or more of the types above. Moreover, the networks in a particular organization are interrelated and may vary from well-structured networks carrying regular task-related messages to loose, informal networks (Guetzkow & Simon, 1955).

In real-world organizations, communications are involved in the exercise of authority, the exchange of information, the completion of specific tasks, friendship, and status. In communication networks based on authority and those based on information, the information typically flows in opposite directions. That is, information in networks that are based on authority flows from the persons who are in positions of authority down to subordinates. In contrast, in many networks that are based on information, the information flows primarily upward from those who provide information to those who collect that information for use in decision making; as a consequence, the potential for conflict is great.[15]

Uses. Network experiments can be used to simulate some particular organizational problem. In one such simulation by Hesseling and Kormen (1969), five participants represented each of five separate departments of a manufacturing company: sales, R & D, planning and production, organizational methods, and purchasing and subcontracting. All participants received complete information about the procedures of the company and a functional description of their respective departments. They were also given the necessary information to contribute to the decision-making process in their respective departmental roles. The purpose of the simulation was to discover, within a time limit of five 15-minute periods, the best working combination of the product's design, delivery time, and price so they would be able to accept or reject a customer's order. The participants were given sufficient time to discuss as a team how to organize the different departments' roles. Only written communication could be passed among the five department heads. The participants were left to form their own network. The analysis focused on what kinds of networks emerged in such circumstances to yield the best combination of outputs. Centralization might promote speed of decision, but quality of decision depended on other factors.

It may be impossible to translate laboratory and simulation findings directly to large organizations. Yet these experimental networks are analogous to real organizational ones. The chain is seen in the vertical and horizontal serial communication linkages in an organization shown in Figure 29.5. The meeting of the board of directors is an all-channel network. The typical line organization is a yoke. For many specific operations in an organization, persons find themselves at the hub of the wheel (Dubin, 1958).

---

[15] Detailed in Chapter 13.

Figure 29.5 Examples of Operational Networks

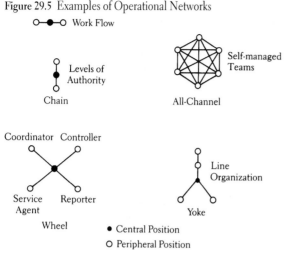

SOURCE: R. Dubin, Stability of human organizations. In M. Haire (ed.), *Modern Organizational Theory.* (New York: Wiley, 1959, 1962)

Statistical Proxies

Kerr (1977) and Kerr and Jermier (1978) reasoned that social, organizational, and physical arrangements can be organized to improve the performance of individuals, teams, and organizations when the demands of a task are known. Also, ways can be found to provide mechanisms and alternatives for the various functions of the formal leader.

Proxies for Leadership: Forms of Circumstantial Moderators

Howell, Dorfman, and Kerr (1986) classified moderators of leadership performance and its effects as neutralizers, enhancers, supplements, and substitutes for leadership.[16] *Neutralizers* do not directly correlate with the outcomes but cancel the leader-outcome relationship. *Enhancers*

---

[16] In terms of multiple regression analysis, employed to test for these moderators of the effects of leadership on outcomes, if $y = ax + bz$, when x is leadership behavior, z is the moderator, and y is predicted subordinate performance, then:

    z is a *neutralizer* if b is negative and z, although correlated with x, does not correlate with y;

    z is an *enhancer* if b is positive and z does not correlate with y;

    z is a *supplement* if it correlates with y, adding to the correlation of x with y;

    z is a *substitute* if it correlates with y while x adjusted for z does not.

augment the leader-outcome relationship. *Supplements* contribute to effects on the subordinates' performance but do not cancel out or augment the leader's direct effects. Of most interest to subsequent research were *substitutes* for leadership, variables that make the leadership impossible or unnecessary.

Neutralizers. Neutralizers make it impossible for leaders to influence the outcomes of subordinates' performance (Howard & Joyce, 1982). For instance, a leader who is supportive and considerate may have little or no impact on highly authoritarian subordinates. The subordinates' authoritarianism neutralizes the leader's support. Supportive leadership would ordinarily promote better performance outcomes (Weed, Mitchell, & Moffitt, 1976). In examining data from 558 staff members of 25 nursing homes, Sheridan, Hogstel, and Fairchild (1985) expected and found that the effects of the supervisors' leadership activities were neutralized. They were significantly weaker in nursing homes with policies and practices that resulted in uncertain work goals and the lack of sufficient rewards for the subordinates' good performance. Another potential neutralizer was the location of the nursing home. The responses of staff members to poor leadership behavior, such as quitting, were expected to be neutralized in small-town locations because there were few alternative jobs available to staff members. Other neutralization of supportive leadership might occur when: (1) cohesive work groups had antimanagement norms; (2) subordinates failed to respect the leader's competence; (3) subordinates were antiauthoritarian with an internal locus of control and a strong need for independence; (4) subordinates did not share the leader's or the organization's goals and objectives; (5) subordinates did not depend on the leader for resources; (6) subordinates worked at a physical distance from the leader; (7) the supportive leader lacked upward influence; and (8) union, civil service, or other institutional constraints prevented the leader from influencing the distribution of organizational rewards (Howell, Bowen, Dorfman, Kerr & Podsakoff, 1990).

Enhancers. A supportive leader who also has influence with a higher authority will have more of an impact on the outcomes of subordinates' performance than one who does not have such influence. Influence with higher-ups will enhance the effect of supportive leadership on the subordinates' performance.

The same variables, such as the norms of a cohesive work group, may neutralize or enhance the leader's effect. If the cohesive group's norms are counter to the leader's and the organization's objectives, the cohesion will offset the effect of the leader on the member's performance. If the cohesive group's norms are in alignment with the leader's and the organization's objectives, the cohesive norms should enhance the leader's effects on the members. Summarizing research through 1988, Howell, Bowen, Kerr, et al. (undated) concluded that the following enhancers should increase the impact of supportive leaders: (1) cohesive work groups with promanagement norms; (2) the leader with important, highly visible organizational responsibility; (3) leaders with a great deal of upward and lateral influence; (4) leaders with a strong resource base; (5) subordinates who are highly dependent on the leaders for resources; and (6) an organizational culture that is supportive of management. The effects on outcomes of the leaders' task-oriented guidance should be enhanced by (7) the subordinates' respect for the leaders' competence; (8) the leaders' reward power; (9) visible, influential champions of the leaders within or outside the organization;[17] (10) a crisis atmosphere; and (11) superordinate goals. Dorfman, Howell, Cotton, et al. (1992) found that the higher rank and expertise of company-grade commissioned officers supervising NCOs in the air defense artillery could enhance the impact of the COs' supportive leadership.

Supplements. Computerized decision support systems exemplify designed supplements to leadership. These are preplanned approaches to solving designated kinds of problems that attempt to parallel systematically the behavior and thought processes of decision makers and can be used to supplement leaders' judgments. They do not substitute completely for the leaders. Rather, they are used by leaders to make a final integrated decision (Wedley & Field, 1984). Howell and Dorfman (1981) demonstrated that for 220 hospital workers, such supplements could be seen in the extent to which their intrinsic

task satisfaction, routinization, and task feedback contributed directly to the employees' commitment or satisfaction or both without inhibiting or augmenting the leaders' more direct influence on the same outcomes. Again, in a study of university counselors, Howard and Joyce (1982) demonstrated that good peer relationships supplemented the leaders' consideration and initiation.

Substitutes. When substitutes for leadership are present, they replace supportive leadership. Leadership by itself will be expected to be of little or no consequence to the satisfaction and performance of subordinates. Logically and empirically, substitutes directly affect the performance of subordinates, while the leadership does not. The substitutes act like neutralizers to cancel the leader's effect on the outcomes of subordinates' performance (Howell, Dorfman, & Kerr, 1986). Interviews with those who were responsible for supervisory professionals, such as research directors and nursing supervisors, talked repeatedly about substitutes for leadership in professional settings. The work itself emerged and directed the professional worker without the need for the leaders to intervene (Wall, 1986). A highly predictable work flow, as a consequence of bureaucratization and centralization, could substitute for control by supervisors (Comstock & Scott, 1977).

In predicting subordinates' commitment to an organization, both Kerr and Jermier (1978) and Howell and Dorfman (1982) found that the formalization of an organization is a strong substitute for the leader's assigning of work. Dorfman, Howell, Cotton et al. (1992) showed that organizational formalization could substitute for directive, participative, and representative leadership of previously mentioned air defense artillery commissioned officers. Formalization is less of a substitute for the leader's specification of the rules. It is also less of a substitute for role clarification by the leader in the prediction of employees' satisfaction. Howell and Dorfman (1986) ascertained that organizational formalization was a weak substitute for the leader's specification of procedures in the prediction of the satisfaction of professionals. Further indirect support showing that organizational formalization could moderate and substitute for leadership in affecting outcomes for subordinates was obtained by Freeston (1987) and Podsakoff, Todor, Grover, and Huber (1984). Kerr and Jermier (1978) and Kerr and

---

[17]Both J. Edgar Hoover's and Hyman Rickover's postponed retirement and continued success as leaders over many decades within the FBI and the U.S. Navy, respectively, depended, in great part, on the extent to which they had many congressmen to champion their causes.

Slocum (1981) found that the subordinates' ability, professional orientation, and desire for autonomy made the addition of task direction from the leader counterproductive. In the same way, Sheridan, Vredenburgh, and Abelson (1984) reported that for 98 supervisors and head nurses and their 670 nurses in four hospitals, the nurses' education, group cohesion, and available work technology substituted for the head nurses' leadership in directly and indirectly affecting the nurses' job performance. The administrative climate of the hospitals acted as a neutralizer.

Other Substitutes. Much of what are considered conscious acts of leadership today were attributable in static traditional societies to highly internalized norms, rules, and values. Compliance was a matter of habit, as was the avoidance of guilt or shame. Except for outlaws, one did what one was expected to do, without explicit direction, monitoring, and reinforcement by a leader (Gardner, 1986a).

Group processes could substitute for leadership. P. B. Smith (1984) found that the manager's role in area management teams of British social workers was relatively unimportant in predicting the effectiveness of the team compared to group process variables such as the personal involvement of members and the low denial of conflict. Substitutes for leadership were also seen as possible when reward systems could operate independently of the leader based on commissions, piecework, incentives, and profit sharing for work done. Also, expert staff personnel could serve as substitutes directly to subordinates without the leader's intervention (Howell, Bowen, Kerr, et al., undated).

Pitner (1988) validated 11 of 13 hypotheses concerning possible substitutes for leadership in the educational context. Staff contributions, differences in teaching, and the structure of the organization could serve as substitutes for leadership in affecting subordinates' performance and attitudes, according to 450 surveyed teachers from 47 schools.

The features of sociotechnological jobs and organizational designs like those advanced by Cherns (1976) are a particularly important source of substitutes for leadership. The computer display itself can give immediate, direct feedback to the employee who is working at a computer terminal about the employee's absolute speed and errors as well as the employee's performance. The display can be contrasted with previous work, standards, and norms. Organizational feedback about performance, which is ordinarily transmitted through supervision, can be sent directly to the employee to promote self-monitoring and self-evaluation. Team operations in which members share responsibility for achieving team objectives can be rewarded on the basis of the team's productivity without supervisory intervention. The team as a whole and its individual members, instead of a supervisor, become the substitute sources for planning, directing, and controlling.

Jones (1983) showed that workflow could be controlled as much by the task structure of the role formalization as by the leader's use of reinforcement. In a study of 220 hospital personnel, Howell and Dorfman (1981) dealt with role ambiguity and conflict. They used the subordinates' ability and experience and the formal organization to substitute for specific supportive leadership behaviors that ordinarily boost the subordinate's job satisfaction and organizational commitment.

Other Analyses of Proxies for Leadership. Proxies for leadership were analyzed as moderators of leader-outcome relationships. Podsakoff, Todor, Grover, and Huber (1982) used moderated regression analysis to test for the effects of substitutes for leadership on the relationship between leaders' contingent reward behavior and subordinates' satisfaction. Change in the variance explained by the addition of the interaction term (leadership behavior multi substitute) to the regression equation was an indicator of the effect of substitution. In line with suggestions of Howard and Joyce (1982) Sheridan, Vredenburgh, and Abelson (1984) used path analysis to detect substitutes for leadership. To obtain path coefficients, they treated leadership as a function of expected substitutes and outcomes, as a function of leadership, of substitutes, and of substitutes combined with leadership. Thus, they used substitutes as a predictor of both the leadership behavior itself and of the outcomes. Posdsakoff, MacKenzie, and Bommer (1996) showed, in a hierarchical regression analysis for 1,539 employees of the statistical proxies for transformational leadership, that a few substitutes had unique effects on follower job attitudes, role perceptions, and citizenship behaviors. The employees came of various industries, levels, and organizational settings.

Applications

Neutralizers, enhancers, supplements, and substitutes can be designed into systems as needed. Jacobs and Jaques (1987) pointed to the extent to which supervision can be more effective if, independent of supervision, the structure in the situation is designed to exert demands on the individual employee that are relevant to accomplishing the work to be done. Howell, Dorfman, and Kerr (1986) suggested that coercive, autocratic leadership can be neutralized by removing the control of rewards and penalties from the leader. Inadequate leadership can be enhanced by team building to increase supportive norms. Selecting mature subordinates may provide a substitute for stable leadership. Assigning an assistant to a manager may supplement the manager's leadership.

A study by Tyagi (1985) of 168 life insurance salespersons showed that variations in jobs, such as in the opportunities they provided for using a variety of skills, enhancing the significance of the task, and allowing for autonomy, combined to account for 47% of the variance in the intrinsic motivation of the salespersons. But these variations in jobs had far less effect on the salespersons' extrinsic motivation, accounting for only 18% of it. In contrast, the leaders' trust and support, interaction facilitation, and psychological and hierarchical influence combined to account for 38% of the salespersons' extrinsic motivation but only 16% of their intrinsic motivation. The variety of skills, significance of the task, and autonomy that were built into the job could substitute more for the leadership in intrinsically motivating the salespersons and less in extrinsically motivating them. Both types of motivation contributed to improvements in the salespersons' work performance.

Self-Management

Autonomous Work Groups

Self-managing teams were discussed in Chapter 12 as illustrative of redistributing power, and again in Chapter 26 for converting the leader to becoming an external consultant and advisor to the self-managing team. Substitution for formal supervision and leadership occurs when autonomous work groups are created and self-management is introduced. Autonomous work groups and self-management by individual members of an organization are two ways in which group processes and individual dynamics are structured to eliminate formal supervision, yet achieve or better the results obtained with formally assigned leaders.

Autonomous work groups can operate without direct supervision. For the omitted supervisor's contribution, they substitute collective control by the work group members of the pace of work, distribution of tasks, and training of new members (Gulowsen, 1972). The supervisor is made redundant if the members of the work group have functionally interrelated tasks and are collectively responsible for the end products. Roles may still be differentiated. One member may still be central, others peripheral. The members must have a variety of skills so they can handle many or most of the groups' tasks. Feedback, along with evaluation of the work group as a whole, is also necessary. Wall, Kemp, Jackson, and Clegg (1986) completed a study of the long-term effects of using such autonomous work groups in manufacturing in Britain. They found that supervisory routines could be eliminated with no noticeable effects on subordinates' motivation or performance. They also found enhanced intrinsic job satisfaction among the members but only temporary increases in extrinsic job satisfaction.

Self-Managing Individuals

Building on Bandura's (1977) social learning theory, Manz (1986) argued for fostering self-planning, self-direction, self-monitoring, and self-control, which could replace otherwise needed supervision. For both the individual and the group, self-management calls for self-observation, specification of goals, cuing strategies, rehearsal, self-evaluation, and self-reinforcement (Manz & Sims, 1980). After difficult or unappealing but necessary tasks are identified, each of these processes can be incorporated into an individual's everyday job performance. Self-observation can be promoted by keeping a daily log of what one has discussed with others by e-mail or telephone. Goal specification occurs when one sets schedules and priorities for oneself. Cuing is illustrated by the example of a checkout board that was placed at the exit of a manager's office to remind her to leave word for her secretary where she was going and when she would be back. Rehearsal occurs when one records a sales presentation on a tape recorder and then listens to one's performance, correcting it as necessary. Self-evaluation is aided by keeping charts of one's progress in improving the quality or quantity of one's performance. Self-reinforcement is accomplished by building natural rewards for the performance of tasks. It may be done by searching for features of the task activities that give one a feeling of purpose, competence, and self-control (Manz, 1983). Contrary to what might have been expected, Manz and Angle (1985) noted from what was seen in an insurance firm that such self-management resulted in increased compliance by sales personnel with the company's procedures and goals.

The Paradox: Higher Authority Is Required for Self-Management

To a considerable degree, self-management by groups and individuals requires considerable delegation by a higher authority. Furthermore, higher-ups provide examples, guidance, encouragement, and support. Manz and Sims (1986b) note that self-managed autonomous groups require a *superleader* who is external to the groups. Such an external leader helps the groups become self-monitoring, set their own goals, criticize and reinforce themselves, and plan and assign tasks by themselves instead of depending on the superleader.

Helping others to shift to self-control from external control requires dealing with a variety of problems. There is a self-serving bias in attributing one's poor performance to situational rather than personal factors. Coordination may suffer. Individuals differ in their need for autonomy. Whether the concern is about the employee's developing proficiencies or the employee's current results makes a difference. Self-control with guidance from an external leader is likely to be more directly relevant to the individual's development and internalization of the desired and required job behavior. External control may be sufficient for monitoring results (Manz, Mossholder, & Luthans, 1983). With no formally appointed leader in each group, members have to be willing and able to take on the leadership task and maintenance functions as needed by the group.

Summary and Conclusions

Physical, organizational, and spatial factors have direct and indirect influence on leader-member relationships. Advances in electronic communication have made virtual leadership common. Studies of interpersonal space indicate that individuals interact more frequently with those who are located close to them than with those who are farther away. The member who occupies the head position at the table tends to assume leadership. Leaders tend to gravitate toward head positions and are expected to do so. Members who occupy head positions tend to be more influential than do those who occupy side or peripheral positions. Members tend to maintain greater physical distance between themselves and members who are of a higher or lower status than between themselves and their peers in status. Differences in status and social distance tend to be valued when the consequences of social interaction may be unpleasant and when effective group performance is desired by group members. Sociometric preferences for contact, communication, and work map the actual patterns of influence in an organization. They may be quite independent of the authority structure and are more likely to correspond with friendship, familiarity, and mutual esteem. Sociometric descriptions of actual contacts, communicants, and work partners do the same.

Individuals who live or work in close proximity to one another also exhibit a higher rate of mutual sociometric choice than do those who are situated at a greater distance from one another. At the same time, the quality of personal interaction in and achievement by the group may be facilitated by some degree of psychosocial distance between the leader and the followers. Individuals prefer greater social distance between themselves and their competitors than between themselves and those with whom they cooperate.

Virtual leadership and virtual teams are replacing face-to-face arrangements on a global scale. Electronic networking between e-leaders and their virtual teams has increased rapidly with the advent of the Internet and the personal computer. Experiments pointed to advantages and disadvantages of e-networking and e-leadership compared to face-to-face (FTF) meetings and leadership. Compared to FTF leaders, e-leaders need to have particular capabilities and to carry out particular actions. Efficient computerized group decision support systems (GDSS) have become available.

Networks are replacing hierarchical communications in importance to organizations. Research on networks in organizations and in experimental communication networks has indicated that the member who occupies a position of centrality tends to emerge as the leader. That member has greater access to communication than do other members and is thus better able to coordinate and direct the group's activities. Groups with positions of centrality within them are more efficient than those with undifferentiated role structures. The openness of network channels is directly related to the information available to a leader and therefore to the leader's ability to exert influence. Regular meetings usually (but not always) provide more continuing communications and promote the group's performance. The member who occupies a position of centrality is better satisfied with the group than are members in peripheral positions. Personal factors, such as the need for autonomy and ascendancy, moderate these effects. The experimental results tend to confirm parallel real-world organizational networks.

Experimental groups with a member in a position of centrality are more efficient than groups without differentiated role structures. Members who occupy positions of centrality that enable them to exercise control over the flow of information are most likely to emerge as leaders. They are also better satisfied with their groups than are the peripheral members. Several studies have suggested that personality factors might be influenced by the relationship between centrality and leadership. A highly submissive member was likely to become a more active participant in the group's activities when placed in a position of centrality.

Social, organizational, and physical rearrangements of how work is accomplished can be used to neutralize, enhance, supplement, or substitute for leadership. Such rearrangements may include setting up autonomous work groups and encouraging self-management. These rearrangements can benefit organizations by reducing the costs of supervision and increasing the employees' commitment and contribute to the persistence and transfer of leadership.

CHAPTER
30

Transfer and Succession

The efforts of many leaders to reach the top begin with initiatives displayed in childhood that continue unabated through adolescence into adulthood. Lyndon Johnson and Margaret Thatcher are illustrative. As adults, they obtained their reputations as successful leaders in one situation and then transferred that reputation for successful leadership to other similar situations. They and some others gained sufficient esteem and experience in their early efforts to succeed as leaders in almost any situation they entered (Bogardus, 1928; Cowley, 1931). Success in one political office served as a stepping-stone to other offices. But failure in one office could destroy one's political career (Burns, 1978), although before Abraham Lincoln was elected president, he suffered a number of defeats in earlier campaigns for lesser offices. The persisting effects of charismatic founders can dominate an organization's culture long after the founders are gone. Salaman (1977) illustrated this effect in a small, successful manufacturing firm that continued to be influenced by a charismatic leader even after he had retired and was no longer on the scene.

Although tasks and goals can be different from situation to situation, some amount of interpersonal competence is required from any leader. So there is likely to be some amount of transfer of who emerges as leader in different situations. In the same way, personal characteristics, such as energy, intelligence, assertiveness, task orientation, need for power, and other personal traits promote the persistence of the same persons emerging as leaders in a variety of times and places. Since considerable consistency is found in intelligence and various personality traits from childhood to adulthood, consistency will also be found in children's trait-associated tendencies to become leaders and their potential to become leaders as adults. For example, C. M. Cox's (1926) analyses of the biographies of 300 outstanding military, religious, and political leaders frequently found above-normal behavior traits in their childhoods, such as the desire to excel, intelligence, in-

sight, self-esteem, and forcefulness—traits usually related to leadership. Analyses that followed subjects from early childhood to retirement found that conscientiousness and mental ability predicted career success, while neuroticism was contraindicated (Judge, Higgins, Thoresen, et al., 1999).

Persistence

The persistence of an individual's attempts, success, and effectiveness as a leader across situations and time periods may be augmented by a consistent "ability to perceive the needs and goals of a constituency and to adjust one's personal approach to group action accordingly" (Kenny & Zaccaro, 1983, p. 678). It is also strengthened by the continuous power that a leader may hold during the various stages in a group's development (Quiggins & Lashbrook, 1972). In 36 firms, Miller (1993), as expected, found that long-tenured executives accumulate power and legitimacy. Their long-term followers respond more favorably to them. Persistence in leadership is further bolstered by the implicit beliefs of followers that regardless of the environmental complexities to be faced, more persistence is a virtue in leaders and shows their sense of responsibility (Graves, 1985). Such persistence in leadership behavior is often seen as characteristic of successful chief executives, manifested in their consistent support of a theme, shifting attention to that theme, granting authority down the line to support the theme, encouraging experimentations about the theme, and developing and maintaining contacts about it throughout the system (Peters, 1980). Such persistence may pay off. Staw and Ross (1980) found that marketing managers whose scenarios revealed a persistence in the same strategy as situations changed were evaluated more favorably by practicing administrators than managers whose scenarios showed that they tended to shift strategies to try to accommodate transient changes in conditions. Nevertheless, by 2006, the persistence of President G. W. Bush to "stay the course" in Iraq and his continuing support for many of his policy advisors despite their many mistakes had lost him much of his popularity with his party and the public.

The Behavior of Newly Appointed CEOs

The political behavior of newly appointed CEOs and how they restructure control within the organization, protect their own position, and implement strategy reflected their leadership in previous positions (House & Singh, 1987). Helmich (1974b) established that the origin and style of successors to 140 presidents of manufacturing firms influenced the changes and improvements that occurred in the organization. The task-oriented leadership behavior of the successors was greater than that of the predecessors, particularly during the early days of the successors' tenure. Zhang and Rajagopalan (2003) observed that strategic change was less likely in manufacturing organizations led by CEOs with long tenure in office. Some began by holding meetings with their new people; others did not. Some were more aware of the social dynamics involved in the succession; others were not. Some might bring allies and assistants with them; others entered the new post alone (Grusky, 1969). Some utilized the formal system and depended on their own authority, with a resulting increase in tension; others relied more on informal contacts to learn about what was needed to guide future actions (Gordon & Rosen, 1981). The personal learning opportunities for the successors were also likely to be of consequence (Hall, 1986). Some failed to consider individual, group, and organizational dynamics, which resulted in conflict, defensiveness, and organizational regression (Oskarsson & Klein, 1982). In a study of 227 successions over a 25-year period (Vancil, 1987) noted that the CEO served also as board chair, shared leadership with the future successor or board chair in a dual arrangement, or was a member of a team of executives. Or else the new CEO was a symbolic figurehead without real power.

Effects of the Ages of Leaders and Followers

Although there is persistence in leadership, systematic changes occur as a function of age. That is, the require-ments for success as a leader are likely to mirror the developmental stages of the leaders and the led. Early on, immaturity, raucousness, and playfulness are required. Later, these characteristics are replaced by demonstrated task and interpersonal competence. The playboy Prince Hal turned into the persuasive and determined King Henry V.

These changes have been demonstrated in studies of children at various ages. For example, observations of the spontaneous play of nursery school children by a one-minute sampling procedure indicated the existence of two approaches to leading others: persuasion and coercion. Such authoritative leadership behavior continued to be seen among three-to-five-year-olds by Barner-Berry (1982) in the ongoing informal leadership of a child even after the succession of a new formal leader. The emerging leader was also readily observed in primary school at an early age (Mey, 1936). At this age, children attempt to become leaders to satisfy their desire to influence others. Such emergent leaders tend to be tyrants or stimulators. But later, attempts to organize become more common. With continuing maturation, consistency in attempts and successful leadership increase, while rivalry decreases among would-be leaders (Toki, 1935). Increasing age brings further changes in the behavior that contributes to the success of a leader. Tryon (1939) found that among 12-year-old girls, the leaders were daring and humorous, but among 15-year-old girls, the friendly, enthusiastic, happy ones were more successful leaders. Among European adolescents, the emphasis on coercion was observed to change with maturation to a persuasive appeal to ideals (Winkler-Hermaden, 1927). Horrocks and Thompson (1946) studied the friendship choices of boys and girls aged 10 to 17 by administering sociometric tests two weeks apart. They discovered that the fluctuation in the choices of boys and girls of the same age did not differ. However, older boys and girls tended to name the same individual both times as friends, while younger children showed less overlap on the two lists. These results suggested that sociometric choices tended to stabilize in later adolescence.[1]

---

[1] The specific traits that are important to leadership are likely to change with changes in society. The pattern has to be rechecked for each generation. Therefore, the results reported here are valid only for the generation in which the data were collected; they may not apply to other generations.

Persistence in School and Onward

I. J. Levi (1930) obtained a correlation of .19 in the leadership activity of the same group of students in elementary school and later in high school. But the correlation was .52 when these children's leadership performance in junior high school was compared with their performance in high school. And D. P. Page (1935) found that the first-year leadership rank of cadets at West Point correlated .67 with fourth-year leadership rank.

Several early studies also determined that leadership in elementary school, high school, and college was predictive of later leadership in adult business and social activities. Courtenay (1938), for example, found that leadership in extracurricular activities as an adolescent was more highly related to various criteria of success as an adult than was scholarship or academic achievement. In other words, leadership, rather than scholarship, was the best predictor of later leadership.[2] Williams and Harrell (1964) reported a significant correlation of .24 between leadership in undergraduate activities and later success in business five years later, as measured by the salary level achieved. Roskens (1958) found significant correlations, ranging from .37 to .63, between college leadership and postcollege leadership. At the same time, postcollege leadership was not highly related to grades in college or to parents' occupational status.

Russell, Mattson, Devlin, and Atwater (1986) obtained a correlation of .18 between high school leadership, as measured by a self-report biodata questionnaire, and subsequent peer ratings as a midshipman leader at the U.S. Naval Academy. Similarly, Yammarino and Bass (1989) found that grades for military proficiency of students at the U.S. Naval Academy correlated with the successful patterns of leadership behavior of the same personnel as shipboard lieutenants as much as eight years later, but their academic grades at the academy were not correlated with their subsequent leadership performance.

Persistence of Leadership in Experimental Groups

As early as 1904, Terman (1904) reported an experimental verification of the consistency of leadership behavior in schoolchildren from one problem to the next. Bor-

gatta, Couch, and Bales (1954) observed that new experimental groups were more effective if they contained "great men" who had been identified in former groups for their ability, assertiveness, and social success. The "great men" continued to be influential in the new groups. Highly esteemed, active, able individuals continued to succeed as leaders in groups with different members that were faced with similar tasks. Blake, Mouton, and Fruchter (1954) reported that the leaders' contribution to the groups' decisions and dominance, as rated by different observers in different situations, yielded consistent individual differences among raters, despite the variation in the situation and the groups' composition. They also noted that as the task and groups were altered, self-ratings and others' ratings were most consistent when they were concerned with leadership and interest. They were less consistent when they were concerned with the rated effectiveness and satisfaction of others.

Borgatta, Couch, and Bales (1954) found that initially effective leaders tended to emerge as leaders in group after group to which they were assigned. Bass and Norton (1951) analyzed test-retest performance in initially leaderless discussions held a week apart. The test-retest measure of successful leadership was .90. Carter, Haythorn, and Howell (1950) studied the emergence of leaders in groups of college students who were performing the same task again after about four months. The test-retest correlations depended on the nature of the task. They ranged from .39 for discussion tasks to .88 for motor coordination tasks.

Rosenberg, Erlick, and Berkowitz (1955) studied small experimental groups that were required to cooperate in tilting an apparatus in such a manner as to move a small ball up a ramp. The persistence of leadership was highly significant among the various regroupings of members. Gordon and Medland (1965a) obtained peer nominations and ratings in small military units before and eight weeks after the reconstitution of the units. Peer nominations for leadership correlated .80 to .90 between the two situations.

Attempted leadership also showed consistencies across different task conditions. Hemphill, Pepinsky, Shevitz, et al. (1954) found an average correlation of .45 between assessments of attempted leadership by the same members of experimental groups engaged in four different tasks: reasoning, instruction, assembly, and strategy. This

---

[2] See also Clem and Dodge (1933), I. J. Levi (1930), D. P. Page (1935), and J. R. Shannon (1929).

consistency across tasks depended on the similarity of the tasks. For example, as groups developed, the same successful leaders reemerged as the same developmental tasks needed to be completed. Sterling and Rosenthal (1950) reported that when leaders and followers changed roles in different phases of their groups' development, the same leaders tended to emerge as similar phases of development recurred.

Persistence of Leadership in Industry and Elsewhere

The consistencies in leadership behavior found among developing individuals and groups and in small experimental groups were also observed among supervisors, managers, and other institutional leaders across times and places. Furthermore, those who were more effective in one situation and time were likely to be more effective at other times and in similar kinds of locations.

Consistency of Leadership Behavior. Holloway and Wolleat (1981) examined the interaction styles and supervisory behavior of trainees and concluded that individual preferences for different kinds of supervisory interactions were stable. Over a three-month period, Greene (1976a) reported rate-rerate coefficients of .60 and above for contingent reward behavior and for contingent punitive behavior by supervisors. Similar results were found for contingent reward by Szilagyi (1980b) and Sims (1977) over 3-, 6-, and 12-month intervals. Sakamaki (1974) studied the descriptions of 339 Japanese first-level bank supervisors and second-level bank managers by their more than 1,800 subordinates and colleagues. The managers remained in the same positions in the two successive years. Rate-rerate correlations of .35 and .74, respectively, were found for their leaders' orientation toward performance. The corresponding correlations for orientation toward maintenance leadership were .53 and .59.

Similar evidence about the consistency of transformational and transactional leadership was obtained for a small sample of executives with a six-month test-retest analysis of their subordinates' descriptions of their behavior (Bass & Avolio, 1989). The mass of case and anecdotal evidence available on world-class leaders also supported the contention that leadership behavior is consistent across times and similar situations.

Persistence of Effective Leadership. Considerable evidence is available concerning the tendency of the same leaders to be effective, given the same task requirements with new work groups. The impressive set of field studies of first-line supervisors is illustrative. H. Feldman (1937) studied 22 work groups that shared in savings on operating costs. One year after the project began, supervisors of groups with high savings in operations were assigned to groups with low savings, and vice versa. The order of merit of the supervisors remained practically the same despite the change in assignments. Many of the differences among groups were associated with the leaders—not with the groups they were leading. The supervisors' assignments were then shifted by chance, and the same results occurred. The relative order of performance of the groups depended on who led the groups. The groups with previously weak savings records that were subsequently led by high-savings leaders later had strong savings, while those with previous strong savings that were subsequently led by low-savings leaders later had weak savings. In the same way, J. M. Jackson (1953b) arranged for the supervisors of telephone line crews with high morale to change places with the supervisors of crews with low morale. A retest of the crews four months later showed a significant shift in the scores for morale, with the previously low groups scoring high and the previously high groups scoring low. Each supervisor tended to receive a score in his second group that was similar to that obtained in his first group. No such significant changes occurred in a set of control groups. Wyndham and Cooke (1964) also studied work groups in which the supervisors exchanged places. They found that the performance of previously ineffective groups improved under previously effective supervisors, but the performance of previously effective groups declined under supervisors of previously ineffective groups.

F. L. W. Richardson (1961) studied work groups in which the only way found to improve productivity and morale was by transferring troublesome leaders out of their groups. N. A. Rosen (1969) obtained ratings of workers' preferences for eight supervisors in an upholstering shop. Supervisors who were high and low in preference then changed places. The greater the workers' consensus in the first and tenth weeks that the new supervisor "is our leader," the greater was the increase in productivity and cohesiveness in the eleventh and sixteenth weeks.

The findings suggested that the new supervisors were evaluated in terms of their ability to help the group. In another experiment by N. A. Rosen (1970b), large changes in the preference for supervisors were associated with large gains in productivity following reassignment. Small changes in preference were associated with small gains or losses in productivity.

Transfer of Leadership

Borrowing from the general psychology of transfer, Bass (1960) developed a model to account for the conditions in which the positive and negative transfer of leadership behavior occurs. Among the major propositions were that *positive transfer* (transfer that facilitates performance) from an old to a new situation will be greater the more the new situation is similar to the old one and the more the new situation calls for the same leadership behavior as the old one to attain goals. *Negative transfer* (transfer that is detrimental to performance) will be greater the more the new situation, different from the old one and requiring new modes of leadership, is responded to with the old ways of behaving to achieve goals. The new situation is responded to as if it were similar to the old, when it actually is not. It is perceived as requiring the old ways of leadership behavior, when actually new ways are necessary.

The transfer of leadership and management at lower levels becomes increasingly difficult from one situation to another as the positions call for different technical knowledge, different human relations skills, and different required participation in planned change. Successful positive transfer requires recognition of the differences in the organizational norms. Positive transfer is easier at higher levels but may have ineffective results if the new situation turns out to have different requirements from the old one. A senior executive with the needed conceptual and organizational skills is able to transfer leadership from one organization to another but may still suffer from negative transfer effects due to differences in markets, products, traditions, and technologies (Yukl, 1998).

Military-to-Civilian Transfer

As many as 70 U.S. Army generals retire annually to enter civilian life at an age and with the skills and experience commensurate with the civilian executive levels into which they move. Ordinarily, the transfers are successful, despite the failure to prepare adequately for the transfer by careful self-analysis and an analysis of the situation into which they transfer (Whelan, 1981).

Like George Marshall before him, Colin Powell, who retired as a general and Chief of Staff, was appointed civilian Secretary of State in 2001. Starting with George Washington, many generals have been elected president. Like many military leaders before him such as Douglas MacArthur, retired general Wesley Clark sought the presidential nomination in 2004. Considerable experimental evidence confirms the positive transfer of leadership.

What transfers positively, say, if one examines the move from high-level military leadership to civilian leadership? Hill (1984) mentioned these characteristics: (1) contacts with top government and foreign officials and specialists; (2) relevant experience in dealing with boards and staffs; (3) effective skills in presentation, persuasion, and communication; (4) experience in strategic planning and decision making; (5) emphasis on clear definitions of authority and responsibility; and (6) experience with integrating operations, such as planning with research and development. Dwight D. Eisenhower illustrated the transfer that is possible from a successful military career to performance as university president and president of the United States.

But military-civilian differences may also be a source of negative transfer effects for military officers taking senior civilian executive positions.

1. A less authoritarian and more collegial style is required.
2. Civilian employees have a great deal more latitude (say, to strike) than do military personnel.
3. Delegation and coordination in civilian business and industry require much more than giving orders and expecting unqualified compliance.
4. The lack of cost control in the military and the profit orientation of civilian firms may be problems for ex-military leaders.

5. The ex-military leader may lack experience in assessing and making calculated marketing risks.

The career of Ulysses S. Grant illustrated this negative transfer. Grant was successful as the commander of the victorious wartime Union Army, although he had previously been a repeated failure in business. Later, he was also a failure as U.S. president (McFeely, 1981).

Transfer of Specialists

Administrators in one specialty readily transfer to another position in the same specialty area. For example, deans of medical schools who change jobs move into other deanships or vice presidencies at their own or other medical schools. A few return to faculty positions, retire, or take up administrative posts outside medical schools (Wilson & McLaughlin, 2001). Some scientists and technologists who wanted to transfer eventually into management positions revealed that they were motivated by needs for upward mobility, power, influence, dominance, security, and respect.

What is learned about leadership of sports teams can be transferred to leading work teams. Healthy competition among members may contribute to overall team performance if they work together effectively and do not try to undermine each other (as candidates frequently did while seeking the 2004 Democratic Party nomination for U.S. president). As shown by professional hockey teams, early experiences of success are encouraging and predictive of better subsequent performance. Taking time out in team sports for feedback, learning, and review benefits subsequent performance. The more time team members have together, learning about one another's roles and team processes and how to anticipate one another's actions, the more team performance is benefited (Katz, 2001).

However, specialization may result in negative transfer effects. Kotter (1982b) noted that when general managers adapt themselves to one specific context, they will find it difficult to transfer to a different context. For a general manager in one organization and industry to become a general manager in another organization and industry requires the ability to learn new things rapidly and to establish new relationships.

Experience as a manager, per se, is not what is important. Rather, whether the transfer of experience will be positive or negative depends on the relevance of the experience of the old position to the new position. Kennedy (1985) found that while time in service and the number of previous positions held added less than 1% to the accuracy of predicting successful leadership performance as a military officer, the assessed *relevance* of the previous positions added 20% to the accuracy in predicting successful leadership performance.

Evidence of the Effects of Positive Transfer

Positive transfer of attempted and successful leadership has been seen when groups move from one similar situation to another and if the issues they face are similar. Even if the membership changes, the same leadership may persist.

Effects of Similar Tasks. Katz, Blau, Brown, and Strodtbeck (1957) reported that groups exhibited a tendency to return to the same leader when the task performed in time 2 was similar to that performed in time 1. As reported in Chapter 6, Bass and Norton (1951) reported a correlation of .90 between successful leadership displayed by members of leaderless group discussions held a week apart. The composition of the groups and the problems discussed were the same. When one discussion was an examination and the other was not, the correlation remained as high as .86 (Bass, 1954a), but the correlation dropped to .75 when two members of each group of seven were coached between the test and retest situations on how to lead (Klubeck & Bass, 1954).

An examination of situational data collected in the screening of candidates for the Office of Strategic Services (OSS, 1948)[3] further illustrated the effects of similar tasks. Positive transfer was evidenced by the increasing correlation of leadership ratings of candidates' performance on other situational tests with their rated performance in leaderless discussions as the other situational tests became more similar to open discussions. The correlation with leadership in discussions was .30 with leadership in cooperatively constructing a giant toy, .47 with leadership in solving a problem of crossing a brook, .48

[3]The OSS was the forerunner of the U.S. Central Intelligence Agency (CIA).

with leadership in a personal interview; and .56 with leadership displayed in a debate.

As posited by the transfer model, the transfer of leadership behavior decreases when tasks differ from an old to a new situation, especially when a change from a purely intellectual activity to purely manual-mechanical activities is involved. Thus, Carter, Haythorn, and Howell (1950) found that although leaders in reasoning tasks also tended to emerge as leaders in intellectual and clerical tasks, they did not do so in mechanical tasks. Leaders in mechanical tasks tended to emerge as leaders in motor coordination tasks, but not in intellectual tasks. In an earlier study, Carter and Nixon (1949a) found a tendency for the same person to emerge as leader in clerical and intellectual tasks, but not in mechanical tasks. Thus, no transfer or even a negative transfer seems most likely when the transfer of leadership is from group tasks of the "head" to tasks of the "hand."

Effects of Similarity of Issues. The positive transfer of successful opinion leadership was reported by Jacoby (1974), who found that opinion leaders' influence overlapped in different areas. The degree of overlap of influence increased with the increase in the similarity of issues about which opinions were sought.

Effects of Changes in Membership. As long as the task stays the same in a new situation, recomposing the group membership does not seem to reduce the positive transfer effects greatly. Various experimental attempts have been made to determine whether the same individuals will emerge as leaders when members are reassigned to new groups with different combinations of leaders and followers. Bass (1949) found a correlation of .72 between the initial leadership status attained by group members in leaderless discussion groups and leadership status attained in reassembled discussion groups. Bass and Wurster (1953a) obtained correlations ranging from .51 to .66 between measures of leadership status in groups that differed in the composition of members and the problems to be discussed. Even when, in addition to changing the groups' composition, a year instead of a week intervened between the test and retest, the tendency to emerge as a discussion leader on the test and the retest correlated .53 (Bass & Coates, 1952). Arbous and Maree (1951) obtained a median correlation of .67 between the extent to which administrative candidates displayed successful leadership when they were appointed discussion leaders and the extent to which they displayed successful leadership in initially leaderless discussions. Similar research by Carter, Haythorn, Meirowitz, and Lanzetta (1951) yielded a correlation of .55. When, in addition to changing the composition of the membership, the type of discussion problem was varied systematically, the correlation in consistency of success was still .58 (Bass & Coates, 1953). Nevertheless, subtle effects can be seen when the composition of the members of a group is changed. Cloyd (1964) found that the same members tended to perform the same function in successive groups but that different functions, if needed, could be performed by the same members. An analysis of leaders' comments in discussions that had different purposes indicated to J. T. Wood (1977) that the same leaders can be successful in a variety of discussion situations with divergent goals, members, and constraints if they adapt their oral behaviors to meet varying goals and compensate for failures at previous meetings. Other members also readjust.

Members adjust for each other's behavior when they find themselves in new groups. For example, Haythorn (1952) combined and recombined the members of experimental groups. Members were rated on aggressiveness, initiative, confidence, submissiveness, sociability, leadership, and the like. Haythorn found that when one member in a group was rated high on one of these variables, other members were all rated low. It appeared that when one member exhibited a high degree of a given behavior, the other members attempted to adapt to the situation by reducing their behaviors in the same area of role performance. Similarly, Bernstein (1964) removed the dominant male from a group of rhesus monkeys. During the month he was away, the remaining males increased their dominance and social activities. Upon his return, the dominant male assumed his former position and the social activities of the other males were reduced.

Effects of Changing Task and Organizational Location. Bass (1960) analyzed the results of eight studies that reported 18 correlations between successful performance in initially leaderless group discussions and successful performance as a leader in real life. Although the median correlation was .38, the 18 correlations ranged from −.25 to .68. Correlations were higher, the more similar the real-life situation was to a leaderless group discussion. In the study mentioned earlier, Sakamaki (1974) found that the performance (P) orientation scores (according to subordinates) of 121 first-line Japanese supervisors who were not transferred correlated .35 from one year to the next. For maintenance (M) orientation, the rate-rerate correlation was .53. For nontransferred second-line supervisors, the respective correlations were .74 and .59. But for 133 transfered first-line supervisors, the corresponding correlations dropped to .03 and to −.07; and for 19 transferred second-line managers, the corresponding correlations dropped to .29 and −.08. The lack of consistency in leadership orientation for the transferred supervisors compared with those who did not transfer could be attributed to a change in the composition of the subordinates who rated them, as well as to a change in their position and social context. Misumi and Mannari (1982) clarified the importance of the similarity or difference between the old and new situations of transferred supervisors. When 67 Japanese bank managers were transfered to jobs with similar work content and social context, they tended to exhibit the same P and M orientations, as revealed in rate-rerate correlations by subordinates of .56 and .42, respectively. But when 23 other bank managers were transferred to different kinds of departments in different branches, the rate-rerate correlations dropped to .10 and −.06, respectively.

Evidence of the Effects of Negative Transfer

For Henry Ford, the automobiles he produced could be any color as long as they were black. The very successful Model T was black, but the public finally turned to his competitors for cars in different colors. Early success in situation fixates the behavior of the rigid, stubborn leader, making him or her less effective in a new, different situation that requires a new approach to problems. For example, a technical supervisor who has been a successful leader in a situation that demands precision exactness may fail to deal with the challenge of decision making in the absence of complete information when promoted to the position of general manager (Pearse, Worthington, & Flaherty, 1954). Similarly, many examples can be found of a business executive transferring his successful profit-making practices to running a government agency with disastrous results (e.g., Fishman, 1952). The political

appointees of the Environmental Protection Agency (EPA) and the Federal Emergency Management Agency (FEMA) provide illustrations.

Negative transfer can also occur for the career bureaucrat. Measures are adopted in keeping with past training. Under new conditions, not recognized as significantly different, the very soundness of the training leads to the bureaucrat's adoption of the wrong procedures. Furthermore, continued success in day-to-day routines makes the bureaucrat unable to change or see the need to change when the conditions under which the bureaucracy was organized change (Merton, 1940). Negative transfer may explain the ill-fated attempt at administrative reform in Zaire in 1973, in which the local chieftaincies were changed by rotating the chiefs outside their areas of origin. The failure of the policy was attributed by Schatzberg (1982) to the lack of timely consultation. Nonetheless, it would seem that there must have been considerable negative transfer because of the loss of legitimacy, understanding, and applicability of a chief's approach when he was moved from his home area to another.

Maladaptation. As might be inferred from Fiedler's (1967) Contingency Theory,[4] shifting leaders from situations that are favorable to them and in which they have experienced effectiveness to situations that are unfavorable to them is likely to produce negative transfer. The leaders' earlier success can result in their continuing to attempt the same leadership in the new situation, with a consequential decrement in effective outcomes. The garrison commander may not do as well when in a front-line command. The effective leader in emergencies may be unsuccessful and ineffective elsewhere. Elkin, Halpern, and Cooper (1962) observed that individuals who emerged as leaders in experimentally created mobs were not popular under other circumstances. Likewise, what is likely to make a leader effective in the early stage of development of a sensitivity training group seems to reverse in later stages of development. Data from 158 members and leaders of 20 such groups showed that trainers who were considered to have little need for control and affection tended to elicit the most favorable reactions during an early period of a group and the

---

[4]See Chapter 21.

most negative reactions at a later time (Schutz & Allen, 1966).

Negative transfer occurs when a new situation requires values different from or opposite to those fitting the old situation. Thus, the political appointments of conservative private sector executives to administer public housing programs to which they were ideologically opposed resulted in their corrupt and wasteful violations of the barest minimum standards of public service (Montgomery, 1989). A well-documented case of negative transfer of leadership was that of a school district superintendent in a midwestern suburban community. She gained a statewide reputation in educational and business circles as an energetic, innovative, and visionary leader who had converted the threat of a budgetary crisis into an opportunity to make improvements in the district. Her transformational leadership had a dramatic impact on the district. Her charisma resulted in some of her followers becoming cultlike. However, when she subsequently served for two years as state commissioner of education, none of the successful transformational leadership was seen. No cultlike following developed. No attributions of extraordinary talents and abilities were heard; no strong bonds of affection were forged with constituents. Instead, there was strong criticism of her leadership style and actions. What had worked well in a school district in crisis was counterproductive in the larger state system (Roberts & Bradley, 1987). Lombardo, Ruderman, and McCauley (1987) examined what "derailed" the promising careers of junior executives who had failed after promotion to senior levels. Derailment occurred for some who liked to work alone and couldn't build a staff if placed in a senior position. Some lacked a strategic perspective, were too controlling and results-oriented, and had trouble starting in new and more complex situations. Some who were conceptually strong and creative lacked sufficient attention to detail and follow-through.

Succession

The process of succession is an examination of the transfer process from another vantage point. Antecedents that promote the more effective replacement of one leader by another and the consequences of replacing one leader with another provide a further opportunity to see how the posi-

tive and negative transfer of leadership may occur (Gordon & Rosen, 1981). This implies that leaders make a difference to the performance of their groups and organizations, although as was noted in earlier chapters, organizational variables may be more important (Pfeffer, 1977). Meindl and Ehrlich (1987) argued that the effects of leadership on organizations were a romantic fiction, a misperception of cause and effect, which attributed the success or failure of organizations to their leaders. Nevertheless, who succeeds as leader is important to group and organizational performance, even though other variables may be more important (Thomas, 1988). Succession planning has been a major strategy for many boards, CEOs, and their organizations since before the 1970s. Some new practices are emerging (Beeson, 1998) to form an effective pipeline of potential CEOs. At each successive career stage, each potential successor needs to develop skills, use time effectively, and adjust values in meeting different leadership challenges and managing others. At each transition, fewer old tasks and more new ones need to be handled (Charan, Drotter, & Noel, 2001).

House and Singh (1987) pointed to the importance of the executive succession process—a phenomenon in all groups and organizations that survive. In the succession process, much power is transferred, along with control of the organization's relationship with its outside environment. A change of executives is often associated with major changes in the organization (Virany, Tushman, & Romanelli, 1985). The succession is a focal point of political processes within the organization (Zald, 1965). Decisions about the succession express the particular political preferences of the organization's constituencies (Pfeffer & Salancik, 1974; Salancik & Pfefer, 1974). The change of leaders is often accompanied by a change in the political environment that casts the replaced leader in an unfavorable light (Rockman, 1984). It is no wonder that most incumbent chief executives give top priority to the question of succession (Bruce, 1986). Except for a major reorganization, the retirement of the chief executive probably causes more job changes down the line than does any other event.

The average tenure in office of chief operating executives in industry appears similar to that in higher education and hospital administration. The *median* tends to be little more than five years, but the *mean* is much longer (weighted by those in office for a lifetime). The expected mean term of office often used to be close to 10 years (Wilson & McLaughlin, 2001). The median was shortened to seven years in the 1990s and in 2005 was closer to four to five years. If the successor comes from within the organization, there may be a wave of other promotions at lower levels. If the successor comes from outside, the organization that supplied the successor must find a replacement, so it, too, will be engaged in a succession process. The rate of succession increases with the rate of organizational acquisitions, expansion, mergers, takeovers, and bankruptcies.

Purposes Served by the Succession Process

There has been increased concern about the need for accountability of top executives for corporate performance and ethics and their appropriate selection and compensation in alignment with stakeholder interests. Replacing a CEO of a poorly performing firm is an effort to regain stakeholder confidence (Puffer & Weintrop, 1995). A survey of 711 Australian human resource business professionals indicated that the purposes of succession management programs were to improve business results and to meet new skill requirements. Efforts were linked, to a considerable degree, with strategic business plans, a broader management strategy, and unique organizational needs (Taylor & Ross-Smith, 2003). Each organization needs to tailor-make the process to fit its culture and support its systems and resources (Berke, 2002).

Some CEOs, like many political leaders, refuse to retire. Their "personal identity is so intertwined with . . . [their] role that retirement represents a personal void." They will have to give up power, status, and perquisites (Sonnenfeld, 1988, p. 264). Term limit rules have to be enforced, or countervailing power will be required for the succession. Saddam Hussein was removed by military force. Coalitions of revolutionaries force resignations. Castro overthrew Batista. In the United States, following the institutionalized rules, the electors from each state choose the next president. Boards of directors, representing the shareholders, legally choose the next CEO, although as will be discussed later, corporate succession in the United States has to be seen as matters of politics, power, shareholder interests, governance rules, government regulations, and laws. In Japan, organizational rules represent the interests of the employees and

institutionalized changes in CEOs are more frequent (Kim, 2000).

Although Flament (1956) and Pryer, Flint, and Bass (1962) reported that experimental groups tended to remain effective as long as they did not change leaders, in the political arena, in particular, the choosing of new leaders is an occasion for renewal. In both capitalist and socialist countries, innovations, new policies, new priorities, and revised budgets usually accompany the succession of new leadership. Some leaders may be chosen as caretakers. When a change of leaders is mandated, such as at the end of four or eight years for a U.S. president, the successor may be chosen to provide continuity. Thus, Blake and Mouton (1985b) showed that four twentieth-century U.S. presidents who chose their successors tended to choose a leader similar to themselves in management style. But the styles of the nine successors who were not chosen by the previous president tended to be different from those of their predecessors.

A change in management because of poor organizational performance is a way in which the organization attempts to be adaptive (Helmich & Brown, 1972). Failure to change the leadership will reduce such adaptivity. Failing firms have lower rates of succession than do nonfailing firms (Schwartz & Menon, 1985).

In choosing the top managing successors of an organization, one is likely to be contributing to changes in the organization's strategies and to what is to be valued by the organization. In searching for successors for the chief executive, organizational renewal is sought. There may be a need to dip down into the next generation of managers with less seniority to find the leadership required for such changes. The organization's structure is likely to be affected by the succession. For example, Hambrick and Mason (1984) hypothesized that if the successors are highly educated professional managers, the organization is likely to see them introduce more thorough planning systems, complex coordination devices, budgeting details, and complex incentive-compensation schemes.

Succession is an opportunity for organizational members to participate in a process that may significantly shift the organization's direction. The expenditure of time and effort in the process reaffirms the importance of the position to the organization and adds to the power of the position (Pfeffer, 1981b). Succession offers opportunities for coalitions of interests within organizations to communicate, exercise preferences, and negotiate the organization's future (Gephart, 1978). According to Boeker's (1997) study of 67 semiconductor producers, the movement of senior management from one organization to another brings managers into the new firm with prior experience with different products and strategies, reflected in the new firm's market entry decisions.

Antecedents of the Succession

Between 1957 and 1981, corporations tended to concentrate on choosing successor CEOs with the same career specialization as before. However, between 1981 and 1997, they were more likely to choose successors from different career specializations, probably to help reduce organizational inertia and to reflect the need for change (White, Smith, & Barnett, 1997). As Trow (1960) noted, it is difficult to sort out the antecedents from the consequences of the succession in leadership. Many successions are routine, due to rules regarding retirement or disability. From an examination of 13 CEO successions in the 1990s in firms such as Corning and Glaxo Wellcome, Spitzer and Evans (1998) inferred that successions worked well if thinking about the succession began with the accession of the previously selected executive, the process was well defined and articulated, the board of directors was involved early, the field of candidates was not narrowed too quickly, and the candidate was first placed and observed for style, values, and vision in a chief operating role for a period. At Ameritech, formerly part of Bell Telephone, the installation of the new CEO was accompanied by the creation of four planning teams of younger executives to assist in the necessary organizational and personnel developments (Tichy, 1996).

In the 1980s, the average CEO could expect to be in office for a decade. But in the 1990s and 2000s, succession events due to dismissals increased substantially as a consequence of poor organizational performance. Increasingly, CEOs were held accountable for an organization's performance; although the evidence is not always supportive, the disruption caused by the succession may outweigh its benefits (Wiersema, 2002). Repetitive executive turnover and leadership discontinuity often result (Krug & Nigh, 2001, 2002). Poor profitability is likely to result in the selection of an outsider as the successor (Cannela & Lubatkin, 1993).

Numerous events affect the succession (Kesner & Sebora, 1994). For instance, product completion and new financing from outside investors may be the reason for a change at the top (Wasserman, 2002). Or the change may be induced by mergers or when one firm acquires another in a takeover. Senior managers in the acquired firm leave at higher-than-normal rates in the years following the acquisition (Hambrick & Cannella, 1993). On the other hand, internal reorganization and organic expansion reduce turnover of CEOs (Vermeulen & Berkema, 2003). There are other reasons that CEOs leave acquired firms and require successors. They may feel their status has been lost and want to avoid conflicts with the acquirers. Their age, tenure, and specific knowledge and skills may be of importance in the decision to be retained or dismissed (Buchholtz, Ribbens, & Houle, 2003).

The turnover of senior executives may be due to disabling ill health, death, or unexpected voluntary retirements and resignations for other personal reasons. When Campion and Mitchell (1986) compared 140 former executives and managers with 143 current ones in the same organization, the leavers reported less satisfying job characteristics, more problems of adjustment and socialization, unmet job expectations, and more job stress than did those currently in the organization. House and Singh (1987) listed personal traits that help to reduce such turnover: psychological hardiness, optimism, vigorous involvement, commitment, the need for achievement, and the ability to cope with stressful conditions. Particularly important contributors to voluntary resignations are the executives' perceptions of their own lack of power to influence their organization and their felt need for such power. Firms that lack internal consensus exhibit more internal conflict, resulting in higher rates of executive turnover than in organizations with internal consensus. Turbulent environments are antecedents of executive turnover. Such turbulence doubled annual voluntary resignations of chief executives between 1974 and 1984 (Weschler, 1984).

Rules of Succession. Herrity (2003) looked at the institutionalized rules in the largest publicly traded U.S. firms between 1975 and 1994 and concluded that the rules were determined by the power and competing interests of the executives, board members, owners, and other stakeholders. But based on an analysis of 216 insider and outsider successions in 108 firms between 1960 and 1990, Ocasio (1999) noted that the boards of directors were both enabled and constrained in their selection process by the institutionalized rules for succession. They relied on the rules as well as past precedents and the availability of internal candidates in choosing a successor.

Determinants of Choice. Santora and Sorros (1995) observed that longevity, specialized competence, and loyalty determined the choice of the successor of a charismatic leader of 24 years. Campbell, Sessa, and Taylor (1995) reported that according to interviews with 327 executives about the succession process, candidates external to the organization were more prevalent but less likely to be appointed. Compared to rejectees, selected candidates were seen to fit the positions and the organizational culture better. They also were more likely to have better interpersonal skills and compatible values. However, they did not have more business or technical experience. They were more likely to be selected for political reasons.

Politics was also seen by Cannela and Lubatkin (2003) in 472 CEO successions in a Forbes list of 800 large publicly traded firms. The results indicated that between 1971 and 1985, poor organizational performance brought on a selection of an outsider successor mainly if there was no heir apparent and the incumbent lacked the ability to influence the selection of the successor. According to an analysis of 220 successions in industry by Zhang and Rajagopalan (2003), an insider was more likely to be chosen if there was an heir apparent. Welsh and Dehler (1988) observed the lobbying, bargaining, forming of coalitions, and other organizational politicking that was present in 36 colleges that were searching for a new dean. Deshpande, Schoderbek, and Joseph (1994) analyzed the promotion decisions of 197 managers and found that subordinates could influence the recommendation process favorably if they had organizational connections known to the manager.

The Search Committee. The particular representation of organizational members on the search committee for the successor enhances the status of their various constituencies in the organization. The quality of the committee's search process adds legitimacy to the chosen successor's leadership (Hollander, 1985). The search committee is an important source of information to the successor about the organization's current normative expectations, values, and distribution of power (Birnbaum, 1987a). Less recognized is that meeting with outside prospects can provide new objectives, values, information, and methods.

Powerful boards of directors tend to favor a successor CEO who is an external candidate and more like them than like the incumbent CEO (Zajac & Westphal, 1996). More outside directors have been appointed to the search committee, presumably so the selection decision will be less influenced by identification with management (Sherman, 1992).

The Founder's Influence. Compared to successions at later stages in a firm's history, the first succession after the retirement of the founder is likely to be strongly affected by the incumbent founder. A founder is more likely to have a strong attachment to the firm, as well as large equity holdings that may control the firm. A founder's values and ideology can exert strong influence on the succession, according to Wasserman's (2001) event-history analysis of successions in 202 Internet firms. But successors may not cling to the same goals as tenaciously as the founders (DiMaggio & Anheier, 1990). Compared with the founders, the successors are more likely to have functional backgrounds in administration rather than technology (Drazin & Kazanjian, 1993).

The Predecessor. According to Sonnenfeld and Ward (1995), the self-concept of the departing chief executive could make the succession process easy or difficult for the organization and the successor. Departing executives varied in whether they saw themselves as having a heroic stature and heroic mission with a unique commanding role that could not be carried out by anyone else. Four types of departing executives were recognized: monarch, general, ambassador, and governor. The *monarch*, with both heroic stature and mission—such as Edwin Land of Polaroid—has to be forced out of office; a palace revolt may be required to replace the monarch. The *general*, with heroic stature but not mission—such as William Paley of CBS—leaves office reluctantly but might return as organizational savior to rescue it from the successor. The *ambassador*—such as Thomas Watson, Jr., of IBM—is heroic neither in stature nor in mission, leaves office gracefully, mentors the successor, and subsequently serves on the board of directors. The *governor*, like the ambassador—such as Stanley Gault of Goodyear—is not heroic, serves a limited term, takes other positions of senior leadership elsewhere afterward, and does not maintain continuing contact with the organization. Successors have many difficulties replacing monarchs and generals. On the other hand, ambassadors remain a source of advice and service to the organization, while governors often develop strong internal successors. Ambassadors who serve as mentors for their successors may obtain vicarious satisfaction and a sense of achievement from their successors' successful performance (Lipman-Blumen, 1996).

Musteen, Barker, and Baeten (2003) surveyed 280 chief executives of nonprofit organizations. They found that long-tenured CEOs were likely to have less favorable attitudes toward organizational change.

The Heir Apparent. This is a future successor who has already been identified but not installed. The wait for the succession to occur depends on the power of the predecessor, the outside board members, and the *heir apparent*. Cannella and Shen (2001) studied what happened to 152 such heirs to the incumbent CEO's position. A powerful incumbent CEO might stall the selection process indefinitely. If the firm is doing poorly, the heir might leave for another position elsewhere. On the other hand, powerful outside directors may try to keep the discouraged heir from leaving, or force the succession to occur. If the firm is doing well, the heir is likely to wait longer. Forty-three percent were actually elevated to CEO, but 20% left the firm. The traditional model of succession that is likely to be favored starts grooming a manager identified early on as a potential heir apparent. Years before succeeding as CEO of Exxon, one young plant superintendent was already being called the crown prince.

Grooming the Successor. Except when seeking to seriously refocus the organization, as when Lou Gerstner, a former marketing executive from American Express, was chosen as CEO of IBM, firms pursue traditional succession strategy and promote most of their chief executives from within the firm. Potential successors are assessed, developed, and coached for numerous senior leadership positions with opportunities for internal and external training. Individual career plans are matched with succession plans and monitored by top management (Gratton & Syrett, 1990). The traditional succession strategy has been increasingly jeopardized by societal and technological change, corporate mergers and acquisitions, globalization, flattening of hierarchies, early retirements, work family considerations, and the effects of the glass ceiling (the numbers of women matching those of men in middle and lower management but not in senior management).

Family Firms. Family-controlled firms are common throughout the world and almost the rule in many developing countries. Family members are crucial in the succession process and, as successors to top executive positions, must be committed to the business. The next generation of family members must be assessed by the family entrepreneurs for their interest in the firm. Some are committed through desire for the top posts, some out of a sense of obligation, some based on the opportunity costs of doing otherwise, and some based on need (Sharma & Rao, 2000).

Involuntary Change. Forced departures were seen by Sonnenfeld (1988) as due to organizational effects ranging from political scheming to mandatory retirement. Phan (1995) and Lee obtained mixed results when examining the forced exits of 26 CEOs in 255 successions reported between 1975 and 1991. CEOs who had to resign were in one or more of the following circumstances: (1) they were entrenched in social networks; (2) they were insiders rather than outsiders; (3) they had more personal prestige; (4) their board of directors was larger; and (5) they owned substantial blocks of the firm's shares. The antecedent condition that most often precipitated an involuntary change of leadership was failure by the organization attributed to the leadership. Sometimes the attribution was accurate, but other times, the CEO was the scapegoat for the organization's shortcomings. Considerable evidence supported the contention that an organization's failure stimulated a change of its leaders. This was found in 172 top management successions in China in companies that also had fewer insiders on the board and had a dominant shareholder. The dominant shareholder was also likely to have a heavy influence on who was chosen as successor (Yue, 2003).

Effects of Poor Corporate Performance. According to an analysis of 240 firms by Puffer and Weintrop (1995), the poor performance of a firm's securities resulted in forced retirement of a CEO and replacement with an external successor. Firms with solvency problems (increased debt-to-equity ratios) changed leadership more frequently than did firms without such problems (Pfeffer & Leblebici, 1973). The high turnover of 576 top managers in 31 Fortune 500 firms was associated with the firms' poor financial performance (Wagner, Pfeffer, & O'Reilly, 1984). Osborn, Jauch, Martin, et al. (1981) demonstrated that the rate of executive succession increased with the firms' volatility in profitability and unstable financial strategies. As with turbulent economic environments, the rate of succession was greater for organizations in more turbulent ownership, supplier relationships, and socioeconomic environments. While 45% of bankrupt firms changed chief executives, only 19% of a comparable sample of healthy firms did so (Schwartz & Menon, 1985). Increasingly, CEOs are held accountable for the poor performance of their firms. The rate of dismissals of CEOs of Fortune 500 firms doubled in the 1990s from what it had been in the 1980s. Such dismissals were signals to the stock market (Moliterno & Wiersema, 2003). Corporate raiders were a source of change in corporate control of firms with a history of poor financial performance. Hostile takeover activity by a raider was followed by changes in corporate officers and directors (Walsh & Kosnick, 1993). When persistent organizational problems remain unmanaged and when there is a failure to cope with critical contingencies, the chief executive loses support and is likely to be replaced (Thompson, 1967). Along with the declining performance of CEO's and their organizations, increasing difficulties in management increase the rate of succession (James & Soref, 1981). Thus Helmich (1978), in a study of 54 petrochemical firms, found that the rate of presidents' turnover was increased with mergers, acquisitions, and the increased dispersal of operations.

Strategic Influences. Virany, Tushman, and Romanelli (1985) concluded, from an analysis of the succession events of corporate-level executives in 37 firms, that although performance was most important in generating the change of executives, such changes were actually driven by strategic reorientations in high-performance firms. Consistent with this finding, Smith and White's (1987) analysis of the succession of 370 chief executive officers in the 25-year history of 173 Fortune 1000 firms showed that the current strategy of the firm tended to dictate the career specialty from which the new chief executive was drawn. Graham and Richards (1979) reached similar conclusions for the railroad industry. It is not surprising that the increased movement of marketing executives into top management coincides with the firms' increased focus on marketing. When there is increased emphasis on cost containment, accountants come to the fore. Increased strategic concern for production and the quality of products brings engineers into top management. The efforts to flatten and downsize organizations have led to more loss of jobs of managers proportionately than of employees in general and have been a major source of turnover of managers (Capelli, 1992). They transfer into staff positions, become consultants, start new businesses, find employment elsewhere, take early retirement, and/or join the ranks of the unemployed.

Other Institutions. The heads of educational institutions are less likely to be ousted because of the institutions' poor financial performance. Instead, a change of president may more likely be a consequence of mismanagement of resources or extreme dissatisfaction of powerful political officials, trustees, alumni, or faculties. Financial failures may play a role in private profit-making educational institutions. Replacements of presidents, deans, and directors also may be initiated as a consequence of disability, competitive job offers, and changes in mission and programs (Cohen & March, 1986). The extent to which managers of baseball teams with the poorest season's records are most likely to be changed is well known (Grusky, 1963a). Path analyses by Allen, Panian, and Lotz (1979) confirmed that poor records, rather than other related elements, resulted in the replacement of managers of baseball teams. In the same way, Hamblin (1958b) demonstrated that groups change leaders informally if the leaders do not have a way of helping the groups out of crises. Such changes in leaders will be accelerated if the members have complex rather than simple personalities (Schroder, Streufert, & Welden,

1964). Conversely, Goldman, and Fraas (1965) found that subordinates were more likely to choose leaders who had been more successful earlier with the group's task. But Daum (1975) failed to find such results.

Organizational Influences. Among the possible antecedents of the rate of executive succession is the size of the organization. Grusky (1961) reported that the rate of succession of chief executive officers was directly related to the firm's size. But when Salancik and Pfeffer (1980) examined the tenure of the chief executives of 84 U.S. corporations, the executives' tenure was unrelated to the corporations' size. Gordon and Becker (1964) suggested that the relationship of organizational size to the rate of executive succession was complicated by other factors. For instance, larger firms have more ready inside replacements and would be expected to exhibit higher rates of succession as a consequence. However, insiders who reach the top serve longer terms in their positions (Helmich, 1976). Kriesberg (1962, 1964) further suggested that the differences among industries and in technology have to be taken into account.

Salancik, Staw, and Pondy (1980) examined the turnover of the heads of 20 university departments. They found that turnover increased with a department's size but was lower if the department had been more successful in receiving outside grants. Turnover was also lower in departments in which there was agreement about how knowledge in one area was relevant in another area, as reflected in the departments' ability to organize long lists of courses in their curricula. Zhang and Rajagopalan (2003) completed an analysis of 206 manufacturing executives who left their positions between 1993 and 1997 and showed that turnover was lower if organizational sales growth and short-term profitability were greater. In another study, Pfeffer and Moore (1980) also found that the size of a department was of consequence. They also obtained positive associations between the length of tenure of its heads, departmental consensus, and the seniority of its faculty. Datta and Rajagopalan (1997) showed that for 134 CEO succession events in manufacturing, there was a modest association between their industry's product differentiation and the length of successor CEOs' organizational tenure. Industry growth rate had the reverse effect on CEO tenure.

Succession in higher education appears to be followed by similar stages in taking charge by the successor (Gmelch, 2000) as in industry (Gabarro, 1985): taking hold, immersion, reshaping, consolidating, and refining. Similarly, the choice of successor university presidents for their previous effective financial performance seems to becoming closer to the choice of new CEOs in industry.

Effects of Age. Differences in the age of top managers and others in a firm contributed to more rapid turnover of top management (Wagner, Pfeffer, & O'Reilly, 1984). Evidently, the increasing age gap, presumably due to older-than-ordinary senior managers, creates pressure to accelerate the succession process. Older CEOs who were turned out of office were more likely to take on advisory roles or to retire from any active role in the firm. Younger CEOs were more like to take on new active roles (Ward, Sonnenfeld, & Kimberly, 1995).

Concentration of Ownership. Although tenure was related to changes in profit margins, Salancik and Pfeffer (1980) found that it depended on the concentration of stock ownership. Tenure was unrelated to the corporation's performance for owner-managed firms but was related positively to profit margins for externally controlled firms and to stock market rates of return for management-controlled firms. According to McEachern (1975) and Allen and Panian (1982), in general, the rate of succession was likely to be greater if the management was under external control than if it was freewheeling and in control of itself.

Effects of the Succession of Insiders or Outsiders. While bureaucratic maintenance is thought to be favored by the succession of an insider, more organizational change may be obtained by the succession of an outsider. A progression of insider successors is seen to slow adaptation (Carlson, 1961) and organizational growth (Helmich, 1974a). After bankruptcies, outside successors appointed as both CEOs and chairs of the board induce more strategic change, according to an analysis of 47 organizations (Dawley, Hoffman & Brockman, 2003).

Conflict inside the organization may be reduced by choosing an outsider. For example, upon winning their independence from Turkey in the nineteenth century, the Balkan countries—Greece, Bulgaria, and Romania—

chose petty German princes as their new kings to avoid conflict among the leading indigenous noble families, as well as to obtain support from the great powers of Britain, Austria-Hungary, France, and Russia. Similarly, Birnbaum (1971) showed that state universities tend to recruit their presidents from the lower administrative levels of other state universities, rather than from their own universities or from nearby colleges in the state, thus both promoting the transfer of knowledge from elsewhere and restricting conflict inside their own universities. (At the same time, the main source of lower-level administrators was promotion from within the universities.)

Nevertheless, Lubatkin and Chung (1985) found no particular differences in the subsequent performance of successors who were insiders or outsiders. Likewise, Chung, Lubatkin, Rogers, et al. (1987) concluded, after comparing 80 appointments of insiders to 19 appointments of outsiders as chief executive officers, that although long-term profitability after a succession depended mainly on the firm's profitability before the succession, rather than on the change of leaders, stock prices went up when outsiders but not insiders were hired by high-performing firms. However, only the exceptional new leader from the outside could successfully turn around the poorly performing firm.

Clearly, contextual moderating variables must be examined before one can reach conclusions about the extent to which better organizational performance results from a choice of an insider or an outsider. One needs to know if the outsider has a mandate for change, particularly to change top management and its strategies. One needs to know whether inside successors have been chosen by default because desired outsiders could not be recruited in the face of the organization's poor history of conflict and performance (House & Singh, 1987).

The succession of insiders provides for the continuity of existing programs, management practices, and organizational stability (House & Singh, 1987). Lack of continuity is seen when outsiders are appointed to senior leadership posts in a new presidential administration. Its effects on the U.S. State Department were a loss of coherence in policy making (Bloomfield, 1984). A change of administration in the Environmental Protection Agency likewise promoted greater distrust between career employees and political appointees, less effective communication, and the inability to handle routine business or to improve the agency's performance over time (Gaertner, Gaertner, & Devine, 1983).

In their survey of senior-ranking human resources officers in 235 Fortune 500 firms, Friedman and Saul (1988) confirmed that the appointment of outside successors to the post of chief executive officer resulted in more post-succession disruption and turnover of lower-level executives than did the appointment of inside successors. However, overall, outside and inside successors did not appear to have different effects on morale.

In an analysis of the impact of 477 successions, Lubatkin, Chung, Rogers, and Owers (1989) concluded that share price is generally depressed by the occurrence of a succession. However, the price of the stock is enhanced (indicating that investors are favorably impressed) when the successor is an outsider and the firm is above average in its performance. For the 15% of 136 successors in Friedman and Singh's (1986) analysis who were outsiders, the market value of the parent firm's shares increased. But the value of shares was unaffected if the successor was an insider. Insider-outsider effects of the predecessor were more complex. The forced resignation of a predecessor who was an insider had a more positive effect than forced resignation of a predecessor who was an outsider, although both events had positive effects. The voluntary resignation of an executive who originally was an outsider resulted in a much greater increase in the market value of the parent firm's shares than did the voluntary resignation of one who was originally from the inside. Although the expected retirement of an insider had no effect, the expected retirement of an outsider did have a positive effect on the market value of the parent firm's shares.

Welsh and Dehler (1986) questioned a random stratified sample of 960 faculty members from 40 professional colleges of business, education, agriculture, and engineering. They followed up the survey with telephone interviews and questionnaires three years later. They found that when consensus about issues was low among the faculty of a college, those colleges that selected a dean from the inside experienced greater turnover of deans. Conversely, when consensus was high among the faculty, colleges that chose a dean from the outside experienced greater turnover. The lowest turnover of deans occurred in colleges with high faculty consensus who selected a dean from the inside.

Reasons for Choosing an Insider or Outsider. Insiders are expected to already know the organization well. Outsiders, chosen from elsewhere, are expected to bring in new ideas, knowledge, attitudes, and changes (Vancil, 1987). Some investigators have concluded that poor organizational performance moves an organization to choose an outsider more often. Other investigators have concluded the opposite. Still others have found middle-range organizational success to be most conducive to choosing an outsider. The differences may be explained partly by the nature of the organizations involved and the measures of financial success or failure (Puffer & Weintrop, 1995). In 85 firms, Schwartz and Menon (1985) found that external successors were appointed in 65% of those that were failing and 44% that remained in business. Allen, Panian, and Lotz (1979) found that outside succession was more disruptive to the performance of a baseball team than was bringing up a new manager from the inside. Nonetheless, there was a greater tendency to go outside for a new manager when the previous year's performance had been poor. In the same way, Virany and Tushman (1986) showed that of the 59 minicomputer firms that were performing poorly tended to make more senior management appointments from the outside than did those firms whose performance was better. Likewise, Otten and Teulings (1970) found, in an analysis of the succession histories of 34 department heads in various Dutch organizations, that poor departmental performance was an incentive to select outsiders as successors. D. R. Dalton and Kesner (1985) observed that outside successors were most often chosen by companies that were middle-range in performance. However, for a sample of 166 large firms, Lubatkin and Chung (1985) noted that in a crisis of falling profits, fewer outsiders were chosen as successors. Chung, Lubatkin, Rogers, et al. (1987) obtained results indicating that in 99 firms, outsiders were chosen in the highly performing firms but in only 14% of the poorly performing ones. These results were explained partly by the nature of the organizations involved and the measures of financial success or failure (Puffer & Weintrop, 1995). Perhaps there was more willingness by outsiders to accept a senior appointment in a prosperous firm than a failing one. Nonetheless, when corporate performance has been good, Brady and Helmich (1984) reported, insiders were more likely to be chosen as they represented stability, continuity, and experience with policies and practices. As mentioned earlier, outsiders are more likely to be chosen when there is no heir apparent and the incumbent is unable to influence the selection (Cannella & Lubatkin, 1993).

In some firms of sufficient age, long-standing policies, management development, and manpower planning, inside heirs are identified early and groomed for the succession. Larger and older firms develop their own chief executives who rise from the ranks and are familiar with the firms' people, markets, and products (Pfeffer & Moore, 1980; Tsurumi, 1983b). Appointment of insiders signals continuity and stability. Appointment of outsiders signals change (Pfeffer & Salancik, 1978).

In the political arena, outsiders are chosen to exemplify the "new broom sweeping clean." Best (1981) contrasted the original appointments of cabinet members and their replacements for the U.S. presidential administrations between 1952 and 1976 in terms of whether they came from inside or outside the government. Only 35% were original appointments at the beginning of a presidential term of office; 65% were replacements during a term of office. The original appointees were chosen to generate legitimacy and to form a cabinet that the president could trust. They were mainly outsiders to the Washington bureaucracy. However, their replacements later in the same presidents' administrations were more often insiders with Washington experience and managerial ability.

Consequences of Succession

Can the benefits of change in executive leadership outweigh the disruptions caused by the change? The answer depends on a variety of considerations. Just as poor organizational performance may be an antecedent of succession, so succession is often associated with greater organizational mortality.

On Organizational Performance. Turnover of key executives can disrupt work routines, interrupt command, diffuse authority, and increase employees' feelings of insecurity (Haveman, 1993). Gordon and Rosen (1981) proposed a model for the dynamics of succession that takes into account variables antedating the arrival and entry of the new leader into the organization, postarrival variables of consequence, and the interaction between the two sets of variables. Included in the prearrival variables are: (1) the successor's background, competence, motivation, and orientation; (2) whether the successor came from inside or outside the organization; (3) how well the successor was known in advance by the organization; (4) the organization's previous general experience with the succession process; and (5) how much the organization was specifically involved in selecting the new leader. The new leader's mandate is also important. Postarrival variables include much of what was identified in preceding chapters about the factors that influence leader-follower relationships and how they, in turn, affect productivity and satisfaction. Ziller (1965b) obtained results suggesting that the rapid replacement of small-group leaders provides a means of creating new ideas that lead to the continued success of the group. But changing leaders can result in a group's decreased performance and high personnel turnover costs (Rogers, Ford, & Tassone, 1961). However, the change in leaders need not be disruptive, especially when it is planned and expected. It may actually result in the improved performance of a group or organization in some instances and no change or reduced performance in others. Boal and Hooijberg (2000) suggested that succession might result in a number of different possibilities: (1) a honeymoon early on due to novelty and temporarily looser reins; (2) an early decline in organizational performance due to the successor's need for time to learn; (3) a reinforcement of the same positive or negative effects over time; (4) effects on organizational performance depending mainly on the personalities and situations involved; (5) eventual declines in performance due to the inability of the successor to adapt to changing environments; and (6) no real effects of the successor on organizational performance, only a fictional "romance of leadership." Different dynamics may be involved in the short-term and long-term consequences of a succession (Zaheer, Albert, & Zaheer, 1999). Jeffrey and Lee (1996) analyzed the consequences of succession and CEOs' tenure in 2,780 community hospitals between 1984 and 1991. They found that failure declined initially with the tenure of the successor, but after six years in office, failure increased steadily with tenure. A meta-analysis of succession outcomes explained the effects as due to differences in measurement, operationalization, and organizations (Tzabbar, 2003).

On Board Members. Ward, Bishop, and Sonnefeld (1999) looked at the consequences to members of the boards of directors in 144 companies between 1988 and 1992 when the CEO was dismissed, retired, or remained in office. With successions, peripheral directors left the board. The board became more involved in the succession when the dismissal was due to strategic disagreement, but directors who were CEOs elsewhere became more involved regardless of the reasons for the dismissal. Ward, Sonnenfeld, and Kimberly (1995) followed up dismissed CEOs and noted that older ones were likely to take advisory roles rather than new executive positions, but this did not affect their various board memberships.

On Personnel. Friedman and Saul (1988) surveyed respondents from 235 Fortune 500 firms. They showed that the morale of a firm's personnel decreased with the succession of a new chief executive officer. Taking into account the successor's age, origin, and position, morale was lower particularly if the predecessor had been in office for many years. But shareholder reactions were usually positive when successions were announced (Davidson, Worrell, & Cheng, 1990). However, Lieberson and O'Connor (1972) found that changes in the corporate sales, profit, and profit margins of 167 corporations in 13 industries over a 20-year period (1946 to 1965) were not closely related to changes in their corporate presidents or chairmen of the boards.

On Managerial and Organizational Performance. The results were different when the effects of changes elsewhere in management were analyzed. Lieberson and O'Connor concluded that the succession of new presidents or board chairmen accounted for less variance in sales, earnings, and profits than differences in either industry or company. But Day and Lord (1986) pointed out that the effects of the change of these top executives increased with time, accounting for 15.2% to 31.7% of the profit margins when the time lag between the change of management and its subsequent effects was increased to three years. Changes in top business management did have important, practical effects on the firms' performance. Thomas (1988) reported in a study of large retail firms in Britain. Changes in the alignment of executives and organizational strategies were seen to have positive effects on organizational performance (Thomas,

Litschert, & Ramaswamy, 1991). Friedman and Saul (1991) surveyed the consequences of changes at the top of the Fortune 500 firms from about 170 replies. If the board initiated the succession, morale was enhanced ($r = .24$) although greater also were disruption ($r = .38$) and executive turnover ($r = .26$). However, if the succession was initiated by the incumbent CEO, there was little effect on disruption, turnover, or morale. When other variables were taken into account, disruption was particularly greater when the successor was an outsider and the incumbent was disabled. Eitzen and Yetman (1972) and Trow (1961) thought that there was an optimal rate of turnover of leaders. Nevertheless, Schendel, Patton, and Riggs (1976) found that 80% of turnaround strategies were associated with the replacement of top managers. Similar results were reported by Graham and Richards (1979) for the railroad industry.

On Sports Teams. Gamson and Scotch (1964) concluded that the impact of the change in managers of a baseball team was minimal; the firing of a baseball manager was only a ritual for, as noted before, Grusky (1963) had found that baseball teams with the highest rates of change in managers had the poorest performance records. Allen, Panian, and Lotz (1979) confirmed that the higher rates of change *subsequently* resulted in poorer performance by the teams. Additionally, their path-analytic examination of managerial succession for 54 seasons showed that baseball teams that replaced a manager during the season subsequently performed worse. According to Smart and Wolfe (2003) winning baseball games was accounted for primarily by individual players' pitching and batting records, not team leadership. Nevertheless, particularly in a circumstance of high rivalry, a baseball team manager with a record of competence and experience could increase a team's successful performance (Cannella & Rowe, 1995).

While Eitzen and Yetman (1972) found no relation between the turnover of coaches of basketball teams and the teams' performance records over 40 years, Giambatista (2004) reported that with National Basketball Association teams from 1980 to 1989, the disruption of in-season replacement of coaches compared to out-of-season successions did result in poorer performance. Brown (1982) concluded that in the case of 26 National Football League teams from 1970 to 1978, there was no difference in the recovery of teams that had steep declines in performance to better winning records when coaches were replaced in midseason because of the teams' poor performance than when the same coaches were retained. Brown inferred that the changing of coaches in midseason was a scapegoating mechanism that had little subsequent effect on the teams' performance.

On Other Entities. Salancik and Pfeffer (1977) studied the influence of 172 successive mayors on the revenues, debt, and expenditures of 30 U.S. cities from 1951 to 1968. As Day and Lord (1986) noted, an adjustment had to be made for the size of the cities to reveal the effect of the succeeding mayors on expenditures and indebtedness. Changes in mayors accounted for about 19% of the variance in financial outcomes. The succession of a new pope, such as John XXIII, brought much change and liberalization worldwide in the Roman Catholic Church. John Paul II returned to a more conservative stance in the Church's teachings on sex, became a bridge for political democracy into Eastern Europe, and brought an increase in the recognition of the importance of Catholicism in Latin America, Africa, and elsewhere in the developing world. Benedict XVI is so far maintaining the changes instituted by his predecessors.

Moderators of the Effects of Succession

As already noted, whether replacing the leader will contribute to a team's or organization's subsequent performance is affected by a variety of moderating variables (Gephart, 1978). The reasons for the succession make a difference in its effects on future performance, as does the mode of analysis, whether the succession is voluntary or forced, and whether the departing chief executive is the firm's founder (Reinganum, 1985). The effects of succession are moderated by whether the successor brings more specialized competence to the position and what changes occur in the style and power of the leadership. The suddenness of the succession, whether the successor is an insider or outsider, and whether there is a consensus in the group or organization will affect whether the change of leadership is beneficial to the group, team, or organization. The industry in which the succession occurs also moderates its effects.

In Business. In an analysis of 136 successions, Friedman and Singh (1986) compared the stock market value of shares of firms from 300 days before the announcement of each succession to 100 days after it. The market value declined when the announced reason for the departure of the chief executive was an unexpected disability. The market value was unaffected if the retirement was expected. It increased if the departure was voluntary or forced because of poor performance. The market value of shares of subsidiary firms that performed poorly for 300 days before the succession increased during the next 100 days with announcement of a new chief executive. But the succession had no effect on the parent firm's shares if they had already been doing well. Ndofor and Rathbun (2003) reported that the effectiveness of the succession in making changes depended on the executive's timing and experience in formulating and implementing change. Shetty and Perry (1976) found that executives had more of a postsuccession effect on their organizations in a new industry if they possessed the necessary knowledge and relevant influence. The succession of executives with prior experience with different products and strategies made for greater success in the entry of these products into the market by their new employers (Boeker, 1997). Day and Lord (1986) noted that it was necessary to take monetary inflation and the size of the organization into account, in addition to allowing sufficient lag-time for the effects of the new management on the firm's performance to be seen. But the effects of changes in management have been most understated by analyses such as those of Lieberson and O'Connor (1972), because the best predictor of future performance is past performance. When the effect of the company's past performance on its future performance is added first in the multiple regression analysis, it takes with it much of the effect of the changes in management on future performance. However, as Weiner and Mahoney (1981) demonstrated for a comparable sample of firms, when the management succession variable is entered into the equation first, it accounts for 75% to 95% of the explained variance. The same is true for studies of the performance of baseball teams.

In Sports Teams. Pfeffer and Davis-Blake (1986) showed, for 22 teams in the National Basketball Association, that when prior performance is controlled, replacing the coach, in general, had no effect on a team's subsequent performance. However, the new coach's greater competence did make a positive contribution to improving the team's performance. A team that replaced its coach with one who had a good prior record and relevant experience or who had brought about improved performance in other teams performed better than did a team whose new coach lacked experience or had performed less adequately in his previous assignments. The succession of coaches of National Hockey League teams from 1942 to 2002 was found by Rowe and Rankin (2003) to be consistent with findings from other professional sports: midseason changes of leaders worsened team performance in that season. However, successions that had occurred in the previous season had a positive consequence on current season performance.

In Religious and Educational Institutions. Smith, Carson, and Alexander (1984) found comparable results with their sample of Methodist ministers. Incoming ministers with a previous record of competence had more positive effects on their new church's performance than did those without such a record. In the same vein, controversial new professional programs were likely to be adopted by liberal arts colleges when incoming college presidents had had previous experience in professional schools (Kraatz & Moore, 2002). In examining the performance of newly appointed deans in 36 colleges, Welsh and Dehler (1988) found that if a lot of preselection politicking occurred among college faculty, in a college with abundant resources, as would be expected, the new successor expended much less effort to acquire resources than did a successor in a college with scarce resources. But unexpectedly, if political activity was low, there were no differences in the activities of the successor. If there was a lot of political activity among the faculty, the successor was expected to engage in more administrative activity if resources were scarce than if they were abundant. However, if resources were abundant, nonadministrative activity was required of the successor if there was little politicking among the faculty.

The Transition

How the transition is handled by organizations and successors is also important. For instance, an organization may resort to an acting appointee before selecting a permanent successor (Gordon & Rosen, 1981). The transition process itself has become an important subject of study to determine whether it foreshadows things to come. From the November election through the first day following the inauguration of the new president on January 20, the transition is carefully watched by journalists for signs of what lies ahead during the new administration. Gilmore (1988) pointed out that the successor, whether in government or in industry, needs to consider the past leader's performance, entrenched interests, and the resistence to change in the agency or firm. A new team has to be assembled, agendas changed, a new vision of the organization created, and a reorganization accomplished that is consistent with the new vision. Change must be realistic and balanced. Productive working alliances need to be negotiated to provide for the organization's effective management.

Abruptness of the Succession. In this regard, Friedman and Singh's (1986) demonstration of the negative impact of an unexpected succession on stock prices was already mentioned. Jackson (1953b) reported finding a work group emotionally disturbed by the unexpected replacement of its valued supervisor. Top management was excoriated, and the new supervisor was overly devalued. Gordon and Rosen (1981) also noted that changes in leadership that come with little advance notice are especially detrimental to the effectiveness of factory work groups.

The sudden death of an executive—particularly one who is highly visible to the public—that forces an unexpected succession, results in a decline in the market value of the firm (Worrell, Davidson, Chandy, & Garrison, 1986). Trow (1961) concluded that the effects of executive succession on organizational performance will be more positive if the succession is orderly and planned than if the succession is unexpected and the selection of the new chief executive has to be made under time pressure. Sorcher (1985) agreed that careful succession planning is needed at each organizational level and must be encouraged by boards of directors (Carey, 1997). Betts and Huntington (1986) noted that long-term instability follows the death of an authoritarian leader if a country is already unstable, if the authoritarian ruler was in office for a long period, and if there is strong social organization

to facilitate antigovernment actions following the death of the ruler. The continuing instability and insurgency in Iraq in 2007 following the termination in 2003 of the 24 years of dictatorship of Saddam Hussein was thus to be expected.

Differences among Industries. Durbrow (1971) analyzed the biographical sketches of some 5,300 executives in 429 organizations in 10 major industries. Mobility rates were highest in the aerospace, electronics, and office equipment industries and lowest in the gas utility, electric utility, and chemical industries. Durbrow found that firms with low rates of executive turnover made the highest profits in high-mobility industries and those with high rates of executive turnover made the highest profits in low-mobility industries. Thus, for instance, utility firms were more profitable if they had high rates of succession, but aerospace firms did best if there was a low turnover among their executives.

Summary and Conclusions

Given its consistency and personal antecedents, it is not surprising that leadership is persistent to some degree among children and more so among adolescents and adults. Both logic and empirical results attest to the persistence of leadership behavior and its effects from childhood onward. However, such persistence depends, to some extent, on the occurrence of leadership in past, present, and future situations that are similar in leadership requirements. It transfers from one situation to another if the new situation is similar in relations and task requirements to the old one. But transfer can be negative if the responses to the old situation are contraindicated. The nature of the demands of the task determines whether the effects of the transfer will be positive or negative. But, in all, there is a tendency for the leader of one group to emerge as the leader when placed in other groups.

Leadership in high school and college tends to be predictive of leadership in adult life. When members of experimental groups are successively reassigned to new groups, the same individuals tend to emerge as leaders. This effect is enhanced when the task is similar from group to group.

When effective and ineffective leaders change places, the performance and morale of formerly ineffective groups tend to improve under effective leaders, but the formerly effective groups suffer from such a change in leaders. The productivity of groups that change leaders frequently or experience high rates of succession of new leaders tend to decline. But such reductions may be the cause rather than the effect of the rapid turnover of leaders. Antecedents affecting the succession of senior executives and CEOs include the composition of the succession committee, the board of directors, the size of the organization, and family ownership. Moderators of the effect include preselection politics, whether successors are insiders or outsiders, how abruptly the changes are made, and the chosen successor's agenda. Another moderator is whether the successor is of the same or opposite sex.

Diversity and Cultural Effects

PART

VII

Diversity and Cultural Effects

CHAPTER 31

Women as Leaders and Followers

Prominent leaders in previous centuries included Cleopatra; Joan of Arc; Eleanor of Aquitaine; Margaret of Denmark, Norway, and Sweden; Isabella of Spain; Elizabeth I of England; Catherine the Great of Russia; Sacajawea of the Lewis and Clark expedition; Harriet Tubman of the Underground Railroad; Susan B. Anthony of the women's suffrage movement; and Carrie Nation of the temperance movement. Earlier in the twentieth century, prominent female leaders included Jane Addams, Emily Pankhurst, Marie Curie, Rosa Luxemburg, Aimee Semple McPherson, and Eleanor Roosevelt, the wife of President Franklin Delano Roosevelt. Mrs. Roosevelt acted as an extension of FDR at times when it was politically difficult for him to operate directly. For example, among her many assignments by the president was her role as unofficial adviser, investigator, and publicist for the National Youth Administration (Abramowitz, 1984). After her husband's death, she became an early ambassador to the United Nations, which she helped shape.

Two Examples

Margaret Thatcher

The most prominent modern British woman leader was Prime Minister Margaret Thatcher, who assumed office in 1979 when the British economy, dominated by nationalized industries, was in poor shape. She turned it around. She had strong convictions. She inspired her middle-class constituents and opposed nationalization of industry and strong unions, promising fair wages for a fair day's work, reduction of taxes, privatization of national industries, support for the police, and reduction in the size of government. Her determined effort to turn Britain back to a market-driven economy succeeded. She followed three principles that seeped into the national consciousness; you can only spend what you earn; keep your guard up—it's a dangerous world; actions have consequences.

She had a commanding presence in Parliament. The "Iron Lady" and her party were reelected three times, and she remained in office until 1991, a record in modern times. Britain's economy in the 1980s became the fastest-growing among the industrialized nations. Unlike her predecessors, she made a dent in the British class system, coming as she did from the lower middle class. She showed her resolve in the national coal strike and the Falklands War, when a more ordinary prime minister might have continued to negotiate a settlement with Argentina rather than strive for total victory (Elliot, 1990). She helped in the liberalization of the Soviet Union when she established good relations with Mikhail Gorbachev in 1984, before he became that country's head. She restored the power of the upper and middle classes at the expense of the labor unions, gave Britons a greater sense of purpose, and was willing to make unpopular decisions such as instituting a poll tax. Just as her father had set high standards for her, she set high standards for herself and her country. For her, leaders did not have to be popular, but they did have to be respected for what they stood for and what they could accomplish. Leadership provided direction and purpose. Decisions were based on principles, supported by the majority who empower the leader to carry out decisions. She was willing to compromise, but only up to a certain point (Holmes, 1993).

Hillary Clinton

In the early twenty-first century, the most prominent woman political leader in the United States is Senator Hillary Clinton, the wife of former president Bill Clinton. Currently a senator from New York, she had the potential in 2008 to be nominated by the Democrats for election as the first woman president. She has already sought and wielded power as first lady in the Clinton administration. Although generally liberal in outlook, she endorses elements of a conservative outlook. She comes from an activist religious background. And she thinks the public good would be best served by marrying the best of liberalism with the best of conservatism. For instance, she sees room for compromise on abortion, between women's right to choose and the right to life position. For Clinton, politics is about how people should behave, as well as how the government should behave. Hers is a message combining values from the nineteenth-century social gospel and from women reformers like Jane Addams; the Methodism of the early twentieth century; liberation theology; and "multiculturally correct" religious leftism (Kelly, 1993). Clinton has an international reputation for speaking out on the rights of minorities and women, religious values, and democratic approaches to solving the problems of health, poverty, and ethnic and national conflicts.

Interest in Woman Leaders

Accompanying the rise of women leaders, owners, and managers in the last quarter of the twentieth century was the expansion of research, studies, and commentary on the gender[1] and biological sex of leaders. Gender was hardly discussed in Stogdill's (1948) review and in the first edition of this handbook (Stogdill, 1974). Many popular books that first appeared during this period argued that women leaders were different from their male counterparts but that to succeed as managers they had to behave like men. Brenner (1982) could report that women managers adopted a masculine orientation. Likewise,

[1] Languages, particularly English, evolve because of usage, not because of logic or consistency. Hence, words that are used incorrectly often come into vogue. Such has been the case with the use of "gender" to mean one of the two sexes.

Men and women are two clearly different biological types, distinguished by a variety of physical and physiological differences. They are the two—the only two—different sexes. Their social and behavioral similarities and differences are looked at in terms of their membership in one sex rather than the other.

Until it was incorrectly applied by social scientists, "gender" was only a grammatical term. In English, there are three grammatical genders: masculine, feminine, and neuter. Nonetheless, by the 1980s, "gender differences," a term that probably originated as a Victorian euphemism, had supplanted "sex differences" in the social sciences. Although differences between the two sexes are now most often relabeled differences between two genders and the social and behavioral blends are *androgynous*, not *neuter*, I have chosen to remain in the minority and continue to call male-female differences differences between the sexes rather than differences between the genders.

McBroom (1987) reported that women learned to act like men as they advanced their careers in management. Without such adjustment, women managers and leaders were seen as more nurturing, considerate, cooperative, and participative. Male managers and leaders were seen as more competitive, controlling, impersonal, and analytic. The traditional hierarchical organization required both female and male managers to act like men. But the accumulated research evidence suggests some merit for a distinct woman's leadership style in the less hierarchical twenty-first-century organization.

Then and Now

In 1972, women held 17% of managerial positions; in 1995, nearly 43% (U.S. Department of Labor, 1996). In 2005, the numbers reflected the proportion of women in the workforce (46%). Nonetheless, women managers remain concentrated in lower and middle management. A female university vice president who had recently attended several executive management sessions afterward wrote that she "was amused to discover that much of what they were teaching were things that women automatically pay attention to" (Swain, 1993). In education, women dominate positions as schoolteachers and school principals, although not superintendents of schools. In the U.S. military, leadership positions have opened for women at all levels from corporal to general. Fifteen percent of all U.S. military officers are women (Kantrowitz & Juarez, 2005). Women have been appointed chiefs of police, a role traditionally reserved for men, in the cities of Detroit, Milwaukee, San Francisco, and Boston (Paul, 2004). Currently, in San Francisco, the three most senior police officials are women (Breslau, 2005a). In the 50 states, women make up approximately 23% of state legislators and 26% of executive officers. In 1999, they were serving as 18 lieutenant governors, 14 secretaries of state, 10 attorneys general, 10 treasurers, and 10 chief state education officers (Anonymous, 1999). In 2005, in Washington state, the governor, the state's two U.S. senators, and four of its nine State Supreme Court justices were women (Breslau, 2005b). In 2000, Mississippi had a state low in the proportion of women elected to political office: 22 women were in the state legislature, 32 were justice court judges, 44 were mayors, and 339 were elected members of city councils (Kimmel, 2002). Significant numbers of women now play important leadership roles in U.S. business, health care, and government agencies. In the mid-1980s, two of the 100 members of the U.S. Senate were women. But by 2005, 14 were women and 81 of the 435 members of the U.S. House of Representatives were women. In 1999, women held at least one statewide office in 42 of the 50 states. In future we should expect to see more women in chief political roles in the United States, as we now see in the parliamentary democracies abroad. Elizabeth Dole was a candidate for president in 2000, and Senator Hillary Clinton was campaigning to become the Democratic candidate in 2008. The gender distribution among office holders has become more equitable in local governments. Women city mayors, county council members, and judges at all levels are now commonplace. One effect of the increasing numbers of women in political office has been the increasing advocacy of and consideration for the welfare of women, family, and children. "Women in Congress have different priorities, raise different issues, and operate differently than their male colleagues" (Walsh, 2002, p. 6).

As of 2007, even larger percentages of women are serving in many other countries as heads of state, prime ministers, and other positions of government leadership. By the mid-1990s, women prime ministers or presidents had been chosen in Britain, France, Ireland, Canada, Portugal, Iceland, Norway, Argentina, Nicaragua, Bolivia, Haiti, Dominica, the Dutch Antilles, Turkey, Israel, India, Pakistan, Bangladesh, Sri Lanka, and the Philippines (Harwood & Brooks, 1993). In 2005, Germany joined the many countries abroad by electing its first women chancellor, Angela Merkel, as head of government.

Women who rose to the top of their political systems in developing countries tended to have a close attachment to their fathers and did not challenge their patriarchical society. They came from elite political families and were widows, sisters, or daughters of male political leaders. But the best-known women who led democracies in the developed world were Golda Meir and Margaret Thatcher, who came from more humble beginnings. They shared deep convictions about their causes. They were known for their determination and self-confidence and were driven by ideology. They had a low tolerance for disagreement (Genovese, 1995). Women are serving in increasing numbers in the cabinets and ministries of the world's

democracies. The first to do so in the United States was Frances Perkins, who served in F. D. Roosevelt's cabinet starting in 1933. Thirteen women served in Bill Clinton's cabinet between 1992 and 2000. By 2002, 37% of the Norwegian Parliament and 42% in ministerial posts were women (Goldsmith, 2002). Women leaders of sociopolitical movements, such as Margaret Sanger, Emma Goldman, Simone de Beauvoir, and Betty Friedan have been but a small number in comparison with the men who have sparked and organized social revolutions and reforms (Apfelbaum & Hadley, 1986). Nonetheless, a substantial number of leaders of nonprofit and volunteer organizations are women.

Increase in Management and Administration

Early on, women worked as supervisors mainly of other women in offices, in hospitals, or in the telephone industry (Northouse, 2001). However, these women were only a small percentage of all the women in the population and a small percentage in contrast to men in leadership positions in general. There was a marked increase in the proportion of women in managerial and leadership positions after 1970. Although women made up less than 5% of middle managers and less than 2% of executives in business in the early 1970s (M. W. Meyer, 1975), between 1970 and 1980, gains for women in top leadership roles were apparent, especially in the mass media, universities, private foundations, and cultural institutions (Dye & Strickland, 1982). Between 1970 and 1980, the total number of women managers and administrators in the U.S. workforce increased by more than 100%. Between 1972 and 1986, the percentage of women in managerial positions rose from 19% to over 30% (Hymowitz & Schellhardt, 1986). In the military, 10% of the U.S. naval officers by 1987 were women, and by 1980, a woman was serving as the commanding general of a large U.S. army post (Beck, 1980). But by and large, more women in proportion to men were concentrated in the lower levels of management. No women entered AT&T in 1960, for instance, as first-level managers. But by 1985—while only 2.7% of the top executives and directors of AT&T were women, and 8.3% and 15% were division and district managers, respectively—22% were second-level supervisors and 38.7% were first-level supervisors (Hymowitz &

Schellhardt, 1986). Proportionately more women than men had attained management jobs in service firms, such as AT&T, rather than in industrial firms, such as DuPont, Exxon, and General Motors, where the percentage hovered around 8%.

The percentages were generally much higher in retail and trade. For instance, in 1985, the proportion of women managers reached 61% in Federated Stores and 64% in Bank of America. Nonetheless, overall Northouse (2001) estimated that in 1998, in the Fortune 1000 firms, women occupied only 11% of managerial and administrative positions, 6% of line positions, and approximately 11% as corporate officers and members of the boards of directors.

By 1981, firms in consumer-related industries were most likely (5 of 10) to have a woman on the board of directors, while holding companies and firms in the extraction industries had none. Also, women had more opportunities to become insider directors (managers elevated to the board of directors in the same firm) in small than in large firms (Harrigan, 1981). By 1990, women managers had reached parity in numbers with men in finance, insurance, real estate, and services but were much less present in manufacturing, mining, and construction (Women's Bureau, 1991). Women CEOs like Carly Fiorina of Hewlett-Packard were still rare in 2004 in America's largest firms. In 2002 only 9% of CEOs, 14% of board members, and 16% of corporate officers of Fortune 500 firms were women (Kantrowitz & Juarez, 2005). But there was a sharp increase in the number of women who owned their own business. In the United States by 1992, 6.4 million women were business owners, mainly of small businesses. During the preceding five years, nationally, 43% of firms were owned by women; and there was an almost 95% increase in women owners of construction companies and an almost 78% increase in women owners of transportation firms (Department of Commerce, 1996). Between 1990 and 2000, women started businesses at twice the rate of men (Northouse, 2001).

Increase in MBAs

In 1964, the first woman enrolled in the MBA program at the University of Pittsburgh. In 1974, Michigan State University reported twice the proportion of women students in business as it had had in 1969. Stanford University noted a similar doubling in the three-year period 1971–1974 (Chambers, 1974). From 1971 to 1976, the number of women enrolled in MBA programs in American universities tripled (L. Werner, 1979). There was a sharp rise in the absolute and proportional numbers of women who received MBA degrees or the equivalent between 1956 and 2000. By the 1990s, parity of the sexes had been reached in many business schools. Today, many programs contain more women than men. The same trend has occurred for undergraduate business majors as well as in law schools, whose graduates ultimately become business, government, and political leaders.

A law degree is a route into political leadership and another preparation for organizational management. Women increased from 10% of first-year law students in 1970 to 49.4% in 2000. Woman now form the majority in many law schools. By 2005, 65% of law school deans and administrators were women.

Society in Transition

Except when such male-favored characteristics as upper body strength are required, the roles of women in society are primarily culturally determined. Biology has some effects; women live longer. And childbearing has its obvious universal effects; but most of what women can do is culture-based. In a survey of 224 mainly subsistence-level societies, Murdock (1937) showed that although men generally hunted and trapped and women usually gathered and prepared food, few occupations were entirely relegated anywhere to only one sex. (An exception was hunting sea mammals, which would be hard on pregnant women.) More than 99% of positions in the U.S. Air Force can be filled by women, who by 2000 made up 18% of its personnel.

We are in a period of transition. Much cultural support for maintaining sex differences in leadership and, more important, different attitudes, beliefs, and values about women leaders is diminishing. The need for a family to have two wage earners to maintain a desired standard of living, as well as equal employment legislation and U.S. Supreme Court decisions, have had dramatic effects. Almost all adult women have been moved to seek part- or full-time employment. Women today constitute 48% of the U.S. workforce. More women than men are applying to, entering, and graduating from college. But some jobs are still seen as more male-relevant and others as more female-relevant, and in many firms the sexes are still segregated according to their positions. Nonetheless, by 1977, more than 75% of women disagreed that some work is meant for men and other work is meant for women—an increase of 21 percentage points from 1962. Younger women in 1977 were even more likely to disagree, which suggests that even more extreme rejection by women of the duality of work roles is becoming the norm (Thornton & Freedman, 1979). In a 1950 Gallup poll, the top recommendations for young women seeking to prepare for careers were nursing, teaching, secretarial or clerical work or the roles of dietician, home economist, and social worker. In 2001, the Gallup poll response to the same question was that women were preparing for careers in the field of computers or medicine (Gallup Tuesday Briefing, 2001).

Early research by Hall and Locke (1938) and E. Livingstone (1953) found that women, particularly in industry, were often reluctant to assume supervisory responsibilities. The times, indeed, are "a-changing." The rise to parity came after years of social turbulence, the women's liberation movement, cultural changes, and legislation prohibiting sex discrimination in employment practices (Title VII of the Civil Rights Act of 1964 and the affirmative action program of the Equal Employment Opportunity Commission). Along with the increase in the proportion of women in the work world, the issue of women as leaders now looms large in research and policy considerations. One indication of the change in attitudes toward women has been steadily increasing percentage of people between 1937 and 1978 in Gallup polls who were willing to vote for a woman for president—in 1937, 31%; in 1949, 48%; in 1958, 52%; in 1967, 57%; and in 1978, 76% (Anonymous, 1983). The upward trend continues.

Attitudes and sex-related stereotypes about women as managers among both women (Kravetz, 1976) and men (Tavris, 1977) have changed. M. M. Wood's (1976) survey of approximately 100 male and female managers found that most managers thought that women were winning increased acceptance in the business environment. A comparison of 1965 and 1985 studies of executives' attitudes about women in business showed that executives' perceptions had changed greatly. In the 1985 survey, ex-

ecutives were more likely to think that women wanted positions of authority and felt more comfortable about working for a female boss (Sutton & Moore, 1985). Many commentators saw the need for more women managers as a consequence of the need for organizations to adapt to new technologies. Women managers were seen as more cooperative and participatory in leading efforts to make changes (Morris, 1988). By 2001, Vinkenbut, Johannesen-Schmidt, and Eagley (2001) could report that, compared to behavioral norms for transformational leadership—usually found at slightly higher levels in women and correlated with successful and effective leadership (Bass, 1998)—effects were exaggerated when participants estimated how frequently male and female managers displayed transformational leadership.

Data from Powell, Posner, and Schmidt (1984) illustrate the changes that have occurred. In contrast to stereotypic expectations, they found that the 130 women managers in their sample placed a greater emphasis on their careers than on their family life and had a greater concern for production than for social relationships. Furthermore, the women managers rated ambition, ability, and skill as more important than did the 130 male managers in the sample. Nevertheless, in many instances, women still face disadvantages in opportunities for managerial and leadership positions.

Constraints on Opportunities for Leadership

Leadership opportunities for women in the past tended to be limited to women's issues and jobs in particular institutions such as sororities, convents, all-girl schools, and telephone operations. Even presidents of women's colleges were often men. Although the vast majority of public school teachers were women, they remained a minority among top-level school administrators (Estler, 1975). According to Sutton and Moore's (1985) survey of executives' attitudes about women as leaders in business, most respondents in 1985, male or female, still believed that women had to be exceptional to succeed in business. Moreover, the women in the poll were less optimistic about their opportunities than were the men queried. The women thought they still had to struggle more to rise in the business world and were likely to earn less than their male counterparts. Nevertheless, despite Litterer's

(1976) finding that in almost all samples, women executives reported that they had suffered from discrimination, women who were managers (as well as men who were managers) had a higher degree of job satisfaction than their nonsupervisory counterparts (Keaveny, Jackson, & Fossum, 1976). These women appeared to enjoy their positions and to hold the same job expectations as male supervisors (Brief & Oliver, 1976). Many other studies have found little or no difference in the job satisfaction of female vs. male leaders.[2]

Obstacles and Conflicts

Even when women are promoted to managerial positions, they continue to face a variety of barriers to their upward mobility. Almost half of respondents to a Gallup poll said they would prefer to work for a man, compared to 22% who preferred to work for a woman (Gallup Poll, 2001, January 11). Salaries for women tended to be less than those for men in comparable positions. In 2001, women executives earned a median of $188,000; men, $257,000. Affirmative action laws calling for equity in hiring men and women have had both positive and negative effects. The numbers of women in leadership positions have increased as women have had to be considered for selection and promotion instead of being excluded. But even if their merit justifies their selection and promotion, their merit may be questioned by others in the organization. They may be seen as having gained their positions as a consequence of legally required preferences for women over men to correct past injustices (Singer, 1994). When 150 undergraduate women were asked whether they had benefited because of legal preference rather than merit, they felt they would be seen as less competent and would produce timid, performance-limiting task decisions. Their self-regard would be lowered. Nevertheless, if they knew they were highly competent and wanted to make a good impression, they would make the best possible task decision (Heilman & Alcott, 2001). The obstacle of discrimination is greater in male-dominated industries, according to an Australian study (Gardiner & Tiggemann, 1999). In some jobs, the obstacle may be the reluctance to send women on business trips with men (Donnelly, 1976). The rotation of

jobs for managerial development may require a woman and her family to relocate, which means that either her husband must also relocate or the couple must live apart in a "commuter marriage." Family relocation may be less necessary when husbands are rotated.

Work/Family Balance. Carroll (1987) argued that the biggest obstacle married women leaders face is coping with the conflict between career and family. It is not surprising that among the few sex differences found by Morrison, White, and Van Velsor (1987), women executives felt less equal than did their male counterparts to the demands placed on their time and energy in their daily lives. In 1989, 83% of working women reported conflicts between their job and the well-being of their children. One of the fastest-growing segments in the workforce is mothers with preschool-age children (Hewlett, 1998).

Many companies and agencies have developed family support policies. When the directors of a large hospital discovered that the primary reason for employees' absenteeism was to take care of ill children, they created an infirmary to care for the children. Supportive husbands may be especially important. Husbands now share homemaking duties. Househusbands and working wives are no longer rare. Among 657 Israeli managers and human service professionals, 57% of whom were women, the burnout and exhaustion from stress at work for the women were ameliorated by the amount of support they received in their lives in general; but for the men, it was support at work that helped prevent burnout from stress. (Etzioni, 1984). Compared to their male counterparts, women professionals in a Swedish insurance company were equally satisfied with their work situations but not their life situations. They reported spending twice as much time on household chores as their spouses and were less able to relax after work. Children added to the work overload and impeded career opportunities. Both men and women at work showed physiological symptoms of stress, yet at home, only the women, especially those with children, continued to show elevated stress levels of epinephrine and norepinephrine (Lundberg & Frankenhaeuser, 1999). A majority of Hollywood TV women executives have eliminated work/family conflict by rejecting the norm of typical family life, marriage, and children (Ensher, Murphy, & Sullivan, 2002).

The success of married managers in foreign assign-

---

[2] See, e.g., Bartol (1974, 1975), Bartol and Wortman (1976), Herrick (1973), and Jacobson and Effertz (1974).

ments depends strongly on the support and satisfaction of the manager's spouse, who is usually female (Brett & Stroh, 1995). Her adjustment to the foreign culture is critical (Black & Gregersen, 1991). A survey of 427 international managers and their 167 spouses found in multiple regression analysis that a manager's willingness to assume a foreign assignment long-term correlated .55 with the spouse's willingness. This, in turn, correlated .44 with the spouse's adventurousness and correlated negatively (−.22) with lack of career support for the spouse (Konopaske, Robie, & Ivancevich, undated).

Comparable Pay. Even in Norway, a country with a high degree of political equality and an egalitarian culture (Goldsmith, 2002), women earned 75% to 76.6% of men doing the same work in investment, banking, insurance, and business services. In central government and municipal government, women working in the same jobs earned 88% and 89%, respectively, of their male counterparts (Moen, 1995).

Fewer Opportunities for Necessary Experience and Contacts. In 2000, only 13% of men and 30% of women said in a representative sample that women who do the same job were paid less than their male counterparts (Gallup, 2000) But Lyness and Thompson (1997) found that even when 51 women made the same pay and bonuses as their male counterparts in similar executive positions, the women managed fewer people and received fewer overseas assignments. Women's lesser experience with team sports in the past limited their ability to participate effectively in management teams (Hennig & Jardim, 1977). Women did not know the rules (Harragan, 1977). "Old boy" networks made it more difficult for women executives to obtain the information necessary to fulfill the manager's monitoring role effectively.

Women do not frequent men's athletic clubs, they may be excluded from some social clubs, and they may be unable to entertain visitors there. These are all situations in which important information may be gathered and important decisions may be made. In Finland, for example, male executives may gather in a sauna to negotiate with male union leaders. Above and beyond this social exclusion, women may remain outsiders in a male-dominated organization. In a survey of 76 men and 64 women in a newspaper publishing firm, Brass (1985) found that on the average, women were rated as less influential than the men, though they did not differ in the number of others whom they had to contact at work or in their centrality to the formal networks. However, they were not well integrated into the men's networks, including the organization's dominant coalition. According to Symons (1986), who interviewed 67 women professionals and managers in France and Canada, gaining entry, establishing credibility, and managing sex identification in the "corporate tribe" is a process of being continuously retested. (The situation is different for men, who need to pass their test of admission and acceptance only once.) Such testing is particularly salient for the token woman middle manager when feminist issues surface in the organization (Rose, 1980).

Fraker (1984) noted a number of other more subtle obstacles for women trying to move up the corporate ladder. Women may be seen as unable to "fit in" with the small informal, all-male group that constitutes upper management. In addition, they may be delegated less authority than are their male counterparts for assigned responsibilities, according to a survey by Sherman, Ezell, and Odewahn (1987). They may not receive the same constructive feedback from their male superiors as their male counterparts. And they may feel uncomfortable and reluctant to discuss personal matters. Furthermore, Bayes and Newton (1978) observed that a woman leader and her subordinates ordinarily have little social experience regarding a woman's possession of the legitimate power to control and protect the boundaries of an adult group, to stand alone as a figure of authority, and to evaluate the output of other adults.

Naiveté. A survey by Radin (1980) of 100 women in upper-, middle-, and entry-level positions in state and local government agencies found that the women overrated education and hard work as prerequisites for advancement and underestimated political awareness. The women tended to be ignorant of the political games played within an organization. Yet a woman's success as a manager, argued Hermig and Jardim (1977) and Trahey (1977), requires competing with men in a system that the men understand better and in which they are more familiar and comfortable.

Conflicting Stereotypes of
Women and Managers

Sixty-eight percent of a representative sample of Americans in a 2001 Gallup poll viewed men as more aggressive than women; 90% viewed women as more emotional than men. Women were seen as more affectionate, talkative, patient, and creative; men were regarded as more courageous (Gallup, 2001, February 21). The men's traits better fit those of the traditional manager and leader. Among 101 male bank managers in India, satisfaction with their interaction with women managers depended on their attitude toward women as managers (Bhatnagar & Swamy, 1995).

Seifert (1984) illustrated the pervasive stereotyping of the inadequacy of females for leadership. Seifert led male and female participants to believe they were working with male and female leaders, when they were all receiving the same standardized communications from the experimenter. The male and female participants who received the notes from the supposed male leaders rated the notes as clearer than did participants who received notes from the supposed female leaders. Carpeno (1976) found that for 100 professional staff members of a regional high school system, statements about female leaders indicated doubt and uneasiness about their future. Frank and Katcher (1977) concluded, from a survey of 104 male and 44 female medical students, that the men tended to stereotype the women's behavior and to exclude them from positions of leadership in dissection groups in anatomy courses. Among 1,000 male executives who were surveyed by Bowman, Worthy, and Greyser (1965), 44% expressed mildly unfavorable to strongly unfavorable attitudes toward women in management. In general, these men believed that women were temperamentally ill-suited for leadership positions. In the same way, a survey of 2,000 executive readers of the *Harvard Business Review* (Bowman, Worthy, & Greyser, 1965) reported that 41% of the men were opposed to women in executive roles. Many readers thought that women were not suitable. Both men and women in the sample believed that women's opportunities for advancement were limited. Similarly, a 1971 Louis Harris poll of representative working women showed a strong preference for a male boss over a female boss (White, 1981). Brenner (1970) found,

in a nationwide survey of managers, that the four traits regarded as most important for an upper-management position were deemed more likely to be found in men than in women. Consistent with both these results, in a study of German students, Kruse and Wintermantel (1986) found that in describing male leaders, the students took it for granted that the leaders would be dominant and competitive, take risks, and be able to make decisions on their own; but for women leaders, these traits had to be stated explicitly. The male leader was the normative one; the female leader had to fit the male schematic. In a second study, Kruse and Wintermantel (1986) found that for male students, the concept of man correlated .9 with the concept of manager and .8 with the concept of leadership. The concept of woman correlated $-.4$ with the concept of manager and $-.5$ with the concept of leadership. The results for the female students were similar.

When they completed self-reports, both male and female managers showed a preference for stereotypic male (task-oriented) management behaviors (Brenner & Bromer, 1981). Similarly, 1,161 students, using the Bem Sex-Role Inventory (Bem, 1970), chose masculine rather than feminine traits to be sought in the good manager, the good president, and even the female political activist. There was a lack of *stereotype fit* between the stereotypical feminine role and the steretypical role of leader. It is suggested that male leaders are "in role" and women leaders are "out of role" and therefore, compared to men, women are likely to receive lower leadership ratings from those susceptible to stereotypical thinking (Atwater & Roush, 1994).[3]

A survey of 320 college students found that the successful leader was perceived to have a masculine orientation (Linimon, Barron, & Falbo, 1984). Four beliefs that reinforce unfavorable attitudes toward women as prospects for managerial positions were revealed in a factor analysis of 176 male managers' responses to a survey of their attitudes toward women in the world of work. The factors extracted about women were: (1) lack of career orienta-

---

[3] A *stereotype* is "a generalized perception ascribing particular traits, characteristics, values, or behavior . . . without regard to accuracy or applicability." It is a judgment with "an inability or unwillingness to alter a personal point of view" (Corsini, 1999). In reading this chapter, the reader will consider the years in which various research studies were published. Nonetheless, stereotypes about women in management may still apply after a half-century or more.

tion, (2) lack of leadership potential, (3) lack of dependability, and (4) lack of emotional stability (Bass, Krusell, & Alexander, 1971). The perceived lack of career orientation is linked to the stereotype that women are less concerned about their jobs. The other stereotypes are built around a mixture of fact and fancy. According to Heilman, Block, Simon, et al. (1989), men perceive the successful manager as a man. Male cadets regarded their own success as leaders as due to their own abilities, but they attributed the successful leadership of women cadets to the efforts of their followers (Rice, Instone, & Adams, 1984). Male stereotyping of women was singled out by 52% of 461 women executives as an important reason for blocking women's advancement in corporate leadership (Catalyst, 1996).

Although women may benefit from some positive stereotyping, such as being expected to be more considerate than their male counterparts (Pearson & Serafini, 1984), Heller (1982) found that female leaders are stereotyped negatively at two ends of a continuum. At one extreme, as mother, pet, or sex object, women are considered too submissive or emotional to be effective leaders. At the other extreme, women violate what is expected of them as women and are seen as "iron maidens," aggressive workaholics, and domineering and manipulative.

Women are likely to have more difficulty than men in obtaining the same role legitimacy as leaders. For instance, unlike their male counterparts, new female professors have to establish their legitimacy among students (Richardson & Cook, 1980). Women are faced with the conflict between the stereotypic expectations of them as women and the stereotypic expectations of them as leaders—the latter identified more with maleness. Maleness is associated with the initiation of structure (Pearson & Serafini, 1984).

The female sex-role stereotype labels women as less competent but emotionally warmer than men. The stereotype of the effective manager matches the masculine stereotype of the effective manager: competent, tough, and emotionally cold. Miner (1965) reflected the accepted stereotype that there are parallel role requirements for being a manager and being a man.[4] Both a manager and a man need to be able to take charge, make decisions, be assertive, and take disciplinary action, but

women managers in hierarchical organizations must follow masculine behavior patterns. During the early years of their managerial experience, women tend to identify with the masculine stereotype of a successful manager to overcome their perceived female inadequacies (Hennig, 1971).

The stereotypic concepts of being a woman and of being a leader were viewed as incompatible (V. E. Schein, 1973, 1975). Surveys tended to report large differences in the traits attributed to women and to successful middle managers. Survey data also indicated the popular belief that women make inferior leaders (Bowman, Worthy, & Greyser, 1965). Women themselves tended to subscribe early on to the different stereotypes of managers and of women. O'Leary (1974) and McClelland (1965b) both found that women as a group described themselves as different from or even opposite to men as a group on traits that are supposedly required for management. As confirmation, Frantzve (1979) found a positive relation between masculinity scores on the Bem Sex-Role Inventory and the tendency to emerge as a leader in 49 initially leaderless discussions in groups of men and women. Again, Brenner and Bromer (1981) found, in self-reports by 66 male and 66 female managers in metropolitan New York, that both sexes had a significant preference for behaviors reflecting the male stereotype. By 1989, however, female managers', but not male managers', views had changed. Thus, 420 male middle managers surveyed by Brenner, Tomkiewicz, and Schein (1989) still clung to the male managerial stereotype reported 15 years earlier by Schein (1973, 1975), while 173 female counterparts no longer equated management with masculine traits.

Broverman, Vogel, Broverman, et al. (1972) asked 100 college students to indicate the characteristics, attitudes, and behaviors in which men and women differed. A second group then rated the extent to which the traits mentioned most frequently by the first group were typical of adult men or women. The female role stereotype that emerged did not fit with what is usually deemed important for effective leadership and management. A woman was regarded as less aggressive, more dependent, and more emotional. She did not hide her emotions and was subjective, easily influenced, and submissive. She enjoyed art and literature, but not mathematics and science. She was excitable in minor crises, passive, uncom-

---

[4]See Chapter 6.

petitive, illogical, home-oriented, unskilled in business, sneaky, and unfamiliar with the ways of the world. Her feelings were easily hurt. She was unadventurous and indecisive, cried easily, rarely acted like a leader, and lacked self-confidence. She was uncomfortable about being aggressive, unambitious, unable to separate feelings from ideas, conceited about her appearance, talkative, tactful, gentle, aware of others' feelings, religious, interested in her own appearance, neat, and quiet and had a strong need for security. She also easily expressed tender feelings.

Such stereotypes resulted in self-imposed attitudinal barriers to women's entrance into positions of leadership. They also caused women to be reluctant to: (1) assert themselves out of fear of being seen as aggressive; or (2) to display their ambition to achieve out of fear of failure (Heller, 1982). *Stereotype threats* also affected women, who felt that the evaluation of their behavior might be used to confirm the negative stereotypes of women as a whole (Steele & Aronson, 1995).

Female leaders were supposedly more attentive to upward communications from their subordinates; males were expected to be more effective in downward directiveness. Stereotyped female leaders were expected to be more indirect and nonconfrontational and to use influence tactics such as helplessness, personal reward, and hints, whereas leaders were expected more often to use direct, forthright influence strategies based on expertise, authority, and logic. Generally, these stereotypes did not necessarily reflect reality (Hall & Donnell, 1979; Rice, Instone, & Adams, 1984; Szilagyi, 1980a). Male candidates for managerial positions were rated as more promising than were equally qualified female candidates on such dimensions as acceptability and potential for service (Gutek & Stevens, 1979; Rosen, Jerdee, & Prestwich, 1975). When Ezell, Odewahn, and Sherman (1982) surveyed 360 male and female managers in state public welfare organizations, they found that on their entry into management and their promotion to higher levels, women's leadership potential was more likely to be judged on their past performance and men's according to future expectations about them, even though the men's and women's competencies and motivation were seen as identical. As a consequence, judgments about the men could be more subjective.

If a woman leader adopted more accommodative, par-

ticipative leadership behavior, she faced criticism for being too passive. But if she adopted an autocratic or task-oriented leadership behavior or a more directive style, she was seen as too aggressive and masculine. Powell (1982), among others, showed that sex differences, as such, were related not to being a good manager but to differences in sex-role identities—how women and men are supposed to differ in the way they behave. For example, in mixed company, a woman was likely to be inhibited by the attitudes she held about the appropriateness of women attempting to take the initiative in such a situation (O'Leary, 1974). Her inhibitions were likely to be reinforced by the mixed reaction of others if she succeeded (Jacobson & Effertz, 1974). Nevertheless, Hyman (1980) suggested that people still perceived woman managers to be either tough, aggressive, unyielding, and autocratic or unassertive, good workers. As a consequence, women leaders were able to use their power as directly as men could (Johnson, 1976). Nevertheless, although women were expected to display less dominance and competitiveness in mixed-sex groups, Bunker and Bender (1980) suggested that female managers were as competitive as their male counterparts, but they competed in different ways. At the same time, Hollander and Yoder (1980) concluded, from a research review, that observed differences in the leadership behavior of women and men could be attributed mainly to the interrelationship of the role expectations, style, and task demands of particular circumstances.

According to Bayes and Newton (1978), subordinates responded to a woman leader partly as an individual and partly according to the cultural stereotype of women. The responses of many subordinates to a woman leader reflected their socialized expectations about women in general, which were likely to conflict with the more appropriate response to a woman who was a manager, and hence involved in a role that they considered to be primarily masculine.

There was disagreement between men and women as subordinates about the perceived characteristics of the prototypical manager, according to a study of the opinions of 702 undergraduates. For instance, male undergraduates were more likely to perceive the prototypical manager as aggressive and competitive, with feelings that were less easily hurt. (Deal & Stevenson, 1998). Women leaders themselves were in conflict when they faced a divergence in what was expected from them in their roles as managers and as females. But do the stereotypes reflect reality? Do women actually differ from men in traits that are of consequence to leadership even as they differ from the stereotype? A variety of answers emerge. For example, women are supposed to be less task-oriented than men. This was actually found to be true when the Orientation Inventory (Bass, 1967), a direct measure, was used for male and female counterparts from adolescence to middle age and for many student and occupational groups, except for one group of senior women at the University of California, Berkeley. But no sex differences appeared when the Least Preferred Co-worker (LPC) score,[5] a more disguised measurement, was used by Chapman (1975) and by J. M. Ward (1977) to determine the task and relations orientation of male and female students, and by Schneier (1978) in a study of emerging leaders. Okanes and Murray (1980) found that the scores of 51 female managers on the Mehrabian achievement scale were significantly higher than those of 51 male managers. Furthermore, evidence has accumulated that the need to achieve is a complex of styles and orientations and that men score higher mainly in the competitive aspects of achievement. The differences in men's and women's scores for the desire for mastery (a component of achievement)—that is, the higher scores of men than of women—tend to diminish with experience. The same happens to the higher scores of women on orientation to work, another component of achievement (Deaux, 1985). Also, male executives are more comfortable than female executives about achievement when the criteria for excellence are clearly specified and when conformity to authority is desirable (Morrison, White, & Van Velsor, 1987).

Hostile sexism and *benevolent sexism* are brought into play to justify the stereotyped justification of the inappropriateness and inadequacy for leadership of the "weaker" sex. Hostile sexism sees women as usurping men's status and power in their traditional role as leader. Benevolent sexism offers chivalrous protection and affection to women who continue in their traditional role. Benevolent sexism also rewards women for conforming to the patriarchical status quo, but inhibits gender equality (Glick & Fiske, 2001).

[5] See Chapter 17.

Caveat

The voluminous research on sex stereotypes in the twentieth century suggests a continuing perception that management and leadership are masculine attributes. This does not seem to fit with the increasing parity occurring in the rise for women in management and leadership. It will take a replication of much of this research in the twenty-first century to see if the stereotypes remain and have a more subtle influence on the now-common presence of women as managers and leaders.

Advantageousness of the Stereotypes

Describing the good manager in masculine terms, as Miner (1974) did in his conception of the motivation to manage (which Powell and Butterfield [1979] also found among 694 business students), reveals stereotypes that may have worked to a woman manager's advantage. If women managers are not expected to perform well and are seen as operating under handicaps (Terborg & Ilgen, 1975), then if they do perform well, their performance may be attributed to extra effort and competence and considered more worthy of reward than that of comparable male managers. Kanter (1977b) and Alban and Seashore (1978) argued that the stereotypic female role requirement that women deal effectively with people offsets the disadvantages to a woman of the stereotypic submissive, nurturing role requirements. Similarly, Larwood and Wood (1977) pointed out, in agreement with what was detailed in preceding chapters, that the effective manager can make use of both the supposedly more masculine traits of competence, task orientation, and initiative and the supposedly more feminine concern for people, feelings, and relationships. Since then, as we have already noted, the stereotypical concerns of women for nurturing and consideration have increasingly appeared as requirements for the good manager in the postindustrial organization. For instance, Schmidt and Eagley (2001) found that estimates of the higher transformational leadership of female than male managers (involving concern for followers) were exaggerated in comparison to the norms for actual managers.

Harassment

Despite its illegality, sexual harassment is experienced by a sizable proportion of women in the workplace (Graham, 1986). For instance, in the U.S. federal government over a period of two years, 44% of women employees reported some form of unwanted sexual attention at work. Sexual harassment is consistently found to contribute to women personnel's loss of job satisfaction and psychological well-being (Offerman & Malamut, 2001). Based on a nationally representative Swedish sample of 594 male and 430 female medical doctors, Konrad and Cannings (2002) found that women reported more sexual harassment in medical units with large proportions of men.

The severity of sexual harassment ranges from teasing and unwanted touching and jokes to rape. Sexual favors may be demanded for women's advancement, and sexual threats may force women into resigning their positions. Sexual harassment may be a hostile response, unrelated to the quality of a woman's job performance, whose goal is to eliminate her as a competitor for advancement. It may be a form of displaced aggression, in which the woman colleague is seen as the weaker and safer target of hostility than the powerful male colleague who has caused the frustration. Both men and women in the workplace have to learn how to relate to each other comfortably without the usually more powerful men misinterpreting women's friendliness and sociability as readiness for sexual intimacy.

Harassers are typically older, married, and of the same race as the target (Seppa, 1997). In civilian organizations, sexual advances to women are usually made by superiors; sexual advances to men are usually made by subordinates (Zanville, 1997). Leadership makes a difference. Sexual harassment was less in army units where confidence in the leader and support from him or her was high, and where the commanding officer spoke out rather than seemed to encourage it. Sexual harassment may be declining in the military, perhaps because the leadership has been paying more attention to it and punishing the perpetrators instead of the victims (Shenon, 1997) and because women are increasingly being admitted to combat units, facing the same risks as their male counterparts. Offerman and Malamut (2001) analyzed military surveys completed in 1995 of 5,629 women from the Army, Air Force, Navy, Marine Corps, and Cost Guard. Women were freer to report harassment incidents when they felt that an adequate complaint process was available and that their hierarchically close superiors and organization were less tolerant of harassment. Both leadership and organizational policy were needed. Using data from 8,093 women in the same 1995 military surveys, Murray, Sivasubramanian, and Jacques (2001) demonstrated that the perceptions of immediate supervisors' trust, fairness, and support in preventing sexual harassment were enhanced when there were women in higher authority. In all five U.S. military services between 1988 and 1995, there were declines in the percentage of women personnel who experienced unwanted sexual attention, ranging from 49% in the air force to 61% in the army.

Response to Sexual Harassment. In two controlled experiments, when women were asked what they would do when sexually harassed during a job interview, they indicated that they would feel angry and confrontative. But when actually faced with such an interview for a research assistantship, they tended to remain nonconfrontational, polite, and respectful. They did express some concern, but would not jeopardize their opportunity for employment (Woodzicka & LaFrance, 2001).

Sexual Relationships

Real and imagined love affairs between men and women in the same corporation are seen as sexual opportunism and are likely to affect the performance of and the favoritism shown to the junior partner—usually the woman. Collins (1983) noted that love between managers is dangerous because it may challenge formal superior-subordinate and customary peer relationships. The dominant male–submissive female personal relationship may take precedence over formal organizational requirements and affect political alliances. According to a survey of offices by Quinn (1977), two thirds of 130 employees believed office romances to cause much gossip; one third, to provoke complaints and hostilities; and one fifth, to result in distorted communication and threats to the unit's reputation. They lowered morale and output. While one third of the female supervisors of the men who were involved in these affairs openly discussed the situation, only 6% of the male supervisors of the women who were involved said they did so.

Executives' Reaction. According to Quinn's 130 respondents, once executives learned that coworkers were romantically entangled, they were twice as likely to fire the women involved. Female executives were less forgiving in this regard than male executives. Foley and Powell (1999) argued that management intervention was justified if the romance created a conflict of interest and if it interfered with work.

Segregation of Work Roles by Sex

Coser (1980) noted that half of all women at work could be found in just 21 occupations. Many studies showed that it was common to find jobs held either by women only or by men only within firms (Bielby & Baron, 1984; Gutek, 1985). This phenomenon occurred in Portugal, Britain, Russia, Ireland, and elsewhere, as well as in North America. The jobs held exclusively by women were likely to be both lower-paid and less likely to lead to advancement into administrative or executive positions. They were more likely to be transient opportunities and to call for less training and commitment. When women sought to enter or be promoted into a position, such as a managereal one, from which they had previously been excluded, they were likely to be judged to be less suitable for such a position if it had been male-dominated (Gutek, 1988). This likelihood was not necessarily due to a personal bias of the decision maker but rather a result of actual or assumed pressure from higher authority (Larwood, Gutek, & Gattiker, 1984).

The more one sex dominates an occupation, the more that performance in it is expected to conform to stereotypes about the sex of the occupants. As long as most nurses are women, expectations continue about their low pay and the warm, loving care expected from them. As long as management in industries and institutions remains male-dominated, high pay, task orientation, aggressiveness, and competitiveness are expected. Women are seen as better suited for traditional woman's work, such as nurse, and less well suited for traditional man's work, such as manager (Konrad & Gutek, 1987). The stereotypes of male competitiveness, adventuresomeness, and assertiveness fit with the stereotypical image of manager, in contrast to the stereotypical feminine qualities of consideration, supportiveness, and affection. What's reflected are the loving mother and the stern father. Suc-

cessful managers were expected to be masculine when Powell and Butterfield (1979) asked college students to describe a good manager. The effect was the same a quarter of a century later (Powell, Butterfield, & Parent, 2002). Despite this effect, by 2006, due to affirmative action, fair employment policies, and greater numbers of management-educated women and career women, many more women had joined management, as both supervisors and CEOs, although they were still concentrated at lower levels.

Women in Assistant and Service Roles. The sex segregation of work has accustomed us to see women in auxiliary and service roles. Numerous surveys and observers' analyses substantiate that being a woman legitimates the performance of a service role as a nurse, secretary, or administrative assistant (O'Leary, 1974; Schein, 1973). R. S. Weiss (1956) noted this linkage of women to service roles in a study of the allocation and acceptance of responsibility in a governmental agency. Reinforcing this linkage is men's preference for receiving nurturance and emotional support from women rather than other men, according to a survey by Burda and Vaux (1987).

Women tended to be counseled accordingly. Weisman, Morlock, Sack, and Levine (1976) observed that the counseling of women who were denied entry into medical school was different from the counseling of men who were denied entry. Men were encouraged to reapply to other medical schools or to try to obtain a doctorate in a related field. Women were reminded of the obstacles they would continue to face if they tried to continue in medicine. They were encouraged to change to more sex-role-accepted professions such as nursing. Such inadequate career counseling and the lack of successful female role models were seen as key factors in reducing women's choice of higher-status careers (Heinen, McGlauchin, Legeros, & Freeman, 1975; Lannon, 1977).

Women in Solo Roles. Women often find themselves the only member of their sex in a group or organization of men. This solo status further handicaps their integration into networks of consequence. A female senior vice president commented about serving solo with 13 men on a management committee: "It was very awkward at first. (After two years) what I have found is that they are never truly comfortable. . . . And it is not because they don't like me. . . . It's that certain guard, that what they might say in a roomful of men will be taken wrong when a woman is there" (Ragins, Townsend, & Mattis, 1998, p. 31).

Tokenism. The effects of being a token woman or man were observed by Berle, Biscone, Katz, et al. (1981) in 26 leaderless group discussions in which one member was of one sex and the rest of the members were of the other. Often, the woman in the solo role is a token of simulated enlightenment. She is at a considerable disadvantage in trying to succeed (Izraell, 1983; Spangler, Gordon, & Pipkin, 1978). Her performance is under closer scrutiny. She is under more pressure to conform to stereotypic expectations about women. Differences between men and women are exaggerated. The token woman is fitted into preexisting stereotypes of what is expected from her (Kanter, 1977b).

As a token, a woman may be thought to have been hired because of affirmative action guidelines rather than her qualifications (Northcraft & Martin, 1982). In blue-collar jobs, a token woman may experience considerable hostility (O'Farrell & Harlan, 1982). Furthermore, token women are more likely to be sexually harassed (Gutek & Morasch, 1982). Nevertheless, only 23% of 400 women executives agree that an obstacle to success for women in their firm was putting women in token positions without real power or operating authority (Segal & Zellner, 1992). In all, tokenism generates many questions about the solo woman leader in a male-dominated organization. How much does the visibility and pressure to perform result in more insecurity and resentment in the token woman? How often do the token woman's attempts to lead meet with resistance from the dominant males because of her token status (Adams & Yoder, 1985)?

Stereotyped Expectations of the Solo Woman. Men are likely to attribute a solo woman's success to her sexuality (Lockheed, 1975). When many men and few women are available, the women are expected to fall into their service and assisting roles (Guttentag & Secord, 1983). Frantzve's (1982) analysis of leaderless group discussions found that when men and women were systematically placed in solo roles among members of the opposite sex, the isolation from others of the same sex particularly inhibited a woman in an otherwise male group, but not vice versa. Solo females, but not solo males, were least likely to initiate proposals, were inter-

rupted most, and were most often ignored. However, according to a survey by Frantzve (1985), women in solo status learn to cope with their isolation by using humor, "playing the game," working hard and competently, and relying on outside support systems. And being distinctive may have its advantages at times. If the group's task appears to be more relevant to the experience of the woman as a woman, she may become the resident expert on the subject for the men who make up the remainder of the group. The choice of task can result in a bias in favor of the woman in the situation (Maccoby & Jacklin, 1974).[6] As the only woman in her cabinet, Margaret Thatcher enjoyed role flexibility. When necessary, she could enact the role of traditional male manager, mother, nanny, dominatrix, or androgeneous leader. Thatcher chose only men for her cabinet, men who were rarely strong and independent. While her colleagues might have known how to handle a male domineering prime minister, they were at a loss with how to deal with a domineering woman. They took the Iron Lady's orders and public humiliations (Genovese, 1995, p. 205).

Status, Sex, and Leadership

The lower status of women in American society is illustrated by what has usually happened when a large number of women entered an occupation: the occupation's prestige and desirability were lowered (Touhey, 1974). The high prestige of an occupation was linked to the presence of a large majority of men in it (Bartol & Bartol, 1975). Thus, the prestige of clerical work declined when women replaced men in it during the American Civil War. The prestige of physicians and lawyers may be affected by the large increase of women in those professions.

Lockheed (1975) noted that women's lack of influence, found in small-group research, has been attributed to sex-role socialization. Yet much of it is really a consequence of women's lower status. The conflict can be observed in stereotyped expectations of dominant male and subservient female that occur when women are assigned to lead men. Chapter 10 noted the extent to which one's success as a leader is associated with the status one is ac-

---

[6]Witness the rapid movement of women into management in consumer-oriented and service-oriented industries, such as banking, publishing, cosmetics, and retailing, in contrast to their much lower participation in management in manufacturing, chemicals, and mining.

corded. Women in our society remain handicapped in their efforts to become leaders by their lower status. Illustrative of the impact of sex status was Megargee's (1969) finding that when participants were paired with their own sex, those who scored high in dominant personality tended to assume leadership, but males, when paired with the opposite sex, assumed leadership even when they were submissive personalities. Presumably, as women's status has increased relative to that of men's since 1969, much less difference in influence is now likely to be found between the sexes, all else being equal.

Cultural Effects. In most cultures, the male's position has higher status than the female's. But considerable variation exists, ranging from societies in which men and women are almost equal in status, as is the case among the Arapesh, to those in which women are higher in status, as, for example, among the Tchambuli. When women are higher in status than men, they were more likely to lead. Higher-status women are dominant; men are less responsible and more dependent. Women make the choice; men are chosen (Mead, 1935). Strodtbeck (1951) contrasted three cultural groups within the United States—Navajo, Mormon, and mainstream American—by arranging discussions between husbands and wives from the three groups. Mormon husbands were most likely to lead discussions, reflecting the higher status of men than women in the patriarchal Mormon culture. Navajo husbands were least likely to lead discussions because women traditionally have more status and are more active and demanding in the Navajo culture. Results for the mainstream American spouses were in between the Mormons and the Navahos. Even among two different geographic regions that presumably have the same general culture, differences in status and leadership appeared. For example, women undergraduates in New York reported "playing dumb" much more frequently when on a date than did women undergraduates from the West Coast (Wallin, 1950). Such regional differences are likely to have decreased, if not disappeared, since 1950. As will be discussed in Chapter 33, the Anglo-American world and the traditional Muslim world differ greatly in status, education, and masculinity, which affects the extent to which Muslim women can participate in management or even work outside their homes.

Stress

Women have to cope, more than men, with career handicaps, conflicts, and disadvantageous stereotypes. A longitudinal study by Cooper and Davidson (1982) compared 135 top female executives in Britain with their 500 male counterparts. The women executives revealed more symptoms of stress such as migraine headaches, increased cigarette smoking, use of drugs, excessive drinking, and marital problems. Men benefit more than women from the social support of coworkers and supervisors, which can alleviate stress on the job (Geller & Hobfoll, 1994). Consistent with these findings, Ottaway and Bhatnagar (1988) reported that both U.S. and Indian female managers described themselves as more conflicted and hard-driving than did their male counterparts. Similarly, Greenglass (1988) found, among 114 Canadian first-level supervisors in government social services, that the women were much more likely than the men to describe themselves as stress-prone Type A personalities. In coping with stress, especially if they were Type As, the women engaged in more wishful thinking as well as more effort to change the situation or their own behavior than did the men. Azar (2000) suggests that unlike men, who fight or flee from stressful interactions, women convert them into "tend-and-befriend" caring, which counters the potential fight or flight with nurturing, affiliative behavior. Women in management may experience more stress than their male counterparts, but they also may cope with it better. Reports of disasters have noted that although women are generally more open in revealing their emotions, they appear to survive the stress of prolonged isolation, cold (or heat), and hunger. On occasion, only the women walked out alive from disastrous crossings of the Mojave Desert in the covered wagon days. Again, women fared better when the Donner Pass wagon train was trapped by winter snows in the High Sierras and with the stress of prolonged siege during the bombings of London in World War II.

Socialization, Sex, and Leadership

In our society, we are socialized primarily within the nuclear family in a culture that defines sex roles as total roles that define our sense of self and our behavior. The sex role pertains to all aspects of life and takes precedence over situation-specific work roles if they are incompatible. Dominance and independence are associated with masculine roles. Submissiveness, passivity, and nurturance are associated with feminine roles. Desirable femininity, culturally defined, emphasizes giving and the avoidance of aggressiveness and domination (Broverman, Broverman, Clarkson, et al., 1970). On the basis of a meta-analytic review of 172 social psychology studies, Eagly and Crowley (1986) concluded that the male helping role is to be chivalrous and heroic, whereas the female helping role is to be caring and nurturing. Riger and Galligan (1980) pointed out that socialization may account for the development in females of traits and behaviors, such as an unwillingness to take risks, that are counter to the demands of the management role. Men learn to see risk taking as an opportunity for success as well as failure, whereas women focus more on the failure aspect of risk taking (Henning & Jardim, 1977).

Importance of the Family. Even the exceptions among women seem to be a consequence of the differences in the nuclear family in which the women were raised. Vogel, Broverman, Broverman, et al. (1970) and Alinquist (1974) found that women who chose nontraditional careers—those historically occupied by men— were raised in families in which the mother worked full-time. In the past, the nuclear family was often likely to discourage women from choosing nontraditional careers. In addition, even if high school students of both sexes had similar aspirations for college and the choice of careers, the male students received significantly more parental attention and pressure to pursue their aspirations (Goodale & Hall, 1976).

Family Influences on Daughters. The different socialization of men and women may explain why being firstborn was more helpful to women's than to men's subsequent attainment of positions of leadership. For women, but not for men, Sandler and Scalia (1975) found a significantly greater likelihood for firstborn women to serve as presidents or other officers of organizations. Particularly in large families (Bossard & Boll, 1955) and families with working mothers, the eldest daughters were delegated authority and expected to take on many family responsibilities, such as caring for younger siblings (Clausen & Clausen, 1973). Klonsky (1978) found that the eldest daughters in large lower-class families received significantly higher-than-average leadership ratings in

high school sports from their coaches. In Puerto Rican families, the eldest daughter was expected to take on the leadership of her siblings. In the same way, Hennig and Jardim (1977) observed in a sample of 25 successful top-level women leaders that being firstborn was a common characteristic.

Other parental practices in rearing daughters were also seen as making a difference in the subsequent leadership of the girls as adolescents and adults. Parental warmth and discipline contributed to the development of a girl's subsequent performance as a leader, especially if leadership was fostered by the mother as the family's authority figure (Bronfenbrenner, 1961). However, Hennig and Jardim (1977) found that fathers' encouragement was important to women who achieved success in management.

Psychosocial Development. For Freud (1922), the sex difference in psychosocial development was the reason for the maleness centering of leadership in the family, culture, art, and civilization. Miller (1976) saw that in addition to biological differences in males, women were delegated—because of the cultural domination of men— not humanity's higher needs for achievement and success, but its lower needs for affiliation, cooperation, and attachment. Differential psychosocial development was also the cause of the more passive life goals of females. Grant (1988) suggested that women developed a higher value on connectedness than men did. According to Bernardez (1983), differences in socialization between males and females result in some males' unconscious fear of females' power. This fear bars such males from submission, passivity, and dependence on women. But other males create fantasies that woman leaders are perfect mothers who are selfless, totally accepting, abnegating, nurturing, and without aggression or criticism. When women do not fulfill these expectations, such men direct irrational anger and criticism toward them. To avoid this reaction, some female leaders unconsciously try to minimize their ability and visibility. Chodorow (1978) argued that girls are socialized with greater relational potential and empathy. They see themselves as less separated from others and more connected to the world. They value intimacy and and closeness more (J. Miller, 1976). Males tend to emerge as leaders more than females, according to numerous studies of mixed-sex groups (Aries, 1976), and females tend to differ from men in their activity and influence in small-group experiments (Lockheed & Hall, 1976). Status and sex-role stereotyping handicap the elevation of women to leadership positions. Moreover, one's socialization as a female itself contributes to the reduced motivation to lead (Estler, 1975). But which observed differences in traits affect men's and women's respective tendencies to attempt to lead and to succeed as leaders? Are the differences observed in adolescent girls retained by adult women, particularly women who have chosen to enter management and have become experienced managers? Do systematic changes in male-female differences in such traits occur that are associated with societal change? These are some of the questions I will now try to answer.

Differences in the Leadership Potential of Women and Men

Women and men may differ in general in their leadership potential as a consequence of genetics, socialization, and situational circumstances. The differences may be affected by differences in skills, values, motives, reactions to conflict, sex-role identification, self-confidence, and power and its uses.

Verbal and Nonverbal Communication Skills

There are systematic differences between men's and women's styles of conversation and communication, much as a consequence of their different socialization (Gray, 1992). There is a lot of room for misinterpretation when leaders and followers are of opposite sexes (Atwater & Yammarino, 1994). There are also sex differences in cultural stereotypes about communication skills. Women tend to be seen as better communicators (Hyman, 1980). A study of senior executives by Menkes (1999) found that women executives had better communication skills than their male counterparts. Grant (1988) explained this as a matter of women, at an early age, needing to use conciliation instead of confrontation. Their communication networks serve as the foundation for social interaction. In group discussions, men vie to speak, while women take turns. Case (1985) intensively analyzed tapes of mixed-sex meetings of management students and identified

speech that was assertive and authoritative as a male style. Such speech featured informal pronunciation, imperative construction, interjections, competitive/aggressive talk, slang, depersonalization, and use of the third person. The female style was personal and facilitative and characterized by intensifiers, conjunctions, passive agreement, tag questions, and proof from personal experience. Speech that combined elements of each style, which was supportive and assertive in language, was most influential. Bligh and Kohles (2003), using a dictionary-based language analysis, found that U.S. women senators differed from political norms. They were significantly less aggressive and more ambivalent. They used less praise and human interest in their public discourse.

In an assessment of 422 AT&T managers reported by Howard and Bray (1988), women were superior in one of their oral presentations and scored still significantly higher than the men on a test of verbal ability. The women assessees also had better written communication skills, but no differences were observed for other oral presentations dealing with solutions to stimulated managerial problems.[7] Maccoby and Jacklin (1974) also reported that women were superior to men in communication skills, but subsequent analyses have suggested that this difference was weak (Hyde, 1981). According to a laboratory experiment by Steckler and Rosenthal (1985), the voices of females were perceived as sounding more competent when women were speaking to their peers.

Communicative Cues. Women have been found to be superior in encoding and decoding nonverbal cues (Hall & Halberstadt, 1981). Howard and Bray (1988) found that their woman assessees were judged to be more sensitive and socially objective. Deaux (1976b) concluded, from a review of studies, that they are more sensitive to nonverbal cues. Women try to minimize social distance while men use nonverbal behavior to maintain social distance and assert their status (Denmark, 1977). Men more frequently initiate nonreciprocated touching of women, which declares their dominance or higher status. Women look more at the speaker than do men. But in a mutual gaze, women lower their eyes first. Men more frequently use the direct stare as a threat, while women use it as sexual provocation. Smiling, often a submissive

[7] See Chapter 34.

gesture, is more frequent among women. The use of non-verbal power plays is unacceptable if used by women (Henley, 1973a, b).

Cognitive and Noncognitive Skills

Howard and Bray (1988) concluded, from their intensive assessment of AT&T managers, that in addition to the just-mentioned slight but significant superiority of women in verbal ability, men scored higher on a test of general information but both men and women contributed equally to the functioning of discussion groups and did equally well in the planning, organizing, and decision making aspects of an in-basket test. The women were somewhat more creative on the in-basket test. Similarly, strengths likely to contribute to effective leadership, such as goal setting and teamwork, tended to be higher for the women among 2,482 managers rated 360 degrees with the Manager-Leadership Practices Inventory (Pfaff, 1999).

Reviews by Shields (1975) and Wittig (1976) and a meta-analysis by Hyde (1981) found some support for sex differences favoring men in spatial visualization. Block and Kolakowski (1973) attributed this difference to a sex-linked chromosome. Maccoby and Jacklin (1974) concluded that particularly from adolescence onward, males are superior to females in mathematical ability, but a meta-analysis of studies suggested that the effects were small (Hyde, 1981), although males dominated in the achievement of extremely high scores in mathematics (Benbow & Stanley, 1983). However, 20 years later, Spelke (2005) completed a critical review on whether cognitive sex differences result in men having more talent in mathematics than women and more often attaining careers in mathematics and science. She found no difference between the sexes. Rosenthal and Rubin (1982) pointed out that in the preceding 20 years, females had shown significant gains relative to their male counterparts in verbal, numerical, and spatial skills. In the past several decades, the attraction of women into higher education and careers in mathematics, science, and engineering has been marked.

Socioemotional Skills. Groves (2003) used the Riggio (1989) Social Skills Inventory, a somewhat disguised self-assessment, to analyze self-rated differences between 41 female senior managers and 67 male counterparts from universities, government, and business. The women saw themselves as stronger in socioemotional competencies than did the men. Results were similar when Groves (2005) expanded the study to 108 managers and their 325 direct subordinates in four public institutions, agencies, and programs. Women were higher than men in social skills (r = .24), social sensitivity (.22), and social expressivity (r = .20). They were higher in overall emotional skills (r = .32), in emotional sensitivity (r = .30), and emotional expressivity (r = .33). They were also higher in social control (r = .32) but not emotional control (r = −.09). Women managers were also described by their subordinates on the Conger and Kanungo (1994) scale as more charismatic (r = .22). However, Gardiner and Tiggermann (1999) found no sex difference in the interpersonal orientation of Australian managers if their industry was male-dominated. Only in female-dominated industries were female managers more interpersonally oriented than male managers.

Ways of Thinking. Women may consider their thought processes as different from those of men. Myers and McCaulley (1985) reported systematic differences on the Myers-Briggs Type Inventory of the self-descriptions of 1,051 men and 181 women who attended management development programs at the Center for Creative Leadership between 1979 and 1983. Some of the differences may have been due to the greater proportion of men in upper management and the greater proportion of women in middle management and staff positions. More women than men frequently typed themselves as intuitive and feeling. Men more frequently typed themselves as sensing and thinking than women.

Women managers use different constructs to describe managers than do men. Alimo-Metcalfe (1994) subjected male and female managers in the British National Health Service to Kelly's (1955) repertorial grid, in which they generated constructs to describe the two designated managers with whom they could be compared in communication and interpersonal skills. The male managers' constructs dealt with the ability to influence, with confidence, and with the ability to communicate effectively with a wide audience. The female managers' constructs were about being approachable, fun to be with, sensitive and supportive, and helping someone who feels intimidated at meetings.

Other Consistent Differences between the Sexes

Tannen (1991) suggested that women and men talk and listen differently. Women need to learn not to be threatened by conflict and differences of opinion. Conflict may also arise about the intimacy of talk. Sharing details about their personal lives is more common between women than between men, who see such intimacy as a breach of trust. Often women talk to affirm their similarities and reinforce intimacy; men talk to define their independence and establish their status. Other small but real sex differences that affect leadership potential are in identification, self-confidence, moral values, interpersonal concerns, and use of power. Differences in attitudes toward authority, tendencies to conform, sex-role orientation, and attitudes toward oneself are involved. These may be continuing differences in traits between the sexes that are ordinarily of consequence to leadership. But they may still fail to result in differences between men's and women's attempts to lead and their success and effectiveness as leaders. For instance, although the women in a mixed-sex group may not be as assertive as the men, they may attempt as much leadership as the men because they are equal in experience or expertise in the task at hand. They may be as successful leaders as the men because followers happen to be more attentive to the members' knowledge. Although female executives may prefer to take fewer risks than do male executives, Muldrow and Bayton (1979) demonstrated that their effectiveness was as good as their male counterparts'. The quality of their decisions matched those of the male executives.

Differences in Personality and Motivation.

A meta-analysis of 63 social psychology studies by Eagly and Steffen (1986) found that, on average, men were more aggressive than women. But the results for many other differences in traits between the sexes may appear more frequently for students and inexperienced adults and disappear among more mature adults and managers. Thus Morrison, White, and Van Velsor (1987) could find few sex differences in a large data bank of interviews and assessments of male and female executives. Only trivial differences were reported in four large samples of men and women, in the effects of race, age, and ethnicity, but women job applicants scored higher on overt integrity tests (Ones & Viswesvaran, 1998). Female MBA students,

in four periods between 1960 and 1980, obtained mean scores that were lower than their male counterparts', in their motivation to manage: orientation toward authority, competitiveness, assertiveness, comfort with exercising power, efforts to obtain visibility, and ability to take care of detail (Miner & Smith, 1982). Among 232 MBA students, the mean score for the motivation to manage was 7.04 for males and 3.24 for females (Bartol & Martin, 1986). But for samples of male and female store managers and school administrators, Miner (1974a) could find no differences between the men's and women's motivation to manage. Further illustrating the impermanence of sex differences in personality, Miner (1965) found that the motivation of women changed with training and experience in a way similar to that of men. Comparable results were reported by Morrison and Sebald (1974). Female executives were similar to male executives in self-esteem, motivation, and mental ability. In a number of additional studies,[8] female executives differed from female employees in general in the same way that male executives differed from male employees in general. Again, after reviewing the evidence, Terborg (1977) concluded that, on the whole, women who become managers have motives that are similar to those of male managers. Concomitantly, women who are experienced managers show no differences from their experienced male counterparts in leadership abilities (Caudrea, 1975). At the same time, Pfeffer and Shapiro (1978) observed that managerial women differ from women in general. They are less likely to have traditional female characteristics and more likely, either by temperament or accomodation to the stereotyped male role (Hennig, 1971), to be analytical, rationally oriented, and personally competitive (Lannon, 1977). In a study of 27 women in middle management in a variety of organizations, Banfield (1976) found that all but two incorporated masculine characteristics; 17 were identified as masculine in self-concept and role behavior, only one was identified as feminine; and the other nine were identified as androgynous. Consistent with the masculine stereotype of the good manager (Powell & Butterfield, 1979), Schein (1975) found that, compared to men, women thought a good manager was more unlike themselves.

In developing a leadership orientation scale for the

---

[8] Bartol (1976a); Brief and Aldag (1975); Brief and Oliver (1976); and Matteson, McMahon, and McMahon (1974).

Women's Strong Vocational Interest Blank, Casey (1975) found that the interests of women leaders varied significantly from those of women nonleaders. The leaders indicated a preference for positions of eminence, freedom of thought, challenge, and interpersonal contact; the nonleaders favored artistic activities. Konrad, Corrigall, Lieb, et al. (2000) completed a meta-analysis of 31 studies of what managers and business students preferred in jobs. Men significantly regarded earnings and responsibilities as more important than women did. For women, prestige, challenge, task, significance, variety, growth, job security, good coworkers, and good supervisors were more important, as was the work environment. Jensen, White, and Singh (1990) found women to be significantly more concerned about the work environment. Larwood and Wood (1977) agreed that women in general have been found to differ from men in traits of consequence to leadership. These differences may include men's greater need for achievement, assertiveness, self-esteem, power, dominance, self-reliance, dependence and their preference for taking risks, and competitiveness and women's greater fear of success. These differences may result in women's failure, when they are first placed in leadership roles, to seek their maximum advantage. They may also fail because of their tendency to seek compromises too quickly when cooperation is required. But Larwood and Wood interpreted the results of experimental findings of such sex differences as transitory evidence of the women's relative lack of familiarity with the leadership tasks involved. With experience, the sex differences disappear. At the same time the differences in traits of men and women, in general (even among adolescents), that are of consequence to leadership may be disappearing with societal change. By 1986, Santner (1986) found no differences in the cognitive skills, dominance, friendliness, task orientation, and motivation to achieve of male and female high school leaders, although female students were more likely to head formal groups and male students were more likely to lead informal groups. The generation from which data have been collected to analyze male-female differences is likely to be an important modifier of these kinds of results. An exception is male-female differences in interests. There has been surprisingly little change in the patterns of males' and females' interests. Hansen (1988) compiled analyses of the Women's Strong Vocational Interest patterns of 500 women in the 1930s;

1,000 in the 1960s; 300 in the 1970s; and 500 in the 1980s. Through all these decades, women tended to be more interested than men in art, music, drama, writing, social science, and nature, and less interested in realistic and mechanical activities. The only areas in which formerly sizable male-female differences disappeared in the 1980s were in teaching, mathematics, and scientific activities. This finding may have some implications for the movements of women into positions of leadership in finance, science, and high tech.

Women are thought to overemphasize the task at hand rather than its implications for future achievement. They concentrate on their current activities either because they personally have not learned to set goals or because they believe they are unlikely to be promoted. Also, they remain more concerned than men about their interpersonal relations, either because of socialization or because they must remain in the same "dead-end" position (Kanter, 1977b).

Reactions to Conflict. A study by Beatty (1996) of 193 Canadian professional women in their mid-30s to late 40s recognized the possibilities of family-work conflict but found that professional women did not reveal higher levels of anxiety, depression, hostility, or physical symptoms of stress. Results were similar for senior executives and those with children. But for a larger representative sample of women, their genetics and experiences handicap leadership performance, as they suffer from depression 1.7 times as much as men. Also, negative thinking and sad feelings are more common among women than men, according to the 1994 National Morbidity Survey. Women are more likely than men "to dwell on petty slights and to mentally replay testy encounters" (Gilbert, 2004). Consistent with Gilligan (1982), that women are more caring than men, Gibson, Mainiero, and Sullivan (2004) found in an online national survey three months after the September 11, 2001, terrorist destruction of the World Trade Center, involving 5,860 full-time workers (63.7% women, 36.2% men) that the women respondents expressed more caring and sensitivity than the men. But unlike earlier scholarly expectations, the women also expressed somewhat more desire than the men to seek justice.

Women may differ from men in how they react to obstacles and conflicts not faced by men that affect their potential as leaders. Heinen, McGlauchin, Legeros, and Freeman (1975) suggested that women managers have particular difficulty dealing with interpersonal conflict among subordinates because their socialization encourages them to avoid confrontation. Larwood and Wood (1977) saw that women were more likely to withdraw psychologically from organizations when they faced obstacles to their promotion to higher management levels. Role conflict with homemaking may be a second source of psychological withdrawal from the organization. When faced with opportunities to share a reward, men may be more likely than women to initiate competition for the whole reward. In comparison, women may first try to cooperate. They will enter competition only in retaliation when others reject their initial efforts to cooperate (Terhune, 1970; J. A. Wall, 1976).

In the 1960s, the implication was that women had to adapt to a managerial model that conformed to the male stereotype of our culture. Women's traits had to be altered so they could become more consistent with those of male managers. But subsequently it was noted that if and when there are personality differences between men and women, the two sexes could complement each other in management. Mixed-sex teams could be more creative than same-sex teams (Loden, 1985). The leadership behavior of women, in contrast to that of their male counterparts in the same situation, could be positively enhanced by their greater recognition of and response to the needs of others, and greater sensitivity to interpersonal cues. To the degree that women, in general, are less assertive, they may make better leaders in situations in which such assertiveness would be threatening and likely to arouse competitiveness and defensiveness in followers (Larwood & Wood, 1977). Perhaps this may explain why women supervisors who expressed anger in video vignettes were rated higher by 370 undergraduates and 265 employees although supervisors as a whole who expressed anger were rated lower (Glomb & Hulin, 1997).

Reactions to Feedback. In laboratory studies, women were found more responsive to feedback than their male counterparts. Compared to men, they were more likely to alter their self-appraisals based on the feedback they received and to find feedback meaningful. Men remained more confident about their competencies despite the negative feedback they received (Roberts & Nolen-

Hoeksema, 1989). The same male-female difference was also detected among male and female midshipmen at the U.S. Naval Academy, but the difference was not significant (Atwater & Roush, 1994).

Differences in Sex-Role Identification. An obvious difference between the sexes that remains at all levels of maturity and experience is sex-role identification. Each sex engages in different role activities. Men are more likely to pay attention to business affairs and sports. Women are more likely to pay more attention to friends and children. Male managers who choose to spend considerable time at household tasks are penalized in the workplace (Konrad & Cannings, 1997). Howard and Bray (1988) found sex-role identification to be the biggest difference in their personality assessments of male and female managers at AT&T. Such sex-role identification, if masculine, predicts stronger aspirations for management (Powell & Butterfield, 1981). It seems to have taken more than two decades of research to recognize that the various available masculinity and femininity scales appear to measure, respectively, the tendencies to be directive and assertive and to be nurturing and interpersonally concerned. Men score higher on the former scales, and women higher on the latter. But the best supervisors score higher on both scales (Motowidlo, 1981, 1982). However, even this positive association of androgyny with successful leadership in small groups seems to dissipate as groups continue to develop over time, according to a study of the development of ten groups by Spillman, Spillman, and Reinking (1981).

The identification of 68 Israeli women managers compared to 84 male equivalents was seen when they were presented with a brief incident of political influence. Generally, political behavior was less acceptable to the women but was tolerated more if the target was a man. Political behavior was generally more acceptable to the men, particularly if the target was a woman (Drory & Beaty, 1991). Seifert (1984) completed a contrived experiment in which male and female participants were led to believe they were working with male or female leaders. But all communications (by note) had been prewritten by the experimenter. The female participants rated themselves as less competent than did the male participants. When the outcome of the task was "successful," compared to the males, the females attributed more of the reason for success to the "leader" than to themselves. The male participants gave themselves relatively lower ratings and their "leaders" relatively higher ratings when their "leaders" supposedly were male.

Differences in Self-Confidence. An exception to the general reduction in the effects of differences between sexes, from adolescent students to experienced managers, is the continued lower self-confidence of females compared to males (White, 1981). This lower self-confidence is correlated with relatively lower self-esteem and less willingness to take risks because of a greater fear of failure. Females may also feel uncomfortable with too much success, although this issue has remained controversial.[9] These propensities may contribute to a lower career orientation and a lower desire to compete for advancement (Hennig & Jardim, 1977), as well as a greater tendency to conform (Eagly & Carli, 1981) and to avoid attempting to be influential (Eagly, 1983). According to a meta-analysis by Kling, Hyde, Showers, et al. (1999) with 216 effect sizes for 97,121 respondents, the difference ($d = .33$) favoring males in self-esteem is greatest in late adolescence. Results were replicated in a second analysis with three other large, nationally representative samples, although the differences found were not as large.

Maccoby and Jacklin (1974) obtained findings indicating that females had less confidence in their abilities across a wide variety of activities, such as achieving good grades in tasks requiring manual dexterity, solving puzzles, and the ability to deal with emergencies. In the past, possibly out of a desire to project stereotyped femininity (Ireson, 1976), females, more than males, tended to predict lower performance for themselves than was warranted by their intelligence (Crandall, Katkovsky, & Preston, 1962), and they presented themselves as dependent and incompetent (Vaught, 1965). Although the results were not uniform (Morrison, White, & Van Velsor, 1987; R. S. Schuler, 1975), typical reports like those of Schwartz and Waetjen (1976) and Hennig and Jardim (1977) concluded that women managers were observed by their own supervisors to be less confident, more conservative, and less likely to take risks than their male counterparts. The lack of confidence in themselves was seen in woman managers' tendencies to attribute their

personal failures to their own lack of ability rather than to luck or to external forces. Despite these findings, Spence, Helmreich, and Stapp (1975) concluded that women's self-confidence was increasing with the incorporation into their own self-concepts of more stereotyped masculine traits. At the same time, in comparison with men, women appeared to be better able to express their vulnerability and acknowledge instances when they lacked self-confidence (Grant, 1988).

Differences in Moral Values. Another difference between the sexes that is of consequence to leadership is men's and women's values, how they develop, and the attitudes associated with them (Gilligan, 1982). For example, public opinion polls always show women, compared with men, as more supportive of peace and less supportive of militarism. Men's competitiveness shows up in the greater importance they attach to equity and fairness in the allocation of rewards. For women, valuing such equity is weaker than, say, valuing need (Brockner & Adsit, 1986). Consistent with this finding, Gilligan (1982) argued that the sexes differ in moral reasoning. Women focus on care and responsibility, while men are preoccupied with rights and justice. For a total sample of 187 people faced with real-life dilemmas, 92% of the women and 62% of the men were found to show care for others in their reasoning. None of the men ignored justice, while 23% of the women did (Gilligan, 1982). A meta-analysis of moral reasoning by Jafee and Hyde (2000) confirmed that women were slightly more oriented toward caring than men, while men were slightly more oriented toward justice (See Chapter 9).

Women are more concerned with seeing that no one is hurt and that everyone involved in a situation can be accommodated. Men attach more importance to hierarchical relationships; women, to networks and "webs of connection." Chodorow (1985) added that the separation of self from others is valued more by men, while the connection of self to others is valued more by women. Furthermore, when Powell, Posner, and Schmidt (1984) compared the reported values of 130 male and 130 female managers aged 34 to 45, they obtained results indicating that the women showed more concern for others with respect to ethical issues and religious values. Stamper and Van Dyne (1999) surveyed the organizational citizen behavior of 257 restaurant workers and

---

[9]See, e.g., Horner (1970), O'Leary (1974), Tresemer (1976), Wood and Greenfeld (1976), and Zuckerman and Wheeler (1975).

their supervisors. They found the women to be more loyal, altruistic, and obedient than the men, but no difference appeared in their advocacy participation.

Differences in Power and Using Power. Historically, men have dominated business and government organizations. Even in nonprofit organizations two-thirds of which are based on a paid and unpaid female workforce, men have often dominated the leadership. Women came to the fore as leaders only on such specific national issues as women's rights and child welfare. At the local level, women concentrated as leaders of nonprofit social service, community, and volunteer organizations. More often, they served in supportive rather than leadership roles (O'Neill, 1994).

The sexes differ systematically in their respective relationships to power and therefore in their emergence as successful and effective leaders (Eagly, 1983; Henley, 1973). Women's status, relative to men, and their legitimacy as leaders reduce their power to lead, as does their supposed lack of expertise. In the past, male leaders could more readily use power to induce members to conform to group norms without losing favor than could female leaders (Denmark & Diggory, 1966). However, when Ragins (1987, 1991) carefully matched male and female leaders by rank, department, and specialization, she found no difference in the evaluations of the leaders' effectiveness because of their sex. But she did find strong differences in the evaluations due to the perceived power of the leaders. In reviewing earlier studies on the subject, she noted that similar results had been reported by many other investigators,[10] who had controlled power-related variables. Sex differences appeared only when power-related variables could enter the picture.[11]

Differences in Leadership Style between Women and Men

Differences in leadership styles between the sexes tend to be significant but small. Irwin (1988) found, in a large

sample of U.S. firms, large and small, that female managers used a more participative, interactive style in working with others, while male managers more often tended to employ a more "directive" command and control style. This was to be expected from their known differences in traits and in male-female socialization.

Chapman (1975) reported no sex differences in leadership styles among noncoms to majors in the military or among civilian middle managers. However, differences in leadership style were found in laboratory and assessment studies but not in organizational studies. Bender (1979) inferred from laboratory studies that the leadership process was different with female and male leaders. However, Osborn and Vicars (1976) concluded that in leadership studies similarities rather than differences in style between the sexes appeared most frequently. Rosener (1990) argued that in the past, to advance in management, women had to adopt the masculine style of command and control. But "a second wave of women is making its way to the top, not by adopting the styles that have proved successful for men but by drawing on the skills and attitudes they developed from their shared experience as women" (p. 119). Statham (1987) reported that women managers depended for their leadership more on their social power, nurturing, and relations orientation. Men's leadership depended more on their personal power, individualism, and task orientation. Jago and Vroom (1982) found, among 483 students and managers, that when queried about what decisions they would make in various circumstances, the women chose to be more participative than the men did. Blanchard and Sargent (1984) obtained parallel results for situational leadership choices. Morrison, White, and Van Velsor (1987) found that female executives did more to personalize their experiences than did male executives. On the other hand, Boulgarides (1984) could find no differences in the personal values or preferred decision making styles of 108 male and 108 female business managers of the same age. Epstein (1991) argued that both men and women tend to describe their own style to match the stereotypes—what the culture says they should be like. Self-descriptions are suspect. Nevertheless, there is now considerable evidence of gender differences, often small, based on others' ratings. Eagly and Johnson (1990) completed a definitive meta-analysis of male-female comparisons in leadership styles in 329 comparisons, half of

---

[10] The studies included Adams (1978); Day and Stogdill (1972); Dobbins and Platz (1986); Osborn and Vicars (1976); Rice, Instone, and Adams (1984); and Terborg and Shingledecker (1983).

[11] The studies included Bartol and Butterfield (1976); Haccoun, Haccoun, and Sallay (1978); Jacobson and Effertz (1974); Petty and Lee (1975); and Rosen and Jerdee (1973).

which had been published after 1981. No average significant difference was obtained for 269 organizational studies. The role of manager had more effect on style than did differences in sex (Eagly, 1991). However in the aforementioned meta-analysis by Eagly and Johnson, significant results fitting the stereotypical differences in interpersonal style, task orientation, and directive style were found for 43 personal assessment studies and 17 laboratory studies.

Transformational and Transactional Leadership

Women leaders seem to be more transformational; men, more transactional (Bass, Avolio, & Atwater, 1996). In their transactional styles, women tend to be more humane and more appreciative of situational circumstances when correcting subordinates (Murphy, Eckstat, & Parker, 1995). Rosener (1990) obtained survey results suggesting that her "new wave" of female executives were likely to be more transformational than their male counterparts. Instructors were rated as more transformational as leaders by their female students, than by their male students (Walumbwa & Wu, undated). Another 262 teachers were rated by 101 vocational administrators. The women teachers were seen as more transformational (Daughtry, 1997). A small overall effect favoring women was found between male and female leaders in a meta-analysis by Van Engen and Willemsen (2004) of leadership studies between 1987 and 2000. Southwick (1998) reported that a large sample of female managers surveyed with the Multifactor Leadership Questionnaire (MLQ) were higher than men on all the transformational leadership scales and on contingent reward (which contains a transformational component). Men were higher than women on all the transactional leadership scales. The same was reported by Bass, Avolio, and Atwater (1996), regardless of whether the subordinate raters were men or women. In subsequent meta-analyses, Eagly and Johanneson-Schmidt (1995, 2001) extended the results to find mean differences indicating that 2,874 women leaders were somewhat more transformational and less transactional and less laissez-faire than their 6,126 male counterparts. Female leaders were more transformational than male leaders and also practiced more contingent reward. Male leaders were more likely to be transactional and laissez-faire in style (Eagly, 2002; Eagly & Johannesen-Schmidt, 2002). However, Yammarino, Dubinsky, Comer, et al.

(1997) established with WABA analysis that the transformational or contingent style of each woman's leadership varied from one individual follower to another and was not generalizable to her group of followers as a whole. Consistent with Southwick and with Bass, Avolio and Atwater (1996), Carless (1998) found for Australian managers, in an Australian experiment, that males acting as supervisors were more likely than females to use transactional messages of correction when faced with supposedly poorly performing subordinates.

Subscale Differences

In 1984, I observed in workshops for business and public agency managers in New Zealand and the United States that the MLQ subscale scores of charismatic leadership were higher among women than men. This was consistent with Grove's (2003) finding that women leaders were higher in charisma on Conger and Kanungo's (CK) scale. Telephone interviews of more than 100 state and national elected officials and legislators ascertained that the women were more transformational but they also rated themselves higher in active managing by exception, which the men practiced more passively (Bass & Harding, 1999). Tucker (1994) obtained similar results for 430 of the 1,517 women serving in U.S. state legislatures in 1993–1994.

A total of 120 junior and middle-level Australian female branch bank managers were rated on various instruments as more transformational than their 184 male peers by both their 32 superiors and their 588 subordinates. The differences appeared to center mainly around individualized consideration from the MLQ, enabling others to act and encouraging the heart from the LPI, and from interpersonal leadership responses to the Global Transformational Leadership Scale (GTL) (Carless, 1995). Thirty-one male hall directors were rated significantly higher in intellectual stimulation than their women peers, but the other expected scale differences for MLQ scores in transformational and transactional differences were too small to be significant (Komives, 1991). Instructors were rated as more transformational leaders by their female but not their male students (Walumbwa & Wu, undated). Again, 262 teachers were rated by 101 vocational administrators. The women teachers were seen as more transformational (Daughtry, 1997). At a New Zealand polytech, 153 students used the MLQ and the Bem Sex-Role Inventory (SRI) to describe a leader "of whom they had vivid recollections." Business, social, sports and other leaders' SRI ratings in *femininity* correlated significantly higher with MLQ consideration (.56) and charisma (.57) than with SRI *masculinity* (.22 versus .43), and significantly lower (.29 versus .46) with MLQ intellectual stimulation (.29 versus .46).

Relations versus Task Style. Women leaders tend to be higher in concern for interpersonal relationships; male leaders, for task achievement. Such was the case for the just-mentioned hall directors (Komives, 1991). Likewise, an Eagley and Johnson (1990) meta-analysis indicated that male leaders were more task-oriented than women leaders. Also, women leaders were more concerned about relationships, but only in laboratory and assessment studies. No such differences appeared in organizational studies. In some samples but not others, Petty and Bruning (1980) reported, female supervisors displayed more consideration than male supervisors. Bowes-Sperry, Veiga, and Yanouzas (1997) found that women managers more than male peers tended to respond with understanding when employees sought help. Male managers did more evaluating, but both males and females relied more on evaluating for helping. With reference to emerging leadership, Deaux (1976b) suggested that women were more likely to seek interpersonal success, in contrast to men's greater concern for being successful in the task. Similarly, Eskilson and Wiley (1976) reported that women attempted to create a more positive group affect than did men. In allocating resources, Vinacke (1969) inferred that women focus more on maintaining harmony, whereas men concentrate on the quality of individual performance.

Preferences in Ideal Leaders. In a survey by Denmark and Diggory (1966), sorority leaders were likely to be described as displaying less authoritarian behavior than fraternity leaders. Consistent with this finding, schoolteachers described female principals as exhibiting less coercive behavior than male principals (Kappelman, 1981). On the other hand, when a much broader set of studies was considered in Eagley and Johnson's (1990) meta-analysis, women leaders were found to be more participative and democratic, men more directive and autocratic. In a study by Rosenfeld and Fowler (1976), some differences emerged among the self-described

scores for "ideal democratic leader" of 89 men and 89 women. But the results for preferred ideal autocratic leaders were the same for both groups. Women emphasized being helpful, affectionate, nurturing, and open-minded, and accepting blame; men emphasized being mature, forceful, competent, moral, utilitarian, and analytical, and valuing people.

Administrative Styles. Morsink (1966) found that when female principals were described by both male and female staff members, they were significantly higher on Leader Behavior Description Questionnaire (LBDQ-XII) factors than male principals were in representing their people, persuasiveness, emphasis on production, predictive accuracy, integration of the group, and influence with superiors. Kappelman (1981) obtained similar results in another survey of male and female principals. Millard (1981) obtained results indicating that 38 female managers, compared to a matched sample of male managers, in a large government agency, were described by subordinates as scoring higher on production and orientation toward superiors but lower on tolerance for freedom and uncertainty. Sleeth and Humphreys (undated) found differences between 122 men and 122 women students at a large urban university in self-descriptions of their leadership behavior, as scored on the LBDQ and Hersey and Blanchard's (1977) Leader Effectiveness and Adaptability Description (LEAD), as well as their self-descriptions of assertiveness and endorsement of the work ethic. The women reported themselves as slightly higher in consideration and the men reported themselves as higher in task than relations orientation. Similarly, more consideration than initiation of structure was seen in the self-descriptions of 51 first- and second-level women supervisors (DiMarco & Whitsitt, 1975).

Involvement. Eskilson (1975) reported that the women who emerged as leaders of three-person laboratory groups showed more intensive involvement with the task than did the men who emerged as leaders. Similar results appeared for coalition-forming in a competitive, high-risk game (Lirtzman & Wahba, 1972). The female executives were thought to be more concerned than their male counterparts about achieving organizational goals and following rules and policies (Hyman, 1980), but the male executives were more comfortable with intellectual authority (Morrison, White, & Van Velsor, 1987). Bass

(1985a) reported that women managers display less management by exception than their male counterparts. This may point to women's greater tendency to be involved in their subordinates' activities. Associated with this tendency may be the different ways in which female and male supervisors appear to view poor performance by their subordinates. In a laboratory simulation of a workplace, Dobbins (1985) found that women supervisors were more supportive in their leadership if the subordinates were women. Male supervisors were supportive only if they had inferred that the cause of the poor performance was stable and due to causes beyond the subordinate's personal control. They thought that close monitoring of a poorly performing subordinate was more appropriate if the subordinate was lazy and incompetent.

Little or No Difference Due to Differences Between the Sexes

The preceding studies found some tendencies for women leaders to be more relations-oriented and involved than their male counterparts. However, a large array of evidence has failed to establish any consistent differences. Many male managers are caring and considerate; many female managers are controlling and autocratic. Management training now "preaches the importance of nurturing, cooperation, and consensus" (McKee, 1992, p. 5).

Girls and women do differ from boys and men on many attributes. These attributes may be associated with one's emergence as a leader. But the differences between the sexes blur if one contrasts women and men who have already achieved status as leaders. Once they are legitimated as leaders, the preponderance of research suggests that women actually do not behave much differently from men in the same kind of positions. Most often, reviews and analyses of both field and laboratory studies have concluded that few or no effects of sex on leadership style were obtained, whether the leaders were describing themselves or being described by their subordinates.[12] Thus among 100 male and 100 female executives at the same middle-management level in federal agencies, Muldrow and Bayton (1979) found no differences in the

handling of six personnel decisions, although the women described themselves as less likely to take risks. And Carpeno (1976) found no differences due to sex on the Leadership Opinion Questionnaire. Sonnenfeld (1995) found little significant difference in the behaviors of 220 male and 30 female CEOs described by an average of six members of their management teams. Southwick (1998) reported no gender differences in perceptions of transformational or transactional leadership when MLQ ratings were obtained from leaders' supervisors, although these differences had been found in subordinates' ratings of the same leaders.

Michener and Schwertfeger (1972) reported no differences between men's and women's preference for the use of coercive power or for withdrawing from a situation, although men, if they were liked, were more likely to be persuasive. In a study of a simulated work setting, Baker, DiMarco, and Scott (1975) obtained no significant differences between the way men and women allocated rewards or penalties. In a longitudinal field study, Szilagyi (1980a) failed to discern any differences in men's or women leaders' administration of rewards or punishments, according to their subordinates of both sexes. Likewise, Butterfield and Powell (1981) obtained no differences in the ratings of the styles of male and female managers. Osborn and Vicars (1976) also found no sex differences in initiation of structure or the amount of consideration of supervisors, according to their subordinates in men's residences. Similarly, Thomas (1982) reported no differences in the supervisory orientations of 252 male and 285 female business students or in the students' responses on in-basket tests. No sex differences in preferred solutions to the LEAD situational leadership questionnaire appeared among the male and female management students. Also, Birdsall (1980) reported that both men and women managers used the same masculine communication style.

Androgyny. According to Murphy, Eckstat, and Parker (1995), women leaders are no longer adopting a completely masculine orientation as in the past but are using a feminine or, better yet, androgynous orientation. They can be both nurturing and task-oriented; as was advised 44 years ago by Blake and Mouton (1964): to be the best, managers must have strong concern for performance and concern for people. Both male and female leaders are

---

[12]See, e.g., Bartol (1973, 1974); Bartol and Butterfield (1976); Bartol and Wortman (1975, 1976); Chapman (1975); Day and Stogdill (1972); Martin (1972); Remland, Jacobson, and Jones (1983); Roussel (1974); and Wexley and Hunt (1974).

adopting androgyneous approaches, reducing the differences in style between them (Ballard-Reich & Elton, 1992). Androgynous leaders use masculine styles in some situations and feminine styles in other situations (Vonk & Ashmore, 1993). They integrate rather than polarize the masculine and feminine styles (Park, 1997). Androgynous women leaders rated themselves higher than did their peers, which male leaders were less prone to do (Gurman & Long, 1993). However, women leaders are more likely to adopt androgynous styles accompanied by more flexibility in response to different situations. Male managers still tend to concentrate more on performance and less on people (Stern, Dietz, & Kalof, 1993). And for 1979 and 1989 samples of undergraduate and graduate business students, the good manager was still being described as masculine rather than androgynous (Powell & Butterfield, 1989). Nevertheless, it is the androgynous leader—both task- and relations-oriented—who tends to be the most effective (see below).

Success and Effectiveness of Women Leaders

When women rather than men are placed in supervisory and leadership roles, how well are they accepted and followed by their subordinates? How meritorious is their performance, as appraised by their superiors? How good is the performance of the groups they lead? How satisfied are their subordinates? Does the sex of the leader make a difference in whether the group attains its objectives and satisfies its needs? Are the productivity and satisfaction of the group affected by the sex of the leader? Rice, Bender, and Vitters (1980) commented that these questions are complicated when answers depend on subjective ratings that may reflect sex bias. However, at the beginning of the twenty-first century, the organizational requirements for more consensus and cooperation and less "command and control" styles of leadership, more common among women, are giving them greater success and effectiveness. This is despite the fact that women in the same leadership roles as men often tend to be less valued (Adams & Yoder, 1985). Powell (1993) concluded from a review that although there were differences in traits and styles of men and women leaders, the differences disappeared when one examines the effectiveness of their actual performance. In all, the evidence is mixed. Some

studies show that groups and organizations do better with female leaders; some studies show that groups and organizations do better with male leaders; and still others find no differences due to the sex of the leader. In the aggregate, meta-analyses give a slight edge to the women. Ballard (1992) concurs that overall, women make better managers. Whether or not women managers are accepted as role models by their subordinates depends much more on their effectiveness than their sex, according to a survey of 1,579 Canadian public senior managers (Javidan, Bemmels, Devine, et al., 1995).

When Women Leaders Are More Effective

Contrary to what they had hypothesized, Eskilson and Wiley (1976) found, in a study with 144 undergraduates, that groups led by females were more productive than those led by males. And from a review of the literature between 1979 and 1984, Smith (1986) concluded that on creative tasks, groups led by women outperformed groups led by men. Bass and Avolio (1994) confirmed the slightly greater effectiveness of women manager, saying it could be attributed to their being more transformational than their male counterparts. The results were the same for ratings from both male and female subordinates. According to Zimmerman-Treichel, Dunlap-Hinkler, and Washington (2003), firms were more effective when women served on boards of directors and in senior management.

Irwin (1998) inferred from the profiling of 360-degree ratings from a large sample of managers from Fortune 100 corporations and small businesses that women managers were somewhat more effective. Women were stronger on such performance factors as communicating, planning, controlling, leading, problem solving, and managing relationships.

Androgynous Leaders May Be Most Effective

Park (1996) agreed (as was noted in earlier chapters) that the best leaders tend to be both task- and relations-oriented. The blending of the more masculine task orientation and the more feminine relations orientation by both men and women may make for the most effective leadership style. Thus the "one-minute manager" was seen as androgynous by Blanchard and Sargent (1984).

Kaplan and Sedney (1980) suggested that an androgynous style allowed for broader, more flexible leadership. Women managers' leadership styles reveal more willingness to consider circumstances when rewarding or correcting subordinates.

When Women Leaders Are Less Effective

Several studies pointed to the negative effects of women in leadership posts. Baril, Elbert, Mahar-Potter, et al. (1989) found, contrary to the above, that for 65 first-line supervisors administered the Bem Sex-Role Inventory, the androgynous supervisors were rated least effective by their superiors. Their successful women supervisors were rated higher in masculinity. In an employee attitude survey, Hansen (1974) found that women supervisors had less impact than men supervisors on the climate of their departments, as evidenced by the correlations between supervisors' attitudes and ratings of the groups' climate. Roussel (1974) examined the effects of the sex of 40 department heads on teachers' ratings of the departmental climate in 10 high schools. Departments headed by men were rated higher in esprit and intimacy; departments headed by women were rated higher in hindrances. Atwater, Carey, and Waldman (2001) interviewed 163 subordinates about their supervisors' workplace disciplinary behavior. Women supervisors were judged to be less effective in disciplinary actions and less effective overall. Hutchinson, Valentino, and Kirkner (1998) surveyed 91 employees and their leaders. Employees' commitment to the organization was higher if their male, but not their female, supervisor was high in consideration and initiating structure.

Yerby (1975) assigned 192 male and female undergraduates to small problem-solving groups according to their positive or negative attitudes toward female leaders. All groups were led by women. The groups' performance correlated with the attitudes of their members toward females as leaders. Such attitudes also resulted in the lower group morale of male subordinates under female leaders. Rice, Bender, and Vitters (1980) completed a laboratory study of 288 West Point cadets assigned to 724-person groups led by females and males with all subordinate roles filled by males. They found that groups with male leaders did better on two assigned tasks than groups led by females. When 312 Israeli soldiers rated 82 unit lead-

ers, satisfaction was lowest in units led by women (Gavrieli, 2003).

Null Evidence

Bartol (1978) concluded, in a review of the results of laboratory studies, that in general the sex of the leader was not a consistent factor in determining a group's productivity. Nor, according to Larwood, Wood, and Inderlied (1978), did the effectiveness of the performance of managers in field studies appear to be associated consistently with their sex. B. A. Hall (1975) reported no difference in the effectiveness of the assertiveness training of women as a function of the sex of the group leader.

Emergence as a Leader

Ross, Davidson, and Graham (1985) reported that 165 women who worked for a major domestic airline scored higher in their performance at centers to assess their management and leadership potential than 215 men did. These results were attributed to the relatively bias-free situation.

Men came to the fore more often as leaders than women of initially leaderless groups, according to a meta-analysis of 75 studies by Eagley and Karau (1991). They analyzed mainly college-age samples from four preceding decades of laboratory studies and from few natural studies, with a median size of four members. The mixed-sex groups were composed of an average of 53% males and 47% females. Male leadership was more pronounced if sessions were shorter than 20 minutes, if the tasks were masculine, if the groups were smaller, if the subjects were older, if the studies had been completed years farther back in the past, if general and task measures of leadership were used, and if respondents of both sexes thought men would be more likely than women to lead the groups performing the tasks. Consistent with social role expectations, women led if more social complexity was present and if social measures of leadership were used.

In all-male and all-female groups, members high in in dominance, intelligence, general self-efficacy, and self-monitoring tended to emerge as leaders (Foti & Gershenoff, 1999). Masculine and androgynous-gendered individuals more frequently emerged as leaders of small mixed-sex groups, although biological sex was not significant (Kolb, 1997). Some earlier studies pointed to the biological sex difference in emergence between women and men in mixed-sex groups. Women were socialized to hold back from attempting leadership because of sex-role expectations (Eagley, 1983). When paired with men in work dyads, they were less likely to come to the fore as leaders even when they had the strengths to fit the requirements for leadership (Carbonell, 1984). No doubt this difference will disappear with the liberation of women and their efforts to increase assertiveness. For some tasks and for the continuing expectations of participants about the appropriateness of the leadership role for women (Hollander, 1983), men are seen as more likely to attempt leadership or emerge as leaders in mixed-sex circumstances (Eskilson & Wiley, 1976). As noted earlier, even when women are generally more dominant, they have tended to defer to men for leadership (Megargee, 1969). Attempts to lead, as seen in the initiation of structure and the amount of talking, were found by Strodtbeck and Mann (1956), in jury deliberations, to be greater for men. At a Mormon institution, Brigham Young University, Oddou (1983) found that men came to the fore more frequently than women as leaders of mixed-sex work groups. However, at a nonsectarian school, while Kent and Moss (1993) found sex differences in leadership emergence among 122 undergraduates favoring men, they also noted that but men with an androgynous orientation were more likely to emerge as leaders.

Many studies failed to find any differences that could be attributed to gender differences. For instance, Schneler and Bartol (1980) examined sex differences in the appearance of leaders in 52 task groups participating in a personnel administration course over 15-weeks. They found no significant differences when leadership was assessed by sociometric choice or when it was based on observational data from Bales's interaction process analyses.

Subordinates' Satisfaction and the Sex of the Leader

The expected conflict between fulfilling the stereotyped role of a woman and fulfilling the role of a manager has already been noted. Yet the satisfaction of subordinates appears to be unrelated to whether supervisors fulfill appropriate sex-role stereotypes (Bartol & Wortman, 1975; Millard, 1981; Osborn & Vicars, 1976). It is difficult to divorce subordinates' attitudes and expectations about

women leaders from the subordinates' job satisfaction under female or male leaders. Nevertheless, many studies have reported little difference in the job satisfaction of subordinates as a function of the sex of their supervisor.[13] For instance, Terborg and Shingledecker (1983) could find no differences about staying in or quitting a job between 331 male and female employees under female supervisors and 132 employees working for male supervisors, except that of all the employees, the male subordinates under male supervisors were the most unclear about how their own performance was evaluated. Adams's (1976) survey of the 276 subordinates of 18 chain store managers failed to find differences in the subordinates' satisfaction with supervision that were due to the sex of the managers. But numerous other studies[14] have reported a preference for male supervisors, again with other relevant factors affecting the preference. For example, among blue-collar employees surveyed by Haccoun, Haccoun, and Sallay (1978), satisfaction of subordinates was higher with male supervisors.

Confounding Factors. In a study, Goetz and Herman (1976), looked at subordinates of department managers in a large retail store chain and found that employees working for women managers were more satisfied with their supervision than employees working for men. Yet, there the effects of sex could be accounted for mainly by other differences, such as commission versus noncommission payment plans and the composition of the work units. In the same way, Osborn and Vicars (1976) reported that the effects of the sex of the supervisor could be explained by other factors. One such factor may be the duration of the leader-subordinate relationship. In a short-term laboratory study, Rice, Bender, and Vitters (1980) showed that male West Point cadets holding traditional attitudes toward women as army officers were less satisfied in their interactions in a short exercise with appointed female leaders than were egalitarian male or female subordinates. But in summer training, an experience of longer duration, the correlation disappeared (Adams, Prince, Instone, & Rice, 1984). In cadet-training programs that lasted six weeks, no consistency in the correla-

---

[13] See, e.g., Bartel (1974, 1975), Bartol and Wortman (1975), N. R. E Maier (1970a), Millard (1981), and Osborn and Vicars (1976).
[14] Brief and Oliver (1976), Osborn and Vicars (1976), and Renwick and Tosi (1978).

tion of these attitudes with satisfaction was obtained, regardless of the sex of the leader or the subordinate (Rice, Instone, & Adams, 1984).

The leader's influence "upstairs" is another confounding factor. Trempe, Rigny, and Haccoun (1985) demonstrated, from their findings with 197 semiskilled employees, 52% of whom were women, that although the sex of a supervisor was irrelevant to an employee's satisfaction, the supervisor's influence with a higher authority was important and male supervisors were seen to have greater influence (Terborg, 1977). Similarly, Taylor and Ilgen (1979) completed a survey of employees with female and male supervisors and could find no difference in the employees' satisfaction with their supervisors that was associated with sex. But in comparison to employees working under male supervisors, the employees working for female managers thought that their supervisors had less reward power.

Revealed wisdom and early research hinted that even women workers generally preferred male superiors. As White (1981) noted, a 1971 poll of working women showed that they strongly preferred a male rather than female boss. But by the 1980s, studies of college women were suggesting that women preferred women as bosses. The same changes were occurring for preferred opinion leaders. By 1975, men, on most topics, revealed no preferences in selecting opinion leaders on the basis of the leaders' sex, but women exhibited a distinct preference for women leaders, except on political issues (Richmond & McCroskey, 1975). As shall be seen later, bettereducated subordinates had become more favorably inclined toward women as leaders than had less-educated subordinates. But male subordinates' attitudes toward women superiors have remained less sanguine.

Performance Appraisals of Women Managers and Professionals

Again, the evidence is mixed. On the one hand, as has already been noted, there is a bias toward men in positions of leadership. Nevertheless, such distortion tends to dissipate with performance appraisals based on intensive observation or extensive experience. Laboratory studies have tended to find no difference in the performance appraisals assigned to men and women (e.g., Gianantonio, Olian, & Carroll, 1995), although such findings have not been uniform. Some have favored women (e.g., Bigoness, 1976); others, men (e.g., Woehr & Roch, 1996).

In field studies, Powell and Butterfield (1994) found that higher evaluations were received by women applicants for executive service in a federal agency. Schwartz and Waetjen (1976) reported that 95 percent of employers of female managers rated their job performance as excellent, very good, or good (probably no different from their leniency-prone ratings of male managers). But according to a review by J. E. Smith (1986), when managers were rated by their peers or superiors, no consistent sex differences appeared. Again, Tsui and Gutek (1984) could find no differences between the sexes in performance appraisals of middle-level managers in a corporation. This finding was confirmed in a meta-analysis by Dobbins and Platz (1986), who felt the search for such differences should be abandoned.

Deaux (1976a) obtained no difference in the rated performance of men and women retail store managers. M. M. Wood (1975, 1976) and Wood and Greenfeld (1976) also found little difference in the rated performance of men and women managers in several field analyses. Likewise, the AT&T assessment center's predictions of the managerial potential of 1,097 women were similar to those for men. The distribution of the assessors' ratings for men and women were similar (Ritchie & Moses, 1983). No difference was found in the leadership evaluations of male and female management students using the same style of leadership (Butterfield & Powell, 1981). On the other hand, making use of a professional accounting association, Griffith and Bedeian (1989) found that male supervisors in 464 dyads rated their male subordinates lower than their female subordinates.

Some Differences on Specific Aspects of Performance. In a few studies, women leaders received higher or lower ratings than male leaders on some particular kinds of performance. M. M. Wood (1976) surmised from a survey that male managers tended to rate their female peers more highly in decision making, competence, and ability to handle emotions. Women were seen as bringing a fresh outlook to business problems and as offering useful insights into marketing problems involving female customers. They were regarded as tending to reduce intense feelings of competition among male managers.

Rosen and Jerdee (1973) completed three experiments with in-basket evaluations to examine cross-sex role behavior by women supervisors. Although friendly, helpful leadership was rated as more effective whether the supervisor was male or female, a reward style was evaluated as more effective for male than female supervisors. At the same time, Petty and Lee (1975) obtained results suggesting that consideration by female supervisors is more highly related to the satisfaction of subordinates than the same consideration by male supervisors. Petty and Lee inferred that because more consideration is expected from women, when it fails to materialize, it is more likely to result in subordinates' dissatisfaction.

In an analysis using 192 male middle managers, R. A. Patterson (1975) found that females received lower ratings than males on evaluations of performance and promotability. As mentioned earlier, male cadets were satisfied to serve under female cadet leaders in summer training. But female cadet leaders at West Point earned lower staff appraisals than male cadet leaders for their performance in summer camp. The performance appraisals of 86 female cadets during summer training, compared to those for a random sample of male cadets, were found by Adams and Hicks (undated) to show that in assigned formal leadership roles, female leaders were rated more poorly in overall performance. Rice, Instone, and Adams (1984) reported these same results for larger samples. The female leaders were rated as having less capacity for increased responsibility, less ability to organize and coordinate the efforts of others, less initiative, forcefulness, and aggressiveness, and less ability to adjust to new or changing situations and stresses than the male leaders.

Same Behavior but Evaluated Differently. Although women leaders may behave in a way similar to their male counterparts and have similar effects on their groups, they are likely to be evaluated differently (Seifert, 1984). Van Nostrand (1993) argued that the culture plays favorites. Men are more privileged and entitled. Women are less favored by higher authority. They are evaluated slightly less favorably, according to a meta-analysis by Eagley, Makhijani, & Klonsky (1992). This occurs especially when the women are autocratic, directive, and stereotypically masculine when they occupy masculine-dominated roles, and when the evaluators are men. But an earlier

meta-analysis by Dobbins and Platz (1986) of studies comparing male and female leaders on the LBDQ measures of initiation and consideration did not reveal significant mean effects owing to sex differences. Findings by Ziegert and Hanges (2002) suggested that stereotyped attitudes affect what happens, whether they are measured implicitly or explicitly and regardless of efforts to statistically control the attitudes.

Differences in sex moderated the evaluation of the same expressive emotional leadership behavior in a laboratory study by Sherony (2003). Men's emotional expressiveness received higher ratings than women in positive, creative, and task situations, and lower ratings in negative situations; but Ashkanasy and Newcombe (2001) found otherwise. Women leaders on videotape received lower evaluations than men after being viewed giving the same negative feedback with negative affect.

Wheelan (1975) reported that for 72 female and 72 male undergraduates, women were ranked lower than men in leadership in mixed-sex, six-person groups, despite the women's greater participation, ordinarily predictive of leadership. In the same way, subordinates may be less satisfied with women supervisors who display the same styles as male supervisors (Petty & Lee, 1975; Rosen & Jerdee, 1973). Hansen (1974) could find no significant differences in support or goal facilitation by supervisors that were associated with the women's gender; nevertheless, subordinates of both sexes were more dissatisfied if their supervisor was a woman. This finding may have been due to the reports by women supervisors themselves that they had less autonomy or, as was found in other studies, that as women supervisors they had less influence with higher authority (South, Bonjean, Corder, & Markham, 1982). Subordinates may also favor male managers because male managers are generally more experienced (Liden, 1985). In all, one is forced to conclude, as did Denmark (1977), that in a majority of cases, differences between male and female leaders are more a matter of stereotyped expectations than actual fact.

One reason for the perceptions of the differences between the leadership of men versus women in the absence of actual differences in behavior between the sexes was demonstrated by Ceis, Boston, and Hoffman (1985). These researchers contrasted how viewing all-male and all-female authority role models in television commercials affected the subsequent leadership performance and leadership evaluations of 276 undergraduates in four-person mixed-sex discussions. The men and women performed equally as leaders in the discussion, but their equal performance was recognized only by those subjected to the all-female TV authority figures. Those who viewed the all-male authority figures recognized only the males as leaders in their own discussions.

As noted before, females who were perceived to be directive were negatively evaluated, while males perceived to be directive received positive evaluations (Jago & Vroom, 1982). Again, illustrating the difference in evaluations, Denmark (1980) contrasted the reaction of 384 students to a hypothetical male or female professor who had written an outspoken or a conciliatory letter in response to a suggestion made at a faculty meeting. Although the conciliatory style was favored by the students, the conciliatory female professor was rated as less of a leader, less interesting, less sophisticated, less strong, and less fair than her male counterpart. The outspoken woman professor was particularly downgraded by the female students. In the same way, Moore (1984) found that in evaluations of performance, masculine behaviors (ambition, self-reliance, independence, and assertiveness) were valued more highly than feminine behaviors (affection, gentleness, and understanding), especially in female high performers.

Different Reasons Applied. There are also differential attributions for why men and women succeed or fail. A man's success is more likely to be attributed to ability, but a woman's success is attributed to hard work, good luck, or an easy task (Deaux & Emswiller, 1974). Conversely, a woman's failure will be attributed to her lack of ability, but a man's failure will be attributed to bad luck, task difficulty, or lack of effort (Cash, Gillen, & Burns, 1977; Feather & Simon, 1975). Forsyth and Forsyth (1984) used female confederates as leaders who behaved either in a task-oriented or interpersonally concerned way in mixed-sex groups. When the group was successful with a female leader, both the leader and the male subordinates attributed the success to luck. With a male leader, the group attributed the success to the leader's ability.

The attributions for the successful and unsuccessful leadership of women by men are related to men's attitude toward women as managers. For 143 male participants who evaluated a scenario of the performance of a woman manager, those with more favorable attitudes toward women as managers were more likely to attribute success to the woman's ability and effort rather than to luck or the value of the job. With such favorable attitudes, they were less likely to attribute failure to the woman's lack of ability or effort (Garland & Price, 1977; Stevens & DeNisi, 1980).

Other Distorting Factors. As noted earlier, men are more likely to explain a woman's success as a leader as due to her sex rather than to her job-relevant competencies if she is in a solo position (Lockheed, 1975). Devaluations of a woman's successful performance are also more likely if the job appears to be inappropriate for women or the outcome of the work effort is ambiguous.

When 96 experienced managers were asked by Wiley and Eskilson (1982) to evaluate the performance of a hypothetical male or female supervisor who used his or her expert or reward power to influence a subordinate successfully, the managers evaluated the male supervisor more favorably when he employed expert rather than reward power. But the female supervisor was evaluated more favorably when she used her reward-based power. The investigators thought these results were due possibly to the greater credibility of men as experts.

Evaluations come closer to reality when work objectives are clear and the job fits sex-appropriate stereotypes. For example, evaluations are closer to reality for female nursing administrators than for female engineering supervisors. Discrimination disappears if objective reasons for success are available (Riger & Galligan, 1980). In fact, with equally high levels of objective performance by men and women, participants explicitly evaluated women more favorably than they did men in overreaction to women's unexpected success (Bigoness, 1976). Distortions favoring the woman leader were seen by Jacobson and Effertz (1974) in subordinates' and peers' evaluations of leadership performance. They found that women leaders in experimental small groups were judged less harshly than male leaders when performance levels did not meet the groups' expectations. And unexpected success by a woman was seen as deserving more praise than the same unexpected success by a man (Taynor & Deaux, 1973).

Moderating Effects

Despite their claims to the contrary, both male and female owners did not manage their small businesses using a masculine or femininine style. They actually practiced both styles. The results seen in a Canadian study by Cliff, Langton, and Aldrich (2003) of 229 small businesses depended on what the owners did rather than what they said.

Effects of the Sex of Subordinates

After a review of the available evidence, Chapman and Luthans (1975) concluded that sex differences in leadership depended on the group and the situation involved. For instance, in a survey of 1,137 employees in three organizations, compared to men, the women preferred consideration from their supervisors. Nevertheless, both men and women with more education and tenure preferred less structuring from their leaders (Vecchio & Boatwight, 2002). Haccoun, Haccoun, and Sallay (1978) found that although nondirective styles were favored for women, the sex of both the supervisor and the subordinate determined the group's performance. Differences between the sexes in the leadership of men and women occur that may be due partly to other moderating factors, such as differences in men's and women's age, education, seniority, experience, level in the organization, and professional training.

Pygmalion Effect. When supervisors, teachers, and leaders are led to believe that their subordinates, students, and followers are highly competent, improved performance results, according to experimental research on the "Pygmalion effect" (Eden, 1993). But the Pygmalion effect appears to work better for men than women, as seen in a meta-analysis of 19 studies (McNutt, 2000). Successful induction of the Pygmalion effect occurs when leaders' low expectations of subordinates are raised to high expectations.[15] Lees-Hotton and Syantek (2002) reported inducing the Pygmalion effect with women, although most other attempts with women have failed. Followers of control leaders who don't change their low expecta-

[15] See Chapter 17.

tions perform poorly compared to those for whom there are natural or induced expectations of better performance. The controls are an illustration of the "golem effect," in which leaders with low expectations generate or maintain poor follower performance (Eden & Davidson, 1997).

Success of the Leader of the Same or Opposite Sex of Followers. Whether the subordinate and the leader are of the same or opposite sex affects the leader's likelihood of success. Thus in trios, female leaders were least likely to succeed when the other two members were men; they were most likely to succeed when the other two members were women (Eskilson, 1975). Consistent with these results, Aries (1976) observed that males displayed more leadership than females in mixed groups of males and females than in same-sex situations. Likewise, Megargee, Bogart, and Anderson (1966) examined various combinations of dominant and submissive men and women in two experimental tasks. Dominant men paired with submissive men and women, and dominant women paired with submissive women tended to appoint themselves as leaders. But dominant women paired with submissive men tended to appoint the men as leaders. The dominant women avoided attempting to lead male partners. Among 144 undergraduates in 48 trios, Eskilson and Wiley (1976) observed that although typical sex-role expectations resulted in male leaders receiving more requests for direction, both sexes addressed more directive behavior toward groups of their own sex.

As was noted early in the chapter, the placement of women in leadership positions over men generates status-reversal conflict, particularly for men with traditional attitudes toward the role of women. The consequence is a negative impact on the men's performance (Yerby, 1975). Early on, Whyte (1949) described such a status reversal in restaurants in which waitresses gave orders to counter men. Although the counter men accepted such orders, they did so with resentment and hostility. Despite the continuing stereotypes, it is expected that greater acceptance of women as leaders has occurred since these studies were completed. Yet men who work for women may still feel a greater reluctance to disclose difficulties because they want to protect their own feelings of superior status and not be seen as lacking strength. Zammuto, London, and Rowland (1979) studied how resident advisory assistants in dormitories dealt with their supervisors as a consequence of whether the assistants and the supervisors were men or women. Both female and male assistants were less likely to withdraw when they were in conflict with female rather than male supervisors. Also, highly committed male assistants were more likely to try to smooth over differences, to compromise, or to confront their female supervisors.

But contrary to expectations, Frantzve (1979) failed to find much effect on whether males or females emerged as leaders in initially leaderless groups when she systematically varied the number of females from one to six in six-person groups. Opposite results were found in the field studies of West Point cadets by Rice, Instone, and Adams (1984). Similarly, Lonetto and Williams (1974) found that regardless of the sex of the group, the same personal factors, such as a member's intelligence and self-orientation, were related to the men's and women's emergence as leaders for 31 males and 31 females in three-person undergraduate groups. In the same way, Kanter (1977b) noted that when all-male and all-female groups were given a specific assignment, the interactional patterns and leadership styles within each group were similar. Likewise, in a group of experienced managers, Gaudreau (1975) could find no differences in leaders' competencies associated with their sex. But compared to male cadet subordinates under male or female cadet leaders, female cadet subordinates under female cadet leaders generally described their leaders less favorably. They attributed greater influence to hard work by subordinates and less to the leaders' skill.

Effectiveness of the Leader of the Same or Opposite Sex.

Eisman (1975) found that in marathon encounter groups of one sex or the other, in which a goal is to promote self-disclosure for therapeutic purposes, more such disclosure occurred when groups were led by a person of the opposite rather than the same sex. But most studies that dealt with short-term, less emotionally involved performances found the contrary to be true: same-sex supervision was better. Females supervised by a woman rather than a man performed better on mechanical tasks (Larwood, O'Carroll, & Logan, 1977), standard mathematics tests (Pheterson, Goldberg, & Keisler, 1971), and mathematical word problems (Hoffman & Maier, 1967). Groups with same-sex leaders were reported by Bullard

and Cook (1975) to develop a better group atmosphere than groups led by opposite-sex leaders. However, no differences in productivity were found.

Attitudes toward the Leader by the Same or Opposite Sex.

Subordinates' sex and other personal characteristics moderate the difference in the attitudes of subordinates toward female or male supervisors. Subordinates' attitudes are a complex interaction of the sex composition of the subordinate groups and the leader's sex (Yerby, 1975). Male subordinates looked less favorably on their women superiors than did women subordinates (Jacobson, Antonelli, Winning, et al., 1977). Subordinates received better performance ratings and were better liked in same-sex leader-subordinate dyads than in opposite-sex dyads (Tsui and O'Reilly, 1989). Compared with men, women were more favorably disposed toward women managers (Stevens & DeNisi, 1980). Male midshipmen subordinates led by women rated their leaders slightly lower than male leaders. The women subordinates evaluated their leaders equally whether their leaders were male or female (Atwater & Roush, 1994). But in another military school study, female cadets reacted more favorably to female cadet leaders (Larwood, Glasser, & McDonald, 1980). In all, according to Helland, Barksdale, and Peat (2005), women have an advantage in subordinates' and peer ratings, but not in self-, supervisor or assessment center ratings of leadership.

In their laboratory study of 72 teams of male cadets led by males or females, Rice, Bender, and Vitters (1980) found that the male subordinates with traditional attitudes toward women were lower in overall team morale when led by women. When led by women, traditionalists attributed their groups' success more to luck and less to the leaders' shared work. For subordinates with liberal attitudes, the leaders' sex did not matter as much. Nevertheless, male subordinates, as a whole, thought that women leaders contributed more to the group's performance but that the expert ability of male leaders was more important to their own individual performance. In agreement, Garland and Price (1977) found that men with favorable views toward women managers attributed the managers' success to factors such as ability and effort and avoided attributions of success to luck and the difficulty of the task. These attributions differed from those of more traditional men that women succeed because of good luck, easy tasks, or extra effort (Deaux & Ernswiller, 1974). They subscribed to the stereotype that men with masculine characteristics make better managers. But women looked on successful managers as having both masculine and feminine characteristics (Brenner, Tomkiewicz & Schein, 1989).

Vecchio and Bullis (2002) examined the appraisal by U.S. Army officers of their satisfaction with their 2,883 supervising U.S. Army officers. Satisfaction with one's supervisor generally decreased over time. The largest decrease occurred for women supervised by women. The most consistently satisfied were men supervised by men. Petty and Lee (1975) found that male subordinates of female supervisors rated their supervisors as lower in consideration and higher in initiating structure than did female subordinates of female supervisors or subordinates of either sex of male supervisors. But it is not known whether the ratings reflected the actual differences in the behavior of the female supervisors toward female and male subordinates or differences in the way subordinates perceived the same behavior by female and male supervisors. The male subordinates with female supervisors felt less satisfied with their work and with their supervisors. Since women are expected to exhibit more consideration, and generally do, Petty and Lee suggested that when female supervisors display a lack of consideration, their inconsiderate behavior has more of an effect on their subordinates' dissatisfaction than similar inconsiderate behavior by a male supervisor.

Differential Effects of Leaders' Behavior. Petty and Lee (1975) reported the tendency for male subordinates to be more dissatisfied with female supervisors who were high in initiation of structure and to be more satisfied when both male and particularly female supervisors were more considerate. Petty and Miles (1976) noted that considerate leadership behavior by female supervisors of social service agencies (as well as initiation of structure by male supervisors) was most conductive to the subordinates' satisfaction with supervision. But when larger samples were employed, Bowman, Worthy, and Greyser (1965) found that among 2,000 active executives, 86% of the men and 77% of the women reported that men were uncomfortable working for women executives. Consistent with what was reported earlier about stereotypes of women's lack of leadership potential (Bass, Krusell, &

Alexander, 1971), 41% of the men were unfavorable toward women as managers; women respondents were less unfavorable.

Effects of Marriage. Career women executives are more likely to be divorced or never married. A national sample of male managers and executives in 1975 revealed negative expectations about married women executives. They felt that married women could not handle the responsibilities of both home and career (Rosen, Jerdee, & Prestwich, 1975). On the basis of field research using participant observations, S. S. Mayes (1979) concluded that women in authority elicited hostility and dependence in men. Men resist the changes in sex-role behavior involved in promoting women to positions of authority over them. The men fear such change will destroy the traditional norms of family and relations between the spouses. Few men talk openly about such hostility, but they continue to harbor much resentment. "Behind every woman manager is a man who thinks she got the job only because she's a woman" (Wessel, 1986, p. 20D). When competing for a job, it is difficult for a man to accept defeat on the basis of qualifications; it is easier for him to blame the woman's success on affirmative action. (Attitudes and expectations may have changed in the last 20–plus years.)

Effects of Subordinates' Age and Education. Often women have been found to prefer working for a man (Ferber, Huber, & Spitze, 1979; Robic, 1973). However, women with higher levels of education were more favorable toward women managers. And younger college women indicated they were looking forward to working for a woman (Koff, 1973; Terborg, Peters, Ilgen, & Smith, 1977). Undergraduate women appeared to be more favorable toward working for women leaders than male students, who were slower to change their outlook (Welsh, 1979). Wheeless and Berryman-Fink (1985) suggested that, compared to male respondents, female respondents perceive female managers as more competent communicators, regardless of their previous experience in working for a woman manager. Yet Hollander and Neider (1978) found that women, but not men, generated more negative critical incidents about female leaders. When Petty, Odewahn, Bruning, and Thomason (1976) employed larger samples, they found that, regardless of the sex of the supervisor or the subordinates, the subordinates' satisfaction with supervision was positively correlated with all leadership behaviors except emphasis on production. Similarly, Bartol (1974), in a study of 100 undergraduates in 24 same-sex and mixed-sex teams of four members playing a business game, failed to find that dominant (counter-stereotype) women had a detrimental effect on the subordinates' satisfaction. Again, Fallon and Hollander (1976) reported no difference in the satisfaction of undergraduate males and females with their elected male and female leaders of mixed-sex groups. But the male leaders were seen by both male and female members as more influential and better able to deal with tasks.

Effects of the Task

According to social role theory, people are expected to pursue activities that are congruent with their culturally defined gender roles (Eagley, 1987). Hollander and Yoder (1980) pointed out that some tasks, such as mechanical construction, are seen as masculine, while others, such as child care, are seen as feminine. Men are more likely to take the lead in dealing with stereotypically masculine tasks, and women are likely to do so with feminine ones. In the latter case, women who ordinarily might not accept leadership roles will think it is legitimate to do so when dealing with a task that is relevant to them.

Congeniality of Tasks and Sex Roles. Since leadership in a mixed-sex group is less customary for women, women may be more sensitive to the need to be competent in dealing with the task (Eskilson & Wiley, 1976). Beckman (1984) found that with married couples, in general, it was the wife who tended to dominate the decision processes about fertility and contraception. However, interviews with 376 Egyptian villagers indicated that it was the husband who dominated the basically economic decision for the family to migrate to better employment opportunities (McDevitt & Gadalla, 1985–1986).

Similarly, Bass (1965a) reported in an experiment that *directive* and persuasive wives were more acceptable as leaders in working with their husbands on a task that dealt with household issues. At the same time, they were unacceptable as *directive* and persuasive leaders if the task involved issues within the organization in which

the husband worked. Carbonell (1984) demonstrated that females with leadership ability were less likely to display leadership in interactions with males when they were dealing with masculine tasks. Musham (1980) found that women, in general, and men whose role preferences were androgynous were more likely to emerge as leaders if the tasks were socioemotional. Men, in general, and androgynous women emerged as leaders when task-oriented leadership was required. The intention of female and male Japanese university students to lead in a laboratory situation depended on whether the task was customary for their sex—feminine (doing embroidery) or masculine (making frequent decisions in an adventure computer game) (Sakata & Kurokawa, 1992). For a meta-analysis to show the effects of task-sex congeniality to effective leadership, Eagley, Makhijani, and Karau (1992) asked 306 undergraduates to rate 119 leadership roles for congeniality to men or women. A leadership task congenial to men was coaching a football team; a leadership task congenial to women was editing a women's fashion magazine. Gender match with sex role affected leaders' effectiveness. The meta-analysis of 56 organizational and 20 laboratory comparisons found that men were more effective in "masculine" leadership tasks; women were more effective in "feminine" leadership tasks.

Career Advancement of Women Leaders and Managers

"Doctor Asserts Women Are Unfit for Top Jobs" was a headline on July 26, 1970, in *The New York Times*. Dr. Edgar Berman declared that "raging hormonal influences" of the menstrual cycle as well as menopause disqualified women for key executive jobs because they had the potential to disrupt crucial decisions. Some selection committees might still be influenced by such considerations. But according to a review by Vecchio (2002) of leadership research on sex differences, the claims of women being less successful leaders and the weaker sex have been seriously overstated. Their role as mothers is more influential than the father's role, according to a Gallup poll. While 53% of Americans said their mother had more influence on their life growing up, only 28% chose their father. The relationship with the mother was very positive for 75%, less so with the father. Klein

(2000) notes that the advent of the information technology of the Internet and computer communications has leveled the playing field, increasing the opportunities for women's advancement in management. "Old-boy" networks are less important for information, and virtuality has increased in decision making when awareness of the sex of other members may be obscured.

The Glass Ceiling

Lyness and Schrader (2002) compared announcements in 1998 in *The Wall Street Journal* of the appointments of men and women to senior management positions; women received 6% of the appointments. They were severely underrepresented in appointments to top management in business and industry but not in federal government administration. (Powell and Butterfield [1994] studied promotion decisions for senior executive service positions in the U.S. federal government and found that being a woman was advantageous.)

In business and industry, staff women, compared to men, were more likely to be appointed to new staff rather than line positions and to remain at the same management level with no increase in job scope. Stroh, Brett, and Reilly (1992) looked at the career advancement of 795 male and 223 female managers in 20 Fortune 500 firms. The women lagged behind the men in the progression of their salaries and job promotions. The women were comparable with the men in education, industry, contributions to the family, steady employment, and apparent readiness to transfer, but they were actually less geographically mobile. In the same way, Kirchmeyer (1998) found that experience, tenure, career continuity, and professional degree had stronger effects on men's than women's management career success. Women had to be better than their male counterparts to be promoted (Baumgardner, Lord, & Maher, 1991). Women's entry into management was handicapped by male administrators' tendencies to discriminate against women in personnel decisions involving promotion (Gutek & Stevens, 1979).

Gradually, women are reaching parity with men in middle-management but not higher-level management positions. Except for selected industries such as publishing, cosmetics, and retailing, a "glass ceiling" still keeps women from advancing to top management (Ragins,

Townsend, & Mattis, 1998). They have the necessary abilities but may lack the network required (Adler & Izraeli, 1994). To be promoted to senior levels, senior women executives in Fortune 100 firms have to have fewer weaknesses and more strengths than their male peers (Morrison, White, & Van Velsor, 1987).

Ann Hopkins. Her failure to fit the male stereotype of a woman was enough to block her promotion. Ann Hopkins, a successful manager at PriceWaterhouse, was the only woman nominee for promotion into partnership. She had brought into the accounting firm more new business—over $40 million—than any of the other 87 nominees, but she was denied promotion, while 47 of the 87 men were promoted. Her supporters described her as courageous, self-confident, assertive, independent, and outspoken—traits ordinarily seen as important for leadership. But her detractors interpreted the same behavior as being overbearing, arrogant, self-centered, abrasive, and lacking in interpersonal skills. She used profanity. She did not fit the stereotype for a woman. Her behavior was interpreted differently "because she (was) a woman and leadership is a (cognitive) categorization less likely to be applied to women" (Lord & Maher, 1991, p. 5).

Such discriminatory practices have been justified on the basis of women's higher absenteeism and turnover and their lack of geographic mobility, particularly if they are married or have children (Robie, 1973). Absenteeism and turnover rates of women used to be far higher than those of men at all age levels (U.S. Department of Labor, 1977), often as a consequence of child care problems and their husbands' relocation. In the movement to upgrade women at work, it has been especially important to provide adequate day care for their children, more challenging jobs, and the opportunity for individual women to decide about relocation instead of being treated as a class who follow in the wake of their husbands' career moves.

A Glass Ceiling Commission was created by the U.S. Congress as an amendment to the 1991 Civil Rights Act. In a 1992 *BusinessWeek* interview poll of 400 women executives in corporations with $100 million in annual sales, 56% agreed that a glass ceiling, a point beyond which women never seem to advance, was an obstacle to success in their company (Segal & Zellner, 1992). This was abetted by the unfavorable view that the stock market takes upon the announcement of the appointment of a women CEO, although the negative effect is lessened if the promotion is from within the firm (Lee & James, 2003). The glass ceiling has been pervasive in U.S. corporations, according to a 1990 mail survey of executive women and CEOs. In 1995, women accounted for 10% of corporate officers and 2.4% of corporate leadership in Fortune 1000 firms.

The Myth about Quitting. The glass ceiling is costly. Eighty percent of women middle managers reported quitting their organization for another. Many leave to start their own competitive business (Ragins, Townsend, & Mattis, 1998). The revealed wisdom is that women managers voluntarily quit their jobs more readily than men. However, women's turnover among 26,359 managers in a financial services organization proved to be somewhat lower than the rates for their male counterparts. Also, women promoted in the previous 11 months were less likely to quit than their counterpart promoted men (Lyness & Judiesch, 2001). The early-21st-century economy requires a two-income family. Both spouses in middle-class families must usually remain gainfully employed.

Shattering the Glass Ceiling. To be able to shatter the glass ceiling, it is necessary to understand the barriers to promotion of women to top positions and the strategies of women who succeed in overcoming the barriers. In addition, corporate leaders, male and female, need to understand the barriers and corporate climate, unfavorable to women's advancement to the top, faced by their female employees. In a survey of male CEOs in 1990, the lack of women in top management was blamed on too few having line experience (82%) and too few women being in the pipeline long enough (64%). Among women executives, only 29% and 47%, respectively, agreed. They saw, as the reasons for the glass ceiling, male stereotyping and preconceptions (52%), exclusion from informal networks (49%), and inhospitable cultures (35%) (Ragins, Townsend, & Mattis, 1998). In a Korn Ferry International survey (1990), half the CEOs saw opportunities for women to advance to senior management as having improved greatly in the preceding five years; but only 23% of the women executives agreed. In a survey of 708 employees, 33% of them women, in a large insurance firm, the scaled perception of six items that a glass ceiling was present correlated .81 with the scaled perception of nine items that men and women employees were treated differently (example: "At our company, men are assumed to be competent, but women must prove their competence"). Perceptions of a glass ceiling correlated .59 with the perceived existence of an old-boys' network and the importance of having decision makers as friends. However, perceived upward mobility was viewed as aided by the firm's standard promotion procedures, by mentoring one's immediate manager, and by special career development programs for women (Elacqua, Beehr, & Curtiss, undated).

"Queen Bees." Fewer high-level women are available to serve as mentors. Their number is reduced further by "queen bees," who are uninterested in or unsuited to such mentoring (Riger & Galligan, 1980). Queen bees tend to be antifeminine. They are interested primarily in preserving their unusual high-level status in a world of men (Staines, Tavris, & Jayaratne, 1974).

Mentoring. Fortunately, queen bees do not represent the majority of high-level woman executives, more of whom are supportive of their younger junior women managers (Terborg, Peters, Ilgen, & Smith, 1977). Bowen (1985) compared 18 male with 14 female mentors of female protégés. Although the cross-sex pairing created problems, such as jealousy among spouses, the most salient problem, regardless of the sex of the mentor, was the resentment of coworkers.[16] Women indicated that they needed more help than men to rise in the organization (Van Velsor, 1987). Men, who occupy most of the higher-level positions, are thought to be less willing to serve as mentors for young women managers. Nevertheless, women reported having received more help from mentors than their male manager counterparts did, according to Shapiro's (1985) survey of 75 middle and senior male managers and 67 comparable female managers.

Hoffmann and Reed (1981) concluded, from interviews of both clerks and supervisors in a Fortune 500 firm, that the lower rate of promotion of women was self-imposed rather than due to discrimination. They found that promotion was directly dependent on both men's and women's motivation for advancement. However, al-

---

[16]See Chapter 34 for a detailed discussion about mentoring.

though marriage increased the motivated men's efforts to be promoted into management, it decreased such efforts to be promoted, among similarly motivated women. Women who sought and accepted promotion were disproportionately those who had rejected marriage and parenthood. The societal change in delaying marriage and parenthood and the increased career orientation and higher education of women in the past few decades have changed the calculus and considerably increased women's motivation for careers in management. Hymowitz (1997) argued that many women in exit interviews may give as their reason for leaving the need to return home full-time but in fact may be quitting to accept another job elsewhere. Maintaining both family and job provides more income, opportunities to experience success, and an expanded frame of reference, but it may also bring occasions of failure, frustration, and increased distress.

Personal and Family Factors. Women leaders are less likely to explicitly orient themselves toward careers as leaders. In interviews by Apfelbaum and Hadley (1986) and a 1999 Gallup poll, women were less likely than men to consider themselves leaders. Nonetheless, Fagenson's (1986) survey of 260 women entrepreneurs and managers found that women advanced in their careers because of personal orientation as well as organizational opportunities. Those who were higher in their organizations gave more weight to their careers than to their personal lives and were more committed to their organizations. Also, they were more satisfied with their jobs than those at a lower level. At the same time, those in higher-level positions thought their organization was more concerned about the growth of their careers. In addition, they felt that they were included in the informal power structure in after-hours activities.

Family Considerations among Political Leaders. Carroll (1987) examined the personal and family factors that were of consequence to a sample of 609 women and a comparable representative sample of 365 men who were in state legislatures or the federal administration. Although 24% and 31%, respectively, of the female political appointees in the Carter and Reagan administrations had never been married, the corresponding figures for the male appointees were 4% and 12%, respectively. Over 80% of the men but only half the women appointed were currently married. The pattern was the same for state senators and state representatives, although the differences due to sex were not as extreme. On the other hand, while 80% to 100% of the married women officials reported having very supportive husbands, only 58% to 72% of their male counterparts indicated that they had very supportive wives. The men were more likely than the women to have at least one child under age 12. The women who were elected to the state legislatures, compared to the men, more often felt it was important "to my running for office that my children were old enough for me to feel comfortable about not being home as much." However, family and job roles were the single largest source of conflict for women in politics. Nevertheless, Barnett and Hyde (2001) argued that the multiple roles that have to be enacted do not mean less commitment to one role or the other.

Affiliations. Personal affiliations were also important for the career women professionals. From 64% to 81% were members of at least one major women's organization, such as the American Association of University Women. Many federal appointees, especially in Democratic administrations, were also members of at least one feminist organization, such as the National Organization for Women. Regardless of political party, they tended to belong to organizations of women public officials and women's business and professional organizations.

Attractiveness. Riger and Galligan (1980) noted that personal attractiveness may be disadvantageous for female applicants seeking managerial positions that are believed to require predominantly male attributes such as ambition, decisiveness, and rationality (Heilman & Saruwatari, 1979). But countering this "dumb blonde" syndrome is the fact that physically attractive women are likely to find more office doors readily open to them and to be granted longer interviews. Then (1988) found that, in the judgments of 35 male and 37 female students in a simulation experiment, very attractive women were rated higher than average-looking or unattractive women in their potential for promotion to top management. The unattractive women received the lowest ratings, despite being seen as more "masculine" in their potential for promotion, as well as more suitable as a coworker or friend. Among 285 female and 452 male MBA graduates surveyed over a period of 10 years, the attractiveness of women's faces contributed to their salaries in later years, but not when they started their careers, while attractiveness helped men both at the start and in later years (Frieze, Olson, & Russell, 1991).

Competence, Personality, and Advancement. Larwood and Kaplan (1980) surveyed 80 women bank officers concerning the reasons for their success. These women thought that their ability to make decisions and their demonstration of competence were most important. Successful officers were distinguished from unsuccessful ones by their greater interest in learning from male models and their decision-making ability. They reported themselves to be successful, despite their lower evaluation of their self-confidence. At the same time, the women middle managers studied by Banfield (1976) emphasized their human relations skills, participative decision making, sacrifice of femininity, and reluctance to assert themselves. As a group, they revealed well-integrated personalities with high levels of self-esteem. According to Litterer (1976), the successful woman executive was characterized by the ability to move socially between informal male and female groups. She could be part of the important informal communication. Similarly, Bartol (1978) distinguished between women managers and women in general, finding that, compared to non-career-oriented women managers, the career-oriented women managers saw themselves as more broad-minded, dominating, efficient, and independent.

Motivation, Support, and Advancement. A survey of 1,087 Australian managers and their 1,000 subordinates indicated that career advancement was predicted by managerial aspirations and masculine traits (Tharenou, 2001). According to Koff and Handlon (1975), women who were more likely to advance were motivated to do so. Their motivation is evidenced by their desire to achieve, their previous successes, and their personal commitment to develop their careers. Those who are career-oriented are pioneers, climate sensitives, or support seekers. *Pioneers* are innovators, initiators, risk takers, and high achievers. They enjoy challenges and are not easily

discouraged. They have a positive sense of self-worth and expect to be successful. They also expect to operate independently and autonomously and to be rewarded for their achievements. They feel a sense of accomplishment from handling increased responsibilities. *Climate sensitives* are more responsive to the psychological climate around them and to approval and recognition from top management. *Support seekers* need stroking and hand-holding. Their upward path needs to be cleared of external obstacles and resistance. These women are easily discouraged, readily lose confidence, and do not like to take risks. But support from a higher authority is important for most women for successful careers in management.

Organizational Factors. Organizations may foster or deny opportunities for women to advance. They may have developmental systems such as career counseling for women, networking groups, mentoring programs, and diversified job assignments. They may provide training programs. On the other hand, they may deny women opportunities by excluding them from the inner circles of management, from opportunities to earn rewards and recognition, and from entry into development programs (Ruderman, 2002). Wood (1975) argued that women have to be more competent and work harder to rise in a corporation than do their male counterparts. Although women have been concentrated at the lower levels of management, their failure to advance may be due partly to the fact that in the past, many have had less seniority and experience than their male counterparts. Contrary to expectations, when Tsui and Gutek (1984) examined a representative sample of 217 male and 78 female middle managers in a large corporation with business in computers, education, and finance, they found that the women had a faster rate of promotion, higher performance appraisals, and more merit pay increases.

A further illustration of the organizational aspect of women's careers is that, historically, women in smaller firms have been more likely to advance (Bowman, Worthy, & Geyser, 1965). However, it is the larger firms that have the best-developed affirmative action programs and more standardized promotion plans that constrain sex biases (Donnelly, 1976). Probably, as a consequence of affirmative action programs in larger organizations, Dreher, Dougherty, and Whitely (1988) found that for 486 business school alumni, the typical lower management salaries for women were less common in larger organizations.

Despite affirmative action programs, Gutek (1988) noted that women appear to have only one real route to high-level positions. They must enter the organization with a professional job of reasonably high status—one that traditionally has gone to men. Such an opportunity in the twenty-first century is a realistic expectation. Graves and Powell (1988) found no sex discrimination in 483 campus interviews by outside organizational recruiters. The results were the same for both male and female recruiters. But affirmative action is unlikely to help women move up the corporate ladder from female-dominated, low-status jobs. Furthermore, according to a survey by Chacko (1982), affirmative action programs are a mixed blessing. Women managers who thought they had been hired because of affirmative action by the organization instead of their abilities were less committed to the organization. Also, they were less satisfied with their work, supervision, and coworkers. They experienced more role conflict and role ambiguity than the women managers who believed that their status as women had not been important to their selection.

In larger firms, most women enter managerial ranks in staff rather than line positions. In these positions, they can become specialists and earn credit and acceptance from male colleagues for their skills, expertise, and competence in performing tasks (Hennig & Jardim, 1977; Jacobson & Kock, 1977). But to advance, they usually need to move into more general management. In an Australian study, a mailed survey was completed at three time periods by 1,399 female and 1,431 male employees. Some could be tracked as they were promoted into various levels of management. Compared to the men, advancement of the women from nonmanager to lower-middle and senior management, ocurred in organizations less dominated by a male hierarchy (Tharenou, 2001).

Foreign Assignments. Women are less likely than men to be offered, to seek, and to accept foreign assignments (Adler, 1986–1987; Adler, 1994). They are often pioneers when they accept such assignments. They report feeling more isolated and excluded, according to Linehan (2001), who interviewed 50 senior Western European and North American female managers experienced in at least one international career move. They mentioned the difficulties involved with trailing male spouses; work family conflicts; lack of mentors, career planning, networks and female role models; and tokenism. Almost all reported that, upon return, they had more difficulty in reentering their home organization. They felt a loss of status and autonomy. Needed support was unavailable.

Support and Encouragement. Kimmel (2002) found that women elected to political office in Mississippi particularly owed their career to family encouragement, family financial responsibility, and the power of their connections. But generally, men benefited even more from social support.

Support from Higher Authority. In Tharenon's (2002) Australian survey, women were more likely to be promoted into management early if they had worked closely with a female manager. Especially for advancement into middle and senior management, women, compared to men, were helped more by a sponsoring mentor's encouragement, coaching, and challenging assignments. Hennig and Jardim (1977) found that 25 women who had reached the higher executive level in major corporations were similar to one another in many respects. All were firstborn children.[17] Their fathers, with whom they tended to be close, had encouraged them to be independent, self-reliant, and risk-taking. As children, they had been active in team games. The encouragement, support, and help of a male superior with whom they had developed a close relationship tended to be crucial to their success. Morrison, White, and Van Velsor (1987) confirmed the importance, to the success of the careers of 22 women executives, of help from above. Ruderman (2002) reported that for women in a firm, lack of promotion opportunities correlated −.51 with being supervised by an unsupportive boss. The support of a higher authority is, no doubt, of considerable consequence to the advancement of men, but the powerful person of consequence to a woman's promotion usually has to be an enlightened male manager. Protégés of male mentors obtained greater financial reward than protégés of female mentors (Dreher & Cox, 1996). Male protégés of female mentors had the lowest rate of promotion.

[17]This finding is consistent with earlier discussions about the greater responsibilities parents place on their eldest daughters and the effects on the daughters' subsequent performance as leaders.

Reasons for the Failure of Careers

Driscoll and Goldberg (1993–1994) advised that having a woman senior executive meet with clients at breakfast outside the "comfort zone" of some senior male executives. Failure of women to be promoted has been attributed to biased selection committees. But Powell and Butterfield (1994) could find no such tendency in the U.S. Senior Executive Service. And Knott and Natalle (1997) found that sex differences did not account for benchmark skills, in a sample of 400 managers at medium and upper levels rated by their superiors. It may be that some of the women with the necessary seniority and experience who fail to rise prefer to avoid increased responsibility, challenges, and risks. Or possibly they are passive and lack ambition and energy. They may lack self-esteem and be motivated mainly by the need for security. They may view their peers as family. Or promotion may conflict with their loyalty to their peers, since it may mean the need to sever relations with friends.

Failure to perform effectively as a manager results in reduced self-confidence and motivation. And that failure reinforces the negative stereotypes about women's potential for management (Schwartz & Waetjen, 1976). The two main reasons for women's failure as managers, according to a survey of 100 male managers, were the women's unwillingness to help other women and their tendency to be overdemanding at times, particularly of other women (M. M. Wood, 1976). Women are expected to behave in a feminine manner by showing their subordinates more consideration and less direction than would be expected from male leaders (Bartol & Butterfield, 1976). But, as mentioned earlier, some women who achieve high status exhibit a "queen bee syndrome" and downgrade their women associates (Staines, Tavris, & Jayaratne, 1973). As noted earlier, women managers who attributed their hiring to their status as women rather than to their potential contribution to the firm suffered more role conflict and role ambiguity, which interfered with their effectiveness as leaders (Chacko, 1982). But this cannot account for the small proportion of women in upward movement from middle to top management blocked by the glass ceiling.

Tactics and Strategies for Women

Some women, such as Cynthia Trudell at Saturn, do manage to reach the top even in traditional male-dominated industries such as the automobile industry. Argentina's Maria Lacroze de Fortabat took over a cement company on the death of her husband and built a large conglomerate enterprise. When South African's Wendy Lomathemba Luhabe hit a glass ceiling at BMW, she formed her own training organization (Crowe & Wucker, 1999).

Credentialing. According to a mailed survey of 486 business school alumni by Dreher, Dougherty, and Whitely (1988), no differences appeared in the upward-influence tactics and strategies of women and men. But Larwood and Wood (1977) suggested strategies women managers should use to promote their success in an organization. Even more than male managers, women managers should assure their superiors of their competence by earning the right credentials and by receiving competitive job offers and outside acclaim (M. M. Wood, 1975). Mainiero (1994) agreed and, based on 55 successful women executives, added that women especially need to be assigned high-visibility projects, attract high-level support, accurately identify what their organization values, and display entrepreneurial inititive and critical skills for effective job performance. Parents should encourage sports-mindedness and self-reliance in their daughters (Fierman, 1990). And although early socialization correlates with women's entry into management, it does not predict their further advancement (Tharenou & Conroy, 1994). Nonetheless, as with men, career encouragement of women predicts more engagement and training, leading to advancement in management (Tharenou, Latimer, & Conroy, 1994).

Interviews with and surveys of managers in a Fortune 100 firm by Lauterbach and Weiner (1996) indicated that the women were more likely to involve others in planning. They were more likely to act out of organizational interests, consideration of others' points of view, and concerns for both task and relationships. Men were more concerned about their self-interests and the task, showed less concern for others' feelings, and planned alone in their upward-influence efforts.

More than their male counterparts, women managers

need to have the opportunity to demonstrate their abilities in successive organizational experiences (Konrad & Cannings, 1997). Learning how to befriend and give and receive help from men without letting that experience turn into a sexual encounter is important. Pearson (1980) concluded, from a study of the choices of 60 employers in the human services field who had viewed videotapes of six employment interviews, that female applicants who combined a warm, cooperative style with goal-oriented leadership skills were most preferred.

Suggested Strategies to Advance Careers. Four strategies stood out in a national survey of 461 female executives and 325 CEOs reported by Raggins, Townsend, and Mattis (1998). To achieve status as executives, 77% said it was crucial to consistently exceed performance expectations, 61% said it was crucial to develop a style that men were comfortable with; and 50% said it was crucial to seek high-visibility "stretch" assignments. Other less crucial, but still fairly important strategies included having an influential mentor, networking with influential colleagues, gaining line management experience, changing functional areas, initiating discussions about career aspirations, having the ability to relocate, upgrading educational credentials, changing organizations, developing leadership on the outside, and gaining international experience. A poll by Segal and Zellner (1992) found 83% of the 400 women interviewed agreeing that women should build networks with other women to help each other; 76% of those polled agreed that women should take legal action against discrimination, and 70% agreed that women should take a strong public stand on hiring and promotion of women executives.

Networking. It is important not just for women to be in a network but to have the right network of contacts relevant to their profession, business, and interests. Pragmatic business contacts are likely to be more useful than general meetings with other women managers (Cox, 1986). Interviews with 15 women TV industry executives suggested that a woman manager needs to network 360 degrees—with her superiors, peers, and subordinates (Ensher, Murphy, & Sullivan, 2002). The woman manager needs to act and dress more like a manager and less like a secretary. She can take a visible seating position at meetings (Donnelly, 1976). She can make sure to inform superiors about her activities. Like the male manager, the woman manager can profit from an apprentice role with several superiors. Sometimes she may find it useful to exploit her stereotypic differences by requesting assignments to ensure that "the woman's point of view is represented." Depending on the situation, the woman manager needs to be able to play the female role or the managerial role, whichever is appropriate (Trahey, 1977). As was already mentioned, she needs to know how to deal with sexual advances and sexual harassment. Almost all the women executives surveyed by Litterer (1976) had experienced sexual advances from male executives, but practically none reported having had an affair with someone in their own organization. The traditional "casting couch" demand on an entertainer for a successful career is obviously present but not required for success as a woman manager. Women need to learn how to use and react to power effectively (Instone, Major, & Bunker, 1983). They must convert aggressiveness into assertiveness and initiation. They need to appreciate their own competencies better (Wood, 1975).

Constraints on Acceptable Behavior. After a review of interview and assessment data on more successful and less successful women executives, Morrison, White, and Van Velsor (1987) concluded that executive women may actually differ little from their male counterparts on most matters that count, but, unlike the men, they must confront two sets of demands. To be successful, "[they have] to show their toughness and independence and at the same time count on others. They [must] contradict the stereotypes that their male executives and coworkers have about women—they [must] be seen as different, 'better than women' as a group [yet they must not] . . . forfeit all traces of femininity, because that would make them too alien to their superiors and colleagues. . . . [They must] do what wasn't expected of them, while doing enough of what was expected of them as women to gain acceptance. The capacity to combine the two consistently, to stay within a narrow band of acceptable behavior, is the real key to success" (p. 4).

Women in leadership positions need to make special adjustments that are not required of their male counterparts. Satisfaction with one's job and one's life in general tend to be correlated. However, Kavanagh and Halpern (1977) found them uncorrelated for women at higher levels of university leadership. This lack of correlation may be due partly to the fact that, as was mentioned earlier, women executives are less likely to have husbands to assist with the social and home care demands on their time (Harlan, 1976). But for a majority of women managers, work/family conflict is regarded as inevitable. They need to ask for programs like flexible work arrangements (Nelson & Burke, 2000).

Dealing with Conflicting Roles. As Hall (1972) noted, women managers who are married and mothers face role conflicts that are best handled by *structural role redefinition*—changing the demands within the conflicting roles of homemaker and manager—rather than trying to meet the conflicting demands of both. Unlike the glass ceiling they encounter in large firms, women have fewer such obstacles starting small businesses. Often these are in the service sector in new industries. Women's decision to start such businesses may reflect family considerations, the desire to make better use of their knowledge and abilities, the desire to restart interrupted careers, less discrimination, more control of their own fate, and greater financial opportunities (Bowen & Hirsch, 1986). In all, a resilient woman will treat perceived obstacles with a sense of realistic optimism. Potential threats will be converted into challenges to be overcome (Nelson & Burke, 2000). Tharenou and Conroy (1994) found that while career advancement for Australian women managers continued to be impeded by the smaller degree of mobility they had compared to men, they were able to adequately handle their home responsibilities. Their educational level was not as important to their advancement as it was for their male counterparts. They appeared to have an advantage in advancement in the public sector due to equal opportunity legislation. Their advancement was disadvantaged, compared to men, by their greater unavailability for training. But they reported more career encouragement from organizational peers and seniors than men did.

Summary and Conclusions

Surprisingly, the research results about the stereotyping of women in conflict with the "male" factor in manage-
ment have continued into the twenty-first century. Nevertheless, because changes are rapidly occurring for women in leadership roles, earlier research may need to be discounted. Progress toward seeing women as compatible with management continues, despite the handicaps of socialization, status conflicts, and stereotyping. Some consistent differences in traits between boys and girls remain as they do, to a lesser extent, among adult men and women managers and leaders. Characteristics that are usually linked to masculinity are still demanded for effective management, though most differences between male and female leaders tend to be accounted for by controllable or modifiable factors. Still, women continue to face conflicts in their decisions about their roles as wives and mothers, and managers and leaders.

When it comes to the traits underlying the potential to lead, women benefit by having slightly better verbal skills, but differences in cognitive skills are generally small. With reference to personality traits and the use of power, women may suffer from a lack of self-confidence; but this trait, along with other personality differences in the needs, values, and interests that are of consequence to leadership, appears to evaporate for women who move up the corporate ladder and gain positions of power. For instance, Menkes (1999) found that senior executive women were as comfortable wielding power as their male peers and were no more democratic in doing so.

The rise of feminism and affirmative action has been accompanied by a flood of analyses of sex differences in leadership, to the point where, by 1985, Dobbins called for a moratorium on such studies. Publications since then may reflect societal and institutional changes. Society is changing from a time when smart women played dumb, to a time when assertiveness training for women is commonplace. Yet it seems necessary to continue to give careful consideration to the underlying dynamics and dimensions of the success and effectiveness of women leaders. The same careful consideration is necessary to the development of a new appreciation of racial and ethnic differences in leadership.

Minorities as Leaders and Followers

Four criteria distinguish a minority from the dominant mainstream group of white Americans: (1) visible differences from the mainstream; (2) differential power; (3) differential and pejorative treatment (discrimination); and (4) group awareness (Dworkin & Dworkin, 1999). In addition to the various nonwhite and ethnic groups, older persons, the disabled, and the obese also meet some of the criteria of disadvantaged groups. Attention to diversity tends to pay off. Between 1986 and 1992, organizations recognized by awards from the U.S. Department of Labor for having excellent affirmative action programs showed greater increases in stock prices after the award than they had experienced before. Those settling lawsuits for discrimination showed losses in stock prices following the news. According to a survey of 242 employees in an office of a federal agency, in general, the diverse groups do not share a common culture. Each group, including both men and women, organizes its experience differently (Fine, Johnson, & Ryan, 1990). Socially, as they have assimilated, they have been able to increasingly identify as both Americans and members of a minority. Differences among the races in attitudes and values tend to be social rather than genetic. There is more genetic variation within racial groups than between them (Tomes, 2004).

The racial and ethnic composition of the American workforce is continuing to change. The Hispanic population gained 9.8% in a little over two years between 2000 and 2002 and became the largest minority of 38.8 million, passing the 36.6 million African American population, which grew only 3.1%. The 12.7 million U.S. Asian minority also grew fast at 9.0%, compared to the 200 million whites, who increased by only 0.7% (Armas, 2003). An important factor in this population growth has been immigration, which has increased the diversity of race and ethnicity. In California and Florida, there are now fewer whites than nonwhites. Pursuing diversity has become an important organizational goal for three reasons:

(1) diverse insights and skills are potentially valuable resources; (2) diversity enables organizations to gain legitimacy and access to diverse markets, and (3) fairness and avoidance of discrimination are moral imperatives (Slay, 2003). But diversity has its costs. It is both an emotional issue and an intellectual one. It can be divisive and a cause of conflict among leaders and followers (Cox & Beale, 1997). Until the mid–twentieth century, assimilation into the mainstream was generally sought by diverse minorities. But increasingly, there is an effort of those not in the mainstream to honor their racial or ethnic roots and to maintain some of their traditions.

There is much diversity within the various groups. Black Americans vary from purely Negro African ancestry to almost purely white European forebears. They may be partly American Indian. Their ancestors may have arrived as slaves from 1619 on, or they may be recent immigrants from Africa, Haiti, the Dominican Republic, or Jamaica or from elsewhere in the West Indies. Hispanics or Latinos include Mexican Americans (Chicanos), Puerto Ricans, Cuban Americans, and Central and South Americans. Asian Americans range from Koreans to Vietnamese. American Indians come from more than 500 tribes. The disabled include both the physically disabled and the mentally impaired.

The Current Situation in America. Affirmative action regulations inhibit gross discrimination in hiring, promotion, and benefits for disadvantaged minorities and women. Yet there remain subtle and sometimes not so subtle biases when leaders and followers are of different races and ethnicities. Biases may be automatic, unintentional, and unconscious when we compare people like "them" with people like "us." Intergroup biases create a hostile environment for out-groups with "awkward social interactions, embarrassing slips of the tongue, unchecked assumptions, stereotypic judgments, and spontaneous neglect." Stereotypes are primed. Open hostility is not expressed, but in-group comfort and out-group discomfort are felt. Liking and respect are missing (Fiske, 2002). Research by Heilman, Block, and Stathatos (1997) suggested that affirmative action hires are stigmatized as less competent. Some minority department chairs in educational institutions complain that because of lack of respect for them (1) they are not taken seriously, (2) they face continuous end runs to higher administration, (3) their initiatives are blocked, and (4) all discussions with them are reduced to routine business (E. Smith, 1996). Often the biases against another race or ethnicity are mixed, both favorable and unfavorable, associated with the perceived competition and status of the out-group (Fiske, 2002, p. 124). Because of earlier experiences of unfair treatment, minority subordinates have greater expectations than subordinates in the mainstream majority of being treated unfairly by their superiors and are more likely to reject rational explanations for perceived discrimination (Davidson & Friedman, 1998). Organizations differ in how much their human resources policies and practices comply with affirmative action and equal opportunity legislation. Lawsuits and compliance reviews are highest for organizations lacking identity-conscious policies and practices. Such organizations also have the lowest percentages of disadvantaged minorities and women (Konrad & Linnehan, 1995).

The Rising Status of Minorities. Thousands of African Americans have sought and been elected or appointed to public office. They have been mayors of Los Angeles; Detroit; Washington, D.C.; Chicago; Philadelphia; Atlanta; New Orleans; and New York City. Hispanics have achieved similar success in San Antonio, Miami, Los Angeles, and elsewhere. Black general officers are no longer unusual. Blacks are taking leading roles in sports, entertainment, and the Democratic Party, and served in high-ranking positions in Republican administrations. Ethnics, blacks, Asian Americans, and Indian Americans serve in the U.S. Senate and state governorships. Blacks, Hispanics, Asian Americans, Indian Americans, and members of ethnic minorities have achieved prominence as political, governmental, business, and professional leaders. But in comparison with mainstream Americans, members of these minority groups face systematic differences in the likelihood of their emerging as leaders and the probabilities of their success. Minorities are under-represented in top management in business. In 2003, although they comprised 27% of all personnel, only 3% of blacks or women occupied senior executive positions (Bell, Gilley, & Coombs, 2003). But diversity may have unexpected effects on decision making. For instance, 26 new Internet-based ventures developed with "ethnic presence" in their teams were more likely to pursue strategies as prospectors than did 26 matched mainstream teams (Chaganti, Watts, Chaganti, et al., 2003). Firms such as Allstate Insurance may turn diversity to comparative advantage by maintaining a highly diverse organization to link their business to their diverse customer base. Such firms can better understand, attract, and handle the needs of customers outside the mainstream (Wan, 1999).

Affirmative Action. It is clear that the pressure of legislation promoting equal employment opportunities has brought marked increases in employment and advancement of women and minorities. But organizations differ in the extent to which their human resources management practices are fully supportive of affirmative action. As noted before, according to Konrad and Linnehan (1995), the practices of less supportive firms are revealed in both fewer women and minority members and a history of more lawsuits and legal bouts with government equal opportunity regulators.

Research on Leading Diverse Groups. Diversity of organizations' personnel has increased substantially, but leadership research in the past has been concentrated on white leaders and white followers (Offerman & Gowing, 1990). Most of the research on leadership on minorities has dealt with blacks as leaders or subordinates. Considerably less has been done with Hispanic, Asian American, and other racial and ethnic minorities. There is also a dearth of information on the movement of Jewish Americans, Italian Americans, Polish Americans, Greek Americans, American Indians, and other minorities into top-level positions of leadership, although highly visible members of these groups continue to appear in industry, government, education, and nonprofit organizations. Much of the available diversity research hinges on objective demographic diversity, which has weaker effects than the subjective sense of being a member of a particular race and ethnicity and the value and emotional significance of that membership (Phinney, 1990). Initially, ethnically diverse teams, compared with nondiverse teams, may have different perspectives about the same issue. They may perform less adequately due to greater difficulties in coordination (Cox, 2003). This tends to dissipate over longer periods of time (Wagner, 1995). Watson, Johnson, and Merritt (1998) found more self-orientation than team orientation in ethnically diverse student problem-solving groups. Such teams remained more self-oriented over time. Nevertheless, the ethnically diverse teams, "regardless of the extent of cultural diversity, . . . learn to perform better with periodic feedback about performance and how to improve interpersonal processes for better performance" (p. 185). Sensitivity to race or ethnicity may disappear with time in a supervisor-subordinate relationship as both become accustomed to each other, especially if the relationship becomes a high-quality exchange.

The Challenge of Diversity

In 2002, the 815 hotel workers in the Washington Hilton spoke 36 languages. About 65% were foreign-born (Offerman & Phan, 2002). Diversity is a challenge to their supervisors. Mayo, Pastor, and Meindl (1996) found that diversity in race, age, sex, and tenure in 68 work groups, combined with poorer performance, resulted in the leaders' loss of feelings of self-efficacy. Although diversity may enhance the social processes of a group, more often, according to Williams and O'Reilly (1998) who reviewed the results of 80 studies, it had adverse effects on social processes. Reskin, McBrier, and Kmec (1999) reached a similar conclusion in their review. More specifically, Foley, Linnehan, Greenhaus, et al. (2003) reported that racial dissimilarity of subordinates and supervisor was likely to reduce family-supportive supervision. Vecchio and Bullis (2001) collected surveys from 2,883 U.S. Army officers and noncoms about the leadership of their officer supervisors, who ranged in rank from second lieutenant to general. An analysis focused on the demographic similarity of each subordinate rater and rated supervisor. The respondents included 23% blacks, 13% women, 12% Hispanics, 3% Asian/Pacific Islanders, and 2% American Indians and Eskimos. The officer supervisors were 13% black, 10% female, 9% Hispanic, 2% Asian/Pacific Islander, and 1% American Indians and Eskimos. Female

and Hispanic supervisors received slightly less favorable ratings than did their male and non-Hispanic counterparts. A stronger effect emerged when it was found that white subordinates were least satisfied under nonwhite supervisors. Managing diversity needs to be part of an organization's reward structure.

Based on interviews with managers and executives, a review of the literature, and their own experience in various organizations, Joplin and Daus (1997) detailed six "preeminent" challenges confronting leaders of a diverse workforce:

1. *Changes in power.* Mainstreamers may try to bolster and retain power at the expense of promoted minority newcomers. Leaders must avoid showing favoritism. Mainstreamers may feel an erosion in their power. They may feel less attached and committed to the organization and more uncertain about how they fit in. They may become more negative in attitudes if forced to attend diversity training. Tensions increase as minorities gain voice and express opinions.

2. *Diversity of opinions.* Leaders must be prepared for the exponential increase in the number and range of perspectives of a workforce with an increased range of values and norms. Leaders need to be able to recognize the different frames of reference of minority members. They need to synthesize diverse opinions and get to the crux of issues, while maintaining the respect and dignity of their diverse constituents. Visible disdain must be avoided.

3. *Perceived lack of empathy in the leader.* Leaders must sense the feelings of others and anticipate reactions to proposals. They must understand "where others are coming from, what they have been through, and where they are going" (p. 41).

4. *Real and perceived tokenism.* An organization with tolerant policies will find it less necessary to fill quotas rather than hiring and promoting based on candidates' merits. It will achieve fair representation through active recruitment in diverse categories. Perceived tokenism is likely to be greater in intolerant organizations that hire to fill quotas, causing more resentment and attributions of failure to race or ethnicity.

5. *Participation.* Minority participation needs to be encouraged to capitalize on new, different, and creative ways of thinking. Leaders need to ensure than everyone has a voice in reaching solutions to problems. This will require a lot of a leader's time.

6. *Overcoming inertia.* The leader needs a strong and clearly communicated vision and goals. If the organization is in a state of intolerance of diversity, the leader needs to communicate the advantages of diversity. If diversity is already appreciated, the leader needs to integrate ideas into implementation plans and action to avoid relapses into inertia and malingering.

Effects of Demographic Similarity and Dissimilarity

Supervisory support for equal opportunity affects majority and minority groups differently. The majority look on their supervisors more favorably if they feel their supervisor does *not* support equal opportunity. The minority are more favorable if they feel their supervisor supports equal opportunity. Over time, satisfaction of subordinates with their supervisor drops if they are different in race. Tsui and Reilly (1989) reported that demographic dissimilarity between supervisor and subordinate resulted in less supervisor attraction to the subordinate, lower supervisor rating of the subordinate, and more role ambiguity for the subordinate. In New Zealand, Chong and Thomas (1997) noted that dissimilarity between whites and Maoris produced less satisfied followers. On the other hand, Wright, Ferris, and Hiller (1995) compared organizations that had won awards for affirmative action programs with organizations that had had to settle discrimination lawsuits. The stock prices of those that had promoted diversity increased in the days surrounding the awards, while the stock prices of those having to settle discrimination lawsuits declined. Simmons and Nelson (1997) found that the performance of 30 firms identified as "better for minorities and women" was slightly better than their industry average for the years 1985 to 1994. Clark and Clark (1994) proposed that for an organization to benefit from diversity, common ground and true integration needed to be established and overtly supported by its leadership. Organizational support for diversity for 90 solo minority managers correlated .37 with job satisfaction and −.31 with intention to quit. Solos were the lone representatives of their race or ethnicity in their work group (Wagner, Rosek, DePuy, et al., 2001).

Military Integration. In 1948, President Truman ordered the integration of the U.S. military. In 1973, a worldwide leadership survey was completed by the U.S. Army in each of its major commands (Penner, Malone, Coughlin, et al., 1973). Data were obtained by asking about one third of the 30,735 respondents to complete a written questionnaire describing the leadership of their immediate superior; another third, to complete a questionnaire describing the leadership of one of their immediate subordinates; and the final third, to complete a questionnaire describing their own leadership. In addition to various demographic items and a single measure of satisfaction with the overall performance of the individual described, the questionnaire used in the study included a list of 43 specific items of behavior that are commonly observed in U.S. Army leaders. About half these 43 behaviors were derived fairly directly from the SBDQ and LBDQ. For each behavior, three questions were asked: "How often does he . . . ?", "How often should he . . . ?", and "How important was this to you?" The first question was a measure of perceived actual performance; the second, a statement of expectations; and the third, an indicator of the criticality of the behavior according to the respondent. Surveyed were the differences among supervisors', self, and subordinates' overall satisfaction with U.S. white and nonwhite field-grade officers and company-grade commissioned and senior and junior noncommissioned officers.

All but the junior noncoms gave higher evaluations to white than to nonwhite leaders, while the subordinates did the reverse, favoring nonwhites. Self-ratings of satisfaction were generally the same for whites and nonwhites. White and nonwhite field-grade officers differed in the list of behaviors that correlated most highly with how satisfied they were with their own overall performance. The list for nonwhite field-grade officers contained seven negative items to be avoided. The list for white field-grade officers contained only one such negative item of behavior. Thus, in evaluating themselves, the nonwhite field-grade officers were satisfied with their own overall performance if they avoided doing negative things such as "hesitating to take action," "failing to show appreciation for priorities of work," or "making it difficult for subordinates to use initiative." On the other hand, the white field-grade officers were satisfied with their own overall performance if they did positive things such as "being technically competent to perform their duties," "seeking additional and more important responsibilities," and "being aware of the state of their unit's morale and doing all they can to make it high." The investigators attributed this difference to the discrimination experienced by the nonwhite officers in the 1950s and early 1960s when they first entered service, when it was more important for nonwhite officers to avoid making mistakes than it was for them to stand out in a positive manner. Consistent to some degree with these results, Sackett and DuBois (1989) combined civilian data from U.S. firms with military data and found that both nonwhites and whites gave lower ratings to nonwhites.

Networking of Minority Managers. Revealed wisdom suggests that corporate advancement depends on whom you know as much as what you know. Minority managers are seen to have more difficulty gaining support (Thomas & Alderfer, 1989). Minorities' advancement is handicapped by their exclusion from social networks (Morrison & Van Glinow, 1990). To study this issue, Ibarra (1995) examined the contacts outside their business unit of 17 minority middle managers (12 black, 3 Hispanic, and 2 Asian American) with a survey and interviews, and compared them with the contacts of 46 white middle managers. Altogether, 20 were women, but sex was statistically controlled when the results were extracted. Compared to white managers, minority managers felt that networking was less important to their advancement. The managers reported more racially mixed networks but fewer intimate ones. Minority managers with high potential balanced same and cross-race contacts rather than being dominated by whites. They had more contacts outside their groups.

Effects of Marginality. Marginality can be an asset. A marginal person who lives at the boundary of two worldviews has two ways of looking at problems and of finding answers to them. The acculturation of black or Hispanic subordinates to the mainstream varies. High "biculturals" have their feet planted firmly in both the mainstream and the minority. According to an experiment by Carza, Romero, Cox, and Ramirez (1982), high biculturals, whether they are Chicano (Mexican American) or black, attempt more leadership in simulated, nonsupportive groups with a mix of Chicanos, blacks, and whites if they are externally oriented. They ask for more opinions and evaluations and make more clarifying remarks. But minority status may be a liability. Lovelace and Rosen (1996) compared perceptions of a group of 157 white, 35 black, and 24 Hispanic of the managers' organizational fit. The blacks perceived themselves as significantly lower in fitting into the organization than did the whites and Hispanics. Poor fit was correlated with job dissatisfaction, intention to leave, and more stress.

Marginality as a source of stress was seen by Ford (1985), who analyzed job stress in five empirical studies of black, American Indian, and Mexican American professionals and found that they experienced more job stress than their white counterparts. They experienced less stress when supervised by nonwhites and when given emotional and structural support.

Leading and Managing Diversity

Diversity can be effective if it is well managed (Adler, 1990). Well-managed top-management teams with diversity in members can achieve greater performance and cohesion (Elron, 1997). Creativity can be increased by using people from different perspectives. Turnover can be reduced among minorities with good leadership (Cox & Blake, 1991). To lead and manage a diverse workforce, constituency, or organizational membership, and to avoid hindering follower performance, leaders need to identify and understand what disturbs individuals from minority backgrounds. They need to appreciate the stress and conflict that may be created in multicultural settings of implicit and explicit organizational policies. These negative influences need to be removed (Mai-Dalton, 1993). Findings from 200 interviews and surveys of 450 employees by Gordon and Loden (1989) suggested that in addition to awareness of multicultural issues, management needs to be open to change and actively create opportunities for minority employees. They need to be ethically committed to fairness and to mentoring and empowering minority employees, and need to be models and catalysts for organizational change. Offerman and Phan (2002) added that leaders need to facilitate implementation of diversification policies and the flow of information, set high expectations, provide for continuing education and training, and watch out for backlash from mainstreamers. Pastors of urban churches support diversity by (1) raising awareness of diverse racial and ethnic groups in the organization; (2) using cognitive dissonance between biases and brotherhood; (3) providing expertise and credibility in introducing change; (4) providing a voice for different stories; and (5) connecting experience with transcendental vision.

Cultural Competence. Management of diversity calls for cultural competence: attitudes, practices, and policies that respect different cultures and people. Culturally competent leaders seek advice and consultation from diverse racial and ethnic groups and communities and actively incorporate the information into their behavior and commitment (Cross, Bazron, Dennis, et al., 1989). Such leaders are able to leave behind intelligent behaviors learned in one cultural context for what is intelligent in a new context (Offerman & Phan, 2002). Del Castillo (undated) associated transformational leadership with cultural competence. The transformational leader appreciates and adapts to the diversity of followers, and understands her or his own culture and the dynamics of cultural differences.

Programmatic Efforts. Ellis and Sonnenfeld (1994) noted that brief "one-shot" contacts to propagandize for diversity may hinder rather than help manage diversity by reinforcing stereotypes, hostility, and misunderstanding of other races and ethnicities. They listed eight programmatic approaches that firms have used to encourage and support diversity: (1) multicultural workshops; (2) meetings on a monthly basis to confront stereotypes and personal biases; (3) minority support groups, networks, and advisory councils that report directly to senior management; (4) reward systems for training and promotion of minorities; (5) fast-track programs for minorities who demonstrate exceptional talent and potential; (6) mentoring of minorities by senior managers; (7) corporate announcements of appreciation; and (8) commitment to diversity. Few evaluations of the effects of these approaches have appeared.

Allstate Insurance is an example of a program that enhanced diversity relations and its effects. When employees join Allstate Insurance they receive the message, accompanied by an informational booklet, that they can expect to enjoy a bias-free environment. In the 1960s and 1970s, the emphasis was on assimilating differences. In 1993, it became a strategic initiative to accept differences and to incorporate them into all business processes. This initiative increased Allstate's customer base and satisfaction. Twenty-five percent of the merit pay or compensation of leaders at all levels is tied to their upholding diversity in their workplace or business unit. A diversity index asks respondents to what extent (1) quality service is delivered to customers regardless of their background; (2) respondents are treated with respect and dignity at work; (3) their managers and team leaders seek out and utilize the diverse backgrounds and perspectives in their group; (4) they observe insensitive behavior at work such as inappropriate comments or jokes; and (5) they work in an environment of trust (Anonymous, 1999).

Chen and Van Velsor (1996) suggested that diversity leadership needs to consider the impact of sociopsychological processes and minority group identities embedded in organization group identities. DiTomaso and Hooijberg (1996) point to the need for leaders involved in managing diversity and multiculturalism to remain conscious of their effects on various racial and ethnic groups and to provide role models. The leaders need

> To create bridges, channels, pathways, connections, perhaps "safe passages" for those who have been hindered, excluded or constrained from participating to maximum effect, and they . . . [ought to] . . . require the same of other organizational leaders. They [should] be inclusive, while expecting and then supporting superior achievement. (p. 170)

Strategic planning and initiatives should take diversity into account. Structures should be adapted to enable equal access to the organizational networks. Ethical considerations need to be kept in mind.

Caveat. Fairholm (1994a) declared that leadership is impossible outside of a community of individuals with shared values and vision. Leaders need not accept unreservedly the values of every racial and ethnic group. Instead, they need to use the mainstream American culture as a foundation on which to build the basis for their leadership. E pluribus unum—one from many. Much is held in common by Americans, regardless of their diverse group identities. For instance, according to overt integrity tests of 724,806 job applicants, although women scored higher than men, age and racial or ethnic identity made little difference in scores (Ones & Viswesvaran, 1998). Leaders need to create unity out of diversity. Similarities, not differences, need to be highlighted. A leader needs to create a group that is more than just an amalgam of diverse views. The leader needs to bring the followers together in a common work culture to fit "the work done and the character and capacities of the stakeholders to the benefit of all concerned. . . . Leaders create a set of group values that supersede organizationally inappropriate ones and replace them with values all can accept and work under" (p. 88). Leaders build unified groups from diverse individuals in alignment with organizational goals (Fairholm, 1994b). Since 2006, in order to win the presidential election in 2008, the Democratic Party has been asked to appeal more to the common economic and social interests of both the mainstream and minorities.

African Americans and Leadership

A system of prejudice has built up over the centuries. Although socially and politically we have agreed to get rid of this system, its effects still linger, often in subtle ways. A supervisor may fail to see what he is doing to a black employee or black fellow manager. . . . In turn, the African American may feel prejudice from the supervisor when it is not present. (Bass, Cascio, & McPherson, 1977)

African Americans as a Subculture

Of minorities in America, black Americans have been among the most negatively stereotyped (T. W. Smith, 1990). Blacks in the United States are not members of another culture. Rather, they form an American subculture that is tied to the majority white cultural institutions without clear boundaries to mark off their society from the larger white society (Liebow, 1967). Increasingly, their norms and values are influencing the majority culture, and vice versa. Blacks have adopted the cultural patterns of the dominant white society (Baldwin, Glazer, Hook, et al., 1966). The social groups they identify with

are American and black. Being black and being American has significance both emotionally and in values. They span two worlds (Slay, 2003). Unlike other minorities, African Americans' perceptions of family, friends, society, love, work, and money are fairly similar to those of white Americans. Blacks and whites are psychoculturally close (Cunningham, 1984). In fact, Pinkney (1969) found that middle-class blacks tended to overconform to white middle-class standards of behavior. As Bass, Cascio, McPherson, and Tragash (1976) noted, in a study of 315 managers' responses to a racial awareness questionnaire, many agreed that the "system" is biased against blacks and that blacks are still often excluded from the mainstream. Even potential black leaders may restrict themselves. Thus Gump (1975) found that black female college students were more likely to see their future roles as wives and mothers, whereas white female college students were oriented more toward their own career development than toward fulfilling the traditional woman's role. But this has changed with the large increase in black women attending college and seeking careers.

Among 359 black executives surveyed by E. E. Jennings (1980), 45% still believed that racial prejudice was the most important impediment to further progress in their careers. Nevertheless, the legacy of the master-slave relationship is giving way—by fits and starts prompted by war, civil strife, civil rights legislation, and education—to the rise of a large number of black Americans into positions of leadership. By 2007, two blacks were successively U.S. secretaries of state. The CEO of TIAA, the country's largest nonprofit organization, is black. The 359 black executives in Jennings's (1980) survey were located primarily in large organizations, mainly in manufacturing, real estate, insurance, or finance. They performed the same organizational functions that provide for the faster advancement of whites: marketing, manufacturing, and finance. Their higher education and personal contacts were important to their being recruited.

Race Relations in Transition

Experimental, observational, and survey research lags behind the changes in attitudes and behavior since the 1940s resulting from desegregation, the civil rights movement, affirmative action, and the increased visibility of blacks in politics, athletics, and entertainment. Moreover, the scant research that was available prior to the mid-1960s is of less relevance to an understanding of the attitudes and behavior of minorities and whites in the twenty-first century. For example, consider Goode and Fowler's (1949) finding that the tough, autocratic, punitive supervisor was most effective for maximizing productivity among marginal[1] predominantly black workers in a Detroit bumper-grinding and polishing shop. Today, large numbers of African Americans are present in the workforce, including in manufacturing, service, sports, education, government, law enforcement, and the armed forces. Black line workers, army privates, teaching assistants, and government personnel would not expect nor accept white leadership that was overtly coercive. Black women have almost reached parity with white women in employment and earned income, and proportionately surpassed white male students in entering higher education. Nevertheless, 30% of black men are unemployed or not in the labor force. One of seven has spent time in prison.

The Gallup Poll Social Audit (1997) interviewed by telephone a nationally representative sample of 1,269 blacks and 1,767 whites. In 1965, 54% of blacks and 93% of whites were satisfied with their jobs. In 1997, 73% of blacks and 86% of whites were satisfied with their jobs. The gaps between blacks and whites tend to disappear for those with high levels of education and income. In 1965, 53% of whites said they would vote for a black person for president; in 1997, 93% said they would do so.

Emergence of African Americans as Leaders

There is a rich store of biographical literature on the emergence of black political, community, educational, and religious leaders, ranging from the leaders of slave insurrections such as Nat Turner to reform leaders Frederick Douglass and Martin Luther King, Jr. To work within "the system" like Booker T. Washington, to modify it like W. E. B. DuBois, to attempt to destroy it like Malcolm X, or to lead it like Jesse Jackson have been the different goals of emergent, charismatic political leaders. There is continuity in leadership among blacks. According to a longitudinal study by Tripp (1986), the black student activists of the 1960s continued to be involved in community activities in 1969 and 1978. But entry into

[1] Marginal workers, in this context, were the last hired by and first fired from the automobile assembly plants, the source of better-paying jobs.

leadership positions in business and industry, except for a few black service-oriented industries, such as insurance and undertaking, is mainly a consequence of the equal opportunities legislation of the 1960s. The entry of blacks into military leadership was stimulated by President Harry S. Truman's order to integrate the armed forces in the late 1940s, which was followed by continuing increases in the proportion of blacks, particularly in the all-volunteer army. By the end of the twentieth century, according to Oscar Williams, the Southeastern Training of Trainers Program had been responsible for the training of roughly 10,000 black leaders (approximately 65% female) in five southern states, in empowering others, and in long-range planning and implementation.

When legislation, higher authority, or political climate demands it, such as occurred earlier in the military and more recently in industrial and educational organizations, blacks have advanced into higher-level positions. There are numerous black generals, CEOs, presidential candidates, police chiefs, government executives, judges, and university chancellors. School desegregation and affirmative action have opened opportunities for education and advancement of blacks and made visible the movement of blacks into higher-status positions. Formalized recruitment procedures and personnel policies with responsible documentation have resulted in large increases in the advancement of minorities, particularly in larger organizations (Braddock, 1984). The legal impediments to political leadership have changed drastically since the restrictions on black voting rights were lifted in 1964. Especially where blacks form a majority of large minority voting blocs, such as in the Deep South and the inner cities, blacks have succeeded in being elected to office in large numbers. Some black politicians have gained large white constituencies. They have become prominent in federal, state, and local government.

In a laboratory experiment using pairs of high- and low-dominant white and black coeds performing a clerical task in which one participant had to assume the role of leader and the other of follower, Fenelon (1966) found, contrary to expectations, that black women assumed the role of leader twice as often as did white women, no matter what their relative assessment scores in dominance. The white women with high scores in dominance thought it more important to show their egalitarian attitudes than to become leaders.

Group Membership. Although white Americans tend to be addicted to joining groups and associations, black Americans are even more extreme in this regard. Membership in associations is a springboard to leadership experiences and political influence. Concrete, visible issues, such as the right to vote, integration of schools, and lack of access to public accommodations mobilized black followers. But when these concrete issues were resolved and when only more amorphous or less visible issues remained, such as whites-only school board membership, leadership and organization become blunted and the willingness of individuals to be followers declined (Davis, 1982). Without salient black issues, blacks are less likely to assume leadership roles even when they form a sizable proportion of the membership of an organization.

Underrepresentation. Despite their high proportions in some types of organizations such as labor unions, blacks were often underrepresented in positions of leadership. For example, Lamm (1975) found that among 30 union locals with black members in the San Francisco Bay area, only 10 had blacks in leadership positions in proportion to their number in the membership. In 10 locals, blacks were proportionally underrepresented among the leaders, and in the remaining 10 locals, there were no black leaders. Similarly, despite their overrepresentation in excellence in athletics, blacks remain underrepresented in sports leadership positions such as football quarterbacks or team coaches.

Blacks remain underrepresented in management in both the public and private sectors, except in special circumstances. In a study of black MBAs, Brown and Ford (1977) found that relative to their white counterparts, black MBAs had lower opportunities for promotion and advancement. Again, Fernandez (1981) found the biggest gap between aspirations and expectations of upward mobility among black male managers. And according to Jones (1986), 84% of the black MBAs from the top five graduate business schools reported that considerations of race had a negative impact on their performance appraisals, pay, assignments, recognition, and promotions. Nonetheless, black managers could advance when conditions were favorable. For 194 black managers with MBAs who were working in larger organizations, advancement occurred more often when they had more seniority, were in line rather than staff positions, and had

help from mentors. They were also helped by their social activities (Nkomo & Cox, 1987).

The entry of blacks and whites into positions of leadership is likely to follow different paths. The importance of a religious ministerial practice as a route to leadership for black men is well known. What is less well known is how the route to leadership often differs for black and white women. Mottl's (1977) interview study of the different career paths of white and black women reform leaders found that the school bureaucracy was immediately more accessible to white women, who became involved as teachers and middle-class mothers. Their ease of entry from home into school politics was related to the closeness of the schools, particularly the elementary schools, to family life.

African Americans remain underrepresented as small-business owners in America's inner cities. Earlier in the twentieth century, Jews were inner-city small-business owners; currently it is the immigrant Asian Americans, such as Koreans, who do so. Unlike Koreans, blacks often lack stable families working together and the rotating credit associations that are often required to start and maintain these small businesses (Fukuyama, 1997). African Americans also face additional constraints.

Constraints on African Americans as Leaders in America

Lower rates of achievement and leadership can be attributed to personal deficits or to educational or cultural deprivation due to blocked opportunities because of cultural conflict and discrimination (Bowman, 1964). Much of black's experience and how they feel about it is invisible to whites, according to a survey of 270 black professionals and 39 in-depth interviews with black executives. Whites need to understand how their black colleagues experience the organizational environment. What is invisible to whites needs to be made visible. Nearly 90% of the black professionals feel that if they are successful, other blacks will be seen in a better light by whites, but half of those surveyed said that if they are failures, other blacks will be seen unfavorably. They remain ambivalent about networking and confiding in white managers because they are not unsure if they can trust white managers (Livers & Caver, 2002). Overtly racist expressions, such as racial slurs, have become less socially acceptable and more politically incorrect, but more subtle discrimination still exists. Discrimination has been outlawed in the workplace and public facilities by government legislation and regulation. Nevertheless, blacks' encounters with understated slights and devaluations are still common (Essed, 1991; Stone, Stone, & Dipboye, 1992). The continuation of such incidents can have a dehabilitating effect (Swim, Cohen, & Hyers, 1998), be a source of physiological stress (Miller & Kaiser, 2001), and result in feelings of hopelessness (Branscombe, Schmitt, & Harvey, 1999).

The differing perspectives were seen in public opinion polling in 1997. Blacks were treated unfairly on the job, according to 45% of blacks but only 14% of whites in a national representative sample. From 42% to 46% of the blacks also felt that they were treated unfairly in shops and malls and in restaurants, while only 12% to 19% of whites agreed that blacks were treated unfairly in those situations. Sixty percent of blacks and 30% of whites agreed that blacks were treated unfairly by the police (Gallup, 1997). Arguing that perceived mistreatment was a more valid measure of discrimination and prejudice on the part of their superiors, Deitch, Barsky, Butz, et al. (2003) analyzed the responses of 314 line workers, 5,483 navy personnel, and 8,311 U.S. Army personnel who were questioned on the extent to which they had been victims of mistreatment. Questions included "Has anyone has set you up for failure?" "given others privileges you didn't get?," "failed to provide you with the information to do your job?" In the military samples, blacks reported more mistreatment than did whites, resulting in lower job satisfaction and felt physical well-being.

Black Women Managers. Black women are less disadvantaged than black men. The 2000 Census indicated that black women outnumbered black men in professional and managerial work by approximately 800,000. But only 3% held managerial positions. They said that racism is more of a barrier to their opportunities in a mainstream organization than is sexism (Delany & Delany, 1993). But compared to white men and women, "black women executives are more likely to suffer from the interactive effects of racial and gender discrimination" (Parker & Ogilvie, 1996, p. 201).

Black women managers display some of the same feminine leadership style as white women noted in the previous chapter, such as emphasis on interpersonal relations, empathy, and collaboration. But more often than white women managers, they also tend to observe the traditional masculine style of command, control, and competitiveness. They are likely to be androgynous in their leadership, both task and relations oriented (Parker & Ogilvie, 1996). Their socialization contributes to this tendency as adults. Much is due to dominant and protective disciplinarian mothers (Parker & Ogilvie, 1996). In comparison to white girls, black girls are expected to become self-assertive and independent. Their parents expect them to mature earlier. Even as preschoolers, black girls may already be required to carry considerable responsibility for younger siblings. Early on, they are exposed to strong, dominant mothers as role models (Baumrind, 1972).

"Black mothers . . . raise daughters who are self-reliant and assertive" (Collins, 1990), and "not socialized to be 'passive' or 'irrational' . . . but rather independent, strong . . . and self-actualizing in a society that devalues black women" (Parker & Ogilvie, 1996, p. 195). The daughters are socialized to resist the standards of mainstream culture and its ideology about race. They are enabled to hold on to a positive sense of self. They have equal or higher educational and career aspirations than white adolescents (E. Smith, 1982). Proportionately more black women now enter college than do white men.

Black women managers need to offset the stereotype by whites that they are too direct, assertive, and flashy; black men need to offset the stereotype as angry and intimidating. About half believe that their own mistakes will reflect badly on other black managers in the organization and that they will be affected adversely by the mistakes of other black managers (Livers & Caver, 2002b).

Succession Problems. Black leaders, whether of social movements or in politics, have often been highly charismatic. One has only to think of Martin Luther King Jr., Jesse Jackson, and Malcolm X. But as often occurs with many charismatic leaders,[2] they seldom leave strong organizations behind them. Because of this, their successor can ordinarily command little of their predecessor's influence (Davis, 1982).

Financial Support. In contrast to comparable white leaders, black leaders usually run underfunded organi-

[2] See Chapter 21.

zations that limit their growth. They must concentrate their efforts on raising money, face bankruptcy, and curtail their programs. By the 1980s, a number of traditional black organizations experienced reductions of up to 90% in their operating capital. Many newer black organizations (and subsidized black businesses as well) have collapsed in proportionately greater numbers than was expected from the experience of mainstream organizations. Funds to support black organizations have shifted since 1970 from predominantly black to primarily mainstream corporate sources. The influence of the mainstream on black organizational development is also seen in the extent to which mainstream organizations select and identify black leaders of assimilation rather than leaders of protest or black nationalism (Davis, 1982).

Cognitive and Interpersonal Abilities

In Chapters 4 and 5, it was concluded that leaders need to be more intelligent (but not too much more) than those they lead. Whatever the reason, blacks score lower on tests of general cognitive ability. Although more than 30% of whites score in the 108 to 134 IQ range, only 3.3% of blacks do the same. Blacks with the same amount of education as whites (but not necessarily the same quality of education) who apply for the same jobs or admission to the same colleges score considerably lower in general cognitive abilities, and these black-white differences are resistant to change (Gottfredson, 1986). Meta-analyses of studies of black-white differences in tests for college admission and applying for jobs indicate that black applicants are about a standard deviation lower in mean than white applicants (Roth, Bevier, & Bobko, 2001). More intellectually demanding jobs tend to employ proportionately fewer blacks. Reviewing the research evidence, Schmidt and Hunter (1974) concluded that the lower average job performance of blacks from cognitive ability tests is accurately predicted from their lower average test scores. The lower scores of blacks than whites are not due to test biases. In fact, if anything, the job performance of blacks has been overestimated based on their test results.

Howard and Bray (1988) reported a similar amount of black-white differences in their large-scale manager assessment project. Minorities, mainly black employees of AT&T, were in the 22nd percentile in tested cogni-

tive abilities, while whites were at the 57th percentile. Whites also scored better in general information and on in-basket decision making. But the minorities did just as well as the whites on interpersonal skills, oral presentations, and group participation exercises. In all, compared to 50% of the whites, 29% of the minorities were seen as having middle-management potential. For 13 management competency assessments of 545 whites and 88 blacks, the *cognitive* differences, such as in assessment of judgment, showed up as expected, but most of the *noncognitive* black-white differences, such as assessment of human relations, were not significant (Goldstein, Yusko, & Nicolopoulos, 2001).

Despite these continuing black-white differences, it is clear that a sizable percentage (29% in this instance) of blacks have the potential to be leaders. More generally, 25% of blacks are still higher in tested intelligence than 50% of whites. Although they may be proportionately fewer than the number of whites who are available, a substantial number of blacks with the necessary cognitive skills are on hand for positions of leadership (Elliot & Penner, 1974). And such leadership, for instance in the black community, is related to ability, as reflected in the educational level that is attained.

Education. J. J. Cobb (1974) showed that blacks who were nominated as the most influential members in their black communities were well educated in diverse fields. The educational levels of black executives who were surveyed by E. E. Jennings (1980) were similar to those of their white counterparts. Social class was an important determinant of educational level attained (Bell & Nkomo, 2001) and no doubt affected social class attainment.

In 1970, one in 10 whites had completed at least four years of college, but fewer than one in 20 blacks had done so. Only 15% of blacks aged 55 to 64 had completed high school, compared to 45% of whites. Among those aged 20 and 21, 82% of whites and 50% of blacks had completed high school. But the educational gap between blacks and whites has narrowed considerably since 1970. By the 1980s, blacks were actually entering college in greater numbers and obtaining more years of education than were whites of the same intelligence level of (Manning & Jackson, 1984). Nevertheless, it is the lack of educational attainment, reflected in large dropout rates, coupled with the often inferior quality of the education that is available, that continue to be factors in keeping lesser proportions of blacks than whites in positions of political, educational, military, and industrial leadership.

Socioeconomic Status

Socioeconomic status, one key to leadership, remains lower for blacks than for whites. Blacks' incomes are lower and their unemployment rates higher than those of whites. Nevertheless, it is a mistake to equate impoverishment with race. Half of all blacks do not live in slums. And there is a small black upper class. This "high society" of black professionals and businessmen is characterized by conspicuous consumption and the excessive formation of clubs because of their exclusion from the counterpart white society (Frazier, 1966). Increasingly, however, social exclusion is diminishing. There is a larger black middle class, although the plurality of blacks falls into the lower class. The black class structure is unlike the white structure. Whites see themselves mainly as middle class, with small proportions in the upper and lower classes (Drake & Cayton, 1966).

The Slum Subculture. Any study of blacks as leaders would be incomplete if it ignored the large subset of blacks who are the disadvantaged poor. The slum subculture contains its own ethos, which is a more important determinant of behavior than is being black. The characteristics of this subculture include the absence of a sheltered childhood, early initiation into sex, female-centered families, authoritarianism, marginality, helplessness, resignation, fatalism, dependence, feelings of inferiority, lack of impulse control, inability to defer gratification, belief in the superiority of males, and tolerance of psychological pathology (H. Lewis, 1965).

There are strategies for survival in the slums, according to Rainwater (1966), and presumably black leaders in the ghetto become masters of such strategies. First, to obtain immediate gratification, one needs to make oneself interesting and attractive to others to manipulate and seduce them, even though one really has little to exchange. The second strategy is to resort to force and violence. Getting into trouble with the law is a rite of passage for some. Blacks constitute half the inmate population of Ameri-

can prisons. Toughness and masculinity are sought, along with cleverness in manipulating others, excitement and thrills, and luck and autonomy (W. B. Miller, 1965). At the same time, lower-class black youths, particularly the boys, miss the socialization experiences to prepare them for the world of work that are obtained by white working-class youths (Himes, 1965). Lower-class blacks have a generalized distrust of mainstream organizations. The contingencies between effective work and its positive outcomes are weak. They see considerate and supportive supervisors as hostile and untrustworthy—evaluations that are unlikely to foster success in an organization (Triandis, 1984).

Family Life. For the population as a whole, black family life is less stable than white family life. Black children are much less likely to live with both parents, and black women are more likely to encounter marital discord than are white women. Moynihan's (1965) well-publicized analysis concluded, from these types of differences, that black fathers, often transient, failed to provide their children with support, discipline, or direction. Hill (1971) countered by pointing with pride to five strengths of intact black families: the adaptability of family roles, strong kinship bonds, a strong work orientation, a strong religious orientation, and a strong achievement orientation.

An interesting question is whether the absence of fathers as role models for children who are raised only by their mothers reduces their leadership potential in either childhood or later life. Actually, strong, dominant mothers have been most significant for many world leaders. Fatherless children may have to take on responsibilities earlier, although evidence suggests that fatherless boys who lack a masculine role model with which to identify develop personalities that are marked by impulsivity, academic failure, indifference, immature dependence, and effeminacy (I. Katz, 1974). Role models for black boys are often provided by older street gang leaders and older brothers. In urban inner-city ghettos, being arrested and going to prison are viewed by many black adolescent boys as a rite of passage into adulthood.

The educational impact of fatherlessness seems minimal. Whiteman and Deutsch (1968) found no relationship between black children's reading skills and the intactness of their families. Similarly, the national survey by Coleman, et al. (1966) found that the presence or absence of a father was not a factor in the scholastic attitudes or achievement of lower-class black or white students. Also, Feld and Lewis (1967) found practically no relationship between family intactness and school anxiety.

Relevant to their adolescent and adult tendencies to influence rather than to be influenced, young black girls, especially those in lower-middle-class black families, are likely to become highly self-assertive and independent, despite authoritarian treatment by their parents. In particular, their mothers provide strong, dominant role models. Parental warmth is moderate, but the parents discourage infantile behavior. As noted before, early maturity of behavior is expected of the daughters, who are required to assume considerable responsibility for the care of younger siblings at an early age (Baumrind, 1971; Billingsley, 1968; Ladner, 1971).

Black Stress Due to Marginality. As noted earlier, minorities often live marginal lives, in between the mainstream and their own minority world. To capture the constraining effects on individual blacks who attempt to succeed as leaders, particularly in a white world, one must attend to the stress created by marginality. At the extreme, black managers, particularly female black managers, may be alone in a white-dominated organization, solo pioneers seen by many as tokens of integration (Bell & Nkomo, 2001). They face anxieties from internal conflicts (such as between their higher visibility and their lower social status) and confusion from external inconsistencies (such as policies of racial equality but incidents of apparent prejudice). They lack exposure to the informal networks of consequence (Jones, 1973). They may lack accessibility to superiors and respect, appreciation, and encouragement from them (Human & Hofmeyr, 1984). Many black managers feel isolated and alienated. They may suffer a loss of identity. They report difficulties in adjusting to the cues and norms of the corporate environment. They experience value conflicts and may feel uncomfortable among whites. Even though mentoring or counseling might be helpful, they avoid getting involved for fear that the information they reveal may be used against them. As with other disadvantaged groups, their families are unlikely to understand what they do. They often feel rage against some whites' subtle devaluation of them. Therefore, it is not surprising that blacks suf-

fer from high blood pressure at twice the rate of whites (B. M. Campbell, 1982).

Personal Attributes Associated with Black Leadership

As with whites, leadership potential shows up early in the lives of black individuals. According to personal interviews and surveys of 221 black men and women who were serving in elected positions in North Carolina in 1977, evidence of leadership within the black community began as early as elementary school. Each experience as a leader or a follower in the family, school, church, or community was seen as an opportunity for learning and developing leadership potential (Buie, 1983). But there are also systemic aspects that are particular to black leaders.

Black Values and Black Leadership. As was indicated in Chapter 10, individuals who "typify the group norm" are more esteemed than are those who reject or depart from it. Grossack (1954a) found that blacks who were attracted to black activities and who valued the Negro race, as such, were more esteemed by fellow blacks than were those who were indifferent to black activities, who rejected blacks, or who disliked black heroes. Thus it follows, as Kirkhart (1963) showed that college students who were accepted for group leadership and external leadership positions were those who identified themselves with their own racial group. Dellums (1977) thought that black political leaders must fully identify with "black politics," a commitment to the eradication of the oppression of minorities.

Lamm (1975) noted that black union leaders, despite their own higher incomes, identified themselves with the black working class and had more favorable attitudes toward blacks. They were also antiwhite and anti-Semitic in attitude. Fifty percent were identified as "Race Men." Compared with 27% of the members of the black middle class who were identified as "Uncle Toms" (subscribing to the white value structure), only 6% of black union leaders could be so identified. On this question of values, blacks who aspire to positions of leadership may be faced with a conflict between the black movement's concerns for social, political, and economic equality and the achievement and individualism that are likely to be of more importance in mainstream organizational life.

Differences in the leadership potential of blacks and whites are likely to accrue from the differences in personal values expressed by black and white college students. According to Fichter (1966) and Bayer and Boruch (1969), in comparison to white college students, black students placed a greater emphasis on being helpful to others and to society. They were less concerned than whites about experiencing leadership, making money, and being autonomous. Traditionally, blacks sought high-status open occupations with little interaction and competition with whites, such as teaching in all-black schools (Porat & Ryterband, 1974). But the occupations they sought broadened by the late 1960s (Bayer & Boruch, 1969) as affirmative action opened new opportunities in the professions and industry. Nevertheless, educated blacks continue to concentrate much more than their white counterparts in education and social service occupations. They favor law over medicine. They remain underrepresented in engineering, science, and medicine. The differences in aspirations and access are reinforced by the different networks of contacts and information that are available to blacks and whites and by continued segregated living (Spilerman, 1977). Black managers remain convinced of the importance of "the system" to their own job satisfaction. Wright, King, Berg, and Creecy (1987) found that organizational rather than personal factors most accounted for the job satisfaction of black managers.

Job Satisfaction of Black Leaders. Overall, satisfaction that their needs were being met was lower among black leaders and professionals than among their white counterparts. Slocum and Strawser (1972) found that black certified public accountants (CPAs) reported more deficiencies in the fulfillment of their needs than did other CPAs. Black CPAs felt significantly more deprived in compensation, opportunities to help people and to make friends, independent thought and action, and feelings of self-fulfillment and self-esteem. E. E. Jennings (1980) reported that black executives felt their progress as a group had been slower than that of women and was likely to be slower over the next 15 years. Nonetheless, a correlation of .37 was found between support of black managers for diversity and job satisfaction and −.37 between support for diversity and intention to quit. O'Reilly and Roberts (1973) reported that overall job

satisfaction was significantly higher for white than for nonwhite female registered nurse supervisors. On the other hand, contrary to King and Bass's (1974) prediction, Scott and Moore (1981) discovered in a survey of the assessed value of management by objectives (MBO) to 77 black managers and 61 white managers, supervisors, and professionals, that although both blacks and whites were favorable toward the use of MBO, blacks found more value in MBO than did whites for doing their jobs and for the organization. Again, Alper (1975) observed that, compared with white newly hired college graduates, black graduates gave the contextual rather than the intrinsic elements of work significantly higher ratings in importance.

Motivational Differences. Watson and Barone (1976) noted that black managers were lower in power motivation. Yet in a study of 23 black and 75 white supervisors, Miner (1977c) found the black supervisors to be higher than their white counterparts in the motivation to manage (good relations with superiors, competitiveness, masculinity, assertiveness, visibility, and willingness to deal with routines). Consistent with Miner, Thomas (1982) obtained results indicating that black male and female business students were more task oriented in their supervisory orientation than were comparable white students. Black leaders of U.S. Navy squads scored lower than did white squad leaders on Rotter's Internal-External Control Scale (W. R. Allen, 1975b). Vinson and Mitchell (1975) showed that black managers assigned higher ratings than did white managers to the importance of obtaining autonomy, self-fulfillment, friendship, and promotion.

These results may reflect the extent to which middle-class blacks conform to mainstream norms more than do their white counterparts. Black-white values and orientation probably depend more on the segments of the respective professional groups from which they are drawn. Black managers may be more task-oriented than their mainstream counterparts, whereas black ministers may be more concerned about social issues than their mainstream counterparts.

Differences in Self-Esteem. Studies in the 1960s found that, on the average, blacks had lower self-esteem than did whites (Ruhe, 1972) even when they were given evidence that their abilities were equal to those of whites

(Lefcourt & Ladwig, 1965). Such lack of self-esteem affected their assertiveness, desire to be integrated, and expectations of success in their careers (Crain & Weisman, 1972). However, in a large-scale study of more than 5,000 blacks and whites in 25 northern metropolitan areas, Crain and Weisman (1972) found that the lower self-esteem of blacks was more common among blacks who were born in the South. The self-esteem of blacks who were born in the North tended to be as high as or higher than that of whites. Furthermore, the lack of self-esteem among blacks and its implication for black leadership (Proshansky & Newton, 1968) had to be discounted, to some extent, as a factor. Since the 1960s, there has been a rapid increase of successful black models in sports, television, movies, the military, government, and politics. Opportunities for qualified black professionals and managers in the white world of work have opened, stimulated by programs to foster diversity. With the rise of the black movement, the "new" black person has come to value assertiveness and a feeling of having greater control over fate (Ruhe, 1972). The findings of L. Campbell's (1983) survey of 20 black women leaders in rural southern communities illustrate the changes that have occurred in the South. On various self-report instruments, these leaders described themselves as high in self-esteem and feelings of expertise, competence, and internal control. They were high in the need for achievement and felt they had the concrete personal resources to influence others and to fulfill their groups' expectations. Another sign of higher self-esteem was seen in a study of U.S. Navy squad leaders. Black leaders chose themselves as the best squad leader in their company more often than did white leaders (W. R. Allen, 1975a). Gray-Little and Hofdahl (2000) confirmed a full turnabout with a meta-analysis of 261 comparisons of the self-esteem of blacks and whites involving more than 500,000 individuals. Higher self-esteem was found in black than white children, adolescents, and young adults. The black-white difference increased with age and more for females rather than for males.

Disappearing Differences. A number of older studies also reported little or no personal differences owing to race. For instance, Dexter and Stein (1955) found little difference among women leaders on campuses as a function of race in masculinity, personality, and speed of association. And Barati (1981) could find no significant differences in the preferred leadership styles or attitudes toward subordinates of 160 black and white undergraduates of both sexes. In better-controlled subsequent studies, especially studies of individuals who have already achieved positions of leadership, black-white differences in values, motivation, and other personal attributes have tended to disappear. For example, among blacks who have attained leadership and management positions, less difference has been found between their values and the values of their white counterparts. Watson and Barone (1976) failed to detect such differences in self-concept on England's (1967a) Personal Values Questionnaire or in the need for achievement and affiliation. And W. R. Allen (1975b) could find no significant differences between black and white naval squad leaders' levels of aspiration and expectancy of success.

Performance of Blacks and Whites as Leaders

Shull and Anthony (1978) found that among 21 black and 56 white participants in a supervisory training program, the blacks were less willing to support harsh punishment for violation of organizational rules than were the whites, especially when the subordinates had a history of good performance. Otherwise, there was little difference in the way blacks and whites thought they would handle disciplinary problems and role conflicts. Somewhat different findings emerged when Stogdill and Coady (1970) used the Ideal Form of the Leadership Behavior Description Questionnaire (LBDQ) in a study of two vocational high schools. The white students thought that consideration was the most highly regarded factor for ideal leaders, whereas the black students thought that initiating structure was most important.

The importance of the race of the supervisor was shown by Richards and Jaffee (1972), who completed a laboratory study in which groups consisting of two white undergraduate males and a black or white supervisor played a business game. Trained observers rated the white supervisors significantly higher than the black supervisors on human relations skills and administrative-technical skills. Their ratings were based on checklists of effective and ineffective behaviors, as well as overall graphic ratings. The observers also used Bales's Interaction Process Analysis to assess the leaders' and subordinates' behavior. The white supervisors of the all-white groups of subordinates engaged in significantly more signs of solidarity, giving suggestions, and giving orientation, which lent support to King and Bass's (1974) hypothesis that white supervisors are more directive and less passive about relationships than are black supervisors when dealing with predominantly white subordinates. However, Bartol, Evans, and Stith (1978) argued that the evaluative data may have been biased, since all the observers were white.

Experiments before the early 1960s with biracial teams working on intellectual-type problem-solving tasks showed that blacks spoke less and, therefore, exerted less effort to be influential than did whites (Katz & Benjamin, 1960; Katz, Goldston, & Benjamin, 1958). But, possibly reflecting societal shifts in the 1960s, Fenelon and Megargee (1971) obtained contrary results with female college students who had described themselves as either high or low in dominance. Despite the white women's personal dominant tendencies, the white women yielded to the black women with whom they interacted, apparently to avoid the implication of prejudice.

Charismatic-Transformational Black Leaders

Bass, Avolio, and Goodheim (1987) asked sets of students to describe the transformational and transactional leadership behavior of world leaders. Among the 69 leaders, three were black and almost all the rest were white. Martin Luther King, Jr., was at the top of the scale in charisma, and Malcolm X was not far behind. The two were also near the top of the sample in intellectual stimulation. For Davis (1982), this finding was to be expected, for he felt that "the needs and experiences of the black population may dictate a greater emphasis on transformational leadership" (p. 194). Jesse Jackson illustrated these charismatic and transformational tendencies in the 1984 and 1988 presidential election campaigns. Consistent with this was an MLQ survey and interviews of 17 black women college presidents whom Jones (1992) found tended to be transformational, empowering, envisioning, and directly involved in whatever work needed to be done.

Martin Luther King, Jr., a national icon, was a profound, provocative, emotionally powerful orator. Although charismatic in most respects, he was filled with self-doubts, and was never able to gain mass support for

nonviolent struggle to achieve radical social change. He used black Christian idiom to advocate unconventional political ideas. He galvanized black protest activists with his oratory, but the actual protest movement was more often led by self-reliant local and student black leaders. He served as a conciliator among them in strategy sessions. His influence with public officials was based on his moral and intellectual clarity. He articulated blacks' concerns to white audiences and mobilized black community institutions, financial resources, regional networks of black churches, grassroots leaders through his emphasis on nonviolence and received much positive press coverage (Carson, 1987).

Malcolm X attacked three myths that denigrated blacks and justified racism by whites, and resulted in blacks demeaning themselves: (1) blacks were animals, (2) blacks were a minority, and (3) blacks supported and would be benefited by integration. He instilled a sense of history and racial pride in blacks. He noted that colored races were in the majority in the world. Their cultures predated the European. Integration would weaken black identity and reinforce the belief in white superiority (Flick, 1981). Like other leaders of black movements, Malcolm X focused on group identity and the need for a sense of community. Though leaders in the white mainstream more often direct their attention to conserving resources and the status quo, leaders of minorities, such as blacks, must more often be transformational in their concern for social change (Burns, 1978), as well as for unmet social needs and for inequities in the distribution of opportunities (Thompson, 1963).

Importance of the Leader's and Subordinates' Race

A study of black and white supervisors is likely to require knowledge of whether the subordinates are black or white. Wesolowski and Mossholder (1997) surveyed 170 subordinates and their immediate superiors according to whether each dyad was the same or demographically different in age, sex, race, and education. With an 87% return rate, the subordinates reported that differences in race correlated with their perceptions of job satisfaction and procedural justice, but not with job burnout. Again, a study by Rosen and Jerdee (1977) illustrated the expectation that a leader's effective supervisory style depends on the racial composition of the group he or she is supervising. Rosen and Jerdee administered a decision-making exercise to 148 business students. The students evaluated the extent to which participative decision-making styles were appropriate when supervising work groups of various organizational statuses and minority compositions. Significantly less participation was seen as likely to be efficacious with minority subordinates. Such subordinates were judged to be less competent and less concerned with the organization's goals.

A line of evidence that indirectly indicates that race affects interactions between leaders and subordinates comes from studies reviewed by Sattler (1970) on the influence of race on behavior in interviews. Respondents tended to give socially desirable responses to interviewers of races other than their own, responses that were socially "correct" or acceptable, whether or not they reflected the respondents' true feelings. Lower-class respondents were even more likely to be sensitive to the interviewer's race than were middle- and upper-class respondents.

Black Supervisor with Black Subordinates. Traditionally, blacks were limited to leading other blacks. Black supervisors with mainly black subordinates were expected by King and Bass (1974) to be highly concerned about how their subordinates felt about them. Therefore, although in general black leaders were more directive, they were expected to be less directive than were white supervisors of blacks. Adams (1978) reported that both black and white subordinates perceived their black supervisors to be more considerate. The 11% of the subordinates in a retail organization who were black gave their black superiors particularly higher ratings for consideration over their white counterparts. However, as noted in Chapter 28, for 19 black social service agency heads supervising 54 counselors of black inner-city clients, Schriesheim and Murphy (1976) found that more consideration was helpful mainly in low-stress job settings. When blacks supervised blacks and stress was high, more initiation of structure was helpful.

Black leaders often face the problem of having to earn the trust of their black subordinates, since the latter see them as having been co-opted into the white power structure (M. L. King Jr., 1968). Delbecq and Kaplan (1968) studied the managerial effectiveness of local leaders in neighborhood opportunity centers in an urban ghetto. Clients served by the centers thought that the directors were conservative, unwilling to permit the community to be involved in decision making, and ineffective in negotiations with leaders in the larger community. Subordinates in the centers sought immediate change and action through social protest, marches, and rallies. The directors tended to see such activism by subordinates as a threat to their own self-esteem and to their leadership position. They knew that higher authority was opposed to demonstrations and therefore felt in the middle between conflicting demands from subordinates and from the higher authority. At the same time, King and Bass (1974) suggested that in comparison to white supervisors, black supervisors of black subordinates may have more difficulty identifying with a white higher authority than with their black work group. A black supervisor may need additional symbols of authority as well as higher-level support to make his or her position credible.

Black supervisors of black subordinates in particular may have to be able to converse fluently in the street language ("Ebonics" or black English) of their subordinates and the general American English of their superiors and to be flexible about using both (Kochman, 1969).

Black Supervisor with White Subordinates. King and Bass (1974) suggested that, in comparison with whites supervising whites, black supervisors with mainly white subordinates would be expected to engage more often in general rather than close supervision and to allow or encourage subordinates to initiate boss-subordinate interactions. Doing so would reduce the possible feelings of status incongruity[3] among the white subordinates. The minority-majority status inversion that occurs when blacks supervise whites may generate, for status-conscious whites, a conflict between wanting to avoid the black supervisor and the need to interact with him or her (Blalock, 1959). Such whites may also suffer from a sense of lost status as a consequence of the required interaction with a black superior (Blalock, 1967). Even if the black leader has status as an expert, hostility and loss of status may be experienced, particularly by lower-status white subordinates (Winder, 1952). In a retail organization in which 88% of 406 subordinate managers were white, the black male bosses, as predicted by King and Bass, were perceived by the white subordinate managers to exhibit

[3] See Chapter 13.

more consideration than did their white male counterparts. But as was noted earlier, their black subordinates were more extreme in perceiving the black superiors as more considerate (Adams, 1978).

The job of black supervisors of white subordinates may be made more difficult, according to Richards and Jaffee (1972), by white subordinates who go out of their way to hinder their effectiveness. For this and other reasons, King and Bass (1974) suggested that it is particularly important for black supervisors of whites to have the full support of higher authority.

King and Bass (1974) also noted that the small number of black leaders in organizations, particularly blacks who supervise whites, makes them more visible than their white counterparts. This visibility, King and Bass advised, should cause the black supervisors to have more anxiety about succeeding, a greater sensitivity to negative data regarding the activities they supervise, a possible overreaction to such data, and a greater need for external confirmation of the value of the group's and the leader's performance.

White Supervisor with Black Subordinates. King and Bass (1974) suggested that white supervisors were likely to be more *directive*[4] and less consultative when supervising groups with predominantly black subordinates than when supervising groups of white subordinates. They would be more likely to undervalue the capabilities of black subordinate. Their rejection of black workers, in turn, would cause the workers to perform poorly (I. Katz, 1968, 1970). White supervisors would want black subordinates to respect them rather than to like them and to be concerned primarily with pleasing (probably white) higher authority. Furthermore, King and Bass (1974, p. 256) noted

Whites supervising blacks often reflect . . . in private conversations, a feeling of walking on eggs. This feeling may well be reflected in (1) greater censoring of responses and reactions by white supervisors when most of their subordinates are black, (2) less spontaneity in supervisory-subordinate relations, and (3) less certainty on the part of white supervisors as to how rigidly to enforce company rules or procedures. . . . Reciprocally, black subordinates may be less willing to

discuss personal problems with a white as opposed to a black supervisor.

Consistent with this comment was Sattler's (1970) research review, which indicated that black clients preferred black counselors. Also consistent was the finding among 1,944 workers in various hotels that, compared to other nonwhite workers, the African Americans were more sensitive to their white supervisors and management and felt the supervisors showed less behavioral integrity. The black workers were also lower in commitment, trust, and satisfaction with supervision. They revealed more intention to quit (Friedman, Simons, & Liu, 2003). And in agreement with King and Bass's (1974) suggestion that white supervisors would be more *directive* with their black subordinates, Kipnis, Silverman, and Copeland (1973) found that although they mentioned similar kinds of problems with their black and white subordinates, white supervisors reported using more coercion, such as suspensions, more frequently when dealing with black than with white subordinates. Kraut (1975a) also noted that white managers are often apprehensive about supervising new black subordinates, but they frequently react by giving special help to new black employees. White supervisors may be concerned about how white clients will react to black subordinates. Also, they may worry about how to handle mixed-race social events.

Indirect confirmation of the possible subtle effects of a white leader–black subordinate interaction came in an experiment. White interviewers deliberately treated the white job applicants to the same subtle features of the negative interaction by not leaning forward, sitting farther away, and making the interviews shorter. The white job applicants reported that they were more nervous and performed less effectively in the interview than did the white applicants who were treated to a positive interaction with the interviewers. This study corroborated commentary that new black professional employees experience many stresses above and beyond what would be expected for white employees and their new, usually white, superiors.[5]

When blacks were involved in intellectual-type experiments, their performance was affected adversely especially if anxiety levels were high and if they were led to believe that they were being compared with equivalent

---

[4]As defined in Chapter 18, *direction* or *directive* (italic) refers only to giving orders with or without explanation.

[5]See, for instance, E. W. Jones (1973), T. R. Mitchell (1969), Nason (1972), and C. H. Williams (1975).

whites (Katz, Epps, & Axelson, 1964; Katz & Greenbaum, 1963)

The Hard-Core Unemployed as Subordinates. Although many whites are numbered among the hard-core unemployed, blacks are heavily overrepresented. Therefore, the literature about their supervision has relevance, particularly the possible extra need for supervisors to be generally both supportive and controlling. This need was demonstrated by Friedlander and Greenberg (1971) and by the National Industrial Conference Board (1970). Both studies found that the hard-core unemployed wanted supervisory support in terms of friendliness, courtesy, and encouragement. The need for supervisors to intervene with the interpersonal difficulties of the hard-core unemployed (Goodman, 1969; Hodgson & Brenner, 1968; Morgan, Blonsky, & Rosen, 1970) and possibly to provide close supervision (Triandis & Malpass, 1971) was suggested, even though such close supervision might prove dissatisfying (Goodale, 1973).

Beatty (1974) found generally positive correlations between the extent to which 21 hard-core unemployed black women described their supervisor's consideration on the Supervisory Behavior Description Questionnaire (SBDQ) and their earnings and performance over a two-year period. But supervisory initiation of structure on the SBDQ[6] was negatively associated with the black women's work performance. W. S. MacDonald (1967b) found somewhat different results in Job Corps centers with large percentages of black trainees. Positive incentives had little value in shaping behavior. Nor was verbal reproof of much use in contrast to setting and policing goals and applying sanctions for infractions by the group. Infractions dropped 60% in two weeks.

Similar in many respects are unskilled and precariously employed black day laborers. Still lingering are some of the master-slave effects of black slavery in America of white bosses and black day laborers hired and paid for the day. Soaries (2003) found the similar themes in 10 interviews recorded in the 1930s with former slaves and 10 interviews of blacks hired and paid for the day from a day-labor pool. The similarities included themes of superior master (boss) and inferior slave (laborer), a sense of paternalism, and coercive leadership.

Black or White Leaders with Mixed Racial Groups. No simple generalizations are possible here. Some studies reported that whether the supervisor was black or white did not matter. For instance, in groups of mixed racial composition, Adams (1978) could find no differences in satisfaction or job problems among 406 subordinates in a retail organization (88% of whom were white) that were associated with whether their supervisor was a black male, a white male, or a white female. Nor did the subordinates' satisfaction depend on whether the subordinates were black or white. The specific behavior of leaders, rather than their race or the race of their subordinates, may be a much more important influence on subordinates' performance and satisfaction. Schott (1970) found that among nonwhite school principals with integrated staffs, job satisfaction of faculty members was highly related to the principals' reconciliation of demands, tolerance of uncertainty, persuasiveness, tolerance of freedom, assumption of roles, consideration, predictive accuracy, and integration of the group, as measured by the LBDQ-XII.

When subordinates comprise a mixed group of black and white employees, King and Bass (1974) suggested, the group will lack cohesion, which should result in the need for more directive behavior by supervisors, black or white.[7] Conversely, when groups of subordinates are racially homogeneous, cohesion will probably be higher and will result in the possibility of more participative supervisory styles by both black and white supervisors. But experiments failed to support these conjectures. Hill and Hughes (1974) and Hill and Ruhe (1974) conducted a laboratory experiment in which undergraduate student participants had to compare black and white leaders under conditions in which the subordinate dyads were black, white, or both. Black and white observers were employed. The one significant difference in Bales Interaction Process Analyses observations showed that both the black and the white leaders of the black dyads were less *directive* than were the leaders of the white or mixed dyads on a fairly structured knot-tying task. (Of the three tasks, the knot-tying task was expected to require the most *directive* behavior from the leaders who possessed the knot-tying knowledge.) Hill and Ruhe (1974) reported no difference in the total time each supervisor talked during the three tasks, regardless of the racial composition of

---

[6] SBDQ initiation includes autocratic items (see Chapter 20).

[7] See Chapter 18.

the subordinate pairs, and Allen and Ruhe (1976) found no difference in the supervision of mixed dyads involved in ship-routing and knot-tying tasks.

But some investigations did show that it made a difference whether a black or white was in charge of a mixed-race group and that subordinates acted differently depending on the supervisor's race. According to Mayhand and Grusky (1972), when black supervisors adopt a close and punitive style of leadership with a mixed group of black and white subordinates, the black subordinates are likely to be more vocal than are the white subordinates in opposing the leaders. But the white subordinates may show their dissatisfaction by reducing their output. Whites in this situation may be more accommodating in attitude but not in behavior to coercive black supervisors. Hill and Fox (1973) noted, on the basis of a study of 17 racially mixed rifle squads in a training battalion of the U.S. Marines, that white squad leaders reported giving proportionately more reprimands, but also more praise, to white subordinates than to black subordinates. And the praise white leaders reported giving to white subordinates was more than that given by black leaders to white subordinates.

In a previously mentioned study of 288 male naval recruits, W. R. Allen (1975a) formed 64 experimental groups of four members each, 25% black, 50% black, and 75% black. The supervisors were black or white. The leaders, regardless of whether they were black or white, experienced increasing supervisory difficulties as the relative proportion of blacks increased in the groups they were supervising. But the subordinates' SBDQ descriptions of the consideration or initiation of their leaders failed to account for any of the results. Furthermore, black leaders were less expressive in their behavior and were generally more inhibited. White-supervised groups performed tasks faster than did black-supervised groups. Allen explained that these results were because of status incongruence and social stress.

In another previously cited study, W. S. Parker (1976) administered the Survey of Organizations[8] to a sample of 17 white supervisors and all of the 16 black supervisors in three plants with a total of 427 supervisors and 7,286 hourly employees. A total of 72 black and 36 white subordinates described the 33 supervisors. Smaller percentages

[8] See Chapter 17.

of Chicano supervisors and subordinates were also involved in the racially mixed work groups. When the four leadership effectiveness measures derived from the Survey of Organizations were examined, significant differences were found between black and white supervisors. Compared to the white supervisors, the black supervisors were rated significantly more favorably by their subordinates on managerial support, emphasis on goals, and facilitation of work. The difference for facilitation of interaction was in the same direction but was not statistically significant. Furthermore, according to Parker, blacks achieved higher ratings from their black and white subordinates because black supervisors were seen as giving more support, stimulating a contagious enthusiasm for doing a good job, emphasizing the task to be completed, and removing roadblocks to doing a good job. Also, when white subordinates were the minority in their work group, they tended to rate their white supervisor more favorably on managerial support than did white subordinates who were in the majority in their own work group. This finding was an exception to the general finding, to be discussed next, that subordinates did not give more favorable ratings to supervisors of their own race.

Are Performance Evaluations of Black Leaders Biased?

A variety of different kinds of bias have been demonstrated, but the effects have been decidedly mixed. Hammer, Kim, Baird, and Bigoness (1974) asked participants to rate workers who were shown performing on videotape according to an objective criterion of effectiveness. The raters and workers included whites and blacks of both sexes. Although high performers were generally rated as more effective than low performers, blacks rated blacks higher than whites, whites rated whites higher than blacks, and greater differences were seen between high- and low-performing whites than between high- and low-performing blacks. A total of 22,431 managers were rated, 73% of them white, in a meta-analysis by Mount, Fisher, Holt, et al. (1995). It was concluded that black superiors, peers, and subordinates rated black managers more favorably than they rated white managers. White superiors rated white managers more favorably than they did black managers, but white peers and white subordinates were not inclined to do the same. Black raters were more lenient in their ratings of managers of both races.

Explanations for the good or poor performance of blacks and whites are systematically different. Similar to what was found for the performance of women compared to that of men in the previous chapter, the attributions given blacks for high performance were that they were lucky or highly motivated. Equally high-performing whites were seen as able and well educated. Poorly performing blacks were perceived as showing their lack of ability and education; poorly performing whites, their anxiety and lack of luck or motivation (Pettigrew, Jernmott, & Johnson, 1984).

Bigoness (1976) found that raters tended to give higher ratings to poorly performing blacks than to poorly performing whites yet rated high-performing whites and blacks similarly. Bartol, Evans, and Stith (1978) concluded after a review of studies [9] that there was a tendency to evaluate black leaders more positively on relations-oriented than task-oriented factors.

For example, Beatty (1973) found that sponsoring employers' perceptions of social behaviors, such as friendliness and acceptance by others, had a greater influence on the employers' performance ratings of new black supervisors than did employers' perceptions of the new black supervisors' task-related behaviors. At the same time, Richards and Jaffee (1972) obtained results suggesting that subordinates with more liberal attitudes were more likely to give their black supervisors higher ratings, especially on human relations skills, than were subordinates with less liberal attitudes. This finding may account for the different results obtained in field and laboratory studies by Kraiger and Ford (1985), who completed a meta-analysis of 59 studies involving almost 15,000 black and white ratees. Whites tended to give higher ratings to white supervisors; blacks tended to give higher ratings to black supervisors. The effects of race were substantial in the field studies but close to zero in the laboratory studies. (Most laboratory studies are done in college settings, where norms for racial equality and against racial bias are likely to be greater than in the field.) Nonetheless, reports of bias have not been uniform in either setting. There has been a considerable variation in findings.

Burroughs (1970) studied black and white girls in discussion groups. White followers rated black leaders higher when they exhibited a high quality of performance. But Hall and Hall (1976) found no differences due to race or sex in undergraduates' ratings of a case of an effective personnel administrator. And Durojaiye (1969) studied the effects of sex and race on sociometric choice among schoolchildren aged 8 to 11. Although these children preferred friends of their own sex and race, neither sex nor race influenced their choice of leaders. However, Richards and Jaffee (1972) found that, as a whole, white trained observers judged black leaders more severely than they did white leaders. But Vinson and Mitchell (1975) reported the opposite. They noted that from mostly white superiors, black managers received higher performance ratings than did white managers. Schmidt and Johnson (1973) found no differences in peer evaluations among supervisory trainees, whereas among naval squad leaders, W. R. Allen (1975b) found that white leaders received significantly higher ratings from white subordinates than from black subordinates. Similarly, black subordinates chose their black leader as best squad leader in the company more often than they chose their white leader. Finally, Cox and Krumboltz (1958) and Dejung and Kaplan (1962) found, in early nonsupervisory situations, that ratees received significantly higher evaluations from persons of their own race. In the same way, Flaugher, Campbell, and Pike (1969) found that black medical technicians were rated significantly higher by black than by white supervisors.

Some Implications. No simple answers emerge to the question of whether racial considerations bias evaluations of performance. As long as one must depend on subjective evaluations of black and white leaders, one must be sensitive to the potential for bias in their evaluations, although such biases may fail to show up in particular instances. One can imagine some circumstances in which superiors will bend over backward to give unearned higher evaluations to black supervisors, but other situations in which prejudice may cause lower-than-deserved ratings. Black subordinates and superiors may feel the need to overvalue members of their own race or may set extra-high standards for them. Student participants' ratings in transitory experimental settings may be freer or more biased by the students' generalized feelings about race in comparison to the ratings by long-time organiza-

[9] The studies were by Beatty (1973), Drucker and Schwartz (1973), Huck and Bray (1976), and Richards and Jaffee (1972).

tional colleagues of the performance of familiar associates. But such colleagues also may be more biased or less biased, depending on their general racial attitudes.

Individual differences may override any possible generalizations. Thus Bass, Cascio, McPherson, and Tragash (1976) collected the responses of 315 managers and professional employees in a large light-manufacturing establishment on 109 racial awareness items. A factor analysis revealed that the respondents differed reliably among themselves to the extent to which they agreed that the effectiveness of blacks in leadership and management is generally influenced by five factors: (1) bias in the system, (2) limited implementation of affirmative action policies, (3) incompetence of black employees, (4) failure to include black employees in the system in a real way, and (5) need for black employees to build self-esteem.

Personal Strategies for Black Managers and Professionals

Among the personal strategies that African Americans can adopt is to make themselves more valued. They can enhance their competence through higher education, particularly in fields such as engineering or business. They can avoid resegregating themselves within white schools, to develop as much experience and comfort working in a white as in a black world. As Ken Chenault, the black CEO of American Express, noted, "I learned very early to move between both (black and white worlds) and develop a level of confidence no matter what world I am operating in" (Slay, 2003, p. 56). African Americans can seek entry into firms with good track records for developing and promoting blacks. They can seek sponsors and mentors in those firms. They can prepare themselves to be at the margin of two influences, accepting and maintaining both the desirability of their black identity and the organization's values.

Henderson (1986) suggested that individual African Americans need such specific strategies to anchor themselves in corporate America. They must strengthen their leadership skills and develop a healthy and secure home life. Bowman (1964) used the path-goal hypothesis to sum up what African Americans need to consider in their efforts to succeed. In addition to pursuing education, they must believe that their efforts will pay off for them

and they must learn to cope with the various social and organizational barriers that stand in their way. Black social identity may need to be emphasized in a black organization but deemphasized in a mainstream organization. Colin Powell, when faced with racism early in his army career, chose to be successful rather than to become enraged by racism (Slay, 2003).

African-American leaders as a group can assist in the process of upgrading those who follow them. Black leaders in the emerging black middle class need to channel their political energy, talent, and imagination to constructive ends, particularly to help cope with the problems of lower-class blacks (Loury, 1985).

Walters (1985) called for a shift in political strategy from the protest movements of the 1960s and 1970s. Much of this has occurred in the past 30 years. Consultation has replaced confrontation. The black community has been reconstructed internally by strengthening its common resource base and its common frame of reference. The newer strategy is harder to pursue as the issues have become so complex that black leaders may have difficulty with their constituencies because of the additional information and comprehension required (Davis, 1987). African American leaders continue to face a strong challenge in unifying the diverse sectors of their community (Jacob, 1985), but signs of their success are prevalent in higher education, suburban living, and leading roles in politics, government, business, religion, sports, entertainment, and the military. Nevertheless, the success is not shared by the one-third or more who remain mired in poverty, unemployment, and slum housing.

Hispanics

Hispanics are the most rapidly increasing minority in the United States. As noted at the beginning of this chapter, they have passed African Americans as the largest minority in the United States and are expected to continue to grow at a faster rate than the mainstream, increasing from over 40 million in 2005 to 88 million by 2050, when one of every four to five Americans is expected to be Hispanic. Sixty percent of the Hispanic population are descendants of the Mexican settlers and American Indians of formerly Mexican territory from Texas to California, but the remaining 40% are divided among recent immigrants from

Mexico (66%), Puerto Rico, (9%), Cuba (4%) and from 21 other countries of the Caribbean and Central and South America (21%). Hispanics are far from homogeneous. Many Cubans came from middle-class backgrounds and have moved much more rapidly into positions of political and business leadership than those who came from the Mexican peasant and labor class. The long-established Hispanics of New Mexico contain a small elite of Spanish descent from whom some of the governors of the state have come; they are far different from working-class Puerto Ricans or Dominicans of New York City. An immigrant Chilean engineer of European descent has little in common with the former Indian peasant from Nicaragua or El Salvador (Estrada, undated). Hispanics are concentrated in New Mexico (41% of the population), California (32%), Texas (30%), Arizona (23%), Nevada (17%) and 15% in Florida, New York, and Colorado. They are highly urbanized. Forty-five percent live in Los Angeles, New York, Miami, San Francisco, San Jose, and Chicago. "To build a political base and influence, (many) Latino leaders concentrate their work in populated areas dealing with critical issues that proliferate in urban settings" (Bordas, 2001, p. 125). But they have also led the unionizing of agricultural workers. The rate of employment for Hispanics without college is about the same as for mainstreamers (Boo, 2004).

Socioeconomic Status

Half of Hispanics are less than 25 years old. Education is a critical issue. Their average educational attainment is low, and their high school dropout rate is high. Latino students have the highest high school dropout rate of all racial and ethnic groups. Disparities in educational attainment begin in kindergarden. Hispanics are handicapped by family responsibilities, poverty, poor schools, placement in lower-track classes, poor self-image, limited neighborhood resources, lack of role models, and negative gender role attitudes (Zambrana & Zoppi, 2002). According to the 2000 U.S. Census, 57% of Hispanics had graduated from high school and 10% from college, compared to 88% of whites graduating from high school and 28% of whites graduating from college. The figures for blacks were 79% and 17%, respectively. Females headed 24% of Hispanic families, compared to 13% of white families. Poverty rates are disproportionately high. In 1999, median family income for Hispanic married couples was $37,132, for non-Hispanic whites was $59,697, and for blacks was $50,656. Most generally, Hispanics are employed in manual labor, service, and support, although in 2000, 15% of Hispanics were employed as executives, administrators, or managers and another 13% as professionals (National Council of La Raza, NCLR, 2004). An estimated 11 million Hispanics have entered the United States illegally in 2006, mainly by crossing the porous border with Mexico. These work as unskilled labor in agriculture and industry, often for less than the legally required minimum wages.

Despite their diversity of race, origin, and socioeconomic status, Hispanics share cultural commonalities that are likely to affect their emergence and success as leaders, as well as their attitudes and performance as subordinates. They are more likely to be found in service and manual labor jobs and to face poverty and language barriers. In large proportions, they are newcomers, and average nine years younger than the general population. We can infer how Hispanics differ from Anglo mainstreamers in their attitudes and behavior as leaders and subordinates from how they differ from mainstreamers in selected attitudes and values that are likely to affect leader-subordinate interactions (Bordas, 2001)

Attitudes and Values

"Three dynamics . . . position Latinos for leadership. *Personalismo* is . . . needed to earn the trust and respect of followers. *Tejando lazos* (weaving connections) describes leaders as storytellers, keepers of cultural memory, dream weavers, and dream makers . . . The third dynamic . . . is knowing how to foster consensus and encouraging collective action" (Bordas, 2001, p. 112). Hispanics are diverse in history and color. Their classification requires answers to two questions, since they can vary in identification in both race and ethnicity (Kirnan, Bragge, DeNicolis, et al., 2001) But they are bound together by the Spanish language, colonization, the Catholic Church, and diverse indigenous roots. They value *confianza, respeto,* and being *simpático*. A leader with *confianza* is trustworthy, someone in whom you can confide. A survey of 3,000 Latinos by the National Community for Latino Leadership (NCLL) found that keeping one's word, doing what you say you will do, and fulfilling promises were the most valued qualities in Latino leaders. Traditionally, *respeto*, deference and respect, was shown to those of higher status and authority by body language, tone of voice, and manners and by offering profuse thanks, praise, and apologies. According to the NCLL survey, leaders need to be unselfish, empathetic, courteous, and respectful. Latino leaders are expected to be *simpático*. Their social relations should be congenial and pleasant. They relate first on a personal level, focusing on "the individual, the family, where people are from, and personal preferences. . . . Being polite and gracious . . . are just as important as having many achievements" (Bordas, 2001, pp. 116–117). More collectivistic than individualistic,[10] compared to mainstream Americans, an individual Hispanic who is faced with a decision such as whether to join the U.S. Navy will worry about how other Hispanics view the action. Other Hispanics are not likely to favor such a decision, and the individual will worry about how this disfavor will affect his family. Ridicule and the loss of cultural identity may be seen as the price of entry into mainstream organizations (Triandis, 1981).

Importance of la Familia. Leaders of Hispanics must shape organizations to retain relations and personal connections. Of particular importance is the family. In contrast to mainstream Americans, Hispanics are more intensely attached to their nuclear and extended families and more concerned about meeting family obligations and sacrificing their own interests for the sake of their families. Compared to the strong pull of the family, they are ambivalent about work environments (Triandis, Marin, Hui, et al., 1982). They do not separate their professional and personal lives. Trusted leaders are regarded as part of their extended family of intimate friends and godparents. Leaders of Hispanics "are challenged to fashion" organizations that remain "user friendly" and keep the family as the "bridge . . . to the impersonal institutions of society" (Bordas, 2001, p. 125).

Collectivism. In her dissertation survey of 377 Latina U.S. Army officers, Zoppi (2004) found that collectivistic attitudes headed one of two canonical roots (correlations with other variables). Hispanics have difficulty separating

[10]Collectivism versus individualism will be discussed in more detail in the Chapter 33.

the person from the role taken by the person (Rojas, 1982). Likely to affect their performance as leaders, they tend to emphasize cooperation and assistance as opposed to competition and rivalry (Triandis, Ottati, & Marin, 1982). They are more optimistic about interpersonal interactions but less likely to feel that criticism by another person will be constructive (Triandis, Marin, Lisansky, et al., 1984). Latino leaders have a sense of destiny. They feel that chance, unforeseen events, and outside forces govern their lives. A greater power guides their efforts, unlike mainstream leaders who are more likely to value self-determination and their own individual efforts (Bordas, 2001).

The collectivist values to which Hispanics subscribe, more than do those in the mainstream, that are likely to affect their performance as leaders include being sensitive, loyal, respected, dutiful, gracious, and conforming. Mainstreamers are more likely to emphasize being honest and being moderate (Triandis, Kashima, Lisansky, et al., 1982). Hispanics have the highest participation of any minority in the U.S. labor force. They do not shy away from manual labor as beneath their dignity. Leaders are expected to help with onerous work when necessary. Other important values for Latino leaders include making time for socializing, and sharing. The NCLL survey indicated that Latino leaders needed to express compassion, kindness, and affection. Other ethnics and mainstreamers might be made uncomfortable by the extent to which Latinos are encouraged to express their feelings and emotions, which can result in misunderstandings (Bordas, 1994). To enjoy life is an important value. They commemorate many occasions and spend more on entertainment, movies, food, and eating out than do mainstreamers. They arrange community celebrations and fiestas, and entertain family and friends. They try to balance work with time for having fun (Bordas, 2001). At the same time, there is considerable spirituality among them. "Spirituality for traditional Latinos is a mixture of indigenous beliefs and the influence of the Catholic Church. . . . When Latinos marched in support of the farm workers' rights . . . they went in procession with a statue of Our Lady of Guadalupe leading the way" (p. 127).

The attitudes and values of loyalty of Mexican Americans to their ethnic group are factorially independent of their cultural awareness. Arbona, Flores, and Novy (1995) surveyed 364 technical college and university students in south Texas. Two factors emerged in their responses to the questionnaire: (1) ethnic loyalty concerned the students' preference for one culture over another, (2) cultural awareness involved knowledge and practice of cultural traits.

These analyses, mainly of male Hispanics, do not account for the greater acceptance of responsibilities and leadership in school sports by lower-class Puerto Rican girls in comparison to their matched black or white lower-class counterparts. Klonsky (1987) attributed such results to the closer attention that Puerto Rican girls receive from their overprotective mothers (as observed by Cahill, 1967) and less neglect of them by their fathers than is true for other lower-class children. In general, socialization is greater among Puerto Rican girls than among their black or white classmates.

Leadership. Hispanics are more likely than mainstreams to favor supervisors who provide social support and consideration even if the supervisors are not well organized (Triandis, Hui, Lisansky, et al., 1982). Supervisors are likely to find it useful to keep in mind that some Hispanic subordinates may be hostile to and distrustful of non-Hispanics and the establishment. According to a survey of 139 Hispanic workers by Sanchez and Brock (1996), they may feel discriminated against, resulting in tensions at work, job dissatisfaction, and lack of organizational commitment. For Hispanic workers, links between behavior and reward are less clear. They are likely to be ambivalent about their self-esteem and see themselves as a bundle of roles, rather than as a bundle of traits. They tend to accept and favor social, sex, and power differentiation and will tolerate inefficiency. Furthermore, they are likely to view competence in a task to be less important than agreeableness, conscientiousness, and getting along with others, and will favor equality over equity. In addition, they will tend to favor group over individual assignments but may not necessarily value participative decision making (Triandis, 1984). Consistent with finding that like leadership in many collectivistic cultures, Zoppi (2004) showed that Latina army officers described themselves as more transformational than U.S. norms. They also said they were less passive leaders.

Some evidence has accrued about the impact of black or white supervisors on mixed Hispanic-mainstream groups. For example, Hill and Fox's (1974) examination of the extent to which black and white squad leaders reprimanded or praised their black, white, and Puerto Rican subordinates found that the squad leaders treated all their subordinates similarly. As was noted earlier, although it was expected that one minority group would favor another, Parker (1976) found that Mexican-American subordinates of black and of white industrial supervisors gave the white supervisors significantly higher ratings on support, emphasis on goals, and facilitation of work and interaction than they did their black supervisors.

Among the best-known Hispanic leaders was César Chávez. He embodied leadership that was attuned to the needs of the Hispanic farmworker. As a child, he followed his parents into the fields as a migratory farmworker and witnessed the inhumane treatment of farm labor. He believed strongly in participative leadership. To be successfully unionized, he believed, farmworkers must build and control their organization. There had to be collaboration between the leader and the led. He adapted Saul Alinsky's approach that workers themselves could identify problems and come together to solve them. They could be the source of new ideas and directions. He encouraged workers to take on leadership roles, telling them that good organizers were not afraid to make mistakes. He uplifted the Latinos as no one had before. He made use of Latino rituals, ceremonies, language, dress, religious ceremonies, and prayer meetings (Martinez-Cosio, 1996).

Other Ethnic Minorities

East Asian Americans: Chinese, Japanese, and Koreans

Considered our model minority, Asian Americans have burst into the U.S. scientific and professional community in record numbers, although they made up only 1.5% of the population in 1980. Asian Americans are likely to be as collectivistic as Hispanics (Hsu, 1981), with a strong sense of family obligations and concerns about their own acculturation. Again, they are diverse in national origin and ethnicity. But Asian Americans suffered from institutionalized legal impediments of state and national restrictions and still suffer from the stereotype that all Asian Americans are foreigners (Locke, 2000). J. Tang (1997) argues that despite their success in science and professional careers, they remain less able to move into management compared to African Americans and whites. In surveys, like Hispanics and blacks they reported more discrimination against them than whites and were more favorable to affirmative action programs than were mainstream whites (Bell, Harrison, & McLaughlin, 1997).

Chinese immigrants first arrived in California in the early 1800s. In the 1848 gold rush, they prospected, mined, and formed a significant source of labor and services. They set up the first school for Chinese children in San Francisco in 1857. The Naturalization Law of 1790 had reserved naturalized citizenship for whites only, and beginning in 1882, further immigration of Chinese and their naturalization were prohibited by the Chinese Exclusion Act. Citizenship was restricted to those of Chinese descent born in the United States until that act was repealed in 1943. (The Cable Act of 1922 had declared that any American woman who married an alien ineligible for citizenship would lose her own.)

The Japanese first immigrated as contract laborers to the then-independent Hawaii after the Chinese, and later followed them to the U.S. West. However, all Asians were excluded from immigration in 1924. During World War II, 120,000 Japanese Americans, two thirds of them citizens born in the United States, were interned in detention camps.

The first Korean workers arrived in Hawaii in 1900; the preponderance of Koreans came to the U.S. mainland during and after the Korean War, which ended in 1953. The same was true for the Vietnamese during and after the end of the war in Vietnam, which ended in 1975 (Chan, 1991). Between 1944 and 1952, all the exclusion orders were repealed. Small quotas were established for Asian Indians and Filipinos, 5,000 highly educated Chinese residing in the United States, and war brides of Asian-American veterans. Not until 1965 was immigration based on national origin abolished. Other immigrants from Asia, such as the Vietnamese, share many values with the Chinese and have similar cultural attitudes.

Management and Leadership. In 1985, Asian Americans constituted 8% of the professionals and technicians in the United States but made up only 1.3% of the managers and executives. Some of this difference may be due to racial prejudice, but some may also be due to the ambivalence of Asian Americans toward integration and so-cialization into the American mainstream's values, attitudes, and behaviors. Conflict is due to a cultural background that stresses modesty and the stereotype of Asian Americans as being passive and retiring rather than having the assertiveness needed for leadership (Yu, 1985). Kelsey (1998) found that when she studied small mixed groups of Chinese and white males, in all the groups, the Chinese had less influence than the whites. Whites were more talkative than the Chinese Americans and whites became the leaders. Nonetheless, in 1946, Wing F. Ong became the first Asian American to be elected to a state office (the Arizona House of Representatives). Starting in the 1960s, Daniel Inouye began a long career as a U.S. senator and Spark Matsunaga and Patsy Mink as representatives from Hawaii in the U.S. Congress (Chan, 1991). Asian Americans serve in state legislatures and as governors from Alaska to California.

With their family and peer support for education, their large overrepresentation at leading American universities, and their acceptance as professionals and technicians, they are likely to experience an upward trend in such employment unless a backlash occurs. But their movement into management in proportions representative of their numbers in technical and professional work is likely to lag, despite Agor's (1986a) finding that, along with women, Asian Americans in general have more intuitive ability than mainstreamers, which is critical for decision making at higher levels of management. As managers, compared to whites, they reported using less self-disclosure, less self-focused impression management, and less supervisor-focused management. Instead, they tended to employ job-focused impression tactics, but their supervisors said they were not impressed. Furthermore, Asian Americans don't do as much impression management to improve supervisor-subordinate relations as do whites (Xin, 1997). According to Yammarino and Jung (1998), Asian American collectivism is likely to show up in the better or worse treatment of the entire group of followers by their leader, rather than as in each different dyad formed by a white leader with different individual white followers. Jung (1997) compared the performance of 153 Asian American and 194 white American undergraduate students by subjecting them to transformational and transactional leadership simulated by trained actors. Along with the expected positive direct effects on both cultural groups, transformational leadership had indirect effects mediated by the collective efficacy among the Asian Americans, while transactional leadership had stronger effects on the performance of the white students.

Jung and Yammarino (2001) compared 105 Asian American business students in 30 groups and 31 white American business students in a group task to prepare an essay recommending how to improve the quality of the education provided by the business school so it could be reaccredited. A project manager was provided to each group, whose style and effects were rated by the students afterward. As hypothesized, the correlation between the rated transformational leadership of the manager and the perceived potency of the group and effectiveness of the manager were much stronger for the Asian American students than for the white students, whereas the correlation between the transformational leadership of the manager and the followers' self-efficacy was much stronger for the whites than for the Asian Americans. Jung and Avolio (1998) subjected 153 Asian Americans and 194 whites (mainly students) to a brainstorming task. Compared to whites, Asian Americans generated more ideas when working with a transformational leader than did whites. Collective efficacy mediated the impact of transformational leadership on the Asian Americans but not the whites.

More Asian American leaders are needed in both the public and private sectors, according to the state of Washington's first Chinese American governor, Gary Locke (2000). They are needed: (1) to fight for education, (2) to combat the collective punishment of an entire racial or ethnic group for individuals' actions, (3) to combat hate crimes, (4) to speak out against prejudice, and (5) to protect the rights of immigrants. More leadership is needed to provide "a more vibrant and healthy Asian American community" (p. 1).

South Asian Americans: Indians and Pakistanis

Along with many other important immigrant groups to the United States, we will have to depend mainly on Chapter 33 to consider how the nationality of their origins affects their attitudes and behaviors as leaders and followers. South Asian Americans have become prominent as small-business entrepreneurs and in the health care industries. Additionally, Indian immigrants have become important to U.S. high tech and higher education.

Native Americans: American Indians, Inuits, and Aleuts

The Iroquois constitutional arrangement for a council of representatives from the six tribes was well known to Benjamin Franklin and provided him with a model at the U.S. Constitutional Convention in 1787. Prominent American Indian leaders were Chief Sitting Bull, medicine man of the Lakota Sioux; Chief Joseph of the Nez Percé; Chief Seattle of the Suquamish and Duwamish; Chief Tecumseh of the Shawnee; Chief Pontiac of the Ottawa, Potawatomi, and Ojibwa confederacy. They were were known for their eloquence, political acumen, strategic thinking, and ability to mobilize movements.

Billy Frank Jr., a Nisqually tribal elder, is a wide-ranging contemporary Indian leader and visionary. Starting as a youth, he was active in the "fishing wars" with state game wardens and police until the historic 1974 Boldt decision in U.S. District Court upheld Indian treaty fishing rights. As of 2003, he was serving as the chairman of the Northwest Indian Fisheries Commission, which he cofounded. He presided over the restoration of the salmon industry, essential to tribal tradition (Adams, 1984, p. 1). The commission represents 20 tribes in Washington state. His peacemaking program has been a model for several other states. He has also played an important role in the WaHeLut school with students from 22 Indian nations. He was involved as a leader in cooperative management environmental agreements dealing with wildlife and water resource planning. In 1976 he worked with the timber industry and the Washington state government to change logging and spraying practices, which helped the comeback of the bald eagle. In 1984, he helped found the Northwest Renewable Resources Center, which mediates natural resources conflicts in six states. In 1989, as chairman of the Native American Committee of the Washington State Centennial Commission, he argued for celebrating future rather than past Indian interests. In 2003, he declared that Indian tribes have emerged as a political force to be reckoned with.

Identity. Native Americans are extremely varied in cultures and values, although they have some values in common. They now constitute more than 300 self-determined nations with sovereignty, and many smaller tribes. They vary in race from white to black because of their traditional tendency toward inclusiveness and interbreeding. Cheyennes intermarried with Arapahoes, Ojibways with Crees, Choctaws with Chickasaws, and so on. One of the spouses would join the other tribe's family, depending on whether it was patrilinear or matrilinear. It was the same for offspring. Adoption of outsiders, individual or groups, was widely practiced. One third of Seminoles are partly descendents of runaway black slaves. Many Indians have English or French surnames going back to early colonial times. Those of mixed race sometimes identify with Indians, sometimes with whites or blacks. John Ross, the seventh-eights white son of a Cherokee and a fully white mother, led the Cherokees for 20 years in their losing effort to avoid forced resettlement in Oklahoma by the federal government in 1838. John Ridge, one-eighth white and seventh-eighths Cherokee, opposed Ross and led the accommodationist faction supporting the move. This was a cause of divisiveness lasting for several generations. Jim Beckworth, a full-blooded black adopted by the Crows, eventually became a chief.

Nevertheless, strongly influenced by Bureau of Indian Affairs (BIA) personnel, the 1934 Indian Reorganization Act called for constitutions for each tribe that defined as Indian racially those at least one fourth Indian in ancestry. In the 1960s, the U.S. government turned many Indians into non-Indians by unilaterally dissolving 103 Indian groups, such as the Mission Bands of California. Enacted in 1990 but not enforced was congressional legislation to limit Indian identity for arts and crafts to only those created by members of federally recognized tribes. The 1975 constitution of the Cherokee Nation of Oklahoma was the only one to abandon race as a criterion for tribal membership and to return to the traditional Indian openness to enrollment as a tribal member. Formal Cherokee membership grew from 10,000 in 1950 to over 300,000 in 1998. In 1990, self-identification as an Indian could range from 2 million, based on the 1990 U.S. Census, to an unofficial 30 million (Churchill, 1998).

Deculturation and Assimilation. Until the 1930s, federal policy was directed toward deculturation and assimilation. While most Indians lived on reservations in 1900, less than 45% do so now. Some now live on farms

and ranches. A larger portion live in cities. Many whose homes are on reservations work in the cities. The movement from reservations was encouraged by the 1887 General Allotment Act, which replaced collective ownership of land with individual allotments. Of the 150 million acres of Indian lands, 50 million were allocated to Indians and 100 million were opened to others (Churchill, 1998). No provision was made for any increase in population. Many Indians were completely impoverished. According to Adams (1984), many living on reservations became depressed and apathetic. Many others assimilated and faded into the general population. But the change in America in attitudes toward minorities beginning with the Roosevelt administration (1933–1945) and developments such as fair employment practices, racial integration of the U.S. Army in 1948, and the civil rights legislation of 1965 improved their chances for better incomes, social, and educational condition. Recent years have seen marked improvements, but Native Americans' health, educational levels, and incomes still fall below the mainstream. Many state, federal agencies and NGOs are still directed at the uplift of Native Americans.

Native American names and cultural and spiritual symbols have been adopted by professional sports teams, schools, universities, Hollywood, and corporations. The Washington Redskins and the Atlanta Braves were seen as racist and belittling to Indians by the National Coalition on Racism in Sports and the Media. Students on college campuses helped eliminate attaching the name "Indian" to the Dartmouth and Stanford University teams. Unfair stereotypes and disrespect for Indian nation sovereignty are fostered by the Cleveland Indians baseball fans' supportive gesturing of "scalping" and Braves fans "tomahawk chop." Treating Indians as mascots, and offensive usage of Indian names and symbols are being fought in courts and boardrooms (Teters, 1999). Until the 1950s, Indians were portrayed in the movies and on television as treacherous villains.

Education. Pavel (1999) commented that starting in the 1860s, federal boarding schools were inaugurated to convert Indians from their tribal cultures to the mainstream culture. The model was Carlisle, founded in Pennsylvania in 1875. The students, all male, were expected to learn Christian morality and the benefits of private property. They had to cut their long hair and dress in mainstream clothes. They were forbidden to speak their native tongue and were taught English, mathematics, and a trade to instill the work ethic. The forced transfer of children from tribal homes to boarding schools was strongly resisted. By 1997, this model had long since been abandoned. A comprehensive survey completed by the National Center for Education Statistics (1997) found that 47% of the almost half-million Indian and Alaskan Native American youth were concentrated in 1,244 public schools and 170 BIA schools, out of approximately 82,900 schools nationwide. "This relatively small number of schools enrolling a relatively large number of Native American students has provided fertile ground to improve Indian education. Exemplary programs have advanced Indian education throughout the nation. . . . A growing number of schools have dramatically improved academic achievement among Native students" (p. 2). BIA students are required to pass more coursework in English, mathematics, social studies, and the sciences than are public school students. Stricter graduation requirements are observed. In 1989, graduation rates were 82% in BIA schools and 91% in public schools with concentrations of native students. Thirty-three percent of BIA graduates applied for admission to college. The marked advances in native education in the 1980s and 1990s are seen by Pavel, Swisher, and Ward (1996) as a consequence of tribal self-governance and national school movements.

In BIA tribal schools, traditional culture and values are incorporated into the curriculum. One-third of BIA students speak their native language at home; 16% in public schools with high concentrations of natives do so, as well. Almost half of teachers and principals are cultural role models as they identify as American Indians or Alaska natives, and virtually all of them are enrolled in a state or federally recognized tribe. In public schools with high concentrations of native students, 13% identify themselves as tribal members. Thirty-eight percent of BIA teachers are native, most of them members of a tribe. In schools with concentrations of native students, 15% of the teachers are natives, a majority enrolled as tribal members (Pavel, 1999).

A number of major universities such as Penn State, Ohio State, and Arizona State now offer graduate education to prepare American Indians and Alaska natives for leadership in their nations. Harvard University's John F. Kennedy School of Government offers a graduate program dealing with research and executive education to take account of Indian nation sovereignty, institutions, culture, and social and economic development.

Leadership and Management. More than 300 self-governing sovereign Indian nations within the 50 states are federally recognized as democratic entities with their own constitutions. Only the federally recognized tribes can participate in federal housing, health, and education programs and maintain their government-to-government relation with the federal government (Echohawk, 1990). Such recognition of sovereignty has permitted the establishment of gambling casinos on tribal land when it is illegal elsewhere in a state. Gambling casinos have turned poor Indian nations into wealthy ones (*Wall Street Journal*, 2004) and enhanced resources for health, education, and welfare. The often large casino revenues have also increased the potential for corrupt leadership. There have been abuses of power by the governing bodies of reservations. They have muffled criticism of mishandling millions of dollars of tribal money. A report by *The Detroit News* (2001) detailed abuses of democracy, judicial process, and financial benefits by the leaders. They used their power to expel political opponents and to change the election rules to favor themselves.

The observed leadership tends to differ from one Native American tribal culture to another. Although in most tribes men are the leaders, women play a more important role among the matrilinear tribes such as the Navajo. Warner (1989) completed a study of American Indian female supervisors and their stereotypes.

Anthropological reports sift out the patterns of consequence. Illustrative was a study by Dekin (1985) of the Inupiat of northern Alaska, who live in the Point Barrow area.[11] Dekin observed that in community meetings, Inupiat leaders need to conform to Inupiat social norms, which would confuse unsophisticated mainstream Americans. Indulgence, indifference, acquiescence, noncompetitiveness, and tolerance are highly valued among the Inupiat and socialized in childhood. These deeply held values are reflected in the unwillingness to impose one's will on others to divert or correct them, particularly if

---

[11] The Inupiat are an Inuit (Eskimo) people.

others have already expressed their points of view. Community development and planning among the Inupiat are particularly difficult because of traditional leadership patterns; whoever speaks first determines what will be accepted. Avoidance of conflict and an unwillingness to impose on others or to correct them are the rule. Those with recognized leadership roles, such as the city mayor, must speak first. In public meetings, others are reluctant to disagree with the leaders, so all acquiesce even though they do not privately agree. The followers are tolerant but uncommitted. Elections and secret balloting can produce results that diverge markedly from what was expressed openly at public meetings. Some politicians and administrators take advantage of these norms by obtaining a false consensus in public hearings, despite the fact that if private voting had been allowed, quite different opinions would have been revealed.

The Inupiats' tolerance and indulgence of deviation by followers may be misinterpreted by outsiders as apathy. Rather, these traits represent their reluctance to impose decisions on others, if decisions are made at all. Decisions, which must be made by a single leader, are consciously avoided, if possible, even if doing so means delays or inaction. The Inupiat norms also mean that public safety officers, clerks, and accountants, who must abide by impersonal rules of enforcement in the face of differences of opinion, cannot be selected from among the Inupiat.

Italian Americans

To the original European immigrants to North America from the British Isles and northern Europe have been added diverse ethnic groups from southern and eastern Europe. Prominent among these immigrants and their descendants are Italian Americans. More than five million Italians emigrated to the United States, mainly from the south of Italy and Sicily, fewer from Rome and the North. In the 1990 Census, the approximately 16 million Italian Americans formed 6% of the U.S. population. Although a majority of the first generation were manual laborers, by 1990 two thirds held white-collar jobs and had moved rapidly into positions of leadership in government and industry. This section points to some elements that may continue to contribute to the leadership and follower performance of Italian Americans. There is a pau-

city of controlled research on what may distinguish their leadership from the mainstream. Just as American Indians were stereotyped until the 1950s as villains in the movies and television, so Italian Americans were stereotyped in entertainment and by widely publicized accounts of the Mafia as members of organized crime families. Although there has been some immigration of educated middle-class Italian professionals from northern Italy, the large preponderance of Italian immigrants were uneducated peasants from southern Italy and Sicily whose children in the United States moved rapidly into the middle class and a broad range of occupations and professions.

Social Beliefs. Prud'homme and Baron (1988) found that Italian Canadians have a pattern of irrational beliefs that are likely to influence their interactions with others and that are different from the beliefs of English Canadians. Social approval ("It is essential that one be loved or approved of by virtually everyone in his community") was more fully endorsed by the Italian Canadians than the English Canadians in their study. This need for social approval is consistent with Rutonno and McGoldrick's (1982) finding that Italian Americans tend to build a network with relatives of the same age, however distant. In contrast to the beliefs of English Canadians, those of Italian Canadians contained more irrational fatalism ("Unhappiness is caused by outside circumstances, and the individual has no control over it"). This finding by Prud'homme and Baron fit with the sense of resignation to events that Spiegel (1982) observed among Italian ethnics. Prud'homme and Baron also found irrationally high self-expectations in their Italian Canadian sample ("One must be perfectly competent, adequate, and achieving to consider oneself worthwhile") and a necessity for perfect solutions ("There is always a right or perfect solution to every problem, and it must be found or the results will be catastrophic"). There are other elements that may be of consequence to leadership among those who identify with their Italian American heritage. For example, the Italian American community tends to be as cohesive as is the Italian American family, with its emphasis on strong family ties (Ziegler & Richmond, 1972).

Leadership Status. Italian Americans have moved into top leadership positions in every walk of American life, as witnessed by Lee Iacocca in industry; Amadeo Giannini in banking; football coach Vince Lombardi; Antonin Scalia on the Supreme Court; Mario Cuomo in politics; Francis Ford Coppola, Martin Scorsese, and Frank Capra as movie directors; Arturo Toscanini as a symphony orchestra conductor; and A. Bartlett Giamatti, as both president of Yale University and commissioner of Major League Baseball. On the local level there are many Italian Americans politicians, such as Fiorello La Guardia, who became mayor of New York with the help of a strong Italian American voting bloc but was reelected on his own merits alone. Former Mayor Rudolph Giuliani of New York City attained his political success by his performance as U.S. Attorney and his national prominence by his pseudotransformational leadership following the destruction of the World Trade Center on September 11, 2001. Italian Americans played an important role in Franklin D. Roosevelt's Democratic Party coalition of ethnic groups, but by the years following World War II, as their social and economic status rose, they became equally likely to support Republican politicians.

Italian Americans have showed up in leadership roles in increasing numbers. In 1950, 6% of the members of the New York State legislature were Italian Americans; in 1994, they made up 34% of the members, far exceeding their proportion of the state's population (Primo, 2003). Italian Americans elected as U.S. Republican and Democratic senators in recent years include Peter Domenici, Alfonse D'Amato, and Rick Santorum. State governors include Ella Grasso of Connecticut and Richard Celeste of Ohio. In addition to New York City, other cities that have elected Italian Americans as mayors include San Francisco (George Mosconi), Philadelphia (Frank Rizzo), and Boston (Thomas Menino). Geraldine Ferraro, a U.S. congress member, was the first woman to be nominated as a vice presidential candidate in 1984.

There are curious anomalies. For example, Italian Americans constitute 26% of Roman Catholic Church membership but only 8% of its leadership. In the private sector, 12% of the CEOs in the Fortune 500 firms have Italian surnames, twice their proportion in the general population, but they total only 3% of senior managers and are overrepresented in middle management. Corporations founded by Italian Americans, such as Bank of America and Planters Peanuts, have none on their executive boards. Chains featuring Italian American food products, such as the Olive Garden and Domino's Pizza, were not founded by Italian Americans, nor do they have any Italian-surnamed senior executives (Italic Institute of America, 2004). In the 1960s, Italian Americans were considered a potent source of elected political leaders. However, assimilation, unrelenting media defamation, and stereotyping in the movies (*The Godfather*) and television (*The Sopranos*) have drained away their potential. Mario Cuomo, an exceptional speaker and popular reelected New York governor, was reported to have turned down the nomination for presidential candidate in 1988 because he didn't think anyone with an Italian name could be elected (Italic Institute of America, 2002).

Jewish Americans

A national Jewish population survey (2000–2001) estimated that 2.2% to 2.5% of Americans were Jewish. This was much lower than the median estimate of 18% believed to be the case by both Jews and non-Jews, according to a 1990 national Gallup sampling of the general population. Three percent estimated that 50% or more were Jewish. Even 18% of Jews projected themselves as making up more than 15% of the U.S. population. Except for the recent immigration of Russian Jews, their numbers are not likely to grow much. As of 1996, 53% to 54% had intermarried with gentiles. Three quarters of the children of mixed marriages are not raised as Jewish, and 86% of these children marry gentiles. From colonial times, Jews have been disappearing into the American mainstream culture. Much of the overestimation is probably due to their eminence in science, medicine, law, education, literature, art, music, entertainment, and communications, and their prominence in American life as candidates for national office, such as Joseph Leiberman, as secretaries of state, such as Henry Kissinger, as senators, such as Dianne Feinstein, as governors, such as Herbert Lehman, as financiers, such as George Soros, and as program directors, such as Robert Oppenheimer and Hyman Rickover of applications of nuclear energy.

Identity. Identity is a problem. Jews are an ethnic group supposedly identified by religion, yet the 2001 national survey found that 27% of those who identified themselves as Jews said they had no religious preference, compared to 14% of non-Jews who said the same. Only

51% believed in Judaism. Younger Jews want to identify as an ethnic rather than a religious group. The percentage of Zionists had fallen from 90% in 1948 to 22% in 1995. Only 9.7% were Orthodox in religious practice.

Korman (1988) reviewed the research evidence on the Jewish experience in America and concluded that despite the liberalization that has occurred in the mainstream in the past half century, despite the fact that Jews have built and managed many successful organizations, despite their prominence and visibility, and despite strong family support in their development, Jewish Americans remained absent from managerial and executive roles in many of the largest and most important American industries, ranging from oil and chemicals to foods and commercial banking. Paradoxically, they serve in these same industries as professionals, staff personnel, and consultants. There is a parallel here to the experience of women in general, Asian Americans, and other minorities in the past several decades. Although American Jews have reached positions of leadership in government and in selected industries, such as retailing and the communications media, that far exceed their small percentage of the population, they still remain outsiders in their access to careers in line management in many other industries. Although Jews make up less than 2.5% of the U.S. population, 10% of college graduates identify themselves as Jewish, so it would be expected that they would be overrepresented rather than underrepresented in management positions. Four decades ago, Powell (1969) found in a survey of 239 executives from a variety of industries that more than 23% said that being Jewish hindered an executive's career, but less than 2% said that being gentile had the same impact. More than 63% thought being Jewish kept one from being promoted, compared to the 24% and 20%, respectively, who said the same about being Mormon or Roman Catholic. But the comparable figures for lack of promotability were less than 4% for Episcopalians, Methodists, Congregationalists, Lutherans, and Presbyterians.

These executives did not base their opinions on lack of competence, morality, or motivation, or on outright discrimination. However, they believed that Jews, Mormons, and Catholics could not develop the network of necessary friendships inside and outside the firm as easily as could a Protestant mainstreamer and could not meet the criteria of social acceptability, compatability, and "fitting in" in the company. These beliefs, in turn, may have been supported by stereotypes, such as that Jews are overly aggressive. The continued exclusion of qualified Jews as well as Asian Americans and other ethnic minorities from line management appeared to be based primarily on the belief that they were not socially acceptable, which, in turn, reinforced the self-perceptions of the ethnics that they were outside the mainstream. Jews remained outsiders in a "Catch-22" bind: they were excluded from higher levels of management because they were not members of the right social clubs, and they were excluded as members of the clubs because they were Jews and partly because they had not attained the higher levels of management (Zweigenhaft, 1980). Quinn, Kahn, Tabor, and Gordon (1968) found that although 139 executives in the Cleveland-Akron area were generally unprejudiced in the abstract in that they agreed that Jewish persons should be hired or promoted to important management positions on the same basis as everyone else, when it came to a concrete decision, a fifth indicated that they would choose a gentile over a Jew with equal qualifications. There also was systematic exclusion from entering the corporation at the bottom. When it was still legal to do so, 50% of the requests for management applicants to the California Public Employment Service explicitly discriminated against Jews, as did 27% in Chicago (Waldman, 1956). Most public and private employment agencies in many other cities continued to accept such open discriminatory requests well into the 1960s.

Jewish executives are likely to be found in representative numbers more often in sales functions and in states such as New York, New Jersey, Pennsylvania, and Illinois that have large Jewish populations. But they were less likely to be promoted to higher positions in corporate headquarters in the 1960s and 1970s. And they were still highly underrepresented on corporate boards of directors (Korman, 1988). However, by the mid-1980s, much depended on differences in industries and specific firms. For example, 27% of senior managers in the apparel industry are Jewish, as are 21% in retail and supermarket chains and 10% in textiles and publishing, but 8% in the aerospace industry and the soap and cosmetics industries, and less than 1% in the petroleum industry. Within industries, they were more prevalent in the smaller firms. And when they did attain top management positions, it was because of their status as founding entrepreneurs or investors, or their staff or outside status and professional accomplishments as lawyers, accountants, scientists, or engineers, not their promotion through line management (Korman, 1988).

Despite all the progress of the past half-century in moving minorities into positions of business and industrial leadership, company policies can still account for much of the continuing discrimination. The exclusion of Jews from entry into line management in industries with few Jewish executives can also occur as a consequence of a corporate policy not to recruit graduates from even highly prestigious schools with more than 30% Jewish enrollment (Slavin & Pradt, 1982) in contrast to recruiting graduates from comparable schools with low percentages of Jewish students. Corporate policy also modifies the potential of prejudicial managers to make biased decisions. Although only 29% of the managers who would prefer to discriminate against Jews in recruiting, hiring, and promotion to management positions said they would act on their biases even if they believed their company was concerned about equal opportunity, 68% would do so if they thought their company did not care (Quinn, Kahn, Tabor, & Gordon, 1968).

There is only indirect evidence about differences in the leadership and leadership preferences of Jews and gentiles. For instance, Jewish Americans are more likely to support liberal political leaders and are much less affected by their income levels in this regard than are gentiles. Higher incomes of mainstreamers ordinarily reduce liberal preferences. Ward (1965) found that when the top management of a firm was composed of Jews rather than of gentiles, the firm's personnel policies and practices were likely to be more liberal. However, firms that had both Jewish and gentile senior managers were even more liberal.

Arab Americans

From 1960 to 1980, an elite class of Arab Muslims immigrated to the United States from Syria, Jordan, Lebanon, Saudi Arabia, Egypt, Yemen, and other parts of the Middle East. After 1980, they came more from the middle class, and were more alienated from Western values. They and their descendents were more interested in maintaining an Islamic way of life. By 2000, Islamic student associations were common on many college campuses. Some remained more connected to Islamic countries and under the influence of foreign imams in spirituality, culture, and politics. Alienation and discrimination increased with the "war on terror." Younger Muslim Americans became more observant Muslims than their parents. They began to pursue Islamic traditions and practices with a social and political agenda (Abdo, 2004). More will be said about the cultural elements of Arab leadership in the next chapter.

Other Minorities

The Physically Impaired

Legally, a person has a real or perceived disability if it limits major life activities. Likely to affect the performance of physically impaired people, both as leaders and as followers, is the tendency for impaired people to cut short and distort interactions with them. Presumably, such behavior may reduce the success of handicapped people in leadership positions.[12] Nonetheless, a physical impairment need not be an impediment. Franklin D. Roosevelt still provides an inspiring model of a person who lost the use of his legs at 39 years of age, midway in his political career, but was able to overcome the adversity. The deaf-blind Helen Keller is another such inspiration.

According to Bell, McLauglin, and Sequeira (2002), the U.S. workforce includes more than 4.5 million adults with disabilities. In 1986, of these, 46% with disabilities were able to work. By 1995, 15% were telecommuting (Kugelmass, 1995). According to Bell et al., 56% were employed in 2000. Federal legislation was enacted in 1973 to protect against discrimination of disabled government employees. The Americans with Disabilities Act (1990) did the same for all employees in the private sector. Nonetheless, people with disabilities work in less challenging jobs than unimpaired persons. Thirty-six percent of the disabled report having been denied an interview, promotion, or job for which they were qualified and being paid less for work similar to that of those without disabilities. But among 61 managers in the Chicago area, those who had experience hiring people with disabilities said they were more likely to hire physically

[12] See Chapter 6.

impaired applicants. The disabled seen as personally responsible for their disability (e.g., deafness after playing in a rock band) are seen more negatively than people with congenital disabilities or those caused by accidents. A model of what coworkers judge as fair for accommodating workers with disabilities based on equity and need has been proposed. Managers with previous experience with the physically impaired say they are more likely to hire disabled job applicants (Messina, Roberts, & Becker, 2004), although there is consistent evidence of pervasive discrimination against highly overweight job applicants and employees (Roehling, 2002). Obese people are subjects of discrimination and are looked on less favorably by employers because of their appearance and their greater health risks. They are not shielded by federal anti-discrimination laws unless they can prove that their obesity comes from physiological causes (Roehling, 2002). Except for a few states including Michigan and California, the obese are not legally protected against discrimination by state laws. Most tend to be excluded from higher-paying occupations. Being obese is perceived by employers and supervisors as self-caused due to lack of self-control, lack of discipline, incompetence, and laziness—traits unfavorable to being recruited, hired, or promoted (Bell, McLaughlin, & Sequeira, 2002).

Some Evidence. Few controlled studies have been unearthed that compared impaired and unimpaired supervisors in their leadership of impaired and unimpaired subordinates. When 133 deaf subordinates of 21 deaf and 21 hearing supervisors described the supervisors on the LBDQ-XII in a survey analyzed by Sutcliffe (1980), no differences were revealed except that the deaf subordinates rated their deaf supervisors higher in orientation to higher authority. But Sutcliffe found in interviews that the deaf supervisors achieved the same quality of leadership as the hearing supervisors by keeping their communications short and to the point. They avoided communicating over the heads of their subordinates. Furthermore, the deaf supervisors tended to be more charismatic than the hearing supervisors.

Baker, DiMarco, and Scott (1975) noted a compensatory reaction in supervisory reinforcement of blind workers. In an experiment with subjects who acted as supervisors, the subjects were more likely to administer rewards to blind workers than to sighted workers for iden-

tical performance. In a simulation and in a field study of 41 supervisors and 220 subordinates, Colella and Varma (2001) found that with disabled subordinates, ingratiation was more strongly correlated with supervisors' quality of leader-member exchange (LMX) ratings. The increasing availability of physical and sensory computer aids should lead to more job opportunities for the physically impaired.

The Older Worker

The aging of the U.S. and European populations makes understanding older leaders and supervising older workers of increasing importance. Legislative sanctions against mandatory retirement have increased the average age of managers, supervisors, and employees. The working life of employees and professionals in the past century has increased from 25 to 50 years. Again, discrimination and stereotyping need to be overcome. Leaders need to be mindful of the age of their followers.

The effects of age on leadership and management are found extensively in previous chapters. With the aging of the population, the interest in, need to, and opportunity to continue working part-time or full-time for those who would have retired in their sixties have increased in the past several decades. Many large employers such as Wal-Mart have found it economically advantageous to employ part-time older workers in large numbers, although little has been published about supervising this group.

The Older Leader. Aging has some benefits for leadership. As Simon (1987) concluded, intuition depends directly on the richness of experiences.[13] In a survey of 200 business school alumni, Pinder and Pinto (1974) found that older managers (aged 40 to 55), were less autocratic and more skilled in human relations, compared to younger ones (aged 20 to 29). They were also regarded as more efficient and gathered more information before making a decision. Liden, Stilwell, and Ferris (1996) noted that 122 sales representatives achieved higher levels of performance both objectively and subjectively working under older than younger supervisors. However,

---

[13]Although I presented examples in Chapter 8 of the potential decline in effectiveness of leadership that may accompany advanced age, I can also cite Armand Hammer, Claude Pepper, Konrad Adenauer, and Colonel Sanders as a few examples of effective older leaders.

Campbell (1981), using a mailed survey administration of the LBDQ returned by 127 program supervisors of community mental health centers as well as by their superiors and their subordinates, obtained only slight differences in LBDQ descriptions. According to a survey of 189 nonfaculty staff members at a university, who were aged 18 to 70, LBDQ ratings of their supervisors' initiation of structure were more predictive of the younger employees' satisfaction. For the older workers, their supervisors' consideration was more important (Gallagher, 1983).

The Older Subordinate. Older subordinates are likely to react differently from younger ones to different styles displayed by their leaders. Selvin (1960) examined older and younger military trainees under three types of leadership: persuasive, weak, and arbitrary. For the trainees as a whole, arbitrary leadership generated the most tension and escape activities, and persuasive leadership generated the least. Under persuasive leadership, the younger trainees tended to exhibit aggressive behavior, such as fighting with each other. Under arbitrary leadership, the younger trainees exhibited relatively personal forms of withdrawal behavior, such as attending mass entertainments and sports events and concentrating on their hobbies. Older trainees under the arbitrary leader tended to respond with anger. Liden, Stilwell, and Ferris (1996) reported that older employees performed better on both objective and subjective performance measures, but a meta-analysis by Waldman and Avolio (1986) found little difference in objective performance in studies comparing the job performance of younger and older employees. However, despite the small objective difference between the employees, the subjective performance appraisals by their supervisors were biased in favor of the younger workers. A decrease in sensory and memory functions does accompany aging, but greater experience appears to compensate for these declines.

The Generation Gap. Since the publication of the book by Strauss and Howe (1991) on the historical cycling of successive generations born 20 years apart, there has been considerable popular interest focused on the possibility of systematic changes in the managers, leaders, and followers of the *traditional* generation, born approximately between 1925 and 1945; the *baby boomer* generation, born between 1946 and 1965; *Generation X*, born between 1966 and 1985; and the *millennial*, or *Generation Y*, born between 1986 and 2005, who will be entering the workforce in 2010. Strauss and Howe proposed that the values of a generation were shaped by their first 10 years of life, as a consequence of the generation into which they were born. Most currently available empirical research compares the baby boomers and Generation X. Anecdotal evidence suggests that Gen Xers are expected to show more job mobility than baby boomers, to work to live rather than live to work, as the baby boomers do, and to prefer a relations-oriented rather than a task-oriented work environment. It may be of practical use to determine the generational attitudes and behavior, but the differences are likely to be accounted for by the fact that *at any point in time* baby boomers are 20 years older on average than Gen Xers. Prensky (1998) argued that the generation gap requires that personnel under 30 years of age (late Generation X) have to be treated differently from their parents by supervisors and colleagues. They have grown up with advances in technology and have different cognitive styles than older people.

Studies with No Correction for Age of the Different Generation Members. Dittman (2005) mentioned a study by Ruth Fassinger of 100 prominent women. The younger women were more likely to question workplace expectations that called for taking work home and working long hours. They expressed concern for their parenting obligations and commitments. A hundred fifty baby boomer managers and leaders were compared with 150 Generation Xers on what it took to keep them committed to their organization. The two generations mentioned the same top seven themes in the same order of importance: compensation (45% versus 34%), challenge (40% versus 33%), support (33% versus 25%), advancement (31% versus 29%), recognition (20% versus 27%), values (18% versus 21%), and organizational success (16% versus 11%) (Bryson & McKenna, 2002). A higher percentage of Gen Xers than baby boomers mentioned five of the same themes.

Rodriguez, Green, and Ree (2003) compared Gen Xers and baby boomers on five themes in a mailed survey of a representative sample of 1,000 personnel managers and executives from five levels of leadership in a telecommunications company. The response rate was

81% (805 responded). Fifty-two percent of the respondents were male, 48% female. Whites constituted 46% of the sample; African Americans, 19%; Hispanics, 29%; and Asian Americans, 5%. The survey was made up of 25 forced-choice pairs of statements, each expected to discriminate between the two generations. The statements were suggested by Bass and Avolio's (1994) definition of transformational leadership. One of each pair was expected to be preferred by baby boomers (older in age); the other, by Gen Xers (younger in age) When forced to choose, boomers differed significantly from Gen Xers. Boomers chose tasks accomplished in several days; Gen Xers chose tasks completed in one day. Boomers (especially women and Hispanics) chose the telephone to compare prices; GenXers chose the Internet. Boomers chose regularly scheduled hours; GenXers chose flexible hours. Boomers chose retirement plans with benefits; GenXers chose a portable 401(k) plan with a lump sum distribution. Boomers chose jobs with security; Gen Xers chose jobs with challenge and fun, again not when age was controlled (p. 10). Smola and Sutton surveyed 350 baby boomers and Gen Xers again years later. They found that values changed as each generation matured. The priority given work and sense of pride in it was reduced. Self-orientation and wanting promotion more quickly increased. Loyalty to the firm decreased in the Gen Xers.

Studies Corrected for Age. Hart, Schembri, Bell, et al. (2003) collected survey data from 635 baby boomers (ages 39 to 59) and 382 Gen Xers (ages 21 to 38) from five organizations. Boomers were significantly higher than Gen Xers in organizational commitment, but the results were not at all significant when age was controlled. The same was true for rewards for loyalty, although the Gen Xers were significantly higher in belief in mobility.

Sexual Orientation

Gays and lesbians are a minority protected by antidiscrimination legislation. Organizations are increasingly including sexual orientation in their diversity programs (Raeburn, 2000). Gays and lesbians may represent a larger proportion in the workforce than some other minorities included in diversity efforts (Woods, 1993). They usually discover their identity as homosexual in late adolescence or as young adults. They face societal intolerance, fear, and prejudice. In most states, they cannot marry their domestic partners nor obtain the health and social benefits provided to spouses. Homosexuals often have a negative self-image. They often lack confidence in themselves and self-efficacy and are unwilling to compete for advancement (Boatwright, Gilbert, Forrest et al., 1996). Presumably, they are less likely to attempt leadership in a heterosexual group. They choose to work in organizations that have nondiscriminatory cultures and policies. They are now more likely to be open about their sexual orientation, resulting in their greater commitment to such organizations (Day & Schoenrade, 1997).

Trau and Hartel (2002) were able to survey anonymously online 582 gay working men with the cooperation of an Australian organization of gay men. Their education ranged from high school to PhD. They came from nine states ranging from New South Wales to Western Australia. Thirty-six percent were in management and administration; 18% were in health practice; human services, or education; 9% worked in research and policy; 9% were in sales or marketing; 5% in the police or military; 3% in the arts and writing; and the rest in blue-collar and unskilled jobs. Some had disclosed their sexual orientation in their workplace; others were still closeted. In-depth interviews were also completed with career counselors involved in organizational diversity. Results indicated that gay men reporting more difficulties with their identities had lower career satisfaction and less career encouragement. Those who felt a high degree of support and help from their organization and in their career were more satisfied and committed to both. Those who reported that there was fair treatment of gays were also more committed to their organization and felt more satisfaction with their career. Comfort with their sexual identity and disclosure appeared to have little moderating effect on the results. One expected finding from the interviews was the importance of top management's understanding of diversity issues and leadership in providing fair policies and environment in the organization from top to bottom. Ragins and Cornwall (2001) queried 534 homosexual employees and found that homosexuals were more likely to report discrimination when they had no support from organizational policies, worked in groups that were mainly heterosexual, had negative work attitudes, and received fewer promotions.

Summary and Conclusions

The many changes that have occurred in this area in recent years suggest the need to discount the findings of many of the earlier studies. The mainstream in the millennial generation is likely to be less prejudiced toward minorities than its predecessors. But discriminatory constraints are still apparent among African American leaders and leaders from other minorities. Leadership styles are affected by whether leaders and subordinates each are black or white. Situational constraints and personal factors may be associated with the emergence of blacks as leaders. The performance and satisfaction of black leaders depends on the extent to which their performance is contingent on the racial composition of their subordinates. The supervision of black subordinates by whites calls for whites' understanding of the black subculture. However, more needs to be known about black leaders' supervision of whites or mixed groups. We are just beginning to learn about Hispanics, Asian Americans, and those from other racial and ethnic groups as leaders and as subordinates. In each group, different factors may be important. Hispanics and Asian Americans share an emphasis on collectivism over the mainstream emphasis on individualism. While educational achievement is lower for blacks and Hispanics, it is higher than the mainstream for Asian Americans and for Jewish Americans, and although both groups are prominent in corporate America as staff members and consultants, they remain outsiders and are underrepresented in the seats of power in much of American industry. Equally little known but likely to increase in importance for study is the impact of age and physical impairment on supervisory-subordinate relationships when prejudice may outweigh differences in performance.

From examining leadership in subcultures of the United States, we now move on to consider how leadership and its study are affected by the cultures and nationalities of leaders and their followers.

Globalization and Cross-National Effects

Some questions about cross-cultural leadership are: how much is it possible to generalize the results of leadership research from one country to another? How transferable are managers with experience and education from one country to another? How do managerial decision-making practices and leadership styles vary in different cultures? What dimensions of leadership are universally relevant while others are culturally specific?

The effectiveness of organizations at home and abroad depends much on their leadership (Hodgetts & Luthans, 1994). Multicultural groups can be highly effective or highly ineffective, depending on whether the diversity of cultures within them is effectively managed (Adler, 1990). To meet this challenge, Gordon and Loden (1989) argued that *pluralistic* leaders are required who: (1) recognize and support diversity at all levels of the organization; (2) are ethically committed to fairness and the elimination of prejudice; (3) are broadly aware of multicultural issues, (4) accept feedback and make changes accordingly, (5) are empathic to cultural differences, and (6) create developmental opportunities for their diverse employees.

The internationalization of managing took several new twists in the past 25 years. Multinational businesses and nongovernmental organizations (NGOs) proliferated. European, Japanese, and third-world multinational corporations increased in number and importance relative to the previously dominant U.S.-based multinational corporations. Multinationals increased their presence greatly in the United States itself. This resulted in a much more frequent intercultural mix of foreign ownership and management and North American employees.[1] Thus, Japanese cars began to be assembled in the United States by North American employees under North American and Japanese supervisors and managers for domestic sales and export to Japan and elsewhere. By 2005, China, India, Taiwan, South Korea, and Singapore had become major global players. India had become a telecommunications call center for the English-speaking world. As noted in Chapter 29, a research manager in the United States could be in immediate two-way contact by e-mail and video conference with a sizable number of immediate subordinates in France and China who were engaged in a common project. Such information technology made it possible for one organization to operate continuously on a project 24 hours a day with units located in four locations each successively six time zones apart.

The economies of the former Soviet bloc were built with investment and technology from the first world. Russian gas pipelines became important to industry and heating in western Europe and Japan. The "offshore" relocation of whole plants and industries and the decline of manufacturing from higher-cost-production to lower-cost countries became an important political issue in the first world. Rapidly developing China overtook Japan in production, second only to the United States.

By 2005, the U.S. military had contingents in 130 countries and was trying to establish and maintain peace in Afghanistan, Iraq, the Balkans, and Haiti in collaboration with NATO and other members of the United Nations. Terrorism had taken on a greater international scope from Indonesia and the Philippines to the United States and Great Britain driven by Islamic militants against the Christian "infidels" and Israel. Militant groups such as *Hezbollah* could take over south Lebanon and start a war and, like *Hamas* in Gaza, obtain a significant number of elected seats in the Palestinian parliament.

International organizations such as the United Nations, the International Red Cross, and the World Trade Organization dealt with long-festering disputes within

[1] Publicly owned manufacturing companies in the United States whose headquarters were in Britain, Japan, Germany, the Netherlands, France, and elsewhere were concentrated in such states as California, Connecticut, Illinois, Massachusetts, Michigan, New Jersey, New York, Ohio, Pennsylvania, and Texas.

and between countries. Along with its economic integration, a one-world popular culture has emerged from the world market for television, by rock concerts, and fashions. Multinational military teams and peacekeeping forces have become commonplace. Cross-cultural and multinational research publications on leadership have annually grown more than fourfold in the last half century (Hofstede, 2001, p. 525). First-world universities remain responsible for the advanced education of numerous current and future leaders of third-world nations.

Issues of Consequence

The issues of consequence since 1960 have become more sophisticated. Understanding of universal and culturally specific values and leadership practices has become more complex and realistic. Dimensions of culture have been identified, validated empirically, and replicated in large studies across many countries. The effects of culture on social information processing has been added (Hanges, Dickson, & Lord, 2002). Triandis (1993) observed that parameters can now be established for leadership theories by examining cross-cultural variations.[2]

The internationalization of institutions and their leadership continues to grow. The industrialized societies of Europe, Japan, and the Anglo-American world are converging. The traditional Japanese value of lifetime commitment is becoming less important. In diverse countries such as Argentina, India, Israel, Nigeria, and Pakistan, employment in business and industry has resulted in many converging values (Miner, 1984). A large, affluent middle class with an international outlook is arising in China. Converging values were seen by Podsakoff, Dorfman, Howell, et al. (1986) when they compared Mexican

[2] For additional coverage, particularly on leadership among children, in education, and in small groups, the reader should consult Triandis's (1980) *Handbook of Cross-Cultural Psychology*, volumes 4 and 5. For earlier research reviews, the reader may consult Harbison and Myers (1959), who published a collection of field studies on comparative management and leadership in various countries. This work was followed by Haire, Ghiselli, and Porter's (1966) survey comparison of managers in 14 countries. Available two-country or multiple-country comparisons made possible reviews by Barrett and Bass (1976), Boddewyn and Nath (1970), Nath (1979), and K. H. Roberts (1970). Other works of consequence include those by Farmer and Richman (1964), Fayerweather (1959), and McClelland (1961). Studies generally tended to be based on interviews, but Nath (1969) uncovered 20 survey reports, mostly of comparisons of students in two countries.

and U.S. employees who were working for the same *maquiladora* firms in Mexico that assemble U.S.-made components for distribution of the final products in the United States and elsewhere. They found little difference in the way the Mexican and U.S. employees in the same firms conceptualized leaders' rewarding and disciplinary behaviors and their effects. Similarly, Smith, Tayeb, Peterson, et al. (1986) found that questionnaire items dealing with relationships, such as those on the consideration scale of the Leader Behavior Description Questionnaire (LBDQ) or on Misumi's PM (1985) (M)aintenance orientation scale kept the same factor structure whether in the United States, Britain, Japan, or Hong Kong. Yet there were variations across national boundaries for items on the scales of initiation of structure and (P)erformance orientation. And, as shall be seen from the considerable research on leadership that has been completed in countries ranging from Australia to Zambia, there are differences in the concept and meaning of leadership.

Chemers (1994) proposed an integrated contingency theory of cross-cultural leadership involving three components: (1) projection of a "leaderly" image that instills in followers an acceptance of the leader's influence; (2) motivating relationships based on understanding followers' needs and providing opportunities to meet those needs; and (3) coordinating efforts and followers' capacities to meet those needs. To this should be added that the leadership will be successful to the extent it fits with universal or culture-specific values. Thus, the successful leader values individual merit in North America but in East Asia, must value group merit. To be successful, the leader's style needs to match the culture's dominant themes. Some cultural differences remain strong. Pakistanis born and raised in Britain may still show Pakistani rather than British reactions to power distance and uncertainty avoidance (Shackleton & Ali, 1990).

National Wealth. The global marketplace has increased the spread of income and wealth between the rich and poor nations, both those that can compete successfully and those that fail. Peters (1998) suggested seven determinants that signal nations that fail: (1) restriction on the free flow of information, (2) subjugation of women, (3) inability to accept responsibility for failure, (4) the extended family or clan as the basic unit of social organization, (5) domination by a restrictive religion, (6) a low valuation of education, and (7) low prestige attached to work. Leadership development is handicapped by these same seven national signs. In the poorer of 36 countries, assertive masculine values correlated with well-being. In the wealthier countries, the opposite was true; feminine caring values correlated with well-being ($r = .69$) (Arrindell, 1998).

Subjective Well-Being. In the aggregate, wealthier countries report more subjective well-being. But Latin American countries such as Brazil and Chile report a greater sense of well-being than would be predicted by their wealth. Former Soviet bloc countries and Japan report a lesser sense of well-being than accounted for by income. The sense of well-being has risen in China, India, and Nigeria with increased national development and wealth (Luthans, 2002).

Caveat. People and countries with similar cultures are coming together in the process of globalization. Yet Huntington (1993) foresaw a clash between civilizations of people from the Judeo-Christian world and Islam based on fundamental cultural differences in ideologies. Civilizations in conflict are more intransigent and less compromising than nations divided by different national interests or how to balance power. To paraphrase Haire (1966), exporting democracy from the West to the Arab world may be preaching to people who believe in the divine right of kings.

Methods

Most cross-cultural sampling is a matter of convenience and opportunity. Within countries, samples may be small and unequal in size. Representative sampling may be limited to large polling organizations with proprietary interests. Between-country results may thus reflect differences between organizations rather than between cultures or individuals (Adler, 1984). Data from members of multinational organizations in one country may not be comparable with data from members of local firms in another. Complex designs suitable for research in one country may be unsuitable in others. Research is also ethnocentrically biased; the sources of concepts, theories, models, and methods have been primarily American and secondarily European (Den Hartog & Dickson,

2004). As Hofstede (2001) noted, American concepts and theories fit American value patterns. For instance, Maslow's (1954) hierarchy of needs, from security to self-realization, was found valid for American managers but not necessarily elsewhere. What might be true of value patterns in American and other individualistic cultures might not be true in the collectivistic cultures such as China and Japan (Triandis, 2004). Similarly, factor structures of beliefs and personality traits may differ in collectivistic Eastern countries from the individualistic United States. Clusters in 22 European countries that share the same cultural values also share the same concepts of ideal leadership, according to a survey of 6,052 middle managers using the GLOBE project questionnaire of 112 questions about the traits and behaviors of an outstanding leader (Brodbeck, Frese, Akerblom, et al., 2000).

Language. The same words in a questionnaire for one country, literally translated, may be different in meaning in another. The internal consistency of correlations among items of the authoritarian *F* Scale in the United States break down in Turkey (Kagitçibasi, 1970). As one crosses national and cultural boundaries, the differences in socialization in the various nations of the world give rise to different conceptions of leadership. To avoid the ethnocentrism endemic in the heavy use of American-originated concepts, cross-cultural research must create its concepts cross-culturally, as was done in the GLOBE project (House et al., 1994). What Western Aristotelian thought conceives of as "either/or" opposites such as proactivity or reactivity, action or inaction, work life or family life, and self or other, in China the culture sees as the need for harmonious balance between them (Chin, Gu, & Tubbs, 2001). In Iran, being direct is not a prized principle. Praise is given and promises are made but not meant. Hope is offered when there is no reason. Symbolism and vagueness are inherent. Iran is a poetic culture where "yes" may mean "yes," "no," or "maybe." The practice of insincerity (*taarof*) can be good manners (Slackman, 2006).

Language clearly distinguishes cultures. Needed across cultures are translations that provide equivalent meanings rather than literal translations. The concept of what is good leadership will vary. Even the English word *leader* may not be directly translatable. For instance, it does not easily translate into French, Spanish, or German, so *le leader, el lider,* and *der Leiter* may be used instead of the available French, Spanish, or German words, *le meneur, el jefe,* or *der Führer,* which connote leadership that is only directive (Graumann, 1986). Replications demonstrating the same phenomenon generalized under differing conditions are helpful. Functional equivalence of subsamples from different countries are an ideal requirement. Quantitative analysis needs to be buttressed by qualitative methods (Peng, Peterson, & Shyi, 1991). The mean variance between countries is likely to be greater than the variance within countries among the same respondents, indicating that WABA analysis is likely to be useful. Larger samples for each country studied are needed from the same representative organizations, as well as control of extraneous differences in the data between countries such as age, sex, education, status, and function. The IBM Work Values Survey and the GLOBE project, described below, are two examples of such efforts. Dorfman (2004) suggests that in the future, studies comparing just a few countries will need to be justified by compelling reasons explaining why they were selected for comparison. Assumptions about rapidly changing countries like China will have to be based on recent findings.

Cognitive mapping is an innovative method that Sims and Siew-Kim (1993) applied to studying the tensions involved simultaneously in being a woman, an Asian, and a manager in Singapore. Singaporean women managers used the concepts, beliefs, categories, and ideas in relating anecdotes that were most enlightening in their own language and thought systems. The themes that emerged were integrity, coping with male insecurity, Western versus Taoist-Confucian values, supporting friends and superiors, female leadership, fighting, individual versus group rights, not wishing to undermine others, and high standards for self. On the combined map, for instance, Taoist-Confucian values linked to acting with reticence with seniors, which was seen by Asians as respect. The values also linked with openness and fights, which were enjoyed if they were good fights. Integrity depended on being honest and not on accurate but unsympathetic reporting. Integrity also connected with protecting men from difficult unethical decisions, which indirectly led to coping with male insecurity. As a consequence, men were seen to feel threatened and to become macho and controlling.

Within-Country Differences. There is often a failure to appreciate the regional differences in cultures within countries. For instance, in southern Brazil, Lenaetowicz and Roth (2001) examined the differences in values of kiosk owners in four distinct regional groups: *Mineiros* from the mountains of mineral-rich south-central Brazil, *Cariocas* from around Rio de Janeiro; *Paulistas* from around the high plateau surrounding São Paolo; and *Gauchos* from the plains of southernmost Brazil. The 189 kiosk owners varied regionally in their values. Individualistic *Gauchos* emphasized achievement more than did *Mineiros.* The more introverted and reserved *Mineiros* worried about taking risks more than the business-oriented *Paulistas.* The investigators also correlated their findings with business performance. *Paulistas* demonstrated the best business performance (sales to inventory) over a five-week period. Next best were *Gauchos.* In third place were *Cariocas.* In a separate data analysis, *Paulistas* were also better in business than *Mineiros.* Independence and enjoyment correlated with business performance. Concern for security was negatively related to performance.

Similarities and Differences

Both similarities and differences in leadership are found in cross-cultural research (Dorfman & Ronen, 1991). But there is a tendency to focus more on differences and less on similarities (Fu & Yukl, 2000). For instance, managers in China and the United States view rational persuasion as an effective influence tactic, and pressure as an ineffective tactic. Some behaviors, attributes, causes, and effects are found everywhere. But other elements tend to be concentrated in some cultures and countries rather than others. Executives are faced with the challenge of the global marketplace and what strategy to use in entering a particular local market. They must consider how much they can remain consistent in practices from one country to another and how much they need to consider local uniqueness (Peterson & Hunt, 1997). North American leaders need to consider how adaptable are American leadership theories and styles as they move abroad (Dorfman, Howell, Hibino, et al., 1997).

Cross-Cultural Variables of Consequence

The values, beliefs, norms, and ideals embedded in a culture affect the leadership behavior, goals, and strategies of organizations (Dill, 1958; Negandhi & Relmann, 1972). Thus Smith and Whitehead (1984) found that North Americans emphasized individual ability and effort as the bases for promotions. In India, advancement was attributed to externalities such as marriage, friends, family, and corruption. Linked with these values and ideals are attributes of cultures such as traditionalism versus modernity, particularism versus universalism, idealism versus pragmatism, cooperativeness versus competitiveness, the sense of duty and obligation, interpersonal competencies, communication skills, effective intelligence, liberalism versus conservatism (political, religious, and social) and needs for achievement, affiliation, and power. Interests, goals, and objectives also differ and likewise contribute to differences in leadership style (Dawson, Haw, Leung, & Whitney, 1971; Negandhi & Estafen, 1967).

Hofstede Indexes

For his IBM Values Survey, Hofstede (1980) began with 126 survey questions to be asked of individual middle managers, technical professionals, and sales personnel about their personal goals and beliefs. Forty-four questions were extracted from the larger set and subjected to oblique factor analyses. Hofstede conceived five conceptually based indexes of value: **(1) power distance (PDI), (2) uncertainty avoidance (UAI), (3) individualism versus collectivism (IDV), (4) masculinity versus femininity (MAS). A fifth index, long-term versus short-term orientation (LTO),** was added later. (Hofstede, 2001). The indexes were based on brainstorming of IBM staff with multinational experience, the author's familiarity with the subject, and post hoc factor analyses of data collected from IBM personnel in 50 countries and three regions. The indexes were hypothesized to represent, for each given country, the normative beliefs and personal goals of the average member of the country's middle class. The indexes tended to be independent of one another except that national income had to be controlled to achieve independence between PDI and IDV. This independence disappeared for the other four indexes unless a wide range of rich and poor countries was included in

the analysis (Hofstede, 2001). For the index scores and ranks of the 50 countries and three regions (Arab World, East Africa, and West Africa) on the five indexes PDI, UAI, IDV, MAS, and LTO, see Hofstede (2001, p. 500).

1. *Power distance (PDI)* is an index of inequality and dependency in a country or culture. It is based on perceptions of the superior's decision making, the type of decision making preferred by subordinates, and whether they fear disagreeing with their superior. Malaysia, Guatemala, Panama, the Philippines, and Mexico were highest in PDI; Austria, Israel, Denmark, New Zealand, and Ireland were lowest. In countries with high power distance, discipline was high but with less acceptance of responsibility.

2. *Uncertainty avoidance (UAI)* is an index of the average respondents' belief about uncertainty in the future. It was assessed by rule orientation, employment instability, and stress. It correlated with the national anxiety level. Greece, Portugal, Belgium, Japan, and Peru were highest in uncertainty avoidance; Singapore, Denmark, Sweden, Hong Kong, and Ireland were lowest.

3. *Individualism versus collectivism (IDV)* is an index of the prevailing relationship between the individual and the collective. It was assessed by the perceived importance of personal time versus the importance of company time. Favoring collectivism correlated with acquiescence. Collectivism related to the easy integration of the individual into primary groups. Individualism was was highest in the United States, Australia, Britain, Canada, and the Netherlands; collectivism was highest in Venezuela, Columbia, Pakistan, Peru, and Taiwan.

4. *Masculinity versus femininity (MAS)* is an index of the extent to which respondents in a country endorsed work goals usually more popular among men than women. It correlated with greater preference for risk, need for achievement, and differences in values between men and women working at the same jobs. It related to the differences in emotional roles between men and women in a country. Japan, Austria, Venezuela, Italy, and Switzerland were highest in masculinity; Denmark, the Netherlands, Norway, and Sweden were highest in femininity.

5. Long-term versus short-term orientation (LTO) This dimension, well known to managers and to scholars of organization and strategy, was a fifth index added later. Long-termers are persistent; short-termers expect quick results. LTO is related to focus on the future or focus on the present. LTO was evidenced in a Chinese Value Survey completed by students in 23 countries (Bond & Smith, 1996). The highest factor loading on long-term orientation was on perseverance (.76). The highest factor loading on short-term orientation was on personal steadiness and stability (−.76). Adaptation was likely to be faster.

The gaps in the indexes between Hong Kong and Britain shifted considerably between 1970 and 1993. PDI increased more in Hong Kong than in Britain; UAI decreased more in Britain than in Hong Kong. The gap in IDV decreased between the more individualistic Britain and the more collectivistic Hong Kong. The gap in MAS between Britain and Hong Kong disappeared (Lowe, 1996). Hoppe (1990) replicated the findings among predominantly European leaders. A review by Søndergaard (1994) of 61 binational and multinational comparative reports found IDV nearly universally applicable, and PDI, UAI, and MAS relevant in many nations in the reports.

Long-term orientation (LTO) predicted transformational leadership in Russia (Ardichvili, 2001). LTO correlated .70 with a World Bank index of national economic growth between 1985 and 1995. National wealth moderated the indexes and their effects. In the wealthier nations, although the indexes were conceptual, only UAI could be extracted as a factor. In 23 countries, the direction of correlation of IDV with MAS reversed in poorer compared to wealthier countries (Hofsteded, 2001).

Caveat. Hofstede's indexes are widely cited and used in cross-cultural research. Nevertheless, they have been criticized. The 1980 version was dependent on a single source—IBM middle managers working in 50 countries—and on questions not necessarily relevant to non-IBM personnel. They were not a representative sample of a country's middle managers nor of the general population. The 2001 version was enlarged to include non-IBM managers. It ignored within-country hetero-geneity. The content of some of the survey items lacked face validity and was a mixture of different matters. For instance, the masculinity-femininity score of cultures on the MAS was high if cultures were seen as assertive and tough, interested in money, materialistic, uncaring about people or the quality of life, and oriented toward performance and achievement. MAS was low if the culture valued modesty and tenderness, warm social relations, and caring for the weak (Den Hartog, 2004) and in countries where opportunities for women had increased, as, for instance, in Israel, where

women, flextime, and child care and its publicized positive attitudes toward women rapidly increased the opportunities for women and their supply in administration and management from hardly any to 18 percent. By 1982, in Israel, proportionately more female than male supervisors were being elected to offices of blue-collar unions. (Izraeli, 1982).

The indexes are correlated. Country IDV is negatively correlated with PDI. Individualism predicts lack of power distance. France and Belgium are exceptions that are strong in individualism but high in power distance. Costa Rica is also an exception: collectivistic, yet low in power distance.

Gerstner and Day (1994) failed to corroborate the existence of an MAS factor. House, Wright, and Aditya (1997) noted that the five scales are not independent of one another and lack face validity. As with the MAS scale, the uncertainty avoidance items include perceived stress, length of time the respondent expects to remain with the company, and whether rules can be broken. All individualism-collectivism items are about the respondent's job goals. Nevertheless, the ranking of the 50 countries on the dimensions has not changed much in 25 years, and several studies have verified the rankings for independent smaller sets of countries (e.g., Ralston, Gustafson, Elsass et al., 1992; Morris, Davis, & Allen, 1993; Smith & Peterson, 1994), as has Hofstede (2001) for the 50 countries from before 1980 to 1990 and beyond.

A Chinese Value Survey (CVS) was administered by Hofstede and Bond (1988) in 20 countries. Its items came from 22 scholars' opinions about Chinese values, and were factored into four dimensions (Chinese Culture Connection, 1987). (1) Integration correlated .65 with

Hofstede's country rankings of collectivism (IDV) and −.58 with power distance (PDI). (2) Human-heartedness correlated .67 with femininity (MAS). But (3) Confucian work dynamism was low in correlation with any of the Hofstede dimensions. Hofstede and Bond (1988) used results from countries such as Brazil and India without Confucian or Chinese connections; they felt that the factor was about valuing entrepreneurship. Ng, Akhtar, Ball, et al. (1982) calculated discriminant functions of 100 student-rated values. Two functions emerged matching PDI and IDV; a third function correlated with both UAI and MAS; and a fourth function failed to match any of the Hofstede dimensions. Different questions have been substituted within an index, so that one has to be careful about referring to the same index in different studies. For instance, a question about the importance of earnings and advancement was introduced in 1982 to contribute to the Masculinity-Femininity Index, but the importance of earnings was dropped in 1994 when earnings were negatively correlated with advancement among Eastern European students (Hofstede, 2001). Helmreich and Merritt (1998) obtained Work Values Survey question responses from 15,000 commercial airline pilots from 23 countries. PDI and IDV fit expectations, UAI less so, and MAS not at all. Commenting on these results, Hofstede (2001, p. 67) noted that the "underlying syndrome (of four indexes) can still be universal . . . and permanent, but the measuring instruments have to be adapted to the population . . . and the times. . . . When correlating the country (index) scores, I always include GNP/capita as a (control) variable." For 18 eastern and western nations (nine rich and nine poor), Franke, Hofstede, and Bond (1991) showed that 77% of the growth in GNP between 1965 and 1980 could be accounted for by collectivism (IDV) combined with Confucian dynamics; 81% of the growth in GNP could be accounted for by collectivism combined with competitiveness, Confucian dynamics, and lack of power distance (PDI).

Stability of Answers to Survey Questions. Hofstede (2001) found the mean country correlations between responses to 44 questions completed four years apart by IBM employees in 19 to 29 countries to range from .12 (unclear on duties) to .95 (importance of freedom). Responses to individualism (IDV) question items were less stable, ranging from .09 to .76. Country rankings based on mean responses to questions of satisfaction had a median rate-rerate correlation of only .39. Country rankings based on mean personal goals and beliefs had a median rate-rerate ranking of .76.

The GLOBE Project

The GLOBE project studied middle managers in the same industries from 62 nations in more than 800 organizations. A coordinating team headed by Robert House collaborated with more than 180 internationally representative investigators! More than 15,000 middle managers participated. A meeting of 84 scholars reached consensus on a universal definition of organizational leadership as "the ability of an individual to influence, motivate, and enable others to contribute toward the effectiveness and success of the organizations of which they are members" (House, Wright & Aditya, 1997). For GLOBE, data were extracted from three industries in all the countries studied: food processing, financial services, and telecommunications. All regions of the world were represented: eastern Europe, Latin America, Germanic Europe, Nordic Europe, Far East, northern Arab, central and southern Arab, Anglo, and Latin European. At least three countries represented each region. India, Pakistan, Japan, and the United States were treated separately. At least 150 middle managers were surveyed in each sector and each country. The unit of analysis for a country was the aggregated responses of middle managers and, wherever possible, from two echelons in the organizational hierarchy above and below them.

Quantitative surveys were combined with narrative case materials. Unobtrusive measures and participant observation were also employed. Data were collected over a three-year period between 1993 and 1995 on leadership preferences, attributes and behavior of outstanding leaders, and organizational and societal culture (House, 1998). The dimensions that emerged from analyses of the data on which countries differed in culture expanded from those of Hofstede's. They depended on the purposes of the analyses. Some were focused on the effects of societal practices; others on the effects of societal values. Some concerned leaders behavior; others implicit theories of leadership. Attributes of leadership compared included autocratic and domineering, decisive, diplomatic, face-saving, self-concerned, inspirational, methodical, performance-oriented, self-concerned, status-conscious, and visionary. Additionally, it was expected that some attributes of leaders, such as integrity, administerial competence, and charisma, would be universally endorsed. However, leader attributes were also expected to reflect societal and organizational culture (House, Agar, Hanges, et al., 1994). Each country's investigators participated in scale development and validation. They also arranged for the translation and back translation of the survey questions, scale development, validation, and collection of data. International meetings of the investigators provided additional sharing of ideas. The GLOBE constructs and model aimed to incorporate thinking about leadership on a global basis (House, Javidan, & Dorfman, 2001).

The 112 leadership items factored into 21 correlated scales. The scales yielded six second-order factors: (1) charismatic (integrity, decisive, performance-oriented); (2) self-protective (self-centered, status-conscious, face saving); (3) humane (modest, humane-oriented); (4) team-oriented (diplomatic, not malevolent, administratively competent); (5) participative (not autocratic, not nonparticipative, delegative); and (6) individualistic (independent, unique) (Den Hartog, House, Hanges et al., 1999). The first of several volumes began to appear summarizing the empirical findings of the GLOBE project (House, Hanges, Javidan, et al., 2004).

Culture, Country, and Attributes of Leadership

Some aspects of leadership are universal (*etic*); they are found in all countries and regions studied. Other aspects are specific (*emic*) to countries and cultures and vary from one country to another. For instance, as nations become industrialized, their leaders come to share many values in common. At the same time, they may continue to maintain some of the values specific to their culture. For instance, 567 managers from 12 nations all agreed that being broad-minded, capable, and courageous was more important to a manager than being forgiving, helpful, and loving. Although the 12 socialist republics of the former Soviet Union entered the market economy, by 1998 only 20% of the GNP of Belarus was due to private enterprises, while 60% of Armenia's GNP was from the private sector. In Eastern Europe, the respective percent-

ages in 14 former Communist countries varied from 35% in Bosnia and Herzgovina to 80% in Hungary.

Universality

Universal leadership tendencies are common to a wide variety of cultures and countries although, at the same time, unique or unusual leadership practices may appear in a particular culture and its institutions (Smith, Misumi, Tayeb, et al., 1989). According to Triandis (1993), one must look hard to find a culture where the high-performance and high-maintenance leader (Misumi's PM leader) is not effective. Again, using standard survey procedures in 12 countries and clusters of countries ranging from the United States and Britain to India and Japan, Bass, Burger, Doktor, et al. (1979) found that managers everywhere wanted to be more proactive and to get work done by using less authority. In the same way, managers with higher rates of career advancement everywhere saw themselves as having higher effective intelligence. The GLOBE project identified 22 universal positive attributes of leadership such as trustworthy, just, dynamic, dependable, and informed. Yet Latin Americans place more emphasis on relationships than do North Americans, who are more task-oriented. In a 24-nation comparative study, Spector, Cooper, Sanchez, et al. (in press), reported that in all 24 nations from Ukraine to Japan and from the United States to China, widely varying in culture, 5,185 managers' sense of well-being at work was directly related to their perceived control.

Types. Dorfman and Ronen (1991) suggested four kinds of possible regularities across all cultures: (1) *Simple universals* are illustrated by parenting; humans require parenting for survival. (2) *Variform universals* are regularities such as single parenting, which is frequent in countries with high divorce rates. (3) *Functional universals* such as laissez-faire leadership are seen almost everywhere as dissatisfying and ineffective. (4) *Systematic behavioral universals* are whole theories of leadership that explain a web of relationships across cultures. The effects of transformational leadership on followers' evaluations of their leaders tend to be positive everywhere (Bass, 1997).

Helping to wash out cross-cultural effects may be the

more powerful transcending organizational effects of the multinational corporation. For example, to see if the original Early Identification of Management Potential assessment program in the United States could be validated cross-nationally, the analyses were replicated with 800 Exxon managers from Norway, Denmark, and the Netherlands (Laurent, 1970). Success as a manager was measured by salary, adjusted for age and the organization's salary structure. Table 33.1 shows the extent to which the results generalized across the four countries.

The same traits and measurements of ability in Norway, Denmark, and the Netherlands were predictive of the success of North American managers, as well as of managers in other countries who were working in the same multinational corporation. Cassens (1966a, b) obtained similar results using the same biographical information blank for selecting Exxon executives with samples of nearly 400 Latin Americans working in their native country (Venezuela and elsewhere) and 200 North American managers. There may be several reasons for this similarity. First, universal traits may be involved for relatively uniform tasks. Second, Exxon may tend to recruit "Americanized" Europeans and Latin Americans. Third, socialization processes that occur after one enters an organization may result in uniform requirements that transcend cultures. Another reason that indigenous values are washed out is the convergence in values that occurs among Asians, Africans, and Arabs who have had a westernized MBA education (Mellahi, 2000).

The GLOBE project identified, for 53 countries, 22 of 112 attributes that were universally endorsed as contributing to outstanding leadership (House, Hanges, & Javidan, 2004, p. 677). The criteria for choosing the attributions were that they achieved a country mean of 6 on a 7-point scale (7 = highest endorsement) and that 95% of a country's respondents gave them at least a score of 5. These were items such as being positive, just, trustworthy, intelligent, encouraging, confidence building, honest, informed, dynamic, and dependable. They were attributions associated with charisma, inspiration, and vision. Eight attributions were universally condemned in a leader: ruthless, asocial, irritable, egocentric, nonexplicit, noncooperative, dictatorial, and a loner. Such leaders were self-centered, malevolent, face-saving, and autocratic (Den Hartog, House, & Hanges, 1999). Dorfman, Hanges, and Brodbeck (2004) considered 21 dimensions and six higher-level factors attributed to outstanding leaders drawn from the GLOBE data. Team-oriented leadership was universally endorsed, as were vision and inspirational leadership.

For eight countries with widely differing cultures, Carl (1999) used GLOBE data from more than 2,300 middle managers to find a highly effective, universal, culture-free profile of charisma: vision, motivation, and proactivity. GLOBE data confirmed, in a multigroup analysis of eight countries, that charismatic leadership revealed a universal profile of visionary, inspirational, and performance-oriented attributes (Carl & Javidan, 2002). In the same way, the GLOBE project established that entrepreneurship had universal appeal in its 62 countries (Gupta, MacMillan, & Surie, 2002).

Robie, Johnson, Nilsen, et al. (2001) found that among various competencies *drive for results* and *analyzing issues* were highly regarded as critical management skill dimensions in the United States and all seven European countries using a managerial performance feedback system. When leaders were assessed by their subordinates in Japan, South Korea, Taiwan, Mexico, and the United States, charismatic leadership, supportiveness, and contingent reward were endorsed in all six countries. On the other hand, directive leadership was country-specific. It yielded positive effects in Taiwan and Mexico, while par-

Table 33.1 The Forecasting Accuracy of a Common Battery of Tests and Measurements for the Early Identification of Exxon Managers in Four Countries

Test	United States	Norway	Denmark	The Netherlands
Part A	.44	.59	.61	.55
Part B	.64	.65	.57	.62
Part C	.33	.29	.34	.27
Part D	.52	.43	.34	.45

SOURCE: Adapted from Laurent (1970).

ticipative leadership yielded positive effects in South Korea and the United States.

Country and Culture Specificity

Although leadership, management, and management education have universal characteristics, they also reflect a country's culture (Thornhill, 1993). GLOBE attributions in the 53-country analysis reported by Den Hartog, House, and Hanges were deemed country-specific if they were seen to contribute to outstanding leadership in some countries and impede such leadership in other countries. They were identified by the intraclass correlations and within-group variance compared to between-group variance for the 53 countries. For example, the attribute *individualistic* had a mean range among countries from 1.67 (moderately impedes outstanding leadership) to 5.10 (moderately contributes to outstanding leadership). Thirty-five of the 112 attributes were identified. They included *evasive* ranging from 1.52 to 5.57; *independent*, ranging from 1.67 to 5.32; and *cautious*, ranging from 1.26 to 5.78.

According to Dorfman, Hanges, and Brodbeck's (2004) examination of GLOBE attributions, being self-protective (self-centered, status-conscious, face-saving, and conflict-inducing) was counterproductive for outstanding leadership in the Scandinavian and German cultures but much less so in Asian cultures. The pattern of attributes specific to German culture and German leadership included a strong orientation toward performance, uncertainty avoidance, and assertiveness, along with low levels of humane orientation. In the workplace, interpersonal relations were stern and straightforward. Compassion was low. German leaders were low in self-protection and team orientation, but at the same time they favored participation and autonomy. "German leaders are tough on the issue, and tough on the person" (Brodbeck, Frese, & Javidan, 2002). Other examples specific to countries and cultures are listed next.

Family Ownership. Specific to Indians, overseas Chinese, and many other national groups is the extent that to which their large corporations are owned by a single family. Middle managers can aspire to senior management only if they are members of the family through birth, marriage, or adoption. In China and for overseas Chi-

nese, Hofstede (2001) labels the personal intervention of the owner and his relatives in family-owned businesses "direct supervision." There are many, mostly smaller corporations elsewhere whose shares are owned by a single family. Where trust is low, for example in countries or regions such as Taiwan and southern Italy, small family-owned companies are the rule and large investor-owned corporations are the exception. The leader is the family head, usually the oldest male of the extended family. Criminal gangs like the tongs and the Mafia mirror family enterprises (Fukuyama, 1997).

Leader Behavior Matches Cultures. Jackovsky, Slocum, and McQuade (1988) reported that in general the leadership styles of samples of French, West German, Swedish, and Taiwanese CEOs matched the values of their own culture. Bass, Burger, Dokter, et al. (1979) concluded that, more often than not, national boundaries did make a difference in managers' goals, preferences for taking risks, pragmatism, interpersonal competence, effective intelligence, emotional stability, and leadership style. National boundaries also affected the degree to which these attributes were associated with the speed of promotion. Consistent with these findings, on the basis of a survey of 1,768 managers in a single multinational firm, Griffeth, Hom, DeNisi, et al. (1980) found that 52% of the variance in managers' attitudes could be accounted for by their nationality.

Implementing Plans by Self and Others. Bass (1977) demonstrated by using exercise organization (Bass, 1975d) that in general, for North American managers, productivity and satisfaction are greater when they complete plans developed in their own group than when they carry out plans assigned by another group. North Americans are extreme in this regard, compared to nationals from selected countries of Europe, Latin America, and Japan. Objective efficiency was 14% higher for North Americans carrying out their own rather than others' plans. Similar results were obtained for Irish (13%) and French (12%) managers but not for Danish or German managers, for whom it did not make any difference whose plans were followed. In between in these effects were British, Colombian, Italian, Swiss, Belgian, Dutch, and Japanese managers. Although the managers from all the countries studied rated their own plans as better than those assigned to their group by others, the French managers were most exaggerated in this competitive effect.

Leadership Requirements. The same method may place a greater burden on leaders in one country than in another. For example, Miskin and Gmelch (1985) contrasted the requirements for leadership of quality control teams in Japan and the United States and argued that Japan's organizational culture (mainly in its larger and better firms and agencies) of entire careers spent in the same organization, security of employment, gradual upward mobility, strong familial relationships, and collective decision making provides more ready-made support for quality control efforts than does the U.S. organizational culture with its short-term company loyalty, tough-minded management, rugged individualism, and ambitious upward mobility. In the United States, the leader of a quality control team needs to place more emphasis on the socioemotional components of the group's cooperation, involvement, commitment, and long-term loyalty, which are already present in Japanese teams. When data derived from Misumi's PM theory were obtained from shop floor work teams in individualistic work teams and their supervisors in individualist Britain and the United States and in collectivist Hong Kong and Japan, Smith, Misumi, Tayeb, et al. (1989) noted that although the PM dimensions were reliably identified in all four locations, there were systematic differences in the behaviors that fit the dimensions and the way they were applied by the supervisors. Furthermore, although Misumi's Japanese PM theory is applicable universally, there are specific behaviors that differentiate collectivist Japanese and individualist American respondents. For instance, only for Americans is "checking on the quality of a person's work" a behavior contributing to the P(roduction) scale score. Only for Japanese is "waiting longer for tardy employees before showing disapproval" a behavior contributing to the M(aintenance) scale score. Other items are ambiguous in translation and for equivalence need modification before use in the West (Peterson, Brannen, & Smith, 1994). The interaction of P and M is less consistent and clear in the United States than in Japan (Peterson, Maiya, & Herreid, 1993).

Ubuntu. Specific to sub-Saharan Africa is *ubuntu*, a way of living. Relationships are reciprocal rather than instrumental. One should treat others as brothers and sisters. "I am because I belong." The extended family is important. To name is to create. Poetry and wordplay are signs of wisdom, as are gray hair and age, which are respected. Time heals. Allow enough for reaching a decision and restoring harmony. Rewards are shared; so is suffering. Solidarity and spirituality are important, as is support for complex consensus (Hampden-Turner & Trompenaar, 1993). Ubuntu is ordinarily collectivistic, but in postapartheid South Africa, blacks are surprisingly individualistic. They are likely, at the managerial level, to be acculturated to the common national culture, which resembles that of the Netherlands and the Anglo-American cluster of nations (Thomas & Bendixen, 2000).

Islamic Concepts. Specific to leadership in Islamic countries still influenced by the fourteenth-century Ibn Khaldun's concept is *asabiya*, the cohesiveness that was found in tribal society but not in cities, where coexistence was enforced by a ruling dynasty. After several generations, each dynasty was overthrown by a new dynasty, which began with a new set of rules based on interpretations of the Koran. Muhammed, a religious leader of an autonomous group of followers in Mecca, was inspired by revelation of God's purpose and determined to lead his followers to assert that purpose among the surrounding Jews, Christians, and pagans. The commands imposed on believers on how to live in a community dealt with the many problems, public and private, from commercial to family "in a disordered but consistent set of absolutes . . . everything is owed to God, nothing is owed to Caesar." The vision in the Koran is one of seventh-century Arabia—loyalty is to the family and the tribe, but accountability for one's actions is only to God. The threat of punishment or the promise of reward by God is ever-present (Scruton, 2002).

Those matters which in Western societies are resolved by negotiation, compromise, and the laborious work of offices and committees, are the object of eternal decrees, either laid out explicitly in the holy book, or discerned there by some religious leader whose authority, however, can always be questioned by a rival *imam* or jurist, since the *sharia* recognizes no office or institution as endowed with any independent lawmaking power. (Scruton, 2002, p. 5)

Among the Sunnis, the imam leads the community in prayer and is selected for his personal qualities and religious knowledge. Among the Shia, the imam is a descendant of Ali, a first cousin of Muhammed. Arab and Muslim countries are high in power distance and moderately high in collectivism, masculinity, and uncertainty avoidance. Voters in Pakistan and political party holders, using a list of 30 traits, preferred their leaders to be helpful to people, politically aware and reliable, nationalist, and patriotic. Postgraduates highly rated "places country before life," as did military officers and other ranks. However, unlike civilians, the Pakistani military placed democratic, politically aware, helpful to people, and business awareness at the bottom of the list of 30 preferred traits (Akhtar, 1997).

Sources of Specificity. The cultures and nation states that tend to be compared are somewhat arbitrary. In the aggregate, countries and cultures differ from one another in the environments that systematically affect leader-follower relations. They may differ from each other in language, religion, values, attitudes, beliefs, education, social organization, technology, wealth, politics, and law (Terpstra, 1978). National boundaries make a convenient difference. But they may or may not be coterminous with cultural boundaries. The Dutch-speaking Flemish are culturally closer in many respects to their Dutch neighbors in the Netherlands than to their French-speaking Wallonian Belgian countrymen. Nevertheless, it is the national boundaries between the Netherlands and Belgium, not the cultural boundaries between the Dutch and French speakers, that determine the educational institutions, legal forces, political effects, and economic considerations that are of consequence to understanding leadership and management. On the other hand, cultural boundaries are likely to have a greater impact on values, sentiments, ideals, language, and role models.

The combined culture-country effect can be seen when persons from one culture move into a country dominated by another culture. Kelley and Worthley (1981) found that Japanese Americans in financial institutions in Hawaii have managerial attitudes that lie between those of Japanese and American managers. The same kind of result was reported by Zurcher, Meadow, and Zurcher (1965) for Mexican bank officers and employees who were working in Mexico and comparable Chicanos and Anglos who were working in the United States.

Countries Clustered by Cultures

The universal and specific cultural tendencies are seen in the extent to which countries can be clustered by culture. Thus, North American managers (excluding those in French Canada) tend to cluster with their British cousins on numerous dimensions of leadership behavior and attitudes. Together, they form part of an even larger Anglo-American cluster that includes Australia, Canada, New Zealand, and South Africa. With more than 190 countries in the world, containing several hundred cultures, it is important to try to merge comparisons into a framework of fewer but larger clusters of nations and cultures. Clusters of countries provide a way to display cross-cultural results in summary form. The labels provide a preliminary identification of the leadership patterns that are likely to be found and the basis for predictions and explanations of what will be found. They may have practical value. For example, they make it possible to determine relevant policies for a country cluster. Preliminary comparisons can concentrate on a dozen clusters, rather than on 192 individual countries.

Ronen and Shenkar (1985) synthesized eight previous efforts[3] to cluster countries according to their similarities and differences in the importance of work, satisfaction with work, autocratic versus democratic attitudes toward work, personal values (such as pragmatism, achievement, decisiveness, and orderliness), and interpersonal values (such as conformity, recognition, and benevolence). Geography, history, language, religions, and technological development strongly influenced the clustering.

The Anglo-American Cluster. There are more commonalities than differences among the Anglo countries, for example, in the importance they attach to the individual. In addition to language, these countries also have in common high per capita wealth, democratic forms of government, and a British heritage. Anglo countries differ in particular from the Far Eastern, Middle Eastern, and Arab clusters of countries, which, for instance, place much more of a premium on authority than do Anglos. The Anglo-American cluster places more of a premium on individualism, merit, willingness to take calculated risks, profitability, and productivity. Anglos are more as-

[3] See, for example, Haire, Ghiselli, and Porter (1966, 1980) and Ronen and Kraut (1977).

sertive, pragmatic, and trusting of their subordinates to display initiatives. They are more self-determined and imaginative and less judgmental. They are more open and prefer general to close supervision. They engage in more short-term objectives. Compared to other clusters, they place relatively less emphasis on family and employee welfare. They are more ready to compromise than to prolong conflict. Self-control and equality are valued more than in some other clusters.

The Anglo cluster was studied by Kipnis, Schmidt, Swaffin, Smith, and Wilkinson (1984), who found no differences in the various strategies used by 360 American, Australian, and English managers to achieve their personal objectives. Posner and Low (1988) reported more similarities than differences in the value placed on organizational stakeholders and personal traits by 426 Australian and 1,498 U.S. managers. However, Kabanoff and Daly (2000) found that while their leadership and collegiality value structures were similar, elite value structures were more common in the annual reports of 77 Australian firms; meritocratic value structures were more prevalent in the annual reports of 55 U.S. organizations.

The Scandinavian and Germanic Clusters. In addition to geographic, historical, religious, and (except for Finland) linguistic affinities, the Scandinavian countries, even more than the Anglo-American countries, strongly support parliamentary democracy in government and industrial democracy in the workplace. Language, industrial development, and attitudes toward work, among other things, tie together the Germanic nations of central Europe. Weissenberg (1979) reported that German-speaking managers varied significantly in their judgments of the importance of 6 of 11 life goals, depending on whether they came from Austria, West Germany, or German Switzerland. The Austrians placed relatively more emphasis on service; the West Germans on leadership, independence, and prestige; and the Swiss Germans, on wealth and duty. Weibler, Brodbeck, Szabo, et al. (2000) found communalities and differences in a survey of 900 Germans, Austrians, and Swiss Germans on leadership attributes, behavior, and leadership schemas. Szabo, Reber, Weibler, et al. (2001) and Brodbeck, Frese, Reber, et al. (2000) found the differences among German, Austrian, and Swiss managers in leadership values and be-

havior to be much smaller than the differences found among managers elsewhere.

Latin Europe. The cluster of Latin Europe—France, Italy, Portugal, and Spain—is separated from its Germanic neighbors by history, language, generally later technical development, and more uniformity in Catholicism. The distinctiveness of the difference is evidenced in the much slower introduction of organizational development and related participative leadership practices.

The Latin European and Latin American clusters separate the colonizers from the colonized. The Latin European countries are more advanced in their development and more stable politically, for the most part. France, Italy, and Spain have accelerated in technical development. They also tend to be more homogeneous ethnically and racially in their populations than are the Latin American countries, although the numbers of their African immigrants have increased substantially. Common to the Latin European and the Latin American cultures are Roman law and the lack of a consensual basis, which are seen to strengthen the centralization of the state's authority (Faucheux & Rojot, 1979). The Latin cultures also share a lower capacity for openness, trust, and the rational expression of feelings, in contrast to the Anglo cluster. Competence is more likely to be overruled by considerations of formal status in the Latin than in the Anglo cluster. The tolerance for uncertainty and ambiguity is likely to be lower. The transfer of programs and practices, such as management by objectives or organizational development, from the Anglo to the Latin world is fraught with impediments, including the greater Latin than Anglo institutionalized centralization of decision making, bureaucratic protection, state intervention. Lesser importance is attached to internal organizational processes in comparison to the class struggle and to social movements that are external to the individual organization (Faucheux, Amado, & Laurent, 1982). There is also more hidden game playing in the Latin than in the Anglo organization.

Latin America. In addition to sharing a common Spanish language and colonial heritage, Spanish America has common patterns of leadership and decision making. For instance, Heller (1969b) stated that South American boards of directors do not seem to abide by standards of

Anglo-American efficiency. He also saw common values and habits in Argentina and Chile, each with its own different Latin American subculture, that were deleterious to the effectiveness of organizations. In 59 of 68 business organizations, he observed, board meetings were held without precirculated minutes and agendas. Consequently, the boards spent some 38% of their time reexamining the same subject matter that they had previously discussed. Furthermore, the organizations did not carry out decisions that had been reached by the boards. Heller also noted that managers in these countries tended to equate authority with rapid decision making and to stress its importance. Anglo-American managers commonly try to gather more information before they make a decision. But Heller sensed that in Argentina, Chile, and Uruguay, senior managers were expected to make quick decisions. Adding to the inefficiency of decision making is the Latin American propensity to rely on intuition, emotional arguments, and justifications (McCann, 1964). Thought proceeds in a series of direct perceptions of truths. The truths concern the object being contemplated, independent of any demonstrated reasoning process. The truths are neither verifiable nor repeatable. The tendency is toward action that is improvised—undertaken without conscious planning. When planning is done, projects may be considered completed after they have been planned (*projectismo*).

East Asia. Japan, China, and Korea have common roots in the Confucian ideology of harmony through proper obedient behavior according to one's prescribed role in one's family, village, and society. East Asians tend to focus more on social roles and obligations (Fukada, 1983; Markus, Kitayama, & Heiman, 1996). The countries in the East Asian cluster build on their shared Confucian heritage and "shame" culture. Unlike the West's "guilt" culture, in which individuals are accountable mainly to themselves, in the "shame" culture, interpersonal behavior is more restrained. The verdicts of others are more acceptable, as is parental authority (Ronen, 1986). In the Confucian tradition, the stability of society is based on unequal relationships between those unequal in status. Seniors owe juniors consideration and protection; juniors owe seniors respect and obedience. The family is the model for all social organizations. The Confucian Golden Rule, while like Hillel's, is worded nega-

tively: Do not unto others as you would not have them do to you. The virtuous person works hard, is patient and devoted to becoming educated, and practices moderation (King & Bond, 1985). The boundaries between self and others are unclear. Challenge is less of a personal and more of a collective goal (Metzger, 1977). Little importance is attached to having sufficient time for personal and family life. One's obligation to the family is strong, but being the family breadwinner is what is important, not spending time with the family (Eberhard, 1971). Work and duty are more important than are leisure and enjoyment (Dawson, Haw, Leung, et al., 1971). It is more important to comply with legitimate authority. Personal aggrandizement and advancement are valued less than is recognition by one's peers. Achievement is tied to team efforts (Shenkar & Ronen, 1987). More than for Americans or Europeans, it is important to do things right and to comply with legitimate authority (Latham, 1988). The shared Confucian-principled culture goes a long way toward explaining the rapid ecnomic growth of the "Five Tigers"—China, Taiwan, Hong Kong, South Korea, and Singapore—between 1965 and 1995 (Hofstede & Bond, 1988), despite the setbacks of the Cultural Revolution in China and of the continued recession in the 1990s in Japan. In the early twenty-first century, China has passed Japan and is now second only to the United States in gross national production.

The Arab Cluster. The Arab countries form a distinct cluster of countries with authoritarian regimes that resist political liberalization, remain unaccountable to their people, and pocket public assets. Civil liberties are repressed, and the state is controlled by force and and conspiracy. Support comes from their common enmity toward Israel. A rich, urban, educated elite and the majority of the both urban and rural agricultural poor prefer strong leaders and remain beholden to their tribal chiefs. But in the past several decades, literacy rates have improved, public administrations have been modernized, women's rights have improved in some Arab countries such as Egypt and declined in others such as Iran, and the structures of tribal societies have changed. The mass media have provided competition with state propaganda. Morocco, Egypt, and Lebanon have become freer (Kubler, 2000). Saddam Hussein's repressive dictatorship was forcefully replaced in Iraq by a coalition force led by the United States with a constitutional government, which had been absent for 35 years. But terrorism, instability, insurrection, and civil war between Sunnis and Shias threaten stability. Islamists remain a threat in many of these countries, as occurred in Iran of a return to the medieval laws and government of religious fundamentalism ruled by the imams, Koran, and *sharia.*

Eastern Europe. The countries of Eastern Europe are mainly Slavic and were socialist under Soviet hegemony. Citizens of the former Communist countries were more likely to regard compromise as a personal loss and perhaps unethical as well. They were more supportive of the use of punishment as a deterrent (Cunningham, 1984). As will be noted later, the former Soviet economic system and the Russian historical heritage resulted in different supervisor-subordinate relationships from those in western Europe and North America.

The Sub-Saharan Cluster. The sub-Saharan African countries like Angola, Uganda, and Rwanda form a cluster of former European colonies. They remain poor and underdeveloped, scourged by civil wars, corruption, and the AIDS epidemic. Nonetheless, the rural peasants in particular share cultural traits of hospitality and *ubuntu,* a form of collectivism and sociability.

Other Countries. Brazil, India, and Israel do not fall into any of the clusters. India's different technological development, colonial history, and heterogeneity of ethnic and language groups and Israel's unique history and development keep them separate from the Anglo cluster. Unlike in Spanish America, in Brazil, Portuguese, Indian, and African influences have had the strongest impact. In contrast to the overly rapid decision making observed by Heller in Spanish-American Argentina, Chile, and Uruguay, Harbron (1965) noted the opposite tendency in Portuguese-American Brazil. Traditional Brazilian managers running inherited family factories practice *jeitinhos,* finding solutions to small problems and avoiding dealing with big problems with which they have had no experience. They are characterized by languid, compromising, "wait and see" attitudes. Despite this type of leadership, Brazil has undergone a remarkable economic expansion since 1965 that has involved robust (and sometimes ruthless) enterpreneurial activity not often seen in Spanish America.

Cluster and Country Differences

Within-Cluster Differences. Despite these cultural clusters, considerable differences exist among the countries that are clustered on the basis of similar cultures. For example, Hines and Wellington (1974) found that both entrepreneurs and middle managers in New Zealand who were native to Britain had a much higher need for achievement than did those who were native to Australia and New Zealand. Shouksmith (1987) further pointed to the sharp cultural differences in work values and social orientation of the Europeans (*pakehas*) and Maori in New Zealand. The same can be said for the growing number of black leaders and managers in South Africa, in contrast to their white counterparts (Hofmeyer, 1987).

Although the United States and Britain are both in the Anglo cluster, considerable differences are often noted between managers in the two countries. In the United States, it is polite to be friendly whether you mean it or not; in Britain, it is impolite to be friendly if you do not mean it (Terry, 1979). With respect to the firm and the job, in the United States, the shop supervisor, who represents management, is more important to workers' performance than is the shop steward, who represents the union; the reverse is true in Britain (Earley, 1986).

In an in-basket simulation, U.S. management trainees responded more favorably than did their English counterparts to both praise and criticism, and attached more value to social interaction (Earley, 1985). The results suggest that a contingent reinforcement style of leadership is likely to be more effective with U.S. than with English subordinates.

In particular, Britons are more class conscious. Speech, dress, and style limit mobility and acceptance. It is still much more unusual in Britain than in the United States to move out of the working class into the higher ranks of political and business leadership (Newman, 1985). Nor are leaders likely to be as oriented to the postindustrial world as are their counterparts in the United States, Europe, or Japan. Public school education (actually private, elitist boarding schools) stresses the need for middle- and upper-class Britons to develop a commanding social presence with grace, wit, eloquence, self-possession, and subtlety. Technical and business education are considered to be of less value (Hampden-Turner, 1983).

Although the U.S. and British cultures are similar in

many respects, British managers are regarded as less aggressive and less ambitious than their North American cousins. British employees are more likely to regard their jobs as a right and privilege, not something to be earned. Work is less of a focal point in their lives than it is for Americans. British employees see themselves as members of their community; Americans see themselves as members of their company. British managers are more likely than their American counterparts to dislike and distrust foreigners, to be more averse to risk taking, to be fonder of tradition and formality and less accepting of change, to be more class conscious, to want to see more structure, and to follow precedents rather than written codes (Terry, 1979).

The countries in the Latin American cluster vary widely in many ways that are of consequence to leadership. Mexico is characterized by its mestizo majority; Argentina, by its diverse European ethnic groups. Venezuela is thoroughly Latin; Chile is more northern and Latin European. Starting with Cuba in 1959, Latin American and Brazilian governments have moved from rightist dictatorships to populist leftist democracies. In 18 countries of Latin America, most of which had democratized in the past 25 years, a poll of 18,643 citizens and intense interviews with 231 political, economic, and social leaders, including 41 current or former presidents and vice presidents, found much disillusionment with democracy. Fifty-five percent said they would support a return to an authoritarian regime (Hoge, 2004).

The East Asian cultures also differ in many respects. Confucianism took a different path in Japan than in Korea or China. The result is that in China and Korea, people feel a more personalized loyalty to individuals, family, and kinship, whereas in Japan, people have a greater loyalty to an organization. (The role of the samurai, *joeishikimoku*, formulated in the twelfth century, placed more emphasis on ability and common causes than on blood relations.) There is a greater acceptance of top-down leadership in China and Korea and a greater acceptance of bottom-up leadership in Japan. In Japan, by being competent in playing one's proper role in the organization and being committed to it, one can aspire to rise to the top. Among South Koreans and Chinese in Singapore, Taiwan, and Hong Kong, only members of the family clan who own a firm can aspire to top positions. In Japan, harmony is achieved with leadership that

fosters consensus through much participation; harmony is achieved among Koreans and Chinese by leadership that seeks consensus through much more planning and control by the leader (Castaldi & Soerjanto, 1988).

Japan's history and technological development have diverged widely from those of other Far Eastern countries. Professional management appeared earlier in Japan, even earlier than in the West. The history of entrepreneurial activity in Japan was likewise quite different from that found elsewhere in Asia.

Japanese, Korean, and Chinese leadership and management practices are different in numerous ways, despite their common emphasis on collective responsibility and the in-group. Likewise, the preferred management styles of Japanese business students were found to differ significantly from those of Thai business students (Neranartkomol, 1983). In Japan, the East Asian collectivistic loyalty to the family is converted into loyalty to the organization.

Aside from the obvious effects on them of the differences in their economic, political, and social systems, the Chinese in the People's Republic of China diverge from the Chinese in Hong Kong, Taiwan, and Singapore. Unlike those in offshore locations, Selden (1971) found that subordinate officials in mainland China were expected to interpret, modify, and adapt policies that were initiated higher up in the system. Another difference is the greater stress in the People's Republic of China on cooperation among workers and less emphasis on the promotion of managers. These differences were revealed in surveys of Chinese managers' judgments of the importance of various work goals in the People's Republic of China, Hong Kong, Taiwan, and Singapore (Shenkar & Ronen, 1987). They were also seen between 49 managers in the People's Republic of China and 49 managers in Hong Kong by Birnbaum and Wong (undated). Managers in the People's Republic of China valued power differences, risk taking, individualism, and assertive masculinity considerably less than did their Hong Kong counterparts. Consistent with this finding, according to Lindsay and Dempsey (1985), collectivism is shown in the attention that managers of firms China pay to the lower-level needs of workers and by the managers' holistic concern for workers and for their lifetime employment. Korea is the most Confucian of the countries; by the thirteenth century, Confucianism had replaced Buddhism. Nam (1991) found that Korean managers, following Confucian tradition, accepted responsibility for group failure instead of blaming the group members. Nonetheless, by the 1950s, 20% of Koreans were Protestant Christians. Syngman Rhee, who became the first president of South Korea following the departure of the Japanese colonizers in 1945, was a Christian.

As it did in China, a mandarin bureaucracy emerged with Confucianism. Rules and regulations became de rigueur. Illustrative are the rules for court officials displayed in office hangings in the Duksu royal palace in Seoul, Korea: REGARDLESS OF YOUR RANK, DON'T ENTER THIS OFFICE WITHOUT PERMISSION. ONLY OFFICIALS ASSIGNED TO THIS OFFICE ARE ALLOWED TO ENTER. DO NOT LEAVE THE OFFICE UNLESS ON OFFICIAL BUSINESS.

While Taiwan and Hong Kong have a very large number of small private firms, Korea has extremely large corporations and a highly concentrated industrial structure. Unlike Japan and more like Taiwan, in Korea families dominate private enterprise, but Korea differs from Taiwan and Hong Kong in its gigantic networked conglomerates, *chaebols*, such as Samsung and Hyundai. The *chaebol* bears some similarity to Japan's *zaibatsu*. In 1988, three *chaebols* were networks for 672 companies in many different industries that produced 36% of Korea's GNP. *Chaebol* member firms own shares in one another and collaborate on a nonprice basis. They were instituted as government policy by President Park Chung Hee to promote Korean economic development.

The patriarchical family tradition translates into hierarchical and authoritarian leadership in business. Kinship and class are important. Korean entrepreneurs are likely to come from the *yangban* gentleman-scholar class. Although collectivistic like the other Tigers, they also can be more individualistic, and their labor-management relations are more adversarial as in North America and Europe. Investigators are sometime surprised when they fail to find expected differences between Korean and American leadership scale scores (Chah & Locke, 1996). Education and literacy are prized, and managers are recruited mainly from prestigious universities (Fujiyama, 1997).

Within-Country Differences. Within-country differences in the cultural orientation of leaders were seen as significant in Italy by Gallino (1975). Three types of Italian managers were observed: the liberal, the lay humanist, and the Christian socialist. These types varied in how they conceived the manager's role and functions, how

subordinates should be trained, their use of formal organizational techniques, their models of economic development, their investment preferences, and their attitudes toward the workforce and the representation of workers. Liberal managers were more often found in older, established private companies operating in relatively traditional productive and technological sectors; lay humanists in newer, recently established private companies operating in the advanced production and technological sectors; and Christian socialists in companies run fully or partly by the state. The liberal managers were task-oriented and profit-maximizing, the lay humanists were more concerned about relations and people, and the Christian socialists were oriented toward the public good and the collectivity.

Chowdhry and Pal (1960) also warned against focusing on an overall pattern of values among people within one country, such as India, which could obscure the differences between subgroups in that country. Furthermore, emphasizing the overall patterns of values among countries could miss the commonalities among similar subgroups within these countries. Thus, Singh, Arya, and Reddy (1965) reported that patterns of leadership behavior in Indian villages differed systematically with the leaders' socioeconomic status, caste, and occupation. Similarly, Gopala and Hafeez (1964) reported, for a sample of Indian supervisors, that high educational attainment was associated with favorable attitudes toward employees, while lack of education was associated with a production orientation. But what is of as much or more consequence to leadership in countries such as India are the divisions among communities caused by religion, language, and region.

Origins of Leaders

Differences among countries are the rule rather than the exception when one investigates the origins of their leaders in the public and private sectors.[4] Thus countries may vary in the extent to which their managements are drawn from all social classes or from the upper or lower portions

---

[4]An exception was seen in nonindustrial societies, where Greenbaum (1977), in an analysis of 616 societies, described in *Murdock's Ethnographic Atlas* (1967), found that whether the village head inherited or was elected or appointed to the post was unrelated to family, economic, or other societal factors.

of society. Japan is an almost classless society, in that one can climb to positions of leadership through demonstrated capabilities certified by admission and passage through elite universities. At the other extreme, McClelland (1961) noted that 54% of Turkey's business leaders came from the upper-middle and upper classes. In Turkey, managers in the public sector come from much different class backgrounds than do managers in the private sector; in contrast, managers in both sectors in Italy have much more similar backgrounds. In Poland, a former socialist country, 96% of the managers reported that they came from the working or lower middle classes. In a country like the United States, managers are drawn somewhat more uniformly from all classes. Neither the working classes nor the aristocracy and upper classes are the prime sources of managers in the private sector in Mexico or Italy.

Curiously, despite their public service leadership, it was not the established landed gentry in Britain who sparked industrialization and the moves toward modernity. Generally, the founders of new industry came from dissenting minorities. In England, the leaders of the industrial revolution were drawn disproportionately from the Methodist and other dissenting religious groups. In Roman Catholic France, until the revocation of the Edict of Nantes in 1685, the source was Protestant Huguenots. In Colombia, much business development was due more to the minority of Antioquian miners than to the landowning latifundists. In India, it was due to the Parsee minority, and in Southeast Asia, to the Chinese minority. In the Western world, the Jewish minority played an important entrepreneurial role (Hagen, 1962).

Differences in History, Climate, and Institutions

Cross-country comparisons of the differences in the leaders' origins need to consider what are often almost unique circumstances within a given country. For instance, religion and history (the Roman Catholic ethos and the return of French entrepreneurs to France after the British takeover of Canada in 1763) were seen to have retarded the emergence of French Canadians as leaders in Canadian industry and business (Pelletier, 1966). Studies of leadership in the United States, with its cultural emphasis on individualism, action rather than contemplation, pragmatism, and egalitarianism, cannot capture the diversity of relationships found in other countries, which are influenced by their own histories, climates, and institutional peculiarities. In many ways, the U.S. experience has been unique for the development of leadership. Alexis de Tocqueville drew attention to this uniqueness in *Democracy in America* (1832/1966), based on his travels in the United States:

> These Americans are the most peculiar people in the world. You'll not believe it when I tell you how they behave. In a local community in their country a citizen may conceive of some need which is not being met. What does he do? He goes across the street and discusses it with his neighbor. Then what happens? A committee comes into existence and then the committee begins functioning on behalf of that need. . . . All of this is done without reference to any bureaucrat. All of this is done by the private citizens on their own initiative (quoted in Miller & Hofstedde, 1987, p. 91).

The military historian S. L. A. Marshall (1964) noted the surprise in 1917 of the European trainers of the American Expeditionary Force to be sent to France that the U.S. draftees responded naturally to discipline and that a high percentage of them were potential leaders. Getting this army ready was not the formidable task they had originally envisaged on the basis of their European experience.

An institutional peculiarity of the United States is its litigiousness. The country has about 18 lawyers for every 10,000 inhabitants. Legal education is an important source of American leaders in government and business, but it is much less important in most other first-world countries. Japan, in contrast, has one lawyer per 10,000 people. In Japan, one's behavior following an ambiguous agreement is much more important than is the written contract, whose words are critical for the American. Close attention must be paid to the Japanese intimations of their needs without explicit statements of them. To the Japanese, qualifiers are more important than are definite positives and negatives (Morita, 1981). Nor do France (two lawyers per 10,000) or West Germany (four lawyers per 10,000), whose languages are more explicit, depend as much on lawyers as a source of their leaders as does the United States (Lee & Schwendiman, 1982).

In decided contrast to the United States, in Britain managing in business or industry (other than finance) was not historically the occupation of a gentleman. The eldest son inherited the estate; the younger sons went into the armed services or the church. Middle-class sons went into the professions, the civil service, or the family business. Until recently, a businessman who wanted a title had to work hard for public causes, devoting less time to business and more to public service. But business has finally become respectable; finance always was (R. Stewart, 1966).

In Britain, public school education followed by matriculation at Oxford or Cambridge University was the basis for careers in finance, the civil service, foreign service, the military, and the Church of England (Copeman, 1955). According to an analysis of the educational backgrounds of 3,682 of the British elite by D. P. Boyd (1974), the importance of the public schools and Oxford and Cambridge Universities to careers changed little between 1939 and 1971. Social class traditions and entrance into management as a consequence of social class and academic (nonmanagement) education continue to remain strong.

In Britain, the importance of class and the "right" schools has been coupled with a lack of mobility within the firm. In the traditional British firm, each department was a self-contained unit in which members frequently spent much of their whole careers. In consequence, the members of a department were exposed to a limited range of management attitudes and ideas. They became so immersed in their department's way of thinking that they were unlikely to be able to think outside this pattern of beliefs (R. Stewart, 1966).

In France, the major route to political leadership and ministerial office is not, as in Britain or in present-day Germany, through election to Parliament; rather, it is often through experience in the civil service and the French president's or premier's confidence in the official with such experience. This same source of government leaders was seen in Bismarck's Germany (Dogan, 1979). But as was noted in Chapter 30, only later in their administration do U.S. presidents draw their cabinet officers from within the government. Early on, presidents seek politically acceptable leaders, for the most part, from business, education, agriculture, and other nonpolitical institutions.[5]

In the Netherlands, participative leadership is an im-

portant correlate of transformational leadership. Heroes are less likely to be acknowledged as they are in the United States or Britain. Supposedly, fewer statues of heroes are erected in the Netherlands than in the United States and Britain. In Australia a particularly high value is placed on egalitarianism—a successful leader must remain "one of the boys." In Mexico, a particularly high value is placed on social status; competent applicants for leadership positions are rejected because of their lower-class status (Den Hartog, House, & Hanges, 1999). This hurts the country's economic competitiveness. Mexican firms need to become more competitive since they joined the North American Free Trade Agreement, and need to avoid blocking the upward flow of information that is likely when subordinates are afraid to disagree with their superiors (Sibeck & Stage, 2001).

Leadership in the Public and Private Sectors

Some common patterns have been observed across what at first would appear to be extremely different cultural settings. Wilkinson (1964) noted that Confucian China and Victorian England emphasized the same developmental requirements for leaders in the public sector. Good manners, good form, and classical cultural training better fitted amateurs for government service in comparison to experts with technical or professional education. Civil servants were drawn from the landed gentry and those of middle-class origin who went to the same schools and adopted the accent, dress, and mannerisms of the upper class. Of course, particularly in the People's Republic of China, leadership in the public sector now originates quite differently. A detailed study by M. Sheridan (1976) of five prominent women party leaders in the People's Republic of China indicated that they came from families of manual and service workers. They earned merit in their political, familial, and work roles and became models for others. But by the 1990s, as in the former Soviet Union, the new leaders were increasingly likely to come from the favored classes of party officials, military officers, managers, business owners, and intellectuals.

Meritocracies. In France and Belgium, educational achievement, a source of income from property, and bourgeois origins underlie the leadership of industry and government. Elite cadres dominate the management of business and government on the basis of an educational level that is not ordinarily attained by children from the working classes. Particularly important is a degree from one of the highly selective *grandes écoles* of technology, administration, and the military. Leadership in nonremunerative high-prestige fields is pursued by those with income from property. In Japan as well, educational achievement, based on graduation from the highly selective and prestigious Tokyo University, is a key to success in business or government.

Strong class divisions characterized the former Soviet Union. Party officials, the military, intellectuals, and industrial and scientific technocrats were the upper classes. The workers and peasants were the lower classes. In a production-oriented economy, engineering or technical training was almost mandatory for advancement in industry. Still a different and changing pattern is seen in Germany. Since World War II, there have been increasing opportunities for people of working-class origins to advance into positions of top leadership in business and governmental service. Before 1945, such leadership was dominated by the landed, business, and military aristocracy (Granick, 1962b).

Family Control. A high degree of authority is exercised and obedience demanded in the Indian family system. Children are taught obedience to their elders. This obedience continues into adulthood, as is seen in the lack of delegation in management. Yet subtle constraints prevent the head from giving directions without consulting with senior family members (Chowdhry & Tarneja, 1969). At the same time, it is difficult for nonfamily members to advance into upper-management positions. There is a sharp gap between middle and upper management, unlike, say, the situation in firms in the United States. In India, the managing agency system was the basis for the development of large-scale indigenous private and public enterprise, as well as of foreign subsidiaries. The agency promoted, financed, and managed the reorganization of India with capital from London. It was rigidly structured, highly characterized, personal, and likely to be a family unit dominated by one person, the *karta* or head of the extended Indian family, responsible for its other members and with authority over them.

The leadership of a country by the few large landown-ing families, *latifundismo*, is still strong in many Latin American countries and is a prime cause of revolutionary action. The leaders of business and government in Chile sprang from such a landed aristocracy (Harbron, 1965). In other Latin American countries, the technocrats of public and private enterprise, who are of middle-class backgrounds, are leading social change efforts. Thus, Mexico is a "guided democracy" run by self-made millionaires, an industrial elite, top government bureaucrats, and political figures with middle-class origins. In countries such as Argentina and Peru, the rise of industrial managers from the middle classes occurred with the post-1945 industrial expansion. Lauterbach (1963) observed, in interviews in 13 Latin American countries, that family relationships are important to the emergence as a leader, particularly outside the major industrial centers. There is a lack of specialization. The same person, family, or executive office can administer a wide variety of enterprises. Immediate objectives predominate. Competition is accepted in the abstract, but in practice is considered a bothersome condition to be restrained by public or private action.

Cultural and Institutional Changes

A common set of antiauthoritarian values emerged in the developed nations following World War II. These values emphasized democratic participation in the decisions of organizations and government. According to repeated national surveys, the postwar generation remained more oriented toward freedom of opportunity. It represented a systematic change from the preceding generation, particularly in Germany and Italy. Elsewhere, privileged classes were the rule (Inglehart, 1981). However, although sharp social, economic, and political changes may occur in a country, strong underlying historical continuities remain. For instance, Shouksmith (1987) pointed to the changes in the meaning of work in New Zealand in the 1980s. After a history of full employment, New Zealand faced a situation in which disadvantaged, older, and unskilled workers were finding it increasingly difficult to obtain and keep jobs. And jobs themselves were being deskilled by automation. The social values of the Maori were becoming increasingly important in the work force, as were women.

France. Centralization is still characteristic in France. Its most recent appearance occurred with the accession of the socialist president François Mitterrand and the nationalization of 90% of France's banking, its entire steel industry, half of its major electrical, data-processing, and pharmaceutical industries, and its public works construction. Since the Middle Ages and the Counter-Reformation, there has been a centralized government and industry, submission to hierarchy, lack of autonomy, antieconomic attitudes, and a strong civil service in France. Today, centralization continues, with its top management originating in three *grandes écoles* and the meritocracy of the *grand corps.* The favored few remain the symbolic expression of society, whether they work in the public or private sector (Aubert, Ramanantsoa, & Reitter, 1984).

Japan. In Japan, economic stagnation set in 1990. The structure of its economy is changing. The close ties in Japan among government, business, and workers are being replaced by increased entrepreneurism, concern for shareholder value, and divestment of unprofitable activities. Lifetime employment has been replaced by layoffs of workers. The low unemployment rate has doubled. Foreign multinational firms such as Ford and Renault are gaining control of failing Japanese corporations. The financial markets are being overhauled. Venture capital firms have appeared (Chandler & Tolbert, 2000). The decline in the industrial base has reduced employment particularly for men aged 24 and under (Struck & Tolbert, 2000).

The downturn of the Japanese economy in the 1990s and beyond radically changed Japanese business practices (Onishi, 2003). The *keiretsu,* large groups of companies that agreed to buy from one another and exclude competition, created inefficiencies in a global economy where firms buy supplies based on price and quality. More innovation and flexibility were needed. Banks continued to carry bankrupt companies on their books. The country now had to face strong competition from China, South Korea, Taiwan, and the other surging Asian Tigers, not to mention the reawakened North American and western European economies. It is particularly in its domestic market that it needed to overcome protectionism, deals made on the basis of personal connections and favoritism, copycat strategies, and corruption (Behr, 1998).

The Japanese population needs to shift its emphasis from personal savings to investment, which may in turn mean more old-age insurance and social security. Japan has the highest longevity rate of any nation.

Other East Asian Countries. Hong Kong, Chinese values were strongly affected by Western values. Although ethnically Chinese, Hong Kong managers' values were in between those of Chinese and American managers (Ralston, Gustafson, Elsass, et al., 1992). In 1997, the British lease ended and capitalist Hong Kong became part of the Communist mainland. However, Hong Kong was able to continue its successful economy. Meanwhile, the opening of the People's Republic of China to capitalistic enterprise in 1980 resulted in an explosion of private companies side by side with continuing state enterprises. China rapidly overtook Japan as the world's second largest economy. Its middle management and professionals became mobile. Instead of being assigned to a state enterprise and remaining with it, as in the socialist system, the annual turnover among middle managers is now up to 20% in multinational firms. In 1995, firms were offering 50% or more increases in salaries to retain managers who were threatening to leave (Kaye, 1995).

South Korea and the other East Asian Tigers suffered an economic downturn in the late 1990s and had to make major reforms. In South Korea, to reduce expenses, more flexible union-management agreements were introduced, including wage reductions of 10% to 30%, unpaid leave, and a return of bonuses (Joon-Hun, 1998). The many *chaebol,* large family-founded and family-controlled conglomerates holding companies with diverse interests ranging from electronics to shipbuilding, followed the Confucian principle of deference to the family elder and promotion based on age and seniority. Their productivity was considerably lower than that of their competitors. By the late 1990s, merit increasingly replaced age, seniority, personal relations, and politics, providing opportunities for younger, well-educated managers and professionals and more democratic leadership (M. Baker, 1998).

Russia. Tuller (2001) found that early in Russia's transformation from a planned to a market economy, norms for American managers were significantly higher than those of 120 Russian managers who wanted to start a business. But four years later, the national differences between

58 Russians and 59 Americans had almost disappeared. Puffer (1994) noted that market-oriented Russia replaced centralized leadership with shared power; micromanaging with delegation; service to the party and to the collective with individual success; following rules with chasing opportunities; struggling to accomplish the routine with struggling to accomplish the new; two sets of books with wild capitalism; and greasing the wheels of the state with greasing palms with gratuities (*blat*). They learned to do business straight, with less cynicism, overpromising, and emphasis on bigness and quantity. The new Russia and its Confederation of Independent States (CIS) continues to be different in leadership and management ideology from Western countries. Nonetheless, many of the practices of the former Soviet Union are still seen to affect management and leadership in Russia and the CIS.

Successful Russian managers see themselves as working in a collective with community spirit. Authoritarianism is still acceptable if it includes some of the human side of enterprise, paternalism, and egalitarianism. Impersonal group meetings are less valued than one-to-one relations. Productivity per employee is much less than in the West, since there are still many more employees to do the same tasks than in firms in the First World. The law is regarded as having been created to protect those in charge rather than to safeguard personal and intellectual property (Holden, Cooper, & Carr, 1999). There was a decline in personal and political freedom between 1991 and 2004. The authoritarian president Vladimir Putin's administration became increasingly repressive; nonetheless, his approval rating remained at 70% (J. Taylor, 2005).

Spain. In Spain in 1975, there was a rapid shift from a highly controlled authoritarian government, which had ruled for almost 40 years, to a liberal parliamentary democracy. The protection and regulation of business of the Franco regime were replaced by the need for leaders of business to survive in the new, highly competitive environment of aggressive unions, changing political ideologies, and autonomous regional governments. Spain's joining the European Common Market added a new challenge of foreign competition and the opportunity of an enlarged market. In Spain, leaders who were adaptable were seen to be of particular importance (Anzizu & Nuenos, 1984).

Changes in Origins and Opportunities for Women Leaders

The origins of women leaders and their opportunities for leadership can be quite different in different countries. For example, in Egypt, women leaders seem to come from wealthy families, in which females had the requisite educational opportunities and could obtain social prominence and visibility by being active in social work (Khuri, 1981). In Italy, the small percent of business executives who are women is likely to come from families who own their own businesses; nevertheless, a woman headed Italtel, the top telecommunications company in the country. In Britain, the universities are becoming a source of women managers. Between 1965 and 1983, Singapore's national policy of support for training programs for women, flextime, and child care, and its publicized attitudes, greatly increased the percentage of woman leaders from almost zero to 18% in administration and management. The percentage continues to increase. By 1982 in Israel, many more women were being elected to offices of blue-collar unions (Israeli, 1982). Women serve as prime ministers and occupy other important political offices around the world, as already noted in Chapter 31. In parliamentary democracies, they sometimes constitute more than 40% of the members of a national legislature. In the GLOBE data, Bajdo and Dickson (2001) found that the estimated percentage of women in management in a country was correlated with country means of gender egalitarianism and humane management.

Socioeconomic Development, Climate, and Delegative Leadership

Historians have noted the success or failure of societies at the societal level. Thus, for Toynbee (1987), civilization developed and thrived where the climate was neither too severe nor too mild. This was corroborated by Van de Vliert, Huang, and Parker (2001). However, leadership style appears to be affected in the opposite way when it results in leaders' relying for guidance on their subordinates' judgments and decisions. Reliance on subordinates' judgments by 4,022 senior executives in 59 countries correlated nonlinearly .43 and .76 with national development. National development was correlated with Hofstede's (2001) cultural indexes of power distance (PDI) and individualism (IDV). Willingness to delegate authority was greatest in underdeveloped and highly developed countries where the climate was uncomfortably cold or hot, as in Estonia, Iceland, Thailand, and Hong Kong. Moderate willingness to delegate was intermediate in countries with moderate levels of development regardless of their climate, such as Brazil, Lithuania, South Korea, and South Africa. Willingness to delegate was lowest in the least and most developed countries with comfortable climates, such as Guatemala, Zimbabwe, Greece, and Uruguay. An explanation of these results was offered by Van de Vliert and Smith (2002) as follows: (1) Basic human needs make life in uncomfortable climates more demanding. (2) The development of societies in uncomfortable climates make their members more interdependent. (3) Leaders in such societies experience more interdependence between their own goals and their subordinates' goals. (4) Greater development provides more resources to meet the demands of the uncomfortable climate. (5) Underdevelopment in uncomfortable climates results in negative interdependence and more willingness to delegate. (6) Greater development produces positive independence and more willingness to delegate in uncomfortable climates.

Cross-Cultural Differences in Planning, Control, and Accounting

Horovitz (1980) noted the systematic cultural differences in planning and control among Great Britain, France, and Germany, with British managers doing a better job than the Germans. Hofstede (2001) suggested that personal rather than impersonal planning and control are higher with more power distance (PDI). Cultures and organizations higher in uncertainty avoidance (UAI) want more short-term feedback. Although it was expected that more information and detail in planning and control was desired where UAI was high, Hofstede cited the research of Zaheer and Zaheer (1997) that found the opposite to be true. They examined the number of conversations in an electronic network originated by currency traders from more than 3,000 banks in 23 countries. Information was less likely to be sought by the traders in high-UAI countries. They preferred to rely on set procedures.

Hofstede (2001) regarded accounting systems as culture-based rituals with underlying values. For in-stance, in Germany and France, accounting is theoretically based on general economic principles; in the United States, accounting is more a matter of traditions seen as established facts. In Germany, annual reports to shareholders offering valuations are the same as those provided to tax authorities. In Holland, Britain, and America, where highly profitable corporations can avoid or defer taxes, they are quite different. In high-PDI countries, accounting is used more often to justify the decisions of those at the top in status and power. In high-UAI countries, accounting systems contain more detailed rules; in low-PDI countries, more decisions are left to the discretion of the organization. The focus on achievement of purely financial targets is higher in masculine (MAS) countries such as the United States and Germany than in feminine countries such as the Netherlands and Sweden. In the West, the managerial or administrative decision itself is much more discrete and separable from the implementation that is to follow. In Japan, the making of the decision is seen as the beginning of a search for the best way to implement it. In the West, a decision is ordinarily identified with an individual; in Japan, it is more often a collective action (P. B. Smith, 1984a). More will be said about this difference later in the chapter.

Traditionalism versus Modernity

The strength of traditionalism in Pakistan, the strength of modernism in Sweden, and the mix of the two in Japan are well known. Traditionalism emphasizes the family, class, revealed truths, reverence for the past, and an ascribed status hierarchy in which everyone has a rightful place. Modernism stresses merit, rationality, and progress (Inkeles, 1966). Traditionalism takes different forms in Moslem, Hindu, and Buddhist societies. Traditional Muslim Arabs turn the clock back to conform to its medieval culture and the seventh-century Koran, to be learned by heart in the *madrasa*—often the only available education. Modernity is a threat. Traditional Hindu Indians integrate spiritualism and a sense of detachment into their everyday life, but this does not preclude modern education and modern development. In the World Value Survey of 43 countries, Inglehart (1997) found a cultural factor of secular rationality versus traditional authority. The traditional leader is likely to be the oldest—usually male—head of the family. The status of women is relatively low. Corruption may be a way of life and an accepted means of supplementing a bureaucrat's income (Davis, Ming, & Brosnan, 1986). As the members of a society receive more modern education, the society shifts toward modern attitudes. At a certain point, the most educated may revert to a semitraditional point of view and lead a revival of traditionalism, such as has been seen in Iran and elsewhere in the Islamic world.

In traditional societies, such as in rural Indonesia, time is preindustrial and agricultural in orientation. There is no sense of urgency or time pressure. Life is paced naturally; punctuality and long-range planning are unimportant (Davis, Ming, & Brosnan, 1986). There is a multiple instead of a single time frame (E. T. Hall, 1976). In a multiple time frame, the explicit and implicit times to meet may be different, making coordination and decentralization more difficult (Ronen, 1986). Traditional societies are more responsive to authoritative leadership. A modernist leader like Kemal Atatürk in a traditional society like the former Osmanli Turkey often had to resort to autocratic and coercive methods to promote change. Such a response to authority could be the cause of delay in modernization. Moreux (1971) observed that progress in a traditional semirural French Canadian community was held back by its one wealthy, charismatic leader. Valuing modernity rather than tradition is likely to be accompanied by a reduction in the sense of obligations to family and friends. More traditional French Canadian managers are likely to choose family over business obligations when they are in conflict, whereas the less traditional English Canadians do the reverse (Auclair, 1968). Differential effects on successful leadership are likely to follow. Strong traditionalists are unlikely to be willing or able to lead their followers toward modernity but will be more influential when attempting to turn back the clock.

Within societies that were changing from traditionalism to modernity, systematic differences among students and managers could be observed. Along with the traditionalism of 138 Botswanan students, Ulin (1976) measured their elitism, prejudice, anomie, and authoritarianism. Ulin found that the students were ambivalent about traditionalism and authoritarianism but showed weakened social norms, anomie, and elitist convictions; they held strong anti-Asiatic prejudices and weaker antiwhite attitudes, but they were not biased against other tribes of Africans. In Iraq, a survey of 232 managers by Ali (1982) found that traditional tribalisms were more common in smaller organizations, among older managers, and among those with a lower income.

Particularistic versus Universalistic Orientation

A particularistic value orientation implies institutionalized obligations to friends, whereas a universalistic value orientation stresses institutionalized obligations to society and places lesser emphasis on interpersonal considerations (Parsons & Shils, 1959). In the particularistic value orientation, family relations and friendships take precedence over considerations of merit and equity. Particularism with reference to work is likely to be more common in a Latin American country; universalism, in the Anglo-American world. As mentioned before, Zurcher (1968) contrasted Mexican, Mexican American, and American bank officers and employees. As expected, the Mexicans were more particularistic than were the Mexican Americans, and the Mexican Americans were more particularistic than were the Anglo Americans. Beyond this, the bank officers, as a whole, were more universalistic than line employees of the same ethnicity. Such universalism correlated with job satisfaction and plans to continue working in the bank (Zurcher, Meadow, & Zurcher, 1965).

Decisions about Compensation

Schuler and Rogovsky (1998) reported that lack of power distance (PDI) correlated with signs of modernity such as child care at the work site, stock options, and ownership for managers and employees. Evidence of cross-cultural differences in particularism versus universalism among managers was seen in an analysis by Bass, Burger, et al. (1979) of the responses to Exercise Compensation (Bass, 1975b) of 4,255 managers from the same 12 national groups. The respondents had to decide the percentage salary increase to recommend for each of 10 engineers who differed in merit, job context, and personal problems. A universalistic response was seen in managers who awarded salary increases only for merit. Particularism was noted by the respondents' focus on various personal problems rather than on merit as the basis for awarding an increase. Although the 4,255 managers as a whole recommended only 82% as much of an increase for the engineer in the tenth percentile in merit as for the engineer at the fiftieth percentile, the Indian managers gave him 103% of the average-performing engineer's increase. Only in India was the poor performer given more of an increase than the average performer. Ryterband and Thiagarajan (1968) suggested that in India, a salary increase is seen as a stimulator, rather than as a reward for meritorious performance as is the case in developed countries. They reported a similar tendency for Colombians in contrast to U.S. and Scandinavian managers. For each individual manager in the sample of 4,255, the standard deviation in his recommendations for eight engineers in the fiftieth percentile in merit was calculated by Bass, Burger, et al. (1979). The results confirmed the earlier findings by Ryterband and Thiagarajan that in the less developed countries, family, job insecurity, alternative offers, lack of job prestige, and so on justified such differentials. However, managers from more developed countries (except from Japan) tended to justify salary differentials for people doing the same job only by merit differences among the job occupants. In Bass, Burger, et al.'s (1979) analysis of the results for Exercise Compensation, discussed earlier, Japanese managers stood apart from the managers in the other developed countries in that they awarded a hypothetical engineer in the ninetieth percentile in merit only 138% of the average salary increase, in contrast to the 162% favored by managers from elsewhere, and paid more attention to the engineer's personal problems. However, when Howard, Shudo, and Umeshima (1983) compared the surveyed attitudes and values of Japanese and American managers, they inferred that although the Japanese attached greater importance to socially beneficial values in contrast to the Americans' emphasis on individuality and being straightforward, the Japanese had a higher motivation for money and advancement, but these were to be achieved through collective action. Japanese managers may score puzzlingly low in their preference for good relations with their colleagues (Hofstede, 1980) because such collective feeling is a matter of obligation to them, not a personal preference (Atsumi, 1979).

Japan differed from the West in that salary increases did not accompany merit promotions. Westerners have difficulty appreciating such "empty promotions" (Yokochi, 1989a). Consistent with these conclusions, Beatty,

McCune, and Beatty (1988) delineated the policies that differentiated 41 Japanese from 63 U.S. managers. Again, U.S. managers emphasized job performance while the Japanese focused on other elements in deciding on pay increases. Similar to Bass, Burger, et al.s' (1979) findings, the Japanese managers were much less likely to vary the increases for the different employees than were the American managers. Respect for money differed in Taiwan, Britain, and the United States. Chinese employees in Taiwan endorsed the money ethic the most and Americans viewed money as relatively least in importance. At the same time, Americans were most in agreement that money was good (Tang, Furnham, & Davis, 2003).

Attitudes toward merit and competence were also reflected in the differential decisions of more particularistic Greek and more universalistic U.S. personnel directors and students when rating hypothetical applicants for positions in accounting and finance. Triandis (1963) asked 100 American students, 100 Greek students, 32 American personnel directors, and 20 Greek personnel directors to rate 32 candidates who differed systematically in competence, age, sex, race, religion, sociability, and wealth. For the American personnel directors, 54% of the variance in the ratings of the candidates was accounted for by whether the candidates were described as highly competent or barely competent. But such competence accounted for only 24.8% of the ratings of the Greek personnel directors. Competence was even more important to the American students, whereas sociability was particularly important to the Greek students.

Idealism versus Pragmatism

Pragmatists look for what will work; idealists search for the truth. Pragmatists are opportunistic (England, 1967a). Idealism is greatest and the pragmatic orientation is rare among theology students, regardless of their cultural background (England, 1970). *Webster's Third International Dictionary* of 1933 included "active and skilled in business" in the definition of "pragmatic." Managers from different countries are more like one another in pragmatism than like compatriots who are not managers (England, 1970). Nonetheless, national differences in judging what is right, good, and important to managers showed up strongly in England, Dhingra, and Agarwal's (1974) survey of more than 2,600 managers in five countries. The primary orientation of 66% of the Japanese, 61% of the Koreans, and 58% of Americans was pragmatic. But it was pragmatic for only 40% of the Australians and 34% of the Indians. Moralism (idealism) was the primary value orientation only for 11% of the Koreans and 12% of the Japanese. However, it was much higher among the Australians (40%) and the Indians (44%).

Variations across countries in pragmatism as opposed to idealism were seen in a multinational survey of IBM personnel completed by Hofstede (1978). Factor scores varied greatly in national norms for personal acquisitiveness in contrast to social concerns. Japanese personnel were most acquisitive, and Scandinavians were most socially concerned. The factor scores were as follows: Japan, 95; Germany, 73; Italy, 70; Britain, 66; United States, 62; Latin America, 61; Belgium 54; India, 50; France, 43; Spain and Portugal, 37; the Netherlands, 14; Scandinavia, 10. (The factor scores for 50 nations can be found in Hofstede, 2001.)

The relatively greater extent of pragmatism among Japanese managers underlies their task and relations orientation toward employees, based on pursuing leadership that works (Yokochi, 1989b). Similarly, for the 5,122 managers in 12 countries who were administered Exercise Objectives (Bass, 1975a) by Bass, Burger, et al. (1979), there were wide variations among the managers of different nationalities on budgeting decisions in their willingness to spend money to deal with problems of social responsibility. Whereas 71% of Latin American managers chose to clean up a stream the company was polluting, only 46% of Japanese managers did so. In a replication by Palmer, Veiga, and Vora (1981), 82% of the Indian managers chose to clean up the stream, but only 61% of U.S. managers did. And the decision of Indian and U.S. managers to reject such expenditures in Exercise Objectives was higher among those with stronger pragmatic values (economic, political, and theoretical) and lower among those with altruistic or idealistic values (social, aesthetic, and religious).

Relation to Advancement. England and Lee (1974) found pragmatism, as measured by their Personal Values Questionnaire, to be related to the success of managers in the United States, Australia, India, and Japan. The success of the careers of these approximately 2,000 managers was indexed by their income adjusted for their age. In all four countries, successful managers were more likely to hold pragmatic values emphasizing productivity, profitability, and achievement. Among the managers studied by Bass, Burger, et al. (1979), significant relations were found between nationality and the managers' rate of advancement and the tendency to be idealistic or pragmatic about two of the budgeting decisions. For instance, in general, the slower-climbing managers favored the idealistic decision to accept a costly wage agreement to settle a strike immediately, whereas in India, the faster-climbing managers did so more frequently than did the slower-rising managers. It may be that in India, idealism is more favored for leadership than is pragmatism. In a study of student leaders and nonleaders in India, Kumar (1965) found that unlike the usual results for American or European students, Indian student leaders scored high on theoretical and religious interests, while nonleaders scored high on economic and social values. But Govindarajan (1964) observed that Indian high school leaders were more interested in professional and technical jobs than were nonleaders. They more frequently mentioned salary, prestige, and status as reasons for choosing a job.

Individualism versus Collectivism

Based on a review of the literature, Triandis (1995) pointed to four ways in which individualism differs from collectivism: (1) Conceptions of the self are different. For the individualist, the self is independent of groups; for collectivists the self is connected to others in various in-groups. (2) Goals differ. Personal goals have priority for the individualist and self-interest overrides collective interests; for the collectivist, personal goals are subordinated to collective goals. (3) Acceptance of prevailing attitudes and norms differ. For individualists, their own beliefs, values and attitudes are more important to their behavior than the prevailing social norms, beliefs, values, and attitudes that drive the collectivists. (4) Orientation toward tasks and relationships differ. Individualists are oriented toward task accomplishment, sometimes at the expense of relationships; collectivists emphasize harmonious relationships, sometimes at the expense of task accomplishment. Additionally, individualists draw a boundary between themselves and others; collectivists distinguish between those who are personally related to them and those who are not. Individualists are more comfortable moving into and out of groups depending on needs and objectives; collectivists are more attached to fewer, more stable, and more closely knit groups. According to Schaubroeck and Lam (2002), in individualist cultures advancement in a unit is related to similarity of personality with that of one's peers. On the other hand, in collectivist cultures, advancement is related to the similarity of the personality of the subordinate to that of the unit supervisor. Earlier, Triandis (1993) had suggested that compared to the individualist, the collectivist (1) bases success on help received rather than own ability; (2) attributes failure to lack of effort rather than difficulties or bad luck; (3) interprets the self in terms of the in-group rather than traits; (4) attaches more importance to group than individual goals; (5) favors interdependence rather than independence; (6) values security, obedience, duty, and intimate relations rather than pleasure, achievement, competition, autonomy, and freedom; and (7) has a few important in-groups in which harmony is valued and social behavior is different from that in many less important out-groups.

Other Consequences. When the Schwartz Value Survey (SVS) was administered to participants in 20 countries, Schwarz (1992) found that individualism-collectivism was a higher-order factor. Individualism was composed of the primary factors of (1) power, (2) achievement, (3) hedonism, (4) stimulation, and (5) self-direction. Collectivism, as opposed to individualism, was composed of the factors of (1) benevolence, (2) tradition, and (3) conformity. Individualists were more open to change and would follow their own emotional and intellectual interests. Collectivists are motivated to maintain the status quo and the stability of personal relationships. People in individualistic societies find meaning in life through their uniqueness; people in collectivistic societies find meaning in belonging to their society and identifying with its goals (Schwartz, 1999). Ralston, Holt, Terpstra, et al. (1995) found that mean individualism scores were highest on the SVS for 166 U.S. managers, next highest for 156 Russian managers, next to lowest for 130 Japanese, and lowest or most collective for 152 Mainland Chinese managers. The Americans were highest and the Chinese lowest on openness to change, with the Russians and Japanese in between. Schwartz and Sagie

(2000) found in 47 countries that democracy and socioeconomic development enhanced independent thinking and general concern for others, not just close friends and family members. Conformity, tradition, and security became less important. On the other hand, in collectivist societies, more favoritism was observed in evaluations of in-group members and more acceptance of team reward (Kirkman & Shapiro, 2000). In the GLOBE data for individualist countries, outstanding leaders were autonomous, independent, and unique, but these same traits were contraindicated for outstanding leaders in collectivist countries (Den Hartog, House, Hanges, et al., 1999). In 10 countries, Jackson (2001) found systematic differences in ethical judgments, attitudes, and subsequent decisions between individualist and collective countries. In the same way, the local firms of collectivist Asia were more likely to share the burden than to downsize in dealing with a downturn in the economy in 1997 to 1998. The more individualistic foreign multinational firms with subsidiaries in the same area of Asia were more likely to downsize (Wyatt, 1999).

In her seminal study of 13 primitive societies, Mead (1939) contrasted those societies that were cooperative or collective with those that were individualistic or competitive. In cooperative societies, one is more concerned with one's relations with others, and the achievement of the team and one's group is more important than one's personal achievement. In individualistic societies, self-interest dominates. Earley (1993) conducted an experiment using 60 Chinese, 45 Israeli, and 60 American managers. The more individualistic managers performed better if they thought they were working alone. The more collectivistic managers did better if they thought they were working in their own in-group of nationals than by themselves or in a foreign out-group.

Individualism was correlated with compensation for individual performance in the 24 countries studied by Schuler and Rogovsky (1998). In China, collectivism made it possible to maintain the system of regular meetings of workers to critique state-owned company performance. In a quantitative survey of 46 U.S., 203 Mexican, and 503 Taiwan Chinese employees working in the same electronics manufacturing plants in Taiwan and on the U.S.-Mexican border, Dorfman and Howell (1988) found, as expected, that the Mexican and Taiwanese employees were more collectivistic in their beliefs than were the U.S. employees. Paşa, Kabasakal, and Bodur (2001) ascertained in surveys of Turkish managers that collectivism was dominant in organizational norms and practices. The same was true for ideal and observed leadership. Team leadership in Turkey satisfied the need for belonging in collectivistic Turkey (Paşa, Kabasakal, & Bodur, 2001).

An analysis of GLOBE data from 24 countries involving 5,185 middle managers found that the mean level of individualism in a nation or region predicted internal locus of control, which in turn correlated with sense of well-being, job satisfaction, and absence of strain. But individualism failed to predict well-being (Spector, Cooper, Sanchez, et al., 2001). When Smith, Peterson, and Wang (1996) asked 78 managers from the United States, 88 from Britain, and 132 from China how they would deal with nine risky events such as changing work procedures, choosing new subordinates, and improving communications with senior executives, the U.S. and British managers were more likely than the Chinese managers to rely on their own experience. The Chinese preferred to rely on rules, procedures, and their superiors.

Turkish and Dutch high school students living in the Netherlands considered the same scenario of an altercation between a Turkish boy and a Dutch boy. The Turks, from a collectivist culture, attributed the fight to a provocation by the Dutch boy. The Dutch, from an individualist culture, were more willing to blame the Dutch boy. The Turks, but not the Dutch, were willing to engage in in-group favoritism (Schruijer & Lemmers, 1996).

Horizontal versus Vertical Relations. Triandis (1995) suggested that the social relations in individualist and collectivist cultures may be horizontal or vertical. In *individualist-horizontal* cultures, self-reliance is prized but status remains unimportant. In *individualist-vertical* societies, individuals compete for high status. In *collectivist-horizontal* societies, emphasis is on common goals, connectiveness, interdependence, and similarity to others in the in-group. Authority is not readily accepted. In *collectivist-vertical* societies, there is a willingness to sacrifice for the good of the in-group. The in-group is supported in competition with out-groups. Tradition and authority are respected. Social relations in the United States are more vertically oriented; in Denmark, they are more horizontally oriented. Although both countries are individualistic, this may explain the greater valuation in America than in Denmark of achievement and the display of success (Nelson & Shavitt, 2002).

Individualism in the United States. Among 50 countries, the United States ranked the highest in individualism, according to Hofstede's (1980, 2002) surveys. Hofstede (1993) further noted that North American theories emphasized market processes and managers more than workers. The "take charge, individual initiative" of U.S. managers contrasts with the more collegial approaches preferred elsewhere (Bennett, 1986). The participation of individual students is prized in the North American classroom but not as much in classrooms elsewhere. Among the IBM employees and supervisors in 50 nations surveyed by Hofstede (1980), those in the United States were most extreme in their individualism, which was seen as a contributor to greatness. Elsewhere, for example among the Chinese, it was not. Individualism was high in the Anglo cluster of countries and lowest in some of the Latin American and Far Eastern countries and Pakistan.

Foreign managers who work in the United States see this difference from their own cultural backgrounds. Repeated apologies for a late report by a Japanese may produce anger in a North American. An Iranian's polite social circumlocutions may produce frustration in a North American. A Latin American's small talk and socializing to enhance relations before getting down to work is seen as time-wasting by a North American. North American managers are likely to want more autonomy than Swiss superiors want to give them.

Collectivism in Japan. The collectivistic, cooperative Japanese downplay their own individual intelligence. To make much of it would be a threat to the group's harmony, equality, and achievement and would meet with criticism. In Japan, one's concern is for members of one's in-group, not for those in temporary groups or out-groups. But the importance of group and collective action in collective societies fails to materialize in the ordinary laboratory studies in which unacquainted U.S. students are temporarily brought together. In such studies, loyalty to the team and acceptance of its influence will not necessarily be seen because the team may not be a real in-group for the participants. Nevertheless, Klauss and Bass

(1974) found the greatest conformity in such temporary groups of Japanese managers compared to 12 other nationalities. Frager (1970) did likewise in studying conformity and anticonformity in Japan with students as subjects.

Collectivism in Japan is reflected in the structure of corporations. Individual stock ownership is small and of little consequence, and the corporation's board of directors is often identical with its management. What is stressed are cooperation, consensus, and working for the goals of the majority of company members and optimizing benefits for all. Promotion is from inside. The organization is expected to defend its employees' interests. Loyalty to the firm and a sense of duty are paramount. Collectivism is expressed in Japanese, Chinese, and Korean family-owned companies as loyalty to one's family. In addition to being born or marrying into the family, future company leaders may be legally adopted as sons and heirs (Abegglen, 1984).

Quality Control Circles. Collectivism in Japan goes a long way toward explaining the greater success in Japan of an American idea, the quality control circle. According to a 1983 survey by the Union of Japanese Scientists and Engineers, such small-group activities were in effect in more than 80% of Japanese companies with more than 1,000 employees and in 50% of companies with 100 to 1,000 employees. Attendance was 90% (Ishikawa, 1985). In turn, the Japanese attention to quality was dramatized by Gavin (1983), who compared nine U.S. and seven Japanese manufacturers of room air conditioners. The technology, equipment, and product were identical. During the period studied, the U.S. firms averaged 6.3 defects per 100 units on the assembly line and the Japanese firms averaged .95 defects. The U.S. firms averaged 10.5 service calls the first year per 100 units, whereas Japanese firms averaged 0.6. The cost of failures for the U.S. firms was 4.0% of sales, but 1.3% for the Japanese firms. At the same time, the Japanese firms' output was higher. Productivity in the U.S. firms averaged 1.3 units per labor hour, compared to the Japanese average of 1.8 units per labor hour. Comparisons of the printed circuit board industry in the two countries unearthed similar results. The error rate in American firms averaged 5%, but in the Japanese firms, it averaged .05%. The error rates were lower in the Japanese firms, even though the Japanese produced more complex boards that are ordinarily more prone to errors. The Japanese also dealt with much more variety in the product. The yield was 70% in the United States but 92% in Japan. The U.S. firms produced approximately 1,200 styles, whereas the Japanese firms produced approximately 17,000 styles. At that time, the refinement of the printed circuits in the United States was 15-millimeter spacing compared to Japan, where it was 4-millimeter spacing. However, in many ways, by 2000, the United States had caught up with and passed Japan in quality and quantity of productivity.

Antipathy to Individualism. Collectivism explains the antipathy of Japanese managers toward individualistic behavior. "Scapegoating" is avoided by collective responsibility, even though ultimate responsibility rests with the highest-ranking overseer of a project or enterprise. Criticism of performance is for the betterment of the organization and is seen to be directed toward the task or project for which the group has accepted responsibility, although the leader remains ultimately responsible (Yokochi, 1989b). Even the introduction of a new idea that does not emanate from one's group may be seen as selfish or inconsiderate. Innovators may resign because their successful, accepted ideas were embarrassing and disruptive (Hornstein, 1986). In contrast to the results for Britain and the Netherlands, cooperativeness is more likely to be rewarded with advancement in Japan, according to Rosenstein's (1985) analysis of the results of the performance of several thousand managers on selected exercises that were correlated with their rates of advancement.

Role Concepts. Organizational role concepts are different in Japan than in the West. The Japanese operate their large organizations with a lack of specificity about the nature of each member's job and area of authority and responsibility. According to a 1960 survey, one-quarter of the larger Japanese firms had no organizational chart, and only one-third had rules delineating the authority for the chief of the general affairs division or for the chief of the accounting division (Keizal Doyukai, 1960). When Japanese were asked what their job was, they were likely to reply that they were members of a particular company instead of saying what they did (Tsutomu, 1964). Associated with this lack of specificity was a lack of career specialization (Mannari & Abegglen, 1963). The ambiguous organization worked effectively because of the group orientation of its members, the members' willingness to work organically with one another, and their taking into account not only a particular role requirement but who was filling it. The group orientation was accompanied by strong peer pressure (Abegglen, 1958). Hesseling and Kormen (1969) reported that during a decision-making simulation, the Japanese managers were extremely critical of their peers compared to the Dutch managers. In this situation, the Japanese managers appeared to combine behaviors that Westerners would consider to be incompatible.

Commitment, Involvement, Loyalty, and Collectivism. Collectivistic values strengthen commitment, involvement, and loyalty. Collectivism is high in Mexico, as in many other Latin American countries, and lowest in the United States on Hofstede's index. Although, after hearing bad news about an investment, 168 Mexicans and 153 Americans both escalated their commitment to the investment, the Mexicans were much more inclined to do so (Greer & Stevens, 2001).

The lifetime employment assignments in Japan were well known. However, what may be less well known is that, as Abegglen (1958) noted, the employer was generally more obligated than was the employee. Complicating the issue of lifetime employment were the two levels of discourse in Japan. *Tatemae* is the polite, open communication; *honne* is when the communication expresses true feelings about the matter. Lifetime employment was expected at the time of employment. Employees continually express, as required, the sense of lifetime commitment to their organization, which is *tatemae*, and only reveal their true feelings, *honne*, on the day before they leave to take a job with another firm (Yokochi, 1989b). According to Marsh and Mannari (1971), quitting rates and piracy of managers indicated that there is actually considerable movement from one firm to another among Japanese employees. For example, during one decade, one-fourth of the Japanese manufacturing employees left their place of employment annually, and two-thirds of those did so voluntarily. Despite these facts, both Japanese managers and workers tended to believe and act as if they had permanent employment. Organizational loyalty was high. Anyone who was not loyal would be regarded

as a person of lesser moral principles and deserving of punishment (Yokochi, 1989b). Promotions took place at regular intervals, but an "up-or-out" policy actually resulted in either continued promotion upward or early retirement (Kezai Doyukal, 1960). Many exceptions to lifetime arrangements could be found even in well-known larger Japanese firms (Pucik, 1981). In an analysis of the personnel records of the Kikkoman Shoyu Company over 60 years beginning in 1918, Lawrence (1984) found considerable variation in the provision for lifetime employment, compensation based on seniority, and ideological identification with the firm as one's family. The practices and beliefs were transitory, rather than deeply fixed, and depended much on economic effects, especially the effects of World War II. The continuing recession in Japan in the 1990s led to a decline in lifetime arrangements in many firms. Although many of the practices and beliefs in lifetime commitments remain true for the largest and wealthiest Japanese firms and agencies, they have disappeared in smaller firms that are less secure economically, such as job shops that depend on maintaining contract work for the larger organizations.

Nonetheless, in comparison to the responses of successful U.S., Australian, and Indian managers, England and Lee (1974) found that successful Japanese managers were most likely to emphasize loyalty. Among the 12 nationalities studied by Bass, Burger, et al. (1979), the life goal of duty—dedication to ultimate values, ideals, and principles—was among the top three in importance for 46% of the Japanese and 34% of Indian managers at one extreme, and 7% to 9% of the German, Austrian, Scandinavian, and British managers at the other. Japanese workers tended to merge their company and family life. Thus whereas 56% of the Japanese workers in the early 1960s perceived the company to be at least equal in importance to their personal lives, only 24% of the North Americans felt the same way (Whitehill, 1964). According to a questionnaire administered by Whitehill and Takezawa (1968) to approximately 2,000 Japanese workers, 57% thought of their company as "a part of my life at least equal in importance to my personal life," whereas only 22% of U.S. workers responded similarly.

In-group Loyalty

In collective societies, people see themselves as members of in-groups and extended families who protect their interests in exchange for their loyalty. Satisfaction for doing a job well that is recognized by one's peers is sought, in contrast to doing a job well by one's own standards. Job and family life are more closely linked (Hofstede, 1984). Collectivist Hong Kong Chinese students used equality in rewarding in-group members but equity (each according to his or her contribution) in rewarding out-group members. Individualistic American students, consistent with the universalism of reward for merit, used the equity to reward both in-group and out-group members (Leung, 1983).

The values of a culture affect individual expectations of organizational rewards (England & Koike, 1970). In the individualistic United States, workers believe they receive wages in exchange for their performance and seniority. However, in the collectivistic East compensation is considered to be an obligation of the employer, who is responsible for the employees' welfare; thus compensation is less likely to be related to the services performed than to each individual's needs. Under such circumstances it is difficult to introduce performance appraisal (Gellerman, 1967). In the same way, Russian students raised in a traditionally communal and collectivist society feel that needs should be heavily weighted when allocating bonuses. American students were opposed to considering needs (Giacobbe-Miller & Miller, 1995).

Loyalty to close friends takes on special relationships in a number of countries and can markedly affect patterns of influence. Particularism flourishes. For example, in the Philippines, *pakkisama*, which expresses all-encompassing friendship, results in intense loyalty to one's boss and the formation of cliques. In Greece, one speaks of *philotimo*—the strong bond of affection and loyalty between friends—that fosters the formation of cliques. In Nigeria, loyalty to other members of one's tribe transcends objective considerations. In this situation, as in those in which employers feel more obligated to satisfy the needs of their employees than to provide rewards for merit, objective merit ratings, promotions, and salary recommendations based on performance become impossible, as ratings reflect tribal relationships rather than performance.

Ingelhart, Basanez, and Moreno (1998) obtained a multiple correlation of .86 among 43 countries for well-being and survival in countries on the MAS index that valued feminine caring rather than masculine assertiveness and those on the IDV index that valued individualism rather than collectivism.

Personal Values, Motives, and Goals

Although managers tested in many countries tended to score high on achievement and recognition, Page and Baron (1995) reported that Scandinavian managerial assessments were also higher in commercial interests than were those of British and French managers. The British preferred a more structured environment; the French were more motivated by a flexible environment. Nowotny (1964) called attention to the differences between European and U.S. management philosophies at that time. Nowotny attributed the emphasis on stability, convention, quality, and diversity to the European respect for the past. U.S. management's focus on the future resulted in an emphasis on vitality, mobility, informality, abundance, quantity, and organization. But these differences lessened as U.S. management was made less secure by the growth in industrial and economic power of Europe, East Asia, and India and the loss of many whole industries to them, as well as by the dislocations and vast restructurings of U.S. firms. Certainly, U.S. management has become much more concerned about the quality of its products. Many more now work in mature firms that had been growing in the 1960s. In turn, European and Asian firms have adopted many of the practices of U.S. management in their own efforts to internationalize.

By 1998, formerly Communist countries differed considerably in how much they had shifted to market economies. The percent of firms in the private sector in Hungary was 80%, in the Czech Republic, 75%; and in Estonia, 70%; but in Belarus, only 20%. The speed of adaptation of European former Communist countries to market economies was shown by Franke (1999) to depend on their different cultures and modal values. Those with Western Christian cultures adapted more successfully than those with Orthodox Christian and Muslim cultures. For example, GNP between 1993 and 1995 grew in Roman Catholic Poland by 6.25% and Slovakia by 5.89%, while in Orthodox Bulgaria it grew by 1.54%, and in Macedonia it declined by 4.85%. Barrett and Ryterband (1968) found that managers from developing countries such as Colombia and India assigned less importance to meeting competition than did managers from the United States, Britain, and the Netherlands. Managers from developed countries placed greater stress on the objectives of growth and competition. Conversely, the maintenance of satisfactory organizational operations appeared to be more important to those from the developing countries. England, Dhingra, and Agarwal (1974) noted that for North American managers, organizational stability was a means to attain the objective of profitability; for Indian managers, organizational stability was an end in itself. When state-owned companies in formerly socialist Hungary became privatized, foreign-owned, reorganized, and reequipped in the 1990s, supervisors gained more authority but workers appeared to maintain control of how they operated on the job, according to a survey of 385 employees in 13 industrial firms (Whitley & Czaban, 1998).

The Need for Achievement, Affiliation, and Power

Illustrative of the many available studies, McClelland (1961) reported systematic differences among approximately 200 managers from the United States, Italy, Turkey, and Poland in their achievement, affiliation, and power need scores. The rankings for the four countries, from highest to lowest, were as follows: achievement— the United States, Poland, Italy, and Turkey; affiliation— Italy, Turkey, the United States, and Poland; and power—the United States, north Italy, Turkey, south Italy, and Poland. Kanungo and Wright (1983) found that British managers had a greater need for achievement than did French managers. R. G. Hunt and Meindl (1991) showed that achievement was the most important work value for Chinese and Americans. The Chinese expressed stronger collectivistic values and the importance of friendships in the workplace. However, regardless of national differences, a high need for achievement contributed to entrepreneurial drive, as evidenced in analyses in Turkey (Bradburn, 1963), Nigeria (LeVine, 1966), Brazil (Angelini, 1966), Iran (Tedeschi & Kian, 1962), South Africa (Morsbach, 1969), India (Singh, 1969, 1970), and Trinidad (Mischel, 1961). McClelland and Winter (1969)

were also able to demonstrate that a program that increased achievement needs also resulted in increased entrepreneurial activity by Indian and Mexican businessmen. McClelland (1961) analyzed the themes in children's books from 1925 and 1950 for achievement, affiliation, and power needs to show how they predicted subsequent motivation patterns in adult managers and later gross national product in 23 and 32 countries, respectively. National correlations of themes were negatively correlated with power distance (PDI) and uncertainty avoidance (UAI) and positively correlated with individualism (UAI) in the books from 1925 but not the 1950 books (Hofstede, 2001).

Entrepreneurial Motivation. In 1999, one in 12 Americans was attempting to start a business, compared to one in 67 Finns. The average rate of 6.9 start-ups per 100 businesses in the United States, Canada, and Israel was the highest; it was intermediate at a rate of 3.4 per 100 in Britain and Italy, and lowest at an average rate of 1.8 per 100 in Denmark, Finland, France, Germany, and Japan, in countries surveyed by the Global Entrepreneurship Monitor Study. Starting a business was seen as legitimate in some countries but was a cultural anomaly in many others (Campbell, 1999). Of course, many institutional factors made opening a new business possible, such as the availability of bank loans and government regulations. McClelland (1985) succeeded with a training program to stimulate need achievement to increase entrepreneurship in developing countries such as Mexico and India.

Personal Goals

In Exercise Life Goals (Bass, 1975e), 3,082 managers from the 12 nationalities surveyed by Bass, Burger, et al. (1979) rated the importance of 11 life goals to themselves. Although high percentages of managers everywhere ranked self-realization as first, second, or third, the Japanese were highest (74%) and the Indians were lowest (42%) in this tendency. Leadership was ranked first, second, or third by 51% of the Germans and Austrians and least frequently by the Dutch (20%) for whom expertise (50%) was most important. Expertise was lowest for the Italians (22%) than for any of the other 11 groups. Stereotypes to the contrary, the British managers were highest in emphasizing pleasure (29%), followed by the Scandinavians (26%), and the Dutch (20%). The Indians (6%), Germans (4%), and Japanese (2%) were the lowest in this regard.

When nationalities were compared, wealth—amassing a personal fortune—was most important to the Indian and North American managers and least important to the Japanese. Independence was most important to the Germans and Austrians and least important to the Indians. Prestige was most important to the Latin Americans and least important to the Japanese, for whom duty was most important. Service was most important to the Scandinavians (31%), French (30%), and Spaniards (29%) and security was most important to the Scandinavians (36%), British (34%), and Italians (32%).

According to a survey of 23 countries, Confucian-principled China, Hong Kong, Taiwan, Japan, and South Korea ranked highest in long-term orientation (LTO); Western countries were more short-term in goals; and in between were the developing non-Western countries of Zimbabwe, the Philippines, Nigeria, and Pakistan (Chinese Culture Connection, 1987). In poorer countries, LTO correlated $-.27$ with power distance (PDI); in wealthier countries, LTO correlated .72 with PDI. In poorer countries, LTO correlated insignificantly with individualism (1DV) compared to a correlation of $-.77$ in wealthier countries. In 15 countries, LTO correlated .49 with the propensity to save (Hofstede, 2001).

Kanungo and Wright (1983) surveyed managers' attitudes in Canada, France, Japan, and Britain to determine the job outcomes the managers sought. The British and French managers were most different. The British sought self-actualization, and the French sought security and good working conditions. The British-French distinctness was seen within Canada in a survey by McCarrey, Gasse, and Moore (1984) of the difference in work values between Anglophone managers on the west coast of Canada and their francophone counterparts in Quebec. The francophone managers attached greater importance to being loving and helpful. They also placed more emphasis on work that allowed them to be creative and imaginative. The anglophones attached more importance to work that provided independence and prestige and allowed them to be clean, neat, and tidy. According to England, Dhingra, and Agarwal's (1974) survey, dignity, prestige, security, and power were far more important to

Indian than to American or Australian managers. Al-Hajjeh (1984) found that Middle Eastern managers placed more emphasis on security than did a comparable sample of Americans.

Smallest-space mapping of the personal goals of managers of various nationalities by Shenkar and Ronen (1987) showed that the meaning of a particular goal may be different in various countries. For instance, attaining higher earnings was seen as both an intrinsic and extrinsic goal in Western countries such as Canada, Britain, West Germany, and France but was a purely extrinsic goal for managers in state industries in China. Shenkar and Ronen attributed this attitude of Chinese managers at that time both to Confucian philosophy and to Maoist admonitions that material incentives are likely to lead to anticollective self-interest, power, and privileges.

Business Objectives. Lodge and Thurow (1999) obtained results for the performance of 114 firms from the United States, European Union, and Japan showing that they were significantly different in their objectives, which affected their performance. Profits were the main objectives in the United States and European Union. They were short-term objectives for the the U.S. firms and long-term for the E.U. companies. The Japanese placed more importance on growth. Forced to have short-term objectives in order to satisfy investors, U.S. firms adopt a strategy of substituting capital for labor resulting in higher wages and greater efficiencies (Katz, Werne & Brouthers, 1999).

Personal Values

For 12 countries, Bigoness and Blakely (1989) extracted four factors from the rankings by managers of the importance of 18 Rokeach (1973) instrumental values. The four factors were: (1) supportiveness (cheerful, forgiving, helpful, and loving), (2) dependability (clean, obedient, polite, responsible, and self-controlled), (3) strength (broad-minded, capable, and courageous), and (4) intelligence (imaginative, independent, and intellectual). Overall there was considerable agreement among the managers from the 12 countries about the relative order of value of the factors: (1) strength, (2) intelligence, (3) dependability, and (4) supportiveness. Nevertheless, there remained sizable mean divergences of opinion according to nationality. Thus, consistent with Bass, Burger, et al.'s (1979) observation about the Japanese strong concern for peers and the French lack of such concern, the Japanese managers were the highest of 12 nationalities in their relative ranking of the importance of supportiveness; the lowest were the French. Again, the Japanese tied the Brazilians in valuing dependability most highly; the Swedes were least concerned with the value of such dependability. Strength was of prime importance to the Brazilians and of least consequence to the U.S. managers. The Brazilians and Italians valued intelligence most highly; the Danes and Australians attached least value to intelligence. The Britons, Germans, Dutch, and Norwegians were at neither extreme on any of the four factors.

Beliefs. India is a country where many strongly held beliefs are counterproductive. Sinha, Singh, and Gupta (undated) obtained six factors from 20 items in a survey of 522 middle managers from eight organizations located in the widely separated Indian cities of Jamshedpur, Patna, Ahmedabad, and Harirar. The factors and the highest loadings on the factors were (1) selfishness—people try to get ahead at the expense of others (.68); (2) status and power—people in the society are highly conscious of their status and position (.73); (3) emotionality—people react emotionally rather than rationally to societal problems (−.61); (4) familism—people value family more than work requirements (.62); (5) traditionalism—people have high respect for their tradition (.68); and (6) sociability—people seek and get help on social occasions (.74).

Business Ethics. In contrast to Europe and Japan, Vogel (1992) suggested that business ethics were unusually visible in the United States because of its distinctive institutional, legal, social, and cultural context and its individualistic approach to business ethics compared to other capitalist societies.

Americans are more concerned with the ethics of business because they have higher expectations of business conduct. Not only is more business conduct considered unethical but unethical behavior is more likely to be exposed, punished, and thereby become a "scandal" in America than in other capitalist nations. (Vogel, p. 36)

But according to an index of national business ethics, the Transparency International Corruption Index (Transparency International, 1998), in 26 wealthier countries, the index ranged from highest in Denmark (10.0) to lowest in South Korea (4.3). The Index score for the United States was 7.5. It was higher than 7.5 in the Nordic countries, Germany, Switzerland, New Zealand, Canada, Britain, Ireland, Singapore, and Hong Kong. Generally it was lower in poorer countries, ranging from highest in Chile (6.8) to lowest in Nigeria (1.9). For the 26 wealthier countries, the Transparency Index score correlated −.78 with uncertainty avoidance, −.55 with power distance, .47 with individualism-collectivism, and −.33 with masculinity-femininity.

Although the norms of ethical behavior vary in different capitalist societies, globalization is slowly forcing a convergence. For instance, 194 Russian managers and owners in private enterprises showed no difference in advocacy of Machiavellianism than American norms. But they did feel that Russian organizations fostered structurally opportunistic climates (Sommer, Welsh, & Gubman, 2000). In a 28-nation interview survey by Parboteeah and Cullen (2002) of the effects of national social institutions, a random and quota sample of 3,450 managers was asked the extent to which seven unethical behaviors could be justified. The behaviors were subsequently found to form a single factor. The highest loading, .72, was on "buy something you knew was stolen." The next highest loading, .70, was on "cheat on tax if you have the chance." Other unethical behaviors included "lying in your own interest" and "accepting bribes in the course of your duty" with loadings of .67 and .64 respectively. Hierarchical linear modeling (Bryk & Raudenbush, 1989) made it possible to intercorrelate variables across two levels of analysis, individual and national. Regression analyses of individual and national variables showed that in countries with greater social inequality, managers were more likely to consider that unethical behavior was more acceptable. Inequity could be reduced by breaking social norms, such as behaving unethically. In nations higher in religiosity and access to higher education, managers could more readily justify unethical behavior. From the same data, Cullen, Parboteeah, and Hoegl (2004) found that the willingness to justify ethically suspect behaviors in the 28 countries was related to cultural dimensions proposed by Tropenaars and Hampden-Turner (1998) of individualism, achievement, pecuniary materialism, and equality of opportunity. Contrary to expectations, hierarchical linear modeling indicated that national characteristics of individualism and achievement negatively predicted justifying unethical behaviors but equality of opportunity and pecuniary materialism were positive predictors of justifying unethical behavior.

Masculinity-Femininity (MAS)

MAS was Hofstede's (1980) Index of country norms about men and women's job preferences and the dominant role patterns of masculine assertiveness and femininine nurturing. Japan, Austria, Venezuela, Italy, and Switzerland ranked highest in masculinity (MAS) and Sweden, Norway, Netherlands, Denmark, and Costa Rica ranked highest in femininity. Women in the same occupations scored higher in preference for *social* goals like friendly atmosphere and cooperation in the workplace; men scored higher in preference for *ego* goals such as recognition and earnings. MAS correlated .84 with a factor of assertiveness-service, one of two factors Hofstede (2001) extracted from Exercise Life Goals completed by 3,082 managers from 12 countries (Bass & Burger, 1979). Assertiveness was high when managers ranked leadership, independence, and self-realization highest and service and duty lowest. Schein, Mueller, and Lituchy (1996) found that in both China and Japan, 361 male and 228 female students agreed that successful middle managers generally possess characteristic, attitudes, and temperaments ascribed to men rather than women.

Hostile and Benevolent Sexism. Facets of MAS are *hostile sexism*, the dislike of women who are seen as usurping men's roles, and *benevolent sexism*, an ideology of chivalry, protection, and affection for women who embrace conventional roles. Glick and Fiske (2001) used the Ambivalent Sexism Inventory to query more than 15,000 respondents in 19 countries. The highest six countries in hostile sexism, in order, were Cuba, South Africa, Nigeria, Botswana, Colombia, and Chile. In between were South Korea, Turkey, Portugal, Italy, Brazil, Spain, and Belgium. Lowest in hostile sexism were Japan, Germany, the United States, Australia, England, Australia, and the Netherlands. The order is almost the same for benevolent sexism, except that Japan and Germany

moved to the middle and Italy moved into the lowest countries. Hostility toward career women, feminists, and seductresses appeared to be the belief that they were stealing men's power. Patronizing of women who serve men as mothers and wives and in romantic affairs was benevolent sexism. The hostile and benevolent beliefs were likely to influence the interpersonal relations of leaders and followers of both men and women.

Uncertainty Avoidance (Aversion to Risk Taking)

Risk differs in concept from uncertainty. We avoid risks when we have some knowledge of the probabilities of failure, harm, or negative outcomes. We avoid uncertainty when we lack knowledge about the outcomes (Cyert & March, 1963). We fear taking risks; we are anxious about uncertainties. At the country level, if we avoid risk and uncertainty we are, authoritarian, ethnocentric, rigid, dogmatic, superstitious, racist, and intolerant of ambiguities.

Risk Taking. Bass, Burger, et al. (1979) noted which of 12 nationalities were above or below the median on 18 indicators of the tendency to take risks and the preference for doing so when managers were engaged in various training exercises. U.S. managers were least averse to taking risks; the Austrians and Germans were most cautious. Cummings, Harnett, and Stevens (1971) also ordered nationalities according to their preferences for avoiding financial or physical risks. Again, managers in the United States had the least aversion to taking risks. Managers in Greece, Scandinavia, and central Europe were the most risk-averse, while Spanish managers were in between.

Hornstein (1986) illustrated the propensity of North American managers to take risks in contrast to the Japanese managers' aversion to doing so. Only 15% of the American managers but 40% of the Japanese managers said they had never acted courageously during their careers. Ronen (1986) also concluded that North American managers are much more aggressive risk takers than are their counterparts elsewhere, such as in Indonesia, Burma, Turkey, and Egypt. Americans may misinterpret when Japanese fall silent in negotiations about a proposal with Americans. The Americans may perceive that the Japanese are not interested in the proposal when in fact they may just be thinking about it (Anonymous, 1989).

Uncertainty Avoidance (UAI). A somewhat different picture emerged in Hofstede's (1980, 2001) 50-nation survey of the avoidance of personal uncertainty and discomfort in unpredictable and unclear situations. Greece, Portugal, and the Latin American countries of Panama, Peru, El Salvador, Uruguay, and Guatemala were particularly high in this tendency. Most tolerant of uncertainty were the Southeast Asian countries of Singapore, Hong Kong, and Malaysia; the Scandinavian countries of Sweden and Denmark; and the Commonwealth-linked Jamaica, Great Britain, and Ireland. In the GLOBE project, attributions of outstanding leaders varied with societal uncertainty avoidance. Offerman and Hellman (1997) noted that in countries high in avoiding uncertainty, managers were more controlling, less willing to delegate, and less easy to approach. Also, they were less innovative. Champions were expected to promote innovation without violating organizational rules and norms (Shane, 1993, 1995). In countries tolerant of uncertainty, champions of innovation were expected to break rules to deal with organizational inertia (Shane, Venkataraman, & MacMillan, 1995).

Uncertainty Avoidance Index (UAI) scores for 26 countries correlated with dissatisfaction with family, work, health, and happiness and lack of well-being (Inglehart, Basañnez, & Moreno, 1998). Ethical decision making was found to be different in countries high and low in uncertainty avoidance (Jackson, 2001). In a 1990–1993 World Values Survey (1994), a country's UAI was negatively correlated with normative willingness to trust others. In Sweden, low in UAI, 66% said people can be trusted; only 7% in Brazil saw people as worthy of trust (Hofstede, 2001). In 30 countries, UAI correlated negatively with a factor of independence from existing rules (Shane, Venataraman, & MacMillan, 1995). Low-UAI countries revealed higher rates of innovation (Shane, 1993). Hofstede (2001) suggested that countries high in UAI are inclined to reduce uncertainty with rules, rituals, laws, faith, and fatalism. Furthermore, the ability to cope with uncertainty is an important source of power in countries high in UAI.

Other Personal Traits

Numerous other cross-cluster and cross-country similarities and differences in norms of personality have been reported. Consistent with the generally obtained differences between the East Asian and Anglo clusters, Gill (1983), using Cattell's Sixteen Personal Factors Questionnaire, found that Singapore Chinese managers described themselves as significantly more reserved, serious, conservative, assertive, expedient, trusting, group-dependent, and relaxed than did comparable North American or British managers. They also saw themselves as significantly less imaginative and tough-minded. Effective managers in Thailand, China, and the United States all scored low in neuroticism and high in extroversion on the "Big Five" personality inventory, but only in the United States did effective managers score high in open-mindedness (Silverthorne, 2001). Scores on the Myers-Briggs Type Indicator for 206 Latin American and 875 U.S. managers were in line with expected Anglo–Latin American differences, according to Osborn and Osborn (1986), who reported that 78% of the Latin Americans described themselves as sensory-intuitives, while only 52% of the North Americans did so. The Latin Americans also saw themselves as more judgmental (87%) than did the North Americans (70%) and less perceptive. In addition, compared to North Americans the Latin Americans tended to express their desire for inclusion with and control of others and affection from them significantly more on Schutz's FIRO-B. Management controlling skills in high–power distance (PD) countries like Malaysia and managerial interactive skills in lower-PD countries like the United States supported the positive relationship between self-awareness and managerial effectiveness (Shipper, Rotondo, & Hoffman, 2003). In their comparison of the attitudes of executives from five countries or clusters, Cummings, Harnett, and Stevens (1971) found Spanish managers to be fatalistic, somewhat suspicious, and conciliatory. North Americans were at the other extreme: self-determined, trusting, and belligerent. Scandinavians and central European executives were in between in these attitudes. Greek managers were highly suspicious and conciliatory but more like North Americans in believing they were the masters of their own fate.

In a study of 329 managers and technicians from 22 countries in South and Central America, Africa, Asia, and the Middle East, Gruenfeld and MacEachron (1975) found that managers from the less developed countries were more field-dependent than were managers from the developed countries. Gruenfeld and MacEachron concluded that since they were more field-dependent, those from the developing countries were likely to be more conforming to authority and more personal and attentive rather than impersonal. According to Yokochi (1989b), Japanese managers were unusual in the extent to which they repeatedly express appreciation for long-past services to indicate that they remain indebted for favors rendered to them. They also repeat apologies for their inadequacies. However, these are *tatemae*, not deep-seated feelings (*honne*).

Satisfaction of Needs

Haire, Chiselli, and Porter (1966) surveyed approximately 3,600 managers from 14 countries on how important each of the needs in Maslow's hierarchy was and how much each of the needs was fulfilled. Mozina (1969) used the same questionnaire to survey 500 managers from the former Yugoslavia, as did Clark and McCabe (1970) for more than 1,300 Australian managers and Badawy (undated) for middle managers in Saudi Arabia. In agreement with Bass, Burger, et al.'s (1979) findings, all these studies found that Maslow's (1954) higher-level needs, such as for self-actualization and esteem, were judged important by managers everywhere. But generally, the fulfillment of these higher-level needs was deemed inadequate. The lowest-level basic needs were seen to be fairly well satisfied. The need for security, considered to be important, was relatively highly fulfilled. (No doubt this has been less true in recent years as a consequence of the downsizing of managements and the increase in industrial change.) Again, broad national variations emerged. Managers from the developing countries perceived all the needs to be more important to them than did managers from developed countries and reported a greater sense of nonfulfillment. At the other extreme, managers from the northern European countries tended to place the least importance on all the needs. Consistent with what was concluded in Chapter 8 about the greater job satisfaction of those at higher levels in their organization, the managers' perceptions of the fulfillment of their needs depended everywhere on their hierarchical rank in their organizations. Upper-level managers, especially in Japan before 1990, consistently indicated more fulfillment of all the needs compared to lower-level managers.

Stress and Conflict

Peterson, Smith, Akande, et al. (1995) analyzed data reported by middle managers from 21 countries dealing with perceived role conflict, role ambiguity, and role overload. The mean data for each country were correlated with national scores on power distance (PDI), individualism-collectivity (IDV), uncertainty avoidance (UAI), and masculinity-femininity (MAS). Role stresses varied more by country than individual or organizational variables. Power distance (PDI) was negatively related to role ambiguity and positively related to role overload. Individualism was positively related to role ambiguity and negatively related to role overload. Rogers (1977) found in a U.S.-Canadian comparison that whereas both workload and decision making were equally frequent sources of stress for Canadian managers, decision making alone was the more important source of stress for U.S. managers. But even sharper differences appeared when English and French Canadian managers were analyzed by Auclair (1968). Male French Canadian managers placed a higher value on their role as the head of the family than did English Canadian managers. Consequently, the French-Canadian managers perceived more stress from the conflicting role demands of family and business. In comparison, the English Canadian managers placed relatively less value on their role in the family and experienced less conflict with the role demands of their business organization. Spector, Cooper, and Aguilar-Vafaie (2002), in a survey of 207 Iranian and 120 U.S. managers, found that the Iranians were significantly higher in mental job stresses and physical strains than the Americans. In France, an in-depth interview survey of 30 managers in the Paris area was conducted by COF-REMCA (1978). What seemed particularly salient in the French managers' attitudes and values was the conflict between valuing their own work and their self-actualization as professionals, the lack of warmth and understanding in work relations, insecurity among the older managers, and competitiveness, particularly in large firms.

Indian supervisors may face various kinds of role conflict specific to the Indian scene. Although industrial supervisors were observed to be more production oriented than human relations oriented (Bhatt & Pathak, 1962). Indian workers expected their supervisors to do more in the way of settling personnel problems and grievances, clarifying work difficulties, and improving work methods and conditions. In other respects, as well, supervisors perceived that they were required to perform duties that were not legitimately part of their jobs, such as training new workers on the job, arranging wage agreements, and checking supplies (Sequeira, 1964). Yoga (1964) obtained such results in 11 Indian plants in three types of industries (textiles, food processing, and engineering). Nonetheless, Ivancevich, Schweiger, and Ragan (1986) found that a sample of approximately 300 Indian managers reported little difference from their approximately 175 North American counterparts in their felt global stress, job stress, or somatic symptoms of stress. If anything, the Indian managers felt less daily stress and were less anxious. In fact, it was a comparable sample of over 200 Japanese managers who felt significantly more global stress, more daily stress, more job stress, more somatic symptoms of stress, and more anxiety than did their Indian or North American counterparts.

National Differences in Conflict Resolution. Another source of failure may be due to differences in handling cross-national disagreements. Tinsley (1998) expected that Japanese managers would defer to status in dealing with disagreements, German managers would fall back on regulations and to a lesser extent try to integrate the interests of opposing parties, and American managers would seek personal gain and reaching a compromise that integrated the interests of the disputants. She provided Japanese, German, and American managers with a hypothetical management conflict and asked them to rate the importance to them of various ways to resolve the hypothetical conflict. As expected, compared with the Germans and Americans, the Japanese managers felt that they needed to consult with their higher-status superiors. Compared with the Japanese and the Americans, the German managers preferred that they apply regulations but that, in doing so, it was important for them to integrate the interests of the parties in conflict. The Americans wanted to integrate conflicting interests even more than did the Germans. Tinsley suggested that American managers may become frustrated when trying to reach agreement with Japanese who wish to consult with their superiors and with Germans who argue for a resolution based on applying the rules.

International Problem Solving, Conflict, and Cooperation. Toshiba, Siemens and IBM brought together a total of a hundred Japanese, German and American scientists to an IBM facility in Fishkill, New York, to work together on a project to develop a revolutionary memory chip. And just as I was disturbed when lecturing to 200 Japanese managers who closed their eyes, the German research personnel were shocked at those meetings by the Japanese thinking about the issues by closing their eyes and looking as though they were sleeping. Liking to review ideas with others, the Japanese were pained by having to work alone in small windowless offices in Fishkill instead of the customary large "tank" room accommodating the whole group, where they could more easily consult with one another and discuss both research and personal matters. In Japan, their supervisor's desk was in the same room; the supervisor walked around, looking over their shoulders, and was immediately accessible. The Germans were equally unaccustomed to working in offices with small windows where they could be watched by anyone. Compared to Americans, they are more likely to keep their office doors closed. English was a problem for the Japanese. The Americans complained that the Japanese did not make clear decisions and wanted to revise them constantly. The Americans felt the Germans planned too much. There was suspicion by some personnel that information was being withheld from the group, perhaps because they came from different and competitive firms. By 7 or 8 P.M., the Americans were gone, as were most of the Germans, but half the Japanese were in the hall in unplanned informal discussion. Despite the cross-cultural discomforts and problems, sufficient progress was made and the project continued into a second year (Browning, 1994).

According to Tinsley and Brett (2001), 94 American and 120 Hong Kong Chinese students differed in approaches to a simulated conflict. Compared to the Chinese, the Americans focused more attention on each party's interests and tried to synthesize multiple issues. The Chinese focused more than the Americans on collective interests and authority. They were more likely to consult with higher-ups. The Americans reached more integrative outcomes and resolved more issues. In another simulation study, Brett and Okumura (1998) found that in cross-cultural "buy-sell" negotiations between 30 American and Japanese negotiators, 47 Americans negotiating with each other, and 18 Japanese negotiating with each other, the individualistic Americans espoused self-interest schemata; the hierarchical Japanese pursued power schemata in their tactics. Although Schmidt and Yeh (1992) found that British, Australian, Japanese, and Taiwanese managers shared common influence tactics, they differed in interpretations and perceived importance of the tactics. Deutsch's (1949) theory of cooperation and competition was applied successfully in various countries such as Hong Kong to understanding constructive discussion between employees and management when they had cooperative goals. Empowerment, productive work, and stronger work relations followed (Tjosvold, Hui, & Law, 1995).

Conflicts in the Former Soviet Union. The Soviet manager in state enterprises faced fundamental conflicts in contradictory demands from an inflexible system of production quotas and rewards and punishments for performance. This began to be ameliorated by Gorbachev's efforts to reform the system with glasnost (openness) and perestroika (restructuring), followed by Boris Yeltsin's revolution in 1991 and continued under Putin. Central state planning was replaced by a market economy and privatization of many large state enterprises. Capitalism produced new corruption and conflict to replace the conflicts and defenses that were rooted in Russia's Mongol, Byzantine, tsarist, and Soviet past with an entrenched bureaucracy and an emphasis on secrecy that had long been part of the Russian culture (Pipes, 1974). The Soviet leader-follower relationship was reflected in Lenin's model of close-knit, mutually supportive working relationships with immediate subordinates whose advice might be sought but who were expected to conform to their superiors' dictates (Bass & Farrow, 1977a). Loyalty to and support for one's superiors were exchanged for the protection of workers from the larger outside system (Ryapolov, 1966). Leaders and their immediate subordinates become excessively dependent on each other to buffer the demands of the larger system (Granick, 1960). The need to "beat the system" produced mutual suspicion between superior and subordinate. Both faced cuts in pay to 25% below base salary if their performance was not up to expectations (Anonymous, 1970).

After Russia joined the market economy, managers in the private sector became more externally oriented, attending more to their markets and customers. Managers of state enterprises remained more focused internally on their own operations and production (Shama, 1993). They were were perceived by their employees to continue to have more power than those in the private sector (Banai & Teng, 1996). Public opinion surveys in the 1990s suggested that less than 50% supported a market economy, normative democracy, and building a civil society. They want strong leadership. Private ownership is still seen to be accompanied by greed, stinginess, cruelty, bribery, and extortion (Samsonova, 1998).

Soviet central planning pitted the managers in state enterprises and their immediate subordinates against the arbitrary, distant, demanding central authority. To survive within the system, the managers and subordinates had to back up each other, for they had to engage in unauthorized activities, such as falsifying plans to meet quotas. For example, central planning overestimates of available supplies resulted in shortages of vital parts. The factory that needed the supplies had to hire *tolkhachi*, who lived permanently near the bases of supply, to obtain necessary materials, even shipping them by briefcase if necessary (Ryapolov, 1966). Assembled items were declared ready for shipment and distribution even though parts were missing. If a higher-up in the larger system wanted to "get" the plant director, the success of the director's cover-up depended on his immediate subordinates' loyalty to him.

Conflicts in China. Unlike his Soviet counterpart, who had to conceal productive capacity, hoard resources, sacrifice product quality, or falsify reports to meet inflexible production quotas from central planning, the plant director in the People's Republic of China, prior to the privatization of many enterprises, did not face the same demands from central authority. Rather, more such pressures were likely to arise from the plant's workforce, coupled with much greater flexibility to adjust plans on the basis of experience, even weekly. "Democratic" centralism in China involved massive participation by workers in the management of the enterprises (Richman, 1967). The post-Maoist reforms that moved China into a market economy added to the pressure on private sector managers, who now had to make a profit or be shut down. The pressure has spilled over to the managers of the remaining state enterprises.

National Differences in Competencies and Behavioral Patterns

Various abilities and patterns of behavior associated with leadership have been found to differ across countries. Cross-cultural differences have been observed in social perceptual skills, interpersonal competence, effective intelligence, and efficient work habits. Thus, Britons were found to be more realistic about their own performance than were Southeast Asians; they were more accurate in estimating how correct they had been in answering questions (Wright et al., 1977). When 359 managers from collectivistic Hong Kong and China and individualistic America were subjected to a laboratory and field experiment, results demonstrated that self-focused training improved individualists but not collectivists in self-efficacy and performance. On the other hand, compared to individualists, collectivists profited more in self-efficacy and performance from group-based training (Earley, 1994).

Use of Time. Seven Korean, five Hong Kong Chinese, eight Japanese, and five American CEOs worked alone and in groups for about the same amount of time. The Hong Kong Chinese spent their time in short, fragmented activities, mostly much less than one hour per activity. This was in contrast to the Japanese and Korean CEOs, who concentrated more time in fewer, less fragmented activities, longer meetings, and contact with more employees and made more use of delegation than did their Hong Kong and American counterparts (Doktor, 1990).

Social Perceptions: Empathy, Similarity, Projection. Bass, Alexander, Barrett, and Ryterband (1971) calculated empathy and projection scores for managers from 12 national groupings based on the managers' rankings of their own life goals, as well as those of the other members of their training group. The similarity of their self-rankings was also obtained. With an index of 1.00 implying perfect empathic matching of estimates with actualities and zero implying no matching, the British (.35) and Japanese (.30) were highest in empathic matching and the Latin Americans (.03) were the lowest. The British (.62) and Dutch (.62) were highest in the projection of their own rankings onto others, and the Indians (.31) and Spanish and Portuguese (.34) were lowest. To some extent, the results were attributable to the usual

similarity among the participants' self-rankings. The average similarity of participants in their self-rankings was only .15 in India, with its 16 major language groups and many religions and castes. It was even lower for the United States (.11), with its multiplicity of ethnic, racial, and religious groups, and lowest for Latin America (.05), where data included managers drawn from recent European immigrant groups from many countries, those of old Spanish or Portuguese stock, and mestizos and multiethnics. In general, in Europe, with its greater uniformity of religion, language, and centralized education, the average similarities ranged from .23 for France to .39 for Britain. Japan (.27) was also more homogeneous. Managers everywhere assumed themselves to be more similar to their colleagues than they actually were. The distortion was greatest for U.S. managers and Latin Americans. At the other extreme, the Spanish and Portuguese managers' projections of similarity were closest to their actual similarity.

Self-Appraisals of Interpersonal Behavior. A factor analysis of 60 self-ratings on Exercise Self-Appraisals (Bass, 1975f) of actual and preferred behavior by Bass, Burger, et al. (1979) revealed, for more than 1,000 managers, seven factors that are involved in interpersonal competence: (1) preferred awareness, (2) actual awareness, (3) submissiveness, (4) reliance on others, (5) favoring group decision making, (6) concern for good human relations, and (7) cooperative relationships with peers. With reference to the first factor, which deals with preferences for awareness of the feelings of others, self-understanding, accepting feedback from others, listening to others, and concern for the welfare of subordinates, the Spanish and Portuguese managers were the highest and the Germans and Austrians were the lowest among the 12 national groupings. The Germans and Austrians were also lowest on the second factor of actual awareness. On the third factor, submissiveness, Indian managers were the most concerned about rules and Japanese managers were the least concerned. The Japanese felt the least conflict about the more ambiguous organizational arrangements to which they are accustomed. (Unspoken rules must be understood; otherwise one is regarded as an "untrained person" [Yokochi, 1989b].) As for the fourth factor, reliance on others, the Indian managers saw themselves as most dependent on a higher authority; the

German and Austrian managers saw themselves as the least dependent. The Italian managers saw themselves as being lowest in depending on others in problem solving, and, as expected, the Japanese were highest in this regard, as well as in the preference to imitate others when solving problems. As for the fifth factor, U.S. managers stood out in their preference for group decision making, whereas the Spanish, Portuguese, and Italian managers were lowest. On factor 6, Concern for Human Relations, the Dutch were highest and the Germans were lowest. On factor 7, French managers were the lowest in their reported actual cooperative peer relations and the Dutch were the highest. On other specific ratings, such as the willingness to discuss feelings with others, the French managers again were lowest among the 12 national groupings and the Italian and Japanese managers were the highest.

Self-appraisals that discriminated faster- from slower-climbing managers varied from one country to another. For example, in France, Spain, and Portugal especially, the faster-climbing managers were more concerned than the slower climbers about their dependence on a higher authority.

Cultural Awareness. To understand and effectively relate to others, leaders need to be aware of cultural specificities in acceptable interpersonal relations (Javidan & House, 2001). In eastern European and Middle Eastern countries, where power distance is high, communication is top down. Subordinates expect that their superior knows more than they do and that they will be directed without being consulted. They want and expect guidance. They are less likely to challenge their superiors, and fear disagreeing with them (Adsit, London, Crom, et al., 1997). Where power distance is low, such as in Nordic, Germanic, and Anglo countries, participative leadership is endorsed and subordinates expect to be consulted by their leaders in two-way communications (Dorfman, Hanges, & Brodbeck, 2004).

CEO Task Competence. Hambrick (1989) reported on a 20-country Korn-Ferry survey of 1,508 primarily senior managers and CEOs about CEOs. Fifty-eight percent were CEOs, and 26% of senior managers were their direct reports. They were asked to consider what would be needed by CEOs a decade ahead. While 65% of the

respondents from other countries regarded a finance background as important, only a little over half of the Japanese agreed. But over half of the Japanese felt that an R&D background was important. On the other hand, while over half of the Americans felt that experience in operations or production was important, just a little over 30% of the other nationalities agreed. Only about 20% of Americans called for foreign language training; elsewhere 65% did. Close to 30% of Americans felt that experience outside the headquarters country was needed by the CEO, while close to 75% of all other nationalities agreed about the need for such experience. In characterizing their ideal CEO for the year 2000, the Japanese—in contrast to the other 19 nationalities—placed a greater emphasis on technological and international capabilities than did the respondents from the United States, Western Europe, and Latin America. The respondents from western Europe but not from the United States agreed with the Japanese about the emphasis on international competence. But O'Roark (2001) pointed out the overriding importance of international competence for the Anglo American who is consulting professionally with foreign management.

Other Desired and Actual Competencies. In Bass, Burger, et al.'s (1979) analysis, the Japanese were highest in the desire to be objective rather than intuitive, and their preference for persistence was even more extreme relative to that of other nationalities. Furthermore, they strongly favored being proactive rather than reactive and preferred long-term to short-term views. Moreover, the Japanese managers also saw themselves as very high (in comparison to the results for 11 other nationalities) in actual objectivity, persistence, proactivity, and long-term thinking. On the other hand, the French tended to be most critical of themselves in their self-appraisals of their actual objectivity, persistence, proactivity, and long-term thinking.

In Exercise Communication (Bass, 1975g), Leavitt's one-way/two-way problem is completed. Senders verbally transmit a pattern of six dominoes when two-way communications are permitted. If communications are one way only, receivers must reconstruct the pattern without seeing the original and cannot ask questions. Consistent with their actual and preferred self-appraisals, the objective results of Exercise Communication for 12 nationalities showed the Japanese managers to be highest in the number of correct placements, in both one-way and two-way communications (Bass, Burger, et al., 1979). This finding is consistent with the higher mean scores on intelligence tests reported for the Japanese compared to other nationals (Hathaway, 1984). The faster-climbing Japanese managers, in particular, were able to achieve this degree of accuracy in the fastest time for one-way communications. Close behind them in accuracy with one-way communications were the Germans and the Austrians. Indian managers did the poorest; they were relatively slow and inaccurate. These results may be attributable to the Japanese familiarity with ideographic communication and to the fact that for Indian managers, English, the language of business, is usually their second or third language.

Differences in Leadership Across Cultures

Requisites of Leadership

House, Wright, and Aditya (1997) advanced the *cultural congruence* hypothesis. For effective leadership, there must be a match between the leader's values and behavior and the culture's values. Innovative leaders can depart somewhat but not too much from what is required of them by the culture. In an individualist culture like that of the United States, the leader can make more use of public recognition of good individual employee performance, whereas in a collective culture such as Japan's, it might cause the employee embarassment to be singled out from his work group for praise. Dickson, BeShears, and Gupta (2004) offered interesting notions about the likely mechanisms underlying cultural congruence, such as the socialization of the leader to the dominant values of the culture or the leader's response to societal pressures. Additionally, self-selection and formal selection procedures may improve the match in values of the leader and the led. The individualistic Canadian may choose or be chosen to work in the individualist Netherlands more than in the collectivist Uruguay. Hofstede (2001) suggested that in masculine cultures like those of Japan, Austria, Venezuela, and Italy, to be successful, leaders need to be assertive; in feminine countries such as the Netherlands, Denmark, Norway and Sweden, leaders have to be modest. A content analysis of publica-

tions about managing directors and CEOs by Jackofsky and Slocum (1988) showed that in a high-power-distance country such as France, such leaders took autocratic initiatives. In Japan, high in long-term orientation, leaders had to practice patience. In Sweden, low in uncertainty avoidance and high in femininity, leaders took a lot of entrepreneurial risks and also showed concern for their employees' quality of life. According to Hofstede (1980) the high-uncertainty-avoiding (UAI) French and Germans preferred a boss who had an unambiguous style of resolving problems—by hierarchical means in high-power-distance (PDI) France and through consensus in low-PDI Germany. When power distance (PDI) and uncertainty avoidance (UAI) are low, as in the Anglo-American cluster, Scandinavia, and the Netherlands, participative leadership is practiced on the shop floor. When PDI is low and UAI is higher, as in Germany, Austria, and Switzerland, participation matches the culture with industrial democracy—legalized forms of worker representation in management. When the PDI score is high, as in Latin America and the Middle East, authoritarian and directive leadership is expected.

Differences in Prototypes. As noted earlier, there are both universalities and specifics in the requirements for leadership across cultures and countries. Images of the ideal leader, *prototypes*, tend to vary from one culture and country to another. Prototypes are more widely shared within strong cultures than weak ones (Hunt, Boal, & Sorenson, 1990). Using 59 possible traits of leadership, Lord, Foti, and DeVader (1984) found that the prototypical American leader was intelligent, understanding, honest, and determined. The prototypical Japanese leader was fair, flexibile, outgoing, and responsible (O'Connell, Lord, & O'Connell, 1990). Gerstner and Day (1994) reported similar differences for prototypes in Asian compared to American and European countries. At the same time, some prototypical traits generalize across countries. Instant communication, worldwide media, trade, travel, multinational enterprises, and the transfer of technology have increased the convergence of requirements for leadership on a worldwide basis. Even in widely disparate cultures, such as Zambia and Bangladesh, Ali, Humbalo, Khaleque, and Rahman (1982) found that managers shared common concerns about their salaries, political pressures, regionalism, communication breakdowns, and ways of coping with conflict. I have already alluded to the more general pragmatism of business and industrial managers compared to the idealism of leaders of social movements. A survey of 115 white (*pakeha*) male and female managers and 19 Maori male managers in New Zealand, reported by L. R. Anderson (1983), found that the degree of *pakeha*-Maori mix of their work groups did not influence how their leadership behavior contributed to the effectiveness of the work groups but only to the difficulty of its implementation. In a simulation experiment, Ensari and Murphy (2003) demonstrated that attributions of charisma in collectivistic Turkey and individualistic America occurred based on similar processes. However, in Turkey, forming a leadership impression was affected more by leaders' organizational performance outcomes than prototypical traits. In the individualistic United States, the impression of charisma was due mainly to stereotyped traits.

Differences in Self-Management. Receptivity to working in self-managed teams is greater in collectivistic than in individualistic countries, according to observations, interviews, and surveys of 378 work teams in 11 countries ranging from the individualistic United States to the collectivistic Indonesia. Receptivity was also greater where team members valued equity rather than status and power differences and believed that they had more control over personal and organizational outcomes (Kirkman, Gibson, & Shapiro, 2001).

Differences in Primitive Cultures. Particularly in the less developed areas of the world as well as those with the strongest local traditions, there are still other important differences in what is required for leadership. Mead's (1930, 1935, 1939) anthropological comparisons clearly showed that what it takes to be a leader varies across primitive cultures. The aggressive, efficient, ambitious Manus leader in Oceania would have been rejected by the Dakota Indians, who valued generosity, hospitality, mutual welfare, and conforming to the group. Individualism, the lack of political integration, and lack of need to comply with leadership characterized the Bachiga of central Africa. Obedience, respect for the chief, and cooperative effort with little room for rivalry were the norms among the Bathonga. With their consciousness of position and conformity to rank in a clear hierarchy, the Sa-

moans followed a completely different style of leadership from that pursued by the individualistic Inuits, who considered no person's importance relative to another. Leadership among the Iroquois was achieved through behavior that was socially rewarding to others, such as generosity, cooperation, and hospitality. But among the Kwakiutl, the ideal chieftain was one who could successfully compete financially against other chiefs. What appeared to be demanded of the leader was quite different among the Arapesh of New Guinea, who had no strict ownership of land or scale of success, and the Ifugao of the Philippines, where land ownership was concentrated and the landowner was the ideal of success. Thus it is not surprising that the patterns of leader-subordinate behavior in industrialized societies vary considerably across countries and across cultures. Although such extreme effects of cultural differences may not be seen in the modern industrialized world, nevertheless considerable differences emerge in what managers think is required for success in the top, middle, and lower levels of management

Differences in Explicit and Implicit Theories of Leadership. As we move from one culture or country to another, we see systematic differences in what is regarded as important for effective leadership and explanations for why this is so. An important source of differences in leadership among countries is a consequence of these different explicit and implicit theories about leader-subordinate relationships. It was to be expected that the belief in participative management would originate in Scandinavia and North America—countries in which political democracy and the importance of the individual are deeply embedded. According to Lau (1977), East Asian cultures have a less differentiated view of reality: X does not cause Y; rather, X and Y affect each other. There is also less abstract thinking. The consequences are a less clear allocation of responsibilities and less organized planning in Chinese firms. At the same time, Confucian principles in China resulted in perceptions of managers as linchpins, mediating the effects of the work environment on their subordinates (Shenkar & Ronen, 1987).

Beliefs about leadership in Japan are embedded in a cultural matrix of beliefs about the important relations between members of a group. The concept of *amae*, dependence on another person's kindness and goodwill, is central to leadership in Japan. It places a debt on the person who is loved that must be repaid and binds the leader to the group. Subordinates would be angered by a leader who failed to provide *amae*. *Wa*, group harmony, that balances individual needs and desires with the good of the group and fosters mutual cooperation, would be lost. It is appropriate for superiors to look to subordinates for advice (Lee & Schwendiman, 1982).

Consistent with what has just been said was Sullivan, Suzuki, and Kondo's (1984) survey of responses by 100 U.S. and 266 Japanese managers to designed scenarios. The Japanese, more than the Americans, subscribed to an implicit social model to control performance rather than to an implicit model of the rational-economic individual. In the social model, the individual is thought to be submerged in the work group. The social entity—the group rather than the individual—must be assigned responsibility, monitored, and rewarded. At the same time, Japanese tradition called for leaders to be persons of exemplary moral courage, self-sacrifice, and benevolence. To this list was added the now widely accepted espousal of Charles Protzman's[6] requirement in post–World War II Japan that the leader be transformational in securing the faith and respect of those under him (Tsurumi, 1982).

Post–World War II Germany saw the rejection of the *Führerprincip* of omniscient command and unquestioning obedience to orders espoused by the Nazis. As a counter, the Allied military occupation imposed industrial democracy which, coupled with the growth of participatory education, resulted in the current German norm for subordinates to expect to be consulted about decisions. Yet consistent with the earlier German tradition, once the leader has made the decision, subordinates expect to carry it out to the best of their ability. At the same time, the explicit Harzburg model (Hohn, 1962) appeared in post–World War II Germany—a model that was more consistent with the *Führerprincip*. According to the model, the leader must be directive. However, the leader is required to delegate permanent areas of task responsibilities to coworkers, rather than to give short-term orders. Job descriptions must be carefully written. Subordinates must assume responsibilities within their prescribed area of consequence, along with accepting 315 organizational rules. The approach replaced patriarchical-authoritarian direction with bureaucratic-authoritarian direction. It al-

lowed for little subordinate participation or upward influence. Only economic goals were seen as legitimate. The Harzburg model has been replaced among German scholars and managers with the espousal of participative management and emphasis on human relations (Grunwald & Bernthal, 1983). Nevertheless, along with its use in Austria and Switzerland, the popularity of the Harzburg model was evidenced in a survey by Topfer (1978), who found that 16% of 355 West German firms were using it at that time.

More implicit in India was the preference of many subordinates for a dependent personal relationship with their leader rather than a contractual one. Such subordinates sought a nurturant leader and accepted authority and status differences (Sinha, 1984). Endemic underemployment until the boom of the 1990s resulted in overstaffing, and leadership that had to take cognizance of legitimate inefficiencies. At that time, Sinha suggested that the effective leader in India started by being nurturant and then followed with how to get the work done. Much needs to be learned about how leader-subordinate relations are changing in India to reflect the rising significance of India as a center of electronic manufacturing, research and development, and global communications. Triandis (1993) conceived nurturance as playing an important role in effective leadership in collectivistic cultures. However, Geben and Steinkamp (1991) found that while manager production orientation was positively related to a firm's economic success in Taiwan and Nigeria, patriarchical caring was contraindicated.

Modern Egypt is a rapidly industrializing, urbanizing amalgam of cultures—Pharoanic, Arab, Turkish, Levantine, and European. The favorite expression is the fatalistic *"inshallah,"* "If God wills." On the one hand, an easygoing attitude about work, relationships, and accomplishments dominates leader-subordinate relations. On the other hand, Egyptian leadership in organizations has been strongly affected by Egypt's widespread use of large public organizations to pursue its development. These organizations follow the higher-structured and centralized bureaucratic patterns in socialist and other developing countries (Badran & Hinings, 1981).

Differences in Trust. Nationalities vary in their willingness to trust others and the way in which they deal with lack of trust. Trust is the key to the quality of rela-

---

[6]One of the U.S. consultants who introduced statistical quality control in Japan in the 1950s.

tions between the leader and the led in different cultures. If the leader trusts the follower, the leader can be open with information. The leader is likely to be more closed if the leader distrusts the follower. With trust in the follower, the leader can be more democratic, participative, and delegative. If the leader is trusted by the follower, the leader can take more risks, share more information, and display more discretionary behavior.

Trust influenced the willingness of subordinates to work with democratic leaders, according to Williams, Whyte, and Green (1966), who found that the level of trust among Peruvians was generally low. The GLOBE project found distrust of managers to be widespread in the former Soviet bloc of nations. In Italy, trust may be publicly expressed but privately denied, for Italy's history has been characterized by oppressive surface regimentation, first by foreign occupiers, then by domestic autocratic governments. But a strong defense of the liberty of the individual and the family has been maintained. Outer and inner acceptance have been separated by making the world truly a stage in which the relations between the leader and the led play a dramatic part in Italy (Barzini, 1964). Within countries, organization and status affect the willingness to trust others. For example, Senner (1971) obtained results showing that Brazilian bankers were similar to American college students in that both groups were more trusting than were Peruvian white-collar workers. The bankers' levels of trust reflected their above-average socioeconomic status in Brazil. Likewise, Negandhi and Prasad (1971) found that Indian managers in U.S. subsidiaries in India showed more trust in their subordinates than did Indian managers in indigenous Indian firms.

Traits Judged Important for Top, Middle, and Lower Management.
Bass, Burger, et al. (1979) analyzed the choices of managers in their selection, from a list of 25 traits, of the five most important traits and the five least important traits required for top, middle, and lower managers using Exercise Supervise (Bass, 1975c), developed from original lists by L. W. Porter (1959). Indexes reflecting the choices of 3,401 managers yielded significant variations across 12 countries in many of the attributes for the three management levels. For example, Dutch managers saw no difference in the *imagination* needed for lower and middle managers, but managers everywhere else called for more imagination in successively higher levels

of management. Being *systematic* was judged most important for lower-level managers in Italy, Spain, Portugal, and Latin America but more necessary for middle managers everywhere else. Managers everywhere were expected to be more *careful* the lower their organizational level. But the Dutch thought it was most important for middle managers. The French judged it most important for lower and middle managers to be *sharp-witted*. The U.S. and British managers put a premium on being *resourceful*; the Japanese saw *intuition* as far more important for them than *logic*. *Sociability* was seen as important for top managers by faster-accelerating managers in their careers more than by slower ones in the Netherlands, Belgium, Italy, Spain, Portugal, Latin America, and India. Slower-rising managers saw sociability as more important for top management in Britain, Scandinavia, and France.

In the previously mentioned Korn/Ferry International survey of senior management in 20 countries of the personal characteristics required of a CEO, in the United States, the most important were *ethicality, intelligence,* and *enthusiasm*. In western Europe, they were *enthusiasm, intelligence,* and *inspiration*. In Latin America, they were *ethicality, creativity,* and *intelligence*.

Superior-Subordinate Relations.
Germany, Japan, the United States, and the former Soviet bloc illustrate the systematic differences that are likely to appear in different countries. Luther's concept of the "calling," to serve God by doing one's best in one's occupation, was a strong influence on the extent to which German subordinates expected to carry out decisions once they had been reached. The required informal mutual defense pacts that provided for the survival of both superiors and subordinates in the Soviet system have already been mentioned. For the Japanese, the organization assumes a particular importance in one's life. In turn, the importance of the organization affects what is required of Japanese superior-subordinate relations. The supervisor has different relevance to the worker in Japan than elsewhere. Not only is the supervisor likely to be more involved in the subordinate's off-the-job life, but the supervisor is accorded more status off the job. Whereas 44% of Japanese workers would offer their supervisor their seat on a crowded bus, only 2% of Americans said they would do so (Whitehill & Takezawa, 1968).

Van de Vliert (2003) reported that among 18,767 managers, those most likely to rely on their subordinates came from countries that were uncomfortably cold or hot and highly developed or underdeveloped

Differences in Required Masculinity. National boundaries produce different conclusions about the importance of masculinity to management. The stereotype of a successful manager was found by Schein (2001) to be male in the United States, Britain, Germany, Japan, and China. Chapter 31 reported Bartol and Butterfield's (1976) finding that sex-role stereotypes biased the performance evaluation of U.S. managers' behavior and that masculinity was favored. But Israeli and Israeli (1985) found no such bias when the study was replicated with Israeli instead of American managers.

Consistent differences among 30 countries appeared in the strength of masculine and feminine traits. Williams and Best (1982) found instrumental traits linked with masculinity and expressive traits linked with femininity. Chapter 31 noted that the U.S. data strongly indicated that both male and female respondents thought that masculinity (assertiveness, ambition, and task orientation) is required for success in management. Yet among 1,600 Australian high school students, Bottomley and Sampson (1977) reported comparable results only for male respondents. Unlike the boys, a majority of the Australian girls believed that the attributes of both men and women contribute to one's competence in dealing with leadership tasks.

In Hofstede's (1980) survey, masculinity scores (MAS) were high among IBM personnel in countries in which roles were clearly differentiated for men and women. In these countries such as Japan, assertive and dominant men, along with nurturing women, were favored. Work, money, material goods, and performance were emphasized, rather than play. There was admiration for machismo, for the successful achiever, for speed, and for size. In countries that were low in masculinity, like Sweden, there was endorsement of the attitudes that men can be nurturant, sex roles are fluid, there should be equality between the sexes, unisex and androgeny are ideal, the quality of life is important, work is a means to the good life, people and the environment are important, interdependence is valued, being of service is more important than being ambitious, and small and slow are beautiful. Highest in MAS mean scores were IBM respondents

from Japan, followed closely by the Germanic cluster; Jamaica; the Latin American countries of Venezuela, Ecuador, Mexico, and Colombia; and Catholic Italy and Ireland. Lowest in masculinity were IBM personnel from the Scandinavian countries of Sweden, Norway, Denmark, and Finland and from the Netherlands. More job stress was likely for leaders in countries with a high masculinity index. In addition, leadership was likely to be more caring and relations oriented in countries with personnel who are low in masculinity (high in femininity), and less in countries with personnel who are high in masculinity (Hofstede, 1980, 2001).

Critique of MAS. After noting that Australia and New Zealand scored only a little above the mean in Hofstede's masculinity-femininity (MAS) index, Shouksmith (1987) suggested that MAS was mislabeled, since the pattern of life in Australia and New Zealand is traditionally so masculine in orientation. Shouksmith suggested that the MAS dimension really describes the extent to which good living rather than work is valued, along with compatibility with coworkers. If one looks at the country-by-country results, one sees that the complex mixture of questioned attitudes resulted in the differences among countries due to different elements. The MAS index is derived from too many unrelated topics, such as sex roles, dominance in social relations, being humane, and performance orientation. The scale responses concern assertiveness, toughness, acquisition of money and materials, quality of life and people, and not caring for others. Low scores are derived from caring for the weak, warm social relations, and other traditionally feminine values. Japan's high masculinity index fits with its emphasis on the importance of work over leisure and the strong belief in sex-role differentiation. Sweden accepts the equality of the sexes, giving it its low masculinity index, and may have as strong an interest in recreation as does New Zealand.

High MAS scores generally indicate countries in which men are expected to be assertive and tough and women are expected to be tender and modest. If MAS in a country is high, a smaller percentage of women will reach positions of leadership. The low masculinity index score obtained for Sweden is reflected in the highest labor participation rate of females in the world. And in the past several decades, opportunities for higher-level positions in government for women have opened in Sweden. Over 40% of the Swedish legislature were women in 2000, as was the foreign minister. Although they are well represented in lower and middle management in private industry, as in many other countries, such as Britain, France, and the United States, the glass ceiling keeps their numbers in top management proportionately lower. The GLOBE project saw fit to measure gender role egalitarianism, assertiveness, performance orientation, and humane orientation separately (Den Hartog, House, Hanges, et al., 1999).

Styles of Leadership

Considerable national and cultural differences have been found in required, preferred, and observed leadership that is autocratic or democratic, participative or directive, relations oriented or task oriented, considerate or structuring, and active or laissez-faire—the styles discussed earlier in Chapters 6 and 17 through 20. The cultural differences become even more apparent if the data are gathered from those who are most freely socialized within a given culture—that is, from those who endorse the core beliefs of the culture. Thus, Dorfman and Howell (1988) demonstrated that in Taiwan, directive leadership displayed by one's superiors correlated .44 with subordinates' satisfaction with work for subordinates who had strong beliefs in the key cultural values of the Chinese culture. The correlation was only .19 for those who did not have such strong beliefs in their culture.

Autocratic versus Democratic Leadership

R. Likert (1963) argued that democratic leadership and System 4, as described in Chapter 21, is most likely to be effective in any productive organization, regardless of the culture or the country. Despite the wide variations in leadership preferences and behavior, Likert's argument was that regardless of culture, there was a best way to organize and lead. The System 4 participatory approach was successfully introduced into Japan, whose management had ordinarily been seen as a benevolent autocracy (System 2) practicing System 3 consultation (Sakano, 1983). In support of Likert's contention, Misumi (1974) applied a System 4 strategy in 1970 in a large shipyard in Japan, using group meetings for group problem solving,

goal setting, and decision making in an effort to reduce accidents among 4,000 workers. Accidents per man-hours worked ($\times$ 10) declined from 30 in 1969 to 12 in 1973.

Close rather than general supervision was found to be favored by workers in countries that are high in power distance and authoritarianism, such as Peru (Whyte, 1963) and Thailand (Deyo, 1978). Among North American workers and others in the Anglo-American cluster, however, the opposite was usually the case. Thus at the other end of the spectrum, as expected, 500 Australian managers from the Anglo cluster indicated their strong endorsement of democratic managerial beliefs, such as the capacity of subordinates to display initiative, the utility of sharing information, and the importance of self-control (Stening & Wong, 1983).

In the role playing in Exercise Supervise (Bass, 1975c), an equal number of contrived "passive," "moderately involved," or "vitally interested" subordinates meet in a counterbalanced order with a contrived democratic, autocratic, or persuasive "supervisor." Although on a chance basis, 33% of the participants should prefer to work with a democratic supervisor again, Bass, Burger, et al. (1979, p. 167) found that 63% of French managers were most in favor of doing so and 40% of Japanese managers least in favor among 12 nationalities. The other 10 European, American, and Asian nationalities were in between in their favoring of the democratic leader. Latin Americans (19%) differed in their preference from Latin Europeans (33%). Likewise, North Americans (32%), Germans (33%), and Scandinavians (31%) differed from Britons (22%) in this regard. In this same analysis, the preference of the participants who played the supervisory roles to work again with passive, uninvolved subordinates was highest among Indian managers (47%) and lowest among the Japanese (12%).

Power Distance. Among the 50 countries in the IBM survey, those highest in reported Power Distance Index (PDI) scores included Malaysia, Indonesia, Singapore, and the Philippines from Southeast Asia; the Spanish-American countries of Mexico, Guatemala, Panama, Ecuador, Colombia, Venezuela, and Peru; India; the Middle Eastern countries; and the west African countries. At the lower end of the spectrum in the PDI were the Anglo, Nordic, and Germanic clusters of countries, Israel, and Costa Rica. Greater acceptance of an autocratic style of leadership was to be expected and found in the countries that were high in power distance and acceptance of a democratic style, in the countries that were low in power distance. Somewhat consistent with Hofstede's results was the conclusion reached by Redding and Casey (1975) that managers in Malaysia, Indonesia, Thailand, and the Philippines favored an autocratic style, those in Singapore and Hong Kong were somewhat less favorable toward it, and those in Western countries favored it the least. Al-Hajjeh (1984) concluded from a survey of 25 North American and 25 Middle Eastern managers that the Middle Easterners supported more autocratic leadership and the North Americans did the reverse. Compared to the North Americans, the Middle Easterners felt less positive about the capacity of subordinates and saw a greater need to provide them with detailed instructions. Gebert and Steinkamp (undated) found from 218 interviews with representative indigenous manufacturers in Nigeria in West Africa that economic success was thought to depend on discipline and obeying rules whenever possible. Kenis (1977) compared the attitudes toward leadership of 150 Turkish and 147 American first-line supervisors in bank branches in Ankara and Istanbul. The Turks favored more autocratic leadership, in contrast to the Americans who favored more democratic leadership. Kenis attributed his results to the authoritarianism inherent in the Turkish culture. In a country high in power distance, such as Mexico, direction,[7] coupled with supportive (caring) leadership, contributed directly to effective performance. In a country low in power distance like the United States, participation made a direct contribution to effective performance (Dorfman, Howell, et al., 1997). Eylon and Au (1999) found that MBA students in a management simulation were more satisfied with their jobs if they were empowered rather than disempowered. But only in low-PDI countries did they perform better. In a firm with operations in the United States, Poland, Mexico, and India, Robert, Probst, Martocchio, et al. (2000) found that continuous improvement related positively to job satisfaction in all four locations. However, empowerment, related

positively to job satisfaction in the United States and Poland, was negatively associated with higher PDI in India but not in Mexico, also high in PDI. Huang (2003) found that empowerment and management openness worked to increase 136,018 employees' willingness to voice their opinions about organizational issues in 24 countries low in PDI.

Chapter 12 discussed the extent to which greater power differences between the leader and the led accent the greater potential for the leader to be authoritarian, directive, persuasive, or coercive. Smith, Peterson, Schwartz, et al. (2002) found in GLOBE data in 47 countries that in high-PDI countries, managers used more rules generated from above to handle daily events. Compared to U.S. employees, Chinese employees were shown by Bu, Craig, and Peng (2001) to be more willing to accept direction from supervisors. In line with this hypothesis, Mulder (1976) saw a large power distance between the leader and the led associated with the fear of disagreeing with one's superior. In Hofstede's (1980) survey, the same connections were revealed. Coercive, autocratic leadership was more common in countries in which the power distance between superiors and subordinates was high. When PDI is high, children greatly respect parents, elders, and teachers. Teachers initiate all communications. In countries with a high PDI, decision making is more centralized and authority is concentrated. Organizations are tall. Ideal leaders are directive, benevolent autocrats who rely on formal rules. Subordinates expect to be told what to do. Superior-subordinate relations are polarized and emotional. Subordinates are influenced by formal authority and sanctions.

More democratic styles are practiced in countries with low power distance. National elites are egalitarian rather than authoritarian. Authority is based on secular-rational arguments rather than tradition. Top leaders are younger rather than older. Children treat parents and teachers as equals. In work organizations, in countries with low PDI, decision making is likely to be decentralized and authority is less concentrated. Organizations are flatter. Supervisors have a wide span of control, ideal leaders are resourceful democrats, practical, orderly, and rely on experience and subordinates. Subordinates expect to be consulted. Superior-subordinate relations are pragmatic. Subordinates are influenced by reasoning and bargaining (Hofstede, 2001, pp. 107–108).

---

[7]The convention was introduced in Chapter 18. Participation (in roman) includes consultation (the superior decides); *participation* (in italic) is limited to joint decision making by superiors and subordinates. Direction (in roman) refers to initiatives by a leader that involve telling, persuading, selling, and bargaining; *direction* (in italics) is limited to telling and giving orders.

Authoritarianism. Authoritarianism, as measured by the *F* Scale, influences the acceptance of autocratic rather than democratic behavior.[8] The *F* Scale has been administered to student groups in many different countries. As previously noted, Turkish students were likely to score higher and American students lower on the scale. Indian students usually scored high as well (Meade & Whittaker, 1967). Meade's (1967) experimental replication in India of the classic Lewin, Lippitt, and White (1939) study of leadership found that both productivity and satisfaction in boys' groups were higher under autocratic than under nonautocratic leadership in India.

In Arab and other Muslim countries, family and tribal traditions result in benevolent, paternal, autocratic leadership. The leader is expected to be a father who cares more about his own followers than outsiders. In Arab organizations, this is combined with bureaucratic leadership left over from colonial days, the promulgation of many rules—which are ignored due to favoritism—and personal connections. Traditionally, each new ruler made new rules to replace the old ones. Conformity to rules depends on the power and personality of the rule makers. The typical organization is a strong patriarchical authority. Leaders are either prophets who depend on their personal charisma or caliphs who must rule by coercive power (Dorfman, 1996). The most desirable leadership in Qatar and Kuwait, according to surveys of 179 middle managers and interviews with another 21 upper-middle managers, were charismatic, self-protective, and considerate (Abdalla & Al-Homoud, 2001). According to 300 Iranian middle managers (Muslim but not Arabic) in the GLOBE project, effective leadership was helped or hindered by being supportive, autocratic, planful, familial, humble, faithful, and receptive.

Sinha (1976) agreed that authoritarian leadership is optimum in Hindu India. Such leadership features task orientation, strong personal involvement and effort by the leader. More democratic processes are possible only after the structure has become firm for the employees and moderate productivity has been achieved. In support, Singh and Arya (1965) studied 40 sociometrically identified leaders in a village in India. Given the strong authoritarian norm, it was not surprising that leaders were found to be significantly more authoritarian than

were nonleaders. Leaders preferred task-oriented leaders to other types, but both leaders and nonleaders rejected the self-interested leader. However, neither Kakar (1971) nor Jaggi (1977) could find similar support for favoring the autocratic mode in India. According to Fujiyama (1997), Korean business leaders favor hierarchical, authoritarian, and centralized leadership, unlike Japan's focus on consensus in reaching decisions after considerable deliberation. This enables Korean companies to take actions more quickly than can comparable Japanese firms. Variations have also been observed within Asia in the perceived power distance and in autocratic leadership behavior. The specific issues involved in a given country are likely to make a difference as well. Ishikawa (1986) compared the favored and perceived distribution of power of managers and employees in nine Asian countries. Employers viewed participation by workers more favorably in India and Japan than in Pakistan and Taiwan. Power distance regarding decisions about management policy, personnel, working conditions, and workplace issues generally was greatest in Thailand and least in Sri Lanka. In Japan, power distance was seen as being lower on workplace issues and higher on questions of management policy. In India and elsewhere, perceived power distance also depended on which issues were involved. But in general, workers in Taiwan perceived the strongest relation between one's position in the hierarchy and one's power.

The subscription to democratic leadership was found to be surprisingly high by Haire, Ghiselli, and Porter (1966) across the 14 countries they studied. But compared to U.S. managers, managers elsewhere indicated little acceptance of what would be required for such democratic leadership, such as agreement that employees as well as supervisors have the potential to exhibit initiative, share leadership, and contribute to the problem-solving process. The researchers concluded, on the basis of data from the early 1960s, that introducing democratic leadership into most other countries at that time would be "a little like building the techniques and practices of a Jeffersonian democracy on a basic belief in the divine right of kings" (p. 130). The proposition still seems to contain some truth in 2006, although fragile democracies have struggled to be established in countries as diverse as Ukraine and Nepal and much of Latin America. Autocratic charisma was regarded strongly pejoratively

---

[8] See Chapter 7.

by managers from countries that experienced autocratic charismatic dictators.

Paternalism. The degree of paternalism in a culture affects the acceptance of benevolent authoritarian leadership and taking care of employees and their families. Failure of subordinates to comply with the wishes of the patron is seen as disloyalty. Paternalism was a dimension of consequence in Georgia, Russia, Kazakhstan, and the Kyrgyz Republic (Ardichvili, 2001) The sense of paternalism was higher among Taiwan Chinese and Mexican employees than among U.S. employees working for the same company. Using data on employees in Taiwan, Mexico, and the United States, Dorfman and Howell (1988) emerged with a factor of paternalism. When paternalism was strong, employees subscribed to expecting job security and to be looked after by their company as a person, not only as a worker. Lincoln, Hanada, and Olson (1981) found that Japanese and Japanese-American employees in 28 Japanese-owned firms in the United States valued paternalistic company behavior more than did American employees of the same firms. A 30-year survey of the literature on leadership in Korea by Baik (1999) found paternalism, "hierarchical structures where elders, predecessors, and patriarchs exert significant influence in Korean society" still a norm. In comparison to 235 German managers, 306 Korean managers more strongly valued family, authority, and paternalistic leadership, according to a study by Park in 1984 reported by Baik.

Farmer and Richman (1965) rated a number of countries on paternalism, using a review of the literature and reports from experts. They concluded that Japan was most strongly paternalistic, as evidenced by policies of lifetime employment, age-grade lockstep promotions and salary increases, and the companies' provision of housing, recreational facilities, and shrines for worship for their employees. Other countries that were high in paternalism included Egypt, Chile, Germany, India, France, Mexico, and Saudi Arabia. At the other end of the spectrum were the United States, Britain, the former Soviet Union, and the former Yugoslavia.

In developing countries, paternalism featured autocratic patrons and compliant followers. Power distance was high. Patrons were expected to care for workers and their families (Dickson, Den Hartog & Mitchelson, 2003). In indigenous Brazilian industry, the traditional worker identified with the *patrão*, the patriarchial owner, to whom he was a ward, not just a member of an organization headed by the patron. In rural Guatemalan factories, immediate supervisors were of local origin. As members of the *padrone's* workforce, they had limited authority; they could only suggest, not order. On the other hand, if the workers were not unionized, the foreign engineer and the owner or his white-collar surrogates treated workers like children, physically abusing them as well as dealing directly with their complaints (M. Nash, 1958). In India, Sinha (1980, 1994) found that both Indian managers and subordinates preferred as leaders benevolent autocrats who were nurturing and paternalistic if the subordinates were obedient, respectful, and task-oriented.

Participative versus Directive Leadership

Smith, Peterson, and Schwartz (2002) found that western European managers preferred to rely more on subordinates for information about events than did managers from African countries, who preferred information provided by superiors and rules. A survey by Sirota (1968) of the attitudes of IBM employees in 46 countries toward supervision indicated their preference for consultation (the leader makes a decision after discussion with the subordinate) and *participative* joint decision making, although directive leadership was seen as being more common. In other studies, Israeli managers revealed more actual participatory leadership than they said they supported ideologically (Vardi, Shirom, & Jacobson, 1980). Australian managers were the reverse; they endorsed participatory practices ideologically but were actually less supportive of them in practice (Clark & McCabe, 1970). On the other hand, Australian managers more often chose *participation* among the Vroom and Yetton (1973) alternatives to handling problems than did managers from the Pacific Islands and Africa (Borttger, Hallein, & Yetton, 1985). Given the same Vroom-Yetton set of problems, Austrian managers, compared to American managers, chose group *participation* in making decisions. Consistent with these methods and results, German and Swiss managers also favored *participation*, in contrast to Polish and Czech managers, who were inclined to choose *directive* decisions (Reber, Jago, & Böhnisch, 1993). As would be expected from Chapter 18, the managers who consulted were viewed most favorably by subordinates. Leaders who practiced a lot of persuasion, especially the ones with "no style," were viewed least favorably, particularly in Britain. In Britain, participative managers were not seen as good counselors; many subordinates objected to the number of meetings they called (Sadler, 1970). Consistent with these results, Chaney (1966) found that whereas more productive U.S. scientists had more frequent communications with their superiors and their colleagues, the reverse was true for British scientists—the more productive ones had less frequent communications with their superiors. In Israel, participation suppressed social loafing; in the United States, participation increased social loafing. The difference was associated with more collectivism in Israel and more individualism in the United States (Earley, 1993).

An analysis by Sadler and Hofstede (1972) of IBM employees from Australia, Brazil, Britain, and Japan showed that the preferred style by the employees was consultative, 65% to 45%, but only in Brazil was there a sizable preference also for *participation* (29%). These results were consistent with data gathered through the Management Styles Survey in the United States, Spain, Sweden, Finland, and India (Bass, Valenzi, Farrow, & Solomon, 1975). Consultation was preferred over *participation* everywhere and was more frequently seen everywhere. In all the countries in the IBM survey and in those just mentioned *directive* supervision was in little favor with the vast majority of subordinates. Although as noted in Chapter 18, the leader's direction tended to correlate positively with the subordinates' satisfaction with the leader, it did not do so as strongly as did participation. According to Bass, Burger, et al. (1979), the relative preference for participative leadership in decision making was highest among the Italians and the Japanese. Participative leadership was self-appraised (in exercise self-appraisal) as highest among the Italian managers and lowest among the Dutch and Japanese managers. Differences were found among eight countries in observed participation and direction by senior executives (Sweden was more participative; Israel was more directive). The differences were outweighed by which types of decisions were involved (Heller & Wilpert, 1981).

Howell and Dorfman (1988) found that participative leadership had stronger effects on the satisfaction and commitment of U.S. employees than on their Mexican counterparts. The correlations for the North Americans

were .49 with satisfaction with work, .69 with satisfaction with supervision, and .65 with satisfaction with job performance. The comparable correlations for the Mexican employees were .26, .49, and .09, respectively. At the same time, as Dorfman and Howell (1988) hypothesized, *directive* leadership correlated between .38 and .50 with the Taiwan Chinese and Mexican employees' satisfaction with the leader and commitment to the organization. For the North Americans, working in similar settings, the correlations of *direction* and the subordinates' satisfaction were only .22 and .25 (Howell & Dorfman, 1988). Differences in the cohesiveness of the work groups could not substitute for the effects of differences in the leaders' *direction*.

Consultation and Two-Way Communication. A multinational sample of IBM managers thought they did more consulting than their subordinates thought they did. Of the 178 managers, 71% saw themselves as using a consulting leadership style, but only 29% of their employees agreed with them (Sadler & Hofstede, 1972). A contradiction probably contributed to the discrepancy. In Haire, Ghiselli, and Porter's (1966) 14-country study noted earlier, whereas 3,600 managers professed favorable attitudes toward participative leadership and sharing information, they also believed that the average individual preferred to be directed and wanted to avoid responsibility. Similar results were reported by Clark and McCabe (1970) for an additional 1,300 managers in Australia and by Cummings and Schmidt (1972) for a small sample of Greek managers.

These national differences in preferences for certain styles of leadership were seen with considerable consistency across studies. The percentages of managers in a country who preferred two-way over one-way communication in doing Exercise Communication (Bass, 1975g) correlated across nationalities .82 with Haire, Ghiselli, and Porter's (1966) survey measure of the propensity to share information and objectives (Barrett & Franke, 1969). Consultation is the most popular style of decision making among U.S. and Japanese managers. U.S. and Japanese managers were also the highest among those of 12 nationalities in seeing two-way communications as less frustrating than one-way communications. The relatively least frustrated by one-way communications were the Belgians, the Germans, Austrians, and the French. All the Japanese managers who were sampled preferred two-way communications, as both senders and receivers. Almost identical results occurred for the U.S. managers. The Dutch, Belgians, German, Austrians, French, and Indians seemed somewhat more tolerant of one-way communications as senders, but not as receivers (Bass, Burger, et al., 1979).

A. S. Tannenbaum (1974) contrasted the extent to which employees participated both informally and formally in decision making in Italy, Austria, the United States, Yugoslavia, and an Israeli kibbutz. As expected, subordinates and superiors were closest in agreement about their job satisfaction and mental adjustment in Yugoslavia and in the Israeli kibbutz, where workers formally participated in organizational decision-making processes. They were farthest apart in Italy, where employees did not participate in decisions, either formally or informally, despite Italian legislation supporting such participation.

Legislatively Mandated versus Actual Participation. According to the International Research Group on Democracy in Europe (IDE), the percentage of decisions for which formal rules of *participation* apply was seen to vary in what had been legalized as of 1981 within 12 European countries and Israel. The European countries that were the highest in these percentages were the former Yugoslavia (76%), Italy (66%), Norway (64%), and Sweden (61%). The countries that were lowest were Britain (21%) and Israel (23%) (IDE, 1981). Elden (1986) argued that in countries with highly legislated programs for industrial democracy, such as Norway, participative decision making in the workplace may be preached more often than practiced. In the former Yugoslavia, with its strong legislative support for the participation of workers through workers' councils, Kolaja (1965) observed that actually only about 40% of the decisions were instituted by workers and supervisors and 60% of the decisions were initiated by higher-level managers. This situation may be contrasted to that of the United States where, without such legislation, it was possible to find establishments that held participatory meetings in which blue-collar supervisors and workers initiated 52% of decisions and management was responsible for introducing only 48% of the ideas (Rosenberg, 1977). When Jacob and Ahn (1978) examined the participation of workers in six socialist and nine nonsocialist countries, they found that whether a country was socialist had little

effect. Nor was the technological level of the workers in the different countries of any consequence. Rather, participation in influencing decisions depended on whether the management style, work culture, and formal industrial relations system of the country gave individual workers the feeling that they had the power to determine their work conditions.

Legally required formal codetermination in corporate decision making by worker representatives and management reduces the power distance in organizations and promotes democracy. Franke (1997) found differences among 11 European nations, Israel, and Japan in the extent to which national legislation and practices provided workers with decision-making rights. In 1980, the nations ranged in ratings of industrial democracy from Finland (2.88) to Belgium (1.36). These ratings strongly correlated with economic growth rates of the countries between 1980 and 1990 corrected for their levels of economic development in 1980. (Those at lower levels in 1980 gained more.)

Legislatively Mandated Participation and Perceived Influence. Comparisons were made in the perceived influence of workers and supervisors among 12 European countries and Israel with surveys by the IDE (1979) where participation was nationally legislated. Although perceived influence by workers was lowest for the Israelis and highest for the Yugoslavs, legalized participation was not strongly associated with actual perceived influence on the decision-making process in most of the other European countries (IDE, 1981a, 1981b). In Israel and Belgium, workers felt relatively less influential in comparison to workers elsewhere in Europe about 16 decisions. In the former Yugoslavia, workers felt relatively more influential in comparison to workers elsewhere. Danish supervisors perceived themselves as being highest in influence compared to supervisors elsewhere; Belgian supervisors felt the least influential. German and French top managers thought they were the most influential, while Scandinavian and Yugoslavian top managers felt the least influential.

When Participation Is Not Legally Required. In a comparison by Lam, Chen, and Schaubroeck (2002) of American and Chinese American workers in a multinational bank in an individualistic culture, the workers were more likely to participate if they felt self-efficacious. In a collectivist culture, they were more likely to participate if they felt their group was efficacious. This was affirmed in a study of 402 Chinese and Indian banking and finance employees. Collective efficacy but not self-efficacy mediated the effects of transformational leadership on work-related outcomes. Transformational leadership had more of a positive effect on organizational commitment and job satisfaction when self-efficacy was high (Walumbwa, Lawler, Avolio et al., 2005). For 387 students of Australian and Chinese background, Weirter, Ashkanasy, and Callan (1997) showed that high self-monitors were more affected by the message than the personal charisma of the leader. Additionally, the Chinese high self-monitors were more affected than the Australians.

Hierarchical Influences. Top-down decision making accompanies the power distance that is prevalent in West Africa and in the Arab countries of the Middle East even in minor matters (Pezeshkpur, 1978), as well as in Turkey. Ottih (1981) observed a low level of delegation and participation by subordinates in decision making in Nigerian banks, where decision making was highly centralized as favored by management. Ergun and Onaran (1981) suggested that *direction* and negotiation were "natural" in Turkey. As mentioned before, Kenis (1977) concluded that Turks favored directive leadership. Nonetheless, in the survey of Turkish electric utility employees by Ergun and Onaran (1981), the employees reported similar satisfaction whether their supervisors were directive or participative. Correlations ranged between .32 and .42 in the satisfaction of subordinates and the tendencies of their supervisors to be more active in any one of five styles ranging from *directive* to delegative.

Manipulative versus Participative Tactics. Bass and Franke (1972) administered the Organizational Success Questionnaire to 1,064 university students from six countries in their native languages. The students were applying for summer jobs in other countries. The students' nationality strongly influenced how they varied in their endorsement of political manipulative approaches to success in getting ahead in management, such as bluffing, rather than social participative approaches, such as openly committing oneself.[9] All six nationalities tended

[9]See Chapter 7.

to favor the participative approaches and to reject the political manipulative ones. In addition, the Germans were highest among the six nationalities in their endorsement of openly committing themselves, but they were lowest in finding it important to share in decision making. The Swedes were highest in endorsing the fostering of mutual trust and leveling with others and lowest in the political withholding of information, maintaining social distance, compromising for delay, and initiating but retarding actions. Students from the United States were highest in endorsing the establishment of mutual objectives and lowest in endorsing bluffing and making political alliances. The French were highest in supporting the participative arranging of group discussions and sharing in decision making, as in the making of political alliances.

Although they were relatively high in their willingness to share in decision making, the British were lowest in their endorsement of openly committing themselves and fostering mutual trust. They were also highest in their endorsement of withholding information for release when it would do the most good. The Dutch were next to the highest among the six nationalities in favoring the fostering of mutual trust; they were the lowest in endorsing the establishment of mutual objectives, leveling with others, and arranging for group decisions. They also were the highest in their support for maintaining social distance and initiating actions but then retarding their progress.

The participative endorsements for the six countries as a whole correlated .89 with Haire, Ghiselli, and Porter's (1966) managers' preferences in the same countries for sharing information and objectives. Furthermore, endorsement of the participative approaches for the six countries correlated .77 with the countries' national wealth, as measured by the per capita gross national product.

National Differences in the Meaning and Practice of Participation

Personality Influences. DeFrank, Matteson, and Schweiger (1985) surveyed 107 Japanese and American CEOs and found some personality differences between them that may influence their leadership style and how they look at participation and direction. The Japanese CEOs were less ambitious, hard-driven, and impatient (less Type A). However, compared to American CEOs, the Japanese CEOs reported feeling more stressed in their daily activities and less able to relieve the stress. They were also less satisfied with their pay, position, and discretionary freedom on the job.

Personnel Practices. To create better problem finding, important to the applicability of creative thinking, Japanese firms are likely to provide their scientific and engineering personnel in their first six months with positions in the sales department to give them an understanding of the firm's customers problems and needs. The next 18 months are spent rotating through manufacturing and engineering before taking up their work in R & D. Suggestions from all employees and problem finding are strongly encouraged. In contrast to 2.3 suggestions per employee annually from the typical leading U.S. firm, suggestion rates in the largest Japanese leading companies, each receiving more than a million suggestions per year, range from Mazda's rate of 126.5 per employee to Nissan's 38.5 per employee. Employees post perceived problems ("golden eggs") on a wall and their group and relevent others proceed to try to solve and implement them (Basadur, 1992).

Country Differences in the Meaning and Practices of Participation and Direction

Japan. Franke (1984) compared 149 Japanese managers' and 1,373 U.S. managers' tendency to endorse these same participative and political approaches. The Japanese significantly endorsed all the political approaches to a much greater degree than did the North American managers. Although they agreed that their success could be enhanced by participative decision making with subordinates, it was the Americans who were more in favor of leveling with others, openly committing themselves, establishing mutual objectives, fostering mutual trust, and arranging for group discussions.

Some of these differences between the Japanese and Americans' endorsements of participative decisions may have been due to the extent to which such practices are discretionary for American leaders but institutionalized, as the *ringi* method in Japan. Participation may take on a different character in a country like Japan from what is ordinarily practiced elsewhere. In traditional Japan, negative votes in a group were rare. The members of a group

faced loss of esteem, ridicule, and causing offense to others if they deviated from the "will of the group," as announced by the group leader. The leader, in turn, had to divine intellectually and emotionally "with his belly," *haragei*, what the group needed and wanted as a group (Kerlinger, 1951). Supervisory leaders play a more important role in Japanese organizations than in the United States (Smith & Misumi, 1989). To a Western observer, leader-subordinate relations in which complete subordinate obedience is given to decisions announced by the leader may seem authoritarian-submissive in style. Actually, leadership in Japan, as seen in the *ringi* method, is a blend of full consultation all around and a seeming intolerance for deviation when consensus has been reached. In the West, consultation is initiated by the leader, who asks for the subordinates' opinions and suggestions before deciding. In Japan, consultation, as seen in the *ringi* system, begins with *nemawashi*, the informal sounding out of opinions of colleagues about ideas, then formally submitting to one's superior what has emerged in consultation with them (P. B. Smith, 1984a). *Nemawashi* may also involve middle managers talking to subordinates individually about how upper management really feels about an issue before it is to be discussed in public by their group of subordinates (Yokochi, 1989b). Long-term planning and collective responsibility are the rule rather than the exception (Keys & Miller, 1984). Yet Japanese leaders can structure their relations with their subordinates to some extent rather than depend solely on tradition (Durphy, 1987).

Misumi (1984) noted several important features of *ringi*. First, many people, whether directly or indirectly involved, learn about the proposal. Consensus has developed among many in the organization before the decision reaches the top management. The experience and knowledge of all who are involved are applied to the decision, which enhances its quality. (Thus, Maguire and Pascale [1978] found that the quality of decisions in Japanese firms was correlated with the extent to which the decisions came from below. This was not true for American firms, in which the quality of the decision was better if more time was spent studying the issues.) Second, the wide involvement in the process of people at all levels in the organization means that the decision can be implemented quickly if it is authorized. (This was of great assistance in Japan's rapid change over the last century.)

Third, the originator of the idea receives training in management development. Fourth, the *ringi* method fits large firms as well as smaller, family-owned, paternalistic companies. However, when Japanese supervise North American workers, they are less consultative than are American supervisors. Communication difficulties and cultural barriers inhibit implementing the *ringi* practice with American workers (Beatty, Owens, & Jenner, undated).

China. Lindsay and Dempsey (1985) suggested that leadership in state enterprises in China can only be described as "semiparticipative." It blends group criticism and group discussion without group decision making. There is an avoidance of strong public disagreements, a strictly patterned discussion flow, and a strong dependence on authority. In private enterprises, we need to add an understanding of the varieties of leadership and decision making in China. Tsui, Wang, Xim, et al. (2003) collected descriptions of the behavior of 550 Chinese CEOs provided by 1,500 professional employees and middle managers in their firms. The descriptions were converted into questionnaires, which were then factor-analyzed into six dimensions and clustered into four types of leadership styles. The dimensions were: (1) articulating vision (communicating a future to followers), (2) monitoring operations (setting context, shaping decisions, and controlling managerial and operational systems), (3) being creative and risk-taking (in thinking and formulating strategies), and (4) relating and communicating (maintaining harmonious interpersonal relationships with employees and outsiders), (5) showing benevolence (doing personal favors, showing concern for the well-being of and demonstrating generosity toward employees and their families), and (6) being authoritative (emphasizing personal dominance over subordinates, centralizing authority, being the "father figure," and making unilateral decisions). Many of these dimensions in the Chinese context go beyond their meanings in the West. For instance, showing benevolence is not necessary for achieving instrumental or immediate objectives, but is intrinsically valued. It reflects the Confucian virtue that superiors should treat subordinates with kindness. In return, subordinates should respect their superiors with filial duty, deference, loyalty, and obedience. (Consistent with these findings, an interview survey of 50 workers and 120 managers noted that managers in China offer favors,

develop warm relationships with workers, loosen the operating rules, and request assistance from the workers and their families [Wall, 1989].)

The Chinese CEOs were clustered into four leadership styles according to their distance from one another on scores on the six dimensions: (1) *Advanced leaders* were highest on all except the authoritative dimension, where they were moderate in score. (2) *Authoritative leaders* were highest on the authority dimension but in between the other three types on the other dimensions. (3) *Invisible leaders* were lowest on all the dimensions except for being authoritative, on which they were moderate in score. (4) *Progressing leaders* were moderate on all six dimensions. To illustrate, S. M. Zhang of the Neptunus Group, an advanced leader, is highly intelligent and creative, incorporates Western practices with Chinese values, and is regarded as a hero. Yue Zhang of Shanghai Broad Air-Conditioning, an authoritative leader, is rule-driven, hardworking, and extremely task-oriented. His subordinates are intimidated and highly controlled by him.

Russia. Participative approaches in Russia's largest textile factory resulted in a decrease in performance (Welsh, Luthans, & Sommer, 1993). This could be explained by Russian national norms favoring the use of authority and direction from above. According to numerous Russian opinion polls since the demise of the Soviet Union, their allegiance is to family and friends. Trust in outsiders is low. Compared to multinational polls showing Swedes as most trusting of their government, Russians are least trusting of their government. In 2003, 78% of respondents agreed that democracy is a façade for government control by rich and powerful cliques. A majority said that multiparty elections did more harm than good. In one province, 88% indicated they would choose order over freedom. Most said they would be willing to give up freedom of speech, press, or movement in exchange for stability, and 76% favored restoring censorship over the mass media (Pipes, 2004).

Britain and France. Decision-making processes take a different form in Britain than in France. According to Graves (1973), British managers do not consider all alternatives. Greater conflict occurs in regard to the value of various alternatives; nevertheless, once a decision is reached, there is more commitment to it. French managers place more weight on alternatives but may be less committed to the alternative selected for implementation. Subordinates' felt pressure to participate in decisions may depend more on individual differences. It may be a more impersonal matter in Britain and more personal in France (Inzerilli & Laurent, 1983).

Multinational Subsidiaries versus Indigenous Firms.
Heller and Wilpert (1981) surveyed the extent to which decision making was directive (with or without explanation), consultative, joint, or delegative among 625 boss-subordinate dyads in 29 firms in eight countries. The results varied by country from most directive to most participative. Israel was most directive, and Sweden was most participative. But the authors noted that the type of firm had to be taken into account. For example, more direction was found in indigenous German firms than in German multinational corporations. German subsidiaries of multinational firms headed by other nationals were the most participative. Similarly, Negandhi and Prasad (1971) obtained results indicating that managers in North American subsidiaries in Argentina, Brazil, India, the Philippines, and Uruguay found it more comfortable to delegate than did indigenous managers in locally owned firms in the same countries. Whether employees in North American subsidiaries of Japanese multinationals were satisfied or tended to quit appeared to depend on whether the management was under more Japanese or American influence. Japanese employees were more satisfied with Japanese managers and practices than were U.S. employees (Yokochi, 1989b).

Influences of Power, Legitimacy, and Expectations.
Although a participatory style may work well for leaders and with subordinates in low power distance, as in the United States where it is culturally legitimate, considerably less effective outcomes may be found in high-PDI countries in which participation is less expected and appreciated. For example, in Saudi Arabia, Algattan (1985) compared the effectiveness of participatory leadership on U.S. and mainly Asian and African workers. Participatory leadership was more effective with the U.S. workers and was related to their greater need for the scope of the task, growth, and inner locus of control in comparison to Asian and African employees. The *referent* power of U.S. supervisors, their esteem and popularity, enhanced the performance of their subordinates, but *legitimate* power was more important to Bulgarian supervisors in contributing to their subordinates' effectiveness. In Bulgaria, the supervisor was seen to have the right to control subordinate behavior (Rahim, Antonioni, Krumov, et al., 2000).

In a seminal field experiment, Coch and French (1948) found a marked increase in productivity by North American work groups that were permitted to participate in goal-setting decisions that affected them. This was in contrast to findings with control groups that were not permitted to participate. But the same experiment failed with Norwegian factory workers because Norwegian workers were thought to have a lower need for autonomy and did not see participation as legitimate to the extent that American workers did (French, Israel, & As, 1960). Locke, Latham, and Erez (1987) showed in laboratory comparisons that group participation in goal setting was unnecessary in the United States, where (serendipitously) the experimenter had been friendly and supportive when instructing the subjects. In Israel, the experimenter had been more curt. In Puerto Rico, when the manager of a new Harwood Manufacturing plant began to encourage employees to participate in problem-solving meetings, turnover increased sharply! It was found that the workers in Puerto Rico had decided that if the management was so ignorant of the answers to its problems that it had to consult employees, the company was poorly managed and unlikely to survive (Marrow, 1964b). In the same way, Israeli sailors were more satisfied with expected legitimate directive leadership than with participative leadership (Foa, 1957).

Relations-Oriented and Task-Oriented Leadership [10]

Considerable agreement across countries was reported by Blake and Mouton (1970) in what managers regard as ideal. Among almost 2,500 managers from the United States, South Africa, Canada, Australia, the Middle East, and South America in GRID seminars, most agreed that the "9,9 management style" (integrated concern with both production and people), as defined in Chapter 19, was the ideal for their company. But much of the uniformity across countries could be attributed to indoctrina-

[10] See Chapter 19.

tion in the GRID seminars. There was more concern in general for productivity when managers described their own actual behavior. In the same way, Howell and Dorfman (1988), comparing Chinese, Mexican, and American employees in electronics manufacturing plants, concluded that supportive leadership generally had similar positive effects on satisfaction and commitment in all three samples. Moreover, the cohesiveness of the work groups could often substitute for the supportive leadership in generating the satisfaction and commitment Ayman and Cherners (1983) and Kakar (1971) reached similar conclusions.

The relations orientation and task orientation (Bass, 1967b) of leaders and nonleaders have been studied in many different countries, including Poland (Dobruszek, 1967), Britain (Cooper, 1966; R. Cooper & Payne, 1967), India (Muttayya, 1977) and Hong Kong (Lomas, 1997). Lomas found that Hong Kong Chinese project managers, in comparison to their Western counterparts, placed more emphasis on personal relationships than on the task. Muttayya observed that among 275 diverse formal and informal Indian leaders and nonleaders that the leaders were more task oriented, as expected. Lindell and Arvonen (1996) obtained results indicating that Latin European managers were somewhat higher in task orientation than Scandinavian and Hungarian managers. Employee orientation was higher in Scandinavian than Latin European managers. Likewise, the importance of the vertical dyad linkage on the quality of superior-subordinate relationships was as applicable in Japan and elsewhere as in the United States (Wakabayashi & Graen, 1984).

Dorfman (1996) concluded from a review of the literature that the importance of task orientation and its contribution to subordinate satisfaction and effectiveness did vary somewhat from one culture to another. A third dimension needed to be introduced to account for the fuller orientation of the leader toward the task and relationships. Such a third dimension dealing with character and morals had to be added to P(roduction) and M(aintenance) to describe Chinese leaders in the application of Misumi's PM theory. According to Peterson (1988), PM theory, which was developed and validated in collectivist Japan, may be improved in the individualist United States with some modification of this type.

The Japanese Example. As noted earlier, the Japanese place a particular premium on the quality of relationships with others. A variety of empirical studies and case analyses have corroborated this finding. Among the 12 national groups studied by Bass, Burger, et al. (1979), the Japanese managers were relatively high or highest in preferred awareness of self-understanding, listening to others with understanding, and accepting warmth and affection from others. They were also highest in their willingness to discuss feelings with others and to cooperate rather than to compete with their peers, and in seeing the need for top management to be tolerant. At the same time, they remained relatively high among the nationalities in their actual and preferred task orientation relative to their human relations orientation, which admittedly was also strong in an absolute sense. The task centeredness of the Japanese managers appeared more acceptable than it would for British managers, according to White and Trevor (1983), for the Japanese were considered more committed, expert, and socially close (P. B. Smith, 1984a).

Task orientation was expected to be high in organization members in Japan, for it is directly connected with acceptance of the organization's mission and goals. Relations orientation was beyond discussion, for it was assumed on the Japanese scene that organizational survival and success depended on it as well as concerns for the task (Yokochi, 1989b). The same emphasis on task orientation was seen in Japanese-owned plants in Britain, the United States, and Hong Kong, even when a majority of supervisors were not Japanese (Smith, Paterson, Misumi, et al., 1992).

Bolon and Crain (1985) compared the responses of 40 Japanese and 39 U.S. managers and executives in how they would handle a problem subordinate. The Japanese were found to take significantly more steps in dealing with the subordinate. They invested more effort in trying to understand the situation. On the other hand, U.S. male managers (but not female managers) more often attempted to resolve the situation by firing the subordinate or forcing him or her to quit. When American, Indian, and Japanese managers were compared by Ivancevich, Schweiger, and Ragan (1986), it was found that the Japanese felt they obtained more social support from their bosses than did the Indian or American managers. For Indians and Americans, spouses and relatives were more important providers of such social support.

The greater emphasis on the human side of enterprise by Japanese compared with American managers in large firms was seen in their differential response to intensified price competition. Americans cut their human resources expenditures while maintaining their capital equipment, plant, and material resources. They sought financial and legal solutions to deal with the competition rather than technical ones. Before the economic recession in the 1990s, the Japanese tried to save their human resources. They avoided layoffs, discharges, and wage reductions to reduce labor costs, although they did withhold bonuses. If personnel costs had to be cut, they reduced their own salaries and made use of quality circles and other "bottom-up" suggestions to reduce costs. They reduced the costs of production by increasing the flexibility of their operations. When they replaced workers with automation, they transferred and retrained the displaced workers. The Japanese approach required a high degree of coordination and good working relations among R & D, manufacturing, and marketing, as well as commitment, loyalty, and employees' involvement (Tsurumi, 1983).

The Japanese attention to relationships was made more specific by Hall and Hall (1987), who pointed to the unusual degree to which the Japanese place a premium on listening and the value of agreement. Questions should not be posed unless they have answers or the answers can be found beforehand by asking the questions in advance of a meeting. Proposals should not be refused outright, but should be taken under consideration. If a proposal is finally rejected, the reasons need to be fully stated with politeness and apologies. The transformational factor of individualized consideration, as measured by the Multifactor Leadership Questionnaire, emerges from a different set of items in Japan because such consideration is expected from one's supervisor even though it remains unspoken. Guidance by the supervisor and acceptance by the subordinate is an unsaid rule governing their relationship (Yokochi, 1989a).

Westerners who interact with Japanese will be more successful if they pay attention to the need for patience. Impatient behavior will be interpreted as bad manners and a lack of sincerity. Uncontrolled emotion will be considered as weakness and in bad taste. But patience may not help the Western negotiator. Until the economic downturn in the 1990s, the Japanese remained ethnocentric in their domestic business activities in Japan itself. They made special efforts to buy Japanese products whenever possible rather than buying them abroad. They infringed on Western patents (not infringement, according to Japanese law) and continued to rely on more expensive Japanese suppliers. The "old-boy" networks were particularly strong in Japan and difficult for foreigners to penetrate.

Initiation and Consideration

Cultures differ in what is seen as considerate behavior. In the West, it is considerate for a leader to praise publicly but criticize privately. In Japan, criticism from a leader comes indirectly through a peer since direct criticism from the leader would cause the follower to lose face (Smith & Peterson, 1988). Substantial differences in the initiation of structure and consideration have been found among managers from different countries. For instance, Anderson (1983) did not find that consideration by leaders contributed to the effectiveness of managers in New Zealand as was usually found elsewhere. In the Bass, Burger, et al. (1979) 12-nation data for Exercise Self-Appraisal, although there was an overall trend to see the need to be more considerate by leaders at lower levels of management, the French and Latin countries regarded being considerate as relatively unimportant at all levels of management; Northern Europeans, British, and Americans thought it more important. On the other hand, consideration was emphasized by fast-rising but not by slow-climbing managers in Italy, Spain, Portugal, and the United States; it was deemphasized by those with accelerated careers in Belgium, Scandinavia, France, Latin America, and India. Tscheulin (1973) found positive effects of consideration on satisfaction for a German sample, as did Rim (1965) for Israeli nurses and industrial supervisors and Fleishman and Simmons (1970) for Israeli supervisors. But L. R. Anderson (1983) reported the opposite for middle managers in New Zealand.

L. R. Anderson (1966a, 1966b) studied discussion groups composed of American and Indian graduate students. The leader's effectiveness, as rated by the American students, was positively correlated with both the leader's consideration and initiation of structure. But Indian students' ratings of leader effectiveness were correlated only with the leader's consideration scores. When the initiation of structure scores eliminated the coercive items such as "pushing for production," initiation of structure also correlated positively with leader effectiveness.

Differences in Psychometric Properties. Culture may affect the psychometric properties involved in measuring initiation and consideration. As noted earlier, the factor structures of leadership behavior descriptions in the United States, Britain, Japan, and Hong Kong systematically differed, especially in which questionnaire items correlated with initiation of structure (Smith, Tayeb, Peterson, et al., 1986). Ayman and Cherners (1982) emerged with a single factor instead of the two factors of initiation and consideration for European in contrast to U.S. managers, as described by their respective subordinates. When K. F. Mauer (1974) administered the Leadership Opinion Questionnaire to a sample of 190 mine overseers and shift bosses in the South African gold-mining industry, neither a varimax rotation nor an orthogonal target rotation of the two extracted factors approximated the findings of U.S. and Canadian researchers. An oblique target rotation produced a South African solution that was closest to the North American solution.

The correlation between the factors was much higher than that found in other studies. Nevertheless, Matsui, Ohtsuka, and Kikuchi (1978) were able to replicate and extend Fleishman and Peters's (1962) U.S. results with 79 Japanese supervisors. As with the U.S. results, they found that considerate Japanese supervisors (as seen by their subordinates on the Supervisory Behavior Description Questionnaire) were higher in self-inventoried benevolence on L. V. Gordon's Survey of Interpersonal Values. The supervisors' initiation of structure, as described by their subordinates, was lower if the supervisors reported themselves to be higher in valuing independence.[11]

Laissez-Faire Leadership versus the Motivation to Manage [12]

In data collected between 1968 and 1972, the preference to be more influential was high among managers from all 12 nations studied by Bass, Burger, et al. (1979). But it was highest among Japanese, Spanish, and German managers and lowest among French and Dutch managers. During this same period, the endorsement of active intervention by the leader, in contrast to laissez-faire behavior, was seen by Bass and Franke (1972) to relate to a country's rate of economic growth. Bass and Franke obtained a correlation of .93 in the ranking of six industrialized countries between the rate of economic growth of the country for the preceding nine years and the extent to which students from those countries endorsed a manager's being both more participative and more political to achieve success in a career.

Some consistency with these results was obtained by Keys, Edge, Heinz, et al. (1986), who compared the self-descriptions of 214 Korean, 101 Filipino, and 97 American middle managers about how active they were in their relations with others in dealing with various issues. The issues were expected to make a difference, since the Asians were more likely to be more collectivistic and the Americans more individualistic. The Americans reported themselves as being more likely than did the Filipinos or Koreans to threaten their subordinates to obtain compliance with requests. Americans also more frequently ordered subordinates to "do what I want done." Furthermore, the U.S. middle managers were most likely to say that they would disagree openly with their boss and remind the boss about matters if he or she procrastinated. However, the Korean managers were most likely to indicate that they would confront their boss if treated unfairly, while the Filipinos were most likely to indicate a reluctance to go over the boss's head to a higher authority. Less collectivistic than the Filipinos or Koreans, the Americans were more likely to actively complain to their boss if their peers got out of line. They were most likely to remind their peers of rules and policies.

Motivation to Manage. Collectivisim and individualism had different effects on the motive to manage others in hierarchical settings. Projective results on the strength of the motivation to manage within bureaucracies, as revealed by scores on the Miner Sentence Completion Scale (MSCS)[13] by foreign and U.S. students in American schools, were quite different. Consistent with the decline in American MSCS scores between 1960 and 1980 (Miner & Smith, 1982; Miner, Smith, & Ebrahimi, 1985), American students were found to score much lower than Asian or African students. Also, Ebrahimi (1985c) noted that the motivation to manage, as measured by the MSCS, was significantly higher in a combined sample of Japanese, Korean, Taiwanese, Philippine, Ma-

---

[11] See Chapter 8.
[12] See Chapter 6.

[13] See Chapters 17 to 19.

laysian, and Chinese students and a separate sample of Thai students than in a sample of American students. Also, the MSCS scores were successively higher for students from India, Iran, Thailand, and Nigeria. Some of these differences could be attributed to personal differences among the students. The foreign students studying in the United States were likely to be more ambitious, adventuresome, assertive individuals, who were more highly socialized to Western mores and higher in class and education than those who remained at home. At the same time, the results suggested, these Asian and African students would fit more readily into management in the highly bureaucratized organizations in which they were likely to find employment when they returned home. Consistent with these results, Wachtel (1988) found that prospective managers from Mexico were higher in managerial motivation than were their American counterparts.

National Influences on Transformational and Charismatic Leadership

With few exceptions, transformational leadership is universal in its greater success and effects on positive follower outcomes in comparison with management by exception and laissez-faire leadership (Bass, 1997, 1998). Yet there are cultural contingencies. Yan and Shi (2003) set forth that each of Hofstede's (2001) five dimensions differentially relate to the adoption of Bass's (1985) original dimensions of transformational leadership and acceptance by followers. Jung, Bass, and Sosik (1995) argued that transformational leadership was more likely to appear in collectivistic than individualistic cultures. In the collective cultures like those of China, Japan, and Korea, individuals more readily identify with a group, share responsibility for goal attainment, try to maintain a harmonious group, and emphasize mutual interdependence in organizations. These behaviors are consistent with what a transformational or charismatic leader tries to accomplish.

Davis, Guan, Luo, et al. (1997) distributed the Multifactor Leadership Questionnaire in Mandarin to all managers and their subordinates in a state department store in central China. A 65% response rate provided 241 completed questionnaires. Stepwise regression analyses with transactional scores and then transformational

scores were added as predictors of outcomes. An index of transformational leadership added significantly to transactional leadership scores in the prediction of effectiveness ($R^2 = .43$); individual effort ($R^2 = .65$), satisfaction with the leadership ($R^2 = .31$) and intention to quit ($R^2 = -.20$). Contrary to Bass (1997), Ardichvili (2001) found more country specificity than universality in transformational leadership in Georgia, Kazakhstan, Russia, and the Kyrgyz Republic. Koh (1990) reported the same kind of results for school principals in Singapore, which is also high in collectivism and mainly Chinese in culture. Chiu (1997) compared results obtained with 233 part-time MBA students working in collectivist Hong Kong and the sample of individualist Americans used by Bycio, Hackett, & Allen (1985). He also compared in-group members in Hong Kong, those who looked out for the welfare for each individual member in the group, with out-group members. Hong Kong Chinese leaders were more likely to use intellectual stimulation and individualized consideration with their in-group members. American leaders were less likely than Chinese leaders to show individualized consideration to their subordinates. Compared to Americans, Hong Kong Chinese subordinates and members of the in-group were more likely to perceive their leaders as charismatic. Howell, Dorfman, Hibino, et al. (1994) reported that charismatic leadership correlated with subordinate satisfaction in Korea, Taiwan, Mexico, and the United States, but not in Japan.

Japanese leaders take full responsibility for organizational outcomes. They make extra effort to understand their followers' needs and feelings. In turn, they are treated with respect and trust. According to Yokochi (1989a), in collectivist Japan, managers at the CEO level and several rungs below are much more transformational than transactional. Their subordinates are likely to indicate on the Multifactor Leadership Questionnaire that their leaders take full responsibility for their actions (as a matter of tradition) and are generous in giving concrete guidance. The leaders are highly respected and trusted. The leaders encourage sacrifice by subordinates and at the same time make extra efforts to assure subordinates of their feelings and concern for the welfare of the subordinates and their families. Subordinates are challenged with new ideas and tasks. As noted elsewhere, it is the firm or agency, not the leaders, that provides unspoken rewards and promotions.

Yokochi (1989b) completed an MLQ survey of three hierachical levels in 14 Japanese firms involving 66 executives, 44 managers, and 194 subordinates. She concluded that Japanese leaders take readily to transformational leadership as a consequence of their humanistic values and corporate goals. Intellectual stimulation is comfortable due to the culture's emphasis on continuous learning and pursuit of intellectual activities. Strong adherence to company management philosophy is attributed to the desire to emulate senior management behavior. Adherence to hierarchy does not mean autocratic leadership but is rather symbolic. The emperor is highly revered as a figurehead in a constitutional monarchy. Legimate hierarchical orders are usually consensual; decision making is widely shared. The preference is for working in groups. Standing alone for personal freedom is not admired.

Pereira (1986) found similar results in collectivist India for 58 senior and middle-level managers from Larsen and Toubro, an engineering firm. Again, Echevarria and Davis (1997) in the collectivist Dominican Republic reported similarly high correlations of transformational leadership with effectiveness, satisfaction, and extra effort for 402 employees from two newspapers.

Walumba and Lawler (2000, 2003) collected survey data from 745 employees in banking and finance in China, India, Japan and Kenya. They confirmed that transformational leadership contributed to job satisfaction and commitment in all four collectivist countries. In low-power-distance countries such as Australia, transformational leaders are participative in style (Ashkanasy & Falkus, 2004). In high-power-distance countries, they tend to be more directive (Den Hartog, House, Hanges, et al., 1999). Howell and Dorfman (1988) expected charismatic leadership to have a considerable impact on Mexican and American employees' satisfaction with work and with supervision. Although the expected effects were positive on both samples, the impact of charismatic leadership was greater on the American employees. Correlations of .50 and .70 were found, compared to the Mexican employees, for whom the correlations were .29 and .57. Some of the darker history of charismatic Mexican political leaders may have been a drag on the Mexican results. This may partly explain why Ardichvili (2001) found more country specificity than universality in transformational leadership in Georgia, Kazakhstan, Russia, and the

Kyrgyz Republic. Although Australia and the United States belong to the same Anglo-American cluster of countries, Australians put even more of a premium on equality and individualism. Transformational leadership had the same effects in both countries, but Australians varied more in attributing it to their leaders. Transformational factors in Australia are 0.7 to 1.1 lower in standard deviation (Parry, 1994). However, according to Parry (1996), Australians, more than Americans, expect charismatic leaders to take an interest in the welfare of their followers—to be individually considerate. Australians expect a lot more from their leaders than do Americans. High status is not enough to create respect; respect has to be earned.

Transactional Leadership: Contingent Reinforcement. Transactional leadership has many elements that fit better with an individualistic society. Rather than endorsement of shared purposes and identification with group goals, leaders and subordinates are motivated by personal goals. Individual initiatives and self-interest are more important (Jung & Avolio, 1999). Early (1988) pointed to important cross-cultural differences in the effectiveness of contingent rewarding. He noted that since workers in individualist England did not value praise, criticism, or general conversation with their superiors, as did American or Ghanaian workers (Early, 1984), English workers would be less likely to be influenced by contingent rewarding. The English workers, particularly those in heavy industry, would distrust feedback from their supervisors (Blumberg, 1968; Goodman & Whittingham, 1969). In the same way, individualistic U.S. worker samples generated higher correlations between transactional contingent rewarding and measures of satisfaction with work and with supervision (.48 and .73) than Howell and Dorfman (1988) found in collectivist Mexican workers (.19 and .57). Likewise, the effects of contingent punishment were greater for the U.S. than the Mexican samples. Nonetheless, contingent reinforcement was found to have positive effects on satisfaction and organizational commitment in collectivist Taiwan (Dorfman & Howell, 1988). Similar correlations were found by Peterson, Peng, Hunt, et al. (1994) when they compared 447 middle managers and supervisors working in local city government (.54) in the individualistic United States with their 196 counterparts in city government in the collectivist Japan. While noncontingent punishment correlated negatively with job satisfaction in the United States (−.39), it had no effect in collectivist Japan (−.05).

The transactional factor of contingent reward is complicated in Japan by unspoken expectations of reward as well as obligations. For example, the failure to be promoted would be a consequence of failure to meet unspoken expectations. Strict rules of *tatamae* prohibit explicitly seeking rewards or professing open expectations of them. Unspoken needs are those that will be fulfilled with successful leader-follower performance. This *honne* is well understood, although not by those unaccustomed to the system (Yokochi, 1989a). Even more complicating is the fact that Japanese employees do not differentiate themselves from their supervisors and managers but see all collectively as members of the company. Promotion is from within the organization, so that shared common mottos, values, and goals are maintained by workers and management. Pay differentials are small and are decided (along with promotions) not by one's immediate superior but by the amorphous company, consistent with its standards, values, history, and traditions. Even more of a problem for the Japanese is management by exception, since it is difficult for them to appreciate such a supervisory-subordinate relationship. For them, it would be a matter of custom and tradition for a supervisor to be more concerned about the subordinate.

Howell, Dorfman, Hibino, et al. (1994) reported that contingent reward, praise, approval, and recognition by the leader for good performance universally generated follower commitment, satisfaction with supervision, and satisfaction with the leader. (This is not surprising since Antonakis and Avolio (2004) found that contingent reward such as recognition is both transformational and transactional.) Material rewards are transactional. However, contingent reproof and disapproval for poor performance had more of an impact in individualistic countries like the United States than in the collectivistic countries of Asia. The same should be true for management by exception. Parry (1996) set forth the idea that monitoring and controlling subordinates' interpersonal behavior is indicative of less effective leadership, more in Australia than in the United States. Subordinates are more cynical about authority and likely to reject influence based only on the status of the source.

Leadership in the Multinational Firm

Multinational Corporations (MNCs)

International organizations, both collegial and hierarchical, have been around for a long time, dating back to the ancient world. Currently, executives, managers, and employees from the world's different nations work together in the United Nations, the World Bank, the World Court, and a host of other international agencies and private enterprises. Among these international organizations, much of the available research on leader-subordinate relations appeared in studies of multinational corporations that began with management and industrial activities in one country and spread to others as they went beyond importing and exporting to manufacturing, marketing, and research in the other countries through developing, purchasing and franchising subsidiaries organized for these purposes. Many MNCs have recognized that increasingly their sales and revenues are coming from foreign sales and services. For instance, Avon Products, a U.S. firm, was making 65% of its sales abroad by the mid-1990s (Henson, 1996).

The Growth of MNCs. Direct investment in development or acquisition of foreign subsidiaries or merging with other companies across borders came when import or export alone failed to meet supplies, sales, or service objectives domestically or as a result of the personal predilictions of senior management of the MNC. An MNC may develop and provide funding for a new start-up subsidiary headed by a parent-company executive and some staff who will mainly hire and train host-country nationals. It may purchase a local firm for cash or stock in whole or in part. If integration with the parent company or domestic and other foreign subsidiaries is sought, parent-country or third-country executives, managers, and supervisors may be placed in key positions. MNC mergers involve creating one company out of two by one company taking over another across borders. Development of a foreign start-up contains the fewest cross-cultural problems and is likely to be successful. Mergers encompass the most cross-cultural problems and are least likely to be successful (Hofstede, 2001). Deals may fail as a consequence of misunderstanding one's own culture or the other party's culture (Kemper, 1997). Often, mergers and joint ventures face conflicts in the distribution of power and agreement about the criteria on which to judge performance. For instance, in Chinese and American joint ventures, the Chinese favor evaluating the technology; Americans favor evaluating operations (Zhao & Culpepper, 1997). Cultural proximity between the MNC and the subsidiary increased the chances for Dutch MNCs' success in start-ups, acquisitions, and mergers (Barkema, Bell, & Pennings, 1996) and likewise for Chinese joint ventures with foreign MNCs (Luo, 1999).

International Strategic Alliances. These are formal contracts or understandings between partner firms across borders. They provide linkages of resources for joint accomplishment of objectives. In 1983 to 1986, such cooperative arrangements were likely to generate cross-cultural conflicts. For instance, Americans want frequent interactions in alliances and explicit understandings in formal contracts; Japanese are satisfied with more implicit agreements. The Americans are comfortable with vigorous conflict; the South Koreans and the Middle Easterners find conflict distasteful. A survey of cross-border alliances with American firms had a failure rate of 70%. Nevertheless, Americans felt that alliances provided important information. European and Japanese firms emphasized the strategic needs met by alliances (Parkbe, 1993).

The United States dominated the multinational scene in the 1960s. European MNC parent countries included Germany, Britain, Sweden, and Italy. MNCs also originated in Japan, Korea, India, and Arab countries as well as in Australia, South Africa, and elsewhere. Regardless of origins, MNCs become truly globalized, with shares owned, components assembled, markets, personnel, and research deriving increasingly from many countries. In 1991, 4.1 million Americans were working for foreign multinationals in the United States (Eunni & Post, 2002). Their headquarters are in Britain, the Netherlands, Germany and Japan. For instance, in 1992, Japanese nationals with subsidiaries in the United States employed an estimated 850,000 Americans and about 27,000 Japanese expatriates. About three-fourths of the 7,000 businesses were small or medium-sized. They were owned by 2,000 Japanese firms. They tried to minimize layoffs, provide 20% more pay, and hire as many women and minorities as their American counterparts. Americans participate as managers at all levels, but much more at lower levels.

The Americans had to adapt to the more flexible Japanese management system (Tsurumi, 1992).

Approaches to Management. MNCs, such as General Motors (United States), L. M. Ericsson (Sweden), Mitsubishi (Japan), and Ciba-Geigy (Switzerland), originating as they did in different countries, vary considerably in their approaches to coordination, the balancing of requirements, promotion of host country nationals, decision making, and power relationships (Doz & Prahalad, 1984). On the one hand, we have seen, for instance, in the Exxon studies that forecast success as a manager (Laurent, 1970) and the Arab-American homogenization of perceived leadership styles within their multinational firms (Algattan, 1985), that multinational firms are a force for global convergence. At the same time, the GLOBE studies confirmed both the similarities and differences among managers from different countries (House, Hanges, & Javidan, 2004).

Fitting the Culture. Management and leadership in multinational corporations (MNCs) need to fit more with the host country than with the parent-country culture. For instance, Newman and Nollen (1996) found that among 176 business units in 18 Asian and Western foreign subsidiaries of a U.S. MNC, unit and subsidiary profitability as measured by returns on sales and assets was higher if practices in the unit matched whether the host country was high or low in Hofstede's (2001) dimensions. Nevertheless, the American MNC Procter & Gamble introduced a U.S. code of ethics into its Asian and African subsidiaries. The subsidiaries, unlike the ones in the United States, were all high in power distance, collectivism, uncertainty avoidance, and masculinity. P&G expected to see some adaptation in the subsidiaries of reduced collectivism and masculinity (Reeves-Ellington, 1995).

Management controls tend to reflect more the culture of the parent company's home-country culture. According to a study of 75 foreign acquisitions, American MNCs tend to emphasize more informal control and the use of teams; British and French MNCs tend to stress more formal control (Calori, Lubatkin, & Very, 1994). In general, the greater the cultural distance between the parent and host country, the more likely is control to be personalized and centralized (Harzing, 1999) and the more likely is the CEO to be from the parent country, according to a study of 287 subsidiaries of 104 MNCs in nine parent countries and 22 host countries by Harzing (1999).

The cultural adaptation of the parent-country manager to the host country may make a difference. A videotape of a Japanese parent-company national interacting with host-country national subordinate in the United States was shown to 223 employees of Japanese manufacturing firms in the United States. Management effectiveness and intentions to trust were positively related when the manager was shown as being culturally adapted to the United States (Thomas & Ravlin, 1995). Nationals of a country may differ in what they do when they are at home and when they go abroad. Takamiya (1979) observed that Japanese firms in the United States and in Europe were not providing lifetime job security or Japanese-style company welfare programs for their employees. Nonetheless, the Japanese firms abroad were found to be highly productive and to maintain the same high-quality standards they did at home. The success of the firms appeared to be more a consequence of their attention to production management and high-quality standards than to Japanese-style human relations practices (Hayes, 1981). Pascale and Maguire (1980) came to similar conclusions from a study of 13 Japanese firms operating in both Japan and the United States. They found that the location of Japanese plants in Japan or the United States was more important to supervisor-subordinate relations than the fact that the management was Japanese. Absenteeism was lower in Japan; more was spent on employee benefits in the United States. According to a study of 126 firms, they were more likely to expand and diversify internationally if their top management team was younger, longer-tenured, higher in elite education, and more experienced internationally (Tihanyi, Ellstrand, Daily, et al., 2000).

Parent, Host, and Third-Country Nationals

Little has been reported about the specific leader-subordinate relationships of supervisors of one nationality and subordinates of another. They may be operating together at the headquarters in the parent country, in a host country, or in a third country. The leader or the subordinate may be a parent-country national (PCN), a host-country national (HCN), or a third-country national (TCN).

Developing International Managers. Oddou and Derr (1991) examined 55 Anglo American, Scandinavian, German, Dutch, and Latin European MNCs ranging in size from under 1,000 to over 200,000 employees. The functions internationalized in order from most to least were marketing, finance, manufacturing, R & D, and human resources. Fifty-three percent of the top 50 line managers had experienced at least one international assignment, as had 48% of the staff managers. The two most frequent means of developing international managers were moving PCNs to foreign offices and conducting international seminars with PCNs, HCNs, and TCNs. More needed to be done by developing international task forces and bringing HCNs and TCNs to a major parent-country national office Additionally, to meet the needs for more expertise about the host countries and international issues, the firms planned to: (1) hire more HCNs, (2) use more specialized consultants, (3) increase use of HCNs in other countries, (4) send top managers to international seminars, and (5) create international networks with friendly firms. Company inattention to proper selection and training of PCNs was a particularly important source of failure. In another study of 105 MNCs, ratings of the reported lack of rigor of selection, training, and preparation of personnel for overseas assignment correlated .63 with personnel failure rates (Tung, 1979).

Decision Making, Status, and Power. Of considerable importance to the leader-subordinate relationship in the MNC is its method of decision making and the differential status and power of its PCNs, HCNs, and TCNs. Perlmutter (1969) saw three possibilities: (1) *ethnocentric*—the PCN in all respects and all decisions and methods is controlled by the PCN. PCNs monopolize the power and status; (2) *polycentric*—the organization is host-oriented. Local HCNs are seen able to make the best decisions. HCNs are more equal in power to PCNs; and (3) *geocentric*—the organization is world-oriented, and a balanced view of decision making takes account of local and national interests and the objectives of the multinational firm. Managerial positions are filled by people having the most talent, regardless of their national background. TCNs have as much status and power as PCNs and HCNs.

As a multinational organization matures, it moves from ethnocentric to geocentric organizational patterns. Presumably, cultural origins become less significant in the decision-making process with increasing maturity. Ethnocentricity may be maintained longer by Japanese firms. Polycentrism may be the only stage for some service firms, such as convenience foods franchises; geocentrism may be reached early in other industries that find comparative advantages in integrating activities in different countries to obtain their financing and supplies, their research, development, and manufacturing, and marketing their products. But empirically, according to their CEOs, Japanese parent company headquarters exert little influence on leadership style in American subsidiaries. On the other hand, the leadership style in Japanese foreign subsidiaries are influenced by TCNs and HCNs in their corporate headquarters (Justin & Jones, 1995).

Differences in Satisfaction, Perspective, and Valuation.

A job satisfaction survey completed by Peter (1969) for Shell, a British-Dutch multinational corporation, illustrated the significance of employees' identification as PCNs, HCNs, or TCNs. Non-Europeans were much more dissatisfied with the company's image than were Europeans. Moreover, among all the nationals, the PCN British and Dutch were relatively most satisfied with the company as a place to work and with opportunities to obtain responsibility and authority.

The managers' work location, their willingness to work abroad, and their experience in working abroad are likely to affect their attitudes. Positive experiences are likely to generate more favorable attitudes and satisfaction with foreign assignments. The turnover rates of American PCNs ranged from 16% to 40%, compared to 5% to 15% for Americans who remained in the United States (Eunni & Post, 2002). Their intention to quit the job in the foreign location was greater than to leave their organization (Birdseye & Hill, 1995). But Yeh (1988) generally did not find differences in power distance, avoidance of uncertainty, individualism, and masculinity when PCN and TCN managers (63 American and 356 Japanese) were compared with HCN managers (2,237 Taiwanese) working for firms in Taiwan.

Possibly reflecting MNCs in general, Swedish and Dutch MNCs top management teams have not internationalized as have their employees (Eunni, 2002). When a team is international in composition, the perspectives of the different members need to be understood. Mem-

bers may vary in whether they are oriented toward the mastery of nature and its control with technology, are oriented to subjugation of nature with a predestined plan and unavoidable constraints, or are oriented toward living in harmony with nature and a balance of self and environment. Humans are seen as basically good or evil. If good, they can be trusted; if evil, they are untrustworthy. Their perspectives also differ if they come from countries high rather than low in PDI, UAI, IDV, MAS, and/or LTO. International teams need to *decenter*—change from blaming others for the differences and developing an understanding that the differences are due to different perspectives. Then they can *recenter*—build a common view of the situation to better deal with it (Maznevski & Peterson, 1997).

Uniformity.

According to interviews with 248 HCNs and PCNs by Zeira (1975), PCNs and TCNs tend to impose parent-country headquarters' managerial patterns on their host-country peers and subordinates. This finding was corroborated by Al-Jafari and Hollingsworth (1983). But although an Arab organization, as such, would have been expected to operate more autocratically than a U.S. or European multinational firm, among 337 managers of 10 multinational organizations in the Persian Gulf region, both U.S. and Arab managers saw their organizations operating in a Survey of Organizations Systems 3 (consultative) mode and leaning toward Systems 4, an even more participative style (Al-Jafari & Hollingsworth, 1983).

According to headquarters' PCN personnel directors, multinational uniformity facilitated comparisons of managers in subsidiaries in different countries (Zeira, 1975). Uniformity was also thought to keep up the firm's reputation in different countries and to make it easier to introduce policy changes. HCNs disagreed. A majority thought that PCNs maintain uniformity of policies and practices for their own self-interest. The HCNs believed that the PCNs (and the TCNs) at higher management levels in the local subsidiaries were not motivated to make local improvements or to meet local needs. They thought that the PCNs' insensitivity to the expectations of local HCNs resulted in many conflicts. The HCNs were particularly critical of the tendency of multinational firms to centralize decisions, which made it impossible to adapt to the needs of the local marketplace. They mistrusted their PCN superiors and believed that their promotion to a higher level was prevented by their not being nationals of the parent country (Zeira, 1975).

PCN Benefits. Because the PCNs are representative of their multinational corporations, they can achieve entry into the upper-class social life of the local communities beyond what they could reach in their previous positions at international headquarters at home. PCNs obtain special benefits as part of their compensation abroad. This makes it possible for them to enjoy a standard of living that is considerably higher than that of their local peers and higher than what they can expect when they return home.

Why PCNs Fail or Succeed. Despite the extra benefits of working abroad, the failure rates of PCNs are high. More than one third return from overseas assignments prematurely. The incidence of divorce, alcoholism, and drug abuse is high (Chesanow, 1984). PCNs may experience anxiety over their transfer, disorientation as a result of culture shock, social dislocation, anxiety about being separated from family and friends, and feelings of having been abandoned by headquarters. They may sense that they lack the necessary influence and local technical assistance. They may have physical problems. Reentry problems on returning home also need to be faced (Ronen, 1986).

A survey of 321 American managers on international assignment found a correlation of .71 between commitment to both the parent and host companies with how much discretion they had in their roles, .47 with adjustment to the host country, and .33 with how much they interacted with host nationals. They were commited to their parent company rather than their host country company to the extent they had predeparture training ($r = .60$) and if they were not adjusted to the host country ($r = .53$) (Gregersen & Black, 1992). Among 109 British managers, willingness to work abroad depended on the country to which they might be assigned. On a scale of 1 to 7, among 22 countries, they were most willing to serve in the Netherlands (5.11), France (5.01), northwestern European countries (4.67), North America (4.64), and Australia (4.40). They were less willing to serve in southern Europe (3.77), eastern Europe (2.84), South America (2.77), and Japan (2.71), and least willing to serve in

Africa (2.36), China (2.21), and the Middle East (1.92). They were most willing to go abroad for a British parent organization (6.53) and least willing to go abroad for a Japanese parent organization (2.28). The willingness to accept a foreign assignment was correlated with viewing a life goal of independence as highly important and a life goal of security as less important.

The spouse's willingness to relocate, short- and long-term, was seen to be a function of individual, family, and organizational circumstances according to a questionnaire survey of 427 international managers and their 167 spouses by Konopaske, Robie, and Ivancevich (2003). A survey of 105 U.S. multinational firms by Tung (1979) suggested that the most important reasons for a PCN's failure to function effectively in a foreign environment were: (1) the inability of the manager's spouse and family to adjust to a different physical or cultural environment; (2) the manager's inability to adapt to a different physical or cultural environment; (3) the manager's emotional immaturity; (4) the manager's inability to cope with the larger responsibilities posed by the overseas work; (5) the manager's lack of technical competence for the job assignment; and (6) the manager's lack of motivation to work overseas.

Hechanova, Beehr, and Christianson (2003) completed a meta-analysis of 42 empirical studies involving 5,210 PCNs and TCNs demonstrating that general, interactional, and work adjustment were predicted by self-efficacy. The mean correlations ranged from .27 to .41. Path analysis indicated that the three adjustments reduced stress and increased job satisfaction with the foreign assignment. Finally, job satisfaction and lack of stress both contributed to organizational commitment, job performance, and intention to stay.

PCNs can fail because their customary back-home autocratic or democratic style of leadership may be a poor match for the host culture (M. G. Harvey, 1996). Or they can fail because they erroneously adopt the wrong leadership style for the host country. For instance, probably because of their low estimation of the capabilities and discipline of their Melanesian host employees in Papua New Guinea, an Australian firm adopted a rational-economic, authoritarian, hierarchical leadership approach that was incompatible with traditional styles of Melanesian leadership. Performance and job satisfaction suffered, and the project had to be abandoned following large sunk costs (Ronen, 1986). In England, Holland, Belgium, and West Germany, most HCNs felt that to avoid failure, PCNs need to adapt their leadership style to fit the prevailing pattern in the host country, rather than to emphasize uniformity with the multinational parent country. PCNs need to understand the local nonverbal language and clients' and employees' expectations. A sore point is the larger benefit package often provided to the PCN than to HCNs (Zeira & Banai, 1981).

Stolin (1997) suggested that North American executives fail in selecting competent managers in Russia because the PCNs tend to choose those with whom they will be more comfortable, that is, those with a good command of English and a Westernized persona. Such managers may be less respected by subordinates than those who pursue a more Russian leadership style. For instance, in Canada and the United States, a manager's delegation is seen as a sign of trust and confidence. In Russia, it is perceived that by delegating, the manager is avoiding the risk that he is imposing on the subordinate.

Repatriation. Most PCNs experience problems when in returning to their parent country. Positions similar to their status and responsibility abroad need to be found. Visibility and promotional opportunities in the home office may be lost while the PCN is away (Gregerson & Black, 1996). There may be a loss of autonomy, career direction, and a feeling that the foreign experience was undervalued (Scullion, 1992). Reintegration into the firm was seen as more difficult by most expatriates than the original move abroad (Linehan, 2001). Many chose to resign from the organization and take jobs with other firms (Black & Gregersen, 1998).

Conflicting National Values. Despite globalization and convergence, large differences in national values can be continuing sources of stress and conflict when managers work outside their own country. Japanese value patience, harmony, and hierarchy; Americans value action, freedom, and equality. According to an eight-country multinational survey of 2,514 senior managers, 50.4% rated their top-management teams as insensitive to internal issues within their corporation and 27.8% as divergent in vision rather than sharing in vision of internal issues (McMahon & Myers, 1995).

The newly arrived Japanese manager in the United States may be shocked by American social diversity, violence and crime, poverty and homelessness, inadequate service, hasty deal making, legal minefields, lack of spiritual organizational quality, individual careerism, narrow job focus, political confrontation, and employee disloyalty. The Japanese manager may also be shocked by American assertiveness, frankness, egoism, glibness, and impulsiveness (Linowes, 1993). I asked a group of Japanese managers working for various firms in New York City about their biggest surprise in their American assignment. They all said that they were most surprised by how the American experience had changed their wives.

Suggested Remedial Actions. A survey of 402 corporate employees with overseas experience concluded that selection based on interviews and psychological analyses of the candidates and their families is likely to be more useful in placing employees in foreign assignments than is depending on training alone to provide employees with the means to cope with cultural problems and communication barriers (Dotlich, 1982).

At the same time, a phenomenon that may help PCNs in a foreign assignment is the socialization process in shifting attitudes from the norms of the parent country toward the norms of the host country. For example, Lee and Larwood (1983) found that a sample of 33 U.S. expatriate managers in Korea shifted significantly closer to the mean of 105 native Korean managers and away from the mean of 74 U.S. managers in the United States in favoring more nonmaterialism, less materialism, more security, less achievement, less competition, more reflectiveness, less activity, and more subjectivity in relationships.

Expatriate managers agreed that the adaptability of families, interpersonal and leadership skills, and technical and language competence are required for the success of PCN managers. They also pointed to the importance of respect for the laws and people of the host country (Gonzalez & Negandhi, 1967). In a policy-capturing analysis, Russelli and Dickinson (1978) identified, from among 75 attributes, what it takes to be successful in work in other countries: the acceptability of the assignment to the candidate and the family, skill in interpersonal relations, skill in planning and organizing, and linguistic and technical ability. Thirty-nine upper-middle managers in international divisions of their companies used these attributes to judge 60 profiles, half of which were of candidates for jobs in hardship posts, the other half in relatively comfortable foreign assignments. The acceptability of the assignment to the candidate and the family weighed more heavily in the decisions of the 39 managers than all the other attributes. Skill in interpersonal relationships weighed more heavily than skill in planning and organizing, proficiency in the language of the host country, and technical ability. Adaptability weighed more heavily than did technical ability and proficiency in the language of the host country.

Staffing with HCNs. A survey of PCN West German male middle managers in a German multinational corporation found them likely to doubt the competence of their HCN subordinates (more particularly in Latin America and Europe, rather than in the United States) but not the competence of their own peers or supervisors (Miller & Cattaneo, 1982). Consistent with this finding, more HCNs are used in developed countries than in developing countries, where qualified HCNs are less readily available. Nevertheless, when efforts are made to locate, select, and train HCNs, dramatic increases can be achieved in the percentage of HCN managers in a developing country, as was illustrated by Nestlé, the Swiss multinational firm, in its Ivory Coast subsidiary (Salmons, 1977).

Multinational firms can attract potentially more productive and accommodating types of HCNs into their ranks than can comparable domestic firms. For example, Vansina and Taillieu (1970) showed that highly task-oriented Flemish business school graduates preferred to work for U.S. or German companies than for their own Belgian organizations.

North American and European multinationals employ HCNs at all levels of management, particularly in developed countries. The reasons for management staffing with HCNs include familiarity with the culture, knowledge of the local language, reduced costs, and good public relations (Tung, 1979). TCNs are most likely to be used as a consequence of their competence and technical expertise. PCNs, likewise, are selected for technical competence and are more likely to be used when starting up a foreign enterprise.

Japanese multinationals are most likely to continue to employ PCNs for top- and middle-management positions in their foreign operations (Tung, 1982), in the belief that HCNs or TCNs will not be able to understand, transmit, and maintain the desired organizational culture and policies and communicate easily with the Japanese home office. However, the interest of U.S. multinational corporations in the local employment of HCNs, rather than PCNs, has increased, and their interest in training PCNs for work abroad has decreased. It is uncertain how this change in interest will influence the movement of local HCNs into the headquarters offices and into top-management positions (Latham, 1988), but it does suggest that fewer U.S. PCNs will be able to have experience in foreign assignments as they move up the corporate ladder—an important aspect of management development in any firm in the global market for suppliers and customers. In the long term, developing HCNs as managers is less expensive than continuing to depend on PCNs abroad, but it requires good communications, decentralization of decision making, and prospects of career advancement similar to those enjoyed by PCNs, thereby making the multinational more attractive to HCNs (Rosenzweig, 1994).

Summary and Conclusions

The exponential increase in cross-cultural research in leadership in the past 25 years led Dickson, Den Hartog, and Michelson (2004) to suggest that it would be impossible to cover the topic with one chapter. I have tried and hope I did not leave out too much. Although internationalization proceeds apace as we become a unified global economy, cultural and national differences affect leader-follower relationships. Nevertheless, there is considerable universality in traits, origins, and requirements for leadership.

Countries and cultures can be clustered to provide the bases for useful classifications. The unit of study one uses to examine how nationality and culture affect leadership may be clusters of countries with cultural affinities, individual countries within the same or different clusters, and subgroups within countries. Different conclusions may be reached, depending on which unit is used. The cultural dimensions of consequence to leadership in a given society include traditionalism, particularism, collectivism, and idealism, compared to modernity, universalism, individualism, and pragmatism. In the same way, the needs for achievement, affiliation, and the power of subordinates and supervisors have different effects on leader-follower relations in different cultures. The meaning and practice of styles of leadership such as participation differ considerably when studied in China rather than in Britain or France.

Although some argue that there is one best way to manage, considerable evidence points to the greater effectiveness of autocratic leadership behavior in authoritarian cultures and of democratic leadership behavior in democratic cultures. The same is seen for direction versus participation, task orientation versus relations orientation, and initiation versus consideration. Within the multinational firm, leader-subordinate relations will be affected by whether the firm is ethnocentric, polycentric, or geocentric and whether the individuals involved are from the parent country of the organization, the host country, or a third country. The success rate of managers in foreign assignments can be improved considerably by assessment and training, as will be discussed next for leaders in general.

Development and Identification of Leaders and Leadership

Training and Development

"Teach and institute leadership" was among W. Edwards Demings's 14 principles of quality control. Moreover, the importance of leadership training was implicit in many of his other principles, such as the need to set up a climate for innovation and to remove barriers that rob people of pride in workmanship. Between 1980 and 1998, the Kellogg Foundation funded 31 community, high school, and college projects to test and support models of leadership development for young adults. Evidence was obtained that such programs were effective in developing the leadership potential of participants which persisted (Zimmerman-Oster & Burkhart, 1999). During the years that followed, Kellogg carried on the effort with higher education organizations, professional associations, and other institutions (Foster, 1998). The Kravis Leadership Institute identified 49 institutions with formal academic training in leadership. Of 10 of these, all had community service requirements and most offered specific courses in leadership (Ayman, Adams, Fisher, et al., 2003).

Approaches. Wren (1994) proposed a model course for teaching leadership drawn from history, political science, philosophy, psychology, and anthropology. McGill and Slocum (1994) suggested learning to lead from modeling mentoring, managing, and monitoring learning—"the most powerful ways that leaders can exert influence on the behavior of people in their organization" (p. 7). Leaders themselves learn in a variety of ways, such as (1) modeling themselves after esteemed persons; (2) adopting an implicit idea about what to do and trying to do it; (3) observing how to solve a problem as an opportunity for experience; and (4) seeking truth through observation, conceptualization, deduction, and/or experimentation (Bennis & Goldsmith, 1997). Six organizations, including the World Bank, General Electric, and Shell International, were studied, from a total of 35 organizations, and identified by a surveying research team as having the best practices in developing leaders.

These best practices were (1) leadership development has been aligned with corporate strategy; (2) leadership development has mixed educational and business interests; (3) the particular competencies and characteristics of successful leaders in their own organization have been defined; (4) development of leaders is emphasized, rather than recruitment from outside; (5) action learning and real-time business issues are the basis of leadership development; (6) leadership development is linked to succession planning; (7) leadership development is supported by top management throughout the success of the effort; and (8) evaluations of the leadership development effort, from quantitative to anecdotal, are ongoing (Fulmer & Wagner, 1999). B. Lee (1996) added that leadership development programs should focus on universal principles of vision, trust, and feedback, the core of personal change. It should be a continuing rather than a onetime process. The design of leadership learning in the postindustrial world must reflect advances in technology, globalization, and societal developments. The design should emphasize process, action, discovery, virtuality, and practical outcomes (Fulmer, 1997).

Development of Leadership

C. M. Cox's (1926) study of 300 eminent historical personages noted the appearance among them in childhood of leadership traits of intelligence, self-confidence, and assertiveness. Likewise, Barton (1984) commented that as children, those who subsequently became community leaders displayed greater-than-ordinary role diversity, flexibility in dealing with others, and other signs of leadership potential.

Nature or Nurture? "Are leaders born or made?" has been the age-old question. Indeed, one's genes contribute to one's intelligence and activity levels, which in turn contribute to leadership. As noted in Chapter 5, according to comparisons of identical and fraternal twins, heritability plays a significant role. Childhood experiences make their mark. Developing facility with language is of consequence to leadership. To some extent, leaders are "born" and developed at an early age. But at the same time, much can be done with children's development, education, and training to "make" them leaders. Understanding the performance of leaders requires an examination of their family background, early childhood development, education, and role models, along with the social and political learning experiences, informal and formal, that they personally encounter as an adult that shape their performance as leaders.

Personal and Sociological Differences. Differences in individual development formed the basis of a theory of transformational leadership by Kuhnert and Lewis (1987), who proposed that such leadership reflects the mature adult development of personal standards and transcendental values in the leader. In contrast, those who pursue only transactional approaches have been arrested at lower levels of development that are built around their own needs, feelings, and interpersonal connections.

Rejai and Phillips (1979, 1988, 1996, 1998) studied the development of 135 revolutionary, 50 loyalist, and 45 military leaders from four centuries and four continents. They concluded that the three kinds of leaders were remarkably similar in sociodemographic backgrounds, psychological dynamics, and situational conditions regardless of time, place, culture, and national frontiers. The leaders tended to be (1) native-born men; (2) born into a political or military family; (3) mainstream in ethnicity and religion; (4) well educated; (5) urbanized, cosmopolitan, and widely traveled; (6) stimulated by relative deprivation of the values and status they sought; (7) culturally marginal in norms; (8) vain and egotistical; (9) either a nationalist or an imperialist; and (10) verbally and organizationally skilled. Nevertheless, some differences also appeared. Revolutionaries were more likely to be from the middle class (50%) than the upper (20%) or lower class (30%). They were motivated by a sense of justice, subscribed to a spartan lifestyle, and resisted colonization and occupation. Loyalists were uniformly nationalistic and patriotic but lacked a commitment to social justice. They were mainly upper or middle class.

Their fathers held prestigious occupations. Military leaders were likely to be born in rural areas before becoming urbanized. They distinguished between their own people as good and other people as bad. In more recent times, they were most likely to come from the middle or lower class.

Organizational Differences. A 1997 survey of 540 organizations, ranging in size from 50 to 2,000 employees or more, obtained findings indicating that "leading edge" firms, compared with ordinary firms, spend more money on training and tend to be leaders in technology. They are more likely to make use of newer practices such as 360-degree feedback, individual feedback, mentoring, and coaching. Successful organizations, compared with unsuccessful organizations, use more learning technologies and are influenced more by innovative training. The health care industry had the highest rate of employee training (82%). Ninety-three percent of the 540 organizations engaged in management and supervisory skills training, and 63% provided for executive development. The management and supervisory training were almost equally split between inside and outside courses, but executive development was mainly outside. Management and supervisor training included conducting employee appraisals, implementing rules and policies, managing projects and processes, planning, and budgeting. Computer literacy and applications were also important. Executive development included leadership, envisioning, strategic planning, policy making, and goal setting (Anonymous, 1998).

Changes in management and leadership development need to reflect the challenges of the postindustrial world, the changing marketplace, and new technologies. Globalization and the changing workforce will require more sensitivity to diversity and community and more interpersonal competence (Conger, 1993a).

Developmental Issues in Leadership

Stages in Developing Leaders

Chapter 30 alluded to the persistence of leadership tendencies from childhood to adolescence and from adolescence to adulthood. This chapter looks at the factors that contribute to such persistence. Adult development appears to follow along the lines described in theories of childhood development. For instance, the constructive developmental theory of Kegan (1982) focused on a series of developmental experiences in adolescence and adulthood. Kegan and Lacey (1984) showed that the theory could be applied to adult leadership development. As do children, adults continue to learn to integrate new information into schemata of subjective and objective reality that influence their maturing behavior. As an individual develops, subjective understanding becomes objective. Development occurs in stages of differentiation and integration of empathy and principled decision making. At lower stages, little empathy is shown for another person's perspectives and feelings. The individual is self-oriented. At the middle level, the individual is guided by principles of relationships and interaction with others. At maturity, the individual is guided by principles of integrity, fairness, and trust. The theory explains the emergence of transformational leadership (Kuhnert & Lewis, 1987). Lucius (1997) validated the theory empirically for 32 military cadet undergraduate juniors. Four interviewers rated the cadets' demonstrated initiatives, peer rankings of esteem, and the cadets' responses to the Rest (1986) Defining Issues Test of stages in moral development. Constructive development significantly correlated .34 with the cadets' demonstrated initiatives, .35 with their esteem, and .34 with their moral development.

The succession, tenure, and performance of owners and coaches of National Basketball Association teams appear to go through stages of disruption, learning, and stagnation. Disruption is most prevalent when coaches are changed during the season (Giambatista, 2004). According to Quinn (1988) and Dryfus and Dryfus (1986), managers and leaders evolve in five stages, from novice to expert. The *novice* learns facts and rules to be followed. With some experience, the *advanced beginner* in the second stage starts to pay attention also to basic norms and values in the situation. In the third stage, *competence as a leader*, the complexity of the task is appreciated, and a large set of cues is recognized. Calculated risks are taken. Reliance on rules begins to disappear. In the fourth, *proficiency*, stage, rules, calculation, and rational analysis are replaced by an unconscious, fluid, and effortless flow. Finally, in the fifth or *expert* stage, the leader uses a holistic recognition based on a full understanding of the situation. Cognitive maps are mentally programmed. The leader has an intuitive grasp of the situation and can change strategies as cues change.

Family Influences

The Adams family illustrates family influence in the dynasties of leaders who continue for a number of generations. John Adams, founding father and second president of the United States; his son John Quincy, the fourth president; his grandson Charles Francis, congressman and diplomat; and his great-grandson Henry played leading roles in politics, literature, and journalism (Brookhiser, 2002). The two presidents Roosevelt, Theodore and Franklin, and Franklin's wife, Eleanor, were cousins from an elite New York family. They fought against the economic privileges of their own class, championed reform and progressivism, and transformed the political landscape of America. Franklin and especially Eleanor also played important roles in the creation of the United Nations. Other American dynasties have been the Kennedys—brothers John, Robert, and Edward, their father (an ambassador) and grandfather (a mayor), and their sons (state and federal representatives); the Longs of Louisiana—Huey, Earl, and Russell (governors and senators); and the Bushes—Senator Prescott Bush of Connecticut; his son the forty-first president, George Herbert Walker Bush; his grandson the forty-third president, George W. Bush; and George's brother, Florida governor Jeb Bush. The Nehrus and Gandhis are well-known examples from India. In dynastic dictatorship, political power and position are passed on to spouses, siblings, and children, as occurs in hereditary monarchies. Family influence in Britain was examined by C. J. Cox and Cooper (1988). They found that successful British managers in larger "blue-chip" organizations came from high-status public school (that is, U.S. private school) and "Oxbridge" backgrounds; those in smaller and local firms attended grammar (U.S. public) and professional schools. Of course, the British hereditary monarchy ensures family influences on its royalty.

Each girl in H. H. Jennings's (1943) sociometric analysis[1] was asked to describe the different members of her family and to name the member whom she most closely resembled. The leaders (in terms of sociometric choice

---

[1] See Chapter 10 for more details.

and offices held) were found to identify themselves with the member of the family whom they described as sociable, reliable, and encouraging. Nonleaders identified themselves with the family members who they said tended to express discouragement, anxiety, and worry.

Birth Order. Childhood and adolescent relationships at home result in tendencies of some to emerge as a leader during these formative years. Of significance are birth order, family size, family socioeconomic status, and parental treatment. Some studies, such as Day's (1980) analysis of promotion of 116 health care professionals, found that being either firstborn or lastborn was conducive to advancement, compared with being born in between. To explain such results, theorists attributed different personality developments to the eldest and youngest children and those born in between. Compared with his or her siblings, the oldest child in a family was thought to be less dominant, less aggressive, less self-confident, and less inclined toward leadership because of the inexperience and insecurity of the parents with their firstborn child and the need for the oldest child to adjust from an only-child family to a family in which attention toward children is divided (Goodenough & Leahy, 1927). Nonetheless, the firstborn has the advantage of more early interaction with adults and adult language. As was noted in Chapter 31, firstborn children are also likely to be given family responsibilities earlier and are expected to mature faster. In comparison with their siblings, youngest children were reported to be more disobedient, more persistent, and more likely to be pampered and helped when help is no longer necessary, as well as disregarded when family or personal decisions are to be made (Hurlock, 1950). In all, taken by itself, it would seem that birth order may or may not make a difference, depending on other aspects of family life, such as the family's income, parental expectations, a full-time working mother, and so on. In low-income families or families with working mothers, the firstborn, particularly girls, tend to be given considerable responsibility for caring for their siblings early on.

Family Size. Maller (1931) found that the tendency of a child to work in a group for a group goal, rather than alone for an individual prize, is greatest among children with three or four siblings and is less among children of

smaller or larger families. Cooperativeness was rated highest among children from families with the optimal number of children, but persistence was greatest among children from the larger families.

Treatment by Parents. Jane Addams, Clara Barton, the Mayo brothers, William E. Gladstone, Robert E. Lee, Woodrow Wilson, Benjamin Franklin, and George Washington are among the many historical leaders whose lives illustrate the significance of either a mother or father in determining the career of the future leader (Bogardus, 1934). Among more recent political leaders, parents, particularly mothers, have had a strong positive influence on the development of the leadership potential of their children. Using the Multifactor Leadership Survey (Bass & Avolio, 1991) and the Life History Survey (Owens & Schoenfeldt, 1979), Avolio (1994) obtained significant correlations of .20 and .19, respectively, between their parents' interest in the development of 182 leaders from various sectors of a community and the leaders' inspirational and individually considerate leadership. Leaders are likely to have had parents who allowed more independence and freedom and were less punitive and critical (Snell, Stokes, Sands, et al., 1994). A review in Britain by C. J. Cox and Cooper (1988) found that as children, successful managers had to make use of their own resources and take responsibility for themselves and others. Often they were separated from their parents for schooling or other reasons. Again, Cox and Jennings (1995) found that successful senior executives and self-made entrepreneurs tended to have had a childhood of adversity. Mary Kay Ash, founder and CEO of Mary Kay Cosmetics, is an American example. However, a comparison of children reared in orphanages with children reared by parents suggested that parental interaction was important in fostering childhood leadership behavior. H. H. Anderson (1937) found that nursery school children who were living with their parents interacted more with others and initiated and attempted more leadership than did children from a nursery in an orphanage. But I did not find a statistically significant relationship between college students' success as leaders in initially leaderless discussions and the extent to which each of their parents had been considerate of them or had initiated interactions with them when they were children (Bass, 1954a).

B. M. Bishop (1951) noted that when interacting with

a neutral adult, children tend to transfer to the new situation the pattern of interaction they have developed with their mothers. If their mothers are directive, interfering, and critical, the children tend to be inhibited, reluctant, or noncooperative in their interactions with others. If negativism and rebellion against authority are fostered in interactions with parents, they will be reflected in aggressive behavior against others, such as fighting, threatening, and boasting. Or they may result in a withdrawal into fantasy. The normal maturing child can accept parental and school authority and is cooperative with his or her family and teachers (L. B. Murphy, 1947).

Children from homes in which the children participate in decisions were found by A. L. Baldwin (1949) to be more active, socially outgoing, intelligent, curious, original, constructive, and domineering. C. T. Meyer (1947) concluded that sociability and cooperativeness were greater when parents were clear and consistent, explained decisions to their children, offered opportunities for decision making, had rapport with their children, and better understood their children's problems. Summers (1995) added that warm, supportive, nurturant, conscientious parents who set rational expectations give rise to offspring who are mature for their age, socially responsive, friendly, purposive, and achievement oriented, all characteristics of potential leaders. On the other hand, authoritarian, demanding, physically punitive, and unsympathetic parents give rise to children who are withdrawn, discontented, distrustful, and lacking in social responsibility. Indulgent, neglectful, overprotective parents who deny their children opportunities to experience risks and mistakes commensurate with their maturity seem to restrict their children's development. Such children may, as adults, exhibit irresponsibility, carelessness, overconfidence, and other characteristics that are likely to interfere with their success as leaders. Experiences of success and failure that promote the learning of social skills, of what can and cannot be done in most groups, are missed by such children.

Parents who neglect or ignore their children create a pattern of behavior in children that is also likely to interfere with their leadership potential (except possibly in an antisocial group, such as a group of delinquents). Such children often exhibit symptoms such as stealing, lying, cruelty, and other attention-getting behavior. Rejected children are often distrustful, are strongly motivated to seek praise, and feel persecuted and indulge in self-pity (Bass, 1960). Conformity was more the norm in 1960 than in 2005. At that time, respect for authority was taught more by parents. Questioning of authority is now more common.

Conflicting demands by the mother and father promote behavior in their children that is detrimental to the children's effective and successful interaction with others. The most nervous behavior in children occurs when parents issue conflicting negative demands. Disobedience is greatest when parents issue conflicting positive demands (Meyers, 1944). Consistency from parents and the high standards set by them may be important clues to the early development of future leaders.

Attachment to Parents. Attachment theory holds that attachment figures, usually parents, create either a secure or insecure model of relations of self and others. Relations are seen as positive by secure children and negative by insecure children (Bowlby, 1982). Securely attached individuals generally trust others and are comfortable with being close to others. Secure children, as adults, are more likely to exhibit transformational leadership. Popper, Maiseles, and Kastelnuvo (2000) demonstrated this with 86 Israeli cadets in three courses for police officers. The correlation, corrected for social desirability, was .31 between secure attachment and the combined transformational leadership score for charisma, intellectual stimulation, and individualized consideration, and ranged from .21 to .36. For those insecurely attached to their parents (ambivalent, dismissive, and fearful), the comparable correlations ranged from −.04 to −.30. Popper (2000) assumes that *socialized* charismatic leaders will be adults with secure attachments as children. They are likely as adults to be more self-assured and self-esteemed. *Personalized* charismatic leaders are more likely to have had an avoidant attachment from their parents. As adults, they do not have a keen interest in others. They are reluctant to maintain intimate relationships. If narcissistic, they seek admiration, which does not require closeness and intimacy.

The Importance of Strong Mothers. In the late 1980s, about 25% of American children were being raised by one parent—in 90% of these cases by the mother, who was divorced or had never been married. The divorced or unwed father may still play an important amicable role, but one may speculate that if single parenthood results in a strong mother and a weak or absent father, the pattern replicates the family conditions that gave rise to many prominent world-class leaders, whose fathers were weak, absent, or died early. Many of the modern U.S. presidents' fathers were business failures. The importance of maternal authority was noted in Chapter 31 (Bronfenbrenner, 1961). Dominant mothers whose sons remained attached and close to them figured in the lives of Presidents Warren Harding, Calvin Coolidge, Franklin D. Roosevelt, Harry Truman, Dwight Eisenhower, Lyndon Johnson, Richard Nixon, Bill Clinton, Douglas MacArthur, Winston Churchill, Henry Ford, and Robert Moses, as well as many Mafia leaders (Odom, 1990) and Benedict Arnold. Consistent with this, interviews with 30 CEOs who were selected because of their success as business leaders found that they tended to have strong role models. Most of these models were their mothers, not their fathers (Piotrowski & Armstrong, 1987). V. and M. G. Goertzel (1962), reviewing case histories in *Cradles of Eminence*, found that 109 mothers of 413 eminent men and women of the twentieth century were described as dominating, overwhelming, determined, and strong-willed. But only 21 fathers were so described. Rather, 384 of the fathers were described as failure-prone, improvident, alcoholic, and/or deserters of their families. Freud was quoted as saying "A man who has been the indisputable favorite of his mother keeps for life the feeling of a conqueror, that confidence of success that often induces real success" (Jones, 1953, p. 5). For 24 British prime ministers between 1804 and 1937, 15% and 66% had lost a father in childhood due to death or divorce. The same was true for only 2% of the population as a whole (Iremonger, 1970). Zaleznik (1992) noted that the leaders he analyzed suffered from "father deprivation" due to the father's detachment, absence, or unavailability.

Parents as Models. W. A. Anderson (1943) showed that parents' leadership behavior was a model for their children. In a rural New York area, Anderson found that the social participation of an individual is a family tendency. If the father participated, so did the mother. If both participated, the children usually did also. Keller (1999) showed for 78 college seniors (a majority were women) positive correlations between their prototypical

or implicit model of leaders and how they described their parents' leadership behavior. The correlation with their idea of a prototypical leader's charisma and how they described their mother's charisma was .32. For their father, the comparable correlation was .28. For the trait of tyranny, the correlation with the implicit leader was .31 for the father and .27 for the mother. For the trait of dedication, the figures were .31 for the father but only a nonsignificant .08 for the mother. For the trait of sensitivity, the figures for father and mother were positive (.16 and .10).

Family Status. To add to what was said in the preceding chapter about the importance of socioeconomic background to the emergence of leaders in different countries, the father's occupation and background make a distinct difference in whether their sons emerge as loyalist political leaders such as Ngo Dinh Diem, Fulgencio Batista, Lázaro Cárdenas, and Jacques Necker, or as revolutionary political leaders such as Ho Chi Minh, Fidel Castro, Pancho Villa, and Maximilien Robespierre.[2] A comparison of 50 loyalist leaders with 50 revolutionary leaders by Rejai and Phillips (1988) found that the loyalists' fathers were much more likely than the revolutionaries' fathers to have been government officials, military officers, bankers, industrialists, professionals, or members of the landed gentry. Children from higher-class family backgrounds were also likely to have had a wider range of experiences. Prior to the advent of universal education and class mobility, upper- and middle-class family backgrounds were ordinarily requisite for the emergence of leaders even of the proletariat. As was concluded in Chapter 4, socioeconomic status contributes to one's emergence as a leader, and, as was noted in Chapter 33, the middle and upper classes generally provide a majority of the world's future managers. Until recently, America's labor leaders seldom came from working-class backgrounds. Leaders of the "workers'" revolutions, from Lenin to Castro, came from middle-class, not working-class or peasant, backgrounds. Orlans (1953) observed that many of our great presidents (such as Washington, Jefferson, and both Roosevelts) came from an aristocratic class, from a background that provided them with a great deal of opportunity to examine and evaluate new ideas as

---

[2]Loyalists, in the sense used here, were those leaders best known for their efforts to maintain old, unreconstructed regimes. Revolutionaries were leaders best known for their efforts to overthrow the old regimes.

well as the freedom to pursue a political career. Despite the high status of one's family, children can feel *relatively* deprived in what they want. Such children may grow up to become more successful as leaders than those who are overprotected and pampered.

Parental Standards. Avolio (1994) reported that the moral standards of parents correlated .16 and .20 with inspirational and considerate leadership when their children became leaders as adults. Day (1980) compared 58 health care professionals who were promoted and 58 who were not. Those who were promoted were much more likely to express a recurring theme in interviews about having had a family background that emphasized a strong work ethic. Gibbons's (1986) in-depth interviews with transformational and transactional managers found that the transformational executives were much more likely to describe parents who set high educational standards and provided a family life that was neither extremely lavish nor extremely disadvantaged. And in the just-mentioned study of 30 CEOs, Piotrowski and Armstrong (1987) found that of those who discussed their childhood, most said that they had had favorable family conditions during childhood and adolescence. In line with these findings, Hall (1983) observed that charismatic leaders were given more responsibilities as children and felt a lot of respect from their elders. As may be seen most clearly with Charles de Gaulle's childhood, conviction, ideology, and the need to restore *la gloire de la France* were instilled in him by his early family life just after the ignominious defeat of France by the Germans in 1870. The values and goals of the future French leader were strongly affected for life (Hoffman & Hoffman, 1970).

Leadership was more likely to be displayed by elementary-school boys whose parents instilled high standards as well as granted them responsibilities and scope for independent action (Hoffman, Rosen, & Lippitt, 1960). Consistent with this finding, Klonsky (1983) noted that occupants of leadership positions on boys' teams had parents who made more demands for achievement and provided more discipline accompanied by more maternal warmth. Girls who became team leaders were given more responsibilities by their families but less parental warmth. Parental ambitions may also direct the child toward social success and influence. A family atmosphere of high-quality relationships with parents and siblings

also makes a difference (Bass, 1960). Leaders are more likely to make the transition into adolescence without the pains of separation from family, without a sense of becoming isolated, and without the need to compensate for feelings of helplessness (Levinson & Rosenthal, 1984).

Opportunities in Childhood and Adolescence

Murphy (1947) suggested that adult performance in groups was likely to be affected by children's security or anxiety, developed in their relations with other children in school. The emergence or reinforcement of authoritarian or democratic tendencies was a matter of respect for others fostered in school or neighborhood, frustration or happiness in peer groups, and/or feelings of being respected or excluded from school and social groups.

Practice in leadership is afforded by both school and outside activities. Such experiences in solving problems can enhance a person's esteem with other members of the group. They provide opportunities to interact with the opposite sex in a socially approved manner and enable the individual to learn more about following, cooperation, competition, and leading others. Adolescence affords the developing leader the opportunity to learn to change his or her behavior as situational demands change to maintain success and effectiveness in interactions with others. Social proficiencies learned during adolescence can foster an individual's success in interacting with others as an adult. Social and athletic proficiencies may make a difference in an adolescent's success as an adult leader, depending on the adult environment. The social graces, etiquette, and grooming learned in childhood and adolescence may also prove significant. Finally, experiences in extracurricular activities and dating afford opportunities to practice and transfer leadership and to see the success or failure of different attempts to lead (Bass, 1960). Gibbons's (1986) transformational managers had a lot of experience as leaders in high school and college. Likewise, Hall (1983) noted that charismatic leaders reported more childhood experiences as leaders. Extracurricular experiences in high school tend to predict subsequent leadership activities in college and in military academies (Yammarino & Bass, 1989a). Participation in varsity sports in the naval academy is also predictive of subsequent success as a naval officer (Atwater & Yammarino, 1989). Parents' and teachers' guidance and enlarging of responsibilities can be important to the developing leader. The encouragement of intellectual self-exploration and increasing equalization of power relations with parents and teachers will also contribute (Bass, 1960).

Marginality. After examining the childhood environment of 15 twentieth-century world-class charismatic leaders, Willner (1968) concluded that almost all were socially and psychologically at the margins of several classes, religions, or ethnic affiliations. For example, Kemal Atatürk, the founding father of modern Turkey, grew up at the borders of the Christian Greek and Muslim Turkish cultures. The 15 leaders were also likely to have plural identifications that gave them multiple perspectives, a more flexible view of society, and ways of communicating with and responding more convincingly and empathically to a broad spectrum of people. This heterogeneity in background was likely to be augmented by a wider range of experience, by the mobility of the family, and by the exposure to various environments during childhood and adolescence.

Educational Institutions

Primary and Secondary Education

Illustrating the shaping of future leaders was Britain's educational system. The leaders and administrative officials of the British Empire at its zenith received from their public schools, such as Eton and Harrow, a general education in self-discipline, teamwork, and group loyalty that created an aura of command and habits of superiority with "a facade of crisp decisiveness." Their classical education included nothing about modern science, technology, modern languages, or the social sciences. Little attention was paid to innovation and creativity. Skill in and capacity for social role taking, a sense of self-esteem and a need for achievement were sufficient to create reasonably effective leaders and officials for the world arena (Burns, 1978). The 1,200 members of the Indian Civil Service, most of them British, were of this elite. Their public school and university education had imbued them with a contempt for moneymaking and corruption, pride in the ideals of fair play and open justice, and the sense of duty to make improvements and maintain an efficient

and properly recorded administration. "They were Plato's guardians—a caste apart, bred and trained to be superior" (Lapping, 1985). But they were also handicapped by the class consciousness instilled in them by family and schooling.

The satisfaction of future leaders with their educational experiences in school correlated with all four components of the leaders' transformational leadership, ranging from .19 to .24 (Avolio, 1994). Higher occupational attainment was predicted by very high academic standing and positive attitudes towards high school teachers (Snell, Stokes, Sands, et al., 1994). Large-scale efforts to provide leadership training for high school students have been conducted by the American Management Association, the Center for Creative Leadership, the 4-H program, and other organizations that are interested in the development of young people. Athletic teams, interest clubs, and student government provide leadership experiences. A formal source of leadership training and practice in high school is the 3,000 Junior Reserve Officer Training Corps programs (Funk, 2002).

It was among educators in primary and secondary school settings that evaluative research on leadership education first appeared. For example, Fretwell (1919) gave elected leaders in junior high school responsibility for managing athletic and playground activities. A leadership club was formed to plan and discuss the activities. Fretwell concluded that such experience provided opportunities for leadership and initiative. In the same way, Mayberry (1925) observed that participation in student government provided training in social purpose, initiative, and cooperation.[3]

Controlled Experiments. Eichler and Merrill (1933) asked each member of high school classes to rate the others on leadership. Experimental and control groups were paired on the basis of the ratings. Experimental groups were given lectures on leadership methods or participated in discussions about leadership. New ratings were then collected. The experimental groups gained more than the control groups in such ratings of leadership, but not to a significant degree. Similarly, G. G. Thompson (1944) studied nursery school children under two programs. In one, the teacher acted in an impersonal man-

[3]For other early examples, see E. W. Hastings (1926), Lavoy (1928), G. C. Meyers (1923), A. M. Nash (1927), and E. L. Thorndike (1916).

ner and gave help only when needed. In the second, the teacher took an active part in play and helped the children to adjust to one another. The children in the second group showed significant gains in ascendance, social participation, and leadership. McCandless (1942) studied two residential groups of boys in a training school. Both began with adult supervisors, but the experimental group became self-governing. Sociometric ratings of intermember popularity were highly correlated with dominance at the beginning. Four months later, the most dominant boys lost in popularity in the experimental group but not in the control group. Zeleny (1940b) compared recitation and group discussion as methods of teaching sociology. Students in the discussion classes gained more in dominance and sociability than did those in the recitation classes and recorded slightly greater gains in knowledge of the subject. Again, Zeleny (1941, 1950) gave student leaders instruction in techniques of leadership and guided practice in the use of these techniques. Students found the training interesting and thought it helped them adapt better to the social demands made on them.

Higher Education

Importance of a College Education to Career Success. A college degree, a college education, and socioeconomic status are confounded in their effects on the subsequent emergence of persons in managerial and leadership positions. Nevertheless, there is value in the actual education beyond just being identified as a college graduate. In the Management Progress Study (Bray, Campbell, & Grant, 1974), 274 college graduates who had been hired for first-level management jobs at AT&T and 148 who had been hired without college degrees participated in a three-day assessment center. The college graduates were judged by the assessors to have a higher potential for middle management. After 20 years, the modal college graduate had reached the third level of management, but the modal noncollege graduate had reached only the second level of management. Furthermore, those who had come from better-rated colleges were at a higher level of management (Howard, 1986). This finding was consistent with a correlation of .32 between the ranking of the universities from which 80 Japanese graduates came and the appraisals for their potential

for promotion that they received after three years (Wakabayashi & Graen, 1984). Altemeyer (1966) compared engineering and science majors with students in the fine arts during their four years matriculating at Carnegie Mellon University and found that the engineering students, who were likely to be future leaders in industry, increased in analytical ability but decreased in imagination. The reverse was true for the arts students.

Education for leadership is implicit although not always explicit in higher education. College catalogues often mention as one of their important missions preparing the future leaders of society. Cleveland (1980) argued that "equipping minds for leadership ought to be what's 'higher' about higher education." According to the results of a survey,

> Between 500 and 600 campuses are paying attention to developing their students as leaders, either in the classroom or in extracurricular activities and programs [that] . . . originate either in a student development office or in direct student initiative. The academic courses . . . draw mainly on social psychological and management studies . . . and the liberal arts . . . humanities and social sciences. (Spitzberg, 1987, p. 4)

Community leadership education is often an important aspect in two-year community colleges (Gardner, 1987).

Examples. LeaderShape, a curriculum-based leadership development program, was conducted in 2002 for 2000 participants at 31 colleges and universities across the United States. A pre-post study by Thoms and Blasko (undated) at Penn State–Erie University showed that LeaderShape increased general transformational leadership skills and the ability to create organizational vision. An unusual leadership educational effort focused on gifted children to help them to perform better as leaders. Familiarity with the characteristics of leaders, creativity, and divergent thinking were followed by role playing, observing, and analyzing the leadership of others. Then came practice in exercises and real-life leadership experiences (Black, 1984). At the College of Wooster, in addition to formal course work, students spend three to five days observing national leaders on the job. A consortium of universities in North Carolina conducts a fellows program that includes summer internships and attendance at an annual leadership training program at the Center for Creative Leadership. Mentoring programs are provided at the University of California at Irvine. The ethical responsibilities of leadership are stressed in a sequence of courses at the University of San Diego (Spitzberg, 1987). Harvard's John F. Kennedy School of Government sponsors leadership education with faculty scholars and government leaders in residence. Binghamton University's School of Management offers a three-course sequence on the individual, the group, and the organization at undergraduate and graduate levels. An integrated four-year undergraduate leadership studies program is offered at the Jepson School of Leadership Studies at the University of Richmond. In addition to coursework in leadership, Claremont McKenna College provides a job shadow program for students to learn leadership by following around business, health care, or government managers and executives on the job (R. E. Riggio & H. R. Riggio, 1999).

College student leadership data from 10 institutions were followed from 1994 to 1998. Self-reports from 875 students participating in leadership courses and activities sponsored by the Kellogg Foundation were compared with students from nonparticipating colleges. The results indicated that participating college students increased their ability to set goals, sense of personal ethics, and willingness to take risks, along with leadership motivation, skills, and understanding. Also increased were multicultural awareness, community orientation, and civic responsibilities (Astin & Cress, undated). Top American universities such as Stanford, Harvard, and U.C. Berkeley offer programs in leadership (Riggio, undated).[4] Olson (undated) described 49 undergraduate programs in leadership at institutions such as Rice, Kansas State, and Northwestern. Five programs offered majors, 21 offered minors, and 23 offered concentrations and certificates. Telephone interviews about 10 of the programs indicated that: (1) all but one had been established in the 1990s; (2) all were interdisciplinary, comprising three or more courses; one, at least, experiential; another, a capstone seminar to integrate the coursework; and (3) community service was required in all 10 of the programs. Student internships were included in 80%; senior projects were required in 50%; and faculty-student research

was conducted in 40% of the programs. Some common practices in the 10 undergraduate programs were (1) self-assessment and reflection, (2) skill building, (3) problem solving, (4) intercultural understanding, (5) outdoor leadership, (6) self-initiated and self-sustained learning, (7) mentoring, (8) community involvement, and (9) public policy. In 1992, the Jepson School of the University of Richmond was the first to start a Bachelor of Arts in Leadership Studies. It integrated cognitive, affective, and behavioral leadership learning with a developmental component of leadership effectiveness. Studies combine academic knowledge with experiential learning during four years in which the student progresses from novice to expert (Klenke, 1993).

Professional School Education. Increasingly, schools, of business, education, administration, social welfare, health, and government are providing graduate education in leadership and related behavior and skills to increase the students' capacity to exert personal influence, make proper use of power, motivate others, negotiate and mediate effectively, and take initiatives. The American Assembly of Collegiate Schools of Business completed a ten-year project to assist schools of management in programmatic efforts in this regard (Zoffer, 1985). Orpen (1982) showed that MBAs had achieved a higher level of position and salary after five years than had a matched sample of non-MBAs. Hurley-Hanson, Wally, Sonnenfeld, et al. (2003) examined the career attainment of a first cohort of 540 managers and a second cohort of 968 more recent arrivals in the same firm. The prestige of their school forecast career attainment in the first but not the second cohort. However, possessing an MBA was associated with career success. Baruch and Bell (2003) obtained survey responses from more than 300 managers indicating the value they had received from graduate management education. Competencies and skills gained were associated with internal and external criteria of their career success. Nonetheless, whether the 100,000 MBAs annually awarded and the education associated with the MBA degree are of consequence to careers remains unknown. The schools face increasing competition from one another, as well as from distance learning—instruction over the Internet—and in-house corporate training programs (Jones, 2000). Their value is still questioned (Pfeffer & Fong, 2002).

[4]For more details about curricula and programs, see Clark, Freeman, and Britt (1987).

Crawford, Brungardt, Scott, et al. (2002) reviewed more than 40 university degree programs and found that colleges and universities were increasingly serving non-traditional students. They were also making more use of distance learning.

Executive Education Programs. The business schools at Harvard early in the twentieth century and the University of Pittsburgh in the 1940s pioneered postgraduate executive education programs. They are now commonplace in colleges, universities, and individual free-standing institutions in the United States and abroad. Experienced executives are on campus for extended periods of time. Military, government, and nonprofit executives attend these programs along with business executives. The Center for Creative Leadership provides one-week or longer courses in leadership to more than 20,000 managers and executives in the United States and abroad each year.

Military Institutions. The U.S. military academies invest a considerable amount of their students' time in education for leadership. Students begin by learning to work effectively in highly disciplined subordinate roles before being given positions of increasing leadership responsibility. These opportunities for leadership are experienced in their campus lives and in summer field and sea settings. These experiences add to the formal study of the subject, observational study, self-study, and reflection. The students' development as leaders is appraised periodically, and feedback is provided for remedial efforts (Katz, 1987; Prince, 1987). The intellectual content in the teaching of leadership in the behavioral science departments of the U.S. military academies requires the students to use higher-order cognitive skills such as the discovery of conflicting assumptions and values. Students need to apply logic to identify what is happening in the task facing the leader in a problem or case, account for what is happening, and formulate and apply what the leader should do in the situation (Shulman & Jones, 1996). Atwater, Dionne, Avolio, et al. (1999) followed 236 Virginia Military Institute cadets from entrance to graduation. Data from the first year on cognitive ability, physical fitness, and prior leadership experience predicted who subsequently rose to be formally appointed leaders in the fourth year and to be effective leaders.

Physical fitness and moral reasoning increased with time, but self-esteem did not. These results were consistent with empirical findings in the U.S. Army, Navy, and Air Force military academies.

Adult Continuing Education and Development

Education for leadership occurs in the context of the current stage of development in which the leader is found. On the basis of analogies from developmental learning over the adult life cycle, Bryson and Kelley (1978) suggested that adult leaders go through stages, just as children do. Ideally, a developmental learning process occurs in which capacities and skills that are gained in one stage should prepare the adult leader for new and bigger tasks and responsibilities in later stages. An adult should learn to be a leader by receiving appropriate feedback while serving as a leader and be promoted to higher levels of leadership responsibilities because of past performance as a leader and promise of future performance.

The development of executives is a logical progression over time. The nature of this progression and how to manage it needs to be understood. The progression of abilities needs to be specified. There should be a conceptual linkage between leadership at lower levels of an organization and at more senior levels. The executive's development can be conceived of as a process of acquiring successively more complex cognitive maps and other necessary competencies over time. As the skills required for successful operation at a higher level are accumulated, the executive becomes ready to move to that level (Jacobs & Jaques, 1987). However, there may be innate limits on the conceptual and cognitive skills that can be developed through education and experience.

Continuous Learning

Increasingly recognized is the need for managers and leaders to engage in continuous learning, both for their own sake as well as for their organization. Learning and teaching are part of their job, particularly if they are in industries with rapidly changing technologies, processes, products, services, and markets or in agencies facing new regulations, new problems, and new demands. With managers likely to engage in several successive careers and two retirements (in countries without mandatory retirement) instead of one organization over the working years, maintaining learning skills will be essential for continuing career success. Continuous learning is helped by a development orientation (Maurer, 2002), belief in self-efficacy (Maurer, 2001), taking advantage of new on-the-job challenges (Ohlott, 1998), and realistic knowledge of one's own competencies (Maurer & Tarulli, 1994). According to a survey of 906 managers in 50 different positions in a telecommunications firm, competence in continuous learning is needed, particularly about networking, company service, technical problem solving, and dealing with information and subordinates. Frequent and important tasks were seen most to require continuous learning. Information gathering and synthesis, dealing with subordinates, and technical problem-solving design correlated most highly with the need for competence in continuous learning (Maurer & Weiss, 2003). Continous learning and the ability to learn quickly have become essential for career success with the need to make several career moves as a result of the reduced opportunity to rise in one organization over one's working life (Hall & Mervis, 1995). Competence in continous learning calls for a development orientation, motivation to expand one's skill or knowledge (London, 1983), and being challenged by the opportunity to learn new ideas and ways (Dweck & Leggett, 1988). There is a need to know one's strengths, weaknesses, and need for self-development and to do one's best (Maurer & Tarulli, 1994). One must be able to replace routine old-role behavior with more complex new-role behavior (Hooijberg & Quinn, 1992). One must also be aware of new competencies required in rapidly changing environments, know how to learn these new competencies, and embed the knowledge in the organization to increase its adaptability (Briscoe & Hall, 1999). Continous learning contributes to increased productivity and the ability to meet organizational goals (Van Velsor, 1998).

Paradoxically, the additional power that accrues with rising status in the organization may increasingly inhibit continued learning. Rising power may bring about reduced negative feedback from colleagues. It may also bring about greater monopolization of discussions and decisions by the leader, induction of fear in others by the leader's aura of power, distancing of relationships with others, isolation from below, and exemption from appraisal by others. All these problems can be avoided by the rising executive's consciousness of them and their effects (Kaplan, Drath, & Kofodimos, 1985).

Technical and professional competence often tend to be valued over competence as a supervisor and leader. The successful engineer who moves into a management position or the successful teacher who becomes a school principal frequently continues to focus on the technical aspects of the work to be done and does poorly in getting colleagues to function at their full potential (Kotter, 1985b). Subsequent progress in management appears to be much more a matter of general higher education than specialization in business, engineering, social science, or the humanities. For example, little difference in the level achieved after 20 years at AT&T was found among those who entered the firm with different educational majors (Howard, 1986). Although engineering majors earn higher grades than do nonengineering majors while they are midshipmen at Annapolis, they do not appear to perform any better as leaders when they subsequently serve as naval officers (Yammarino & Bass, 1989).

Virtual Leadership Training and Development

Most managers have been introduced to computer-mediated communications technology, but many managers and executives still need to develop specific skills in using computers, the Internet and intranets, as described in Chapter 29, when they want to engage in distance learning, use specialized new programs in computer decision making, and lead virtual teams, to avoid being dependent on more computer-literate assistants. It is now common for executives, when traveling, to carry their own laptop computers with them or to use publicly available computers. Many such training programs are available on the Internet and company intranet and can be used by managers as they have the time to do so. Testing and feedback can also be provided online (Spreitzer, 2002).

Development of Leaders to Use Computer-Mediated Communications. Virtual leaders, as detailed in Chapter 29, have to learn how to quickly diagnose what is happening based on a limited amount of information from a follower and to be of assistance if needed (Thompsen, 2000). Informal learning from chance, unscheduled encounters with followers, such as in the lunchroom, is lacking. Lack of such spontaneous interactions makes it necessary for the virtual leader to learn how to keep abreast of what is happening in the distant follower's site and to develop a close personal relationship with the follower (Cooper & Kurland, 2002). The virtual leader may find it useful to make more unplanned e-mails and telephone calls inquiring about how things are going (Speitzer, 2002). Virtual leaders must eschew joking and sarcasm to avoid being misunderstood by the distant follower. The leaders need to carefully verify their interpretations of communications to avoid ambiguities. They and their distant followers need to learn how to use and interpret symbols in e-mails that can be used to express emotions (Spreitzer, 2000). Leaders must develop a willingness to spend more time in reaching consensus with followers because it may be more difficult to reach closure (O'Mahoney & Barley, 1999). Virtual leaders can be developed by giving them assignments to be members of a virtual team. They can learn how to use computer mediation for brainstorming and decision making. They will need to learn to give discretion to distant followers and do without continuous monitoring of followers. But they can learn to use archived recordings of virtual meetings to assess follower contributions and progress. Organizations and virtual leaders need to formulate and control privacy policies so followers are assured that computer-mediated communications are safe for sharing concerns. Organizations can provide distant personnel with company portals and intranet to provide access to all necessary information about career opportunities. Virtual leaders need to establish expectations for distant followers about the criteria for judging their performance. Mutual trust between leaders and distant followers is essential (Spreitzer, 2002).

Developing Leaders of Virtual Teams. According to reviews by Cascio (2000) and Spreitzer (2002), to build cohesive virtual teams, the leader must learn how to create a shared mental model to provide a shared sense of purpose (London, 2000). Virtual leaders help virtual team members to overcome a sense of isolation by beginning communications about the team, its mission, and its members and their competencies (Cascio, 2000; Moreland, 1999). The leaders need to transmit a clear, inspiring vision and ensure that members are kept up to date

on what is going on in the organization. Group norms must be set to guide interactions. The leaders need to have learned and transmitted a role model for establishing and adhering to the rules and expectations for working together, about schedules, and appropriate response times. They also need to be sensitive to cultural and individual differences and how the team can take advantage of these differences.

Career Issues

Individual and Organizational Alignment

The education and development of adult leaders require the combined efforts of the individual and the organization. The development of adult leaders is largely a matter of self-development, abetted by opportunities provided by the organization. An individual needs a personal awakening to enhance effectiveness as a leader. Our leadership is an expression of who we are. Thus, to grow as leaders, we need to grow as persons (Cashman, 1998). Federal Express provides a program, LEAP (Leadership Evaluation and Awareness Process), to aspiring managers to examine their interests and aptitudes for management (AMA, 1990).

Avoiding Obsolescence. Both individual motivation and organizational stimulation are involved in the avoidance of managerial and professional obsolescence. An individual's need for achievement and opportunities for organizational participation were the two most important among 12 possible determinants for avoiding obsolescence, according to a survey of 451 U.S. Air Force officers and civilian personnel (Shearer & Steger, 1975). To avoid obsolescence, Shearer and Steger deemed experience to be more important for managers and continuing education more important for professionals. Managers also need to maintain clear perspectives about their organization. For instance, those who work in senior civil service positions in the government must understand the historical, social, and political context of their jobs. The Federal Executive Institute for training senior managers places a heavy emphasis on this objective (Wood, 1985).

The Need for Flexibility. Careers need to fit purposes that are aligned with the organization's strategic direction. At the same time, managers should be flexible in the face of shifts in opportunities and conditions. They need to be flexible about making tentative choices and evaluations that are subject to revision, to engage in multiple small careers at low levels, to experience a few plateaus in career advancement, to continue on to new challenging assignments, to take risks, and to experience small failures (Gaertner, 1988).

The alignment of career and organization has become much more difficult as organizations change internally to cope with the changes occurring in a turbulent environment and societal change. As Conger (1993b, p. 203) noted, organizations are facing "heightened competitive pressures." Genentech reduced the time from ten to seven years to introduce the first engineered successfully therapeutic anticancer drug, which rose to over a billion dollars in sales, but it soon faced 18 firms hoping to gain FDA approval to introduce competing drugs. From 2001 to 2003, it instituted extensive organizational, strategic, and cultural changes to position its hematology business unit for continuous and rapid growth (Ahn, Adamson, & Dornbusch, 2004).

Many people experience difficulties in their attempts to adapt their careers to organizational restructuring, downsizing, delayering, hierarchical flattening, teaming, and outsourcing. No longer can they count on one career with one organization. They need to take charge of their own careers by being more versatile in their skills, accepting change, remaining flexible, and being ready to adapt to new technologies and job requirements. They can expect a career of working sequentially for a number of different organizations. The informal employment covenant between organization and employee and the loyalty to each other has been corroded. "Responsibility for career development must lie with the individual, not the organization" (Brousseau, Driver, & Larsson, 1996, p. 52).

Career Planning. Effective career planning is interactive. Career development is enhanced by the joint efforts that develop leaders' resilience in the face of adversity. An organization can encourage such resilience with feedback and positive reinforcement. The developing leader needs career resilience, career insight, and career identity. These are furthered by creating and implementing a vision of his or her future in the context of expectations about the organization's future. Contingency plans are needed to maintain flexibility (London, 1985). Thus 77 middle managers who were judged by a higher-level committee to be more adaptive to changing role demands demonstrated more openness to different ideas and used simpler decision-making processes than did those who were judged to be less adaptive. They were higher in self-esteem and presumably more likely to attempt leadership (Morrison, 1977).

Expectations reflect promotion to higher levels or the failures to do so. For example, the expectations of all 270 managers whose careers at AT&T were studied measured annually over 20 years declined sharply during the first five years of employment. However, after the fifth year, the expectations of those who subsequently attained fourth- to sixth-level executive positions by the end of the 20-year period turned around and began a steady movement upward. The expectations of those who attained only third-level positions after 20 years remained about the same after the fifth year, while the expectations of those who ended their 20 years at the first or second levels of management continued to decline steadily after the fifth year (Howard & Bray, 1988).

Leader-Subordinate Relations

The prospective leader's behavior develops in concert with those who are directly above and below him or her in the hierarchy. The leader may develop different interlocking behaviors with each of his or her subordinates. Along with a general normative relationship, the roles played by both will be worked out for designated situations (Graen, 1976). The quality of this leader-member exchange early in one's career contributes to one's successful movement up the corporate ladder later on. Early promotion is an important predictor of future success (E. H. Schein, 1985).

Latitude and Challenges. Of particular consequence will be the latitude granted subordinates, the leader's support of subordinates' activities, and the leader's attention to subordinates' development (Graen & Cashman, 1975). Challenging assignments provided early contribute to one's success at subsequent stages of one's career as a manager (Vicino & Bass, 1978). Bray and Howard (1983) found that only 30% of the college recruits at AT&T who were predicted to reach middle management actually attained it eight years later if they had not experienced a challenging job early on. Of those who had been predicted to fail to reach middle management, 61% attained it if they had earlier experienced a more challenging job.

Quality of Relation. The superior-subordinate exchange develops into a role relationship that may rigidify or be flexible, depending on a variety of individual and organizational factors. Some people engage in role-making experiences; others do not. The quality of the relationships becomes even more important to one's success in a career than one's initially tested ability. According to a 13-year panel study by Wakabayashi and Graen (1984) of 85 Japanese college graduates, those who had higher-quality vertical superior-subordinate exchange relationships in their first years of employment, as reflected in their speed of promotion and bonuses, were most likely to demonstrate greater progress at seven and 13 years of employment. Those with a lower tested ability on entrance to their firms could make up for it in their advancement by early higher-quality dyadic relationships.

Travel Experiences. The importance of travel experiences to the development and personal change of political leaders has been overlooked. When Rejai and Phillips (1988) contrasted 50 loyalist political leaders with 50 revolutionaries, they found that travel experiences reinforced the politicization of the loyalists that had begun at home and in school. For the revolutionaries, travel was radicalizing and transforming, and helped them to develop standards against which to measure their own countries. However, travel may become of less consequence in a world linked by television and instant communication.

Career Paths

As already noted, careers depend on both the individual and the organization. In some kinds of organizations, only one route is open. One must enter at the bottom to climb to the top. For example, entry into the U.S. military officer corps requires admission to and graduation from a military academy, ROTC, or an officer candidate school. Promotion is from within; a direct transfer from civilian life to a high-level position in the military is not possible (except during wartime). Career paths in business and industry are much less circumscribed. As noted in Chapters 31 and 32, women and ethnic minorities who become senior executives are less likely to rise through the ranks of line management and more likely to emerge into top management from staff, technical, or professional careers inside or outside the organization. Union leaders can come from the rank and file, from staff professional service, or directly from the outside (Schwartz & Hoyman, 1984). Educational leaders ordinarily begin as teachers. Loyalist political leaders are much more likely than revolutionary leaders to have been employed in governmental service early on (Rejai & Phillips, 1988).

Careers of U.S. Presidents. Currently, voters pay little attention to the job experience of candidates for the most important job in the world, president of the United States. Although candidates talk much about it, voters are more attentive to the emotional uplift provided by the candidates, party identification, and the credibility of their promises. Nonetheless, 10 of 14 presidents since 1898 who had been state governors were elected, compared to four who had been in Congress. Presidents who have had experience as state governors tend to earn higher ratings for their performance as leaders and crisis managers than do those who have served as senators or representatives.

Career Mobility. Mobility is valued. Managers measure their success in terms of their rate of mobility and advancement. They fear stagnation if they remain too long in one position (Veiga, 1981). Rapid organizational change has led to more movement of managers within and between organizations (Brousseau, Driver, Larssen, et al. 1996). It used to be unusual for a manager to be fired. Poor performers "were locked in an office and the key thrown away until retirement." Now, with organizations in a more turbulent and competitive market, managers may find themselves out of a job. Unemployed, they may need to start a new career in another organization or start their own organization. But mobility may be deterred for many individual and organizational reasons. Older people may feel less mobile and more concerned about their job security (J. Hall, 1976). They are likely to perceive themselves as less marketable. Company benefits that cannot be transferred will hamper the consideration of job changes (Albrook, 1967). Community ties also inhibit one from moving away, which may be required when one changes jobs. Other deterrents to geographic mobility are a spouse's career requirements and children's educational needs. Veiga (1983) studied the mobility of 1,216 managers in three manufacturing firms. The average time the managers spent in a particular position, as expected, was affected by their own perceived marketability, the value of company benefits, and the importance of job security, and somewhat less by their and their families' ties to their communities. Dissatisfaction with their current position, as expected, increased the managers' willingness to consider changing employers. Likewise, in a study of 283 managers by Campion and Mitchell (1986), such dissatisfaction predicted the managers' resignation from managerial positions and from the organization. But quitting was also predicted by lack of socialization into the firm, lack of adjustment, unmet job expectations, and being under more stress. With a survey of almost 4,000 U.S. Air Force personnel, a good percentage of whom were noncommissioned officers, Watson (1986) showed that both opportunities elsewhere and commitment to the U.S. Air Force were important. The lack of commitment and the availability of civilian opportunities together correlated .74 with thoughts of leaving the Air Force and searching elsewhere. The lack of commitment and thoughts of leaving combined to correlate .79 with intentions to leave the Air Force, and these intentions correlated .71 with actual quitting.

Mount (1984) surveyed 483 managers of a multinational corporation who were working in the same metropolitan area about their job satisfaction and whether they were establishing their career, advancing in it, or maintaining a well-established career. Managers who were getting established were more satisfied than those who were further along in their careers.

Career Change. Low current satisfaction may be a reason for changing careers. For example, engineers who are seeking more important and better-paying positions shift into line management or become responsible for training, quality control, or research. The change is ordinarily a promotion within the same organization (Bain, 1985). They are more likely to switch into management if they have entrepreneurial, affiliative, and assertive interests. They are less likely to switch if they have strong investigative and artistic interests (Sedge, 1985).

Better opportunities may cause people to change careers. Thus, whether U.S. Air Force officers intend to remain in service or become civilians depends on how attractive they viewed civilian life and how oriented they were toward their occupation (O'Connell, 1986). Personnel may become alienated from their current organizational and professional responsibilities as a consequence of violated and unmet expectations; loss of satisfaction with colleagues; and changes in their own beliefs, interests, values, and maturation (Korman, Wittig-Berman, & Lang, 1981). But Schein (1996) argued that the choice of career is a matter of motivation. Persons are anchored to careers by personal interests and values. The work itself may be the anchor. They prefer to advance in a career in their own technical or functional competencies. Management may be the anchor, as they are motivated by being able to take calculated risks and achieve common goals. They may be anchored in a preference for stability and security, be willing to conform, and be socialized into an organization's values. They may enjoy entrepreneurial activities and moving from project to project. They may prefer a career that provides autonomy and independence. They may be dedicated to a cause or pure challenge and winning in competition. Or they may want a career that makes for a satisfying lifestyle.

Careerism. Managers who were on a career plateau (a long period without promotion) were found to have timed their career moves less adequately than did those who did not experience such plateaus (Veiga, 1981). For the highly ambitious, it is argued, career development is enhanced by the ability to move within three to four years into different areas of management and leadership in different organizations. Such movement is seen to pay off in more rapid advancement to higher organizational levels. For the ambitious, concern for career advancement takes precedence over loyalty and commitment to their current organization (Feldman, 1985). Such careerism is a serious threat to organizational effectiveness. Feldman sees in it anticipatory dissatisfaction with jobs that do not contribute to the advancement of one's career, lack of involvement in one's job and loyalty to one's organization, increased job turnover, inauthentic interpersonal relationships, and absorption in self-interest.

Career Success. Career advancement in an organization may be due to unusual talents, reputation for excellent performance, or sponsorship by a champion in senior management. Some managers are singled out early for rapid promotion. They are high flyers who are identified as having a lot of managerial talent. Since they have been identified as talented, subsequent self-fulfilling prophecy maintains their high-flying evaluation. Their career moves are planned for them to reach senior management while still young (Hirsh, 1985). McCall (1998) agrees that developing managers into high flyers is a responsibility of leadership, which must to provide opportunities for learning on-the-job through challenging assignments and experiences so that their talents can grow. Baltes and Dickson (2001) theorize that leaders with successful careers, when faced with limited resources, will optimize their choices. For instance, they reward subordinates selectively for meritorious performance. Faced with functional losses over time, such as losses in market share or of valued employees, they compensate with impression management. Or there is the example of the young employee promoted rapidly from line employee to senior management who walks into the CEO's office and asks, "Okay, Dad, what do I do next?" Career success can be a matter of family connections.

Career Failure. Careerism may result in fast-track rapid promotions and short-term job assignments but derailment later at higher levels because of failure to develop competencies to perform at higher levels of management and to align self-interests with the needs of the organization (Kovach, 1986). According to a comparison by their superiors of 86 successful senior managers and 83 who had been derailed, Lombardo, Ruderman, and McCauley (1987) found that the termination of career advancement was seen to be due to personal flaws that did not show up quickly as the fast tracker moved from one assignment to another but became visible only when higher-level complexities were faced. These managers may not have been politically astute, able to think strategically, or able to make high-quality decisions in the face of ambiguous conditions, or they may have lacked leadership competencies. Also, the derailed managers were more likely to be abrasive, untrustworthy, and unstable. Early remedial action, feedback, coaching, and mentoring might have helped some of those who were side-tracked. Along with personal development, haphazard, short-time job-hopping needs to be discouraged. Instead, systematic moves are needed to increase one's experience in various aspects of an organization, with successive broadening increases in responsibility lasting up to two years (Reibstein, 1986). Leaves of absence can prove costly to a manager regardless of the reason, whether due to illness, family responsibilities, education, or the call to active duty of a military reservist or a member of the National Guard. Among 11,815 managers, leaves of absence subsequently resulted in fewer promotions and smaller salary increases (Judiesch & Lyness, 1999).

Costs to the Organization. Careerism among an organization's personnel can create a heavy burden, in both the private and public sectors. For example, careerism was seen by Hauser (1984) to degrade the effectiveness of the U.S. military services. In peacetime, there is an absence of lateral entry from higher-level civilian positions into the military, which results in a shortage of credible challenges to whatever is the conventional wisdom in the military. Careers tend to be short. The ideal officer is a generalist, not a specialist. Transfers are frequent; advancement is rapid for many. Coupled with early retirement, the transitory aspects of military careers contribute to conformity and avoidance of risks. These tendencies are further reinforced by the military's centralization of evaluation and "whole man" concepts of promotion.

A career in a bureaucracy can be hurt by one bad mistake. Career-oriented managers have to avoid "rocking the boat." Few dare to be whistle-blowers who may be ostracized or lose their jobs. As a consequence, the organization may suffer from failure to uncover a serious problem.

Value of Training and Development in Leadership

The Kellogg Foundation invested heavily in its National Fellowship Program under the assumption that leadership skills can be taught, learned, and developed. Leaders can benefit from exposure to diverse ideas, cultures, and approaches to problem solving and time for disciplined reflection (Sublett, 1995–96, pp. 1, 2). The widespread belief in leadership training was noted by Alpander

(1986), who found that more than 80% of the first-level supervisors in 155 Fortune 500 companies are asked to attend in-house training programs of one to four hours at least once a year; 75%, programs that last 5 to 12 hours; and 37%, programs that last 13 to 40 hours. Almost all the supervisors participate in such a longer program at least once in five years. Thirty-four low-performance Indian employees and their 12 supervisors showed improvements in pre-post assessments from a program that featured an awareness effort followed by personal workshops for the low-performing employees and training for the supervisors in mentoring, counseling, and supervision. The employees improved in overall job performance, discipline, adaptability, morale, interpersonal relations, and self-esteem (Subramanian & Rao, 1997).

Without taking the trouble to examine the available research, critics continue to argue that leadership training lacks theoretical or empirical grounding, is seldom evaluated, and is faddish, depending more on faith than on facts (Rice, 1988). Following a comprehensive review, Latham (1988, p. 574) strongly disagreed:

> The scientific leadership training literature is not dominated by fads.... [S]elf-regulation techniques, Leader Match, role motivation theory, LMX, and double-loop learning have been systematically evaluated for more than a decade, and their evaluation is on-going ... these leadership training programs are grounded in theory ... the training programs have been subject to repeated investigations; and ... the training has been evaluated empirically. Many of the evaluations included follow-up data collected from three months to five years subsequent to the training. Moreover, the dependent variables for evaluating the training programs included observable behaviors.

Numerous scientific comparisons of trained and untrained managers have been completed to ascertain the extent to which the trained but not the untrained managers changed their attitudes and behaviors, used what they learned, and contributed to more effective operations of their organization. Nevertheless, it may be that the perception that there has been little evaluation of leadership training is due to the large amount of training that occurs and the extent to which most such training is evaluated cursorily by asking the trainees how satisfied they were with the experience. So although the number of published research comparisons is large, it seems small in

contrast to the actual amount of training that is provided. The large body of published research provides confidence in the theoretical underpinnings and factual substantiation of the conclusions reached. We have come a long way from the earliest reports of leadership training in industry and the armed services, which were primarily statements about the value of leadership training, descriptions of programs, and discussions of problems.[5]

What about the Bottom Line?

Are the returns on investment worth the costs of training? Keith and Gresso (1997) found a higher objective profitability for the firms among 57 Fortune 500 organizations that used newer training methods. Watson Wyatt Worldwide (Anonymous, 1999) completed an analysis of the increase in market value for three and five years of 405 large companies linked to their improvements in their human resources, much of it associated with their leadership. Greater shareholder value accrued 10.1% from improved recruiting excellence; 9.2% from improvements in clear rewards and accountability; 7.8% from enhanced teamwork, workplace collegiality, and flexibility; and 4.0% from the increased integrity of its communications. But increasing the amount of general training programs and 360-degree feedback resulted in reduced market value. General training was thought to prepare trainees for their next job rather than their current one.

What do managers say they want from a training session? An unexpected answer was obtained by one study. Using Kirkpatrick's 1959 rubric for valuing training (content applicability and importance), Lingham (2003) found, to his surprise, according to regression analysis, that managers regarded gaining new knowledge as four times as important as the applicability of the learning.

Assessing Organizational and Individual Needs

Whatever the education or training effort, its effectiveness in improving leadership performance depends first on identifying what needs improvement and then demonstrating or helping trainees or students learn how to

---

[5] See, for example Dietz (1943), W. I. Foster (1929), Greenly and Mapel (1943), MacKechnie (1944), McFeely and Mussman (1945), and R. S. Miller (1943).

change their perceptions, cognitions, attitudes, and behavior. Experiences must be provided in which the trainees can exhibit the appropriate leadership. Instructors, observers, and other trainees can give the trainees feedback about the adequacy and effects of their efforts (Bass & Vaughan, 1966). But much hinges on the correct identification of the trainees' needs for learning. Moreover, there are two other necessary prelearning conditions: the trainees' desire to know and the trainees' sense of role (Akin, 1987). The organization will benefit if the leadership training begins at the top and works its way downward. Karseras (1997) suggests that this is even more important when transformational rather than transactional leadership is being taught. Dealing with what learning is needed has to be continuing. Competence in the activity is an important aspect of performing well as a manager, according to 906 incumbents in 50 different managerial positions in a telecommunications company. Leadership training calls for more than just learning concepts but concepts that are put into practice in observable behaviors that can generate feedback from others (Howard & Wellins, 1994, p. 33). Needs assessment must reflect the extent to which the organization has been delayered, networked, and increased in horizontal relations (Bartlett & Goshal, 1997).

Top-Down and Bottom-Up Approaches. The assessment of needs can be initiated in the organization from the top down or from the bottom up. An illustrative top-down approach began with informal meetings with senior management to identify the training and developmental needs of British social work managers. Priorities were then established among the 15 identified skills by the 66 managers below them. Sharp differences had to be taken into account between the openness of the subordinate managers and their superiors (Leigh, 1983). The training requirements for transformational leadership by high-flying middle managers in financial institutions in London were identified by 20 senior training managers. They cited the need for enhancement of coaching skills, creativity, production and communication of vision, generation of trust and respect, and a balance in risk taking (Karseras, 1997). An illustrative bottom-up approach began in a large Texas human resources agency with a survey of 636 subordinates' evaluations of the supervisory styles of their immediate superiors. From these evaluations, a plan for improved supervision was extracted

(Russell, Lankford, & Grinnell, 1984). The importance of using both superiors' and subordinates' assessments of needs was seen in a survey of approximately 7,000 first- and second-level white- and blue-collar supervisors that found the supervisors to be overly confident about their own human relations skills (Bittel & Ramsey, 1983). Supervisors have biased perceptions of consideration; subordinates' descriptions tend not to be as favorable as the supervisors' self-descriptions (Weissenberg & Kavanagh, 1972; Bass & Yammarino, 1989). At the same time, the supervisors were much less confident about how well they could stimulate improvements in productivity.

Training officers differ considerably about the appropriate source of the assessment of their needs of their higher-ups or their subordinates. The previously mentioned 155 training officers in different Fortune 500 companies were surveyed by Alpander (1986) concerning the training needs of first-line supervisors. A third of the respondents thought that the need of a given supervisor for training should be decided by his or her immediate boss; 18% felt the decision should be made by higher-ups; and 14%, by the staff. Others mentioned volunteering and various forms of joint decision making. Clearly, some combination of sources makes the most sense. Peterson and McClear (1990) conducted a multilevel, multimethod approach of felt needs for training, starting with 23 senior managers who completed career plots for themselves and listed critical incidents of effective and ineffective middle managers that showed they were more in agreement than they thought. In both methods, they averaged 50% of their time using human skills and the other time split between using technical and conceptual skills. The average human skills at work for critical incidents were judged as close to 60%, with 40% again split between technical and conceptual skills. The results were consistent with a survey of the 449 usable responses of midlevel and lower-level managers. They ranked "acting consistently and inspiring subordinates" among the first three most important training needs. Included by management levels in the first ten training needs in importance were emphasizing performance, communication, planning, and organizing.

Needed Contents of Training and Development Programs. Although one might argue that some of the contents of most or all of the preceding chapters should be included in leadership training, the programs are much more limited. For instance, Alpander asked the training officers to indicate what should be and has been included in first-line supervisory training programs. According to the officers and 155 respondents, the content actually included in their own first-line supervisory training programs was as follows: how to feed back the results of performance evaluations to employees (92%), how to delegate (90%), how to improve listening skills (83%), how to improve personal leadership effectiveness (80%), and how to encourage and obtain subordinates' participation in decision making (74%). At least 70% also identified as most representative of the content of their training program: how to make the work environment conducive to self-motivation, how to improve the quality of the product, how to ensure that established goals are perceived as realistic and relevant by employees, how to assign specific duties to employees, and how to assist employees to understand their role in relationship to the company's overall objectives.

Programs to teach particular concepts and models of leadership such as those described in earlier chapters clearly include content about the concepts and models being taught. Many of these will be discussed later. Joynt (1981–1982) expressed an additional educational requirement for managers: they need to learn how to do research and become "intelligent consumers." They need to be able to examine which theories are relevant and applicable to their own circumstances and which are not.

Accentuate the Positive. Thirty years before Martin Seligman (1998) pointed out the advantages of positive psychology in place of emphasizing the negative approach to stimulating and guiding behavior by reducing needs, Don Clifton stressed concentrating on one's strengths rather than weaknesses. Building on personal strengths rather than managing around weaknesses was a direction in training supported by interviews with 2 million managers in 63 countries by the Gallup Organization. Remediation of weaknesses is not strength-building. The greatest room for growth is not in the areas of greatest weaknesses, but rather in strengths. Strengths include talents that often appear early in life. They reflected what we will strive for, what we do best, what work gives us the most satisfaction, and what we can learn most quickly. Gallup provided a standardized instrument, the StrengthsFinder, to assess strengths in terms of 34 themes

from *achiever* to *woo* (the desire to win over other people to your side) (Buckingham & Clifton, 2001).

Luthans, Luthans, Hodgetts, et al. (2001) accented the positive in a formalized program (PAL) of four components of would-be effective leaders: realistic optimism, emotional intelligence, confidence, and hope. *Confidence* and self-efficacy from previous successes and vicarious modeling of other successful leaders moved leaders to choose stretch goals, perseverance, and resilience. From *hope* came a sense of agency or determination to succeed in achieving selected goals and the belief in the ability to generate alternative ways to reach the goals

According to Schneider (2001), *realistic optimism* called for (1) being lenient about past failures to meet expectations and accepting what cannot be changed; (2) appreciation for the present, concentrating on the positive aspects of the current situation; and (3) opportunity seeking for the future. The leader's assignment was a challenge rather than a problem. Seligman (1998) added that when faced with a severe challenge the leader needed to deal with self-defeating beliefs by identification, reflection, and diagnosis to prove the belief inaccurate according to reliable information or to replace the disturbing belief with a more constructive, accurate one.

Emotional intelligence was considered in Chapter 5 as a complex trait. But it can also be a state of mind. Faced with problem situations, leaders can learn to cope effectively by using emotional intelligence. Goleman (2000) suggested that emotional intelligence was central to effective leadership. Emotionally intelligent leadership, self-aware and empathic, creates a climate of trust.

Extraneous Factors

Training may not be needed as much as a change of facilities, resources, or organizational policies. Organizational policies and practices may be at fault, not the performance of individual leaders. The burden for improvement should not be shifted to individual managers, who will be frustrated only because their attempts to improve themselves do not matter as long as the organization as a whole remains unchanged (Dreilinger, McElheny, Rice, & Robinson, 1982).

Off-the-Job Leadership Training and Development

Off-the-job leadership training can be obtained from didactic and experiential training. Didactic training includes lectures and readings. Experiential training includes discussions and role playing. Games and simulations can be used along with management in-baskets to provide scenarios of mock or real situations. Computer-assisted interactive programs can be applied, as well as much less structured sensitivity training. Stimulated by social learning theory, behavior role modeling can provide an integration of didactic and experiential approaches.

Lectures and Discussions

Among the methods to be examined here, lectures are the least popular with training directors (Carroll, Paine, & Ivancevich, 1972). Nonetheless, a meta-analysis of the effectiveness of management training programs by Burke and Day (1986) found that lectures had a positive value. Discussion groups are relied on heavily in most leadership programs even when many lecture, film, and other didactic presentations are used. Lectures (or their off-the-job leadership training surrogates—films, audio programs, videotapes, video discs, Web-based programs, and television) can arouse audiences, provide information, and stimulate thinking. These prepared programs have the advantage of making use of master lecturers and performers, carefully worked-out scripts, and standardization and development based on evaluative tests.

Audiovisual aids to lectures have improved greatly in the past half century. Close detail can be shown. Animation and special effects can be put to good use. Music and artwork can provide desired emphases. Interviews with real model leaders can be presented. But without an interactive program, the easy interaction of discussion is absent. A broad range of leadership cases is found in the library of 80 films at Hartwick College drawn from great works of drama, philosophy, history, and biography. Participants write down the leadership issues and themes they observe, which are then discussed (Clemens, 2000). Films and videotapes are also prepared with vignettes to illustrate behaviors fitting with concepts of leadership

such as the four factors of transformational leadership (Bass & Avolio, 1992).

Most comparisons of lecture versus discussion approaches to instructing leaders to change their ways of behaving suggest that lectures and surrogates are more effective if combined with guided discussion of the issues in small groups, particularly if attitudes have to change before the new ways of leading are accepted and adopted by trainees. Discussion provides experience in working with others to reach decisions (L. A. Allen, 1957). The experience can promote the potential leadership of the members by preparing them to use group discussion to reach effective decisions. Again, Riegel (1952) suggested that case discussions, in particular, can provide experience in objective ways of thinking about common leadership problems. The need to study issues in terms of possible causes and effects is emphasized. Trainees exchange and evaluate each other's solutions to such problems. They develop an awareness of the need for more than single, simple answers to complex problems.

Maier (1953), among others, demonstrated the effectiveness of training using problem-solving discussions. He compared the performance of 176 trained supervisors with 144 untrained ones. The supervisors with eight hours of training in groups were found to be more likely to bring about acceptance of change in their groups. Argyris (1965) used lectures and case discussions in the laboratory training of senior executives. No significant change followed the lectures, but some measures of skill in interpersonal relations improved after the case discussions.

Discussions may be ineffective poolings of ignorance, or they can be adequately stimulated, directed, and provided with resources to promote learning. Mann and Mann (1959c) compared the effects of free-discussion groups and task-directed groups on behavior as described by members. Members of task-directed discussion groups changed significantly more than did those in free-discussion groups in friendliness, desirability as a friend, leadership, attainment of goals, cooperativeness, and general adjustment. Nevertheless, numerous reports failed to confirm the expectation that discussions were more effective than lectures. Early on, DiVesta (1954) compared lectures and group discussions as vehicles for training in human relations and found them to be equally effective. However, the discussion groups did show slight gains in favorable attitudes toward initiating structure. Mahoney, Jerdee, and Korman (1960) compared case analyses, group discussions, and lectures as methods for training in management development and likewise found no significant difference among the methods. All the groups gained in a test of knowledge as a result of practice.

Both Discussions and Lectures Can Be Useful. Experiments have focused on the wrong issue. Discussions and lectures are suitable for different objectives, different situations, and different personnel. As a result of a research survey on leadership training, Filley and Jesse (1965) developed a set of hypotheses setting forth the conditions under which more didactic, *trainer-oriented*, training and more discussion-like, *trainee-oriented*, training are effective. Burke and Day's (1986) meta-analysis found that both lectures and a combination of lectures and discussions could be useful in management education. House (1965) studied the attitudes of 43 managers toward trainee-oriented (more discussion) and trainee-oriented (more lecture) training and found that 24 preferred a combination of the two methods, while 12 preferred trainee-oriented and seven preferred trainer-oriented training.

Discussions reinforce lectures. Discussions are useful when a lecture needs clarification and amplification. Learning from a lecture or surrogate is facilitated if it is followed by small "buzz groups" to share opinions, raise questions, and consider alternatives. The conclusions of each buzz group can be be shared with the other buzz groups and the trainer. This promotion of two-way communication increases trainees' motivation and enables them to test their understanding. Teleconferencing makes it possible for one instructor to lecture or to conduct training discussions with groups of leadership trainees at different sites. However, what is needed for such teleconference training is ways to maintain the trainees' attention in the absence of personal contact with the trainer. The trainees have to be willing and able to communicate back to the distant trainer and to learn from what has happened in other groups. High-quality graphics are also required, and a face-to-face meeting with the trainer is desirable (Smeltzer & Davey, 1988).

Role Playing

Various methods of social and behavioral adjustments, developed by psychiatrists and social and clinical psychologists, were adapted to the training of leaders. Psychodrama and sociodrama, originated by Moreno (1955) in the 1930s, require participants (alone or with other actors) to act out various leadership problems under different conditions of audience participation in discussion groups (Lippitt, Bradford, & Benne, 1947). Role playing is a variant. It requires one member to play the role of leader and other members to play the roles of followers. The purpose of playing a role, rather than reading or talking about a solution to an interpersonal problem without a script, is to improve learning and retention and to promote transfer from the learning situation to the leadership performance on the job. Bradford and Lippitt (1952) suggested that interpersonal skills may be hard to teach by providing only verbal or intellectual reasons for behaving in a certain way without actually helping to produce the ability to behave in the desired way. Didactic approaches, by themselves, may reduce successful leadership behavior by adding to anxiety rather than to understanding.

Benefits. Role playing quickly became one of the most popular leadership training methods. Many possible uses were seen for it. Trainees could practice what they eventually had to do. Role playing could serve as a diagnostic technique. Group discussion following the role playing might focus on examining specific interchanges experienced in the role plays. Different ways of solving problems could be tested by role players. Other trainees could gain vicariously from observing the success or failure of various attempts during role plays. Standards could be set for handling specific situations (J. R. P. French, 1944b).[6]

As expected, Lonergan (1958) and Lawshe, Brune, and Bolda (1958) observed that participants in role playing tended to regard it as beneficial in increasing their understanding of human relations problems. Furthermore, the latter found that about twice as many par-

[6] See also Corsim, Shaw, and Blake (1961); A. F. Klein (1956); Speroff (1957); Stahl (1953, 1954); Symonds (1947); Wolozin (1948); and Zander (1947). Corsini, Shaw, and Blake's (1961) survey of the various role-playing methods included an annotated bibliography of 102 references.

ticipants preferred the leader role to the follower role. Similarly, Mann and Mann (1959a, b) demonstrated that experience in role playing improved role-playing ability, as judged by the individual, other role players, and observers. When they compared ratings of participants' behavior during role playing and group discussions, they found that the participants improved more in interpersonal adjustment after role playing than after group discussion.

Role playing appears to add to leaders' skills in dealing with human relations problems. For example, Solem (1960) arranged for small teams drawn from 440 supervisors to meet either in 22 case discussion groups or in 23 multiple role-playing exercises. They role-played or discussed one of two problems concerning either the assignment of a new truck to a crew of utility repair personnel or how to change a work procedure. When role-playing the new-truck problem, a participant took the part of the crew's supervisor and another acted as a repair employee. In the new-truck case discussion, the teams talked about solutions to the problem. The change-of-work-procedure problem was handled similarly as a role play or case discussion. Among the role-playing teams, 46% developed integrated new solutions to the problems. That is, instead of assigning the new truck to the employee with the oldest truck, they replaced the oldest truck but enabled each employee to switch to a newer truck. But only 15% of the case discussants did likewise. More integrated solutions were also developed for the role played change-of-work procedures than for the case discussion.

Contingencies. The positive effects of role playing depended on a variety of circumstances. For instance, Lawshe, Bolda, and Brune (1959) studied five groups under different conditions of feedback. They found that role playing and subsequent discussion increased the participants' sensitivity and orientation toward employees when the participants were required to criticize their own performance and when the human relations point of view was presented to them in a strong, emotional manner. Similarly, Harvey and Beverly (1961) found that role playing had a significant positive effect on changes of opinion, but authoritarian participants gained more from role playing than did those who were not authoritarian. However, Elms and Janis (1965) found that counternorms were accepted to a high degree only under conditions of overt role playing (as opposed to nonovert role

playing) and only if large monetary rewards were paid. Trittipoe and Hahn (1961) studied participants in role-playing groups and problem-solving groups. Both observers and followers rated participants higher in role playing if they also rated them higher in problem solving. In turn, those who were rated higher in both were rated higher in leadership and class standing.

Some experiments that were less favorable to role playing were also completed. Mann and Mann (1960) compared the experience of participants in role-playing and task-oriented groups. Contrary to their hypothesis, they observed that participants in the task-oriented problem-solving groups changed more in leadership and general adjustment than those in the role-playing groups. In addition, Hanson, Morton, and Rothaus (1963) found that role-playing situations involving the evaluation of followers' personality traits induced a critical posture in the leader and a submissive role for followers, whereas working on a problem in goal setting and planning permitted followers to be more active. In a study of 200 military officer trainees, Tupes, Carp, and Borg (1958) noted that the ability to play roles was not related to ratings of leadership effectiveness but to personality scores. In the aforementioned experiments, both role reversal and multiple role playing were used extensively.

Role Reversal. When supervisors appear to be unable to appreciate the views of subordinates, they may be asked to play the role of subordinate while someone else plays the role of supervisor. Supervisors in such role reversals may gain insight into what is affecting their subordinates. Furthermore, having to verbalize an opposing position promotes the shift toward that new viewpoint (Bradford & Lippitt, 1952; Speroff, 1954).

Multiple Role Playing. An audience is divided into small teams, and each team member receives instructions to play a particular role. Following the role plays within each team, the audience reassembles and shares experiences (Maier & Zerfoss, 1952). The different teams can be given different instructions, and the effects of these differences on what occurs during the interactions among the players are then revealed during the critique by the audience after the groups reassemble as a whole.

Role Playing Combined with Video Feedback. Video feedback of role plays has become commonplace in leadership training. Illustrative of the use of video replay was a training program of American overseas advisers. They viewed a video of their interactions with an actor who was trained to play the role of a foreigner. The trainees' performance was critiqued as they watched the video. Learning was more effective and was retained longer in the videotaped role-playing group than in a control group that only read the training manual about the same issue (P. H. King, 1966).

Ivancevich and Smith (1981) compared role playing and videotaped feedback with a lecture and role playing without videotaping and with a control group without training. They evaluated the performance of 60 sales managers in dealing with their sales representatives in clarifying goals, openness, giving information, and supportiveness in simulated goal-setting interviews before and after training. In addition, surveys of the 160 sales representatives three months after training found that improvement had indeed been greatest for the managers who were trained with video feedback in clarifying goals and supportiveness. But role playing without video feedback was as successful as role playing with videotaped feedback in improving openness and the giving of information. And according to the representatives, both training groups of managers did equally better than the control group in giving feedback and challenging the representatives. The sales representatives in the trained groups also did better than the sales representatives of the control group of untrained managers in increasing orders they received per sales presentation, but no differences were obtained in the new accounts generated by the sales representatives of the trained and untrained groups of managers. In all, video feedback following training appeared to do as well as or better than traditional role playing in improving the managers' performance in its effects on the sales representatives. Both trained groups of managers generally showed such improvements in contrast to the untrained control groups of managers. Videotaping provides models for role plays. Models in supportive environments are important for learning desired performance from role playing (Sims & Lorenzo, 1992).

Availability. Role plays can be packaged for self-administration by the role players.[7] For example, Shack-

[7] Such "off-the-shelf" leadership training materials are widely distributed by commercial publishers.

leton, Bass, and Allison (1982) provided participants with a booklet of self-administering instructions that made it possible for them to experience and obtain results comparing the five leadership styles: *directive*, negotiative, consultative, *participative*, and delegative—presented in Chapter 18. Packaged video programs and interactive computer programs can create highly realistic settings and role requirements for training.

Simulations and Games

Facsimiles of real organizations and managerial work are created figuratively and literally as reproductions that sample real or fictitious processes. Organizational games are simulations with rules in which one can compete with opposing players against standards. The simulations and games can be used as learning experiences, assessment, and research.

In-Baskets. Participants are given a booklet that essentially reproduces the contents of a manager's in-basket, along with some general information about the organization in which the manager is located. Each participant has to decide what actions to take to dispose of the items before leaving on a trip (Frederiksen, 1962a, b). Good performance is associated with a good sense of priorities, planning ahead, and the appropriate use of available information (Zoll, 1969). Discussions can be held about the responses to the in-basket items. Butler and Keys (1973) reported comparisons between 33 first-line supervisors who took a traditional course on the fundamentals of supervision and 30 supervisors who carried out a series of group discussions based on their handling of in-basket items. The traditional course resulted in no significant improvement in tested knowledge on the How Supervise? (File & Remmers, 1971) or the Supervisory Inventory on Human Relations (Kirkpatrick, 1954). But the in-basket discussion group improved significantly on both instruments. Commensurate with the significant gains in knowledge registered by the in-basket participants in the next several months back on the job, their subordinates reported more changes for the in-basket discussion participants in their behavior as supervisors, particularly in their "people orientation" and in innovation on Marvin's (1968) Management Matrix. Little or no such change was found for those who took the traditional course on the principles of leadership. Cases can be recast into in-basket tests and games. For example, ED/AD/EX, used in training programs in the United States, Spain, and India, incorporates interpersonal, strategic, and value aspects of the environment in which a school principal has to operate (Immegart, 1987).

Games and Simulations. Organizational, institutional, and business games are living cases. Trainees must make sequential decisions and then live with them (Leavitt & Bass, 1964). Outcomes from leadership performance have fairly rapid consequences. Success and failure are more fully objective and observable than is true for role playing in general. More than 30,000 executives participated in one or more of the hundred or so business games that appeared in the first five years following the introduction by the American Management Association of its Top Management Decision Simulation in 1956 (L. Stewart, 1962). The Carnegie Mellon game was an early example of a business simulation of three soap companies working in competition with each other in a common market. These prototype business games and most of their successors confront teams of players with sets of decisions that require them to decide at each successive play how much to budget for raw materials, plant, equipment, advertising, research, and labor. Computer assistance helps register the distribution of players' quarterly expenditures and investments for each company as well as calculate their stock prices and return on assets (ROA) as they compete. Players usually need to make decisions on what prices to set for their products, whether to borrow money, and whether to build plants. They may negotiate with "suppliers" and "union officials." When the game is used for leadership training, teams may compete against one another or against a computer model. Videotapes were made of the elected presidents of 27 "companies," each with eight MBA students who took other management positions. The simulated companies ran for 12 quarters. Companies with transformational presidential leadership produced higher ROAs. A bankruptcy could be attributed to poor presidential leadership.

Organizational simulations such as UPPOE create leadership problems. For instance, player-managers literally have to obtain the cooperation of player-workers to produce, for a "market," paper products made by cutting, assembling, and stapling. Players can be hired and fired; they can speed up, slow down, or strike. Tangible products and raw materials can be processed, bought, and sold (Bass, 1964).

MG 101. Closer to real management is MG 101, an undergraduate course created at Bucknell University (J. A. Miller, 1991, 1995a). Half the course time and grade is spent in the usual readings and lecture-discussions of an introductory management class. In coordination, the other half is dedicated to twice-weekly laboratories. Technical manuals are provided in accounting, finance, marketing, operations, and personnel, supported by guest lecturers. Each company organizes itself to choose and complete a real community service, such as designing and constructing a county storage and distribution center for food and clothing. Or the company chooses a business project that will be financed to produce and/or sell real items, such as T-shirts, calendars, or coffee, profitably. A business plan is prepared and presented to a board of directors for approval. The activity is completed with the presentation of a final report to a large audience of students and faculty. The course was begun in the early 1980s; by 1995, more than 4,000 undergraduates at Bucknell and other institutions had completed it (J. A. Miller, 1995b).

The Looking Glass. The Looking Glass, developed by the Center for Creative Leadership (McCall & Lombardo, 1982), is a carefully constructed simulation of the organization of a real glass manufacturer. It attempts to reproduce faithfully in simulation the required arrangements among the managers of the real company. Relevant financial data and information about products are included and must be factored into communications and decision making. Up to 20 executive positions are filled in the top four levels of the simulated glass manufacturer. The training involves a period, such as a day, to complete the simulation exercise and a subsequent period for individual and group feedback. Learning is enhanced by systematic feedback of the performance of participants in the simulation. But here there is a need to "teach for transfer," with structure to support the transfer to the back-home job of what has been learned in the simulation, according to Kaplan, Lombardo, and Mazique's (1985) six-month follow-up evaluation back on the job.

Howell (1991) presented a case of a class of MBA students who were managing the Looking Glass Company when, unknown to Howell (the instructor), one student decided on his own to be so disruptive that he would be "fired." Howell discussed what was learned from the case and the feedback afterward.

War Games. These have been used by the military to identify hypotheses and challenging assumptions as well as for training (Killebrew, 1998). War games can vary from board games and computer games to complex simulations with high fidelity and real soldiers in training to engage trained soldiers acting as enemies. An example is the Joint Readiness Training Center (JRTC) at Fort Polk in Louisiana. Whole U.S. Army infantry battalions spend 11 days and nights in the field in a "battle" with a highly trained "enemy." It is almost like real combat except that hits are registered electronically, determining "wounds" and "kills." The platoons have to move into defensive positions, defend them, and then attack. If they are airborne battalions, they may parachute or helicopter into the area. Each platoon and unit at higher and lower levels is shadowed by a trained observer-controller, who provides coaching and feedback. After-action reviews are held frequently (Avolio, 1999).

Evaluations. Despite the widespread use of games and simulations, evaluations of them are hard to come by. However, Raia (1966) showed that a business game, simple or complex, can add more to performance on a final examination about case problems than can discussions and reading about the cases. In addition to providing training opportunities for participants, simulations and games can generate valid research about the processes used by the players and the results can suggest real-life outcomes depending on the fidelity of the simulation — that is, how accurately it matches real life.

Programmed Instruction, E-Learning, and Computer-Assisted Instruction

Programmed Instruction. With this application, instruction is programmed into concrete steps. Trainees must generate or choose the correct answer to a question before proceeding to the next question. Efforts have been made to use programmed instruction to teach effective

human relations. For example, the American Management Association has sponsored PRIME, a programmed textbook for training supervisors. Other examples are "cultural assimilators," programmed texts that have been developed and evaluated to teach leadership and good human relations relevant to a designated culture (Fiedler, 1968).

It is difficult to write an effective program if what is to be taught involves shades of opinion, sensitivity to fuzzy socioemotional issues, and unclear ideas about the order of steps in which learning can take place (Bass & Barrett, 1981). Nevertheless, Hynes, Feldhusen, and Richardson (1978) obtained positive results in a controlled experimental study of a three-stage program to train high school students to be better leaders. Programmed instruction, coupled with lectures, yielded improvements in understanding and attitudes in the first stage, whereas experiential approaches failed to do so in the second and third stages. Positive effects have also been obtained with cultural assimilators (Fiedler, 1968).

Electronic Learning (E-Learning). This is learning using the Web, computers, virtual classrooms, distance learning, and/or digital collaboration. In the twenty-first century, e-learning has become the new form of correspondence course. Videotapes and films can be included as part of computer-regulated programs and can be incorporated in training as stimuli, response alternatives, and feedback.[8] For instance, Decision Point: A Living Case Study is an interactive computer program that provides the trainee with a high-fidelity audiovisual simulation of the different phases of managerial experiences. It begins with the trainee being offered and accepting a position with a firm to help manage its marketing problems. Political issues arise, along with personnel grievances, conflicts among departments, and questions of credit policy. Ten decisions need to be made. In each instance, four alternatives are provided. A written debriefing is provided by the computer about the adequacy of each of the chosen decisions, along with explanations.

Preston and Chappel (1988) contrasted randomly assigned groups of undergraduates to computer-based training, computer-based training with videotaped vignettes, and group discussions with the videotaped vignettes.

---

[8] The NeXt personal computer was an elegant effort to exploit this multimedia process.

They found that any one of the three training methods could improve performance on tests of knowledge about principles of leadership equally well. DeRouin, Fritzsche, and Salas (2003) have offered research-based guidelines for learner control and learner-led instruction in e-learning. Learner control can include pacing, number of examples and practice, sequence of topics, and course content and context. The amount of control should be limited to that required for effective instruction. Too much control, requiring too many decisions, may distract the learner from the subject matter to be learned. Guidelines include: (1) Learners need to spend enough time to understand how much control they have. (2) Learners need to understand that learner-led instruction is challenging. (3) Help needs to be provided by self-tests and feedback. (4) Learners differ in ability and experience and how well they can e-learn. (5) Learners should be allowed to skip rather than add extra instruction about the same content. Instead, the extra time should be spent on new instruction. (6) Learners should be allowed to choose their own real contexts for examples. (7) Learners need to be able to navigate backward and forward through the training program, with key links connecting directly to all the nodes or segments. (8) All the information necessary to solve a problem in a node should be provided in that node. (9) Connections between nodes may need to be explained with text to be understood. (10) Formatting needs to be consistent throughout the program. E-learning at the workplace or school may promote self-regulated lifelong learning.

Computer-Assisted Instruction (CAI). Hausser, Blaiwes, Weller, and Spencer (1974) described computer-assisted instruction (CAI), a technically advanced version of programmed instruction, to teach interpersonal skills to U.S. Navy commanders. Using the PLATO system and an instructional programming language, TUTOR, Hausser and Spencer (1975) applied CAI to interpersonal skill training in feedback, communication, goal setting, problem solving, decision making, effective rewards and punishments, and the use of power and authority. Compared to controls who received the same pre- and posttest assessments and were involved in the same duties as recruiting officers, those who were trained with CAI learned considerably more. By 1985, a survey of Fortune 500 firms indicated that more than half of them were already beginning to make use of CAI (Hassett & Dukes, 1986).

Behavior Modeling

Behavior modeling involves instructions for mastering a skill demonstrated by a competent model (live or video) of mental and physical practice, follow-up, and overlearning to assist long-term retention. It is based on social learning theory. In contrast to the more "mindless" Skinnerian operant learning or the emphasis on insightful discovery in learning, Bandura (1977) argued with experimental support that learning is facilitated if learning models are provided with information in advance of the consequences of engaging in a specific behavior. Action can be taken with foresight. People are more attentive and active in organizing what is to be learned if they are provided with models to follow. In observational learning, anticipation of a reinforcer influences not only what is observed but what goes unnoticed. Learning from the model is increased when the consequences of the model's behavior are highly valued. To illustrate, videotapes of a positive model of leadership, obtained by Pescuric and Byam (1996) from interview information about the skills to be learned, were followed by a one-to-one practice and feedback on how well the skills were used. Groups of learners discussed how they would use the skills on the job.

Goldstein and Sorcher (1974) showed how, in theory, this approach could be applied to training first-line supervisors. Pilot experiments followed. Results were generally supportive (Kraut, 1976).[9] For instance, in an experiment by Latham and Saari (1979), for two hours each week for nine weeks, 20 supervisors engaged in training that dealt with (1) orienting a new employee, (2) giving recognition, (3) motivating a poor performer, (4) correcting poor work habits, (5) discussing a potential disciplinary action, (6) reducing absenteeism, (7) handling a complaining employee, (8) decreasing turnover, and (9) overcoming resistance to change. Each session followed the same plan after an introduction of (1) a film showing a model supervisor effectively handling a situation, followed by a set of three to six learning points that were shown in the film immediately before and after the model was pre-

---

[9] See also King and Arlinghaus (1976) and Moses and Ritchie (1976).

sented; (2) group discussion of the effectiveness of the model in exhibiting the desired behaviors (to promote retention); (3) practice in role-playing the desired behaviors in front of the entire class; and (4) feedback from the class about the effectiveness of each trainee in demonstrating the desired behaviors. The learning points shown in the film were posted in front of the trainee who played the role of supervisor. Points to use when handling a complaint included (1) avoiding responding with hostility or defensiveness; (2) asking for and listening openly to the employee's complaint; (3) restating the complaint to achieve a thorough understanding of it; (4) recognizing and acknowledging the employee's viewpoint; (5) stating one's position nondefensively, when necessary; and (6) setting a specific date for a follow-up meeting. Positive reactions to the program were sustained over an eight-month period. In contrast to 20 supervisors in a control group, the experimental trainees scored significantly higher on a test of the knowledge necessary to transfer the principles learned in class to different types of job-related problems. The experimental trainees were also more effective in role plays resolving supervisor-employee problems and in earning higher evaluations of their job performance from their superiors one year after training than were the supervisors in the control group. They had been equivalent in rated performance with the control group one month before training.

Burke & Day (1986) concluded from a meta-analysis of evaluative studies, and a review by Latham (1989) showed that behavior modeling was an effective management training method. However, Yukl (1998) pointed out the many limitations of the research and applications. He suggested that behavior modeling was likely to work better for learning concrete behavior in a specific situation rather than developing flexible, adaptive behavior in a variety of situations. More studies are needed about whether the learning facilitated actual behavioral change back on the job.

Computer-Assisted Behavioral Modeling. Because behavioral modeling has discrete components and pursues a systematic series of steps, it lends itself readily to computer assistance. CAI behavioral modeling programs have been developed to help train supervisors. In these programs, supervisors operate interactively with a computer to learn how to orient new employees, deal with

resentment, resolve conflicts, inform the union of a change, and terminate employees (Development Dimensions International, 1983).

Caveat. Fox (1989) unearthed 13 reports of the positive effects of using behavioral modeling to improve supervisory skills. Yet despite its effectiveness in promoting the learning of leadership behavior, behavioral modeling may produce varied and unwanted results. Manz and Sims (1986a) contrasted three separate modeling interventions for leadership behavior. Videotapes provided models of contingent-reward leadership, contingent-reprimand leadership, and goal-setting leadership for randomly selected students assigned to 10 leader-subordinate dyads. A fourth control group did not view any tape. Pre-post measures of the three styles of leadership behavior and the controls' performance were obtained. Overall, modeling generated significantly more improvement than was observed under the control condition. As expected, the subordinates' satisfaction with the leader increased with increased contingent reward (.61) and increased goal setting (.35) but not with the increased contingent reprimand. Moreover, the coefficients from path analyses showed that the contingent-reward model directly promoted contingent-rewarding leadership behavior (.21). However, the contingent-reprimand model not only resulted in increased reprimanding (.16) but also *reduced* contingent rewarding $(-.55)$ and goal setting $(-.43)$. Finally, the goal-setting model failed to enhance goal-setting leadership significantly and increased reprimanding leadership (.22). Thus the theoretical basis for the modeling has to be considered in determining whether behavioral role modeling may be productive or counterproductive. Hakel (1976), Locke (1977), and McGehee and Tullar (1978) cautioned against its uncritical adoption.

Training in Specific Leadership Skills

In addition to behavioral role modeling to cope with specific leadership problems, there is much training in the skills that are necessary to fulfill a leader's responsibilities adequately. Goldstein (1980) noted the continuing work on the training of raters and the improving of performance evaluations by supervisors. He also found that much of what is available for evaluating training in leadership skills, such as how to handle disciplinary problems, is anecdotal. But illustrative of controlled experimental evaluations of such training was a small sample investigation by Douglas (1977), who examined the efficacy of the systematic training of group leaders using operationally defined leadership skills in a group interaction. Compared to the leaders in an alternate placebo group, those who were trained to use both the reflective-supportive (considerate) and the command-response (directive) styles employed these styles consistently and appropriately. The trained leaders also used the associated verbal responses more consistently and appropriately than did the leaders under the placebo condition. As with Manz and Sims's (1986a) results, another finding was that the effects on the leaders' behaviors overlapped regardless of the theoretical orientation, which suggests that when leadership skills are being taught, there are likely to be spillover effects across skills and orientations. Training leaders in one skill, such as how to use a particular verbal response style, may reduce or increase their ability to use another leadership style. Conceivably, leaders can simultaneously increase their integration of their task and relations orientation (as advocated in Chapter 19).

Sensitivity Training

It was at a social workers' conference on leadership in 1946 that Kurt Lewin and his graduate students at the Massachusetts Institute of Technology stumbled serendipitously into sensitivity training. The conferees found the students' observations about the interpersonal processes that occurred during the conference to be more valuable to the conferees' learning than the formal leadership topics that the conferees had discussed. The idea took root that all participants in discussion groups could become observers and that the sharing of their observations would provide insight into leadership processes in general. In addition, participants could learn about their adequacy in interaction with others and what they might do to improve. Subsequently, the learning process was facilitated by eliminating the formal agenda before a group convened (Bradford, Gibb, & Berme, 1964).

The group leader became a trainer. And, on the surface at least, the trainer abdicated the leadership role. The social vacuum that was created as a consequence of beginning without an agenda or a group leader revealed the individual participants' differences in ability and willingness to attempt and succeed in initiating structure. The ambiguous situation gave participants the opportunity to try out new ways of carrying out various task and maintenance leadership activities that were of use to the group. The feedback from the other participant-observers reinforced the new attempts that worked well and indicated the inadequacy of other, less successful attempts to lead. For this reason, the situation was seen as a "laboratory," a place for experimenting.

Trainers established themselves as ambiguous authority figures, provided group members with the information needed to analyze group processes, and encouraged participation and openness. They did not structure the group discussion; instead, they threw the entire burden of initiative back on the group members. Feedback sessions were used to suggest that the participants' demands for direction and structure from the trainer inhibited the examination of group processes and the development of insight into role relationships.

Theory. Theoretical supports for sensitivity training and its variants are diverse. In addition to Lewin's (1939) topological existentialism, they include analytic theory, Bion's (1948, 1961) fight-or-flight analyses, Moreno's (1955) sociopsychological focus, Berne's (1964) transactional analysis, Perls's (1969) gestalt therapy, Maslow's (1965) humanistic psychology and Argyris's (1976) single- and double-loop learning. In *single-loop learning*, leaders as well as followers seek little feedback from their environment that might confront their fundamental beliefs and behavior. The beliefs are self-sealing and self-fulfilling. There is little testing of them. Leaders learn only about what is comfortable for them to discuss. In *double-loop learning*, they are willing to confront their own perspectives and invite others to do so. They work through blind spots. They can learn through listening and reflecting on questions around their assumptions about their roles in the organization and their own and the organization's goals.

Variants of Sensitivity Training. Numerous variants have been developed. Sensitivity (or laboratory) training using the T- (for training) group, focused on interpersonal learning during the 1950s and onward. The encounter group, which arose in the 1960s, provided a more intensive experience in openness; the self-examination of hostilities, defenses, and feelings; self-awareness; and personal growth. Also in the 1960s, personal growth programs took on a life of their own to improve self-awareness and overcome personal obstacles to developing competence in leadership (Yukl, 1998). To increase transfer of training to the work situation, team building engaged people who work as a group, along with their supervisor, as a T-group in sensitivity training, but with issues relevant to work and organization.

Sensitivity training may begin with a task and structure, then gradually become less structured. A marathon nonstop training weekend may be used. Two or more trainers who meet with a much larger than ordinary cluster group may be employed. Many organizations developed unique programs, incorporating some aspects of the sensitivity training laboratory (Morton & Bass, 1964). Actually, many of the elements of sensitivity training, such as participation and feedback, have found their way into training and human resources management in general. They also can be seen in numerous self-development programs, ranging from group therapy to the physically demanding Outward Bound challenge programs. Sensitivity training has also been instrumented so that no trainer is needed. In such a case, all instructions come from written materials or directions, or directors outside the training group (Blake & Mouton, 1964). Sensitivity programs may require three hours to three weeks. They may run with once-a-week sessions. The numerous variants of sensitivity training all attempt to accomplish one or more of the following changes in attitude or behavior by the trainee-leaders: (1) greater sensitivity to the needs and desires of followers; (2) greater openness and sharing of information; (3) greater sharing of decision-making responsibilities with followers; (4) more intimate, friendly, and egalitarian interaction with followers; and (5) less structuring, personal dominance, and pushing exclusively for productive output.

Instrumented and Packaged Sensitivity Training. The standardization of techniques can increase the reliability and reduce the variability of results with sensitivity training. Groups can undergo standardized processes that involve instrumented, self-administered, repeated questionnaires for data gathering; analysis; discussion; role plays; in-basket simulations; cases; audiotaped or vid-

eotaped instructions; and other types of experiential exercises for sensitivity training. The instruments either create a process similar to a T-group, or focus on more specific socioemotional learning experiences. Seven standards are proposed for developing such "ready-to-use" learning programs: (1) a scientific review of what is known about the processes; (2) identification of the behavioral dimensions of consequence that are to be the subjects of learning; (3) effective reinforcement; (4) reliable and valid measures of change; (5) adequate follow-up; (6) the control of necessary antecedent conditions and associated consequences; and (7) adequate norms (Bass, 1977).

Blake and Mouton (1962a) pioneered the instrumentation of sensitivity training, the "most radical innovation in T-group training" (Weschler & Schein, 1962): they removed the trainer. The managerial grid training (Blake & Mouton, 1964) that emerged was widely adopted as a substitute for sensitivity training with trainers. Self-administered instrumental training was seen to give trainees greater responsibility for learning. It was expected to be more likely to be transferred. It gave participants more respect for systematic data analysis. It was cheaper to conduct (Shepard, 1964). Its content fit with theory and research on the need and ways for supervisors to integrate task-and-relations orientation.

Berzon, Reisel, and Davis (1969) evaluated a 10-session instrumented audiotape program for self-directed personal growth groups entitled Planned Experiences for Effective Relating (PEER). They reported a positive change in self-concept. Worden (1976) found that although no immediate personality differences could be detected between the experimental and control subjects, 25 of 67 youths who were subjected to PEER reported, in a six-month follow-up, that they had made use of leadership skills learned in PEER. Similarly, Vicino, Krusell, Bass, et al. (1973) evaluated the effects of PROCESS (Krusell, Vicino, Manning, et al., 1971, 1982), a program of eight exercises (12 in the 1982 revision), self-administered by booklet, for personal and interpersonal development. A field experiment using a holdout control procedure yielded results indicating that the undergraduate participants improved their concept of themselves, were more able to see themselves as their peers did, and reacted favorably to the total experience. Similar results were obtained with 219 members of a women's religious order.

It would seem that less expensive instrumented approaches can be substituted for the more expensive T-group without much loss of effect. Whether either approach should be included in a leadership training program must take into account the question of whether the learning, even if it has salutary effects on the individual trainee, can be applied in the real-life setting to which the trainee returns. If not, it may be that Bamforth's (1965) solution of incorporating sensitivity training and process learning into on-the-job activities is more efficacious.

Learning Outdoors. In 1941, a large merchant shipping line asked Kurt Hahn to set up a training program to try to reduce the poor survival rate of young sailors. He created an outdoor training program structured to help individuals discover and realize the potential of their inner resources, to reflect the dangerous environment in which they operated (Anonymous, 1995a). The leadership and team development of four six-man teams of Norwegian naval cadets were enhanced considerably by four days of experience in sinking boats and survival experience with limited resources. They were challenged with a variety of military and social problems (Polley & Eid, 1990).

The Office of Strategic Services assessment staff (1948) set up outdoor physical problems for assessment purposes that were adapted to sensitivity training, team building, and personal growth. Problems for the group and its leadership included figuring out how to safely cross a deep stream or how to get the entire group over a high wall without a ladder. Each member of the group might take a turn falling off a wall, depending on the group to break the fall. These kinds of outdoor situations were adopted for sensitivity training.

In sensitivity training outdoors, participants face psychological but not physical risks such as cliff climbing with ropes, so they have novel experiences they did not realize they could do. The novel tasks and the unusual environment make for readily remembered events for discussion and feedback about performance under stress. Focus is on management competencies. Connections are made to the workplace (Anonymous, 1995b). To increase the scope and realism of training, groups are taken to the outdoors, where physical problems need to be considered. Obviously, military training groups and sports teams practice outdoors. A wilderness experience can provide safe risk taking. Team building for an intact management team was expected to accrue from the cohesiveness developed from learning to trust others, sharing risks, and overcoming challenges. Personal growth was expected to accrue from increased confidence in success in dealing with risks (Williams, Graham, & Baker, 2002). Also expected was development of commitment to the organization and awareness of mutual strengths and weaknesses (McAvoy, Cragun, & Appleby, 1997) and improved conflict management (Wagner, Baldwin, & Roland, 1991). Outward Bound is an example of a physically challenging outdoor program that involves a group in increasingly difficult physical activities such as cooperating in scaling a wall, crossing a stream, or rappelling down a cliff in real or simulated wilderness conditions. Feedback after the activity discusses feelings and behavior with implications for leadership and organizational life (Yukl, 1998). Evaluations have reported improvement back home in participants' self-concept (Marsh, Richards, & Barnes, 1987), teamwork (Baldwin, Wagner, & Roland, 1991), and retention of personnel (Gall, 1987).

Evaluations of Sensitivity Training. Most of the research concerned with the effects of sensitivity training has attempted to determine whether change has occurred. Although testimonials do not constitute evidence of consequence, Wedel (1957) surveyed 333 former participants in sensitivity training and found that they tended to regard the training as valuable in improving their human relations skills. Nonetheless, critics continually questioned whether these objectives were being met in sensitivity-training programs. Studies of the impact of sensitivity training on trainees' attitudes, perceptions, and behavior yielded a mix of results. Likewise, the detailed examination of the impact of sensitivity training on the groups and organizations to which the trainees returned resulted in a complex of conclusions concerning the costs and benefits of the training. Cohesiveness may be increased, but performance may be impaired. It may be difficult to transfer what is appropriate in training to what is appropriate back on the job (Bass, 1968). Generalizations about the effects of sensitivity training are made difficult because of its many variations.

Changes in Trainees' Attitudes. Although the results have been somewhat mixed, the majority of evaluations have indicated that sensitivity training results in significant changes in interpersonal attitudes: more favorable attitudes toward subordinates, a stronger human relations orientation, and greater awareness of interpersonal dynamics. For example, Bunker and Knowles (1967) and P. B. Smith (1964, 1975) reported significant changes in the attitudes of participants as a consequence of laboratory training. Schutz and Allen (1966) found that the effects of laboratory training resulted in more changes in the attitudes and personality of those in the experimental group than of those in the control group. Tests administered before and six months after training indicated more changes in feelings and behavior toward other people and toward themselves and more changes in the perceptions of others' behavior and feelings toward themselves than occurred for control groups. The participants indicated greater friendliness, sensitivity, and tolerance toward others after training. When Golembiewski and Carrigan (1970) conducted a mild reinforcement session one year after the initial sensitivity training of managers, they found that changes in attitudes persisted over a period of 18 months for the group that received reinforcement. But Belasco and Trice (1969b) reported that the changes associated with training alone were small, whereas training combined with testing was more effective in producing changes. The most significant changes were in morale, self-concept, and role expectations. Asquith and Hedlund (1967) administered a before-and-after questionnaire to 20 management trainees in a chemical firm. They noted that although improvements in attitudes toward human relations practices were obtained, the participants exhibited no significant changes in attitudes toward consideration, initiation of structure, supervision, or management. Blake and Mouton (1966) studied managers and union officers from the same plant and found that instrumental sensitivity training resulted in significant improvements in the attitudes of both groups. But H. B. Stephenson (1966); Biggs, Huneryager, and Delaney (1966); and Asquith and Hedlund (1967) all obtained results indicating that laboratory training produced no significant changes in attitudes toward leadership behaviors, as measured by such instruments as the Leadership Opinion Questionnaire (LOQ).[10] Similarly, Kernan (1963) obtained before-and-after responses to at-

titude and personality items from two experimental groups and a control group but found no significant changes in the attitudes or personalities of those in the T-groups or the control group.

Changes in Trainees' Perceptions. In line with the primary objective of training to increase perceptual sensitivity, a content analysis by R. H. Solomon (1976) found leaders' statements of the effects of the laboratory training of undergraduates to include increased personal awareness, improved interpersonal relations, and improvements, as well as frustrations, in their leadership skills. Bass (1962b) asked members of a training group to record their self-rated moods at five different intervals during sensitivity training. He found that skepticism decreased and depression increased for a while and then leveled off, but anxiety did not increase as expected.

Several studies were concerned with changes in self-concept and in perceptions of others. T. Gordon (1955) found that leader-trainees tended to describe their behavior in terms that were similar to their conception of an ideal leader. They stated that laboratory training produced changes toward greater conformity with such ideal behavior. Burke and Bennis (1961) reported that perceptions of actual self and ideal self were closer at the end than at the beginning of training. Bass (1962a) noted significant increases in perceptual sensitivity to interpersonal relations after training. Sensitivity was positively related to peer ratings of influence in the group. But Greiner, Leitch, and Barnes (1968) were unable to demonstrate that instrumented sensitivity training produced significant changes in trainees' perceptions. Likewise, Kassarjian (1965) reported no significant changes in orientation toward self or others as a result of sensitivity training. A central problem here is that as trainees become more sensitive to the issues and dimensions of consequence, they also become much more modest about the adequacy of their attitudes and behavior. Thus, after a week of feedback from colleagues in instrumented sensitivity training workshops about their own concerns for people and productivity, there is a sharp decline from preworkshop self-ratings about the extent to which the trainees are 9,9, highly concerned in an integrated way about the productivity of people and their well-being. Among 647 participants, 59.8% saw themselves as 9,9 be-

---

[10] See Chapter 20.

fore the workshop but only 13.4% saw themselves as 9,9 at the end of the week (Blake, 1986).

Changes in Trainees' Behavior. Typical of improvements reported were those found by Boyd and Ellis (1962). Each trainee's supervisor, two of his peers, and two of his subordinates were interviewed in the sixth week and again in the sixth month following training at the Hydroelectric Power Commission of Ontario. Controls were also interviewed in the same manner. Improvements were noted in 64% of the sensitivity trainees but in only 23% of the controls. The trainees changed more than the controls in increased listening; better interpersonal understanding; better contributions at meetings; increased tolerance and flexibility; and, to a lesser extent, self-confidence and effective expression. Similarly, Bunker (1965b) questioned trainees and their coworkers one year after participation in a laboratory training program. The coworkers reported that the participants gained significantly more than did a control group in interpersonal skills, openness, and understanding of social relationships. Likewise, Morton and Bass (1964) studied 97 managers who listed more than 350 incidents of behavioral change during the six months following an instrumented laboratory experiment in management development. The most frequently mentioned changes dealt with improved working relationships and self-understanding.

M. B. Miles (1965) obtained results showing that sensitivity training resulted in the unfreezing of participation and greater receptivity to feedback. Change was also found in consideration and initiating structure (M. B. Miles, 1960). Buchanan and Brunstetter (1959) used T-group methods to train 60 engineers in supervisory positions. Afterward, subordinates evaluated the supervisors from the trained group as being more desirable supervisors than they did those from the control group. R. Harrison (1962) asked participants in laboratory training to describe themselves and 10 associates before and after training. The trained group increased the number of interpersonal and emotional words they used to describe themselves but not others.

In another study, R. Harrison (1966) found that 115 laboratory trainees, three months after training, used more terms indicating their awareness of interpersonal relations and fewer terms expressing the manipulation of behavior. In a similar fashion, Oshry and Harrison (1966) administered before-and-after tests to middle managers. The items in which changes occurred suggested that after training, the managers viewed themselves as more human and less impersonal, saw a closer connection between meeting personal needs and getting work done, and understood that they were a significant part of the problem, yet saw no connection between their new perceptions and how to translate them into action. These effects were strongest for those who participated most intensely in the laboratory training.

Harrison and Lubin (1955b) studied person-oriented and work-oriented participants in homogeneous and heterogeneous training groups. Person-oriented members were rated as behaving more expressively and warmly and as forming stronger ties to their homogeneous group. Contrary to the hypothesis, work-oriented members were perceived as learning more than person-oriented members. Members who preferred low structure exceeded those who preferred high structure in "understanding self" and "understanding others." The members of the high-structure group believed themselves to be capable and active in discussion but avoided the examination of interpersonal relations. Although a majority of studies have shown that sensitivity training can induce changes in behavior, the effects appear to be moderated by the personalities of the trainees.

Effects on Group and Organizational Performance. The preceding studies were designed to determine whether sensitivity training results in changes in the attitudes or behavior of the trainees themselves. The most pragmatic criterion of the effect of training, however, is whether it results in changes in the performance or responses of the groups supervised by the leaders who have received sensitivity training. Unfortunately, the outcomes are complex and multiple. Thus when Blake, Mouton, and Fruchter (1962) factor-analyzed various measures of instrumented T-group outcomes, they found that group cohesion and group accomplishment loaded on separate factors. T-groups could increase cohesion at the expense of productivity. Blake, Mouton, Barnes, and Greiner (1964) studied the management of a large petroleum company engaged in instrumented training. They concluded that the employees' productivity increased as a result of changes in the managers toward a 9,9 leadership style after they were trained. Miles, Milavsky, Lake, and

Beckhard (1965) found that sensitivity training resulted in both changes in managers' attitudes and the improved productivity of departments. Beckhard (1966) and Kuriloff and Atkins (1966) also attributed improved operating efficiency to the effects of T-group programs. Unfortunately, the controls in these studies were inadequate. The research was conducted during a long economic upswing when business profits were increasing in general.

The Trainee and the Back-Home Organization Differences. Zenger (1974) made a strong case for integrating the assessment of managers with their training. L. R. Anderson (1990) suggested that high self-monitors could be more successful if they were taught how to improve their social and task skills and learn how their own behavior affects their followers. They needed to learn about team building, process consultation, and ways of improving their relations with others. For instance, high self-monitors would be expected to profit more as leaders from Hersey and Blanchard's training in situational leadership. On the other hand, Anderson suggested that low self-monitors will profit more from changing their organizational environments. They should do better by training to change their relationships upward and downward to be compatible with their own dispositions. Learning about leader match (Fiedler & Maher, 1979) is illustrative.

Lennung and Ahlberg (1975) compared the gains of 17 managers who received sensitivity training with an untrained control sample five to seven months after training. Most striking were the greater variances of the trained compared to the untrained samples in attitudes, awareness, and observed and objectively measured behaviors. This variance suggested that the effects of training depended on individual differences and differences in the work and organizational situations to which trainees returned. Schein and Bennis (1965) studied a complex of organizational and personal variables related to perceived and observed change following sensitivity training. Verified change was defined as change reported by the trainee and two associates in the organization. The security and power of the trainee's position in the organization and unfreezing by the trainee during training were significantly related to verified behavioral change. Prior anticipation of change by the trainee was negatively related to verified change.

Composition of the Training Group. The composition of sensitivity training groups has figured strongly in evaluative experiments. Illustrating this type of experiment, Harrison and Lubin (1965b) studied participants in groups that were homogeneous or heterogeneous in the personal attributes of the members. The finding that most learning occurred in heterogeneous groups was interpreted as suggesting that members' feelings of cohesiveness and emotional satisfaction may not be appropriate criteria for evaluating the effects of training groups, since ordinarily, much more conflict tends to be experienced in heterogeneous groups once the polite facades have been removed. On the other hand, a number of commentators and a survey of participants and their superiors by Williams (1982) strongly advocated the need for a women-only management course in which many of the more subtle issues of socialization, discrimination, harassment, and influence can be discussed more openly than when both men and women are participants and instructors.

Attributes of the Trainer. Psathas and Hardert (1966) obtained results indicating that trainers in sensitivity training groups formulate implicit norms that indicate to members what the groups' norms should be. Thus the trainers play a significant role in determining the groups' values and norms. According to C. L. Cooper (1969), participants in sensitivity training tended to identify with the trainers when they thought the trainers were attractive. As a result, they became more like the trainers in attitude and behavior as training progressed. Zigon and Cannon (1974) found similarly that students in group discussions whose appointed leaders were seen as genuine and respected were more likely to transfer what was learned in the groups. Rosen, Georgiades, and McDonald (1980) found that the gain in a multiple-choice examination of leadership knowledge and principles among 39 groups of U.S., British, and Canadian trainees from the profit and nonprofit sectors was correlated with the instructors' experience (.31) and professional academic training (.20), specific training to teach the course (.65), and the status of the instructor as an outside professor or consultant (.59). Also contributing to the gain were the support provided by the organization (.38), the price paid for the course (.37), and the number of hours allocated to the course (.45).

Bednar and Heisler (1985) contrasted 38 more effective and less effective industrial training instructors who described their own communication styles. The instructors' effectiveness was judged by their management and professional trainees. Instructors who were judged more effective saw themselves as more open, dramatic, animated, and relaxed than those who judged themselves less effective. They also thought they left more of a lasting impression about what they had said and how they had said it.

Casualties. The trainer was likely to be particularly important to the outcomes of sensitivity training. Much of the rationale for instrumented self-guided training is based on the known variance in outcomes that are due to differences in trainers' motivation and skills. The amount of learning was similarly affected by trainers. Lieberman, Yalom, and Miles (1973) studied 206 trainees led by different types of encounter group trainers. They found that casualties among trainees were greatest (12%) when the trainers were autocratic, aggressive, charismatic, and convinced of their own beliefs. Other types of trainers with high casualty rates were impersonal, uncaring trainers (11%); highly controlling trainers (10%); and laissez-faire trainers (8%). On the other hand, there were few or no casualties when the laboratory was trainerless and conducted by instrumented audiotape or when trainers were benevolent, caring, group-oriented, or participative. Learning was also likely to be greater with such trainers. Learning correlated −.33 with casualty rates, contrary to the expectations of those who see value in making the learning a highly stressful experience.

Caveat. Many published studies of sensitivity training have ended in mixed evaluations. Problems remain in the transfer of sensitivity training to the back-home situation. Sensitivity training also raises ethical concerns.

Mixed Conclusions. Friedlander (1967) compared four work groups that participated in team training with eight similar groups that did not. The trained groups improved in problem solving, mutual influence, and personal involvement more than did the control groups. But there were no significant differences in changes in interpersonal trust, the approachability of leaders, or the evaluation of training sessions. Weschler and Reisel (1959)

studied a sensitivity training group over a period of one year. An emotionality index increased steadily through 30 sessions, but group productivity varied from week to week. Less salutary effects of sensitivity training on effectiveness and productivity were seen by Mosvick (1971), who analyzed eight studies of scientists and engineers that used control groups. In four of the studies[11] the subjects were trained by lectures and discussions. In the four other studies,[12] the groups were given T-group training. Mosvick found that the standard methods of training in human relations were more effective than were the T-group methods with technically oriented supervisors. Similarly, in a massive analysis of field data, D. G. Bowers (1973) found strong indications in 23 organizations of less positive effects of T-group training on the subsequent improvements of the organization's performance, in contrast to survey feedback without the T-group experience. Despite the plethora of empirical research on the effects of sensitivity training, Goldstein (1980) complained about the absence of an adequate theory to account for the various results, such as those reported by P. B. Smith (1975, 1976), who had concluded that it is not known if the effects occur in all types of groups, why effects are detected with some measures but not with others, and why certain effects occur at all.

Additional evidence suggested that sensitivity training may improve the relations within a group at the expense of impairing the group's subsequent performance of a task. For example, Deep, Bass, and Vaughan (1967) studied 93 business students who were assigned to simulated companies to play a business game. Some had undergone sensitivity training as intact groups 15 weeks earlier, while others came from diverse sensitivity training groups. The intact groups performed significantly more poorly than did those composed of separately trained members, but they described themselves as higher in cooperation and openness. In the same way, Stinson (1970) studied five control groups, five groups trained as intact teams, and five composed of members assigned to different training groups that were equated on the basis of gross profits earned in a prior business game. The fragmented and control groups outperformed the intact groups in gross

[11]Carron (1964), Miner (1960b), Moon and Hariton (1958), and Mosvick (1966).
[12]Asquith and Hedlund (1967), Buchanan and Brunstetter (1958), Kernan (1963), and Underwood (1965).

profit but declined in cohesiveness, whereas the intact groups were highest in cohesiveness but lowest in productivity. Likewise, Underwood (1965), in a study of 15 training and 15 control groups, found that the T-groups changed more than did the controls, but training had an adverse effect on productivity. Hellebrandt and Stinson (1971) reported similar findings.

To a considerable degree, the belief that organizational productivity increases as a result of sensitivity training tends to rely on inadequately controlled studies. When controls are more adequate, sensitivity-trained groups and their trainees may prove no different or less productive than control groups (Weschler & Reisel, 1959). Subsequent group learning and problem solving may be lower under some previously sensitivity-trained leaders but not among others (Maloney, 1956). Reviews by House (1967, 1968) and findings presented by Goodall (1971) agreed that sensitivity training induces changes, particularly in attitudes, but it can also induce anxiety, confusion, and uncertainty.

Buchanan (1969) found that only two of 66 analyzed studies made adequate use of control groups. However, from a review of the literature, Campbell and Dunnette (1968) concluded that laboratory training did change behavior in the laboratory, but there was less conclusive evidence for the transfer of such training to the job situation. P. B. Smith (1975) was able to collect a sufficient number of studies that had satisfactory controls, repeated measure designs, and a minimal duration of 20 hours of training. Unfortunately, the pretest sensitization of participants and the raters' awareness of who participated in training could still not be controlled in most of these studies. Although Smith found 78 reports of significant effects of training on one or more scores after training, only 31 studies employed designs that assessed the persistence of the effects. But 21 studies did report long-term effects, supporting the conclusion that a high degree of cohesiveness usually appeared at the end of sensitivity-training groups (Stinson, 1970). However, the impact on productivity is more problematic, depending on individual differences (Cooper & Levine, 1978) and the back-home circumstances to which the training is to be transferred (Argyris, 1969; Bass, 1967c).

Problems in the Transfer of Sensitivity Training.

Pugh (1965), among others, called attention to the problem of transferring what is learned in the artificially contrived T-group setting to the real world. Thus Oshry and Harrison (1966) found that the new diagnostic orientations that middle managers learned during sensitivity training could not be converted into action back on the job because the managers saw no clear connection between their new perceptions and their jobs. To promote the positive transfer of training, Bass (1967c) advised that in parallel with sensitivity training groups, simulations of the back-home organization involving supervisory, managerial, and organizational issues should be brought into the training laboratory. Bamforth (1965) went farther. As a consequence of the failure of the within-plant T-group members to transfer their learning to on-the-job problems, Bamforth changed the role of the T-group trainer to that of a consultant to regularly functioning, formal work-group meetings. In these meetings, he helped the groups to recognize their boss-subordinate difficulties, anxieties about using or not using authority, relationships with colleagues, role classifications, difficulties in communication, resistance to the disclosure of initially unrecognized dynamics, and other sociopsychological problems. To prevent fade-out of the effects of an offsite team-building program, A. R. Bass (1983) organized regular private follow-up meetings between the supervisor and each subordinate. The 135 participants who had such individual follow-ups with their supervisors exhibited less loss of learning than did 71 controls who did not have such individual follow-up meetings.

Ethical Concerns.

K. F. Taylor (1967) charged that sensitivity training is based on questionable objectives: development of group cohesiveness, confidence in compliance with the norms of the training culture, and disruption of the trainees' personal integrity. Similarly, Lakin (1969) questioned the ethical basis of laboratory training on the ground that untrained and improperly trained trainers are often employed. Also, the method takes advantage of group pressure to impose the trainers' values on the trainees, uses scapegoating, and demands for consensus and conformity to accomplish its objectives. It invades the individual's privacy. The sensitivity-training experience can be a highly stressful one for some participants. It may result in psychological casualties. However, these are infrequent and controllable with an ethical training staff. But the slight risk of such occurrences needs to be offset, from an ethical point of view, by large benefits for most other participants (Cooper, 1975).[13] Sensitivity training is a double-edged sword: participants can learn how to be more empathic and understanding of others, but they can also learn how to be Machiavellian, how to disguise their true feelings, and and how to promote a false sense of confidence in their leadership.

On-the-Job Leadership Training and Development

According to Hultman (1984), since leaders are action-oriented, the educational methods used should stress action, not theory. The methods employed should reflect the participants' working conditions. Particularly if the leaders and managers have considerable power, opportunity must be afforded them for reflection on their style of leadership. The leaders and managers may confuse power with leadership and fail to lead others because of their power and interest in maintaining their power (Maccoby, 1982). In the same vein, J. G. Anderson (1984) argued that leaders can learn to identify their own workplace behaviors that help or hinder them in reaching their goals. They can be systematically aided in this endeavor with appropriate methods. Leadership learning and development may occur during the performance of regularly assigned duties and may be as effective as formalized training programs.

Training for leadership in any organizational context can be provided in many different ways. Individuals may receive training on or near their jobs. They may be coached by their immediate superiors. They may be given guided job experience on a planned basis. They may train as understudy-assistants to those in a higher position. They may serve a formal management apprenticeship or internship. They may rotate through a variety of jobs by planned transfers. They may be placed in a special trainee position or be given special project assignments. They may be provided feedback from surveys and process consultation. They may learn leadership from self-study, special assignments, on-the-job coaching, mentoring,

[13] For further critiques along these lines, the reader may wish to consult Back (1972), Coghill (1967), Golembiewski and Blumberg (1970), Marrow (1964b), Odiorne (1963), and Stock (1964).

and attendance at meetings of professional associations (Phillips, 1986). Most important, they can learn from their experiences.

Learning from Experience

It is evident that much learning can accrue from experience. J. B. Hunt (2000) commented on how much the travel experiences of John Quincy Adams, Frederick Douglass, and Jane Addams as young adolescents or young adults had influenced their perspectives, self-confidence, leadership skills, and sense of purpose. Other world-class leaders significantly affected in similar ways by their travels as youths were Franklin and Eleanor Roosevelt, Mahatma Gandhi, John F. Kennedy, Theodore Roosevelt, Benjamin Franklin, and John Kerry. Parks (1996) found that 72% of more than 100 leaders oriented toward the public good had had travel experiences as young adults. Bennis and Thomas (2002) suggested from interviews with 43 leaders that a pivotal experience was crucial to their careers, sometimes with a mentor, sometimes climbing a mountain or doing some other extreme physical activity.

Members of the English Institute of Personnel and Development are encouraged to document and reflect on their key learning experiences. These are shared with peers to foster their personal development by exposing them to wider perspectives and new ideas (Beardwell, Evans, & Collard, 1998). Among the experiences managers listed as major influences in their development were working with a wide variety of people, early overall responsibility for important tasks, achieving results, leadership opportunities, wide experience in many functions, being stretched by immediate bosses, and having a manager who acted as a role model early in their careers (Margerison, 1980). According to Lombardo (1986), 86 senior executives who were interviewed were able to list 286 key events in their careers that generated 529 lessons. The findings from these lessons, as well as from interviews with more than 300 executives, suggested that although everyone appears to value learning from mistakes, successful executives admit making them. Unsuccessful executives try to hide or deny their failures or blame them on others. It is necessary for successful executives to understand what went wrong, to accept the consequences, and to avoid similar circumstances in the future. High performers drew many more lessons from these events than did low performers. They learned skills and attitudes that they needed to overcome obstacles to complete their work. Involvement with others forced an examination of their personal values. Failures led successful managers to confront their own limitations. Five types of assignments were seen to have special importance for the development of managers: project assignments, line-to-staff shifts, start-ups, fix-its, and assignments involving a major change in scope.

Developmental Opportunities. Rudman, Ohlott, and McCauley (1988) surveyed 346 midlevel managers and executives from nine Fortune 500 companies to identify and classify the on-the-job developmental opportunities they had experienced. The 103 descriptive items were correlated with global ratings of the jobs' developmental potential and then factor analyzed. Particularly important to development were a supportive boss and opportunities to establish personal credibility. Having to deal with intense pressure and with responsibilities for downsizing were also seen as important opportunities. These sources of development were linked to from 5 to 31 specific lessons unearthed by Lindsey, Holmes, and McCall (1987) that were learned from the opportunity. For example, learning how to be comfortable with ambiguous situations appears to accrue from the lesson learned in holding a job for which there is an absence of strategic direction.

Interviews and questionnaires with 41 New York Telephone managers revealed numerous on-the-job events and developmental opportunities that provided important lessons. A quarter to a half of the respondents mentioned increased responsibilities, special projects, exposure to role models, self-initiated activities, and learning from negative experiences as being most salient for their learning of skills and broader perspectives (Valerio, 1988).

Copeman (1971) collected detailed experiences from 109 CEOs about the experiences they felt had contributed most to the development of various competencies, such as their ability to negotiate or formulate policies. On-the-job assignments, such as taking charge of a division or serving as assistant to the president, were often mentioned. Similar results were reported by Davies and Easterby-Smith (1984) for 60 British managers. A study at Honeywell (1981) indicated that on-the-job experiences

were the primary source of development of much managerial knowledge, skill, and ability, including effective decision making, problem solving, communication, delegation, empathy, resolution of conflicts, knowledge about business, knowledge of the products, business, trends, and knowledge of costs. Baxter (1953) found such on-the-job opportunities for learning to be as effective as formal supervisory training.

To examine the development of junior- to senior-grade U.S. Army officers, Mumford, Marks, Connelly, et al. (2000) assessed the leadership skills of officers who were serving at six grade levels. They tested knowledge about leadership, complex problem-solving skills, solution construction, creative thinking, and social judgment. It was assumed that it might take as much as 20 years of experience for a senior officer to develop the skills to solve a novel, ill-defined organizational problem. Also assumed was that the kinds of experiences that promoted learning at one hierarchical level could be different from those at another level. Such level effects were seen when expertise learned at a lower level was required for dealing with complex problems at a higher level. Twenty types of experiences were identified, ranging from combat and negotiation to administration and systems maintenance. For instance, between junior and midlevel officers, the increase in required complex problem solving involved in boundary spanning correlated .32 with performance. For the changes between midlevel and senior level, the correlation was .29. Higher scores in creative problem solving, social judgment, systems skills, and expertise in leadership were seen as officers moved into more responsible assignments. As Mumford, Zaccaro, Harding, et al. (2000) theorized, different aspects of expertise and leadership skills need to be mastered at different grade levels. Senior officers generally require more in dealing with critical incidents and creating higher-quality solutions to ill-defined leadership problems.

Relevant Experience. Not just any experience will do. Bettin and Kennedy (1990) rated the previous work and training experiences of 84 U.S. Army captains rated for relevance to their current positions. Relevance of experiences was found to be the most important predictor of their current leadership performance. Time in service and number of positions previously held did not matter. Avery, Tonidandel, Griffith, et al. (1999) used the statistics from the 1997–1998 National Basketball Association's Official Guide and the NBA Register to determine the effect of four types of experience of 29 NBA coaches on the percentage of games won by their teams, controlling for team ability from rankings of team members. Regression analysis indicated that the previous years of experience in coaching NBA teams was relevant ($p < .06$) but the years coaching non-NBA teams was unrelated to games won in the 1997–1998 season. The coach's years of experience as a player was also predictive of games won ($p < .02$). Another significant predictor was years of experience in the stressful playoffs ($p < .01$).

McCall and McCauley (1986) summarized other features of jobs that help develop leaders. Important characteristics are assignments with broad responsibilities, troubleshooting assignments, early experience in leadership positions, and staff positions at corporate headquarters. Also valuable are assignments with project task forces and newly created departments. In addition, career development is enhanced by working in the mainline functional areas that are central to the organization's business (Kotter, 1982a). Moreover, although moving among important job assignments is essential, sufficient time has to be spent in an assignment for it to contribute to the development of one's career (Gabarro, 1985).

Lindsey, Holmes, and McCall (1987) examined the extent to which job assignments differ in their developmental potential by identifying the kinds of experiences that more than 400 executives said provided them with lessons and changed them. For instance, one experience the executives thought made a big difference in their development was their move into staff jobs, such as business or product planning, that forced them to develop new ways of thinking about some strategic element of the business. These jobs often involved exposure to top executives and the executives' assignment to corporate headquarters. (This is despite the tendency to view staff positions as less powerful and important as stepping-stones to higher line positions.[14])

Learning and Development from Challenging Assignments.

Learning and Development from Challenging Assignments. Jobs enhance development if they are challenging. Challenges can be set up as assignments for

---

[14]Staff assignments after line experience are advantageous, but being limited only to staff positions, as Chapters 31 and 32 noted, limits advancement for women and minorities.

learning leadership (Lombardo, 1985), since experience seems to be the best way to learn leadership (McCall, Lombardo, & Morrison, 1988). Exxon managers whose entry-level jobs provided such challenges were more likely to be seen as meritorious six years later (Vicino & Bass, 1978) than were those whose jobs did not provide such challenges. In the AT&T assessment program (Bray & Howard, 1983), candidates with assessed potential were more likely to reach middle management if they were assigned challenging jobs. In a questionnaire survey of 118 managers, McCall and McCauley (1986) found that assignments involving overcoming the past and dealing with inadequate, resistant staffs contributed to perceived growth as a manager. The less experienced the manager, the more the assignment was seen to have the potential for development.

McCauley, Ruderman, Ohlott, et al. (1994) created and validated the Developmental Challenge Profile (DCP), which assessed the jobs of 692 managers for the components which were challenging and developmental for the managers. It was assumed that on-the-job learning was most likely to occur when managers were faced with these components. They provided learning opportunities to try out new behaviors and to reframe old ways of thinking or acting. Novel, ambiguous situations and situations with incompatible demands are illustrative, as are demands to take action with feedback about the action. Challenging situations can also provide motivation to learn to be more competent, to earn a significant reward, or to avoid a negative outcome. The most central of the 15 factored scales of developmental challenges were developing new directions, inherited problems, problems with employees, managing business diversity, job overload, influencing without authority, and lack of top management support. The scales correlated with reports of on-the-job learning and how the job incumbents felt about them.

Challenges can be too great. Assignment to a difficult boss appeared to detract from a job's developmental value for a manager. Challenging assignments may fail in their utility for development because of inadequate feedback and an insufficient variety of assignments (Lindsey, Homes, & McCall, 1987).

Meta-challenge. Vaill (1996) postulated a learning premise that might be called a "meta-challenge." Given the rapidity of change in the physical, economic, political, and social forces on organizations in many industries, managerial leadership is not learned, it *is* learning. In real time, a condition is faced by the leader that is problematic for the objectives being pursued. Changes in conditions and objectives as well as resources may be difficult to predict. Leaders needs to adapt their skills as each new problematic situation evolves. Leaders are continually confronted with new problems, ideas, techniques, possibilities, and limits and must remain in a learning mode to deal with them. They need to avoid the error of military planners who ignore new developments and plan for the last war. Learning from each *new* experience followed by feedback, review, and reflection may contribute to insight, wisdom, and intuition.

Action Learning

In the 1930s, Reginald Revans (1982) pioneered action learning, which combined training with learning from experience and carried it forward into the 1990s. Barker (1998) profiled Revans's career from a physics student assisting Einstein, Thompson, and Rutherford to management consultant and business school dean. With action learning, projects in the field are coordinated with skill-training seminars conducted by a facilitator. For instance, the managers in training may role-play how they might have better handled problems that arose in the field. Action learning concentrates on developing interpersonal and cognitive rather than technical skills for dealing with complex organizational problems. Seminars are held periodically to discuss, analyze, and learn from the project experience. New skills learned in the seminar compete with the old habitual routines, so the transfer from training sessions needs repetition and generalization, promoted by asking participants to write down new situations in which the transfer will be effective (Yukl, 1998, p. 481). The Federal Aviation Administration organized the Leadership Linkages program, which promoted action learning by providing FAA supervisors with a choice of six of 13 structured projects to be completed in conjunction with skills learned in classroom leadership training. An experienced manager coached and advised the supervisor about the project task and gave insights and feedback to the supervisor. Afterward, both debriefed the performance (Marson & Bruff, 1992).

The after-action review in the military of leaders with the groups they lead illustrates using experience as a basis for learning. The review is a debriefing by all those involved that looks back at an experience. It is a discussion directed toward examining how the leader, the group, and its individual members could improve by providing each other with positive and negative feedback about what they did well and what they could improve on in their skills and actions. They might consider the most effective way they could have reacted, what skills and equipment were missing, and how good the coordination with units was. Lessons can suggest new training efforts.

Learning from One's Superior. Superiors are likely to have a positive influence on their subordinates' managerial styles (Marshall & Stewart, 1981), as was noted earlier in describing the "failing dominoes" effect (Bass, Waldman, Avolio, & Bebb, 1987). Subordinates are more likely to model their own leadership style on that of their superiors if they perceive their immediate supervisors to be successful and competent. Aspiring military cadets are likely to select for role models those superiors whom they believe are charismatic (Clover, 1989). Also, they parallel their superior's occupational values if they think their superiors are considerate (Weiss, 1978). At Illinois Tool Works, managers were trained to train others in leadership skills (Cusimano & Stalcup, 1993).

Job Rotation

One of the oldest and most favored developmental programs used by business, industry, and the military rotates managers and management trainees through a set of job assignments, each held from six months to several years. The jobs provide experience in and familiarity with various functions of the organization, various markets, and various locations. Personnel may rotate as assistants to managers and executives in charge of different units, or they may take charge themselves as they move from one unit to another. Yukl (1998) noted that rotation tends to follow a pattern regardless of the developmental needs of the learner and be similar for each rotating manager. Or the rotation may be more carefully individualized to satisfy familiarization as well as organizational purposes. Rotation may come with promotion. It may be limited to high flyers.

Rotation can have negative effects. Nonrotators and supervisors may resent the continued burden of training newcomers to their unit. It may entail heavy personal and moving costs and relocations of families, particularly if overseas assignments are involved. It may occur at the expense of initially poor performance as the rotator learns the new work. The change of management could also be detrimental to the unit (Cheraskin & Stevens, 1994).

Coaching and Mentoring

Coaching refers to guidance and feedback about specific knowledge, skills, and abilities involved in a task, the performance of a job, and the handling of assignments; *mentoring* refers to advising and guiding education, relationships, and career development. A coach is likely to be one's immediate superior or a consultant or staff member, although peers can coach each other. Staff professionals and subordinates may also serve as coaches.

A mentor is likely to be an immediate supervisor of the protégé but may be found at higher levels in the organization or outside the organization among those with more experience and influence than the protégé. Immediate supervisors serve as mentors for their protégés in about half of all mentoring programs. Peers may mentor one another. For instance, one director in a British firm may pair with another to provide a focus on personal development (Beardwell, Evans, & Collard, 1998).

Some of the differences in coaching and mentoring are that coaches provide support and help managers and executives to analyze, improve, and practice; mentors provide career advice and opportunities for skill development on the job, identify needs for improvement, and promote the protégé's reputation (Yukl, 1998, p. 102).

Coaches and mentors need to respect their protégés and have self-awareness, credibility, and empathy. They need to listen actively and react verbally and nonverbally that the protégés are being understood. They need to ask questions to verify understanding and to encourage further explanations (Anonymous, 1997). The relationship with the coach or mentor may be informal or formally assigned. Of a random sample of 246 corporate staff interviewed by telephone by Douglas and McCaully (1997), 60 formal coaching and mentoring programs were reported in 52 firms. In 22 firms, the programs were for new managers; in 18, they were for high flyers. They were less frequently arranged for senior managers. Larger firms were more likely to use them.

Effective Coaching. The administrations of Ronald Reagan and George H. W. Bush (1981 to 1992) ran up huge budget deficits, as has the administration of George W. Bush since 2001. In 1999, partway through the Bill Clinton administration, Larry Summers—a world-class academic economist but a novice in financial markets and rough around the edges—replaced the financially astute fiscal disciplinarian Robert Rubin as Secretary of the Treasury. The succession was greeted with a 200-point drop in the Dow Jones Industrial Average. Yet much of the large surplus seen in 2000 at the end of the Clinton administration could be attributed to Rubin and his coached successor and protégé, Summers (Hirsh, 1999).

Coaching is likely to work well if the learner can identify with the coach and the coach provides a good model, if both the coach and the learner are open and trusting with each other, if both accept responsibilities fully, and if the learner is provided with suitable rewards and recognition for his or her improvement (H. Levinson, 1962). In addition, coaches are more effective if they set clear standards, appreciate their learner's interests and abilities, practice delegation coupled with appropriate follow-up, and encourage learners to complete assignments (Goodacre, 1963). Coaching thrives in a climate of confidence in which trainees respect the integrity and capability of their coaches. Coaching is expected to take greatest advantage of the possibilities of individualized instruction. It can concentrate on the specific problems that learners find hardest to deal with. It can attend to the specific performances that learners find hardest to improve. It may provide the kind and quality of feedback that can have a great impact on learning (Mace, 1950).

Mills (1986) asked 207 subordinate managers to use a 25-item questionnaire to describe the coaching practices of their immediate superiors. The practices that emerged emphasized (1) self-development and self-discovery, (2) offering constructive ways to improve, (3) conducting regular coaching interviews, (4) good listening, (5) delegating and challenging subordinate managers to perform, (6) and setting realistic standards. All these coaching behaviors contributed to the subordinate managers' satisfaction with the coaching. Coaching was likely to be ineffective if relations between the coached learner and the coach were ambiguous because the learner did not trust the coach; the coach regarded the learner as a rival; the learner's need for dependence was ignored; the coach was intolerant or did not allow sufficient time for coaching; the coach withheld information to maintain power or to feel more secure; or the coach was hostile toward the learner (Tannenbaum, Kallejian, & Weschler, 1954).

Experimental Evaluation of Coaching. Several experiments provided evidence that, as expected, coaching could improve leadership performance. Wexley and Jaffee (1969) compared 10 control groups, 10 groups with approval of the leader "as is" after the first session, and 10 groups with early coaching of the leader. Both observers and followers reported significant changes in the coached leaders in the direction of greater human relations orientation. Maloney (1956) reported that group cohesiveness and participation but not group learning were improved when a leader followed a precisely coached method for implementing discussion.

Some individuals profited more from leadership training than did others. Klubeck and Bass (1954) studied 140 women from seven sororities who were divided into 20 groups composed of one member from each of the seven sororities. The groups engaged in leaderless discussion problems. Observers rated each girl on leadership, influence on the discussion, and other behaviors. The average leadership ratings were used to rank the women from first to seventh in each group. Between the first and second leaderless group discussion sessions, some of the women were given private instruction on how leaders behave. Women who were initially ranked higher in leadership profited more from training than did those who ranked lower. Coached women who initially ranked third in their groups gained significantly more than did those who received no coaching. Coached women who initially ranked sixth in their groups did not gain significantly more than those without coaching.

Edelstein (2001) described the success of a 12-session yearlong coaching program for 37 executives. But no control was reported. After 360-degree assessment with and feedback from the Management Factors Survey and discussions with staff and boss, learners developed a plan (which was also shared) for their current position or for transition to a position of increased scope and responsi-bility. Plans were implemented with logs of activities and experiences. The executives were coached in flexibility to manage as situations varied. Following experience with their revised management behaviors, they were again assessed 360 degrees and surveyed on the perceived benefits of the program. The pre and post-360-degree assessments showed statistically significant increases from 4% to 9% in avoiding premature closure, soliciting and openness to feedback, taking a corporate perspective, working as a team player, learning from experience, synthesizing data and finding solutions, delegating effectively, and utilizing empathy constructively. The increase in making good decisions was problematic. All the executives said the experience was valuable to extremely valuable. None said the coaching failed to change their managerial behavior, but 3% said the change had faded over time. Consistent change was perceived by 83%.

Effective Mentoring. In a majority of cases examined, the mentors of the protégés are their immediate supervisors (Roche, 1979; Burke, 1964; Ragins & Sandstrom, 1990). The other mentors may be of higher rank or in the same or different units of the organization. Kram (1983) described the process involved in 18 mentor-protégé relationships as beginning with phased-in initiation, followed by cultivation, separation, and redefinition. During the process, the mentors provided protégés with sponsorship, exposure and visibility, coaching, counseling, protection, friendship, and challenging assignments. The mentors acted as role models and as a source of acceptance and confirmation.

The intention of 607 state government supervisors to be mentors and the barriers involved were not affected by whether they were men or women. Willingness to mentor (strong intentions and weak barriers) was correlated with educational level. Age was unrelated to perceived barriers. Nevertheless, older supervisors revealed little intention to mentor. Supervisors with experience as mentors or protégés were more willing to mentor. Internal locus of control, upward striving, and quality of the relationship with prospective protégés contributed to the willingness to serve as a mentor (Allen, Poteet, Russell, et al., 1995).

Mentoring tends to be paternalistic in that it provides a role model for the protégé to follow (Levinson, Darrow, Klein, et al., 1978). Mentors use their greater knowledge, experience, and status to help their protégés and do more than merely act supportive or give advice. They may assist in the organizational visibility and advancement of the protégés by informing higher-ups about how good a job the protégés are doing (M. C. Johnson, 1980; Shapiro, 1985).

A survey of 1,736 managers at Kaiser Permanente Medical Care Program found that women were more likely than men to have mentors, perhaps because they had more desire for a mentor. Woman with mentors perceived more sponsorship, guidance, and networking. Men with mentors saw more opportunities for contact with senior management. Promotion of protégés with less than four years and more than 10 years of tenure was enhanced if their mentor was of the opposite sex (Bachman & Gregory, 1993).

Sosik, Godshalk, and Yammarino (2004) completed WABA analyses of 217 pairs of mentors and protégés who worked full-time in firms in 11 different industries. The protégés were also part-time MBA students. Data were collected by mail from the mentors and directly from the protégés. Almost half the mentors were supervisors of the protégés. Measures of the mentors' transformational leadership (by self and protégé) and learning goal orientation, expected career success, career balance, and developmental relationships were also collected from mentors and protégés. The results indicated that transformational leadership of mentors, learning goal orientation, expected career success, expected career achievement, and developmental relations were based on differences between individuals. But differences between the dyads were also involved. Mentors and protégés were in agreement about the mentor's transformational leadership.

Benefits of Mentoring. Of 122 persons who had recently been promoted, two-thirds indicated that they had mentors (M. C. Johnson, 1980). Mentored personnel earned higher overall compensation than did those without mentors (Roche, 1979). Personnel with mentors in a large health business firm believed they had more career opportunities, promotions, security, and recognition than did those without mentors (Fagenson, 1989). Zey's (1984) more than 100 interviews with middle and senior managers found about a third reporting that their careers had benefited from the opportunity. The popularity of mentoring reflects the interest, both of individual

employees and of their organizations, in the career development of individual employees (Clutterbuck, 1982b; Collins & Scott, 1978).

Mentoring can help to retain subordinates. It is likely to increase the subordinates' self-esteem and satisfaction with their work and with the progress of their careers. Shelton (1982) noted that protégés were recognized as more promotable by organizational leadership. Mentoring can also help protégés to cooperate in joint efforts (Hunt & Michael, 1983) and to use their intelligence more fully to make a contribution to the organization's success (Fiedler & Leister, 1977a). Mentoring provides time for some executives to develop an understanding of the mixed messages they are receiving about their roles and performance. Mentoring is particularly helpful to executives who have recently shifted from technical or professional positions to managerial business positions (Hyman & Cunningham, 1998).

The mentors' own advancement is facilitated if their replacements are considered to be adequately prepared to step into their shoes. Advancement is also facilitated if the performance of developing subordinates is used as a criterion for evaluation and reward by the mentors' superiors (Jennings, 1967a). In addition, mentors accumulate respect, power, and future access to information from individuals they have helped to develop. They spread their influence elsewhere, both inside and outside their organization, through their former protégés. Successful mentors are also likely to gain esteem among their peers (Kram, 1980). Mentoring can be a creative, satisfying, and rejuvenating experience for the mentors (Levinson, Darrow, Klein, et al., 1978).

Mentors can inform protégés about how the organization works (Johnson, 1980) and about the uses of power, integrity, and the artistic and craftsmanlike elements in effective management (Zaleznik, 1967). They can help women protégés, in particular, to integrate their career and family responsibilities. Mentors are particularly important to the success of the careers of women managers without family connections in the firm (Kram, 1980). At the same time, mentoring appears to be more helpful in the early careers of young managers and college faculty members from higher socioeconomic backgrounds (Whitely, Dougherty, & Dreher, 1991). A survey of 1,320 faculty members (43% female, 57% male) was conducted by van Emmerick (2003). Fifty-eight percent had mentors. Having a mentor was significantly but weakly related to intrinsic job satisfaction (.17), career satisfaction (.13), increased personal accomplishment (.11), lack of emotional exhaustion (.10) and depersonalization (.11). Regression analyses showed that after controlling for sex, hierarchical level, working status, role conflict, and work pressure, the modest relations remained significant. In a sample of 1,334 U.S. Army officers, 81% reported having had at least one mentor. Of these, 85% had provided career or job guidance; the remainder, psychological or social support. Immediate supervisors formed 68% of the mentors. In a two-year period, mentoring was found to contribute to commitment and reduced turnover (Payne & Huffman, 2005).

Conditions for Effective Mentoring. Numerous publications (see, for example, Tyson & Birnbrauer, 1983) have laid out the prescriptions for good mentoring. But there have been some changes in the past 30 years that need to be taken into account. Earlier, more women needed mentoring and the mentors were more often men. Cross-sex mentoring was the rule rather than the exception. More women mentors have now become available as they have risen in rank and seniority, and same-sex mentoring may now be more effective. As Clawson (1980) observed in 38 superior-subordinate relationships, some mentor-protégé arrangements work well, while others do not. Effective mentoring requires executives who can tolerate emotional interchanges and who are able to accept conflict as a dispute over substance, not as a personal attack (Zaleznik, 1967). Sosik and Lee (2002) theorized that effective mentorship depends on the mentor's ability to help solve complex social problems that occur in a protégé's career.

In addition to being sufficiently empathic to the needs of protégés, according to Levinson, Darrow, Klein, et al. (1978), mentors should be older and have about eight to 15 years more experience than their protégés. The authors argued that a greater disparity in age results in a generation gap that interferes with mentoring, while less disparity gives rise to a peer relation rather than a mentoring relation. Bowen and Zollinger (1980) suggested that mentors should be of the same sex, if possible (although female mentors were likely to be scarce at that time). Nevertheless, male mentors reacted more favorably to female protégés, particularly if the female protégés were unmarried, but they were more willing to act as mentors

toward married than unmarried men. Mentors were also more favorable toward protégés whom they regarded as good in job performance.

Hunt and Michael (1983) argued that mentors should be highly placed, powerful, and knowledgeable. They needed to be executives who would not be threatened by their protégés' potential to equal or surpass them. Such mentors would be more effective, since individuals value the positive feedback they receive from those they esteem much more than that from those they do not value (Bass, Wurster, & Alcock, 1961). Protégés place a premium on feedback from mentors who are higher in authority and whom they believe are experienced, knowledgeable, and esteemed (Bass, 1985a).

Successful competent and considerate mentors were believed to serve as role models for their protégés. Results from studies of leader-subordinate modeling (Adler, 1982; Korman, 1976) suggested that protégés would model themselves after mentors if they regarded the mentors as competent and if they believed their mentors were in control of the protégés' paths to valued rewards and to organizational advancement. Furthermore, protégés were more likely to model the leadership styles of their mentors if the mentors were easy to identify with and personally attractive to the protégés (Bass, 1985a). Sosik and Godshalk (2000) found that mentors who overrated their transformational leadership, compared to their subordinates' ratings of them, exhibited less effective mentoring than those mentors who were more accurate in self-awareness. Mentors had to take the protégés' feelings into account as a valued person sharing the relationship (Gold & Roth, 1999). In addition to self-awareness, to be effective mentors needed to be familiar with the networks of influence in the organization to be able to serve as sponsors of their protégés (Ibarra, 1993). In two organizations with mentoring, the best time for mentoring was seen to be early in the protégé's career. But for 129 former protégés, only modest benefits were seen by them, nor did they increase with how long the relationship lasted. However, the benefits were greater if the mentor was influential and in greater contact with higher-ups (Arnold & Johnson, 1997).

Clawson (1979) listed the characteristics of superiors that were likely to contribute to the subordinates' ability to learn a lot from their superiors. Effective superiors who acted informally as coaches and mentors more often were relations oriented and even tempered, tolerated ambiguity, valued the organization, liked the protégés, and respected the protégés' intelligence. Effective superiors saw themselves as teaching, setting examples, being directive and instructive, providing clear feedback, and avoiding being too critical. The superiors, as effective coaches and mentors, took the time to understand their subordinates, listen with understanding, and provide new perspectives, and they sponsored subordinates with higher management. Clawson's subordinates were likely to say they learned a lot from their superiors if they, the subordinates, were also more relations oriented, if they respected and liked their superior and perceived themselves in the role of a learner dealing with relevant assignments. Subordinates showed their interest by responding enthusiastically and adaptively to the superior's guidance; similar requirements and benefits were suggested for effective cross-sex mentoring (Clawson & Kram, 1984)—women managers were thought to need and benefit more from mentoring from men (Warihay, 1980). (Perhaps this is less of an issue in 2008.) Women managers found male mentors useful because the women were less likely than were men to have access to information networks (Rosen, Templeton, & Kirchline, 1981). They still may need to learn their way around a male-dominated organization with male-oriented norms and standards of behavior (Noe, 1988). However, more recently, when 138 MBA students returning from international internships were mentored by either men or women, the protégés were less likely to receive task-related, social-related, or career-related support if they differed in sex or nationality (Feldman, Folks, & Turnley, 1999). While women still experienced less benefit from formal mentoring than did their male counterparts, they did earn more afterward if they had male rather than female mentors (Ragins & Cotton, 1999). Career mentoring was more beneficial to early career progress for those from higher socioeconomic backgrounds.

Formality of Programs. Mentoring programs may be formally organized or remain informal. In the formal program, mentors are matched with protégés by third parties. Informal matching occurs when mentor and protégé select each other. Ragins, Cotton, and Miller (2000) surveyed 1,162 protégés working as engineers, journalists, and social workers who had been mentored in formal programs or informally. Informal mentoring was much more beneficial. Informal mentors provided more coach-

ing, challenging assignments, and increases in the protégé's visibility. They were more likely to become supportive friends, facilitate social interactions, and act as role models. Protégés were more satisfied with their informal mentors and received more compensation than formally mentored protégés. Ragins and Cotton (1999) suggested that informal mentoring was favored because protégés chose, as their mentor, a person whom they thought was expert and well connected; protégés and mentors could more readily identify with each other; and mentors could choose protégés they thought had more potential. Additionally, informal mentoring could last for years, while formal mentoring lasts for less than a year; mentors may choose to join the formal effort because of commitment to the organization, not the protégé. Full trust may be missing in the formal relationship. Formal programs tend to concentrate on short-term career goals; informal relations, on long-term career objectives. Ragins, Cotton, and Miller (2000) pointed to the need to formally recruit skilled and motivated mentors, train the participants, and create a satisfying organizational environment for the mentoring relationship. Cunningham (1993) suggested that in order to be successful, a formal program needs to have top management support, careful matching of mentors and protégés, an extensive orientation program, clearly stated responsibilities for mentors and protégés, and criteria for the frequency and duration of contact between them. These points were supported empirically by Lyons and Oppler (2003), who found that the satisfaction of 565 protégés with a formal mentoring program in a U.S. federal agency was determined more by the frequency of meetings and feedback about assignments than by demographic data.

E-Mentoring. The availability of e-mentoring or virtual mentoring has increased mentoring opportunities, flexibility, and maintenance of the relationship. Mentors and protégés do not have to be in the same location; more mentors can be available. The distractions of visual cues can be avoided. Cross-sex and cross-racial relationships can be more comfortable (Hamilton & Scandura, 2003).

Mentoring Personal Development. Learning to learn about self-reflection, self-disclosure, self-direction, self-reliance, and relationships in the work situation can be mentored (Uhl-Bien, 2003). Their expansion in meaning recognizes leadership beyond the formal and informal to include relationships with the organization and the environment (Hunt & Dodge, 2001). Personal skill development includes communicating effectively, listening attentively, solving problems, and creatively achieving better working relations. Landau and Scandura (2002) conducted a multivariable survey of the effects of mentoring on personal development learning, relational job learning, and personal skill development of 440 employees of a nonprofit hospital. More than three-fourths of the respondents were women and over half currently had mentors. Just under half of the mentors were the immediate supervisors of the protégés. Landau and Scandura concluded from regression analyses, in agreement with Kram & Hall (1996), that mentors were valuable resources for learning organizations. Mentoring provided vocational support positively related to relational job learning. Vocational support from mentors helped protégés increase their understanding of the context of their jobs, reduced the ambiguity of their roles in the organization, and increased their job satisfaction. Landau and Scandura inferred that protégés challenged by assignments that increase their exposure to other people in their organization develop a better understanding of the organization and, at the same time, increase their visibility. However, personal learning was not advanced with mentoring. Skill development depended on role modeling. Mentors needed to be proactive in fostering personal learning. Some kinds of mentoring were not beneficial to personal learning and yielded negative outcomes (Scandura, 1998).

Counseling. In addition to receiving coaching and mentoring from superiors and peers, subordinates may obtain counseling from staff professionals in individual and group sessions. Smith, Organ, and Near (1983) considered this behavior to be good organizational citizenship. Furthermore, leaders and managers can learn from colleagues and their own subordinates as well as from others whom they may encounter in their work (McCall & McCauley, 1986). The careers of leaders within the organization may be influenced by consultants, advisers, HR staff, and sponsors who are not necessarily coaches or mentors. Advisors can provide specific information and facilitate the solution of specific problems; sponsors can use their power to provide opportunities for experiences

that are necessary for advancement (Wood & Hertz, 1982).

Other Developmental Relationships

McCauley and Young (1993) pointed to other developmental relationships useful to a manager. Colleagues in a developmental relationship with a manager may serve in roles as (1) *assignment brokers*, who can arrange challenging assignments that will fit the learner's developmental needs; (2) *counselors*, trusted individuals who can help deal with emotional issues and personal feelings such as frustrations or fear of failure; (3) *feedback providers* of information on how well the learner is doing in developing a skill or changing behavior; (4) *role models*, to emulate; (5) *friends*, for support; (6) *cheerleaders*, for encouragement; and (7) *reinforcers*, to provide rewards for progress toward developmental goals. A reinforcer may serve (1) as a "sounding board" for strategic decision making and for managing decisional uncertainties, (2) as a coach of a newly appointed supervisor who has never supervised before, (3) to help managers deal with stress, and (4) to help a team resolve conflicts fairly (Foxhall, Chamberlin, and Smith, 2002). Counseling psychologists may advise managers about the managers' mentoring or coaching.

Giving and Receiving Feedback

The considerable hortatory literature about giving and receiving feedback can be summarized as suggesting that feedback should be about the recipient's observed behavior, not the recipient's personality, motivation, or intentions. The receipt of adequate feedback from others and from one's environment requires that the recipient solicit or be open to accepting it. Often the reverse is true: managers are prone to close out opportunities for learning when faced with difficult and threatening problems (Argyris, 1982). But instead of shutting out, ignoring, or denying such inputs, it is important to examine in what ways changes can be made to improve the situation. Feedback, coupled with personal reflection, can be used to expand self-awareness and to strengthen relationships with colleagues (May & Kruger, 1988). Survey feedback can be used to communicate performance expectations, set development goals, establish a learning culture, and register the effects of organizational change (Tornow, London, et al. 1999–2000). Facteau, Facteau, Schoel, et al. (1998) found an insignificant correlation of .14 between acceptance of subordinate and peer feedback of 49 supervising managers of a large public utility. On the other hand, the correlation was .54 between the perceived usefulness of subordinate and peer feedback.

Yukl (1982) fed back more specifically observable leadership behavior in 23 categories using subordinates', peers', and superiors' descriptions of what they regarded as optimal behavior for effectiveness in the position occupied by the leader. Again, the focus of training was on the discrepancies between actual and desired behaviors. A similar strategy was adopted by Bass and Avolio (1989) for feeding back to managers, on an item-by-item and factor-by-factor basis, their transformational and transactional leadership as seen by their subordinates. The salutary effects obtained will be discussed later. For three successive years, a sample of 148 Xerox managers received feedback on 44 behaviors from their subordinates on their management of tasks, management of change, communication, leadership, and delegation, as well as how much they involved their employees and helped to develop them. Eighty-three percent of the managers used the feedback to create action plans for improvement. Subsequently, their management style was judged by their employees to be improving (Deets & Morano, 1986).

Feedback activities are not always beneficial. A meta-analysis by Kluger and DeNisi (1996) found that performance appraisal feedback in one-third of the cases decreased performance. Atwater, Waldman, Atwater, et al. (2000) found that the performance of only 50% of the managers receiving feedback improved. Atwater, Brett, and Waldman (2003) concluded from a review of feedback studies, mainly from subordinates to their supervisors, that feedback could improve self-awareness of supervisors' and customers' loyalty. But negative feedback was more likely to reduce effort and organizational commitment and decrease satisfaction with the raters. Cynics were more likely to reject the results. A total of 142 supervisors received feedback about their work-unit climate, communications, and management relations from 1,450 military personnel. This was followed by action planning. When resurveyed a year afterward, the supervisors with initially higher ratings had improved; those initially lower had not.

Survey Feedback

Feedback about leadership performance on the job is crucial if learning from work experiences is to occur. This is why survey feedback from peers, subordinates, and clients, as well as superiors, based on standardized questionnaires, can play an important part in leadership development. Such feedback has been practiced for half a century in leadership training and education programs. R. D. Mann (1961) found more change in supervisors of experimental than of control departments as a consequence of survey feedback. D. G. Bowers (1973) reported that survey feedback promoted more improvement than did other developmental interventions such as sensitivity training or individual consultation.

360-Degree Feedback. Military organizations began making use of formal ratings by superiors of their subordinates in the early nineteenth century, and educational and business institutions began later on. Peer (buddy) ratings were found to be good predictors of performance by the military in World War II. It was the advent in the late 1930s of the human relations movement and group dynamics theory that called attention for leaders to get feedback from their subordinates, not only for research but also for the leaders' own edification (Lewin, 1939). However, there are still many executives who cannot accept the idea of their subordinates rating them. It was the military who made research use of superiors', peers', subordinates' and self ratings of the same leaders in a single survey report (Penner, Malone, Coughlin, et al., 1973) Comparisons of subordinates' and self-ratings of leaders were fed back to leaders in a single report (Bass, 1976). Attention was focused on which data and discrepancies were important to try to change and how change might be attempted and evaluated. R. J. Solomon (1976) showed that such feedback could result in the improved performance of library departments supervised by department heads who received the feedback. The feedback instrument, Profile, was one of 16 multirater leadership survey programs evaluated by Van Velsor and Leslie (1991). To round out feedback, Church and Waclawski (1996) suggested that the ratings of direct reports (subordinates) also need to be added to peers' and superiors' data.

Feedback of ratings of a single focal leader from superiors, peers, subordinates or clients, and self, 360-degree feedback, became popular. For example, feedback information was obtained for 538 senior service providers from 4,446 coworkers and supervisors and 1,617 clients. Each source of the multiple ratings revealed different rates of rater response and ratee acceptance (Church, Rogelsberg, & Waclawski, 2000). Each type of rater could provide a different perspective on a variety of criteria of the focal person's performance. The learning of the focal person accrues from feedback before and after self-awareness obtained from self-ratings and the survey feedback from others. Anonymity of subordinates and peers is maintained by feeding back to the focal person only the average and variance in ratings from subordinates and peers.

Facteau, Facteau, Curtis, et al. (1998) argued that 360-degree feedback will work only if the focal person finds the feedback valid. Otherwise, there is little chance than they will want to make changes in their behavior. Although we might expect that high self-monitors could manipulate the ratings, such was not the case. Higher ratings were not obtained by focal persons who attempt to manipulate others (Warech, Smither, Reilly, et al., 1998).

Dalton (1998) and Tornow and London (1998) listed the characteristics of effective 360-degree feedback: (1) Raters and ratees have been trained. (2) A plan for development can be constructed. (3) Following the plan will depend on the ratee's boss. (3) The ratee must be ready to receive the feedback. (4) Results can be used for coaching, mentoring, training, and self-development. (5) A question remains as to whether the collected information should be shared or remain anonymous by reporting only group results to all but the ratee. (6) Adequate sample sizes make for reliable measurements. (7) There is adequate support at higher management levels (Dalton, 1999; Nowack, Hartley, & Bradley, 1999; Tornow & London, 1998). Waldman, Atwater, and Antonioni (1998) question whether many organizations use 360-degree feedback for political reasons and to create a favorable impression about their human relations. Ratings are biased if it is thought they might be used for personnel decisions instead of personal development. A supervisor may detract from his unit performance by relaxing requirements in order to maintain favorable ratings. Care needs to be taken in creating the feedback measurements and the training of the raters.

Electronic Facilitation. A near-360-degree program, Profile, was the computerized feedback of subordinates, anonymous descriptions of their leaders' *directive*, negotiative, consultative, *participative*, and delegating behavior; the leader's power to decide relative to the subordinates; and various perceptions about the organization and the group in which they worked.[15] The subordinates' satisfaction with and perceptions of the effectiveness of the leaders' performance were also appraised. The leaders' self-perceptions were obtained on the same variables. No peer ratings were obtained. Feedback by individual counselors or in workshops provided the leaders with a profile of the data and discrepancies from norms among their own, subordinates', and normative descriptions of their performance (Bass, 1976).

Web-based rating and scoring facilitates 360-degree survey assessment and feedback of ratings of the same leader from subordinates, peers, superiors, and self to appear in the same report to the leader. MLQ ratings are computer-scored on effectiveness and satisfaction with the leader and items of leadership factors ranging from leadership behavior that is idealized laissez-faire (Bass & Avolio, 2002). Over 5,000 managers and professionals in diverse business, military, and educational organizations in the United States and abroad have received MLQ feedback (Bass & Riggio, 2005) and is the underlying measurement for the program, the Full Range of Leadership Development (Avolio, 1999).

Expected Effects of Leadership Training and Education

Application of Theory

Following Ellis's rational theory of therapy, an example of theory-based training was conducted by R. E. John-

[15] As defined in Chapters 22 and 23, *direction* (italic) refers only to giving orders with or without explanation. Direction (roman) included ordering, persuading, and manipulating. *Participation* (italic) refers only to sharing in the decision process. Participation (roman) includes consulting, sharing, and delegating.

son (1980), who showed, with a controlled training experiment, that beliefs in "rational leadership" could be inculcated. Theories of vision, organizational learning, cultural consequences, and transformational leadership may be the basis of a leadership training effort. However, as Tetrault, Schriesheim, and Neider (1988) pointed out, it is necessary to separate the question of the utility of the training effort based on a theory and the validity of the theory. It is possible to observe a training program that improves the performance of the leaders even though it is based on an invalid theory or a theory about which positive evidence is lacking. In research reports, training procedures can seldom be described in complete detail. For this reason, it is difficult to determine the particular methods that participants have learned in the training that they may use to gain and hold a position of leadership. Nonetheless, a number of studies have shown that direct training in the techniques of leadership can improve trainees' leadership and effectiveness in groups.

Training to Improve Leaders' Attitudes, Skills, and Knowledge

Early leadership training programs [16] stressed increasing the supervisor's human relations knowledge, skills, and ability, especially with reference to problems of interaction among his or her subordinates, as one of the basic goals of training. A meta-analysis by Burke and Day (1986) almost two decades ago found mixed results for the effects of management training, and only 2 of 70 evaluations considered organizational performance as a criterion of effectiveness. Rummler and Brache (1995) suggested that emphasis in developing individual leaders had shifted toward improving organizational performance. By 2000, 16 newer management development studies were found by Collins (2001) that focused on the effects of leadership development on organizational improvement that implicitly resulted from individual leadership improvement. The contents of leadership development have shifted with globalization, rapid technological change, organizational delayering, and restructuring. It is not surprising that she found strategic leadership to be the most popular, 33%, among the 54 published research studies she located. Next most frequent was employee develop-

[16] For example, Canter (1949), Katzell (1948), Maier (1948), Mold (1947), and Voriachen et al. (1946).

ment (20%). Only three of these published reports were of negative findings. (But for both journal editors and investigators, there is an unfortunate propensity to publish only positive findings.) Most depended on survey evaluations, but five were qualitative. Training evaluations dealt with improving attitudes, knowledge, self-perception, decision making, broader patterns of leadership behavior, and discussion leadership.

Attitudes and Knowledge. Katzell (1948) found that 73 supervisors scored significantly higher on a test of human relations attitudes (How Supervise) after an eight-week training course. Canter (1951), using the same test, studied supervisors in insurance companies. He found significant gains in scores on how to supervise, general facts about and principles of supervision, and estimates of the group's opinion. He also found that large gains in understanding the psychological principles of supervising others and better insight into subordinates' attitudes were obtained through supervisory training. Similarly, Goodacre (1955) and Neel and Dunn (1960) administered tests of knowledge of human relations practices to members of training groups; significant gains in knowledge were obtained in both studies. But Hand and Slocum (1970) reported no change in knowledge of human relations, self-actualization, motivation, interpersonal relations, or participation as a consequence of a training program for middle managers.

Results obtained by R. D. Miller (1969) indicated that leadership training also improved attitudes toward the importance of the leadership role. Papaloizos (1962) reported that about one-third of the participants in a human relations training program exhibited favorable changes in attitude toward subordinates. Following similar training, Mayo and Dubois (1963) found that the gain in leadership ratings was correlated positively with final course grades but not with other criteria. Likewise, Cassel and Shafer (1961) gave students direct training in human relations and leadership. Test scores revealed significant gains in leadership and social insight but not in sociometric preference or personality tensions and needs. But House and Tosi (1963) found that a 40-week training course produced no important advantages for management trainees in job satisfaction and other measures of performance over a control group. Because of the substantive and process differences in the contents of different leadership and human relations training programs, no single generalization about their efficacy is possible.

Self-Perceptions. As noted before, programs that provide feedback purported to increase the accuracy of a leader's self-image. Trice (1959) reported significant changes in self-perception in a trained group but not in a control group. Members of the experimental group who changed the most described themselves as more flexible after training. In a study of human relations training for middle managers, Hand and Slocum (1970) obtained results indicating that acceptance of oneself and others was significantly improved in a immediate posttest, but the significance had disappeared 90 days later. To improve self-perception was the objective of several democratic leadership training studies. Although Gassner, Gold, and Snadowsky (1964) found no significant increase between the actual and ideal self for members of either the experimental or control groups, they found that the experimental group increased significantly in knowledge of democratic leadership, but the control group did not.

Decision Making. Decision making was also often targeted for improvement. For instance, employing 83 undergraduates trained in human relations techniques and 75 who were not, Madden (1977) reported that leaders who received human relations training made significantly more accurate postdiscussion decisions than did untrained leaders, but they were no different in their satisfaction with the decision-making process.

Broader Role Patterns. Hooijberg and Quinn (1992) described a leadership development program in which leaders were taught to abandon routine roles in favor of broader ones that provided for more autonomy and bigger jobs for their subordinates and themselves. The leaders considered the customary way they did things and how they could become more effective. For instance, they could have more time for themselves for planning ahead if their subordinates could decide for themselves what supplies were needed to do their work or how absences could be handled through cross-training. The new patterns were to be tried for a period of time and then reexamined in a follow-up workshop.

Discussion Leadership. Training can also improve the likelihood that discussions will be effective. Maier

(1953) demonstrated that discussion groups with skilled leaders produced better decisions than did those with unskilled leaders. Maier (1950) studied groups of foremen with a leader and three followers with and without training. The leaders of the 44 experimental groups were given eight hours of lectures, discussions, and role playing, whereas the leaders of the 36 control groups were untrained. Maier found that the trained leaders had more success than the untrained leaders in inducing their groups to accept change and compromise. Subsequently, Maier and Hoffman (1960a) demonstrated that groups with trained leaders produced discussions of higher quality than did those with untrained leaders. Again, Maier and Hoffman (1964) and Maier and Solem (1962) found that leaders who used a problem-solving approach helped their groups achieve higher-quality solutions than did leaders who applied financial incentives or concentrated on a solution. Barnlund (1955) demonstrated that trainees who were given discussion leadership training regulated participation more and exhibited a greater ability to resolve conflict in group discussions. Mere practice as a discussion leader also made a difference. Jennings (1952b) studied two groups of 20 production supervisors over 16 training sessions. The experimental group was subdivided into discussion groups to solve case problems. At the end of the first session, the emergent leaders were removed and placed in a separate group. Thus new leaders were forced to emerge in the second session. These leaders were also removed and placed in the leadership pool. Successive sessions permitted the rise of new leaders. In the control group, the appointed discussion leader presented a problem and helped the group arrive at a solution. Six months later, more members of the experimental group than of the control group were rated above average in effectiveness as leaders.

Training and Education in Leadership Styles

Training and education programs, both off the job and on the job, have been developed and evaluated to train individuals to be more successful leaders on the job. The University of Michigan's pioneering survey research feedback programs reduced autocratic and increased democratic leadership behavior. Likert (1977b) summarized the many completed evaluations of the approach Vroom and Yetton (1973) created and subsequently evaluated programs that teach when various forms of participation or direction are rationally more appropriate. Blake and Mouton's (1964) Managerial Grid Training and Hersey and Blanchard's (1982a) situational leadership programs centered on the development of improved task and interpersonal relationships. Fiedler and Mahar (1979b) developed a program to train managers to deal with the situations they face as a function of their scores on the Least Preferred Coworker (LPC) questionnaire and summarized 12 validity studies of the efficacy of the program. Numerous programs, beginning with Fleishman's (1953b), focused on increasing the consideration of supervisors and evaluations of the efforts. Miner (1965) trained managers in how to increase their motivation to manage. The Full Range of Leadership Development program is an attempt to develop transformational and transactional leadership (Avolio, 1999).

Training in Democratic Leadership

Eichler and Merrill (1933) and Zeleny (1941) found that students gained from direct training in democratic leadership and ways to improve human relations. In the same way, A. K. Healy (1962) noted that training in democratic leadership enabled schoolchildren to gain in carrying out the leadership role and in their sociometric scores. The status of sociometric isolates was improved in the democratic setting, as was academic achievement. Similarly, Spector (1958) obtained significant improvement in human relations attitudes among U.S. Air Force cadets as a result of such training. Bavelas (1942) trained three adult leaders in the democratic leadership of community center activities; three controls received no training. The trained leaders greatly reduced the number of leader-initiated activities and the giving of orders and increased the number of activities in which children exercised responsibility, but the control group made no such changes. Under trained leaders, the children showed more interest, enthusiasm, and initiative in planning projects.

Lippitt (1949) gave community leaders in intergroup relations a two-week workshop in democratic leadership, group discussion, role playing, and sociodrama. Both the participants and the observers reported that the trainees became more proficient in handling problems of intergroup relations as a result of the workshop. Likewise, Maier and Hoffman (1961) demonstrated that supervisors who were trained to pursue democratic solutions led

groups to a more effective and creative solution of a problem in changing work methods than did those without such training. Similarly, Baum, Sorensen, and Place (1970) found that workers said they had increased in actual and desired organizational control after their supervisors had completed a course about the need for more democratic control.

Training in Participation and Direction

Participative Leadership Training Sensitivity training was seen by Argyris (1969) as key to the development in leaders of receptivity to participative leadership. Sensitivity training, according to Argyris, moves people to become trusting and open, to experiment with their own ideas and feelings, and to own up to them. Moreover, such people can help others to become more so. Without sensitivity training, supervisors will be more inclined to remain directive in their leadership. The argument is that those who have been through sensitivity training will be more comfortable with participative approaches with their subordinates. But others believe that sensitivity training can produce more manipulative leaders as well (Bass, 1967c).

Training efforts to promote participative or directive leadership were described by A. J. Franklin (1969), Herod (1969), and House (1962). Franklin administered a test of knowledge of group theory to groups of disadvantaged youths. Test scores after training were related to the groups' cohesiveness, but not to a significant degree. Herod (1969) demonstrated that a group-centered training program for college women resulted in the enhancement of participative leadership practices after training. At the end of four months, however, the leaders had regressed to their original positions. House (1962) trained one group in a participative style of leadership and another in a directive style. The more directive method, along with elevated course requirements, was associated with a significant decrease in trainee absences and a significant increase in the number of trainees who completed the course. In an evaluation of the Hersey-Blanchard situational leadership model, 60 executive managers completed a training course about when it was appropriate to tell, sell, participate, or delegate. After completing training, they scored significantly higher on a situational leadership examination than did a control group (Hersey, Angelim, & Carakushansky, 1982). By means of a controlled experiment with workshop supervisors, Crookall (1989) obtained positive results in a more comprehensive evaluation of a group of correctional inmates trained in situational leadership, in contrast to a control group.

Vroom-Yetton Deductive Model. Chapter 22 described Vroom and Yetton's deductive model for choosing which leadership style to use. Seven decision rules provided guidance to the leader on how directive or participative to be. The Vroom and Yetton training program encourages trainees to see the discrepancies between their way of dealing with a set of standardized cases and the rational model's solution. Detailed analyses are also provided to trainees in answer to such questions as: What circumstances cause the trainee to behave in a directive fashion, and what circumstances cause the trainee to behave participatively? What rules of the model do trainees violate most frequently and least frequently? Jago and Vroom (1975) also provided feedback to the focal trainees with data from their subordinates about how they think their superior would respond to each Vroom-Yetton case problem.

The Vroom-Yetton model has been found useful in teaching leaders to use different decision processes in different situations and as a way of increasing effectiveness of decisions. Training involves teaching trainees how to analyze various situations to choose the amount of direction or participation that is likely to produce that best decision. Managers who are trained to use the model are more likely to select an appropriate decision-making style (Field, 1982; Vroom & Jago, 1978). The model requires learning to make it useful in everyday situations (Wexley & Latham, 1981). Performance aids can be provided. Personal computer programs furnish instant profiles of rules violated by a decision, feasible alternatives, and qualitative effects of the decision for sets of problems of the expanded Vroom-Jago (1988) model. Nonetheless, questions about the Vroom-Yetton training model remain because of its extensive dependence on leaders' self-reports (Schriesheim & Kerr, 1977b). Field (1979) added a number of other problems that weaken confidence in Vroom and Yetton's conclusions, including the effects of social desirability, the lack of external validity, and the biases of experimenters (see also Tetrault, Schriesheim, & Neider, 1988).

Training in Task and Relations Orientation

PM Leadership Training. For P(erformance)-M(aintenance) leadership training, the ideal leader is "an adaptive perceiver of employees' needs and a diagnostician of how these needs can be met. Feedback processes from employees to their supervisors are central" (Peterson, 1989, p. 34). Supervisors must focus on whether their behavior is experienced by employees as having sufficient planning, performance, and maintenance content. Misumi (1985) reported that a program to teach Japanese shipyard supervisors his theory of performance-maintenance (PM) leadership stressing the need for both task and relations orientation resulted in a reduction of accidents at work. Cognitive discrepancies on P and M scores between self-ratings and others' ratings decreased. Although the morale and PM scores of nontrained supervisors dropped because of deleterious changes in the company, the PM scores of the trainees did not. Their superiors judged that the performance of 56 of the 71 trained supervisors showed considerable to substantial improvement.

Leader Match Training. According to Fiedler's contingency model, the leaders' effectiveness depends on the leaders' LPC scores and on whether the situation is favorable. Since LPC is seen as a kind of invariant personality attribute, it follows that leadership effectiveness can best be increased by teaching leaders how to make situations more favorable to themselves. Fiedler, Chemers, and Mahar (1976) developed a self-paced programmed instruction workbook, *Leader Match*, that teaches leaders how to (1) assess their own leadership style based on their LPC scores, (2) assess the amount of situational favorability, and (3) change the situation so it matches their style.

Fiedler and Mahar (1979b) reviewed 12 studies that demonstrated the validity of the training effort. Five studies were conducted in civilian organizations, and seven in military settings. The performance evaluations were collected from two to six months after training. Some included measures before and after training. The performance evaluations of 423 trained leaders were compared with those of 484 leaders without Leader Match training randomly assigned to control groups. Partially supportive results were obtained. In Fiedler and Mahar's (1979b) field experiment with 190 ROTC cadets, Leader Match training was administered to the cadets before they attended four weeks of advanced summer camp, where they were selected at random to serve in several different leadership positions for 24-hour periods. An analysis was completed of officers' and peer evaluations of the cadets' performance. The 155 male and 35 female cadets with training tended to perform better than did the 176 male and 39 female cadets in the control group.[17] A meta-analysis by Burke and Day (1986) lent some confidence that Leader Match generalized in its effectiveness across situations, as measured by superiors' ratings. In a study of the effects of leadership training on productivity and safety, Fiedler, Bell, Chemers, and Patrick (1984) combined Leader Match training, which emphasizes the need to change situations, and behavioral modeling training, which teaches leadership behavior that is independent of the situation. No attempt was made to separate the effects of the two types of training. The two training methods together increased productivity and decreased accidents. A five-year follow-up evaluation showed a continuation of the positive effects of the combined training on productivity and safety (Fiedler, Wheeler, Chemers, & Patrick, 1988).

Caveat. Schriesheim and Hosking (1978) were troubled with Leader Match because they found too many problems in the contingency model itself to warrant using it for remedial actions by specific individuals in specific situations. And Jago and Ragan (1986b) used a computer simulation to show that Leader Match was inconsistent with the contingency model. But Chemers and Fiedler (1986) argued that the wrong assumptions had been made. Jago and Ragan (1986b) disagreed. Kabanoff (1981) also noted that Leader Match was inconsistent with the contingency model and suggested alternative explanations for the results of using Leader Match. Rice and Kastenbaum (1983) inferred that the positive effects of Leader Match are due to its sensitizing leaders to the possibility that they can change their situations. Leader Match, like many other kinds of training, may exert its positive effects because it bolsters the confidence of leaders who receive the training. Frost (1986) evaluated Leader Match against an alternative training method and

a control group. As with other studies, experienced managers who received Leader Match training changed their situational control in accordance with the Leader Match prescriptions. In the alternative method, trainees were also taught successfully how to change their situation control, but no mention was made of their LPC score or its implications. The performance of the trainees in this alternative condition improved in the same way as did the performance of those who received regular Leader Match training. Frost suggested that the results were due to increases in the leaders' confidence, not to feedback about their leadership style (LPC) around which Leader Match training is organized. Frost concluded, from the results of his aforementioned experiment, that for experienced managers, at least, behavioral modeling or other methods of teaching that require leadership behavior that is independent of the situation are likely to be more effective than is Leader Match.

Leader-Member Exchange Training.[18] LMX training is aimed at improving the dyadic exchange relations of leaders with members of the group. A controlled experiment completed by Graen, Novak, and Sommerkamp (1982) showed that supervisors who were specifically trained in maintaining high-quality leader-member exchange relationships, in contrast to supervisors who received a placebo experience, improved the productivity of their subordinates more than 16%; their subordinates' motivation and loyalty were increased, and their role conflict and role ambiguity were reduced. Similarly, Scandura and Graen (1984) found that LMX training compared to a control group improved the level of reciprocal understanding and helpfulness between supervisors and subordinates. As a consequence of LMX training, initially outgroup subordinates perceived increased support from their supervisors. The weekly productive output and job satisfaction of the subordinates were also increased.

Cogliser & Scandura (2003) suggested that LMX relations could be improved in the line of hierarchy between each leader and each follower if (1) each leader develops and communicates to followers a vision consistent the organization's; each follower becomes a leader in the next level below and passes the vision on to the followers in the level below; (2) the leader's behavior is consistent

[17] Similar findings were obtained by Chemers and Mahar (1978); Csoka and Bons (1978); Fiedler, Mahar, and Schmidt (1976); and Leister, Borden, and Fiedler (1977).

[18] See Chapter 18.

with the organization's values; (3) the leader's values are consistent with the organization's and are communicated clearly to the followers; (4) each leader has a teachable point of view that is communicated candidly with followers; (5) each leader is a role model for followers; and (6) at every level, each leader and follower become more effective in their relationships.

Training in Consideration and Initiation of Structure

Efforts here have been twofold, to show, first, that supervisors' attitudes toward initiation and consideration, as measured by the LOQ, can be changed with training and, second, that this change can also be measured by the Leader Behavior Description Questionnaire (LBDQ). As was noted in Chapter 20, coercive elements were involved in earlier versions of the SBDQ and the LBDQ. As a consequence, reductions in initiation and increases in consideration were sought in training.

The results of numerous controlled experiments using the LOQ and the LBDQ to measure improvements have been mixed. Comparisons were difficult because of the extent to which the training itself varied in emphasis, quality, and extent, for there is no single standardized program about how to teach leaders to change their initiation and consideration. Stroud (1959) reported that after training, supervisors were described by their superiors as more considerate Fleishman (1953b) and Harris and Fleishman (1955) examined the initiation and consideration scores of 39 International Harvester supervisors following a training program. The supervisors' consideration scores increased in means and variances, but the supervisors maintained their heightened consideration scores only if they returned to superiors who were similarly higher in consideration. At the same time, the questionnaire was administered to a control group of supervisors who had not taken the course. Compared to the controls, the trainee group exhibited more of a reduction in initiating structure and more of an increase in consideration.

Fifty supervisors of an Australian government railway department were randomly selected and assigned by Tharenou and Lyndon (undated) to receive training, and 50 were similarly selected and assigned to a control group. A two-week residential course trained participants in the skills of planning and relating. Measures of consideration and initiation were obtained before and after training from the supervisors, as well as from 100 male subordinates of the supervisors. Compared to those of the untrained controls, the trainees' self-rated and subordinate-rated consideration and initiation were both increased. Similarly, Deitzer (1967) studied experimental and control groups of district sales managers in an insurance company before, four weeks after, and 12 weeks after a training program to increase consideration and initiation of structure. The experimental group outperformed the control group after training on all criterion variables—the number of new agents recruited, the volume of new policies sold by the agent working under the manager, and the like. The managers' consideration was positively related to the volume of sales, both 4 and 12 weeks after training; the managers' initiation of structure was related to sales 12 weeks later. However, Bendo (1984) failed to find any significant changes in the LBDQ scores of 126 supervisors who were subjected to Leader Effectiveness Training, a standardized training program. However, in the aggregate, training programs can increase considerate behavior in leaders, as measured by the LBDQ. And when the measurement of initiation includes coercive behavior as with the SBDQ, reductions in initiation can be brought about with training.

Savan (1983) contrasted trained and control groups of supervisors and found that a simulation exercise dealing with initiation and consideration conducted between immediate pre- and postmeasurements failed to shift LOQ scores. Nevertheless, six months after training, there was a notable improvement in the job performance of the trained supervisors compared with the control group. On the other hand, Painter (1984) measured the LOQ scores of public welfare supervisors and their subordinates' descriptions of the supervisors on the LBDQ two months before and after training in interpersonal skills but failed to find any significant effects of the training. Likewise, in a similar pre-post LOQ measurement of 40 restaurant managers and LBDQ assessments of them by their 380 subordinate employees, Anghelone (1981) was unable to find much change in the attitudes or performance of the managers as a consequence of a management training program.

Hand and Slocum (1972) conducted a training program to raise supervisors' consideration scores; 18 months later, they found the supervisors' job performance more highly rated as a consequence. Biggs, Huneryager, and

Delaney (1966) found that a two-week training course resulted in more favorable attitudes toward consideration and less favorable attitudes toward initiating structure. Carron (1964) also obtained data indicating that supervisors became less strongly oriented toward structuring and authoritarianism as a result of a training effort. Schwartz, Stillwell, and Scanlon (1968) studied two groups of insurance supervisors, one of which whose score moved toward more consideration and less emphasis on production after training and the other of which moved toward more initiation of structure. And although Herod (1969) and M. B. Miles (1965) obtained results from a training program that produced a more considerate attitude toward group processes, they found no significant change in attitudes toward consideration and initiation of structure. Carron (1964) noted that although attitudes toward initiation of structure and authoritarianism decreased immediately after training, no significant changes were apparent 17 months later. Ayers (1964) found that feedback did little to enhance the effects of training, as measured by changes in attitudes toward consideration and initiation of structure. Similarly, H. B. Stephenson (1966) observed that the training of 449 management trainees in management development produced no significant change in their attitude scores on the LOQ initiation of structure and consideration.

Stogdill (1970) developed a set of films, each depicting one of four different patterns of LBDQ-XII leadership behavior: consideration, initiation of structure, tolerance of freedom, and production emphasis. The films were shown to 35 sorority presidents. Each film was followed by a discussion period that was designed to induce insight into the whys and wherefores of the patterns of behavior. Leaders were described by five sorority members before training and three months after on the LBDQ-XII. The results suggested that leadership behavior was more logically related to the performance of groups after training than before. Stogdill and Bailey (1969) showed the four films to small groups of boys in three vocational high schools, along with a fifth film on representation. After seeing each movie, the groups discussed the supervisor's behavior. The investigators found that the discussion of the movies exerted a favorable effect on the groups' responses to supervision. In another experiment, Stogdill, Coady, and Zimmer (1970) attempted to influence students' attitudes toward the different supervisory roles by using the films. The results suggested that discussion of the films affected the students' adjustment to supervision. Insight and understanding facilitated favorable responses to supervision.

Training Motivation to Manage. By means of a lecture, Miner (1961b) successfully increased the favorableness of the attitudes of 72 research and development supervisors, as measured by the Miner Sentence Completion Scale,[19] to accepting responsibility for their leadership role above and beyond their professional roles. He further reported that training resulted in more favorable attitudes to supervisory work. He obtained a small positive correlation between favorable changes in attitudes to and changes toward more effective supervisory performance (Miner, 1960b, 1965). Finally, both college students and business managers who took a course with Miner (1965) improved their attitudes toward the acceptance of responsibility and authority and the willingness to initiate remedial action. Five years later, the business managers who had taken the course had significantly better promotion records than did a control group.

Miner (1988) reviewed previous research on training to increase the motivation of managers and noted its uniqueness in emphasizing how to deal with ineffective subordinates. He further argued that the effectiveness of other training programs, such as Leader Match or behavioral modeling, as seen in Frost's (1986) experiment, depended on their sensitizing trainees to the management role.

Training in Transformational and Charismatic Leadership

Although specific behavioral skills can be taught in training and actresses have been taught how to display charismatic behaviors in laboratory situations (Howell & Frost, 1988), the emphasis in developing charismatic-transformational[20] leaders needs to be on education and development, not on skill training alone (Avolio & Gibbons, 1988). Gibbons (1986) reported that in contrast to managers who were transactional, managers who were nominated by their colleagues and described by their subordinates as transformational on the Multifactor

[19] See Chapter 6.
[20] See Chapters 21 and 22.

Leadership Questionnaire said that their performance primarily reflected their whole integrated person, not specific skills taught in brief workshops that may or may not fit their deeply held values and self-concepts. Transformational leadership requires a broad educational process. Such leadership cannot be manipulated; it must be a joint search for truth by the teacher and the students in which the students are moved "to higher stages of moral reasoning and hence to higher levels of principled judgment" (Burns, 1978, p. 449). The *persona* or *aura* of a leader who is more likely to be seen as charismatic can be learned by being optimistic and passionate in generating enthusiasm, using the body language of a charismatic with appropriate gestures and stance, and inspiring appropriate emotions in followers (Richardson & Thayer, 1993). Fidel Castro learned to imitate Benito Mussolini's speech making in gestures and stance to captivate his audiences.

Feedback is essential in programs of education in transformational leadership, as in many other management development approaches. In this instance, the feedback from colleagues is about one's transformational performance as a charismatic, inspirational, individually considerate, and intellectually stimulating leader and how much one practices the transactional processes of contingent reward and management by exception (Bass & Avolio, 1989). Discrepancies between self and colleagues and self and norms are used to generate ideas and plans for improvement. In an illustrative program, feedback of MLQ results was used to increase the transformational leadership behavior of 250 executives and their direct reports (including the chief executive officer and top four levels of management) of a large Canadian financial institution (Howell & Avolio, 1989). In this program emphasis was also placed on examining the organization's culture as it is and envisioning what it and its goals and objectives should be.

Concentration on developing followers was seen by Dvir (1998) as making the difference between charismatic and transformational leadership, though they have many attributes in common. Charismatic leaders, particularly self-serving ones, are interested in exploiting their subordinates, not developing them, while Dvir saw that the development of followers is at the core of transformational leadership. Followers are developed into leaders. Bass (1985a) found charisma to be the largest among the

factors in transformational leadership, accounting for 66% of it. House and Shamir (1993) preferred to see the two concepts integrated as charismatic-transformational. In the education and training effort, meaning is provided about organizational considerations. Long-term strategies are articulated, along with how implementation is to be achieved. New organizations are considered, along with rearrangements of social roles and networks (Tichy & Devanna, 1986). Personal and organizational visions are shared, along with their planned implementation in organizational planning simulations or by a review and discussion of testimonials of what leaders have said about how they do it (Kouzes & Posner, 1985).

Experimental Evaluations. Controlled experiments have been completed in correctional institutions, industry, colleges, and the military. Crookall (1989) compared the transactional and transformational leadership training of shop work supervisors of the Canadian correctional service. The supervisors were employed for their trade skills and supervised the shop work for inmates, who are ordinarily low in education and motivation. Twenty of the supervisors completed a three-day program on the Hersey-Blanchard situational leadership model (Hersey & Blanchard, 1977). Another 20 supervisors received three days of education about transformational and transactional leadership (Avolio & Bass, 1989). Still another 20 supervisors served as an untrained control group. The situational leadership training was seen by the supervisors and their bosses as a review of good basic supervisory practices; the transformational leadership training was considered to be more of a personal development experience. Three months before training and three months after training of the supervisors, the inmates were rated on their work habits and productivity. Both groups of inmates with trained supervisors significantly improved, but not those of the control group. The length of the inmates' voluntary stay in the shop programs increased by 50% for both sets of trained supervisors and remained unchanged for the control group. Pre and post changes in inmates' case descriptions prepared by their case managers who did not know about the training experiment registered significant improvement in the inmates' personal growth and development, but no changes occurred for the control group. However, only the transformational program significantly improved the inmates' citizenship behavior and respect for the supervisors. No significant reduction in disciplinary offenses was reported in any of the three groups, although the inmates' supervisors reported the need to intervene less often as a consequence of training. They also reported less contraband, sabotage, and complaints from inmates about the staff. In addition, transformational leadership education resulted in dramatic changes in some of the supervisors. One supervisor changed from a chronic complainer to a problem solver. Another had inmates asking to be assigned to him for the first time in ten years. Complaints about another supervisor for being boring and repetitive were no longer made. And a fourth supervisor broke with the tradition of his discipline to take the lead in introducing computerized equipment.

The results of this experiment suggest that transformational leadership education is not a substitute for situational or transactional leadership training. Rather, as is argued elsewhere (Bass, 1985a), transformational leadership can augment transactional leadership. Training in situational leadership can profitably be followed by education in transformational leadership. Gillis, Gitkate, Robinson, et al. (undated) completed an MLQ questionnaire study in the same correctional system using 35 shop work instructors, 143 inmates, and seven managers of the instructors. The managers reported that supervisors with transformational training were more effective in obtaining extra effort from the inmates. Inmates who rated their supervisors as transformational rather than transactional had more positive attitudes and work motivation. They were also more punctual. As expected, supervisors rated as laissez-faire generated lower inmate motivation and job involvement, and less extra effort.

Barling, Weber, and Kelloway (1996) conducted a one-day training workshop in transformational leadership for nine managers, along with four booster sessions on a monthly basis. They were compared with a control group of 11 managers. All were rated by their subordinates before and after the training of the nine managers. A multivariate analysis of variance accounted for significant effects in subordinate ratings in transformational leadership when trainees were compared with controls.

Kirkpatrick and Locke (1996) conducted an experiment to simulate visionary and charismatic leadership for 282 student participants. High-quality envisioning increased trust in the leader and shared attitudes with those

in the vision, and had a minor impact on participants' performance. Implementation of the vision with task cues also had an impact on performance, but charismatic communications influenced only affected perceptions of charismatic leadership.

Popper, Landau, and Gluskinos (1992) evaluated the effectiveness of a three-day training program in transformational leadership for Israel Defense Forces cadets with surveys over 18 months. Most of the cadets said that the program was inspiring and important and that they would try to implement what they had learned when they became commanders. This was followed up in a controlled experiment by Dvir (1998). As part of an Israeli infantry officer course, the experimental cadets completed workshops in transformational leadership while the controls completed an eclectic leadership program as usually taught by consultants and trainers. As the 49 cadets assumed the role of platoon commanders, data were collected about their performance from themselves, their 46 company commanders, their 89 NCOs, and 724 recruits. Objective tests were completed after the training of 40 of the 49 platoons, each led by one of the trainees as platoon commanders responsible for the development of the performance of their recruits. The platoons led by the experimentals were significantly better on all the objective tests: written light weapons, practical light weapons, physical fitness, obstacle course, and shooting after exertion. The recruits led by the experimentals, but not the controls, correlated significantly in the development of attitudes closer to those of the NCOs. The attitudes of the experimentally led recruits shifted toward a more collectivistic orientation, active engagement in the task, perceived effectiveness of the platoon commander, and perceived similarity to the leader.

Organizational Vision Training. Thoms and Greenberger (1998) provided training in organizational vision, a component of transformational leadership. The 111 participants were 58 men and 53 women, all but two at management levels ranging from first-line supervisor to CEO. Visioning ability was judged from writing about a future image of the organizational unit the participant managed. Visioning ability correlated with positivism and future time perspective. Mean results improved from 3.5 to 4.0 from before to after the training for the trained managers, compared to a group of 50 control participants who attended a management program of the same length in personnel law. The controls' mean results changed from 3.4 to 3.5. The differences between the changes in the trainees and the controls were highly significant.

Motivation to Learn Leadership

Trainees are motivated to attend, to learn from training courses, and to transfer the knowledge, skills, and abilities (KSAs) they have learned to their work when they see that positive transfer from training to their job will be beneficial to them. It has further been suggested that trainees will be motivated to learn about leadership if (1) they are confident about using what they have learned, (2) they are aware that the new KSAs are appropriate to their job, (3) they believe the new KSAs would be helpful in dealing with job demands (Noe & Schmitt, 1986), (4) they respect the reputation of the trainers or the training organization, and (5) they value the managerial training courses and would recommend them to peers (Facteau, Dobbins, Russell, et al., 1995). Also important to trainee motivation are perceived task characteristics that facilitate or block the transfer of training such as new equipment. Social support may also make a difference (Noe, 1986). Particularly salient is the support or lack of it by the trainee's immediate superior (Clark, Dobbins, & Ladd, 1993). Additionally, trainees' belief in their self-efficacy mediates the effects of training (Saks, 1995).

Switzer (2003) surveyed the motivation of 93 managers of a large nationwide insurance company before training. In agreement with hypotheses, pretraining motivation correlated .48 with the perceived reputation of the training program; .39 with perceived managerial support; and .55 with self-efficacy. Noe's (1986) model of requirements for effective training suggested that leadership trainees need to believe in the assessments of their strengths and weaknesses. They must value the outcomes of training and believe they can achieve the outcomes. They must believe that the training fits with the resources they have available on the job and that the organization will support them if they make use of their learning. Differences in trainees' motivation figured in Gruenfeld's (1966) report that participants who paid part of their tuition devoted themselves more intensely to the program,

found it more difficult, and benefited more, as measured by a rating scale and test of values. Avolio and Bass (1998) demonstrated that 66 managers improved MLQ subordinates' ratings from before to after a training program, but only on those transformational leadership factors they said they would try to improve.

Stages

Motivation and readiness to learn about leadership and development as a leader can be seen to evolve in stages. Borrowing from the Prochaska, DiClemente, & Norcross (1992) model of stages in the therapeutic process, Harris and Cole (1999) proposed a four-factor model of stages for which they developed a 21-item factored survey questionnaire: (1) *pre-contemplation* ("I don't have any leadership development needs"), (2) *general contemplation* ("It might be worthwhile to work on improving my leadership skills"), (3) *specific program contemplation* ("Maybe this leadership development program . . . will help me to become a better leader"), and (4) *action* ("I am actively working on my leadership shortcomings"). Between 75 and 80 managers and engineering project heads in a manufacturing division in an MNC in the southeastern United States completed the survey as they attended different sessions of the training program. Using five anchors from 1 = strongly disagree to 5 = strongly agree, the mean responses for the four factors were as follows: precontemplation = 1.76; general contemplation = 4.25; specific program contemplation = 4.20; and Action = 3.68. Readiness to change correlated −.56 with pre-contemplation, .70 with general contemplation, .63 with specific program contemplation, and only .29 with action. Only those at the specific and general contemplation stages tended to specify needing to learn about managing conflict, budgeting, quality management, visionary leadership, and team building but not stress management.

The Learning Organization. Senge (1990) described the ideal learning organization. Motivation to learn and adaptivity to changes in conditions arise when (1) previous fragmentary thinking becomes systematic thinking, (2) personal visions are continually clarified and reality is seen objectively, (3) competition between members becomes cooperation in helping each other to excel, (4) reactivity becomes proactivity, (4) thinking about inquiry and advocacy becomes open to influence by others, and (5) shared visions arise through dialogue. The members become communities of commitment (Kofman & Senge, 1993). Newkirk-Moore and Backer (1998) studied the commitment to strategic planning of 157 small financial businesses as gauged by the frequency senior managers in the firms attended strategic management training programs. The frequency of attendance was significantly related to greater return on stockholders' equity.

Programmatic Applications

PepsiCo, General Electric, Hewlett-Packard, and ServiceMaster were cited by Cohen and Tichy (1997) for having the best practices for leadership development in training and education programs both on and off the job similar to those presented above.

Management Development Programs

Management development programs usually refer to the total long-term off-the-job and on-the-job educational process; management training refers to shorter courses. A full-blown program may accomplish much more than what may be possible with shorter independent training courses. Thus Guetzkow, Forehand, and James (1962) reported that a one-year management development course changed behavior significantly more than did training courses of short duration.

Management development programs serve other organizational functions. Recruitment of personnel is facilitated if prospective applicants know that such a program is available. An organizational growth strategy can be maintained efficiently when candidates for newly opening positions are already in training. In turn, the growth strategy provides for more possibilities for promotion as a source of reward for managers at lower levels and may reduce defensive competition for promotion (Luttwak, 1976). Two of the many available management development programs are LeaderLab and Full Range of Leadership Development.

LeaderLab.
The purpose of this program is to provide leadership training in action learning with realism, sim-

plicity, relevance, the actions of leading, and the intellect and emotions involved, and the time to plan, act, reflect, and learn to learn. The program is aimed at dealing with the leadership challenges of rapid change, diversity of people and views, and developing a shared sense of purpose. Participants develop an action plan to improve their leadership, then return after three months to review their progress. Participants keep a journal. A process advisor remains in contact. A partner in the course and another partner back home help with troubleshooting, analysis, and guiding the process forward (Burnside & Guthrie, 1992).

Full Range of Leadership Development (FRLD).
This is one program among many that have been created since the 1940s to teach leadership, deriving from a particular set of concepts. Other examples include the GRID (Blake & Mouton, 1964), Likert's (1967) Systems 1 to 4, Fiedler's (1967) program and others presented in previous chapters on styles of leadership. FRLD illustrates some of the common characteristics to be found in these programs, such as well-researched concepts that need to be differentiated by trainees, a theory to explain their connections to performance and satisfaction, measurements of progress, and feedback. FRLD has the theory, empiricism, and empirical support for differentiating between transformational and transactional leadership. FRLD introduces the MLQ model in a basic two- to three-day workshop, after which trainees are provided with their own nine-factor, 360-degree feedback of their transformational, active, and passive transactional leadership behaviors. They are provided comparisons of their own ratings with norms and ratings by others above, below, and at the same organizational level. Focus is on the discrepancies between their self-rated profile of ratings and others' ratings. Lectures, discussions, and coaching assist the participants. Each participant prepares a leadership development plan and its implementation to practice on the job some of the learnings from the workshop. Also, they examine the obstacles that need to be overcome before they can implement their plan in their organization. In two to three months, they return for an advanced two-day workshop. This second workshop begins with sharing experiences about what new leadership behaviors they tried and how they were received. Exercises on transformational factors come next; participants

in small discussion groups give feedback to one another on the factors. This peer feedback is followed by lectures and readings on ways to be more intellectually stimulating. The workshop concludes with each participant making a presentation on videotape that aims to inspire those in the envisioned organization the participant hopes to lead in two to five years. A selection of these tapes are then reviewed and commented upon in an assembly of the participants.

In the past 15 years, the FRLD program and modifications have been conducted in a variety of organizations in various locations from North America and Europe to Australia and Singapore, and industries ranging from insurance firms and automobile manufacturing conglomerates to cable companies and NGOs. In all, several thousand managers and executives in many different countries have completed the program (Avolio & Bass, 1991, 2002).

Self-ratings of transformational leadership increase from before to after training. Transactional management by exception decreases. However, those initially lower tend to show more improvement. When 43 participants from health care, education, business, government, and nonprofit agencies in a public workshop were asked afterward if FRLD had met their personal objectives, 54% said "a great deal" and 37% said "fairly much." Similar results were obtained in response to whether FRLD had met their career objectives and their objectives for community leadership. All but 3% felt that FRLD was worth their investment in time and energy. When 213 participants were asked at the end of the overall program how satisfied they were with it, 92% were satisfied a great deal or fairly much and 89% agreed that the leadership could be applied to their development. Among 87 participants, their subordinates' ratings from before to after FRLD, idealized influence, inspirational leadership, and intellectual stimulation factor scores increased significantly, but not individualized consideration. Management by exception and laissez-faire leadership decreased. Those with initially lower transformational leadership increased more than those with initially higher transformational leadership ratings.

For 66 trainees who returned for a follow-up session from six months to two years later, their subordinates reported significant improvements in transformational leadership data, but only on those factors that the 66 had

said in their plans they wanted to improve (Bass & Avolio, 1996). The largest improvement was in the reduction of transactional management by exception and passive-avoidant leadership. Critical incident reviews following training mentioned increased inspirational leadership (e.g., communicating a clearer sense of mission), increased intellectual stimulation (e.g., determining opportunities in challenges), and increased individualized consideration (e.g., developing the ability to lead in others) (Avolio & Bass, 1993, 1994). Between 1998 and 2002, 86 managers in New Zealand completed the FRLD program. An increase of 10% to 15% in their leadership effectiveness was reported (Parry, 2003). For a review of research and applications of FRLD, see Avolio, (1999).

Specialized Leadership Training and Education

Much specialized effort has been devoted to training programs about how to lead scientists, engineers, technicians, entrepreneurs, military personnel, nurses, schoolteachers, sales personnel, and so on. The MBA curriculum at universities is another specialized program aimed at preparing students for general business leadership. Entrepreneurial motivation has also been promoted through achievement training. Other specialized programs prepare leaders to work with labor union members and minorities and in other cultures. Many of these specialized efforts are now discussed briefly.

Science and Engineering Leadership. Many new supervisors enter a technical firm with insufficient education in science, so remedial programs are made available for them. Although supervision and leadership often become major responsibilities for engineers and scientists as they progress in their organizations, their preparation for these responsibilities is left until they have graduated from their professional schools and are at work. Considerable evidence has been obtained that such postgraduate efforts are generally efficacious. Moon and Hariton (1958) gave 50 engineering supervisors 30 hours of instruction on methods of self-improvement and greater job efficiency. Lectures were followed by role-playing sessions in which each participant acted out problems in human relations. A questionnaire administered to 67 subordinates of the trained group and to 67 subordinates of untrained supervisors indicated greater improvement for the trained group in understanding subordinates as individuals, expressing recognition for good work, giving subordinates an opportunity to express their side of a story, and showing more interest in employees' progress. Carton (1964) administered training over a six-month period to 23 scientists in supervisory positions using lectures, discussions, and role playing. A battery of tests was administered to the experimental group and a control group immediately before and after training and again 17 months later. The experimental group decreased significantly in authoritarianism and initiation of structure, whereas the control group did not. Mosvick (1966) examined four different training methods in a study of 55 engineers in supervisory positions. Three attitude scales and two behavioral measures were administered to experimental and control groups before and after training. Members of the trained group showed significant improvement in behavior and their ability to analyze a simulated communication conflict situation but not in their attitudes.

Educational Leadership. A school principal's leadership is strongly connected with the school's educational effectiveness. "Principals remain key individuals as instructional leaders, initiators of change, school managers, personnel administrators, problem solvers and boundary spanners for the school" (Portin & Shen, 1998, p. 34). But it is a difficult position, fraught with potential conflicts of goals. Principals are supposed to maximize their teachers' ability to teach and students' ability to learn, but they also have to deal with other diverse priorities, such as student discipline, safety, the physical plant, and the satisfaction of the students' parents, as well as national testing, state government regulations, and school board mandates. Their accountability is increased, but their authority is downgraded. Their compensation may not match their responsibilities. Many ask to return to teaching or to leave the school system.

Turnover and population expansion require preparation of new assistant principals and principals. The shortage of principals in many California school districts, such as Glendale and Santa Monica, resulted in specialized training programs to foster the professional growth of teachers and future principals. Similar developments have occurred in New York State; the Academy of Lead-ership of the Center for Leadership Studies at Binghamton University assessed and trained teachers and staff members in the Full Range of Leadership Development for Broome and Tioga Counties (Bass, 2000).

Military Leadership. U.S. military officers form an elite profession with its own code and customs and its own politics and culture. They study, train, and prepare for armed conflicts, ranging from terrorist attacks to conventional national invasions. They maintain a worldwide surveillance of military threats (Morganthau & Horrock, 1984). The amount of required training in the military is also greatly increased by the demand that the military continue to be at the cutting edge of new technology, as well as by the steady stream of military personnel to civilian life who need to be replaced.

There is a heavy continuing investment in leadership training for military leaders at all levels to compare with controlled untrained comparison groups. Typical examples have compared U.S. Army squad leaders who received leadership preparation training with a control group of leaders who did not. The trained leaders received higher effectiveness ratings, their squads showed higher spirit, and their followers scored higher on proficiency tests. Descriptions by followers indicated that trained leaders initiated more structure, exercised better control of field exercises, and demonstrated more adequacy in briefing and giving information. Their subordinates were less willing to reenlist, however, and showed less favorable attitudes toward the army (Hood, Showel, & Stewart, 1967). Again, infantry graduates of schools for noncommissioned officers exceeded a control group in their rate of promotion and number of awards, but not in leadership evaluations (Rittenhouse, 1968). In another typical analysis, films of leadership situations followed by group discussion were used to train military leaders. The groups that discussed the films were more effective than the control groups in solving leadership problems (Lange, Rittenhouse, & Atkinson, 1968). Many other examples of effective military leadership training have been discussed in earlier chapters as demonstrations of various principles of consequence (see, for example, Eden & Sham, 1982; Fiedler & Garcia, 1987).

Over a thousand cadets are trained each year in the four-year leadership program at the U.S. Military Academy at West Point. Among a number of innovative courses are those dedicated to intellectual procedure (McNally, Gerras, & Bullis, 1996). To enhance the cadets' cognitive skills in leadership, they learn 22 theories of leadership and apply each of them to a case requiring military leadership. Being an intelligent, thoughtful, and reflective leader is encouraged. The cadets need to identify what is happening, account for it, and formulate the action that the leader should take. Cases are actual experiences of the military faculty. The importance of understanding subordinates, peers, superiors, and the organization is encompassed in a set of systems. Individual systems focus on attribution theory (Kelly, 1955). The group system discusses organizational socialization (Van Maanen & Schein, 1979), cohesion (Cartwright, 1965), group development (Bennis & Shepard, 1965), and group decision making (Vroom & Yetton, 1974). The leadership system concentrates on the differences between transformational and transactional leadership (Bass, 1985). Integration efforts follow.

MBA Education. Education for up to two years that leads to the Master of Business Administration is broadly based in institutions that follow the guidelines of the American Assembly of Collegiate Schools of Business. In these schools, students receive instruction in applied behavioral science, management information systems, business policy and planning, applied mathematics, and applied economics, as well as in the functional areas of production, human resources management, marketing, finance, and accounting. MBA programs have increased dramatically since the mid-1950s, when approximately 3,200 MBA degrees were awarded per year. By 1998, more than 102,000 were being awarded annually in North America (Pfeffer & Fong, 2002). Similar rapid growth has followed in Europe and elsewhere (Anonymous, 1991; Berger & Watts, 1992).

Herbert (1972) found no clear effect of MBA education on job performance. But according to Herbert (1977), 82 supervisors of MBAs and non-MBAs gave MBAs better reputational ratings on technical skills, initiative, responsibility, motivation, judgment, and problem solving but not on better human relations or supervisory skills. The results were not affected by whether the rates were in staff or line positions. Jenkins, Reizenstein, and Rodgers (1984) surveyed 110 presidents of Fortune 500 companies and 124 personnel directors from the same firms,

along with 450 business school alumni, 93 deans, and 302 faculty members. They found that 57% to 60% of the respondents believed the program should focus strongly on quantitative analysis and that an even greater percentage supported an emphasis on decision making. But 32% to 45% of these samples thought that MBA programs should deemphasize short-term decision making in favor of long-term strategic planning. The percentage who were satisfied with the extent to which leadership skills were developed among MBAs ranged from 36% to 50%. The deans, personnel directors, and alumni were more satisfied, and the presidents and faculty members were less satisfied. Satisfaction with MBAs' interpersonal skills ranged from 28% to 46%; those in the business community were less satisfied and the academics more satisfied. Only pluralities of 21% to 43% were satisfied with the managerial skills of MBAs.

Interviews with 600 senior executives tended to be consistent with the foregoing findings. Seventy percent thought that business school education was pretty good, and 49% regarded the MBA degree as somewhat or very important to getting ahead in their own company, although 86% thought that too much theory and too little application were taught. However, Pfeffer and Fong (2002) questioned whether business schools will survive without major changes. They argued that the curricula have little relation to what is important to business. The greater success in business of graduates can be accounted for by the characteristics of the students admitted to the schools. The curricula lack the focus on practices found in other professional schools. Academic research has little effect on business. Needed are ways of integrating academic knowledge with active experience.

Executive Development Programs. Executive development is a career-long process. Zaccaro (1999) suggested that basic to any healthy organization is a climate that nurtures leaders and prospective executives. Any developmental program must attend to the cognitive and social capacities and skills required by executives for effective leadership and work performance. The cognitive competencies needed by executives include intelligence, analytical reasoning, flexible integrative complexity, and verbal and writing skills. Executives need to be able to deal with organizational contradictions, as well as with cognitive and behavioral complexity (Streufert & Swezey,

1988). As detailed in Chapter 20, the required social competencies include social reasoning, behavioral flexibility, and competence in persuasion, negotiation, and managing conflict. The ideal executive is open, curious, disciplined, flexible, self-efficacious, and a calculated risk taker, with a need for achievement and socialized rather than personalized power. Executive development is a slow process. Development of competencies should be focused on the requirements of the next higher level of position in the organization. According to interviews with 40 executives by Kaplan, Drath, and Kofodimos (1985), the criticism received and accepted by the executive is affected by job demands and the power of the executive. The need for mastery, the acceptance of criticism, and earlier history of success determine whether the executive will attempt to change. Improvement in performance will depend on the open flow of information, the ability to look inward, the ability to accept criticism, and the ability to change (Kaplan, Kofodimos, & Drath, 1987).

Formal university executive development programs lasting a few weeks to a semester or more are popular in the industrialized world. They are helping countries from Chile to Norway and formerly Communist countries to cope with the global marketing economy. Course content parallels that to be covered in the MBA program with variations, depending on the management level of the trainees, the length of the program, and whether a certificate or degree will be awarded. The programs can be made more effective with commitment from outside sponsors to continued executive development and its importance to executive career planning, the use of assessment centers[21] to provide individualized developmental guidance, effective needs analysis, computer networks to link executives in their offices with university faculties, more attention to executive leadership and self-development, and an international perspective, along with custom-made programs for individual organizations (Watson, 1988). Executives need to be prepared for discontinuous change and the adoption of a "leap ahead" strategy (F. J. Brown, 2000). Zsambok (1993) designed a program for senior managers working for the U.S. Air

Force that incorporated a model of effective team strategic decision making. Included in the program were envisioning time horizons, avoiding micromanaging, and using diverging and converging in situational assessment. Comparisons of trained with control groups have been promising.

Executive development programs are not for future senior executives alone. Many managers are enrolled in such programs to make contributions to strategic planning and help their organizations change from traditional ones to ones more suitable to meeting competition, taking advantage of new technological advances and the best human resources practices (Hoffman, 1996).

Fellowship Programs. Illustrative and mentioned earlier is the Kellogg Fellows Program, which is international in scope. The fellows are established leaders from governmental, educational, nongovernmental, and philanthropic institutions and agencies. They are committed to advancing social change. Kellogg supports them for a number of years to help them access individuals, organizations, and programs for further development of the leadership skills to improve people's lives in their communities and to broaden their understanding of community change (Webb-Petett, undated).

Entrepreneurial and Achievement Motivation. Building on earlier theory and research about the need for achievement, McClelland and Winter (1969) designed workshops to instill a greater need for achievement in entrepreneurs. These workshops were conducted in developed as well as in developing countries such as Mexico and India. Black entrepreneurs in South Africa were also singled out for attention. Increasing the entrepreneurs' need for achievement was expected to increase their willingness to expand their spheres of activity and their willingness to take on more challenges and responsibility.

The workshops involved showing how the need for achievement is revealed in its projections in the Thematic Apperception Test and how one could increase the achievement thematic content in responding to the test. Generalization about achievement and entrepreneurial activities followed. Positive effects of the training were reported (McClelland & Winter, 1969). Since the need for achievement is of consequence to management in general, achievement training has been applied to managers.

---

[21]Other similar kinds of evaluative studies were reported by K. R. Andrews (1966), Basil (1964), Habbe (1950), Jerkedal (1967), Merrell (1965), Oberg (1962), Roethlisberger (1954), and Wikstrom (1961). A handbook (Taylor & Lippitt, 1975) and texts (see, for example, Herbert & Yost, 1978) on management education and development are also available.

Illustrative were results reported by Boer (1985) in a study of the effects of achievement training on the performance of South African factory management teams (in contrast to control teams who were not trained). Labor productivity was increased and turnover and absenteeism were reduced in the trained but not in the control groups.

Leadership of Minorities and Women. "Awareness" training, mainly for white male managers about special issues of working with women, blacks, and the disadvantaged, became commonplace following the passage of affirmative action legislation (Anonymous, 1968b). In some instances, heightened awareness produced overreactions and backlash (L. A. Johnson, 1969). An extensively evaluated program was reported by Bass, Cascio, McPherson, and Tragash (1976). Following the identification of five factors differentiating issues of awareness of managers about affirmative action for black employees (Bass, Cascio, & McPherson, 1972), PROSPER, a self-administered program, was developed. The booklet for PROSPER that each participant received began with a pretraining assessment on the five factors. Next, a case of an insubordinate black engineer was presented, and the participants had to make in-basket decisions. Each participant then was assigned a role as one of five different managers in a firm gathered to discuss the case; each of the roles was built around one of the five factors. The participants verbalized favorable positions on one of the factors while they heard favorable information about the others. Significant increases in the scores for more favorable attitudes toward working with black employees were achieved by 2,293 managers. After three to five months, 298 managers still showed some of the increase on all five factors. Cascio and Bass (1976) further analyzed the specific role-playing effects of PROSPER and found that the results were in the direction of expectations. PROFAIR, a comparable attitude change program for supervisors of women (Bass, 1971), was developed out of a survey of attitudes toward working with women.

Special programs to train black leaders were illustrated by Katz and Cohen's (1962) *assertion training* to increase self-confidence among blacks. Beatty (1973) completed a study about the training of black supervisors and the importance of their superiors' expectations. Assertiveness training for women became popular in the 1970s. For example, Heinen, McGlauchin, Legeros, and Freeman (1975) increased the self-awareness and self-confidence of 19 of 20 women managers with such training. Numerous other programs to train women as leaders have been conducted, predicated on the supposition that women have unique problems which could be effectively resolved only through changing the organizational culture. Woman as leaders need to adjust to the organization as well. Nevertheless, a survey of 101 female and 121 male managers by Alpander and Gutman (1976) indicated that both sexes perceived similar training needs. Hart (1975) designed and evaluated a training program in leadership for adult women based on Hersey and Blanchard's life-cycle theory. Training that focused on interpersonal skills, leadership theory, lifestyles, and the importance of motivation to being a leader resulted in increasing the self-esteem and self-confidence of the trainees in contrast to the controls. Compared to the controls, the trainees also perceived themselves as better able to make decisions, as more active, as more in control of their lives, and as having a greater knowledge of listening skills.

Development and Training of Labor Leaders. The role of union leaders handling relations with management was presented in Chapter 13. As organized labor membership in the United States has declined in the past half century, so have empirical studies of union leaders. An example of a recent study was by Skarlicki and Latham (1997), who examined the effects of training 25 union leaders on how they administered principles of organizational justice, according to 177 union members. The leaders were perceived to have increased in fairness, while the members were perceived to have increased in citizenship behavior involving the union. Forty-five years earlier, despite generally favorable attitudes toward their union local, only half of 140 rank-and-file members felt that the local was fair in assigning jobs; 18% felt it was unfair (Davis & St. Germain, 1952). Barkin (1961) noted the greater difficulty organizers had in persuading workers in the rural South to form a union compared to those in urban areas. Uphoff and Dunnette (1956) found that among 1,251 union officers, activists, and members, the members were less fully committed to the union movement. Before 1945, a majority of union leaders came from middle-class backgrounds; after 1945, 60% came from working-class backgrounds. The leaders were likely to be better educated than the rank and file but of the same religion and political affiliation. Although they might begin as blue-collar workers, leaders move on to union positions early in their careers to become professionals (Mills & Atkinson, 1945).

Samuel Gompers and John L. Lewis are the two leaders who shaped the labor movement in the United States. Their development is instructive. Gompers, as a boy, emigrated to the United States with his Dutch-Jewish working-class family from the East End of London to the Lower East Side of New York City. With only four years of education, Gompers began working as an apprentice shoemaker at the age of 10. At age 14 he joined his father as a cigar maker and as a member of the Cigar Makers' International Union (CMIU). He remained in the union, but since it enrolled only skilled cigar makers, Gompers formed the United Cigar Makers, which included the less skilled. It became the largest local of CMIU in 1875, when the latter agreed to enroll members of families of varying skills who did their work at home in tenement apartments leased by the cigar companies. (The firms bought the production from the families.) The craft unions encouraged training members and provided apprenticeship programs in their crafts (Mandel, 1963; Neumann, 2004). That same year, Gompers became an official unpaid but successful organizer. He continued to work in a cigar-rolling factory. His education was furthered by the custom of cigar makers' taking advantage of their quiet workplaces to hire a reader who read aloud to them from books and newspapers about current political conditions, labor conditions elsewhere in the world, and political economics. He overcame a speech impediment to become a prominent orator. He found employment again only after having been blacklisted by many employers. Unlike the national Knights of Labor, which encompassed many diverse social and political causes, he rejected the socialist movement and political agitators, and focused narrowly on "bread-and-butter issues" of wages, work hours, and benefits. In 1886, he helped found the American Federation of Labor, which aimed to control job opportunities and conditions in each craft. Each craft had its own organization. Under his leadership, the AFL had 1.7 million members by 1904. Although theoretically open to all, its membership was limited to white males. High dues built up strike funds to assist striking workers. But he required that any strike proposal be approved by secret ballot in the shop organiza-

tion as well as the local union, and he came down hard on "wildcat" strikes. He tended to avoid strikes when possible, as well as involvement in political actions such as legislation for old-age pensions, employers' responsibility for worker safety, and compulsory health insurance.

It was left to the creation of industrial unions such as the mine workers' and automobile workers' unions to organize around all workers in the same industry rather than the same craft. The most prominent leader in organizing industrial unions for 40 years was John L. Lewis. He was the eldest of six sons, born in 1880 to Welsh immigrant parents from coal-mining families. He had only a seventh-grade education, but he continued his education with extensive reading. He joined his father and brother working in the coal mines at the age of 15. His father was blacklisted for union activities and eventually took a job as a jail custodian. In his youth, Lewis also acted and managed a local theater and a baseball team. His acting skills stood him in good stead during his many negotiations and public appearances. Before he was 27 years old, he had also tried farming, construction work, and small business. Joined by his family, Lewis built a local power base of Welsh immigrant coal miners. He became a member of the United Mine Workers in 1907 and in 1909 became a successful union organizer. In the next 11 years, he became the secretary-treasurer and delegate to the UMWA national convention, and in 1917 he was elected president of his union local. In 1920, he was elected president of the UMWA, in which office he served until 1960, retiring at the age of 80. He successfully unionized many of the nonunion coal regions. He was a founder of the Congress of Industrial Organizations (CIO) and was instrumental in the organizing of many major industrial unions, such as the United Steelworkers of America (USWA), Communications Workers of America (CWA), and United Auto Workers (UAW). He regularly advised U.S. presidents and the U.S. Congress, and challenged America's corporate leaders. He improved health care for miners and their families with a fund that built eight hospitals and many clinics in Appalachia, paid for from UMW contracts with the coal companies that set aside royalties for a workers' pension fund.

Lewis was a charismatic leader. He had self-taught rhetorical skills and readily quoted from the Bible, Shakespeare, Plato, and Homer. His grandiloquent oratory made him a most effective political spokesman. He was a

230-pound bear with a volcanic personality. He was a fearsome adversary, cunning, ruthless, and opportunistic, had a colossal ego, and felt his supporters wanted someone like him who could stand up to the bosses of big business. He was autocratic and considered a demagogue by many. He was a despot who expelled his rivals from his organization. But he actually pursued moderate objectives, including the right to organize labor unions, shorter work hours, prohibition of child labor, equal pay for men and women doing the same comparable jobs, and steady employment.

He was admired by business leaders and Republicans in the 1920s but switched to the Democratic Party when President Franklin Roosevelt was elected in 1932 with a policy promoting and legalizing collective bargaining. By 1937, Lewis had succeeded in unionizing the two largest firms in the United States, General Motors and U.S. Steel. But in 1940, when Roosevelt ran for a third term, he switched back to the Republicans. His popularity declined after 1937 and even further during the war years and afterward, when he practically shut down American industry with national coal strikes, since American manufacturing, transportation, utilities, and home heating were fueled mainly by coal. When he called out the miners in 1943, during the middle of World War II, 87% of a national sample said they had an unfavorable opinion of him. Between 1943 and 1946, there was much loss of public and political support for labor as a consequence of the strikes, which was ultimately reflected in the decline of national union membership. States passed "right to work" laws and Congress, the antilabor Taft-Hartley Act. Nonetheless, following federal intervention, the miners' incomes and benefits were substantially increased by the strike settlements (Dubofsky & Van Tine, 1986).

Training Leaders for Foreign Assignments. Preparing managers for overseas assignments is costly, but the lack of such preparation is more costly (Tung, 1979). On the basis of surveys and interviews, Zeira (1975) suggested that multinational firms need to equip parent-country nationals and third-country nationals to serve as managers abroad. They need adequate knowledge of the complex human problems of international enterprises. They need self-confidence to adapt their leadership behavior to the needs of the subsidiary. Education, training, and assign-

ments are needed early in a manager's career to learn the critical nuances in international business. As parent companies expand into increasing numbers of countries, there is a need to train the executives who have to visit numerous countries for short periods of time in cross-cultural sensitivity as well as briefings on the specific countries. Those who work in multinational councils and projects need similar general as well as specific cultural training (Ezzedean, Swiercz, & Holt, 2003).

Tung (1979) found that 26 of 105 U.S. multinationals ran training programs to prepare personnel for overseas assignments. About half these programs used environmental briefings, cultural orientations, and language training. A few used culture assimilators, sensitivity training, and field experience.

Universities provide courses and curricula. Illustrative is the Global Leadership Program at the University of Michigan. Teams of students spend two weeks in a designated country to identify business opportunities. They tour businesses and meet with corporate and business leaders, visit homes and marketplaces, and use public transportation. On their return, they prepare reports. At many universities, student interns spend a semester in a foreign country to develop a business plan for a foreign firm as an action learning experience.

Seminal experiments were completed in the 1960s. Mitchell and Foa (1969) studied American leaders with non-American followers. They found that leaders were rated as more effective when they were trained in the norms of their followers. Chemers, Fiedler, Lekhyananda, and Stolurow (1966) demonstrated that training leaders in the culture of a foreign nation, as opposed to training them in the geography of the nation, resulted in higher levels of group performance and rapport in tasks involving subjects from two different cultures. L. R. Anderson (1965) trained leaders in their own culture's style of leadership or in the style characteristic of another culture, and then assigned them to intercultural task groups. Those who were trained in other cultural styles led groups that were more effective in creativity tasks but not in negotiation tasks. In line with Fiedler's contingency model, Chemers (1969) found that intercultural training tended to modify the situation in the direction of making it more favorable for the low-LPC (task-oriented) leader, who then showed more consideration than did the high-LPC (relations-oriented) leader.

Training Community Leaders. Training community leaders is a well-established strategy. In the late 1990s, the number of community leadership programs approached 700 (Fredericks, 1998). Among their purposes were to foster critical thinking in the public domain and to examine alternative solutions to civic problems (Reed, 1996). In five counties of New York State, the problems included youth violence, declining water resources, waste management, urban/rural competition for resources, overstressed family resources, dealing with neighborhoods at risk, and empowering community leaders (Avolio, Bass, Miles, et al., 1994). Rossing and Heasley (1987) described a design for rural and agricultural leadership training programs. Similarly, Miller (1986) detailed West Virginia University's plan, in which its faculty contributes directly to the community. Community development was the objective of Ohio's cooperative extension leadership workshops (Long, 1986). The Kansas Community Leadership Initiative aimed to help directors and board members of 17 local community leadership programs gain new insights and skills in personal relationships, as well as to foster improvement in leadership programs (Wituk, Warren, Heiny, et al., 2003). Increased numbers of civic leaders was a goal of 72 California civic leadership development programs (Azzam & Riggio, 2003). While 85% of community leadership programs have structured classroom instruction, they also provide familiarization visits with community institutions and meetings with prominent citizens. In addition, they work on community problems and projects. They are a form of action learning (Conger & Toegel, 2004). Leadership development programs have also been designed to prepare retirees to become volunteer community leaders (Brungardt, 1996).

Contributions to Networking. Community leadership training programs have been sparked by a national effort of the U.S. Chamber of Commerce to furnish cross-fertilizing education and training grounded in workshops for prospective leaders from a single community. The trainees are drawn from local industry, government, unions, law enforcement agencies, agriculture, hospitals, and volunteer and welfare agencies. In addition to the informational learning that is possible, important lasting networks can be established across organizational boundaries that will benefit the community and its development. For instance, such a leadership educational program was provided to 227 rural citizens of Montana. Classroom and on-site experiences were both useful in enhancing the leaders' self-image, skills, and understanding (Williams, 1981). Brown and Detterman (1987) agreed and added that participation in community leadership classes promoted increased contacts among the community leaders. In turn, Rossing and Heasley (1987) noted that involvement in public affairs was promoted by such community leadership training.

There is evidence that communities with more civic involvement and stronger local leadership have better schools, lower crime rates, more effective government, and greater sense of personal ownership (Rossing, 1998). Training programs are needed to replace retiring civic leaders. Program alumni remain active in the civic affairs of their communities. They help followers without the training experience to take on initiatives and become project leaders (Daugherty & Williams, 1997).

Azzam and Riggio (2003) surveyed by telephone 72 of 83 directors of civic leadership programs in California. The oldest program had been started in 1980. The average age of the programs was 10.7 years. Almost half of the participants came from the private sector (48%) while most of the other half came from the nonprofit (23%) and government sectors. Twenty-one percent of the programs concentrated on orientation visits and visits to local institutions. Seventy-six percent received both classroom instruction and orientation (close to the national pattern). Meetings were held usually once a month for 12 months. Alumni were followed up with newsletters (28%) and social events (45%). Alumni associations were formed by 38% that might engage in long-term projects, raise money, and advise the program.

Evaluation of Leadership Training and Education

Evaluative Impressions

Information was provided by Russon and Rainelt (2004) about the desired and unintended outcomes of 55 leadership development programs sponsored by the W. K. Kellogg Foundation from the 1930s onward and alternatives to approaches, methods, and data collection. By the 1960s, attendance at leadership development programs was routine for both novice and experienced managers.

The National Industrial Conference Board (1963) surveyed 1,074 recently recruited college graduates who had attended management development programs sponsored by their employees. About 40% of those who had hoped that the programs would prepare them for promotion felt disappointed and regarded the programs as of little value to themselves or the company. They preferred instruction that would prepare them for the tasks of specific jobs rather than for better human relations and general management. Organizational experience made a difference. Executives with experience had a different point of view. K. R. Andrews (1966) received 6,000 replies from executives who had attended one of 39 different university programs in management development. Although about 85% saw no relationship between attending the courses and their subsequent advances in salary, the benefits they most frequently mentioned were increased understanding of self and others, greater tolerance for differences in opinion, and heightened awareness of alternative solutions to problems. Structured lectures and didactic teacher-led classwork were regarded as more valuable than unstructured group discussions and informal contacts with faculty and students. The National Industrial Conference Board (1964) surveyed 167 firms' experience with management development. In evaluating the effectiveness of such programs, 57% of the firms expressed the belief that the programs were valuable, but only 14% reported evidence in support of this belief.[22]

Evaluating Changes

Attitudes and Self-Reported Changes. Leadership training of some sort figures strongly in most management development programs, although training is likely to be provided in many other nonsupervisory management functions. In fact, M. W. McCall (1976) suggested that too much emphasis has been placed on leadership training and not enough on the many other varied aspects of a manager's work, although the opposite can also be argued.

Despite the previously noted evidence to the contrary that training fails to shift Leadership Opinion Questionnaire scores (Anghelone, 1981; Savan, 1983; Painter, 1984), numerous other examples of successful changes

---

[22] Discussed in Chapter 36.

in attitudes as a consequence of longer-term development programs have appeared. For instance, C. W. Nelson (1967) conducted a training course for top-level managers in a plant, who in turn conducted a similar course for their lower-level managers. Nelson found that not only did significant changes in attitude occur, but that a retest one year later showed that the effects persisted. Similarly, E. H. Schein (1967) demonstrated that a two-year course in management education produced a significant change in attitudes toward human relations. Valiquet (1968) reported a significant change in attitudes and behavior among managers who participated in a one-year training program. R. S. Barrett (1965) found significant change in attitudes, but not in performance, following the completion of an executive development program. Blake's (1960) study of a management development program in Norway found that the 67 participants reported a greater understanding of other people, themselves, and social trends and more self-confidence in dealing with superiors, peers, and subordinates. Waaler (1962) studied another 194 executives in a management development program in Norway. Participants from the firms with the "best" programs, when compared with those in firms with the "poorest" programs, reported greater nearness to, warmth toward, and understanding of their employees; more informality with employees; greater predictability of behavior; more frequently letting employees know what to expect; and reduced pressure on subordinates.

Training to overcome resistance to change by developing a better understanding of change is key to bringing about organizational change. Vision 2016 was a program to directly train 2,000 senior government officials in Botswana that indirectly impacted 50,000 citizens. The program concentrated on developing "knowledge checks" to ensure that managers and their subordinates understood the change program and its implications (Washington & Hacker, 2003). Executives need to be prepared for discontinuous change and the adoption of a "leap ahead" strategy (F. J. Brown, 2000).

Factors That Affect Training Outcomes

Personal attributes of trainees, the composition of the training group, follow-up strategies, the behavior of the trainer, the congeniality of the environment to which the person returns, and the criterion outcomes themselves affect training results.

Criteria of Effective Training

The strength of the effects of training that are found depends on the criteria employed to assess the effects. Burke and Day (1986) completed meta-analyses of the results of 70 managerial training studies. They contrasted four types of criteria employed in the studies: subjective learning, objective learning, subjective behavior, and objective results. Subjective learning was obtained from the trainees' self-reports about what they thought they had learned from the training. Objective learning was based on tests or measurements of learning during and after training. Subjective behavior was taken from self-reports about the trainee's performance after training, and objective results were based on independent measures of the trainee's performance as a consequence of training. For all four criteria as a whole, the authors concluded that managerial training is moderately effective, and that the effectiveness of training methods can be generalized to new situations.

When the measured learning outcomes were subjective, the effects were all positive for general management, self-awareness, and human relations training. Nonetheless, self-awareness and human relations training generated stronger effects of subjective learning outcomes than did general management training.

When learning outcomes were measured objectively, positive effects were also obtained for all four types of training. But training in motivation emerged as relatively most effective and training in problem solving as relatively least effective.

With subjective behavioral outcomes, the effects of general management, human relations, and self-awareness training were again all positive, and self-awareness was the greatest in this regard.

When objective results were used as criteria, the effects of training were again all positive, and human relations training showed the strongest of these positive effects.

When subjective learning outcomes were the criterion, positive outcomes were seen to have been achieved with sensitivity training, behavioral modeling, and lecture–discussion–role play or practice. Similarly, positive effects

on objective learning criteria were obtained for lecture, lecture-discussion, and lecture–discussion–role play or practice. Against subjective behavior outcomes, positive effects were obtained for lecture and lecture-discussion, Leader Match, sensitivity training, behavioral modeling, and combinations of these methods. Sensitivity training and behavioral modeling demonstrated the strongest positive effects.

In all, it would seem that regardless of how training outcomes are measured, the average study reveals a positive effect. However, different types of training will emerge as stronger or weaker in effect, depending on the outcome measures employed.

Follow-Up Reinforcing Practice and Feedback

To transfer to the job what has been learned during training, trainees need to be given continuing opportunities to practice what has been learned. This practice, in turn, needs to be coupled with feedback or self-reinforcement about the trainees' practice efforts. The need for reinforcing booster programs is well recognized (Avolio, 1999). One of many examples was provided by Wexley and Nemeroff (1975), who described a self-feedback mechanism for promoting the transfer of leadership training to the job. For six weeks following training, supervisory trainees completed a daily behavioral checklist to record their supervisory behaviors. On each day, they noted whether they had (1) praised subordinates, (2) thanked subordinates for suggestions, (3) told them how they would be followed up, (4) called subordinates together to discuss mutual assistance, (5) given help as requested, (6) assigned jobs without interfering until the jobs were completed, (7) consulted individually with trainees on the job to review progress, and (8) arranged for trainees to try out and evaluate the effects of newly learned behaviors.

Congruence of Training and the Organizational Environment

By the 1950s, organizational factors had been recognized to have an important impact on the effectiveness of supervisory training. These included the organizational climate, the trainee's immediate superior, and upper management. Zaleznik (1951) explained the failure of a human relations training program to help trainees solve their work problems as due to an inadequate initial diagnosis of supervisory difficulties and to the irrelevance of the training to the problems. Sykes (1962) conducted a case study of a firm in which participants in a management development program regarded the training as unsuccessful because top management was unwilling to correct grievances and unsatisfactory conditions. Again, a deterioration in human relations resulted from an attempt at supervisory training when a program conflicted with unionism, when recruitment for a program was inadequate, and when a program itself was seen as an effort to indoctrinate a captive audience (Form & Form, 1953).

Supervisory training to increase considerate behavior resulted in a much greater shift in some trainees' behavior when organizational conditions were taken into account (Harris & Fleishman, 1955). Baumgartel and Jeanpierre (1972) queried 240 managers from 200 different industrial and commercial firms who had participated in a management development program. The respondents indicated whether they could apply what they had learned in training depended on (1) the freedom they had to set personal goals, (2) consideration by higher management of the feelings of lower management, (3) the organization's stimulation and approval of innovation and experimentation, (4) the organization's desire for executives to make use of information given in management courses, and (5) free and open communication among management groups.

Immediate Supervisor. Most important to whether training modified behavior back on the job was the trainee's immediate supervisor. F. C. Mann (1951) found that supervisors who changed more as a consequence of training in leadership (1) received more encouragement from their superiors, (2) expected greater personal benefit from training, (3) felt more secure in their relations with their superiors, and (4) felt that they had a greater opportunity to try out new ideas on the job. Consistent with this finding, Hariton (1951) observed that supervisory training increased employees' satisfaction when the supervisors were encouraged by their superiors to use the principles they had learned in training.

Slightly later, Harris and Fleishman (1955) reported that supervisors who were trained in a human relations orientation appeared to experience role conflict when

they returned to their jobs to work under superiors who exhibited a markedly different pattern of behavior. Supervisors who returned to their work after human relations training tended to endorse a more considerate attitude toward employees, and to be described by employees as high in consideration if the superiors of the supervisors endorsed considerate attitudes and behaved in a considerate manner. There was a nonsignificant tendency for supervisors to be described as high in initiating structure when their superiors exhibited a similar pattern of behavior.

Supervisors who returned from training to work under a superior who was low in consideration and high in initiating structure (including being coercive) experienced the greatest role conflict, as measured by the discrepancy between their observed behavior and their ideas about how they ought to behave. No such relationship was found for control supervisors who had not taken the training course in human relations. Thus, the supervisors' leadership behavior tended to be highly conditioned by the attitudes and behavior of their superiors (Fleishman, Harris, & Burtt, 1955).

Haire (1948), W. Mahler (1952), and many others since have argued that for leadership training to be effective, the entire management of the organization should be subjected to the same or a similar program. It is self-defeating to train lower-level managers in an approach to leadership that is incompatible with that of their superiors.

Other Organizational Constraints. Despite the generally observed positive effects of leadership training programs, the effects can be constrained or nullified by various organizational conditions, according to an interview study by Campisano (1984). The content of the program may be irrelevant to the daily activities of the supervisor or may suffer from redundancy. Furthermore, the interviewees stated that technical competence and management structure were more critical to performance in their organization than was training in leadership skills. Steele, Zane, and Zalkind (1970) reported that perceived pressures from associates, particularly peers, reduced the trainees' involvement (according to consultants) as their activities changed 20 months after instruction. On the other hand, Carroll and Nash (1970) reported that 45 foremen in a management development program thought the training was more applicable to the job if they were more highly motivated toward promotion, were more satisfied with the organization, and had sufficient freedom to perform their functions.

Training must often be supported by other specific organizational actions to result in the desired effects. Specific organizational practices, congruent with the training effort, need to be developed and institutionalized on the basis of a comprehensive analysis of organizational, managerial, and technical/professional needs (Dreilinger, McElheny, Robinson, & Rice, 1982). Thus a supervisory training program to reduce employee absenteeism actually lowered absenteeism only when quantitative data about the absences of the supervisors own subordinate personnel were fed back to supervisors following training (Mann & Sparling, 1956). Similarly, training programs for women managers require buttressing by encouraging senior managers to be supportive of female middle-level managers and by helping husbands to understand the importance of their support in ensuring the success of their wives on the job (Brenner, 1972).

The Need for Programmatic Integration. Van Velsor (1984) summarized what is needed for leadership training and education to have an impact. The organization must show that it supports what is to be learned. The trainee must be willing to participate in the training. The need for training must be perceived. The program should deal with relevant problems and should provide sufficient interaction with peers and valid feedback. Follow-up activities should include postsession debriefing, maintenance of alumni groups, consultation, follow-up training as needed, and reward for improvement and the application of what has been learned. The promotion of the trainees should be integrated with their development and focused on individualized needs that are aligned with those of the organization (Cunningham & Leon, 1986).

Day's (1980) interview survey of 116 health care professionals showed that the professionals tended to connect promotion with training. Of those interviewed, 67 percent noted that following promotion, their organizations made an effort to prepare them for their new responsibilities with training (mostly on-the-job training). At the same time, Alpander's (1986) survey of 155 corporate training officers found that less than 1% reported a direct relationship of promotion to undergoing super-visory training. However, 52% reported some indirect contribution of training to the trainees' subsequent advancement. But 31% reported that training was of little or no consequence to promotion.

At the upper level of an organization, Hall (1986) noted the difficulties involved in connecting executive succession with the learning of individual executives. Most planned executive development focuses on tasks rather than personal learning. Classroom activities, rather than the exploitation of learning from experience, are emphasized. But such learning from educational and personal experiences needs to be integrated into planning for succession.

Bunker (1986) attributed the success of management training in Japan to the firms' subscription to the proposition that their employees need to be developed before the firms can make a profit. Except for firms that suffered during the depressed economy in the 1990s, employees and their development are valued. Japanese firms see themselves as educational institutions engaged in learning with their employees. "The company is the business school!" Training is "just in time," that is, it is systematically provided just as managers need new skills to take on new roles. Much attention is paid to socialization to the organization. New recruits of Japanese firms receive up to eight weeks of initial residential training. This training is followed by extensive job rotation during the next two years to develop familiarity with various functions and departments. Later on, training is provided to deal with obsolescence and burnout, along with new challenges. Training provides the basis for employees at all levels to fit into and make contributions in a consultative organizational culture.

Summary and Conclusions

Leadership education begins early in childhood and continues through adolescence and adulthood. Early developments contribute to a leader's subsequent success. Of importance are one's parents, the standards they set, and the challenges they provide, commensurate with one's maturation. Equally important are the leadership opportunities and experiences one has in childhood, adolescence, and adulthood. Education also plays an important role. Leadership training and education need to be designed around what will be required when trainees and students take on leadership responsibilities.

Experiential training approaches have been favored over highly structured didactic lectures alone for leadership education and training, but new kinds of highly structured experiences, such as those provided by behavioral modeling, have demonstrated the desired training effects. Nevertheless, sensitivity training or its variants, such as team building, continues to be widely practiced. Considerable research is available about its effects.

Research indicates, not unexpectedly, that the effectiveness of training, particularly sensitivity training, depends on the trainee, the trainer, the composition of the training group, follow-up reinforcement and feedback, and particularly whether there is congruence between the training and the organizational environment for which the trainee is being prepared. Positive results depend, to some extent, on opportunities for the transfer of learning into appropriate organizational settings.

Training proceeds both off the job, such as in special seminars and workshops, as well as on the job in action learning, coaching, mentoring, and various forms of performance feedback, including 360-degree survey feedback. Well researched are the evaluations of programs to teach the various styles of leadership presented in earlier chapters. Coaching, on-the-job leadership training by the learner's immediate supervisor, and mentoring of junior by senior executives are widely practiced. Special attention is also given to examining ways to train leaders to work effectively with minorities and the disadvantaged. Specific programs prepare people for foreign assignments. Numerous leadership and management training and education programs have their benefits and limitations.

In all, meta-analyses of available evaluative studies have provided evidence that leadership and management training, education, and development are usually effective. Effective training and education add to valid assessment in fostering effective leadership and management.

CHAPTER 35

Assessment, Appraisal, and Selection

Assessments based on tests and judgments as well as appraisals of current performance can be used for leadership and management-development purposes. They can be used to modify current performance and predict future performance. The judgments and their combinations can forecast success and effectiveness as leaders. Such predictive data can be extracted from assessments of personal backgrounds, psychological tests of ability and motivation, and current performance in contrived and real-life settings. Forbes and Piercy (1991) examined the backgrounds and careers of 250 CEOs and emphasized the importance of early career success. In mid-career, alternate routes to the top were movement into general management or functional specialization. Background and experience influenced early promotion into middle and senior management. Credibility and visibility were enhanced by level of education, breadth of experience, entry from a prestigious university and its advanced management training programs, service on the staff of a senior executive, work in a powerful department, and functional understanding of the corporate organization's critical problems. It also could help to be a member of the family that controlled the corporation.

Business and industry were quick to adapt the intelligence tests developed for selection by the U.S. Army in 1917, in World War I, to assess 1.7 million draftees. (Portions of these tests can be found in the current, commercially available Wonderlic Personnel Test.) Development of personality inventories for assessment soon followed. The first modern standardized attitude surveys were completed by employees in the U.S. Department of Agriculture in the early 1930s (Likert, 1932).

Purposes of Assessment

The uses of assessment are twofold. By whatever means it is done, assessment provides the basis for choosing from among candidates for leadership and management posts. It also provides useful information for the counseling and further development of incumbent leaders. The organization clearly benefits from using valid selection processes for its leaders rather than relying on haphazard processes, ranging from casual and ill-formed choices to those involving favoritism, prejudice, politics, nepotism, and bribery (Immegart, 1987). Organizational effectiveness is enhanced by the increased assignment of those best able to fill leadership posts. A valid assessment increases the tendency of the status of organization members to be correlated more highly with their ability and esteem. Also, it reduces potential conflicts caused by incongruities among status, esteem, and ability.[1] In the same way, counseling and development based on valid measurements rest on much firmer ground than do management counseling and development based exclusively on impressions and feelings. Thus Knight and Weiss (1980) demonstrated in an experiment that leaders perceived to have been chosen by a competent agent were judged by other group members to have greater expertise than those selected by a less competent agent. These leaders were also more influential.

Varieties of Available Assessment Information

Personal traits related to leadership have included tests and judgments of capacity, achievement, and verbal and nonverbal communication styles; interests, attitudes, and

[1] See Chapter 13.

values; sociability, initiative, confidence, and popularity; task and relations orientation; status, family, educational background, and work history. For example, Miner (1960a) and Nash (1966) reported patterns for forecasting managerial success that were consistent with the personal factors connected with leadership discussed in earlier chapters. These patterns involved energy, risk taking, verbal fluency, confidence, independence, and the desire to be persuasive. Mahoney, Jerdee, and Nash (1960, 1961) showed that the success of 468 managers in Minnesota-based companies was predicted by work-related, business-related, and higher-level occupational interests. These concerned interests in leadership, independence, moderate risk, and work that were not closely detailed. Also predictive were intelligence, solid education, activities in more organizations, and self-reported dominance. In the same way, Ghiselli (1971) predicted managers' progress based on a battery of tests of intelligence, supervisory ability, self-assurance, decisiveness, self-actualization, and motivation to achieve.

In addition to information generated from tests and simulations, the predictive data have been supplied by observers, interviewers, outsiders, superiors, peers, subordinates, and the assessees themselves. Assessment centers (discussed in detail below) have become a popular way of systematically gathering and pooling such multiple and diverse sources of information. The sources of information may be either subjective judgments about candidates for selection, development, and promotion or objective work samples, tests, and inventories. Often, both sources will be combined for a prediction. Naive observers may do just as good a job as trained process observers in identifying which individuals in a group are emerging as its leaders (Stein, 1977). The methods of combining the predictors for success as a leader are either statistical, judgmental, or both. Clinical judgment or mechanical pooling of the information in some objective systematic way may be used. To aid judgment, objective or subjective information or both may be displayed in profiles or printed in narrative reports. The mechanical combining may be based on unit or differential weighting of the information. The weighting can be a matter of judgment, or multiple regression analysis may be used to minimize error in the predictions (Sawyer, 1966).

Importance of Effective Assessment and Appraisal

"We bet on people, not strategies," declared Larry Bossidy, CEO of Allied Signal. Many senior managers fail to have a "talent mind-set" that can maintain the quality of an organization. Only 23% of top executives agreed that their firm brought in highly talented people, and even fewer (16%) said they could identify the high and low performers. Only 11% agreed that they could retain almost all high performers; only 5% said they could remove low performers quickly (Michaels, 1998). Yet talent needs to be identified early in high flyers' careers in order to provide rapid promotion into leadership positions and avoid losing the high flyers to competing firms (Gratton, 1992). Early experiences in team sports and business and early identification are seen as important for the development of business leaders (Benton, 1990).

Importance of Acceptability of Appraisals and Feedback for Development

Increasingly, performance appraisals, especially from multiple sources, are being used for development as well as placement and advancement. Their acceptability is important in determining how much they can change behavior (Taylor, Masterson, & Renard, 1988). This depends on the willingness of the rater to provide unbiased appraisals, and that of the ratee to accept and make use of the feedback (Waldman & Bowen, 1998). (The importance of feedback of appraisals to leaders' development and training, especially 360-degree feedback, was mentioned in earlier chapters.)

CEO Performance Evaluation

Truskie (1995) presented the results of a survey of appraisal practices of more than 600 large firms, by the chief executives. Thirty-eight percent had formalized oral and written processes; 78% had preset performance objectives; 75% of the boards used the evaluations for compensation purposes. All CEOs were held accountable for the company's financial performance. Boards of directors were supposed to be able to justify CEOs' compensation. CEOs could use the evaluations for personal improvement and for building relations with the board. However, boards considered short-term, quarterly, and yearly goals as more important than long-term ones. Qualitative goals such as leadership might be considered, but only informally, and they were unlikely to be factored into compensation. In most cases, the evaluations were based on formal performance reviews.

Judgmental Approaches

Pure judgments of the readiness of job incumbents for promotions into positions that require more leadership are commonly used. These judgments may be obtained from observers. More often, they are obtained from the supervisors of the incumbents or from higher management. Such judgments can be a part of standard performance appraisals, and, as was noted in Chapter 30, such early appraisals of performance as a leader are likely to predict subsequent success as a leader. They also can be based on observations of leaders' performance in work samples and situational tests, as well as in the actual performance of a job. Simulations of management situations, paper-pencil simulations in the form of standardized managerial basket tests, initially leaderless group discussions (LGDs), and other small-group exercises can be used to generate the observations from which judgments are derived. Other ways of judging the potential for leadership are supervisors' opinions and performance appraisals, interviews, references, and recommendations. In addition to judgments of an assessee's overall leadership performance, discrete elements can be singled out for examination and decision. These elements can then be formed into scores for standardized processing.

Judgments Based on Simulations

In-basket Tests. These tests simulate the typical contents of a manager's in-basket. The items may include telephone messages, brief memos, detailed reports, letters, directives, complaints, and junk mail about a recently vacated management position. The examinee is instructed to imagine that he or she has just taken over

the position and has limited time, such as one hour, to decide how to handle each item (Frederiksen, 1962b, 1966; Frederiksen, Saunders, & Ward, 1957). Realism can be added with telephone calls and visual presentations (Lopez, 1966). An element that is deemed important in the test is ambiguity (Gill, 1979), although the common problems faced by all managers need to be sampled (Stewart & Stewart, 1976). Brass and Oldham (1976) argued that the more representative and appropriate the in-basket sample to the examinee's particular future management situation, the better the test results predict that performance.

As many as nine independent factors were uncovered in a Sears in-basket test (Bentz, 1967), but Gill (1979) concluded that most factor analyses of in-basket results, including Meyer's (1970a), emerge with just two factors: a relations dimension of supervision and an intellectual dimension of planning and administration. Highly reliable results can be obtained with standardized scoring procedures by adequately trained judges of the examinee's responses (Richards & Jaffee, 1972). Interviews with the examinees after they complete the in-basket test can augment the accuracy of the predictions obtained (Clutterbuck, 1974).

The results of the in-basket tests of IBM supervisors were found by Wollowick and McNamara (1969) to correlate .32 with increases in management responsibility during the three years following testing. Judgments of the examinees' organizing and planning ability and work standards, garnered from an in-basket test, correlated .27 and .44, respectively, with the managerial level they achieved at AT&T eight years later (Bray & Grant, 1966) and .19 and .24 with the level they achieved 20 years later (Howard & Bray, 1988). Similar findings were reported by Meyer (1963) for manufacturing supervisors at General Electric and by Lopez (1966) for managers at the Port Authority of New York and New Jersey. These investigators agreed that judgments and scores from in-basket tests add considerably to the accuracy of forecasting success as a manager that is not possible with ordinary paper-pencil tests of capacity and interests.

Leaderless Group Discussion (LGD). In the simplest form of small-group exercise, the initially leaderless discussion group (LGD) is assigned a problem to discuss to reach a group decision. Observers judge who emerges as a leader, initiatives displayed by each participant, and other aspects of interpersonal performance, such as motivation of others, persuasiveness in expression, and skills in dealing with others to handle the problems to be solved. Bass (1954a) reported correlations of these observers' judgments of LGDs of .44, .53, and .38 with rated merit among the 348 ROTC cadets as cadet officers obtained six months to a year later. A similar correlation of .47 was found in predicting subsequent nominations for positions of fraternity leadership from earlier performance in an LGD. Similarly, Arbous and Maree (1951) obtained a correlation among 168 South African administrative trainees of .50 between an LGD and the trainees' rated capacity a year later as administrators. Vernon (1950) found, among 123 personnel, a correlation of .33 between an LGD and their rated suitability for foreign service. The LGD was validated in the same way for shipyard supervisors (Mandell, 1950b), military officers (Weisloge, 1953), U.S. Army personnel (Gleason, 1957), and British supervisors who were followed up for four years (Handyside & Duncan, 1954). The LGD became a routine part of many assessment centers. Vernon (1950) found a correlation of .75 between judgments based on a one-hour LGD and judgments by assessors after three days of activities at an assessment center. Although the quantity of talk in an LGD reflects *attempts* to lead, its quality affects a person's *success* in leading (Bottger, 1984). Participants who are highly rated by observers see themselves as more assertive, competitive, self-confident, and willing to function autonomously. Those rated less effective view themselves as cooperative, disciplined, and tactful (Hills, 1985).

Small-Group Simulations. Complex simulations are specifically constructed exercises for small groups of candidates that can be observed by assessors whose judgments are shaped by what they see. Roskin and Margerison (1983) presented examples of simulations that involved organizing a team effort among managers whose problem required little special information or experience but could bring out differences in participants' leadership, managerial skills, and attitudes. These simulations were: (1) the production of a set of prototype greeting cards; (2) the building of a "monument" from material provided; (3) the solution of a case problem, at both individual and corporate levels; (4) the construction and fly-

ing of paper airplanes; (5) the selection of an employee from a number of candidates. Assessors' judgments were based on observations of 39 elements in the assessees' behavior. The assessments were related to the compatibility of the behavior with the situation and how the assessments dealt with cognitive and perceptual complexity. Managers were detected who were most likely to be high achievers. Scores of leadership attitudes and opinions on paper-and-pencil tests alone failed to relate to the managers' performance.

Dunnette (1970) described two simulated business situations from which judgments of performance could be gleaned for predictions of leadership. Six participants were told they were managing an investment fund and had to buy and sell stocks to make profits for their investors. Stock quotations were changed every five minutes, and other information was presented at predetermined intervals. Organizing skillfully, working cooperatively with other people, handling a large amount of information, and other group process and cognitive variables were judged from each participant's behavior. In the second simulated business situation, the six participants were asked to play roles as managerial trainees. Each participant had to plan a project and make a 10-minute presentation justifying the project and its budget. After the six presentations, the participants engaged in an hour's discussion about the merits of the various projects. Skills in judgment, planning, and organizing, proficiency in oral communication, and effectiveness at working in competitive situations could be judged with some accuracy from the emergent behaviors.

Cognitive Tests. Organizational leadership is characterized as social problem solving in ill-defined, usually novel domains (Mumford, Zaccaro, Harding, et al., 2000). Cognitive and metacognitive abilities are needed to solve the problems of executive leadership. Cognitive abilities include intelligence, general reasoning skills, divergent thinking, and oral and written expression and comprehension (Connelly, Gilbert, Zaccaro, et al., 2000). Cognitive abilities are needed to get things done. Metacognitive abilities guide the problem-solving process and enhance choosing, planning, monitoring, and evaluating what to do. Such abilities include verbal fluency, information-processing skills, and inductive and deductive reasoning (Marshal-Mies, Fleishman, Martin, et al., 2000). Cognitive and metacognitive tests of executive leadership skills have been conducted by both conventional and computer methods. A battery of these complex problem-solving measures was administered at the National University, in San Diego, to senior military officers.

Problem-Solving Scenarios. Zaccaro, Mumford, Connelly, et al. (2000) administered a set of psychometric tests to tap the problem-solving capabilities of 1,807 U.S. Army officers ranging in rank from 597 second lieutenants to 37 colonels, most with experience serving in leadership roles from platoon to brigade commanders; 80% were men, and 20% were women. The first tests administered were either cued or uncued scenarios calling for creative problem-solving and processing of complex problems. (Half the samples underwent cued scenarios; the other half, uncued scenarios.) Next, military scenarios required the construction of solutions to assess attention to the constraints on and understanding of the context. Scenarios calling for social judgments tested the understanding of people. Knowledge of the roles of a leader in dealing with various tasks, writing skills (rewriting headlines), and divergent thinking about the consequences of unlikely events were also examined, using similarly brief 10- to 15-minute tests. Responses were constructed by the examinees rather than chosen by them. Cued and uncued complex problem-solving scenarios correlated with knowledge of leadership, .32, .33; understanding leadership as problem solving, .22, .41; divergent thinking, .49, .51; verbal reasoning, .18, .14; and creative writing, .30, .33. Cued problem solving correlated .55 with solution construction; uncued problem solving correlated .50 with social judgment.

Judgments Based on Speeches and Essays

Essays written by candidates, managers, and leaders and their speeches can provide the basis of judgments about their future performance. Winter (1987) demonstrated that the contents of the inaugural addresses of U.S. presidents could be judged and coded to obtain valid inferences of their leadership motivation patterns. Such patterns, in turn, were predictive of the success of their administrations. Speechwriters provided the specific words, but the leaders reviewed and modified the text.

House, Woycke, and Fodor (1988) extended the work to Canadian prime ministers.[2]

Judgments Based on Appraised Performance

Superiors' appraisals, evaluations by peers, and self-reports of leaders about their own performance may all be employed as predictors of future leadership success. Generally, consistencies are likely to fall between superiors' and peers' ratings, although superiors are prone to emphasize getting work done and peers are more likely to emphasize cooperativeness. Self-reports tend to be inflated (although some managers may have better insight into themselves than others do). Self-reports may be unrelated to judgments obtained from peers or superiors. For example, Lawler (1967a) found a correlation of .52 between superiors' and peers' ratings of the job ability of 113 middle and top managers. Agreement on the rated quality of the managers' job performance was .38. On the other hand, correlations were close to zero between the managers' self-reports and the peers' or superiors' ratings of the managers' ability and performance. A meta-analysis by Harris and Schaubroeck (1988) of 11 to 36 reported correlations found a high correlation, on average, between peers' and superiors' ratings but much lower correlations between self-reports and superiors' ratings, or between self-reports and peers' ratings. Agreement between self-reports and others' ratings was lower for managers and professionals than for blue-collar and service employees. Whether the rating format was dimensional or global had little effect on the agreement.

Judgments by Superiors

Organizations commonly use supervisors' and superiors' judgments to decide whom to hire, transfer, and promote. The judgments are attempts to forecast future success as a leader and manager in the positions for which the candidates are to be chosen. Equally common are teachers' and trainers' appraisals of prospective future position holders while they are enrolled in training and education programs. When 493 to 631 U.S. Army soldiers were rated by their supervisors and peers, 13% of the variance in the supervisors' appraisals was accounted for by

[2]The results of work with this approach were discussed in Chapters 7 and 21.

the soldiers' scores in ability, job knowledge, and proficiency. But only 7% could be accounted for by peers. When interpersonal factors were included, the percentages rose to 28% and 19% (Borman, White, & Dorsey, 1995). The cumulative military performance grades awarded by superiors at Annapolis correlated .25 with subsequent fitness reports of 186 U.S. Navy officers serving in the fleet as much as a decade later. They also predicted the tendency of subordinates to describe the officers as charismatic (Yammarino & Bass, 1989).

Academic Performance Grades. Cumulative academic performance grades at Annapolis were not predictive (Yammarino & Bass, 1989) of success. This finding was consistent with the failure, more often than not, to find significant correlations between undergraduate college grades and success in business and industry (see, e.g., Schick & Kunnecke, 1982) or better ratings of job performance (Pallett & Hoyt, 1968). The record for postgraduate grades has been somewhat better (Weinstein & Srinivasan, 1974), although in general, postgraduate grades of any consequence emerged mainly in specific elective courses (Marshall, 1964). As the importance of technology increases, so may the importance of academic performance if grade inflation is not too severe. In special circumstances, academic performance may be predictive. In one study, academic performance predicted teachers' ratings of the leadership of high school students (Schneider, Paul, White, et al., 1999). The school was a magnet school focusing on leadership development, and these students spent most of two years of their class time together, confirming the data gathered about them. Grade point average (GPA) correlated .59 with task-goal teacher ratings of leadership and .48 with peers' nominations of leadership (Schneider, Ehrhart, & Ehrhart, 2002). Generally, results lagged over the two-year period. They showed more modest correlations among teachers' and peers' appraisals and the Myers-Briggs Type Indicator, the Campbell Interest and Skill Survey, and leadership in an initially leaderless group discussion.

From the research on the persistence of leadership in Chapter 30, it can be inferred that superiors' performance appraisals of managers' behavior as leaders furnish a greater opportunity to observe the managers in action than when the managers are observed in diverse positions by different superiors, peers, and subordinates. At the same time, the predictive validity of superiors' judgments

suffers to the extent that they overweight the candidates' technical proficiency and manipulative styles (Farrow, Valenzi, & Bass, 1981); the requirements of the new positions are also different from those of the old ones. Furthermore, successful performance in a lower-level position may not necessarily predict performance in a higher-level position that requires more cognitive complexity (Jacobs & Jaques, 1987).

Brush and Schoenfeldt (1980) proposed a procedure that would direct superiors' ratings toward a systematic evaluation of their current subordinates on dimensions of consequence to future positions the subordinates might hold. They argued that it is even possible to evaluate blue-collar workers, based on their observed behavior on the job, on dimensions relevant to supervisory positions to which they might aspire. Schippmann and Prien (1986) obtained such judgments of 47 candidates for first-level supervisory jobs in a steel company from 29 supervisors. The dimensions arranged for the supervisors' judgments included: (1) representational skills, (2) supervisory ability, (3) ability to analyze and evaluate information to define problems, (4) knowledge about and ability to work with mechanical devices, (5) ability to manage/orchestrate current activities effectively, (6) ability to decide and act, (7) ability to follow through to achieve closure on a task, (8) administrative ability. Satisfactory reliabilities were achieved, but self-assessed merits were much more lenient than the supervisors' ratings.

Superiors' Intentions in Appraising Subordinates. What stimulates superiors to appraise subordinates? In one study, 73 subordinates were rated by 32 supervisors. Some were rated by 25 of the supervisors, and none were rated by 16 supervisors. Supervisors who rated all the subordinates differed significantly from those who rated only some or none. According to the subordinates, the 32 supervisors were higher in initiating structure; they came from more formal departments; their work groups were more cohesive; their subordinates were better educated; and they had more confidence in the appraisals (Fried, Fried, Tiegs, & Bellamy, 1992).

Superiors may intend to try to rate subordinates' performance accurately or to inflate or deflate subordinates for political, social, or personal reasons. Davis (2000) queried the intentions of law enforcement superiors in appraising the performance of subordinates. A total of 266 superiors (captains, lieutenants, and sergeants in a county sheriff's department) completed the questionnaire. The superiors indicated their intention to be more accurate in their performance appraisals of their subordinates if they felt that the appraisals: (1) enabled employees to participate in the process; (2) contributed to developmental purposes; (3) served to reward employees. Also, intentions to be accurate were greater if the supervisors had better relations with their subordinates and were more satisfied with the performance appraisal system.

Peer Appraisals. Consistent with other analyses of "buddy ratings," peer ratings by cadets at West Point and at officer candidate schools (OCS) were found to be the best single predictor of subsequent success as a regular U.S. Army officer (Haggerty, Johnson, & King, 1954). A correlation of .51 was obtained between peers' ratings at West Point and the rated success of infantry officers 18 months later. A correlation of .42 was obtained between peers' ratings in OCS and officers' combat performance in World War II (Baier, 1947). Similar results were reported for the U.S. Marine Corps (Wilkins, 1953; Williams & Leavitt, 1947b) and the U.S. Air Force (USAF 1952a, b). Ricciuti (1955) found fellow midshipmens' ratings of aptitude for service more predictive of the subsequent performance of naval officers than ratings made at the U.S. Naval Academy by their navy officers. Hollander (1965) and Amir, Kovarsky, and Sharan (1970) applied peer ratings to accurately predict the success of junior officers. Downey, Medland, and Yates (1976) extended the findings to senior officers. They found that ratings by 1,656 colonels of each other forecast who would be promoted to general. The correlation was .47. Peer nominations among 133 women soldiers in the U.S. Army were found to generate two distinct factors, professional and social, but parallel ratings yielded only one general factor, suggesting the ratings were subject to halo bias (Schwartzwald, Koslowsky, & Mager-Bibi, 1999).

Judgments by peers are often in the form of nominations of one or several associates with whom the rater is acquainted (see Chapter 10). Nominations of the most and least valued have been employed. But to be predictive of subsequent success, the nominations must be positive. Kaufman and Johnson (1974) showed, in two studies of ROTC cadets, that being nominated as the most effective cadet officer during the school year correlated between .36 and .43 with independent criteria of performance as a platoon leader at summer camp. But

being nominated for the least effective performance officer did not correlate as negatively as expected with such leadership at summer camp. For this, correlations were .03 and .16 in the two studies.

In business, Kraut (1975b) obtained peers' ratings from 156 middle-level IBM managers and 83 higher-level executives attending a monthlong training program. Two factors emerged from 13 ratings: (1) impact; and (2) tactfulness. These factors correlated .35 and .37, respectively, with the performance appraisals of the higher-level executives, but close to zero with the performance appraisals of the middle managers once they were back on the job. However, the peers' ratings of impact correlated with the subsequent number of promotions received by both the middle managers and the executives. These predictions from peer judgments were much more likely to be correlated with subsequent success than predictions obtained from the training staff of the monthlong program.

Are peer ratings biased by friendship? Mumford (1983) was impressed with the validity of peer ratings but found a need for a better theoretical understanding of the reasons for it. It would seem that peer ratings are valid because they are likely to be influenced by many of the persistent traits that contribute to success as a leader, such as competence and esteem not necessarily due to friendship.

Subordinates' Appraisals. With the increase in participative management has come an increase in the acceptance of subordinates' ratings of their bosses. Anecdotal evidence suggests that some managers learn from their subordinates that they talk too much or are not good listeners. Some receive better ratings than they expected. Reasons for discrepancies between ratings from the different sources can also be examined and action planning undertaken. Bob Myers, a vice president at the Limited, discovered that his colleagues wanted him to be more open to different views. Ellen Walton, at AT&T Network Systems, found out that she did not always listen. CEO Lawrence Bossidy of Allied Signal was not surprised to learn that his subordinates agreed with him that he was opinionated (Maynard, 1994). In 1992, the motorcycle manufacturer Harley-Davidson began an upward feedback program to its executive committee members from their direct reports. Increasingly, in many firms such as General Electric and IBM, feedback programs for developing managers are surveying the managers' subordinates, as well as their peers and superiors (Gunn, 1992). Information from subordinates is also likely to be predictive of future success as a manager. However, the accuracy of the predictions derived from such information may suffer to the degree that the subordinates overweigh sentimentality, the superior's likability and the extent to which the future position's requirements differ from the current one. Nevertheless, Hater and Bass (1988) showed that among 56 Federal Express managers, those who were rated higher in transformational leadership and lower in laissez-faire leadership by their subordinates were significantly more likely to be judged by senior managers as having a greater potential for leadership. Similar results were found by Yammarino and Bass (1989) for junior naval officers.

Of course, it is one thing to use superiors', peers', and subordinates' ratings in research; it is another thing to use them in operations. The colleagues' and candidates' resistance and distortions are likely to increase when the ratings are to be employed by a higher authority to decide on a promotion for which the colleagues are also competing.

Self-Ratings. Objective personality tests and inventories may provide assessments for personal leadership development as well as selection of leaders. Most survey feedback asks managers to describe their own behavior. These results are then fed back to the managers relative to the average group results. The self-ratings are not likely to be as useful to the prediction of future success as the discrepancies between theirs and others' judgments. But the discrepancies are especially useful for developmental counseling and training. Most answers to questionnaires that ask managers to describe or evaluate their own behavior suffer from a variety of errors. Nevertheless, autobiographical material dealing with a person's early history of the challenge of important life decisions can be the basis of valid judgments by trained reviewers (Ezekiel, 1968). Assessees may be asked to write about their high school and college experiences, their peak experiences, their jobs and organizations five years into the future, and their obituaries (what they expect and hope will be said about them and their performance). Anonymity is often important, using coded names for feedback and correlated research. Nonetheless, when it was optional for U.S. Army officers to sign their names to their answers to a personnel survey, most signed, wanting to indicate that they were cooperating.

Self-ratings tend to be inflated compared to other ratings sources. They may be accurate, especially when they are not being used for administrative purposes or when they are verifiable statements of intention. Again, some attributes that are self-rated, such as commitment, may be accurate rather than biased, as was found for 79 public service administrative staff (Goffin & Gellatly, 2001). Toegel and Conger (2003) argued that two kinds of 360-degree assessments are needed: one that provides more qualitative assessment and feedback for management development; the other, more quantitative assessment feedback for performance appraisal and performance outcomes.

Multiple Rating Sources

The validity, accuracy, and relevance of ratings and other subjective judgments can be improved in a variety of ways. These include changes in format—by rater selection and training, by corrections for biases and expectations, and in particular by the use of multiple sources for ratings. The overall agreement among raters and the reliability and accuracy of the results are likely to increase with the number of independent raters judging the same ratee. To add validity to performance appraisals, ratings may be obtained from more than one source. Multisource ratings may be any combination of ratings of leaders from superiors, peers, subordinates, and self, as well as other sources such as clients, customers, and members of the same organization from different departments. A common multisource research plan is to obtain ratings of leaders from three or more subordinates and peers. As many as five observers may be employed by assessment centers and then compared with self-ratings. A plethora of studies has been completed on comparisons between self-rating and ratings by others.

Self-Ratings versus Others' Ratings
Oh, wad some power the giftie gie us
To see oursels as others see us,
It wad frae monie a blunder free us
An' foolish notion
(Burns, R., 1785/1974, pp. 43–44)

Poets, among others, have long been aware of the inaccuracy of self-appraisal. At the same time, many studies have shown that leaders are more accurate in their self-appraisals than are nonleaders; that is, leaders are in higher agreement with others' ratings of them (e.g., Gallo & McClintock, 1962). Baril, Ayman, & Palmiter (1994) examined the agreement between the self-ratings of 92 supervisors and their 853 subordinates. There was only minor agreement, but the agreement correlated with raters' situational control in Fiedler's (1967a) contingency model of leadership. Atwater and Yammarino (1992) looked at the self-other agreement of 92 midshipmen leaders with their subordinates and with the officers they reported to at the U.S. Naval Academy's summer camp. Using the Multifactor Leadership Questionnaire, subordinates and supervising officers rated the transformational leadership of each self-rating leader. As is usually found, mean self-ratings were higher than mean subordinates' ratings. Nevertheless, some leaders could be classified as overestimators or underestimators based on their deviations from the means. *Overestimators* were defined as more than half a standard deviation above the mean; *underestimators* were defined as more than half a standard deviation below the mean. For the remainder, self-ratings were defined as being in agreement with subordinates' or superiors' ratings. Approximately half of the 61 leaders were categorized in the same way by subordinates and superiors. Underestimators were seen more favorably by others. Self-ratings correlated .35 with superiors' ratings, but only .19 with subordinates' ratings. Bass and Yammarino (1991) obtained comparable data about 155 U.S. navy officers in the surface fleet. Again, mean self-ratings were inflated. The officers were classified in the same way as the midshipmen. Those officers who were less likely to be overestimators were more likely to obtain recommendations for promotion and better performance appraisals from their superiors. Self-ratings were unrelated to the superiors' performance appraisals and recommendations for promotion. Using differences between self-ratings and subordinates' ratings, of 2,056 managerial raters, the in-agreement raters and the underestimators were regarded by their superiors as more effective than overestimators. Yammarino and Atwater (1997) inferred that overestimators compared to underestimators and individuals *in agreement* were more likely to misdiagnose their strengths and weaknesses, make less

effective decisions, suffer from career derailment, be resentful and hostile, see no need for training and development, be absent and get into conflicts with colleagues more frequently, and quit. They lowered their self-evaluations and improved their performance when feedback from others was received and accepted. Underestimators are likely to be more successful but are lower in self-esteem, set low aspirations, underachieve, and avoid attempting leadership. Individuals in agreement and rated as good are likely to be the best performers; make effective decisions; develop favorable expectations and achievement; be most promotable; be successful, effective leaders; be low in absenteeism, turnover, and conflicts with others; and accept and use feedback from others constructively. Those who agreed they were poor performers were likely to be poor decision makers; lack competencies, self-esteem, motivation, and a positive outlook; and take few actions to improve their performance. When subordinate-peer agreement was used to predict superiors' ratings, overestimation, underestimation, or agreement of self and peers' ratings correlated with superiors' evaluations of the leadership effectiveness of 2,292 focal managers, but only if the self- and peers' ratings were not in between favorable or unfavorable. Actually, it was mainly the peers' ratings that provided the best prediction. Peers' ratings correlated .40 with superiors' evaluations; self-ratings correlated only .17 with superiors' evaluations (Brutus, Fleenor, & Taylor, 1966).

According to a meta-analysis by Harris and Schaubroeck (1988), self-ratings were much less in agreement with peers' ($r = .36$) and supervisors' ratings ($r = .35$) than peers' and supervisors' ratings were with each other ($r = .62$). Shipper and Davy (2002) compared five peers' and immediate subordinates' evaluations with self-evaluations. The questionnaire ratings dealt with the interactive and initiating skills of 1,125 middle managers in various facilities of a high-tech company. The peers' and immediate subordinates' ratings of interactive skills ($r = .69$) and initiating skills ($r = .33$) predicted the attitudes of the professional employees serving in the managers' units. In turn, the professional employees' attitudes significantly predicted the managers' performance. On the other hand, the self-evaluations of interactive skills were actually *negatively* related ($r = .15$) to managerial performance.

Inflated self-evaluations can cause careers to derail.

The discrepancy in what leaders think of themselves and what their colleagues think of them may be seen by colleagues and others as arrogance (McCall & Lombardo, 1983). The absence of such a discrepancy benefits manager-subordinate relationships (Wexley, Alexander, Greenwalt, et al., 1980).

Adding Self-Ratings and Others, Ratings for Predicting Performance. Atwater, Ostroff, Yammarino, et al. (1998) obtained self- and peers' Benchmarks ratings on 1,460 managers in leadership development programs as well as on-the-job performance appraisals from their direct supervisors. Correlations with the supervisors' ratings were .25 with self, .33 with subordinates, .37 with peers, and .50 between subordinates and peers. When subordinates' and peers' ratings were added in a linear regression equation, a multiple R of .40 was obtained. When curvilinearity was introduced by adding to the equation the squares and cross-products of self- and peers' ratings to predict supervisors' effectiveness ratings, the multiple correlation rose to only .41, but numerous other conclusions were able to be drawn about extreme underestimators and extreme overestimators from the three-dimensional equation.

Moderators of Self-Other Agreement. Becker, Ayman, & Korabik (2002) found complex effects when men and women, either high or low self-monitors, were compared as to their agreement with their subordinates in male-dominated industrial and educational organizations rather than in organizations balanced in the sexes. Atwater and Yammarino (1997) reviewed the literature and noted that students rated their scholastic ability higher than their peers' ability as they increased in age (Bailey & Bailey, 1974). Older and longer-tenured adults tended to inflate their own ratings (Ferris, Yates, Gilmore, et al., 1985). Intelligence, achievement, and internal locus of control correlate with more accurate self-evaluation (Mabe & West, 1982). Cognitively complex raters demonstrate more accurate self-assessments (Nydegger, 1975). Self-other ratings of MBTI types are higher in agreement for introverts than for extroverts, for feelers than for thinkers (Roush & Atwater, 1992), and for those higher in self-awareness (Van Velsor, Taylor, & Leslie, 1993). Accurate expectations increase the accuracy of self-assessments (Beyer, 1990) as do experiences with feedback of self-ratings (Kooker, 1974). Self-ratings will be inflated if they are to be used for personnel decisions or to manage impressions (Ferris & Judge, 1991). They also will be inflated by both subordinates and peers if they are used as recommendations for promotion rather than for developmental feedback (Gregura & Robie, 2001).

360-Degree Ratings

When ratings for an executive or manager by subordinates, peers, superiors, and self are determined, there exists a 360-degree report that can be used for administrative purposes, promotion from within, succession planning, self-development, coaching, or training and development. Though anonymity usually is initially maintained for subordinates' ratings, when they are used for development, it is not uncommon for leaders to discuss their 360-degree report with subordinates as well as with peers and boss. Although the increase in 360-degree reporting paralleled the delayering of organizations and the increase in participative management and teamwork, it is not new. The Center for Creative Leadership introduced the 360-degree format in 1974, and Personnel Decisions did the same in 1984 (Maynard, 1994). A 360-degree analysis for managers and leaders can be obtained from sources such as Personnel Decisions and the Center for Creative Leadership. A 360-degree report can be obtained for the Full Range of Leadership Development; from charismatic to laissez-faire; in Web or paper format (Avolio & Bass, 2004). (For a list of 10 commercially available 360-degree programs and their validity, languages, Web feedback availability, and other characteristics, see Morical, 1999.)

Alimo-Metcalfe and Metcalfe (1998) enumerated the advantages of 360-degree appraisals: (1) The data are more valid since they include observations by subordinates, who are in closer contact with the manager than is the manager's boss. (2) Subordinates see how the manager reacts in day-to-day situations as well as crises. (3) Subordinates are on the receiving end of managers' practices. Their ratings may provide greater validity than top-down ratings. (4) The subordinates, peers, and bosses observe and rate different aspects of the manager's behavior. (5) The reliability and fairness and the manager's acceptance of the data are greater. (6) With peer ratings, the organization shows its interest in horizontal relations.

The Metcalfes collected 360-degree data at a university management development program for British National Health Service middle managers (212 males, 263 females), their bosses, two to three peers each, and two to three subordinates each. The data included ratings of 41 competencies. Up to nine factors emerged in the different subsets of raters, but the factor performance management was usually the first and largest factor to emerge in the sets of women and men from the different sources analyzed. Other factors included presentation/communication skills, enterpreneurial innovation, and analytical ability. The variance in ratings accounted for by the six to nine factors per set ranged from 53% to 61%. There appeared to be more similarities than differences between the sexes and the sources of the appraisals.

Scullen, Mount, and Sytsma (1996) selected 2,297 managers from 22,431 in a personnel decisions data set from a variety of firms and industries. Along with self-ratings, each manager had been rated by two others at organizational levels above them, at the same level, and below them. The ratings were based on the Management Skills Profile (MSP) of 18 skills measured by 122 items. According to a Principles Components factor analysis, responses to the items formed three factors: (1) interpersonal skills (listening and human relations); (2) administrative skills (delegating, personal organization, and time management); (3) planning and general supervisory skills (occupational and technical knowledge, problem analysis, and financial and quantitative skills). As expected, mean self-ratings were higher than those of any other type of rater for interpersonal skills but not the other two factors. Reliabilities of the three factored scales ranged for superiors from .84 to .87; for peers, .82 to .86; and for subordinates, .76 to .82. Agreement between the pairs of superior raters ranged from .41 to .45; for pairs of peers, .31 to .35; and for pairs of subordinates, .31 to .36. Correlations were as follows among the types of raters: superiors-peers, .34; superiors-subordinates, .26; superiors-self, .17; subordinates-peers; .27; peers-self, .19; and subordinates-self, .34. These results indicated that there was modest agreement between and within the different levels of raters. Each rater was providing a somewhat different snapshot of the ratee. No rater level was redundant. A composite based on 360-degree ratings was needed to provide a fuller picture of the ratee's performance. Considerable training was needed to increase the correlations between raters at the same level. As was usually found across organizational levels, correlations were higher between peers and superiors and lower between self and

others (Harris & Schaubroeck, 1988; Erisman & Reilly, 1996).

Conway and Huffcutt (1997) calculated for 319 managers from a Fortune 500 company how much unique variance would be found in the 360-degree ratings from different organizational levels and a customer assessment. They determined how much each source contributed to a multiple correlation when combined with the other sources. The results confirmed that each source was contributing mainly unique or nonredundant variance.

Multisource ratings are essential to provide a complete appraisal for developmental purposes, as each source of ratings comes from a different perspective of the same ratee. At the same time, although rating-point interpretations will differ among different groups of raters, the construct validity of most of the dimensions rated by different groups of raters holds up well on such 360-degree instruments as Benchmarks (Wise, 1998). An average predictive validity of .30 was obtained for the 360-degree ratings of 62 to 65 general managers of district retail stores. The ratings predicted their district discount retail stores' sales-to-goals ratio for four business quarters (Healey & Rose, 2003).

Judgments Based on Organizational and Personnel Procedures

Personnel procedures upon which judgments are based include interviews, projective testing, board meetings, and references and recommendations.

Judgments Based on Interviews. The standardized interview from which the interviewer forms judgments about the assessee ordinarily covers the candidate's family, education, and work history. Also often discussed are the candidate's expressed objectives, strong and weak points, hopes and fears, social values, interests, attitudes toward the organization, and attitudes toward interpersonal relationships. The accuracy of these self-descriptions is higher for the information that the candidate believes can be independently corroborated (Cascio, 1975).

The interviews vary widely in how they are organized in the time devoted to them, in the probing skills of the interviewer, in the extent to which the interviewer is trained to provide a similar stimulating situation for each candidate, and so on. A deliberate effort may be made to place stress on the candidate to observe his or her ability to cope. Admiral Hyman Rickover conducted more than 20,000 such stressful interviews in the process of choosing personnel for the nuclear surface ship and submarine program. However, there appeared to be little standardization in what he did. Furthermore, anecdotal evidence suggests that what he did do contributed little to his accuracy in predicting the subsequent performance of officers in the nuclear fleet (Polmar & Allen, 1981).

Early reviews of the validity of interviews for predicting performance were not supportive (Wagner, 1949). Upward of 80 studies led Mayfield (1964) to conclude that mainly intelligence could be satisfactorily predicted from an interview. However, subsequent improvements in the interview process, especially when combined with other personnel procedures, have revealed that interviews, properly designed, can be valid and useful. Wiesner and Cronshaw (1988) completed a meta-analysis of 150 reported efforts to validate the interview. *Structured interviews* produced validity coefficients twice as high, on average, as *unstructured interviews*. In the structured interview, the interview proceeded in an orderly manner and was programmed with specific areas to probe, and specific questions to be answered and recorded.

Huse (1962) compared the ratings made by interviewers of 107 managers in 37 firms and the ratings of the same managers by the managers' superiors. Consistent with Mayfield's findings, the interviewers' and superiors' ratings of the intellectual capacity of the managers correlated .26. But they also correlated on various other aspects as well: leadership, .38; creativeness, .27; and overall effectiveness, .16. When the interviewers' leadership judgments were combined with the results of projective and objective tests, the multiple prediction of the superiors' ratings of the managers' leadership reached .44. Likewise, 20 experienced supervisors who were rated as highly effective by their superiors were matched by Glaser, Schwartz, and Flanagan (1958) with 20 less effective supervisors of similar experience, age, and scores on a paper-and-pencil test. The judgments combined with the test scores correlated .34 with discriminating between more effective and less effective supervisors. The results of the interview added to the accuracy of the discrimination. Similarly, Howard and Bray (1988) reported that interviews with assessment center candidates, assessed 20 years earlier, could detect a number of attributes of consequence to the managers' success at AT&T.

They found a correlation of .30 between the interviewers' judgments of the interviewees' range of interests and the managerial level attained by the assessees 20 years later. The interviewers' judgments of the assessees' need for advancement correlated .44 with the level attained by the assessees 20 years later.[3]

Careful attention to the job requirements of the position for which candidates are being considered and the use of multiple trained interviewers appear to make a difference in the validity of the interview. Russell (1978) arranged for five trained interviewers to assess 66 senior manager candidates in a Fortune 500 firm for positions as general managers. The candidates were assessed on nine dimensions generated by a focus group to describe the task and process responsibilities of the desired positions. Accomplishments, disappointments, and developmental activities were discussed in the interviews. The interviewers prepared a report on the candidates for discussion at a meeting to reach consensual decisions about the candidates' readiness for promotion to the positions and the candidates' developmental needs. The consensual judgments of understanding, analyzing, and setting direction for a business correlated .32 with the bonuses that were awarded, .26 with the quality of the candidates' relations with customers and other outsiders, and .23 with staffing performance. The pooled interview judgments of organizational acumen (understanding of the corporate environment to achieve both individual and unit objectives) also correlated .36 with superiors' appraisals of the candidates' nonfiscal performance. In another vein, Herriot and Rothwell (1983) found that the judgments of recruiters, based on their interviews with graduating students, added to the accuracy of predictions of the applicants' suitability above what was obtained from the applicants' résumés alone.

Other studies pointed to what was important in the interviews. For instance, Rasmussen (1984) observed that credentials listed on résumés and verbal behavior had more influence than nonverbal behavior on judgments of qualifications. Singer and Bruhns (1991) found, in an experiment comparing job selection interview scenarios,

---

[3]This research on the value of the interview for predicting managers' performance appeared in the context of its use in assessment centers. More will be said later about the validity of the interview for forecasting the subsequent performance of leaders when the validity and utility of assessment centers are examined.

that students' decisions gave more weight to academic qualifications, while managers emphasized work experience in their choices. Still other studies pointed to ways of improving the assessment of judgments from interviews. For example, Dipboye, Fontenelle, and Garner (1984) found that reading the candidate's application before the interview increased the amount of correct information collected during the interview. Huffcutt, Weekley, J. A. Weisner, et al. (2001) showed that responses to interview questions about the actual past behavior of interviewees were more predictive of subsequent job performance than questions about how the candidate would respond to a hypothetical job situation. Having the interviewee describe his or her past behavior generated more information about the interviewee. Long-term memory, needed to select alternatives to a hypothetical problem, was less informative.

Virtual Interviews. Straus, Miles, and Levesque (2001) arranged for 59 MBA students to serve as simulated job applicants for interviews by video, by telephone, and face-to-face (FTF) with interviewers. Interviewers assessed "applicants" more favorably by telephone than FTF, particularly if the applicants were less physically attractive. Interviewers had more difficulty regulating and understanding discussions by video than FTF, and applicants were less favorable to video interviewing.

Career Path Appreciation Interviews. Zaccaro (1996) summarized research studies about these two-hour sessions to assess an interviewee's conceptual capacity. The scores predicted insight, self-confidence, creativity, intuitive thinking, innovative-adaptive thinking, breadth of perspective, skill in strategic thinking, ability to handle ambiguity, ability to work simultaneously on several projects, military officer potential, and attained level of management.

Objective Tests. We have described aptitude, attitude, personality tests, and behavioral inventories of individual differences that have been found predictive of current and future leadership performance combined. With good judgment, these criteria can be used for assessment in the context of normative standards. Many objective tests use special keys to forecast leadership potential. Some generate scores that can be combined to optimize

predictions of performance for future leaders and managers. These methods will be discussed later.

Projective Tests. Responses to projective tests can also form the basis of valid judgments by trained clinicians. The relationship of Miner's sentence completion test to managerial performance was noted in Chapter 6. Huse (1962), for example, found that the results of projective tests correlated with the ratings of 107 managers by their superiors as follows: persuasiveness, .33; leadership, .26; overall effectiveness, .21; social skills, .18; planning, .18; creativeness, .17; intellectual capacity, .13; and motivation and energy, .03.

Judgments by Boards. It is centuries-old military and naval practice to have candidates appear before boards of officers to present their credentials and be interviewed, after which the combined judgments of the board members are used to decide whether to accept or reject the candidates for selection or promotion. Such boards are also used to screen teachers and managers in civil service systems. Selection committees are the rule rather than the exception for selecting faculty and administrators in colleges and universities. However, some of the processes that affect the decisions of such boards and committees are just beginning to be known.[4] For purposes of simulation, Day and Sessa (2001) created videotapes of four candidates differing in "hard" and "soft" skills. Hard skills are the concrete task-oriented skills contributing to handling the core technology of the organization. Soft skills are relations-oriented skills, leadership, and teamwork, as judged by inference. The candidates were finalists for president of a division of a medium-sized glass company. The candidates varied in negative attributions around an average of 21.5%, for leadership styles, competencies, decisiveness, vision, and experience. The tapes were viewed individually by 819 senior executives, who the next day were formed into 145 selection committees to achieve a consensus ranking of the four candidates during a 45-minute discussion. The committees significantly underreported candidates' strengths and overreported weaknesses. They reported more hard strengths and more soft weaknesses. Among key words for explanations of support for candidates were: teamwork (70%), leadership (66%), in-

---

[4] To be discussed later in the context of assessment centers.

ternational (65%), marketing (63%), visionary (56%), technological (44%), risk taking (32%), and interpersonal skills (23%). The more the respondents' explanations used these prototypical key words, the lower was the correlation with the average ranking of the candidates ($r = .31$).

Judgments from References, Recommendations, and Search Firms. The judgments of former superiors, colleagues, and acquaintances are routinely and almost universally used. Yet little has been published on their validity as predictors of success as leaders and managers. Illustrative of what is possible, however, was G. W. McLaughlin's (1971) predictions of the first year of success of cadets at West Point based on ratings about them by their high school teachers and coaches. Ratings of charisma (personal magnetism, bearing, and appearance) and situational behavior (moral and ethical values, cooperation and teamwork, common sense and judgment) were the best predictors of the cadets' leadership and followership performance during their first year at the academy. Athletic coaches and mathematics teachers provided the most valid ratings. References and recommendations about candidates from outside an organization have become more suspect and invalid due to the threat of lawsuits as sources increasingly avoid making accurate negative appraisals; recommenders have become legally responsible for their information.

Cox (1986) surveyed more than a thousand executives from 13 U.S. service, consumer, and business corporations. They appeared somewhat more favorable to executives nominated by a search firm than by their own corporation's personnel department.

Online versus Paper-and-Pencil Questionnaires. Traditional paper-and-pencil formats are being replaced by e-mail questionnaires sent via the Worldwide Web or via intranets, responses collected from raters in the same way. Large firms, with facilities at different locations, find the Web approach more efficient in a number of ways. In comparison to paper and pencil and regular mail, the Web reaches more respondents quickly, and response rates are increased, while costs, missing data, and turnaround time are reduced (Yost & Homer, 1998; Frame & Beatty, 2000). Of 12,111 PepsiCo managers in 40 countries who rated 4,063 managers, 69.4% chose to complete

the survey online; 30.6% chose mailing back paper *opscan* recommendations. The 87% choosing the Web actually completed the survey while 40% choosing paper did not. There was little difference in the overall outcomes, although the Web users skipped more items and paper users marked "Don't know" more frequently. Online users provided more comments on developmental needs than did paper users (Church, 2002). Richmond, Keisler, Weisband, et al. (1999) completed a meta-analysis that showed hardly any difference between Web and paper in the effect of social desirability. After controlling for rater and ratee characteristics, Smither and Walker (2002) obtained no difference in results from paper and intranet arrangements.

Donovan, Drasgow, and Probst (2000) found that computerization did not affect item or test functioning. Stanton (1998) reported similar results for several tests of fairness. The Web is an obvious facilitator of 360-degree ratings, multiple raters, and feedback for development. Yet despite the advantages of using the Web for development, it also has problems. Everyone involved needs to have access to a computer. Addresses may be wrong. Poor page design and format can frustrate raters. Security must be provided so that only the correct raters are able to enter the system and ensure that the correct ratees are included. And results need to be transmitted to those with a need to know, for development or personnel decision purposes (Summers & Fleenor, 1998).

Measurement Equivalence. Measurements are equivalent among multiple raters rating the same ratees if they produce the same confirmatory factor patterns and factor loadings (Cheung, 1999). Web and paper measures have equal scale reliabilities and equal construct validities (King & Miles, 1995). Equivalence was found for Web and paper surveys across four of five countries (Spera & Moye, 2001). Smither and Walker (2003) found at first that the upward ratings of 789 employees who used an intranet rather than paper and pencil were more favorable, but equivalence between raters appeared when the results were controlled for rater and ratee characteristics.

Lack of equivalence between sources of ratings may occur for many reasons: (1) differences in raters biases (Harris & Schaubroack, 1988); (2) self-serving and felt need for self-enhancement (Fahr & Dobbins, 1989a); (3) opportunities to observe different behavior (Landy &

Farr, 1980; Murphy & Cleveland, 1995); (4) differences in concerns and social comparison information at different organizational levels (Fahr & Dobbins, 1989b); (5) differences in understanding the scale items; (6) ratees' different behavior around different raters; (7) different experiences or training with the scales or format (Diefendorff & Silverman, 2001); (8) different models of effectiveness (Facteau & Smith, 2000); (9) the importance attributed to some roles rather than to others (Tsui & Ohlott, 1988); (10) the inclusion, importance, and weighting of some dimensions rather than others (Campbell & Lee, 1988; Facteau & Smith, 2000); (11) the manager's need to meet the expectations of different ratees (Tsui, 1984).

Repertory Grid. This method of appraisal was developed by an American clinical psychologist, George Kelly, in 1955. Since 1980, in Britain, it has become a general approach to appraising team members by comparing them on elements designated by the rater, along with a paired member judged to be most opposite to the first. A grid can be formed showing the pattern for each ratee on each element. There are many variations of the method that can be used to appraise individuals, groups, and systems (Easterby-Smith, Thorpe, & Holman (1996).

Classification and Narrative Description. Here the information obtained mechanically from tests and measures is combined into a display, summarized into a categorical type by its pattern, or reported in a narrative. From these displays, categorizations or narratives—judgments about the potential or performance of leaders—can be made. For instance, the results of the Myers-Briggs test are arranged to sort examinees into various combinations of sensors, feelers, thinkers, and judges; then the different types are related to the managers' and leaders' performance (McCaulley, 1989).

The individual examinee's capacity, interest, and personality scores are typically categorized, profiled, or converted into narratives. The scores are shown in contrast to norms for the individual's class, organization, occupation, and so on. Then judgments are made based on the profiles. For example, Dicken and Black (1965) administered a test battery to candidates for promotion. The battery included the Otis Quick Scoring Mental Ability Test, the Strong Vocational Interest Blank, the Minnesota Multiphasic Personality Inventory, and other measures of aptitude and knowledge. Narrative reports of about 500 words were written for each candidate based on the results. After reading the reports, four psychologists rated each candidate on effective intelligence, personal soundness, drive and ambition, leadership and dominance, likableness, responsibility and conscientiousness, ability to cooperate, and overall potential. Three to seven years later, officials from the two firms in which the examinees worked rated them on the same variables. The median correlations between the psychologists' and the officials' follow-up ratings were .38 and .33 in the two firms.

In similar fashion, Albrecht, Glaser, and Marks (1964) had three psychologists rank the potential of 31 prospective district marketing managers in budgeting effectiveness, sales performance, interpersonal relationships, and overall. Their rankings were clinical judgments based on combining objective and projective test results, as well as results from an interview and a personal history form. Although the test scores alone correlated .20, on average, with subsequent success as a manager, the psychologists' predictions, based on the combined results of tests, interviews, and personal history, correlated between .43 and .58 with the managers' subsequent job performance. When tests, interviews, and personal history are combined in this way with individual and small group exercises to make integrated judgments, the total illustrates what can be accomplished in an assessment center.

Mechanical Methods of Combining Assessments

Objective tests provide samples or signs of individual differences in cognition and behavior related to leadership that aim to predict leaders' subsequent performance. Responses to the test items are unit-weighted rather than differentially weighted when they are totaled to form a score, since identical results will be obtained when more than four or five items are to be summed (Gulliksen, 1950). Keys are developed to score those items that correlate with emergent, successful, or effective leadership.

Special Keys. It has often been possible to develop an especially cross-validated key for the Strong Campbell Vocational Interest Blank to discriminate among those who subsequently achieve more success as leaders in their organizations. The inventory is examined item by item (Laurent, 1968). This takes advantage of the extent to which values and interests are important to success as a leader. For example, Harrell and Harrell (1975) developed such a key with the Strong Campbell for predicting high- and low-earning managers among MBAs from Stanford University five years after graduation. They also keyed responses to the Guilford-Zimmerman Personality Inventory and a survey of personal history in the same way. The total high earners key predicted earnings of the graduates at 5, 10, 15, and 20 years after graduation. The correlations were .52, .39, .33 and .44, respectively (Harrell & Harrell, 1984). For 443 Exxon managers, a key was developed from answers to the Guilford-Zimmerman Temperament Survey that correlated .31 with their success, as measured by their salaries adjusted for their age, education, seniority, and function. The key correlated .23 with their effectiveness as ranked by their superiors (Laurent, 1968).

Goodstein and Schrader (1963) developed a managerial potential key using the items of the California Psychological Inventory (CPI), a collection of personality items. The items included in the key that were found valid in differentiating managers from nonmanagers were consistent with much of what was said in earlier chapters about the personality requirements for successful leadership. The items were about masculinity, need for achievement, dominance, status, self-acceptance, and tolerance. In support, Rawls and Rawls (1968) compared 30 high-rated executives with 30 low-rated utilities executives using the CPI. High-rated executives scored higher than low-rated executives in dominance, status, sociability, and self-acceptance. Subsequently, the 206 items of the key were reduced to 34 by Gough (1984) in a study evaluating the items against measures of the success of military officers and bank managers. The reduced management potential key correlated .88 and .89 with Goodstein and Schrader's much longer version. The most positive items in the revised management potential scale were also consistent with the discussions in earlier chapters. They dealt with optimism about the future, ability to create a good impression, interpersonal effectiveness, self-confidence, relative freedom from instability and conflict, and realism in thinking and social behavior. Gough (1984) also reported considerable consistency between the keyed management potential

scores and descriptions of the respondents by their fellow college students, by their spouses, and by assessment staffs.

Scored Application and Biodata Blanks. Responses to standardized operational questions on application blanks and biographical information blanks can be similarly keyed to forecast leadership and management performance. The blanks may focus on personal characteristics, events, and experiences at work, school, and home. Kirkpatrick (1960, 1966) constructed such a key from an 11-page biographical questionnaire. The key was constructed to sort out above-average, average, and below-average chamber of commerce executives. A five-year follow-up study demonstrated the ability of the key to discriminate 80 high-salary from 81 low-salary managers matched in age and the size of their employing organizations. Along with higher salaries, as evidence of greater success as an executive, it was observed that the higher-salaried executives were more likely to place a heavy emphasis on their careers, participate actively in community affairs, and enjoy excellent health. Again, the items that formed the key and discriminated more successful from less successful executives of the chamber of commerce were consistent with general findings about the antecedents and concomitants of successful leadership discussed earlier. According to the key, the more successful chamber of commerce executives: (1) came from a middle-class background; (2) had spent a happy childhood in a stable family; (3) had received a good education; (4) had engaged in many extracurricular activities in high school and college; (5) had held leadership positions in many of the organizations to which they belonged; (6) displayed communication skills in debating, dramatics, and editorial work.

A similar type of key, developed for scoring the biographical information blanks of 443 Exxon managers, correlated above .50 with their success and above .30 with their ranked effectiveness (Laurent, 1968). Drakeley and Herriot (1988) used data from 41 scorable items of a biographical inventory completed by 420 officers of the British Royal Navy and then cross-validated on a further sample of 282 officers. Three separate keys could be constructed to predict ratings for professional performance, leadership, and commitment. When cross-validated, the professional performance key correlated .50 with appraised professional performance; the leadership key correlated .20 with appraised leadership; and the commitment key correlated .24 with remaining in the program. Russell and Domm (2007) found four factors for 748 cases in responses to biodata questions (1) problems and negative toning; example: "How often have you found yourself making assumptions about other people only to find out you were very wrong?"; (2) dealing with groups or information; example: "How often have you been part of a team or group that developed team spirit?"; (3) focused work efforts; example: "How often have you felt involved and constantly 'on the go' in your job?"; (4) rules and regulations; example: "Have you ever had to participate on a jury that actually deliberated some decision in a court of law?"

A promising biodata blank variant is one that emphasizes past accomplishments. The Accomplishment Record developed and validated by Hough (1984) correlated with subsequent job success (Hough, Keyes, & Dunnette, 1983). Biographical information—generated from retrospective life history essays primarily about past accomplishments and completed by first-year Annapolis midshipmen—was used to develop a biodata questionnaire of life history events. In constructing this questionnaire, Kuhnert and Russell (1990) were guided by Kegan's (1982) six stages of constructive development, from the reflexivity and impulsivity of immaturity to interpersonal maturity and interindividuality. They suggested that the answers to the questions could help to explain the meanings that leaders derive from their life experiences. A total of 917 midshipmen who were entering Annapolis completed a scored and keyed biodata questionnaire. The biodata scales predicted, in cross-validation, subsequent military performance, academic performance, and peer ratings of leadership at the U.S. Naval Academy (Russell, Mattson, Devlin, et al., 1986; Stricker, 1987). Russell (1990) assessed previous life experiences of 66 candidates for a position of division general manager in a Fortune 50 multinational firm and suggested that the assessments could contribute to senior managers' performance.

Data from Small-Group Exercises. Small-group exercises also generate objective leadership results that can be mechanically correlated with the future performance of leaders or managers. For example, in Bass, Burger, et al.'s (1979)[5] large-scale study of managers from 12 national clusters, Exercise Life Goals was administered to 3,082 managers who were above or below the median in their own rate of advancement. In this exercise, the managers had to rank the importance to themselves of 11 life goals. The *high flyers*, managers who had advanced more rapidly in their careers, attached more importance to leadership, expertise, prestige, and duty, whereas the slower-climbing managers favored self-realization, affection, security, and pleasure.

In a small-group budgeting exercise, the high flyers in all 12 nations studied were more cautious about allocating funds for safety, labor relations, management development, research and development, and controlling water pollution. Nevertheless, in another small-group exercise that asked for recommendations about salary increases, the high flyers granted larger increases than the slow-track managers. In Exercise Supervise, the high flyers gave more weight to the importance of generosity, honesty, and fair-mindedness.

In other small-group exercises, fast-track, compared with slow-track, managers rated themselves higher in self-understanding and preference for being more task-oriented. They also saw themselves as interpersonally competent. In addition, the high flyers revealed more objective signs of effective intelligence, objectivity, proactivity, and long-term views. They were more accurate and slower in a two-way communication exercise. Many other objective signs obtained from the exercises differentiating fast-track from slow-track managers were country-specific.

Rank and Salary Information. To assess managers' success, Farrow, Valenzi, and Bass (1982) used salary information to compare 159 managers' predicted salary grade and actual salary grade, arguing that salaries reflected managerial merit. To predict expected salary grade, the multiple regression equation was as follows: $.56 \times$ (starting salary grade level) $+ 1.24 \times$ (years of service) $+ .041 \times$ (department size) $- .93$ (male) $+ .472 \times$ (educational level). Overachievement was seen if a manager's actual salary grade was higher than predicted; underachievement, when actual salary grade was lower than predicted.

[5] Detailed in Chapter 33.

Multiple Cutoffs, Unit Weighting, and Optimal Weighting

When multiple cutoffs are employed, only applicants or candidates whose scores on selected tests are above a certain level are accepted; all other applicants are rejected. When scores are unit-weighted, they are merely added together in a combined prediction—the scores need to be standardized with means of 0 and standard deviations of 1 to give them equal weighting if they are added together to form a single prediction. Such standardized scores can be differentially weighted on the basis of a multiple regression equation or can be accepted or rejected for inclusion, as well as differentially weighted, by a stepwise regression process to optimize the prediction of effectiveness.

Multiple Cutoffs. Mahoney, Sorenson, Jerdee, and Nash (1963) administered the Wonderlic Intelligence Test, an empathy test, the Strong Vocational Interest Blank, the CPI, and a personal history questionnaire to 468 managers from 13 Minnesota-based firms. Panels of executives ranked the examinees on global, or overall, effectiveness in carrying out their functions as managers. For half the sample, the ability of each of the 98 measures from the test battery was analyzed to discriminate between the top and bottom thirds of the managers in ranked effectiveness. These managers were grouped into six discriminating clusters. One cluster that separated effective from ineffective managers rated them on whether, or not they had the interests of a sales manager, a purchasing agent, and the president of a manufacturing firm. The second cluster dealt with their lack of interest in dentistry, printing, and farming. A high score on the intelligence test and self-rated dominance on the CPI formed the bases of the third and fourth clusters. One's educational level and one's spouse's educational level and type of work were in the fifth cluster. Engagement in many sports and hobbies, offices held, and high school memberships were the sixth cluster. An optimum cutoff was determined for deciding whether a manager "passed" or "failed" each cluster. To be predicted "acceptable," a manager had to score above the cutoff point for five of the six clusters. For example, an acceptable manager was one scoring above the cutoffs in the interests of a sales manager, intelligence, dominance, education, and extracurricular activities.

The other half of the sample was held out for cross-validation. The same multiple cutoffs were used; 45.5% of the managers in the cross-validation sample were accepted and 54.5% were rejected. Of those who were accepted, 62% had been ranked high in effectiveness on the job and 29% had been ranked low. But of those who were rejected, only 38% had been ranked high in effectiveness while 71% had been ranked low.

Unit Weighting. Campbell, Dunnette, Lawler, et al. (1970) reviewed studies of the value of various measures that are usually included in test batteries—such as intelligence, interests, personality, and biographical information—for predicting leadership and management potential in designated locations. Salaries of supervisors and executives, adjusted for length of service and age, were predicted with correlations above .20 at Minneapolis Gas on scale scores of 15 to 18 (Jurgensen, 1966). The promotability of managers at Jewel Tea (Meyer, 1963) and sales managers at the American Oil Company (Albright, 1966) could similarly be predicted. But mixed results were reported by Tenopyr and Ruch (1965) for various technical managers at North American Aviation.

Selover (1982) combined into a single advancement potential score five measures obtained from newly hired personnel at Prudential Insurance that had been found to predict the rate of advancement four to five years later. Correlations ranging from .35 to .40 were found between the advancement potential scores, similarly derived, and the rate of advancement in three additional samples of newly hired employees. Ghiselli (1971) identified 13 traits of managerial talent and developed a questionnaire, the Self Description Inventory, to measure them. He then related the scores on the 13 traits to supervisors' ratings of effectiveness. Ten of the 13 scores related significantly to the criteria. These predictive scores dealt with supervisory ability, the need for occupational status, intelligence, self-actualization, self-assurance, decisiveness, and lack of the need for security. These scores could then be combined into a single score.

Basically negative conclusions about the value of tests and biographical information for predicting general success as a manager were reached by Brenner (1963) at Lockheed Aircraft. But with managers in the same company, Flanagan and Krug (1964) showed that it was necessary to differentiate between whether one was trying to predict success and effectiveness in supervision, creativity, organization, research, engineering, or sales. For each, a differently weighted optimization was required.

Multiple Regression: Optimal Weighting of Predictions

An illustration of the use of optimal weighting was created by Atwater and Yammarino (1997), who obtained a stepwise multiple regression coefficient of .53 when predicting the perceived transformational leadership of squad leaders of USNA plebes in summer camp from eight personal measures. The highest standardized beta weights were for engagement in varsity sports, .31; MBTI thinking/feeling, −.21; and intelligence, .22. The use of stepwise multiple regression for predicting performance has become a common practice, as research is directed not only at optimal weighting of the predictors but also optimizing the number of predictors.

Sears Program. The Sears program for predicting managerial performance extended over a period of 35 years. The test battery that evolved tapped intellectual abilities, personality, values, and interests. Its results predicted the promotability of executives and the satisfaction of subordinates with operating efficiency, relationships, and their own personal satisfactions. Multiple regression

was used to weight the test scores optimally to minimize the errors of the predictions. Illustrative are the results for 48 store managers and 42 higher-level managers, shown in Table 35.1.

The Sears battery of psychological tests for predicting executives' performance included measures to tap flexible intellectual functioning by using the Sears adaptation of the California F Scale of authoritarianism. The battery included a number of tests constructed to measure creative ingenuity and ability to initiate change, tests for preference for complexity, a scored biographical history form, an adjective checklist, a verbal fluency test, and a self-rating of role definition.

To assess administrative skill and decision making, Sears devised a special in-basket test, along with two leaderless group problem-solving situations. In addition, three problem-solving simulations were designed. The Guilford Martin Personality Inventory was specially modified to measure emotional stability and competitive drive. The multiple correlation of the combination of predictor measures with various criteria, such as superiors' ratings, ranged from .49 to above .80.

The Thurstone Test of Mental Ability, the Guilford Martin Personality Inventory, the Allport Vernon Study of Values, and the Kuder Interest Inventory were used to

Table 35.1 Multiple Correlations between Scores for the Morale of Sears Employees and Scores on the Test Battery for Executives Who Were Responsible for Supervising the Employees

Areas of Employee Morale	Multiple Correlations with Executive Test Battery Scores[a]	
	48 Store Managers	*42 Executives*
I. Operating Efficiency		
a. Effectiveness of administration	.77	.51
b. Technical competence of supervision	.74	.43
c. Adequacy of communication	.59	.61
II. Personal Relations		
a. Supervisor-employee relations	.68	.54
b. Confidence in management	.59	.52
III. Individual Satisfactions		
a. Status and recognition	.69	.62
b. Identification with the company	.51	.52
IV. Job and Conditions of Work		
a. Working conditions	.36	.40
b. Overall morale score	.47	.54

[a]All correlations are significant at the 1 or 5 percent level of confidence.

Source: Adapted from Bentz (1968, p. 71).

predict success as a Sears purchasing manager. Multiple correlations ranging from .32 to .57 were obtained against various criteria of job performance and management potential. A similar battery for predicting the long-term performance of managers of Sears stores yielded measures that correlated from .37 to .61 when optimally combined (Bentz, 1983, 1987, 1992).

EIMP. Exxon's Early Identification of Management Potential (EIMP) is another prominent effort to use multiple regression to optimize the prediction of managers' success from a battery of predictors. The combination of tests includes the Miller Analogies Test, the Strong Vocational Interest Inventory, the Guilford-Zimmerman Temperament Inventory, and a specially keyed and scored biographical information blank (Laurent, 1968). In the United States, the multiple predictions correlated between .33 and .64 with managers' success (salary adjusted for age, seniority, and function). In Norway, Denmark, and the Netherlands, the comparable multiple correlations ranged from .27 to .65 (Laurent, 1970). A multiple correlation of .70 was obtained in predicting performance appraisals from the EIMP battery.

Similar correlations were obtained in predicting examinees' subsequent overall managerial effectiveness, according to their rankings by higher-level executives. For predicting managerial effectiveness, the multiple correlations ranged from .37 for managers in oil exploration and production to .66 for managers in traffic and purchasing. The multiple correlations predicted success as a manager (suitably adjusted for education, seniority, and function), from .67 for marketing managers to .82 for employee relations managers. The predictive validity of the EIMP battery appeared to increase steadily with the years between testing and the measurement of the criteria during 3- to 12-year follow-ups. Sparks (1989, 1992) attributed the increase to improvements in the criteria of managerial effectiveness. He inferred that the EIMP measures of reasoning, judgment, and temperament contribute more to predicting performance at higher levels of management.

A derivative of the EIMP battery is the Manager Profile Record (MPR), based on the biographical data, the keyed Guilford Zimmerman Temperament Inventory, and other tested judgmental elements. The MPR makes use of computer scanning, scoring, and output of results.

Its measures include: (1) academic and extracurricular achievements, self-worthiness, and social and work orientation; and (2) judging typical management situations either needing solutions or calling for value judgments about staff communication, employee motivation and development, and decision-making style. Different scoring was provided for younger inexperienced candidates and for older, more experienced candidates. The profile indicated the similarity of the candidate to highly successful managers. It could be used to validate predictions specific to an organization. It excluded traditional intelligence and reasoning-ability tests of concern to civil rights agencies. New item analyses and new validations were completed for the MPR against criteria for the level of responsibility attained by more than 15,000 managers in a variety of industries. Rated potential job level attainable correlated .52 with the MPR total scores. The same correlations ranged from .50 for 86 administrative staff to .70 for 90 manufacturing personnel. In subsequent validation studies, rank and/or salary already achieved were correlated similarly with the MPR total scores of 446 managers and supervisors in a steelworks, 310 in a coal company, 2,205 in a baked goods firm, 361 in an urban utility firm, 592 in a national insurance company, 221 in an office equipment manufacturer, 478 in two chemical-processing firms, 416 in a hotel chain, and 4,856 managers and professionals in 14 southwestern banks. The work was repeated for first-level supervisors across a variety of situations, from utilities plants to data-processing offices. Validations for 8,765 first-level supervisors yielded correlations ranging from .25 to .37 between the derived Supervisory Profile Record and supervisors' appraisal on job performance as meeting or exceeding the requirements of the job[6] (Richardson, Bellows, Henry, & Company, undated).

A set of multiple regression predictions was developed by Saville (1984) for the Occupational Personality Questionnaire (OPQ) to measure the potential for a variety of different team roles and leader/subordinate types of roles. The output was standardized against a norm group of 527 British managers and professionals. Meaningful correlations were found between supervisors' appraisals of the

---

[6]Drawn from the manuals and Technical Reports 1, 2, and 3 for the Manager Profile Record and the Supervisory Profile Record of Richardson, Bellows & Henry Company. Although by no means identical, similar results were obtained in different functional areas.

performance of 440 British managers and OPQ predictive scores. For instance, a score on persuasiveness, extracted from optimally weighted scoring of the OPQ results, as predicted, correlated .27 with being appraised as having a commercial flair and .28 with being appraised as a good negotiator.

Benchmarks. A product of the Center for Creative Leadership, Benchmarks is a 360-degree appraisal whose multiple scales in combination can predict managers' performance. Managers are rated 360 degrees to form 16 positive scores about resourcefulness, being a quick study, doing whatever it takes, and leading subordinates. Additionally, six negative scores are included, such as difficulty molding a staff, difficulty making strategic transitions, and lack of follow-through. For 336 managers, an optimally weighted multiple regression accounted for 46% of the variance in bosses' ratings of the managers (McCaulley & Lombardo, 1990).

Specifications Equations. If we have the multiple regressions for predicting a criterion of leadership performance from a set of factored ratings or test scores, and for predicting the same criterion from scores based on situational variables, we can develop a specification equation for predicting the leadership criterion from the beta weights of predictors X, Y, Z. The specification equation is given by the sum of the products of every situational beta weight with the standardized rating or test score (means of zero and standard deviations of 1). For each individual case, the specification provides the best possible prediction of the criterion of leadership performance. Cattell (1980) provided specification equations for the Sixteen Personality Factor Questionnaire (16 PF) of 16 traits and various situations and Saville (1984) for occupational profiles.

Moderators of Judgments and Their Predictive Validity

Moderators are analogous to Einstein's theory that gravity is a phenomenon due to the warping of space around stars, planets, and moons. Newton's laws have to be moderated to predict more accurately the force of gravitational attraction between them.

Some of the moderating conditions are primarily associated with the rater, some with the ratee, and some with both. Some methods are moderators. Waldman, Yammarino, and Avolio (1990) completed a WABA analysis of 140 managers in a large mining company paired with their immediate bosses. They were imbedded in 39 work groups. Individual differences were common in the various types of performance and skill ratings received by the managers. Their bosses varied in the average ratings they assigned to the managers. The dyadic matches were also of consequence.

Personal Moderating Conditions

Rater's Training and Competence. The effects of rater training to produce more reliability and validity of the ratings and greater agreement among raters are well known. A rater of leaders needs perceptive skills, cognitive ability, and reflective thinking to make good judgments. This can be helped by the quality of the cues provided by the rating method and the research that has been completed to develop the procedure. Global assessments that are based on broad aspects of performance and can be used to make explicit comparisons between ratees provide the greatest differential accuracy, but more priming of the rater may be needed to provide for useful diagnostic feedback (Blake & Goffin, 2001).

Biases in Perceptions and Ratings. Both predictions and criteria of success are often subjective managerial ratings and assessments. Expectations bias ratings. When rating others, people tend to confirm rather than disconfirm their expectations (Copeland, 1993). In addition, ratings are biased by the effects of leniency, response set, halo effects, and implicit theories of leadership (Bass & Avolio, 1989). Starbucks and Mezias (1996) reviewed other distortions in management perceptions. For instance, correlations were close to zero between managers' perceptions of the uncertainties in their business environments and the objective volatility of the environment as measured by financial reports and industry statistics (Tosi, Aldeg, & Story, 1973; Downey, Hellriegel, & Slocum, 1975). Payne and Pugh (1976) found little agreement among managers describing their own organizations. Subsequent studies led Starbuck and Mezias to conclude that average senior managers' judgments about their firms' performance could be accurate, but their individual judgments varied greatly (Sutcliffe, 1994). Salam, Cox, and Sims (1997) found that leaders who were rated as challenging the status quo and encouraging their subordinates to act independently were rated lower by their superiors and higher by their subordinates. The fairness seen by ratees of the performance appraisal and feedback system was greater when the ratees felt they could voice their opinions about it (Cawley, Keeping, & Levy, 1998; Folger & Cropanzano, 1988). When 208 employees responded in a survey about the voice they had in an appraisal system ("I felt I could have influenced the review discussion"), those impressions correlated .59 with perceived accuracy, .43 with perceived utility, .52 with procedural justice, and .59 with satisfaction with the system (Keeping, Brown, Scott, et al., 2003).

Feedback to leaders and managers of subordinates' average judgments about performance can be misleading because they mask large differences among the subordinates' judgments. The subordinates may not be, for example, able to discriminate between a manager's personal idiosyncrasies and the requirements of the manager's role (Herold, Fields, & Hyatt, 1993).

Raters' Age. Benchmarks were completed by superiors, peers, subordinates, and self for more than 2,000 focal managers. While favorable superiors' and self-ratings by the managers increased with age, subordinates' and peers' ratings did not. Brutus, McCaully, and Fleenor (1996) offered several explanations, but the most plausible one was that managers behave differently toward their superiors than toward others and have a better rapport with them. Also, managers may engage in more impression management with their superiors than with peers and subordinates.

Raters' Choose Raters. When leaders select those who are to rate them, the results are likely to be inflated. For instance, the norms for the Multifactor Leadership Questionnaire ratings when raters are selected by ratees are likely to be one point higher on a five-point scale of the transformational and contingent reward factor scores (Avolio & Bass, 2004). At the same time, O'Leary, Harkom, et al. (2003) reported that moderate positive correlations of .30 to .53 were found between ratee-selected and nonselected raters of the performance of 96 professional education students.

Confidence in the Ratings. Harper, Maurer, and Tross (1988) examined the 360-degree ratings of 1,852 aggregations of raters evaluating the teamwork, character, learning, vision, and leadership skills of 463 leaders. Raters also indicated their confidence in the accuracy of their ratings. More confident supervisors and more confident self-raters were slightly more likely to connect teamwork and character with leadership skills. More confident peers added vision to the prediction of leadership. Gabris and Ihrke (2001) showed that the job satisfaction of 134 professional county government employees was related to the perceived fairness and validity of the performance appraisals they received.

Moderating Conditions

Ratees' Early Career Experience. Berlew and Hall (1966) showed that the degree of first-year challenge sensed by managers added to the prediction of their subsequent success. Within an Exxon U.S. subsidiary, Vicino and Bass (1978) showed that the accuracy of the predictions could be substantially enhanced by adding attending information about what happened subsequently to 140 newly hired managers. Six years after employment, the managers were more successful and effective than predicted by the EIMP battery if they (1) had initially been assigned to a supervisor with influence "upstairs"; (2) had a personality different from that of their first supervisor; (3) were more satisfied with the challenges of their first task; (4) were under less stress in the two years before their measured success and effectiveness.

Ratees' Motivation and Needs. Ghiselli (1968a) reported results demonstrating that motivational factors interacted with personality traits that were predictive of managers' job success. The need for job security was the strongest and the need for power was the weakest moderator in producing interactions between traits and success. Thus, whether managers had a low or a high need for security affected the extent to which their assertiveness correlated with their success as managers. In the same way, whether a score showing a high need or power forecast success as a leader depended on whether it was coupled with a strong sense of responsibility (Winter, 1989).

Ratees' Seniority. Although Moore (1981) found that it did not matter whether librarians came to their assignments as a first or second career choice, the librarians' patterns of personality and leadership were closer to norms for the general population than they had been 20 years earlier. Similarly, when Harrell and Harrell (1984) applied stepwise regression equations to ability and personality predictions of the success of MBAs from Stanford University in achieving high salaries 5, 10, 15, and 20 years after graduation, different predictors emerged. For example, high earnings at the end of five years were predicted by orientation to high earnings, but after 20 years, the best combination of predictors of high earnings from the measures obtained 20 years earlier were youth, interest in sales management, a projective measure of the need for power, and a scored background survey that was favorable.

Age. Baltes and Staudinger (1993) noted that aging into older adult years modifies the relations between intelligence and leadership effectiveness. On the one hand, there is a decline in mental fluid mechanics. Leadership tasks depending on speed of reaction, processes of sensory information input, visual and motor memory, and processes of discrimination, categorization, and coordination decline with aging. On the other hand, older age increases wisdom, good judgment, and advice on uncertain but important aspects of life, based on expert knowledge. Such expert knowledge includes factual knowledge about the fundamental pragmatics of life, the contexts and uncertainties of life and societal change, and the competing relativism of values, life goals, and moral absolutes. While much of the decline in fluid mechanics is heavily influenced by biology, expert wisdom is more a matter of cultural inheritance, cultural innovation, and facilitative experiences. The wise person is open to new facilitative experiences. Nevertheless, Irwin (1998) reported that when 915 members (30% women) of teams in a variety of U.S. firms rated each other on 31 behaviors, and sex, education, ethnicity and job level were controlled, older members were rated as less effective by their peers. They were also rated less effective as managers. However, those of high status in their own organizations

were rated more positively, as were women, especially black women. Peers also rated others as more effective if they had known them longer. According to Ferris, Yates, Gilmore, et al. (1985), age also influenced performance ratings of subordinates.

Sex and Race. The effects of sex and race of assessment center examinees may be of limited consequence in moderating predictive accuracy. Women do about as well as men when undergoing assessment, according to an analysis by Ritchie and Moses (1983) of the overall scores obtained by 1,097 female managers at AT&T. The assessment center's predictions for the progress of their careers at the end of seven years were as valid as those for male managers. Similar results for women and for men were reported by Moses and Boehm (1975) and for black women compared to white women (Huck & Bray, 1975). But, subsequently, a meta-analysis (to be discussed later) found that the predictive validity of assessment programs was higher when the percentage of women assessees was higher. A validity of .38 based on multiple correlations of the Exxon EIMP battery and managerial success was found for 67 black males; of .31, for 80 white females; and .53 for 685 white males (Sparks, 1989).

Coaching of Ratees. In a meta-analysis of 131 controlled studies of feedback, by DeNisi and Kluger (2000), coaching to accompany feedback to those working at tasks was beneficial to more favorable appraisals of ratees' subsequent performance. In a different circumstance, 213 candidates for promotion in city fire and police departments were coached prior to being interviewed. The coached and better-prepared candidates gave more organized responses to the interviewers, who judged them as being better in performance in the interview (Maurer, Solomon, Andrews, et al., 2001).

Personality of Ratees. McCarthy & Garavan (2003) found that among 520 managers in a large Irish firm who received 360-degree feedback, belief in procedural justice and lack of cynicism accounted for 51.3% of the variance in the extent to which they accepted the feedback.

Situational Moderating Conditions

Organization. A modifier of regression predictions is organizational purpose. Szilagyi and Schweiger (1984) pointed to the need to keep an organization's strategies in mind when trying to forecast the patterns of ability, personality, and experience that will best match candidates with the requirements of a job. Hambrick and Mason (1984) argued that an organization's character and performance and the particular personal attributes and experience of its senior managers will be correlated. The differential weights in multiple regression predictions of success in a rapidly growing organization are likely to be different from those in a mature or declining organization. The weights of predictors of success as a combat officer are likely to be different from the weights for optimizing the prediction of success as a garrison officer.

Feedback Environment. Feedback ratings may be moderated by an organization's business and human resource strategy. Firms with *prospector* strategies may place more of a premium on involved, innovative leadership; firms with *defender* strategies may focus more attention on inducements (Sivasubrahmanium & Kroeck, 1995). Employees who see a favorable feedback environment are more likely to use feedback from 360-degree ratings (Steelman & Levy, 2001).

DeNisi and Kluger (2000) concluded from a meta-analytic analysis of 131 evaluated controlled studies of feedback from 3,000 reports that 38% was harmful to performance rather than likely to improve it. The investigators assumed that attention was limited to gaps from feedback to standards. Little attention was paid where gaps were not present. Subsequent behavior was affected by this attention. They found that attention focused on task performance and resulted in improvement only if sufficient details for improvement were provided. Otherwise, the focus remained on the details of the feedback, not on improving performance. If multisource messages were in disagreement, more attention was focused on self-rating. If the feedback, particularly negative feedback, focused on the self and the self-concept rather than the task, performance suffered. Whether a ratee wants to work on a task or had to work on the task affected whether performance improved or declined with feedback. A goal-setting plan needed to be provided with feedback if

subsequent performance was to improve. As much as possible, information provided with feedback should be about improving performance and not about the relative performance of others, as the latter can increase anxiety and a decline in performance. Feedback may be more harmful than beneficial to people working on complex tasks.

Culture. Given the cultural specificity of some leadership phenomena, as seen in Chapter 33, as one moves from one culture and country to another, it is not surprising that culture moderates the relationship between performance appraisal procedures and effectiveness. When ratees in work units in countries with *individualistic* cultural norms are similar in personality to their peers, the peers' ratings predict the promotion of the ratees in work units, but in work units in countries with *collectivistic* norms, the supervisor's ratings predict the promotion (Schaubroeck & Lam, 2002).

Milliman, Nason, Lowe, et al. (1995) asked 237 South Koreans, 241 Taiwanese, 223 Japanese, and 144 Americans what purposes were served by performance appraisals. Most were managers, engineers, and professionals. Questionnaire items were about performance appraisal practices, performance appraisal effectiveness, organizational effectiveness, job satisfaction, and five possible purposes: pay, promotion, development, enabling subordinates to express themselves, and documentation of performance. LISREL analyses revealed, as expected, significant cultural differences in the relationships among the variables. In South Korea, only the purposes of documentation, promotion, and development were seen as contributing to appraisal effectiveness, which, in turn, contributed to organizational effectiveness and job satisfaction. In Japan, all five purposes contributed to appraisal effectiveness, which in turn related to organizational effectiveness and job satisfaction. In Taiwan, only documentation, pay, and development were seen to directly affect appraisal effectiveness and, indirectly, organizational effectiveness and job satisfaction. Finally, among Americans, a considerably different path model emerged. Documentation, promotion, and enabling subordinate expression were the chosen purposes. Appraisal effectiveness was positively related to job satisfaction but negatively related to organizational effectiveness.

Methods as Moderators

Criteria of Success. Obviously, how success is measured affects the differential weightings that optimize a multiple regression prediction of success. A majority of studies have depended on subjective evaluations of success as a leader provided by superiors and a higher authority. These evaluations may suffer from various sources of bias by raters, such as the halo effect and leniency. They may be subject to the quirks of memory and different raters' values.

Objective approaches to measuring success have also varied and, as a consequence, have led to different prediction results. At one extreme, as was noted in Chapter 4, many investigations before 1948 defined success as occupying a position of leadership, that is, holding an office or some position of responsibility. The level reached by a manager in an organization was often seen as an appropriate measure of success. This definition was improved by adjustments. Blake and Mouton (1964) used a managerial achievement quotient to evaluate the progress of managers' careers in a single organization; the level of the positions was corrected by the managers' chronological age: younger managers at higher organizational levels were seen as more successful than older managers at lower levels. Hall and Donnell (1979) modified the formula slightly. They continued to assume that regardless of the actual organization, managers worked in organizations of eight levels. To generate a realistic index number, they further assumed that all managers' careers are in eight-level organizations. Bass, Burger, et al. (1979) adjusted the quotient by dividing a manager's current level by the actual number of levels in the organization, then multiplying by the size of the organization. They argued that managers of larger organizations who are at the same place on their respective organizational ladders as managers of smaller organizations are more successful.

Another criterion of managers' success was the amount of salary or compensation earned (Harrell & Harrell, 1975). But the compensation had to be adjusted for age, function, experience, seniority, inflation, and other moderators when used to forecast managerial success (Farrow, Bass & Valenzi, 1977; Sparks, 1966). When performance quality was the main criterion of success, Deming (1986) argued, performance appraisal programs were detrimental to the quality of the performance because: (1) They

held the ratee responsible for mistakes that could be due to faults in the system; (2) When their rewards were contingent on appraisals, the employees were directed toward short-term targets and quotas; (3) Ratees who fell at the lower end of the distribution of the appraisals were discouraged from trying to excel. Ghorpede and Chen (1995) suggested that the performance appraisal system would contribute to performance quality if: (1) The primary purpose of performance appraisal was the improvement of the ratee; (2) Everyone affected by the appraisal system was involved in improving it; (3) Opportunities for improvement and reduction of systematic errors were examined; (4) The focus of the performance appraisal was on behavior using input and output for diagnosis and development of the ratee; (5) For each dimension of performance, both task accomplishment and task improvement were considered; (6) Absolute rather than relative standards of performance were used.

Single-Source Errors. Single-source bias arises when data are collected from one source or method about two or more variables, such as self-report survey questionnaires (D. T. Campbell & Fiske, 1959). The same leader provides a self-report of influence, X, and a rating of job satisfaction, Y. The correlation of X and Y will be inflated by single-source variance. Sometimes it cannot be helped, but a correction is needed. The correlation may reflect a generalized response set and form a general factor in a factor analysis whose effect can be subtracted. But new errors are then introduced (Kemery & Dunlap, 1996). Within-and-Between Analysis (WABA) may be used to determine and correct same-source variance and error in self-reports (Avolio, Bass, & Yammarino, 1988). Performance appraisal becomes overshadowed in the case of CEOs rated by biased compensation committees, which may award extremely high annual CEO compensation for continuously failing performance.

Assessment Centers

In the European tradition, the identification of potential leaders tended to make use of inferences based on observations, personality tests, and interviews. The assessment center fit readily with the European approach. As early as 1923, following experience in World War I, boards of psychologists and officers formed judgments of candidates for leadership positions in the German army from observing the candidates in a roundtable discussion and from other tests and methods (Simoneit, 1944). Comparable developments took place in Great Britain (Garforth, 1945). By the 1940s, the British had organized country house retreats for civil service and industrial candidates to meet with assessors. The candidates were then observed by psychologists and a management assessor in formal exercises and in informal interactions. The results provided valid assessments for choosing candidates (Vernon, 1948, 1950).

During World War II, the Office of Strategic Services (1948), the forerunner of the Central Intelligence Agency (CIA), created a similar assessment program for candidates for assignments as special agents and spies, based on the psychological theories of Henry Murray (1938). In addition to the usual testing, the candidates were systematically subjected to cognitive and physical group exercises, along with stress interviews. Decisions were made on the basis of the assessors' ratings, which were formed from their observations of the candidates' performance in the various exercises (Murray & MacKinnon, 1946). The interest in assessment programs generated the establishment, in 1949, of a civilian assessment center at the University of California, Berkeley (MacKinnon, 1960); at Standard Oil of Ohio (SOHIO) in 1953 (Finkle & Jones, 1970); at IBM (Kraut, 1972); at General Electric (Meyer, 1972); and at Sears (Bentz, 1971). The modern assessment center approach spread rapidly around the world (Thornton & Byham, 1982). But most prominent was the assessment center program launched in 1956 at AT&T as a long-term research study of the development of the managers' careers (Bray, Campbell, & Grant, 1974).

As MacKinnon (1975) noted, "assessment center" may refer to a physical facility, such as Berkeley's Institute of Personality Assessment Research; a standardized assessment program, such as SOHIO's Formal Assessment of Corporate Talent; or the bringing together of a group of candidates for assessment. By the end of the 1970s, several thousand centers and programs were in operation.

Methods

Ideally, the procedures and variables to be assessed in a particular assessment center should stem from an analysis of the requirements of the jobs for which the candidates are being considered. Assessment procedures to tap the identified dimensions that match these requirements should then follow (Thornton & Byham, 1982). Worbois (1975) selected 12 assessment variables in this way and predicted supervisory ratings of the subsequent performance of candidates with a correlation of .39. As noted in the preceding meta-analyses, specific dimensions of a candidate's current performance are harder to predict than the candidate's overall future performance or potential as a manager.

All the individual and group testing activities discussed so far in this chapter have been used in assessment centers and take from a half day to five days. These activities may include paper-and-pencil and projective tests of values, interests, and personality; tests of cognitive abilities and reading and writing skills; and observers' judgments of performance on in-basket tests, interviews, role-playing exercises, organizational simulations, work samples, and leaderless group discussions requiring cooperation or competition. What is special about the assessment center is its use of the pooled judgments of staff psychologists and managers from the organization who have been assigned as observers. The judgments are based on their observations of the candidates in action and the inferences they draw from the test results to reach consensual decisions about the leadership potential of each candidate. The observers also use consensus to predict each candidate's likely performance as a manager and other aspects of the candidate's future performance. From 10 to 52 variables, assumed to be related to managerial performance, may be judged and pooled by the team of observers in this way (Howard, 1974). According to a survey of assessment centers by Bender (1973), the typical center uses six assessors, including psychologists and managers at several levels above the candidates. Usually, candidates are processed in multiples of six, which is seen as an optimal number for interactions and observations. For example, 12 candidates at a time were processed by Macy's in interviews, group discussions, and in-basket tests. Six executives from top and middle management formed the assessment team (Anonymous, 1975). Unless the information is withheld to avoid contaminating follow-up research, feedback of the consensual judgments is given to candidates in most centers to contribute to the candidates' developmental efforts. Assessment centers have demonstrated moderate validities for predicting job performance and leadership potential.

Virtual Assessment Centers

The spread of firms nationally as well as globally has sparked the need for assessment of managers for development and promotion at a distance from each other, to enhance a firm's quality of management. The Internet makes it possible to administer simulations and batteries of individual and group tests to managers in different locations. Virtuality eliminates extensive travel time, costs, and absence from work. It realistically simulates real business challenges (Smith, Rogg, & Collins, 2001). The investigators described a virtual assessment center for 78 senior managers in a global organization, 39% based in the United States and 61% in Britain, France, Germany, and the Netherlands. The AON virtual assessment center simulated a work environment in which the candidate had to analyze problems, make decisions, take appropriate actions, and move issues forward with e-mails, voice mails, timed interruptions, and role plays. Also included in the assessments were a work accomplishment record, structured interviews, a 360-degree survey, and the 16 PF Questionnaire. Higher convergent validities were obtained from assessment constructs that were alike than from divergent validities obtained for constructs that were unalike.

Variables

Because of the prominence of the AT&T Management Progress Study and the availability of materials from Development Dimensions International (DDI) derived from it, the 25 variables deemed important for success at AT&T have been incorporated, as a whole or in part, into many assessment programs elsewhere. These variables are: general mental ability, oral and written communication skills, human relations skills, personal impact, perception of threshold social cues, creativity, self-objectivity, social objectivity, behavioral flexibility, need for the approval of superiors, need for the approval of peers, inner work standards, need for advancement, need for security, goal flexibility, primacy of work, value orientation, realism of expectations, tolerance of uncertainty, ability to delay gratification, resistance to stress, range of interests, energy, organization and planning, and decision making (Bray, Campbell, & Grant, 1974, pp. 19–20).

The 25 AT&T assessment variables were logically grouped into seven categories, as follows: (1) administrative skills—a good manager has the ability to organize work effectively and to make high-quality decisions; (2) interpersonal skills—a forceful personality makes a favorable impression on others with good oral skills; (3) intellectual ability—a good manager learns quickly and has a wide range of interests; (4) stability of performance—a good manager is consistent in his or her performance, even under stressful conditions or in an uncertain environment; (5) motivation to work—a good manager will find positive areas of satisfaction in life; he or she is concerned with doing a good job for its own sake; (6) career orientation—a good manager wants to advance quickly in the organization but is not as concerned about a secure job; the manager does not want to delay rewards for too long a time; (7) lack of dependence on others—a good manager is not as concerned about getting approval from superiors or peers and is unwilling to change his other life goals.

Administrative skills were found to be assessed best by a manager's performance on the in-basket test. An evaluation of interpersonal skills was procured from the observer teams' judgment of the manager's performance in group exercises. A measure of intellectual ability was reliably obtained from standardized general ability tests. A measure of stability of performance was acquired from the individual's performance in the simulations. A motivation work measure was obtained from projective tests and interviews, with some contribution from the simulations. Career orientation was seen in both interviews and projective tests and, to some extent, in the personality questionnaires. A measure of dependence was gained mostly from the projective tests (Bray, Campbell, & Grant, 1974).

Dunnette (1971) concluded, from a review of factor analyses of these variables not only for the AT&T assessment programs but for those at IBM, SOHIO, and elsewhere, that the underlying factors included overall activity and general effectiveness, organizing and planning, interpersonal competence, cognitive competence, motivation to work, personal control of feelings, and resistance to stress.[7] Empirical studies by Sackett and Hakel (1979) and Tziner (1984) also led to questioning whether more than just a few dimensions could account for all 25 variables or their factor clusters. Despite this questioning,

---

[7]Note the similarity of these factors with much of what was presented in earlier chapters on personal factors associated with leadership.

the surplus of variables may be useful for diagnosis and counseling (Thornton & Byham, 1982).

Moreover, the correlations between the ratings of the dimensions on the same exercise are often much higher than the correlations for ratings of any one of the dimensions between exercises (Sackett & Dreher, 1982), which suggests that just a few global measures are involved. In 10 sessions, 149 government agency managers examined personal effects, effects of an exercise with nine behavioral dimensions, and assessors' effects on the assessments. Multiple assessors were used for four exercises: a competitive allocation exercise, an in-basket test, a written test, and a noncompetitive management problems exercise. Differences among the individual assessees accounted for 60% of the assessments, whereas only 11% of assessments were accounted for by the differences between exercises and between assessors. From a study of 19 managers in three days of assessment and four months of follow-up training, Cunningham and Olshefski (1985) concluded that assessment centers, as ordinarily constituted, were better detectors of socioemotional leadership skills than of task leadership skills, but the two tended to be correlated. Bycio (1988) found little effect on ratings earned by participants at an assessment center due to one of 11 orders in which the participants completed assessment activities.

Prescreening

Much prescreening of candidates occurs for the expensive assessment center. For instance, in one year, 1974, Macy's interviewed 2,000 prospective candidates for participation in an assessment center in New York City. Of these prospective candidates, only 500 were processed through the assessment center (Anonymous, 1975). Self-selection also served as prescreening. Ordinarily, participation from within an organization is voluntary after candidates (such as those at Michigan Bell) have learned that they have been nominated for participation in the assessment center by their supervisors, sometimes with higher-level approval. Self-nominations are also possible.

Psychometric testing can be used advantageously to prescreen candidates before involving them in the expense of the total assessment process. For example, for a sample of 80 AT&T prospects, the Gordon Personality Profile and Gordon Personality Inventory tests were administered before the prospective candidates could participate in an assessment center. Four of the scores on the tests correlated with the subsequent assessment based on the full three-day program, as follows: ascendancy, 46; sociability, .32; original thinking, .37; and vigor, .21. A specially scored biographical questionnaire alone correlated .48 with the results of the three days of assessments. If a composite score based on the biographical questionnaire and the measures of ascendancy and original thinking had been in effect, 84% of those scoring in the lowest or "D" category would have been detected as not acceptable to the assessors after three days, while only 16% would have been deemed acceptable. It was reckoned that more than $2,000 per successful candidate was saved by the installation of such a screening program (Moses & Margolis, 1979). In the same way, Dulewicz and Fletcher (1982) found that scores on an intelligence test, but not previous specialized experience, contributed to candidates' performance and assessment based on the situational exercises of an assessment center. Thus, preassessment intelligence tests could be used to screen prospects for assessment. The possibilities of prescreening with a single LGD have been ignored, although, as mentioned earlier, a correlation of .75 was reported by Vernon (1950) between the results about candidates obtained in a one-hour LGD and the results of a full assessment at an assessment center.

Reliability of Assessments

Agreement among assessors in assessment centers has been subjected to numerous analyses to provide estimates of the reliability of the assessments. Fewer rate-rerate estimates are available.

Agreement among Assessors. Observers' independent ratings of assessees correlated .74 in their ratings on average and .76 in the corresponding rankings of 12 participants in the various segments of a two-day IBM assessment program (Greenwood & McNamara, 1967). Comparable median correlations of .68 and .72 were reported for AT&T's program (Grant, 1964). For the SOHIO program, correlations of assessments between psychologists and managers who served as assessors ranged from .74 for the assessment of the drive of assessees to .93 for the judgment of the amount of assessees' participation.

Correlations among raters were increased most by the consensual discussions they held. Before such discussions, median correlations ranged from .50 (Tziner & Dolan, 1982) to .76 (Borman, 1982). After the discussions, the median correlations rose to .80 or above (Sackett & Dreher, 1982) and as high as .99 (Howard, 1974). Schmitt (1977) reported that when a team of four assessors evaluated 101 middle-management prospects over a four-month period, mean interrater correlations before the raters' discussion of the ratings ranged from .46 for the rating of assessees' inner work standards to .88 for the rating of assessees' oral communication skills. After the assessors discussed their first ratings, the intercorrelations rose to .74 and .91, respectively, but the opinion of no one assessor shifted more than that of any other (Schmitt, 1977), which suggested that mutual influence had occurred. However, in an analysis of the participation of 2,640 candidates in an assessment program to determine their suitability for training as U.S. Navy officers, Herriot, Chalmers, and Wingrove (1985) found that a discussion changed the opinions of the assessors if they: (1) were deviates from the majority opinion; (2) depended on their rank as officers for their influence; (3) were above or below the majority in the rating they had initially given a candidate. This increase may reflect more shared information, or it may be a matter of the raters' influence on one another. In an overall review, Howard (1984) concluded that correlations among assessors tended to be at least .60 in most cases, rising to as high as .99. This agreement was not affected by whether the assessors were psychologists or managers; but, as will be noted later, meta-analytic results from 47 assessment studies (Gaugler, Rosenthal, Thornton, & Bentson, 1987) showed that psychologists were more valid assessors than managers were.

Agreement among assessors depends on how much training they have received in making ratings in general and in making ratings about performance in specific exercises. For example, Richards and Jaffee (1972) obtained an increase in interrater agreement as a result of the assessors' training in rating the performance on in-basket tests. They found increases in interrater agreement from .46 to .78 on ratings of human relations skills and of .58 to .90 on ratings of administrative/technical skills. On the other hand, as noted in an examination of self-ratings and multiple raters, there was little correlation found by Clapham (1998) between the self-ratings of 167 assessment center participants and the ratings they received from five assessors. Randall, Ferguson, & Patterson (2000) noted that accurate self-assessments might add to the validity of psychometric tests in assessment center decisions.

Rate-Rerate Reliability. A rate-rerate retest reliability of .77 was reported for the AT&T assessment center's testing of men one month apart. The rate-rerate agreement obtained for women candidates was .70, .68 for black candidates of both sexes, and .73 for white candidates of both sexes (Moses & Boehm, 1979; Moses & Margolis, 1979).

Predictive Validity

Jansen and Stoop (2001) found that Dutch assessment center ratings, based on group discussion and presentation of analysis, predicted the average salary growth of 679 academic graduates over seven years. The correlation was .39 when corrected for starting salary and restriction in range. Reviews by Huck (1973) and Klimoski and Strickland (1977) concluded that assessment centers generated valid predictive information. This conclusion was corroborated in a meta-analysis by Hunter and Hunter (1984), which obtained median corrected correlations of .63 for predicting managerial potential from assessments and .43 for predicting on-the-job performance. But these findings appeared to be inflated according to a more extended meta-analysis by Gaugler, Rosenthal, Thornton, et al. (1987) based on 47 studies of assessment centers involving 12,235 participants. The 107 validity coefficients between the assessment centers' forecasts for candidates and criterion appraisals of candidates' managerial performance and advancement (corrected for sampling error, restrictions in range, and unreliability of the criteria) averaged .37. In the Management Program Study at AT&T, assessments were followed up for eight years to see if they predicted the promotion of assessees into middle management. Assessment results were kept unknown to promotion decision makers. At AT&T and IBM, the assessment center's results for each candidate were not subsequently seen by their superiors, who were responsible for the on-the-job appraisals and promotions of the candidates; so the validity correlations could not be inflated by such contamination, as they might have been in other studies.[8]

Consensual Discussions among Raters. Correlations among raters were increased most by the consensual discussions they held. Before such discussions, median correlations ranged from .50 (Tziner & Dolan, 1982) to .76 (Borman, 1982). After discussions, median correlations were likely to rise to .80 or above (Sackett & Dreher, 1982) and as high as .99 (Howard, 1974).

Predictions of Career Advancement. At AT&T, of those assessees who were predicted to succeed, 42% did succeed, while only 7% of those predicted to fail actually attained middle-management positions (Bray, Campbell, & Grant, 1974). A correlation of .44 was found among 5,943 men designated as "more than acceptable," "acceptable," "less than acceptable," or "not acceptable" by the consensus of the assessors' judgments and information whether the men had subsequently earned two promotions in the eight years following the assessment. The overall managerial level the candidates achieved at the end of 20 years continued to be accurately forecast by the assessments obtained 20 years earlier. Intelligence scores and motivation and personality measures obtained from psychometric instruments, and the results of interviews and in-basket tests, all contributed positively to the accuracy of the predictions (Howard & Bray, 1988). The assessments collected 20 years previously also predicted satisfaction, self-confidence, and emotional adjustment.

At IBM, Wollowick and McNamara (1969) found a correlation of .37 between the assessment by the assessment center and increased responsibility assigned to candidates. In a follow-up, Hinrichs (1978a) obtained a correlation of .46 between the overall judgments of the assessment center and the level of management reached by candidates after eight years. At SOHIO, a correlation of .64 was achieved between the assessments and superiors' appraisals of the candidates' potential 6 to 27 months afterward. The correlation remained stable in forecasting appraisals up to 5 years later (Carleton, 1970).

Howard (1974) noted that the components of various assessment centers differed in the contributions they

made to the accuracy of forecasts. For example, at AT&T, the overall assessment and situational tests had the highest predictive validities; at SOHIO, projective and psychometric tests were particularly important overall; at IBM, some elements in each of the procedures tended to contribute to the prediction of promotion. Arthur, Woehr, & Maldegen (2000) analyzed the convergent and divergent validities of an assessment center for two federal agencies. In 10 sessions, 149 government agency managers examined personal effects, effects of an exercise with nine behavioral dimensions, and assessors' effects on the assessments. Multiple assessors were used for four exercises: a competitive allocation exercise, an in-basket test, a written test, and a noncompetitive management problems exercise. Differences among the individual assessees accounted for 60% of the assessments, whereas only 11% of assessments were accounted for by the differences between exercises and between assessors.

Moderating Effects on the Validities

Purposes Served. The purpose of the validation effort makes a difference. According to the extended meta-analysis by Gaugler, Rosenthal, Thornton, and Bentson (1987), the validity of an assessment center's forecast depends on the criterion of success predicted by the assessment. On average, according to the validities obtained (weighted by sample size and corrected for attenuation and the unreliability of the criterion), candidates' potential for promotion, rated by supervisors and a higher authority, was better predicted (.53) than was their rated current performance (.36), rated performance in training (.35), or advancement in their careers (.36). The least valid predictions were for appraisals by supervisors of the same on-the-job dimensions rated at the assessment center (.33). The assessment center's focus on candidates' current job requirements appeared to be less useful than its concentration on the candidates' possible future job assignments. An extreme case was illustrated by Turnage and Muchinsky (1984), who found no validity in a one-day program for predicting candidates' currently appraised job performance, but did find valid predictions of the candidates' potential after five years and their appraised career potential.

When the effort was for research purposes, the correla-

---

[8]As will be noted later, even when it is possible, such contamination does not appear to occur.

tion between assessment predictions and subsequent appraisals of success was .48. However, the correlation was lower if the purpose of the effort was for administration of selection (.41), early identification of promise (.46), or promotion (.30). Overall judgments of candidates' participation in an assessment center's activities appeared to be better predictors of their advancement and salary increases than were the performance appraisals they received from their supervisors. In turn, the assessments appeared to be better predictors of the appraised on-the-job performance than objective measures of such performance (Turnage & Muchinsky, 1984). Nevertheless, it seems that the pooled ratings and consensual decisions of assessors may yield a less accurate prediction than one made by optimally weighing the independent assessors' ratings and using mechanical pooling of the assessors' ratings by means of multiple regression analysis (Tziner, 1987).

Some assessment centers have been aimed at development of leaders rather than selection. They provide feedback to participants for coaching and self-learning. For instance, an MBA program may conduct such a center for new entrants into the program. Engelbrecht and Fischer (1995) compared an experimental group with a control group of randomly selected first-line supervisors (56 white, 20 nonwhite; 38 men, 38 women) in a South African insurance firm. The 41 in the experimental group received assessment and feedback; the 35 in the control group did not. Three months afterward, the experimentals were significantly higher than the controls in action management, human resources management, information management, and problem resolution. Similarly, Fleenor (1988) found that, compared to results observed from a control sample, career development was significantly advanced by attendance at an assessment center for development.

Individual Raters' Differences in Validity. Borman, Eaton, Bryan, and Rosse (1983) could find no evidence of significant individual differences in the validity of raters' judgments. However, the aforementioned meta-analyses suggested that validities were higher if the assessors were psychologists rather than managers, if the percentage of female assessees was greater, and if the percentage of minority assessees was smaller. Some exercises generated ratings with higher predictive validities than others

did (Sackett & Dreher, 1982). Validities were also higher when a broader array of exercises were employed and when peer ratings of one another were provided by the assessees. On the other hand, the validity of assessment center predictions was little affected by other expected influences such as the ratio of assessees to assessors, the number of days of observation, the number of days the assessors were trained, and number of hours the assessors spent in integrating information. Criterion contamination accruing from providing feedback to assessees and their supervisors also had little of the expected effect on the validities.

Transparency of Constructs. Ninety-nine students were rated by assessors in a Dutch assessment center based on four types of simulated individual interviews. In one interview, they were assessed in their efforts to get a subordinate to work overtime. The experimental students were told in advance about the constructs being assessed (sensitivity, analytical skills, and persuasiveness); 50 control students were not so informed. Contrary to expectations, there were no differences in the validity of the outcomes. The study was replicated with the assessment of 297 job applicants (mostly for management) who were told about the constructs, and of 393 controls, who were not told. Group exercises were added. Predictive validity significantly improved with the transparency of the constructs to the 297 applicants, compared to the lack of information for 393 control applicants. At the same time, in both studies, no differences appeared in the mean ratings between the transparent and nontransparent methods (Kolk, Born, & van der Flier, 2003).

Validity of Other Applications. Specialized assessment centers have been created and found valid for predicting successful performance in various institutional settings. Centers were found to be valid and useful for assessing military recruits (Borman, 1982), naval officers (Gardner & Williams, 1973), Canadian female military officers (Tziner & Dolan, 1982), managers of law enforcement agencies (McEvoy, 1988), and civil service and foreign service administrators (Anstey, 1966; Vernon, 1950; Wilson, 1948). Schmitt, Noe, Merrit, and Fitzgerald (1984) extended the use of assessment centers to forecast candidates' success as a school administrator. The specially developed assessment center featured activities and exercises relevant to schools, rather than business and industry. The assessments correlated between .20 and .35 with appraisals of the job performance of the administrators by teachers and administrative staff. However, the assessments failed to correlate with subsequent promotions or salary increases.

Utility. Because thousands of dollars may have to be spent per candidate, many essays on the cost-effectiveness of assessment centers have been produced (see, e.g., Byham & Thornton, 1970). Cascio and Sibley (1979) calculated the quantitative analysis of the hypothetical utility of assessment centers based on assumptions about the costs, validities, and gains to the organization as a consequence of improvements in the accuracy of prediction provided by the assessment center. The authors showed the numerous parameters that had to be considered and the optimal arrangements that were possible if the designated costs, validities, and benefits were involved.

Dunnette (1970) initially raised the question of whether the additional cost of assessment center procedures, in contrast to less expensive mechanical methods, added sufficiently to the validity of prediction. For instance, Glaser, Schwartz, and Flanagan (1958) had determined that assessments of 227 supervisors from individual interviews, an LCD session, a role-playing situation, and a simulated management-work situation, when combined with two paper-and-pencil tests, yielded multiple correlations of only .30 to .33. Yet the two paper-and-pencil tests alone correlated .23 and .25 with the appraised effectiveness of the supervisors on the job. On the other hand, the AT&T, SOHIO, and particularly the IBM studies showed considerable augmentation of the validity of predictions (up to multiple correlations of .62) when the results of an in-basket test, LGD, and biographical information inventory were added to information gained from a personality test (Wollowick & McNamara, 1969). But such augmentation did not occur in an assessment of 37 prospects for supervisory positions at Caterpiller Tractor (Bullard, 1969).

Cost estimates have ranged up to $5,000 per assessment center examinee,[9] including space and materials as well as the assessors' and assessees' time and travel costs,

without even considering staff salaries. Much less expensive alternatives use standardized machine-scored cognitive and personality psychometric tests. However, the validities of these tests are less likely to reach as high as what is possible when they are combined with the situational tests and other procedures of the assessment center. Another alternative is to rely on recommendations, individual interviews, committee reviews of credentials, and previous performance appraisals. Again, such approaches are unlikely to yield the same accuracies of prediction. Nor does actuarial prediction based on multiple regression yield more accurate predictions than assessors' ratings, according to an analysis based on 24 predictors of the growth of the salaries of 254 managers one, three, and five years after the managers were assessed (Howard, 1984).

Still, the benefits outweigh the costs. One mistake in the selection or promotion of a manager may cost an organization grievously. The validity of decisions about selection and promotion of managers may be raised from .25 to .50 or higher by using assessment centers instead of less thorough efforts. Hogan and Zenke (1986) showed that with a sample of 115 persons applying for seven school principalships, selected exercises at an assessment center yielded a large gain in performance (valued in dollars) over the traditional interview procedures. Nevertheless, Tziner (1987) suggested that it is still an open question whether much less expensive alternatives can achieve sufficiently accurate predictions of future managerial performance to justify using them instead of the procedures of full-blown assessment centers.

MacKinnon (1975) enumerated a number of other benefits that may be obtained from an assessment center. The assessment center is an educational experience for the assessees and even more so for the managers who serve as observers. Both assessees and assessors may perform better after returning to their jobs (Campbell & Bray, 1967). Lorenzo (1984) demonstrated that experience as an assessor resulted in proficiency in interviewing others, as well as obtaining and presenting relevant information about candidates and their managerial qualifications. Assessors also increased their proficiency in preparing concise written reports about this information.

Intangible costs also need to be considered. The centers may promote organizational stagnation in that assessees will be favored who are most similar in attitudes and

[9]In 1980 dollars.

values to current managers, hence stifling organizational change. Another possible negative effect is that the assessment center may establish "crown princes" whose future success becomes a self-fulfilling prophecy of the organization. Conversely, a candidate who receives a poor assessment may be denied opportunities to show what he or she can really do in an organization. In addition, the stressfulness of the assessment experience may invalidate it for some candidates. Finally, those who are not nominated for participation at an assessment center may feel abandoned in the advancement of their careers in an organization (Howard, 1974; MacKinnon, 1975).

Summary and Conclusions

The traits that predict a person's performance as a leader, which were discussed in previous chapters, can be assessed and combined in various ways to forecast success and effectiveness. Pure judgment and the expectations of supervisors and higher authority figures on the basis of current on-the-job performance are commonly used, often as part of performance appraisals; the judgments of peers and subordinates can also be considered, as can references from sources outside the organization. Clinical judgments based on psychological instruments and interviews with employees are another alternative. The reliability and validity of forecasting success with such pure judgments can be increased through standardization of judgmental requirements, the pooling of judgments, and the training of the judges.

Simulations make it possible to observe and judge employees' performance in standardized problem settings. These simulations include managerial in-basket tests, small-group exercises, and LGDs. High-fidelity simulation and virtual assessment centers are now possible with computerization and the Internet. Complex data processing has been facilitated.

Valid scores from psychometric tests, application blanks, and biographical information blanks can be obtained, often through the use of specially constructed discriminating keys. The scores can be combined mechanically with or without the use of multiple regression. They also can be combined mechanically with judgments. Conversely, judgments can be formed from observations and information obtained from such tests and measurements. The procedures of assessment centers have become a popular means of combining scores on psychometric tests with observations of candidates in a variety of simulations that are relevant to current and future positions. The increased accuracy of predictions from the pooling of data gathering in assessment centers appears to justify the expense entailed. The centers usually provide more accurate predictions of the future potential of leaders and managers than do predictions of future performance of leadership candidates obtained by less expensive alternatives. The search for improvements and alternatives will be an issue for future research on leadership.

The Future

Looking Ahead

Robert Crandall, as chairman and president of American Airlines, once opined, "I think the ideal leader in the 21st Century will . . . create an environment that encourages everyone in the organization to stretch their capabilities and achieve a shared vision . . . give people the confidence to run farther and faster . . . and establish the conditions for people to be more productive, more innovative, and feel more in charge of their own lives" (McFarland, Senn, & Childress, 1993). The twenty-first century might well be called the Age of Peter Drucker. Because of him, organizational leaders scan their environments; revisit their missions; decide who are the customers and clients they serve; ban hierarchy; arrange flexible, fluid management systems; replace up-down vocabulary with team vocabulary; reject the status quo and policies that work for today and not for tomorrow; and communicate with clear, consistent mission-focused messages. Leadership is dispersed and highly involved, and responsibilities are shared. The moral compass of leaders works full-time by voice and example. Results are measured by objectives reached. The journey is celebrated (Hesselbein, November 4, 2000).

At the beginning of the second millennium, after reviewing what has happened in leadership research over the preceding 33 years, I looked forward 33 years and forecast that: in the year 2034, leaders will pay more attention to each follower than to the group they lead. Individualized consideration will have become routine. Leaders will be developed primarily online. Full second careers in management lasting 20 years will be commonplace. Women will dominate as MBA students and as educational, government, nonprofit, and service organization leaders. Empirically based ethical codes will have been established for management. Artificial intelligence will be a basis of management decision making. Biotechnology, such as genetic profiling and brain scanning, will be employed in assessing managers and leaders. There will be more concentration on leaders' strengths than

weaknesses. Mathematical operations will be used to optimize outcomes in negotiations. Leadership fads will be as strong as ever. Virtual teams and e-leadership will be the rule rather than the exception in large organizations (Bass, 2002).

The ideal twenty-first-century organizational leader will think locally and act globally, replace a bureaucratic hierarchy with a community of responsibility, communicate a strong sense of mission, and value the distribution of power, diversity, and inclusiveness (Leadership IS, 1994). Leadership research and its applications will continue to expand. Their effects will be seen in the ever-increasing attention to the "people" side of enterprise—in corporate mission statements, military doctrine, educational curricula, and nationwide community programs.

Caveat. It is impressive how wrong we can be about the future. In 1903, just before the Wright Brothers' flight at Kitty Hawk, physicists were writing that heavier-than-air aircraft would never fly. Walter Lippmann commented in his column of April 27, 1948, in *The New York Times* that the Arab-Israeli conflict was "one of the simplest and most manageable."

We can only speculate about how much the results of studies of leadership, popularized in college courses, best-selling books, and the mass media, contribute to the implicit theories of leadership espoused by college graduates—our future leaders. For the students believe that the productivity and morale of workers depend on leaders who express concern about the work to be done, are participatory, and offer praise and rewards for good performance (Graves, 1983). Would these same three clusters of leadership behavior have emerged among college students in 1950? In 1950, whatever was produced profitably could be sold. The largest companies were manufacturers, such as General Motors. In 2007, the profitability of the largest firms—retailers like Wal-Mart—depended on satisfied customers and the ability to negotiate lower prices with suppliers. Would students today have the same prosocial attitudes and the same cynicism were it not for continuing scandals in business and government? The predictions about leadership and management in the year 2000 made in the mid-1960s and a few years later erred mainly in that the predicted developments came sooner than expected (Bass, 1967c; Bass & Ryterband, 1974). The predictions made today are likely to be equally conservative. Evaluation of past national growth rates by Franke, Hofstede, and Bond (1991) showed that individualistic, entrepreneurial, and innovative societies such as the United States tend to be disadvantaged in growth rate, compared with more collectivistic and bureaucratic societies such as Japan. However, since the 1990s it has been the latter type of society that has been disadvantaged compared to the former (Franke & Barrett, 2004).

Expected Developments in Leadership Research

Paradigm shifts that took place between 1975 and 2005 are likely to settle into new concentrations of research effort. For instance, there is likely to be more research on transformational factors such as charismatic and inspirational leadership and on the cognitive processes involved in leader-subordinate relationships. In addition, there is likely to be much more sorting out of the personal and situational processes that influence leaders and followers, leading to the possibility of finding generalizations that apply to any leader and to any follower. Controlled survey and laboratory studies will increasingly extend to a wider array of methods. In the same way, issues will be broadened by the cross-fertilization of interests of the behavioral, social, and political sciences. Contributions to the field of both substance and methods from sources outside North America will increase. Concerns about the equitable distribution of power will be increasingly shared with concerns about the equitable distribution of information.

There is also likely to be increasing consolidation, as well as reanalysis, of earlier findings about leadership and the outcomes of leadership that questioned whether various contingencies were merely transient phenomena. The cultural, social, and economic changes that took place in the last half of the past century may require, as

Tucker (1983) suggested, a reexamination of the instruments, structures, and relationships established earlier. Leadership researchers will need to consider whether their purpose is to make a contribution to theory or to application. If their intended audience is academia and their purpose is to make a rigorous addition to understanding, they may find there is less application of their work to human resources management, in contrast to possibly more messy broader empirical results (Weibler & Wald, 2004). Researchers will be paying more attention to the substance than the shadows (Bass, 1974). *Anything that can be meta-analyzed will be meta-analyzed.* Van de Vall and Bolas (1997) looked at the extent to which 120 Dutch policy research projects had an impact on organizational decisions. According to interviews, the impact of the findings had more effect on decisions if they were empirically grounded rather than based on theoretical constructs.

As new nations become complex industrialized societies, much will be learned about the leadership and management that emerge. These factors will need to fit with the cultural realities of the different nations. For instance, the new leadership styles emerging in China as a leading global market economy will be affected by the collectivism inherent in China's rich 3,000-year-old philosophical heritage (Liancang, 1987).

Considerations in Looking Ahead

Six considerations guide our peek into the future of research on leadership and its applications: (1) extrapolation from the past, (2) societal changes, (3) new technologies, (4) organizational trends, (5) changes in organizations, (6) changes in personnel practices, (7) new paradigms.

Extrapolation

First, we look ahead by extrapolation from the past. For example, much of the course in the 2000s and beyond has been set by the trend that began in the 1950s and 1960s toward more longitudinal research rather than onetime, cross-sectional studies. Already confirmed in the 1950s and 1960s were the importance of the computer; the needs for challenging work and flexible organizations; faster communications; and more teamwork, diversity, temporary organizations, and simulation for decision making and training. Mass production and large inventories were beginning to be replaced by deliveries of just-in-time supplies and production for specific customer orders. Drucker (1994) noted that in the developed countries during the twentieth century, both qualitative and quantitative transformations occurred in the nature of work and in social, economic, and political systems. These transformations will continue through the twenty-first century. By 2010, Drucker (1998) foresaw, there will be no single dominant world economic power like the United States. To remain competitive, company leaders will need to have as good information about events and conditions outside their firms as internal reports and surveys provide about what is happening inside the firms. Retirement age will go up in developed countries, but the workforce will decrease in size as the productivity of knowledge and knowledge work continues to increase and provides the decisive competitive advantage.

Societal Changes

The substance of research on leadership is influenced considerably by what is happening in society as a whole. Leaders will have to adapt to the changing roles and relationships in society. Will government continue to enlarge despite the efforts to reduce it? (Beckhard, 1995). The majority of the American workforce has shifted from manufacturing to service and information work. Will manufacturing, services and information work continue to move offshore? More work is being done in smaller companies (Cascio, 1995). Organizational life in the public sector and health care have become of increasing interest. Opportunities to increase productivity, particularly its quality, have become more dependent on effective human relationships and the development of personnel. In the same way, when humans are replaced with robots and computers, more high-level personnel specialists, supervisors, and team development are likely to be required. Mandated in much of western Europe, industrial democracy remains voluntary in the United States, where it is increasingly becoming a fact of life through enlightened managements and employee ownership plans. At the same time, the percentage of the workforce in U.S. labor unions continues to decline, particularly in the private sector. Labor unions remain stronger in Europe,

Australia, and the U.S. public sector. Nevertheless, despite unionization, affective organizational commitment to their firms by 635 Australian employees of Generation X, born between 1960 and 1975, when controlled for age, appears no different from that of 382 Australian baby boomers born between 1941 and 1959 (Hart, Schembri, Bell, et al., 2003). Low wages (paid in the United States to 25% of workers in 2004) remain acceptable to families because both spouses tend to be working. But the many scandalous threats to the United States' civic infrastructure have resulted in a sharp reduction of public trust in government and business institutions (Gill, 1996).

Demographics are inexorably working their will. The current generation of U.S. employees is older and more diverse in sex, color, race, and foreign birth than the preceding one. Unlike in Europe, Japan, China, and parts of the Middle East, the United States' birth rate is not declining, and its population is continuing to increase very quickly due to continuing immigration. The trend continues toward more automation and self-service, and many immigrants are needed to fill lower-paying jobs in construction, manufacturing, agriculture, and service. Russian and other Eastern European professionals and skilled employees have migrated west in significant numbers. Illegal immigration of cheap labor from Mexico and elsewhere has reached crisis proportions. Flows of illegal immigrants from undeveloped Africa to developed Europe are occurring in the same way. Lower-paying jobs and the income gap between the rich and the poor continue to increase in the United States. The percentage of more relations-oriented personnel in the U.S. labor force has increased with the sharp rise in the employment of women. A plural society of varied ethnicity and race is replacing the ideal of a single melting pot.

The multinational firm, with its worldwide outlook, continues to expand. Multinational firms are just as likely to be headquartered in Japan, Britain, Germany, or elsewhere as in the United States. Dual careers and wage earners in the family are now the rule. Five of every six men over age 65 are moving into a new long-lived class of retirees. By 2010, Drucker (1998) expects, healthy people will stop working at 75. Foreign investment in the United States has risen sharply, particularly since 1985. A considerable percentage of U.S. personnel are now working for foreign-owned firms. There is an increasing need to remain competitive in the world marketplace with the

Pacific Rim nations and with the rapidly growing European Union. The developed countries can remain competitive for a few more decades in the productivity of knowledge work (Drucker, 1998), although India and China are catching up fast.

Forms of government and economic systems from Chile to the Russian Federation changed in the 25 years from 1980 to 2005. Japan's industry is maturing; Britain's class structure is shifting. Ireland has gone from being one of the poorest to one of the wealthiest countries in Europe. The U.S. hegemony in 1945 in economic power is being challenged in 2008 by the European Union and East Asia. The expansion in international trade has been accompanied by rapid changes in exports and imports. In 2003, developing China exported $30 billion in manufactured and high-tech goods to the developed United States; the developed United States exported $3 billion in agricultural products to developing China. These economic and political changes are bringing new, continuing challenges for leaders at many levels in both countries in government, industry, and education. Continued social change is foreseen in the coming years.

The world climate continues to warm. The failure to control agricultural and industrial pollution continues, along with threats of pandemics of AIDS and avian influenza, a new strain of influenza resistant to medication available in 2008. Other threats include worldwide terrorism and the exploding populations in developing countries. Concern about corruption, business ethics, and the social responsibility of large corporations continues.

Leadership research and development reflect these societal developments. Mentoring will play an increasingly important role (Zey, 1988). Furthermore, a premium will be placed not only on junior managers' abilities to deal with the human factor but on attention to quality and costs. More statesmanship and an international outlook will increasingly be required of senior executives, who also will need to remain vigilant in the face of mergers and hostile corporate takeovers. Political leaders will increasingly need to learn how to negotiate and cooperate internationally in a competitive and sometimes hostile world.

Work/Life Balance. Households with both husband and wife working full-time as well as households with single parents have focused attention on balancing the needs of work with those of home and family. Johnson & Johnson introduced its Balancing Work and Family program in 1988. It was seen as beneficial for recruiting and retention (Cole, 1998). In 1996, of 1,050 employers surveyed, 68% provided flexible scheduling; 86%, child care; 30%, elder care; and 23%, adoption benefits. Other firms were arranging job sharing and compressed workweeks, help for spouses of relocated employees finding employment, and other benefits for help with home and family. Family friendliness was seen as a strategic objective (Vincola, 1998). Family-friendly corporations have been found to increase shareholder returns, according to an analysis by Cascio and Young (2005) of the 100 Best Companies for Working Mothers. Fathers are taking on more household and child care duties. A combined work and family life is an increasingly common experience for children that is shaping their attitudes (Riggio & Desrochers, 2005).

National Security. The increased importance of the highly equipped and trained individual soldier and small teams in the all-volunteer armed services will continue the need to promote stability and cohesiveness through effective leadership. In 2025, U.S. military thinking will need to make strong use of the political, economic, and social aspects of national security. Training and resources will need to be invested in peacekeeping as well as fighting war. More focus will be needed on small-scale interventions with greater mobility, agility, flexibility, and speed of strategy and decision making. Unless the major confrontation in the Middle East continues, overall, the active U.S. defense forces could be limited to three army divisions, three aircraft carrier battle groups, and four fighter wings. Much more may be invested in small, mobile special operations teams. A robust reserve force may be necessary, as might strong intelligence and understanding of foreign cultures and governments. What is predictable is less dependence on big force-on-force threats and conflicts and more dependence on special operations, airlifting, and close air support, together with diplomacy that integrates the use of U.S. and allied forces. These changes will make us well prepared to deal with the threats of terrorism and guerrilla warfare (Bass, 1998; D. Smith, Corbin, & Hellman, 2002).

Special operations teams in large numbers will replace the big military forces. Their missions are intensive, often secret, highly focused, and usually swift, stressful, and hazardous. Their members are cohesive "bands of brothers"–style heroes who are daring, imaginative, highly trained, and highly disciplined. They exploit short-term opportunities, surprise, weaknesses, and unpublicized vulnerabilities in the well-defended, much larger, and stronger-opposing forces. Whether army Rangers, navy Seals, British SAS (or guerrillas as in Spain or Russia in the past), the teams are led by extraordinary leaders who think "out of the box." Their leaders need to learn more without postponing decisions, to adapt shrewdly without losing focus, to understand their opponents as well as themselves, and to command while maintaining authority and mutual loyalty. Both teams and leaders need to combine intellectual with physical courage, daring with patience, sacrifice with achievement, endurance with change, and attention to detail with openness to new approaches (Leebaert, 2006, pp. 7–11, 585–587).

International cooperation, multinational alliances, and astute diplomacy will be needed more than ever. Competitive market forces, population pressures, accelerating technological advances, and rapid societal changes further reduce the tolerance for laissez-faire leadership. But care has been taken to avoid a drift back to the promotion of autocratic behavior in the guise of active leadership. Presidents Ronald Reagan and George W. Bush both breached the constitutional limits on the powers of the president in the name of defending the nation against threats to national security. Paradoxically, they both sought to promote democracy abroad by upsetting the constitutional balance of the courts, Congress, and the executive branch at home.

New Technologies

A new managerial mindset is needed. The diffusion of new technologies makes innovation a competitive requirement. A premium has been placed on organizational learning. E-commerce, e-retailing, and online transactions with suppliers and customers increase revenues and reduce costs (Hitt, 2000). Networks of personal computers and interactive programming greatly increase the speed and opportunities for survey studies and the experimental manipulation of leader-follower variables. Advances in miniaturization and telemetry will no doubt be put to good use in the direct observation of neural reactions and nonverbal leader-follower interactions (Schyns & Mohr, 2004). As electronic mail crosses oceans and cultural boundaries instantly, leaders face new opportunities and challenges. Behavioral research on information systems is stimulated. Complexity theory suggests that the order, innovation, fitness, and decline of an organization depend on its networks inside and outside the organization, whether they are closer to or farther from the organization's technological core. Leaders should help to build and maintain these networks (Marion, 1999). Kahi, Sosik, and Avolio (2003) predicted that with the Internet, some organizational boundaries will disappear. Increasingly, consumers will communicate directly with peer suppliers through networks such as eBay. Hierarchical systems will be revolutionized by networking.

E-technology can bring both positive and negative consequences. It can foster e-leadership and virtual teamwork and promote close monitoring of employees. Spreitzer (2003) sees virtual teamwork continuing to replace face-to-face supervision with more remote management. Virtuality reduces the need to travel, increases round-the-clock operations in different time zones without the need for shift work, and minimizes diversity problems. But it may foster feelings of isolation, cross-cultural misunderstanding, and reduced identification.

Computerization. Fifty years ago, Leavitt and Whisler (1958) predicted that by the 1980s, computerization would change the role of management and leadership in organizations. Much of the routine decision making and reporting by middle management would be computerized. Information technology would replace much of the need for the traditional middle management role. Much of what was predicted came to pass. The world of computerized management information systems and the change in organizations came by the 1980s, as forecast. Middle management was squeezed out, as Leavitt and Whisler predicted, because senior management could be linked by computer directly to lower levels of supervision and to operations. Employee empowerment, collaboration, and teamwork also reduced the need for frequent managerial decision making and intervention (Kielson, 1996). Byrne and Zellner (1988) estimated that more than a million U.S. managers and staff professionals lost their jobs during the 1980s and that more than a third of middle-management positions were eliminated. The tenure of the average manager in a single firm, which was 12 years in 1970, had been reduced to seven years by 1990. By that year, much of the information processing formerly done by management and staff had been taken over by computers. Information technology departments were organized to maintain and modify what was needed.

Leadership and the Information Revolution. According to Cleveland (1985), the character of the leadership role is systematically changing under the shock of the information revolution. This revolution is evidenced by the rapidly changing distribution of the U.S. workforce. In 1920, 9% of the workforce was engaged in knowledge and educational services; in 1955, 29%; and in 1975, 50%. In 2000, it was estimated that 66% of the workforce was involved in such services. The generation, communication, storage, and retrieval of information have been increasing exponentially in speed and amount. Older approaches to getting work done may provide little guidance for the future.

Six interlinked characteristics of information have radically altered the leader-follower relationship. The agenda for research on leadership entails dealing with these properties of information: (1) Information is expandable. The more we have, the more we use and the more useful it can become. Information is not a scarce resource; only time and the capacity of people limit its growth. (Of course, it is possible to be overloaded with information so that decisions based on it become delayed or less than optimum.) (2) Information is compressible. It can be concentrated, integrated, summarized, and miniaturized in its manipulation and storage. It requires little energy and the depletion of few physical resources. (3) Information can replace land, labor, and capital. Whole libraries can be packed into a computerized data bank. Automation replaces people. Organized data reduces localized inventory requirements. (4) Information is highly transportable. Telecommunications makes physical meeting sites unnecessary. People geographically distant from one another can work together in virtual teams. According to Kahai's (2000) surveys of senior executives, virtual teams are among the top five challenges for organizations to address in the future, along with the search for workers best suited to staff virtual projects. (5) Information is diffusive. It leaks. Despite efforts

to maintain secrecy, the leakage may be wholesale and pervasive. (6) Information is shareable. An information-rich environment is "a sharing environment . . . the standards, rules, conventions, and codes are . . . different from those created to manage the zero-sum bargains of market economics" (Cleveland, 1985, p. 32).

The information technology revolution enables organizations to solve problems and share innovations with agility and speed by connecting the collective knowledge of their members. Ready access to marketing, production, employee, and customer information will be important for businesses to remain competitive. By 2025, it is estimated that 60% of work will use equipment and operations that did not exist in 2000. Future managers will attend more to operations, products, and outputs. They will coordinate their subordinates rather than telling them what to do. Again, they will coordinate rather than direct consultants, contract workers, and temporary employees outside the organization (Kahai, 2000). Networks of inside and outside organizational members will become more important to managers and leaders (Ronfeldt 1993). Before the information revolution, managers faced the possibility of too little information; now they are faced with information overload. In managing operations, information about objectives without clear boundaries as they affect decision-making processes can be treated as "fuzzy sets" of objectives instead of the less realistic single objective function. When involved with different sources of information, the multiscaling of categorizations can be applied. Computer mediation enhances the speed of communication and interaction between leaders and followers (Fischer & Manstead, 2004).

Age-Status Imbalance. Younger managers and junior officers are likely to have grown up with the rise of information technology. Older senior executives and senior officers are less likely to have developed "hands-on" experience with the personal computer, the Internet, and the Web. Older executives grew up with relative information scarcity. Now they have to deal with an overload of information. Computer-challenged managers and leaders who are not young enough to have grown up with computers are being helped with short courses, self-training, and coaching (Fleener, 2004). Computer literacy is becoming universal and is being instituted faster in the developed world, more slowly in the developing nations. Computer training is furnished in elementary, secondary, and higher education as well as virtually and at workplaces.

Changes in Organizations

The Future of the Hierarchical Organization. Like many, Helgeson (2005) argued that top-down power is obsolete and will be replaced by networking. Nonetheless, in agreement with Leavitt (2005), some form of top-down hierarchy will remain in most organizations into the foreseeable future. As Leavitt noted, such hierarchies will persist even though we don't like them. They will continue to be further modified substantially by the humanist movement and strengthened substantially by the systems movement. We need to learn how to live with them as they are softened by the humanizing changes occurring; at the same time, the controls are being hardened in organizations by modern information technology. We need to reconcile personal growth and fulfillment inside the hierarchy with the "roiling, multidirectional storms" of internal and external "storms of change" (Leavitt, 2005, p. 11). Hierarchy is unpopular in democratic societies because it generates dependence and mistreatment, blocks interpersonal relationships, and provides those at the top with power to become greedy and corrupt. Hierarchies may be slow, unresponsive, and inflexible. Those at the bottom may suffer from violation of democratic values, while those at the top may suffer from intrigues and conspiracies, cronyism, and personal and physical insecurities. Nevertheless, organizational hierarchies are here to stay. In contrast to the alternatives, they are efficient. Yet research continues to be needed on how they can be improved by further humanization and systemization.

Organizational Change. The very purpose of an organization is to provide reliability, predictability, and coordination to its constituent parts. Nevertheless, its environment continues to increase in turbulence, and continuing responsiveness, flexibility, and change are required. Attention to both stability and change in organizations will continue to be required, with efforts held together by good communications. Hierarchy has been changed with the participative management and the

team approach of the *humanizers*, and with the rise of operations research, information technology, and analytical managing by the *systemizers*.

The Case for Further Humanizing. Although humanizing and systemizing are two opposing approaches to modifying organizations, both are needed for improvement. "Organizations used to be [discussed] as pieces of engineering, flawed pieces maybe but capable of perfection, of precision, of full efficiency designed, planned and managed . . . [with] control backed by authority. . . . The new language of organization is about networks and alliances, adhocracy and federalism, shared values . . . and consensus . . . options not plans, the possible rather than the perfect, involvement instead of compliance, political systems (rather than) engineering . . . leadership rather than management" (Handy, 1994, p. 7).

Humanizers push for less hierarchy. As predicted by Bennis (1992, p. 3), traditional hierarchies are being modified by "networks, clusters, cross-functional teams, temporary systems, *ad hoc* task forces, lattices, modules, matrices." Tall organizational structures are flattened. Combined with cost-cutting efforts, mergers, and acquisitions, the flatter structures have contributed to a decrease in the number of managers in the resulting new type of organization (Tomasko, 1987). The number of layers in management hierarchies continues to decrease, with larger spans of control for those who remain.

In an expanding economy, newly formed firms can absorb most of the managers made redundant in their former companies. But the decline of the percentage of managers in the U.S. workforce from its high of above 10% in 1980 is expected to continue well into the twenty-first century, exacerbated by the stock market bubble at the beginning of the millennium and the downturn in the economy in the three subsequent years. A career in a single firm from entry to retirement can no longer be counted on. Managers are redirecting their attention more toward personal goals and capabilities. The psychological contract of managers' loyalty to the firm and the firm to the managers will continue to erode (R. Hirsch, 1987; Marks, 1988). The new contract provides managers with career-enhancing but impermanent opportunities. Managers need to take responsibility for their own careers. There is less status than before in working for a Fortune 500 company. Although 2,000 managers from many different corporations said that there was more than a 100% difference between the top performers and those below average in performance, the actual difference in pay between those at the same organizational level was 5% to 10%. Opportunities for promotion have decreased as layers of management have been reduced. To replace these motives for remaining with an organization, an organization needs to identify whom it wants to retain. Opportunities for involvement, recognition, and development need to be provided. For example, younger managers can be assigned to action learning projects. Organizations can be made more attractive through less bureaucracy, more flexible hours, and a greater sense of ownership (Mason, 1996). Among others, Clegg (1990) saw the need for organizations to move away from rationalistic, deterministic, and bureaucratic forms of organizing, toward more flexible, fluid, and values-driven forms. Decisions have to take into account individuals' values, emotions, and preferences as well as logic and empirical considerations. The individuals include suppliers and consumers outside the organization (Maas & Graf, 2004).

The Case for Further Systemizing. Systemizers support hierarchy, consistency, discipline, and order. Humans are just another resource amid these factors for the organization. Systemizers want to control, regulate, and reduce variability. They prefer to substitute machine performance for human performance and artificial intelligence for human thinking. They favor managing over leading. They are more supportive of hierarchies as the natural way to get things done than are humanizers. Both will contribute to effective organizational change into the foreseeable future. Boundaryless organizations illustrate a compromise between humanizing and systemizing. Such organizations contain fewer fixed structures and more temporary systems. Technology and systems are assembled as needed for specific projects (Davis, 1995). Boundaryless organizations are clusters of activities whose members and their goals are continually changing. Projects are more significant than positions (Kanter, Stein, & Jick, 1991). *Dejobbing*, or unbundling of work, illustrates another such compromise. Instead of a permanent position—a bundle of tasks—to be performed by one person, various necessary tasks are done by people inside and outside the organization. The individual member is assigned various tasks at different times (Bridges, 1995). Generally, changes in organization—following sociotechnical theory—encompass both systemizing and humanizing efforts to improve a system and employees' work satisfaction.

Issue Management. During changes in an organization, an underresearched area is leaders' role in building the momentum of key issues critical to the change process and reducing the attention to other issues by manipulating the dimensions of the issues. As a big change occurs, members are cognizant of a stream of issues flowing continually and competing with other issues for members' attention. These issues of organizational change often involve internal changes rather than changes in the external environment. For organizational change to occur, leaders need to move members to attend to the important issues inside the organization in order to solve the problems they present (Dutton, 1988). Leaders can do this by increasing the *salience* of an issue in an ongoing stream of issues by emphasizing and publicizing it; the *ambiguity* of an issue by clarifying it; the *immediacy* of an issue by setting deadlines; the *interdependence* of an issue by incorporating others' objectives; and the *scope* of an issue by broadening its range of activities (Hietapelto, 1994). In nonprofit organizations, Hesselbein (2004), as leader of the Girl Scouts for 13 years and leader of the Peter Drucker Foundation for the same time span, noted three particular challenging issues for nonprofit organizations. First, leaders of change must be developed with a moral compass that works full-time; they must be healers and unifiers who embody the mission, live the values, keep the faith, and remain fully responsible. Second, such leaders need to reflect and embrace diversity in the board, management, workforce, clients, and customers. Third, such leaders need to be open to collaboration, alliance, and partnerships. Nonprofits need to be in equal partnerships with government and private corporations. A more general question for nonprofit organizations is why there has been so little controlled leadership research about them. Many nonprofit foundations are dedicated to leadership development yet provide relatively little for formal leadership research in the nonprofit sector (Riggio & Orr, 2004).

Changes in Personnel Practices

Another consideration that may help predict likely future developments in substantive research on leadership and its applications is the discernment of dissatisfaction with the adequacy of current personnel practices. According to a survey in early 1988 (Anonymous, 1988b), the needs of human resource management that were not being handled well at that time and were seen as requiring emphasis were succession planning, human resource productivity, and organizational design. Less important practices that also needed improvement were team building, the measurement of morale, performance aids, job design, the stress of career development, and outplacement.

Matching Practice with Theory and Doctrine. The importance of a trusting relationship between leaders and their subordinates has been stressed as a principle for effective leadership in many previous chapters. It has been U.S. Army doctrine since 1775, but practice has often failed to match theory and doctrine. For instance, mentoring of junior officers by superiors is a well-established doctrine, but 85% of junior officers reported that they had received their support from such counseling less than a week before the Officer Evaluation Report was due (Bass, 1998).

Practices Endorsed by Popular Books. Academics are often asked what they think about a popular best-selling book on leadership and are likely to regard it with disdain, as anecdotal and not as rigorous as academic research published in peer review journals. But practicing leaders and managers are more likely to have read or heard about the popular book. Fortunately, Dickson, BeShears, Borys, et al. (2003) found that the gap between popular and academic literature on leadership was closing. They summarized the models of leadership themes they found in 30 best-selling books on leadership. At least 10 of the books were written by prominent academics. As seen in the preceding chapters, the themes in the popular press are readily found in the academic literature. They include the importance to leadership of goal orientation, self-awareness, visionary leadership, building of teamwork, development of others, assessment of the organization and environment, and management of organizational culture. Followers also read the popular literature and may expect their leaders to behave accordingly.

New Paradigms

A last consideration is the possibility of new paradigms that can affect both future methods and the content of leadership research. In looking to the future, we must not forget the past. Leadership is a mature field of study (Hunt & Dodge, 2001, p. 436). Concepts such as transformational leadership have evolved through stages (Reichers & Schneider, 1990): introduction and elaboration, evaluation and augmentation, and consolidation and accommodation. We have already seen the rapid impact on leadership theory and research of the cognitive revolution in psychology. Of the most prominent academic theories of leadership from 1900 into the twenty-first century, information processing became very active only in the 1990s; charismatic-transformational leadership (the "new leadership") became very active only in the 1980s; and trait theories, which had been very active before 1920, reemerged as very active in the 1990s (Antonakis, Cianciolo, & Sternberg, 2004). Developments in the mathematics of dealing with irregularities, reversals in trends, and seemingly chaotic conditions may be applied to modeling the natural discontinuities in leader-follower relationships (Lord & Maher, 1991, p. 195). The physical sciences may suggest new ways of looking at short-lived phenomena—for example, the emergence of instant leadership in a crisis followed by its equally instant disappearance. The willingness to accept two distinct ways of dealing with the same phenomenon, as is common in wave and particle physics, may lead leadership theorists to simultaneously treat the leader's and subordinates' different rationales for what is happening around them. Cause-and-effect analyses may be seen as the exception to mutual effects between the leader and the led. The 1980s saw an upsurge in interest in upward influence (see, for example, Kipnis & Schmidt, 1983), which has continued. It is likely that a greater number of future studies will be conducted of the reciprocity involved in the effects of upward and downward influence, as was done by Deluga (1988–1988a), who showed that subordinates' upward influence is depressed more by transactional than by transformational leaders. Generally, we are likely to see more work on how leaders influence *and are influenced* by the individuals and teams they have been elected or appointed to lead. Hollander (1958) focused importance on the follower in the emergence of the leader. But the follower needed to be active, not passive (Offerman, 1997). "We are content to follow when we lead the way" (Homer, c. 750 B.C.E.).

Societal, technological, and organizational changes call for new ways of thinking, the importance of creating new knowledge, and its diffusion and utilization in the organization. Many organizations consider their personnel as human capital assets accruing from their investment in human resources (Hitt, 2000). In contrast to regarding employees as assets to be developed and retained, another strategy is hiring temporary workers. A firm's workforce and costs can be expanded or contracted depending on its needs. Or whole functions such as payrolls can be contracted out. The workplace can be replaced by work at home, with subordinates linked to supervisors and colleagues by e-mail and telephone (Challenger, 1998). Faced with global competition, firms will put an emphasis on innovation, flexibility, and responsiveness. Leaders' attention will shift from tangible to intellectual resources (Dess & Picken, 2000). Attention will also continue to be paid to the company image, reputation, political connections, and strategic flexibility (Hitt, 2000). Methodological and substantive issues will broaden. Korukanda and Hunt (1991) see conflicting paradigms about leadership that may be combined. For instance, leadership research can be objective or subjective. The *objectivist* view assumes that leadership is a natural object—a concrete reality amenable to quantification. Understanding accrues from the discovery of facts about leadership and its processes and relationships. Inferences are drawn about the statistics of the average individual. The *subjectivist* view is that leader and leadership are convenient labels or fictions that facilitate sense making for the observer or for introspection. Results are usually qualitative. Self-awareness and self-improvement are of central importance to the information gathered. *Holistic* leadership demonstrates the subjectivist approach. The leaders of the Body Shop, for instance, focus on organizational processes with a systems view of interactions between people in their various roles and relationships. They keep the big picture in mind and practice empowerment. The senior managers refer to themselves as support staff. What the people in their franchised stores do is more important to the business than they are. Self-awareness and self-improvement are stressed. A new paradigm may combine the objectivist and subjectivist views to help understand the phenomenon better.

In the public sector, government agencies will ideally become more empowering and supportive rather than serving; competitive but not monopolizing of the delivery of services; mission-driven rather than rule-driven; results-oriented; meeting the needs of the client rather than the needs of the bureaucracy; likely to run surpluses rather than deficits; market-oriented, anticipatory, participative, and decentralized (Gore, 1993; Osborne & Gaebler, 1993). Change is also appropriate if it is creative and humane and there is a dedication to public service (Denhardt, 1993). Research, graduate education, and empirical studies in the United States have had strong influences on public administration in Britain, Belgium, the Netherlands, Germany, and Scandinavia but not in France, Spain, or Italy (Nelissen, 1998). It is proposed that by 2015 diplomacy between nations will not be limited to diplomats, but, thanks to the Internet, "diplomacy" will include governments and NGOs as well as individual citizens from the general public of the nations involved. Efforts to promote such virtual diplomacy have already been initiated (United States Institute of Peace, 2002).

Changes in the Prominence of Leadership Theories. From 1991 to 2000, of the 188 articles published in *The Leadership Quarterly*, the most prominent were those dealing with charismatic and transformational leadership (34%), contingency theories (25%), and other, newer directions such as political leadership, strategic leadership, top-management teams, leader-member exchange, and other multiple-level approaches. This was in contrast to fewer articles on trait theories and behavior theories of leadership. No doubt some of these will continue in prominence in the twenty-first century, while some will be replaced by newer entries stemming from new developments in genetics, technology, and European and Asian influences. In looking ahead from 1975 and 1995, Phillips (1995) suggested that, increasingly, theories and research about leadership schemas and cognition will modify trait, behavioral, and situational contingency theories.

Methodological Issues

Causal Relations

In examining how leadership relates to outcomes, we continue to be faced with the question of what is cause and what effect. Thus, Kernberg (1984) stated that breakdowns in work effectiveness are erroneously attributed to failures of leadership. Yet often they are due to failures in systems and environmental, organizational, and group factors. Ineffective leadership is an effect rather than a cause. Supervisors may be supportive because they have productive subordinates, or subordinates may be productive because they have supportive supervisors (Bass, 1965c). Some investigations (see, for example, Greene, 1974) have shown that subordinates cause their leader's behavior. Other studies (see, for instance, Dawson, Messick, & Phillips, 1972) have found that the leader's behavior is a cause of the subordinates' performance. Still others (such as Jacobs, 1970) have pointed to mutual causality in an exchange in which subordinates comply because of the leader's promise and the leader rewards subordinates for the compliance.

Although they still form a distinct minority, a sizable number of causal studies of leadership have appeared since 1970. Of 89 studies of leadership between 1970 and 1975 reviewed by Hunt, Osborn, and Schriesheim (1977), almost all the 17 laboratory studies but only 24% of the 72 field studies concentrated on causal relations. Despite the shortcomings of laboratory studies, they still make collecting causal data convenient—something that is much more difficult to accomplish in the field. However, it is edifying to see the increasing efforts to combine laboratory experiments with field studies and to search the field for corroboration of laboratory findings. But care is required, especially about the need for highly reliable measures. Regression strategies to determine cause and effect, such as path analysis, require highly reliable measures and strong enough relationships to permit the testing of alternative models.

Laboratory versus Field Studies

The five-year review by Hunt, Osborn, and Schriesheim (1977) of six major journals found that 72 field studies and 17 laboratory investigations focused mainly on su-

pervisors' behavior and reactions to it. In the field, managers and their associates in a wide variety of organizations were the subjects of inquiry. In the laboratory, superior-subordinate relations were simulated by students. A fundamental question was whether the temporary nature of laboratory situations could faithfully represent the real-world relationship. Osborn and Vicars (1976) noted a particular source of error in trying to generalize from laboratory studies of leader-follower relations: short-term laboratory situations tend to evoke the behavior of participants on the basis of available stereotypes. Extensive interpersonal contact in real life provides a more realistic basis for behavior.

Field studies, by their very nature, are fraught with internal and external threats to the validity of their data and measurements. Nonetheless, although laboratory experiments provide rigor and control, relying exclusively on laboratory studies should be avoided. As Meehl's (1967) paradox indicates, the more aseptic and controlled the laboratory study, the greater the precision of its outcome. In physics, greater precision increases confidence in the generality of the finding; in the social sciences, it does just the opposite. Ideally, laboratory studies should be planned in conjunction with fieldwork.

In controlled laboratory experiments, students are usually the subjects. When there is disagreement between the findings from such experiments and field studies of operating supervisors and employees, the greater rigor and control of the experiments often leads to greater confidence in their conclusions. They are preferred to field studies, although at times, field studies may obtain results that are closer to the truth. Thus, Fodor (1976) showed that the results of laboratory experiments, with practicing supervisors instead of students as participants, may be quite different from the results obtained in the field. In a rare laboratory study that utilized industrial supervisors as participants, Fodor found that, in comparison to control subjects, supervisors who were exposed to a group stress situation responded by giving significantly fewer pay raises and lower performance evaluations to compliant workers. However, field studies (such as Goodstadt & Kipnis, 1970) earlier found just the opposite; in those studies, compliant workers received significantly more pay increases under group stress than under control conditions. Nor were the laboratory results with supervisors consistent with the results that Fodor (1974) obtained with students. In all, we can expect to see an increase in efforts to examine and report laboratory experiences jointly with tests of the same hypotheses in the field.

The Erroneous Law of Small Numbers

The law of large numbers states that large random samples will be highly representative of the population from which they are drawn. The law of small numbers assumes erroneously that small samples will be similarly representative. If you have a sufficiently large sample, any difference is likely to be statistically significant. Testing the null hypothesis with a small sample of differences is a meaningless ritual (Cohen, 1994). Critics continue to voice their objections, but statistical significance testing of differences in results remains strong. Tversky and Kahneman (1971) demonstrated that the belief in the law of small numbers leads to highly inflated estimates of the amount of information contained in studies that use small samples. Schmidt and Hunter (1980) thought that much of the variation in the observed relationships in small samples could be considered random departures from a relatively simple overall generalization. The overall generalization does not need to be qualified by the particular situation involved. For example, in examining the relationship between individual competence and job performance, Schmidt, Hunter, and Urry (1976) showed that the samples were usually too small to produce acceptable levels of statistical power. Thus, if the true correlation between, say, scores on intelligence tests and the success of leaders is really about .35, any sample of 30 to 50 would yield a result that was statistically significant, from zero only 25% to 50% of the time. For a statistical power of .90, in order to reject statistically the zero relationship 90% of the time when the true correlation is .35, sample sizes of 200 or more are needed.

Erroneous Interpretations of Small Differences. In organizational research, we ordinarily measure the responses of individuals nested in their work groups. They are not random and are likely to be influenced by their groups. In the same way, if the groups are nested in different organizations and influenced by their organizational membership, they are not random (Hanges & Shteynberg, 2004). They need to be treated by the variant approach (Dansereau, Alutto, & Yammarino, 1984), by

hierarchical linear modeling (Hofmann, 1997), or by factor analysis (Muethen, 1994).

We may look at ten small-sample studies of scores on intelligence tests as they relate to leadership performance and find that half are statistically significant and half are not. Then we try to infer a reason for the different findings, when in fact the differences in the various samples are null and can be accounted for by the law of large numbers. The obvious implication is our need to be cautious in interpreting the meaning of situational variance when the data from the different situations are based on small samples. With contingent analyses using small samples, we will err considerably in rejecting the null hypothesis at the 5% level of confidence that no differences exist between different contingencies. Thus, Hunter and Schmidt (1978) noted that 28% of the time (at the 5% level of confidence) we could erroneously infer differential relationships between, say, intelligence and performance for 30 black leaders compared with 30 white leaders when no true difference exists.

The problem is far from academic. Hunt, Osborn, and Schriesheim's (1977) review of 89 reports found that 20% used samples as small as 30 or even fewer in analyses of data. The problem is compounded when we deal with leadership because ordinarily only small samples of leaders are available unless an organization is very large. Thus, we may need to reexamine carefully how much contingent results occur because of the low power of the sampling on which many are based.

Meta-analysis offers the opportunity to test how random are the various results obtained from the pool of small-sample studies of the same relationship and to arrive at a mean effect size for a given relationship. Here, however, we have to be cognizant of the inflation in the estimated effect size resulting from the adjustments for criterion unreliability and restriction in range. These adjustments may be highly unrealistic because they are based on assumptions about infinitely repeated measurements and samples with the full range of possibilities. Nevertheless, as has been noted, meta-analysis helps to tease out reliable contingent effects from those that are ephemeral, transient, or a consequence of random variation from a true mean relationship.

Erroneous Conclusions from Small Effects. Exacerbating the problem of small samples is the small size of many of the mean effects that emerge. It requires little in the way of systematic errors to distort or confound them. Systematic errors creep into the scene for a number of reasons (Webster & Starbuck, 1987). There are broad characteristics of people, such as intelligence, that appear to correlate with leadership and with outcomes when it is possible that there may be no direct relationship between the leadership and the outcomes. It may be that leaders tend to be more intelligent and that better outcomes require more intelligence, but there may be no direct link between the leadership and the outcomes. The failure to consider a contaminating third variable may result in the unwarranted blowing up of the importance of many small mean effects. Thus Woodward (1965) found that decision-making processes within an organization depended on the organization's technology and structure. Many subsequent studies elaborated on this finding. However, Gerwin (1981) showed that the modest results obtained tended to disappear when the size of the organization was held constant. Multiple-regression control variables are likely to become the rule, rather than the exception, in future research.

Erroneous Conclusions from Convenience Sampling

Convenience and feasibility have often dictated that a sample studied was actually a selected complete subpopulation, rather than a random representation of a complete population. For example, all the supervisors in one Canadian department store are surveyed or interviewed, rather than a representative sample of all Canadian retail sales supervisors. Researchers still have to rely too much on convenience samples—samples that are most often obtained from larger rather than smaller organizations. The organizations must be cooperative and supportive or the data can be collected only on the outside or by an unobtrusive participant-observer. The combination of large organizations with accessible personnel systems, data banks, mailed surveys, and telephone interviewing will increase the possibilities of large-scale representative sampling.

Single-Source Variance. Convenience also leads to reliance on the same respondent for descriptions or evaluations of a leader's behavior and the outcomes of the leadership. Methods for correcting for the built-in corre-lation that is due to such single-source variance have been developed. They include removing from the data the first general factor that is assumed to be due to the rater's propensities (Podsakoff & Organ, 1986), using one respondent to describe the leader and another to describe the outcome, and the varient approach of breaking the analysis of covariance into that among leaders and among between multiple respondents rating the same leader (Avolio, Bass, & Yammarino, 1988). However, so far, no one corrective action seems to be free of problems.

Measurement Problems

Lord Kelvin overreacted when he declared that in the pursuit of understanding, "if you can't measure it, you don't know what you are talking about." Handy (1994) retorted that when you cannot easily measure the phenomenon you wish to understand, it is wrong to disregard it if the phenomenon is difficult to measure or to argue that it is unimportant or that it doesn't exist.

Need for Balanced Use of Standardized Measures. A wide diversity of environmental, task, group, interpersonal, and personal variables have been employed in leadership research, each to a lesser extent, usually in multivariate fashion, as antecedent conditions, correlates, or moderators. Standardized scales for some variables, such as role clarity and role conflict, have been adopted, despite the many different but closely parallel conceptualizations of leadership style. Instruments such as Fiedler's Least Preferred Co-worker (LPC) scale and some form of the Leader Behavior Description Questionnaire (LBDQ) have dominated research on leadership in the past 40 years. This use of common standardized instruments has made possible a great deal of comparison across studies. It has already been noted how even small changes in instruments may lead to large differences in outcomes. But this concentration of leadership measures has kept the research establishment from looking at many other, possibly more important, aspects of leadership behavior. A balance is needed. On the one hand, researchers need to avoid inventing new measures of the same attributes when old ones with satisfactory reliability and validity are available. On the other hand, concentrated efforts with measures other than the most popular ones are needed, particularly if they can be joined in a nomothetic network with the well-used instruments.

Limitations. Elaborate theories may spin out tales of curvilinear complexity and multiplicative effects. Yet analyses over 50 years based on such efforts have usually added little beyond error to the prediction equation, even though the record is improving with more sophisticated measurements. Theory building should not go too far beyond what is empirically possible. Although contingency models are intuitively appealing (Yntema & Torgerson, 1961), contingency hypotheses (how X relates to Y depends on Z), Korman (1973) noted, should be entertained in a theory only if they are empirically supported and necessary. Consistent with what has already been said about the erroneous interpretation of small differences, we may see a return to the positing of simpler relations based on larger samples.

Most observational studies use the single, mutually exclusive coding of the various categorizations of observed data. But such coding is no longer necessary. Statistical and computer programs are now available to analyze the multiple coding of multipurpose activities, multiple contacts, and simultaneous roles played (Martinko & Gardner, 1985).

Cross-lagged correlational analyses to demonstrate leader-subordinate relationships also have their limitations. For instance, Greene (1976a) noted that initial changes in leadership behavior between Time 1 and Time 2 may fail to be associated with parallel changes in subordinates during that same period, but they may show up between Time 2 and Time 3. Thus, three, not two, data collection points are needed. In addition, it is difficult, if not impossible, to rule out the possibilities of confounding uncontrolled changes in third variables on both the leader and the subordinate. Hence, the increased use of repeated measurements over many time periods, such as that reported by Howard and Bray (1988), is needed.

Yukl (1982) noted that factor-scaled questionnaires fail to include important items of leadership behavior that are correlated with two or more factors. Infrequent behaviors are also likely to be missed. Frequency is overemphasized while the leader's sequencing, timing, and style of execution are neglected. Often, the context in which the behavior appears is also missed. Richer information is also likely to be obtained from questionnaires if in addition to the items that purport to be objective behavioral descriptions, researchers use more items that tap the observers' gut feelings and estimates about the potential for future assignments of the leader being observed. We need to avoid, because of special interest in the leader-subordinate dyad, eliminating descriptions and evaluations of overall leader-group relations, for it is clear that both are important. Conversely, items about the interaction of the leader with the whole group fail to provide information about the leader's dyadic relationship with each individual member of the group (Yammarino & Bass, 1988).

Simple versus Complex Hypothesis Testing. We face a dilemma. On the one hand, "the chain of relationships between leader behavior and outcome is long and complex" (Lieberman, 1976a). Much of what needs to be understood is missed if we simply try to relate leadership behavior, particularly generalized leadership behavior, to final group outcomes. The relationship must be considered in terms of the group's norms, cohesiveness, and so on, as well as of the leader's characteristics. Members' expectations may be more important in determining group outcomes than anything the leader can do. Multivariate analyses, complex models, and contingent and moderator analyses need to be used. On the other hand, the limitations that have been noted in the measurements available, and the extent to which situational variations from one small sample to another, are likely to be random rather than true effects. At the same time, second- or higher-order interactions are likely to render inconsistent simple moderator effects from large sample to large sample. Thus, when faced with complex models, we need to be more open to experience and greater clinical understanding of data that demand less mathematical rigor (Bass, 1974; L. G. Cronbach, 1975). On the other hand, *structural equation models* (Gavin & Cheung, 2004) have become increasingly popular in dealing with both the direct and indirect paths between independent, intervening, and dependent variables. Each path or partial correlation corrects for the other paths and helps understand the network of relations.

Models may be built a priori on the basis of logic and prior information, and then tested to see if they fit the data obtained in the test. Or models can be built a posteriori to fit the obtained data. There are problems with each approach. Korman and Tanofsky (1975) pointed out that a priori models are hard to use because of the difficulties of accurately estimating the necessary parameters. Yet a posteriori empirical models may be fraught with psychometric error. They may be likely to exploit random effects. Both kinds of models may be more helpful in identifying the important elements for study rather than discerning the final true relationships.

Field studies can reflect the complexities of the real world, but laboratory studies and their controls do not provide the solution to dealing with complexity. For instance, in the study of the effects of sex differences on leadership, the short-term, artificial nature of leadership created in the laboratory results in participants' relying on stereotypes that influence their responses to the leader. This reliance on stereotypes is less likely to occur in field studies in which leader-subordinate relations are long-term. The laboratory engenders exaggerated sex-role demands, and thus the effects of sex differences in the laboratory are not replicated in the field setting (Osborn & Vicars, 1976).

Need for Qualitative Methods. These methods may be more suitable for providing confidence in the results when complex hypotheses are involved. Bryman (2004) was able to enumerate 65 acceptable published qualitative studies of leadership between Pettigew (1979) and Vangen and Huxham (2003), although the historical and management literatures are replete with many more qualitative comparisons. Additionally, Amabile, Schatzel, Moneta, et al. (2004) completed analyses of daily diary narratives written by leaders' subordinates.

Bryman, Bresnen, Beardsworth, and Keil (1988) examined the situational factors that construction project leaders take into account when deciding what style of leadership to adopt. Interviews revealed that site managers continually adjusted their leadership styles to suit varying circumstances, such as time pressure, their subordinates' personalities, and the degree of control they had. The authors suggested that qualitative research can uncover a wider array of contextual variables. Such variables are grounded in people's experiences and therefore are more accessible to leaders and researchers alike. The search for meaning and significance in the behaviors of leaders and their followers, as well as in related events, is aided by qualitative research (Van Maanen, 1979).

People's actions can be explained in terms of the total context in which they occur instead of the isolated or manipulated elements within the situation (H. Smith, 1975).

Qualitative research is likely to begin with deductions from a theory or a set of general propositions (Orpen, 1987) and then to proceed as a detective might to track down patterns, searching for consistencies in the qualitative information. Qualitative research need not begin with precoded systems but can depend on analytic inductions (Strong, 1984). Creativity and controlled imagination are required to move from specific findings to general conclusions (Mintzberg, 1979). Thus, the movement is a circular process involving the search for and collection of specific data, development of crude hypotheses, and then the examination of the data (or new data) to see how well the inferred hypotheses fit the data (Brogdan & Taylor, 1975). More such qualitative research is needed and is likely to find its way into the study of leadership as the limitations of quantitative methods in dealing with organizational complexities become increasingly apparent (Orpen, 1987).

McCall and Lombardo (1978) advocated more leadership research using the ethnographic methods of nonstatistical naturalists to detect the subtleties and nuances involved in the leadership process. Greater attention needs to be paid to unconscious motives that affect leaders' and followers' perspectives. Often, qualitative research can deal better with the art and craft of leadership than more objective qualitative analyses. That is, there is much art in leadership that is difficult or impossible to put into a test tube. Nevertheless, there is much regularity in this art that can be made understandable by detecting and describing the patterns that appear. Orpen (1987) regretted that, for the most part, qualitative and quantitative research are likely to parallel or remain independent of each other, rather than being integrated, even though they could do much to complement each other. This was demonstrated by Gibbons (1986), for example, who made use of both quantitative surveys and in-depth interviews of the same executives.

A risk in qualitative research is that we may learn more about the investigator than about the complex scene being investigated. Chafee (1987) noted the divergent conclusions reached by four investigators who looked at the same qualitative data about college presidents. The investigators' conclusions diverged, she argued, because the investigators came from different theoretical traditions: organizational theory, leadership theory, strategic theory, and anthropological theory. The same key words had different meanings for them. That is, the researchers used the same terminology but drew different inferences from the same qualitative database. Ideally, studies need to *triangulate* qualitative with quantitative methods. They need to check the results of one against the other. Bryman (2003) was able to enumerate 11 such studies between Rosener (1990) and Voelek (2003). Rosener followed up a quantitative survey of woman managers to generate research questions that became the basis of a full qualitative study that followed. Voelek used qualitative data about university library managers to support and expand quantitative results about them.

Webster and Starbuck (1987) pointed to another handicapping bias in research on leadership. Within each research discipline—industrial/organizational psychology, social psychology, sociology, political science, educational administration, and so on—there are shared sets of beliefs, values, and techniques. The empiricists in each discipline prefer to measure certain sets of variables of consequence. Thus, the dimensions of leaders' and subordinates' behavior examined and the methods employed to do so continue to be narrow (Greene, 1976c). The narrowness depends on the disciplinary background of the investigator. There appears to be relatively little consensus on substantive issues of consequence (Campbell, 1982), especially across interdisciplinary boundaries. Despite this lack of consensus, we are likely to see, in this century, an increase in the use of common methods in the study of leadership, depending on whether the investigator is a behavioral, social, or political scientist or an historian, but one with a continuing wide range of substantive foci.[1]

Dealing with Systematic Biases

Leniency. The need will remain in future leadership practice and research to guard against leniency bias. Perlmutter (1954) found that the greater leaders' abilities to influence other group members, the greater the number of favorable traits applied to the leaders—and

the more socially desirable the traits attributed to them. Schriesheim, Kinicki, and Schriesheim (1979) demonstrated the strong leniency effect in the LBDQ-XII consideration scale. A specific leader will earn higher LBDQ scores from respondents who give favorable ratings to leaders in general. Similar leniency is likely to be found in related measures of leaders' relations orientation, participation, and support. Leniency may account for much of the association between subordinates' descriptions of their leaders' consideration and the subordinates' satisfaction. Measures of the initiation of structure that are free of coercive items and measures of consideration that are free of leniency (if such is possible) will provide more precise measurements against which to pit situational and personal variables for study. The Multifactor Leadership Questionnaire's scales to measure transformational and transactional leadership appear to be relatively free of leniency effects (Bass & Avolio, 1989).

Errors in Leaders' Self-Ratings. Except for using it for personal development and expectations and exposing the gap between self- and others' ratings, future leadership research needs to avoid depending on self-ratings, as many studies still do. In earlier chapters, it was repeatedly pointed out that there is little or no relationship between leaders' self-descriptions and descriptions of them by their subordinates or superiors. Leaders' self-ratings and self-reports are suspect. Thus, in an intensive interview study and work flow analysis of 34 pairs of supervisors and subordinates, Webber (1980) found that the supervisors reported that they initiated almost twice as much verbal interaction with their subordinates as the subordinates perceived had occurred. At a considerably lower level, subordinates also overestimated the extent to which they initiated interactions with their superiors. Leaders' self-ratings have consistently been found to relate poorly or not at all to various dependent variables (Schriesheim & Kerr, 1977b). Most are probably contaminated by social desirability (Schriesheim & Kerr, 1974). They contain self-serving, self-vindicating biases and are likely to generate descriptions of what leaders think is expected of them in their organization and society, rather than an accurate portrayal of their behavior relative to other leaders'. The manager who assures everyone that there is always full consultation on subordinates' problems since the manager's door is "always open" is not uncommon. Then

---

[1] *The Leadership Quarterly* has as one of its purposes to provide a single forum for research on leadership from the different disciplines.

there is the self-described "democratic" manager who announces that the organization is going to be democratic or else sanctions will be imposed.

No wonder so little correlation is found between subordinates' perceptions of what the leader does, what they think he will do, and what he should do, on the one hand, and the leader's self-reports on the same issues, on the other. Thus Rees and O'Karma (1980) observed that city department managers and their subordinates differed significantly in how the managers would behave in different situations described by the LEAD questionnaire. Holton (1984) reported similar discrepancies between leaders of a Cooperative Extension Service program and their staff subordinates. Nanko (1981) noted that although 1,800 elementary school teachers, using the LBDQ, judged that their supervisor was doing a poor job, each of the supervisors saw him- or herself as doing a good job. The correlations of responses from the two sources were close to zero. Burt (1984) found that 32 heads of hospital departments gave themselves better ratings on the LBDQ than their 379 employees gave them. In the same way, according to Dalessio (1983), working business students and their bosses disagreed about their bosses' leadership. As was noted earlier, supervisors see themselves as having bigger and more important jobs than their bosses say the supervisors have (Haas, Porat, & Vaughan, 1969). Leaders generally see themselves as more transformational than subordinates see them (Bass & Avolio, 1988). According to a survey using the Multifactor Leadership Questionnaire of a representative sample of 186 surface fleet officers in the U.S. Navy, the correlations of the self- versus subordinates' ratings of leadership were only .21 for charismatic leadership and .21 for individualized consideration (Bass & Yammarino, 1989). The self-subordinate correlations for the remaining five scales were close to zero.

In Birnbaum's (1986) survey of 252 college presidents about the effectiveness of the institutional leadership of the average presidents, their predecessors, and themselves, the presidents gave themselves a mean rating of 77.3; the average president, 65.6; and his or her predecessor, 52.0, on a scale of 0 to 100. A serious issue raised by these discrepant results is the reliance that so many studies of chief executive officers (CEOs) place on interviews with CEOs about themselves. Given the low or even zero correlations between what leaders do and their col-

leagues' descriptions of their behavior, we need to proceed with great care in drawing any inferences from leader-only data. In meeting with small informal groups of CEOs, I found that CEOs are likely to be highly and selectively biased in their self-descriptions. This is not to say that the leaders' self-descriptions are necessarily incorrect and the colleagues' descriptions of the leaders are necessarily correct. Rather, it is important for researchers to avoid depending solely on leaders' self-descriptions. Moreover, leaders obviously differ. Some are much more congruent than others in the extent to which their self-reports match those provided by their colleagues. Such congruence with their subordinates can increase the subordinates' morale (Browne & Neitzel, 1952), the quality of the leader-subordinate relationships (Graeri & Schiemann, 1978), satisfaction with communications (White, Crino, & Hatfield, 1985), and superiors' evaluations of the leaders (Bass & Yammarino, 1989).

Increasing the Validity of Self-Ratings. Various techniques help curb inflated self-ratings: (1) In forced-choice methods, a self-rater chooses from pairs of self-descriptions that appear equally favorable or socially desirable but in which only one of the pair is valid for prediction or assessment purposes. (2) Self-raters may be asked to complete a questionnaire as if they were applying for a job. Then they are asked to complete the same questionnaire as if it were to be used by a trusted adviser. (3) Self-raters are attached to a *bogus pipeline*, a physiological apparatus that purportedly is able to register their genuine responses. A meta-analysis of 31 studies demonstrated that, compared to a control group without the bogus pipeline, socially desirable self-ratings were lower (Roese & Jamieson, 1993).

Training and research efforts will, over time, make greater use of superiors', peers', and subordinates' ratings and less of leaders' self-ratings of their purported behavior. But, as will be discussed later, leaders' own perceptions, attributions, cognitions, and opinions will continue to be of considerable research importance as a link to what leaders actually do.

Other Systematic Errors. Ratings of leaders and followers are built around memories of their behavior. What leaders or followers have actually done may register less in current evaluations of them than false memories of what they did. Past events may be remembered as far more important than they actually were. The "Rashomon effect" is illustrative: four people witness the same violent event; each later recalls a highly differing version of the same event. In future, we should expect further studies of the effects of false memories on ratings and evaluations.

Among all the biases in perceptions and ratings, a few are most salient in the study of leadership. One such tendency is for subordinates to see more good in their own relations with their leader than in the quality of leader-subordinate relations they observe elsewhere. Adams, Prince, Instone, and Rice (1984) found that when 400 freshman cadets at West Point described good leadership incidents, the incidents usually involved their interactions with their leaders, whereas the cadets perceived bad leadership as occurring mainly in other units. This perception may be part of the larger phenomenon of "we-they" bias, that is, seeing "our group" as better than "their group." In the future, the use of multiple sources of information with demonstrable convergent validity and suitable corrections of such self-other bias will be more routine.

Consistent with earlier work,[2] Larson (1982) and Larson, Lingle, and Scerbo (1984) demonstrated that raters' responses to LBDQ descriptions of leaders who were viewed in action on a videotape were affected by whether the respondents were cued before viewing the tape about whether the leader they were looking at was considered effective or ineffective. Such cuing before they observed the videotape of the leader in action moved them to selectively encode into memory different kinds of information. Given their implicit theories about the effects of initiation and consideration, the raters saw the supposedly effective leader as higher in both. Binning and Fernandez (1986) showed that another bias in the LBDQ descriptions was due to the differential availability to the rater's memory of the different items. The availability of items to the rater's memory is greater the more familiar, dramatic, specific, positively salient, retrievable, and imaginable the items of leadership behavior in the LBDQ are. An average correlation of 48 was found between the extent to which an item of leadership behavior was seen as descriptive of a leader and the availability of the item to memory. The correlation was higher if information about the leader

was more limited. In the future, standardized corrections in the LBDQ and similar questionnaires are likely to be introduced to adjust for these availability biases.

An aspect of the bias in self-fulfilling prophecy was detected by Schoorman (1988), who verified that the supervisors of 354 subordinates who had originally participated in the decision to hire them tended to bias their subsequent performance appraisals in a favorable direction if they had supported the decision to hire. They tended to do the reverse if they had opposed the decision.

These consistencies among persons because of their individual predilections and the tendency to be influenced by personal memories reinforce the need to have multiple sources of data about leaders and outcomes attributed to the leaders. Or else, as was mentioned earlier, corrections need to be made to allow for single-source bias when only a single source of information is possible. An example is when a dyadic analysis of the leader with each subordinate calls for each subordinate to describe both the felt quality of relations with the leader and how much the subordinate is committed to the organization's goals.

Phillips and Lord (1986) noted that leadership questionnaires need to be designed according to the type of accuracy being sought, that is, whether it is behavioral or classificatory. Also, the theory (or lack of it) underlying the questionnaire needs to be taken into account when the questionnaire is employed, to assess interventions that attempt to change leadership behavior.

Dyadic versus Group Relations

At times, the need to describe leaders' performance in terms of their one-on-one relationships with each of their subordinates is more conceptually pleasing than empirically fruitful. However, the dyadic approach can be applied with considerable utility to a variety of research questions. For example, sanctioning, punitive leadership behavior seems to be the result, rather than the cause, of the inadequate performance of specific subordinates. It follows that dyadic analysis should reveal strong differential dealings of supervisors with their subordinates on the basis of leaders' differential judgments about each of their subordinates.

Indeed, we are likely to find a variety of important consequences stemming from Hollander's (1978) obser-

[2]See Binning and Lord (1980).

vation that leaders have "A" lists and "B" lists of subordinates. The As are closer, and the Bs are more distant. Work-oriented leaders are likely to relegate the more incompetent of their subordinates to the B list and to treat them more punitively. But the As will be expected to be more loyal and obedient and will be required to maintain higher standards of performance. However, person-oriented leaders may exert extra effort with their black sheep and may even think that their most competent subordinates are sources of conflict because their performance exceeds the group's norms. The linkages to Least Preferred Co-worker need to be investigated.

Several different approaches have originated, to tease out individual, dyadic, and group effects. One approach is to hold leader-group effects constant to see what happens within each leader's group. Vecchio (1982) obtained data on attitudes and performance from in-group and out-group members of 48 four-man military groups. Within-group leader-member differences predicted attitudes, but only after between-group leader differences were held constant. Performance outcomes appeared to be unaffected by dyadic or group leadership. Katerberg and Hom (1981) used a stepwise hierarchical regression analysis. They first determined the contribution of each of 31 U.S. Army National Guard units to LBDQ descriptions of the units' leaders, then the contribution of the individuals within the units. Although the effects of within-unit variations in LBDQ scores were stronger than between-unit variations, both significantly predicted the subordinates' reactions.

Still another approach uses an *adaptive process regression* technique that determines the artificially assembled groups of an original pool of subordinates that will result in the best possible predictions. The nature of these groups then gives the investigator an idea of which possible groupings may moderate the dyadic leader-subordinate relationship. Berkes and Rauch (1981) found such artificial clusters among 800 police officers. One moderating cluster of those officers operated under less specified procedures. Another cluster was younger, better educated, and more interdependent in their work. Less role clarifying and more participative leadership were required for satisfying the young, educated, interdependent officers.

The use of dyadic analyses of leaders' relations with individual peers, individual superiors, and relevant others will continue to increase owing to the continuing interest in leader-member exchange theory (Graen, 1976) and its quantitative possibilities. However, allowance clearly has to be made for leaders not only to relate on some dimensions, at least, in the same way to every group member, but to the generation of effects that transcend the average member. For instance, an *assembly bonus effect* in productivity may be due to a leader's structuring the group as a whole, which goes beyond the contributions of the group's members.

The Variant Approach. As was noted in earlier chapters, the most ambitious, comprehensive, and possibly defensible effort, the varient[3] approach, was developed by Dansereau, Alutto, and Yammarino (1984), who used this method to reexamine the reports that originally supported the importance of the individual leader-member exchange dyad over the leader-group relationship in how much negotiating latitude the leader provides each member and the group as a whole. The analyses concluded that both individual member effects and group effects may be equally salient (Nachman, Dansereau, & Naughton, 1983).

The varient approach is a paradigm for formulating and testing theories that explicitly consider both the involved variables and entities—the individual, the group, and/or higher levels of analysis (Yammarino, 1988). The future will increasingly see its use to clarify: (1) the differences among leaders in their average leadership style (ALS); and (2) their vertical dyad linkages (VDL) or leader-member exchanges (LMX), as was done by Markham, Dansereau, Alutto, and Dumas (1983). More superior-subordinate communications will be profitably analyzed by the varient method (Dansereau & Markham, 1987). A higher level of effects may be examined, such as the effects of whole departments or organizations and their different policies on the leaders' relations with their group members as a whole, as well as with various individual members.

New nomological networks of variables will be clarified by WABA procedures. For example, a leadership behavior may be related or unrelated to two outcomes. Or the two outcome variables may be related, but the leadership behavior may be related to one outcome, not to the

---

[3] *Varient* is not a misspelling of *variant*; it stands for *vari(able) ent(ities)*.

other. Another possibility is that the two outcome variables may be unrelated and leadership behavior may be related to one outcome, but not to the other. The leader's dyadic and group relations may affect the members' satisfaction but not the members' productivity, for instance. New moderator variables and contingency effects will be identified with WABA. One possibility is that variables are directly related; that leaders' behavior, for instance, directly affects outcomes. Another possibility is that a relationship between two variables (leadership behavior and an outcome, for example) is dependent or contingent on the values of a third variable, such as company regulations. This indirect contingency is a moderated effect. Here, leaders' behaviors could relate strongly to dyadic and group outcomes in departments with few regulations but not in departments with many regulations (Dansereau, Alutto, Markham, & Dumas, 1982).

A Future of Variety

New approaches to the study of leadership will continue to proliferate. The method of choice for study and application depends on the way the leader-follower phenomenon is conceptualized. Among the most likely approaches are cognitive and information processing, phenomenology, motivation, psychodynamics, and behavioral observations and reports. At the one extreme are cognitive investigators who focus on perceptions, causal attributions, and expectations. At the other are behavioral investigators who concern themselves with stimulating conditions, behavioral repertoires, and reinforcements that are contingent on subordinates' performance. The vast array of possible variables to study must continually be pruned. For surveys and experiments to be manageable, researchers must single out for study different aspects of the total process of leader-follower interactions. But the models they construct that focus on one aspect or another are not necessarily inconsistent with each other. The potential exists for considerable integration of the models.

As noted in Chapter 4, by the 1940s, a variety of methods was available to study leadership, including observation and time sampling, sociometry, position and office holding, analysis of biographies and case histories, and judged requirements for leadership. Measurements were being obtained from psychological tests, questionnaires, rating scales, and interviews. Dimensionalizing by factor analysis was possible (but time-consuming). Along with refinements in these procedures since the 1940s, promising new methods have emerged.

Cognitive and Information-Processing Methods

Applications of new methods (or new applications of old methods) have accompanied the emergence of interest in cognitive and information processes in lieu of descriptions of the behavior of leaders and followers. Since 1970, empirical examination has found a decline in behavioral and an increase in cognitive studies (Robins, Gosling, & Craik, 1999). In leadership reports, the focus is on leaders' and followers' schemas for actively organizing information and the scripts they employ to give specific meanings to situations. The making of meaning or sense making "is the process of arranging our understanding of experience so we can know what has happened . . . what is happening, so we can predict what will happen" (Drath & Palus, 1994, p. 2). Prototypes help interpret the world of leadership. Information about specific situations is encoded, stored in memory, and retrieved in terms of category structures and inferential strategies (Pervin, 1985). Galbraith and De Noble (2004) presented a cognitive framework for historical leadership stories.

Cognitive-perceptual methods, first developed in the 1940s and 1950s to study learning and decision-making processes, the dynamics of personality, and counseling, were subsequently introduced into the study of leadership. These methods include protocol analysis, stimulated recall, and the repertory grid. In protocol analysis, individuals' thoughts, feelings, and emotions are recorded as they engage in the activity under investigation. With stimulated recall, an audio or video record of the activity or the protocol is played back, and the individuals describe more fully the thoughts, ideas, and feelings they had when the activity was in progress (Burgoyne & Hodgson, 1984). To construct a repertory grid, a respondent sorts colleagues, noting the categories used to differentiate them (Kelly, 1955). Coghill (1981) showed the profitability of studying the perceptual categories that managers naturally use to assess one another. He applied Kelly's repertory grid method with 90 managers to provide data to illustrate the importance of perceptual mediation, personal constructs, and implicit theories.

Phenomenological and Perceptual Methods

The methodology of another line of cognitive inquiry has been phenomenological. The inability to resolve the controversy surrounding Fiedler's (1967a) Contingency Theory after more than three decades of theorization and empirical research led Bar-Tal (1989) to argue that what may be most important in understanding leadership is to determine leaders' and followers' phenomenological fields rather than to continue to pursue a positivistic, mechanistic, or statistical explanation of their interaction. To expedite this methodology, the researcher may disclose as much about himself or herself to the focal leader as the leader does to the researcher. Basic emotional processes can then be explored, along with remote and accessible aspects of their respective lives. Barriers between the researcher and the leader to knowing and sharing are expected to be minimized in this way (Massarik, 1983).

If the focus is on perception or cognition rather than behavior, methods that exploit attribution phenomena can be applied with profit to the leader-follower relationship. As noted in earlier chapters, the behavior of leaders toward their subordinates appears to be strongly determined by the reasons (ability or motivation) the leaders give for their subordinates' performance—how much it is a matter of luck or of the situation or whether it is under the subordinates' control. In the same way, the subordinates' attributions of the reasons for the leaders' behavior will strongly relate to the subordinates' satisfaction. Leaders whom subordinates perceive to be incompetent but willing seem to be more forgivable than leaders whom subordinates perceive to be competent but unwilling.

As already noted, conscious perceptions can determine a leader's subsequent efforts. Thus Nebeker and Mitchell (1974) found that differences in leaders' behavior could be explained by the leaders' expectations that a certain style of leadership would be effective in a given situation. At the same time, subordinates' descriptions of their leaders' behavior may be distorted by their implicit theories about leadership, particularly when they lack real information about the situation and are therefore inclined to fall back on stereotypes (Schriesheim & deNisi, 1978).

The use of cognitive, as opposed to exclusively behavioral, methods is likely to parallel the same continuing developments in psychology in general.

Still underutilized are sociometric designs, such as the "Work with" sociometry[4] of Stogdill and Haase (1957), which provides a measure of interaction structures that can be applied to a variety of research designs. Three-dimensional holographic sociometry (Bradley, 1987) is in its infancy. It is likely to have a promising future as it opens up the contributions of the sociometric structure of triadic relationships within an organization to the performance of leaders.

Motivational and Psychodynamic Methods

Documents, recordings, and protocols can be analyzed from particular theoretical perspectives and coding models based on motivational and psychoanalytical theories. Keyword coding of protocols provides a powerful tool. The projective inferential methodology, pioneered by Winter (1973) to analyze the needs and values of leaders from their speeches, documents, and biographical materials, was detailed in Chapter 8. The approach is likely to provide important empirical support for and understanding of studies of charismatic and inspirational leadership. Less prominent is the inductive methodology that Demause (1982) derived from psychoanalysis. Demause argued that a group's fantasies, shared by the leader and his or her followers, which play a crucial role in charismatic leadership, can be detected from a psychoanalytic examination of the leader's and followers' speeches, documents, and body language. The group's fantasies can be teased out from the metaphors and similes that the leader and followers use, and body language, feeling tones, and emotional states can be significant. Thus the "killing" of bills and "dead" halts in negotiations are relevant to the psychohistorian, as are unusual or gratuitous word usages (in the 2004 presidential campaign, saying "the 'L word,'" for example, implied that "liberal" was a dirty word). Unusual repetition and phrasing in discussions, speeches, documents, and minutes of meetings imply potent messages for the psychoanalyst. Symbolism has obvious implications; even its absence during long peri-

---

[4]Sociograms plot the choices by organizational members of those with whom they would most prefer to work.

ods without imagery may be symptomatic of the severe repression of the group's fantasy (Scheidlinger, 1980).

Increasingly, metaphors from science will be used for taxonomies, as, for example, Field (1989b) did in likening leaders to stars, pulsars, quasars, and black holes. (Stars communicate positive expectations to followers and induce positive performance. Pulsars communicate positive, but unsustainable and unrealistic, expectations. Quasars are pessimistic, but followers succeed despite them. Black holes' pessimism is a drag on followers.)

Zaleznik (1984) reviewed a number of promising schemes for looking at the "text" of leadership—the meanings, intentions, and motives that are subconscious as well as conscious in the spoken or written words employed. The deeper structure underlying the surface interactions of the leader and the followers can be discerned from thematic interpretation. Such interpretation requires grasping a multiplicity of complex conceptual structures in the text. These structures may be cultural or social forces or individual values, meanings, and intentions. They may be seen in the linguistic study of speech patterns or of the formation of symbols. Hidden meanings and unconscious ideas and fantasies are brought to light. Clues to what is hidden in the text may include: the percentage of positive, neutral, and negative words and phrases, emotional or nonemotional; the percentage of references to the past, present, conditional, or future; the percentage of action verbs; the percentage of interruptions, hidden reversals, or recycling; and delayed responses and silences.

The formation of groups and movements can be organized around such shared fantasies and provide the basis for displacing personal inadequacies. For instance, Demause (1982) applied a psychoanalytical coding scheme to the Nixon tapes to complete a fantasy analysis of them. The analysis found that a leader's personal embarrassments can become substitutes for policy; goals can disappear, while actions become irresistible.

Psychohistory has been the psychoanalysts' exclusive turf. However, documentary analyses (House, 1988b) and survey methodology (Bass, Avolio, & Goodheim, 1987) are beginning to be applied to psychohistory. Indeed, if motivational analysis is to move off the psychoanalyst's couch, it will need to take individual, political, and social psychology, as well as relevant aspects of sociology and anthropology, into account to elucidate the per-

formance of historical figures (Strozier & Offer, 1985). In the hands of psychoanalysts, psychohistory has been limited to an understanding of collective actions from an individualistic orientation. It has focused too much on neurotic mechanisms and the inner person, whose ideas and thoughts are interpreted by an analyst who is far distant in place and time from the leader (Gay, 1985).

Recourse to more objective methods that are also projective techniques is likely to move researchers toward establishing more confidence in the findings about the hidden and unconscious motives and the implicit theories of leadership that affect interactions. For example, Boal, Hunt, and Sorenson (1988) constructed a "Leadership Quotes" questionnaire. Respondents indicated whether each of 133 famous quotations (such as "People are more easily led than driven," "The world needs able men who can create and lead others," and "Happy the kings whose thrones are founded on their peoples' hearts" were related to leadership and whether the leadership was effective or ineffective. Multiple factors emerged that dealt with the direction of activities, influential interactions, legitimate power to lead, and initiation of structure.

In the future, we are likely to see more joining of motivational analyses of the biographies of world-class leaders, analyses of their speeches and writings, news accounts of their performances, and evaluations of them by historians and political scientists. Much of this joining is already to be seen, for example, in the work of House, Woycke, and Fodor (1988).

Behavioral Methods

Behavioral accounts are still the most popular. Purely behavioral explanations cannot be dismissed. One can look at leadership as a perceptual phenomenon under certain conditions or as a behavioral phenomenon under other conditions and accurately explain what is happening in both instances. Research on leadership has been heavily dependent on subordinates' reported perceptions of their leaders' behavior. Yet Gilmore, Beehr, and Richter (1979) demonstrated, in a laboratory setting, that participants failed to perceive that their leaders (who had been instructed to be high or low in initiation and consideration) actually differed in their behavior. Nevertheless, higher-quality work by the subordinates resulted if the leaders' behavior was actually high rather than low in initiation and consideration. The lowest-quality work occurred when the leader's initiation of structure was high but consideration was low. It is clear that studies that do not depend solely on perceptions are still needed.

Among the promising behaviorally-oriented methods is one that shifts attention away from the leader's *frequency* of behavior to the leader's *intensity* of behavior. Influenced by opponent process theory, Sheridan, Kerr, and Abelson (1982) examined the intensity, rather than the frequency, of a leader's actions. Seven dimensions of leadership behavior were scaled: task direction, participation, consideration, performance feedback, integrity, performance reward, and representation. Intensive task direction was illustrated by "taking time to instruct subordinates in proper work techniques in their jobs." The lack of intensive task direction was illustrated by "bringing new employees into the group without providing any direction or indication of their job responsibilities."

Multidimensional Scaling

The use of multidimensional scaling in the study of leadership also has not been exploited as much as it could be. One example was provided by Misumi (1985), who described the use of the Quantification of Pattern Classification as a multidimensional scaling method for assigning quantitative values to categorizations of leadership and their effects. At the same time, not to be ignored are old methods that can be applied to new taxonomies of leadership behavior. For example, Van Fleet and Yukl (1986b) trained students to code more than 2,500 entries for each of 23 behavior categories as the students encountered them in biographies and autobiographies of military leaders. Clarifying work roles, setting goals, monitoring the environment, planning, and inspiration were the most frequent entries. Bass, Avolio, and Goodheim (1987) asked students to complete the Multifactor Leadership Survey questionnaire about the world-class leaders whose biographies they read. Inspirational leadership emerged as an important factor, along with other transformational factors.

Observation of Behavior

Davis and Luthans (1984) demonstrated the usefulness of idiosyncratic observational efforts. They observed over time what happens when a single leader, in this case a production manager, takes a specific action: the introduction of a new scheduling form with complete instructions and deadlines. The investigators found that the new form resulted in improvements in the quality and quantity of production that could be explained from the cause-effect linkages in what they were able to observe in detail. The Leadership Observation System (LOS) was developed by Luthans and Lockwood (1984) to be used by trained participants and observers to record independently the behavior of managers using time sampling. Twelve leadership behavior categories with numerous subcategories emerged from a Delphi process that began with 100 categories of possible managerial behaviors. A typical category was planning/coordinating. Within this category were subcategories, such as setting goals and objectives. In a study of 120 managers in a number of organizations, Lockwood (1981) found that LOS had greater convergent and discriminant validity than parallel descriptions of the same managers with the LBDQ-Form XII or the Managerial Behavior Scales. Different conclusions about managers' consideration and initiation of structure were reached when the different methods were applied.

At odds with Strong's atheoretical approach (1984) to ethnographic analysis has been the construction of new observational procedures based on explicit theories and models. Although observational studies of leadership are not new, among the most promising current approaches are those that use observations of leadership based on a formal model of interrelated measurements. Particularly notable has been the emergence of increasingly sophisticated methodologies to observe behaviors and their linkage to theory in their construction. SYMLOG (Bales, Cohen, & Williamson, 1979) uses teams of up to five observers, each of whom is on his or her own time schedule. The observers pick out salient acts of the members of academic self-study groups. Twenty-six general behaviors of a member, such as "active, dominant, talks a lot," and 26 value descriptions, such as "making others feel happy," can be recorded and profiled in terms of three dimensions: friendly versus unfriendly, dominant versus submissive, and instrumentally controlled versus emotionally expressive. Members rate one another on these dimensions. Their images of one another reflect the polarization or unification of the group. The observed leadership behaviors and inferred values are examined for their decisive influence on the polarization or unification.

Even more closely tied to theory, Komaki, Zlotnick, and Jensen (1986) began with a theory-based taxonomy of supervisory behavior and then proceeded to develop appropriate observational measures. The taxonomy included three categories based on the theory of operant conditioning: antecedents, monitoring, and consequences of performance. Further classification broke down the observed supervisory behavior into own and solitary performance and work and nonwork-related behavior. Archival records could be consulted in addition to observed work samples and others' reports and self-reports about designated actions. Satisfactory interrelated reliabilities were obtained, along with differential patterns of effective and ineffective supervisory behavior (Komaki, 1986). The results were particularly promising because they can be linked to the voluminous psychological research that deals with operant conditioning.

Martinko and Gardner (1984a) designed and utilized a model involving field observation of leaders' external and work environments, competencies, needs, and causal attributions. Also included were categories of behavior (such as planning, organizing, directing, and rewarding) and outcomes. With the procedures and model, the time and event patterns of more effective and less effective school principals could be readily distinguished. For instance, in comparison to principals who were low performers, those who were high performers used more diverse media for communication and initiated more contacts with teachers and students. Metcalfe (1984) analyzed the behavior of leaders in taped appraisal interviews. A behavior that distinguished effective from ineffective interviewers was the greater frequency with which leaders invited participation from their followers.

Simulation and Games

Increasingly, along with the theory-based observations of behavior for research on leadership, simulations that feature interactive computer programs portraying problem situations likely will become common. Research on maximizing the utility of such programs and evaluating their impact on the performance of leaders will be likely in the decades ahead. Simulation offers the opportunity to examine perceptions, cognitions, motivations, and behaviors simultaneously. In a live field study, observers have no control over what they are observing. This fact places a premium on high-fidelity simulation as a method of inquiry. With high-fidelity simulation, the antecedent conditions and contingencies can be controlled, to a considerable degree, and time can be compressed to facilitate the observational processes and linkages to outcomes. The future is likely to see increasing reliance on simulations to provide opportunities for research on cognitive processes as well as on observed behavior.

Developed from earlier attempts with small-group exercises, in-basket tests, computerized business games, and larger organizational games, high-fidelity simulations have become a fine art that provides opportunities to manipulate variables experimentally in laboratory conditions that approach field studies. Subjects may be hired for a week to do, as far as they know, real clerical work in a seemingly real office. Computer simulations provide complete visual and auditory displays in which leader-subordinate relations can be examined. Complex business games that last for many months are conducted, in which many of the elements of real-world decisions must be dealt with satisfactorily and in which leaders may find themselves involved in labor negotiations and with real boards of directors. Complex military and political games played by real military and political leaders can both provide training and clarify the most probable effects on decisions for the real world. The future will bring increasing fidelity to the games.

As illustrated in Chapter 35, the Looking Glass is a finely developed simulation and parallel-in-miniature to managing Corning Glass. The Looking Glass re-creates for players the hierarchy of positions, necessary requirements, and interactions to running a sample organization. Salient variables can be manipulated in a collapsed time frame. Follow-up critiques of players in these simulations make it possible to gain insight into the processes and relationships perceived to be of consequence to the players (McCall & Lombardo, 1982). Videotaping can store the experience for later intensive analysis.

Mathematical Modeling

Mathematical modeling is another approach to simulation that has a great deal of unexploited potential for leadership research. Zahn and Wolf (1981) used the Markov model to chain events that related the current hypothetical task-oriented or relations-oriented performance of supervisors to future states of supervisory-subordinate relationships. The model could be manipulated to see designed hypothetical effects on outcomes. Long-term behavior was determined to be highly variable and versatile. Both the leader and the subordinates could influence the system.

What If?

What if? is a thought experiment or a mental simulation of possible events at turning points of history and its leaders. It is counterfactual. What if Lee Harvey Oswald's bullet had missed John F. Kennedy in 1963? Would Lyndon Johnson's reforms have been delayed? Would the United States still be entangled in Vietnam? What if the Germans had not arranged in 1917 for Lenin to go by train from his exile in Switzerland through Germany and German-occupied land, to emerge in St. Petersburg? Would the Bolsheviks have taken over from the Democratic Kerensky regime for the next 70 years following the October Revolution? Would the monarchy have been restored? Would fascism have taken over, so that Russia would have been allied with Germany, Italy, and Japan in World War II? How different would world history have been if the Supreme Court's 5–4 decision had not terminated the reexamination of the Florida balloting and given the 2000 presidential election to the less experienced, conservative Republican George W. Bush instead of to the more experienced Al Gore, a liberal Democrat who had won the popular vote but not the electoral college vote?

The Need to Use Multiple Methods

No one approach is fully adequate, by itself, to understand the leadership process. Yukl (1982) pointed out that cognitive processes, for instance, are unlikely to be reliably detected from observation alone. Yukl and Van Fleet (1982) found, when analyzing four studies to identify effective patterns of leadership behavior among military cadets and U.S. Air Force officers, that different results materialize when nonquestionnaire methods, such as the critical incidents technique, are employed than when questionnaires are used in the same situation. They noted that leadership consideration was important to effective leadership in the critical incidents analyses but not in the questionnaire surveys, whereas coordination was important to effective leadership in the questionnaire surveys but not in the critical incidents studies.

There will continue to be proponents of one method over another. For instance, there will continue to be proponents of a *cognitive-perceptual* approach and advocates of a *behavioral* approach to understanding. Still others will emphasize social factors. Hooijberg, Hunt, and Dodge (1997) suggested that a full account of leader-outcome results would require the use of more complex approaches—cognitive, behavioral and social—for comprehensive explanations of leadership, followership, and their interaction.

Substantive Issues

In a discipline, consensus about a new paradigm usually develops slowly. Nevertheless, a number of new substantive issues quickly aroused attention in the last quarter of the twentieth century and the twenty-first century. For example, charismatic and transformational leadership can be studied in small groups and in the histories of world-class leaders with the same theoretical framework. Historical studies of leaders in the past were stories about prominent figures who had influenced events (Luecke, 1994). Relatively recent and continuing cultural, behavioral, social, and/or political science explanations of institutions, followers, leaders, and events are in force. More than just narratives of the past, they are stories about elites and ordinary people, individual choices and collective experiences, unusual and normal events, and social, political, educational, and economic problems. Historians provide descriptive statistics and maps to buttress their propositions. In the future, some may analytically test the validity of hypotheses about qualitative and quantitative changes linked to the leaders (Fischer, 1989). Illustrative is the investigation of the constructiveness and destructiveness of charismatic leaders by psychologists (O'Connor, Mumford, Clifton, Gessner & Connelly, 1995). The centuries-old person-versus-situation controversy is likely to remain with us, with more attention in the future to genetics and hormonal effects. New co-twin studies are to be expected of the heritability of leadership behavior. Hormonal levels will also be considered. Thus

Dabbs (2000) suggested that testosterone level is a biological aspect of temperament. Coupled with a proclivity for action, this factor has predicted firefighting and emergency medical performance. It may predict a leader's power, motivation, dominance, boldness, focused attention, frame of mind, and leadership style, along with the emergence of violent or conciliatory behavior. Hormonal levels may become increasingly important as women take more positions of leadership.

Jago (1982) believed that much more needed to be done to compare the validity of universal and contingent theories of leadership. Since then, mounting evidence has supported the point of view that both personal factors and contingencies are involved. How much of each is important is an empirical question for continuing research (Bass, 1997).

Personal Factors Associated with Leadership

There has been a renewal of interest in the personal factors of leadership. Although research designed solely to isolate the characteristics of leaders was thought to have reached the point of diminishing returns, it has been revived in a new form with the emergence of interest in the life-span development of leaders, particularly transformational leaders. The need to learn more about what contributes to the self-confidence, self-determination, and freedom from inner conflict of the charismatic leader is apparent. The quest for a greater understanding of personality and the personality dynamics that affect leaders' performance transcends situational considerations. Programmatic efforts to look at personality, as such, are also suggested by the developments of assessment centers, as well as long-term predictions of success as a manager. Increasingly, character is seen as of prime importance to leadership.

Paige (1977) proposed a hypothesis that still awaits empirical confirmation: leaders choose tasks and engage in them on the basis of personal considerations, such as their age. Thus, what could be a tempting challenge to a 40-year-old executive might be sidestepped by his or her 60-year-old counterpart. More often than not, even when there is a lack of supporting evidence, personality is seen as interacting with situational variables to account for leadership and group performance. It may be more important in some situations than others and with some

people more than others. It may be dominant in cultural settings where, to be a leader, one must epitomize the authoritarianism rooted in the culture. Autocrats may behave the way they do because of their personalities; democrats may behave the way they do as a consequence of both their personalities and other immediate situational and personal considerations (Farrow & Bass, 1977).

Research that is designed to test the effects on the group of the interaction of the characteristics of the leader and the followers has generally been effective in producing valuable insights into leader-follower relations. Research in the 1950s and 1960s on different combinations of authoritarian leaders and followers continues to suggest designs that could be used to test the effects of other leader-follower characteristics. Although much has been done with reference to the need for achievement, the need for affiliation, internal and external loss of control, and so on, many other personality dimensions can be examined in the same way to test the interaction of the leader's personality, values, and behaviors with the followers' personalities, values, and behaviors and the effect of such interaction on the group. Interest is strong in examining how the leader's style of thinking, as measured by the Myers-Briggs Type Inventory, interacts with the followers' styles. To be kept in mind is the likelihood that extreme homogeneity in leader-follower characteristics may be dysfunctional to satisfactory problem solving by the group that requires flexibility and creativity. With increased interest in charismatic-transformational leadership, *time orientation* of leaders to the past, present, or future is an underresearched issue likely to be examined more frequently in the future (Daltrey & Langer, 1984).

The Leader's and Manager's Role

Suggestions continue to be made that research on leadership—in addition to its narrowness—has been concentrating on the wrong thing. The aim of science is to understand. Understanding is checked by prediction. Adequate prediction can produce control. Practitioners are anxious to provide such control when their understanding is far from perfect. Research on leadership is faulted when it fails to improve such control immediately. Basic research should be judged on whether it contributes to understanding.

The failure of adequate prediction to make the suitable control of behavior possible may also be partly a consequence of the unpredictable and uncontrollable elements in the real-world performance of leaders. Mintzberg (1973) and many others since have concluded that instead of a systematic, steady, orderly attack on one problem at a time, the practicing manager is more likely to be observed devoting short bursts of time to different problems. Frequently interrupted, the manager unsystematically responds to a diversity of demands from superiors, peers, clients, and subordinates. (This behavior helps explain the popularity of management training in time management.) Given the large array of diverse situations that are the daily regimen of the general manager, M. W. McCall (1977) suggested that much of the research to determine which type of leadership style is most effective in particular conditions may remain an impractical academic exercise because the demand characteristics of the manager's role result in the manager optimizing his or her performance by "proficient superficiality" (Mintzberg, 1973). Insufficient time is given to different problems to deal with each of them fully and adequately.

A promising approach looks at how the leader's identity, prototypicality, and representativeness of the team, the followers' social identification with the team, and team members' desires for closure to reduce uncertainty contribute to various criteria of satisfaction and effectiveness. Pierro, Cicero, Bonaiuto, et al. (2005) surveyed 242 manager professionals and white-collar and blue-collar employee members of three Italian firms in petrochemicals, manufacturing, and electronics. Leader prototypicality correlated .41 with perceived leader effectiveness and .20 with job satisfaction. Intentions to quit were high when leader prototypicality was low, but only when members were also high in preference for closure. The members' self-rated performance was high when the leader's prototypicality was high, but only when members were high in preference for closure.

Innovation and Creativity. Mumford, Connelly, and Gaddis (2003) concluded from a set of experiments that for leaders to promote creativity and innovation, they must possess creative thinking skills. These may provide a critical perspective in evaluative operations in collaboration with followers. More needs to be learned about the leader's contribution to the followers' creativity. The leader's competence in this regard may depend

on: (1) his or her awareness of temporal complexity in a "knowledge-rich," hypercompetitive technological environment (Halbesleben, Novicevic, Harvey, et al., 2003); (2) whether the leader accepts, challenges, or synthesizes different ways of doing things (Sternberg, Kaufman, & Pretz, 2003); (3) how transformational leadership contributes to innovation (Jung, Chow, & Wu, 2003); (4) how the transformational leader's unconventional behavior can add to the group's creativity (Jaussi & Dionne, 2003); (5) how transformational leadership and members' anonymity can make a difference (Kahai, Sosik, & Avolio, 2003); (6) the leader's emotional intelligence (Zhou & George, 2003).

We need to learn more about why, when jobs are routine, extrinsic rewards contribute to the innovativeness of cognitively adaptive followers but, when jobs are complex, the results of extrinsic rewards may be negative (Baer, Oldham, and Cummings, 2003). Mumford and Licuan (2004) concluded that further research is needed on: (1) how leaders choose the performance strategies that influence the innovations they are willing to support; (2) how leaders establish a creative group identity; (3) how leaders need to understand the importance of emotions in the leadership of creativity in the groups they lead. Research is also needed that distinguishes: (1) leading idea generation and idea implementation; (2) leadership of routine groups and leadership of creative groups; (3) leadership of groups working on significant innovations being implemented. We need to learn the cognitive requirements that contribute to a follower's creativity (Reiter & Illies, 2004). Further evidence needs to be found about how a leader's consultation increases followers' creativity and how clarification of roles and objectives affects it (Amabile, Schatzel, Moneta, et al., 2004). Such clarity provides clear objectives, commitment to excellence, and support for innovation (West, Borrill, Dawson, et al., 2003). Research is needed on: (1) how to be participative and delegative leaders and yet be able to impart expert knowledge to promote subordinates' creativity (Krause, 2004); (2) about what contextual features in the leader-subordinate relationship promote followers' creativity (Shalley & Gilson, 2004); (3) how team members with different preferences in the creative process can be brought to think together innovatively (Basadur, 2004). Further studies are also required of the champions of innovation, how they informally influence idea generation in the organization and pursue a flexible role orientation. Cognitive mapping of their mental models is needed (Howell & Boies, 2004).

Leader-Member Exchange. In addition to seeing the leader's role as less orderly, Graen (1976) shifted attention away from the unilateral and consistent group-oriented behavior of the leader toward a focus on the mutual role relationships of the leader with each different member of the group. The quality of this reciprocal relationship contains considerable explanatory value, and researchers should continue to explore its antecedents and consequences with methods described earlier, to ascertain its importance relative to average leader-group effects. Nonetheless, Dienesch and Liden (1986) argued that to be more fully utilized, leader-member exchange needs to be conceived of as a multidimensional variable involving perceived contributions, loyalty, and affect. Research is needed on the different ways in which the leader-member relationship varies, and the different outcomes that will occur as a consequence.

Succession and Retention of the Leadership Position

Various personal characteristics—rates of talking and interaction, capacity to interact, ability to perform a task, dominance, exclusive possession of information, initiation of spontaneity, provision of freedom to the group, and acceptance of group members—have been found to be associated with emergence as a leader. It has not been demonstrated, however, that these are the same variables that enable the leader to retain his or her role. There is a need for research that isolates the factors that facilitate retention of a position of leadership once it has been attained. There is an abundance of evidence about factors that contribute to the emergence of a leader; there is a dearth of research on factors that enable a leader to consolidate his or her position once it has been obtained. In the same way, the characteristics required to win election to political office may be quite different from those required for success and effectiveness as an officeholder. An important problem that has been ignored concerns the effects of training on the retention of the leadership role. What kind of training strengthens or weakens an individual's chances of retaining the leadership position?

Issues of Succession. Increasing empirical attention to the replacement and succession problem would seem to have great utility. There are many issues to be explored in this regard. Nathan (1989) concluded that whether a succession had a positive or negative effect or no effect on an organization depended on the study's method, the criterion of effectiveness, and the level of analysis. Continuing good organizational performance will slow successions; continuing poor organizational performance will speed up successions. Several questions needing future research include: What are the optimum rates of succession for different types of groups, organizations, or institutions? How is the succession used as a tool of strategic change? How do successors cope best with initial resistance? Do the dynamics of the succession process change over time? Is the cost of accelerating the recruitment and compensation of successor CEOs justified? (In 1965, the compensation of CEOs of major U.S. corporations averaged 24 times that of their average worker. The ratio was 38 times in 1978, 71 times in 1989, and 262 times in 2005–$10.9 million for the average CEO compared to $41,861 for the average worker.)

Many other questions about the succession process can also be posed: Does a successor executive ignore the former occupant's performance in an executive position, see it competitively, or attempt to build on it? Should the former occupant be involved in the choice of the successor? Does the former occupant help or hinder the succession process? When occupants are "lame ducks" and must give up office in a designated amount of time, how does the time limit shape their objectives, planning, and power? How does the loss of institutional knowledge affect legislatures whose members cannot run for reelection after two or three terms?

Types of Successors. Sonnenfeld (1988) was able to interview 50 CEOs and their senior management about the CEOs' retirement experience and succession plans—interviews that were difficult to obtain. Four types of CEOs were identified: (1) *Monarchs* did not leave office willingly but were overthrown. (2) *Generals* left office reluctantly but instituted campaigns to return to office. (3) *Ambassadors* remained active in the firm after leaving office and supported their successors; (4) *Governors* left the firm cleanly and cut all formal contact with it. Each type had advantages and disadvantages. The *monarch* had brilliant visions, assumed personal responsibility for problems, created order in the face of environmental disturbances, and was completely dedicated. The firm grew in assets, sales, employees, and shareholder support. At the same time, the monarch stubbornly defended old strategies and was reluctant to develop the next generation of leadership. The *general* was capable of building strong leaders but was cautious about leadership transitions and was ready to return to office if needed. But the general fueled internal rivalries, encouraged resistance to successors, and even undermined them. The *ambassador* provided long service, continuity of command, and wisdom as an elder statesman. As a member of many outside boards, with wide contacts and community interests, the ambassador remained available for assignment as an external representative of the firm and was familiar with other approaches to management. But his continued presence became awkward, he supported inappropriate fads, and he needed to defend his record. He wanted to remain available to give advice that was unwanted. The *governor* was in office for only a short time. His organization was a large, stable, and formal bureaucracy. He had a wide range of outside business interests, which may have distracted him from his responsibilities of office. The firm's performance lagged. He gave his successor little help except for the freedom to revamp his strategy. When he retired, he completely cut connections with his organization. Many of Sonnenfeld's qualitative conclusions and typology can form the basis of future quantitative studies of executive retirement and succession.

Leadership and Power

Those who tend to conceive leadership as nothing but a form of social power obscure important relationships between leadership and power and restrict the range of research on the problem. More research is needed on the interaction of power with leadership behavior and personality. Questions remain: (1) Will followers respond positively to a leader with power who exhibits task-oriented rather than relations-oriented behavior? (2) How will the personality of the followers and the urgency to complete the task affect their response? (3) Are there patterns of a leader's personality that may mitigate the adverse effects of coercive power? (4) Can a sense of humor exert a strong moderating effect? (5) Will coercive power

and strong control be more readily accepted when the leader's and followers' values are highly similar than when they are not? (6) What factors tend to legitimate different forms of power among members of a group? (7) What factors tend to legitimate different forms of power in the eyes of observers who are not members of the group? (8) What contributes to a leader's continuing to be held in high regard despite his making one mistake after another? (9) How do presidents and television evangelists maintain their power and charisma regardless of the quality of their performance? (10) What are the limits to the possibilities of "damage control"? (11) When does reward power become adverse in its effects?

Power Equalization. Research on the equalization of power has been attended by serious difficulties. Appropriate control organizations are seldom available for comparative purposes when some form of power equalization is introduced into an organization. External forces are almost impossible to control. The effects of social, political, and economic factors may be stronger than any variations that can be introduced. Simulated organizations may provide a better setting for the study of the equalization of power in the large organization.

Conflict of Roles and Ideas. Research on role conflict, conducted primarily in formal organizations, is deficient in experimental controls. Here again, it would be advantageous to study role conflict in simulated organizations in which conflict-inducing demands can be varied and controlled. Research is needed to determine the extent to which various styles of the personality and behavior of leaders are subject to role conflict. We need to know more about how controversy—conflicts of ideas—can result in creative outcomes. Tjosvold (1985d) pointed to the importance of goal interdependence, confirmation, and collaborative influence in this regard. These factors would be relevant to strategic decision making, policy setting, and participative leadership. A small number of competently executed studies are available on the legitimization of the leadership role. More studies are needed. Little is yet known about what makes a leader legitimate and why and what the effects of such legitimacy are. The importance of the subject merits a much higher rate of activity in this area. In future research, it would be desirable to determine the effect of variations in the followers' characteristics, as well as variations in a leader's characteristics. One would like to know, for example, for what types of follower a given characteristic or pattern of behavior tends to legitimate the leadership role. In addition, it would be useful to know under what conditions a given pattern of leadership behavior is regarded as legitimate or illegitimate and by what type of follower. From a practical point of view, the problem of the legitimization of leaders is one that should be given high priority in future research. With the expected continued increase in knowledge work, the formal leader of a knowledge work group needs to share leadership. Leadership in knowledge work done in teams should rotate to the worker with the knowledge, skills, and abilities for the work at hand. Leadership will rotate when knowledge tasks are highly complex and interdependent and when much creativity is required (Pearce, 2004). Much is still to be learned about how *superleaders* (see Chapter 20) share their power by converting and legitimatizing others to lead themselves (Goel, Manz, Neck, et al., 1995). They convert leaders into self-leaders. The suppressive effects of power on followers suggest the need for more subtle approaches to data collection than direct questioning. We should also be seeing more multiple methods examining the same power and leadership issues. Authority and responsibility, linked to power but conceptually different, could be examined more fully in their distribution as sources of organizational pathology.

Conflict Management. What should be done for managers who want to be participative but have poor skills in conflict management? Are there high costs for such managers who bring their subordinates together to resolve conflicts among them? (Crouch & Yetton, 1987). Burgess, Salas, Cannon-Bowers, et al. (1992) prepared training guidelines for teams under stress. To correct errors leaders needed to learn transactional practices such as contingent rewarding and management by exception (MBE). MBE included troubleshooting and double-checking of team members' performance focused on the immediate task. Transformational leadership was suggested for handling future crises, understanding the mission, aligning individual and team goals, providing support, and establishing trust and cooperation.

Empirical studies are needed of the mathematical approach that Brams (1993) developed for resolving con-

flicts. Opportunities should be expanded for learning more about crisis management based on the increased willingness of decision makers to air their mistakes. The disclosure by U.S. and Soviet decision makers in 1989, 27 years after the Cuban missile crisis in 1962, of how each side misread the other's intentions and almost jointly precipitated World War III is illustrative (Keller, 1989). Likewise, Whyte's (1989) addition to the factors that underlie "groupthink" may further elucidate events when leadership fails during a crisis. Whyte noted the tendency for a group to polarize around the point of view initially dominant in the group. This tendency usually frames the leader's and group's decision as a choice between two or more unattractive options. Threats are not seen as possible opportunities. Risk seeking occurs as a way of gambling for a reasonable chance to avoid the certain losses. Much still has to be learned about the U.S. leadership's initiating a preemptive war against Iraq, a secular state, when it was fundamentalist religious Muslims in Saudi Arabia who were mainly responsible for the 2001 terrorist attacks on the United States. How much was due to the groupthink of the neoconservative advisers in the Bush administration? How much was due to the false intelligence that the Iraqis had weapons of mass destruction? How much did Saddam Hussain's game-playing behavior about inspections contribute to the sense of threat from Iraq? How much was due to failures, secrecy, and poor communications among the 15 U.S. security agencies? How much did the excessive layers of bureaucracy affect decision making? How much did the destruction of the World Trade Center on September 11, 2001, and the desire for retaliation contribute (*The 9/11 Commission Report,* 2004)? The mishandling of the Hurricane Katrina disaster in 2005 and its flooding of New Orleans and the Gulf Coast will be the subject of studies for years to come.

In the business world we need to learn more about the human costs and benefits of acquisitions and mergers. A great many fail to achieve the expected benefits from the combining of firms. Failures are estimated to be as high as 80% due to choice of partners, lack of clarity of strategy, incompatibility of organizational cultures, and inadequate preparation of their organizations' members for the event (Marks & Mirvis, 2000).

Leadership Styles

To some degree, all research on leadership styles prior to Burns's (1978) introduction of the concepts of transformational versus transactional leadership could be conceived of as being about democratic, autocratic, or laissez-faire leadership, which takes us back to where it all began, in 1938 with Lewin and Lippitt's seminal experiment. Each of these three styles is described by either the amount of overall activity of the leaders or the extent to which the leaders are oriented toward being completely work-oriented or completely person-oriented.

Ordinarily, leaders' performance will be better if they are more active than inactive. But activity does not guarantee effective, satisfied, and cohesive groups. A number of hypotheses need to be tested further. For instance, it has been suggested that leaders tend to be more autocratic and directive when it is easier and more comfortable for them to be so because of their own personalities and because goals are clear and structure is given. But it has also been proposed that leaders really need to be directive and structuring when goals are not clear and structure is not given. Another suggestion is that leaders tend to be more democratic, participative, relations-oriented, and considerate when they are concerned about the need for input and reactions from subordinates. Again, how different personalities and situational demands play their parts can be tested in designated organizational settings to determine the importance of selection in contrast to training of leaders.

Dimensions. Many dimensions of autocratic and democratic leadership have been proposed to describe leaders' different styles. The relationships among some of the dimensions have been clarified and altered. Borrowing from work motivation theory, researchers have purged the initiation-of-structure scales of their coercive components and have relabeled them instrumental (to the success of the task). Similarly, consideration is now seen as supportive leadership, and its focus is now on leaders' attention to the different needs of individual subordinates rather than to the use of group methods.

The situational leadership approach, as in the Hersey-Blanchard model, and an approach to the best way of integrating task and relations orientation, as advocated by Blake and Mouton, need to be compared with a variety of methods and measurement instruments. Studies ought to be conducted that make the comparisons in simulated organizations and in controlled laboratory settings, as well as in content analyses of documents and time-sampling observations in the field.

It should be clear that factor analyses can establish only how leaders are distributed empirically in the eyes of observers of their performance on given dimensions, such as *directive*, negotiative, consultative, *participative*, and delegative.[5] However, leaders in real-life positions tend to reveal performance on all the dimensions but in different amounts, although the dimensions are conceptually distinct but not empirically uncorrelated.

One can stress the utility of consultation (the manager's most frequent style) as a useful style in general. But, as Vroom (1976b) noted, concrete situations may demand otherwise. And leaders do change their styles in response to situational conditions (Hill & Hughes, 1974).

The differential effects of task-related and person-related clusters of leadership styles suggest that two central needs are: a response allocation analysis, to sort out the different styles from one another conceptually; and more factorial analyses to determine the empirical communalities among the styles. Researchers need to take into account the well-established negative impact on the group of the inactivity of a laissez-faire leader with the possibly but not necessarily positive impact of various types of active intervention by the leader.

Theory and research are needed about the various kinds of considerate behavior. Consideration, as measured by the LBDQ, tends to be noncontingent, unlike the contingent rewarding of the MLQ. For instance, LBDQ items about how much the leader helps and does favors for the group do not refer to the group's performance. Nor does LBDQ consideration correlate highly with the individualized consideration factor score of the MLQ (Seltzer & Bass, 1990), which tends to concentrate on how much the leader is concerned about followers' differential development needs.

---

[5] As detailed in Chapters 18 and 19, *direction* (italicized) refers only to giving orders with or without explanation. Direction (romanized) includes ordering, persuading, and manipulating. *Participation* (italicized) refers only to sharing in the decision process. Participation (romanized) includes consulting, sharing, and delegating.

Transformational and Transactional Leadership

Before the 1980s, behavioral research on leadership concentrated on the transactional exchange between the leader and the led. The leader clarified what needed to be done and the benefits of compliance to the self-interests of the followers. In the new paradigm, the transformational leader moves followers to transcend their own interests for the good of the group, organization, or society (Burns, 1978; Bass, 1985a). Paraphrasing Zaleznik (1977), transformational leaders, like charismatics, attract strong feelings of identification from their subordinates.

The 1980s were a decade in which empirical research was initiated with this new paradigm in mind. As noted in Chapter 25, a number of survey questionnaires, such as the Multifactor Leadership Questionnaire (MLQ), were used extensively in a variety of organizations and countries (Bass, 1997). In the twenty-first century, the work has expanded into new areas, such as the empirical connection of transformational leadership with corporate social responsibility (Waldman, Siegel, & Javidan, 2004).[6] Much more still needs to be done, especially in teasing out the dynamics involved. Some empirical support has been obtained of followers' strong beliefs in the leader as a person. Do these beliefs go beyond the leader's actual competence? Followers have faith that the leader will make it possible for the group to succeed. Are they justified in their faith? Do the followers willingly give the leader too much power to act in crises? Do such leaders transform followers into leaders? Podsakoff, MacKenzie, Moorman, and Fetter (1990) have shown the importance of *trust* as a variable intervening between transformational leadership and outcomes in performance and satisfaction.

Generally, transformational leadership augments transactional leadership (Waldman, Bass, & Yammarino, 1988). But under what conditions do they conflict? How can one add the fostering of the pursuit of group and organizational goals (in transformational leadership) to the promotion of self-interest (in transactional leadership)? Much more research lies ahead about the components of transformational and transactional leadership: charisma and inspiration, intellectual stimulation, individualized

---

[6]See Chapter 14.

---

consideration, contingent rewarding, and active management by exception (which includes contingent but not noncontingent punishment).

> Transformational leadership theory has now gone from being novel and interesting to initial acceptance; to critiques of what is missing . . . a much deeper investigation [is needed] of what constitutes the constructs of transformational leadership and how it can be measured, developed, and projected through technology in virtual teams and organizations. (Avolio & Yammarino, 2002, p. 388)

Charisma and Inspirational Leadership. Leaders of political, social, and labor and student movements as well as managers, ministers, battalion commanders, teachers, coaches, and directors can be found who fit the description of persons to whom followers form deep emotional attachments and who, in turn, inspire their followers to go beyond their own interests for superordinate goals, higher goals than the followers previously recognized. Even in hardened bureaucracies, there are leaders with knowledge of the system, good connections, and the ability to mobilize and husband resources. Such leaders keep their eyes on the bigger issues and take the risks required for "creative administration," which gives them the large amount of *idiosyncrasy credit* necessary to arouse in subordinates complete faith and trust in them and a willingness to strive for the higher goals they set forth as challenges for the group.

To understand the high expectations of success generated by the charismatic leader, we can look at Field and Van Seters' (1989) proposal to combine the self-altering prophecies of the Pygmalion and Galatea effects to generate an energized group, organization, or society of high expectations in which members act with positive expectations about one another. This group is labeled the "Metharme effect" by Field (1989), after the daughter of Pygmalion and Galatea (Field & Van Seters, 1989). House and Shamir (1993) and Shamir, House, and Arthur (1993) began a theoretical explanation of the effects of transactional and transformational leadership. Transactional leaders focus on pragmatic paths and goals that can be reached by followers. Transformational leaders produce in their followers a greater sense of: (1) collective identity in their self-concepts; (2) consistency between their self-concepts and their actions for the leader; (3) self-worth and self-esteem; (4) similarity between their self-concept and perception of the leader; (5) collective efficacy; (6) meaning in their work and lives. Charismatic/transformational leaders arouse in followers unconscious motives of achievement, power, and affiliation.

Idealized Influence. Handy (1994) noted that Maslow's (1954) hierarchy of needs from safety and security to self-realization failed to include a need for *idealization*, a higher need than self-realization, not as self-centered as the rest of the hierarchy. Bass and Avolio (1989–2003) began to substitute *idealized influence* for charismatic leadership because of charisma's popular association with flamboyance and malevolent dictators. Idealized influence was thought, like inspirational leadership, to correlate highly with charismatic leadership. For Handy (1994, p. 275), Maslow's hierarchy was all self-centered. At a higher level was idealization, "the pursuit of an ideal or a cause that is more than oneself." Handy's concept may relate better to Howell and House's (1992) concept of *socialized* charisma than to *personalized* charisma. Is this also true for idealized influence?

Collective Motivation. An interesting research issue is raised by the question of how collective motivation is promoted in organizations. Collective motivation on the part of employees was seen by Lawler (1982) to be a matter of outcomes that they valued occurring from the performance of the organization and their own contributions to that performance. But Staw (1984) argued that collective motivation depends on employees' identification with the organization and their contributions to the organization's performance. Transformational leadership theory would go further and imply that collective motivation is generated by the employees' identification with their leader and the employees' and their leader's identification with the organization and its goals and values. This requires fuller testing empirically.

The Importance of Identification. House, Howell, & Shamir (2002) use the identification of followers with a transformational/charismatic leader to explain why the followers are willing to forgo their own self-interests for the collective mission. The theory they present raises

many questions for the future, including the evolutionary processes that have made social identification such a strong force. In what ways is identification with a charismatic leader and his or her organization important to members' decision making, sense making, satisfaction, and commitment? Why do strong emotions accompany identification with the charismatic leader and mission? How and when does identification cause conformity, groupthink, blind obedience, and abandonment of rationality?

The themes of neo-Weberian charismatic leadership research that are likely to continue are: (1) charisma in everyday life of work, care, friendship, and leisure; (2) focus on the relationships between the leaders and the led, with special emphasis on emotional interactions; (3) a determination of the extent to which the charismatic leader or the charismatic mission drives followers; (4) an explanation of the charismatic mission is institutionalized, routinized, and maintained in the succession (Jermier, 1993). Additionally, research is needed on: (5) how the charismatic leader influences followers' self-concept, self-efficacy, and social identification (Yukl, 1994); (6) how much motivational impetus and routinization in the mission is lost in a succession when the charismatic is replaced, departs, or dies; (7) how much the routinization of the charismatic mission impedes needed organizational changed to facilitate adaptation to the changed environment; (8) how much is lost in the succession without the driving force of the departed charismatic leader (Bryman, 1993).

Intellectual Stimulation. As noted earlier, innovation and creativity often depend on leadership (Mumford & Licuan, 2004). Mueller (1980) described the "leading-edge" leader who deals with "fuzzy futures." This type of leader is able to simplify problems and to get to the crux of complex matters while the rest of the crowd is still trying to identify the problem.[7] Research is needed on this "rapid reification" and how to integrate and relate intellectual stimulation with the logical and intuitive attributes of leadership. With the continuing importance of technological innovation in the twenty-first century, we will see more research on the subject, such as that by Berson, Dionne, and Jaussi (2002) connecting task, technol-

---

[7]This type of leadership is discussed in Chapter 14 as intellectual stimulation, one of the factors in transformational leadership.

ogy, people, and innovative processes both quantitatively and qualitatively.

Individualized Consideration. Future questions to be answered are: How do leaders maintain their recognition for fairness when they treat each of their followers individually? How much do the effects of individualized consideration using the MLQ correlate with the effects of consideration using the LBDQ? When is an individually considerate leader seen by followers as weak? How different is individualized consideration from relations-oriented leadership? Can participation proceed without individualized consideration?

Management by Exception: Contingent Reward and Punishment. Podsakoff and Schriesheim (1985) enumerated a number of unanswered questions about a leader's use of contingent reinforcement for which research is needed. What is the best sequencing of contingent and noncontingent rewards and punishments (when necessary)? How do they interact? Can contingent punishment for poor performance work if it is offset by promises of rewards for appropriate performance? What rewards make promises more or less effective? How important are specificity and focus on the subordinate's performance or products to the efficacy of contingent praise for good performance (as Kanouse, Gumpert, and Canavan-Gumpert [1984] suggested)? How does contingent reinforcement of the individual affect the group? How does contingent reinforcement of the group affect the individual? Further exploration is needed about the conditions when active management by exception is successful and/or effective and when it is not. Is there evidence of its changing in practice when followers are novices versus when they are experts?

The Hierarchy of Effectiveness. A hierarchy of leader-outcome relationships based on survey questionnaire methods and routines has been established in a number of industrial, educational, and military settings. Transformational leadership, particularly charismatic leadership, correlates above .70 with subordinates' satisfaction with the leader and the leader's perceived effectiveness. The transactional contingent reward correlates closer to .40 with these same outcomes in satisfaction, as can the transformational aspect of contingent rewarding of psychological benefits (Antonakis, 2000). Transactional pas-

sive management by exception correlates closer to zero with these outcomes (Yammarino & Bass, 1989). Studies of the more conceptually differentiated personal communication style of the transformational leader, along with his or her mastery of impression management and authenticity, will be important. Will Handy's (1994) *idealization*, the pursuit of ideals, help or hinder effectiveness? Researchers need to examine the conditions that promote the emergence of a transformational leader and how to facilitate this emergence. They need to determine the consequences of moving from an emphasis on social exchange, which characterizes the transactional leader, to leadership that mobilizes and directs members toward higher objectives. They need to study the costs and obvious dangers, as well as the benefits, of transformational leadership. A step in this direction will be to examine further the communication differences between self-oriented and prosocial leaders.

Handling Stress and Conflict. Investigators should be searching for how a transformational or transactional leader moves followers toward acceptance of superordinate goals. How can followers be aroused to self-transcendence? How can a leader move a group from complacency, hasty responses, inertia, or defensiveness in the face of threats to complete and adequate vigilance? If a group is focused primarily on its lower-level needs for safety and security, how can a leader move it toward concern for recognition and achievement? If a group is under stress that is too high for coping with the complexity of the situation, how can the leader steady and calm the group?

Micro-Macro Linkage. Hollander (1985) remained dissatisfied with the overconcentration of research on the microleadership of small groups. More macroleadership studies are needed of how leaders affect the strategic functions of institutions and organizations. For instance, Khan (2002) reported on the transformational and transactional leadership of the executives in 157 sponsoring high-tech Japanese-U.S. alliances, finding that, as predicted, transformational leadership by both the Japanese and American executives resulted in lower innovative effectiveness in the alliance.

The transformational-transactional distinction offers an avenue for tying together research on microleadership and macroleadership. Gordon and Yukl (2004) see the need to link microleadership with strategic leadership. As noted in Chapter 12, transformational leadership—charismatic, intellectually stimulating, inspirational leadership—can be manipulated in the laboratory, reliably observed in small groups playing business games, rated reliably in large organizations at all levels, and used to differentiate among world-class leaders. At the same time, the paradigm lends itself to investigations across the disciplines of political science, organizational science, anthropology, sociology, and psychology.

Selection and Training. We need to be able to train the average supervisor in the sensitivities and interpersonal competencies that are required of a transformational leader. We need to be able to select potential transformational leaders who may not show up well on many currently available predictors of transactional leadership. It may be less difficult to enable leaders to learn how and when to be constructive with contingent rewards or corrective with management by exception. Self-reports, incidents, and 360-degree ratings from 200 executives and 500 leaders in one community were collected during and after their participation in Full Range Leadership Development programs, indicating modest improvements by the trainees in transformational leadership and reduced management by exception. Similar results were found for U.S. Army platoon sergeants and lieutenants from 72 platoons rated by their more than 3,000 subordinates, peers, and superiors (Avolio & Bass, 1996).

Contraindications. Theory and research are needed on the costs and dangers of transformational leaders. Thus Bennis (1989) pointed to the destructive consequences of considering only such successful transformational leaders as Steve Jobs and Lee Iacocca as heroes. Lippman-Blumen (2005, p. 220) warned against heroes with noble visions who are actually toxic for us. We need to "escape the magnetic pull of subtle toxic leaders . . . heroes [who] . . . attract us with challenges and visions that entrap us before we perceive their negative potential, . . . their dark call to battle, genocide, and unjust war." The *toxic leader* is pseudotransformational. Toxic leaders consciously feed followers with illusions that enhance the leaders' power and impair followers' capacity to act independently. They play to followers' basic fears and needs. They mislead followers through deliberate untruths. They treat their own followers well but persuade them to hate others. They are amoral and lack integrity. Their egos and arrogance blind them to their own faults that limit the possibilities of their self-improvement (Lipman-Blumen, 2005, pp. 20–21). Much needs to be learned about the moral development of the toxic pseudotransformational leader when the charismatic leader is a false messiah.

Bass (1985a) speculated on organizational and societal circumstances that might militate against the success and effectiveness of transformational leaders. Spangler and Braiotta (1990) located such an example. Chairmen of audit committees of boards of directors need to be more concerned about good monitoring, auditing, and controlling. For them, transactional leadership may be as effective as transformational leadership. Contingent reward and active management by exception correlated .43 and .39, respectively, with effectiveness judged by colleagues in accounting and auditing inside and outside the firm. Parallel correlations with effectiveness of individualized consideration, intellectual stimulation, and inspirational leadership were .40, .30, and .25 respectively.

Laissez-Faire Leadership

Questions for the future: What makes laissez-faire leadership ineffective and empowerment effective? When is laissez-faire leadership appropriate and effective?

Political Leadership

Political leadership needs to be seen in a positive light as well as a Machiavellian one. Although the evidence (possibly as a consequence of social desirability) points to a general rejection of Machiavellian approaches (withholding information, bluffing, agreeing but delaying, and maintaining social distance), organizational and social decisions can often be understood as a consequence of coalition formation, negotiations, and other beneficial political processes. Decisions are based on the relative power of those involved rather than the merits of the issue.[8] Ammeter, Douglass, Gardner, et al. (2004) agreed that since organizations are an arena for politics (Mintzberg, 1983), they can be beneficial as well as harmful. They can be altruistic as well as self-serving. Ammeter et al. (2002) theorized that the effects of political leadership

[8]Chapter 7, in particular, looked at individual differences in this regard.

in organizations were to be studied, not deprecated Like Cyert & March (1963), they took a neutral stance on organizational politics. Their model proposed that the antecedents and outcomes of political influence depend on many intervening variables, such as the combinations of tactics used, the need to justify decisions, the facilitators of political effectiveness, and the leader's motivation, reputation, and interpersonal style. Also important were the status of the leaders and followers and the question of whether the political behavior was directed toward individuals on a one-to-one basis, in coalitions, or in networks.

Culbert and McDonough (1980) considered effective brokering inside and outside their own groups as a challenge for leaders. Inside the group, the leader should try to negotiate arrangements with the members that make for the best possible mix of members' serving their own interests and meeting the needs of the group. Externally, the leader as a representative can often do much to increase the group's resources and opportunities through effective negotiations with higher authority, with constituencies, and with opposition. Whereas, within organizations such negotiating behavior with individual subordinates may be a counterproductive leadership style,[9] the leader's successful playing of the role of broker is worthy of further exploration.

The effective political use of authority and power is still a highly underresearched area. Particularly important and underresearched is how the would-be organizational politician can be converted into an organizational statesman. It is possible to be an "honest broker," for whom the marshaling of evidence becomes as significant as the relative interests of the parties in a negotiation. In this regard, the similarities and differences between legislative leadership and executive leadership need to be examined more fully. We are likely to see a continuing interest in the specifics of the influence tactics employed by leaders and managers to obtain desired outcomes from their superiors, their subordinates, their organization, and outsiders (Kipnis, Schmidt, Swaffin-Smith, & Wilkinson, 1984), as well as the use of increasingly refined instruments to do so (Schriesheim & Hinken, 1986). Hermann, Snyder, and Cunningham (1980) posed a number of questions about the way the organizational politician uses

staffs, advisers, and confidants: How are they chosen? To what extent do they insulate the leader from the rest of the organization? To what extent do they amplify, distance, or reduce incoming and outgoing communications by the leader?

Drake and Moberg (1986) called for research on how leaders modify their language to create consistent forms of calibration and impression. Contingencies in the phrasing of requests need to be examined. Tactics need to be related to desired outcomes. The effective use of disclaimers needs to be better understood, along with other ways in which the forms of language can foster interaction.

> It is not feasible for even the most active leader of a complex business to have a hand on every lever . . . not practical to juggle with a fast-moving present . . . and the imponderable forces of the future. . . . The direct order [needs to be] replaced by a framework—a set of values to guide the independent actions [of others]. Devising that framework needs sympathetic thought, specific to the objective. . . . The well-tempered leader . . . will combine tactical skill, judgment, and the ability to coalesce the intentions [of others]. . . . [He will be] an *impresario* skilled in generating enthusiasm and . . . the aspirations of [people with talent]. (Benton, 1990, p. 349)

Ethics

Ciulla (2004) suggested that the writings of classical philosophers such as Plato and Confucius contained many principles of ethics worthy of modern empirical research. These classics contain themes and values that offer well-grounded ideas about who we are, what we should be like, and how we should live. In reviewing the ethics of leadership, Bennis (2004) concluded that particularly significant for further study will be the continuing examination of leadership from a cross-cultural perspective. We need to understand each other's symbols, values, and mind-sets. For instance, Westerners need to develop a better understanding of leadership in the Islamic world, especially its tribalism, a handicap to globalization. Bennis also suggested that future efforts need to focus on leadership that continues to involve rhetoric, artifice, and perceived authenticity. The public figure is mainly a vir-

---

[9]Chapters 10 and 11 discussed the more general issues involved.

tual leader, depending on the media to carry his or her message to the public. Impressions from the media create the perceived character of the political leader. We need to do more research about how the media affect the reputation and behavior of public leaders. *Spin* begins where reality ends. Trust in leaders falls as belief in the media's manipulation of reality increases. Instant polling allows leaders to change their positions in midspeech. More must be learned about how modern leadership is affected by the Internet as it grows in size and importance as an informal channel of information, rumor, and gossip (Bennis, 2004, pp. 340–341). Much of this has equal relevance to political leadership in the private sector, about which little is known (House, 1999)

Both legislative and the organizational politicians may adopt influence tactics that border on the unethical. Flagrant lying, cheating, and stealing are clearly unethical managerial practices. But the extent to which telling white lies, cutting corners on standards, and making unauthorized use of company or government property are clearly unethical varies with the circumstances and individual differences in the concepts of right and wrong. Despite the importance that it should have, this is a severely underresearched area of empirical research on managerial and leadership behavior. A 1988 Louis Harris poll of 1,031 office workers and 150 senior executives reported that while 89% of the employees thought that it was very important for managers to be honest, upright, and ethical in their dealings with employees and the community, only 41% said this was actually true of their current employers (Anonymous, 1988a).

Weber (1989) found in interviews with 37 managers that they reasoned morally in order to conform to majority opinion and their organization's rules rather than due to any universal principles of morality. For Burns (1978), the fostering of moral virtue was fundamental to being a transformational leader. The self-seeking charismatic, by definition, could not truly be a transformational leader. But Howell (1988) and Bass (1989) suggested that many charismatic leaders have two faces. They can show their prosocial one, which is transforming, and keep their self-aggrandizing face from interfering with the process.

For Kuhnert and Lewis (1987), the transformational leader develops from having a concern for personal goals and agendas to having more mature, higher levels of values and obligations. At the highest level of development

are to be found the endorsement of universal ethical principles of justice, the equality of human rights, and respect for human dignity. There is a belief in and a commitment to these principles as valid and as an end in themselves. Thus, the values of life and liberty led Paige (1977) to argue that the pursuit of nonviolent means for dealing with problem solving has to be a central focus in the education of political leaders. Somewhat less idealistic is the extent to which values are relative to the group and circumstance; sometimes they may conflict with one another. But the organization and society are maintained by the decision to do what is right. At the other extreme, if the ethical sense is absent, one obeys the rules to avoid being punished (Kohlberg, 1969).[10]

Chapter 11 reviewed the few studies that could be found that dealt with managers' attitudes toward corrupt practices. Revealing to a competitor one's own company's bid for a payoff was almost universally condemned, but taking petty payoffs from outside contractors for awarding them contracts was much less frowned upon. Insider trading is seen as more a matter of illegality[11] than immorality (Pitt, 1985). The Enron scandal of 2001 showed how widespread and devastating corruption could be, as it involved fraudulent behavior by the CEO, vice presidents, leading financial officers, accountants, and outside auditing agencies. It resulted in the bankruptcy of the firm, the destruction of the auditing agency, the loss of employment by thousands of employees, and the employees' loss of pensions and savings. Thousands of shareholders were left with worthless shares (*St. Petersburg Times*, 2006).

An experimental program was launched in 1986 to apply Misumi's (1985) PM leadership in seven Chinese factories, hospitals, and agencies. An idiographic character function of leadership was added to the survey feedback process with emphasis on the moral character of the leader. Along with elements of effective human relations familiar to the West was included in moral character "the commitment to remain within the law and resist temptations for personal gain" (Peterson, 1989, p. 33). Also included was willingness to follow the Communist Party line even when one's personal views conflicted with it.

In the West, professional organizations, such as those in the health professions or in public accounting, tend to

---

[10] Illustrative of people at this level are those who faulted President Richard M. Nixon not for trying to subvert the law but for getting caught.
[11] In some countries, such as Japan, it is not even illegal.

monitor violations of their rules on a case-by-case basis. But beyond this monitoring, critical-incidents survey methods used by the American Psychological Association (1953) are available for gathering both clear-cut and borderline incidents of immoral behavior by managers and the various alternative ways in which managers and leaders could have acted that would have been morally acceptable in terms of informed consensual opinion or universal standards. We are still waiting to see such an effort in the fields of organizational management, led by the accounting profession. But we are more often likely to see questions of commitment to ethical behavior added to survey feedback.

A Model for Ethical Analysis. For Socrates, ethics was the search for the good life in which one's actions are in accord with the truth. According to Steidlmeier (1987), ethics is creative—the search for human fulfillment and the choosing of it as good and beautiful. Ethics is practical in purpose. It seeks the full flowering of the human person and excellence in the actualization of the human capacity. Moral virtues are life-giving patterns of behavior; moral vices are destructive ones.

Most discussions of professional ethics focus on the destructive vices. They are negative and guilt-ridden. The focus is on what should not be, rather than on what should be. Discussions are defensive and dogmatic. Steidlmeir accented the positive. He suggested that we need to clarify our worldview and our principles, which should be integrated into our educational and developmental processes. Unfortunately, principles of self-regulation and codes of conduct often conflict with the avoidance of costs and the maintenance of one's competitive edge. There is a need to recognize the costs and to share them with public officials, stockholders, management, employees, and the public to gain societywide benefits. Weber (1989) pointed to the need to examine how the organization impinges on the manager's maturity of moral reasoning. Beyond this, there is a need to determine the connection between moral reasoning and moral behavior and how each depends on the issue involved.

What's needed is a model that can fit both the hortatory literature on business and political leaders' ethics and social responsibility and the survey evidence of current leaders' and managers' beliefs and practices. Forrest,

Cochran, Ray, and Robin (1989) made such an attempt but were unable to account for the ethical opinions of 315 surveyed managers and 577 surveyed teachers. The investigators extracted four bipolarities from the prescriptive literature: (1) economic versus social purpose, (2) company policy versus individual managers' discretion, (3) recurring versus one-time problems, (4) utilitarian versus ideological decision-making rules.

Organizational Citizenship. Conceptualizing organizations as a collection of constituencies (March & Simon, 1958) remains a powerful source for understanding the individual organizational leader's performance. Much of the success of leaders with their subordinates may depend on how well they negotiate arrangements with other units. By now, the need to focus more attention on the manager's horizontal interactions with peers in other units and with clients (Dubin, 1962b) has become a platitude. However, these leader-leader interactions could be studied with considerable profitability (Hermann, Snyder, & Cunningham, 1980).

Whistle-blowers. In opposition to the political balancing of self-interest, a new concept is taking shape that transcends the formal horizontal or vertical relationship. It is that of the good organizational citizen who goes beyond his or her immediate self-interest to promote the well-being of the organization, its members, and society as a whole. "Whistle-blowers" are illustrative. There is a need in both the public and private sectors to provide more support for valid whistle-blowers and less for their corrupt superiors. More often than not, the whistle-blower is likely to suffer more punishment than the corrupt superior. Nonetheless, big rewards are being paid to whistle-blowers based on how much money was earned and how much in fines was assessed in the fraud or other crimes. What may follow the "me-too" generations of the past 40 years is more good organizational citizenship. Or there may be a reversion to the "my-group" generation of the 1950s (like the East Asians of today), which was concerned primarily with peer pressure. What happens will have considerable implications for leadership.

Ethical resolve continues to remain more important than philanthropical concerns to senior management, according to surveys of several hundred CEOs in 1988 and 1989; but ethics are less important to them than legal or economic considerations. Nor does ethical resolve appear to relate one way or another to a corporation's financial performance (Aupperle & Simmons, 1989). Nevertheless, research on the morality of business leaders and the citizenry is likely to increase substantially in the twenty-first century if the continuing political lobbying scandals and the power of money to win elections are any indication. The increase in the consideration of the effects of spirituality and religious orientation on transformational leadership also may have ethical implications (Twigg, 2004).

Criteria of Effective Leadership

In a review of 89 studies published between 1970 and 1975, Hunt, Osborn, and Schriesheim (1977) reported that 61% used only a single criterion of effective leadership and 43% of that group emphasized performance. However, a greater use of multiple criteria was noted in field studies. Most field studies (81%) used criteria obtained from a different informational source than the predictors.

Studies have been conducted on followers' beliefs, satisfaction, and behavior, as well as productivity, drive, and cohesiveness. However, certain variables, such as group productivity and followers' satisfaction, have been overemphasized at the expense of other variables. For instance, the mean true correlation was .30 between job performance and job satisfaction for 54,417 individuals in 312 samples, according to a meta-analysis by Judge, Thoresen, Bono, et al. (2001). Followers' efforts, which presumably should be affected by leadership, have been neglected as an outcome due to leadership.

Use of a Supermeasure. Morgan and Rao (2002) advocated using one single criterion of effectiveness in service organizations that align their strategy with operating systems serving well-defined markets. One supermeasure focuses the attention of these service firms on their customers' needs better than a complex set of criterion measures does. For instance, Continental Airlines found that on-time performance of its flights encompassed an effective incentive system that was simple to implement, communicate, and build a strategy around—one that provided a feeling of success when Continental's on-time arrivals ranked highest among airlines. Nordstrom, a department

store, identified customer satisfaction as its supermeasure, Marriott supported careful, selective hiring of staff for its economy service. Fairfield Inns selected its supermeasure of cleanliness, friendliness, and efficiency.

Consecutive Criteria. Anderson, Lievens, van Damm, et al. (2004) noted that flexible forms of work teams and rapidly changing organizations mean that the criteria for a single leadership job are less relevant to predicting performance than are the criteria for a role involving a multiplicity of assignments (Howard, 1995). Instead of predicting person-job fit, the effort has to be in two stages. First, there is a need to determine the composition of a changeable job role; then there is a need to predict the person-role fit. Person-role fit may entail considering, along with aptitude predictors of adaptability, flexibility, innovativeness, openness to change, and skills needed for the future (Herriot & Anderson, 2004).

Evaluations Are Relative and Subject to Change. Evaluations of leaders are subject to revision. Shartle (1956) observed that ten years too late, a firm might discover it had fired its most effective manager. Often vilified while he was in office, President Harry S. Truman's performance was upgraded considerably in the years that followed. Seen as being more interested in playing golf than in taking decisive actions, President D. Eisenhower was later found to have played an active role in substituting clandestine forces in Iran, Central America, and elsewhere for open displays of U.S. military power actions. These actions had delayed and devastating effects on those countries and on subsequent U.S. relations with them. Donald Burr, at first evaluated as a hero who devised a radical new approach to managing airlines, became the villain who failed to consult with others and overexpanded PEOPLExpress to the point where it was thrust into bankruptcy.

Evaluations are relative. Well known are the stories about executives who introduce belt-tightening measures into a department, ride roughshod over subordinates to reduce costs, maximize immediate productivity, and are then promoted to repeat the process higher up. They leave behind a shambles of dissatisfaction and conflict to be blamed on their successors. Peters and Waterman's (1982) popular assessment of exemplary firms that represented excellence in management was based on a highly subjective evaluation of excellent management. When a fuller analysis of the firms' financial performance was compared with those of 1,000 firms evaluated by *Forbes*, the performance of the first group of firms was seen as not particularly better (Aupperle, Acar, & Booth, 1986).

What scholars view as effective leadership and how followers view the same performance may be quite different. In contrast to presidents from Woodrow Wilson through Richard M. Nixon, who fulfilled nearly 75% of their campaign pledges, Jimmy Carter did almost as well but was seen as a failure by the public because he did not fulfill the major campaign promises that were important to voters: reducing unemployment and inflation (Krukones, 1985). Despite many mistakes made in his first administration, George W. Bush won reelection in 2004. But his popularity fell from 90% to 30% as his administration's mistakes continued; and by 2006 he could not figure out how to withdraw from the war in Iraq he had started in 2003. The discrepancies between scholarly appraisals and the public's evaluation of a leader's performance are particularly apparent in the case of demagogues.

There is a need to distinguish between the successful influence of a leader and his or her long-term effectiveness, as determined by the contribution that the "influence" makes to attaining the long-term goals and well-being of the organization or nation. For instance, researchers need to broaden the criteria of consequence and to attach the appropriate longer-term value of leadership to the development of followers, the organization, and the nation (McCall, 1977). Human resources accounting is an effort in this direction. As managerial accountants increasingly become interested in the behavioral side of a firm's assets and liabilities, there should be increasing opportunities to measure such effects (Caplan & Landekich, 1974). Utility analysis is a promising tool (Cascio & Ramos, 1986). But considerable care will be required to weed out the cause-effect relationships. First Lady Nancy Reagan was effective in the short run in the nation with her campaign "Just say no to drugs," which was largely forgotten once her husband left office, but Eleanor Roosevelt had lasting effects on the world with her influence as an advocate for human rights and the United Nations (Wills, 1994).

Additional questions about the evaluations of the effectiveness of leaders were posed by Hermann, Snyder, and Cunningham (1980). Who determines the criteria for effective leadership, and what difference does it make? (Shareholders will emphasize stock prices; employees, job satisfaction.) Are output measures, such as the size of profits, votes obtained, or church membership, sufficient measures of the effectiveness of leaders, or are leadership-process variables more important? How do researchers avoid having leaders directly influence the raters to render favorable judgments about their effectiveness, a phenomenon examined by Dubin (1979)?

Linkages, Moderators, and Substitutes

Why does a leader's behavior affect the group's outcomes? Why do the group's outcomes affect a leader's behavior? The leadership roles serve the necessary functions of maintaining role structure, role freedom, goal direction, and cohesive group action in the performance of a task. These roles do not necessarily specify the patterns of behavior required but, rather, the purposes they serve. These purposes include dealing with goal direction, individual members' goals, and relations within the group; maintaining the group's role structure, constraints and freedom; and promoting individual and group motivation, individual satisfaction and group cohesion, and the group's norms and requirements.

In the emergent situation, leadership is created by the group in response to its own necessities even though an impatient member may impose himself or herself upon the group before the group expresses a demand for such services. In formal organizations, the necessity is acknowledged by the appointment or election of leaders. The effective performance of a task is usually dependent on the appointed or emergent leader's enactment of the leadership roles to carry out the necessary functions. How are the role enactments affected by changes in membership, task, and organization? Are there satisfactory substitutes for leadership, such as overtraining of followers, computerization and automation, or policies and regulations? How far can self-management be taken with such substitutes?

Computers can be substituted for a supervisor for monitoring of and feedback (to both employees and a higher authority) about an individual employee's productivity, wasting of time, frequency of errors, and presence at or absence from the workstation. Computers can troubleshoot and inform employees about corrections they should make and how to make them. Are such monitoring and feedback likely to be favorably accepted by the employee, in contrast to less close human monitoring? Are some aspects more coercive than others? What if this type of monitoring and feedback represents a diminution of the job for the employee, with the associated effects of increased boredom, dissatisfaction, and loss of self-esteem?

A Systems Approach

Katz and Kahn (1966) pointed the way. A systems approach looks at the leader as someone imbedded in a system with multiple inputs from the environment, the organization, the immediate work group supervised, the task and the leader's behavior. Other factors include his or her relationships with subordinates and outputs in terms of effective performance and satisfactions (Bass, 1976). Hunt, Osborn, and Schriesheim (1977) thought this kind of systems view of contingent variables was particularly important for future research. For instance, studies of military leadership confirmed that combat and noncombat conditions require different patterns of effective leadership behavior. Such differences are likely to vary by the officers' level. Upward and lateral influence in the system can be as important as downward influence to the accomplishment of missions (Van Fleet & Yukl, 1986). Gal (1989) argued that military leadership in the future will be derived from the commitment of subordinates to rise to the challenge of complex, risky, uncertain, and dangerous situations.

According to Demming (1986), managers need to know whether the system in which they are involved is stable and predictable. Are the system's goals and norms stable? Inefficiencies that show up repeatedly call for managers' efforts to improve the situation. Any one positive outcome by itself, such as the satisfaction of customers or meeting the competition, may mean little to the overall health of the system. Zero-defects programs or new equipment alone may also be of little consequence to the system. Management needs to focus proactively on the constant improvement of the design and processes of the system that lie within its capabilities.

Much needs to be learned about how leaders manage the boundary between what is inside and outside their mission in the larger organization and how to protect it. How do they create the necessary environment for productivity within their boundaries? To what must they attend, and what can they ignore? How do they help others to make sense of arrangements and situations (Gilmore, 1982)?

Adams and Yoder (1985) advocated that particular attention be paid to the need to consider leader-subordinate relations in the broader setting in which actions take place—the wider organization and external environment—as was done in Chapter 25. Hermann, Snyder, and Cunningham (1980) noted the absence of research about how a leader's behavior is affected by a variety of specific contextual issues. Will a number of groups need to be coordinated, or can one group handle the problems? Is the organizational problem a crisis, or is it routine? Is the problem familiar or unfamiliar to the organization? Is the leadership operating with immediate subordinates or at a distance? Similarly, Behling and Schriesheim (1976) and Schriesheim and Neider (1988a) saw the need for more future research about the externally oriented activities of managers with higher authority, other department heads, clients, and the community. In all, a more complex set of roles will be seen as part of managerial leadership.

The application of a systems approach to leadership was reflected in the principles set forth for senior executives by the Center for Creative Leadership. Executive leaders need to get in touch with "what is really going on" at different levels in the organization. They need to articulate a vision with clear goals, standards, and priorities, along with a plan for developing a climate that will support the effort. Key leaders at various levels of the organization will need to set examples of such support. Periodic measurements of the effort and its success are required. Risk taking and trust building need to be encouraged. Competitiveness that reduces information sharing needs to be discouraged. Suitable appraisal and reward systems for outstanding individual and team accomplishments should follow, with continuing attention to effective personnel staffing, development, and succession to fit the programmatic effort.

In contrast to *microlevel* research on the leader in relation to his or her subordinates and immediate superiors and to *macrolevel* research on the aggregated data that relate to the total organization and its environment, *me-*

solevel research involves the individual leader, on the one hand, and the total organization and environment surrounding the leader, on the other. More such mesolevel research is needed (House, 1988a).

The Learning Organization. Senge (1990) introduced the concept of the *learning organization.* It adapts to the changes in its environment. Its leaders learn how to move its members to adjust to needed changes. The leaders and members learn to be more flexible. New perspectives are adopted when the organization moves from national to global markets. Leaders and members adapt to the needs to diversify the workforce and customers. In the learning organization, the permanent bundle of specific tasks that form a job is replaced with a temporary combination of tasks. Some tasks may be shifted to others in the organization or outsourced. Needed also in the learning organization is consultative leadership that articulates what needs to change, careful listening, the giving and accepting of feedback, coaching, mentoring, calculated risk taking, and careful experimentation (Bass, 2000).

Discretionary Possibilities and Nondiscretionary Requirements

A few efforts have been made to identify the discretionary opportunities that shape a leader's behavior. Much more study is needed to determine what is and is not under a leader's control. Such knowledge should reduce subordinates' unrealistic expectations about the leader, as well as the leader's own experiences of violated expectations. In selection and placement testing, researchers should be able to generate higher validity coefficients between personality attributes and the portion of a leader's behavior that is discretionary.

Delegation

Delegation remains a relatively unexplored management option despite the evidence of its important contribution to the leader's and the organization's effectiveness. Miller and Toulouse (1986) showed that the extent to which delegation of authority was practiced in 97 small businesses in Quebec correlated .31 with profitability and .34 with sales growth of the business relative to others in the same industry. The effects of delegation were stronger

than any others examined, such as the business strategies employed, how they were devised, and the CEO's personal characteristics.

Studies of the delegative process are likely to be important in future research on leadership, with more fine-tuning of delegation as a style of leadership. Delegation is clearly not participation. Although Vroom and Yelton (1973); Bass, Valenzi, Farrow, and Solomon (1975); and Leana (1986, 1987), among others, contributed to some understanding of delegation, it still remains the least researched style.

As a step forward in the research effort, Schriesheim and Neider (1988) conceived of three forms of delegation instead of one. Research is needed to learn whether each of the forms is likely to interact differently with the motivation, commitment, satisfaction, and performance of the leaders and subordinates: (1) *advisory* delegation, in which the subordinate makes a decision after first getting a recommendation from the leader; (2) *informed* delegation, in which the subordinate makes the decision after first getting needed information from the leader; (3) *nonsuggestive* delegation, in which the subordinate makes the decision without any input from the leader. Of the three forms, advisory delegation is likely to coincide with a strong commitment from the subordinates.

Delegation has been regarded as the style at the other end of the continuum of styles from autocratic directive leadership. Yet an autocrat may delegate because of lack of interest or time to handle the problem directly. A transactional leader may delegate in exchange for subordinate support. A transformational leader will use delegation to develop his or her subordinates. A consultative leader may delegate after being convinced of the subordinate's competence and motivations to handle the problem. Delegation may be the choice of a participant consensus. A laissez-faire leader may delegate to avoid taking the blame for a possible failure.

There is a need to conceptualize delegation as a process and to research what makes it effective or ineffective.

Contingent Models

Personal traits that are associated with the emergence of a leader appear to transcend situational demands. It is still axiomatic that some of the variance in the emergence and effectiveness of leadership is due to personal traits, and some is due to situational and interactive factors. Nevertheless, a meta-analysis by Lord, DeVader, and Alliger (1986) of data from Mann (1959) and additional data suggested that both Stogdill (1948) and Mann seriously underestimated the importance of personal traits relative to situational effects. The meta-analysis showed that the theoretical mean correlations predicting emergence as a leader between such traits as intelligence, extroversion, and assertiveness, and actual emergence as a leader were much higher than had been realized. These high correlations occurred even when suitable adjustments were made for restrictions in the range of the subjects of the studies and for the unreliability of the measures employed. Also taken into account in the meta-analysis was the likelihood of random variation from one study to the next, which explained much of the situational variance and argued against the need for contingent explanations. Assertiveness, for example, is necessary for leaders, regardless of the situation.

Contingent models are still required to explain how the styles required for effective leadership vary with the demands of a situation. For example, Barbieri (1983) used path analyses to show that much of the 39% of the variance in revenues from the sales of mature products generated by marketing managers and their sales representatives could be accounted for by the managers' extroversion, relations orientation, and intuitive thinking. But revenues from the sales of innovative products were accounted for by the managers' task orientation and the sales representatives' experience, practical orientation, and intelligence. At the same time, the branch managers' unwillingness to delegate was not a contingent effect; it contributed positively to the sales of both kinds of products.

In sum, despite meta-analytic support for generalizing across situations about personal traits associated with the emergence of leadership, such as intelligence, assertiveness, and extroversion, applications of contingent models of leadership are likely to remain prolific sources of further examination and validation. This occurs particularly with reference to the styles of leadership that are most effective in designated circumstances. More causal, longer-term, larger-scale contingent studies of styles of leadership and their effectiveness are likely to appear during the coming decades.

Assessment

Research on the various assessment methods employed and their integration into decisions about assessees need to be studied further. The phrasing of more than 100 such research questions emerged from a brainstorming session on the subject (Jeswald, 1971), and most of them still remain unanswered or partly unanswered almost four decades later. For example, much more remains to be learned about the kinds of biodata and biometric data that can be profitably used for assessment.

The development and evaluation of more sophisticated theory-based, in contrast to empirically-originated, biodata forms of greater validity are needed. These forms can be developed and evaluated by asking questions that generate responses more likely to relate to the personal styles that are of consequence to subsequent performance as a leader. Thus researchers can ask questions about how the applicant coped with "the most important challenge you faced" or "your most disappointing experience." Appropriate scoring, consistent with theoretical expectations, can be developed (Kuhnert & Russell, 1989). A list of such dynamic items for application blanks was suggested by Bass and Barrett (1972) — for example, "May we consult your present employer?"

In this endeavor, as well as in the development of new psychological tests and measurements, experimental findings about personality and social psychology can be put to better use. More complex simulations that duplicate critical aspects of on-the-job performance should be employed. The subtleties of the deep structures involved can be introduced into such simulations. More should be done to assess creative, flexible intelligence, as well as less socially desirable aspects of personality, such as dogmatism and authoritarianism, that may influence leadership behavior. More research is needed on newer personality dimensions that are of consequence, such as the tolerance for ambiguity. A lot more needs to be known about the abilities needed to cope with higher-level managerial responsibilities, including the ability to translate ideas into actions. More sophisticated assessments of leaders' performance in decision-making processes are desirable. Justification of the greater expense of assessment centers over ordinary selection methods calls for more utility analyses such as the one presented by Cascio and Ramos (1986). The contextual conditions surrounding the assessment process also need to be taken into account more fully (Bentz, 1987). For example, Kleinmann, Kuptsch, and Köller (1996) showed that for 119 students in a German assessment center, construct validity was higher if the dimensions on which they were being assessed were transparent, that is, if the students were informed in advance about the assessment dimensions and the behavior that was required of them. In the same way, McClelland (1998) noted that for good competency assessment in interviews, the competencies assessed and how they may be improved should be made public instead of kept secret as in the case of traditional testing of traits.

Expected Developments in Assessment. Fernándes-Ballester (1995) suggested that in the coming decades, new evaluations of mental processes will appear that examine human cognitive functioning, the dynamic assessment of intelligence, and applications of Item Response Theory to computerized and adaptive intelligence tests and personality inventories. Also, new ways of reducing biases in self-reports will emerge. New biophysical measurements of emotion and new ways of assessing person-situation interactions will appear. Many uses for assessment will accrue from the availability of virtual reality. Further studies will be needed in the utility of cognitive, social, and emotional assessment by individual tests in comparison to group situational tests. Assessment technology will have spread to many more countries in many more languages. Further developments can be expected in controlling response set, faking, and desirability of responses.

Leadership Development, Training, Persistence, and Succession

On one hand, researchers can point with pride to the large array of positive evidence about the efforts to train and educate leaders and the success that has been experienced.[12] On the other, it is still possible to decry the many continuing inadequacies of leadership training and education. Kerr (2004) summarized the results of a symposium of book authors on the subject of how organizations can best prepare leaders to lead and manage. All four authors agreed, and argued convincingly, that developing

leader-managers early in their careers is important. But this effort has to be limited, for their turnover is much greater than those of long-term employees and so much less is known about them. This places a premium on careful selection and appraisal. Secondly, work assignments have to be seen as a developmental tool. An assignment should provide a learning opportunity. But more often, an already experienced employee is given an assignment to ensure its successful completion.

Leadership development is a continuing process. Researchers need to learn a lot more about how experience with subordinates, peers, and superiors, as well as with family and friends, shapes one's subsequent performance as a leader. Research on the persistence and transfer of leadership has produced a convincing body of evidence indicating that one's past success as a leader contributes to one's future success as a leader.

What experiences are necessary to make an effective leader? Does one need to be trained in business to be an effective industrial leader? Does one need to be trained in theology to make an effective pope? Does one need to be a lawyer to be an effective legislative leader? Does one need legislative experience to be an effective state governor or president?

Innovative and creative approaches for teaching leadership using films, classics, and fiction are provided by Pillai and Stites-Doe (2003). For instance, some of the subjects covered in college courses include: (1) What is leadership, and is it learned or innate? (2) What are the qualities and behaviors of a great leader, and are they the same for all cultures? (3) Are political leaders history's slaves? (4) Are there unique challenges for women leaders? (5) How do great leaders handle mistakes and failures? (Nathan, 2003).

Based on a review of 20 studies, Atwater, Brett, and Waldman (2003) see both benefits and risks in multirater feedback. Improvement based on feedback was not uniformly found. Negative feedback was likely to result in reduced performance and commitment, anger, questioning of the validity of the feedback process, and discouragement. To be useful, rating systems need to be ongoing and integrated with a means of training and development. Conger and Toegel (2003) foresee a systematic set of action projects being assigned to an employee so that learning from them can build and be integrated. Qualitative data needs to be included. (In the future, we will see

---

[12] See Chapter 34.

more analyses of qualitative data for feedback.) For Uhl-Bien (2003), relationship skills are the social capital that organizations need. Awareness of the other person's needs, mutual obligation, trust, and respect are present in high-quality relationships. Without them, teamwork suffers. Leadership development requires more attention in the future to training in relations skills.

Kuhnert and Lewis (1987) raised a number of unanswered substantive questions about the development of transformational leadership. Are there observable changes in transformational leaders' behavior as a function of the leaders' personalities? Is transactional leadership a less mature developmental phase than transformational leadership? Are leaders' developmental phases invariant? Does one have to be a transactional leader before he or she can become transformational? What happens when leaders and followers operate at different developmental levels?

The Genetic Factor. The nature-nurture controversy is by no means settled. Advances in genetics and biology need to be incorporated into leadership models. Large-scale studies of heredity suggest that genes contribute to energy levels, intelligence, long life, interests, assertiveness, a sense of well-being, the ability to take risks, and even job satisfaction. The genetic factor needs to be taken into account in any complete examination of leadership. There are remarkable correlations in these kinds of traits and outcomes among identical twins reared apart, in contrast to people who are genetically unrelated.

Purposes of Leadership Education and Training. Stogdill (1974) faulted research on training for focusing too much on the extent to which training produces attitudinal and behavioral changes in trainees. He demanded more evidence on the impact of the training of leaders on followers. Yet researchers still need to link particular training efforts with particular behavioral changes. For instance, training may understandably increase a trainee's sensitivity; nevertheless, increased sensitivity may be counterproductive on the job. Sensitivity training may incapacitate the leader for coping with strong opposition, threats, and challenges to the legitimacy of his or her status. What is at fault here is not the training as such, but an inadequate analysis of the situational demands on the leader. We are beginning to see much greater precision

in such analyses. Over time, it is expected that the application of sophisticated analyses of managers', administrators', and leaders' roles to training will be much more intensive.

For Rost and Barker (2000), leadership education, such as that furnished by secondary and higher education, needs to be distinguished from organizational leadership training. Leadership education should produce citizens for a democratic society who understand the dynamics of the change process and the politics of distributing scarce resources to facilitate change. Participants need to learn how: to get into the decision-making process; collect, interpret, and disseminate information about the issues involved; develop a reputation; think critically in public discourse; and confront opposition. Cherrey and Isgar (1998) propose as goals for teaching students leadership in the twenty-first century: (1) understanding the complexity of an interrelated system such as a multinational NGO with many alliances and diverse units; (2) continually reflecting and learning with a commitment to the greater good; (3) valuing diversity and embracing inclusiveness; (4) practicing collective leadership; (5) focusing on the leadership process, not on the leader; (6) linking academic and extracurricular activities that provide opportunities to learn about leadership. For Ayman, Adams, Fisher, et al. (2003), who evaluated the leadership development programs at 63 U.S. universities, fewer than 10% appear to offer the complete program envisaged: (1) long-term involvement, (2) the facts about what works, (3) insights gained from reading and case discussions, (4) opportunities for reflection, (5) opportunities to lead, (6) increased self-awareness as a result of personal feedback. The attention to the importance of individual merit, competitiveness, and the "bottom line" needs to be leavened with the importance of cooperation, corporate social responsibility, and ethics (Berry, 1997). Aupperle and Simmons (1989) compared the forced-choice tested attitudes of 245 CEOs in 1981 and 1988 and found there was no change in how much emphasis they placed on their corporate social responsibility. In order of importance, from most to least important, were economic, legal, ethical, and philanthropic responsibilities. The U.S. Army, Navy, and Air Force military academies come closer to meeting Ayman, Adams, and Fisher et al.'s (2003) requirements for leadership education. Also closer to the requirements are colleges such as

Jepson, which offer a four-year curriculum in leadership. In 1998, there were almost 700 leadership development programs in U.S. academic institutions (Honan, 1998). With increasing recognition of the importance of leadership, we can expect more to appear in the future, as well as full four-year programs in leadership.

Increased Reliance on Intuition. While new and better techniques for analytical decision making will be developed in the coming years, we will also learn and be trained in how to make better use of intuition—apprehending something without completely understanding it. Intuition is based on experiences and reflective thinking about the experiences. It uses metaphors and imagery. There will be less reluctance to depend on intuition if reflection connects the known information, perspectives, and feelings about the issue. It can add to what analysis can provide for making a decision in the absence of complete information (Cartwright, 2004).

Improvements in Evaluation. Evidence of the utility of focusing on specific behavioral training and its specific effects is to be found in the attention now being paid to behavioral objectives, behavioral modeling, and applications of social learning theory. But in many evaluative studies of leadership training, it is impossible to determine the method or combination of methods employed. Evaluative reports need to describe in detail both the method of training and the content taught. In addition, more attention needs to be paid to the threats to the validity of training designs and their evaluations (Kane, 1976). For example, for the purposes of unbiased evaluations, if possible, superiors should not know who has received training and who has not after trainees return to their jobs. Likewise, trainees should not be told whether they are serving as experimental subjects or controls (as in holdout designs).

Multinationalism and Diversity. The globalization of industry will mean increasing attention to international managers, as such, with the probable submergence of surface differences in national styles and performance, but with needed increases in attention to underlying differences in institutions, cultures, and governments. At the same time, with the rise in power and influence and

the further economic development of countries whose cultures are alien to the West, attitudes, values, interests, and beliefs that are different from those in the West and that affect leader-follower relations will emerge. They are likely to emphasize tradition and collectivism more heavily. Globalization has been accompanied by the emergence of a global civil society whose problems challenge the international community. Learning from the experiences of corporations and institutions can be helpful in satisfying the "need for leadership to promote peace, democracy, and development within (nations) and between (nations) . . . the national leader's (has a) responsibility to serve his people . . . and global civil society's efforts to promote peace and development worldwide . . . without losing sight of the larger picture linking leadership to human development" (Safty, 2000).

In the United States, studies of black, Hispanic, Asian-American, and women leaders will continue to increase, reflecting their movement into higher levels of leadership and management in industry, government, and education. A greater openness to line management by Jewish Americans, Asian Americans, and other minorities is likely to increase with the increasing technological requirements for remaining competitive. As more women move into the higher reaches of management, we may see more of an emphasis on androgyny than on masculinity as being favorable to effective management (Adams & Yoder, 1985). Extensive commentaries will be replaced by more empirical studies. More empirical studies will also be needed, considering how quickly outdated conclusions from them can become.

Because of the emotional content involved, care needs to be taken not to accept at face value leaders' and subordinates' cross-race and cross-sex opinions and descriptions. At the same time, more attention has to be paid to the underlying feelings of rejection, contempt, guilt, and threat in mainstreamers and outsiders that do not surface because of superficial socialization, socially desirable responses, or mistrust of the investigators. This is another reason why empirical monitoring of such dimensions as the self-confidence of blacks, women, Hispanics, and particularly Asian Americans is essential. It should be recognized that an effective, polite, mutual acceptance can be maintained at one level while underneath, a wall of misunderstanding still exists.

Little is known about Anglo-Hispanic leader-subordinate relations. Yet Latinos are now the largest U.S. minority. Research here will be made particularly difficult by the wide differences among Mexican Americans, Puerto Ricans, Cuban Americans, and the large immigrant groups from the central Caribbean and elsewhere in Latin America.

So far, the preponderance of evidence endorses the need for minority members serving as leaders in majority environments to emulate the original white male manager. However, more and timely research will be needed on the accommodations made by minority members to the duality of their roles as both managers and members of a minority group. Leadership is also a completely different matter for minority community leaders, who ordinarily need to identify more with their own subculture than do their followers.

Work/Family Balance. There will be more focus on family-friendly policies. More will need to be learned about the policies needed for the different types of child care by single mothers and single fathers, divorcées, homosexual couples, and grandparents. More research is needed on the full range of working family forms and incomes for policies across socioeconomic levels. Beyond this can lie a future where families engage in educational experiences for mutual benefit, from learning computer programs to learning foreign languages. Increasingly, we are likely to see government policies toward families becoming friendlier, with more flexible work weeks, longer part-time hours and more sharing of the costs of child care as well as greater portability of pension benefits, care for parents, and solutions to the problems of overscheduled lives. Globalization may bring the United States closer to many European nations in family friendliness (Murphy & Halpern, 2005).

Criminal Leadership

One of the areas of leadership among many that I have neglected is leadership of organized criminal gangs such as the Mafia, Colombian drug lords, and the Japanese Yakuza. The gangs pursue a variety of illegal activities and also invest in legal businesses. Their leadership tends to be autocratic and coercive, supported by disciplinary rules and codes of honor. Informants and undercover agents unveil the secrets of their operations. Fictional portrayals are common in literature and TV and, like *The Sopranos,* can be used to propose principles of leadership, but can serve only as illustrations (Yammarino, 1996).

Summary and Conclusions

Many important issues remain relatively unexplored. Others have been overworked. Much original, creative leadership research has appeared since the early twentieth century and especially since the 1940s. But it has also been accompanied by a wasteful repetition of tests of shopworn hypotheses. The atheoretical research published before 1965 was too unfocused, but much of the research that followed was based on naive, uncritical theorizing and retarded the process of new discoveries. Nevertheless, much has been accomplished. Based on his 32 years as a military leader and 10 years directing the Center of Creative Leadership, Ulmer (1997) found that much had been accomplished in leadership research by then, although there had been diversions. Yukl (1998, p. 508) concluded that the field "has witnessed an increase in the richness of research questions and the variety of approaches used to study them, and . . . appears to be undergoing an accelerating pace of discovery."

Accomplishments

Critics complain that leadership is fundamentally antidemocratic and antithetical to nonleaders' rights of expression and power sharing. Other critics complain that despite all the research, nothing is known about leadership! Still others declare that leadership is a figment of the imagination or that leadership as a research subject is moribund and has reached a "dead end." Nonetheless, this and the preceding chapters attest to the health and well-being of the subject. A wide range of new and challenging substantive issues have been created: implicit leadership, substitutes for leadership, prototypicality effects, neocharismatic and transformational leadership, strategic leadership, virtual leadership, leader-member exchange, impression management, self-management, and upward influence. Among the methodologies introduced have been analysis by WABA, meta-analysis, and triangulation of quantitative and qualitative findings.

More replicated studies have made possible many more meta-analyses to increase confidence in results. Both personal traits *and* situations have been shown to be important to leadership.

Considerable advances have occurred in the development and use of theories. Linkages have been forged to general theories, for example, between contingent reinforcement leadership and the general theory of reinforcement. Testable theories have been constructed and tested. No longer does one have to wait for the demise of the theorist before a theory of leadership is abandoned or modified because of its failure to be supported empirically.

The ability to predict future leadership performance accurately has increased substantially during the past half century. Many studies have taken advantage of the miniaturization of wireless physiological recording and the personal computer. More will be doing so in the future. The same is true for electronic mail, videoconferencing, and other forms of telecommunication, which will also increase in importance in linking leaders and subordinates who are distant from each other.

New complex and effective research designs are now available. These designs would be equally useful for testing other relationships that have not been explored. The production of critically needed information could be greatly accelerated by feeding new combinations of variables into research designs that have been demonstrated to be effective. Efforts are increasing to bring together active leaders, organizational consultants, and research investigators to discern common problems and interests and to increase the focus of this research on realities and the application of research results (see, e.g., Clark & Clark, 1989).

In the social sciences, old theories used to wither away with the retirement of the originators and their disciples. However, although some theories of leadership have gone or are going this route, other theories of leadership, such as path-goal theory, the contingency theories, and charismatic/transformational leadership have by no means withered. Rather, they have been systematically tested and reshaped as a consequence of the results of tests. And new models have been fashioned on top of them.

The preceding suggestions for future research indicate that the possibilities are far from exhausted. Leadership presents a lively, challenging field for research and innovative applications.

Optimism or Pessimism? The optimist sees the wine bottle as half full; the pessimist sees it as half empty (and sour to boot). It is easier to be destructive than constructive, particularly when one lacks information. "Know-nothings" argue that the past years have essentially been a waste and it is now necessary to start afresh. Miner (1975) proposed that the concept of leadership be abandoned altogether. Since then, he has changed his mind. M. W. McCall (1977) thought that leadership would remain an enigmatic subject because of its many definitions, but in Chapter 1, I noted that the definitions were evolving in a systematic fashion and that, at any rate, the diverse definitions do not seem to detract from model and theory building. The many models and theories that have sprung forth in the past five decades are not as divergent and conflicting as one might expect from the diverse definitions of leadership on which they may be built. Ways are needed to juxtapose one model with another to test which one yields more plausible explanations. Fiedler and associates tested Fiedler's contingency theory; Vroom and associates tested their deductive model; Likert and his associates produced massive amounts of support for System 4. Points of theoretical disagreement can be found and critical experiments developed, as was done by Locke, Latham, and Erez (1987) and Blake and Mouton (1985) to determine which model best fits the data.

To some extent, the problem may be that each theoretical point of view is supported by a different array of measurements and situational circumstances. Part of the problem may also be that situational factors determine some kinds of leadership behavior but not others. Autocratic leaders—rigid, inflexible, and self-assured—may try to lead in any situation in which they are placed. Democratic leaders may attempt to lead only if they feel competent and supported in the particular situation. The nondiscretionary behavior of leaders will be determined by organizational and environmental matters that are not within their control. But leaders' discretionary performance will be much more a matter of their personal predilections than of situational differences alone.

It is one thing to say that researchers know nothing because they do not obtain consistent results. The lack of consistency may be attributed to a lack of knowledge. Yet it may be that to achieve consistent results requires accounting for a complexity of variables and that, as researchers do so, they increase their understanding of what is happening. What is needed are better measurements; a broader appreciation of which situational variables are more important and which are less so (Korman, 1974); and, as was noted earlier, larger samples. Calas (1986) and Calas and Smircich (1987) joined the "cry and dismay" about the narrow substantive themes and methodological means of the past in what has been published about leadership by its establishment of scientific investigators. Nevertheless, the researchers believe that the field has the potential to become: much more open to broader approaches in the search for understanding; accepting of expanded horizons; reflective of more adequate connections with salient substantive issues of the real world outside the community of researchers; and populated with researchers learning from experience, observation, and narrative interpretations of meaning about what they write, as well as from continued dependence on field surveys and controlled experiments. Historians, anthropologists, and political scientists have much to say about leadership in their narrative reports. Illustrative is Schruijer's (1997) historical essay on the early-medieval Christian bishops' management of meaning between the fourth and eighth centuries. They carefully substituted and imitated pagan practices and beliefs to satisfy people's need for miracles in a dangerous world. And because they tolerated and encouraged magical practices, they succeeded in redirecting loyalty and commitment from pagan gods to Christian saints.

The choice of topics needs to be broadened to reflect more of the long-lasting issues that leaders, as well as the leadership research establishment, confront. However, one side of the establishment has continued to complain about the substantive and methodological narrowness of research in the field. The other side has been equally vociferous about the need for more rigor and discipline. Both types of investigators make contributions, particularly when they can join forces or pursue the expansion of horizons from a disciplinary or interdisciplinary basis. New lines of investigation should be expected and welcomed. For instance, Morgeson (2005) demonstrated the utility of examining the impact of novel and disruptive events on self-managing teams. This was followed shortly by Morgeson and DeRue (2006) demonstrating the impact of criticality, urgency, and duration on the disruption of teams, and influence on the intervention by the team leader. The future should see more efforts to develop understanding of how leadership is affected by events. The future should also see more research on developing, in both leaders and followers, positive psychological capacities such as hope, optimism, confidence, and resiliency (Anonymous, 2006).

Some collectively disparage the thousands of research studies of leadership.[13] But T. R. Mitchell (1979) concluded that theory and research were continuing to develop and that much of what had been done was being used in practice: "There was reason for controlled optimism. Yet the challenges are still there for the years ahead." His words are even truer a quarter of a century later. At the end of the twentieth century, House (1999) concluded that, "there is a substantial amount of available knowledge concerning the exercise and effectiveness of leadership, and there are sufficient number of remaining issues and questions to occupy the time of social scientists for a considerable, and indefinite duration."

This book should provide an antidote for the arguments of those continuing to bemoan the supposedly unknowable, elusive, mysterious nature of leadership. I expect and hope that I have been able to show that a considerable body of theory, method, evidence, and understanding is available about how, why, and under what conditions leadership, in all its rich variations—implied, observed, described, and/or evaluated—energizes and exerts its influence—sometimes for the worse, more often for the better.

Past and Future Developments

In 1967, I looked ahead to the year 2000 and forecast accurately that organizations would be more flexible, that providing challenging work would be a more common practice, and that online computers would greatly facilitate management. Sensitivity training would be more proficient; and knowledge would be more important to management. There would be increased attention to the behavioral and social sciences and a decline in middle

---

[13] About 7,500 have been cited here.

management (Bass, 1967, Wilcox & Bush, 2003). In 1998, I speculated about the U.S. Army in 2025 (Bass, 1998). In 2002, I looked ahead to 2034 and suggested what future leadership research and applications might be like. Many of these predictions are noted next (Bass, 2002).

Methodological Trends. More studies will combine data from individual, team, and organizational levels for within and between analyses (WABA). Old fads will decline, but new ones may take their place, thanks to newspaper and magazine articles, journals and books on the subject. The fads are well known by managers. As noted earlier, academic researchers are now often the source of the information, so that we can expect an increasing coalescence of the fads and scientific literature (Gibson & Tesone, 2001; Gill, 1992). With the increase in more reliable and valid measurements, mathematical operations and model testing will increase in application. Organizational charts will describe networks of leadership, communications, responsibility, and accountability. We will have seriously underestimated developments in information technology, nanotechnology, biotechnology, and electronic brain and body scanning applicable to understanding leaders' and followers' cognitions, behavior, and perceptions. Genetic profiling and hormone levels will have been introduced into the study of leadership. Artificial intelligence will assist managerial decision making. More longitudinal studies contrasting and combining economic, social, and behavioral studies will have been completed.

Substantive Trends. Coaching, mentoring, and individualized consideration will have become routinized, much of it available for delivery online. Most training will be delivered from Web sites, the Internet, and intranets. The "not invented here" syndrome will disappear in a global economy. Most industries and businesses will be dominated by a few gigantic multinational corporations. Purely transactional bureaucratic organizations will have given way to more transformational ones. In the developed world, women will be in the majority in legislatures, government, and business management and ownership. They will foster more networking, relationships, and concerns for social justice, equity, and fairness. In the United States, more Hispanics, Blacks, Asian Americans, and American Indians, as well as those of southern and eastern European ancestry, will have increased proportionately in senior management. Second careers for leaders after retirement will be commonplace. Working to the age of 85 will not be unusual.

Ethical codes will be constructed empirically, based on experience with borderline cases and judgments about them by managers, ethicists, and workers. Changes in the environment will be mirrored in changes in the organization. At all levels, adaptability will be essential. Leaders will be prized for their innovativeness, responsiveness, and flexibility and their greater frequency of transformational leadership. Improvements in health and medical care will make diseases such as cancer, Alzheimer's, stroke, and heart disease less likely to disrupt careers acting as Robert Crowley's "wild cards in history."

As Aelfric, a schoolteacher and abbot (c. 955–1020), said, "We dare not lengthen this book much more, lest it . . . stir up men's antipathy because of its size" (Lacy & Danziger, 1999).

Glossary

This glossary has been prepared because some readers may be unfamiliar with particular specialized terms in statistics, management, and the behavioral, social, and political sciences that were mentioned in the text but not defined or fully discussed. The glossary may also be helpful to readers from outside the United States who are less familiar with some American colloquialisms that appear in the text. The terms that are discussed more fully in the text are likely to be found in the subject index rather than in this glossary.

A

Accountability Members of an organization who are given responsibility and authority are held answerable for the results.

Achievement motive (nAch) Motivation to seek high performance and success.

Acquiescent response set Agreement with statements, regardless of their content.

Action research Research whose objective includes the implemented solution of the research problem using the diagnosis of the problem, the collection of data, and the analysis and feedback of data.

Adaptation level An individual's expectations and experience set a standard against which events or objects are perceived.

Ad hoc group A temporary group established to deal with a problem or problems (also *Task force*).

Affect (noun) Feeling; emotional reaction.

Affiliation motive (nAff) The motivation to belong and to be with other people.

Affirmative action Positive programs to increase opportunities for the employment and promotion of members of disadvantaged groups.

Algorithm A procedure used to solve a set of problems by an explicit formula.

Alienation A generalized sense of meaninglessness, helplessness, and social isolation that contributes to the disinhibition of personal controls against engaging in deviant behavior.

Altruism Helping others with no obvious benefit to oneself and with few expectations for personal gain.

Analog A physical, mechanical, or electrical model of an object or concept about which measurements and calculations can be made.

Androgynous Combining attitudes and behavior of both males and females.

Anglos Mainstreamers in the southwest region of the United States.

Anomie The reduced social control against deviant behavior that is due to a disregard of norms and standards.

Anxiety Generalized, diffuse apprehension.

A posteriori Explanations are offered after the facts are known.

Application blank A personnel form to elicit information about an individual's personal characteristics, background, and experience.

A priori Hypotheses are formulated before the facts are known.

Arbitration A situation in which a third party renders a decision for two parties who are in conflict.

Artifact The results of an arbitrary method, rather than the true state of affairs.

Artificial intelligence The emulation of the problem-solving, linguistic, and other capabilities of human beings by means of a computer.

Assumed similarity We assume that we are like other people in values, interests, beliefs, and personality (see *Projection*).

Attenuation Reduction from a theoretically true correlation because of the unreliability of one or both measures correlated.

Attitude An affective, evaluative, relatively enduring reaction, positive or negative, toward an object or proposition.

Attribution theory A theory of the way people impute intentions to other persons or situations.

Auditing Verification of the validity of data, statements, and records.

Autokinetic effect A stationary light that, when viewed in a dark room, appears to move.

Autonomy The degree of freedom in carrying out an assignment.

Aversive reinforcement Reinforcing conditions that inhibit the reinforced behavior; also *Negative reinforcement*.

B

Batch production The production of quantities of similar items, rather than mixes of items.

Behavior modification Changing behavior by changing the consequences of that behavior. Desired new behavior is rewarded (*positively reinforced*); undesired old behavior is punished or positive consequences are removed (*negatively reinforced*).

Behavior shaping *Behavior modification* in which small increments of behavior are reinforced in the direction of the desired behavior until a final desired result is achieved.

Biased sample A sample that is unrepresentative because of one or more sources of systematic error.

Binary Involving two digits or states.

Biographical information blank See *Application blank*.

Boundary-spanning roles Liaison roles that connect departments or organizations with each other and with the environment.

Bounded rationality Managers make the best decisions they can within the constraints of limited information about possible alternatives and the consequences of the alternatives.

Brainstorming The generation of ideas without evaluating them; a maximum number of ideas can be generated in a limited time.

Buffering Actions or events to seal off processes from external variations.

Bureaucracy An organization that is operated on the basis of rules, regulations, and orderliness and that focuses on legitimacy, the duties of jobs, and the rights of office. It is characterized by standardization, hierarchical control, specified authority, and responsibilities.

Bureaucratic personality The preference for rules, regulations, and order in running organizations.

Burnout Emotional, mental, and physical exhaustion resulting from continuing exposure to stress.

Business game A simulation of a business operated by two or more players competing with other businesses in a common market.

C

Career plateau A prolonged halt in promotion up the corporate ladder.

Centralization The degree of concentration of authority in a central location at the top of the organization.

Chain of command The hierarchy of authority in an organization from top to bottom. Members are supposed to know to whom they should report and who reports to them.

Change agent An individual who guides the process of group or organizational change.

Channel The communication path along which information flows.

Chicano American of Mexican descent.

Classical organization theory Early efforts to identify the principles of effective management.

Code A system for representing information and rules.

Coefficient alpha The internal consistency or reliability of a test or measure based on the average intercorrelation among its items.

Cognition A mental event in which perceptions, memories, beliefs, and thoughts are processed; the sensing of many narrow segmented categories in behavior or events, rather than a few broad classifications.

Cognitive dissonance The holding of incompatible beliefs and cognitions.

Cognitive dissonance theory The theory that it is unpleasant to maintain strongly held beliefs that clash with facts, and that people

are motivated to resolve the incompatibility by maintaining the beliefs and denying the facts.

Cognitive framework The categories and their connections into which individuals place events, behaviors, objects, attributes, and concepts.

Cohesiveness The forces that hold a group together; the attractiveness of a group for its members and the members for one another.

Collective bargaining The negotiation and administration of agreements between labor and management about wages, working conditions, benefits, and other labor-management issues.

Commitment Strong, positive involvement; continuing concern.

Common factor The statistical representation of a factor underlying two or more variables.

Communality The sum of squares of *factor loadings* for a designated variable; the total variance that is due to the factors that this variable shares with all other variables in an intercorrelated set.

Communication overload The receipt of excessive amounts of information such that the information cannot be processed satisfactorily.

Complexity leadership Leaders go beyond ordinary management to coordinate the complexities of the organization.

Compliance Acting that is consistent with rules, norms, or influence by others.

Compression of salaries Because of changes in labor market conditions, newly hired employees may begin employment at salaries that are near to or the same as those with seniority, more experience, but similar other credentials.

Compulsory arbitration A negotiation in which the arbiter's decision is binding on the parties in conflict.

Computer-assisted instruction (CAI) Instruction by computers that substitutes for human instruction.

Computer program A set of instructions, arranged in proper sequence, to cause a computer to perform a desired set of operations.

Concept A mental image formed from a set of observations; a definition that labels and provides meaning to the observed reality.

Conflict management Intervening as needed to avoid, reduce, or resolve conflicts.

Confrontation A situation in which parties in conflict directly face, oppose, and resist each other on the issues.

Connective leadership Achieving styles (behavioral strategies) to deal with a changing environment.

Consensus An emotionally and intellectually acceptable group decision.

Construct See *Concept*.

Content analysis An objective, systematic, and usually quantitative description of communications as observed, recorded, or documented.

Contingency table A display of the frequency of individuals or cases, classified according to two or more attributes.

Continuous processing Inputs of energy and materials are transformed into products in a flow for a period of time, such as occurs in a petrochemical refinery.

Controlling The process of monitoring and correcting organizational activities to see that they conform to plans.

Co-optation A situation in which authorities choose their successors, colleagues, and assistants.

Coordination Integration of the activities of the separate parts of a group or organization.

Correlation coefficient The relationship between two variables obtained from the same set of cases. It can range from $+1.00$ through 0.00 to -1.00. It is the ratio of how much one (standardized) variable's changes coincide with the changes in the other (standardized) variable.

Counterculture A culture that is radically divergent from the mainstream culture of the society of which it is a part.

Coup Illegitimate, sudden seizure of power; also, a sudden, surprising victory.

Covariance The mean of the products of the deviations of each of two variables from its own mean.

Criterion A standard of performance; the measure against which other measures are calibrated.

Critical incidents method A performance appraisal in which the supervisor keeps a record over a period of time of the behaviors of each subordinate that are critical to the performance of the job. Also, a survey method for collecting desired and undesired critical behaviors from a sample of employees.

Cross-lag The correlation of earlier data on one variable with later data from another variable and vice versa.

Cross-lagged correlational analysis Correlations between variables X and Y are obtained at time 1 and time 2. The correlations between X1 and Y2 and X2 and Y1 are contrasted with the correlations between X1 and Y1 and X2 and Y2.

Cross-validation Scoring keys developed using a first sample are validated using a second sample.

D

Damage control Explanations to offset the effects of a leader's failures and mistakes.

Decentralization The delegation of power and authority from a central, higher authority to lower levels of the organization, which often results in smaller, self-contained organizational units.

Decision making Identifying and selecting a course of action to solve a problem.

Decode To convert coded data into readable and meaningful information.

Deep change The process of radical alteration or transformation that occurs infrequently and with profound effects on the individual or group.

Deindividuation A state of being in which an individual in a collection of people does not feel personally identifiable by others.

Dejobbing An individual worker is assigned to complete a variety of tasks at different times rather than a bundle of the same tasks.

Delphi method A method by which expert opinion is surveyed and compiled, and then each expert evaluates the compilation.

Demand characteristics Explicit and implicit perceptual cues of what behavior is expected in a situation.

Departmentalization The grouping into departments of similar, logically connected work activities.

Dependent variable A variable whose changes are the consequences of changes in other variables.

Dialectical inquiry method A method in which decision makers first examine their assumptions, then negate their assumptions, and then create countersolutions that are based on the negated assumptions.

Differentiation Separating and focusing on the differences between individuals, groups, and the activities in an organization.

Discriminant function An optimal weighting of a set of variables to show the maximum statistical discrimination between two groups.

Discrimination (social) The acceptance or rejection of people solely on the basis of their age, sex, race, ethnicity, or membership in a particular group or organization.

Division of labor The breakdown of a complex task into components so that different individuals are responsible for a limited set of more closely connected or similar activities, instead of the task as a whole.

Dogmatism A close-minded rigid style with beliefs that are authoritarian in content.

Double-loop learning Errors are corrected, resulting in a change of values about what is important to change; actions are then taken accordingly. In single-loop learning, values remain unchanged and no actions are taken.

Downsizing Making smaller.

Dramaturgy Managing impressions by controlling information or cues to be imparted to others.

Dual-career family A family in which both the husband and wife hold jobs or otherwise pursue careers.

Dyad A two-person group.

Dynamic correlation A correlation of a predictor with successive criteria that change as the criteria change in time.

Dyzygotic Fraternal twins from two eggs. Less common inheritance than identical twins but more than ordinary siblings.

E

Efficiency The use of minimum costs and resources in achieving organizational objectives.

Ego The part of one's personality that is oriented toward acting reasonably and realistically (see *Id* and *Superego*).

Ego ideal A partly conscious image of oneself at one's future best.

Empathy The internalization of the feelings of another person.

Empirically-oriented leadership Relies on data and information.

Encoding The translation of information into a series of symbols for communication.

Equity The fairness of rewards and punishments; a situation in which the ratio of outcomes to inputs for a person is equal to the same ratio for comparison persons.

Ethicality Implied standards of morally acceptable conduct with emphasis on moral principles.

Ethnocentrism The rejection of foreigners, aliens, and outgroups; the extreme favoring of one's own group. Also belief that the home country is superior to other countries and that

methods that work at home can be exported elsewhere (see *Geocentrism* and *Polycentrism*).

Expectancy An estimate or judgment of the likelihood that some outcome or event will occur.

Expectancy theory The theory that an effort to achieve high performance is a function of the perceived likelihood that high performance can be achieved and will be rewarded if achieved and that the reward will be worth the effort that is expended.

Experiment The manipulation of one or more independent variables and the control of other related variables to observe one or more dependent variables.

Experimental control The elimination or holding of some variables constant, to examine the effects of other variables that are allowed to vary.

External environment The environment outside the organization or the independent group.

External validity The conclusiveness with which findings can be generalized to other populations and settings.

Extrinsic rewards Pay, promotion, and fringe benefits, apart from the satisfaction that is derived from the work itself.

F

F test A test that determines whether the greater variance in the means among groups compared to the variance within the groups cannot be accounted for by chance.

Factor analysis A statistical technique to extract the smallest number of underlying factors accounting for a larger set of variables.

Factor loading The correlation of any particular variable with an extracted factor.

Factor matrix A matrix whose entries are the *factor loadings* obtained from a factor analysis.

Factor validation The validity of scores derived from a *factor analysis*.

Fear of success The fear that envy and dislike by others will accompany one's success.

Feedback The receiver's expression of her or his reaction to the sender's message or actions. Also, information about the results of one's behavior, efforts, or performance that can result in correction and control.

Field experiment The use of the controlled laboratory method in a real-life setting.

Field study The examination of the relations and interactions among variables in real-life settings, without the manipulation of variables as in a field experiment.

Field theory The theory that social behavior is a function of one's environment, as well as of one's attitudes and personality.

First impression One's impression of others that is formed early in a relationship, that often has a lasting impact.

First-line managers Managers who are at the lowest level in the management hierarchy and who are responsible only for the work of operating employees, not for the work of other managers.

First-order factors Factors that are extracted from an original set of variables.

Flexible organization An organization in which the policies, structure, relationships, and jobs are loosely defined and open to alteration.

Forecasting The prediction of outcomes and future trends.

Formal authority Legitimate or position power; the right to exert influence because of one's hierarchical position in the organization.

Formal group A group that is created by a *formal authority* and is directed toward achieving specific objectives.

Formalization A situation in which rules, policies, and procedures in organizations are written and institutionalized (see *Bureaucracy*).

Functional organization An organization that is departmentalized so that those engaged in the same functional activity, such as marketing, are grouped into one department.

G

Game theory The explanation of the behavior of rational people in competitive and conflict situations.

Gender Grammatical categories, male, female, and neuter, such as he, she, and it. Commonly misapplied to the two biologically distinct sexes, male and female.

General factor The factor present in every variable of the set.

General manager An individual who is responsible for all departments within a larger division, such as a manufacturing plant.

Geocentrism A world view of management, operations, and opportunities rather than one limited to a single nation or nationality (*Eth-*

nocentrism) or an independent collection of countries (*Polycentrism*).

Grapevine The paths through which informal communications are passed in an organization.

Group decision support system (GDSS) A computerized information system in a group meeting to make better use of information for group decisions.

Groupthink Faulty processes resulting in group decisions that are poorer than those of the individual members working alone.

H

Habituated followers Blindly trusting followers of the charismatic or pseudotransformational leader.

Halo effect The influence of overall impressions on the rating of a specific characteristic.

Hawthorne effect The performance of employees who receive special attention will be better simply because the employees received that attention.

Hedonism Motivation that is attained by gaining pleasure and avoiding pain.

Heuristics "Rule of thumb" solutions to problems that are based on past experience rather than explicit formulas.

Hierarchical factor analysis The systematic organization of a factor solution from the simplest two-factor solution to a complex of many factors.

Hierarchical organization In a hierarchical organization, except for the member at the top, each member has a superior; and except for those at the bottom, each member has one or more subordinates.

Higher-order factors Factors that are extracted from a set of first-order factors (also called *second-order factors*).

Higher-order interactions The analysis of the interacting effects of three or more independent variables.

Hollistic hunch Intuition.

Human resource information system A computerized collection, storage, maintenance, and retrieval system for an organization's information about its personnel.

Hygiene factors Benefits that cause dissatisfaction with the job if they are not present but that do not add to satisfaction if they are present.

Hypothesis A conditional prediction about the relationship among concepts or among

variables, often generated from a theory, that is subjected to empirical verification.

I

Id The part of the personality that is the repository of basic drives and unsocialized impulses, including sex and aggression.

Idealistic leadership Relies on intuition and a minimum of data and information.

Ideologue A convinced advocate of a specific set of doctrines, attitudes, and beliefs.

Ideology A strongly held set of values, attitudes, and beliefs that explain the world.

Implicit theories The tendencies of individuals to weave characteristics of others or characteristics of events into explanatory patterns.

In-basket test A test in which an examinee is given a booklet that contains a sample of memos, bulletins, notes, letters, and reports representing a manager's in-basket; the test is scored on the way the individual prepares to deal with various issues contained in the material.

Incremental adjustments Problem solving in which each successive action represents a small change.

Independent variable A variable that is manipulated in an experiment whose changes are considered to be the cause of changes in other variables (the dependent variables); variables selected in a survey for the same purpose.

Inflection point Major change in technology, business, or performance evidenced in a changing trend in a graph.

Informal communication Communication that is not officially sanctioned (see *Grapevine*).

Informal group A group that voluntarily arises from the needs of individuals and the attraction of people to one another because of common values and interests; an unofficial group that is created without the sanction of a higher organizational authority.

Informal organization The relationships between members of an organization that are based on friendship, propinquity, and personal and social needs.

Ingratiation An attempt to influence other persons by flattering them.

Insider trading Trading of stocks and bonds on knowledge from inside the firm that is not available to the public.

Integration The joining of elements to work together in a unified way.

Internal environment Workers, managers, technology, working conditions, and the culture in the organization.

Internalized Behavior, compliance, and conformity are consistent with one's beliefs and values.

Internal locus of control The belief that the rewards one receives result from one's own efforts, rather than because of chance or the effects of others.

Internal validity The conclusiveness with which the effects of the experimental treatments are established in an experiment.

Interpretive strategy Attention placed on perceptions, feelings, values, symbols, and nuances rather than simple realities.

Intrapsychic tension Conflicts within an individual.

Intrinsic rewards Satisfaction from doing the work itself apart from the pay, promotion, and benefits; feelings of growth, esteem, and achievement from doing a job well.

Introjection The unconscious or subconscious attribution of others' motives to oneself.

Ipsative scores A set of scores generated for the same person, rather than a single score per person generated for a set of persons.

J, K

Job A collection of tasks grouped together similarly in a number of similar positions in a given organization.

Job enlargement The combining of various operations at a similar level into one job to provide more variety for workers.

Job enrichment Providing a job with more challenge, meaning, *autonomy*, and responsibility.

Job satisfaction Attitudes and feelings about one's job.

Job scope The number of separate operations a particular job requires before a cycle is repeated.

Job specialization The division of work into standardized, simplified tasks.

L

Laboratory study Research in which the effects of extraneous factors that are irrelevant to the problem are minimized by isolating the research in an artificial setting; elements thought to be important in real life are re-

produced and manipulated under controlled conditions.

Lame duck A leader whose power has declined because his or her tenure in the leadership position is near its end.

Lateral (or horizontal) communication Communication between departments of an organization that generally follows the work flow, thus providing a direct channel for coordination and problem solving.

Lateral (or horizontal) relationship Direct contact between members of different departments at the same hierarchical level that bypasses the chain of command in their own department.

Leader-member exchange (LMX) Interaction of a leader with an individual member of the group or the average member of the group in contrast to the interaction of a leader with the group of members.

Learned helplessness A condition in which persons become passive, depressed, and unable to learn to cope with the situation.

Leniency bias The tendency to be more favorable and positive than is justified by evidence.

Libido Psychic energy that is expended in satisfying different needs.

Likert scale A scale in which respondents are asked to indicate how much they agree or disagree with an attitudinal statement.

Linear programming A method for the optimal allocation of limited resources to attain a goal.

Line personnel Those managers and workers who are directly responsible for achieving organizational goals (in contrast to staff personnel, who provide support services for the line personnel).

Linguistics The scientific study of language.

LMX See *Leader-member exchange.*

Locus of control The degree to which individuals are controlled by their internal motives, habits, and values, rather than by external forces.

Logic Principles and criteria of validity in thought and demonstration; the application of truth tables, the relations of propositions, and the consistency of deductions and assumptions.

Long-linked technology Serial interdependence between work activities; one task can be performed only after another task has been completed.

M

Management by objectives (MBO) A formal set of procedures to review the progress toward common goals of organizational superiors and their immediate subordinates.

Management information system (MIS) A formal, usually computerized, system to provide management with information.

Management science See *Operations research.*

Manipulation An attempt to influence others in which the manipulator tries to conceal the effort from the target of the influence.

Marginality The position of people at the boundary between two societies, who are often uncertain about their identity and status.

Markov model The mathematical transformation of one set of states and events into another.

Mathematical model A facsimile of reality in mathematical terms; a description of a process and parameters and their relationships to one another and to environments.

Matriarchal A female-dominated family or society in which the woman (wife or mother) is most influential.

Matrix organization An organization in which each subordinate reports to both a functional (or divisional) manager and to a project (or group) manager.

MBA Master of Business Administration.

Mechanistic organization An organization in which the operations are rule based.

Mediating variable Its correlation with the criterion in a multiple regression serves to add to the multiple effect by its linkage to the other predictor variables.

Mediation A situation in which a third party assists two parties in conflict to reach agreement.

Mentors Individuals who pass on the benefits of their knowledge and experience to younger and less experienced individuals.

Message Encoded information sent by a sender to a receiver.

Mestizo Of mixed Indian-Native American and European descent.

Meta-analysis Statistical method for estimating the true correlation between two variables from the distribution of sample correlations corrected for the different size of samples, restrictions in range, and its limits from the results obtained from several individual samples or studies.

Middle managers Managers at the middle levels of the organizational hierarchy, who are responsible for the direction of the lower level supervisors reporting to them.

Mission The stated purposes of the organization.

Model A facsimile that captures the important essentials of reality; may be conceptual, mathematical, or physical.

Modeling Learning by imitation; behaving in the same way as observed in another person to make a certain response.

Moderated regression analysis An optimal prediction equation that includes the effects of *moderator variables.*

Moderator variable Unrelated by itself to the criterion variable in a multiple regression, its correlation with predictor variables adds to the multiple prediction of the criterion.

Monotonic Numbers arranged so that each is larger (or smaller) than the one preceding it in the sequence.

Monozygotic Identical twins from one egg. The closest in heritability of the same traits.

Moral identity Awareness of one's own moral beliefs and ethical behavior, and of their imortance to oneself.

Morality Set of social beliefs and values of right conduct.

Multinational corporation (MNC) A corporation with operations and divisions in numerous countries, but that is controlled by headquarters in one country.

Multinational firm An organization that locates, trades, or produces products or offers services in several countries.

Multiple regression The optimal weighting of a set of predictor variables to minimize the error of prediction of a criterion.

Myth A dramatic narrative of imagined events and fantasies, usually to explain origins and developments.

N

Negative reinforcement See *Aversive reinforcement.*

Network A pattern of interconnections among individuals, groups, or organizations.

Nominal group technique The pooling of the ideas of individuals without their meeting to generate or accumulate the pool of ideas.

Nomological network The web of logical connections among constructs.

Nomothetical network See *Nomological network.*

Nonprogrammed decisions Specific solutions that emerge from unstructured processes to deal with nonroutine problems.

Normative model A model that prescribes a solution to a problem.

Normative scores Raw scores scaled in relation to those of the rest of the population, for example percentiles and standard scores.

Norms Shared group expectations about behavior; socially defined and enforced standards about how the world should be interpreted and how one should behave in it.

NROTC Naval Research Officers Training Corps, for the U.S. Navy.

O

Objectives The targeted goals of individuals, groups, or organizations toward which resources and efforts are channeled.

Oblique dimensions Dimensions inclined toward each other at some angle other than 90°, representing their correlation; not orthogonal.

Occupation A collection of similar jobs existing in different firms.

One-way communication Any communication from the sender without a reply from the receiver.

Open system A system that transforms inputs from its environment to outputs to its environment; its general principles may explain organizational behavior.

Operant conditioning A behavioral modification technique in which cued responses are strengthened (more likely to be repeated) as a result of reinforcements (consequences of the behavior).

Operational definition A specification of the procedures or operations by which a concept is sensed and measured.

Operations research Mathematical techniques for modeling, analysis, and solution of management problems.

Organic organization An organization in which operations are subject to modification through learning from *feedback.*

Organizational climate Employees' attitudes toward the organization and their satisfaction with it.

Organizational conflict Disagreement between organizational members and groups over the allocation of scarce resources, or how to engage in interdependent work activities; disagreements arising from different assumptions, goals, identifications, or statuses.

Organizational culture The norms, values, attitudes, and beliefs, evidenced in myths, stories, jargon, and rituals that are shared by organizational members.

Organizational design The creation of the organizational structure that is most appropriate for the strategy, people, technology, and tasks of the organization.

Organizational development A long-range effort to improve an organization's problem solving and renewal process.

Organizational goals An organization's purpose, mission, and objectives that form the bases of its strategy.

Organizational structure The arrangement and interrelationship of the various components and positions in a organization.

Organization chart A diagram displaying the functions, departments, and positions in an organization.

Orthogonal dimensions Dimensions that are at right angles to each other; uncorrelated, independent dimensions.

Overload The lack of capacity to meet performance expectations.

P

Parsimonious The simple but accurate explanation of a phenomenon that avoids more complicated explanations because the simplified one is adequate.

Partial reinforcement A schedule of reinforcement in which rewards are given intermittently.

Path-goal analysis The means and ways that describe what objectives can be reached.

Patriarchal A male-dominated family or society in which the men are much more in power and control than are the women.

Perception An immediately sensed experience of other persons or objects, modified and organized by the perceiver's personal characteristics and by social influences.

Perceptual defense A selective perception in which a person substitutes innocuous perceptions for unpleasant stimuli.

Performance appraisal The evaluation of an individual's performance by comparing it to standards or objectives.

Peripheral routing Persuading people unable or unmotivated to accept the idea.

Personal construct A concept that is used by a particular individual to categorize events and other persons' behaviors.

Personality The dynamic organization of

the abilities, attitudes, beliefs, and motives of a particular individual that contribute to the individual's reaction to his or her environment.

Phenomenological Of or related to comprehending the environment above and beyond the objective environment.

Placebo A substance or a condition used as an experimental control, which should have no effects relevant to the experiment.

Policy General guidelines for decision making.

Policy capturing A multiple regression procedure in which the regression weights underlying the policies that influenced the decision makers are determined.

Polycentrism The view that because countries are different, local control is best for organizing operations.

Population The total collection of people or cases from which a sample is drawn.

Position power Power that is inherent in the formal position occupied by the incumbent.

Positive reinforcer The consequence of behavior that is desirable, pleasant, or needed. When linked to the behavior, the positive reinforcer increases the probability that the behavior will be repeated in the same or similar situations.

Post hoc analysis A statistical analysis that is chosen after the experimental data have been collected, not as a part of the original design of the experiment.

Power structure A set of relationships among different members or units of an organization that is based on the differences in power among them.

Prejudice A negative evaluation of a person because of the person's sex, age, race, ethnicity, or membership in another group or organization.

Primary effect The predominant effect of the first information received about persons, objects, or issues upon learning, retention, judgment, or opinion about them.

Principled moral reasoning Application of general rules to decide on a just solution.

Prisoner's dilemma The choice when a better outcome for one player is incompatible with the choice resulting in a better outcome for a competing player. This dilemma leads to both players making choices that have unfavorable results for both of them.

Probability estimate Probability of success.

Probability sample A sample chosen in such a way that every member of the population has a known, usually equal, probability of being included.

Process consultation Consultation in which members of an organization are helped to understand and change the ways in which they work together.

Productivity Performance relative to resources; output divided by input; quantity and quality of output in a given period.

Programmed decisions Solutions to routine problems determined by rules, procedures, or habits.

Projection The attribution of one's own motives to others, usually unconsciously or subconsciously (see *Assumed similarity*).

Propinquity Physical proximity.

Prototype An idealized image or the first of its kind on which copies are based.

Prospectors Strategists who search for new opportunities.

Pseudotransformational leadership A false messiah who appears to act like a transformational leader but is actually inauthentic and self-interested and leads the group, organization, or society astray.

Psychological contract Mutual expectations between an individual and an organization or between subordinates and superiors of how work is to be performed and how they will relate to each other; the rights, privileges, and obligations of each to each other.

Psychosocial Psychological elements combine with social aspects to affect relationships.

Purpose The primary role of an organization in society in producing goods or services.

p value The probability of a given outcome or event, on a scale from 0.00 (not possible) to 1.00 (certain).

Q

Q-technique A technique in which a set of paired scores is correlated across different variables for two persons or cases.

Quality circles Periodic meetings of employees and management personnel to solve quality, production, and related problems.

Quality control The process that ensures that goods and services meet predetermined standards.

Quality of work life The value of work that takes into account the well-being of the employee as well as that of the organization.

R

R & D Research and development.

Random sample A probability sample in which members are drawn in a random manner from a list of prospects that enumerates the population.

Rational approach An approach in which conclusions are arrived at by reasoning.

Rational-economic man A theory that fully informed people are motivated primarily by money and self-interest.

Rationally-oriented leadership Relies on logical and methodical reasoning.

Real-time operation An operation in which an event is controlled by information generated by the event.

Recency effect The predominant effect of the most recent information received on learning, retention, judgment, or opinion about persons, objects, or issues.

Reference group A group with whom a person identifies and compares him or herself.

Reflect The sign of a variable is changed so the variable is now opposite in meaning.

Refreezing A process in which new behavior becomes the norm through support and *reinforcement*.

Reinforcement The consequence of behavior that influences whether the behavior will be evoked again under the same or similar stimulus conditions.

Reinforcement schedule The pattern of *reinforcement* that can affect how quickly behavior is modified, shaped, and learned, and how resistant it is to change or extinction.

Relative deprivation The tendency to be dissatisfied with one's own status and compensation relative to that of those with whom one compares oneself, to expectations, and to comparable conditions.

Reliability The consistency of measurement, as seen in the stability of scores over time or in the equivalence of scores on two forms of a test of the same attributes (see *Coefficient alpha*).

Representative sample A sample that is composed of different members proportionate to their types in the population.

Reputational capital Intangible corporate value enhanced by executive leadership, quality of products, publicized awards, and rankings.

Resilience Ability to deal with adversity.

Response sets A systematic way of answering a question that is not directly related to the content of the question but to the form of the question and the alternative answers.

Risk ratio   Maximum risk compared with probability of success.

Risky shift   The tendency for groups to make a decision that is less conservative than one that would be made alone by each of its individual members.

Rite   An elaborate, dramatic, ceremonial activity that consolidates cultural expressions into a social event.

Rites of passage   Rites in which a person passes from an organizational outsider to an organizational insider. They convey the organization's norms and values symbolically. In society, they include confirmation, graduation, and marriage.

Ritual   A fixed way of enacting a set of rites within an *organizational culture*.

Role   A socially defined pattern of behavior that is expected of an individual in a designated function in a particular position within a group, organization, or society.

Role ambiguity   A condition of uncertainty about what is expected and what role behavior will be accepted and rewarded.

Role boundaries   Limits of the role behavior that are expected.

Role conflict   A situation in which persons are faced with meeting conflicting demands. Conflict can arise between values within a role, between competing roles, or from the demands of others.

Role overload   A situation in which role requirements exceed the limits of time, resources, and capabilities.

Role perception   What an individual sees are the behaviors needed to enact a role.

Rotation   Moving factor axes and their hyper-planes around the 0,0 coordinate to allow more points representing *factor loadings* to fall in these hyper-planes.

ROTC   Reserve Officers Training Corps for the U.S. Army or U.S. Air Force.

R-technique   A technique in which the paired scores on two variables are correlated for a number of persons or cases.

S

Sample   A portion of a population that is selected for study in lieu of the complete population.

Sampling error   Deviation of any sample statistic from the population value.

Satisfice   The choice of a suboptimal alternative that meets some minimal criteria of acceptance, when making a decision.

Scapegoating   The displacement of hostility toward a weaker available target when the source of frustration is too powerful or not available for attack.

Scientific method   The systematic use of deduction, induction, and verification of predictions by the collection of relevant data.

Selective perception   Sensing some aspects.

Self-actualization   Using one's capacities fully in meaningful, personally satisfying endeavors.

Self-concept   The way people perceive and evaluate themselves.

Self-fulfilling prophecy   The expectation of a reality influences the fulfillment of that reality.

Self-serving bias   Bias to judge oneself favorably, crediting oneself for successes but blaming others and external factors for failures.

Semantic differential rating   Graphic scale with defined extremes, such as a term at one end and its antonym at the other, but undefined anchors in between.

Sense making   Attributing meaning to experience.

Significance   See *Statistical significance*.

Simple structure   A structure in which a *rotation* solution is achieved so that each variable is maximally correlated with as few factors as possible; the variance of the *factor loadings* is maximized in the *VARIMAX* solution.

Simulation   The representation of the necessary elements of some object, phenomenon, system, or environment to facilitate control and study. The representation mirrors or maps the effects of various changes in the original, enabling the researcher or trainee to study, analyze, and understand the original by means of the behavior of the model.

Single-loop learning   See *Double-loop learning*.

Single-source bias   An inflated value that occurs when the same rater supplies the information for the pairs of variables to be correlated.

Smallest-space analysis and mapping   The mathematical procedure to locate and display optimally in two dimensions, a sample of individuals or cases according to their respective distances in measurements from each other.

Social desirability   A response set to answer

questions about oneself in the socially approved manner.

Social determinism   The view that the course of history emerges only as an expression, instrument, or consequence of historical laws.

Social distance   The acceptable degree of closeness (physical, social, or psychological) between leaders and subordinates and between members of particular ethnic groups.

Socialization   Learning the norms of one's group, organization, or society and acquiring its distinctive values, beliefs, and characteristics.

Social loafing   A condition in which workers reduce or withhold effort on a group task.

Socioemotional   Interpersonal; dealing with the social and emotional aspects of the relations between people.

Sociometric measure   A measure based on the nominations of peers; who chooses whom can provide a display of the informal structure of relations in a group.

Specialization   The performance of only some specific part of a whole collection of tasks by an individual worker.

Specification equation   An equation that indicates a designated individual's performance on a test in terms of factor sub-scores weighted by *factor loadings*.

Specific factor   The statistical representation of some variable based on only one variable in contrast to common factors which are based on two or more variables.

Staff   Individuals or groups who provide line personnel with advice and services.

Staff personnel   See *Line personnel*.

Stakeholders   Individuals and groups who gain from the organization's successes and lose from its failures.

Standard deviation   A measure of how much variability is present in a set of scores. It is the square root of the variance.

Statistical prediction   Objective judgments about people based on data combined by means of formulas or mechanical methods.

Statistical significance   The probability that a given mean statistic could not have occurred by chance alone.

Statistical test   A mathematical procedure for determining the probability that obtained results are due to chance.

Stepwise multiple regression analyses   Analyses in which one predictor variable at a time is added to the regression equation.

The process is halted when the next step adds more error than predictive value to the optimal combination of predictors.

Stereotype A standard image applied to all members of the same group that ignores the variations among them.

Strategic planning The formulation of an organization's objectives and how to achieve them.

Stratified random sample A probability sample whose members are selected by dividing the population into several categories, then selecting respondents randomly from each category (see *Representative sample*).

Structure A pattern of prescribed or observed consistencies in relations among members of a group or organization.

Sunk costs Money spent or resources already used.

Superego The part of the personality that is oriented toward doing what is regarded as morally right and proper: one's conscience, *ego ideal*, and ideal self-image.

Superordinate goals Goals around which divergent parties can rally to collaborate to achieve the goals.

Switch hitter Ambidextrous; one who can respond in alternative ways.

Symbols Emblems, tokens, and signs representing ideas, terms, and objects.

Synergy Cooperative efforts among people or units that generate more motivation than would the isolated operation of the units or people.

System boundary The boundary between the system and its environment. It is rigid in a closed system (not interactive with its environment) and flexible in an *open system* (interactive with its environment).

T

Task force A temporary group established to address a specific problem (also *Ad hoc group*).

Tautology Circular reasoning; for example, arguing that A caused B because B caused A.

Team building Improving relationships among members and the accomplishment of the task by diagnosing problems in team processes affecting the team's performance.

Territoriality An innate drive in many species of animals to defend their own habitat.

Theory A system of concepts, rules about the interconnections of the concepts, and ways of linking the concepts to observed facts.

Theory X A theory that assumes that the average worker dislikes work, is lazy, has little ambition, and must be directed or threatened with punishment to perform adequately.

Theory Y A theory that assumes the average worker can enjoy work and be committed, involved, and responsible.

Transformational leadership The leader elevates the follower morally about what is important, valued, and goes beyond the simpler transactional relationship of providing reward or avoidance of punishment for compliance.

Triad A three-person group.

t-test A test that determines whether the average statistics for two samples of subjects cannot be accounted for by chance.

U

Unfreezing Making old ways unacceptable so that changes are readily accepted and can occur.

Unobtrusive measures Measures obtained without the knowledge of the persons studied.

V

Valence The values or motivating strength of a reward to an individual.

Validity The accuracy or correctness of a method or measurement according to expert opinion, its predictive ability, or its correlation with a construct representing its true meaning.

Values What people consider right, good, and important.

Variable Any quantity that may take on several points on a dimension.

Variance The mean of the sum of squares of the deviations of each of a set of scores from its mean; the square of the standard deviation.

Varimax A solution in factor analysis in which the rotation achieves a maximum variation among the *factor loadings* so that variables correlate as highly as possible with as few factors as possible and as low as possible with as many other factors as possible.

Verification The collection of facts to support or refute hypotheses.

Vertical communication Communication up or down the chain of command.

Visionary Leadership Planning and forming policy that is farsighted and future-oriented, and provides direction for future actions.

W, X, Y

Walk-around management Top managers visit with employees at their workplace.

Whistle blower Employee who voluntarily reports infractions of the rules, violations of ethics, or illegal actions by other members of the organization.

Z

Zero loading A loading in a *factor analysis*, a correlation between a variable and a factor so small that it can be attributed to a chance difference from zero.

References

Aaronovich, G. D., & Khotin, B. L. (1929). The problem of imitation in monkeys. *Novoye v Refleksologii i Fiziologii Nervnoy Systemi, 3,* 378–390.

Abbe, E. (1900). *Motive und Erlauterungen zum Entwurf eines Statuts der Carl Zeiss-Stiftung. (Motive and explanation of the plan and regulations of the Carl Zeiss establishment.)* Reprinted in 1989 as part of a complete treatise of lectures, reports and works on sociopolitical and related subjects by Ernst Abbe. Hildesheim, Zurich, New York: Olms, 330–403.

Abdel-Halim, A. A. (1981). Personality and task moderators of subordinate responses to perceived leader behavior. *Human Relations, 34,* 73–88.

Abdel-Halim, A. A. (1983a). Effects of task and personality characteristics on subordinate responses to participative decision making. *Academy of Management Journal, 26,* 477–484.

Abdel-Halim, A. A., & Rowland, K. M. (1976). Some personality determinants of the effects of participation: A further investigation. *Personnel Psychology, 29,* 41–55.

Abdalla, A., & Al-Homoud, M. A. (2001). Exploring the implicit leadership theory in the Arabian Gulf states. *Applied Psychology: An International Review, 50,* 506–531.

Abdo, G. (2004). Alienated Muslims. In T. Halstead (ed.), *The real state of the union.* New York: Basic Books.

Abegglen, J. C. (1958). *The Japanese factory: Aspects of its social organization.* New York: Free Press.

Abels, M. (1996). The local government manager as a transformational leader. *The Journal of Leadership Studies, 3s,* 97–98,105, 108–109.

Abelson, R. P. (1981). Psychological status of the script concept. *American Psychologist, 36,* 715–729

Abernathy, D. J. (1999). The human side of the net. *Training & Development,* March 16–17.

Abrahamsen, D. (1977). *Nixon vs. Nixon: An emotional tragedy.* New York: Farrar, Straus, & Giroux.

Abrahamson, M. (1969). Position, personality, and leadership. *Psychological Record, 19,* 113–122.

Abramowitz, M. W. (1984). Eleanor Roosevelt and the National Youth Administration 1935–1943—An extension of the presidency. *Presidential Studies Quarterly, 14(4),* 569–580.

Abramson, L. Y., Seligman, M. E. P., & Teasdale, J. D. (1978). Learned helplessness in humans: Critique and reformulation. *Journal of Abnormal Psychology, 87,* 49–74.

Accenture, E. L., & Williams, J. R. (2000). *An empirical examination of accountability perceptions within a multi-source feedback system.* Paper, Society for Industrial and Organizational Psychology, San Diego, CA.

Accoce, P., & Rentchnick, P. (1994). The president's illness: Culture, politics, and fetishism in Benin. *Culture, Medicine and Psychiatry, 18(1),* 61–81. (Original book published in 1988.)

Accoce, P., & Rentchnick, P. (2003). The president's illness: Talked about in T. J. Coffey, *A better democratic model.* Trafford Publishing.

Ace, G., & Emerman, E. (1999). *Watson Wyatt Worldwide study: Superior human capital practices linked to superior shareholder returns.* Special report.

Ackermann, F., & Eden, C. (2003). *Powerful and interested stakeholders matter: Their identification and management.* Paper, Academy of Management, Seattle, WA.

Ackerson, L. (1942). *Children's behavior problems: Relative importance and intercorrelations among traits.* Chicago: University of Chicago Press.

Adair, J. (1973). *The Action-Centered Leader.* London: McGraw-Hill.

Adair, J. (1989). *Great leaders.* London: Talbot Adair Press.

Adams, E. F. (1976). *Influences of minority supervisors on subordinate attitudes.* Unpublished manuscript.

Adams, E. F. (1978). A multivariate study of subordinate perceptions of and attitudes toward minority and majority managers. *Journal of Applied Psychology, 63(3),* 277–288.

Adams, H. (1984). Red powerlessness: Bureaucratic authoritarianism on Indian reservations. *Cornell Journal of Social Relations, 18(1),* 28–40.

Adams, J. (2004). American Indian visionary award: Indian country today recognizes Billy Franks, Jr. www.msnbc.msn.com/id/3881595.

Adams, J., Instone, D., Rice, R. W., & Prince, H. T, II. (1981). *Critical incidents of good and bad leadership.* Paper, American Psychological Association, Los Angeles.

Adams, J., Prince, H., II, Instone, D., & Rice, R. W. (1984). West Point: Critical incidents of leadership. *Armed Forces and Society, 10,* 597–611.

Adams, J., & Yoder, J. D. (1985). *Effective leadership for women and men.* Norwood, NJ: Ablex Publishing.

Adams, J. S. (1963). Wage inequities, productivity and work quality. *Industrial Relations, 3,* 9–16.

Adams, J. S., & Romney, A. K. (1959). A functional analysis of authority. *Psychological Review, 66(4),* 234–51.

Adams, S. (1952). Effect of equalitarian atmospheres upon the performance of bomber crews. *American Psychologist, 7,* 398.

Adams, S. (1953). Status congruency as a variable in small group performance. *Social Forces, 32,* 16–22.

Adler, A. (1954). *Understanding human nature.* New York: Fawcett.

Adler, N. (1984). Understanding the ways of understanding: cross-cultural management methodology reviewed. In R. N. Farmer (ed.), *Advances in international comparative management* (Vol. 1). Greenwich, CT: JAI Press.

Adler, N. J. (1986–1987). Women in management worldwide. *International Studies of Management and Organization, 16*, 3–32.

Adler, N. J. (1990). International dimensions of organizational behavior. Boston: PWS-KENT.

Adler, N. J. (1993). An international perspective on the barriers to the advancement of women managers. *Applied Psychology: An International Review, 42*, 289–300.

Adler, N. J. (1994). Competitive frontiers: Women managing across borders. In N. J. Adler & D. N. Izraeli (eds.), *Competitive frontiers: Women managers in a global economy*. Oxford, U.K.: Basil Blackwell.

Adler, N. J. (1996). Global women political leaders: An invisible history, an increasingly important future. *Leadership Quarterly, 7*, 133–161.

Adler, N. J., & Izraeli, D. N. (1994). Where in the world are the women executives? *Business Quarterly, 159*(1), 89–94.

Adler, R. (1995). *International dimensions of organizational behavior* (2nd ed.) Boston: Kent.

Adorno, T. W., Frenkel-Brunswik, E., Levinson, D. J., & Sanford, R. N. (1950). *The authoritarian personality*. New York: Harper.

Adsit, D.J., London, M., Crom, S., and Jones, D. (1997). Cross-cultural differences in upward ratings in a multinational company. *International Journal of Human Resource Management, 8*(4), 385–401.

Agle, B. R. (1993). *Charismatic chief executive officers: Are they more effective? An empirical test of charismatic leadership theory*. Doctoral dissertation, University of Washington, Seattle, WA.

Agle, B. R., Mitchell, R. K., & Sonnenfeld, J. A. (1999). Who matters to CEOs? An investigation of stakeholder attributes and salience, corporate performance, and CEO values. *Academy of Management Journal, 42*, 507–525.

Agle, B. R., & Sonnenfeld, J. A. (1994). *Charismatic chief executive officers: Are they more effective? An empirical test of charismatic leadership theory*. Paper, Academy of Management, Dallas, TX.

Agor, W. H. (1984). Using intuition to manage organizations in the future. *Business Horizons, 27*(4), 49–54.

Agor, W. H. (1986a). *The logic of intuitive decision-making: A research-based approach for top management*. New York: Quorum Books.

Agor, W. H. (1986b). The logic of intuition: How top executives make important decisions. *Organizational Dynamics, 14*(3), 5–18.

Aguinis, H., Nesler, M. S., Quigley, B. M., et al. (1996). Power bases of faculty supervisors and educational outcomes for graduate students. *Journal of Higher Education, 67*, 267–297.

Ahn, M. J., Adamson, J. S. A., & Dornbusch, D. (2004). From leaders to leadership: Managing change. *Journal of Leadership & Organizational Studies, 10*(4), 112.

Ahuja, M. K., Robert, L., Chudoba, K. M., et al. (2003). *Identity formation among virtual workers*. Paper, Academy of Management, Seattle, WA.

Aiken, E. G. (1965a). Changes in interpersonal descriptions accompanying the operant conditioning of verbal frequency in groups. *Journal of Verbal Learning and Verbal Behavior, 4*, 243–247.

Aiken, E. G. (1965b). Interaction process analysis changes accompanying operant conditioning of verbal frequency in small groups. *Perceptual and Motor Skills, 21*, 52–54.

Aiken, M., & Bacharach, S. B. (1985). Environmental influences on authority and consensus in organizations. *Research in the Sociology of Organizations, 4*, 351–377.

Akhtar, T. (1997). *A comparative psychological profile of political, organizational, and military leadership in Pakistan*. Doctoral dissertation, Quaid-al-Azam University, Islamabad, Pakistan.

Akhtar, S. S., & Haleem, A. (1980). Differences between newly-promoted supervisors and workers with regard to "consideration" and "initiating structure." *Journal of Psychological Researches, 24*, 90–95.

Akin, G., & Hopelain, D. (1986). Finding the culture of productivity. *Organizational Dynamics, 14*(3), 19–32.

Alban, B. T., & Seashore, E. W. (1978). Women in authority: An experienced view. *Journal of Applied Behavioral Science, 14*, 21.

Alban-Metcalfe, R. J., & Alimo-Metcalfe, B. (2000). An analysis of the convergent and discriminant validity of the transformational leadership questionnaire. *International Journal of Selection & Assessment, 8*(3), 158.

Albaum, G. (1964). Horizontal information flow: An explanatory study. *Academy of Management Journal, 7*, 21–33.

Albino, J. E. N. (1999). Leading and following in higher education. *The Psychologist-Manager Journal, 3*(1), 27–40.

Albrecht, P. A., Glaser, E. M., & Marks, J. (1964). Validation of a multiple assessment procedure for managerial personnel. *Journal of Applied Psychology, 48*, 351–360.

Albright, L. (1966). *A research study of the Vernon Psychological Laboratory Test Battery and other measures for field sales managers*. Chicago: American Oil Co. (Reported in Campbell, Dunnette, et al., 1970, 191.)

Albright, M. D., & Levy, P. E. The effects of source credibility and performance rating discrepancy on reactions to multiple raters. *Journal of Applied Social Psychology, 25*, 577–600.

Aldag, R. J., & Brief, A. P. (1977). Relationships between leader behavior variability indices and subordinate responses. *Personnel Psychology, 30*, 419–426.

Aldag, R. J., & Brief, A. P. (1981). *Managing organizational behavior*. St. Paul, MN: West Publishing.

Alexander, E. (1942). *Our age of unreason*. Philadelphia: Lippincott.

Alexander, E. R. (1979). The design of alternatives in organizational contexts: Pilot study. *Administrative Science Quarterly, 24*, 382–404.

Alexander, J. A., & Lee, S. D. (1996). The effects of CEO succession and tenure on failure of rural community hospitals. *Journal of Applied Behavioral Science, 32*, 70–88.

Alexander, L. D. (1979a). The effect of level in the hierarchy and functional area on the extent to which Mintzberg's managerial roles are required by managerial jobs. *Proceedings, Academy of Management*, Atlanta, GA, 186–189.

Alexander, L. D. (1979b). The effect of level in the hierarchy and functional area on the extent to which Mintzberg's managerial roles are required by managerial jobs. *Dissertation Abstracts, 40*, 2156A.

Alford, R. R., & Scoble, H. M. (1968). Community leadership, education, and political behavior. *American Sociological Review, 33*, 259–272.

Algattan, A. A. (1985). *The path-goal theory of leadership: An empirical and longitudinal analysis*. Unpublished manuscript.

Ali, A. J. (1982). An empirical investigation of managerial value systems for working in Iraq. *Dissertation Abstracts International, 43*(7A), 2429.

Ali, M. R., Humbalo, R., Khaleque, A., & Rahman, A. (1982). *Intergroup conflict in industry: A cross-cultural study*. Paper, International Congress of Applied Psychology, Edinburgh, Scotland.

Alimo-Metcalfe, B. (1993). Women in management: Organizational socialization and assessment practices that prevent career advancement. *International Journal of Selection and Assessment, 1*(2), 68–83.

Alimo-Metcalfe, B. (1994). Gender bias in the selection and assessment of women in management. In M. J. Davidson & R. Burke (eds.), *Women in management: Current research issues*. London: Paul Chapman.

Alimo-Metcalfe, B. (1994). *An investigation of female and male constructs of leadership and empowerment*. Paper, International Congress of Applied Psychology, Madrid, Spain.

Alimo-Metcalfe, B., & Metcalfe, S. J. (1998). *Do managers, their bosses, direct reports, and colleagues agree as to the nature of effectiveness, and does gender make a difference? Factor analysis of 360 degree/multi-rater feedback*. Paper, International Congress of Applied Psychology, San Francisco, CA.

Alimo-Metcalfe, B., & Alban-Metcalfe, A. (1999). *The development of a new transformational leadership questionnare*. Leeds, U.K.: University of Leeds, Nuffield Institute Centre for Leadership.

Alinsky, S. (1971). *Rules for radicals: a practical primer for realistic radicals*. New York: Random House, Inc.

Al-Jafary, A., & Hollingsworth, A. (1983). An exploratory study of managerial practices in the Arabian Gulf region. *Journal of International Business Studies, 14*(2), 143–52.

Al-Kubaisy, A. (1985). A model in the administrative development of Arab Gulf countries. *The Arab Gulf, 17*(2), 29–48.

Allee, W. C. (1945). Social biology of subhuman groups. *Sociometry, 8*, 2129.

Allee, W. C. (1951). *Cooperation among animals, with human implications*. New York: Schuman.

Allen, F. (1981). Managers at work: A large-scale study of the managerial job in New York City government. *Academy of Management Journal, 24*, 613–619.

Allen, M. P., & Panian, S. K. (1982). Power, performance and succession in the large corporation. *Administrative Science Quarterly, 27*, 538–547.

Allen, M. P. (1974). The structure of interorganizational elite cooptation. *American Sociological Review, 39*, 393–406.

Allen, M. P., Panian, S. K., & Lotz, R. E. (1979). Managerial succession and organizational performance: A recalcitrant problem revisited. *Administrative Science Quarterly, 24*, 167–180.

Allen, T. H. (1981). Situational management roles: A conceptual model. *Dissertation Abstracts International, 42*(2A), 465.

Allen, T., Katz, R., Grady, J. J., et al. (1988). Project team aging and performance: The roles of project and functional managers. *R&D Management, 18*, 295–308.

Allen, T. D., Poteet, M. L., Russell, et al. (1995). A field study of factors related to supervisors' willingness to mentor others. *Journal of Vocational Behavior, 50*, 1–22.

Allen, T. J. (1966). Studies of the problem-solving process in engineering design. *IEEE Transactions on Engineering Management, EM-13*(2), 72–83.

Allen, T. J., & Cohen, S. I. (1969). Information flow in research and development laboratories. *Administrative Science Quarterly, 14*, 12–19.

Allen, T. J., & Gerstberger, R. C. (1973). A field experiment to improve communications in a product engineering department: The non-territorial office. *Human Factors, 15*(5), 487–498.

Allen, T. J., Lee, D. M. S., & Tushman, M. L. (1980). R & D performance as a function of internal communication, project management, and the nature of the work. *IEEE Transactions on Engineering Management, 27*(l), 2–12.

Allen, W. R. (1975a). Black and white leaders and subordinates: Leader choice and ratings, aspirations and expectancy of success. In D. Frederick & J. Guiltinan (eds.), *New challenges for the decision sciences*. Amherst, MA: Northeast Region of the American Institute for Decision Sciences.

Allen, W. R. (1975b). A comparative analysis of black and white leadership in a naturalistic setting. *Dissertation Abstracts International, 36*, 2516.

Allen, W. R., & Ruhe, J. A. (1976). Verbal behavior by black and white leaders of biracial groups in two different environments. *Journal of Applied Psychology, 61*, 441–445.

Allender, H. D. (1993) Self-directed work teams: How far is too far? *Industrial Management, 35*(5), 13–15.

Alliger, G. M., & Dwight, S. A. (2000). A meta-analytic investigation of the susceptibility of integrity tests to faking and coaching. *Educational and Psychological Measurement, 60*(1), 59–72.

Allinson, R. E. (1995). A call for ethically-centered management. *Academy of Management Executive, 9*(1), 73–76.

Allison, M., Armstrong, G., & Hayes, G. (2001) The effects of cognitive style on leader-member-exchange. *Journal of Occupational & Organizational Psychology, 74*, 201–220.

Alloy, L. B., & Abramson, L. Y. (1982). Learned helplessness, depression, and the illusion of control. *Journal of Personality and Social Psychology, 42*,1114–1126.

Allport, G. W., & Vernon, P. E. (1933). *Studies in expressive movement*. New York: Hafner Publishing.

Allport, F. H. (1924). *Social psychology*. Boston: Houghton Mifflin.

Almquist, E. M. (1974). Sex stereotypes in occupational choice: The case for college women. *Journal of Vocational Behavior 5*(1),13–21.

Alonso, F. M. (1994). *Carisma y liderazgo carismatico: Una aproximación empírica desde las perspectivas de Bass y Friedman*. Tesis doctoral, Universidad Nacional de Educación a Distancia, Madrid, Spain.

Alpander, C. C. (1974). Planning management training programs for organizational development. *Personnel Journal, 53*, 15–21.

Alsikafi, M., Jokinen, W. J., Spray, S. L., & Tracy, C. S. (1968). Managerial attitudes toward labor unions in a southern city. *Journal of Applied Psychology, 52*, 447–453.

Altemeyer, B. (1998). The other "authoritarian personality." In M. Zanna (ed.), *Advances in Experimental Social Psychology* (vol. 30). San Diego: Academic Press.

Altemeyer, R. A. (1981). *Right wing authoritarianism*. Winnipeg: University of Manitoba.

Altemeyer, R. A. (1966). *Education in the arts and sciences: Divergent paths*. Doctoral dissertation, Carnegie Institute of Technology, Pittsburgh, PA.

Altieri, L. B. (1995). Transformationaland transactional leadership in hospital nurse executives in the Commonwealth of Pennsyvania: a descriptive study. Dissertation. Fairfax, VA: College of Nursing and Health Science, George Mason University.

Alutto, J. A., & Acito, F. (1974). Decisional participation and sources of job satisfaction: A study of manufacturing personnel. *Academy of Management Journal, 17*, 160–167.

Alutto, J. A., & Belasco, J. A. (1972). A typology for participation in organizational decision making. *Administrative Science Quarterly*, 17, 117–125.

Alutto, J. A., & Hrebimak, L. G. (1975). *Research on commitment to employing organizations: Preliminary findings on a study of managers graduating from engineering and MBA programs.* Paper, Academy of Management, New Orleans.

Alvarez, R. (1968). Informal reactions to deviance in simulated work organizations. *American Sociological Review*, 33, 895–912.

Alwon, G. J. (1980). Response to agencywide crisis: A model for administrative action. *Child Welfare*, 59, 335–346.

Amabile, T. M., & Gryskiewicz, S. S. (1987). *Creativity in the R & D laboratory* (Tech. Rep. No. 30). Greensboro, NC: Center for Creative Leadership.

Amabile, T. M., Schatzel, E. A., Moneta, G. B., et al. (2004). Leader behaviors and the work environment for creativity: Perceived leader support. *Leadership Quarterly*, 15, 5–32.

Amason, A. C. (1996). Distinguishing the effects of functional and dysfunctional conflict on strategic decision making: Resolving the paradox for top management teams. *Academy of Management Journal*, 39, 123–148.

Amason, A. C., Thompson, K. R., Hochwarter, W. A., et al. (1995). An important dimension in successful management teams. *Organizational Dynamics*, 24(2), 20–35.

Ambrose, M. L., & Schminke, M. (2003). Organization structure as a moderator of the relationship between procedural justice, interactional justice, perceived organizational support, and supervisor trust. *Journal of Applied Psychology*, 88, 295–305.

Ambrose, S. E. (1987). *The education of a politician, 1913–1962.* New York: Simon & Schuster.

American Management Association (1990). Blueprints for service quality. AMA *Management Briefing*, 21–35.

American Psychological Association (1953). *Ethical standards of psychologists.* Washington, DC: American Psychological Association.

Amir, Y., Kovarsky, Y., & Sharan, S. (1970). Peer nominations as a predictor of multistage promotions in a ramified organization. *Journal of Applied Psychology*, 5, 462–469.

Ammeter, A. P., Douglas, C., Gardner, W., et al. (2004). Toward a political theory of leadership. *Leadership Quarterly*, 13, 751–796.

Anand, V., Ashforth, B. E., & Joshi, M. (2004). Business as usual: The acceptance and perpetuation of corruption in organizations. *Academy of Management Executive*, 18, 39–55.

Ancona, D. G. (1987). Groups in organizations: Extending laboratory models. In C. Hendrick (ed.), *Group processes and intergroup relations.* Newbury Park, CA: Sage Press.

Ancona, D. G., & Caldwell, D. F. (1988). Beyond task and maintenance: Defining external functions. *Group and Organization Studies*, 13, 468–494.

Anderhalter, D. E, Wilkins, W., & Rigby, M. K. (1952). *Peer rating relationships between officer and peer-candidate predictions of effectiveness as a company grade officer in the U.S. Marine Corps and the ability to predict estimated officer effectiveness of peers* (Tech. Rep. No. 2). St. Louis, MO: Washington University, Department of Psychology.

Anderson, B., & Nilsson, S. (1964). Studies in the reliability and validity of the critical incident technique. *Journal of Applied Psychology*, 48, 398–413.

Anderson, C. R. (1977). Locus of control, coping behaviors, and performance in a stress setting: A longitudinal study. *Journal of Applied Psychology*, 62, 446–451.

Anderson, C. R., & Schneier, C. E. (1978). Locus of control, leader behavior and leader performance among management students. *Academy of Management Journal*, 21, 690–698.

Anderson, C. R., Hellriegel, D., & Slocum, J. W., Jr. (1977). Managerial response to environmentally induced stress. *Academy of Management Journal*, 20, 260–272.

Anderson, D. F. (1982). The legacy of William Howard Taft. *Presidential Studies Quarterly*, 12(1), 26–33.

Anderson, D. F., & Wasserman, D. P. (2001). Choosing leaders: A group interactional approach. *Journal of Leadership Studies*, 8(2), 38–51.

Anderson, H. H. (1940). An examination of the concepts of domination and integration in relation to dominance and ascendance. *Psychological Review*, 47, 21–37.

Anderson, J. (1983). Why presidents stumble. *Parade* magazine, March 23, 4–6, 8.

Anderson, L. E., & Balzer, W. K. (1988). *The effects of timing of leaders' opinions on problem solving groups: A field experiment.* Paper, Society for Industrial and Organizational Psychology, Dallas.

Anderson, L. M. (1985). *A kind of wild justice: Revenge as theme and device in Shakespeare's comedies.* Doctoral dissertation.

Anderson, L. R. (1964). *Some effects of leadership training on intercultural discussion groups* (Tech. Rep.). Urbana: University of Illinois, Group Effectiveness Research Laboratory.

Anderson, L. R. (1966a). *Initiation of structure, consideration, and task performance in intercultural discussion groups.* Urbana: University of Illinois, Group Effectiveness Research Laboratory. Unpublished report.

Anderson, L. R. (1966b). Leader behavior, member attitudes, and task performance of intercultural discussion groups. *Journal of Social Psychology*, 69, 305–319.

Anderson, L. R. (1983). Management of the mixed-cultural work group. *Organizational Behavior and Human Performance*, 31, 303–330.

Anderson, L. R. (1990). Toward a two-track model of leadership training: Suggestions from self-monitoring theory. *Small Group Research*, 21(2), 147–167.

Anderson, L. R., & Fiedler, F. E. (1964). The effect of participatory and supervisory leadership on group creativity. *Journal of Applied Psychology*, 48, 227–236.

Anderson, L. R., Karuza, J., & Blanchard, R N. (1977). Enhancement of leader power after election or appointment to undesirable leader roles. *Journal of Psychology*, 97, 59–70.

Anderson, L. R., Tolson, J., Fields, M. W., et al. (1990). Extension of the Pelz Effect: The impact of leader's upward influence on group members' control within the organization. *Basic & Applied Social Psychology*, 11, 19–32.

Anderson, M. (2000). Leaders and leadership as a competitive edge. *Canadian HR Reporter*, 13(13), 8–9.

Anderson, N. (1923). *The hobo: The sociology of the homeless man.* Chicago: University of Chicago Press.

Anderson, N., Lievens, F., van Dam, K., et al. (2004). Future perspectives on employee selection: Key directions for future research and practice. *Applied Psychology: An International Review*, 53, 487–501.

Anderson, N., Herriot, P., and Hodgkinson, G. P. (2001). The practitioner-researcher divide in industrial, work and organizational (IWO) psychology: Where are we now, and where do we go from here? *Journal of Occupational & Organizational Psychology*, 74(4), 391–411.

Anderson, P. (2000). Does the new economy require a new type of leadership? *Journal for Quality and Participation*, 23(3), 12–13.

Anderson, R. C. (1959). Learning in discussions: A résumé of the authoritarian-democratic studies. *Harvard Educational Review*, 29, 201–215.

Anderson, R. M. (1964). Activity preferences and leadership behavior of head nurses. *Nursing Research*, 13, 239–242, 333–337.

Anderson, T. D. (1998). *Transforming leadership*. St. Lucie, FL: St. Lucie Press.

Andrews, F. M. Creative ability, the laboratory environment, and scientific performance. *IEEE Transactions in Engineering Management*, 14, 76–83.

Andrews, F. M., & Farris, G. F. (1967). Supervisory practices and innovations in scientific teams. *Personnel Psychology*, 20, 497–515.

Andrews, I. R., & Henry, M. (1963). Management attitudes toward pay. *Industrial Relations*, 3, 29–40.

Andrews, J. D. W. (1967). The achievement motive and advancement in two types of organizations. *Journal of Personality and Social Psychology*, 6, 163–168.

Andrews, K. R. (1994). The concepts of corporate strategy. In B. De Wit & B. Meyer (eds.), *Process, content and context*. New York: West.

Andrews, M. C., & Kacmar, K. M. (2001). Impression management by association: Construction and validation of a scale. *Journal of Vocational Behavior*, 58, 142–161.

Andrews, P. (1984). Performance, self-esteem and perceptions of leadership emergence: A comparative study of men and women. *Western Journal of Speech Communication*, 48, 1–13.

Andrews, R. E. (1955). *Leadership and supervision, a survey of research findings: A management report*. Washington, DC: U.S. Civil Service Commission.

Angelini, A. L. (1966). Measuring the achievement motive in Brazil. *Journal of Social Psychology*, 68, 35–44.

Anikeeff, A. M. (1957). The effect of job satisfaction upon attitudes of business administrators and employees. *Journal of Social Psychology*, 45, 277–281.

Anonymous (1945/1946). Informal social organizations in the Army. *American Journal of Sociology*, 51, 365–370.

Anonymous (1970). Russia sets program of wage incentives in scientific work. *Wall Street Journal*, June 11, 12.

Anonymous (1975). *Romantic progression: The psychology of literary history*. Washington, DC: Hemisphere.

Anonymous (1978, May/June). The only way. Execu-Time: *The Newsletter on Effective Use of Executive Time*, 25.

Anonymous (1985). *OPQ Manual*. Esher, Surrey, England: Saville & Holdsworth.

Anonymous (1987). Notre Dame's "Father Ted" bids farewell. *Newsweek*, May 11, 75.

Anonymous (1988a). Managers need to be tougher on workplace slackers. *Success*, 35(5), 30.

Anonymous (1988b). Survey says staffing issues big concern for next 5 years. Decisions. *Newsletter*, Management Decision Systems, Boston, September 1.

Anonymous (1989). Blunders abroad. *Nation's Business*, March, 56.

Anonymous (1989). Employee involvement and the supervisor. *Worklife Report*, 7(1), 6–7.

Anonymous (1991). *Human development report*. New York: United Nations.

Anonymous (1991). Management education: Passport to prosperity. *The Economist*, March 2, 5–7.

Anonymous (1992). *Statistical yearbook*. New York: United Nations.

Anonymous (1992). *Supervisory process and functions for operations manager, team leader, team associate, and supervisor*. Binghamton, NY: Workforce Dynamics Associates.

Anonymous (1994). *World Values Survey, 1981–1984, 1990–1993*. Ann Arbor, MI: Inter-University Consortium for Political and Social Research, World Values Study Group.

Anonymous (1995a). Skills shortages and training: Highlights the importance of improvement in output and productivity. *Journal of European Industrial Training*, 19(6), 22–23.

Anonymous (1995b). Outdoor management development: Reality or illusion? *Journal of European Training*, 19(6), 20–21.

Anonymous (1995). Changing scene. *Fast Facts*, 4(2), 5.

Anonymous (1997). *Army leadership field manual* (FM 22–100). Initial draft, April 4, 7–4, 11.

Anonymous (1997). *Army leadership*. (FM 22–100). Initial draft, April 3, 4, 10.

Anonymous (1998). Transparency International corruption perception index. www.gwdg.de/~uwvw/icr.htm.

Anonymous. (1999). *Telecommuting option preferred*. Woodcliff Lake, NJ: Lee Hecht Harrison.

Anonymous (1999). *Women in statewide offices*. New Brunswick, NJ: Rutgers University, Center for Women in Statewide Politics.

Anonymous (1999). Diversity at Allstate. *Management Review*, 88(7), 25–30.

Anonymous (1999a). Dale Sundby: Power agent. In Avolio, B., & Bass, B. M. (eds.), *Developing potential across a full range of leadership: Cases on transactional and transformational leadership*. Mahwah, NJ: Lawrence Erlbaum & Associates.

Anonymous (1999b). Compensation fit for a king. *Forbes*, 163(10), 202–203.

Anonymous (1999c). *Grassroots leaders: Growing healthy and sustainable communities*. Battle Creek, MI: W. K. Kellogg Foundation.

Anonymous. (2001) The Mideast: No clear successor to Arafat exists. *Dallas Morning News*.

Anonymous (2004a). *American Indian Leadership Program*. www.personal.psu.edu/users/j/y/yyz101/deptweb6/eps/programs.html.

Anonymous (2004b). *The Harvard Project on American Indian economic development*. www.ksg.harvard.edu/edu/hpaied/overview.

Anonymous (2004). History now: Leadership lessons from Warren Harding . . . and other unlikely sources. *American Heritage*, June–July, 16.

Anonymous (2006). Market watch. *St. Petersburg Times*, July 9, D1.

Anonymous (2006). Psychological capital (PsyCAP): Measurement, development, and performance impact. Lincoln, NE: Gallup Leadership Institute, Briefings Report 2006–01.

Anonymous (undated, a). *Participants' perceptions of inter-organizational relations*. Unpublished manuscript.

Anonymous (undated). *Some key features of the Full Range Leadership Development Program*. Binghamton, NY: Binghamton University, Center for Leadership Studies.

Anonymous (undated, b). *Stability of managerial values*. Unpublished manuscript.

Anonymous (undated). *The Federal Express approach: Blueprints for service quality*. AMA Management Briefing, New York, NY.

Ansari, M. A. (1988). *Leadership styles and influence strategies: Moderating effect of organizational climate*. Paper, International Congress of Psychology, Sydney, Australia.

Ansari, M. A., Baumgartel, H., & Sullivan, G. (1982). The personal orientation–organizational climate fit and managerial success. *Human Relations*, 35, 1159–1177.

Ansbacher, H. L. (1948). Attitudes of German prisoners of war: A study of the dynamics of national-socialistic followership. *Psychological Monographs*, 62, 1–42.

Ansbacher, H. L. (1951). The history of the leaderless group discussion technique. *Psychology Bulletin*, 48(5), 383–391.

Anstey, E. (1966). The civil service administrative class and the diplomatic service: A follow-up. *Occupational Psychology*, 40, 139–151.

Anthill, J. K., & Cunningham, J. D. (1979). Self-esteem as a function of masculinity in both sexes. *Journal of Consulting and Clinical Psychology*, 47, 783–785.

Anthony, L. V. L. (1994). Private communication, April 4.

Anthony, L. V. L. (1994). *The relationship between transformational leadership and organizational culture, employee performance, and employee attrition*. Doctoral dissertation, University of Miami, Miami, FL.

Anthony, W. P. (1978). *Participative management*. Reading, MA: Addison-Wesley.

Antonakis, J. (2000). *On transformational/transactional leadership*. Predoctoral paper, Lausanne, Switzerland.

Antonakis, J. (2001). *The validity of the transformational, transactional, and laissez-faire leadership model as measured by the Multifactor Leadership Questionnaire (MLQ 5X)*. Doctoral dissertation, Yale University, New Haven, CT.

Antonakis, J. (2003). Why "emotional intelligence" does not predict leadership effectiveness: A comment on Prati, Douglas, Ferris, Ammeter, and Buckley. *International Journal of Organizational Analysis*, 11, 355–361.

Antonakis, J. (2004). On why "emotional intelligence" will not predict leadership effectiveness beyond IQ or the "Big Five": An extension and rejoinder. *Organizational Analysis*, 12(2), 171–182.

Antonakis, J., & Atwater, L. (2002). Leader distance: a review and a proposed theory. *Leadership Quarterly*, 13, 673–704.

Antonakis, J., Ciancolo, A. T., & Sternberg, R. J. (2004). *The nature of leadership*. Thousand Oaks, CA: Sage.

Antonakis, J., Cianciolo, A. T., & Sternberg, R. J. (2004). Leadership, past, present, and future. In J. Antonakis, A. T. Cianciolo, & R. J. Sternberg (eds.), *The nature of leadership*. Thousand Oaks, CA: Sage Publications.

Antonakis, J. and House, R. J. (2002). The full-range leadership theory. In Avolio, B. J. & Yammarino, F. J. (eds.) *Transformational and charismatic leadership: the road ahead*. Amsterdam: JAI Press.

Antonini, D. (1994). The effects of feedback accountability on upward appraisal ratings. *Personnel Psychology*, 47, 349–356.

Antonini, J. E. (1994). Focus on renewal. *Journal of Business Strategy*, 15(1), 12.

Anzizu, J. M., & P. Nuenos (1984), *Leadership under sociopolitical change: Business enterprise in Spain*. Paper presented at the 75th Anniversary Colloquium on Leadership, Harvard Business School, Boston.

Apfelbaum, E., & Hadley, M. (1986). Leadership MS-qualified: II. reflections on initial case study investigation of contemporary women leaders. In C. F. Graumann & S. Moscovici (eds.), *Changing Conceptions of Leadership*. New York: Springer, 199–221.

Applebaum, H. A. (1982). Construction management: Traditional versus bureaucratic methods. *Anthropological Quarterly*, 55, 224–234.

Applebaum, S. H. (1977). The motivation of government administrators within a closed climate. *Akron Business and Economic Review*, 8, 26–32.

Aquino, K. (2000). Structural and individual determinants of workplace victimization: The effects of hierarchical status and conflict management style. *Journal of Management*, 26, 171–193.

Aquino, K., Ray, S., & Reed, A. (2003). *The self-importance of moral identity as a predictor of lying in negotiations*. Paper, Academy of Management, Seattle, WA.

Arad, S., Arnold, J. A., Rhoades, J. A., & Drascow, F. (1995). *The Empowering Leadership Questionnaire: The construction of a new scale for measuring leader behaviors*. Paper, Society for Industrial and Organizational Psychology, Orlando, FL.

Arbona, C., Flores, C. L., & Novy, D. M. (1995). Cultural awareness and ethnic loyalty: Dimensions of cultural variability among Mexican American college students. *Journal of Counseling and Development*, 73, 610–614.

Arbous, A. G., & Maree, J. (1951). Contributions of two group discussion techniques to a validated test battery. *Occupational Psychology*, 25, 7389.

Ardichvili, A. (2001). Leadership styles and work-related values of managers and employees of manufacturing enterprises in post-communist countries. *Human Resource Development Quarterly*, 12(4), 363–383.

Arensberg, C. M., & McGregor, D. (1942). Determination of morale in an industrial company. *Applied Anthropology*, 1, 12–34.

Arenson, K. W. (2005). Presidents of colleges cite finance as main issue. *New York Times*, October 31, A11.

Argyle, M., Gardner, C., & Ciofi, E. (1958). Supervisory methods related to productivity, absenteeism, and labour turnover. *Human Relations*, 11, 23–40.

Argyris, C. (1954). Human relations in a bank. *Harvard Business Review*, 32, 63–72.

Argyris, C. (1960). *Understanding organizational behavior*. Homewood, IL: Dorsey.

Argyris, C. (1957). *Personality and organization*. New York: Harper.

Argyris, C. (1962). *Interpersonal competence and organizational effectiveness*. Homewood, IL: Irwin-Dorsey.

Argyris, C. (1964a). *Integrating the individual and the organization*. New York: Wiley.

Argyris, C. (1982). *Learning and action: Individual and organizational*. San Francisco: Jossey-Bass.

Argyris, C. (1983). Action science and intervention. *Journal of Applied Behavioral Science*, 19, 115–140.

Arias, O. (2005). *Management of leadership and lechnology for the 21st century*. Address, Symposium, Istanbul, Turkey, May 3–4.

Aries, B. (1976). Interaction patterns and themes of male, female, and mixed groups. *Small Group Behavior, 7*, 7–18.

Aries, C. (1976). Interaction patterns and themes of male, female, and mixed groups. *Small Group Behavior, 7*, 7–18.

Aries, E. (1976). *Sex differences in small group behavior.* Paper presented at the Conference on Sex Roles in American Society: A Psychological Perspective, Troy, New York, May 1.

Arindell, W. A. (1998). Femininity and subjective well-being. In G. Hofstede et al. (eds.), *Masculinity and femininity: The taboo dimensions of national cultures.* Thousand Oaks, CA: Sage.

Aristotle (324 B.C./1981). *Politics.* London: Penguin

Armas, G. C. (2003). Hispanics largest minority group: Hispanics show the most growth. *Binghamton Press & Sun-Bulletin,* June 19, 3a.

Armilla, J. (1967). Predicting self-assessed social leadership in a new culture with the MMPI. *Journal of Social Psychology, 73,* 219–225.

Armstrong, P. (1983). Class relationships at the point of production: A case study. *Sociology, 17,* 339–358.

Armstrong, J. S., & Collopy, F. (1996). Competitor orientation: Effects of objectives and information on managerial decisions and profitability. *Journal of Marketing Research, 33,* 188–199.

Armstrong, J. and Green, K. 2005. Competitor-oriented objectives: The myth of market share. *International Journal of Business, 12.*

Armstrong, J. S., & Green, K. C. (2007). Competitor-oriented objectives: The myth of market share. *International Journal of Business, 12*(1), 117–136.

Army Personnel Research Establishment, U.K. (undated). Part I: *Combat stress and battle: A guide for NCOs and junior commanders.*

Arnaud, A., Ambrose, M., & Schminke, M. (2002). *Individual moral development and ethical climate: The influence of person-organization fit on job attitudes.* Paper presented at the Academy of Management Annual Meeting, Denver, CO.

Arnold, J., & Johnson, K. (1997). Mentoring in early career. *Human Resource Management, 7*(4), 61–70.

Arnott, D. H. (1995). The five lenses of leadership. *The Journal of Leadership Studies, 2,* 137–141.

Aronson, E., & Worchel, F. (1966). Similarity versus liking as determinants of interpersonal attractiveness. *Psychonomic Science, 5,* 157–158.

Arrington, R. E. (1943). Time sampling in studies of social behavior: A critical review of techniques and results with research suggestions. *Psychological Bulletin, 40,* 81–124.

Arsenault, P. M. (1998). Using the social constructive perspective to investigate charismatic leadership. Doctoral dissertation, Temple University, Philadelphia, PA.

Arthur, J. B. (1994). Effects of human resource systems on manufacturing performance and turnover. *Academy of Management Journal, 37,* 670–687.

Arthur, W., Jr., Woehr, D. J., & Moldegen, R. (2000). Convergent and discriminant validity of assessment center dimensions: A conceptual and empirical reexamination of the assessment center construct validity paradox. *Journal of Management, 26,* 813–835.

Arvey, R., Davis, G., & Nelson, S. (1984). Use of discipline in an organization: A field study. *Journal of Applied Psychology, 69,* 448–460.

Arvey, R. D., & Ivancevich, J. M. (1980). Punishment in organizations: A review, propositions, and research suggestions. *Academy of Management Review, 5,* 123–132.

Arvey, R. D., & Neel, C. W. (1974). Moderating effects of employee expectancies on the relationship between leadership consideration and job performance of engineers. *Journal of Vocational Behavior, 4,* 213–222.

Arvey, R. D., Rotundo, M., Johnson, W., Zhang, Z., and McGue, M. The determinants of leadership role occupancy: genetic and personality factors. *Leadership Quarterly, 17*(1), 1–20.

Arvonen, J. (1995) *Leadership behavior and coworker health: A study in the process industry* (Report No. 801). Reports from the Department of Psychology, Stockholm University, Stockholm, Sweden.

Arvonen, J. (2002). *Change, production and employees: An integrated model of leadership.* Doctoral dissertation, Stockholm University, Stockholm, Sweden.

Aryee, S., Tan, H. H., & Budhwar, P. (2002). Antecedents of leader-member exchange and explanation of its relationship with organizational citizenship behavior. Paper, Academy of Management, Denver, CO.

Asch, S. E. (1946). Forming impressions of personalities. *Journal of Abnormal and Social Psychology, 41,* 258–290.

Asch, S. E. (1952). *Social psychology.* New York: Prentice-Hall.

Ascher, W., & Hirschfelder-Ascher, B. (2005). *Revitalizing political psychology: The legacy of Harold D. Lasswell.* Mahwah, NJ: Lawrence Erlbaum & Associates.

Ash, M. K. (1981). *Mary Kay.* New York: Harper & Row.

Ashby, W. R. (1957). *An introduction to cybernetics.* New York: Wiley.

Ashby, W. R. (1960). *Design for a brain.* New York: Wiley.

Ashford, S. J., & Cummings, L. L. (1981). Strategies for knowing: When and from whom do individuals seek feedback. Proceedings, *Academy of Management, 41,* 161–165.

Ashford, S. J., & Cummings, L. L. (1983). Feedback as an individual resource: Personal strategies of creating information. *Organizational Behavior and Human Performance, 32,* 370–398.

Ashford, S. J., & Northcraft, G. B. (1992). Conveying more (or less). than we realize: The role of impression-management in feedback seeking. *Organizational Behavior and Human Decision Processes, 53,* 310–334.

Ashford, S. J., & Tsui, A. S. (1991). Self-regulation for managerial effectiveness: the role of active feedback seeking. *Academy of Management Journal, 34*(2), 251–280.

Ashforth, B. (1989). The experience of powerlessness in organizations. *Organizational Behavior and Human Decisions Processes, 43,* 207–242.

Ashforth, B. (1994). Petty tyranny in organizations. *Human Relations, 47,* 755–778.

Ashforth, B. (1997). Petty tyranny in organizations: A preliminary examination of antecedents and consequences. *Canadian Journal of Administrative Sciences, 14,* 126–140.

Ashkanasy, N. M., & Dasborough, M. T. (2002). *Emotional intelligence and leadership: Concepts and controversies.* Symposium introduction, Academy of Management, Denver, CO.

Ashkanasy, N. M., & Newcombe, M. J. (2000). *An experimental study of affect and gender in leader-member-exchange.* Paper, Society for Industrial and Organizational Psychology, New Orleans, LA.

Ashkanasy, N. M., & O'Connor, C. (1997). Value congruence in leader-member exchange. *Journal of Social Psychology, 137*(5), 647–662.

Ashkanasy, N. M., & Falkus, S. (2004). The Australian enigma. In Chhokar, J., Brodbeck, F. C., & House, R. J. (eds.) *Cultures of the world, A GLOBE anthology of in-depth descriptions of the cultures of 14 countries.* Thousand Oaks, CA: Sage.

Ashkanasy, N. M., & Tse, B. (2000). Transformational leadership as a management of emotion: A conceptual review. In N. Ashkanasy, C. E. J. Hirtel, & W. J. Zerbe (eds.), *Emotions in the workplace: Research, theory and practice.* Westport, CT: Quorum Books.

Ashkanasy, N. M., Windsor, C. A., and Trevino, L. K. (2001). Bad apples in bad barrels revisited: cognitive moral development, just world beliefs, rewards, and ethical decision making. *Business Ethics Quarterly, 16*(4), 449–473. Also: (2001), New York: Alfred Knopf.

Ashour, A. S. (1973a). The contingency model of leadership effectiveness: An evaluation. *Organizational Behavior and Human Performance, 9,* 339–355.

Ashour, A. S. (1973b). Further discussion of Fiedler's contingency model of leadership effectiveness. *Organizational Behavior and Human Performance, 9,* 369–376.

Ashour, A. S., & England, C. (1971). Subordinate's assigned level of discretion as a function of leader's personality and situational variables. *Experimental Publications System, American Psychological Association, 12,* No. 466–1.

Aspegren, R. E. (1963). A study of leadership behavior and its effects on morale and attitudes in selected elementary schools. *Dissertation Abstracts, 23,* 3708.

Astin, A. W., & Scherrei, R. A. (1980). *Managing leadership effectiveness.* San Francisco: Jossey-Bass.

Astin, H. S., & Cress, C. M. (1998). *A national profile of academic women in research universities.* Paper presented at the Conference of Women in Research Universities, Harvard University, Cambridge, MA, November.

Astin, H. S., Cress, C. M., Zimmerman-Oster, K., & Burkhardt, J. C. (2001). Developmental outcomes of college students' involvement in leadership activities. *Journal of College Student Development, 42*(1), 15–27.

Atkinson, J. W. (1964). *An introduction to motivation.* Princeton, NJ: Van Nostrand.

Atsumi, R. (1979). Tsukiai: Obligatory personal relationships of Japanese white-collar company employees. *Human Organization, 38,* 63–70.

Atwater, L. (1988). The relative importance of situational and individual variables in predicting leader behavior: The surprising impact of subordinate trust. *Group & Organization Studies, 13*(3), 290–310.

Atwater, L. E. (1995). The relationship between supervisory power and organizational characteristics. *Group & Organizational Management, 20,* 460–485.

Atwater, L. E., Brett, J. F., & Waldman, D. (2003). Understanding the benefits and risks of multisource feedback. In S. E. Murphy & R. E.Riggio (eds.), *The future of leadership development.* Mahwah, NJ: Lawrence Elbaum Associates.

Atwater, L. E., Carey, J. A., & Waldman, D. A. (2001). Gender and discipline in the workplace: Wait until your father gets home. *Journal of Management, 27,* 537–561.

Atwater, L. E., Dionne, S. D, Avolio, B. J., et al. (1996). *Leader attributes and behaviors predicting emergence of leader effectiveness* (Tech. Rep.

1044). Alexandria, VA; United States Army Research Institute for the Behavioral and Social Sciences.

Atwater, L. E., Dionne, S. D., Avolio, B. J., et al. (1999). A longitudinal study of the leadership development process: Individual differences predicting leader effectiveness. *Human Relations, 52,* 1543–1562.

Atwater, L. E., Dionne, S. D. Camobreco, J. E., et al. (1998). Individual attributes and leadership style: Predicting the use of punishment and its effects. *Journal of Organizational Behavior, 19,* 559–576.

Atwater, L. E., Lau, A., Bass, B., et al. (1994). *The content, construct and criterion-related validity of leader behavior measures* (ARI Research Note). Alexandria, VA: U.S. Army Research Institute for the Behavioral and Social Sciences. Also: Army Research Institute, Technical Note, Contract #MDA-903–91–0131, Arlington, VA.

Atwater, L. E., Ostroff, C., Yammarino, F. J., et al. (1992). Self-other agreement: Does it really matter? *Personnel Psychology, 45,* 141–163.

Atwater, L. E., Ostroff, C, Yammarino, F. J., et al. (1998). Self-other agreement: Does it really matter? *Personnel Psychology, 51,* 577–598.

Atwater, L. E, & Roush, P. (1994). An investigation of gender effects on followers' ratings of leaders, leaders' self-ratings and reactions to feedback. *Journal of Leadership Studies, 1*(4), 37–52.

Atwater, L., & Waldman, D. (1998). 360 degree feedback and leadership development. *Leadership Quarterly, 9,* 423–426.

Atwater, L. E., Waldman, D. A., Atwater, D., et al. (2000). An upward feedback field experiment: Supervisors' cynicism, reactions, and commitment to subordinates. *Personnel Psychology, 53,* 275–297.

Atwater, L., Waldman, D., Carey, J., & Cartier, P. (2001). Subordinate and observer reactions to discipline: Are managers experiencing wishful thinking? *Journal of Organizational Behavior, 22,* 249–270.

Atwater, L. E., Waldman, D. A., Carey, J. A., et al. (2001). Recipient and observer reactions to discipline: Are managers experiencing wishful thinking? *Journal of Organizational Behavior, 22,* 249–270.

Atwater, L., & White, M. (1985). *Behavior and effectiveness of first-line supervisors* (NPRDC Tech. Rep. 86–5). San Diego, CA: Navy Personnel Research and Development Center.

Atwater, L., & Yammarino, F. J. (1989). *Predictors of military leadership. A study of midshipmen leaders at USNA* (ONR Tech. Rep. 7). Binghamton: State University of New York, Center for Leadership Studies.

Atwater, L. E., & Yammarino, F. J. (1989). *Personal attributes as predictors of military leadership* (ONR Tech. Rep. 7). Binghamton, NY: Binghamton University, Center for Leadership Studies.

Atwater, L. E., & Yammarino, F. J. (1992). Does self-other agreement on leadership perceptions moderate the validity of leadership and performance predictions? *Personnel Psychology, 45,* 141–164.

Atwater, L. E., & Yammarino, F. J. (1993). Personal attributes as predictors of superiors' and subordinates' perceptions of military academy leadership. *Human Relations, 46,* 645–667.

Atwater, L. E., & Yammarino, F. J. (1996). Bases of power in relation to leader behavior: A field investigation. *Journal of Business and Psychology, 11*(1), 3–22.

Atwater, L. E., & Yammarino, F. J. (1997). Self-other agreement: A review and model. *Research in Personnel and Human Resources Management, 15,* 121–174.

Aubert, N., Ramanantsoa, B., & Reitter, R. (1984). *Nationalization, managerial power and societal change: A field study in France 1982–*

1983. Paper, 75th Anniversary Colloquium on Leadership, Harvard Business School, Boston.

Auclair, G. (1968). *Managerial role conflict: A cross-cultural comparison.* Paper, American Psychological Association, San Francisco.

Auerbach, P. (2002). *Lessons from the E.R.: Prescriptions for success in managing your business.* New York: Free Press.

Aupperle, K. E. (1996). Spontaneous organizational reconfiguration: a historical example based on Xenophon's *anabasis. Organizational Science,* 7(4), 445–460.

Aupperle, K. E. (1999). *Xenophon's* Anabasis *and the strategic importance of culture: An examination through the use of Gareth Morgan's metaphor.* Paper, Academy of Management, Atlanta, GA.

Aupperle, K. E., Acar, W., & Booth, D. E. (1986). An empirical critique of *In Search of Excellence*: How excellent are the excellent companies? *Journal of Management, 12,* 499–512.

Aupperle, K. E., & Simmons, F. B., III (1989). *Have CEOs of large companies changed the CSR orientations during the Reagan presidency?* Paper, Academy of Management, Washington, D.C.

Austin, G., & Reynolds, D. (1990). Managing for improved school effectiveness: an international survey. *School Leadership & Management,* 10 (2), 167–178.

Austin, T. W. (1981). What can managers learn from leadership theories? *Supervisory Management, 26*(7), 22–31.

Ausubel, D. P., & Schiff, H. M. (1955). Some intrapersonal and interpersonal determinants of individual differences in socioemphatic ability among adolescents. *Journal of Social Psychology, 41,* 39–56.

Avant, X. (1994). *Political institutions and military change.* Ithaca, NY: Cornell University Press.

Avery, D. R., Tonidandel, S., Griffity, K. L., & Quinones, M. A. (2000). *Is all experience created equal? The impact of experience type on leader effectiveness.* Presentation at the Academy of Management Conference. Toronto, Canada, August.

Avolio, B. J. (1994). The "natural": Some antecedents of transformational leadership. *International Journal of Public Administration, 17,* 1559–1581.

Avolio, B. J. (1997). *The great leadership migration to a full range leadership development system.* Working paper, Kellogg Leadership Studies Project, University of Maryland, College Park, MD.

Avolio, B. J. (1999–1999a). *Full leadership development: Building the vital forces in organizations.* Thousand Oaks, CA: Sage Publications.

Avolio, B. J. (1999b). *Reflections on JRTC: JRTC review.* Unpublished memo, March 22.

Avolio, B. J., & Bass, B. M. (1986). Transformational leadership, charisma and beyond. In J. G. Hunt, H. R. Baliga, & H. P. Dachler (eds.), *Emerging leadership vistas.* Lexington, MA: Heath.

Avolio, B. J., & Bass, B. M. (1988). Transformational leadership, charisma, and beyond. In J. G. Hunt, B. R. Baliga, H. P. Dachler, & C. A. Schriesheim (eds.), *Emerging Leadership Vistas.* Lexington, MA: D. C. Heath

Avolio, B.J. and Bass, B.M. (1989). Potential biases in leadership measures: How prototypes, leniency, and general satisfaction relate to ratings and rankings of transformational and transactional leadership constructs. *Educational and Psychological Measurement, 49,* 509–527

Avolio, B. J., & Bass, B. M. (1991). *Full-range of leadership development.* Binghamton, NY: Bass, Avolio & Associates.

Avolio, B. J., & Bass, B. M. (1991). *Manual for the full range of leadership.* Binghamton, NY; Binghamton University.

Avolio, B. J., & Bass, B. M. (1991). *Manual for the full range of leadership development.* Redwood City, CA: Mindgarden.

Avolio, B. J., & Bass, B. M. (1993). *Transforming communities through effective leadership.* Binghamton, NY: Binghamton University, Center for Leadership Studies.

Avolio, B. J., & Bass, B. M. (1994). *Evaluate the impact of transformational leadership training at individual, group, organizational, and community levels.* Binghamton, NY: Binghamton University, Center for Leadership Studies.

Avolio, B. J., & Bass, B. M. (1995). *Building highly developed teams: An application of the full range of leadership practices.* Paper, Academy of Management, Vancouver, BC.

Avolio, B. J., & Bass, B. M. (1995). Individualized consideration viewed at multiple levels of analysis: A multi-level framework for examining the diffusion of transformational leadership. *Leadership Quarterly, 6,* 199–218.

Avolio, B. J., & Bass, B. M. (1996). *A new paradigm of leadership*: An inquiry into transformational leadership. Alexandria, VA: U.S. Army Research Institute in the Behavioral and Social Sciences.

Avolio, B. J., & Bass, B. M. (1998). You can drag a horse to water but you can't make it drink unless it's thirsty. *Journal of Leadership Studies,* 5(1), 4–17.

Avolio, B. J., & Bass, B. M. (eds.). (2002). *Developing potential across a full range of leadership: Cases on transactional and transformational leadership.* Mahwah, NJ; Lawrence Erlbaum Associates.

Avolio, B. J., & Bass, B. M. (2004). *Multifactor Leadership Questionnaire: Manual and sampler set* (3rd ed.). Redwood City, CA: Mind Garden.

Avolio, B. J., Bass, B. M., Atwater, L. E., et al. (1994). *Antecedent predictors of the "full range of leadership" and management styles.* Interim report to the Army Research Institute in the Behavioral and Social Sciences, Arlington, VA, July 30.

Avolio, B. J., Bass, B. M., & Berson, Y. (1998). *Team leadership and its impact on platoon readiness and Joint Readiness Training Center (JRTC) performance.* Paper, Society for Industrial and Organizational Psychology, New Orleans, LA.

Avolio, B. J., Bass, B. M., & Berson, Y. (2000). *Leadership and its impact on platoon readiness at Joint Readiness Training Center (JRTC).* Paper, Society of Industrial and Organizational Psychology, New Orleans. LA.

Avolio, B. J., Bass, B. M., & Dong, I. J. (1999). Re-examining the components of transformational and transactional leadership using the multifactor leadership questionnaire. *Journal of Occupational and Organizational Psychology, 72*(4), 441–462.

Avolio, B. J., Bass, B. M., & Jung, D. I. (1995–1996). *Examining the construct validity of the Multifactor Leadership Questionnaire (MLQ 5X): Refinements and extension.* San Diego, CA: SIOP.

Avolio, B. J., Bass, B. M., & Jung, D. I. (1999). Reexamining the components of transformational and transactional leadership using the Multifactor Leadership Questionnaire. *Journal of Occupational and Organizational Psychology, 72,* 441–462.

Avolio, B. J., Bass, B. M., & Miles, S. E. (1994). *Transforming community leaders: An active paradigm for changing leaders and organizations at the organizational level.* Grant proposal to the Mott Foundation, Flint, MI.

Avolio, B. J., Bass, B. M., & Yammarino, F. J. (1988). *An alternative strategy for reducing biases in leadership ratings.* Paper, Academy of Management, Anaheim, CA.

Avolio, B. J., Bass, B. M., & Yammarino, F. J. (1988). *A strategy for assessing single-source bias* (CLS Report 88–3). Binghamton, NY: Binghamton University, Center for Leadership Studies.

Avolio, B., Dionne, S. D., Atwater, L. E., Lau, A. W., Camobreco, J. F., Whitmore, N., & Bass, B. (1996). *Antecedent predictors of a "full range" of leadership and management styles.* Publication No. ARI TR 1104. Alexandria, VA: U.S. Army Research Institute for the Behavioral and Social Sciences.

Avolio, B. J., Gardner, W. L., Walumbwa, F. O., et al. (2004). Unlocking the mask: A look at the process by which authentic leaders impact follower attitudes and behaviors. *Leadership Quarterly, 15,* 801–824.

Avolio, B. J., & Howell, J. M. (1993). The effects of leadership behavior and leader-follower congruence on predicting follower satisfaction and consolidated unit performance. In K. E. Clark, M. B. Clark, & D. P. Campbell (eds), *The impact of leadership.* Greensboro, NC: Center for Leadership Studies.

Avolio, B. J., & Howell, J. M. (1993). The impact of leadership behavior and leader-follower personality match on satisfaction and unit performance. In K. E. Clark, M. B. Clark, & D. P. Campbell (eds), *The impact of leadership.* Greensboro, NC: Center for Leadership Studies.

Avolio, B. J., Howell, J. M., & Sosik, J. J. (1999). A funny thing happened on the way to the bottom line: Humor as a moderator of leadership style effects. *Academy of Management Journal, 42,* 219–227.

Avolio, B. J., Howell, J. M., & Sosik, J. (1999). A funny thing happened on the way to the bottom line: Humor as a moderator of leadership style effects. *Journal of Applied Psychology, 42,* 219–227.

Avolio, B. J., Jung, D. I., Murray, W., et al. (1996). Building highly developed teams: Focusing on shared leadership processes, efficacy, trust, and performance. *Advances in Interdisciplinary Studies of Work Teams, 3,* 173–209.

Avolio, B. .J., Jung, D. I., Sivasubramanian, N., et al. (2002). *A preliminary validation of the Team Multifactor Leadership Questionnaire.* Binghamton, NY: Binghamton University, Center for Leadership Studies.

Avolio, B. J., & Kahai, S. S. (2003a). Adding the "e" to e-leadership: How it may impact your leadership. *Organizational Dynamics, 31,* 325–338.

Avolio, B. J., & Kahai, S. (2003b). Placing the "e" in e-leadership: Minor tweak of fundamental change. In S. Murphy & R. Riggio (eds.), *The future of leadership development.* Mahwah, NJ: Lawrence Erlbaum Associates.

Avolio, B. J., Kahai, S., & Dodge, G. E. (2001). E-leadership: Implications for theory, research, and practice. *Leadership Quarterly, 11,* 615–658.

Avolio, B. J., & Maritz, D. (2000). E-leading.com: Anywhere, anytime, at any level. *Management Today,* August, 14–16.

Avolio, B. J. & Locke, E. E. (2002). Contrasting different philosophies of leader motivation: Altruism versus egoism. *Leadership Quarterly, 13,* 169–191.

Avolio, B. J., Sivasubramaniam, N., Murry, W. D., et al. (2002). Assessing shared leadership: Development and preliminary validation of a Team Multifactor Leadership Questionnaire. In C. I. Pearce & J. A. Conger (eds.), *Shared Leadership: Reforming the hows and whys of leadership.* Thousand Oaks, CA: Sage.

Avolio, B. J., Sosik, J. J., Jung, D. I., & Berson, Y. (2003). Leadership models, methods, and applications. In W. C. Borman, D. R. Ilgen, & R. J. Klimoski (eds.), *Handbook of psychology* (vol. 12). Hoboken, NJ: Wiley.

Avolio, B. J., Waldman, D. A., & Einstein, W. O. (1988). Transformational leadership in a management game simulation. *Group & Organization Studies, 13,* 59–80.

Avolio, B. J., & Yammarino, F. J. (1990). Operationizing charismatic leadership using a levels-of-analysis framework. *Leadership Quarterly, 1,* 345–373.

Avolio, B. J., & Yammarino, F. J. (2002). Reflections, closing thoughts, and future directions. In B. J. Avolio & F. J. Yammarino (eds.), *Transformational and charismatic leadership: The road ahead.* New York, NY: JAI Elsevier.

Avolio, B. J. & Yammarino, F. J. (2002). *Transformational and charismatic leadership: The road ahead.* New York: JAI Press.

Avolio, B. J., Yammarino, F. J., & Bass, B. M. (1991). Identifying common methods variance with data collected from a single source: An unresolved sticky issue. *Journal of Management, 17,* 571–587.

Awamleh, R., & Gardner, W. L. (1999). Perceptions of leader charisma and effectiveness: The effects of vision content, delivery, and organizational performance. *Leadership Quarterly, 10,* 345–373.

Ayer, J. G. (1968). *Effects of success and failure of interpersonal and task performance upon leader perception and behavior* (Tech. Rep. No. 26). Urbana: University of Illinois, Group Effectiveness Research Laboratory.

Ayman, R., & Chemers, M. M. (1982). *The relationship of managerial behavior to effectiveness and satisfaction in Mexico.* Paper, International Congress of Applied Psychology, Edinburgh.

Ayman, R., & Chemers, M. M. (1983). Relationship of supervisory behavior ratings to work group effectiveness and subordinate satisfaction among Iranian managers. *Journal of Applied Psychology, 68(2),* 338–341.

Ayman, R., & Chemers, M. M. (1986). *The emic/etic approach to leadership orientation job satisfaction of Mexican managers.* Paper, International Congress of Applied Psychology, Jerusalem.

Ayman, R. (2002). Contingency model of leadership effectiveness. In L. Neider & C. A. Schreisheim (eds.), *Leadership.* Greenwich, CT: Information Age Publishing.

Ayman, R., Adams, S., Fisher, B., et al. (2003). Leadership development in higher education institutions: A present and future perspective. In S. E. Murphy & R. E. Riggio (eds.), *The future of leadership development.* Mahwah, NJ: Lawrence Erlbaum Associates.

Ayman, R., & Chemers, M. M. (1991). The effect of leadership match on subordinate satrisfaction in Mexican organizations: Some moderating influences of self-monitoring. *Applied Psychology: An International Review, 40,* 299–314.

Azar, B. (2000). A new stress paradigm for women: Rather than fighting or fleeing, women may respond to stress by tending to themselves and their young and befriending others. *APA Monitor,* July–August, 42–43.

Azzam, T., & Riggio, R. (2003). Community based civic leadership programs: Descriptive investigation. *Journal of Leadership and Organizational Studies,* 10(1), 55–67.

Baba, V. V., & Ace, M. E. (1989). Serendipity in leadership: Initiating structure in the classroom. *Human Relations,* 42, 509–525.

Babad, E., Inbar, J., & Rosenthal, R. (1982). Pygmalion, Galetea, and the Golem investigation of biased teachers. *Journal of Educational Psychology,* 74, 459–474.

Babbitt, B. (1987). To delegate or not to delegate. *Across the Board,* 24(9), 56–57.

Babiak, P. (1995). When psychopaths go to work: A case study of an industrial psychopath. *Applied Psychology: An International Review,* 44, 171–188.

Babikan, K. (1981). The leader-entrepreneur in the public sector. In F. I. Khuri (ed.), *Leadership and Development in Arab Society.* Beirut: American University of Beirut, Center for Arab and Middle East Studies.

Bachand, C. (1981). Boards of directors in Canadian government enterprises: An exploratory research. *Dissertation Abstracts International,* 42(3A), 1289.

Bachman, J. G., Smith, C., & Slesinger, J. A. (1966). Control, performance, and satisfaction: An analysis of structural and individual effects. *Journal of Personality and Social Psychology,* 4, 127–136.

Bachman, S. I., & Gregory, K. (1993). *Mentor and protégé gender: Effects on mentoring roles and outcomes.* Paper, Society for Industrial and Organizational Psychology, San Francisco, CA.

Bachrach, A. J., Candland, D. K., & Gibson, J. T. (1961). Group reinforcement of individual response experiments in verbal behavior. In I. A. Berg & B. M. Bass (eds.), *Conformity and deviation.* New York: Harper.

Bachrach, P., & Botwinick, A. (1992). *Power and empowerment: A radical theory of participatory democracy.* Philadelphia: Temple University Press.

Back, K. W. (1948). Interpersonal relations in a discussion group. *Journal of Social Issues,* 4, 61–65.

Backman, C. W., & Secord, P. F. (1959). The effect of perceived liking on interpersonal attraction. *Human Relations,* 12, 713–715.

Bacon. N., & Blyton, P. (2000). High road and low road teamworking: Perceptions of management rationales and organizational and human resource outcomes. *Human Relations,* 53, 1425–1458.

Badin, I. J. (1974). Some moderator influences on relationships between consideration, initiating structure, and organizational criteria. *Journal of Applied Psychology,* 59, 380–382.

Badran, M., & Hinings, B. (1981). Strategies of administrative control and contextual constraints in a less-developed country: The case of Egyptian public enterprise. *Group & Organization Studies,* 2(1), 3–21.

Baehr, M. E. (1992). *Predicting success in higher level positions: A guide to the system for testing and evaluation of potential.* New York: Quorum.

Baer, M., Oldham, & Cummings, A. (2003). Rewarding creativity: When does it really matter? *Leadership Quarterly,* 14, 569–586.

Baier, D. E. (1947). Note on "A review of leadership studies with particular reference to military problems." *Psychological Bulletin,* 44, 466–467.

Baik, K. (1999). Thirty years of leadership research in Korea: A literature review and critique. *Korean Social Science Journal,* 26(1), 101–130.

Bailey, F. G. (1969). *Stratagems and spoils: A social anthropology of politics.* New York: Schocken Books.

Bailey, F. G. (1983). *The tactical uses of passion.* Ithaca, NY: Comell University Press.

Bailey, H. D. (1966). *An exploratory study of selected components and processes in educational organizations.* Doctoral dissertation, University of California, Berkeley.

Bailey, R., & Baily, K. (1974). Self-perceptions of scholarly ability at four grade levels. *Journal of Genetic Psychology,* 124, 197–212.

Bain, P. G., Mann, C., & Piolo-Merlo, A. (2001). The innocent imperative: The relationship between team climate, innovation, and performance in research and development teams. *Small Group Research,* 32, 55–73.

Baird, J. E., Jr. (1977). Some nonverbal elements of leadership emergence. *The Southern Speech Communication Journal,* 42, 352–361.

Baird, J. E., Jr., & Wieting, G. K. (1979). Nonverbal communication can be a motivational tool. *Personnel Journal,* 58(9), 607–610, 625.

Bajdo, L., & Dickson, M. W. (2001). Perceptions of organizational culture and women's advancement in organizations: a cross-cultural examination. *Sex Roles,* 45 (5/6), 399–414.

Baker, A. J. (1982). The problem of authority in radical movement groups: A case study of lesbian-feminist organization. *Journal of Applied Behavioral Science,* 18, 323–341.

Baker, H., & France, R. R. (1954). *Centralization and decentralization in industrial relations.* Princeton, NJ: Princeton University, Industrial Relations Section.

Baker, L. D, DiMarco, N., & Scott, W. E. (1975). Effects of Supervisors' Sex and Level of Authoritarianism on Evaluation and Reinforcement of Blind and Sighted Workers. *Journal of Applied Psychology,* 60(1), 28–32.

Baker, M. (1998). Out with Confucius in Korea's big firms. *Christian Science Monitor,* March 11, 1, 9.

Balcazar, F E., Hopkins, B. L., & Suarez, Y, (1985–86). A critical objective review of performance feedback. *Journal of Organizational Behavior Management,* 7(3–4), 65–89.

Balcom, J., & Brossy, R. (1997). Executive pay—then, now and ahead. *Directors & Boards,* 22(1), 55.

Baldwin, I., Glazer, N., Hook, S., et al. (1966). Liberalism and the Negro: A round-table discussion. In B. E. Segal (ed.), *Racial and ethnic relations.* New York: Thomas Y, Crowell.

Baldwin, L. E. (1932). *A study of factors usually associated with high school male leadership.* Master's thesis, Ohio State University, Columbus.

Baldwin, T. T., Wagner, R. J., & Roland, C. C. (1991). *Effects of outdoor challenge program on group and individual outcomes.* Paper, Society for Industrial and Organizational Psychology, St. Louis, MO.

Bales, R. F (1950). *Interaction process analysis.* Reading, MA: Addison-Wesley.

Bales, R. F. (1958a). Task roles and social roles in problem-solving groups. In E. E. Macoby, T. M. Newcomb, & E. L. Hartley (eds.), *Readings in social psychology.* New York: Holt.

Bales, R. F., Cohen, S. P., & Williamson, S. A. (1979). *SYMLOG: A system for the multiple level observation of groups.* New York: Free Press.

Bales, R. F., & Slater, P. E. (1955). Role differentiation in small decision-making groups. In T. Parsons & R. F. Bales (eds.), *Family, socialization, and interaction processes*. New York: Free Press.

Bales, R. F., & Strodtbeck, F. L. (1951). Phases in group problem-solving. *Journal of Abnormal and Social Psychology, 46*, 485–495.

Bales, R. F., Strodtbeck, F., Mills, T., & Roseborough, M. E. (1951). Channels of communication in small groups. *American Social Review, 16*, 461–468.

Baliga, B. R., & Hunt, J. C. (1988). An organizational life cycle approach to leadership. In J. C. Hunt, B. R. Baliga, H. R. Dacher, & C. A. Schriesheim (eds.), *Emerging leadership vistas*. Lexington, MA: D. C. Heath.

Balkin, D. B., Markman, G. D., & Gomez-Mejia, L. R. (2000). Is CEO pay in high-technology firms related to innovation? *Academy of Management Journal, 43*, 1118–1129.

Balkundi, P., & Harrison, D. A. (2006). Ties, leaders, and time in teams: Strong inference about network structure's effects on team viability and performance. *Academy of Management Journal, 49*, 49–68.

Ball, G. A., & Trevino, L. K. (1990). *Leader reactions to punishing subordinates: Justice evaluations and emotional responses*. Paper, Academy of Management, San Francisco, CA.

Ball, K. L. (1999). The psychologist president: Some afterthoughts about getting and being there. *The Psychologist-Manager Journal, 5*(1), 41–48.

Ball, R. S. (1938). The predictability of occupational level from intelligence. *Journal of Consulting Psychology, 2*, 184–186.

Ballard, R. (1992). Short forms of the Marlowe-Crowne social desirability scale. *Psychological Reports, 71*(3), December, 1155–1160.

Ballard-Reisch, D., & Elton, M. (1992). Gender orientation and the Bem sex role inventory: A psychological construct. *Sex Roles, 27*, 291–306.

Balma, M. J., Maloney, J. C., & Lawshe, C. H. (1958a). The role of the foreman in modern industry. II. Foreman identification with management, work group productivity, and employee attitude toward the foreman. *Personnel Psychology, 11*, 367–378.

Balma, M. J., Maloney, J. C., & Lawshe, C. H. (1958b). The role of the foreman in modem industry. III. Some correlates of foreman identification with management. *Personnel Psychology, 11*, 535–544.

Baltes, B. B., & Dickson, M. W. (2001). Using life-span models in industrial-organizational psychology: The theory of selective optimization with compensation. *Applied Developmental Science, 5*(1), 51–62.

Baltes, P. B., & Staudinger, U. M. (1993). The search for a psychology of the wisdom. *Current Directions in Psychological Science, 2*(3), 75–80.

Baltzell, E. D. (1958). *Philadelphia gentlemen: The making of a national upper class*. New York: Free Press.

Baltzell, E. D. (1980). *Puritan Boston and Quaker Philadelphia*. New York: Free Press.

Banai, M., & Teng, B.-S. (1996). Comparing job characteristics, leadership style, and alienation in Russian public and private enterprises. *Journal of International Management, 2*, 201–224.

Bandura, A. (1977). Self-efficacy: Toward a unifying theory of behavioral change. *Psychological Review, 84*, 191–215.

Bandura, A. (1977). *Social learning theory*. Englewood Cliffs, NJ: Prentice Hall.

Bandura, A. (1982). Self-efficacy mechanism in human agency. *American Psychologist, 37*, 122–147.

Bandura, A. (1985). Explorations in self-efficacy. In Sukemune, S. (ed.) *Advances in social learning theory*. Tokyo: Kaneko-shoho.

Bandura, A. (1986) *Social foundations of thought and action*. Englewood Cliffs, NJ: Prentice Hall.

Bandura, A. (1989). Perceived self-efficacy in the exercise of personal agency. *The Psychologist: Bulletin of the British Psychological Society, 2*, 411–424.

Bandura, A. (ed.). (1995). *Self-efficacy in changing societies*. New York: Cambridge University Press.

Bandura, A. (1997). *Self-efficacy: The exercise of control*. New York: H. W. Freeman.

Bandura, A. (2000). Exercise of human agency through collective efficacy. *Current Directions in Psychological Science, 9*(3), 75–78.

Bane, M. J. (2005). The mixed legacy of John Paul II. *Compass*, 10–14.

Banfield, E. (1976). *Women in middle management positions*. Ph.D. dissertation, United States International University.

Banfield, E., & Wilson, J. Q. (1963). *City politics*. Cambridge, MA: Harvard University Press.

Bankart, C. P., & Lanzetta, J. (1970). Performance and motivation as variables affecting the administration of rewards and punishments. *Representative Research in Social Psychology, 1*, 1–10.

Banks, H. (1984). General Electric: Going with the winners. *Forbes*, March 26.

Bansal, P., & Roth, K. (2000). Why companies go green: A model of ecological responsiveness. *Academy of Management Journal, 43*(4), 717–736.

Banta, T. J., & Nelson, C. (1964). Experimental analysis of resource location in problem-solving groups. *Sociometry, 27*, 488–501.

Bantel, K. A., & Jackson, K. E. (1989). Top management and innovations in banking: Does the composition of the top team make a difference? *Strategic Management Journal, 10*, 117–124.

Barati, M. E. (1981). Comparison of preferred leadership styles, potential leadership effectiveness, and managerial attitudes among black and white, female and male management students. *Dissertation Abstracts International, 43*(4A), 1271.

Barber, H. F. (1990). Some personality characteristics of senior military officers. In K. E. Clark & M. B. Clark (eds.), *Measures of leadership*. Greensboro, NC: Center for Creative Leadership.

Barber, J. D. (1965). *The law makers*. New Haven, CT: Yale University Press.

Barber, J. D. (1966). *Power in committees: An experiment in the government process*. Chicago: Rand McNally.

Barber, J. D. (1968). Classifying and predicting presidential styles: Two "weak" presidents. *Journal of Social Issues, 24*, 51–80.

Barber, J. D. (1977). *The presidential character: Predicting performance in the White House*. Englewood Cliffs, NJ: Prentice Hall.

Barber, J. D. (1985). *Presidential character: Predicting performance in the White House* (3rd ed.). Englewood Cliffs, NJ: Prentice Hall.

Barber, J. D. (1991). *The prime minister since 1945*. Oxford, U.K.: Basil Blackwell.

Barbieri, E. A. (1983). Trait patterns for effective marketing performance. *Dissertation Abstracts International, 44*(12A), 3790.

Barbuto, J. E., Jr., (2000). Influence triggers: A framework for understanding follower compliance. *Leadership Quarterly, 11*, 365–387.

Barbuto, J. E., Jr., & Scholl (1998). Motivation Sources Inventory: Development and validation of new scales to measure an integrative taxonomy of motivation. *Psychological Reports*, 82, 1011–1022.

Barenboim, D. (2001). On music: Germans, Jews, and music. *New York Review of Books*, 48, March 29, 50–51.

Barge, J. K. (1994). *Leadership: Communication skills for organizations and groups*. New York: St. Martin's Press.

Barge, J. K., & Hirokawa, R. Y. (1989). Toward a communication competency model of leadership. *Small Group Behavior*, 20, 167–189.

Baril, G. L., Ayman, R., & Palmiter, D. J. (1994). Measuring leader behavior: Moderators of discrepant self and subordinate descriptions. *Journal of Applied Social Psychology*, 24, 189–217.

Baril, G. L., Elbert, N., Maher-Potter, S., et al. (1989). Are androgenous managers really more effective? *Group & Organization Studies*, 14, 234–249.

Barkema, H. G., Bell, J. H. J., & Pennings, M. (1996). Foreign entry, cultural barriers, and learning. *Strategic Management Journal*, 17, 151–166.

Barkema, H. C., & Gomez-Mejia, L. R. (1998) Managerial compensation and firm performance: A general research framework. *Academy of Management Journal*, 41, 135–145.

Barker, A. E. (1998). Action learning: Profile of action learning's principal pioneer: Reginald W. Revans. *Performance Improvement Quarterly*, 11(1), 9–22.

Barker, J. R. (1993). Tightening the iron cage: Concertive control in self-managing teams. *Administrative Science Quarterly*, 38, 408–437.

Barker, J. R. (1996). Communal-rational authority as the basis for leadership on self-managing teams. *Advances in Interdisciplinary Studies of Work Teams*, 3, 105–126.

Barker, R. A. (1994). The rethinking of leadership. *Journal of Leadership Studies*, 1, 47–48 (46–64)

Barker, R. G. (1942). The social interrelations of strangers and acquaintances. *Sociometry*, 5, 169–179.

Barker, R. G. (1968). *Ecological psychology*. Stanford, CA: Stanford University Press.

Barkin, S. (1961). *The decline of the labor movement and what can be done about it?* Santa Barbara, CA: Center for the Study of Democratic Institutions.

Barksdale, J. L. (1998). Communications technology in dynamic organizational communities. In F. Hesselbein, M. Goldsmith, R. Beckhard, et al. (eds.), *The community of the future*. San Francisco: Jossey-Bass.

Barling, J., Weber, T., & Kelloway, E. K. (1996). Effects of transformational leadership on attitudinal and financial outcomes: A field experiment. *Journal of Applied Psychology*, 81, 827–832.

Barlow, J. A. (1981). Mass line leadership and thought reform in China. *American Psychologist*, 36, 300–309.

Barnard, C. I. (1938). *The functions of the executive*. Cambridge, MA: Harvard University Press.

Barnard, C. I. (1946b). The nature of leadership. In S. D. Hoslett (ed.), *Human factors in management*. New York: McGraw-Hill.

Barnard, C. I. (1948). *Organization and management*. Cambridge, MA: Harvard University Press.

Barnard, C. I. (1951). Functions of status systems in formal organizations. In R. Dubin (ed.), *Human relations in administration*. Englewood Cliffs, NJ: Prentice Hall.

Barnard, C. I. (1952). A definition of authority. In R. K. Merton, A. P. Cray, B. Hockey, & H. C. Selvin (eds.), *Reader in bureaucracy*. New York: Free Press.

Barner-Berry, C. (1982). An ethological study of a leadership succession. *Ethology & Sociology*, 3, 199–207.

Barness, Z. I., Diekmann, K. A., & Seibel, M. L. (2002). *Out of "sight," not out of mind: The impact of diminished organizational visibility on impression management*, Paper, Academy of Management, Denver, CO.

Barnlund, D. C. (1962). Consistency of emergent leadership in groups with changing tasks and members. *Speech Monographs*, 29, 45–52.

Bar-On, R. (1997). *Bar-On Emotional Quotion Inventory: A measure of emotional intelligence*. Toronto: Multi-Health Systems.

Barnett, R. C., & Hyde, J. S. (2001). Women, men, work, and family: An expansionist theory. *American Psychologist*, 56, 781–796.

Barnett, T., Bass, K., & Brown, G. (1996). Religiosity, ethical ideology, and intentions to report a peer's wrongdoing. *Journal of Business Ethics*, 15(11), 1161–1174.

Baron, R. A. (1984). Reducing organizational conflict: An incompatible response approach. *Journal of Applied Psychology*, 69, 272–279.

Baron, R. A. (1989). Personality and organizational conflict: Effects of the Type A behavior pattern and self-monitoring. *Organizational Behavior and Human Decision Processes*, 44, 281–296.

Baron, R. A. (2000). Psychological perspectives on entrepreneurship: cognitive and social factors in entrepreneurs' success. *Current Directions in Psychological Science*, 9(1), 15–18.

Barr, M. D. (2000). *Lee Kuan Yew: The beliefs behind the man*. Washington, DC: Georgetown University Press.

Barr, M. D. (2002). *Cultural politics and Asian values: The tepid war*. Routledge Curzon.

Barr, M. D. (2002). Security, democracy, and economic liberalization: Completing priorities in U.S. Asian policy: A set of papers. *Analysis*, 7, 2.

Barrett, G. V., & Franke, R. H. (1969). *Communication preference and performance: A cross-cultural comparison*. Paper, American Psychological Association, Washington, DC.

Barrett, G. V., & Ryterband, E. C. (1968). *Cross-cultural comparisons of corporate objectives on exercise objectives*. Paper, American Psychological Association, San Francisco.

Barrett, R. S. (1963). Performance suitability and role agreement: Two factors related to attitudes. *Personnel Psychology*, 16, 345–357.

Barrick, M. R., Day, D. V., Lord, R. G., & Alexander, R. A. (1991). Assessing the utility of executive leadership. *Leadership Quarterly*, 2, 9–22.

Barrick, M. R., & Mount, M. K. (1991). The Big Five personality dimensions and job performance: A meta-analysis. *Personnel Psychology*, 44(1), 1–26.

Barrick, M. R., & Mount, M. K. (1993). Autonomy as a moderator of the relationship between the Big Five personality dimensions and job performance. *Journal of Applied Psychology*, 78(1), 111–118.

Barrionuevo, A. (2005). The rise of the boards: As directors feel their oats, chiefs are put out to pasture. *New York Times*, March 15, C1.

Barrionuevo, A. (2006). 2 Enron chiefs are convicted in fraud and conspiracy trial; appeals expected. Case becomes a symbol of corporate excess in the 1990's. *New York Times*, May 26, A1, C4.

Barrow, J. C. (1975). An empirical framework of leadership effectiveness and investigation of leader-subordinate-task causality relationships. *Dissertation Abstracts International*, 35, 3631.

Barrow, J. C. (1976). Worker performance and task complexity as causal determinants of leader behavior, style, and flexibility. *Journal of Applied Psychology*, 61, 433–440.

Barrow, J. C. (1977). The variables of leadership: A review and conceptual framework. *Academy of Management Review*, 2, 231–251.

Barry, D. (1991). Managing the bossless team: Lessons in distributed leadership. *Organizational Dynamics*, 21(2), 31–47.

Barry, D. (1997). Navigating the garbage can: How agendas help managers cope with job realities. *Academy of Management Executive*, 11(2), 26–42.

Barsade, S. G., Ward, A. J., Turner, J. D. F., et al. (2000). To your heart's content: A model of affective diversity in top management teams. *Administrative Science Quarterly*, 45, 802–836.

Bar-Tal, Y. (1989). What can we learn from Fiedler's contingency model? *Journal for the Theory of Social Behaviour*, 19(1), 79.

Bartlett, C. A., & Ghoshal, S. (1997). The myth of the generic manager: New personal competencies for new management roles. *California Management Review*, 92–116.

Bartlett, F. C. (1926). The social psychology of leadership. *Journal of National Institutional and Industrial Psychology*, 3, 188–193.

Bartol, K. M. (1974). Male versus female leaders: The effect of leader need for dominance on follower satisfaction. *Academy of Management Journal*, 17(2), 225–233.

Bartol, K. M. (1975). The effect of male versus female leaders on follower satisfaction and performance. *Journal of Business Research*, 3(1), 33–42.

Bartol, K. M. (1978). The sex structuring of organizations: A search for possible causes. *Academy of Management Review*, 3(4), October, 805–815.

Bartol, K. M., Anderson, C. R., & Schneier, C. E. (1980). Motivation to manage among college business students: A reassessment. *Journal of Vocational Behavior*, 17, 22–32.

Bartol, K. M., & Bartol, R. A. (1975a). Women in managerial and professional positions: The United States and the Soviet Union. *Industrial and Labor Relations Review*, 28(4), 524–534.

Bartol, K. M., & Bartol, R. A. (1975b). Women in managerial and technical positions: The United States and the Soviet Union. *Industrial Labor Relations Review*, 28, 524–534.

Bartol, K. M., & Butterfield, D. A. (1976a). Sex effects in evaluating leaders. *Journal of Applied Psychology*, 61, 446–454.

Bartol, K. M., & Butterfield, D. A. (1976b). Sex effects in evaluating leaders. *Journal of Applied Psychology*, 61(4), 446–454.

Bartol, K. M., Evans, C. L., & Stith, M. T. (1978). Black vs. white leaders: A comparative review of the literature. *Academy of Management Review*, 3, 293–304.

Bartol, K. M. and Martin, D. C. (1982) Managing information systems personnel: a review of the literature and managerial implications. *MIS Quarterly*, 6, special issue, 49–70.

Bartol, K. M., & Martin, D. C. (1990). When politics pays: factors influencing managerial compensation decisions. *Personnel Psychology*, 43(3), 599–614.

Bartol, K. M., & Wortman, M. S. (1975). Male versus female leaders: Effects on perceived leader behavior and satisfaction in a hospital. *Personnel Psychology*, 28(4), 533–547.

Bartol, K. M., & Wortman, M. S. (1976a). Sex effects in evaluating leaders. *Journal of Applied Psychology*, 61(4), 446–454.

Bartol, K. M., & Wortman, M. S. (1976b). Sex effects in leader behavior self descriptions and job satisfaction. *Journal of Psychology*, 94(2), 177.

Bartone, P. T. (2001). Personality hardiness as a predictor of officer cadet leadership performance.

Bartone, P. T., & Dardis, G. J. (2001). *Transformational leadership predicts leaders performance in cadets.* Paper, International Association Conference, Miami, FL.

Bartone, P. T., & Kirkland, F. R. (1991). Optimal leadership in small Army units. In R. Gal & A. D. Mangelsdorff (eds.), *Handbook of military psychology.* New York: John Wiley & Sons.

Bartunek, J. M., Gordon, J. R., & Weathersby, R. P. (1983). Developing "complicated" understanding in administrators. *Academy of Management Review*, 8, 273–284, 550.

Baruch, Y. (1998). Leadership: Is that what we study? *The Journal of Leadership Studies*, 5, 104–105, 112, 114

Baruch, Y., & Bell, M. P. (2003). *Graduate degrees in business: Tangible and intangible added value of management education.* Paper, Academy of Management, Seattle, WA.

Barzini, L. (1964). *The Italians.* London: Atheneum.

Basadur, M. (1992). Managing creativity: A Japanese model. *Academy of Management Executive*, 6(2), 29–40.

Basadur, M. (2004). Leading others to think innovatively together: Creative leadership. *Leadership Quarterly*, 15, 103–122.

Basik, K. J., Gershenoff, A., & Foti, R. J. (1999). *Leader assignment in small groups and task interdependence.* Paper, Society for Industrial and Organizational Psychology, Atlanta, GA.

Bass, A. R., Fiedler, F. E., & Krueger, S. (1964). *Personality correlates of assumed similarity (ASo) and related scores* (Tech. Rep. No. 19). Urbana: University of Illinois, Group Effectiveness Research Laboratory.

Bass, B. M. (1949). An analysis of the leaderless group discussion. *Journal of Applied Psychology*, 33, 527–533.

Bass, B. M. (1952). *Supervisory judgement of employee ability and employee job satisfaction.* Unpublished report.

Bass, B. M. (1952). Ultimate criteria of organizational worth. *Personnel Psychology*, 5, 157–173.

Bass, B. M. (1953). Effects of the nature of the problem on LGD performance. *Journal of Applied Psychology*, 37, 96–99.

Bass, B. M. (1954a). The leaderless group discussion. *Psychological Bulletin*, 51, 465–492.

Bass, B. M. (1954b). Feelings of pleasantness and work group efficiency. *Personnel Psychology*, 7, 81–91.

Bass, B. M. (1955a). Authoritarianism or acquiescence? *Journal of Abnormal and Social Psychology*, 51, 616–623.

Bass, B. M. (1955b). *Interrelations among measurements of leadership and associated behavior.* Baton Rouge: Louisiana State University. Unpublished report.

Bass, B. M. (1955c). *Behavior in groups. III. Consistent differences in the objectivity measured performance of members and groups.* Baton Rouge: Louisiana State University. Unpublished report.

Bass, B. M. (1956). Leadership opinions as forecasts of supervisory success. *Journal of Applied Psychology*, 40, 345–346.

Bass, B. M. (1957a). Leadership opinions and related characteristics of salesmen and sales managers. In R. M. Stogdill & A. E. Coons (eds.), *Leader behavior: Its description and measurement.* Columbus: Ohio State University, Bureau of Business Research.

Bass, B. M. (1957b). *Behavior in groups.* Third Annual ONR Report. Baton Rouge: Louisiana State University

Bass, B. M. (1958). Leadership opinions as forecasts of supervisory success: A replication. *Personnel Psychology, 11,* 515–518.

Bass, B. M. (1960). *Leadership, psychology, and organizational behavior.* New York: Harper.

Bass, B. M. (1960). Measures of average influence and change in agreement of rankings by a group of judges. *Sociometry, 23,* 195–202.

Bass, B. M. (1961c). Some observations about a general theory of leadership and interpersonal behavior. In L. Petrullo & B. M. Bass (eds.), *Leadership and interpersonal behavior.* New York: Holt, Rinehart & Winston.

Bass, B. M. (1962b). *Orientation Inventory.* Palo Alto, CA: Consulting Psychologists Press.

Bass, B. M. (1963). Amount of participation, coalescence, and probability of decision making discussions. *Journal of Abnormal and Social Psychology, 67,* 92–94.

Bass, B. M. (1964). Business gaming for organizational research. *Management Science, 10,* 545–556.

Bass, B. M. (1965a). *Orientation and reactions to coercive, persuasive, and permissive leadership* (Tech. Rep. No. 4). Pittsburgh: University of Pittsburgh, Office of Naval Research.

Bass, B. M. (1965b). *Social behavior and the orientation inventory* (Tech. Rep. No. 9). Pittsburgh: University of Pittsburgh, Office of Naval Research.

Bass, B. M. (1965c). *Organizational psychology.* Boston: Allyn & Bacon.

Bass, B. M. (1966b). Effects on the subsequent performance of negotiators of studying issues or planning strategies alone or in groups. *Psychological Monographs, 80,* No. 6.

Bass, B. M. (1967a). Combining management training and research. *Training 6 Development Journal, 21*(4), 2–7.

Bass, B. M. (1967a). *Implications of behavioral science in the year 2000.* Paper, American Management Association, New York.

Bass, B. M. (1967b). Some effects on a group of whether and when the head reveals his opinion. *Organizational Behavior and Human Performance, 2,* 375–382.

Bass, B. M. (1967c). Social behavior and the orientation inventory: A review. *Psychological Bulletin, 68,* 260–292.

Bass, B. M. (1968). How to succeed in business according to business students. And managers. *Journal of Applied Psychology, 32,* 254–262.

Bass, B. M. (1970a). When planning for others. *Journal of Applied Behavioral Science, 6,* 151–171.

Bass, B. M. (1970b). Errata: How to succeed in business according to business students and managers. *Journal of Applied Psychology, 54,* 103.

Bass, B. M. (1974). The substance and the shadow. *American Psychologist, 29,* 870–886.

Bass, B. M. (1975a). *Exercise objectives.* Scottsville, NY: Transnational Programs.

Bass, B. M. (1975c). *Exercise supervise.* Scottsville, NY: Transnational Programs.

Bass, B. M. (1975d). *Exercise organization.* Scottsville, NY: Transnational Programs.

Bass, B. M. (1975e). *Exercise life goals.* Scottsville, NY: Transnational Programs.

Bass, B. M. (1975f). *Exercise self appraisal.* Scottsville, NY: Transnational Programs.

Bass, B. M. (1975g). *Exercise communication.* Scottsville, NY: Transnational Programs.

Bass, B. M. (1976). A systems survey research feedback for management and organizational development. *Journal of Applied Behavioral Science, 12,* 215–229.

Bass, B. M. (1977). Utility of managerial self-planning on a simulated production task with replications in twelve countries. *Journal of Applied Psychology, 62,* 506–509.

Bass, B. M. (1978). *What the Ergom exercises tell us about management career advancement in twelve country groups.* Plenary Session address, International Congress of Applied Psychology, Munich, Germany.

Bass, B. M. (1980). Team productivity and individual member competence. *Small Group Behavior, 11,* 431–504.

Bass, B. M. (1981). Individual capability, team response, and productivity. In E. A. Fleishman & M. D. Dunnette (eds.), *Human performance and productivity.* New York: Erlbaum.

Bass, B. M. (1982). Intensity of relation, dyadic-group considerations, cognitive categorization, and transformational leadership. In J. G. Hunt, U. Sekaran, & C. A. Schriesheim (eds.), *Leadership beyond establishment views.* Carbondale: Southern Illinois University Press.

Bass, B. M. (1983). *Organizational decision making.* Homewood, IL: Irwin.

Bass, B. M. (1983). *The black minority in high-technology organizations: Interpersonal relationships, management, and supervision* (CLS Report 83–64). Binghamton, NY: BinghamtonUniversity, School of Management.

Bass, B. M. (1983a). Leadership and management in the 1980's. In A. Glickman (ed.), *The changing composition of the work force.* New York: Lawrence Erlbaum.

Bass, B. M. (1983b). *Organizational decision-making.* Homestead, IL: Richard D. Irwin.

Bass, B. M. (1983c). Issues involved in relations between methodological rigor and reported outcomes in evaluation of organizational development. *Journal of Applied Psychology, 68,* 197–199.

Bass, B. M. (1983d). Leadership, participation and non-trivial decisionmaking. In J. G. Hunt & C. A. Schriesheim (eds.), *New frontiers in leadership research.* New York: Oxford University Press.

Bass, B. M. (1985a). *Leadership and performance beyond expectations.* New York: Free Press.

Bass, B. M. (1985b). Leadership: Good, better, best. *Organizational Dynamics, 13*(3), 26–40.

Bass, B. M. (1985c). *The multifactor leadership questionnaire: Form 5.* Binghamton: State University of New York.

Bass, B. M. (1987). *Charismatic and inspirational leadership: What's the difference?* Symposium, Charismatic Leadership in Management. Faculty of Management, McGill University, Montreal, QU, May.

Bass, B. M. (1988). The inspirational processes of leadership. *Journal of Management Development, 7,* 21–31.

Bass, B. M. (1988). *Transformational leadership and coping with crisis and stress conditions.* Paper, International Congress of Psychology, Sydney, Australia.

Bass, B. M. (1989). The two faces of charismatic leadership. *Leaders Magazine, 12*(4), 44–45.

Bass, B. M. (1990). From transactional to to transformational leadership: Learning to share the vision. *Organizational Dynamics, 18*(3), 19–36.

Bass, B. M. (1990a) Editorial: Toward a meeting of minds. *Leadership Quarterly, 1,* 145.

Bass, B. M. (1992). Stress and leadership. In F. Heller (ed.). *Decision-making and leadership.* Cambridge, U.K.: Cambridge University Press.

Bass, B. M. (1993). A seminal shift: the impact of James Burns' leadership. *The Leadership Quarterly, 4*(3), 375.

Bass, B. M. (1994). Commentary: The leadership question. *Wilson Quarterly, 18*(3),154.

Bass, B.M. (1995) Concepts of leadership: The beginnings. In J. T. Wren, (ed.), *The leader's companion: insights on leadership through the ages.* New York: Free Press.

Bass, B. M. (1995). The meaning of leadership. In J. T. Wren (ed.). *The Leader's Companion: Insights on Leadership through the Ages.* New York: Free Press, 33–36.

Bass, B. M. (1995). Does the transactional/transformational paradigm transcend organizational and national boundaries? *American Psychologist, 9,* 11.

Bass, B. M. (1996). Is there universality in the full range model of transformational leadership? *International Journal of Public Administration, 19,* 731–762.

Bass, B. M. (1996). *A new paradigm of leadership: An inquiry into transformational leadership.* Alexandria, VA: U.S. Army Research Institute in the Behavioral and Social Sciences.

Bass, B. M. (1997). Concepts of leadership. In R. P. Vecchio (ed.), *Leadership: understanding the dynamics of power and influence in organizations.* Notre Dame, IN: University of Notre Dame Press.

Bass, B. M. (1997). Does the transactional/transformational leadership paradigm transcend organizational and national boundaries? *American Psychologist, 52,* 130–139.

Bass, B. M. (1998). Leading in the Army after Next. *Military Review,* March–April, 46–57.

Bass, B. M. (1998). *Transformational leadership: Industrial, military, and educational impact.* Mahwah, NJ: Lawrence Erlbaum & Associates.

Bass, B. M. (1999). Early history of work in teams. In M. Beyerlein (ed.), *Work teams, past, present, and future.* New York: Klewer Academic Publications.

Bass, B. M. (1999). The ethics of transformational leadership. In J. B. Ciulla (ed.), *Ethics, the heart of leadership.* Westport, CT: Praeger.

Bass, B. M. (1999). *Leadership in a technology-enabled environment.* Binghamton, NY: Binghamton University, Center for Leadership Studies.

Bass, B. M. (1999). On the taming of charismas: A reply to Janice Beyer. *Leadership Quarterly, 10,* 541–553.

Bass, B. M. (1999a). Current developments in transformational leadership: Research and applications. *Psychologist-Manager Journal, 3,* 5–21.

Bass, B. M. (1999b). Two decades of research and development in transformational leadership. *European Journal of Work and Organizational Psychology, 8*(1), 9–32.

Bass, B. M. (2000). The future of leadership in learning organizations. *Journal of Leadership Studies, 7,* 18–40.

Bass, B. M. (2002). Forecasting organizational leadership from back (1967) to the future (2034). In B. J. Avolio & F. J. Yammarino (eds.). *Transformational and charismatic leadership: The road ahead.* New York: JAI Elsevier.

Bass, B. M. (2005). *Leadership and management in the information age: Communications, networking, and leadership.* Address, International Symposium on Society, Governance, Management and Leadership in the Information Age. Istanbul, Turkey, May 12–13.

Bass, B. M., Alexander, R. A., Barrett, G. V., & Ryterband, E. C. (1971). Empathy, projection and negation in seven countries. In L. E. Abt & B. F. Reiss (eds.), *Progress in clinical psychology: Industrial applications.* New York: Grune & Stratton.

Bass, B. M., & Avolio, B. J. (1987). *Biases in leadership ratings* (Working Paper No. 87–124). Binghamton: State University of New York.

Bass, B. M., & Avolio, B. J. (1988). *Prototypicality, leniency and generalized response set in rated and ranked transformational and transactional leadership descriptions.* (Report Series 88–2), Binghamton: State University of New York, Center for Leadership Studies.

Bass, B. M., & Avolio, B. J. (1989). Potential biases in leadership measures: How prototypes, leniency, and general satisfaction relate to ratings and rankings of transformational and transactional leadership constructs. *Educational and Psychological Measurement, 49,* 509–527.

Bass, B. M., & Avolio, B. J. (1989). *Manual: The Multifactor Leadership Questionnaire.* Palo Alto, CA: Consulting Psychologists Press.

Bass, B. M., & Avolio, B. J. (1990). Developing transformational leadership: 1992 and beyond. *Journal of European Industrial Training, 14*(5), 21–27.

Bass B. M. & Avolio, B. J. (1991). *The multifactor leadership questionnaire: Form 5x.* Binghamton, NY: Binghamton University, Center for Leadership Studies.

Bass, B. M., & Avolio, B. J. (1992). *Multifactor Leadership Questionnaire; 6S,* Redwood City, CA: Mindgarden.

Bass, B. M., & Avolio, B. J. (1993a) Transformational leadership: A response to critiques. In M. M. Chemers & R. Ayman (eds.), *Leadership theory and research: Perspectives and directions.* San Diego, CA: Academic Press.

Bass, B. M., & Avolio, B. J. (1993b). Transformational leadership and organizational culture. *Public Administration Quarterly, 17,* 112–122.

Bass, B. M., & Avolio, B. J. (eds.). (1994). *Improving organizational effectiveness through transformational leadership.* Thousand Oaks, CA: Sage.

Bass, B. M., & Avolio, B. J. (1994). Shatter the glass ceiling: Women may make better managers. *Human Resources Management Journal, 33,* 549–560.

Bass, B. M., & Avolio, B. J. (1995). *The Multifactor Leadership Questionnaire.* Redwood City, CA: Mind Garden.

Bass, B. M., & Avolio, B. J. (1995) *Manual for the Multifactor Leadership Questionnaire.* Redwood City, CA: Mind Garden.

Bass, B. M., & Avolio, B. J. (1996, 2002). Multifactor Leadership Questionnaire feedback report.

Bass, B. M., & Avolio, B. J. (1996). *Transformational Leadership Development: Manual for the Multifactor Leadership Questionnaire.* Palo Alto, CA: Consulting Psychologists Press.

Bass, B. M., & Avolio, B. J. (1997). *Full range of leadership: Manual for the Multifactor Leadership Questionnaire.* Redwood City, CA: Mind Garden.

Bass, B. M. & Avolio, B. J. (1999). Training full range leadership. Redwood City, CA: Mind Garden.

Bass, B. M., Avolio, B. J., & Atwater, L. E. (1996). The transformational and transactional leadership of men and women. *Applied Psychology: An International Review, 45,* 5–34.

Bass, B. M., Avolio, B. J., & Goodheim, L. (1987). Biography and the assessment of transformational leadership at the world-class level. *Journal of Management, 13,* 7–19.

Bass. B. M., Avolio, B. J., & Jung, D. I. (1999). Reexamining the components of transformational and transactional leadership using the Multifactor Leadership Questionnaire (Form 5X). *Journal of Organizational and Occupational Psychology, 72,* 441–462.

Bass, B. M., Avolio, B. J., Jung, D. I., & Berson, Y. (2003). Predicting unit performance by assessing transformational and transactional leadership. *Journal of Applied Psychology, 88*(2), 207–218.

Bass, B. M., & Barrett, G. V.(1972). *Man, work and organizations: An introduction to industrial and organizational psychology.* Boston: Allyn & Bacon.

Bass, B. M., & Barrett, G. V. (1981). *People, work and organizations: An introduction to industrial and organizational psychology* (2nd ed.). Boston: Allyn & Bacon.

Bass, B. M., Binder, M. J., & Breed, W. (1967). *Profitability and good relations: Which is cause and which is effect?* (Brief No. 4). Pittsburgh: University of Pittsburgh, Management Research Center.

Bass, B. M., Burger, R. C., Doktor, R., & Barrett, G. V. (1979). *Assessment of managers: An international comparison.* New York: Free Press.

Bass, B. M., Cascio, W. F., & McPherson, J. W. (1972). *PROSPER: An affirmative action for black employees.* Scottsville, NY: Transnational Programs.

Bass, B. M., Cascio, W. F., McPherson, J. W., & Tragash, H. J. (1976). PROSPER: Training and research for increasing management awareness about affirmative action in race relations. *Academy of Management Journal, 19,* 353–369.

Bass, B. M., & Coates, C. H. (1952). Forecasting officer potential using the leaderless group discussion. *Journal of Abnormal and Social Psychology, 47,* 321–325.

Bass, B. M., & Coates, C. H. (1953). *Situational and personality factors in leadership in ROTC.* Baton Rouge: Louisiana State University.

Bass, B. M., Cooper, R. C., & Haas, J. A. (eds.). (1970). *Managing for accomplishment.* Lexington, MA: Heath Lexington Books.

Bass, B. M., & Dunteman, G. (1963). Behavior in groups as a function of self, interaction, and task orientation. *Journal of Abnormal and Social Psychology, 66,* 419–428.

Bass, B. M., & Farrow, D. L. (1977a). Quantitative analyses of biographies of political figures. *Journal of Psychology, 97,* 281–296.

Bass, B. M., & Farrow, D. L. (1977b). *A phoenix arises: The importance of manager and subordinate personality in contingency leadership analysis.* Paper, Western Academy of Management, Sun Valley, ID.

Bass, B. M., Farrow, D. L., & Valenzi, E. R. (1977). *A regression approach to identifying ways to increase leadership effectiveness* (Tech. Rep. No. 77–3). Rochester, NY: University of Rochester, U.S. Army Research Institute for the Behavioral and Social Sciences.

Bass, B. M., & Flint, A. W. (1958a). *Some effects of power, practice and problem difficulty on success as a leader* (Tech. Rep. No. 18). Baton Rouge: Louisiana State University.

Bass, B. M., Flint, A. W., & Pryer, M. W. (1957b). *Effects of status-esteem conflict on subsequent behavior in groups.* Baton Rouge: Louisiana State University.

Bass, B. M., & Franke, R. H. (1972). Societal influences on student perceptions of how to succeed in organizations: A cross-national analysis. *Journal of Applied Psychology, 56,* 312–318.

Bass, B. M., Gaier, E. L., & Flint, A. W. (1956). *Attempted leadership as a function of motivation interacting with amount of control.* Baton Rouge: Louisiana State University.

Bass, B. M., Gaier, E. L., Farese, F. J., & Flint, A. W. (1957). An objective method for studying behavior in groups. *Psychological Reports, 3,* 265–280. Also: Bass, B. M. (1960). Measures of average influence and change in agreement of rankings by a group of judges. *Sociometry, 23,* 195–202.

Bass, B. M., & Harding, D. (1999). *Transformational and transactional leadership behavior of female and male legislators.* Paper, Conference of National Foundation of Women Legislators, Pasadena, CA, August 21.

Bass, B. M., Hurder, W. P., & Ellis, N. (1954). *Human stress tolerance* (Final Tech. Rep.). Baton Rouge: Louisiana State University, USAF Aero-Medical Lab.

Bass, B. M., Krusell, J., & Alexander, R. A. (1971). Male managers' attitudes toward working women. *American Behavioral Scientist, 15,* 221–236.

Bass, B. M., McGehee, C. R., Hawkins, W. C., et al. (1953). Personality variables related to leaderless group discussion behavior. *Journal of Abnormal and Social Psychology, 48,* 120–128.

Bass, B. M., & Mitchell, C. W. (1976). Influences on the felt need for collective bargaining by business and science professionals. *Journal of Applied Psychology, 61,* 770–773.

Bass, B. M., & Norton, F. M. (1951). Group size and leaderless discussions. *Journal of Applied Psychology, 35,* 397–400.

Bass, B. M., Pryer, M. W., Gaier, E. L., & Flint, A. W. (1958). Interacting effects of control, motivation, group practice, and problem difficulty on attempted leadership. *Journal of Abnormal and Social Psychology, 56,* 352–358.

Bass, B. M., & Riggio, R. E. (2006). *Transformational leadership* (2nd ed.). Mahwah, NJ: Lawrence Erlbaum Associates.

Bass, B. M., & Ryterband, E. C. (1979). *Organizational psychology* (2nd ed.). Boston: Allyn & Bacon.

Bass, B. M., & Shackleton, V. J. (1979). Industrial democracy and participative management: A case for synthesis. *Academy of Management Review, 4,* 393–404

Bass, B. M., & Steidlmeier, P. (1999). Ethics, character, and authentic transformational leadership behavior. *Leadership Quarterly, 10,* 181–217.

Bass, B. M., & Valenzi, E. R. (1973). PROFILE. Scottsville, NY: Transnational Programs.

Bass, B. M., & Valenzi, E. R. (1974). Contingent aspects of effective management styles. In J. G. Hunt & L. L. Larson (eds.), *Contingency approaches to leadership.* Carbondale: Southern Illinois University Press.

Bass, B. M., Valenzi, E. R., & Farrow, D. L. (1977). External environment related to managerial style (Tech. Rep. No. 77–2). Rochester, NY: University of Rochester, U.S. Army Research Institute for the Behavioral and Social Sciences. Also: (1977). Proceedings, International Conference on Social Change and Organizational Development, Dubrovnik, Yugoslavia.

Bass, B. M., Valenzi, E. R., Farrow, D. L., & Solomon, R. J. (1975). Management styles associated with organizational, task, personal, and interpersonal contingencies. *Journal of Applied Psychology, 60,* 720–729.

Bass, B. M., Waldman, D. A., Avolio, B. J., & Bebb, M. (1987). Transformational leadership and the falling dominoes effect. *Group & Organization Studies, 12,* 73–87.

Bass, B. M., & White, O. L. (1951). Situation tests. III. Observers' ratings of leaderless group discussion participants as indicators of external leadership status. *Educational and Psychological Measurement, 11,* 355–361.

Bass, B. M., & Wurster, C. R. (1953a). Effects of the nature of the problem on LGD performance. *Journal of Applied Psychology, 37,* 96–99.

Bass, B. M., & Wurster, C. R. (1953b). Effects of company rank on LCD of oil refinery supervisors' performance. *Journal of Applied Psychology, 37,* 100–104.

Bass, B. M., Wurster, C. R., & Alcock, W. (1961). A test of the proposition: We want to be esteemed most by those we esteem most highly. *Journal of Abnormal and Social Psychology, 63,* 650–653.

Bass, B. M., Wurster, C. R., Doll, P. A., & Clair, D. I. (1953). Situational and personality factors in leadership among sorority women. *Psychological Monographs, 67,* 1–23.

Bass, B. M., & Yammarino, F. J. (1988). *Leadership: Dispositional, situational, or both?* Report 88–5, Binghamton, NY: Binghamton University, Center for Leadership Studies.

Bass, B. M., & Yammarino, F. J., (1989). *Transformational leaders know themselves better* (ONR Tech. Rep. No. 5). Binghamton: State University of New York, Center for Leadership Studies.

Bass, B. M., & Yammarino, F. J. (1991). Congruence of self and others' leadership ratings of naval officers for understanding successful performance. *Applied Psychology: An International Review, 40,* 437–454.

Bass, B. M., & Yokochi, N. (1990). *Charisma among senior executives and the special case of Japanese CEO's.* Invited address, Institute for Group Dynamics, Kyushu University, Fukuoka, Japan.

Bassett, G. A., & Meyer, H. H. (1968). Performance appraisal based on self-review. *Personnel Psychology, 21,* 421–430.

Basu, R. (1991). *An empirical of leader-member exchange and transformational leadership as predictors of innovative behavior.* Doctoral dissertation, Purdue University, Lafayette, IN.

Basu, R., & Green, S. G. (1995). Subordinate performance, leader-subordinate compatibility, and exchange quality in leader-member dyads. *Journal of Applied Social Psychology, 25,* 77–92.

Basu, R., Simmons, B. L., & Kumar, M.S. (1997). *Performance satisfaction, absenteeism, and turnover in self-led work groups.* Paper, Academy of Management, Boston.

Bateman, T., Strasser, S., & Dailey, R. (1982). Toward proper specification of the effects of leader punitive behavior: a research note. *Journal of Management 8,* 83–93.

Bates, A. F. (1952). Some sociometric aspects of social ranking in a small, face-to-face group. *Sociometry, 15,* 330–342.

Bates, F. L. (1953). *The coordination of maintenance activities in bomb wings: Synchronization and performance.* Chapel Hill: University of North Carolina, Institute for Research in Social Science.

Batkins, J. F. (1982). A descriptive study of power: Exploring directors' styles, staff climates and organizational efficiency in human services. *Dissertation Abstracts International, 43*(2B), 505.

Batson, C. D. (1991). *The altruism question: Toward a social psychological answer.* Hillsdale, NJ: Lawrence Erlbaum Associates.

Batson, C. D., & Shaw, L. L. (1991). Evidence for altruism: Toward a pluralism of social motives. *Psychological Inquiry, 2,* 107–122.

Baucus, M. S., & Near, J. P. (1991). Can illegal corporate behavior be predicted? An event history analysis. *Academy of Management Journal, 34*(1), 9–36.

Bauer, R., Collar, T., Tang, V. & Wind, J. (1992). *The Silverlake Project: Transformation at IBM.* New York: Oxford University Press.

Baum, B. H. (1961). *Decentralization of authority in a bureaucracy.* Englewood Cliffs, NJ: Prentice-Hall.

Baum, B. H., Sorensen Jr., P. F. & Place, W. S. (1969). Patterns of consensus in the perception of organizational control. *The Sociological Quarterly 10* (3), 335–340.

Baum, B. H., Sorensen, P. F., & Place, W. S. (1970). The effect of managerial training on organizational control: an experimental study. *Organizational Behavior and Human Performance, 5,* 170–182.

Baum, J. R., Locke, E. A., & Kirkpatrick, S. A. (1998). A longitudinal study of the relation to vision and vision communication to venture growth in entrepreneurial firms. *Journal of Applied Psychology, 83,* 43–54.

Baumgardner, T. L., Lord, R. G., & Maher, K. J. (1991). Perceptions of women in management. In R. Lord & K. J. Maher (eds.) *Leadership and information processing: Linking perceptions and performance.* Boston: Unwin Hyman.

Baumgartel, H. (1956). Leadership, motivations, and attitudes in research laboratories. *Journal of Social Issues, 12,* 23–31.

Baumgartel, H. (1957). Leadership style as a variable in research administration. *Administrative Science Quarterly, 2,* 344–360.

Baumrind, D. (1971). Current patterns of parental authority. *Developmental Psychology Monographs, 4*(2), 103.

Baumrind, D. (1972). An exploratory study of socialization effects on black children: Some black-white comparisons. *Child Development, 43,* 261–267.

Bavelas, A. (1950). Communication patterns in task-oriented groups. *Journal of Acoustical Society of America, 22,* 725–730.

Bavelas, A. (1960). Leadership: Man and function. *Administrative Science Quarterly, 4,* 491–498.

Bavelas, A., Hastorf, A. H., Gross, A. E., & Kite, W. R. (1965). Experiments on the alteration of group structure. *Journal of Experimental Social Psychology, 1,* 55–70.

Bayer, A. E., & Boruch, R. F. (1969). *The black student in American colleges, Research Report No. 4*(2). Washington, DC: American Council on Education.

Bayes, M., & Newton, P. M. (1978). Women in Authority: A Sociopsychological Analysis. *Journal of Applied Behavioral Science, 14*(1), 7–20.

Bazerman, M. H. and Messick, D. M. (1996). Ethical leadership and the psychology of decision making. *Sloan Management Review,* 37(2), 9–22.

Bazerman, M. H., White, S. B., & Lowenstein, G. F. (1995). Perceptions of fairness in interpersonal and individual choice situations. *Current Directions in Psychological Science,* 4(2), 39–43.

Beach, B. H., & Beach, L. R. (1978). A note on judgments of situational favorableness and probability of success. *Organizational Behavior and Human Performance,* 22, 69–74.

Beal, R. M., & Yasai-Ardekani, M. (2000). Performance implications of aligning CEO functional experiences with competitive strategies. *Journal of Management,* 26, 733–762.

Beam, H. H. (1975). *Effectiveness and satisfaction as a function of managerial style and technological complexity in a Navy work environment.* Doctoral dissertation, University of Michigan, Ann Arbor.

Bean, A. S. (ed.). (1997). Managing breakthrough innovation demands: Methods that are fundamentally different—and generally unfamiliar! *CIMS Technology Management Report,* 3, 1–2.

Beardwell, I., Evans, J., & Collard, R. (1998). Learned responses: recording and reviewing your key learning experiences is a useful exercise, whatever the level your career has reached. *People Management,* 4(8), 43–46.

Beatty, C. A. (1996). The stress of managerial and professional women: Is the price too high? *Journal of Organizational Behavior,* 17, 233–251.

Beatty, J. R., McCune, J. T., and Beatty, R. W. (1988). A policy-capturing approach to the study of United States and Japanese managers' compensation decisions. *Journal of Management,* 14, 465–474.

Beatty, J. R., Owens, A. E., & Jenner, S. R. (undated). *Perceptual differences of leadership styles between Japanese supervisors and U. S. subordinates.* Unpublished manuscript.

Beatty, R. W. (1973). Blacks as supervisors: A study of training job performance and employer expectations. *Academy of Management Journal,* 10, 191–206.

Beatty, R. W. (1974). Supervisory behavior related to job success of hardcore unemployed over a two-year period. *Journal of Applied Psychology,* 59, 38–42.

Beauchamp, T. L., Faden, R. R., Wallace, R. J., Jr., & Walters, L. (eds.). (1982). *Ethical issues in social science research.* Baltimore: Johns Hopkins University Press.

Bechterew, W., & Lange, A. (1924/1931). Die Ergebnisse des Experiments auf dem Gebiete der kollektiven Reflexologie. *Zeitschrift for Angewandte Psychologie,* 24, 224–254. (Reported in G. Murphy & L. Murphy, *Experimental social psychology.* New York: Harper, 1931.)

Beck, L. (1994). *Reclaiming educational administration as a caring profession.* New York: Teachers College Press.

Becker, J., Ayman, R., & Korabik, K. (2002). Discrepancies in self/subordinates' perceptions of leadership behavior: Leader's gender, organizational context, leader's self-monitoring. *Group & Organization Management,* 27(2), 226–245.

Becker, M. H. (1970). Sociometric location and innovativeness: Reformulation and extension of the diffusion model. *American Sociological Review,* 35, 267–304.

Becker, S. W., & Baloff, N. (1969). Organization structure and complex problem solving. *Administrative Science Quarterly,* 14, 260–271.

Becker, T. E. (1992). Foci and bases of commitment: Are they distinctions worth making? *Academy of Management Journal,* 35, 232–244.

Becker, T. E. (1998). Integrity in organizations: beyond honesty and conscientiousness. *Academy of Management Review,* 23, 154–161.

Becker, T. E., Billings, R. S., et al. (1996). Foci and bases of employee commitment: Implications for job performance. *Academy of Management Journal,* 39, 464–482.

Beckhard, R. (1966). An organization improvement program in a decentralized organization. *Journal of Applied Behavioral Science,* 2(1), 3–25.

Beckhard, R. (1995). On future leaders. In F. Hesselbein, M. Goldsmith, & R. Beckhard (eds.), *The leader of the future.* San Francisco: Jossey-Bass.

Beckhard, R. (1997). On future leaders. In F. Hesselbein, M. Goldsmith, & R. Beckhard (eds.), *The leader of the future: New visions, strategies and practices for the next era.* San Francisco: Jossey-Bass.

Beckman, L. J. (1984). Husbands' and wives' relative influence on fertility decisions and outcomes. *Population & Environment: Behavioral & Social Issues,* 7, 182–197.

Bedore, G. L. (1993) Technology: The critical role in organizational, work, and management change. *Journal of Leadership Studies,* 1, 1–44.

Beebe, R. J. (1975). The least preferred coworker score of the leader and the productivity of small interacting task groups in octants II and IV of the Fiedler contingency model. Dissertation. *Abstracts International,* 35, 3642.

Beehr, T. A., & Gupta, N. (1987). Organizational management styles, employee supervisory status, and employee responses. *Human Relations,* 40(1), 45–57.

Beehr, T. A., Weisbrodt, D. M., & Zagumny, M. J. (1994). Satisfaction with subordinates: A neglected research issue concerning supervisors. *Journal of Applied Social Psychology,* 24, 1665–1684.

Beer, M. (1964). *Leadership, employee needs, and motivation.* Doctoral dissertation, Ohio State University, Columbus.

Beer, M. (1988). The critical path for change: Keys to success and failure in six companies. In R. H. Kilmann & T. J. Covin (eds.), *Corporate transformation: Revitalizing organizations for a competitive world.* San Francisco: Jossey-Bass.

Beer, M. (1994). *Developing an organization capable of implementing strategy and learning* (Working Paper 395–037). Boston: Harvard Business School.

Beer, M. (1997). *Leading learning and learning to lead: An approach to developing organizational fitness.* Working paper, Harvard Business School, Boston.

Beer, M., Buckhout, R., Horowitz, M. W., & Levy, S. (1959). Some perceived properties of the differences between leaders and nonleaders. *Journal of Psychology,* 47, 49–56.

Beer, M., & Eisenstat, R. A. (2000). The silent killers of strategy implementation and learning. *Sloan Management Review,* Summer, 29–40.

Beer, M., Eisenstat, R. A., & Spector, B. (1990). Why change programs don't produce change. *Harvard Business Review,* 68(5), 158–166.

Beer, M., & Nohria, N. (2000). Cracking the code of change. *Harvard Business Review,* 80(3), 133–141.

Beer, S. (1966). *Decision and control.* New York: Wiley.

Beeson, J. (1988). Succession planning: Building the management corps. *Business Horizons, 41*(5), 61–66.

Behling, O., Gifford, W. E., & Tolliver, J. M. (1980). Effects of grouping information on decision making under risk. *Decision Sciences, 11,* 272–283.

Behling, O., & McFillen, J. M. (1996). A syncretical model of charismatic/transformational leadership. *Group & Organizational Management, 21,* 163–191.

Behling, O., & Schriesheim, C. (1976). *Organizational behavior: Theory, research, and application.* Boston: Allyn & Bacon.

Behr, E. T. (1997). Acting from the center. *Monthly Labor Review, 120*(12), 51–55.

Behr, R. (1998). Whatever happened to Japan? *Press & Sun-Bulletin* (Binghamton, NY), January 15, 8B.

Bekson, T., & Eveland, J. D. (1990). The interplay of work group structures and computer support. In J. Galegher, R. Kraut, & C. Egido (eds.), *Intellectual teamwork: Social and technological foundations of cooperative work.* Hillsdale, NJ: Lawrence Erlbaum Associates.

Belasco, J. A. (1973). Educational innovation: The impact of organizational and community variables on performance contract. *Management Science, 20,* 498–506.

Bell, G. B. (1951). *The relationship between leadership and empathy.* Doctoral dissertation, Northwestern University, Evanston, IL.

Bell, G. B. (1967). Determinants of span of control. *American Journal of Sociology, 73,* 100–109.

Bell, G. B., & Hall, H. E. (1954). The relationship between leadership and empathy. *Journal of Abnormal and Social Psychology, 49,* 156–157.

Bell, J. B. (2002). The organization of Islamic terror: The global jihad. *Journal of Management Inquiry, 11,* 261–266.

Bell, M. P., Gilley, K. M., & Coombs, J. E. (2003). *Diversity at the top: Effects of women and minority CEOs and directors on organizational diversity.* Paper, Academy of Management, Seattle, WA.

Bell, M. P., Harrison, & Mclaughlin, M. E. (1997a). *Diversity at the top: Effects of women and minority CEOs and directors on organizational diversity.* Paper, Academy of Management, Boston.

Bell, M. P., Harrison, & McLauglin, M. E. (1997b). Asian American attitudes toward affirmative action in employment: Implications for the Model Minority Myth. *Journal of Applied Behavioral Science, 33,* 356–377.

Bell, M. P., McLaughlin, & Sequeira, J. M. (2002). *Age, disability, and obesity: Similarities, differences and common threads.* Paper, Academy of Management, Denver, CO.

Bell, T. O. (1969). A study of personality characteristics of school superintendents in relation to administrative behavior. *Dissertation Abstracts, 29A,* 2049–2050.

Bell, W., Hill, R. J., & Wright, C. R. (1961). *Public leadership: A critical review with special reference to adult education.* San Francisco: Chandler.

Bellingrath, C. C. (1930). *Qualities associated with leadership in extracurricular activities of the high school.* New York: Teachers College Contributions to Education.

Bellow, A. (2003). In praise of nepotism. *Atlantic Monthly,* July–August, 98–105.

Bellows, R. M. (1959). *Creative leadership.* Englewood Cliffs, NJ: Prentice Hall.

Bem, D. J. (1970). *Beliefs, attitudes and human affairs.* Belmont, CA: Brooks/Cole.

Benbow, C. P., & Stanley, J. C. (1983). Sex differences in mathematical reasoning ability: More facts. *Science, 222,* 1029–1031.

Bendapudi, V., Bendipudi, N., & Ballam (2002). *Individual differences in psychological contracts: An attachment style perspective.* Paper, Academy of Management, Denver, CO.

Bender, I. E., & Hastorf, A. H. (1950). The perception of persons: Forecasting another person's responses on three personality scales. *Journal of Abnormal and Social Psychology, 45,* 556–561.

Bender, J. M. (1973). What is "typical" of assessment centers? *Personnel, 50*(4), 50–57.

Bendix, R. (1974). *Work and authority in industry.* Berkeley: University of California Press.

Benezet, L. T., Katz, J., & Magnusson, F. W. (1981). *Style and substance: Leadership and the college presidency.* Washington, DC: American Council on Education.

Benne, K. D., & Sheats, P. (1948). Functional roles of group members. *Journal of Social Issues, 4,* 41–49.

Benner, P. E. (1984). *Stress and satisfaction on the job.* New York: Praeger.

Bennett, A. (1986). American culture is often a puzzle for foreign managers in the U.S. *Wall Street Journal,* February 12, 33.

Bennett, E. B. (1971). Discussion, decisions, commitment, and consensus in "group decision." *Human Relations, 8*(2), 251–273.

Bennett, W. J. (1994). *Book of Virtues.* New York: Simon & Schuster.

Bennis, W. G. (1959). Leadership theory and administrative behavior: The problems of authority. *Administrative Science Quarterly, 4,* 259–301.

Bennis, W. G. (1961). Revisionist theory of leadership. *Harvard Business Review, 39*(l), 26–36, 146–150.

Bennis, W. G. (1964). Goals and meta-goals of laboratory training. In W. C. Bennis (ed.), *Interpersonal dynamics, essays and readings on human interaction.* Homewood, IL: Dorsey.

Bennis, W. G. (1965). Theory and method in applying behavioral science to planned organizational change. *Journal of Applied Behavioral Science, 1,* 337–360.

Bennis, W. G. (1966c). Organizational developments and the fate of bureaucracy. *Industrial Relations Review, 7,* 41–55.

Bennis, W. G. (1970). *American bureaucracy.* Chicago: Aldine.

Bennis, W. G. (1982). Warren Bennis on . . . the art form of leadership. *Training & Development Journal, 36*(4), 44–46.

Bennis, W. G. (1983). Transformative leadership. *Harvard University Newsletter,* April.

Bennis, W. G. (1984). The 4 competencies of leadership. *Training & Development Journal, 38*(8), 14–19.

Bennis, W. G. (1989). *Why leaders can't lead: The unconscious conspiracy continues.* San Francisco: Jossey-Bass.

Bennis, W. (1991). Creative leadership. *Executive Excellence,* August, 5–6.

Bennis, W. (1992). *Leaders on leadership: Interviews with top executives.* Boston: Harvard University Business School Press.

Bennis, W. (1997). Cultivating creative leadership. *Industry Week,* August 18, 84–88.

Bennis, W. (1997). The secrets of great groups. *Leader-to-Leader*, Winter 29–33.

Bennis, W. (1999). The leadership advantage, *Leader-to-Leader, 12*, Spring, 18–23.

Bennis, W. (1999). The end of leadership: Exemplary leadership is impossible without full inclusion, initiatives, and cooperation of followers. *Organizational Dynamics, 28*(1), 71–80.

Bennis, W. G. (2004). *On becoming a leader: The leadership classic*. New York: HarperCollins.

Bennis, W. G., Berkowitz, N., Affinito, M., & Malone, M. (1958). Authority, power, and the ability to influence. *Human Relations, 11*, 143–155.

Bennis, W., & Biederman, P. W. (1997). *The secrets of creative collaboration*. New York: Addison Wesley Longman.

Bennis, W. G., and Goldsmith, (1997). *Learning to lead: A workbook on becoming a leader*. New York: Perseus.

Bennis, W. G., & Nanus, B. (1985). *Leaders: The strategies for taking charge*. New York: Harper & Row.

Bennis, W., Parikh, J., & Lessem, R. (1995). *Beyond leadership: Balancing economics, ethics, and ecology*.

Bennis, W. G., & Shepard, H. A. (1956). A theory of group development. *Human Relations, 9*, 415–437.

Bennis, W., & Thomas, R. (2002). *Geeks and geezers*. Boston: Harvard Business School Press.

Benoit-Smullyan, E. (1944). Status, status types, and status interrelations. *American Sociological Review, 9*, 151–161.

Bensahel, J. C. (1981). Are you ready to cope with those minor crises? *International Management, 36*(2), 24–25.

Bensimon, E. M. (1987). *The meaning of good presidential leadership: A frame analysis*. Paper, National Meeting of the Association for the Study of Higher Education, Baltimore.

Bensimon, E. M. (1988). *On becoming a college president* (OERI/Ed Report). New York: Columbia University, Teachers College.

Bensimon, E. M. (1990). Viewing the presidency: Perceptual congruence between presidents and leaders on their campuses. *Leadership Quarterly, 1*, 71–90.

Bensimon, R. (1990). *Will you love me in December as you do in May?: Why experienced college presidents lose faculty support*. Paper, Association for the Study of Higher Education, University of Maryland, College Park, MD.

Bensman, J., & Givant, M. (1975). Charisma and modernity: The use and abuse of a concept. *Social Research, 42*, 570–614.

Bensman, J., & Rosenberg, B. (1960). The meaning of work in bureaucratic society. In M. R. Stein, A. J. Vidich, & D. M. White (eds.), *Identity and anxiety: Survival of the person in mass society*. Glencoe, IL: Free Press.

Benson, P. G., Kemery, E. R., Sauser, W. L, & Tankesley, K. E. (1985). Need for clarity as a moderator of the role ambiguity–job satisfaction relationship. *Journal of Management, 11*, 125–130.

Benson, T. E. (1992). A braver new world? Stories abound of self-directed work teams cutting costs and raising productivity, but some seasoned business people are reserving judgment. *Industry Week*, August 24, 8–54.

Bentham, Jeremy (1789). *An introduction to the principles of morals and legislation*. (1748–1831) "The object of the law is to achieve the greatest happiness of the greatest number." *Encyclopaedia Britannica, 1*.

Benton, P. (1990). *Riding the whirlwind: Benton on managing turbulence*. London, U.K.: Basil Blackwell.

Bentz, V. J. (undated). *Leadership, a study of social interaction*. Unpublished manuscript.

Bentz, V. J. (1964). *The Sears experience in the investigation, description, and prediction of executive behavior*. Chicago: Sears, Roebuck. Unpublished report.

Bentz, V. J. (1987). *Explorations of scope and scale: The critical determinant of high-level effectiveness* (Tech. Rep. No. 31). Greensboro, NC: Center for Creative Leadership.

Bentz, V. J. (1990). Contextual issues in predicting high level leadership performance: Contextual richness as a criterion consideration in personality research with executives. In K. E. Clark & M. B. Clark (eds.), *Measures of leadership*. West Orange, NJ: Leadership Library of America.

Ben-Yoav, O., Hollander, E. P., & Carnevale, R. J. D. (1983). Leader legitimacy, leader-follower interaction, and followers' ratings of the leader. *Journal of Social Psychology, 121*, 111–115.

Benze, J. G., Jr. (1981). Presidential management: The importance of presidential skills. *Presidential Studies Quarterly, 11*, 470–478.

Benze, J. G., Jr. (1985). Presidential reorganization as a tactical weapon: Putting politics back into administration. *Presidential Studies Quarterly, 15*, 145–157.

Berenson, P. (1997). *The biological roots of human behavior*. Unpublished manuscript.

Berenson, P. J. (1998, 24 February). U.S. Army values: The "C" words. Fort Monroe, VA: United States Army Training and Doctrine Command.

Berg, A. S. (1989). *Goldwyn: A Biography*. New York: Alfred A. Knopf.

Bergen, S. A. (1986). *Project Management*. New York: Basil Blackwell.

Berger, A. M. (1997). *Public leaders and multi-sectional collaborations: Assessing the influence of leaders on partnership outcomes*. Paper, Academy of Management, Boston.

Berger, C., & Braduc, J. (1982). *Language and social knowledge: Uncertainty in interpersonal relations*. London: Arnold.

Berger, M., & Watts, P. (1992). Management development in Europe. *Journal of European Industrial Training, 16*(6), 13–21.

Berger, P. L. (1963). Charisma and religious innovation: The social location of Israelite prophecy. *American Sociological Review, 28*, 940–950.

Bergh, D. D. (2001). Executive retention and acquisition: A test of opposing views on the influence of organizational tenure. *Journal of Management, 27*, 603–622.

Bergum, B. C., & Lehr, D. J. (1963). Effects of authoritarianism on vigilance performance. *Journal of Applied Psychology, 47*, 75–77.

Berke, D. (2002). Finding success at successions. *Issues & Observations, 22*(5), 20–21.

Berkes, L. J., & Rauch, C. F., Jr. (1981). The use of the adaptive process regression program to analyze leadership effectiveness in a police organization. *Proceedings, Academy of Management*, San Diego, CA.

Berkowitz, L. (1953a). An exploratory study of the roles of aircraft commanders. USAF *Human Resources Research Center and Research Bulletin*, No. 53–65, 1–27.

Berkowitz, L. (1953b). Sharing leadership in small, decision–making groups. *Journal of Abnormal and Social Psychology, 48*, 231–238.

Berkowitz, L. (1957). Liking for the group and the perceived merit of the group's behavior. *Journal of Abnormal and Social Psychology, 54*, 353–357.

Berkowitz, L., & Connor, W. H. (1966). Success, failure, and social responsibility. *Journal of Personality and Social Psychology, 4*, 664–669.

Berkowitz, L., & Daniels, L. R. (1963). Responsibility and dependency. *Journal of Abnormal and Social Psychology, 66*, 429–436.

Berkowitz, L., & Howard, R. C. (1959). Reactions to opinion deviates as affected by affiliation need (n) and group member interdependence. *Sociometry, 22*, 81–91.

Berkowitz, L., & Lundy, R. M. (1957). Personality characteristics related to susceptibility to influence by peers or authority figures. *Journal of Personality, 25*, 306–316.

Berle, A. A., & Means, G. C. (1932). *The modern corporation and private property.* New York: Macmillan, 501.

Berle, N. S., Biscone, C. G., Katz, B., et al. (1981). *Gender isolation: All alone in a crowd.* Paper, Academy of Management, San Diego, CA.

Berlew, D. E. (1974). Leadership and organizational excitement. In D. A. Kolb, I. M. Rubin, and J. M. McIntyre (eds.), *Organizational psychology.* Englewood Cliffs, NJ: Prentice-Hall.

Berlew, D. E., & Hall, D. T. (1966). The socialization of managers: Effects of expectations on performance. *Administrative Science Quarterly, 11*, 207–223.

Berlew, D. E., & Hall, D. T. (1979). Leadership and organizational excitement. In D.A. Kolb, I. M.Rubin, & J. M. McIntyre (eds.), *Organizational psychology: A book of readings.* Englewood Cliffs, NJ: Prentice-Hall.

Berlew, D. E., & Heller, D. (1983). Style flexibility-tools for successful leaders. *Legal Economics, 9*(6), 34–37.

Berlyne, D. E. (1967). Arousal and reinforcement. In D. Levine (ed.), *Nebraska Symposium on Motivation,* Lincoln: University of Nebraska Press. *15*, 1–110.

Berman, E. M., & Van Wart, M. (1999). The ethics of productivity toward increased dialogue and customer-based accountability. *International Journal of Organizational Theory & Behavior, 2*(3–4), 413–430.

Bernard, C. (1938). *The Functions of an Executive.* Cambridge, MA: Harvard University Press.

Bernard, J. (1928). Political leadership among North American Indians. *American Journal of Sociology, 34*, 296–315.

Bernard, L. L. (1926). An *introduction to social psychology.* New York: Holt.

Bernard, L. L. (1927). Leadership and propaganda. In J. Davis & H. E. Barnes (eds.), *An introduction to sociology.* New York: Heath.

Bernardez, T. (1983). Women in authority: Psychodynamic and interactional aspects. *Social Work with Groups, 6*(3–4), 43.

Bernardin, H. J. (1976). The influence of reinforcement orientation on the relationship between supervisory style and effectiveness criteria. *Dissertation Abstracts International, 37*, 1018.

Bernardin, H. J., & Alvares, K. M (1975). The effects of organizational level on perceptions of role conflict resolution strategies. *Organizational Behavior and Human Performance, 14*, 1–9.

Bernardez, T. (1983). Women in Authority: Psychodynamic and Interactional Aspects. *Social Work with Groups, 6*(3–4), 43.

Bernath, S. B. (1991). *Leadership: The road to coaching excellence.* Master's thesis, Binghamton University, Binghamton, NY.

Berne, E. (1964). *Games people play.* New York: Grove Press.

Bernhard, L. A., & Walsh, M. (1981). *Leadership: The key to the professionalization of nursing.* New York: McGraw-Hill.

Bernhardt, R. C. (1972). *A study of the relationships between teachers' attitudes toward militancy and their perceptions of selected organizational characteristics of their schools.* Doctoral dissertation, Syracuse University, Syracuse, NY.

Bernstein, B. L., & Lecomte, C. (1979). Supervisory-type feedback effects: Feedback discrepancy level, trainee psychological differentiation, and immediate responses. *Journal of Counseling Psychology, 26*, 295–303.

Bernstein, I. S. (1964). Group social patterns as influenced by removal and later reintroduction of the dominant male rhesus. *Psychological Reports, 14*, 3–10.

Berrien, F. K. (1961). Homeostasis theory of groups—implications for leadership. In L. Petrullo & B. Bass (eds.), *Leadership and Interpersonal Behavior,* New York: Holt, Rinehart & Winston.

Berry, A. J. (1997). Approaching the millennium: Transforming leadership education for stewardship of the planet's resources. *Leadership & Organization Development Journal, 18*(2/3), 86–92.

Berry, D. S., & McArthur, L. Z. (1986). Perceiving character in faces: The impact of age-related craniofacial changes on social perception. *Psychological Bulletin, 100*, 3–18.

Berscheid, E., & Walster, E. (1969). *Interpersonal attraction.* Reading, MA: Addison-Wesley.

Berson, Y. (undated). *Transformational leaders as mediators of the social environment: How military commanders make their soldiers perform beyond social expectation.* Unpublished manuscript.

Berson, Y. (1999). *A comprehensive assessment of leadership using triangulation of qualitative and quantitative methods.* Doctoral dissertation, Binghamton University, Binghamton, NY.

Berson, Y., & Avolio, B. J. (2001). *Contribution of triangulating qualitative, quantitative and unobtrusive methods in the measurement of charismatic/transformational leadership.* Paper, Society for Industrial and Organizational Psychology, San Diego, CA.

Berson, Y., & Avolio, B. J. (2004). Transformational leadership and the dissemination of organizational goals: A case study of a telecommunication firm. *The Leadership Quarterly, 15*, 625–646.

Berson, Y., Dionne, S. D., & Jaussi, K. S. (2002). *Intellectual stimulation of senior executives: Triangulation evidence from the U.S. and Israel.* Paper, Academy of Management, Denver, CO.

Berson, Y., Jung, D. I., & Termiza, S. A. (1997). *A framework for a measure of the Full Range of Leadership: Applying the principles of triangulation and levels of analysis.* Paper, Academy of Management, Boston.

Berson, Y., & Linton, J. D. (2003). *An examination of the relationship between leadership style, quality, and employee satisfaction in R & D environments.* Engineering Management Conference, 2003. IEMC '03. Managing Technologically Driven Organizations: The Human Side of Innovation and Change, 410–414.

Berson, Y., Shamir, B., Avolio, B. J., et al. (2001). The relationship between vision strength, leadership style, and context. *Leadership Quarterly, 12*, 53–73.

Berson, Y., & Yammarino, F. J. (1998). *Followership, leadership, and attachment styles: A development approach.* Paper, Society for Industrial and Organsizational Psychology, Dallas, TX.

Besco, R. O., & Lawshe, C. H. (1959). Foreman leadership as perceived by superiors and subordinates. *Personnel Psychology, 12*, 573–582.

Beshers, J. (1962). *Urban social structure.* New York: Free Press of Glencoe.

Bess, J. L., & Goldman, P. (2001). Leadership ambiguity in universities and K–12 schools and the limits of contemporary leadership theory. *Leadership Quarterly, 12*, 419–450.

Best, J. J. (1981). Presidential cabinet appointments: 1953–1976. *Presidential Studies Quarterly, 11*, 62–66.

Bettin, P. J., & Kennedy, J. K., Jr. (1990) Leadership experience and leadership performance: Some empirical support at last. *Leadership Quarterly, 1*, 219–228.

Betts, R. K., & Huntington, S. P. (1986). When a dictator dies, how much turmoil will follow? *Wall Street Journal*, August 13, 22.

Betz, B., & Fry, W.R. (1995). The role of group schema in the selection of influence attempts. *Basic & Applied Social Psychology, 16*, 351–365.

Beu, D. S., & Buckley, M. R. (2004a). Using accountability to create a more ethical climate. *Human Resource Management Review, 14*, 67–83.

Beu, D. S., & Buckley, M. R. (2004b). This is war: How the politically astute achieve crimes of obedience through the use of moral disengagement. *Leadership Quarterly, 15*, 551–568.

Beutler, L. E., Jobe, A. M., & Elkins, D. (1974). Outcomes in group psychotherapy: Using persuasion theory to increase treatment efficiency. *Journal of Consulting and Clinical Psychology, 42*, 547–553.

Beyer, J. M. (1981). Managerial ideologies and the use of discipline. *Proceedings, Academy of Management*, San Diego, CA, 259–263.

Beyer, J. M. (1999). Taming and promoting charisma to change organizations. *Leadership Quarterly, 10*, 307–330.

Beyer, J. M., & Trice, H. M. (1984). A field study of the use and perceived effects of discipline in controlling work performance. *Academy of Management Journal, 27*, 743–764.

Beyer, S. (1990). Gender differences in the accuracy of self-evaluations of performance. *Journal of Personality and Social Psychology, 59*(5), 960–970.

Bhaskar, R. (1978). *Problem solving in semantically rich domains.* Doctoral dissertation, Carnegie-Mellon University, Pittsburgh.

Bhatia, K. (1995). Leadership & leaders are on their way. What do we need to appreciate? *Journal of Leadership Studies, 2*(2), 66–72.

Bhatnagar, D., & Swamy, R. (1995) Attitudes toward women as managers: Does interaction make a difference? *Human Relations, 48*, 1285–1307.

Bhatt, L. I., & Pathak, N. S. (1962). A study of functions of supervisory staff and the characteristics essential for success as viewed by a group of supervisors. *Manas, 9*, 25–31.

Biddle, B. J., French, J. R. P., & Moore, J. V. (1953). *Some aspects of leadership in the small work group.* Ann Arbor: University of Michigan, Institute of Social Research.

Biddle, T., & Fisher, C. D. (1987). *Performance appraisal interview: A review of research* (ONR Tech. Rep. No. 8). College Station: Texas A&M University, Department of Management.

Bielby, W. T., & Baron, J. N. (1984). A woman's place is with other women: Sex segregation within organizations. In B. F. Reskin (ed.), *Sex segregation in the workplace: Trends, explanations, remedies.* Washington, DC: National Academy Press.

Bielby, W. T., & Baron, J. N. (1984). The organization of work in a segmented economy. *American Sociological Review, 49*(4), 454–473.

Bierstedt, R. (1950). An analysis of social power. *American Sociology Review, 15*, 730–736.

Bies, R. J. (2000). Interactional (in)justice: The sacred and the profane. In J. Greenberg & R. Cropanzano (eds.), *Advances in organizational psychology.* Stanford, CA: Stanford University Press.

Bies, R. J., & Shapiro, D. L. (1986). *It's not my fault, but it's for the greater good: The influence of social accounts on perceptions of managerial legitimacy.* Paper, Academy of Management, Chicago.

Bies, R. J., & Shapiro, D. L. (1988). Voice and justification: Their influence on procedural fairness judgments. *Academy of Management Journal, 31*, 676–685

Biggart, B. W., & Hamilton, C. C. (1987). An institutional theory of leadership. *Journal of Applied Behavioral Science, 23*, 429–441.

Biggart, N. (1981). Management style as strategic interaction: The case of Governor Ronald Reagan. *Journal of Applied Behavioral Science, 17*, 291–308.

Bigoness, W. J. (1976). Effect of applicant's sex, race, and performance on employers' performance ratings: Some additional findings. *Journal of Applied Psychology, 61*, 80–84.

Bigoness, W. J., & Blakely, G. L. (1996). A cross-national study of managerial values. *Journal of International Business Studies, 27*, 739–752.

Bigoness, W. J., Ryan, R., & Hamner, W. C. (1983). Moderators of leader reward behavior. In G. R. Reeves & J. R. Sweigert (eds.), *Proceedings, American Institute for Decision Sciences*, Boston, 412–414.

Billard, M. (1992). Do women make better managers? *Working Woman, 3*, 68–71, 106.

Binder, A., Wolin, B. R., & Terebinski, S. J. (1965). Leadership selection when uncertainty is minimal. *Psychonomic Science, 3*, 367–368.

Binder, A., Wolin, B. R., & Terebinski, S. J. (1966). Learning and extinction of leadership preferences in small groups. *Journal of Mathematical Psychology, 3*, 129–139.

Bingham, W. V. (1927). Leadership. In H. C. Metcalf, *The psychological foundations of management.* New York: Shaw.

Binning, J. F., & Fernandez, G. (1986). *Heuristic processes in rating of leader behavior: Assessing item-induced availability biases.* Paper, American Psychological Association, Washington, DC.

Binning, J. F., & Lord, R. G. (1980). Boundary conditions for performance cue effects on group process ratings: Familiarity versus type of feedback. *Organizational Behavior & Human Performance, 26*, 115–130.

Bion, W. R. (1948). Experiences in groups. *Human Relations, 1*, 314–320, 487–496.

Bion, W. R. (1961). *Experiences in groups.* New York: Basic Books.

Bird, C. (1940). *Social psychology.* New York: Appleton-Century.

Birden, L. (1992). *Leadership behavior styles of administrators and school climate in area vocational technical schools in Oklahoma as perceived by teachers.* Doctoral dissertation, Oklahoma State University, Norman, OK.

Birdseye, M. G., & Hill, J. S. (1995). Individual, organizational work and environmental influences on expatriate turnover tendencies: An empirical study. *Journal of International Business Studies, 26,* 787–813.

Birdwhistell, R. L. (1970). *Kinesis and context.* Philadelphia, PA: University of Pennsylvania Press.

Birkeland, S. A., Borman, W. C., & Brannick, M. T. (2003). *Using personal construct theory to investigate 360-degree source effects.* Paper, Society for Industrial and Organizational Psychology, Orlando, FL.

Birnbaum, P. H., & Wong, G. Y. Y. (undated). *Cultural values of managers in the People's Republic of China and Hong Kong.* Unpublished manuscript.

Birnbaum, R. (1971). Presidential succession: An inter-institutional analysis. *Educational Record,* Spring, 133–145.

Birnbaum, R. (1986). Leadership and learning: The college president as intuitive scientist. *Review of Higher Education,* 9(4), 381–395.

Birnbaum, R. (1987a). *Presidential searches and the discovery of organizational goals.* Paper, Leadership Research Conference, Council for Liberal Learning of the Association of American Colleges, Wingspread, Racine, WI.

Birnbaum, R. (1987c). *The implicit leadership theories of college and university presidents.* Paper, Association for the Study of Higher Education, Baltimore.

Birnbaum, R. (1988a). *Responsibility without authority: The impossible job of the college president.* National Center for Postsecondary Governance and Finance, Teachers College, Columbia University, New York.

Birnbaum, R. (1988) *How colleges work: The cybernetics of academic organization and leadership.* San Francisco: Jossey-Bass.

Birnbaum, R. (1990). *Leadership and campus productivity* (Executive Summary No. 26). New York: Columbia University, Teachers College, Institutional Leadership Project.

Birnbaum, R., Bensimon, E. M., & Neumann, A. (1989). Leadership in higher education: A multi-dimensional approach to research. *Review of Higher Education, 12,* 101–105.

Birnbrauer, H., & Tyson, L. A. (1984). Flexing the muscles of technical leadership. *Training & Development Journal,* 38(8), 48–52.

Bish, J., & Schriesheim, C. (1974). *An exploratory dimensional analysis of Form XII of the Ohio State leadership scales.* Paper, Academy of Management, Seattle, WA.

Bishop, D. W. (1967). *Group member adjustment as related to interpersonal and task success and affiliation and achievement motives* (Tech. Rep. No. 23). Urbana: University of Illinois, Group Effectiveness Research Laboratory.

Bizman, A., & Fox, S. (1984). Managers' perception of the stability of workers' positive and negative behaviors. *Journal of Applied Psychology,* 69, 40–43.

Bjerstedt, A. (1956). The interpretation of sociometric status scores in the classroom. *Nordisk Psykologi,* 1(2), 8–14.

Black, C. H. (1981). *Managerial motivation of hospital chief administrators in investor-owned and not-for-profit hospitals.* Doctoral dissertation, Georgia State University, Atlanta.

Black, L. D., & Härtel, C. E. J. (2002). *Towards a typology of corporate sosial responsibility orientations.* Paper, Academy of Management, Denver, CO.

Black, J. S., & Gregersen, H. B. (1991). When Yankee comes home: Factors related to expatriate and repatriate spouse adjustment. *Journal of International Business Studies,* 22, 671–694.

Black, J. S., & Gregerson, H. B. (1998). *So you going overseas: A handbook for personal and professional success.* San Diego, CA: Global Business Publishers.

Blackburn, D. A. (1992). *Trust in manager-subordinate relationships.* Johannesburg, South Africa: University of Witwatersrand.

Blackmar, E. W. (1911). Leadership in reform. *American Journal of Sociology, 16,* 626–644.

Blades, J. W. (1976). The influence of intelligence, task ability and motivation on group performance. *Dissertation Abstracts International,* 37, 1463.

Blades, J. W., & Fiedler, F. E. (1973). *Participative management, member intelligence, and group performance* (Tech. Rep. No. 73–40). Seattle: University of Washington, Organizational Research.

Blades, J. W., & Fiedler, F. E. (1976). *The influence of intelligence, task ability, and motivation on group performance.* Technical Report No. 76–78.

Blaihed, S. A. (1982). The relationship between leadership behavior of the chief executive officer in the hospital and overall hospital performance. *Dissertation Abstracts International,* 43(7A), 2169.

Blake, J. R., & Goffin, R. D. (2001). Can performance-feedback accuracy be improved? Effects of rater priming and rating-scale format on rating accuracy. *Journal of Applied Psychology,* 86, 134–144.

Blake, R. J., Potter , E. H. , Jr., & Slimak, R. E. (1993). Validation of the structural scales of the cpi for predicting the performance of junior officers in the U. S. coast guard. *Journal of Business and Psychology,* 7, 431–448.

Blake, R. R., & McCanse, A. A. (1991). *Leadership dilemmas—grid solutions.* Houston, TX: Gulf Publishing.

Blake, R. R., & McKee, R. K. (1993). The leadership of corporate change. *Journal of Leadership Studies,* 3, 71–84.

Blake, R. R., & Mouton, J. S. (1962b). The intergroup dynamics of win-lose conflict and problem-solving collaboration in union-management relations. In M. Sherif (ed.), *Intergroup relations and leadership.* New York: Wiley.

Blake, R. R., & Mouton, J. S. (1964). *The managerial grid.* Houston, TX: Gulf.

Blake, R. R., & Mouton, J. S. (1965). A 9,9 approach for increasing organizational productivity. In E. H. Schein & W. G. Bennis (eds.), *Personal and organizational change through group methods.* New York: Wiley.

Blake, R., & Mouton, J. S. (1972). *The managerial grid: Key orientations for achieving production through people.* Houston, TX: Gulf.

Blake, R. R., & Mouton, J. S. (1978). *The new managerial grid.* Houston, TX: Gulf.

Blake, R. R., & Mouton, J. S. (1981a). Management by grid principles or situationalism: Which? *Group & Organization Studies,* 6, 439–455.

Blake, R. R., & Mouton, J. S. (1981b). Theory and research for developing a science of leadership. *Journal of Applied Behavioral Science, 18,* 275–291.

Blake, R. R., & Mouton, J. S. (1985a). Effective crisis management. *New Management*, 3(1), 14–17.

Blake, R. R., & Mouton, J. S. (1985b). Presidential (grid). styles. *Training & Development Journal*, 39(3), 30–34.

Blake, R. R., & Mouton, J. S. (1985c). *The managerial grid III*. Houston, TX: Gulf.

Blake, R. R., Mouton, J. S., Barnes, L. B., & Greiner, L. E. (1964). Breakthrough in organization development. *Harvard Business Review*, 42(6), 133–155.

Blake, R. R., Mouton, J. S., & Fruchter, B. (1954). The consistency of interpersonal behavior judgments made on the basis of short-term interactions in three-man groups. *Journal of Abnormal and Social Psychology*, 49, 573–578.

Blalock, D. (1996). Study shows many execs are quick to write off ethics. *Wall Street Journal* (26 March 1996), C1, C5.

Blalock, H. M. (1959). Status consciousness: A dimensional analysis. *Social Forces*, 37, 243–248.

Blalock, H. M., Jr. (1967). *Toward a theory of minority-group relations.* New York: Wiley.

Blanchard, K., & Johnson, S. (1982). *The one minute manager.* New York: William Morrow.

Blanchard, K., & Sargent, A. G. (1984). The one minute manager is an androgynous manager. *Training and Development Journal*, 38(5), 83–85.

Blanchard, K. H., Zigarmi, D., & Nelson, R. B. (1993). Situational leadership after 25 years: A retrospective. *Journal of Leadership Studies*, 1, XX–36.

Blank, W., Weitzel, J. R., & Green, S. G. (1987). Situational leadership theory: A test of underlying assumptions. *Journal of Management.*

Blank, W., Weitzel, J. R., & Green, S. G. (1990). A test of the sotiatopmal leadership theory. *Personnel Psychology*, 43(3), 579–597.

Blankenship, L. V., & Miles, R. E. (1968). Organizational structure and managerial decision behavior. *Administrative Science Quarterly*, 13, 106–120.

Blasé, J., & Blasé, J. R. (1997). The micropolitical orientation of facilitative school principals and its effect on teachers' sense of empowerment. *Journal of Educational Administration*, 35, 138–164.

Blasi, A. (1980). Bridging moral cognition and moral action: A critical review of the literature. *Psychological Bulletin*, 88(1), 1–45.

Blau, P. M. (1954). Patterns of interaction among a group of officials in a government agency. *Human Relations*, 7, 337–348.

Blau, P. M. (1960). Patterns of deviation in work groups. *Sociometry*, 23, 245–261.

Blau, P. M. (1964). *Exchange and power in social life.* New York: Wiley.

Blau, P. M. (1968). The hierarchy of authority in organizations. *American Journal of Sociology*, 73, 453–467.

Blau, P. M., & Scott, W. R. (1962). *Formal organizations.* San Francisco: Chandler.

Bleda, P. R., Gitter, C. A., & D'Agostino, R. B. (1977). Enlisted men's perceptions of leader attributes and satisfaction with military life. *Journal of Applied Psychology*, 62, 43–49.

Bledsoe, J. C., Brown, S. E., & Dalton, S. L. (1980). Perception of leadership behavior of the school business manager. *Perceptual and Motor Skills*, 50, 1147–1150.

Bliese, P. D., Bienvenu, R. V., Castro, C. C., et al. (2002). *Leadership support in an austere and dangerous environment.* Paper, Society for Industrial and Organizational Psychology, Toronto.

Bliese, P. D., & Halverson, R. R. (2002). Using random group resampling in multilevel research: An example of the buffering effects of leadership climate. *Leadership Quarterly*, 13, 53–68.

Bliese, P. D., Halverson, R. R., & Schriesheim, C. A. (2002). Benchmarking multilevel methods in leadership: The articles, the model, and the data set. *Leadership Quarterly*, 13, 3–14.

Bliese, P. D., Ritzer, D. & Thomas, J. L. (2001). *Supervisory support and stressor-commitment relations: A multi-level investigation.* Paper, Society for Industrial and Organizational Psychology, San Diego, CA.

Bligh, M. C., & Kohles, J. C. (2003). *Negotiating gender role expectations: Rhetorical leadership and women in the Senate.* Paper, Academy of Management, Seattle, WA.

Bligh, M. C., Kohles, J. C., & Meindl, J. R. (2004). Charisma under crisis: Presidential leadership, rhetoric, and media responses before and after the September 11th terrorist attacks. *Leadership Quarterly*, 15, 211–239.

Block, C. J., & Kennedy, J. K., Jr. (1986). *The effects of variations in leader behavior.* Paper, American Psychology Association, New York.

Block, N. J., & Kolakowski, D. (1973). Further evidence of sex-linked major gene influence on human spatial visualizing ability. *American Journal of Human Genetics*, 25, 1–14.

Block, P. (1986). *The empowered manager.* San Francisco: Jossey-Bass.

Block, P. (1987). *The empowered manager: Positive political skills at work.* San Francisco: Jossey-Bass.

Block, P. (1993). *Stewardship.* San Francisco: Barrett-Koehler.

Blood, M. R., & Hulin C. L. (1967). Alienation, environmental characteristics, and worker responses. *Journal of Applied Psychology*, 51, 284–290.

Bloomfield, L. P. (1984). What's wrong with transitions. *Foreign Policy*, 55, Summer, 23–39.

Bloskie, C. (1995). Leadership and integrity. *Optimum*, 26(2), 37.

Blum, L. A. (1980). *Friendship, altruism, and morality.* London: Routledge & Kegan Paul.

Blumberg, P. (1968). *Industrial democracy: The sociology of participation.* London: Constable.

Blumenthal, A. (1932). *Small townstuff.* Chicago: University of Chicago Press.

Blyth, D. E. (1987). *Leader and subordinate expertise as moderators of the relationship between directive leader behavior and performance.* Doctoral dissertation, University of Washington. (Reported in F. E. Fiedler & R. J. House [1987] *Leadership theory and research*: A *report of progress.* International Reviews of 1/0 Psychology. New York: Wiley.)

Boal, K. B., & Bryson, J. M. (1988). Charismatic leadership: A phenomonological and structural approach. In J. G. Hunt, et al. (eds.), *Emerging leadership vistas.* Lexington, MA: Lexington Books.

Boal, K. B., & Hooijberg, R. (2000). Strategic leadership research: Moving on. *Leadership Quarterly*, 11, 515–549. (Available online.)

Boal, K. B., Hunt, J. G., & Sorenson, R. L. (1988). *Leadership folk theories and second phase development work on the Leadership Quotes Questionnaire.* Paper, Western Academy of Management, Big Sky, MT.

Boatwright, K. J., Gilbert, M. S., Forrest, L., et al. (1996). Impact of identity development upon career projectory. Listening to the voices of lesbian women. *Journal of Vocational Behavior, 48,* 210–228.

Bobo, L., & Gilliam, F. D., Jr. (1990). Race, sociopolitical participation, and black empowerment. *The American Political Science Review, 84,* 377–393.

Boccialetti, G. (1995). *It takes two.* San Francisco: Jossey-Bass.

Boccialetti, G. (1996). Making authority relationships reciprocal. *Training and Development Journal, 50*(6), 34–40.

Bochner, A. P., DiSalvo, V., & Jonas, T. (1975). A computer-assisted analysis of small group process: An investigation of two Machiavellian groups. *Small Group Behavior, 6,* 187–203.

Bockman, S., & Cayk, W. F. (1977). Political orientations and political ideologies. *Pacific Sociological Review, 20,* 536–552.

Bodycombe, B. (1982). How to manage disasters—in advance. *Management Today, 41,* November, 44, 46.

Boeker, W. (1992). Power and managerial dismissal: Scapegoating at the top. *Administrative Science Quarterly, 27,* 538–547.

Boeker, W. (1997). Executive migration and strategic change: The effect of top management movement on product-market entry. *Administrative Science Quarterly, 42,* 213–236.

Bogard, H. M. (1960). Union and management trainees: A comparative study of personality and occupational choice. *Journal of Applied Psychology, 44,* 56–63.

Bogardus, E. S. (1918). *Essentials of social psychology.* Los Angeles: University of Southern California Press.

Bogardus, E. S. (1928). World leadership types. *Sociology and Social Research, 12,* 573–599.

Bogardus, E. S. (1929). Leadership and attitudes. *Sociology and Social Research, 13,* 377–387.

Bogardus, E. S. (1934). *Leaders and leadership.* New York: Appleton-Century.

Boies, K., & Corbett, R. (2005). *Relations between leadership styles and subordinates' perceptions of leaders' trustworthiness.* Paper, Society for Industrial and Organizational Psychology, Los Angeles, CA.

Boise, W. B. (1965). Supervisors' attitudes toward disciplinary actions. *Personnel Administration, 28,* 24–27.

Boje, D. M. (1995). Stories of the storytelling organization: A postmodern analysis of Disney as "Tamara-Land." *Academy of Management Journal, 38,* 997–1035.

Bolino, M. C. (1999). Citizenship and impression management: Good soldiers or good actors. *Academy of Management Review, 24*(1), 82–98.

Bolino, M. C., Turnley, W. H., & Bloodgood, J. M. (2002). Citizenship behavior and the creation of social capital in organizations. *Academy of Management Review, 27,* 505–522.

Bolman, L. G. (1973). Some effects of trainers on their groups: A partial replication. *Journal of Applied Behavioral Science, 9,* 534–539.

Bolman, L. G. (1986). *Concepts of leadership and power in innovating organizations: Machines, families, jungles and theatres.* Paper, Conference on Innovations & Management in the 1990's. Carlsbad, Czechoslovakia.

Bolman, L. G., & Deal, T. E. (1984). *Modern approaches to understanding and managing organizations.* San Francisco: Jossey-Bass.

Bolman, L. G., & Deal, T. E. (1995). *Leading with soul.* San Francisco: Jossey-Bass.

Bolman, L. G., & Deal, T. E. (2001). *Leading with soul: An uncommon journey of spirit, new & revised.* San Francisco: Jossey-Bass.

Bolon, D. S., & Crain, C. R. (1985). *Decision sequence: A recurring theme in comparing American and Japanese management.* Proceedings, Academy of Management, San Diego, CA, 88–92.

Bommer, W. H., & Rubin, R. S. (2001). *Antecedents and consequences of transformational leadership behaviors: The role of leader attitudes and social context upon leader behavior and performance outcomes.* Washington, DC: Academy of Management.

Bommer, W. H., Rubin, R. S., & Baldwin, T. T. (2004). Setting the stage for effective leadership: Antecedents of transformational leadership behavior. *Leadership Quarterly, 15*(2), 195–210.

Bond, M. H., & Smith, P. B. (1996). Cross-cultural social and organizational psychology. *Annual Review of Psychology, 47,* 205–35.

Bono, J. E. & Judge, T. A. (2003). Core self-evaluations: A review of the trait and its role in job satisfaction and job performance. *European Journal of Personality, 17*(S1), S5–S18.

Bononno, G. A. (2005). Loss, trauma, and human resilience: Have we underestimated the human capacity to thrive after extremely adverse events? *American Psychologist, 59,* 20–28.

Bons, P. M. (1974). *The effect of changes in leadership environment on the behavior of relationship and task-motivated leaders.* Doctoral dissertation, University of Washington, Seattle.

Bons, P. M., Bass, A. R., & Komorita, S. S. (1970). Changes in leadership style as a function of military experience and type of command. *Personnel Psychology, 23,* 551–568.

Bons, P. M., & Fiedler, F. E. (1976). Changes in organizational leadership and the behavior of relationship—and task-motivated leaders. *Administrative Science Quarterly, 21,* 433–472.

Boo, K. (2004). The black gender gap. In T. Halstead. *The real state of the union.* New York: Basic Books.

Boon, S. D., & Holmes, J. G. (1991). The dynamics of interpersonal trust: Resolving uncertainty in the face of risk. In R. A. Hinde & J. Groebel (eds.), *Cooperation and prosocial behavior.* Cambridge, U.K.: Cambridge University Press.

Booz, Allen & Hamilton. (2002). When and why do CEOs leave? *Wall Street Journal* September 18, B3.

Bord, R. J. (1975). Toward a social-psychological theory of charismatic social influence processes. *Social Forces, 53,* 486–497.

Bordas, J. (1994). *Passion and power: Finding personal purpose: An essay on reflections on leadership.* New York: John Wiley & Sons.

Bordas, J. (2001). Latino leadership: Building a humanistic and diverse society. *Journal of Leadership Studies, 8*(2), 114–133.

Borden, D. F. (1980). *Leader-boss stress, personality, job satisfaction, and performance: Another look at the interrelationship of some old constructs in the modern large bureaucracy.* Doctoral dissertation, University of Washington, Seattle.

Borg, W. R. (1956). Leadership reactions in situational tests. *American Psychologist, 11,* 379.

Borg, W. R., & Tupes, E. C. (1958). Personality characteristics related to leadership behavior in two types of small group situational problems. *Journal of Applied Psychology, 42,* 252–256.

Borgatta, E. F. (1954). Analysis of social interaction and sociometric perception. *Sociometry, 17,* 7–32.

Borgatta, E. F. (1955b). Attitudinal concomitants to military statuses. *Social Forces, 33,* 342–347.

Borgatta, E. F., & Bales, R. F. (1953b). Task and accumulation of experience as factors in the interaction of small groups. *Sociometry, 16*, 239–252.

Borgatta, E. F., Cottrell, L. S., & Wilker, L. (1959). Initial expectation, group climate, and the assessments of leaders and members. *Journal of Social Psychology, 49*, 285–296.

Borgatta, E. F., Couch, A. S., & Bales, R. F. (1954). Some findings relevant to the great man theory of leadership. *American Sociological Review, 19*, 755–759.

Borland, C. (1974). *Locus of control, need for achievement and entrepreneurship.* Doctoral dissertation, The University of Texas, Austin.

Borowiec, W. A. (1975). Persistence and change in the gatekeeper role of ethnic leaders: The case of the Polish-American. *Polish Anthropology, 1*, 21–40.

Borman, W. C. (1982). Validity of behavioral assessment for predicting military recruiter performance. *Journal of Applied Psychology, 67*, 3–9.

Borman, W. C., Eaton, N. K., Bryan, J. D., & Rosse, R. L. (1983). Validity of Army recruiters behavioral assessment: Does the assessor make a difference? *Journal of Applied Psychology, 68*, 415–419.

Borman, W., & Motowidlo, S. (1993). Expanding the criterion domain to include elements of contextual performance. In N. Schmitt & W. Borman (eds.), *Personnel selection in organizations.* San Francisco: Jossey-Bass.

Borman, W. C., White, L. A., & Dorsey, D. W. (1995). Effects of ratee task performance and interpersonal factors on supervisor and peer performance ratings. *Journal of Applied Psychology, 80*, 168–177.

Born, D. H., & Mathieu, J. E. (1996). Differential effects of survey-guided feedback: The rich get richer and the poor get poorer. *Group & Organizational Management, 21*, 388–403.

Bornstein, E., & Zajonc, R. B. (1965a). Individual task performance in a changing social structure. *Sociometry, 28*, 16–29.

Bose, S. K. (1955). Employee morale and supervision. *Indian Journal of Psychology, 30*, 117–125.

Boss, R. W. (1978). The effects of leader absence on a confrontation team-building design. *Journal of Applied Behavioral Science, 14*, 469–478.

Boss, R. W., & Golembiewski, R. T. (1995). Do you have to start at the top? The chief executive's role in successful organizational development efforts. *Journal of Applied Behavioral Science, 31*, 259–277.

Boss, R. W., & McConkie, M. L. (1976). *An autopsy and an OD failure.* Boulder: University of Colorado. (Reported in Boss, 1978.)

Bossard, J. H. S., & Boll, E. S. (1955). Personality roles in the large family. *Child Development, 26*, 71–78.

Bossard, J. H. S., and Boll, E. S. (1956). *The large family system: An original study in the sociology of family behavior.* Philadelphia: University of Pennsylvania Press.

Bossidy L. (1977). In McClenehen, J. S. *Jack's men.* (1977). *Industry Week,* July 7, 12–17.

Bottger, P. C. (1984). Expertise and air time as bases of actual and perceived influence in problem-solving groups. *Journal of Applied Psychology, 69*, 214–221.

Bottger, P. C., Hallein, L. H., & Yetton, P. W. (1985). A cross-cultural study of leadership: Participation as a function of problem structure and leader power. *Journal of Management Studies, 22*, 358–368.

Bottomley, M., & Sampson, S. (1977). The case of the female principal: Sex role attitudes and perceptions of sex differences in ability. *Australian and New Zealand Journal of Sociology, 13*, 137–140.

Bouchard, T. J., & McGue, M. (1981). Familial studies of intelligence: A review. *Science, 212*(4498), 1055–1059.

Boulgarides, J. D. (1984). A comparison of male and female business managers. *Leadership and Organizational Development Journal, 5*(5), 27–31.

Bouty, I. (2000). Interpersonal and interaction influence on informal resource exchanges between R&D researchers across organizational boundaries. *Academy of Management Journal, 43*, 50–65.

Bovard, E. W. (1951a). Group structure and perception. *Journal of Abnormal and Social Psychology, 46*, 398–405.

Bovard, E. W. (1951b). The experimental production of interpersonal affect. *Journal of Abnormal and Social Psychology, 46*, 521–528.

Bovard, E. W. (1952). Clinical insight as a function of group process. *Journal of Abnormal and Social Psychology, 47*, 534–539.

Bowden, A. O. (1926). A study of the personality of student leaders in the United States. *Journal of Abnormal and Social Psychology, 21*, 149–160.

Bowen, D. D. (1985). Were men meant to mentor women? *Training & Development Journal, 39*(2), 30–35.

Bowen, D. D., & Hirsch, R. D. (1986). The female entrepreneur: A career development perspective. *Academy of Management Review, 11*, 393–407.

Bowers. C. A., Pharmer, J. A., & Salas, E. (2000). When member homogeneity is needed in work teams: A meta-analysis. *Small Group Research, 31*, 305–327.

Bowers, D. G. (1963). Self-esteem and the diffusion of leadership style. *Journal of Applied Psychology, 47*, 135–140.

Bowers, D. G. (1964a). Self-esteem and supervision. *Personnel Administration, 27*, 23–26.

Bowers, D. G. (1964b). Organizational control in an insurance company. *Sociometry, 27*, 230–244.

Bowers, D. G. (1969). *Work organizations as dynamic systems* (ONR Tech. Rep.). Ann Arbor; University of Michigan.

Bowers, D. G. (1975). *Navy manpower: Values, practices, and human resources requirements.* Ann Arbor: University of Michigan, Institute for Social Research.

Bowers, D. G. (1976). *Systems of organization.* Ann Arbor: University of Michigan Press.

Bowers, D. G., & Franklin, J. (1975). *Survey guided development: Data based organizational change.* Ann Arbor, MI: University of Michigan, Institute for Social Research.

Bowers, D. G., & Seashore, S. E. (1966). Predicting organizational effectiveness with a four-factor theory of leadership. *Administrative Science Quarterly, 11*, 238–263.

Bowers, D. G., & Seashore, S. E. (1967). Peer leadership within work groups. *Personnel Administration, 30*, 45–50.

Bowers, M. (1997). *The will to lead: Running a business network of leaders.* Boston: Harvard Business School Press.

Bowes-Sperry, L., & Powell, G. N. (1999). Observers' reactions to social-sexual behavior at work: An ethical decision making perspective. *Journal of Management, 25*(6), 779.

Bowes-Sperry, L., Veiga, J. F., & Yanouzas, J. N. (1997). An analysis of managerial helping responses based on social role theory. *Group and Organization Management, 22*, 445–459.

Bowlby, J. (1982). *Attachment and loss.* Vol. 1: *Attachment.* New York: Basic Books.

Bowie, N. E. (1998). A Kantian theory of meaningful work. *Journal of Business Ethics, 17*(9–10), 1083.

Bowman, G. W., Worthy, N. B., & Greyser, S. A. (1965). Are women executives people? *Harvard Business Review, 43*(4).

Bowman, H. J. (1964). Perceived leader behavior patterns and their relationships to self-perceived variables—responsibility, authority, and delegation. *Dissertation Abstracts, 25,* 3340.

Bowman, M. A. (1997). Popular approaches to leadership. In P. G. Northouse (ed.), *Leadership theory and practice.* Thousand Oaks, CA: Sage.

Boyatsis, R. R. (1982). *The competent manager.* New York: John Wiley.

Boyd, N. K. (1972). *Negotiation behavior by elected and appointed representatives serving as group leaders or as spokesmen under different cooperative group expectations.* Doctoral dissertation, University of Maryland.

Boyd, J. T., Jr. (1988). *Leadership extraordinary: A cross national military perspective on transactional versus transformational leadership.* Doctoral dissertation, Nova University, Ft. Lauderdale, FL.

Boyd, J. T., Jr. (1989a). *Are military leaders more or less transformational than their superiors?* Unpublished manuscript.

Boyd, J. T., Jr. (1989b). *Are military leaders becoming more or less transformational?* Unpublished manuscript.

Bracey, H., Rosenblum, J., Sanford, A., & Trueblood, R. (1990). *Managing from the heart.* New York: Delacorte Press.

Bradburn, N. M. (1963). N achievement and father dominance in Turkey. *Journal of Abnormal and Social Psychology, 67,* 464–468.

Braddock, J. H., II (1984). *Recruitment and selection of minorities in high-tech organizations: A sociological perspective.* Paper, ONR Conference on Minorities Entering High Tech Careers, Pensacola, FL.

Bradford, D. L., & Cohen, A. R. (1984). The postheroic leader. *Training & Development Journal, 38*(1), 40–49.

Bradford, L. R., & French, J. R. R. (1948). Introduction: The dynamics of the discussion group. *Journal of Social Issues, 4,* 2–8.

Bradford, L. R, & Lippitt, R. (1945). Building a democratic work group. *Personnel, 22*(3), 142–148.

Bradley, G. W. (1978). Self-serving biases in the attribution process: A reexamination of the fact or fiction question. *Journal of Personality and Social Psychology, 36,* 56–71.

Bradley, R. T. (1984). *Charisma and social structure: A relational analysis of power and communion in communes.* Unpublished working manuscript, University of Minnesota. (Cited in Trice & Beyer, 1984.)

Bradley, R. T. (1987). *Charisma and social structure: A study of love and power. Wholeness and transformation.* New York: Paragon House.

Bradshaw, H. H. (1970). Need satisfaction, management style, and job level in a professional hierarchy. Experimental Publications System, *American Psychological Association, 8,* No. 289–1.

Brady, G. F., & Helmich, D. L. (1982). Leadership style in the boardroom. *Directors & Boards, 6*(3), 46.

Brady, G. F., & Helmich, D. L. (1984). *Executive succession.* Englewood Cliffs, NJ: Prentice Hall.

Brainard, S. R., & Dollar, R. J. (1971). Personality characteristics of leaders identifying with different student subcultures. *College Student Personnel, 12,* 200–203.

Bramel, D., & Friend, R. (1987). The work group and its vicissitudes in social and industrial psychology. *Journal of Applied Behavioral Science, 23,* 233–253.

Brams, S. J. (1990). *Negotiating games: Applying game theory to bargaining and arbitration.* New York: Routledge.

Brams, S. J. (1993). *Fair division: From cake-cutting to dispute resolution.* New York: W. W. Norton.

Bramwell, A. (1991). *Charismatic leadership and group performance: When is charisma not a good idea?* Paper, Western Academy of Management, Santa Barbara, CA.

Brandon, A. C. (1965). Status congruence and expectations. *Sociometry, 28,* 272–288.

Brandon, N. (1998). *Self-esteem at work: How confident people make powerful companies.* San Francisco: Jossey-Bass.

Branscombe, N. R., Schmitt, M. T., & Harvey, R. D. (1999). Perceiving pervasive discrimination among African Americans: Implications for group identification and well-being. *Journal of Personality and Social Psychology, 77,* 135–149.

Brass, D. J. (1984). Being in the right place: A structural analysis of individual influence in an organization. *Administrative Science Quarterly, 29,* 518–539.

Brass, D. (1985). Men's and women's networks: A study of interaction patterns and influence in an organization. *Academy of Management Journal, 28*(2), June 85, 327–343.

Brass, D. J. (1992). Power in organizations: A social network perspective. *Research in Politics and Society, 4,* 295–323.

Brass, D. J., & Burkhardt, M.E. (1992). Centrality and power in organizations. In N. Nohria & R. Eccles (eds.), *Networks and organizations: Theory and practice.* Cambridge, MA: Harvard University Press.

Brass, D. J., & Oldham, G. R. (1976). Validating an in-basket test using an alternative set of leadership scoring dimensions. *Journal of Applied Psychology, 61,* 652–657.

Bratton, V. K., Carlson, D. S., Witt, L. A., et al. (2003). *Impression management as a moderator of the politics-performance relationship.* Paper, Society for Industrial and Organizational Psychology, Orlando, FL.

Braun, D. D. (1976). Alienation and participation: A replication comparing leaders and the "mass." *Journal of Political and Military Sociology, 4,* 245–259.

Bray, D. W., Campbell, R. J., & Grant, D. L. (1974). *Formative years in business: A long-term AT&T study of managerial lives.* New York: Wiley-Interscience.

Bray, D. W., & Grant, D. L. (1966). The assessment center in the measurement of potential for business management. *Psychological Monographs, 80*(17), No. 625.

Bray, D. W., & Howard A. (1983). The AT&T longitudinal studies of managers. In K. W. Shaiel (ed.), *Longitudinal studies of adult psychological development.* New York: Guilford Press.

Brenner, L. (2003). *The demographics of American Jews: "My people are American. My time is today." Counterpunch,* October 18–19. www.counterpunch.org/brenner10242003.html.

Brenner, M. H. (1963). *Management selection test validation.* Lockheed California Company, Industrial Relations Research Department. (Reported in Campbell, Dunnette, et al., 1970, 1973.)

Brenner, M. H. (1970). *Management development activities for women.* Paper, American Psychological Association, Miami, FL.

Brenner, M. H. (1972). Management development for women. *Personnel Journal, 51*, 165–169.

Brenner, O. C. (1982). Relationship of education to sex, managerial status, and the managerial stereotype. *Journal of Applied Psychology, 67*, 380–383.

Brenner, O. C., & Bromer, J. A. (1981). Sex stereotypes and leaders' behavior as measured by the agreement scale for leadership behavior. *Psychological Reports, 48*, 960–962.

Brenner, O. C., Tomkiewicz, J., & Schein, V. E. (1989). The relationship between sex role stereotypes and requisite management characteristics revisited. *Academy of Management Journal, 32*, 662–669.

Breslau, K. (2005). A new team in town: In San Francisco, women are in charge of the public's safety . . . *Newsweek*, October 24, 64–66.

Bresnen, M. J. (1995). All things to all people? Perceptions, attributions, and constructions of leadership. *Leadership Quarterly, 6*, 495–513.

Brett, J. M., & Okumura, T. (1998). Inter- and intracultural negotiation: U.S. and Japanese negotiators. *Academy of Management Journal, 41*, 495–510.

Brett, J. M., Stroh, L., Tenbrunsel, A., et al. (1995). Dynamic and static work-family relationships. *Organizational Behavior & Human Decision Processes, 63*(3), 233–246.

Brewer, E., & Tomlinson, J. W. C. (1964). The manager's working day. *Journal of Industrial Economics, 12*, 191–197.

Brewer, N., & Ridgeway, T. (1998). Effects of supervisory monitoring on productivity and quality of performance. *Journal of Experimental Psychology: Applied, 4*, 211–227.

Brewer, N., Socha, L., & Potter, R. (1996). Gender differences in supervisors' use of performance feedback. *Journal of Applied Social Psychology, 26*, 786–803.

Brewster, C., & Larsen, H. H. (1992). Human resource management in Europe: Evidence from ten countries. *International Journal of Human Resource Management, 3*, 409–434.

Bridges, E. M., Doyle, W. F., & Mahan, D. F. (1968). Effects of hierarchical differentiation on group productivity, efficiency, and risk taking. *Administrative Science Quarterly, 13*, 305–319.

Bridges, W. (1995). Leading the de-jobbed organization. In F. Hesselbein, M. Goldsmith, & R. Beckhard (eds.), *The leader of the future*. San Francisco: Jossey-Bass.

Brief, A. P, Aldag, R. J., Russell, C. J., & Rude, D. E. (1981). Leader behavior in a police organization revisited. *Human Relations, 34*, 1037–1051.

Brief, A. P., Dukerich, J. M., and Doran, L. I. (1991). Resolving ethical dilemmas in management: Experimental investigations of values, accountability, and choice. *Journal of Applied Social Psychology, 21*, 380–396.

Brief, A. P., & Oliver, R. L. (1976). Male-female differences in work attitudes among retail sales managers. *Journal of Applied Psychology, 61*, 526–528.

Brief, A. P., & Hollenbeck, J. R. (1985). An exploratory study of self-regulating activities and their effects on job performance. *Journal of Occupational Guidance, 6*, 197–208.

Briggs, S. R., Cheek, J. M., & Buss, A. H. (1980). An analysis of the self-monitoring scale. *Journal of Personality and Social Psychology, 38*, 679–686.

Brillhart, J. K., & Jochem, L. M. (1964). Effects of different patterns on outcomes of problem solving discussions. *Journal of Applied Psychology, 48*, 175–179.

Brindle, L. 1992. How do executives get better jobs? *Executive Development, 5*, 1.

Brim, O. G. (1954). The acceptance of the new behavior in child-rearing. *Human Relations, 7*, 473–491.

Brindisi, J. G. (1976). *Role satisfaction of community school council members*. Doctoral dissertation, Florida Atlantic University, Boca Raton.

Brinker, F. A. (1955). Supervisor's and foremen's reasons for frustration. *Personnel Journal, 34*, 101–103.

Briscoe, J. P., & Hall, D. T. (1999). Grooming and picking leaders using competency frameworks: Do they work? Alternative approach and new guidelines for practice. *Organizational Dynamics, 28*(2), 37–52.

Brockhaus, R. H. (1975). I-E locus of control scores as predictors of entrepreneurial intentions. *Proceedings, Academy of Management*, New Orleans, LA, 433–435.

Brockhaus, R. H. (1980). Risk taking propensity of entrepreneurs. *Academy of Management Journal, 23*, 509–520.

Brockman, E. N., Hoffman, J. J. & Dawley, D. D. (2003). Do size and diversification type matter? An examination of post-bankruptcy outcomes. *Journal of Managerial Issues*, Winter 2003.

Brockman, E., Hoffman, J. J., & Fornaciari, C. J. (2003). *The impact of CEO duality and prestige on a bankrupt organization*. Paper, Academy of Management. Seattle, WA.

Brockner, J., & Adsit, L. (1986). The moderating impact of sex on the equity-satisfaction relationship: A field study. *Journal of Applied Psychology, 71*(4), 585–590.

Brockner, J., Siegel, P. A., Daly, J. P., et al. (1997). When trust matters: The moderating effect of outcome favorability. *Administrative Science Quarterly, 42*, 558–583.

Brodbeck, F. C., Frese, M., Akerblum, S., et al. (2000). Cultural variation of leadership prototypes across 22 Euopean countries. *Journal of Occupational & Organizational Psychology, 73*, 1–29.

Brodbeck, F. C., Frese, M., & Javidan, M. (2002). Leadership made in Germany: Low on compassion, high on performance. *Academy of Management Executive, 16*(1), 16–29.

Brodbeck, F. C., Frese, M., Reber, G., et al. (2000). Cultural variation of leadership prototypes across 22 European countries. *Journal of Occupational and Organizational Psychology, 73*, 1–29.

Brogden, H. E., & Thomas, W. F. (1943). The primary traits in personality items purporting to measure sociability. *Journal of Psychology, 16*, 85–97.

Broich, K. (1929). Fiffireranforderungen in der Kindergruppe. *Zeitschrift ffir angervarulte Psychologie, 32*, 164–212.

Brollier, C. L. (1984). Managerial leadership in hospital-based occupational therapy. *Dissertation Abstracts International, 45*(5B), 1433.

Broman, W. K. (1974). *The relationship of administrative processes to the innovativeness of public secondary schools*. Doctoral dissertation, State University of New York, Buffalo.

Bronfenbrenner, U. (1961). Some familial antecedents of responsibility and leadership in adolescents. In L. Petrullo & B. M. Bass (eds.), *Leadership and interpersonal behavior*. New York: Holt, Rinehart & Winston.

Brogdan, R., & Taylor, S. J. (1975). *Introduction to qualitative research methods.* New York: Wiley.

Bronson, G. (1997). Warden: An impossible job. In T. Clear & G. Cole (eds.). *American corrections* (4th ed.). Belmont, CA: Wadsworth.

Brookhiser, R. (2002). *America's first dynasty: The Adamses, 1735–1918.* New York: Free Press.

Brooks, D. (2003). The transformer. *Atlantic Monthly,* July–August, 27–29.

Brooks, E. (1955). What successful executives do. *Personnel, 32,* 210–225.

Brooks, J. H. (1999). *Personal characteristics and rater congruence in multi-rater feedback.* Paper, Society for Industrial and Organizational Psychology, Atlanta, GA.

Brooks, T. (1995). *Accountability: It all depends on what you mean.* Clifton, NJ: Akkad Press.

Brossoit, K. B. (2001). *Empowerment to work: The role of transformational leadership and relationships to work outcomes.* San Diego, CA: Society for Industrial and Organizational Psychology.

Brousseau, K.R., Driver, M., Eneroth, K., et al. (1996). Career pandemonium: Realigning organizations and individuals. *Academy of Management Executive, 10*(4), 52–88.

Broverman, I., Broverman, D. M., Clarkson, F., et al. (1970). Sex-role stereotypes and clinical judgments of mental health. *Journal of Consulting and Clinical Psychology, 34,* 1–7.

Brower, H. H., Schoorman, F. D., & Tan, H. H. (2000). A model of relationship: The integration of trust and leader-member exchange. *Leadership Quarterly, 11,* 227–250.

Brown, A. D., & Thornborrow, W. T. (1996). Do organizations get the followers they deserve? *Leadership & Organization Development Journal, 17*(1), 5–11.

Brown, A. F. (1967). Reactions to leadership. *Educational Administrative Quarterly, 3,* 62–73.

Brown, D. (1987). *Leadership and organization transformation: A competency model.* Doctoral dissertation, Fielding Institute, Santa Barbara, CA.

Brown, D. J., & Keeping, L. M. (1999). Examining the role of affect in transformational leadership.

Brown, D. J. & Lord, R.G. (1999). The utility of experimental research in the study of transformational/charismatic leadership. *Leadership Quarterly, 10,* 531–539.

Brown, D. S. (1964). Subordinates' views of ineffective executive behavior. *Academy of Management Journal, 7,* 288–299.

Brown, F. J. (2000). *Preparation of leaders* (IDA Document D-2382). Washington, DC: Institute for Defense Analyses.

Brown, F. W., & Moshavi, D. (2002). Herding academic cats: Faculty reactions to transformational and contingent reward leadership by department chairs. *Journal of Leadership Studies, 8,* 79–93.

Brown, H. A., & Ford, D. L., Jr. (1977). An exploratory analysis of discrimination in the employment of black MBA graduates. *Journal of Applied Psychology, 62,* 50–56.

Brown, J. F. (1936). *Psychology and the social order.* New York: McGraw-Hill.

Brown, J. (1993). *Leadership for change in secondary schools: A team effort.* Paper presented at the Annual Meeting of the American Educational Research Association, Atlanta, GA, April 12–16, 1993.

Brown, J. (1993). Leadership for school improvement. *Emergency Librarian, 20*(3), 8–20.

Brown, J. S. (1970). Risk propensity in decision making: A comparison of business and public school administrators. *Administrative Science Quarterly, 15,* 473–481.

Brown, K. A., & Mitchell, I. R. (1986). Influence of task interdependence and number of poor performers on diagnoses of causes of poor performance. *Academy of Management Journal, 29,* 412–424.

Brown, L. D., & Detterman, L. B. (1987). Small interventions for large problems: Reshaping urban leadership networks. *Journal of Applied Behavioral Science, 23,* 151–168.

Brown, M. (1933). *Leadership among high school principals.* New York: Teachers College Contribution to Education.

Brown, M. (1934). Leadership among high school pupils. *Teachers College Record, 35,* 324–326.

Brown, M. C. (1982). Administrative succession and organizational performance: The succession effect. *Administrative Science Quarterly, 27,* 1–16.

Brown, M. E. (2003). *The influence of leadership styles on unethical conduct in work groups: An empirical test.* Paper, Academy of Management, Seattle, WA.

Brown, M. E., & Gioia, D. A. (2002). Making things click: Distributive leadership in an online division of an offline organization. *Leadership Quarterly, 13,* 397–419.

Brown, M. E. & Trevino, L. K. (2002). Conceptualizing and measuring ethical leadership: Development of an instrument. *Academy of Management Proceedings, Social Issues in Management,* D1–D6, Denver, CO.

Brown, M. E., & Trevino, L. K. (2003). The influence of leadership styles on unethical conduct in work groups. *Academy of Management Proceedings, Social Issues in Management,* B1–B6, Seattle, WA.

Brown, S. C. (1931). Some case studies of delinquent girls described as leaders. *British Journal of Educational Psychology, 1,* 162–179.

Browne, C. G. (1949). A study of executive leadership in business. I. The R, A, and D scales. *Journal of Applied Psychology, 33,* 520–526.

Browne, C. G. (1950a). An exploration into the use of certain methods for the study of executive function in business. *Dissertation Abstracts, 58,* 51–57.

Browne, C. G. (1950b). Study of executive leadership in business. II. Social group patterns. *Journal of Applied Psychology, 34,* 12–15.

Browne, C. G (1950c). Study of executive leadership in business. III. Goal and achievement index. *Journal of Applied Psychology, 34,* 82–87.

Browne, C. G., & Neitzel, B. J. (1952). Communication, supervision, and morale. *Journal of Applied Psychology, 36,* 86–91.

Browne, M. A., & Mahoney, M. J. (1984). Sport psychology. *Annual Review of Psychology, 35,* 605–625.

Browne, R. J., & Golembiewski, R. T. (1974). The line-staff concept revisited: An empirical study of organizational images. *Academy of Management Journal, 17,* 406–417.

Browning, E. S. (1994). Side-by-side: Computer chip project brings rivals together, but the cultures clash. *Wall Street Journal,* May 3, A1, A8.

Browning, R. R., & Jacob, H. E. (1964). Power motivation and political personality. *Public Opinion Quarterly, 28*, 75–90.

Bruce, J. S. (1986). *The intuitive pragmatists: Conversations with chief executive officers* (Special Report). Greensboro, NC: Center of Creative Leadership.

Bruce, W., & Plocha, E. (1999). Reflections on maintaining a spirituality in the government workplace: What it means and how to do it. *International Journal of Organizational Theory and Behavior, 1999.*

Brungardt, C. (1996). The making of leaders: A review of the research in leadership development and education. *Journal of Leadership Studies, 3*(3), 81–95.

Bruns, G. H., & Shuman, I. G. (1988). Police managers' perceptions of organizational leadership styles. *Public Personnel Management, 17*(2), 145–157.

Brutus, S., Fleenor, J. W., & Taylor, S. (1996). *Methodological issues in 360-degree feedback research.* Paper, Society for Industrial and Organizational Psychology, San Diego, CA.

Brutus, S., McCauley, C. D., & Fleenor, J. W. (1996). Age and managerial effectiveness: Some interesting trends. *Issues & Observations, 16*(1), 1–2.

Bryans & Wilson (2000). *A view from the trenches: A manual for wardens by wardens.* A review by Morganbesser. NAAWS.

Bryant, G. W. (1968). Ideal leader behavior descriptions of appointed and sociometrically chosen student leaders. *Dissertation Abstracts, 28,* 3497.

Bryant, S. E. (2003). The role of transformational and transactional leadership in creating, sharing and exploiting organizational knowledge. *Journal of Leadership and Organizational Studies, 9*(4), 32–44.

Bryant, S. E., & Gurman, E. B. (1996). Contingent supervisory behavior: A practical predictor of performance. *Group & Organization Management, 21,* 404–413.

Bryk, A. S., & Rauderbush, S. W. (1989). Methodology for cross-cultural organizational research. *Research in the Sociology of Organizations, 7,* 233–273.

Bryk, A. S., & Raudenbush, S. W. (1992). *Hierarchical linear models.* Newbury Park, CA: Sage.

Bryman, A. (1992). *Charisma and leadership in organizations.* London: Sage.

Bryman, A. (1993). Charismatic leadership in business organizations: Some neglected issues. *Leadership Quarterly, 4,* 289–304.

Bryman, A. (2004). Qualitative research on leadership: A critical but appreciative review. *Leadership Quarterly, 15,* 729–770.

Bryman, A., Bresnen, M., Beardsworth, A., & Keil, T. (1988). Qualitative research and the study of leadership. *Human Relations, 4*(1), 13–30.

Bryson, J., & Kelley, G. (1978). A political perspective on leadership emergence, stability, and change in organizational networks. *Academy of Management Review, 3,* 712–723.

Bryson, K., & McKenna, K. (2002). A retention strategy for the ages. *Leadership in Action, 22*(4), 7–10.

Bu, N., Peng, T. K. & Craig, T. J. (2001). Employee reactions to supervisory direction in four types of firms in Taiwan: The effects of company policy, peer consensus, and independent assessment. *Asia-Pacific Journal of Management, 18*(1).

Buchan, I. H. (1998). Servant leadership: A model for future faculty and future institutions. *Journal of Leadership Studies, 5,* 128–131.

Buchanan, B. (1974). Government managers, business executives, and organizational commitment. *Public Administration Review, 34,* 339–347.

Buchanan, P. C., & Brunstetter, P. H. (1959). A research approach to management improvement. *Journal of the American Society of Training Directors, 13,* January 1959, 9–18; February, 18–27.

Buchholtz, A. K., Ribbens, B. A., & Boule, I. T. (2003) The role of human capital in postacquisition CEO departure. *Academy of Management Journal, 46,* 506–514.

Buckingham, M., & Clifton, D. O. (2001). *Now, discover your strengths.* New York: Free Press.

Buckley, W. F. (1979). Let's define that "leadership" that Kennedy says we need. *Press-Bulletin* (Binghamton, NY), September 22, 4A.

Buenstorf, G., & Murmann, J. P. (2003). *Ernst Abbe's Scientific Management: A 19th century forerunner of the resource-based theory?* Paper, Academy of Management, Seattle, WA.

Buerge, D. M. (2004). *Chief Seattle and Chief Joseph: From Indians to icons.* University of Washington Libraries Digital Collections. http://content.lib.washington.edu/aipnw/buerge2/html.

Bugental, D. E. (1964). A study of attempted and successful social influence in small groups as a function of goal-relevant skills. *Dissertation Abstracts, 25,* 660.

Bugental, J. F., & Lehner, G. F. J. (1958). Accuracy of self-perception and group-perception as related to two leadership roles. *Journal of Abnormal and Social Psychology, 56,* 396–398.

Bui, K. V. T., Raven, B. H., & Schwarzwald, J. (1994). Influence strategies in dating relationships: The effects of relationship satisfaction, gender and perspective. *Journal of Social Behavior and Personality, 9,* 429–442.

Buie, S., Jr. (1983). The emergence process of black elected leadership in North Carolina. *Dissertation Abstracts International, 44*(3A), 620.

Bullard, J. F. (1969). *An evaluation of the assessment center approach to selecting supervisors.* Peoria, IL: Caterpillar Tractor, Corporate Personnel.

Bullard, R. D., & Cook, P. E. (1975). Sex and workstyle of leaders and followers: Determinants of productivity. *Psychological Reports, 36*(2), 545–546.

Bullis, R. C., Kane, T., & Tremble, T. R. (1997). *Multifactor leadership; The factor structure of the Questionnaire (MLQ): An investigation across organizational levels.* Paper, Academy of Management, Boston.

Bunce, V. (1981). *Do new leaders make a difference?: Executive succession and public policy under capitalism and socialism.* Princeton, NJ: Princeton University Press.

Bundel, C. M. (1930). Is leadership losing its importance? *Infantry Journal, 36,* 339–349.

Bunderson, J. S. (2003). Team members functional background and involvement in management teams: Direct effects and the moderating role of power centralization. *Academy of Management Journal, 46,* 458–474.

Bunker, B. B. (1986). Management training in Japan: Lessons for America. *Proceedings, OD Network Conference,* New York.

Bunker, B., and Bender, L. (1980). How women compete: A guide for managers. *Management Review, 69*(8), 55–62.

Burda, P. C., & Vaux, A. C. (1987). The social support process in men: Overcoming sex-role obstacles. *Human Relations, 40,* 31–43.

Burdett, J. O. (1991). What is empowerment anyway? *Journal of Industrial Training, 15*(6), 23–30.

Bureau of Labor Statistics (2006). *Occupational Employment Statistics: All Occupations.* Updated: May 10, 2007.

Burgess, K. A., Riddle, D. D., Hall, J. K., et al. (1992). *Principles of team leadership under stress.* Paper, Southeastern Psychological Association, Knoxville, TN.

Burgess, K. A., Salas, E., Cannon-Bowers, J. A., et al. (1992). *Training guidelines for team leaders under stress.* Paper, Human Factors Society, Atlanta, GA.

Burgess, R. (1969). Communication networks and behavioral consequences. *Human Relations, 22,* 137–159.

Burgoyne, J. G., & Hodgson, V. E. (1984). An experiential approach to understanding managerial action. In J. G. Hunt, D. Hosking, C. A. Schriesheim, & R. Stewart (eds.), *Leaders and managers: International perspectives on managerial behavior and leadership.* New York: Pergamon.

Burke, C. S., Fiore, S. M., & Salas, E. (2002). The role of shared cognition in enabling shared leadership and team adaptability. In J. Conger & C. Pearse (eds.), *Shared leadership: Reframing the how's and why's of leadership.* Sage.

Burke, C. S., Stagl, K. C., Klein, C., et al. (2006). What type of leadership behaviors are functional in teams? A meta-analysis. *Leadership Quarterly, 17,* 288–307.

Burke, E. (1790). *Reflections on the revolution in France: And on the proceedings in certain societies in London.* Printed for J. Dodsley.

Burke, L. A., & Miller, M. K. (1999). Taking the mystery out of intuitive decision making. *Academy of Management Executive, 13*(4), 91–99.

Burke, P. J. (1966a). Authority relations and disruptive behavior in the small group. *Dissertation Abstracts, 26,* 4850.

Burke, P. J. (1966b). Authority relations and disruptive behavior in small discussion groups. *Sociometry, 29,* 237–250.

Burke, P. J. (1971). Task and social-emotional leadership role performance. *Sociometry, 34,* 22–40.

Burke, M. J., & Day, R. R. (1986). A cumulative study of the effectiveness of managerial training. *Journal of Applied Psychology, 71,* 232–246.

Burke, R. J. (1969). A plea for systematic evaluation of training. *Training & Development Journal, 23,* 24–29.

Burke, R. J. (1970) Methods of resolving superior-subordinate conflict: The constructive use of subordinate differences and disagreements. *Organizational Behavior and Human Performance, 5,* 393–411.

Burke, R. J., Weitzel, W., & Weir, T. (1978). Characteristics of effective employee performance review and development interviews: Replication and extension. *Personnel Psychology, 31,* 903–919.

Burke, R. J., & Wilcox, D. S. (1971). Bases of supervisory power and subordinate job satisfaction. *Canadian Journal of Behavioral Sciences, 3,* 183–193.

Burke, W. (1986). Leadership as empowering others. In S. Srivastra (ed.), *Executive power.* San Francisco: Jossey-Bass.

Burke, W., Richley, E. A., & DeAngelis, L. (1985). Changing leadership and planning processes at the Lewis Research Center, National Aeronautics and Space Administration. *Human Resource Management, 24*(1), 81–90.

Burke, W. W. (1965). Leadership behavior as a function of the leader, the follower, and the situation. *Journal of Personality, 33,* 60–81.

Burke, W. W. (1998). On leadership. *The Industrial-Organizational Psychologist, 35*(3), 60–61.

Burke, W. W., Trahant, W., & Koonce, R. (1999). *Business climate shifts: Profiles of change makers.* Boston: Butterworth Heinemann.

Burks, F. W. (1938). Some factors related to social success in college. *Journal of Social Psychology, 9,* 125–140.

Burnett, C. W. (1951b). Validating campus leadership. *Educational Research Bulletin, 30,* 67–73.

Burner, D. (1979). *Herbert Hoover.* New York: Knopf.

Burnham, J. (1941). *The managerial revolution.* Bloomington: Indiana University Press.

Burns, J. H. (1934). *Psychology and leadership.* Fort Leavenworth, KS: Command and General Staff School Press.

Burns, J. M. (1956). *Roosevelt: The lion and the fox.* New York: Harcourt Brace.

Burns, J. M. (1976). *The wellsprings of political leadership.* Presidential address, American Political Science Association, Chicago, IL.

Burns, J. M. (1978). *Leadership.* New York: Harper & Row, 3.

Burns, J. M. (1996). *Empowerment for change: A conceptual working paper.* College Park, MD: University of Maryland, Kellogg Leadership Studies Project.

Burns, J. M. (2003). *Transforming leadership: A new pursuit of happiness.* New York: Grove Press.

Burns, J. M., & Dunn, S. (2001). *The three Roosevelts: Patrician leaders who transformed America.* Boston: Atlantic Monthly Press.

Burns, J. M., & Sorenson, G. J. (2000). *Dead center: Clinton-Gore leadership and the perils of moderation.* New York: Scribner.

Burns, R. (1785/1974). To a louse (Stanza 8). *Poetical works of Burns.* Boston: Houghton-Mifflin.

Burns, T. (1954). The directions of activity and communication in a departmental executive group: A quantitative study in a British engineering factory with a self-recording technique. *Human Relations, 7,* 73–97.

Burns, T. (1957). Management in action. *Operational Research Quarterly, 8,* 45–60.

Burns, T., & Stalker, G. M. (1961). *The management of innovation.* Chicago: Quadrangle Books.

Burnside, R. M., & Guthrie, V. A. (1992). *Training for action: A new approach to executive development.* Report No. 153, Center for Creative Leadership, Greensboro, NC.

Burnstein, E. (1969). An analysis of group decision involving risk ("the risky shift"). *Human Relations, 22,* 381–395.

Burnstein, E., & Zajonc, R. B. (1965a). Individual task performance in a changing social structure. *Sociometry, 28,* 16–29.

Burnstein, E., & Zajonc, R. B. (1965b). The effect of group success on the reduction of status incongruence in task-oriented groups. *Sociometry, 28,* 349–362.

Burpitt, W. J., & Bigoness, W. J. (1997). Leadership and innovation among teams: The impact of empowerment. *Small Group Research, 28,* 414–423.

Burroughs, W. A. (1970). The study of white females' voting behavior toward two black female collaborators in a modified leaderless group discussion. *Dissertation Abstracts International, 30,* 5063.

Burt, J. M. (1984). Relationships between leadership behavior and employee absenteeism and turnover in community hospitals' departments. *Dissertation Abstracts International, 45*(6B), 1723.

Burwen, L. S., & Campbell, D. T. (1957a). A comparison of test scores and role-playing behavior in assessing superior vs. subordinate orientation. *Journal of Social Psychology, 46,* 49–56.

Busch, P. (1980). The sales manager's bases of social power and influence upon the salesforce. *Journal of Marketing, 44,* 91–101.

Busche, G. R. (1987). Temporary or permanent middle management groups?: Correlates with attitudes in QWL change projects. *Group & Organization Studies, 12,* 23–37.

Butler, D. C., & Miller, N. (1965). Power to reward and punish in social interaction.

Butler, J. K. (1991). Toward understanding and measuring conditions of trust: Evolution of a Condition of Trust Inventory. *Journal of Management, 17,* 643–663.

Butler, M. C., & Jones, A. P. (1979). Perceived leader behavior, individual characteristics, and injury occurrence in hazardous work environments. *Journal of Applied Psychology, 64,* 299–304.

Butt, D. S., & Fiske, D. W. (1968). Comparison of strategies in developing scales of dominance. *Psychological Bulletin, 70*(6), 505–19.

Butt, D. S., & Fiske, D.W. (1969). Differential correlates of dominance scales. *Journal of Personality, 37,* 415–428.

Butterfield, D. A., & Bartol, K. M. (1977). Evaluators of leader behavior: A missing element in leadership theory. In J. C. Hunt & L. L. Larson (eds.), *Leadership: The cutting edge.* Carbondale: Southern Illinois University Press.

Butterfield, D. A., & Powell, G. N. (1981). Effect of group performance, leader sex, and rater sex on ratings of leader behavior. *Organizational Behavior and Human Performance, 28,* 129–141.

Butterfield, D. A., & Powell, G. N. (1985). *Leadership in the public sector: Presidential candidates as chief executive officers.* Paper, Academy of Management, San Diego, CA.

Butterfield, K. D., Trevino, L. K., & Ball, G. A. (1996). Punishment from the manager's perspective: A grounded investigation and inductive model. *Academy of Management Journal, 39,* 1479–1512.

Buttgereit, H. (1932). Fiffirergestalten in der Schulklass. *Zeitschrift ffir angewardte Psychologie, 43,* 369–413.

Button, S. B. (2001). Organizational efforts to affirm sexual diversity: A cross-level examination. *Journal of Applied Psychology, 86,* 17–28.

Bychowski, G. (1948). *Dictators and disciples from Caesar to Stalin.* New York: International Universities Press.

Bycio, P. (1988). Exercise order and assessment center performance. *Proceedings, Academy of Management,* 264–267.

Bycio, P., Hackett, R. D., & Allen, J. S. (1995). Further assessments of Bass's (1985) conceptualization of transactional and transformational leadership. *Journal of Applied Psychology, 80,* 468–478.

Byrne, D. (1961). Interpersonal attraction and attitude similarity. *Journal of Abnormal and Social Psychology, 62,* 713–715.

Byrne, D. (1965). Authoritarianism and response to attitude similarity-dissimilarity. *Journal of Social Psychology, 66,* 251–256.

Byrne, D., & Griffitt, W. (1966a). A developmental investigation of the law of attraction. *Journal of Personality and Social Psychology, 4,* 699–703.

Byrne, D., & Griffitt, W. (1966b). Similarity versus liking: A clarification. *Psychonomic Science, 6,* 295–296.

Byrne, D., Griffitt, W., & Golightly, C. (1966). Prestige as a factor in determining the effect of attitude similarity-dissimilarity on attraction. *Journal of Personality, 34,* 434–444.

Byrne, J. A., & Zellner, W. (1988). Caught in the middle: Six managers speak out on corporate life. *Business Week,* September 12, 80–88.

Cader, J., Eby, L. T., Noble, C. L., et al. (1999). *Self-monitoring and leader emergence: A perceptual not a behavioral process.* Society for Industrial and Organizational Psychology, Atlanta, GA.

Cahill, I. D. (1967). Child-rearing practices in lower socioeconomic ethnic groups. *Dissertation Abstracts, 27*(9A), 31–39.

Calas, M. B. (1986). *The unavoidable contextual and cultural bases of attribution of leadership research: A literature/literary critique.* Chicago: Academy of Management.

Calas, M. B. (1993). Deconstructuring charismatic leadership: Rereading Weber from the darker side. *Leadership Quarterly, 4,* 305–328.

Calas, M. B., & Smircich, L. (1987). Reading leadership as a form of cultural analysis. In J. C. Hunt, B. R. Baliga, H. F. Dachler, & C. A. Schriesheim (eds.), *Emerging leadership vistas.* Lexington, MA: D.C. Heath.

Calder, B. J. (1977). An attribution theory of behavior. In B. M. Staw & G. R. Salancik (eds.), *New Directions in Organizational Behavior.* Chicago: St. Clair.

Caldwell, D. F., & O'Reilly, III (undated). *Matching individual skills to job requirements.* Unpublished manuscript.

Caldwell, O. W. (1920). Some factors in training for leadership. In *Fourth Yearbook, National Association of Secondary School Principals,* Washington, DC.

Caldwell, O. W., & Wellman, B. (1926). Characteristics of school leaders. *Journal of Educational Research, 14,* 1–15.

Caligiuri, P. M. (2000). The Big Five personality characteristic as predictors of expatriate's desire to terminate the assignment and supervisor-rated performance. *Personnel Psychology, 53,* 67–88.

Calloway, D. W. (1985). The promise and paradoxes of leadership. *Directors and Boards, 9*(2), 12–16.

Calori, R., Johnson, G., & Sarnin, P. (1994). CEO's cognitive maps and the scope of the organization. *Strategic Management Journal, 15,* 437–457.

Calori, R., Lubatkin, M., & Very, P. (1994). Control mechanisms in cross-border acquisitions. *Organizational Studies, 15,* 361–379.

Calvin, A. D., Hoffmann, F. K., & Harden, E. D. (1957). The effect of intelligence and social atmosphere on group problem-solving behavior. *Journal of Social Psychology, 45,* 61–74.

Cameron, K., & Caza, A. (2002). Organizational and leadership virtues and the role of forgiveness. *Journal of Leadership and Organizational Studies, 9*(1), 33.

Cameron, K. S., & Ulrich, D. O. (1986). Transformational leadership in colleges and universities. In J. C. Smart (ed.), *Higher education: Handbook of theory and research,* vol. 2. New York: Agathon Press.

Cammalleri, J. A., Hendrick, H. W., Pittman, W. C., Jr., et al. (1973). Effects of different leadership styles on group accuracy. *Journal of Applied Psychology, 57,* 32–37.

Cammann, C., & Nadler, D. A. (1976). Fit control systems to your managerial style. *Harvard Business Review, 54,* 65–72.

Campbell, A. (1991). Brief case: Strategy and intuition—A conversation with Henry Mintzberg. *Long Range Planning, 24,* 108–110.

Campbell, B. M. (1982). Black executives and corporate stress. *New York Times Magazine,* December 12, 100, 102, 104–107.

Campbell, C. R., & Martinko, M. J. (1998). An integrative attributional perspective and learned helplessness: A multimethod field study. *Journal of Management, 24,* 173–200.

Campbell, D. P. (1980). *If I'm in charge here why is everybody laughing?* Niles, IL: Argue Communications.

Campbell, D. (1987). *The psychological test profiles of brigadier generals: Warmongers or decisive warriors?* Paper, American Psychological Association, New York, NY.

Campbell, D. P. (1991). The challenge of assessing leadership characteristics. *Issues and Observations, 2*(2), 1–5.

Campbell, D. P. (1992). *The leadership characteristics of leadership researchers.* In K. E. Clark, M. B. Clark, & D. P. Campbell (eds.), *The impact of leadership.* Greensboro, NC: Center for Creative Leadership.

Campbell, D. J. (2000). The proactive employee: Managing workplace initiative. *Academy of Management Executive, 14*(3), 52–66.

Campbell, D. J., & Lee, C. (1988). Self-appraisal in performance evaluation: Development versus evaluation. *Academy of Management Review, 13*(2), 302–314.

Campbell, D. T. (1953). *A study of leadership among submarine officers.* Columbus: Ohio State University, Personnel Research Board.

Campbell, D. T. (1955). An error in some demonstrations of the superior social perceptiveness of leaders. *Journal of Abnormal and Social Psychology, 51,* 694–695.

Campbell, D. T. (1956). *Leadership and its effect upon the group.* Columbus: Ohio State University, Bureau of Business Research.

Campbell, D. T. (1991). The challenge of assessing leadership characteristics. *Issues and Observations, 2*(2), 1–5.

Campbell, D. T., Burwen, L. S., & Chapman, J. P. (1955). *Assessing attitudes toward superiors and subordinates through direct attitude statements.* Evanston, IL: Northwestern University, Department of Psychology.

Campbell, D. T., & Damarin, F. L. (1961). Measuring leadership attitudes through an information test. *Journal of Social Psychology, 55,* 159–176.

Campbell, D. T., & Fiske, D. W. (1959). Convergent and discriminant validation by the multi-trait multi-method matrix. *Psychological Bulletin, 55,* 81–105.

Campbell, D. T., & McCormack, T. H. (1957). Military experience and attitudes toward authority. *American Journal of Sociology, 62,* 482–490.

Campbell, E. (undated). *A sociometric study of day care children.* Unpublished manuscript.

Campbell, J. D. (1952). Subjective aspects of occupational status. *American Psychologist, 7,* 308.

Campbell, J. D., Trapnell, P. D., Heine, S. J., et al. (1996). Self-concept clarity: Measurement, personality correlates, and cultural boundaries. *Journal of Personality and Social Psychology, 70,* 141–156.

Campbell, J. J., Dunnette, M. D., Lawler, E. E., & Weick, K. E. (1970). *Managerial behavior, performance, and effectiveness.* New York: McGraw-Hill.

Campbell, J. P. (1977). The cutting edge of leadership. An overview. In J. C. Hunt & L. L. Larson (eds.), *Leadership: The cutting edge.* Carbondale: Southern Illinois University Press.

Campbell, J. P. (1982). Editorial: Some remarks from the outgoing editor. *Journal of Applied Psychology, 67,* 691–700.

Campbell, J. P., Dunnette, M. D., Lawler, E. E., & Weick, K. E. (1970). *Managerial behavior, performance, and effectiveness.* New York: McGraw-Hill.

Campbell, J. (2002). *Inner reaches of outer space: Metaphor as myth and as religion.* New York: New World Library.

Campbell, J., & Moyers, B. (1988). *The power of myth* (B. S. Flowers, ed.). New York: Doubleday.

Campbell, J., & Moyers, B. (1991). *The power of the myth.* Knopf. (Published in paperback on May 1, 1988. New York: Doubleday.)

Campbell, K. (1999). Various states of start-up business: Attitudes to entrepreneurialism differ between countries, a new study reports. *Financial Times,* June 22.

Campbell, L. (1983). Black women community leaders in the rural South: A study in power and influence. *Dissertation Abstracts International, 45*(2B), 719.

Campbell, M. V. (1958). *Self-role conflict among teachers and its relationship to satisfaction, effectiveness, and confidence in leadership.* Doctoral dissertation, University of Chicago, Chicago.

Campbell, O. L. (1961). The relations between eight situational factors and high and low scores on the leadership behavior dimensions of instructional supervisors. *Dissertation Abstracts, 22,* 786.

Campbell, R. J., & Bray, D. W. (1967). Assessment centers: An aid in management selection. *Personnel Administration, 30*(2), 6–13.

Campbell, R. J., Bray, D. W., & Grant, D. L. (1974). *Formative years in business: A long-term AT&T study of managerial lives.* New York: Wiley.

Campbell, R. J., Sessa, V. I., & Taylor, J. (1995). Choosing top leaders: Learning to do better. *Issues & Observations, 15* (4), 1–5

Campbell T. S., & Marino A. M., (1994). Myopic investment decisions and competitive labor markets. *International Economic Review, 35,* 855–875.

Campion, J. E. (1969). Effects of managerial style on subordinates' attitudes and performance in a simulated organization setting. *Dissertation Abstracts International, 30,* 881.

Campion, M. A., Cheraskin, L., & Stevens, M. J. (1994). Career-related antecedents and outcomes of job rotation. *Academy of Management Journal, 37,* 1518–1542.

Campion, M. A., & Mitchell, M. M. (1986). Management turnover. Experiential differences between former and current managers. *Personnel Psychology, 39,* 57–69.

Campion, M. A., Pappar, E. M., & Medsker, G. J. (1996). Relations between work team characteristics and effectiveness: A replication and extension. *Personnel Psychology, 49,* 429–452.

Cannella, A. A., & Lubatkin, M. (1993). Succession as a sociopolitical process: Internal impediments to outsider succession. *Academy of Management Journal, 36,* 763–793.

Cannella, A. A., Jr., & Monroe, M. J. (1997). Contrasting perspectives on strategic leaders: Toward a more realistic review of top managers. *Journal of Management, 23,* 213–237.

Cannella, A. A., & Rowe, W. G. (1995). Leader capabilities, succession and competitive context: A study of professional baseball teams. *Leadership Quarterly, 1995, 6,* 69–88.

Cannella, A. A., & Shen, W. (2001). So close and yet so far: Promotion versus exit for CEO heirs apparent. *Academy of Management Journal, 44,* 252–270.

Cannon, L. (1982). *Reagan.* New York: Putnam.

Capelle, M. H. (1967). Concurrent validation of the Leadership Opinion Questionnaire for college student leadership. *Dissertation Abstracts, 27,* 3607.

Capelli, P. (1992). Examining managerial displacement. *Academy of Management Journal, 35,* 203–217.

Caplan, E. H., & Landekich, S. (1974). *Human resource accounting: Past, present and future.* New York: National Association for Accountants.

Caplan, R. D., Cobb, S., French, J. R. R, Jr., Harrison, V., & Pinneau, S. R., Jr. (1975). *Job demands and workers' health,* Washington, DC: U.S. Government Printing Office.

Caplow, T. (1968). *Two against one: Coalitions in triads.* Englewood Cliffs, NJ: Prentice-Hall.

Caplow, T., & Forman, R. (1950). Neighborhood interaction in a homogeneous community. *American Sociological Review, 15,* 357–366.

Capozzoli, T. K. (1995). Managers and leaders: A matter of cognitive difference. *Journal of Leadership Studies, 2*(3), 20–29.

Caprera, G. V., & Zimbardo, P. G. (2004). Personalizing politics: A congruency model of political preferences. *American Psychologist, 59,* 581–594.

Carbone, T. C. (1981). Theory X and theory Y revisited. *Managerial Planning, 29*(6), 24–27.

Carbonell, J. L. (1984). Sex roles and leadership revisited. *Journal of Applied Psychology, 69,* 44–49.

Carey, D. C. (1997). Where the board drives succession planning. *Directors and Boards, 21*(3), 54–56.

Carey, M. R. (1992). Transformational leadership and the fundamental option for self-transcendence. *Leadership Quarterly, 3,* 217–236, p. 217.

Carl, D. E. (1999). *The robustness of charismatic leadership as a universal paradigm.* Doctoral dissertation, University of Calgary, Calgary, Alberta, Canada.

Carl, D. E., & Javidan, M. (2002). *Universality of charismatic leadership.* Paper, Academy of Management, Denver, CO.

Carl, J., & Stokes, G. (1991). Ordinary people, extraordinary organizations. *Nonprofit World, 9*(6), 21–26.

Carless, S. A. (1995). *Transformational leadership and Australian bank managers.* Doctoral dissertation, University of Melbourne, Australia.

Carless, S. A. (1998). Gender differences in transformational leadership: An examination of superior, leader and subordinate perspectives. *Sex Roles, 39,* 887–902.

Carless, S. A. (2001). Assessing the discriminant validity of the Leadership Practices Inventory. *Journal of Occupational & Organizational Psychology, 74,* 233–239.

Carless, S. A., Mann. L., & Wearing, A. (1995). *An empirical test of the transformational leadership model.* Paper, Inaugural Australian Industrial and Organizational Psychology Conference, Melbourne.

Carli, L. L. (1990). Gender, language, and influence. *Journal of Personality and Social Psychology, 59,* 941–9515.

Carlopio, J. R. (1994). Holism: A philosophy of organizational leadership for the future. *Leadership Quarterly, 5,* 297–307.

Carlson, D. S., Kacmar, K. M., & Wadsworth, L. L. (2001). The impact of moral intensity dimensions on ethical decision making: Assessing the relevance or orientation. *Journal of Managerial Issues, 14*(1), 15.

Carlson, E. R. (1960). Clique structure and member satisfaction in groups. *Sociometry, 23,* 327–337.

Carlson, H. B., & Harrell, W. (1942). An analysis of *Life's* "ablest congressman" poll. *Journal of Social Psychology, 15,* 153–158.

Carlson, P. J., & Burke, F. (1998). Lessons learned from ethics in the classroom: Exploring student growth in flexibility, complexity, and comprehension. *Journal of Business Ethics, 17,* 1179–1187.

Carlson, R. E., & James, L. R. (1971). *Sampling managerial behavior: A functional time analysis.* Life Insurance Agency Management Association. Unpublished report.

Carlson, R. O. (1961). Succession and performance among school superintendents. *Administrative Science Quarterly, 6,* 210–227.

Carlson, S. (1951). *Executive behavior: A study of the workload and working methods of managing directors:* Stockholm, Sweden: Strombergs.

Carlyle, T. (1841/1907). *Heroes and hero worship.* Boston: Adams.

Carmel, E., & Bird, B. J. (1997). Small is beautiful: A study of packaged software development teams. *Journal of High Technology Management Research, 8,* 129–148.

Carney, R. W. (1982). A call for authority. *Management World, 11*(10), 41–44.

Caro, R. A. (1982). *The Years of Lyndon Johnson.* Vol. 1: *The Path to Power.* New York: Knopf.

Caro, R. A. (1982). *The Years of Lyndon Johnson.* Vol. 2: *Means of Ascent.* New York: Knopf.

Carp, F. M., Vitola, B. M., & McLanathan, F. L. (1963). Human relations knowledge and social distance set in supervisors. *Journal of Applied Psychology, 47,* 78–80.

Carpeno, L. (1976). Expectations of male/female leadership styles in an educational setting. *Dissertation Abstracts International, 37,* 1482.

Carr, R. W. (1971). *A study of the job satisfaction of high school principals.* Doctoral dissertation, University of Michigan, Ann Arbor.

Carrier, H. D. (1984). An empirical investigation of the competing values of leadership. *Dissertation Abstracts International, 45*(3B), 1051.

Carroll, A. (2004). Pressure may force ethical hand. *Athens Banner-Herald,* October 24. Reprinted in *BGS International Exchange,* Fall, 5.

Carroll, G. R., & Teo, A. C. (1996). On the social networks of managers. *Academy of Management Journal, 39,* 421–440.

Carroll, L. B. (1865). *Through the looking glass.* London: Macmillan.

Carroll, S. J. (1987). *Gender difference and the contemporary leadership crisis.* Paper, Wingspread Seminar on Leadership Research, Racine, WI.

Carroll, S. J., & Gillen, D. J. (1987). Are the classical management functions useful in describing managerial work? *Academy of Management Review, 12,* 38–51.

Carroll, S. J., & Taylor, W. H. (1968). The study of the validity of a self-observational central-signaling method of work sampling. *Personnel Psychology, 21,* 359–364.

Carroll, S. J., & Taylor, W. H. (1969). Validity of estimates by clerical personnel of job time estimates. *Journal of Applied Psychology, 53,* 164–166.

Carron, A. V., & Chelladurai, P. (1978). Psychological factors and athletic success: An analysis of coach-athlete interpersonal behaviour. *Canadian Journal of Applied Sport Sciences, 3,* 43–50.

Carson, A. (1985). Participatory management beefs up the bottom line. *Personnel, 4*(7), 45–48.

Carson, C. (1987). Martin Luther King, Jr: Charismatic leadership in a mass struggle. *Journal of American History, 74,* 448–454.

Carson, J. O., & Schultz, R. E. (1964). A comparative analysis of the junior college dean's leadership behavior. *Journal of Experimental Education, 32,* 355–362.

Carsten, K. W. D., Evers, Beersma, et al. (2001). A theory-based measure of conflict management strategies in the workplace. *Journal of Organizational Behavior, 22,* 645–668.

Carsten, K. W. D., & Weingart, L. R. (2002). *Task versus relationship conflict, team performance, and team member satisfaction.* Paper, Academy of Management, Denver, CO.

Carter, L. F. (1953). Leadership and small group behavior. In M. Sherif & M. O. Wilson (eds.), *Group relations at the crossroads.* New York: Harper.

Carter, L. F., Haythorn, W., & Howell, M. (1950). A further investigation of the criteria of leadership. *Journal of Abnormal and Social Psychology, 45,* 350–358.

Carter, L. F., Haythorn, W., Meirowitz, B., & Lanzetta, J. T. (1951). The relation of categorizations and ratings in the observation of group behavior. *Human Relations, 4,* 239–254.

Carter, L. F., Haythorn, W., Shriver, B., & Lanzetta, J. T. (1951). The behavior of leaders and other group members. *Journal of Abnormal and Social Psychology, 46,* 589–595.

Carter, L. F., & Nixon, M. (1949a). An investigation of the relationship between four criteria of leadership ability for three different tasks. *Journal of Psychology, 27,* 245–261.

Carter, L., & Nixon, M. (1949b). Ability, perceptual, personality, and interest factors associated with different criteria for leadership. *Journal of Psychology, 27,* 377–388.

Cartwright, D. (1951). Achieving change in people: Some applications of group dynamics theory. *Human Relations, 4,* 381–393.

Cartwright, D. (1959a). A field theoretical conception of power. In D. Cartwright (ed.), *Studies in social power.* Ann Arbor: University of Michigan, Institute for Social Research.

Cartwright, D. (1959b). *Studies in social power.* Ann Arbor, MI: University of Michigan, Institute for Social Research.

Cartwright, D. (1965). Influence, leadership, control. In J. G. March (ed.), *Handbook of organizations.* Chicago: Rand McNally.

Cartwright, D., & Zander, A. (1960). *Group dynamics: Research and theory.* Evanston, IL: Row, Peterson.

Cartwright, T. (2004). Feeling your way: Enhancing leadership through intuition. *Leadership in Action, 24*(2), 8–9.

Caruso, D. R., Mayer, J. D., & Salovey, P. (2002). Emotiopnal intelligence and emotional leadership. In R. E. Riggio, S. E. Murphy, & F. J. Pirozzzolo (eds.), *Multiple intelligences and leadership.* Mahwah, NJ: Lawrence Erlbaum Associates.

Carzo, R., & Yanouzas, J. N. (1969). Effects of flat and tall organization structure. *Administrative Science Quarterly, 14,* 178–191.

Cascio, W. F. (1995–1995a). *Guide to responsible structuring.* Washington, DC: U.S. Department of Labor, Office of the American Workplace.

Cascio, W. F. (1995b). Whither industrial and organizational psychology in a changing world of work. *American Psychologist, 50,* 928–939.

Cascio, W. F. (1998). The virtual workplace: A reality now. *The Industrial-Organizational Psychologist, 35*(4), 32–36.

Cascio, W. F. (2000). Managing a virtual workplace. *Academy of Management Executives, 14*(3), 81–90.

Cascio, W. F. (2000). The changing world of work: Preparing yourself for the road ahead. In J. M. Kummerow (ed.), *New Directions in Career Planning and the Workplace* (2nd ed.). Palo Alto, CA: Davies-Black Publishing.

Cascio, W. F. (2001). Knowledge creation for practical solutions appropriate to a changing world of work. *SA Journal of Industrial Psychology, 27*(4), 14–16.

Cascio, W. F. (2003). Responsible restructuring: Seeing employees as assets, not costs. *Ivey Business Journal,* November/December 2003, reprint # 9B03TF06.

Cascio, W. F., & Ramos, R. A. (1986). Development and application of a new method for assessing job performance in behavioral/economic terms. *Journal of Applied Psychology, 71,* 20–28.

Cascio, W. F., & Shurygailo, S. (2002). E-leadership and virtual teams. *Organizational Dynamics, 31,* 362–376.

Cascio, W. F., & Sibley, V. (1979). The utility of the assessment center as a selection device. *Journal of Applied Psychology, 64,* 107–118.

Case, C. M. (1933). Leadership and conjuncture. *Sociology and Social Research, 17,* 510–513.

Case, S. S. (1985). A sociolinguistic analysis of the language of gender relations, deviance, and influence on managerial groups (intergroup language differences). *Dissertation Abstracts International, 46*(7A), 2006.

Casey, T. J. (1975). The development of a leadership orientation scale on the SVIB for women. *Measurement and Evaluation Guide, 8,* 96100.

Cash, T. F., Gillen, B., & Burns, D. S. (1977). Sexism and "beautyism" in personnel consultant decision making. *Journal of Applied Psychology, 29,* 80–85.

Cashman, J., Dansereau, F., Graen, G., et al. (1976). Organizational understructure and leadership: A longitudinal investigation of the managerial role-making process. *Organizational Behavior and Human Performance, 15,* 278–296.

Cashman, J. F., & Snyder, R. A. (1980). Perceptions of leaders' behavior: Situational and personal determinants. *Psychological Reports, 46,* 615–624.

Cashman, K. (1998). *Leadership from the inside out.* Provo, UT: Executive Excellence Publishing.

Casimir, G. (2001). Combinative aspects of leadership style: The ordering and temporal spacing of leadership behaviors. *Leadership Quarterly, 12,* 245–278.

Cassel, R. N., & Stancik, E. J. (1982). *The leadership ability evaluation-revised: Manual.* Los Angeles: Western Psychological Services.

Cassens, F. P. (1966a). Cross cultural dimensions of executive life history antecedents (biographical information). *Dissertation Abstracts, 27,* 291.

Cassens, F. P. (1966b). *Cross cultural dimensions of executive life history antecedents (biographical information).* Greensboro, NC: Creativity Research Institute, Richardson Foundation.

Casserly, J. J. (1977). *The Ford White House: The diary of a speech writer.* Boulder, CO: Colorado Associated University Press.

Castaldi, R. M. (1982). An analysis of the work roles of chief executive officers in small furniture manufacturing firms. *Dissertation Abstracts International, 44*(4A), 1184.

Castaldi, R. M., & Soerjanto, T. (1988). *Post-Confucianism management practices and behaviors: A comparison of Japan versus China and South Korea.* Paper, Western Academy of Management, Big Sky, MT.

Castro, S. L. (2002). Data analytic methods for the analysis of multilevel questions: A comparison of intraclass correlation coefficients, rwg[J], hierarchical linear modeling, within—and between—analysis, and random group resampling. *Leadership Quarterly, 13,* 69–93.

Catalyst. (1996). *Women in corporate leadership: Progress and prospects.* New York: Catalyst.

Catanyag, D. V. (1995). *Effects of the transformational leadership behaviors of public secondary school principals in the national capital region on school effectiveness.* Doctoral dissertation, University of the Philippines, Manila.

Cattell, R. B. (1942). The concept of social status. *Journal of Social Psychology, 15,* 293–308.

Cattell, R. B. (1946). *Description and measurement of personality.* New York: World Book.

Cattell, R. B. (1950). *Personality: A systematic theoretical and factual study.* New York: McGraw-Hill.

Cattell, R. B. (1951). New concepts for measuring leadership in terms of group syntality. *Human Relations, 4,* 161–184.

Cattell, R. B. (1953). On the theory of group learning. *Journal of Social Psychology, 37,* 27–52.

Cattell, R. B. (1957). A mathematical model for the leadership role and other personality-role relations. In M. Sherif & M. O. Wilson (eds.), *Emerging problems in social psychology.* Norman: University of Oklahoma.

Cattell, R. B. (1980). *Handbook for the Sixteen Personality Factor Questionnaire.* Champaign, IL: Institute for Personality and Ability Testing.

Cattell, R. B., & Stice, G. F. (1954). Four formulae for selecting leaders on the basis of personality. *Human Relations, 7,* 493–507.

Cattell, R. B., Saunders, D. R., & Stice, C. F. (1953). The dimensions of syntality in small groups. *Human Relations, 6,* 331–356.

Cattell, R. B., Saunders, D. R., & Stice, G. F. (1957). *The sixteen personality factors questionnaire.* Champaign, IL: Institute for Personality and Ability Testing.

Caudrea, P. A. (1975). Investigation of sex differences across job levels. *Dissertation Abstracts International, 36,* 1957

Caudron, C. (1995). Open the corporate closet to sexual orientation issues. *Personnel Journal, 74*(8), 42–47.

Caulkin, S. (1993). Incentive pay—the management myth. *New Zealand Herald,* December 21, Section 1, 8. (Originally in the London *Observer.*) Also see A. Kohn (1993).

Cauldron, S. (1998). Keeping team conflict alive. *Training and Development,* September, 48–52.

Cavenaugh, M. S., Goldberg, A., & Larson, C. (1979). *Power Orientation Scale.* Denver, CO: University of Denver, Department of Speech.

Cawley, B. D., Keeping, L. M., & Levy, P. E. (1998). Participation in the performance appraisal process and employee reactions: A meta-analytic review of field investigations. *Journal of Applied Psychology, 83,* 615–633.

Ceballos, A. (1999). Leadership issues. *The Mezzanine.* September–October, 1–5.

Cederblom, D. (1982). The performance appraisal interview: A review, implications and suggestions. *Academy of Management Review, 7,* 219–227.

Cell, C. F. (1974). Charismatic heads of state: The social context. *Behavioral Science Research, 4,* 255–304.

Centers, R. (1948). Motivational aspects of occupational stratification. *Journal of Social Psychology, 28,* 187–217.

Certo, S. T., Lester, R. H., Daily, C. A., et al. (2003). *Meta-analysis of top management team demographics: Do top executives matter?* Paper, Academy of Management, Seattle, WA.

Chacko, H. E. (1990). Methods of upward influence, motivational needs, and administrators' perceptions of their supervisors, leadership styles. *Group & Organizational Studies, 15,* 253–265.

Chacko, T. J. (1982). Women and equal employment opportunity: Some unintended effects. *Journal of Applied Psychology, 67,* 119–123.

Chafetz, J. S., & Dworkin, A. G. (1984). Work pressure similarity for homemakers, managers and professionals. Free Inquiry in *Creative Sociology, 12*(1), 47–50.

Chaffee, E. E. (1985). Three models of strategy. *Academy of Management Review, 10,* 89–98.

Chafee, E. E. (1987). *Variations on a theme: Leadership.* Paper, Association for the Study of Higher Education, Baltimore.

Chaganti, R., & Sambharya, R. (1987). Research notes and communications: Strategic orientation and characteristics of upper management., *Strategic Management Journal, 8,* 393–401.

Chaganti, R., Watts, A. D., Chaganti, R., et al. (2003). *Ethnicity and new ventures: Prospector strategy and performance of Internet-based IPOs.* Paper, Academy of Management, Seattle, WA.

Chah, D. O., & Locke, E. (1996). Correlates of leadership effectiveness in the United States and Korea. *Current Topics in Management, 1,* 201–223.

Chakravarthy, B., & Gargiulo, M. (1998). Maintaining leadership legitimacy in the transition to new organizational forms. *Journal of Management Studies, 35,* 437–456.

Challenger, J. A. (1998). There is no future for the workplace. *The Futurist,* October16–18.

Chambers, P. (1974). No easy path for women managers. *International Management, 2,* 46–48.

Chan, K., & Drasgow, R. (2001). Toward a theory of individual differences and leadership: Understanding the motivation to lead. *Journal of Applied Psychology, 86,* 481–498.

Chan, S. (1991). *Asian Americans: Interpretive history*. Boston, MA: Twayne Publishers.

Chandler, A. D., Jr. *The visible hand: The managerial revolution in American business*. Cambridge, MA: Harvard University Press.

Chandler, A. D. (1956). Management decentralization: A historical analysis. *Business History Review, 30*, 111–174.

Chandler, A. D., Jr. (1962). *Strategy and structure: Chapters in the history of the industrial enterprises*. Cambridge, MA: M.I.T. Press.

Chandler, C., & Tolbert, K. (2000). In a changing Japan, echoes of the U.S. on competition and profits. *International Herald Tribune*, January 4, 11.

Chaney, F. B. (1966). A cross-cultural study of industrial research performance. *Journal of Applied Psychology, 50*, 206–210.

Chang, C. H., & Rosen, C. C. (2003). *A meta-analytic review of perceived organizational politics and its outcomes*. Paper presented at the meeting of the Society for Industrial and Organizational Psychology, Orlando, FL, April.

Chang, M. (1982). *A re-examination of Weber's theory of charismatic authority: The case of Mao Tse-tung and the Chinese Communist Party*. Paper, North Central Sociological Association Conference.

Chanin, M. N., & Schneer, J. A. (1984). A study of the relationship between Jungian personality dimensions and conflict-handling behavior. *Human Relations, 37*, 863–879.

Chapin, F. S. (1924a). Socialized leadership. *Social Forces, 3*, 57–60.

Chapin, F. S. (1924b). Leadership and group activity. *Journal of Applied Sociology, 8*, 141–145.

Chapin F. S. (1945). *Community leadership and opinion in Red Wing*. Minneapolis: University of Minnesota Press.

Chapin, F. S., & Tsouderos, J. E. (1955). Formalization observed in ten voluntary associations: Concepts, morphology, process. *Social Forces, 33*, 306–309.

Chapman, G. B., & McCauley, C. (1993). Early career achievements of National Science Foundation (NSF) graduate applicants: Looking for Pygmalion and Galetea effects on NSF winners. *Journal of Applied Psychology, 78*, 815–820.

Chapman, J. B. (1975). Comparison of male and female leadership styles. *Academy of Management Journal, 18*, 645–650.

Chapman, J. B., & Luthans, F. (1975). The female leadership dilemma. *Public Personnel Management, 4*, 173–179.

Chapman, L. J., & Campbell, D. T. (1957a). An attempt to predict the performance of three-man teams from attitude measures. *Journal of Social Psychology, 46*, 277–286.

Chapman, L. J., & Campbell, D. T. (1957b). Response set in the F scale. *Journal of Abnormal and Social Psychology, 54*, 129–132.

Chapman, M., & Antoniou, C. (2003). *Gifts, favors, trust and transaction costs in Greek business*. Paper, Academy of Management, Seattle, WA.

Chapple, E. D., & Donald, G., Jr. (1946). A method of evaluating supervisory personnel. *Harvard Business Review, 24*, 197–214.

Charon, R., Drotter, S., & Noel, J. (2001). *The leadership pipeline: How to build the leadership-powered company*. San Francisco: Jossey-Bass.

Charon, R., Rosen, N., & Abarbanel, J. (1991). *Energizing the corporation through organizational information*. Unpublished manuscript.

Chassie, M. B. (1984). Vertical dyadic linkage information: Predictors and processes determining quality superior-subordinate relationships. *Dissertation Abstracts International, 46*(IA), 199.

Chatman, J. A., & Barsade, S. G. (1995). Personality, organizational culture, and cooperation: Evidence from a business simulation. *Administrative Science Quarterly, 40*, 423–443.

Chee, K. (2002). *Growing differentiated leaders at Microsoft Corporation*. Paper, Society for Industrial and Organizational Psychology, Toronto.

Cheek, S. K. (1987). *Recent state initiatives: The governor as policy leader: The governor as chief administrator*. Paper, Academy of Management, New Orleans.

Chelladurai, P., & Saleh, S. D. (1980). Dimensions of leader behavior in sports: Development of a leadership scale. *Journal of Sport Psychology, 2*(1), 34–45.

Chemers, M. M. (1969). Cross-cultural training as a means for improving situational favorableness. *Human Relations, 22*, 531–546.

Chemers, M. M. (1993). An integrative theory of leadership. In M. M. Chemers & R. Ayman, (eds.), *Leadership theory and research: Perspectives and directions*. New York: Academic Press.

Chemers, M. M. (1994). *A theoretical framework for examining the effects of cultural differences on leadership*. Paper, International Congress of Applied Psychology, Madrid, Spain.

Chemers, M. M., & Ayman, R. (1993). *Leadership theory and research: Perspectives and directions*. New York: Academic Press.

Chemers, M. M., Rice, R. W., Sundstrom, E., & Butler, W. (1975). Leader esteem for the least preferred co-worker score, training, and effectiveness: An experimental examination. *Journal of Personality and Social Psychology, 31*, 401–409.

Chemers, M. M., & Skrzypek, G. J. (1972). Experimental test of the contingency model of leadership effectiveness. *Journal of Personality and Social Psychology, 24*, 172–177.

Chemers, M. M., Watson, C. B., & May, S. T. (2000). Dispositional affect and leadership effectiveness: A comparison of self esteem, optimism, and efficacy. *Personality and Social Psychology Bulletin, 26*, 267–277.

Chen, C. C., Chen, X.-P., & Meindl, J. R. (1998). How can cooperation be fostered? The cultural effects of individualism-collectivism. *Academy of Management Review, 23*, 285–304.

Chen, C. C., Choi, J., and Chi, S. (2002). Making justice sense of local-expatriate compensation disparity: Mitigation by local referents, ideological explanations, and interpersonal sensitivity in China-foreign joint ventures. *Academy of Management Journal, 45*(4), 807–817.

Chen, C. C., & Van Velsor, E. (1996). New directions for research and practice in diversity leadership. *Leadership Quarterly, 7*, 285–302.

Cheng, Y. C. (1994). Teacher leadership style: A classroom-level study: *Journal of Educational Administration, 32*(2), 54–71.

Cherniss, C., & Goleman, D. (eds.). (2001). *The emotionally intelligent workplace: How to select for, measure, and improve emotional intelligence in individuals, groups, and organizations*. San Francisco: Jossey-Bass.

Cherns, A. (1976). The principles of sociotechnical design. *Human Relations, 29*, 783–792.

Cherry, C., & Isgar, R. (1998). Leadership education in the context of the new millennium. *Concepts & Connections: A Newsletter for Leadership Educators, 6*(1), 5–11.

Cherulnik, P. D., Donley, K. A., Tay, Wiewel, T. S. R., et al. (2001). Charisma is contagious: The effect of leader's charisma on observer's affect. *Journal of Applied Social Psychology, 31,* 2149–2159.

Chesanow, N. (1984). Getting cultured: Class acts for foreign-bound. *Savvy,* April, 72–77.

Chesterfield, R., & Ruddle, K. (1976). A case of mistaken identity: Ill-chosen intermediaries in a Venezuelan agricultural extension programme. *Community Development journal, 11,* 53–59.

Cheung, G. W. (1999). Multifaceted conceptions of self-other disagreement. *Personnel Psychology, 52,* 1–36.

Chevaleva-Ianovskaia, E., & Sylla, D. (1929). Essai d'une étude sur les enfants meneurs. *Journal of Psychology, 26,* 604–612.

Chhokar, J. S., & Wallin, J. A. (1984). A field study of the effect of feedback frequency on performance. *Journal of Applied Psychology, 69,* 524–530.

Child, J. (1974). Managerial and organizational factors associated with company performance. *Journal of Management Studies, 11,* 13–27.

Child, J., & Ellis, T. (1973). Predictors of variation in managerial roles. *Human Relations, 26,* 227–250.

Child, J., Pearce, S., & King, L. (1980). Class perceptions and social identification of industrial supervisors. *Sociology, 14,* 363–399.

Chiles, A. M., & Zorn, T. E. (1995). Empowerment in organizations: Employees' perceptions on the influences on empowerment *Journal of Applied Communication Research, 23,* 1–25.

Chin, C. O., Gu, J., & Tubbs, S. L. (2001). Developing global leadership competencies. *Journal of Leadership Studies, 7*(4), 20–31.

Chinese Culture Connection. (1997). Chinese values and the search for culture-free dimensions of culture. *Journal of Cross-Cultural Psychology, 18,* 143–164.

Chisister, J. (1992). *The rule of Benedict: Insight for the ages.* New York: Crossroads.

Chitayat, G., & Venezia, J. (1984). Determinants of management styles in business and nonbusiness organizations. *Journal of Applied Psychology, 69,* 437–447.

Chittister, J. (1992). *The rule of Benedict: Insight for the ages.* New York: Crossroads.

Chiu, J. C. (1997). *Transformational and transactional leadership in a collectivist context.* Paper, Academy of Management, Boston, MA.

Chodorow, N. (1978). *The reproduction of mothering: Psychoanlysis and the sociology of gender.* Berkeley: University of California Press.

Chodorow, N. (1985). Gender, relation, and difference in psychoanalytic perspective. In H. B. Eisenstein & A. Jardine (eds.), *The future of difference.* New Brunswick, NJ: Rutgers University Press.

Chodorow, N. J. (1985). Beyond drive theory: Object relations and the limits of radical individualism. *Theory & Society, 14*(3), 271.

Choi, T.Y, & Behling, O.C (1997). Top managers and team success: One more look after all these years. *Academy of Management Executive, 11,* 37–47.

Choi, Y., & Mai-Dalton, R. (1998). On the leadership function of self-sacrifice. *Leadership Quarterly, 9,* 475–501.

Choi, Y., & Mai-Dalton, R. R. (1999). The model of followers' responses to self-sacrificial leadership: An empirical test. *Leadership Quarterly, 10,* 397–421.

Chong, L. M. A., & Thomas, D. C. (1997). Leadership perceptions in cross-cultural context. *Leadership Quarterly, 8,* 275–293.

Chow, E. N., & Crusky, O. (1980). Productivity, aggressiveness, and supervisory style. *Sociology and Social Research, 65,* 23–36.

Chowdhry, K., & Newcomb, T. W. (1952). The relative abilities of leaders and nonleaders to estimate opinions of their own groups. *Journal of Abnormal and Social Psychology, 47,* 51–57.

Chowdhry, K., & Pal, A. D. (1960). Production planning and organizational morale. In J. A. Rubenstein & C. J. Haberstroh (eds.), *Some theories of organization.* Homewood, IL: Dorsey.

Chowdhry, K., & Tarneja, R. (1961). India. In *Developing better managers: An eight-nation study.* New York: National Industrial Conference Board.

Christie, P., Lessem, R., & Mbigi, L. (1993). *African management philosophies, concepts and appliations.* Randburg, South Africa: Knowledge Resources.

Christie, R. (1952). Changes in authoritarianism as related to situational factors. *American Psychologist, 7,* 307–308.

Christie, R. (1954). Authoritarianism re-examined. In R. Christie & M. Jahoda (eds.), *Studies in the scope and method of "The Authoritarian Personality."* New York: Free Press.

Christie, R., & Cook, R. (1958). A guide to published literature relating to the authoritarian personality through 1956. *Journal of Psychology, 45,*171–179.

Christie, R., & Geis, F. (1970). *Studies in Machiavellianism.* New York: Academic Press.

Christner, C. A., & Hemphill, J. K. (1955). Leader behavior of B-29 commanders and changes in crew members' attitudes toward the crew. *Sociometry, 18,* 82–87.

Chun, R. (2003). *The positioning of global 500 firms' ethical character: Japan, US, and UK.* Paper, Academy of Management, Seattle, WA.

Chung, K. H., Lubotkin, M., Rogers, R. C., et al. (1987). Do insiders make better CEO's than outsiders? *Academy of Management Executive, 1,* 323–329.

Chung, K. S. (1970). *Teacher-centered management style of public school principals and job satisfaction of teachers.* ERIC Document Reproduction Service (Ms. No. ED042–259).

Church, A. H. (1998). From both sides now: Leadership—So close and yet so far. *Industrial-Organizational Psychologist, 35*(3), 57–69

Church, A. H. (1997). Do you see what I see? An exploration of congruence in ratings from multiple perspectives. *Journal of Applied Social Psychology, 27*(11), 983–1020.

Church, A. H. (2002). Does method matter?: On-line vs. paper effects in multisource (360-degree). feedback. Paper, Academy of Management, Denver, CO.

Church, A. H., Rogelberg, S. G., & Waclawski, J. (2000). Since when is no news, good news? The relationship between performance and response rates. *Personnel Psychology, 53,* 435–451.

Church, A. H., & Waclawski, J. (1993). Making multirater feedback systems work. *Organizational Dynamics, 21*(3), 46–58.

Church, A. H., & Waclawski, J. (1996). *The impact of leadership style on global management practices.* Unpublished paper.

Churchill, W. (1998). The crucible of American Indian identity: Native tradition versus colonial imposition in postconquest North America.

Z Magazine: A Political Monthly. www.zmag.org/Zmag?articles/jan98ward.htm

Cialdini, R. B. (2001). *Influence: Science and practice* (4th ed.). Boston, MA: Allyn & Bacon.

Cialdini, R. B., Petty, R. E., & Cacioppo, J. T. (1981). Attitude and attitude change. *Annual Review of Psychology, 32,* 357–404.

Cialdini, R. B., Sagarin, B. J., & Rice, W. E. (2001). Training in ethical influence. In J. Darley, D. Messick, and T. Tyler (eds.), *Social influences on ethical behavior in organizations.* Mahwah, NJ: Erlbaum, 137–153.

Ciulla, J. B. (1995). Leadership ethics: Mapping the territory. *Business Ethics Quarterly, 5,* 5–28.

Ciulla, J. B. (1996). Ethics and critical thinking in leadership education. *Journal of Leadership Studies, 3*(3), 110–119.

Ciulla, J. B. (ed.). (1998, 2004). *Ethics, the heart of leadership.* Westport, CT: Praeger.

Ciulla, J. B. (1998, 2004). Leadership ethics: Mapping the territory. In Ciulla, J. B. *Ethics: The heart of leadership.* Westport, CT: Praeger.

Ciulla, J. B. (2004). Ethics and leadership effectiveness. In J. Antonakis, A. T. Cianciolo, & Sternberg (eds.), *The nature of leadership.* Thousand Oaks, CA: Sage Publications.

Ciulla, J. B & Burns, J. M. (1998). *Ethics, the heart of leadership.* Westport, CT: Quorum Books.

Clapham, M. M. (1998). A comparison of assessor and self dimension ratings in an advanced management assessment center. *Journal of Occupational & Organizational Psychology, 71,* 193–203.

Clark, A. W., & McCabe, S. (1970). Leadership beliefs of Australian managers. *Journal of Applied Psychology, 54,* 1–6.

Clark, B. R. (1956). Organizational adaptation and precarious values: A case study. *American Sociological Review, 21,* 327–336.

Clark, C. S., Dobbins, G. H., & Ladd, R. T. (1993). Exploratory field study of training motivation. *Group & Organization Management, 18,* 292–307.

Clark, J. K. (1986). Anticipating chain reactions. *Public Relations Journal, 42*(8), 6–7.

Clark, K. E., & Clark, M. B. (eds.). (1989). *Measures of leadership.* Greensboro, NC: Center for Creative Leadership.

Clark, K. E., & Clark, M. B. (eds.). (1990). *Measures of leadership* (2nd ed.). West Orange, NJ: Leadership Library of America.

Clark, K. E., & Clark, M. B. (1994). *Choosing to lead.* Greensboro, NC: Center for Creative Leadership Press.

Clark, M. B., Freeman, F. H., & Britt, S. K. (1987). Leadership education '87: A source book. Greensboro, NC: Center for Creative Leadership.

Clarke, H. I. (1951). Definition of a leader: Roosevelt? Toscanini? Hitler? Adams? Dillinger? *Group, 13,* 7–11.

Clause, R. W., & Spurgeon, K. L. (1995). Corporate analysis of humor. *Psychology: A Quarterly Journal of Human Behavior, 32,* 1–24.

Clausen, J. A., & Clausen, S. R. (1973). The effects of family size on parents and children. In J. T. Fawcett (ed.), *Psychological perspectives on population.* New York: Basic Books.

Claxton, M., & Puls, M. (2001). American Indian rule: Sovereignty abused. *Detroit News,* August 5–6, November 11, December 30, 58.

Cleeton, G. U., & Mason, C. W. (1934). *Executive ability: Its discovery and development.* Yellow Springs, OH: Antioch Press.

Clegg, C. W., Gray, M. O., & Waterson, P. E. (2000). The "Charge of

the Byte Brigade" and a socio-technical response. *International Journal of Human-Computer Studies, 52,* 235–251.

Clegg, S. R. (1990). *Modern organization: Organization studies in the post-modern world.* London: Sage.

Clem, O. M., & Dodge, S. B. (1933). The relation of high school leadership and scholarship to post-school success. *Peabody Journal of Education, 10,* 321–329.

Clemens, J. K. (2000). Using film as a leadership development medium. In B. Kellerman & L. R. Matusik (eds.), *Cutting edge leadership.* College Park, MD: University of Maryland, Center for the Advanced Study of Leadership.

Clement, F. A. (1983). An investigation on the validity of the Vroom-Yetton model of leadership. *Dissertation Abstracts International, 45*(3B), 994.

Clement, J. K., & Mayer, D. F. (1987). *The Classic Touch: Lessons in Leadership from Homer to Hemingway.* Homewood, IL: Dow Jones–Irwin.

Cleveland, H. (1980). *Learning the art of leadership: The worldwide crisis in governance demands new approaches.* Unpublished manuscript.

Cleveland, H. (1985). *The knowledge executive: Leadership in an information society.* New York: Dutton.

Cleven, W. A., & Fiedler, F. E. (1956). Interpersonal perceptions of open-hearth foremen and steel production. *Journal of Applied Psychology, 40,* 312–314.

Cliff, J. E., Langton, N., & Aldrich, H. (2003). *On their own terms? Gendered rhetoric versus business behavior in small firms.* Paper, Academy of Management, Seattle, WA.

Clifford, C., & Cohn, T. S. (1964). The relationship between leadership and personality attributes perceived by followers. *Journal of Social Psychology, 64,* 57–64.

Clifton, D. O. (1999). Guiding principles for a growing company. *The Psychologist-Manager Journal, 3,* 49–56.

Clifton, D. O. (2000). Signature themes of leadership: The language of leaders. In B. Kellerman & L. R. Matusak (eds.), *Cutting edge leadership.* College Park, MD: University of Maryland, Center for the Advanced Study of Leadership.

Clifton, D. O., & Nelson, P. (1992). *Soar with your strengths.* New York: Delacorte.

Cline, T. A. (1974). *A study of the relationships between Colorado Community College faculty members' attitudes toward collective negotiations and their perceptions of the management styles used in their colleges.* Doctoral dissertation, University of Colorado, Boulder.

Cline, V. B., & Richards, J. M. (1960). Accuracy of interpersonal perception—a general trait? *Journal of Abnormal and Social Psychology, 60,* 1–7.

Cline, V. B., & Richards, J. M. (1961). The generality and accuracy of interpersonal perception. *Journal of Abnormal and Social Psychology, 62,* 446–449.

Clouse, R. W. & Spurgeon, K. L. (1995). Corporate analysis of humor. *Psychology: A Journal of Human Behavior, 32*(3/4), 1–24.

Clover, W. H. (1988). *Personality attributes of transformational AOCs.* Paper presented to the U.S. Air Force Academy, Colorado Springs, CO.

Clover, W. H. (1989). Transformational leaders: Team performance, leadership ratings and first hand impressions. In K. E. Clark & M. B. Clark (eds.), *Measures of Leadership*. West Orange, NJ: Leadership Library of America.

Clutterbuck, D. (1974). Acid test for management potential. *International Management*, May, 54–57.

Clutterbuck, D. (1982a). How much does success depend upon a helping hand from above? *International Management*, 37, 17–19.

Coad, A. F., & Berry, A. J. (1998). Transformational leadership and learning orientation. *Leadership & Organizational Development Journal*, 19, 164–172.

Coates, J. (1984). *Personality and situational variables as determinants of the distribution of power in a company organization*. Doctoral dissertation, University of Toronto.

Coch, L., & French, J. R. R (1948). Overcoming resistance to change. *Human Relations*, 1, 512–532.

Cobb, J. J. (1974). Leadership and decision-making in a black community: An inter-disciplinary analysis and study. *Dissertation Abstracts International*, 34, 4451.

Coffey, J. W. (1985). The statesmanship of Harry Truman. *Review of Politics*, 47(2), 231–252.

Coffin, T. E. (1944). A three-component theory of leadership. *Journal of Abnormal and Social Psychology*, 39, 63–83.

COFREMCA (1978). A psychological study of the attitudes of French managers. *International Study of Management and Organization*, 8, 22–38.

Coghill, C. J. (1981). *Managerial role perception in organization*. Doctoral dissertation, University of the Witwatersrand, Johannesburg, South Africa.

Cogliser, C. C. (2002). *Rethinking leadership from a strategic view*. Paper, Academy of Management, Denver, CO.

Cogliser, C. C., & Scandura, T. A. (2003). Waterfalls, snowballs, and scuzzballs: Does leader-member exchange up the line influence leader development? In S. L. Murphy & R. H. Riggio (eds.), *The future of leadership development*. Mahwah, NJ: Lawrence Erlbaum & Associates.

Cogliser, C. C., & Schriesheim, C. A. (2000). Exploring work unit context and leader-member exchange: A multi-level perspective. *Journal of Organizational Behavior*, 21(5), 487–511.

Cohen, A. M. (1962). Changing small group communication networks. *Administrative Science Quarterly*, 6, 443–462.

Cohen, A. M., & Bennis, W. G. (1961). Continuity of leadership in communication networks. Human *Relations*, 14, 351–367.

Cohen, A. M., Bennis, W. C., & Wolkon, C. H. (1961). The effects of continued practice on the behaviors of problem-solving groups. *Sociometry*, 24, 416–431.

Cohen, A. M., & Foerst, J. R. (1968). Organizational behaviors and adaptations to organizational change of sensitizer and represser problemsolving groups. *Journal of Personality and Social Psychology*, 8, 209–216.

Cohen, A. M., Robinson, E. L., & Edwards, J. L. (1969). Experiments in organization embeddedness. *Administrative Science Quarterly*, 4, 208–221.

Cohen, A. R. (1953). *The effects of situational structure and individual self-esteem on threat-oriented reactions to power*. Unpublished doctoral dissertation, University of Michigan.

Cohen, A. R. (1958). Upward communication in experimentally created hierarchies. *Human Relations*, 11, 41–53.

Cohen, A. R. (1959). Situational structure, self-esteem, and threat-oriented reactions to power. In D. Cartwright (ed.), *Studies in social power*. Ann Arbor: University of Michigan, Institute for Social Research.

Cohen, A. R. (1964). Communication networks. *Personnel Administration*, 27, 18–24.

Cohen, D., & March, J. G. (1974). *Leadership and ambiguity*. New York: McGraw-Hill.

Cohen, E., & Tichy, N. (1997). How leaders develop leaders. *Training and Development Journal*, 51(5), 58.

Cohen, D. J., & Lindsley, O. R. (1964). Catalysis of controlled leadership in cooperation by human stimulation. *Journal of Child Psychology*, 5, 119–137.

Cohen, E. (1956). Stimulus conditions as factors in social change. *American Psychologist*, 11, 407.

Cohen, G. B. (1969). *The task-tuned organization of groups*. Amsterdam: Swets Zeitlinger.

Cohen, J. (1994). The earth is round. *American Psychologist*, 49, 997–1003

Cohen, M. D., & March, J. G. (1974). *Leadership and ambiguity*. New York: McGraw-Hill.

Cohen, M. D., & March, J. G. (1986). *Leadership and ambiguity: The American college president* (2nd ed.). Boston: Harvard Business School Press.

Cohen, P. (1996). The shape of things to come: An interview with Peter Drucker. *Leader to Leader*, 1, 12–18.

Cohen, S. G., Chang, L., & Ledford, G. E. (1997). Self-management leadership and its relation to quality of work life and perceived work group effectiveness. *Personnel Psychology*, 50, 275–308.

Cohen, S. G., & Gibson, C. B. (2000). *Virtual teams pose special challenges—Here's how to make them work in your organization*. CIMS Technology Management Report, Center for Innovation Management Studies, Lehigh University, Bethlehem, PA.

Cohen, S. G., & Ledford, G. E. (1994). The effectiveness of self-managed teams: A quasi-experiment. *Human Relations*, 47, 13–43.

Cohen, W. M., & Levinthal, D. A. (1990). Absorptive capacity: A new perspective on learning and innovation. *Administrative Science Quarterly*, 35, 128–152.

Cohn, T. S., Fisher, A., & Brown, V. (1961). Leadership and predicting attitudes of others. *Journal of Social Psychology*, 55, 199–206.

Colby, A. H., & Zak, R. E. (1988). *Transformational leadership: A comparison of Army and Air Force perceptions* (Report 88–0565). Air Command and Staff College, Air University, Maxwell AFB, AL.

Cole, J. F. (1984). High school reform. *Educational Leadership*, 41, 38–40.

Cole, J. (1993). Gentle persuasion: New CEO at Hughes studied its managers, got them on his side that let Armstrong move fast to reshape GM unit as more market driven: IBM executive makes good. *Wall Street Journal*, March 30, A1, A6.

Cole, J. (1998). Building heart and soul. *HRfocus*, October, 9–10.

Colella, A. (2001). Coworker distributive fairness judgments of the workplace accommodation of employees with disabilities. *Academy of Management Review*, 26, 100–116.

Colella, A., & Varma, A. (2001). The impact of subordinate disability on leader-member exchange relationships. *Academy of Management Journal*, 44, 304–315.

Colella, A., Zardkoohi, A., Paetzold, R., et al. (2003). *Pay secrecy revisited: An integrative model.* Paper, Academy of Management, Seattle, WA.

Coleman, E. P., Patterson, J., Fuller, J. B., et al. (1995). A meta-analytic examination of leadership style and selected follower compliance outcomes. Paper, Society for Industrial and Organizational Psychology, Orlando, FL.

Coleman, J. S., et al. (1966). *Equality of educational opportunity.* Washington, DC: U.S. Department of Health, Education, and Welfare, U.S. Government Printing Office.

Collaros, F. A., & Anderson, L. R. (1969). Effect of perceived expertness upon creativity of members of brainstorming groups. *Journal of Applied Psychology*, 2, 159–163.

Collins, B. E., & Guetzkow, H. (1964). *A social psychology of group processes for decision-making.* New York: Wiley.

Collins, D. (1995). Death of a gainsharing plan: Power politics and participative management. *Organizational Dynamics*, 24(1), 23–38.

Collins, D. (1998). Knowledge work or working knowledge? Ambiguity and confusion in the analysis of the "knowledge age." *Journal of Systemic Knowledge Management*, 1(1).

Collins, D., Ross, R. A., & Ross, T. L. (1989). Who wants participative management? *Group & Organization Studies*, 14(4), 422–445.

Collins, D. B. (2001). Organizational performance: The future focus of leadership development programs. *Journal of Leadership Studies*, 7(4), 44–54.

Collins, E. G. C. (1983). Managers and lovers. *Harvard Business Review* 61(5), 142–153.

Collins, H. P. (1990). *Black feminist thought: Knowledge, consciousness, and the politics of empowerment.* Boston: Unwin Hyman.

Collins, J. (1996). Aligning action and values. *Leaders to Leaders*, 1(1), 19–14.

Collins, J. C., & Porras, J. I. (1994). *Built to last: Successful habits of visionary companies.* New York: HarperCollins.

Collins, N. W. (1983). *Professional women and their mentors.* Englewood Cliffs, NJ: Prentice-Hall.

Collins, O. F., & Moore, D. G. (1970). *The organization makers: A behavioral study of independent entrepreneurs.* New York: Appleton-Century-Crofts.

Collins, O. F., Moore, D. G., & Unwalla, D. (1964). The enterprising man and the business executive. *MSU Business Topics*, 12(1), 19–34.

Collins, O. F., Moore, D. G., & Unwalla, D. B. (1970). *The enterprising man.* East Lansing, MI: Bureau of Business and Economic Research, Michigan State University.

Colmen, J. G., Fiedler, C. O., & Boulger, J. R. (1954). Methodological considerations in determining supervisory training needs. *American Psychologist*, 9, 350.

Colquitt, & Shaw, J. C. (2003). *The importance of team commitment and team cognitive ability in parallel teams.* Paper, Society for Industrial and Organizational Psychology, San Francisco, CA.

Colvin, R. E. (1996). *Transformational executive leadership.* Doctoral dissertation, Virginia Commonwealth University, Richmond, VA.

Colvin, R. E. (2001). *Leading from the middle: A challenge for middle*

managers. Festschrift for Bernard Bass. Binghamton, NY: Binghamton University, Center for Leadership Studies.

Colyer, D. M. (1951). The good Foreman-as his men see him. *Personnel*, 28, 140–147.

Combs, J. G., & Skill, M. S. (2003). Managerialist and human capital explanations for key executive pay premiums. A contingency perspective. *Academy of Management Journal*, 46, 63–73.

Comrey, A. L., High, W. S., & Wilson, R. C. (1955a). Factors influencing organizational effectiveness. VI. A survey of aircraft workers. *Personnel Psychology*, 8, 79–99.

Comrey, A. L., High, W. S., & Wilson, R. C. (1955b). Factors influencing organizational effectiveness. VII. A survey of aircraft supervisors. *Personnel Psychology*, 8, 245–257.

Comrey, A. L., Pfiffner, J. M., & Beem, H. P, (1952). Factors influencing organizational effectiveness. I. The U.S. Forest Survey. *Personnel Psychology*, 5, 307–328.

Comstock, D. E., & Scott, W. R. (1977). Technology and structure of subunits: Distinguishing individual and work efforts. *Administrative Science Quarterly*, 22, 177–202.

Conger, J. A. (1989). *The charismatic leader: Behind the mystique of exceptional leadership.* San Francisco: Jossey-Bass.

Conger, J. A. (1990). The dark side of leadership. *Organizational Dynamics*, 19(2), 44–55.

Conger, J. A. (1991). Inspiring others: The language of leadership. *Academy of Management Executive*, 5(1), 31–45

Conger, J. A. (1992). *Learning to lead: The art of transforming managers into leaders.* San Francisco: Jossey-Bass.

Conger, J. A. (1993a). Training leaders for the twenty-first century. *Human Resources Management Review*, 3(3), 203–218.

Conger, J. A. (1993b). The brave new world of leadership training. *Organizational Dynamics*, 21(3), 46–58.

Conger, J. A. (1998). The folly of knowing an elephant by its tail: Why the field needs multiple levels of analysis. In F. Dansereau and F. J. Yammarino (eds), *Leadership: The Multiple Level Approachs.* Greenwich, CT: JAI Press, 77–84.

Conger, J. A. (1998). Qualitative research as the cornerstone methodology for understanding leadership. *Leadership Quarterly*, 9, 107–121.

Conger, J. A. (1999). Charismatic and transformational leadership in organizations: An insider's perspective on these developing streams of research. *Leadership Quarterly*, 10, 145–179.

Conger, J. A. (2000). The vision thing: Explorations into visionary leadership. In Kellerman, B., & Matusak, L. (eds.), *Cutting edge: Leadership 2000.* Center for the Advanced Study of Leadership, University of Maryland.

Conger, J. A. (2003b). The brave new world of leadership training. *Organizational Dynamics*, 21(3), 46–58.

Conger, J. A. (2005). "Oh Lord, won't you buy me a Mercedes-Benz?": How compensation practices are undermining the credibility of executive leaders. In J. B. Ciulla, T. L. Price, & S. E. Murphy (eds.), *The quest for moral leaders: Essays on leadership ethics.* Cambridge, U.K.: Edward Elgar.

Conger, J. A., & Kanungo, R. N. (1987). Toward a behavioral theory of charismatic leadership in organizational settings. *Academy of Management*, 12, 637–647.

Conger, J. A., & Kanungo, R. N. (1988). Behavioral dimensions of charismatic leadership. In J. A. Conger & R. N. Kanungo (eds.), *Charismatic leadership: The elusive factor in organizational effectiveness.* San Francisco: Jossey-Bass, 78–97.

Conger, J. A., & Kanungo, R. N. (1994). Charismatic leadership in organizations: Perceived behavioral attributes and their measurement. *Journal of Organizational Behavior, 15,* 439–452.

Conger, J. A. & Kanungo, R. N. (1998). *Charismatic leadership: The elusive factor in organizational effectiveness* (2nd ed.). San Francisco: Jossey-Bass.

Conger, J. A., & Kanungo, R. N. (1998). *Charismatic leadership in organizations.* Thousand Oaks, CA: Sage Publications.

Conger, J. A., Kanungo, R. N., & Menon, S. T. (2000). Charismatic leadership and follower effects. *Journal of Organizational Behavior, 21,* 747–767.

Conger, J. A., & Pearce, C. L. (1998). A landscape of opportunities: Future research on shared leadership. In C. L. Pearce & J. A. Conger (eds.), *Shared leadership: Reframing the how's and why's of leadership.* Thousand Oaks, CA: Sage.

Conger, J. A., & Toegel, G. (2003). Action learning and multi-rater feedback as leadership development interventions: popular but poorly deployed. *Journal of Change Management, 3*(4), 332–348.

Conger, J. A., & Toegel, G. (2005). Actions learning and multi-rater feed back: Pathways to leadership development? In S. L. Murphy & R. H. Riggio (eds.), *The future of leadership development.* Mahwah, NJ: Lawrence Erlbaum Associates.

Connelly, M. S., Gilbert, J. A., Zaccaro, S. J., et al. (2000). Exploring the relationship of leadership skills and knowledge to leader performance. *Leadership Quarterly, 11,* 65–86.

Connelly, S., Gaddis, B., & Helton-Fauth, W. (2002). A closer look at the role of emotions in transformational and charismatic leadership. In Avolio, B. J., & Yammarino, F. J. (eds.), *Transformational and charismatic leadership: The road ahead.* New York: Elsevier Science.

Conway, C. (1993). The customer comes first. *Sunday Times* (London), October 17.

Conway, J. M., & Huffcutt, A. I. (1997). Psychometric properties of multisource performance ratings: A meta-analysis of subordinate, peer, supervisor, and self-ratings. *Human Performance, 10,* 331–360.

Conway, M. (1915). *The crowd in peace and war.* New York: Longmans, Green.

Conover, P. J., Mingst, K. A., & Sigelman, L. (1980). Mirror images in Americans' perceptions of nations and leaders during the Iranian hostage crisis. *Journal of Peace Research, 17,* 325–337.

Conyon, M. J., & Peck, S. I. (1998). Board control, remuneration committees, and top management compensation. *Academy of Management Journal, 41,* 146–157.

Cook, D. M. (1968). The impact on managers of frequency feedback. *Academy of Management Journal, 11,* 263–277.

Cook, S. (1994). The cultural implications of empowerment. *Empowermenrt in organizations, 2*(1), 9–12.

Cooke, R. A., & Lafferty, J. C. (1983). *Level V: Organizational culture inventory—form l.* Plymouth, MI: Human Synergistics.

Cooke, R. A., & Saumal, J. (1992). *Measuring normative beliefs and shared behavioral expectations in organizations: The reliability and*

validity of the Organizational Culture Inventory. Plymouth, MI: Human Synergistics, Inc.

Cooley, C. H. (1902). *Human nature and the social order.* New York: Scribner's.

Cooley, C. W. (1956). *Social organization.* Glencoe, IL: Free Press.

Cooper, C. D., & Kurland, N. B. (2002). Telecommuting , professional isolation, and employee development in public and private organizations. *Journal of Organizational Behavior, 23,* 511–532.

Cooper, C. L., & Davidson, M. J. (1982). *High pressure: Working lives of women managers.* Fontana, London.

Cooper, G. L., & Davidson, M. J. (1982). The high cost of stress on women managers. *Organizational Dynamics, 1*(4), 44–5 3.

Cooper, R. (1966). Leader's task relevance and subordinate behavior in industrial work groups. *Human Relations, 19,* 57–84.

Cooper, R., & Payne, R. (1967). *Personality orientations and performance in football.*

Coovert, M. D., Campbell, G. E., Cannon-Bowers, J. A., et al. (1995). *A methodology for a team performance measurement system.* Paper, Society for Industrial and Organizational Psychology, Orlando, FL.

Copeland, J. T. (1993). Motivational approaches to expectancy confirmation. *Current Directions in Psychological Science, 2*(4), 117–121.

Copeland, M. A., & Mcglaughlin, M. W. (2000). *Rethinking school leadership: Moving from role to function in abn An inquiry-based model of school reform.* Proceedings, III International Conference on School Management, Bilbao, Spain, September 12–15.

Copeland, N. (1942). *Psychology and the soldier.* Harrisburg, PA: Military Service Publishing.

Copeman, C. H. (1955). *Leaders of British industry: A study of the careers of more than a thousand public company directors.* London: Gee.

Cordery, J. L., Mueller, W. S., & Smith, L. M. (1991). Attitudinal and behavioral effects of autonomous group working: A longitudinal field study. *Academy of Management Journal, 34,* 464–476.

Cordiner, R. J. (1952). *Problems of management in a large decentralized organization.* New York: American Management Association.

Cornelius, E. T., III, & Lane, K. B. (1984). The power motive and managerial success in a professionally oriented service industry organization. *Journal of Applied Psychology, 69,* 32–39.

Cornell, W. B. (1928). *Industrial organization and management.* New York: Ronald Press.

Cornwell, J. M. (1983). *A meta-analysis of selected trait research in the leadership literature.* Paper, Southeastern Psychological Association, Atlanta, GA.

Corrigan, P. (1999). *Shakespeare on management: Leadership lessons for today's managers.* London: Kogan Press.

Corrigan, P. W., Kwartarini, W. Y., & Pramana, W. (1992). Staff perception of barriers to behavior therapy at a psychiatric hospital. *Behavior Modification, 16*(1), 132–144.

Corrigan, P. W., Lickey, S. E., McCracken, S. G., et al. (2001). Organizational correlates to staff attitudes about behavioral programs. *Behavioral Change, 18,* 114–123.

Cornell, W. B. (1928). *Industrial organization and management.* New York: Ronald Press.

Corsini, R. J. (1999). Stereotype. In *The dictionary of psychology.* Philadelphia, PA: Brunner/Mazel.

Corsini, R. J., Shaw, M. E., & Blake, R. R. (1961). *Roleplaying in business and industry.* New York: Free Press.

Corsino, L. (1982). Malcolm X and the Black Muslim movement: A social psychology of charisma. *Psychohistory Review, 10,* 165–184.

Cortes, J., & Gatti, F. M. (1972). *Delinquency and crime: A biopsychological approach.* New York: Seminar Press.

Coser, L. (1956). *The functions of social conflict.* Glencoe, IL: Free Press.

Coser, R. L. (1980). Women and work. *Dissent, 27,* 51–55.

Cosier, R. A., & Aplin, J. C. (1980). Effects of delegated choice on performance. *Personnel Psychology, 33,* 581–593.

Costa, P. T., Jr. (1994). *Work and personality: Use of the NEO PI-R in Industrial/Organizational Psychology.* Paper, International Congress of Applied Psychology, Madrid, Spain.

Costa, P. T., Jr., & McCrae, R. R. (1992). *The NEO–PI–R professional manual.* Odessa, FL: Psychological Assessment Resources.

Costa, P. T., Jr., & McCrae, R. R. (1995). Domains and facets: Hierarchical personality assessments using the revised NEO personality inventory. *Journal of Personality Assessment, 64,* 21–50.

Costa, P. T., Jr., & McCrae, R. R. (1999). Stability and change in personality assessment: The revised NEO personality inventory in the year 2000. *Journal of Personality Assessment, 68,* 86–94.

Cotton, E. H. (1932). *William Howard Taft: A character study.* Boston, MA: Beacon Press.

Cotton, G. C., & Cotton, E. G. (1982). *Marginality orientation and LPC: Evidence that task-oriented persons are more "marginal."* Paper, International Congress of Applied Psychology, Edinburgh, U.K.

Cotton, J. L., Vollrath, D. A., Froggatt, K. L., Lengnick-Hall, M. L., & Jennings, K. R. (1988). Employee participation: Diverse forms and different outcomes. *The Academy of Management Review, 13*(1), 8–22.

Courtenay, M. E. (1938). Persistence of leadership. *School Review, 46,* 97–107.

Courtney, D., Greer, F. L., & Masling, J. M. (1952). *Leadership identification and acceptance.* Philadelphia: Institute for Research in Human Relations.

Courtney, D., Greer, F. L., Masling, J. M., & Orlans, H. (1953). *Naval, neighborhood, and national leadership.* Philadelphia: Institute for Research in Human Relations.

Courtright, J. A., Fairhurst, G. T., & Rogers, L. E. (1989). Interaction patterns in organic and mechanistic systems. *Academy of Management Journal, 32,* 773–802.

Couto, R. A. (1992). *Grassroots policies of empowerment.* Paper, American Political Science Association, Chicago, IL.

Couto, R. A. (1993). Narrative, free space, and political leadership in social movements. *The Journal of Politics, 55*(1), 57–79.

Couto, R. A. (1997). *Social capital and leadership.* University of Maryland, College Park: Transformational Leadership Focus Group. Kellogg Leadership Studies Project.

Covey, S. (1997). In F. Hesselbein, M. Goldsmith, & R. Beckhard (eds.), *The Leader of the Future: New Visions, Strategies and Practices for the Next Era.* San Francisco: Jossey-Bass.

Covin, T. J., Kolenko, T. A., Sightler, K. W., et al. (1997). Leadership style and post-merger satisfaction. *Journal of Management Development, 16*(1), 22–33.

Cowen, S. S. (1990). *A study of the relationships between perceived leadership behaviors of presidents at public 4-year institutions of higher education in the U.S.* Doctoral dissertation, Gonzaga University, Spokane, WA.

Cowley, W. H. (1928). Three distinctions in the study of leaders. *Journal of Abnormal and Social Psychology, 23,* 144–157.

Cowley, W. H. (1931). Traits of face-to-face leaders. *Journal of Abnormal and Social Psychology, 26,* 304–313.

Cox, C. J., & Cooper, C. L. (1988). *High flyers.* London: Basil Blackwell.

Cox, C. J., & Cooper, C. L. (1989). The making of the British CEO: Childhood, work experience, personality, and management style. *Academy of Management Executives, 3*(3), 241–245.

Cox, C. J., & Jennings, R. (1995). The foundations of success: The development and characteristics of British entrepreneurs and intrapreneurs. *Leadership and Organizational Development Journal, 16*(7), 4–9.

Cox, C. M. (1926). *The early mental traits of three hundred geniuses.* Stanford, CA: Stanford University Press.

Cox, J. A., & Krumboltz, J. D. (1958). Racial bias in peer ratings of basic airmen. *Sociometry, 21,* 292–299.

Cox, M. (1986). Clearer connections: The nebulous networks of the 70's give way to pragmatic business contacts. *Wall Street Journal,* March 24, 19D.

Cox, T. (1993). *Cultural diversity in organizations.* San Francisco: Berrett-Koehler.

Cox, T., & Beale, R. L. (1997). *Developing competency to manage diversity.* San Francisco: Berrett-Koehler.

Cox. T., & Blake, S. (1991). Managing cultural diversity: Implications for organizational competitiveness. *Academy of Management Executive, 5,* 45–56.

Coye, R. W. (1982). Subordinate responses to ineffective leadership. *Dissertation Abstracts International, 43*(6A), 2070.

Coyle, G. L. (1948). *Group work with American youth.* New York: Harper.

Craig, J. G., & Jull, G. W. (1974). *Teleconferencing studies: Behavioral research and technological implications.* Ottawa, Canada: Communications Research Centre.

Craig, R. D. (1983). Policy capturing in the evaluation of self-esteem as a moderator of the relationship between supervisory style and subordinate satisfaction in the path-goal theory of leadership. *Dissertation Abstracts International, 44*(9B), 2928.

Craig, S. B., & Gustafson, S. B.(1998). Perceived leader integrity scale: An instrument for assessing employee perceptions of leader integrity. *Leadership Quarterly, 9,* 127–145.

Crain, R. L., & Weisman, C. S. (1972). *Discrimination, personality, and achievement.* New York: Seminar Press.

Crampton, S. M., & Wagner, J. A. (1994). Percept-percept inflation in microorganizational research: An investigation of prevalence and effect. *Journal of Applied Psychology, 79,* 67–76.

Crandall, V. J., Katkovsky, W., & Preston, A. (1962). Motivational and ability determinants of young children's intellectual achievement behaviors. *Child Development, 33,* 643–661.

Crant, J. M., & Bateman, T. S. (2000). Charismatic leadership viewed from above: The impact of proactive personality. *Journal of Organizational Behavior, 21,* 63–75.

Crawford, C. B. (1994). Theory and implications regarding the utilization of strategic humor by leaders. *Journal of Leadership Studies, 1,* 53–67.

Crawford, C. B. (1995). Socially supportive transformational leaders: Paradigm and prescription for organizational stress management. *Journal of Leadership Studies, 2,* 75–85.

Crawford, C. B., Brungart, C. L., Scott, R. F., et al. (2002). Graduate programs in organizational leadership: A review of programs, faculty, costs, and delivery methods. *Journal of Leadership Studies, 5*(4), 64–74.

Crawford, K. S., Thomas, E. D., & Fink, J. J. (1980). Pygmalion at sea: Improving the work effectiveness of low performers. *Journal of Applied Behavioral Science, 16,* 482–505.

Creglow, A. (1998). *Updated research on the relationship between core GWA employee perceptions with business outcomes.* Thesis, Gallup University, Lincoln, NE.

Cribbin, J. I. (1981). *Leadership: Strategies for organizational effectiveness.* New York: AMACOM.

Crockett, W. H. (1955). Emergent leadership in small, decision-making groups. *Journal of Abnormal and Social Psychology, 51,* 378–383.

Crockett, W. J. (1981). Dynamic subordinancy. *Training & Development Journal, 35,* 155–164.

Cronbach, L. G. (1975). Beyond the two disciplines of scientific psychology. *American Psychologist, 30,* 116–127.

Cronbach, L. J., & Glaser, G. C. (1953). *Psychological tests and personnel decisions.* Urbana: University of Illinois Press.

Cronbach, L. J., Hartmann, W., & Ehart, M. E. (1953). *Investigation of the character and Properties of assumed similarity measures* (Tech. Rep. No. 7). Urbana: University of Illinois, Group Effectiveness Research Laboratory.

Cronin, I. E. (1984), Thinking and learning about leadership. *Presidential Studies Quarterly, 14*(1), 22–34.

Cronin, T. (1980). *The state of the presidency* (2nd ed.). Boston: Little, Brown.

Cronshaw, S. F., & Lord, R. G. (1987). Effects of categorization, attribution, and encoding processes of leadership perceptions. *Journal of Applied Psychology, 72,* 97–106.

Crookall, P. S. (1989). *Leadership in prison industry.* Doctoral dissertation, University of Western Ontario, London, ON.

Cropanzano, R., Howes, J. C., Grandey, A. A., & Toth, P. (1997). The relationship of organizational politics and support to work behaviors, attitudes, and stress. *Journal of Organizational Behavior, 18,* 159–180.

Crosby, P. B. (1990). *Leading: The art of becoming an executive.* New York: McGraw-Hill.

Cross, T. L., Bazios, B. J., Dennis, K. W., et al. (1989). *Toward a community competent system of care.* Washington, DC: Child Development Center.

Cross, W. E., Jr. (1978). Models of psychological nigrescence: A literature review. *Journal of Black Psychology, 5,* 13–31.

Crouch, A. (1986). *Effects of manager and subordinate needs for dominance on manager willingness to legitimize conflict and subordinate performance.* Paper, Academy of Management, Chicago.

Crouch, A. (1987). An equilibrium model of management group performance. *Academy of Management Review, 12,* 499–510.

Crouch, A. G., Yetton, R., & Yetton, P. (1987). Manager behavior, leadership style, and subordinate performance: An empirical extension of the Vroom-Yetton conflict rule. *Organizational Behavior & Human Decision Processes, 39,* 384–396.

Crouch, A. G., & Yetton, P. (1988). Manager-subordinate dyads: The relationships among social contact, manager friendliness and subordinate performance in management groups. *Organizational Behavior and Human Decision Processes, 41,* 65–82.

Crow, W. J., & Hammond, K. R. (1957). The generality of accuracy and response sets in interpersonal perception. *Journal of Abnormal and Social Psychology, 54,* 384–390.

Crowe, B. J., Bochner, S., & Clark, A. W. (1972). The effects of subordinates' behavior on managerial style. *Human Relations, 25,* 215–237.

Crowe, S., & Wucker, M. (1999). The 20 most powerful international business women: Africa, Latin America. *Working Woman,* November, 58–66.

Crowne, D. P. (2000). *Social desirability.* In Kazdin, A.E. (ed.), *Encyclopedia of psychology.* American Psychological Association: Oxford University Press.

Crowther, F., & Olsen, P. (1997). Teachers as leaders: An exploratory framework. *International Journal of Educational Management, 11*(1), 6–13.

Crozier, M. (1984). *The bureaucratic phenomenon.* Chicago: University of Chicago Press.

Csikszentmihalyi, M. (1996). *Creativity: Flow and the psychology of discovery and invention.* New York: HarperCollins.

Csikszentmihalyi, M. (1997). *Finding flow: The psychology of engagement with everyday life.* New York: Basic Books.

Csoka, L. S. (1974). A relationship between leader intelligence and leader rated effectiveness. *Journal of Applied Psychology, 59,* 43–47.

Csoka, L. S. (1975). Relationship between organizational climate and the situational favorableness dimension of Fiedler's contingency model. *Journal of Applied Psychology, 60,* 273–277.

Csoka, L. S. (1993). Psychological profiles for predicting leader performance. *Human Resource Management Review, 3*(4), 255–270.

Culbert, S. A., & McDonough, J. (1980). *The invisible war: Pursuing self-interests at work.* New York: Wiley.

Culbert, S. A., & McDonough, J. (1985). *Radical management: Power politics and the pursuit of trust.* New York: Free Press.

Cullen, F. (1993). Prison wardens' job satisfaction, *Prison Journal, 73,* 141–161.

Cullen, J. B., Parbotreeah, K. P., & Hoegl, M. (2004). Cross-national differences in managers' willingness to justify ethically suspect behaviors: A test institutional anomie theory. *Academy of Management Journal, 47,* 411–431.

Cullers, B., Hughes, C., & McGreal, T. (1973). Administrative behavior and student dissatisfaction: A possible relationship. *Peabody Journal of Education, 50,* 155–163.

Cummin, P. C. (1967). TAT correlates of executive performance. *Journal of Applied Psychology, 51,* 78–81.

Cummings, J. N. (2001). *Symposium introduction: Real evidence from virtual teams: Five mechanisms for overcoming physical distance.* Paper, Academy of Management, Washington, DC.

Cummings, L. L., & ElSalmi, A. M. (1970). The impact of role diversity, job level, and organizational size on managerial satisfaction. *Administrative Science Quarterly, 15,* 1–10.

Cummings, L. L., Harnett, D. L., & Stevens, O. J. (1971). Risk, fate conciliation and trust: An international study of attitudinal differences among executives. *Academy of Management Journal, 14,* 285–304.

Cummings, L. L., & Schmidt, S. M. (1972). Managerial attitudes of Greeks: The roles of culture and industrialization. *Administrative Science Quarterly, 17,* 265–272.

Cummings, L. L., & Schwab, D. P. (1973). *Performance in organizations: Determinants and appraisal.* Glenview, IL: Scott, Foresman.

Cummings, L. L., & Schwab, D. P. (1978). Designing appraisal systems for information yield. *California Management Review, 20,* 18–25.

Cummings, L. L., & Scott, W. E. (1965). Academic and leadership performance of graduate business students. *Business Perspectives, 1,* 11–20.

Cummins, R. C. (1970). An investigation of a model of leadership effectiveness. *Proceedings, American Psychological Association,* 599–600.

Cummins, R. C. (1971). Relationship of initiating structure and job performance as moderated by consideration. *Journal of Applied Psychology, 55,* 489–490.

Cummins, R. C. (1990). Job stress and the effect of supervisory support. *Group & Organization Studies, 15,* 92–104.

Cunningham, C. J. (1964). *Measures of leader behavior and their relation to performance levels of county extension agents.* Doctoral dissertation, Ohio State University, Columbus.

Cunningham, I., & Leon, P. (1986). Focusing managerial development. *Journal of European Industrial Training, 10*(8), 23–26.

Cunningham, J. B. (1993). Facilitating a mentorship program. *Leadership & Organization Development Journal, 14*(4), 15–21.

Cunningham, R. B., & Olshfski, D. F. (1985). Evaluating task leadership: A problem for assessment centers. *Public Personnel Management, 14,* 293–299.

Cunningham, S. (1984). Culture plays important role in our beliefs. *APA Monitor,* September 8–9.

Cuny, K. (1983). *Disasters and development.* Oxford, U.K.: Oxford University Press.

Curfman, M. (1939). *An experimental investigation of some of the influences of authoritarian and democratic atmospheres on the behavior of small groups.* Master's thesis, Stanford University, Palo Alto, CA.

Curphy, G. J. (1985). *An empirical investigation of Bass' theory of transformational and transactional leadership.* University of Minnesota, Minneapolis.

Curphy, G. J. (1990). *An empirical evaluation of Bass's (1985) theory of transformational and transactional leadership.* Doctoral dissertation, University of Minnesota, Minneapolis, MN.

Curphy, G. J. (1992). An empirical investigation of the effects of the transformational and transactional leadership on organisational climate, attrition and performance. In Clark, E. (ed.), *Impact of Leadership,* The Centre for Creative Leadership, Greensboro, NC.

Curphy, G. (2000). *The role of personality in leadership emergence.* Paper, Society for Industrial and Organizational Psychology, San Diego, CA.

Curtis, B., Smith, R. E., & Smoll, F. L. (1979). Scrutinizing the skipper: A study of behaviors in the dugout. *Journal of Applied Psychology, 64,* 391–400.

Curtis, Q. F., & Gibbard, H. A. (1955). *The acquiring of membership in established groups* (Final Tech. Rep.). Morgantown: West Virginia University.

Cushman, J. H. (1989). Air traffic controllers and U.S. reach accord. *New York Times,* January 14, 6.

Cusimano, J., & Stalcup, G. (2000). Managing five paradoxes of 360-degree feedback. *Industrial Engineering, 28*(11), 58–60.

Cycyota, C. S., & Harrison, D. A. (2002). Top manager responses to organizational surveys: When questioning executives, are networks the answer? *Academy of Management Best Papers Proceedings.*

Cyert, R. M., & March. J. G. (1963). *A behavioral theory of the firm.* Englewood Cliffs, N.J.: Prentice-Hall.

Czarniawska-Joerges & Wolff (1991). Leaders, managers, entrepreneurs on and off the organizational stage. *Organizational Studies, 12*(4), 529–546.

Dabbs, J. (2000). *Testosterone, temperament, and leadership: A proposal on hormones and heroes.* Private communication, July 11.

Daboub, A. J., Rasheed, A. M. A., Priem, R. L., & Gray, D. A. (1995). Top management team characteristics and corporate illegal activity. *Academy of Management Review, 20*(1), 138–170.

Daft, R. L. (1983). *Organizational theory and design.* St. Paul, MN: West Publishing.

Daft, R. L., & Weick, K. E. (1984). Towards a model of organizations as interpretation systems. *Academy of Management Review, 9,* 284–295.

Dagirmanjian, S. (1981). The work experience of service staff in mental health service organizations and its relationship to leadership style and organizational structure. *Dissertation Abstracts International, 43*(5B), 1609.

Dahl, R. A. (1957). The concept of power. *Behavioral Science, 2,* 201–215.

Dahl, R. A. (1961). *Who governs?* New Haven, CT: Yale University Press.

Dahl, R. A., March, J., & Nastair, D. (1957). Influence ranking in the United States Senate. Cited in R. A. Dahl, The concept of power, *Behavioral Science, 2,* 201–215.

Daigneault, M. G. (1997). Why ethics?: Defining ethical behavior may feel like a slippery slope, but having clear values is a must for success. *Association Management, 49*(9), 28–37.

Daily, C. M., & Johnson, J. L. (1997). Sources of CEO power and firm financial performance: A longitudinal assessment. *Journal of Management, 23,* 97–117.

Dalessio, A. (1983). Subordinates' leadership preferences and leader-subordinate understanding. *Dissertation Abstracts International, 45*(5B), 1611.

Dalessio, A., & Davis, D. D. (1986). *Predicting innovation among R & D scientists and engineers.* Paper, American Psychological Association, Washington, DC.

Daley, D. M. (1986). Humanistic management and organizational success: The effect of job and work environment characteristics on organizational effectiveness, public responsiveness, and job satisfaction. *Public Personnel Management, 15*(2), 131–142.

Dallas Morning News. (1997) Palestinians unbowed in refugee camp where uprising began. *Dallas Morning News,* December 11. Laura King Associated Press. Document ID: 0ED3D96CE585B784.

Daloz, L. A. P., Keen, C. H., Keen, J. P., & Parks, S. D. (1997). *Common fire: Leadership lives of commitment in a complex world.* Boston: Beacon Press.

Dalton, D. R., Daily, C. M., Ellstrand, A. E., et al. (1998). Meta-analytic reviews of board composition, leadership structure, and financial performance. *Strategic Management Journal, 19*, 269–290.

Dalton, D. R., & Kesner, I. F. (1985). Organizational performance as an antecedent of inside/outside chief executive succession: An empirical assessment. *Academy of Management Journal, 28*, 749–762.

Dalton, G. W., Barnes, L. B., & Zaleznik, A. (1968). *The distribution of authority in formal organizations.* Boston: Harvard University, Graduate School of Business Administration.

Dalton, M. (1950). Conflicts between staff and line managerial officers. *American Sociological Review, 15*, 342–351.

Dalton, M. (1959). *Men who manage: Fusions of feelings and theory in administration.* New York: John Wiley & Sons.

Daltry, M. H., & Langer, P. (1984). Development and evaluation of a measure of future time orientation. *Perceptual & Motor Skills, 58*, 719–725.

D'Angelo, R. V. (1973). *The influence of three styles of leadership on the process and outcome of an organization development effort.* Doctoral dissertation, University of California, Berkeley.

Daniel, T. (1985). Managerial behaviors: Their relationship to perceived organizational climate in a high-technology company. *Group & Organization Studies, 10*, 413–428.

Daniels, C. S., Leritz, L. E., & Mumford, M. D. (2003). *When is planning necessary: A study of planning skills and emergent leaders.* Paper, Academy of Management, Seattle, WA.

Daniels, L. R., & Berkowitz, L. (1963). Liking and response to dependency relationships. *Human Relations, 16*, 141–148.

Dansereau, F. (1995). A dyadic approach to leadership: Creating and nurturing this approach under fire. *Leadership Quarterly, 6*, 479–490.

Dansereau, F., Alutto, J. A., Markham, S. E., & Dumas, M. (1982). Multiplexed leadership and supervision: An application of within and between analysis. In J. G. Hunt, U. Sekaran, & C. A. Schriesheim (eds.), *Leadership: Beyond establishment views.* Carbondale: Southern Illinois University Press.

Dansereau, F., Alutto, J. A., & Yammarino, F. J. (1984). *Theory testing in organizational behavior: The varient approach.* Englewood Cliffs, NJ: Prentice-Hall.

Dansereau, F., & Dumas, M. (1977). Pratfalls and pitfalls in drawing inferences about leadership behavior in organizations. In J. G. Hunt & L. L. Larson (eds.), *Leadership: The cutting edge.* Carbondale: Southern Illinois University Press.

Dansereau, F., Cashman, J., & Graen, G. (1973). Instrumentality theory and equity theory as complementary approaches in predicting the relationship of leadership and turnover among managers. *Organizational Behavior and Human Performance, 10*, 184–200.

Dansereau, F., Graen, G., & Haga, W. (1975). A vertical dyad approach to leadership within formal organizations. *Organizational Behavior and Human Performance, 13*, 46–78.

Dansereau, F., & Markham, S. E. (1987). Superior-subordinate communication: Multiple levels of analysis. In F. Jablin, L. Putnam, K. Roberts, & L. Porter (eds.), *Handbook of organizational communication.* Newbury Park, CA: Sage.

Dansereau, F., & Yammarino, F. J. (1998) (eds.). Leadership: The multiple-level approaches. Part A: Classical and new wave. Part B: Contemporary and alternatives. *Monographs in organizational behavior and industrial relations.* Stanford, CT: JAI Press.

Dansereau, F., Yammarino, F. J., & Markham, S. E. (1995). Leadership: The multiple level approaches. *Leadership Quarterly, 6*, 97–109.

Dansereau, F., Yammarino, F. J., Markham, S. E., et al. (1995). Individualized leadership: A new multiple level approach. *Leadership Quarterly, 6*, 413–450.

Darley, J. M. (2001). The dynamics of authority influence in organizations and the unintended action consequences. In J. M. Darley, D. M. Messick, & T. R. Tyler (eds.), *Social influences on ethical behavior in organizations.* Mahwah, NJ: Lawrence Erlbaum Associates.

Darley, J. M., & Berscheid, R. (1967). Increased liking as a result of the anticipation of personal contact. *Human Relations, 20*, 29–40.

Dasborough, M. T., & Ashkanasy, N. M. (2002). *Emotion and attribution of intentionality in leader-member relationships.* Paper, Academy of Management, Denver, CO.

Dasborough, M. T., & Ashkanasy, N. M. (2002). Emotion and attribution of intentionality in leader-member relations. *Leadership Quarterly, 13*, 615–634.

Dasborough, M. T., & Ashkanasy, N. M. (2003). *A qualitative study of cognitive and employee affective reactions to leadership behaviors.* Paper, Academy of Management, Seattle, WA.

Dastmalchian, A., Javidan, M., & Kamrun, A. (2001). Effective leadership and culture in Iran. *Applied Psychology: An International Review, 50*, 532–558.

Datta, D. K., & Rajagopalan, N. (1997). Industry structure and CEO characteristics: An empirical study of succession events. *Strategic Management Journal, 19*(9), 833–852.

Daugherty, R., & Williams, S. (1997). The long-term impact of leadership development: An assessment of a state wide program. *Journal of Leadership Studies, 4*(2), 101–114.

Daughtry, L. (1995). *Vocational administrator leadership effectiveness as a function of gender and leadership style.* Unpublished doctoral dissertation, Virginia Polytechnic Institute and State University, Blacksburg, VA.

Daughtry, L. H. & Finch, C. R. (1997). Effective leadership of vocational administrators as a function of gender and leadership style. *Journal of Vocational Educational Research, 22*(3), 173–186.

Daum, J. W. (1975). Internal promotion: A psychological asset or debit? A study of the effects of leader origin. *Organizational Behavior and Human Performance, 13*, 404–413.

Daus, C. S., & Ashkanasy, N. M. (2003). Will the real emotional intelligence please stand up? On deconstructing the emotional intelligence "debate." *The Industrial/Organizational Psychologist, 41*, 69–72.

D'Aveni, R. A. (1994). *Hypercompetition: Managing the Dynamics of Strategic Manoeuvring.* New York: Free Press.

D'Aveni, R. A., & MacMillan, I. (1990). Crisis and the content of management communications: A study of the focus of attention of top managers in surviving and failing firms. *Administrative Science Quarterly, 35*, 634–657.

Davidson, J. E., Deuser, R., & Sternberg, R. J. (1994). The role of meta-cognition in problem solving. In J. Metcalf & A. P. Shimamura (eds.) *Metacognition: Knowing about knowing.* Cambridge, MA: MIT Press.

Davidson, M. N., & Friedman, R. A. (1998). When excuses don't work: The persistent injustice effect among black managers. *Adminisrative Science Quarterly, 43,* 154–183.

Davidson, O. B., & Eden, D. (1997). *Golem effects among underprivileged women: Mediating role of leadership, subordinate expectations and motivation.* Paper, Academy of Management, Boston, MA.

Davidson, W. N., Worrell, D. L., & Cheng, L. (1990). Key executive succession and stockholder wealth: The influence of successor's origin, position, and age. *Journal of Management, 36,* 647–664.

Davidson, R. J. (2001). Toward a biology of personality and emotion. *Annals of the New York Academy of Sciences, 935*(1), 191–207.

Davies, J. C. (1954). Charisma in the 1952 campaign. *American Political Science Review, 48,* 1083–1102.

Davies, J. C. (1963). *Human nature in politics.* New York: Wiley.

Davis, D. D. (1995). Form, function, and strategy in a boundaryless organizations. In A. Howard (ed.), *The changing nature of work.* San Francisco: Jossey-Bass.

Davis, D. D., & Bryant, J. L. (2003). Influence at a distance: Leadership in global virtual teams. *Advances in Global Leadership, 3,* 303–339.

Davis, D. D., Guan, P., Luo, Y., et al. (1997). *Need for continuous improvement, organization citizenship, and service climate in a Chinese state enterprise.* Paper, Society for Organizational and Industrial Psychology, St. Louis, MO.

Davis, D. D., & Polonko, K. A. (2003). *Distributed work in the virtual office: A network study of telework and work outcomes.* Paper, Society for Industrial and Organizational Psychology, Orlando, FL.

Davis, F. J. (1954). Conceptions of official leader roles in the air force. *Social Forces, 32,* 253–258.

Davis, G. (1975). The maturation of Theodore Roosevelt: The rise of an "affective leader." *The History of Childhood Quarterly, 3,* 43–74.

Davis, H. J., Ming, L. W., & Brosnan, I. F. (1986). *The Farmer-Richman model: A bibliographic essay emphasizing applicability to Singapore and Indonesia.* Paper, Academy of Management, Chicago.

Davis, J. A. (1929). A study of 163 Communist leaders. *American Sociological Society, 24,* 42–45.

Davis, J. H., Schoorman, F. D., & Donaldson, L. (1997). Toward a stewardship theory of management. *Academy of Management Review, 22,* 20–47.

Davis, K. (1951). Learning to live in informal groups. *Advanced Management, 16,* 17–19.

Davis, K. (1962). *Human relations at work.* New York: McGraw-Hill.

Davis, K. (1968b). Success of chain of command oral communications in a manufacturing management group. *Academy of Management Journal, 11,* 379–387.

Davis, K. E. (1982). The status of black leadership: Implications for black followers in the 1980s. *Journal of Applied Behavioral Science, 18,* 309–322.

Davis, L. T. (2000). *The effect of organizational factors on intended behavior.* Poster, Society for Industrial and Organizational Psychology, New Orleans, LA.

Davis, R. A. (1987). *Consensus and neoconservatism in the black community: A theoretical analysis of black leadership.* Paper, American Sociological Association, Chicago

Davis, R. C. (1942–1951). *The fundamentals of top management.* New York: Harper.

Davis, T. R., & Luthans, F. (1984). Defining and researching leadership as a behavioral construct: An idiographic approach. *Journal of Applied Behavioral Science, 20,* 237–251.

Davis, T. R. V., & Luthans, F. (1979). Leadership reexamined: A behavioral approach. *Academy of Management Review, 4,* 237–248.

Davis, W. D., & Gardner, W. L. (2004). Perceptions of politics and organizational cynicism: An attributional and leader-member exchange perspective. *Leadership Quarterly, 15,* 439–465.

Dawe, H. C. (1934). The influence of size of kindergarten group upon performance. *Child Development, 5,* 295–303.

Dawley, D. D., Hoffman, J. J., & Brockman, E. N. (2003). Do size and diversification type matter? An examination of post-bankruptcy outcomes. *Journal of Managerial Issues, 15*(4), 413–429.

Dawson, C. A. (1969). Leadership and achievement: The effects of teaching styles on first-grade children. *Dissertation Abstracts, 29,* 2648–2649.

Dawson, J. E., Messick, L. A., & Phillips, J. L. (1972). Effect of instructor-leader behavior on student performance. *Journal of Applied Psychology, 56,* 369–376.

Dawson, J. L. M., Haw, H., Leung, A., & Whitney, R. E. (1971). Scaling Chinese traditional-modern attitudes and the CSR measurement of "important" versus "unimportant" Chinese concepts. *Journal of Cross-Cultural Psychology, 2,* 1–27.

Day, C. (1909). Industrial leadership. *Yale Review, 18,* 21–33.

Day, C. M. (1980). Promotions of health care personnel in hospitals: Heuristic decision-making. *Dissertation Abstracts International, 42*(3A), 1290.

Day, D. R. (1961). Basic dimensions of leadership in a selected industrial organization. *Dissertation Abstracts, 22,* 3760.

Day, D. R. (1968). *Descriptions of male and female leader behavior by male and female subordinates.* Urbana: University of Illinois, Department of Industrial Administration.

Day, D. V. (2002). Leadership development: A review in context. *Leadership Quarterly, 11,* 581–613.

Day, D. V., Gronn, P., & Salas, E. (2004). Leadership capacity in teams, *Leadership Quarterly,* 857–880.

Day, D. V., & Lord, R. G. (1986). *Executive leadership and organizational performance: Suggestions for a new theory and methodology.* Paper, Academy of Management, Chicago. Also: (1988). *Journal of Management, 14,* 453–464.

Day, D. V., & Lord, R. G. (1988). Executive leadership and organizational performance: Suggestions for a new theory and methodology. *Journal of Management, 14,* 453–464.

Day, D. V., & Lord, R. G. (1992). Expertise and problem categorization: The role of expert processing in organizational sense-making. *Journal of Management Studies, 29,* 35–47.

Day, D. V., & Sessa, V. I. (2001). *Group social accounts in executive selection.* Poster, Society for Industrial Organizational Psychology, San Diego, CA.

Day, N. E., & Schoenrade, P. (1997). Staying in the closet versus coming out: Relationships about communication about sexual orientation and work attitudes. *Personnel Psychology, 50,* 147–163.

Day, R. C., & Hamblin, R. L. (1964). Some effects of close and punitive styles of supervision. *American Journal of Sociology, 69*, 499–510.

Deal, J. J., & Stevenson, M. A. (1998). Perceptions of female and male managers in the 1990's. *Sex Roles, 38*, 287–300.

Deal, T. E., & Kennedy, A. A. (1982). *Corporate cultures: The rite and rituals of corporate life.* Reading, MA: Addison-Wesley.

Dean, J. W., Jr. & Scharfman, M. P. (1996). Does decision process matter? A study of strategic decision-making effectiveness. *Academy of Management Journal, 39*, 368–396.

DeAngelis, T. (1993) Psychologists aid victims of violence in post office. *Psychology Monitor, 24* (10), 44–45.

DeAngelis, T. (1997). Stereotypes still stymie women managers. *Monitor,* American Psychological Association, August, 41–42.

Dearborn, D. C., & Simon, H. A. (1958). Selective perception: A note on the departmental identifications of executives. *Sociometry, 21*, 140–144.

Deaux, K. (1976a). *Self-evaluations of male and female managers.* Unpublished manuscript.

Deaux, K. (1976b). *The behavior of women and men.* Monterey, CA: Brooks/Cole.

Deaux, K. (1985). Sex and gender. *Annual Review of Psychology, 36*, 4981.

Deaux, K., & Ernswiller, T. (1974). Explanations of successful performance on sex-linked tasks: What is skill for the male is luck for the female. *Journal of Personality and Social Psychology, 29*, 80–85.

DeBolt, J. W., Liska, A. E., & Weng, B. R. (1976). Replications of associations between internal locus of control and leadership in small groups. *Psychological Reports, 38*, 470.

deCharms, R. (1968). *Personal causation.* New York: Academic Press.

deCharms, R., & Hamblin, R. I. (1960). *Structural factors and individual needs in group behavior.* St. Louis, MO: Washington University.

Deci, E. L. (1972). The effects of contingent and noncontingent rewards and controls on intrinsic motivation. *Organizational Behavior and Human Performance, 8*, 217–229.

Deckop, J. (1987). Top executive compensation and the pay-for-performance issue. In D. B. Balkin & L. R. Gomez-Mejia (eds.), *New perspectives in compensation.* Englewood Cliffs, NJ: Prentice-Hall.

DeCrane, A. C. (1997). A constitutional model of leadership. In F. Hesselbein, M. Goldsmith, & R. Beckhard (eds), *The leader of the future: New visions, strategies and practices for the next era.* San Francisco: Jossey-Bass. p.249.

Deep, S. D., Bass, B. M., & Vaughan, J. A. (1967). Some effects on business gaming of previous quasi-T-group affiliations. *Journal of Applied Psychology, 51*, 426–431.

Deets, N., & Morano, R. (1986). Xerox's strategy for changing management styles. *Management Review, 75*(3), 31–35.

Deets, N. R., & Tyler, D. (1986). How Xerox improved its performance appraisals. *Personnel Journal, 65*(4), 50–52.

de Forest, M. E. (1994) Thinking of a plant in Mexico? *Academy of Management Executive, 8*(1), 33–40.

DeFrank, Konopaske, R., & Ivancevich, J. M. (2000). Executive travel stress: Perils of the road warrior. *Academy of Management Executive, 14*(3), 58–71.

DeFrank, R. S., Matteson, M. T., Schweiger, D. M., & Ivancevich, J. M.

(1985). The impact of culture on the management practices of American and Japanese CEOs. *Organizational Dynamics,* Spring 1985, 62–76.

DeGroot, T., Kiker, D. S., & Cross, T. C. (2000). A meta-analysis to review organizational outcomes related to charismatic leadership. *Canadian Journal of Administrative Sciences, 17*, 356–371.

De Hoogh, A. H. B., Den Hartog, D. N., Koopman, P. L., et al. (2005). Leader motives, charismatic leadership, and subordinates' work attitude in the profit and voluntary sector. *Leadership Quarterly, 16*, 17–38.

Deitch, E. A., Barsky, A., Butz, R. M., et al. (2003). *Subtle yet signficant: The existence and impact of racial discrimination in the workplace.* Paper, Society for Industrial ands Organizational Psychology, Orlando, FL.

Dejung, J. W., & Kaplan, H. (1962). Some differential effects of race of rater and ratee on early peer ratings of combat attitude. *Journal of Applied Psychology, 26*, 370–374.

Dekin, A. (1985). *Planning input from communities: politics and participation.* Paper, Alaska Anthropological Association, Anchorage.

Dekmeiian, R. H., & Wyszomirski, M. J. (1972). Charismatic leadership in Islam: The Mahdi of the Sudan. *Comparative Studies in Society and History. 14*, 193–214.

Delbecq, A. L., & Kaplan, S. J. (1968). The myth of the indigenous community leader: A case study of managerial effectiveness within the "War on Poverty." *Academy of Management Journal, 11*, 11–25.

Delbecq, A. L., & Mills, P. K. (1985). Managerial practices that enhance innovation. *Organizational Dynamics, 14*, 24–34.

DelCostillo, S. W. (undated). *An historical development of the principle of equal opportunity from implementing affirmative action in becoming culturally competen .* Unpublished manuscript.

Dellums, R. V. (1977). Black leadership: For change or for status quo? *Black Scholar, 8*, 2–5.

Dellva, W. L., McElroy, J. C., & Schrader, C. B. (1987). *A longitudinal network analysis of formal versus emergent leadership.* Paper, Academy of Management, New Orleans.

Delson, S. (1986). *Leadership in a public institution of higher education during a period of declining enrollment and declining resources.* Doctoral dissertation, Columbia University Teacher's College, New York.

Deluga, R. (1986). *Employee influence strategies as possible coping mechanisms for role conflict and role ambiguity.* Paper, Eastern Psychological Association, New York.

Deluga, R. J. (1988–1988a). Relationship of transformational and transactional leadership with employee influencing strategies. *Group & Organization Studies, 13*, 456–467.

Deluga, R. (1988b). The politics of leadership: The relationship between task-people leadership and subordinate influence strategies. *Journal of Organizational Behavior, 9*, 359–366.

Deluga, R. J. (1989). Employee influence strategies as possible stress-coping mechanisms for role conflict, and role ambiguity. *Basic and Applied Psychology, 10*(4), 329–335.

Deluga, R. J. (1991a) The relationship of upward-influencing behavior and subordinate-impression management. *Journal of Applied Social Psychology, 21*, 1145–1160.

Deluga, R. J. (1991–1991b). The relationship of leader and subordinate influencing activity in naval environments. *Military Psychology, 3,* 25–39.

Deluga, R. J. (1992) The relationship of leader-member exchanges with laissez-faire, transactional, and transformational leadership in the naval environment. In K. E. Clark, M. B. Clark, & D. P. Campbell (eds.), *Impact of leadership.* Greensboro, NC: Center for Creative Leadership.

Deluga, R. J. (1995). The relationship between attributional charismatic leadership and organizational citizen behavior. *Journal of Applied Social Psychology, 26,* 1642–1669.

Deluga, R. J. (1997a). *Relationship among American presidential proactivity, charismatic leadership, and rated performance.* Paper, Society for Industrial and Organizational Psychology, St. Louis, MO.

Deluga, R. J. (1997b). Relationship among American presidential charismatic leadership, narcissism, and rated performance. *Leadership Quarterly, 6,* 49–65.

Deluga, R. J. (2001). American presidential Machiavellianism: Implications for charismatic leadership and performance. *Leadership Quarterly, 12,* 339–363.

Deluga, R. J. & Perry, J. T. (1991). The relationship of subordinate upward influencing behavior, satisfaction, and perceived superior effectiveness with leader-member exchanges. *Journal of Occupational Psychology, 64,* 239–252.

Deluga, R. J., & Souza, J. (1990–1991). The effects of transformational and transactional leadership styles on the influencing behavior of subordinate police officers. *Journal of Occupational Psychology, 64*(1), 49–55.

Delunas, E. E. (1983). Temperament, personality, and managerial effectiveness: Keirsey-Myers leadership styles. *Dissertation Abstracts International, 44*(4A), 1027.

DeMause, L. (1982). *Foundations of Psychohistory.* New York: Creative Roots.

DeMeuse, K. P. (1986). A compendium of frequently used measures in industrial/organizational psychology. *The Industrial-Organizational Psychologist, 23*(2), 53–59.

De Meuse, K. P., & Tornow, W. W. (1993). Leadership and the changing psychological contract between employer and employee. *Issues & Obervations, 13*(2), 2–6.

De Meyer, A., Loch, C. H., & Pich, M. (2002). Managing project uncertainty: From variation to chaos. *MIT Sloan Management Review,* Winter, 60–64.

Deming, W. E. (1986). *Drastic changes for Western management.* Madison, WI: Center for Quality and Productivity Improvement.

Deming, W. E. (1986). *Out of the crisis.* Cambridge, MA: Center for Advanced Engineering Study, Massachusetts Institute of Technology.

Denenberg, D. (1997). Move over Barney: Make way for real heroes. *American Educator,* Fall, 18, 23.

Denhardt, R. B. (1987). Images of death and slavery in organizational life. *Journal of Management, 13*(3), 529–541.

Denhardt, R. B. (1993). *Theories of Public Organization.* Belmont, CA: Wadsworth Publishing.

Denhart, R. B. (2000). *The pursuit of significance: Strategies for managerial organizations.* Prospect Heights, IL: Waveland Press.

Den Hartog, D. N. (1997). *Inspirational leadership.* Academisch Proefschrift, Vrije Universiteit te Amsterdam, Netherlands.

Den Hartog, D. N. (2004). Assertiveness. In R. J. House, P. A. Hanges, M. Javidan, et al. (eds.), *Leadership, culture, and organizations.* Thousand Oaks, CA: Sage Publications.

Den Hartog, D. N., & Dickson, M. W. (2004). Leadership and culture. In Antonakis, J., Cianciolo, A. T. & Sternberg, R. J. (eds.), *The nature of leadership.* Thousand Oaks, CA: Sage.

Den Hartog, D. N., Dickson, M. W., & Mitchelson, J. (2003). Research on leadership in a cross-cultural context: Making progress and raising new questions. *Leadership Quarterly, 14*(6), 729–768. (See Dickson.)

Den Hartog, D. N., House, R. J., Hanges, P. J., et al. (1999). Culture specific and cross-culturally generalizable implicit leadership theories: Are attributes of charismatic/transformational leadership universally endorsed? *Leadership Quarterly, 10,* 219–256.

Den Hartog, D. N., & Koopman, P. L. (2001). Leadership in organizations. In Anderson, N., Ones, D. S., Kepir-Sinangil, H., & Viswesvaran, C. (eds.), *International handbook of industrial, work and organizational psychology,* vol. 2. London: Sage.

Den Hartog, D. N., Koopman, P. L., & Van Muijen, J. J. (1995). Charismatic leadership: State of the art. *Journal of Leadership Studies, 2,* 35–50.

Den Hartog, D. N., Van Muijen, P. L., & Koopman, P. L. (1994). *Transactional versus transformational leadership: An analysis of the MLQ in the Netherlands.* Paper, International Congress of Applied Psychology, Madrid, Spain.

Den Hartog, D. N., van Muijen, J. J., & Koopman, P. L. (1996). Linking transformational leadership and organizational culture. *Journal of Leadership Studies, 3*(4), 68–83.

Den Hartog, D. N., Van Muijen, J. J. & Koopman, P. L. (1997). Transactional and transformational leadership: An analysis of the MLQ. *Journal of Occupational and Organizational Psychology, 70,* 19–34.

Den Hartog, D. N. & Verburg, R. M. (1997). Charisma and rhetoric: Communicative techniques of international business leaders. *Leadership Quarterly, 8,* 355–391.

DeNisi, A. S., & Kluger, A. N. (2000). Feedback effectiveness: Can 360-degree appraisals be improved? *Academy of Management Executive, 14*(1), 129–139.

DeNisi, A. S., & Pritchard, R. D. (1978). Implicit theories of performance as artifacts in survey research: A replication and extension. *Organizational Behavior and Human Performance, 21,* 358–366.

DeNisi, A. S., Randolph, W. A., & Blencoe, A. G. (1983). Potential problems with peer feedback. *Academy of Management Journal, 26,* 457–464.

Denison, D. R. (1984). Bringing corporate culture to the bottom line. *Organizational Dynamics, 13*(2), 5–22.

Denmark, F. L. (1977). Styles of leadership. *Psychology of Women Quarterly, 2,* 99–113.

Denmark, F. L. (1980). Psyche: From rocking the cradle to rocking the boat. American *Psychologist, 35,* 1057–1065.

Denmark, F. L. (1993). Women, leadership, and empowerment. *Psychology of Women Quarterly, 17,* 343–356.

Denmark, F. L., & Diggory, J. C. (1966). Sex differences in attitudes toward leaders' display of authoritarian behavior. *Psychological Reports, 18,* 863–872.

Dennis, A. R., George, J. F., Jessup, L., et al. (1988). Information technology to support electronic meetings. *MIS Quarterly, 12,* 591–624.

Dennis, A. R., & Valacich, J. S. (1993). Computer brainstorms: More heads are better than one. *Journal of Applied Psychology, 78,* 531–537.

Densten, I. L., & Gray, J. H. (1998). The case for using both latent and manifest variables to investigate management-by-exception. *Journal of Leadership Studies, 5*(3), 80–92.

Denston, I. L., & Sarros, J. C. (1995). *Leadership and burnout in an Australian law enforcement organization.* Paper, Inaugural Australian Industrial and Organizational Psychology Conference, Sydney, Australia.

Dent, J. K. (1959). Organizational correlates of the goals of business managements. *Personnel Psychology, 12,* 365–396.

Denton, R. T. (1976). The effects of differing leadership behaviors on the job satisfaction and job performance of professional mental health workers. *Dissertation Abstracts International, 37,* 3183.

DePaulo, B. M., & Rosenthal, R. (1979). Telling lies. *Journal of Personality and Social Psychology, 37,* 1713–1722.

DeRouin, R. E., Fritsche, B. A., & Salas, E. (2003). *Optimizing e-learning: Research based guidelines for learner-controlled training.* Paper, Society of Industrial and Organizational Psychology, Orlando, FL.

Derber, M., Chalmers, W. E., Edelman, M. T., & Triandis, H. C. (1965). *Plant union-management relations.* Urbana: University of Illinois Press.

Derr, B. C. (1972). Successful entry as a key to successful organization development in big city school systems. In W. Burke & H. A. Hornstein (eds.), *The social technology of organization development.* Fairfax, VA: NTL Learning Resources.

DeSanctis, G., & Poole, M. S. (1997). Transitions in teamwork in new organizational forms. *Advances in group processes, 14,* 157–176.

Deshpande, S. P., Schoderbek, P. P., & Joseph, J. (1994). Promotion decisions by managers: A dependency perspective. *Human Relations, 47,* 223–232.

Desmond, R. E., & Seligman, M. (1977). A review of research on leaderless groups. *Small Group Behavior, 8,* 3–24.

Dess, G. G., & Pickens, J. C. (2000). Changing Roles: Leadership in the 21st century. *Organizational Dynamics, 28*(3), 18–34.

Dessler, G. (1973). *An investigation of the path-goal theory of leadership.* Doctoral dissertation, Baruch College, City University of New York.

Dessler, G., & Valenzi, E. R. (1977). Initiation of structure and subordinate satisfaction: A path analysis test of path-goal theory. *Academy of Management Journal, 20,* 251–259.

De Souza, G., & Klein, H. J. (1995). Emergent leadership in the group goal setting process. *Small Group Research, 26,* 475–496.

De Toqueville, A. (1832/1966). *Democracy in America.* New York: Harper & Row.

Dess, G. G. & Picken, J. C. (2000). Changing roles: Leadership in the 21st century. *Organizational Dynamics, 28*(3), 18–34.

Deutsch, M. (1949). An experimental study of the effects of cooperation and competition upon group process. *Human Relations, 2,* 199–232.

Deutsch, M. (1962). Cooperation and trust: Some theoretical notes. In M. R. Jones (ed.), *Nebraska Symposium on Motivation.* Nebraska University Press.

Deutsch, M. (1973). *The resolution of conflict: Constructive and destructive processes.* New Haven, CT: Yale University Press.

Deutsch, M., & Gerard, H. B. (1954). *A study of normative and informational social influences upon individual judgment* (Tech. Rep.), Contract NONR-285(10). New York: New York University.

Deutsch, R. (1962). *Nonlinear Transformations of Random Processes* Englewood Cliffs, NJ: Prentice-Hall.

Deutschberger, P. (1947). The structure of dominance. *American Journal of Orthopsychiatry, 17,* 343–351.

Development Dimensions International. (1983). *Behavior modeling through computer-assisted instruction, 2*(3), 1–3.

Devereaux, C. (1955). Charismatic leadership and crisis. In W. Muensterberger & S. Axelrod (eds.), *Psychoanalysis and the Social Sciences.* New York: International University Press.

Devine, R. P. (1977). Opinion influence roles: Opinion leaders, opinion followers, and isolates. *Dissertation Abstracts International, 37*(12A), 7977.

DeVries, D. L. (1992). Executive selection: Advances but no progress, *Issues & Observations, 12*(4), 1–5.

DeVries, D. L. (1993). *Executive selection: A look at what we know and what we need to know.* Greensboro, NC: Center for Creative Leadership.

De Vries, R. E. (1997). *Need for leadership: A solution to empirical problems in situational theories of leadership.* Doctoral dissertation, University of Tilburg, Tilburg, Netherlands.

De Vries, R. E., Roe, R. A., & Taillieu, T. C. B. (1998). Need for supervision: Its impact on leadership effectiveness. *Journal of Applied Behavioral Science, 34*(4), 486–501.

De Vries, R. E., Roe, R. A., & Taillieu, T. C. B. (2002). Need for leadership as a moderator of the relationship between leadership and individual outcomes. *Leadership Quarterly, 13,* 121–137.

Dewhirst, H. D. (1971). *Use of communications sources: An intercultural investigation.* New York: Haworth Press.

Dewhirst, H. D. (1971b). Influence of perceived information-sharing norms on communication channel utilization. *Academy of Management Journal, 14,* 305–315.

Dewhirst, H. D., Metts, V., & Ladd, R. (1987–8). *Exploring the delegation decision: Managerial responses to multiple contingencies.* Paper, Academy of Management, New Orleans.

Dexter, E. S., & Stein, B. (1955). The measurement of leadership in white and Negro women students. *Journal of Abnormal and Social Psychology, 51,* 219–221.

Deyo, F. C. (1978). The cultural patterning of organizational development: A comparative case study of Thailand and Chinese industrial enterprises. *Human Organization, 37,* 68–72.

Dicke, L. A. (2002). Ensuring accountability in human services contracting: can strewardship theory fill the bill? *The American Review of Public Administration, 32*(4), 455.

Dicken, C. F., & Black, J. D. (1965). Predictive validity of psychometric evaluations of supervisors. *Journal of Applied Psychology, 49,* 34–37.

Dickerson, A., & Taylor, M. A. (2000). Self-limiting behavior in women: Self-esteem and self-efficacy as predictors. *Group & Organization Management, 25,* 191–210.

Dickinson, Z. C. (1937). *Compensatory industrial effort.* New York: Ronald Press.

Dickson, M. W., Den Hartog, D. N., & Mitchelson, J. (2003). Research on leadership in a cross-cultural context: Making progress and raising new questions. *Leadership Quarterly, 1*(6), 729–768.

Dickson, M. W. (1998). *Differences within-organization agreement when describing the organization—and implications of those differences.* Paper, Society for Industrial Organizational Psychogy, Dallas, TX.

Dickson, M. W., BeShears, R. S., Borys, J., et al. (2003). *The popular and academic literatures on leadership: Different messages or different packaging?* Paper, Society for Industrial and Organizational Psychology. Orlando, FL.

Dickson, M. W., BeShears, R. S., & Gupta, V. (2004). The impact of societal culture and industry on organizational culture: theoretical explanations. In House, R. J., Hanges, P. J., Javidan, M., Dorfman, P. W. & Gupta, V. (eds.), *Culture, leadership, and organizations: The GLOBE study of 62 societies.* Thousand Oaks, CA: Sage. p. 74–90.

Dickson, M. W., Smith, D. B., Grojean, M. W., Ehrhart, M. (2001). An organizational climate regarding ethics: the outcome of leader values and the practices that reflect them. *Leadership Quarterly, 12*(2), 197–217.

Diefendorf, J. M., & Silverman, S. B. (2001). *Examining the equivalence of 360° ratings across sources: Recommendations for research and practice.* Paper, Society for Industrial and Organizational Psychology, San Diego, CA.

Diener, E. (2000). Subjective well-being; the science of happiness and a proposal for a national index. *American Psychologist, 55,* 34.

Diener, E., Diener, M., & Diener, C. (1995). Factors predicting the subjective well-being of nations. *Journal of Personality and Social Psychology, 69,* 851–864.

Dienesch, R. M. (1985). *A three dimensional model of leader-member exchange: An empirical test.* Paper, Academy of Management, Chicago.

Diemer, H. (1914). *Factory organization and administration* (2nd ed.). New York: McGraw-Hill.

Dienesch, R. M., & Liden, R. C. (1986). Leader-exchange model of leadership: A critique and further development. *Academy of Management Review, 11,* 618–634.

Dietz, W. (1943). Training new supervisors in the skill of leadership. *Personnel, 19,* 604–608.

Digman, J. M. (1990). Personality structure: Emergence of the five-factor model. *Annual Review of Psychology, 41,* 417–440.

Digman, J. M. (1996). The curious history of the five-factor model of personality.: Lexical perspectives of the five-factor model. In J. S. Wiggins (ed.), *Theoretical perspectives for the five-factor model of personality.* New York: Guilford Press.

Dill, D., & Pearson, A. W. (1984). The effectiveness of project managers: Implications of a political model of influence. *IEEE Transactions on Engineering Management, 31*(3), 138–146.

Dill, W. R. (1958). Environment as an influence on managerial autonomy. *Administrative Science Quarterly, 2,* 409–443.

Dilulio, J. (1987). *Governing prisons: Comparative study of correctional management,* New York: Free Press.

DiMaggio, P. J. (1995). Comments on "What theory is *not*." *Administrative Scheince Quarterly, 40,* 391–397.

DiMaggio, P. J., & Anheier, H. K. (1990). The sociology of nonprofit organizations and sectors. *Annual Review of Sociology, 16,* 137–159.

DiMarco, N., & Whitsitt, S. E. (1975). A comparison of female supervi-

sors in business and government organizations. *Journal of Vocational Behavior, 6,* 185–196.

DiNisi, A. S., & Kluger, A. S. (2000). Feedback effectiveness: Can it be improved? *Academy of Management Executive, 14*(1), 129–139.

Dionne, S. D., Yammarino, F. J., Atwater, L., et al. (2002). Neutralizing substitutes for leadership theory: Leadership effects and common-source bias. *Journal of Applied Psychology, 87,* 454–464.

Dionne, S. D., Yammarino, F. J., Comer, L. B., et al. (1996). Transformational and transactional leadership of female managers: Predicting subordinate effectiveness and performance. *Journal of Leadership Studies, 3,* 134–147.

Dipboye, R. L., Fontenelle, G. A., & Garner, K. (1984). Effects of previewing the application on interview process and outcomes. *Journal of Applied Psychology, 69,* 118–128.

Dirks, K. T. (2000). Trust in leadership and team performance from NCAA basketball. *Journal of Applied Psychology, 85,* 1004–1012.

Dirks, K. T., & Skarlicki, D. (2004). Trust in leaders: Existing research and emerging issues. In R. Kramer, & K. Cook (eds.), *Trust within organizations.* Russell Sage Foundation.

DiThomaso, N. (1993). Weber's social history and Etzioni's structural theory of charisma in organizations: Implications for thinking about charismatic leadership. *Leadership Quarterly, 3,* 257–275.

DiThomaso, N., & Hooijberg, R. (1996). Diversity and the demands of leadership. *Leadership Quarterly, 7,* 163–187.

Dittman, M. (2005). Generational differences at work: A psychologist studies ways to help traditionalists, baby boomers, gen Xers and millenials work better together, despite their generational differences. *Monitor on Psychology,* June, 34–35.

DiVesta, F. J. (1954). Instructor-centered and student-centered approaches in teaching a human relations course. *Journal of Applied Psychology, 38,* 329–335.

Dixon, N. (1976). *On the psychology of military incompetence.* London: Jonathan Cape.

Dixon, N. (1997). *On the psychology of military incompetence.* New York: Basic Books.

Dobbins, G. H. (1985). Effects of gender on leaders' responses to poor performers: An attributional interpretation. *Academy of Management Journal, 28,* 587–598.

Dobbins, G. H., & Platz, S. J. (1986). Sex differences in leadership: How real are they? *Academy of Management Review, 11*(1), 118–127.

Dobbins, G. H., Sgro, J. A., & Smith, E. (1990). The effects of attributions and costs of corrective actions on leaders' implementation of control policy: An extension of the attributional model of leadership. *Basic & Applied Social Psychology, 11,* 49–60

Dobbins, G. H., & Russell, J. M. (1986). The biasing effects of subordinate likeableness of leaders' responses to poor performers: A laboratory and a field study. *Personnel Psychology, 39,* 759–777.

Dobbins, G. H., & Zaccaro, S. J. (1986). The effects of group cohesion and leader behavior on subordinate satisfaction. *Group & Organization Studies, 11,* 203–219.

Dobruszek, Z. (1967). Badanie postaw kierowniczych za pomoca "Inwentarza postaw i pogladow" B. M. Bassa. [A study on leadership attitudes with "Orientation Inventory" of B. M. Bass.] *Przeglad Psychologiczny, 15.*

Dockery, T. M. (1993). *Subordinate independence: a boundary condi-*

tion on the effectiveness of transformational leadership? Baton Rouge, Louisiana State University.

Dodge, C. (1995). Ethics watch: Jerry's kids. *Ethics: Easier said than done, 29,* 3.

Dodge, G. E. (1998). *Leader-teams role paper,* September 4. otdod@ttacs.ttu.edu.

Dogan, M. (1979). How to become a minister in France: Career pathways 1870–1978. *Comparative Politics, 12*(1), 1–26.

Dogan, M., & Rokkan, S. (1969). *Quantitative ecological analysis in the social sciences.* Cambridge, MA: MIT Press.

Doktor, R. H. (1990). Asian and American CEOs: A comparative study. *Organizational Dynamics,18*(3), 46–56.

Doloff, P. G. (1999). Beyond the org chart. *Across the Board,* February, 43–47.

Donaldson, L. (1990). The ethereal hand: Organizational economics and management theory. *Academy of Management Review, 15,* 369–381.

Donaldson, T., & Dunfee, T. W. (1994). Toward a unified conception of business ethics: Integrative social contracts theory. *Academy of Management Review, 19*(2), 252–284.

Donnelly, C. (1976). Keys to the executive powder room. *Money,* August, 28–32.

Donovan, M. A., Drasgow, F., & Probst, T. M. (2000). Does computerizing paper-and-pencil job attitude scales make a difference? New IRT analyses offer insight. *Journal of Applied Psychology, 85,* 305–313.

Dooley, R. S. & Fryxell, G. E. (1999). Attaining decision quality and commitment from dissent: The moderating effects of loyalty and competence in strategic decision-making teams. *Academy of Management Journal, 42,* 389–402.

Dorfman, P. (2004). International and cross-cultural leadership research. In Pennet, B.J. & Shenkar, O. (eds.). *Handbook for international research* (2nd ed). Ann Arbor, MI: University of Michigan, 265–355.

Dorfman, P., Hanges, P. J., & Brodbeck, F. C. (2004). Leadership and cultural variation: The identification of culturally endorsed leadership profiles. In House, R. J., Hanges, P. J., Javidan, M., Dorfman, P., & Gupta, V. (eds.), *Leadership, culture, and organizations: The GLOBE study of 62 societies.* Thousand Oaks, CA: Sage Publications, Inc., 667–718.

Dorfman, P. W. (1996). International and cross-cultural leadership. In H. B. Pennett & O. Shenkar (eds.). *Handbook of international business research.* Cambridge, MA: Blackwell.

Dorfman, P. W., & Howell, J. P. (1988). Dimensions of national culture and effective leadership patterns. *Advances in International Comparative Management, 3,* 127–150.

Dorfman, P. W., Howell, J. P., Cotton, B., & Tate, U. (1992). Leadership within the "discontinuous hierarchy" structure of the military: Are effective leadership behaviors similar within and across command structures? In K. E. Clark, M. B. Clark, & D. P. Campbell (eds.), *Impact of Leadership.* Greensboro, NC: Center for Creative Leadership.

Dorfman, P. W., Howell, J. P., Hibino, S., et al. (1997). Leadership in Western and Asian countries: Commonalities and differences in effective leadership processes across cultures. *Leadership Quarterly, 8,* 233–275.

Dorfman, P. W., & Ronen, S. (1991). *The universality of leadership theories: Challenges and paradoxes.* Paper, Academy of Management, Miami, FL.

Dorfman, R. H. (1994a). *Cross-cultural leadership research: Issues and assumptions.* Paper, Society for Industrial and Organizational Psychology, Nashville, TN.

Dorfman, R. H. (1994b). *Lessons learned from international and cross-cultural research.* Paper, International Congress of Applied Psychology, Madrid, Spain.

Dossett, D. L., Cella, A., Greenberg, C. I., & Adrian, N. (1983). *Goal setting, participation and leader supportiveness effects on performance.* Paper, American Psychological Association, Anaheim, CA.

Dotlich, D. L. (1982). International and intercultural management development. *Development journal, 3*(10), 26–31.

Dougherty, D., & Hardy, C. (1996). Sustained product innovation in large, mature organizations: overcoming innovation-to-organization problems. *Academy of Management Journal, 39*(5), 1120–1153.

Dougherty, D. E. (1999). Dialogue through standpoint: Understand women's and men's standpoints of sexual harassment. *Management Communication Quarterly, 12,* 436–468.

Douglas, C. A., & McCaulley, C. D. (1997). A survey on the use of formal developmental relationships in organizations. *Issues & Obervations, 17*(1–2), 5–10.

Douglas, W. S. (1977). An evaluation of experimental procedures for the systematic training of group leaders. *Dissertation Abstracts International, 36,* 4255.

Dover, K. (1999). Avoiding empowerment traps. *Management Review, 88*(1), 51–55.

Dow, T. E., Jr. (1969a). The theory of charisma. *Sociological Quarterly, 10,* 306–318.

Dow, T. E., Jr. (1969b). The role of charisma in modern African development. *Social Forces, 46,* 328–336.

Dowd, A. R. (1986). What managers can learn from manager Reagan. *Fortune,* September 15, 33–41.

Dowd, J. (1936). *Control in human societies.* New York: Appleton-Century.

Dowell, B. E., & Wexley, K. N. (1978). Development of a work behavior taxonomy for first-line supervisors. *Journal of Applied Psychology, 63,* 563–572.

Downey, H. K., Hellriegel, D., & Slocum, J. W., Jr. (1975). Environmental uncertainty: The construct and its application. *Administrative Science Quarterly, 20,* 613–629.

Downey, H. K., Sheridan, J. E., & Slocum, J. W., Jr. (1975). Analysis of relationships among leader behavior, subordinate job performance and satisfaction: A path goal approach. *Academy of Management Journal, 18,* 253–262.

Downey, H. K., Sheridan, J. E., & Slocum, J. W., Jr. (1976). The path-goal theory of leadership: A longitudinal analysis. *Organizational Behavior and Human Performance, 16,* 156–176.

Downey, R. C., Medland, F. F., & Yates, L. C. (1976). Evaluation of a peer rating system for predicting subsequent promotion of senior military officers. *Journal of Applied Psychology, 61,* 206–209.

Downs, A. (1967). *Inside bureaucracy.* Boston: Little, Brown.

Downton, J. V. (1973). *Rebel leadership: Commitment and charisma in the revolutionary process.* New York: Free Press.

Doyle, W. J. (1971). Effects of achieved status of leader on productivity of groups. *Administrative Science Quarterly, 16,* 40–50.

Drachkovitch, M. M. (1964). Succession and the charismatic leader in Yugoslavia. *Journal of International Affairs, 18*(1), 54–66.

Drach-Zahavy, A., & Somech, A. (2003). *Towards supportive teams: The role of team's design, culture, and leadership.* Paper, Academy of Management, Seattle, WA.

Dragon, A. C. (1979). Leader behavior in changing libraries. *Library Research, 1*(1), 53–66.

Drake, St. C., & Cayton, H. (1966). The world of the urban lower-class Negro. In R. J. Murphy & H. Elinson (eds.), *Problems and prospects of the Negro movement.* Belmont, CA: Wadsworth.

Drake, B. H., & Moberg, D. (1986). Communicating influence attempts in dyads: Linguistic sedatives and palliatives. *Academy of Management Review, 11,* 567–584.

Drake, R. M. (1944). A study of leadership. *Character & Personality, 12,* 285–289.

Drakeley, R. J., & Herriot, P. (1988). Biographical data, training successes and turnover. *Journal of Occupational Psychology, 61,* 145–152.

Draper, N. R., & Smith, H. (1966). *Applied regression analysis.* New York: Wiley.

Drath, W. H., & Palus, C. J. (1994). *Making common sense: Leadership as meaning–making in a community of practice.* Greensboro, NC: Center for Creative Leadership.

Drazin, R., & Kazanjian, R. K. (1993). Applying the DEL technique to the analysis of cross-classification data: A test of CEO succession and top management team development. *Academy of Management Journal, 36,* 1374–1399.

Dreher, G., & Cox, T. H., Jr. (1996). Race, gender, and opportunity: A study of compensation attainment and the establishment of mentoring relationships. *Journal of Applied Psychology, 81,* 297–308.

Dreher, C. F., Dougherty, T. W., & Whitely, W. (1988). Influence tactics and salary attainment: A study of sex-based salary differentials. *Proceedings,* Academy of Management, Anaheim, CA, 346–350.

Dreher, G. F., Dougherty, T. W., & Whitely, B. (1988) *Influence tactics and salary attainment: A study of sex-based salary differentials.* Paper presented at the Academy of Management, 48th Annual National Meeting, Anaheim, CA.

Dreilinger, C., McElheny, R., Rice, D., & Robinson, B. (1982). The promise of leadership-style training: An outdated myth? *Training 6, Development Journal, 3*(8), 69–71.

Drenth, P. J. D. (1986). *The university and its leadership: A look from the rector's office.* Presidential address, Division of Organizational Psychology, International Association of Applied Psychology, Jerusalem, Israel.

Dreyfus, H. L., & Dreyfus, S. E. (1986). *Mind over machine: The power of human intuition and expertise in the era of the computer.* New York: Free Press.

Driscoll, D. M., & Goldberg, C. R. (1993). Women and work. *Harvard Business Review, 71*(5), 178–180.

Driscoll, D. M., & Goldberg, C. R. (1993). *Members of the club: Coming of age of executive women.* New York: Free Press.

Driscoll, D. M., & Goldberg, C. R. (1994). Personal power. *Executive Female, 17*(5), 46.

Drory, A., & Beaty, D. (1991). Gender differences in the perception of organizational influence tactics. *Journal of Organizational Behavior, 12,* 249–258.

Drory, A., & Gluskinos, V. M. (1980). Machiavellianism and leadership. *Journal of Applied Psychology, 65,* 81–86.

Drucker, E. H., & Schwartz, S. (1973). *The prediction of AWOL, military skills, and leadership potential.* Alexandria, VA: Human Resources Research Organization.

Drucker P, (1986). A crisis of capitalism. *Wall Street Journal,* September 30, p. 31.

Drucker, P. F. (1946). *Concept of the corporation.* New York: John Day.

Drucker, P. F. (1954). *The practice of management.* New York: Harper & Row.

Drucker, P. F. (1991). The discipline of innovation. In J. Henry & D. Walker (eds.), *Managing innovation.* San Francisco: Sage.

Drucker, P. F. (1994). The age of transformation. *The Atlantic Monthly,* November.

Drucker, P. F. (1998). *The profession of management.* Boston, MA: Harvard Business School Press.

Drucker, P. F. (1999). Managing oneself. *Harvard Business Review,* (2), 65–74, p. 73.

Drucker, P. F. (1999). *Management challenges for the 21st century.* New York: HarperCollins.

Druckman, D. (1994). Determinants of compromising behavior in negotiation. *Journal of Conflict Resolution, 38,* 507–556.

Druskat, V. U., & Wheeler, J. V. (2001). *Managing from the boundary: The effective leadership of self-managing work teams.* Paper, Academy of Management, Washington, DC.

Druskat, V. U., & Wheeler, J. V. (2003). Managing from the boundary: The effective leadership of self-managing work teams. *Academy of Management Journal, 46,* 435–457.

Duarte, D. L., & Snyder, N. T. (1999). *Mastering virtual teams.* San Francisco: Jossey-Bass.

Duarte, N. T., Goodson, J. R., & Klich, N. R. (1994). Effects of dyadic quality and duration on performance appraisal. *Academy of Management Journal, 37,* 499–521.

Dubin, R. (1958, 1962). *The world of work.* Englewood Cliffs, NJ: Prentice Hall.

Dubin, R. (1962b). Stability of human organizations. In M. Haire (ed.), *Modern organizational theory.* New York: Wiley.

Dubin, R. (1979). Metaphors of leadership: An overview. In J. C. Hunt & L. L. Larson (eds.), *Crosscurrents in leadership.* Carbondale: Southern Illinois University Press.

Dubin, R., & Spray, S. L. (1964). Executive behavior and interaction. *Industrial Relations, 3,* 99–108.

Dubnick, M. J. (1998). Clarifying accountability: An ethical theory framework. In C. N. P. Samford & C. A. Bois (eds.). *Public sector ethics. Finding and implementing values.* Leichhardt, NSW, Australia: Federation Press/Routledge.

Dubnick, M. J. (2003). Accountability and ethics: Reconsidering the relationships. *International Journal of Organizational Theory and Behavior, 6,* 405–441.

Dubinsky, A. J., Yammarino, F. J., & Jolson, M. A. (1995). An examination of linkages between personal characteristics and dimensions of transformational leadership. *Journal of Business and Psychology, 9*(3), 315–335.

Dubno, P. (1963). Decision time chartacteristics of leaders and group problem solving behavior. *Journal of Social Psychology, 59*, 259–282.

Dubno, P. (1968). Group congruency patterns and leadership characteristics. *Personnel Psychology, 21*, 335–344.

Dubofsky, M., & Van Tine, W. (1986). *John L. Lewis: A biography.* Champaign, IL: University of Illinois Press

Dubofsky, M., & Van Tine, W. (1987). *Labor leaders in America.* Urbana, IL: University of Illinois Press.

DuBrin, A. J. (1963). Trait and situational approaches in the development of a leadership inventory. *Journal of Industrial Psychology, 1*, 28–37.

Duchon, D., Green, S. G., & Tabor, T. D. (1986). Vertical dyad linkage: A longitudinal assessment of antecedents, measures, and consequences. *Journal of Applied Psychology, 71*, 56–60.

Duke, L. (1988). *Relationships between nurse education administrators' leadership and empowerment of nursing faculty and students.* Salt Lake City, UT: Brigham Young University.

Dukerich, J. M., Nichols, M. L., Elm, D. R., & Vollrath, D. A. (1990). Moral reasoning in groups: Leaders make a difference. *Human Relations, 43*(5), 473–493.

Dulebohn, J. H., & Ferris, G. R. (1999). The role of influence tactics in perceptions of performance evaluation fairness. *Academy of Management Journal, 42*, 288–303.

Dumaine, B. (1990). Who needs a boss? *Fortune*, May 7, 52–55.

Duncan, W. J. (1982). Humor in management: Prospectus for administrative practice and research. *Academy of Management Review, 7*, 136–142.

Duncan, W. J. (1984). Perceived humor and social network patterns in a sample of task-oriented groups: A re-examination of prior research. *Human Relations, 37*, 895–907.

Duncan, P. K., & Bruwelheide, L. R. (1985–86). Feedback: Use and possible behavioral functions. *Journal of Organizational Behavior Management, 7*(3–4), 91–114.

Dunegan, K. J., Duchon, D., & Uhl-Bien, M. (1992). Examining the link between leader-member exchange and subordinate performance. The role of task analyzability and variety as moderators. *Journal of Management, 18*, 59–76.

Dunfee, T. W. (2001). Marketlike morality within organizations. In J. M. Darley, D. M. Messick, and T. R. Tyler (eds.), *Social influences on ethical behavior in organizations.* Mahwah, NJ: Lawrence Erlbaum Associates.

Dunford, B. B., & Williams, J. (1999). *Feedback seeking and the relationship between self-supervisor performance ratings.* Paper, Society for Industrial and Organzational Psychology, Atlanta, GA.

Dunkerley, M. D. (1940). A statistical study of leadership among college women. *Student Psychology and Psychiatry, 4*, 1–64.

Dunlap, A. J., & Andelman, B. (1996). *Mean business: How I save bad companies and make good companies great.* New York: Fireside.

Dunnette, M. D. (1967). The motives of industrial managers. *Organizational Behavior and Human Performance, 2*, 176–182.

Dunnette, M. D. (1970). *Multiple assessment procedures in identifying and developing managerial talent* (ONR Tech. Rep. 4000). Minneapolis: University of Minnesota.

Dunnette, M. D. (1971). Multiple assessment procedures in identifying and developing managerial talent. In P. McReynolds (ed.), *Advances in psychological assessment*, vol. 1. Palo Alto, CA: Science and Behavior Books.

Dunnette, M. D. (1986). *Describing the role of the middle manager. Is the role of the middle manager really different?* Symposium, American Psychological Association, New York.

Dunphy, D. C. (1963). The social structure of urban adolescent peer groups. *Sociometry, 26*, 230–246.

Dunteman, G. H. (1966). Self, interaction, and task-orientation scores and their relationship to promotability ratings. *Journal of Industrial Psychology, 4*, 20–26.

Dunteman, G. H., & Bass, B. M. (1963). Supervisory and engineering success associated with self, interaction, and task orientation scores. *Personnel Psychology, 16*, 13–22.

Dupuy, R. E., & Dupuy, T. N. (1959). *Brave men and great captains.* New York: Harper & Row.

Durand, D. E., & Nord, W. R. (1976). Perceived leader behavior as a function of personality characteristics of supervisors and subordinates. *Academy of Management Journal, 19*, 427–438.

Durand, D. E., & Shea, D. (1974). Entrepreneurial activity as a function of achievement motivation and reinforcement control. *Journal of Psychology, 88*, 57–63

Durant, W. (1957). *The reformation.* New York: Simon & Schuster.

Durbrow, B. R. (1971). *Inter-firm executive mobility.* Doctoral dissertation, Ohio State University, Columbus.

Durojaiye, M. O. (1969). Patterns of friendship and leadership choices in a mixed ethnic junior school: A sociometric analysis. *British Journal of Educational Psychology, 39*, 88–89.

Dustin, D. S., & Davis, H. F (1967). Authoritarianism and sanctioning behavior. *Journal of Personality and Social Psychology, 6*, 222–224.

Dutton, J. E. (1988). Understanding strategic agenda building in organizations and implications for management change. In L. R. Pondy, R. J. Boland, Jr., & H. Thomas (eds.), *Managing ambiguity and change.* Chichester, U.K.: Wiley.

Dutton, J. E., Dukerich, J. M., & Harquail, C. V. (1994). Organizational images and member identification. *Administrative Science Quarterly, 39*, 239–263.

Dutton, J. E., Frost, P. J., Worline, M. C., et al. (2000). Leading in times of trauma. *Harvard Business Review, 80*(1), 54–61.

Duxbury, M. L., Armstrong, G. D., Drew, D. J., & Henly, S. J. (1984). Head nurse leadership style with staff nurse burnout and job satisfaction in neonatal intensive care units. *Nursing Research, 33*(2), 97–104.

Dvir, T. (1998). The impact of transformational leadership training on follower development and performance: A field experiment. Doctoral dissertation, Tel Aviv University, Israel. See also Dvir, T., Eden, D., Avolio, B. J., & Shamir, B. (2002). *Academy of Management Journal, 45*, 735–744.

Dvir, T., Eden, D, & Banjo, M. L. (1995). Self-fulfilling prophesy and gender: Can women be Pygmalion and Galetea? *Journal of Applied Psychology, 80*, 253–270.

Dvir, T., & Shamir, B. (2002). *Transformational followership: Longitudinal study of follower characteristics as predicting leadership.* Paper, Society for Industrial and Experimental Psychology, Toronto.

Dweck, C., & Leggett, E. (1988). A social-cognitive approach to motivation and personality. *Psychological Review, 95,* 256–273.

Dwivedi, R. S. (1983). Management by trust: A conceptual model. *Group & Organization Studies,* 8, 375–405.

Dworkin, A. G., & Dworkin, R. J. (1999). *The minority report: An introduction to racial, ethnic, and gender relations,* 3rd ed. Wadsworth Publishing.

Dworkin, R. H. (1979). Genetic and environmental influences on person-situation interactions. *Journal of Research in Personality,* 13(3), 279–293.

Dwyer, D. C. (1984). The search for instructional leadership: Routines and subtleties in principal's role. *Educational Leadership, 4,* 32–37.

Dyck, B. (1994). Build in sustainable development and they will come: A vegetable field of dreams. *Journal of Organizational Change Management,* 7(4), 47–63.

Dye, T. R., & Strickland, J. (1982). Women at the top: A note on institutional leadership. *Social Science Quarterly, 63,* 333–341.

Dyer, J. L., & Lambert, W. E. (1953). *Coordination of flying activities in bomb wings: Integration and performance.* Chapel Hill: University of North Carolina, Institute for Research in Social Science.

Dyer, W. G., & Dyer, J. H. (1984). The M*A*S*H generation: Implications for future organizational values. *Organizational Dynamics* 13(l), 66–79.

Dynes, R. R. (1970). *Organized behavior in disasters.* Lexington, MA: D. C. Heath.

Dyson, J. W., Godwin, P. H., & Hazelwood, L. A. (1976). Group composition, leadership orientation, and decisional outcomes. *Small Group Behavior,* 7, 114–128.

Eagly, A. H. (1970). Leadership style and role differentiation as determinants of group effectiveness. *Journal of Personality, 38,* 509–524.

Eagly, A. H. (1983). Gender and social influence: A social psychological analysis. *American Psychologist, 38,* 971–981.

Eagly, A. H. (1987). *Sex differences in social behavior.* Hillsdale, NJ: Lawrence Erlbaum & Associates.

Eagly, A. H. (1991). *Gender and leadership.* Address, American Psychological Association, San Francisco, CA.

Eagly, A. H. (1995). The science and politics of comparing women and men. *American Psychologist, 50,* 145–158.

Eagly, A. H. (2001). *Differences and similarities in the leadership styles of women and men: Transformational, transactional, and laissez faire leadership:* Paper, Festschrift for Bernard M. Bass. Binghamton University, Binghamton, NY.

Eagly, A. H., & Carli, L. L. (1981). Sex of researchers and sex-typed communications as determinants of sex differences in influenceability: A meta-analysis of social influence studies. *Psychological Bulletin,* 90, 1–20.

Eagly, A. H., & Crowley, M. (1986). Gender and helping behavior: A meta-analytic review of the social psychological literature. *Psychological Bulletin, 100,* 283–308.

Eagly, A. H., & Johannesen-Schmidt, M. C. (2001). The leadership styles of women and men. *Journal of Social Issues,* 57(4), 781–797.

Eagly, A. H., Johannesen, M. C., & van Engen (2002). *Transformational, transactional and laissez-faire leadership styles.* Paper, Academy of Management, Denver, CO.

Eagly, A. H., & Johannesen-Schmidt, M. (2001). The leadership styles of women and men. *Journal of Social Issues,* 57(4), 781–797.

Eagly, A. H., & Johnson, B. T. (1990). Gender and leadership style: A meta-analysis. *Psychological Bulletin, 108,* 233–256.

Eagly, A. H., & Karau, S. J. (1991). Gender and the emergence of leaders: A meta-analysis. *Journal of Personality and Social Psychology, 60,* 685–610.

Eagly, A. H., & Karau, S. J. (2002). Role congruity theory of prejudice toward female leaders. *Psychological Review, 109,* 573–598.

Eagly, A. H., Karau, S. J., & Makhijani, M. G. (1995). Gender and the effectiveness of leaders: A meta-analysis. *Psychological Bulletin, 117,* 125–145.

Eagly, A. H., Karau, S. J., & Makhijani, M. G. (1995). Gender and leadership style: A meta analysis. *Psychological Bulletin, 111,* 3–22.

Eagly, A. H., Makhijani, M. G., & Klonsky, B. G. (1992). Gender and the evaluation of leaders: A meta-analysis. *Psychological Bulletin, 111,* 3–22.

Eagly, A. H., & Steffen, V. J. (1986). Gender and aggressive behavior: A meta-analytic review of the social psychological literature. *Psychological Bulletin, 100,* 309–330.

Eagly, A. H., & Steffen, V. J. (1986). Gender stereotypes, occupational roles, and beliefs about part-time employees. *Psychology of Women Quarterly, 10,* 252–262.

Earley, P. C. (1984). Social interaction: The frequency of use and valuation in the U.S., England, and Ghana. *Journal of Cross-Cultural Psychology, 15,* 477–485.

Earley, C. R. (1985). The role of praise and criticism across cultures: A study of the U.S. and England. *Proceedings, Academy of Management,* 206–209.

Earley, P. C. (1985). Influence of information, choice and task complexity upon goal acceptance, performance, and personal goals. *Journal of Applied Psychology, 70,* 481–491.

Earley, P. C. (1986a). An examination of the mechanisms underlying the relation of feedback to performance. *Proceedings,* Academy of Management, Chicago, 214–218.

Earley, P. C. (1986b). Supervisors and shop stewards as sources of contextual information in goal setting: A comparison of the United States with England. *Journal of Applied Psychology, 71,* 111–117.

Earley, P. C. (1988). *Contributions of intercultural research to the understanding of performance feedback.* Paper, Society for Industrial and Organizational Psychology, Dallas.

Earley, P. C. (1993). East meets West meets Mideast: Further explorations of collectivistic and individualistic work groups. *Academy of Management Journal, 36,* 319–348.

Earley, P. C. (1994). Self or group? Cultural effects of training on self-efficacy and performance. *Administrative Science Quarterly, 39,* 89–117.

Easterby-Smith, M., Thorpe, R., & Holman, D. (1996). Using repertory grids in management. *Journal of European Industrial Training,* 20(3), 1–30.

Eaton, J. H., Sr. (1977). *The relationship between the superintendent's management behavior, elementary and secondary principal's rule administration behavior, and leadership perception.* Doctoral dissertation, Pennsylvania State College, State College, PA.

Ebrahimi, B. (1985c). Measuring the effects of cultural and other explanatory variables on motivation to manage of potential managers from five countries: A case of theory building and theory testing in cross-cultural research. *Dissertation Abstracts International,* 4(2A), 469–470.

Echavarria, N. U., & Davis, D. D. (1994). *A test of Bass's model of transformational and transactional leadership in the Dominican Republic.* Paper, International Congress of Applied Psychology, Madrid, Spain.

Echohawk, J. E. (1990). The first Californians are still last. *Los Angeles Times,* March 12, 5.

Eckhardt, W. (1965). War propaganda, welfare values, and political ideologies, *The Journal of Conflict Resolution,* 9(3), 345–358.

Eckhardt, W. (1988). Comment on Ray's "Why the F Scale predicts racism: A critical review." *Political Psychology,* 9, 681–691.

Eddleston, K. A., Kidder, D. L., & Litsky, B. E. (2002). Who's the boss? Contending with competing expectations from customers and management. *Academy of Management Executive,* 16, 85–95.

Eddy, E. R., Stone, D. L., & Stone-Romero, E. F. (1999). The effects of information managemnet policies on reactions to human resource information systems: An integration of privacy and procedural justice perspectives. *Personnel Psychology,* 52, 335–358.

Edelstein, B. (2001). *Executive coaching & development: Does it work? What makes it work? What benefits do participants and corporations derive?* Paper, Society for Industrial and Organizational Psychology, San Diego, CA.

Eden, D. (1984). *Pygmalion at work.* Lanham, MD: Lexington Books.

Eden, D. (1984). Self-fulfilling prophecy as a management tool: Harnessing Pygmalion. *Academy of Management Review,* 9, 64–73.

Eden, D. (1988). Pygmalion, goal setting, and expectancy: Compatible ways to boost productivity. *Academy of Management Review,* 13, 639–652.

Eden, D. (1993). Leadership and expectations: Pygmalion effects and other self-fulfilling prophecies in organizations. *Leadership Quarterly,* 3, 271–305.

Eden, D., & Aviram, A. (1993). Self-efficacy training to speed reemployment: Helping people to help themselves. *Journal of Applied Psychology,* 78, 352–360.

Eden, D., & Davidson, O. B. (1997). *Remedial self-fulfilling prophesy: Preventing Golem effects among disadvantaged women.* Paper, Society for Industrial and Organizational Psychology, St. Louis, MO.

Eden, D., Geller, D., Gerwirtz, A., et al. (2000). Implanting Pygmalion leadership through workshop training: Seven experiments. *Leadership Quarterly,* 11, 171–210.

Eden, D., & Kinnar, J. (1991). Modeling Galetea: Boosting self-efficacy to increase volunteering. *Journal of Applied Psychology,* 76, 770–780.

Eden, D., & Leviatan, U. (1975). Implicit leadership theory as a determinant of the factor structure underlying supervisory behavior scales. *Journal of Applied Psychology,* 60, 736–741.

Eden, D., & Ravid, G. (1982). Pygmalion vs. self-expectancy: Effects of instructor—and self-expectancy on trainee performance. *Organizational Behavior and Human Performance,* 30, 351–364.

Eden, D., & Shani, A. B. (1982). Pygmalion goes to boot camp: Expectancy, leadership, and trainee performance. *Journal of Applied Psychology,* 67, 194–199.

Edinger, L. J. (1993). A preface to studies in political leadership. In G. Sheffer (1993). *Innovative leaders in international politics.* Albany, NY: State University of New York Press.

Edmondson, E. L. J. (2001). *Our separate ways: Black and white women and the struggle for professional identity.* Boston: Harvard Business School Press.

Edwards, C., & Heery, E. (1985). The incorporation of workplace trade unionism? Some evidence from the mining industry. *Sociology,* 19, 345–363.

Edwards, J. E., & Rode, L. G. (1986). *A path analytic approach to the construct validation of selected leadership scales.* Paper, Academy of Management, Chicago.

Edwards, J. R. (2001). Alternatives to difference scores: Polynomial regression analysis and response surface methodology. In F. Drasgow & Schmitt (eds.), *Advances in measurement and data analysis.* San Francisco: Jossey-Bass.

Edwards, J. R., & Perry, M. (1993). On the use of polynomial regression equations as an alternative to difference scores in organizational research. *Academy of Management Journal,* 36, 1577–1613.

Edwards, M. T. (1973). *Leader influence and task set.* Master's thesis, State University of New York, Buffalo.

Efron, B., & Tibshirani (1993). *An introduction to bootstrap.* New York: Chapman & Hall.

Egan, R. F. C., Sarros, J. C., & Santora, J. C. (1995). Putting transactional and transformational leadership into practice. *Journal of Leadership Studies,* 2, 100–123.

Egbert, R. L., Meeland, R., Cline, V. B., et al. (1957). *Fighter 1: An analysis of combat fighters and non-fighters* (HumRRO Tech. Rep. No. 44). Presidio of Monterey, CA: U.S. Army Leadership Human Research Unit.

Eggleston, K. K., & Bhagat, R. S. (1993). Organizational contexts and contingent leadership roles: A theoretical explanation. *Human Relations,* 46, 1177–1192.

Egri, C. P., & Frost, P. J. (1994). Leadership for environmental and social change. *Leadership Quarterly,* 5, 195–200.

Egri, C. P., & Herman, S. (2000). Leadership in the North American environmental sector: Values, leadership styles, and contexts of environmental leaders and their organizations. *Academy of Management Journal,* 43, 571–604.

Ehrhart, M. G., & Klein, K. J. (2001). Predicting followers' preferences for charismatic leadership: The influence of followers' values and personality. *Leadership Quarterly,* 11, 153–179.

Ehrhart, M. G., & Klein, K. J. (2001). Predicting followers' preferences for charismatic leadership: The influence of follower values and personality. *Leadership Quarterly,* 12, 153–179.

Ehrlich, H. J. (1973). *The social psychology of prejudice.* New York: Wiley.

Eichenwald, K. (2006). Enron: Beyond the verdicts Enron's name is mud, but some of its ideas are still golden—and are making other companies billions. *Newsweek,* international edition, 11 December 2006, 64–65.

Eichler, G. A. (1934). *Studies in student leadership.* Doctoral dissertation, Pennsylvania State College, State College, PA.

Eichler, C. A., & Merrill, R. R. (1933). Can social leadership be improved by instruction in its technique? *Journal of Educational Sociology,* 7, 233–236.

Eisenberger, R., Armeli, S., & Pretz, J. (1998). Can the promise of reward increase creativity? *Journal of Personality and Social Psychology,* 74, 704–714.

Eisenberger, R., & Cameron, J. (1998). Reward, intrinsic interest and creativity: New findings. *American Psychologist,* 53, 676–678.

Eisenstadt, S. N. (1952). The process of absorption of new immigrants in Israel. *Human Relations,* 5, 223–246.

Eisenstadt, S. N. (1954). Studies in reference group behavior. 1. Reference norms and the social structure. *Human Relations,* 7, 191–216.

Eisman, B. (1975). *The effects of leader sex and self-disclosure on member self-disclosure in marathon encounter groups.* Unpublished doctoral dissertation, Boston University.

Eisman, E. J. (1975). The effects of leader sex and self-disclosure on member self-disclosure in marathon encounter groups. *Dissertation Abstracts International,* 36, 1429.

Eitzen, R., & Yetman, N. (1972). Managerial change, longevity, and organizational effectiveness. *Administrative Science Quarterly,* 17, 110–116.

Ekvall, G. (1988). *Förneyelse och friktion. Om organisation, kreativitet och innovation, nature och culture.* Stockholm. Sweden.

Ekvall, G., & Arvonen, J. (1984). *Leadership styles and organizational climate for creativity: Some findings in one company* (Report 1). Stockholm: Faradet.

Ekvall, G., & Arvonen, J. (1991). Change-centered leadership: An extension of the two-dimensional model. *Scandinavian Journal of Management,* 7, 17–26.

Elenkov, D. S., & Judge, W. (2002). *Strategic leadership behaviors and innovation influence: An empirical international study.* Paper, Academy of Management, Denver, CO.

Eley, T. C. (1997). General genes: A new theme in developmental pathology. *Current Directions in Psychological Science,* 6, 90–92.

Elgie, D. M., Hollander, E. P, & Brice, R. W. (1988). Appointed and elected leaders' responses to favorableness of feedback and level of task activity from followers. *Journal of Applied Social Psychology,* 18, 1361–1370.

El Haddad, C. M. (undated). *How leaders shape group efficacy: The role of psychological state and nonverbal expression.* University of Southern California; Management and Organization Department.

El Salmi, A. M., & Cummings, L. L. (1968). Managers' perceptions of needs and need satisfactions as a function of interactions among organizational variables. *Personnel Psychology,* 21, 465–477.

Elkin, F., Halpern, G., & Cooper, A. (1962). Leadership in a student mob. *Canadian Journal of Psychology,* 16, 199–201.

Elkins, T., & Keller, R. (2003). Leadership in research and development organizations: A literature review and conceptual framework. *Leadership Quarterly,* 14, 587–2003.

Ellerman, D. P. (1999). Global institutions: Transforming international development agencies into learning organizations. *Academy of Management Executive,* 13, 25–35.

Elliot, M. (1990). Thatcher's stormy term ends abruptly: British life won't be quite the same. *Press & Sun-Bulletin* (Binghamton, NY), November 25 1E, 5E.

Elliott, O., & Penner, D. D. (1974). The impact of social structure and organizational change. In H. L. Fromkin & J. J. Sherwood (eds.), *Integrating the organization.* New York: Free Press.

Elliott, R. (1996). *Leadership, teams, and outcomes: Two associated measures.* Paper, Australian Psychological Society, Sydney.

Elliott, R. (1997). Leadership and team performance measurement. *Magazine: Australian Institute of Management,* March, 1–7.

Ellis, A., & Ilgen, D. R. (undated). *Race and ratings in a team situation: An attributional perspective.* Unpublished manuscript.

Ellis, C., & Sonnenfeld, J. A. (1994). Diverse approaches to managing diversity. *Human Resource Management,* 33(1), 79–109.

Ellis, C. A. (undated). *Computer supported cooperative work.* MCC, Austin, Texas.

Ellis, R. A. (1956). Social status and social distance. *Sociology and Social Research,* 40, 240–246.

Ellis, S., Nadler, A., & Rabin, A. (1996). Political leaders in the : SYMLOG space: Perceptions of right and left wing leaders by right and left wing constituencies. *Leadership Quarterly,* 7, 507–526.

Elms, A. C., & Janis, I. L. (1965). Counter-norm attitudes induced by consonant vs. dissonant conditions of role-playing. *Journal of Experimental Research in Personality,* 1, 50–60.

Elron, E. (1997). Top management teams within multinational corporations. *Leadership Quarterly,* 8, 393–412.

Elsbach, K. D., & Elofson, G. (2000). How the packaging of decision explanations affects perceptions of trustworthiness. *Academy of Management Journal,* 43, 80–89.

Elshtain, J. B. (1995). *Democracy on trial.* New York: Basic Books.

Ely, R. J. (1990). *The role of women in relationships among professional women at work.* Paper, Academy of Management, San Francisco, CA.

Ely, R. J. (1995). The power in demography: Women's social construction of gender identity at work. *Academy of Management Journal,* 38, 589–634.

Emans, B. J. M., Munduate, L., Klaver, E., & Van de Vliert, E. (2003). Constructive consequences of leaders' forcing influence styles. *Applied Psychology: An International Review,* 52(1), 36–54.

Emerson, R. M. (1964). Power-dependence relations: Two experiments. *Sociometry,* 27, 282–298.

Emery, F. E. (1959). *Characteristics of socio-technical systems.* Document no. 527. London: Tavistock Institute of Human Relations.

Emery, F. E . (1967) The next thirty years: Concepts, methods and anticipations. *Human Relations,* 20, 199–237.

Emery, F. E. (1987). *Paper No. 24, Strategies for work and learning—1999.* Einar Thorsrud Memorial Seminar, Work Research Institute, Oslo, Norway.

Emery, F. E., & Trist, E. L. (1965). The causal texture of organizational environments. *Human Relations,* 18, 21–32.

Emmons, R. A. (1987). Narcissism: Theory and measurement. *Journal of Personality and Social psychology,* 52, 11–17.

Emmons, R. A. (1999). *The psychology of ultimate concerns: Motivation and spirituality in personality.* New York: Guilford Press.

Emrich, C. G, Brower, H. H., Feldman, J. M., et al. (2001). Images in words: Presidential rhetoric, charisma, and greatness. *Administrative Science Quarterly,* 46, 527–557.

Engel , C. V (1970). Professional autonomy and bureaucratic organization. *Administrative Science Quarterly,* 15, 12–21.

Engelbrecht, A. S., & Cloete, B. E. (2000). An analysis of a supervisory-subordinate relationship. *Journal of Industrial Psychology,* 26(1), 24–28.

Engelbrecht, A. S., Erasmus, R. G., & Sivasubramaniam, N. (1999). Validating a typology of fit between strategic resource management and organizational performance. *Management Dynamics*, 8(2), 40–57.

Engelbrecht, A. S., & Fischer, A. H. (1995). The managerial performance implications of a developmental assessment center process. *Human Relations*, 48, 387–404.

Engelbrecht, A. S., & Murray, W. D. (1995). *The influence of leader-subordinate work value congruence on the performance and satisfaction outcomes of transactional and transformational leaders*. Binghamton, NY: Binghamton University.

England, C. W. (1967a). Personal value systems of American managers. *Academy of Management Journal*, 10, 53–68.

England, G. W. (1967b). Organizational goals and expected behavior of American managers. *Academy of Management Journal*, 10, 107–117.

England, C. W. (1970). *Personal value systems analysis as an aid to understanding organizational behavior: A comparative study in Japan, Korea, and the United States*. Paper, Exchange Seminar on Comparative Organizations, Amsterdam.

England, C. W., Dhingra, O. P., & Agarwal, N. C. (1974). *The manager and the man: A cross-cultural study of personal values*. Kent, OH: Kent State University Press.

England, C. W., & Koike, R. (1970). Personal value systems of Japanese managers. *Journal of Cross-Cultural Psychology*, 1, 21–40.

England, C. W., & Lee, R. (1974). The relationship between managerial values and managerial success in the United States, Japan, India, and Australia. *Journal of Applied Psychology*, 59, 411–419.

England, C. W., & Weber, M. L. (1972). *Managerial success: A study of value and demographic Correlates* (ONR Tech. Rep.). Minneapolis: University of Minnesota, Center for the Study of Organizational Performance and Human Effectiveness.

Engle, E. M., & Lord, R. G. (1997). Implicit theories, self-schemas, and leader-member exchange. *Academy of Management Journal*, 40, 988–1010.

Enright, R. D., Freedman, S., & Rique, (1998). The psychology of interpersonal forgiveness In R. D. Enright & J. North (eds.), *Exploring forgiveness*. Madison, WI: University of Wisconsin Press.

Ensari, N., & Murphy, S. (2003). Cross-cultural variations in leadership perceptions and attributions of charisma to the leader. *Organizational Behavior and Human Decision Processes*, 92, 52–56.

Ensari, N., & Riggio, R. E. (2005). *Personality and leadership emergence in leaderless group discussions: A meta-analysis*, Paper, Society for Industrial and Organizational Psychology, Los Angeles, CA.

Ensari, N., & Riggio, R. E. (2005b). *Emergence in leaderless group discussions: A meta-analysis*. Paper, Society of Industrial and Organizational Psychology, Los Angeles, CA.

Ensher, E. A., Murphy, S. E., & Sullivan, S. E. (2002). Reel women: Lessons from female TV executives on managing work and real life. *Academy of Management Executive*, 16(2), 108–119.

Ensley, M. D., Hmieleski, K. M., & Pearce, C. L. (2006). The importance of vertical and shared leadership within new venture top management teams: Implications for the performance of startups. *Leadership Quarterly*, 17, 217–231.

Ensley, M. D., & Pearce, C. L. (2001). Shared cognition in top management teams: Implications for new venture performance. *Journal of Organizational Behavior*, 22, 145–160.

Ensley, M. D., Pearce, C. L., & Hmieleski, K. M. (2006). The moderating effect of environmental dynamism on the relationship between entrepreneur leadership behavior and new venture performance. *Journal of Business Venturing*, 21(2), 243–263.

Entwisle, D. R., & Walton, J. (1961). Observations on the span of control. *Administrative Science Quarterly*, 5, 522–533.

Eoyang, C. K. (1983). Symbolic transformation of belief systems. In L. Pondy, R. Frost, E. Morgan, & T. Dandridge (eds.), *Organizational symbolism*. New York: JAI Press.

Epitropaki, O., & Martin, R. (2001). *"Getting my way with my manager . . .": Transformational leadership, upward influence tactics and employee outcomes*. Paper, Academy of Management, Washington, DC.

Epitropaki, O., & Martin, R. (2005). The moderating role of individual differences in the relation between transformational/transactional leadership perceptions and organizational identification. *Leadership Quarterly*, 16(4), 569–589.

Epstein, G. F. (1969). Machiavelli and the devil's advocate. *Journal of Personality and Social Psychology*, 11, 38–41.

Epstein, C. F. (1991). Debate: Ways women lead. *Harvard Business Review*, 69(1), 150–151.

Epstein, S. (1994). Integration of the cognitive and the psychodynamic unconscious. *American Psychologist*, 49, 709–724.

Eran, M. (1966). Relationship between self-perceived personality traits and job attitudes in middle management. *Journal of Applied Psychology*, 50, 424–430.

Erdogan, B. (2002). Antecedents and consequences of justice perceptions in performance appraisals. *Human Resource Management Review*, 12(4), 555–578.

Erdogan, B., Kraimer, M. L., & Liden, R. C. (2002). *Person-organization fit and work attitudes: The moderating role of leader-member exchange*. Poster, Academy of Management, Denver, CO.

Erez, M. (1979). *Correlates of leadership style: Field-dependence and social intelligence versus social orientation*. Unpublished manuscript.

Erez, M. (1980). Correlates of leadership style: Field-dependence and social intelligence versus social orientation. *Perceptual and Motor Skills*, 50, 231–238.

Erez, M. (1986). The congruence of goal-setting strategies with sociocultural values, and its effects on performance. *Journal of Management*, 12, 83–90.

Erez, M., & Arad, R. (1986). Participative goal-setting: Social, motivational, and cognitive factors. *Journal of Applied Psychology*, 71, 591–597.

Erez, M., Earley, P. C., & Huhn, C. L. (1985). The impact of participation on goal acceptance and performance: A two-step model. *Academy of Management Journal*, 28, 50–66.

Erez, M., & Kanfer, F. H. (1983). The role of goal acceptance in goal setting with task performance. *Academy of Management Review*, 8, 454–463.

Erez, M., & Rim, Y. (1982). The relationships between goals, influence, tactics, and personal and organizational variables. *Human Relations*, 35, 871–878.

Ergun, T., & Onaran, O. (1981). Managerial styles as a means of improving an organization: The Turkish Electricity Authority case. *Turkish Public Administration Annual, 8,* 45–67.

Ericksen, J. (2003). *Exploring variations in team development across high and low performing project teams.* Paper, Academy of Management, Seattle, WA.

Erikson, E. C. (1969). *Gandhi's truth: On the origins of militant nonviolence.* New York: Norton.

Erikson, E. (1968). *Identity: Youth and crisis.* New York: W. W. Norton.

Erikson, E. (1964). *Insight and responsibility.* New York: W. W. Norton.

Erikson, E. (1958, 1968). *Young man Luther: A study in psychoanalysis and history.* New York: Norton.

Ericsson General Electric. (1993). The evolution of empowerment. *Training, 30*(9), 21–27.

Erisman, M. S., & Reilly, N. P. (1996). *The 360 degree performance evaluation: Unique or redundant information?* Paper, Society for Industrial and Organizational Psychology, San Diego, CA.

Erwin, P. (1995). *The role of leadership in developing work teams.* Inaugural Australian Industrial and Organizational Psychology Conference, Melbourne.

Eskilson, A. (1975). Sex composition and leadership in small groups. *Dissertation Abstracts International, 35,* 5694.

Eskilson, A., & Wiley, M. G. (1976). Sex composition and leadership in small groups. *Sociometry, 39,* 183–194.

Essa, L. M. (1983). Expectations of the head nurse's qualifications, leadership behavior and role in Egyptian hospitals. *Dissertation Abstracts International, 44*(6B), 1780.

Essed, P. (1991). *Understanding everyday racism.* Newbury Park: Sage

Esser, N. J., & Strother, C. B. (1962). Rule interpretation as an indicator of style of management. *Personnel Psychology, 15,* 375–386.

Estler, S. E. (1975). Women as leaders in public education. *Signs, 1,* 363–386.

Ettle, J. (1986). *The first-line supervisor and advanced manufacturing technology.* Ann Arbor, MI: Industrial Technology Institute.

Etzioni, A. (1961). *A comparative analysis of complex organizations.* New York: Free Press.

Etzioni, A. (1965). Dual leadership in complex organizations. *American Sociological Review, 30,* 688–698.

Etzioni, A. (1984). Moderating effect of social support on the stressburnout relationship. *Journal of Applied Psychology, 69,* 615–622.

Etzioni, A. (2002). When it comes to ethics, b-schools get an f. *The Washington Post,* 4 August.

Eunni, R.V., & Post, J. E. (2002). *What matters most? A review of MNE literature, 1990–2000.* Paper, Academy of Management, Denver, CO.

Evan, W. M., & Simmons, R. G. (1969). Organizational effects of inequitable rewards: Two experiments in status inconsistency. *Administrative Science Quarterly, 4,* 224–237.

Evan, W. M., & Zelditch, M. (1961). A laboratory experiment on bureaucratic authority. *American Sociological Review, 26,* 883–893.

Evans, M. G. (1968). *The effects of supervisory behavior upon worker perception of their path-goal relationships.* Doctoral dissertation, Yale University, New Haven, CT

Evans, M. G. (1970a). The effects of supervisory behavior on the path-goal relationship. *Organizational Behavior and Human Performance, 5,* 277–298.

Evans, M. G. (1973). A leader's ability to differentiate: The subordinate's perception of the leader and subordinate's performance. *Personnel Psychology, 26,* 385–395.

Evans, M. G. (1974). Extensions of a path-goal theory of motivation. *Journal of Applied Psychology, 59,* 172–178.

Evans M. G., & Dermer, J. (1974). What does the least preferred coworker scale really measure? A cognitive interpretation. *Journal of Applied Psychology, 59,* 202–206.

Exline, R. V. (1960). Interrelations among two dimensions of sociometric status, group congeniality and accuracy of social perception. *Sociometry, 23,* 85–101.

Exline, R. V., & Ziller, R. C. (1959). Status congruency and interpersonal conflict in decision-making groups. *Human Relations, 12,* 147–162.

Eylon, D., & Au, K.Y. (1999). Exploring empowerment cross-cultural differences along the power distance dimension. *International Journal of Intercultural Relations, 23*(3), 373–385.

Eysenck, H. J. (1967). *The biological basis of personality.* Springfield: C. C. Thomas.

Eysenck, H. J. (1970). *The structure of human personality* (3rd ed.). London: Methuen.

Eysenck, H. J. (1985). *Personality and individual differences: A natural science approach.* New York: Plenum.

Eysenck, H. J., & Wilson, G. D. (1978). *The psychological basis of ideology.* Lancaster, U.K.: MTP Press.

Ezekiel, R. S. (1968). The personal future and Peace Corps competence. *Journal of Personality and Social Psychology Monograph Supplement,* Part 2, 8, 1–26.

Ezell, H. F., Odewahn, C. A., & Sherman, J. D. (1982). Women entering management: Differences in perceptions of factors influencing integration. *Group & Organization Management, 7*(2), 243–253.

Ezzedeen, S. R., Swiercz, P. M., & Holt, H. W. (2003). *Global executive socialization: A model and research agenda for executive development.* Paper, Academy of Management, Seattle, WA.

Faber, D. (1978). *The presidents' mothers.* New York: St. Martin's Press.

Facteau, C. L., Facteau, J. D., Schoel, L. C., et al. (1998). Reactions of leaders to 360-degree feedback from subordinates and peers. *Leadership Quarterly, 9,* 427–448.

Facteau, J. D., Dobbins, G. H., Russell, J. E. A., et al. (1995). The influence of general perceptions of the training environment on pretraining motivation and perceived training transfer. *Journal of Management, 21,* 1–25.

Facteau, J. D., & Smith, W. G. (2000). *A comparison of managerial effectiveness models across four rating sources.* Paper, Society for Industrial and Organizational Psychology, San Diego, CA.

Fagenson, E. A. (1986). Women's work orientations: Something old, something new. *Group & Organization Studies, 11*(1–2), 75–100.

Fagenson, E. A. (1989). *The mentor advantage: Career and job attributes considered.* Unpublished manuscript.

Fahey, W., & Harris, R. (1987). *Excellence in Command. Conference on Military Leadership: Tradition and Future Trends.* Annapolis, MD: U.S. Naval Academy.

Fairholm, G. W. (1994a) *Leadership and a culture of trust.* New York: Praeger.

Fairholm, G. W. (1994b). Leading diverse followers. *Journal of Leadership Studies, 1*(4), 82–93.

Fairholm, G. W. (1995). Leadership: A function of interactive trust. *Journal of Leadership Studies, 2*(2), 9–19, p. 11.

Fairhurst, G. T., Green, S. C., & Snavely, B. K. (1984). Face support in controlling poor performance. *Human Communication Research, 11,* 272–295.

Falbe, C. M., & Yukl, G. A. (1992). Consequences for managers of using single tactics and combinations of tactics. *Academy of Management Journal, 35,* 638–652.

Fallon, B. J., & Hollander, E. P. (1976). *Sex-role stereotyping in leadership: A study of undergraduate discussion groups.* Paper, American Psychological Association, Washington, DC.

Farina, A., Allen, J., & Saul, C. (1966). The role of the stigmatized person in affecting social relationships. *Journal of Personality, 71,* 421–428.

Farkus, C. M., & De Backer, P. (1996). *Maximum leadership: Five strategies for success from the world's leading CEOs.* London: Perigee.

Farling, M. L., Stone, A. G., & Winston, B. E. (1999). Servant leadership: Setting the stage for empirical research. *Journal of Leadership Studies, 6,* 49–72.

Farmer, R. N., & Richman, B. M. (1965). *Comparative management and economic progress.* Homewood, IL: Irwin.

Farmer, S. M., & Maslyn, J. M. (1999). Why are styles of upward appraisal neglected? Making the case for a configurational approach to influences. *Journal of Management, 25,* 653–682.

Farquhar, K. W. (1995). Not just understudies: The dynamics of short-term leadership. *Human Resource Management, 34,* 51–70.

Farr, J. I., & Dobbins, G. H. (1989a). Effects of self-esteem on leniency bias in self-reports of performance: A structural model equation. *Personnel Psychology, 42,* 835–850.

Farr, J. I., & Dobbins, G.H. (1989b). Effects of comparative performance information on the accuracy of self-ratings and agreement between self- and supervisor ratings. *Journal of Applied Psychology, 74,* 606–610.

Farren, C., & Kaye, B. L. (1996). New skills for new leadership roles. In F. Hesselbein, M. Goldsmith, & R. Beckhard (eds.), *The Leader of the Future: New Visions, Strategies and Practices for the Next Era.* San Francisco: Jossey-Bass.

Farris, G. F. (1971a). *Colleagues' roles and innovation in scientific teams* (Working Paper No. 552–71). Cambridge, MA: Alfred F. Sloan School of Management, MIT.

Farris, G. F. (1972). The effect of individual roles on performance in innovative groups. *R&D Management,* No. 3.

Farris, G. E., & Lim, F. G. (1969). Effects of performance on leadership, cohesiveness, influence, satisfaction, and subsequent performance. *Journal of Applied Psychology, 53,* 490–497.

Farrow, D. L. (1984). *Impact of authoritarianism on organizational functioning.* Paper, International Conference on Authoritarianism and Dogmatism, Potsdam, NY.

Farrow, D. L., & Bass, B. M. (1977). *A phoenix emerges: The importance of manager and subordinate personality in contingency leadership analyses.* (Tech. Rep. 77–1). Rochester, NY: University of Rochester.

Farrow, D. L., Valenzi, E. R., & Bass, B. M. (1980). *A comparison of leadership and situational characteristics within profit and non-profit organizations.* Paper, Academy of Management, Detroit.

Farrow, D. L., Valenzi, E. R., & Bass, B. M. (1981). *Managerial political behavior, executive success and effectiveness.* Paper, Academy of Management, San Diego, CA.

Fast, R. C. (1964). *Leader behavior of principals as it relates to teacher satisfaction.* Master's thesis, University of Alberta, Edmonton.

Fattah, H. M. (2006). Kuwaiti women join the voting after a long battle for suffrage. *New York Times,* June 30, A9.

Faucheux, C. (1984). *Leadership, power and influence within social systems.* Paper, Symposium on the Functioning of Executive Power, Case Western University, Cleveland, OH.

Faucheux, C., Amado, G., & Laurent, A. (1982). Organizational development and change. *Annual Review of Psychology, 33,* 343–370.

Faucheux, C., & Rojot, J. (1979). Social psychology and industrial relations: A cross-cultural perspective. In G. M. Stephenson & C. J. Brotherton (eds.), *Industrial relations: A social psychological approach.* New York: Wiley.

Faunce, D., & Beegle, J. A. (1948). Cleavages in a relatively homogeneous group of rural youth: An experiment in the use of sociometry in attaining and measuring integration. *Sociometry, 11,* 207–216.

Fauquier, W., & Gilchrist, J. (1942). Some aspects of leadership in an institution. *Child Development, 13,* 55–64.

Fay, R. J., & Middleton, W. C. (1943). Judgment of leadership from the transmitted voice. *Journal of Social Psychology, 17,* 99–102.

Fayol, H. (1916). *Administration industrielle et générale.* Paris: Dunod.

Feather, N. T., & Simon, J. G. (1975). Reactions to male and female success and failure in sex-linked occupations: impressions of personality, causal attributions, and perceived likelihood of different consequences. *Journal of Personality and Social Psychology, 31,* 20–31.

Fedor, D. B., Buckley, M. R., & Eder, R. W. (1990). *Subordinate perceptions of supervisor feedback intentions.* Unpublished manuscript.

Fedor, D. B., Buckley, M. R., & Eder, R. W. (1990). Measuring subordinate perceptions of supervisor feedback intentions: Some unsettling results. *Educational and Psychological Measurement, 50,* 73–89.

Fedor, D. B., Davis, W. D., Maslyn, J. M., et al. (2001). Performance improvement efforts in response to negative feedback: The roles of source power and recipient self-esteem. *Journal of Management, 27,* 79–97.

Fedor, D. B., Goodman, J. S., & Maslyn, J. M. (1992). *Factors affecting the use of upward influence structures.* Paper, Academy of Management, Las Vegas, NV.

Feierabend, R. L., & Janis, I. L. (1954). An experimental comparison of two ways of organizing positive and negative arguments in persuasive communications. *American Psychologist, 9,* 362–363.

Feil, M. H. (1950). *A study of leadership and scholastic achievement in their relation to prediction factors.* Doctoral dissertation, Ohio State University, Columbus.

Feinberg, M. R. (1953). Relation of background experience to social acceptance. *Journal of Abnormal and Social Psychology, 48,* 206–214.

Feitler, F. C., & Blumberg, A. (1971). Changing the organizational character of a school. *Elementary School Journal, 71,* 206–215.

Feld, S., & Lewis, J. (1967). *The assessment of achievement anxieties in children*. Washington, DC: National Institute of Mental Health, Mental Health Study Center. National Institute of Mental Health.

Feldman, D. C. (1985). The new careerism: Origins, tenets and consequences. *Industrial-Organizational Psychologist, 23*, 39–44.

Feldman, D. C. (1986). Why no good deed goes unpublished. *The Industrial-Organizational Psychologist, 24*, 39–41.

Feldman, D. C., Folks, W. R., & Turnley, W. H. (1999). Mentor-protégé diversity and its impact on international internship experiences. *Journal of Organizational Behavior, 20*, 597–611.

Feldman, R. A. (1967). Three types of group integration: Their relationship to power, leadership, and conformity behavior. *Dissertation Abstracts, 27*, 2202–2203.

Fellner, D. J., & Sulzer-Azaroff, B., (1985). Occupational safety: Assessing the impact of adding assigned or participative goal-setting. *Journal of Organizational Behavior Management*, 3–24.

Fenchel, G. H., Monderer, J. H., & Hartley, E. L. (1951). Subjective status and the equilibration hypothesis. *Journal of Abnormal and Social Psychology, 46*, 476–479.

Fenelon, J. R. (1966). *The influence of race on leadership prediction.* Master's thesis, University of Texas, Austin.

Fenelon, J. R., & Megargee, E. I. (1971). The influence of race on the manifestation of leadership. *Experimental Publications System, American Psychological Association, 10*, No. 380–12.

Fenichel, O. (1945). *The psychoanalytic theory of neurosis.* New York: W. W. Norton.

Fenton-O'Creevy, M. (1998). Employee involvement and the middle manager. *Journal of Organizational Behavior, 19*, 67–84.

Ferber, M., Huber, J., & Spitze, C. (1979). Preference for men as bosses and professionals. *Social Forces, 58*(2), 466–476.

Fermi, L. (1966). *Mussolini.* Chicago: University of Chicago Press.

Fernándes-Ballester, R. (1995). Crucial issues in the field of psychological assessment and evaluation during the next decades. *International Association of Applied Psychology Newsletter, 7*(2), 13–20.

Fernandez, C. F., & Vecchio, R. P. (1997). Situational test theory revisited: A test of an across-jobs perspective. *Leadership Quarterly, 8*, 67–84.

Fernandez, R. (1981). *Racism and sexism in corporate life: Changing values in American business.* Lexington, MA: D. C. Heath.

Fernberg, O. F. (1979). Regression in organizational leadership. *Psychiatry, 42*(1), 24–39.

Ferraro, F., Pfeffer, J., & Sutton, R. L. (2005). Economics language and assumptions: How theories can become self-fulfilling. *Academy of Management Review, 30*, 8–24.

Ferrell, O. C., & Fraedrich, J. P. (1994). *Ethics: Ethical decision making and cases.* Boston, MA: Houghton Mifflin.

Ferris, A. E. (1965). *Organizational relationships in two selected secondary schools: A comparative study.* Doctoral dissertation, Columbia University, New York.

Ferris, C. R. (1985). Role of leadership in the employee withdrawal process: A constructive replication. *Journal of Applied Psychology, 70*, 777–781.

Ferris, G. R., Bhawuk, D.P. S., Fedor, D. F., & Judge, T. A. (1995). Organizational politics and citizenship: attributions of intentionality and construct definition. In M. J. Martinko (ed.), *Advances in attribution theory: An organizational perspective.* Delray Beach, FL: St. Lucie Press.

Ferris, G. R., & Judge, T. (1991). Personnel/human resources management: A political influence perspective. *Journal of Management, 17*, 447–488.

Ferris, G. R., & Kacmar, K. M. (1992). Perceptions of organizational politics. *Journal of Management.* Sage.

Ferris, G. R., Hochwarter, W. A., Douglas, C., et al. (2002). Social influence processes in organizations. Sage.

Ferris, G. R., & Rowland, K. M. (1981). Leadership, job perceptions, and influence: A conceptual integration. *Human Relations, 34*, 1069–1077.

Ferris, G. R., Russ, G. S., & Fandt, P. M. (1989). Politics in organizations. In R. A. Giacalone & P. Roenfield (eds.), *Impression management in the organization.* Hillsdale, NJ: Lawrence Erlbaum.

Ferris, G. R., Treadway, D. C., Kolodinsky, R. W., et al. (2005). Development and validation of the Political Skill inventory. *Journal of Management, 31*, 126–152.

Ferris, G., Yates, V., Gilmore, D., et al. (1985). The influence of subordinate age on performance ratings and causal attributions. *Personnel Psychology, 38*, 545–557.

Festinger, L. (1949). The analysis of sociograms using matrix algebra. *Human Relations, 2*, 153–158.

Festinger, L. (1950). Informal social communication. *Psychological Review, 57*, 271–282.

Festinger, L. (1954). A theory of social comparison processes. *Human Relations, 7*, 117–140.

Festinger, L., Cartwright, D., Barber, K., et al. (1947). A study of a rumor: Its origin and spread. *Human Relations, 1*, 464–486.

Festinger, L., & Hutte, H. A. (1954). An experimental investigation of the effect of unstable interpersonal relations in a group. *Journal of Abnormal and Social Psychology, 49*, 513–522.

Festinger, L., & Kelley, H. H. (1951). *Changing attitudes through social contact.* Ann Arbor, MI: Research Center for Group Dynamics.

Festinger, L., Pepitone, A., & Newcomb, T. (1952). Some consequences of de-individuation in a group. *Journal of Abnormal and Social Psychology, 47*, 382–389.

Feyerherm, A. E. (1994). Leadership in collaboration: A longitudinal study of two interorganizational rule-making groups. *Leadership Quarterly, 5*, 253–270.

Fichter, J. H. (1966). Career preparation and expectations of Negro college seniors. *Journal of Negro Education, 35*, 322–335.

Fiedler, F. E. (1953a). Quantitative studies in the role of therapists' feelings toward their patients. In O. H. Mowrer (ed.), *Psychotherapy: Theory and research.* New York: Ronald Press.

Fiedler, F. E. (1953b). The psychological distance dimension in interpersonal relations. *Journal of Personality, 22*, 142–150.

Fiedler, F. E. (1954a). Interpersonal perception and sociometric structure in prediction of small team effectiveness. *American Psychologist, 8*, 365.

Fiedler, F. E. (1954b). Assumed similarity measures and predictors of team effectiveness. *Journal of Abnormal and Social Psychology, 49*, 381–388.

Fiedler, F. E. (1955). The influence of leader-keyman relations on combat crew effectiveness. *Journal of Abnormal and Social Psychology, 51*, 227–235.

Fiedler, F. E. (1956). *Social perception and group effectiveness* (Annual Technical Report). Urbana: University of Illinois.

Fiedler, F. E. (1957). A note on leadership theory: The effect of social barriers between leaders and followers. *Sociometry, 20,* 87–94.

Fiedler, F. E. (1958). *Leader attitudes and group effectiveness.* Urbana: University of Illinois Press.

Fiedler, F. E. (1962). Leader attitudes, group climate, and group creativity. *Journal of Abnormal and Social Psychology, 65,* 308–318.

Fiedler, F. E. (1964). A contingency model of leadership effectiveness. In L. Berkowitz (ed.), *Advances in experimental social psychology,* vol. 1. New York: Academic Press.

Fiedler, F. E. (1966). The effect of leadership and cultural heterogeneity on group performance: A test of the contingency model. *Journal of Experimental Social Psychology, 2,* 237–264.

Fiedler, F. E. (1967a). *A theory of leadership effectiveness.* New York: McGraw–Hill.

Fiedler, F. E. (1967b). The effect of inter-group competition on group member adjustment. *Personnel Psychology, 20,* 33–44.

Fiedler, F. E. (1968). The effect of culture training on leadership, organizational performance, and adjustment. *Naval Research Review,* 7–13.

Fiedler, F. E. (1970a). Leadership experience and leader performance: Another hypothesis shot to hell. *Organizational Behavior and Human Performance, 5,* 1–14.

Fiedler, F. E. (1971a). *Leadership.* New York: General Learning Press.

Fiedler, F. E. (1971b). Note on the methodology of the Graen, Orris, and Alveres studies testing the contingency model. *Journal of Applied Psychology, 55,* 202–204.

Fiedler, F. E. (1971c). Validation and extension of the contingency model of leadership effectiveness: A review of empirical findings. *Psychological Bulletin, 76,* 128–148.

Fiedler, F. E. (1971d). *Personality and situational determinants of leader behavior* (Tech. Rep.). Seattle: University of Washington, Department of Psychology.

Fiedler, F. E. (1972a). Personality, motivational systems, and behavior of high– and low-LPC persons. *Human Relations, 25,* 391–412.

Fiedler, F. E. (1973). The contingency model–a reply to Ashour. *Organizational Behavior and Human Performance, 9,* 356–368.

Fiedler, F. E. (1977b). A rejoinder to Schriesheim and Kerr's premature obituary of the contingency model. In J. C. Hunt & L. L. Larson (eds.), *Leadership: The cutting edge.* Carbondale: Southern Illinois University Press.

Fiedler, F. E. (1978). The contingency model and the dynamics of the leadership process. In L. Berkowitz (ed.), *Advances in Experimental Social Psychology,* vol. 2. New York: Academic Press.

Fiedler, F. E. (1982). *Are leaders an intelligent form of life? The role of cognitive processes in leadership performance* (Organizational Research Tech. Rep. 82–1). Seattle: University of Washington.

Fiedler, F. E. (1984). *The contribution of cognitive resources and leader behavior to organizational performance* (Organizational Research Tech. Rep. 84–4). Seattle: University of Washington.

Fiedler, F. E. (1986). The contribution of cognitive resources and leader behavior to organizational performance. *Journal of Applied Social Psychology, 16*(6), 532–548.

Fiedler, F. E. (1995). Cognitive resources and leadership performance. *Applied Psychology, 44*(1), 5–28.

Fiedler, F. E., & Garcia, J. E. (1987). *New approaches to effective leadership: Cognitive resources and organizational performance.* New York: Wiley.

Fiedler, F. E., Bell, C. H., Chemers, M. M., & Patrick, D. (1984). Increasing mine productivity and safety through management training and organization development: A comparative study. *Basic & Applied Social Psychology, 5,* 1–18

Fiedler, F. E., Bons, P. M., & Hastings, L. (1975). The utilization of leadership resources. In W. T. Singleton & P. Spurgeon (eds.), *Measurement of human resources.* London: Taylor & Francis.

Fiedler, F. E., & Chemers, M. M. (1974). *Leadership and effective management.* Glenview, IL: Scott, Foresman.

Fiedler, F. E., Chemers, M. M., & Mahar, L. (1976). *Improving leadership effectiveness: The LEADER MATCH concept.* New York: Wiley.

Fiedler, F. E., Fiedler, I., & Camp, S. (1971). Who speaks for the community? *Journal of Applied Social Psychology, 1,* 324–333.

Fiedler, F. E. & Garcia, J. E. (1987). *New approaches to effective leadership: Cognitive resources and organizational performance.* New York: Wiley.

Fiedler, F. E., & Hoffman, E. L. (1962). Age, sex, and religious background as determinants of interpersonal perception among Dutch children: A cross-cultural validation. *Acta Psychologica, 20,* 185–195.

Fiedler, F. E., & House, R. J. (1988). Leadership: A report of progress. In C. Cooper (ed.), *International review of industrial and organizational psychology.* Greenwich, CT: JAI Press.

Fiedler, F. E., & Leister, A. F. (1977). Leader intelligence and task performance: A test of a multiple screen model. *Organizational Behavior and Human Performance, 20,* 1–14.

Fiedler, F. E., & Mahar, L. (1979a). A field experiment validating contingency model leadership training. *Journal of Applied Psychology, 64,* 247–254.

Fiedler, F. E., & Mahar, L. (1979b). The effectiveness of contingency model training: Validation of LEADER MATCH. *Personnel Psychology, 32,* 45–62.

Fiedler, F. E., & McGuire, M. A. (1987). Paper, Third Army Leadership Conference, Kansas City, MO.

Fiedler, F. E., & Meuwese, W. A. T. (1963). Leaders' contribution to task performance in cohesive and uncohesive groups. *Journal of Abnormal and Social Psychology, 67,* 83–87.

Fiedler, F. E., Meuwese, W. A. T., & Oonk, S. (1961). An exploratory study of group creativity in laboratory tasks. *Acta Psychologica, 18,* 100–119.

Fiedler, F. E., & Nealey, S. M. (1966). *Second-level management.* Washington, DC: U.S. Civil Service Commission.

Fiedler, F. E., O'Brien, C. E., & Ilgen, D. R. (1969). The effect of leadership style upon the performance and adjustment of volunteer teams operating in successful foreign environment. *Human Relations, 22,* 503–514.

Fiedler, F. E., Potter, E. H., & McGuire, M. A. (1988). *Stress and effective leadership decisions.* Paper, International Congress of Psychology, Sydney, Australia.

Fiedler, F. E., Potter, E. H., Zais, M. M., et al. (1979). Organizational stress and the use and misuse of managerial intelligence and experience. *Journal of Applied Psychology, 64,* 635–647.

Fiedler, F. E., Warrington, W. G., & Blaisdell, F. J. (1952). Unconscious attitudes as correlates of sociometric choice in social groups. *Journal of Abnormal and Social Psychology, 47,* 790–796.

Fiedler, F. E., Wheeler, W. A., Chemers, M. M., & Patrick, D. (1987). Structured management training in underground mining: A five year follow-up. *Training &Development Journal, 4* (9), 40–43.

Field Manual FM *22–100*, 7–22.

Field, R. H. G. (1979). A critique of the Vroom-Yetton contingency model of leadership behavior. *Academy of Management Review, 4,* 249–257.

Field, R. H. G. (1982). A test of the Vroom-Yetton normative model of leadership. *Journal of Applied Psychology, 67,* 523–532.

Field, R. H. G. (1989a). The self-fulfilling prophecy leader: Achieving the metharme effect. *Journal of Management Studies, 26,* 151–175.

Field, R. H. G. (1989b). Leaders as stars, pulsars, quasars, and black holes. *Business Horizons,* May–June, 1–5.

Field, R. H. G., & Van Seters, D. A. (1988). Management by expectations: The power of positive prophecy. *Journal of General Management, 1*(2), 19–33.

Field, S. (1984). Leadership style and job satisfaction among human service workers. *Dissertation Abstracts International, 45*(7A), 2255.

Fields, D. L., & Herold, D. M. (1997). Using the leadership practices inventory to measure transformational and transactional leadership. *Educational and Psychological Measurement, 57*(4), 569.

Fields, W. (1994). *Union of words: A history of presidential eloquence.* New York: Free Press.

Fierman, J. (1990). Why women still don't hit the top. *Fortune, 122*(3), 40–62.

File, Q. W., & Remmers, H. H. (1971). *How supervise?* New York: Psychological Corporation.

Filella, J. F. (1971). *Exercise lifegoals: Guess work or interpersonal perception?* (Tech. Rep. No. 40). Rochester, NY: University of Rochester, Management Research Center.

Filipczak, R. (1993). Ericsson General Electric: The evolution of empowerment. *Training (USA), 30*(9), 21–27.

Filley, A. C., & Grimes, A. J. (1967). *The bases of power in decision processes.* Paper, Academy of Management, New York.

Filley, A. C., House, R. J., & Kerr, S. (1976). *Managerial process and organizational behavior* (2nd ed.). Glenview, IL: Scott, Foresman.

Filley, A. C., House, R., & Kerr, S. (1979). *Managerial process and organizational behavior* (2nd ed.) Glenview, IL: Scott, Foresman.

Filley, A. C., & Jesse, F. C. (1965). Training leadership style: A survey of research. *Personnel Administration, 28,* 14–21.

Finch, F. H., & Carroll, H. A. (1932). Gifted children as high school leaders. *Pediatrics Seminar, 41,* 476–481.

Fine, B. D. (1970). Comparison of work groups with stable and unstable membership. Experimental Publications System, *American Psychological Association, 9*(333), 1.

Fine, M. G., Johnson, F. L., & Ryan, M. S. (1990). Cultural diversity in the workplace. *Public Personnel Management, 19,* 305–319.

Fine, S. E. (1977). *Job analysis for heavy equipment operators.* Washington, DC: International Union of Operating Engineers.

Fineman, H. (1994). The virtuecrats. *Newsweek, 123*(24), 30.

Fineman, S. (1998). Street-level bureaucrats and the social construction of environmental control. *Organization Studies, 19*(6), 953–974.

Fineman, S. (2006). On being positive: Concerns and counterpoint. *The Academy of Management Review (AMR), 331*(2) 270–291.

Finkelstein, S. (1992). Power in top management teams: Dimensions, measurement, and validation. *Academy of Management Journal, 35,* 535–508.

Finkelstein, S., & Boyd, B. K. (1998). How much does the CEO matter?: The role of managerial discretion in the setting of CEO compensation. *Academy of Management Journal, 41,* 179–199.

Finkelstein, S., & Hambrick, D. C. (1990). Top-management team tenure and organizational outcomes: The moderating role of managerial discretion. *Administrative Science Quarterly, 35,* 484–503.

Finkelstein, S., & Hambrick, D. C. (1996). *Strategic leadership: Top executives and their effects on organizations.* St. Paul, MN: West Educational Publishing.

Finkle, R. B., & Jones, W. S. (1970). *Assessing corporate talent: A key to managerial manpower planning.* New York: Wiley-Interscience.

Fiol, C. M., Harris, D., & House, R. (1999). Charismatic leadership: Strategies for effecting social change. *Leadership Quarterly, 10,* 449–482.

Fiorelli, J. S. (1988). Power in work groups: Team members' perspectives. *Human Relations, 41,* 1–12.

Firestone, I. J, Lichtman, C. M., & Colamosca, J. V. (1975). Leader effectiveness and leadership conferral as determinants of helping in a medical emergency. *Journal of Personality and Social Psychology, 31,* 243–248.

Firestone, W. A., & Wilson, B. L. (1985). Using bureaucratic and cultural linkages to improve instruction: The principal's contribution. *Educational Administrative Quarterly, 21*(2), 7–30.

Fischer, P. H. (1953). An analysis of the primary group. *Sociometry, 16,* 272–276.

Fischer, D. H. (1989). *Albion's seed: Four British folkways in America.* New York: Oxford University Press.

Fischer, O. & Manstead, A. S. R. (2004). Computer-mediated leadership: Deficits, hypercharisma, and the hidden power of social identity. *German Journal for Human Resource Research, 18,* 306–328.

Fischman, J. (1987). Type A on trial. *Psychology Today, 21*(2), 42–50.

Fishbein, M., Landy, E., & Hatch, G. (1969a). Some determinants of an individual's esteem for the least preferred co-worker: An attitudinal analysis. *Human Relations, 22,* 173–188.

Fishbein, M., Landy, E., & Hatch, G. (1969b). A consideration of two assumptions underlying Fiedler's contingency model for prediction of leadership effectiveness. *American Journal of Psychology, 82,* 457–473.

Fishel, J. (1985). *Presidents and promises: From campaign pledge to presidential performance.* Washington, DC: Congressional Quarterly Press.

Fisher, B. M., & Edwards, J. E. (1988). Consideration and initiating structure and their relationships with leader effectiveness: A meta-analysis. *Best Paper Proceedings, Academy of Management,* 201–205.

Fisher, C. (1998). Business on the road. *American Demographics, 20,* 44–47.

Fisher, C. D. (1979). Transmission of positive and negative feedback to subordinates: A laboratory investigation. *Journal of Applied Psychology, 64,* 533–540.

Fisher, J., Tack, M., & Wheeler, K. (1988). *The effective college president.* New York: Macmillan.

Fisher, K. (1993). *Leading self-directed work teams.* New York: McGraw-Hill.

Fisher, S. C. (1982). *Institutions, authority and the structure of doctor-patient communication*. Paper, Society for the Study of Social Problems.

Fisher-McAuley, G., Stanton, J. M., Jolton, J. A., & Gavin, J. (2003). *Modeling the relationship between work/life balance and organizational outcomes*. Paper presented at Society for Industrial and Organizational Psychology, Orlando, FL.

Fishman, A. Y. (2003). *Leading innovation: Assessing the impact of top management teams on boundary-spanning innovation*. Paper, Academy of Management, Seattle WA.

Fishman, L. (1952). Limitations of the business executive as government administrator. *Journal of Business, 25,* 89–94.

Fiske, S. T. (2002). What we know now about bias and intergroup conflict, the problem of the century. *Current Directions in Psychological Science, 11,* 123–128.

Fitness, J. (2000). Anger in the workplace: An emotion script to anger episodes between workers and their supervisors, coworkers and subordinates. *Journal of Organizational Behavior, 21,* 147–162.

Fitzgerald, T. H. (1988). Can change in in organizational culture really be managed? *Organizational Dynamics, 17*(2), 5–15.

Flament, C. (1956). Changements de rôles et adaptation la tache dans des groupes de travail utilisant divers riseaux de communications. *Années Psychologia, 56,* 411–431.

Flanagan, J. C. (1951). Defining the requirements of the executive's job. *Personnel, 28*(1), 28–35.

Flanagan, J. C. (1954). The critical incident technique. *Psychology Bulletin, 51,* 327–358.

Flanagan, J. C., & Krug, R. E. (1964). Testing in management selection: State of the art. *Personnel Administration, 27*(2), 3–5.

Flanagan, J. C., Levy, S., et al. (1952). *Development of an objective form of the leaders reaction test*. Pittsburgh, PA: American Institute for Research.

Flannery, B. L., & May, D. R. (1994). Prominent factors influencing environmental activities: Application of the environmental leadership model (ELM). *Leadership Quarterly, 5,* 201–221.

Flannery, B. L. & May, D. R. (2000). Environmental ethical decision making in the U.S. metal-finishing industry. *Academy of Management Journal, 43*(4), 642–662.

Flaugher, R. L., Campbell, J. T., & Pike, L. W. (1969). *Ethnic group membership as a moderator of supervisor's ratings*. ETS Bulletin PR69–5. Princeton, NJ: Educational Testing Service.

Flax, S. (1984). The toughest bosses in America. *Fortune*, August 6, 1–5

Fleenor, J. W. (1988). *The utility of assessment centers for career development*. Doctoral dissertation, North Carolina State University, Raleigh, NC.

Fleenor, J. W. (2004). Making it click: Strategies for helping computer-challenged leaders. *Leaders in Action, 24*(2), 13–15.

Fleenor, J. W., McCauley, C. D., & Brutus, S. (1996). Self-other rating agreement and leader effectiveness. *Leadership Quarterly, 7,* 487–506.

Fleishman, E. A. (1951). *Leadership climate and supervisory behavior*, Personnel Research Board, Columbus: Ohio State University.

Fleishman, E. A. (1953a). The measurement of leadership attitudes in industry. *Journal of Applied Psychology. 37,* 153–158.

Fleishman, E. A. (1953b). Leadership climate, human relations training, and supervisory behavior. *Personnel Psychology, 6,* 205–222.

Fleishman, E. A. (1953c). The description of supervisory behavior. *Journal of Applied Psychology, 37,* 1–6.

Fleishman, E. A. (1956). Differences between military and industrial organizations. In R. M. Stogdill & C. L. Shartle (eds.), *Patterns of administrative performance*. Columbus: Ohio State University, Bureau of Business Research.

Fleishman, E. A. (1957a). A leader behavior description for industry. In R. M. Stogdill & A. E. Coons (eds.), *Leader behavior: Its description and measurement*. Columbus: Ohio State University, Bureau of Business Research.

Fleishman, E. A. (1957b). The leadership opinion questionnaire. In R. M. Stogdill & A. E. Coons (eds.), *Leader behavior: Its description and measurement*. Columbus: Ohio State University, Bureau of Research.

Fleishman, E. A. (1960). *Leadership opinion questionnaire*. Chicago: Science Research Associates.

Fleishman, E. A. (1972). *Examiner's manual for the supervisory behavior description questionnaire*. Washington, DC: Management Research Institute.

Fleishman, E. A. (1973). Twenty years of consideration and structure. In E. A. Fleishman & J. G. Hunt (eds.), *Current developments in the study of leadership*. Carbondale: Southern Illinois University Press.

Fleishman, E. A. (1989a). *Examiner's manual for the Leadership Opinion Questionnaire (LOQ)* (revised). Chicago: Science Research Associates.

Fleishman, E. A. (1989b). *Examiner's manual for the Supervisory Behavior Description (SBD) Questionnaire* (Revised). Chicago: Science Research Associates.

Fleishman, E. A., & Harris, E. F. (1962). Patterns of leadership behavior related to employee grievances and turnover. *Personnel Psychology, 15,* 43–56.

Fleishman, E. A., Harris, E. F., & Burtt, H. E. (1955). *Leadership and supervision in industry*. Columbus: Ohio State University, Bureau of Educational Research.

Fleishman, E. A., Mumford, M. D., Zaccaro, S. J., et al. (1991). Taxonomic efforts in the description of leader behavior: A synthesis and functional interpretation. *Leadership Quarterly, 2*(4), 245–287.

Fleishman, E. A., Harris, E. F., & Burtt, H. E. (1955). *Leadership and supervision in industry*. Columbus: Ohio State University, Bureau of Educational Research.

Fleishman, E. A., & Peters, D. R. (1962). Interpersonal values, leadership attitudes, and managerial "success." *Personnel Psychology, 15,* 127–143.

Fleishman, E. A., & Quaintance, M. K. (1984). *Taxonomies of human performance*. New York: Academic Press.

Fleishman, E. A., & Salter, J. A. (1963). Relation between the leader's behavior and his empathy toward subordinates. *Journal of Industrial Psychology, 1,* 79–84.

Fleishman, E. A., & Simmons, J. (1970). Relationship between leadership patterns and effectiveness ratings among Israeli foremen. *Personnel Psychology, 23,* 169–172.

Fleishman, E. A., & Zaccaro, S. J. (1992). Toward a taxonomy of team performance functions. In R. W. Sweezy & E. Salas (eds.), *Teams: Their training and performance*. Norwood, NJ: Ablex.

Flemming. (1935). A factor analysis of the personality of high school leaders. *Analysis of Personality, 5,* 596–605.

Fletcher, C., & Williams, R. (1976). The influence of performance feedback in appraisal interviews. *Journal of Occupational Psychology, 49,* 75–83.

Flick, H. (1981). Malcolm X: The destroyer and creator. *Journal of Black Studies, 12*(2), 166–181.

Flint, A. W., Bass, B. M., & Pryer, M. W. (1957a). *Esteem and successful leadership* (Tech. Rep. No. 11). Baton Rouge: Louisiana State University.

Flint, A. W., Bass, B. M., & Pryer, M. W. (1957b). *Esteem, status, motion, and attraction to the group* (Tech. Rep. No. 9). Baton Rouge: Louisiana State University.

Flocco, E. C. (1969). An examination of the leader behavior of school business administrators. *Dissertation Abstracts International, 30,* 84–85.

Floyd, S. W. (1992). Managing strategic consensus: The foundation of effective implementation. *Academy of Management Executive, 6*(4), 27–39.

Foa, U. G. (1956). A test of the foreman-worker relationship. *Personnel Psychology, 9,* 469–486.

Foa, U. G. (1957). Relation of worker's expectation to satisfaction with supervisor. *Personnel Psychology, 10,* 161–168.

Foa, U. G., Mitchell, T. R., & Fiedler, F. E. (1971). Differential matching. *Behavioral Science, 16,* 130–142.

Fodor, E. (1987). *Motive pattern as an influence on leadership in small groups.* Paper, American Psychological Association. New York.

Fodor, E. M. (1973a). Group stress, ingratiation, and the use of power. *Journal of Social Psychology, 91,* 345–346.

Fodor, E. M. (1973b). Disparagement by a subordinate, ingratiation, and the use of power. *Journal of Psychology, 84,* 181–186.

Fodor, E. M. (1974). Disparagement by a subordinate as an influence on the use of power. *Journal of Applied Psychology, 59,* 652–655.

Fodor, E. M. (1976). Group stress, authoritarian style of control, and use of power. *Journal of Applied Psychology, 61,* 313–318.

Fodor, E. M. (1978). Simulated work climate as an influence on choice of leadership style. *Personality and Social Psychology Bulletin, 4,* 111–114.

Fodor, E. M. (1984). The power motive and reactivity to power stresses. *Journal of Personality and Social Psychology, 47,* 853–859.

Fodor, E. (1987). *Motive pattern as an influence on leadership in small groups.* Paper, American Psychological Association. New York.

Fodor, E. M., & Farrow, D. L. (1979). The power motive as an influence on the use of power in an industrial simulation. *Journal of Personality and Social Psychology, 37,* 2091–2097.

Fodor, E. M., & Smith, T. (1982). The power motive as an influence on group decision making. *Journal of Personality and Social Psychology, 42,* 178–185.

Foley, S., Linnehan, F., Greenhaus, J., et al. (2003). *The relation of gender and racial similarity to family-supportive supervision.* Paper, Academy of Management, Seattle, WA.

Foley, S., & Powell, G. N. (1999). Not all is fair in love and work: Coworkers preferences for and responses to management interventions regarding workplace romances. *Journal of Organizational Behavior, 20,* 1043–1056.

Folger, R., & Cropanzano, R. (1998). *Organizational justice and human resource management.* Thousand Oaks, CA: Sage.

Follert, V. (1983). Supervisors' power: An exchange model of leadership. *Psychological Reports, 52,* 740.

Follett, M. P. (1918). *The new state.* Gloucester, MA: Peter Smith.

Follett, M. P. (1918). *The new state: Group organization—The solution of popular government.* New York: Longmans Green.

Folkman, S., & Moskowitz, J. T. (2000). Stress, positive emotion, and coping. *Current Directions in Psychological Science, 9*(4), 115–118.

Foote, A. E. (1970). *Managerial style, hierarchical control, and decision making in public television stations.* Doctoral dissertation, Ohio State University, Columbus, OH.

Forbes, J. B. (1985). The relationship between management styles and functional specialization. *Group & Organization Studies, 10,* 95–111.

Forbes, J. B., & Piercy, J. E. (1991). *Corporate paths to the top: Studies for human resource and management development specialists.* New York: Quorum Books.

Ford, C. M., & Gioia, D. A. (2000). Factors influencing creativity in the domain of discussion making. *Journal of Management, 25,* 705–732.

Ford, D. L. (1985). Job-related stress of the minority professional: A exploratory analysis and suggestions for future research. In T.A. Beehr, & R. S. Bhagat (eds.), *Human stress and cognition in organizations.* New York: Wiley, 287–323.

Ford, J. B. (1980). The effects of covert power on the inhibition of structural change. *Dissertation Abstracts International, 41*(5A), 2316.

Ford, J. D. (1981). Departmental context and formal structure as constraints on leader behavior. *Academy of Management Journal, 24,* 274–288.

Ford, J. M., & Greguras, G. J. (2001) *An examination of the multidimensionality of supervisor perceptions of leader-member exchange.* Paper, Society for Industrial and Organizational Psychology, San Diego, CA.

Ford, L. (1981). Evangelism and social responsibility. *Evangelical Newsletter, 1981.*

Ford, L. (1991). *Transforming leadership: Jesus' way of creating vision, shaping values & empowering change.* Downers Grove, IL: InterVarsity Press.

Ford, R. C. (1983). Delegation without fear. *Supervisory Management, 28*(7), 2–8.

Ford, R. C., & Fottler, M. D. (1995). Empowerment: A matter of degree. *Academy of Management Executive, 9*(3), 21–31.

Form, W. H. (1945). Status stratification in a planned community. *American Sociological Review, 10,* 605–613.

Form, W. H., & Form, A. L. (1953). Unanticipated results of a foreman training program. *Personnel Journal, 32,* 207–212.

Form, W. H., & Nosow, S. (1958). *Community in disaster.* New York: Harper.

Forrest, P. J., Cochran, D. S., Ray, D. F, & Robin, D. P. (1989). *Factors which influence ethical business judgments: A managerial and societal comparison.* Paper, Academy of Management, Washington, DC.

Forrester, J.W. (1961). *Industrial dynamics.* Cambridge, MA: Wright-Allen Press.

Forrester, R. (2000). Empowerment: Rejuvenating a potent idea. *Academy of Management Executive, 14*(3), 67–80.

Forsyth, D. R., & Forsyth, N. M. (1984). *Subordinates' reactions to female leaders.* Paper, Eastern Psychological Association, Baltimore.

Fortune (1946). *The management poll.* 34(4), 5–6.

Forward, J., & Zander, A. (1971). Choice of unattainable group goals and effects on performance. *Organizational Behavior and Human Performance*, 6, 184–199.

Foster, R. M. & Imig, G. L. (1998). *Leadership in the making: Impact and insights from leadership development programs in U.S. colleges and universities.* W.K. Kellogg Foundation Memo to Kellogg President's Commission (unpublished).

Foster, W. T. (1929). Education for leadership in business. *School Society*, 29, 734–736.

Foti, R. J., & Cohen, B.A. (undated) *Self-monitoring and leadership emergence.* Unpublished manuscript.

Foti, R. J., Fraser, S. L., & Lord, R. G. (1982). Effects of leadership labels and prototypes on perceptions of political leaders. *Journal of Applied Psychology*, 67, 326–333.

Foti, R. J., & Gershenoff, A. (1999). *Female leader emergence: A pattern approach.* Paper, Society for Industrial and Organizational Psychology, Atlanta, GA.

Foti, R. J., & Hauenstein, M. A. (2005). Linking leadership emergence to leadership effectiveness in a military context. *Paper, Society for Industrial and Organizational Psychology*, Los Angeles, CA.

Fowler, E. M. (1982). Careers: Discontent of middle managers. *New York Times*, December 15, D17.

Fowler, R. (1999). Managing a professional association. *The Psychologist-Manager Journal*, 3, 57–69.

Fox, D., Lorge, I., Weltz, P., & Herrold, K. (1953). Comparison of decisions written by large and small groups. *American Psychologist*, 8, 351.

Fox, T. G. (1973). *The influence of manifest and latent social identities on medical school faculty attitudes.* Doctoral dissertation, University of Michigan, Ann Arbor.

Fox, W. M. (1954). *An experimental study of group reaction to two types of conference leadership.* Doctoral dissertation, Ohio State University, Columbus.

Fox, W. M. (1957). Group reaction to two types of conference leadership. *Human Relations*, 10, 279–289.

Fox, W. M. (1974). *Least preferred coworker scales: Research and development* (Tech. Rep. No. 70–5). Gainesville, FL: University of Florida, College of Business Administration.

Fox, W. M. (1976). Reliabilities, means, and standard deviations for LPC scales: Instrument refinement. *Academy of Management Journal*, 19, 450–461.

Fox, W. M. (1982). A test of Octant I of Fiedler's contingency model with training dependent coaching task groups. *Replications in Social Psychology*, 2(1), 47–49.

Fox, W. M. (1987–88, Winter). Improving performance appraisal systems. *National Productivity Review*, 7(1), 20–27.

Fox, W. M. (1989). *Behavior modeling: An overview.* Unpublished manuscript.

Fox, W. M. (2000). *Assertive values in decline.* Gainsville, FL: First Books.

Fox, W. M. (1988). Getting the most from behavior modeling training. *National Productivity Review*, 7(3), 238–245.

Fox, W. M. (1994). Developments toward viable control theory. *International Journal of Public Administration*, 17, 1369–1369.

Fox, W. M. (1995). Sociotechnical system principles and guidelines: Past and present. *Journal of Applied Behavioral Science*, 31(1), 91–105.

Fox, W. M., Hill, W. A., & Guertin, W. N. (1973). Dimensional analyses of least preferred co-worker scales. *Journal of Applied Psychology*, 57, 192–194.

Foxhall, K. (2002). More psychologists are attracted to the executive coaching field: Psychologists in executive coaching say joining the field requires business and psychological know-how. *Monitor on Psychology*, 33(4), 52–53.

Fraedrich, J. P., & Ferrell, O. C. (1992). The impact of perceived risk and moral philosphy type on ethical decison making in business organizations. *Journal of Business Research*, 24(4), 283–295.

Frain, E. H., & DuBrin, A. J. (1981). Time-span orientation: A key factor of contingency management. *Personnel Journal*, 60(1), 46–48, 61.

Fraker, S. (1984). Why women aren't getting to the top. *Fortune* (April 16, 1984), 40–45.

Frame, J. H., & Beaty, J. C.(2000). *An investigation of high-technology survey methods at Hewlett-Packard.* Paper, Society for Industrial and Organizational Psychology, New Orleans, LA.

Francois, P. (1993). *Representations sociales et contingencies du leadership en milieu organisationnel.* Doctoral Dissertation, University of Bordeaux, Bordeaux, France.

Frank, E. J. (1971–1973). *Cognitive complexity and leadership: The effect of perceptual sensitivity on leadership success.* Doctoral dissertation, Purdue University, Lafayette, IN.

Frank, H. H., & Katcher, A. H. (1977). The qualities of leadership: How male medical students evaluate their female peers. *Human Relations*, 30(5), 403.

Frank, L. K. (1939). Dilemma of leadership. *Psychiatry*, 2, 343–361.

Frank, L. L., & Hackman, J. R. (1975). A failure of job enrichment: The case of the change that wasn't. *Journal of Applied Behavioral Science*, 11, 413–436.

Franke, R. H. (1984). *Contrasts and changes in Japanese and American managerial attitudes between 1960 and 1980.* Paper, Academy of Management, Boston.

Franke, R. H. (1997). Industrial democracy and convergence in economic performance: Comparative analysis of industrial nations in the 1970's and 1980's. *Research in the Sociology of Work*, 6, 95–108.

Franke, R. H. (1999). Transformation of the Second World from plan to market: Economic effects of culture, convergence, and investment. *International Journal of Business*, 4(1), 39–52.

Franke, R. H. (2005). Introduction. Taking business seriously. *International Journal of Business*.

Franke, R. H., & Barrett, G. V. (2004). *A new strategic era: Beyond the computer and innovation paradoxes.* Paper, Strategic Management Society, San Juan, PR.

Franke, R. H., Hofstede, G., & Bond, M. H. (1991). Cultural roots of economic performance. *Strategic Management*, 12, 165–173.

Franke, R. H., Hofstede, G., & Bond, M. H. (2001). National culture and economic performance. In M. J. Gannon & K. L. Newman (eds.), *Handbook of Cross-Cultural Management.* Oxford, England: Blackwell.

Franke, R., & Kaul, J. (1978). The Hawthorne experiments revisited: First statistical interpretation. *American Sociological Review*, 43, 623–643.

Franke, R., & Miller, J. (2007). Capital investment and utilization in business performance and economic growth. *International Journal of Business*, 12(1).

Franke, R. H., & New, J. R. (1984). *Presidential personality and national economic performance*. Paper, American Association for the Advancement of Science, New York, NY.

Franke, V. C. (1997). Warriors for peace: The next generation of military leaders. *Armed Forces & Society*, 24, 33–57.

Franklin, A. J. (1969). The relationship between leadership training in group dynamics and the development of groups among disadvantaged youth. *Dissertation Abstracts*, 29, 2090–2091.

Franklin, J. L. (1975). Relations among four social-psychological aspects of organizations. *Administrative Science Quarterly*, 20, 422–433.

Frantzve, J. (1979). *The influence of gender composition of leaderless group discussions on ratings of effectiveness*. Doctoral dissertation, University of Georgia, Athens.

Frantzve, J. L. (1982). *Gender isolation as an influence on behavior*. Paper, International Congress of Applied Psychology, Edinburgh.

Frantzve, J. L. (1985). *Organizational women: Fiction and fact*. Paper, American Psychological Association, Los Angeles.

Frazier, E. .F (1966). "Society": Status without substance. In R. J. Murphy & H. Elinson (eds.), *Problems and prospects of the Negro movement*. Belmont, CA: Wadsworth.

Fredericks, S. (1998). Exposing and exploring statewide community leadership training programs. *Journal of Leadership Studies*, 5(2), 129–142.

Frederiksen, N. (1962a). In-basket tests and factors in administrative performance. In H. Guetzkow (ed.), *Simulation in social science: Readings*. Englewood Cliffs, NJ: Prentice-Hall.

Frederiksen, N. (1962b). Factors in in-basket performance. *Psychological Monographs*, 76(22), No. 541.

Frederiksen, N. (1966). Validation of a simulation technique. *Organizational Behavior and Human Performance*, 1, 87–109.

Frederksen, N., Saunders, D. R., & Ward, B. (1957). The in-basket test. *Psychological Monographs: General and Applied*, 71(9), whole no. 438.

Free, V. (1983). CEOs and their corporate cultures—new game plans. *Marketing Communications*, 8(6), 21–27.

Freedman, DiMatteo, & Tarant (1980). In *Doctors talking with patients: patients talking with doctors. Improving communication in medical visits*, by D. L. Roter & J. A. Hall. Connecticut: Greenwood Publishing Group. Also reprinted in 2006 by Praeger Publishers.

Freeman, C. L., & Taylor, E. K. (1950). *How to pick leaders*. New York: Funk & Wagnalls.

Freeman, L. C., Fararo, T J., Bloomberg, W., & Sunshine, M. H. (1963). Locating leaders in local communities: A comparison of some alternative approaches. *American Sociological Review*, 28, 791–798.

Freeman, R. E. (1984). *Strategic management: A stakeholder approach*. Boston: Pitman.

Freemesser, G. F., & Kaplan, H. B. (1976). Self-attitudes and deviant behavior: The case of the charismatic religious movement. *Journal of Youth and Adolescence*, 5(1), 1–9.

French, J. R. P. (1950). Field experiments: Changing group productivity. In J. C. Miller (ed.), *Experiments in social process*. New York: McGraw-Hill.

French, J. R. P. (1956). A formal theory of social power. *Psychological Review*, 63, 181–194.

French, J. R. P., Kay, E., & Meyer, H. H. (1966). Participation and the appraisal system. *Human Relations*, 19, 3–20.

French, J. R. P., & Zander, A. (1949). The group dynamics approach. In A. Kornhauser (ed.), *Psychology of labor-management relations*. Champaign, IL: Industrial Relations Research Association.

Freeston, K. (1987). Leader substitutes in educational organizations. *Educational Administration Quarterly*, 23(2), 45–59.

French, J. R. P. (1941). The disruption and cohesion of groups. *Journal of Abnormal and Social Psychology*, 36, 361–377.

French, J. R. P. (1944b). Retraining an autocratic leader. *Journal of Abnormal and Social Psychology*, 39, 224–237.

French, J. R. P. (1956). A formal theory of social power. *Psychological Review*, 63, 181–194.

French, J. R. P., Israel, J., & As, D. (1960). An experiment on participation in a Norwegian factory. *Human Relations*, 13, 3–19.

French, J. R. P., Morrison, W., & Levinger, G. (1960). Coercive power and forces affecting conformity. *Journal of Abnormal and Social Psychology*, 61, 93–101

French, J. R. P., & Raven, B. (1959). The bases of social power. In D. Cartwright (ed.), *Studies in social power*. Ann Arbor: University of Michigan, Institute for Social Research.

French, R. L. (1951). Sociometric status and individual adjustment among naval recruits. *Journal of Abnormal and Social Psychology*, 46, 64–72.

Fretwell, E. K. (1919). Education for leadership. *Teachers College Record*, 20, 324–352.

Freud, S. (1910/1964). *Leonardo da Vinci and a memory of his childhood* (tr. A. Tyson). New York: Norton.

Freud, S. (1913/1946). *Totem and taboo*. New York: Vintage Books.

Freud, S. (1922). *Group psychology and the analysis of ego*. London: International Psychoanalytical Press.

Freud, S. (1922/1939). *Moses and monotheism*. London: Hogarth Press. New York: A. A. Knopf.

Freud, S., & Bullitt, C. (1932). *Thomas Woodrow Wilson: A psychological study*. New York: Houghton Mifflin.

Frew, D. R. (1977). *Management of stress*. Chicago, IL: Nelson-Hall.

Frey, M. W. (1963). An experimental study of the influence of disruptive interaction induced by authoritarian-equalitarian, leader-follower combinations upon the decision-making effectiveness of small groups. *Dissertation Abstracts*, 25, 897.

Fried, B. J. (1988). Power acquisition in a health care setting: An application of strategic contingencies theory. *Human Relations*, 41, 915–927.

Fried, Y., Tiegs, R. B., & Bellamy, A. R. (1992). Personal and contextual predictors of supervisors' avoidance of evaluating subordinates. *Journal of Applied Psychology*, 77, 462–468.

Friedland, W. H. (1964). For a sociological concept of charisma. *Social Forces*, 43(1), 18–26.

Friedlander, F. (1963). Underlying sources of job satisfaction. *Journal of Applied Psychology*, 47, 246–250.

Friedlander, F. (1966). Importance of work versus nonwork among socially and occupationally stratified groups. *Journal of Applied Psychology*, 50, 437–441.

Friedlander, F. (1967). The impact of organizational training laboratories upon the effectiveness and interaction of ongoing work groups. *Personnel Psychology, 20,* 289–307.

Friedlander, F., & Greenberg, S. (1971). Effect of job attitudes, training, and organizational climate on performance of the hard-core unemployed. *Journal of Applied Psychology, 55,* 287–295

Friedlander, F., & Margulies, N. (1969). Multiple impacts of organizational climate and individual value systems upon job satisfaction. *Personnel Psychology, 22,* 171–183.

Friedman, H. S., DiMatteo, M. R., & Taranta, A. (1980). A study of the relationship between individual differences in nonverbal expressiveness and factors of personality and social interaction. *Journal of Research in Personality, 14,* 351–364.

Friedman, H. S., Hall, J. A., & Harris, J. M. (1985). Type A behavior, nonverbal expressive style, and health. *Journal of Personality and Social Psychology, 48,* 1299–1315.

Friedman, H. S., Prince, L. M., Riggio, R. E., & DiMatteo, M. R. (1980). Understanding and assessing nonverbal expressiveness: The affective communication test. *Journal of Personality and Social Psychology, 39,* 331–351.

Friedman, H. S., & Riggio, R. E. (1981). Effect of individual differences in nonverbal expressiveness on transmission of emotion. *Journal of Nonverbal Behavior, 6,* 96–104.

Friedman, M., & Rosenman, R. H. (1974). *Type A behavior and your heart.* New York: Knopf.

Friedman, R. A., Simons, T. L., & Liu, L. A. (2003). *Racial differences in sensitivity to behavioral integrity.* Paper, Academy of Management, Seattle, WA.

Friedman, S. D., & Saul, K. (1988). *Internal consequences of CEO succession events in large corporations.* Paper, Academy of Management, Anaheim, CA.

Friedman, S. D., & Saul, K. (1991). A leader's wake: Organization member reactions to CEO succession. *Journal of Management, 17,* 619–642.

Friedman, S. D., & Singh, H. (1986). *CEO succession events and market reactions: The effects of reason, successor origin, and contact.* Unpublished manuscript.

Friedman, T. (2005). *The world is flat: A brief history of the twenty-first century.* New York: Farrar, Straus & Giroux.

Friedrich, C. J. (1961) Political leadership and the problem of the charismatic power. *Journal of Politics, 23,* 3–24.

Friesen, B. J. (1983). Organizational and leader behavior correlates of the line worker job satisfaction and role clarity. *Dissertation Abstracts International, 44*(8A), 2581.

Frieze, I. H., Olson, J. E., & Russell, J. (1991). Attractiveness and income for men and women in management. *Journal of Applied Social Psychology, 21,* 1039–1057.

Frischer, J. (1993). Empowering management in new product development units. *Journal of Product Innovation Management, 10,* 393–401.

Fritz, R. (1986). The leader as creator. In J. D. Adams (ed.), *Transforming leadership.* Alexandria, VA: Miles River Press.

Fritzsche, D. J., & Becker, H. (1984). Linking management behavior to ethical philosophy: an empirical investigation. *Academy of Management Journal, 27,* 166–175.

Fromm, E. (1941). *Escape from freedom.* New York: Farrar & Rinehart.

Frost, D. E. (1983). Role perceptions and behavior of the immediate superior: Moderating effects of the prediction of leadership effectiveness. *Organizational Behavior and Human Performance, 31,* 123–142.

Frost, D. E. (1986). A test of situational engineering for training leaders. *Psychological Reports, 59,* 771–782.

Frost, D. E., Fiedler, F. E., & Anderson, J. W. (1983). The role of personal risk–taking in effective leadership. *Human Relations, 36,* 185–202.

Frost, P. J. (1986). Power, politics and influence. In L. W. Porter, L. L. Putnam, K. H. Roberts, & E. M. Jablin (eds.), *The handbook of organizational communication.* Beverly Hills, CA: Sage.

Frost, P. J. (1987). Power, politics, and influence. In F. M. Jablin, L. L. Roberts, & L. W. Porter (eds.), *Handbook of organizational communication.* Newbury Park, CA:

Frost, P. J., & Hayes, D. C. (1979). An exploration in two cultures of a model of political behavior in organizations. In C. W. England, A. R. Negandhi, & B. Wilpert (eds.), *Organizational functions in a cross-cultural perspective.* Kent, OH: Kent State University Press.

Fruchter, B., & Skinner, J. A. (1966). Dimensions of leadership in a student cooperative. *Multivariate Behavioral Research, 1,* 437–445.

Fry, L. W. (2003). Toward a theory of transformational leadership. *Leadership Quarterly, 14,* 657–692.

Fry, L. W., Kerr, S., & Lee, C. (1986). Effects of different leader behaviors under different levels of task interdependence. *Human Relations, 39,* 1067–1082.

Fry, L. W., & Malone, P. N. (2003). *Transforming schools through spiritual leadership: A field experiment.* Paper, Academy of Management, Seattle, WA.

Fry, L. W., Scott, W. G. & Mitchell, T. R. (1987). *Organizational and contextual causes of variation in the performance appraisal process used in schools of business.* Paper, Academy of Management, Anaheim, CA.

Frye, R. L., & Spruill, J. (1965). Type of orientation and task completion of elementary-grade students. *Journal of Genetic Psychology, 106,* 45–49.

Fu, P. P., & Yukl, G. (2000). Perceived effectiveness of influence tactics in the United States and China. *Leadership Quarterly, 11,* 251–256.

Fuess, C. M. (1940). *Calvin Coolidge: The man from Vermont.* Boston: Little, Brown & Co.

Fujishima, Y., & Morata, K. (1998). *Impact of CMC and/or FtF on impression formation.* Paper, International Congress of Applied Psychology, San Francisco, CA.

Fujita, E. (1990). *The evaluation of college presidents: Dimensions used by campus leaders* (Executive Summary No. 34). National Center for Postsecondary Governance and Finance..

Fukami, C. V., & Hopkins, D. M. (1990). *The role of contextual factors in disciplinary judgements.* Paper, Academy of Management.

Fukuda, K. (1983). Japanese and Chinese management practices: Uncovering the differences. *Mid-Atlantic Journal of Business, 21*(2), 3544.

Fukuyama, F. (1997). Falling Tide. *Harvard International Review,* Winter 97, 20(1).

Fukuyama, F. (1995). *Trust: The social virtues and the creation of prosperity.* New York: Free Press.

Fulk, J., Schmitz, J. & Ryu, D., and Steinfield, C. W. (1989). *Communication in R D via electronic mail.* III: *Final report.* University of Southern California, Annenberg School of Communications.

Fulk, J., & Wendler, E. R. (1982). Dimensionality of leader-subordinate interactions: A path–goal investigation. *Organizational Behavior and Human Performance, 30,* 241–264.

Fulker, D. W. & Cardon, L. R. (1993). What can twin studies tell us about structure and correlates of twin studies? In T. J. Bouchard, Jr., & P. Propping (eds.), *Twins as a tool of behavioral genetics.* West Sussex, U.K.: Wiley.

Fullan, M. (1991). *The new meaning of change,* London: Sage.

Fullan, M. G. (1992). *Successful school improvement: The implementation perspective and beyond.* Buckingham, UK: Open University Press.

Fulmer, R. M. (1997). The evolving paradigm of leadership development. *Organizational Dynamics, 25*(4), 59–72.

Fulmer, R. M., & Wagner, S. (1999). The evolving paradigm of leadership development. *Organizational Dynamics, 25*(4), 59–72.

Funk, R. C. (2002). Developing leaders through high school junior ROTC: Integrating theory with practice. *Journal of Leadership Studies, 8*(4), 43–53.

Furst, S. A., Cable, D. M., & Edwards, J. R. (2001). *Walking the talk: Managers' reactions to espoused and enacted values.* Paper, Academy of Management, Washington.

Furst, S., Reeves, M., Rosen, B., et al. (2003). *A longitudinal study of virtual team effectiveness.* Paper, Academy of Management, Seattle, WA.

Furukawa, H. (1981). Management objectives, conditions in workunit, and leadership behavior. *Psychologia: An International Journal of Psychology in the Orient, 24,* 176–184.

Gabarro, J. J. (1978). The development of trust influence expectations. In A. G. & J. J. Gabarro (eds), *Interpersonal behavior: Communication and understanding in relationships.* Englewood Cliffs, NJ: Prentice-Hall.

Gabarro, J. J. (1979). Socialization at the top: How CEO's and subordinates evolve interpersonal contracts. *Organizational Dynamics, 7,* 323.

Gabarro, J. J. (1985). Taking charge: Stages in management succession. *Harvard Business Review, 64*(3), 110–123.

Gabarro, J. J. (1985). When a new manager takes charge. *Harvard Business Review, 63,* May–June, 110–123.

Gabarro, J. J. (1987). *The dynamics of taking charge.* Boston: Harvard Business School Press.

Gabarro, J. J., & Kotter, J. F. (1980). Managing your boss. *Harvard Business Review, 58,* 92–100.

Gabris, G. T., & Ihrke, D. M. (2001). Does performance appraisal contribute to heightened level of employee burnout? The results of one study. *Public Personnel Management, 30*(2). 157–172.

Gabris, J. J., & Ihrke, D. M. (2003). Unanticipated failures of well-intentioned reforms: Some lessons from federal and local governments. *International Journal of Organizational Theory and Behavior, 6,* 195–225.

Gaddis, B., Connelly, S., & Mumford, M. D. (2004). Failure feed-

back as an affective event: Influences of leader affect on subordinate attitudes and performance. *Leadership Quarterly, 15,* 663–686.

Gaertner, G. H., Gaertner, K. N., & Devine, I. (1983). Federal agencies in the context of transition: A contrast between democratic and organizational theories. *Public Administration Review, 43,* 421–432.

Gaertner, K. N. (1988). Managers' careers and organizational change. *Academy of Management Executive, 2,* 311–318.

Gaertner, K. N., & Gaertner, C. H. (1985). Performance-contingent pay for federal managers. *Administration and Society, 17*(l), 7–20.

Gage, N. L., & Exline, R. V. (1953). Social perception and effectiveness in discussion groups. *Human Relations, 6,* 381–396.

Gaines, C. W. (1992). *An investigation of the relationship between self-perceived pastoral styles and growing churches in the Arizona Southern Baptist Convention.* Doctoral dissertation, New Orleans Baptist Theological Seminary, New Orleans, 348.

Gaines, J. (1993). "You don't necessarily have to be charismatic ..." An interview with Anita Roddick and reflections on charismatic leadership in the Body Shop International. *Leadership Quarterly, 4,* 347–359.

Gal, R. (1983). *Courage under stress.* In S. Breznitz (ed.), *Stress in Israel.* New York: Van Nostrand Reinhold.

Gal, R. (1985a). *Combat stress as an opportunity: The case of heroism.* Paper, Northeast Regional Conference of the Inter–University Seminar on Armed Forces and Society, Albany, NY

Gal, R. (1985b). Commitment and obedience in the military: An Israeli case study. *Armed Forces and Society, 11,* 553–564.

Gal, R. (1986). Unit morale: From a theoretical puzzle to an empirical illustration: An Israeli example. *Journal of Applied Social Psychology, 16,* 549–564.

Gal, R. (1987). *Yesterday's conventional warfare—Tomorrow's nuclear warfare? Lessons from the Israeli experience.* Paper, Conference on Military Leadership, Annapolis, MD.

Gal, R. (1989). *Military leadership for the 1990's: Commitment-derived leadership.* Unpublished manuscript.

Gal, R., & Jones, F. O. (1985). *Psychological aspects of combat stress: A model derived from Israeli and other combat experiences.* Unpublished manuscript.

Gal, R., & Lazarus, R. S. (1975). The role of activity in anticipating and confronting stressful situations. *Journal of Human Stress, 1*(4), 4–20.

Gal, R., & Manning, F. (1984). *Correlates of unit cohesion and morale in the US and Israeli armies.* Paper presented at the annual meeting of the American Psychological Association, Toronto.

Galagan, P. (1987). Between two trapezes. *Training and Development Journal, 41*(3), 40–53.

Galanter, M. (1982). Charismatic religious sects and psychiatry: An overview. *American Journal of Psychiatry, 139,* 1539–1548.

Galaskiewicz, J., & Shatin, D. (1981). Leadership and networking among neighborhood human service organizations. *Administrative Science Quarterly, 26,* 434–448.

Galbraith, C. S., & De Noble (2004). *Memory, cognition, and metacognition: A framework for history's stories.* Paper. Academy of Management, New Orleans, LA.

Gall, A. L. (1987). You can take the manager out of the woods, but ... *Training and Development Journal, 41*(3), 54–61.

Gallagher, A. (1983). The older worker: The relationship between job satisfaction and supervisor style. *Dissertation Abstracts International, 45*(2A), 460.

Galinsky, M. J., & Schopler, J. H. (1980). Structuring co-leadership in social work training. *Social Work with Groups, 3*(4), 51–63.

Gallino, L. (1975). Three types of Italian top managers. *International Student Management Organization, 5,* 43–70.

Gallo, P. S., & McClintock, C. G. (1962). Behavioral, attitudinal, and perceptual differences between leaders and non-leaders in situations of group support and non-support. *Journal of Social Psychology, 56,* 121–133.

Gallup (1997). *Black/white relations in the United States, 1997.* Gallup Poll Social Audit.

Gallup (2001, February 21). *Americans see women as emotional and affectionate, men as more aggressive.* www.gallup.com/poll//pr010221 .asp.

Gallup Organization. (1999). *A leadership style study of female and male legislators.* Lincoln, NE, August.

Gallup Poll (2000, January 25). *The gender gap.* www.Gallup.com/poll/ releases.

Gallup Poll (2001, January 11). *When it comes to choosing a boss, Americans still prefer men.* www.gallup.com/poll/releases/pr010111.asp.

Gallup Poll (2001, April 24). Tuesday Briefing.

Gallup Poll (2001, May 8). *Mother's Day.* list-admin@gallup.com.

Gallup Tuesday Briefing (2001).

Gallupe, R. B., DeSanctis, G., & Dickson, G. W. (1988). Computer-based support for group problem-finding: An experimental investigation. *Management Information Systems Quarterly, 12,* 277–296.

Galton, F. (1869). *Hereditary genius.* New York: Appleton.

Galvin, J. (2000). The new business ethics. *Smart Business for the New Economy, 13*(6), 86.

Gamson, W. A., & Scotch, N. (1964). Scapegoating in baseball. *American Journal of Sociology, 70,* 69–70.

Ganster, D. C. (2005). Executive job demands: Suggestions from a stress and decision-making perspective. *Academy of Management Review, 30.* 492–502.

Ganster, D. C., Fusilier, M. R., & Mayes, B. T. (1986). Role of social support in the experience of stress at work. *Journal of Applied Psychology, 71,* 102–110.

Gantz, B. S., Erickson, C. O., & Stephenson, R. W. (1977a). Measuring the motivation to manage in a research and development population. In J. B. Miner (ed.), *Motivation to manage.* Atlanta, GA: Organizational Measurement Systems Press.

Garcia, J. L. (1995). *Transformational leadership processes and salesperson performance: A field experiment.* Doctoral dissertation, Fielding Institute, Santa Barbara, CA.

Garcia, M. M., Shaw, D. S., Winslow, E. B., & Yaggi, K. E. (2000). Destructive sibling conflict and the development of conduct problems in young boys. *Developmental Psychology, 36,* 44–53.

Gardiner, M., & Tiggemann, M. (1999). Gender differences in leadership style, job stress, and mental health in male- and female-dominated industries. *Journal of Occupational and Organizational Psychology, 72,* 301–315.

Gardner, B. B., & Whyte, W. F. (1945). The man in the middle. *Applied Anthropology, 4,* 1–28.

Gardner, G. (1956). Functional leadership and popularity in small groups. *Human Relations, 9,* 491–509.

Gardner, H. (1985). *The mind's new science: A history of the cognitive revolution.* New York; Basic Books.

Gardner, J. W. (1961). *Excellence: Can we be equal and excellent too?* New York: Harper.

Gardner, J. W. (1963). *Self-renewal: The individual and the innovative society.* New York: Harper & Row.

Gardner, J. W. (1965b). *Self-renewal.* New York: Harper & Row.

Gardner, J. W. (1986a). *The nature of leadership: Introductory considerations* (Leadership Paper 1). Washington, DC: Independent Sector.

Gardner, J. W. (1986b). *The tasks of leadership* (Leadership Paper No. 2). Washington, DC: Independent Sector.

Gardner, J. W. (1987). *Attributes and context.* Leadership Studies Program, Independent Sector, Leadership Papers.

Gardner, J. W. (1987b). Leaders and followers. *Liberal Education, 73*(2), 4–8.

Gardner, J. W. (1988). *The changing nature of leadership.* (Leadership Paper No. 11). Washington, DC: Independent Sector.

Gardner, J. W. (1988). Leadership: An overview. *Leadership Papers, 12,* 3–28.

Gardner, J. W. (1988b). *Renewing: The leader's creative task* (Leadership Paper No. 10). Washington, DC: Independent Sector.

Gardner, J. W. (1988a). *The task of motivating* (Leadership Paper No. 9). Washington, DC: Independent Sector.

Gardner, J. W. (1989). *On leadership.* New York: Free Press

Gardner, J. W. (1990). *On leadership.* New York: Free Press.

Gardner, J.W. (1993). *On leadership.* New York: Free Press.

Gardner, J. W. (1997). Boundary crossers: Community leadership in a global age. Foreword. In J. W. Gardner & G. Sorenson (eds.), *Citizen participation & political leadership focus group.* Kellogg Leadership Studies Project, University of Maryland, College Park, MD.

Gardner, J. W. (2003). *Living, leading and the American dream.* New York: Jossey-Bass.

Gardner, J. W. (2003). *On leadership* (2nd ed.). New York: Free Press.

Gardner, K. E., & Williams, A. P. O. (1973). A twenty-five year follow-up of an extended interview selection procedure in the Royal Navy. *Occupational Psychology, 47,* 1–13.

Gardner, W. L., & Avolio, B. J. (1998). The charismatic relationship: A dramaturgical perspective. *Academy of Management Review, 23,* 32–58.

Gardner, W. L., & Cleavenger, D. (1996). *Impression management behaviors of transformational leaders at the world-class level: A psychohistorical assessment.* Paper, Southern Management Association, New Orleans.

Gardner, W. L., & Martinko, M. J. (1988). Impression management: An observational study linking audience characteristics with verbal selfpresentations. *Academy of Management Journal, 31,* 42–65.

Garforth, F. I. de la P. (1945). War office selection boards. *Occupational Psychology, 19,* 97–108.

Garland, H., & Beard, J. F. (1979). Relationship between self-monitoring and leader emergence across two task situations. *Journal of Applied Psychology, 64,* 72–76.

Garland, H., & Price, K. H. (1977). Attitudes toward women in management and attributions for their success and failure in managerial positions. *Journal of Applied Psychology, 62*, 29–33.

Garlitz, G. K (1983). Learning from worksite traumas. *Personnel Administrator, 28*(4), 28–34.

Garrison, K. C. (1933). A study of some factors related to leadership in high school. *Peabody Journal of Education, 11*, 11–17.

Gartner, D., & Iverson, M. A. (1967). Some effects of upward mobile status in established and ad hoc groups. *Journal of Personality and Social Psychology, 5*, 390–397.

Garza, R. T., Romero, G. J., Cox, B. G., & Ramirez, M. (1982). Biculturalism, locus of control, and leader behavior in ethnically mixed small groups. *Journal of Applied Social Psychology, 12*(3), 237–253.

Gassner, S. M., Gold, J., & Snadowsky, A. M. (1964). Changes in the phenomenal field as a result of human relations training. *Journal of Psychology, 58*, 33–41.

Gast, J. F. (1984). Leader discretion as a key component of a manager's role. In J. C. Hunt, D. Hosking, C. A. Schriesheim, & R. Stewart (eds.), *Leaders and managers: International perspectives on managerial behavior and leadership.* New York: Pergamon.

Gaston, I. L. (1983). *Factors enabling psychologically healthy individuals (managers) to function in the less-than-optimal organizational system.* Doctoral dissertation, George Washington University, Washington, DC.

Gates, D. (1989). The faking of the President. Did the Reagan years really happen? *Newsweek*, November 27, 84–85.

Gaudreau, P. A. (1975). Investigation of sex differences across job levels. *Dissertation Abstracts International, 36*, 1957B.

Gaugler, B. B., Rosenthal, D. B., Thornton, C. C., & Bentson, C. (1987). Meta-analysis of assessment center validity. *Journal of Applied Psychology, 72*, 493–511.

Gautschi, F. H., III, & Jones, T. M. (1998). Enhancing the ability of business students to recognmize business issues: An empirical assessment of the effectiveness of a course in business ethics. *Journal of Business Ethics, 17*, 205–216.

Gavin, D. A. (1983). Quality on the line. *Harvard Business Review, 61*(5), 65–75.

Gavin, M. B., & Cheung, G. W. (2004). *Structural equation modeling with LISREL.* Presentation, Academy of Management, New Orleans.

Gavin, M. B., Green, S. G., & Fairhurst, G. T. (1995). Managerial control strategies for poor performnce over time and the impact on subordinate reactions. *Organizational Behavior & Human Decision Processes, 63*, 207–221.

Gavrieli, D. A. (2003). *Gender and leadership in the Israeli Defense Forces.* Paper, Academy of Management, Seattle, WA.

Gay, P. (1985). Foreword. In C. B. Strozier & D. Offer (eds.), *The leader: Psychohistorical Essays.* New York: Plenum.

Gebert, D., & Steinkamp, T. (1991). Leadership style and economic success in Nigeria and Taiwan. *Management International Review, 31*, 161–171

Geertz, C. (1977). Centers, kings and charisma: Reflections on the symbolics of power. In J. Ben-David & T. N. Clark (eds.), *Culture and its creators: Essays in honor of Edward Shils.* Chicago: University of Chicago Press.

Geertz, C. (1983). *Reflections on the symbolics of power.* In C. Geertz (ed.), *Local knowledge.* New York: Basic Books.

Gehrman, C. H. (1970). *An investigation of the relationship between participation and organizational climate: An empirical study of the perceptions of high school senior students, teachers, principals and district superintendents in innovative vs. noninnovative schools.* Doctoral dissertation, University of Massachusetts, Amherst.

Geier, J. G. (1963). A descriptive analysis of an interaction pattern resulting in leadership emergence in leaderless group discussion. *Dissertation Abstracts, 26*, 2919–2920.

Geier, J. C. (1967). A trait approach to the study of leadership in small groups. *Journal of Communication, 17*, 316–323.

Geijsel, F., Sleegers, P., & van den Berg, R. (1999). Transforming leadership and the implementation of large-scale innovation programs. *Journal of Educational Administration, 37*, 309–328.

Geijsel, F., Sleegers, P., van den Berg, R., & Kelchtermans, G. (2000). Conditions fostering the implementation of large-scale innovation programs in schools: Teachers' perspectives. *Educational Administration Quarterly, 37*, 130–166.

Geijsel, F., van den Berg, R., & Sleegers, P. (1999). The innovative capacity of schools in primary education: A qualitative study. *Qualitative Studies in Education, 12*, 175–191.

Geis, F. L., Boston, M. B., & Hoffman, N. (1985). Sex of authority role models and achievement by men and women: Leadership performance and recognition. *Journal of Personality and Social Psychology, 49*(3), 636–653.

Geissler, E. M. (1984). Personality characteristics and feelings of power-powerlessness in nurse and non-nurse leaders. *Dissertation Abstracts International, 45*(7B), 2101.

Gekoski, N. (1952). Predicting group productivity. *Personnel Psychology, 5*, 281–291.

Geller, P. A., & Hobfell, S. E. (1994). Gender differences in job stress, tedium and social support in the workplace. *Journal of Personal and Social Relationships, 11*, 555–572.

Gellerman, S. W. (1967). Passivity, paranoia, and "pakikisama." *Columbia Journal of World Business, 2*, 59–66.

Gellert, E. (1961). Stability and fluctuation in the power relationships of young children. *Journal of Abnormal and Social Psychology, 62*, 815.

Gelman, E., Hughey, Tsuruoka, et al. (1984). Macho men of capitalism: In the nation's executive suites, some strong leaders can be hard to follow. *Newsweek*, October 15, 8–59.

Gemmill, C. R., & Thamhain, H. J. (1974). Influence styles of project managers: Some project performance correlates. *Academy of Management Journal, 17*, 216–224.

Gemmill, G. R., & Heisler, W. J. (1972). Fatalism as a factor in managerial job satisfaction, job strain, and mobility. *Personnel Psychology, 25*, 241–250.

Gemmill, G. R., & Oakley, J. (1992). Leadership: An alienating social myth. *Human Relations, 45*, 113–129.

Geneen, H., & Moscow, A. (1984). *Managing.* New York: Doubleday.

General Electric Company (1957). *The effective manufacturing foreman.* Schenectady, NY: General Electric Company.

Genovese, M. (1993). Margaret Thatcher and the politics of conviction leadership. In Genovese, M. (ed.), *Women as national leaders.* Newbury Park, CA: Sage.

Genovese, M. A. (1995). *The presidential dilemma: Leadership in the American system.* New York: HarperCollins.

George, A. L., & George, G. L. (1956). *Woodrow Wilson and Colonel House: A personality study*. New York: Macmillan. (See Wilson in text).

George, C. S., Jr. (1972). *The history of management thought*. Englewood Cliffs, NJ: Prentice-Hall.

George, J. F., Easton, G. K., Nunamaker, J. F., Jr., et al. (1990). A study of collaborative group work with and without computer-based support. *Information Systems Research, 1*, 394–413.

George, J. M. (1995). Leader positive mood and group performance: The case of customer service. *Journal of Applied Social Psychology, 25*, 778–794.

George, J. M. (1996). Trait and state affect. In K. Murphy (ed.), *Individual differences and behavior*. San Francisco: Jossey-Bass.

George, J. M. (2000). Emotions and leadership: The role of emotional intelligence. *Human Relations, 53*. 1027–1055.

Georgopoulos, B. S. (1965). Normative structure variables and organizational behavior. *Human Relations, 18*, 155–169.

Georgopoulos, B. S., Mahoney, G. M., & Jones, N. W. (1957). A path-goal approach to productivity. *Journal of Applied Psychology, 41*, 345–353.

Georgopoulos, B.S., & Seashore, S.E. (1961). Superior-subordinate relationships and performance. *Personnel Psychology, 14*, 357–375.

Gephart, R. P., Jr. (1978). Status degradation and organizational succession: An ethnomethodological approach. *Administrative Science Quarterly, 23*, 553–581.

Gerard, H. B. (1953). The effect of different dimensions of disagreement on the communication process in small groups. *Human Relations, 6*, 249–271.

Gerard, H. B. (1957). Some effects of status, role clarity, and group goal clarity upon the individual's relations to group progress. *Journal of Personality, 25*, 475–488.

Gerdes, D. A. (1994). *Morality, leadership, and excellence: A naturalistic study of collegiate men's basketball coaching*. Thesis, University of Kansas, 1994.

Gergen, K. J., & Taylor, M. G. (1969). Social expectancy and self-presentation in a status hierarchy. *Journal of Experimental Social Psychology, 5*, 79–92.

Gersick, C. J. G. (1985). *Time and transition in work teams: Towards a new model of group development*. [Reported in B. B. Morgan, A. S. Glickman, et al. (1986). *Measurement of team behaviors in a Navy environment*. Orlando, FL: Center of Excellence for Simulation and Training Technology, Naval Training Systems Center.]

Gerstberger, P. G., & Allen, T. J. (1968). Criteria used by research and development engineers in the selection of an information source. *Journal of Applied Psychology, 52*, 272–279.

Gerstein, M. S., & Shaw, R. B. (1992). Organizational architectures for the 21st century. In D. A. Nadler, M. S. Gerstein, & R. B. Shaw (eds.), *Organizational architecture: Design for changing organizations*. San Francisco: Jossey-Bass.

Gerstner, C. R., & Day, D. D. (1994). Cross-cultural comparison of leadership prototypes. *Leadership Quarterly, 5*, 121–134

Gerstner, C. R., & Day, D. V. (1997). Meta-analysis review of leader-member exchange theory: Correlates and construct ideas. *Journal of Applied Psychology, 82*, 827–844.

Gerth, H., & Mills, C. W. (1952). A sociological note on leadership. In J. E. Hulett & R. Stagner (eds.), *Problems in social psychology*. Urbana: University of Illinois Press.

Gerth, H., & Mills, C. W. (1953). *Character and social structure*. New York: Harcourt, Brace.

Gerwin, D. (1981). Relationships between structure and technology. In R. C. Nystrom & W. H. Starbuck (eds.), *Handbook of organizational design*. New York: Oxford University Press.

Getzels, J. W. (1963). Conflict and role behavior in an educational setting. In W. W. Charters, & N. L. Gage (eds.), *Readings in the social psychology of education*. Boston: Allyn & Bacon.

Getzels, J. W., & Cuba, E. G. (1954). Role, role conflict, and effectiveness: An empirical study. *American Sociological Review, 19*, 164–175.

Getzels, J. W. & Cuba, E. G. (1957). Social behavior and the administrative process. *School Review, 55*, 423–441.

Geyer, A. L., & Steyrer, J. (1998). Transformational leadership, classical leadership dimensions and performance indicators in savings banks. *Leadership Quarterly, 47*, 397–420.

Geyer, L. J., & Steyrer, J. M. (1998). Transformational leadership and objective performance in banks. *Applied Psychology: An International Review, 47*, 397–420.

Ghiselli, E. E. (1959). Traits differentiating management personnel. *Personnel Psychology, 12*, 535–544.

Ghiselli, E. E. (1963b). Intelligence and managerial success. *Psychological Reports, 12*, 898.

Ghiselli, E. E. (1964). Maturity of self-perception in relation to managerial success. *Personnel Psychology, 17*, 41–48.

Ghiselli, E. E. (1966a). Psychological properties of groups and group learning. *Psychological Reports, 19*, 17–18.

Ghiselli, E. E. (1968a). Interaction of traits and motivational factors in the determination of the success of managers. *Journal of Applied Psychology, 52*, 480–483.

Ghiselli, E. E. (1971). *Explorations in managerial talent*. Pacific Palisades, CA: Goodyear.

Ghiselli, E. E., & Barthol, R. P. (1956). Role perceptions of successful and unsuccessful superiors. *Journal of Applied Psychology, 40*, 241–244.

Ghiselli, E. E., & Johnson, D. A. (1970). Need satisfaction, managerial success, and organizational structure. *Personnel Psychology, 23*, 569–576.

Ghiselli, E. E., & Lodahl, T. M. (1958a). The evaluation of foremen's performance in relation to the internal characteristics of their groups. *Personnel Psychology, 11*, 179–187.

Ghodsian-Carpey, J., & Baker, L. A. (1987). Genetic and environmental influences on aggression in 4 to 7 year old twins. *Aggressive Behavior, 13*(4), 173–186.

Ghorpade, J. (2000). Managing five paradoxes of 360-degree feedback. *Academy of Management Executive, 14*(1), 140–150.

Ghorpede, J., & Chen, M. M. (1995). Creating quality-driven performance appraisal systems. *Academy of Management Executive, 9*(1), 32–39.

Ghoshal, S. (2005). Bad management theories are destroying good management practices. *Academy of Management Learning & Education, 4*, 75–91.

Ghoshal, S., & Bartlett, C. A. (1997). *The individualized corporation.* New York: Harper.

Ghoshal, S., & Moran, P. (1996). Bad for practice: A critique of transaction cost theory. *Academy of Management Review, 21,* 13–47.

Giacobbe-Miller, J. K., & Miller, D. J. (1995). *A comparison of U.S. and Russian pay allocation decisions and distributive justice judgments.* Paper, Academy of Management, Vancouver, BC.

Giambatista, R. C. (2004). Jumping through hoops: a longitudinal study of leader life cycles in the NBA. *Leadership Quarterly, 15*(5), 607–624.

Giampetro-Meyer, A., Brown, T., Browne, M. N., & Kubasek, N. (1998). Do we really want more leaders in business? *Journal of Business Ethics, 17,* 1727–1736.

Giannantonio, C. N., OIian, J. D., & Carroll, S. J. (1995). An experimental study of gender and situational effects in a performance evaluation of a manager. *Psychological Reports, 76,* 1004–1006.

Gibb, C. A. (1947). The principles and traits of leadership. *Journal of Abnormal and Social Psychology, 42,* 267–284.

Gibb, C. A. (1949). Some tentative comments concerning group Rorschach pointers to the personality traits of leaders. *Journal of Social Psychology, 30,* 251–263.

Gibb, C. A. (1950). The sociometry of leadership in temporary groups. *Sociometry, 13,* 226–243.

Gibb, C. A. (1954). Leadership. In G. Lindzey (ed.), *Handbook of social psychology.* Cambridge, MA: Addison-Wesley.

Gibb, C. A. (1958). An interactional view of the emergence of leadership. *Australian Journal of Psychology, 10,* 101–110.

Gibb, C. A. (1969a). Leadership. In G. Lindzey & E. Aronson (eds.), *The handbook of social psychology* (2nd ed., vol. 4). Reading, MA: Addison-Wesley.

Gibb, J. R. (1961). Defense level and influence potential in small groups. In L. Petrullo & B. M. Bass (eds.), *Leadership and interpersonal behavior.* New York: Holt, Rinehart & Winston.

Gibb, J. R. (1964). The T-group as a climate for trust formation. In L. P Bradford, J. R. Gibb, & K. D. Berme (eds.), *T-group theory and laboratory methods: Innovation in re-education.* New York: Wiley.

Gibbons, T. C. (1986). *Revisiting the question of born vs. made: Toward a theory of development of transformational leaders.* Doctoral dissertation, Fielding Institute, Santa Barbara, CA. Also: Paper, OD Network Conference, New York.

Gibson, A. K. (1974). *The achievement of sixth grade students in a midwestern city.* Doctoral dissertation, University of Michigan, Ann Arbor.

Gibson, C. B. (1999). Do they do what they believe they can? Group efficacy and group effectiveness across tasks and cultures. *The Academy of Management Journal, 42*(2), 138–152.

Gibson, D., Mainero, L., & Sullivan, S. E. (2004). *Do men and women react differently in crisis events? An examination of care and justice response orientations.* Paper, Academy of Management, New Orleans, LA.

Gibson, F. W., Fiedler, F. E., & Barrett, K. M. (1993). Stress, babble, and the utilization of the leader's intellectual abilities. *Leadership Quarterly, 4,* 189–208.

Gibson, J. E. (1968). *Introduction to engineering design.* New York: Holt, Rinehardt, & Winston.

Gibson, J. W., Blackwell, C. W., Dominicus, P., et al. (2002). Telecommuting in the 21st century: Benefits, issues, and a leadership model which will work. *Journal of Leadership Studies, 8*(4), 75–86.

Gibson, J. W., & Tesone, D. V. (2001). Management fads: Emergence, evolution, and implications for managers. *Academy of Management Executive, 15*(4), 122–133.

Gide, C. (1930). *Communist and cooperative colonies.* New York: Crowell.

Giestland, D. S. (1982). *Leadership and the bases of power.* Doctoral dissertation, University of California, Santa Barbara.

Giffort, D., & Ayman, R. (1988). *Leadership style, situational control and subordinate job satisfaction.* Paper, Academy of Management, Anaheim, CA.

Gilbert, E. M. (1972). *Teaching styles prevalent in satisfying and dissatisfying college credit courses as perceived by adult students.* Doctoral dissertation, Ohio State University, Columbus.

Gilbert, G. R. (1985). Building highly productive work teams through positive leadership. *Public Personnel Management, 14,* 449–454.

Gilbert, J. A., & Ones, D. S. (1998). *Heritability of job involvement: Implications for industrial-organizational psychology.* Paper, International Congress of Psychology, San Francisco.

Gilbert, S. (2004). New clues to women veiled in black. *New York Times,* March 16, D1, D7.

Gilchrist, J. C. (1952). The formation of social groups under conditions of success and failure. *Journal of Abnormal and Social Psychology, 47,* 174–187.

Gilchrist, J. C., Shaw, M. E., & Walker, L. C. (1954). Some effects of unequal distribution of information in a wheel group structure. *Journal of Abnormal and Social Psychology, 49,* 554–556.

Gill, J. (1992). Management by panacea: Accounting for transience. *Journal of Management Studies, 30,* 281–295.

Gill, J. (1996). Leadership and Ethics. In K. Smith and P. Johnson (eds.), *Business ethics and business behavior.* International Thomson Publishing.

Gill, R. W. T. (1979). The in-tray (in-basket) exercise as a measure of management potential. *Journal of Occupational Psychology, 52,* 185–197.

Gill, R. W. T. (1983). *Personality profiles of Singapore–Chinese, British and American managers: A cross-cultural comparison.* Paper, Third Asian Regional Conference on Cross-Cultural Psychology, Bangi, Malaysia.

Gill, R. W. T. (1996). Japanese-style management Singapore: Some perceptions, problems and prescriptions. *Today's Manager,* Singapore, May–July, 26–28.

Gill, R. W. T. (1998). Leadership and organizations for the new millennium. *Journal of Leadership Studies, 4,* 46–59.

Gillen, D. J., & Carroll, S. J. (1985). Relationship of managerial ability to unit effectiveness in more organic versus more mechanistic departments. *Journal of Management Studies, 22,* 668–676.

Gillespie, D. F., & Cohen, S. E. (1984). Causes of worker burnout. *Children and Youth Services Review, 6,* Fall, 115–124.

Gillespie, D. F., & Numerof, R. E. (1984). The Gillespie-Numerof burnout inventory: Technical manual. St. Louis, MO: Washington University.

Gillespie, H. R. (1980). An investigation of current management/

leadership style of manufacturing executives in American industry. *Dissertation Abstracts International, 41*(7A), 3177.

Gillespie, J. B. (1980). The phenomenon of the public wife: An exercise in Coffman's impression management. *Symbolic Interaction, 3*(2), 109–126.

Gilligan, C. (1982). *In a different voice*. Cambridge, MA: Harvard University Press.

Gillis, C., Getkate, M., Robinson, D., et al. (1995). Correctional work supervisor leadership and credibility: Their influence on offender work motivation. *Research in Brief*, 15–17.

Gilmore, D. C., Beehr, T. A., & Richter, D. J. (1979). Effects of leader behaviors on subordinate performance and satisfaction: A laboratory experiment with student employees. *Journal of Applied Psychology, 64*, 166–172.

Gilmore, T. N. (1982). Leadership and boundary management. *Journal of Applied Behavioral Science, 18*, 343–356.

Gilmore, T. N. (1988). *Making a leadership change: How organizations and leaders can handle leadership transitions successfully*. San Francisco: Jossey-Bass.

Gilovich, T., & Savitzky (1999). The spotlight effect and the illusion of egocentric assessments of how we are seen by others. *Current Directions in Psychological Science, 8*, 165–168.

Gini, A. (1995). Too much to say about something. *Business Ethics Quarterly, 5*, 143–155.

Gini, A. (1996). *Moral leadership and business ethic*. College Park, MD: Center for Political Leadership and Participation.

Ginnett, R. C. (1993). Crews as groups: Their formation and their leadership. In E. L. Wiener, B. G. Kanki, & R. L. Helmreich (eds.), *Cockpit resource management*. Orlando, FL: Academic Press.

Gintner, G., & Lindskold, S. (1975). Rate of participation and expertise as factors influencing leader choice. *Journal of Personality and Social Psychology, 32*, 1085–1089.

Gioia, D. A., & Sims, H. P. (1985). On avoiding the influence of implicit leadership theories in leader behavior descriptions. *Educational and Psychological Measurement, 45*, 217–232.

Gioia, D. A., & Sims, H. P (1986). Cognition-behavior connections: Attribution and verbal behavior in leader-subordinate interactions. *Organizational Behavior and Human Decision Processes, 37*, 197–229.

Gitter, A. G., Black, H., & Fishman, J. E. (1975). Effect of race, sex, nonverbal communication and verbal communication on perception of leadership. *Sociological and Social Research, 60*, 46–57.

Gist, M. E., & Gerson, D. S. (1998). *In the eyes of the beholder: A structural model of strategic leadership and executive effectiveness*. Unpublished manuscript.

Gist, M. E. & Mitchell, T. R. (1992). Self-efficacy: A theoretical analysis of its determinants and malleability. *Academy of Management Review, 17*, 183–211.

Glad, B. (1980). *Jimmy Carter: In search of the great White House*. New York: W. W. Norton.

Gladstein, D. L., & Reilly, N. R. (1985). Group decision making under threat: The tycoon game. *Academy of Management Journal, 28*, 613–627.

Gladstone, R. (1989). Auto unions and companies lose to Japan. *Binghamton Press & Sun-Bulletin*, July 31, Business Section, 5.

Glanzer, M., & Glaser, R. (1961). Techniques for the study of group structure. II. Empirical studies of the effects of structure in small groups. *Psychological Bulletin, 58*, 1–27.

Glaser, B. G., & Strauss, A. L. (1967). *The discovery of grounded theory*. Chicago: Aldine.

Glaser, R., Schwartz, F. A., & Flanagan, J. C. (1958). The contribution of interview and situational performance procedures to the selection of supervisory personnel. *Journal of Applied Psychology, 42*, 69–73.

Glassman, E. (1989). Creative problem solving: Your role as leader. *Supervisory Management, 34*(4), 37–42.

Gleason, W. J. (1957). Predicting Army leadership ability by modified leaderless group discussion. *Journal of Applied Psychology, 41*, 231235.

Glick, P., & Fiske, S. T. (2001). An ambivalent alliance: Hostile and benevolent sexism as complementary justifications for gender inequality. *American Psychologist, 56*(2), 109–118.

Glickman, A. S., Hahn, C. R, Fleishman, E. A., & Baxter, B. (1969). *Top management development and succession: An exploratory study*. New York: Macmillan.

Glickman, C. D. (1990). Pushing reform to a new edge: The seven ironies of school empowerment. *Phi Delta Kappa, 72*, September, 68–75.

Glomb, T. M., & Hulin, C. L. (1997). Anger and gender effects in observed supervisor-subordinate interactions. *Organizational Behavior & Human Decision Processes, 72*, 281–307.

Glynn, M. A., & Slepian, J. (1992). Leaders and transitions: The role of leadership in corporate name change. In K. E. Clark, M. B. Clark, & D. P. Campbell (eds.), *Impact of leadership*. Greensboro, NC: Center for Creative Leadership.

Gmelch, W. H. (2000). Leadership succession: How new deans take charge and learn the job. *Journal of Leadership Studies, 7*(3), 68–87.

Godfrey, E. P, Fiedler, F. E., & Hall, D. M. (1959). *Boards, management, and company success*. Danville, IL: Interstate.

Godschalk, V. M., & Sosik, J. J. (2000). Does mentor-protégé agreement on mentor leadership behavior influence the quality of the mentoring relationships? *Group and Organization Management, 25*, 291–317.

Goeglein, A. T. (1997). *Values-based transformational leadership; the relationship between consciousness, values, and skills*. Doctoral dissertation, California School of Professional Psychology at Alameda, Alameda, CA.

Goel, S., Manz, C. C., Neck, C. P., et al. (1995). Beyond traditional leadership: Leading others to lead themselves. *Journal of Leadership Studies, 2*(1), 81–92.

Goertzel, V. & Goertzel, M.G. (1962). *Cradles of Eminence*. Little Brown: Boston, MA.

Goetz, T. E., & Herman, J. B. (1976). *Effects of supervisor's sex and subordinate sex on job satisfaction and productivity*. Washington, DC: American Psychological Association.

Goffin, R. D., & Gellatly, I. R. (2001). A multi-rater assessment of organizational commitment: Are self-report measures biased? *Journal of Organizational Behavior, 22*, 437–451.

Goffman, E. (1959). *The presentation of self in everyday life*. Garden City, NY: Doubleday.

Goitein, B. (2004). *Open book management.* Paper, Academy of Management, New Orleans.

Golb, E. F, & Fiedler, F. E. (1955). *A note on psychological attributes related to the score assumed similarity between opposites (ASo).* (Tech. Rep. No. 12). Urbana: University of Illinois, Group Effectiveness Research Laboratory.

Gold, R. (1951–1952). Janitors versus tenants: A status-income dilemma. *American Journal of Sociology, 57,* 486–493.

Gold, Y., & Roth, R. A. (1999). *Transformational helping professional: A new vision, mentoring and supervising reconsidered.* Needham Heights, MA: Allyn & Bacon.

Goldberg, C. (1995). Psychologist posits the origins of evil. *APA Monitor,* October.

Goldberg, H., & Iverson, M. A. (1965). Inconsistency in attitude of high status persons and loss of influence: An experimental study. *Psychological Reports, 16,* 673–683.

Goldberg, L. R. (1993). The structure of phenotypic personality traits *American Psychologist, 48,* 26–34.

Goldberg, M. (1984). The essential points of a nation at risk. *Educational Leadership, 41,* 15–16.

Goldberg, M. L. (1955). Leadership and self-attitudes. *Dissertation Abstracts, 15,* 1457–1458.

Goldberg, R. (1983). *The intuitive edge: Understanding and developing intuition.* Boston: Houghton Mifflin.

Goldberg, S. C. (1954). Three situational determinants of conformity to social norms. *Journal of Abnormal and Social Psychology, 49,* 325–329.

Goldman, M., & Fraas, L. A. (1965). The effects of leader selection on group performance. *Sociometry, 28,* 82–88.

Goldsmith, C. (2002). Norway plans to put gender equality on the boardroom table: Oslo wants women to be 40% of corporate board; move is first in Europe. *Wall Street Journal,* July 19, A9.

Goldsmith, H. H. (1983). Genetic influences on personality from infancy to adulthood. *Child Development, 54*(2), 331–355.

Goldsmith, M. (1996). Retaining high-impact performers. *Leader-to-Leader, 1*(1), 6–8.

Goldstein, A. P., & Sorcher, M. (1974). *Changing supervisory behavior.* New York: Pergamon.

Goldstein, H. W., Hoffman, M. P., & Yusko, K. P. (1995). *Crisis leadership: The role of follower efficacy perception.* Paper, Academy of Management, (Call 212–387 1557).

Goldstein, H. W., Yusko, K. P., & Nicopoulos, V. (2001). Exploring black-white subgroup differences of managerial competencies. *Personnel Psychology, 54,* 783–807.

Goldstein, I. L. (1980). Training in work organizations. *Annual Review of Psychology, 31,* 229–272.

Goleman, D. (1995). *Emotional intelligence.* New York: Bantam Books.

Goleman, D. (1998). *Working with emotional intelligence.* New York: Bantam Books.

Goleman, D. (2000). Leadership that gets results. *Harvard Business Review,* March–April, 78–90.

Golembiewski, R. T. (1967). *Organizing men and power.* Chicago: Rand McNally.

Golembiewski, R. T., Billingsley, K., & Yeager, S. (1976). Measuring change and persistence in human affairs: Types of change generated by OD designs. *Journal of Applied Behavioral Science, 12,* 133–157.

Golembiewski, R. T., & Carrigan, S. B. (1970). The persistence of laboratory-induced changes in organization styles. *Administrative Science Quarterly, 15,* 330–340.

Gomez, C., & Rosen, B. (2001). The leader-member exchange as a link between management trust and employee empowerment. *Group & Organization Management, 26,* 53–69.

Gomez-Mejia, L. R., Page, R. C., & Tornow, W. W. (1982). A comparison of the practical utility of traditional statistical, and hybrid job evaluation approaches. *Academy of Management Journal, 25,* 790–809.

Gomez-Mejia, L. R., Tosi, H., & Hinkin, T. R. (1987). Managerial control, performance, and executive compensation. *Academy of Management Journal, 30,* 51–70.

Gonzalez, R. F., & Negandhi, A. R. (1967). *The United States overseas executive: His orientations and career patterns.* East Lansing, MI: Michigan State University.

Goodacre, D. M. (1951). The use of a sociometric test as a predictor of combat unit effectiveness. *Sociometry, 14,* 148–152.

Goodacre, D. M. (1953). Group characteristics of good and poor performing combat units. *Sociometry, 16,* 168–179.

Goodacre, D. M. (1955). Experimental evaluation of training. *Journal of Personnel Administration and Industrial Relations, 2,* 143–149.

Goodacre, D. M. (1963). Stimulating improved management. *Personnel Psychology, 16,* 133–134.

Goodale, J. G. (1973). Effects of personal background and training on work values on the hard-core unemployed. *Journal of Applied Psychology, 57,* 1–9.

Goodale, J. G., & Hall, D. T. (1976). Inheriting a career: The influence of sex, values, and parents. *Journal of Vocational Behavior, 8,* 19–30.

Goodall, K. (1971). Casualty lists from group encounters. *Psychology Today, 5,* 28.

Goode, W. J., & Fowler, I. (1949). Incentive factors in a low morale plant. *American Sociological Review, 14,* 618–624.

Goodenough, F. L. (1930). Inter-relationships in the behavior of young children. *Child Development, 1,* 29–48.

Goodenough, F. L., & Leahy, A. M. (1927). The effects of certain family relationships upon the development of personality. *Pedagogical Seminary, 34,* 45–71.

Goodman, J. F. B., & Whittingham, I. G. (1969). *Shop stewards in British industry.* London: McGraw-Hill.

Goodman, P. S. (1967). An empirical examination of Elliott Jaques' concept of time span. *Human Relations, 20,* 155–170.

Goodman, P. S. (1969). Hiring, training, and retaining the hard-core. *Industrial Relations, 9,* 54–66.

Goodsell, C. T. (1983). *The case for bureaucracy: A public administration, polemic.* Chatham, NJ: Chatham House.

Goodson, J. R., McGee, G. W., & Cashman, J. F. (1989). Situational leadership theory: A test of leadership prescriptions. *Group & Organizational Studies, 14,* 446–461.

Goodstadt, B. E., & Hjelle, L. A. (1973). Power to the powerless: Locus of control and the use of power. *Journal of Personality and Social Psychology, 27,* 190–196.

Goodstadt, B. E., & Kipnis, D. (1970). Situational influences on the use of power. *Journal of Applied Psychology, 54,* 201–207.

Goodstein, L. D., & Schrader, W. (1963). An empirically-derived managerial key for the California Psychological Inventory. *Journal of Applied Psychology, 47*, 42–45.

Goodwin, V. L., Wofford, J. C., & Whittington, J. L. (2001). A theoretical and empirical extension to the transformational leadership construct. *Journal of Organizational Behavior, 22*, 759–774.

Gopala, K. K. M., & Hafeez, A. (1964). A study of supervisors' attitude towards employees and production in relation to some personal factors. *Indian Journal of Applied Psychology, 1*, 78–83.

Gorbachev, M. (1988, December 8). Excerpt from speech to U.N. on major Soviet military cuts. *New York Times*, A16.

Gorden, R. L. (1952). Interaction between attitude and the definitions of the situation in the expression of opinion. *American Sociological Review, 17*, 50–58.

Gordon, G. E., & Becker, C. (1964). Organization size and managerial succession: A re–examination. *American Journal of Sociology, 70*, 215–222.

Gordon, G. E., & Rosen, N. (1981). Critical factors in leadership succession. *Organizational Behavior and Human Performance, 27*, 227–254.

Gordon, G.. and Yukl, G. (2004). The future of leadership research: challenges and opportunities. *German Journal of Human Resource Research, 18*, 359–365.

Gordon, L. V. (1952). Personal factors in leadership. *Journal of Social Psychology, 36*, 245–248.

Gordon, L. V. (1963a). *Manual, Gordon personal profile*, rev. ed. New York: Harcourt Brace Jovanovich.

Gordon, L. V. (1963). *Gordon personal inventory: Manual.* New York: Harcourt, Brace & World.

Gordon, L. V., & Medland, F. F. (1965a). The cross-group stability of peer ratings of leadership potential. *Personnel Psychology, 18*, 173–177.

Gordon, R. A. (1961). *Business leadership in the large corporation.* Berkeley: University of California Press.

Gordon, R. D. (2002). Conceptualizing leadership with respect to its historical–contextual antecedents to power. *Leadership Quarterly, 13*, 151–167.

Gordon, T. (1955). *Group-centered leadership: A way of releasing the creative power of groups.* Boston: Houghton Mifflin.

Gordon, T. A., & Loden, M. (1989). *Pluralistic leadership survey.* Copyrighted by Loden Associates, Inc. and Interface Associates. All rights reserved.

Gore, A. (1993). *From red tape to results: Creating a government that works better & costs less. Report of the national performance review.* Washington, DC: Office of the Vice President.

Gore, A., Jr. (1993). An open letter to public managers. *The Public Manager: The New Bureaucrat, 22*(4), 3.

Gorn, G. J., & Kanungo, R. N. (1980). Job involvement and motivation: Are intrinsically motivated managers more job involved? *Organizational Behavior and Human Performance, 26*, 265–277.

Gottfredson, L. S. (1986). Societal consequences of the g factor in employment. *Journal of Vocational Behavior, 29*, 379–410.

Gottheil, E., & Lauterbach, C. G. (1969). Leader and squad attributes contributing to mutual esteem among squad members. *Journal of Social Psychology, 77*, 69–78.

Gottheil, E., & Vielhaber, D. P. (1966). Interaction of leader and squad

attributes related to performance of military squads. *Journal of Social Psychology, 68*, 113–127.

Gottlieb, T. W. (1990). *Transactional and transformational leadership styles of chief and associate chief nurses in department of veterans' affairs medical centers: A descriptive study.* Doctoral dissertation, Columbia University, DC.

Gough, H. G. (1957). *Manual for the California Psychological Inventory.* Palo Alto, CA: Consulting Psychologists Press.

Gough, H. G. (1969). A leadership index on the California psychological inventory. *Journal of Counseling Psychology, 16*, 283–289.

Gough, H. G. (1984). A managerial potential scale for the California Psychology Inventory. *Journal of Applied Psychology, 69*, 233–240.

Gough, H. G. (1988–1989). *Administrator's guide for the California psychological inventory.* Palo Alto, CA: Consulting Psychologists Press.

Gough, H. G., & Heilbrun, A. B. (1983). *The Adjective Checklist Manual.* Palo Alto, CA: Consulting Psychologists Press.

Gouldner, A. W. (1950). *Studies in leadership.* New York: Harper.

Gouldner, A. W. (1954). *Patterns of industrial bureaucracy.* New York: Free Press. Also: (1965). Yellow Springs, OH: Antioch Press.

Govindarajan, I. N. (1964). Vocational interests of leaders and nonleaders among adolescent school boys. *Journal of Psychological Research, 8*(3), 124–130.

Gowin, E. B. (1915). *The executive and his control.* New York: Macmillan.

Gowin, E. B. (1918). *The selection and training of the business executive.* New York: Macmillan.

Gracian, B. (1658/1992). *The art of worldly wisdom.* New York: Barnes & Noble.

Graeff, C. L. (1983). The situational leadership theory: A critical view. *Academy of Management Review, 8*, 285–291.

Graeff, C. L. (1997). Evolution of situational leadership theory: A critical review. *Leadership Quarterly, 8*, 153–170.

Graen, G. (1976). Role making processes within complex organizations. In M. D. Dunnette (ed.), *Handbook of industrial and organizational psychology.* Chicago: Rand McNally.

Graen, G. (1978). *Role-making processes of leadership development.* Paper, American Association for the Advancement of Science, Washington, DC.

Graen, G., Alvares, K., Orris, J. B., & Martella, J. A. (1970). Contingency model of leadership effectiveness: Antecedent and evidential results. *Psychological Bulletin, 74*, 285–296.

Graen, G., & Cashman, J. F. (1975). A rolemaking model of leadership in formal organizations: A developmental approach. In J. G. Hunt & L. L. Larson (eds.), *Leadership frontiers.* Kent, OH: Kent State University Press.

Graen, G., Cashman, J. F., Ginsburgh, S., & Schiemann, W. (1977). Effects of linking-pin quality upon the quality of working life of lower participants: A longitudinal investigation of the managerial understructure. *Administrative Science Quarterly, 22*, 491–504.

Graen, G., Dansereau, F., & Minami, T. (1972a). Dysfunctional leadership styles. *Organizational Behavior and Human Performance, 7*, 216–236.

Graen, G., Dansereau, F., & Minami, T. (1972b). An empirical test of the man-in-the-middle hypothesis among executives in a hierarchical organization employing a unit-set analysis. *Organizational Behavior and Human Performance, 8,* 262–285.

Graen, G., Dansereau, F., Minami, T., & Cashman, J. (1973). Leadership behaviors as cues to performance evaluation. *Academy of Management Journal, 16,* 611–623.

Graen, G. B., Liden, R. C., & Hoel, W. (1982). Role of leadership in the employee withdrawal process. *Journal of Applied Psychology, 67,* 868–872.

Graen, G., Novak, M. A., & Sommerkamp, P. (1982). The effects of leadership-member exchange and job design on productivity and satisfaction: Testing a dual attachment model. *Organizational Behavior and Human Performance, 30,* 109–131.

Graen, G., Orris, J. B., & Alvares, K. M. (1971). Contingency model of leadership effectiveness: Some experimental results. *Journal of Applied Psychology, 55,* 196–201.

Graen, G., Orris, J., & Johnson, T. (1973). Role assimilation in a complex organization. *Journal of Vocational Behavior, 3,* 395–420.

Graen, G., & Scandura, T. A. (1986). Toward a psychology of dyadic organizing. In B. M. Staw & L. L. Cummings (eds.), *Research in organizational behavior,* vol. 9. Greenwich, CT: JAI Press.

Graen, G., & Schiemann, W. (1978). Leader-member agreement: A vertical dyad linkage approach. *Journal of Applied Psychology, 63,* 206–212.

Graen, G., & Uhl-Bien, M. (1991). The transformation of professionals into self-managing and partially self-designing contributors: Toward a theory of leadership-making. *Journal of Management Systems, 3,* 25–39.

Graen, G., & Uhl-Bien, M. (1995). Relationship-based approach to leadership: Development of leader-member exchange (LMX) theory over 25 years: Applying a multi-level multi-domain perspective. *Leadership Quarterly, 6,* 219–247.

Graen, G. B., & Wakabayashi, M. (1992). Adapting Japanese leadership techniques to their transplants in the United States. *Japanese Direct Investment in the United States.* JAI Press.

Graham, E. (1986). My lover, my colleague: As on the job romance flourishes firms finding adapting touchy but essential. *Wall Street Journal,* March 24, Section 4, 25–26.

Graham, F. C. (1982). Job stress in Mississippi cooperative extension service county personnel as related to age, gender, district, tenure, position and perceived leadership behavior of immediate supervisors. *Dissertation Abstracts International, 43*(7A), 21–80.

Graham, G. H. (1969). Theories X and Y in the teaching of management. *Collegiate News Views, 22,* 15–18.

Graham, J. W. (1987). The essence of leadership: Fostering follower autonomy, not automatic followership. In J. C. Hunt (ed.), *Emerging leadership vistas.* Elmsford, NY: Pergamon.

Graham, J. W. (1991). Servant-leadership in organizations: Inspirational and moral. *Leadership Quarterly, 2,* 105–119.

Graham, J. W. (1995). Leadership, moral development, and citizenship behavior. *Business Ethics Quarterly, 5,* 43– 54.

Graham, W. K. (1968). Description of leader behavior and evaluation of leaders as a function of LPC. *Personnel Psychology, 21,* 457–464.

Graham, W. K. (1969). Comparison of job attitude components across three organizational levels. *Personnel Psychology, 22,* 33–40.

Graham, W. K. (1970). Leader behavior, esteem for least preferred co-worker, and group performance. *Experimental Publications System,* *American Psychological Association,* No. 192A. Also: Graham, W. K. (1973). *Journal of Social Psychology, 90,* 59–66.

Graham, W. K., & Gleno, T. (1970). Perception of leader behavior and evaluation of leaders across organizational levels. *Experimental Publications System, American Psychological Association,* No. 144A.

Graicunas, V. A. (1937). Relationship in organization. In L. Gulick & L. Urwick (eds.), *Papers on the science of administration.* New York: Institute of Public Administration.

Granick, D. (1960). *The red executive.* Garden City, NY: Doubleday.

Granick, D. (1962). Business and class in Europe. In D. Granick (ed.), *The European executive.* New York: Doubleday.

Granovetter, M. S. (1973). The strength of weak ties. *American Journal of Sociology, 78,* 1360–1380.

Granovetter, M. S. (1982). The strength of weak ties: A network theory revisited. In P.V. Marsden & N. Lin (eds.), *Social structure and network analysis.* Beverly Hills, CA: Sage Publications.

Grant, D. L. (1964). Situational tests in the assessment of managers. Part II: Contributions to the assessment process. In *The Executive Study Conference: Management games in selection and development.* Princeton, NJ: Educational Testing Service.

Grant, J. (1988). Woman as managers: What they can offer organizations. *Organizational Dynamics,* Winter, 56–63.

Grant, K. P., Graham T. S., & Heberling, M. E. (2001). The project manager and project team involvement: Implications for project leadership. *Journal of Leadership Studies, 7,* 32–42.

Gratton, L. (1992). Selecting leaders: Practices and trends. In M. Syrett, & C. Hogg (eds.), *Frontiers of leadership: An essential reader.* London, Basil Blackwell.

Gratton, L., & Syrett, M. (1990). Heirs, apparent: Succession strategies for the 90's. *Personnel Management,* January, 34–38.

Graumann, C. E. (1986). Changing conceptions of leadership: An introduction. In C. F. Graumann & S. Moscovici (eds.), *Changing conceptions of leadership.* New York: Springer-Verlag.

Graves, D. (1973). The impact of culture upon marginal attitudes, beliefs and behavior in England and France. In D. Graves (ed.), *Management research: A cross cultural perspective.* San Francisco: Jossey-Bass.

Graves, L. M. (1983). Implicit leadership theory: A comparison to two-dimensional leadership theory. *Proceedings, Eastern Academy of Management,* Pittsburgh, PA, 93–95.

Graves, L. M. (1985). Effects of leader persistence and environmental complexity on leadership perceptions: Do implicit beliefs discourage adaption to complex environments? *Group & Organization Studies, 10,* 19–36.

Graves, L. M., & Powell, G. N. (1988). An investigation of sex discrimination in recruiters' evaluations of actual applicants. *Journal of Applied Psychology, 73,* 20–29.

Gray, J. (1992). *Men are from Mars, women are from Venus.* New York: HarperCollins.

Gray-Little, B., & Hafdahl, A. R. (2000). Factors influencing racial comparisons of self-esteem: A quantitative review. *Psychological Bulletin, 126,* 26–54.

Gray, S. T. (1994). 12 characteristics of the 21st century leader. *Leadership IS: Independent sector, 3*(1), 1.

Greco, S., Caggiano, C., & Ballon, M. (1999). "I was seduced by the new economy," *Inc.,* February, 34–57.

Green, G. H. (1948). Insight and group adjustment. *Journal of Abnormal and Social Psychology, 43,* 49–61.

Green, S. G., Anderson, S. E., & Shivers, S. L. (1996). Demographic and organizational influences on leader-member exchange and related work attitudes. *Organizational Behavior and Human Decision Processes, 66,* 203–214.

Green, S. G., & Liden, R. C. (1980). Contextual and attributional influences on control decisions, *Journal of Applied Psychology, 65,* 453–458.

Green, S. G., & Mitchell, T. R. (1979). Attributional processes of leaders in leader-member interactions. *Organizational Behavior and Human Performance, 23,* 429–458.

Green, S. G., & Nebeker, D. M. (1977). The effects of situational factors and leadership style on leader behavior. *Organizational Behavior and Human Performance, 19,* 368–377.

Green, S. G., Nebeker, D. M., & Boni, M. A. (1974). *Personality and situational effects in leader behavior* (Tech. Rep. No. 74–55). Seattle: University of Washington, Organizational Research.

Greenberg, J. (1978). Equity, motivation, and the effects of past rewards on allocation decisions. *Personality and Social Psychology Bulletin, 4,* 131–134.

Greenberg, J. (1988). Cultivating an image of justice: Looking fair on the job. *Academy of Management Executive, 2*(2),155–157.

Greenberg, J. (1990). Looking fair vs. being fair: managing impressions of organizational justice. In B. M. Staw & L. L. Cummings (eds.), *Research in organizational behavior,* vol. 12, 111–157. Greenwich, CT: JAI Press.

Greenberg, L., & Barling, J. (1999). Predicting employee aggression against coworkers, subordinates, and supervisors: The rules of person behaviors and perceived workplace factors. *Journal of Organizational Behavior, 20,* 897–913.

Greene, C. N. (1972). Relationships among role accuracy, compliance, performance, evaluation, and satisfaction within managerial dyads. *Academy of Management Journal, 15,* 205–215.

Greene, C. N. (1973). *A longitudinal analysis of relationships among leader behavior and subordinate performance and satisfaction.* Proceedings, Academy of Management, Boston, 438–439.

Greene, C. N. (1974). *The path-goal theory of leadership: A replication and an analysis of causality.* Proceedings, Academy of Management, Seattle, Washington.

Greene, C. N. (1975). The reciprocal nature of influence between leader and subordinate. *Journal of Applied Psychology, 60,* 187–193.

Greene, C. N. (1976a). A longitudinal investigation of performance–reinforcing behaviors and subordinate satisfaction and performance. *Proceedings,* Midwest Academy of Management, St. Louis, MO, 157–185.

Greene, C. N. (1976c). Disenchantment with leadership research: Some causes, recommendations, and alternative directions. In J. G. Hunt & L. L. Larson (eds.), *Leadership: The cutting edge.* Carbondale: Southern Illinois University Press.

Greene, C. N. (1979a). Questions of causation in the path-goal theory of leadership. *Academy of Management journal, 22,* 22–41.

Greene, C. N. (1979b). A longitudinal investigation of modifications to a situational model of leadership effectiveness. *Proceedings,* Academy of Management, Atlanta, GA.

Greene, C. N., & Podsakoff, R M. (1979). *Effects of withdrawal of a performance-contingent reward on supervisory influence and power.* Indiana University, Bloomington, IN, working paper. Also: (1981). *Academy of Management Journal, 24,* 527–542.

Greene, C. N., & Schriesheim, C. (1977). *Causal paths among dimensions of leadership, group drive, and cohesiveness: A longitudinal field investigation.* Paper, Academy of Management, Orlando, FL.

Greene, C. N., & Schriesheim, C. A. (1980). Leader-group interactions: A longitudinal field investigation. *Journal of Applied Psychology, 65,* 50–59.

Greenfield, M. (1990). Mandela's discipline: Confident of his political beliefs and goals, he forced us to deal with him on his own terms. *Newsweek,* July 9, 68.

Greenfield, T. B. (1968). Research on the behavior of educational leaders: Critique of a tradition. *Alberta Journal of Educational Research, 14,* 55–76.

Greenfield, T. B., & Andrews, J. H. M. (1961). Teacher leader behavior. *Alberta Journal of Educational Research, 7,* 92–102.

Greenglass, E. R. (1988). Type A behavior and coping strategies in female and male supervisors. *Applied Psychology: An International Review, 37,* 271–288.

Greenhalgh, L., McKersie, R. B., & Gilkey, R. W. (1986). Rebalancing the workforce at IBM: A case study of redeployment and revitalization. *Organizational Dynamics, 14*(4), 30–47.

Greenleaf, R. K. (1970, 1991). *The servant as leader.* Essay, Robert K. Greenleaf Center. Indianapolis, IN.

Greenleaf, R. K. (1977). *Servant leadership.* Essay, Robert K. Greenleaf Center, Indianapolis, IN.

Greenleaf, R. K. (1979). *Servant leadership: A journey into the nature of legitimate power and greatness.* New York: Paulist Press.

Greenly, R. S., & Mapel, E. B. (1943). The development of executive talent. *Personnel, 19,* 628–634.

Greenwald, A. G. (1980). The totalitarian ego: Fabrication and revision of personal history. *American Psychologist, 35,* 603–618.

Greenwald, A. G. (1985). *Totalitarian egos in the personalities of democratic leaders.* Paper, International Society of Political Psychology, Washington, DC.

Greenwood, J. M., & McNamara, W. J. (1967). Interrater reliability in situational tests. *Journal of Applied Psychology, 51,* 101–106.

Greenwood, J. M., & McNamara, W. J. (1969). Leadership styles of structure and consideration and managerial effectiveness. *Personnel Psychology, 22,* 141–152.

Greer, C. R., & Labig, C. E. (1987). Employee reactions to disciplinary action. *Human Relations, 40,* 507–524.

Greer, C. R. & Stephens, G. K. (2001). Escalation of commitment: A comparison of differences between Mexican and U.S. decisionmakers. *Journal of Management, 27,* 51–78.

Greer, F. L. (1953). Neighborhood leaders. In D. Courtney et al. (eds.), *Naval, neighborhood, and national leadership.* Philadelphia: Institute for Research in Human Relations.

Greer, F L. (1954, May). *Leadership identification and acceptance.* Status Report. Washington, DC: Institute for Research in Human Relations.

Greer, F. L. (1960). *Leader indulgence and group performance.* Washington, DC: General Electric Company.

Greer, F. L. (1961). Leader indulgence and group performance. *Psychological Monographs, 75,* No. 516.

Greer, F L., Galanter, E. H., & Nordlie, P. G. (1954). Interpersonal knowledge and individual and group effectiveness. *Journal of Abnormal and Social Psychology, 49*, 411–414.

Greer, M. (2003). When intuition misfires: Intuition helps us to understand the world—except when it's wrong. What are the causes and consequences of its faults? *Monitor on Psychology*, March, 58.

Gregersen, H. B., & Black, J. S. (1992). Antecedents to commitment to a parent company and a foreign operation. *Academy of Management Journal, 35*, 65–90.

Gregory, R. A. (1986). *Leadership education in institutions of higher education: An assessment*. Greensboro, NC: Center for Creative Leadership.

Gregory & Stone (1999). *Self-schema*. Paper, Society for Industrial and Organizational Psychology, New Orleans.

Greguras, G. J., & Robie, C. (2001). *Effects of rating purpose on the quality of multi-source ratings*. Symposium Paper, Society for Industrial and Organizational Psychology, San Diego, CA.

Greiner, L. E., Leitch, D. F., & Barnes, L. B. (1968). The simple com. plexity of organizational climate in a government agency. In R. Tagliuri & C. H. Litwin (eds.), *Organizational climate*. Boston: Harvard University, Graduate School of Business Administration.

Greller, M. M. (1978). The nature of subordinate participation in the appraisal interview. *Academy of Management Journal, 21*, 646–658.

Greller, M. M. (1980). Evaluation of feedback sources as a function of role and organizational development. *Journal of Applied Psychology, 65*, 24–27.

Greller, M. M., & Herold, D. M. (1975). Sources of feedback: A preliminary investigation. *Organizational Behavior and Human Performances, 13*, 244–256.

Grensing-Pophal, L. (1998). Walking the tightrope, balancing risks & gains. *HR Magazine, 43*(11), 112.

Grey, R. J., & Kipnis, D. (1976). Untangling the performance appraisal dilemma: The influence of perceived organizational context on evaluative processes. *Journal of Applied Psychology, 61*, 329–335.

Griffeth, R. W., & Bedeian, A. G. (1989). Employee performance evaluations: effects of rate age, rater age, and rate gender. *Journal of Organizational Behavior, 10*, 83–90

Griffin, M., Burley, I., & Neal, A. (2000). *The impact of supportive leadership and conscientiousness on safety behavior at work*. Academy of Management symposium, Canada.

Griffeth, R. W., Hom, F. W., DeNisi, A., & Kirchner, W. (1980). A multivariate multinational comparison of managerial attitudes. *Proceedings, Academy of Management*, Detroit, 63–67

Griffin, M. A., & Mathieu, J. E. (1997). Modeling organizational processes across hierarchical levels: Climate, leadership, and grouip process in wirk groups. *Journal of Organizational Behavior, 18*, 731–744.

Griffin, R. W. (1979). Task design determinants of effective leader behavior. *Academy of Management Review, 4*, 215–224.

Griffin, R. W. (1980). Relationships among individual, task design, and leader behavior variables. *Academy of Management Journal, 23*, 665–683.

Griffin, R. W., & Bedeian, A. G. (1989). Employee performance evaluations: Effects of ratee age, rater age, and ratee gender. *Journal of Organizational Behavior, 10*, 83–90.

Griggs, D. F. (1985). Police stress and management style. *Dissertation Abstracts International, 46*(4A), 1094.

Grigorenko, E. L., Gil, G., Jarvin, L., & Sternberg, R. J. (2000). *Toward a validation of aspects of the theory of successful intelligence*. Unpublished manuscript.

Grinnell, J. P. (2001). To be or not to be? The existential implications of organizational meaning systems. *Journal of Management Inquiry*.

Grinnell, J. P. (2002). Effects of leaders' and evaluators' sex on sex-role stereotyping on charismatic leaders. *Psychological Reports, 91*, 1247–1252.

Groh, D. (1986). The dilemma of unwanted leadership in social movements: The German example before 1914. In G. F. Graumann & S. Moscovici (eds.), *Changing conception of leadership*. New York: Springer-Verlag.

Gronlund, N. E. (1955a). Acquaintance span and sociometric status. *Sociometry, 18*, 62–68.

Gronlund, N. E. (1955b). Sociometric status and sociometric perception. *Sociometry, 18*, 122–128.

Gronn, P. (1995). *From transactions to transformations: A new world order in the study of leadership?* Lecture, Educational and Administration Society, Balliol College, Oxford University, Oxford, England.

Gronn, P. (1997). Leading for learning: Organizational transformation and the formation of leaders. *Journal of Management Development, 16*(4), 274.

Gronn. P. (1999). Substituting for leadership: The neglected role of the leadership couple. *Leadership Quarterly, 10*, 41–62.

Grosch, N, Salter, R. S. & Smith, W. G. (2000). *Leadership—and goal-oriented correlates of leadership self-schema*. Paper, Society for Industrial and Organizational Psychology, New Orleans.

Gross, E. (1961). Dimensions of leadership. *Personnel Journal, 40*, 213–218.

Gross, N., Martin, W. E., & Darley, J. G. (1953). Studies of group behavior: Leadership structures in small organized groups. *Journal of Abnormal and Social Psychology, 48*, 429–432.

Gross, N., Mason, W. S., & McEachern, A. W. (1958). *Explorations in role analysis*. New York: Wiley.

Gross, N., McEachern, A. W., & Mason, W. S. (1966). Role conflict and its resolution. In B. J. Biddle & E. J. Thomas (eds.), *Role theory: Concepts and research*. New York: Wiley.

Grossack, M. M. (1954) Some effects of cooperation and competition on small group behavior. *Journal of Abnormal and Social Psychology, 49*, 341–348.

Grossack, M. M. (1954a). Perceived Negro group belongings and social rejection. *Journal of Psychology, 38*, 127–130.

Grosser, D., Polansky, N., & Lippitt, R. (1951). A laboratory study of behavioral contagion. *Human Relations, 4*, 115–142.

Grossman, W., & Hoskinsson. (1998). CEO pay at the crossroads of Wall Street and Main: Toward the strategic design of executive compensation. *Academy of Management Executive, 12*(1), 43–56.

Grove, A. S. (1986). Tapping into the leader who lies within us. *Wall Street Journal*, April 7, 22.

Groves, K. (2003). *Gender differences in social and emotional skills in charismatic leadership*. Paper, Academy of Management, Seattle, WA.

Groves, K. S. (2005). Linking leader skills, followers attitudes, and contextual variable via an integrated model of charismatic leadership. *Journal of Management, 31*(2), 255–277.

Group for the Advancement of Psychiatry (1974). *Problems of Psychiatric Leadership* (GAP Report No. 90). Formulated by the Committee on Therapy.

Gruber, J. E. (1987). *Controlling bureaucracies: Dilemmas in democratic governance.* Berkeley, CA: University of California Press.

Gruenfeld, L. W. (1962). A study of the motivation of industrial supervisors. *Personnel Psychology, 15,* 303–314.

Gruenfeld, L. W. (1966). Effects of tuition payment and involvement on benefit from a management development program. *Journal of Applied Psychology, 50,* 396–399.

Gruenfeld, L. W., & Arbuthnot, J. (1968). Field independence, achievement values and the evaluation of a competency related dimension on the least preferred coworker (LPC) measure. *Perceptual and Motor Skills, 27,* 991–1002.

Gruenfeld, L. W., & Kassum, S. (1973). Supervisory style and organization effectiveness in a pediatric hospital. *Personnel Psychology, 26,* 531–544.

Gruenfeld, L. W., & MacEachron, A. E. (1975). A cross national study of cognitive style among managers and technicians. *International Journal of Psychology, 10*(1), 27–55.

Gruenfeld, L. W., Rance, D. E., & Weissenberg, F. (1969). The behavior of task oriented (low LPC) and socially oriented (high LPC) leaders under several conditions of social support. *Journal of Social Psychology, 79,* 99–107.

Gruner, C. R. (1965). An experimental study of satire as persuasion. *Speech Monographs, 32,* 149–153.

Gruner, C. R. (1997). *The game of humor: A comprehensive theory of why we laugh.* New Brunswick, NJ: Transaction Publications.

Grunwald, W., & Bernthal, W. F. (1983). Controversy in German management: The Harzburg model experience. *Academy of Management Review, 8,* 233–241.

Grusky, O. (1961). Corporate size, bureaucratization, and managerial succession. *American Journal of Sociology, 67,* 261–269.

Grusky, O. (1963). The effects of formal structure on managerial recruitment: a study of baseball organization. *Sociometry, 26*(3), 345–353.

Grusky,O. (1963a). Managerial succession and organizational effectiveness. *American Journal of Sociology, 69,* 21–31.

Grusky, O. (1969). Succession with an ally. *Administrative Science Quarterly, 14,* 155–170.

Guest, R. H. (1956). Of time and the foreman. *Personnel, 32,* 478–486.

Guest, R. H. (1962a). *Organizational change: The effect of successful leadership.* Homewood, IL: Irwin-Dorsey.

Guetzkow, H. (1951). *Groups, leadership, and men: Research in human relations.* Pittsburgh: Carnegie Press.

Guetzkow, H. (1954). *Organizational development and restrictions in communication.* Pittsburgh: Carnegie Institute of Technology.

Guetzkow, H. (1954). *Restrictions in communication.* Pittsburgh, PA: Carnegie Institute of Technology.

Guetzkow, H. (1960). Differentiation of roles in task-oriented groups. In D. Cartwright & A. Zander (eds.), *Group dynamics.* Evanston, IL: Row, Peterson.

Guetzkow, H. (1961). Organizational leadership in task-oriented groups.

In L. Petrullo & B. M. Bass (eds.), *Leadership and interpersonal behavior.* New York: Holt, Rinehart & Winston.

Guetzkow, H., & Cyr, J. (1954). An analysis of conflict in decision-making groups. *Human Relations, 7,* 367–382.

Guetzkow, H., & Dill, W. R. (1957). Factors in the organizational development of task–oriented groups. *Sociometry, 20,* 175–204.

Guetzkow, H., Forehand, C. A., & James, B. J. (1962). An evaluation of educational influence on administrative judgment. *Administrative Science Quarterly, 6,* 483–500.

Guetzkow, H., & Kriesberg, M. (1950). *Executive use of the administrative conference.* New York: American Management Association.

Guetzkow, H., & Simon, H. A. (1955). The impact of certain communication nets upon organization and performance in task oriented groups. *Management Science, 31,* 43–49.

Guilford, J. P. (1967). *The nature of human intelligence.* New York: McGraw-Hill.

Guilford, J. P. (1975). Factors and factors of personality. *Psychological Bulletin, 82,* 802–814.

Guilford, J. P., & Guilford, R. B. (1939). Personality factors D,R,T, and A. *Journal of Abnormal and Social Psychology, 34,* 21–36.

Guilford, J. S. (1952). Temperament traits of executives and supervisors measured by the Guilford Personality Inventories. *Journal of Applied Psychology, 36,* 228–233.

Gulley, K. M., Coombs, J. E., Parayitam, et al. (2003). *CEO compensation and the influence of comparable firms.* Paper, Academy of Management, Seattle, WA.

Gullahorn, J. T. (1952). Distance and friendship as factors in the gross interaction matrix. *Sociometry, 15,* 123–134.

Gulliksen, H. (1950). *Theory of mental tests.* New York: Wiley.

Gully, S. M., Beaubien, J. M., & Incalcaterra, K. A. (1998). *A meta-analytic investigation of the relationship between perceived collective capability and performance.* Paper, Society for Industrial and Organizational Psychology, New Orleans, LA.

Gulowsen, J. (1972). A measure of work group harmony. In L. E. Davis & J. C. Taylor (eds.), *Design of jobs.* Harmondsworth, U.K.: Penguin.

Gummer, B. (1988). Post-industrial management: Teams, self-management, and the new interdependence. *Administration in Social Work, 12*(3), 117–132.

Gump, J. R. (1975). Comparative analysis of black women's and white women's sex-role attitudes. *Journal of Consulting and Clinical Psychology, 43,* 858–863.

Gundlach, M. J., Douglas, S. C., & Martinko, M. J. (2003). The decision to blow the whistle: A social information processing framework. *Academy of Management Review, 28,* 107–123.

Gunn, E. (1992). Rating the boss: Companies see positive effects as workers critique managers. *Milwaukee Journal,* March 15, 1–2.

Gupta, A. K. (1988) Contingency perspectives on strategic leadership: Current knowledge and future research directions. In D.C. Hambrick (ed.), *The executive effect: Concepts and methods for studying top managers.* Greenwich, CT: JAI Press.

Gupta, A. K., & Govindarajan, V. (1984). Build, hold, harvest: Converting strategic intentions into reality. *The Journal of Business Strategy, 4*(3), 34–47.

Gupta, V., MacMillan, J. C., & Surie, G. (2002). *Entrepreneurial lead-*

ership: A cross-cultural construct. Paper, Academy of Management, Denver, CO.

Gurin, G., Veroff, J., & Feld, S. (1960). *Americans view their mental health: A nationwide interview study.* New York: Basic Books.

Gurman, E. B., & Long, K. (1992). Gender orientation and emergent leader behavior. *Sex Roles, 27*(7–8). 391–400.

Gurman, E. B., & Long, K. (1993). Emergent leadership and female sex role identity. *Journal of Psychology, 126*(3), 309–316.

Guskin, A. (1999). On being a pragmatic idealist: A social psychologist's reflections on his role as a university president. *The Psychologist-Manager Journal, 3,* 84–96.

Gustafson, D. P. (1968). The effect of commitment to the task on role differentiation in small unstructured groups. *Academy of Management Journal, 11,* 457–458.

Gustafson, D. P., & Harrell, T. W. (1970). A comparison of role differentiation in several situations. *Organizational Behavior and Human Performance, 5,* 299–312.

Gustafson, L. (1999). How to measure success. *Leader to Leader,* No. 12, Spring, 14–17.

Gutek, B. A. (1985). *Sex and the workplace: Impact of sexual behavior and harassment on women, men and organizations.* San Francisco: Jossey-Bass.

Gutek, B. A. (1988). Sex segregation and women at work: A selective review. *Applied Psychology: An International Review, 37*(2), 103–120.

Gutek, B. A., & Morasch, B. (1982). Sex ratios, sex role spillover and sexual harassment of women at work. *Journal of Social Issues, 38*(4), 55–74.

Gutek, B. A., & Stevens, D. A. (1979). Differential responses of males and females to work situations which evoke sex role stereotypes. *Journal of Vocational Behavior, 14,* 23–32.

Guttentag, M., & Secord, P. F. (1983). *Too many women? The sex ratio question.* Beverly Hills, CA: Sage.

Guyot, J. F. (1962). Government bureaucrats are different. *Public Administration Review, 22,* 195–202.

Guzzo, R., Yost, P., Campbell, R., et al. (1993). Potency in groups: Articulating a construct. *British Journal of Social Psychology, 32,* 87–106.

Gwertzman, B. (1983, March 17). Reagan reaffirms goal for Lebanon. *New York Times,* A9.

Haas, J. A., Porat, A. M., & Vaughan, J. A. (1969). Actual versus ideal time allocations reported by managers: A study of managerial behavior. *Personnel Psychology, 22,* 61–75.

Haass, R.N. (1995). Are presidents good managers? Strategies from the Oval Office to sharpen leadership skills. *USAIR Magazine,* March, 55, 57, 59.

Habbe, S. (1947). Job attitudes of life insurance agents. *Journal of Applied Psychology, 31,* 111–128.

Habbe, S. (1952). Does communication make a difference? *Management Record, 14,* 414–416, 442–444.

Haccoun, D. M., Haccoun, R. R., & Sallay, C. (1978). Sex differences in the appropriateness of supervisory styles: A nonmanagement view. *Journal of Applied Psychology, 63,* 124–127.

Hackett, R. D., Farh, J. L., & Song, L. J. (2003). *The LMX-OCB relationship revisited: A quantitative and qualitative review.* Paper, Academy of Management, Seattle, WA.

Hackman, J. R. (1990). *Teams that work (and some that don't).* Englewood Cliffs, NJ: Prentice-Hall.

Hackman, J. R., & Oldham, G. R. (1975). Development of the job diagnostic survey. *Journal of Applied Psychology, 60,* 159–170.

Hackman, J. R., & Walton, R. E. (1986). Leading groups in organizations. In P. S. Goodman (ed.), *Designing effective work groups.* San Francisco, CA: Jossey-Bass. 72–119.

Hackman, M. Z. & Johnson, C. E. (1991). *Leadership: A communication perspective.* Waveland Press.

Hackman, M. Z., Furness, A. H., Hills, M. J., et al. (1992). Perceptions of gender role characteristic and transformational and transactional leadership behaviours. *Perceptual and Motor Skills, 75,* 311–319.

Haeggberg, D., & Chen, P.Y. (2000). *Effects of subordinate ratings on subsequent supervisor ratings: Does anonymity matter?* Paper. Society for Industrial and Organizational Psychology, New Orleans, LA.

Hage, J. (1974). *Communication and organizational control: Cybernetics in health and welfare settings.* New York: Wiley.

Hagen, E. (1962). *On the theory of social change.* Homewood, IL: Dorsey Press.

Haggerty, H. R., Johnson, C. C., & King, S. H. (1954). Evaluation of ratings on combat performance of officers, obtained by mail. *American Psychologist, 9,* 388 (Abstract).

Hahn, C. P., & Trittipoe, T. G. (1961). *Situational problems for leadership training: III. Review for petty officers of leadership research.* Washington, DC: Naval Contract Report, Institute for Research.

Haiman, F. S. (1951). *Group leadership and democratic action.* Boston: Houghton Mifflin.

Hain, T. (1972). *Determinants of changes in supervisory styles: An empirical test.* Paper, Midwest Academy of Management, Notre Dame, IN.

Hain, T., & Tubbs, S. (1974). *Organizational development: The role of communication in diagnosis, change and evaluation.* Paper, International Communication Association.

Haire, M. (1948). Some problems of industrial training. *Journal of Social Issues, 4,* 41–47.

Haire, M., Ghiselli, E. E., & Porter, L. W. (1966). *Managerial thinking: An international study.* New York: Wiley.

Haislip, O. L., Jr. (1986). C4 = effective leadership. *Supervision, 48*(4), 14–16.

Hakel, M. D. (1976). Some questions and comments about applied learning. *Personnel Psychology, 29,* 361–369.

Hakel, M. D., Hollman, D., & Dunnette, M. D. (1968). Stability and change in the social status of occupations over 21 and 42 year periods. *Personnel and Guidance Journal, 46,* 762–764.

Halal, W. E. (1974). Toward a general theory of leadership. *Human Relations, 27,* 401–416.

Halberstam, D. (1983). *The best and the brightest.* New York: Penguin.

Halbesleben, J. R. B., Novecevic, M. M., Harvey, M. G., et al. (2003). Awareness of temporal complexity in leadership of creativity and innovation: A competency-based model. *Leadership Quarterly, 14,* 433–454.

Haleblian, J., & Finkelstein, S. (1993). Top management team size, CEO dominance, and firm performance: The moderating roles of environmental turbulence and discretion. *Academy of Management Journal, 36,* 844–863.

Hales, C. P. (1986). What do managers do? A critical review of the evidence. *Journal of Management Studies, 23,* 88–115.

Haley, M. J. (1983). Relationship between internal-external locus of control beliefs, self-monitoring and leadership style adaptability. *Dissertation Abstracts International, 44*(11B), 35–63.

Hall, A. T., Blass, F. R., & Ferris, G. R. (2003). *Leader reputation and accountability in organizations: Implications for leader behavior.* Paper, Academy of Management, Seattle, WA.

Hall, A. T., Blass, F. R, Ferris, G. R., et al. (2004). Leader reputation and accountability: Implications for dysfunctional leader behavior. *Leadership Quarterly, 15,* 515–536.

Hall, A. T., Hochwarter, & Ferris, G. R. (2003). *The interactive effects of accountability and job efficacy on organizational citizenship behavior and on political behavior.* Paper, Society for Industrial and Organizational Behavior, Orlando, FL.

Hall, B. A. (1975). *The effect of sex of the leader on the development of assertiveness in women undergoing group assertive training.* Doctoral dissertation, University of Missouri, Kansas City.

Hall, B. P. (2000). *Values development and learning organizations.* Paper presented at III International Conference on School Management, Bilbao, Spain, September 12–15.

Hall, D. T. (1972). A model of coping with role conflict: The role behavior of college educated women. *Administrative Science Quarterly, 17,* 471–486.

Hall, D. T. (1986). Dilemmas in linking succession planning to individual executive learning. *Human Resource Management, 25,* 235–265.

Hall, D. T., Bowen, D. D., Lewicki, R. J., & Hall, F. F. (1975). *Experiences in management and organizational behavior.* Chicago: St. Clair Press.

Hall, D. T., & Lawler, E. E. (1970). Job characteristics and pressures and the organizational integration of professionals. *Administrative Science Quarterly, 15,* 271–281.

Hall, D. T., & Lawler, E. E. (1971). Job pressures and research performance. *American Scientist, 59*(1), 64–73.

Hall, D. T., & Mansfield, R. (1971). Organizational and individual response to external stress. *Administrative Science Quarterly, 16,* 533–547.

Hall, D. T., & Mervis, P. T. (1995). The new career contract: Developing the whole person at midlife and beyond. *Journal of Vocational Behavior, 47,* 269–289.

Hall, D. T., Schneider, B., & Nygren, H. T. (1970). Personal factors in organizational identification. *Administrative Science Quarterly, 15,* 176–190.

Hall, E. T. (1976). *Beyond culture.* New York: Doubleday.

Hall, E. T. (1983). *The dance of life.* New York: Doubleday.

Hall, E. T., & Hall, M. R. (1987). *Hidden differences: Doing business with the Japanese.* New York: Doubleday.

Hall, F. S., & Hall, D. T. (1976). Effects of job incumbents' race and sex on evaluations of managerial performance. *Academy of Management Journal, 19,* 476–481.

Hall, H. E. (1953). *Empathy, leadership and art.* Master's thesis, Louisiana State University, Baton Rouge, LA.

Hall, J. (1976). To achieve or not: The manager's choice. *California Management Review, 18,* 5–18.

Hall, J. (1979). Student preference for leadership styles. *Assistant Librarian, 72*(6), 86–88.

Hall, J., & Donnell, S. M. (1979). Managerial achievement: The personal side of behavioral theory. *Human Relations, 32*(1), 77–101.

Hall, J. A., & Halberstadt, A. C. (1981). Sex roles and nonverbal communcation skills. *Sex Roles, 7,* 273–287.

Hall, L. K. (1983). *Charisma: A study of personality characteristics of charismatic leaders.* Doctoral dissertation, University of Georgia, Athens.

Hall-Merenda, K., & Howell, J. M. (undated). *Network organizations: A theoretical discussion of the provenance and a process model of their creation and operation.* Unpublished.

Hall, M. S. (1994). Core competencies for effective nonprofit managers. *Leadership IS,* 7–15.

Hall, R. J., & Lord, R. G. (1995). Multi-level information processing explanations of followers' leadership perceptions. *Leadership Quarterly, 6,* 265–287.

Hall, R. H. (1962). Intraorganizational structural variation: Application of bureaucratic model. *Administrative Science Quarterly, 7,* 295–308.

Hall, T. (1984). For a company chief, when there's a whim, there's often a way. Thus, a stop at a coffee shop leads to an acquisition; Greyhound's move West. When Wickes took up golf. *Wall Street Journal,* October 1, 1, 20.

Hallock, K. F. (2004). Managerial pay in nonprofit and for-profit organizations. In R. E. Riggio & S. S. Orr (eds.), *Improving leadership in nonprofit organizations.* San Francisco, CA: Jossey-Bass.

Hallowell, E. M. (1999). The human moment at work. *Harvard Business Review, 77,* January–February, 58.

Halmish, H. (2000). *The model of the Full Range of Leadership as related to individual variables among cadets.* Paper, Academy of Management, Dallas, TX.

Halperin, K., Synder, C. R., Shenkel, R. I., & Houston, B. K. (1976). Effect of source status and message favorability on acceptance of personality feedback. *Journal of Applied Psychology, 61,* 85–88.

Halpern, D., & Osofsky, S. (1990). A dissenting view of MBO. *Public Personnel Management,* Fall, 321–330.

Halpin, A. W. (1954). The leadership behavior and combat performance of airplane commanders. *Journal of Abnormal and Social Psychology, 49,* 19–22.

Halpin, A. W. (1955b). The leader behavior and leadership ideology of educational administrators and aircraft commanders. *Harvard Educational Review, 25,* 18–32.

Halpin, A. W. (1956a). *The leader behavior of school superintendents.* Columbus: Ohio State University, College of Education.

Halpin, A. W. (1957a). The leader behavior and effectiveness of aircraft commanders. In R. M. Stogdill & A. E. Coons (eds.), *Leader behavior: Its description and measurement.* Columbus: Ohio State University, Bureau of Business Research.

Halpin, A. W. (1957b). *Manual for the leader behavior description questionnaire.* Columbus: Ohio State University, Bureau of Business Research.

Halpin, A. W. (1957c). The observed leader behavior and ideal leader behavior of aircraft commanders and school superintendents. In R. M. Stogdill & A. E. Coons (eds.), *Leader behavior: Its description and measurement.* Columbus: Ohio State University, Bureau of Business Research.

Halpin, A. W., & Croft, D. B. (1962). *The organizational climate of schools.* St. Louis, MO: Washington University.

Halpin, A. W., & Winer, B. J. (1957). A factorial study of the leader behavior descriptions. In R. M. Stogdill & A. E. Coons (eds.), *Leader behavior: Its description and measurement.* Columbus: Ohio State University, Bureau of Business Research.

Halverson, S. K., Holladay, C. L., Kazama, S. M., et al. (2004). Self-sacrificial behavior in crisis situations: The competing roles of behavioral and situational factors. *Leadership Quarterly, 15,* 263–275.

Hambleton, R. K., & Gumpert, R. (1982). The validity of Hersey and Blanchard's theory of leader effectiveness. *Group & Organization Studies, 7,* 225–242.

Hamblin, R. L. (1958b). Leadership and crises. *Sociometry, 21,* 322–335.

Hamblin, R. L., Miller, K., & Wiggins, J. A. (1961). Group morale and competence of the leader. *Sociometry, 24,* 295–311.

Hambrick, D. C. (1981a). Environment, strategy, and power within top management teams. *Administrative Science Quarterly, 26,* 253–276.

Hambrick, D. C. (1981). Strategic awareness within top management teams. *Strategic Management Journal, 2,* 263–279.

Hambrick, D. C. (1989). Guest editor's introduction: Putting top managers back in the strategy picture. *Strategic Management Journal, 10,* 5–15.

Hambrick, D. C., & Abrahamson, E. (1995). Assessing managerial discretion across industries: A multimethod approach. *Academy of Management Journal, 38,* 1427–1441.

Hambrick, D. C., & Cannelli, A. A. (1993). Relative standing: A framework for understanding departures of acquired executives. *Academy of Management Journal, 36,* 733–762.

Hambrick, D. C., & Cannella, A. A., Jr. (2004). CEOs who have COOs: contingency analysis of an unexplored structural form. *Strategic Management Journal, 25,* 959–979.

Hambrick, D. C., & Finkelstein, S. (1987). Managerial discretion: A bridge between polar views of organizational outcomes. In L. L. Cummings & B. M. Staw (eds.), *Research in Organizational Behavior,* vol. 9. Greenwich, CT: JAI Press.

Hambrick, D. C., Finkelstein, S., & Mooney, A. C. (2005). Reply: Executives sometimes lose it, just like the rest of us. *Academy of Management Review, 30,* 503–508.

Hambrick, D. C., & Fukutomi, G. D. (1991). The seasons of a CEO's tenure. *Academy of Management Review, 16,* 719–742.

Hambrick, D. C., & Mason, P. (1984). Upper echelons: The organization as a reflection of top managers. *Academy of Management Review, 9,* 193–206.

Hamel, G. (2000) (with the assistance of Schonfeld). Waking up IBM: How a gang of unlikely rebels transformed big blue. *Harvard Business Review, 78*(4), 137–146.

Hamer, D. H. (1997). The search for personality genes: Adventures of a molecular biologist. *Current Directions in Psychological Science, 6,* 111–116.

Hamer, D. H., & Copeland, P. (1998). *Living with our genes.* New York: Doubleday.

Hamilton, B. A., & Scandura, T. (2003). E-mentoring: Implications for organizational learning and development in a wired world. *Organizational Dynamics, 31,* 388–402.

Hamm, S. (2003). Borders are so 20th century: High tech transactionals take "stateless" to the next level. *Business Week,* September 22, 68, 70, 72.

Hammer, M. (1997). The neural basis of associative reward learning in honeybees. *Trends in Neurosciences, 20*(6), 245–252.

Hammer, S. (1978). When women have power over women. *Ms. Magazine, 7*(3), 49.

Hammer, T. H., & Dachler, R. (1973). *The process of supervision in the context of motivation theory* (Tech. Rep. No. 3). College Park, MD: University of Maryland, Department of Psychology.

Hammer, T. H., & Turk, J. (1985). *Organizational determinants of leader behavior and authority.* Paper, Academy of Management, San Diego. Also: (1987). *Journal of Applied Psychology, 71,* 674–682.

Hammer, W. C., Kim, J. S., Baird, L., & Bigoness, W. J. (1974). Race and sex as determinants of ratings by potential employers in a simulated work-sampling task, *Journal of Applied Psychology, 59,* 705–711.

Hammerschlag, C. A., & Astrachan, B. M. (1971). The Kennedy airport snow-in: An inquiry into intergroup phenomena. *Psychosomatics, 34,* 301–308.

Hammonds, K. H. (2002) Michael Porter, big ideas. *Fast Company,* March, 150–154, 156.

Hampden-Turner, C., & Trompeneer, A. (1993). *The seven cultures of capitalism.* New York: Currency/Doubleday.

Hanaway, J. (1985). Managerial behavior, uncertainty and hierarchy. *Human Relations, 38,* 1085–1100.

Hand, H. H., & Slocum, J. W. (1970). Human relations training for middle management: A field experiment. *Academy of Management journal, 13,* 403–410.

Hand, H. H., & Slocum, J. W. (1972). A longitudinal study of the effects of a human relations training program on managerial effectiveness. *Journal of Applied Psychology, 56,* 412–417.

Handy, C. B. (1976). *Understanding organizations.* Baltimore: Penguin Books.

Handy, C. (1987). *The language of leadership.* Paper, 34th National Management Conference, Irish Management Institute.

Handy, C. (1994). *Age of paradox.* Cambridge, MA: Harvard Business School Press.

Handyside, J. D., & Duncan, D. C. (1954). Four years later: A follow-up of an experiment in selecting supervisors. *Occupational Psychology, 28,* 9–23.

Hanfmann, E. (1935). Social structure of a group of kindergarten children. *American Journal of Orthopsychiatry, 5,* 407–410.

Hanges, P. J., & Dickson, M. W. (2004). The development and validation of GLOBE leadership. In R. J. House, P. J. Hanges, & M. Javidan (eds.), *Culture, leadership, and organizations.* Thousand Oaks, CA: Sage.

Hanges, P. J., Dickson, M. W., & Lord, R. G. (2002). *Trends, developments, and gaps in cross-cultural research on leadership.* Paper, International Congress of Applied Psychology, Singapore.

Hanges, P. J., House, R. J., Dickson, M., et al. (1997). *Development and validation of scales measuring organizational culture, societal culture, and preferences for leaders behaviors and attributes.* College Park: University of Maryland.

Hanges, P. J., & Shteynburg, G. (2004). Methodological challenges and solutions for leadership researchers. *German Journal of Human Resource Research, 18,* 346–358.

Hanna, N. E. (1973). *Organizational variables and innovativeness in collegiate nursing institutions: A comparative study.* Doctoral dissertation, University of Michigan, Ann Arbor.

Hansen, J. C. (1988). Changing interests of women: Myth or reality? *Applied Psychology: An International Review, 37,* 133–150.

Hansen, P. (1974). *Sex differences in supervision.* Paper, American Psychological Association, New Orleans.

Hanson, P. G., Morton, R. B., & Rothaus, P. (1963). The fate of role stereotypes in two performance appraisal situations. *Personnel Psychology, 16,* 269–280.

Harari, O. (1997). Looking beyond the "vision thing." *Management Review, 86*(6), 26.

Harbron, J. D. (1965). The dilemma of an elite group: The industrialist in Latin America. *Inter-American Economic Affairs, 19,* 43–62.

Harding, L. W. (1949). Twenty-one varieties of educational leadership. *Educational Leadership, 6,* 299–302.

Hardingham, A. (1998). Moments of clarity. *People Management, 4,* 31.

Hardy, R. C. (1971). Effect of leadership style on the performance of small classroom groups: A test of the contingency model. *Journal of Personality and Social Psychology, 19,* 367–374.

Hardy, R. C. (1975). A test of poor leader-member relations cells of the contingency model on elementary school children. *Child Development, 45,* 958–964.

Hardy, R. C., & Bohren, J. F. (1975). The effect of experience on teacher effectiveness: A test of the contingency model. *Journal of Psychology, 89,* 159–163.

Hardy, R. C., Sack, S., & Harpine, K. (1973). An experimental test of the contingency model on small classroom groups. *Journal of Psychology, 85,* 3–16.

Harland, L., Harrison, W., Jones, J. R., & Reiter-Palmon, R. (2005). Leadership behaviors and subordinate resilience. *Journal of Leadership & Organizational Studies, 11*(2), 2.

Hare, A. P. (1952). A study of interaction and consensus in different sized groups. *American Sociological Review, 17,* 261–267.

Hare, A. P. (1953). Small group discussions with participatory and supervisory leadership. *Journal of Abnormal and Social Psychology, 48,* 273–275.

Hare, A. P. (1957). Situational differences in leader behavior. *Journal of Abnormal and Social Psychology, 55,* 132–135.

Hare, A. P, & Hare, R. T. (1948). Family friendship within the community. *Sociometry, 11,* 329–334

Hare, A. P., Hare, S. E., & Blumberg. (1998). Wishful thinking: Who has the least preferred coworker? *Small Group Research, 29,* 419–435.

Har-Evan, S. (1992). *Four models of leadership persuade you.* Paper, Seminar on Leadership. Tel Aviv: Open University.

Hargrove, E. C. (1987). *Jimmy Carter as President.* Paper, Conference on the Presidency, Princeton University, Princeton, NJ.

Hargrove, E. C. (1988). Two conceptions of institutional leadership. In B. Jones (ed.), *Political leadership from political science perspectives.* Lawrence: University of Kansas Press.

Hargrove, E. C., & Nelson, M. (1984). *Presidents, politics, and policy.* Baltimore: Johns Hopkins University Press.

Harlan, A. (1976). *Psychological coping patterns of male and female managers.* Paper, Academy of Management, Kansas City, MO.

Harman, D. (1984). Lessons learned about emergency preparedness. *Public Management, 66*(3), 5–8.

Harnquist, K. (1956). *Adjustment: Leadership and group relations in a military training situation.* Stockholm: Almquist & Wiksell.

Harper, J. P., Maurer, T. J., & Tross, S. A. (1998). *Differential leadership perceptions: The impact of the rater-ratee relationship.* Paper, Society for Industrial and Organizational Psychology, Dallas, TX.

Harper, S.C. (1992). The challenges facing CEOs: Past, present, and future. *Academy of Management Executive, 6*(3), 7.

Harragan, B. L. (1977). *Games mother never taught you: Corporate gamesmanship for women.* New York: Rawson Associates.

Harrell, A. M., & Stahl, M. J. (1981). A behavioral decision theory approach for measuring McClelland's trichotomy of needs. *Journal of Applied Psychology, 66,* 242–244.

Harrell, A. M., & Stahl, M. J. (1986). Additive information processing and the relationship between expectancy of success and motivational force. *The Academy of Management Journal, 29*(2), 424–433.

Harrell, M. S., Harrell, T. W., McIntyre, S. H., & Weinber, C. B. (1977). Predicting compensation among MBA graduates five and ten years after graduation. *Journal of Applied Psychology, 62*(5), 636–640.

Harrell, T W. (1966). *Personality differences between extreme performers during a fourth discussion session* (Tech. Rep. No. 12). Stanford, CA: Stanford University, Graduate School of Business.

Harrell, T. W., & Alpert, B. (1979). The need for autonomy among managers. *Academy of Management Review, 4,* 259–267.

Harrell, T. W., Burnham, L. E., & Lee, H. E. (1963). *Correlations between seven leadership criteria* (Tech. Rep. No. 4). Stanford, CA: Stanford University, Graduate School of Business.

Harrell, T. W., & Gustafson, D. P. (1966). *Division groups with a trend away from role differentiation* (Tech. Rep. No. 13). Stanford, CA: Stanford University, Graduate School of Business.

Harrell, T. W., & Harrell, M. S. (1975). *A scale for high earners* (ONR Tech. Rep. No. 7). Stanford, CA: Stanford University, Graduate School of Business.

Harrell, T. W., & Harrell, M. S. (1984). *Stanford MBA careers: A 20 year longitudinal study.* Stanford, CA: Stanford University, Graduate School of Business.

Harrell, T. W., & Lee, H. E. (1964). *An investigation of the product moment intercorrelations among small group leadership criteria* (Tech. Rep. No. 6). Stanford, CA: Stanford University, Graduate School of Business.

Harrigan, K. R. (1981). Numbers and positions of women elected to corporate boards. *Academy of Management Journal, 24,* 619–625.

Harris, E. F., & Fleishman, E. A. (1955). Human relations training and the stability of leadership patterns. *Journal of Applied Psychology, 39,* 20–25.

Harris, L. (1987). *Inside America.* New York: Vintage Press.

Harris , J. F. (2005). *The survivor: Bill Clinton in the White House.* New York: Random House.

Harris, K. W. (1968). *Change in role requirements of superintendents over the last quarter-century.* Doctoral dissertation, Ohio State University, Columbus.

Harris, M. A., Schiller, Z., Mitchell, R., et al. (1986). The dynamo: Jack Welch is often described in three words: tough, tough and tough.

He's determined to transform GE. So far, so good. *Business Week*, June 30, 60–67.

Harris, M. M., & Schaubroeck, J. (1988). A meta-analysis of self-supervisory, self-peer, and peer-supervisor ratings. *Personnel Psychology, 41*, 43–62.

Harris, P., & Lucas, K.W. (1991). *Executive leadership: Requisite skills and developmental processes for three- and four-star assignments.* US Army Research Institute for the Behavioral and Social Sciences, Alexandria, VA.

Harris, R. (1987). Excellence in command. *Conference on military leadership: Traditions and future trends.* U.S. Naval Academy, Annapolis, MD.

Harris, S. C., & Cole, M. S. (1999). *A stages of change perspective on motivation to learn in a leadership development context: An empirical investigation.* Paper, Academy of Management, Chicago, IL.

Harrison, I. M. (1985). Communication and participative decision making: An exploratory study. *Personnel Psychology, 38*, 93–116.

Harrison, R. (1962). The impact of the laboratory on perceptions of others by the experimental group. In C. Argyris (ed.), *Interpersonal competence and organizational effectiveness.* Homewood, IL: Dorsey.

Harrison, R. (1966). Cognitive change and participation in a sensitivity training laboratory. *Journal of Consulting Psychology, 30*, 517–520.

Harrison, R., & Lubin, B. (1965b). Personal style, group composition, and learning. Part II. *Journal of Applied Behavioral Science, 1*, 294–301.

Harsanyi, J. C. (1962a). Measurement of social power, opportunity costs, and the theory of two-person bargaining games. *Behavioral Science, 7*, 67–80.

Harsanyi, J. C. (1962b). Measurement of social power in n-person reciprocal power situations. *Behavioral Science, 7*, 81–91.

Hart, L. B. (1975). Training women to become effective leaders: A case study. *Dissertation Abstracts International, 35*, 69–77.

Hart, P., & Mellons, J. (1970). Management youth and company growth: A correlation? *Management Decision, 4*, 50–53.

Hart, P., & Saunders, C. (1996). *Computer nets demand more, not less interaction.* CIMS Technology Management Report, Center for Innovation in Management Studies, Lehigh University, Bethlehem, PA.

Hart, P. M., Schembri, C., Bell, C. A., et al. (2003). *Leadership, climate, work attitudes and commitment: Is Generation X really that different?* Paper, Academy of Management, Seattle, WA.

Hart, R. K., & McLeod, P. L. (2003a). *Personal relationships in geographically dispersed work teams: Leading through everyday communications.* Paper, Academy of Management, Seattle, WA.

Hart, R. K., & McLeod, P. L. (2003). Rethinking team building in geographically dispersed teams: One message at a time. *Organizational Dynamics, 31*, 352–361.

Hart, S. L., & Quinn. (1993). Roles executives play: CEOs, behavioral complexity, and firm performance. *Human Relations, 46*, 543–574.

Hartmann, R. (1980). *Palace politics: An inside account of the Ford years.* New York: McGraw-Hill.

Harvey, M. G. (1996). Developing leaders rather than managers for the global market place. *Human Resource Management Review, 6*, 279–304.

Harvey, O. J. (1953). An experimental approach to the study of status relations in informal groups. *American Sociological Review, 18*, 357–367.

Harvey, O. J. (1960). Reciprocal influence of the group and three types of leaders in an unstructured situation. *Sociometry, 23*, 57–68.

Harvey, O. J., & Beverly, C. D. (1961). Some personality correlates of concept change through role playing. *Journal of Abnormal and Social Psychology, 63*, 125–130.

Harvey, O. J., & Consalvi, C. (1960). Status and conformity to pressure in informal groups. *Journal of Abnormal and Social Psychology, 60*, 182–187.

Harvey, S., Kelloway, E. K., & Duncan-Leiper, L. (2003). Trust in management as a buffer of the relationships between overload and strain. *Journal of Occupational Health Psychology, 8*, 306–315.

Harvey, S. S., Royal, M., & Stout, D. (2003). *Instructor's transformational leadership: University student attitudes and ratings.*

Harville, D. L. (undated). *A model of communication apprehension, job level, communication requirements of the job, job satisfaction, and career change activities.* Air Force Human Resources Laboratory, Training Systems Division, Brooks AFB, San Antonio, TX.

Harville, D. L. (1969). Early identification of potential leaders. *Journal of College Student Personnel, 10*, 333–335.

Harwood, J., & Brooks, G. (1993) Ms. President: Other nations elect women to lead them, so why doesn't the U.S.? *Wall Street Journal*, December 14, A1,A9.

Harzing, A. W. K., & Hofstede. (1999). *Managing the multinational: An international study of control mechanisms.* Cheltenham, England: Edward Elgar.

Hassett, J., & Dukes, S. (1986). The new employee trainer: A floppy disk. *Psychology Today, 20*(9), 30–32.

Hastings, E. W. (1926). Is pupil training for leadership a worthwhile feature? *American Physical Education Review, 31*, 1080–1085.

Hastings, R. E. (1964). Leadership in university research teams. *Dissertation Abstracts, 24*, 23–27.

Hastorf, A. H. (1965). The reinforcement of individual actions in a group situation. In L. Krasner & L. R Ullmann (eds.), *Research in behavior modification.* New York: Holt, Rinehart & Winston.

Hatch, M. J. (1987). Physical barriers, task characteristics, and interaction activity in research and development firms. *Administrative Science Quarterly, 32*, 387–399.

Hatch, M. J. (1993). The dynamics of organizational culture. *Academy of Management Review, 18*, 657–693.

Hatch, R. S. (1962). *An evaluation of a forced-choice differential accuracy approach to the measurement of supervisory empathy.* Englewood Cliffs, NJ: Prentice-Hall.

Hater, J. J., & Bass, B. M. (1988). Supervisors' evaluations and subordinates' perceptions of transformational and transactional leadership. *Journal of Applied Psychology, 73*, 695–702.

Hatfield, E., Cacioppo, J. T., & Rapson, R. L. (1993). Emotional contagion. *Current Directions in Psychological Science, 2* (3), 96–98.

Hathaway, B. (1984). Question value of IQ tests. *ARA Monitor*, September, 10.

Hauser, W. L. (1984). Careerism vs. professionalism in the military. *Armed Forces and Society, 10*, 449–463.

Hausser, D., Blaiwes, A. S., Weller, D., & Spencer, G. (1974). *Appli-*

cations of computer-assisted instruction to interpersonal skill training (Tech. Rep. 74-C-0100–1). Orlando, FL: NAVTRAEQUIPCEN.

Haveman, H. A. (1993). Ghosts of managers past: Managerial succession and organizational mortality. *Academy of Management Journal*, 36, 864–881.

Havighurst, R. J., & Taba, H. (1949). *Adolescent character and personality*. New York: Wiley.

Havron, M. D., & McGrath, J. E. (1961). The contribution of the leader to the effectiveness of small military groups. In L. Petrullo & B. M. Bass (eds.), *Leadership and interpersonal behavior*. New York: Holt, Rinehart & Winston.

Hawkins, C. H. (1962). A study of factors mediating a relationship between leader rating behavior and group productivity. *Dissertation Abstracts*, 23, 733.

Hay, R., & Gray, E. (1974). Social responsibilities of business managers. *Academy of Management Journal*, 17, 135–143.

Hayashida, C. T. (1976). The isolation of leadership: A case study of precarious religious organization. *Review of Religious Research*, 17, 141–152.

Hayes, R. H. (1981). Why Japanese factories work. *Harvard Business Review*, 5(4), 56–66.

Hayes, R. H., & Abernathy, W. J. (1980). Managing our way to economic decline. *Harvard Business Review*, 58, 67–77.

Haynes, F. D. (1972). *A comparison of perceived organizational characteristics between selected work stoppage and non–work stoppage school districts in the state of Michigan*. Doctoral dissertation, Western Michigan University, Kalamazoo.

Haythorn, W. W. (1952). *The influence of individual group members on the behavior of coworkers and on the characteristics of groups*. Doctoral dissertation, University of Rochester, Rochester, NY.

Haythorn, W. W. (1954a). *Relationships between sociometric measures and performance in medium bomber crews in combat* (AFPTRC-TR-54-101). San Antonio, TX: Lackland Air Force Base Crew Research Laboratory, AF Personnel & Training Reserve Center.

Haythorn, W. W., Couch, A., Haeffier, D., Langham, P., & Carter, L. F. (1956a). The behavior of authoritarian and equalitarian personalities in groups. *Human Relations*, 9, 57–74.

Haythorn, W. W., Couch, A., Haefner, D., Langham, R., & Carter, L. F (1956b). The effects of varying combinations of authoritarian and equalitarian leaders and followers. *Journal of Abnormal and Social Psychology*, 53, 210–219.

Hayward, M., & Hambrick, D. C. (1997). Explaining the premiums paid for large acquisitions: Evidence of CEO "hubris." *Administrative Science Quarterly*, 42, 103–127.

Hays, S., & Thomas, W. N. (1967). *Taking command*. Harrisburg, PA: Stackpole.

Hazan, C. & Shaver, P. (1987). Romantic love conceptualized as an attachment process. *Journal Personality and Social Psychology*, 52(3), 511–524.

Healy, A. K. (1962). Effects of changing social structure through child leaders. *Dissertation Abstracts*, 23, 22–33.

Healy, J. H. (1956). *Executive coordination and control*. Columbus: Ohio State University, Bureau of Business Research Monograph.

Healy, M. C., & Rose, D. S. (2003). *Validation of a 360-degree feedback instrument against retail sales performance: Content matters*.

Poster, Society for Industrial and Organizational Psychology, Orlando, FL.

Heath, M. R., & Bekker, S. J. (1986). *Identification of opinion leaders in public affairs educational matters and family planning in the township of Atteridgeville* (Research Finding Comm. N-142). Pretoria, South Africa: Human Sciences Research Council.

Hechanova, R., Beehr, T. A., & Christiansen, N. D. (2003). Antecedents and consequences of employees' adjustment to overseas assignment: a meta-analytic review. *Applied Psychology: An International Review*, 52(2), April 2003, 213–236.

Heclo, H. (1974). *Modern social politics in Britain and Sweden*. New Haven, CT: Yale University Press.

Hedberg, B. (1981). How organizations learn and unlearn. In P. C. Nystrom & W. H. Starbuck (eds.), *Handbook of organizational design*, vol. 1. London: Oxford University Press.

Hedberg, B., Nystrom, R. C., & Starbuck, W. H. (1976). Camping on seesaws: Prescriptions for a self-designing organization. *Administrative Science Quarterly*, 21, 41–65.

Hedges, L.V., & Olkin, I. (1985). *Statistical methods for meta-analysis*. Orlando, FL: Academic Press.

Hedlund, J., Forsythe, G. B., Horvath, J. A., Williams, W. M., Snook, S., Dennis, M., & Sternberg, R. J. (1999). *Identifying and assessing tacit knowledge: A method for understanding leadership*. Unpublished manuscript.

Hegarty, W. (1974) Using subordinate ratings to elicit behavioral changes in supervisors. *Journal of Applied Psychology*, 59, 764–766.

Hegarty, W. H., & Sims, H. P. (1978). Some determinants of unethical decision behavior: An experiment. *Journal of Applied Psychology*, 63, 451–457.

Hegel, C. F. (1830/1971). Philosophy of mind. (Tr. W. Wallace.). In *Encyclopedia of the philosophical sciences*. Oxford, U.K.: Clarendon Press.

Heifitz, R. (1994). *Leadership without easy answers*. Cambridge, MA: Harvard University Press.

Heifitz, R. (1998). *Leadership without easy answers*. Cambridge, MA: Belknap Press.

Heifetz, R. L., & Sinder, R. M. (1987). Political leadership: Managing the public's problem solving. In R. B. Reich (ed.), *The power of public ideas*. New York: Ballinger.

Heilman, M. E., & Alcott, V. B. (2001). What I think you think of me: Women's reactions to being viewed as beneficiaries of preferential selection. *Journal of Applied Psychology*, 86, 574–582.

Heilman, M. E., Block, C. J., Simon, M. C., et al. (1989). Has anything changed? Current characteristics of men, women, and managers. *Journal of Applied Psychology*, 74, 935–942.

Heilman, M. E., Block, C. J., & Strathatos, P. (1997). The affirmative action stigma of incompetence: Effects of performance information ambiguity. *Academy of Management Journal*, 40, 603–625.

Heilman, M. E., Cage, J. H., Hornstein, H. A., & Herschlag, J. K. (1984). Reactions to prescribed leader behavior as a function of role perspective: The case of the Vroom-Yetton model. *Journal of Applied Psychology*, 69, 50–60.

Heilman, M. E., & Guzzo, R. A. (1978). The perceived cause of work success as a mediator of sex discrimination in organizations. *Organizational Behavior and Human Performance*, 21, 346–357.

Heilman, M. E., Hornstein, H. A., Cage, J. H., & Herschlag, J. K.

(1984). Reactions to prescribed leader behavior as a function of role perspective: The case of the Vroom-Yetton model. *Journal of Applied Psychology, 69,* 50–60.

Heilman, M. E., & Saruwatari, L. R. (1979). When beauty is beastly: The effects of appearances and sex on evaluations of job applicants for managerial and nonmanagerial jobs. *Organizational Behavior and Human Performance, 23*(3), 360–372.

Heinen, H. A., McGlauchin, D., Legeros, C, and Freeman, H. Developing the woman manager. *Personnel Journal, 54,* 282–28.

Heinen, J. S., & Jacobsen, E. (1976). A model of task group development in complex organizations and a strategy of implementation. *Academy of Management Review, 1,* 98–111.

Heinen, J. S., McGlauchin, D., Legeros, C., & Freeman, J. (1975). Developing the woman manager. *Personnel Journal, 54,* 282–286.

Heinicke, C., & Bales, R. F. (1953). Developmental trends in the structure of small groups. *Sociometry, 16,* 7–38.

Heise, G. A., & Miller, G. A. (1951). Problem-solving by small groups using various communication nets. *Journal of Abnormal and Social Psychology, 46,* 327–335.

Heizer, J. H. (1969). A study of significant aspects of manager behavior. *Academy of Management Journal, 3,* 386–387.

Helfrich, M. L., & Schwirian, K. P. (1968). The American businessman—entrepreneur or bureaucrat? *Bulletin of Business Research, 1,* 6–9.

Helgeson, S. (1995). Leading from the grass roots. In F. Hesselbein, M. Goldsmith, & R. Beckhard (eds.), *The leader of the future.* San Francisco: Jossey-Bass.

Helland, K., Barksdale, C. D., & Peat, J. A. (2005). *Examining the female leadership advantage across multiple rating sources.* Paper, Society for Industrial and Organizational Psychology, Los Angeles, CA.

Helland, K., & Blair C. A. (2005). *Leaders behaving badly: The relationship between narcissism and unethical leadership.* Paper, Society for Industrial and Organizational Psychology, Los Angeles, CA.

Hellebrandt, E. T., & Stinson, J. E. (1971). The effects of T-group training on business game results. *Journal of Applied Psychology, 77,* 271–272.

Heller, F. A. (1969a). *Managerial decision making.* London: Human Resources Center, Tavistock Institute of Human Relations.

Heller, F. A. (1969b). The role of business management in relation to economic development. *International Journal of Comparative Sociology, 10,* 292–298.

Heller, F. A. (1972a). *Managerial decision making: A study of leadership styles and power sharing among senior managers.* New York: Harper & Row.

Heller, F. A. (1976). The decision process: An analysis of power-sharing at senior organizational levels. In R. Dubin (ed.), *Handbook of work, organization, and society.* Chicago: Rand McNally.

Heller, F. A. (1994). Leadership. In *International encyclopedia of business management.* London: Routledge.

Heller, F. A., Drenth, P., Koopman, P., et al. (1988). *Decisions in organizations.* London: Sage.

Heller, F. A., & Wilpert, B. (1981). *Competence and power in management decision-making: A study of senior levels of organization in eight countries.* London: Wiley.

Heller, F. A., & Yukl, C. (1969). Participation, managerial decision-making, and situational variables. *Organizational Behavior and Human Performance, 4,* 227–241.

Heller, T. (1982). *Women and men as leaders.* New York: Praeger.

Heller, T. (1985). Changing authority patterns: A cultural perspective. *The Academy of Management Review, 10*(3), 488.

Heller, T., & Stein, F. T. (1978). Explaining the relationship of leadership status to high verbal participation. *Personality and Social Psychology Bulletin, 4,* 356.

Heller, T., & Van Til, J. (1982). Leadership and followership: Some summary propositions. *Journal of Applied Behavioral Science, 18,* 405–414.

Helmich, D. L. (1974a). Predecessor turnover and successor characteristics. *Cornell Journal of Social Relations, 9,* 249–260.

Helmich, D. L. (1974b). Organizational growth and succession patterns. *Academy of Management Journal, 17,* 771–775.

Helmich, D. L. (1976). Succession: A longitudinal look. *Journal of Business Research, 4,* 335–364.

Helmich, D. L. (1978). Leader flows and organizational process. *Academy of Management Journal, 21,* 463–478.

Helmich, D. L., & Brown, W. (1972). Successor type and organizational change in the corporate enterprise. *Administrative Science Quarterly, 17,* 371–381.

Helmich, D. L., & Erzen, F. E. (1975). Leadership style and leader needs. *Academy of Management Journal, 18,* 397–402.

Helmreich, R. L., & Collins, B. E. (1967). Situational determinants of affiliative preference under stress. *Journal of Personality and Social Psychology, 6,* 79–85.

Helmreich, R. L., & Merritt, A. C. (1998) *Culture at work in aviation and medicine: National, organizational, and professional influences.* Aldershot, U.K.: Ashgate.

Hemming, E. C. (1935). A factor analysis of the personality of high school teachers. *Journal of Applied Psychology, 19,* 596–605

Hemphill, J. K. (1949a). The leader and his group. *Journal of Educational Research, 28,* 225–229, 245–246.

Hemphill, J. K. (1949b). *Situational factors in leadership.* Columbus: Ohio State University, Bureau of Educational Research.

Hemphill, J. K. (1950a). *Leader behavior description.* Columbus: Ohio State University, Personnel Research Board.

Hemphill, J. K. (1950b). Relations between the size of the group and the behavior of "superior" leaders. *Journal of Social Psychology, 32,* 11–22.

Hemphill, J. K. (1952). *Leadership in small groups* (Tech. Rep.). Columbus: Ohio State Leadership Studies.

Hemphill, J. K. (1954). A *proposed theory of leadership in small groups* (Tech. Rep.). Columbus: Ohio State University, Personnel Research Board.

Hemphill, J. K. (1955). Leadership behavior associated with the administrative reputations of college departments. *Journal of Educational Psychology, 46,* 385–401.

Hemphill, J. K. (1959). Job descriptions for executives. *Harvard Business Review, 37*(5), 55–67.

Hemphill, J. K. (1960). *Dimensions of executive positions.* Columbus: Ohio State University, Bureau of Business Research.

Hemphill, J. K., & Coons, A. E. (1957). Development of the leader behavior description questionnaire. In R. M. Stogdill & A. E. Coons (eds.), *Leader behavior: Its description and measurement.* Columbus: Ohio State University, Bureau of Business Research.

Hemphill, J. K., & Pepinsky, P. N. (1955). *Leadership acts.* Columbus: Ohio State University, Personnel Research Board.

Hemphill, J. K., Pepinsky, P. N., Kaufman, A. E., & Lipetz, M. E. (1956). *Leadership acts: III. The effects upon attempts to lead of task motivation and the expectancy of accomplishment of the task.* Ohio: The Ohio State University Research Foundation, 1955.

Hemphill, J. K., Pepinsky, P. N., Shevitz, R. N., et al. (1954). *Leadership acts. I. An investigation of the relation between possession of task relevant information and attempts to lead.* Columbus: Ohio State University, Personnel Research Board.

Hemphill, J. K., Pepinsky, P. N., Shevitz, R. N., et al. (1956). The relation between possession of task relevant information and attempts to lead. *Psychological Monographs, 70*(7), 414.

Hemphill, J. K., Seigel, A., & Westie, C. W. (1951). *An exploratory study of relations between perceptions of leader behavior, group characteristics, and expectations concerning the behavior of ideal leaders.* Columbus: Ohio State University, Personnel Research Board.

Hemphill, J. K., & Westie, C. M. (1950). The measurement of group dimensions. *Journal of Psychology, 29*, 325–342.

Henderson, D. B. (1977). Identification and analysis of the relationship between self-actualization and leadership style in selected graduate students in educational administration. *Dissertation Abstracts International, 37*, 4894.

Henderson, E. (1986). Blacks in corporate America: Is there a future? *Personnel Journal, 65*(1), 12–14.

Henderson, J. C., & Nutt, P. C. (1980). The influence of decision style on decision-making behavior. *Management Science, 26*, 371–386.

Henderson, J. E., & Brookhart, S. M. (1996). Leader authenticity: Key to organizational climate, health and perceived leader effectiveness. *Journal of Leadership Studies, 3*(4), 87–103.

Henderson, J. E., & Hoy, W. K. (1982). Leader authenticity: The development and test of an operational measure. *Educational and Psychological Research, 3*, 63–75.

Henderson, J. E. and Hoy, W. K. (1982). *Leader authenticity: the development and test of an operational measure.* Paper presented at the 66th Annual Meeting of the American Educational Research Association, New York, March 19–23, 1982.

Hendrick, C., & Brown, S. R. (1971). Introversion, extraversion, and interpersonal attraction. *Journal of Personality and Social Psychology, 20*, 31–35.

Hendrickson, P., & Torrance, E. P. (1960) *School discipline and the creative personality.* Bureau of Educational Research, University of Minnesota

Hendrix, W. H., & McNichols, C. W. (1982). Organizational effectiveness as a function of managerial style, situational environment, and effectiveness criterion. *Journal of Experimental Education, 52*, 145–151.

Hendry, L. (1974). Coaches and teacher of physical education: A comparison of the personality dimensions underlying their social orientation. *International Journal of Sport Psychology, 5*(1), 40–53.

Hendry, L. B. (1974). Human factors in sports systems: Suggested models for analyzing athlete-coach interaction. *Human Factors, 16*(5), 528–44.

Heneman, H. G., III. (1973). Impact of performance on managerial pay levels and pay changes. *Journal of Applied Psychology, 58*, 128–130.

Heneman, R. L., Greenberger, D. R., & Anonyuo, C. (1989). Attributions and exchanges: The effects of interpersonal factors on the diagnosis of employee performance. *Academy of Management Journal, 32*, 466–476.

Henley, N. M. (1973). The politics of touch. In P. Brown (ed.), *Radical psychology.* New York: Harper & Row.

Henley, N. M. (1973a). Status and sex: Power, sex and nonverbal communication. *Bulletin of the Psychonomic Society.*

Henley, N. M. (1973b). Status & sex: Some touching observations. *Bulletin of the Psychonomic Society, 2*, 91–93.

Hennig, M., & Jardin, A. (1977). *The Managerial Woman.* Garden City, NY: Anchor Press/Doubleday.

Hennigar, J., & Taylor, R. G. (1980). A study of the correlation between general administrative style and openness to change. *Journal of Instructional Psychology, 7*(1), 6–12.

Henry, D. (1998). GE's Welch sees opportunity in Asia crisis: CEO's letter spells out how to be an "A" player. *USA Today*, February 2, 7A, 8B.

Henry, W. E. (1949). The business executive: The psycho-dynamics of a social role. *American Journal of Sociology, 54*, 286–291.

Henson, R. (1996). *Applying I/O practices globally at Avon.* Invited address, Society for Industrial and Organizational Psychology, San Diego, CA.

Hepperlin, T. M., & Reiter-Palmon, R. (2000). *The evolution of LMX relationships: Development of a temporal scale.* Paper, Society for Industrial and Organizational Psychology, New Orleans, LA.

Hepperlin, T. M., & Reiter-Palmon, R. (2001) *The influence of the temporal nature of relationship development on LMX, OCBs, and performance.* Paper, Society for Organizational and Industrial Psychology, San Diego, CA.

Herbert, T. T. (1972). *Philosophy and design of graduate business programs: Evaluative feedback and implications.* Paper, Midwest Academy of Management, Notre Dame, IN.

Herbert T. T. (1977). The MBA and job performance: Evidence from appraisals. *Akron Business and Economic Review, 8*, 35–40.

Herbert, T. T., & Deresky, H. (1987). General managers should match their missions. *Organizational Dynamics, 15*(3), 40–51.

Herman, A. (2001). *How the Scots invented the modern world: The true story of how Western Europe's poorest nation created our world & everything in it.* New York: Three Rivers Press.

Herman, S. M. (1994). *A force of ones: Reclaiming individual power in a time of teams, work groups, and other crowds in a time of teams, work groups and other crowds.* San Francisco: Jossey-Bass.

Hermann, C. P. (1963). Some consequences of crisis which limit the viability of organizations. *Administrative Science Quarterly, 8*, 61–82.

Hermann, M. (1980). Explaining foreign policy behavior using the personal characteristics of political leaders. *International Studies Quarterly, 24*, 7–46.

Hermann, M. G. (1986). Ingredients of leadership. In M. G. Hermann (ed.), *Political psychology:* San Francisco: Jossey-Bass.

Hermann, M. G. (1993). *Leaders and foreign policy decision making. Essays in honor of Alexander George.* Boulder, CO: Westview Press.

Hernandez, S. R., & Kaluzny, A. D. (1982). Selected determinants of performance within a set of health service organizations. *Proceedings, Academy of Management*, New York, 52–56.

Herod, J. (1969). Characteristics of leadership in an international fraternity for women and influence on the leaders' attitudes of a group centered leader training experience. *Dissertation Abstracts, 29*, 3461–3462.

Herold, D. M. (1974). *Mutual influence processes in leader-follower relationships*. Doctoral dissertation, Yale University, New Haven, CT.

Herold, D. M. (1977). Two-way influence processes in leader-follower dyads. *Academy of Management Journal, 20*, 224–237.

Herold, D. M., Fields, D. L., & Hyatt, C. W. (2003). *Using leadership instruments in a management development context: What are we measuring?* Paper, Academy of Management, Atlanta, GA.

Herold, D. M., & Greller, M. M. (1977). Feedback. The definition of a construct. *Academy of Management journal, 20*, 142–147.

Heron, A. R. (1942). *Sharing information with employees*. Stanford, CAN: Stanford University Press.

Herrenkohl, R. C., Judson, G. T., Heffner, J. A., et al. (1999). Defining and measuring employee empowerment. *Journal of Applied Behavioral Science, 35*, 373–389.

Herrick, J. S. (1973). Work motives of female executives. *Public Personnel Management, 2*, 380–388.

Herriot, P., & Anderson, N. (1997). Selecting for change: How will personnel and selection psychology survive? In N. Anderson & P. Herriot (eds.), *International handbook of selection and assessment*. Chichester, U.K.: Wiley.

Herriot, P., & Rothwell, C. (1983). Expectations and impressions in the graduate selection interview. *Journal of Occupational Psychology, 56*, 303–314.

Herriot, R., Chalmers, C., & Wingrove, J. (1985). Group decision-making in an assessment centre. *Journal of Occupational Psychology, 58*, 309–312.

Herrity, A. C. (2003). *Power and institutionalized rules of CEO succession at U.S. industrial corporations, 1975–1994*. Paper, Academy of Management, Seattle, WA.

Hersey, J. (1975). *The president*. New York: A. A. Knopf.

Hersey, P., Angelini, A. L., & Carakushansky, S. (1982). The impact of situational leadership and classroom structure on learning effectiveness. *Group & Organization Studies, 7*, 216–224.

Hersey, P., & Blanchard, K. H. (1969a). Life cycle theory of leadership. *Training & Development Journal, 23*, 26–34.

Hersey, P., & Blanchard, K. H. (1969b). *Management of organizational behavior*. Englewood Cliffs, NJ: Prentice-Hall.

Hersey, P., & Blanchard, K. H. (1972). The management of change. Change and the use of power. *Training & Development Journal, 26*(1); (2), 20–24; (3), 6–10.

Hersey, P., & Blanchard, K. H. (1973). *Leader effectiveness and adaptability description–self*. Escondido, CA: Center for Leadership Studies.

Hersey, P., & Blanchard, K. H. (1974). So you want to know your leadership style? *Training & Development Journal, 28*(2), 22–37. Also: (1981). *35*(6), 34–54.

Hersey, P., & Blanchard, K. H. (1977). *Management of organizational behavior: Utilizing human resources*. Englewood Cliffs, NJ: Prentice-Hall.

Hersey, P., & Blanchard, K. H. (1982b). Leadership style: Attitudes and behaviors. *Training & Development journal, 36*(5), 50–52.

Hertzler, J. O. (1940). Crises and dictatorships. *American Sociological Review, 5*, 157–169.

Herzberg, F. I. (1966). *Working and the nature of man*. New York: Crowell.

Heslin, P. A. (1999). Boosting empowerment by developing self-efficacy. *Asia Pacific Journal, 37*(1), 52–64.

Heslin, P. A., & Latham, G. P. (2004). The effect of upward feedback on managerial behavior. *Applied Psychology: An International Review, 59*, 23–37.

Heslin, J. A., Jr. (1966). *A field test of the Likert theory of management in an ADP environment*. Master's thesis, American University, Washington, DC.

Heslin, R., & Dunphy, D. (1964). Three dimensions of member satisfaction in small groups. *Human Relations, 17*, 99–112.

Hespe, C., & Wall, I. (1976). The demand for participation among employees. *Human Relations, 29*, 411–428.

Hesselbein, F. (2000). *Peter Drucker on management and leadership*. Address, International Leadership Association, Toronto, November 4.

Hesselbein, F. (2004). Circles of inclusion. *Leader to Leader, 32*, 4–6.

Hesselbein, F. (2004). The indispensable partnership. *Leader to Leader, 33*, 4–7.

Hesseling, P., & Konnen, E. E. (1969). Culture and subculture in a decision-making exercise. *Human Relations, 22*, 31–51.

Heuerman, T. (2001). *The new leaders' relationships and results*. Pamphlet 6, >http://www.amorenaturalway.com<

Heuerman, T. (2002). *Spirit at work* (3): *Leaders who care*. Pamphlet 61, TomHeu@cableone.net.

Heuerman, T. & Olson, D. (1999). *Connections: Is anyone out there?* Pamphlet 29, TomHeu@aol.com.

Heuerman, T. & Olson, D. (1999). *Leading in chaos*. Pamphlet 23.

Hewitt, R., & Stokes, R. (1975). Disclaimers. *American Sociological Review, 40*, 1–11.

Hewlett, S. (1998). The feminization of the workforce. *New Perspectives Quarterly, 15*(3), 66–69.

Heyns, R. W. (1948). *Effects of variation in leadership on participant behavior in discussion groups*. Doctoral dissertation, University of Michigan, Ann Arbor, MI.

Heyns, R. W. (1950). *Factors determining influence and decision satisfaction in conferences requiring pooled judgments*. Proceedings, Administrative Conference, University of Michigan, Ann Arbor.

Hickman, C. R., & Silva, M. A. (1984). *Creating excellence: Managing corporate culture, strategy, and change in the New Age*. New York: New American Library.

Hicks, D. A. (2002). Spiritual and religious diversity in the workplace. Implications for leadership. *Leadership Quarterly, 13*, 379–396.

Hicks, D. A. (2005). Ethical diversity and the leader's religious commitments. In J. Ciulla, T. L. Price, & S. E. Murphy (eds.), *The quest for moral leaders: Essays on leadership ethics*. Cheltenham, U.K.: Edward Elgar.

Hicks, J. A., & Stone, J. B. (1962). The identification of traits related to managerial success. *Journal of Applied Psychology, 46*, 428–432.

Hicks, R. S. (1990). *Effectiveness of transactional and transformational leadership in turbulent and stable conditions.* Doctoral dissertation, Claremont Graduate School, Claremont, CA.

Hickson, D. J., Hinings, C. R., Less, C. A., Schneck, R. E., & Permings, J. M. (1971). A strategic contingencies theory of intraorganizational power. *Administrative Science Quarterly, 16,* 216–229.

Hietafelto, A. B. (1994). *Dynamic attributes of issue enactment.* Paper, Academy of Management, Dallas, TX.

Higgins, K., Jones, J. W., & Paddock, W. A. (2002). *E-leaders versus traditional leaders: A qualitative biographical analysis.* Paper, Society for Industrial Organizational Psychology, Toronto.

Hill, C. W. L., & Phan, P. (1991). CEO tenure as a determinant of CEO pay. *The Academy of Management Journal, 34,* 3, 707–717.

Hill, E. J., Miller, B. C., Weiner, S. P., et al. (1998). Influence of the virtual office on aspects of work/life balance. *Personnel Psychology, 51*(3), 667–683.

Hill, J. W., & Hunt, J. G. (1970). *An investigation of the relationship between employee need satisfaction and perceived leadership of two levels of management.* Carbondale: Southern Illinois University, Department of Management.

Hill, K. D., & Kerr, S. (1984). The impact of computer integrated manufacturing systems on the first-line supervisor. *Journal of Organizational Behavior Management, 6,* 81–97.

Hill, M., Mann, L., & Wearing, A. (1996). The effects of attitude, subjective norm, and self-efficacy on intention to benchmark: A comparison between managers with experience and no experience in benchmarking. *Journal of Organizational Behavior, 17,* 313–327.

Hill, N. (1976). Self-esteem: The key to effective leadership. *Administrative Management, 31*(8), 24.

Hill, R. (1984). From war room to boardroom. Professional soldiers excelling as managers. *International Management, 39*(4), 22–28.

Hill, R. (1985). The business leader with the Shakespearean touch. *International Management, 40*(9), 71–76.

Hill, R. B. (1971). *The strength of black families.* New York: National Urban League.

Hill, T. A. (1973). *An experimental study of the relationship between the opinionatedness of a leader and consensus in group discussions of policy.* Doctoral dissertation, Indiana University, Bloomington, IN.

Hill, T. E., & Schmitt, N. (1977). Individual differences in leadership decision making. *Organizational Behavior and Human Performance, 19,* 353–367.

Hill, W. (1969a). The validation and extension of Fiedler's theory of leadership effectiveness. *Academy of Management Journal, 12,* 3347.

Hill, W. A. (1973). Leadership style: Rigid or flexible? *Organizational Behavior and Human Performance, 9,* 35–47.

Hill, W. H., & Fox, W. A. (1973). Black and white marine squad leaders' perceptions of racially mixed squads. *Academy of Management Journal, 16,* 680–686.

Hill, W. H., & Hughes, D. (1974). Variations in leader behavior as a function of task type. *Organizational Behavior and Human Performance, 11,* 83–96.

Hill, W. H., & Ruhe, J. A. (1974). Attitudes and behaviors of black and white supervisors in problem solving groups. *Academy of Management Journal, 17,* 563–569.

Hiller, N. J., Day, D. V, & Vance, R. J. (2003). *Enacted shared leadership roles and team effectiveness: A field study.* Paper, Society for Industrial and Organizational Psychology, Orlando, FL.

Hiller, S., Jr. (1988). *Corporate governance: The flaw in America's reconstruction.* Address, Commonwealth Club, San Francisco, CA, May 21.

Hillery, J. M., & Wexley, K. N. (1974). Participation effects in appraisal interviews conducted in a training situation. *Journal of Applied Psychology, 59,* 168–171.

Hills, D. A. (1985). Prediction of effectiveness in leaderless group discussions with the adjective check list. *Journal of Applied Social Psychology, 15,* 443–447.

Hills, F. S. (1979). The pay-for-performance dilemma. *Personnel, 56*(5), 23–31.

Hiltz, S. R., Johnson, K., & Turoff, M. (1991). Group decision support: The effects of designated human leaders and statistical feedback in computerized conferences. *Journal of Management Information Systems, 8*(2), 81–107

Himes, J. S. (1965). Some work-related deprivations of lower-class Negro youths. In L. A. Ferman, J. A. Kornbluh, & A. Haber (eds.), *Poverty in America.* Ann Arbor: University of Michigan Press.

Himsel, D. (2004). *Leadership Sopranos style: How to become a more effective boss.* Dearborn Trade Publishing: Chicago, IL.

Hines, C. H., & Wellington, V. U. (1974). Achievement motivation levels of immigrants in New Zealand. *Journal of Cross-Cultural Psychology, 5,* 37–47.

Hinings, C. R., Hickson, D. J., Permings, J. M., & Schneck, R. E. (1974). Structural conditions of intraorganizational power. *Administrative Science Quarterly, 19,* 22–44

Hinkin, T. R., & Schriescheim, C. A. (1989). Development and application of new scales to measure the French and Raven (1959) bases of social power. *Journal of Applied Psychology, 74,* 561–567.

Hinkin, T. R., & Schreisheim, C. A. (1990). Relationships between subordinate perceptions of supervisor influence tactics and attributed bases of supervisory power. *Human Relations, 43,* 221–237.

Hinkin, T.R., & Tracey, J.B. (1999). The relevance of charisma for transformational leadership in stable organizations. *Journal of Organizational Change Management, 12,* 105–119.

Hinrichs, J. R. (1978a). An eight-year follow-up of a management assessment center. *Journal of Applied Psychology, 63,* 596–601.

Hinton, B. L., & Barrow, J. C. (1975). The superior's reinforcing behavior as a function of reinforcements received. *Organizational Behavior and Human Performance, 14,* 123–149.

Hinton, B. L., & Barrow, J. C. (1976). Personality correlates of the reinforcement propensities of leaders. *Personnel Psychology, 29,* 61–66.

Hirsch, J. (1987). College leaders read "how to." *New York Times,* August 2, Education section, 9.

Hirsch, W. (1985). *Flying too high for comfort. Manpower policy and practice. Career management in the organization: A guide for developing manpower policy and practice* (Report No. 16). London: Institute of Manpower Studies.

Hirsch, W., & Fonda, N. (1984). *Career management in the organization: A guide for developing manpower policy and practice* (Report No. 16). Institute of Manpower Studies, University of Sussex, London.

Hirschhorn, L. (1990). Leaders and followers in a postindustrial age:

A psychodynamic view. *Journal of Applied Behavioral Science, 26,* 529–542.

Hirsh, M. (1999). Grooming Mr.Summers: One of outgoing Secretary Bob Rubin's moves was prepping his successor. *Newsweek,* May 24, 53–55.

Hirst, G., & Mann, L. (2003). *A model of R & D leadership and team communication: The relationship with project performance.* Paper, Academy of Management, Seattle, WA.

Hise, R. T. (1968). The effect of close supervision on productivity of simulated managerial decision-making groups. *Business Studies,* North Texas State University, Fall, 96–104.

Hites, R. W. (1953). A questionnaire for measuring leader-identification. *American Psychologist, 8,* 368.

Hites, R. W., & Campbell, D. T. (1950). A test of the ability of fraternity leaders to estimate group opinion. *Journal of Social Psychology, 32,* 95–100.

Hitt, M. A. (2000). The new frontier: Transformation of management for the new millennium. *Organizational Dynamics, 28*(3), 7–17.

Hitt, M. A., Hoskisson, R. E., & Harrison, J. S. (1991). Strategic competitiveness in the 1990s: Challenges and opportunities for U.S. executives. *Academy of Management Executive, 5*(2), 7–21.

Hitt, M. A., Keats, B. W., Harback, F., et al. (1994). Rightsizing: Building and maintaining strategic leadership and long-term competitiveness. *Organizational Dynamics, 23,* 18–32.

Hitt, M. A., & Tyler, B. B. (1991). Strategic decision models: Integrating different perspectives. *Strategic Management Journal, 12,* 327–351.

Ho, T. H., & Raman, K. S. (1991). The effect of GDSS and elected leadership on small group meetings. *Journal of Management Information Systems, 8*(2), 109–133.

Hobbes, T. (2003). *Leviathan.* In L. P. Pojman (ed.), *Classics of Philosophy* (2nd ed.). New York: Oxford University Press.

Hobert, R., & Dunnette, M. D. (1967). Development of moderator variables to enhance the prediction of managerial effectiveness. *Journal of Applied Psychology, 51,* 50–64.

Hobhouse, L. T., Wheeler, G. C., & Ginsberg, M. (1930). *The material culture and social institutions of the simpler peoples.* London: Chapman & Hall.

Hochwarter, W. A., Kacmar, C., Ferris, G. R., et al. (2003). *Accountability at work: An examination of antecedents and consequences,* Paper, Society for Industrial and Organizational Psychology, Orlando, FL.

Hocking, W. E. (1924). Leaders and led. *Yale Review, 13,* 625–641.

Hodge, J. W. (1976). The relationship between styles of supervision and need satisfaction of two levels of management employees. *Dissertation Abstracts International, 37,* 1987.

Hodgetts, R. M., & Luthans, F. (1994). *International management* (2nd ed.). New York: McGraw-Hill.

Hodgson, J. D., & Brenner, M. H. (1968). Successful experience: Training hard-core unemployed. *Harvard Business Review, 46*(5), 148–156.

Hoffmann, C., & Reed, J. S. (1981). Sex discrimination? The XYZ affair. *Public Interest, 62,* Winter 1981, 21–39.

Hofmann, D. A. (1997). An overview of the logic and rationale of hierarchical linear models. *Journal of Management, 23,* December, 723–744.

Hoff, J. (1975). *Herbert Hoover: Forgotten progressive.* Boston: Little, Brown and Co.

Hoffer, E. (1951). *The true believer: Thoughts on the nature of mass movements.* New York: Harper & Row.

Hoffman, E. (1996). Not for future CEO's alone: Executive education courses now target more levels of management and help managers create strategies their companies need to grow. *Business Traveler, 3*(4), 18, 20, 22, 25.

Hoffman, E. L., & Rohrer, J. H. (1954). An objective peer evaluation scale: Construction and validity. *Educational and Psychological Measurement, 14,* 332–341.

Hoffman, L., Rosen, S., & Lippitt, R. (1960). Parental coerciveness, child autonomy, and the child's role at school. *Sociometry, 23,* 15–22.

Hoffman, L. R., Burke, R. J., & Maier, N. R. F. (1965). Participation, influence, and satisfaction among members of problem-solving groups. *Psychological Reports, 16,* 661–667.

Hoffman, L. R., Harburg, E., & Maier, N. R. F. (1962). Differences and disagreement as factors in creative group problem solving. *Journal of Abnormal and Social Psychology, 64,* 206–214.

Hoffman, L. R., & Maier, N. R. F. (1967). Valence in the adoption of solutions by problem-solving groups: 11. Quality and acceptance as goals of leaders and members. *Journal of Personality and Social Psychology, 6,* 175–182.

Hoffman, M. L. (1956). Conformity to the group as a defense mechanism. *American Psychologist, 11,* 375.

Hoffman, P. I., Festinger, L., & Lawrence, D. H. (1954). Tendencies toward group comparability in competitive bargaining. *Human Relations, 7,* 141–159.

Hoffman, R., & Hegarty, W. (1993). Top management influence on innovations: Effects of executive characteristics and social culture. *Journal of Management, 19,* 3, 549–574.

Hoffman, S., & Hoffman, I. (1970). The will to grandeur: De Gaulle as political artist. In D. A. Rustow (ed.), *Philosophers and kings: Studies in leadership.* New York: George Braziller.

Hofmeyer, K. (1987). Training and development of black management. In B. M. Bass & P. J. D. Drenth (eds.), *Advances in organizational psychology: An international review.* Beverly Hills, CA: Sage.

Hofstede, G. (1978). Private correspondence, January 20.

Hofstede, G. (1980). *Culture's consequences: international differences in work related values.* Beverly Hills, CA: Sage.

Hofstede, G. (1984). The cultural relativity of the quality of life concept. *Academy of Management Review, 9,* 389–398.

Hofstede, G. (1993). Cultural constraints in management theories. *Academy of Management Executive, 7*(1), 81–94.

Hofstede, G. (1997). *Cultures and organizations: The software of the mind.* New York: McGraw-Hill.

Hofstede, G. (2001). *Culture's consequences: Comparing values, behaviors, institutions, and organizations across nations* (2nd ed.). Thousand Oaks, CA; Sage.

Hofstede, G., & Bond, G. H. (1988). IDV, PDI, UAI, MAS

Hofstede, G., & Bond, G. H. (1998). The Confucius connection: From cultural roots to economic growth. *Organizational Dynamics, 16,* 4–21.

Hogan, J., & Hogan, R. (1996). *Motives, Values, and Preferences Inventory.* Tulsa, OK: Hogan Assessment Systems.

Hogan, J., & Hogan, R. (2002). Leadership and sociopolitical intelligence. In R. E. Riggio, S. E. Murphy, & F. J. Pirozzolo (eds.), *Multiple intelligences and leadership.* Mahwah, NJ: Lawrence Erlbaum Associates.

Hogan, J., & Holland, B. (1998). *Validity of the Hogan personality inventory for identifying effective retail managers.* Tulsa, OK: Hogan Assessment Systems.

Hogan, J., & Zenke, L. (1986). Dollar-value utility of alternative procedures for selecting school principals. *Educational and Psychological Measurement, 46,* 935–945.

Hogan, R. (1969). Development of an empathy scale. *Journal of Consulting and Clinical Psychology, 33,* 307–316

Hogan, R. (1994). Trouble at the top: Causes and consequences of managerial incompetence. *Consulting Psychology Journal, 46,* 9–15.

Hogan, R. (1998). What we know about leadership. *The Industrial-Organizational Psychologist, 35*(3), 62–63

Hogan. R. (2003). *Leadership and values.* Orlando, FL: Society for Industrial and Organizational Psychology.

Hogan, R., Curphy, G. J. & Hogan, J. (1994). What we know about leadership: Effectiveness and personality. *American Psychologist, 49,* 493–504.

Hogan, R., Jones, W. H., & Cheek, J. M. (1985). Socioanalytic theory: An alternative to armadillo psychology. In B. Schlenker (ed.), *Self and social life.* New York: McGraw-Hill.

Hogan, R., Raskin, R., & Fazzini, D. (1990). The dark side of charisma. In K. E. Clark & M. B. Clark (eds.), *Measures of leadership.* West Orange, NJ: Leadership Library of America.

Hogan, R., Raskin, R., & Fazzini, D. (1990). The dark side of charisma. *Leadership Quarterly, 5,* 3–23. And in Clark, K. E., Hollenbeck, J. R., Ilgen, D. R., & Sego, D. J. (1994). *Repeated measures regression and mediational tests: Enhancing the power of leadership research.*

Hogarth, R. M. (2001). *Educating intuition.* Chicago and London: University of Chicago Press.

Hoge, W. (2004). Latin America losing hope in democracy, report says. *New York Times,* April 22, A3.

Hogg, M. A. (2001). A social identity theory of leadership. *Personality & Social Psychology Review, 5*(3), 184–200.

Hogue, M. B., Ludwig, J., & Yoder, J. D. (submitted). *Increasing initial leadership effectiveness: Assisting both women and men.*

Hohn, R. (1962). *Menschenführung im Handel.* Bad Harzburg: Verlag für Wissenschaft, Wirtschaft, und Technik.

Holden, R. (1954). Relationships between perceived leadership perceptions of the ideal, and group productivity in small classroom groups. *Dissertation Abstracts, 14,* 1994.

Holden, N., Cooper, G., & Carr, J. (1998). *Dealing with the new Russia.* Chichester, U.K.: Wiley.

Holladay, S. J. & Coombs, W. T. (1993). Communicating visions: An exploration of the role of delivery in the creation of leadership charisma. *Management Communication Quarterly, 6,* 405–427.

Holladay, S. J. & Coombs, W. T. (1994). Speaking of visions and visions being spoken: An exploration of content and delivery in perceptions of leader charisma. *Management Communication Quarterly, 8,* 165–189.

Holland, P. W., & Leinhardt, S. (1976). Local structure in social networks. In D. R. Heise (ed.), *Sociological Methodology.* San Francisco: Jossey-Bass.

Hollander, E. P. (1954). Authoritarianism and leadership choice in a military setting. *Journal of Abnormal and Social Psychology, 49,* 365–370.

Hollander, E. P. (1958). Conformity, status, and idiosyncrasy credit. *Psychological Review, 65,* 117–127.

Hollander, E. P. (1960). Competence and conformity in the acceptance of influence. *Journal of Abnormal and Social Psychology, 61,* 365–369.

Hollander, E. P. (1961a). Some effects of perceived status on responses to innovative behavior. *Journal of Abnormal and Social Psychology, 63,* 247–250.

Hollander, E. P. (1961b) Emergent leadership and social influence. In L. Petrullo & B. M. Bass (eds.), *Leadership and interpersonal behavior.* New York: Holt, Rinehart & Winston.

Hollander, E. P. (1964). *Leaders, groups, and influence.* New York: Oxford University Press.

Hollander, E. P. (1965). Validity of peer nominations in predicting a distance performance criterion. *Journal of Applied Psychology, 49,* 434–438.

Hollander, E. P. (1966). *Leadership style, competence, and source of authority as determinants of active and perceived influence* (tech. rep.). Buffalo: State University of New York.

Hollander, E. P. (1978). *Leadership dynamics: A practical guide to effective relationships.* New York: Free Press.

Hollander, E. P. (1983). Women and leadership. In H. H. Blumberg, A. P. Hare, V. Kent, & M. Davies (eds.), *Small Groups and Social Interaction,* vol. 1. New York: Wiley.

Hollander, E. P. (1985). Leadership and power. In G. Lindzey and E. Aronson (eds.), *The handbook of social psychology.* New York: Random House.

Hollander, E. P. (1986). On the central role of leadership processes. *International Review of Applied Psychology, 35,* 39–52.

Hollander, E. P. (1987). *College and university leadership from a social psychological perspective: A transactional view.* Paper, Invitational Interdisciplinary Colloquium on Leadership in Higher Education, National Center for Postsecondary Governance and Finance, Columbia University, New York.

Hollander, E. P. (1992). The essential interdependence of leadership and followership. *Current Directions in Psychological Science, 1*(2), 71–75.

Hollander, E. P. (1993). Legitimacy, power, and influence: A perspective on relational features of leadership. In M. M. Chemers & R. Ayman (eds.), *Leadership theory and research: Perspectives and directions.* New York: Academic Press.

Hollander, E. P. (1995). Ethical challenges in the leader-follower relationship. *Business Ethics Quarterly, 5,* 54–65.

Hollander, E. P. (1996). *How and why active followers matter in leadership.* Paper, American Psychological Association, Toronto, Ontario.

Hollander, E. P. (1997). How and why active followers matter in leadership. In *The balance of leadership & followership: Working papers.* Academy of Leadership Press.

Hollander, E. P., & Bair, J. T. (1954). Attitudes toward authority-figures as correlates of motivation among aviation cadets. *Journal of Applied Psychology, 38,* 21–25.

Hollander, E. P., Fallon, B. J., & Edwards, M. T. (1977). Some aspects of influence and acceptability for appointed and elected leaders. *Journal of Psychology, 95,* 289–296.

Hollander, E. P., & Julian, J. W. (1969). Contemporary trends in the analysis of leadership processes. *Psychological Bulletin*, 71, 387–397.

Hollander, E. P., & Julian, J. W. (1970). Studies in leader legitimacy, influence, and innovation. In L. Berkowitz (ed.), *Advances in experimental social psychology*, Vol. 5. New York: Academic Press.

Hollander, E. P., & Kelly, D. R. (1990). *Rewards from leaders as perceived by followers*. Paper presented at the meeting of the Eastern Psychological Association, Philadelphia, PA.

Hollander, E. P., & Neider, L. L. (1978). *Critical incidents and rating scales in comparing "good"-"bad" leadership*. Paper, American Psychological Association, Toronto.

Hollander, E. P., & Webb, W. B. (1955). Leadership, followership, and friendship: An analysis of peer nominations. *Journal of Abnormal and Social Psychology*, 50, 163–167.

Hollander, E. P., & Yoder, J. (1980). Some issues in comparing women and men as leaders. *Basic Applied Social Psychology*, 1, 267–280.

Hollenbeck, J. R., Ilgen, D. R., & Sego, D. J. (1994). Repeated measures regression and mediational tests: Enhancing the power of leadership research. *Leadership Quarterly*, 5, 3–23.

Hollie, P. (1980). Officers recapture New Mexico prison without resistance. *New York Times*, February 4, A1, D9.

Hollingshead, A. B. (1949). *Elmtown's youth: The impact of social classes on adolescents*. New York: Wiley.

Hollingsworth, A. T., & Al-Jafary, A. R. A. (1983). Why supervisors don't delegate and employees won't accept responsibility. *Supervisory Management*, 28(4), 12–17.

Hollingworth, L. S. (1926). *Gifted children*. New York: Macmillan.

Hollman, R. W. (1973). *A study of the relationships between organizational climate and managerial assessment of management by objectives*. Doctoral dissertation, University of Washington, Seattle.

Holloman, C. R. (1967). The perceived leadership role of military and civilian supervisors in a military setting. *Personnel Psychology*, 20, 199–210.

Holloman, C. R. (1968). Leadership and headship: There is a difference. *Personnel Administration*, 31(4), 38–44.

Holloman, C. R. (1986). "Headship" vs. leadership. *Business and Economic Review*, 32(2), 35–37.

Holloway, E. L., & Wolleat, F. L. (1981). Style differences of beginning supervisors: An interactional analysis. *Journal of Counseling Psychology*, 28, 373–376.

Holmes, J. S. (1969). Comparison of group leader and nonparticipant observer judgments of certain objective interaction variables. *Psychological Reports*, 24, 655–659.

Holt, R. (1952a). *An exploratory study of the French cabinets of the first legislature of the Fourth Republic* (Tech. Rep. No. 2). Minneapolis: University of Minnesota.

Holt, R. (1952b). *An analysis of the problem of stability and cohesive membership in coalitions* (Tech. Rep. No. 3). Minneapolis: University of Minnesota.

Holton, P. B. (1984). *Leadership styles of program leaders in the Cooperative Extension Service in New England*. Ph.D. thesis, University of Connecticut, New Haven.

Holusha, J. (1991). Grace Pastiak's "web of inclusion." *New York Times*, May 5, Business Section, 1–3.

Homans, G. C. (1950). *The human group*. New York: Harcourt, Brace.

Homans, G. C. (1958). Social behavior as exchange. *American Journal of Sociology*, 63, 597–606.

Homans, G. C. (1961). *Social behavior: Its elementary forms*. New York: Harcourt, Brace.

Homer (ca. 750 B.C.). *The Iliad*, Book X, line 14.

Honan, W. (1998). Programs that make leadership their goal. *New York Times*, September 30.

Honeywell Corporate Human Resources and Corporate Employee Relations. (1981). *Honeywell management development survey: Corporate findings*. Minneapolis, MN: Honeywell.

Hood, R. D., Showel, M., & Stewart, E. C. (1967). *Evaluation of three experimental systems for noncommissioned officer training*. Washington, DC: George Washington University, Human Resources Office.

Hooijberg, R. (1996). A multidirectional approach toward leadership: An extension of the concept of behavioral complexity. *Human Relations*, 49, 917–946.

Hooijberg, R., & Choi, J. (2000). Which leadership roles matter to whom? An examination of rater effects on perceptions of effectiveness. *Leadership Quarterly*, 11, 341–364.

Hooijberg, R., Hunt, J.G., & Dodge, G. E. (1997). Leadership complexity and the development of the Leaderplex Model. *Journal of Management*, 23, 375–408.

Hooijberg, R., & Quinn, R. E. (1992). Behavioral complexity and the development of effective managers. In R. L. Phillips & J. G. Hunt (eds), *Strategic leadership: A multiorganizational perspective*. Westport, CT: Quorum Books.

Hook, C. M., Rollinson, D. J., Foot, M., & Handley, J. (1996). Supervisor and manager styles in handling discipline and grievance: Part one comparing styles in handling discipline and grievance. *Personnel Review*, 25(3), 20–34.

Hook, S. (1943). *The hero in history*. New York: John Day.

Hooker, E. R. (1928). Leaders in village communities. *Social Forces*, 6, 605–614.

Hooper, D. B. (1969). Differential utility of leadership opinions in classical and moderator models for the prediction of leadership effectiveness. *Dissertation Abstracts International*, 30, 13.

Hoover, N. R. (1987). *Transformational and transactional leadership: A test of the model*. Doctoral dissertation, University of Louisville, Louisville, KY

Hoppe, M. H. (1990). *A comparative study of country elites: International differences in work-related values and learning and their implications for management training and development*. Doctoral dissertation, University of North Carolina, Chapel Hill, N.C.

Hoppock, R. (1935). *Job satisfaction*. New York: Harper.

Hord, S. M., Hall, G. E., & Stiegelbauer, S. M. (1984). How principals work with other change facilitators. *Education and Urban Society*, 17, 89–109.

Horn, J. M., Plomin, R., & Rosenman, R. (1976). Heritability of personality traits in adult male twins. *Behavior Genetics*, 6, 17–30.

Hornaday, J. A., & Bunker, C. S. (1970). The nature of the entrepreneur. *Personnel Psychology*, 23, 47–54.

Horne, J. H., & Lupton, T. (1965). The work activities of "middle" management: An exploratory study. *Journal of Management Studies*, 2, 14–33.

Hornstein, H. (1986). *Managerial courage: Revitalizing your company without sacrificing your job.* New York: Wiley.

Horovitz, J. (1980). *Top management control in Europe.* London: Macmillan.

Horwitz, M. (1954). The recall of interrupted group tasks: An experimental study of individual motivation in relation to group goals. *Human Relations, 7,* 3–38.

Horwitz, M., Goldman, M., & Lee, F. J. (1955). *Effects of two methods of changing a frustrating agent on reduction of hostility* (preliminary report). Urbana: University of Illinois, Bureau of Educational Research.

Horrocks, J. E., & Thompson, G. G. (1946). A study of the friendship fluctuations of rural boys and girls. *Journal of Genetic Psychology, 69,* 189–198.

Horsfall, A. B., & Arensberg, C. M. (1949). Teamwork and productivity in a shoe factory. *Human Organization, 8,* 13–26.

Hosking, D. M., & Hung, J. G. (1982). Leadership research and the European connection: an epilogue. In J. G. Hunt, U. Sekaran, & C. E. Shriesheim (eds.), *Leadership: Beyond establishment views.* Carbondale, IL: Southern Illinois University Press, 278–289.

Hosmer, L. T. (1982). The importance of strategic leadership. *Journal of Business, 3*(2), 47–57.

Hosmer, L. T. (1995). Trust: The connecting link between between organizational theory and philosophical ethics. *Academy of Management Review, 20,* 379–403.

Hough, L. M. (1984). Development and evaluation of the "accomplishment record" method of selecting and promoting professionals. *Journal of Applied Psychology, 69,* 135–146.

Hough, L. M. (1992). The "Big Five" personality variables—construct confusion: Description versus prediction. *Human Performance, 5, 1 & 2,* 139–155.

Hough, L. M., Keyes, M. A., & Dunnette, M. D. (1983). An evaluation of three "alternative" selection procedures. *Personnel Psychology, 36,* 261–276.

House, R., J. (1962). An experiment in the use of management training standards. *Academy of Management Journal, 5,* 76–81.

House, R. J. (1965). Managerial reactions to two methods of management training. *Personnel Psychology, 18,* 311–320.

House, R. J. (1967). T-group education and leadership effectiveness: A review of the empiric literature and a critical evaluation. *Personnel Psychology, 20,* 1–32.

House, R. J. (1971). A path goal theory of leader effectiveness. *Administrative Science Quarterly, 16,* 321–338.

House, R. J. (1972). *Some new applications and tests of the path-goal theory of leadership.* Unpublished manuscript.

House, R. J. (1977) A 1976 theory of charismatic leadership. In J. G. Hunt & L. L. Larson (eds.), *Leadership: The cutting edge.* Carbondale, IL: Southern Illinois University Press.

House, R. J. (1984). *Power in organizations: A social psychological perspective.* Toronto: University of Toronto. Unpublished manuscript.

House, R. J. (1985). *Research contrasting the behavior and effect of reputed charismatic Versus reputed non-charismatics.* Paper, Administrative Science Association of Canada, Montreal.

House, R. J. (1988a). Leadership research: Some forgotten, ignored, or overlooked findings. In J. G. Hunt, B. R. Baliga, H. P. Dachler, & C. A. Schriesheim (eds.), *Emerging leadership vistas.* Lexington, MA: D. C. Heath.

House, R. J. (1988b). Power and personality in complex organizations. In B. M. Staw & L. L. Cummings (eds.), *Research in organizational behavior.* Greenwich, CT: JAI Press.

House, R. J. (1991). The distribution and exercise of power in complex organizations: A meso theory. *Leadership Quarterly, 2,* 23–58.

House, R. J. (1992). A theory of charismatic leadership: Extensions and evidence. In A. Howard (ed.), *The Changing Nature of Work.* San Francisco, CA: Jossey-Bass.

House, R. J. (1992) (House, R. J. (1977)). A theory of charismatic leadership: Extensions and evidence. A 1976 theory of charismatic leadership. In L. G. Hunt & L. L. Larson (eds.), *Leadership: The cutting edge.* Carbondale: Southern Illinois University Press.

House, R. J. (1992). The distribution and exercise of power in mechanistic and organic organizations. In H. L. Tosi (ed.), *The environment/organization/person contingency model: A meso approach to the study of organizations.* Greenwich, CT: JAI Press.

House, R. J. (1995). Leadership. In N. Nicholson (ed.), *The Blackwell Encyclopedic Dictionary of Organizational Behavior.* Cambridge, MA: Blackwell Publishers, 284–288.

House, R. J. (1995). Leadership in the twenty-first century: A speculative inquiry. In A. Howard (ed.), *The changing nature of work.* San Francisco, CA: Jossey-Bass.

House, R. J. (1996). Path-goal theory of leadership: Lessons, legacy, and a reformulated theory. *Leadership Quarterly, 7,* 323–352.

House, R. J. (1998). Leadership. In C. L. Cooper & C. Argyris (eds.), *The concise Blackwell encyclopedia of management.* Oxford, U.K.: Oxford University Press.

House, R. J. (1999). Weber and the neo-charismatic paradigm: A response to Beyer. *Leadership Quarterly, 10,* 563–574.

House, R. J., & Aditya, R. (1997). The social scientific study of leadership Quo vadis? *Journal of Management Yearly Review, 23,* 409–473.

House, R. J., Agar, M., Hanges, P., et al. (1995). GLOBE. *The global leadership & organizational behavior research program: A multinational study of cultures, organizational practices, and leadership.* Prospectus.

House, R. J., & Dessler, G. (1974). The path goal theory of leadership: Some post hoc and a priori tests. In J. G. Hunt & L. L. Larson (eds.), *Contingency approaches to leadership.* Carbondale: Southern Illinois University Press.

House, R. J., Filley, A. C., & Gujarati, D. N. (1971). Leadership style, hierarchical influence, and the satisfaction of subordinate role expectations: A test of Likert's influence proposition. *Journal of Applied Psychology, 55,* 422–432.

House, R. J., Filley, A. C., & Kerr, S. (1971). Relation of leader consideration and initiating structure to R and D subordinates' satisfaction. *Administrative Science Quarterly, 16*(1), *Organizational Leadership* (Mar. 1971), 19–30.

House, R. J., Gupta, V., & Ruiz-Quintanilla, S. A. (1998). *Unobtrusive measures and participant observation measures in GLOBE.* Paper, Academy of Management, San Diego, CA.

House, R. J., Hanges, P. J., Dickson, M. & Ruiz-Quintanilla, S. A. (1996). *The development and cross-cultural validation of scales measuring societal culture, organizational culture and prototypical leadership attributes.* GLOBE working paper. Philadelphia, PA: University of Pennsylvania Press.

House, R. J., Hanges, P. J., Dickson, M.W., Ruiz-Quintanilla, S. A., & Globe CCIs (1998). *Culture and leadership scales.* Unpublished manuscript.

House, R. J., Hanges, P. J., & Javidan, M., et al. (2004). *Culture, leadership, and organizations: The Globe study of 62 societies.* Thousand Oaks, CA: Sage.

House, R. J., & Howell, J. M. (1992). Personality and charismatic leadership. *Leadership Quarterly,* 3, 81–108.

House, R. J., & Howell, J. M. (1992). *Socialized and personalized charisma: An essay on the bright and dark sides of charisma.* Paper, University of Western Ontario, Canada.

House, R. J., Howell, J. M., & Shamir, B. (2002). *Leadership: Values, identities, and potency.* Thousand Oaks, CA: Sage Publications.

House, R. J., Howell, J. M., Shamir, B., et al. (1992). *Charismatic leadership: A 1992 theory and five empirical tests.* Unpublished manuscript.

House, R. J., & Javidan, M. (2004). Overview of GLOBE. In R. House, P. J. Hanges, M. Javidan, et al. (eds), *Culture, leadership, and organizations.* Thousand Oaks, CA; Sage.

House, R. J., Javidan, M., & Dorfman, P. (2001). Project GLOBE: An introduction. *Applied Psychology: An International Review,* 50, 489–505.

House, R. J., & Miner, J. B. (1969). Merging management and behavioral theory: The interaction between span of control and group size. *Administrative Science Quarterly,* 14, 451–464.

House, R. J., & Mitchell, T. R. (1974). Path-goal theory of leadership. *Journal of Contemporary Business,* 3, 81–97.

House, R. J. & Podsakoff, P. M. (1994). Leadership effectiveness and future research direction. In G. Greenberg (ed.), *Organizational behavior: The state of the science.* Hillsdale, NJ: Lawrence Erlbaum Associates.

House, R. J., & Rizzo, J. R. (1972a). Toward the measurement of organizational practices: Scale development and validation. *Journal of Applied Psychology,* 56, 388–396.

House, R. J., & Rizzo, J. R. (1972b). Role conflict and ambiguity as critical variables in a model of organizational behavior. *Organizational Behavior and Human Performance,* 7, 467–505.

House, R. J., & Shamir, B. (1993). Towards the integration of transformational, charismatic, and visionary theories. In M. M. Chemers & R. Ayman (eds.), *Leadership theory and research: Perspective and directions.* New York: Academic Press.

House, R. J., & Singh, J. V. (1987). Organizational behavior. Some new directions for I/O psychology. *Annual Review of Psychology,* 38, 669–718.

House, R. J., Spangler, W. D., & Woycke, J. (1989). *Personality and charisma in the U.S. presidency.* Unpublished manuscript.

House, R. J., Spangler, W. D. & Woyke, J. (1991). Personality and charisma in the U.S. presidency: A psychological theory of leader effectiveness. *Administrative Science Quarterly,* 36, 364–396.

House, R. J., & Tosi, H. L. (1963). An experimental evaluation of a management training program. *Academy of Management Journal,* 6, 303–315.

House, R. J., Woycke, J., & Fodor, E. (1986). *Research contrasting the motives and effects of reputed charismatic versus reputed non-charismatic U.S. presidents.* Paper, Academy of Management, Chicago.

House, R. J., Woyke, J., & Fodor, E. M. (1987). *Perceived behavior and effectiveness of charismatic and non-charismatic U.S. presidents.* Paper, International Symposium on Leadership and Management, McGill University, Montreal.

House, R. J., Woycke, J., & Fodor, E. M. (1988). Charismatic and non-charismatic leaders: Differences in behavior and effectiveness. In J. A. Conger & R. N. Kanungo (eds.), *Charismatic leadership: The elusive factor in organizational effectiveness.* San Francisco: Jossey-Bass.

House, R. J., Wright, N. S., & Aditya, R. N. (1997). Cross-cultural research on organizational leadership: A critical analysis and a proposed theory. In P. C. Early & M. Erez (eds.), *New perspectives on international industrial/organizational behavior.* San Francisco: New Lexington Press.

Hovey, D. E. (1974). The low-powered leader confronts a messy problem: A test of Fiedler's theory. *Academy of Management Journal,* 17, 358–362.

Howard, A. (1974). An assessment of assessment centers. *Academy of Management Journal,* 17, 115–134.

Howard, A. (1986). College experiences and managerial performance. *Journal of Applied Psychology,* 71, 530–552.

Howard, A. (1995). A framework for change. In A. Howard (ed.), *The changing nature of work.* San Francisco: Jossey-Bass.

Howard, A., & Bray, D. W. (1988). *Managerial lives in transition: Advancing age and changing times.* New York: Guilford Press.

Howard, A., Shudo, K., & Umeshima, M. (1983). Motivation and values among Japanese and American managers. *Personnel Psychology,* 36, 883–98.

Howard, A., & Wellins, R. S. (1994). *High-involvement leadership: Changing roles for changing times.* Leadership Research Institute, Development Dimensions International.

Howard, D. S. (1968). Personality similarity and complementarity and perceptual accuracy in supervisor-subordinate relationships. *Dissertation Abstracts,* 28, 4789–4790.

Howard, P. W., & Joyce, W. F. (1982). *Substitutes for leadership: A statistical refinement.* Paper, Academy of Management, New York.

Howat, G., & London, M. (1980). Attributions of conflict management strategies in supervisor-subordinate dyads. *Journal of Applied Psychology,* 65, 172–175.

Howell, J. M. (1985). *A laboratory study of charismatic leadership* (Working Paper No. 85–35). London, ON: School of Business Administration, University of Western Ontario.

Howell, J. M. (1986). *Charismatic leadership: Effects of leadership style and group productivity on individual adjustment and performance.* Doctoral dissertation, University of British Columbia, Vancouver, BC.

Howell, J. M. (1988). Two faces of charisma: Socialized and personalized leadership in organizations. In J. Conger & R. Kanungo (eds.), *Charismatic leadership: The illusive factor in organizational effectiveness.* San Francisco: Jossey-Bass.

Howell, J. M. (1991). Through the looking glass: Reflections on a disruptive experience. *Journal of Management Education,* 15, 415–427.

Howell, J. M. (1997). *Organization contexts, charismatic and exchange leadership.* Kellogg Leadership Studies Monograph, Center for Political Leadership and Participation, University of Maryland.

Howell, J. M. (2003). *Organization contexts, charismatic and exchange leadership.* Paper, Society for Industrial Organizational Psychology, Orlando, FL.

Howell, J. M., & Avolio, B. J. (1989). *Transformational versus transactional leaders: How they impart innovation, risk-taking, organizational structure and performance.* Paper, Academy of Management, Washington, DC.

Howell, J. M., & Avolio, B. J. (1992). The ethics of charismatic leadership: Sumission or liberation? *Academy of Management Executive,* 6(2), 43–54.

Howell, J. M., & Avolio, B. J. (1993). Transformational leadership, transactional leadership, locus of control, and support for innovation: Key predictors of consolidated-business-unit performance. *Journal of Applied Psychology,* 78, 891–902.

Howell, J. M., & Boies, K. (2004). Champions of technological innovation: The influence of contextual knowledge, role orientation, idea generation on champion emergence. *Leadership Quarterly,* 15, 123–144.

Howell, J. P., Bowen, D. E., Dorfman, P. W., Kerr, S., and Podsakoff, P. M. (1990). Substitutes for leadership: Effective alternatives to ineffective leadership. *Organizational Dynamics,* 19(1), 20–38.

Howell, J. M., & Costley, D. L. (eds.). (2001, 2006) *Understanding behaviors for effective leadership.* Upper Saddle River, NJ: Pearson Prentice-Hall.

Howell, J. P., & Dorfman, P. W. (1981). Substitutes for leadership: Test of a construct. *Academy of Management Journal,* 24, 714–728.

Howell, J. P., & Dorfman, P. W. (1986). Leadership and substitutes for leadership among professional and nonprofessional workers. *Journal of Applied Behavioral Science,* 22, 29–46.

Howell, J. P., & Dorfman, P. W. (1988). *A comparative study of leadership and its substitutes in a mixed cultural work setting.* Unpublished manuscript.

Howell, J. R., Dorfman, P. W., & Kerr, S. (1986). Moderator variables in leadership research. *Academy of Management Review,* 11, 88–102.

Howell, J. P., Dorfman, P. W., Hibino, J. K., et al. (1994). *Leadership in Western and Asian countries: Commonalities and differences in effective leadership processes and substitutes.* Las Cruces, NM: New Mexico State University, Center for Business Research.

Howell, J. M., & Frost, P. J. (1989). A laboratory study of charismatic leadership. *Organizational Behavior and Human Decision Processes,* 43, 243–269.

Howell, J. M., & Hall-Merenda, K. E. (1999). The ties that bind: Impact of leader-member exchange, transformational and transactional leadership, and distance on predicting follower performance. *Journal of Applied Psychology,* 84, 680–694.

Howell, J. M., & Higgins, C. A. (1990). Leadership behaviors, influence tactics, and career experiences of technological innovation. *Leadership Quarterly,* 1, 249–264.

Howell, J. M., & House, R. (1992). *Socialized and personalized charisma: An essay on the bright and dark side of leadership.* Unpublished manuscript.

Howell, J. M., Neufield, D. J., & Avolio, B. J. (1998). *Leadership at a distance: The effects of physical distance, charismatic leadership, and communication style in predicting business unit performance.* London, ON: University of Western Ontario.

Howell, J. M., Neufield, D. J., & Avolio, B. J. (2005). Examining the relationship of leadership and physical distance with business unit performance. *Leadership Quarterly,* 16, 273–285.

Howell, J. M. & Shamir, B. (2005). The role of followers in the charismatic leadership process: Susceptibility, social construction and leader empowerment. *Academy of Management Review,* 30, 96–112.

Howell, J. M., Shea, C. M., & Higgins, C. A. (1998). Champions of product innovations: Defining, developing, and validating a measure of champion behavior. *Journal of Business Venturing,* 20(5), 641–661.

Hoxie, R. G. (1983). Eisenhower and presidential leadership. *Presidential Studies Quarterly,* 13, 589–612.

Hoy, W. K., & Brown, B. L. (1988). Leadership behavior of principals and the zone of acceptance of elementary teachers. *Journal of Educational Administration,* 26, 23–38.

Hoy, W. K., & Ferguson, J. (1985). A theoretical framework and exploration of organizational effectiveness of schools. *Educational Administrative Quarterly,* 21(2), 117–134.

Hoy, W. K., Tarter, C. J., & Forsyth, F. (1978). Administrative behavior and subordinate loyalty: An empirical assessment. *Journal of Educational Administration,* 16, 29–38.

Hoyt, C. C., & Stoner, J. A. (1968). Leadership and group decisions involving risk. *Journal of Experimental and Social Psychology,* 4, 275–284.

Hoyt, P. D., & Garrison, J. A. (1997). Political manipulation within small group: Foreign policy advisers in the Carter administration. In P. Hart, E. K. Stern, & B. Sundelius (eds.), *Beyond groupthink: Political group dynamics and foreign policy-making.* Ann Arbor: University of Michigan Press.

Hsu, C. C., & Newton, R. R. (1974). Relation between foremen's leadership attitudes and the skill level of their work groups. *Journal of Applied Psychology,* 59, 771–772.

Hsu, F. L. K. (1981). *American and Chinese: Passage to differences* (3rd ed.). Honolulu: University of Hawaii Press.

Hu, S., Pattatucci, A. M. L., Patterson, C., et al. (1995). Linkage between sexual orientation and chromosome Xq28 in males but not in females. *Nature Genetics,* 11, 248–256.

Hua, W. (2003). *A social exchange model of subordinate's trust in supervisors.* Paper, Academy of Management, Seattle, WA.

Huber, V. L. (1986). Effects of cognitive heuristics and goals on negotiator performance and subsequent goal setting. *Organizational Behavior and Human Decision Processes,* 38, 342–365.

Huber, V. L., & Neale, M. A. (1986). Effects of cognitive heuristics and goals on negotiating performance and subsequent goal setting. *Organizational Behavior and Human Decision Processes.* 38, 342–365.

Huck, J. R. (1973). Assessment centers: A review of external and internal validities. *Personnel Psychology,* 26, 191–212.

Huck, J. R., & Bray, D. W. (1976). Management assessment center evaluations and subsequent job performance of white and black females. *Personnel Psychology,* 29, 13–30.

Hudson, G. (1979). *The role of humor in John F. Kennedy's presidential campaign.* Doctoral dissertation, Southern Illinois University, Carbondale, IL.

Huertas, S. C., & Powell, L. (1986). Effect of appointed leadership on conformity. *Psychological Reports, 59,* 679–682.

Huffcott, A. I., Weekley, J. A., Wiesner, W. H., et al. (2001). Comparison of situational and behavior description interview questions for higher level positions. *Personnel Psychology, 54,* 619–644.

Huffcutt, A. I, Roth, P. L. & McDaniel, M. A. (1996). A meta-analytic investigation of cognitive ability in employment interview evaluations: moderating characteristics and implications for incremental validity. *Journal of Applied Psychology, 81*(5), 459–473.

Hughes, E. C. (1946). The knitting of racial groups in industry. *American Sociological Review, 11,* 512–519.

Hughes, G. D. (1990). Managing high-tech product cycles. *Academy of Management Executive, 4,* 44–55.

Hughes, R. L., Ginnett, R. C., & Curphy, G. J. (1993). *Leadership: Enhancing the lessons of experience.* Homewood, IL: Irwin.

Hughes, R.L., Ginnett, R. C., & Curphy, G. J. (1993). Power, influence, and influence tactics. In R. L. Hughes, R. C. Ginnett, & Curphy, G. J. *Leadership: Enhancing the lessons of experience.* Homewood, IL: Irwin.

Hughes, R. L., Ginnett, R. C., et al. (1996). *Leadership: Enhancing the lessons of experience* (2nd ed.). Boston: Irwin/McGraw-Hill.

Hulin, C. L. (1962). The measurement of executive success. *Journal of Applied Psychology, 46,* 303–306.

Hulin, C. L. (1987). A psychometric theory of evaluations of item and scale translations. *Journal of Cross-Cultural Psychology, 2,* 115–142.

Hult, G. T. M. (1995). Managing the international strategic sourcing process as a market-driven organizational learning system. *Decision Sciences, 29*(1), 193–216.

Hultman, C. (1984). Managerial work, organizational perspectives, and the training of managers. *Scandinavian Journal of Educational Research, 28,* 199–210.

Human, L., & Hofmeyr, K. (1984). Black managers in a white world: Strategy formulation. *South African Journal of Business Management, 15,* 96–104.

Hummel, R. P. (1973). *Charisma in politics: Psycho-social causes of revolution as pre-conditions of charismatic outbreaks within the framework of Weber's epistemology.* Master's thesis, New York University, New York.

Hummel, R. P. (1975). Psychology of charismatic followers. *Psychological Reports, 37,* 759–770.

Humphry, S. E., Hollenbeck, J. R., Meyer, C. J., et al. (2003). *Conscientious extroverts, agreeable extroverts and self-managed teams: A configural approach.* Paper, Society for Industrial and Organizational Psychology, Orlando, FL.

Hunt, D. M., & Michael, C. (1983). Mentorship: A career training and development tool. *Academy of Management Review, 8,* 475–485.

Hunt, J. B. (2000). Travel experience in the formation of leadership: John Quincy Adams, Frederick Douglass, and Jane Adams. *Journal of Leadership Studies, 7*(1), 92–106.

Hunt, J. E. (1968). Expectations and perceptions of the leadership behavior of elementary school principals. *Dissertation Abstracts, 28,* 4852–4853.

Hunt, J. G. (1967). Fiedler's leadership contingency model: An empirical test in three organizations. *Organizational Behavior and Human Performance, 2,* 290–308.

Hunt, J. G. (1971). Leadership-style effects at two managerial levels in a simulated organization. *Administrative Science Quarterly, 16,* 476–485.

Hunt, J. G. (1991). *Leadership: A new synthesis.* Newbury Park: Sage Publications.

Hunt, J. G. (1999). Transformation/charismatic leadership's transformation of the field: A short, historical essay. *Leadership Quarterly, 10,* 129–144.

Hunt, J. G., Boal, K. B., & Dodge, G. E. (1999). The effects of visionary and crisis-responsive charisma on followers: An experimental examination of two kinds of charismatic leadership. *Leadership Quarterly, 10,* 423–448.

Hunt, J. G., Boal, K. B., & Sorenson, R. L. (1990). Top management leadership: Inside the black box. *Leadership Quarterly, 1,* 41–65.

Hunt, J. G., & Conger, J. A. (1999). Charismatic and transformational leadership in organizations: an insider's perspective on these developing streams of research. *Leadership Quarterly, 10*(2), 145.

Hunt, J. G., & Dodge, G. E. (2001). Leadership déjà vu all over again. *Leadership Quarterly, 11,* 435–458.

Hunt, J. G., & Hill, J. W. (1971). *Improving mental hospital effectiveness: A look at managerial leadership* (Tech. Rep. No. 71–4). Carbondale: Southern Illinois University.

Hunt, J. G., Hill, J. W., & Reaser, J. M. (1971). *Consideration and structure effects in mental hospitals: An examination of two managerial levels* (Tech. Rep. No. 71–1). Carbondale: Southern Illinois University.

Hunt, J. C., Hill, J. W., & Reaser, J. M. (1973). Correlates of leadership behavior at two managerial levels in a mental institution. *Journal of Applied Psychology, 3,* 174–185.

Hunt, J. G., & Larson, L. L. (1975). In J. G. Hunt & L. L. Larson (eds.), *Leadership frontiers.* Kent, Ohio: Kent State University Press.

Hunt, J. G., & Liebscher, V. K. C. (1973). Leadership preference, leadership behavior, and employee satisfaction. *Organizational Behavior and Human Performance, 9,* 59–77.

Hunt, J. G., & Meindl, J. R. (1991). Chinese political economic reforms and the problem of legitimizing leader roles. *Leadership Quarterly, 2,* 189–204.

Hunt, J. G., Osborn, R. N., & Larson, L. L. (1975). Upper level technical orientation and first level leadership within a noncontingency and contingency framework. *Academy of Management Journal, 18,* 476–488.

Hunt, J. G., Osborn, R. N., & Martin, H. J. (1979). A *multiple influence model of leadership.* Unpublished manuscript. Also: Hunt, J. G., Osborn, R. N., & Martin, H. J. (1981). Tech. Rep. No. 520. Carbondale: Southern Illinois University Press.

Hunt, J. G., Osborn, R. N., & Schriesheim, C. A. (1977). *Omissions and commissions in leadership research.* Unpublished manuscript.

Hunt, J. G., Osborn, R. N., & Schriesheim, C. A. (1978). Some neglected aspects of leadership research. *Proceedings, Midwest Academy of Management Meetings,* 364–375.

Hunt, J. G., Osborn, R. N., & Schuler, R. S. (1978). Relations of discretionary and nondiscretionary leadership performance and satisfaction in a complex organization. *Human Relations, 31*(6), 507–523.

Hunt, J. G., & Peterson, M. F. (1997). International and cross-cultural research: Overview. *Leadership Quarterly, 8,* 201–202.

Hunt, J. G., & Phillips, R. L. (1991). Leadership in battle and garrison: A framework for understanding the differences and preparing for both. In R. Gal & A. D. Mangelsdorff (eds.), *Handbook of military psychology.* New York: Wiley

Hunt, J. G., & Ropo, A. (1995). Multi-level leadership: Grounded theory and mainstream theory applied to the case of General Motors. *Leadership Quarterly, 6,* 379–412.

Hunt, J. G., & Schuler, R. S. (1976), *Leader reward and sanctions: Behavior relations criteria in a large public utility.* Carbondale: Southern Illinois University. Department of Administrative Sciences.

Hunt, M. (1999). Leading with vision and values. *Leader to Leader, 1999(12),* 11.

Hunter, A., & Fritz, R. (1985). Class, status, and power structures of community elites: A comparative case study, *Social Science Quarterly, 66,* 602–616.

Hunter, E. C., & Jordan, A. M. (1939). An analysis of qualities associated with leadership among college students. *Journal of Educational Psychology, 30,* 497–509.

Hunter, F. (1953). *Community power structure.* Chapel Hill: University of North Carolina Press.

Hunter, J. E. (1986). Cognitive ability, cognitive aptitudes, job knowledge, and job performance. *Journal of Vocational Behavior, 29,* 340–362.

Hunter, J. E., & Hunter, R. F. (1984). Validity and utility of alternative predictors of job performance. *Psychological Bulletin, 96,* 72–98.

Hunter, J. E., & Schmidt, F. L. (1978). Differential and single group validity of employment tests by race: A critical analysis of three recent studies. *Journal of Applied Psychology, 63,* 1–11.

Hunter, J. E., & Schmidt, F. L. (1990). *Methods of meta analysis: Correcting error and bias in research findings.* Newbury Park, CA: Sage.

Huntford, R. (1984). *Scott and Amundsen: The race to the South Pole.* London: Pan.

Huntington, S. P. (1993). *The clash of civilizations and the remaking of the world order.* New York: Simon & Schuster.

Hurley, A. E., & Sonnenfeld, J. A. (1995). *The rise to the top: Is it really the cream?* Paper, Academy of Management, Vancouver, BC.

Hurley-Hanson, A. E., Stefan, W., Sonnenfeld, J., et al. (2003). *The impact of formal education on managerial career attainment.* Paper, Academy of Management, Seattle, WA.

Hurlock, E. B. (1950). *Child development.* New York: McGraw-Hill.

Hurwitz, J. I., Zander, A. F., & Hymovitch, B. (1953). Some effects of power on the relations among group members. In D. Cartwright & A. Zander (eds.), *Group dynamics.* Evanston, IL: Row, Peterson.

Husband, R. W. (1940). Cooperative versus solitary problem solution. *Journal of Social Psychology, 11,* 405–409.

Huse, E. F. (1962). Assessments of higher level personnel: IV. The validity of assessment techniques based on systematically varied information. *Personnel Psychology, 15,* 195–205.

Hutchins, E. B., & Fiedler, F. E. (1960). Task-oriented and quasi-therapeutic role functions of the leader in a small military group. *Sociometry, 23,* 393–406.

Hutchinson, S., Valentino, K., & Kirkner, S. L. (1998). What works for

the gander does not work as well for the goose: The effects of leader behavior. *Journal of Applied Social Psychology, 28,* 171–182.

Hyde, J. S. (1981). How large are cognitive gender differences? A meta-analysis using w2 and d. *American Psychologist, 36,* 892–901.

Hyman, B. (1980). Responsive leadership: The woman manager's asset or liability? *Supervisory Management, 25(8),* 40–43,

Hyman, H. H. (1942). The psychology of status. *Archives of Psychology,* No. 269.

Hyman, J., & Cunningham, I. (1998). Managers as developers: some reflections on the contribution of empowerment in Britain. *International Journal of Training and Development, 2(2),* 41–107.

Hyman, S. (1954). *The American presidency.* New York: Harper & Row.

Hymowitz. C. (1997a). Colleagues often have the wrong idea about why women quit. *Wall Street Journal,* January 11, B1.

Hymowitz, C. (1997b). Managing your career. *Wall Street Journal,* November 25, B1.

Hymowitz, C. (2003). In the lead: Innovative leadership and lofty goals cure ailing medical center. *Wall Street Journal,* August 26, B1.

Hymowitz, C., & Schellhardt, T. D. (1986). The glass ceiling: Why women can't seem to break the invisible barrier that blocks them from the top jobs. *Wall Street Journal,* March 24, Section 4, 1, 4–5.

Hynes, K., Feldhusen, J. F., & Richardson, W. B. (1978). Application of a three-stage model of instruction to youth leadership training. *Journal of Applied Psychology, 63,* 623–628.

Iacocca, L. (1984). *Iacocca: An autobiography.* New York: Bantam Books.

Ibarra, H. (1993). Personal networks of women and minorities in management: A conceptual framework. *Academy of Management Review, 18.* 56–87.

Ibarra, H. (1995). Race, opportunity, and diversity of social circles in managerial networks. *Academy of Management Journal, 38,* 673–703.

Ickes, W. J., & Barnes, R. D. (1977). The role of sex and self-monitoring in unstructured dyadic interactions. *Journal of Personality and Social Psychology, 35,* 315–330.

IDE (Industrial Democracy in Europe), International Research Group. (1979). Participation: Formal rules, influence, and involvement. *Industrial Relations, 18,* 273–294.

IDE (Industrial Democracy in Europe), International Research Group. (1981a). Industrial democracy in Europe: Differences and similarities across countries and hierarchies. *Organization Studies, 2,* 113–129.

IDE (Industrial Democracy in Europe), International Research Group. (1981b). *Industrial democracy in Europe.* Oxford: Clarendon Press.

Ilchman, W. F., & Uphoff, N. T. (1969). *The political economy of change.* Berkeley: University of California Press.

Ilgen, D. R. (1999). Teams embedded in organizations: Some Implications. *American Psychologist, 54,* 129–139.

Ilgen, D. R. & Davis, C. (2000). Bearing bad news: Reactions to negative performance feedback. *Applied Psychology: An International Review, 49,* 550–565.

Ilgen, D. R., Fisher, C. D., & Taylor, M. S. (1979). Consequences of individual feedback on behavior in organizations. *Journal of Applied Psychology, 64,* 349–371.

Ilgen, D. R., & Fujii, D. S. (1976). An investigation of the validity of leader behavior. *Journal of Applied Psychology, 61(5),* 642–651.

Ilgen, D. R., & Knowlton, W. A., Jr. (1980). Performance attributional effects on feedback from superiors. *Organizational Behavior and Human Performance, 25,* 441–456.

Ilgen, D. R., Mitchell, T. R., & Frederickson, J. W. (1981). Poor performers: Supervisors' and subordinates' responses. *Organizational Behavior and Human Performance, 27,* 386–410.

Ilgen, D. R., & O'Brien, G. (1974). Leader-member relations in small groups. *Organizational Behavior and Human Performance, 12,* 335–350.

Ilgen, D. R., Peterson, R. B., Martin, B. A., & Boeschen, D. A. (1981). Supervisor and subordinate reactions to performance appraisal sessions. *Organizational Behavior and Human Performance, 28,* 311–330.

Immegart, G. (1987). *Selection and training of headmasters.* Paper, 11th World Basque Congress, Bilbao, Spain.

Immelman, A. (1998). The political personalities of 1996: U.S. presidential candidates Bill Clinton and Bob Dole. *Leadership Quarterly, 9,* 335–366.

Inderrieden, E. J. (1984). Empirical investigation of the expanded work group structure model: The effects of leader needs and behavioral characteristics (technology, size, environment). *Dissertation Abstracts International, 46*(2A), 470.

Indik, B. P. (1963). Some effects of organization size on member attitudes and behavior. *Human Relations, 16,* 369–384.

Indik, B. P. (1964). The relationship between organization size and supervisory ratio. *Administrative Science Quarterly, 9,* 301–312.

Indik, B. P. (1965a). Organization size and member participation: Some empirical tests of alternative explanations. *Human Relations, 18,* 339–350.

Indik, B. P. (1965b). *Three studies of organizational and individual dimensions of organizations* (Tech. Rep. No. 15). New Brunswick, NJ: Rutgers, The State University.

Indik, B. P, Georgopoulos, B. S., & Seashore, S. E. (1961). Superior-subordinate relationships and performance. *Personnel Psychology, 14,* 357–374.

Indvik, J. (1985). *A path-goal theory investigation of superior-subordinate relationships.* Doctoral dissertation, University of Wisconsin, Madison.

Indvik, J. (1986a). Path-goal theory of leadership: A meta-analysis. *Proceedings, Academy of Management,* Chicago, 189–192.

Indvik, J. (1986b). *A path-goal theory investigation of achievement-oriented and participative leader message behaviors.* Paper, Academy of Management, Chicago.

Indvik, J. (1988). *A more complete testing of path-goal theory.* Paper, Academy of Management, Anaheim, CA.

Indvik, J. (2001). Women and leadership. In P. Northouse (ed.), *Leadership theory and practice.* Thousand Oaks, CA: Sage Publications.

Infante, D. A., & Gordon, W. E. (1985). Superiors' argumentativeness and verbal aggressiveness as predictors of subordinates' satisfaction. *Human Communication Research, 12,* 117–125.

Inglehart, R. (1981). Value change in the uncertain 1970's. In G. Dlugos & K. Weiermair (eds.), *Management under differing value systems: Political, social, and economical perspectives in a changing world.* Berlin: deGruyter.

Inglehart, R. (1997). *Modernization and postmodernization: Cultural,* economic, and political change in 43 societies. Princeton, NJ: Princeton University Press.

Inglehart, R., Basañez, M., & Moreno, A. (1998). *Human values and beliefs: Cultural values and beliefs: A cross-cultural source-book.* Ann Arbor, MI: University of Michigan Press.

Ingoldsby, E. M., Shaw, D. S., & Garcian, M. M. (2001). Intrafamily conflict in relation to boys' adjustment at school. *Development and Psychopathology, 13,* 35–52

Ingraham, L. C. (1981). Leadership, democracy, and religion: Role ambiguity among pastors in Southern Baptist churches. *Journal for the Scientific Study of Religion, 20,* 119–129.

Inkeles, A. (1966). The modernization of man. In M. Weiner (ed.), *Modernization.* New York: Basic Books.

Insch, G. S., Moore, J. E., & Murphy, L. D. (1997). Content analysis in leadership research: Examples, procedures, and suggestions for future use. *Leadership Quarterly, 8,* 1–25.

Inskon, A., Thibaut, J. W., Mochle, D., et al. (1980). Social evolution and the emergence of leadership. *Journal of Personality and Social Psychology, 39,* 431–448.

Institute for Social Research. (1954). *Task order 2* (annual report). Ann Arbor: University of Michigan.

Instone, D., Major, B., & Bunker, B. B. (1983). Gender, self confidence, and social influence strategies: An organizational simulation. *Journal of Personality and Social Psychology, 44,* 322–333.

Inzerilli, C., & Laurent, A. (1983). Managerial views of organization structure in France and USA. *International Studies of Management and Organization, 13,* 97–118.

Ippoliti, P. (1989). *The transformational transactional differences between new business and established business leaders.* Doctoral dissertation, Temple University, Philadelphia.

Ireland, R. D., & Miller, C. C. (2004). Decision-making and firm success. *Academy of Management Executive, 18*(4), 8–12.

Ireland, R. D., & Hitt, M. A. (1999). Achieving and maintaining strategic competence in the 21st century: The role of strategic leadership. *Academy of Management Executive, 13,* 43–57.

Iremonger, L. (1970). *The fiery chariot: A study of British prime ministers and the search for love.* London: Secker & Warburg.

Iremonger, L. (1970). *Political psychology, 21,* 729–744.

Ireson, C. J. (1976). *Effects of sex role socialization on adolescent female achievement.* Paper, Pacific Sociological Association, San Diego, CA.

Irvine, W. B. (2000–2001). Confronting relativism. *Academic Questions, 14*(1), 42–49.

Irwin, J. (1988). *Findings from the analysis of the effects of gender, ethnicity, personality, and degree of rater-ratee familiarity on 360-degree feedback assessments.* Paper, International Congress of Applied Psychology, San Francisco, CA.

Isenberg, D. G. (1981). Some effects of time-pressure on vertical structure and decision-making accuracy in small groups. *Organizational Behavior and Human Performance, 27,* 119–134.

Isenberg, D. G. (1984). How senior managers think. *Harvard Business Review, 62,* 81–90.

Ishikawa, K. (1985). *What is total quality control?* (Trans. D. J. Lu.) Englewood Cliffs, NJ: Prentice-Hall.

Italic Institute of America. (2002). *Italian surnames fail to reach the top.* http://italic.org/gianelle.

Ivancevich, J. M. (1970). An analysis of control, bases of control, and satisfaction in an organizational setting. *Academy of Management Journal, 13,* 427–436.

Ivancevich, J. M. (1974). A study of a cognitive training program: Trainer styles and group development. *Academy of Management Journal, 17,* 428–439.

Ivancevich, J. M. (1976). Effects of goal setting on performance and job satisfaction. *Journal of Applied Psychology, 61,* 605–612.

Ivancevich, J. M. (1979). An analysis of participation in decision making among project engineers. *Academy of Management Journal, 22,* 253–269.

Ivancevich, J. M. (1983). Contrast effects in performance evaluation and reward practices. *Academy of Management Journal, 26,* 465–476.

Ivancevich, J. M., & Donnelly, J. H. (1970a). Leader influence and performance. *Personnel Psychology, 23,* 539–549.

Ivancevich, J. M., & Donnelly, J. H. (1974). A study of role clarity and need for clarity for three occupational groups. *Academy of Management Journal, 17,* 28–36.

Ivancevich, J. M., & McMahon, J. T. (1982). The effects of goal setting, external feedback, and self generated feedback on outcome variables: A field experiment. *Academy of Management Journal, 25,* 359–372.

Ivancevich, J. M., Schweiger, D. M., & Ragan, J. W. (1986). *Employee stress, health, and attitudes: A comparison of American, Indian, and Japanese managers.* Paper, Academy of Management, Chicago.

Ivancevich, J. M., & Smith, S. V. (1981). Goal setting interview skills training: Simulated and on-the-job analyses. *Journal of Applied Psychology, 66,* 697–705.

Iverson, M. A. (1964). Personality impression of punitive stimulus persons of differential status. *Journal of Abnormal and Social Psychology, 68,* 617–626.

Izraeli, D. N. (1983). Sex effects or structural effects? An empirical test of Kanter's theory of proportions. *Social Forces, 62,* 153–165.

Jaap, T. (1982). Trends in management development: Introducing theory "P"—A British organizational model. *Training & Development Journal, 36*(10), 57–62.

Jablin, F. M. (1980). Superior's upward influence, satisfaction, and openness in superior-subordinate communication: A reexamination of the "Pelz effect." *Human Communication Research, 6,* 210–220.

Jablin, F. M. (1981). An exploratory study of subordinates' perceptions of supervisory politics. *Communication Quarterly,* 269–275.

Jablin, F. M. (1985). Task/work relationships: A life-span perspective. In M. L. Knapp & G. R. Miller (eds.), *Handbook of interpersonal communication.* Beverly Hills, CA: Sage.

Jackofsky, E. F., Slocum, J. W. Jr., McQuade, S. A. (1988). Cultural values and the CEO: Alluring companies? *The Academy of Management Executive, 2*(1), 39–49.

Jackson, E. M., & Hambrick, D. C. (2003). *Prestigious executives, directors, and backers of IPOs: Enduring advantage or fading gloss?* Paper, Academy of Management, Seattle, WA.

Jackson, J. M. (1953a). *The relation between attraction, being valued, and communication in a formal organization.* Ann Arbor: University of Michigan, Institute for Social Research.

Jackson, J. M. (1953b). The effect of changing the leadership of small work groups. *Human Relations, 6,* 25–44.

Jackson, J. M. (1960). Structural characteristics of norms. In G. E. Jensen (ed.), *Dynamics of instructional groups.* Chicago: University of Chicago Press.

Jackson, M. L., & Fuller, V. F. (1966). Influence of social class on students' evaluations of their teachers. *Proceedings, American Psychological Association,* New York, 269–270.

Jackson, P. B., & Wall, T. D. (1991). How does operator control enhance performance of advance manufacturing technology? *Ergonomics, 34,* 1301–1311.

Jackson, T. (2001). Cultural values and management ethics. *Human Relations, 54,* 1267–1302.

Jacob, F. E., & Ahn, C. (1978). *Impetus for worker participation.* Paper, International Sociological Association, Uppsala, Sweden.

Jacob, J. E. (1985). Black leadership in a reactionary era. *Urban League Review, 9*(1), 42–45.

Jacobs, H. L. (1976). A critical evaluation of Fiedler's contingency model of leadership effectiveness in its application to interdisciplinary taskgroups in public school settings. *Dissertation Abstracts International, 36,* 4912.

Jacobs, M., Jacobs, A., Feldman, G., & Cavior, N. (1973). Feedback II—the credibility gap: Delivery of positive and negative and emotional and behavioral feedback in groups. *Journal of Consulting and Clinical Psychology, 41,* 215–223.

Jacobs, M. T. (1991). *Short term America: The causes and cures of our business myopia.* Boston: Harvard Business School Press.

Jacobs, T. O. (1970). *Leadership and exchange in formal organizations.* Alexandria, VA: Human Resources Research Organization.

Jacobs, T. O., & Jaques, E. (1987). Leadership in complex organizations. In J. A. Zeidner (ed.), *Human productivity enhancement,* vol. 2. New York: Praeger.

Jacobs, T. O., & Jaques, E. (1990). Military executive leadership. In K. E. Clark & M. B. Clark (eds.), *Measures of leadership.* Greensboro, NC: Center for Creative Leadership.

Jacobsen, C., & House, R. J. (2001). Dynamics of charismatic leadership: A process theory, simulation model, and tests. *Leadership Quarterly, 12,* 75–112.

Jacobsen, E. N. (1984). The subordinate: A moderating variable between leader behavior and effectiveness. *Dissertation Abstracts International, 45*(7B), 2296.

Jacobson, E. (1951). Foremen and stewards, representatives of management and the union. In H. Guetzkow (ed.), *Groups, leadership, and men.* Pittsburgh: Carnegie Press.

Jacobson, E. (1971). *Depression.* New York: International Universities Press.

Jacobson, E., Charters, W. W., & Lieberman, S. (1951). The use of role concept in the study of complex organizations. *Journal of Social Issues, 7,* 18–27.

Jacobson, M. B., Antonelli, J., Opeil, D., & Winning, P. U. (1977). Women as authority figures: The use and nonuse of authority. *Sex Roles, 3*(4), 365

Jacobson, M. B., & Effertz, J. (1974). Sex roles and leadership: Perceptions of the leaders and the led. *Organizational Behavior and Human Performance, 12,* 383–396.

Jacobson, M. B., & Kock, W. (1977). Women as leaders: Performance evaluation as a function of method of leader selection. *Organizational Behavior and Human Performance, 20,* 149–157.

Jacoby, J. (1968). Creative ability of task-oriented versus person-oriented leaders. *Journal of Creative Behavior, 2,* 249–253.

Jacoby, J. (1974). The construct validity of opinion leadership. *Public Opinion Quarterly, 38,* 81–89.

Jacoby, J., Mazursky, D., Troutman, T., & Kuss, A. (1984). When feedback is ignored: Disutility of outcome feedback. *Journal of Applied Psychology, 69,* 531–545.

Jacofsky, E. F., & Slocum, J. W. (1988). CEO roles across cultures. In D. C. Hambrick (ed.), *The executive effect: Concepts and methods for studying top managers.* Greenwich, CT: JAI Press.

Jacques, D. (2000). *Learning in groups: A handbook for improving group work.* New York: Routledge.

Jaeger, D., & Pekruhl, U. (1998). Participative company management in Europe: The new role of middle management. *New Technology, Work and Employment, 13*(2), 94–103.

Jaffee, C. L. (1968). Leadership attempting: Why and when? *Psychological Reports, 23,* 939–946.

Jaffee, C. L., & Skaja, N. W. (1968). Conditional leadership in a two-person interaction. *Psychological Reports, 23,* 135–140.

Jaffe, D. T., & Scott, C. D. (1998). Reengineeering in practice: Where are the people? Where is the learning? *Journal of Applied Behavioral Science, 34,* 250–267.

Jaffee, S., & Hyde, J. S. (2000). Gender differences in moral orientation: A meta-analysis. *Pschological Bulletin, 126,* 703–726.

Jaggi, B. (1977). Job satisfaction and leadership style in developing countries: The case of India. *International Journal of Communication Sociology, 3,* 230–236.

Jago, A. G. (1978a). A test of spuriousness in descriptive models of participative leader behavior. *Journal of Applied Psychology, 63,* 383–387.

Jago, A. G. (1978b). Configural cue utilization in implicit models of leader behavior. *Organizational Behavior and Human Performance, 22,* 474–496.

Jago, A. G. (1982). Leadership: Perspectives in theory and research. *Management Science, 28,* 315–336.

Jago, A. G., & Ragan, J. W. (1986b). Some assumptions are more troubling than others: Rejoinder to Chemers and Fiedler. *Journal of Applied Psychology, 71,* 564–565.

Jago, A. G., Reber, G., Bohnisch, W., et al. (1993). *Cultures consequences? A seven-nation study of participation.* Proceedings, Decision Sciences Institute, Washington, D.C.

Jago, A. G., & Vroom, V. H. (1980). An evaluation of two alternatives to the Vroom/Yetton normative model. *Academy of Management Journal, 23,* 347–355.

Jago, A. G., & Vroom, V. H. (1982). Sex differences in the incident and evaluations of participative leader behavior. *Journal of Applied Psychology, 67,* 776–783.

Jambor, H. (1954). *Discrepancies in role expectations for the supervisory position.* Doctoral dissertation, University of Minnesota, Minneapolis.

James, D. (1995). Follow the leader: Some thoughts on leadership. *Journal of Leadership Studies, 2,* 162–164.

James, D. R., & Soref, M. (1981). Profit constraints on managerial autonomy: Managerial theory and the unmaking of the corporation president. *American Sociological Review, 46,* 1–18.

James, G., & Lott, A. J. (1964). Reward frequency and the formation of positive attitudes toward group members. *Journal of Social Psychology, 62,* 111–115.

James, L. R., Demaree, R. G., & Wolf, G. (1984). Estimating within-group interrater reliability with and without response bias. *Journal of Applied Psychology, 69*(1), 85–98.

James, L. R., & White, J. E. (1983). Cross-situational specificity in managers' perceptions of subordinate performance, attributions, and leader behavior. *Personnel Psychology, 36,* 809–856.

James, W. (1882). Great men, great thoughts, and their environment. *Atlantic Monthly, 46,* 441–459.

James, W. (1917). *Selected papers on philosophy.* New York: E. P. Dutton.

Jameson, S. H. (1945). Principles of social interaction. *American Sociological Review 10,* 6–12.

Janda, K. F. (1960). Towards the explication of the concept of leadership in terms of the concept of power. *Human Relations, 13,* 345–363.

Janis, I. L. (1972). *Victims of groupthink: A psychological study of policy decisions and fiascos.* Boston: Houghton Mifflin.

Janis, I. L. (1982). *Groupthink* (2nd ed.). Boston: Houghton Mifflin.

Janis, I. L., & Feshbach, S. (1953). Effects of fear-arousing communications. *Journal of Abnormal and Social Psychology, 48,* 78–92.

Janis, I. L., & Mann, L. (1977). *Decision making: A psychological analysis of conflict, choice, and commitment.* New York: Free Press.

Jansen, P. G. W., & Stoop, B. A. M. (2001). The dynamics of assessment center validity: Results of a 7-year study. *Journal of Applied Psychology, 86,* 741–753.

Janson, R. (1989). Achieving service excellence. *National Productivity Review, 8*(2), 129–143.

Janson, R. (undated). Eight steps toward company wide change. *Executive Excellence: Newsletter of personal development, managerial effectiveness, and organizational productivity.*

Janssen, O., & Van Yperen. (2004). Employees' goal orientations, the quality of leader-member exchange, and outcomes of job performance and job satisfaction. *Academy of Management Journal, 47,* 368–384.

Jaques, E. (1952). *The changing culture of a factory.* New York: Dryden Press.

Jaques, E. (1956). *Measurement of responsibility.* Cambridge, MA: Harvard University Press.

Jaques, E. (1966). Executive organization and individual adjustment. *Journal of Psychosomatic Research, 10,* 77–82.

Jaques, E. (1978). *General theory of bureaucracy.* Exeter, NH: Heinemann Books.

Jaques, E. (2001). *The great social power of the CEO.* Unpublished Draft.

Jaques, E., & Clement, S. D. (1991). *Executive leadership.* Cambridge, MA: Blackwell.

Jarvenpaa, S. L., Knoll, K., & Leidner, D. E. (1998). Is anybody listening out there? Antecedents of trust in global virtual teams. *Journal of Management Information Systems, 14*(4). 29–64.

Jarvenpaa, S. L., & Tanriverdi, H. (2003). Leading virtual networks. *Organizational Dynamics, 31*(4), 403–412.

Jassawalla, A. R., & Sashittal, H. C. (1999). Building collaborative cross–functional new product teams. *Academy of Management Executive, 13*(3), 50–63.

Jaussi, K. S., & Dionne, S. D. (2003). Leading for creativity: The role of unconventional leader behavior. *Leadership Quarterly, 14,* 475–498.

Jaussi, K. S., & Dionne, S. D. (2004). Unconventional leader behavior, subordinate satisfaction, effort and perception of leader effectiveness. *Journal of Leadership & Organizational Studies, 10*(3), 15.

Javidan, M. (1992). Managers on leaders: Developing a profile of effective leadership in top management. In K. E. Clark, M. B. Clark, & D. P. Campbell (eds.), *Impact of leadership.* Greensboro, NC: Center for Creative Leadership.

Javidan, M., Bemmels, B. V., Devine, K. S., et al. (1995). Superior and subordinate gender and the acceptance of superiors as role models. *Human Relations, 48,* 1271–1284.

Javidan, M., & Dastmalchian, A. (1993). Assessing senior executives: The impact of context on their roles. *The Journal of Applied Behavioral Science, 29,* 328–342.

Javidan, M., & House, R. J. (2001). Cultural acumen for the global manager: Lessons from Project GLOBE. *Organizational Dynamics, 29*(4), 289–305.

Javidan, M., & Waldman, D. A. (2001). *Exploring charismatic leadership in the public sector: Measurement and consequences.* Paper, Academy of Management, Washington, DC.

Javier, E. O. (1972). *Academic organizational structure and faculty/administrator satisfaction.* Doctoral dissertation, University of Michigan, Ann Arbor, MI.

Jaynes, W. E. (1956). Differences between jobs and between organizations. In R. M. Stogdill & C. L. Shartle (eds.), *Patterns of administrative performance.* Columbus: Ohio State University, Bureau of Business Research.

Jeannot, T. M. (1989), Moral leadership and practical wisdom. *International Journal of Social Economics, 16*(6), 14–38

Jeffrey, A. A., & Lee, S. D. (1996). The effects of CEO succession and tenure on failure in small organizations. *Journal of Applied Behavioral Science 32* (1): 70–88.

Jehn, K. A. (1995). A multimethod examination of the health benefits and detriments of intragroup conflict. *Administrative Science Quarterly, 40,* 256–282.

Jencks, C., Bartlett, S., Corcoran, M., et al. (1979). *Who gets ahead? The determinants of economic success in America.* New York: Basic Books.

Jenkins, C. D. (1976). Recent evidence supporting psychologic and social risk factors for coronary disease. *New England Journal of Medicine, 294,* 987–994, 1033–1038.

Jenkins, C. D. (1978). Behavioral risk-factors in coronary artery disease. *Annual Review of Medicine, 29,* 543–562.

Jenkins, C. D., Zyzanski, S., & Rosenman, R. H. (1976). Risk of new myocardial infarction in middle-aged men with manifest coronary heart disease. *Circulation, 53,* 342–347.

Jenkins, J. G. (1948). The nominating technique, its uses and limitations. In D. Krech & R. S. Crutchfield (eds.), *Theory and problems of social psychology.* New York: McGraw-Hill.

Jenkins, R. L., Reizenstein, R. C., & Rodgers, E. C. (1984). Probing opinions: Report cards on the MBA. *Harvard Business Review, 62*(5), 20–30.

Jenkins, W. O. (1947). A review of leadership studies with particular reference to military problems. *Psychological Bulletin, 44,* 54–79.

Jennings, C. (1999). *The time lord: The psychology of punctuality.* Sunday Daily Mail, London, 18–20.

Jennings, E. E. (1952a). The frustrated foreman. *Personnel Journal, 31,* 86–88.

Jennings, E. E. (1952b). Forced leadership training. *Personnel Journal, 31,* 176–179.

Jennings, E. E. (1960). *An anatomy of leadership: Princes, heroes, and supermen.* New York: Harper.

Jennings, E. E. (1967a). *Executive success: Stresses, problems, and adjustments.* New York: Appleton-Century-Crofts.

Jennings, E. E. (1980). *Profile of a black executive.* Cited in *World of Work Report,* April, 28.

Jennings, H. H. (1943). *Leadership and isolation.* New York: Longmans, Green.

Jennings, H. H. (1944). Leadership: A dynamic re-definition. *Journal of Educational Sociology, 17,* 431–433.

Jennings, H. H. (1947). Leadership and sociometric choice. *Sociometry, 10,* 32–49.

Jensen, M. B., & Morris, W. E. (1960). Supervisory ratings and attitudes. *Journal of Applied Psychology, 44,* 339–340.

Jensen, S. M. (2003). *Entrepreneurs as leaders.* Paper, Academy of Management, Seattle, WA.

Jensen, T. D., White, D. D., & Singh, R. (1990). Impact of gender, hierarchical position, and leadership styles on work-related values. *Journal of Business Research, 20,* 145–152.

Jenson, M. C., & Meckling, W. H. (1976). Theory of the firm: Managerial behavior, agency costs, and ownership structure. *Journal of Financial Economics, 3,* 305–360.

Jerdee, T. H. (1964). Supervisor perception of work group morale. *Journal of Applied Psychology, 48,* 259–262.

Jermier, J. M. (1993). Introduction. Charismatic leadership: Neo-Weberian perspectives. *Leadership Quarterly, 3–4,* 217–233.

Jermier, J. M. (1996). The path-goal theory of leadership: A subtextual analysis. *Leadership Quarterly, 7,* 311–316.

Jeswald, T.A. (1971). Research needs in assessment: A brief report of a conference. *Industrial Psychologist, 9*(1), 12–14.

Jiambalvo, J., & Pratt, J. (1982). Task complexity and leadership effectiveness in CPA firms. *Accounting Review, 57,* 734–750.

Jick, T. D. (1979). Mixing qualitative and quantitative methods: Triangulation in action. *Administrative Science Quarterly, 24,* 602–611.

Joe, V. C. (1971). Review of the internal-external control construct as a personality variable. *Psychological Reports, 28,* 619–640.

Johns, C. (1978). Task moderators of the relationship between leadership style and subordinate responses. *Academy of Management Journal, 21,* 319–325.

Johnson, A. C., Peterson, R. B., & Kahler, G. E. (1968). Historical changes in characteristics of foremen. *Personnel Journal, 47,* 475–481, 499.

Johnson, A. L., Luthans, F., & Hennessey, H. W. (1984). The role of locus of control in leader influence behavior. *Personnel Psychology, 37,* 61–75.

Johnson, A. M., Vernon, P. A., McCarthy, J., et al. (1998). *Born to lead: A behavior genetic investigation of leadership ability.* Paper, Society for Industrial and Organizational Psychology, Dallas, TX.

Johnson, A. M., Vernon, P. A., Harris, J. A., & Jang, K. L. (2004). A behavior genetic investigation of the relationship between leadership and personality. *Twin Research*, 7(1), 27–32.

Johnson, B. T., Mullen, B., & Salas, E. (1995). Comparison of three major meta-analytic approaches. *Journal of Applied Psychology*, 80, 94–106.

Johnson, C. (2000). Taoist leadership ethics. *The Journal of Leadership Studies*, 7(1), 82–91.

Johnson, C. E. (2001). *Meeting the ethical challenges of leadership: Casting light or shadow*. Thousand Oaks, CA: Sage Publications.

Johnson, D. E. (1969). *A comparison between the Likert management systems and performance in Air Force ROTC detachments*. Doctoral dissertation, University of Minnesota, Minneapolis.

Johnson, D. E. (1970). *Concepts of air force leadership*. Maxwell AF Base, AL: Air University.

Johnson, D. M., & Smith, H. C. (1953). Democratic leadership in the college classroom. *Psychological Monographs*, 67, No. 11.

Johnson, E. W. (1988). *Management and labor: Breaking away*. Chicago: DePaul University.

Johnson, F. (1976). Women and power: Toward a theory of effectiveness. *Journal of Social Issues*, 32, 99–110.

Johnson, J. R. (1998). Embracing change: A leadership model for the learning organisation. *International Journal of Training and Development*, 2, 141–150.

Johnson, L. A. (1969). *Employing the hard-core unemployed*. New York: American Management Association.

Johnson, M. (1993). *Moral imagination: implications of cognitive science for ethics*. Chicago: University of Chicago Press.

Johnson, M. C. (1980). Speaking from experience: Mentors—the key to development and growth. *Training & Development Journal*, 34(7), 55–57.

Johnson, R. E. (1980). A significance of rational behavior training in the leadership development of first-line supervisors. *Dissertation Abstracts International*, 41(2A), 597.

Johnson, R. H. (1973). *Initiating structure, consideration, and participative decision making: Dimensions of leader behavior*. Doctoral dissertation, Michigan State University, East Lansing.

Johnson, S. D., & Bechter, C. (1998). Examining the relationship between listening effectiveness and leadership emergence: Perceptions, behaviors, and recall. *Small Group Research*, 29, 432–471.

Johnson, V. E., & Brennan, L. L. (2002). *Building effective networks for corporate social responsibility*. Paper, Academy of Management, Denver.

Johnston, G. (undated). *A study of teacher loyalty to the principal: Rule administration and hierarchical influence of the principal*. Unpublished manuscript.

Johnston, G. (undated, b). *Relationships among teachers' perceptions of the principal's style, teachers' loyalty to the principal*. Unpublished manuscript.

Johnston, M. A. (2000). Delegation and organizational structure in small businesses: Influences of manager's attachment patterns. *Group & Organizational Management*, 25, 4–21.

Johnston, R. W. (1981). Leader-follower behavior in 3-D. Part 1. *Personnel*, 5(4), 32–42.

Jolson, M. A., Dubinsky, A. J., Yammarino, F. J., & Comer, L. B. (1993).

Transforming the salesforce with leadership. *Sloan Management Review*, 34(3), 95.

Jonas, H. S., Fry, R. E., & Srivestva, S. (1990). The office of the CEO: Understanding the executive experience. *Academy of Management Executive*, 4, 36–67.

Jone, G. R., & George, J. M. (1998). The experience and evolution of trust: Implications for cooperation and teamwork. *Academy of Management Review*, 23, 531–546.

Jones, D. (2000). Will business schools go out of business? E-learning, corporate academies change the rules. *USA Today*, May 24, 9A–10A.

Jones, A. R, James, L. R., & Bruni, J. R. (1975). Perceived leadership behavior and employee confidence in the leader as moderated by job involvement. *Journal of Applied Psychology*, 60, 146–149.

Jones, E. (1953). *The life and work of Sigmund Freud*, vol. 1. New York: Basic Books.

Jones, E. E. (1954). Authoritarianism as a determinant of first-impression formation. *Journal of Personality*, 23, 107–127.

Jones, E. E. (1964). *Ingratiation*. New York: Appleton-Century-Crofts.

Jones, E. E., & deCharms, R. (1957). Changes in social perception as a function of the personal relevance of behavior. *Sociometry*, 20, 7585.

Jones, E. E., Gergen, K. J., Cumpert, R., & Thibaut, J. W. (1965). Some conditions affecting the use of ingratiation to influence performance evaluation. *Journal of Personality and Social Psychology*, 1, 613–625.

Jones, E. E., Gergen, K. J., & Jones, R. E. (1963). Tactics of ingratiation among leaders and subordinates in a status hierarchy. *Psychological Monographs*, 77, No. 566.

Jones, E. E., & Pittman, T., S. (1982). Toward a general theory of strategic self-preservation. In J. Suls (ed.), *Psychological perspectives on the self*. Hillsdale, NJ: Erlbaum

Jones, E. E., & Wortman, C. (1973). *Ingratiation: An attributional approach*. Morristown, NJ: General Learning Press.

Jones, E. W. (1973). What it's like to be a black manager. *Harvard Business Review*, 51(3), 108–116.

Jones, E. W. (1986). Black managers: The dream deferred. *Harvard Business Review*, 64(3), 84–93.

Jones, G. R. (1983). Forms of control and leader behavior. *Journal of Management*, 9, 159–172.

Jones, R. E., & Jones, E. E. (1964). Optimum conformity as an ingratiation tactic. *Journal of Personality*, 32, 436–458.

Jones, R. E., & Melcher, B. H. (1982). Personality and the preference for modes of conflict resolution. *Human Relations*, 35(8), 649–658.

Jones, T. M. (1986). Corporate board structure and performance: Variations in the incidence of shareholder suits. In L.E. Preston (ed.), *Research in corporate social performance and policy*, vol. 8. Greenwich, CT: JAI Press.

Jones, T. M. (1991). Ethical decision making by individuals in organizations: An issue-contingent model. *Academy of Management Review*, 16, 366–395.

Jongbloed, L., & Frost, P. J. (1985). Pfeffer's model of management: An expansion and modification. *Journal of Management*, 11, 97–110.

Joon-hun, N. (1998). Flexible labor management spreading. *Korea Times*, January 25, 7.

Joplin, J. R.W., & Daus, C. S. (1997). Challenges of leading a diverse workforce. *Academy of Management Executive*, 11(3), 32–47.

Jordan, H. (1982). *Crisis: The last year of the Carter Presidency.* New York: G. P. Putnam & Sons.

Jordan, P. C. (1986). Effects of an extrinsic reward on intrinsic motivation: A field experiment. *Academy of Management Journal, 29,* 405–412.

Jöreskog, K. G., & Sorbos, D. (1978). LISREL VI: Analysis of linear structure. See J. S. Long, (1983). *Covariance Structure models: An introduction to LISREL.* Beverly Hills, CA: Sage.

Joynt, R. (1981–1982). Contingency research as a management strategy. *Journal of General Management, 7*(2), 24–35.

Judge, T. A., & Bono, J. E. (2000). Five-factor model of personality and transformational leadership. *Journal of Applied Psychology, 85,* 751–765.

Judge, T. A., & Bono, J. E. (2001). Relationship of core evaluations traits—self-esteem, generalized self-efficacy, locus of control, and emotional stability—with job satisfaction, and job performance: A meta-analysis. *Journal of Applied Psychology, 86,* 80–92.

Judge, T. A., Bono, J. E., Ilies, R., & Gerhardt, M. W. (2002). Personality and leadership: A qualitative and quantitative review. *Journal of Applied Psychology, 87*(4), 765–780.

Judge, T .A., Bono, J. E., Ilies, R., et al. (2000, 2001). *Personality and leadership: A review.* Paper, Society for Industrial and Organizational Psychology, New Orleans, LA. Also (2001). *Personality and leadership: A qualitative and quantitative review.* Paper, Academy of Management, Washington, DC.

Judge, T. A., Boudreau, J. W., & Bretz, R. D., Jr. (1994). Job and life attitudes of male executives. *Journal of Applied Psychology, 79,* 767–782.

Judge, T. A., Colbert, A. E., Ilies, R. (2004). Intelligence and leadership: A quantitative review and test of theoretical propositions. *Journal of Applied Psychology, 89,* 542–552.

Judge, T. A., Higgins, C. A., Thoresen, C. J., et al. (1999). The big five personality traits, general mental ability, and career success across the life span. *Personnel Psychology, 52,* 621–652.

Judge, T. A., Ilies, R., Bono, J. E., & Gerhardt, M. W. (2002). Personality and leadership: A qualitative and quantitative review. *Journal of Applied Psychology, 87,* 765–780

Judge, T. A., Piccolo, R. F., & Ilies, R. (2004). The forgotten ones? The validity of consideration and initiating structure in leadership research. *Journal of Applied Psychology, 89,* 36–51.

Judge, T. A., Thoresen, C. J., Bono, J. E., et al. (2001). The job satisfaction and job performance relationship. A qualitative and quantitative review. *Psychological Bulletin, 127,* 408–423.

Judge, W. O., Gryxell, G. E., & Dooley, R. S. (1997). The new tasks of R&D management: Creating goal-directed communities for innovation. *California Management Review, 39,* 72–85.

Judge, W. Q. (1999). *The leader's shadow: Exploring and developing the executive character.* Thousand Oaks, CA: Sage.

Judge, W. Q. (2001). Is a leader's character culture-bound or culture free? An empirical comparison of the character traits of American and Taiwanese CEOs. *Journal of Leadership Studies, 8*(2), 63–78.

Judiesch, M., & Lyness, K. (1998). Left behind: The impact of leaves of absence on managers' career success. *Academy of Management Journal, 42,* 41–851.

Julian, J. W. (1964). Leader and group behavior as correlates of adjust-

ment and performance in negotiation groups. *Dissertation Abstracts, 24,* 646.

Julian, J. W., & Hollander, E. R. (1966). *A study of some role dimensions of leader-follower relations* (Tech. Rep. No. 1). Buffalo, NY: State University of New York.

Julian, J. W., Hollander, E. P., & Regula, C. R. (1969). Endorsement of the group spokesman as a function of his source of authority, competence, and success. *Journal of Personality and Social Psychology, 11,* 42–49.

Jung, C. G. (1971). *Psychological types.* (Trans. R. F. C. Hall.) Princeton, NJ: Princeton University Press.

Jung, C. K. (1968). *Analytical psychology: Its theory and practice.* New York: Pantheon Books.

Jung, D. I. (1997). *Effects of different leadership styles and followers' cultural orientations on performance under various task structure and reward allocation conditions.* Binghamton, NY: Doctoral dissertation, State University of New York at Binghamton.

Jung, D. I. (2000–2001). Transformational and transactional leadership and their effects on creativity in groups. *Creativity Research Journal, 13*(2), 185.

Jung, D. I., & Avolio, B. J. (1998). Examination of transformational leadership and group process among Caucasians and Asian-Americans: Are they different? *Research in International Business and International Relations, 7,* 29–66.

Jung, D. I., & Avolio, B. J. (2000). Opening the black box: An experimental investigation of the mediating effects of trust and value congruence on transformational and transactional leadership. *Journal of Organizational Behavior,* in press.

Jung, D. I., Bass, B. M., & Sosik, J. J. (1995). Bridging leadership and culture: A theoretical consideration of transformational leadership and collectivist culture. *Journal of Leadership Studies, 2*(4).

Jung, D. I., Butler, M. C., & Ki Bok Baik. (1998). *Effects of transformational leadership on group members collective efficacy and perceived performance.* Paper, Society for Industrial and Organizational Psychology, New Orleans, LA.

Jung, D. I., Chow, C., & Wu, A. (2003). The role of transformational leadership in enhancing organizational innovation: Hypotheses and some preliminary findings. *Leadership Quarterly, 14,* 525–544.

Jung, D. I., & Yammarino, F. J. (2001). Perceptions of transformational leadership among Asian Americans and Caucasian Americans: A level of analysis perspective. *Journal of Leadership Studies, 8*(1), 3–21.

Juola, A. E. (1957). Leaderless group discussion ratings. What do they measure? *Educational and Psychological Measurement, 17,* 499–509.

Jurgensen, C. E. (1966). *Report to participants on adjective Word sort. Minneapolis: Minneapolis Gas Company.* Unpublished manuscript. Reported in Campbell, Dunnette, Lawler, & Weick (1970), 188–190.

Jurkiewicz, C. L., & Massey, T. K., Jr. (1997). What motivates municipal employees?: A comparison of supervisory and non-supervisory personnel. *Public Personnel Management, 26,* 367–377.

Jurma, W. E. (1978). Leadership structuring style, task ambiguity, and group member satisfaction. *Small Group Behavior, 9,* 124–134.

Justis, R. T. (1975). Leadership effectiveness: A contingency approach. *Academy of Management Journal, 18,* 160–167.

Kaarbo, J., & Hermann, M. G. (1998). Leadership styles of prime ministers: How individual differences affect the foreign policymaking process. *Leadership Quarterly, 9*, 243–263.

Kabanoff, B. (1981). A critique of LEADER MATCH and its implications for leadership research. *Personnel Psychology, 34*, 749–764.

Kabanoff, B. (1985a). *Do feelings of cooperativeness and assertiveness affect the choice of conflict management mode?* Paper, Academy of Management, San Diego, CA.

Kabanoff, B. (1985b). Potential influence structures as sources of interpersonal conflict in groups and organizations. *Organizational Behavior and Human Decision Processes, 36*, 113–141.

Kabanoff, B., & Daly, J. P. (2000). Values espoused by Australian and U.S. organizations. *Applied Psychology: An International Review, 49*, 284–314.

Kabanoff, B., & O'Brien, G. E. (1979). Cooperation structure and the relationship of leader and member ability to group performance. *Journal of Applied Psychology, 64*, 526–532.

Kacmar, K. M., Witt, L. A, & Zivnuska, S. (2001). *The impact of leader-member exchange on communication type, frequency, and performance.* Paper, Academy of Management, Washington, DC.

Kacmar, K. M., & Carlson, D. S. (1997). Further validation of the perceptions of politics scale: A multiple sample investigation—POPS—includes appendix. *Journal of Management*, 9–10.

Kaczka, E. E., & Kirk, R. V. (1967). Managerial climate, work groups, and organizational performance. *Administrative Science Quarterly, 12*, 253–272.

Kadushin, A. (1968). Games people play in supervision. *Social Work, 13*, 23–32.

Kagitçibasi, Ç. (1970). Social norms and authoritarianism: A Turkish-American comparison. *Journal of Personality and Social Psychology, 16*, 444–451.

Kahai, S. S. (2000). Challenges of the cyber-workplace. *Inside Binghamton University*, April 13, p. 10.

Kahai, S. S., Avolio, B. J., & Sosik, J. J. (1998). Effects of source and participant anonymity and difference in initial opinions in an EMS context. *Decision Sciences, 29*, 427–460.

Kahai, S. S., Sosik, J. J., & Avolio, B. J. (1997). Effects of leadership style and problem structure on work group process and outcomes in an eletronic meeting system environment. *Personnel Psychology, 50*, 121–146.

Kahai, S. S., Sosik, J. J., & Avolio, B. J. (2003). Effects of leadership style, anonymity, and rewards on creativity-relevant processes and outcomes in an electronic meeting system context. *Leadership Quarterly, 14*, 499–524.

Kahn, R. L. (1956). The prediction of productivity. *Journal of Social Issues, 12*, 41–49.

Kahn, R. L., & Katz, D. (1953, 1960). Leadership practices in relation to productivity and morale. In D. Cartwright & A. Zander (eds.), *Group dynamics.* New York: Harper & Row.

Kahn, R. L., & Quinn, R. P. (1970). Role stress: A framework for analysis. In A. McLean (ed.), *Mental health and work organizations.* Chicago: Rand McNally.

Kahn, R. L., & Tannenbaum, A. S. (1957). Leadership practices and member participation in local unions. *Personnel Psychology, 10*, 277–292.

Kahn, R. L., Wolfe, D. M., Quinn, R. R., Shoek, J. D., & Rosenthal, R. A. (1964). *Organizational stress: Studies in role conflict and ambiguity.* New York: Wiley.

Kahn, S. (1970). *How people get power.* New York: McGraw-Hill.

Kaiser, R. B., & Kaplan, R. E. (2001). *A new look at leadership versatility: Assessing the forceful and enabling polarity to executive development.* Unpublished manuscript.

Kakar, S. (1971). Authority patterns and subordinate behavior in Indian organizations. *Administrative Science Quarterly, 16*, 295–307.

Kakutani, M. (2006). Disparate conservative assessments of Bush. *New York Times*, February 21, Books of the Times.

Kalay, E. (1983). *The commander in stress situations in IDF combat units during the Peace for Galilee campaign.* Paper, Third International Conference of Psychological Stress and Adjustment in Time of War and Peace, Tel-Aviv, Israel.

Kalma, A. P., Visser, L., & Peeters, A. (1993). Sociable and aggressive dominance: Personality differences in leadership style? *Leadership Quarterly, 4*, 45–64.

Kamano, D. K., Powell, B. J., & Martin, L. K. (1966). Relationship between ratings assigned to supervisors and their ratings of subordinates. *Psychological Reports, 18*, 158.

Kamensky, J. M. (1996). The role of reinventing government movement in federal management reform. *Public Administration Review, 56*, 247–255.

Kamerman, J. B. (1981). A "scrutinization" of charisma: Charismatic authority and control in the work of the symphony orchestra conductor. Paper, Eastern Sociological Society, New York.

Kaminitz, H. (1977). The employers' approach to participation. In O. Karmi & A. Saar (eds.), *Proceedings, International Seminar on Workers Participation.* Israel: Bar Ilan University, The Israel Institute of Productivity and the Institute for the Advancement of Labor Relations.

Kan, M. M., & Parry, K.W. (2004). Identifying paradox: A grounded theory of leadership in overcoming resistance to change, *Leadership Quarterly, 15*, 467–491.

Kanaga, K., & Browning, H. (2003). Keeping watch: How to monitor and maintain a team. *Leadership in Action, 23*(2), 3–8.

Kanareff, V. T., & Lanzetta, J. T. (1960). Effects of task definition and probability or re-enforcement upon the acquisition and extinction of imitative responses. *Journal of Experimental Psychology, 60*, 340–348.

Kane, D. E. (1984). *A General Electric case study: Four critical steps to cultural change.* Unpublished manuscript.

Kane, J. D. (1976). The evaluation of organizational training programs. *Journal of European Training, 5*, 289–338.

Kane, T. D., & Baltes, T. R. (1998). *Efficacy assessment in complex social domains: Leadership efficacy in small task groups.* Paper, Society for Industrial and Organizational Psychology, Dallas, TX.

Kanouse, D. E., Gumpert, P., & Canavan-Gumpert, D. (1984). The semantics of praise. In J. H. Harvey, W. Ickes, & R. F. Kidd (eds.), *New directions in attributional research*, vol. 3. Hillsdale, NJ: Erlbaum.

Kanov, J. (undated). *Compassion as an organizational virtue.* Unpublished manuscript.

Kant, I. (1785/1959). *Foundations of the metaphysics of morals*, L. W. Beck, (trans.). New York: Notre Dame Press.

Kanter, R. M. (1976). Why bosses turn bitchy. *Psychology Today, 11*(5), 56–59, 88–91.

Kanter, R. M. (1977a, 1993). *Men and women of the corporation*. New York: Basic Books.

Kanter, R. M. (1977b). Some effects of proportions on group life: Skewed sex ratios and responses to token women. *Journal of Sociology*, 82, 965–990.

Kanter, R. M. (1982a). Dilemmas of participation: Issues in implementing participatory quality-of-work-life programs. *National Forum*, 62(2), 16–19.

Kanter, R. M. (1982b) Dilemmas of managing participation. *Organizational Dynamics*, 11(1), 5–27.

Kanter, R. M. (1983). *The change masters: Keys to successful innovation*. New York: Simon & Schuster.

Kanter, R. M. (1989). The new managerial work. *Harvard Business Review*, 67(6), 85–92.

Kanter, R. M., Stein, B. A., & Jick, T. D. (1991–1992). *The challenge of organizational change: how organizations experience it and leaders guide it*. New York: Free Press.

Kantrowitz, B., & Juarez, V. (2005). As growing numbers of female executives rise to the top, how will they change the culture of the workplace? *Newsweek*, October 24, 46–47.

Kanungo, R. N., & Conger, J. A. (1993). Promoting altruism as a corporate goal. *Academy of Management Executive*, 7(3), 37–48.

Kanungo, R. N., & Mendonca, M. (1996). *Ethical dimensions of leadership*. Thousand Oaks, CA: Sage.

Kanungo, R. N. & Mendonca, M. (1997). Ethics of leadership. *Encyclopedia of Applied Ethics*. Academic Press.

Kanungo, R. N., & Wright, R. (1983). A cross-cultural comparative study of managerial job attitudes. *Journal of International Business Studies*, 14, 115–129.

Kaplan, A. G., & Sedney, M. A. (1980). *Psychology and sex roles: An androgynous perspective*. Boston, MA: Little, Brown.

Kaplan, E. M., & Cowen, E. L. (1981). Interpersonal helping behavior of industrial foremen. *Journal of Applied Psychology*, 66, 633–638.

Kaplan, R. E. (1986). The warp and woof of the general manager's job. In B. Schneider & D. Schoorman (eds.), *Facilitating work effectiveness*. Lexington, MA: Lexington Books.

Kaplan, R. E., Drath, W. H., & Kofodimos, J. R. (1985). *High hurdles: The challenge of executive self-development* (Tech. Rep. No. 25). Greensboro, NC: Center for Creative Leadership.

Kaplan, R. E., Lombardo, M. M., & Mazique, M. S. (1985). A mirror for managers: Using simulation to develop management teams. *Journal of Applied Behavioral Science*, 21, 241–253.

Kaplan, R. E., & Mazique, M. (1983). *Trade routes: The manager's network of relationships* (Tech. Rep. No. 22). Greensboro, NC: Center for Creative Leadership.

Kaplan, R. E., Kofododimos, J. R., & Drath, W. H. (1987). Development at the top: A review and a prospect. *Research in Organizational Change and Development*, 1, 229–273.

Kappelman, S. K. (1981). *Teachers' perceptions of principals' bases of power in relation to principals' styles of leadership*. Doctoral dissertation, University of New Orleans, New Orleans.

Kappelman, S. K. (1981). Teachers' perceptions of principals' bases of power·in relation to principals' styles of leadership. *Dissertation Abstracts International* 42, 2405A. University Microfilms No. 81–25, 884.

Kark, R., & Shamir, B. (2002). The dual effect of transformational leadership: Priming relational and collective selves and further effects on followers. In B. J. Avolio & F. J. Yammarino (eds), *Transformational and charismatic leadership: The road ahead*. New York: JAI Press, New York.

Kark, R., & Shamir, B. (2002). *The influence of transformational leadership on followers' relational versus collective self-concept*. Paper. Academy of Management, Denver, CO.

Kark, R., Shamir, B., & Chen, G. (2003). The two faces of transformational leadership: Empowerment and dependency. *Journal of Applied Psychology*, 88(2), 246–255.

Karmel, B. (1978). Leadership: A challenge to traditional research methods and assumptions. *Academy of Management Review*, 3, 475–482.

Karren, R., & Zacharias, L. (2003). *The case against integrity tests*. Paper, Academy of Management, Seattle, WA.

Karseras, G. F. (1997). *Transformational leadership training in the financial services industry: A Delphi application*. Master's thesis, College of Cardiff, University of Wales, Cardiff, U.K.

Karson, S. C. (1979). Insurance industry and social responsibility. *Journal of Contemporary Business*, 8, 103–114.

Kash, D. E., & Rycroft, R. W. (1996). *Technology in a complex world*. Unpublished manuscript.

Kash, D. E., & Rycroft, R. W. (1997). Synthetic technology-analytic governance: the 21st century challenge. *Technological Forecasting and Social Change*, 54(1), 17–27.

Kasriel, J., & Eaves, L. (1976). The zygosity of twins: Further evidence on the agreement between diagnosis by blood groups and written questionnaires. *Journal of Biosocial Science*, 8(3), 263–266.

Kass, S. (1999). Employees perceive women as better managers than men, finds five-year study. *APA Monitor*, 30(8), 5.

Kassarjian, H. H. (1965). Social character and sensitivity training. *Journal of Applied Behavioral Science*, 1, 433–440.

Katerberg, R., & Hom, P. W. (1981). Effects of within-group and between-groups variation in leadership. *Journal of Applied Psychology*, 66, 218–223.

Kates, S. L., & Mahone, C. H. (1958). Effective group participation and group norms. *Journal of Social Psychology*, 48, 211–216.

Katner, G. (1996). Examining and confronting the esoteric leadership of militia groups in the United States. *Journal of Leadership Studies*, 3(3), 60–71.

Katz, D. (1951). Survey research center: An overview of the human relations program. In H. Guetzkow (ed.), *Groups, leadership and men*. Pittsburgh: Carnegie Press.

Katz, D., & Kahn, R. L. (1966, 1978). *The social psychology of organizations*. New York: Wiley.

Katz, D., Maccoby, N., Gurin, G., & Floor, L. (1951). *Productivity, supervision, and morale among railroad workers*. Ann Arbor: University of Michigan, Institute for Social Research.

Katz, D., Maccoby, N., & Morse, N. C. (1950). *Productivity, supervision, and morale in an office situation*. Ann Arbor: University of Michigan, Institute for Social Research.

Katz, D. J. (1987). *Introduction. Conference on Military Leadership: Traditions and Future Trends*. U.S. Naval Academy, Annapolis, MD.

Katz, E., Blau, P. M., Brown, M. L., & Strodtbeck, F. L. (1957). Leadership stability and social change: An experiment with small groups. *Sociometry*, 20, 36–50.

Katz, E., & Lazarsfeld, P. F. (1955). *Personal influence: The part played by people in the flow of mass communications.* New York: Free Press.

Katz, E., Libby, W. L., & Strodtbeck, F. L. (1964). Status mobility and reactions to deviance and subsequent conformity. *Sociometry, 27,* 245–260.

Katz, I. (1968). Factors influencing Negro performance in the desegregated school. In M. Deutsch, I. Katz, & A. R. Jensen (eds.), *Social class, race, and psychological development.* New York: Holt, Rinehart & Winston.

Katz, I. (1970). Experimental studies of Negro-white relationships. In L. Berkowitz (ed.), *Advances in experimental social psychology,* vol. 5. New York: Academic Press.

Katz, I. (1974). Cultural and personality factors in minority group behavior: A critical review. In M. L. Fromkin & J. J. Sherwood (eds.), *Integrating the organization.* New York: Free Press.

Katz, I., & Benjamin, L. (1960). Effects of white authoritarianism in biracial work groups. *Journal of Abnormal and Social Psychology, 61,* 448–456.

Katz, I., & Cohen, M. (1962). The effects of training Negroes upon cooperative problem solving in biracial teams. *Journal of Abnormal and Social Psychology, 64,* 319–325.

Katz, I., Epps, E. G., & Axelson, L. J. (1964). Effect upon Negro digit-symbol performance of anticipated comparison with whites and with other Negroes. *Journal of Abnormal and Social Psychology, 69,* 77–83.

Katz, I., Goldston, J., & Benjamin, L. (1958). Behavior and productivity in biracial work groups. *Human Relations, 11,* 123–141.

Katz, I., & Greenbaum, G. (1963). Effects of anxiety, threat, and racial environment on task performance of Negro college students. *Journal of Abnormal and Social Psychology, 66,* 562–567.

Katz, J. P., Werner, S., & Brouthers, L. (1999). Does winning mean the same thing around the world? National ideology and the performance of global competitors. (Derived from Lodge, G. C., & Thurow, L. (1999). *Journal of Business Research, 44,* 117–126.)

Katz, N. (2001). Sports teams as a model of workplace teams: Lessons and liabilities. *Academy of Management Executive, 15*(3), 56–67.

Katz, R. (1977). The influence of group conflict on leadership effectiveness. *Organizational Behavior and Human Performance, 20,* 265–286.

Katz, R., & Allen, J. J. (1985). Project performance and the locus of influence in the R & D matrix. *Academy of Management Journal, 28,* 67–87.

Katz, R., & Farris, G. (1976). *Does performance affect LPC?* Boston: Massachusetts Institute of Technology. Unpublished manuscript.

Katzell, R. (1987). *How leadership works.* Paper, Conference on Military Leadership: Traditions and Future Trends, United States Naval Academy, Annapolis, MD.

Katzell, R. A., & Guzzo, R. A. (1983). Psychological approaches to productivity improvement. *American Psychologist, 38,* 468–472.

Katzell, R. A., Barrett, R. S., Vann, D. H., & Hogan, J. M. (1968). Organizational correlates of executive roles. *Journal of Applied Psychology, 52,* 22–28.

Katzell, R. A., Miller, C. E., Rotter, N. G., & Venet, T. G. (1970). Effects of leadership and other inputs on group processes and outputs. *Journal of Social Psychology, 80,* 157–169.

Katzenbach, J. R. (1997). *Teams at the top.* Boston, MA: Harvard Business School Press.

Katz, R., Phillips, E., & Cheston, R. (1976). *Methods of conflict resolution: A re-examination.* Boston: Massachusetts Institute of Technology. Unpublished manuscript.

Katzenbach, J. R. (1997). *Teams at the top: Unleashing the potential of both teams and individual leaders.* Boston, MA: Harvard Business School Press.

Katzenbach, J. R. & Smith, D. K. (1994). The delicate balance of team leadership. *McKinsey Quarterly, 4,* 148–142.

Kaufman G. G., & Johnson, J. C. (1974). Scaling peer ratings: An examination of the differential validities of positive and negative nominations. *Journal of Applied Psychology, 59,* 302–306.

Kavanagh, M. J. (1975). Expected supervisory behavior, interpersonal trust and environmental preferences. Some relationships based on a dyadic model of leadership. *Organizational Behavior and* Human *Performance, 13,* 17–30.

Kavanagh, M. J., & Halpern, M. (1977). The impact of job level and sex differences on the relationship between life and job satisfaction. *Academy of Management Journal, 20,* 66–73.

Kavanagh, M. J., MacKinney, A. C., & Wolins, L. (1970). Satisfaction and morale of foremen as a function of middle manager's performance. *Journal of Applied Psychology, 54,* 145–156.

Kawasaki, G. (1992). Inspiration, inspiration, inspiration works. *Boardroom Reports,* November 15.

Kay, B. R. (1959). Key factors in effective foreman behavior. *Personnel, 36,* 25–31.

Kay, E., & Meyer, H. H. (1962). The development of a job activity questionnaire for production foremen. *Personnel Psychology, 15,* 411–418.

Kay, E., Myer, H. H., & French, J. R. P. (1965). Effects of threat in a performance appraisal interview. *Journal of Applied Psychology, 49,* 311–317.

Kaye, L. (1995). No time like the present: Management training finds home in China. *Far Eastern Review,* August 10, 65–66.

Kean, T. H., Hamilton, L. H., & Staff (2004). *The 9/11 Commission report: Final report of the National Commission on Terrorist Attacks.* New York: W. W. Norton.

Kearns, K. P. (1996). *Managing for accountability.* San Francisco: Jossey-Bass.

Kearny, W. J. (1979). Pay for performance? Not always. *MSU Business Topics, 27,* 5–16.

Keaveny, T. J., Jackson, I. H., & Fossum, J. A. (1976). *Sex differences in job satisfaction.* Paper, Academy of Management, Kansas City, MO.

Keeler, B. T., & Andrews, J. H. M. (1963). Leader behavior of principals, staff morale, and productivity. *Alberta Journal of Educational Research, 9,* 179–191.

Keeping, L. M., Brown, D. J., Scott, K., et al. (2003). *The effects of uncertainty and voice on performance appraisal reactions.* Paper, Society for Industrial and Organizational Psychology, Orlando, FL.

Kegan, R. (1982). *The evolving self: Problem and process in human development.* Cambridge, MA: Harvard University Press.

Kegan, R., & Lahey, L. L. (1984). Adult leadership and adult development: A constructivist view. In B. Kellerman (ed.), *Leadership: Multidisciplinary perspectives.* Englewood Cliffs, NJ: Prentice Hall.

Keichel, W., III. (1983). Wanted: Corporate leaders. *Fortune*, May 30, 135–140.

Keidel, R. (1990). The triangular approach to organizational design. *Academy of Management Executive, 4*(4), 21–37.

Keidel, R. W. (1984). Baseball, football, and basketball: Models for business. *Organizational Dynamics, 12*(3), 5–18.

Keiser, J. D. (2004). Chief executives from 1960–1989: A trend toward professionalization. *Journal of Leadership and Organizational Studies, 10*(3), 52–68.

Keiser, N. M., & Shen, J. (2000). Principals' and teachers' perceptions of teacher empowerment. *Journal of Leadership Studies, 7*, 115–121.

Keith, J. D., & Grasso, D. W. (1997). The relationships among leadersip in training organizations, training methods, and organization profitability. *Performance Improvement Quarterly, 10*(3), 56–66.

Keizal Doyukai 1958 Survey Report (1960). The structure and function of top management of large enterprises in Japan. In N. Kazuo (ed.), *Big business executives in Japan*. Tokyo: Diamond Press.

Keller, R. T. (1987). *A test of the path-goal theory of leadership with need for clarity as a moderator in research and development organizations*. Paper, Academy of Management, New Orleans.

Keller, R. T. (1989a). A test of the path-goal theory of leadership with need for clarity as a moderator in research and development organizations. *Journal of Applied Psychology, 74*, 208–212.

Keller, R. T. (1989b). *Toward a contingency theory of leader behavior and creative versus incremental innovative outcomes in research and development project groups: Report on the first wave of data*. Bethlehem, PA: Lehigh University, Center for Innovation Management Studies.

Keller, R. T. (1992). Transformational leadership and the performance of research and design project groups. *Journal of Management, 18*, 489–501.

Keller, R. T., & Szilagyi, A. D. (1976). Employee reactions to leader reward behavior. *Academy of Management Journal, 19*, 619–627.

Keller, T. (1999). Images of the familiar: Individual differences and implicit leadership theories. *Leadership Quarterly, 10*, 589–607.

Keller, T. (undated). *The self as guiding leadership sensemaking: An attachment perspective*. Jepson School of Leadership Studies, University of Richmond, Richmond, VA. Unpublished manuscript.

Keller, T., & Dansereau, F. (1995). Leadership and empowerment: A social exchange perspective. *Human Relations, 48*, 127–146.

Keller, W. (1989). '62 missile crisis yields new puzzle. *New York Times*, January 30, A2.

Kellerman, B. (1987). *The politics of leadership in America: Implications for higher education in the late 20th century*. Paper, Invitational Interdisciplinary Colloquium on Leadership in Higher Education, National Center for Postsecondary Governance and Finance, Teachers College, Columbia University, New York.

Kellerman, B. (2004). *Bad leadership: What it is, how it happens, why it matters*. Boston: Harvard Business School Press.

Kellerman, B., & Webster, S. W. (2001). The recent literature on public leadership: Reviewed and considered. *Leadership Quarterly, 12*, 485–514.

Kellett, J. B., Humphrey, R. H., & Sleeth, R. G. (2002). Empathy and complex task performance: Two routes to leadership. *Leadership Quarterly, 13*, 523–544.

Kelley, H. H. (1950). The warm-cold variable in the first impressions of persons. *Journal of Personality, 18*, 431–439.

Kelley, H. H. (1973). The processes of causal attribution. *American Psychologist, 28*, 107–128.

Kelley, H. H., & Arrowood, A. J. (1960). Coalitions in the triad: Critique and experiment. *Sociometry, 23*, 231–244.

Kelley, H. H., & Michela, J. L. (1980). Attribution theory and research. *Annual Review of Psychology, 31*, 457–501.

Kelley, L., & Worthley, R. (1981). The role of culture in comparative management: A cross-culture perspective. *Academy of Management Journal, 24*, 164–173.

Kelley, M. R. (1995). Productivity and information technology: The exclusive connection. *Management Science*.

Kelley, R. (1992). *The power of followership*. New York: Currency.

Kelley, W. R. (1968). The relationship between cognitive complexity and leadership style in school superintendents. *Dissertation Abstracts, 28*, 4910–4911.

Kellogg, C. E., & White, D. D. (1987). *Leader behaviors and volunteer satisfaction with work: The effect of volunteer motivation level*. Paper, Academy of Management, New Orleans.

Kelloway, E. K., & Barling, J. (1993). Members' participation in local union activities: Measurement, prediction, and replication. *Journal of Applied Psychology, 78*(2), 262.

Kelly, G. (1955). *Psychology of personal constructs*. New York: Norton.

Kelly, J. (1964). The study of executive behavior by activity sampling. *Human Relations, 17*, 277–287.

Kelly, M. (1993). Hillary Clinton and the politics of doing good. *International Herald Tribune*, May 25, 17.

Kelman, H. C. (1953). Attitude change as a function of response restriction. *Human Relations, 6*, 185–214.

Kelman, H. C. (1958). Compliance, identification, and internalization: Three processes of attitude change. *Journal of Conflict Resolution, 2*, 51–60.

Kelman, H. C. (1970). A social-psychological model of political legitimacy and its relevance to black and white student protest movements. *Psychiatry, 33*, 224–246.

Kelman, H. C. (1999). The interdependence of Israeli and Palistinian interdepence: The role of the other in existential conflicts. *Journal of Social Issues, 55*, 581–600.

Kelman, H. C. (2001). Ethical limits on the use of influence in hierarchical relationships. In J. M. Darley, D. M. Messick, & T. R. Tyler (eds.), *Social influences on ethical behavior in organizations*. Mahwah, NJ: Lawrence Erlbaum Associates.

Kelman, H. C., & Hamilton, V. L. (1989). *Crimes of obedience: Towards social psychology of authority and responsibility*. New Haven, CT: Yale University Press.

Kelsey, B. L. (1998). The dynamics of multicultural groups: Ethnicity as a determinant of leadership. *Small Group Research, 29*, 502–623.

Kemp, R. L. (1984). The city manager's role in emergency management. *Public Management, 66*(3), 9–12.

Kemp, R. M. (1983). Effective management of high technology projects. *Dissertation Abstracts International, 43*(12A), 4017.

Kemper, C. (1997). Culture counts in deals: International mergers fouled by missed small points. *Denver Post*, March 23.

Kenan, T. A. (1948). *A method of investigating executive leadership.* Doctoral dissertation, Ohio State University, Columbus.

Kenis, P. (1977). *A cross-cultural study of personality and leadership.* CA: Sage Publications.

Kennedy, J. (1985). *Measuring leadership experience based on relevant work history.* Paper, American Psychological Association, Los Angeles.

Kennedy, J. K. (1982). Middle LPC leaders and the contingency model of leadership effectiveness. *Organizational Behavior and Human Performance, 30,* 1–14.

Kennedy, M. M. (1995). Political mistakes of the newly promoted. *Across the Board, 32*(9), 52–54.

Kenney, R., Blascovich, J., & Shaver, P. R. (1994). Implicit leadership theories: Prototypes for new leaders. *Basic & Applied Social Psychology, 15,* 409–437.

Kenny, R. A., Blascovich, J., & Shaver, P. R. (1994). Corporate transitions, Lynchburg, Va. *Basic & Applied Social Psychology, 15,* 409–437.

Kenny, D. A., & Hallmark, B. W. (1992). Rotational designs in leadership research. *Leadership Quarterly, 3,* 25–41.

Kenny, D. A., & Zaccaro, S. J. (1983). An estimate of variance due to traits in leadership. *Journal of Applied Psychology, 68,* 678–685.

Kent, R. L., & Moss, S. E. (1994). Effects of sex and gender role on leader emergence. *Academy of Management Journal, 37*(5), 1335–1346.

Kerber, K. W., & Buono, A. F. (2003). *Leading a team of change agents in a global corporation: Leadership challenges in a global world.* Paper, Academy of Management, Seattle, WA.

Kerlinger, F. N. (1951). Decision-making in Japan. *Social Forces, 30,* 3641.

Kerman, N., & Hadley, M. (1986). The creation of political leaders in the context of American politics in the 1970s and 1980s. In C. F. Graumann & S. Moscovici (eds.), *Changing conceptions of leadership.* New York: Springer-Verlag.

Kern, A. G., & Bahr, H. M. (1974). Some factors affecting leadership climate in a state parole agency. *Pacific Sociological Review, 17,* 108–118.

Kernan, J. P. (1963). *Laboratory human relations training—its effects on the personality of supervisory engineers.* Doctoral dissertation, New York University, New York.

Kernberg, O. F. (1979). Regression in organizational leadership. *Psychiatry, 42*(1), 24–38.

Kernberg, O. F. (1984). Regression in organizational leadership. In M. F. R. Kets de Vries (ed.), *The irrational executive: Psychoanalytic explorations in management.* New York: International Universities Press.

Kerr, I. L. (1985). Diversification strategies and managerial rewards: An empirical study. *Academy of Management Journal, 28,* 155–179.

Kerr, J., & Slocum, J. W., Jr. (1987). Managing corporate culture through reward systems. *Academy of Management Executive, 1*(2), 99–108.

Kerr, S. (1975). On the folly of rewarding A, while hoping for B. *Academy of Management Journal, 18,* 769–783.

Kerr, S. (1977). Substitutes for leadership: Some implications for organizational design. *Organization and Administrative Sciences, 8,* 135–146.

Kerr, S. (1995). On the folly of rewarding A, while hoping for B. *Academy of Management Executive, 9*(1), 7–14. (Originally published in the *Academy of Management Journal,* (1975), *18,* 769–783.)

Kerr, S. (2004). Executives ask: How can organizations best prepare people to lead and manage others? *Academy of Management Executive, 18*(3), 118–120.

Kerr, S., Hill, K. D., & Broedling, L. (1986). The first-line supervisor: Phasing out or here to stay? *Academy of Management Review, 11,* 103–117.

Kerr, S., & Jermier, J. (1978). Substitutes for leadership: Their meaning and measurement. *Organizational Behavior and Human Performance, 22,* 374–403.

Kerr, S., & Schriesheim, C. (1974). Consideration, initiating structure, and organizational criteria—an update of Korman's 1966 review. *Personnel Psychology, 27,* 555–568.

Kerr, S., Schriesheim, C. A., Murphy, C. J., & Stogdill, R. M. (1974). Toward a contingency theory of leadership based upon the consideration and initiating structure literature. *Organizational Behavior and Human Performance, 12,* 62–82.

Kerr, S., & Slocum, J. W., Jr. (1981). Controlling the performances of people in organizations. In P. C. Nystrom & W. H. Starbuck (eds.), *Handbook of organizational design,* vol. 2. New York: Oxford University Press.

Kerr, W. A., & Speroff, B. J. (1951). *Measurement of empathy.* Chicago: Psychometric Affiliates.

Kersting, K. (2004). Accenting the positive: A new classification of positive personality traits paves the way for further research and implementation of the subfield. *Monitor on Psychology, 35*(7), 64–65.

Kesner, I. F., & Sebora, T. C. (1994). Executive succession: Past, present & future. *Journal of Management. 20*(2), 327.

Kessing, F. M., & Kessing, M. M. (1956). *Elite communication in Samoa: A study of leadership.* Stanford, CA: Stanford University Press.

Kessler, C. C. (1968). Differences between subordinates who are successful and less successful in meeting superiors' demands. *Dissertation Abstracts, 28,* 3866–3867.

Kessler, T. G. (1993). *The relationship between transformational, transactional, and laissez-faire leadership behaviors and job satisfaction in a research environment.* Ft. Lauderdale, FL: Nova University.

Ketchel, J. M. (1972). *The development of methodology for evaluating the effectiveness of a volunteer health planning organization.* Doctoral dissertation, Ohio State University, Columbus.

Ketchen, D. J., Jr., Snow, C. C., & Hoover, V. L. (2004). Improving firm performance by matching strategic decision-making processes to competitive dynamics. *Academy of Management Executive, 18*(4), 29–43.

Kets de Vries, M. F. R. (1980). *Organizational paradoxes. Clinical approaches to management.* London: Tavistock.

Kets de Vries, M. F. R. (1984). Managers can drive their subordinates mad. In M. F. R. Kets de Vries (ed.), *The irrational executive. Psychoanalytic explorations in management.* New York: International Universities Press.

Kets de Vries, M. F. R. (1988). Prisoners of leadership. *Human Relations, 41,* 261–280.

Kets de Vries, M. F. R. (1989). Leaders who self destruct: The causes and cures. *Organizational Dynamics, 17*(4), 5–17.

Kets de Vries, M. F. R. (1989). *Prisoners of leadership.* New York: Wiley.

Kets de Vries, M. F. R. (1994). The leadership mystique. *Academy of Management Executive, 8,* 73–92.

Kets de Vries, M. F. R. (1995). Leaders who go off the deep end: Narcissism and hubris. In M. F. R. Kets de Vries (ed.), *Life and death in the executive fast lane.* San Francisco: Jossey-Bass.

Kets deVries, M. F. R. (1997). The leadership mystique. In K. Grint (ed.), *Leadership: Classical, contemporary and critical approaches.* Oxford, England: Oxford University Press.

Kets de Vries, M. F. R. (2001). *The leadership mystique.* London: Prentice Hall.

Kets de Vries, M. F. R., & Miller, D. (1984). *The neurotic organization.* San Francisco: Jossey-Bass.

Kets de Vries, M. F. R., & Miller, D. (1984a). Group fantasies and organizational functioning. *Human Relations, 37,* 111–134.

Kets de Vries, M. F. R., & Miller, D. (1984b). *Leadership in organizations: Review, synthesis and application.* Paper, 75th Anniversary Colloquium Series, Harvard Business School, Boston.

Kets de Vries, M. F. R., & Miller, D. (1986). Personality, culture, and organization. *Academy of Management Review, 11,* 266–279.

Key, R. C. (1974). *A study of perceived organizational characteristics in persistent disagreement school districts and nonpersistent disagreement districts in the San Francisco Bay area.* Doctoral dissertation, University of Southern California, Los Angeles.

Keys, J. B., & Miller, T. R. (1984). The Japanese management theory jungle. *Academy of Management Review, 9*(2), 342–353.

Keys, B., Edge, A. G., Heinz, D. D., et al. (1986). *A cross-national study to evaluate differences between leadership relationships of managers in the U.S., Philippines, and Korea.* Paper, Academy of Management, Chicago.

Khadra, B. (1990). The prophetic-caliphal model of leadership. An empirical study. *International Studies of Management and Organization, 20*(3), 37–51.

Khaire, M. (2002). *Survival beyond succession: The impact of founder ideological zeal and organizational mortality.* Paper, Academy of Management, Denver, CO.

Khan, R., Dharwadkar, R., Brandes, P., et al. (2002). *Do institutional owner characteristics predict CEO compensation? A longitudinal explanation.* Paper, Academy of Management, Denver, CO.

Khan, R. H. (2002). *The strategic leadership of international alliances and their innovative performance.* Paper, Academy of Management, Denver, CO.

Khandwalla, R. (1973). Effect of competition on the structure of top management control. *Academy of Management Journal, 16,* 285–295.

Khatri, N., Ng, H. A., & Lee, T. H. (2001). The distinction between charisma and vision: An empirical study. *Asia Pacific Journal of Management, 18*(3), 373–393.

Khoubesserian, L. (1987). *Mikhail Gorbachev's leadership style.* Student paper, Binghamton University, Binghamton, NY.

Khurana, R. (2002). *Searching for a corporate savior: The irrational quest for charismatic CEOs.* Princeton, NJ: Princeton University Press.

Khuri, F. I. (ed.). (1981). *Leadership and development in Arab society.* Beirut, Lebanon: American University of Beirut, Center for Arab and Middle East Studies.

Kidd, J. S. (1958). Social influence phenomena in a task-oriented group. *Journal of Abnormal and Social Psychology, 56,* 13–17.

Kiefer, C. (1986). Leadership in metanoic organizations. In J. D. Adams (ed.), *Transforming leadership.* Alexandria, VA: Miles River Press.

Kiefer, C., & Senge, P. (1984). Metanoic organizations. In J. D. Adams (ed.), *Transforming Work.* Alexandria, VA: Miles River Press.

Kielson, D. C. (1996). Leadership: Creating a new reality. *Journal of Leadership Studies, 3*(4), 104–106.

Kiernan, J. P. (1975). A critical appreciation of Sundkler's leadership types in the light of further research. *African Studies, 34,* 193–201.

Kiggundu, M. N. (1983). Task interdependence and job design: Test of a theory. *Organizational Behavior and Human Performance, 31,* 145–172.

Kilbourne, C. E. (1935). The elements of leadership. *Journal of Coast Artillery, 78,* 437–439.

Kilcourse, T. (1985). A framework for training influential managers. *Journal of the European Industrial Training, 9*(4), 23–26.

Kilduff, M., & Day, D.V. (1994). Do chameleons get ahead? The effects of self-monitoring on managerial careers. *Academy of Management Journal, 37,* 1047–1060.

Kilinski-Dupuis, H., & Kottke, J. L. (1999). *Perceptions of personal and supervisor humor at work.* Paper, Western Psychological Association, Irvine, CA.

Killebrew, R. B. (1998). Learning from war games: A status report. *Parameters,* Spring, 122–132.

Kilmann, R. H., & Saxton, M. J. (1983). *Organizational cultures: Their assessment and change.* San Francisco: Jossey-Bass.

Kilmann, R. H., & Thomas, K. W. (1975). Interpersonal conflict-handling behavior as a reflection of Jungian personality dimensions. *Psychological Reports, 37,* 971–980.

Kim, H. (2000). *When will my boss step down?: Tenure rules in top management executive change in Japanese firms.* Doctoral dissertation, Massachussetts Institute of Technology, Cambridge, MA.

Kim, H. (2001). *Succession rules for CEOs in large Japanese institutions and agencies.* Doctoral dissertation. Massachussetts Institute of Technology, Cambridge, MA.

Kim, H., & Yukl, G. (1995). Relationships of self-reported and subordinate-reported leadership behaviors in managerial effectiveness and advancement. *Leadership Quarerly, 6,* 361–377.

Kim, J. (1993). Trimmer GE is making strides: Welch thinks small, acts big. *USA Today,* 2B.

Kim, K. I., & Organ, D. W. (1982). Determinants of leader-subordinate exchange relationships. *Group & Organization Studies, 7,* 77–89.

Kimball, L., & Eunice, A. (1999). The virtual team: Strategies to opimize performance. *Health Forum Journal, 42*(3), 58–62.

Kimberly, J. R., & Evanisko, M. J. (1981). Organizational innovation: The influence of individual organizational and contextual factors on hospital adoption of technological and administrative innovations. *Academy of Management Journal, 24,* 689–713.

Kimmel, S. B. (2002). *Sources of interpersonal power and barriers to female candidacy for political office.* Doctoral dissertation, University of Southern Mississippi, Hattiesburg, Mississippi.

Kincheloe, S. C. (1928). The prophet as a leader. *Sociology and Social Research, 12,* 461–468.

Kinder, B. N., & Kolmann, R. R. (1976). The impact of differential shifts in leader structure on the outcome of internal and external group participants. *Journal of Clinical Psychology, 32,* 857–863.

Kinder, D. R. (1981). President, prosperity, and public opinion. *Public Opinion Quarterly, 45*(1), 1–21.

Kindler, H. S. (1996). More ways to manage conflict and disagreement. In E. Beich & J. E. Jones (eds), *The HR Handbook,* vol. 1. Amherst, MA: HRD Press.

King, A. S. (1971). Self-fulfilling prophecies in training the hard-core: Supervisors' expectations and the underprivileged workers' performance. *Social Science Quarterly, 52,* 369–378.

King, A. Y. C., & Bond, M. H. (1985). The Confucian paradigm of man: A sociological view. In W. Tseng & D. Wu (eds.), *Chinese culture and mental health: An overview.* New York: Academic Press.

King, D. C., & Bass, B. M. (1974). Leadership, power, and influence. In H. L. Fromkin & J. J. Sherwood (eds.), *Integrating the organization.* New York: Free Press.

King, H. D., & Arlinghaus, C. G. (1976). *Interaction management validated in the steel industry.* Unpublished manuscript.

King, M. L., Jr. (1968). The role of the behavioral scientist in the civil rights movement. *Journal of Social Issues, 24,* 1–12.

King, W. C., & Miles, E. W. (1995). A quasi-experimental assessment of the effect of computerizing non-cognitive paper-and-pencil measurement: A test of measurement equivalence. *Journal of Applied Psychology, 80,* 643–651.

Kingsbury, K. (2006). Losing our faith: At the World Economic Forum, leaders will try to understand why people no longer trust authority. *Time,* Bonus Section, January 30, A7, A10.

Kingsley, L. (1967). Process analysis of a leaderless counter-transference group. *Psychological Reports, 20,* 555–562.

Kinicki, A. J., & Schriesheim, C. A. (1978). Teachers as leaders: A moderator variable approach. *Journal of Educational Research, 70,* 928–935.

Kinicki, A. J., & Vecchio, R. P. (1994). Influences on the quality of supervisor-subordinate relations: The role of time-pressure, organizational commitment, and locus of control. *Journal of Organizational Behavior, 15*(1), 75–82.

Kinlaw, D. C. (1991). *Developing superior work teams: Building quality and the competitive edge.* Lexington, MA: Lexington Books.

Kipmis, D. (1958). The effects of leadership style and leaderless power upon the inducement of an attitude change. *Journal of Abnormal and Social Psychology, 57,* 173–180.

Kipnis, D. (1964). Mobility expectations and attitudes toward industrial structure. *Human Relations, 17,* 57–72.

Kipnis, D. (1972). Does power corrupt? *Journal of Personality and Social Psychology, 24,* 33–41.

Kipnis, D. (1976). *The powerholders.* Chicago: University of Chicago Press.

Kipnis, D. (1984). Technology, power and control. *Research in the Sociology of Organizations, 3,* 125–156.

Kipnis, D. (1987). Psychology and behavioral technology. *American Psychologist, 42,* 30–36.

Kipnis, D. (1993). Unanticipated consequences of using behavior technology. *Leadership Quarterly, 4,* 149–171.

Kipnis, D., Castell, R. J., Gergen, M., & Mauch, D. (1976). Metamorphic effects of power. *Journal of Applied Psychology, 61,* 127–135.

Kipnis, D., & Cosentino, J. (1969). Use of leadership powers in industry. *Journal of Applied Psychology, 53,* 460–466.

Kipnis, D., & Lane, W. P. (1962). Self-confidence and leadership. *Journal of Applied Psychology, 46,* 291–295.

Kipnis, D., & Schmidt, S. M. (1983). Upward Influence styles: Relationship with performance evaluations, salary, and stress. *Administrative Science Quarterly, 33,* 528–542.

Kipnis, D., & Schmidt, S. M. (1983). An influence perspective on bargaining within organizations. In M. H. Bazerman & R. I. Lewicki (eds.), *Negotiating in organizations.* Beverly Hills, CA: Sage.

Kipnis, D., Schmidt, S. M., Price, K., & Stitt, C. (1981). Why do I like thee: Is it your performance or my orders? *Journal of Applied Psychology, 66,* 324–328.

Kipnis, D., Schmidt, S. M., Swaffin-Smith, C., & Wilkinson, I. (1984). Patterns of managerial influence: Shotgun managers, tacticians, and bystanders. *Organizational Dynamics, 12*(3), 58–67.

Kipnis, D., Schmidt, S. M., & Wilkinson, I. (1980). Intraorganizational influence tactics: Explorations in getting one's way. *Journal of Applied Psychology, 65,* 440–452.

Kipnis, D., Silverman, A., & Copeland, C. (1973). Effects of emotional arousal on the use of supervised coercion with black and union members. *Journal of Applied Psychology, 57,* 38–43.

Kipnis, D., & Vanderveer, R. (1971). Ingratiation and the use of power. *Journal of Personality and Social Psychology, 17,* 280–286.

Kipnis, D., & Wagner, C. (1967). Character structure and response to leadership. *Journal of Experimental Research in Personality, 1,* 16–24.

Kirby, P. C., Paradise, L. V., & King, M. I. (1992). Extraordinary leaders in education: Understanding transformational leadership. *Journal of Educational Research, 85*(5), 303.

Kirchmeyer, C. (1990). A profile of managers active in office politics, *Basic & Applied Social Psychology, 11,* 339–356.

Kirchmeyer, C. (1998). Determinants of managerial career success: Evidence and explanation of male/female differences. *Journal of Management, 24,* 673–692.

Kirchner, W. K. (1961). Differences between better and less effective supervisors in appraisal of their subordinates. *American Psychologist, 16,* 432–433 (Abstract).

Kirchner, W. K., & Reisberg, D. J. (1962). Differences between better and less effective supervisors in appraisal of subordinates. *Personnel Psychology, 15,* 295–302.

Kirke, L. B., & Aldrich, H. E. (1983). Mintzberg was right!: A replication and extension of the nature of managerial work. *Management Science, 29,* 975–984.

Kirke, L. B., & Stein, A. W. (1986). *What made Alexander great? Strategy and tactics.* Paper, Academy of Management, Chicago; IL.

Kirkhart, R. O. (1963). Minority group identification and group leadership. *Journal of Social Psychology, 59,* 111–117.

Kirkman, B. L., Gibson, C. B., & Shapiro, D. L. (2001). "Exporting" teams: Enhancing the effectiveness of work teams in global affiliates. *Organizational Dynamics, 30*(1), 12–29.

Kirkpatrick, D. L. (1954). *Evaluating human relations programs for industrial foremen and supervisors.* Doctoral dissertation, University of Wisconsin, Madison.

Kirkpatrick, D. L. (1976). Evaluation of training. In R. L. Craig (ed.),

Training and development handbook: A guide to human resource development (2nd ed.). New York: McGraw-Hill.

Kirkpatrick, J. J. (1960). *Background history factors that lead to executive success.* Paper, American Psychological Association, Chicago.

Kirkpatrick, J. J. (1966). *Five-year follow-up study of the American Chamber of Commerce standard application for employment form.* Washington, DC: U.S. Chamber of Commerce.

Kirkpatrick J. P., et al. (1999). The policy termination process. *Policy Studies Review 16*, 209–216.

Kirkpatrick, S. A. & Locke, E. A. (1991). Leadership: Do traits matter? *Academy of Management Executive, 5*, 48–60.

Kirkpatrick, S. A., & Locke, E. A. (1996). Direct and indirect effects of three core charismatic leadership components on performance and attitudes. *Journal of Applied Psychology, 81*(1), 36–51.

Kirkpatrick, S. A., Wofford, J. C., & Baum, J. R. (2002). Measuring motive imagery contained in the vision statement. *Leadership Quarterly, 13*(2), 139–150.

Kirmeyer, S. L., & Lin, T. (1987). Social support: Its relationship to observed communication with peers and superiors. *Academy of Management Journal, 30*, 138–151.

Kirnan, J,. Bragge, J. D., Brecher, E., et al. (2001). What race am I? The need for standardization in race question wording. *Public Personnel Management, 30*, 211–220.

Kirton, M. J. (1976). Adaptors and innovators: A description and measure. *Journal of Applied Psychology, 61*, 622–629.

Kirton, M. J. (1980). Adaptors and innovators in organizations. *Human Relations*, 213–224.

Kirton, M. J. (1989). *Adaptors and innovators: Styles of creativity and problem solving.* London: Routledge.

Kirton, M. J., & DeCiantis, S. M. (1986). Cognitive style and personality: The Kirton adaptation and Cattell's sixteen personality factor inventories. *Personality and Individual Differences, 7*(2), 141–146.

Kissinger, H. (1994). *Diplomacy.* New York: Simon & Schuster.

Klagge, J. (1995). Unity or diversity: A two-headed opportunity for today's leaders. *Leadership and Organization Development Journal, 16*(4), 45–47.

Klagge, J. (1995). Leadership: A notion come of age. *Journal of Leadership Studies, 2*(2), 20–26.

Klagge, J. (1996). The leadership role of today's middle manager. *Journal of Leadership Studies, 3*(3), 11–19.

Klauss, R. (1981). *Senior executive service competencies: A superior manager's model.* Unpublished manuscript.

Klauss, R., & Bass, B. M. (1974). Group influence of individual behavior across cultures. *Journal of Cross-cultural Psychology, 5*, 236–246.

Klauss, R., & Bass, B. M. (1981). *Impact of communication.* New York: Academic Press.

Klauss, R., & Bass, B. M. (1982). *Interpersonal communication in organizations.* New York: Academic Press.

Klauss, R. Flanders, L., Fisher, D., & Carlson, D. (1981b). *Analyzing managerial roles in the federal government.* Paper, Academy of Management, San Diego, CA.

Klebanoff, H. E. (1976). Leadership: An investigation of its distribution in task-oriented small groups. *Dissertation Abstracts International, 36*, 3614.

Kleck, B., Ono, H., & Hastorf, A. H. (1966). The effects of physical space upon face-to-face interaction. *Human Relations, 19*, 425–436.

Kleck, R. E., & Nuessle, W. (1968). Congruence between the indicative and communicative functions of eye contact in interpersonal relations. *British Journal of Social and Clinical Psychology, 7*, 241–246.

Klein, A. F. (1956). *Role playing in leadership training and group problem solving.* New York: Association Press.

Klein, A. L. (1976). Changes in leadership appraisal as a function of the stress of a simulated panic situation. *Journal of Personality and Social Psychology, 34*, 1143–1154.

Klein, E. E. (2000). The impact on information technology on leadership opportunities for women: The leveling of the playing field. *Journal of Leadership Studies, 7*(3), 88–98.

Klein, H. J., & Kim, J. S. (1998). A field study of the influence of situational constraints, leader-member exchange, and goal commitment on performance. *Academy of Management Journal, 41*, 88–95.

Klein, K. J., & House, R. J. (1995). On fire: Charismatic leadership and levels of analysis. *Leadership Quarterly, 6*, 183–198.

Klein, K. J., & Ralls, R. S. (1994). The organizational dynamics of computerized technology implementation: A review of the empirical literature. In L. Gomez-Meija & M. W. Lawless (eds.), *Implementation and management in high technology.* Greenwich, CT: JAI Press.

Klein, M. I. (1992). *Corporate culture and store performance: Differences among high performance and low performance stores.* Doctoral dissertation, Temple University, Philadelphia, PA.

Klein, S. M., & Maher, J. R. (1966). Education and satisfaction with pay. *Personnel Psychology, 18*, 195–208.

Klein, S. M., & Maher, J. R. (1968). Educational level, attitudes, and future expectations among first-level management. *Personnel Psychology, 21*, 43–53.

Klein, S. M., & Maher, J. R. (1970). Decision-making autonomy and perceived conflict among first-level management. *Personnel Psychology, 23*, 481–492.

Kleinmann, M., Kuptisch, C., & Köller, O. (1996). Transparency: A necessary requirement for the construct validity of assessment centers. *Applied Psychology: An International Review, 45*(1), 67–84.

Klenke, K. (1993). Leadership education at the great divide: Crossing into the twenty-first century. *Journal of Leadership Studies, 1*(1), 111–127.

Klepinger, B. W. (1980). The leadership behavior of executives of social service organizations as related to managerial effectiveness and employee satisfaction. *Dissertation Abstracts International, 41*(5A), 2295.

Klimoski, R. (2005). There is nothing as dangerous as a bad theory. *Academy of Management Learning & Education, 4*, 74.

Klimoski, R. J., Friedman, B. A., & Weldon, E. (1980). Leader influence in the assessment of performance. *Personnel Psychology, 33*, 389–401.

Klimoski, R. J., & Hayes, N. J. (1980). Leader behavior and subordinate motivation. *Personnel Psychology, 33*, 543–555.

Klimoski, R. J., & Strickland, W. J. (1977). Assessment centers: valid or merely prescient. *Personnel Psychology, 30*, 353–361.

Kline, B. E., & Martin, N. H. (1958). Freedom, authority, and decentralization. *Harvard Business Review, 36*(3), 69–75.

Kling, K.C., Hyde, J. S., Showers, C. J., et al. (1999). Gender differences in self-esteem: A meta-analysis. *Psychological Bulletin, 125,* 470–500.

Klofper, P. H. (1969). *Habitats and territories: A study of the use of space by animals.* New York: Basic Books.

Klonsky, B. G. (1978). *Family structure, socialization, and aspects of female social and personality development: Some neglected leads and unfinished business.* Paper, American Psychological Association, Toronto.

Klonsky, B. G. (1983). The socialization and development of leadership ability. *Genetic Psychology Monographs, 108,* 95–135.

Klonsky, B. G. (1987). *The socialization and development of leadership ability and responsibility in female adolescents: A multi-ethnic analysis.* Unpublished manuscript.

Klopp, H., & Tarey, B. (1991). *The adventure of leadership.* Stamford, CT: Longmeadow Press.

Klubeck, S., & Bass, B. M. (1954). Differential effects of training on persons of different leadership status. *Human Relations, 7,* 59–72.

Kluger, A. N., & DeNisi, A. (1996). The effects of feedback interventions on performance: A historical review, a meta-analysis, and a preliminary feedback intervention theory. *Psychological Bulletin, 119,* 254–284.

Kmetz, J. T., & Willower, D. J. (1982). Elementary school principals' work behavior. *Educational Administration Quarterly, 18,* 62–78.

Knapp, D. E., & Knapp, D. (1966). Effect of position on group verbal conditioning. *Journal of Social Psychology, 69,* 95–99.

Knapp, M. L., Stohl, C., & Reardon, K. (1981). Memorable messages. *Journal of Communication, 31,* 27–42.

Knickerbocker, I. (1948). Leadership: A conception and some implications. *Journal of Social Issues, 4,* 23–40.

Knight, D., Pearce, C. L., Smith, K. G., et al. (1999). Top management team diversity, group process, and strategic consensus. *Strategic Management Journal, 20*(5), 445–465.

Knight, P. A. (1984). Heroism versus competence: Competing explanations for the effects of experimenting and consistent management. *Organizational Behavior and Human Performance, 33,* 307–322.

Knight, P. A., & Weiss, H. M. (1980). Effect of selection agent and leader origin on leader influence and group member perceptions. *Organizational Behavior and Human Performance, 26,* 7–21.

Knights, E., & Morgan, G. (1992). Leadership and corporate strategy: Toward a critical analysis. *Leadership Quarterly, 3,* 186.

Knott, K. B., & Natalle, E. J. (1997). Sex differences, organizational level, and superiors' evaluation of managerial leadership. *Management Communication Quarterly, 10,* 523–540.

Knowlton, W. (1979). *The effects of stress, experience, and intelligence on dyadic leadership performance.* Doctoral dissertation, University of Washington, Seattle.

Knowlton, W., & McGee, M. (1994). *Strategic leadership and personality: Making the MBTI relevant.* National Defense University, Washington, DC.

Knowlton, W. A., & Mitchell, T. R. (1980). Effects of causal attributions on a supervisor's evaluation of subordinate performance. *Journal of Applied Psychology, 65,* 459–466.

Kobasa, S. C., Maddi, S. R., & Puccetti, M. C. (1982). Personality and exercise as buffers in the stress-illness relationship. *Journal of Behavioral Medicine, 5*(4), 391–404.

Kobasa, S. C., Maddi, S. R., & Kahn, S. (1982). Hardiness and health: A prospective study. *Journal of Personality and Social Psychology, 42,* 168–77.

Koberg, C. S., Boss, R. W., Senjem, J. C., et al. (1999). *Group and Organizational Management, 24,* 71–91.

Kochan, T. A., Cummings, L. L., & Huber, G. P. (1976). Operationalizing the concepts of goals and goal incompatibilities in organizational behavior research. *Human Relations, 29,* 527–544.

Kochan, T. A., Schmidt, S. M., & de Cotiis, T. A. (1975). Superiorsubordinate relations: Leadership and headship. *Human Relations, 28,* 279–294.

Koene, B. A. S., Vogelaar, A. L. W., & Soeters, J. L. (2002). Leadership effects on organizational climate and financial performance: Local leadership effect in chain organizations. *Leadership Quarterly, 13,* 193–215.

Koff, L. A. (1973). Age, experience and success among women managers. *Management Review, 62,* 65–66.

Koff, L. A., & Handlon, J. H. (1975). Women in management—key to success or failure. *Personnel Administration, 20*(2), 24–28.

Kofman, F., & Seege, P. (1993). Communities of commitment: The heart of learning organizations. *Organizational Dynamics, 22*(2), 5–23.

Kofodimos, J. R., Kaplan, R. E., & Drath, W. H. (1986). *Anatomy of an executive: A close look at one executive's managerial character and development* (Tech. Rep. No. 29). Center for Creative Leadership, Greensboro, NC.

Koford, C. B. (1963). Group relations in an island colony of Rhesus monkeys. In C. H. Southwick (ed.), *Primate social behavior.* Princeton, NJ: Van Nostrand.

Koh, W. L. (1990). *An empirical validation of the theory of transformational leadership in secondary schools in Singapore.* Doctoral dissertation, University of Oregon, Eugene, OR.

Koh, W. L., Terborg, J. R., & Steers, R. M. (1991). *The impact of transformational leaders on organizational commitment, organizational citizenship behavior, teacher satisfaction and student performance in Singapore.* Academy of Management Meetings, August, 1991, Miami, FL.

Kohlberg, L. (1969). Stage and sequence: The cognitive-developmental approach to socialization. In D. A. Goslin (ed.), *Handbook of socialization theory and research.* Skokie, IL: Rand-McNally.

Kohlberg, L. (1981). *The meaning and measurement of moral development.* Worcester, MA: Clark University Press.

Kohn, A. (1986). How to succeed without even vying. *Psychology Today, 20*(9), 22–28.

Kohn, A. (1993). Why incentive plans cannot work. *Harvard Business Review,* September–October, 1–7.

Kohn, M. L. (1971). Bureaucratic man: A portrait and an interpretation. *American Sociological Review, 36,* 461–474.

Kohs, S. C., & Irle, K. W. (1920). Prophesying army promotion. *Journal of Applied Psychology, 4,* 73–87.

Kohut, G. F. (1983). Women in management: Communicative correlates of sex role identity and leadership style toward the development of a managerial self–concept. *Dissertation Abstracts International, 44*(6A), 1625.

Kohut, H. (1976). Creativeness, charisma, group psychology. In J. E.

Gedo & C. H. Pollock (eds.), *Psychological issues 34/35.* New York: International Universities Press.

Kohut, H. (1977). *The restoration of the self.* New York: International Universities Press.

Kokkelenberg, E. (1988). An economic investigation into the determinants of CEO compensation, *Forefronts,* 3, December,

Kolaja, J. (1965). *Workers' councils: The Yugoslav experience.* London: Tavistock.

Kolb, C. (1993). *White House daze: The unmaking of domestic policy in the Bush years.* New York: Free Press.

Kolb, J. A. (1997). Are we still stereotyping leadership? A look at gender and other predictors of leader emergence. *Small Group Research,* 28, 370–393.

Kolb, J. H. (1933). *Trends of country neighborhoods.* Madison: University of Wisconsin, Agriculture Experimental Station.

Kolb, J. H., & Wileden, A. F. (1927). *Special interest groups in rural society.* Madison: University of Wisconsin, Agriculture Experimental Station.

Kolk, N. J., Born, M. P., & van der Flier (2003). The transparent assessment center: The effects of revealing dimensions to candidates. *Applied Psychology: An International Review,* 52, 648–668.

Komaki, J. L. (1981). Applied behavior analysis. *The Industrial Psychologist,* 19, 7–9.

Komaki, J. L. (1982). Why we don't reinforce: The issues. *Journal of Organizational Behavior Management,* 4(3–4), 97–100.

Komaki, J. L. (1986). Toward effective supervision: An operant analysis and comparison of managers at work. *Journal of Applied Psychology,* 71, 270–278.

Komaki, J. L., & Citera, M. (1990) Beyond effective supervision: Identifying key interaction between superior and subordinate. *Leadership Quarterly,* 1, 91–105.

Komaki, J. L., Collins, R. L., & Penn, P. (1982). The role of performance antecedents and consequences in work motivation. *Journal of Applied Psychology,* 67, 334–340.

Komaki, J. L., Deselles, M. L., & Bowman, E. D. (1989). Definitely not a breeze: Extending an operant model of effective supervision to teams. *Journal of Applied Psychology,* 74, 522–529.

Komaki, J. L., Zlotnick, S., & Jensen, M. (1986). Development of an operant-based taxonomy and observational index of supervisory behavior. *Journal of Applied Psychology,* 71, 260–269.

Komives, S. R. (1991). Gender differences in the relationship of hall directors' transformational and transactional leadership and achieving styles. *Journal of College Student Development,* 32, 155–165.

Komives, S. R. (1991). The relationship of same and cross-gender work pairs to staff performance and supervisor leadership in residence hall units. *Sex Roles,* 24, 355–363.

Konar-Goldband, E., Rice, R. W., & Monkarsh, W. (1979). Time-phased interrelationships of group atmosphere, group performance, and leader style. *Journal of Applied Psychology,* 64, 401–409.

Konczak, L. J., Stelly, D. J., & Trusty, M. (1996). *Measuring empowering behaviors of managers: Some preliminary construct validity eveidence.* Paper, Society for Industrial and Organizational Psychology, San Diego, CA.

Konopaske, R. U., Robie, C., & Ivancevich, J. M. *A preliminary model of spouse influence on managerial global assignment willingness.* Paper, Academy of Management, Seattle, WA.

Konovsky, M. A. (1986). *Antecedents and consequence of informal leader helping behavior: A structural equation modeling approach.* Doctoral dissertation, Indiana University, Bloomington.

Konovsky, M. A., & Folger, R. (1991). The effects of procedures, social accounts, and benefits level on victims' layoff reactions. *Journal of Applied Social Psychology,* 21(8), 630.

Konrad, A. M., & Cannings, K. (1997). The effects of gender role congruence and statistical discrimination on managerial advancement. *Human Relations,* 50, 1305–1328.

Konrad, A. M., & Cannings, K. (2002). *Asymmetrical demography effects on perceived reward and social outcomes: Differential effects of leader gender and work unit gender effects.* Unpublished manuscript.

Konrad, A. M., Corrigall, E., Lieb, P., et al. (2000). Sex differences in job attribute preferences among managers and business students. *Group & Organization Management,* 25(2), 108–131.

Konrad, A. M., & Cummings, K. (1997). The effects of gender role congruence and statistical discrimination on managerial advancement. *Human Relations,* 50, 1305–1328.

Konrad, A. M., & Gutek, B. A. (1986). Impact of work experiences on attitudes toward sexual harassment. *Administrative Science Quarterly,* 31, 422–38.

Konrad, A. M., & Gutek, B. A. (1987). Theory and research on group composition: Applications to the status of women and ethnic minorities. In S. Oskamp & S. Spacapan (eds.), *Interpersonal processes: The Claremont symposium on applied social psychology.* Newbury Park, CA: Sage.

Konrad, A. M., & Linnehan, F. (1995). Formalized HRM structures: Coordinating equal employment opportunity or concealing organizational practices? *Academy of Management Journal,* 38, 787–820.

Kooker, E. (1974). Changes in ability of graduate students in education to assess own test performance as related to their Miller Analogies Test scores. *Psychological Reports,* 35, 97–98.

Koontz, H. (1958). A preliminary statement of principles of planning and control. *Academy of Management Journal,* 1, 45–61.

Koontz, H., & O'Donnell, C. (1955). *Principles of management.* New York: McGraw-Hill.

Koontz, H., O'Donnell, C., & Weihrich, H. (1958). *Management.* New York: McGraw-Hill.

Koopman, P. L. (1991). Charistisch leiderschap motivatie en presatie. *Gedrag en Organisatie,* 5, 357–368.

Kopelman, R. E., & Reinharth, L. (1982). Research results: The effect of merit-pay practices on white collar performance. *Compensation Review,* 14(4), 30–40.

Kor, Y. (2002). *Direct and interaction effects of top management team attributes and corporate governance on R&D Investment strategy.* Paper, Academy of Management, Denver, CO.

Korman, A. K. (1966). "Consideration," "initiating structure," and organizational criteria. *Personnel Psychology,* 18, 349–360.

Korman, A. K. (1968). The prediction of managerial performance: A review. *Personnel Psychology,* 21, 295–322.

Korman, A. K. (1973). On the development of contingency theories of leadership: Some methodological considerations and a possible alternative. *Journal of Applied Psychology,* 58, 384–387.

Korman, A. K. (1974). Contingency approaches to leadership: An overview. In J. C. Hunt & L. L. Larson (eds.), *Contingency approaches to leadership.* Carbondale: Southern Illinois University Press.

Korman, A. K. (1976). A hypothesis of work behavior revisited and an extension. *Academy of Management Review, 1,* 50–63.

Korman, A. K. (1988). *The outsiders: Jews and corporate America.* Lexington, MA: Lexington Books.

Korman, A. K., & Tanofsky, R. (1975). Statistical problems of contingency models in organizational behavior. *Academy of Management Journal, 18,* 393–397.

Korman, A. K., Wittig-Berman, U., & Lang, D. (1981). Career success and personal failure: Alienation in professionals and managers. *Academy of Management Journal, 24*(2), 342–360.

Korn/Ferry International (1988, 1990). *Reinventing the CEO.* Graduate School of Business, Columbia University, New York.

Korn/Ferry International (1995). *International executive profile: A survey of corporate leaders in the eighties.* New York, NY.

Korotkin, A. L., & Yarkin-Levin, K. (1985). *A study of leadership competency requirements and job performance dimensions.* Unpublished manuscript.

Korotov, K., & Onyemah, V. (2003). *Social network position and employee leadership potential: An empirical study.* Paper, Academy of Management, Seattle, WA.

Korten, D. C. (1962). Situational determinants of leadership structure. *Journal of Conflict Resolution, 6,* 222–235.

Korten, D. C. (1968). Situational determinants of leadership structure. In D. Cartwright & A. Zander (eds.), *Group dynamics: Research and theory.* New York: Harper & Row.

Korten, D. (1996). Let's get real about business responsibility. *Business Ethics, 61.*

Korukonda, A. R., & Hunt, J. G. (1989). Pat on the back versus kick in the pants: An application of cognitive inference to the study of leader reward and punishment behaviors. *Group & Organizational Studies, 14,* 299–324.

Korukonda, A. R., & Hunt, J. G. (1991). Premises and paradigms in leadership research. *Journal of Organizational Change Management, 4*(2), 19–33.

Kossek, E. E., & Ozeki, C. (1998). Work-family conflict, policies and the job-life relationship: A review and directions for organizational behavior-human resources research. *Journal of Applied Psychology, 83,* 139–149.

Koslowsky, M., & Schwarzwald, J. (1993). The use of power tactics to gain compliance: Testing aspects of Raven's (1998) theory in conflictual situations. *Social Behavior and Personality, 21,* 135–144.

Kotter, J. P. (1978). Power, success and organizational effectiveness. *Organizational Dynamics, 6,* 26–40.

Kotter, J. P (1979). *Power in management.* New York: AMACOM.

Kotter, J. P. (1982a). *The general managers.* New York: Free Press.

Kotter, J. P. (1982b). What effective general managers really do. *Harvard Business Review, 60*(6), 156–167.

Kotter, J. P (1985a). Never underestimate the power of your subordinates. *Working Woman, 10*(12), 19–22.

Kotter, J. P. (1985b). Looking for more Iacoccas. Why business has so few leaders. *New York Times,* October 20, 2E.

Kotter, J. P. (1988). *The leadership factor.* New York: Free Press

Kotter, J. P. (1990). *A force for change: How leadership differs from management.* New York: Free Press.

Kotter, J. P. (1999). *On what leaders really do.* Boston, MA: Harvard Business School Press.

Kotter, J. P., & Heskett, J. L. (1992). *Corporate culture and performance.* New York: Free Press.

Kotter, J. P., & Lawrence, P. R. (1974). *Mayors in action.* New York: Wiley.

Koulack, D. (1977). Effect of outgroup responses on perceptions of leader effectiveness. *Social Forces, 55,* 959–965.

Kouzes, J. M., & Posner, B, Z. (1985). When are leaders at their best? *Santa Clara Magazine, 27*(3), 2–6.

Kouzes, J. M., & Posner, B. Z. (1987). *The leadership challenge: How to get extraordinary things done in organizations.* San Francisco: Jossey-Bass.

Kouzes, J. M., & Posner, B. Z. (1992). *The leadership challenge: How to get extraordinary things done in organizations.* San Francisco, CA: Jossey-Bass.

Kouzes, J. M., & Posner, B. Z. (1993). *Credibility: How leaders gain and lose it, why people demand it.* San Francisco: Jossey-Bass.

Kouzes, J. M., & Posner, B. Z. (1995). *The leadership challenge. How to keep getting extraordinary things done in organizations.* San Francisco: Jossey-Bass.

Kouzes, J. M., & Posner, B. Z. (2001). Bringing leadership lessons from the past into the future. In W. Bennis, G. M. Spreitzer, & T. G. Cummings (eds.), *The future of leadership: Today's top leadership thinkers speak to tomorrow's leaders.* San Francisco, CA: Jossey-Bass, 81–90.

Kouzes, J. M., & Posner, B. Z. (2002). *The Leadership Challenge* (3rd ed.). San Francisco, CA.: Jossey-Bass.

Kovach, B. E. (1986). The derailment of fast-track managers. *Organizational Dynamics, 15*(2), 41–48.

Koze, S., & Masciale, E. (1993). Why teams don't work and how to fix them. *Canadian Manager,* Spring, 8–11.

Kozlowski, S. W., & Doherty, M. L. (1989). Integration of climate and leadership: Examination of a neglected issue. *Journal of Applied Psychology, 74,* 546–553.

Kozlowski, S. W. J., Gully, S. M., Salas, E., et al. (1996). Team leadership and development: Theory, principles, and guidelines for training leaders and teams. In M.M. Beyerlein, D. Johnson, & S. T. Beyerlein (eds.), *Team leadership: Interdisciplinary studies of work teams,* vol. 3. Greenwich, CT: JAI Press.

Kraatz, M. S., & Moore, J. H. (2002). Executive migration and institutional change. *Academy of Management Journal, 45,* 120–143.

Krackhardt, D. (1990). Assessing the political landscape: Structure, cognition, and power organizations. *Administrative Science Quarterly, 35,* 342–369.

Krackhardt, D., & Kilduff, M. (1999). Whether close or far: Social distancer effects on perceived balance to friendship networks. *Journal of Personality and Social Psychology, 76,* 770–782.

Krackhardt, D., & Stern, D. (1988). Informal networks and organizational crises: An experimental simulation. *Social Psychology Quarterly, 51*(2), 123–140.

Kraemer, K. L., & Danziger, J. N. (1984). Computers and control in the work environment. *Public Administration Review, 44*(1), 32–42.

Kraft, M. E., & Vig, N. J. (1984). Environmental policy in the Reagan presidency. *Political Science Quarterly, 99,* 415–439.

Kraiger, K., & Ford, J. K. (1985). A meta-analysis of ratee race effects in performance ratings. *Journal of Applied Psychology, 70,* 56–65.

Kraitem, M. H. (1981). An investigation of current management/leadership style of top financial executives in the United States. *Dissertation Abstracts International, 42*(2A), 774.

Kram, K. E. (1980). *Mentoring process at work: Developmental relationships in managerial careers.* Doctoral dissertation, Yale University, New Haven, CT

Kram, K. E. (1983). Phases of the mentor relationship. *Academy of Management Journal, 26,* 608–625.

Kram, K. E., & Hall, D. T. (1996), Mentoring in a context of diversity and turbulence. In S. Lobel, & E. E. Kossek (eds.), *Human resource strategies for managing diversity.* London: Blackwell Publishers.

Krantz, J., & Gilmore, T. (1990). The splitting of leadership and management as a social defense. *Human Relations, 43,* 183–204.

Krause. D. E. (2004). Influence-based leadership as a determinant of the inclination to innovate and of innovation-related behaviors: An empirical investigation. *Leadership Quarterly, 15,* 79–102.

Kraut, A. I. (1972). A hard look at management assessment centers and their future. *Personnel Journal, 51,* 317–326.

Kraut, A. I. (1975a). The entrance of black employees into traditionally white jobs. *Academy of Management Journal, 18,* 610–615.

Kraut, A. I. (1975b). Prediction of managerial success by peer and training-staff ratings. *Journal of Applied Psychology, 60,* 14–19.

Kraut, A. I. (1976). Developing managerial skills via modeling techniques: Some positive research findings—a symposium. *Personnel Psychology, 29,* 325–369.

Kraut, A. I., Pedigo, P. R., McKenna, D. D., & Dunnette, M. D. (1989). The role of the manager: What's really important in different management jobs. *Academy of Management Executive, 3,* 286–293.

Kravetz, D. (1976). Sex role concepts of women. *Journal of Consulting Clinical Psychology, 44,* 437–443.

Krech, D., & Crutchfield, R. S. (1948). *Theory and problems of social psychology.* New York: McGraw-Hill.

Krejci, J. (1976). Leadership and change in two Mexican villages. *Anthropological Quarterly, 49,* 185–196.

Kriesberg, L. (1962). Careers, organization size, and succession. *American Journal of Sociology, 68,* 355–359.

Kriesberg, L, (1964). Reply. *American Journal of Sociology, 70,* 223.

Kristof, N. D. (1996). Koreans search for infiltrators from wrecked sub. *New York Times,* September 18, A1, 11.

Krohe, J., Jr. (1997). Ethics are nice, but business is business. *Across the Board, 34*(4), 16–22.

Kroll, K., & Vandenberg, L. (1996). Community centered organizational leadership: Challenges for practice. *Journal of Leadership Studies, 3.*

Kroll, M. J., & Pringle, C. D. (1985). Individual differences and path goal theory: The role of leader directiveness. *Southwest Journal of Business and Economics, 2*(3), 11–20.

Kroll, M. J., Toombs, L. A., & Wright, P. (2000). Napoleon's tragic march home from Moscow: lessons in hubris. *Academy of Management Executive, 14*(1), 117–128.

Krout, M. H. (1942). *Introduction to social psychology.* New York: Harper.

Krug, J. A., & Nigh, D. (2001). Executive perceptions in foreign and domestic acquisitions: An analysis of foreign ownership and its effect on executive fate. *Journal of World Business, 36,* 85–105.

Krug, J. A., & Nigh, D. (2002). *Mergers and acquisitions: Long-term leadership continuity and the effect of foreign ownership.* Paper, Academy of Management, Denver, CO.

Kruglanski, A. W. (1969). Some variables affecting interpersonal trust in supervisor-worker relations. *Dissertation Abstracts, 29,* 3219.

Krugman, P. (2006). Osama, Saddam, and the ports. *New York Times,* February 24, A27.

Kruisinga, H. J. (1954). *The balance between centralization and decentralization in managerial control.* Oxford, U.K.: Blackwell.

Krukones, M. C. (1985). The campaign promises of Jimmy Carter: Accomplishments and failures. *Presidential Studies Quarterly, 15*(1), 136–144.

Krumboltz, J. D., Christal, R. E., & Ward, J. H. (1959). Predicting leadership ratings from high school activities. *Journal of Educational Psychology, 50,* 105–110.

Krupp, J. A. (1986). Using the power of the principalship to motivate experienced teachers. *Journal of Staff Development, 17,* 100–110.

Kruse, L., & Wintermantel, M. (1986). Leadership Ms-Qualified: 1. The gender bias in everyday and scientific thinking. In C. F. Graumann & S. Moscovici (eds.), *Changing conceptions of leadership.* New York: Springer-Verlag.

Krusell, J., Vicino, F. L., Manning, M. R., et al. (1972). *PROCESS: A program of self-administered exercises for personal and interpersonal development.* Scottsville, NY: Transnational Programs.

Krusell, J., Vicino, F., Manning, M. R., et al. (1982). *Personal and interpersonal development: A self-administered workbook.* San Diego, CA: University Associates.

Kugelmass, J. (1995). *Telecommuting: A manager's guide to flexible work arrangements.* New York: Lexington Books.

Kugihara, N., & Misumi, J. (1984). An experimental study of the effect of leadership types on followers' escaping behavior in a fearful emergency maze-situation. *Japanese Journal of Psychology, 55,* 214–220.

Kugihara, N., Misumi, J., Sato, S., & Shigeoka, K. (1982). Experimental study of escape behavior in a simulated panic situation: II. Leadership in emergency situation. *Japanese Journal of Experimental Social Psychology, 21,* 159–166.

Kuhn, M. H. (1964). Major trends in symbolic interaction theory in the past twenty-five years. *The Sociological Quarterly, 5*(1), 61–68.

Kuhn, T. (1970). *The structure of scientific revolutions.* Chicago: University of Chicago Press.

Kuhnert, K. W. (1994) Transforming leadership: Developing people through delegation. In B. M. Bass & B. J. Avolio (eds.), *Improving organizational effectiveness through transformational leadership.* Thousand Oaks, CA: Sage.

Kuhnert, K. W., & Lewis, P. (1987). Transactional and transformational leadership: A constructive developmental analysis. *Academy of Management Review, 12,* 648–657.

Kuhnert, K. W., & Russell, C. J. (1989). Theory and practice in the selection and development of organizational leaders. *Journal of Management,* in press.

Kuhnert, K. W., & Russell, C. J. (1990). Using constructive developmental theory and biodata to bridge the gap between personnel selection and leadership. *Journal of Management, 16,* 598–607.

Kuiper, N. A., & Martin, R. A. (1993). Humor and self-concept. *International Journal of Humor Research, 6,* 251–270.

Kumar, F. (1965). A study of value-dimensions in student leadership. *Psychological Studies, 10,* 73–79.

Kumar, P. (1966). Certain personal factors in student leadership. *Journal of Psychological Researches, 10,* 37–42.

Kunczik, M. (1976a). Empirische Überprüfung des Kontingenzmodells effektiver Führung. Teil 1. [Empirical test of the contingency model of leadership effectiveness. Part 1.] *Kölner Zeitschrift für Soziologie und Sozialpsychologie, 28,* 517–536.

Kunczik, M. (1976b). Empirische Überprüfung des Kontingenzmodells effektiver Führung. Teil 2: Beprüfing anhand von Ausbildungsgruppen der Bundeswehr. [Empirical test of the contingency model of leadership effectiveness. Part 2: Examination with the aid of the training groups of the federal armed services.] *Kölner Zeitschrift für Soziologie und Sozialpsychologie, 28,* 738–754.

Kung, M. C., & Steelman, L. A. (2003). *A cross-cultural study in feedback-seeking.* Paper, Society for Industrial and Organizational Psychology, Orlando, FL.

Kunich, J. C., & Lester, R. I. (1996). Leadership and the art of feedback: Feeding the hands that back us. *Journal of Leadership Studies, 3,* 4–22.

Kupperman, J. J. (1991). *Character.* New York: Oxford University Press.

Kureshi, A., & Fatima, B. (1984). Power motive among student leaders and non-leaders: Testing the affective-arousal model. *Journal of Psychological Researches, 28*(1), 21–24.

Kuriloff, A. H., & Atkins, S. (1966). T-group for a work team. *Journal of Applied Behavioral Science, 2,* 63–93.

Kurke, L. B., & Aldrich, H. E. (1979). *Mintzberg was right!: A replication and extension of "the nature of managerial work."* Paper, Academy of Management, Atlanta, CA. Also: (1983). *Management Science, 29*(8), 975–984.

Kurke, L. B., & Brindle, (1999). *The cognitive processes of enactment: Evidence from Alexander the Great.* Paper, Academy of Management, Chicago, IL.

Kurland, N. B. (1996). Sales agents and clients: Ethics, incentives, and a modified theory of planned behavior. *Human Relations, 49,* 51–74.

Kurland, N. B., & Bailey, D. E. (1999). When workers are here, there and everywhere: A discussion of the challenge of the advantages and disadvantages of telework. *Organizational Dynamics, 28*(5), 53–68.

Kurland, N. B., & Bailey, D. E. (2002) A review of telework research, findings, new directions, and lessons for the study of modern work. *Journal of Organizational Behavior, 23,* 383–400.

Kuster, R., & Jones, R. (1995). The influence of corporate headquarters on Japanese and U.S. subsidiary companies. *Leadership & Organization Development Journal, 16*(5), 11–15.

Kuykendall, J., & Unsinger, R. C. (1982). The leadership styles of police managers. *Journal of Criminal Justice, 10,* 311–321.

Labak, A. S. (1973). The study of charismatic college teachers. *Dissertation Abstracts International, 34,* 1258B.

Lacey, L. (1977). Discriminability of the Miner sentence completion

scale among supervisory and nonsupervisory scientists and engineers. In J. B. Miner (ed.), *Motivation to manage.* Atlanta, CA: Organizational Measurement Systems Press.

Lacey, R., & Danziger, D. (1999). *The year 1000.* London: Little, Brown & Co.

Labich, K. (1994). Is Herb Kelleher America's best?: Behind his clowning is a people-wise manager who wins when others can't. *Fortune,* May 2, 44–52.

Labovitz, C. H. (1972). More on subjective executive appraisal: An empirical study. *Academy of Management Journal, 18,* 289–302.

Lachman, R. (1985). Public and private sector differences: CEOs' perceptions of their role environments. *Academy of Management Journal, 28,* 671–680.

LaCour, J. A. (1977). Organizational structure: Implications for volunteer program outcomes. *Journal of Voluntary Action Research, 6,* 41–47.

Ladner, J. A. (1971). *Tomorrow's tomorrow: The black woman.* New York: Doubleday.

Ladouceur, J. (1973). *School management profile and capacity for change.* Doctoral dissertation, University of Toronto, Toronto, ON.

LaGumina, S. J. (1998). Sicilian culture: News and views. *Altreitalie,* 17. agnelli.it:altreitalie/17/–saggild.htm

Lake, D. G., & Martinko, M. J. (1982). *The identification of high performing principals* (working paper). Tallahassee: Florida State University. (Cited in Martinko & Gardner, 1984.)

Lakin, M. (1969). Some ethical issues in sensitivity training. *American Psychologist, 24,* 923–928.

Lam, S. S. K., Chen, X. P., & Schaubroeck, J. (2002). Participative decision making and employee performance in different cultures: The moderating effects of allocentrism/idiocentrism and efficacy. *Academy of Management Journal, 45,* 905–914.

Lambert, R. A., Larker, D. F., & Weigelt, K. (1991). How sensitive is executive compensation to organizational size? *Strategic Management Journal, 12,* 395–402.

Lamm, H. (1973). Intragroup effects on intergroup negotiation. *European Journal of Social Psychology, 3,* 179–192.

Lamm, R. (1975). Black union leaders at the local level. *Industrial Relations, 14,* 220–232.

Lana, R. E., Vaughan, W., & McGinnies, E. (1960). Leadership and friendship status as factors in discussion group interaction. *Journal of Social Psychology, 52,* 127–134.

Lanaghan, R. C. (1972). *Leadership effectiveness in selected elementary schools.* Doctoral dissertation, University of Illinois, Urbana-Champaign.

Lancaster, H. (2002). *Promoting yourself: 52 lessons for getting to the top . . . and staying there.* New York: Wall Street Journal Books.

Landau, M. J., & Scandura, T. A. (2002). An investigation of personal learning in mentoring relationships: Content, antecedents, and consequences. *Academy of Management Journal, 45,* 779–790.

Landau, S. B., & Leventhal, G. S. (1976). A simulation study of administrators' behavior toward employees who receive job offers. *Journal of Applied Social Psychology, 6,* 291–306.

Landsberger, H. A. (1961). The horizontal dimension in bureaucracy. *Administrative Science Quarterly, 6,* 299–332.

Landy, F. J., Barnes, J. L., & Murphy, K. R. (1978). Correlates of perceived fairness of performance evaluation. *Journal of Applied Psychology*, 63, 751–754.

Landy, F. J., & Farr, J. (1980). Performance rating. *Psychological Bulletin*, 87, 72–107.

Lane, R. E. (1961). *Political life*. Glencoe, IL: Free Press.

Lane, T. F. E. (1985). Take a lead from your followers. *Chief Executive*, October, 11.

Lange, C. J., Campbell, V., Katter, R. V., & Shanley, F. J. (1958). *A study of leadership in army infantry platoons*. Washington, DC: Human Resources Research Office.

Lange, C. J., & Jacobs, T. O. (1960). *Leadership in army infantry platoons: Study II*. Washington, DC: Human Resources Research Office.

Lange, C. J., Rittenhouse, C. H., & Atkinson, R. C. (1968). *Films and group discussions as a means of training leaders*. Washington, DC: Human Resources Research Office.

Langer, E. J., Blank, A., & Chanowitz, B. (1978). The mindlessness of ostensibly thoughtful action. *Journal of Personality and Social Psychology*, 36, 635–642.

Langenderfer, H. Q., and Rockness, J. W. (1989). Integrating ethics into the accounting curriculum: issues, problems, and solutions. *Issues in Accounting Education* 4(1), 58–69.

Langfred, C. W. (2004). Too much of a good thing? Negative effects of high trust and individual autonomy in self-managing teams. *Academy of Management Journal*, 47, 385–399.

Langhoff, J. (1996). *The telecommuter's advisors: Working in the fast lane*. Providence, RI: Aegis Press.

Langley, P., & Jones, R. (1988). A computational model of scientific insight. In R. J. Sternberg (ed.), *The nature of creativity*. New York: Cambridge University Press.

Lankau, M. J., & Scandura, T. A. (2002). An investigation of personal learning in mentoring relationships: Content, antecedents, and consequences. *Academy of Management Journal*, 43, 779–790.

Lannon, J. M. (1977). Male and female values in management. *Management International Review*, 17, 9–12 (United Kingdom only).

Lannon, J. M. (1977). Male vs. female values in management. *Management International Review*, 17, 9–12.

Lansing, F. W. (1957). Selected factors of group interaction and their relation with leadership performance. *International Journal of Sociometry*, 1, 170–174.

Lanzara, G. E. (1983). Ephemeral organizations in extreme environments: Emergence, strategy, and extinction. *Journal of Management Studies*, 20(1), 71–95.

Lanzetta, J. T. (1953). *An investigation of group behavior under stress* (Task Order V). Rochester, NY: University of Rochester.

Lanzetta, J. T., Haeffier, D., Langham, P., & Axelrod, H. (1954). Some effects of situational threat on group behavior. *Journal of Abnormal and Social Psychology*, 49, 445–453.

Lanzetta, J. T., & Hannah, T. E. (1969). Reinforcing behavior of naive trainers. *Journal of Personality and Social Psychology*, 11, 245–252.

Lanzetta, J. T., & Haythorn, W. W. (1954). *Instructor-crew influence on attitude formation in student crews* (TR-54-79). San Antonio, TX: Crew Research Laboratory, Air Force Personnel and Training Reserve Center.

Lanzetta, J. T., & Roby, T. B. (1955). *Group performance as a function of work–distribution patterns and task load* (CRL-LN-55-4). San Antonio, TX: Crew Research Laboratory, Air Force Personnel and Training Reserve Center.

Lanzetta, J. T., & Roby, T. B. (1960). The relationship between certain group process variables and group problem-solving efficiency. *Journal of Social Psychology*, 52, 135–148.

Lapiere, R. T. (1938). *Collective behavior*. New York: McGraw-Hill.

Lapiere, R. T., & Farnsworth, F. R. (1936). *Social psychology*. New York: McGraw-Hill.

LaPolice, C. C., & Costanza, D. P. (2003). *Change-related leader behaviors: When task and relations just aren't enough*. Paper, Society for Industrial and Organizational Psychology, Orlando, FL.

Lapping, B. (1985). *End of empire*. London: Grenada.

Larkin, R. W. (1975). Social exchange in the elementary school classroom: The problem of teacher legitimation of the social power. *Sociological Education*, 48, 400–410.

Larmore, A., & Ayman, R. (1998). *Empowering leadership, transformational leadership, and feelings of empowerment*. Paper, Society for Industrial and Organizational Leadership, Dallas, TX.

LaRocco, J. M., & Jones, A. P. (1978). Co-worker and leader support as moderators of stress-strain relationships in work situations. *Journal of Applied Psychology*, 63, 629–634.

Larson, A. (1968). *Eisenhower: The president nobody knew*. New York: Popular Library.

Larson, C. E., & LaFasto, F. M. J. (1989). *Teamwork: What must go right; what can go wrong*. Newbury Park, CA: Sage.

Larson, C. E., & Luthans, K. W. Potential added value of psychological capital in predicting work attitudes. *Journal of Leadership and Organizational Studies*, 13, 75–92

Larson, J. R. (1980). *Some hypotheses about the causes of supervisory performance feedback behavior*. Paper, Academy of Management, Detroit, MI.

Larson, J. R. (1982). Cognitive mechanisms mediating the impact of implicit theories of leader behavior on leader behavior ratings. *Organizational Behavior and Human Performance*, 29, 129–140.

Larson, J. R., Jr. (1984). The performance feedback process: A preliminary model. *Organizational Behavior and Human Performance*, 33, 42–76.

Larson, J. R., Jr. (1986). Supervisors' performance feedback to subordinates: The impact of subordinate performance valence and outcome dependence. *Organizational Behavior and Human Decision Processes*, 37, 391–408.

Larson, J. R. (1989). The dynamic interplay between employees' feedback-seeking strategies and supervisors' delivery of performance feedback. *Academy of Management Review*, 14, 408–422.

Larson, J. R., Jr., Glynn, M. A., Fleenor, C. D., & Scontrino, M. P. (1986). Exploring the dimensionality of managers' performance feedback to subordinates. *Proceedings, Academy of Management*, San Diego. Also: (1986). *Human Relations*, 39, 1083–1102.

Larson, J. R., Jr., Lingle, J. H., & Scerbo, M. M. (1984). The impact of performance cues on leader–behavior ratings: The role of selective information availability and probabilistic response bias. *Organizational Behavior and Human Performance*, 33, 323–349.

Larson, L. L., Hunt, J. C., & Osborn, R. N. (1974). Correlates of leadership and demographic variables in three organizational settings. *Journal of Business Research, 2*, 335–347.

Larson, L. L., & Rowland, K. M. (1974). Leadership style and cognitive complexity. *Academy of Management Journal, 17*, 37–45.

Larwood, L., Glasser, E., & McDonald, R. (1980). Attitudes of male and female cadets toward military sex integration. *Sex Roles, 6*, 381–390.

Larwood, L., Gutek, B. A., & Cattiker, U. (1984). Perspectives on institutional discrimination and resistance to change. *Group & Organization Studies, 9*(3), 333–352.

Larwood, L., & Kaplan, M. (1980). Job tactics of women in banking. *Group & Organization Studies, 5*, 70–79.

Larwood, L., O'Carroll, M., & Logan, J. (1977). Sex role as a mediator of achievement in task performance. *Sex Roles, 3*, 109–114.

Larwood, L., and Wood, M. M. (1977). *Women in Management.* Lexington, MA: Lexington Books.

Larwood, L., Wood, M. M., & Inderlied, S. D. (1978). Training women for management: New problems, new solutions. *Academy of Management Review, 3*, 584–593.

Laschinger, H. K. S., Finegan, J., Shamian, J., et al. (2002). The impact of workplace empowerment and organizational trust on staff nurses' work satisfaction and organizational commitment. *Health Care Management Review, 26*(3), 7–23

Lasher, W. F. (1975). *Academic governance in university professional schools.* Doctoral dissertation, University of Michigan, Ann Arbor.

Laskey, K. B., Leddo, J. M., & Bresnick, T. A. (1990). *Executive thinking and decision skills: A characterization and implications for training.* ARI Research Note 91–07, U.S. Army Research Institute for the Behavioral and Social Sciences, Alexandria, VA.

Lasswell, H. (1948). *Power and personality.* New York: W. W. Norton.

Latack, J. C. (1986). Coping with job stress: Measures and future directions for scale development. *Journal of Applied Psychology, 71*, 377–385.

Latham, G. P. (1988). Human resource training and development. *Annual Review of Psychology, 39*, 545–582.

Latham, G. P. (1988). Behavior approaches to the training and learning process. In I. L. Goldstein (ed.), *Training and development in organizations.* San Francisco: Jossey-Bass.

Latham, G. P., & Baldes, J. J. (1975). The "practical significance" of Locke's theory of goal setting. *Journal of Applied Psychology, 60*, 122–124.

Latham, G. P., & Lee, T. W. (1986). Goal setting. In E. A. Locke (ed.), *Generalizing from laboratory to field settings.* Lexington, MA: Lexington Books.

Latham, G. P., & Saari, L. M. (1979). Importance of supportive relationships in goal setting. *Journal of Applied Psychology, 64*, 151–156.

Latham, G. R., & Steel, T. P. (1983). The motivational effects of participation versus goal setting on performance. *Academy of Management Journal, 26*, 406–417.

Latta, J. A., & Emener, W. G. (1983). State vocational rehabilitation agency leadership behavior styles. *Journal of Rehabilitation Administration, 7*, 141–148.

Lau, A. W., Newman, A. R., & Broedling, L. A. (1980). The nature of managerial work in the public sector. *Public Administration Review, 40*(5), 513–520.

Lau, A. W., & Pavett, C. M. (1980). The nature of managerial work: A comparison of public and private sector managers. *Group & Organization Studies, 5*, 453–466.

Lau, S. (1977). *Managerial styles of traditional Chinese firms.* Doctoral dissertation, University of Hong Kong, Hong Kong.

Laughlin, R. A. (1973). *A study of organizational climate perceived by faculty in Colorado community junior colleges.* Doctoral dissertation, University of Colorado, Boulder.

Laurent, H. (1970). Cross-cultural cross-validation of empirically validated tests. *Journal of Applied Psychology, 54*, 417–423.

Lauterbach, A. (1963). Management aims and development needs in Latin America. *Business History Review, 39*, 557–572, 577–588.

Lauterbach, K. E., & Weiner, B. J. (1996). Dynamics of upward influence: How male and female managers get their way. *Leadership Quarterly, 7*, 87–107.

Lavagnino, D. (2001). The 2001 salary survey. *Working Woman,* July/August, 44–48.

Lavelle & Folger (2002). See Turillo, C. J., Folger, R. Lavelle, J. J. & Umphress, E. E. (2002).

Laverty, K. J. (1996). Economic "short-termism": The debate, the unresolved issues, and the implications for management practice and research. *Academy of Management Review, 21*, 825–860.

Lavoie, D., & Culbert, S. A. (1978). Stages in organization and development. *Human Relations, 31*, 417–438.

Lawler, E. E., III (1965). Managers' perceptions of their subordinates' pay and of their superiors' pay. *Personnel Psychology, 18*, 413–422.

Lawler, E. E., III (1966c). Managers' attitudes toward how their pay is and should be determined. *Journal of Applied Psychology, 50*, 273–279.

Lawler, E. E., III (1967a). Management performance as seen from above, below, and within. *Journal of Applied Psychology, 51*, 247–253.

Lawler, E. E., III (1967b). How much money do executives want? *Personnel Management Abstracts, 12*, 1–8.

Lawler, E. E., III (1982). Increasing worker involvement to enhance organizational effectiveness. In P. S. Goodman (ed.), *Changes in organizations.* San Francisco: Jossey-Bass.

Lawler, E. E., III (1985). Education, management style, and organizational effectiveness. *Personnel Psychology, 38*, 1–26.

Lawler, E.E., III (1986). *High involvement management.* San Francisco: Jossey-Bass.

Lawler, E. E., III (1988). Substitutes for hierarchy. *Organizational Dynamics, 17*, 4–1X.

Lawler, E. E., III (1998). *Strategies for high performance oranizations.* San Francisco, CA: Jossey-Bass.

Lawler, E. E., III, & Cohen, S. (1992). *Designing pay systems for teams.* CEO Publication T 92–12.

Lawler, E. E., III, & Mohrman, S. A. (1987). Unions and the new management. *Academy of Management Executive, 1*, 293–300.

Lawler, E. E., III, & Hackman, J. R. (1969). Impact of employee participation in the development of pay incentive plans: A field experiment. *Journal of Applied Psychology, 53*, 467–471.

Lawler, E. E., III, Mohrman, A. M., Jr., & Resnick, S. M. (1984). Performance appraisal revisited. *Organizational Dynamics, 13*(1), 20–35.

Lawler, E. E., III, & Mohrman, S. A. (1987). Quality circles after the honeymoon. *Organizational Dynamics, 1*, 42–54.

Lawler, E. E., III, Mohrman, S. A., & Ledford, G. E. (1995). *Creating high performance organizations, practices, and results of employee involvement and Total Quality Management in Fortune 1000 companies.* San Francisco: Jossey-Bass.

Lawler, E. E., III, & Porter, L. W. (1966). Predicting managers' pay and their satisfaction with their pay. *Personnel Psychology, 19,* 363–374.

Lawler, E. E., III, & Porter, L. W. (1967). The effect of performance on job satisfaction. *Industrial Relations.*

Lawler, E. E., III, & Porter, L. W. (1967b). Antecedent attitudes of effective managerial performance. *Organizational Behavior and Human Performance, 2,* 122–142.

Lawler, E. E., III, Porter, L. W., & Tannenbaum, A. (1968). Managers' attitudes toward interaction episodes. *Journal of Applied Psychology, 52,* 432–439.

Lawler, E. J., (1975). An experimental study of factors affecting the mobilization of revolutionary coalitions. *Sociometry, 38,* 163–179.

Lawler, E. J., (1983). Cooptation and threats as "divide and rule" tactics. *Social Psychology Quarterly, 46,* 89–98.

Lawrence, B. S. (1984). Historical perspective: Using the past to study the present. *Academy of Management Review, 9,* 307–312.

Lawrence, L. C., & Smith, P. C. (1955). Group decision and employee participation. *Journal of Applied Psychology, 39,* 334–337.

Lawrence, P. R., & Lorsch, J. W. (1967a). *Organization and environment.* Cambridge, MA: Harvard University Press.

Lawrence, F. R., & Lorsch, J. W. (1967b). Differentiation and integration in complex organizations. *Administrative Science Quarterly, 1,* 47.

Lawrence, P. (1997). *Toward a unified theory of organizational life.* Working Paper. Division of Research, Harvard Business School, Cambridge, MA..

Lawrence, P., & Nohria, N. (2002). *Driven: How human nature shapes our choices.* San Francisco: Jossey-Bass.

Lawrie, J. W. (1966). Convergent job expectations and ratings of industrial foremen. *Journal of Applied Psychology, 50,* 97–107.

Lawshe, C. H., Bolda, R. A., & Brune, R. L. (1959). Studies in management training evaluation: 11. The effect of exposures to role playing. *Journal of Applied Psychology, 43,* 287–292.

Lawshe, C. H., Brune, R. L., & Bolda, R. A. (1958). What supervisors say about role playing. *Journal of American Social Training of Directors, 12,* 3–7.

Lawshe, C. H., & Nagle, B. F. (1953). Productivity and attitude toward supervisor. *Journal of Applied Psychology, 37,* 159–162.

Lazar, I. (1953). *Interpersonal perception: a selected review of the literature.* Urbana: University of Illinois.

Lazarsfeld, R., Berelson, B., & Gaudet, H. (1948). *The people's choice* (2nd ed.). New York: Columbia University Press.

Lazarus, R. S. (1966). *Psychological stress and the coping process.* New York: McGraw-Hill.

Leana, C. (1983). *The effects of group cohesiveness and leader behavior on defective decision processes: A test of Fanis' groupthink model.* Paper, Academy of Management, Dallas.

Leana, C. R. (1984). *Antecedents and consequences of delegation.* Doctoral dissertation, University of Houston, Houston, TX.

Leana, C. R. (1985). A partial test of Janis' groupthink model: Effects of group cohesiveness and leader behavior on defective decision making. *Journal of Management, 11,* 5–17.

Leana, C. R. (1986). Predictors and consequences of delegation. *Academy of Management Journal, 29,* 754–774.

Leana, C. R. (1987). Power relinquishment vs. power sharing: Theoretical clarification and empirical comparison of delegation and participation. *Journal of Applied Psychology, 72,* 228–233.

Learned, E. P., Ulrich, D. N., & Booz, D. R. (1951). *Executive action.* Boston: Harvard University Press.

Leary, M. R., & Kowalski, R.M. (1990). Impression management: A literature review and two-component model. *Psychological Bulletin, 107,* 34–47.

Leavitt, H. J. (1951). Some effects of certain communication patterns on group performance. *Journal of Abnormal and Social Psychology, 46,* 38–50.

Leavitt, H. J. (1986). *Corporate pathfinders.* New York: Dow Jones–Irwin and Penguin Books.

Leavitt, H. J. (2005) *Top down: Why hierarchies are here to stay and how to manage them more effectively.* Boston: Harvard Business School Press.

Leavitt, H. J., & Bass, B. M. (1964). Organizational psychology. *Annual Review of Psychology, 15,* 371–398.

Leavitt, H. J., & Whisler, T. L. (1958). Management in the 1980's. *Harvard Business Review, 36,* 41–48.

Leavy, B. (1996) On studying leadership in the strategy field. *Leadership Quarterly, 7,* 435–454.

LeBon, C. (1897). *The crowd.* New York: Macmillan.

Lécuyer, R. (1976). Social organizations and spatial organization. *Human Relations, 29,* 1045–1060.

Lee, B. (1996). In the center. *Issues & Observations, 16,* (2–3), 1.

Lee, C., & Zemke, R. (1993). The search for spirit in the workplace. *Training, 30*(6), 21.

Lee, D. M. (1976). Subordinate perceptions of leadership behavior: A judgmental approach. *Dissertation Abstracts International, 37,* 2555–2556.

Lee, F. J., Horwitz, M., & Goldman, M. (1954). Power over decision making and the response to frustration in group members. *American Psychologist, 9,* 413–414 (Abstract).

Lee, I. J., & Lee, L. L. (1956). *Handling barriers in communication.* New York: Harper.

Lee, P. M., & James, E. H. (2003). *She CEOs: Gender effects and stock price reactions to announcements of top executive appointments.* Paper, Academy of Management, Seattle, WA.

Lee, P. M., & James, E. H. (2007). She CEOs: Gender effects and investor reactions to the announcements of top executive appointments. *Strategic Management Journal, 28*(3), 227–241.

Lee, S. M., & Schwendiman, G. (eds.). (1982). *Japanese management: Cultural and environmental considerations.* New York: Praeger.

Lee, Y., & Larwood, L. (1983). The socialization of expatriate managers in multinational firms. *Academy of Management Journal, 26,* 657–665.

Leebaert, D. (2006). *To dare to conquer: Special operations and the destiny of nations, from Achilles to Al-Qaeda.* New York: Little, Brown & Co.

Lees-Hutton, C. A., & Syvantek, D. J. (2002). *The influence of gender and the Pygmalion effect on performance.* Paper, Society for Industrial and Organizational Psychology, Toronto.

Lefcourt, H. M., & Ladwig, G. W. (1965). The effect of reference groups upon Negroes' task persistence in a biracial competitive game. *Journal of Personality and Social Psychology, 1,* 668–671.

Lefcourt, H. M., & Martin, R. A. (1986). *Humor and life stress: Antidote to adversity.* Berlin: Springer.

Lefebvre, M., & Singh, J. B. (1996). A comparison of the contents and foci of Canadian and American corporate codes of ethics. *International Journal of Management, 13*(2), 156–170.

Lefkowitz, M., Blake, R. R., & Mouton, J. S. (1955). Status factors in pedestrian violation of traffic signals. *Journal of Abnormal and Social Psychology, 51,* 704–706.

Lehman, H. C. (1937). The creative years in science and literature. *Science Monitor, 45,* 65–75.

Lehman, H. C. (1942). Optimum ages for eminent leadership. *Science Monitor, 54,* 162–175.

Lehman, H. C. (1947). The age of eminent leaders, then and now. *American Journal of Sociology, 52,* 342–356.

Lehman, H. C. (1953). *Age and achievement.* Princeton, NJ: Princeton University Press.

Lehnen, L. P., Ayman, R., & Korablik, K. (1995). *The effects of transformational leadership and conflict management styles on subordinate satisfaction with supervision.* Paper, Society for Industrial and Organizational Psychology, Orlando, FL.

Lei, D., & Slocum, J. W. (2005). Strategic and organizational requirements for competitive advantage. *Academy of Management Executive, 19*(1), 31–45.

Leib, A. (1928). Vorstellungen und Urteile von Schülern über Fiffirer in der Schulklass. *Zeitschrift für Angewandte Psychologie, 30,* 241–346.

Leigh, A. (1983). Analyzing management training needs in British social work. *Social Policy and Administration, 17,* 249–259.

Leighton, A. H. (1945). *The governing of men: General principles and recommendations based on experiences at a Japanese relocation camp.* Princeton, NJ: Princeton University Press.

Leipold, W. E. (1963). *Psychological distance in diadic interview.* Doctoral dissertation, University of North Dakota, Grand Forks.

Leithwood, K. (1994). Leadership for school restructuring. *Educational Administration Quarterly, 30*(4), 498–518.

Leithwood, K. (1995). *Effective school district leadership: transforming politics into education.* SUNY Press.

Leithwood, K. A., & Montgomery, D. J. (1984). Obstacles preventing principals from becoming more effective. *Education and Urban Society, 17*(1), 73–88.

Leithwood, K., & Steinbach, R. (1991). Indicators of transformational leadership in the everyday problem solving of school administrators. *Journal of Personnel Evaluation in Education, 4*(3), 221–244.

Leithwood, K., Tomlinson, D., & Genge, M. (1996). Transformational school leadership. In K. Leithwood, J. Chapman, D. Corson, et al. (eds.), *International Handbook of Educational Leadership and Administration.* Dortrecht: Klewer.

Lemann, N. (1990). Moynahan is again ahead of his time. *New York Times,* February 18, 1E, 4E.

Lemann, T. B., & Solomon, R. L. (1952). Group characteristics as revealed in sociometric patterns and personality ratings. *Sociometry, 15,* 7–90.

Lenartowicz, T., & Roth, K. (2001). Does subculture within a country matter? A cross-cultural study of motivational domains and business performance in Brazil. *Journal of International Business Studies, 32*(2), 305–325.

Lennerlöf, L. (1965a). The formal authority of the supervisor. *Psychology Research Bulletin, 5,* 22–31.

Lennox, R. D., & Wolfe, R. N. (1984). Revision of the self-monitoring scale. *Journal of Personality and Social Psychology, 46,* 1349–1364.

Lennung, S. A., & Ahlberg, A. (1975). The effects of laboratory training: A field experiment. *Journal of Applied Behavioral Science, 11,* 177–188.

Lenski, C. E. (1956). Social participation and status crystallization. *American Sociological Review, 21,* 458–464.

Leopold, L. (1913). *Prestige.* London: Fisher & Unwin.

LePine, J. A., & Van Dyne, L. (1998). Predicting voice behavior in work groups. *Journal of Applied Psychology, 83,* 853–868.

Lepkowski, M. L., Sr. (1970). *Cooperative decision making as related to supportive relations and communication in the senior high school.* Doctoral dissertation, University of Buffalo, Buffalo, NY.

Lesser, J. V. (1994). *Working women and their families.* Thousand Oaks, CA: Sage.

Lester, D., & Genz, J. L. (1978). Internal-external locus of control, experience as a police officer, and job satisfaction in municipal police officers. *Journal of Police Science and Administration, 6,* 479–481.

Lester, J. T. (1965). *Correlates of field behavior. Behavioral research during the 1963 Mount Everest expedition* (Tech. Rep. No. 1). San Francisco: Berkeley Institute of Psychological Research.

Lester, R. I. (1981), Leadership: Some principles and concepts. *Personnel Journal, 60,* 868–870.

Leuchauer, D. L., & Shulman, G. M. (1996). Training transformational leaders: A call for practicing empowerment in the classroom. *International Journal of Public Administration, 19,* 827–848.

Leung, K. (1983). *The impact of cultural collectivism on reward allocation.* Master's thesis, University of Illinois, Urbana.

LeVay, S., & Hamer, D. H. (1994). Evidence for a biological influence in male homosexuality. *Scientific American, 270*(5), 44–49.

Level, D. A. (1972). Communication effectiveness: Method and situation. *Journal of Business Communication, 10,* 19–25.

Level, D. A., & Johnson, L. (1978). Accuracy of information flows within the superior/subordinate relationship. *Journal of Business Communication, 15*(2), 12–22.

Leventhal, G. S. (1980). What should be done with equity theory?: new approaches to the study of fairness in social relationships. In K. J. Gergen, M. S. Greenberg, & R. H. Willis (eds.), *Social exchange: Advances in theory and research.* New York: Plenum, 27–55.

Leventhal, G. S., Michaels, J. W., & Sanford, D. (1972). Inequity and inter-personal conflict: Reward allocation and secrecy about rewards as methods of preventing conflict. *Journal of Personality and Social Psychology, 23,* 88–102.

Leventhal, G. S., & Whiteside, H. D. (1973). Equity and the use of reward to elicit high performance. *Journal of Personality and Social Psychology, 25,* 75–88.

Levering, R., Moskowitz, M., & Katz, M. (1984). *The 100 best companies to work for in America.* Reading, MA: Addison-Wesley.

Levi, A. M., & Benjamin, A. (1977). Focus and flexibility in a model of conflict resolution. *Journal of Conflict Resolution, 21,* 405–423.

Levi, A. S., & Mainstone, L. E. (1992). Breadth, focus, and content in leader priority-setting: Effects on decision quality and perceived leader performance. In K. E. Clark, M. B. Clark, & D. C. Campbell (eds.), *Impact of management.* Greensboro, NC: Center for Creative Leadership.

Levi, I. J. (1930). Student leadership in elementary and junior high school and its transfer into senior high school. *Journal of Educational Research, 22,* 135–139.

Levi, M. (1991). *Marxism.* Aldershot, England: Elgar.

Levi, M. A. (1954). *A comparison of two methods of conducting critiques* (AFPTRC-TR54-108). San Antonio, TX: Lackland AFB, Crew Research Laboratory, AF Personnel & Training Reserve Center.

Levi, M. A., Torrance, E. R, & Pletts, C. O. (1954). Sociometric studies of combat air crews in survival training. *Sociometry, 17,* 304–328.

Levine, J., & Butler, J. (1952). Lecture vs. group discussion in changing behavior. *Journal of Applied Psychology, 36,* 29–33.

Levine, J. M., & Moreland, R. L. (1990). Progress in small group research. *Annual Review of Psychology, 41,* 585–634.

LeVine, R. (1966). *Dreams and deeds: Achievement motivation in Nigeria.* Chicago: University of Chicago Press.

Levine, S. (1949). An approach of constructive leadership. *Journal of Social Issues, 5,* 46–53.

Levine, S. (1988). Scoops of fun. *Philadelphia Inquirer,* July 3, 10C.

Levinger, G. (1959). The development of perceptions and behavior in newly formed social power relationships. In D. Cartwright (ed.), *Studies in social power.* Ann Arbor: University of Michigan, Institute for Social Research.

Levinger, G., Morrison, H. W., & French, J. R. P. (1957). Coercive power and forces affecting conformity. *American Psychologist, 12,* 393 (Abstract).

Levinson, D. J. (1959). Role, personality, and social structure in the organizational setting. *Journal of Abnormal and Social Psychology, 58,* 170–180.

Levinson, D. J., Darrow, C. M., Klein, E. C., Levinson, M. H., & McKee, B. (1978). *The seasons of a man's life.* New York: Knopf.

Levinson, H. (1962). A psychologist looks at executive development. *Harvard Business Review, 40,* 69–75.

Levinson, H. (1970). *Executive stress.* New York: Harper & Row.

Levinson, H. (1980b). Power, leadership, and the management of stress. *Professional Psychology, 11,* 497–508.

Levinson, H. (1981). *Executive.* Cambridge, MA: Harvard University Press.

Levinson, H. (1984). Management by guilt. In M. F. R. Kets de Vries (ed.), *The irrational executive. Psychoanalytic explorations in management.* New York: International Universities Press.

Levinson, H. (1988). You won't recognize me: Predictions about changes in top-management characteristics. *Academy of Management Executive, 2*(2), 119–125.

Levinson, H. (1994). Why the behemoths fell: The psychological roots of corporate failure. *American Psychologist, 49,* 428–436.

Levinson, H., & Rosenthal, S. (1984). *CEO: Corporate leadership in action.* New York: Basic Books.

Levinson, H. (1980). Criteria for choosing chief executives. *Harvard Business Review, 58*(4), 113–120.

Levit, R. A. (1992). Meaning, purpose, and leadership. *International Forum on Logotherapy, 15.*

Levy, B. I. (1954). *A preliminary study of informal crew conferences as a crew training adjunct* (AFPTRC-TR-54-87). San Antonio, TX: Lackland AFB, Crew Research Laboratory, AF Personnel & Training Reserve Center.

Levy, P. E., Miller, T., & Cober, R.T. (2000). *The effect of leadership perceptions in feedback-seeking intentions.* Paper, Society for Industrial and Organizational Psychology, New Orleans, LA.

Levy-Leboyer, C., & Pineau, C. (1981). Caractéristiques organisationnelles, style de leadership et réussite dans la recherche bio-médicale. *Revue de Psychologie Appliquée, 31,* 201–235.

Lewicki, R. J. (1983). Lying and deception: A behavioral model. In M. Bazerman & R. J. Lewicki (eds.), *Negotiating in organizations.* Beverly Hills, CA: Sage Publications.

Lewicki, R. J., Stevenson, M. A., & Bunker, B. B. (1997). *The three components of interpersonal trust: Instrument development and differences across relationships.* Paper, Academy of Management, Boston.

Lewin, K. (1939). Field theory and experiment in social psychology: Concepts and methods. *American Journal of Sociology, 44,* 868–896.

Lewin, K. (1947a). Frontiers in group dynamics: Concept, method and reality in social science, social equilibria and social change. *Human Relations, 1,* 5–41.

Lewin, K. (1947b). Group decision and social change (1944). In I. Newcomb & E. Hartley (eds.), *Readings in social psychology.* New York: Holt.

Lewin, K., & Lippitt, R. (1938). An experimental approach to the study of autocracy and democracy: A preliminary note. *Sociometry, 1,* 292–300.

Lewin, K., Lippitt, R., & White, R. K. (1939). Patterns of aggressive behavior in experimentally created social climates. *Journal of Social Psychology, 10,* 271–301.

Lewis, D. R., & Dahl, T. (1976). Time management in higher education administration: A case study. *Higher Education, 5,* 49–66.

Lewis, F. L. (1982). *Facilitator: A micro computer decision support systems for small groups.* Doctoral dissertation, University of Louisville, Louisville, KY.

Lewis, G., Morkel, A., & Hubbard, G. (1993). *Australian strategic management: Concepts, context and cases.* Sydney: Prentice Hall.

Lewis, H. (1965). Child rearing among low-income families. In L. A. Ferman, J. L. Kornbluh, & A. Haber (eds.), *Poverty in America.* Ann Arbor: University of Michigan Press.

Lewis, H. S. (1974). Leaders and followers: Some anthropological perspectives. *Addison-Wesley Module in Anthropology No. 50.* Reading, MA: Addison-Wesley.

Lewis, K. M., & Gibson, C. B. (1998). *The efficacy advantage: Observing and modeling the relationship between team heterogeneity, group efficacy, and outcomes.* Paper, Society for Industrial and Organizational Psychology, New Orleans, LA.

Lewis, P., & Jacobs, T. O. (1992). Individual differences in strategic leadership capacity: A constructive development review. In R. L. Phillips & J. G. Hunt (eds.), *Strategic leadership: A multiorganizational-level perspective.* Westport, CT: Quorum Books.

Lewis, P., Kuhnert, K., & Maginnis, R. (1987). Defining military character. *Parameters: U.S. Army War College Quarterly, 17*(2), 33–41.

Lewis, R. T. (2002). *New York Times* President and Chief Executive Officer Russell Lewis on "The CEO's lot is not a happy one . . ." with apologies to Gilbert and Sullivan. *Academy of Management Executive, 16*, 37–42.

Ley, R. (1966). Labor turnover as a function of worker differences, work environment, and authoritarianism of foremen. *Journal of Applied Psychology, 50*, 497–500.

Li, A., & Butler, A. B. (2004). The effects of participation in goal setting and goal rationales on goal commitment: An exploration of justice mediators. *Journal of Business and Psychology,19*, 37–51.

Liancang, X. (1987). Recent developments in organizational psychology in China. In B. M. Bass, R. J. D. Drenth, & R. W. Weissenberg (eds.), *Advances in organizational psychology: An international review.* Beverly Hills, CA: Sage.

Liang, X., Ndofor, H. A., & Picken, J. C. (2003). *Top management team communication, Environmental uncertainty, and organizational performance.* Paper, Academy of Management, Seattle, WA.

Lichtenberg, P., & Deutsch, M. (1954). *A descriptive review of research on the staff process of decision-making* (AFPTRC-TR-54-129). San Antonio, TX: Air Force Personnel & Training Reserve Center.

Lichtenstein, B. M., Smith, B. A., & Torbert, W. R. (1995). Leadership and ethical development: balancing light and shadow. *Business Ethics Quarterly, 5*(1), 97–116.

Lichtheim, M. (1973). *Ancient Egyptian literature. Vol. 1: The old and middle kingdoms.* Los Angeles: University of California Press.

Liden, R. C. (1981). *Contextual and behavioral factors influencing perceptions of ineffective performance and managerial responses.* Doctoral dissertation, University of Cincinnati, Cincinnati, OH.

Liden, R. C. (1985). Female perceptions of female and male managerial behavior. *Sex Roles, 12*, February, 3–4.

Liden, R. C., Ferris, C. R., & Dienesch, R. M. (1988). The influence of causal feedback on subordinate reactions and behavior. *Group & Organization Studies, 13*, 348–373.

Liden, R. C., & Graen, G. (1980). Generalizability of the vertical dyad linkage model of leadership. *Academy of Management Journal, 23*(3), 451–465.

Liden, R. C., & Maslyn, J. M. (1998). Multidimensionality of leader–member exchange: An empirical assessment through scale development. *Journal of Management, 24*, 43–72.

Liden, R. C., & Mitchell, I. R. (1985). Reactions to feedback: The role of attributions. *Academy of Management Journal, 28*, 291–308.

Liden, R. C., Stilwell, D., & Ferris, G. R. The effects of supervisors and subordinates on objective and subjective performance ratings. *Human Relations, 49*, 327–347.

Liden, R. C., Wayne, S. J., & Sparrowe, R. T. (2000). An examination of the mediating role of psychological empowerment on the relations between the job, interpersonal relationships, and work outcomes. *Journal of Applied Psychology, 85*, 407–416.

Liden, R. C., Wayne, S. J., & Stilwell, D. (1993). A longitudinal study on the early development of leader-member exchanges. *Journal of Applied Psychology, 78*, 662–674.

Lieberman, M. A. (1976a). Change induction in small groups. *Annual Review of Psychology, 27*, 217–250.

Lieberman, M. A., Yalom, I. D., & Miles, M. B. (1973). *Encounter groups: First facts.* New York: Basic Books.

Lieberson, S., & O'Connor, J. F. (1972). Leadership and organizational performance: A study of large corporations. *American Scoiological Review, 37*(2), 117–130.

Liebow, E. (1967). *Tally's corner.* Boston: Little, Brown.

Liem, M. A., & Slivinski, L. W. (1975). A comparative study of middle and senior management dimensions and job types in the Canadian public service. *Studies in Personnel Psychology, 6*, 21–34.

Lien, N., Kottke, J. L., & Agars, M. D. (2003). *Cultural predictors of interpersonal conflict in the workplace.* Paper, Society for Industrial and Organizational Psychology, Orlando, FL.

Lievens, F. (2001). Assessors and the use of assessment center dimensions: A fresh look at a troubling issue. *Journal of Organizational Behavior, 22*, 203–221.

Lievens, F., Van Geit, P., & Coetsier, P. (1997). Identification of transformational leadership qualities: An examination of potential biases. *European Journal of Work and Organizational Psychology, 6*, 415–430.

Lifton, R. J. (1967). *Death in life: Survivors of Hiroshima.* New York: Random House.

Likert, R. (1932). A technique for the measurement of attitudes. *Archives of Psychiatry, 52*, 140.

Likert, J. (1958). *Leadership for effective leagues.* Washington, DC: League of Women Voters.

Likert, R. (1959). Motivational approach to management development. *Harvard Business Review, 37*, 75–82.

Likert, R. (1961a). *New patterns of management.* New York: McGraw-Hill.

Likert, R. (1961b). An emerging theory of organizations, leadership and management. In L. Petrullo & B. M. Bass (eds.), *Leadership and interpersonal behavior.* New York: Holt, Rinehart & Winston.

Likert, R. (1963). Trends toward a world-wide theory of management. *Proceedings, International Management Congress, 2*, 110–114.

Likert, R. (1967). *The human organization.* New York: McGraw-Hill.

Likert, R. (1975). Improving cost performance with cross-functional teams. *Conference of Board of Records, 92*, 51–59.

Likert, R. (1977a). Management styles and the human component. *Management Review, 66*, 23–28, 43–45.

Likert, R. (1977b). *Past and future perspectives on system 4.* Paper, Academy of Management, Orlando, FL.

Likert, R., & Fisher, S. (1977). MBGO: Putting some team spirit into MBO. *Personnel, 54*(1), 41–47.

Likert, R., & Likert, J. G. (1976). *New ways of managing conflict.* New York: McGraw-Hill.

Likert, R., & Likert, J. G. (1978). A method for coping with conflict in problem-solving groups. *Group & Organization Studies, 3*, 427–434.

Lim. B.-C., & Ployhart, R. (2000). *Transformational leadership: Relations to FFM, typical and maximum performance.* Paper, Society for Industrial and Organizational Psychology, Toronto.

Lim, L. H, Raman,K. S., & K. K., Wei (1994). Interacting effects of GDSS and leadership. *Decision Support Systems, 12*, 199–211.

Limerick, D. C. (1976). Authority: An axis of leadership role differentiation. *Psychologia Africana, 16*, 153–172.

Lincoln, J.R., Hanada, M., & Olson, J. (1981). Cultural orientations and individual reactions to organizations: A study of employees of Japanese-owned firms. *Administrative Science Quarterly, 26*, 93–114.

Lind, E. A., & Tyler, T. R. (1988). *The social psychology of procedural justice.* New York: Plenum.

Lind, M. (2004). Are we still a middle-class nation? In T. Halstead (ed.), *Real state of the union.* New York: Basic Books.

Lindell, M. (1989). *Förändringsorienterad ledarstil I finländska företag.* Helsinki, Finland: Swedish School of Economics and Business Administration.

Lindell, M., & Arvonen, J. (in press). The Nordic management style in a European context. *International Studies on Management and Organization, 26,* 73–92.

Lindell, M., & Rosenqvist, G. (undated). *Is there a third management style?* Stockholm, Sweden: Swedish School of Economics and Business Administration.

Lindemuth, M. H. (1969). *An analysis of the leader behavior of academic deans as related to the campus climate in selected colleges.* Doctoral dissertation, University of Michigan, Ann Arbor.

Lindsay, C. P., & Dempsey, B. L. (1985). Experiences in training Chinese business people to use U.S. management techniques. *Journal of Applied Behavioral Science, 21,* 65–78.

Lindsey, E., Holmes, V., & McCall, M. W., Jr. (1987). *Key events in executive lives* (Tech. Rep. No. 32). Greensboro, NC: Center for Creative Leadership.

Lindzey, G., & Kalnins, D. (1958). Theoretic apperception test: Some evidence bearing on the "hero assumption." *Journal of Abnormal and Social Psychology, 57,* 76–83.

Linehan, M. (2001). *An empirical study of the repatriation of female managers: An emerging issue for European managers.* Paper, Academy of Management, Washington, D.C.

Lingham, T. (2003). *Evaluating leadership training: Content and applicability in managerial learning and development.* Paper, Academy of Management, Seattle, WA.

Linimon, D., Barron, W. L., III, & Falbo, T. (1984). Gender differences in perceptions of leadership. *Sex Roles, 11,* 1075–1089.

Linowes, R. G. (1993). The Japanese manager's entry into the United States: Understanding the American-Japanese cultural divide. *Academy of Management Executive, 7*(4), 21–37.

Linton, R. (1945). *The cultural background of personality.* New York: Appleton-Century-Crofts.

Linville, P. W., & Jones, E. E. (1980). Polarized appraisals of outgroup members. *Journal of Personality and Social Psychology, 38,* 689–703.

Lipetz, M. E., & Ossorio, F. G. (1967). Authoritarianism, aggression, and status. *Journal of Personality and Social Psychology, 5,* 468–472.

Lipham, J. M. (1960). *Personal variables related to administrative effectiveness.* Doctoral dissertation, University of Chicago, Chicago.

Lipman-Blumen, J. (1996). *The connective edge: Leading in an interdependent world.* San Francisco: Jossey-Bass.

Lipman-Blumen, J. (2005). *The allure of toxic leaders: How we follow destructive bosses and corrupt politicians—and how we can survive them.* Oxford, U.K.: Oxford University Press.

Lippa, R. (1978). The effect of expressive control on expressive consistency and on the relation between expressive behavior and personality. *Journal of Personality, 46,* 438–461.

Lippitt, M. (1999). How to influence leaders. *Training & Development,* March, 19–22.

Lippitt, R. (1940a). *An analysis of group reaction to three types of experimentally created social climates.* Doctoral dissertation, State University of Iowa, Iowa City.

Lippitt, R. (1940b). An experimental study of the effect of democratic and authoritarian group atmospheres. *University of Iowa Studies in Child Welfare, 16,* 43–95.

Lippitt, R. (1949). *Training in community relations.* New York: Harper.

Lippitt, R., Bradford, L. P., & Berme, K. D. (1947). Sociodramatic clarification of leader and group roles as a starting point for effective group functioning. *Sociatry, 1,* 82–91.

Lippitt, R., Polansky, N., Redl, F., & Rosen, S. (1952). The dynamics of power. *Human Relations, 5,* 37–64.

Lippitt, R., Thelen, H., & Leff, E. (undated). Unpublished memorandum.

Lippitt, R., & White, R. K. (1943). The social climate of children's groups. In R. C. Baker, J. S. Kounin, & H. F. Wright (eds.), *Child behavior and development.* New York: McGraw-Hill.

Lippmann, W. (1922). *Public opinion.* New York: Harcourt, Brace.

Lippmann, W. (1945). Roosevelt has gone. *New York Times,* April 14.

Lipset, S. M. (1985). Feeling better: Measuring the nation's confidence. *Public Opinion, 8*(37), 6–9, 56–58.

Lirtzman, S., & Wahba, M. (1972). Determinants of coalitional behavior of men and women: Sex roles or situational requirement? *Journal of Applied Psychology, 56,* 406–411.

Litman-Adizes, T., Raven, B. H., & Fontaine, G. (1978). Consequences of social power and causal attributions for compliance as seen by powerholder and target. *Personality and Social Psychological Bulletin, 4*(2), 260–264. (cited in House, 1974.)

Litterer, J. A. (1976). *Life cycle changes of career women: Assessment and adaptation.* Paper, Academy of Management, Kansas City, MO.

Little, K. B. (1965). Personal space. *Journal of Experimental Social Psychology, 1,* 237–247.

Littler, C., & Hede, A. (1995). *Downsizing organizations.* News release, Department of Human Resource Management and Employee Relations, University of Southern Queensland, Australia, June 25.

Litwin, G. H. (1968). Climate and motivation: An experimental study. In R. Tagiuri & C. H. Litwin (eds.), *Organizational climate.* Boston: Harvard University, Graduate School of Business Administration.

Litwin, G. H., & Stringer, R. A. (1966). *The influence of organizational climate on human motivation.* Paper, Conference of the Foundation for Research on Human Behavior, Ann Arbor, MI.

Litwin, G. H., & Stringer, R. A. (1968). *Motivation and organizational climate.* Boston: Harvard University, Graduate School of Business Administration, Division of Research.

Litzinger, W. D. (1965). Interpersonal values and leadership attitudes of branch bank managers. *Personnel Psychology,18,* 193–198.

Litzinger, W. D. (1965b). The motel entrepreneur and the motel manager. *Academy of Management Journal, 8,* 268–281.

Litzinger, W. D., & Schaefer, T. E. (1982). Leadership through followership. *Business Horizons, 25*(5), 78–81.

Litzinger, W. D., & Schaefer, T. E. (1986). Something more: the nature of transcendent management. *Business Horizons, 29*(2), 68–72.

Livers, A. B., & Caver, K. A. (2002). Across the divide: Grasping the black experience in corporate America. *Leadership in Action, 22*(5), 7–11.

Livingstone, E. (1953). Attitudes of women operatives to promotion. *Occupational Psychology*, 27, 191–199.

Livingstone, S. (1969). Pygmalion in management. *Harvard Business Review*, 47, 81–89.

Lobban, S. (1988). *An analysis of the relationships between clinical supervision and situational leadership: The development process to to increase clinical supervsion effectiveness.* Doctoral dissertation, University of Massachusetts, Amherst.

Lock, J. D., & Thomas, L. E. (1998). *The effects of leaders' values on group citizenship.* Paper, Society for Industrial and Organizational Psychology, San Diego, CA.

Locke, E. A. (undated). The traits of American business heroes in fact and fiction—drawn from Ayn Rand (1957) *Atlas Shrugged.* New York: Signet.

Locke, E. A. (1968). Toward a theory of task motivation and incentives. *Organizational Behavior and Human Performance*, 3, 157–190.

Locke, E. A. (1977). The myths of behavior mod in organizations. *Academic Management Review*, 4, 131–136.

Locke, E. A., Kloberdanz, K., Hilton, H., et al. (2006). Getting smart at being good. *Inside Business, Time Bonus Section*, January, A1–A22.

Locke, E. A., & Latham, G. P. (1990). Work motivation: The high performance cycle. In U. Kleinbeck, H. Quast, H. Thierry, et al. (eds.), *Work motivation.* Hillsdale, NJ: Lawrence Erlbaum Associates.

Locke, E. A., Latham, G. P, & Erez, M. (1987). *3-way interactive presentation & discussion: A unique approach to resolving scientific disputes: Designing crucial experiments.* Paper, Conference of the Society for Industrial and Organizational Psychology, Atlanta, GA.

Locke, E. A., Latham, G., Saari, L. M., & Shaw, K. N. (1981). Goal setting and task performance: 1969–1980. *Psychological Bulletin*, 90, 125–152.

Locke, E. A., Motowidlo, S. J., & Bobko, R. (1986). Using self-efficacy theory to resolve the conflict between goal-setting theory and expectancy theory in organizational behavior and industrial/organizational psychology. *Journal of Social and Clinical Psychology*, 4, 328–338.

Locke, E. A., & Schweiger, D. M. (1979). Participation in decision making: one more look. In B. Staw & L. L. Cummings (eds.), *Research in organizational behavior*, Vol. 1. Greenwich, CT: JAI Press.

Locke, E. A., Schweiger, D. M., & Latham, G. P. (1986). Participation in decision making: When should it be used? *Organizational Dynamics*, 14(3), 65–79.

Locke, E. A., & Woiceshyn, J. (1995). Why businessmen should be honest: The argument from rational egoism. *Journal of Organizational Behavior*, 16, 405–414.

Locke, G. (2000). The need for Asian American leadership: A call to action. *Asian American Policy Review*, 9, 1–4.

Locke, J. (1960). *The two treatises of government.* Cambridge, U.K.: Cambridge University Press.

Lockheed, M. E. (1975). Female motive to avoid success: A psychological barrier or a response to deviancy? *Sex Roles*, 1, 41–50.

Lockheed, M. E., & Hall, K. P. (1976). Conceptualizing sex as a status characteristic: Applications to leadership training strategies. *Journal of Social Issues*, 32, 111–124.

Lockman, N. (1995). American ignorance, American hate. *Press & Sun Bulletin*, (Binghamton, NY), December 19, 9a.

Lockwood, D. L. L. (1981). The assessment of an observational system to measure leadership behaviors. *Dissertation Abstracts International*, 42(11 A), 4870.

Lodahl, A. (1982). *Crisis in values and the success of the Unification Church.* Bachelor of Arts thesis in sociology, Cornell University, Ithaca, NY (cited in Trice & Beyer, 1986).

Loehlin, J. C. (1992). *Genes and environment in personality development.* Newbury Park, CA: Sage.

Lohmann, D. (1992). The impact of leadership on corporate success: A comparative analysis of the American and Japanese experience. In K. E. Clark, M. B. Clark, & D. P. Campbell (eds.), *Impact of leadership.* Greensboro, NC: Center for Creative Leadership.

Lomas, D. W. (1997). Leadership styles of project managers in Hong Kong: An empirical study. *International Journal of Management*, 14, 667–672.

Lombardo, M. M. (1983). I felt it as soon as I walked in. *Issues & Observations*, 3(4), 7–8.

Lombardo, M. M. (1985). *Executive inventory.* Greensboro, NC: Center for Creative Leadership.

Lombardo, M. M. (1986). Questions about learning from experience. *Issues & Observations*, 6(1), 7–10.

Lombardo, M. M., & Eichinger, R. W. (1989), *Preventing derailment: What to do before it's too late.* Center for Creative Leadership, Greensboro, NC.

Lombardo, M. M. & McCall, M. W., Jr. (1978). Leadership. In M. W. McCall, Jr., and M. M. Lombardo (eds.), *Where else can we go?* Duke University Press.

Lombardo, M. M., & McCauley, C. D. (1999). *BENCHMARKS: A guide to its development and use.* Greensboro, N.C.: Center for Creative Leadership.

Lombardo, M. M., Ruderman, M. N., & McCauley, C. D. (1987). *Explanations of success and derailment in upper-level management positions.* Paper, Academy of Management, New York.

London, M. (1983). Toward a theory of career motivation. *Academy of Management Review*, 8, 620–630.

London, M. (1985). *Developing managers.* San Francisco: Jossey-Bass.

London, M. (1995). Giving feedback: Source-centered antecedents and consequences of constructive and destructive feedback. *Human Resource Management Review*, 5, 159–188.

London, M. (2002). *Leadership development: Paths to self-insight and professional growth.* Mahwah, NJ: Lawrence Erlbaum & Associates.

London, M., & Smither, J. (1995). Can multi-source feedback change perceptions of goal accomplishment, self-evaluations and performance related outcomes? Theory-based applications and directions for research. *Personnel Psychology*, 48, 803–839.

Lonergan, W. G. (1958). Management trainees evaluate role playing. *Journal of American Society of Training Directors*, 12, 20–25.

Lonetto, R., & Williams, D. (1974). Personality, behavioral and output variables in a small group task situation: An examination of consensual leader and non-leader differences. *Canadian Journal of Behavioral Sciences*, 6, 59–74.

Long, R. J. (1979). Desires for and patterns of worker participation in decision making after conversion to employee ownership. *Academy of Management Journal*, 22, 611–617.

Long, R. J. (1988). Factors affecting managerial desires for various types of employee participation in decision making. *Applied Psychology: An International Review, 37*, 15–34.

Long, R. L. (1986). An evaluation of Ohio Cooperative Extension Service leadership workshops in a community development context. *Dissertation Abstracts International, 46*, 1899–1900.

Longnecker, C. O., Sims, H. P., & Gioia, D. A. (1987). Behind the mask: The politics of employee appraisal. *Academy of Management Executive, 1*(3), 183–193.

Lopez, F. M. (1966). *Evaluating executive decision making: The in-basket technique* (AMA Research Study 75). New York: American Management Association.

Lord, R. G. (1975). Group performance as a function of leadership behavior and task structure. *Dissertation Abstracts International, 35*, 6155.

Lord, R. G. (1976). Group performance as a function of leadership behavior and task structure: Toward an explanatory theory. *Organizational Behavior and Human Performance, 17*, 76–96.

Lord, R. G. (1977). Functional leadership behavior: Measurement and relation to social power and leadership perceptions. *Administrative Science Quarterly, 22*, 114–133.

Lord, R. G. (1985). An information processing approach to social perception, leadership perceptions, and behavioral measurement in organizational settings. In L. L. Cummings & B. M. Staw (eds.), *Research in organizational behavior,* vol. 7. Greenwich, CT: JAI Press.

Lord, R. G., & Alliger, G. M. (1985). A comparison of four information processing models of leadership and social perceptions. *Human Relations, 38*, 47–65.

Lord, R. G., Binning, J., Rush, M. C., & Thomas, J. C. (1978). Effect of performance and leader behavior on questionnaire ratings of leader behavior. *Organizational Behavior and Human Performance, 21*, 27–39.

Lord, R. G., Brown, D. J., & Freiberg, S .J. (1999). Understanding the dynamics of leadership: The role of follower self-concepts in the leader/follower relationship. *Organizational Behavior & Human Decision Processes, 78*, 167–203.

Lord, R. G., Brown, D. J., Harvey, J. L., et al. (2001). Contextual constraints on prototype generation and their multilevel consequences for leadership perceptions. *Leadership Quarterly, 12*, 311–338.

Lord, R. G., DeVader, C. L., & Alliger, G. M. (1986). A meta-analysis of the relation between personality traits and leadership perceptions: An application of validity generalization procedures. *Journal of Applied Psychology, 71*, 402–410.

Lord, R .G., & Emerich, C. G. (2001). Thinking outside the box by looking inside the box: Extending the cognitive revolution in leadership research. *Leadership Quarterly, 11*, 551–579.

Lord, R. G., Foti, R. J., & Devader, C. (1984). A test of leadership categorizations: Internal structure, information processing and leadership perceptions. *Organizational Behavior and Human Performance, 34*, 343–378.

Lord, R. G., Foti, R. I., & Phillips, J. S. (1982). A theory of leadership categorization. In J. G. Hunt, U. Sekaran, & C. Schriesheim (eds.), *Leadership: Beyond establishment views.* Carbondale: Southern Illinois University.

Lord, R. G., & Kerman, M. C. (1978). Scripts as determinants of goal commitment. *Academy of Management Review, 12*, 235–249

Lord, R. G., & Maher, K. J. (1990). Alternative information processing models and their implications for theory, research, and practice. *Academy of Management Review, 15*, 9–28.

Lord, R. G., & Maher, K. J. (1991). *Leadership and information processing: Linking perceptions and performance.* Boston: Unwin Hyman.

Lord, R. G., & Maher, K. J. (1993). *Leadership and information processing: Linking perceptions and performance.* New York: Routledge.

Lord, R. G., & Rowzee, M. (1979). Task interdependence, temporal phase, and cognitive heterogeneity as determinants of leadership behavior and behavior-performance relations. *Organizational Behavior and Human Performance, 23*, 182–200.

Lorenzo, R. V. (1984). Effects of assessorship on managers' proficiency in acquiring, evaluating, and communicating information about people. *Personnel Psychology, 37*, 617–634.

Lorge, I., Fox, D., Davitz, J., & Brenner, M. (1958). A survey of studies contrasting the quality of group performance and individual performance, 1920–1957. *Psychological Bulletin, 55*, 337–370.

Lott, D. F., & Sommer, R. (1967). Seating arrangements and status. *Journal of Personality and Social Psychology, 7*, 90–95.

Loury, C. C. (1985). The moral quandary of the black community. *Public Interest, Spring, 79*, 9–22.

Lovelace, K., & Rosen, B. (1996). Differences in achieving person-organization fit among diverse groups of managers. *Journal of Management, 22*, 703–722.

Lowe, K. B., & Gardner, W. L. (2000). Ten years of the Leadership Quarterly: Contributions and challenges for the future. *Leadership Quarterly, 11*, 459–514.

Lowe, K. B., Kroeck, K. G., & Sivasubrahaniam, N. (1996). Effectiveness correlates of transformational and transactional leadership: A met-analytic review of the MLQ literature. *Leadership Quarterly, 7*, 385–425.

Lowe, S. (1996). Hermes revisited: A replication of Hofstede's study in Hong Kong and the UK. *Asia and Pacific Business Review, 2*(3), 101–119.

Lowin, A. (1968). Participative decision making: A model, literature, critique, and prescription for research. *Organizational Behavior and Human Performance, 3*, 68–106.

Lowin, A., & Craig, J. R. (1968). The influence of level of performance on managerial style: An experimental object-lesson in the ambiguity of correlation data. *Organizational Behavior and Human Performance, 3*, 440–458.

Lowin, A., Hrapchak, W. J., & Kavanagh, M. J. (1969). Consideration and initiating structure: An experimental investigation of leadership traits. *Administrative Science Quarterly, 14*, 238–253.

Lubatkin, M. H., & Chung, K. H. (1985). *Leadership origin and organizational performance in prosperous and declining firms.* Paper, Academy of Management, San Diego, CA.

Lubatkin, M. H., Chung, K. H., Rogers, R. C., & Owers, J. E. (1989). Stockholder reactions to CEO changes in large corporations. *Academy of Management Journal, 32*, 47–68.

Lucas, C. (1965). Task performance and group structure as a function of personality and feedback. *Journal of Social Psychology, 66*, 257–270.

Lucas, K. W., & Makessini, J. (1993). *Senior leadership in a changing world order: Requisite skills for U.S. Army one- and two-star generals.* ARI Technical Report No. 976, U.S. Army Research Institute for the Behavioral and Social Sciences.

Lucius, R. H. (1997). *Adult development and leadership: An empirical investigation of the constructive-development theory.* Society for Industrial and Organizational Psychology, St. Louis, MO.

Luckie, W. R. (1963). Leader behavior of directors of instruction. *Dissertation Abstracts, 25,* 1960.

Ludwig, D. C., & Longenecker, C. O. (1993). The Bathsheba syndrome: the ethical failure of successful leaders. *Journal of Business Ethics, 12*(4), 265–273.

Lueck, T. J. (1985). Why Jack Welch is changing G.E. *New York Times,* May 5.

Luechauer, D. L., & Shulman, G. M. (1996). Training transformational leaders: A call for practicing empowerment in the classroom. *International Journal of Public Administration, 19,* 827–848.

Luecke, R. A. (1994). *Scuttle your ships before advancing (and other lessons from history on leadership and change in today's managers).* New York: Oxford University Press.

Lundberg, U., & Frankenhauser, M. (1999). Stress and the workload of women in high ranking positions. *Journal of Occupational Health Psychology, 4,* 142–151.

Lundquist, A. (1957). *Arbetsledare och arbetsgrupp.* Stockholm: Personal Administrativa Ridet.

Lundy, R. M. (1956). Assimilative projection and accuracy of prediction in interpersonal perceptions. *Journal of Abnormal and Social Psychology, 52,* 33–38.

Luo, Y. (1999). Time-based experience and international expansion: The case of an emerging economy. *Journal of Management Studies, 36,* 505–534.

Luong, A., & Rogelberg, S. G. (1998). How to increase your survey response rate. *The Industrial-Organizational Psychologist, 36,* 61–65.

Lupfer, M. B. (1965). Role enactment as a function of orientation, expectations, and duration of interaction. *Dissertation Abstracts, 25,* 5376–5377.

Luthans, F. (1977). *Organizational behavior* (2nd ed.). New York: McGraw-Hill.

Luthans, F. (1986). *Fifty years later: What do we know about managers and managing.* Presidential address, Academy of Management, Chicago.

Luthans, F. (1988). Successful versus effective real managers. *Academy of Management Executive, 2*(2), 127–132.

Luthans, F. (2002). Positive organizational behavior (POB): Developing and managing psychological strengths. *Academy of Management Executive, 16,* 57–72

Luthans, F. (2002). The need for and meaning of positive organizational behavior. *Journal of Organizational Behavior, 23*(6), 695–706.

Luthans, F., & Kreitner, R. (1975). *Organizational behavior modification.* Glenview, IL: Scott, Foresman.

Luthans, F., & Larsen, J. K. (1986). How managers really communicate. *Human Relations, 39,* 161–178.

Luthans, F., & Lockwood, D. L. (1984). Toward an observation system for measuring leader behavior in natural settings. In J. G. Hunt, D. Hosking, C. A. Schriesheim, et al. (eds.), *Leaders and managers: International perspectives on managerial behavior and leadership.* New York: Pergamon Press.

Luthans, F., Luthans, K. W., Hodgetts, R,M., et al. (2001). Positive approach to leadership (PAL): Implications for today's organizations. *Journal of Leadership Studies, 8*(2), 3–20.

Luthans, F., & Martinko, M. J. (1978). *The power of positive reinforcement: a workshop on organizational behavior modification.* New York: McGraw-Hill.

Luthans, F., Peterson, S. J., & Ibrayeva, E. (1998). The potential for the "dark side" of leadership in post Communist countries. *Journal of World Business, 33*(2), 185–201.

Luthans, F., & Riolla, L. T. (1997) Albania and the Bora Company: Lessons learned before the recent chaos. *Academy of Management Executive, 11*(3), 61–71.

Luthans, F., Rosenkrantz, S. A., & Hennessey, H. W. (1985). What do successful managers really do? An observation study of managerial activities. *Journal of Applied Behavioral Science, 21,* 255–270.

Luthans, K. (2000). Recognition: A powerful, but often overlooked, leadership tool to improve employee performance. *Journal of Leadership Studies, 7,* 33–39.

Luttwak, E. N. (1976). *The grand strategy of the Roman empire.* Baltimore, MD: Johns Hopkins University Press.

Lydon, C. (1970). Doctor asserts women are unfit for top jobs. *New York Times,* July 26.

Lyle, J. (1961). Communication, group atmosphere, productivity, and morale in small task groups. *Human Relations, 14,* 369–379.

Lynd, R. S., & Lynd, H. M. (1929). *Middletown.* New York: Harcourt, Brace.

Lyness, K .S., & Judiesch, M. K. (2001). Are female managers quitters? The relationships of gender, promotions, and family leaves of absence to voluntary turnover. *Journal of Applied Psychology, 86,* 1167–1178.

Lyness, K. S., & Schrader, C. A. (2002). *How much progress have women made? Announcements of women's and men's job moves in The Wall Street Journal.* Paper, Academy of Management, Denver, CO.

Lyness, K. S., & Thompson, D. E. (1997). Above the glass ceiling? A comparison of matched samples of female and male executives. *Journal of Applied Psychology, 82,* 359–375.

Lyon, B., & Oppler, E. (2004). The effects of structural attributes and demographic characteristics on protege satisfaction in mentoring programs. *Journal of Career Development, 30* (3), 215–229.

Lyons, B. D. (2003). *Determinants of protégé satisfaction in formal mentoring programs.* Paper, Society for Industrial and Organizational Psychology, Orlando, FL.

Maas, A., & Graf, P. (2004). Leadership by customers? New roles of service companies.

Maas, H. S. (1950). Personal and group factors in leaders' social perception. *Journal of Abnormal and Social Psychology, 45,* 54–63.

Mabe, P., & West, S. (1982). Validity of self-evaluation of ability: A review and meta-analysis. *Journal of Applied Psychology, 67,* 280–296.

Maby, R., & Brady, G. (1996). Sports related leadership. *Journal of Leadership Studies, 3,* 131–137.

MacCallum, R. (1998). Commentary on quantitative methods in I/O research. *The Industrial-Organizational Psychologist, 35*(4).

Macaulay, S. (1963). Noncontractual relations in business. *American Sociological Review, 28,* 55–67.

Maccoby, E. E., & Jacklin, C. N. (1974). *The psychology of sex differences.* Stanford, CA: Stanford University Press

Maccoby, M. (1976/1978). *The gamesman.* New York: Simon & Schuster. Also (1974). New York: Bantam Books.

Maccoby, M. (1979). Leadership needs of the 1980's. *Current Issues in Higher Education, 2,* 17–23.

Maccoby, M. (1981). *The leader: A new face for American management.* New York: Ballantine.

Maccoby, M. (1982). The leader. *NABW (National Association of Bank Women) Journal, 58*(3), 2, 5–28.

Maccoby, M. (1983). Management: Leadership and the work ethic. *Modern Office Procedures, 28*(5), 14, 16, 18.

Maccoby, M. (1988). *Why work: Leading the new generation.* New York: Simon & Schuster.

Macdonald, D. A. (1969). The relationship between leadership orientation and group productivity and satisfaction: The residence hall adviser and his section. *Dissertation Abstracts International, 30,* 391.

MacDonald, W. S. (1967a). Responsibility and goal establishment: Critical elements in Job Corps programs. *Perceptual and Motor Skills, 24,* 104.

MacDonald, W. S. (1967b). Social structure and behavior modification in Job Corps training. *Perceptual and Motor Skills, 24,* 142.

Mace, M. L. (1950). *The growth and development of executives.* Boston, MA: Harvard Business School, Division of Research.

MacFarlane, B. (2001). Developing reflective students: Evaluating the benefits of learning logs within a business ethics programme. *Teaching Business Ethics, 5,* 375–387.

Machiavelli, N. (1513/1952/1961). *The prince.* (Rev. trans. E. R. P. Vincent). New York: Mentor Press.

Mack, W. P., & Konetzni, A. H., Jr. (1982). *Command at sea* (4th ed.). Annapolis, MD: Naval Institute Press.

MacKechnie, A. R. (1944). Importance and development of leadership in our small unit commanders. *Military Review, 24,* 9–12.

MacKenzie, R. A. (1969). The management process in 3-D. *Harvard Business Review, 47*(6), 80–87.

MacKinney, A. C., Kavanagh, M. J., Wolins, L., & Rapparlie, J. H. (1970). *Manager development project: Summary of progress through June 1969.* Ames: Iowa State University.

MacKinnon, D. W. (1960). The highly effective individual. *Teachers College Record, 61,* 367–378.

MacKinnon, D. W. (1975). *An overview of assessment centers* (Tech. Rep. No. 1). Greensboro, NC: Center for Creative Leadership.

MacIver, R. M. (1947). *The web of government.* New York: Macmillan.

MacMillan, I. C., & George, R. (1975). Corporate venturing: Challenges for senior managers. *Journal of Business Strategy, 5,* 34–43.

Madden, F. M. (1977). The effect of human relations training on group leaders' decisions and members' satisfaction. *Dissertation Abstracts International, 38,* 52.

Maddi, S. (1989). *Personality theories: A comparative approach.* Pacific Grove, CA: Brooks/Cole Publishing.

Madique, M. A. (1980). Entrepreneurs, champions, and technological innovation. *Sloan Management Review, 21*(2), 59–76.

Madison, D. L., Allen, R. W., Porter, L. W., Renwick, F. A., & Mayes, B. T. (1980). Organizational politics: An exploration of managers' perceptions. *Human Relations, 33,* 79–100.

Madsen, D., & Snow, P. G. (1983). The dispersion of charisma. *Comparative Political Studies, 16,* 337–362.

Madzar, S. (2001). Subordinates' information inquiry: Exploring the effect of perceived leadership style and individual differences. *Journal of Occupational and Organizational Psychology, 74,* 221–232.

Mael, F. (1986). *Trading latitude for lieutenancy: The exchange component of the leader member exchange model of leadership.* Masters thesis, Wayne State University, Detroit, MI.

Mael, F. A. & Alderks, C. (1993). Leadership Team Cohesion and Subordinate Work Unit Morale and Performance. *Military Psychology, 5,* 18.

Mael, F. A., Waldman, D. A., & Mulqueen, C. (2001). From scientific work to organizational leadership: Predictors of management aspiration among technical personnel. *Journal of Vocational Behavior, 59,* 132–148.

Maguire, M. A., & Pascale, R. T. (1978). Communication, decision-making and implementation among managers in Japanese and American managed companies in the United States. *Sociology and Social Research, 63,* 1–22.

Maher, J. P. (1976). Situational determinants of leadership behavior in task-oriented small groups. *Dissertation Abstracts International, 37,* 693–694.

Mahler, F. W. (1961). The span of control in sixty Australian undertakings. *Personnel Practice Bulletin, 17,* 35–40.

Mahler, W. (1952). Trends in management training: A composite training and development program. In M. J. Dooher & V. Marquis (eds.), *The development of executive talent.* New York: American Management Association.

Mahoney, G. M. (1953). *Supervisory and administrative practices associated with worker attitudes toward an incentive system.* Ann Arbor: University of Michigan, Institute for Social Research.

Mahoney, T. A. (1955). *What do managers do?* Minneapolis: University of Minnesota, Industrial Relations Center.

Mahoney, T. A. (1961). *Building the executive team.* Englewood Cliffs, NJ: Prentice-Hall.

Mahoney, T. A. (1967). Managerial perceptions of organizational effectiveness. *Management Science, 14,* 76–91.

Mahoney, T. A., Jerdee, T. H., & Carroll, S. I. (1965). The job(s) of management. *Industrial Relations, 4,* 97–110.

Mahoney, T. A., Jerdee, T. H., & Korman, A. (1960). An experimental evaluation of management development. *Personnel Psychology, 13,* 81–98.

Mahoney, T. A., Jerdee, T. H., & Nash, A. N. (1960). Predicting managerial effectiveness. *Personnel Psychology, 13,* 147–163.

Mahoney, T. A., Jerdee, T. H., & Nash, A. N. (1961). *The identification of management potential.* Dubuque, IA: W. C. Brown.

Mahoney, T. A., Sorenson, W. W., Jerdee, T.H., & Nash, A. N. (1963). Identification and prediction of managerial effectiveness. *Personnel Administration, 26,* 12–22.

Mai-Dalton, R. R. (1975). *The influence of training and position power on leader behavior* (Tech. Rep. No. 75–72). Seattle: University of Washington, Organizational Research.

Mai-Dalton, R. R. (1993). Managing cultural diversity on individual, group, and organizational levels. In M. M. Chemers & R. Ayman (eds.), *Leadership theory and research: Perspectives and directions.* San Diego, CA: Academic Press.

Maier, N. R. F. (1950). The quality of group decisions as influenced by the discussion leader. *Human Relations, 3,* 155–174.

Maier, N. R. F. (1953). An experimental test of the effect of training on discussion leadership. *Human Relations, 6,* 161–173.

Maier, N. R. F. (1960). Screening solutions to upgrade quality: A new approach to problem-solving under conditions of uncertainty. *Journal of Psychology, 49,* 217–231.

Maier, N. R. F. (1963). *Problem-solving discussions and conferences: Leadership methods and skills.* New York: McGraw-Hill.

Maier, N. R. F. (1965). *Psychology in industry.* Boston: Houghton Mifflin.

Maier, N. R. F. (1967). Assets and liabilities in group problem solving: The need for integrative function. *Psychological Review, 74,* 239–249.

Maier, N. R. F. (1970b). *Problem solving and creativity in individuals and groups.* Belmont, CA: Brooks/Cole.

Maier, N. R. F., & Danielson, L. E. (1956). An evaluation of two approaches to discipline in industry. *Journal of Applied Psychology, 40,* 319–323.

Maier, N. R. F., & Hoffman, L. R. (1960a). Using trained "developmental" discussion leaders to improve further the quality of group decisions. *Journal of Applied Psychology, 44,* 247–251.

Maier, N. R. F., & Hoffman, L. R. (1960b). Quality of first and second solutions to group problem-solving. *Journal of Applied Psychology, 44,* 278–283.

Maier, N. R. F., & Hoffman, L. R. (1961). Organization and creative problem solving. *Journal of Applied Psychology, 45,* 277–280.

Maier, N. R. F., & Hoffman, L. R. (1964). Financial incentives and group decision in motivating change. *Journal of Social Psychology, 64,* 355–368.

Maier, N. R. F., & Hoffman, L. R. (1965). Acceptance and quality of solutions as related to leaders' attitudes toward disagreement in group problem solving. *Journal of Applied Behavioral Science, 1,* 373–386.

Maier, N. R. F., Hoffman, L. R., & Read, W. H. (1963). Superior-subordinate communications: The relative effectiveness of managers who held their subordinates' positions. *Personnel Psychology, 16,* 1–12.

Maier, N. R. F., & Maier, R. A. (1957). An experimental test of the effects of "developmental" vs. "free" discussions on the quality of group decisions. *Journal of Applied Psychology, 41,* 320–323.

Maier, N. R. F., & McRay, F. (1972). Increasing innovation in change situations through leadership skills. *Psychological Reports, 31,* 343–354.

Maier, N. R. F., & Sashkin, M. (1971). Specific leadership behaviors that promote problem solving. *Personnel Psychology, 24,* 35–44.

Maier, N. R. F., & Solem, A. R. (1952). The contribution of a discussion leader to the quality of group thinking: The effective use of minority opinions. *Human Relations, 5,* 277–288.

Maier, N. R. F., & Solem, A. R. (1962). Improving solutions by turning choice situations into problems. *Personnel Psychology, 15,* 151–158.

Maier, N. R. F., & Thurber, J. A. (1969). Problems in delegation. *Personnel Psychology, 22,* 131–139.

Maier, N. R. F, & Zerfoss, L. F. (1952). MRP: A technique for training large groups of supervisors and its potential use in social research. *Human Relations, 5,* 177–186.

Mailer, J. B. (1931). Size of family and personality of offspring. *Journal of Social Psychology, 2,* 3–25

Mainiero, L. A. (1994). Getting anointed for advancement: The case of the executive woman. *Academy of Management Executive, 8*(2), 53.

Mair, J. (2002). *How much do middle managers matter, really? An empirical study on their impact on sustained superior performance.* Paper, Academy of Management, Denver.

Maissonneuve, J. (1952). Selective choices and propinquity. *Sociometry, 15,* 135–140.

Majchrzak, A. (1987). Effects of management policies on unauthorized absence behavior. *Journal of Appied Behavioral Science, 23*(4), 501–523.

Major, K. D. (1988). *Dogmatism, visionary leadership, and effectiveness of secondary schools.* Doctoral dissertation, University of LaVerne, LaVerne, CA.

Major, M. (1984). Delegating authority without losing control. *Today's Office, 19*(5), 45–46.

Makiney, J. D., Marchioro, C. A., & Hall, R. J. (1999). *Relations of leaders perceptions to personality, leadership style and self–schema.* Paper, Society for Industrial and Organizational Psychology, Boston.

Maloney, F. C. (1979). A study of the relationship between leadership behavior and particular personality characteristics of women elementary principals in public and Roman Catholic schools. *Dissertation Abstracts International, 39*(8A), 4633.

Maloney, R. M. (1956). Group learning through group discussion: A group discussion implementation analysis. *Journal of Social Psychology, 43,* 3–9.

Manasse, A. L. (1984). Principals as leaders of high performing systems. *Educational Leadership, 41,* 42–46.

Manchester, W. (1967). *Death of a president.* Harper Row, NY.

Manchester, W. (1978). *American Caesar: Douglas MacArthur, 1880–1964.* Boston: Little, Brown.

Manchester, W. (1988). Manchester on leadership. *Modern Maturity, 3*(5), 40–46, 108–111.

Manchester, W. (1992). *A world lit only by fire: The medieval mind and the Renaissance; Portrait of an age.* Boston: Little, Brown.

Mandel, B. (1963). *Samuel Gompers: A biography.* Yellow Springs, Ohio: Antioch Press.

Mandell, M. M. (1950a). The administrative judgment test. *Journal of Applied Psychology, 34,* 145–147.

Mandell, M. M. (1950b). Validation of group oral performance test. *Personnel Psychology, 3,* 179–185.

Mandell, M. M., & Duckworth, P. (1955). The supervisor's job: A survey. *Personnel, 31,* 456–462.

Mandell, M. P. (2000). A revised look at management network structures. *International Journal of Organizational Theory & Behavior, 3,* 185–209.

Mangaliso, M. P. (2001). Building competitive advantage from ubuntu: Management lessons from South Africa. *Academy of Management Executive, 15*(3), 23–33.

Manheim, H. L. (1960). Intergroup interaction as related to status and leadership differences between groups. *Sociometry, 23,* 415–427.

Mankiewicz, F. (1973). *Perfectly clear.* New York: New York Times.

Mankiewicz, F. (1973). *Perfectly clear: Nixon from Whittier to Watergate.* New York: Quadrangle.

Mann, F. C. (1951). Changing superior–subordinate relationships. *Journal of Social Issues*, 7–8, 56–63.

Mann, F. C. (1965). Toward an understanding of the leadership role in formal organization. In R. Dubin (ed.), *Leadership and productivity.* San Francisco: Chandler.

Mann, F. C., & Baumgartel, H. (1952). *Absences and employee attitudes in an electric power company.* Ann Arbor: University of Michigan, Survey Research Center.

Mann, F. C., & Dent, J. K. (1954b). *Appraisals of supervisors and attitudes of their employees in an electric power company.* Ann Arbor: University of Michigan, Survey Research Center.

Mann, F. C., & Hoffman, L. R. (1960). *Automation and the worker: A study of social change in power plants.* New York: Holt, Rinehart & Winston.

Mann, F. C., Indik, B. R, & Vroom, V. H. (1963). *The productivity of work groups.* Ann Arbor: University of Michigan, Survey Research Center.

Mann, F. C., & Sparling, J. E. (1956). Changing absence rates: An application of research findings. *Personnel*, 32, 392–408.

Mann, J. H., & Mann, C. H. (1959a). The effect of role-playing experience on role-playing ability. *Sociometry*, 22, 64–74.

Mann, J. H., & Mann, C. H. (1959b). Role playing and interpersonal adjustment. *Journal of Counseling Psychology*, 6, 148–152.

Mann, J. H., & Mann, C. H. (1959c). The importance of group task in producing group-member personality and behavior changes. *Human Relations*, 12, 75–80.

Mann, J. W. (1961). Group relations in hierarchies. *Journal of Social Psychology*, 54, 283–314.

Mann, R. D. (1959). A review of the relationships between personality and performance in small groups. *Psychological Bulletin*, 56, 241270.

Mann, R. D. (1961). Dimensions of individual performance in small groups under task and social-emotional conditions. *Journal of Abnormal and Social Psychology*, 62, 674–682.

Mann, R. D., Gibbard, G. S., & Hartman, J. J. (1967). *Interpersonal styles and group development: An analysis of the member–leader relationship.* New York: Wiley.

Mann, W. C. & Gruner, C. R. (1981). "Sick jokes," speaker sex, and informative speech. *Southern Speech Communication Journal*, 46, 411–418.

Mannari, H., & Abegglen, J. (1963). The educational background of Japan's industrial leaders. *Bessatsu chuo koron: Keiei mondai*, Winter, 190–197.

Mannheim, B. F., Rim, Y., Grinberg, B. (1967). Instrumental status of supervisors as related to workers' perceptions and expectations. *Human Relations*, 20, 387–396.

Manning, F. J. (1991). Morale, cohesion, and esprit de corps. In R. Gal & A. D. Mangelsdorff (eds.), *Handbook of Military Psychology.* New York: John Wiley & Sons.

Manning, W. H., & Jackson, R. (1984). College entrance examinations: Objective selection or gatekeeping for the economically privileged. In C. R. Reynolds & R. I Brown (eds.), *Perspectives on bias in mental testing.* New York: Plenum.

Manogran, P., & Conlon, E. J. (1993) *A leader-member-exchange approach to explaining organizational citizenship behavior.* Paper, Academy of Management, Atlanta, GA.

Manor, J. (1993). Mahatma Gandhi as architect capturing and sustaining the British Raj in Indian government. In G. Sheffer, *Innovative leaders in international politics.* Albany, NY: State University of New York at Albany Press

Mansor, N., & Asri Mohd Ali, M. (1998). An exploratory study of organizational flexibility in Malaysia. *International Journal of Human Resource Management*, 9, 506–515.

Mansour, J. M. (1969). Leadership behavior and principal-teacher interpersonal relations. *Dissertation Abstracts International*, 30, 526.

Manz, C. C. (1983). Improving performance through self-leadership. *National Productivity Review*, 2(3), 288–297.

Manz, C. C. (1986). Self-leadership: Toward an expanded theory of self-influence processes in organizations. *Academy of Management Review*, 11, 585–600.

Manz, C. C. (1992). Self-leading work teams: Moving beyond self-management myths. *Human Relations*, 45, 1119–1140.

Manz, C. C., Adsit, D. J., Dennis, J., Campbell, S., & Mathison-Hance, M. (1988). Managerial thought patterns and performance: A study of perceptual patterns of performance hindrances for higher and lower performing managers. *Human Relations*, 41, 447–465.

Manz, C. C., & Angle, H. L. (1985). *Does group self-management mean a loss of personal control?: Triangulating a paradox.* Paper, Academy of Management, San Diego, CA.

Manz, C. C., Mossholder, K. W., & Luthans, F. (1983). *A contemporary perspective of control in organizations: A social learning view.* Paper, Academy of Management, Dallas.

Manz, C. C., & Sims, H. P., Jr. (1980). Self-management as a substitute for leadership: A social learning theory perspective. *Academy of Management Review*, 5, 361–367.

Manz, C. C., & Sims, H. P., Jr., (1984). Searching for the "Unleader": Organizational member views on leading self-managed teams. *Human Relations*, 37, 409–424.

Manz, C. C., & Sims, H. P., Jr. (1986a). Beyond imitation: Complex behavioral and affective linkages resulting from exposure to leadership training models. *Journal of Applied Psychology*, 71, 571–578.

Manz, C. C., & Sims, H. P., Jr. (1986b). Leading self-managed groups: A conceptual analysis of a paradox. *Economic and Industrial Democracy*, 7, 141–165.

Manz, C. C., & Sims, H. P., Jr. (1987). Leading workers to lead themselves: The external leadership of self-managing work teams. *Administrative Science Quarterly*, 32, 106–129.

Manz, C., & Sims, H. P., Jr. (1989). *Superleadership: Leading others to lead themselves.* New York: Simon & Schuster.

Manz, C. C., & Sims, H. P., Jr. (1991). Superleadership: Beyond the myth of heroic leadership. *Organizational Dynamics*, 19(4), 18–35.

Manz, C. C., & Sims, H. P., Jr. (1993). Superleadership: Beyond the myth of heroic leadership. In D. Bohl (ed.), *New Dimensions in Leadership.* New York: American Management Association.

Manz, C. C., & Sims, H. P., Jr. (1993). *Business without bosses.* New York: John Wiley & Sons.

Manz, C. C., & Sims, H. P. (2001). *The new Superleadership: Leading others to lead themselves.* San Francisco, CA: Berrett-Koehler.

Marak, G. E. (1964). The evolution of leadership structure. *Sociometry*, 27, 174–182.

Maranell, G. M. (1970). The evaluation of presidents: An extension of the Schlesinger polls. *Journal of American History, 57,* 104–113.

Maraniss, D. (1998). Past a predictor of Clinton's present. *Press & Sun-Bulletin* (Binghamton, NY), February 12, 9A.

March, J. C. (1955). Group autonomy and internal group control. *Social Forces, 33,* 322–326.

March, J. C., & Olsen, J. P. (1984). The new institutionalism: Organizational factors in political life. *American Political Science Review, 78,* 734–749.

March, J. C., & Simon, H. A. (1958). *Organizations.* New York: Wiley.

Marchant, M. P. (1976). *Participative management in academic libraries.* Westport, CT: Greenwood.

Marchetti, P. V. (1953). Some aspects of the manager-employee relationship in the retail grocery. *American Psychologist, 8,* 402.

Marcus, J. 1 (1961). Transcendentalism and charisma. *Western Political Quarterly, 14,* 237.

Marder, E. (1960). *Leader behavior as perceived by subordinates as a function of organizational level.* Master's thesis, Ohio State University, Columbus.

Margerison, C., & Glube, R. (1979). Leadership decision making: An empirical test of the Vroom and Yetton model. *Journal of Management Studies, 16,* 45–55.

Margerison, C. J. (1988). Action learning and excellence in management development. *Journal of Management Development, 7,* 43–54.

Margiotta, K. D. (1976). A military elite in transition: Air Force leaders in the 1980's. *Armed Forces and Society, 2,* 155–184.

Margolis, J. D., Walsh, J. P. (2001). *People and Profits?: The search for a link between a company's social and financial performance.* Mahwah, NJ: Lawrence Erlbaum Associates.

Margolis, H. (1982). *Selfishness, altruism, and rationality: A theory of social choice.* Cambridge: Cambridge University Press.

Marion, R. (1999). *The edge of organization: Chaos and complexity theories of formal social systems.* Thousand Oaks, CA: Sage Publications.

Marion, R., & Uhl-Bien, M. (2001). Leadership in complex organizations. *Leadership Quarterly, 12*(4), 389–418.

Marks, J. B. (1959). Interests and group formation. *Human Relations, 12,* 385–390.

Marks, M. L. (1988). The disappearing company man. *Psychology Today, 22*(9), 34–39.

Marks, M. L. & Mirvis, P. H. (2000). Managing mergers, acquisitions, and alliances: Creating an effective transition structure. *Organizational Dynamics, 28*(3), 35–47.

Marks, M. R., & Jenkins, L. W. (1965). *"Initiate structure" and "Consideration"—their surprising and general relation to global ratings or rankings* (Tech. Rep.). Rochester, NY: University of Rochester.

Markessini, J., Lucas, K. W., Chandler, X., et al. (1994). *Executive leadership: Requisite cognitive skills and developmental processes for the U.S. Army civilian executives.* Research Note 94–26, Alexandria VA: U.S. Army Institute for the Behavioral and Social Sciences.

Markham, S. E. (1988). The pay-for-performance dilemma revisited: An empirical example of the importance of group effects. *Journal of Applied Psychology, 73,* 172–180.

Markham, S. E., Yammarino, F. J., Murry, W. D., & Palanski, M. E. (in press). Leader-member exchange, shared values, and performance: Agreement and levels of analysis do matter. *Leadership Quarterly,* forthcoming.

Markoff, J. (2005). When + adds up to minus: Fiorina's confrontational tenure at Hewlett-Packard comes to a close. *New York Times,* February 10p. C1, C7.

Marks, M., & Mirvis, P. H. (2000). Managing mergers, acquisitions, and alliances: Creating an effective transmission structure. *Organizaional Dynamics, 28*(3), 35–47.

Marks, M. A., Zaccaro, S. J., & Mathieu, J. E. (2000). Performance implications of leader briefings and team-interaction training for team adaptation to novel environments. *Journal of Applied Psychology, 85,* 971–986.

Markus, H. R., Kitayama. S., & Heiman, R. (1996). Culture and "basic" psychological principles. In E. T. Higgins & A. W. Kruglanski (eds.), *Social psychology: Handbook of basic principles.* New York: Guilford Press.

Markus, H., Smith, X., & Moreland, X. (1977). Self-schemata and processing information about the self. *Journal of Personality and Social Psychology, 35,* 63–78.

Marquis, D. G. (1962). Individual responsibility and group decisions involving risk. *Industrial Management Review, 3,* 8–23.

Marrow, A. J. (1964b). Risks and uncertainties in action research. *Journal of Social Issues, 20,* 5–20.

Marrow, A. J., Bowers, D. C., & Seashore, S. E. (1968). *Management by participation.* New York: Harper & Row.

Marschall, D. E., Saftner, J., and Tangney, J. P. (1994). *The state shame and guilt scale.* Fairfax, VA: George Mason University.

Marsh, H. W., Richards, G. E., & Barnes, J. (1987). A long-term followup of the effects of participation in an outward bound program. *Personality and Social Psychology Bulletin, 12,* 475–492.

Marsh, M. K., & Atherton, R. M., Jr. (1981–1982). Leadership, organizational type, and subordinate satisfaction in the U.S. Army: The hi-hi paradigm sustained. *Journal of Social Relations, 9,* 121–143.

Marsh, R. M., & Mannari, H. (1971). Lifetime commitment in Japan: Roles, norms, and values. *American Journal of Sociology, 76,* 795–812.

Marshall, G. L. (1964). *Predicting executive achievement.* Doctoral dissertation, Harvard University, Cambridge, MA.

Marshall-Mies, J. C., Fleishman, E. A., Martin, J. A., et al. (2000). Development and evaluation of cognitive and meta-cognitive measures for predicting leadership potential. *Leadership Quarterly, 11,* 135–153.

Marshall, J., & Stewart, R. (1981). Managers' job perceptions: Their overall frameworks and working strategies. *Journal of Management Studies, 18,* 177–190.

Marshall, S. L. A. (1964). *World War I.* New York: American Heritage.

Marson, P. P., & Bruff, C. D. (undated). *The impact of classroom leadership training on managerial/supervisory job performance.* Leadership Developmental Program, Federal Aviation Administration, Washington, DC.

Marston, A. (1964). Personality variables related to self-reinforcement. *Journal of Psychology, 58,* 169–175.

Martin, D. C. (1987). Factors influencing pay decisions: Balancing managerial vulnerabilities. *Human Relations, 40,* 417–430.

Martin, H. J., & Hunt, J. G. (1981). *Discretionary leadership: Theory and measurement.* Paper, Midwest Academy of Management, Carbondale, IL.

Martin, J., & Harder, J. (1988). *Bread and roses: Justice and the distribution of financial and socio-emotional rewards in organizations* (Research Paper No. 1010). Stanford, CA: Stanford University, Graduate School of Business.

Martin, J., Feldman, M. S., Hatch, M. J., & Sitkin, S. B. (1983). The uniqueness paradox in organizational stories. *Administrative Science Quarterly, 28,* 438–453.

Martin, J., Scully, M., & Levitt, B. (1988). *In justice and the legitimation of revolution: Damning the past, excusing the present, and neglecting the future.* Unpublished manuscript

Martin, J., & Siehl, C. (1983). Organizational culture and counterculture: An uneasy symbiosis. *Organizational Dynamics, 12*(2), 52–64.

Martin, J., Sitkin, S. B., & Boehm, M. (1985). Founders and the elusiveness of a cultural legacy. In P. J. Frost, L. F. Moore, M. R. Louis, C. C. Lundberg, & J. Martin (eds.), *Organizational culture.* Beverly Hills, CA: Sage.

Martin, M. M. (1996). *Leadership in a cultural trust chasm: An analysis of trust directed behaviors and vision directed behaviors that lead to positive follower attitude responses.* Doctoral dissertation, Virginia Commonwealth University, Richmond, VA.

Martin, N. H. (1959). The levels of management and their mental demands. In W. L. Warner & N. H. Martin (eds.), *Industrial man.* New York: Harper & Row.

Martin, N. H., & Sims, J. H. (1956). Thinking ahead: Power tactics. *Harvard Business Review, 34*(6), 25–36, 140.

Martin, W. E., Gross, N., & Darley, J. G. (1952) Studies of group behavior: Leaders, followers, and isolates in small organized groups. *Journal of Abnormal and Social Psychology, 47,* 838–842.

Martin, W. J., & Willower, D. J. (1981). The managerial behavior of high school principals. *Educational Administration Quarterly, 17,* 69–90.

Martindale, C. (1975). *Romantic progression: The psychology of literary history.* Washington, DC: Hemisphere

Martinez-Cosio, M. (1996). Leadership in communities of color: Elements and sensitivities of a universal model. *Journal of Leadership Studies, 3*(1), 71–77.

Martinko, M. J. (2002). *Thinking like a winner: A guide to high performance.* Tallahassee, FL: Gulf Coast Publishing.

Martinko, M. J. (1995). *Attribution theory: An organizational perspective.* Delray Beach, FL: St. Lucie Press.

Martinko, M. J., & Gardner, W. L. (1984a). The observation of high performing educational managers: Methodological issues and managerial implications. In J. G. Hunt, D. Hosking, C. A. Schriesheim, & R. Stewart (eds.), *Leaders and managers: International perspectives on managerial behavior and leadership.* New York: Pergamon.

Martinko, M. J., & Gardner, W. L. (1984b). *The behavior of high performing educational managers: An observational study.* Department of Management, Florida State University, Tallahassee, FL.

Martinko, M. J., & Gardner, W. L. (1985). Beyond structured observation: Methodological issues and new directions. *Academy of Management Review, 10,* 676–695.

Martinko, M. J. & Gardner, W. L. (1987) The leader/member attributional process. *Academy of Management Review, 12,* 235–249.

Martins, L. L., & Kambil, A. (1999). Looking back and thinking ahead: Effects of prior success on managers' interpretations of new information technologies. *Academy of Management Journal, 42,* 652–661.

Martinsen, O. L. (2000). *The Big Five and 360 degree evaluations of leadership behavior.* Paper, Academy of Management, Washington, D.C.

Marvin, P. (1968). *Management goals: Guidelines and accountability.* Homewood, IL: Dow Jones–Irwin.

Marwell, G. (1966). Types of past experience with potential work partners: Their effects on partner choice. *Human Relations, 19,* 437–447.

Marwell, G., & Schmitt, D. (1967). Dimensions of compliance-gaining behavior: An empirical analysis. *Sociometry, 30,* 350–364.

Masi, R. (1994). *Transformational leadership and its roles in empowerment, productivity and commitment to quality.* Doctoral dissertation, University of Illinois, Chicago.

Masi, R., & Cooke, R. A. (2000). Effects of transformational leadership on subordinate motivation, empowering norms, and organizational productivity. *International Journal of Organizational Analysis, 8*(1), 16–47.

Maslach, C., & Jackson, S. E. (1986). *Manual: Maslach Burnout Inventory.* Palo Alto, CA: Consulting Psychologists Press.

Masling, J. M. (1953). The Bainbridge study. In D. Courtney (ed.), *Naval, neighborhood, and national leadership.* Philadelphia: Institute for Research in Human Relations.

Masling, J. M., Greer, F. L., & Gilmore, R. (1955). Status, authoritarianism, and sociometric choice. *Journal of Social Psychology, 41,* 297–310.

Maslow, A. H. (1954). *Motivation and personality.* New York: Harper.

Maslow, A. H. (1965). *Eupsychian management: A journal.* Homewood, IL: Dorsey.

Maslyn, J. M., & Uhl-Bien, M. (2001). Leader-member exchange and its dimensions: Effects of self and other effort on relationship quality. *Journal of Applied Psychology, 86,* 697–708.

Mason, E. S., & Mudrack, P. E. (1997). Are individuals who agree that corporate social responsibility is a "fundamentally subversive doctrine" inherently unethical? *Applied Psychology: An International Review, 46,* 135–152.

Mason, J. (1996). *Qualitative Researching.* London: Sage.

Mason, J. C. (1992). Leading the way into the 21st century. *Management Review,* October, 16–19.

Mason, J. (1996). *Qualitative Researching.* London: Sage.

Maas, A., & Graf, P. (2004). Leadership by customers? New roles of service companies' customers. *German Journal of Human Resources Research, 18*(3), 329–345.

Massarik, F. (1983). Searching for essence in executive experience. In S. Srivastva (ed.), *The executive mind.* San Francisco: Jossey-Bass.

Massarik, F., Tannenbaum, R., Kahane, M., & Weschler, I. R. (1953). Sociometric choice and organizational effectiveness: A multi-relational approach. *Sociometry, 16,* 211–238.

Mathews, J. E. (1963). Leader behavior of elementary principals and the group dimensions of their staffs. *Dissertation Abstracts, 25,* 2318.

Matthews, K. A., Batson, C. D., Horn, J., & Rosenman, R. H. (1981). Principles in his nature which interest him in the fortune of other: The heritability of empathic concern for others. *Journal of Personality, 49*(3), 237–247.

Matthews, S. (1980). The gentle art of delegation. *Accountancy (UK),* 91, 104–106, 122, 124.

Mathieu, J. E. (1990). A test of subordinates' achievement and affiliation needs as moderators of leader path goal relationships. *Basic & Applied Social Psychology,* 11, 179–189.

Mathieu, J. E., Tannenbaum, S. I., & Salas, E. (1992). Influences of individual and situational characteristics on measures of training effectiveness. *Academy of Management Journal,* 35, 828–847.

Matsui, T., Ohtsuka, Y., & Kikuchi, A. (1978). Consideration and structure behavior as reflections of supervisory interpersonal values. *Journal of Applied Psychology,* 63, 259–262.

Matthes, K. (1992). Telecommuting: Balancing business and employee needs. *HR Focus,* 69(3), December, 3.

Matteson, M. T., & Ivancevich, J. M. (1982). Stress and the medical technologist: 1. A general overview. *American Journal of Medical Technology,* 48, 163–168.

Matusak, L. R. (1997). *Finding your voice: Learning to lead . . . anywhere you want to make a difference.* San Francisco: Jossey-Bass.

Mauer, J. C. (1969). *Work role involvement of industrial supervisors.* East Lansing: Michigan State University, Bureau of Business and Economic Research.

Mauer, K. F. (1974). The utility of the leadership opinion questionnaire in the South African mining industry. *Journal of Behavioral Science,* 74, 67–72.

Maurer, T. J. (2001). Career-relevant learning and development, worker age, and beliefs about self-efficacy for development. *Journal of Management,* 27, 123–140.

Maurer, T. J. (2002). Employee learning and development orientation: Toward an integrative model of involvement in continuous learning. *Human Resource Development Review,* 1(1), 9–44.

Maurer, T. J., Solomon, J. A., Andrews, K. D., et al. (2001). Interviewee coaching, preparation strategies, and response strategies in relation to performance in situational employment interviews: An extension of Maurer, Solamon, and Troxtel (1998). *Journal of Applied Psychology,* 86, 709–717.

Maurer, T. J., & Tarulli, B. (1994). Perceived environment, perceived outcome, and person variables in relationship to voluntary development activity by employees. *Journal of Applied Psychology,* 79, 3–14.

Maurer, T. J. & Weiss, E. (2003). *Continuous learning skill demands associated with dimensions of managerial work.* Paper, Academy of Management, Seattle, WA.

Mausner, B. (1953). Studies in social interaction. III. Effect of variation in one partner's prestige on the interaction of observer pairs. *Journal of Applied Psychology,* 37, 391–393.

Mausner, B. (1954a). The effect of prior reinforcement on the interaction of observer pairs. *Journal of Abnormal and Social Psychology,* 49, 65–68.

Mausner, B. (1954b). The effects of one partner's success in a relevant task on the interaction of observer pairs. *Journal of Abnormal and Social Psychology,* 49, 557–560.

Mausner, B., & Bloch, B. L. (1957). A study of the additivity of variables affecting social interaction. *Journal of Abnormal and Social Psychology,* 54, 250–256.

Mawhinney, I. C., & Ford, J. D. (1977). The path goal theory of leader effectiveness: An operant interpretation. *Academy of Management Review,* 2, 398–411.

Mawhinney, T. C. (1982). Maximizing versus matching in people versus pigeons. *Psychological Reports,* 50, 267–281.

May, G. D., & Kruger, M. J. (1988). The manager within. *Personnel Journal,* 67(2), 56–65.

May, M. A., & Doob, L. W. (1937). *Competition and cooperation* (Bulletin No. 25). New York: Social Science Research Council.

May, O. P., & Thompson, C. L. (1973). Perceived levels of self-disclosure, mental health, and helpfulness of group leaders. *Journal of Counseling Psychology,* 20, 349–352.

May, R. C., & Whittington, J. L. (2003). *The gospel of affirmation: A model for spiritual leafership.* Paper, Academy of Management, Seattle, WA.

Mayberry, B. A. (1925). Training for leadership by means of student government. *Journal of the National Educational Association,* 14, 186.

Mayer, R. J., & Schoorman, F. D. (1995). An integrative model of organizational trust. *Academy of Management Review,* 20, 709–734.

Mayes, B. T. (1979). *Leader needs as moderators of the subordinate job performance–leader behavior relationship.* Paper, Academy of Management, Atlanta, GA.

Mayes. S. F. (1979). Women in positions of authority: A case study of changing sex roles. *Signs; Journal of Women in Culture and Society,* 4(3), 556–568.

Mayfield, E. C. (1964). The selection interview: A re-evaluation of published research. *Personnel Psychology,* 17, 239–260.

Mayfield, J., & Mayfield, M. (1998). Increasing worker outcomes by improving leader follower relations. *Journal of Leadership Studies,* 5, 72–81.

Mayhand, E., & Crusky, O. (1972). A preliminary experiment on the effects of black supervisors on white and black subordinates. *Journal of Black Studies,* 2, 461–470.

Maynard, M. (1994). Evaluations evolve from bottom up: Workers, peers rate managers. *USA Today,* August 3, 6B.

Maynard, M. T. (2003). *The ethical implications of virtual team membership.* Paper, Academy of Management, Seattle.

Mayo, E., & Lombard, G. F. F. (1944). *Teamwork and labor turnover in the aircraft industry of Southern California* (Report No. 32). Cambridge, MA: Harvard Business School.

Mayo, G. C., & DuBois, R. H. (1963). Measurement of gain in leadership training. *Educational Psychology Measurement,* 23, 23–31.

Mayo, M., Pastor, J. C., & Meindl, J. R. (1996). The effects of group heterogeneity on the self-perceived efficacy of group leaders. *Leadership Quarterly,* 7, 265–284.

Mazlish, B. (1976). *The revolutionary ascetic: Evolution of a political type.* New York: Basic Books.

Mazlish, B., & Diamond, E. (1979). *Jimmy Carter: A character portrait.* New York: Simon & Schuster.

Maznevski, M., & Chudoba, K. (2000). Bridging space over time: Global virtual team dynamics and effectiveness. *Organizational Science,* 11, 473–492.

Maznevski, M., & Peterson, M. F. (1997). Societal values, social interpretation, and multinational teams. In C. Beranrose & E. S. Oskampe (eds.), *Cross-cultural work groups.* Thousand Oaks, CA: Sage .

McAllister, D. W., Mitchell, T. R., & Beach, L. R. (1979). The contingency model of decision strategies: An empirical model of the effects of significance, accountability, and reversibility. *Organizational Behavior and Human Performance, 24,* 228–244.

McBroome, W. H. (1987). Longitudinal change in sex role orientations: Differences between men and woman. *Sex Roles, 16,* 439–452.

McCall, M. W., Jr. (1974). *The perceived cognitive role requirements of formal leaders.* Paper, American Psychological Association, New Orleans, LA.

McCall, M. W., Jr. (1977). *Leaders and leadership: Of substance and shadow* (Tech. Rep. No. 2). Greensboro, NC: Center for Creative Leadership.

McCall, M. W., Jr. (1978). Conjecturing about creative leaders. *Journal of Creative Behavior, 14,* 225–234.

McCall, M. W., Jr. (1998). *High flyers: Developing the next generation of leaders.* Boston, MA: Harvard Business School Press.

McCall, M. W., Jr., & Lombardo, M. M. (eds.). (1978). *Leadership: Where else can we go?* Durham, NC: Duke University Press.

McCall, M. W., Jr., & Lombardo, M. M. (1982). Using stimulation for leadership and management research: Through the looking glass. *Management Science, 28,* 533–549.

McCall, M. W., Jr., & Lombardo, M. M. (1983). *Off the track: Why and how successful executives get derailed* (Tech. Rep. No. 21). Greensboro, N.C.: Center for Creative Leadership.

McCall, M. W., Jr., & McCauley, C. D. (1986). *Developmental experiences in managerial work: A literature review* (Tech. Rep. No. 26). Greensboro, NC: Center for Creative Leadership.

McCall, M. W., Jr., Morrison, A. M., & Hanman, R. L. (1978). *Studies of managerial work: Results and methods* (Tech. Rep.). Greensboro, NC: Center for Creative Leadership.

McCall, M. W., Jr., & Segrist, C. A. (1980). *In pursuit of the manager's job: Building on Mintzberg* (Tech. Rep. No. 14). Greensboro, NC: Center for Creative Leadership.

McCandless, B. R. (1942). Changing relationships between dominance and social acceptability during group democratization. *American Journal of Orthopsychiatry, 12,* 529–535.

McCann, E. C. (1964). An aspect of management philosophy in the United States and Latin America. *Academy of Management Journal, 7,* 149–152.

McCarrey, M. W., Gasse, Y., & Moore, L. (1984). Work value goals and instrumentalities: A comparison of Canadian west-coast Anglophone and Quebec City Francophone managers. *International Review of Applied Psychology, 33,* 291–303.

McCarthy, A., & Garavan, T. (2003). *Predicting 360-degree feedback acceptability: The role of procedural justice, employee cynicism and locus of control.* Paper, Society for Industrial and Organizational Psychology, Orlando, FL.

McCarthy, D. J. (2000). View from the top: Henry Mintzberg on strategy and management. *Academy of Management Executive, 14*(3), 31–35.

McCarthy, J. F. (1993). *Short stories at work: Organizational storytelling as a leadership conduit dying turbulent times.* Paper, Academy of Management, San Francisco, CA.

McCartney, K., Harris, M. J., & Bernieri, F. (1990). Growing up and growing apart: A developmental meta-analysis of twin studies. *Psychological Bulletin, 107*(2), 226–37.

McCauley, C. D. (1987). Stress and the eye of the beholder. *Issues & Observations, 7*(3), 1–16.

McCauley, C. D., & Lombardo, M. M. (1990). BENCHMARKS: An instrument for diagnosing management strength and weaknesses. In K. E. Clark & M. B. Clark (eds.), *Measures of leadership.* West Orange, NJ: Leadership Library of America.

McCauley, C. D., Ruderman, M. N., Ohlott, P. J., et al. (1994). Assessing the developmental components of managerial jobs. *Journal of Applied Psychology, 79,* 544–560.

McCauley, C. D., & Young, D. P.(1993). Creating developmental relationships, roles and strategies. *Human Resources Management Review, 3*(3), 219–230.

McCaulley, M. H. (1989). *The Myers-Briggs type indicator and leadership.* Gainesville, FL: Center for Applications of Psychological Type.

McCaulley, M. H. (1989). "Those who were involved in the production of tangible products or in following established procedures tended to be practical sensing types. Those who provided long-range vision tended to be the imaginative, theoretical, intuitive types." M. H. McCaulley & Staff, 1989.

McClelland, D. C. (1961). *The achieving society.* Princeton, NJ: Van Nostrand.

McClelland, D. C. (1965b). Achievement motivation can be developed. *Harvard Business Review, 43*(6), 6–24, 178.

McClelland, D. C. (1965c). N achievement and entrepreneurship: A longitudinal study. *Journal of Personality and Social Psychology, 1,* 389–392.

McClelland, D. C. (1975a) How motives, skills and values determine what people do. *American Psychologist, 40,* 55–58.

McClelland, D. C. (1975). *Power: The inner experience.* New York: Irvington Publishers (distributed by Halstead Press).

McClelland, D. C. (1980). Motive dispositions: The merits of operant and respondent measures. In L. Wheeler (ed.), *Review of personality and social psychology.* Beverly Hills, CA: Sage.

McClelland, D. C. (1985). How motives, skills, and values determine what people do. *American Psychologist, 40,* 812–825.

McClelland, D. C. (1985). *Human motivation.* Glenview, IL: Scott, Foresman.

McClelland, D. C. (1998). Identifying competencies with behavioral event interviews. *Psychological Science, 9,* 331–339.

MClelland, D. C., & Boyatzis, R. E. (1982). Leadership motive pattern and long-term success in management. *Journal of Applied Psychology, 67,* 737–743.

McClelland, D. C., & Burnham, D. H. (1976). Power is the great motivator. *Harvard Business Review, 54*(2), 100–110.

McClelland, D. C., & Pilon, D. (1983). Sources of adult motives in pattern of parent behavior in early childhood. *Journal of Personality and Social Psychology, 44,* 564–574.

McClelland, D. C., & Winter, D. G. (1969). *Motivating economic achievement.* New York: Free Press.

McClintock, C. G. (1966). The behavior of leaders, non-leaders, non-joiners, and non-leader joiners under conditions of group support and non-support. In R. V. Bowers (ed.), *Studies on behavior in organizations.* Athens: University of Georgia Press.

McColl-Kennedy, J. R., & Anderson, R. D. (2002). Impact of leadership style and emotions on subordinate performance. *Leadership Quarterly, 13*(5), 545–559.

McComb, S., Green, S. G., & Compton, W. D. (2003). *The relationship between team context and the team leader's linking pin quality.* Paper, Academy of Management, Seattle, WA.

McConkie, M. L. (1979). A clarification of the goal setting and appraisal, process in MBO. *Academy of Management Review, 4,* 29–40.

McConkie, M. L. (1984). *The symbolic meanings of leadership.* Paper, International Congress of Psychology, Acapulco.

McCormick, J., & Powell, B. (1988). Management for the 1990's. *Newsweek,* April, 47–48.

McCormick, M. J. (2001). *Applying social cognitive theory in leadership: A new paradigm.* Paper, Society of Industrial Organizational Psychology, San Diego, CA.

McCormick, M. J., & Martinko, M. J. (2004). Identifying leader social cognitions: Integrating the causal reasoning perspective into social cognitive theory. *Journal of Leadership & Organizational Studies, 10*(4), 2–11.

McCoy, D. (1967). *Calvin Coolidge: The quiet president.* New York: Macmillan.

McCrae, R. R., & Costa, P. T., Jr. (1987). Validation of the five-factor model of personality across instruments and observers. *Journal of Personality and Social Psychology, 52,* 81–90.

McCrae, R. R., & Costa, P. T., Jr., (1990). *Personality in adulthood.* New York: Guilford.

McCrae, R. R., & Costa, P. T., Jr., (1992). Discriminant validity of NEO-PIR facet scales. *Educational & Psychological Measurement, 52*(1), 229.

McCrae, R. R., & Costa, P. T., Jr. (1997). Personality trait structure as a human universal. *American Psychologist, 52,* 509–516.

McCrae, R., Zonderman, A. B., Costa, P. T. Jr., Bond, M. H., & Paunone, S. V. (1996). Evaluating replicability of factors in the revised NEO personality: Confirmatory factor analysis versus Procrustes rotation. *Journal of Personality & Social Psychology, 70*(3), 552–566.

McCroskey, J. C. (1977). *Oral communication apprehension: A summary.* Unpublished manuscript.

McCroskey, J. C., & Richmond, V. (1979). The impact of communication apprehension on individuals in organizations. *Communication Quarterly, 27,* 55–61.

McCroskey, J. C., & Young, T. J. (1981). Ethos and credibility: The construct and its measurement after three decades. *Speech Monographs, 41,* 261–266.

McCullough, C. E. (1975). The effects of changes in organizational structure: Demonstration projects in an oil refinery. In L. E. Davis & A. B. Cherns (eds.), *The quality of working life.* Vol. 2: *Cases and commentary.* New York: Free Press.

McCullough, D. (1992). *Truman.* New York: Simon & Schuster.

McCullough, M. E. (2000). Forgiveness as human strength: theory, measurement, and links to well-being. *Journal of Social and Clinical Psychology, 19,* 43–45.

McCullough, M. F. (2001). Forgiveness: Who does it and how do they do it? *Current Directions in Psychological Sciences, 10,* 194–197.

McCurdy, H. G., & Eber, H. W. (1953). Democratic versus authoritarian: A further investigation of group problem-solving. *Journal of Personality, 22,* 258–269.

McCurdy, H. G., & Lambert, W. E. (1952). The efficiency of small human groups in the solution of problems requiring genuine cooperation. *Journal of Personality, 20,* 478–494.

McDevitt, T. M., & Gadalla, S. M. (1985–1986). Special issue: Migration intentions and behavior: Third World perspectives. *Population & Environment: Behavioral & Social Issues, 8,* 98–119.

McDonald, F. (1994). *The American presidency: An intellectual history.* Lawrence: Kansas University Press.

McDonnell, J. F. (1974). An analysis of participative management as a choice of leadership style. *Dissertation Abstracts International, 35,* 1339.

McDonough, E. F., III & Kinnunen, R. M. (1984). Management control of new product development projects. *IEEE Transactions on Engineering Management, 31*(1), 18–21.

McEachern, W. A. (1975). *Managerial control and performance.* Lexington, MA: D. C. Heath.

McElroy, J. C. (1982). A typology of attribution leadership research. *Academy of Management Review, 7,* 413–417.

McElroy, J. C. (1985). Inside the teaching machine: Integrating attribution and reinforcement theories. *Academy of Management, 11,* 123–141.

McElroy, J. C., & Schrader, C. B. (1986). Attribution theories of leadership and network analysis. *Journal of Management, 12,* 351–362.

McEvoy, G. M. (1988). Predicting managerial performance: A seven year assessment center validation study. *Proceedings,* Academy of Management, Anaheim, CA, 277–281.

McEvoy, G. M., & Beatty, R. (1989). Assessment centers and subordinate appraisals of managers: A seven year examination of predictive validity. *Personnel Psychology, 42,* 37–52.

McEvoy, G. M., Cragun, J. R., & Appleby, M. (1997). Using outdoor training to develop and accomplish organizational vision. *Human Resource Planning, 20*(3), 20–28.

McFarland, L. J., Senn, L. E,, & Childress, J. R. (1993). *Twenty-first century leadership: Dialogues with 100 top leaders,* Long Beach, CA: Leadership Press.

McFeely, W. M., & Mussmann, W. W. (1945). Training supervisors in leadership. *Personnel, 21,* 217–223.

McFillen, J. M. (1977). The organizing and managing of organizational behavior: A review of first edition organizational behavior texts. *Academy of Management Review, 2,* 355–359.

McFillen, J. M. (1978). *The role of power, supervision, and performance in leadership productivity* (Working Paper). Columbus: Ohio State University, College of Administrative Sciences.

McFillen, J. M., & New, J. R. (1978). *Situational determinants of supervisor attributes and behavior* (Working Paper). Columbus: Ohio State University, College of Adminstrative Sciences.

McFillen, J. M., & New, J. R. (1979). Situational determinants of supervisor attributions and behavior. *Academy of Management Journal, 22,* 793–809.

McGee, R. & Cody, H. H. (1995). Cultivating mentors. *Winds of Change, 10*(3), 32–34.

McGehee, W., & Tullar, W. L. (1978). A note on evaluating behavior modification and behavior modeling as industrial training techniques. *Personnel Psychology, 31,* 477–484.

McGill, M. E., & Slocum, J. W. Jr. (1993). Unlearning the organization. *Organizational Dynamics, 22*(2), 67–79.

McGill, M. E., & Slocum, J. W. (1994). Leading learning. *Journal of Leadership Studies, 1*(3), 7–21.

McGill, M. E., & Slocum, J. W. Jr. (1998). A little leadership please? *Organizational Dynamics, 26*(3), 39–49.

McGrath, J. E. (1964). *Leadership behavior: Some requirements for leadership training.* Washington, DC: Office of Career Development, U.S. Civil Service Commission.

McGrath, J. E. (1997). Small group research, that once and future field: An interpretation of the past with an eye on the future. *Group Dynamics, 1,* 7–27.

McGregor, D. (1944). Conditions of effective leadership in the industrial organization. *Journal of Consulting Psychology, 8,* 55–63.

McGregor, D. (1960). *The human side of enterprise.* New York: McGraw-Hill.

McGregor, D. (1966). *Leadership and motivation.* Cambridge, MA: M.I.T. Press.

McGrory, M. (1994). Let Roosevelt fill Clinton's shoes in campaign, *Press & Sun Bulletin* (Binghamton, NY), November 1, 17A.

McGruder, J. (1976). *The community reintegration centers of Ohio: A case analysis in community based corrections.* Doctoral dissertation, Ohio State University, Columbus.

McGuire, C., Lammon, M., & White, G. D. (1953). Adolescent peer acceptance and valuations of role behaviors. *American Psychologist, 8,* 397 (Abstract).

McGuire, M. A. (1987). *The contribution of intelligence to leadership performance on an in-basket test.* Master's thesis, University of Washington, Seattle.

McHenry, J. J. (1986). *Activity and responsibility differences between first-level and middle managers: The effects of job function.* Paper, American Psychological Association, Washington, DC.

McHoskey, J. W., Worzel, W., & Szyarto, C. (1998). Machiavellianism and psychopathy. *Journal of Personality and Social Psychology, 74,* 192–210.

McInerney, T. J. (1981). Eisenhower Governance and the power to command: A perspective on presidential leadership. *Presidential Studies Quarterly, 11,* 262–270.

McKeachie, W. J. (1954). Individual conformity to attitudes of classroom groups. *Journal of Abnormal and Social Psychology, 49,* 282–289.

McKee, V. (1992). Managing without the charisma. *Times* (London), October 4, Section 5, p.5.

McKenna, J. F. (1991). Bob Galvin: Predicts life after perfection. *Industry Week,* January 21, 12–14.

McKinley, W., Sanchez, C. M., & Schick, A. G. (1997). Organizational downsizing: constraining, cloning, learning. *IEEE Engineering Management Review, 25*(1)16–23.

McKenna, P. J. & Maister, D. (2002). *First among equals.* New York: Free Press.

McLachlan, J. F. (1974). Therapy strategies, personality orientation and recovery from alcoholism. *Canadian Psychiatric Association Journal, 19,* 25–30.

McLaughlin, G. W. (1971). *The use of high school faculty ratings to predict USMA fourth class performance.* West Point, NY: United States Military Academy, Office of Institutional Research.

McMahon, J. T. (1972). The contingency theory: Logic and method revisited. *Personnel Psychology, 25,* 697–710.

McMartin, J. A. (1970). Two tests of an averaging model of social influence. *Journal of Personality and Social Psychology, 15,* 317–325.

McNally, J. A., Gerras, S. J., & Bullis, R. C. (1996). Teaching leadership at the U.S. Military Academy at West Point. *Journal of Applied Behavioral Science, 32,* 175–187.

McNamara, V. D. (1968). *Leadership, staff, and school effectiveness.* Doctoral dissertation, University of Alberta, Alberta, Canada.

McNatt, D. B. (2000). Ancient Pygmalion joins contemporary management: A meta-analysis of the result. *Journal of Applied Psychology, 85*(2), 314–322.

McNeese-Smith, D. K. (1999). The relationship between managerial motivation, leadership, nurse outcomes and patient satisfaction. *Journal of Organizational Behavior, 20,* 243–259.

McNeilly, M. R. (1996). *Sun Tzu and the art of business.* Oxford, U.K.: Oxford University Press.

McPherson-Frantz, C. & Janoff-Bulman, R. (2000). Considering both sides: The limits of perspective taking. *Basic and Applied Social Psychology, 22,* 31–42.

McSweeney, J. P. (1976). Rumors—enemy of company morale and community relations. *Personnel Journal, 55,* 435–436.

Mead, G. H. (1934). *Mind, self and society from the standpoint of a social behaviorist.* Chicago: University of Chicago Press

Mead, M. (1930). *Growing up in New Guinea—A comparative study of primitive education.* New York: Morrow.

Mead, M. (1935). *Sex and temperament in three primitive societies.* New York: Morrow.

Mead, M. (1939). *From the South Seas: Coming of age in Samoa.* New York: Morrow.

Mead, M., Mirsky, M., Landes, R., et al. (1937). *Cooperation and competition among primitive peoples.* New York: McGraw-Hill.

Meade, R. D. (1967). An experimental study of leadership in India. *Journal of Social Psychology, 72,* 35–43.

Meade, R. D., & Whittaker, J. D. (1967). A cross-cultural study of authoritarianism. *Journal of Social Psychology, 72,* 3–7.

Mechanic, D. (1962). Sources of power of lower participants in complex organizations. *Administrative Science Quarterly, 7,* 349–364.

Medalia, N. Z. (1954). Unit size and leadership perception. *Sociometry, 17,* 64–67.

Medalia, N. Z. (1955). Authoritarianism, leader acceptance, and group cohesion. *Journal of Abnormal and Social Psychology, 51,* 207–213.

Medalia, N. Z., & Miller, D. C. (1955). Human relations leadership and the association of morale and efficiency in work groups: A controlled study with small military units. *Social Forces, 33,* 348–352.

Medcof, J. W., & Evans, M. G. (1986). Heroic or competent? A second look. *Organizational Behavior and Human Decision Processes, 38,* 295–304.

Medow, H., & Zander, A. (1965). Aspirations for the group chosen by central and peripheral members. *Journal of Personality and Social Psychology, 1,* 224–228.

Meehl, P. (1967). Theory testing in psychological physics. *Philosophy of Science, 34,* 103–115.

Megargee, E. I. (1969). Influence of sex roles on the manifestation of leadership. *Journal of Applied Psychology*, 53, 377–382.

Megargee, E. I., Bogart, P., & Anderson, B. J. (1966). Prediction of leadership in a simulated industrial task. *Journal of Applied Psychology*, 50, 292–295.

Meglino, B. M., Ravlin, E. C., & Adkins, C. L. (1992). The measurement of work value congruence: A field study comparison. *Journal of Management*, 18, 33–43.

Meheut, Y., & Siegel, J. P. (1973). *A study of leader behavior and MBO success*. Toronto: University of Toronto, Faculty of Management Studies. Unpublished manuscript.

Mehrabian, A. (1968a). Inference of attitude from the posture, orientation, and distance of a communicator. *Journal of Consulting Clinical Psychology*, 32, 296–308.

Mehrabian, A. (1968b). Communication with words. *Psychology Today*, 2(4), 53–56.

Meindl, J. R. (1990). On leadership: An alternative to conventional wisdom. In B. M. Straw & H. H. Cummings (eds.), *Research in organizational behavior*, 12, 159–204. Greenwich, CT: JAI Press.

Meindl, J. R. (1993). Reinventive leadership: A radical social psychological approach. In J. K. Murningham (ed.), *Social psychology in organizational advances in theory* A. Englewood Cliffs, NJ: Prentice Hall.

Meindl, J. R. (1995). The romance of leadership as a follower-centric theory: A social constructionist approach. *Leadership Quarterly*, 6, 329–341.

Meindl, J. R. (1998). Appendix: Measures and assessments for the romance of leadership approach. *Monographs in organizational behavior and industrial relations*, 24(B), 299–302.

Meindl, J. R., & Ehrlich, S. B. (1987). The romance of leadership and the evaluation of organizational performance. *Academy of Management Journal*, 30, 91–109.

Meindl, J. R., Ehrlich, S. B., & Dukerich, J. M. (1985). The romance of leadership. *Administrative Science Quarterly*, 30, 78–102.

Melcher, A. J. (1976). Participation: A critical review of research findings. *Human Resources Management*, 15(2), 12–21.

Mellahi, K. (2000). The teaching of leadership on UK MBA programmes: A critical analysis from an international perspective. *Journal of Management Development*, 19(4), 297–308.

Meltzer, L. (1956). Scientific productivity in organizational settings. *Journal of Social Issues*, 12, 32–40.

Mendell, J. S., & Gerjuoy, H. C. (1984). Anticipatory management or visionary leadership: A debate. *Managerial Planning*, 33(3), 28–31, 63.

Mendenhall, M. E. (1983). Self-monitoring as a determinant of leader emergence. *Dissertation Abstracts International*, 44(7B), 2284.

Menkes, J. (1999). *Gender differences in management styles*. Paper, Society for Industrial and Organizational Psychology, Atlanta, GA.

Menon, S. T. (2003). *Task focus: A meta-competence for career success?* Paper, Academy of Management, Seattle, WA.

Merei, F. (1949). Group leadership and institutionalization. *Human Relations*, 2, 23–39.

Merriam, C. E. (1926). *Four American party leaders*. New York: Macmillan.

Merriam, C. E., & Gosnell, H. E. (1929). *The American party system*. New York: Macmillan.

Merron, K., Fisher, D., & Torbert, W. R. (1987). Meaning making and management action. *Group & Organization Studies*, 12, 274–286.

Merton, R. K. (1940). Bureaucratic structure and personality. *Social Forces*, 18, 560–568.

Merton, R. K. (1949, 1957). *Social theory and social structure*. New York: Free Press.

Merton, R. K. (1969). The social nature of leadership. *American Journal of Nursing*, 69, 2614–2618.

Merton, R. K., & Kitt, A. S. (1950). Contributions to the theory of reference group behavior. In R. K. Merton, & P. F. Lazarsfeld (eds.), *Studies in the scope and method of "The American Soldier."* New York: Free Press.

Messick, D. M., & Bazerman, M. H. (1996). Ethical leadership and the psychology of decision making. *Sloan Management Review*, 37(2), 9–22.

Messina, J. L., Roberts, W., & Becker, G. A. (2004). *Manager attitudes toward persons with disabilities as measured by two attitudinal instruments*. Paper, Academy of Management, New Orleans, LA.

Metcalfe, B. A. (1984). Microskills of leadership: A detailed analysis of the behaviors of managers in the appraisal interview. In J. Hunt, D. M. Hosking, C. A. Schriesheim, & R. Stewart (eds.), *Leaders and managers: International perspectives on managerial behavior and leadership*. New York: Pergamon.

Metzger, T. A. (1977). *Escape from predicament*. New York: Columbia University Press.

Meuwese, W. A. T., & Fiedler, F. E. (1965). *Leadership and group creativity under varying conditions of stress* (Tech. Rep.). Urbana: University of Illinois, Group Effectiveness Research Laboratory.

Mey, W. (1936). Spontaneous and elective leadership in school classes. *Pidagogische Studien und Kritiken*, 12, 1–82.

Meyer, C. T. (1947). The assertive behavior of children as related to parent behavior. *Journal of Home Economics*, 39, 77–80.

Meyer, E.C. (1982). The unit. *Defense*, 82, 1–9.

Meyer, E. C. (1980). Leadership: A return to the basics. *Military Review*, 60(7), 4–9.

Meyer, E. C. (1983). Leadership: A soldier's view. *Washington Quarterly*, 6(3), 169–174.

Meyer, H. D. (1961). *An exploratory study of the executive position description questionnaire in the Jewel Tea Co., Inc.* Paper, Conference on the Executive Study, Princeton, NJ.

Meyer, H. D. (1963). *A four year study of management promotions in the Jewel Tea Co. as related to three measures of achievement motivation*. Chicago: Jewel Tea Co. (Reported in Campbell, Dunnette, et al., 1970, 190–191.)

Meyer, H. H. (1951). Factors related to success in human relations aspect of work-group leadership. *Psychological Monographs*, 65, No. '320.

Meyer, H. H. (1959). A comparison of foreman and general foreman conceptions of the foreman's job responsibility. *Personnel Psychology*, 12, 445–452.

Meyer, H. H. (1968). Achievement motivation and industrial climates. In R. Tagiuri & G. H. Litwin (eds.), *Organizational climate*. Boston: Harvard University, Graduate School of Business Administration.

Meyer, H. H. (1970a). The validity of the in-basket test as a measure of managerial performance. *Personnel Psychology*, 23, 297–307.

Meyer, H. H. (1970b). *Improving supervisor-employee relations in the shop.* Unpublished manuscript.

Meyer, H. H. (1972). *Assessment centers at General Electric.* Paper, Development Dimensions Orientation Conference, San Francisco.

Meyer, H. H. (1975). The pay for performance dilemma. *Organizational Dynamics, 3*(3), 39–50.

Meyer, H. H., Kay, E., & French, J. R. P. (1965). Split roles in performance appraisal. *Harvard Business Review, 43*(1), 123–129.

Meyer, H. H., & Walker, W. B. (1961). Need for achievement and risk preferences as they relate to attitudes toward reward systems and performance appraisal in an industrial setting. *Journal of Applied Psychology, 45,* 251–256.

Meyer, J. P., & Allen, N. J. (1991). *Commitment to the workplace: Theory, research, and application.* Thousand Oaks, CA: Sage Publications.

Meyer, M. W. (1968). The two authority structures of bureaucratic organization. *Administrative Science Quarterly, 13,* 211–228.

Meyer, M. W. (1975). Leadership and organizational structure. *American Journal of Sociology, 81,* 514–542.

Meyers, C. E. (1944). The effect of conflicting authority on the child. *University of Iowa Study on Child Welfare, 20,* 31–98.

Meyers, G. C. (1923). Training for leadership. *School and Society, 17,* 437–439.

Meyrowitz, J. (1980). *Carter and the evolution of political image.* Paper, Eastern Communication Association, Ocean City, MD.

Meznar, M. B. (2003). *Top management philosophy a a predictor of corporate social performance: An empirical examination.* Paper, Academy of Management, Seattle, WA.

Michaels, E. (1998). The hunt for talent. *Leader to Leader, 10,* Fall, 10–13.

Michaelson, F. J. (1951). *Some motivational aspects of leadership.* Doctoral dissertation, Ohio State University, Columbus, OH.

Michaelson, L. K. (1973). Leader orientation, leader behavior, group effectiveness, and situational favorability: An empirical extension of the contingency model. *Organizational Behavior and Human Performance, 9,* 226–245.

Michaelsen, L. K., Watson, W. E., & Black, R. H. (1989). A realistic rest of individual versus group consensus decision making. *Journal of Applied Psychology, 74,* 834–839.

Michel, J. G., & Hambrick, D. C. (1992). Diversification posture and top management team characteristics. *Academy of Management Journal, 35,* 9–37.

Michener, A., Fleishman, J., Elliot, G., & Skolnick, J. (1976). Influence use and target attributes. *Journal of Personality and Social Psychology.*

Michener, A., & Schwertfeger, M. (1972). Liking as a determinant of power tactic preference. *Sociometry, 35,* 190–202.

Michener, H. A., & Burt, M. R. (1975a). Components of "authority" as determinants of compliance. *Journal of Personnel Psychology, 31,* 606–614.

Michener, H. A., & Burt, M. R. (1975b). Use of social influence under varying conditions of legitimacy. *Journal of Personality and Social Psychology, 32,* 398–407.

Michener, H. A., & Lawler, E. J. (1975). Endorsement of formal leaders: An integrative model. *Journal of Personality and Social Psychology, 31,* 216–223.

Michie, S. G., Dooley, R. S., & Fryxell, G. E. (2003). *Top management team heterogeneity, consensus, and collaboration: A moderated mediatopn model of decision quality.* Paper, Academy of Management, Seattle, WA.

Miklos, E. (1963). *Dimensions of conflicting expectations and the leader behavior of principals.* Doctoral dissertation, University of Alberta, Edmonton.

Miles, A. S. (1970). Dimensions of student leadership at Cornell University. *Dissertation Abstracts International, 30,* 2856.

Miles, C. S. (1985). *Leadership effectiveness of professional home economists in Cornell cooperative extension.* Doctoral dissertation, Cornell University, Ithaca, NY

Miles, M. B. (1965). Changes during and following laboratory training: A clinical experimental study. *Journal of Applied Behavioral Science, 1,* 215–242.

Miles, M. B., Milavsky, J. R., Lake, D. C., & Beckhard, R. (1965). *Organizational improvement: Effects of management team training in Bankers Trust.* New York: Bankers Trust Company, Personnel Division.

Miles, R. E. (1964a). Attitudes toward management theory as a factor in managers' relationship with their superiors. *Academy of Management Journal, 7,* 308–314.

Miles, R. E., & Ritchie, J. B. (1968). Leadership attitudes among union officials. *Industrial Relations, 8,* 108–117.

Miles, R. E., & Snow, C. C. (1978). *Organizational strategy, structure, and process.* New York: McGraw-Hill.

Miles, R. H., & Petty, M. M. (1977). Leader effectiveness in small bureaucracies. *Academy of Management Journal, 20,* 238–250.

Mileti, D. S., Drabek, T. E., & Haas, J. E. (1975). *Human systems in extreme environments: A sociological perspective.* Boulder: University of Colorado, Institute of Behavioral Science.

Milewicz, J. C. (1983). *An exploratory study in the behavioral dimensions of a channel of distribution: An assessment of the power, leadership, control, and performance linkages.* Doctoral dissertation, University of Alabama, Tuscaloosa.

Milgram, S. (1965b). Some conditions of obedience and disobedience to authority. *Human Relations, 18,* 57–76.

Milgrim, S. (1974). *Obedience to authority: An experimental view.* New York: Harper & Row.

Miliffe, K., Piccolo, R. F., & Judge, T. A. (2005). *Consideration, initiating structure, and transformational leadership.* Paper, Society for Industrial and Organizational Psychology, Honolulu, HI.

Mill, John Stewart. (1859). *Ethics and politics.*(1806–1873)

Millard, R. J. (1981). A comparative analysis of male and female management style and perceived behavior patterns. *Dissertation Abstracts International, 42*(3B), 1219.

Miller, C. C. (2002). *Effective use of intuition in strategic decision making.* Paper, Academy of Management, Denver, CO.

Miller, C. C., & Ireland, R. D. (2005). Intuition in strategic decision making: Friend or foe in the fast-paced 21st century. *Academy of Management Executive, 19*(1), 19–30.

Miller, C. T., & Kaiser, C. R. (2001). A theoretical perspective in coping with stigma. *Journal of Social Issues, 57,* 73–92

Miller, D. (1983). The correlates of entrepreneurship in three types of firms. *Management Science, 29,* 770–791.

Miller, D. (1993). Some organizational consequences of CEO succession. *Academy of Management Journal,36,* 644–659.

Miller, D., & Friesen, P. (1980). Momentum and revolution in organizational management. *Academy of Management Journal, 23,* 591–614.

Miller, D., & Toulouse, J. M. (1986). Strategy, structure, CEO personality and performance in small firms. *American Journal of Small Business,* Winter, 47–62.

Miller, D. C., & Schull, F. A. (1962). The prediction of administrative role conflict resolutions. *Administrative Science Quarterly, 7,* 143–160.

Miller, D. B. (1986). *Managing professionals in research and development.* San Francisco: Jossey-Bass.

Miller, D. T., & Ross, M. (1975). Self-serving biases in the attribution of causality: Fact or fiction? *Psychological Bulletin, 82,* 213–225.

Miller, E. L. (1966). Job attitudes of national union officials: Perceptions of the importance of certain personality traits as a function of job level and union organizational structure. *Personnel Psychology, 19,* 395–410.

Miller, E. L., & Cattaneo, R. (1982). Some leadership attitudes of West German expatriate managerial personnel. *Journal of International Business Studies, 13*(1), 39–50.

Miller, F. G., & Remmers, H. H. (1950). Studies in industrial empathy. II. Management's attitudes toward industrial supervision and their estimates of labor attitudes. *Personnel Psychology, 3,* 33–40.

Miller, G. J. (1987). *Administrative dilemmas: The role of political leadership.* Working paper. St. Louis, MO: Washington University.

Miller, J. (1976). *Psychology of women.* London: Penguin.

Miller, J. A. (1973a). *Structuring/destructuring: Leadership in open systems* (Tech. Rep. No. 64). Rochester, NY: University of Rochester, Management Research Center.

Miller, J. A. (1973b). *A hierarchical structure of leadership behaviors* (Tech. Rep. No. 66). Rochester, NY: University of Rochester, Management Research Center.

Miller, J. A. (1974). *Leadership in open systems.* Doctoral dissertation, University of Rochester, Rochester, NY

Miller, J. A. (1991). Experiencing management: A comprehensive "hands-on" model for the introductory undergraduate management course. *Journal of Management Education, 15,* 151–169.

Miller, J. A. (1992). *Responsible management: Effectiveness, efficiency, community.* Bucknell University, Lewisburg, PA.

Miller, J. A. (1995). *Project manual for MG 101: Introduction to organization and management.* Lewisburg, PA.: Bucknell University, 26th edition.

Miller, J. S., Wiseman, R. M., & Gomez-Mejia, L. R. (2002). The fit between CEO compensation design and firm risk. *Academy of Management Journal, 45,* 745–756.

Miller, K. I., & Monge, P. R. (1986). Participation, satisfaction, and productivity: A meta-analytic review. *Academy of Management Journal, 29,* 727–753.

Miller, L., & Hamblin, R. L. (1963). Interdependence, differential rewarding, and productivity. *American Sociological Review, 28,* 768–778.

Miller, L. C., & Hofstedde, R. J. (1987). Group approaches. In D. E. Johnson, L. R. Meiller, & G. F. Summers (eds.), *Needs assessment: Theory and methods.* Ames: Iowa State University Press.

Miller, R. D. (1969). A systems concept of training. *Training & Development Journal, 23,* 4–14.

Miller, R. S. (1943). Developing leadership in young officers. *Military Review, 23,* 11–12.

Miller, R. W. (1986). Extending university resources in support of volunteer development: Evaluation of a pilot effort. *Journal of Voluntary Action Research, 15*(1), 100–115.

Miller, S. J. (1970). *Prescription for leadership: Training for the medical elite.* Chicago: Aldine-Atherton.

Miller, W. B. (1965). Focal concerns of lower-class culture. In L. A. Ferman, J. L. Kornbluh, & A. Haber (eds.), *Poverty in America.* Ann Arbor: University of Michigan Press.

Milliman, J. F., Nason, S., Lowe, K., et al. (1995). *An empirical study of performance appraisal practices in Japan, Korea, Taiwan, and the U.S.* Paper, Academy of Management, Vancouver, BC.

Milliman, J. F., & Neck, C. P. (1994). Thought self-leadership: Finding spiritual fulfillment in organizational life. *Journal of Managerial Psychology, 9*(6), 9–16.

Millon, T. (1990). *Toward a new personology: An evolutionary model.* New York: Wiley.

Mills, J. (1986). Subordinate perceptions of managerial coaching practices. *Proceedings,* Academy of Management, Chicago, 113–116.

Milton, O. (1952). Presidential choice and performance on a scale of authoritarianism. *American Psychologist, 7,* 597–598 (Abstract).

Miner, J. B. (1960a). The Kuder preference record in management appraisal. *Personnel Psychology, 13,* 187–196.

Miner, J. B. (1960b). The effect of a course in psychology on the attitudes of research and development supervisors. *Journal of Applied Psychology, 44,* 224–231.

Miner, J. B. (1962a). Conformity among university professors and business executives. *Administrative Science Quarterly, 7,* 96–109.

Miner, J. B. (1962b). Personality and ability factors in sales performance. *Journal of Applied Psychology, 46,* 6–13.

Miner, J. B. (1965). *Studies in management education.* New York: Springer-Verlag.

Miner, J. B. (1967). *The school administrator and organizational character.* Eugene: University of Oregon, Center for the Advanced Study of Educational Administration.

Miner, J. B. (1968). The early identification of managerial talent. *Personnel and Guidance Journal, 46,* 586–591.

Miner, J. B. (1973). *The management process: Theory, research and practice.* New York: Macmillan.

Miner, J. B. (1974a). Motivation to manage among women: Studies of college students. *Journal of Vocational Behavior, 5, 2,* 241–50.

Miner, J. B. (1974b). Student attitudes toward bureaucratic role prescriptions and the prospects for managerial talent shortages. *Personnel Psychology, 27,* 605–613.

Miner, J. B. (1975). The uncertain future of the leadership concept: An overview. In J. G. Hunt & L. L. Larson (eds.), *Leadership frontiers.* Kent, OH: Kent State University Press.

Miner, J. B. (1977c). Motivational potential for upgrading among minority and female managers. *Journal of Applied Psychology, 62,* 691–697.

Miner, J. B. (1982a). The uncertain future of the leadership concept: Revisions and clarifications. *Journal of Applied Behavioral Science, 18*(3), 293–307.

Miner, J. B. (1982b). A note on theory and research for developing a science of leadership. *Journal of Applied Behavioral Science, 18*(5), 365–38.

Miner, J. B. (1982). *Theories of organizational structures and process.* Chicago, IL: The Dryden Press.

Miner, J. B. (1984). Participation and management. In B. Wilpert & A. Sorge (eds.), *International perspectives on organizational democracy.* New York: Wiley.

Miner, J. B., & Crane, D. F. (1977). The continuing effects of motivational shifts among college students. In J. B. Miner (ed.), *Motivation to manage.* Atlanta, CA: Organizational Measurement Systems Press.

Miner, J. B., & Crane, D. P. (1981). Motivation to manage and the manifestation of a managerial orientation in career planning. *Academy of Management Journal, 24,* 626–633.

Miner, J. B., Rizzo, J. R., Harlow, D. N., & Hill, J. W. (1974). Role motivation theory of managerial effectiveness in simulated organizations of varying degrees of structure. *Journal of Applied Psychology, 59,* 31–37. Also: Hill, J. W. (1977). In J. B. Miner (ed.), *Motivation to manage.* Atlanta, GA: Organizational Measurement Systems Press.

Miner, J. B., & Smith, N. R. (1982). Decline and stabilization of managerial mmotivation over a 20-year period. *Journal of Applied Psychology.*

Miner, J. B., Smith, N. R., & Ebrahimi, B. (1985). Further considerations in the decline and stabilization of managerial motivation: A rejoinder to Bartol, Anderson, and Schneier (1980). *Journal of Vocational Behavior, 26,* 290–298.

Miner, J. B., Smith, N. R., & Bracker, J. S. (1994). Role of entrepreneurial task in the growth of technologically innovative firms: Interpretations from follow-up data. *Journal of Applied Psychology, 79,* 627–630.

Ministry of Health Canada. Science & Research. Science Advisory Board. Home, >www.hc-sc.gc.ca<

Mintz, A. (1951). Non-adaptive behavior. *Journal of Abnormal and Social Psychology, 46,* 150–159.

Mintzberg, H. (1970). Structured observation as a method to study managerial work. *Journal of Management Studies, 7,* 87–104.

Mintzberg, H. (1973). *The nature of managerial work.* New York: Harper & Row.

Mintzberg, H. (1975). The manager's job: Folklore and fact. *Harvard Business Review, 53*(4), 49–61.

Mintzberg, H. (1979). An emerging strategy of "direct" research. *Administrative Science Quarterly, 26,* 583–589.

Mintzberg, H. (1983). The organization as political arena. *Journal of Management Studies, 22,* 133–154.

Mintzberg, H. (1983). *Power in and around organizations.* Englewood Cliffs, NJ: Prentice-Hall.

Mintzberg, H., & James, J. A. (1985). Of strategies, deliberate and emergent. *Strategic Management Journal, 6,* 257–272.

Mintzberg, H., & Jorgenson, J. (1987). Emergent strategy for public policy. *Canadian Public Administration, 30,* 214–229.

Mintzberg, H., & Waters, J. A. (1982). Tracking strategy in an entrepreneurial firm. *Academy of Management Journal, 25,* 465–499.

Mischel, W. (1961). Preference for delayed reinforcement and social responsibility. *Journal of Abnormal and Social Psychology, 62,* 1–7.

Mischel, W. (1977). The interaction of person and situation. In D. Magnusson and N. S. Endle (eds.), *Personality at the crossroads: Current issues in interactional psychology.* Hillsdale, NJ: Erlbaum.

Miskin, V. D., & Gmelch, W. H. (1985). Quality leadership for quality teams. *Training & Development Journal, 39*(5), 122–129.

Misumi, J. (1974). *Action research on the development of leadership, decision-making processes and organizational performance in a Japanese shipyard.* Paper, International Congress of Applied Psychology, Liege, Belgium.

Misumi, J. (1984). Decision making in Japanese groups and organizations. In B. Wilpert & A. Sorge (eds.), *International yearbook of organizational democracy,* vol. 2. Chichester, U.K.: Wiley.

Misumi, J. (1985). *The behavioral science of leadership: An interdisciplinary Japanese research program.* Ann Arbor: University of Michigan Press.

Misumi, J., & Mannari, N. (1982). The empirical study concerning the validity of the measurement of the leadership behavior in industrial organizations. *Proceedings, Japanese Organizational Science Association.* (Cited in J. Misumi, 1985, 284–290.)

Misumi, J., & Peterson, M. F. (1985). The performance-maintenance (PM) theory of leadership: Review of a Japanese research program. *Administrative Science Quarterly, 30,* 198–223.

Misumi, J., & Peterson, M. F. (1987). Supervision and leadership. In B. M. Bass, P. J. D. Drenth, & P. Weissenberg (eds.), *Advances in organizational psychology: An international review.* Beverly Hills, CA: Sage.

Misumi, J., & Sako, H. (1982). An experimental study of the effect of leadership behavior on followers' behavior of following after the leader in a simulated emergency situation. *The Japanese Journal of Experimental Social Psychology, 22,* 49–59.

Misumi, J., & Seki, F. (1971). Effects of achievement motivation on the effectiveness of leadership patterns. *Administrative Science Quarterly, 16,* 51–59.

Mitchell, B. N. (1969). The black minority in the CPA profession. *Journal of Accounting, 128*(3), 41–48.

Mitchell, T. R. (1970a). The construct validity of three dimensions of leadership research. *Journal of Social Psychology, 80,* 89–94.

Mitchell, T. R. (1970b). Leader complexity and leadership style. *Journal of Personality and Social Psychology, 16,* 166–174,

Mitchell, T. R. (1972). Cognitive complexity and group performance. *Journal of Social Psychology, 86,* 35–43.

Mitchell, T. R. (1979). Organizational behavior. *Annual Review of Psychology, 30,* 243–281.

Mitchell, T. R. (1981). *Leader attributions and leader behavior: First stage testing of theoretical model* (Tech. Rep. No. 522). Seattle: University of Washington, School of Business.

Mitchell, T. R. (1985). Review of *In search of Excellence* versus *The 100 Best Companies to Work for in America:* A question of perspective and values. *Academy of Management Review, 10,* 350–355.

Mitchell, T. R. (1993). Leadership, values, and accountability. In M. M. Chemers & R. Ayman (eds.), *Leadership theory and research: Perspectives and directions.* New York: Academic Press.

Mitchell, T. R., Biglan, A., Oncken, G. R., & Fiedler, F. E. (1970). The Contingency Model: Criticism and suggestions. *Academy of Management Journal, 13,* 253–267.

Mitchell, T. R., & Foa, U. G. (1969). Diffusion of the effect of cultural training of the leader in the structure of heterocultural task groups. *Australian Journal of Psychology, 21*, 31–43.

Mitchell, T. R., & Kalb, L. S. (1982). Effects of job experience on supervisor attributions for a subordinate's poor performance. *Journal of Applied Psychology, 67*, 181–188.

Mitchell, T. R., Larson, J. R., & Green, S. C. (1977). Leader behavior, situational moderators and group performance: An attributional analysis. *Organizational Behavior and Human Performance, 18*, 254–268.

Mitchell, T. R., & Scott, W. G. (1987). Leadership failures, the distrusting public, and prospects of the administrative state. *Public Administration Review, 47*, 445–452.

Mitchell, T. R., & Scott, W. G. (1990). America's problems and needed reforms: Confronting the ethic of personal advantage. *Academy of Management Executive, 4*, 23–35.

Mitchell, T. R., Smyser, C. M., & Weed, S. E. (1975). Locus of control: Supervision and work satisfaction. *Academy of Management journal, 18*, 623–630.

Mitchell, T. R., & Wood, R. E. (1979). *An empirical test of an attributional model of leaders' responses to poor performance.* Paper, Symposium on Leadership, Duke University, Durham, NC.

Mitchell, T. R., & Wood, R. E. (1980). Supervisor's responses to subordinate poor performance: A test of an attributional model. *Organizational Behavior and Human Performance, 25*, 123–138.

Mitchell, V F. (1968). The relationship of effort, abilities, and role perceptions to managerial performance. *Dissertation Abstracts, 29*, 360.

Mitchell, V. F., & Porter, L. W. (1967). Comparative managerial role perceptions in military and business hierarchies. *Journal of Applied Psychology, 51*, 449–452.

Mitroff, I. I. (1978). Systematic problem solving. In M. W. McCall & M. M. Lombardo (eds.), *Leadership: Where else can we go?* Durham, NC: Duke University Press.

Mitroff, I. (1983). *Stakeholders of the organization mind.* San Francisco: Jossey-Bass.

Mitroff, I. I., & Kilmann, R. H. (1976). On organization stories: An approach to the design and analysis of organization through myths and stories. In R. H. Kilmann, L. R. Pondy, & D. P. Slevin (eds.), *The management of organization design,* Vol. 1. New York: Elsevier North Holland.

Mitroff, I. I., Shrivastava, P., & Udwadia, F. E. (1987). Effective crisis management. *Academy of Management Executive, 1*, 283–292.

Mitscherlich, A. (1967). Changing patterns of authority: A psychiatric interpretation. In L. I. Edinger (ed.), *Political leadership in industrialized societies.* New York: Wiley.

Moen, J. K. (1995). Women in leadership: The Norwegian example. *Journal of Leadership Studies, 2*(3), 3–19.

Mohanna, A. I., & Argyle, M. (1960). A cross-cultural study of structured groups with unpopular central members. *Journal of Abnormal and Social Psychology, 60*, 139–140.

Mohr, L. B. (1971). Organizational technology and organizational structure. *Administrative Science Quarterly, 16*, 444–459.

Mohr, L. B. (1977). Authority and democracy in organizations. *Human Relations, 30*, 919–947.

Mohrman, A., & Lawler, E. (1983). Motivation and performance appraisal behavior. In F. Landy, S. Zedeck & J. Cleveland (eds.), *Performance measurement and theory.* Hillsdale, NJ: Erlbaum.

Mold, H. P. (1952). Management builds itself—a case study in conference training. In M. J. Dooher & V. Marquis (eds.), *The development of executive talent.* New York: American Management Association.

Molero, R., & Morales, J. F. (1994). *A study on leadership in a health-care organization using Bass' multifactor leadership questionnaire (mlq).* Paper presented at the meeting of the International Congress of Applied Psychology. Madrid, Spain.

Moliterno, T. P., & Wiersema, M. F. (2003). *Human and social capital as market signals: Implications for CEO selection.* Paper, Academy of Management, Seattle, WA.

Mollenhoff, C. R. (1980). *The President who failed: Carter out of control.* New York: Macmillan.

Monge, R. R., & Kirste, K. K. (1975). *Proximity, location, time, and opportunity to communicate.* San Jose: California State University.

Montagner, H., Arnaud, M., Jeandroz, M., et al. (1973). Les activités ludiques de jeune enfant: Jeu ou ontogenese? *Vers l'education nouvelle,* numéro hors série (special issue), 3–32.

Montefiore, S. S. (2004). Tyrants on trial: What Stalin taught Sadaam about public relations. *New York Times,* July 2, op–ed.

Montgomery, R. (1989). Inside job: How a HUD program grew into a slush fund for Republican insiders. *Common Cause, 15*(4), 17–20.

Montoya-Weiss, M. M., Massey, A. P., & Song, M. (2001). Getting it together: Temporal coordination and conflict management in global virtual teams. *Academy of Management Journal, 44*, 1251–1262.

Moon, C. G., & Hanton, T. (1958). Evaluating an appraisal and feedback training program. *Personnel, 35*, 37–41.

Moon, H. (2001). The two faces of conscientiousness: Duty and achievement striving in escalation of commitment dilemmas. *Journal of Applied Psychology, 86*, 535–540.

Mooney, A. C. (2003). *What makes a top management group a top management team?* Paper, Academy of Management, Seattle, WA.

Mooney, J. D., & Reiley, A. C. (1931). *Onward industry: The principles of organization and their significance to modern industry.* New York: Harper.

Moore, B. V. (1927). The May conference on leadership. *Personnel Journal, 6*, 124–128.

Moore, D. P. (1984). Evaluating in-role and out-of-role performers. *Academy of Management Journal, 27*, 603–618.

Moore, H. T. (1921). The comparative influence of majority and expert opinion. *American Journal of Psychology, 32*, 16–20.

Moore, J. C. (1968). Status and influence in small group interactions. *Sociometry, 31*, 47–63.

Moore, J. C. (1969). Social status and social influence: Process considerations. *Sociometry, 32*, 145–158.

Moore, J. V. (1953a). *A factor analysis of subordinate of noncommissioned officer supervisors* (Research Bulletin No. 53–6). San Antonio, TX: USAF Human Resources Research Center.

Moore, J. V. (1953b). *Factor analytic comparisons of superior and subordinate ratings of the same NCO supervisors* (Tech. Rep. No. 53–24). San Antonio, TX: USAF Human Resources Research Center.

Moore, J. V., & Smith, R. G. (1953). Some aspects of noncommissioned officer leadership. *Personnel Psychology, 6*, 427–443.

Moore, L. L. (1976). The FMI: Dimensions of follower maturity. *Group 6 Organization Studies, 1,* 203–222.

Moore, M. M. (1981). First career, second career, and alternative career academic librarians: A study in personality and leadership differentials as related to managerial talent. *Dissertation Abstracts International, 42*(1A), 7.

Moore, M. M. (1983). "New blood" and managerial potential in academic libraries. *Journal of Academic Librarianship, 9*(3), 142–147.

Moore, W. E. (1970). *The professions: Roles and rules.* New York: Russell Sage Foundation.

Moos, M., & Koslin, B. (1951). Political leadership reexamined: An empirical approach. *Public Opinion Quarterly, 15,* 563–574.

Morales, J. F., & Molero, F. (1995). Leadership in two types of healthcare organization. In J. M. Peiro, F. Prieto, et al. (eds.), *Work and organizational psychology: European contributions of the nineties.* Hove, UK: Taylor & Francis, 209–221.

Morall, H. H. (1974). *The relationship between perceived participation in school management and morale of selected black and non-black teachers and students in Volusia County, Florida senior high schools.* Doctoral dissertation, University of Miami, Miami, FL.

Moran, B. B. (1992). Gender differences in leadership. *Library Trends, 40,* 475–491.

Moreland, R. L. (1999). Transactive memory: Learning who knows what in workgroups and organizations. In L. Thompson, J. Levine, & D. Messick (eds.), *Shared cognition in organizations: The management of knowledge.* Mahwah, NJ: Lawrence Erlbaum & Associates.

Moreno, J. L. (1934/1953). *Who shall survive?* Beacon, NY: Beacon House.

Moreno, J. L. (1955). *Sociodrama: A method for the analysis of social conflicts.* Beacon, NY: Beacon House.

Moreux, C. (1971). Spécificité culturelle du leadership en milieu rural canadien-français. *Sociologie et Sociétés, 3,* 229–258.

Morgan, B. S., Blonsky, M. R., & Rosen, H. (1970). Employee attitudes towards a hard-core hiring program. *Journal of Applied Psychology, 54,* 473–478.

Morgan, G. (1986). *Images of organizations.* London: Sage.

Morgan, I., & Rao, J. (2002). Aligning service strategy through super-measure management. *Academy of Management Executive, 16* (4), 121–131.

Morgan, W. R., & Sawyer, J. (1967). Bargaining, expectations, and the preference for equality over equity. *Journal of Personality and Social Psychology, 6,* 139–149.

Morganthau, T., & Hager, M. (1981). The "Ice Queen" at E.P.A. *Newsweek,* October 19, 67–68.

Morganthau, T., & Horrock, N. (1984). The new warriors. *Newsweek,* July 9, 32–33.

Morgenbesser, L. I. (1999). *A view from the trenches: A manual for wardens by wardens.* Lanham, MD: American Correctional Association. (Book review.)

Morgenbesser, L. I. (2000). The prison governor: Theory and practice. *The Grapevine,* 5–6. (Book review.)

Morgeson, F. P. (2000). *Team leaders as event managers.* Unpublished manuscript.

Morgeson, F. P. (2005). The external leadership of self-managing teams: Intervening in the context of noveland disruptive events. *Journal of Applied Psychology, 90,* 497–508.

Morgeson, F. P., & DeRue, D. S. (2006). Event criticality, urgency, and duration: Understanding how events disrupt teams and influence team leader intervention. *Leadership Quarterly, 17,* 272–287.

Morical, K. E. (1999). A product review: 360 assessments. *Training & Development,* April, 43–47.

Morita, A. (1981). Yes, no, or the importance of however. *Industrial Management, 23*(4), 12–15.

Morley, M. J., & Garavan, T. (1995). Current themes in organizational design: Implications for human resource development. *Journal of European Industrial Training, 19*(11), 3–13.

Morphet, E. L., Johns, R. L., & Reller, T. L. (1982). *Educational organization and administration: Concepts, practices and issues.* Englewood Cliffs, NJ: Prentice-Hall.

Morris, C. G. (1966a). Task effects on group interaction. *Journal of Personality and Social Psychology, 4,* 545–554.

Morris, C. G. (1966b). Effects of task characteristics on group process. *Dissertation Abstracts, 26,* 7477.

Morris, C. G., & Hackman, J. R. (1969). Behavioral correlates of perceived leadership. *Journal of Personality and Social Psychology, 13,* 350–361.

Morris, M. H., Davis, D. L., & Allen, J. W. (1993). Fostering corporate entrepreneurship: Cross-cultural comparison of the importance of individualism versus collectivism. *Journal of International Business Studies, 25,* 65–89.

Morris, R. (1988). Management: Why women are leading the way. *Options,* December, 307–312.

Morris, W. T. (1967). *Decentralization in management systems: An introduction to design.* Columbus: Ohio State University Press.

Morrison, A. M., White, R. P, & Van Velsor, E. (1987). The narrow band. *Issues & Observations, 7*(2), 1–7.

Morrison, A. M., White, R. P., & Van Velsor, E. (1987). *Breaking the glass ceiling: Can women reach the top of America's largest corporations?* Reading, MA: Addison-Wesley.

Morrison, E. W., & Phelps, C. C. (1999). Taking charge at work: Extrarole efforts to initiate workplace change. *Academy of Management Journal, 42,* 403–419.

Morrison, E. W., & VanGlinow, M. A. (1990). The glass ceiling: are women where they should be? *American Psychologist, 45,* February, 200–208.

Morrison, R. F. (1977). Career adaptivity: The effective adaptation of managers to changing role demands. *Journal of Applied Psychology, 62,* 549–558.

Morrison, R. F., & Sebald, M. L. (1974). Personal characteristics differentiating female executives from female nonexecutive personnel. *Journal of Applied Psychology, 59*(5), 656–59.

Morrow, I. J., & Stern, M. (1990). Stars, adversaries, producers, and phantoms at work: A new leadership typology. In K. E. Clark & M. B. Clarke (eds.), *Measures of leadership.* West Orange, NJ: Leadership Library of America.

Morsbach, H. (1969). A cross-cultural study of achievement motivation and achievement values in two South African groups. *Journal of Social Psychology, 79,* 267–268.

Morse, J. J., & Wagner, F. R. (1978). Measuring the process of managerial effectiveness. *Academy of Management Journal, 21,* 23–35.

Morse, N. C. (1953). *Satisfactions in the white collar job.* Ann Arbor: University of Michigan, Institute for Social Research.

Morse, N. C., & Reimer, E. (1956). The experimental change of a major organizational variable. *Journal of Abnormal and Social Psychology, 52,* 120–129.

Morse, N. C., Reimer, E., & Tannenbaum, A. S. (1951). Regulation and control in hierarchical organizations. *Journal of Social Issues, 7,* 41–48.

Morsink, H. M. (1966). *A comparison of the leader behavior of fifteen men and fifteen women secondary school principals in Michigan.* Unpublished manuscript.

Mortensen, M. (2001). *Fighting conflict: Shared identity formation in geographically dispersed teams.* Paper, Academy of Management, Washington, DC.

Morton, R. B., & Bass, B. M. (1964). The organizational training laboratory. *Training Directors Journal, 18,* 2–18.

Moseley, A. L. (1998). A behavioral approach to leadership: Implications for diversity in today's organizations. *Journal of Leadership Studies, 5*(1), 38–50.

Moses, J. L., & Boehm, V. R. (1975). Relationship of assessment-center performance to management progress of women. *Journal of Applied Psychology, 60,* 527–529.

Moses, J. L., & Margolis, J. P. (1979). *Assessing the assessor.* Paper, International Congress of Assessment Center Method, New Orleans, LA.

Moses, J. L., & Ritchie, R. J. (1976). Supervisory relationships training: A behavioral evaluation of a behavioral modeling program. *Personnel Psychology, 29,* 337–343.

Moses, L. L., & Lyness, K. S. (1988). Individual and organizational responses to ambiguity. In F. D. Schoorman & B. Schneider (eds.), *Facilitating work effectiveness.* Lexington, MA: Lexington Books.

Moskowitz, J. T., Folkman, S., Collette, L., et al. (1996). Coping and mood during AIDS-related caregiving and bereavement. *Annals of Behavioral Medicine, 18,* 49–57.

Moss, G. (1974). How community leaders view extension. *Journal of Extension, 13*(3), 8–15.

Moss, S. E., & Martinko, M. J. (1988). The effects of performance attributions and outcome dependence on leader feedback behavior following poor subordinate performance. *Journal of Organizational Behavior, 19,* 259–274.

Mossholder, K. W., & Dewhurst, H. D. (1980). The appropriateness of management by objectives for development and research personnel, *Journal of Management, 6,* 145–156.

Mosvick, R. K. (1966). *An experimental evaluation of two modes of motive analysis instruction in an industrial setting.* Doctoral dissertation, University of Minnesota, Minneapolis.

Mosvick, R. K. (1971). Human relations training for scientists, technicians, and engineers: A review of the relevant experimental evaluations of human relations training. *Personnel Psychology, 24,* 275–292.

Motowidlo, S. J. (1981). A scoring procedure for sex-role orientation based on profile similarity indices. *Educational and Psychological Measurement, 41,* 735–744.

Motowidlo, S. J. (1982). Sex role orientation and behavior in a work setting. *Journal of Personality and Social Psychology, 42,* 935–945.

Mottl, T. L. (1977). School movements as recruiters of women leaders: Boston's school movements of the 1960's and 1970's. *Urban Education, 12,* 3–14.

Mount, M. K. (1984). Managerial career stage and facets of job satisfaction. *Journal of Vocational Behavior, 24,* 340–354.

Mount, M. K., Barrick, M. R., & Strauss, J. P. (1999). The joint relationship of conscientiousness and ability with performance: Test of the interaction hypothesis. *Journal of Management, 25*(5), 707–721.

Mount, M. K., Hazacha, J. F., Holt, K. E., et al. (1995). *Rater-ratee race effects in performance ratings of managers.* Paper, Academy of Management, Vancouver, BC.

Mowday, R. T. (1978). The exercise of upward influence in organizations. *Administrative Science Quarterly, 23,* 137–156.

Mowday, R. T. (1979). Leader characteristics, self-confidence, and methods of upwards influence in organizational decision situations. *Academy of Management Journal, 22,* 709–725.

Mowday, R. T., & Sutton, R. I. (1993). Organizational behavior: Linking individuals and groups to organizational contexts. *Annual Review of Psychology, 44,* 195–229.

Mowli, C. A. (1989). Successful management based on key principles. *Healthcare Financial Management, 43*(6), 122, 124.

Mowrer, O. H. (1938). Authoritarianism vs. self government in the management of children's aggressive (anti-social) reactions as a preparation for citizenship in a democracy. *Journal of Social Psychology, 10,* 121–127.

Moyle, P., & Parkes, K. (1999). The effects of transition stress: A relocation study. *Journal of Organizational Behavior, 20,* 625–646.

Moynihan, D. P. (1965). Employment income, and ordeal of the Negro family. In I. Parsons & K. B. Clark (eds.), *The Negro American.* Boston: Houghton Mifflin.

Mozina, S. (1969). Management opinion on satisfaction and importance of psychosocial needs in their jobs. *Proceedings,* International Congress of Applied Psychology, Amsterdam.

Muczyk, J. P., & Reimann, B. C. (1987). The case for directive leadership. *Academy of Management Executive, 11,* 301–311.

Muczyk, J. P., & Steel, R. P. (1998). Leadership style and the turnaround executive. *Business Horizons, 41*(2), 39–46.

Mudrack, P. E. (2002). *Utilizing moral reasoning in decision making: a closer look.* Paper presented at the Academy of Management meeting, Denver.

Mueller, R. K. (1980). Leader-edge leadership. *Human Systems Management, 1,* 17–27.

Mulder, M. (1960). Communication structure, decision structure, and group performance. *Sociometry, 23,* 1–14.

Mulder, M. (1963). *Group structure, motivation and group performance.* The Hague: Mouton.

Mulder, M. (1971). Power equalization through participation? *Administrative Science Quarterly, 16,* 31–38.

Mulder, M. (1976). Reduction of power differences in practice: The power instance reduction theory and its applications. In G. Hofstede & M. S. Kassem (eds.), *European contributions to organization theory.* Assen, Netherlands: Van Corcum.

Mulder, M., van Dijk, R., Stirwagen, T., Verhagen, J., Soutendijk, S., & Zwerzeriinen, J. (1966). Illegitimacy of power and positiveness of attitude towards the power person. *Human Relations, 19,* 21–37.

Mulder, M., de Jong, R. D., Koppelaar, L., & Verhage, J. (1986). Power, situation, and leaders' effectiveness: An organizational field study. *Journal of Applied Psychology, 71,* 566–570.

Mulder, M., & Stemerding, A. (1963). Threat, attraction to group, and need for strong leadership. *Human Relations, 16,* 317–334.

Mulder, M., van Eck, R., & de Jong, R. D. (1971). An organization in crisis and non-crisis situations. *Human Relations, 24,* 19–41.

Muldrow, I. W., & Bayton, J. A. (1979). Men and women executives and processes related to decision accuracy. *Journal of Applied Psychology, 64,* 99–106.

Mullen, B., & Rosenthal, R. (1985). *BASIC Meta-analysis.* Hillsdale, NJ: Lawrence Erlbaum Associates.

Mullen, B., Salas, E., & Driscoll, J. E. (1988). *Salience, motivation, and artifact as contributions to the relation between participation and leadership.* Paper, 11th Nags Head Conference on Groups, Networks, and Organizations, Nags Head, NC, June.

Mullen, J. H. (1954) The supervisor assesses his job in management. *Personnel, 31,* 94–108.

Mullen, J. H. (1965). Differential leadership modes and productivity in a large organization. *Academy of Management Journal, 8,* 107–126.

Mullen, J. H. (1966b). *Personality and productivity in management.* New York: Columbia University Press.

Mulligan, L., & Mulligan, G. (1981). Reconstructing restoration science: Styles of leadership and social composition of the early royal society. *Social Studies of Science, 11,* 327–364.

Multivariate Software, Inc. (undated). *Structural equation modeling has never been easier!*

Mumford, E. (1906/1907). Origins of leadership. *American Journal of Sociology, 12,* 216–240, 367–397, 500–531.

Mumford, E. (1909). *The origins of leadership.* Chicago: University of Chicago Press.

Mumford, E. M. (1959). Social behavior in small work groups. *Sociological Review, 7,* 137–157.

Mumford, E. (2000). Socio-technical design: an unfulfilled promise or a future opportunity. In R. Baskerville, J. Stage, and J. I. DeGross (eds.), *Organizational and social perspectives on information technology.* Boston: Kluwer Academic Publications.

Mumford, M. D. (1983). Social comparison theory and the evaluation of peer evaluations: A review and some applied implications. *Personnel Psychology, 36,* 867–881.

Mumford, M. D., Connelly, S., & Gaddis, B. (2003). How creative leaders think: Experimental findings and cases. *Leadership Quarterly, 14,* 411–432.

Mumford, M. D., Fleishman, E. A., Levin, K. Y., et al. (1988). *Taxonomic efforts in the description of leadership behavior: A synthesis and cognitive interpretation.* Fairfax, VA: George Mason University Center for Behavioral and Cognitive Studies.

Mumford, M. D., Gessner, T. L., Connelly, M. S., et al. (1993). Leadership and destructive acts: individual and situational influences. *Leadership Quarterly, 9(2),* 115–147.

Mumford, M. D., & Gustafson, S. B. (1988). Creativity syndrome: Integration, application, and innovation. *Psychological Bulletin, 103(1),* 27–43.

Mumford, M. D., & Licuanan, B. (2004). Leadership for innovation: Conclusions, issues, and directions. *Leadership Quarterly, 15,* 163–171.

Mumford, M. D., Marks, M., Connelly, M. S., et al. (2000). Development of leadership skills: Experience and timing. *Leadership Quarterly, 11,* 87–114.

Mumford, M. D., O'Connor, J., Clifton, T., et al. (1993). Background data constructs as predictors of leadership behavior. *Human Performance, 62,* 41–53.

Mumford, M. D., Scott, G., Gaddis, B., et al. (2002). Leading creative people: Orchestrating expertise and relationships. *Leadership Quarterly, 13,* 705–750.

Mumford, M. D., & Gustafson, S. B. (1988). Creativity syndrome: Integration, application, and innovation. *Psychological Bulletin, 103(1):* 27–43.

Mumford, M. D., Zaccaro, S. G., Harding, F. D., et al. (1993). *Cognitive and temperment predictors of executive ability: Principles for developing leadership capacity.* (Technical Report 977.) US Army Research Institute for the Behavioral and Social Sciences. Alexandria VA.

Mumford, M. D., Zaccaro, S. J., Harding, F. D., et al. (2000). Leadership skills for a changing world: Solving complex social problems. *Leadership Quarterly, 11,* 11–35.

Mumford, M. D., Zaccaro, S. J., Johnson, J. F., et al. (2000) Patterns of leader characteristics: Implications for performance and development. *Leadership Quarterly, 11,* 115–133.

Mumford, T. V. (2003). *A leadership skills strategaplex: Leadership skill requirements, across organizational levels.* Paper, Academy of Management, Seattle, WA.

Munch, F. A. (1945). *Sociology of Tristan da Cunha: Results of the Norwegian scientific expedition to Tristan da Cunha, 1937–1938.* Oslo: I Kommisjon Hos Jacob Dybwad, No. 13.

Munn, W. C., & Gruner, C. R. (1981). "Sick" jokes, speaker sex, and informative speech. *Southern Speech Communication Journal, 46,* 411–418.

Munro, W. B. (1930). Civic organization. In *Encyclopaedia of the social sciences.* New York: Macmillan.

Munson, C. E. (1981). Style and structure in supervision. *Journal of Education for Social Work, 17,* 65–72.

Munson, E. L. (1921). *The management of men.* New York: Holt.

Munson, E. (2004). *Where do we go from here? A BGS look at business ethics after Enron, Tyco, Martha Stewart, et al.* BGS International Exchange. www.betagammasigma.org.

Murakami, T. (1997). The autonomy of teams in the car industry: A cross national comparison. *Work Employment and Society, 11,* 749–758.

Murata, K., & Fujishima, Y. (1998). *Long-term computer-mediated communication and friendship.* Paper, International Association of Applied Psychology, San Francisco, CA.

Murdock, G. P. (1937). Comparative data on the decision of labor by sex. *Social Forces, 15,* 551–553.

Murdock, G. P. (1967). *Ethnographic atlas.* Pittsburgh: University of Pittsburgh Press.

Murnighan, J. K., & Leung, T. K. (1976). The effects of leadership involvement and the importance of the task on subordinates' performance. *Organizational Behavior and Human Performance, 17,* 299–310.

Murninghan, J. K., & Mowen, J. C. (2002). *The art of high-stakes decision-making: Tough calls in a speed-driven world.* New York: Wiley.

Murphy, A. J. (1941). A study of the leadership process. *American Sociological Review, 6,* 674–687.

Murphy, E. C., & Snell, M. (1993). *The genius of Sitting Bull.* Englewood Cliffs, NJ: Prentice–Hall.

Murphy, E. F., Jr., Ekstat, A., & Parker, T. (1995). Sex and gender differences in leadership. *Journal of Leadership Studies, 2*(1), 116–131.

Murphy, K. R., & Cleveland, J. N. (1995). *Understanding performance appraisal: Social, organizational, and goal based perspectives.* Thousand Oaks, CA: Sage.

Murphy, L. B. (1947). Social factors in child development. In T. M. Newcomb & E. L. Hartley (eds.), *Readings in social psychology.* New York: Holt.

Murphy, P. E. & Enderly, G. (1995). Managerial ethical leadership: Examples do matter. *Business Ethics Quarterly,* 117–128.

Murphy, S. E. (2002). Leader self-regulation: The role of self-efficacy and multiple intelligences. In R. Riggio, S. Murphy, & F. J. Pirozzolo (eds.), *Multiple intelligences and leadership.* Mahwah, NJ: Lawrence Erlbaum Associates.

Murphy, S. E, Blyth, D., & Fiedler, F. E. (1992). Cognitive resource theory and the utilization of the leader's and the group members' technical competence. *Leadership Quarterly, 3*(3), 235–255.

Murphy, S. E., & Ensher, E. A. (1999). The effects of leader and subordinate characteristics in the development of leader-member exchange quality. *Journal of Applied Social Psychology, 29,* 1371–1394.

Murphy, S. E., & Halpern, D. F. (2005). Vision for the future of work and family interaction. In D. F. Halpern & S. E. Murphy (eds.), *From work-family balance to work family interaction.* Mahwah, NJ: Lawrence Erlbaum Associates.

Murphy, S. E., & Macaulay, J. (1992). *Leadership experience under evaluative apprehension.* Unpublished working paper.

Murphy, V. V., & Corenblum, A. F. (1966). Loyalty to immediate superior at alternate hierarchical levels in a bureaucracy. *American Journal of Sociology, 72,* 77–85.

Murray, F. (1988). *A study of transformational leadership and organizational effectiveness in selected small college settings.* Doctoral dissertation, Kent State University, Kent, OH.

Murray, H. A., & MacKinnon, D. W. (1946). Assessment of OSS personnel. *Journal of Consulting Psychology, 10,* 76–80.

Murray, R. K. (1969). *The Harding era.* St. Paul, MN: University of Minnesota Press.

Murray, R. K., & Blessing, T. H. (1983). The presidential performance study: A progress report. *Journal of American History, 70,* 535–555.

Murray, W. D. (1993). *Leader-member exchange and work value congruence: A multiple levels approach.* Doctoral Dissertation, Virginia Polytechnical Institute, Blacksburg, VA.

Murray, W. D., Sivasubramanian, N., & Jacques, P. H. (2001). Supervisory support, social exchange, and sexual harassment consequences: A test of competing models. *Leadership Quarterly, 12,* 1–29.

Musham, C. (1980). The relationship between leadership emergence, sex-role adaptability and interpersonal behavior. *Dissertation Abstracts International, 41*(11B), 4310.

Mussen, P. H., & Porter, L. W. (1959). Personal motivations and self-conceptions associated with effectiveness and ineffectiveness in emergent groups. *Journal of Abnormal and Social Psychology, 59,* 23–27.

Musser, S. J. (1987). *Charismatic empowerment: Stimulating self-actualization or creating dependency.* Paper, Academy of Management, New Orleans, LA.

Musser, S. J., & Martin, Y. (1988). *An initial study of the influence and conflict management strategies employed by socialized charismatic leaders.* Unpublished manuscript.

Musteen, M., Barker, V. L., & Baeton, V. (2003). *A peek into the black box: The relationship between CEO tenure and attitude toward change.* Paper, Academy of Management, Seattle, WA.

Muthen, B. (1994). Multilevel covariance structure analysis. *Sociological Methods and Research, 22*(3), 376–398.

Muttayya, B. C. (1977). Personality and value orientations of Panchayat leaders, informal leaders and non-leaders: A comparative study. *Behavior Science Community Development, 11,* 1–11.

Myers, I. B. (1962). *The Myers-Briggs type indicator.* Palo Alto, CA: Consulting Psychologists Press.

Myers, I. B., & McCaulley, M. H. (1985). *Manual: A guide to the development and use of the Myers-Briggs type indicator.* Palo Alto, CA: Consulting Psychologists Press.

Nachman, S., Dansereau, F., & Naughton, T. J. (1983). Negotiating latitude: A within- and between-groups analysis of a key construct in the vertical dyad linkage theory of leadership. *Psychological Reports, 53,* 171–177.

Nachman, S., Dansereau, F., & Naughton, T. J. (1985). Levels of analysis and the vertical dyad linkage approach to leadership. *Psychological Reports, 57,* 661–662.

Nadler, D. A., & Tushman, M. L. (1990). Beyond the charismatic leader: Leadership and organizational change. *California Management Review, 32,* 77–97.

Nafe, R. W. (1930). A psychological description of leadership. *Journal of Social Psychology, 1,* 248–266.

Nagata, Y. (1965). The effects of task structure upon group organization process in terms of the relevance of the individual's goal oriented activities. *Japanese Journal of Psychology, 36,* 56–66.

Nagata, Y. (1966). Effects of task structure on the process of group organization in terms of the difficulty of the task. I. *Psychological Reports, 18,* 566.

Nagle, B. F. (1954). Productivity, employee attitude, and supervisor sensitivity. *Personnel Psychology, 7,* 219–232.

Nance, J. J. (1984). *Splash of colors: The self-destruction of Braniff International.* New York William Morrow.

Nahabetian, H. J. (1969). *The effects of a leader's upward influence on group member satisfaction and task facilitation.* Doctoral dissertation, University of Rochester, Rochester, NY.

Nahavandi, A., & Aranda, E. (1994). Restructuring teams for the reengineered organization. *Academy of Management Executive, 8*(4), 58–68.

Nahavandi, A., & Malekzadeh, A. R., (1993a). Leader style in strategy and organizational performance: An integrative network. *Journal of Management Studies, 30,* 405–425.

Nahavandi, A., & Malekzadeh, A. R. (1993b). *Organizational culture in the management of mergers.* Westport, CT: Quorum Books.

Nam, S. (1991). *Cultural and managerial attributions for group performance.* Doctoral dissertation, University of Oregon, Eugene, OR.

Nance, J. (1984). *Splash of colors: The self-destruction of Braniff International*. New York: William Morrow, Inc.

Nanko, R. A. (1981). The relationship between the perceptions of leadership behavior of supervisors and anxiety levels of teachers. *Dissertation Abstracts International*, 42(5A), 1949.

Nanus, B. (1992). *Visionary leadership: Creating a sense of direction in your organization*. San Francisco: Jossey-Bass.

Narayanan, S., Venkatachalam, R., & Bharathiar, U. (1982). Leadership effectiveness and adaptability among small hosiery units. *Managerial Psychology*, 3(2), 40–47.

Nash, A. M. (1927). Training for leadership here and now. *Training School Bulletin*, 24, 10–14.

Nash, A. N. (1966). Development of an SVIB key for selecting managers. *Journal of Applied Psychology*, 50, 250–254.

Nash, J. B. (1929). Leadership. *Phi Delta Kappan*, 12, 24–25.

Nash, M. (1958). *Machine age Maya: The industrialization of a Guatemalan community* (Memoirs No. 87). Menasha, WI: American Anthropological Association.

Nason, R. W. (1972). Dilemma of black mobility in management. *Business Horizons*, 15, 57–68.

Natarajan, R., & Rashee, A. (2003). The role of CEO characteristics and incentives in corporate disclosures: An empirical examination.

Nathan, B. R. (1989). *CEO succession and organizational performance: Towards an integrative resolution of a recalcitrant problem*. Unpublished manuscript.

Nathan, B. R., & Alexander, R. A. (1985). The role of inferential accuracy in performance rating. *Academy of Management Review*, 10, 109–115.

Nathan, B. R., Hass, M. A., & Nathan, M. L. (1986). *Meta-analysis of Fiedler's leadership theory: A figure is worth a thousand words*. Paper, American Psychological Association, Washington, DC.

Nathan, M. (2003). All my best (leadership). thoughts were stolen by the ancients. In R. Pillai & S. Stites-Doe (eds.), *Teaching leadership: innovative approaches for the 21st century*. Greenwich, CT: Information Age Publishing.

Nathan, R. P. (1983). *The administrative presidency*. New York: Wiley.

National Business Ethics Survey. (2000). *Report Summary*. Ethics Resource Center.

National Community for Latino Leadership (NCLL). (2001). *Reflecting an American vista: The character and impact of Latino leadership*.

National Council of La Raza (NCLR). (2001). Twenty most frequently asked questions about the Latino Community. Updated March 2001. www.nclr.org/about/nclrfaq.html.

National Industrial Conference Board. (1963). *College graduates assess their company training*. New York: National Industrial Conference Board.

National Industrial Conference Board. (1964). *Developing managerial competence: Changing concepts and emerging practices*. New York: National Industrial Conference Board.

National Industrial Conference Board. (1970). *Managing programs to employ the disadvantaged* (Studies in Personnel Policy No. 219). New York: National Industrial Conference Board.

National Research Council. (1943). *Psychology for the fighting man*. New York: Penguin Books.

Naumann-Etienne, M. (1975). *Bringing about open education: Strategies for innovation and implementation*. Doctoral dissertation, University of Michigan, Ann Arbor.

Naylor, J. C., & Dickinson, T. L. (1969). Task structure, work structure, and team performance. *Journal of Applied Psychology*, 3, 167–177.

Naylor, J. C., Pritchard, R. D., & Ilgen, D. R. (1980). *A theory of behavior in organizations*. New York: Academic Press.

Ndofor, H. A., & Rathburn, J. A. (2003). *Executive succession and organizational performance: Temporal pacing and the experience contingency*. Paper, Academy of Management, Seattle, WA.

Nealey, S. M., & Blood, M. R. (1968). Leadership performance of nursing supervisors at two organizational levels. *Journal of Applied Psychology*, 52, 414–422.

Nealey, S. M., & Fiedler, F. E. (1968). Leadership functions of middle managers. *Psychological Bulletin*, 5, 313–329.

Near, J. R., & Miceli, M. P. (1986). Retaliation against whistle blowers: Predictors and effects. *Journal of Applied Psychology*, 71, 137–145.

Near, D., Wilson, D. S., & Miller, R. R. (1995). *Exploitative and cooperative strategies of social conduct: An approach from elementary game theory*. Unpublished manuscript.

Nebeker, D. M. (1975). Situational favorability and environmental uncertainty: An integrative study. *Administrative Science Quarterly*, 20, 281–294.

Nebeker, D. M., & Hansson, R. O. (1972). *Confidence in human nature and leader style* (Tech. Rep. No. 72–37). Seattle: University of Washington, Organizational Research.

Nebeker, D. M., & Mitchell, T. R. (1974). Leader behavior: An expectancy theory approach. *Organizational Behavior and Human Performance*, 11, 355–367.

Neck, C. P., & Cooper, K. H. (2000). The fit executive: Exercise and diet guidelines for enhancing performance. *Academy of Management Executive*, 14(2), 72–82.

Neel, R. G., & Dunn, R. E. (1960). Predicting success in supervisory training programs by the use of psychological tests. *Journal of Applied Psychology*, 44, 358–360.

Negandhi, A. R., & Estafen, B. D. (1967). A research model to determine the applicability of American management know-how in differing cultures and/or environments. In S. B. Prasad (ed.), *Management in international perspective*. New York: Appleton-Century-Crofts.

Negandhi, A. R., & Prasad, S. B. (1971). *Comparative management*. New York: Appleton-Century-Crofts.

Negandhi, A. R., & Reimann, B. C. (1972). A contingency theory of organization re-examined in the context of a developing country. *Academy of Management Journal*, 15, 137–146.

Neider, L. L. (1980). An experimental field investigation utilizing an expectancy theory view of participation. *Organizational Behavior and Human Performance*, 26, 425–442.

Neider, L. L., & Schriesheim, C. A. (1988). Making leadership effective: A three stage model. *Journal of Management Development*, 7(5), 1020.

Neilsen, E. H., & Rao, M. V. H. (1987). The strategy-legitimacy nexus: A thick description. *Academy of Management Review*, 12, 523–533.

Neisser, U., Boodoo, G., Bouchard, T. J., et al. (1996). Intelligence: Knowns and unknowns. *American Psychologist*, 51, 77–101.

Nel, C. (1993). Value-centered leadership: The journey to becoming a world-class organization. In P. Christie, R. Lessem & L. Mbigi

(Eds), *African Management*. Randsburg. South Africa: Knowledge Resources.

Nelissen, N. J. M. (1998). Public administration at the edge of a new millennium: Mega trends in the science of public administration in Western Europe. *International Journal of Organizational Theory & Behavior, 1,* 255–278.

Nelson, C. W. (1950). *Differential concepts of leadership and their function in an industrial organization.* Paper, American Psychological Association, State College, PA.

Nelson, C. W. (1967). A new approach to the development of institutional leadership and communication: A challenge to deans. *Journal of National Association of National Deans' Counselors, 30,* 132–137.

Nelson, D. L., & Burke, R. (2000). Women executives: Health, stress, and success. *Academy of Management Executive, 14*(2), 107–121.

Nelson, J. E. (1978). Child care crises and the role of the supervisor. *Child Care Quarterly, 7,* 318–326.

Nelson, M. R., & Shavitt, S. (2002). Horizontal and vertical individualism and achievement values: A multimethod examination of Denmark and the United States. *Journal of Cross-Cultural Psychology, 22*(5), 439–458.

Nelson, P. D. (1964b). Supervisor esteem and personnel evaluations. *Journal of Applied Psychology, 48,* 106–109.

Nelson, R. B. (1993). The leader's use of informal rewards and reward systems in obtaining organizational goals. *Journal of Leadership Studies, 1,* 148–158.

Nemetz, P. L., & Christensen, S. L. (1996). The challenge of cultural diversity: Harnessing a diversity of views to understand multiculturalism. *Academy of Management Review, 21,* 431–462.

Neranartkomol, P. (1983). Attitudes toward managerial styles and need satisfaction: A comparison of Thai and Japanese business students. *Dissertation Abstracts International, 45*(6A), 1813.

Nessen, R. (1978). *It sure looks different from the inside.* Chicago: Playboy Press.

Neubauer, W. (1982). Dimensionale Struktur der impliziten Fuhrungstheorie bei Vorgesetzten. [Dimensional structure of the implicit leadership theory among supervisors.] *Psychologie und Praxis, 26*(1), 1–11 (Abstract).

Neuberger, O. (1983). Fuhren als widerspruchliches Handeln. [Leadership and its dilemmas.] *Psychologie und Praxis, 27*(1), 22–32.

Neubert, M. (1999). Too much of a good thing or the more the merrier? Exploring the dispersion and gender composition of informal leadership in manufacturing teams. *Small Group Research, 30,* 635–646.

Neuman, J. H., & Baron, R. A. (1997). Aggression in the workplace. In R. A. Giacalone & J. Greenberg (eds.), *Antisocial behavior in organizations.* Thousand Oaks, CA: Sage.

Neumann, A. (1987). *Strategic leadership: The changing orientations of college presidents.* Paper, Association of the Study of Higher Education, Baltimore, MD.

Neumann, A., & Bensimon, E. M. (1990). *Constucting the presidency: College presidents' image of their leadership roles: A comparative study.* New York: Teachers College, Columbia University.

Neumann, C. E. (2004). *Samuel Gompers (1850–1929): Leaders in the early U.S. labor movement.* In G. R. Goethals, G. Sorenson, & Burns, J. M. (eds.), *Encyclopedia of Leadership. 2,* 585–589.

Neustadt, R. (1960). *Presidential power.* New York: Wiley.

Neustadt, R. E. (1980). *Presidential power: The politics of leadership from FDR to Carter.* New York: Wiley.

Nevans, R. (1979). T. Wilson of Boeing: The CEO of the year. *Financial World, 148,* March, 26–28.

Newall, S. E., & Stutman, R. K. (1991). The episodic nature of social confrontation. *Communication Yearbook, 14,* 359–392.

Newcomb, T. M. (1943). *Personality and social change.* New York: Holt, Rinehart & Winston.

Newcomb, T. M. (1956). The prediction of interpersonal attraction. *American Psychologist, 11,* 575–586.

Newcomb, T. M. (1961). *The acquaintance process.* New York: Holt, Rinehart & Winston.

Newcomb, T. M., Turner, R. H., & Converse, P. E. (1965). *Social psychology.* New York: Holt, Rinehart & Winston.

Newcombe, M. J., & Ashkanasy, N. M. (2002). The role of affect and affective congruence in perceptions of leaders: An experimental study. *Leadership Quarterly, 13*(5), 601–614.

Newell, A., & Simon, H. A. (1972). *Human problem solving.* Englewood Cliffs, NJ: Prentice-Hall.

Newkirk-Moore, S., & Bracker, J. S. (1998). Strategic management training and commitment to planning: Critical partners in stimulating firm performance. *International Journal of Training and Development, 2*(2), 82–90.

Newman, B. (1985). A Briton needn't pay much heed to class; he knows his place. *Wall Street Journal,* May 6, 1, 26.

Newman, K. L., & Nollen, S. D. (1996). Culture and congruence: The fit between management practices and national culture. *Journal of International Business Studies, 27,* 753–779.

Newman, R. C. (1983). Thoughts on superstars of charisma: Pipers in our midst. *American Journal of Orthopsychiatry, 53,* 201–208.

Newman, W. H., & Logan, J. (1965). *Business policies and central management.* Cincinnati, OH: Southwestern.

Newman, W. H., & Summer, C. E. (1961). *The process of management: Concepts, behavior, practice.* Englewood Cliffs, NJ: Prentice-Hall.

Newport, G. (1962). A study of attitudes and leadership behavior. *Personnel Administration, 25,* 42–46.

Newstetter, W. I., Feldstein, M. J., & Newcomb, T. M. (1938). *Group adjustment.* Cleveland, OH: Western Reserve University Press.

Ng, S. H., Akhtar-Hossein, A. B. M., Ball, A. B., et al. (1982). Human values in nine countries. In R. Rath, J. B. P. Sinha, & H. S. Asthana (eds.), *Diversity and unity in cross-cultural psychology.* Lisse, Netherlands: Swets & Zeitlinger.

Nguyen, N. T., & McDaniel, M. A. (2001). *The influence of impression management on organizational outcomes: A meta-analysis.* Paper, Society for Industrial and Organizational Psychology, San Diego, CA.

Nice, D. C. (1998). The warrior model of leadership: Classical perspectives and contemporary relevance. *Leadership Quarterly, 9,* 321–332.

Nicol, J. H. (1983). Video-mediated communication and leadership emergence in small groups. *Dissertation Abstracts International, 44*(11A), 3196.

Nicholls, J. R. (1985). A new approach to situational leadership. *Leadership and Organization Development Journal, 6*(4), 2–7.

Nicholls, J. (1990). Rescuing leadership from Humpty Dumpty. *Journal of General Management, 16*(2), 76–89.

Nichols, R., & Bilbro, (1966). The diagnosis of twin zygosity. *Acta Genetica, 16,* 265–275.

Nicholson, R. (1983). Managing emerging businesses. *Managing, 3*(3), 21–25.

Nie, N. H., Powell, C. B., Jr., & Prewitt, K. (1969). Social structure and political participation: Developmental relationships. *American Political Science Review, 63,* 361–378, 808–832.

Niebuhr, R. E., Bedeian, A. C., & Armenakis, A. A. (1980). Individual need states and their influence on perceptions of leader behavior. *Social Behavior and Personality, 8,* 17–25.

Niehoff, B. P., Enz, C. A., & Grover, R. A. (1989). *The impact of top management actions on employee attitudes.* Paper, Academy of Management, Washington, DC.

Niehoff, B. P., Enz, C. A., & Grover, R. A. (1990). The impact of top-management actions on employee attitudes and perceptions. *Group & Organizational Studies, 15,* 337–352.

Niehoff, B. P., Moorman, R. H., Blakely, G., et al. (2001). The influence of empowerment and job enrichment on employee loyalty in a downsizing environment. *Group & Organization Management, 26,* 93–113.

Nietzsche, F. (1883/1974). Thus spake Zarathustra. In O. Levy (ed.), *The complete works of Friedrich Nietzsche.* New York: Gordon Press.

Nietzsche, F. (1888/1936). *The Antichrist.* Magdeburg: Nordland-Verlag.

Nisbett, M. A. (1986). The leader: Boss or coach? *Canadian Banker, 93*(1), 54–57.

Nix, H. L., Dressel, P. L., & Bates, F. L. (1977). Changing leaders and leadership structure: A longitudinal study. *Rural Sociology, 42,* 2241.

Nix, H. L., Singh, R. N., & Cheatham, P. L. (1974). Views of leader respondents compared with random respondents' views. *Journal of Community Development and Society, 5,* 81–91.

Nkomo, S. M., & Cox, T., Jr.(1987). *Individual and organizational factors affecting the upward mobility of black managers.* Paper, Academy of Management, New Orleans, LA.

Nocera, J. (1996). Confessions of a corporate killer. *Fortune, 134*(6), September 30, 200.

Noe, R. A. (1986). Trainees' attributes attitudes: Neglected influences on training effectiveness. *Academy of Management Review, 11,* 736–749.

Noe, R. A. (1988). Women and mentoring: A review and research agenda. *Academy of Management Review, 13,* 65–78.

Noe, R. A., & Schmitt, N. (1986). The influence of trainee attitudes on training effectiveness: Test of a model. *Personnel Psychology, 39,* 497–523.

Noer, D. (1993). *Healing the wounds: Overcoming the trauma of layoffs and revitalizing downsized organizations.* San Francisco, CA: Jossey-Bass.

Norburn, D., & Birley, S. (1988). The top management team and corporate performance. *Strategic Management Journal, 9,* 225–237.

Norman, W. T. (1963). Toward an adequate taxonomy of personality attributes: Replicated factor structures in peer nomination personality ratings. *Journal of Abnormal and Social Psychology, 66,* 574–583.

Normann, R. (1977). *Management for growth.* New York: Wiley.

Norrgren, F. (1981a). *Managers' beliefs, behavioral intentions and evaluations with respect to participation* (Report No. 6, 3). Göteborg, Sweden: University of Göteborg, Department of Applied Psychology.

Norrgren, F. (1981b). *Subordinate reactions to different managerial beliefs about participation* (Report No. 6, 2). Goteborg, Sweden: University of Goteborg, Department of Applied Psychology.

Norris, M. (1992). Warren Bennis on rebuilding leadership. *Planning Review,* September–October, 13–15.

Norris, W. R., & Vecchio, R. P. (1992). Situational leadership theory: A replication. *Group & Organizatio Management, 17,* 331–342.

Northcraft, G., & Martin, J. (1982). Double jeopardy: Resistance to affirmative action from potential beneficiaries. In B. A. Gutek (ed.), *Sex-role stereotyping and affirmative action policy.* Los Angeles: University of California, Institute for Industrial Relations.

Northouse, P. G. (2001). *Leadership theory and practice* (2nd ed.). Thousand Oaks, CA: Sage.

Northway, M. L. (1946). Some challenging problems of social relationships. *Sociometry, 9,* 187–198.

Northway, M. L., Frankel, E. B., & Potashin, R. (1947). Personality and sociometric status. *Sociometry Monographs, 11.*

Northwood, L. K. (1953). The relative ability of leaders and non-leaders as expert judges of fact and opinions held by members of the community of which they are a part. *Dissertation Abstracts, 13,* 898.

Novak, M. A., & Graen, G. B. (1985). *Perceived leader control as a moderator of personal leader resources contributing to leader-member exchange.* Paper, Academy of Management, San Diego, CA.

Nowack, K. M., Hartley, J., & Bradley, W. (1999). How to evaluate your 360 feedback efforts. *Training and Development,* April, 48–53.

Nowotny, O. H. (1964). American vs. European management philosophy. *Harvard Business Review, 42*(2), 101–108.

Numerof, R. E., Cramer, K. D., & Shachar-Hendin, S. A. (1984). Stress in health administrators: Sources, symptoms, and coping strategies. *Nursing Economics, 2,* 270–279.

Numerof, R. E., & Seltzer, J. (1986). *The relationship between leadership factors, burnout, and stress symptoms among middle managers.* Paper, Academy of Management, Chicago.

Numerof, R. E., Seltzer, J., & Bass, B. M. (1989). Transformational leadership: Is it a source of more burnout and stress? *Journal of Health and Human Resources Administration, 12,* 174–185.

Nutt, P. C. (1986). Decision style and strategic decision of top executives. *Technological Forecasting and Social Change, 30,* 39–62.

Nutt, P. C. (1986). Tactics of implementation. *Academy of Management Journal, 29,* 230–261.

Nutt, P. C. (1999). Surprising but true: Half of organizational decisions fail. *Academy of Management Executive, 13*(4), 75–90.

Nutt, P. C. (2001). Decision debacles and how to avoid them. *Business Strategy Review, 12*(2), 1–14.

Nutt, P. C. (2002). *Why decisions fail: Avoiding the blunders and traps that lead to debacles.* San Francisco, CA: Berrett-Koehler.

Nutt, P. C. (2004). Expanding the search for alternatives during strategic decision-making. *Academy of Management Executive, 18*(4), 13–28.

Nutt, P. C., & Backoff, R. W. (1993). Transforming public organizations with strategic management and strategic leadership. *Journal of Management, 19,* 299–347.

Nuttin, J. R. (1984). *Motivation, planning and action: A relational theory of behavioral dynamics.* Hillsdale, NJ: Erlbaum.

Nydegger, R. (1975). Developmental stages in moral reasoning. *Dissertation Abstracts International, 32,* 4109A.

Nygren, D. J., & Ukeritis, M. D. (1993). *The future of religious orders in the US: Transformation and commitment.* Westport, CT: Praeger.

Nystrom, P. C. (1978). Managers and the hi-hi leader myth. *Academy of Management Journal, 21,* 325–331.

Nystrom, P. C. (1986). Comparing beliefs of line and technostructure managers. *Academy of Management Journal, 29,* 812–819.

Nystrom, P. C., & Starbuck, W. H. (1984). To avoid organizational crises, unlearn. *Organizational Dynamics, 12*(4), 53–65.

Oaklander, H., & Fleishman, E. A. (1964). Patterns of leadership related to organizational stress in hospital settings. *Administrative Science Quarterly, 8,* 520–531.

O'Barr, W. M. (1982). *Linguistic evidence: Language, power, and strategy in the courtroom.* New York: Academic Press.

Oberg, W. (1972). Charisma, commitment, and contemporary organization theory. *Business Topics, 20,* 18–32.

Obradovic, J. (1970). Participation and work attitudes in Yugoslavia. *Industrial Relations, 9,* 161–169.

O'Brien, G. E. (1969b). Leadership in organizational settings. *Journal of Applied Behavioral Science, 5,* 45–63.

O'Brien, G. E., & Harary, F. (1977). Measurement of the interactive effects of leadership style and group structure upon group performance. *Australian Journal of Psychology, 29,* 59–71.

O'Brien, W. J. (1986). *A philosophy to live by.* Worcester, MA: Hanover Insurance Companies.

Obrochta, R. J. (1960). Foreman-worker attitude patterns. *Journal of Applied Psychology, 44,* 88–91.

Ocasio, W. (1999). Institutionalized action and corporate governance: The reliance on rules on CEO succession. *Administrative Science Quarterly, 44,* 384–416.

O'Connell, J. J. (1968). *Managing organizational innovation.* Homewood, IL: Irwin.

O'Connell, M. J. (1986). *The impact of institutional and occupational values on Air Force officer career intent.* Paper, Academy of Management, Chicago, IL.

O'Connell, M. S., Lord, R. G., & O'Connell, M. A. (1990). *Differences in Japanese and American prototypes: Implications for cross–cultural training.* Paper, Academy of Management, San Francisco, CA.

O'Connell, S. E. (1996). The new workplace. *Business Week,* April 29, 105–113.

O'Connor, E. J., & Farrow, D. L. (1979). A cross-functional comparison of prescribed versus preferred patterns of managerial structure. *Journal of Management Studies, 16,* 222–234.

O'Connor, E. J., Peters, L. H., Pooyan, A., Weekley, J., Blake, F., & Erenkrantz, B. (1984). Situational constraint effects on performance, affective reactions, and turnover: A field replication and extension. *Journal of Applied Psychology, 69,* 663–672.

O'Connor, J., Mumford, M. D., Clifton, T. C., et al. (1995). Charismatic leaders and destructiveness: An historiometric study. *The Leadership Quarterly, 6*(4), 529–555.

O'Connor, J. P., Jr., & Priem, R. L. (2003). *Do CEO stock options prevent or promote corporate accounting irregularities?* Paper, Academy of Management, Seattle, WA.

O'Connor, M., Foch, T., Sherry, T., and Plomin, R. (1980). A twin study of specific behavioral problems of socialization as viewed by parents. *Journal of Abnormal Child Psychology, 8*(2), 189–199.

O'Dempsey, K. (1976). Time analysis of activities, work patterns and roles of high school principals. *Administrators Bulletin, 7,* 1.

Oddou, G. R. (1983). The emergence of leaders in natural work groups: A test of self-monitoring theory. *Dissertation Abstracts International, 4*(7B), 2284.

Oddou, G. R., & Derr, C. D. (1991). *European MNC strategies for internationalizing managers: Current and future trends.* Paper, Academy of Management, Miami, FL.

Odier, C. (1948). Valeur et valence du chef. *Schweizerisches Archiv fïir Neurologisches Psychiatrie, 61,* 408–410.

Odom, G.R. (1990). *Mothers, leadership, and success.* Houston, TX: Polybius Press.

O'Farrell, B., & Harlan, S. L. (1982). Craftworkers and clerks: The effect of male co-worker hostility on women's satisfaction with nontraditional jobs. *Social Problems, 29*(3), 252–264.

Offerman, L. R. (1984). Short-term supervisory experience and LPC score: Effects of leader's sex and group sex composition. *Journal of Social Psychology, 23,* 115–121.

Offerman, L. R. (1997). *KLSP Leadership and followership group summary.* Battle Creek, MI: Kellogg Leadership Studies Project.

Offerman, L. R. (2000). Leadership and followership 2000: Different faces, different places. In B. Kellerman & L. R. Matusak (eds.), *Cutting Edge Leadership.* College Park, MD: University of Maryland, Center for the Advanced Study of Leadership.

Offerman, L. R., & Gowing, M. K. (1993). Personnel selection in the future: the impact of changing demographics and the nature of work. In N. Schmitt, & W. C. Borman (eds.), *Personnel selection in organizations.* San Francisco, CA: Jossey-Bass, 385–417.

Offerman, L. R., & Hellman, P. S. (1997). Culture's consequences for leadership behavior: National values in action. *Journal of Cross-Cultural Psychology, 28,* 342–351.

Offermann, L. R., Kennedy, J. K., Jr., & Wirtz, P. W. (1994). Implicit leadership theories: Content, structure, and generalizability. *Leadership Quarterly, 5*(1), 43–58.

Offerman, L. R., & Malamut, A. B. (2001). *When leaders harass: The role of organizational leadership in managing sexual harassment within its ranks.* Paper, Academy of Management, Washington, DC.

Offerman, L., & Phan, L. U. (2002). Culturally intelligent leadership for a diverse world. In R. E. Riggio, S. E. Murphy, & F. J. Pirozzolo, (eds.), *Multiple intelligences and leadership.* Mahwah, NJ: Lawrence Erlbaum & Associates.

Offerman, L. R., Schroyer, C. J., & Green, S. K. (1998). Leader attributions to subordinate performance: Consequences for subsequent leader interactive behaviors and ratings. *Journal of Applied Social Psychology, 28,* 1125–1139.

Office of Strategic Services (O.S.S.) Assessment Staff. (1948). *Assessment of men: Selection of personnel for Office of Strategic Services.* New York: Rinehart.

Ogbuehi, D. A. (1981). The correlates of leadership effectiveness of managers in selected private and semi-public organizations in Nigeria. *Dissertation Abstracts International, 42*(4A), 1383.

Ohlott, P. J. (1988). Job assignments. In C. McCauley, R. Moxley, & E. Van Velsor (eds.), *The Center for Creative Leadership Handbook of Leadership Development.* San Francisco: Jossey-Bass.

Okanes, M. M., & Murray, W. (1980). Achievement and Machiavellianism among men and women managers. *Psychological Reports, 46,* 783–788.

Okanes, M. M., & Stinson, J. E. (1974). Machiavellianism and emergent leadership in a management simulation. *Psychological Reports, 35,* 255–259.

Oldham, G. R. (1975). The impact of supervisory characteristics on goal acceptance. *Academy of Management Journal, 18,* 461–475.

Oldham, G. R. (1976). The motivational strategies used by supervisors: Relationships to effectiveness indicators. *Organizational Behavior and Human Performance, 15,* 66–86.

Oldham, G. R., & Cummings, A. (1996). Employee creativity: Personnel and contextual factors at work. *Academy of Management Journal, 39,* 607–634.

O'Leary, M. B. (2001). *Overcoming distance: Socialization practices in the Hudson's Bay Company, 1670–1826.* Paper, Academy of Management, Washington, DC.

O'Leary, R. S., Harkcom, K. R., Jackson, K., et al. (2003). *Rater selection in performance evaluation. Does it make a difference?* Paper, Society for Industrial and Organizational Psychology, Orlando, FL.

O'Leary, V. E. (1974). Some attitudinal barriers to occupational aspirations in women. *Psychological Bulletin, 81,* 809–28.

O'Leary, V. E. (1989). Ambition and leadership in men and women (excerpt). In A. Campbell (ed.), *The Opposite Sex.* London: Ebury Press.

O'Mahoney, S., & Barley, S. R. (1999). Do digital telecommunications affect work and organization? The state of our knowledge. *Research in Organizational Behavior, 21,* 125–161.

Olien, C. N., Tichenor, P. J., & Donohue, G. A. (1987). Role of Mass Communication. In D. E. Johnson, L. R. Miller, L. C. Miller, & G. F. Summers (eds.), *Needs assessment: Theory and methods.* Ames: Iowa University Press.

Oliver, J. E. (1982). An instrument for classifying organizations. *Academy of Management Journal, 25,* 855–866.

Oliverson, L. R. (1976). Identification of dimensions of leadership and leader behavior and cohesion in encounter groups. *Dissertation Abstracts International, 37,* 136–137.

Olmsted, D. W. (1957). Inter-group similarities of role correlates. *Sociometry, 20,* 8–20.

Olmstead, M. S. (1954). Orientation and role in the small group. *American Sociological Review, 6,* 741–751.

Olsen, M. E. (1968). *The process of social organization.* New York: Holt, Rinehart & Winston.

Olson, B. J. (2003). *Diversification and CEO compensation: Direct effects and moderating effects of CEO power.* Paper, Academy of Management, Seattle, WA.

Olson, D. A. (1999). *Overview of undergraduate leadership studies programs: Preparing tomorrow's leaders.* Claremont, CA: Claremont McKenna College, Kravis Leadership Institute.

O'Neill, M. (1994). The paradox of women and power in the nonprofit sector. In T. Odendahl & M. O'Neill (eds.), *Women & Power in the Nonprofit Sector.* San Francisco: Jossey-Bass.

Ones, D. S., & Viswesvaran, C. (1998). Gender, age, and race differences in overt integrity tests: Results across four large-scale job applicant data sets. *Journal of Applied Psychology, 83,* 35–42.

Onishi, N. (2003). With all due respect, Japanese are dropping titles: A nationwide emphasis on efficiency and merit has relaxed old rules about how to address authority figures. *St. Petersburg Times,* November 1, 1A–D1.

Onnen, M. K. (1987). *The relationship of clergy leadership characteristics to growing or declining churches.* Doctoral dissertation, University of Louisville, Louisville, KY

Opsahl, R. L., & Dunnette, M. D. (1966). Role of financial compensation in industrial motivation. *Psychological Bulletin, 66,* 94–118.

O'Regan, N., & Ghobadian, A. (2003). *Refocusing performance: A strategy-centered approach in small and medium sized enterprises.* Paper, Academy of Management, Seattle, WA.

O'Reilly, C. A. (1977). Supervisors and peers as information sources, group supportiveness, and individual decision-making performance. *Journal of Applied Psychology, 62,* 632–635.

O'Reilly, C. A. (1977). Person-job fit: Implications for individual attitudes and performance. *Organizational Behavior and Human Performance. 18,* 36–46.

O'Reilly, C. A. (1984). *Charisma as communication: The impact of top management credibility and philosophy on employee involvement.* Paper, Academy of Management, Boston, MA.

O'Reilly, C. A., III, Chatman, J., & Caldwell, D. F. (1991). People and organizational culture: A profile comparison approach to assessing person-organization fit. *Academy of Management Journal, 34,* 487–516.

O'Reilly, C. A., III, & Puffer, S. M. (1983). *Positive effects from negative sanctions: The impact of rewards and punishments in a social context.* Paper, Academy of Management, San Diego, CA.

O'Reilly, C. A., III, & Roberts, K. H. (1973). Job satisfaction among whites and nonwhites: A cross-cultural approach. *Journal of Applied Psychology, 57,* 295–299.

O'Reilly, C. A., & Roberts, K. H. (1974). Information filtration in organizations: Three experiments. *Organizational Behavior and Human Performance, 11,* 253–265.

O'Reilly, C. A., III, & Weitz, B. A. (1980). Managing marginal employees: The use of warnings and dismissals. *Administrative Science Quarterly, 25,* 467–484.

O'Reilly, T. A. (1988) Does leadership make a difference to organizational performance? *Administrative Science Quarterly, 33,* 388–400.

Orlans, H. (1953). *Opinion polls on national leaders* (Report No. 6). Washington, DC: Institute for Research on Human Relations.

Orlikowski, W. J. (1992). The duality of technology: Rethinking the concept of technology in organizations. *Organization Science, 3,* 398–427.

O'Roark, A. M. (1986). *Bass-Valenzi decision modes and Myers-Briggs dominant functions: Management perspectives and preferences.* Paper, International Congress of Applied Psychology, Jerusalem.

O'Roark, A. M. (1995). Job stress survey results and informed interventions: Follow-through methods for business settings. *Stress & Emotion. 15*

O'Roark, A. (2000). *The quest for executive effectiveness: Turning vision inside-out: Charismatic-participatory leadership.* Nevada City, CA: Blue Dolphin Publishing.

O'Roark, A. M. (2001). Assessment and intervention issues in international organizational consulting. In R. L. Lowman (ed.), *Organizational Consulting Handbook*. San Francisco: Jossey-Bass.

Orpen, C. (1982). Effects of MBA training in managerial success. *Journal of Business Education*, 57(l), 152–154.

Orpen, C. (1987). The role of qualitative research in management. *South African Journal of Business*, 18, 250–254.

Osborn, A. R. (1953). *Applied imagination: Principles and procedures of creative thinking*. New York: Scribner.

Osborne, D. (1988). *Laboratories of democracy*. Harvard Business School Press, Boston, MA.

Osborne, D., & Gaebler, T. (1993). *Reinventing government: How the entrepreneurial spirit is transforming the public sector*. New York: Plume.

Osborn, R. N., & Ashforth, B. E. (1990). Investigating the challenges to senior leadership in complex high-risk technologies. *Leadership Quarterly*, 1, 147–163.

Osborn, R. N., & Hagedoorn, J. (1997). The institutionalization and evolutionary dynamics of interorganizational alliances and networks. *Academy of Management Journal*, 40, 261–278.

Osborn, R. N., & Hunt, J. G. (1975a). An adaptive-reaction theory of leadership: The role of macro variables in leadership research. In J. C. Hunt & L. L. Larson (eds.), *Leadership frontiers*. Carbondale: Southern Illinois University Press.

Osborn, R. N., & Hunt, J. G. (1975b). Relations between leadership, size, and subordinate satisfaction in a voluntary organization. *Journal of Applied Psychology*, 60, 730–735b.

Osborn, R. N., & Hunt, J. G. (1979). *Environment and leadership: Discretionary and nondiscretionary leader behavior and organizational outcomes*. Unpublished manuscript.

Osborn, R. N., Hunt, J. G., & Bussom, R. S. (1977). On getting your own way in organizational design: An empirical illustration of requisite variety. *Organization and Administrative Sciences*, 8, 295–310.

Osborn, R. N., Hunt, J. G., & Jauch, L. R. (1980). *Organization theory: An integrated approach*. New York: Wiley.

Osborn, R. N., Hunt, J. C., & Skaret, D. J. (1977). Managerial influence in a complex configuration with two unit heads. *Human Relations*, 30, 1025–1038.

Osborn, R. N., & Jackson, D. H. (1988). Leaders, riverboat gamblers, or purposeful unintended consequences in the management of complex, dangerous technologies. *Academy of Management Journal*, 31, 924–947.

Osborn, R. N., Jauch, L. R., Martin, I. N., & Glueck, W. F. (1981). The event of CEO succession, performance, and environmental conditions. *Academy of Management Journal*, 24, 183–191.

Osborn, R. N., & Vicars, W. M. (1976). Sex stereotypes: An artifact in leader behavior and subordinate satisfaction analysis. *Academy of Management Journal* 19, 439–449.

Osborn, T. N., & Osborn, D. B. (1986). Leadership profiles in Latin America: How different are Latin American managers from their counterparts? *Issues & Observations*, 6(2), 7–10.

Oshry, B. L., & Harrison, R. (1966). Transfer from here-and-now to there-and-then: Changes in organizational problem diagnosis stemming from T-group training. *Journal of Applied Behavioral Science*, 2, 185–198.

Oskarsson, H., & Klein, R. H. (1982). Leadership change and organizational regression. *International Journal of Group Psychotherapy*, 32, 145–162.

Osterloh, M., & Frey, B. S. (2003). *Corporate governance for crooks? The case for corporate virtue*. Zurich, Switzerland: University of Zurich. Unpublished manuscript.

Oswald, S. L., Mossholder, K. W., & Harris, S. G. (1997). Relations between strategic involvement and managers' perceptions of environment and competitive strengths: The effect of vision salience. *Group & Organization Management*, 22, 343–365.

O'Toole, J. (1985). *Vanguard management*. New York: Doubleday.

O'Toole, J. O. (1995). *Leading change: Overcoming the ideology of comfort and the tyranny of custom*. San Francisco: Jossey-Bass.

O'Toole, J. O. (2000). Researching the organizational dimensions of leadership. In B. Kellerman & L. R. Matusak (eds.), *Cutting Edge Leadership*. College Park, MD: University of Maryland, Center for the Advanced Study of Leadership.

Ottaway, R. N., & Bhatnagar, D. (1988). Personality and biographical differences between male and female managers in the United States and India. *Applied Psychology: An International Review*, 37, 201–212.

Otteri, A. J. W., & Teulings, A. W. M. (1970). Buitenstaanders en Krachtfiguren. [Outsiders and power figures]. *Mens en Onderneming*, 24, 296–313.

Ottih, L. O. (1981). Managerial decentralization in Nigerian banks: Case studies of selected banks. *Dissertation Abstracts International*, 42(7A), 3280.

Ouchi, W. (1981). *Theory Z: How American business can meet the Japanese challenge*. Reading, MA: Addison-Wesley.

Ouchi, W. G., & Maguire, M. A. (1975). Operational control: Two functions. *Administrative Science Quarterly*, 20, 559–569.

Overholser, G. (2000). But we need ideas, debate: Spice in the race. *International Herald Tribune*, January 8–9, 6.

Owens, W. A., & Schoenfeldt, L. F. (1979). Toward a classification of persons. *Journal of Applied Psychology Monograph*, 65, 569–607.

Pace, L., Hartley, D., & Davenport, L. (1992). Beyond situationalism: Subordinate preference and perceived leader impact. *Impact of Leadership*. Greensboro, NC: Center for Creative Leadership.

Page, B. I. (1984). Presidents as opinion leaders: Some new evidence. *Policy Studies Journal*, 12, 649–661.

Page, D. P. (1935). Measurement and prediction of leadership. *American Journal of Sociology*, 41, 31–43.

Page, E. C. (1985). *Political authority and bureaucratic power. A comparative analysis*. Brighton, Sussex: Wheatsheaf Books.

Page, R., & Tornow, W. W. (1987). *Managerial job analysis: Are we farther along?* Paper, Society for industrial and Organizational Psychology, Atlanta, GA.

Page, R. C. (1987). The position description questionnaire. In S. Gael (ed.), *Handbook of job analysis*. New York: Wiley.

Page, R. C., & Baron, H. B. (1995). *Identifying what motivates managers*. Paper, Society for Industrial and Organizational Psychology, Orlando, FL.

Page, R. H., & McGinnies, E. (1959). Comparison of two styles of leadership in small group discussion. *Journal of Applied Psychology*, 43, 240–245.

Pagery, F. D., & Chapanis, A. (1983). Communication control and leadership in telecommunications by small groups. *Behavior and Information Technology, 2*(2), 179–196.

Paige, G. D. (1977). *The scientific study of political leadership.* New York: Free Press.

Paine, F. T., Carroll, S. J., & Leete, B. A. (1966). Need satisfactions of managerial level personnel in a government agency. *Journal of Applied Psychology, 50,* 247–249.

Paine, L. S. (1997). *Cases in leadership, ethics, and organizational integrity: A strategic perspective.* Chicago: Irwin

Painter, L. C. (1984). Leadership orientation and behavior following interpersonal skill training: Perceptions of supervisors and subordinates (Consideration, structure, management). *Dissertation Abstracts International, 45*(6A), 1631.

Palgi, M. (1984). *Theoretical and empirical aspects of workers' participation in decision-making: A comparison between kibbutz and non-kibbutz industrial plants in Israel.* Doctoral dissertation, Hebrew University, Jerusalem.

Pallett, J. E., & Hoyt, D. P. (1968). College curriculum and success in general business. *Journal of College Personnel, 9*(4), 238–245.

Palmer, D. D., Veiga, J. F., & Vera, J. A. (1981). Personal values in decision making: Value-cluster approach in two cultures. *Group and Organizational Management, 6*(2), 224–234.

Palmer, D. D., Veiga, J. F., & Vera, J. A. (1998). Differences in value systems of Anglo-American and Far Eastern students: Effects of American business education. *Journal of Business Ethics, 17*(3), February, 253–262.

Palmer, G. J. (1962a). Task ability and effective leadership. *Psychological Reports, 10,* 863–866.

Palmer, G. J. (1962b). Task ability and successful and effective leadership. *Psychological Reports, 11,* 813–816.

Palmer, I., & Byrne, D. (1970). Attraction toward dominant and submissive strangers: Similarity versus complementarity. *Journal of Experimental Research in Personality, 4,* 108–115.

Palmer, I., & King, A. W. (2003). *Listening to Jack: GE's change conversations with shareholders.* Paper, Academy of Management, Seattle, WA.

Palmer, F. H., & Myers, T. I. (1955). Sociometric choices and group productivity among radar crews. *American Psychologist, 10,* 441–442.

Pandey, J. (1976). Effects of leadership style, personality characteristics and methods of leader selection on members' leaders' behavior. *European Journal of Social Psychology, 6,* 475–489.

Pandey, J., & Bohra, K. A. (1984). Ingratiation as a function of organizational characteristics and supervisory styles. *International Review of Applied Psychology, 33,* 381–394.

Paolillo, J. G. (1981). Managers' self-assessments of managerial roles: The influence of hierarchical level. *Journal of Management, 7,* 43–52.

Paolillo, J. G. (1981b). Role profiles for managers at different hierarchical levels. *Proceedings,* Academy of Management, San Diego, CA, 91–94.

Papaloizos, A. (1962). Personality and success of training in human relations. *Personnel Psychology, 15,* 423–428.

Parameshwar, S. (2006). Inventing higher purpose through suffering: The transformation of the transformational leader. *Leadership Quarterly, 17*(5), 454–474.

Parboteeah, K. P., & Cullen, J. B. (2002). *Managers' justifications of unethical behaviors: A 28 nation social institutions approach.* Paper, Academy of Management, Denver, CO.

Parboteeah, K. P., & Cullen, J. B. (2003). Social institutions and work centrality: Explorations beyond national culture. *Organization Science, 14*(2), 137–148.

Park, B. E. (1988). When world leaders get sick—Disease, disability and danger. *Leaders, 11*(2), 36–38.

Park, D. (1996). Sex-role identity and leadership style: Looking for an androgynous leadership style. *Journal of Leadership Studies, 3*(3), 49–59

Park, D. (1997). Androgynous leadership style: An integration rather than a polarization. *Leadership & Organization Development Journal, 18*(2–3), 166–171.

Parke, A. (1993). Partner nationality and the structure-performance relationship in strategic alliances. *Organization Science, 10*(5), 301–302.

Parker, F. E. (1923). *Consumers' cooperative societies in the United States in 1920.* Washington, DC: U.S. Department of Labor Bulletin No. 313.

Parker, F. E. (1927). *Cooperative movements in the United States in 1925 (other than experimental).* Washington, DC: U.S. Department of Labor Bulletin No. 437.

Parker, L. E., & Price, R. H. (1994) Empowered managers and empowered workers: The effects of managerial support and managerial perceived control on workers' sense of control over decision making. *Human Relations, 47,* 911–928.

Parker, P. S., & Ogilvie, D. T. (1996). Gender, culture, and leadership: Toward a culturally distinct model of African-American women executives' leadership strategies. *Leadership Quarterly, 7,* 189–214.

Parker, S. (1958). Leadership patterns in a psychiatric ward. *Human Relations, 11,* 287–301.

Parker, T. C. (1963). Relationships among measures of supervisory behavior, group behavior, and situational characteristics. *Personnel Psychology, 16,* 319–334.

Parker, W. S., Jr. (1976). Black-white differences in leader behavior related to subordinates' reactions. *Journal of Applied Psychology, 61,* 140–147.

Parks, B. (1998). Telecommuting brightens the future for Florida Power and Light. *Employment Relations Today, 24,* 65–72.

Parks, J. M., Conlon, D. E., Aug, S., et al. (1999). The manager giveth, the manager taketh away: Variation in distribution/recovery rules due to resource type and cultural orientation. *Journal of Management, 25,* 723–757.

Parry, K. W. (1994). Transformational leadership: An Australian investigation of leadership behavior. In A. Kouzmin, L. Still, & P. Clarke (eds.), *New directions in management.* Sydney: McGraw-Hill, 82–114.

Parry, K. W. (1996). *Transformational leadership: Developing an enterprising management culture.* Pitman Publishing, South Melbourne: Australia.

Parry, K. W. (1998). Grounded theory and social process: A new direction for leadership research. *Leadership Quarterly, 9,* 85–105.

Parry, K. W. (1999). Enhancing adaptability: Leadership strategies to accommodate change in local government settings. *Journal of Organizational Change Management, 12*(2), 134–156.

Parry, K. W. (2002). Four phenomenologically determined social processes of organizational leadership: Further support for the construct of transformational leadership. In B. J. Avolio, & F. J. Yammarino (eds.), *Transformational and charismatic leadership: The road ahead.* Oxford: Elsevier Science.

Parry, K. W. (2003). *Chief executive summary: Report on outputs for the period 1998–2003.* Wellington, New Zealand: Victoria University, Centre for the Study of Leadership.

Parry, K. W., & Proctor, S. B. (1999).*The New Zealand Leadership Survey.* Wellington, New Zealand: New Zealand College of Management and Victoria University, Centre for the Study of Leadership.

Parry, K. W., and Proctor-Thompson, S. B. (2002). Perceived integrity of transformational leaders in organizational settings. *Journal of Business Ethics, 35*(2), 75–96.

Parry, K. W., & Sinha, P. (2005). Researching the trainability of transformational organizational leadership. *Human Resources Development International, 8*(2), 165–183.

Parry, K. W., & Sorros, J. (1994). Transformational leadership in Australia and the United States? *Working Paper Series, 4*(2). University of Southern Queensland, Brisbane, Australia.

Parsons, C. K., Herold, D. M., & Leatherwood, M. L. (1985). Turnover during initial employment: A longitudinal study of the role of causal attributions. *Journal of Applied Psychology, 70,* 337–341.

Parsons, C. K., Herold, D. M., & Turlington, B. (1981). *Individual differences in performance feedback preferences.* Paper, Academy of Management, San Diego, CA.

Parsons, T. (1937). *The structure of social action.* New York: Free Press.

Parsons, T. (1951). *The social system.* New York: Free Press.

Parsons, T., & Shils, E. A. (eds.). (1959). *Toward a general theory of action.* Cambridge, MA: Harvard University Press.

Parten, M. B. (1932). Social participation among preschool children. *Journal of Abnormal and Social Psychology, 27,* 243–269

Pasa, S. F., Kabasakal, H., & Bosur, M. (2001). Society, organizations, and leadership in Turkey. *Applied Psychology: An International Review, 50,* 559–589.

Pascal, B. (1660/1950). *Pensées.* New York: Pantheon.

Pascale, R. T., & Maguire, M. A. (1980). Comparison of selected work factors in Japan and the United States. *Human Relations, 33,* 433–455.

Pastor, J. C. & Mayo, M. (2006) *Transformational and transactional leadership: An examination of managerial cognition among Spanish upper echelons* (Working Paper No. WP06–13). Instituto de Empresa Business School. Available at SSRN.

Pastor, J. C., Meindl, J. R., & Mayo, M. C. (2002). A network effects model of charisma attributions. *Academy of Management Journal, 45,* 410–420.

Pastor, J., & Nebeker, D. M. (2002). *Emotional intelligence and leadership effectiveness.* Paper, Academy of Management, Denver, CO.

Patchen, M. (1962). Supervisory methods and group performance norms. *Administrative Science Quarterly, 7,* 275–294.

Patchen, M. (1970). *Participation, achievement, and involvement on the job.* Englewood Cliffs, NJ: Prentice-Hall.

Patchen, M. (1974). The locus and basis of influence on organizational decisions. *Organizational Behavior and Human Performance, 11,* 195–221.

Pate, L. E., & Heiman, D. C. (1981). *A test of the Vroom-Yetton decision model in seven field settings.* Paper, Academy of Management, San Diego, CA.

Patten, T. H. (1968b). Merit increases and the facts of organization life. *Management of Personnel Quarterly, 7,* 30–38.

Patterson, C. E. P. (1995). Transformational teaching: An examination of classroom leadership. *The Journal of Leadership Studies, 2*(2), 42–50.

Patterson, J., & Kim, P. (1991). *The day America told the truth: What people really believe about everything that really matters.* New York: Prentice Hall.

Patterson, M. (1968). Spatial factors in social interactions. *Human Relations, 21,* 351–361.

Patterson, R. A. (1975). *Women in management: An experimental study of the effects of sex and marital status on job performance ratings, promotability ratings, and promotion decisions.* Dissertation Abstracts International, 1975 (Dec), Vol. 36 (6-B), 3108–3109.

Pattie, M. W. (2004). *Leadership development: The developmental difference between socialized and personalized leaders.* Paper, Society for Industrial and Organizational Psychology, New Orleans, LA.

Pauchant, T.C. (1991). Transferential leadership. Towards a more complex understanding of charisma in organizations, *Organization Studies, 12*(4), 507–527.

Paul, N. C. (2004). The woman chosen to lead Boston's police. *Christian Science Monitor,* March 16, 2, 4.

Paul, R. J., & Ebadi, Y. M. (1989). Leadership decision making in a service organization: A field test of the Vroom-Yetton model. *Journal of Occupational Psychology,62,* 201–211.

Paul, T., Schyns, B., Mohr, et al. (2000). *What does the leader-member exchange scale measure?* Paper, European Association of Work and Organizational Psychology, Prague, Czech Republic.

Pavel, D. M. (1999). American Indians and Alaska Natives in higher education: Promoting access and achievement. In K. G. Swisher & J. W. Tippeconic (eds.), *Next steps: Research and practice to advance Indian education.* Charleston, WV: Eric Clearing House on Rural Education and Small Schools.

Pavel, D. M., & Curtain, T. R. (1997). *Characteristics of American Indian and Alaska Native education results from the 1990–91 and 1993–94 schools and staffing surveys.* Washington, DC: Department of Education, National Center for Educational Statistics.

Pavel, D. M., Swisher, K. G., & Ward, M. (1996). Special focus: American Indian and Alaska Native demographics and education trends. In D. J. Carter & R. Wison (eds.), *Minorities in higher education.* Washington, DC: American Council on Higher Education.

Pavett, C. M. (1983). Evaluation of the impact of feedback on performance and motivation. *Human Relations, 36,* 641–654.

Pavett, C. M., & Lau, A. W. (1983). Managerial work: The influence of hierarchical level and functional specialty. *Academy of Management Journal, 26,* 170–177.

Pawar, B. S., & Eastman, K. K. (1997). The nature and implications of contextual influences on transformational leadership: A conceptual examination. *Academy of Management Review, 22,* 80–109.

Payne, B. (2000). *Shakespeare on leadership*: Durham, NC: Duke University, Hart Leadership Program.

Payne, R. G., & Hauty, C. T. (1955). The effect of psychological feedback upon work decrement. *Journal of Experimental Psychology, 50,* 343–351.

Payne, R. L., & Pugh, D. S. (1976). *Organizational structure and climate.* In M. D. Dunnette (ed.), *Handbook of Industrial and Organizational Psychology.* Chicago: Rand McNally.

Payne, S. C., & Huffman, A. H. (2005). A longitudinal examination of the influence of mentoring on organizational commitment and turnover. *Academy of Management Journal, 48,* 158–168.

Peabody, D., & Goldberg, L. R. (1989). Some determinants of factor structures from personality-trait descriptors. *Journal of Personality and Social Psychology, 57,* 552–567.

Peabody, R. L. (1962). Perceptions of organizational authority: A comparative analysis. *Administrative Science Quarterly, 6,* 463–482.

Peabody, R. L. (1964). *Organizational authority: Superior-subordinate relationships in three public organizations.* New York: Atherton Press.

Peabody, R. L. (1976). *Leadership in Congress.* Boston: Little, Brown.

Pearce, C. L. (2004). The future of leadership: Combining vertical and shared leadership to transfer knowledge work. *Academy of Management Executive, 18*(1), 47–57.

Pearce, C. L., & Conger, J. A. (2002). Introduction. In C. L. Pearce & J. A. Conger (eds.), *Shared leadership: Reframing the hows and whys of leadership.* Thousand Oaks, CA: Sage Publications.

Pearce, C. L., & Ensley, M. D. (2003). A reciprocal and longitudinal investigation of the innovation process: The central role of shared vision in product and process innovation teams (PPITs). *Journal of Organizational Behavior, 24,* 1–20.

Pearce, C. L., Rode, G., & Kohut, G. F. (2001). *Enhancing team development: The role of managerial enablement.* Paper, Academy of Management, Washington, DC.

Pearce, C. L., & Sims, H. P., Jr. (2002). Virtual versus shared leadership as predictors of the effectiveness of change management teams: An examination of aversive, directive, transactional, transformational, and empowering leaders behaviors. *Group Dynamics: Theory, Research, and Practice, 6,* 172–197.

Pearce, C. L., Sims, H. P., Cox, J. F., Ball, G., Schnell, E., Smith, K. A., et al. (2003). Transactors, transformers and beyond: A multi-method development of a theoretical typology of leadership. *Journal of Management Development, 22,* 273–307.

Pearce, C. L., Yoo, Y., & Alavi, M. (2003–2004). Leadership, social work, and virtual teams: The relative influence of vertical vs. shared leadership in the nonprofit sector. In R. Riggio & S. S. Orr (eds.), *Improving leadership in nonprofit organizations.* San Francisco: Jossey-Bass (Wiley).

Pearce, J. L. (1982). Leading and following volunteers: Implications for a changing society. *Journal of Applied Behavioral Science, 18,* 385–394.

Pearce, J. L. (1983). Comparing volunteers and employees in a test of Etzioni's compliance typology. *Journal of Voluntary Action Research, 12*(2), 22–30.

Pearce, J. L., & Porter, L. W. (1986). Employee responses to formal performance appraisal feedback. *Journal of Applied Psychology, 71,* 211–218.

Pearce, J. L., Stevenson, W. B., & Perry, J. L. (1985). Managerial compensation based on organizational performance: A time series analysis of the effects of merit pay. *Academy of Management Journal, 28,* 261–278.

Pearse, R. F., Worthington, E. I., & Flaherty, J. J. (1954). A program for developing tools engineers into manufacturing executives. *ASTE Tool Engineering Conference Papers,* 22T5, Detroit.

Pearson, B. E. (1980). Women's entry into managerial positions at human service agencies: Effect of applicant's locus of control and leadership style on employer preference for applicants. *Dissertation Abstracts International, 41*(5A). 1958.

Pearson, C. M., & Clair, J. A. (1998). Reframing crisis management. *Academy of Management Review, 23,* 59–76.

Pearson, J. C., & Serafini, D. M. (1984). Leadership behavior and sex role socialization: Two sides of the same coin. *Southern Speech Communication Journal, 49,* 396–405.

Pearson, W. M., & Sanders, L. T. (1981). State executives' attitudes toward some authoritarian values. *State and Local Government Review, 13*,1(2), 73–79.

Peck, S. M. (1966). *The rank-and-file leader.* New Haven, CT: College & University Press.

Pedigo, P. R. (1986). *Impact of information technology on middle management.* Paper, American Psychological Association, Washington, DC.

Peirce, N., & Johnson, C. (1997). *Boundary crossers: Community leadership for a global age.* College Park, MD: University of Maryland, James MacGregor Academy of Leadership.

Pellegrin, R. J. (1952). *Status achievement in youth groups: Elements of group adjustment in relation to social mobility.* Doctoral dissertation, University of North Carolina, Chapel Hill.

Pellegrin, R. J. (1953). The achievement of high status and leadership in the small group. *Social Forces, 32,* 10–16.

Pelletier, G. (1966). Business management in French Canada. *Business Quarterly–Canada Management Journal,* Fall, 56–62.

Pelz, D. C. (1949). The effect of supervisory attitudes and practices on employee satisfaction. *American Psychologist, 4,* 283–284.

Pelz, D. C. (1951). Leadership within a hierarchical organization. *Journal of Social Issues, 7,* 49–55.

Pelz, D. C. (1952). Influence: A key to effective leadership in the first-line supervisor. *Personnel, 29,* 209–217.

Pelz, D. C. (1960). Conditional effects in the relationship of autonomy and motivation to performance. In E. Litwak, Models of bureaucracy which permit conflict. *The American Journal of Sociology, 67*(2), September 1961, 177–184.

Pelz, D. C. (1963). Relationships between measures of scientific performance and other variables. In C. W. Taylor & F. Barron (eds.), *Scientific creativity: Its recognition and development.* New York; Wiley.

Pelz, D. C., & Andrews, F. M. (1966a). *Scientists in organizations: Productive climates for research and development.* New York: Wiley.

Pelz, D. C., & Andrews, F. M. (1966b). Autonomy, coordination, and stimulation in relation to scientific achievement. *Behavioral Science, 11,* 89–97.

Pence, K. R., & Dilts, D. M. (2003). *The decision to fail: Bias and uncertainty in terminated technology projects.* Paper, Academy of Management, Seattle, WA.

Penfield, R. V. (1975). Time allocation patterns and effectiveness of managers. *Personnel Psychology, 27,* 245–255.

Peng, T. K., Peterson, M. F., & Shyi, Y. P. (1991). Quantitative methods in cross-national management research: Trends and equivalence issues. *Journal of Organizational Behavior, 12,* 87–107.

Penn, W. Y., Jr., & Collier, B. D. (1985). Current research in moral development as a decision support system. *Journal of Business Ethics, 4,* 131–138.

Penner, D. D., Malone, D. M., Coughlin, T. M., & Herz, J. A. (1973). Satisfaction with U.S. Army leadership. U.S. Army War College, *Leadership Monograph Series No. 2.*

Pennings, J. M. (1975). The relevance of the structured-contingency model for organization effectiveness. *Administrative Science Quarterly, 20,* 393–407.

Pennington, D. F., Haravey, F., & Bass, B. M. (1958). Some effects of decision and discussion on coalescence, change, and effectiveness. *Journal of Applied Psychology, 42,* 404–408.

Penzer, W. N. (1969). Educational level and satisfaction with pay: An attempted replication. *Personnel Psychology, 22,* 185–199.

Pepinsky, P. N., Hemphill, J. K., & Shevitz, R. N. (1958). Attempts to lead, group productivity, and morale under conditions of acceptance and rejection. *Journal of Abnormal and Social Psychology, 57,* 47–54.

Pepitone, E. (1952). *Responsibility to the group and its effect on the performance of the members.* Doctoral dissertation, University of Michigan, Ann Arbor.

Pepitone, A. (1958). Attributions of causality, social attitudes, and cognitive matching processes. In R. Tagiuri and L. Petrullo (eds.), *Person perception and interpersonal behavior.* Stanford, CA: Stanford University Press.

Peppers, L., & Ryan, J. (1986). Discrepancies between actual and aspired self: A comparison of leaders and nonleaders. *Group & Organization Studies, 11,* 220–228.

Pereira, D. F. (1986). *Transformational and transactional leadership: Applicability in an Indian engineering firm.* Paper, International Congress of Applied Psychology, Jerusalem, Israel.

Perlmutter, H. V. (1954). Impressions of influential members of discussion groups. *Journal of Psychology, 38,* 223–234.

Perlmutter, H. V. (1969). The tortuous evolution of the multinational corporation. *Columbia Journal of World Business, 4(1),* 9–18.

Perloff, R. (1999) What would Barnard say?: Self-reports of six psychologists: CEOs and their use of psychology in the CEO role. *The Psychologist-Manager Journal, 3,* 397–104.

Perlow, L. (1997). *Finding time: How corporations, individuals, and families can benefit from new work practices.* Ithaca, NY: Cornell University.

Perlow, L. A. (1998). Boundary control: The social ordering of work and family time in a high-tech organization. *Administrative Science Quarterly, 43,* 328–357.

Perls, F. (1969). In John O. Stevens (ed.), *Gestalt theory verbatim.* Layfayette, CA: Real People Press.

Perreault, G. (1997). Ethical followers: A link to ethical leadership. *Journal of Leadership Studies, 4(1),* 78–89.

Perrowe, P. L., Ferris, G. R., Frink, D. D., et al. (2000). Political skill: An antidote of workplace stressors. *Academy of Management Executive, 14(3),* 115

Perrucei, R., & Pilisak, M. (1970). Leaders and ruling elites: The interorganizational bases of community power. *American Sociological Review, 35,* 1040–1057.

Person, H. S. (1928). Leadership as a response to environment. *Educational Record Supplement No. 6, 9,* 10–21.

Pervin, L. A. (1985). Personality: Current controversies, issues and directions. *Annual Review of Psychology,* 83–114.

Pescosolido, A. (2002). Emergent leaders as managers of group emotions. *Leadership Quarterly, 13,* 583–599.

Pescuric, A., & Byham, W. C. (1996). The new look of behavioral modeling. *Training & Development, 50(7),* 24–30.

Peter, H. (1969). *Cross-cultural survey of managers in ten countries.* Paper, American Psychological Association, Washington, DC.

Peters, L. H., Fisher, C. D., & O'Connor, E. J. (1982). The moderating effect of situational control of performance variance on the relationship between individual differences and performance. *Personnel Psychology, 35,* 609–621.

Peters, L. H., Hartke, D. D., & Pohlmann, J. T. (1985). Fiedler's contingency theory of leadership: An application of the meta-analysis procedure of Schmidt and Hunter. *Psychological Bulletin, 97,* 274–285.

Peters, L. H., & O'Connor, E. J. (1980). Situational constraints and work outcomes: The influences of a frequently overlooked construct. *Academy of Management Review, 5,* 391–397.

Peters, R. (1998). Spotting the losers: Seven signs of non-competitive states. *Parameters, 28(1),* 36–39.

Peters, T. J. (1979). Leadership: Sad facts and silver linings. *Harvard Business Review, 57(6),* 164–172.

Peters, T. J. (1980). A style for all seasons. *Executive, 6(3),* 12–16.

Peters, T. J., & Austin, N. K. (1985). Managing by walking around. *California Management Review, 28,* 9–34.

Peters, T. J., & Waterman, R. H. (1982). *In search of excellence.* New York: Harper & Row.

Petersen, E., Plowman, E. G., & Trickett, J. M. (1962). *Business organization and management.* Homewood, IL: Irwin.

Peterson, C., & Seligman, M. E. P. (eds.) (2004). *Character strengths and virtues: A handbook and classification.* Washington, DC: American Psychological Association.

Peterson, M. F. (1985a). Experienced acceptability: Measuring perceptions of dysfunctional leadership. *Group & Organization Studies, 40,* 447–477.

Peterson, M. F. (1985b). *Paradigm struggles in leadership research: Progress in the 1980's.* Paper, Academy of Management, San Diego, CA.

Peterson, M. F. (1988). *PM theory in Japan and China: What's in it for the United States?* New York: American Management Association.

Peterson, M. F. (1988). PM theory in Japan and China: What's in it for the United States? *Organizational Dynamics, 31,* 22–38.

Peterson, M. F. (1995). Role conflict, ambiguity, and overload: A 21-nation study. *Academy of Organizational Management Journal, 38,* 429–452.

Peterson, M. F., Brannen, M. Y., & Smith, P. B. (1994). Japanese and United States leadership: Issues in current research. *Advances in International Comparative Management, 9,* 57–82.

Peterson, M. F., & Hunt, J. G. (1997). International perspectives on international leadership. *Leadership Quarterly, 8,* 203–232.

Peterson, M. F., Maiya, K., & Herreid, C. (1993). Adapting Japanese PM leadership field research for use in western nations. *Applied Psychology: An International Review. 43,* 70–74.

Peterson, M. F., Peng, T. K., Hunt, J. G., et al. (1994). *Leadership, style, attitudes, and evaluated performance in local governments: Japan–United States comparisons.* Paper, International Congress of Psychology, Madrid, Spain.

Peterson, M. F., Phillips, R. L., & Duran, C. A. (1989). A comparison of Japanese performance-maintenance measures with U.S. leadership scales. *Psychologia: An International Journal of Psychology in the Orient, 32,* 58–70.

Peterson, M. F., Smith, P. B., Akande, A., Ayestaran, S., Bochner, S., Callan, V., et al. (1995). Role conflict, ambiguity and overload: A 21-nation study. *Academy of Management Journal, 38,* 429–452.

Peterson, M. F., Smith, P. B., & Tayeb, M. (1993). Development and use of English versions of Japanese PM leadership measures in electronics plants. *Journal of Organizational Behavior, 14,* 251–267.

Peterson, M. F., & Sorenson, R. L. (1990). Cognitive processes in leadership: Interpreting and handling events in an organizational contest. *Communication Yearbook, 14*(11), 501–534.

Peterson, R. S. (2001). Toward a more deontological approach to the ethical use of social influence. In J. M. Darley, D. M. Messick, & T. R. Tyler (eds.), *Social influences on ethical behavior in organizations.* Mahwah, NJ: Lawrence Erlbaum Associates.

Peterson, T. O., & McAlear, D. L. (1990). *A multi-method multi-sample approach for assessing managerial development needs: From felt need to actual need. Proceedings,* Academy of Management, San Francisco, CA.

Petrick, J. A. (1999). Global leadership skills and reputational capital: Intangible resources for sustainable competitive advantage. *Academy of Management Executive 13*(1), 58–69.

Petrick, J. A., Scherer, R. F., Brodzinski, J. D., et al. (1999). Global leadership skills and reputational capital: Intangible resources for sustainable competitive advantage. *Academy of Management Executive, 13*(1), 58–69.

Pettigrew, A. (1972). Information control as a power resource. *Sociology, 6,* 187–204.

Pettigrew, A. M. (1973). *The politics of organizational decision-making.* London: Tavistock.

Pettigrew, A. M. (1979). On studying organizational cultures. *Administrative Science Quarterly, 24,* 570–581.

Pettigrew, T. F., Jemmott, J. B., & Johnson, J. T. (1984). *Race and the questioner effect: Testing the ultimate attribution error.* University of California, Santa Cruz. Unpublished manuscript.

Pettigrew, T. F., & Martin, J. (1987). Shaping the organizational contexts for Black American inclusion. *Journal of Social Issues, 43,* 41–47.

Petty, M. M., & Bruning, N. S. (1980). A comparison of the relationships between subordinates' perceptions of supervisory behavior and measures of subordinates' job satisfaction for male and female leaders. *Academy of Management Journal, 23,* 717–725.

Petty, M. M., & Lee, C. K. (1975). Moderating effects of sex of supervisor and subordinate on relationships between supervisory behavior and subordinate satisfaction. *Journal of Applied Psychology, 60,* 624–628.

Petty, M. M., & Miles, R. H. (1976). Leader sex-role stereotyping in a female-dominated work culture. *Personnel Psychology, 29,* 393–404.

Petty, M. M., Odewahn, C. A., Bruning, N. S., & Thomason, T. L. (1976). *An examination of the moderating effects of supervisor sex and subordinate sex upon the relationships between supervisory behavior*

and subordinate outcomes in mental health organizations. Unpublished manuscript.

Petty, R. E., & Cacioppo, J. T. (1980). *Attitudes and persuasion. Classic and contemporary approaches.* Dubuque, IA: W. C. Brown.

Pezeshkpur, C. (1978). Challenges to management in the Arab world. *Business Horizons, 21,* 47–55.

Pfeffer, J. (1972b). Interorganizational influence and managerial attitudes. *Academy of Management Journal, 15,* 317–330.

Pfeffer, J. (1977). The ambiguity of leadership. *Academy of Management Review, 2,* 104–112.

Pfeffer, J. (1981a). Management as symbolic action: The creation and maintenance of organizational paradigms. In L. L. Cummings & B. Staw (eds.), *Research in organizational behavior,* Vol. 3. Greenwich, CT: JAI Press.

Pfeffer, J. (1981b). *Power in organizations.* Boston: Pitman.

Pfeffer, J. (1995). Producing sustainable competitive advantage through the effective management of people. *Academy of Management Executive, 9*(1), 55–69.

Pfeffer, J., Cialdini, R. B., Hanna, B., et al. (1998). Faith in supervision and self-enhancement bias: Two psychological reasons why managers don't empower workers. *Basic and Applied Social Psychology, 20,* 313–321.

Pfeffer, J., & Davis-Blake, A. (1986). Administrative succession and organizational performance: How administrator experience mediates the succession effect. *Academy of Management Journal, 29,* 72–83.

Pfeffer, J., & Fong, C. T. (2002). The end of business schools? Less success than meets the eye. *Academy of Management Learning and Education, 1*(1), 78–95.

Pfeffer, J., & Leblebici, H. (1973). Executive recruitment and the development of interfirm organizations. *Administrative Science Quarterly, 18,* 449–461.

Pfeffer, J., & Moore, W. L. (1980). Average tenure of academic department heads: The effects of paradigm, size, and departmental demography. *Administrative Science Quarterly, 25,* 387–406.

Pfeffer, J., & Salancik, G. R. (1974). Organizational decision making as a political process: The case of a university budget. *Administrative Science Quarterly, 19,* 135–151.

Pfeffer, J., & Salancik, G. R. (1975). Determinants of supervisory behavior: A role set analysis. *Human Relations, 28,* 139–153.

Pfeffer, J., & Salancik, G. R. (1978). *The external control of organizations.* New York: Harper & Row.

Pfeffer, J., & Shapiro, S. J. (1978). Personnel differences in male and female MBA candidates. *Business Quarterly, 43,* 77–80.

Pfiffner, J. M. (1951). *The supervision of personnel: Human relations in the management of men.* Englewood Cliffs, NJ: Prentice-Hall.

Pfiffner, J. M., & Sherwood, F. P. (1960). *Administrative organization.* Englewood Cliffs, NJ: Prentice-Hall.

Pfiffner, J. M., & Wilson, R. C. (1953). "Management-mindedness" in the supervisory ranks: A study of attitudes in relation to status. *Personnel, 30,* 122–125.

Phan, P. H., & Lee, S. H. (1995). *Human capital or social networks: What constrains CEO dismissals?* Paper, Academy of Management, Vancouver, BC.

Phares, E. J. (1973). *Locus of control: A personality determinant of behavior.* Morristown, NJ: General Learning Press

Phelps, J. A., Davis, J. D., & Schartz, K. M. (1997). Nature, nurture, and twin research strategies. *Current Directions in Psychological Science,* 6, 117–121.

Pheterson, F. L., Kiesler, S. B., & Goldberg, P. A. (1971). Evaluation of the performance of women as a function of their sex, achievement, and personal history. *Journal of Personality and Social Psychology,* 19, 114–118.

Pheysey, D. C., Payne, R. L., & Pugh, D. S. (1971). Influence of structure at organizational and group levels. *Administrative Science Quarterly,* 16, 61–73.

Philbin, L. P. (1997). *Transformational leadership and the secondary school principal.* Doctoral dissertation, Purdue University, Lafayette, IN.

Philip, H., & Dunphy, D. (1959). Developmental trends in small groups. *Sociometry,* 22, 162–174.

Philips, J. M. (2001). The role of decision influence and team performance in member self-efficacy, withdrawal, satisfaction with the leader, and willingness to return. *Organizational Behavior and Human Decision Processes,* 84, 122–142.

Phillips, J. M. (1995). Leadership since 1975: Advancement or inertia? *Journal of Leadership Studies,* 2, 71–80.

Phillips, J. J. (1986). Training supervisors outside the classroom. *Training & Development Journal,* 40(2), 46–49.

Phillips, J. S., & Lord, R. C. (1981). Causal attributions and perceptions of leadership. *Organizational Behavior and Human Performance,* 28, 143–163.

Phillips, J. S., & Lord, R. C. (1982). Schematic information processing and perceptions of leadership in problem-solving groups. *Journal of Applied Psychology,* 67, 486–492.

Phillips, J. S., & Lord, R. C. (1986). Notes on the practical and theoretical consequences of implicit leadership theories for the future of leadership measurement. *Journal of Management,* 12, 31–41.

Phillips, T. R. (1939). Leader and led. *Journal of the Coast Artillery,* 82, 45–58.

Philipsen, H. (1965a). Het meten van leiderschap. *Mens en Onderneming,* 19, 153–171.

Philipsen, H. (1965b). Medezeggenschap in de vorm van werkoverleg. In C. J. Lammers (ed.), *Medezeggenschap en overleg in het bedriif.* Utrecht: Het Spectrum.

Philipsen, H., & Cassee, E. T. (1965). Verschillen in de wijze van leidinggeven tussen drie typen organisaties. *Mens en Onderneming,* 19, 172–174.

Phinney, J. S. (1990). Ethnic identity in adolescents and adults: A review of research. *Psycholgical Bulletin,* 108, 499–514.

Piaker, P. M. (2002). Back to accounting bedrock. *Christian Science Monitor,* July 17, 9.

Piedmont, R. L., & Weinstein, H. P. (1993). A psychometric evaluation of the new NEO-PI-R facet scales for agreeableness and conscientiousness. *Journal of Personality Assessment,* 60, 302–318.

Piedmont, R. I., & Weinstein, H. P. (1994). Predicting supervisor ratings of job performance using the NEO Personality Inventory. *Journal of Psychology,* 128, 255–265.

Pielstick, D. (2000). Formal vs. informal leading: A comparative analysis. *Journal of Leadership & Organizational Studies,* 7(3), 99–114.

Pierro, A., Cicero, L., Bonaiuto, M., et al. (2005). Leader group proto-typicality and leadership effectiveness: The moderating role of need for cognitive closure. *Leadership Quarterly. Special Issue: Leardership, Self, and Identity,* 16(4), 503–516.

Piersol, D. T. (1958). Communication practices of supervisors in a midwestern corporation. *Advanced Management,* 23, 20–21.

Pierson, J. F. (1984). Leadership styles of university and college counsel center directors: Perspectives from the field (personality type, job satisfaction, consideration, initiation of structure). *Dissertation Abstracts International,* 45(2A), 418.

Pigors, P. (1935). *Leadership or domination.* Boston: Houghton Mifflin.

Pigors, P (1936). Types of leaders in group work. *Sociology and Social Research,* 21, 3–17.

Pillai, R. (1993). *The role of structural, contextual, and cultural factors in the emergence of charismatic leadership in organizations.* Doctoral dissertation, Buffalo, NY: State University of New York at Buffalo.

Pillai, R. (1996). Crisis and the emergence of charismatic leadership in groups: An experimental investigation. *Journal of Applied Social Psychology,* 26, 543–562.

Pillai, R., & Meindl, J. R. (1991). *The effect of crisis on the emergence of charismatic leadership: A laboratory study.* Academy of Management Best Papers Proceedings, Miami, FL

Pillai, R., & Meindl, J. R. (1998). Context and charisma in a meso level examination of the relationship of organic structure, collectivism and crisis to charismatic leadership. *Journal of Management,* 24, 643–671.

Pillai, R., & Stites-Doe, S. (2003). *Introduction.* In R. Pillai & S. Stites-Doe (eds.), Greenwich, CT: Information Age Publishing.

Pillai, R., & Williams, E. A. (1998). Does leadership matter in the political arena? Voter perceptions of candidates' transformational and charismatic leadership and the 1996 U.S. presidential vote. *Leadership Quarterly,* 9, 397–416.

Pillai, R., Williams, E. A., Lowe, K. B., et al. (2002). *Personality, transformational leadership, trust, and the 2000 U.S. presidential vote.* Paper, Academy of Management, Denver, CO.

Pinchot, J., III. (1985). *Intrapreneuring.* New York: Harper & Row.

Pincus, J. D. (1986). Communication satisfaction, job satisfaction, and job performance. *Human Communication Research,* 12, 395–419.

Pines, M. (1980). Psychological hardiness. *Psychology Today,* 14(2), 38–39.

Pinder, C., Pinto, P. R., & England, G. W. (1973). *Behavioral style and personal characteristics of managers* (tech. rep.). Minneapolis: University of Minnesota, Center for the Study of Organizational Performance and Human Effectiveness.

Pinder, C. C., & Pinto, P. R. (1974). Demographic correlates of managerial style. *Personnel Psychology,* 27, 257–270.

Pinkney, A. P. (1969). *Black Americans.* Englewood Cliffs, NJ: Prentice-Hall.

Pinnell, R. L. (1984). *The relationships between locus of control, communication apprehension, power orientations and leadership styles.* Doctoral dissertation, University of Denver, Denver, CO.

Piotrowski, C., & Armstrong, T. R. (1987). Executive leadership characteristics portrayed on CNN's pinnacle. Reported in *Behavioral Science Newsletter, Vol.* 23, Book XVI.

Piotrowski, C., & Armstrong, T. R. (1989). The CEO: An analysis of the CNN telecast "Pinnacle." *Psychological Reports, 65,* 435–438.

Pipes, D. (2004). Flight from freedom. *Foreign Affairs, 33(3),* 9–15.

Pipes, R. (1974). *Russia under the old regime.* New York: Weidenfeld & Nicolson.

Pirola-Merlo, A., Hartel, C., Mann, L., et al. (2002). How leaders influence the impact of affective events on team climate and performance in R&D teams. *Leadership Quarterly, 13,* 561–581.

Pitcher, P. (1997). *The drama of leadership. Artists, craftsmen and technocrats and the power struggle that shapes organizations and societies.* New York: John Wiley & Sons.

Pitman, B. (1993). *The relationship between charismatic leadership behaviors and organizational commitment among white-collar workers.* Doctoral dissertation, Georgia State University, Atlanta, GA.

Pitner, N. J. (1988). Leadership substitutes: Their factorial validity in educational organizations. *Educational and Psychological Measurement, 48,* 307–315.

Pitt, L. F. (1985). Managerial attitudes towards corruption—A pilot study. *South African Journal of Business Management, 16,* 27–30.

Plato. (1945). *The republic.* (Trans. F. M. Comford.) New York: Oxford University Press.

Playhart, R. E., Lim, B., & Chan, K. (2001). Exploring relations between typical and maximum performance ratings and the five factor model of personality. *Personnel Psychology, 54,* 809–843.

Plomin, R. (1997). Current directions in behavioral genetics: Moving into the mainstream. *Current Directions in Psychological Science, 6,* 85–88.

Plomin, R., DeFries, J. C., & McClearn, G. E. (1990). *Behavioral genetics: A primer,* 2nd ed. New York: W. H. Freeman.

Plott, C. (1998). The 1998 ASTD state of the industry report. *Training and Development,* January, 22–43.

Plutarch. (1932). *Lives of the noble Grecians and Romans.* New York: Modern Library.

Podsakoff, P. M. (1982). Determinants of a supervisor's use of rewards and punishments: A literature review and suggestions for further research. *Organizational Behavior and Human Performance, 29,* 58–83.

Podsakoff, P. M., Dorfman, P. W., Howell, J. R., & Todor, W. D. (1986). Leader reward and punishment behaviors: A preliminary test of a culture-free style of leadership effectiveness, *Advances in International Comparative Management, 2,* 95–138.

Podsakoff, P. M., MacKenzie, S. B., & Ahearne, M. (1997). Moderating effects of goal acceptance on the relationship between group cohesiveness and productivity. *Journal of Applied Psychology, 82(3),* 764–383.

Podsakoff, P. M., MacKenzie, S. B., & Bommer, W. H. (1996a). Meta-analysis of the relationships between Kerr and Jermier's substitutes for leadership and employee job attitudes, role perceptions, and performance. *Journal of Applied Psychology, 81(4),* 380–399.

Podsakoff, P. M., MacKenzie, S. B., & Bommer, W. H. (1996–1996b). Transformational leader behaviors and substitutes for leadership as determinants of employee satisfaction, commitment, trust, and organizational citizenship behaviors. *Journal of Management, 22,* 259–298.

Podsakoff, P. M., MacKenzie, S. B., & Fetter, R. (1993). Substitutes for leadership and the management of professionals. *Leadership Quarterly, 4,* 1–44.

Podsakoff, P. M., MacKenzie, S. B., Moorman, R. H., et al. (1990). Transformational leader behaviors and their effects on follower's trust in the leader, satisfaction, and organizational citizenship behaviors. *Leadership Quarterly, 1,* 177–192.

Podsakoff, P. M., Niehoff, B. P., MacKenzie, S. B., et al. (1993). Do substitutes for leadership really substitute for leadership? An empirical examination of Kerr and Jermier's leadership model. *Organizational Behavior and Human Decision Processes, 54,* 1–44.

Podsakoff, P. M. & Organ, D. W. (1986). Self-reports in organizational research: Problems and prospects, *Journal of Management, 12,* 31–41.

Podsakoff, P. M., & Schriesheim, C. A. (1985a). Field studies of French and Raven's bases of social power: Critique, reanalysis and suggestions for future research. *Psychological Bulletin, 97,* 387–411.

Podsakoff, P. M., & Schriesheim, C. A. (1985b). Leader reward and punishment behavior: A methodological and substantive review. In B. Staw & L. L. Cummings (eds.), *Research in organizational behavior.* San Francisco: Jossey-Bass.

Podsakoff, P. M., & Todor, W. D. (1983a). *Individual differences as moderators of leader reward and punishment behaviors* (Working Paper). Bloomington: Indiana University.

Podsakoff, P. M., & Todor, W. D. (1983b). *An analysis of the nature of the moderators of leader reward and punishment behaviors.* Bloomington: Indiana University. Unpublished manuscript.

Podsakoff, P. M., & Todor, W. D. (1985). Relationships between leader reward and punishment behavior and group processes and productivity. *Journal of Management, 11,* 55–73.

Podsakoff, P. M., Todor, W. D., Grover, R. A., & Huber, V. L. (1984). Situational moderators of leader reward and punishment behaviors: Fact or fiction? *Organizational Behavior and Human Performance, 34,* 21–63.

Podsakoff, P. M., Todor, W. D., & Schuler, R. S. (1983). Leader expertise as a moderator of the effects of instrumental and supportive leader behaviors. *Journal of Management, 9,* 173–185.

Podsakoff, P. M., Todor, W. D., & Skov, R. (1982). Effect of leader contingent and non-contingent reward and punishment behaviors on subordinate performance and satisfaction. *Academy of Management Journal, 25,* 810–821.

Polansky, N., Lippitt, R., & Redl, F. (1950a). An investigation of behavioral contagion in groups. *Human Relations, 3,* 319–348.

Polis, T. (1964). A note on crisis and leadership. *Australian Journal of Psychology, 16,* 57–61.

Pollard, C. W. (1996). The leader who serves. In F. Hesselbein, M. Goldsmith, & R. Beckhard (eds.), *The Leader of the Future: New Visions, Strategies and Practices for the Next Era.* San Francisco: Jossey-Bass.

Polley, B. & Eid, J. (1990). Leadership training on the Bergen Fjord: A case study and evaluation. *Group & Organization Management, 15,* 2, 192–211).

Polley, R. B. (1990). Leadership training in the Bergen Fjord. *Group & Organization Studies, 15,* 192–211.

Polmar, N., & Allen, T. B. (1981–1982). *Rickover: Controversy and genius. A biography.* New York: Simon & Schuster.

Polodney, J. M., & Page, K. L. (1998). Network forms of organizations. *Annual Review of Sociology, 24,* 57–76.

Ponder, Q. D. (1958). *Supervisory practices of effective and ineffective foremen.* Doctoral dissertation, Columbia University, New York.

Pondy, L. (1983). Union of rationality and intuition in management action. In S. Srivastva & Associates (eds.), *The executive mind.* San Francisco: Jossey-Bass.

Pondy, L. R. (1967). Organizational conflict: concepts and models. *Administrative Science Quarterly, 12,* 296–320.

Ponemon, L. A. (1992). Ethical reasoning and selection-socialization in accounting. *Accounting, Organizations and Society, 17*(3–4), 239–258.

Ponemon, L. A. (1993). Can ethics be taught in accounting? *Journal of Accounting Education, 11,* 185–209.

Ponemon, L. A. (1993). Ethical reasoning in accounting education. *The Auditor's Report, 16,* 6–7.

Popper, M. (2000). The development of charismatic leaders. *Political Psychology, 21,* 729–744.

Popper, M. (2001). *Hypnotic leadership: Leaders, followers and loss of self.* Westport, CT: Praeger.

Popper, M. (2002). Hypnotic leadership: Leaders, followers, and the loss of self. *American Psychologist, 49,* 709–724.

Popper, M., Meiseles, O., & Castelnuvo, O. (2000). Attachment and transformational leadership. *Leadership Quarterly, 11,* 267–289.

Popper, M., Landau, O., & Gluskinos, U. (1992). The Israeli Defence Forces: An example of transformational leadership. *Leadership and Organization Development Journal, 13*(1), 3–8.

Popper, M., Mayseless, O., & Castelnovo, O. (2000). Transformational leadership and attachment. *Leadership Quarterly, 11,* 267–289.

Porat, A. M., & Ryterband, E. C. (1974). Career performance, choice and attainment for members of minority groups. In H. L. Fromkin & J. J. Sherwood (eds.), *Integrating the organization.* New York: Free Press.

Porter, G. (1997). Employees' perceptions of management: A case for leadership training. *International Journal of Training and Developmennt 1,* 271–286.

Porter, L. W. (1959). Self-perceptions of first-level supervisors compared with upper-management personnel and operative line workers. *Journal of Applied Psychology, 43,* 183–186.

Porter, L. W. (1961b). Perceived trait requirements in bottom and middle management jobs. *Journal of Applied Psychology, 45,* 232–236.

Porter, L. W. (1963a). Job attitudes in management: II. Perceived importance of needs as a function of job level. *Journal of Applied Psychology, 47,* 141–148.

Porter, L. W. (1963b). Job attitudes in management: III. Perceived deficiencies in need fulfillment as a function of line versus staff type of job. *Journal of Applied Psychology, 47,* 267–275.

Porter, L. W., Allen, R. W., & Angle, H. L. (1981). The politics of upward influence in organizations. In B. Staw & L. Cummings (eds.), *Research in organizational behavior.* Greenwich, CT: JAI Press.

Porter, L. W., & Ghiselli, E. E. (1957). The self perceptions of top and middle management personnel. *Personnel Psychology, 10,* 397–406.

Porter, L. W., & Kaufman, R. A. (1959). Relationships between a top-middle management self-description scale and behavior in a group situation. *Journal of Applied Psychology, 43,* 345–348.

Porter, L. W., & Lawler, E. E. (1964). The effects of "tall" versus "flat" organizational structures on managerial job satisfaction. *Personnel Psychology, 17,* 135–148.

Porter, L. W., & Lawler, E. E. (1965). Properties of organization structure in relation to job attitudes and behavior. *Psychological Bulletin, 64,* 23–51.

Porter, L.W., & Lawler, E. E. (1968). *Managerial Attitudes and Performance.* Irwin.

Porter, L. W., Lawler, E. E., & Hackman, J. R. (1975). *Behavior in organizations.* New York: McGraw-Hill.

Porter, L. W., & Mitchell, V. F. (1967). Comparative study of need satisfactions in military and business hierarchies. *Journal of Applied Psychology, 51,* 139–144.

Porter, L. W., & Siegel, J. (1965). Relationships of tall and flat organization structures to the satisfaction of foreign managers. *Personnel Psychology, 18,* 379–392.

Porter, M. E. (1979). How competitive forces shape strategy. *Harvard Business Review, 57*(2), 137–145.

Porter, M. E. (1980). *Competitive strategy: Techniques for analyzing industries and firms.* New York: Free Press.

Porter, R. B. (1989). Ford's presidency: Brief but well run. *New York Times, 29.*

Portin, B. S., & Shen, J. (1998). The changing principalship: Its current status, variability, and impact. *Journal of Leadership Studies, 5*(3), 93–113.

Posner, B. Z., & Kouzes, J. M. (1988a). Development and validation of the Leadership Practices Inventory. *Educational and Psychological Measurement, 48,* 483–496.

Posner, B. Z., & Kouzes, J. M. (1988b). Relating leadership and credibility. *Psychological Reports, 63,* 527–530.

Posner, B. Z. & Kouzes, J. M. (1996). Ten lessons for leaders and leadership developers. *The Journal of Leadership Studies, 3*(3), 3–10.

Posner, B. Z. & Schmidt, W. H. (1984). Values and the American manager: An update. *California Management Review, 3,* 202–216.

Posthuma, A. B. (1970). *Normative data on the least preferred coworkers scale (LPC) and the group atmosphere questionnaire (GA)* (Tech. Rep. No. 70–8). Seattle: University of Washington, Organizational Research.

Potter, E. H. (1978). *The contribution of intelligence and experience to the performance of staff personnel.* Doctoral dissertation, University of Washington, Seattle, WA.

Potter, E. H., III, & Fiedler, F. E. (1981). Stress and the utilization of staff member intelligence and experience. *Academy of Management Journal, 24,* 361–376.

Potter, E.H., III, & Fiedler, F. E. (1993). Selecting leaders: Making the most of previous experience. *Journal of Leadership Studies, 1*(1), 61–71.

Potter, J. (1994). Tapping the iceberg: How to get the best out of your people through empowerment. *Empowerment in Organizations, 2*(1), 4–8.

Powell, C. L. (with Persico, J. E.). (1995). *My American journey.* New York: Ballantine Books.

Powell, G. N. (1982). Sex-role identity and sex: An important distinction for research on women in management. *Basic and Applied Social Psychology, 3,* 67–79.

Powell, G. N. (1993). *Women and men in management* (2nd ed). Newbury Park, CA: Sage.

Powell, G. N., & Butterfield, D. A. (1979). The "good manager": Masculine or androgynous? *Academy of Management Journal, 22,* 395–403.

Powell, G. N., & Butterfield, D. A. (1981). A note on sex-role identity effects on managerial aspirations. *Journal of Occupational Psychology, 54,* 299–301.

Powell, G. N., & Butterfield, D. A. (1989). The "good manager": Did androgyny fare better in the 1980's? *Group & Organization Studies, 14,* 216–233.

Powell, G. N., & Butterfield, A. (1994). Investigating the "glass ceiling" phenomenon: An empirical study of actual promotions to top management. *Academy of Management Journal, 37,* 68–86.

Powell, G. N., Butterfield, D. A., & Mainiero, L. A. (1981). Sex-role identity and sex as predictors of leadership style. *Psychological Reports,49,* 829–830.

Powell, G. N., Butterfield, D. A., & Parent, J. D. (2002). Gender and managerial stereotypes: Have the times changed? *Journal of Management, 28,* 177–193.

Powell, G. N., Posner, B. Z., & Schmidt, W. H. (1984). Sex effects on managerial value systems. *Human Relations, 37,* 909–921.

Powell, R. M. (1969). *Race, religion, and the promotion of the American executive.* Columbus: Ohio State University Press.

Pratt, J., & Jiambalvo, J. (1982). Determinants of leader behavior in an audit environment. *Accounting, Organizations and Society, 7,* 369–379.

Prensky, M. (1998). Twitch speed. *Across the Board, 35*(1), 14–10.

Presthus, R. V. (1960). Authority in organizations. *Public Administration Review, 20*(2), 86–91.

Preston, J. C., & Chappel, K. E. (1988). *Assessment of three training methods used to teach managers leadership.* Paper, International Congress of Psychology, Sydney, Australia.

Preston, M. C., & Heintz, R. K. (1949). Effects of participatory vs. supervisory leadership on group judgment. *Journal of Abnormal and Social Psychology, 44,* 345–355.

Presthus, R. (1964). *Men at the top: A study in community power.* New York: Oxford University Press.

Previde, G. P., & Rotondi, P. (1996). Leading and managing change through adaptors and innovators. *Journal of Leadership Studies, 3,* 120–134.

Price, J. (1993). *An investigation of the relationship between the perceived leadership and management effectiveness in matrix organizations.* Doctoral dissertation, George Mason University, Fairfax, VA.

Price, K. H., & Garland, H. (1981). Compliance with a leader's suggestions as a function of perceived leader/member competence and potential reciprocity. *Journal of Applied Psychology, 66,* 329–336.

Price, M. A. (1948). *A study of motivational factors associated with leadership behavior of young women in a private school.* Doctoral dissertation, Ohio State University, Columbus.

Price, T. L. (2003). The ethics of authentic transformational leadership. *Leadership Quarterly, 14,* 67–81.

Prien, E. P. (1963). Development of a supervisor position description questionnaire. *Journal of Applied Psychology, 47,* 10–14.

Prien, E. P., & Culler, A. R. (1964). Leaderless group discussion participation and inter-observer agreements. *Journal of Social Psychology, 62,* 321–328.

Priest, R. F., & Sawyer, J. (1967). Proximity and peership: Bases of balance in interpersonal attraction. *American Journal of Sociology, 72,* 633–649.

Prieto, A. C. (1975). *An investigation of the relationship between participative group management in elementary schools and the needs satisfaction of elementary classroom teachers.* Doctoral dissertation, University of New Orleans, New Orleans, LA.

Prince, H. T. (1987). *Leader development at the U.S. Military Academy.* Paper, Conference on military leadership: Traditions and trends. United States Naval Academy, Annapolis, MD.

Pritchard, A. (1983). Presidents do influence voting in the U.S. Congress: New definitions and measurements. *Legislative Studies Quarterly, 8,* 691–711.

Pritchard, R., & Karasick, B. (1973). The effects of organizational climate on managerial job performance and job satisfaction. *Organizational Behavior and Human Performance, 9,* 110–119.

Prochaska, J. O., DiClemente, C. C., & Norcross, J. C. (1992). In search of how people change: Applications to addictive behaviors. *American Psychologist, 47,* 1102–1114.

Proctor-Thomson, S. B., & Parry, K. W. (2000). What the best leaders look like . . . leadership in the Antipodes. In K. W. Parry (ed.), *Institute of Policy Studies.* Victoria University of Wellington. Wellington, New Zealand. 166–91.

Proshansky, H., & Newton, P. (1968). The nature and meaning of Negro self-identity. In M. Deutsch, I. Katz, & A. Jensen (eds.), *Social class, race, and psychological development.* New York: Holt, Rinehart & Winston.

Prothero, J., & Fiedler, F. E. (1974). *The effects of situational change on individual behavior and performance: An extension of the contingency model* (Tech. Rep. No. 74–59). Seattle: University of Washington, Organizational Research.

Prud'homme, L., & Baron, P. (1988). Irrational beliefs and ethnic background: Ellis' theory revisited. *Applied Psychology: An International Review, 37,* 301–310.

Prussia, G. E., Anderson, J., Joe, S., et al. (1998). Self-leadership and performance outcomes: The mediating influence of self-efficacy. *Journal of Organizational Behavior.19,* 523–538.

Pruzan, P. & Thyssen, O. (1994). The Renaissance of ethics and the ethical accounting statement. *Educational Technology, 34*(1), 23–28.

Pryer, M. W., & DiStefano, M. K. (1971). Perceptions of leadership behavior, job satisfaction, and internal-external control across three nursing levels. *Nursing Review, 20,* 534–537.

Pryer, M. W., Flint, A. W., & Bass, B. M. (1962). Group effectiveness and consistency of leadership. *Sociometry, 25,* 391–397.

Psathas, G., & Hardert, R. (1966). Transfer interventions and normative patterns in the T group. *Journal of Applied Behavioral Science, 2,* 149–169.

Pucik, V. (1981). Promotions and intraorganizational status differentiation among Japanese managers. *Proceedings,* Academy of Management, San Diego, CA, 59–62.

Puffer, S. M. (1994). Understanding the bear: A portrait of Russian business leaders. *Academy of Management Executive, 8*(1), 41–54.

Puffer, S. M., & Weintrop, J. B. (1995). CEO and board leadership: The influence of organizational performance, board composition, and retirement on CEO successor origin. *Leadership Quarterly, 6*, 49–68.

Pugh, D. (1965). T-group training from the point of view of organizational theory. In G. Whitaker (ed.), *ATM Occasional Papers*, vol. 2. Oxford: Basil E. Blackwell.

Pugh, D. S., Hickson, D. J., Hinings, C. R., & Turner, C. (1968). Dimensions of organization structure. *Administrative Science Quarterly, 13*, 65–105.

Pulakos, E. D., & Wexley, K. N. (1983). The relationship among perceptual similarity, sex, and performance ratings in manager-subordinate dyads. *Academy of Management Journal, 26*, 129–139.

Punch, K. F. (1967). *Bureaucratic structure of schools and its relationship to leader behavior*. Toronto: Ontario Institute for Studies in Education. Unpublished manuscript.

Purcell, T. V. (1953). *The worker speaks his mind on company and union*. Cambridge, MA: Harvard University Press.

Purcell, T. V. (1954). Dual allegiance to union and management (a symposium). 2. Dual allegiance to company and union packinghouse workers. A Swift-UPWA Study in a crisis situation (1949–1952). *Personnel Psychology, 7*, 45–58.

Puryear, E. F. (1971). *Nineteen stars*. Washington, DC: Coiner.

Putnam, R. D. (2000). *Bowling alone: The collapse and revival of American community*. New York: Touchstone.

Quaglieri, P. L., & Carnazza, J. P. (1985). Critical inferences and the multidimensionality of feedback. *Canadian Journal of Behavioral Science, 17*, 284–293.

Quarantelli, E. L. (1954). The nature and conditions of panic. *American Journal of Sociology, 60*, 267–275.

Quetelet, L. A. J. (1835/1968). *A treatise on man and the development of his faculties*. Brussels.

Quick, J. C. (1994). Crafting an organizational culture: Herb's hand at Southwest Airlines. *Organizational Dynamics, 21*, 45–56.

Quick, J. C., Gavin, J. H., Cooper, C. L., et al. (2000). Executive health: Building strength, managing risks. *Academy of Management Executive, 14*(2), 34–43.

Quiggins, J. G., & Lashbrook, W. B. (1972). *Task and socio-emotional leadership in ongoing groups: A theoretical perspective*. Paper, Western Speech Communication Association, Honolulu.

Quinn Mills, D. (1991). *Rebirth of the corporation*. John Wiley & Sons, Inc.

Quinn, J. B., Anderson, P., & Finkelstein, S. (1996). Leveraging intellect. *Academy of Management Executive, 10*(3), 7–25+.

Quinn, R. E. (1977). Coping with Cupid: The formation, impact, and management of romantic relationships in organizations. *Administrative Science Quarterly, 22*, 30–45.

Quinn, R. E. (1984). Applying the competing values approach to leadership: Towards an integrative framework. In J. C. Hunt, D. Hosking, C. A. Schriesheim, & R. Stewart (eds.), *Leaders and managers: International perspectives on managerial behavior and leadership*. New York: Pergamon.

Quinn, R. E. (1988). *Beyond rational management: Mastering the Paradoxes and competing demands of high performance*. San Francisco: Jossey-Bass.

Quinn, R. E. (1996). *Deep change: Discovering the leader within*. San Francisco: Jossey-Bass.

Quinn, R. E., & Cameron, K. (1983). Organizational life cycles and shifting criteria of effectiveness: Some preliminary evidence. *Management Science, 29*, 33–51.

Quinn, R. E., Dixit, N., & Faerman, S. R. (1987). *Perceived performance: Some archetypes of managerial effectiveness and ineffectiveness*. Albany, NY: State University of New York at Albany, Nelson A. Rockefeller College of Public Affairs and Policy, Institute for Government and Policy Studies.

Quinn, R., Faerman, S., Thompson, M., & McGrath, M. (1996). *Becoming a master manager: A competency framework*. New York: John Wiley and Sons.

Quinn, R. E., & Hall, R. H. (1983). Environments, organizations, and policy makers: Towards an integrative framework. In R. H. Hall & R. E. Quinn (eds.), *Organization theory and public policy: Contributions and limitations*. Beverly Hills, CA: Sage.

Quinn, R. P., Kahn, R. K., Tabor, J. M., & Gordon, L. K. (1968). *The chosen few: A study of discrimination in executive selection*. Ann Arbor: University of Michigan, Institute for Social Research.

Quirk, M. P. & Fandt, P. (2000). *The 2nd language of leadership*. Mahway, N.J: Lawrence Erlbaum Associates.

Rabi, M. M. (1967). *The political theory of Ibn Khaldun*. Leiden: Brill.

Radin, B. A. (1980). Leadership training for women in state and local government. *Public Personnel Management, 9*(2), 52–60.

Radke, M., & Klisurich, D. (1947). Experiments in changing food habits. *Journal of American Diet Association, 23*, 403–409.

Raeburn, N. C. (2000). *The rise of lesbian, gay, and bisexual rights inb the workplace*. Doctoral dissertation, Ohio State University, Columbus, OH.

Ragins, B. R. (1987). *Power and leadership effectiveness: A study of subordinate evaluations of male and female leaders*. Doctoral dissertation, University of Tennessee, Knoxville, TN.

Ragins, B. R. (1991). Gender effects in subordinate evaluations of leaders: Real or artifact? *Journal of Organizational Behavior, 12*, 259–268.

Ragins, B. R., & Cornwell, J. M. (2001). Pink triangles: Antecedents and consequences of perceived workplace discrimination against gay and lesbian employees. *Journal of Applied Psychology, 86*, 1244–1261.

Ragins, B. R., & Cotton, J. L. (1999). Mentor functions and outcomes: A comparison of men and women in formal and informal mentoring relationships. *Journal of Applied Psychology, 84*(4), 529–550.

Ragins, B. R., Cotton, J. L., & Miller, J. S. (2000). Marginal mentoring: The effects of type of mentor, quality of the relationship, and program design on work and career attitudes. *Academy of Management Journal, 43*, 117X–1194.

Ragins, B. R., & Sundstrom, E. (1990). Gender and perceived power in manager-subordinate relations, *Journal of Occupational Psychology, 63*, 273–288.

Ragins, B. R., Townsend, B., & Mattis, M. (1998). Gender gap in the executive suite: CEOs and female executives report on breaking the glass ceiling. *Academy of Management Executive, 12*(1), 28–42.

Rahim, A., & Buntzman, G. F. (1989). Supervisor power bases, styles of handling conflict with subordinates, and subordinate compliance and satisfaction. *Journal of Psychology, 123,* 195–210.

Rahim, M. A. (1982). Measurement of organizational conflict. *Journal of General Psychology, 109,* 189–199.

Rahim, M. A. (1983). A measure of styles of handling interpersonal conflict. *Academy of Management Journal, 26,* 368–376.

Rahim, M. A. (1986). *A new measure of bases of leader power.* Paper, Academy of Management, Chicago.

Rahim, M. A. (1988). The development of a leader power inventory. *Multivariate Behavioral Research, 23,* 491–503.

Rahim, M. A. (1989). Relationships of leader power to compliance and satisfaction with supervision: Evidence from a national sample of managers. *Journal of Management, 15,* 545–556.

Rahim, M. A., Antonioni, D., Krumov, K., & Ilieva, S. (2000). Power, conflict, and effectiveness: A cross cultural study in the United States and Bulgaria. *European Psychologist, 5*(1), 28–33.

Rahim, M. A., Kim, N. H., & Kim, J. S. (1994). Bases of leader power, subordinate compliance, and satisfaction with supervision: A cross-cultural study of managers in the U.S. and South Korea. *International Journal of Organizational Analysis, 2,* 136–154.

Raia, A. P. (1966). A study of the educational value of management games. *Journal of Business, 39,* 339–352.

Rainey, H. C. (1979). Reward expectancies, role perceptions, and job satisfaction among government and business managers: Indications of commonalities and differences. *Proceedings,* Academy of Management, Atlanta, CA, 357–361.

Rainey, H. G. (1983). Public agencies and private firms. *Administration and Society, 15,* 207–242.

Rainio, K. (1955). *Leadership qualities: A theoretical and an experimental study on foremen.* Helsinki: Academiae Scientiarum Fermicae.

Rainwater, L. (1966). Crucible of identity: The Negro lower-class family. *Daedalus, 95,* 172–216.

Raja, U., Ntalianis, F., Johns, G. (2002). *The role of personality in psychological contracts: From formation to violation.* Paper, Academy of Management, Denver, CO.

Ralls, S. (1994) *Integrating technology with workers in the new American workplace.* Washington, DC: U.S. Department of Labor, Office of the American Workplace.

Ralston, D. A. (1985). Employee ingratiation: The role of management. *Academy of Management Review, 10,* 477–487.

Ralston, D. A., Gustafson, D. J., Elsass, P. M., et al. (1992). Eastern values: A comparison of managers in the United States, Hong Kong, and the People's Republic of China. *Journal of Applied Psychology, 77,* 664–671.

Ralston, D. A., Holt, D. H., Terpstra, R. H., et al. (1995). *The impact of culture and ideology on managerial work values: A study of the United States, Russia, Japan, and China.* Paper, Academy of Management, Vancouver, BC.

Rambo, W. W. (1958). The construction and analysis of a leadership behavior rating form. *Journal of Applied Psychology, 42,* 409–415.

Ramus, C. A., & Steger, U. (2000). The roles of supervisory support behaviors and environmental policy in employee "ecoinitiatives" at leading-edge European companies. *Academy of Management Journal, 43,* 605–626.

Rand, A. (1959). *Atlas shrugged.* New York: Random House.

Rand, A. (1964). *The virtue of selfishness.* New York: New American Library.

Randall, R., Ferguson, E., & Patterson, F. (2000). Self-assessment accuracy and assessment center decisions. *Journal of Occupational & Organizational Psychology, 73,* 443–459.

Randolph, W. A. (1995). Navigating the journey to empowerment. *Organizational Dynamics, 23*(4), 19–32.

Randolph, W. A., & Finch, F. E. (1977). The relationship between organization technology and the direction and frequency dimensions of task communications. *Human Relations, 30,* 1131–1145.

Rankin, D. K., & Golden, B. R. (2002). *Minding the minders: CEO-Directors as catalysts for substantive or symbolic change in boardroom self-governance?* Paper, Academy of Management, Denver, CO.

Rao, A., Schmidt, S.M., & Murray, L. H. (1995). Upward impression management: Goals, influence strategies, and consequences. *Human Relations, 48,* 147–167.

Rao, N. R. K. (1982). An investigation of the impact of the supervisor's reinforcement contingency on his behavior in a dyadic interaction with a subordinate. *Dissertation Abstracts International, 43*(2A), 497.

Raskin, R., & Hall, C. S. (1979). A Narcissistic Personality Inventory. *Psychological Reports, 45,* 55–60.

Raskin, R., & Hall, C. S. (1981). The Narcissistic Personality Inventory: Alternate form reliability and further evidence of construct validity. *Journal of Personality Assessment, 43,* 159–162.

Rasmussen, C., & Zander, A. (1954). Group membership and self-evaluation. *Human Relations, 7,* 239–251.

Rasmussen, K. G., Jr. (1984). Nonverbal behavior, verbal behavior, resume credentials, and selection interview outcomes. *Journal of Applied Psychology, 69,* 551–556.

Rasmussen, R. L. (1976). The principal's leadership behavior in unusually successful and unsuccessful elementary schools. *Education Research Quarterly, 1,* 18–29.

Rath, K. C., & Sahoo, M. S. (1974). Socio-economic status of Panchayat leaders and their role in agricultural production. *Social Cultural, 5,* 25–28.

Rathbun, J. A., Miller, J. S., & Aniolek, K. (2003). *Organizational culture and ethical ambivalence as determinants of escalation of commitment.* Paper, Academy of Management, Seattle, WA.

Raudsepp, E. (1981). Delegate your way to success. *Computer Decisions, 13*(3), 157–158, 163–164.

Raven, B. H. (1959a). The dynamics of groups. *Review of Education Research, 29,* 332–343.

Raven, B. H. (1965b). Social influence and power. In I. D. Steiner & M. Fishbein (eds.), *Current studies in social psychology.* New York: Holt, Rinehart & Winston.

Raven, B. H. (1992) A power/interaction model of interpersonal influence: French and Raven thirty years later. *Journal of Social Behavior and Personality, 7,* 217–244.

Raven, B. H. (1993). The bases of power: origins and recent developments. *Journal of Social Issues, 49,* 227–251.

Raven, B. H., & Eachus, H. T. (1963). Cooperation and competition in means-interdependent triads. *Journal of Abnormal and Social Psychology, 67,* 307–316.

Raven, B. H., & French, J. R. P. (1957). An experimental investigation of legitimate and coercive power. *American Psychologist, 12,* 393.

Raven, B. H., & French, J. R. P. (1958a). Group support, legitimate power, and social influence. *Journal of Personality, 26,* 400–409.

Raven, B. H., & French, J. R. P. (1958b). Legitimate power, coercive power, and observability in social influence. *Sociometry, 21,* 83–97.

Raven, B. H., & Kruglanski, A. W. (1970). Conflict and power. In P. Swingle (ed.), *The structure of conflict.* New York: Academic Press.

Raven, B. H., Schwarzwald, J., & Kozlowsky, M. (1998). Conceptualizing and measuring a power/interaction model of interpersonal influence. *Journal of Applied Social Psychology, 28,* 307–332.

Rawlins, C. L. (1983). Teleconferencing and the leadership of small groups. *Dissertation Abstracts International, 44*(8A), 2562.

Rawlins, C. L. (1989). The impact of teleconferencing on the leadership of small groups. *Journal of Organizational Behavior Management, 10*(2), 37–52.

Rawls, J. (1971). *A theory of justice.* Cambridge, MA: Harvard University Press.

Rawls, J. (1985). Justice as fairness: Political not metaphysical. *Philosophy and Public Affairs, 14,* 223–251.

Rawls, J., Ulrich, R., & Nelson, O. (1973). A comparison of managers entering or re-entering the profit and non-profit sectors. *Academy of Management Journal, 3,* 616–623.

Ray, B. (1989). *The relationship of job satisfaction, individual characteristics, and leadership behaviors to corporate culture beliefs and climate for change.* Doctoral dissertation, East Texas State University, Commerce, TX

Ray, D., & Bronstein, H. (1995). *Teaming up: Making the transition to a self-directed team-based organization.* New York: McGraw-Hill.

Ray, R. G., Ugbah, S. D., Brammer, C., & DeWine, S. (1996). Communication behaviors, innovation, and the maverick leader. *Journal of Leadership Studies, 3*(3), 20–30.

Read, P. B. (1974). Source of authority and the legitimation of leadership in small groups, *Sociometry, 37,* 180–204.

Read, W. H. (1962). Upward communication in industrial hierarchies. *Human Relations, 15,* 3–15.

Reall, M. J., Bailey, J. J., & Stoll, S. K. (1998). Moral reasoning "on hold" during a competitive game. *Journal of Business Ethics, 17*(11), 1205–1210.

Reardon, K. K., & Rowe, A. J. (2000). The leader style inventory: A test of assessing leadership strengths. In B. Kellerman & L. R. Matusak (eds.), *Cutting Edge Leadership.* College Park, MD: University of Maryland, Center for the Advanced Study of Leadership.

Reaser, J. M., Vaughan, M. R., & Kriner, R. E. (1974). *Military leadership in the seventies: A closer look at the dimension of leadership behavior.* Alexandria, VA: Human Resources Research Organization.

Reavis, C. A., & Derlega, V. J. (1976). Test of a contingency model of teacher effectiveness. *Journal of Educational Research, 69,* 221–225.

Reber, G., Jago, A. G., & Bohnisch, W. (1993). Interkulturelle unterschiede im Fürungsuerhalten. *Globalisierierung der Wirtschaft-Einvirkungen auf die Betreibwirtschaftslebre.* Verlag Paul Haupt Bern, Stuttgart.

Reddin, W. J. (1967). The 3-D management style theory. *Training and Development Journal, 23*(5), 8–17.

Reddin, W. J. (1977). An integration of leader-behavior typologies. *Group & Organization Studies, 2,* 282–295.

Redding, S. G., & Casey, I. W. (1975). Managerial beliefs among Asian managers. *Proceedings,* Academy of Management, New Orleans, 351–355.

Redding, W. C. (1972). *Communication within the organization: An interpretive review of theory and research.* New York: Industrial Communications Council.

Redl, F. (1942). Group emotion and leadership. *Psychiatric, 5,* 573–596.

Redl, F. (1948). Resistance in therapy groups. *Human Relations, 1,* 307–313.

Reed, D. B., & Himmler, A. H. (1985). The work of the secondary assistant principalship: A field study. *Education and Urban Society, 18*(1), 59–84.

Reed, H. D., & Janis, I. L. (1974). Effects of a new type of psychological treatment on smokers' resistance to warnings about health hazards. *Journal of Consulting and Clinical Psychology, 42,* 748.

Reed, T. K. (1996). A new understanding of "followers" as leaders: Emerging theory of civic leadership. *Journal of Leadership Studies, 3,* 95–104.

Reeder, R. R. (1981). The importance of the superior's technical competence in the subordinates' work. *Dissertation Abstracts International, 42*(6A), 2830.

Reedy, G. (1982). *Lyndon B. Johnson: A memoir.* Kansas City, MO: Andrews McNeel.

Rees, R. T., & O'Karma, J. G. (1980). Perception of supervisor leadership style in a formal organization. *Group & Organization Studies, 5,* 65–68.

Reeves, R. (1995). *The character of John F. Kennedy.* Austin, TX: LBJ School of Public Affairs.

Reeves-Ellington, R. H. (1995). Organizing for global effectiveness: Ethnicity and organizations. *Human Organization., 54,* 249–262.

Reeves-Ellington, R. H. (1998). Leadership for socially responsible organizations. *Leadership & Organization Development Journal, 19*(2), 97–105.

Reibstein, L. (1986). The not-so-fast track: Firms try promoting hotshots more slowly. *Wall Street Journal,* March 24, 23.

Reich, R., & Copening, L. (1994) Empowerment without the rhetoric. *Quality Progress,* June, 35–37.

Reichers, A. E., & Schneider, B. (1990). Climate and culture: An evolution of constructs. In B. Schneider (ed.), *Organizational climate and culture.* San Francisco: Jossey-Bass.

Reichers, A. E., Wanous, J. P., & Austin, J. T. (1997). Understanding and manufacturing cynicism about organizational change. *Academy of Management, 11*(1), 48–X.

Reider, N. (1944). Psychodynamics of authority with relation to some psychiatric problems in officers. *Bulletin of the Menninger Clinic, 8,* 55–58.

Reilly, A. H. (1990). *Effective crisis management: More than the daily routine.* Doctoral dissertation, Northwestern University, Evanston, IL.

Reinganum, M. R. (1985). The effect of executive succession on stockholder wealth. *Administrative Science Quarterly, 30,* 46–60.

Reingold, J., & Jespersen, F. (2000). Executive pay. *BusinessWeek Online,* April 17, 1–8.

Reiss, D. (1997). Mechanisms linking genetic and social influences in adolescent development: Beginning a collaborative search. *Current Directions in Psychological Science, 6,* 100–105.

Reiss, S. (2000). *The 16 basic desires that motivate our actions and define our personalities.* New York: Tarcher, Putnam.

Reiter-Palmon, R., & Illies, J. J. (2004). Leadership and creativity: Understanding leadership from a problem-solving perspective. *Leadership Quarterly, 15*, 55–78.

Reitz, H. J. (1971). Managerial attitudes and perceived contingencies between performance and organizational response. *Proceedings, Academy of Management*, Atlanta, GA, 227–238.

Reitz, H. J. (1977). *Behavior in organizations.* Homewood, IL: Richard D. Irwin.

Rejai, M. (1980). Theory and research in the study of revolutionary personnel. In T.R. Gurr (ed.), *Handbook of Political Conflict: Theory and Research.* New York: Free Press.

Rejai, M. (1980). The professional revolutionary: A profile. *Air University Review, 31*(3), 87–90.

Rejai, M., & Philips, K. (1979). *Leaders of revolution.* Beverly Hills, CA: Sage Publications.

Rejai, M., & Philips, K. (1983). *World revolutionary leaders.* New Brunswick, NJ: Rutgers University Press.

Rejai, M., & Phillips, K. (1988). *Loyalists and revolutionaries: Political leaders compared.* New York: Praeger.

Rejai, M., & Phillips, K. (1988). Loyalists and revolutionaries: Political elites in comparative perspective. *International Political Science Review, 9*, 107–118.

Rejai, M., & Phillips, K. (1996). *World military leaders: A collective and comparative analysis.* Westport, CT: Praeger.

Rejai, M., & Philips, K. (1998). Comparing leaders: An interactional theory. *Journal of Leadership Studies, 5*(1), 62–71.

Remdisch, S. (1995). *Implementing group work in the car manufacturing industry.* Doctoral Dissertation, Department of Work-Psychology, Justis-Liebig-University, Glessen, Germany.

Remland, M. S. (1984). Leadership impressions and nonverbal communication in a superior-subordinate interaction. *Communication Quarterly, 32*(l), 41–48.

Renn, R.W. (1998). Participation's effect on task performance: Mediating roles of goal acceptance and procedural justice. *Journal of Business Research, 41*(2), 115–125.

Reskin, B. F., McBrier, D. B., & Kmec, J. A. (1999). The determinants and consequences of workplace sex and race composition. *Annual Review of Sociology, 25*, 335–361.

Rest, J. R. (1979). *Development in judging moral issues.* Minneapolis, MN: University of Minnesota Press.

Rest, J. R. (1984). The major components of morality. In W. Kurtines, & J. Gewirtz (eds.), *Morality, moral behavior, and moral development.* New York, NY: Wiley. p. 24–40.

Rest, J. (1986). *Moral development: Advances in research and theory.* New York: Prager.

Rest, J. R. (1988). Why does college promote development in moral judgment? *Journal of Moral Education, 17*(3), 183–194.

Rest, J. R. (1990). *DIT manual: Manual for the defining issues test* (rev. ed.). Center for the Study of Ethical Development, Minneapolis, MN: University of Minnesota.

Revans, R. W. (1982). *The origins and growth of action learning.* Bromley, UK: Chartwell Bratt Ltd.

Reykowski, J. (1982). Social motivation. *Annual Review of Psychology, 33*, 123–154.

Reynolds, J. (1994). *Out front leadership: Discovering, developing, & delivering your potential.* Austin, TX: Mott & Carlisle.

Rhinehart, J. B., Barrell, R. P., DeWolfe, A. S., et al. (1969). Comparative study of need satisfaction in government and business hierarchies. *Journal of Applied Psychology, 53*, 230–235.

Ricciuti, H. N. (1955). Ratings of leadership potential at the U.S. Naval Academy and subsequent officer performance. *Journal of Applied Psychology, 39*, 194–199.

Rice, B. (1986). Dealing with difficult bosses. *U.S. Air*, December, 32–39.

Rice, B. (1988). Work or perk? *Psychology Today, 22*(11), 26, 28–29.

Rice, R. W. (1976). The esteem for least preferred co-worker (LPC) score: What does it measure? *Dissertation Abstracts International, 36B*, 5360–5361.

Rice, R. W. (1978a). Psychometric properties of the esteem for least preferred co-worker (LPC scale). *Academy of Management Review, 3*, 106–118.

Rice, R. W. (1978b). Construct validity of the least preferred co-worker score. *Psychology Bulletin*, 85i 1199–1237.

Rice, R. W. (1979). Reliability and validity of the LPC scale: A reply. *Academy of Management Review, 4*, 291–294.

Rice, R. W. (1981). Leader LPC and follower satisfaction: A review. *Organizational Behavior and Human Performance, 28*, 1–25.

Rice, R. W., Bender, L. R., & Vitters, A. G. (1980). Leader sex, follower attitudes toward women, and leadership effectiveness: A laboratory experiment. *Organizational Behavior and Human Performance, 25*, 46–78.

Rice, R. W., & Chemers, M. M. (1973). Predicting the emergence of leaders using Fiedler's contingency model of leadership effectiveness. *Journal of Applied Psychology, 57*, 281–287.

Rice, R. W., & Chemers, M. M. (1975). Personality and situational determinants of leaders' behavior. *Journal of Applied Psychology, 60*, 2027.

Rice, R. W., Instone, D., & Adams, J. (1984). Leader sex, leader success, and leadership process: Two field studies. *Journal of Applied Psychology, 69*, 12–32.

Rice, R. W., & Kastenbaum, D. R. (1983). The contingency model of leadership: Some current issues. *Basic and Applied Social Psychology, 4*, 373–392.

Richards, S. A., & Jaffee, C. L. (1972). Blacks supervising whites: A study of interracial difficulties in working together in a simulation organization. *Journal of Applied Psychology, 56*, 234–240.

Richardson, Bellows, Henry & Co., Inc. (1981). *Supervisory Profile Record Technical Reports* (Vols. 1, 2, & 3). Washington, DC: Richardson, Bellows, Henry & Co., Inc.

Richardson, Bellows, Henry & Co. (undated). *Manager Profile Record: Executive summary.* National Computer Systems. Unpublished manuscript.

Richardson, F. L. W. (1961). *Talk, work, and action.* Ithaca, NY: Cornell University, New York State School of Industrial and Labor Relations.

Richardson, F. L. W., & Walker, C. R. (1948). *Human relations in an expanding company.* New Haven, CT: Yale University, Labor and Management Center.

Richardson, L. W., & Cook, J. A. (1980). *Classroom authority management of male and female university professors.* Paper, American Sociological Association, New York.

Richardson, M. D., Short, P. M., & Prickett, R. L. (1993). *School principals and change.* New York: Garland.

Richardson, R. (1971). *Fair pay and work.* London: Heinemann.

Richardson, R. J., & Thayer, K. T. (1993). *The charisma factor: How to develop your natural leadership ability.* Englewood Cliffs, NJ: Prentice Hall.

Richey, B. E., Garbi, E., & Bernardin, H. J. (2002). *Is alternative justice just: ADR program characteristics and employee fairness and trust perceptions.* Unpublished manuscript. Florida Atlantic University.

Richie, R. J. (1994). Using the assessment center method to predict senior management potential: Issues in the assessment of managerial and executive leadership. *Consulting Psychology Journal*, 46, 16–23.

Richman, B. (1967). Capitalists and managers in Communist China. *Harvard Business Review*, 45, 57–71, 78.

Richman, J. A., Flaherty, J. A., Rospenda, K. M., et al. (1992). Mental health consequences and correlates of reported medical student abuse. *Journal of the American Medical Association*, 267, 692–694.

Richmond, V. P., & McCroskey, J. C. (1975). Whose opinion do you trust? *Journal of Communication*, 25(3), 42–50.

Richmond, W. L., Kiesler, S., Weisband, S., et al. (1999). A meta-analytic study of social desirability distortion in computer-administered questionnaires, traditional questionnaires, and interviews. *Journal of Applied Psychology*, 84i 754–775.

Ricks, T. E. (1997). Deep trouble: A skipper's chance to run a trident sub hit stormy waters. *Wall Street Journal*, November 20, A1, A2, A6.

Ridings, W. J., Jr., & McIver, S. B. (1997). *Rating the presidents: A ranking of U.S. leaders from the great and honorable to the dishonest and incompetent.* Secaucus, NJ: Citadel.

Riecken, H. W. (1952). Some problems of consensus development. *Rural Sociology*, 17, 245–252.

Riedel, J. E. (1974). *A comparison of principal, teacher and student perceptions of selected elementary school principals' effectiveness.* Doctoral dissertation, University of Southern California, Los Angeles, CA.

Riegel, J. W. (1952). *Executive development: A survey of experience in fifty American corporations.* Ann Arbor: University of Michigan Press.

Riegel, J. W. (1955). *Employee interest in company success—how can it be stimulated and maintained?* Ann Arbor: University of Michigan, Bureau of Industrial Relations.

Riger, S., & Calligan, P. (1980). Women in management: An explanation of competing paradigms. *American Psychologist*, 35, 902–910.

Riggio, H. R., & Desrochers, S. (2005). The influence of maternal employment on the work and family expectations of offspring. In D. F. Halpern & S. E. Murphy (eds.), *From work-family balance to work-family interaction: Changing the metaphor.* (177–196). Mahwah, NJ, U.S.: Lawrence Erlbaum Associates, Publishers.

Riggio, R. E. (undated). *Top liberal arts colleges and national colleges and universities.* Claremont, CA: Claremont McKenna College, Kravis Leadership Institute.

Riggio, R. E. (1986). Assessment of basic social skills. *Journal of Personality and Social Psychology*, 51, 649–660.

Riggio, R. E. (1989). *Manual for the Social Skills Inventory.* Palo Alto, CA: Consulting Psychologists Press.

Riggio, R. E. (2005). It's the leadership, stupid: An I-O psychology perspective on the 2004 U.S. presidential election. *The Industrial-Organizational Psychologist*, 42(3), 21–26.

Riggio, R. E., Bass, B. M., & Orr, S. S. (2004). Transformational leadership in nonprofit organizations. In R. E. Riggio & S. S. Orr (eds.), *Improving leadership in nonprofit organizations.* San Franscisco: Jossey-Bass.

Riggio, H. R., & Desrochers, S. (2005). The influence of maternal employment on the work and family expectations of offspring. In D. F. Halpern & S. E. Murphy (eds.), *From work-family balance to work-family interaction: Changing the metaphor.* Mahwah, NJ: Lawrence Erlbaum Associates.

Riggio, R. E., Murphy, S. B., & Pirozzolo, F. J. (eds.). (2002). *Multiple intelligences and leadership.* Mahwah, NJ: Lawrence Erlbaum Associates.

Riggio, R. E., & Riggio, H. R. (1999). *Evaluation of school-to-work programs using the NLSY97 data base: Report prepared for the Groundhog Job Shadow Day Coalition.* Claremont, CA: Claremont McKenna College, Kravis Leadership Institute.

Riggio. R. E., Riggio, H. R., & Salinas, C. C. (2003). The role of social and emotional communication skills in leader emergence and effectiveness. *Group Dynamics: Theory, Research, and Practice*, 7, 83–103.

Riker, W. H. (1986). *Art of political manipulation.* New Haven, CT: Yale University Press.

Riley, M. W., & Flowerman, S. H. (1951). Group relations as a variable in communications research. *American Sociological Review*, 16,174–176.

Rim, Y. (1965). Leadership attitudes and decisions involving risk. *Personnel Psychology*, 18, 423–430.

Rim, Y. (1981). Childhood, values and means of influence in marriage. *International Review of Applied Psychology*, 30, 507–520.

Rinne, C., & Karl, K. (1990). *Leadership for the new age.* Dubuque, IA: William C. Brown Publishers.

Ringer, R. C. (1996). *Lessons in leadership: Robert Oppenheimer and the Los Alamos Laboratory.* Proceedings of the Academy of Management.

Ringer, R. C. (2002). Change at Los Alamos. *Strategic Direction*, 18(6), 12–14.

Ritchie, J. B., & Miles, R. E. (1970). An analysis of quality and quality of participation as mediating variables in the participative decision making process. *Personnel Psychology*, 23, 347–359.

Ritchie, R. J., & Moses, J. L. (1983). Assessment center correlates of women's advancement into middle management: A 7-year longitudinal analysis. *Journal of Applied Psychology*, 68, 227–231.

Ritscher, J. A. (1986). *Spiritual leadership.* In J. Adams (ed), *Transforming leadership: From vision to results.* Alexandria, VA: Miles River Press.

Rittenhouse, C. H. (1968). *A follow-up study of NCO leaders school graduates.* Washington, DC: Human Resources Research Office.

Rittenhouse, J. D. (1966). Conformity behavior in sixth grade leaders. *Dissertation Abstracts*, 26, 6212.

Rivenbeck, L. (2000). Employees want more opportunities to telecommute, report reveals. *HRNews*, 14–16.

Rivera, J. B. (1994). *Visionary versus crisis-induced charismatic leadership: An experimental test.* Doctoral dissertation, Texas Tech University, Lubbock, TX.

Rivlin, G. (2005). Hewlett's board forces chief out after rocky stay. Grumbling over profits, Fiorina and directors at odds on how to steer the computer giant. *Wall Street Journal*, February 10, 1A, 6–7C.

Rizzo, J. R., House, R. J., & Lirtzman, S. I. (1970). Role conflict and ambiguity in complex organizations. *Administrative Science Quarterly,* 15, 150–163.

Robbins, S. R (1983). The theory Z organization from a power-control perspective. *California Management Review,* 25, 67–75.

Robert, C., Probst, T. M., Martocchio, J. J., et al. (2000). Empowerment and continuous improvement in the United States, Mexico, Poland, and India: Predicting fit on the basis of the dimensions of power distance and individualism. *Journal of Applied Psychology,* 85, 643–658.

Roberto, M. A. (2002). Lessons from Everest: The interaction of cognitive bias, psychological safety, and system complexity. *California Management Review,* Fall. In press.

Roberts, A. H., & Jessor, R. (1958). Authoritarianism, punitiveness, and perceived social status. *Journal of Abnormal and Social Psychology,* 56, 311–314.

Roberts, B. B. (1969). The leader, group, and task variables of leader selection in college. *Dissertation Abstracts,* 29, 2360–2361.

Roberts, J. (2001). Trust and control in Anglo-American systems of corporate governance: The individualizing and socializing effects of processes of accountability. *Human Relations,* 54, 1547–1572.

Roberts, B. B., & Thorsheim, I. (1987). *Empowering leadership.* Northfield, MN: St. Olaf College, Social Ecology Research.

Roberts, B. W., & DelVecchio, W. F. (2000). The rank-order consistency of personality traits from childhood to old age: A quantitative review of longitudinal studies. *Psychological Bulletin,* 126, 3–25.

Roberts, K. A., Blankenship, L. V., & Miles, R. E. (1968). Organizational leadership, satisfaction, and productivity. *Academy of Management Journal,* 11, 401–422.

Roberts, N. C. (1986). Organizational power styles: Collective and competitive power under varying organizational conditions. *Journal of Applied Behavioral Science,* 22, 443–458.

Roberts, N. C., & Bradley, R. T. (1987). *Limits to charisma.* Paper, Conference on Charisma, McGill University, Montreal.

Roberts, N., & Bradley, R. T. (1988). Limits to charisma. In J. Conger & R. Kanungo (eds.), *Charismatic leadership in management.* San Francisco, CA: Jossey-Bass.

Roberts, T., & Nolen-Hoeksema, S. (1989). Sex differences in reactions to evaluative feedback. *Sex Roles,* December, 21(11–12), 725–747.

Robertson, I.T., Baron, H., Gibbons, P., MacIver, R., & Nyfield, G. (2000). Conscientiousness and managerial performance. *Journal of Occupational & Organizational Psychology,* 73(2), 171–180.

Robie, E. A. (1973). Challenge to management. In E. Ginzberg & A. M. Yohalem (eds.), *Corporate lib: Women's challenge to management.* Baltimore: Johns Hopkins University Press.

Robins, A. R., Willemin, L. P., & Brueckel, J. E. (1954). Exploratory study of echelon differences in efficiency ratings. *American Psychologist,* 9, 457b.

Robins, R. W., Gosling, S. D., & Craik, K. H. (1999). An empirical analysis of trends in psychology. *American Psychologist,* 54, 117–128.

Robinson, R. J., Lewicki, R. J., & Donahue, E. M. (2000). Extending and testing a five factor model of ethical and unethical bargaining tactics: Introducing the sins scale. *Journal of Organizational Behavior,* 21(6), 649–664.

Robinson, S. L., & Bennett, R. J. (1995) A typology of deviant workplace behaviors: A multidimensional scaling study. *Academy of Management Journal,* 38, 555–572.

Robinson, S. L., & O'Leary-Kelly, A. M. (1998) Monkey see, monkey do: The influence of work groups on the antisocial behavior of employees. *Academy of Management Journal,* 41(6), 658–672.

Roby, T. B. (1953). *Relationships between sociometric measures and performance in medium-bomber crews* (Res. Bull. No. 53–18). San Antonio, TX: Lackland Air Force Base, Human Resources Research Center.

Roby, T. B. (1961). The executive function in small groups. In L. Petrullo & B. Bass (eds.), *Leadership and interpersonal behavior.* New York: Holt, Reinhart & Winston.

Roby, T. B., & Forgays, D. G. (1953). *A problem solving model of communication in B-29 crews* (Tech. Rep. No. 53–32). San Antonio, TX: Lackland Air Force Base, Human Resources Research Center.

Roby, T. B., Nicol, E. H., & Farrell, F. M. (1963). Group problem solving under two types of executive structure. *Journal of Abnormal and Social Psychology,* 67, 550–556.

Roche, C. R. (1979). Much ado about mentors. *Harvard Business Review,* 57(1), 17–28.

Rock, M. L., & Hay, E. N. (1953). Investigation of the use of tests as a predictor of leadership and group effectiveness in a job evaluation situation. *Journal of Social Psychology,* 38, 109–119.

Rockman, B. A. (1984). *The leadership question: The presidency and the American system.* New York: Praeger.

Rodgers, C., & Teicholz, E. (2001). Telecommuting and the computer . . . here today, home tomorrow. *Facilities Design & Management,* 20, 22–24.

Rodgers, R., & Hunter, J. E. (1991). Impact of management by objectives on organizational productivity. *Journal of Applied Psychology,* 76(2), 322–336.

Roddick, A. (2000). *Business as unusual.* Bath, U.K.: Bath Press.

Rodgers, R., Hunter, J. E., & Rogers, D. L. (1993). The influence of top management commitment on program success. *Journal of Applied Psychology,* 78, 151–155.

Rodrigues, A., & Lloyd, K. L. (1998) Reexamining bases of power from an attributional perspective. *Journal of Applied Social Psychology,* 28, 973–997.

Rodriguez, R. O., Green, M. T., & Ree, M. J. (2003). Leading generation X: Do the old rules still apply? *Journal of Leadership and Organizational Studies,* 9(4), 67–75.

Roehling, M. V. (2002). *Weight discrimination in the American workplace.* Paper, Academy of Management, Denver, CO.

Roese, N. J., & Jamieson, D. W. (1993). Twenty years of bogus pipeline research: A critical review and meta-analysis. *Psychological Bulletin,* 114, 363–375.

Roethlisberger, F. J. (1945). The foreman: Master and victim of double talk. *Harvard Business Review,* 23, 283–298.

Roethlisberger, F. J., & Dickson, W. J. (1947). *Management and the worker.* Cambridge, MA: Harvard University Press.

Roethlisberger, F. J., Lombard, C. F. F., & Renken, H. O. (1954). *Training for human relations: An interim report.* Boston: Harvard University, Graduate School of Business Administration

Rogelberg, S. G., & Luong, A. (1998). Nonresponse to mailed surveys: A review and guide. *Current Directions in Psychological Science,* 7(2), 60–65.

Rogers, C. R. (1951). *Client-centered therapy.* Boston: Houghton Mifflin.

Rogers, C. R. (1959). A theory of therapy, personality, and interpersonal relationships as developed in the client-centered framework. In S. Koch (ed.), *Psychology: A study of a science* (vol.3). New York: McGraw-Hill.

Rogers, M. S., Ford, J. D., & Tassone, J. A. (1961). The effects of personnel replacement on an information-processing crew. *Journal of Applied Psychology, 45*, 91–96.

Rogers, R. E. (1977). Components of organizational stress among Canadian managers. *Journal of Psychology, 95*, 265–273.

Rohde, K. J. (1952). The relation of authoritarianism of the aircrew member to his acceptance by the airplane commander. *American Psychologist, 7*, 310–311.

Rohde, K. J. (1954a). *Individual executive ability as a factor in the performance of small groups* (Tech. Rep. No. 17). Columbus: Ohio State University, Personnel Research Board.

Rohde, K. J. (1954b). *Variations in group composition with respect to individual task ability as a factor in group behavior* (Tech. Rep. No. 18). Columbus: Ohio State University, Personnel Research Board.

Rohde, K. J. (1954c). An evaluation of the extent to which task ability of the man in charge of a group is determinative of that group's success in performing the task. *American Psychologist, 9*, 569 (Abstract).

Rohde, K. J. (1958). Theoretical and experimental analysis of leadership ability. *Psychological Reports, 4*, 243–278.

Rohricht, M. T., & Rush, M. C. (1977). *Leadership styles, pressure of change, and stress resiliency from the leader's perspective.* University of Tennessee, Memphis, TN.

Rojas, L. (1982). *Salient mainstream and Hispanic values in a Navy training environment: An anthropological description* (ONR Tech. Rep. No. 22). Champaign: University of Illinois, Department of Psychology.

Roff, M. (1950). A study of combat leadership in the air force by means of a rating scale: Group differences. *Journal of Psychology, 30*, 229–239.

Rokeach, M. (1960). *The open and closed mind.* New York: Basic Books.

Rokeach, M. (1971). Long-range experimental modification of values, attitudes and behavior. *American Psychologist, 26*, 453–459.

Rokeach, M. (1972). A theory of organization and change within value/attitude systems. In C. D. Paige (ed.), *Political leadership: Readings for an emerging field.* New York: Free Press.

Rokeach, M. (1973). *The nature of human values.* New York: Free Press.

Rollinson, D., Hook, C., Foot, M., et al. (1996) Supervisor and manager styles in handling discipline and grievances: II. Approaches to handling discipline and grievance. *Personnel Review, 23*(4), 38–55.

Roloff, M. E., & Paulson, G. D. (2001). Confronting organizational transgressions. In J. M. Darley, D. M. Messick, & T. R. Tyler, (eds.), *Social influences on ethical behavior in organizations.* Mahwah, NJ: Lawrence Erlbaum Associates. 53.

Romanelli, E., & Tushman, M. L. (1983). *Executive leadership and organizational outcomes: An evolutionary perspective* (Rep. No. 130). New York: Columbia University, Center for Career Research and Human Resources Management

Ronan, W. W. (1970). Individual and situational variables relating to job satisfaction. *Journal of Applied Psychology, 54*, 1–3 1.

Ronen, S. (1986). *Comparative and multinational management.* New York: Wiley.

Ronen, S., & Shenkar, O. (1985). Clustering countries on attitudinal dimensions: A review and synthesis. *Academy of Management Review, 10*, 435–454.

Ronfeldt, D. (1993). *Institutions, markets, and networks: A framework about the evolution of societies.* Report DRU-590-FF. Santa Monica, CA: RAND

Ronken, H. O., & Lawrence, P. R. (1952). *Administering changes.* Boston: Harvard University, Graduate School of Business Administration.

Roof, W. C. (1999). *Spiritual marketplace: Baby boomers and the remaking of american religion.* Princeton, NJ: Princeton University Press.

Rosch, E. (1975). Cognitive representations of semantic categories. *Journal of Experimental Psychology, 104*, 192–233.

Rose, E. (1982). The anatomy of mutiny. *Armed Forces and Society, 11*, 561–574.

Rose, M. R., & Nelson, C. E. (1998). *Relationship between subordinate health outcomes under varying conditions.* Paper, Society for Industrial and Organizational Psychology, Dallas, TX.

Rose, R. J. (1995). Genes and human behavior. *Annual Review of Psychology, 46*, 625–54.

Rose, S. O. (1980). *Betwixt and between: Women and the exercise of power in middle management positions.* Paper, Eastern Sociological Society, Philadelphia, PA.

Rosen, B., & Jerdee, I. H. (1973). The influence of sex-role stereotypes on evaluations of male and female supervisory behavior. *Journal of Applied Psychology, 57*, 44–48.

Rosen, B., & Jerdee, T. H. (1977). Influence of subordinate characteristies on trust and use of participative decision strategies in a management simulation. *Journal of Applied Psychology, 62*, 628–631.

Rosen, B., & Jerdee, T. H. (1978). Effects of decision permanence on managerial willingness to use participation. *Academic Management Journal, 21*, 722–725.

Rosen, B., Jerdee, T. H., & Prestwich, T. L. (1975). Dual-career marital adjustment: Potential effects of discriminatory managerial attitudes. *Journal of Marriage and the Family, 37*(3), 565–572.

Rosen, B., Templeton, M. E., & Kirchline, K. (1981). First few years on the job: Women in management. *Business Horizons, 24*, 26–29.

Rosen, H. (1961a). Managerial role interaction: A study of three managerial levels. *Journal of Applied Psychology, 45*, 30–34.

Rosen, H. (1961b). Desirable attributes of work: Four levels of management describe their job environments. *Journal of Applied Psychology, 45*, 156–160.

Rosen, H., &. Weaver, C. G. (1960). "Motivation in management: A study of four managerial levels." *Journal of Applied Psychology 44*(6), 386–392.

Rosen, M. (1985). Breakfast at Spiro's: Dramaturgy and dominance. *Journal of Management, 11*(2), 31–48.

Rosen, N. A. (1969). *Leadership change and work-group dynamics.* Ithaca, NY: Cornell University Press.

Rosen, N. A. (1970b). Demand characteristics in a field experiment. *Journal of Applied Psychology, 54*, 163–168.

Rosen, N. A., Georgiades, N. J., & McDonald, G. (1980). An empirical test of a leadership contingency model for teaching behavioral science concepts to managers. *Journal of Occupational Psychology, 53*, 1–10.

Rosen, S., Levinger, G., & Lippitt, R. (1961). Perceived sources of social power. *Journal of Abnormal and Social Psychology, 62*, 439–441.

Rosenbach, W. E., & Mueller, R. (1988). *Transformational and transactional leadership effectiveness.* Paper, International Congress of Psychology, Sydney, Australia.

Rosenbaum, D. E. (1988). Democrats keep solid hold on Congress. *New York Times,* November 9, A24.

Rosenbaum, L. L., & Rosenbaum, W. B. (1971). Morale and productivity consequences of group leadership style, stress, and type of task. *Journal of Applied Psychology, 55,* 343–348.

Rosenbaum, M. E. (1959). Social perception and the motivational structure of interpersonal relations. *Journal of Abnormal and Social Psychology, 59,* 130–133.

Rosenberg, M. (1956). Misanthropy and political ideology. *American Sociological Review, 21,* 690–695.

Rosenberg, M., & Pearlin, L. I. (1962). Power-orientations in the mental hospital. *Human Relations, 15,* 335–350.

Rosenberg, R. D. (1977). *A dual process model of worker participation at the blue–collar level.* Doctoral dissertation, Technion–Israel Institute of Technology, Haifa.

Rosenberg, S., Erlick, D. E., & Berkowitz, L. (1955). Some effects of varying combinations of group members on group performance measures and leadership behaviors. *Journal of Abnormal and Social Psychology, 51,* 195–203.

Rosener, J. B. (1990). Ways women lead. *Harvard Business Review, 68*(6), 119–125.

Rosenfeld, E. (1951). Social stratification in a "classless" society. *American Sociological Review, 16,* 766–774.

Rosenfeld, J. M., & Smith, M. J. (1967). Participative management: An overview. *Personnel Journal, 46,* 101–104.

Rosenfeld, L. B., & Fowler, C. D. (1976). Personality, sex, and leadership style. *Communications Monographs, 43,* 320–324.

Rosenfeld, P., Giacalone, R. A., & Riordan, C. A. (1995). *Impression management in organizations. Theory, measurement, and practice.* London: Routledge.

Rosenstein, E. (1985). Cooperativeness and advancement of managers: An international perspective. *Human Relations, 38,* 1–22.

Rosenthal, A. (1974). *Legislative performance in the states: Explorations in committee behavior.* New York: Free Press.

Rosenthal, D., & Frank, J. D. (1956). Psychotherapy and the placebo effect. *Psychological Bulletin, 53,* 294–302.

Rosenthal, R. (1974). *On the social psychology of the self-fulfilling prophesy: Further evidence for Pygmalion effects and their mediating mechanisms.* (Module 53). New York: MSS Modular Publications.

Rosenthal, R. (1978). Combining results of independent studies. *Psychological Bulletin, 85,* 185–193.

Rosenthal R. (1979a). The "file-drawer" problem and tolerance for null results. *Psychological Bulletin, 86,* 638–641.

Rosenthal, R. (ed.). (1979b). *Skill in nonverbal communication.* Cambridge, MA: Oelgeschlarger, Gunn, & Hain.

Rosenthal, R. (1991). *Meta-analytic procedures for social research* (rev. ed.). Beverly Hills, CA: Sage.

Rosenthal, R. (1994). Interpersonal expectancy effects: A thirty-year perspective. *Current Directions in Psychological Science, 3,* 3–12.

Rosenthal, R., & Jacobson, L. (1968). *Pygmalion in the classroom: Teacher expectation and pupils' intellectual development.* New York: Holt, Rinehart & Winston.

Rosenthal, R. & Rubin, D. B. (1978). Interpersonal expectancy effects: The first 345 studies. *Behavioral and Brain Sciences, 3,* 379–415.

Rosenthal, R., & Rubin, D. B. (1982). Further meta-analytic procedures for assessing cognitive gender differences. *Journal of Educational Psychology, 74,* 708–712.

Rosenthal, R., & Rubin, D. B. (1982). A simple, general-purpose display of magnitude of experimental effect. *Journal of Educational Psychology, 74,* 166–169.

Rosenthal, R., & Rubin, D. B. (1988). Comment: Assumptions and procedures in the file drawer problem. *Statistical Science, 3,* 120–125.

Rosenzweig, P. M. (1994). The new "American challenge": Foreign multinationals in the United States. *California Management Review, 36*(3), 107–123.

Roskens, R. W. (1958). The relationship between leadership participation in college and after college. *Dissertation Abstracts, 19,* 473.

Roskies, E., & Louis-Guerin, C. (1990). Job insecurity in managers: Antecedents and consequences. *Journal of Organizational Behavior, 11,* 345–359.

Roskin, R., & Margerison, C. (1983). The effectiveness of some measures of managerial effectiveness. *Human Relations, 36,* 865–882.

Ross, J. D., Davidson, S., & Graham, W. K. (1986). *Sex differences in pre and mid–management assessment center performance.* Paper, Academy of Management, San Diego, CA.

Ross, M. G., & Hendry, C. E. (1957). *New understandings of leadership.* New York: Association Press.

Ross, R. B. (1982). Emergency planning paid off. *Security Management, 26*(9), 62–65.

Ross, R. R., & Gendreau, P. (1980). *Effective correctional treatment.* New York: Butterworth.

Ross, S. M., & Offerman, L. R. (1997). Transformational leaders: Measurement of personality attributes and work group performance. *Personality and Social Psychology Bulletin, 23,* 1078–1086.

Rosse, J. G., & Kraut, A. I. (1983). Reconsidering the vertical dyad linkage model of leadership. *Journal of Occupational Psychology, 56,* 63–71.

Rossing, B. (1998). Learning laboratories for renewed community leadership: Rational programs and challenges. *Journal of Leadership Studies, 5*(4), 68–81.

Rossing, B. E., & Heasley, D. K. (1987). Enhancing public affairs participation through leadership development education: Key questions for community development research and practice. *Journal of the Community Development Society, 18*(2), 98–116.

Rost, J. C. (1991). *Leadership for the twenty-first century.* Westport, CT: Greenwood Publishing.

Rost, J. C. (1993). Leadership development in the new millennium. *Journal of Leadership Studies, 1,* 92–110.

Rost, J. C. (1993). *Leadership for the twenty-first century.* Westport, CT: Praeger.

Rost, J. C. (1996). *Leadership and democracy in the twenty-first century.* Paper, Kellogg Leadership Studies Project, University of Maryland, College Park, MD.

Rost, J. C., & Barker, R. A. (2000). Leadership education in colleges: Toward a 21st century paradigm. *Journal of Leadership Studies, 7*(1), 10–12.

Rotberg, R. I. (2000). Africa's mess: Mugabe's mayhem. *Foreign Affairs, 5,* 47–61.

Roth, P. L., Bevier, C. A., Bobko, P., et al. (2001). Ethnic group differences in cognitive ability in employment and educational settings. *Personnel Psychology, 54,* 297–330.

Rothbart, M. (1968). Effects of motivation, equity, and compliance on the use of reward and punishment. *Journal of Personality and Social Psychology, 8,* 143–147.

Rothe, H. F. (1960). Does higher pay bring higher productivity? *Personnel, 37,* 20–38.

Rothe, H. F. (1961). Output rates among machine operators: III. A nonincentive situation in two levels of business activity. *Journal of Applied Psychology, 45,* 50–54.

Rothschild, W. E. (1993). *Risktaker, Caretaker, Surgeon, Undertaker: The Four Faces of Strategic Leadership.* New York: John Wiley & Sons.

Rothwell, R., Freeman, C., Horsley, A., et al. (1974). SAPPHO updated: Project SAPPHO phase II. *Research Policy, 3,* 258–291.

Rotter, J. B. (1966). Generalized expectancies for internal versus exter-nal control of reinforcement. *Psychological Monographs, 80,* No. 609.

Rouhana, N. N., & Bar-Tel, D. (1998). Psychological dynamics of intractable ethnonational conflicts: The Israeli-Palestinian case. *American Psychologist, 53,* 761–770.

Roure, J. B., & Keeley, R. H. (1990). Predictors of success in new technology-based ventures. *Journal of Business Venturing, 5,* 201–220.

Roush, P., & Atwater, L. (1992). Using the MBTI to understand transformational leadership and self-perception accuracy. *Military Psychology, 4,* 17–34.

Rousseau, D. M. (1990). New hire perspectives of their own and their employer's obligations: a study of psychological contracts. *Journal of Organizational Behavior, 11,* 389–400.

Rousseau, D.M. (1995). *Psychological contracts in organizations: Understanding written and unwritten agreements.* Thousand Oaks, CA: Sage.

Rousseau, D. M., & Schalk, R. (2000). *Psychological contracts in employment: Cross-national perspectives.* Thousand Oaks, CA: Sage Publications

Rousseau, D. M., & Tijoriwala, S. A. (1998). Assessing psychological contracts: Issue, alternatives and measures. *Journal of Organizational Behavior, 19,* 731–744.

Roussel, C. (1974). Relationship of sex of department head to department climate. *Administrative Science Quarterly, 19,* 211–220.

Rowan, R. (1986). *The intuitive manager.* Boston: Little, Brown

Rowe, P. A., Christie, M., & Martin, J. F. (2003). *Leadership support: A necessary condition to open the "black box" of sharing tacit knowledge.* Paper, Academy of Management, Seattle, WA.

Rowe, W. G. (2001). Creating wealth in organizations: The role of strategic leadership. *Academy of Management Executive, 15*(1), 81–94.

Rowe, W. G., & Rankin, D. (2003). *Leader succession: An examination using coaches and general managers in the National Hockey League.* Paper, Academy of Management, Seattle, WA.

Rowland, K. M., & Scott, W. E. (1968). Psychological attributes of effective leadership in a formal organization, *Personnel Psychology, 21,* 365–377.

Rowney, J. I. A., & Cahoon, A. R. (1988). *A preliminary investigation of burnout dimensions in intact work groups.* Paper, International Congress of Psychology, Sydney, Australia.

Rubenowitz, S. (1962). Job-oriented and person-oriented leadership. *Personnel Psychology, 15,* 387–396.

Rubenstein, G. (2002). The Soviet man and the authoritarian personality. *International Psychology Reporter, 6*(3–4), 20, 34.

Rubenzer, S. J., Faschingbauer, T. R., & Ones, D. S. (2000). Assessing the U.S. presidents using the Revised NED Personality Inventory. *Assessment, 7*(4),403–420.

Rubin, I. M., & Berlew, D. E. (1984). The power failure in organizations. *Training & Development Journal, 38*(l), 35–38.

Rubin, I. M., & Goldman, M. (1968). An open system model of leadership performance. *Organizational Behavior and Human Performance, 3,* 143–156.

Rubin, J. Z., Lewicki, R. J., & Dunn, L. (1973). *The perception of promisors and threateners.* Paper, American Psychological Association, Montreal.

Ruble, M. R. (1984). *An empirical test of a decision support system in a group decision making environment.* Unpublished doctoral dissertation, Arizona State University, Tempe, AZ.

Ruderman, M. N., & Ohlott, P. J. (2002). *Organizational climate and the effective inclusion of women managers.* Paper, Academy of Management, Denver, CO.

Ruderman, M. N., Ohlott, P. J., & McCauley, C. D. (1989). Assessing opportunities for leadership development. In K. E. Clark & M. B. Clark (eds.), *Measures of leadership.* West Orange, NJ: Leadership Library of America.

Rudin, S. A. (1964). Leadership as a psychophysiological activation of group members: A case experimental study. *Psychological Reports, 15,* 577–578.

Ruhe, J. A. (1972). *The effects of varying racial compositions upon attitudes and behaviors of supervisors and subordinates in simulated work groups.* Doctoral dissertation, University of Florida, Gainesville.

Ruland, R. G. (1993). Book review. *Journal of Business Ethics, 12*(3), 178.

Rumelt, R. F. (1987). Theory, strategy and entrepreneurship. In D. J. Treece (ed.), *The competitive challenge.* New York: Harper & Row.

Rummler, G. A., & Brache, A. P. (1995). *Improving Performance* (2nd ed.). San Francisco, CA.: Jossey-Bass.

Runyon, K. E. (1973). Some interactions between personality variables and management styles. *Journal of Applied Psychology, 57,* 228–294.

Rusaw, A. C. (1996). All God's children: Leading diversity in churches as organizations. *Leadership Quarterly, 7,* 229–241.

Rusaw, A. C. (2000). The ethics of leadership trust. *International Journal of Organizational Theory and Behavior. 3,* 547–569.

Rush, C. H. (1957). Leader behavior and group characteristics. In R. M. Stogdill & A. E. Coons (eds.), *Leader behavior: Its description and measurement.* Columbus: Ohio State University, Bureau of Business Research.

Rush, C. H., Jr. (undated). *Group dimensions of air crews.* Columbus: Ohio State University, Personnel Research Board.

Rush, M. C., Thomas, J. C., & Lord, R. G. (1977). Implicit leadership theory: A potential threat to the internal validity of leader behavior questionnaires. *Organizational Behavior and Human Performance, 20,* 93–110.

Rushton, J. P., Fulker, D. W., Neale, M. C., Nias, D. K. B., & Eysenck, H. J. (1986). Altruism and aggression: The heritability of individual differences. *Journal of Personality and Social Psychology, 50*(6), 1192–1198.

Rusmore, J. T. (1961). Use of the executive position description questionnaire in a study of managers in the Pacific Telephone and Telegraph Company. *Proceedings,* Conference on the Executive Study, Princeton, NJ.

Rusmore, J. T.(1984). *Executive performance and intellectual ability in organizational levels.* San Jose, CA: San Jose State University, Advanced Human Systems Institution.

Russell, B. (1938). *Power.* London: Allen & Unwin.

Russell, C. J. (1990). Selecting top corporate leaders: An example of biographical information. *Journal of Management, 16,* 73–86.

Russell, C. J., & Domm, D. R. (undated). *On the construct validity of biographical information: Evaluation of a theory based method of item generation.* Unpublished manuscript.

Russell, C. J., & Domm, D.R. (2007). Is personality related to assessment center performance? That depends on how old you are. *Journal of Business and Psychology, 22*(1), 21–33.

Russell, C. J., Mattson, J., Devlin, S. E., & Atwater, D. (1986). *Predictive validity of biodata items generated from retrospective life experience essays.* Paper, Society for Industrial and Organizational Psychology, Chicago, IL.

Russell, P. A., Lankford, M. W., & Grinnell, R. M., Jr. (1984). Administrative styles of social work supervisors in a human service agency. *Administration in Social Work, 8*(l), 1–16.

Russelli, P. W., Jr., & Dickinson, T. L. (1978). *Factors affecting overseas success in industry.* Paper, Society for Intercultural Education, Training and Research, Phoenix, AZ.

Russon, C., & Reinelt, C. (2004). The results of an evaluation scan of 55 leadership development programs. *Journal of Leadership Studies, 10,* 104–107.

Rutherford, W. L. (1984). Styles and behaviors of elementary school principals: Relationship to school improvement. *Education and Urban Society, 17*(1), 9–28.

Rutonno, M., & McGoldrick, M. (1982). Italian families. In M. McGoldrick, J. K. Pearce, & J. Giordano (eds.), *Ethnicity and family therapy.* New York: Guilford Press.

Ryan, A. M., Chan, D., Ployhart, R. E., et al. (1999). Employee attitude surveys in a multinational organization: Considering language and culture in assessing measurement equivalence. *Personnel Psychology, 52,* 37–58.

Ryapolov, G. (1966). I was a Soviet manager. *Harvard Business Review, 44*(1), 117–125.

Ryterband, E. C., & Thiagarajan, K. M. (1968). *Managerial attitudes toward salaries as a function of social and economic development* (Tech. Rep. No. 24). Rochester, NY: University of Rochester, Management Research Center.

Sabath, G. (1964). The effect of disruption and individual status on person perception and group attraction. *Journal of Social Psychology, 64,* 119–130.

Sablynski, C. J. (2002). *Social effects of destructive leadership.* Showcase Symposium, Academy of Management Conference, Denver, Colorado, August 2002.

Sackett, P. R., & Dreher, C. F. (1982). Constructs and assessment center dimensions: Some troubling empirical findings. *Journal of Applied Psychology, 67,* 401–410.

Sackett P. R., & DuBois, C. L. (1991). Rater-ratee race effects on performance evaluation: challenging meta-analytic conclusions. *Journal of Applied Psychology, 76,* 873–877.

Sackett, P. R., & Hakel, M. D. (1979). Temporal stability and individual differences in using assessment information to form over-all ratings. *Organizational Behavior and Human Performance, 23,* 120–137.

Sadler, P. J, & Hofstede, G. H. (1972). Leadership styles: Preferences and perceptions of employees of an international company in different,countries. *Mens en Onderneming, 26,* 43–63.

Sadler-Smith, E., & Shefy, E. (2004). The intuitive executive: Understanding and applying "gut feel" in decision-making. *Academy of Management Executive, 18*(4), 76–91.

Safire, W. (1975). *Before the fall: An inside view of the pre-Watergate White House.* New York: Doubleday.

Safty, A. (2001). *Leadership in the age of globalization.* 21 June 2001, Copyright (c) Turkish Daily News.

Sager, D. J. (1982). *Participatory management in libraries.* Metuchen, NJ: Scarecrow Press.

Sagie, A. (1994). Organizational attitudes and behaviors as a function of participation in strategic and tactical change decisions: An application of path-goal theory. *Journal of Organizational Behavior, 15,* 37–47.

Sagie, A. (1997). A leader direction and employee participation in decision making: Contradictory or compatible practices, *Applied Psychology, 46,* 387–416.

Sakano, N. (1983). Leadership styles: Japanese school administrators and Japanese corporate managers. *Dissertation Abstracts International, 45*(IA), 77.

Sakata, K., & Kurokawa, M. (1992). Sex differences in leader behavior from the perspective of attitudes toward sex roles and influence strategies. *Japanese Journal of Experimental Social Psychology, 31,* 187–202.

Saks, A. M. (1995). Longitudinal field investigation of the moderating and mediating effects of self-efficiency on the relationships between training and newcomer adjustment. *Journal of Applied Psychology, 80,* 211–225.

Saks, A. M. (1997). Transfer of training and self-efficacy: What is the dilemma? *Applied Psychology: An International Review, 46,* 365–370.

Salam, S., Cox, J. F., & Sims, H. P., Jr. (1997). In the eye of the beholder: How leadership relates to 360-degree performance ratings. *Group and Organization Management, 22,* 185–209.

Salaman, G. (1977). A historical discontinuity: From charisma to routimzation. *Human Relations, 30,* 373–388.

Salancik, G. R., & Meindl, J. R. (1984). Corporate attributions to strategic illusions of management control. *Administrative Science Quarterly, 29,* 238–254.

Salancik, G. R., & Pfeffer, J. (1974). The bases and use of power in organizational decision making: The case of a university. *Administrative Science Quarterly, 19,* 453–473.

Salancik, G. R., & Pfeffer, J. (1977). Constraints on administrator discretion: The limited influence of mayors on city budgets. *Urban Affairs Quarterly, 12,* 475–498.

Salancik, C. R., & Pfeffer, J. (1980). Effects of ownership and performance on executive tenure in U.S. corporations. *Academy of Management Journal, 23,* 653–664.

Salancik, C. R., Staw, B. M., & Pondy, L. R. (1980). Administrative turnover as a response to unmanaged organizational independence. *Academy of Management Journal, 10,* 422–437.

Salas, E. (1993). Team training and performance., *Psychological Science Agenda,* January–February, 9–11

Salas, E., Mullen, B., Rozell, D., et al. (1997). *The effects of team building on performance: An integration.* Paper, Society for Industrial and Organizational Psychology, St. Louis, MO.

Saleh, S. D., & Otis, J. L. (1964). Age level and job satisfaction. *Personnel Psychology, 17,* 425–430.

Sales, J. R. (1964). *Managerial behavior: Administrators in complex organizations.* New York: McGraw-Hill

Sales, S. M. (1964). *A laboratory investigation of the effectiveness of two industrial supervisory dimensions.* Master's thesis, Cornell University, Ithaca, NY.

Sales, S. M. (1972). Authoritarianism: But as for me, give me liberty, or give me a big, strong leader I can honor, admire, respect and obey. *Psychology Today, 8,* 94, 143.

Salmons, S. (1977). Africans get a taste for the top. *International Management, 32,* 39–41.

Salovey, P., & Mayer, J.D. (1990). Emotional intelligence. *Imagination, Cognition, and Personality, 9,* 185–211.

Salzman, H. (1992). Skill-based design: Productivity, learning, and organizational effectivenessa. In P. S. Adler & T. Winograd (eds.), *Usability: Turning technology into tools.* London: Oxford University Press.

Samelson, F. (1986). Authoritarianism from Berlin to Berkeley: On social psychology and history. *Journal of Social Issues, 42,* 191–208.

Samonova, T. (1998). Current shifts in Russian national mentality: The new versus the old. *International Psychology Reporter,* November, 17.

Sample, J. A., & Wilson, T. R. (1965). Leader behavior, group productivity, and rating of least preferred co-worker. *Journal of Personality and Social Psychology, 1,* 266–270.

Sanchez, J. I., & Brock, P. (1996). Outcomes of perceived discrimination among Hispanic employees: Is diversity management a luxury or a necessity? *Academy of Management Journal, 39,* 704–719.

Sanders, G. S., & Malkis, E. S. (1982). Type A behavior, need for control, and reactions to group participation. *Organizational Behavior and Human Performance, 30,* 71–86.

Sanders, J. E., Hopkins, W. E., & Geroy, G. D. (2003). From transactional to transcendental: Toward an integrated theory of leadership. *Journal of Leadership and Organizational Studies, 9(4),* 21–31.

Sanders, W. G. (1995). *Prizes with strings attached: Determinants of the structure of CEO compensation.* Paper, Academy of Management, Vancouver, BC.

Sanders, W. G. (2001). Behavioral responses of CEOs to stock ownership and stock option pay. *Academy of Management Journal, 44,* 477–492.

Sanderson, D., & Nafe, R. W. (1929). Studies in rural leadership. *American Sociological Review, 23,* 163–175.

Sandler, B. E., & Scalia, F. A. (1975). The relationship between birth order, sex, and leadership in a religious organization. *Journal of Social Psychology, 95,* 279–280.

Sanford, F. H. (1950). *Authoritarianism and leadership: A study of the follower's orientation to authority.* Philadelphia, PA: Institute for Research in Human Relations.

Sanford, F. H. (1951). Leadership identification and acceptance. In H. Guetzkow (ed.), *Groups, leadership, and men.* Pittsburgh: Carnegie Press.

Sanford, N. (1956). The approach of the authoritarian personality. In J. L. McCary (ed.), *Psychology of Personality.* New York: Grove Press.

Sanford, N. (1986). A personal account of the study of authoritarianism: Comment on Samelson. *Journal of Social Issues, 42,* 209–214.

Sankar, Y. (2003). Character, not charisma is the critical measure of leadership excellence. *Journal of Leadership and Organizational Studies, 9(4),* 45–55.

Sankowski, D. (1995). The charismatic leader as narcissist: Understanding the abuse of power. *Organizational Dynamics, 23(4),* 57–71.

Santee, R. T., & Vanderpol, T. L. (1976). Actors status and conformity to norms–Study of student evaluations of instructors. *Sociological Quarterly, 17,* 378–388.

Santner, B. (1986). *The relationship of dominance, friendliness, task orientation, achievement motivation, intelligence, gender, and race to high school student leadership.* Doctoral dissertation, Fordharn University, New York, NY.

Santora, J. C., & Sarros, J. C. (1994). Leadership: 1993–1994: A selected guide to the literature. *Journal of Leadership Studies, 1(4),* 161–174.

Santora, J. C., & Sarros, J. C. (1995). Mortality and leadership succession: A case study. *Leadership & Organizational Development Journal, 16(7),* 29–32.

Sarachek, B. (1968). Greek concepts of leadership. *Academy of Management Journal, 11,* 39–48.

Sarbin, T. R., & Jones, D. S. (1955). The assessment of role-expectations in the selection of supervisory personnel. *Educational and Psychological Measurement, 15,* 236–239.

Sargent, J. F., & Miller, G. R. (1971). Some differences in certain communication behaviors of autocratic and democratic leaders. *Journal of Communication, 21,* 233–252.

Saris, R. J. (1969). *The development of a l3th subscale to the Leader Behavior Description Questionnaire–Form XII entitled "Responsibility Deference."* Doctoral dissertation, University of Idaho, Moscow.

Sarkesian, S. C. (1985). Leadership and management revisited. *Bureaucrat, 14(1),* 201–224.

Sarsar, S., & Stunkel, K. R. (1994). Political leaders and followers: Two sides of the same coin? *Journal of Leadership Studies, 1(4),* 94–103.

Sashkin, M. (1972). Leadership style and group decision effectiveness: Correlational and behavioral tests of Fiedler's contingency model. *Organizational Behavioral and Human Performance, 8,* 347–362.

Sashkin, M. (1986). The visionary leader. *Training & Development Journal, 40(5),* 58–61.

Sashkin, M. (1988). The visionary leader. In J. A. Conger & R. N. Kanungo (eds.), *Charismatic leadership: The elusive factor in organizational effectiveness.* San Francisco: Jossey-Bass.

Sashkin, M. (1991). *Strategic leadership competencies: What are they? How do they operate? What can be done to develop them?* Conference Paper, Army War College, Carlisle, PA, February 12–15.

Sashkin, M., & Burke, W. W. (1989). Understanding and assessing organizational leadership. In K. E. Clark & M. B. Clark (eds.), *Measures of leadership.* West Orange, NJ: Leadership Library of America.

Sashkin, M., & Fulmer, R. M. (1985). *Toward an organizational leadership theory.* Paper, Biennial Leadership Symposium, Texas Tech University, Lubbock, TX.

Sashkin, M., & Sashkin, M. (1990). *Leadership and culture building in schools: Quantitative and qualitative understandings.* Paper presented at the Annual Meeting of the American Educational Research Association, Boston, MA.

Sashkin, M., Taylor, F. C., & Tripathi, R. C. (1974). An analysis of situational moderating effects on the relationships between least preferred co-worker and other psychological measures. *Journal of Applied Psychology, 59,* 731–740.

Sattler, J. M. (1970). Racial "experimenter effects" in experimentation, testing, interviewing, and psychotherapy. *Psychological Bulletin, 73,* 137–160.

Saucier, G. (1994). Mini-markers: A brief version of Goldberg's unnipolar big-five markers. *Journal of Personality Assessment, 6,* 506–516.

Saunders, J., Davis, J., & Monsees, D. M. (1974). Opinion leadership in family planning. *Journal of Health and Social Behavior, 15,* 217–227.

Saunders, R. M. (1985). Military force in the policy of the Eisenhower administration. *Political Science Quarterly, 100*(1), 97–116.

Saudino, K. J., & Cherny, S. S. (2001). Sources of continuity and change in observed temperament. In R. Emde (ed.), *The transition from infancy to early childhood: Genetic and environmental influences.* New York: Cambridge University Press.

Saunders, C. S., & Scamell, R. (1982). Intraorganizational distributions of power: Replication research. *Academcy of Management journal, 25,*192–200.

Savage, G. T., Nix, T. W., Whitehead, C. J., et al. (1991). Strategies for assessing and managing organizational stakeholders. *Academy of Management Executive, 5*(2), 61–74.

Savan, M. (1983). The effects of a leadership training program on supervisory learning and performance. *Dissertation Abstracts International, 45*(4A), 1193.

Savard, C. J., & Rogers, R. W. (1992). A self-efficacy and subjective expected utility theory analysis of the selection and use of influence strategies. *Journal of Social Behavior and Personality, 7,* 273–292.

Savery, L. K., & Waters, H. J. (1989). Influence and trust in a multinational company. *Journal of Managerial Psychology* (U.K.), *4*(3), 23–26.

Saville, P. (1984). Occupational personality questionnaires. *Personnel Management, 16*(2), 47.

Sayles, L. R. (1958). *Behavior of industrial work groups.* New York: Wiley.

Sayles, L. R. (1964). *Managerial behavior: Administration in complex organizations.* New York: McGraw-Hill.

Sayles, L. R. (1979). *Leadership: What effective managers really do and how they do it.* New York: McGraw-Hill.

Sayles, L. R. (1984). The unsung profession. *Issues & Observations, 4*(2), 1–4.

Sayles, L. R. (1999). Managerial behavior and a journey through time. *Leadership Quarterly 10,* 7–11. (Reprinted from L. R. Sayles, 1979).

Sayles, L. R., & Wright, R. V. L. (1985). The use of culture in strategic management. *Issues & Observations, 5*(4), 1–9.

Scandura, T. A. (1998). Dysfunctional mentoring relationships and outcomes. *Journal of Management, 24,* 449–467.

Scandura, T. A., & Dorfman, P. (2004). Leadership research in an international and cross-cultural context. *Leadership Quarterly, 15,* 277–307.

Scandura, T. A., Graen, G. B., & Novak, M. A. (1986). When managers decide not to decide autocratically: An investigation of leader-member exchange and decision influence. *Journal of Applied Psychology, 71,* 579–585.

Scandura, T. A., & Schriesheim, C. A. (1994). Leader-member exchange and supervisor career mentoring as complementary constructs in leadership research. *Academy of Management Journal, 37,* 1588–1602.

Scandura, T. A., & Tejeda, M. J. (2003). *An investigation of leader-member-exchange: Organizational justice and performance.* Paper, Society for Industrial and Organizational Psychology, Orlando, FL.

Schachter, S. (1951). Deviation, rejection, and communication. *Journal of Abnormal and Social Psychology, 46,* 190–207.

Schachter, S., Willerman, B., Festinger, L., & Hyman, R. (1961). Emotional disruption and industrial productivity. *Journal of Applied Psychology, 45,* 201–213.

Schanck, R. L. (1932). A study of a community and its group and institutions conceived of behavior of individuals. *Psychological Monographs, 43,* No. 2.

Schatzberg, M. G. (1982). *Le mal Zairois:* Why policy fails in Zaire. *African Affairs, 81,* 337–348.

Schaubroeck, J., & Lam, S. S. K. (2002). How similarity to peers and supervisors influences organizational advancement in different cultures. *Academy of Management Journal, 45*(6), 1120–1136.

Scheffler, I., & Winslow, C. N. (1950). Group position and attitude toward authority. *Journal of Social Psychology, 32,* 177–190.

Scheidlinger, S. (1980). The psychology of leadership revisited: An overview. *Group, the Journal of the Eastern Group Psychotherapy Society, 4,* 1–17.

Schein, E. H. (1965). *Organizational psychology.* Englewood Cliffs, NJ: Prentice-Hall.

Schein, E. H. (1967). Attitude change during management education. *Administrative Science Quarterly, 11,* 601–628.

Schein, E. H. (1983). The role of the founder in creating organizational culture. *Organizational Dynamics, 12,* 13–28.

Schein, E. H. (1985). *Organizational culture and leadership: A dynamic view.* San Francisco: Jossey-Bass.

Schein, E. H. (1990). *Career anchors: Discovering your real values.* San Diego, CA: Pfeiffer & Co.

Schein, E. H. (1992). *Organizational culture and leadership.* San Francisco: Jossey-Bass.

Schein, E. (1995). *Organizational and managerial culture as a facilitator or inhibitor of organizational transformation.* Cambridge, MA: MIT Sloan School of Management, Working Paper 3831, July.

Schein, E. H. (1996). Career anchors revised: Implications for career development in the 21st century. *The Academy of Management Executive. Briarcliff Manor, 10*(4), 80–88.

Schein, E. H., & Bennis, W. C. (1965). *Personal and organizational change through group methods.* New York: Wiley.

Schein, E. H., & Lippitt, G. L. (1966). Supervisory attitudes toward the legitimacy of influencing subordinates. *Journal of Applied Behavioral Science, 2,* 199–209.

Schein, E. H., & Ott, J. S. (1962). The legitimacy of organizational influence. *American Journal of Sociology, 67,* 682–689.

Schein, V. E. (1973). The relationship between sex role stereotypes and requisite management characteristics. *Journal of Applied Psychology, 57*, 95–100.

Schein, V. E. (1975). The relationship between sex role stereotypes and requisite management characteristics among female managers. *Journal of Applied Psychology 60*, 340–44.

Schein, V. E. (1989). Would women lead differently? In W. E. Rosenbach & R. L. Taylor (eds.), *Contemporary Issues in Leadership* (2nd ed.). Boulder, CO: Westview Press.

Schein, V. E., Mueller, R., Lituchy, T., et al. (1996). Think manager—think male: A global phenomenon? *Journal of Organizational Behavior, 17*(1), 33–41.

Schell, H. (1951). *Technique of administration: Administrative proficiency in business.* New York: McGraw-Hill.

Schendel, D. G., Patton, C. R., & Riggs, J. (1976). Corporate turnaround strategies: A study of profit decline and recovery. *Journal of General Management, 3i* 3–11.

Schenk, C. (1928). Leadership. *Infantry Journal, 33*, 111–122.

Schere, J. L. (1981). Tolerance of ambiguity as a discriminating variable between entrepreneurs and managers. *Proceedings, Academy of Management,* San Diego, CA, 404–408.

Schiffer, I. (1973). *A psychoanalytic look at mass society.* Toronto: University of Toronto Press.

Schiffer, I. (1983). *Charisma: A psychoanalytic look at mass society.* Toronto: University of Toronto Press.

Schiffman, L. G., & Gaccione, V. (1974). Opinion leaders in institutional markets. *Journal of Marketing, 38*, 49–53.

Schilit, W. K. (1987). Upward influence activity in strategic decision making: An examination of organizational differences. *Group & Organization Studies, 12*, 343–368.

Schilit, W. K., & Locke, E. A. (1982). A study of upward influence in organizations. *Administrative Science Quarterly, 27*, 304–316.

Schippmann, J. S., & Prien, E. P. (1986). Psychometric evaluation of an integrated assessment procedure. *Psychological Reports, 59*, 111–122.

Schippmann, J. S., Prien, E. P., & Hughes, G. L. (1991). The content of managerial work: Formation of task and job skill composite classifications. *Journal of Business and Psychology, 5*, 723–736.

Schlenker, B. (1980). *Impression management: The self-concept, social identity, and interpersonal relations.* Monterey, CA: Brooks/Cole.

Schlesinger, A., Jr. (1999). Witness to the century: The glorious and the damned. *AARP Bulletin, 40*, 11, 15.

Schlesinger, L., Jackson, J. M., & Butman, J. (1960). Leader-member interaction in management committees. *Journal of Abnormal and Social Psychology, 61*, 360–364.

Schmidt, F. L., & Hunter, J. E. (1977). Development of a general solution to the problem of validity generalization. *Journal of Applied Psychology, 62*, 529–540.

Schmidt, F. L., & Hunter, J. E. (1974). Racial and ethnic bias in psychological tests: Divergent implications of two definitions of test bias. *American Psychologist, 28*, 1–8.

Schmidt, F. L., & Hunter, J. E. (1980). The future of criterion-related validity. *Personnel Psychology, 33*, 41–58.

Schmidt, F L., Hunter, J. E., & Urry, V. W. (1976). Statistical power in criterion-related validity studies. *Journal of Applied Psychology, 61*, 473–485.

Schmidt, F. L., & Johnson, R. H. (1973). Effect of race on peer ratings in an industrial setting. *Journal of Applied Psychology, 57*, 237–241.

Schmidt, L. L., Wood, J., & Lugg, D. (2003). *A hierarchical model of team climate in an extreme climate.* Paper, Society for Industrial and Organizational Psychology, Orlando, FL.

Schmidt, R. E. (1985). Management in a leaderless environment. *Bureaucrat, 14*(3), 30–32.

Schmidt, S. M., & Kipnis, D. (1984). Managers' pursuit of individual and organizational goals. *Human Relations, 37*, 781–794.

Schmidt, S. M., & Yeh, R. (1992). The structure of leader influence: A cross-national comparison. *Journal of Cross-cultural Psychology, 23*, 251–264.

Schmidt, W. H., & Posner, B. Z. (1986). Values and expectations of federal service executives. *Public Administration Review, 46*(5), 447–454.

Schmitt, N. (1977). Interrater agreement in dimensionality and combination of assessment center judgments. *Journal of Applied Psychology, 62*, 171–176.

Schmitt, N. (1982). The uses of analysis of covariance structures to assess beta and gamma change. *Multivariate Behavioral Research, 17*, 343–358.

Schmitt, N., Noe, R. A., Merrit, R., & Fitzgerald, M. P. (1984). Validity of assessment center ratings for the prediction of performance ratings and school climate of school administrators. *Journal of Applied Psychology, 69*, 207–213.

Schnaars, S. (1994). *Managing imitation strategies.* New York: Free Press.

Schnake, M. E. (1986). Vicarious punishment in a work setting. *Journal of Applied Psychology, 71*, 343–345.

Schneer, J. A., & Reitman, F. (1997). *Women in the executive suite: Are they different from the good old boys?* Paper, Academy of Management, Boston, MA.

Schneider, B. (1973). The perception of organizational climate: The customer's view. *Journal of Applied Psychology, 57*, 248–256.

Schneider, B., Ehrhart, K. H., & Ehrhart, M. G. (2002). Understanding high school student leaders II. Peer nominations of leaders and their correlates. *Leadership Quarterly, 13*, 275–299.

Schneider, B., Paul, M. C., White, S. S., et al. (2002). Understanding high school leaders I. Predicting teacher ratings of leader behavior. *Leadership Quarterly, 13*, 609–636.

Schneider, D. J. (1973). Implicit personality theory: A review. *Psychological Bulletin, 79*, 294–309.

Schneider, D. J. (1981). Tactical self–presentations: Toward a broader conception. In J. T. Tedeschi (ed.), *Impression management and social psychological research.* New York: Academic Press.

Schneider, D. M. & Goldwasser, C. (1998). Be a model of change. *Management Review, 87*(3), 41–45.

Schneider, D. J., Hastorf, A. H., & Ellsworth, P. C. (1979). *Person perception.* Reading, MA: Addison-Wesley.

Schneider, J. (1937). The cultural situation as a condition for the achievement of fame. *American Sociology Review, 2*, 480–491.

Schneider, J., & Mitchel, J. O. (1980). Functions of life insurance agency managers and relationships with agency characteristics and managerial tenure. *Personnel Psychology, 33*, 795–808.

Schneider, S. L. (2001). In search of realistic optimism: Meaning, knowledge, and warm fuzziness. *American Psychologist, 56*, 250–263.

Schneier, C. E. (1978). The contingency model of leadership: An extension to emergent leadership and leader's sex. *Organizational Behavior and Human Performance, 21*, 220–239.

Schneier, C. E., & Bartol, K. M. (1980). Sex effects in emergent leadership. *Journal of Applied Psychology, 65*, 341–345.

Schon, D. A. (1963). Champions for radical new inventions. *Harvard Business Review, 41*(2), 77–86.

Schott, J. L. (1970). *The leader behavior of non-white principals in inner-city elementary schools with integrated teaching staffs under conditions of high and low morale.* Doctoral dissertation, Purdue University, Lafayette, IN.

Schrag, C. (1954). Leadership among prison inmates. *American Sociological Review, 19*, 37–42.

Schrage, H. (1965). The R & D entrepreneur: Profile of success. *Harvard Business Review, 43*(6), 56–61.

Schrank, W. R. (1968). The labeling effect of ability grouping. *Journal of Educational Research, 62*, 51–52.

Schriesheim, C. A. (1979a). The similarity of individual directed and group directed leader behavior descriptions. *Academy of Management Journal, 22*, 345–355.

Schriesheim, C. A. (1979b). Social desirability and leader effectiveness. *Journal of Social Psychology, 108*, 89–94.

Schriesheim, C. A. (1982). The great high consideration–high initiating structure leadership myth: Evidence on its generalizability. *Journal of Social Psychology, 116*, 221–228.

Schriescheim, C. A. (1995). Multivariate and moderated within—and between—entity analysis (WABA) using hierarchical linear multiple regression. *Leadership Quarterly, 6*, 1–18.

Schriesheim, C. A. (2003). Why leadership research is generally irrelevant for leadership development. In S. E. Murphy & R. E. Riggio (eds.), *The future of leadership development.* Mahwah, NJ: Lawrence Erlbaum & Associates.

Schriesheim, C. A., Bannister, B. D., & Money, W. H. (1979). Psychometric properties of the LPC scale: An extension of Rice's review. *Academy of Management Review, 4*, 287–290.

Schriesheim, C. A., Castro, S. L., & Cogliser, C. C. (1997). *Leader-member-exchange (LMX). research: A comprehensive review of theory, measurement, and data-analytic practices.* Paper, Society for Industrial and Organizational Psychology, Boston, MA.

Schriesheim, C. A., Castro, S. L., Zhou, X. T., et al. (2002). The folly of theorizing "A" but testing "B": A selective level-of-analysis review of the field and a detailed leader-member exchange illustration. *Leadership Quarterly, 12*, 515–555.

Schriesheim, C. A., Castro, S. L., & Yammarino, F. J. (2000). Investigating contingencies: An examination of the impact of span of supervision and upward controllingness on leader-member exchange using traditional and multivariate within- and between-entities analysis. *Journal of Applied Psychology, 85*, 659–677.

Schriesheim, C. A., & DeNisi, A. S. (1978). *The impact of implicit theories on the validity of questionnaires.* Unpublished manuscript.

Schriesheim, C. A., & DiNisi, A. S. (1981). Task dimensions as moderators of the effects of instrumental leadership: A two-sample replicated test of path-goal leadership theory. *Journal of Applied Psychology, 66*, 589–597.

Schriesheim, C. A., & Hinken, T. R. (1986). *Influence tactics used by subordinates: A theoretical and empirical analysis and refinement of the Kipnis, Schmidt, and Wilkinson subscales.* Paper, Academy of Management, San Diego, CA.

Schriesheim, C. A., Hinken, T., & Podsakoff, P. M. (1991). Can ipsative and single-item measures produce erroneous results in French and Rasven's (1959) five bases of power? An empirical investigation. *Journal of Applied Psychology, 76*, 106–114.

Schriesheim, C. A., Hinken, T. R., & Tetrault, L. A. (1988). *The validity of measuring "leader" reinforcement behavior by questionnaire: An examination of the leader reward and punishment questionnaire (LRPQ).* Unpublished manuscript.

Schriesheim, C. A., & Hosking, D. (1978). Review essay of Fiedler, F. E., Chemers, M. M., & Mahar, L. Improving leadership effectiveness: the leader match concept. *Administrative Science Quarterly, 23*, 496–505.

Schriesheim, C. A., House, R. J., & Kerr, S. (1976). Leader initiating structure: A reconciliation of discrepant research results and some empirical tests. *Organizational Behavioral and Human Performance, 15*, 297–321.

Schriesheim, C. A., & Kerr, S. (1974). Psychometric properties of the Ohio State leadership scales. *Psychological Bulletin, 81*, 756–765.

Schriesheim, C. A., & Kerr, S. (1977b). Theories and measures of leadership: A critical appraisal of present and future directions. In J. G. Hunt & L. L. Larson (eds.), *Leadership: The cutting edge.* Carbondale: Southern Illinois University Press.

Schriesheim, C. A., Kinicki, A. J., & Schriesheim, J. F. (1979). The effect of leniency of leader behavior descriptions. *Organizational Behavioral and Human Performance, 23*, 1–29.

Schriesheim, C. A., Mowday, R. T., & Stogdill, R. M. (1979). Crucial dimensions of leader-group interactions. In J. G. Hunt & L. L. Larson (eds.), *Cross-currents in leadership.* Carbondale: Southern Illinois University Press.

Schriesheim, C. A., & Murphy, C. J. (1976). Relationship between leader behavior and subordinate satisfaction and performance: A test of some situational moderators. *Journal of Applied Psychology, 61*, 634–641.

Schriesheim, C. A., & Neider, L. L. (1988a). *The coming new phase of leadership theory and development.* Unpublished manuscript.

Schriesheim, C. A., and Neider, L. L. (1988). Making leadership effective: A three stage model. *Journal of Management Development. Special Issue: Developing leadership excellence 7*(5), 10–20.

Schriesheim, C. A., & Neider, L. L. (1988b). *Distinctions among subtypes of perceived delegation and leadership decision making: A theoretical and empirical analysis.* Paper, Society for Industrial and Organizational Psychology, Atlanta, GA.

Schriesheim, C. A., & Neider, L. L. (1988c). *Subtypes of management delegation: An extension of the Vroom and Yetton conceptualization.* Unpublished manuscript.

Schriesheim, C. A., Neider, L., & Scandura, T. A. (1998). Delegation and leader-member exchange: Main effects, moderators, and meadurement scales. *Academy of Management Journal, 41*, 298–318.

Schriesheim, J. F. & Schriesheim, C. A. (1980). A test of the path-goal theory of leadership and some suggested directions for future research. *Personnel Psychology 33*(2), 349–370.

Schriesheim, C. A., & Stogdill, R. M. (1975). Differences in factor structure across three versions of the Ohio State leadership scales. *Personnel Psychology, 28*, 189–206.

Schriesheim, C. A., Tepper, B. J., & Tetrault, L. A. (1988). *The validity of drawing across-octant conclusions from the contingency model of leadership effectiveness: Critique and analysis.* Unpublished manuscript.

Schriesheim, C. A., & Von Glinow, M. A. (1977). The path goal theory of leadership: A theoretical and empirical analysis. *Academy of Management journal, 20,* 398–405.

Schriesheim, J. F. (1980). The social context of leader–subordinate relations: An investigation of the effects of group cohesiveness. *Journal of Applied Psychology, 65,* 183–193.

Schroder, H. M., Driver, M. J., & Streufert, S. (1967). *Human information processing.* New York: Holt, Rinehart, & Winston.

Schroder, H. M., Streufert, S., & Welden, D. C. (1964). *The effect of structural abstractness in interpersonal stimuli on the leadership role* (Tech. Rep. No. 3). Princeton, NJ: Princeton University, Office of Naval Research.

Schruijer, S. G. L. (1997). Management of meaning in early medieval Europe. In D. Cariani & A. Delle Fratte (eds.), *Quaderni di Psicologia del Lavoro, 5,* 55–59.

Schruijer, S. G. L., & Hendriks, M. (1996). Managers' life goals and their wiliness to accept an international assignment. *European Journal of Work and Organizational Psychology, 5,* 541–554.

Schruijer, S. G. L., & Lemmers, L. (1996). Explanations and evaluations of Turks and Dutchmen of norm violating ingroup and outgroup behavior. *Journal of Community and Applied Social Psychology, 6,* 101–107.

Schubert, A., & Arline, F. (1974). *A study of nonverbal communication and leadership emergence in task-oriented and informal small group discussions.* Paper, International Communication Association, New Orleans, LA.

Schuler, R. S. (1975). Sex, organizational level, and outcome importance: Where the differences are. *Personnel Psychology, 28,* 365–376.

Schuler, R. S., & Rogovsky, N. (1998). Understanding compensation practice variations across firms: The impact of national culture. *Journal of International Business Studies, 29*(1), 159–77.

Schumer, H. (1962). Cohesion and leadership in small groups as related to group productivity. *Dissertation Abstracts, 22,* 3735–3736.

Schutz, W. C. (1955). What makes groups productive? *Human Relations, 8,* 465–499.

Schutz, W. C. (1961b). The ego, FIRO theory, and the leader as completer. In L. Petrullo & B. M. Bass (eds.), *Leadership and interpersonal behavior.* New York: Holt, Rinehart & Winston.

Schutz, W. C., & Allen, V. L. (1966). The effects of a T-group laboratory on interpersonal behavior. *Journal of Applied Behavioral Science, 2,* 265–286.

Schwartz, A. R., & Hoyman, M. M. (1984). The changing of the guard: The new American labor leader. *Annals of the American Academy of Political and Social Science, 473,* 64–75.

Schwartz, B. (1983). George Washington and the Whig conception of heroic leadership. *American Sociological Review, 48,* 18–33.

Schwartz, E. B. & Waetjen, W. B. (1976). Improving the Self-Concept of Women Managers. *Business Quarterly, 41*(4), 20–27.

Schwartz, F. C., Stillwell, W. P., & Scanlon, B. K. (1968). Effects of management development on manager behavior and subordinate perception. *Training & Development Journal, 22*(4), 38–50.

Schwartz, K. B., & Menon, K. (1985). Executive succession in failing firms. *Academy of Management Journal, 28,* 680–686.

Schwartz, M. M., Jenusaitis, E., & Stark, H. F. (1966). A comparison of the perception of job-related needs in two industry groups. *Personnel Psychology, 19,* 185–194.

Schwartz, M. M., & Levine, H. (1965). Union and management leaders: A comparison. *Personnel Administration, 28*(3), 44–47.

Schwartz, S. H. (1992). Universals in the content and structure of values: Theoretical advances and empirical tests in 20 countries. In M. P. Zanna (ed.), *Advances in experimental social psychology.* San Diego: CA: Academic Press.

Schwartz, S. H. (1999). Cultural value differences: Some implications for work. *Applied Psychology: An International Review, 48,* 23–47.

Schwartz, S. H., & Sagie, G. (2000). Value consensus and importance: A crossnational study. *Journal of Cross-Cultural Psychology, 31*(4), 465–97.

Schwartzbaum, A., & Gruenfeld, L. (1969). Factors influencing subjec-tobserver interaction in an organizational study. *Administrative Science Quarterly, 14,* 443–449.

Schwarzwald, J., & Koslowsky, M. (1998). *Captain's leadership type and police officers' compliance to power sources.* San Francisco, CA: American Psychological Association.

Schwarzwald, J., Koslowsky, M., & Mager-Bibi, T. (1999). Peer ratings versus peer nominations during training as predictors of actual performance criteria. *Journal of Applied Behavioral Science, 35,* 360–372.

Schweiger, D. M., Ivancevich, J. M., & Power, F. R. (1987). Executive actions for managing human resources before and after acquisition. *Academy of Management Executive, 1*(2), 127–138.

Schweiger, D. M., & Jago, A. G. (1982). Problem-solving styles and participative decision making. *Psychology Reports, 50,* 1311–1316.

Schweitzer, A. (1984). *The age of charisma.* Chicago: Nelson-Hall.

Schyns, B., & Mohr, G. (2004). Non-verbal elements of leadership behaviour. *German Journal of Human Resources Management, 18,* 1–17.

Scioli, F. P., Dyson, J. W., & Fleitas, D. W. (1974). The relationship of personality and decisional structure to leadership. *Small Group Behavior, 5,* 3–22.

Scott, D., & Moore, M. L. (1981). An assessment of a management by objectives program by black and white managers, supervisors, and professionals. *Proceedings, Academy of Management,* San Diego, CA, 219–223.

Scott, E. L. (1956). *Leadership and perceptions of organization.* Columbus: Ohio State University, Bureau of Business Research.

Scott, K. A., & Brown, D. J. (2006). Female first, leader second: Gender bias in the encoding of leadership behavior. *Organizational Behavior and Human Decision Processes, 101*(2), 230–242.

Scott, K. L. (2003). *CEOs and effective strategic leadership: A matter of cognitive differences?* Paper, Academy of Management, Seattle, WA.

Scott, L. K. (1978). Charismatic authority in the rational organization. *Educational Administration Quarterly, 14*(2), 43–62.

Scott, M. D., McCroskey, J. C., & Sheahan, M. E. (1978). Measuring communication apprehension. *Journal of Communication, 28*(1), 104–111.

Scott, S. G., & Bruce, R. A. (1994). Determinants of innovative behavior: A path model of individual innovation in the workplace. *Academy of Management Journal, 37,* 580–607.

Scott, S. G., & Bruce, R. A. (1998). Following the leader in R&D: The joint effect of subordinate problem-solving style and leader-member relations on innovative behavior. *IEEE Transactions in Engineering Management, 45,* 3–10.

Scott, W. A. (1967). *Organizational theory: A behavioral analysis for management.* Homewood, IL: Irwin.

Scott, W. E. (1965). Some motivational determinants of work behavior. *Indiana Business Information Bulletin, 54,* 116–131.

Scott, W. E. (1977). Leadership: A functional analysis. In J. G. Hunt & L. L. Larson (eds.), *Leadership: The cutting edge.* Carbondale: Southern Illinois University Press.

Scott, W. E., Jr., & Podsakoff, F. M. (1982). Leadership, supervision and behavioral control: Perspectives from an experimental analysis. In L. Frederickson (ed.), *Handbook of organizational behavior management.* New York: Wiley.

Scott, W. G., & Hart, D. K. (1991). The exhaustion of managerialism. *Society,* March–April, 39–48.

Scruton, R. (2002). The political problem of Islam. *The Intercollegiate Review, 38*(1), 3–16.

Scullen, S. E., Mount, M. K., & Sytsma, M. R. (1996). *Comparisons of self, peer, direct report and boss ratings of managers' performance.* Poster, Society for Industrial and Organizational Psychology, San Diego, CA.

Scullion, H. (1992). Strategic recruitment and development of the international manager: Some European considerations. *Human Resources Management Journal, 3,* 57–69.

Scully, J. A., Sims, H. P., Olian, J. D., et al. (1994). Tough times make tougher bosses: A MESO analysis of CEO leader behavior. *Leadership Quarterly.*

Scully, M. (1973). The 55 sheepish goats of Dr. Fox. *Chronicle of Higher Education, 8*(4), 1–5.

Seaman, D. F. (1981). *Working effectively with task-oriented groups.* New York: McGraw-Hill.

Seashore, S. E. (1954). *Group cohesiveness in the industrial work group.* Ann Arbor: University of Michigan, Institute for Social Research.

Seashore, S. E., & Bowers, D. G. (1963). *Changing the structure and functioning of an organization.* Ann Arbor: University of Michigan, Institute for Social Research.

Seashore, S. E., & Bowers, D. G. (1970). Durability of organization change. *American Psychologist, 25,* 227–233.

Seath, I., & Clark, J. (1993). A clean cut vision of progression. *Managing Service Quality, 9*(7), 11–13.

Sedge, S. K. (1985). A comparison of engineers pursuing alternate career paths. *Journal of Vocational Behavior, 27,* 56–70.

Sedring, D. D. (1969). Models and images of man and society in leadership theory. *Journal of Politics, 31*(1), 1–31.

Seeman, M. (1950). Some status correlates of leadership. In A. G. Grace (ed.), *Leadership in American education.* Chicago: University of Chicago Press.

Seeman, M. (1953). Role conflict and ambivalence in leadership. *American Sociological Review, 18,* 373–380.

Seeman, M. (1957). A comparison of general and specific leader be-

havior descriptions. In R. M. Stogdill & E. A. Coons (eds.), *Leader behavior: Its description and measurement.* Columbus: Ohio State University, Bureau of Business Research.

Seeman, M. (1960). *Social status and leadership—the case of the school executive.* Columbus: Ohio State University, Educational Research Monograph No. 35.

Seers, A. (1989). Team-member exchange quality: A new construct for role-making research. *Organizational Behavior and Human Decision Processes, 43,* 118–135.

Seers, A., Petty, M. M., & Cashman, J. F. (1995). Team-member exchange under team and traditional management: A naturally occurring quasi-experiment. *Group & Organization Management, 20*(1), 18–38.

Seers, A. (2002). *Rethinking leadership in self-directing teams.* Paper, Academy of Management, Denver, CO.

Seers, A., & Graen, G. B. (1984). The dual attachment concept: A longitudinal investigation of the combination of task characteristics and leader-member exchange. *Organizational Behavior & Human Performance, 33,* 283–306.

Segal, A. T., & Zellner, W. (1992). Corporate women: Progress? Sure, but the playing field is still far from level. *Business Week,* June 8, 74–78.

Seibert, S., & Sparrowe, R. T. (2002). *A group exchange structure approach to leadership in groups.* Paper, Academy of Management, Denver, CO.

Seifert, C. M. (1984). Reactions to leaders: Effects of sex of leader, sex of subordinate, method of leader selection and task outcome. *Dissertation Abstracts International, 45*(12B), 3999.

Selekman, B. M. (1947). *Labor relations and human relations.* New York: McGraw-Hill.

Selden, M. (1971). *The Yenan way in revolutionary China.* Cambridge, MA: Harvard University Press.

Seligman, M. E. P. *Learned optimism.* New York: Pocket Books.

Seligman, M. E. P. (1998). The president's address. In APA 1998 Annual Report at www.positivepsychology.org.

Sells, S. B. (1968). The nature of organizational climate. In R. Tagiuri & G. L. Litwin (eds.), *Organizational climate: Explorations of a concept.* Cambridge, MA: Harvard University Press.

Sels, L., Janssens, M., et al. (2000). Belgium: A culture of compromise. In D. M. Rousseau & R.Schalk (eds.), *Psychological contracts in employment: Cross-national perspectives.* Thousand Oaks, CA: Sage Publications.

Seltzer, J., & Bass, B. M. (1987). *Leadership is more than initiation and consideration.* Paper, American Psychological Association, New York, NY.

Seltzer, J., & Bass, B. M. (1990). Transformational leadership: Beyond initiation and consideration. *Journal of Management, 16,* 693–703.

Seltzer, J., & Miller, L. E. (1990). *Leader behavior and subordinate empowerment in a human service organization.* Paper, Academy of Management, San Francisco, CA.

Seltzer, J., & Numerof, R. E. (1988). Supervisory leadership and subordinate burnout. *Academy of Management Journal, 31,* 439–446.

Seltzer, J., Numerof, R. E., & Bass, B. M. (1987). *Transformational leadership: Is it a source of more or less burnout or stress?* Paper, Academy of Management, New Orleans. Also: *Journal of Health and Human Resources Administration* (in press).

Seltzer, J., Numerof, R., & Bass, B. M. (1989). Transformational leadership: Is it a source of more burnout and stress? *Journal of Health and Human Resources Administration, 12,* 174–185.

Selvin, H. C. (1960). *The effects of leadership.* New York: Free Press.

Selznick, P. (1943). An approach to a theory of bureaucracy. *American Sociological Review, 8,* 47–54.

Selznick, F. (1957). *Leadership in administration: A sociological interpretation.* Evanston, IL: Row, Peterson.

Senge, P. (1980). *System dynamics and leadership* (Working Paper D3263). Cambridge: Massachusetts Institute of Technology, System Dynamics Group.

Senge, P. (1984). *Systems thinking and the new management style* (Working Paper D-3586–2). Cambridge, MA: Massachusetts Institute of Technology, System Dynamics Group.

Senge, P. (1986). Systems principles for leadership. In J. D. Adams (ed.), *Transforming leadership.* Alexandria, VA: Miles River Press.

Senge, P. M. (1995). Robert Greenleaf's legacy: A new foundation for twenty-first century institutions. *Reflections on leadership: How Robert K. Greenleaf's theory of servant-leadership influenced today's top management thinkers.* New York, NY: John Wiley and Sons, 217–40.

Senge, P. M. (1990). *The fifth discipline: The art and practice of the learning organization.* New York: Doubleday.

Senge, P. (1997). Communities of leaders and learners. *Harvard Business Review, 75* (5), 30–32.

Senger, J. (1971). Managers' perceptions of subordinates' competence as a function of personal value orientation. *Academy of Management Journal, 14,* 415–423.

Senneker, P., & Hendrick, C. (1983). Androgyny and helping behavior. *Journal of Personality and Social Psychology, 45,* 916–925.

Senner, E. E. (1971). *Trust as a measure of the impact of cultural differences on individual behavior in organizations.* Paper, American Psychological Association, Washington, DC.

Seppa, N. (1997). Sexual harassment in the military lingers on. *APA Monitor, 28*(5),

Sequeira, C. E. (1964). Functions of a supervisor. *Indian Journal of Applied Psychology, 1,* 46–54.

Serafini, D. M., & Pearson, J. C. (1984). Leadership behavior and sex role socialization: Two sides of the same coin. *Southern Speech Communication Journal, 49,* 396–405.

Sergiovanni, T. J. (1992). Why we should seek substitutes for leadership. *Educational Leadership,* February, 41–45.

Sessa, V. (1999). *Interpersonal skills: The sine qua non factor in the success of executives at the very top.* Paper, Society for Industrial and Organizational Psychology, Atlanta, GA.

Severance, L. (1988). How two fat guys got a big scoop of a hot market. *Chicago Tribune,* July 10, Section 5, 6.

Seversky, P. M. (1982). Trust, need to control, and the tendency to delegate: A study of the delegation behavior of superintendents. *Dissertation Abstracts International, 43*(9A), 2851.

Sexton, W. P. (1967). Organizational and individual needs: A conflict? *Personnel Journal, 46,* 337–343.

Sgro, J. A., Worchel, P., Pence, E. C., & Orban, J. A. (1980). Perceived leader behavior as a function of the leader's interpersonal trust orientation. *Academy of Management Journal, 23,* 161–165.

Shackleton,V. J. (1995). *Business Leadership.* Part of the Essential Business Psychology Series. UK: Cengage Learning.

Shackelton, V. J. (2001). *Business leadership.* London: Routledge-Paul.

Shackleton, V. J. (1990). *How to pick people for jobs.* London: Fontana.

Shackleton, V. J., Bass, B. M., & Allison, S. N. (1975). *PAXIT.* Scottsville, NY: Transnational Programs.

Shackleton, V. J., Bass, B. M., & Allison, S. E. (1982). *Survival: The impact of leadership style.* San Diego, CA: University Associates.

Shalley, C. E., & Gilson, L. L. (2004). What leaders need to know: A review of social and contextual factors that can foster or hinder creativity. *Leadership Quarterly, 15,* 33–54.

Shama, A. (1993). Management under fire: The transformation of managers in the Soviet Union and Eastern Europe. *Academy of Management Executive, 7*(1), 22–35.

Shamir, B. (1990). Calculations, values and identities: The sources of collectivistic work motivation. *Human Relations, 43,* 313–332.

Shamir, B. (1991). The charismatic relationship: Alternative explanations and predictions. *Leadership Quarterly, 2,* 81–104.

Shamir, B. (1992). Attribution of influence and charisma to the leader: The romance of leadership revisited. *Journal of Applied Social Psychology, 22,* 386–407.

Shamir, B. (1993). *Kellogg leadership program.* Unpublished evaluation.

Shamir, B. (1994). Ideological position, leaders' charisma, and voting preferences: Personal vs. partisan elections. *Political Behavior, 16,* 265–287.

Shamir, B. (1995). Social distance and charisma: Theoretical notes and an exploratory study. *Leadership Quarterly, 6,* 19–47.

Shamir, B. (1999) Leadership in boundaryless organizations: Disposable or indipensible? *European Journal of Work and Organizational Psychology, 8,* 49–72.

Shamir, B., Arthur, M. B., & House, R. J. (1994). The rhetoric of charismatic leadership: Theoretical extension and a case study. *Leadership Quarterly, 5,* 25–42.

Shamir, B., House, R. J., & Arthur, M. B. (1988). *The transformational effects of charismatic leadership: A motivational theory.* Unpublished manuscript.

Shamir, B., House, R. J., & Arthur, M.B. (1993). The motivation effects of charismatic leadership: A self-concept based theory. *Organization Science, 4,* 584–594.

Shamir, B., & Howell, J. M. (1999). Organizational and contextual influences on the emergence and effectiveness of charismatic leadership. *Leadership Quarterly, 10,* 257–283.

Shamir, B., & Howell, J. M. (2005). The role of followers in the charismatic leadership process: Susceptibility, social construction, and leader empowerment. *Academy of Management Review,* 96–112.

Shamir, B., Zakay, E., Breinin, E., et al. (1998). Correlates of charismatic leadership behavior in military units: Subordinate attitudes, unit characteristics and superiors' assessments of leaders' performance. *Academy of Management Journal, 41,* 387–409.

Shamir, B., Zackay, E., Breinin, E., et al. (2000). Leadership and social identification in military units: Direct and indirect relationships. *Journal of Applied Social Psychology, 30,* 612–640.

Shane, S. A. (1993). Cultural influences on national rates of innovation. *Journal of Business Venturing, 8,* 59–73.

Shane, S. A., Venkataraman, S., & MacMillan, I. C. (1995). Cultural influences in innovation championing strategies. *Journal of Management, 21,* 931–952.

Shapira, Z. (1975). *Expectancy determinants of intrinsically motivated behavior.* Doctoral dissertation, University of Rochester, Rochester, NY.

Shapira, Z. (1976). A facet analysis of leadership styles. *Journal of Applied Psychology, 61,* 136–139.

Shapira, Z. (1997). *Risk taking: A managerial perspective.* New York: Russell Sage Foundation.

Shapira, Z. (2000). Governance in organizations; A cognitive perspective. *Journal of Management and Governance, 4,* 53–67.

Shapira, Z. (in press). Behavioral decision theory and organizational decision making. In G. Hodgkinson & W. Starbuck (eds.), *Handbook of organizational decision making.* Oxford University Press.

Shapira, Z., & Dunbar, R. L. M. (1978). Testing Mintzberg's managerial roles classification using an in-basket simulation. In B. M. Bass (ed.), *Stogdill's Handbook of leadership: A survey of theory and research.* New York, NY: The Free Press, 283.

Shapiro, D. L., Lewicki, R. J., & Devine, P. (1995). When do employees choose deceptive practices to stop unwanted change? A relational perspective. In R. J. Lewicki, B. Sheppard, & R. Bies (eds.), *Research on negotiations in organizations,* vol. 5. Greenwich, CT: JAI Press.

Shapiro, G. L. (1985). *Sex differences in mentoring functions received and valued by managers.* Paper, Academy of Management, San Diego, CA.

Shapiro, R. J., & Klein, R. H. (1975). Perceptions of the leaders in an encounter group. *Small Group Behavior, 6,* 238–248.

Sharf, B. F. (1978). A rhetorical analysis of leadership emergence in small groups. *Communication Monographs, 45,* 156–172.

Sharma, C. L. (1955). *Practices in decision-making as related to satisfaction in teaching.* Doctoral dissertation, University of Chicago, Chicago.

Sharma, P., & Rao, S. A. (2000). Successor attributes in Indian and Canadian family firms: A comparative study. *Family Business Review, 13,* 313–330.

Sharma, S. L. (1974). Social value orientations of activist student leaders: A comparative study. *Indian Journal of Social Work, 35,* 67–71.

Sharp-Paine, L. (1994). Managing for organizational integrity, *Harvard Business Review, 72*(2), March-April, 106–117.

Sharpe, R. T. (1956). Differences between perceived adminstrative behavior and role: Norms as factors in leadership evaluation and group morale. *Dissertation Abstracts, 16,* 57.

Shartle, C. L. (1934). A clinical approach to foremanship. *Personnel Journal, 13,* 135–139.

Shartle, C. L. (1949b). Leadership and executive performance. *Personnel, 25,* 370–380

Shartle, C. L. (1950b). Studies of leadership by interdisciplinary methods. In A. G. Grace (ed.), *Leadership in American education.* Chicago: University of Chicago Press.

Shartle, C. L. (1951a). Leader behavior in jobs. *Occupations, 30,* 164–166.

Shartle, C. L. (1951b). Studies in naval leadership. In H. Guetzkow (ed.), *Groups, leadership, and men.* Pittsburgh, PA: Carnegie Press.

Shartle, C. L. (1956). *Executive performance and leadership.* Englewood Cliffs, NJ: Prentice-Hall.

Shartle, C. L., Stogdill, R. M., & Campbell, D. T. (1949). *Studies in naval leadership.* Columbus: Ohio State University Research Foundation.

Shaw, C. E. (1976). *A comparative study of organizational climate and job satisfaction at selected public and Catholic secondary schools in Connecticut.* Doctoral dissertation, University of Connecticut, Storrs.

Shaw, E. R. (1965). The social distance factor and management. *Personnel Administration, 28,* 29–31.

Shaw, J. B., & Fisher, C. D. (1986). *Supervisor-subordinate agreement on performance feedback: A field study* (ONR Tech. Rep. No. 7). College Station, TX: Texas A & M University, Department of Management.

Shaw, J. B., & Weekley, J. A. (1985). The effects of objective work-load variations of psychological strain and post-work-load performance. *Journal of Management, 11,* 87–98.

Shaw, M. E. (1954a). Some effects of unequal distribution of information upon group performance in various communication nets. *Journal of Abnormal and Social Psychology, 49,* 547–553.

Shaw, M. E. (1954b). Some effects of problem complexity upon problem solving efficiency in different communication nets. *Journal of Experimental Psychology, 48,* 211–217.

Shaw, M. E. (1960). A note concerning homogeneity of membership and group problem solving. *Journal of Abnormal and Social Psychology, 60,* 448–450.

Shaw, M. E. (1961). A serial position effect in social influence on group decisions. *Journal of Social Psychology, 54,* 83–91.

Shaw, M. E. (1963a). Some effects of varying amounts of information exclusively possessed by a group member upon his behavior in the group. *Journal of General Psychology, 68,* 71–79.

Shaw, M. E., & Ashton, N. (1976). Do assembly bonus effects occur on disjunctive tasks? A test of Steiner's theory. *Bulletin of the Psychonomic Society, 8,* 469–491.

Shaw, M. E., & Blum, J. M. (1964). *Effects of leadership style upon group performance as a function of task structure.* Gainesville: University of Florida.

Shaw, M. E., & Blum, J. M. (1966). Effects of leadership style upon group performance as a function of task structure. *Journal of Personality and Social Psychology. 3*(2) 238–42.

Shaw, M. E., & Harkey, B. (1976). Some effects of congruency of member characteristics and group structure upon group behavior. *Journal of Personality and Social Psychology, 34,* 412–418.

Shaw, M. E., & Penrod, W. T. (1962). Does more information available to a group always improve group performance? *Sociometry, 25,* 377–390.

Shaw, M. E., & Rothschild, C. H. (1956). Some effects of prolonged experience in communication nets. *Journal of Applied Psychology, 40,* 281–286.

Shaw, M. E., Rothschild, C. H., & Strickland, J. F. (1957). Decision processes in communication nets. *Journal of Abnormal and Social Psychology, 54,* 323–330.

Shea, C. M. (1990). Who are the real leaders? There are natural, charismatic types and there are puppets manipulated by PR men: . . . the visionaries are sorted from the cardboard cutouts. *Evening Standard* (London), 24 September.

Shea, C. (1999). The effect of leadership style on performance improvement on a manufacturing task. *Journal of Business, 72,* 407–422.

Shea, C. M., & Howell, J.M. (1992). *Reconceptualizing the empowerment process.* Paper, Association des Sciences Administratives, Quebec, Canada.

Shea, C. M. & Howell, J. M. (1998). Organizational antecedents to the successful implementation of total quality management: A social cognitive perspective. *Journal of Quality Management, 3,* 3–24.

Shea, C. M., & Howell, J. M. (1999). Charismatic leadership and task feedback: Study of their effects on self-efficacy and task performance. *Leadership Quarterly, 10,* 375–396.

Shearer, R. L., & Steger, 1. A. (1975). Manpower obsolescence: A new definition and empirical investigation of personal variables. *Academy of Management Journal, 18,* 263–275.

Sheffer, G. (1993). *Innovative leaders in international politics.* New York: State University of New York Press.

Shelley, H. P. (1960a). Focused leadership and cohesiveness in small groups. *Sociometry, 23,* 209–216.

Shelley, H. P. (1960b). Status consensus, leadership, and satisfaction with the group. *Journal of Social Psychology, 51,* 157–164.

Shelton, C. K. (1982). *The relationship of mentoring and behavioral style to selected job success variables.* Unpublished Ph.D dissertation, University of Southern Illinois.

Shen, W. (2003). The dynamics of the CEO-board relationship: An evolutionary perspective. *Academy of Management Review.* 466–476.

Shenkar, O., Ronen, S. Shefy, E., et al. (1998). The role structure of Chinese managers. *Human Relations, 51,* 51–72.

Shenon, P. (1997). Sex harassment in Army "common": Leaders to blame says study team. *Denver Post,* September 12, 2a.

Shepard, H. A. (1964). Explorations in observant participation. In L. R Bradford, J. R. Gibb, & K. D. Berme (eds.), *T-group theory and laboratory method.* New York: Wiley.

Shepherd, C., & Weschler, I. R. (1955). The relation between three interpersonal variables and communication effectiveness: A pilot study. *Sociometry, 18,* 103–110.

Sheppard, B. H., & Sherman, D. M. (1998). The grammars of trust: A model and general implications. *Academy of Management Review, 23,* 422–437.

Shepperd, J. A. (1995). Remedying motivation and productivity loss in collective settings. *Current Directions in Psychological Science, 4*(5), 131–134.

Sheridan, J. E., Hogstel, M., Fairchild, I. J. (1985). *Contextual model of leadership influence on the job performance, absenteeism and turnover of nursing home staff* (Working Paper No. 2). Dallas: TX: Christian University, McNeeley School of Business.

Sheridan, J. E., Kerr, J. L., & Abelson, M. A. (1982). Leadership activation theory: An opponent process model of subordinate responses to leader behavior. In J. C. Hunt, V. Sekarian, & C. A. Schriesheim (eds.), *Leadership: Beyond establishment views.* Carbondale: Southern Illinois University Press.

Sheridan, J. E., & Vredenburgh, D. J. (1978a). Usefulness of leadership behavior and social power variables in predicting job tension,

performance, and turnover of nursing employees. *Journal of Applied Psychology, 63,* 89–95.

Sheridan, J. E., & Vredenburgh, D. J. (1979). Structural model of leadership influence in a hospital organization. *Academy of Management Journal, 22,* 6–21.

Sheridan, J. E., Vredenburgh, D. J., & Abelson, M. (1984). Contextual model of leadership influence in hospital units. *Academy of Management Journal, 27,* 57–78.

Sheridan, M. (1976). Young women leaders in China. Signs. *Journal of Women in Culture and Society, 2,* 59–88.

Sherif, D. R. (1969). *Administrative behavior: A quantitative case study of six organizations.* Iowa City: University of Iowa, Center of Labor and Management.

Sherif, M. (1936). *The psychology of social norms.* New York: Harper.

Sherif, M., & Sherif, C. W. (1964). *Reference groups: Explorations into conformity and deviations of adolescents.* New York: Harper & Row.

Sherif, M., & Sherif, C. W. (1953). *Groups in harmony and tension.* New York: Harper.

Sherif, M., & Sherif, C. W. (1956). *An outline of social psychology.* New York: Harper.

Sherif, M. (1967). *Social interaction: Process and products.* Chicago: Aldine.

Sherif, M., White, B. J., & Harvey, O. J. (1955). Status in experimentally produced groups. *American Journal of Sociology, 60,* 370–379.

Sherman, J. D., Ezell, H. F., & Odewahn, C. A. (1987). Centralization of decision making and accountability based on gender. *Group & Organization Studies, 12,* 454–463.

Sherony, K. M. (2003). *Leader emotional expression, leader gender and leader-member exchange.* Paper, Academy of Management, Seattle, WA.

Sherwood, C. E., & Walker, W. S. (1960). Role differentiation in real groups: An extrapolation of a laboratory small-group research finding. *Sociology and Social Research, 45,* 14–17.

Shields, S. A. (1975). Functionalism, Darwinism, and the psychology of women. *American Psychologist, 30,* 739–754.

Shiflett, S. C. (1973). The contingency model of leadership effectiveness: Some implications of its statistical and methodological properties. *Behavioral Science, 18,* 429–440.

Shiflett, S. C. (1974). Stereotyping and esteem for one's best preferred co-worker. *Journal of Social Psychology, 93,* 55–65.

Shiflett, S. C., & Nealey, S. M. (1972). The effects of changing leader power: A test of situational engineering. *Organizational Behavior and Human Performance, 7,* 371–382.

Shils, E. A. (1954). Authoritarianism: "right" and "left." In R. Christie & M. Jahoda (eds.), *Studies in the scope and method of "the authoritarian personality."* New York: Free Press.

Shils, E. A. (1965). Charisma, order, and status. *American Sociological Review, 30,* 199–213.

Shils, E. A., & Janowitz, M. (1948). Cohesion and disintegration of the Wehrmacht in World War II. *Public Opinion Quarterly, 12,* 280–315.

Shima, H. (1968). The relationship between the leader's modes of interpersonal cognition and the performance of the group. *Japanese Psychology Research, 10,* 13–30.

Shimada, H., & MacDuffie, J. P. (1986). *Industrial relations and "hu-*

manware": Japanese investments in automobile manufacturing in the United States. Working Paper No. 1855–87, Sloan School of Management, Massachusetts Institute of Technology, Cambridge, MA.

Shimizu, K., & Hitt, M. A. (2004). Strategic flexibility: Organizational preparedness to reverse ineffective strategic decisions. *Academy of Management Executive*, 18(4), 44–59.

Shipper, F., & Davy, J. (2002). A model and investigation of managerial skills, employees' attitudes, and managerial performance. *Leadership Quarterly*, 13, 95–120.

Shipper, F. M., Rotondo, D. M., & Hoffman, R. C. (2003). *A cross-cultural study of linkage between emotional intelligencew and managerial effectiveness*. Paper, Academy of Management, Seattle, WA.

Shipper, F., & Wilson, C. L. (1992). The impact of managerial behaviors on group performance, stress, and commitment. In K. E. Clark, M. B. Clark, & D. P. Campbell (eds.), *Impact of leadership*. Greensboro, NC: Center for Creative Leadership.

Shore, L. M., & Barksdale, K. (1988). Examining the degree of balance and level of obligation in the employment relationship: A social exchange approach. *Journal of Organizational Behavior*, 19, 731–744.

Shorey, P. (1933). *What Plato said*. Chicago: University of Chicago Press.

Short, J. A. (1973). *The effects of medium of communication on persuasion, bargaining, and perceptions of the other*. Cambridge, England: Post Office, Long Range Intelligence Division.

Shostrom, E. L. (1974). *POI manual: An inventory for the measurement of self-actualization*. San Diego, CA: Educational and Industrial Testing Service.

Shouksmith, C. (1987). Emerging personnel values in changing societies. In B. M. Bass, P. J. D. Drenth, & P. Weissenberg (eds.), *Advances in organizational psychology*. Beverly Hills, CA: Sage.

Shrivastava, P., & Nachman, S. A. (1989). Strategic leadership patterns. *Strategic Management Journal*, 51–66.

Shriver, B. (1952). *The behavioral effects of changes in ascribed leadership status in small groups*. Doctoral dissertation, University of Rochester, Rochester, NY.

Shull, F., & Anthony, W. P (1978). Do black and white supervisory problem solving styles differ? *Personnel Psychology*, 31, 761–782.

Shulman, K. R., & Jones, G. E. (1996). The effectiveness of massage therapy intervention on reducing anxiety in the workplace. *Journal of Applied Behavioral Science*, 32, 160–173.

Sibeck, G. P., & Stage, H. D. (2001). Aspects of comparative management in selected Mexican and Peruvian firms. *International Journal of Organizational Theory & Behavior*, 4(1–2), 91–101.

Siegall, M., & Cummings, L. L. (1986). Task role ambiguity, satisfaction, and the moderating effect of task instruction source. *Human Relations*, 39, 1017–1032.

Siegel, J., Dubrovsky, V., Kiesler, S., & McGuire, T. W. (1986). Group processes in computer mediated communication. *Organizational Behavior and Human Decision Processes*, 37, 157–187.

Siegel, J. P. (1973). *Reconsidering "consideration" in a leadership-path-goal interpretation of satisfaction and performance*. Toronto: University of Toronto. Unpublished manuscript.

Sievers, B. (1986). Beyond the surrogate of motivation. *Organization Studies*, 7, 335–351.

Silver, W. S., Mitchell, T. R., & Gist, M. E. (1991). *Interpreting performance information: The influence of self-efficacy on causal attributions for successful and unsuccessful performance*. Seattle, WA: University of Washington. Unpublished manuscript.

Silverman, B. R. (1983). Why the merit pay system failed in the federal government. *Personnel Journal*, 62, 294–302.

Silverthorne, C. (2001). Leadership effectiveness and personality: A cross-cultural evaluation. *Personality and Individual Differences*, 30, 303–310.

Simmons, B. L., & Nelson, D. L. (1997). *The diversity advantage?* Paper, Academy of Management, Boston, MA.

Simmons, R. C. (1968). The role conflict of the first-line supervisor: an experimental study. *American Journal of Sociology*, 73, 482–495.

Simon, H. (1987). Making management decisions: The role of intuition and emotion. *Academy of Management Executive*, 1(1), 57–64.

Simon, H. A. (1947). *Administrative behavior: A study of the decision-making process in administrative organization*. New York: Macmillan.

Simon, H. A. (1957). *Models of man*. New York: Wiley.

Simoneit, M. (1944). *Grundriss der charakterologischen Diagnostik*. Leipzig: Teubner.

Simons, H. W. (1970). Requirements, problems, and strategies: A theory of persuasion for social movements. *Quarterly Journal of Speech*, 56(1), 1–11.

Simons, T., Pelled, L. H., & Smith, K. A. (1999). Making use of difference, diversity, debate, and decision comprehension in top management teams. *Academy of Management Journal*, 42, 662–673.

Simonton, D. K. (1986). Presidential personality: Biographical use of the Gough Adjective Check List. *Journal of Personality and Social Psychology*, 51, 149–160.

Simonton, D. K. (1987). *Why presidents succeed: A political psychology of leadership*. New Haven: Yale University Press.

Simonton, D. (1988). Presidential style: Personality, biography, and performance. *Journal of Personality and Social Psychology*, 55, 928–936.

Simonton, D. K. (1999). Significant samples: The psychological study of eminent individuals. *Psychological Methods*, 4, 425–451.

Simpson, W. G., & Ireland, T. C. (1987). Managerial excellence and shareholder returns. *American Association of Individual Investors Journal*, 9, 4–8.

Sims, D., & Siew-Kim, J. L. (1993). Discovering an alternative view of managing: A study with Singaporean woman managers. *Applied Psychology: An International Review*, 42, 365–377.

Sims, H. P. (1977). The leader as manager of reinforcement contingencies: An empirical example and a model. In J. G. Hunt & L. L. Larson (eds.), *Leadership: The cutting edge*. Carbondale: Southern Illinois University Press.

Sims, H. P. (1980). Further thoughts on punishment in organizations. *Academy of Management Review*, 5, 133–138.

Sims, H. P., & Manz, C. C. (1981). Social learning theory: The role of modeling in the exercise of leadership. *Journal of Organizational Behavior Management*, 3(4), 55–63.

Sims, H. P., Jr., & Gioia, D. A. (1984). Performance failure: Executive response to self-serving bias. *Business Horizons*, 1, 64–71.

Sims, H. P., Jr., & Lorenzi, P. (1992) *The new leadership paradigm: Social learning and cognition in organizations*. Newbury Park, CA.: Sage.

Sims, H. P., Jr., & Manz, C. C. (1984). Observing leader verbal behavior: Toward reciprocal determinism in leadership theory. *Journal of Applied Psychology, 69,* 222–232.

Sims, H. P, Jr., & Szilagyi, A. D. (1975). Leader reward behavior and subordinate satisfaction and performance. *Organizational Behavior and Human Peformance, 14,* 426–438.

Sims, H. P., & Szilagyi, A. D. (1978). *A causal analysis of leader behavior over three different time lags.* Paper, Eastern Academy of Management, New York.

Sims, H. P., Szilagyi, A. D., & Keller, R. T. (1976). The measurement of job characteristics. *Academy of Management Journal, 19,* 195–211.

Sims, R. R. (1992). Linking groupthink to unethical behavior in organizations. *Journal of Business Ethics, 11*(9), 651.

Sims, R. R.,Veres, J. G., III, Jackson, K. A., et al. (2001). *The challenge of front-line management: Flattened organizations in the new economy.* Westport, CT: Quorum Books.

Singer, J. E. (1966). The effect of status congruence and incongruence on group functioning. *Dissertation Abstracts, 27,* 1932.

Singer, M. S. (1985). Transformational versus transactional leadership: A study of New Zealand company managers. *Psychological Reports, 57,* 143–146.

Singer, M. S. (1994). Mental framing by consequence thinking: Its effects on judgments of gender-based employment selection. *Journal of Economic Psychology, 15,* 149–172.

Singer, M. S., & Bruhns, C. (1991). Relative effect of applicant work experience and academic qualification on selection interview decisions: A study of between-sample generalizability. *Journal of Applied Psychology, 76,* 550–559.

Singer, M. S., & Singer, A. E. (1986). Relation between transformational vs. transactional leadership preference and subordinates' personality: An exploratory study. *Perceptual and Motor Skills, 62,* 775–780.

Singer, P. (1969). Toward a re-evaluation of the concept of charisma with reference to India. *Journal of Social Research, 12*(2), 13–25.

Singh, C. B. P., & Qamar, M. I. U. (1997). Power in Indian organizations: A conceptual inquiry. *Journal of Industrial Relations, 33,* 81–93.

Singh, N. P. (1969). n/Ach among successful-unsuccessful and traditional-progressive agricultural entrepreneurs of Delhi. *Journal of Social Psychology, 79,* 271–272.

Singh, N. P. (1970). n/Ach among agricultural and business entrepreneurs of Delhi. *Journal of Social Psychology, 81,* 145–149.

Singh, R. (1983). Leadership style and reward allocation: Does least preferred co-worker scale measure task and relation orientation? *Organizational Behavior and Human Performance, 32*(2), 178–197.

Singh, R., Bohra, K. A., & Dalal, A. K. (1979). Favourableness of leadership situations studied with information integration theory. *European Journal of Social Psychology, 9,* 253–264.

Singh, S. N., & Arya, H. P. (1965). Value-orientations of local village leaders. *Manas, 12,* 145–156.

Singh, S. N., Arya, H. P., & Reddy, S. K. (1965). Different types of local leadership in two north Indian villages. *Manas, 12,* 97–107.

Singh-Gupta, S. (1997). Leadership: A style or influence process. *Indian Journal of Industrial Relations, 32,* 265–286.

Sinha, J. B. P. (1976). The authoritarian leadership: A style of effective management. *Indian Journal of Industrial Relations, 2,* 381–389.

Sinha, J. B. P. (1980). *The nurturant task leader.* New Delhi, India: Concept.

Sinha, J. B. P. (1994). Cultural embeddedness and the development role of industrial organizations in India. In Dunnette, M. (ed.), *Handbook of industrial and organizational psychology* (2nd ed.). Chicago: Rand McNally.

Sinha, J. B. P., & Chowdry, G. R. (1981). Perception of subordinates as a moderator of leadership effectiveness in India. *Journal of Social Psychology, 113,* 115–121.

Sinha, J. B. P., Singh, S., Gupta, P., et al. (2002). *Relationships among societal, organizational, and managerial beliefs and practices.* Paper, International Congress of Applied Psychology, Singapore.

Sinha, N., & Viswesvaran, C. (1998). *Reliability of autonomy scales: A meta-analysis,* Paper, Society for Industrial and Organizational Psychology, Dallas, TX.

Sirota, D. (1968). *Internatinal survey of job goals and beliefs.* Paper, International Congress of Applied Psychology, Amsterdam.

Sitkin, S. B., & Roth, N. L. (1993). Explaining the limited effectiveness of legalistic remedies for trust/distrust. *Organization Science, 4,* 367–392.

Sivasubrahmaniam, N., & Kroeck, K. G. (1995). *The concept of "fit" in strategic human resource management.* Paper, Academy of Management, Vancouver, BC.

Sivasubrahmaniam, N., Murray. W. D., Avolio, B. J., et al. (1997). A longitudinal model of the effects of team leadership and group potency on performance. *Group & Organization Management, 27,* 66–96.

Skarlicki, D. P., & Latham, G. P. (1997). Leadership training in organizational justice within a labor union: A replication. *Personnel Psychology, 50,* 617–633.

Skinner, B. F. (1969). *Contingencies of reinforcement: A theoretical analysis.* New York: Appleton Century Crofts.

Skinner, E. W. (1969). Relationships between leadership behavior patterns and organizational-situational variables. *Personnel Psychology, 22,* 489–494.

Skipp, C. (2003). Hot bytes by the dozen: Krispy Kreme's Web portal keeps franchises humming. *Newsweek,* April 28.

Slack, K. J., Etchegaray, J. M., Jones, A. P., et al. (2002). *Supervisory support and employee performance: the role of perceived values.* Paper, Society for Industrial and Organizational Psychology, Toronto, Ontario.

Slackman, M. (2006). Iranian 101: A lesson for Americans. The fine art of hiding what you mean to say. *New York Times,* Week in Review, August 6.

Slansky, P. (1989). *The clothes have no emperor: A chronicle of the 80s.* New York: Fireside.

Slater, R. E. (1955). Role differentiation in small groups. *American Sociological, 20,* 300–310.

Slater, R. E. (1958). Contrasting correlates of group size. *Sociometry, 21,* 129–139.

Slavin, S. L., & Pradt, M. S. (1982). *The Einstein syndrome: Corporate anti-Semitism in America today.* Lanham, MD: University Press of America.

Slay, H. S. (2003). Spanning two worlds: Social identity and emergent African-American leaders. *Journal of Leadership and Organizational Studies, 9*(4), 56–66.

Sleeth, R. G., & Humphreys, L. W. (undated). *Differences in leadership styles among future managers: A comparison of males and females.* Unpublished manuscript.

Sleeth, R. G., & Showalter, E. D. (2000). *Addressing time-based breakdowns in leadership.* Paper, Academy of Management, Toronto, Ontario.

Sloan, J. W. (1984). The Ford presidency: A conservative approach to economic management. *Presidential Studies Quarterly, 14,* 526–537.

Slocum, J. W., Jr. (1970). Supervisory influence and the professional employee. *Personnel Journal, 49,* 484–488.

Slocum, J. W. (1984). Commentary: Problems with contingency models of leader participation. In J. G. Hunt, D. Hosking, C. A. Schriesheim, and R. Stewart (eds.), *Leaders and managers: International perspective on managerial behavior and leadership.* New York: Pergamon.

Slocum, J. W., Miller, J. D., & Misshauk, M. J. (1970). Needs, environmental work satisfaction, and job performance. *Training & Development Journal, 24,* 12–15.

Slocum, J. W., & Strawser, R. H. (1972). Racial differences in job attitudes. *Journal of Applied Psychology, 56,* 28–32.

Slusher, A., Van Dyke, J., & Rose, G. (1972). Technical competence of group leaders, managerial role, and productivity in engineering design groups. *Academy of Management Journal, 15,* 197–204.

Slusher, A., Van Dyke, J., & Rose, G. (1998). Technical competence of group leaders, managerial role, and productivity in engineering design groups. *Journal of Leadership Studies, 5,* 197–204.

Smallridge, R. J. (1972). *A study of relationships between perceived management system of elementary schools and the personal needs satisfaction of teachers.* Doctoral dissertation, George Peabody College for Teachers, Nashville, TN.

Smart, D., & Wolfe, R. (2003). The contribution of leadership and human resources to organizational success: An empirical assessment of performance in major league baseball. *European Sport Management Quarterly, 3,* 165–188.

Smelser, W. T. (1961). Dominance as a factor in achievement and perception in cooperative problem solving interactions. *Journal of Abnormal and Social Psychology, 62,* 535–542.

Smeltzer, L. R., & Davey, J. A. (1988). An analysis of management training via telecommunications. *Journal of European Industrial Training, 12*(3), 11–16.

Smircich, L., & Chesser, R. J. (1981). Superiors' and subordinates' perceptions of performance: beyond disagreement. *Academy of Management Journal, 24,* 198–205.

Smircich, L., & Morgan, G. (1982). Leadership: The management of meaning. *Journal of Applied Behavioral Science, 18,* 257–273.

Smith, A. (1775). *An inquiry into the nature and causes of the wealth of nations.* London: Methuen and Co. Edwin Cannan, ed., 1904. Fifth edition. First published 1776.

Smith, A., Pitcher, P., Houghton, S. M., et al. (2003). Power among top management team members in effect on organizational performance. *Journal of Management Studies,* Also Paper, AOM Academy of Management, Seattle, WA.

Smith, A. B. (1971). *Role expectations for and observations of community college department chairmen: An organizational study of consensus and conformity.* Doctoral dissertation, University of Michigan, Ann Arbor.

Smith, A. F. R., Kudish, J. D., & Thibodeaux, H. F. (2000) *Factors associated with willingness to participate in upward feedback.* Paper, Society for Industrial and Organizational Psychology, New Orleans.

Smith, B. J. (1982). *An initial test of a theory of charismatic leadership based on the responses of subordinates.* Doctoral dissertation, University of Toronto, Ontario.

Smith, C., & Elmes, M. (2002) Leading change: Insights from Jungian interpretations of the book of Job. *Journal of Organizational Change Management, 15*(5), 448.

Smith, C. A. (1937). Social selection and community leadership. *Social Forces, 15,* 530–545.

Smith, C. A., & Ellsworth, P. C. (1985). Patterns of cognitive appraisal in emotion. *Journal of Personality and Social Psychology, 48,* 813–838.

Smith, C. A., Organ, D. W., & Near, J. P. (1983). Organizational citizenship behavior: Its nature and antecedents. *Journal of Applied Psychology, 68,* 653–663.

Smith, C. B. (1984). Do legitimacy of supervisor and reward contingency interact in the prediction of work behavior? *Human Relations, 37,* 1029–1046.

Smith, C. G., & Ari, O. N. (1964). Organizational control structure and member consensus. *American Journal of Sociology, 69,* 623–638.

Smith, C. G., & Tannenbaum, A. S. (1963). Organizational control structure: A comparative analysis. *Human Relations, 16,* 299–316.

Smith, C. G., & Tannenbaum, A. S. (1965). Some implications of leadership and control for effectiveness in a voluntary association. *Human Relations, 18,* 265–272.

Smith-Crowe, K., Umphress, E. E., Brief, A. P., et al. (2003). *Cooking the books: The effect of accountability and social dominance.* Paper, Society for Industrial and Organizational Psychology, Orlando, FL.

Smith, D., Corbin, M., & Hellman, C. (2002). *Reforging the sword: Forces for a 21st century security strategy.* Center for Defense Information.

Smith, D. M. (1985). *Cavour.* London: Weidenfeld & Nicolson.

Smith, E. E. (1957). The effects of clear and unclear role expectations on group productivity and defensiveness. *Journal of Abnormal and Social Psychology, 55,* 213–217.

Smith, E. (1996). Leader or manager: The minority department chair of the majority department. *Journal of Leadership Studies, 3*(1), 79–94.

Smith, H. (1975). *Qualitative research methods.* New York: McGraw-Hill.

Smith, H. L., & Krueger, L. M. (1933). *A brief summary of literature on leadership.* Bloomington: Indiana University, School of Education Bulletin.

Smith, J., & Arkless, C. (1993). Guidelines on good practice in foreign-language training. *Journal of European Industrial Training, 17*(7), 14–18.

Smith, J. A., & Foti, R. J. (1998). A pattern approach to the study of leader emergence. *The Leadership Quarterly, 9*(2), 147–160.

Smith, J. E. (1986). *Women in management (1979–1984): A review of the literature.* Paper, American Psychological Association, New York, NY.

Smith, J. E., Carson, K. R., & Alexander, R. A. (1984). Leadership: It can make a difference. *Academy of Management Journal, 27,* 765–776.

Smith, J. H. (1994). Coping with stress: The implications of leaders' personality. *Journal of Leadership Studies, 1*, 26–36.

Smith, K. G., Smith, K. A., & Olian, J. D., et al. (1994). Top management of team demography and process: The role of social integration and communication. *Administrative Science Quarterly, 39*, 3, 412–438.

Smith, K. M. (1983). Harry Truman: Man of his times? *Presidential Studies Quarterly, 13*(1), 70–80.

Smith, L. M. (1967). *Social psychological aspects of school building design.* St. Louis, MO: Washington University.

Smith, M. (1934). Personality dominance and leadership. *Sociology and Social Research, 19*, 18–25.

Smith, M. (1935a). Leadership: The management of social differentials. *Journal of Abnormal and Social Psychology, 30*, 348–358.

Smith, M. (1948). Control interaction. *Journal of Social Psychology, 28*, 263–273.

Smith, M., Thorpe, R., & Lowe, A. (1991). *Management research: An introduction.* London: Sage.

Smith, M. R., Rogg, K. L., & Collins, P. H. (2001). *Challenges and opportunities in creating a virtual assessment center.* Paper, Society for Industrial and Organizational Psychology, San Diego, CA.

Smith, M., & White, M. C. (1987). Strategy, CEO specialization, and succession. *Administrative Science Quarterly, 32*, 263–280.

Smith, N. R., & Miner, J. B. (1984). *Motivational considerations in the success of technologically innovative entrepreneurs.* Paper, Entrepreneurship Research Conference, Babson College and Georgia Institute of Technology.

Smith, P. B. (1964). Attitude changes associated with training in human relations. *British Journal of Social and Clinical Psychology, 3*, 104–112.

Smith, P. B. (1975). Controlled studies of the outcome of sensitivity training. *Psychological Bulletin, 82*, 597–622.

Smith, P. B. (1976). Why successful groups succeed: The implications of T-group research. In C. L. Cooper (ed.), *Developing social skills in managers.* New York: Wiley.

Smith, P. B. (1984a). The effectiveness of Japanese styles of management: A review and critique. *Journal of Occupational Psychology, 57*, 121–136.

Smith, P. B., & Misumi, J. (1989). Japanese management: A sun rising in the West? In C. L. Cooper & I. Robertson (eds.), *International review of industrial and organizational psychology.* London: Wiley.

Smith, P. B., Misumi, J., Tayeb, M., et al. (1989). On the generality of leadership style cultures across culture, *Journal of Occupational Psychology, 62*, 97–109.

Smith, P. B., Moscow, D., Berger, M., & Cooper, C. (1969). Relationships between managers and their work associates. *Administrative Science Quarterly, 14*, 338–345.

Smith, P. B., & Peterson, M. F. (1988). *Leadership, organizations, and culture: An event management model.* London: Sage.

Smith, P. B., & Peterson, M. F. (1994). *Leadership as event management: A cross-cultural survey based on managers from 25 nations.* Paper, International Congress of Psychology, Madrid, Spain.

Smith, P. B., Peterson, M. F., Misumi, J., et al. (1992). A cross-cultural test of the Japanese PM theory. *Applied Psychology: An International Review, 41*, 5–19.

Smith, P. B., Peterson, M. F., & Schwartz, S. H. (2002). Cultural values, sources of guidance, and their relevance to managerial behavior. *Journal of Cross-Cultural Psychology, 33*, 188–208.

Smith, P. B., Peterson, M. F., & Wang, P. (1996). The manager as mediator of alternative meanings: A pilot study from China, the U.S.A. and U.K. *Journal of International Business Studies, 27*(1), 115–29.

Smith, P. B., Tayeb, M., Peterson, M., et al. (1986). *On the generality of leadership style measures.* Unpublished manuscript.

Smith, P. C., Kendall, L. M., & Hulin, C. L. (1969). *The measurement of satisfaction in work and retirement.* Chicago: Rand McNally.

Smith, R. B. (1983). Why soldiers fight. Part I. Leadership, cohesion and fighter spirit. *Quality and Quantity, 18*(1), 1–32.

Smith, R. G. (1974). The effects of leadership style, leader position power, and problem solving method on group performance. *Dissertation Abstracts International, 35*, 773–774.

Smith, S., & Whitehead, G. (1984). Attributes for promotions and demotion in the United States and India. *Journal of Social Psychology, 124*, 27–34.

Smith, T. W. (1990). *Ethnic images.* GSS Topical Report 19, National Opinion Research Center, University of Chicago, Chicago, IL

Smith, W. G., Brown, D. J., Lord, R. G., et al. (1996). *Leadership self-schema and their effect on leadership perceptions.* Unpublished manuscript.

Smith, W. P (1967a). Power structure and authoritarianism in the use of power in the triad. *Journal of Personality, 35*, 65–89.

Smith, W. P. (1967b). Reactions to a dyadic power structure. *Psychonomic Science, 7*, 373–374.

Smither, J. W., & Walker, A. G.(2002). *Examining the equivalence of web vs. upward feedback ratings.* Paper, Society for Industrial Organizational Psychology, Orlando, FL.

Smither, R. D. (1989). *Using social psychology to make quality circles more effective.* Paper, American Psychological Association, Atlanta, GA.

Smither, R. D. (1991). *Authoritarian management revisited : Participation, organizational effectiveness, and the leader's appeal to emotion.* Submitted.

Smither, R. D. (1991). The return of the authoritarian manager. *Training,* November, 40–43.

Smither, R. D. (1993). Authoritarianism, dominance, and social behavior: A perspective from evolutionay personality psychology. *Human Relations, 46*(1), 23–43.

Smola, K. W., & Sutton, C. D. (2002). Generational differences: Revisiting generational work values for the new millennium. *Journal of Organizational Behavior, 23*, 363–382.

Snadowsky, A. M. (1972). Communication network research: An examination of controversies. *Human Relations, 25*, 283–306.

Snell, A. F., Stokes, G. S., Sands, M. M. & McBride, J. R. (1994). Adolescent life experiences as predictors of occupational attainment. *Journal of Applied Psychology, 79*, 131–141.

Snoek, J. D. (1966). Role strain in diversified role sets. *American Journal of Sociology, 71*, 363–372.

Snow, D. A., Rochford Jr., E. B., Worden, S. K., & Benford, R. D. (1986). Frame alignment processes, micromobilization, and movement participation. *American Sociological Review, 51*(4), 464–481.

Snyder, C. R. (1997). Hope: An individual motive for social commerce. *Group Dynamics, 1*, 107–118.

Snyder, C. R. (2000). *Handbook of hope*. San Diego, CA: Academic Press.

Snyder, M. (1974). The self-monitoring of expressive behavior. *Journal of Personality and Social Psychology, 30*, 526–537.

Snyder, M. (1979). Self-monitoring processes. In L. Berkowitz (ed.), *Advances in experimental social psychology, 12*, 86–128. New York: Academic Press.

Snyder, M., & Cantor, N. (1980). Thinking about ourselves and others: self-monitoring and social knowledge. *Journal of Personality and Social Psychology, 39*, 222–234.

Snyder, M., & Mason, T. C. (1975). Persons, situations, and the control of social behavior. *Journal of Personality and Social Psychology, 32*, 637–644.

Snyder, N., & Glueck, W. F. (1977). *Mintzberg and the planning literature: An analysis and reconciliation*. Paper, Academy of Management, Orlando, FL.

Snyder, N., & Glueck, W. F. (1980). How managers plan: The analysis of managers' activities. *Long Range Planning, 13*(1), 70–76.

Snyder, N. H., Dowd, J. J., & Houghton, D. M. (1994). *Vision, values and courage. Leadership for quality management*. New York: Free Press.

Snyder, N. H., & Wheelen, T. L. (1981). Managerial roles: Mintzberg and the management process theorists. *Proceedings*, Academy of Management, San Diego, CA, 249–253.

Snyder, L. (1983). An anniversary review and critique: The Tylenol crisis. *Public Relations Review, 9*(3), 24–34.

Snyder, R. A., & Bruning, N. S. (1985). Quality of vertical dyad linkages: Congruence of supervisor and subordinate competence and role stress as explanatory variables. *Group & Organization Studies, 10*, 81–94.

Snyder, R. A., & Morris, J. H. (1984). Organizational communication and performance. *Journal of Applied Psychology, 69*, 461–465.

Soares, C. E. (2003). *Work or survival? A textual analysis of African-American male slave narratives and contemporary at-risk African-American males*. Paper, Academy of Management, FL.

Sofranko, A. J., & Bridgeland, W. M. (1975). Agreement and disagreement on environmental issues among community leaders. *Cornell Journal of Social Relations, 10*, 151–162.

Solem, A. R. (1953). The influence of the discussion leader's attitude on the outcome of group decision conferences. *Dissertation Abstracts, 13*, 439.

Solem, A. R. (1960). Human relations training: Comparison of case study and role playing. *Personnel Administration, 23*, 29–37.

Solem, A. R., Onachilla, V. J., & Heller, K. Z. (1961). The posting problems technique as a basis for training. *Personnel Administration, 24*(3), 22–31.

Solomon, C. M. (1998). Building teams across borders. *Global Workforce*, November, 12–17.

Solomon, E. E. (1986). Private and public sector managers: An empirical investigation of job characteristics and organizational climate. *Journal of Applied Psychology, 71*, 247–259.

Solomon, L. (1960). The influence of some types of power relationships and game strategies upon the development of interpersonal trust. *Journal of Abnormal and Social Psychology, 61*, 223–230.

Solomon, R. H. (1976). Personality changes in leaders and members

of personality laboratories. *Dissertation Abstracts International, 36*, 5285–5286.

Solomon, R. J. (1976). An examination of the relationship between a survey feedback O. D. technique and the work environment. *Personnel Psychology, 29*, 583–594.

Somech, A., & Drach-Zahavy, A. (2003). Relative power and influence strategy: The effects of agent/target organizational power on superiors' choices of influence strategies. *Journal of Organizational Behavior, 23*(2), 167–179.

Sommer, R. (1961). Leadership and group geography. *Sociometry, 24*, 99–110.

Sommer, R. (1967). Small group ecology. *Psychological Bulletin, 67*(2), 145–152.

Sommer, R. (1969). *Personal space: The behavioral basis of design*. Englewood Cliffs, NJ: Prentice-Hall

Sommer, S. M., Welsh, D. H. B., & Gubman, B. (2000). The ethical orientation of Russian entrepreneurs. *Applied Psychology: An International Review, 49*, 688–708.

Søndergaard, M. (1994). Hofstede's consequences: A study of reviews, citations, and replications. *Organization Studies, 15*, 447–456.

Song, J. H. (1982). Diversification strategies and the experience of top executives of large firms. *Strategic Management Journal, 3*, 377–380.

Sonnenfeld, J. (1981). Executive apologies for price fixing: Role biased perceptions of causality. *Academy of Management Journal, 24*, 192–198.

Sonnenfeld, J. (1988). *What happens when CEOs retire*. Oxford, UK: Oxford University Press.

Sonnenfeld, J. A. (1994). Haiti: Clinton's lessons in leadership. *New York Times*, September 25.

Sonnenfeld, J., & Ward, A. (1995). Being skillful at succession. *Directors & Boards, 19*(4), 17.

Sonnenfeld, J. A., Washington, P. G., Barry, M. S., et al. (1995). *Gender comparison of CEO leadership styles*. Atlanta, GA: Emory University, Center for Leadership & Career Studies.

Sorcher, M. (1985). *Predicting executive success: What it takes to make it into senior management*. New York: Wiley.

Sorenson, G. (1996). *Reconstructing the civic architecture: The historical framework of American civic life*. Kellogg Leadership Studies Program. Transformational Leadership Group.

Sorenson, T.C. (1965). *Kennedy*. New York: Harper & Row.

Sorokin, P. A. (1927b). Leaders of labor and radical social movements in the United States and foreign countries. *American Journal of Sociology, 33*, 382–411.

Sorokin, P. A. (1943). *Man and society in calamity*. New York: Dutton.

Sorrentino, R. M., & Boutillier, R. G. (1975). The effect of quantity and quality of verbal interaction on ratings of leadership. *Journal of Experimental Social Psychology, 11*, 403, 411.

Sosik, J. J. (1996). *Leadership and group creativity: Influencing GDSS process and outcome*. San Diego, CA: SIOP.

Sosik, J. J. (1997). Effects of transformational leadership and anonymity on idea generation in computer-mediated groups. *Group and Organization Management, 22*, 460–487.

Sosik, J. J. (2005). The role of personal values in the charismatic leadership of corporate managers: A model and preliminary field study. *Leadership Quarterly, 16*, 221–244.

Sosik, J. J., Avolio, B. J., & Kahai, S. S. (1997). Effects of leadership style and anonymity on group potency and effectiveness in a decision support system environment. *Journal of Applied Psychology, 82,* 89–103.

Sosik, J. J., Avolio, B. J., & Kahai, S. S. (1998). Inspiring group creativity: Comparing anonymous and identified electronic brainstorming. *Small Group Research, 29*(1), 3–31.

Sosik, J. J., & Dworakivsky, A. C. (1998). Self-concept based aspects of the charismatic leader: More than meets the eye. *Leadership Quarterly, 9,* 503–526.

Sosik, J. J., & Godshalk, V. M. (2000). Leadership styles, mentoring functions received, and job-related stress: A conceptual model and preliminary study. *Journal of Organizational Behavior, 21,* 365–390.

Sosik, J. J., Godshalk, V. M., & Yammarino, F. J. (2004). Transformational leadership, learning goal orientation, and expectations for career success in mentor-protégé relationships: A multiple levels of analysis perspective. *The Leadership Quarterly, 15,* 241–261.

Sosik, J. J., Jung, D. I., Berson, Y., et al. (2001, 2004). *The dream weavers: Strategy-focused leadership in technology-driven organizations.* Greenwich, CT: Information Age Publishing.

Sosik, J. J., Jung, D. I., Berson, Y., et al. (2005). Making all the right connections: The strategic leadership of top executives in high-tech organizations. *Organizational Dynamics, 34*(1), 47–61.

Sosik, J. J., Kahai, S. S., & Avolio, B. J. (1998). Transformational leadership and dimensions of creativity: Motivating idea generation in computer-mediated groups. *Creativity Research Journal, 11,* 111–121.

Sosik, J. J., Kahai, S. S., & Avolio, B. J. (1999). Leadership style, anonymity, and creativity in group decision support systems: The mediating role of optimum flow. *Journal of Creative Behavior, 33,* 227–256.

Sosik, J. J., & Lee, D. L. (2002). Mentoring in organizations: A social judgement perspective for developing tomorrow's leaders. *The Journal of Leadership Studies, 8*(4), 23–32.

Sosik, J. J., & Megerian, L. E. (1999). Understanding leader emotional intelligence and performance: The role of self-other agreement on transformational leadership perceptions. *Group & Organization Management, 24,* 367–390.

South, S. J., Bonjean, C. M., Corder, J., & Markham, W. T. (1982). Sex and power in the federal bureaucracy: A comparative analysis of male and female supervisors. *Work and Occupations, 9*(2), 233–254.

Southern, L. J. F. (1976). *An analysis of motivation to manage in the tufted carpet and textile industry of northwest Georgia.* Doctoral dissertation, Georgia State University, Atlanta.

Spangler, W. D. & Braiotta, L. (1990). Leadership and corporate audit committee effectiveness. *Group & Organization Studies, 15*(2), June, 134–157.

Spangler, W. D., Dubinsky, A. J., Yammarino, F. J., et al. (1997). Impact of personality on sales manager leadership style. *Journal of Business-to-Business Marketing, 3*(4), 27–53.

Spangler, E., Gordon, M. A., & Pipkin, R. M. (1978). Token women: An empirical test of Kanter's hypothesis. *American Journal of Sociology, 84,* 160–170.

Spangler, W. D., & House, R. J. (1991). Presidential effectiveness and the leadership motive profile. *Journal of Personality and Social Psychology, 60,* 439–455.

Sparks, C. C. (1990). Testing for management potential. In K. E. Clark & M. B. Clark (eds.), *Measures of leadership.* West Orange, NJ: Leadership Library of America.

Sparks, C. P. (1966). *Personnel development series.* Houston, TX: Humble Oil & Refining Company. Unpublished report.

Sparks, C. P. (1989). Testing for management potential. In K. E. Clark & M. B. Clark (eds.), *Measures of leadership.* West Orange, NJ: Leadership Library of America.

Sparks, R. (1976). Library management: Consideration and structure. *Journal of Academic Librarianship, 2*(2), 66–71.

Sparrowe, R. T., & Liden, R. C. (1997). Process and structure in leader-member exchange. *Academy of Management Review, 22,* 522–552.

Spaulding, C. B. (1934). Types of junior college leaders. *Sociology and Social Research, 18,* 164–168.

Spector, A. J. (1953). Factors in morale. *American Psychologist, 8,* 439–440.

Spector, A. J. (1958). Changes in human relations attitudes. *Journal of Applied Psychology, 42,* 154–157.

Spector, B. (1987). Transformational leadership: The new challenge for U.S. unions. *Human Resource Management, 26,* 3–16.

Spector, P. E. (1975). Relationships of organizational frustration with reported behavior reactions of employees. *Journal of Applied Psychology, 60,* 635–357.

Spector, P. E. (1986). Perceived control by employees: A meta-analysis of studies concerning autonomy and participation at work. *Human Relations, 39,* 1005–16.

Spector, P. E., Cooper, C. L., & Aguilar-Vafaie, M. E. (2002). A comparative study of perceived job stressor sources and job strain in American and Iranian managers. *Applied Psychology: An International Review, 51*(3), 446–457.

Spector, P. E., Cooper, C. L., Poelmans, S., Allen, T. D., O'Driscoll, M., Sanchez, J. I., et al. (2004). A cross-national comparative study of work-family stressors, working hours, and well-being: China and Latin America versus the Anglo world. *Personnel Psychology, 57*(1), 119–142.

Spector, P. E., Cooper, C. L., Sanchez, J. I., et al. (2001). Do national levels of individualism and internal locus of control relate to well-being: An ecological analysis. *Journal of Organizational Behavior, 22,* 815–832.

Spector, P. E., Cooper, C. L., Paul, C., et al. (2004). A cross-national comparative study of work-family stressors, working hours and well-being: China and Latin America versus the Anglo World. *Personnel Psychology,* Refereed Journal Articles.

Spector, P., & Suttell, B. J. (1956–1957). *Research on the specific leader behavior patterns most effective in influencing group performance.* Washington, DC: American Institute for Research.

Spelke, E. S. (2005). Sex differences in intrinsic aptitude for mathematics and science? *American Psychologist, 60,* 950–958.

Spence, J. T., Helmreich, R., & Stapp, J. (1975). Ratings of self and peers on sex role attributes and their relation to self-esteem and conceptions of masculinity and femininity. *Journal of Personality and Social Psychology, 32*(1), 29–39

Spencer, B. A., & Carte, I. C. (1991). *Captain Rickenbacker's airline.* Paper, Academy of Management, Miami Beach, FL.

Spencer, J. F. (1981). Contingency planning. *Handling & Shipping Management, 22*(11), 58–64.

Spencer, L. M. (undated). *The Navy leadership and management education and training program.* Unpublished manuscript.

Spencer, L. M., Jr., & Spencer, S. M. (1993). *Competence at work: Models for superior performance.* New York: John Wiley & Sons.

Spera, S. D., & Moye, N. A. (2001). *Measurement equivalence between paper and web survey methods in a multinational company.* Paper, Society for Industrial and Organizational Psychology, San Diego, CA.

Speroff, B. J. (1954). Rotational role playing used to develop executives. *Personnel Journal, 33,* 49–50.

Speroff, B. J. (1957). The "behind-the-back" way in training leaders. *Personnel Journal, 35,* 411–412, 435.

Sperry, R. (1985). Managers' job definitions and concepts. *Bureaucrat, 14*(3), 14–18.

Spicochi, R. L., & Tyran, K. L. (2002). *A tale of two leaders: Exploring the role of leader storytelling and follower sensemaking in transforming organizations.* Paper, Academy of Management, Denver, CO.

Spiegel, J. (1982). An ecological model of ethnic families. In M. McGoldrick, J. K. Pearce, & J. Giordano (eds.), *Ethnicity and family therapy.* New York: Guilford Press.

Spielberger, C. D. (1972). Anxiety as an emotional state. In C. D. Spielberger (ed.), *Anxiety: Current trends in theory and research,* vol. 1. New York: Academic Press.

Spielberger, C. D., Gorsuch, R. L., & Lushene, R. E. (1970). *Manual for the state-trait anxiety inventory.* Palo Alto, CA: Consulting Psychologists Press.

Spilerman, S. (1977). Labor market structure, and socioeconomic economic achievement. *American Journal of Sociology, 85,* 551–593.

Spillane, R. (1980). Attitudes of business executives and union leaders to industrial relations: Twenty-three years later. *Journal of Industrial Relations, 22,* 317–325.

Spiller, G. (1929). The dynamics of greatness. *Sociological Review, 21,* 218–232.

Spillman, B., Spillman, R., & Reinking, K. (1981). Leadership emergence dynamic analysis of the effects of sex and androgyny. *Small Group Behavior, 12,* 139–157.

Spitz, C. J. (1982). The project leader: A study of task requirements, management skills and personal style. *Dissertation Abstracts International, 43*(6A), 2073.

Spitzberg, I. (1987). Paths of inquiry into leadership. *Liberal Education, 73*(2), 24–28.

Spitzer, M. E., & McNamara, W. J. (1964). A managerial selection study. *Personnel Psychology, 17,* 19–40.

Spitzer, Q., & Evans, R. (1998). How to succeed at executive succession. *Leader to Leader,* Fall, 47–53.

Spitzmueller, C., Gibby, R. E., & Stanton, J. M. (2003). *Managerial ethics and ethical climate as predictors of job attitudes.* Paper, Society for Industrial and Organizational Psychology, Orlando, FL.

Spranger, E. (1928). *Types of men.* Halle, Germany: Max Niemeyer Verlag.

Spreitzer, G. M. (1995). Psychological empowerment in the workplace: Dimensions, measurement, and validation. *Academy of Management Journal, 38,* 1442–1465.

Spreitzer, G. M. (1996). Social structural characteristics of psychological empowering. *Academy of Management Journal, 39,* 483–504.

Spreitzer, G. M. (2002). *Leadership development in the virtual workplace.* Paper, Academy of Management, Denver, CO.

Spreitzer, G. M. (2003). Leadership development in the virtual workplace. In S. Murphy & R. Riggio (eds.), *Future of leadership development.* Mahwah, NJ: Lawrence Erlbaum Associates.

Spreitzer, G. M., Cohen, S. G., & Ledford, G. E., Jr. (1999). Developing effective self-managing work teams in service organizations. *Group & Organization Management, 24,* 340–366.

Spreitzer, G. M., & de Janasz, S. C. (1994). *The transformational capacities of empowered managers.* Los Angeles, CA: University of Southern California, Department of Management Organization.

Spreitzer, G. M., Kizilos, M. A., & Nason, S. W. (1997). A dimensional analysis of the relationship between psychological empowerment and effectiveness, satisfaction, and strain. *Journal of Management, 23,* 679–704.

Spreitzer, G. M., & Mishra, A. K. (1999). Giving up control without losing control. *Group and Organization Management, 24*(2), 155–187.

Springer, D. (1956). Why employees refuse promotion: A case study. *Personnel, 32,* 457–462.

Springer, R. (2001). *Leadership and organizational climate.* Upper Saddle River, NJ: Prentice Hall.

Sproull, L. S. (1981). Managing education programs: A microbehavioral analysis. *Human Organization, 40,* 113–122.

Sprunger, J. A. (1949). *The relationship of group morale estimates to other measures of group and leader effectiveness.* Master's thesis, Ohio.

Srivastava, S. (1983). Introduction: Common themes in executive thought and action. In S. Srivastva & Associates, *The executive mind.* San Francisco: Jossey-Bass.

Srivastava, S., & Kumar, S. (1984). Leadership style and effectiveness of junior and middle level central government officers: A comparative study. *Psychological Studies. 29,* 136–138.

St. John, W. D. (1983). Successful communications between supervisors and employees. *Personnel Journal, 62*(1), 71–77.

Stagner, R. (1954). Dual allegiance to union and management. 1. Dual allegiance as a problem in modern society. *Personnel Psychology, 7,* 41–46.

Stagner, R. (1969). Corporate decision making: An empirical study. *Journal of Applied Psychology, 53,* 1–13.

Stagner, R., Chalmers, W. E., & Derber, M. (1958). Guttman-type scales for union and management attitudes toward each other. *Journal of Applied Psychology, 42,* 293–300.

Stagner, R., Derber, M., & Chalmers, W. E. (1959). The dimensionality of union-management relations at the local level. *Journal of Applied Psychology, 43,* 1–7.

Stagner, R., Flebbe, D. R., & Wood, E. V. (1952). Working on the railroads: A study of job satisfaction. *Personnel Psychology, 5,* 293–306.

Stahl, G. R. (1953). Training directors evaluate role playing. *Journal of Industrial Training, 7,* 21–29.

Stahl, G. R. (1954). A statistical report of industry's experience with role playing. *Group Psychotherapy, 6,* 202–215.

Stahl, M. J. (1983). Achievement, power and managerial motivation: Selecting managerial talent with the job choice exercise. *Personnel Psychology, 36,* 775–789.

Stahl, M. J. & Harrell, A. M. (1982). Evolution and evaluation of a behavioral decision theory measurement approach to achievement, power, and affiliation. *Journal of Applied Psychology, 67, 744–751.*

Staines, G., Tavris, C., & Jayaratne, T. E. (1973). The Queen Bee Syndrome. In C. Tavris (ed.), *The Female Experience.* Del Mar, CA: CRM Books.

Stajkovic, A. D., & Luthans, F. (1998). Self-sufficiency and work-related performance: A meta-analysis. *Psychological Bulletin, 124,* 240–261.

Stamper, C. L., & Van Dyne, L. (1999). Diversity at work: Do men and women differ in their organizational citizenship behavior? *Performance Improvement Quarterly (Special Issue: Embracing Diversity), 12,* 59–76.

Stampolis, A. (1958). *Employees' atittudes toward unionization, management, and factory conditions.* Atlanta: Georgia State College of Business Administration.

Standard & Poor's (1967). *Register of corporations, directors and executives.* New York: Standard & Poor's.

Stanton, E. S. (1960). Company policies and supervisors' attitudes toward supervision. *Journal of Applied Psychology, 44,* 22–26,

Stanton, J. M. (1998). An empirical investigation of data collected using the internet. *Personnel Psychology, 51,* 709–724.

Staples, D. S. (1999). *A comparison of the impact of employee-manager trust on employees in a remote-management and local-management environment.* Paper, Academy of Management, Chicago, IL.

Starbuck, W. H., & Mezias, J. M. (1996). Opening Pandora's box: Studying the accuracy of managers' perceptions. *Journal of Organizational Behavior, 17(2),* 99–117.

Stark, S. (1969–1970). Toward a psychology of charisma: II. The pathology viewpoint of James C. Davies. *Psychological Reports, 24,* 88–90.

Stark, S. (1970). Toward a psychology of charisma: III. Intuitional empathy, Vorbilder, Fuehrers, transcendence-striving, and inner creation. *Psychological Reports, 26,* 683–696.

Starr, C. G. (1954). *Civilization and the Caesars.* Ithaca, NY: Cornell University Press.

Statham, A. (1987). The gender model revisited: Differences in the management styles of men and women. *Sex Roles, 16,* 409–429.

Staw, B. M. (1984). Organizational behavior: A review and reformulation of the Field's outcome variables. *Annual Review of Psychology, 35,* 627–666.

Staw, B. M., & Sutton, R. I. (1993). Macro organizational psychology. In Murringhan (ed.), *Social psychology in organizations: Advances in theory and research.* Englewood Cliffs, NJ: Prentice-Hall.

Staw, B. M., McKechnie, P. I., & Puffer, S. M. (1982). The justification of organizational performance. *Administrative Science Quarterly, 28,* 562–600.

Staw, B. M., & Ross, J. (1980). Commitment in an experimenting society: A study of the attribution of leadership from administrative scenarios. *Journal of Applied Psychology, 65,* 249–260.

Staw, B. M., Sandelands, L. E., & Dutton, J. E. (1981). Threat-rigidity effects in organizational behavior: A multi-level analysis. *Administrative Science Quarterly, 26,* 501–524.

Stayer, R. (1990). How I learned to let my workers lead. *Harvard Business Review, 68(6),* 66–83.

Stech, E. L. (1981). Leadership has a logic all its own. *Hospital Financial Management, 35(2),* 14–18, 24–25.

Stech, E. L. (1983). *Leadership communication.* Chicago: Nelson-Hall.

Steckler, N. A., & Rosenthal, R. (1985). Sex differences in nonverbal and verbal communication with bosses, peers, and subordinates. *Journal of Applied Psychology, 70,* 157–163.

Steeb, R., & Johnson (1981). A computer-based interactive system for group decision making. *IEEE Transactions on Systems, Man, and Cybernetics, 11,* 544–552.

Steel, R. P., & Mento, A. J. (1986). Impact of situational constraints on subjective and objective criteria of managerial job performance. *Organizational Behavior and Human Decision Processes, 37,* 254–265.

Steele, C. M., & Aronson, J. (1995). Stereotype threat and the intellectual test performance of African Americans. *Journal of Personality and Social Psychology, 69,* 797–811.

Steele, C. M., Spencer, S. J., & Aronson, J. (2002). Contending with group image: The psychology of stereotype and social identity threat. In M. Snyder (ed.), *Advances in Experimental Social Psychology, 34,* 379–440. New York: Academic Press.

Steele, F. I., Zane, D. E., & Zalkind, S. S. (1970). Managerial behavior and participation in a laboratory training process. *Personnel Psychology, 23,* 77–90.

Steele, R. S. (1973). *The physiological concomitants of psychogenic motive arousal in college males.* Doctoral dissertation, Harvard University, Cambridge, MA.

Steele, R. S. (1977). Power motivation, activation, and inspirational speeches. *Journal of Personality, 45,* 53–64.

Steelman, L. A., & Levy, P. E. (2001). *The feedback environment and its potential role in 360-degree feedback.* Paper, Society for Industrial and Organizational Psychology, San Diego, CA.

Steelman, L. A., Williams, J. R., & Levy, P. E. (1996). *The environment for feedback seeking and feedback seeking behavior.* Paper, Society for Industrial and Organizational Psychology, San Diego, CA.

Steger, J. A., Kelley, W. B., Chouiniere, C., & Goldenbaum, A. (1977). A forced choice version of the Miner sentence completion scale and how it discriminates campus leaders and non-leaders. In J. B. Miner (ed.), *Motivation to manage.* Atlanta, GA: Organizational Measurement Systems Press.

Steidlmeier, P. (1987). *The paradox of poverty: A reprisal of economic development policy.* Cambridge, MA: Ballinger.

Steidlmeier, P. (1992). *People and profits.* Englewood Cliffs, NJ: Prentice-Hall.

Stein, S., Dietz, T., & Kalof, L. (1993). Value orientations, gender, and environmental concern. *Environment and Behavior, 25,* 322–348.

Stein, P. C., & Shapiro, S. (1982). Sex differences in personality traits of female and male master of business administration students. *Journal of Applied Psychology, 67,* 306–310.

Stein, R. G., & Pinchot, G. (1995). Building intelligent organizations. *Association Management, 47(11),* November, 32–44.

Stein, R. T. (1971). *Accuracy in perceiving emergent leadership in small groups.* Paper, American Psychological Association, Washington, DC.

Stein, R. T. (1975). Identifying emergent leaders from verbal and nonverbal communications. *Journal of Personality and Social Psychology, 32,* 125–135

Stein, R. T. (1977). Accuracy of process consultants and untrained observers in perceiving emergent leadership. *Journal of Applied Psychology, 62,* 755–759.

Stein, R. T. (1982b). High status group members as exemptors: A summary of field research on the relationship of status to congruence conformity. *Small Group Behavior, 13,* 3–21.

Stein, R. T., Geis, F. L., & Damarin, F. (1973). Perception of emergent leadership hierarchies in task groups. *Journal of Personality and Social Psychology, 28,* 77–87.

Stein, R. T., & Heller, T. (1978). *The relationship of emergent leadership status and high verbal participation in small groups: A review of the literature.* Chicago: University of Illinois at Chicago Circle, Department of Psychology. Unpublished manuscript.

Stein, R. T., Hoffman, L. R., Cooley, S. J., & Pearse, R. W. (1979). Leadership valence: Modeling and measuring the process of emergent leadership. In J. G. Hunt & L. L. Larson (eds.), *Crosscurrents in leadership.* Carbondale: Southern Illinois University.

Stein, Z., Susser, M., Saenger, G., et al. (1975). *Famine and human development: The Dutch hunger winter of 1944–45.* New York: Oxford University Press.

Steinberg, A. G., & Leaman, J. A. (1990). *Dimensions of army commissioned and noncommissioned officer leadership* (Technical Report 879). Alexandria, VA: U.S. Army Research Institute for the Behavioral and Social Sciences.

Steiner, D. D., & Dobbins, G. H. (undated). *The role of work values in leader-member exchange.* Unpublished manuscript.

Steiner, I. D. (1972). *Group process and productivity.* New York: Academic Press.

Steiner, I. D., & McDiarmid, C. G. (1957). Two kinds of assumed similarity between opposites. *Journal of Abnormal and Social Psychology, 55,* 140–142.

Steiner, I. D., & Peters, S. C. (1958). Conformity and the A-B-X model. *Journal of Personality, 26,* 229–242.

Stening, B. W., & Wong, P. S. (1983). Australian managers' leadership beliefs, 1970/82. *Psychological Reports, 53,* 274–278.

Stephan, F. E. (1952). The relative rate of communication between members of small groups. *American Sociological Review, 17,* 482–486.

Stephens, C. R., D'Intino, R. S., & Victor, B. (1995). The moral quandary of transformational leadership. *Research in Organizational Change and Development, 8,* 123.

Stephenson, H. B. (1966). The effect of a management training program on leadership attitude and on-the-job behavior. *Dissertation Abstracts, 27,* 1512.

Sterling, T. D., & Rosenthal, B. G. (1950). The relationship of changing leadership and followership in a group to the changing phases of group activity. *American Psychologist, 5,* 311.

Stern, B. (2007). Tattered standard of duty on wall street. *New York Times,* Business Section: Everybody's business, December 23.

Stern, P., Dietz, T., & Kalof, L. (1993). Value orientations, gender, and environmental concern. *Environment and Behavior, 25,* 322–348.

Sternberg, R. J. (1985). *Beyond IQ.* Cambridge, MA: Cambridge University Press.

Sternerg, R. J. (2007). Successful intelligence: A new approach to leadership. In R. J. Sternberg (ed.), *Handbook of human intelligence.* Cambridge, MA: Cambridge University Press.

Sternberg, R. J., Kaufman, J. C. & Pretz, J. L. (2003). A propulsion model of creative leadership. *Leadership Quarterly, 14,* 455–474.

Sternberg, R. J., Wagner, R. K. & Okagaka, L. (1993). Practical intelligence: The nature and role of tacit knowledge in work and at school. In H. Reese & J. Puckett (eds.), *Advances in lifespan development.* Hillsdale, NJ: Lawrence Erlbaum Associates.

Sterngold, J. (1988). Group bids $20.9 billion for Nabisco. *The New York Times,* November 4, Dl.

Steuer, J. (1992). Defining virtual reality: Dimensions determining telepresence. *Journal of Communications, 42*(4), 73–93.

Stevens, G., & DeNisi, A. (1980). Women as managers: Attitudes and attributions for performance by men and women. *Academy of Management Journal, 23,* 355–361.

Stewart, A., & Stewart, V. (1976). *Tomorrow's men today.* London: Institute of Personnel Management/Institute of Manpower Studies.

Stewart, A. J., & Winter, D. C. (1976). Arousal of the power motive in women. *Journal of Consulting and Clinical Psychology, 44,* 495–496.

Stewart, D. W., & Sprinthall, N. A. (1994). Moral development in public administration. In T. L. Cooper, & K. C. Cooper (eds.), *Handbook of administrative ethics.* New York: Marcel Dekker, Inc. 325–348.

Stewart, G. L., & Manz, C. C. (1995). *Attitude and intention as explanations for supervisor resistance to empowerment.* Paper, Society for Industrial and Organizational Psychology, Orlando, FL.

Stewart, G. T. (1974). Charisma and integration: An eighteenth century North American case. *Comparative Studies in Society and History, 16*(2), 138–149.

Stewart, L. (1962). Management games today. In J. M. Kibbee, C. J. Craft, & B. Nanus (eds.), *Management games.* New York: Rinehart.

Stewart, M. M., & Roberson, Q. M. (2000). *Decoupling elements of negative feedback: Clarifying the effects of credibility, accuracy and fairness on recipients' motivation.* Paper, Society for Industrial and Organizational Psychology, New Orleans, LA.

Stewart, P. A. (1967). *Job enlargement.* Iowa City: University of Iowa, Center for Labor & Management.

Stewart, R. (1965). The use of diaries to study managers' jobs. *Journal of Management Studies, 2,* 228–235.

Stewart, R. (1966). The socio-cultural setting of management in the United Kingdom. *International Labor Review, 94,* 108–131.

Stewart, R. (1967). *Managers and their jobs: A study of the similarities and differences in the way managers spend their time.* London: Macmillan.

Stewart, R. (1976b). To understand the manager's job: Consider demands, constraints, choices. *Organizational Dynamics, 4,* 22–32.

Stewart, R. (1982a). *Choices for the manager: A guide to understanding managerial work and behavior.* Englewood Cliffs, NJ: Prentice–Hall.

Stewart, R. (1982b). A model for understanding managerial jobs and behavior. *Academy of Management Review, 7,* 7–13.

Stewart, R. (1997). *The reality of management.* Oxford, England: Butterworth-Heinemann.

Stewart, T. A. (1994). Managing in a wired company. *Fortune,* July 11, 44–47, 50, 54.

Stewart, W., May, R. C., & Kalia, A. (2003). *Executive perceptions and environmental scanning among managers and entrepreneurs in two countries.* Paper, Academy of Management, Seattle, WA.

Stewart, W. H., Jr., May, R. C., & Arvind, K. (2008). Environmental perceptions and scanning in the United States and India: Convergence in entrepreneurial information seeking? *Entrepreneurship Theory and Practice* 32(1), 83–06.

Steyrer, J. (2002). Stigma and charisma and the narcissistic personality. In B.J . Avolio & F. J. Yammarino (eds), *Transformational and charismatic leadership: The road ahead.* New York: JAI Press.

Stinglhamber, F., & Vandenberghe, C. (2001). *Perceived support and discretionary treatment from organizations and supervisors.* Paper, Society for Industrial and Organizational Psychology, San Diego, CA.

Stierheim, M. R. (1984). Crisis management in metropolitan Dade County. *Public Management,* 66(3), 2–4.

Stimpson, D. V., & Bass, B. M. (1964). Dyadic behavior of self-, and interaction-, and task-oriented subjects in a test situation. *Journal of Abnormal and Social Psychology,* 68, 558–562.

Stinson, J. E. (1970). *The differential impact of Participation in laboratory training in collaborative task effort in intact and fragmented groups.* Doctoral dissertation, Ohio State University, Columbus.

Stinson, J. E. (1972). "Least preferred coworker" as a measure of leadership style. *Psychological Reports,* 30, 930.

Stinson, J. E., & Johnson, T. W. (1975). The path-goal theory of leadership: A partial test and suggested refinement. *Academy of Management Journal,* 18, 242–252.

Stinson, J. E., & Tracy, L. (1974). Some disturbing characteristics of the LPC score. *Personnel Psychology,* 24, 477–485.

Stirling, J. B., II, (1998). The role of leadership in condominium and homeowner associations. *Journal of Leadership Studies,* 5, 148–155.

Stockdale, J. B. (1981). The principles of leadership. *American Educator,* 5(4), 12, 14–15, 33.

Stockdale, J. B. (1987). *Leadership in response to changing societal values.* Paper, Conference on Military Leadership: Traditions and Future Trends. Annapolis, MD: United States Naval Academy.

Stogdill, R. M. (1948). Personal factors associated with leadership: A survey of the literature. *Journal of Psychology,* 25, 35–71.

Stogdill, R. M. (1949). The sociometry of working relations in formal organizations. *Sociometry,* 12, 276–286.

Stogdill, R. M. (1950). Leadership, membership and organization. *Psychological Bulletin,* 47, 1–14.

Stogdill, R. M. (1951a). The organization of working relationships: Twenty sociometric indices. *Sociometry,* 14, 366–374.

Stogdill, R. M. (1951b). Studies in naval leadership, Part II (ed.). In H. Guetzkow (ed.), *Groups, leadership, and men.* Pittsburgh: Carnegie Press.

Stogdill, R. M. (1955). Interactions among superiors and subordinates. *Sociometry,* 18, 552–557.

Stogdill, R. M. (1957a). *Leadership and structures of personal interaction.* Columbus: Ohio State University, Bureau of Business Research.

Stogdill, R. M. (1959). *Individual behavior and group achievement.* New York: Oxford University Press.

Stogdill, R. M. (1963a). *Manual for the Leader Behavior Description Questionnaire Form XII.* Columbus: Ohio State University, Bureau of Business Research.

Stogdill, R. M. (1963). *Team achievement under high motivation.* Columbus, Ohio: Ohio State University, Bureau of Business Research, College of Commerce and Administration.

Stogdill, R. M. (1965a). *Managers, employees, organizations.* Columbus: Ohio State University, Bureau of Business Research.

Stogdill, R. M. (1965b). *Manual for job satisfaction and expectation scales.* Columbus: Ohio State University, Bureau of Business Research.

Stogdill, R. M. (1969). Validity of leader behavior descriptions. *Personnel Psychology,* 22, 153–158.

Stogdill, R. M. (1970). *Effects of leadership training on the performance of sororities.* Columbus: Ohio State University. Unpublished report.

Stogdill, R. M. (1972). Group productivity, drive, and cohesiveness. *Organizational Behavior and Human Performance,* 8, 26–43.

Stogdill, R. M. (1974). *Handbook of leadership* (1st ed.). New York: Free Press.

Stogdill, R. M. (1975). The evolution of leadership theory. *Proceedings,* Academy of Management, New Orleans.

Stogdill, R. M., & Bailey, W. R. (1969). *Changing the response of vocational students to supervision: The use of motion pictures and group discussion.* Columbus: Ohio State University, Center for Vocational and Technical Education.

Stogdill, R. M., & Coady, N. R (1970). Preferences of vocational students for different styles of supervisory behavior. *Personnel Psychology,* 23, 309–312.

Stogdill, R. M., Coady, N. R, & Zimmer, A. (1970). *Response of vocational students to supervision: Effects of reinforcing positive and negative attitudes toward different supervisory roles.* Columbus: Ohio State University, Center for Vocational and Technical Education.

Stogdill, R. M., & Coons, A. E. (1957). *Leader behavior: Its description and measurement.* Columbus: Ohio State University, Bureau of Business Research.

Stogdill, R. M., & Goode, O. S. (1957). Effects of the interactions of superiors upon the performances and expectations of subordinates. *International Journal of Sociometry,* 1, 133–145.

Stogdill, R. M., Goode, O. S., & Day, D. R. (1962). New leader behavior description sub-scales. *Journal of Psychology,* 54, 259–269.

Stogdill, R. M., Goode, O. S., & Day, D. R. (1963a). The leader behavior of corporation presidents. *Personnel Psychology,* 16, 127–132.

Stogdill, R. M., Goode, O. S., & Day, D. R. (1963b). The leader behavior of United States senators. *Journal of Psychology,* 56, 3–8.

Stogdill, R. M., Goode, O. S., & Day, D. R. (1964). The leader behavior of presidents of labor unions. *Personnel Psychology,* 17, 49–57.

Stogdill, R. M., Goode, O. S., & Day, D. R. (1965). *The leader behavior of university presidents.* Columbus: Ohio State University, Bureau of Business Research.

Stogdill, R. M., & Haase, K. K. (1957). Structures of working relationships. In R. M. Stogdill (ed.), *Leadership and structures of personal interaction.* Columbus: Ohio State University, Bureau of Business Research.

Stogdill, R. M., & Koehler, K. (1952). *Measures of leadership structure and organization change.* Columbus: Ohio State University, Personnel Research Board.

Stogdill, R. M., & Scott, E. L. (1957). Responsibility and authority relationships. In R. M. Stogdill (ed.), *Leadership and structures of personal interaction.* Columbus: Ohio State University, Bureau of Business Research.

Stogdill, R. M., Scott, E. L., & Jaynes, W. E. (1956). *Leadership and role expectations.* Columbus: Ohio State University, Bureau of Business Research.

Stogdill, R. M., & Shartle, C. L. (1948). Methods for determining patterns of leadership behavior in relation to organization structure and objectives. *Journal of Applied Psychology, 32,* 286–291.

Stogdill, R. M., & Shartle, C. L. (1955). *Methods in the study of administrative leadership.* Columbus: Ohio State University, Bureau of Business Research.

Stogdill, R. M., & Shartle, C. L. (1958). *Manual for the Work Analysis Forms.* Columbus: Ohio State University, Bureau of Business Research.

Stogdill, R. M., Shartle, C. L., Scott, E. L., Coons, A. E., & Jaynes, W. E. (1956). *A predictive study of administrative work patterns.* Columbus: Ohio State University, Bureau of Business Research.

Stogdill, R. M., Shartle, C. L., Wherry, R. J., & Jaynes, W. E. (1955). A factorial study of administrative behavior. *Personnel Psychology, 8,* 165–180.

Stogdill, R. M., Wherry, R. J., & Jaynes, W. E. (1953). *Patterns of leader behavior: A factorial study of Navy officer performance.* Columbus: Ohio State University, Bureau of Business Research.

Stohl, C. (1986). The role of memorable messages in the process of organizational socialization. *Communication Quarterly, 34,* 231–249.

Stolin, V. (1997). N Stolin, V. (1997). *North Americans managing abroad. A Russian case study.* Paper, Society for Industrial and Organizational Psychology, St. Louis, MO.

Stone, D. L., Gueutal, H. G., & Macintosh, B. (1984). The effects of feedback sequence and expertise of rater on perceived feedback accuracy. *Personnel Psychology, 37,* 487–506.

Stone, E. F., Stone, D. L., & Dipboye, R. L. (1992). Stigmas in organizations: Race, handicaps, and physical unattractiveness, In K. Kelley (ed.), *Issues, theory, and research in industrial organizational psychology: Advances in psychology,* Amsterdam, Netherlands: North Holland.

Stoner-Zemel, M. J. (1988). *Visionary leadership, management, and high performing work units.* Doctoral dissertation, University of Massachusetts, Amherst.

Stonequist, E. V. (1937). *The marginal man.* New York: Scribner's.

Storey, A. W. (1954). A study of member satisfaction and types of contributions in discussion groups with responsibility-sharing leadership. *Dissertation Abstracts, 14,* 737.

Stotland, E. (1954). Peer groups and reactions to power figures. *American Psychologist, 9,* 478.

Stouffer, S. A. (1949). An analysis of conflicting social norms. *American Sociological Review, 14,* 707–717.

Stouffer, S. A., Suchman, E. A., DeVinney, L. C., Star, S. A., & Williams, R. M., Jr. (1949). *The American soldier: Adjustment during army life.* Princeton, NJ: Princeton University Press.

St. Petersburg Times (2001). Most entering law school are women. March 26, 3A.

Strange, J. M., & Mumford, M. D. (2002). The origins of vision charismatic versus ideological leadership. *Leadership Quarterly, 13*(4), 343–377.

Strasser, F. (1983). Techniques: Delicate delegation. *Management World, 12*(4), 32–33.

Straus, S. G., Miles, J. A., & Levesque, L. L. (2001). The effects of videoconference, telephone, and face-to-face media on interviewer and applican judgements to employment interviews. *Journal of Management, 27,* 363–381.

Strauss, A. L. (1944). The literature on panic. *Journal of Abnormal and Social Psychology, 39,* 317–328.

Strauss, A., & Corbin, J. (1990). *Basics of qualitative research: Grounded theory procedures and techniques.* Newbury Park, CA: Sage.

Strauss, G. (1962). Tactics of lateral relationship: The purchasing agent. *Administrative Science Quarterly, 7,* 161–186.

Strauss, G. (1963). Some notes on power-equalization. In H. J. Leavitt (ed.), *The social science of organizations: Four perspectives.* Englewood Cliffs, NJ: Prentice-Hall.

Strauss, G., & Rosenstein, E. (1970). Workers' participation: A critical view. *Industrial Relations, 9,* 197–214.

Streib, G. F., Folts, W. E., & LaGreca, A. J. (1985). Autonomy, power, and decision-making in thirty-six retirement communities. *Gerontologist, 25,* 403–409.

Streufert, S. S. (1965). Communicator importance and interpersonal attitudes toward conforming and deviant group members. *Journal of Personality and Social Psychology, 56,* 242.

Streufert, S., Streufert, S. C., & Castore, C. H. (1968). Leadership in negotiations and the complexity of conceptual structure. *Journal of Applied Psychology, 52,* 218–223.

Streufert, S., & Swezey, R. W.(1986). *Complexity, managers' capacity, and organizations.* New York: Academic Press.

Stricker, L. J. (1989). *Assessing leadership potential at the naval academy with a biographical measure.* Research Report. Princeton, NJ: Educational Testing Service.

Stricker, L. J. & Rock, D. A. (1998). Assessing leadership potential with a biographical measure of personality traits. *International Journal of Selection and Assessment, 6,* 164–184.

Strickland, L. H. (1967). Need for approval and the components of the ASo score. *Perceptual and Motor Skills, 24,* 875–878.

Strickland, L., Guild, P., Barefoot, J., & Paterson, S. (1978). Teleconferencing and leadership emergence. *Human Relations, 31,* 583–596.

Stringer, R. (2001). *Leadership and organizational climate: The cloud chamber effect.* Upper Saddle River, NJ: Prentice Hall.

Strodtbeck, F. L. (1951). Husband-wife interaction over revealed differences. *American Journal of Sociology, 16,* 468–473.

Strodtbeck, F. L., & Mann, R. D. (1956). Sex role differentiation in jury deliberations. *Sociometry, 19,* 3–11.

Stroh, L. K., Brett, J. M., & Reilly, A. H. (1992). All the right stuff: A comparison of female and male managers' career progression. *Journal of Applied Psychology, 77,* 251–260.

Strohmeier, B. R. (1998). Achieving effective technical leadership in today's R&D organizations. *Journal of Leadership Studies, 5,* 29–37.

Stromberg, R. F. (1967). Value orientation and leadership behavior of school principals. *Dissertation Abstracts, 27,* 2811.

Strong, E. K. (1943). *Vocational interests of men and women.* Stanford, CA: Stanford University Press.

Strong, L. (1956). Of time and top management. *Management Review, 45,* 486–493.

Strong, R. M. (1984). On qualitative methods and leadership research. In J. C. Hunt, D. Hosking, C. A. Schriesheim, & R. Stewart (eds.),

Leaders and managers: International perspectives on managerial behavior and leadership. New York: Pergamon.

Stross, R. E. (1996). *The Microsoft way: The real story of how the company outsmarts its competition.* New York: Basic Books.

Stross, R. E. (1998). How Yahoo! won the search wars. *Fortune* (March 2), 137(4), 148–154.

Struck, D., & Tolbert, K. (2000). Japan's economic upheaval takes a toll in lives. *International Herald Tribune,* January 6, 16.

Stroud, P. V. (1959). Evaluating a human relations training program. *Personnel,* 36, 52–60.

Stroup, T. G., Jr. (1996). Leadership and organizational culture: Actions speak louder than words. *Military Review,* January–February, 44–49.

Strozier, C. B., & Offer, D. (1985a). Introduction. In C. B. Strozier & D. Offer (eds.), *The leader: Psychohistorical essays.* New York: Plenum.

Strozier, C. B., & Offer, D. (1985b). Sigmund Freud and history. In C. B. Strozier & D. Offer (eds.), *The leader: Psychohistorical essays.* New York: Plenum.

Strube, M. J., & Garcia, J. E. (1981). A meta-analytical investigation of Fiedler's contingency model of leadership effectiveness. *Psychological Bulletin,* 90, 307–321.

Strube, M. J., & Garcia, J. E. (1983). On the proper interpretation of empirical findings: Strube and Garcia (1981) revisited. *Psychological Bulletin,* 93, 600–603.

Struckman, C., & Yammarino, F. J. (2003). A solution to the enigma of the 21st century. *Organizational Dynamics,* 32, 234–246.

Strumpfer, D. J. W. (1983). How managers describe themselves in a job context. *South African Journal of Business Management,* 14, 45–52.

Stryker, P. (1961). *The character of the executive.* New York: Harper & Row.

Stuart, J. M., Weierter, S. J. M., Ashkanasy, N. M., & Callan, V. (1997). Effect of self-monitoring and national culture on follower perceptions pf personal charisma and charismatic message. *Australian Journal of Psychology,* 49(2), 101–105.

Stuart, R. (1996). The trauma of organizational leadership. *Journal of European Training,* 20(2), 11–16.

Student, K. R. (1968). Supervisory influence and workgroup performance. *Journal of Applied Psychology,* 52, 188–194.

Stumpf, S. (undated). *Leadership behaviors in managing scientists and engineers: A path analytic approach.* Unpublished manuscript.

Sublett, R. H. (1995–1996). The challenge of leadership. *Focus: W. K. Foundation National Fellowship Program,* 1–2.

Subramanian, S., & Rao, K. S. (1997). An integrated training intervention for enhancing work effectiveness of low performers. *Indian Journal of Industrial Relations,* 33(1), 68–80.

Sucharski, I. (2002). Perceived supervisor support: Contributions to perceived organizational support and employee retention. *Journal of Applied Psychology,* 87(3), 565–573.

Suetonius, G. S. T. (c. 122 /1957). *The lives of the Caesars.* (Trans. R. Groes.) London: Penguin.

Sugiman, T., & Misumi, J. (1984). Action research on evacuation method in emergent situation: II. Effects of leader: Evacuee ratio on efficiency of follow-direction method and follow-me method. *Japanese Journal of Experimental Social Psychology,* 23, 107–115.

Sugiman, T., & Misumi, J. (1988). Development of a new evacuation

method for emergencies: Control of collective behavior by emergent small groups. *Journal of Applied Psychology,* 73(1), 3–10.

Sugiman, T., Misumi, J., & Sako, H. (1983). Action research on evacuation method in emergent situations: I. Comparison between follow-direction method and follow-me method. *Japanese Journal of Experimental Social Psychology,* 22, 95–98.

Sujan, H., Weitz, B. A., & Kumar, N. (1994). Learning orientation, working smart, and effective selling. *Journal of Marketing,* 58, 39–52.

Sukel, W. M. (1983). Assessing adults' socialization: Attitudes of top, middle, and supervisory managers. *Psychological Reports,* 52, 735–739.

Sullivan, J., Suzuki, T., & Kondo, Y. (1984). Managerial theories of the performance control process in Japanese and American work groups. *Proceedings,* Academy of Management, Boston, 98–102.

Summers, L., & Fleenor, J. W. (1998). Information technology and 360-degree feedback. *Leadership in Action,* 18(4), 9–13.

Summers, P. P. (1995). Personality, competence, and leadership: The synergism of effective parenting. *The Journal of Leadership Studies,* 2(2), 117–137.

Sun Tzu (c. 400 B.C./1963). *The art of war.* London: Oxford University Press.

Survey Research Center. (1948). *Productivity, supervision, and employee morale.* Ann Arbor: University of Michigan.

Sutcliffe, K. (1994). What executives notice: Accurate perceptions in top management teams. *Academy of Management Journal,* 37, 1360–1378.

Sutcliffe, R. E. (1980). A comparative study of leader behavior among deaf and hearing supervisors. *Dissertation Abstracts International,* 42(2A), 496.

Sutton, C. D., & Moore, K. K. (1985). Executive women—20 years later. *Harvard Business Review,* 63(5), 42–66.

Sutton, C. D., & Woodman, R. W. (1989). Pygmalion goes to work: The effects of supervisory expectations in a retail setting. *Journal of Applied Psychology,* 74, 943–950.

Sutton, R. I., Eisenhardt, K. M., & Jucker, J. V. (1986). Managing organizational decline. *Organizational Dynamics,* 14(4), 17–29.

Sutton, R. I., & Staw, B. M. (1995). What theory is not. *Administrative Science Quarterly,* 40, 371–384.

Swain, M. A. (1993). Personal communication, August 30.

Sward, K. (1933). Temperament and direction of achievement. *Journal of Social Psychology,* 4, 406–429.

Swartz, J. L. (1973). *Analysis of leadership styles of college level head football coaches from five midwestern states.* Doctoral dissertation, University of Northern Colorado, Greeley.

Sweeney, A. B., Fiechtner, L. A., & Samores, R. J. (1975). An integrative factor analysis of leadership measures and theories. *Journal of Psychology,* 90, 75–85.

Sweeney, J. (1982). Research synthesis on effective school leadership. *Educational Leadership,* 39, 346–352.

Swim, J. K., Cohen, L. L., & Hyers, L. L. (1998). Experiencing everyday prejudice and discrimination. In J. K. Swim & C. Stangor (eds.), *Prejudice: The target's perspective.* San Diego, CA: Academic Press.

Swingle, R. C. (1970a). Exploitative behavior in non-zero-sum games. *Journal of Personality and Social Psychology,* 16, 121–132.

Switzer, K. A. (1975). Peasant leadership: Comparison of peasant leaders in two Colombian states. *International Journal of Comparative Sociology, 16*, 291–300.

Switzer, K. (2003). *The influence of training reputation, managerial support, and self–efficacy on pretraining motivation and perceived training transfer.* Paper, Society for Industrial and Organizational Psychology, Orlando, FL.

Sylvia, D., & Hutchison, T. (1985). What makes Ms. Johnson teach? A study of teacher motivation. *Human Relations, 38*, 841–856.

Symonds, P. M. (1947). Role playing as a diagnostic procedure in the selection of leaders. *Sociatry, 1*, 43–50.

Symons, G. L. (1986). Coping with the corporate tribe: How women in different cultures experience the managerial role. *Journal of Management, 12*, 379–390.

Sypher, B. D., & Zorn, I. E., Jr. (1986). Communication-related abilities and upward mobility. *Human Communication Research, 12*, 420–431.

Szabo, E., Reber, G., Weibler, F. C., et al. (2001). Values and behavior orientation in leadership studies: Reflections based on findings in three German-speaking countries. *Leadership Quarterly, 12*, 219–244.

Szilagyi, A. D. (1980a). Reward behavior of male and female leaders: A causal inference analysis. *Journal of Vocational Behavior, 16*, 59–72.

Szilagyi, A. D. (1980b). Causal inferences between leader reward behavior and subordinate performance, absenteeism, and work satisfaction. *Journal of Occupational Psychology, 53*, 195–204.

Szilagyi, A. D., Jr., & Schweiger, D. M. (1984). Matching managers to strategies: A review and suggested framework. *Academy of Management Review, 9*, 626–637.

Szilagyi, A. D., & Sims, H. P. (1974a). The cross–sample stability of the supervisory behavior description questionnaire. *Journal of Applied Psychology, 59*, 767–770.

Szlagyi, A. D. & Simms, H. P. (1978). Causal analysis of a leader behavior over three different time lags. *Eastern Academy of Manaagement Proceedings*, 77–91.

Szymanski, D. M., Bharadwaj, S. G., & Varadarajan, P. R. (1993). An analysis of the market share-profitability relationship. *Journal of Marketing, 57*(7), 1–18.

Tabak, F. (1997). Employee creative performance: What makes it happen? *Academy of Management Executive, 11*(1), 119–120. (From Oldham, G. R., & Cummings, A. (1996). Employee creativity: Personal and contextual factors at work. *Academy of Management Journal, 39*, 607–634.)

Taggar, S. (2001). Group composition, creative energy, and group performance. *Journal of Creative Behavior, 35*, 261–286.

Taggar, S., & Seijts, G. H. (2003). Leader and staff-role efficacy as antecedents of collective-efficacy and performance. *Human Performance, 16*, 131–156.

Tagiuri, R., & Kogan, N. (1957). The visibility of interpersonal preferences. *Human Relations, 10*, 385–390.

Tait, R. (1996). The attributes of leadership. *Leadership & Organization Development Journal, 17*(1), 27–31.

Takamiya, M. (1979). *Japanese multinationals in Europe: Internal operations and their public policy implications.* Berlin: International Institute of Management.

Talland, G. A. (1954). The assessment of group opinion by leaders and

their influence on its formation. *Journal of Abnormal and Social Psychology, 49*, 431–434.

Tang, J. (1997). The Model Minority thesis revisited: (Counter)evidence from the science and engineering fields. *Journal of Applied Behavioral Science, 33*, 291–315.

Tang, T., L.-P., Furnham, A., & Davis, G. M. T. W. (2003). A cross-cultural comparison of the money ethic, the Protestant work ethic, and job satisfaction: Taiwan, the USA, and the UK. *International Journal of Organizational Theory and Behavior, 6*, 175–184.

Tang, T. L., Tollison, P. S., & Whiteside, H. D. (1988). *Top-, middle-, and lower-management attendance and quality circle effectiveness.* Paper, American Psychological Association, Atlanta, CA.

Tanimoto, R. H. (1977). *A field study of MBO in a utility company.* MBA thesis, Pepperdine University, School of Business and Management, Malibu, CA.

Tannen, D. (1991). *You just don't understand: Women and men in conversation.* London: Virago.

Tannenbaum, A. S. (1958). The relationship between personality and group structure. In R. Likert (ed.), Effective supervision: An adaptive and relative process. *Personnel Psychology, 11*, 317–322.

Tannenbaum, A. S. (1956a). The concept of organization control. *Journal of Social Issues, 12*, 50–60.

Tannenbaum, A. S. (1956b). Control structure and union functions. *American Journal of Sociology, 61*, 536–545.

Tannenbaum, A. S. (1963). *Control in organizations: Individual adjustment and organizational performance.* Palo Alto, CA: Stanford University.

Tannenbaum, A. S. (1968). *Control in organizations.* New York: McGraw-Hill.

Tannenbaum, A. S. (1974). *Hierarchy in organizations: An international comparison.* San Francisco: Jossey-Bass.

Tannenbaum, A. S., & Allport, F. H. (1956). Personality structure and group structure: An interpolative study of their relationships through event-structure analysis. *Journal of Abnormal and Social Psychology, 53*, 272–280.

Tannenbaum, A. S., & Bachman, J. G. (1966). Attitude uniformity and role in a voluntary organization. *Human Relations, 19*, 309–323.

Tannenbaum, A. S., & Smith, C. G. (1964). Effects of member influence in an organization: Phenomenology versus organization structure. *Journal of Abnormal and Social Psychology, 69*, 401–410.

Tannenbaum, D. E. (1959). Relation of executive leadership to the factor of external authority: A study of board-executive relationships in five family agencies. *Dissertation Abstracts, 22*, 1239.

Tannenbaum, R. (1950). Managerial decision making. *Journal of Business, 23*, 33–37.

Tannenbaum, R., Kallejian, V., & Weschler, I. R. (1954). *Training managers for leadership. Instructions on Industrial Relations.* UCLA, Los Angeles, No. 35.

Tannenbaum, R., & Massarik, F. (1950). Participation by subordinates in the managerial decision-making process. *Canadian Journal of Economic and Political Science, 16*, 408–418.

Tannenbaum, R., & Schmidt, W. H. (1958). How to choose a leadership pattern. *Harvard Business Review, 36*(2), 95–101.

Tannenbaum, R., Weschler, I. R., & Massarik, F. (1961). *Leadership and organization.* New York: McGraw-Hill.

Tannenbaum, S. L., Smith-Jentsch, K. A., & Behson, S. J. (1998). Training team leaders to facilitate team learning and performance. In J. A. Cannon-Bowers & E. Salas (eds.), *Making decisions under stress: Implications for individual and team training*. Washington, DC: American Psychological Association.

Tarnapol, L. (1958). Personality differences between leaders and non-leaders. *Personnel Journal, 37,* 57–60.

Taussig, F. W., & Joslyn, C. S. (1932). *American business leaders: A study in social origins and social stratification*. New York: Macmillan.

Tavris, C. (1977). Men and women report their views on masculinity. *Psychology Today, 10,* 34–42, 82.

Taylor, C. R., & Wheatley-Lovoy, C. (1998) Leadership lessons from the Magic Kingdom. *Training and Development Journal, 52,* 22–25.

Taylor, F. W. (1911). *Principles of scientific management*. New York: Harper & Brothers.

Taylor, H. (1980). Effective leadership styles. *Canadian Manager, 5(5),* 12–13.

Taylor, J. (2005). Challenge match: How the former world-chess champion Garry Kasparov hopes to unseat Vladimir Putin. *Atlantic Monthly, 296(5),* 48–52.

Taylor, J. C., & Bowers, D. G. (1972). *Survey of organizations: Toward a machine-scored standardized questionnaire instrument*. Ann Arbor: University of Michigan, Institute for Social Research.

Taylor, K. F. (1967). Some doubts about sensitivity training. *Australian Psychology, 1,* 171–179.

Taylor M., Crook, R., & Dropkin, S. (1961). Assessing emerging leadership behavior in small discussion groups. *Journal of Educational Psychology, 52,* 12–18.

Taylor, M. S. (1981). *The effects of feedback consistency: One test of a model*. Paper, Academy of Management, San Diego, CA.

Taylor, M. S., Fisher, C. D., & Ilgen, D. R. (1984). Individuals' reactions to performance feedback in organizations: A control theory perspective. In K. M. Rowland & G. R. Ferris (eds.), *Research in personnel and human resource management*, Vol. 2. Greenwich, CT: JAI Press.

Taylor, M. S., & Ilgen, D. R. (1979). *Employees' reactions to male and female managers: Is there a difference?* Paper, Academy of Management, Atlanta, GA.

Taylor, M. S., Masterson, S., Renard, M., et al. (1998). Managers' reactions to procedurally just performance management systems. *Academy of Management Journal, 41,* 568–580.

Taylor, M. S., & Slania, M. A. (1981). *The moderating effects of chronic self-esteem upon the psychological success cycle*. Paper, Midwestern Psychological Association, Detroit.

Taylor, T., Ross-Smith, A. E., & McGraw, P. (2003). *Succession management practices in Australian organizations*. Paper, Academy of Management, Seattle, WA.

Taynor, J., & Deaux, K. (1973). When women are more deserving than men: Equity, attribution, and perceived sex differences. *Journal of Personality and Social Psychology, 28,* 360–367.

Tead, O. (1929). The technique of creative leadership. *In human nature and management*. New York: McGraw-Hill.

Tead, O. (1935). *The art of leadership*. New York: McGraw-Hill.

Tedeschi, J. T., & Kian, M. (1962). Cross-cultural study of the TAT assessment for achievement motivation: Americans and Persians. *Journal of Social Psychology, 58,* 227–234.

Tedeschi, J. T, Lindskold, S., Horai, J., & Gahagan, J. P. (1969). Social power and the credibility of promises. *Journal of Personality and Social Psychology, 13,* 253–261.

Tekleab, A. G., Yun, S., Tesluk, P., et al. (2001). Are we on the same page? The effects of leaders' self-awareness of their leadership behavior on follower and leader outcomes. *Personnel Psychology* (submitted).

Telligen, A. (1985). Structures of mood and personality and their relevance to assessing anxiety, with emphasis on self-report. In A. H. Truman & J. D. Maser (eds.), *Anxiety and anxiety disorders*. New York: Erlbaum.

Telligen, A., Lykken, T. J., Bouchard, K. J., Jr., et al. (1988). Personality similarity in twins reared apart and together. *Journal of Personality and Social Psychology, 54,* 1031–1039.

Tenbrunsel, A. E., & Messick, D. M. (2001). Power asymmetries and the ethical atmosphere for negations. In J. M. Darley, D. M. Messick, & T. R. Taylor (eds.), *Social influences on ethical behavior in organizations*. Mahwah, NJ: Lawrence Erlbaum.

Tenopyr, M. L., & Ruch, W. W. (1965). *The comparative validity of selected leadership scales relative to success in production management*. Paper, American Psychological Association, Chicago.

Tepper, B. J. (1990). *Influence tactics employed in charismatic leader–follower interaction*. Doctoral dissertation, University of Miami, Miami, FL.

Tepper, B. J. (2000). Consequences of abusive supervision. *Academy of Management Journal, 43,* 178–190.

Tepper, B. J., Duffy, M. K., & Hoobler, J. M. (2002). *Moderating effects of abusive supervision on relationships between coworkerers' organizational citizenship behavior and fellow employees' attitudes*. Paper, Academy of Management, Denver, CO.

Tepper, B. J., Duffy, M. K., & Shaw, J. D. (2001). Personality moderators of the relationship between abusive supervision and subordinates' resistance. *Journal of Applied Psychology, 86,* 974–983.

Tepper, B. J., & Percy, P. M., (1994). Structural validity of the multifactor leadership questionnaire. *Educational and Psychological Measurement 54,* 734–744.

Tepper, B. J., Schriesheim, C. A., Nehring, D., Nelson, R. J., Taylor, E. C., & Eisenbach, R. J. (1998). *The multidimensionality and multifunctionality of subordinates' resistance to downward influence attempts*. Paper presented at the annual meeting of the Academy of Management, San Diego, CA.

Terborg, J. R. (1977). Women in Management: A Research Review. *Journal of Applied Psychology, 62,* 647–664.

Terborg, J. R., Howard, G. S., & Maxwell, S. E. (1980). Evaluating planned organizational change: A method for assessing alpha, beta, and gamma change. *Academy of Management Review, 5,* 109–121.

Terborg, J. R., & Ilgen, D. R. (1975). A theoretical approach to sex discrimination in traditionally masculine occupations. *Organizational Behavior and Human Performance, 13,* 352–76.

Terborg, J. R., and Ilgen, D. R. (1975). Sex discrimination and sex role stereotypes: Are they synonymous? No! *Organizational Behavior and Human Performance, 14,* 154–57.

Terborg, J. R., Peters, L. H., Ilgen, D. R., & Smith, F. (1977). Organizational and personal correlates of attitudes toward women as managers. *Academy of Management Journal 20,* 89–100.

Terborg, J. R., & Shingledecker, P. (1983). Employee reactions to supervision and work evaluation as a function of subordinate and manager sex . *Sex Roles*, 9(7), 813–824.

Terhune, K. W. (1970). The effects of personality in cooperation and conflict. In P. Swingle (ed.), *The structure of conflict.* New York: Academic Press.

Terman, L. M. (1904). A preliminary study of the psychology and pedagogy of leadership. *Pedagogical Seminary*, 11, 413–451.

Terman, L. M. (1925). *Mental and physical traits of a thousand gifted children.* Stanford, CA: Stanford University Press.

Terpstra, V. (1978). *The cultural environment of international business.* Cincinnati, OH: Southwestern.

Terry, L. D. (1995). The leadership-management distinction: The domination and displacement of mechanical and organismic theories. *Leadership Quarterly*, 6, 515–527.

Terry, P. T. (1979). The English in management. *Management Today* 1(11), 90–97.

Tesluk, P. E., & Mathieu, J. E. (1999). Overcoming roadblocks to effectiveness: Incorporating management of performance barriers into models of work group effectiveness. *Journal of Applied Psychology*, 84, 200–217.

Testa, G. (1998). Values, leadership, and change: How to change whilst building on your roots. *ISVOR-FIAT.Training and Education Review*, June, 29–32.

Teters, C. (1999). *American Indians are people, not mascots.* Spokane, WA: National Coalition on Racism in Sports and Media.

Tetlock, P. E. (1985). Accountability: The neglected social context of judgment and choice. In L. L. Cummings & B. M. Staw (eds.), *Research in organizational behavior* (vol. 8). Greenwich, CT: JAI Press

Tetrault, L. A., Schriesheim, C. A., & Neider, L. L. (1988). Leadership training interventions: A review. *Organizational Development Journal*, 6(3), 77–83.

Tetrick, L. (1989). The motivating potential of leaders: A comparison of two models. *Journal of Applied Social Psychology*, 19, 947–958.

Tewel, K. (1986). The urban school principal: The rocky road to instructional leadership. *Carnegie Quarterly*, 31(1), 1–8.

Thakor, A.V. (1990). Shareholder preferences and dividend policy. *The Journal of Finance.*

Tharenou, P. (2001). Going up? Do traits and informal social processes predict advancing in management? *Academy of Management Journal*, 44, 1005–1017.

Tharenou, P. (2002). Receptivity to careers in international work—abroad and at home. *Australian Journal of Management*, 27, Special Issue, 129–136.

Tharenou, P., & Conroy, D. (1994). Men and women managers' advancement: Personal or situational determinants. *Applied Psychology: An International Review*, 43, 5–31.

Tharenou, P., Latimer, S., & Conroy, D. (1994). How do you make it to the top? An examination of influences on women's and men's managerial advancement. *Academy of Management Journal*, 37, 899–931.

Tharenou, P., & Lyndon, J. T. (undated). *The effect of a supervisory development program on leadership style.* Unpublished manuscript.

Thatcher, M. (1993). *Interview by Paul Holmes.* London: British Broadcasting System, December 21.

Thelen, H. A. (1954). *Dynamics of groups at work.* Chicago: University of Chicago Press.

Thelen, H. A., & Whitehall, J. (1949). Three frames of reference: The description of climate. *Human Relations*, 2, 159–176.

Thelen, H. A., et al. (1954). *Methods for studying work and emotionality in group operation.* Chicago: University of Chicago, Human Dynamics Laboratory.

Theodorson, G. A. (1957). The relationship between leadership and popularity roles in small groups. *American Sociological Review*, 22, 58–67.

Thiagarajan, K. M., & Deep, S. D. (1970). A study of supervisor-subordinate influence and satisfacion in four cultures. *Journal of Social Psychology*, 82, 173–180.

Thibaut, J. W., & Coules, J. (1952). The role of communication in the reduction of interpersonal hostility. *Journal of Abnormal and Social Psychology*, 47, 770–777.

Thibaut, J. W., & Faucheux, C. (1965). The development of contractual norms in a beginning situation under two types of stress. *Journal of Experimental Social Psychology*, 1, 89–102.

Thibaut, J. W., & Gruder, C. L. (1969). Formation of contractual agreements between parties of unequal power. *Journal of Personality and Social Psychology*, 11, 59–65.

Thibaut, J. W., & Kelley, H. H. (1959). *The social psychology of groups.* New York: Wiley.

Thibaut, J. W., & Riecken, H. W. (1955a). Some determinants and consequences of the perception of social causality. *Journal of Personality*, 24, 113–133.

Thibaut, J. W., & Riecken, H. W. (1955b). Authoritarianism, status, and the communication of aggression. *Human Relations*, 8, 95–120.

Thibaut, J. W. & Strickland, L. H. (1956). Psychological set and social conformity. *Journal of Personality*, 25, 115–129.

Thibaut, J., & Walker, L. (1975). *Procedural justice: a psychological analysis.* Hillsdale, NJ: Lawrence Erlbaum Associates.

Thibodeaux, H. F., & Kudisch, J. D. (2000). *The effects of source attributes on feedback seeking: A field study.* Paper, Society for Industrial and Organizational Psychology, New Orleans, LA.

Thierry, H., Den Hartog, D. N, Koopman, P., et al. (1997). *Leadership, politics, and culture in the Netherlands.* Unpublished draft.

Thoma, S. J. (1985). *On improving the relationship between moral reasoning and external criteria: The utilizer/nonutilizer dimension.* Unpublished doctoral dissertation, Minneapolis, MN: University of Minnesota.

Thoma, S. J., Rest, J. R., & Davison, M. L. (1991). Describing and testing a moderator of the moral judgment and action relationship. *Journal of Personality and Social Psychology*, 61(4), 659–669.

Thomas, A. B. (1988). Does leadership make a difference to organizational performance? *Administrative Science Quarterly*, 33, 388–400.

Thomas, A., & Bendixen, M. (2000). Management implications of ethnicity in South Africa. *Journal of International Business Studies*, 31, 507–519.

Thomas, A. S., Litschert, R. J., & Ramaswamy, K. (1991). The performance impact of strategy-manager coalignment: An empirical alignment. *Strategic Management Journal*, 12, 509–522.

Thomas, D. C., & Ravlin, E. C. (1995). Responses to employees in cultural adaptation by a foreign manager. *Journal of Applied Psychology*, 80, 133–146.

Thomas, E. J. (1957). Effects of facilitative role interdependence on group functioning. *Human Relations, 10,* 347–366.

Thomas, E. J., & Fink, C. F. (1963). Effects of group size. *Psychological Bulletin, 60,* 371–384.

Thomas, J. L., Dickson, M. W., & Bliese, P. D. (2001). Values predicting leader performance in the U.S. Army Reserve Officer Training Corps Assessment Center: Evidence for a personality mediated model. *Leadership Quarterly, 12,* 181–196.

Thomas, K. W. (1976). Conflict and conflict management. In M. D. Dunnette (ed.), *Handbook of industrial and organizational psychology.* Chicago: Rand McNally.

Thomas, K. W., & Schmidt, W. H. (1976). A survey of managerial interests with respect to conflict. *Academy of Management Journal, 19,* 315–318.

Thomas, K. W., & Tymon, W. G. (1994). Does empowerment always work?: Understanding the role of intrinsic motivation and personal interpretation. *Journal of Management Systems, 6*(2), 1–13.

Thomas, K. W., & Velthouse, B. A. (1990). Cognitive elements of empowerment: An "interpretive" model of intrinsic task motivation. *The Academy of Management Review, 15*(4), 666–681.

Thomas, P. (2002). *Teaching leadership through a series of challenges.* Paper, Academy of Management, Denver, CO.

Thomas, T., Scherman, J. R., & Dienhart, J. W. (2004). Strategic leadership of ethical behavior in business. *Academy of Management Executive, 18*(2), 56–68.

Thomas, V. G. (1982). The relationship of race and gender of supervisor, subordinates, and organization to estimated stress and supervisory style in a simulated organization: A study of business administration and management students. *Dissertation Abstracts International, 44*(12B), 3970.

Thomason, G. F. (1967). Managerial work roles and relationships (Part II). *Journal of Management Studies, 4,* 17–30.

Thoms, P., & Govekar, M. A. (1997). Vision is in the eye of the leader: A control theory model explaining organizational vision. *OD Practitioner, 29,* 15–24.

Thoms, P., & Greenberger, D. B. (1995). The relation between leadership and time orientation. *Journal of Management Inquiry, 44,* 272–292.

Thoms, P., & Greenberger, D. B. (1998). A test of vision training and potential antecedents to leaders' visioning ability. *Human Resource Development Quarterly, 9*(1), 3–19.

Thompsen, J. A. (2000). Effective leadership of virtual project teams. *Futurics, 24*(3–4), 85–91.

Thompson, C. M. (2000). *The congruent life: Following the inward path to fulfilling work and inspired leadership.* San Francisco, CA: Jossey-Bass.

Thompson, D. C. (1963). *The Negro leadership class.* Englewood Cliffs, NJ: Prentice-Hall.

Thompson, D. E. (1971). Favorable self-perception, perceived supervisory style, and job satisfaction. *Journal of Applied Psychology, 55,* 349–352.

Thompson, G. G. (1944). The social and emotional development of preschool children under two types of educational programs. *Psychological Monographs, 56,* 1–29.

Thompson, J. D. (1967). *Organizations in action.* New York: McGraw-Hill.

Thompson, R. C., & Hunt, J. G. (1996). Inside the black box of alpha, beta, and gamma change: Using a cognitive processing model to assess attitude structure. *Academy of Management Review, 21,* 655–690.

Thompson, S. C. (1999). Illusions of control: How we overestimate our personal influence. *Current Directions in Psychological Science, 8,* 187–190.

Thorndike, E. L. (1916). Education for initiative and originality. *Teachers College Record, 17,* 405–416.

Thorndike, E. L. (1940). *Human nature and the social order.* New York: Macmillan.

Thorndike, R. L., & Stein, S. (1937). An evaluation of the attempts to measure social intelligence. *Psychological Bulletin, 23,* 275–285.

Thorne, L. (1998). The role of virtue in auditors' ethical decision making: An integration of cognitive-development and virtue-ethics perspectives. *Research on Accounting Ethics, 4,* 291–308.

Thornhill, A. R. (1993). Management training across cultures: The challenge for trainers. *Journal of European Industrial Training, 17*(7), 43–51.

Thornton, A., & Freedman, D. (1979). Consistency of sex role attitudes of women, 1962–1977: Evidence from a panel study. *American Sociological Review, 44,* 831–842.

Thornton, G. C., III (1980). Psychometric properties of self-appraisals of job performance. *Personnel Psychology, 33,* 263–271.

Thornton, G. C., III, & Byham, W.C. (1982). *Assessment centers and managerial performance.* New York: Academic Press.

Tichy, N. (1973). An analysis of clique formation and structure in organizations. *Administrative Science Quarterly, 8,* 194–208.

Tichy, N. (1996). Simultaneous transformation and CEO succession: Key to global competitiveness. *Organizational Dynamics, 25*(1), 45–59.

Tichy, N., & Devanna, M. (1986). *Transformational leadership.* New York: Wiley.

Tichy, N. M., & Sherman, S. (1993). *Control your destiny or someone else will.* New York: Doubleday.

Tichy, N., & Ulrich, D. (1983). *Revitalizing organizations: The leadership role.* Graduate School of Business Administration, University of Michigan, Ann Arbor. Unpublished manuscript.

Tichy, N. M., & Ulrich, D. O. (1984). The leadership challenge: A call for the transformational leader. *Sloan Management Review, 26*(l), 59–68.

Tierney, P., & Farmer, S. M. (2003) *Leading for creativity: Development of the Creativity Leadership Index.* Paper, Academy of Management, Seattle, WA.

Tierney, P., Farmer, S. M., & Graen, G. (1999). An examination of leadership and employee creativity: The relevance of traits and relationships. *Personnel Psychology, 52,* 591–620.

Tierney, W. G. (1987). *Symbolism and presidential perceptions of leadership.* Paper, Association for the Study of Higher Education, Baltimore.

Tihanyi, L., Ellsrand, A. E., Daily, C. M., et al. (2000). Composition of the top management team and firm international diversification. *Journal of Management, 26,* 1157–1177.

Timasheff, N. S. (1938). The power phenomenon. *American Sociological Review, 3,* 499–509.

Timmons, W. M. (1944). Some outcomes of participation in dramatics:

II. Likeability and cooperativeness: Relationships between outcomes. *Journal of Social Psychology, 19–20,* 35–51.

Tinsley, C. (1998). Models of conflict resolution in Japanese, American, and German cultures. *Journal of Applied Psychology, 83,* 316–323.

Tinsley, C. H., & Brett, J. M. (2001). Managing workplace conflict in the United States and Hong Kong. *Organizational Behavior and Human Decision Processes, 85*(2), 360–381.

Titus, C. H. (1950). *The process of leadership.* Dubuque, IA: W. C. Brown.

Titus, H. E., & Hollander, E. P. (1957). The California F-scale in psychological research. *Psychological Bulletin, 54,* 47–64.

Tjosvold, D. (1984a). Effects of crisis orientation on managers' approach to controversy in decision making. *Academy of Management Journal, 27,* 130–138.

Tjosvold, D. (1984b). Effects of leader warmth and directiveness on subordinate performance on a subsequent task. *Jounal of Applied Psychology, 69,* 422–427.

Tjosvold, D. (1985a). Implications of controversy research for management. *Journal of Management, 11,* 21–37.

Tjosvold, D. (1985b). Stress dosage for problem solvers. *Working Smart,* August, 5.

Tjosvold, D. (1985d). The effects of attribution and social context on superiors' influence and interaction with low performing subordinates. *Personnel Psychology, 38,* 361–376.

Tjosvold, D. (2002). *Effects of viewing power as expandable or limited: Influencing performance.* Paper, Society Industrial and Organizational Psychology, Toronto.

Tjosvold, D., Andrews, L., & Jones, H. (1983). Cooperative and competitive relationships between leaders and subordinates. *Human Relations, 36,* 1111–1124.

Tjosvold, D., Hui, C., & Law, K. S. (1995). *Empowerment in the leader relationship in Hong Kong: Interdependence and controversy.* Unpublished manuscript.

Tjosvold, D., & Tjosvold, M. (2000). *Leading the team organization: How to create an enduring competitive advantage.* New York: Lexington, Macmillan.

Tjosvold, D., Wedley, W. C., & Field, R. H. G. (1986). Constructive controversy, the Vroom-Yetton model, and managerial decision making. *Journal of Occupational Behavior, 7,* 125–138.

Toegel, G., & Conger, J. A. (2003). 360-degree assessment: Time for reinvention. *Academy of Management Learning and Education, 2,* 297–311.

Toki, K. (1935). Führer-Gefolgschaftsstruktur in der Schulklasse. [Leader-follower structure in school classes.] *Japanese Journal of Psychology, 10,* 27–56.

Tolkoff, E. (1998). Andrew Grove: Time Magazine's Man of the Year brings all alumni reason to rejoice. The man who has played a key role in forging the computer revolution has never forgotten "a cataclysmic moment" at City College. *Alumnus, City College of New York,* Spring, 4–5.

Tollgerdt-Andersson, I. (1996). Attitudes, values, and demands on leadership: A cultural comparison among some European countries: In P. Joynt & M. Warner (eds.), *Managing across cultures: Issues and perspectives.* London: Thomson.

Tomasko, R. (1987). *Downsizing.* New York: AMACOM.

Tomassini, L. A., Solomon, I., Romney, M. B., & Krogstad, J. L. (1982). A framework of a cognitive-behavior theory of leader influence and effectiveness. *Organizational Behavior and Human Performance, 30,* 391–406.

Tomekovic, T. (1962). Levels of knowledge of requirements as a motivation factor in the work situation. *Human Relations, 15,* 197–216.

Tomes, H. (2004). Deconstructing race. *Monitor on Psychology,* December, 37.

Toney, F. (1994). CEOs: Actions and traits that result in profitable companies. *Journal of Leadership Studies, 1*(4), 69–81.

Toney, F. (1996). A leadership methodology: Actions, traits, and skills that result in goal achievement. *Journal of Leadership Studies, 3*(2), 107–127.

Toney, F., & Oster, M. (1998). The leader and religious faith: The relationship between the exercise of religious faith by CEOs, and goal achievement, self-fulfillment, and social benefits. *Journal of Leadership Studies, 5,* 135–147.

Topfer, A. (1978). Das Harzburger Modell in der Unternehmungpraxis: Eine Bestandanalyse. *Der Betrieb, 38,* 1802–1803.

Torbert, W. R. (1991). *The power of balance: Transforming self, society and scientific inquiry.* Newbury Park, CA: Sage. (See p. 550.)

Torbert, W. R., Lichtenstein, B., & Smith, B. (1995). Leadership and ethical development: A balance of light and shadow. *Business Ethics Quarterly, 5*(1), 97–116.

Tornow, W. (1998). Comment and conclusions on leadership. *Industrial-Organizational Psychologist, 35*(3), 58–60

Tornow, W. W., & London, M. (1998). 360-degree feedback: The leadership challenges. *Leadership in Action, 18*(1), 1, 12–13.

Tornow, W. W., London, M., & CCL Associates. (1999). *Maximizing the value of 360-degree feedback: A process for successful individual and organizational development.* Greensboro, NC: Center for Creative Leadership.

Tornow, W. W., London, M., & CCL Associates (2000). *Maximizing the value of 360-degree feedback.* San Francisco: Jossey-Bass.

Tornow, W. W., & Pinto, F. R. (1976). The development of a managerial job taxonomy: A system for describing, classifying, and evaluating executive positions. *Journal of Applied Psychology, 61,* 410–418.

Toronto, R. S. (1972). *General systems theory applied to the study of organizational change.* Doctoral dissertation, University of Michigan, Ann Arbor, MI.

Torrance, E. P. (1952). *Survival research* (Rep. No. 29). Washington, DC: Human Resources Research Laboratory.

Torrance, E. P. (1953). Methods of conducting critiques of group problem-solving performance. *Journal of Applied Psychology, 37,* 394–398.

Torrance, E. P. (1954). Some consequences of power differences in decision making in permanent and temporary three-man groups. *Research Studies, 22,* 130–140.

Torrance, E. P. (1954b). The behavior of small groups under the stress conditions of "survival." *American Sociological Review, 19,* 751–755.

Torrance, E. P (1955a). Some consequences of power differences in permanent and temporary three-man groups. In P. Hare, E. F. Borgatta, & R. F. Bales (eds.), *Small groups.* New York: Knopf.

Torrance, E. P. (1955b). Perception of group functioning as a predictor of group performance. *Journal of Social Psychology, 42,* 271–281.

Torrance, E. P. (1959). Explorations in creative thinking in the early school years. In G. Roheim (ed.), *Psychoanalysis and the social sciences.*

Torrance, E. P. (1961). A theory of leadership and interpersonal behavior under stress. In L. Petrullo & B. Bass (eds.), *Leadership and interpersonal behavior.* New York: Holt, Rinehart & Winston.

Torrance, E. P., & Staff. (1955). *Survival research. A report of the fourth year of development.* Reno, NV: Stead AFB, CRL Field Unit No. 2.

Tosi, H. (1970). A reexamination of personality as a determinant of the effects of participation. *Personnel Psychology, 23,* 91–99.

Tosi, H. (1971). Organization stress as a moderator in the relationship between influence and role response. *Academy of Management Journal, 14,* 7–20.

Tosi, H. (1973). The effect of interaction of leader behavior and subordinate authoritarianism. *Personnel Psychology, 26,* 339–350.

Tosi, H., Aldag, R., & Storey, R. (1973). On the measurement of the environment: An assessment of the Lawrence and Lorsch environmental uncertainty subscale. *Administrative Science Quarterly, 18,* 27–36.

Tosi, H. L. (1991). The organization as a context for leadership theory: A multilevel approach. *Leadership Quarterly, 2,* 205–225.

Tosi, H. L. (1992). The organization and the environment: The E/O link in the model. In H. L. Tosi (ed.), *The environment/organization/person contingency model: A meso approach to the study of organizations.* Greenwich, CT: JAI Press.

Tosi, H. L., & Gomez-Mejia, L. R. (1989). The decoupling of CEO pay and performance: An agency theory perspective. *Administrative Science Quarterly, 34,* 169–189.

Tosi, H. L., & Gomez-Mejia, L. R. (1994). CEO compensation monitoring and firm performance. *Academy of Management Journal, 37,* 1002–1016.

Tosi, H. L., Misangyi, V. F., Waldman, D. A., et al. (2004). CEO charisma, compensation, and firm performance. *Leadership Quarterly, 15,* 405–420.

Tosi, H. L., & Werner, S. (1995). *Managerial discretion and the design of compensation strategy.* Paper, Academy of Management, Vancouver, BC.

Tosi, H. L., Werner, S., Katz, J. P., et al. (2000). How much does performance matter? A meta-analysis of CEO pay studies. *Journal of Management, 26,* 301–339.

Touhey, J. (1974). Effects of additional women professionals on ratings of occupational prestige and desirability. *Journal of Personality and Social Psychology, 29,* 86–89.

Tourigny, L. (2000). *Servant-leadership: A study of American presidents.* Paper, International Leadership Association, Toronto.

Tourigny, L. (2002). *Relationship among servant-leadership, altruism and social performance: A study of American presidents.* [Diss.]

Tourigny, L. (2001, February 22). *American Presidential Management Inventory.*

Tourigny, L., Baba, V. V., & Lituchy T. R. (2005). Job burnout among airline employees in Japan: A study of the buffering effects of absence and supervisory support. *International Journal of Cross Cultural Management, 5*(1), 67–85.

Townsend, A. M., DeMarie, S. M., & Hendrickson, A. R. (1998). Virtual teams: Technology and the workplace of the future. *Academy of Management Executive, 12*(3), 17–29.

Townsend, J. C., & Jones, A. P. (2000). *Leader-member similarity and interaction patterns: Supervisory power and employee negotiation.* Paper, Society for Industrial and Organizational Psychology, New Orleans, LA.

Toynbee, A. J. (1987). *A study of history.* New York: Oxford University Press.

Trahey, J. (1977). *Women and power.* New York: Avon Books.

Trani, E. P., & Wilson, D. L. (1977). *The presidency of Warren Harding.* Kansas: Regents Press.

Trapp, E. F. (1955). Leadership and popularity as a function of behavioral predictions. *Journal of Abnormal and Social Psychology, 51,* 452–457.

Trau, R., & Hartell, C. E. J. (2002). *Individual and contextual factors affecting the quality of work life and work attitudes of gay men.* Paper, Academy of Management, Denver, CO.

Treadway, D. C., Hochwarter, W. A., Ferris, G. R., Kacmar, C. J., Douglas, C., Ammeter, A. P., et al. (2004). Leader political skill and employee reactions. *The Leadership Quarterly, 15,* 493–513.

Trempe, J., Rigny, A., & Haccoun, R. R. (1985). Subordinate satisfaction with male and female managers: Role of perceived supervisory influence. *Journal of Applied Psychology, 70,* 44–47.

Trevelyan, R. (2001). The paradox of autonomy: A case of academic research scientists. *Human Relations, 54*(4), 495–525.

Trevino L. K. (1986). Ethical decision-making in organizations: A person-situation interactionist model. *Academy of Management Review, 11,* 601–617.

Trevino, L. K., Brown, M., & Hartman, L. P. (2003). A qualitative investigation of perceived executive leadership: Perceptions from inside and outside the executive suite. *Human Relations, 56,* 5–37.

Trevino, L. K., Hartman, L. P., & Brown, M. (2000). Moral person and moral manager: How executives develop a reputation for ethical leadership. *California Management Review, 42*(4), 128–142.

Trevino, L. K., Weaver, G. R., Gibson, D. G., & Toffler, B. L. (1999). Managing ethics and legal compliance: What works and what hurts. *California Management Review, 41*(2), 131–151.

Triandis, H. C. (1959a). Differential perception of certain jobs and people by managers, clerks, and workers in industry. *Journal of Applied Psychology, 43,* 221–225.

Triandis, H. C. (1960). Comparative factorial analysis of job semantic structures of managers and workers. *Journal of Applied Psychology, 44,* 297–302.

Triandis, H. C. (1963). Factors affecting employee selection in two cultures. *Journal of Applied Psychology, 47,* 89–96.

Triandis, H. C. (1981). *Hispanic concerns about the U.S. Navy* (ONR Tech. Rep.). Champaign: University of Illinois.

Triandis, H. C. (1984). *Selection and retention of minorities in organizations.* ONR Conference on Minorities Entering High Tech Careers, Pensacola, FL.

Triandis, H. C. (1993). The contingency model in cross-cultural perspective. In M. M. Chemers & R. Ayman (eds.), *Leadership theory and research: Perspectives and directions.* San Diego, CA: Academic Press.

Triandis, H. C. (1995). *Individualism and collectivism.* Boulder, CO: Westview Press.

Triandis, H. C. (2004). The many dimensions of culture. *The Academy of Management Executives, 18*(1), 88–93.

Triandis, H. C., Kashima, Y., Lisanky, J., and Marin, G. (1982). *Self-*

concepts and values among Hispanic and mainstream Navy recruits (ONR Tech. Rep. No. 7). Champaign: University of Illinois.

Triandis, H. C., & Malpass, R. S. (1971). Studies of black and white interaction in job settings. *Journal of Applied Social Psychology, 1*, 101–117.

Triandis, H. C., Marin, G., Hui, C. H., Lisansky, J., & Ottati, V. (1982). *Role perceptions of Hispanic and mainstream Navy recruits* (ONR Tech. Rep. No. 24). Champaign: University of Illinois.

Triandis, H. C., Marin, G., Lisansky, J., & Betancourt, H. (1984). Simpatia as a cultural script of Hispanics. *Journal of Personality and Social Psychology, 47*, 1363–1375.

Triandis, H. C., Ottati, V., & Marin, C. (1982). *Social attitudes among Hispanic and mainstream Navy recruits* (ONR Tech. Rep. No. 10). Champaign: University of Illinois.

Triandis, H. C., Mikesell, E. H., & Ewen, R. B. (1962). *Some cognitive factors affecting group creativity* (Tech. Rep. No. 5). Urbana: University of Illinois, Group Effectiveness Research Laboratory.

Trice, H. (1959). The affiliation motive and readiness to join Alcoholics Anonymous. *Quarterly Journal of Studies on Alcohol, 20*, 313–320.

Trice, H. M. (1984). Rites and ceremonials in organizational culture. In S. B. Bacharach & S. M. Mitchell (eds.), *Perspectives on organizational sociology: Theory and research*, vol. 4. Greenwich, CT: JAI Press.

Trice, H. M., & Beyer, J. M. (1984). Studying organizational cultures through rites and ceremonials. *Academy of Management Review, 9*, 653–669.

Trice, H. M., & Beyer, J. M. (1986). Charisma and its routinization in two social movement organizations. *Research in Organizational Behavior, 8*, 113–164.

Trice, H. M., & Beyer, J. M. (1991). Cultural leadership in organizations. *Organizational Science, 2*(2), 146–169.

Trice, H. M., & Beyer, J. M. (1993). *The cultures of work organization.* Englewood Clifs, NJ: Prentice Hall.

Trieb, S. E., & Marion, B. W. (1969). *Managerial leadership and the human capital of the firm.* Columbus: Ohio State University, College of Agriculture.

Trimble, C. (1968). Teachers' conceptions of leadership behavior of principals as related to principal's perception of this involvement in the decision-making process. *Dissertation Abstracts, 28*, 4432–4433.

Tripp, L. (1986). Community leadership and black former activists of the 1960s. *Western Journal of Black Studies, 10*(2), 86–89.

Trist, E. L. (1971). Critique of scientific management in terms of socio-technical theory. *Prakseologia, 39–30*, 159–174.

Trist, E. L. (1981). *The evolution of socio-technical systems: A conceptual framework and action research program.* Occasional Paper No. 2, Ontario Quality of Working Life Centre.

Trist, E. L. (1993). A socio-technical critique of scientific management. In E. Trist & H. Murray (eds.), *The social engagement of social science: A Tavistock anthology.* Philadelphia, PA: University of Pennsylvania Press.

Trist, E. L., & Bamforth,V. (1951). Some social and psychological consequences of the longwall method of coal-getting. *Human Relations, 4*, 3–38.

Tritten, J. J. (1995). *Navy combat leadership for tomorrow: Where will we be able to get such men and woman?* Norfolk, VA: Navy Doctrine Command.

Trittipoe,T. G., & Hahn, C. P. (1961). *Situational problems for leader-ship training. Part I. Development and evaluation of situational problems.* Washington, DC: American Institute for Research.

Trivedi, D. N. (1974). Modernization, rationality, opinion leadership or compartmentalization of spheres of activity. *Man in India, 54*, 271–280.

Troiano, P. (1999). Sharing the throne. *Management Review, 88*(2), 39–43.

Trompenaars, F., & Hampden-Turner, C. (1998). *Riding the waves of culture: Understanding cultural diversity in global business.* New York: McGraw-Hill (2nd ed.).

Tronc, K., & Enns, F. (1969). Promotional aspirations and differential role perceptions. *Alberta Journal of Educational Research, 15*, 169–183.

Tropp, K. J., & Landers, D. M. (1979). Team interaction and the emergence of leadership and interpersonal attraction in field hockey. *Journal of Sport Psychology, 1*, 228–240.

Trotter, R. J. (1987). Stop blaming yourself. *Psychology Today, 21*(2), 30–39.

Trow, D. B. (1957). Autonomy and job satisfaction in task-oriented groups. *Journal of Abnormal and Social Psychology, 53*, 204–209.

Trow, D. B. (1960). Membership succession and team performance. *Human Relations, 13*, 259–269.

Trow, D. B. (1961). Executive succession in small companies. *Administrative Science Quarterly, 6*, 228–239.

Trow, D. B., & Herschdorfer, G. (1965). *An experiment on the status incongruence phenomenon* (tech. rep.). Binghamton, NY: State University of New York.

Trow, D. B., & Smith, D. H. (1983). Correlates of volunteering in advocacy planning: testing a theory. In D. H. Smith, & J. Van Til (eds.), *International perspectives on voluntary action research.* Washington, DC: University Press of America.

Troy, C. J., Smith, K. G., & Gordon, L. A. (2003). *Strategy and accounting fraud.* Paper, Academy of Management, Seattle, WA.

Truskie, S. D. (1995). *CEO performance evaluation: How America's leading companies review and evaluate the performance of their chief executive officers.* Pittsburgh, PA: Management Science & Development.

Tryon, C. M. (1939). Evaluations of adolescent personality by adolescents. *Monographs in Social Research and Child Development, 4*, No. 4.

Tscheulin, D. (1973). Leader behaviors in German industry. *Journal of Applied Psychology, 57*, 28–31.

Tsui, A. S. (1982). *A role set analysis of mangerial reputation.* Paper, Academy of Management, New York.

Tsui, A. S. (1984a). A role set analysis of managerial reputation. *Organizational Behavior and Human Performance, 34*, 64–96.

Tsui, A. S. (1984b). A multiple constituency framework of managerial reputational effectiveness. In J. G. Hunt, D. Hosking, C. A. Schriesheim, et al. (eds.), *Leaders and managers: International perspectives on managerial behavior and leadership.* New York: Pergamon Press.

Tsui, A. S. (1994). Reputational effectiveness: Toward a mutual responsiveness framework. In B. M. Staw & L. L. Commings (eds.), *Research in organizational behavior* (vol.16). Greenwich, CT: JAI Press.

Tsui, A. S., Ashsford, S. J., St. Clair, L., et al. (1995). Dealing with discrepant expectations: Response strategies and managerial effectiveness. *Academy of Management Journal, 38*, 1515–1543.

Tsui, A. S., & Gutek, B. A. (1984). A role set analysis of gender differences in performance, affective relationships, and career success of industrial middle managers. *Academy of Management Journal, 27*, 619–635.

Tsui, A. S., & Ohlott, P. (1986). *Multiple assessment of managerial effectiveness: Consensus in effectiveness models.* Paper, American Psychological Association, Washington, DC. Also: Tsui, A. S., & Ohlott, P. (1988). *Personnel Psychology, 41*, 779–803.

Tsui, A. S., & Ohlott, P. (1988). Multiple assessment of managerial effectiveness: Inter-rater agreement and consensus in effectiveness models. *Personnel Psychology, 41*, 779–803.

Tsui, A., & O'Reilly, C. (1989). Beyond simple demographic effects: The importance of relational demography in superior-subordinate dyads. *Academy of Management Journal, 32*, 402–423.

Tsui, A. S., Pearce, J. L., Porter, L. W., et al. (1997). Alternative approaches to the employee-organizational relationship: Does investment in employees pay off? *Academy of Management Journal, 40*, 1089–1121.

Tsui, A. S., Wang, H., Xin, K. R., Zhang, L. H., & Fu, P. P. (2003). *Let a thousand flowers bloom: Variation of leadership styles in Chinese firms.* Academy of Management meeting, Seattle, August 4, 2003.

Tsur, E. (1983). The kibbutz way of life. Structure and management of the kibbutz. *Kibbutz Studies*, November, 23–31.

Tsurumi, R. (1982). American origins of Japanese productivity: The Hawthorne Experiment rejected. *Pacific Basin Quarterly, 7*, Spring–Summer, 14–15.

Tsurumi, Y. (1983b). U.S. mangers often "technically illiterate" and out of touch. *Washington Post*, July 31.

Tsurumi, Y. (1992). Japanese corporations in America: Managing cultural differences. *Pacific Basin Quarterly, 19*(3), 3–7.

Tubbs, M. E. (1986). Goal setting: A meta-analytic examination of the empirical evidence. *Journal of Applied Psychology, 71*, 474–483.

Tuchman, B. W. (1971). *Stilwell and the American experience in China, 1911–45.* New York: Macmillan.

Tubbs, S. L., & Porter, R. G. (1978). *Predictors of grievance activity.* Detroit, MI: General Motors Corporation. Unpublished report.

Tubbs, S. L., & Widgery, R. N. (1978). When productivity lags, check at the top: Are key managers really communicating? *Management Review, 67*, 20–25.

Tucker, J. H. (1983). Leadership orientation as a function of interpersonal need structure: A replication with negative results. *Small Group Behavior, 14*, 107–114.

Tucker, M. L. (1994). *American 1990's women politicians: Transformational or transactional?* Thibodaux, LA: Nicholls State University, Louisiana Center for Women and Government.

Tucker, R. C. (1968). The theory of charismatic leadership. *Daedalus, 97*, 731–756.

Tucker, R. C. (1970). The theory of charismatic leadership. In D. A. Rustow (ed.), *Philosophers and kings: Studies in leadership.* New York: Braziller.

Tucker, R. C. (1981). *Politics as leadership.* Columbia: University of Missouri Press.

Tuckman, B. W. (1965). Developmental sequence in small groups. *Psychological Bulletin, 63*, 384–399.

Tuckman, B. W., & Oliver, W. F. (1968). Effectiveness of feedback to teachers as a function of source. *Journal of Educational Psychology, 59*, 297–301.

Tullar, W. L. (2001). Russian entrepreneurial motive patterns: A validation of the Miner Sentence Completion Scale in Russia. *Applied Psychology: An International Review, 50*, 422–435.

Tullett, A. D. (1995). The adaptive-innovative (A-I) cognitive styles of male and female managers: Some implications for the management of change. *Journal of Occupational & Organizational Psychology, 68*, 359–365.

Tung, R. (1992). *Universality symposium.* Montreal, Canada: Society for Individual/Organization Psychology.

Tung, R. L. (1979). U.S. multinationals: A study of their selection and training procedures for overseas assignments. *Proceedings*, Academy of Management, Atlanta, GA, 298–301.

Tung, R. L. (1982). Selection and training of US, European and Japanese multinationals. *California Management Review, 25*, 57–71.

Tupes, E. C., Carp, A., & Borg, W. R. (1958). Performance in role playing situations as related to leadership and personality measures. *Sociometry, 21*, 165–179.

Tupes, E. C., & Christal, R. E. (1961). *Recurrent personality factors based on trait ratings.* ASD-TR-61–96, Personnel Laboratory, Aeronautical Systems Division, Lackland Air Force Base, TX.

Turillo, C. J., Folger, R., Lavelle, J. J., & Umphress, E. E. (2002). Is virtue its own reward? Self-sacrificial decisions for the sake of fairness. *Organizational Behavior and Human Decision Processes, 89*(1), 839–865.

Turk, H. (1961). Instrumental values and the popularity of instrumental leaders. *Social Forces, 39*, 252–260.

Turk, H., Hartley, E. L., & Shaw, D. M. (1962). The expectation of social influence. *Journal of Social Psychology, 58*, 23–29.

Turk, T., & Turk, H. (1962). Group interaction in a formal setting: The case of the triad. *Sociometry, 25*, 48–55.

Turnage, J. J., & Muchinsky, P. M. (1984). A comparison of the predictive validity of assessment center evaluations versus traditional measures in forecasting supervisory job performance: Interpretive implications of criterion distortion for the assessment paradigm. *Journal of Applied Psychology, 69*, 595–602.

Turner, A. N. (1954). Foreman: Key to worker morale. *Harvard Business Review, 32*(1), 76–86.

Turner, N., Barling, J., Epitropski, O., et al. (2002). Transformational leadership and moral reasoning. *Journal of Applied Psychology, 87*, 304–310.

Turner, S. (1993). Charisma and obedience: A risk cognition approach. *Leadership Quarterly, 3–4*, 235–256.

Tushman, M. L. (1977). A political approach to organizations: A review and rationale. *Academy of Management Review, 2*, 206–216.

Tushman, M. L., & Newman, W. H. (1986). Technological discontinuities and organizational environments. *California Management Review, 29*(1), 29–44.

Tversky, A., & Kahneman, D. (1971). Belief in the law of small numbers. *Psychological Bulletin, 76*, 105–110.

Twigg, N. W. (2004). *Transformational leadership: The effects of spirituality and religious orientation.* Paper, Academy of Management, New Orleans, LA.

Tyagi, P. K. (1985). Relative importance of key job dimensions and leadership behaviors in motivating salesperson work performance. *Journal of Marketing, 49,* Summer, 76–86.

Tyler, T. R., Rasinski, K. A., & McGraw, K. M. (1985). The influence of perceived injustice on the endorsement of political leaders. *Journal of Applied Social Psychology, 15,* 700–725.

Tyson, L., & Birnbrauer, H. (1983). Coaching: A tool for success. *Training & Development Journal, 37*(9), 30–34.

Tyson, X., et al. (1986). *British derailers: Executives on the 16 PF who lacked "N" political skills, made redundant.* Cranfield School of Management Study Reported by M. Lombardo & C. McCaully, Center for Creative Leadership, Greensboro, NC.

Tzabbar, D. (2003). *When executive change lead to organizational change: An appraisal of empirical evidence.* Paper, Academy of Management, Seattle, WA.

Tziner, A. (1984). Predictor of peer rating in a military assessment center: A longitudinal follow-up. *Canadian Journal of Administrative Sciences, 1,* 146–160.

Tziner, A. (1987). The assessment centre revisited: Practical and theoretical considerations. In S. Dolan & R. S. Schuler (eds.), *Human resource management in Canada.* St. Paul, MN: West Publishing.

Tziner, A., & Dolan, S. (1982). Validity of an assessment center for identifying future female officers in the military. *Journal of Applied Psychology, 67,* 728–736.

Tziner, A., & Elizur, D. (1985). Achievement motive: A reconceptualization and new instrument. *Journal of Occupational Behaviour, 6,* 209–228.

Udell, J. G. (1967). An empirical test of hypothesis relating to span of control. *Administrative Science Quarterly, 12,* 420–439.

Uhl-Bien, M. (2002). *Rethinking leadership from a complex network standpoint.* Paper, Academy of Management, Denver, CO.

Uhl-Bien, M. (2003–2004). Relationship development as a key ingredient for leadership development. In S. L. Murphy & R. E. Riggio (eds.), *The future of leadership development.* Mahwah, NJ: Lawrence Erlbaum Associates.

Uhl-Bien, M., & Maslyn, J. M. (2000). *Examining the exchange in leader-member-exchange (LMX): Identification of dyadic relational styles and their association with key work attitudes and behavioral outcomes.* Paper, Academy of Management, Toronto, Ontario.

Ulmer, W. F. (1994). Inside view. *Issues & Observations, 14*(2), 1–2.

Ulmer, W. F., Jr. (1996). *Leadership learnings and relearnings.* Unpublished manuscript, February 12.

Ulmer, W. F. (1996). *Leadership learnings and unlearnings.* Kellogg Leadership Studies. Unpublished manuscript, July 21.

Ulmer, W. F., Jr. (1996). *Leadership learnings and relearnings.* Paper, Kellogg Leadership Studies Project, Battle Creek, MI.

Ulmer, W. F. (1997). *Leadership learnings and relearnings.* College Park, MD: University of Maryland, Kellogg Leadership Studies Project, Transformational Leadership Focus Group.

Ulmer, W. F. (1997). *Leadership learnings and relearnings.* Transformational Leadership Working Papers. Academy of Leadership Press.

Ulmer, W. F. (1997). *Inside view: A leader's observations on leadership.* Greensboro, NC: Center for Creative Leadership.

Ulmer, W. F., Jr. (1998). Military leadership into the 21st century: Another "bridge too far"? *Parameters,* Spring, 4–25.

Ulmer, W. F., Jr. (1999). *Future directions in military leadership.* Paper, World Conference on transformational leadership, Hammerö, Sweden.

Ulrich, D. N., Booz, D. R., & Lawrence, P. R. (1950). *Management behavior and foreman attitude.* Boston: Harvard University, Graduate School of Business Administration.

Underwood, W. J. (1965). Evaluation of laboratory training. *Training Directors Journal, 19,* 34–40.

Ungson, G. R., James, C., & Spicer, B. H. (1985). The effects of regulatory agencies on organizations in wood products and high technology/electronics industries. *Academy of Management Journal, 28,* 426–445.

Uphoff, W. H., & Dunnette, M. D. (1956). *Understanding the union member.* Minneapolis: University of Minnesota Press.

Upmanyu, V. V., & Singh, S. (1981). Test of contingency model of leadership effectiveness. *Psychological Studies, 26,* 44–48.

Uris, A. (1958). Job stress and the executive. *Management Review, 47,* 4–12.

Urwick, L. F. (1952). *Notes of the theory of organization.* New York: American Management Association.

Urwick, L. F. (1953). *Leadership and morale.* Columbus: Ohio State University, College of Commerce and Administration.

U.S. Air Force, Air Training Command. (1952a). *Aspects of noncommissioned officer leadership* (Tech. Rep. No. 52–3). Lackland Air Force Base, TX: Human Resources Research Center.

U.S. Air Force. (1951). *A preliminary investigation of the relationship of trainees and pilot officer promotions* (HRRL Rep. No. 3). Washington, DC: Human Resources Research Laboratory.

U.S. Air Force, Air Training Command. (1952b). *Research on the evaluation and prediction of officer qualities.* Maxwell Field, AL: Human Resources Research Center.

U.S. Department of Commerce. (1996). Women owned businesses set scorching pace! *The Partnership, 1*(3), 1.

Utecht, R. E., & Heier, W. D. (1976). The contingency model and successful military leadership. *Academy of Management Journal, 19,* 606–618.

Vaill, P. B. (1978). Toward a behavior description of high-performing systems. In M. W. McCall, Jr., & M. M. Lombardo (eds.), *Leadership: Where else can we go?* Durham, NC: Duke University Press.

Vaill, P. B. (1982). The purposing of high-performing systems. *Organizational Dynamics, 10*(2), 23–39.

Vaill, P. (1996). *The learning challenges of leadership.* Paper, American Psychological Association, Toronto.

Valenti, J. (1975). *A very human President.* New York: W. W. Norton

Valenzi, E. R., & Dessler, C. (1978). Relationships of leader behavior, subordinate role ambiguity and subordinate job satisfaction. *Academy of Management Journal, 21,* 671–678.

Valenzi, E. R., Miller, J. A., Eldridge, L. D., et al. (1972). *Individual differences, structure, task, and external environment and leader behavior: A summary* (Tech. Rep. No. 49). Rochester, NY: University of Rochester, Management Research Center.

Valiquet, M. L. (1968). Individual change in management development programs. *Journal of Applied Behavioral Science, 4,* 313–325.

Valle, M., & Davis, K. (1998). Teams and performance appraisal: Using metrics to increase reliability and validity. *Team Performance Management, 5*(8), 238–44.

Valle, M., & Perrewe, P. L. (2000). Do politics perceptions relate to political behaviors? Tests of an implicit assumption. *Human Relations*, 53(3), 359–386.

Vancil, R. F. (1987). *Passing the baton: Managing the process of CEO succession*. Boston, MA: Harvard Business School Press.

Vancouver, J. B., & Morrison, E. W. (1995). Feedback inquiry: The effect of source attributes and individual difference. *Organizational Behavior and Human Decision Processes*, 62, 276–285.

Van den Berg, R., & Sleegers, P. (1996). The innovative capacity of secondary schools: A qualitative study. *Qualitative Studies in Education*, 9, 201–223.

Vandenbosh, B., & Ginzberg, M. J. (1997). Lotus notes and collaboration: Plus ça change. *Journal of Management Information Systems*, 13, 65–81.

Van den Brande, I., Janssens, M., Sels, L., et al. (2002). *Multiple types of psychological contracts: A six cluster solution*. Paper, Academy of Management, Denver, CO.

Vanderslice, V. J. (1988). Separating leadership from leaders: An assessment of the effect of leader and follower roles in organizations. *Human Relations*, 41, 677–696.

Van de Vall, M., & Bolas, C. (1980). Applied social discipline research or social policy research: The emergence of a professional paradigm in sociological research. *American Sociology*, 15, 128–137.

Van de Vall, M., & Bolas, C. (1982). Using social policy research for reducing social problems: an empirical analysis of structure and functions. *The Journal of Applied Behavioral Science*, 18, (1), 49–67.

Van de Ven, A. H. (1976). On the nature, formation, and maintenance of relations among organizations. *Academy of Management Review*, 2, 34–53.

Van de Ven, A. H., & Ferry, D. L. (1980). *Measuring and assessing organizations*. New York: Wiley.

Van de Vliert, E. (2003). Thermoclimate, culture, and poverty as country-level roots of workers' wages. *Journal of International Business Studies*, 34, 40–52.

Van de Vliert, E., Huang, X., & Parker, P. M. (2004). Do colder and hotter climates make richer societies more—but poorer societies less—happy and altruistic? *Journal of Environmental Psychology*, 24, 17–30.

Van de Vliert, E., & Smith, P. B. (2003). *Leader reliance on subordinates' judgements and decisions across nations that differ in socio-economic development and thermoclimate*. Paper, Academy of Management, Seattle, WA.

van Emmerik, I. H. (2003). *For better or for worse: Adverse working conditions and beneficial effects of mentoring*. Paper, Academy of Management, Seattle, WA.

van Engen, M. L., van der Leeden, R., & Willemsen, T. M. (2001). Gender, context, and leadership styles: A field study. *Journal of Occupational and Organizational Psychology*, 74, 581–598.

Van Engen, M. L., & Willemsen, T. M. (2004). Sex and leadership styles: A meta-analysis of research published in the 1990s. *Psychological Reports*, 94(1), 3–18.

Van Fleet, D. D. (1983). Span of management research and issues. *Academy of Management Review*, 26, 546–552.

Van Fleet, D. D. (1995) Career description analysis: A systematic approach for studying qualitative information. *Journal of Leadership Studies*, 2(2), 91–102.

Van Fleet, D. D., & Peterson, T. O. (1995). Career description analysis: A systematic approach for studying qualitative information. *Journal of Leadership Studies*, 2, 91–102.

Van Fleet, D. D., & Yukl, G. A. (1986a). *A century of leadership research*. Paper, Academy of Management, Chicago, IL.

Van Fleet, D. D., & Yukl, C. A. (1986b). *Military leadership: An organizat onal behavior perspective*. Greenwich, CT: JAI Press.

Vangen, S., & Huxham, C. (2003). Nurturing collaborative relations: Building trust in interorganizational collaboration. *Journal of Applied Behavioral Science*, 39(1), 5–31

Van Knippenberg, B., van Knippenberg, D., & Wilke, H. A. (2001). Power use in cooperative and competitive settings. *Basic & Applied Social Psychology*, 23, 291–300.

Van Knippenberg, D., van Knippenberg, B., de Cremer, et al. (2004). Leadership, self, and identity: A review and research agenda. *Leadership Quarterly*, 15, 825–856.

Van Maanen, J. (1979). Reclaiming qualitative methods for organizational research. *Administrative Science Quarterly*, 26, 520–527.

Van Muijen, J., Koopman, P. L., Dondeyne, P., De Cock, G., & De Witte, K. (1992). Organizational culture: The development of an international instrument for comparing countries. In Hunyady, G. (ed.), Proceedings of the 2nd European Congress of Psychology. Budapest: Keszult.

Van Nostrand, C. H. (1993). *Gender responsible leadership*. Newbury Park, CA: Sage.

Vannoy, J., & Morrissette, J. O. (1969). Group structure, effectiveness, and individual morale. *Organizational Behavior and Human Performance*, 4, 299–307.

Vansina, L. S. (1982). *The management practices of top performing managing directors*. Address, Management Conference: High performing organizations and their leaders, Stockholm, Sweden.

Vansina, L. S., & Taillieu, T. C. (1970). Comparative study of the characteristics of Flemish graduates planning their careers in national or international organizations. In B. M. Bass, R. C. Cooper, & J. A. Haas (eds.), *Managing for accomplishment*. Lexington, MA: D. C. Heath.

Van Velsor, E. V. (1984). Can development programs make a difference? *Issues & Observations*, 4(4), 1–5.

Van Velsor, E. V. (1987). *Breaking the glass ceiling; Can women make it to the top in America's largest corporations?* Reading, MA: Addison-Wesley.

Van Velsor, E. (1995). Why executives derail: perspectives across time and culture. *Academy of Management Executive*, 9(4), 62–72.

Van Velsor, E. (1998). The Handbook of assessing the impact of development experiences. In C. McCauley, R. Moxley, & E. Van Velsor (eds.), *The Center for Creative Leadership Handbook of Leadership Development*. San Francisco, CA: Jossey-Bass.

Van Velsor, E., & Leslie, J. B. (1991). *Feedback to managers, Volume II: A review and comparison of sixteen multi-rater feedback instruments*. Greensboro, NC: Center for Creative Leadership.

VanVelsor, E., & Leslie, J. B. (1995). Why executives derail: Perspectives across time and cultures. *Academy of Management Executive*, 9, 62–72.

Van Velsor, E., Taylor, S., & Leslie, J. (1993). An examination of the relationships between self-perception accuracy, self-awareness, gender, and leader effectiveness. *Human Resource Management, 32,* 249–264.

Van Yperen, N., Van den Berg, A., & Willering, M. (1999). Towards a better understanding of the link between participation in decision making and organizational citizenship behavior: A multi-level analysis. *Journal of Occupational and Organizational Psychology, 72,* 377–92.

Van Zelst, R. H. (1951). Worker popularity and job satisfaction. *Personnel Psychology, 4,* 405–412.

Van Zelst, R. H. (1952–1952b). Empathy test scores of union leaders. *Journal of Applied Psychology, 36,* 293–295.

Van Zelst, R. H. (1952a). Sociometrically selected work teams increase production. *Personnel Psychology, 5,* 175–185.

Vara, V. (2002). CEO charm may harm, scholar says. *Denver Post,* August 13, C1, C10.

Vardi, Y., Shirom, A., & Jacobson, D. (1980). A study of the leadership beliefs of Israeli managers. *Academy of Management Journal, 23,* 367–374.

Vaughan, M. B. M. (1981). Project phases and role shifts in the work of overseas project managers: A case study of a California-based multinational firm. *Dissertation Abstracts International, 42(7A),* 3282.

Vecchio, R. P (1977). An empirical examination of the validity of Fiedler's model of leadership effectiveness. *Organizational Behavior and Human Performance, 19,* 180–206.

Vecchio, R. P. (1979). A dyadic interpretation of the contingency model of leadership effectiveness. *Academy of Management Journal, 22,* 590–600.

Vecchio, R. P. (1981). Situational and behavioral moderators of subordinate satisfaction with supervision. *Human Relations, 34,* 947–963.

Vecchio, R. P. (1982). A further test of leadership effects due to between-group variation and within-group variation. *Journal of Applied Psychology, 67,* 200–208.

Vecchio, R. P. (1983). Assessing the validity of Fiedler's contingency model of leadership effectiveness: A closer look at Strube and Garcia. *Psychological Bulletin, 93,* 404–408.

Vecchio, R. P. (1987). Situational leadership theory: An examination of a prescriptive theory. *Journal of Applied Psychology, 72,* 444–451.

Vecchio, R. P. (2002). Leadership and gender advantage. *The Leadership Quarterly, 13(6),* 643–671.

Vecchio, R. P., & Boatwright, K. (2002). Preferences for idealized styles of supervision. *Leadership Quarterly, 13,* 327–342.

Vecchio, R. P., & Bullis, R. G. (2001). Moderators of the influence os supervisor-subordinate similarity on subordinate outcomes. *Journal of Applied Psychology, 86,* 884–896.

Vecchio, R. P, & Gobdel, B. C. (1984). The vertical dyad linkage model of leadership: Problems and prospects. *Organizational Behavior and Human Performance, 34,* 5–20.

Vecchio, R. P., & Norris, W. R. (1996). Predicting employee turnover from performance, satisfaction, and leader-member exchange. *Journal of Business and Psychology, 49,* 436–458.

Vecchio, R. P., & Sussman, M. (1989). Preferences for forms of supervisory social influence. *Journal of Organizational Behavior, 10,* 135–143.

Veiga, J. F. (1981). Plateaued versus nonplateaued managers: Career pa-

terns, attitudes, and path potential. *Academy of Management Journal, 24,* 566–578.

Veiga, J. F. (1983). Mobility influences during managerial career stages. *Academy of Management Journal, 26,* 64–85.

Veiga, J. F. (1986). Propensity to give up control in a decision making group: An explanation and a measure. *Proceedings, Academy of Management, Chicago,* 208–212.

Veiga, J. F. (1988). Face your problem subordinates now! *Academy of Management Executive, 2,* 145–152.

Veiga, J. F., & Dechant, K. (1997). Wired world woes: www.help. *Academy of Management Executive, 11(3),* 73–78.

Veiga, J. F., & Dechant, K. (1993). Fax poll: Altruism in corporate America. *Academy of Management Executive, 7(3),* 89–91.

Veiga, J. F., Golden, T. D., & Dechant, K. (2004). A survey of the Executive's Advisory Panel: Why managers bend the rules: *Academy of Management Executive, 18,* 84–91.

Venable, B. (1983). Principal rule administration behavior, influence, and teacher loyalty. *Dissertation Abstracts International, 44(7A),* 2009.

Vengroff, R. (1974). Popular participation and the administration of rural development: The case of Botswana. *Human Organization, 33,* 303–309.

Ventana Corporation (1990, October 10). *Group SystemsTM: Basic and advanced toolboxes.* Tucson, AZ.

Vermeulen, F., & Barkema, H. G. (2003). *How firms shape managers: The influence of firm development activity on top managers' turnover.* Paper, Academy of Management, Seattle, WA.

Vernon, P. E. (1948). The validation of the civil service observation method in the selection of trained executives. *Occupational Psychology, 22,* 587–594.

Vernon, P. E. (1950). The validation of civil service selection board proedures. *Occupational Psychology, 24,* 75–95.

Vernon, P. E., & Allport, G. W. (1931). A test for personal values. *Journal of Abnormal and Social Psychology, 26,* 231–248.

Vernon, P. A., McCarthy, J. M., & Johnson, A. M. *Individual differences in multiple dimensions of aggression: A univariate and multivariate genetic analysis.* Unpublished manuscript.

Veroff, J. (1957). Development and validation of a projective measure of power motivation. *Journal of Abnormal and Social Psychology, 54,* 1–8.

Vicino, F., & Bass, B. M. (1978). Lifespace variables and managerial success. *Journal of Applied Psychology, 63,* 81–88.

Vicino, F. L., Krusell, J., Bass, B. M., et al. (1973). The impact of PROCESS: Self-administered exercises for personal and interpersonal development. *Journal of Applied Behavioral Science, 9,* 737–757.

Vielhaber, D. P., & Gottheil, E. (1965). First impressions and subsequent ratings of performance. *Psychological Reports, 17,* 916.

Vienneau, J. (1982). A study of leadership behavior of volunteer administrators in amateur sports organizations in the province of New Brunswick, Canada. *Dissertation Abstracts International, 43(9B),* 2931.

Viken, R. J., Rose, R. J., Kaprio, J. et al. (1994). A developmental-genetic analysis of adult personality: extraversion and neuroticism from 18 to 59. *Journal of Personality and Social Psychology, 66,* 722–730.

Villa, J. R., Howell, J. P., Dorfman, P. W., et al. (2003). Problems with detecting moderators in leadership research using moderated multiple regression. *Leadership Quarterly, 14,* 3–23.

Vinacke, W. E. (1969). Variables in experimental games: Toward a field theory. *Psychological Bulletin, 71,* 293–318.

Vinacke, W. E., & Arkoff, A. (1957). An experimental study of coalitions in the triad. *American Sociological Review, 22,* 406–414.

Vincola, A., (1998). Cultural change is the work/life solution. *Workforce, 77*(10), 70.

Vinkenbur, C., Johannesen-Schmidt, M. C., & Eagly, A. H. (2001). *Stereotypes about transformational and transactional styles of leadership.* Paper, Society for Industrial and Organizational Psychology, Toronto.

Vinson, E., & Mitchell, T. R. (1975). *Differences in motivational predictors and criterion measures for black and white employees.* Paper, Academy of Management, New Orleans, LA.

Vinton, K. L. (1989). Humor in the workplace. *Small Group Research, 20*(2), 151–166.

Virany, B., & Tushman, M. L. (1986). *Executive succession: The changing characteristics of top management teams.* Paper, Academy of Management, Chicago, IL.

Virany, B., Tushman, M. L., & Romanelli, E. (1985). A longitudinal study of the determinants and effects of executive succession. *Proceedings,* Academy of Management, San Diego, CA.

Virmani, K. G., & Mathur, P. (1984). Intelligence to use intelligence: Managerial trait theory revisited. *Abhigyan,* Spring, 39–48.

Viteles, M. S. (1953). *Motivation and morale in industry.* New York: W. W. Norton.

Vogel, D. (1992). The globalization of business ethics: Why America remains distinctive. *California Management Review 35*(1), 30–43.

Vogel, S. R., Broverman, I. K., Broverman, D. M., et al. (1970). Maternal employment and perception of sex roles among college students. *Developmental Psychology, 3,* 381–384.

Volkerding, J., & Grasha, A. F. (1988). *Status and affect in manager-subordinate relationships.* Paper, American Psychological Association, Atlanta, GA.

Vonk, R., & Ashmore, R. D. (1993). The multifaceted self: Androgyny reassessed by open-ended questions. *Social Psychology Quarterly, 56,* 278–289.

Vos Strache, C. (1979). Players' perceptions of leadership qualities for coaches. *Research Quarterly, 50,* 679–686.

Voyer, J. J., & Faulkner, R. R. (1986). Cognition and leadership in an artistic organization. *Proceedings,* Academy of Management, Chicago, 160–164.

Vroom, V. H. (1959). Some personality determinants of the effects of participation. *Journal of Abnormal and Social Psychology, 59,* 322–327.

Vroom, V. H. (1960a). *Some personality determinants of the effects of participation.* Englewood Cliffs, NJ: Prentice-Hall.

Vroom, V. H. (1966). Organizational choice: A study of pre- and post-decision processes. *Organizational Behavior and Human Performance, 1,* 212–225.

Vroom, V. H. (1976a). Can leaders learn to lead? *Organizational Dynamics, 4*(3), 17–28.

Vroom, V. H. (1976b). Leadership. In M. D. Dunnette (ed.), *Handbook of industrial and organizational psychology.* Chicago: Rand McNally.

Vroom, V. H. (1984). Reflections on leadership and decision making. *Journal of General Management (UK), 9*(3), 18–36.

Vroom, V. H. (1998). Participative leadership. In F. Dansereau & F. J. Yammarino (eds.), *Leadership: The multiple-level approaches: classical and new wave.* Stanford, CT: JAI Press. 145–189.

Vroom, V. H., & Jago, A. G. (1974). Decision making as a social process: Normative and descriptive models of leader behavior. *Decision Science, 5,* 743–769.

Vroom, V. H., & Jago, A. G. (1978). On the validity of the Vroom-Yetton model. *Journal of Applied Psychology, 63,* 151–162.

Vroom, V. H., & Jago, A. G. (1984). *Leadership and decision making: A revised normative model.* Paper, Academy of Management, Boston.

Vroom, V. H., & Jago, A. G. (1988). *The new leadership: Managing participation in organizations.* Englewood Cliffs, NJ: Prentice-Hall.

Vroom, V. H., & Mann, F. C. (1960). Leader authoritarianism and employee attitudes. *Personnel Psychology, 13,* 125–140.

Vroom, V. H., & Yetton, P. W. (1973). *Leadership and decision-making.* Pittsburgh: University of Pittsburgh Press. Also (1974). New York: Wiley.

Vrugt, A. (undated). *Differential social perception and attribution of intent: Testing the effects of nonverbal rule violation.* Amsterdam: Universiteit van Amsterdam, Subfaculteit Psychologie.

Waaler, R. (1962). *Management development: A Norwegian experiment.* Boston: Harvard University, Graduate School of Business Administration.

Wachtel, J. M. (1988). *The effects of cultural variables on managerial motivation: A cross-cultural study of Mexico and the U.S.* Paper, Western Academy of Management, Big Sky, MT.

Waga, P. (1987). Gerstner's direction of IBM earns colleagues' respect. Shareholders likely to approve stock split at today's meeting. *Binghamton Press & Sun-Bulletin,* April 29, 1A–4A.

Wager, L. W. (1965). Leadership style, hierarchical influence, and supervisory role obligations. *Administrative Science Quarterly, 9,* 391–420.

Wagner, J. A. (1995). Studies of individualism-collectivism: Effects on cooperation in groups. *Academy of Management Journal, 38,* 152–171.

Wagner, J. A., III, & Gooding, R. Z. (1987). Shared influence and organizational behavior: A meta-analysis of situational variables expected to moderate participation-outcome relationships. *Academy of Management Journal, 30,* 524–541.

Wagner, J. S. (1994). Participation's effects on performance and satisfaction: A reconsideration of research evidence. *Academy of Management Review, 19, 2,* 312–30.

Wagner, R. (1949). The employment interview: A critical summary. *Personnel Psychology, 2,* 17–46.

Wagner, R. J., Baldwin, T. T., & Roland, C. C. (1991). Outdoor training: Revolution or fad? *Training & Development Journal, 45*(3), 50–57.

Wagner, R. K., & Sternberg, R. J. (1991). *Tacit knowledge inventory for managers.* San Antonio, TX: Psychological Corporation.

Wagner, S. H., Rozek, R. F., DePuy, A., et al. (2001). *Solo-minority managers' perceptions of support for diversity and turnover intentions.* Paper, Society for Industrial and Organizational Psychology, San Diego, CA.

Wagner, W. G., Pfeffer, J., & O'Reilly, C. A. (1984). Organizational demography and turnover in top-management groups. *Administrative Science Quarterly*, 29(1), 74–92.

Wagstaff, L. H. (1970). *The relationship between administrative systems and interpersonal needs of teachers.* Doctoral dissertation, University of Oklahoma, Norman, OK.

Wahn, J. (2003). *The ethics of the high self-monitor.* Paper, Academy of Management, Seattle, WA.

Wainer, H. A., & Rubin, I. M. (1969). Motivation of research and development entrepreneurs: Determinants of company success. *Journal of Applied Psychology*, 53, 178–184.

Waite, R. C. L. (1977). *The psychopathic god: Adolf Hitler.* New York: Basic Books.

Wakabayashi, M., & Graen, C. B. (1984). The Japanese career progress study: A seven year follow-up. *Journal of Applied Psychology*, 69, 603–614.

Wakabayashi, M., Graen, G., Graen, et al. (1988). Japanese management progress: Mobility into middle management. *Journal of Applied Psychology*, 73, 217–227.

Wald, R. M., & Doty, R. A. (1954). The top executive—a firsthand profile. *Harvard Business Review*, 32, 45–54.

Walder, D. (1978). *Nelson.* New York: Dial Press/James Wade.

Waldersee, R. (1995). *Pluralistic leadership in service change programs: Some preliminary findings.* Paper, Academy of Management, Vancouver, BC.

Waldman, D. A., Atwater, L. E., & Antonioni, D. (1998). Has 360 degree feedback gone amok? *Academy of Management Executive*, 12(2), 86–93.

Waldman, D. A., & Avolio, B. J. (1986). A meta-analysis of age differences in job performance. *Journal of Applied Psychology*, 71, 33–38.

Waldman, D. A., Bass, B. M., & Einstein, W. O. (1985). *Effort, performance and transformational leadership.* Working paper 85–80, Binghamton University, Binghamton, NY.

Waldman, D. A., Bass, B. M., & Einstein, W. O. (1987). Leadership and outcomes of performance appraisal process. *Journal of Occupational Psychology*, 60, 177–186.

Waldman, D. A., Bass, B. M., & Yammarino, F. J. (1988). *Adding to leader-follower transactions: The augmenting effect of charismatic leadership* (ONR Tech. Rep. No. 3). Binghamton, NY: Binghamton University, Center for Leadership Studies.

Waldman, D. A., & Bowen, D. (1998). The acceptability of multi-rater appraisal: A customer-supplier relationship perspective. *Human Resource Management*, 37, 117–129.

Waldman, D. A., & Cullen, T. (2003). *Assessment center performance and learning outcomes.* Paper, Academy of Management, Seattle, WA.

Waldman, D. A., & Javidan, M. (2002). Charismatic leadership at the strategic level: Taking a new look at upper echelons theory. In B. J. Avolio & F. J. Yammarino (eds.), *Transformational and charismatic leadership: The road ahead.* New York: JAI Elsevier Science.

Waldman, D. A., Javidan, M., & Varella, P. (2004). Charismatic leadership at the strategic level: A new application of upper echelon theory. *Leadership Quarterly*, 15, 355–380.

Waldman, D. A., Lituchy, T., Gopalakrishnan, M., et al. (1998). A qualitative analysis of leadership and quality improvement. *Leadership Quarterly*, 9, 177–201.

Waldman, D. A., & Ramirez, G. G. (1992). *CEO leadership and organizational performance. The moderating effect of environmental uncertainty.* Working Paper 92–10–37, Concordia University, Montreal.

Waldman, D. A., Siegel, D. S., & Javidan, M. (2004). *CEO Transformational Leadership and Corporate Social Responsibility.* Rensselaer Working Papers in Economics 0415, Department of Economics, Rensselaer Polytechnic Institute, Rensselaer, NY.

Waldman, D. A., Ramirez, G. G., & House, R. J. (2001). Does leadership matter? CEO leadership attributes and profitability under conditions of perceived environmental uncertainty. *The Academy of Management Journal*, 44, 1, 134–143.

Waldman, D. A., & Yammarino, F. J. (1999). CEO charismatic leadership: Levels-of-management and levels-of-analysis effects. *Academy of Management Review*, 24(2), 266–285.

Waldman, D., Yammarino, F. J., & Bass, B. M. (1990). *Leadership in the Navy: Going beyond leader-follower transactions.* Miami Beach, FL, SIOP, April 21.

Waldman, D., Yammarino, F. J., & Avolio, B. J. (1990). A multiple level investigation of personnel ratings. *Personnel Psychology*, 43, 811–835.

Waldman, L. (1955, 1956). Employment discrimination against Jews in the United States. *Jewish Social Studies*, 18, 3. (Cited in Korman, 1988.)

Walker, A. G., & Smither, J. W. (1999). A five-year study of upward feedback: What managers do with their results matters. *Personnel Psychology*, 52, 393–423.

Walker, C. R., & Guest, R. H. (1952). *The man on the assembly line.* Cambridge, MA: Harvard University Press.

Walker, C. R., Guest, R. H., & Turner, A. N. (1956). *The foreman on the assembly line.* Cambridge, MA: Harvard University Press.

Walker, J. M. (1982). The limits of strategic management in voluntary organizations. *Journal of Voluntary Action Research*, 12, 39–55.

Walker, K. F. (1962). Executives' and union leaders' perceptions of each other's attitudes to industrial relations (the influence of stereotypes). *Human Relations*, 15, 183–196.

Walker, T. G. (1976). Leader selection and behavior in small political groups. *Small Group Behavior*, 7, 363–368.

Wall, C. C. (1970). *Perceived leader behavior of the elementary school principal as related to educational goal attainment.* Doctoral dissertation, University of California, Los Angeles.

Wall, J. (1986). *Bosses.* Lexington, MA: D. C. Heath.

Wall, J. A., Jr. (1976). Effects of success and opposing representatives' bargaining orientation on intergroup bargaining. *Journal of Personality and Social Psychology*, 33, 55–61.

Wall, J. A., Jr. (1989). Managers in the People's Republic of China. *Academy of Management Executive*, 13, 19–32.

Wall, T. D., Corbett, J. M., Clegg, C. W., et al. (1990). Advanced manufacturing technology, work design, and performance: A change study. *Journal of Applied Psychology*, 75, 691–697.

Wall, T. D., Cordery, J. L., Clegg, C. W. (2002). Empowerment, performance, and operational uncertainty: A theoretical integration. *Applied Psychology: An International Review*, 51, 146–159.

Wall, T. D., Kemp, N. J., Jackson, P. R., & Clegg, C. W. (1986). Outcomes of autonomous workgroups: A long-term field experiment. *Academy of Management Journal*, 29, 280–304.

Wall, T. D., Corbett, J. M., Clegg, C. W., et al. (1990). Advanced manufacturing technology, work design, and performance: A change study. *Journal of Applied Psychology, 75,* 691–697.

Wall, T. D., Cordery, J. L., & Clegg, C. W. (2002). Empowerment, performance, and operational uncertainty: A theoretical integration. *Applied Psychology: An International Review, 51,* 146–159.

Wall, T. D., Kemp, N. J., Jackson, P. R., et al. (1986). Outcomes of autonomous work groups: A long-term field experiment. *Academy of Management Journal, 29,* 280–304.

Wallach, M. A., Kogan, N., & Bem, D. J. (1962). Group influence on individual risk takings. *Journal of Abnormal and Social Psychology, 65,* 75–86.

Wallechinsky, D. (2006). *Tyrants: The world's worst living dictators.* New York: Harper.

Wallace, W. L., & Gallagher, J. V. (1952). *Activities and behaviors of production supervisors.* New York: Psychological Corporation.

Wallechinsky, D. (2003). The 10 worst living dictators. *Parade Magazine,* February 16, 4–5.

Waller, M. J., Huber, G. P., & Glick. W. H. (1995). Functional background as a determinant of executives' selective perception. *Academy of Management Journal, 38,* 943–974.

Wallin, P. (1950). Cultural contradictions and sex roles: A repeat study. *American Sociological Review 15, no. 2* (April): 288–295.

Wallis, N. C. (1999). *Follow the leader: Understanding the initiation of individualized leadership from the perspectives of followers and leaders.* Doctoral dissertation, Fielding Institute, Santa Barbara, CA.

Wall Street Journal (1985). *TWIST names Welch best chief executive in electrical equipment industry.* May 20, II–3.

Wall Street Journal (2004). *Two million people on the candidates' minds.* August 17, A4.

Walsh, D. (2002). Women wanted: Women in office change the agenda. *The Executive Female, 14*(5), 6, 17.

Walsh, J. P., & Kosnik, R. D. (1993). Corporate raiders and their disciplinary role in the market for corporate control. *Academy of Management Journal, 36,* 671–700.

Wall, T. D., Corbett, J. M., Clegg, C.W., Jackson, P. R., and Martin, R. (1990). Advanced manufacturing technology and work design: towards a theoretical framework. *Journal of Organizational Behavior, 11*(3), 201–219.

Walter, B. (1966). Internal control relations in administrative hierarchies. *Administrative Science Quarterly, 11,* 179–206.

Walter, N. (undated). *A study of the effects of conflicting suggestions upon judgment.*

Walters, R. (1985). Imperatives of black leadership: Policy mobilization and community development. *Urban League Review, 9*(1), 20–41.

Walton, R. E. (1972). Interorganizational decision making and identity conflict. In M. Tuite, R. Chisholm, & M. Radnor (eds.), Interorganizational decision making. Chicago: Aldine.

Walton, R. E., & McKersie, R. B. (1966). Behavioral dilemmas in mixed motive decision-making. *Behavioral Science, 11,* 370–384.

Walumbwa, F. O., & Lawler, J. J. (2003). Building effective organizations: Transformational leadership, collectivist organization, work-related attitudes, and withdrawal behaviors in three emerging economies. *Journal of Human Resource Management, 14,* 1083–1101.

Walumbwa, F. O., Lawler, J. J., Avolio, B. J., et al. (2005). Transformational leadership and work-related attitudes: The moderating effects of collective and self-efficacy across cultures. *Journal of Leadership and Organizational Studies, 11*(3), 2–16.

Walumbwa, F. O., Wang, P., Lawler, J. J., et al. (2003). *The role of collective and self-efficacy: Transformational leadership and work-related outcomes.* Paper, Academy of Management, Seattle, WA.

Walumba, F. O., & Wu, J.-C. C. (undated). *Followers' perspective: Gender, transformational, and transactional leaderships and their impact on leadership outcomes.* Unpublished manuscript.

Wang, H., Law, K. S., Hackett, R. D., et al. (2005). Leader-member exchange as a mediator of the relationship between transformational leadership and followers' performance and organizational citizenship behavior. *Academy of Management Journal, 48,* 420–432.

Wanous, J. P. (1973). Effects of a realistic job preview on job acceptance, job attitudes, and job survival. *Journal of Applied Psychology, 58,* 327–332.

Ward A., Bishop, K., & Sonnenfeld, J. A. (1999). Pyrrhic victories: The cost to the board of ousting the CEO. *Journal of Organizational Behavior, 20,* 767–781.

Ward, A., Sonnenfeld, J. A., & Kimberly, J. R. (1995). In search of a kingdom: Determinants of career outcomes for chief executives who are fired. *Human Resource Management, 34*(1), 117–139.

Ward, C. D. (1968). Seating arrangement and leadership emergence in small discussion groups. *Journal of Social Psychology, 74,* 83–90.

Ward, J. M. (1977). Normative determinants of leadership. *Dissertation Abstracts International, 37,* 4710.

Ward, L. B. (1965). The ethnics of executive selection. *Harvard Business Review, 43*(2), 6–28.

Ward, S. A. (1981). *Rhetorically sensitive supervisory communication: A situational analysis.* Paper, Speech Communication Association, Anaheim, CA.

Wardlow, M. E., & Greene, J. E. (1952). An exploratory sociometric study of peer status among adolescent girls. *Sociometry, 15,* 311–318.

Warech, M. A., Smither, J.W., Reilly, R. R., Millsap, R. E., & Reilly, S. P. (1998). Self-monitoring and 360-degree ratings. *Leadership Quarterly 9,* 449–473.

Warner, L. S. (1989). *Stereotyping and job satisfaction among American Indian female supervisors.* Doctoral dissertation, University of Oklahoma, Norman, OK.

Warner, W. K., & Hilander, J. S. (1964). The relationship between size of organization and membership participation. *Rural Sociology, 29,* 30–39.

Warner, W. L., Meeker, M., & Eells, K. (1949). *Social class in America.* Chicago: Science Research Associates.

Warihay, P. B. (1980). The climb to the top: Is the network the route for women? *The Personnel Administrator, 25*(4), 55–60.

Warriner, C. K. (1955). Leadership in the small group. *American Journal of Sociology, 60,* 361–369.

Warwick, D. F. (1975). *The public bureaucracy: Politics, personality, and organization in the U.S. State Department.* Cambridge, MA: Harvard University Press.

Washington, M., & Hacker, M. E. (2003). *Why change fails: Understanding the importance of knowledge in implementing change.* Paper, Academy of Management, Seattle, WA.

Wasserman, G. (1985). The presidents' mothers. *Washington Post,* May.

Wasserman, N. (2001). *Founder-CEO succession and the paradox of entrepreneurial success.* NOM Research Paper No. 01–02, Harvard Business School, Boston.

Wasserman, N. T. (2002). *The venture capitalist as entrepreneur: Characteristics and dynamics within VC firms.* Unpublished Ph.D. thesis, Harvard University, Boston, MA.

Watson, A., & Wooldbridge, B. (2001). *The influence of business unit managers on the formulation of corporate level strategy: An empirical test.* Paper, British Academy of Management. Cardiff, Wales.

Watson, B. M., Jr. (1984). Lawrence, Kansas—before and after "The Day After." *Public Management, 66*(3), 13–15.

Watson, D., & Friend, R. (1969). Measurement of social-evaluative anxiety. *Journal of Personality and Social Psychology, 33,* 448–457.

Watson, G. B. (1942). *Civilian morale.* New York: Houghton Mifflin.

Watson, K. M. (1982). An analysis of communication patterns: A method for discriminating leader and subordinate roles. *Academy of Management Journal, 25,* 107–120.

Watson, J. G., & Barone, S. (1976). The self-concept, personal values, and motivational orientations of black and white managers. *Academy of Management Journal, 19,* 36–48.

Watson, P. J., Grisham, S. O., Trotter, M. V., et al. (1988). Narcissism and empathy: Validity evidence for the Narcissistic Personality Inventory. *Journal of Personality Assessment, 48,* 301–308.

Watson, R. (1988). New visions for university sponsored executive education programs. *Academy of Management Executive, 2,* 321–323.

Watson, S. C. (1993). *The effect of transformational and transactional leaders behavior on organizational commitment and turnover in radio stations.* Master's thesis, Texas Tech University, Lubbock, TX.

Watson, T. W. (1986). *Full-scale test of an empirical model of turnover.* Paper, Academy of Management, Chicago, IL.

Watson, W., & Michaelsen, L. (1984). Task performance information and leader participation behavior: Effect on leader-subordinate interaction, frustration, and future productivity. *Group & Organization Studies, 9,* 121–144.

Watson. W. E., Johnson, L., & Merritt, D. (1998). Team orientation, self-orientation, and diversity in task groups. *Group & Organization Management, 23,* 161–188.

Watts, P. (1986). *The wounded leader: Coping with managerial dysfunction.* Paper, OD Network Conference, New York.

Wayne, S. J., & Ferris, G. F. (1988). *Influence tactics, affect, and exchange quality in supervisor-subordinate dyads.* Paper, American Psychological Association, Atlanta, GA.

Wayne, S. J. & Ferris, G. R. (1990). Influence tactics, affect, and exchange quality in supervisor-subordinate interactions: A laboratory experiment and field study. *Journal of Applied Psychology, 75,* 487–499.

Wayne, S. J., Graf, I. K., & Ferris, G. R. (1995). *The role of employee influence tactics in human resources decisions.* Paper, Academy of Management, Vancouver, BC.

Wayne, S. J., & Liden, R. C. (1995). Effects of impression management on performance ratings: A longitudinal study. *Academy of Management Journal, 38,* 232–260.

Wearing, A. J., & Bishop, D. W. (1974). The Fiedler contingency model and the functioning of military squads. *Academy of Management Journal, 17,* 450–459.

Weaver, C. H. (1958). The quantification of the frame of reference in labor-management communication. *Journal of Applied Psychology, 42,* 1–9.

Weaver, D. R. (1991). Liberalism and leadership: Lockean roots. *Leadership Quarterly, 2,* 157–174.

Weaver, G. R., & Agle, B. R. (2002). Religiosity and ethical behavior in organizations: A symbolic interactionist perspective. *The Academy of Management Review, 27*(1), 77–97.

Webb-Petett, F. (undated). *Kellogg International Leadership Program.* Battle Creek MI; W.K. Kellogg Foundation.

Webber, R. A. (1980). Perceptions of interactions between superiors and subordinates. *Human Relations, 23,* 235–248.

Weber, G. (1997). Growing tomorrow's leaders. In F. Hesselbein, M. Goldsmith, & R. Beckhard (eds.), *The Leader of the Future: New Visions, Strategies and Practices for the Next Era.* San Francisco: Jossey-Bass.

Weber, J. (1989). Managers' moral meaning: An exploratory look at managers' responses to the moral dilemmas. *Proceedings,* Academy of Management, Washington, DC, 333–337.

Weber, J. (1990). Managers' moral reasoning: Assessing their responses to three moral dilemmas. *Human Relations, 43,* 687–702.

Weber, J. (1995). Influences upon organizational ethical climates: A multi-departmental analysis of a single firm. *Organization Science 6*(5), 509–523.

Weber, J., & Glyptis, S.M. (2000). Measuring the impact of a business ethics course and community service experience on students' values and opinions. *Teaching Business Ethics, 4,* 341–358.

Weber, M. (1922/1963). *The sociology of religion.* Beacon, NY: Beacon Press.

Weber, M. (1924/1947). *The theory of social and economic organization* (Trans. T. Parsons). New York: Free Press.

Weber, M. (1946). The sociology of charismatic authority. In H. H. Mills & C. W. Mills (eds. and trans.), *From Max Weber: Essays in Sociology.* New York: Oxford University Press.

Webley, S., & More, E. (2003). *Does business ethics pay?* London: Institute of Business Ethics.

Webster, I., & Starbuck, W. H. (1987). Theory building in industrial and organizational psychology. In C. L. Cooper & I. T. Robertson (eds.), *International Review of Industrial and Organizational Psychology,* vol. 3. New York: Wiley.

Wedel, C. C. (1957). *A study of measurement in group dynamics laboratories.* Doctoral dissertation, George Washington University, Washington, DC.

Wedley, W. C., & Field, R. H. (1982). The Vroom-Yetton model: Are feasible set choices due to chance? *Proceedings, Academy of Management,* New York, 146–150.

Wedley, W. C., & Field, R. H. C. (1984). A predecision support system. *Academy of Management Review, 9,* 696–703.

Weed, F. J. (1993). The Madd Queen: Charismatic leadership and the founder of Mothers Against Drunk Driving. *Leadership Quarterly, 3–4,* 329–346.

Weed, S. E., Mitchell, T. R., & Moffitt, W. (1976). Leadership style, subordinate personality, and task type as predictors of performance and satisfaction with supervision. *Journal of Applied Psychology, 61,* 58–66.

Weibler, J. (2004). Discourse ethics. In G. R. Goethals, G. J. Sorenson, & J. M. Burns (eds.), *Encyclopedia of Leadership.* Thousand Oaks, CA: Sage.

Weibler, J. (2004). New perspectives in leadership research. *Zeitschrift für Personalforschung,* 18(3), 257–261.

Weibler, J., Brodbeck, F., Szabo, E., et al. (2000). Führung in kulturverwandten regionen: Gemeinsamkeiten und unterschiede bei Führungidealen in Deutschland, Österreich und der Schweiz. *Die Betriebswirtschaft (DBW),* 60(5), 588–606.

Weibler, J., & Wald, A. (2004). Jahre personalwirtschaftliche Forschung: Ökonommische hegemonie und die Krise einer Disziplin. *Die Betriebswivtschaft,* 64(3), 259–279.

Weick, K. E. (1969, 1979). *The social psychology of organizing.* Reading, MA: Addison-Wesley.

Weick, K. E. (1983). Managerial thought in the context of action. In S. Srivastva (ed.), *The executive mind.* San Francisco: Jossey-Bass.

Weick, K. E. (1988). Enacted sensemaking in crisis situations. *Journal of Management Studies,* 25, 305–317.

Weick, K. (1995). *Sense-making in organizations.* Thousand Oaks, CA: Sage.

Weick, K. E., & Roberts, K. H. (1993). Collective mind in organizations: Heedful interrelating on flight decks. *Administrative Science Quarterly,* 38, 357–381.

Weick, K. E., Sutcliffe, K., & Obstfeld, D. (1999). Organizing for high reliability: Processes of collective mindfulness. *Research in Organizational Behavior,* 21, 81–123.

Weierter, S. J. M. (1997). Who wants to play "follow the leader"?: A theory of charismatic relationships based on routinized charisma and follower characteristics. *Leadership Quarterly,* 8, 171–194.

Weierter, S. J. M., Ashkanasy, N. M., & Callan, V. J. (1997). Effect of self-monitoring and national culture on follower perceptions of personal charisma and charismatic message. *Australian Journal of Psychology,* 49, 101–105.

Weinberg, C. (1965). Institutional differences in factors associated with student leadership. *Sociology and Social Research,* 49, 425–436.

Weinberg, S. B. (1978). A predictive model of group panic behavior. *Journal of Applied Communication Research,* 6(1), 1–9.

Weiner, B., Frieze, I., Kukla, A., Reed, L., Rest, S., & Rosenbaum, R. (1971). Perceiving the causes of success and failure. In E. E. Jones, D. E. Kanouse, H. H. Kelley, R. E. Nesbett, S. Valins, & B. Weiner (eds.), *Attribution: Perceiving the causes of behavior.* Morristown, NJ: General Learning Press.

Weiner, N., & Mahoney, T. A. (1981). A model of corporate performance as a function of environmental, organizational, and leadership influences. *Academy of Management Journal,* 24, 453–470.

Weinstein, A. G., & Srinivasan, V. (1974). Predicting managerial success of master of business administration (MBA) graduates. *Journal of Applied Psychology,* 59, 207–212.

Weisband, S., & Atwater, L. (1999). Evaluating self and others in electronic and face-to-face groups. *Journal of Applied Psychology,* 84, 632–639.

Weislogel, R. L. (1953). The development of situational performance tests for various types of military personnel. *American Psychologist,* 81, 464 (abstract).

Weisman, C. S., Morlock, L. L., Sack, D. G., & Levine, D. M. (1976). Sex differences in response to a blocked career pathway among un-accepted medical school applicants. *Sociology of Work and Occupations,* 3, 187–208.

Weiss, H. M. (1977). Subordinate imitation of supervisor behavior: The role of modeling in organizational socialization. *Organizational Behavior and Human Performance,* 19, 89–105.

Weiss, H. M. (1978). Social learning of work values in organization. *Journal of Applied Psychology,* 63, 711–718.

Weiss, J., Davis, R. V., England, G. W., & Lofquist, L. H. (1961). Validity of work histories obtained by interview. *Minnesota Studies of Vocational Rehabilitation,* 12, No. 41.

Weiss, R. S. (1956). *Processes of organization.* Ann Arbor: University of Michigan, Survey Research Center.

Weiss, T. B. (1997). Show me more than the money. *HR Focus,* 74(11), 3–4.

Weiss, W. (1958). The relationship between judgments of a communicator's position and extent of opinion change. *Journal of Abnormal Psychology,* 56(3), 380–4.

Weiss, W., & Fine, B. J. (undated). *The effect of induced aggressiveness on opinion change* (Tech. Rep. No. 2). Boston: Boston University.

Weissenberg, P. (1979). A comparison of the life goals of Austrian, German-Swiss, and West German (FRG) managers. *Economies et Societies,* 13, 683–693.

Weissenberg, P., & Gruenfeld, L. W. (1966). Relationships among leadership dimensions and cognitive style. *Journal of Applied Psychology,* 50, 392–395.

Weissenberg, P., & Kavanagh, M. J. (1972). The independence of initiating structure and consideration: A review of the literature. *Personnel Psychology,* 25, 119–130.

Weitz, J., & Nuckols, R. C. (1953). A validation of "How Supervise?" *Journal of Applied Psychology,* 37, 7–8.

Welbourne, T. M., & Trevor, C.O. (2000). The roles of departmental and position power in job evaluation. *Academy of Management Journal,* 43, 761–771.

Wellins, R. S., Byham, W. C., & Wilson, J. M. (1991). *Empowerment teams.* San Francisco, CA: Jossey-Bass.

Wellins, R. S., Byham, W. C., & Dixon, G. R. (1996). *Inside teams.* San Francisco, CA: Jossey-Bass.

Wells, L. M. (1963). The limits of formal authority: Barnard revisited. *Public Administration Review,* 23(3), 161–166.

Wells, S. (1997). *From sage to artisan: The nine roles of the value-driven leader.* Davies-Black Publishing.

Welsh, D. H. B., Luthans, F., & Sommer, S. M. (1993). Managing Russian factory workers: The impact of U.S.-based behavioral and participative techniques. *Academy of Management Journal,* 36, 58–79.

Welsh, M. A., & Dehler, G. E. (1986). *The political context and consequences of administrative succession.* Paper, Academy of Management, Chicago, IL.

Welsh, M. A., & Dehler, G. E. (1988). Political legacy of administrative succession. *Academy of Management Journal,* 31, 948–961.

Welsh, M. C. (1979). Attitudinal measures and evaluation of males and females in leadership roles. *Psychological Reports,* 45, 19–22.

Werner, L. (1979). MBA: The fantasy and the reality. *Working Woman,* 4(12), 37–41.

Wernimont, P. F. (1971). What supervisors and subordinates expect of each other. *Personnel Journal,* 50, 204–208.

Weschler, D. (1955). *Weschler adult intelligence scale: Manual.* New York: Psychological Corporation.

Weschler, I. R., Kahane, M., & Tannenbaum, R. (1952). Job satisfaction, productivity, and morale: A case study. *Occupational Psychology, 26,* 1–4.

Weschler, I. R., & Reisel, J. (1959). *Inside a sensitivity training group.* Los Angeles: University of California, Institute of Industrial Relations.

Weschler, I. R., & Shepard, C. (1954). Organizational structure, sociometric choice, and communication effectiveness: A pilot study. *American Psychologist, 9,* 492–493.

Weschler, P. (1984). The long haul to the top. *Dun's Business Month, 123*(4), 52–71.

Wesolowski, M. A., & Mossholder, K. W. (1997). Relational demography in supervisor-subordinate dyads: Impact on subordinate satisfaction, burnout, and perceived procedural justice. *Journal of Organizational Behavior, 18,* 351–362.

Wessel, D. (1986). The last angry men. *Wall Street Journal,* March 20, 20D.

Wessel, D. (2002). The hidden cost of labor strife. *Wall Street Journal,* January 10.

West, C. T., & Schwenk, C. R. (1996). Top management team strategic consensus, demographic homogeneity, and firm performance: a report of resounding nonfindings. *Strategic Management Journal, 17*(7), 571–576.

West, M. A., Borrill, C. S., Dawson, J. F., et al. (2003). Leadership clarity and team innovation in health care. *Leadership Quarterly, 14,* 393–410.

Westburgh, E. M. (1931). A point of view: Studies in leadership. *Journal of Abnormal and Social Psychology, 25,* 418–423.

Westerlund, G. (1952a). *Behavior in a work situation with functional supervision and with group leaders.* Stockholm: Nordisk Rotogravyr.

Westerman, J. W., & Rosse, J. G. (1997). Reducing the threat of rater nonparticipation in 360-degree feedback systems. *Group & Organizational Management, 22*(2), 288–309.

Westfall, J. D., & Zajac, E. J. (1994). Substance and symbolism in CEO's long-term incentive plans. *Administrative Science Quarterly, 39,* 367–390.

Westre, K. R., & Weiss, M. R. (1991). The relationship between perceived coaching behaviors and group cohesion in high school football teams. *The Sport Psychologist, 5*(1), 41–54.

Wexley, K. N., Alexander, R. A., Greenwalt, J. P., et al. (1980). Attitudinal congruence and similarity as related to interpersonal evaluations in manager-subordinate dyads. *Academy of Management Journal, 23,* 320–330.

Wexley, K. N., & Jaffee, C. L. (1969). Comparison of two feedback techniques for improving the human relations skills of leaders. *Experimental Publications System, American Psychology Association,* No. 039.

Wexley, K. N., & Latham, C. R. (1981). *Developing and training human resources in organizations.* Glenview, IL: Scott, Foresman.

Wexley, K. N., & Nemeroff, W. F. (1975). Effectiveness of positive reinforcement and goal setting as methods of management development. *Journal of Applied Psychology, 60,* 446–450.

Wheelan, S. A. (1975). Sex differences in the functioning of small groups. *Dissertation Abstracts International, 35,* 4712–4713.

Wheeless, V. E., & Berryman-Fink, C. (1985). Perceptions of women managers and their communicator competencies. *Communication Quarterly, 33,* 137–148.

Wheeler, L. (1964). Information seeking as a power strategy. *Journal of Social Psychology, 62,* 125–130.

Whelan, W. J. (1981). Senior military leadership and post military careers. *Dissertation Abstracts International, 42*(2A), 839.

White, J. C. (1964). Attitude differences in identification with management. *Personnel Journal, 43,* 602–603.

White, J. C. (1972). Perceptions of leadership by managers in a federal agency. *Personnel Administration and Public Personnel Review, 1,* 51–56.

White, J. E. (1950). Theory and method for research in community leadership. *American Sociological Review, 15,* 50–60.

White, M., & Trevor, M. (1983). *Under Japanese management.* London: Heinemann.

White, M. C. (1981). Achievement, self-confidence, personality traits, and leadership ability: A review of literature on sex differences. *Psychological Reports, 48,* 547–569.

White, M. C., Crino, M. D., & Hatfield, J. D. (1985). An empirical examination of the parsimony of perceptual congruence scores. *Academy of Management Journal, 28,* 732–737.

White, M.C., Smith, M., & Barnett, T. (1997). CEO succession: Overcoming forces of inertia. *Human Relations, 50,* 805–828.

White, M. M., Tansky, J. A., & Baik, K. (1995). Linking culture and perceptions of justice: A comparison of students in Virginia and South Korea. *Psychological Reports, 77,* 1103–1112.

White, R. K., & Lippitt, R. (1960). *Autocracy and democracy: An experimental inquiry.* New York: Harper.

Whitehill, A. M. (1964). Cultural values and employee attitudes: United States and Japan. *Journal of Applied Psychology, 48,* 69–72.

Whitehill, A. M., & Takezawa, S. (1968). *The other worker.* Honolulu: East-West Center Press.

Whitehill, M. (1968). *Centralized versus decentralized decision-making in collective bargaining: Effects on substantive contract language.* Iowa City: University of Iowa, Center for Labor and Management.

Whitelock, D. (1950). *The beginnings of English society.* London: Penguin.

Whitely, W. (1984). An exploratory study of managers' reactions to properties of verbal communication. *Personnel Psychology, 37,* 41–59.

Whitely, W. (1985). Managerial work behavior: An integration of results from two major approaches. *Academy of Management Journal, 28,* 344–362.

Whitely, W., Dougherty, T. W., & Dreher, G. F. (1991). Relationship of career mentoring and socioeconomic origin to managers' and professionals' early career progress. *Academy of Management Journal, 34,* 331–351.

Whiteman, M., & Deutsch, M. (1968). Some effects of social class and race on children's language and intellectual abilities. In M. Deutsch, I. Katz, & A. Jensen (eds.), *Social class, race, and psychological development.* New York: Holt, Rinehart & Winston.

Whitener, E. M., Brodt, S. E., Korsgaard, M. A., et al. (1998). Managers as initiators of trust: An exchange relationship framework for understanding managerial trustworthy behavior. *Academy of Management Review, 23,* 513–530.

Whitley, R., & Czaban, L. (1998). Institutional transformation and enterprise change in an emergent capitalist economy: The case of Hungary. *Organization Studies 19*, 259–280.

Whitson, S. (1980). *Authority on the crisis of confidence*. Paper, Mid-South Sociological Association, Little Rock, AR.

Whitty, M. D., & Butts, D. (1989). A vision of leadership for the 1990s. *Journal of Quality and Participation, 12*(3), 32–35.

Whittington, J. L., Pitts, T. M., Kageler, W. V., & Goodwin, V. L. (2005). Legacy leadership: The leadership wisdom of the apostle Paul. *The Leadership Quarterly, 16*(5), 749–770.

Wituk, S., Warren, M., Heiny, P., et al. (2003). Developing communities of leaders: Outcomes of statewide initiative. *Journal of Leadership and Organiztional Studies, 9*(4), 76–86.

Whyte, G. (1989). Groupthink reconsidered. *Academy of Management Review, 14*, 40–56.

Whyte, G. (1991). Diffusion of responsibility. *Journal of Applied Psychology, 76*, 408–415.

Whyte, W. F (1943). *Street corner society: The social structure of an Italian slum*. Chicago: University of Chicago Press.

Whyte, W. F. (1949). The social structure of the restaurant. *American Journal of Sociology, 54*, 302–310.

Whyte, W. F. (1953). *Leadership and group participation—an analysis of the discussion group*. Ithaca, NY: Cornell University, New York State School of Industrial and Labor Relations.

Whyte, W. F. (1963). Culture, industrial relations and economic development: The case of Peru. *Industrial Labor Relations Review, 16*, 583–593.

Whyte, W. F., & Gardner, B. B. (1945). Human elements in supervision. *Applied Anthropology, 4*(7).

Wicker, A. W. (1985). Getting out of our conceptual ruts. *American Psychologist, 40*, 1094–1103.

Widgery, R. N., & Tubbs, S. L. (1975). *Using feedback of diagnostic information as an organizational development strategy*. Paper, International Communication Association.

Wiebe, R. (1967). *The search for order, 1877–1920*. New York, NY: Hill and Wang.

Wickert, F. (1947). *Psychological research on problems of redistribution* (AAF Aviation Psychology Program Research Report No. 14). Washington, DC: U.S. Government Printing Office.

Wiersema, M. (2002). *CEO dismissal and firm performance. A new look at who's to blame*. Paper, Academy of Management, Denver, CO.

Wiersema, M. E., & Bantel, K. A. (1992). Top management team demography and corporate strategy. *Academy of Management Journal, 55*, 91–121.

Wiesner, W. H., & Cronshaw, S. F. (1988). A meta-analytic investigation of the impact of interview format and degree of structure on the validity of the employment interview. *Journal of Occupational Psychology, 61*, 275–290.

Wiggam, A. E. (1931). The biology of leadership. In H. C. Metcalf (ed.), *Business leadership*. New York: Pitman.

Wikstrom, W. S. (1967). *Managing at the foreman's level*. New York: National Industrial Conference Board.

Wilcox, D. S., & Burke, R. J. (1969). Characteristics of effective employee performance review and development interviews. *Personnel Psychology, 22*, 291–305.

Wilcox, M., & Rush, S. (2003). Power to change: A conversation with Bernard M. Bass. *Leadership in Action. 23*(2), 10–12.

Wilcox, M., & Rush, S. (2004). *The Center for Creative Leadership guide to leadership in action: How managers and organizations can improve the practice of leadership*. SanFrancisco: Jossey-Bass.

Wilcox, R. R. (1998). How many discoveries have been lost by ignoring modern statistical methods. *American Psychologist, 53*, 300–314.

Wilcox, W. H. (1982). *Assistant superintendents' perceptions of the effectiveness of the superintendent, job satisfaction, and satisfaction with the superintendent's supervisory skills*. Doctoral dissertation, University of Missouri, Columbia.

Wilensky, H. L. (1967). *Organizational intelligence: Knowledge and policy in government and industry*. New York: Basic Books.

Wiley, M. G., & Eskilson, A. (1982). The interaction of sex and power base on perceptions of managerial effectiveness. *Academy of Management Journal, 25*, 671–677.

Wilhelm, W. (1992). Changing corporate culture—or corporate behavior? How to change your company. *Academy of Management Executive, 6*(4), 72–77.

Wilken, U. (1967). *Alexander the Great*. New York: Norton.

Wilkinson, R. (1964). *Gentlemanly power*. London: Oxford University Press.

Wilkins, A. L., & Bristow, N. J. (1987). For successful organization culture, honor your past. *Academy of Management Executive, 1*, 221–229.

Wilkins, E. J., & deCharms, R. (1962). Authoritarianism and response to power cues. *Journal of Personality, 30*, 439–457.

Wilkins, W. L. (1953). From symposium: Selection of personnel for hazardous duties. *American Psychologist, 8*, 294 (abstract).

Willerman, B. (1954). *Organizational involvement as reflected in type of member complaint: An indirect method of measurement* (Tech. Rep. No. 4). Minneapolis: University of Minnesota.

Willerman, B., & Swanson, L. (1952). An ecological determinant of differential amounts of sociometric choices within college sororities. *Sociometry, 15*, 326–329.

Willerman, B., & Swanson, L. (1953). Group practice in voluntary organizations: A study of college sororities. *Human Relations, 6*, 57–77.

Williams, A. S. (1981). Training rural citizens: An evaluation of a leadership training program. *Journal of the Community Development Society, 12*(l), 63–82.

Williams, C. H. (1975). Employing the black administrator. *Public Personnel Management, 4*, 76–83.

Williams, E. (1968). *An analysis of selected work duties and performances of the more effective versus the less effective manager*. Doctoral dissertation, Ohio State University, Columbus, OH.

Williams, E. S. (1994). *Tying up loose ends: The role of transformational leadership in OCBS, commitment, trust and fairness perceptions*. Paper presented at the Southern Management Association, New Orleans.

Williams, J. B., Miller, C. E., Steelman, L. A., et al. (1999). Increasing feedback seeking in public contexts: It takes two (or more) to tango. *Journal of Applied Psychology, 84*, 969–976.

Williams, J. E., & Best, D. L. (1982). *Measuring sex stereotypes: A thirty nation study*. Beverly Hills, CA: Sage.

Williams, L. K., Whyte, W. F., & Green, C. S. (1966). Do cultural differences affect workers' attitudes? *Industrial Relations, 5,* 105–117.

Williams, M. L., Podsakoff, P. M., Todor, W. D., et al. (1988). A preliminary analysis of the construct validity of Kerr & Jermier's "Substitutes for Leadership" Scales. *Journal of Occupational Psychology, 61,* 307–333.

Williams, R. E. (1956). *A description of some executive abilities by means of the critical incident technique.* Doctoral dissertation, Columbia University, New York, NY.

Williams, R. L., Verble, J. S., Price, D. E., et al. (1995). Relationship of self-management to personality types and indices. *Journal of Personality Assessment, 64,* 494–506.

Williams, R. S. (1982). *Developing skills for women in middle management: A case study in course evaluation.* Paper, International Congress of Applied Psychology, Edinburgh.

Williams, R. Y., & O'Reilly, C. A. (1998). Demography and diversity in organizations: A review of 40 years of research. *Research on Organizational Behavior, 20,* 77–140.

Williams, S. (1997). Personality and self-leadership. *Human Resource Management Review, 7,* 139–155.

Williams, S. B., & Leavitt, H. J. (1947a). Group opinion as a predictor of military leadership. *Journal of Consulting Psychology, 11,* 283–291.

Williams, S. B., & Leavitt, H. J. (1947b). Methods of selecting Marine Corps officers. In G. A. Kelly (ed.), *New methods in applied psychology.* College Park: University of Maryland.

Williams, S. D. (2001). *Personality, attitude, and leader influences on divergent thinking and creativity in organizations.* Paper, Academy of Management, Washington, D.C.

Williams, S. D., Graham, T. S., & Baker, B. (2003). Evaluating outdoor experiential training for leadership and team building. *Journal of Management Development, 22*(1), 45–59.

Williams, S. D., & Dewett, T. (2005). Yes, you can teach business ethics: A review and research agenda. *Journal of Leadership & Organizational Studies, 12*(2), 109–120.

Williams, T. H. (1952). *Lincoln and his generals.* New York: Vantage.

Williams, V. (1965). Leadership types, role differentiation, and system problems. *Social Forces, 43,* 380–389.

Williamson, I. O., & Cable, D. M. (2003). Organizational hiring patterns, interfirm network ties, and interorganizational imitation. *Academy of Management Journal, 46,* 349–358.

Williamson, O. E. (1975). *Markets and hierarchies: Analysis and antitrust implications.* New York: Free Press.

Willis, F. N. (1966). Initial speaking distance as a function of the speakers' relationship. *Psychonomic Science, 5,* 221–222.

Willits, R. D. (1967). Company performance and interpersonal relations. *Industrial Management Review, 8,* 91–107.

Willner, A. R. (1968). *Charismatic political leadership: A theory.* Princeton, NJ: Princeton University, Center for International Studies.

Willner, A. R. (1984). *The spellbinders: Charismatic political leadership.* New Haven, CT: Yale University Press.

Wills, G. (1994). *Certain trumpets: The call of leaders.* New York: Simon & Schuster.

Wilpert, B. (1995). Organizational behavior. *Annual Review of Psychology, 46*(1), 59–90.

Wilson, B. R. (1975). *The noble savages: The primitive origins of cha-*

risma and its temporary survival. Berkeley: University of California Press.

Wilson, C. L., O'Hare, D., & Shipper, F. (1989). Task cycle theory: The processes of influence. In K. E. Clark, & M. B. Clark (eds.), *Measures of leadership.* West Orange, NJ: Leadership Library of America.

Wilson, D. S., Near, D., & Miller, R. R. (1996). Machiavellianism. A synthesis of the evolutionary and psychological literature. *Psychological Bulletin, 119,* 285–289.

Wilson-Evered, E., Hartel, C. E. J., & Neale, M. (2001). A longitudinal study of work group innovation: The importance of transformational leadership and morale. *Advances in Health Care Management,* vol. 2. New York: Elsevier.

Wilson, H. S., & Hutchinson, S. A. (1991). Trangulation of qualitative methods: Heideggerian hermeneutics and grounded theory. *Qualitative Health Research, 2,* 263–276.

Wilson, J. H. (1975). *Herbert Hoover: Forgotten progressive.* Boston: Little, Brown & Co.

Wilson, J. M. (2001). *Trust and familiarity in distributed groups: Bridging physical distance.* Paper, Academy of Management, Washington, DC.

Wilson, M. P., & McLaughlin, C. P. (2001). *Leadership and management in academic medicine.* San Francisco: Jossey-Bass.

Wilson, N. A. (1948). The work of the Civil Service Selection Board. *Occupational Psychology, 22,* 204–212.

Wilson, R. K., & Rhodes, C. M. (1997). Leadership and credibility in N-person coordination games. *Journal of Conflict Resolution, 41,* 767–791.

Wilson, R. T. (1998). Servant leadership. *The Physician Executive, 24*(5), 6–13.

Wilson, T. P. (1968). Patterns of management and adaptations to organizational roles—a study of prison inmates. *American Journal of Sociology, 74,* 146–157.

Wiltshire, C. E. (1997). Managing risk and risk acceptance: A framework for reconciling empowerment. *Optimum, the Journal of Public Sector Management, 27*(3), 14–23.

Winder, A. E. (1952). White attitudes toward Negro-white interaction in an area of changing racial composition. *American Psychologist, 7,* 330–331.

Winerman, L. (2005). Intuition. *Monitor on Psychology,* March, 51–52.

Winkler-Hermaden, V. (1927). *Zur Psychologie des Zugführers.* Jena, Germany: Fischer.

Winn, A. (1966). Social change in industry: From insight to implementation. *Journal of Applied Behavioral Science, 2,* 170–184.

Winter, D. G. (undated). *Predicting long term management success from TAT measures of power motivation and responsibility.* Unpublished manuscript.

Winter, D. G. (1967). *Power motivation in thought and action.* Doctoral dissertation, Harvard University, Cambridge, MA.

Winter, D. G. (1973). *The power motive.* New York: Free Press.

Winter, D.G. (1978). *Navy leadership and management competencies: convergence among tests, interviews, and performance ratings.* Boston, MA: McBer and Company.

Winter, D. G. (1979a). *Navy leadership and management competencies: Convergence among tests, interviews and performance ratings.* Boston: McBer.

Winter, D. G. (1979b). *An introduction to LMET theory and research.* Boston: McBer.

Winter, D. G. (1987). Leaders appeal, Leaders performance, and the motives profile of leaders and followers: A study of American presidents and elections. *Journal of Personality and Social Psychology, 52,* 196–202.

Winter, D. G. (1991). A motivational model of leadership: Predicting long-term management success from TAT measures of power motivation and responsibility. *Leadership Quarterly, 2,* 67–80.

Winter, D. G. (2002). The motivational dimensions of leadership: Power, achievement, and affiliation. In R.E. Riggio, S. E. Murphy, & F. J. Pirozzolo (eds.), *Multiple intelligences and leadership.* Mahwah, NJ: Lawrence Erlbaum & Associates.

Winter, D. G., John, O. P., Stewart, A. J., et al. (1998). Traits and motives: Towards an integration of two traditions in personality research. *Psychological Review, 105,* 230–250.

Winter, D. G., & Stewart, A. J. (1977). Power motive reliability as a function of retest instructions. *Journal of Consulting and Clinical Psychology, 45,* 436–440.

Winter, G. (1987). *Ronald Reagan.* Student Paper, School of Management, Binghamton University, Binghamton, NY.

Wischmeier, R. R. (1955). Group-centered and leader-centered leadership: An experimental study. *Speech Monographs, 22,* 43–48.

Wise, P. G. (1998). *Rating differences in multi-rater feedback.* Paper, Society for Industrial and Organizational Psychology, Dallas, TX.

Wiseman, R. L., & Schenek-Hamlin, W. (1981). A multidimensional scaling validation of an inductively-derived set of compliance-gaining strategies. *Communication Monographs, 48,* 251–270.

Wispe, L. C. (1955). A sociometric analysis of conflicting role-expectancies. *American Journal of Sociology, 61,* 134–137.

Wispe, L. G. (1957). The success attitude: An analysis of the relationship between individual needs and social role-expectancies. *Journal of Social Psychology, 46,* 119–124.

Wispe, L. G., & Thayer, P. W. (1957). Role ambiguity and anxiety in an occupational group. *Journal of Social Psychology, 46,* 41–48.

Wispe, L. G., & Lloyd, K. E. (1955). Some situational and psychological determinants of the desire for structured interpersonal relations. *Journal of Abnormal and Social Psychology, 51,* 57–60.

Witt, L. A., Kacmar, M., & Andrews, M. C. (2001). The interactive effects of procedural justice and exchange ideology on supervisor-rated commitment. *Journal of Organizational Behavior, 22*(5), 505–515.

Witteman, H. (1991). Group member satisfaction: A conflict-related account. *Small Group Research, 22,* 24–58.

Wittenberg, R. M. (1951). Reaching the individual through the group. *Pastoral Psychology, 2,* 41–47.

Wittig, M. A. (1976). Sex differences in intellectual functioning: How much of a difference do genes make? *Sex Roles, 2,* 63–74.

Wituk, S., Warren, M., Heiny, P., Clark, M. J., & Meissen, G. J. (2003). Developing communities of leaders: Outcomes of a statewide leadership initiative. *Journal of Leadership & Organizational Studies, 9,* 76–86.

Woehr, D. J., & Roch, S. G. (1996). Context effects in performance evaluation: The impact of ratee sex and performance level on performance ratings and behavioral recall. *Organizational Behavior and Human Decision Processes, 66,* 31–41.

Wofford, J. C. (1967). Behavior styles and performance effectiveness. *Personnel Psychology, 20,* 461–495.

Wofford, J. C. (1970). Factor analysis of managerial behavior variables. *Journal of Applied Psychology, 54,* 169–173.

Wofford, J. C. (1971). Managerial behavior, situational factors, and productivity and morale. *Administrative Science Quarterly, 16,* 10–17.

Wofford, J. C. (1981). *An integrative theory of leadership.* Paper, Academy of Management, San Diego, CA.

Wofford, J. C. (1982). An integrative theory of leadership. *Journal of Management, 8*(1), 27–47.

Wofford, J. C. (1982). *Organizational behavior: Foundation for organization effectiveness.* Kent Publishing Co.

Wofford, J. C. (1998). *A cognitive process perspective of leadership behavior and effectiveness.* Paper, Academy of Management, San Francisco, CA.

Wofford, J. C. & Goodwin, V. L. (1990). *Toward a cognitive process model of leadership behavior.* Paper, Academy of Management, San Francisco, CA.

Wofford, J. C., & Goodwin, V. L. (1998). *Toward a cognitive processes model of leadership behavior.* Paper, Academy of Management, San Francisco, CA.

Wofford, J. C., & Liska, L. Z. (1993). Path-goal theories of leadership: A meta-analysis. *Journal of Management, 19,* 857–876.

Wolberg, A. R. (1977). Selecting potential group leaders for training in group techniques. *Transnational Mental Health Newsletter, 19,* 7–8.

Wolcott, C. (1984). The relationship between the leadership behavior of library supervisors and the performance of their professional subordinates (path-goal theory, management). *Dissertation Abstracts International, 45*(5A), 1507.

Wolfe, L. L., Lucius, R. H., & Sonnenfeld, J. A. (1998). *CEO leadership style and the dynamics of their top management team.* Paper, Society for Industrial and Organizational Psychology, St. Louis, MO.

Wolfe, R. A., & Dennis, L. (2003). *The contribution of leadership and human resources to performance in major league baseball.* Paper, Academy of Management, Seattle, WA.

Wolfenstein, E. V. (1967). *Revolutionary personality—Lenin, Trotsky, Gandhi.* Princeton, NJ: Princeton University Press.

Wolfenstein, E. V. (1977). Race, racism, and racial liberation. *Western Political Quarterly, 30,* 163–182.

Wolff, M. F. (1996). Innovation networks call for new management style. *CIMS Technology Management Report, 1,* 1–2.

Wolff, M. F. (1997). Managing "complex" technologies means managing increments, trajectories and translations. *CIMS Technology Management Report, 4,* 1–2.

Wolff, S. B., Pescosolidido, A. T., & Druskat, V. U. (2002). Emotional intelligence as the basis of leadership emergence in self-managing teams. *Leadership Quarterly,* 505–522.

Wolin, B. R., & Terebinski, S. J. (1965). Leadership in small groups: A mathematical approach. *Journal of Experimental Psychology, 69,* 126–134.

Wollowick, H. B., & McNamara, W. J. (1969). Relationship of the components of an assessment centre to management success. *Journal of Applied Psychology, 53,* 348–352.

Wolman, B. (1956). Leadership and group dynamics. *Journal of Social Psychology, 43,* 11–25.

Wolman, B. (ed.). (1971). *The psychoanalytic interpretation of history.* New York: Basic Books.

Wolozin, H. (1948). Teaching personnel administration by role playing. *Personnel Journal, 27,* 107–109.

Wonder, B. D., & Cotton, C. C. (1980). Relation of marginality to extroversion-introversion dimension. *Psychological Reports, 47,* 1015–1021.

Wong, L. (2000). *Generations apart: Xers and boomers in the officer corps.* Strategic Studies Institute, Army War College, Carlisle, PA.

Wood, M. M. (1975). What does it take for a woman to make it in management? *Personnel Journal, 54,* 38–41.

Wood, M. M. (1976). Women in management: How is it working out? *Advanced Mangement Journal, 41,* 22–30.

Wood, M. M., & Greenfeld, S. T. (1976). Women managers and fear of success. *Sex Roles, 2,* 375–87.

Wood, M. T., & Sobel, R. S. (1970). Effects of similarity of leadership style at two levels of management on the job satisfaction of the first level manager. *Personnel Psychology, 23,* 577–590.

Wood, J. A., & Winston, B. E. (2005). Toward a new understanding of leader accountability: Defining a critical construct. *Journal of Leadership and Organizational Studies, 11*(3), 84–94.

Wood, J. T. (1977). Leading in purposive discussions: A study of adaptive behavior. *Communication Monographs, 44,* 152–165.

Wood, R. E., & Bandura, R. E. (1989). Social cognitive theory of organizational management. *Academy of Management Review, 14,* 361–384.

Wood, R. E., Mento, A. J., & Locke, E. A. (1987). Task complexity as a moderator of goal effects: A meta-analysis. *Journal of Applied Psychology,* 416–425.

Wood, R. E., & Mitchell, I. R. (1981). Manager behavior in a social context: The impact of impression management on attributions and disciplinary actions. *Organizational Behavior and Human Performance, 28,* 356–378.

Wood, R. S. (1985). Education for leadership. *Bureaucrat,14*(2), 45–46.

Wood, T. (2006). Globalization or Brazilization? *Academy of Management Perspectives, 20,* 80–82.

Woodham-Smith, C. *The great hunger: Ireland 1845–1849.* London: Penguin Books.

Woods, F. A. (1913). *The influence of monarchs.* New York: Macmillan.

Woods, J. D. (1993). *The corporate closet.* New York: Free Press.

Woods, P. F. (1984). A comparative analysis of supervisory leadership styles in quality circle and non-quality circle groups (manufacturing). *Dissertation Abstracts International, 45*(11A), 3406.

Woodward, B. (2004). *Plan of attack.* New York: Simon & Schuster.

Woodward, C. V. (1974). *Responses of the presidents to charges of misconduct.* New York: Dell.

Woodward, J. (1958). *Management and technology.* London: Her Majesty's Stationery Office.

Woodward, J. (1965). *Industrial organization: Theory and practice.* Oxford: Oxford University Press.

Woodzicka, J., & LaFrance, M. (2001). Real versus imagined sexual harassment. *Journal of Social Issues, 57*(1), 15–30.

Worbois, G. M. (1975). Validation of externally developed assessment procedures for identification of supervisory potential. *Personnel Psychology, 28,* 77–91.

Worchel, P. (1961). Status restoration and the reduction of hostility. *Journal of Abnormal and Social Psychology, 63,* 443–445.

Worden, R E. (1976). The impact of two experimental time-limited leadership training programs on youth. *Dissertation Abstracts International, 36,* 5067.

Worrell, D. L., Davidson, W. N., III, Chandy, F. R., & Garrison, S. L. (1986). Management turnover through deaths of key executives: Effects on investor wealth. *Academy of Management Journal, 29,* 674–694.

Worthy, J. C. (undated). *The first managerial revolution and the origins of civilization.* Unpublished manuscript.

Worthy, J. C. (1950). Organizational structure and employee morale. *American Sociological Review, 15,* 169–179.

Worthy, J. C. (1984). *Shaping an American institution: Robert E. Wood and Sears, Roebuck.* Urbana, IL: University of Illinois Press.

Worthy, M. M., Wright, J. M., & Shaw, M. E. (1964). Effects of varying degrees of legitimacy in the attribution of responsibility for negative events. *Psychonomic Science, 1,* 169–170.

Wortman, M. S. (1982). Strategic management and changing leader-follower roles. *Journal of Applied Behaviorial Science, 18,* 371–383.

Wosinska, W., Dabul, A. J., Whetstone-Dion, R., & Cialdini, R. B. (1996). Self-presentational responses to success in the organization: The costs and benefits of modesty. *Basic and Applied Psychology, 18*(2), 229–242.

Wray, D. E. (1949). Marginal men of industry: The foremen. *American Journal of Sociology, 54,* 298–301.

Wren, J. T. (1994). Teaching leadership: The art of the possible. *Journal of Leadership Studies, 1*(2), 73–93.

Wren, J. T. (1995). The problem of cultural leadership: The lessons of the dead leaders society and a new definition of leadership. *Journal of Leadership Studies, 2,* 122–139.

Wright, D. G. (1946). Anxiety in aerial combat. *Research Publication of the Association of Nervous and Mental Disorders, 25,* 116–124.

Wright, G. N., et al. (1977). *Cultural differences in probabilistic thinking: An extension into South East Asia* (Tech. Rep. No. 77–1). London: Brunel University.

Wright, J. A., Philo, J. R., & Pritchard, R. D. (2003). *Participation, procedural justice, and performance: A multi-organizational student.* Presented at the Society of Industrial Organizational Psychology, Orlando, FL.

Wright, J. D., & Hamilton, R. F. (1979). Education and job attitudes among blue-collar workers. *Sociology of Work and Occupations, 67,* 59–83.

Wright, M. E. (1943). The influence of frustration upon social relations of young children. *Character & Personality, 12,* 111–122.

Wright, N. B. (1984–1985). Leadership styles: Which are best when? *Business Quarterly (Canada), 49*(4), 20–23.

Wright, P., Ferris, S. P., & Hiller, J.S. (1995). Competitiveness through management of diversity: Effects on stock valuation. *Academy of Management Journal, 38,* 272–287.

Wright, R., King, S., Berg, W. E., & Creecy, R. F. (1987). Job satisfaction among black female managers: A causal approach. *Human Relations, 40,* 489–506.

Wrong, D. (1980). *Power: Its forms, bases and uses.* New York: Harper & Row.

Wrong, D. H. (1968). Some problems in defining social power. *American Journal of Sociology, 73*, 673–681.

Wu, M., Cordery, J. & Morrison, D. (2001). *Predicting supervisor support for empowered work teams.* Poster, Society for Industrial and Organizational Psychology, Washington, D.C.

Wu, S., Levitas, E., & Priem, R. L. (2005). CEO tenure and company invention under differing levels of technological dynamism. *The Academy of Mangement Journal, 48*(5), 859–873.

Wurster, C. R., & Bass, B. M. (1953). Situational tests: IV. Validity of leaderless group discussions among strangers. *Educational and Psychological Measurement, 13*, 122–132.

Wurster, C. R., Bass, B. M., & Alcock, W. (1961). A test of the proposition: We want to be esteemed most by those we esteem most highly. *Journal of Abnormal and Social Psychology, 63*, 650–653.

Wyndham, C. H., & Cooke, H. M. (1964). The influence of the quality of supervision on the production of men engaged in moderately hard physical work. *Ergonomics, 7*, 139–149.

Xenophon (c. 400 B.C./1972). *The Persian expedition.* Trans. by R. Warner. London, Penguin.

Xiao, Y. (2002). *Study of team excellence: Practices of teams in high velocity, high–stake environment.* Paper, Academy of Management, Denver, CO.

Xiao, Y., Lasome, C., Moss, J., et al. (2001). *Cognitive properties of a whiteboard: A case study in a trauma center.* Proceedings, European Conference on Computer-supported Cooperative Work, Bonn, Germany.

Xie, X., O'Neill, H., & Cardinal, L. B. (2003). *Boards as agents of innovation, how board characteristics affect R&D intensity and R&D performance in research intensive firms.* Paper, Academy of Management, Seattle, WA.

Xin, K. R. (1997). Asian American managers: An impression gap? *Journal of Applied Behavioral Science, 33*, 335–355.

Xin, K. R., & Pearce, J. L. (1996). *Guanxi:* Connections as substitutes for formal institutional support. *Academy of Management Journal, 39*, 1641–1658.

Xin, K. R., & Pelled, L. H. (2003). Supervisor-subordinate conflict and perceptions of leadership behavior: A field study. *Leadership Quarterly, 14*, 25–40.

Xu, H. (2003). *Break the silence: Do management openness and employee involvement raise employee voice worldwide.* Paper, Academy of Management, Seattle, WA.

Yagil, D. (1998). Charismatic leadership and organizational hierarchy: Attribution of charisma to close and distant leaders. *Leadership Quarterly, 9*, 161–176.

Yagil, D. (2002). Substitutions of a leader's power bases for contextual variables. *International Journal of Organization Theory and Behavior, 5*, 383–399.

Yamagishi, T. & Sato, K. (1986). Motivational bases of the public goods problem. *Journal of Personality and Social Psychology, 50*(1), 67–73.

Yammarino, F. J. (1988). *The varient approach: Variables, levels of analysis, and WABA* (Working Paper 88–142). Binghamton: State University of New York, School of Management.

Yammarino, F. J. (1990). Individual and group directed leader behavior: *Educational and Psychological Measurement, 50*, 739–759.

Yammarino, F. J. (1992). Superior-subordinate relationships: A multiple levels of analysis approach. *Human Relations, 45*, 575–600.

Yammarino, F. J. (1995). Dyadic leadership. *Journal of Leadership Studies, 2*, 50–73.

Yammarino, F. J. (1996). Leadership vistas: An alternative interpretation of the data. *Journal of leadership studies 3*(2), 70–74.

Yammarino, F. J. (1997). "Tight" examination of "loose" levels of analysis in leader direction and employee participation. *Applied Psychology: An International Review, 46*, 434–439.

Yammarino, F. J. (1998). Multivariate aspects of the variant/WABA approach: A discussion and leadership illustration. *Leadership Quarterly, 9*, 203–227.

Yammarino, F. J. (2002) Individualized leadership. *Journal of Leadership and Organizational Studies, 9*(1), 90–99.

Yammarino, F. J., & Atwater, L. (1992). *Male and female leadership development through feedback.* Research proposal. Center for Leadership Studies, Binghamton University, Binghamton, NY.

Yammarino, F. J., & Atwater, L. (1997). Do managers see themselves as others see them? Implications of self-other rating agreement for human resources management. *Organization Dynamics, 25*(4), 35–44.

Yammarino, F. J., & Bass, B. M. (1988). *The variant approach: Variables, levels of analysis, and WABA* (Working paper 88–142). Binghamton: State University of New York, School of Management.

Yammarino, F. J., & Bass, B. M. (1989a). Long term forecasting of transformational leadership and its effects among naval officers: Some preliminary findings. In K. E. Clark & M. B. Clark (eds.), *Measures of leadership.* West Orange, NJ: Leadership Library of America. Also: (1988). ONR Tech. Rep. No. 2. Center for Leadership Studies, Binghamton University, Binghamton, NY.

Yammarino, F. J., & Bass, B. M. (1989b). *Multiple levels of analysis investigation of transformational leadership* (ONR Tech. Rep. No. 4). Center for Leadership Studies, Binghamton University, Binghamton, NY.

Yammarino, F. J., & Bass, B. M. (1990). Transformational leadership and multiple levels of analysis. *Human Relations, 43*, 975–995.

Yammarino, F. J. & Bass, B. M. (1991). Person and situation views of leadership: A multiple levels of analysis approach. *Leadership Quarterly, 2*, 121–139.

Yammarino, F. J., & Bass, B. M. (1996). Group leadership: A level of analysis perspective. In M. A. West (ed.), *Handbook of work group psychology.* Chichester, U.K.: Wiley.

Yammarino, F. J., & Dansereau, F. (2002). Individualized leadership. *Journal of Leadership and Organizational Studies, 9*(1), 90–99.

Yammarino, F. J., Dansereau, F., & Kennedy, C. J. (2001). A multiple-level multidimensional approach to leadership: Viewing leadership through an elephant's eye. *Organizational Dynamics, 29*, 149–163.

Yammarino, F. J. & Dubinsky, A. J. (1992). Superior-subordinate relationships: A multiple levels of analysis approach. *Human Relations, 45*(6), 575–600.

Yammarino, F. J., & Dubinsky, A. J. (1990). Salesperson performance and managerial controllable factors: An investigation of individual and work group effects. *Journal of Management, 16*, 87–106.

Yammarino, F. J., Dubinsky, A. J., & Comer, L. B. (1997). Women and transformational and contingent reward leadership: A multiple-levels-of-analysis perspective. *Academy of Management Journal, 40*, 205–222.

Yammarino, F. I., Dubinsky, A. J., & Hartley, S. W. (1987). An approach for assessing individual versus group effects in performance evaluations. *Journal of Occupational Psychology, 60,* 157–167.

Yammarino, F. J., & Jung. D. I. (1998). Asian Americans and leadership: A levels of analysis perspective. *Journal of Applied Behavioral Science, 34,* 47–67.

Yammarino, F. J., & Naughton, T. J. (1988). Time spent communicating: A multiple levels of analysis approach. *Human Relations, 41,* 655–676.

Yammarino, F. J., & Naughton, T. (1992). Individualized and group-based views of participation in decision-making. *Group and Organization Management, 17,* 398–413.

Yammarino, F. J., Spangler, W. D., & Dubinsky, A. J. (1998). Transformational and contingent reward leadership: Individual, dyad, and group levels of analysis. *Leadership Quarterly, 9,* 27–54.

Yan, J., & Shi, D. (2003). *A cross-cultural model of transformational leadership.* Paper, Academy of Management, Seattle, WA.

Yankelovich, D., & Immerwahr, J. (1983). *Putting the work ethic to work.* New York: Public Agenda Foundation.

Yarmolinsky, A. (1987). *Leadership in crisis situations.* Paper, First Annual Conference on Leadership, Wingfoot, Racine, WI.

Yeh, R. (1988). Values of American, Japanese and Taiwanese managers in Taiwan: A test of Hofstede's framework. *Proceedings,* Academy of Management, Anaheim, CA.

Yerby, J. (1975). Attitude, task, and sex composition as variables affecting female leadership in small problem-solving groups. *Speech Monographs, 42,* 160–168.

Yntema, D. B., & Torgerson, W. S. (1961). Man-machine cooperation in decisions requiring common sense. *IRE Transactions on Human Factors (Electronic), 2,* 20–26.

Yoga, M. (1964). Patterns of supervisory authority. *Journal of the Indian Academy of Applied Psychology, 1,* 44–48.

Yokochi, N. (Bryce) (1989a). *Leadership styles of Japanese business executives and managers: Transformational and transactional.* Doctoral dissertation, United States International University, San Diego, CA.

Yokochi, N. (1989b). Private communication, June 28.

Yorges, S. L., Weiss, H. M., & Strickland, O. J. (1999). The effect of leader outcomes on influence, attributions, and perceptions of charisma. *Journal of Applied Psychology, 84,* 428–436.

York, M. W. (1969). Reinforcement of leadership in small groups. *Dissertation Abstracts International, 30,* 1643.

York, R. O, & Hastings, T. (1985–1986). Worker maturity and supervisory leadership behavior. *Administration in Social Work, 9*(4), 37–47.

Yost, P. R. (1998). *Electronic versus paper survey: Does the medium affect the response?* Paper, Society for Industrial and Organizational Psychology, Dallas, TX.

Yost, P. R., Daum, D. L., Robie, C., et al. (2000). *Paper versus web survey administration: Do methods yield different results?* Paper, Society for Industrial and Organizational Psychology, New Orleans, LA.

Youssef, D. A. (2002). Job satisfaction as a mediator of the relationship between role stressors and organizational commitment: A study from an Arabic perspective. *Journal of Managerial Psychology 17*(4), 250–266.

Youssef & Luthans, F. (2007). Positive organizational behavior in the workplace: The impact of hope, optimism. *Journal of Management, 33,* 774–800.

Yu, W. (1985). Asian-Americans charge prejudice slows climb to management ranks. *Wall Street Journal,* September 11, 35.

Yue, Q. (2003). *Antecedents of top management successor origin in China.* Paper, Academy of Management, Seattle, WA.

Yukl, G. A. (1968). Leader personality and situational variables as codeterminants of leader behavior. *Dissertation Abstracts, 29,* 406.

Yukl, G. A. (1970). Leader LPC scores: Attitude dimensions and behavioral correlates. *Journal of Social Psychology, 80,* 207–212.

Yukl, G. A. (1971). Toward a behavioral theory of leadership. *Organizational Behavior and Human Performance, 6,* 414–440.

Yukl, G. A. (1981, 1989, 1994, 1998, 2001). *Leadership in organizations.* Englewood Cliffs, NJ: Prentice-Hall.

Yukl, G. A. (1982). *A behavioral approach to needs assessment for managers.* Paper, Academy of Management, New York.

Yukl, G. A. (1987a). *A new taxonomy for integrating diverse perspectives on managerial behavior.* Paper, American Psychological Association, New York.

Yukl, G. A. (1987b). *Development of a new measure of managerial behavior: Preliminary report on validation of the MPS.* Paper, Eastern Academy of Management, Boston.

Yukl, G. A. (1988). *Development and validation of the managerial practices questionnaire* (Tech. Rep.). Albany: State University of New York at Albany.

Yukl, G. A. (1989). Managerial leadership: A review of theory and research. *Journal of Management, 15*(2), 251–289.

Yukl, G. A. (1994). *Leadership in organizations* (3rd ed.). Englewood Cliffs, NJ: Prentice Hall.

Yukl, G. (1998). A retrospective on Robert House's "1976 theory of charismatic leadership" and recent revisions. *Leadership Quarterly, 4,* 367–373.

Yukl, G. (1998). *Leadership in organizations* (4th ed.). Englewood Cliffs, NJ: Prentice-Hall.

Yukl, G. (1999). An evaluation of conceptual weaknesses in transformational and charismatic leadership potential. *Leadership Quarterly, 10,* 285–305.

Yukl, G. (2002). *Leadership in organizations* (5th ed.). Upper Saddle River, NJ: Prentice-Hall.

Yukl, G., & Carrier, H. (1986). An exploratory study on situational determinants of managerial behavior. *Proceedings,* Eastern Academy of Management, New York, 40–43.

Yukl, G., & Falbe, C. M. (1990). Influence tactics in upward, downward, and lateral influences attempts. *Journal of Applied Psychology, 75,* 132–140.

Yukl, G. A., & Falbe, C. M. (1991). The importance of different power sources in downward and lateral relations. *Journal of Applied Psychology, 76,* 416–423.

Yukl, G., & Fu, P. P. (1999). Determinants of delegation and consultation by managers. *Journal of Organizational Behavior, 20,* 219–232.

Yukl, G., & Hunt, J. B. (1976). An empirical comparison of the Michigan four-factor and Ohio State LBDQ leadership scales. *Organizational Behavior and Human Performance, 17,* 45–65.

Yukl, G. A., & Kanuk, L. (1979). Leadership behavior and the effectiveness of beauty salon managers. *Personnel Psychology, 32,* 663–675.

Yukl, G. A., Kim, H. & Falbe, C. M. (1996). *Power, influence tactics, and content factors in determinants of influence outcomes.* Paper, Society for Industrial and Organizational Psychology.

Yukl, G. A., & Taber, T. (1983). The effective use of managerial power. *Personnel, 60*(2), 37–44.

Yukl, G., & Tracey, B. (1992). Consequences of influence tactic used with subordinates, peers, and the boss. *Journal of Applied Psychology, 77,* 525–535.

Yukl, G. A., & Van Fleet, D. D. (1982). Cross-situational, multimethod research on military leader effectiveness. *Organizational Behavior and Human Performance, 30,* 87–108.

Yukl, G., Wall, S., & Lepsinger, R. (1989). Preliminary report on validation of the managerial practices survey. In K. E. Clark & M. B. Clark (eds.), *Measures of leadership.* West Orange, NJ: Leadership Library of America.

Zablock, B. (1980). *Charisma and alienation.* New York: Free Press.

Zaccaro, F. J. (1996). *Models and theories of executive leadership: A conceptual/empirical review and integration.* Arlington, VA: U.S. Army Research Institute for the Behavioral and Social Sciences.

Zaccaro, S. J. (1999). *Building and maintaining healthy organizations: The key to future success.* Presentation, Myrer Leadership Symposium, U.S. Army War College, Carlisle, PA.

Zaccaro, S. J. (2002). Organizational leadership and social intelligence. In R. E. Riggio, S. E. Murphy, & F. J. Pirozzolo, (eds.), *Multiple intelligences and leadership.* Mahwah, NJ: Lawrence Erlbaum Associates.

Zaccaro, S. J., & Bader, P. (2003). E-leadership and the challenges of leading e-teams: Minimizing the bad and maximizing the good. *Organizational Dynamics, 31,* 377–387.

Zaccaro, S., Blair, V., Peterson, C., & Zazanis, M. (1995). Collective efficacy. In J. E. Maddux (ed.), *Self-efficacy, adaptation, and adjustment: Theory, research, and application.* New York: Plenum Press, 305–328.

Zaccaro, S. J., Foti, R. J., & Kenney, D. A. (1991). Self-monitoring and trait-based variance in leadership: An investigation of leader flexibility across multiple group situations. *Journal of Applied Psychology, 76,* 308–315.

Zaccaro, S. J., Gilbert, J. A., Thor, K. K., et al. (1991). Leadership and social intelligence: Linking social perspectives and behavioral flexibility to leader effectiveness. *Leadership Quarterly, 2,* 317–342.

Zaccaro, S. J., Marks, M., O'Conner-Boes, J., et al. (1995). *The nature and assessment of leader mental models.* MRI Report 5–3, Management Research Institute, Bethesda, MD.

Zaccaro, S. J., Mumford, M. D., Connelly, M. S., et al. (2000). Assessment of leader problem-solving capabilities. *Leadership Quarterly, 11,* 37–64.

Zaccaro, S. J., Mumford, M. D., Marks, M., et al. (1996). *Cognitive and temperament determinants of Army leadership.* MRI Tech. Rep., Management Research Institute, Bethesda, MD.

Zacarro, S. J., Rittman, A. L., & Marks, M. A. (2001). Team leadership. *Leadership Quarterly, 12,* 451–483.

Zacharatos, A., Barling, J., & Kelloway, E. K. (2000). Development and effects of transformational leadership in adolescents. *Leadership Quarterly, 11,* 211–226.

Zaheer, S., Albert, S., & Zaheer, A. (1999). Time scales and organizational theory. *Academy of Management Review, 24,* 725–741.

Zaheer, S., & Zaheer, A. (1998). Country effects on information seeking in global electronic networks. *Journal of International Business Studies, 28,* 77–100.

Zahn, G. L., & Wolf, G. (1981). Leadership and the art of cycle maintenance: A simulation model of superior-subordinate interaction. *Organizational Behavior and Human Performance, 28,* 26–49.

Zahra, S. A. (1999). The changing rules of global competitiveness in the 21st century. *Academy of Management Executive, 13*(1), 36–42.

Zais, M. M. (1979). The *impact of intelligence and experience on the performance of army line and staff officers.* Master's thesis, University of Washington, Seattle, WA.

Zajac, E. J., & Bazerman, M. H. (1991). Blind spots in industry and competitor analysis: Implications of interfirm (mis)perceptions for strategic decisions. *Academy of Management Review, 16,* 37–56.

Zajac, E., & Westphal, J. D. (1996). Who shall succeed: How power preferences and power affect the choice of new CEOs. *Academy of Management Journal, 39,* 64–90.

Zajonc, R. B. (1969). *Animal social psychology: A reader of experimental studies.* New York: Wiley.

Zajonc, R. B., & Wolfe, D. M. (1966). Cognitive consequences of a person's position in a formal organization. *Human Relations, 19,* 139–150.

Zakaria, F. (2005). An imperial presidency. *Newsweek,* December 19.

Zald, M. N. (1964). Decentralization: Myth vs. reality. *Personnel, 41,* 19–26.

Zald, M. N. (1965). Who shall rule? A political analysis of succession in a large welfare organization. *Pacific Sociological Review, 8,* 52–60.

Zald, M. N. (1967). Urban differentiation, characteristics of boards of directors, and organizational effectiveness. *American Journal of Sociology, 73,* 261–272.

Zaleznik, A. (1951). *Foreman training in a growing enterprise.* Boston: Harvard University, Graduate School of Business Administration.

Zaleznik, A. (1963). The human dilemmas of leadership. *Harvard Business Review, 41*(4), 49–55.

Zaleznik, A. (1965a). The dynamics of subordinacy. *Harvard Business Review, 43*(3), 119–131.

Zaleznik, A. (1965b). Interpersonal relations in organizations. In J. G. March (ed.), *Handbook of organizations.* Chicago: Rand McNally.

Zaleznik, A. (1967). Management disappointment. *Harvard Business Review, 45*(6), 59–70.

Zaleznik, A. (1974). Charismatic and consensus leaders: A psychological comparison. *Bulletin of the Menninger Clinic, 38,* 222–238.

Zaleznik, A. (1977). Managers and leaders: Are they different? *Harvard Business Review, 55*(5), 67–80.

Zaleznik, A. (1980). Why authority fails. *The Executive, 6*(3), 34–40.

Zaleznik, A. (1983). The leadership gap. *Washington Quarterly, 6*(1), 32–39.

Zaleznik, A. (1984). *Leadership as a text: An essay on interpretation.* Paper, 75th Anniversary Colloquium, Harvard Business School, Boston.

Zaleznik, A. (1990). The leadership gap. *The executive, 4,* 7–22.

Zaleznik, A. (1997). Real work. *Harvard Business Review, 6,* 5–11 (reprint 97661).

Zaleznik, A., Christensen, C. R., & Roethlisberger, F. J. (1958). *The motivation, productivity, and satisfaction of workers.* Boston: Harvard University, Graduate School of Business Administration.

Zaleznik, A., & Kets de Vries, M. (1975). *Power and the corporate mind.* Boston: Houghton Mifflin.

Zambrana, R. E., & Zoppi, I. M. (2002). Latina students: Translating cultural wealth into social capital to improve academic success. *Journal of Ethnic & Cultural Diversity in Social Work, 11*(1–2), 33–53.

Zammuto, R. F., London, M., & Rowland, K. M. (1979). Effects of sex on commitment and conflict resolution. *Journal of Applied Psychology, 64,* 227–231.

Zand, D. E. (1997). *The leadership triad: Knowledge, trust, and power.* New York: Oxford University Press.

Zander, A. (1947). Role playing: A technique for training the necessarily dominating leader. *Sociatry, 1,* 225–235.

Zander, A. (1953) *The effects of prestige on the behavior of group members: An audience demonstration.* American Management Association, Personnel Service, No. 155.

Zander, A. (1968). Group aspirations. In D. Cartwright & A. Zander (eds.), *Group dynamics: Research and theory* (3rd ed.). New York: Harper & Row.

Zander, A. (1971). *Motives and goals in groups.* New York: Academic Press.

Zander, A., & Cohen, A. R. (1955). Attributed social power and group acceptance: A classroom experimental demonstration. *Journal of Abnormal and Social Psychology, 51,* 490–492.

Zander, A., Cohen, A. R., & Stotland, E. (1957). *Role relations in the mental health professions.* Ann Arbor: University of Michigan, Institute for Social Research.

Zander, A., & Curtis, L. (1962). Effects of social power on aspiration setting and striving. *Journal of Abnormal and Social Psychology, 64,* 63–74.

Zander, A., & Gyr, J. (1955). Changing attitudes toward a merit rating system. *Personnel Psychology, 8,* 429–448.

Zander, A., & Curtis, T. (1965). Social support and rejection of organizational standards. *Journal of Educational Psychology, 56,* 87–9 .

Zander, A., & Forward, J. (1968). Position in group, achievement motivation, and group aspirations. *Journal of Personality and Social Psychology, 8,* 282–288.

Zander, A., Forward, J., & Albert, R. (1969). Adaptation of board members to repeated failure or success in their organization. *Organizational Behavior and Human Performance, 4,* 56–76.

Zander, A., & Havelin, A. (1960). Social comparison and interpersonal attraction. *Human Relations, 13,* 21–32.

Zander, A., Medow, H., & Dustin, D. (1964). Social influences on group aspirations. In A. Zander & H. Mcdow (eds.), *Group aspirations and group coping behavior.* Ann Arbor: University of Michigan, Institute for Social Research.

Zanville, R. L. (1997). *The sociology of women leaders.* Doctoral dissertation, The Union Institute, Cincinnati, OH.

Zavala, A. (1971). Determining the hierarchical structure of a multidimensional body of information. *Perceptual and Motor Skills, 32,* 735–746.

Zdep, S. M. (1969). Intra group reinforcement and its effects on leadership behavior. *Organizational Behavior and Human Performance, 4,* 284–298.

Zdep, S. M., & Oakes, W. F. (1967). Reinforcement of leadership behavior in group discussion. *Journal of Experimental Social Psychology, 3,* 310–320.

Zeidenstein, H.G. (1983). Varying relationship between presidents' popularity and their legislative success: A futile search for patterns. *Presidential Studies Quarterly, 13,* 530–550.

Zeira, Y (1975). Overlooked personnel problems of multinational corporations. *Columbia Journal of World Business, 10,* 96–103.

Zeira, Y., & Banai, M. (1981). Attitudes of host-country organizations toward MNC staffing policies: Cross-country and cross-industry analysis. *Management International Review, 2*(2), 38–47.

Zeleny, L. D. (1941). Experiments in leadership training. *Journal of Educational Sociology, 14,* 310–313.

Zeleny, L. D. (1946–1947). Selection of compatible flying partners. *American Journal of Sociology, 52,* 424–431.

Zeleny, L. D. (1950). Adaptation of research findings in social leadership to college classroom procedures. *Sociometry, 8,* 314–328.

Zelko, H., & Dance, F. E. X. (1965). *Business and professional speech communication.* New York: Holt, Rinehart & Winston.

Zenger, H. (1974). Third generation manager training. *MSU Business Topics, 21,* 23–28.

Zenter, H. (1951). Morale: Certain theoretical implications of data in the American soldier. *American Sociology Review, 16,* 297–307.

Zerbe, W. J., & Paulhus, D. L. (1985). *Socially desirable responding in organizational behavior.* University of British Columbia, Vancouver. Unpublished manuscript.

Zey, M. G. (1984). *The mentor connection.* Homewood, IL: Dow Jones–Irwin.

Zey, M. G. (1988). A mentor for all reasons. *Personnel Journal, 67*(l), 4651.

Zey-Ferrell, M., & Ferrell, O. C. (1982). Role-set configuration and opportunity as predictors of unethical behavior in organizations. *Human Relations, 35*(7), 587–604.

Zhang, Y. A., & Rangopalan, N. (2003). *Strategic change across CEO tenure: The impact of organizational performance and CEO turnover.* Paper, Academy of Management, Seattle, WA.

Zhao, L., & Culpepper, R. (1997). Performance measurement orientations for Chinese joint ventures: Evidence from American and Chinese managers. *International Journal of Management, 14*(1), 57–69.

Zhou, J., & George, J. (2004). Awakening employee creativity: The role of emotional intelligence. *Leadership Quarterly, 14,* 545–568.

Ziegart, J. C., & Hanges, P. J. (2002). *Evaluation of female leaders: The role of attitudes and motivation.* Paper, Society for Industrial and Organizational Psychology, Toronto.

Ziegart, J., Klein, K., & Xiao, Y. (2002). *Team leadership: A review and extension of existing theory through a qualitative study of shock trauma teams.* Paper, Academy of Management, Denver, CO.

Ziegenhagen, E. A. (1964). *Perceived inconsistencies regarding self and ethnocentric political leadership.* Doctoral dissertation.

Ziegler, S., & Richmond, A. H. (1972). *Characteristics of Italian householders in metropolitan Toronto.* Toronto: Ethnic Research Program, Institute for Behavioral Research Centre.

Zierden, W. E. (1980). Leading through the follower's point of view. *Organizational Dynamics, 8*(4), 27–46.

Zigarmi, D., Edeburn, C., & Blanchard, K.H. (1992). *Managerial self-*

reported effectiveness ratings as compared with employee perceptions of climate and satisfaction. Unpublished manuscript.

Zigon, F. J., & Cannon, J. R. (1974). Processes and outcomes of group discussions as related to leader behaviors. *Journal of Educational Research*, 67, 199–201.

Zigurs, I. (2003). Leadership in virtual teams: Oxymoron or opportunity? *Organizational Dynamics*, 31, 339–351.

Ziller, R. C. (1954). Four techniques of decision making under uncertainty. *American Psychologist*, 9, 498.

Ziller, R. C. (1955). Scales of judgment: A determinant of the accuracy of group decisions. *Human Relations*, 8, 153–164.

Ziller, R. C. (1959). Leader acceptance of responsibility for group action under conditions of uncertainty and risk. *Journal of Psychology*, 47, 57–66.

Ziller, R. C. (1963). Leader assumed dissimilarity as a measure of prejudicial cognitive style. *Journal of Applied Psychology*, 47, 339–342.

Ziller, R. C. (1964). Individuation and socialization: A theory of assimilation in large organizations. *Human Relations*, 17, 341–360.

Ziller, R. C. (1973). *The social self.* New York: Pergamon.

Ziller, R. C. (1965b). Toward a theory of open and closed groups. *Psychological Bulletin*, 64, 164–182.

Zimet, C. N., & Fine, H. J. (1955). Personality changes with a group therapeutic experience in a human relations seminar. *Journal of Abnormal and Social Psychology*, 51, 68–73.

Zimmerman-Oster, K. & Burkhardt, J.C, (1999). *Leadership in the making: Impact and insights from leadership development programs in U.S. colleges and universities.* Battle Creek, MI: W. K. Kellogg Foundation.

Zimmerman-Treichel, M. A., Dunlap-Hinkler, D., & Washington, M. L. (2003). *Top management team diversity: Does gender diversity influence firm performance?* Paper, Academy of Management, Seattle, WA.

Zimmerman, M., Washington, M., & Dunlap, D. (2003). *Top management team diversity: Does gender diversity influence firm performance?* Seattle, WA: Academy of Management.

Zink, H. (1930). *City bosses in the United States: A study of twenty municipal bosses.* Durham, NC: Duke University Press.

Zoffer, H. J. (1985). Training managers to take charge. *New York Times*, October 20, 2F.

Zogby-LeMoybe. (2006). *U.S. Troops in Iraq: Executive Summary.* Zogby-International: http://www.zogby.com/news/readnews.dbm?id=1075.

Zola, E. (1902). *The downfall.* New York: Collier.

Zolembiewski, R. T., Billingsley, K., & Yeager, S. (1976). Measuring change and persistence in human affairs: Types of change generated by OD designs. *Journal of Applied Behavioral Science*, 12, 133–157.

Zoll, A. A. (1969). *Dynamic management education* (2nd ed.). Reading, MA: Addison-Wesley.

Zoppi, I. M. (2004). *The relation of self-perceived leadership and acculturation of Latinas in the U.S. Army.* Doctoral dissertation, University of Maryland, College, Park, MD.

Zorn, T. E. (1988). *Construct system development, transformational leadership and leadership messages among small business owners.* Paper, Speech Communication Association, New Orleans, LA.

Zsambok, C. E. (1993). *Advanced team decision making: A model and training implications.* Research Note 95–02, U.S. Army Research Institute for the Behavioral and Social Sciences, Alexandria, VA.

Zullow, H. M., Oettingen, C., Peterson, C., & Seligman, M. E. R. (1988). Pessimistic explanatory style in the historical record: C. A. Ving, LBJ, presidential candidates, and East versus West Berlin. *American Psychologist*, 43, 673–682.

Zurcher, L. A. (1968). Particularism and organizational position: A cross-cultural analysis. *Journal of Applied Psychology*, 52, 139–144.

Zurcher, L. A., Meadow, A., & Zurcher, S. L. (1965). Value orientation, role conflict, and alienation from work: A cross-cultural study. *American Sociological Review*, 30, 539–548.

Subject Index

Author Index